WHEN THERE IS NO WAY

YOUR SOLUTION IS SISU NA-140.

The SISU NA-140, made by Sisu-Auto of Finland,
offers superior all-terrain properties
for transportation of troops and equipment,
and as a platform for weapons and equipment.
It is a rubber-tracked amphibious vehicle
with articulated steering, constructed for terrains
where wheeled vehicles cannot go.
It also rides smoothly on the road.
Sisu NA-140 is your solution if you require
- high mobility and indifference of conditions
- ease of handling and maintenance
- strong power line
- big payload
- safety and protection
- high battle endurance
- low life-cycle cost.

SISU

SISU DEFENCE
P.O.Box. 189
SF-13101 Hämeenlinna, Finland
Tel. + 358-17-5851
Telefax + 358-17-197 130

OSHKOSH: The Heavy Duty Specialist

Heavy Equipment Transporter (HET) Tractor. Model M1070 prime mover for the M1 main battle tank and other vehicles.

Palletized Load System (PLS). Self-loader cargo transporter.

Heavy Expanded Mobility Tactical Truck (HEMTT). Model M977 series of cargo, wrecker, refueler and tractor vehicles.

Oshkosh, the world's largest producer of heavy duty military trucks, continues to set worldwide performance standards.

Only Oshkosh concentrates its resources totally on heavy duty trucks, and that's why the Oshkosh family of tactical vehicles provides maximum capacity and mobility under the most severe conditions.

As a specialist, Oshkosh has the experience and the technological capability to satisfy tough requirements at the lowest possible cost, and with optimized logistical support.

Oshkosh. A name you can count on for heavy duty technical leadership…leadership made possible by specialized, best value design. Built by people who care.

Oshkosh Truck Corporation
P.O. Box 2566
Oshkosh, WI 54903-2566, U.S.A.
Telephone (414) 235-9150
Fax (414) 233-9540

JANE'S MILITARY VEHICLES AND LOGISTICS

FOURTEENTH EDITION

EDITED BY
CHRISTOPHER F FOSS AND TERRY J GANDER

1993-94

ISBN 0 7106 1064 5
JANE'S DATA DIVISION
"Jane's" is a registered trade mark

British Library Cataloguing-in-Publication Data.
A catalogue record for this book is available from the British Library.

Printed and bound in Great Britain by Butler and Tanner Ltd, Frome and London

79 289 055 X

Gone with the wind.

The desert: Breathtaking silence in the structures of sand to experience long gone cultures of human beings. But it´s still alive. There might also be a mine hiding there.

The AN-19/2 mine detector was specifically developed to meet today's requirements for mine clearance on the battle field. It can detect quite small metallic objects, typical of modern mines containing a very low proportion of metal.

Because of its compact, light-weight design and low mutual interference between two detectors, the mission suitability of the AN-19/2 for fast and accurate terrain reconnaissance is ideal. The equipment will also detect mines at limited depth in fresh or salt water.

The excellent discrimination characteristics of the AN-19/2, independent of ambient temperature, qualifies the equipment for use in all climates and environments.

The AN-19/2 is a rugged, long-life product based on rigorous standards of quality control in the manufacturing process (AQAP-4) and the use of high quality components. The AN-19/2 mine detector is in service in several countries all over the world, including many NATO countries.

Recently it was selected by the U.S. Army over all competitors as its new standard mine detector, under the designation AN-PSS/12.

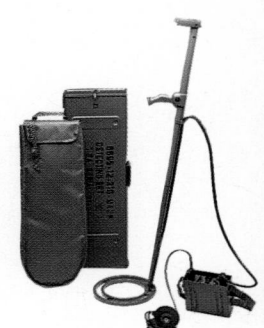

AN-19/2 Mine Detecting Set
For detection of mines
with a very small proportion
of metal content

SCHIEBEL
Security where you need it most.

Dipl. Ing. Hans Schiebel, Elektronische Geräte Gesellschaft m.b.H.
A-1050 Vienna/Austria, Margaretenstraße 112
Telefon (+43 222) 546 26-0, Fax (+43-1) 545 23 39, Telex 136741 schwk a

Contents

ADMINISTRATION

Publishing Director: Robert Hutchinson

Managing Editor: Keith Faulkner

Publishing Supervisor: Ruth Simmance

Publishing Assistant: Lynn Morse

Product Group (Marketing) Manager: Sandra Dawes

EDITORIAL OFFICES

Jane's Information Group Limited, Sentinel House,
163 Brighton Road, Coulsdon, Surrey CR5 2NH, United Kingdom

Tel: 081 763 1030 International +44 81 763 1030
Telex: 916907 Janes G
Fax: 081 763 1006 International +44 81 763 1006

SALES OFFICES

Send enquiries to:
Peter McSherry, Sales Manager,
Jane's Information Group Limited, UK address as above

Send USA enquiries to:
Joe McHale, Senior Vice-President Product Sales,
Jane's Information Group Inc, 1340 Braddock Place, Suite 300,
Alexandria, VA 22314-1651

Tel: +1 703 683 3700
Telex: 6819193
Fax: +1 703 836 0029

ADVERTISEMENT SALES OFFICES

Advertisement Sales Manager: Barbara Urry

Australia: Brendan Gullifer, Havre & Gullifer (PTY) Ltd, 253
Richardson Street, Middle Park, Victoria 3206, Australia

Tel: +61 (3) 6960288
Fax: +61 (3) 6966951

Benelux: Barbara Urry, Jane's Information Group (see United
Kingdom)

Brazil: L Bilyk, Brazmedia International S/C Ltda, Alameda Gabriel
Monteiro da Silva, 366 CEP, 01442, São Paulo

Tel: +55 11 853 4133
Telex: 32836 BMED BR
Fax: +55 11 852 6485

France: Patrice Février, Jane's Information Group – France,
35 avenue Mac Mahon, F-75017 Paris, France

Tel: +33 1 45 72 3311
Fax: +33 1 45 72 1795

Germany and Austria: Rainer Vogel, Media Services International,
Schwabenbergstrasse 12, D-8089 Emmering

Tel: +49 8141 42534
Fax: +49 8141 6706

Greece: Anwar Aswad, A&M Advertising & Marketing Consultants,
Zaimi 7-9, Apt 1, Palaio-Faliron

Tel: +30 1 982 2577
Telex: 218947 GNM
Fax: +30 1 723 2990

Hong Kong: Jeremy Miller, Major Media Ltd, Room 142, 14F Capitol
Centre, 5-19 Jardine's Bazaar, Causeway Bay

Tel: +852 5 890 3110
Fax: +852 5 576 3397

Israel: Oreet Ben-Yaacov, Oreet International Media, 15 Kineret
Street, 51201 Bene Berak

Tel: +972 3 570 6527
Fax: +972 3 570 6526

Italy and Switzerland: Ediconsult Internazionale Srl, Piazza Fontane
Marose 3, I-16123 Genoa

Tel: +39 10 583520, 583684
Telex: 281197 EDINT I
Fax: +39 10 566578

Korea: Young Seoh Chinn, JES Media International, KPO Box 576,
Seoul

Tel: +82 2 545 8001/2
Fax: +82 2 549 8861

Scandinavia: Peter McSherry, Jane's Information Group
(see United Kingdom)

Singapore, Indonesia, Malaysia, Philippines, Taiwan and Thailand:
Hoo Siew Sai, Major Media (Singapore) Pte Ltd, 6th Floor, 52 Chin
Swee Road, Singapore 0316

Tel: +65 738 0122
Telex: RS 43370 AMPLS
Fax: +65 738 2108

Spain: Jesus Moran Iglesias, Varex SA, Modesto Lafuente 4,
E-28010 Madrid

Tel: +34 1 448 7622
Fax: +34 1 446 0198

United States and Canada: Kimberly S. Hanson, Director of
Advertising Sales and Marketing, Jane's Information Group Inc,
1340 Braddock Place, Suite 300, Alexandria, VA 22314-1651

Tel: +1 703 683 3700
Telex: 6819193
Fax: +1 703 836 0029

USA South Eastern Region: Kristin Schulze, Regional Advertising
Manager
(see United States and Canada)

USA North Eastern Region and Canada: Melissa C Gunning,
Regional Advertising Manager
(see United States and Canada)

USA Western Region and Canada: Anne Marie St. John-Brooks,
Regional Advertising Manager, Jane's Information Group, 1523
Rollins Road, Burlingame, CA 94010

Tel: (415) 259 9982
Fax: (415) 259 9751

United Kingdom/Rest of World: Barbara Urry,
Jane's Information Group, Sentinel House, 163 Brighton Road,
Coulsdon, Surrey CR5 2NH

Tel: 081 763 1030 International +44 81 763 1030
Telex: 916907 Janes G
Fax: 081 763 1006 International +44 81 763 1006

Administration: Tara Betts, Jane's Information Group
(see United Kingdom)

IMPROVING OUR POWER

At SANTA BARBARA we are improving and diversifying our range of Armoured Fighting Vehicles in order to meet the requirements of the international market.

The quality of our BLR and BMR vehicles, —tested in combat—; the capability to carry out global upgrading programs, —like the AMX-30—, and the participation in international projects are just a few examples of our expertise.

SANTA BARBARA offers a complete maintenance program for each customer, which now includes our exclusive A.T.I. (Integrated Technical Assistance) system.

SANTA BARBARA.
Now more than ever.

SANTA BARBARA

Grupo INI

Julián Camarillo, 32 • 28037 MADRID (SPAIN)
☎ 34-1-585 01 00 • Telex 44466 ENSB-E • Telefax 34-1-585 02 68

Alphabetical list of advertisers

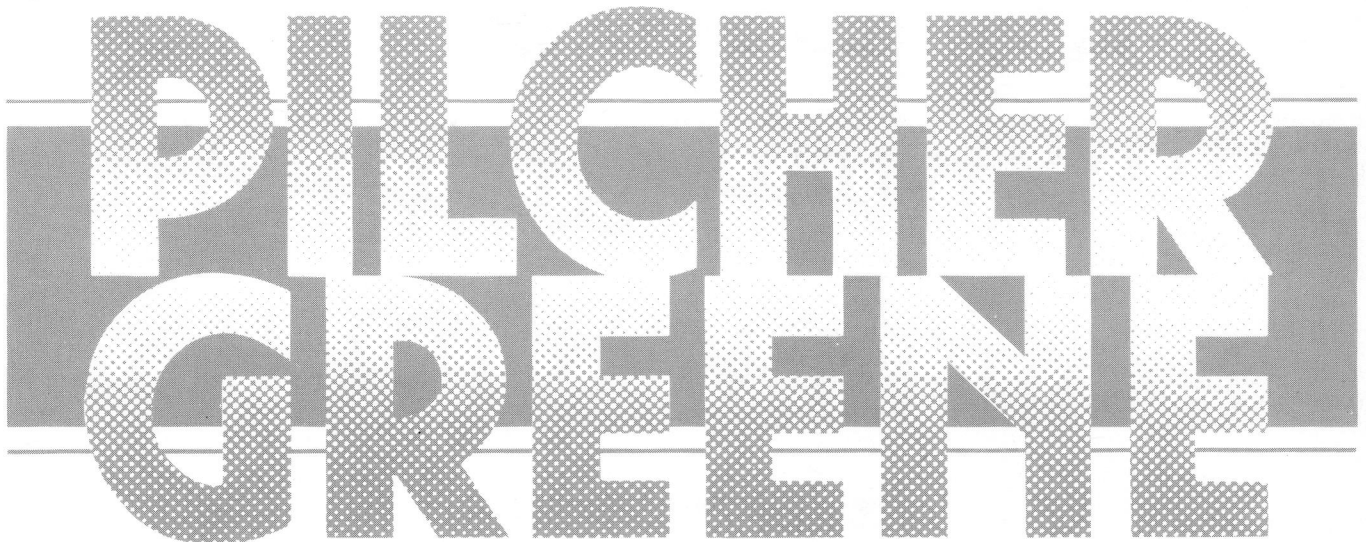

The Specialist Vehicle Builders

People keep coming to us for something special. This is not a single success story - we can tell you many.

For the success of Pilcher-Greene as a company can be clearly seen and accurately measured by the success in service of the many different special-purpose vehicles we build and supply.

People keep coming to us for 'something special'.

And that's exactly what they get.

We have been successful pioneers in the development of specially built vehicles, that are designed and equipped for various specific tasks, for well over sixty years now.

By taking and adapting the rugged and well-tried basic chassis of the world's finest vehicle builders, Pilcher-Greene have built their own success on the

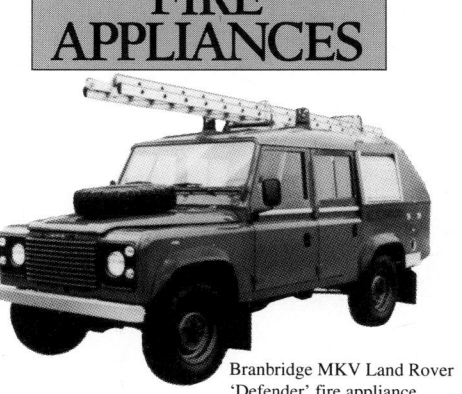

Branbridge MKV Land Rover 'Defender' fire appliance.

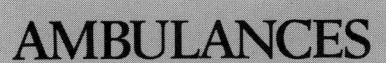

Series 8303 Type S Land Rover 'Defender' ambulance.

careful attention to detail required in creating purpose-made products to meet demanding specifications or fulfil special roles.

So successful have these Pilcher-Greene 'specials' become, that we regularly turn some out as 'standard' vehicles in a highly successful range that offers wide choice to our customers - in many different areas of human activity. But we're ready to build to your specification - if you have something special in mind.

Skilful engineering and craftsmanship, unique bodywork design, great care and attention to meeting performance needs - these are the hallmarks of our success in the creation of vehicles that will match the specific demands of their operators - during a long, reliable, and highly cost-effective service life.

The Specialist Vehicle Builders

PILCHER-GREENE LIMITED, CONSORT WAY, BURGESS HILL, WEST SUSSEX RH15 9NA. TEL: (0) 444 235707/9. TELEX: 877102. TELEFAX: (0) 444 241730. CABLES: AMBULAP BURGESS HILL.

Classified list of advertisers

The companies advertising in this publication have informed us that they are involved in the fields of manufacture indicated below:

Ambulances
Land Rover
Pilcher-Greene
Santa Barbara

Amphibious bridges
CNIM

Armoured bridgelayers
CNIM

Bridgelaying systems
ASTRA
CNIM
Oshkosh

Bridging systems
CNIM

Cargo trucks
Oshkosh
Land Rover
SISU Defence

Container handling equipment
Danish Camp Supply
Oshkosh
SISU Defence

Cranes mounted on military vehicles
Oshkosh

Diesel engines
Hercules Engines
Oshkosh

**Equipment for logistics handling &
transportation of ammunition**
Hydrema
Oshkosh

Explosive ordnance disposal
Explosive Ordnance Disposal World
    Services Incorporated

Fire appliances (4 × 4)
Oshkosh
Pilcher-Greene
SISU Defence

High mobility vehicles
ASTRA
Hydrema
Oshkosh
SISU Defence

Integrated logistics systems
Oshkosh

Jeep and Land Rover type vehicles
Land Rover
Pilcher-Greene

Land mine detection equipment
SCHIEBEL

Military trucks
ASTRA
Hercules Engines
Land Rover
Oshkosh
SISU Defence

Military vehicles
Hercules Engines
Land Rover
Oshkosh
Santa Barbara
SISU Defence

**Military vehicles (tracked &
wheeled)**
ASTRA
Land Rover
Oshkosh
Santa Barbara
SISU Defence

Mobile workshop units
Oshkosh

Multi-purpose military vehicles
Hydrema
Land Rover
Oshkosh
SISU Defence

On/off highway vehicles
Hydrema
Land Rover
Oshkosh
SISU Defence

Pontoon bridges
CNIM

Recovery vehicles
ASTRA
Oshkosh
Santa Barbara

Support vehicles
Land Rover
Oshkosh

Tracked cargo carriers
SISU Defence

Transport vehicles
ASTRA
Land Rover
Oshkosh
SISU Defence

Trucks & variants
Land Rover
Oshkosh
SISU Defence

THE FMTV IS MADE FOR AN EVER CHANGING WORLD.

No matter how quickly the mission, the weather or the terrain changes, the FMTV from Stewart & Stevenson quickly adapts. It's the best of everything the world has to offer in one vehicle, European design technology with U.S. drive train and systems technology.

Key features: the highest horsepower-to-weight ratio and highest ground clearance in its class; push button, automatic tire inflation/deflation for maneuvering from highway to deep sand to roads to swamps; automatic transmission; fastest high-way speed; an advanced computer designed suspension system; multiple configurations; easy to operate.

Add Stewart & Stevenson's 24-hour worldwide parts and service support, and you know why the U.S. Army chose the FMTV to carry it into the changing times of the 21stcentury. Find out more today. For a brochure and spec sheets on the 2.5-ton and 5-ton FMTV, contact:

Stewart & Stevenson Tactical
Vehicle Systems Division
5000 I-10 West
Sealy, Texas 77474
U.S.A.
Telephone: (713) 856-7040
Fax: (409) 885-7910

ENGINEERED POWER STEWART & STEVENSON

Pre-production Unipower M Series (8 × 8) high mobility logistics vehicle undergoing reliability trials late in 1992. The M Series is being developed for a wide range of battlefield missions including logistics, recovery and tank transporter

JANE'S
MILITARY VEHICLES
AND LOGISTICS
1993-94

Jane's Information Group Limited, Sentinel House, 163 Brighton Road, Coulsdon, Surrey CR5 2NH, UK
Jane's Information Group Inc, 1340 Braddock Place, Suite 300, Alexandria, VA 22314-1651, USA

WHERE ARMED FORCES ARE OPERATING THERE IS AN ASTRA TRUCK

BM 314

BM 309 T

BM 318.39

M 113 PIONIER

BM 20

ASTRA long experience in heavy trucks for civil jobs, off road operations, has been transferred in a family of rugged military vehicles, all wheels traction for earth moving, bridging equipment, missiles and special pallettized loads.

ASTRA Veicoli Industriali S.p.A Via Caorsana, 79 - 29100 Piacenza - Italy - Tel. 0523/5431 - Fax. 0523/591773 - Telex 530148 ASTRA I

Foreword

The past military year has been a busy one. Internal warfare in the Balkans has expanded to the point where what (to many outsiders) were long-forgotten republics have once again become the flashpoints of Europe.

There have been sizeable military operations in Somalia as well as campaigns on varying scales throughout other parts of Africa. The Middle East remains a major source of international tension as the continued break-up of the old Soviet empire creates its own fuel for the festering internecine strife among peoples who were once seemingly content to co-exist.

Despite all the hopes that arose once the old Cold War had apparently vanished, the world is still very far from being a peaceful place.

Our television screens have thus continued to display images of war, with all the attendant scenes of strife, human misery and suffering. The cameras have, as usual, seen fit to dwell upon the images which provide the greatest impact on the audiences back home so, apart from the awful human sights that warfare and its aftermath can produce, the main military images of the year have been formed from armoured vehicles patrolling roads and amphibious vehicles emerging from the sea. What these selected images have managed to neglect is the vast backup that these 'glamour' vehicles require.

This is a topic mentioned in these pages on several occasions before now but the importance of logistics to all aspects of military operations is one that many observers still fail to comprehend. Despite the importance of the huge logistic operations that made past campaigns such the Gulf operations of 1990 so successful, it would seem that many observers still tend to overlook the fact that military formations cannot operate without supplies.

Several times during the past year there have been occasions when military operations have not proceeded with the speed that many would like. Two examples spring to mind: the transfer of a relatively small British contingent to carry out peace-keeping operations in Bosnia; and the US Marine Corps intervention in Somalia at the behest of the United Nations. In both cases some political and media observers seemed to think that once a decision had been made to intervene, all that had to happen was a journey and subsequent landing before the required intervention operations could commence. Criticism arose from several quarters that matters were proceeding too hesitantly and that delays were being introduced for various (often unspecified) reasons.

The truth is that any military move, no matter how large or small, takes time and thorough preparation to accomplish with any degree of success. Even relatively minor military upheavals involve logistics from beginning to end. If there is no ready-for-use logistics infrastructure on hand in a proposed theatre of operations, one simply has to be created. That takes time and considerable effort to say nothing of a corresponding investment in logistic hardware and systems, plus personnel trained to operate and utilise both. These all have to be provided and installed before any of the supplies and materiel which will eventually pass through those logistic systems can be considered as even remotely useful. There was no convenient infrastructure awaiting the British in Bosnia but the US Marines did at least have the resources of a naval Task Force not too far away as they prepared for Somalia. Even in the latter case, there were more criticisms when the Marines seemed unable to take over all the trouble spots in that unhappy country within a few days of arrival. Once again the critics failed to accept that the Marines had to build up a sound logistical base before they could proceed. Getting ashore

absorbed just about all the internal resources the Marines had to hand – the rest had to follow later.

Once both the British and the Americans were operational, the media images produced for most audiences were once again misleading. As usual, the cameras tended to concentrate on the armour and the armed men. They overlooked the less glamorous trucks that were really the key vehicles involved and the main reasons for military operations being able to take place at all. In both Bosnia and Somalia it has to be stressed that the trucks were the main reason for military intervention in the first place. They are the ones taking the food, medicines and other supplies to harassed and hungry populations, not the armoured vehicles. The latter have to be there to carry out the necessary function of creating the safety under which logistics operations can progress but they can otherwise accomplish little to further the main objectives of either the Bosnian or Somali operations.

Trucks, by themselves, are perhaps the most important elements in any logistical chain. They have to carry the loads to and from where they are needed, and without them, any military operation would simply grind to a halt. Once again, these simple facts have been mentioned here before but a reminder seems necessary to put the contents of these pages into their true military perspective.

In addition to the vital role played by trucks in Somalia and the former Yugoslavia, mechanical handling equipment of all types has also played a valuable part as has the handling of POL (petrol, oil and lubricants) without which none of the relief operations would have been possible.

Armoured Support Vehicles

In the aftermath of the Gulf conflict, increased emphasis is being placed on armoured engineer vehicles, without which no mechanised force can operate today.

As usual, economic considerations in most western countries have meant that the development and fielding of not only armoured engineer vehicles, but also the equally important armoured vehicle launched bridge, have lagged many years behind that of the Main Battle Tank (MBT) with which they are tasked to operate on the highly mobile battlefield of today.

In the United Kingdom, the Centurion Armoured Vehicle Royal Engineer (AVRE) in now being supplemented by the Chieftain AVRE. But this does not have the cross-country mobility to operate with the current Challenger 1 (or the Challenger 2 when this comes into service) MBT, in fact in a few years' time, all the Chieftain gun tanks will be phased out of service with the British Army.

In the United States, there is a similar situation with the M728 Combat Engineer Vehicle being based on the chassis of the M60 MBT which has now been phased out of front line US Army service. A prototype of Combat Mobility Vehicle (CMV) is, however, under development by BMY Combat Systems. This is based on an M1 MBT chassis and would have the ability to keep up with the M1 series MBT in the forward areas.

There is a very good case for the development and fielding of key MBT support vehicles such as the armoured engineer vehicle, armoured vehicle launched bridge and armoured recovery vehicle at the same time as the MBT and using the same chassis and automotive components.

To its credit, the British Army did fund the development and production of the Challenger Armoured Repair and Recovery Vehicle to support the Challenger MBT. In France, the first production Leclerc MBT has been completed but

there was no funding to develop an armoured recovery vehicle until the UAE ordered 43 units in February 1993.

In the United States, the M1 MBT was fielded as far back as 1980, but still, 13 years later, an armoured recovery vehicle with the capability to recover the M1 family of MBTs has not been fielded, although development work has once again started on yet another improvement to the old M88 whose original design is now over 30 years old.

Anti-personnel Mines

The effects of the large numbers of anti-personnel mines on civilian populations in several parts of the globe have more than once attracted the attentions of organisations such as the International Committee of the Red Cross. This is a result of the sufferings inflicted on civilians who come into contact with what were intended to be weapons of war but have now become indiscriminate sources of danger for all. It is an unfortunate fact that there are significant areas of the globe strewn with anti-personnel mines, originally emplaced to damage an enemy but left to maim and kill innocents once fighting has ceased.

The point has been reached where organisations such as the International Committee of the Red Cross are campaigning to draw up some form of convention or understanding whereby anti-personnel mines will be outlawed as 'A Perverse Use of Technology'. The sheer numbers stockpiled and the ease of manufacture of anti-personnel mines would by themselves seem to mitigate against any success for the proposed convention but, given the right degree of international agreement and a properly drafted programme of implementation, it would seem possible to at least limit the haphazard dispensing of mines other than under accepted circumstances.

Trucks

A number of armies in the world have huge fleets of military vehicles which, for a variety of reasons, cannot be replaced on a regular basis. For this reason some countries, including the United States, have started plans to upgrade parts of their tactical fleet to extend their lives at a fraction of the cost of purchasing a new vehicle.

The modifications normally include the installation of a more fuel efficient engine, improved suspension, new brakes and electrics. New environmental controls mean than some military vehicles no longer meet government guidelines.

In recent years there has been a trend away from developing vehicles specifically for military use with the main emphasis being on developing military vehicles that, wherever possible, are based on standard commercial vehicles, or at least, use commercial components, for example engine, transmission and cab.

Although the Gulf conflict was well over two years ago, it has more recently become apparent that the logistic tail could not always keep up with the front line units. More recent armoured vehicles, such as the General Dynamics, Land Systems M1 Abrams, Giat Industries Leclerc, Krauss-Maffei Leopard 2 and Vickers Defence Systems Challenger 1 and 2 MBTs have a significant increase in cross-country mobility over the vehicles that they have replaced so making it even of greater importance to field logistic vehicles with an adequate cross-country mobility.

There is some indication that more serious consideration is being given to fielding 8 x 8 vehicles for use in the forward areas which would have the capability to keep forward elements supplied with ammunition, fuel and other supplies. The German Army has fielded a family of 8 x 8 MAN vehicles for some time while the United States Army has introduced the Oshkosh Heavy Expanded Mobility Tactical Truck (8 x 8) with a cross-country payload of around 10 tonnes.

Acknowledgements

One of the most pleasant aspects of completing another edition of this Yearbook is being able to thank the many persons and defence organisations who have contributed to its continuing success. The organisations are too many to list here but their names are scattered throughout the entries. The same applies to the many individuals who have given so much of their time and knowledge. Top of the list must come the corps of Jane's Yearbook Editors who, as ever, have contributed a great deal in the spheres of knowledge, information and guidance – once again our thanks are due to them all. More thanks are due to all our other friends who have contributed so much. There are so many of them that we cannot list them all but special thanks must be made to Mick Bell, Kensuke Ebata, Lyn Haywood, Arthur Hogben, Jim Loop, Pierre Touzin, Steve Zaloga and C R Zwart.

On the production side, it is still a constant source of amazement how the Jane's Data Division team manages to get through its workload and complete a yearbook as extensive and complex as this to such a high standard within the required time scale. To produce such a book takes not only hard work but a fair degree of tolerance, humour and self-discipline. All of these factors are well in evidence from the editorial and data input teams lead by Keith Faulkner and Ruth Simmance. Kathy Jones and Carol Horner have ensured that data input has been to their usual high standard and Kevin Borras has been a great help in the later stages of the updating cycle. They have all managed admirably, as always, but special mention must be made to Lynn Morse, our main contact point who has cheerfully been able to handle everything thrown at her.

Once again, we can complete this Edition by expressing our thanks and appreciation to our printers, Butler and Tanner.

Christopher F Foss   February 1993
Terry Gander

Special Notes

The Editors will welcome any extra information, corrections or comments regarding the entries contained in this Yearbook. Please direct all correspondence to the Editors at *Jane's Military Vehicles and Logistics,* Jane's Data Division, Sentinel House, 163 Brighton Road, Coulsdon, Surrey CR5 2NH, United Kingdom.

Please Note

Due to editorial deadlines the Czech Republic and Slovakian entries in this edition of *Jane's Military Vehicles and Logistics* will appear, as before, under the country heading of Czechoslovakia. In the 1994-95 edition the entries will appear under their relevant country heading, Czech Republic or Slovakia.

[18]

Glossary

AARADCOM	Army Armament Research and Development Command	**CKD**	Component knock-down	**FV**	Fighting vehicle
AAT	All arms trencher	**CLAMS**	Clear lane marking system	**FVRDE**	Fighting Vehicles Research and Development Establishment
AAV	Assault Amphibian Vehicle	**CLD**	Camion Lourd de Depannage		
AAVP	Assault Amphibian Vehicle Personnel	**CLEWP**	Cleared lane explosive widening path charge	**FVS**	Fighting vehicle system
				FWAM	Full width attack mine
AAVR	Assault Amphibian Vehicle Recovery	**CMV**	Counter mobility vehicle	**FWD**	Four-wheel drive
		CNIM	Constructions Navales et Industrielles de la Mediterranee	**FY**	Fiscal year
ABLE	Automotive Bridge Launching Equipment			**GCW**	Gross combination weight
		COCT	Cab-over cargo truck	**GEMSS**	Ground-emplaced mine-scattering system
ABS(T)	Amphibious bridging system (tracked)	**COE**	Cab over engine		
		COV	Counter obstacle vehicle	**GIAT**	Groupement Industriel des Armements Terrestres
ACE	Armored Combat Earthmover	**CP**	Command post		
ACPM	Anti Char a Pose Mecanique	**CRB**	Capsill roller beam	**GLCM**	Ground launched cruise missile
ACT	Airportable cargo trailer	**CRRC**	Combat rubber raiding craft	**GMC**	General Motors Corporation
ADAM	Area denial artillery munition	**CSB**	Combat support boat	**GPM**	Gallons per minute; Gepanzerte Pioniermaschine
ADS	Ammunition delivery system	**CSF**	Combined Service Forces		
AEC	Associated Equipment Company	**CST**	Combat support trailer	**GPMG**	General-purpose machine gun
AEV	Armoured engineer vehicle	**CTIS**	Central tyre inflation system	**grp**	Glass-reinforced plastic
AFARV	Armored forward area rearm vehicle	**CUCV**	Commercial utility cargo vehicle	**GV**	Giant Viper
		CVR(T)	Combat vehicle reconnaissannce (tracked)	**GVW**	Gross vehicle weight
AFDE	Arctic fuels dispensing equipment			**GW**	guided weapon
AFV	Armoured fighting vehicle	**DARPA**	Defense Advanced Research Projects Agency	**HAB**	Heavy assault bridge
Ah	Ampere hour			**HB**	Heavy barrel
AHE	Ammunition handling equipment	**dB**	Decibel	**HDRV**	Heavy duty recovery vehicle
AHM	Anti-helicopter mine	**DBP**	Draw bar pull	**HE**	High explosive
ALB	Automatic load-dependent brake	**DCAN**	Direction des Constructions et Arms Navales	**HEAT**	High explosive anti-tank
AM	Anti-material			**HELBAT**	Human Engineering Laboratory, Battalion Artillery Test
AMIDS	Airborne minefield detection system	**DCU**	Dispenser control unit		
		DEF.STAN	Defence Standard	**HEMAT**	Heavy Expanded Mobility Ammunition Trailer
AMS	Air management system	**DIN**	Deutsche Industrie Normen		
AMV	Armored Maintenance Vehicle	**DROPS**	Demountable rack off-loading and pickup system	**HEMTT**	Heavy expanded mobility tactical truck
AMX	Atelier de Construction d'Issy-les-Moulineaux				
		EBG	Engin Blinde de Genie (combat engineer tractor)	**HESH**	High explosive squash head
APC	Armoured personnel carrier			**HET**	Heavy equipment transporter
APFC	Airportable fuel container	**EEC**	European Economic Community	**HGV**	Heavy goods vehicle
APU	Auxiliary power unit	**EFP**	Explosively formed projectile	**HMD**	Helicopter mine dispenser
ARCE	Amphibious river crossing equipment	**EMI**	Electro-magnetic interference	**HMMHE**	High mobility materiel handling equipment
		EMP	Electro-magnetic pulse; Engineering mine plough		
ARE	Atelier de Construction Roanne			**HMMWV**	High-mobility multi-purpose wheeled vehicle
ARM	Artillery rearm module	**EMS**	Enhanced mobility system		
ARMS	Armoured Resupply Maintenance System	**EOD**	Explosive ordnance disposal	**HMRT**	Heavy material recovery team
		EPP	Electric power plant	**HMTT**	High mobility tactical truck
ARRV	Armoured recovery and repair vehicle	**EPU**	Electrical power unit	**hp**	Horse power
		ERAM	Extended range anti-armor munition	**HPD**	Haut pouvoir de destruction
ARV	Armoured recovery vehicle			**HTT**	Heavy tracked tractor
ASF	Army standard family (shelters)	**ERV**	Electronic repair vehicle	**HVSS**	Horizontal volute spring suspension
AT	Anti-tank	**ETAS**	Etablissement Technique d'Angers		
ATAC	All-terrain all climate; All-terrain amphibious carrier	**EWK**	Eisenwerke Kaiserslautern	**Hz**	Hertz
		EWT	Engineer wheeled tractor	**IFV**	Infantry fighting vehicle
ATGW	Anti-tank guided weapon			**IMMLC**	Improved medium mobility load class
ATIS	Anti-tank influence sensor	**FAALS**	Forward Area Armored Logistic System		
ATMDS	Anti-tank mine-dispensing system			**IMP**	Infantry mine project
ATMP	All-terrain mobile platform	**FAASV**	Field Artillery Ammunition Support Vehicle	**IMR**	Inzhenernaia Maschina Razgrazhdeniia
ATS	Atelier de Construction de Tarbes				
ATTD	Advanced technology test demonstrator	**FAC**	Forward air controller; fast attack craft	**IOC**	Initial operational capability
				IR	Infra-red
ATV	All-terrain vehicle	**FAE**	Fuel-air explosive	**IRR**	Infra-red radiation
AVLB	Armoured vehicle-launched bridge	**FAMV**	Forward area multi-purpose vehicle	**IRV**	Improved Recovery Vehicle
AVRE	Assault Vehicle Royal Engineers			**ISC**	Infantry section carrier
		FARE	Forward area refuelling equipment	**ISO**	International Standards Organisation
BAEE	British Army Equipment Exhibition	**FARV-A**	Fully integrated/armored rearm		
BAOR	British Army of the Rhine	**FASCAM**	Family of scatterable mines	**IVECO**	Industrial Vehicle Corporation
BARC	Beach amphibious resupply cargo	**FAST**	Forward area support team	**JATO**	Jet assisted take-off
BARV	Beach armoured recovery vehicle	**FAV**	Fast attack vehicle	**JGSDF**	Japanese Ground Self-Defence Force
BBE	Bridge boat erection	**FAWPSS**	Forward area water point supply system		
BEML	Bharat Earth Movers Limited			**JRA**	Jaguar Rover Australia
BFTA	Bulk fuel tank assembly	**FCS**	Fire control system	**JSFU**	Joint Services flail unit
bhp	Brake horse power	**FCS**	Field-expedient Mineclearing System	**JSOR**	Joint Service operation requirement
BLU	Bomb live unit				
BRE	Battlefield Recovery and Evacuation	**FDC**	Fire direction centre	**KERR**	Kinetic energy recovery rope
		FEBA	Forward edge of the battle area	**KHD**	Klockner-Humboldt-Deutz
CATFAE	Catapult-launched fuel-air explosive	**FFR**	Fitted for radio	**kT**	Kiloton
		FLPT	Fork lift pallet trailer		
CAU	Central alarm unit	**FMS**	Foreign military sales	**LAA**	Light anti-aircraft
CBU	Cluster bomb unit	**FMTV**	Family of Medium Tactical Vehicles	**LAAG**	Light anti-aircraft gun
CCE	Commercial construction equipment			**LAB**	Light assault bridge
		FN	Fabrique Nationale	**LACH**	Lightweight amphibious container handler
cd	Candela	**FNNH**	Fabrique Nationale Nouvelle Herstal		
CEE	Combat explacement excavator			**LAD**	Light aid detachment
CEP	Concept evaluation program	**FOCOS**	Foam overhead cover support system	**LAF**	Light assault ferry
CET	Combat engineer tractor			**LAPES**	Low altitude parachute extraction system
CFM	Crane, field, medium	**FOM**	Forces d'Outre Mer		
CFRP	Carbon fibre reinforced plastic	**FOPS**	Falling object protective structure	**LAR**	Light artillery rocket
CFV	Cavalry fighting vehicle	**FRG**	Federal Republic of Germany	**LARC**	Lighter amphibious resupply cargo
CIS	Chartered Industries of Singapore	**FSB**	Faltschwimmbrucke	**LAV**	Light armoured vehicle

SUPPORTING THE BEST.

For over forty years Land Rover have been proud to be associated with the British Armed Forces. It's a tradition we intend to continue into the twenty first century.

Our versatile family of four wheel drive vehicles have served in all conditions around the world, proving beyond doubt their reliability and ease of maintenance. Tailor-made for a wide variety of roles, from command and communication vehicles to ambulances, from surveillance vehicles to weapons platforms, we have the flexibility and advanced technology to provide vehicles to specifications that meet our customers' exact needs.

Total customer satisfaction is our priority. Throughout the long life of your Land Rover vehicle we'll always be there, with integrated logistic support, wherever you are in the world.

Land Rover supporting Britain's Armed Forces – to meet the challenges of the future and into the next century.

LAND-ROVER

Government & Military Operations, Land Rover, Lode Lane, Solihull, England B92 8NW
Telephone: 021-722 2424. Fax: 021-742 0450.

LAW	Light anti-armour weapon
LCD	Liquid crystal display
LCEE	Low cost emplacement excavator
LED	Light-emitting diode
LHD	Left-hand drive
LIMAS	Lightweight marking system
LMD	Light mobile digger
LMG	Light machine gun
LMTV	Light medium tactical vehicle
LMTVT	Light medium tactical vehicle trailer
LOTS	Logistics over shore
LPC	Launch pod container
LSI	Large-scale integrated
LSV	Logistic supply vehicle; Logistic support vehicle
LSVW	Light support vehicle wheeled
LVS	Logistic vehicle system
LVT	Landing vehicle tracked
LWB	Long wheelbase
MAB	Mobile assault bridge
MACI	Military adaption of commerical items; Mine anti-char indetectable
MACS	Magnetic Countermine System
MAF	Materiel amphibie de Franchissement
MARRS	Modular Armoured Repair and Recovery System
MARS	Military amphibious reconnaissance system
MAV	Maintenance assist vehicle
MBB	Messerschmitt-Bolkow-Blohm
MBT	Main battle tank
MDK	Mashina dorozhnoy kopatelnoy
MDR	Moyen de Deminage Rapide
MERADCOM	Mobility Equipment Research and Development Command
MEV	Medical evacuation vehicle
MEXE	Military Engineering Experimental Establishment
MG	Machine gun
MGB	Medium girder bridge
MHC	Materials handling crane
MIACAH	Mine antichar d'Action Horizontale
MICLIC	Mineclearing line charge
MICV	Mechanised infantry combat vehicle
MIL	Military
MIRADOR	Minefield Reconnaissance and Detector System
MiWS	Minenwerfersystem
MLC	Military load class
MLRS	Multiple launch rocket system
MLVW	Medium logisitic vehicle wheeled
MMLC	Medium mobility load carrier
MMW	Medium multi-purpose wheeled
MoD	Ministry of Defence
MOPMS	Modular pack mine system
MoT	Ministry of Transport
MRT	Mobile repair team
MRTFL	Medium rough terrain forklift
MRV	Maintenance-recovery vehicle
MSG	Minensuchgerat
MSM/W	Minenstreumittel-Werfer
MT	Megaton
MTT	Medium tactical truck
MTU	Motoren-und-Turbinen-Union
MTV	Medium tactical vehicle
MTVT	Medium tactical vehicle trailer
MVEE	Military Vehicles and Engineering Establishment
MVP	Motor vehicle plant
MWT	Medium wheeled tractor
NATO	North Atlantic Treaty Organisation
NBC	Nuclear, biological, chemical
NDI	Non-developmental item
OC & S	Ordnance Center and School
OFC	Overhead foxhole cover

OHC	Overhead cam shaft
OHV	Overhead valve
O & O	Operational and organisational
OP	Observation post
ORATMS	Off-route anti-tank mine system
Pa	Pascal
PAA	Pont Automoteur d'Accompagnement
PADS	Position attack defence system
PARM	Panzerabwehr-richtmine
PDM	Pursuit deterrent mine
PE	Plastic explosive
PETN	Pentaerythritetranitrate
pF	Picofarad
PFC	Parapet foxhole cover
PFM	Pont Flottant Motorisé
PFT	Prefabricated foxhole - twin
PI	Product improvement
PIP	Product improvement programme
PLS	Palletised loading system
POL	Petrol, oil and lubricants
POMINS	Portable mine neutralisation system
POP	Pipeline outfit, petroleum
PSA	Prefabricated surface, aluminium
psi	Pounds per square inch
PTO	Power take-off
pvc	Polyvinyl chloride
RAC	Royal Armoured Corps
RAAC	Royal Australian Armoured Corps
RAAMS	Remote anti-armor mine system
RAE	Royal Australian Engineers; Royal Aircraft Establishment
RAOC	Royal Army Ordnance Corps
RAP	Regimental aid post
RARDE	Royal Armament Research and Development Establishment
RARDE(C)	Royal Armament Research and Development Establishment (Christchurch)
RBEB	Ribbon bridge erection boat
RC/ATV	Remote-control, all-terrain vehicle
RCT	Royal Corps of Transport
R & D	Research and Development
RDJTF	Rapid Deployment Joint Task Force
RE	Royal Engineers
REME	Royal Electrical and Mechanical Engineers
RF	Radio frequency
RFI	Radio frequency interference
RFP	Request for proposals
RHD	Right-hand drive
RLT	Rolling liquid transporter
RMID	Road mine detector
ROMANS	Rapid operational minefield attack and neutralisation system
ROPS	Rollover protective structure
ROWPU	Reverse osmosis water purification unit
rpm	Revolutions per minute
RPV	Remotely piloted vehicle
RRR	Rapid runway repair
RSH	Reservoirs souples heliportable
RSME	Royal School of Military Engineering
RTFL	Rough terrain forklift
SAE	Society of Automotive Engineers
SAM	Surface-to-air missile
SAPLIC	Small arms projected line charge
SAS	Schnellbrucke auf Stutzen
SEE	Small emplacement excavator
SEV	Specially equipped vehicle
shp	Shaft horse power
SICPS	Standardised Integrated Command Post Shelter

SLEP	Service Life Extension Program
SLUFAE	Surface-launched unit, fuel-air explosive
SMS	Scatterable mine system
SPB	Section personnel bridge
SPG	Self-propelled gun
SRDE	Signals Research and Development Establishment
SS	Surface-to-surface
SSM	Surface-to-surface missile
STE/FVS	Simplified Test Equipment/ Fighting Vehicle System
STORM	Sensored tactical off-road mine
SUMB	Simca-Unic Marmon-Bocquet
SUMMADE	System universal modular mine and demolition explosives
SUSV	Small unit support vehicle
SUU	Suspended underwing unit
SWB	Short wheelbase
SWG	Standard wire gauge
TAB	Towed assault bridge
TACOM	Tank-Automotive Command
TAD	Trailing arm drive
TARADCOM	Tank-Automotive Research and Development Command
TD	Tank destroyer
TECOM	Test and Evaluation Command
TEG	Thermo electric generator
TEXS	Tactical explosive system
TFR	Tank ferry raft
TILOS	Tangram Integrated Logistic system
TLB	Trailer-launched bridge
TNT	Trinitrotoluene
TOC	Tactical operations centre
TRM	Toutes Roues Motrices
TROSS	Technical and rear operations support system
TRTG	Tactical radar threat generator
TU	Towed unit
TWDS	Tactical water distribution system
TWMP	Track width mine plough
TWVMP	Tactical Wheeled Vehicle Modernization Plan
UET	Universal engineer tractor
UK	United Kingdom
ULC	Unit load container
UMIDS	Universal mine-dispensing system
VAB	Vehicule de l'Avant Blinde; Vickers Armoured Bridgelayer
VCG	Vehicule de Combat du Genie
VCI	Vehicule de Combat d'Infanterie
VCR-AT	Vehicule de Combat a Roues - Atelier Technique
VEMASID	Vehicle magnetic signature duplicator
VLRA	Vehicule Leger de Reconnaissance et d'Appui
VLTT	Vehicule de Liaison tout Terrain
VMRMDS	Vehicle-mounted road mine detector system
vpm	Vibrations per minute
VRDE	Vehicle Research and Development Establishment
VRRTFL	Variable reach rough terrain forklift
VRRTFLT	Variable reach rough terrain forklift truck
V/STOL	Vertical/short take-off and landing
VTL	Vehicle tactical logistic
VVSS	Vertical volute spring suspension
WAM	Wide area mine
WASPM	Wide area side penetrating mine
WCP	Water carriage pack
ZF	Zahnradfabrik Friedrichshafen

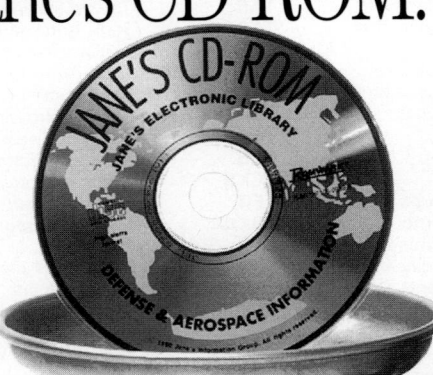

ARMOURED ENGINEER VEHICLES

ARMOURED ENGINEER VEHICLES

AUSTRIA

Steyr Engineer Tank 4KH7FA-AVE

Description

The Steyr Engineer Tank 4KH7FA-AVE is a further development of the Steyr 4KH7FA-B Greif ARV, described and illustrated in the *Armoured recovery vehicles* section. The Engineer Tank entered Austrian Army service in 1988 and is known as the Pionierpanzer 4KH7FA-Pi.

The hull is made of all-welded steel with the fully enclosed crew compartment at the front. Normal means of entry to the crew compartment is by two doors on the left side of the hull but there are additional hatches in the roof. The engine and transmission are at the rear of the hull. The engine compartment is fitted with a fire extinguishing system that can be operated manually or automatically. Over the engine decking is a stowage platform for equipment.

The torsion bar suspension consists of five dual rubber-tyred road wheels with the drive sprocket at the rear and the idler at the front. There are three track return rollers and hydraulic shock absorbers are fitted at the first and fifth road wheel stations.

Mounted on the right side of the superstructure at the front is a hydraulically operated excavation device

(ditcher), the boom of which can be traversed through 234°. Earth drilling equipment with a 350 mm diameter auger can be mounted in place of the bucket, as can a crane hook.

A winch is situated in the lower part of the hull and leads out through the front part of the hull. It is provided with 60 m of 16 mm diameter cable and has a maximum pulling capacity of 8000 kg.

A dozer blade is mounted on the front of the hull. This has a straight motion mechanism and no earth-transporting capability. It is 2.5 m wide when travelling (3 m when working) and 0.9 m high.

A full range of engineer equipment is carried, including cutting and welding equipment. The Engineer Tank does not have an NBC system but the crew compartment is provided with a ventilation and heating unit.

Specifications
Crew: 4
Weight: 22 300 kg
Length: 7.49 m
Width:
(chassis) 2.5 m
(dozer blade in transport position) 2.5 m
(dozer blade in working position) 3 m

Height:
(overall) 3.15 m
(top of hull) 2.3 m
Height transported: 2.8 m
Ground clearance: (loaded) 0.4 m
Track: 2.12 m
Track width: 380 mm
Length of track on ground: 3.037 m
Ground pressure: 0.82 kg/cm^2
Max speed: (road) 65.3 km/h
Range: (road) 600 km
Fuel capacity: 500 l
Fording: 1 m
Gradient: 70%
Side slope: 40%
Trench: 2.1 m
Turning radius: 8 m
Engine: Steyr 7FA 6-cylinder water-cooled 4-stroke turbocharged diesel developing 320 hp at 2400 rpm
Transmission: ZF type 6HP500 with 6 forward and 1 reverse gears
Electrical system: 24 V
Batteries: 2 × 12 V, 180 Ah
Armament:
1 × 12.7 mm M2 HB MG
4 smoke dischargers

Engineer equipment
Crane winch
Winch pull: (1st gear/2nd gear) 80 kN/6.5 kN
Effective cable length: 57 m
Cable diameter: 16 mm

Ditcher
Digging depth: 2.2 m
Dumping height: 4.5 m
Radius of operation: 6.3 m
Area of swivel: 234°

Ground auger
Max torque: 2.17 kNm
Max speed: 125 rpm
Boring diameter: 350 mm

Status
Production as required. In service with Austria (18).

Manufacturer
Steyr-Daimler-Puch Spezialfahrzeug AG, Postfach 100, A-1111 Vienna, Austria.
Tel: 222/76 45 11. Telex: 61 322 1299.
Fax: 222/76 81 49.

Steyr Engineer Tank 4KH7FA-AVE

CANADA

M113 Engineering Specially Equipped Vehicle

Description
The M113 armoured personnel carrier can be converted for basic combat engineering tasks by the addition of a bulldozer blade to the front hull. To increase the combat engineering capabilities of the basic M113 and M113A1 the Diesel Division of General Motors of Canada produced an 'upgrade' kit, known as a specially equipped vehicle (SEV) kit, with five major features. These are an improved interior layout for personnel, supplies, tools and equipment; external fuel tanks; a hydraulic earth auger; a hydraulic-powered tool system; and a ramp restraining device.

The revised interior layout provides space for eight troops plus engineer section stores, combat supplies, NBC protective equipment and weapons. The communications equipment is repositioned to provide easier access for the driver and commander. There are folding seats for the troops. The external fuel tanks are

M113 armoured personnel carrier with engineering SEV kit incorporated

at the rear and have a combined capacity of 360 l. The tanks replace the counter-weights on each side of the rear ramp. The Simcoe hydraulic earth auger is on the

left-hand side of the vehicle, mounted on the roof. It can be set up, operated and stowed by two men in a few minutes and can be used to drill a 203 mm hole in earth, asphalt and frozen ground. Holes up to 3.048 m can be dug with the auger rotating at a speed of 75 rpm. Hydraulic power at a pressure of 138 bars is provided and the same power source is used to power the hydraulic tool system located on the right-hand rear of the vehicle. This has power tools on the end of a 15.24 m twin pressure hose which is normally stowed on a reel. Tools include a chain saw, jack hammer and an impact wrench that can also be used for wood boring. The ramp restraining system is on the rear ramp and allows the ramp to be used either as a working platform or a load-carrying area for weights up to 500 kg.

Status
In service with the Canadian Armed Forces. At the end of 1988 production was complete with a total of 55 vehicles, plus 15 conversion kits. These were delivered to Canadian units stationed in Germany.

Manufacturer
Diesel Division, General Motors of Canada Limited, PO Box 5160, London, Ontario, Canada N6A 4N5. Tel: (519) 452 5184. Fax: (519) 452 5688.

COMMONWEALTH OF INDEPENDENT STATES

Combat Engineer Vehicle based on T-72 (IMR-2)

Description
A Combat Engineer Vehicle (IMR) based on the T-72 MBT chassis has been developed and is understood to be known as the IMR-2. A photograph shows the vehicle to be equipped with a front-mounted dozer blade that can be used in a V-configuration or as a straight dozer blade, and a hydraulic crane. The crane can be fitted with a number of attachments including pincers that can be used to uproot trees.

Status
In service with the CIS.

Manufacturer
State factories.

Combat Engineer Vehicle (IMR-2) based on chassis of T-72 MBT (Jane's Intelligence Review)

BAT-2 Combat Engineer Vehicle

Description
The BAT-2 (*Bul'dozer na Artilleriyskom Tygache 2*) combat engineer vehicle is intended to supplement the BAT-M high speed tractor-mounted bulldozers and similar vehicles (see entry in *Field fortifications and related emplacements equipment* section) but is more readily described as a combat engineer vehicle. In addition to the large dozer blade normally fitted, the BAT-2 has carrying capacity for combat engineer stores behind the forward control cab and also has a crane mounted at the rear of the cab to handle them. The crane can be fitted with pincer-type grabs for clearing obstacles, has a maximum boom outreach of 7.3 m and a load-lifting capacity of 2000 kg. Mounted on the same platform as the crane is a 20 t capacity winch. The armoured cab has seating for the two-man crew and a compartment for an eight-man combat engineer squad.

The BAT-2 is based on the chassis of the MT-T tracked carrier (see entry in *Tracked prime movers* section) which uses suspension and running gear components from the T-64 tank and is powered by a V-64-4 V-12 diesel engine developing 510 hp. Some transmission components are also 'taken from a tank'. Combat weight of the vehicle is 30 000 kg and maximum speed 60 km/h. Length overall is approximately 8.8 m and width overall 3.2 m.

The BAT-2 has the large dozer blade of the earlier vehicles mounted at the front but the hydraulic cylinder actuation system appears to be more powerful and uses a different operating layout. There is also a different system to raise the blade vertically when not in use. The blade has a soil moving capacity of from 300 to 400 m³/h.

Status
In service with the CIS and probably other former Warsaw Pact forces.

Manufacturer
State factories.

BAT-2 combat engineer vehicle in travelling configuration

IRM Engineer Reconnaissance Vehicle

Description
The IRM engineer reconnaissance vehicle (IRM – *Inzhenernaya rezvedivatel 'naya maschina*) was originally known in the West as the IPR amphibious engineer vehicle. It is based on components from the BMP-1 MICV tracked chassis (for details refer to *Jane's Armour and Artillery 1992-93* pages 316 to 321). The IRM is intended for engineer and other reconnaissance over a wide variety of terrain and climatic conditions. It can be carried to its zone of operations by cargo aircraft, assault ships or hovercraft.

The IRM is based on automotive components of the BMP-1 MICV but uses a longer hull with an extra road wheel, making seven road wheels each side; and the engine is located at the rear. There are also five track return rollers. The vehicle is fully amphibious and, when travelling, the hull superstructure may carry a folded-down snorkel mast approximately 10 m long which is erected when the vehicle operates fully submerged; this mast is not always carried. When floating the vehicle is driven and steered by two three-bladed cowled propellers. A trim vane is fitted to the bow.

The crew consists of three or four men, the commander, driver and one or two 'reconnaissance engineers'. The driver and commander are seated towards the

Model of IRM with all equipment stowed

Model of IRM with all equipment stowed

front of the hull and provided with circular hatches; more hatches are provided for the engineers. There is an emergency escape hatch under the hull. The commander is also provided with a small turret at the front of the hull which mounts day and night vision devices and a 7.62 mm PKT machine gun; an infra-red searchlight is mounted next to the machine gun. The only other armament consists of the crew's personal weapons, although a smoke generating apparatus is provided. For closed-down observation the driver is provided with a TNPO-160 observation device for land use; this is changed to a TNP-370 for use when in water. The crew compartment is NBC sealed and supplied with a fire retardant system. The suspension can be locked to withstand blast effects such as those produced by a nuclear explosion. Further crew protection is provided by a radiation detection system that automatically provides a signal when radiation is present outside the hull.

For the reconnaissance role the IRM is provided with a variety of specialised equipment such as an inertial navigation system, a mine detection system, an auger-type sensor for determining the load-bearing capacities of various types of terrain (described as a 'penetrometer' and probably coupled to an onboard computer), an echo sounder, an artificial horizon mounted on the

driver's control panel, a clinometer to measure beach and other terrain angles for the driver, and seven day plus two night vision devices. Also carried are a PIR retractable periscope 1.5 m long (of which 0.75 m can be raised) and a DSP-30 rangefinder to carry out basic survey operations from within the vehicle. Portable equipment carried for use outside the vehicle includes hand-held mine detectors, a device (*ledobur*) for measuring the thickness of ice, and a portable terrain load-bearing measuring instrument.

Mounted at the front of the vehicle, in line with the tracks, are two hydraulically operated arms carrying spade-like units which are mine detectors using the induction principle. The detector units are held parallel to the ground surface by a hydraulic terrain-following mechanism mounted on the arms. If the detector senses a mine the vehicle will stop automatically for the mine to be cleared manually. The vehicle will also stop automatically if the detector strikes an obstacle such as an immovable tree or rock. When not in use the detector arms are folded back onto the roof and sides of the vehicle.

Specifications (provisional)
Crew: 4
Weight: 17 000 kg

Length: 8.2 m
Width: 3.1 m
Height: 2.4 m
Max speed:
(land) 52 km/h
(water) 11 km/h
Range: 500 km
Fuel capacity: 600 l
Endurance afloat: 12 h
Fording: amphibious
Trench: 2.7 m
Engine: Type UTD-20 6-cylinder in-line water-cooled diesel developing 300 hp at 2000 rpm
Transmission: manual, 5 forward and 1 reverse gears
Steering: clutch and brake
Suspension: torsion bar
Electrical system: 24 V
Armament:
1 × 7.62 mm PKT MG
smoke generator

Status
In service with the CIS.

Manufacturer
State factories.

Combat Engineer Vehicle (IMR)

Description
The Combat Engineer Vehicle IMR (*Inzhenernaia Maschina Razgrazhdeniia* – engineer vehicle for the removal of obstacles) was first seen in 1973 and is based on the T-55 MBT chassis. The turret was removed and replaced by a hydraulically operated crane which can be traversed through 360°. The jib of this crane is telescopic and when in the travelling position rests on a cradle at the rear of the hull. The cradle folds down against the engine deck when the crane is being used. The crane is provided with a pair of pincer-type grabs which are used to remove trees and other obstacles. The grab can be replaced by a small bucket which is normally carried above the left rear track when not required. The crane operator is provided with an armoured cupola which has observation windows. A searchlight is mounted on the crane for night operations. At the front of the hull is a hydraulically operated dozer blade which can be used in the straight or V-configuration, but cannot angle doze. An unditching beam is carried at the rear of the hull.

Variant
IWT
The IWT (*inzynieryjny woz torujacy*) is the Polish equivalent of the IMR and shares many of the same features. However the IWT carries a mineclearing rocket system similar to that carried by Polish Army T-55 MBTs (see entry in *Mineclearing equipment* section).

Specifications (provisional)
Crew: 2
Weight: 34 000 kg
Length:
(dozer blade in operating position and crane stowed) 10.6 m
(hull) 6.45 m

Combat engineer vehicle (IMR) stowed for rail transport

Width:
(hull) 3.28 m
(over dozer blade) 3.48 m
Height:
(crane operator's cupola) 2.48 m
(crane in travelling position) 3.37 m
Ground clearance: 0.425 m
Track: 2.64 m
Track width: 580 mm
Length of track on ground: 3.84 m

Ground pressure: 0.76 kg/cm^2
Max speed: (road) 48 km/h
Range: 400 km
Fuel capacity: 812 l
Fording: 1.4 m
Gradient: 60%
Vertical obstacle: 0.8 m
Trench: 2.7 m
Engine: Model V-55 V-12 water-cooled diesel developing 580 hp at 2000 rpm

Transmission: manual with 5 forward and 1 reverse gears
Electrical system: 24 V
Batteries: 4 × 12 V, 280 Ah
Armament: nil

Armour
hull front: 100 mm at 60°

hull sides: 70 mm
hull rear: 60 mm
hull floor: 20 mm
hull roof: 30 mm

Status
In service with the CIS, other members of the former Warsaw Pact and the former Yugoslav Army.

Manufacturer
State factories.

MT-LB Engineer Vehicle

Description
The MT-LB Engineer Vehicle is a variant of the MT-LB multi-purpose tracked vehicle (for full details of this vehicle refer to *Jane's Armour and Artillery 1992-93* pages 327 to 330).

The MT-LB engineer vehicle is similar in appearance to the basic MT-LB but modified to carry a plough blade on the hull roof. This blade is manually fitted to two hydraulic arm assemblies on the hull rear to allow plough blade operations to the rear only. Other combat engineer equipment is carried internally.

The US Army has a number of these vehicles for training purposes. They are based at Fort Irwin, California.

The former East German Army used the MT-LB for combat engineer purposes but their version lacked the plough blade. A rectangular box on the rear upper hull carried engineer equipment.

Status
In service with the CIS and some other countries, including Iraq.

Manufacturer
State factories.

MT-LB engineer vehicle with plough blade raised (Donald C Spaulding)

Tank-mounted Bulldozers BTU and BTU-55

Description
The BTU and BTU-55 tank-mounted bulldozers can both be fitted to either the T-54 or T-55 series of MBTs. The BTU-55 is the more recent version and is an improvement in all aspects. There does not appear to be a bulldozer for the T-62, but the T-64 and T-72 MBTs can each incorporate a form of dozer blade for self-emplacement.

Specifications

Model	BTU	BTU-55
Weight	2300 kg	1400 kg
Width	3.4 m	3.8 m
Clearing speed	1.5-5 km/h	5-7 km/h
(in snow)	4-6 km/h	4-6 km/h
Digging performance	100-200 m³/h	130-250 m³/h
Pushing performance	350 m³/h	—
Mounting time	80-90 mins	60 mins
Dismounting time	30-60 mins	45 mins

Status
Production probably complete. In widespread service.

Manufacturer
State factories.

FRANCE

AMX-13 Engineer Combat Vehicle

Development
The AMX-13 Engineer Combat Vehicle or *Véhicule de Combat du Génie* (VCG) is based on the chassis and hull of the AMX VCI MICV, which in turn is a development of the AMX-13 light tank chassis. The first prototype of the VCG was completed in 1961 and was simply an AMX VCI fitted with a hydraulically operated dozer blade at the front of the hull and was limited to clearing operations. This was followed by a second prototype in 1964 and, after troop trials, series production began in 1969. The vehicle was designed to undertake a wide variety of roles including clearing battlefield obstructions and preparing fire positions. A diesel-engined version is available.

Description
The hull of the VCG is of all-welded steel construction. The driver is seated at the front of the hull on the left side, with a single-piece hatch cover and three periscopes for observation. The engine is mounted on the driver's right, and the commander and gunner are behind him. The armament consists of a standard 7.62 or 12.7 mm machine gun which can be traversed through a full 360°, and can be aimed and fired from

within the vehicle. A white light searchlight is mounted to the right of the machine gun. To the right of the gunner's position is another hatch, with four periscopes mounted to the front and right. The other six members of the crew are seated in the rear of the vehicle and enter and leave by two doors, each with a single firing port, in the rear of the hull. On each side of the personnel compartment are two sets of hatches. Each hatch has an upper part which folds back onto the roof and a lower part which has two firing ports and folds down horizontally.

The suspension of the VCG is of the torsion bar type. There are five road wheels with the drive sprocket at the front and the idler at the rear, and four track return rollers. Shock absorbers are provided on the first and fifth road wheel stations. The manual gearbox has five forward gears (second, third, fourth and fifth have synchromesh) and one reverse gear, and steering is through a Cleveland-type differential.

The VCG is provided with an NBC system and infrared driving lights are standard. It is airportable in the Transall C-160 transport aircraft.

At the front of the vehicle is a hydraulically operated dozer blade 2.85 m wide and 0.7 m high, operated by the driver, which can clear 45 m³/h of soil.

The sheer legs are mounted one each side of the hull and pivoted at the front; when not in use they lie

horizontally along the hull. When assembled, they can lift a maximum of 4500 kg. The winch is also hydraulically operated and the drum is mounted externally on the front of the superstructure, and is provided with 40 m of cable.

Other equipment carried includes eight rifles, two sub-machine guns, one rocket launcher and six projectiles, one metallic mine detector, one non-metallic mine detector, one electric drill, one hammer drill, power saw and demolition equipment. An external electric socket is provided to operate the electric tools carried. The VCG can also tow a four-wheeled trailer which carries additional equipment and weighs 2500 kg unladen. The trailer can be detached from the VCG without the crew leaving the vehicle.

Specifications
Crew: 9 (commander, driver and 7 men)
Weight combat: 17 600 kg
Length:
(dozer blade in travelling position) 6.05 m
(over tracks) 5.364 m
Width:
(overall) 2.995 m
(over tracks) 2.51 m
Height:
(sheer legs in working position) 3.66 m

Véhicule de Combat du Génie with A-frame carrying fascine (ECP Armées)

(sheer legs on tripod) 3.46 m
(sheer legs disassembled and stowed) 2.41 m
Ground clearance: 0.38 m
Track: 2.16 m
Track width: 350 mm
Length of track on ground: 3.012 m
Ground pressure: 0.845 kg/cm²
Max speed: (road, petrol engine) 60 km/h

(road, diesel engine) 65 km/h
Range: (road, petrol engine) 350 km
(road, diesel engine) 500 km
Fuel capacity: 410 l
Fording: 1 m
Gradient: 60%
Vertical obstacle:
(forward) 0.65 m

(reverse) 0.45 m
Trench: (straight sides) 1.6 m
Engine: SOFAM Model 8 GXb, 8-cylinder, water-cooled petrol developing 250 hp at 3200 rpm or GM Detroit Diesel developing 280 hp
Transmission: manual with 5 forward and 1 reverse gears
Electrical system: 24 V
Batteries: 4 × 12 V, 95 Ah
Generator: 4.5 kW
Armament:
1 × 0.50/12.7 mm MG
3 smoke dischargers

Armour
Crew compartment front: 30 mm
Crew compartment side: 20 mm
Crew compartment roof: 15 mm
Hull rear: 15 mm
Hull glacis: 15 mm
Floor forward: 20 mm
Floor rear: 10 mm

Status
In service with the French Army. Production as required.

Manufacturer
Creusot-Loire Industrie, Division Mécanique Spécial-isée, Immeuble Ile de France, Cedex 33, F-92070 Paris La Défense, France.
Tel: (1) 49 00 60 50. Telex: MOTOY 615 638 F. Fax: (1) 49 00 58 99.

AMX-30 Combat Engineer Tractor (EBG)

Development
The AMX-30 *Engin Blindé du Génie* (EBG) was developed by Giat to meet the requirements of the French Engineers and the prototype was shown for the first time in 1981. The EBG entered production during 1987 with the first of a batch of 20 units being completed by the end of that year. A further 16 vehicles were funded in 1989. By September 1991 40 vehicles had been produced. The French Army has a total requirement for 126 EBGs.

Description
The chassis of the EBG is almost identical to that of the AMX-30D ARV described in the following section but uses automotive components of the later AMX-30 B2 MBT including the engine, transmission, torque con-verter and suspension. The three-man crew consists of the vehicle commander, sapper and driver.

Mounted at the front of the hull is a hydraulically operated dozer blade with a capacity of 250 m³/h for transport and filling, or 120 m³/h for excavating. Mounted at the back of the lower part of the dozer blade are six scarifying teeth, these being used for ripping up the surface of roads to a depth of 200 mm when the vehicle is being driven in reverse. The dozer blade is 3.5 m wide when fully extended and 1.1 m high.

The hydraulic winch has a capacity of 20 000 kg, is provided with 80 m of cable and has a winching speed of 0.2 to 0.35 m/s irrespective of traction force. Automatic winding speed is from 0.2 to 1.4 m/s with traction capability interlocked with the speed of the vehicle. The winch, which leads out through the front of the vehicle, can be used during amphibious opera-tions.

Pivoted at the front of the hull on the right side is a hydraulic arm with a maximum lifting torque of 15 000 kg/m; the double-jointed arm can be extended to 7.5 m and traversed through a full 360°. The arm is provided with a lifting hook and pincer-type grab similar to that fitted to the CIS IMR engineer vehicle described elsewhere in this section. The arm can also be fitted with an auger which can drill 220 mm diameter holes in the ground to a depth of 3 m. A 220 mm cutting saw is carried and a 50 kW hydraulic PTO is provided as standard.

Mounted in the centre of the hull, slightly offset to the right, is a two-tier turret. The upper part has a single-piece hatch cover that opens to the rear and is fitted with a 7.62 mm machine gun. To the rear of the turret on either side are two electrically operated smoke dischargers.

Mounted on the forward part of the lower tier is a launching tube for demolition charges and either side of this are two mine launching tubes, each of which has a launching container of five mines.

The 142 mm calibre demolition charge is 800 mm long, weighs 17 kg and contains 10 kg of explosive. The charge is fin-stabilised and fitted with a nose-mounted point detonating fuze; range is between 30 and 300 m.

The mines are 139 mm in diameter, weigh 2.34 kg and contain 0.7 kg of explosive. The launcher dis-charges the mines to a distance of between 60 and 250 m and the mines are then triggered by any vehicle weighing over 1500 kg. According to Giat, the mines will penetrate a tank floor equivalent to 50 mm of armour plate at 500 mm stand-off distance and 60° incidence, or break up a tank's track if the mine is run over. The mines self-destruct after a preset time.

Standard equipment on the EBG includes provision for deep fording with the aid of a snorkel, passive night periscope for the driver, NBC system and a rangefinder telescope for the sapper.

Specifications
Crew: 3
Weight combat: 40 000 kg

AMX-30 combat engineer tractor (EBG)

Length: (dozer blade up) 7.9 m
Width:
(overall) 3.5 m
(without dozer blade extensions) 3.1 m
Height: (overall) 3 m
Ground clearance: 0.45 m
Track: 2.52 m
Track width: 570 mm
Length of track on ground: 4.12 m
Ground pressure: 0.9 kg/cm²
Max speed: (road) 65 km/h
Fording:
(without preparation) 2.5 m
(with preparation) 4 m

Gradient: 60%
Side slope: 30%
Vertical obstacle: 0.9 m
Trench: 2.9 m
Engine: Hispano-Suiza HS 110-2 12-cylinder, water-cooled supercharged multi-fuel developing 700 hp at 2000 rpm, or HS 110-S2 developing 800 hp
Transmission: 5 SD with 5 gears in both directions, or ENC 200 gearbox with lock-up torque converter with 5 forward and 1 reverse gears
Electrical system: 24 V
Armament:
1 × 7.62 mm MG
2 × 2 smoke dischargers

1 × 142 mm demolition charge projector
4 × mine projectors
Ammunition:
(MG) 4000 rounds
(demolition charges) 5
(mines) 40 (8 containers each holding 5)

Status
In production for the French Army.

Manufacturer
Enquiries to Giat Industries, 13 route de la Minière, F-78034 Versailles Cedex, France.
Tel: (1) 30 97 37 37. Fax: (1) 30 97 39 00.

GERMANY

Pionierpanzer 2 Dachs Armoured Engineer Vehicle

Description

Krupp MaK Maschinenbau GmbH, now MaK System Gesellschaft mbH, developed and produced three prototypes of the Pionierpanzer 2 Dachs (Badger) armoured engineer vehicle. A contract award for the conversion of a mix of Leopard ARVs and AEVs was awarded during the early part of 1987 for delivery by December 1990. The conversion price was DM1.3 million per unit. A further nine vehicles, known as the Badger, were produced for the Canadian Armed Forces using new chassis and hulls. The Canadian contract was worth DM49 million and was completed in 1990.

For the German conversion programme MaK stripped down the original vehicles, repaired them where necessary, fitted the dozer blade assembly and hydraulic system and completed the final assembly. Jung Jungenthal GmbH was responsible for hull modifications, Eisenwerke Kaiserslautern for the dredger bucket and traversing turntable, and Wieger Maschinenbau for the telescopic arm assemblies.

The Pionierpanzer 2 is based on the hull, running gear and suspension of the Leopard AEV (see following entry) and the Leopard ARV (see entry under Armoured recovery vehicles). The vehicles have an armoured superstructure situated towards the left-hand side of the vehicle with a telescopic excavator arm located on the right with the traversing turntable situated forward. A straight dozer blade is mounted on the front of the vehicle.

The driver is seated at the front of the superstructure under a hatch cover. He is provided with a number of periscopes and night driving aids and he operates the dozer blade. Behind him is seated the commander with his own cupola and all-round vision periscopes. Periscopes provided for the commander and driver can be tilted. The cupola has provision for mounting a 7.62 mm machine gun. The commander operates the telescopic

excavator arm. There is a third crew member seated within the superstructure.

The telescopic excavator arm is hydraulically operated by a 300 bar system and is electrically controlled. It can be used in a variety of ways and can be elevated or depressed to an angle of ±60°. Its horizontal arc of operation is 196.5°. The bucket on the end of the arm has a capacity of 1.1 m³ and the arm can be extended to a maximum length of 8.3 m. It has an earth working capacity of 140 m³/h. The arm can also be used as a crane jib. If required the excavator arm can be controlled from a remote dismounted position.

The dozer blade has a maximum width of 3.75 m with side extensions fitted and has two scarifiers to rip up road surfaces. Maximum operating speed with the dozer blade in use is 8 km/h and the blade can shift up to 270 m³/h of spoil.

The Pionierpanzer 2 is equipped with a front-mounted hydraulic winch that can be used for self-recovery or the recovery of other vehicles, in which case the dozer blade can be lowered to improve operating stability. The winch, which is sealed, has a cable tensioning system, is supplied with 90 m of 33 mm cable and has a straight pull capacity of 20 000 kg. This can be increased to 35 000 kg by multi-reeving the cable. The vehicle can be used to tow disabled vehicles. Canadian Badger vehicles are fitted with a 35 000 kg capstan winch.

By using a deep wading kit which includes a snorkel tower, the vehicle can be used to prepare underwater approach routes or clear obstacles at depths of up to 4 m. Additional bilge pumps are provided for underwater operations.

Specialist equipment carried on the vehicle includes cutting and welding equipment powered by an integral 50 V generator.

Specifications

Crew: 3
Weight:
(empty) 42 500 kg
(loaded) 43 000 kg

Ground pressure: (combat weight) 0.92 kg/cm²
Length:
(travelling, roads) 8.925 m
(travelling, cross-country) 9.01 m
Width: 3.25 m
Width, dozer blade extended: 3.75 m
Height: (to top of MG mount) 2.57 m
Ground clearance: 0.44 m
Track: 2.7 m
Track width: 550 mm
Length of track on ground: 4.236 m
Ground pressure: 0.92 kg/cm²
Max speed: (road) 62 km/h
Range: approx 650 km
Fuel capacity: 1410 l
Fording:
(normal) 1.2 m
(with preparation) 4 m
Gradient: 50%
Side slope: 30%
Vertical obstacle: 0.9 m
Trench: 2.5 m
Engine: MTU MB 838 Ca M-500 37.4 l V-10 multi-fuel developing 830 hp at 2200 rpm
Transmission: ZF 4 HP 250 planetary-gear shift with hydraulic torque converter, 4 forward and 2 reverse gears
Steering: regenerative double differential
Electrical system: 24 V
Batteries: 6 × 12 V, 300 Ah
Armament:
1 × 7.62 mm MG
6 × smoke dischargers
Dozing capacity: 270 m³/h
Excavating capacity: 140 m³/h
Excavator pull force: 125 kN
Excavator push force: 85 kN
Towing force main winch: 350 kN
Scarifying depth: 0.45 m
Dozing and scarifying speed: 8 km/h (max)
Traverse, excavator arm: 195°
Tilt angle, telescopic arm: ±60°

German Army Pionierpanzer 2 Dachs armoured combat engineer vehicle with snorkel tower fitted preparing river crossing point

Canadian Armed Forces Badger armoured combat engineer vehicle using its telescopic excavator arm

Status
In service with Canada (9) and Germany (137).

Manufacturer
MaK System Gesellschaft mbH, Falckensteiner

Strasse 2, PO Box 9333, D-2300 Kiel 17, Federal
Republic of Germany.
Tel: 431 3995-02. Fax: 431 3995 446.

Leopard Armoured Engineer Vehicle

Development

The Leopard Armoured Engineer Vehicle is a direct
development of the Leopard ARV and differs from it
only in minor details. The first prototype, based on a
design by Dr Ing hc P Porsche KG, was completed by
MaK of Kiel in 1967, with the first production vehicles
completed in 1968. Wherever possible standard
Leopard MBT components were used, for example the
engine, transmission and suspension.

Thirty-three Leopard Armoured Engineer Vehicles
have been converted to Pionierpanzer 2 armoured
engineer vehicles (see previous entry).

Description

The hull is of all-welded construction with the crew
compartment at the front and the engine and transmission at the rear. The driver is seated at the front of the
vehicle to the left of the crane and is provided with a
single-piece hatch cover and three periscopes for
observation, one of which can be replaced by an infra-
red periscope. The commander is seated to the rear of
the driver and has a single-piece hatch cover and eight
periscopes, one of which can be replaced by an infra-
red periscope. There is another hatch to the rear of the
commander's position, and three periscopes provide
vision to the rear of the vehicle. There is a swivelling
periscope in the roof of the superstructure. The crew of
four (commander, driver and two mechanics) can enter
the vehicle either through the roof hatches or through
two doors in the left side of the hull. The suspension is
of the torsion bar type and consists of seven road
wheels with the drive sprocket at the rear and the idler
at the front. There are four track return rollers. The first,
second, third, sixth and seventh road wheel stations
are fitted with hydraulic shock absorbers. The tracks
are of the double-pin type and have rubber pads.

The AEV can carry out similar roles to the ARV
including recovering disabled vehicles and changing
vehicle components (although an auger is carried in
place of the spare engine carried on the ARV).

The dozer blade is mounted at the front of the hull
and operated by two hydraulic cylinders through two
lever arms, and is mechanically locked when not in
use. The dozer blade has a maximum capacity of
200 m³/h and the width of the blade can be extended to
3.75 m by additional side attachments. It can be fitted
with four scarifiers to rip up the surface of roads. The
installation of a heat exchanger enables the vehicle to
perform unlimited bulldozing activities even at high
ambient temperatures. In addition to being used for
dozing operations, the dozer blade is also used to
stabilise the AEV when the crane is in use or when
vehicles are being recovered.

The main winch with its horizontal cable drum is in
the centre of the crew compartment under the floor.
This winch is provided with a total of 90 m of 33 mm
cable. The maximum tractive effort of the main winch in
the lowest cable position is 35 000 kg, which can be
increased to 70 000 kg when using an appropriately
located guide pulley. The exit opening for the main
winch is located at the nose of the vehicle. A
hydraulically driven cable tensioning device is located
immediately behind the opening and automatically
extends or rewinds the cable.

The crane is mounted at the front of the hull on the
right side and when in the travelling position lies
horizontally along the right side of the hull. It has a
maximum lifting capacity of 20 000 kg when used with
the dozer blade as a stabiliser. A scale on the side

Leopard armoured engineer vehicle

plate of the jib shows the allowed load: if it is exceeded
the jib is stopped automatically. The two hydraulic
cylinders for lifting the jib are arranged so that they are
fully splinterproof in the travelling position and extensively splinterproof in the operating position. The jib is
turned by the traversing gearbox directly underneath
the console of the crane. If the hydraulics fail the
traversing gear can be operated by hand. The ladder
mounted on the jib assists in the assembly of the earth
drilling equipment and can also be used for other work
such as overhead lines. The auger is mounted when
required at the end of the jib crane and can drill holes
700 mm in diameter to a maximum depth of 2 m. The
hydraulic oil is supplied to the radial piston motor of the
earth drill through hoses which can be connected to the
jib boom by means of quick-disconnect couplings.

The hoisting winch with a vertical cable drum is
mounted on the right side of the crew compartment. It
is provided with 100 m of 13 mm diameter cable.

Equipment carried on the AEV includes a set of
shackles, tow bar, electric impact wrench, guide pull,
and electric welding and cutting equipment. For demolition work a total of 117 kg of explosives is carried.

Armament consists of a 7.62 mm MG3 machine gun
mounted in the bow of the tank on the left side; this has
an elevation of +15°, a depression of −15°, and a
traverse of 15° left and right. A similar machine gun is
mounted on the commander's hatch for anti-aircraft
defence. Six smoke dischargers are mounted on the
left side of the hull.

The AEV is also provided with an NBC system, crew
heater, fire warning and extinguishing system and a
hull escape hatch. The basic model can ford to a depth
of 2.1 m, but for deep fording operations a snorkel can
be quickly installed.

Specifications

Crew: 4
Weight:
(empty) 40 200 kg
(loaded) 40 800 kg
Length: (with dozer blade raised) 7.98 m
Width:
(with side elements of blade fitted) 3.75 m

(hull) 3.25 m
Height: (with AA MG) 2.69 m
Ground clearance: 0.44 m
Track: 2.7 m
Track width: 550 mm
Length of track on ground: 4.236 m
Ground pressure: 0.86 kg/cm²
Max speed: (road) 65 km/h
Range:
(road) 850 km
(cross-country) 500 km
Fuel capacity: 1410 l
Fording: 2.1 m
(with snorkel) 4 m
Gradient: 60%
Side slope: 30%
Vertical obstacle: 1.15 m
Trench: 3 m
Engine: MTU MB 838 Ca M-500 10-cylinder multi-fuel
developing 830 hp at 2200 rpm
Transmission: ZF 4 HP 250 with 4 forward and
2 reverse gears
Electrical system: 24 V
Batteries: 6 with total capacity of 300 Ah, charged by
3-phase generator driven from main engine
Armament:
1 × 7.62 mm MG3 MG in bow
1 × 7.62 mm MG3 MG on commander's hatch
4250 rounds of 7.62 mm ammunition
6 smoke dischargers

Status

Production complete. In service with Belgium (6),
Germany (36), Italy (40) and the Netherlands (25).
OTO Melara built 28 Leopard AEVs for the Italian
Army.

Manufacturer

MaK System Gesellschaft GmbH, Falckensteiner
Strasse 2, PO Box 9333, D-2300 Kiel 17, Federal
Republic of Germany.
Tel: 431 3995-02. Fax: 431 3995 446.

Leopard Dozer Blade Unit

Description
The Leopard dozer blade unit can be fitted as an optional extra to Leopard 1 and 2 MBTs. The complete dozer blade unit consists of the dozer blade, two pivot-mounted push arms and a hydraulic unit for raising and lowering the blade. A floating capability is available to enable the dozer blade to follow ground contours. Add-on extension elements allow for the dozing of lanes wider than the width of the tank's running gear.

The complete dozer blade can be attached or removed in approximately 10 minutes without recourse to cranes or other equipment and it can be locked in the raised position for travelling. All control elements are packaged into a watertight unit so that the dozer blade can be used during fording operations. A control panel is located in the driver's position and the power supply and control cable passes through one of the slots normally occupied by the vision blocks via a cable adaptor.

For using this dozer blade kit with Canadian Leopard C1 MBTs an Engineer Equipment Interface Modification Kit was developed. This kit allows the tank to operate the dozer blade kit or one of two mineclearing systems, permitting operation with the driver's hatch closed down and all the driver's vision blocks remaining operable.

Status
In production. In service with several nations using Leopard MBTs, including Australia (Leopard 1) and Canada (Leopard C1).

Manufacturer
Krauss-Maffei-Wehrtechnik GmbH, Krauss-Maffei Strasse 2, D-8000 München 50, Federal Republic of Germany.

Tel: (89) 8899-0. Telex: 523 3163-31.
Fax: (89) 812 01 90.

Australian Army Leopard AS 1 MBT equipped with Leopard dozer blade (Australian Army)

ISRAEL

RKM Bulldozer Attachment

Description
The RKM bulldozer attachment was developed jointly by Urdan RKM Limited and the Israeli Army to provide every MBT with the ability to act as an earthmoving vehicle.

The RKM bulldozer attachment has three main assemblies. The first is a standard bulldozer blade modified slightly to improve its performance when working in rocky terrain and sandy soils. The second part is the electro-hydraulic unit which is completely sealed to enable operation under water. It is connected to the vehicle's electrical system to supply hydraulic power to the main cylinder; the unit can be easily and rapidly replaced for maintenance. The electro-hydraulic system and the movements of the blade are controlled from a control box inside the driver's compartment. The third part of the RKM bulldozer attachment is the main structure which includes the adaptor and the arms; it carries the bulldozer blade and the power unit. The structure was designed to withstand vibrations caused by the higher tank driving speeds when crossing difficult terrain. The attachment can be installed on a tank by the normal crew in about 30 minutes; removal takes 15 minutes. If required the blade can be locked in its upper (travel) position manually if the hydraulic system is damaged. The high folding geometry of the attachment enables the carrier tank to negotiate steep banks, terraces and vertical obstacles.

The RKM bulldozer attachment has several operating modes. One is the travel position with the blade in the maximum up position. The bulldozer blade can also be made to 'float' so that the blade rests on the soil, but in the 'blade down' mode the hydraulic cylinder pushes the blade down into the soil for heavy earthmoving. The attachment has automatic hydrostatic locking at

RKM bulldozer attachment fitted to M60 tank showing angle of blade when fully lifted

any given position and a mechanical safety lock (using the travel lock) at the highest position.

The Israeli Army has fitted the RKM to its MBTs but the attachment can also be adapted for other tanks. No modification is required for any MBT to use the RKM attachment.

An earlier version of the RKM was fitted to Israeli Army Centurion tanks.

Status
In production. In service with the Israeli Army.

Manufacturer
Urdan Industries Limited, Industrial Zone, Netanya 42378, Israel.
Tel: 972 53 338074. Telex: 341 822 uasf il.
Fax: 972 53 610274.

ABK-3 Add-on Bulldozer Kit

Description
TAAS – Israel Industries Ltd produces an add-on bulldozer kit known as the ABK-3. This is suitable for use on a range of MBTs including the Centurion, M60 and several other designs. The attachment is joined to the MBT using existing towing and other lugs. Installation takes about 20 minutes without requiring any special tools. When fitted, the dozer blade can dig to 0.25 m below the track level. The blade is 0.99 m high and 3.96 m wide. Weight of the complete kit is approximately 3400 kg and a 24 V DC power supply is required from the carrier vehicle to drive a 10 hp electric motor. The control box is located in the driver's compartment.

The dozer blade operates in four modes: travelling, 'floating' with the blade resting on the soil surface, blade down for digging, and with blade routers lowered for surface ripping. Blade capacity is 3.1 m³. The dozer blade can also be used for clearing scatterable mines from flat surfaces. Tank speed when digging is approximately 5 km/h.

Status
In production. In service with the Israeli Army.

Manufacturer
TAAS – Israel Industries Ltd, POB 1044, Ramat Hasharon 47100, Israel.
Tel: (3) 542 52 22. Telex: 33 719 misbit il.
Fax: (3) 48 96 39.

ABK-3 add-on bulldozer kit mounted on Centurion tank

Bulldozer Protection Kit

Description
Operational experience gained by the Israeli Defence Forces demonstrated that there is a requirement for some form of protection for combat engineer bulldozers working in combat areas. Protection is required from small arms and artillery fire and also for vehicles operating in areas where chemical attack is possible. TAAS – Israel Industries Ltd designed an add-on kit for such situations which has been fitted to Caterpillar D9 bulldozers but it can be adapted to suit other models.

The add-on kit requires no modifications to the basic vehicle structure. The armoured cab is mounted on the vehicle's standard safety frame mounts and the added weight has no effect on overall performance characteristics. The armoured cab has space for an operator/driver and a commander/assistant. Reinforced glass block windows for vision forward, to the sides and to the rear, may be removed leaving an external hardened glass pane to maintain cab isolation and conditioning. Two doors are provided at the front of the cab for entry and exit and an additional door at the rear doubles as a refuelling access point and an emergency exit. The commander has a roof cupola with a full 360° traverse and provision for mounting a machine gun and/or a grenade projector. The cab armour is of a special layered type, and armour plating is provided for the engine compartment on three sides complete with integral air vanes for engine compartment ventilation; servicing access is still possible. Protection is also provided for the hydraulic pistons and tubing and for the fuel and hydraulic fluid tanks.

The cab is equipped with an air conditioning unit driven by the vehicle engine and with an internal and external communications system. Internal lighting is provided and an external light projector may also be fitted. Full convoy and blackout lights are provided and other external additions contained in the kit include weapon mountings, brackets for four fuel containers and a camouflage net and three window wipers.

Bulldozer protection kit fitted to Caterpillar D9

Internal stowage includes water tanks, brackets for personal weapons and equipment, stowage for machine gun ammunition and four spare reinforced glass window blocks. The cab is sealed for operations under NBC conditions.

Specifications
Weight of attachment: approx 6000 kg
Cab dimensions: (internal)
(length) 2 m
(width) 2.6 m
(height) 1.7 m

Air conditioner capacity: 24 000 BTU/h

Status
In production. In service with the Israeli Army.

Manufacturer
TAAS – Israel Industries Ltd, POB 1044, Ramat Hasharon 47100, Israel.
Tel: (3) 542 52 22. Telex: 33 719 misbit il.
Fax: (3) 48 96 39.

ITALY

Astra M113 Combat Engineer Support Vehicle

Description
Astra Veicoli Industriali SpA carried out a repowering and updating project on the M113 APC to enable its combat weight to be of the order of 15 000 kg (for details of the basic M113 refer to *Jane's Armour and Artillery 1992-93* pages 477 to 488). One application for the uprated vehicle is the SIDAM 25 self-propelled air defence vehicle carrying four 25 mm cannon in a turret. A second application is as a combat engineer support vehicle for the Italian Army Engineer Corps.

The Astra conversion involves changes to the hull, engine, transmission, suspension, fuel tanks and armour. Hull alterations involve the relocation of some engine compartment mounts, modifying the top deck to incorporate an improved reverse flow cooling system, reinforcement of the idler wheel mounts and repositioning the shock absorber supports. The existing GMC Detroit Diesel 6V-53 diesel is replaced by a 6V-53T engine developing 265 hp. The cooling system is fitted with a new fan, a reverse air flow system, and a new air cleaner and silencer.

The existing Allison TX-100-1 transmission can either be modified or replaced by the TX-100-1A. The Allison X-200-4 or ZF LSG-1000 transmissions may be fitted as options. New road wheel arms are fitted to the suspension along with new shock absorbers on four wheel arms each side. New and improved torsion bars are also installed.

Two new fuel tanks are fitted to the hull rear,

Basic development vehicle for Astra Veicoli M113-based armoured engineer support vehicle

providing between them a total capacity of 360 l. Optional equipment includes extra light armour on the hull front and sides.

Specialist equipment to be fitted to production vehicles includes a front-mounted, hydraulically operated dozer blade, a roof-mounted 3 t hydraulic crane and twin stabilisers at the rear of the hull. A 10 t capacity recovery winch is located internally with the cable paying out through the rear hatch. A 12.7 mm machine gun can be fitted on a pintle close to the commander's cupola.

Length overall with the dozer blade resting on the ground is 6.32 m.

Status
Under development for the Italian Army.

Manufacturer
Astra Veicoli Industriali SpA, Via Caorsana 79, I-29100 Piacenza, Italy.
Tel: (523) 54 31. Telex: 530 148.
Fax: (523) 6 92 93.

JAPAN

Type 67 Armoured Engineer Vehicle

Description
The Type 67 Armoured Engineer Vehicle is based on the chassis of the Type 61 MBT and was preceded by a trials vehicle based on the Sherman M4A3E8. This had a dozer blade at the front of the hull and a small crane. The Type 67 AEV was designed to clear obstacles from the battlefield and is provided with a dozer blade and crane.

Specifications
Crew: 4
Weight: 35 000 kg
Length: 7.46 m
Width: 3.2 m
Height: 2.9 m
Ground clearance: 0.4 m

Track: 2.45 m
Track width: 500 mm
Length of track on ground: 3.5 m
Ground pressure: 0.95 kg/cm^2
Max speed: (road) 45 km/h
Range: 200 km
Fording: 1 m
Gradient: 60%
Vertical obstacle: 0.8 m
Trench: 2.7 m
Engine: Mitsubishi Type 12 HM 21 WT V-12 direct injection turbocharged air-cooled diesel developing 650 hp at 2100 rpm
Transmission: mechanical with 5 forward and 1 reverse gears, with 2-speed auxiliary reduction unit
Electrical system: 24 V
Batteries: 4 × 12 V, 200 Ah
Armament:
  1 × 0.50/12.7 mm MG
  1 × 0.30/7.62 mm MG

Armour
hull front: 46 mm
hull sides: 25 mm
hull rear: 15 mm

Status
Production complete. In service only with the Japanese Ground Self-Defence Force.

Manufacturer
Production was undertaken at the Maruko, Tokyo, plant of Mitsubishi Heavy Industries, but AFV production is now at the Sagamihara plant near Tokyo. Mitsubishi Heavy Industries, 5-1, Marunouchi 2-chome, Chiyoda-ku, Tokyo, Japan.

Type 75 Armoured Dozer

Development
Development of an armoured dozer began in 1964 and two prototypes were built during FY72 by Komatsu, one with a straight dozer blade and another with an angled blade. After extensive trials the latter was standardised in 1975 and the dozer is in service with the Japanese Ground Self-Defence Force.

The Type 75 armoured dozer can carry out over 90 per cent of the tasks of the D6 medium dozer but has a much higher road speed to enable it to keep up with the leading elements of a convoy.

Description
When the vehicle is travelling the dozer blade is to the rear and the fully armoured crew compartment at the front. The two-man crew can enter either by a door on the right side of the hull or through two circular rear-opening roof hatches. The driver is seated on the left with a rectangular shutter hinged at the top immediately in front of him. This has an integral vision block and can

Type 75 armoured dozer (Kensuke Ebata)

be locked open. The commander is seated to the right of the driver and has a small square shutter hinged at the top, which also has a vision block and can be locked open. Vision blocks are provided in each side of this compartment and there is a shutter with an integral vision block in the rear of the crew compartment for forward vision during dozing operations. There is also a single vision block to the left of the shutter.

The engine and radiator are at the rear of the vehicle. In a combat area they are protected by armoured plates which are removed when the Type 75 is operating in a non-combat area.

The torsion bar suspension consists of five dual rubber-tyred road wheels with the drive sprocket at the front and the idler at the rear. There are also three track return rollers. Hydraulic shock absorbers are fitted at the first, second and fifth road wheel stations.

The hydraulically operated dozer blade is controlled by the driver from inside the armoured cab. The dozer blade is hinged in the middle and a hydraulic winch can be fitted in front of the cab if required.

Specifications
Crew: 2
Weight: 19 200 kg
Length:
(travelling) 6.84 m
(working) 6.3 m
Width:
(travelling) 2.7 m
(working) 3.45 m
Height: 2.79 m

Max speed: 45 km/h
Fording: 1 m
Gradient: 60%
Engine: water-cooled diesel developing 345 hp at 2100 rpm on road and 160 hp at 1850 rpm when working
Armament: none

Status
In service with the Japanese Ground Self-Defence Force.

Manufacturer
Komatsu, 3-6 Akasaka 2-chome, Minato-ku, Tokyo 107, Japan.
Tel: (3) 584 71 11. Telex: 22 812 komatsu j.

POLAND

Armoured Engineering Vehicle

Description
During 1992 the Research and Development Centre of Mechanical Appliances at Gliwice developed and produced the prototype of an armoured engineering vehicle based on the hull of the T-72 MBT and incorporating many features of the WZT-3 armoured recovery vehicle (see entry under *Armoured recovery vehicles*).

The prototype uses many engineering features and components from the T-72/WZT-3 but the main difference from the WZT-3 is the provision of a hydraulically powered heavy jib crane arm located on the right-hand side of the armoured superstructure. The crane arm is provided either with gripper claws intended for the grasping and removal of battlefield obstacles, or a digger bucket. The jib crane arm has a lift capacity of 7000 kg and can extend from 5.94 to 7.94 m over a horizontal working angle of 240°; the maximum vertical working angle is +60° and minimum −55°. The gripper claws fitted to the end of the jib arm can open to a maximum width of 1 m, lift 3000 kg and turn through an angle of 180°. Maximum operating height is 7.5 m and depth 5.5 m. If required the gripper claws can be replaced by a 120 m³ scoop bucket with a maximum cutting depth of 5.5 m.

Located on the front of the vehicle is a V-shaped dozer blade with removable side extensions; the maximum width is 4.2 m. Maximum dozing depth is 0.25 m.

The vehicle is provided with two winches for recovery and other purposes. The main winch has a maximum capacity of 900 kN (with a cable pulley) and is provided with 200 m of rope. An auxiliary winch has a capacity of 20 kN and 400 m of cable.

Other special equipment carried includes an arc welding system. There are stowage bins on the rear upper decking.

The basic crew is the commander and driver although there is internal provision for a combat engineer team of three men. They are provided with an NBC air filtration system and detection equipment. Armament is one 12.7 mm air defence machine gun, a light machine gun for local defence and a shoulder-fired RPG-7 rocket launcher. Smoke grenade launchers and a thermal smoke generator are provided.

If required the vehicle can be provided with deep wading equipment to enable the vehicle to wade through water obstacles up to 5 m for distance up to 1000 m. The normal wading depth is 1.2 m.

Specifications
Crew: 2 + 3
Weight: 44 000 kg
Power-to-weight ratio: 13.3 kW/t
Ground pressure: 0.09 MPa
Length: 8.3 m

Polish armoured engineering vehicle based on chassis of T-72 MBT and WZT-3 ARV

Width:
(over mudguards) 3.6 m
(dozer blade) 4.2 m
Height: 2.7 m
Ground clearance: 0.43 m
Max speed: 60 km/h
Range: 650 km
Fording:
(normal) 1.2 m
(with preparation) 5 m
Gradient: 60%
Vertical obstacle: 0.7 m
Engine: V-12 diesel developing 780 hp at 2000 rpm
Armament:
1 × 12.7 mm NSW MG
1 × 7.62 mm RPK MG
1 × RPG-7

Jib crane
Max lift capacity: 7000 kg
Jib length: (max/min) 7.94/5.94 m
Working slope angle: −55 to +60°
Working traverse: 240°

Jib scoop
Capacity: 120 m³
Cutting depth: 5.5 m

Gripper jaws
Max opening: 1 m

Nominal turn angle: 180°
Lift capacity: 3000 kg
Max operational height: 7.5 m
Max operational depth: 5.5 m

Dozer blade
Width: (with extensions) 4.2 m
Cutting depth: 0.25 m

Main winch
Max towing capacity: (with pulley) 900 kN
Pay-out speed: 0.3 to 0.71 m/s
Winding speed: 0.31 to 0.74 m/s
Rope length: 200 m

Auxiliary winch
Max towing capacity: 20 kN
Max winding and pay-out speed: 1.5 m/s
Rope length: 400 m

Status
Prototype.

Development Agency
Osrodek Badawczo-Rozwojowy Urzadezen Mechanic-zynch, 44-101 Gliwice ul. Toszecka 102, Poland.
Tel: (48) (032) 31 72 41. Telex: 036 197.
Fax: (48) (032) 31 58 87.

MT-LB Armoured Engineer Reconnaissance Vehicle

Description

The Polish Army utilises a version of the MT-LB multi-purpose tracked vehicle developed specifically for the engineer reconnaissance role. The vehicle is intended for the reconnaissance of roads, bridges and their approaches, structures and potential demolition sites, minefields, battlefield obstacles, structures, water resources, and other locations likely to be of interest to combat engineers. The vehicle is also equipped with sensors to detect and plot chemical and nuclear radiation contamination.

The vehicle uses the same general outlines as the conventional MT-LB; for details of the MT-LB refer to *Jane's Armour and Artillery 1992-93* pages 327 to 330. The crew of the reconnaissance vehicle is the commander and driver, with provision internally for a further six men. The additional crew members either operate the various items of reconnaissance or radio equipment or dismount for the close inspection of specific objectives. Most of the additional crew members are seated towards the rear of the vehicle where the specialised role equipment is either located or stowed. The reconnaissance equipment includes photographic and other optical instruments, plus specialised instruments for determining the state or characteristics of roads, ground surfaces and levels, river banks and water obstacles. Reconnaissance data are relayed to higher formations via an R-173 radio system which utilises a rail-type antenna mounted over the right-hand side of the hull; the antenna can be dismounted when not required.

The vehicle is amphibious and is provided with NBC air filtration equipment. Under normal operations the vehicle's various NBC sensors are maintained in a permanently on condition. Automatic and hand-operated fire extinguishers are provided.

The commander's position is covered by a small turret provided with vision devices. Mounted over the turret is a 12.7 mm NSW machine gun for local and air defence; stowage is provided for 240 rounds. Other armament carried includes six RPG-7 rocket launchers and 20 F-1 hand grenades. Eight NDG-2 smoke grenade launchers are mounted on the hull sides towards the rear, four each side.

Polish armoured engineer reconnaissance vehicle based on Polish-produced MT-LB multi-purpose tracked vehicle chassis

Specifications

Crew: 2 + 6
Weight: 12 900 kg ±250 kg
Ground pressure: 0.46 kg/cm²
Length: 6.625 m
Width: (transport condition) 3 m
Height:
(to antenna) 2.7 m
(antenna lowered) 2.35 m
Ground clearance: (max) 0.43 m
Max speed:
(road) 60 km/h
(dirt road) 26-32 km/h
(water) 8 km/h
Range: 500 km
Fording: amphibious

Engine: SW680/167/1 6-cylinder turbocharged diesel developing 245 hp
Armament: 1 × 12.7 mm NSW MG

Status

In service with the Polish Army.

Marketing Agency

Cenzin Co Ltd, 2 Frascati Street, 00-489 Warsaw, Poland.
Tel: 48 22 296738. Telex: 814505 czi pl.
Fax: 48 2 6286356.

UNITED KINGDOM

Chieftain Assault Vehicle Royal Engineers (AVRE)

Development

Following the introduction into service of the Interim Chieftain AVRE (see following entry) Vickers Defence Systems was awarded a contract to convert a number of Chieftain MBTs into a more technically advanced AVRE that better met the British Army's requirements. The combined design, development and production contract was placed with Vickers Defence Systems, covering a total of two prototypes and 46 production vehicles. Vickers Defence Systems initially undertook a four month concept development study during which a full scale wooden mock-up was constructed on a Chieftain hull. This was used to demonstrate to the user the exact position of onboard equipment and systems prior to the manufacture of the prototypes.

The two prototypes were completed in mid 1991 and were extensively trialled by both Vickers Defence Systems and the Royal Engineers at the Armoured Trials and Development Unit at Bovington in Dorset. First-off production was scheduled for late 1992, with production of the full contract quantity proceeding at three units per month until 1994. The two prototypes will be refurbished as production vehicles to bring the total up to 48. In-service date is some time in 1993.

The prime role of the Chieftain AVRE will be to provide mobility support for armoured battlegroups, creating routes through or over natural and man-made obstacles. Typically, breaching of minefields is achieved by using a front-mounted mineplough in

Using a hydraulic loader to position MAXI pipe fascines on the front hamper of a Chieftain AVRE

conjunction with trailer-mounted Giant Viper mineclearing systems. Anti-tank ditches and similar obstacles can be crossed by means of fascines and trackway, both launched from the overhead framework. A dozer blade can be fitted to assist in the clearing of obstructions.

Description

The Chieftain AVRE is built on the chassis of a Chieftain MBT. The running gear remains unchanged apart from the fitment of a hydraulic track tensioner. This is the same as that fitted to the Chieftain ARRV and AVLB and allows the driver to adjust the track

Chieftain AVRE laying MAXI pipe fascines

tension from under armour.

The MBT turret and main armament is removed and replaced by a welded steel armoured superstructure referred to as a penthouse. Seating is provided in the crew compartment for three men abreast, with the commander seated in the centre. The driver's station remains unchanged. The commander is provided with a fixed cupola having a single-piece hatch and seven unitary observation periscopes. The forward periscope is a Helio Type 2100 double prism periscope providing close-in vision to the front of the vehicle. The commander's seat can be raised hydraulically to allow both head out and closed down operation. A further five periscopes are fitted to the penthouse roof for crew vision.

In addition to the cupola hatch there are two further hatches in the penthouse for crew access, one in the left-hand roof plate and another in the front plate. The latter is provided with a foul weather screen with wash/wipe facilities (similar to that provided for the driver on the Warrior APC) to improve crew comfort and forward vision when not in a combat area.

The penthouse is built to be ready to take an NBC pack of Chieftain AVLB dimensions as a Phase Two enhancement. In the interim the vehicle is provided with a three-speed ventilation fan.

Primary hydraulic power for the Special To Role systems is provided by a Commercial Hydraulics HD2-OC-900 pump driven by the main engine via a power take-off. The hydraulic system is load-sensing to optimise power output against power requirements. An electrically driven Commercial Hydraulics PM125 constant horsepower pump is provided as a backup.

Mounted on the hull are two overhead frameworks referred to as hampers. These are tilted hydraulically to launch fascines and trackway and, in the case of the rear hamper, to gain access to the engine decks. The hampers can carry combinations of MAXI pipe fascines and Class 60 trackway up to a maximum distributed load of 14.5 tonnes. Loads are released to the front or rear by means of electrically fired blow-out pins activated by the commander or driver from under armour. The hampers may also be used to transport palletised loads and other engineer equipment.

Mounted on the hull rear plate is a Rotzler 10-tonne hydraulic capstan winch. This can be used to the front or rear with up to 60 m of rope available, depending upon reeving configurations.

A Ferrari hydraulic loader is mounted at the rear of the penthouse, stowed along the engine deck beneath the rear hamper. The lifting capacity is 2.9 tonnes at a maximum extension of 5.45 m. The loader can be operated from controls on the base or from a remote-control connected by a 10 m umbilical. The loader is capable of lifting both fascines and trackway onto the hampers as an alternative to the winch.

The hull front has the necessary attachments to accept a Pearson mineplough or Combat Dozer UDK1. These can be fitted and removed using equipment carried on the vehicle. When not in use, the plough or dozer can be stowed on the rear hamper using the vehicle's hydraulic loader.

A rotatable tow hook, with the necessary electrical connections, is provided at the rear and is designed to tow either two Giant Viper trailers in tandem or a single AVRE trailer.

The defensive armament consists of electrically fired smoke grenade dischargers mounted on the front hamper, and the crew's personal weapons.

Potential Phase Two enhancements include the provision of collective NBC protection for the crew, passive night vision for the commander, and the installation of a minefield marking system.

Status
Prototypes (2); 46 conversions in progress for the British Army.

Manufacturer
Vickers Defence Systems, Scotswood Road, Newcastle upon Tyne NE99 1BX, UK.
Tel: 091 273 8888. Telex: 53104.
Fax: 091 273 2324.

Interim Chieftain Assault Vehicle Royal Engineers (AVRE)

Description
During 1986 a number of early Mark Chieftain MBTs were converted for the armoured combat engineer role by the Engineer Workshops of 40 Army Engineer Support Group at Willich in Germany. Following trials the conversions entered British Army service during 1987 and 18 are used by 32 Armoured Engineer Regiment (RE) in Germany pending the fully developed conversions being produced by Vickers Defence Systems (see previous entry). The Army-converted Chieftain AVREs are interim vehicles pending the development of the more advanced 'production' version.

The Interim Chieftain AVRE conversion involves the removal of the Chieftain MBT turret and armament and installing a steel plate to cover the turret ring. A hatch is provided for the commander and the driver's position is retained unaltered. Two rails are located over the entire length of the vehicle on which up to three maxi-pipe pipe fascines or up to five rolls of Class 60 trackway can be carried. The fascines and trackway are loaded onto the rails with the assistance of a winch. Fascines and trackway are unloaded by raising the rails at the rear. The rails are raised using modified hydraulic jacks taken from M2 bridge/ferry units.

The winch can also be used to load a spare No 9 assault bridge for use with the Chieftain AVLB (see entry in *Mechanised bridges* section).

The Interim Chieftain AVRE carries as standard the dozer blade fitted to some Chieftain MBTs (see entry in this section) but may instead be equipped with mine-ploughs. Current combat engineer trailers can be towed, including the trailer used to carry Giant Viper

Interim Chieftain AVRE laden with pipe fascines and fitted with mine ploughs

mineclearing equipment.

The crew of the Interim Chieftain AVRE consists of three men. No armament is carried other than personal small arms for the crew and a machine gun for local defence.

Interim Chieftain AVREs operating during Operation Desert Storm carried extra side armour and used suspended chain curtains to protect their frontal area.

Status
In service with the British Army (18).

Manufacturer
Army workshops – see text.

Centurion Mk 5 Assault Vehicle Royal Engineers (AVRE)

Development

The Centurion Mk 5 Assault Vehicle Royal Engineers (or AVRE) was developed by the Fighting Vehicles Research and Development Establishment (now the Military Vehicles and Engineering Establishment) to replace the Churchill AVRE which entered service shortly after the end of the Second World War. The first prototype of the Centurion AVRE was completed in 1957 with production being undertaken in the early 1960s.

During 1984 the first of a new variant of AVRE was delivered. This was a conversion of the Centurion MBT once used by Royal Artillery forward observation posts and these tanks retain their main 105 mm L7 guns. They are thus known as AVRE 105s and the existing AVREs fitted with the 165 mm demolition guns are known as AVRE 165s. The AVRE 105s are fitted with the mineplough only, although they are capable of accommodating the dozer blade and towing various trailers. The 105 mm gun is used to fire HESH ammunition only.

The Centurion AVREs are used by only one unit, 32 Armoured Engineer Regiment, Royal Engineers, based in BAOR. Within this regiment the AVREs are used to equip three squadrons, each with three troops. Within each squadron the AVREs are divided into AVRE 165 troops or AVRE 105 troops with three AVREs to a troop.

The Centurion AVRE is being supplemented in service by the Chieftain AVRE (see previous entry) and when sufficient Chieftain AVREs are available the Centurion AVREs will be phased out of service.

Description

The Centurion AVRE (FV4003) is based on a standard Centurion tank hull. The hull is of all-welded construction and the turret is cast with the roof welded in position. The driver is seated at the front of the hull on the right side and is provided with two hatch covers which open left and right, each hatch cover being provided with a periscope. The co-driver is seated to the left of the driver and is also provided with two hatch covers, but only one of these has a periscope. The other three crew members are in the turret, the commander and gunner being on the right and the loader on the left. The commander's cupola can be traversed through a full 360° and has seven periscopes for observation plus a sight linked to the gunner's sight. The loader has a two-piece hatch cover which opens fore and aft. In addition to the stowage boxes on either side of the turret a large wire stowage basket is mounted at the rear of the turret.

The engine and transmission are at the rear of the hull, as are the fuel tanks. The suspension is of the Horstmann type and consists of three units, each with two pairs of road wheels. The drive sprocket is at the rear and the idler is at the front. There are six track support rollers. Shock absorbers are provided for the first and last road wheel stations.

Main armament of the Centurion AVRE 165 consists of a short-barrelled 165 mm L9A1 demolition gun with a fume extractor; the Centurion AVRE 105 has a 105 mm L7A2 tank gun firing HESH only. The 165 mm gun was designed to destroy pillboxes and demolish

Centurion AVRE 165 with turret pannier stowed on hull rear

other targets such as bridges. It fires a HESH projectile weighing 29 kg to a maximum range of 2400 m. However, its effective range is 1200 m as it has a very low muzzle velocity. A 0.30/7.62 mm Browning machine gun is mounted to the left of the main armament and there is a similar weapon on the commander's cupola for anti-aircraft defence. Six smoke dischargers are mounted either side of the turret.

A hydraulically operated dozer blade mounted at the front of the hull can move 229 m³ of soil an hour. A fascine cradle, which can also be used to carry a roll of Class 60 trackway, is also mounted at the front of the vehicle. Full details of this are given in the *Portable roadways* section. Centurion AVRE 105s can be equipped with mineclearing ploughs as an alternative to the dozer blade. Details can be found in the *Mineclearing equipment* section. These mineclearing ploughs can also be fitted to AVRE 165s. The fascine is a 1.828 m diameter bundle of wood or plastic piping and is dropped from a carrying rack on top of the dozer blade into anti-tank ditches and other obstacles, either manually or by releasing lashings using electrically fired blow-out pins. The fascine can also be split to provide 18 m of trackway. A jib can be mounted at the front of the hull for lifting operations if required. At the rear of the hull is a rotatable towing hook which can be jettisoned electrically if required.

AVRE 165s taking part in Operation Desert Storm were fitted with extra armour, with active armour over the turret front.

The Centurion AVRE can tow a two-wheeled trailer carrying the Giant Viper mine clearance system, or a 7.5 t four-wheeled trailer. The latter can carry a variety of equipment including 130 rounds of 165 mm HESH ammunition or 280 jerricans.

The Centurion AVRE is not provided with an NBC system but can be fitted with infra-red night vision equipment. A deep fording kit was developed but was not issued.

Specifications (AVRE 165)

Crew: 5
Weight:
(empty) 49 627 kg

(loaded) 51 810 kg (without fascine)
Length: 8.686 m
Width:
(over hull) 3.39 m
(over dozer blade) 3.962 m
Height: 3.009 m
Ground clearance: 0.46 m
Track: 2.641 m
Track width: 610 mm
Length of track on ground: 4.572 m
Ground pressure: 0.95 kg/cm²
Max speed: (road) 34.6 km/h
Range:
(road) 176 km
(cross-country) 113 km
Fuel capacity: 1037 l
Fording: 1.45 m
Gradient: 60%
Vertical obstacle: 0.941 m
Trench: 3.352 m
Engine: Rolls-Royce Meteor Mk IVB 12-cylinder liquid-cooled petrol developing 650 bhp at 2550 rpm
Transmission: Merritt-Brown Z51R with 5 forward and 2 reverse gears
Electrical system: 24 V
Batteries: 4 × 6 V, 115 Ah
Armament:
1 × 165 mm L9A1 demolition gun
1 × 0.30/7.62 mm Browning MG coaxial with main armament
1 × 0.30/7.62 mm Browning MG
6 smoke dischargers either side of turret
Basic armour
turret front: 152 mm
glacis: 118 mm
nose: 76 mm
hull sides: 51 mm
hull rear upper: 38 mm
hull rear lower: 20 mm
hull floor: 17 mm

Status

In service only with the British Army. Scheduled for replacement by the Chieftain AVRE.

Combat Engineer Tractor (FV180)

Development

In 1962 a General Staff Target (GST 26) was issued for an engineer equipment which would combine the characteristics of an armoured vehicle and an earth mover. Existing commercial earthmoving equipment could not meet this requirement as it had poor mobility, lacked both armour protection and communications equipment and had no amphibious capability.

The following year, three companies, Caterpillar UK, GKN and Vickers, were invited to put forward their proposals for a vehicle to meet the General Staff Target. GKN and Vickers responded but their proposals were not taken up. In 1965 the Military Engineering

Experimental Establishment at Christchurch (now part of the Royal Armament Research and Development Establishment) prepared a design to meet GST 26. At the same time discussions took place between the United Kingdom, France and the then West Germany for the joint development of a Combat Engineer Tractor.

Subsequently, two prototypes were built by the then Royal Ordnance Factory at Leeds, based on a design prepared by the Military Engineering Experimental Establishment. They were powered by a Cummins V-8 diesel which developed 350 hp, were fully amphibious and incorporated some features of the American Universal Engineer Tractor. They were delivered in 1968 but France had meanwhile dropped out of the project as it required a vehicle with a higher water

speed and only limited earthmoving capabilities.

In 1970, after trials with the two test rigs in both Germany and the United Kingdom, the Germans withdrew from the programme as they required a heavier vehicle, without an amphibious capability, mainly for clearing river crossing points.

Meanwhile a major redesign of the vehicle had been carried out with two major objectives: to use standard commercial components wherever possible (engine, transmission, steer unit and winch), and to make the vehicle amphibious with the minimum preparation. In 1969 a General Staff Requirement was issued and the following year Royal Ordnance Factory Leeds was nominated as the prime manufacturer with the Military Vehicles and Engineering Establishment responsible for design work. A contract was awarded to Leeds for

Combat Engineer Tractor (CET) carrying jib crane attachment in digger bucket

seven prototypes, all of which were delivered between February 1973 and January 1974.

Extensive trials were carried out in both the United Kingdom and Germany and in July 1975 the Combat Engineer Tractor (CET) was accepted for service with the British Army. As a result of trials, modifications were incorporated in production vehicles, including improved track tension, replacing the steel-rimmed tyre with a rubber one at the front road wheel station and improvements to the buoyancy system.

Production of the CET began at the Royal Ordnance Factory at Nottingham in 1977 and the first production vehicle was accepted in May 1978. Production was completed in March 1981 after 141 had been built for the British Army but in mid-1984 it was announced that India had ordered the CET. The initial order was for nine vehicles with options (since taken) on a further six. The first vehicle was delivered at the end of 1988 and was first shown publicly during the January 1989 Republic Day parade in New Delhi. The order for 15 was completed by the end of 1990. Reports from India have stated that the final Indian requirement for CETs could be as high as 100.

Description

The CET was designed to provide integral engineer support for the battle group and typical roles include excavating vehicle and gun pits for defensive purposes, repairing and maintaining roads, preparation of river banks, recovering disabled vehicles, and preparing or clearing obstacles.

The hull of the CET is made of all-welded aluminium armour, supplied by Alcan. The vehicle is normally driven with its bucket to the rear, and in this position the crew are seated on the left side. The following description is for the vehicle in this condition.

The driver is seated at the front and also operates the winch, with the bucket operator to his rear. Both crew members can reverse their seats and essential controls are duplicated so that either crew member can operate the vehicle. The crew compartment is provided with two hatch covers which open to the right and a total of 10 vision blocks. The crew compartment is supplied with cooled air via the NBC system from an air-conditioning unit, produced by Gallay Limited. The

unit contains a refrigeration package with a compressor driven from the main gearbox.

The engine and transmission are mounted at the right side of the hull with the final drives being mounted at the front of the hull. From the engine, power is passed through two gearboxes to a steering unit and final drives. The first of these gearboxes, the transfer box, provides PTOs for the water propulsion units and hydraulic pumps. Controlled differential steering is used for road and cross-country drive and skid steering is used for bulldozing operations, and an independent clutch/brake system is provided for this purpose.

The suspension is of the torsion bar type and consists of five road wheels with the fifth road wheel acting as the idler. The drive sprocket is at the front. The tracks are of cast steel with rubber bushes and rubber pads are provided to reduce damage when operating on roads. Hydraulic double-acting ram-type dampers are mounted on the front and rear wheel stations and can be locked from the crew compartment if required.

The CET can ford to a depth of 1.83 m (without preparation), but with preparation the vehicle is fully amphibious. It is propelled in the water by two 330 mm Dowty 40/40B water jets which are mounted one either side of the hull. When in the water, steering is accomplished by deflecting the thrust from the unit on the inside of the turn, and deflecting both units gives reverse. The preparation required before entering the water is to unfold the trim board at the front of the hull and inflate two Hycafloat units to the rear of the trim board. The units were developed by FPT Industries of Portsmouth and replaced the original bellows-type units installed on the prototypes. Two plastic-cased polyurethane foam blocks are fitted into the bucket and held in place by retaining straps.

The bucket is of light alloy construction with steel cutting edges and tines, and has a maximum capacity of 1.72 m³. Its maximum lift height is 1.829 m and its minimum lift height is 102 mm below the track line. This can be used for both digging or bulldozing and can also be used as an earth anchor. Its maximum capacity is 200 m³/h over 100 m hauling distance.

The two-speed winch has a maximum pull of 8000 kg and is provided with 113 m of 16 mm diameter

rope; maximum winching speed is 1.9 m/s. For self-assistance, the winching speed is matched to the speed of the tractor. A high speed winching facility is available for ferrying work. The rope can be led to the front or rear of the vehicle by direction-changing blocks.

A self-emplacing earth anchor is mounted on the top of the hull and this can be rocket-propelled to a maximum distance of 91.4 m. The anchor is attached to the vehicle's winch rope and is used to assist the vehicle when leaving a river with a steep bank.

All CETs are provided with an NBC filtration pack installed at the front of the vehicle, providing clean air to the crew compartment. The filters are changed through an external hatch. If required a passive night vision device can be installed at either crew position. Vehicles produced for India have air-conditioning.

The CET can also be used to tow the trailer-mounted Giant Viper mine clearance system. The vehicle is airportable in C-130 Hercules aircraft.

The following ancillary equipment can be installed on the CET if required:

Pusher bar for launching bridging
Class 30 and Class 60 trackway laying equipment
A jib crane attachment for handling palletised stores up to a maximum weight of 4000 kg can be installed in the bucket.

Specifications

Crew: 2
Weight combat: 18 000 kg
Length:
(overall) 7.3 m
(hull) 5.334 m
Width:
(bucket) 2.921 m
(hull) 2.87 m
(tracks) 2.769 m
Height:
(less RP anchor) 2.83 m
(with RP anchor) 3.41 m
Ground clearance: 0.457 m
Track width: 508 mm
Length of track on ground: 3.76 m
Ground pressure: 0.435 kg/cm²
Max speed:
(road) 52 km/h
(water) 9 km/h
Range: 320 km
Fuel capacity: 418 l
Fording: 1.83 m
amphibious with preparation
Gradient: 60%
Vertical obstacle: 0.61 m
Trench: 2.06 m
Engine: turbocharged Rolls-Royce C6TFR 12.17 l 6-cylinder in-line diesel developing 320 bhp at 2100 rpm
Transmission: TN26 manually controlled power-shift with four gears in each direction coupled to Rolls-Royce CGS 312 steering system
Electrical system: 24 V
Batteries: 4 × 6TN rated at 100 Ah connected in series/parallel giving total capacity of 200 Ah
Armament:
1 × 7.62 mm MG (optional)
6 smoke dischargers
Armour: aluminium

Status

Initial production was completed in 1981 but recommenced for an order from India. In service with the British Army (141) and Indian Army (15).

Manufacturer

Royal Ordnance Guns & Vehicles Division, Kings Meadow Road, Nottingham NG2 1EQ, UK.
Tel: 0602 863341. Fax: 0602 352082.

Chieftain Bulldozer Kit

Description

By fitting a special bulldozer kit, any Mark of Chieftain MBT can be used for basic tactical earthmoving tasks. The kit consists of a hydraulic powerpack with a joystick controller, main linkage assemblies, an aluminium bulldozer blade and protective ducting for the hydraulic linkages. The scale of issue of the kit is variable but is usually of the order of one or two to a troop.

To attach the kit the only part to be removed from the parent tank is the front right-hand trackguard stowage bin. This is replaced by the armoured steel powerpack using the existing attachment points and plugging control and power cables into existing points. This powerpack is in two halves, one with the electrical assemblies and the other with the hydraulic components. The joystick unit for the pack is installed in the driver's compartment to the right of the driver's seat. The front towing eyes are used to mount the main linkage assemblies on the front of the hull and the bulldozer blade is secured to the linkages by its fulcrum pins. The kit can be exchanged from tank to tank with no loss of hydraulic fluid, and all hydraulic hoses are fitted with protective ducts and quick-release, self-sealing couplings.

The tank driver can use the joystick control unit to start and stop the hydraulic motor, raise and lower the blade, or allow the blade to 'float'. The unit has a 'pump-running' indicator lamp and a further indicator for when the fluid filter requires cleaning. Mechanical locks are provided for travelling, one in the highest position for daylight use, and one lower to allow the headlights to function at night.

The power unit operates off the vehicle's 24 V nominal supply which is used to power the hydraulic

Chieftain fitted with bulldozer kit aluminium dozer blade

system 6.5 hp drive motor.

By altering four attachment links, the blade assembly can be fitted to the American M60 MBT attachment points.

Status

In service with the British Army.

Manufacturer

AP Precision Hydraulics Limited, PO Box 1, Shaw Road, Speke, Liverpool L24 9JY, UK. (Hydraulics) Tel: 051 486 2121. Telex: 629394 AP LPL G. Fax: 051 486 2226.

Pearson Combat Dozer UDK1

Description

The Pearson Combat Dozer UDK1 was developed as an add-on attachment for MBTs or armoured engineer vehicles. It can carry out bulldozing tasks such as ground levelling, digging defensive 'tank scrapes', preparing ground for launching bridges, urban obstacle clearance, filling anti-tank ditches, and so on.

The UDK1 incorporates its hydraulic powerpack into the boom arm and is thus a totally self-contained unit. A wedge-block mounting system enables the bulldozer to be removed from one vehicle and fitted to another in under 15 minutes. The bulldozer fits directly to the glacis plate by means of attaching to anchor blocks and lashing eyes pre-welded to the glacis plate. Electrical connection is made between a harness fitted permanently to the bulldozer and a glacis plate harness. The harness passes through armoured ducting to a control box in the driver's compartment. This control box can also be used to control the Pearson Mine Plough (see entry under *Mineclearing equipment*).

The UDK1 unit comprises a blade and boom fitted to a mounting plate, with the blade position controlled by a hydraulic cylinder and top link. The blade is a fabricated steel unit fitted with replaceable hardened steel cutting edges and corner tips. The blade has an extension in the centre that increases dozing capacity and reduces spillage. An electro-hydraulic powerpack is fitted within the boom, along with the drive motor and hydraulic oil reservoir.

The control box in the driver's compartment controls blade lift and lowering functions electrically, using a joystick lever. Cut-out switches in the powerpack provide protection against motor and oil overheating, oil filter blockage and low oil level. These protective switches can be overridden under combat conditions by a 'Battle' switch. The full range of operations are blade up, blade down, float on, float off, the Battle override and a warning light test.

Pearson UDK1 Combat Bulldozer fitted to Challenger MBT

The Pearson Jacklift Pallet (see entry under Pearson Mine Ploughs in *Mineclearing equipment* section) can be used with the UDK1.

Specifications

Weight: 2200 kg
Width: 3.69 m
Height: 1.225 m
Cutting depth: 175 mm
Fitting and removal time: 10 min
Power supply: 24-28 V, 250 A max
Operating pressure: 1250 bar

Power requirements: 250A at 24-28 V DC

Status

In production. Accepted by British Army for use on Challenger MBT and Chieftain AVRE. Also in service with European and Middle East armies.

Manufacturer

Pearson Engineering, Wincomblee Road, Walker, Newcastle upon Tyne NE6 3QS, UK. Tel: 091 234 0001. Telex: 538253. Fax: 091 262 0402.

Pearson Combat Dozer UDK2

Description
The Pearson Combat Dozer UDK2 is a smaller and lighter version of the UDK1 (see previous entry) and can be fitted to light tanks, self-propelled guns and infantry fighting vehicles. It was developed to meet the requirements of the British Army's Future Family Light Armoured Vehicles (FFLAV) programme.

The UDK2 weighs just over 1 tonne and has virtually no effect on vehicle mobility and does not interfere with any main armament. All working parts are identical to those of the UDK1.

Specifications
Weight: 1100 kg
Width: 3.27 m
Height: 1.1 m
Cutting depth: 160 mm
Fitting and removal time: 10 min
Power supply: 24-28 V, 250 A max
Operating pressure: 1250 bar
Power requirements: 250A at 24-28 V DC

Status
In production.

Manufacturer
Pearson Engineering, Wincomblee Road, Walker, Newcastle upon Tyne NE6 3QS, UK.
Tel: 091 234 0001. Telex: 538253.
Fax: 091 262 0402.

Pearson UDK2 Combat Bulldozer fitted to Warrior mechanised combat vehicle

UNITED STATES OF AMERICA

Combat Mobility Vehicle

Development
Following the termination of the Counter-Obstacle Vehicle (COV) project, the US Army has a requirement for a Combat Mobility Vehicle (CMV) as part of their Armored Systems Modernization (ASM) Program. The intention is to provide armoured combat teams with an integrated counter-mine and counter-obstacle capability in a single vehicle. The CMV leads elements of armoured forces to create safe passage lanes for other combat vehicles through complex obstacles such as minefields, craters, anti-tank ditches, and so on.

In April 1991 BMY Combat Systems was awarded a $10 945 000 contract for a single CMV Advanced Technology Transition Demonstrator (ATTD). Under the terms of the contract BMY Combat Systems will produce a single vehicle based on a modified M1 Abrams MBT chassis provided as Government Furnished Equipment (GFE). Following company trials the ATTD will be delivered to the US Army during early 1993. After Army trials the programme is expected to move into full scale engineering development and then production, with both phases open to competition. It is anticipated that the full scale engineering development phase will be completed by the mid-1990s, with production after the turn of the Century.

Major sub-contractors to BMY Combat Systems are Dupont Corporation (analysis of armour package), Mechanical Technologies Inc (depth sensor technology), Gradall Corporation (excavating arm) and Westinghouse Electric Corporation (vetronics).

Description
The CMV has a crew of two, with the commander seated under a cupola in the centre of an armoured superstructure. The commander's cupola is provided with periscopes to provide a full 360° field of vision while the driver, seated to the left front under a hatch, has three forward- and side-facing periscopes. The superstructure uses modular armour panels and is provided with a radiation and spall liner plus an automatic fire extinguisher system; an escape hatch is provided under the hull. The commander's station has a control station to operate all the vehicle's systems. An auxiliary power unit containing the system hydraulics is mounted behind the armoured superstructure along

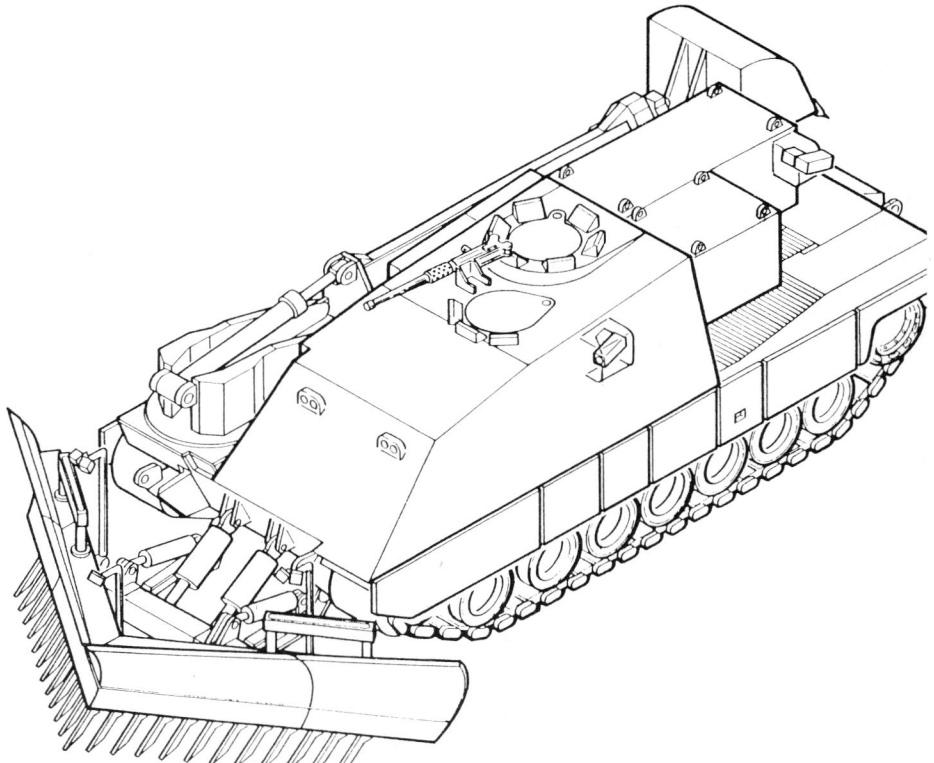

Artist's impression of the CMV ATTD with excavating arm in stowed position and mineclearing blade at front

with an equipment stowage bin. Ballistic protection is provided for hydraulic components and hoses. The track uses T166 track shoes fitted with traction-enhancing grousers.

At the front of the vehicle is a full-width mineclearing blade with automatic depth control and rapid attach/detach features. The blade can clear a path 4.02 m wide, is V-shaped and is provided with 23 replaceable tines. Each tine is 305 mm long, retractable, and is fitted with a shear pin which breaks when hard obstacles such as rocks are struck; should a shear pin

break the tine will rotate to the rear but will remain attached to the blade. The blade also has reversible and replaceable cutting edges while a deflector at the top prevents mines from rolling over the top of the blade. The blade also has a conical cross-section to improve soil curl. Folding wing sections on each side are used to reduce the blade width in less than 5 minutes for transport.

To the right of the superstructure is a hydraulically controlled excavating arm capable of digging, lifting and grappling. The arm is a lightweight single-stage telescopic unit capable of operating in an arc from 46° left and 115° right of the vehicle centreline. The arm has a maximum reach of 9.2 m, a minimum reach of 3.3 m and can dig to a depth of 5.27 m. Maximum lift capacity at full extension is 1814 kg. The digging bucket is detachable.

The vehicle is provided with at least four video cameras to improve vision when operating. One camera is placed under the excavating arm, one is mounted each side of the superstructure to view the extremities of the mineclearing blade, and another provides vision to the rear of the vehicle.

A 0.50/12.7 mm machine gun is provided for local and air defence.

The CMV is air-transportable in C-5A/B and C-17 transport aircraft.

Specifications
Crew: 2
Max combat weight: 64 t
Max vehicle width: 3.657 m
Min range: (secondary roads) 483 km
Max speed: 66.6 km/h
Vertical obstacle: 1.067 m
Trench: 2.74 m
Mineclearing speed: 9.3 km/h
Cleared path:
(lane width) 4.02 m
(depth) 380 mm

Arm reach:
(maximum) 9.2 m
(minimum) 3.3 m
Digging depth: 5.27 m
Lift capacity: (full extension) 1814 kg

Status
Prototype – see text.

Contractor
BMY – Combat Systems Division of HARSCO Corporation, PO Box 15512, York, Pennsylvania 17405-1512, USA.
Tel: (717) 225 4781. Fax: (717) 225 4615.

M728 Combat Engineer Vehicle

Development
In 1959 the M60 was chosen to become the standard MBT of the US Army. Design work on a new CEV based on the M60/M60A1 was soon started and the first prototype was known as the T118E1. After trials this was type classified as the M728 in 1963 and entered production in 1965, entering the US Army inventory in 1968. It is issued to the Engineer Battalions of armoured, mechanised and infantry divisions. Engineer battalions in armoured and mechanised divisions have eight M728s. Infantry division engineer battalions have only three M728s, and separate engineer companies have two M728s each. No funds were requested for the procurement of the M728 in FY76 and FY77. For FY78, the Army requested five M728s at a cost of US $3.4 million, but this request was denied by Congress. In FY79 the US Army requested funds for 51 M728s at a cost of US $31.4 million, but this request was also denied by Congress. In July 1978 the Department of Defense notified congressional committees of its proposed letter of offer to sell the Saudi Arabian government 15 M728s with radios and two years' supply of spare parts at a total cost of $21 million. In FY80 the US Army requested funds for 56 M728s at a cost of US $51.5 million. These two orders were delivered. No funds were requested for M728 production in FY81. Production is complete.

Description
The M728 is based on the M60A1 MBT. The hull is of cast sections welded together while the turret is cast in one piece. The driver is seated at the front of the hull and is provided with a single-piece hatch cover. He has three M27 periscopes for observation purposes, of which the centre one can be replaced by an M24 infra-red periscope on a separate mount for night operations. The other three crew members are in the turret,

with the commander and gunner on the right and the loader on the left. The commander's cupola can be traversed through a full 360° and he is provided with a total of eight vision blocks and an M34 periscope, which can be replaced by an M36 infra-red periscope for night observation. The gunner has an M105 telescope and an M32C periscope. The loader is seated on the left side of the turret and is provided with a single-piece hatch cover that opens towards the rear and an M37 periscope for observation purposes. The engine and transmission are at the rear of the hull as are the fuel tanks.

The suspension of the M728 is of the torsion bar type and consists of six road wheels with the drive sprocket at the rear and the idler at the front; there are three track support rollers. Hydraulic shock absorbers are provided at the first, second and sixth road wheel stations.

The M728 is designed to carry out numerous roles on the battlefield including the destruction of field fortifications and roadblocks, filling in gaps, craters and ditches, preparing fire positions and roadblocks.

Main armament of the M728 consists of an M135 165 mm demolition gun which has an elevation of +20° and a depression of −10°. Turret traverse is a full 360° at 1.6°/s; traverse and elevation are either powered or manual. A 7.62 mm M219 machine gun is mounted coaxially with the main armament (late production vehicles are equipped with an M240 coaxial machine gun) and a 0.50/12.7 mm M85 machine gun is mounted in the commander's cupola; this has an elevation of +60° and a depression of −15°. Totals of 30 rounds of 165 mm, 3600 rounds of 7.62 mm and 600 rounds of 0.50/12.7 mm ammunition are carried.

The A-frame is pivoted from the front of the turret and when not required lies back over the rear of the hull. This has a maximum lifting capacity of 15 876 kg; the two speed winch, which is mounted at the rear of the turret, is provided with 61 m of 19 mm rope and is controlled by the vehicle commander. The dozer blade

is hydraulically operated and is mounted at the front of the hull. (Trials were carried out using a two-part mine-plough in place of the dozer blade.)

The M728 is provided with infra-red night driving equipment and most vehicles have a Xenon infra-red searchlight mounted over the top of the main armament. A central air filtration system pipes fresh air to each crew member.

Specifications
Crew: 4
Weight:
(empty) 50 439 kg
(loaded) 53 200 kg
Length:
(with boom erected) 9.3 m
(with blade and boom in travelling position) 8.91 m
Width:
(including blade) 3.7 m
(hull) 3.631 m
Height:
(travelling) 3.2 m
(lowest operable) 3.257 m
Ground clearance: 0.381 m
Track: 2.921 m
Track width: 711 mm
Length of track on ground: 4.235 m
Ground pressure: 0.89 kg/cm²
Max speed: (road) 48.28 km/h
Range: 450 km
Fuel capacity: 1420 l
Fording: 1.219 m
(with kit) 2.438 m
Gradient: 60%
Vertical obstacle: 0.76 m
Trench: 2.51 m
Engine: Continental AVDS-1790-2A or -2D, 12-cylinder diesel developing 750 bhp at 2400 rpm
Transmission: General Motors Corporation (Allison Division) CD-850-6A with 3 ranges (low, high and reverse)
Electrical system: 24 V
Batteries: 6 × 6TN
Armament:
1 × 165 mm demolition gun
1 × 7.62 mm MG coaxial with main armament
1 × 0.50/12.7 mm AA MG
2 banks of smoke dischargers, 6 in each

Armour
turret front: 120 mm
turret sides: 76 mm
turret rear: 50 mm
turret top: 25 mm
hull front: 120 mm
hull sides, front: 76 mm
hull sides, rear: 51 mm
hull top: 57 mm
hull rear: 44 mm
hull floor: 13.63 mm

Status
Production complete. In service with the US Army, Saudi Arabia and Singapore (8).

Manufacturer
General Dynamics, Land Systems Division, 38500 Mound Road, Sterling Heights, Michigan 48310-3200, USA.

M728 combat engineer vehicle with A-frame in travelling position

Bulldozer, Earthmoving: Tank Mounting M8, M8A1, M8A3 and M9

Description

Differences in these bulldozer kits occur mainly in the details of their mountings. The M8 kit is used with the M48, M48A1 and M48C MBTs. The M8A1 is used only with the M48A2 MBT while the M8A3 is used with the M48A3. The M9 kit is used on the M60 MBTs.

Each bulldozer has a mouldboard with a reversible blade cutting edge supported on a quadrilateral linkage. The linkage has two push beams connected near the bottom of the mouldboard with two inner and outer tilt arms connected at the mouldboard top. Two double-action hydraulic cylinders are provided for raising and lowering. Pressure for the cylinders is provided by a hydraulic pump driven by either the tank engine (M8 series) or a power take-off on the transmission (M9). The location of the control valves and hydraulic reservoir varies between the kits. On the M8 they are mounted on the wall of the tank rear hull; on the M8A1 on the right fender and on the M9 on the left-rear fender.

Status

M8 series no longer in production. M9 in production and in service with the US Army and with many other armies.

M48A2 MBT fitted with M8A1 bulldozer kit (US Army)

Specifications

Tank mounting	M8	M8A1	M8A3	M9
MBT model	M48, M48A1, M48C	M48A2	M48A3	M60
Weight	3981.6 kg	3810 kg	3810 kg	4031 kg
Mouldboard length	3.708 m	3.708 m	3.708 m	3.708 m
Mouldboard height	0.914 m	0.914 m	0.914 m	0.914 m
Blade angle (from horizontal)				
(ground level)	58°	58°	—	58°
(float)	59°	59°	65°	60°
(lowest)	65°	65°	65°	60°
Edge position				
(carrying)	0.787 m	0.686 m	0.736 m	0.736 m
(lowest, below ground)	0.254 m	0.254 m	0.254 m	0.254 m
(highest)	0.762 m	0.762 m	0.762 m	0.762 m
Max rate of lift	267 mm/s	267 mm/s	267 mm/s	165.6 mm/s
Max forward speed, dozing	1.6-4.82 km/h	1.6-4.82 km/h	1.6-4.82 km/h	1.6-4.82 km/h

M9 Armored Combat Earthmover

Development

In 1958 the US Army Mobility Equipment Research and Development Center at Fort Belvoir began work on a vehicle called the All-purpose Ballastable Crawler (ABC). This eventually became known as the Universal Engineer Tractor (UET).

The first prototypes of the Universal Engineer Tractor were built by the Caterpillar Tractor Company and the International Harvester Company. In January 1975 the Pacific Car and Foundry Company completed a further four vehicles, two of which underwent field evaluation at Fort Hood. The result of these trials was considered satisfactory and indicated the vehicle's superiority over available equipment. TECOM testing was completed in August 1976 and type classification (Standard A) was approved in February 1977.

Trials of the M9 were subsequently carried out in both Yuma and Alaska to test modifications made as a result of previous trials and new equipment, such as a winterisation kit. In FY79 $21.1 million was requested for the production of 75 vehicles, but only $10.6 million was authorised for 29 vehicles. Since production of such a small number was not considered an economic proposition, production was delayed in the hope that the FY80 request, for $40.5 million, plus the 1979 allocation, would allow the production of up to 155 vehicles. No M9 funding was made in either the 1980 or 1981 budgets. In November 1982 a revised contract worth $29 million was awarded for the purchase of 15 equipments of which $19.3 million was for the vehicle and the remainder for product improvements (the original contract was to have been $40.4 million for 36 vehicles). All 15 vehicles had been delivered by the end of 1984. Trials with this first batch of vehicles demonstrated that further improvements were required in some areas. Seven of this first batch were modified by PCF Defense Industries and were delivered to the US Army during January 1985. Tests with this batch of vehicles were carried out at Fort Hood.

RFPs were issued to industry during April 1986 and resulted in offers from ADCOR, BMY, FMC, General Motors of Canada, Ingersoll-Rand and PCF Defense Industries. BMY was ultimately awarded a production contract on 25 July 1986. It will build 434 M9s between 1988 and 1993 (provided the last option for 132

M9 Armored Combat Earthmover

vehicles is awarded) at an overall cost of approximately $180 million. The first production examples were delivered to the training base at Fort Leonard Wood during the fourth quarter of FY89. US Army units in Europe started to receive their vehicles during the last quarter of 1990.

The US Marine Corps has a requirement for 202 combat excavators, for which the M9 is understood to be the preferred choice – 30 M9s were loaned to the Marine Corps by the US Army during Desert Shield/ Storm. It is anticipated that funds for Marine Corps M9s will be available during FY93 or 94. The National Guard has also indicated an interest to field the M9 in the Heavy Divisions.

During 1991 two overseas orders were placed for M9s. The first, for 18 units, was from a customer in the Far East. The second order was worth $8 million with deliveries due in late 1992.

Description

The M9 Armoured Combat Earthmover (ACE) is intended to operate in forward areas and due to its high road speed can be located with the lead tanks in a convoy, closer to where it is needed, rather than at the back as is the case with vehicles (such as the D7 medium crawler) which the M9 is intended to replace.

The M9 is a general-purpose engineer vehicle and can carry out tasks in three critical areas, mobility, counter-mobility and survivability. Mobility tasks include filling craters and ditches, assisting fighting vehicles (winching or towing), removing roadblocks, trees, rubble and other battlefield obstacles, preparing access/egress for fording sites and river crossings, preparing and maintaining combat routes and preparing and maintaining assault airfields. Counter-mobility tasks include the construction of anti-armour obstacles, demolishing fords and bridge bypasses, participating in the digging of tank ditches, destroying landing fields and airfields, participating in the preparation of strong points and hauling obstacle materials. Survivability tasks include the digging of hull defilade positions for armour, construction of defensive positions for command and control operations, construction of earth berms for protection, hauling material for protective shelters, clearing fields of fire and digging slots for vehicle-mounted TOWs and other battlefield weapons.

The M9 is airportable in C-130, C-141 and C-5 transport aircraft. It is unarmed but has a smoke grenade launcher. Other equipment includes a standard NBC system (ventilated facepiece), a radio, and the operator can utilise standard night vision goggles. It has a limited amphibious capability and armour protection is provided for the engine, power train and the operator.

The hull of the M9 is made of welded aluminium. At the front of the vehicle is the 6.7 m³ capacity scraper bowl (ballast compartment), hydraulically operated apron and positive load ejector. The driver is seated near the rear of the vehicle on the left side and is provided with a cupola which provides 360° vision. A lighter hatch cover (weight 81.65 kg) than those fitted to early vehicles has been introduced; the hatch incorporates vision blocks in place of the earlier periscopic vision devices. The engine, a variant of that used in the Bradley IFV, is positioned to the right of the driver's compartment. The transmission is below the engine and the steer unit is to the rear. On-vehicle equipment includes a bilge pump and a Carco P30 winch with a line pull of 11 340 kg. The M9 can also be used to tow trailers and other equipment as it has a maximum drawbar pull of 14 059 kg. It is fully amphibious with preparation, being propelled in water by its tracks. The M9 is not suitable for operating in fast-flowing rivers.

The dozer blade is mounted on the apron and dozing and scraping are accomplished by raising and lowering the entire front of the vehicle by means of the hydropneumatic suspension. This consists of eight sets of 711 mm diameter forged aluminium road wheels with the drive sprocket at the rear. The hydropneumatic suspension allows the tractor to be tilted to apply the dozing effort to one corner of the blade. The capability of the vehicle for operations such as dozing can be nearly doubled by self-loading the bowl with approximately 8000 kg of earth which is used as ballast.

Specifications
Crew: 1
Weight:
(travel mode) 16 327 kg
(gross, ballasted) 24 490 kg
Drawbar pull: 14 059 kg
Length: 6.248 m
Width:
(with dozer wings) 3.2 m
(without dozer wings) 2.79 m
(over tracks) 2.692 m
Height:
(windshield raised) 3 m
(windshield stowed) 2.7 m
Ground clearance:
(sprung, engine running) 0.343 m
(unsprung) variable
Track width: 457 mm
Length of track on ground: 2.67 m

Ground pressure: 0.68 kg/cm² (empty)
Max speed:
(road) 48.3 km/h
(water) 4.8 km/h
Range: (secondary roads) 322 km
Fuel capacity: 507 l
Fording: 1.83 m
amphibious with minimum preparation
Freeboard with load of 1814 kg: 0.28 m
Gradient: 60%
Side slope: 20%
Vertical obstacle: 0.457 m
Trench: 1.575 m
Engine: Cummins V903C 14.8 l 8-cylinder diesel developing 295 hp at 2600 rpm
Transmission: Clark Model 13.5 HR 3610-2 with 6 forward and 2 reverse gears. Geared system for high-speed road and cross-country travel, and clutch and brake system for bulldozing operations
Suspension: hydropneumatic
Steering: hydraulic with gears and clutches
Turning radius:
(geared steer mode) 13.7 m
(clutch brake mode) pivots
Armament: nil
Armour: aluminium, Kevlar and steel

Status
In production. Deliveries to the US Army commenced in June 1988. Ordered by an undisclosed Far East nation.

Manufacturer
BMY – Combat Systems Division of HARSCO Corporation, PO Box 15512, York, Pennsylvania 17405-1512, USA.
Tel: (717) 225 4781. Fax: (717) 225 4615.

M113 with Dozer Blade Kit

Description
The M113 armoured personnel carrier can be adapted for general bulldozing work by the addition of a dozer blade kit. Once fitted the kit does not impair the normal capabilities of the vehicle or its load-carrying ability. The vehicle can remain amphibious and the dozer blade acts as a trim vane in the water once the standard trim vane has been removed.

Status
Available.

Manufacturer
FMC Corporation, Ground Systems Division, 1105 Coleman Avenue, San Jose, California 95108, USA.
Tel: (408) 289 2115.

US Army M113 APC fitted with hydraulically operated dozer blade kit

RECOVERY VEHICLES AND EQUIPMENT

Armoured recovery vehicles
Armoured repair vehicles
Recovery vehicles
Recovery equipment

ARMOURED RECOVERY VEHICLES

AUSTRIA

Bergepanzer 4KH7FA-SB 20 Greif Armoured Recovery Vehicle

Description
The Greif armoured recovery vehicle is based on the chassis of the Jagdpanzer SK 105 light tank. The first prototype was completed in 1974 with the first production vehicles following in 1976/77.

The hull is of all-welded construction with the winch and crew compartment at the front. Normal means of entry to the crew compartment is via two doors in the left side of the hull. In addition there are hatches in the roof. The engine and transmission are at the rear of the hull and there is a stowage platform over the engine decking, which is used to carry spare components. The torsion bar suspension consists of five road wheels with the drive sprocket at the rear and the idler at the front. There are three track return rollers. Hydraulic shock absorbers are provided at the first and fifth road wheel stations.

Mounted on the right side of the superstructure, at the front, is a hydraulic crane, which is traversed to the rear for travelling. This crane can be traversed through 234° and its boom elevated from 0 to +60°. The boom can be extended from its normal length of 3 to 3.9 m, and has a maximum lifting capacity of 6000 kg. The crane is provided with 42 m of cable and is capable of lifting the complete turret of the Jagdpanzer SK 105 light tank.

The main winch is in the lower part of the hull and leads out through the front of the hull. This opening can be sealed for fording operations. The winch is provided with 95 m of 24 mm diameter cable and has a maximum pull of 20 000 kg. This enables the Greif to recover both the Jagdpanzer SK 105 light tank and the Steyr APC. A rake blade is mounted at the front of the hull and is used in conjunction with the main winch. A full range of tools is carried as is cutting and welding equipment. The Greif does not have an NBC system, but the crew compartment is provided with a ventilation and heating unit.

Steyr developed a pioneer vehicle based on the chassis of the Greif ARV. Details are given in the *Armoured engineer vehicles* section.

Greif armoured recovery vehicle lifting Steyr 4K 7FA armoured personnel carrier

Specifications
Crew: 4
Weight: 19 800 kg
Length: 6.705 m
Width: 2.5 m
Height:
(overall) 2.74 m
(top of hull) 2.3 m
Ground clearance: 0.4 m
Track: 2.12 m
Track width: 380 mm
Length of track on ground: 3.04 m
Ground pressure: 0.75 kg/cm^2
Max speed: (road) 67.5 km/h
Range: (road) 625 km
Fuel capacity: 500 l
Fording: 1 m
Gradient: 70%
Side slope: 40%
Vertical obstacle: 0.8 m
Trench: 2.1 m

Engine: Steyr Type 7FA 6-cylinder turbocharged diesel developing 320 hp at 2400 rpm
Transmission: ZF manual with 6 forward and 1 reverse gears
Turning radius: 7.25 m
Electrical system: 24 V
Batteries: 2 × 12 V, 180 Ah
Armament:
1 × 0.50/12.7 mm M2 HB MG
4 smoke dischargers
Ammunition: (12.7 mm) 1500 rounds

Status
In production. In service with Argentina (10), Austria (50), Bolivia (2), Morocco (11) and Nigeria (15).

Manufacturer
Steyr-Daimler-Puch Spezialfahrzeug AG, Postfach 100, A-1111 Vienna, Austria.
Tel: 222/76 45 11. Telex: 61 322 1299.
Fax: 222/76 81 49.

BELGIUM

SIBMAS (6 × 6) Armoured Recovery Vehicle

Description
The SIBMAS (6 × 6) armoured recovery vehicle is a conversion of the basic SIBMAS (6 × 6) vehicle range and uses the same basic hull and drive train. No prototype was produced as the first example, produced in mid-1983, retained much of its commonality with the rest of the SIBMAS (6 × 6) range. Full details of the SIBMAS (6 × 6) range can be found in *Jane's Armour and Artillery 1992-93* pages 276 and 277.

The hull is of all-welded steel and is fully watertight. It provides the crew with full protection against 7.62 mm armour-piercing rounds. The driver is seated in the centre of the hull front behind three bulletproof windscreens. Behind him there is a circular hatch for the commander. Mounted on the hatch rail is a 7.62 mm machine gun which can be elevated 65° and depressed 10°. Between the commander's hatch and crane support there is one large roof hatch and another entry hatch on the right of the hull rear. Internally there is rearward-facing seating for three fitters, each side of the commander's position and next to the side doors.

The engine arrangement, type, suspension and drive train are all identical to the rest of the SIBMAS (6 × 6) range.

Specialist recovery equipment mounted externally consists of two hydraulically operated spades, a

SIBMAS (6 x 6) armoured recovery vehicle

hydraulic crane and two winches. The spades are mounted one at the front and the other at the rear and both are fully folding when required. The hydraulic crane is mounted centrally on the hull roof and can be telescopically extended. It has a capacity of 10.5 t/m and can lift loads of up to 3000 kg at a radius of 3.5 m and 8000 kg when used with the crane boom support for suspended towing operations. When extended, a crane jib support is used to secure heavy loads for towing. Of the two winches one is used as the main multi-purpose winch and is centrally mounted to enable guide pulleys for the cable to be extended front or rear. The hydraulically operated main winch has a direct pull of 20 000 kg. The other winch is used as an auxiliary and is mounted behind the main winch. It has a 1500 kg capacity and is used to unwind the main winch cable.

Other external equipment includes towing eyes front and rear, a 360° rotating searchlight on the hull roof, an emergency rotating warning light, a tow rope, a lifting bar, vehicle tool kit and an axe, shovel and pick-axe, sand channels, stowage box, a hydraulic lifting jack with an 8000 kg capacity, fuel and water jerricans, first aid kit, compressor air outlet for tyre inflation, and two six-barrel 76 mm smoke launchers.

Internally, there is stowage capacity for a wide range of specialist equipment including a portable gas welding kit and a hydraulic lifting jack with a 10 000 kg capacity. There is also a VHF communications radio set and full internal communications loudspeakers, only the driver and commander have headsets. The driver has a passive periscope for night driving, and air-conditioning is provided for the full crew.

Specifications
Crew: 2 + 3
Configuration: 6 × 6
Length overall: (travelling) 7.63 m
Width: 2.54 m
Height: (top of crane) 3.2 m
Ground clearance: 0.4 m
Track: 2.066 m
Wheelbase: 2.8 m + 1.4 m
Angle of approach/departure: 35°/35°
Max road speed: 80 km/h
Fuel capacity: 410 l
Max range: (road) 800 km
Fording: 1.07 m
Max gradient: 50%
Side slope: 30%
Vertical obstacle: 0.6 m
Trench: 1.8 m
Engine: MAN D 2566 MK 6-cylinder, in-line, water-cooled turbocharged diesel developing 320 hp at 1900 rpm
Transmission: fully automatic power-shift gearbox with hydrodynamic torque converter type ZF 6 HP-500
Steering: power-assisted
Turning circle: 18 m
Tyres: 14.00 × 20
Electrical system: 24 V

Status
Production complete. In service with Malaysia (24).

Manufacturer
BMF – Belgian Mechanical Fabrication SA, SIBMAS Division, Zoning Industriel, B-4330 – Grace-Hollogne, Belgium.
Tel: (41) 63 99 40. Telex: 42 049.
Fax: (41) 63 65 62.

BULGARIA

MTP-1 Armoured Recovery Vehicle

Description
The MTP-1 armoured recovery vehicle is a variant of the vehicle known in the West as the Armoured Command and Reconnaissance Vehicle (ACRV – actual designation MT-Lbus) as produced in Bulgaria (for details of the ACRV refer to *Jane's Armour and Artillery 1992-93* pages 287 and 288). The MTP-1 is used for the recovery of damaged or disabled vehicles, changing vehicle components, preparing fire positions and vehicle hides, and for general crane lift purposes.

The MTP-1 is virtually identical to the ACRV but mounted on the front right-hand side is a turret identical to that fitted to the MT-LB multi-purpose armoured vehicle (*ibid* pages 327 to 330). This manually operated turret is armed with a 7.62 mm machine gun, although some turrets have been up-gunned to 12.7 mm. Mounted on the roof is a crane with a telescopic jib. When travelling the crane is traversed to the front and the hook is restrained by an eye on the front of the hull. The crane is mounted in a small turret-like cupola with the crane operator being provided with full armour protection. The crane has a lift capacity of 3000 kg with the jib extended to 3.4 m, or 2000 kg extended to the full 5 m.

Mounted at the rear of the vehicle is an entrenching blade similar to that fitted to the engineering variant of the MT-LB (see entry under *Armoured engineer vehicles*). The blade is mounted on hydraulic arms and can prepare a vehicle scrape in about 110 minutes. The blade can also act as an anchor and support when the vehicle's onboard winch is in operation. With the blade lowered the winch has a maximum capacity of 30 tonnes. With the blade raised the winch capacity is

MTP-1 armoured recovery vehicle in travelling configuration

lowered to 10 tonnes.

The MTP-1 is fully amphibious, being propelled in the water by its tracks. An NBC system is fitted. Combat weight is 14 000 kg.

Status
In production.

Contractor
KINTEX, PO Box 209, 66 Anton Ivanov Boulevard, Sofia, Bulgaria.
Tel: 66 23 11. Telex: 22471, 23243.

CHINA, PEOPLE'S REPUBLIC

Type 653 and 653A Armoured Recovery Vehicles

Description
The Type 653 armoured recovery vehicle is based on the chassis and hull of the Type 69 MBT. The Type 653 bears no relationship to a recovery version of the Type 59 MBT which has a tractor-towing role only. The Type 653A is basically a Type 653 with a more powerful crane.

The Type 653 and Type 653A are intended for the field recovery and repair of medium battle tanks and also have a limited combat engineering capability. The basic hull and suspension of the Type 69 are retained but in place of the turret a fixed superstructure is fitted offset to the left and the vehicle also carries a hydraulic crane and an earthmoving dozer blade at the front. The main and auxiliary winches are located within the superstructure. The vehicle has a crew of five with the driver located forward on the left-hand side in an armoured position raised above the normal height of the Type 69 driver's position. The driver has a single forward vision aperture and a circular overhead access hatch. Infra-red lighting and vision devices are provided for night driving. Mounted on the front of the hull and operated by two hydraulic cylinders is the earth-moving dozer blade that can also act as an anchor for heavy winching operations. The dozer blade has an earthmoving capacity of 100 m³/h on dry soil. The main winch access rollers are located between the twin hydraulic cylinders for the dozer blade and the blade has to be in the lower position for recovery. The main winch is hydraulic with a maximum pulling performance of up to 70 000 kg and the effective length of the cable is 130 m (160 m on Type 653A).

To the right of the driver's position is the hydraulic crane jib with its full 360° turntable in line with the driver's position. The crane jib is telescopic and is normally stowed to the rear for travelling. It can be extended to a maximum lifting height of 6 m and has a rated lifting torque (static) of 40 t/m – 70 t/m on Type 653A. The rated lifting capacity is 10 t on the Type 653 and 20 t on the Type 653A. Recovered vehicles can be towed behind the vehicles using a rigid towing trail that is normally carried on the main hull superstructure side. This superstructure has two circular roof hatches and there is provision for a 12.7 mm machine gun mounting on the roof.

The auxiliary winch is located to the left of the driver on the track fenders which also support a number of tool and other stowage boxes. The Type 653 is stated to have a capability of carrying out field repairs and the hydraulic crane can lift an entire tank turret complete with gun. The main communications equipment is the Type 889 radio set and the Type 803 is used as the intercom system.

Type 653 armoured recovery vehicle from right rear

Specifications
Crew: 5
Weight:
(Type 653) 38 000 kg
(Type 653A) 42 000 kg
Length: 7.18 m
Width: (over side skirts) 3.304 m
Height:
(highest point) 3 m
(top of superstructure) 2.34 m
Ground clearance: 0.425 m
Track: 2.64 m
Length of track on ground: 3.845 m
Max speed: 50 km/h
(towing) 18 km/h
Range: (road, normal fuel tanks) 370 km
Fording: 1.4 m
Gradient: 30°
(towing) 15°
Side slope: 30°
Vertical obstacle: 0.7 m
Trench: 2.6 m
Engine power: 580 hp

Main winch
Max towing force: 64 000-70 000 kg
Cable delivery and retract speed:
(without load) 28-30 m/min
(with load) 7 m/min

Crane – Type 653
Rated lifting capacity: 10 000 kg
Rated lifting torque: (static) 40 000 kg/m
Max lifting height: 6 m

Dozer blade
Max digging depth: 200 mm

Digging capacity: (dry earth) 100 m³/h
Max supporting force: 70 000 kg

Status
In production. In service with China, Bangladesh, Iraq, Pakistan and Thailand.

Manufacturer
China North Industries Corporation, 7A Yue Tan Nan Jie, PO Box 2137 Beijing, Beijing, People's Republic of China.
Tel: 867570. Telex: 22339 CNIC CN.
Fax: 867840 Beijing.

COMMONWEALTH OF INDEPENDENT STATES

BREM-1 Armoured Recovery and Repair Vehicle

Description
The BREM-1 (*Bronirovannaya Remontno-evakuatsionnaya-1*) armoured recovery and repair vehicle is based on the T-72B MBT and was first issued during 1984.

The BREM-1 has a crew of three; commander, driver and a vehicle mechanic. Each of the crew is provided with day and night observation equipment.

The BREM-1 is powered by a 840 hp diesel engine providing a maximum road speed of 60 km/h. The fuel tanks give a range of 700 km on paved roads and 500 km on tracks. When towing another tank the road range is reduced to 220 km without refuelling. Long-range fuel tanks are mounted on the rear and can be jettisoned if required. An unditching beam is carried under the rear fuel drums. Ditch-crossing performance is between 2.6 and 2.8 m, depending on the firmness of the banks, and the largest vertical step is 0.85 m. For fording, an OPVT snorkel can be fitted over the crew compartment to enable fording of water obstacles up to 5 m deep and 1000 m wide. When not in use the OPVT snorkel tube is carried at the right rear of the vehicle.

On the left side of the vehicle is a 4.4 m hydro-mechanical crane, used for lifting damaged or ditched vehicles for access or repair. The crane has a lifting capacity of 3000 kg at the full 4.4 m extension or 19 000 kg at 2 m extension. Hydraulic power for the crane is supplied by a pump driven from the vehicle's main engine via an auxiliary gearbox. If the main engine is not running an electrical pump driven from the vehicle's batteries may be used. The crane is controlled from an elevated position that is equipped with all the necessary controls for the operation. With the maximum load suspended from the crane hook the

BREM-1 armoured recovery and repair vehicle in travelling configuration

vehicle may be driven over level ground. If the load exceeds 3000 kg the vehicle suspension is locked automatically. The crane turntable is also lockable. With the crane outrigger extended to 3 m the crane may be used through a full 360°. When extended 3-4 m the crane may only operate between +60 and –10° towards the rear and between +90 and –10° to the front, measured from a line fore and aft. For travelling the outrigger is stowed along the side of the vehicle and held in a special clamp by a screw fitting.

The BREM-1 is equipped with an electric welding system that comprises an SG-10-1S starter/generator, a switch unit, a working position, a welding socket and

a set of welding leads. The maximum welding current is 360 A. Controls for the welding equipment are located on a panel in a hermetically sealed container mounted on a shelf over the left-hand track. Other special tools carried include a universal fitter's tool, spanners and adaptors, all carried in two portable containers on a load platform. In the centre of the roof is a platform 1.706 m long and 1.4 m wide which is provided with removable side flaps; this can accommodate a maximum load of 1500 kg.

For recovery operations the BREM-1 is equipped with hoisting and auxiliary winches, add-on plough and bulldozer blades, towing equipment and a full set of accessories. The mechanical main winch has a capacity of 25 000 kg but this may be increased by using snatch blocks to 100 000 kg. Normally this winch is used forward, in conjunction with the lowered dozer blade, but for self-recovery it may be used to the rear. The length of cable used is 200 m. The winch is power-driven from a 'swing frame' gear via a reduction gearbox. The winch is controlled from the elevated operator's position. A 530 kg auxiliary winch and 400 m of cable are used to pull the cable towards the winch hoist and the speed of winding and unwinding is controlled hydraulically. The winch controls are to the right of the operator's position. A detachable device may be used to clean dirt from the cable. In use, this is placed on the fixed element of the cable feeder and comprises two round revolving brushes, a hydraulic motor, the cable guides and a reduction gear to transmit drive to the brushes. The device is switched on once the cable has been extended.

The bulldozer equipment is mounted on the front of the hull and is hydraulically driven, with control via two push-buttons on the driver's main control handles. The blade is 3.1 m wide and can be used to create an MBT firing position in 20 minutes in heavy soil or 12 minutes in light sandy soil.

The towing equipment consists of two towing rods, each 1.68 m long and with internal shock absorbers, and two 5.5 m long tow lines. Other special equipment carried includes a 30 t capacity hydraulic jack.

The BREM-1 has an R-123U radio installation, a TPU tank telephone system and an overpressure NBC system.

The BREM-1 is stated to have the same degree of armour protection as the T-72 MBT. The only armament carried by the BREM-1 is a single 12.7 mm NSV machine gun and 720 rounds of ammunition. Four forward-firing smoke dischargers may be fitted but smoke screens can be produced by injecting diesel fuel into the exhaust.

Variants

VT-72A and VT-72B

The Czech state factories developed and produced a recovery vehicle based on the T-72 and known as the VT-72B. The main difference from the CIS BREM-1 is that the 18 000 kg capacity extending jib crane is mounted on the right-hand side of the vehicle. The former East German Army received three of these vehicles and planned to purchase more; they were known as the T-72TK.

The Czechs also produced a further variant known as the VT-72A. This differs in having a lighter capacity crane capable of lifting only 7000 kg and intended for component changing and general technical assistance. Other changes from the VT-72B include an additional pulley block for recovery purposes and an internally stowed device for turning over inverted vehicles.

WZT-3

This is a Polish armoured recovery vehicle based on the T-72 MBT chassis. Details are provided in a separate entry in this section.

Specifications

Crew: 3
Weight: 41 000 kg
Power-to-weight ratio: 20.5 hp/t
Ground pressure: 0.83 kg/cm²
Length: 7.98 m
Width: 3.46 m
Height: 2.42 m
Ground clearance: 0.457 m
Max speed: (road) 60 km/h
Range:
  (roads) 700 km
  (tracks) 500 km
  (towing) 220 km
Fording:
  (normal) 1.2 m
  (with preparation) 5 m
Gradient: 60%
Side slope: 40%
Vertical obstacle: 0.85 m
Trench: 2.6 to 2.8 m
Engine: V-12 diesel developing 840 hp
Armament: 1 × 12.7 mm NSV MG

Main winch
Rated line pull: 25 000 kg
With snatch block: 100 000 kg
Usable rope length: 200 m

Auxiliary winch
Max line pull: 530 kg
Usable rope length: 400 m

Jib crane
Lift capacity:
  (at max 4.4 m extension) 3000 kg
  (2 to 3 m extension) 12 000 kg
  (2 m extension) 19 000 kg
Max hook height: 5 m
Traverse: 360°

Status

In production. In service with the CIS. Similar vehicles developed in Czechoslovakia and delivered to former East Germany.

Manufacturer

State factories.

M1977 Armoured Recovery Vehicle

Development/Description

In the 1950s the old Soviet Union developed a tank destroyer based on the chassis of the T-55 MBT. It is believed to have been called the IT-130 and was probably armed with a modified version of the 130 mm M-46 field gun. In concept and appearance it was similar to the earlier SU-100 but was produced only in small numbers as was a similar vehicle based on the chassis of the T-62 MBT. As far as it is known none of these remain in service in their original roles although some have been converted into armoured recovery vehicles which are very similar in appearance to the earlier SU-85-T and SU-100-T ARVs. They are limited to towing operations and as far as it is known they are not fitted with winches or other specialised recovery equipment. The designation for the ARVs based on the T-55 and T-62 assault gun chassis is not known, although the United States calls the T-62 model the M1977 ARV, or the T-62-T ARV.

The M1977 has been used as the basis for a mineclearing vehicle.

Specifications (ARV based on SU-130 chassis)

Crew: 3 or 4
Weight: 36 000 kg
Length: 6.4 m
Width: 3.352 m
Height: 3.438 m
Ground clearance: 0.41 m
Track: 2.64 m
Track width: 580 mm

M1977 ARV clearly showing former space for 130 mm gun in glacis plate

Length of track on ground: 3.84 m
Ground pressure: 0.81 kg/cm²
Max speed: (road) 50 km/h
Range: 500 km
Fuel capacity: 960 l
Fording: 1.5 m
Gradient: 60%
Vertical obstacle: 0.8 m
Trench: 2.7 m

Engine: Model V-55 V-12 water-cooled diesel developing 580 hp at 2000 rpm
Electrical system: 28 V

Status

In service with the CIS.

Manufacturer

State factories.

T-54/T-55 Armoured Recovery Vehicles

Description
The first ARV based on the chassis of the T-54 MBT appeared in the 1950s and was designated the T-54-T. Since then at least seven other T-54/T-55 ARVs have been developed. Most of them have very limited capabilities compared with ARVs developed in the West, and few are equipped with a winch, limiting their capabilities to towing damaged vehicles off the battlefield. These vehicles are known as BTS (medium armoured towers) in the CIS. The T-55-TK is an improvement over the earlier models as it can lift vehicles weighing up to 20 000 kg.

All these ARVs use a T-54 or T-55 MBT chassis with the turret removed. The driver is seated at the front of the hull on the left side and is provided with two periscopes for observation and a single-piece hatch cover. The vehicle commander is normally seated to his right and is provided with a single-piece hatch cover which opens to the right. The other crew members normally sit in the cargo area, which is often cramped as the snorkel and spare fuel drums are usually carried there. An unditching beam is carried on the right side of the hull and tow bars of varying lengths are also carried.

The engine and transmission are at the rear of the hull but unlike the T-54/T-55 MBT there does not appear to be any provision for carrying additional fuel tanks on the rear of the hull. It is assumed that most of these ARVs are provided with an NBC system.

The suspension is of the torsion bar type and consists of five road wheels with the idler at the front and the drive sprocket at the rear. There are no track return rollers.

Variants
T-54-T/T-55-T
This was the first model to enter service and performs a similar role to the T-34-T (B) ARV but is based on a more powerful chassis. A loading platform is mounted in the centre of the vehicle, with sides which can be folded down to facilitate the loading or unloading of spare components such as an engine or a transmission. A large spade is mounted at the rear of the hull and a large diameter snorkel can be installed to the rear of the driver's position for deep fording operations. A jib crane which can lift a maximum weight of 1000 kg is provided. There is no winch, so the vehicle is limited to towing operations. The Finnish Army uses a version of the T-54-T called the BTS-2, which has a winch, spade and a small dismountable crane. Another Finnish ARV based on the T-55 is the KAM-1 for which there is a separate entry in this section.

T-54 (A)
This is a German development and can be fitted with a snorkel for deep fording operations. Standard equipment includes a push/pull bar, full range of tools including both welding and cutting equipment, dismountable crane with a lifting capacity of 1000 kg, radiation warning equipment and a chemical warfare agent detector. This model does not have a winch, nor a spade at the rear. If required PT-54 or PT-55 roller type mineclearing equipment can be installed at the front.

T-54 (B)
This is also a German development and is similar to the T-54 (A) but at the rear of the hull are brackets for

T-54-TK armoured recovery vehicle

securing tow ropes and on the glacis plate at the front of the hull is a protective plate. This model is not provided with a winch or a spade.

T-55-TK (previously known as T-54 (C))
This is another German development and is provided with a stowage platform, snorkel, spade at the rear, dozer blade at the front and a heavy duty crane which is mounted on the right side of the hull. This has a telescopic jib and can lift a maximum weight of 20 000 kg. When not required the crane is traversed to the rear so that its jib rests along the left side of the hull.

Czechoslovak VT-55A ARV
There is a separate entry for this vehicle in this section under Czechoslovakia.

Polish T-54/T-55 ARVs
Poland has developed at least two ARVs based on T-54 or T-55 MBT chassis, designated the WZT-1 and WZT-2.

Specifications
(T-54-T; data in square brackets refer to T-54 (B) and T-55-TK where different)
Crew: 3-5
Weight: (empty) 36 000 [32 000], [34 000] kg
Length: 7.12 [7.05], [9.74] m
Width: 3.23 m
Height: 1.89 [2.2], [2.65] m
Ground clearance: 0.425 m
Track: 2.64 m
Track width: 580 mm
Length of track on ground: 3.84 m
Ground pressure: 0.72 [0.72], [0.77] kg/cm²
Max speed: (road) 48 km/h
Range: 400 km
Fuel capacity: 812 l
Fording: 1.4 m
Gradient: 60%
Vertical obstacle: 0.8 m
Trench: 2.7 m
Engine: Model V-54, V-12, water-cooled diesel developing 520 hp at 2000 rpm
Transmission: manual with 5 forward and 1 reverse gears
Electrical system: 24 V
Batteries: 4 with total capacity of 280 Ah
Armament: nil

Armour
glacis plate: 100 mm at 60°
upper hull sides: 70 mm at 0°

Stripped down T-54 (A) armoured recovery vehicle fitted with snorkel during a training exercise

hull rear: 60 mm
hull floor: 20 mm
hull roof: 30 mm

Note: Models based on a T-55 chassis are powered by a V-55 engine which develops 580 hp at 2000 rpm.

Status
Production complete. The T-54 and T-55 are in service with the following countries so it can be assumed that most of these use the T-54/T-55 ARV: Afghanistan, Albania, Algeria, Angola, Bangladesh, Bulgaria, Cambodia, Central African Republic, China, Congo, Cuba, Czechoslovakia, Egypt, Equatorial Guinea, Ethiopia, Finland, Hungary, India, Indonesia (2 T-54 (A)), Israel, North Korea, Libya, Mali, Mongolia, Morocco, Mozambique, Nicaragua, Nigeria, Pakistan (both Chinese and Soviet models), Peru, Poland, Romania, Somalia, Sudan, Syria, CIS, Vietnam, Yemen, Yugoslavia, Zambia and Zimbabwe. Large numbers also saw service in the former East Germany.

Manufacturer
Czechoslovak, Polish and CIS state factories.

BTR-50PK(B) Amphibious Armoured Recovery Vehicle

Description
The BTR-50PK(B) is a fully amphibious version of the BTR-50 armoured personnel carrier developed especially for the amphibious recovery of AFVs at water obstacles. It retains the basic layout and automotive components of the original vehicle together with the twin hydrojet propulsive units that provide enough thrust to maintain a speed on water of 10 km/h and

sufficient power to tow an amphibious AFV.

For the recovery role the BTR-50PK(B) is equipped with R 123M and R 124 radio sets, a rear-mounted towing coupling, towing gear and hook and two extra towing cables, two special quick-release shackles, standard shackles and snap hooks, a searchlight, two lifebelts, lifejackets and four fenders. Also carried is RG-UF life-saving equipment for use only in an emergency when no qualified divers are available. Other safety equipment includes two PG6Hi hand-held dry fire extinguishers. A set of mechanics' tools is also carried.

The normal crew of the BTR-50PK(B) comprises a commander and driver but there are another four seats for auxiliary personnel. During recovery operations the vehicle can accommodate up to eight rescued personnel. Combat weight of the BTR-50PK(B) is 14 000 kg.

Status
Production complete. In service with various of the former Warsaw Pact armed forces.

Manufacturer
State factories.

CZECHOSLOVAKIA

VPV Armoured Recovery Vehicle

Description

The VPV (*Vyprost'ovaci Pásové Vozidlo*) tracked armoured recovery vehicle is a Czech modification of the BMP-1 infantry fighting vehicle, licence-produced in Czechoslovakia. The VPV is used to support Czech Army motorised infantry units.

The VPV has a crew of three, the commander who also operates the vehicle's crane and winch, the driver, and a recovery fitter. While the BMP-1 chassis, running gear and engine have been retained, the turret is replaced by a cable drum with a hatch at its centre. An extendible traversing crane is installed on top of the hull rear. It has a maximum lifting capability of 5200 kg with the boom extended between 2.9 m and 3.2 m; maximum boom extension is 4.5 m. The vehicle's fuel capacity has been increased to 480 l.

The VPV has a recovery winch with a tractive force of 168 hp although this can be increased by the use of

return pulleys. The winch has 120 m of 19 mm diameter cable. There is also a spade which is hydraulically lowered when the winch is in use. Also carried are tool kits, welding and cutting devices; the commander and driver are both trained welders.

The VPV retains the amphibious characteristics of the BMP-1 but with some restrictions. It can ford water obstacles if the waves are not higher than 100 mm and in current velocities not more than 1.2 m/s.

A version of this vehicle used by Hungary is known as the BMP-1VPV.

The former East German Army received from Czechoslovakia at least three VPVs based on the BMP-2 chassis.

Specifications
Crew: 3
Combat weight: approx 14 000 kg
Length: 6.47 m
Width overall: 2.94 m
Height: (crane lowered) approx 2.5 m

Max speed:
 (road) 70 km/h
 (water) 7 km/h
Range: 500 km
Fuel capacity: 480 l
Engine: V-6 water cooled diesel developing 285 hp
Armament: 1 × 7.62 mm MG

Status
In service with the Czech Army, Hungary and the CIS.

Manufacturer
Czechoslovak state factories.

Top view of VPV armoured recovery vehicle from rear

VPV armoured recovery vehicle

VT-55A Armoured Recovery Vehicle

Description

The VT-55A armoured recovery vehicle was designed in Czechoslovakia and is based on the hull and running gear of the T-55A MBT. An earlier production version (in service with the Czech armed forces) is known as the MT-55 and was based on the T-55: it lacks the forward-mounted dozer blade of the VT-55A. The MT-55 was based on the CIS T-55-T ARV.

Mounted on the right of the hull is a hydraulic crane with a maximum lifting capacity of 1500 kg. On the roof of the ARV, towards the rear, is a 2 × 1.6 m platform which can carry a maximum load, such as a power-pack, of up to 3000 kg.

The VT-55A has two winches. The main winch is mechanically driven by the main engine. It has a

maximum capacity of 25 000 kg and is provided with 28 mm diameter cable. The hydraulically operated auxiliary winch has a capacity of 800 kg and is provided with 400 m of 6.3 mm diameter cable. The seat of the winch operator rotates within a small turret.

At the front of the vehicle is a hydraulically operated dozer blade with a soil-shifting capacity of 150 m³/h.

The vehicle can be fitted with a snorkel tube to allow operations in water obstacles up to 1000 m wide and 5 m deep, and with a stream velocity of 1.5 m/s. Under normal conditions the vehicle can ford water obstacles up to 1.4 m deep.

All vehicles have several tow bars and a tow cable 4.2 m long. Electric welding equipment, a workbench and a vice are mounted above one of the tracks and are pulled out when required. At the rear of the vehicle is a winch anchor spade which can also be used as a dozer blade.

The machine gun turret can be traversed through

360° and the 7.62 mm machine gun can be used against ground and air targets. The vehicle has a three-man crew and standard equipment includes a crew compartment heater, NBC system and infra-red night vision equipment. A snorkel can be fitted for deep fording.

Specifications
Crew: 2
Weight: 36 450 kg
Length overall: 8.3 m
Width:
 (overall) 3.4 m
 (inside track) 2.04 m
Height: (top of stowed crane) 2.52 m
Ground clearance: 0.425 m
Max speed: 50 km/h
Average speed:
 (road) 32-35 km/h
 (towing) up to 18 km/h
Range:
 (road) 270 km
 (cross-country) 100 km
Gradient: 32°
Side slope: 30°
Fording:
 (normal) 1.4 m
 (with preparation) 5 m
Engine power: 570 hp

Status
Available. The earlier MT-55 is in service with Czechoslovakia and may have been exported.

Manufacturer
VOP 025 Nový Jičin, s.p., Dukelská 105, 742 42 Nový Jičin, Czechoslovakia.
Tel: 0656 22919. Telex: 52196.
Fax: 0656 22961.

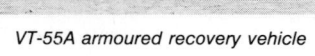

VT-55A armoured recovery vehicle

FINLAND

KAM-1 Armoured Recovery Vehicle

Description
The KAM-1 armoured recovery vehicle was produced during 1984 and is a conversion of a T-55 tank chassis. Only one prototype has been produced and this was handed over to the Finnish Defence Forces in October 1984. The vehicle was developed in answer to a Finnish Defence Forces requirement for a vehicle that would not only act as an armoured recovery vehicle but also as a vehicle that could lift tanks and other vehicles to allow trapped personnel to escape, lift light armoured vehicles onto trailers or railway wagons when disabled for any reason, lift turrets, engines, gearboxes and other heavy vehicle components under field conditions, and tow damaged vehicles.

The KAM-1 conversion involved the removal of the T-55 tank turret and replacing it with a large turntable mounting a hydraulic crane. The interior of the centre of the vehicle is occupied by the hydraulic packs and winch. The driver is seated at the front of the hull on the left-hand side. To his right is the commander in a separate compartment together with a radio and the intercom equipment.

A BTU-55 dozer blade, complete with routing tines, is fitted to the front of the hull. The dozer blade can be used to clear obstacles or for general earthmoving and also acts as an anchor blade for stability while using the recovery winch. It can also be used as a support when the crane is in use. More support is provided by two hydraulically operated support legs at the rear of the vehicle.

The hydraulic crane has a lift moment of 75 t/m and a maximum boom length of 6.7 m. Traverse is unlimited and the maximum load is 22 000 kg. The crane can be controlled by a remote-control box that also controls the hydraulic support legs at the rear. An axial piston pump is used to drive the hydraulic system for the crane and winch at a maximum pressure of 320 bar.

A hydraulic recovery winch is located towards the front of the hull and has a maximum theoretical line pull of 36 000 kg. Using a snatch block this can be doubled to 72 000 kg. The winch is provided with 140 m of cable paying out to the front.

Equipment carried on the vehicle includes a flexible towing device, towing bars, towing ropes, a platform for spare parts and other items, lifting chains, an engine lifting boom, a snatch block and shackles.

Armament carried is limited to crew weapons and a signal pistol. Smoke generators in the engine exhaust manifolds are carried over from the original T-55 design.

Specifications
Crew: 2
Weight: 44 000 kg
Length: 7.6 m
Width: 3.4 m
Height: 3.6 m
Track: 2.64 m
Track width: 580 mm
Max speed: (road) 50 km/h
Engine: V-55 V-12 water-cooled diesel developing 580 hp at 2000 rpm
Transmission: manual with 5 forward and 1 reverse gears

Crane
Lift moment: 75 t/m
Max boom length: 6.7 m
Max load: 22 000 kg
Traverse: unlimited

Winch
Max line pull: (theoretical) 36 000 kg
Max line pull: (with snatch block) 72 000 kg
Cable length: 140 m

Status
Prototype.

Manufacturer
Vammas Limited, PO Box 18, SF-38201 Vammala, Finland.
Tel: (932) 1971. Telex: 22283 vamas sf.
Fax: (932) 41148.

KAM-1 armoured recovery vehicle with crane in travelling position

KAM-1 armoured recovery vehicle in travelling configuration and showing rear crane supports raised

FRANCE

AMX-13 Armoured Recovery Vehicle

Development
The AMX-13 ARV (or *Char de Dépannage* AMX Model 55) is the standard light tracked ARV of the French Army and is based on the chassis of the AMX-13 light tank. Initial production of the AMX-13 ARV was undertaken at the Atelier de Construction Roanne (ARE), but once the ARE became involved in the AMX-30 MBT programme, production was transferred to Creusot-Loire Industrie at Châlon sur Saône.

Early production versions were fitted with a SOFAM petrol engine. This was later changed to a GM Detroit Diesel unit and should production recommence only the latter unit will be available.

Description
The front of the ARV is cast and the remainder of the vehicle is of all-welded construction. The driver is seated at the front of the hull on the left side and is provided with a single-piece hatch cover and three periscopes for observation. The engine is mounted to the right of the driver. The crew compartment is in the centre of the hull. At the front of the superstructure is a

AMX-13 armoured recovery vehicle

hatch cover which opens inwards and on either side of the hull is a single vision port which is covered by a simple swinging type cover when not required. At the rear are twin doors which open outwards. The commander is seated on the left side and is provided with a single-piece hatch cover and eight vision periscopes. To his right is the winch operator who has a single-piece hatch cover that opens to the rear and a single periscope.

The suspension is of the torsion bar type and consists of five road wheels with the drive sprocket at the front and the idler at the rear. There are four track return rollers. Hydraulic shock absorbers are provided for the first and fifth road wheel stations, and the front suspension can be locked when the jib crane is being used. The drive sprocket was modified to assist the vehicle in unditching by winding onto an anchored cable.

At the rear of the hull are four spades which are lowered manually for recovery operations. The main winch is provided with 50 m of 25 mm diameter cable and has a maximum capacity of 17 000 kg. A warning light comes on when a load of 14 000 kg has been reached and the winch stops automatically when 17 000 kg is reached. The secondary winch has a maximum capacity of 11 000 kg and is provided with 120 m of 6 mm diameter cable. The A-frame is pivoted towards the front of the hull and has a maximum capacity of 5000 kg; it can lift components such as AMX-13 tank turrets to a maximum height of 3.4 m. When travelling the A-frame rests over the rear of the hull.

A full range of tools is carried and other equipment includes tow bars, a 250 W searchlight for night work and an 1800 W power unit. The AMX-13 ARV is not provided with an NBC system and does not have any night vision equipment.

Specifications
Crew: 3
Weight in action: 15 300 kg
Length: (outrigger in rear position) 5.6 m
Width:
(overall) 2.59 m
(over tracks) 2.51 m
Height:
(jib stowed) 2.615 m
(jib in use) 4.65 m
(hull) 2.08 m
Ground clearance: 0.43 m
Track: 2.16 m
Length of track on ground: 2.8 m
Ground pressure: 0.76 kg/cm^2
Max speed: (road, petrol engine) 60 km/h
(road, diesel engine) 65 km/h
Range: (road, petrol engine) 400 km
(road, diesel engine) 500 km
Fuel capacity: 480 l
Fording: 1 m
Gradient: 60%
Vertical obstacle:
(forwards) 0.65 m
(rear) 0.45 m
Trench: 1.6 m
Engine: SOFAM Model 8 GXb, 8-cylinder, water-cooled petrol developing 250 hp at 3200 rpm or GM Detroit Diesel developing 280 hp
Transmission: manual with 5 forward and 1 reverse gears (2nd, 3rd, 4th and 5th are synchromesh)
Electrical system: 24 V
Batteries: 4 × 12 V, 95 Ah
Armament:
1 × 7.5 or 7.62 mm MG, 2000 rounds of ammunition

Armour
crew compartment front: 30 mm
crew compartment sides: 20 mm
crew compartment roof: 10 mm
hull rear: 15 mm
hull glacis: 15 mm
floor forward: 20 mm
floor rear: 10 mm

Status
Production complete. Additional production can be undertaken if required. The AMX-13 light tank is used by Argentina, Chile, Dominican Republic, Ecuador, El Salvador, Indonesia (2), Ivory Coast, Djibouti, Lebanon, Morocco, Nepal, Peru, Singapore (no ARV), Tunisia and Venezuela. Many of these countries also have the ARV.

Manufacturer
Creusot-Loire Industrie, Division Mécanique Spécialisée, Immeuble Ile de France, 4 Place de la Pyramide, Cedex 33, F-92070 Paris La Défense, France. Tel: (1) 49 00 57 30. Telex: MOTOY 615 638 F. Fax: (1) 49 00 57 30.

AMX-30D Armoured Recovery Vehicle

Description
The AMX-30D was designed to carry out three basic tasks: recovery of disabled and damaged AFVs, major field repairs such as changing engines, and engineer work.

The chassis of the AMX-30D ARV (or *Char AMX-30 Depanneur-Niveleur*) is identical to that of the basic AMX-30 MBT, but the superstructure is new. Its crew of four consists of commander, driver and two mechanics.

The driver is seated at the front of the hull slightly to the left and is provided with three periscopes for observation. His single-piece hatch cover swings to the left. The commander is seated to his rear and is provided with a TOP 7 cupola. This is similar to that installed on the AMX-30 MBT but does not have the infra-red searchlight or the contra-rotating equipment. The cupola has 10 periscopes for observation and a ×10 sight for the machine gun, which is mounted externally but aimed and fired from within the turret. To the rear of the commander's cupola is the entrance hatch for the engineers which opens to the right. There is a single M336 periscope fore and aft of this hatch cover.

The engine and transmission at the rear of the hull are separated from the crew compartment by a fireproof bulkhead. The suspension is of the torsion bar type and consists of five road wheels with the drive sprocket at the rear and the idler at the front. The first, second, fourth and fifth road wheels are mounted on bogies which are provided with hydraulic shock absorbers. Five rollers support the track.

At the front of the hull is a dozer blade which is hydraulically operated by two cylinders. It is controlled by the driver and is used both for dozing operations and to stabilise the vehicle when the winch crane is being used.

The Griffet crane is mounted at the front right side of the ARV and can lift a load of 12 000 kg through 240°, or 15 000 kg when the crane is towards the front and the dozer blade is in the support position. This crane is normally used for changing major AFV components such as engines and turrets. A spare engine can be carried on the rear of the hull for the rapid replacement of an engine in the field.

The main winch is mounted in the centre of the hull and consists of three subassemblies, frame, transfer gearbox and winch drum with integral reduction gear.

AMX-30D armoured recovery vehicle

The winch cable is led out through the front of the hull. The winch is provided with 100 m of 34 mm diameter cable and is also provided with a safety device which consists of two overload sensing cylinders operated by a pressure switch, which stops the winch automatically when the maximum load of 35 000 kg is reached. The winch has a maximum speed on external layer of 23 m/min and on internal layer of 18.8 m/min.

The auxiliary winch is a Retel TRA 251 mounted at the front of the hull. It is provided with 120 m of 11.2 mm diameter cable and has a maximum capacity of 3500 kg.

The AMX-30D is provided with an NBC system and a crew heater. A snorkel can be installed over the mechanic's hatch enabling the tank to ford to a depth of 4 m.

Variants
The AMX-30D(S) is a special export model for operations in the Middle East with sand shields over the top half of the tracks and a modified gearbox. The engine develops 620 hp at 2400 rpm.

The AMX-30DI was developed by the Pinguely Division of Creusot-Loire. The first prototype was completed in July 1974. This model has a boom which can lift a maximum load of 15 000 kg and slew it through 240°.

Specifications
Crew: 4
Weight: (loaded with spare power plant) 40 000 kg
Length: (dozer blade up, jib in travelling position) 7.53 m
Width: 3.15 m
Height: 2.65 m
(with jib at maximum extension) 6.15 m
(roof) 2.05 m
Ground clearance: 0.45 m
Track: 2.53 m
Track width: 570 mm
Length of track on ground: 4.12 m
Ground pressure: 0.8 kg/cm^2
Max speed: (road) 60 km/h
Range: 650 km

Fuel capacity: 1100 l
Fording: 2 m
(with preparation which takes 5 min) 4 m
Gradient: 60%
Vertical obstacle: 0.93 m
Trench: 2.9 m
Engine: Hispano-Suiza HS-110, 12-cylinder, water-cooled, multi-fuel developing 700 hp at 2400 rpm
Transmission: automatic with 5 forward gears; reverse gear gives same speeds in reverse

Electrical system: 28 V
Batteries: 8 × 12 V, 100 Ah in 2 groups of 4
Armament:
1 × 7.62 mm MG
3 smoke dischargers

Status
In production. In service with the French Army (134) and probably in service with the other countries using the AMX-30 MBT, which include Chile, Cyprus (2), Greece, Iraq, Qatar, Saudi Arabia, Spain (confirmed), Venezuela (4) and the United Arab Emirates.

Manufacturer
Atelier de Construction Roanne (ARE).
Enquiries to Giat Industries, 13 route de la Minière, F-78034 Versailles Cedex, France.
Tel: (1) 30 97 37 37. Fax: (1) 30 97 39 00.

Renault VAB Recovery Armoured Recovery and Repair Vehicle

Description
The Renault VAB Recovery armoured recovery and repair vehicle is under development as a private venture and is available in both 4 × 4 and 6 × 6 configurations. The vehicle was developed for what are described as 'assistance missions' and will be equipped with a crane, recovery winch and repair facilities. For details of the VAB ECH repair vehicle refer to the entry in the *Armoured repair vehicles* section, and for full details of the VAB APC refer to *Jane's Armour and Artillery 1992-93* pages 358 to 362.

The VAB Recovery will have a crew of four; driver and commander in the front compartment and two fitters in the rear. The vehicle will retain the basic layout of the VAB APC but a hydraulically operated telescopic jib crane is mounted on the left-hand side in a recess over the centre of the hull. The 1500 kg capacity crane, which has a traverse of 270°, has a maximum height of 4.4 m and a maximum extension of 4 m. When the crane is in use four stabilisers located at each corner of the hull are lowered hydraulically.

A mechanically powered recovery winch with a 7000 kg capacity is located at the front right-hand side of the vehicle. A block and tackle is carried to increase the winch capacity when required. The winch has a winding speed of 0.27 m/min and is equipped with 60 m of cable. The vehicle is fitted with towing hooks front and rear and a manually operated anchor plate is optional. Among other equipment carried externally are an adjustable floodlight and a ladder.

The rear compartment contains a workbench and to increase internal working height the two rear top hatches can be opened to the vertical position and covered by bows and a tarpaulin cover. Equipment carried, other than tool chests, includes a generating set and oxy-acetylene welding equipment. A removable

Artist's impression of the 6 x 6 version of the VAB Recovery armoured recovery and repair vehicle

stepladder is also provided.

The vehicle commander is provided with a VHF-FM radio set, with a loudspeaker extension to the rear compartment. Armament may be a 7.62 or 12.7 mm machine gun, as required, with internal stowage for 1500 rounds of 7.62 mm ammunition and 500 rounds of 12.7 mm.

Status
Private venture development.

Manufacturer
Renault Véhicules Industriels and Creusot-Loire Industrie.
Enquiries to Société des Matériels Spéciaux Renault V.I. Creusot-Loire Industrie, 316 Bureaux de la Colline, F-92213 Saint-Cloud Cedex, France.
Tel: (1) 46 02 80 33. Telex: 250 662.

GERMANY

Büffel Armoured Recovery Vehicle

Development
Concept studies for a new armoured recovery vehicle capable of recovering up to MLC 70 loads began in 1982, following a series of component studies that commenced in 1977. In 1984 a finalised definition phase contract was placed. This phase was completed in 1986 with the completion of an experimental prototype. A further contract signed in 1987 called for a further two prototypes and the conversion of the experimental prototype.

By 1988 the three prototypes were undergoing technical, tactical and logistic testing. In mid-1990, after an invitation to tender by the Bundesamt für Wehrtechnik und Beschaffung, Krupp MaK (now MaK System Gesellschaft mbH) was selected as the main contractor for series production of the new ARV, named Büffel, for the German Bundeswehr and the Dutch armed forces – the Dutch Army contributed to the development costs.

The order was for 100 vehicles. The original allocation was 75 for the Bundeswehr and 25 for the Dutch armed forces. Manufacture is shared by MaK System at Kiel (55) and Krauss-Maffei (45).

Büffel armoured recovery vehicle

Description

The Büffel ARV is based on the chassis of the Leopard 2 MBT. Its main purpose is the support of the Leopard 2 MBT family of vehicles and can be used for recovery, towing, obstacle removal and crane operations.

The general layout of the Büffel ARV follows that of the earlier Leopard ARV (see following entry).

The Büffel features a traversing crane unit with a maximum capacity of 30 t. Jib traverse is 270°. The crane has an electronic load momentum limiter which computes vehicle tilt, crane jib elevation, load mass, etc, and prevents the crane from being overloaded.

The main winch is a dual capstan unit with an effective cable length of 180 m and a tractive capacity of 35 t. The winch is installed in the hull front plate with direct connection to the cable roller guide so that there is improved distribution of forces directly into the hull structure. The winch has several advanced features such as a constant maximum pulling force and cable speed over the entire cable length, and an absence of cable friction as the cable runs in grooves on the capstans so that the windings do not touch each other. Other features include reduced cable wear, increased cable life, and safe pay-out and pull-in of the cable under all load conditions and varying loads. No cable tensioner is required. This winch is stated to cover 90 to 95 per cent of all military recovery operations as defined by the German Army.

The vehicle is provided with an enlarged dozer/support blade at the front to support and assist during recovery and for obstacle clearing and dozing operations. Other recovery equipment includes an auxiliary winch, a running gear blocking system, a self-recovery system, various couplings and tow bars (including a rapid-recovery bar to be attached to the dozer/support blade) and rapid connect and disconnect couplings for

towing. Electrical cutting and welding equipment is carried. An engine pack may be carried over the engine compartment decking.

Armament carried includes a 7.62 mm machine gun mounted over the commander's cupola and 16 smoke dischargers mounted on the front hull (8) and rear (8). The hull armour is capable of providing protection against 20 mm projectiles.

Specifications (provisional)

Crew: 3 or 4
Combat weight: 54 300 kg
Length: 9.07 m
Width overall: 3.54 m
Height: (less machine gun) 2.735 m
Max speed: 68 km/h
Range: (cruising, road) approx 650 km
Engine: MTU 873 4-stroke exhaust-gas turbocharged diesel developing 1500 hp at 2600 rpm
Transmission: Renk HSWL 284, hydromechanical

Main winch capacity: 35 000 kg
Cable length: 180 m
Crane load:
 (lifting) 30 000 kg
 (pulling) 70 000 kg
Crane traverse: 270°
Towing capacity: 62 000 kg (MLC 70)

Armored Maintenance System
MaK System GmbH has proposed an Armored Maintenance System in which a Büffel ARV is used to tow a tracked field maintenance facility trailer carrying repair and other equipment. The ARV/trailer combination can be used for recovery and the field maintenance and repair support of armoured units. The trailer will use

rubber-belted track running over four idler wheels with air over hydraulic disc brakes on all four wheels. Details of the trailer are as follows:

Weight of trailer:
 (unloaded) 3 t
 (GVW) 10.5 t
Payload: 7.5 t
Length: 4.23 m
Width: 2.4 m
Height: 2.5 m
Ground clearance: 419 mm
Track width: 686 mm
Towed speed:
 (paved road) 80 km/h
 (secondary road) 48 km/h
 (cross-country) 32 km/h

Status

In production (100 ordered) for the Bundeswehr and the Dutch armed forces. The first series vehicles were handed over to both armies at the beginning of August 1992.

Contractors

MaK System Gesellschaft mbH, Falckensteiner Strasse 2, PO Box 9333, D-2300 Kiel 17, Federal Republic of Germany.
Tel: 431 3995-02. Fax: 431 3995 446.
Krauss-Maffei Wehrtechnik GmbH, Krauss-Maffei Strasse 2, D-8000 Munich 50, Federal Republic of Germany.
Tel: 089 8899 2393. Telex: 523163-31.
Fax: 089 8899 2614.

Leopard Armoured Recovery Vehicle

Development

At an early stage in the development of the Leopard MBT the Germans decided to develop an ARV based on its components. Design work was carried out by Porsche with the first prototype being completed by a working group, consisting of Luther and Jordan, Jung Jungenthal and MaK of Kiel, in 1964. The first production ARV (in Germany the Bergepanzer, or BPZ) was completed in September 1966. Production of the ARV and other specialised members of the Leopard family was undertaken by MaK, while production of the MBT was undertaken by Krauss-Maffei of Munich.

The ARV has been designed to undertake the following roles:
 recovering vehicles disabled through enemy action, mechanical failure or which have become bogged down
 towing disabled vehicles
 changing components such as engines and turrets. (A spare Leopard engine pack is carried on the rear decking and a complete engine change can be

carried out in less than 30 minutes. The fastest engine change to date from the tank's stopping to moving off again is 8 minutes.)
 carrying out dozing operations
 refuelling and defuelling other vehicles.

A total of 104 Leopard armoured recovery vehicles has been converted to Pionierpanzer 2 armoured engineer vehicles (see entry in *Armoured engineer vehicles* section).

GLS/Jung Jungenthal are now converting Leopard 1 MBTs to Leopard ARV standard – see following entry.

Description

The Leopard ARV is almost identical to the Leopard AEV, and the reader is referred to this entry for a detailed description of the vehicle. The main differences between the ARV and the AEV are: the ARV carries a spare powerpack and no auger; the ARV carries no explosives for demolition work; no heat exchanger is installed; the dozer blade is not provided with scarifiers to rip up the surface of roads.

In 1978 the German Army took delivery of 100 product-improved Leopard ARVs from MaK. The main improvement is the installation of a hydraulically operated rear support on the right side of the hull at the rear. This relieves the suspension on the crane side

and enables the crane to lift a maximum load of 16 000 kg and traverse it through 270°. In addition the main winch has a higher cable pay-out speed (74 m/min) than the original vehicle's (22 m/min), which corresponds to that of the creeping speed of a Leopard 1 MBT.

The lifting capability of the Product-Improved Leopard ARV compared with the original ARV is as shown in the Specifications below.

Specifications

(data in square brackets relate to product-improved version where different from basic vehicle)
Crew: 4
Weight: (with spare powerpack)
 (empty) 39 200 [39 980] kg
 (loaded) 39 800 [40 580] kg
Length: (spade raised) 7.57 [7.68] m
Width: 3.25 m
Height: (including MG) 2.7 m
Ground clearance: 0.44 m
Track: 2.7 m
Track width: 550 mm
Length of track on ground: 4.236 m
Ground pressure: 0.83 [0.85] kg/cm^2
Max speed: (road) 62 km/h

Leopard armoured recovery vehicle

Dutch Army Leopard armoured recovery vehicle negotiating a dry gap filled with MAXI pipe fascines

Range:
(road) approx 850 km
(cross-country) 500 km
Fuel capacity: 1410 l
Fording: 2.1 m
(with snorkel) 3 m
Gradient: 60%
Side slope: 30%
Vertical obstacle: 1.15 [0.88] m
Trench: 3 m
Engine: MTU MB 838 Ca M-500 10-cylinder multi-fuel developing 830 hp at 2200 rpm
Transmission: ZF 250 with 4 forward and 2 reverse speeds

Electrical system: 24 V
Batteries: 6 with total capacity of 300 Ah, charged by 3-phase generator driven from main engine
Armament:
1 × 7.62 mm MG3 MG in bow
1 × 7.62 mm MG3 MG on commander's hatch
4250 rounds of 7.62 mm ammunition
6 smoke dischargers

Status
Production complete, although conversions from Leopard 1 MBTs are available – see following entry. In service with Australia (6), Belgium (36), Canada (8 – called Taurus), Germany (444 plus 100 product-

improved versions; 104 converted to Pionierpanzer 2), Greece (4), Italy (69), Netherlands (52), Norway (6), and Turkey (4).

Manufacturer
MaK System Gesellschaft mbH, Falckensteiner Strasse 2, PO Box 9333, D-2300 Kiel 17, Federal Republic of Germany.
Tel: 431 3995-02. Fax: 431 3995 446.

GLS/Jung Jungenthal Armoured Recovery Vehicle Conversions

Development
The Gesellschaft für logistischen Service GmbH (a member of the Krauss Maffei group), in conjunction with Jung Jungenthal GmbH, is producing modification kits to convert the M47, M48 and Leopard 1 MBTs into armoured recovery vehicles with a standard virtually identical to that of the Leopard armoured recovery vehicle (see previous entry).

The M47 conversion was developed mainly to meet a Turkish Army requirement. Following testing with an M47 conversion the concept was approved by the Turkish Army in April 1988. The M47 conversion has carried out trials in Pakistan.

The M48 conversion was originally devised in response to a possible Bundeswehr requirement for up to 100 conversions of M48 MBTs. The conversions will involve the armoured recovery vehicle hulls and equipment made available when 104 existing Leopard 1 armoured recovery vehicles were converted into Pionierpanzer 2 armoured engineer vehicles (see entry under *Armoured engineer vehicles* section). A further application is the possible acquisition of 138 M48 ARV conversions by Turkey while Greece is understood to have a requirement for 30 M48 conversions. It is understood that Austria also has a requirement for 25 to 35 M48 conversions. The MBTs used in these conversions will be from German Bundeswehr stocks.

Leopard 1 MBTs are also being used for conversions to ARVs. At least two ex-Bundeswehr MBTs had been converted to ARV standard by mid-1992. It is understood that Denmark has a requirement for 18 ARVs, probably using M48s purchased from Norway.

Description
The conversion involves the removal of the turret from the MBT involved and most of the front hull superstructure and replacing them with a new armoured superstructure, a crane, a winch, a pump drive and a dozer blade system. All are virtually identical to the corresponding components used on the Leopard armoured recovery vehicle and the layout is the same. The M48 conversion also involves the replacement of the Continental main engine by an MTU diesel unit.

The crane has a jib with a six-stage pulley system that can lift loads up to 20 000 kg. The crane can be traversed over an arc of 200° without the support of the dozer blade and 270° with the dozer blade lowered. The maximum hook height is 6.05 m. The crane system has an overload safety switch and a limit switch.

The main winch, powered by two hydraulic motors, has a cable tensioning device and a basic pull capacity of 35 000 kg. By use of a snatch block this can be increased to 70 000 kg. The 33 mm diameter cable length is approximately 90 m long.

The dozer blade is secured to the front hull by two hydraulically powered lever arms and is lifted and lowered by hydraulic cylinders. The blade can be used for earthmoving and can also be used as a stabiliser

GLS armoured recovery vehicle conversion of M48 tank being used to lift Leopard 2 MBT turret

when the crane or main winch is operating. When using the dozer blade the maximum vehicle speed is 8 km/h. The earthmoving capacity when working with heavy soil is 200 m³/h.

The hydraulic system that is used to power the crane, dozer blade and main winch operates at a pressure of 140 bar.

Specifications
(data for M47 conversion – data in square brackets relate to M48 conversion where applicable)
Crew: 4
Weight:
(empty) 43 500 [48 000] kg
(combat) 44 900 [48 500] kg
(max permissible) 47 800 [49 000] kg
Length: 6.998 [7.88] m
Width: 3.59 [3.666] m
Height: 2.985 [2.965] m
Ground clearance: 0.47 [0.46] m
Track: 2.794 m
Track width: 584 mm
Fording: 1.22 m
Gradient: 60%
Vertical obstacle: 0.91 m
Trench: 2.6 m
Engine:
(M47) Continental AV-1790-5B V-12 air-cooled petrol developing 810 bhp at 2800 rpm or
Continental AVDS-1790-2A air-cooled diesel developing 750 hp at 2400 rpm
(M48) MTU MB 837 Ea-501 liquid-cooled diesel developing 750 hp at 2300 rpm
Transmission:
(M47) Allison model CD-850-4, 4A, 4B or 5 cross-drive with 2 forward and 1 reverse ranges

(M48) Allison model CD-850-5 or 6 cross-drive with 2 forward and 1 reverse ranges
Electrical system: 24 V
Armament: smoke dischargers

Boom winch
Cable speed: (with 130 kN) 1.5 to 3.5 m/min
Cable diameter: 13 mm
Cable length: (approx) 100 m

Main winch
Traction in lowest position: 350 to 700 kN
Traction in top position: 200 kN
Cable unwinding speed: approx 22 m/min
Cable winding speed: (1st step) approx 14 m/min
Cable winding speed: (2nd step) approx 44 m/min
Cable length: (approx) 90 m
Cable diameter: 33 mm

Dozer blade
Blade length: 3.25 m
Blade height: 0.591 m
Max dozing speed: 8 km/h
Max dozing capacity: approx 200 m³/h

Status
Ready for production.

Manufacturers
Gesellschaft für logistischen Service GmbH, Allacher Strasse 230e, D-8000 München 50, PO Box 50 02 31, Federal Republic of Germany.
Tel: 0898 899-0. Telex: 5215583. Fax: 0898 126 380.
Jung Jungenthal GmbH, PO Box 20, D-5242 Kirchen, Federal Republic of Germany.
Tel: 02741 683-0. Telex: 875319. Fax: 02741 683 246.

INTERNATIONAL

VCRT Armoured Recovery Vehicle

Description
The VCRT armoured recovery vehicle uses the chassis of the Argentinian VCTP ICV (for details of this vehicle refer to *Jane's Armour and Artillery 1992-93* pages 269 and 270) allied to an armoured superstructure and recovery rig supplied by Krupp MaK. The prototype was ready for initial trials during May 1987.

The VCRT has a crew of four. The driver is positioned in the left of the sloping front hull with the rest of the crew housed in a raised armoured superstructure. On the right of the superstructure is a crane jib with a 213.5° traverse and a maximum lift of 22 t. The main 30 t winch is located within the hull front with a straight dozer blade mounted on the rear to provide extra anchorage when recovering stranded vehicles.

Status
Prototype.

Manufacturers
Chassis: TAMSE, Avenida Rolon 1445, Boulogne Sur Mer, CP 1609, Buenos Aires, Argentina.
Tel: (763) 114/4937/0714. Telex: 26208 TAMSE AR.
Fax: (763) 2624.

Superstructure and recovery rig: Krupp MaK Mas-

Model of VCRT armoured recovery vehicle

chinenbau GmbH, Falckensteiner Strasse 2, PO Box 9009, D-2300 Kiel 17, Federal Republic of Germany.

Tel: (0431) 381 2686. Telex: 02 99 877 mak d.
Fax: (0431) 381 2193.

ITALY

OF-40 Armoured Recovery Vehicle

Description
The OF-40 armoured recovery vehicle is based on the chassis and hull of the OF-40 MBT (for details refer to *Jane's Armour and Artillery 1992-93*, pages 91 to 94). In place of the normal rotating turret the armoured recovery vehicle uses a fixed turret superstructure, and is equipped with a crane, winch and dozer blade.

The driver sits in his normal position offset to the right at the front of the hull. The superstructure houses the commander and two fitters. There is a hydraulic jib crane mounted on the left-hand side of the vehicle with the jib turret providing a 270° traverse. A 6 m boom is fitted with a maximum direct front-lift capacity of 18 000 kg retracted and 5000 kg when fully extended or when traversing with a load. When stowed the crane jib lies along the upper hull of the vehicle and the hydraulic actuating cylinders are arranged so that they are protected from damage by artillery splinters and other such hazards. If the hydraulic system fails the jib can be raised and lowered by hand.

The main winch is installed in the crew compartment and has a direct pull capacity of 36 000 kg although this can be increased to 72 000 kg by use of a pulley block. The winch is normally used in conjunction with the dozer blade which is fully lowered for maximum pull and partially lowered to provide access to the winch hatch at the front of the hull. Power for the winch is hydraulic and a 540 l hydraulic fluid tank is located on the left side of the vehicle – this tank also provides the hydraulic fluid for all other systems such as the crane and the dozer blade. The winch is supplied with 80 m of 32 mm cable.

The dozer blade can be used for field combat engineering tasks but is also used as a support stabiliser for winching operations as described above. The blade is controlled by the driver and can be lowered manually.

The OF-40 armoured recovery vehicle carries recovery and repair tools around the hull and inside the superstructure. Some spares can be carried and a spare engine pack can be carried on the hull decks at the rear. The superstructure interior has an automatic fire-extinguishing system and there is provision for mounting a 7.62 mm machine gun between the commander's and fitter's hatches on the superstructure roof. A bank of six smoke dischargers is located on the right-hand side of the superstructure. The sides of the

OF-40 armoured recovery vehicle with spare powerpack on hull rear

superstructure use armour 50 mm thick, the same thickness as the hull sides.

Specifications
Crew: 4
Weight:
  (combat) 45 000 kg
  (kerb) 43 000 kg
Ground pressure: 0.92 kg/cm^2
Power-to-weight ratio: 18.5 hp/t
Length: (crane stowed) 7.68 m
Width: 2.47 m
Height: (top of superstructure) 2.35 m
Ground clearance: 0.44 m
Max speed:
  (forward) 65 km/h
  (reverse) 24 km/h
Range: (road) 600 km
Fuel capacity: approx 1000 l
Fording: 1.2 m
Gradient: 60%
Side slope: 30%
Vertical obstacle: 0.7 m

Trench: 3 m
Engine: MTU MB 838 Ca M-500 37.4 l V-10 diesel or multi-fuel developing 830 hp at 2200 rpm
Transmission: ZF 4HP 250 with hydraulic torque converter and lock-up clutch and with 4 forward and 2 reverse gears
Suspension: torsion bar
Electrical system: 24 V
Batteries: 8 × 12 V 100 Ah each, total capacity 400 Ah at 24 V
Armament:
  1 × 7.62 mm machine gun
  6 × smoke dischargers

Status
Production complete. In service with United Arab Emirates (4).

Manufacturer
OTO Melara, via Valdilocchi 15, I-19100 La Spezia, Italy.
Tel: 0187 53 01 11. Telex: 270368.
Fax: 0187 53 06 69.

JAPAN

Type 90 Armoured Recovery Vehicle

Description

To support the new Type 90 MBT, Mitsubishi Heavy Industries has developed a prototype of the Type 90 armoured recovery vehicle based on the same hydropneumatic suspension and powerpack but with a new superstructure. On the left-hand front of the upper hull is the pivot for a hydraulically operated crane with a maximum capacity of 25 t and a remote-control facility; for travelling, the crane is stowed facing the rear along the right-hand side of the hull top. Located alongside the crane pivot is the superstructure with accommodation for the driver, commander and two other crew members. The crew commander's cupola is provided with a mounting for a 0.50/12.7 mm machine gun; the superstructure also carries smoke dischargers. Mounted on the front of the vehicle is a hydraulically operated dozer blade that can also be used as a stabiliser during recovery operations. The vehicle is provided with a recovery winch capable of recovering the Type 90 MBT which has a combat weight of 50 t. After recovery the Type 90 armoured recovery vehicle can tow a Type 90 MBT.

The Type 90 armoured recovery vehicle weighs 50 t and has a maximum road speed of 70 km/h. It can pivot turn.

Status
Prototype.

Prototype of Type 90 armoured recovery vehicle

Manufacturer
Mitsubishi Heavy Industries, 5-1 Marunouchi 2-chome, Chiyoda-ku, Tokyo 100, Japan.
Tel: (81 3) 212 31 11. Telex: 22282.
Fax: (81 3) 201 62 58.

Type 78 Armoured Recovery Vehicle

Description

The prototype of an ARV based on the chassis of the Type 74 MBT was completed in 1974 and subsequently standardised as the Type 78 ARV in 1978. The layout of the Type 78 ARV is very similar to that of the German Leopard 1 and French AMX-30D ARVs. Mounted on the right side of the hull at the front is a hydraulically operated crane which is 3.5 m long and has a jib that can be extended a further 1.5 m. The jib can be traversed through 270° and lift a maximum load of 20 000 kg. Mounted at the front of the hull is a hydraulically operated dozer blade which can be used both for dozing operations and as a stabiliser when the winch is being used. The Type 78 retains the hydropneumatic suspension of the Type 74 MBT.

The winch has a maximum capacity of 38 000 kg, is provided with 60 m of 32 mm diameter cable and has two speeds: 6 and 15 m/min. A hydraulic motor is used to extract the cable from the winch at a maximum speed of 30 m/min and there is also a system to apply tension to the cable for rewinding smoothly into the winch when there is no load.

Armament of the Type 78 ARV consists of a pintle-mounted 0.50/12.7 mm M2 HB machine gun and six smoke dischargers.

Specifications
Crew: 4
Weight: 38 000 kg

Type 78 ARV in travelling configuration (Kensuke Ebata)

Length: 7.95 m
Width: (overall) 3.38 m
Height: (to top of hull) 2.4 m
Ground clearance: 0.4 m
Max speed: 53 km/h
Gradient: 60%
Engine: Mitsubishi 10 ZF 2-cycle 10-cylinder air-cooled diesel, developing 720 hp at 2200 rpm
Transmission: Mitsubishi power-shift with 6 forward and 1 reverse gears
Suspension: hydropneumatic with suspension lock at kneeled position
Crane capacity: 20 000 kg
Main winch capacity: 38 000 kg

Armament:
1 × 0.50/12.7 mm MG
6 × smoke dischargers

Status
Production complete. In service with the Japanese Ground Self-Defence Force.

Manufacturer
Mitsubishi Heavy Industries, 5-1 Marunouchi 2-chome, Chiyoda-ku, Tokyo 100, Japan.
Tel: (81 3) 212 31 11. Telex: 22282.
Fax: (81 3) 201 62 58.

Type 70 Armoured Recovery Vehicle

Description

The Type 70 armoured recovery vehicle is based on the chassis of the Type 61 MBT. The turret is replaced by a superstructure which has a winch mounted in a bustle at the rear. The layout of the Type 70 is conventional, with the driver's compartment at the front, crew compartment in the centre and the engine and transmission at the rear. The suspension is of the torsion bar type and consists of six road wheels with the drive sprocket at the front and the idler at the rear. There are three track support rollers and shock absorbers are provided for the first, second, fifth and sixth road wheel stations.

A dozer blade is mounted at the front of the hull for clearing obstacles and for stabilising the vehicle when the A-frame is being used. The latter is pivoted either side of the hull superstructure and is used to change components. A full range of equipment is carried including tow bars, tools and cutting and welding gear.

A 0.50/12.7 mm Browning machine gun is mounted on top of the superstructure for anti-aircraft defence and an 81 mm mortar can be mounted on the front of the hull.

Specifications
Crew: 4
Weight: 35 000 kg
Length: 8.4 m
Width: 2.95 m
Height: 3.1 m
Ground clearance: 0.4 m
Track: 2.45 m

Type 70 ARV with A-frame to rear (K Nogi)

Track width: 500 mm
Length of track on ground: 3.7 m
Ground pressure: 0.95 kg/cm²
Max speed: (road) 45 km/h
Range: 200 km
Fording: 1 m

Gradient: 60%
Vertical obstacle: 0.5 m
Trench: 2.7 m
Engine: Mitsubishi Type 12 HM 21 WT V-12 diesel injection turbocharged, air-cooled developing 650 hp at 2100 rpm

Transmission: mechanical with 5 forward and 1 reverse gears, with 2-speed auxiliary reduction unit
Electrical system: 24 V
Batteries: 4 × 12 V, 200 Ah
Armament:
   1 × 0.50/12.7 mm Browning M2 HB MG
   1 × 81 mm mortar
Armour
hull front: 46 mm
hull sides: 25 mm
hull rear: 15 mm

Status
Production complete. In service only with the Japanese Ground Self-Defence Force.

Manufacturer
Production was undertaken at the Maruko, Tokyo, plant of Mitsubishi Heavy Industries, but AFV production is now at the Sagamihara Plant, near Tokyo. Mitsubishi Heavy Industries, 5-1 Marunouchi 2-chome, Chiyoda-ku, Tokyo 100, Japan.
Tel: (81 3) 212 31 11. Telex: 22282.
Fax: (81 3) 201 62 58.

KOREA, SOUTH

K-1 Armoured Recovery Vehicle

Description
The K-1 armoured recovery vehicle is a derivative of the K-1 MBT, also known as the Type 88 MBT (for details of the Type 88 refer to *Jane's Armour and Artillery 1992-93* pages 101 to 103). The K-1 ARV was developed in co-operation with Krupp MaK of Germany and uses an armoured superstructure and recovery system similar to that of the German Büffel armoured recovery vehicle (see separate entry in this section).

The K-1 ARV is based on the chassis and running gear of the Type 88/K-1 MBT which was developed by the Land Systems Division of General Dynamics in the United States. It is powered by a 1200 hp water-cooled, multi-fuel MTU MB 871 Ka-501 diesel providing a maximum road speed of 65 km/h. A gas turbine auxiliary power unit, developing 112 hp at 9300 rpm, is also provided.

The crew is four men; commander, driver, operator and a mechanic. An integral crew heating system is provided but NBC protection is restricted to individual systems.

The main winch is of the capstan type and is provided with 150 m of usable cable. The winch capacity is 35 tonnes, or 70 tonnes with a guide pulley. There is also an auxiliary winch with 260 m of usable cable.

The hydraulic lifting crane mounted on a turntable to the right of the main superstructure has a maximum lifting capacity of 25 tonnes and can be elevated to an angle of 70°; the crane traverse is 270°. A straight dozer blade is mounted at the front and can be used for obstacle clearing or for support when operating the main winch. The blade's soil-moving capacity is 170 m³/h.

The combat weight of the K-1 armoured recovery vehicle is 51 tonnes, or 56 tonnes when carrying a spare powerpack on the rear decking.

A pintle for a 12.7 mm machine gun is mounted over the commander's cupola on the superstructure roof

K-1 armoured recovery vehicle (left) in action towing Type 88 MBT (right)

and smoke grenade dischargers are mounted on the hull front.

Specifications
Crew: 4
Weight:
   (combat) 51 000 kg
   (with spare powerpack) 56 000 kg
Length: 8.93 m
Width: 3.64 m
Height: 2.65 m
Max speed: (road) 65 km/h
Fording:
   (normal) 1.2 m
   (with kit) 2.2 m
Gradient: 60%
Side slope: 30%
Vertical obstacle: 0.9 m

Trench: 2.74 m
Engine: MTU MB 871 Ka-501 diesel developing 1200 hp at 2600 rpm
Transmission: ZF LSG3000 automatic with 4 forward and 2 reverse gears
Suspension: hydropneumatic and torsion bar
Electrical system: 24 V
Armament: 1 × 12.7 mm MG

Status
Prototype.

Manufacturer
Hyundai Precision & Ind Co Ltd, 140-2, Gye-Dong, Chongro-Ku, Seoul, South Korea.
Tel: (82-2) 746 4010. Telex: HDPIC K23238.
Fax: (82-2) 741 2248.

KIFV Armoured Recovery Vehicle

Description
KIFV stands for Korean Infantry Fighting Vehicle and denotes a family of armoured vehicles. For full details of the KIFV family refer to *Jane's Armour and Artillery 1992-93* pages 408 to 410.

The KIFV family includes an armoured recovery vehicle which is used to support and recover KIFV

units in the field. The KIFV ARV is based on the same chassis, running gear and upper aluminium-armoured hull of the basic IFV version but is provided with a recovery winch and crane together with other equipment and tools to assist in the recovery role. The vehicle can also be used to change components such as powerpacks. There is space inside the vehicle for a crew of up to four.

The recovery winch is located internally and has a capacity of 20 tonnes. When the winch is in use two

stabiliser spades can be lowered from the hull rear.

The hydraulic crane is positioned on the left-hand side of the hull roof, and for transport is stowed with the crane boom facing to the front. The crane has a lifting capacity of 3500 kg.

As with other members of the KIFV family, the KIFV ARV is fully amphibious, being propelled in the water by its tracks.

Specifications

Crew: up to 4
Weight:
  (combat) 14 500 kg
  (empty) 12 800 kg
Power-to-weight ratio: 24.1 hp/t
Ground pressure: (combat) 0.75 kg/cm^2
Length:
  (overall) 5.93 m
  (hull) 5.345 m
Width:
  (overall) 2.91 m
  (over tracks) 2.545 m
Height:
  (top of crane, stowed) 3.05 m
  (hull roof) 1.829 m
Ground clearance: 0.41 m
Track width: 381 mm
Max speed:
  (road) 65 km/h
  (water) 5.6 km/h
Range: (cruising) 480 km
Fuel capacity: 400 l
Fording: amphibious
Gradient: 60%
Side slope: 30%
Vertical obstacle: 0.63 m
Trench: 1.7 m
Engine: MAN (Daewoo) D2848M 14.62 l V-8 diesel developing 280 hp or MAN (Daewoo) D2848T 14.62 l V-8 turbocharged diesel developing 350 hp
Transmission: Self-changing Gears (Daewoo) T-300 semi-automatic with 7 forward and 7 reverse gears or Daewoo X200-5D automatic with 7 forward and 7 reverse gears

KIFV armoured recovery vehicle

Suspension: torsion bar
Electrical system: 28 V
Armament: 1 × 12.7 mm MG

Status
In production. In service with the South Korean Army.

Manufacturer
Special Product Division, Daewoo Heavy Industries Limited, 20th Floor, Daewoo Center, 541, 5ga Namdaemun-ro, Jung-ga, Seoul, South Korea. Tel: (02) 726 3011. Telex: DHILTD K23301. Fax: (02) 756 2679.

POLAND

WZT-3 Armoured Recovery Vehicle

Description

The WZT-3 armoured recovery vehicle is based on the chassis of the T-72 MBT as produced in Poland at the Machinery Industrial Complex 'Bumar-Labedy'. In general layout and appearance it resembles the CIS BREM-1 but there are numerous differences to suit Polish armed forces requirements.

The WZT-3 has a crew of up to four, although only two (the driver and commander) are required during operations. The driver is seated under a hatch cover to the left front of an armoured superstructure with the commander seated on the right under a cupola provided with vision periscopes and a 12.7 mm machine gun pintle. Both the commander and driver are provided with night vision devices. A further crew hatch is provided in the centre of the superstructure roof towards the rear of the superstructure. Behind the superstructure is a load-carrying platform for spare powerpacks or other components. The platform measures 1.91 m long by 2.16 m wide and has side walls 0.62 m high; the load capacity is 3500 kg.

Mounted on a small turntable to the left front of the superstructure is an extending jib crane with a lifting capacity of 15 tonnes. At the front of the vehicle is a 3.605 m wide dozer blade which can be used for earth excavating or anchoring and support during recovery operations. The main recovery winch is mechanically driven and has a maximum pulling capacity, with tackle, of 840 kN. There is also an auxiliary hydraulic winch with a pulling capacity of 20 kN.

Other recovery equipment carried includes rigid tow bars and tow cables. Specialised repair equipment includes electrical and gas welding gear, impact wrenches, chain saws, a tool kit and various special tools, spares and mobile work benches.

The WZT-3 can be fitted with a deep wading kit for water obstacles up to 1000 m wide. Extra fuel can be carried in drums carried on the hull rear.

WZT-3 armoured recovery vehicle

Specifications
Crew: up to 4
Weight: (approx) 42 000 kg
Length overall: 8.3 m
Width:
    (overall) 3.6 m
    (over tracks) 3.37 m
Height: (top of hull) 2.17 m
Ground clearance: 0.428 m
Track: 2.79 m
Length of track on ground: 4.27 m
Max speed: 60 km/h
Range:
    (road) 650 km
    (dirt road) 420 to 600 km

Fuel capacity:
    (basic) 1126 l
    (with extra tanks) 1526 l
Fording:
    (normal) 1.2 m
    (with preparation) 5 m
Vertical obstacle: 0.7 m
Trench: 2.6-2.8 m
Engine: liquid-cooled multi-fuel supercharged diesel developing 780 hp at 2000 rpm
Transmission: synchromesh, hydraulically assisted with 7 forward and 1 reverse gears
Steering: clutch and brake
Suspension: torsion bar
Electrical system: 28.5 V

Armament: 1 × 12.7 mm MG

Status
In production. In service with Polish Army.

Manufacturer
Machinery Industrial Complex 'Bumar-Labedy'.
Marketed by: Machinery Industrial Complex 'Bumar-Labedy', Foreign Trade Bureau, 9 Mechanikow Street, 44-109 Gliwice, Poland.
Tel: 34 58 05. Telex: 036553 bumar pl.
Fax: 34 69 66.

WPT-TOPAS Armoured Recovery Vehicle

Description
The WPT-TOPAS is a Polish modification of the Czechoslovak OT-62A APC, used by the Polish Army under the name of TOPAS (*Transporter Obrneny Pasovy*). The OT-62 is the BTR-50 series APC built in Czechoslovakia with many modifications and improvements. The Polish Army calls the WPT-TOPAS a technical support vehicle and Germany refers to it as a recovery, maintenance and repair vehicle. It is used by units equipped with PT-76 amphibious tanks and TOPAS APCs.

The hull is of all-welded steel armour with the crew compartment at the front and the engine and transmission at the rear. The driver is seated at the front of the hull in the centre and has a one-piece hatch cover that opens outwards with an integral viewing block. There

are a further three viewing blocks below the hatch cover. On the left and right sides of the hull at the front are semi-circular projecting bays, each with three observation blocks. The commander is normally seated in the left bay which has a single-piece hatch cover. Over the right projecting bay is a 7.62 mm machine gun in an armoured mounting, which can be traversed through 360°. The machine gun can be elevated from −15 to +80°. In addition the WPT-TOPAS carries an RPG-7 anti-tank grenade launcher, hand grenades and a signal pistol. Most vehicles have at least two roof hatches and a single door in each side of the hull.

The suspension is of the torsion bar type and consists of six road wheels with the drive sprocket at the rear and the idler at the front. There are no track return rollers. The first and sixth road wheel stations are provided with hydraulic shock absorbers.

The WPT-TOPAS is fully amphibious, propelled in water by two waterjets, one on each side of the hull. Before entering the water a trim board is erected at the

front of the hull and the bilge pumps are switched on.

It is believed that the vehicle has an NBC system as one is installed on the standard APC. Infra-red night vision equipment is provided.

The WPT-TOPAS is provided with a winch with a capacity of 2500 kg and 600 m of cable, a hand-operated crane with a capacity of 1000 kg that can be mounted at various points on the vehicle, spare parts, welding equipment, tools and a four-man tent.

Specifications
Crew: 5
Weight: 15 000 kg
Length: 7 m
Width: 3.14 m
Height: 2.72 m
Ground clearance: 0.41 m
Track: 2.74 m
Track width: 360 mm
Length of track on ground: 4.08 m
Ground pressure: 0.53 kg/cm^2
Max speed:
    (road) 60 km/h
    (water) 10.8 km/h
Range: (road) 500 km
Fuel capacity: 417 l
Fording: amphibious
Gradient: 55%
Vertical obstacle: 1.1 m
Trench: 2.3 m
Engine: PV-6, 6-cylinder in-line diesel developing 300 hp at 1800 rpm with pre-heater for cold starts
Transmission: manual with 5 forward and 1 reverse gears
Electrical system: 24 V
Armament: 1 × 7.62 mm PK MG

Armour
glacis: 11 mm at 80°
upper hull side: 14 mm at 0°
hull roof: 10 mm
hull rear: 10 mm
hull floor: 10 mm (max)

Status
Production complete. In service with the former East German and Polish Army and Marines.

Manufacturer
Czechoslovak state factories with conversion work carried out by Poland.

WPT-TOPAS armoured recovery vehicle with 1000 kg capacity hand-operated crane in position on left side of hull

---

SOUTH AFRICA

Olifant Armoured Recovery Vehicle

Description
The South Africans have converted a number of Centurion tanks to Olifant (Elephant) armoured recovery vehicles. The conversions involve the replacement of the existing powerpack and transmission by the equivalent uprated components fitted into the Olifant tank conversions, also carried out in South Africa. (For details of the Olifant MBT refer to *Jane's*

Armour and Artillery 1992-93 pages 108 and 109).

The structural conversions include removing the tank turret and fitting a fixed armoured superstructure onto the hull. The superstructure houses the crew of at least four men with the driver seated in a position raised from his former driving location to behind a protected window on the right-hand side of the superstructure front. An extending boom crane is positioned to the left of the superstructure; it has a possible traverse of 360°. A front-mounted stabilising spade, which can also be used as an obstacle-clearing dozer

blade, is brought into use when the internally mounted recovery winch is used in the forward-operating mode; the winch cable can also be deployed through a rear-mounted guide assembly primarily for self-recovery to the rear. Various items of recovery equipment are stowed around the superstructure and there are stowage bins provided over the powerpack cover area.

There is provision for machine gun mountings on the cupolas located on the superstructure roof and there are four sets of four-barrelled 81 mm smoke dischargers, one on each corner of the superstructure. No other armament appears to be carried other than the crew's personal weapons.

No further details regarding the Olifant armoured recovery vehicle are available. It has been reported that an armoured repair variant of this vehicle is to be produced. This variant will be able to carry a complete Olifant powerpack. At present this role is carried out within Olifant units by 8 × 8 wheeled vehicles.

Status
In service with the South African Defence Forces.

Manufacturer
Enquiries to: ARMSCOR, Private Bag X337, Pretoria 0001, South Africa.
Tel: (012) 428 1911. Telex: 30217.
Fax: (012) 428 5635.

Olifant armoured recovery vehicle

TFM Gemsbok (4 × 4) Armoured Recovery Vehicle

Development
The TFM Gemsbok (4 × 4) armoured recovery vehicle is a member of the Casspir family of vehicles based on a wheeled armoured personnel carrier, the Casspir Mark 2 (for details refer to *Jane's Armour and Artillery 1992-93* pages 423 to 425). These vehicles have been designed to operate as internal security and riot control vehicles but can also operate over long periods in the bush and desert terrain conditions prevailing in South Africa. The Casspir series, including the Gemsbok armoured recovery vehicle, is operated by the South African Police.

Description
The Gemsbok uses the standard Casspir Mark 2 chassis which in its turn is based on a commercial 15 t 4 × 4 truck. The armoured front cab uses a combination of armour plated and high alloy steels and has a V-shaped monocoque hull to withstand land mine explosions. The hull can withstand three simultaneous TM-57 type anti-tank mine explosions (or an equivalent of between 18 and 20 kg of TNT) without penetration although mechanical component damage may occur. The armour is proof against NATO 7.62 and 5.56 mm ball ammunition and all windows use bullet-resistant glass. Mounted on the roof next to the driver's position is a one-man steel turret that can mount one 7.62 mm machine gun and a further machine gun can be mounted in the front left windscreen.

The armoured cab has seating for three of the crew of a recovered vehicle as well as the recovery vehicle crew of driver and commander. The armoured cab also contains the 185 l fuel tank. Cab ventilation is provided by two impeller fans.

The Gemsbok recovery unit is mounted on the open chassis behind the armoured cab and consists of a twin boom, two service drum recovery hoist with a maximum capacity of 5000 kg. Rectangular section stabilising legs are provided on each side of the chassis for when the hoist is in use. Tool box and other stowage is provided on the rear area for extra recovery equipment and special tools. A standard vehicle tool kit is carried inside the main cab.

Specifications
Cab seating: 2 + 3
Configuration: 4 × 4
Weight:
  (empty) 9600 kg

TFM Gemsbok (4 × 4) armoured recovery vehicle

  (loaded) 14 800 kg
Max load: 5000 kg
Towed load: 15 000 kg
Length: 6.74 m
Width: 2.5 m
Height: 3.12 m
Ground clearance: 0.355 m
Wheelbase: 4.3 m
Angle of approach: 46°
Max speed: 87 km/h
Range:
  (road) 850 km
  (cross-country) 560 km
Fuel capacity: 185 l
Max gradient: 60%
Side slope: 30%
Vertical obstacle: 0.5 m
Trench: 0.95 m
Fording: 1 m
Engine: ADE 352 T 5.675 l 6-cylinder vertical in-line turbocharged diesel developing 162.5 hp at 2800 rpm
Gearbox: Mercedes Benz DB G 3/60 – 5/7, 5 synchromesh with 5 forward and 1 reverse gears
Clutch: single dry plate

Transfer box: Mercedes Benz 2-speed
Steering: ball and nut, power-assisted
Turning circle: 18.3 m
Suspension: semi-elliptic leaf springs on needle roller bearings with telescopic shock absorbers front and rear (double spring pack at rear)
Tyres: 14.00 × 20
Number of tyres: 4 + 1 spare
Brakes:
  (main) dual circuit air-assisted hydraulic with engine-mounted exhaust brake
  (parking) mechanical
Electrical system: 12 V
Battery: 1 × 12 V
Alternator: 55 A
Armament: 2 × 7.62 mm MG

Status
In production. In service with South African Police.

Manufacturer
TFM (Pty) Limited, PO Box 46131, Orange Grove 2119, Transvaal, South Africa.
Tel: 316 2106. Fax: 316 1492.

SPAIN

M-47 E2R Armoured Recovery Vehicle

Development
In 1981 Spain purchased 100 M47 tanks from Italian sources to be modified into special-purpose vehicles. One vehicle, after conversion, was used as a prototype which could later be converted into either a combat engineer vehicle or an armoured recovery vehicle. From this, a further prototype was developed into a full armoured recovery vehicle. The armoured recovery vehicle and the combat engineer vehicle are very similar, both having a front-mounted dozer blade and a swivelling jib crane. To date only the prototypes have been converted from the basic M47 tank; it was anticipated that at least 48 conversions to the armoured recovery vehicle role will be made. The conversion work is being undertaken by Peugeot Talbot España SA, formerly Chrysler España. Before the Chrysler takeover the company was known as Barreiros.

Description
On the M-47 E2R (R – *Recuperacion*) the basic hull of the American M47 tank is retained but the running gear is replaced by M60 components. The transmission has been replaced by an automatic system and the main powerpack is now a Continental V-12 diesel. The main hull superstructure appears to be closely modelled on that of the Leopard 1 armoured engineer vehicle and armoured recovery vehicle as the shape and layout are very similar. The main box-shaped compartment is to the left of a 360° swivelling crane jib with the traversing platform mounted well forward. The box compartment houses the crew of four (commander, driver and two mechanics). Mounted on the front hull is a dozer blade operated via two hydraulic cylinders.

The crane jib of the M-47 E2R has a lift capacity of 56 000 kg and can be elevated to an angle of 71° at which height the hook is 6.34 m above the ground. When traversed directly to the right-hand side of the hull the jib has a length of 6.1 m; fully extended jib length is 8.6 m. The main box compartment houses a winch equipped with 100 m of cable. With a single core of this cable the winch can pull a 35 000 kg load through a port in the bottom front hull. If the cable is doubled using pulleys the load can be increased to 70 000 kg. The dozer blade is used during winching and loads can be pulled from an angle 15° either side of the hull centre line. Loads can also be pulled from 15° above the horizontal and 40° below.

The M-47 E2R carries an electrical generator powered by an 8 hp air-cooled diesel engine and supplying 220/380 V at 5.5 kVA. An air compressor is carried with various items of specialist recovery equipment such as shackles, joists, spare wheels and

M-47 E2R armoured recovery vehicle

tracks, tools, and other such items.

A 0.50/12.7 mm Browning machine gun is mounted on a pintle over the commander's hatch with a 7.62 mm MG1-A3 machine gun to the left of the driver's position, firing through a port in the front hull. Two sets of three-barrelled smoke grenade launchers are carried on the left of the superstructure.

Specifications
Crew: 4
Weight: 47 100 kg
Length:
  (jib rear, dozer blade raised) 7.55 m
  (jib forward, 0° elevation) 11.41 m
Width:
  (overall) 3.65 m
  (over tracks) 3.39 m
  (inside tracks) 2.235 m
Height: (overall) 3.25 m
Ground clearance: 0.47 m
Track width: 580 mm
Length of track on ground: 3.91 m
Ground pressure: 1.02 kg/cm²
Max speed: 56 km/h
Range: 600 km
Fuel capacity: 1500 l
Fording: 1.2 m

Gradient: 60%
Side slope: 30%
Vertical obstacle: 0.9 m
Trench: 2.6 m
Engine: Continental Model AVDS-1790-2D 29.315 l V-12 air-cooled diesel developing 760 hp at 2400 rpm
Transmission: GMC-Allison CD-850-6A with 2 forward and 1 reverse ranges
Electrical system: 24 V
Number of batteries: 6 × 12 V, 300 Ah
Armament:
  1 × 0.50/12.7 mm MG
  1 × 7.62 mm MG
  2 × 3-barrel smoke dischargers
Ammunition:
  (12.7 mm) 600 rounds
  (7.62 mm) 2000 rounds

Status
Prototype completed. Conversion of at least 48 vehicles planned.

Manufacturer/Converter
Peugeot Talbot España, Apartado 140, E-28080 Madrid, Spain.
Tel: 347 20 00. Telex: 27590.
Fax: 347 22 43.

BMR 3560.55 Armoured Recovery and Repair Vehicle

Description
The BMR 3560.55 armoured recovery vehicle is based on the hull and suspension of the BMR 3560.50 armoured personnel carrier and has many components in common with the basic vehicle. It is intended for the recovery of other vehicles in the BMR range (and similar vehicles) and also has some repair capabilities for immobilised vehicles in the field.

The BMR 3560.55 recovery vehicle retains the basic 6 × 6 configuration and hull of the armoured personnel carrier virtually unchanged, the main alteration being the installation of a hydraulic crane on a roof-mounted turntable. This crane has a full 360° traverse and a lifting capacity of 18 000 kg/m. The horizontal reach is 6 m and the maximum hook elevation is 8 m. To stabilise the crane when deployed the BMR 3560.55 has four hydraulically operated stabiliser jacks, two on each side between the first and second set of road wheels and the other two at the rear behind the rear set of wheels. The latter deploy to the rear and are located in place of the water propulsion units fitted to the

BMR 3560.55 armoured recovery vehicle with hydraulic crane deployed and with hydraulic jacks in position

armoured personnel carrier and other vehicles in the BMR series.

Access to the interior of the vehicle is gained via a large single-piece rear ramp that opens downwards. The driver's position may be reached from inside the vehicle main cabin or through a roof hatch. There is another roof hatch for the commander and another for the crane operator towards the rear. The commander's position has a cupola with a machine gun mounting (0.50/12.7 mm or 7.62 mm) that can be operated from within the vehicle. The weapon ports of the basic BMR are retained to allow the crew to use their personal weapons from within and a rack of six Wegmann smoke dischargers is situated on the left-hand side of the hull.

Inside the main vehicle cabin there is provision for various tool cabinets and other special racks but the main space is occupied by a Rotzler winch with a pulling capacity of 7000 kg; by using double pulleys this can be increased to 14 000 kg. The cable length is 100 m. The normal front-mounted winch of the BMR is retained. This has a pulling capacity of 4500 kg. The controls for the main winch are located close to those of the crane, that is, inside the crane-operator's turret hatch. The crane and main winch can both be operated from within the main cabin with the rear door closed. When the rear ramp is closed the main winch cable is passed through the rear door emergency hatch.

To enable the vehicle to be used in the repair role the BMR 3560.55 carries a canvas penthouse and supports on the roof and sides. For this purpose, lighting is supplied by a 50 m long string of lamps with power from a 1.5 kW generator. A workshop tool kit, a welding kit, slings, chains and other recovery and repair equipment are also carried. A lockable tool chest is located just inside the left of the rear door. Radio equipment is located against the engine bulkhead.

The BMR 3560.55 is amphibious and, when in the water, propulsion is obtained from the spinning of the vehicle wheels. Although no water propulsion jets were supplied for versions produced for the Egyptian Army they may be fitted to versions supplied for Marine units.

Specifications
Crew: 5
Configuration: 6 × 6
Combat weight: (APC) 13 750 kg
Length: 6.15 m
Width: 2.5 m
Height: (hull top) 2 m
Ground clearance: 0.45 m (adjustable)
Track: 2.08 m
Wheelbase: 1.65 m + 1.65 m
Angle of approach/departure: 50°/45°
Max speed: 100 km/h
Fuel capacity: 300 l

Max range: 700 km
Fording: amphibious
Gradient: 60%
Side slope: 30%
Vertical obstacle: 0.8 m
Trench: 1.2 m
Engine: Pegaso 6-cylinder in-line diesel developing 310 hp at 2200 rpm
Transmission: ZF 6 HP 500 automatic with 6 forward and 1 reverse gears
Steering: hydraulic
Turning radius: 7.5 m
Suspension: ZF hydropneumatic, independent each wheel
Tyres: 13.00 × 20
Electrical system: 24 V
Batteries: 1 × 12 V, 150 Ah
Armament: 1 × 0.50/12.7 mm or 7.62 mm MG
6 × smoke dischargers

Status
In service with the Egyptian Army.

Manufacturer
Empresa Nacional de Autocamiones SA, Avenida Aragon, 402-Madrid-22, Spain.
Fax: 1/747 80 85.

SWEDEN

Bärgningsbandvagn 82 Armoured Recovery Vehicle

Development
The Bärgningsbandvagn 82 (or Bgbv 82 as it is usually known) was developed by Hägglunds and Söner to meet a Swedish Army requirement for an ARV to recover the S tank and other AFVs. The first prototype was completed in July 1968, and as a result of user trials some modifications were requested by the Swedish Army. The Bgbv 82 was then accepted for service and 24 vehicles were completed between April and December 1973. The vehicle has an almost identical hull to the Brobandvagn 941 (bridgelayer) which was designed at the same time, and to keep costs to a minimum both vehicles share many common components with the Ikv 91 tank destroyer. In addition to being used as a recovery vehicle the Bgbv 82 can also be employed as an engineer vehicle, as for example in clearing river exit points.

Description
The hull of the Bgbv 82 is of all-welded steel construction with the crew compartment at the front and the recovery compartment at the rear. The front of the vehicle is immune to attack from projectiles up to and including 20 mm in calibre, while the sides of the hull, above the tracks, are of a double-skinned construction which gives added protection against attack from HEAT projectiles.

The crew consists of four: commander, gunner, driver and winch operator. The gunner is seated in the turret (which is identical to that fitted on the Pbv 302 APC) on the left side of the hull. This is armed with a 20 mm Hispano 804 cannon which can be elevated from −10 to +50°. Both elevation and traverse are manual. For engaging ground targets the gunner uses a sight with a magnification of ×8 while a special sight is provided for engaging aerial targets, but to use this the gunner has to open his hatch cover and is therefore exposed to small arms fire. Four M17 periscopes are provided in the turret, three to the front and one to the rear. Eight smoke dischargers are mounted on either side of the turret. The driver is seated in the centre of the hull and is provided with three periscopes to his front for observation, and a single-piece hatch cover which opens to the rear. The vehicle commander is seated to the right of the driver and is provided with six periscopes for all-round observation and a single-piece hatch cover. The winch operator is seated to the rear of the commander facing the rear, with his single-piece hatch cover opening to the rear. All the recovery

Bgbv 82 armoured recovery vehicle showing spades in travelling position, crane and recovery equipment

equipment is hydraulically operated from the crew compartment.

The engine, torque converter, clutch, gearbox and steering gearbox (including the bevel gear) can be removed from under the floor of the load/recovery compartment as a complete unit. The fuel tank is also under the floor.

The six road wheels on each side are supported by trailing arms individually suspended by transversal torsion bars. Shock absorbers are mounted on the first and last trailing arms. The idler is at the front and the drive sprocket is at the rear. The track tension is automatically adjusted by a hydraulic system.

The Hägglunds HM 20 winch is mounted to the rear of the crew compartment and is provided with 145 m of wire rope which leads out through the rear of the hull.

Two ground anchor spades are mounted at the rear of the hull and are hydraulically positioned. When in position they can absorb a force of 60 000 kg, the maximum traction for a three-part pull.

The HIAB-Foco 9000 lifting crane is mounted on the right side of the hull and can lift 5000 kg with a jib length of 1.8 m, 3500 kg with a jib length of 2.5 m and 1500 kg with a jib length of 5.5 m. At the front of the hull is a hydraulically operated dozer blade which is normally positioned when the winch or lifting crane is being used.

The Bgbv 82 is fully amphibious being propelled in the water by its tracks. The only preparation required is to erect the trim vane at the front of the hull, switch on the bilge pumps and erect a low flotation screen. If the vehicle is carrying a heavy load, such as a complete powerpack for an S tank, a canvas cover should be erected. The canvas cover should also be fitted when crossing rough water.

The vehicle is not provided with an NBC pack although provision was made in the design for one to be installed at a later date. Infra-red driving lights are provided.

Specifications
Crew: 4
Weight:
(empty) 19 800 kg
(loaded) 26 300 kg (with S tank powerpack)
Length: 7.2 m
Width: 3.25 m
Height:
(top of turret) 2.45 m
(top of spades) 2.63 m

Ground clearance: 0.45 m (centre of hull)
Track width: 450 mm
Length of track on ground: 3.6 m
Ground pressure: 0.82 kg/cm^2
Max speed:
(road) 56 km/h
(water) 8 km/h
Range: 400 km
Fuel capacity: 550 l
Fuel consumption: (road) 1 l/km
Fording: amphibious
Gradient: 60%
Vertical obstacle: 0.6 m
Trench: 2.5 m
Engine: Volvo-Penta Model THD 100C turbocharged 6-cylinder in-line diesel developing 310 bhp at 2200 rpm
Transmission: manual Volvo-Penta R61 with

8 forward and 2 reverse gears
Electrical system: 24 V
Armament:
1 × 20 mm cannon
505 rounds of ammunition
16 smoke dischargers

Status
Production complete. In service only with the Swedish Army.

Manufacturer
Hägglunds Vehicle AB, S-891 82 Örnsköldsvik, Sweden.
Tel: (46) 0660 800 00. Telex: 6051 HAEGG S 6051.
Fax: (46) 0660 151 90.

CV 90 Armoured Recovery Vehicle

Description
During 1991 Hägglunds Vehicle AB produced a prototype of an armoured recovery vehicle intended to provide field recovery and technical support for Swedish Army units operating the Combat Vehicle 90 (CV 90 or Stridsfordon 90) infantry fighting vehicle. Following company trials the vehicle was due to be handed over to the Swedish Defence Material Administration (FMV) for further trials, pending a production order to be placed during 1993. In Swedish Army service the CV 90 ARV will be known as the Bgbv.

The CV 90 ARV is based on the chassis, running gear, powerpack and armoured steel hull of the CV 90 but in place of the usual turret there is a raised cupola for the commander; the rest of the three-man crew comprises the driver and a winch operator. There is also provision for one passenger.

Standard equipment includes a front-mounted stabiliser blade which can also be used for dozing operations. The hull contains two Rotzler hydraulic capstan winches. Each winch has a constant pulling force and cable speed over the entire cable length. Using a four part pull on each winch the CV 90 ARV has a maximum recovery capability of 72 tonnes to the front, enabling it to recover any vehicle in Swedish Army service. The pulling capacity to the rear is 36 tonnes and 9 tonnes to the side. A light crane with a telescopic jib is fitted on the left side of the hull roof towards the rear.

The vehicle has an over-pressure NBC system and an automatic Halon fire detection and suppression system.

A 7.62 mm machine gun with 4000 rounds of ammunition is carried for local defence. A total of 12 smoke dischargers in two groups of six is provided.

Specifications
Crew: 4 + 1
Weight: (combat) 21 500 kg
Length: 7.55 m
Width: 3.1 m

CV 90 ARV with dozer blade lowered and light crane ready for use

Height:
(over cupola) 2.24 m
(roof) 1.73 m
Ground clearance: 0.45 m
Track: 2.47 m
Track width: 533 mm
Length of track on ground: 3.98 m
Max speed: (road) 70 km/h
Fuel capacity: 800 l
Engine: Scania DS-14 diesel developing 550 hp at 2200 rpm
Transmission: Detroit Diesel Allison X 300-5 fully automatic with torque converter and lock-up clutch; 4 forward and 2 reverse gears

Electrical system: 24 V
Armament: 1 × 7.62 mm MG with 4000 rounds
12 smoke dischargers

Status
Prototype.

Manufacturer
Hägglunds Vehicle AB, S-891 82 Örnsköldsvik, Sweden.
Tel: (46) 0660 800 00. Telex: HAEGG S 6051.
Fax: (46) 0660 151 90.

SWITZERLAND

Entpannungspanzer 65/88 Armoured Recovery Vehicle

Development
In 1961 the Swiss Federal Armament Factory at Thun started the development of an armoured recovery vehicle based on the chassis of the Pz 61 MBT. The first prototype was completed in 1967/68 and after trials a modified version, based on the later Pz 68 MBT chassis, was placed in production. First production Entpannungspanzer 65s (or Entp Pz 65 for short) were completed in 1970 and these, together with a quantity of British-supplied Centurion Mk 2 armoured recovery vehicles (called the Entp Pz 56 by the Swiss) are the

standard armoured recovery vehicles of the Swiss Army. Modifications to the hydraulic system and some other changes resulted in a change of designation to Entp Pz 65/88. Each battalion of Pz 61/Pz 68 MBTs has two or three Entp Pz 65/88s in its service company and each 155 mm M109A1 self-propelled artillery battalion has one.

Description
The hull of the Entp Pz 65/88 is of cast sections welded together, with the crew and winch compartment at the front and the engine and transmission at the rear. An entry door is provided in the left side of the hull towards the front. In the crew compartment roof on the left side are two periscopes which provide observation to the

front of the vehicle. To the rear of this position is a cupola with a two-piece hatch cover, which is provided with vision blocks for observation purposes. A 7.5 mm machine gun is mounted externally on this cupola. The driver is seated at the front on the right side and is provided with a one-piece hatch cover which opens vertically to the rear. Three periscopes are mounted to the front of the hatch. To the rear of the driver is another cupola which has vision blocks, a two-piece hatch cover, and four smoke dischargers mounted on its front.

The suspension of the Entp Pz 65/88 is of the Belleville type which consists of six road wheels with the drive sprocket at the rear, the idler at the front, and three track return rollers. Each road wheel is independently sprung by layers of Belleville washers, or conical springs.

The main winch is provided with 120 m of cable and has a maximum capacity of 12 500 kg at high speed, at a maximum speed of 0.4 m/s, and a maximum capacity of 25 000 kg at low speed, at a maximum speed of 0.2 m/s. The capacity at low speed can be increased to 75 000 kg with snatch blocks. The auxiliary winch, which is used to pull out the main cable, is provided with 240 m of cable. Maximum speed on a full drum is 1.79 m/s and on an empty drum is 1.22 m/s. A hydraulically operated dozer blade mounted at the front of the hull is used either to stabilise the vehicle when the A-frame is being used or to clear away obstacles. Maximum height of the cutting edge above surface level is 0.9 m and below surface level 0.49 m. The A-frame is pivoted at the front of the hull and when not required lies back in the horizontal position on the roof. It has a maximum lifting capacity of 15 000 kg which enables it to lift complete tank turrets. An unusual feature of the frame is that at the lower end of each arm is a hydraulic jack, which allows the operator to make minor adjustments when lifting loads such as tank powerpacks into position.

A full range of tools, cutting equipment and tow bars are carried and storage lockers are provided along each side of the hull. The Entp Pz 65/88 has an NBC system.

Specifications
Crew: 5
Weight: 39 800 kg
Length:
(overall) 9.6 m
(hull) 7.57 m
Width:
(hull) 3.15 m
(blade) 3.15 m
Height: (including MG) 3.25 m
Ground clearance: 0.45 m
Track: 2.59 m
Track width: 520 mm

Entp Pz 65/88 armoured recovery vehicle with A-frame lowered

Length of track on ground: 4.23 m
Ground pressure: 0.85 kg/cm^2
Max speed: (road) 60 km/h
Range:
(road) 350 km
(cross-country) 160 km
Fuel capacity: 870 l
Fording: 1.1 m
Gradient: 70%
Vertical obstacle: 0.75 m
Trench: 2.6 m
Engine: German MTU MB 837 8-cylinder diesel developing 660 hp at 2200 rpm
Auxiliary engine: DM OM 836 4-cylinder diesel developing 35 hp at 2800 rpm
Transmission: Schweizerische Lokomotiv und Maschinenfabrik semi-automatic with 6 forward and 6 reverse gears

Electrical system: 24 V
Batteries: 4 × 6 V, 360 Ah
Armament:
1 × 7.5 mm Mg 51 MG
3200 rounds of ammunition
4 smoke dischargers

Status
Production complete. In service only with the Swiss Army.

Manufacturer
Federal Armament Factory, CH-3602 Thun, Switzerland.
Tel: 41 33 28 11 11. Telex: 921256.
Fax: 41 33 28 20 47.

UNITED KINGDOM

Challenger Armoured Repair and Recovery Vehicle

Development
The Challenger Armoured Repair and Recovery Vehicle (CRARRV – named Rhino by the British Army) was designed and developed by Vickers Defence Systems to support the United Kingdom Ministry of Defence's Challenger MBT regiments. The initial production of 80 vehicles was completed by early 1983.

Each Challenger armoured regiment will have five Challenger ARRVs, one with the REME Light Aid Detachment and one with each armoured squadron.

Description
The Challenger ARRV uses the same hydrogas suspension, hull and automotive components as the Challenger MBT (for details of the Challenger 2 MBT refer to *Jane's Armour and Artillery 1992-93* pages 120 to 122) with the David Brown TN54 automatic transmission, and incorporating the Dowty Digital Automotive System Control Unit (DASCU) which carries out the functions of both the previous Main Engine Control Unit and the Gearbox Controller Automatic.

The Challenger ARRV has a basic crew of three (commander, driver and radio operator) but usually carries an additional two fitters. There is seating for a further two passengers in the L-shaped crew compartment. Integral crew heating and cooling facilities are provided along with full NBC collective protection, automatic explosion detection and suppression and a chemical toilet. The ARRV is equipped with welding and air-powered tools, plus onboard spares holding, allowing the vehicle to be used as a field repair vehicle as well as a recovery vehicle.

The Challenger ARRV can tow vehicles of up to 68 000 kg weight on free tracks at speeds of up to 30 km/h. Stability is maintained when retarding the

Challenger ARRV in travelling configuration during Operation Desert Storm

load and when towing at low speeds.

The commander's cupola is a modified (no contra-rotation) AV No 32 Mark 1 (known as the No 36 Mark 1) with a demountable quartz spotlight. For day vision there is a main ×1 wide angle day periscope and a ring of six ×1 day periscopes. For night vision a single ×1 image intensifier periscope is fitted in a rotatable mounting. The driver has a main ×1 day periscope and a ×1 auxiliary day periscope; for night vision a ×1 image intensifier periscope is fitted. The commander is also provided with a single 7.62 mm machine gun on a sliding cradle mounted on a fixed rail around his hatch.

The main winch is a Rotzler Treibmatic hydraulically driven double capstan type with a single line pull of 510 kN. It is controlled from the driver's station and is operable in the closed-down position. The auxiliary winch, a Plumett TL 15, has a maximum line pull of 15 kN and it is also operated from the driver's position. It is independent of the main winch.

The front-mounted blade is a multi-purpose item that can act as an earth anchor, dozer blade or stabiliser blade for the crane. It is controlled from the driver's compartment and, in its role as earth anchor, is capable of withstanding a double reeved main winch pull of 1020 kN.

The repair crane is an Atlas AK6000M8. Hydraulically operated, it has a lift capacity of 6500 kg and is capable of lifting a complete Challenger powerpack. It is driven by an electric motor in turn powering a self-contained hydraulic power system.

Specifications
Crew: 3 + 2 (plus two passengers)
Weight: (combat) 62 000 kg
Ground pressure: 0.99 kg/cm^2
Power-to-weight ratio: 19.35 hp/t
Length: 9.59 m
Width:
   (operating) 3.62 m
   (transport, without blade) 3.51 m
Height: (overall) 3.005 m
Ground clearance: 0.5 m
Max speed: (road) 60 km/h
   (cross-country) 40 km/h
Towing speed: (towing 60 t casualty)
   (road) 30 km/h
   (cross-country, typical) 18 km/h
Range:
   (road) 450 km/h
   (cross-country) 250 km/h
Fording: 1.07 m
Gradient:
   (normal) 58%

(towing 65 t) 25%
Vertical obstacle: 0.85 m
Trench: 2.3 m
Engine: Perkins Engines (Shrewsbury) CV12 TCA 1200 26.1 l V-12 direct injection 4-stroke diesel developing 1200 bhp at 2300 rpm
Transmission: David Brown TN54 automatic with 6 forward and 2 reverse gears
Suspension: hydrogas variable spring rate
Electrical system: 24 V
Main engine generator: 500 A continuous
Auxiliary power unit generator: 350 A continuous
Armament: 1 × 7.62 mm MG
   20 × smoke dischargers (12 front, 8 rear)

Main winch
Speed: variable up to 60 m/min
Max line pull: 510 kN at 9 m/min
Line pull at 60 m/min: 76 kN
Max pay-out rate: 60 m/min
Rope diameter: 35 mm
Rope minimum breaking load: 1000 kN
Rope usable length: (new) 150 m
Winch life: minimum of 720 full load, full length pulls
Rope life: minimum of 120 full load, full length pulls

Auxiliary winch
Max line pull and speed: 15 kN at 60 m/min

Rope diameter: 7 mm
Rope minimum breaking load: 31.4 kN
Rope usable length: 300 m

Crane
Max lift capacity: 6500 kg at 4.9 m reach
Max reach: 5.15 m with 5000 kg
Max hook height of lift: 6.82 m above ground level
Max time to elevate boom without max load: 36 s
Max time to elevate boom with max load: 72 s
Lifting speed of hook, max load: 0-4 m/min
Lifting speed of hook without load: 0-8 m/min
Slewing range: (boom up) 360° continuous
Slew speed: (horizontal, no load) 0 to 6°/s
Max working slope: 6°, vehicle at any orientation to slope
Hook travel: 5 m
Rope diameter: 20 mm
Rope breaking load: 357 kN

Status
In production for the British Army.

Manufacturer
Vickers Defence Systems, Scotswood Road, Newcastle upon Tyne NE99 1BX, UK. Tel: 091 273 8888. Telex: 53104. Fax: 091 273 2324.

Chieftain Armoured Recovery Vehicle

Development
The Chieftain armoured recovery vehicle (FV4204) was developed by the Military Vehicles and Engineering Establishment and the Royal Ordnance Factory at Leeds as the replacement for the Centurion armoured recovery vehicle (FV4006). The final requirement, issued late in 1964, called for a vehicle which could clear obstacles on the battlefield, tow an immobilised Chieftain both on roads and across country, and be fitted with a winch with a capacity of 90 000 kg.

The first of two prototypes (designated R1 and R2) was built and delivered to the School of Electrical and Mechanical Engineering at Bordon late in 1971. Trials with the first prototype resulted in a complete redesign of the hydraulic system of the vehicle, undertaken by Lockheed Precision Products (now AP Precision Hydraulics). This redesign, with a few more modifications, was considered satisfactory and production was authorised. Production of the Chieftain armoured recovery vehicle was undertaken by Vickers at its Elswick facility and the vehicle entered service with the British Army in 1976.

Iran ordered 71 Chieftain ARVs, the last of which was completed early in 1980. About 21 vehicles had been delivered to Iran by the time of the revolution. The remaining 50 vehicles are believed to have been purchased by Jordan.

Production total for the Chieftain ARV was 257.

Description
The Chieftain ARV is based on the chassis of the Chieftain Mk 5 MBT and has three main compartments. The winch compartment is at the front of the vehicle on the right side with the driver seated on the left. To the rear of the driver is a single-piece hatch cover, with a single periscope. The other three crew members are seated in the centre of the vehicle. Provision is made for carrying a fifth man. The commander has a No 17 cupola which can be traversed through a full 360°. In the forward part of the cupola is a No 62 sight periscope with magnifications of ×1 and ×10, and seven No 40 periscopes give the commander vision to the sides and rear. An image intensification sight can be fitted if required and a white/infra-red spotlight is mounted externally. The 7.62 mm L37A1 machine gun can be aimed and fired from inside the cupola. There is a second hatch in the roof of the vehicle, to the rear of the commander's cupola.

The crew compartment has an NBC system and a heater. The engine and transmission at the rear of the

Chieftain armoured repair and recovery vehicle

hull are separated from the crew compartment by a fireproof bulkhead. The crew consists of commander, driver/winch operator, radio operator and a recovery mechanic.

The suspension is of the Horstmann type and consists of three bogies per side, each with two sets of road wheels and a set of three horizontal springs. The first road wheel station has a hydraulic shock absorber. The drive sprocket is at the rear and the idler at the front, with three track return rollers. The top half of the track is covered by armoured skirts, which can be removed for maintenance.

Standard equipment includes a Graviner fire warning, detection and extinguishing system, NBC system, heater and infra-red detection equipment.

The main winch is of the double capstan type with electro-hydraulic controls. It is provided with 122 m of 28 mm diameter cable and has a maximum speed of 13.73 m/min. The auxiliary winch is also of the double capstan type and is hydraulically operated with 295 m of 11 mm diameter cable and a maximum speed of 137 m/min. Power for both winches is taken from a PTO on the main engine.

The front-mounted dozer blade, which weighs 833 kg, is operated by two hydraulic arms. When

lowered it allows the vehicle to exert a pull of up to 90 000 kg.

The vehicle is provided with a full range of recovery equipment including pulleys, cables and tow bars. Some of the Chieftain ARVs for Iran have been fitted with an Atlas AK6000M crane which, in this application, can lift a maximum load of 5803 kg at a reach of 3.62 m. Distance from the hook to the ground at a radius of 3.62 m is 4.67 m and minimum radius with boom extended is 1.445 m. Maximum lifting speed is 3.4 m/min and maximum slewing speed is 9°/s.

Variant
Armoured Repair and Recovery Vehicle
With the introduction of the Challenger MBT into service with the British Army the FV434 (see entry in this section) was unable to service the new vehicle as it cannot lift the engine pack. This has led to the introduction into service of the Chieftain armoured repair and recovery vehicle (ARRV), which has a hydraulic crane boom mounted on the left side of the superstructure with the pivot mounted just behind the commander's hatch. A stand for a spare engine pack is located to the rear and over the vehicle's engine compartment.

Specifications (Vehicle with crane)
Crew: 4
Weight: 55 640 kg
Length: 8.57 m
Width:
  (including blade) 3.53 m
  (tracks) 3.33 m
Height: 3.43 m
Ground clearance:
  (front) 0.5 m
  (rear) 0.58 m
Track: 2.718 m
Track width: 610 mm
Length of track on ground: 4.775 m
Ground pressure: 0.9 kg/cm^2
Max speed: (road) 42.2 km/h

Range:
  (road) 400-500 km
  (cross-country) 200-300 km
Fuel capacity: 955 l
Fording: 1.067 m
Gradient: 70 %
Vertical obstacle: 0.902 m
Trench: 3.15 m
Engine: Leyland L60 No 4 Mark 8A, 2-stroke, compression ignition, 6-cylinder (12 opposed pistons) vertically opposed multi-fuel developing 750 hp at 2250 rpm
Transmission: TN12 with 6 forward and 2 reverse gears plus emergency mechanical selector for second gear forward and low reverse
Electrical system: 28.5 V (24 V nominal) DC

Batteries: 4 × 12 V, 200 Ah
Armament:
  1 × 7.62 mm MG and 1600 rounds
  2 × 6 smoke dischargers (front)
  2 × 4 smoke dischargers (rear)

Status
Production complete. In service with Iran, Iraq (unconfirmed), Jordan and the United Kingdom.

Manufacturer
Vickers Defence Systems, Scotswood Road, Newcastle upon Tyne NE99 1BX, UK.
Tel: 091 273 8888. Telex: 53104.
Fax: 091 273 2324.

Alvis Samson Armoured Recovery Vehicle

Development
The Samson (FV106) is a member of the Scorpion range of light tracked vehicles developed by Alvis Limited and the Military Vehicles and Engineering Establishment. The first prototype was completed in the early 1970s, but as a result of trials some redesign work had to be carried out and the final design entered production in 1977/78.

Description
The hull of the Samson is similar to that of the Spartan APC and is of all-welded aluminium construction. The driver is seated at the front of the hull on the left side and is provided with a single-piece hatch cover which opens to the front and a wide-angle periscope for driving in the closed down position. This can be replaced by a passive night periscope. The engine, mounted to the right of the driver, is common to the Scorpion CVR(T) range.

To the rear of the driver, in the centre of the roof, is a No 27 cupola, which has a single-piece hatch cover that opens to the left and can be traversed manually through 360°. Mounted in the forward part of the cupola is a periscope with a magnification of ×1 which can be replaced by a passive night periscope. There are another five periscopes for all-round vision. Mounted externally on the right side of the cupola is a 7.62 mm GPMG.

The NBC unit, if carried, is on the right-hand sponson plate with the radio in a corresponding position on the left side. Alternatively, an air cooling or through-flow air circulation system can be installed.

At the rear of the hull is the winch compartment and a small door with a built-in vision block. Over the winch compartment is a roof hatch.

The suspension is of the torsion bar type and consists of five road wheels, with the drive sprocket at the front and the idler at the rear. The first and fifth road wheel stations are provided with a hydraulic shock absorber.

The Samson can ford to a depth of 1.067 m without preparation, but with the flotation screen erected it is fully amphibious, being propelled in the water by its tracks at a speed of 6.44 km/h. A propeller kit increases its water speed to 9.6 km/h.

The recovery winch is mounted in the rear of the hull and is driven from a PTO on the main engine. This winch is provided with 229 m of rope and has a variable speed of up to 122 m/min. Maximum pull, with a 4:1 snatch block, is 12 000 kg, and this enables the Samson to recover vehicles such as the FV432 APC. The cable leads out over the top of the hull at the rear. On prototypes this lead-out was through an opening in

Samson armoured recovery vehicle

the lower part of the hull. Two spades at the rear of the hull are released manually. An additional strengthening piece is then added and the Samson is reversed on to the spades. An A-frame can be mounted at the rear of the vehicle to enable the Samson to change light components in the field. A full range of tools, tow bars and blocks is carried.

Specifications
Crew: 3
Weight: (loaded) 8738 kg
Length: 4.788 m
  (including vice and bench) 5.004 m
Width: 2.43 m
Height:
  (top of hull) 1.718 m
  (including MG) 2.254 m
  (including A-frame) 2.83 m
Ground clearance: 0.356 m
Track: 1.7 m
Track width: 432 mm
Length of track on ground: 2.74 m
Ground pressure: 0.358 kg/cm^2
Max speed:
  (road) 72.5 km/h
  (water) 6.44 km/h
Range: 483 km
Fuel capacity: 404.51 l
Fording: 1.067 m
Freeboard with screen raised:
  (front) 0.965 m
  (rear) 0.815 m

Gradient: 60%
Vertical obstacle: 0.5 m
Trench: 2.057 m
Engine: Jaguar J60 No 1 Mark 100B 4.2 l 6-cylinder in-line petrol developing 190 hp at 4750 rpm or Perkins T6-3544 5.8 l 6-cylinder in-line turbocharged diesel developing 200 hp at 2600 rpm
Transmission: TN15 cross-drive, 7 speeds in each direction
Electrical system: 28 V
Batteries: 4 × 6TN, 100 Ah; generator output is 140 A at 28 V
Armament:
  1 × 7.62 mm MG
  2000 rounds of ammunition
  4 smoke dischargers on each side of hull front

Status
The following countries have ordered the Alvis Scorpion: Belgium, Brunei, Honduras, Iran, Ireland, Kuwait, Malaysia, New Zealand, Nigeria, Oman (has 3 Samson ARVs), Philippines, Spain, Tanzania, Thailand, United Arab Emirates, the United Kingdom and Venezuela. Of these, Belgium, Brunei, Oman, Thailand and the United Kingdom are known to use the Samson ARV.

Manufacturer
Alvis Vehicles Limited, The Triangle, Walsgrave, Coventry, CV2 2SP, UK.
Tel: 0203 535455. Telex: 31459.
Fax: 0203 539280.

Vickers Armoured Repair and Recovery Vehicle

Development

Early in 1977 Kenya placed an order with Vickers for 38 Mk 3 MBTs and three ARVs based on the same chassis. First production MBTs were delivered in 1979 and first production ARVs were delivered in 1981. Two of the ARVs have a crane. In 1978 Kenya placed an additional order for 38 MBTs plus four ARVs, two with a crane and two without. In late 1981 Nigeria placed an order for 36 MBTs, five ARVs and six bridgelayers.

Description

The all-welded steel armour hull is divided into three main compartments: front, centre and rear. The front compartment is divided into two, with the driver's compartment on the right and the winch compartment on the left. The driver has a single-piece hatch cover which can be locked open. Mounted in the hatch is a single wide-angle periscope.

The centre compartment accommodates the radio operator, commander and mechanic and also contains the radio sets, batteries, machine gun ammunition stowage and recovery kit. The commander's cupola can be traversed manually through 360° and is provided with a single-piece hatch cover that opens to the rear, periscopes for all-round observation and an externally mounted 7.62 mm MG, which can be aimed and fired from inside the cupola and has an elevation of +90° and a depression of −10°.

The rear compartment houses the power and transmission units. Panniers above each track contain two bag-type fuel tanks. The vehicle is designed to accommodate either the General Motors 12V-71T or the Rolls-Royce Condor V-12 800E engine. Drive is through the TN12 Mark V5 transmission, which combines the Wilson Epicyclic gear change principle with the Merritt steering system.

Suspension is the torsion bar type with each side consisting of six dual rubber-tyred road wheels with the drive sprocket at the rear, idler at the front and three track return rollers. All suspension stations mount a secondary torsion bar within the body of the axle and the first, second and sixth road wheel stations have a hydraulic shock absorber. The tracks are of manganese steel and when new, each track comprises 96 links.

The main winch is operated by the driver and is mechanically driven through an input gearbox with hydraulically operated selector box. The engine PTO, mounted on the rear bulkhead of the winch/crew compartment, is engaged by the driver to provide a drive to the input gearbox and raise hydraulic pressure before the winch can be operated. The twin capstan

Vickers armoured repair and recovery vehicle

winch is equipped with 122 m of 28 mm diameter cable and has a nominal capacity of 25 000 kg when being used in conjunction with an earth anchor spade fitted to the front of the vehicle. The winch, when achieving 25 000 kg direct line pull, is capable of dealing with all normal recovery operations, but where necessary the line pull can be increased to a nominal figure of 75 000 kg by multi-reeving the cable using recovery equipment provided with the vehicle. The hydraulically operated earth anchor enables the maximum pull to be achieved without moving the vehicle.

The Vickers ARV hull is manufactured to accept a hydraulic crane with a lifting capacity of 4000 kg. All vehicles produced to date, other than part of the batch delivered to Kenya, have been fitted with this crane.

Optional equipment for the Vickers ARV includes passive night vision equipment for both the commander and driver, cradle for transporting a complete powerpack and TN12 transmission, auxiliary winch with a capacity of 4060 kg and 250 m of 11 mm diameter cable, smoke grenade launchers, NBC system and a heater.

Specifications

Crew: 4
Weight: 36 800 kg
Length:
  (vehicle) 7.56 m
  (vehicle with spade) 8.38 m
Width: 3.16 m
Height: (top of commander's sight) 2.89 m

Ground clearance: 0.432 m
Track: 2.52 m
Track width: 521 mm
Length of track on ground: 4.28 m
Ground pressure: 0.79 kg/cm^2
Max speed: (road) 50 km/h
Range: (road, at 32.2 km/h) 600 km
Fuel capacity: 1000 l
Fording: 1.1 m
Gradient: 60%
Side slope: 30%
Vertical obstacle: 0.914 m
Trench: 3 m
Engine: General Motors 12V-71T V-12 diesel developing 720 bhp at 2500 rpm or
Perkins CV12 800E V-12 diesel developing 800 bhp at 2300 rpm
Transmission: TN12 Mark V5 automatic
Electrical system: 24 V
Batteries: 4 × 12 V 6TN
Armament: 1 × 7.62 mm L37A1 MG

Status

Production as required. In service with Kenya (7), Nigeria (10) and Tanzania.

Manufacturer

Vickers Defence Systems, Scotswood Road, Newcastle upon Tyne NE99 1BX, UK.
Tel: 091 273 8888. Telex: 53104.
Fax: 091 273 2324.

Centurion Mk 2 Armoured Recovery Vehicle

Development

The standard ARV of the British Army after the Second World War was the Churchill ARV, but it could not handle the heavier Centurion tank. As an interim measure the Centurion Mk 1 ARV was produced; this was the gun tank with its turret removed and a winch with a capacity of 20/30 t installed. The first prototype of the Centurion ARV Mk 2 (FV4006) was completed in 1952/53 and after user trials was adopted with the first production vehicles being completed by Vickers at Elswick in 1956/57. The Centurion ARV is normally issued on the scale of four per armoured regiment. The Mk 2 ARV was to have been followed by the Mk 3 ARV (FV4013) which would have been based on the Mk 7 MBT hull, but it did not enter service.

The production total for the Centurion Mk 2 ARV was 345. Of these 28 were for the Netherlands, 29 for Sweden (Bgbv 81A and 81B), 12 for Switzerland and 9 for Canada.

Description

The hull of the Centurion Mk 2 ARV is of all-welded construction with the driver at the front, crew and winch compartment in the centre and engine and transmission

British Army Centurion Mk 2 ARV with canvas tilt over vehicle rear

at the rear. The driver is seated at the front of the hull on the right side and is provided with a two-piece hatch cover that opens to the left and right, with each piece having an integral periscope. The other three crew members are seated in the crew compartment. The commander's cupola, on top of the crew compartment, can be traversed through 360°, and is fitted with a 0.30 or 7.62 mm machine gun which can be elevated from −15 to +45° and be aimed and fired from inside the vehicle. There are 2000 rounds of machine gun ammunition carried. The engine and transmission are at the rear of the hull.

The suspension is of the Horstmann type and consists of three units per side. Each unit carries two pairs of road wheels which are sprung by one set of concentric springs. The drive sprocket is mounted at the rear and the idler at the front, with six track return rollers. The top halves of the tracks are protected by track skirts which can be removed for maintenance.

The winch has a capacity of 31 000 kg which can be increased, with the aid of snatch blocks, to a maximum of 90 000 kg. A Rolls-Royce B80 petrol engine developing 160 hp at 3750 rpm drives an electric generator, which supplies current to a motor mounted below the winch, and this powers the winch via a chain drive. The winch is provided with 137 m of 88.9 mm diameter rope. At the rear of the ARV are large spades, as the vehicle normally recovers with the winch cable leading out to the rear. A jib crane capable of lifting a maximum

load of 10 000 kg can be erected if required. The vehicle was designed to be fitted with an A-frame but this is seldom used today.

The Centurion ARV does not have an NBC system and has no night vision equipment.

Specifications
Crew: 4
Weight:
(empty) 47 247 kg
(loaded) 50 295 kg
Length: 8.966 m
Width: 3.39 m
Height: 2.895 m
Ground clearance: 0.45 m
Track: 2.641 m
Track width: 610 mm
Length of track on ground: 4.572 m
Ground pressure: 0.9 kg/cm²
Max speed: (road) 34.6 km/h
Range: 102 km
Fuel capacity: 1045 l
Fording: 1.45 m
Gradient: 60%
Vertical obstacle: 0.914 m
Trench: 3.352 m
Engine: Rolls-Royce Meteor Mk IVB 12-cylinder liquid-cooled petrol developing 650 bhp at 2550 rpm
Auxiliary engine: Morris 4-cylinder petrol developing

20 bhp at 2500 rpm
Transmission: manual Merritt-Brown Z51R with 5 forward and 2 reverse gears
Electrical system: 24 V
Batteries: 4 × 6 V
Armament:
1 × 0.30 (7.62 mm) Browning MG
10 smoke dischargers in 2 groups of 5

Armour
glacis: 76 mm
nose: 76 mm
hull sides: 51 mm
hull rear upper: 38 mm
hull rear lower: 20 mm
hull floor: 17 mm
superstructure front, sides and rear: 30 mm

Status
Production complete. The ARV is known to be used by Denmark, Israel, the Netherlands, South Africa, Sweden (called Bgbv 81), and the United Kingdom (107 in 1990). It may also be used by Jordan.

Manufacturer
Vickers, Elswick and Royal Ordnance Factory, Woolwich Arsenal, UK.

Warrior Recovery and Repair Vehicle

Development
The Warrior Recovery and Repair Vehicle is a member of the Warrior mechanised combat vehicle family and uses a basically similar hull and superstructure, and a common power train and running gear. Two variants have been ordered by the British Army including 110 FV512 Mechanised Combat Repair Vehicles (MCRVs) with a crane but no winch and 67 FV513 Mechanised Recovery Vehicles (Repair) (MRV(R)s), with both a winch and crane.

For full details of the Warrior family of vehicles refer to *Jane's Armour and Artillery 1992-93* pages 445 and 449.

Description
The MCRV has a crew of five; commander, driver, gunner and two fitters. The main change to the superstructure is the addition of a hydraulically operated crane on the left of the superstructure and with the

pivot to the rear. This has a capacity of 6500 kg and a maximum reach of 4.52 m. The crane has a full 360° traverse and can lift and replace a Challenger MBT or Warrior powerpack or similar assemblies. A hydraulically actuated stabiliser leg at the left rear of the vehicle is lowered when the crane is in use.

On the MRV(R) a twin capstan winch is carried internally at the rear and has a 20 000 kg capacity, 38 000 kg when double reeved. There is sufficient cable to enable a single line pull of 100 m. The winch can tow a Warrior Section Vehicle over rough terrain up a gradient of 40 per cent. For the recovery role an earth anchor is lowered from the hull rear. A pilot winch is used to raise and lower the earth anchor and is provided with 200 m of cable to provide a capacity of 1250 kg maximum pull.

Internally the vehicle is provided with a fully equipped workshop. The vehicle is fitted with a one-man turret armed with a single 7.62 mm Chain Gun. There is also a collective NBC unit, along with an air-conditioning system.

The vehicle can tow the GKN High Mobility Trailer (for full details see entry in *Trailers* section). This trailer

has been specially designed to operate with the Warrior Recovery and Repair Vehicle and has a gross weight of 10 500 kg. It can carry a Challenger MBT powerpack and employs a four-damper jacking system to maintain a safe level platform when not connected for towing.

Specifications
Crew: 5
Weight: (combat, MRV(R)) 30 000 kg
Length:
(overall) 6.675 m
(over tracks) 5.39 m
Width: 3.13 m
Height:
(over cupola) 2.302 m
(roof) 1.935 m
Ground clearance: 0.49 m
Track: 2.54 m
Track width: 460 mm
Length of track on ground: 3.817 m
Max speed: (road) 71 km/h
Range: (road) 500 km
Fuel capacity: 770 l
Fording: 1.3 m
Gradient: 60%
Side slope: 40%
Vertical obstacle: 0.75 m
Trench: 2.5 m
Angle of approach/departure: 29°/34.5°
Engine: Perkins Engines (Shrewsbury) CV8 TCA V-8 diesel developing 550 hp at 2300 rpm
Transmission: Detroit Diesel Allison X-300-4B fully automatic with torque converter and lock-up clutch, 4 forward and 2 reverse gears
Turning radius: 6 m
Electrical system: 24 V
Armament:
1 × 7.62 mm Chain Gun with 4000 rounds of ammunition
up to 8 banks of smoke dischargers

Armour
hull: aluminium
turret: steel

Status
In production. In service with the British Army.

Manufacturer
GKN Defence, PO Box 106, Hadley Castle Works, Telford, Shropshire TF1 4QW, UK.
Tel: 0952 244321. Telex: 35248 sanhad g.
Fax: 0952 243910.

Rear view of Warrior Mechanised Recovery Vehicle (Repair) (MRV(R))

Saxon Armoured Recovery Vehicle

Description

An armoured recovery vehicle version of the Saxon wheeled armoured personnel carrier has been produced by GKN Defence to support the Saxon infantry battalions allotted to BAOR. The vehicle, known as Saxon Recovery, is basically a converted Saxon APC, with a Williams Fairey Engineering Ltd 5-ton capstan winch mounted on the left-hand side wall of the hull. The winch can operate to either the front or rear of the vehicle using a swivelling fairlead and fixed roller boxes. The cable can be used over a vertical arc of +40° and −10° front and rear and 15° to either side. The cable is stowed on a reel next to the winch. The winch, which can be controlled by a remote-control unit, has a slow speed of 9.1 m/min and a fast speed of 30.84 m/min. By using a block and tackle vehicles of up to 16 000 kg weight can be recovered.

The Saxon ARV has a crew of four and in addition to the usual recovery tools and equipment carried, a lightproof tent can be erected over the rear of the vehicle to act as a temporary repair workshop.

For details of the Saxon APC refer to entry in *Jane's Armour and Artillery 1992-93* pages 460 to 462.

Status

Production complete. In service with the British Army (38).

Saxon armoured recovery vehicle showing winch mounted on the side

Manufacturer

GKN Defence, PO Box 106, Hadley Castle Works, Telford, Shropshire TF1 4QW, UK.

Tel: 0952 244321. Telex: 35248 sanhad g. Fax: 0952 243910.

Vickers Modular Armoured Repair and Recovery System (MARRS)

Development

Recognising the market potential for an armoured recovery vehicle kit, Vickers Defence Systems developed the Modular Armoured Repair and Recovery System (MARRS) in early 1986. It consists of a turret module containing a main winch, crane, auxiliary winch and powerpack, and an earth anchor/dozer blade with its own self-contained hydraulic unit. MARRS is highly adaptable and can be easily fitted to any standard MBT hull such as the M47/M48/M60 series, the Centurion, the T-54/T-55/T-62 series and the Chinese Type 59. With such MBTs, costly hull modifications are avoided by MARRS, and ARV conversions can be made to vehicles where no equivalent ARV variant exists or where the existing ARV has only limited capabilities.

Description

MARRS consists of two self-contained modules, the turret and the blade. The system has been designed to allow the maximum space for crew and equipment stowage, with seating for the commander, a fitter and two passengers in the turret module. The driver continues to use his normal position.

The turret module is constructed from high hardness steel that provides protection from 12.7 mm small arms fire over the frontal arc, and against 7.62 mm small arms fire and shell splinters over the remainder. The turret can be traversed through a full 360° and is attached to the hull, bearing seating normally occupied by the tank turret, by using an adaptor ring. Hull ammunition stowage facilities are removed before the kit is installed. The compact main winch is mounted in trunnion mountings in a similar manner to an MBT gun. The winch has a capacity of up to 50 000 kg (single line pull) and up to 100 000 kg with a double line pull, although this capacity may be derated to avoid overstressing the chassis of some lighter vehicles. The winch storage drum has 120 m of usable rope with the drum mounted on a specially designed turret turntable. If required the main winch can be used for self-recovery.

An auxiliary winch is located in the front left-hand compartment of the turret. It has a 1500 kg capacity and is used to deploy the main winch rope rapidly.

Mounted on the front edge of the turret is an A-frame crane with a capacity of 25 000 kg. In this position the crane allows maximum internal space for the crew and equipment and allows load handling through 360° continuously. A crane hoist winch is mounted on the A-frame and is used to raise and lower the crane hook

Model of Vickers Modular Armoured Repair and Recovery System (MARRS) fitted to M48 MBT chassis

through a pulley block system.

The hydraulic system has been designed to allow combined crane and winch operations at full load to cope with the most difficult of recovery operations. A simple geared hydraulic drive unit is used to drive the turret through 360° continuous rotation and in the event of a hydraulic power failure the turret can still be traversed by means of an emergency electro-hydraulic pump unit. The main hydraulic power unit is driven by a 170 hp air-cooled diesel engine carried in the turret bustle.

The turret electrical system is self-contained, with the exception of the turret communications which interface with the hull rotary base junction, as in the MBT. A control panel at the commander's station contains proportional/electrical joystick controllers to operate the main and auxiliary winches, the crane and turret traverse drive, providing continuously variable speed control from zero to maximum at all design loads.

The blade module is a self-contained unit with its own electrically driven hydraulic system mounted in the back of the blade and is controlled by the driver. Installation is simple being limited to the welding of two brackets to the hull front plate and the connection of a 24 V electrical harness.

The blade module has three functions: earth anchor with up to 100 000 kg capacity; dozer blade; and crane stabiliser, allowing the crane to lift heavy loads in soft soil conditions.

The commander's station may be fitted with a Vickers cupola or a redundant cupola from the MBT involved in the conversion (if possible). A crew access

hatch is located in the turret roof in the rear right-hand corner of the crew compartment. A vision periscope is located in the turret roof to the rear of the crew hatch.

Optional equipment includes a Vickers cupola and machine gun mounting, smoke dischargers, a crew periscope, an NBC system, air-conditioning, a fire suppression system, welding equipment, a compressor and power tools.

Specifications

Crew: 3 + 2
Weight of turret module: approx 11 000 kg
Weight of blade module: approx 2500 kg

Main winch and storage drum
Max load, single line pull: 50 000 kg for MBT weight over 50 000 kg or 40 000 kg for MBT weight under 50 000 kg
Max load, double line pull: 100 000 kg for MBT weight over 50 000 kg or 80 000 kg for MBT weight under 50 000 kg

Auxiliary winch
Main load: 1500 kg
Line speed at max load: 0 to 60 m/min
Usable rope length: 240 m
Rope diameter: 7mm

Crane
Max load over vehicle front: 25 000 kg with MBT weight over 50 000 kg
Max load traversing over vehicle front: 18 000 kg with MBT weight over 50 000 kg or 14 000 kg with

MBT weight under 50 000 kg
Angle of operation: 360° continuous
Max lifting speed:
(crane only) 0 to 8 m/min
(crane and winch operation) 0 to 4 m/min
Max vehicle inclination for crane operation:
(traversing load) 5°
(no traversing) 10°

Blade module
Modes of operation: earth anchor, dozer blade, crane
stabiliser

Earth anchor capability: 100 000 kg
Blade width: 3.4 m
Blade depth: 1.1 m
Crane stabiliser pad dimensions: 3.4 × 0.3 m
Electrical supply: 24 V

Hydraulic powerpack
Location: in turret bustle
Prime mover: air-cooled diesel developing 170 hp
Fuel capacity: 250 l
Main hydraulic pump: 6 output radial piston
Hydraulic cooler: 25 kW at 50°C ambient

Max hydraulic pressure: 275 bar

Status
Development complete. Ready for production.

Manufacturer
Vickers Defence Systems, Scotswood Road,
Newcastle upon Tyne NE99 1BX, UK.
Tel: 091 273 8888. Telex: 53104.
Fax: 091 273 2324.

UNITED STATES OF AMERICA

V-150S and V-300 Commando Recovery Vehicles

Development
The Commando (4 × 4) vehicle was developed as a
private venture by Cadillac Gage with the first production models being completed in 1964. These were
designated the V-100 and were followed a few years
later by the larger V-200. Current production is based
on the V-150S, which has many improvements over
the earlier V-100 and the similar V-150. Over 4000
Commando vehicles of all types have been built.
Similar vehicles called the Chaimite and BRAVIA Mk 1
have been built in Portugal, but not under licence from
Cadillac Gage.

Description
The hull of the Commando V-150S is of all-welded
steel construction which provides the crew with protection from small arms fire. The driver is seated at the
front of the hull on the left side with the co-driver to his
right. Both are provided with vision blocks and a single-
piece hatch cover that opens to the left or right. There
is a further vision block on either side of their positions.

The remainder of the crew is seated to the rear of the
driver's position. The gunner's hatch is in the centre of
the roof and a 7.62 mm machine gun is mounted at this
position.

There is a door in each side of the hull and a third
door in the rear on the right side, all with a vision block
and a firing port. These doors are in two parts, top and
bottom, the bottom part opening downwards to form a
step and the top half opening left or right. There is a
further firing port and vision block in each side of the
hull forward of the side doors. There is also a two-part
roof hatch to the right of the engine compartment.

The engine and transmission are mounted at the
rear of the hull on the left side with access hatches in
the roof and side of the hull. The engine compartment
is provided with a fire suppression system which is
operated by the driver.

The suspension is of the solid axle type with semi-
elliptical springs and heavy duty shock absorbers at
each wheel station. The axles have automatic silent
positive locking differentials. The steering is power-
assisted and the tyres are of the run-flat type and
have a self-cleaning tread. The Commando is fully
amphibious, propelled in the water by its wheels; two
electric bilge pumps are provided.

The A-frame is supported when in operation by two
cables attached to the rear of the vehicle. A hydraulically actuated spade is provided at the front of the hull
and is operated through the same controls used for the
winch and boom. The winch is mounted in the centre of
the hull and leads out through an opening in the
forward part of the commander's roof pod. The winch
has a maximum capacity of 11 348 kg and has 61 m of
19 mm diameter cable. The boom has a maximum
lifting capacity of 4536 kg with the two jack stands in
position. When not in use this rests on the rear of the
hull.

V-150 Commando recovery vehicle in travelling order

Equipment carried on board includes 15.24 m of
hose for the compressor, fuel transfer pump, jacks,
gunner's platform/workbench, portable spotlight, slave
cables, tools and tow bars.

Variant
V-300 Armoured Recovery Vehicle
A 6 × 6 armoured recovery vehicle based on the
V-300 Commando armoured vehicle has been produced. This variant has no turret and has a raised and
fixed superstructure at the rear. An A-frame jib is
mounted on the hull roof front and a folding spade
anchor is located under the vehicle front. An 11 348 kg
capacity winch is fitted and provided with 61 m of
cable. Gross vehicle weight of the V-300 is 14 969 kg,
length is 6.4 m, hull width is 2.54 m and hull height is
1.98 m. Power is provided by a VT-504 turbocharged
V-8 diesel developing 270 hp at 2000 rpm.

For full details of the V-300 Commando armoured
vehicle refer to *Jane's Armour and Artillery 1992-93*
pages 488 and 489.

Specifications (V-150S)
Crew: 4
Configuration: 4 × 4
Combat weight: 10 886 kg
Length: 6.14 m
Width: 2.26 m
Height: (hull) 1.98 m
Ground clearance: (under hull) 0.647 m
Track:
(front) 1.91 m
(rear) 1.94 m
Wheelbase: 3.12 m
Ground pressure: 1.5 kg/cm^2
Max speed:
(road) 100 km/h
(water) 5 km/h
Range: 644 km

Fuel capacity: 302 l
Fording: amphibious
Gradient: 60%
Side slope: 30%
Vertical obstacle: 0.91 m
Engine: 6 CTA 8.3 (turbocharged, after-cooled, in-line
6-cylinder diesel), 186 kW (250 hp) at 2500 rpm
(governed), torque 90 kg-M (650 ft-lbs) at 1584 rpm
Transmission: automatic 6 speed
Transfer box: single speed with spline engagement
clutch for front axle drive
Steering: variable ratio power
Turning radius: 8.5 m
Suspension: Solid axles with semi-elliptic multi-leaf
springs with telescopic direct-acting shock absorbers
at each wheel
Tyres: 395/80 R20 (14.00 R20 optional), radial
Electrical system: 24 V
Batteries: 2 × 12 V, 100 Ah
Alternator: 60 A
Armament:
1 × 7.62 mm MG
2200 rounds of ammunition

Status
In production. Users of the Commando include Bolivia,
Botswana, Cameroon, Chad, Ethiopia, Gabon,
Guatemala, Haiti (ARV confirmed), Indonesia, Jamaica,
Kuwait, Malaysia, Oman, Philippines, Saudi Arabia
(ARV confirmed), Singapore, Somalia, Sudan, Taiwan,
Thailand, Tunisia, Turkey, USA, Venezuela and
Vietnam.

Manufacturer
Cadillac Gage Textron, 25760 Groesbeck Highway,
PO Box 1027, Warren, Michigan 48090, USA.
Tel: (313) 777 7100. Telex: 200707 cgage ur.
Fax: (313) 776 9731.

ARVs and Repair Vehicles based on M113 APC Chassis

Development

The M113 is the most widely used armoured personnel carrier in the world and in addition to being produced in the United States was also built in Italy by OTO Melara. The first M113s were completed in 1960, followed by the M113A1 which has a diesel engine. In the late 1960s a Fitter's Vehicle was developed, fitted with a hydraulic crane and able to change AFV components.

FMC developed a recovery vehicle which became known as the XM806 (gasoline), followed by the XM806E1 (diesel) of which 24 were produced for export. The improved M113A1, the M113A2, is the current production model. It has an improved suspension and cooling system, and a new dual-air personnel heater compatible with NBC protective systems. As the US Army did not purchase the XM806 type recovery vehicle, FMC called the later version the M113A2 Recovery Vehicle. It is in service with several countries.

FMC developed a further vehicle that combines the features of the Recovery Vehicle with the Fitter's Vehicle. It is called the FMC M113A1-B maintenance-recovery vehicle (MRV) and uses the same crane and winch as the Fitter's Vehicle. The first prototype was ready early in 1982; since then it has been produced in Belgium.

The MRV can swim without the need for a water barrier, and it has a buoyant trim vane. The crane is hydraulically operated and has its own winch. The Royal Netherlands Army uses the AIFV recovery vehicle which is similar to the M113A1-B maintenance-recovery vehicle but with torsion bar and tube suspension and a 260 hp turbocharged engine. The FMC MRV weighs approximately 113 kg more than the M113A2 Recovery Vehicle.

Description

M113A2 Recovery Vehicle
The hull of the M113A1/A2 is made of all-welded aluminium. The driver is seated at the front of the hull on the left side and is provided with a single-piece hatch cover that opens to the rear. For observation purposes he has four M17 periscopes and an M19 periscope in his roof hatch and an infra-red periscope for night driving. The engine is mounted to the right of the driver. The commander's cupola has five periscopes and a single-piece hatch cover that opens to the rear. A 0.50/12.7 mm Browning M2 machine gun is mounted on the commander's cupola with an elevation of +53° and a depression of −21°. To the immediate rear of the commander is a rectangular hatch which opens to the rear. Normal means of entry and exit are by a power-operated ramp in the rear of the hull.

The torsion bar suspension consists of five road wheels with the drive sprocket at the front and the idler at the rear. There are no track return rollers.

The vehicle is fully amphibious, being propelled in water by its tracks. Before entering the water the trim vane is extended at the front of the hull and the bilge pumps are switched on. The basic vehicle does not have an NBC system, but this and a variety of other kits are available as optional extras.

The M113A2 recovery vehicle has a P30 (modified) hydraulic winch which is provided with 91.4 m of 16 mm diameter cable, with a capacity on a full drum of 5103 kg and on a bare drum of 9070 kg. A rotating fairlead that guides the cable is at the rear of the

Australian Army M806A1 recovery vehicle (Barry Marriott)

vehicle. A cable tensioner, built into the fairlead, allows free cable to be wound tightly. A level winder keeps the cable properly coiled on the winch drum and heavy shrouds over the winch assembly and a swing-up guard set into the ramp opening protect the operator during winching operations.

A single spade is mounted on each side of the hull at the rear and an additional spade unit can be mounted between the two outer ones for recovery in soft soil.

A manually operated hydraulic crane is mounted on the left side of the vehicle with an extensible arm with two positions for flexibility of use. This crane has a maximum lifting capacity of 1361 kg at a reach of 1.52 m.

Recovery vehicles produced in Belgium incorporate the M113A1 power train and modified (heavy duty) torsion bars. These vehicles are unique to the Belgian Army.

Fitter's Vehicle
This is often incorrectly called the M579, and has an almost identical hull to the M113A2 but does not have the small crane or heavy winch. Mounted on the left side of the roof is a HIAB hydraulic crane which can lift a maximum of 1360 kg at a reach of 3.29 m. The commander's cupola and the hatch to his rear are mounted on a large top hatch that opens to the right. This is 2.39 × 1.37 m and enables a spare M113 engine to be carried inside the vehicle, and to be lifted out with the aid of the crane. The vehicle is also provided with a hydraulic winch which has a maximum capacity on a full drum of 1360 kg, or 1770 kg on a bare drum. For this winch, 15.2 m of 11.1 mm cable is provided.

As of November 1990 488 Fitter's Vehicles had been built, all of them for export.

Specifications

(M113A2 recovery vehicle; data in square brackets relate to Fitter's Vehicle where different)
Crew: 3 [2 + 9 seating]
Weight:
(air transport) 10 834 [10 275] kg

(combat loaded) 11 637 [11 700] kg
Length: 5.34 [4.87] m
Width: 2.69 m
Height: 2.46 [3.15] m
Ground clearance: 0.43 m
Track: 2.159 m
Track width: 381 mm
Length of track on ground: 2.67 m
Ground pressure: 0.57 [0.576] kg/cm²
Max speed:
(road) 67.6 [67.5] km/h
(water) 5.8 km/h
Range: 483 km
Fuel capacity: 363 [360] l
Fording: amphibious
Gradient: 60%
Side slope: 30%
Vertical obstacle: 0.61 m
Trench: 1.68 m
Engine: GMC Diesel Model 6V-53, 6-cylinder, water-cooled developing 215 bhp at 2800 rpm
Transmission: Allison TX-100-1 with 3 forward and 1 reverse gears
Differential: FMC DS200
Electrical system: 24 V
Batteries: 2 × 12 V
Armament:
1 × 0.50/12.7 mm Browning M2 HB MG
2000 rounds of ammunition
Armour: 12-38 mm

Status

Production as required. Both the M113A1/A2 armoured recovery vehicle and the Fitter's Vehicle are known to be in service with the Australian Army. In service with Belgium, Egypt, Israel, Lebanon, the Netherlands (based on AIFV) and Sudan.

Manufacturer

FMC Corporation, Ground Systems Division, Santa Clara, California 95052, USA.
Tel: (408) 289 011. Telex: 6714210.
Fax: (408) 289 2150.

Assault Amphibian Vehicle, Recovery, Model 7A1

Development

The Assault Amphibian Vehicle, Recovery, Model 7A1 (AAVR7A1) was developed from the Landing Vehicle, Tracked, Recovery, Model 7 (LVTR7) and was renamed during 1985. The original LVTR7 was developed by the FMC Corporation under contract to the US Naval Sea Systems Command to recover other members of the LVT7 family (the LVT7 is now known as the Assault Amphibian Vehicle or AAV). The first prototype, designated the LVTRX2, was completed in 1968 and after

trials was standardised as the LVTR7.

Further development by FMC resulted in the LVTR7A1, now known as the AAVR7A1. The AAVR7A1 has improvements to the hull, suspension and power train, and changes to the fuel, hydraulic and electrical systems. The recovery equipment also underwent major modification. Following the completion of US Marine Corps testing in 1981 a contract was awarded to convert the AAVR7 vehicles to AAVR7A1 configuration.

Description

The hull, which is almost identical to that of the AAV, is made of all-welded aluminium. The engine and trans-

mission are at the front of the vehicle and can be removed as a complete unit. The crew compartment and repair area are at the rear of the vehicle.

The driver is seated at the front of the hull on the left side and is provided with a single-piece hatch cover that opens to the rear. Seven vision blocks are provided for observation and for night driving an AN/VVS-2(V)1A periscope can be mounted in the hatch cover. The commander is seated to the rear of the driver and also has a single-piece hatch cover that opens to the rear and seven direct vision blocks. He has an M27 periscope which extends vertically enabling him to see over the driver's position. The winch/crane operator is seated on the right side and

AAVR7A1 in travelling configuration

Width: 3.27 m
Height: 3.28 m
Ground clearance: 0.406 m
Track: 2.609 m
Track width: 533 mm
Length of track on ground: 3.94 m
Ground pressure: 0.55 kg/cm^2
Max speed:
  (road) 72.4 km/h
  (water) 12.9 km/h
Range:
  (land) 482 km at 40 km/h
  (water) 7 h at 2600 rpm
Fuel capacity: 647 l
Fording: amphibious
Gradient: 60%
Side slope: 40%
Vertical obstacle: 0.914 m
Trench: 2.44 m
Engine:
  (LVTR7) Detroit Diesel Model 6V-53
  (AAVR7A1) Cummins VT400
Both are 8-cylinder, water-cooled, turbocharged diesels developing 400 hp at 2800 rpm
Transmission: FMC HS400-3A1 giving 4 forward and 2 reverse gears, manually operated but with power assistance
Electrical system: 24 V
Batteries: 4 × 12 V 6 TN
Armament:
  1 × 7.62 mm M60D MG
  880 rounds of 7.62 mm ammunition

Armour
ramp outer: 25.4 mm
ramp inner: 12.7 mm
hull sides: 31-44.5 mm
hull floor and roof: 30.1 mm
hull rear: 35.4 mm

Status
Production complete. The basic AAV is in service with Argentina, Brazil, Italy, South Korea, Spain, Thailand, the USA and Venezuela.
The AAVR7 and AAVR7A1 are in service with Argentina (1), Brazil (1), South Korea (3), Spain (1), Thailand (1), the USA (54) and Venezuela (1).

Manufacturer
FMC Corporation, Ground Systems Division, Santa Clara, California 95052, USA.
Tel: (408) 289 011. Telex: 6714210.
Fax: (408) 289 2150.

has nine direct vision blocks, with his hatch cover opening to the rear; when operating the crane he uses a seat mounted on the the crane structure.

Over the top of the repair area is a large cargo hatch. Normal means of entry and exit are via the large power-operated ramp in the rear of the hull, which is provided with an integral door.

The torsion bar/tube suspension consists of six dual-tyred road wheels with the idler at the rear and the drive sprocket at the front. The first, second and sixth road wheel stations are provided with a hydraulic shock absorber. The AAVR7A1 is fully amphibious being propelled in the water by two waterjets, one in each side of the hull at the rear. These waterjets are driven through right-angled gearboxes. Deflectors are used for steering and reverse. If these fail, the vehicle can be propelled in the water by its tracks at a slower speed.

Armament consists of a pintle-mounted 7.62 mm M60D machine gun. The AAVR7A1 is not provided with an NBC system but does have infra-red driving lights. Kits for the vehicle include a winterisation kit, visor kit for the driver and a navigation light kit for use when the vehicle is afloat at night.

On the right side of the hull is a hydraulic crane which can be elevated from 0 to +65°. Its boom is telescopic and can lift 2722 kg at 6.553 m reach. A two-speed winch with a maximum capacity of 13 608 kg on a bare drum at low speed and 1878 kg on a full drum at high speed is also installed. Equipment carried includes an air compressor, AC generator, work benches, welding kit and a complete range of tools. If required a tent can be erected at the rear of the vehicle to enable repairs to be carried out in bad weather or under blackout.

Specifications
Crew: 3
Weight:
  (empty) 22 796 kg
  (loaded) 23 834 kg
Length: 8.14 m

M578 Light Armoured Recovery Vehicle

Development
In 1956 the Pacific Car and Foundry Company of Renton, Washington, was awarded a contract to design a new range of self-propelled guns which would all use the same basic chassis. One of the main requirements was to reduce the overall weight of the chassis so that it could be carried by transport aircraft then in service. The following year the programme was expanded to include three armoured recovery vehicles, designated the T119, T120 and T121. The T119 and T121 both had their cranes in an unarmoured mounting, but were not developed beyond the prototype stage. Further development of the T120 (which had a petrol engine) resulted in the T120E1 which had a diesel engine, and was accepted for service as the M578. The contract was awarded to the FMC Corporation, which produced the first production vehicle late in 1962. Production was originally completed in the late 1960s.

In 1971 Bowen-McLaughlin-York (now BMY) won a competitive contract to resume production of the M578 and began production the same year. BMY produced a total of 1018 M578s by the end of 1983, 1844 in all.

The M578 is scheduled to be phased out of US Army service during the early 1990s. It will be replaced by the M88A1, as the light/medium vehicles then in

M578 light armoured recovery vehicle (P Touzin)

service will have outgrown the capabilities of the M578.

Following a Special Mission Adaptation (SMA) a selected number of M578s will be used with Combat Electronic Warfare Intelligence (CEWI) battalions. For details see under Variant in this entry.

During the late 1970s a product improvement programme (PIP) for the M578 was proposed by PCF Defense Systems. It was not adopted, despite testing by the US Army.

Description

The hull of the M578 is similar to that of the 175 mm M107 and 203 mm/8-inch M110 self-propelled guns. The driver is seated at the front of the hull on the left side and is provided with a single-piece hatch cover and three M17 periscopes for driving when closed down. The engine is to his right and the transmission is at the front of the hull.

At the rear of the hull are the turret and crane which can be traversed through 360°. The turret has a door in each side and double doors in the rear. Both the commander and operator are provided with a single-piece hatch cover which opens to the rear and six M17 periscopes for observation.

The torsion bar suspension consists of five road wheels with the drive sprocket at the front, the fifth road wheel acting as the idler. Four of the road wheels have a hydraulic bump-stop and during recovery operations the suspension can be locked to provide a more stable platform.

Armament consists of a single 0.50/12.7 mm Browning M2 HB machine gun mounted at the commander's position. The M578 is provided with infra-red driving lights and has an NBC filter kit option for the driver and cab crew. The vehicle does not have an amphibious capability.

Equipment carried includes tools, tow bars, hydraulic impact wrench, acetylene welding and cutting equipment. A spade is mounted at the rear of the hull. The vehicle has two winches: a tow winch with a maximum capacity of 27 000 kg on a bare drum and a hoisting winch with a maximum capacity of 6750 kg.

Variant

M578 SMA

Following a Special Mission Adaptation (SMA) a selected number of M578s, unofficially known as the M578 SMA, will be used with US Army Combat Electronic Warfare Intelligence (CEWI) battalions. The SMA involves a boom extension of approximately 1.22 m and a lift capacity of 6800 kg, to enable an M578 to lift tactical shelters containing electronic warfare and intelligence equipment from broken-down carrier vehicles and place them on new prime movers. It is believed that the M578 SMA programme will be limited to vehicles assigned to US Army CEWI battalions.

Specifications

Crew: 3
Weight: 24 300 kg
  (air transport) 20 443 kg
Length:
  (overall) 6.426 m
  (hull) 5.588 m
Width: 3.149 m
Height:
  (top of cupola) 2.921 m
  (including MG) 3.416 m
Ground clearance: 0.44 m
Track: 2.692 m
Track width: 457 mm

Length of track on ground: 3.758 m
Ground pressure: 0.7 kg/cm²
Max speed: (road) 54.71 km/h
Range: 725 km
Fuel capacity: 1135.5 l
Fording: 1.066 m
Gradient: 60°
Vertical obstacle: 1.016 m
Trench: 2.362 m
Engine: General Motors Model 8V-71T turbocharged 8-cylinder liquid-cooled diesel developing 425 bhp at 2300 rpm
Transmission: Allison XTG-411-2A cross-drive with 4 forward and 2 reverse gears (automatic)
Electrical system: 24 V with 300 A generator
Batteries: 4 × 6 TN
Armament:
  1 × 0.50/12.7 mm Browning M2 HB MG and 500 rounds of ammunition
  Dutch vehicles have smoke dischargers installed (United Kingdom M578s mount a 7.62 mm L4A4 (Bren) LMG with 1200 rounds)
Armour: steel

Status

In production until end of 1981. In service with Bolivia, Brazil, Canada, Denmark, Egypt, Iran, Jordan, Morocco, Netherlands, Norway, Philippines, Saudi Arabia (88), Spain, United Kingdom and USA.

Manufacturer

BMY Division of HARSCO, PO Box 15512, York, Pennsylvania 17405-1512, USA.
Tel: (717) 225 4781. Fax: (717) 225 4615.

M88, M88A1 and M88A1E1 Armoured Recovery Vehicles

Development

The standard ARV in the US Army immediately after the Second World War was the M74, designed by Bowen-McLaughlin-York (now BMY), which produced over 1000 vehicles. BMY was awarded a contract to build three prototype vehicles under the designation of T88, to use as many components as possible of the M48 tank. These prototypes were followed by 10 pre-production vehicles for troop trials. The production contract was awarded to BMY in 1960 with the first production M88s being completed in February 1961. Final vehicles were completed in 1964, by which time 1075 had been built. The M88 was powered by a Continental AVSI-1790-6A, 12-cylinder, air-cooled supercharged, fuel injection petrol engine.

In April 1972, BMY received a contract from the US Army to design significant improvements for the M88. The basis for these improvements was to change the engine from petrol to diesel fuel to correspond with the US Army's move towards converting all its armoured vehicles to diesel engines. In 1973 an M88 was fitted with a variant of the engine fitted to the M60 MBT. The Teledyne Continental Motors AVDS-1790-2DR 12-cylinder diesel engine produced 750 bhp at 2400 rpm and had a power take-off to facilitate operation of the hydraulic system. Trials demonstrated an increase in operating range from 360 to 450 km. This vehicle also had a modified transmission, a diesel-fired personnel heater and auxiliary power unit, and stowage space for a small quantity of LAW anti-tank weapons. The hydraulic system was redesigned to allow the auxiliary power unit to retrieve the main winch cable as well as stow the boom and spade to prepare the vehicle for recovery, should the main engine fail.

The converted vehicle was designated the M88E1 and BMY built five prototypes for accelerated evaluation. The M88A1 was type classified in March 1975. Due to an increased need for medium recovery vehicles and a desire to improve those already in the field, the US Army contracted in 1975 to re-open the M88 production line at the BMY plant in York, Pennsylvania.

Most of the original M88s (878 of the 1075 produced) were returned to BMY's production facility for overhaul

and conversion. Beginning in 1977 this overhaul/conversion process ran in parallel with new production until early 1982. Production of new M88A1s was then ongoing, with a total of 2167 produced when production ended in early 1989.

When production ended at that stage, and taking into account the overhaul/conversions, the total of M88s was 3244. Of these, 199 were basic M88s, most in service with overseas armies. Although most of the M88A1s are in service with the US armed forces, some 496 were then in service with NATO and allied countries.

In November 1990 it was announced that orders placed by a Far Eastern nation for the M88A1 would involve the re-opening of the production line. Further overseas orders received during 1991 will maintain production until 1994.

During 1981 an Independent Research and Development (IR&D) programme was initiated to investigate improvements necessary for the recovery support of the M1-series Abrams MBT. An initial result was the development of the M88AX automotive demonstrator (see under Variants in this entry), which led to the acceptance by the US Army of a revised version of the M88A1 known as the M88A1E1 (see also under Variants) following testing completed during 1988. The M88A1E1 was expected to be type classified as the M88A2. The US Army re-programmed, with Congress approval, $8 million from FY86 Research and Development funds and further Research and Development funding bringing the total to $25 million, scheduled for FY87 to FY89. A FY88 request for $24.1 million advance procurement funding was made to cover the procurement of long-lead items such as engines, winches and hull components. The first production funding of $79 million was scheduled for FY89 when 80 vehicles were projected. There was no FY90 funding, leading to further work on the M88A1E1 being terminated from April 1989 until early 1991.

It was expected that between 500 and 1300 new M88A2s would be produced by BMY with no conversions from existing vehicles being involved. The M88A2 was to have been used to support US Army M60A3, M1 and M1A1 units. Existing US Army M88A1 assets were then transferred to supporting the Bradley Fighting System and M109-series self-propelled 155 mm howitzers.

In October 1991 it was announced that the US Army

Tank-Automotive Command (TACOM) had awarded BMY Combat Systems Division a contract worth $12.8 million to complete the development and testing of the M88A1E1 Improved Recovery Vehicle (IRV). The five existing M88A1E1 prototypes have been remanufactured and improved in a number of key areas.

Testing restarted during 1992 and will continue into 1993. If the trials are successful a production award could be made, funding permitting, in October 1993. It is not yet certain if new production vehicles will be involved or if current M88A1s will be upgraded to the new standard.

Description

The hull of the M88 and M88A1 is of cast armour and rolled armour welded together with the crew compartment at the front and the engine and transmission at the rear. The driver and mechanic are seated at the front of the hull, each with a single-piece hatch cover and periscopes. The commander was originally provided with a cupola with an internally mounted 0.50/12.7 mm machine gun but this was subsequently replaced by a simple cupola with a pintle-mounted 0.50/12.7 mm machine gun. There is also an entry door in each side of the hull.

The suspension is similar to that used on the M48 MBT and consists of six road wheels, with the drive sprocket at the rear and the idler at the front. There are three track return rollers. Hydraulic shock absorbers are provided for the first, second and sixth road wheel stations.

At the front of the vehicle is a hydraulically operated blade, which stabilises the vehicle when the winch is being used and assists in bulldozing operations. An A-type boom pivoted at the front of the hull can lift a vehicle weighing up to 5443 kg without using the blade or suspension lock-out at the front, or 18 160 kg using lock-out without using the blade. The vehicle can lift 22 700 kg when using the blade. The two winches are in the lower part of the hull.

The M88 is not provided with an NBC system (a kit exists for an M88A1 system incorporating a ventilated face piece) and has no amphibious capability. A fording kit is available for use in water up to 2.6 m deep. Infra-red driving lights are provided and the driver can replace one of his day periscopes with an infra-red periscope. Standard equipment includes tools, tow bars, and an auxiliary fuel pump which allows the vehicle to transfer fuel to other AFVs at 95 l/min.

The M88A1 is fitted with an auxiliary power unit (APU) powered by an Onan 10.8 hp (8.1 kW) diesel, 2-cylinder, 4-cycle engine. The APU powers an auxiliary hydraulic system that can be used to power the boom, spade and main winch and hoist cables if the main hydraulic system is inoperative. It also provides power for the refuelling and fuel transfer pump, which allows the M88A1 to act as a mobile filling station. The hydraulic system also provides power to operate a 19 mm drive hydraulic impact wrench, used for track maintenance and other maintenance and recovery tasks.

Variants

M88AX/M88A1E1

In order to determine the growth potential of the basic M88A1 components, BMY developed an M88AX automotive demonstrator in 1984-85. The demonstrator was an up-powered and up-weighted vehicle powered by a 1050 bhp Teledyne Continental Motors AVDS-1790-8DR diesel engine mated to a slightly modified transmission, the XT-1410-5X. The final drive ratio was changed from 4.63:1 to 4.00:1. During US Army tests held at Aberdeen Proving Ground, Maryland, the 65-tonne M88AX demonstrator recorded a top speed on level ground of 56.8 km/h and towed a 65-tonne load at 46 km/h over the same course. It was also able to tow a 65-tonne load up a 30 per cent slope at 3.38 km/h, and to tow a 65-tonne load over the 6.11 km Churchville 'B' unpaved/hilly course at an average speed 51 per cent greater than an M88A1. The primary purpose of the M88AX was to validate engineering predictions in connection with the US Army search for an armoured vehicle to recover the M1A1 Abrams MBT.

In late 1985 the US Army decided to establish a product improvement programme (PIP) that capitalised on BMY's initial efforts. This programme was overtaken by the introduction of the M88A1E1.

The US Army awarded BMY a research and development contract in January 1987. The fixed-price contract covered the design, construction and testing of five prototype vehicles plus a separate hull for ballistic testing. The prototype vehicles were designated the M88A1E1.

The M88A1E1 was the follow-on from the M88AX programme and featured a 1050 hp Teledyne Continental Motors AVDS-1790-8DR diesel engine coupled to an Allison XT-1410-5A transmission. Improved brakes were fitted along with a brake booster and the sprocket mounting was improved. One of the main changes introduced was a new main winch with a continuous line pull of 63 504 kg, provided with a nominal 100 m of cable. A 1814 kg lead winch was incorporated to allow a single crewman to deploy the main winch cable. The hoist had a capacity (spade down and with a four-part line) of 31 752 kg and was used in conjunction with an A-frame lengthened by 0.84 m to increase the lift height. The lengthened A-frame involved the introduction of increased diameter staylines and an increase in length with the boom stowed to 8.65 m.

Combat loaded weight was 63 141 kg, with most of the weight increase introduced by the addition of overlay armour to the existing M88A1 hull armour, providing ballistic protection against up to 30 mm calibre direct fire and 152 mm indirect fire fragmentation. Ballistic skirts were also provided. The suspension torsion bars, shock absorbers and snubbers were upgraded to cater for the weight increase.

Maximum rated speed was 41.8 km/h and the fuel capacity was increased to 2045 l. The draw bar pull was increased to 48 535 kg compared to 40 824 kg for the M88A1.

The M88A1E1 was selected again by the US Army after competitive testing in 1988. Developmental

M88A1E1 armoured recovery vehicle

testing was nearly complete and over 11 260 km of durability testing had been logged when further work was cancelled by budget cutbacks. Five of the six prototypes produced were used to support activities at Aberdeen Proving Ground. The five prototypes have now been upgraded to M88A1 IRV standard – see separate section in this entry.

M88A2

This would have been the designation of the type classified M88A1E1.

M88 IRV

In January 1991, at the request of the US Army Tank Automotive Command (TACOM), BMY submitted a Phase I M88 IRV (Improved Recovery Vehicle). This would involve the tear-down and inspection of the six M88A1E1 prototypes and some limited engineering to further improve selected areas of the design. Phase II would complete the overhaul and upgrade of the prototypes, conduct the required testing and complete a Technical Data Package.

In October 1991 it was announced that the US Army Tank-Automotive Command (TACOM) had awarded BMY Combat Systems Division a contract worth $12.8 million to complete the development and testing of the M88A1E1 Improved Recovery Vehicle (IRV). The five existing M88A1E1 prototypes have been remanufactured and improved in a number of key areas.

Testing restarted during 1992 and will continue into 1993. If the trials are successful a production award could be made, funding permitting, in October 1993. It is not yet certain if new production vehicles will be involved or current M88A1s will be upgraded to the new standard.

M88A1+ Block 1 IRV

In order to provide the US Army with an M88A1 ARV capable of towing M1 Abrams MBTs under all circumstances, BMY Combat Systems has proposed the M88A1+ or Block I IRV. The intention is to integrate M88A1E1-level armour and automotive improvements into a limited number of M88A1s. As the M88A1s are returned to be modified they would be stripped to the basic hull and receive machining to accept the heavier armour package. A 1050 hp engine would be fitted and the M88A1 winches and hydraulic system would be overhauled. The result, the M88A1+ or Block 1 IRV, would be a vehicle with the towing performance of the M88A1E1 and the lift and winch capabilities of the M88A1. The conversion would retain the ability to grow to the full M88 IRV standard.

Israeli M88

Israeli M88 armoured recovery vehicles are fitted with a Blazer reactive armour package and additional anti-personnel weapons for self and local defence.

Specifications (M88A1)

Crew: 3 or 4
Weight combat: 50 848 kg
Length: (dozer blade raised) 8.267 m
Width: 3.429 m
Height:
(with MG) 3.225 m
(top of commander's hatch) 2.97 m
Ground clearance: 0.43 m
Track: 2.717 m
Track width: 711 mm
Length of track on ground: 4.61 m
Ground pressure: 0.764 kg/cm^2
Max speed: (road) 42 km/h
Range: 483 km
Fuel capacity: 1514 l
Fording: 1.42 m
Gradient: 60%
Vertical obstacle: 1.07 m
Trench: 2.61 m
Engine: Continental AVDS-1790-2DR, 12-cylinder, air-cooled, supercharged fuel injection diesel developing 750 bhp at 2400 rpm
Transmission: XT-1410-4 cross-drive
Electrical system: 24 V
Armament:
1 × 0.50/12.7 mm M2 MG
1500 rounds of ammunition
2 × 6 smoke dischargers
Armour: 12.7-50 mm (estimate)

Status

In production. In service with Bahrain (4 M88A1), Egypt (177 M88A1), Germany (2 M88A1), Greece (27 M88A1), Israel (30 M88A1), Jordan (30 M88A1), South Korea (38 M88A1), Kuwait (10 M88A1), Morocco (18 M88A1), Norway (3 M88A1), Oman (1 M88A1), Pakistan (50 M88A1), Portugal (5), Saudi Arabia (47 M88A1), Spain (1 M88A1), Sudan (2 M88A1), Taiwan (33 M88A1 with 4 on order), Thailand (2 M88A1), Tunisia (6 M88A1) and the USA (US Army (2470), Marine Corps (79)).

Manufacturer

BMY Division of HARSCO, PO Box 1512, York, Pennsylvania 17405, USA.
Tel: (717) 225 4781. Fax: (717) 225 4615.

Abrams Recovery Vehicle (ARV)

Development

When the US Army decided to investigate their requirements for recovery support for the M1 Abrams MBT during the early 1980s, one of the options

available was the development of an armoured recovery variant of the M1 known initially as the RV90. The US Army eventually made a preliminary decision to procure the M88A1E1 recovery vehicle (see previous entry) which would have been type classified as the M88A2. Despite this decision, during 1987 General Dynamics, Land Systems Division, opted to produce

the RV90 and obtained a $1 (one dollar) contract from TACOM in June 1987.

The prototype hull was produced on the M1A1 Abrams MBT production line at the Lima Army Tank Plant, Ohio, in only 23 days. The prototype, known as the Abrams Recovery Vehicle or Abrams RV (ARV), was rolled-out during February 1988 with contractor

Abrams Recovery Vehicle (ARV) prototype with dozer/stabilising blade lowered

trials taking place until mid-March 1988, prior to delivery to Aberdeen Proving Ground in April 1988.

Description

The Abrams RV is automotively identical to the M1 Abrams MBT (over 80 per cent of the Abrams RV chassis is common to the M1A1 Abrams MBT chassis) but uses a new hull armoured superstructure housing a crew of three, with space provided for a further four stranded crewmen. The crew consists of the commander, driver and a fitter/rigger with the driver seated centrally in the upper hull front under a hatch; his field of vision is 167°. The commander is provided with a rotating cupola mounting all-round vision devices and a pintle-mounted 0.50/12.7 mm Browning machine gun.

The superstructure and hull provide at least 30 mm of armour protection for the crew throughout a 360° arc. Located on the left of the superstructure is a hydraulic jib crane with a fixed boom length and a maximum hook height at 70° elevation of 6.49 m. The crane has a capacity of 35 tonnes and a traverse of 270° – this allows the vehicle to change its own power pack if necessary. Mounted at the front of the hull is a hydraulically operated dozer/stabilising blade. In the rear is a 70-tonne winch, the capacity of which can be increased to 140 tonnes by a snatchblock carried on the vehicle. The winch is equipped with 100 m of usable cable. An auxiliary winch has a capacity of 2.5 tonnes and is equipped with 200 m of usable cable. Dual hydraulic circuits are provided throughout.

Other features include an over-pressure NBC system, an automatic Halon fire detection and suppression system (plus two portable fire extinguishers), a 300 hp auxiliary power unit and hydraulic lock-out for the suspension. Equipment carried includes hydraulic tools, a hydraulic fuel/defuel pump and welding and cutting equipment.

Production vehicles could carry a complete M1/M1A1 Abrams powerpack and could be fitted with built-in test equipment (BITE), a transverse-mounted engine, a thermal viewer for the driver, a land navigation system and an inter-vehicular information system.

Specifications (provisional)

Crew: 3 + 4
Weight: 68 500 kg
Length:
  (overall, transport) 9.255 m
  (hull) 7.795 m
Width:
  (maximum) 3.657 m
  (reduced) 3.48 m
Height:
  (maximum, to top of MG) 2.988 m
  (top of superstructure) 2.477 m
Ground clearance: 0.406 m
Track width: 635 mm
Max speed: (governed) 69.2 km/h
Range: between 418 km
Fording: (without kit) 1.22 m
Gradient: (with towed load) 60%
Vertical obstacle: 1.07 m
Trench: 2.74 m
Engine: Textron Lycoming AGT-1500 gas turbine developing 1500 hp at 3000 rpm
Transmission: Detroit Diesel X-1100-3B automatic with 4 forward and 2 reverse gears
Electrical system: 24 V
Armament:
  1 × 12.7 mm MG
  2 × smoke dischargers
Ammunition carried:
  (12.7 mm) 1500 rounds
  (smoke grenades) 24

Status

Prototype.

Manufacturer

General Dynamics, Land Systems Division, PO Box 1743, Warren, Michigan 48090, USA.
Tel: (313) 583 5000.

ARMOURED REPAIR VEHICLES

BRAZIL

ENGESA EE-11 Urutu (6 × 6) Repair and Recovery Vehicle

Description
The ENGESA EE-11 Urutu repair and recovery vehicle uses the same hull and configuration as the basic EE-11 Urutu armoured personnel carrier but has some additional equipment to suit it for its repair and recovery role. The main new features are a front-mounted hydraulic winch and a hydraulic crane with a 360° traverse mounted on top of the hull.

The front-mounted hydraulic winch operates through a plate set into the lower front hull and has a capacity of 5000 kg which can be increased to 10 000 kg by using a pulley block. The winch is supplied with 45 m of 11.1 mm cable. The hydraulic crane has a capacity of 3000 kg and a horizontal reach of 4 m. When travelling the crane arms are carried folded down against the hull rear. When the crane is in use, stabilising jacks can be placed under the hull. A wide range of repair and recovery equipment can be carried internally to allow front-line repairs and maintenance to be carried out.

The vehicle has a basic crew of four: driver, commander, crane operator and a fitter. The commander is provided with a manually operated turret armed with a 0.50/12.7 mm Browning (or other) machine gun and two smoke dischargers are located each side of the turret. The welded steel hull uses 8.5 mm plate that provides protection against 7.62 mm armour-piercing ammunition.

The vehicle can be powered by any one of three diesel engine options developing 190, 212 or 260 hp. The driver is provided with a remote tyre pressure control system to cope with various types of terrain.

For full details of the EE-11 Urutu armoured personnel carrier refer to entry in *Jane's Armour and Artillery 1992-93* pages 282 to 285.

Specifications
Crew: 4
Configuration: 6 × 6
Weight in action: 15 300 kg
Length overall: 6.26 m
Length of hull: 6.1 m
Width: 2.59 m
Height overall: 2.6 m
Height of hull: 2.125 m
Ground clearance: 340 mm
Track: 2.1 m
Wheelbase: 3.05 m
Angle of approach/departure: 60°/58°
Max road speed: 87 km/h
Fuel capacity: 380 l
Max cruising range: 850 km

ENGESA EE-11 Urutu (6 x 6) armoured repair and recovery vehicle with hydraulic crane lifting vehicle engine and transmission

Fording: 1 m
Gradient: 60%
Side slope: 30%
Engine: Mercedes-Benz OM 352-AS 6-cylinder in-line 5.675 l turbocharged diesel developing 190 hp at 2800 rpm or
Detroit Diesel 6V-53N 5.22 l diesel developing 212 hp at 2800 rpm or
Detroit Diesel 6V-53T 5.22 l turbocharged diesel developing 260 hp at 2800 rpm
Transmission: Allison MT-643 automatic with 4 forward and 1 reverse gears
Transfer box: ENGESA 2-speed with PTO
Steering: hydraulic
Suspension:
(front) independent with helical springs and double-action telescopic shock absorbers
(rear) ENGESA 'Boomerang' with walking beams
Tyres: 12.00 × 20 18 PR

Brakes: disc, air over hydraulic
Electrical system: 24 V
Armament:
1 × 0.50/12.7 mm MG
2 × twin-barrel smoke dischargers
Ammunition stowage:
(12.7 mm) 600 rounds
(smoke grenades) 12

Status
In service with Iraq.

Manufacturer
ENGESA Engenheiros Especializados SA, Avda Tucunaré 125/211, PO Box 152/154, 06400 Barueri, SP, Brazil.
Tel: 55 11 421 4711. Telex: 1171302.
Fax: 55 11 421 4445.

CANADA

Husky Armoured Repair Vehicle

Development
In the early 1970s the Swiss MOWAG company developed a range of 4 × 4, 6 × 6 and 8 × 8 vehicles known as the Piranha. These all share many common components such as wheels, suspensions, steering system, hull front and rear, hatches, doors and propellers. In 1977 the Canadian Armed Forces placed an order with the Diesel Division of General Motors of Canada Limited for 350 of the 6 × 6 version. Total value of this order was $52 million and comprised 179 Grizzly APCs, 152 Cougar fire support vehicles (with British-supplied Scorpion turrets) and 19 Husky repair and recovery vehicles. The original order for 350 vehicles was increased to 491 vehicles and final deliveries were made in 1982.

The Canadian Armed Forces call this vehicle the Husky wheeled maintenance and recovery vehicle; 27 are in service.

Description
The hull of the vehicle is of all-welded steel armour; the driver is seated at the front of the hull on the left side and is provided with a single-piece hatch cover and three periscopes. The engine is mounted to the right of the driver and the personnel compartment is at the rear. Entry to this is via two doors in the rear of the hull, each with a MOWAG-designed firing port. Hatches are provided in the roof.

The rear suspension is of the torsion bar type with coil springs and hydraulic shock absorbers at each wheel station. The front suspension is of the coil spring and wishbone type and each wheel station has a hydraulic shock absorber. The tyres have Hutchinson run-flat inner tubes. Brakes are hydraulic on all wheels.

The vehicle is fully amphibious, employing two propellers at the rear. Before entering the water a trim vane is erected at the front of the vehicle. Standard equipment on the Husky includes a HIAB 650 crane with a maximum capacity of 3250 kg.

There is a separate entry for the 8 × 8 recovery vehicle under Switzerland.

Specifications
Crew: 4
Configuration: 6 × 6
Weight: (loaded) 10 500 kg
Length: 5.97 m
Width: 2.5 m
Height: (hull top) 1.85 m
Ground clearance:
(max under hull) 0.5 m
(under differential) 0.39 m
Track:
(front) 2.18 m

(rear) 2.2 m
Tyres: 11.00 × 16
Wheelbase: 2.04 m + 1.04 m
Angle of approach/departure: 40°/45°
Max speed:
  (road) 100 km/h
  (water) 10 km/h
Range: (road) 600 km
Fuel: 210 l
Fording: amphibious
Gradient: 70%
Side slope: 30%
Vertical obstacle: 0.5 m
Engine: turbocharged Detroit Diesel model 6V-53T
developing 300 hp at 2800 rpm
Transmission: Allison MT 650 automatic with
5 forward and 1 reverse gears
Electrical system: 24 V
Armament: 1 × 7.62 mm MG

Status
Production complete in Canada. In service with the
Canadian Armed Forces (27). The MOWAG Piranha is
also used by a number of other countries.

Manufacturers
Canada – Diesel Division, General Motors of Canada
Limited, PO Box 5160, London, Ontario N6A 4N5,
Canada.
Tel: (519) 452 5184. Fax: (519) 452 5688.

Canadian Armed Forces Husky armoured repair vehicle with crane retracted but with stabilisers extended

Switzerland – MOWAG Motorwagenfabrik AG,
CH-8280 Kreuzlingen, Switzerland.
Tel: 072/71 15 15. Telex: 882211 moag ch.
Fax: 072/72 28 86.

General Motors LAV (8 × 8) Armoured Repair and Recovery Vehicle

Development
With the award of a production contract to General
Motors to produce the LAV series of vehicles based on
the MOWAG (8 × 8) Piranha, General Motors developed a repair and recovery version of the basic
vehicle. The LAV recovery was issued to the US
Marine Corps who had an initial requirement for 46 of
these vehicles. They were delivered during 1986.

In July 1989 the Australian Government purchased
an LAV repair and recovery vehicle from the US Marine
Corps as part of an initial purchase of 15 vehicles. The
vehicles entered service with the Australian Army's
2nd Cavalry during 1990.

A maintenance vehicle based on the Infantry Section
Carrier (ISC) was developed for the Canadian Government. For details of this vehicle, which was developed
from the LAV-L armoured logistics carrier, see next
entry.

For details of the LAV-L armoured logistics carrier
based on the same chassis see entry under *Tracked
prime movers, cargo carriers and armoured logistic
vehicles* section.

Description
The LAV (8 × 8) repair and recovery vehicle uses the
basic hull configuration of the original MOWAG Piranha
(for details see entry in this section under Switzerland)
but it is equipped with American cranes and winches.
The vehicle has a crew of four; driver, commander,
rigger and one additional crew member, with the driver
seated forward on the left side and the commander
behind him, seated under a cupola. The roof level of
the rear hull is raised and there is a hatch for the rigger
who controls the hydraulic crane. The HIAB crane has
a 4125 kg lift capacity (1040 kg at maximum extension)
and has a full 360° traverse with the pivoting point just
forward and to the left of the rigger's cupola. The crane
jib reach radius is from 1.37 to 4.7 m. Normally the
crane rests on a support at the rear of the hull. The
additional crew member is seated in the rear compartment which also contains extra tools, floodlights and
cutting equipment. The vehicle also carries a rear-
mounted winch with a 13 608 kg capacity. The vehicle
is amphibious and in the water is driven by two
propeller units at the rear.

The LAV (8 × 8) repair and recovery vehicle has a
fuel transfer subsystem and carries an auxiliary power
unit. If required the crane can be operated using a
remote-control box from outside the vehicle. The

General Motors LAV (8 × 8) armoured repair and recovery vehicle

commander's cupola has a pintle for an M60 7.62 mm
machine gun; 1000 rounds of 7.62 mm ammunition
can be carried. Two M257 smoke grenade dischargers
are carried, one on each side, and are controlled from
the commander's position. A towing hook is fitted at the
rear. Outrigger legs are fitted for use when the crane jib
is extended.

Trials were conducted in order to increase the
mobility of the LAV series over soft terrain. The trials
involved the use of larger tyres producing a 70 per cent
wider footprint and lower ground pressure. The larger
tyres produce a 30 per cent improvement in soft soil
mobility. If the trials result in the adoption of the larger
tyres for the LAV it is anticipated that they will also be
fitted to the LAV armoured repair and recovery vehicle.

Specifications
Crew: 4
Configuration: 8 × 8
Weight: (combat) 12 860 kg
Length:
  (normal) 7.376 m
  (reduced) 6.39 m
Width: 2.5 m

Height:
  (normal) 2.845 m
  (reduced) 2.692 m
Max speed:
  (road) 100 km/h
  (water) 10 km/h
Range: 660 km
Engine: GM Detroit Diesel 6V-53T, 6-cylinder diesel
developing 275 hp at 2800 rpm
Transmission: Allison MT-653 DR automatic,
5 forward and 1 reverse gears
Turning diameter: 15.5 m
Wheel travel: 0.33 m
Armament: 1 × 7.62 mm MG
Ammunition: (7.62 mm) 1000 rounds

Status
In service with the US Marine Corps (45) and the
Australian Army.

Manufacturer
Diesel Division, General Motors of Canada Limited, PO
Box 5160, London, Ontario N6A 4N5, Canada.
Tel: (519) 452 5184. Fax: (519) 452 5688.

General Motors Bison (8 × 8) Mobile Repair Team Vehicle

Development

In July 1989 General Motors of Canada received an order from the Canadian Government for 199 8 × 8 vehicles based on the US Marine Corps LAV, originally known as the Infantry Section Carrier (ISC) and named Bison. The Bison was designed by General Motors during 1988. Four versions of the vehicle were developed, including 16 maintenance vehicles for use by mobile repair teams (MRTs). The other Bison vehicles are the infantry section carrier, a command post and a mortar fire support vehicle. For details of the Bison refer to *Jane's Armour and Artillery 1992-93* pages 294 to 296.

The Bison was developed from the LAV-L armoured logistics carrier by increasing the width of the vehicle at the roof line to create additional internal volume and by adding a hydraulically actuated ramp door at the rear. Other minor changes were made to meet unique Canadian requirements.

The Bison was designed as a common baseline vehicle. By the use of various kits the ISC can be modified for other roles. Each kit is installed in the chassis with a minimum of changes to the hull through the use of a system of integral standard rails to which various components and stowage items can be attached. The vehicle has a flat floor with integral tie-downs and can be used as a cargo carrier.

Description

The Bison Mobile Repair Team vehicle follows the same general lines as the LAV armoured repair and recovery vehicle (see previous entry) but differs in many details to meet Canadian Armed Forces requirements. The vehicle can be made amphibious after 5 minutes' preparation, and may be driven through the water by two propeller units and steered using four rudders.

The Bison Mobile Repair Team vehicle is a basic Bison ISC chassis with the cargo hatch relocated to the rear and with the two troop hatches removed along with two of the four seats. Other additional items include a 265° traverse HIAB crane and stabilisers (the crane is the same as that used on the US Marine Corps repair and recovery vehicle, as are the stabilisers), two detachable floodlights, a utility air line, a machinist's vice, and a quick-release hose for power tools. Provision is made for tool, camouflage net and other equipment stowage.

The vehicle is capable of self-loading and unloading spare wheel assemblies and can carry a complete powerpack internally. The vehicle is capable of towing a similar vehicle and is equipped with a standard tow bar. Although no heavy recovery winch is installed, all Bison vehicles are equipped with a front-mounted 6800 kg dynamic pull hydraulic winch.

The vehicle has a crew of two, a driver and a commander who also acts as a rigger. The driver is seated on the left of the vehicle and when fully closed down he is provided with three M17 periscopes; the commander has five for his position behind the driver. Night vision devices are optional. The vehicle is provided with an M8A1 ventilated face mask NBC system and a VHF radio. A Halon 1301 manual fire suppression system is provided for the crew and engine compartments.

There is provision for a machine gun mounting over the commander's hatch and two Wegmann smoke grenade launchers with eight grenades. An ATGW wire cutter is positioned in front of the driver's position.

Specifications

Crew: 2
Configuration: 8 × 8 or 8 × 4
Weight:
(kerb) 12 055 kg
(max) 13 027 kg
Max load: 973 kg
Length: 7.366 m
Width: 2.5 m
Height: 2.692 m
Max speed:
(road) 100 km/h
(water) 9.7 km/h
Range: 665 km
Gradient: 60%
Side slope: 30%
Fording: amphibious after 5 min prep
Trench: 2.06 m
Engine: Detroit Diesel 6V-53T 6-cylinder diesel developing 275 hp at 2800 rpm
Gearbox: Allison MT-653 DR automatic, 5 forward and 1 reverse gears
Steering: power-assist
Turning radius: 15.5 m
Suspension: independent on all 8 wheels
Electrical system: 24 V
Batteries: 4
Armament: 1 × 7.62 mm MG

Status

In service with the Canadian Armed Forces (16).

Manufacturer

Diesel Division, General Motors of Canada Limited, PO Box 5160, London, Ontario N6A 4N5, Canada. Tel: (519) 452 5184. Fax: (519) 452 5688.

Bison (8 × 8) Mobile Repair Team Vehicle

COMMONWEALTH OF INDEPENDENT STATES

Technical Support Vehicle MTP

Development
This vehicle has been in service since the early 1970s and is used for recovery and repair of armoured personnel carriers and the BMP MICV. It is also used to deliver POL supplies to forward units which are difficult to reach with normal truck-mounted bowsers. Since the vehicle can be hermetically sealed for operation in contaminated terrain it can also be used for NBC reconnaissance.

Description
The MTP has the basic automotive characteristics of the BTR-50P tracked APC and has a maximum road speed of 45 km/h. It is fully amphibious, propelled in the water by its two hydrojets at a maximum speed of 10 km/h. Armour protection is probably similar to that of the BTR-50P.

Recovery equipment consists of anchoring equipment, pushing and towing equipment, tow cables and block and tackle. The drawbar pull of the MTP is 8000 kg which can be increased to 15 000 kg with the aid of block and tackle. The pushing equipment can adjust to the shocks generated by various changes in speed. The crane has a maximum lifting capacity of 1500 kg and can be extended to 2.85 m.

The POL pump, which is reported to be very compact, enables fuel to be transferred from barrels and containers into the fuel tanks of vehicles. Capacity with nozzle is 52 l/min and without nozzle 65 l/min. The pump can be connected to the onboard system of any vehicle with a direct current source of 24 V.

The raised workshop compartment, which is the distinctive feature of the MTP, is high enough to allow the crew to stand while working. It also provides sleeping room for three crew members (two in

Technical support vehicle MTP which is based on the BTR-50P APC chassis

hammocks and one on top of a stowage box). The compartment is heated and hermetically sealed and is also provided with firing ports for the crew's assault rifles and a machine gun which is part of the basic equipment of the MTP.

The repair and maintenance equipment includes a G-74 generator and four 12 V starting batteries, a complete welding set for welding and cutting non-ferrous and ferrous metals, a 40 l oxygen bottle, an acetylene generator, replacement compressed air

bottles, hydraulic press and various other tools and equipment. Sensitive measuring instruments and electrician's tools are stored in a compact metal case which is protected from shock.

Status
Production complete. In service with the CIS.

Manufacturer
State factories.

Technical Support Vehicle MTP-LB

Description
Several variations of the MT-LB multi-purpose tracked vehicle existed before the MTP-LB Technical Support Vehicle was issued to the Technical Emergency Service which has the responsibility of vehicle recovery and repair in the front line.

The basic form of the MT-LB vehicle remains unchanged but several alterations were made to adapt it for recovering armoured fighting vehicles by direct tow or winch, and the recovery of amphibious vehicles from water obstacles. One of the main fitments is an A-frame crane mounted on the front of the vehicle. This has two working positions. One is with the crane jib length at 2.15 m giving a lift height of 3.6 m. The other, with the jib length at 1.35 m gives a lift height of 4.2 m. With the crane under load the vehicle can be driven at speeds up to 5 km/h and with a list of 5°.

The vehicle is also provided with a cable winch, a jacking device, a towing attachment, chocks and other arresting devices, waterborne salvage equipment, and gas welding and oxyacetylene cutting equipment for both steel and aluminium. The hydraulic cable winch is driven by the auxiliary gearbox and drives a cable 85 m long; winching capacity is 67 kN. The jacking device on the front of the vehicle acts not only as an anchor when the cable winch is in use, but also as a metalwork workbench. A hand winch is provided for moving the jacking device from its normal transport position on the vehicle front to the cargo platform when the MTP-LB is afloat. The towing attachment is used for towing armoured fighting vehicles with steering that is out of action.

Other specialised changes to the MTP-LB are the removal of the MT-LB turret and its replacement by an extra hatch and periscope over the commander's position for use when afloat. Extra frames and con-

MTP-LB technical support vehicle with A-frame raised

tainers have been fitted to carry the extra equipment, and apart from the recovery role the MTP-LB carries the equipment required for observation, command, warning, reconnaissance, decontamination and camouflage. Interior lighting is also fitted.

Specifications
Crew: 2
Combat weight: 12 300 kg
Length: 6.8 m
Width: 2.85 m
Height: 2.3 m
Ground clearance: 0.4 m
Track width: 350 mm
Max speed:
  (land) 55 km/h
  (water) 6.5 km/h
Fording: amphibious
Engine: YaMZ 238 V V-8 cylinder diesel developing 240 hp at 2100 rpm

Status
In service with former Warsaw Pact forces.

Manufacturer
State factories.

FRANCE

AMX-10 ECH Repair Vehicle

Description
The AMX-10 ECH is the repair vehicle member of the AMX-10P MICV family which entered service with the French Army in 1973. The vehicle was shown for the first time in 1977. It has no recovery capability and is limited to changing components of other AFVs, for example, the engine of the AMX-10P.

The hull of the AMX-10 ECH is almost identical to that of the AMX-10P and is of all-welded aluminium construction. The driver is seated at the front of the hull on the left side and is provided with a single-piece hatch cover and three periscopes for observation. The engine, which is manufactured under licence by Renault, is mounted to his right. The crew compartment is at the rear of the hull and entrance to it is by the large power-operated ramp at the rear, which is provided with a door in case the ramp fails to open.

The suspension is of the torsion bar type and consists of five road wheels with the drive sprocket at the front and the idler at the rear. There are three track return rollers. Double-acting lever-type shock absorbers are provided for the first and fifth road wheel stations.

The crew of five consists of the driver, the commander in the turret and three mechanics. The AMX-10 ECH is fully amphibious, propelled in water by either its tracks at a speed of 6 km/h, or by two waterjets, one in each side of the hull, giving a maximum water speed of 7.92 km/h. Before entering the water a trim board is erected at the front of the hull.

The vehicle has a Toucan I turret slightly offset to the left side of the hull fitted with a 20 mm cannon and a coaxial 7.62 mm machine gun. The turret can be traversed through 360° and the armament elevated from −13 to +50°. Elevation and traverse are manual, maximum elevation speed is 16°/s and maximum traverse speed is 12°/s. Optical equipment for the turret includes six periscopes, a sight with a magnification of ×6 for engaging ground targets and a separate sight for anti-aircraft fire. A total of 576 rounds of 20 mm and 2000 rounds of 7.62 mm ammunition are carried. The 20 mm cannon can fire a variety of ammunition including HE, HE-I and AP, with a maximum muzzle velocity of 1050 m/s.

On the right side of the roof, at the rear, is the

AMX-10 ECH, a member of the AMX-10P family of tracked combat vehicles

hydraulically operated crane with an extensible jib, which can lift a maximum of 6000 kg. The operator is provided with a small roof hatch. When using this crane jacks are placed under the rear of the hull to support the vehicle. Other equipment carried includes tools, two sheer legs and two jacks, which are used to replace suspension components (for example torsion bars) on other AFVs including the AMX-30 MBT.

Optional kits for the AMX-10 ECH include an NBC system and passive night vision equipment.

Specifications
Crew: 5
Weight:
 (empty) 11 300 kg
 (loaded) 13 800 kg
Length: 5.76 m
Width: 2.78 m
Height:
 (top of hull) 1.92 m
 (overall) 2.62 m
Ground clearance: 0.45 m
Ground pressure: 0.53 kg/cm^2
Max speed: (road) 65 km/h
Range: (road) 600 km
Fording: amphibious

Gradient: 60%
Vertical obstacle: 0.7 m
Trench: 1.6 m
Engine: Hispano-Suiza HS 115-2, V-8, water-cooled supercharged diesel developing 280 hp at 3000 rpm
Transmission: preselective with 4 forward and 1 reverse gears
Electrical system: 24 V
Armament:
 1 × 20 mm cannon
 1 × 7.62 mm MG coaxial with main armament
 2 smoke dischargers either side of turret

Status
In production. In service with Saudi Arabia. The basic AMX-10P is also in service with France, Greece, Mexico, Qatar, Saudi Arabia and the United Arab Emirates.

Manufacturer
Atelier de Construction Roanne (ARE).
Enquiries to Giat Industries, 13 route de la Minière, F-78034 Versailles Cedex, France.
Tel: (1) 30 97 37 37. Fax: (1) 30 97 39 00.

Renault VAB ECH Repair Vehicle

Development
In 1969 the French Army issued a requirement for a new wheeled vehicle called the *Véhicule de l'Avant Blindé* (VAB) which would undertake a wide range of roles including use as an APC, load carrier, ambulance and anti-tank vehicle. Prototypes were built by Panhard and Saviem, and after comparative trials, the Saviem model was adopted by the French Army in 1974. The first production orders were placed the following year and first deliveries of the 4 × 4 version were made to the French Army late in 1976. At least 12 other countries have ordered the VAB and by mid-1990 over 4800 VABs had been completed. About 1000 more VABs of all types were scheduled to be delivered to the French armed forces by 1992. The VAB ECH repair vehicle is one of the many variants offered by Renault/Creusot-Loire Industrie. For details of the basic VAB APC refer to *Jane's Armour and Artillery 1992-93* pages 358 to 362.

In order to cover French Army and export market needs, SMS disclosed the VAB NG (New Generation) during 1990. This will enter production immediately after completion of the current French Army procurement programme. The possibility of refurbishing existing VABs to VAB NG specifications will be offered.

See also the entry for the VAB Recovery in the *Armoured recovery vehicles* section.

Description
The hull of the VAB is of all-welded steel armour with

Renault VAB ECH repair vehicle with hatches and rear doors open

the driver seated at the front of the vehicle on the left and the commander, who also operates the machine gun, to his right. Both the driver and commander have a bulletproof windscreen to their front which can be covered by an armoured plate if required, and a side door with a bulletproof window. The driver has a single-piece hatch cover in the roof which opens to the rear. The armament installation is over the commander/gunner's position.

The engine and transmission are mounted to the rear of the driver's position and are removed as a complete unit through the roof. The engine compartment is provided with a fire-extinguishing system.

The crew compartment is at the rear of the vehicle and there is a connecting corridor between the driver and commanders' compartment at the front, and the rear compartment on the vehicle's right-hand side. At the rear of the vehicle are two doors which open outwards, each with a window with an armoured cover. There is no centre post, therefore bulky equipment can be easily loaded. There are two large roof hatches over the rear compartment and on each side there are three bulletproof windows covered by an armoured shutter.

The VAB ECH can be fitted with at least three different types of armament installation:

Creusot-Loire Industrie CB 52 ring mount with a 7.5 or 7.62 mm machine gun which can be traversed by the gunner's shoulder through 360°. Elevation is from −15 to +45°, and 200 rounds of ready-use ammunition are provided.

Creusot-Loire Industrie TLI 52A turret with a 7.5 or 7.62 mm machine gun. The turret can be traversed through 360°, and the machine gun elevated from −12 to +45°. The gunner is provided with a tilting-head prism periscope with a magnification of ×1, linked to a sight with a magnification of ×5. For observation purposes there are six episcopes. A white light searchlight is mounted externally on the turret and fumes from firing the MG are extracted by

an electric fan system. A total of 200 rounds of ready-use ammunition is provided.

Creusot-Loire Industrie CB127 gun ring shield with 12.7 mm machine gun which can be traversed through a full 360° and elevated from −15 to +65°. 100 rounds of ready-use ammunition are provided.

The steering is power-assisted on the front four wheels (in the case of the 6 × 6 model) and the suspension is of the torsion bar type with telescopic shock absorbers. The tyres are of the run-flat type.

Power is transmitted from the engine to the wheels through a hydraulic torque converter and the gearbox. Gears are selected by means of a short pneumatically assisted lever which also operates the clutch.

The basic vehicle is fully amphibious, propelled in the water by its wheels, but if required the VAB can be delivered with two waterjets mounted in each side of the hull at the rear. Other optional equipment includes infra-red or passive night vision equipment, NBC system, heater and a front-mounted winch with 60 m of cable and a maximum capacity of 7000 kg.

The VAB ECH is provided with the following equipment: a welding station with cylinders of oxygen and acetylene, generator, grinding machine, hand drill, hoist, searchlight, storage cabinets and drawers, water tank, workbench, vice and tool kit. To give the repair crew more headroom a PVC roof extension can be quickly raised over the rear compartment.

Specifications

Crew: 4
Configuration: 6 × 6
Weight:
(empty) 12 000 kg
(loaded) 14 000 kg
Length: 5.98 m
Width: 2.49 m
Height: (top of hull) 2.06 m
Ground clearance: (axles) 0.4 m

Track: 2.035 m
Angle of approach/departure: 45°/45°
Wheelbase: 1.5 m + 1.5 m
Tyres: 14.00 × 20
Max speed:
(road) 92 km/h
(water) 7.2 km/h (with wheels)
Range: (road) 1000 km
Fuel capacity: 300 l
Fording: amphibious
Gradient: 60%
Side slope: 30%
Vertical obstacle: 0.5 m
Trench: 1 m (6 × 6 version only)
Engine: Renault MIDS 06.20.45 6-cylinder diesel developing 220 hp at 2200 rpm
Transmission: semi-automatic with 5 forward and 1 reverse gears
Electrical system: 24 V
Armament: 1 × 7.62 mm MG (see text)

Status

The VAB is in production and in service with the French Army and other countries including Central African Republic, Cyprus, Ivory Coast, Lebanon, Mauritius, Morocco, Oman, Qatar, the United Arab Emirates and other undisclosed countries.

Manufacturers

Renault Véhicules Industriels and Creusot-Loire Industrie, 40 rue Pasteur, BP 302, F-92156 Suresnes Cedex, France.

Enquiries to Société des Matériels Spéciaux Renault V.I Creusot-Loire Industrie, 316 Bureaux de la Colline, F-92213 Saint-Cloud Cedex, France.
Tel: (1) 46 02 80 33. Telex: 250 662 smssacl.
Fax: (1) 46 02 10 27.

Panhard M3 VAT and Buffalo Repair Vehicles

Development

The first prototype of the Panhard M3 APC was completed in 1969 with the first production vehicles following in 1971. The M3 uses 95 per cent of the mechanical components of the Panhard AML light armoured car which is used by many armies. The Panhard M3 VAT (or *Véhicule Atelier*) is basically the standard M3 APC modified to undertake repairs in the field. It has no recovery capability although it can tow other vehicles.

The M3 is no longer in production and has been replaced by the Buffalo.

Description

The hull of the M3 is of all-welded steel construction with the driver seated at the front of the hull. He has a single-piece hatch cover that opens to the right and has three integral periscopes for observation. There

are three small hatch covers which lift upwards and a large door in each side of the hull. At the rear of the hull are two doors, each of which has a firing port. There are two circular hatches in the roof and the 7.62 mm machine gun is normally mounted on the forward hatch cover position.

The engine and transmission are to the rear of the driver. The transmission consists of two gearboxes in one, coupled on both sides of the bevel pinion. The low range box comprises two low gears, top gear, and one reverse, which are used in rough country. The high range box has three low gears and an overdrive. There is no clutch pedal, just a gear selection gate.

The suspension consists of coil springs and hydro-pneumatic shock absorbers acting on suspension arms of the wheel mechanism. Brakes are hydraulic, with separate circuits for front and rear wheels. The tyres have punctureproof Hutchinson inner tubes.

The M3 is fully amphibious, propelled in the water by its wheels. Optional equipment includes a ventilation system and night vision equipment of the infra-red or passive type.

Equipment installed includes a generator, tools, workbenches, inspection lamp, tow bars and tow cables. A penthouse can be erected at the rear to enable repairs to be carried out in bad weather. A block and tackle can be erected at the rear to enable the VAT to carry out engine and other component changes.

Variant

Buffalo
In 1985 the basic M3 series, including the VAT, was replaced in production by a basically similar vehicle known as the Buffalo. The Buffalo series includes a light workshop vehicle but no example has yet been manufactured. The basic Buffalo armoured personnel carrier has a combat weight of 6200 kg and is 4.6 m long, 2 m high and 2.4 m wide. It is powered by a V-6 PRV petrol engine developing 145 hp at 5500 rpm. As an alternative it may be powered by a Peugeot XD 3T diesel engine developing 98 hp at 2250 rpm.

It is expected that the workshop vehicle version of the Buffalo will be very similar to the M3 VAT repair vehicle.

Specifications (M3)

Crew: 5
Configuration: 4 × 4
Weight:
(empty) 5300 kg
(loaded) 6100 kg
Length: 4.45 m
Width: 2.4 m
Height: (without armament) 2 m
Ground clearance: 0.35 m
Track: 2.05 m
Wheelbase: 2.7 m
Max speed:
(road) 90 km/h
(water) 4 km/h
Range: (road) 600 km
Fuel: 165 l
Fording: amphibious
Gradient: 60%
Side slope: 30%
Vertical obstacle: 0.3 m

Panhard M3 VAT repair vehicle showing unditching channels and bench vice at front of vehicle

Trench:
(with 1 channel) 0.8 m
(with 5 channels) 3.1 m
Engine: Panhard Model 4 HD 4-cylinder, horizontally opposed petrol developing 90 hp at 4700 rpm
Transmission: 6 forward and 1 reverse gears (see text)
Armament:
1 × 7.5 or 7.62 mm MG

4 smoke dischargers (optional)

Status
The M3 is no longer in production and was replaced by the Buffalo. The M3 is in service with the following countries, some of which also have the VAT: Angola, Bahrain, Burkina Faso, Gabon, Iraq, Ireland, Ivory Coast, Kenya, Lebanon, Malaysia, Mauritania, Morocco, Niger, Portugal, Rwanda, Saudi Arabia,

Senegal, Spain, Sudan (M3 VAT confirmed), Togo, United Arab Emirates and Zaïre.

Manufacturer
Société de Constructions Mécaniques Panhard et Levassor, 18 avenue d'Ivry, F-75621 Paris, France. Tel: (1) 40 77 40 00. Telex: 270 276.

POLAND

MT-LB Technical Support Vehicle

Description
The Polish Army utilises a locally developed version of the MT-LB multi-purpose tracked vehicle for the front line technical support of armoured units. The vehicle is similar to the basic MT-LB (for details of the MT-LB refer to *Jane's Armour and Artillery 1992-93* pages 327 to 330) but is provided with various items of special equipment for its role. In addition to its technical support role the vehicle can also be used as a general or NBC reconnaissance vehicle.

The vehicle has a basic crew of three but further seating is provided internally for up to four passengers. Its main role is the front line repair and general support of other armoured vehicles, which includes the towing of disabled light vehicles, the evacuation of personnel (including the provision of medical first-aid assistance), and the provision of earth hides or scrapes. For the latter role the vehicle is provided with two hydraulic arms at the rear of the vehicle, onto which a self-entrenching blade can be secured; when not in use the blade is carried on the hull roof on the right-hand side. Also provided for the support role is a light A-frame crane which can be erected over the rear of the hull to assist when handling vehicle components; for transport the crane is stowed folded flat on the hull roof. A comprehensive suite of repair and other tools is carried. The vehicle can be used to tow a trailer carrying spare components or supplies.

The vehicle is amphibious and is provided with NBC air filtration equipment. Under normal operations the vehicle's various NBC sensors are maintained in a permanently on condition.

The commander's position is covered by a small turret provided with vision devices. Mounted over the

Polish MT-LB technical support vehicle showing entrenching blade and A-frame crane stowed on hull roof

turret is a 12.7 mm NSW machine gun for local and air defence.

Specifications
Crew: 3 + 4
Weight: 12 900 kg (±200 kg)
Ground pressure: 0.46 kg/cm^2
Towed load:
(trailer) 6500 kg
(vehicle) 14 000 kg
Length:
(with blade) 7.378 m
(without blade) 7.14 m
(crane extended) 8.72 m
Width: 3.03 m
Height:
(crane stowed) 2.305 m
(crane extended) 4.14 m
Ground clearance: (max) 0.415 m

Max speed:
(road, without trailer) 60 km/h
(road, with trailer) 45 km/h
(when towing vehicle) 6 km/h
(water) 8 km/h
Range: 500 km
Fording: amphibious
Engine: SW680/167/1 6-cylinder turbocharged diesel developing 245 hp
Armament: 1 × 12.7 mm NSW MG

Status
In service with the Polish Army.

Marketing Agency
Cenzin Co Ltd, 2 Frascati Street, 00-489 Warsaw, Poland.
Tel: 48 22 296738. Telex: 814505 czi pl.
Fax: 48 2 6286356.

SOUTH AFRICA

Ratel Armoured Repair Vehicle

Description
The Ratel armoured repair vehicle is a slight variation of the basic Ratel MICV and is a modification that can be carried out on virtually any Ratel MICV although the only examples seen to date have been made to the Ratel 20 version which is armed with a 20 mm cannon. The main armament and layout of the vehicle is retained but a fixed lifting jib made up from four tubular steel posts is mounted on the rear hull. A block and tackle arrangement is used on the jib to raise and carry damaged vehicles which would normally be of the Ratel type. The Ratel armoured repair vehicle carries a variety of repair equipment both internally and in a wire mesh stowage basket mounted on the front hull. An air compressor is carried in a compartment in the hull rear and spare wheels may be carried on the roof. The vehicle retains its full combat capabilities.

Full details of the Ratel MICV can be found in *Jane's Armour and Artillery 1992-93* pages 419 to 422.

Specifications
Crew: (basic) 4
Configuration: 6 × 6
Combat weight: (approx) 18 000 kg
Length: 7.21 m
Width: 2.7 m

Ratel armoured repair vehicle with jib on rear hull

Height: (overall) 3.11 m
Track: 2.08 m
Wheelbase: 4.23 m
Max speed: 105 km/h
Range: (road) 1200 km
Fuel capacity: 480 l
Fording: 1.5 m
Gradient: 60%

Side slope: 30%
Vertical obstacle: 0.35 m
Trench: 1.2 m
Turning radius: 8.5 m
Engine: 6-cylinder, 4-stroke, water-cooled turbocharged diesel developing 230 hp at 2350 rpm
Transmission: automatic with 6 forward and 1 reverse gears

Steering: mechanical recirculating with hydraulic assistance
Armament:
  (main) 1 × 20 mm cannon
  (coaxial) 1 × 7.62 mm MG
  (anti-aircraft) 1 × 7.62 mm MG
Ammunition:
  (20 mm) 500 rounds

(7.62 mm) 900 rounds

Status
Production complete. In service with the South African Army.

Manufacturer
Sandock-Austral Beperk Limited, PO Box 6390, West

Street Industrial Sites, Boksburg, Transvaal, South Africa.
Enquiries to Armscor, Private Bag X337, Pretoria 0001, South Africa.
Tel: (012) 428 1911. Telex: 320217.
Fax: (012) 428 5635.

SWITZERLAND

MOWAG Piranha (8 × 8) Armoured Repair Vehicle

Development
One of the Piranha series of vehicles developed by the Swiss MOWAG concern during the early 1970s is the 8 × 8 armoured repair vehicle, which may also be used if required as an armoured recovery vehicle. It follows the same general lines as the Husky (6 × 6) and Bison (8 × 8) armoured repair vehicles built in Canada (see entries in this section).

Description
The hull of the vehicle is of all-welded steel armour with the front, sides and rear proof against NATO 7.62 mm ball ammunition. The driver is seated at the front of the hull on the left side and is provided with a single-piece hatch cover and three periscopes. The engine is mounted to the right of the driver and the personnel compartment is at the rear. Entry to this compartment is via two doors at the rear of the hull, each with a firing port. Roof hatches are provided.

The rear suspension is of the torsion bar type, and the front suspension has coil springs and wishbone. All wheels are fitted with hydraulic shock absorbers. When the crane is in use, the vehicle is stabilised by hydraulic and mechanical ground supports. All tyres have run-flat cores, and the dual circuit brakes are hydraulic, assisted by compressed air.

The vehicle is also available in a fully amphibious form, driven in the water by two propellers at the rear. Before entering the water a trim vane is erected at the front of the vehicle. The usual crane fitted to the Piranha (8 × 8) is a HIAB unit with a maximum capacity of 3000 kg, although other cranes may be fitted.

The latest version of the MOWAG Piranha is an 8 × 8 vehicle with a revised superstructure to mount a 7000 kg hydraulic crane centrally. This version has several layout changes from the original, one of which is the provision of stabiliser legs inset in the sides in a central position. The centrally mounted crane position allows more internal storage space so that more tools and repair equipment can be carried.

Specifications
Crew: 4 plus
Configuration: 8 × 8
Weight:
  (loaded) 12 300 to 13 000 kg
  (empty) 8800 kg
Length: 6.6 m
Width: 2.5 m
Height:
  (hull top, front) 1.85 m
  (hull top, rear) 2.7 m
Ground clearance: (under hull) 0.5 m
Track:
  (front) 2.18 m

(rear) 2.205 m
Tyres: 11.00 × 16
Wheelbase: 1.1 m + 1.335 m + 1.04 m
Angle of approach/departure: 40°/45°
Max speed:
  (road) 100 km/h
  (water) 10.5 km/h
Range: (road) 780 to 1000 km
Fuel: 300 or 500 l
Gradient: 60%
Side slope: 35%
Vertical obstacle: 0.5 m
Engine: Detroit Diesel 6V-53T developing 300 hp at 2800 rpm
Transmission: Allison MT-653 automatic with 5 forward and 1 reverse gears
Electrical system: 24 V
Armament: pintle-mounted 7.62 mm MG

Status
In production. Known users of the Piranha, some of whom might use the Piranha repair vehicle, include Chile, Ghana, Liberia, Nigeria, Sierra Leone and Switzerland.

Manufacturer
MOWAG Motorwagenfabrik AG, Kreuzlingen, Switzerland.
Tel: 072/71 55 00. Telex: 882211 moag ch.
Fax: 072/72 28 86.

MOWAG Piranha (8 × 8) repair vehicle in travelling configuration

MOWAG Piranha (8 × 8) repair vehicle lifting a powerpack from a Piranha APC

UNITED KINGDOM

FV434 Armoured Repair Vehicle

Development
The FV434 (Carrier, Maintenance, Full Tracked) is a member of the FV432 family of APCs and is operated by the Royal Electrical and Mechanical Engineers (REME). Its primary role is to repair disabled and damaged vehicles, for example changing the complete powerpack of a Chieftain MBT, but it has no recovery capability. The FV434 is unable to handle the power-pack of the Challenger MBT so it has been replaced in

some armoured units by the Chieftain ARRV (see entry in *Armoured recovery vehicles* section), pending the arrival in service of the Challenger ARRV.

Description
The hull of the FV434 is of all-welded steel construction. The crew of four consists of commander, driver (who is also the crane operator) and two fitters. The driver is seated at the front of the hull on the right side and is provided with a single-piece hatch cover that opens to his left and has an integral AFV No 33 Mk 1 periscope which can be replaced by an infra-red

periscope for night driving. To his rear is the commander's cupola, which has a single-piece hatch cover, and three No 32 Mk 1 periscopes for observation. The FV434 is armed with either a 7.62 mm L4A4 (Bren) LMG or a 7.62 mm L7A2 GPMG. To the rear of the commander's position is another hatch which opens to the left. The engine is mounted at the front of the vehicle, to the left of the driver. The load area is at the rear of the hull and is normally covered by bows and a tarpaulin cover.

The suspension is of the torsion bar type and consists of five road wheels with the drive sprocket at the front and the idler at the rear. There are two track return rollers. The first and fifth road wheel stations are provided with hydraulic shock absorbers which are normally locked when the crane is in use.

A flotation screen can be carried around the top of the hull and when erected the FV434 is fully amphibious, propelled in the water by its tracks; this capability is rarely used. The vehicle is provided with a ventilation system and infra-red driving lights.

On the right side of the vehicle is a HIAB crane, which has a lifting capacity of 1250 kg at 3.96 m radius to 3050 kg at 2.26 m radius. A full range of tools is carried, as are a workbench, vice, and tow bars for towing disabled vehicles.

Specifications

Crew: 4
Weight:
    (empty) 15 040 kg
    (loaded) 17 750 kg
Length: 5.72 m
Width: 2.84 m
    (over tracks) 2.527 m
Height:
    (roof) 1.891 m
    (crane travelling) 2.794 m
Ground clearance: 0.35-0.46 m
Track: 2.184 m
Track width: 343 mm
Length of track on ground: 2.819 m
Ground pressure: 0.91 kg/cm^2
Max speed:
    (road) 47 km/h
    (water) 6 km/h
Range: 480 km
Fuel capacity: 454 l
Fording: 1.066 m (amphibious with preparation)
Gradient: 60%
Vertical obstacle: 0.609 m
Trench: 2.05 m
Engine: Rolls-Royce K60 No 4 Mk 4F, 2-stroke,

FV434 armoured repair vehicle

6-cylinder, twin-crankshaft, multi-fuel developing 240 bhp at 3750 rpm
Transmission: GM Allison TX-200-4A semi-automatic with 6 forward and 1 reverse gears
Electrical system: 24 V
Batteries: 6 × 12 V, 100 Ah
Armament:
    1 × 7.62 mm L7A2 GPMG with 1000 rounds or
    1 × 7.62 mm L4A4 LMG with 336 rounds
    2 × 3-barrelled smoke dischargers on hull front
Armour: 6-12 mm

Status

Production complete. In service only with the British Army.

Manufacturer

GKN Defence, PO Box 106, Hadley Castle Works, Telford, Shropshire TF1 4QW, UK.
Tel: 0952 244321. Telex: 35248 sanhad g.
Fax: 0952 243910.

UNITED STATES OF AMERICA

Armored Maintenance Vehicle (AMV)

Development

In 1981 the US Army conducted a Battlefield Recovery and Evacuation (BRE) study to define future guidelines and to analyse the methods of forward area vehicle maintenance and recovery then in use. This BRE study highlighted the fact that the M113 Contact Team repair vehicles then in use were unsuitable for their tasks in forward battle areas. From this the US Army Ordnance Center and School (OC&S), together with the US Army Tank-Automotive Command (TACOM) and Training and Doctrine Command (TRADOC), evolved the concept of a forward-area Armored Maintenance Vehicle (AMV) that would operate in a battle area just short of the Forward Line of Troops (FLOT) to a depth of 6 to 10 km to the rear.

In December 1981 TRADOC included a requirement for the AMV in its Operational and Organizational Plan which in turn led to a Concept Evaluation Program (CEP) study conducted at Fort Hood, Texas, during May 1985. For this study the FMC Corporation supplied two prototype vehicles, one based on the M113A3 chassis (the stretched version with an extra road wheel each side) and the other based on the XM987 Fighting Vehicle System Carrier, used for the Multiple Launch Rocket System (MLRS).

Each vehicle was equipped with a telescopic crane jib capable of lifting a 5- to 6-tonne load such as an M1

Prototype of FMC Corporation Armoured maintenance Vehicle (AMV) based on XM987 Fighting Vehicles System Carrier

Abrams MBT powerpack. Control for the crane could be carried out internally or from a remote-control station box. Both vehicles used a rear-mounted crane

with hydraulically positioned stabiliser legs emplaced when the crane was in use. The XM987-based AMV can carry 3266 kg of tools and spare parts and the crane lift capacity is 6804 kg. The crew of the XM987-based AMV is four men with space for a further four, all with NBC protection. Welding and hydraulically operated tools are provided and the vehicle can be used to tow disabled vehicles.

The report on the Fort Hood trials was published by OC&S in October 1985. Since the trials, the Required Operational Capabilities (ROC) document review process required the BRE study to be updated and a Force Mix analysis to be performed. The results of the studies were proven and exceeded in field trials held during the second CEP conducted in Germany during the Reforger '88 exercise with the 8th and 3rd Infantry Divisions. The report on the Reforger '88 CEP was published by OC&S in September 1989. Production of the AMV awaits future Department of Defense budgets.

The single XM987-based AMV prototype is on lease to the US Army and was deployed to Saudi Arabia during Desert Shield/Storm.

Status

Prototype.

Manufacturer

FMC Corporation, Ground Systems Division, Santa Clara, California 95052, USA.
Tel: (408) 289 0111. Telex: 6714210.
Fax: (408) 289 2150.

RECOVERY VEHICLES

AUSTRIA

Steyr Type 19S25 (4 × 4) Recovery Vehicle

Description

The Steyr Type 19S25 is a development of the Steyr 1291 series of 4 × 4 trucks (see entry in *Trucks* section). The first of these vehicles fitted with recovery equipment was produced in 1984 for the Saudi Arabian National Guard.

The vehicle uses a forward control cab-over-engine design and features a hydraulic tilting cab mechanism to provide maintenance access to the main engine and transmission components. The cab has seating for the driver and two passengers. The chassis is constructed using open channel sections, using a parallel frame design for mounting the recovery equipment. There is a heavy duty suspension to cater for a 13 000 kg rear axle load and 6500 kg lifted towing.

The main recovery component is a 16 t/m crane manufactured by Penz (Austria). Also provided are two Rotzler winches, one 5-tonne, the other 3.5-tonne. There are four square-section outriggers to provide stability during recovery operations and two crane jib support props for towing loads to the rear, each with a 10-tonne pulling capacity. Tools and recovery equipment are located in a large compartment under the crane boom. A spare wheel is carried on the crane boom. A triangular tow bar and lifting tackle is provided for lifted towing.

Specifications
Cab seating: 1 + 2
Configuration: 4 × 4
Weight:
  (kerb) 13 000 kg
  (GVW) 19 000 kg
Length: 7 m
Width: 2.5 m
Height:
  (top of crane) 3.6 m
  (top of cab) 3 m
Ground clearance: 0.35 m
Track:
  (front) 1.958 m
  (rear) 1.8 m
Wheelbase: 3.8 m
Angle of approach/departure: 23°/25°
Max speed: 90 km/h
Fuel capacity: 380 l
Gradient: 60%
Side slope: 30%
Fording: 0.8 m
Engine: Steyr WD 615.74 10 l 6-cylinder in-line water-cooled direct injection diesel developing 250 hp at 2200 rpm or

WD 615.73 developing 290 hp at 2200 rpm or WD 615.78 developing 320 hp at 2200 rpm
Gearbox: ZF 9 S 109 synchromesh or 16 S 130 (for 320 hp engine)
Clutch: single disc dry, hydraulic actuation
Transfer box: Steyr VG 1200 2-speed
Steering: ZF 8046 hydraulic
Suspension: semi-elliptical springs with double-acting hydraulic shock absorbers front and rear
Tyres: 12.00 R 20
Axle loadings:
  (front) 7500 kg
  (rear) 13 000 kg
Brakes: dual circuit air
Electrical system: 24 V
Batteries: 2 × 12 V, 120 Ah
Alternator: 28 V, 30 or 55 A

Status
In production. In service with Cyprus, Ghana, Nigeria and the Saudi Arabian National Guard.

Manufacturer
Steyr Nutzfahrzeuge AG, Schönauerstrasse 5, A-4400 Steyr, Austria.
Tel: 7252/25351-0. Telex: 28200.
Fax: 7252/26746, 28650.

Steyr Type 19S25 (4 × 4) recovery vehicle

Steyr Type 19S25 (4 × 4) recovery vehicle

Steyr Type 32S29 (6 × 6) Recovery Vehicle

Description

The Steyr Type 32S29 recovery vehicle is a development of the Steyr 1491 series of 6 × 6 trucks (see entry in the *Trucks* section). The first of these vehicles fitted with recovery equipment was produced for the Saudi Arabian National Guard.

The vehicle uses a forward control cab-over-engine design and features a hydraulic tilting cab mechanism to provide maintenance access to the main engine and transmission components. The cab has seating for the driver and two passengers. The chassis is constructed using open channel sections, using a parallel frame design for mounting the recovery equipment. There is a bogie suspension to cater for a 2 × 13 000 kg rear load and 7500 kg lifted towing.

The main recovery component is a 30 t/m crane manufactured by Atlas or Penz (Austria). Also provided are two Rotzler winches, one 10-tonne, the other 6.5-tonne. There are four outriggers to provide stability during recovery operations and two crane jib support props for towing loads to the rear, each with a 20-tonne pulling capacity. Tools and recovery equipment are located in a large compartment under the crane boom. A spare wheel is carried on or behind the crane boom. A triangular tow bar and lifting tackle is provided for lifted towing.

Specifications
Cab seating: 1 + 2
Configuration: 6 × 6
Weight:
  (kerb) 18 000 kg
  (GVW) 32 000 kg
Length: 9 m
Width: 2.5 m
Height:
  (top of crane) 3.6 m
  (top of cab) 3 m
Ground clearance: 0.35 m
Track:
  (front) 1.958 m
  (rear) 1.8 m
Wheelbase: 3.5 m + 1.35 m
Angle of approach/departure: 23°/25°
Max speed: 90 km/h
Fuel capacity: 380 l
Gradient: 60%
Side slope: 30%
Fording: 0.8 m

Steyr Type 32S29 (6 × 6) recovery vehicle

Engine: Steyr WD 615.73 10 l 6-cylinder in-line water-cooled direct injection diesel developing 290 hp at 2200 rpm or
WD 615.78 developing 320 hp at 2200 rpm
Gearbox: ZF 9 S 109 synchromesh or 16 S 130 (for 320 hp engine)
Clutch: single disc dry, hydraulic actuation
Transfer box: Steyr VG 1200 2-speed
Steering: ZF 8046 hydraulic
Suspension: semi-elliptical springs with double-acting hydraulic shock absorbers front and rear

Tyres: 12.00 R 20
Axle loadings:
(front) 7500 kg
(rear) 2 × 13 000 kg
Brakes: dual circuit air
Electrical system: 24 V
Batteries: 2 × 12 V, 120 Ah
Alternator: 28 V, 30 or 55 A

Status
In production. In service with Cyprus, Ghana, Lebanon and the Saudi Arabian National Guard.

Manufacturer
Steyr Nutzfahrzeuge AG, Schönauerstrasse 5, A-4400 Steyr, Austria.
Tel: 7252/25351-0. Telex: 28200.
Fax: 7252/26746, 28650.

COMMONWEALTH OF INDEPENDENT STATES

Ural-375D/Ural-4320 (6 × 6) Recovery Vehicle

Description
A recovery vehicle based on the Ural-375D/Ural-4320 (6 × 6) 4000 kg truck was designed to recover vehicles weighing up to 8500 kg in the half-loaded position (for details of the Ural-4320 refer to entry in the *Trucks* section). The vehicle can tow vehicles weighing up to 5000 kg on dirt roads and vehicles of up to 10 000 kg on hard-surfaced roads.

The vehicle is fitted with a winch, half-loaded towing gear, a universal rigid towing blade and a trail spade at the rear. Standard equipment includes a repair kit, entrenching tools, fire extinguishers, a searchlight and pivoting signal lamps. The repair kit is carried to enable a recovered vehicle to be made ready for towing or to make a vehicle ready for transporting.

The power-operated winch is mounted at the chassis rear and has a maximum capacity of 7000 kg. In addition to recovering vehicles it can also load the recovered vehicle onto a transport unit. The transport unit consists of a boom with cross-beam, linking chains, and a longeron frame extension with struts and upper frame members. To couple the recovered vehicle to the transport unit, the boom is lowered to the level of the front bumper and locked in place by a special mechanism. The vehicle is chained to the cross-beam and then raised half-off the ground by the winch cable.

With the trail spade lowered and in position, the winch capacity is increased from 7000 kg to 14 000 kg. The boom is also intended to hold the recovery vehicle down while a vehicle is being recovered. The boom is lowered to the ground and attached to the trail spade which in turn is secured to the upper frame members by two cable braces.

The Ural-375D/Ural-4320 recovery vehicle retains the cab heater, engine heater and central tyre pressure regulation system of the standard cargo truck.

A closely allied variant using the Ural-4320 chassis is known as the MTP-A1.1 Technical Assistance Vehicle. This vehicle is used to carry out first and second line repairs and carries specialised repair equipment, tools, spare parts and materials for body repairs. Also carried are lubricants, electrical equipment and hydraulic jacks. A cargo lifting gantry protrudes over the cab and bonnet and can be used for lifting components. Towing bars and rigs can be used to tow disabled vehicles and a winch is provided.

Status
In service with the CIS.

Manufacturer
Chassis: Ural Motor Vehicle Plant, Miass, CIS.

KET-L (6 × 6) Recovery Truck

Description
The KET-L (6 × 6) recovery truck is based on the chassis of the Ural-375E (6 × 6) 4000 kg truck and for details of this vehicle refer to the entry in the *Trucks* section. For recovery operations the KET-L is fitted with two winches which can be used to either the front or rear and it is recommended that vehicles are recovered when in line with the KET-L recovery truck. The rear-mounted winch has a maximum capacity of 15 000 kg while the front winch has a capacity of 5000 kg. Vehicles up to 1.5 times the weight of the KET-L can be recovered without using supports but for heavier vehicles an anchor plate must be lowered from the rear of the vehicle.

Vehicles weighing up to 5000 kg can be towed on dirt roads using the Type 3108 rigid tow bar carried on the left rear top of the recovery hamper. Vehicles weighing up to 10 000 kg can be towed on paved roads. Mounted on the rear of the chassis is a jib crane with power supplied from the main winch via a power take-off. The crane has a boom 2.4 m long and a hook lift height of 3.5 m. Maximum capacity is 1500 kg.

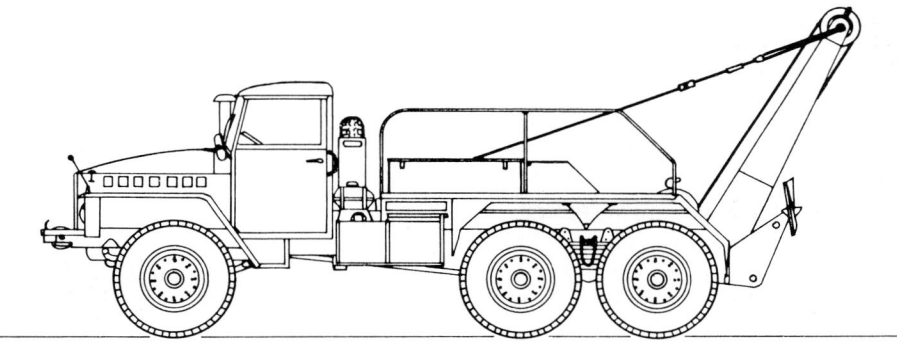

KET-L (6 × 6) recovery truck

Standard equipment carried by the KET-L includes a floodlight at the rear for night recovery operations, timber baulks, a pulley block, two Type OU-2 fire extinguishers (one stowed each side of the cab rear), provision for radio communication systems and metal-cutting equipment.

Status
In service with the CIS and many other armies.

Manufacturer
Chassis: Ural Motor Vehicle Plant, Miass, CIS.

CZECHOSLOVAKIA

AD-090 Wheeled Recovery Vehicle (6 × 6)

Description
This is basically a Tatra 138 (6 × 6) truck chassis fitted with a rear-mounted hydraulically operated crane with a capacity of 9000 kg and a winch with an 8000 kg capacity. It is normally used in conjunction with the PV-10 towing axle which has a capacity of 10 000 kg. An earlier model of the AD-090 is believed to be

designated the AV-8.

Specifications
Configuration: 6 × 6
Weight: 15 900 kg
Length: 9.25 m
Width: 2.45 m
Height: (travelling) 3.08 m
Max road speed:
(without load) 60 km/h
(with 4700 kg load) 40 km/h

Status
Production complete. In service with the Czechoslovak Army.

Manufacturer
(Tatra 138) Tatra, Národini Podnik, Koh privnice, Czechoslovakia.

FRANCE

Renault TRM 10 000 CLD (6 × 6) Heavy Wrecker

Development
The French Army has a requirement for a heavy wrecker truck capable of removing AMX-30 MBT turrets as well as performing the usual range of heavy duty recovery operations. Using the Renault TRM 10 000 as the basic chassis, trials were carried out with two types of hydraulic crane, both with a 15 000 kg lifting capacity and almost identical in appearance. One crane was a PPM product, the other, the GIC 156, a Pinguely product. The Pinguely GIC 156 was selected by the French Army.

Description
For details of the basic Renault TRM 10 000 vehicle refer to the entry in the *Trucks* section. The Pinguely GIC 156 crane is stabilised by smaller legs mounted both at the rear and under the main crane platform, just behind the cab.

The vehicle is fitted with winches with a rearward pull of 15 000/18 000 kg. A forward-mounted winch has a pull of 6000/8000 kg. The crane can be used either for a direct lift or for use with the crane boom extended. As an example the crane can lift a 12 000 kg tank turret to a hook height of 6 m. Heavier loads can be lifted by placing support bars under the crane arm so that loads of up to 18 000 kg can be lifted. The normal towing capacity of the TRM 10 000 is 25 000 kg but on roads this can be increased for short distances to a load of 40 000 kg.

The chassis is used to carry an array of specialist recovery equipment and tools. Numerous optional accessories are available ranging from side-mounted capstans to a cable transfer winch.

Specifications
Cab seating: 1 + 3
Configuration: 6 × 6
Weight:
(complete) 22 570 kg

Renault TRM 10 000 CLD heavy wrecker

(front axle) 7400 kg
(rear axle) 15 170 kg
Towed load: 25 000 kg
Length: (travelling) 9.72 m
Width:
(travelling) 2.48 m
(stabilisers extended) 3.23 m
Height: (overall) 3.08 m
Wheelbase: 4.3 m + 1.4 m
Max speed: 90 km/h
Range: 1000 km
Angle of approach/departure: 45°/45°
Engine: Renault MIDS 06.20-45 6-cylinder diesel developing 275 hp at 2200 rpm
Transmission: ZF 6 HP 500 automatic with torque converter
Transfer box: 2-speed
Steering: hydraulic power-assisted

Tyres: 14.00 × 20
Electrical system: 24 V

Status
In production. In service with the French Army.

Manufacturers
Vehicle: Renault Véhicules Industriels, 40 rue Pasteur, BP 302, F-92156 Suresnes Cedex, France.
Tel: (1) 40 99 71 11. Telex: 620 567 sdce f.
Fax: (1) 40 99 71 08.
Crane: Pinguely, Creusot-Loire, BP 9, F-42152 l'Horme, France.
Tel: (1) 77 22 82 80. Telex: 330 169.
Fax: (1) 77 22 76 22.

Berliet TBC 8 KT (6 × 6) Wrecker

Description
The Berliet TBC 8 KT (6 × 6) CLD (*Camion Lourd de Dépannage*) is a member of the Berliet GBC 8 KT (6 × 6) 4-tonne truck family. The reader is referred to the entry on the latter vehicle for a detailed history of its development and a description of its technical characteristics.

The rear winch is provided with 60 m of cable and has a maximum capacity of 5000 kg which can be increased to 7000 kg with the aid of earth anchors. The crane mounted in the rear is hydraulically operated, and slews through 270°; two stabilisers on each side are lowered to the ground manually. Equipment carried includes two telescopic arm brackets to support the jib, two rear radius rods to support the jib on the ground, tow bars, two earth anchor spades, tackles, one acetylene bottle and hose, one oxygen bottle and hose, and tools.

Variant
A light recovery version of the GBC 8 KT (6 × 6) truck is also in service. This has drop sides and an overhead rail and is provided with a 2000 kg hoist which can be used to lift light vehicles and change components. A winch with a capacity of 5000 kg (or 7000 kg with earth anchors in use) is fitted and can be led out through the front or rear. Loaded weight is 12 600 kg and empty weight is 9600 kg (eg 4400 kg on the front axles, and 2600 kg on each of the rear axles).

Specifications
Cab seating: 1 + 2
Configuration: 6 × 6
Weight: (empty) 13 650 kg
Length: 7.693 m

Berliet GBC 8 KT (6 × 6) wrecker

Width: 2.4 m
Height: 2.97 m
Ground clearance:
(max) 0.515 m
(axles) 0.28 m
Track: 1.86 m
Wheelbase: 3.31 m + 1.28 m
Angle of approach/departure: 45°/45°
Max speed: (road) 80 km/h
Range: 800 km
Fuel capacity: 200 l
Max gradient: 50%
Side slope: 22%

Fording: 1.2 m
Engine: Berliet MK 520 5-cylinder multi-fuel developing 125 hp at 2100 rpm
Transmission: Berliet BDSL with 6 forward and 1 reverse gears, 2-speed transfer case
Turning radius: 10.5 m
Steering: worm gear and nut with servo assistance, turning circle indicator provided
Suspension:
(front) longitudinal leaf springs with hydraulic shock absorbers
(rear) leaf springs
Tyres: 12.00 × 20

Brakes: air with 3 circuits (1 for front, 1 for rear and 1 for trailer) with exhaust retarder
Electrical system: 24 V
Batteries: 4 × 12 V

Status
Production complete. In service with the French Army.

The cargo truck version is also used by Algeria, Austria, China, Iraq, Morocco and Portugal, some of which also use the recovery version.

Manufacturer
Automobiles M Berliet, Bourg. Berliet is now part of the Renault Group. Enquiries to Renault Véhicules

Industriels, 40 rue Pasteur, F-92156 Suresnes Cedex, France.
Tel: (1) 40 99 71 11. Telex: 620 567 sdce f.
Fax: (1) 40 99 71 08.

Berliet TBU 15 CLD (6 × 6) Wrecker

Description
The TBU 15 CLD (*Camion Lourd de Dépannage*) is the recovery member of the GBU 15 (6 × 6) cargo truck family and uses the same basic chassis and cab. The basic truck model entered production in 1959/60 with the wrecker following in 1962.

Mounted at the rear is a hydraulic crane with a maximum lifting capacity of 10 000 kg, which can be swung through 278°. Its telescopic jib has a maximum length when extended of 5.518 m. Two stabilisers on each side of the hull are lowered manually when heavier loads are being lifted. The front-mounted winch has 60 m of 15 mm diameter cable and a capacity of 5000 kg, which can be increased to 7000 kg with the aid of earth anchors. The rear-mounted winch has 60 m of 20 mm diameter cable and a maximum capacity of 8000 kg which can be increased to 12 000 kg with earth anchors. A full range of tools and other equipment is carried including oxygen and acetylene cylinders. Its replacement for the French Army is the Renault TRM 10 000 CLD (6 × 6) heavy wrecker.

Specifications
Cab seating: 1 + 3
Configuration: 6 × 6
Weight: 21 200 kg
Length: 8.88 m
Width: 2.5 m
Height: 3 m
Ground clearance: 0.6 m (max)
Track: 2.04 m
Wheelbase: 3.48 m + 1.45 m
Angle of approach/departure: 45°/45°
Max speed: (road) 68 km/h
Range: 800 km
Fuel capacity: 400 l (2 × 200 l tanks)

Berliet TBU 15 CLD (6 × 6) wrecker

Max gradient: 60%
Max side slope: 30%
Fording: 1 m
Engine: Berliet MK 640 6-cylinder, multi-fuel, water-cooled developing 214 hp at 1800 rpm
Transmission: manual with 5 forward and 1 reverse gears, 2-speed transfer box
Turning radius: 9.2 m
Steering: screw and nut with power assistance
Suspension: longitudinal leaf springs front and rear
Tyres: 14.00 × 20
Brakes: air
Electrical system: 24 V

Batteries: 4 × 6TN

Status
Production complete. In service with the Belgian, French, Irish and other armed forces.

Manufacturer
Automobiles M Berliet, Bourg. Berliet is now part of the Renault Group. Enquiries to Renault Véhicules Industriels, 40 rue Pasteur, F-92156 Suresnes Cedex, France.
Tel: (1) 40 99 71 11. Telex: 620 567 sdce f.
Fax: (1) 40 99 71 08.

GERMANY

MAN Type 27.365 VFAE (8 × 8) Recovery Vehicle (M1002)

Description
The MAN Type 27.365 VFAE is a development from the main line of MAN 15-tonne trucks and was produced for use by the US Army in Europe and the Canadian Armed Forces Europe. The first two examples of this recovery vehicle for the US Army were delivered between July and September 1981 under the designation XM1002. They were later approved for service as the M1002. Production ceased in 1987.

The main engine is situated just behind the tilt-forward cab which has air-assisted suspension seating for the driver and two passengers. The entire chassis frame is constructed from all-welded steel and is a low torsion box structure. A spare wheel is located to the right of the engine. Behind the engine is an open equipment-carrying box with drop sides 2.3 m long. Behind the box is an Atlas crane with a capacity of 20 000 kg which is provided with a remote-control unit; outriggers for stability can be mounted. Directly over the third and fourth axles is a substructure which can either be used as a 'fifth wheel' load-carrying surface or as the position for a recovery assembly capable of lifting up to 11 340 kg and towing 38 556 kg. The recovery assembly may be fitted with a towing bar or other recovery equipment. Other special equipment

MAN recovery vehicle on (8 × 8) Category I A1 chassis

includes a heavy duty recovery winch with a 20 412 kg capacity, and a self-recovery winch with a 9072 kg capacity. Power take-offs for all these equipments can be selected from the main power train. Extra spare wheels can be carried over the main recovery assembly, and the complete vehicle can be finished in an NBC decontaminant-resistant paint. An arctic kit is available.

Specifications
Cab seating: 1 + 2
Configuration: 8 × 8
Weight:
(curb) 20 180 kg
(GCW) 45 300 kg
Length: 8.996 m
Width: 2.5 m

Height:
(top of crane) 3 m approx
(top of cab) 2.921 m
Ground clearance: 0.457 m
Track:
(front) 2.066 m
(rear) 2.072 m
Wheelbase: 1.93 m + 3.2 m + 1.5 m or 1.93 m + 2.77 m +1.5 m
Angle of approach/departure: 42.5°/45°
Max speed: (approx) 90 km/h
Fuel capacity: 600 l
Max gradient: (without towed load) 60%
Side slope: 40%

Fording: 1.22 m
Engine: MAN D 2840 MFG V-10 water-cooled diesel developing 365 hp at 2300 rpm
Gearbox: ZF synchromesh 4S-150 8-speed
Clutch: ZF torque converter clutch 400
Transfer box: ZF-GPA
Steering: recirculatory ball hydro-steering
Suspension: coil springs and telescopic shock absorbers
Tyres: 16.00 × 20
Axle loadings:
(front) 2 × 7500 kg
(rear) 2 × 10 500 kg
Brakes: two circuit air and air over hydraulic

Electrical system: 24 V
Batteries: 4 × 12 V, 125 Ah
Alternator: 28 V, 95 A

Status
Production complete. In service with the US Army, Canadian Armed Forces Europe and other armies. Replaced in production by MAN KAT 1 A – see following entry.

Manufacturer
MAN Nutzfahrzeuge AG, Postfach 500620, D-8000 Munich 50, Federal Republic of Germany. Tel: 89 14 80-1. Telex: 211023.

MAN KAT I A 1 6 × 6 Type 24.260 DFAEG Recovery Vehicle

Description
This recovery vehicle was developed in close co-operation with the British Army and the sub-contractors Atlas Weyhausen and Rotzler. The vehicle has three main components: the chassis supplied by MAN; a self-recovery winch with front pull, provided by Rotzler; and a recovery unit with a crane, heavy towing winch and towing boom, all provided by Atlas Weyhausen.

The MAN KAT I A 1 6 × 6 chassis is powered by a 360 hp six-cylinder in-line engine. It has a low torsion frame and provides stability under military conditions. The hydraulically powered recovery unit was designed for military purposes and can be used on roads as well as extreme off-road conditions. The crane can be used to lift tank engines, containers and so on, without difficulty. Maximum payload moment of the crane is 45 t/m, maximum overhang length is 7.7 m and maximum lift height is 9.25 m. Maximum load on the hook (1st step) is 15 000 kg. The hydraulically extended recovery arm has a maximum carrying capacity of 8000 kg. The tractive force on the recovery cable on the first layer of the heavy towing winch is approximately 250 kN.

Specifications
Cab seating: 1 + 2
Configuration: 6 × 6
Weight: (kerb, with all recovery equipment) 24 700 kg
Axle loadings, technical permissible:
(front) 7500 kg
(rear) 2 × 13 000 kg

MAN KAT I A 1 6 × 6 Type 24.260 DFAEG Recovery Vehicle

Length: (less front counterweight and rear pintle) 8.8 m
Width: 2.5 m
Height: (top of crane) 3.3 m
Wheelbase: 4.25 m + 1.5 m
Angle of approach: 38°
Max speed: (without towed load) approx 95 km/h
Fuel capacity: 400 l
Max gradient: (without towed load) 60%
Side slope: 40%
Engine: MAN D 2866 LXFG 6-cylinder in-line, water-cooled, turbocharged and inter-cooled, developing 360 hp
Gearbox: ZF synchromesh 16S-160A, 16-speed
Clutch: ZF torque converter WSK 400
Transfer box: ZF GPA flanged onto transmission
Steering: recirculatory ball hydro-steering ZF 8046

Suspension: coil springs and telescopic shock absorbers
Tyres: 16.00 × 20
Brakes: dual circuit air and air over hydraulic
Electrical system: 24 V
Batteries: 4 × 12 V, 100 Ah
Alternator 28 V, 120 A

Status
First two units delivered to British Army.

Manufacturer
MAN Nutzfahrzeuge AG, Postfach 500620, D-8000 Munich 50, Federal Republic of Germany. Tel: 89 14 80-1. Telex: 211023.

Faun Recovery Crane Type RTF 25

Description
The Faun Recovery Crane Type RTF 25 was developed for the recovery and repair of wheeled and tracked vehicles as well as for general crane-lifting purposes. The vehicle has a high degree of cross-country mobility using a 4 × 4 drive configuration and with steering on both axles.

The crane uses a forward control cab constructed from steel and glass fibre and with the crane turntable immediately behind the cab. The crane has a telescopic jib with a maximum extension of 22.34 m. Telescopic stabilisers are provided for use when the crane is operating. The crane is stated to have a lifting capacity of 25 000 kg at 7.54 m.

Specifications
Cab seating: 1 + 1
Configuration: 4 × 4
Weight: 21 600 kg
Length: approx 10.45 m
Width: 2.5 m
Height: 3.35 m
Wheelbase: 3.8 m
Max speed: 80 km/h
Fuel capacity: 300 l
Engine: DB OM 366 LA water-cooled diesel developing 240 hp at 2600 rpm
Gearbox: ZF 6 WG 180 power-shift with HN 500

Faun recovery crane Type RTF 25

converter providing 6 forward and 2 reverse gears
Steering: ZF semi-integral power, dual circuit
Tyres: 14.00 R 25
Brakes: compressed air, dual circuit

Status
In production.

Manufacturer
Faun AG, Postfach 10 01 08, D-8560 Lauf ad Pegnitz, Federal Republic of Germany.
Tel: 0 91 23 185-0. Telex: 626093.
Fax: 0 91 23 753 20.

ISRAEL

EYAL Heavy Recovery Vehicles

Description
The EYAL Engineering and Industrial Company Limited produces five models of heavy recovery vehicle. They are the HRV 720 with a lifting moment of 20 t/m, the HRV 930 with a lifting moment of 30 t/m, the HRV 1236 with a lifting moment of 36 t/m and the HRV 1545 with a lifting moment of 45 t/m. The heaviest model is the HRV 1760 with a lifting capacity of 60 t/m.

All these models are produced using a 6 × 6 chassis with the model and make of chassis according to the customer's choice — most examples used by the Israeli armed forces use locally modified M809 series chassis. The recovery hamper is produced as a bolt-on unit and consists of a hydraulic crane, four hydraulically operated outriggers, a main recovery hydraulic winch, a towing hitch, an operating cab and the hydraulic system.

The crane has a full 360° traverse and is equipped with a planetary hydraulic hoisting winch mounted on the main boom. The winch has a built-in automatic brake. Boom operations are carried out by a hydraulic double-acting cylinder with built-in safety devices. The crane block may be assembled with one or two sheaves on a roller bearing and with a swivel hook.

The four outriggers are located with one pair at the front of the upper structure and the other pair at the rear. Each pair is operated separately under hydraulic control and with automatic built-in safety locking valves.

The main recovery winch is mounted on the front of the upper structure and is equipped with 70 m of cable. The winch may have a line pull of 15, 20 or 25 tonnes depending on the model. The cable is drawn under the floor of the recovery unit.

EYAL heavy recovery vehicle lifting recovery frame complete with crane

The towing hitch is mounted at the rear and can tow suspended loads of 6, 7, 8 or 10 tonnes depending on the model involved.

The operating cab is mounted on the right-hand side of the crane boom and levers are used to control the hydraulic system. A rainproof canvas cover is supplied for the operator.

The hydraulic system is driven from the vehicle power take-off.

EYAL also produces a range of hydraulic cranes with varying lift capacities. One of them, the Model 3501, has been mounted on Israeli Army M3 half-tracks.

Status
In production. In service with the Israeli armed forces.

Manufacturer
EYAL Engineering and Industrial Company Limited, POB 374, Herzelia 46103, Israel.
Tel: 052 541111. Telex: 33597.
Fax: 052 541217.

ITALY

IVECO FIAT 6605 AG (6 × 6) Recovery Vehicle

Description
The IVECO FIAT 6605 AG is the recovery member of the 6605 range of vehicles for which there is a separate entry in the *Trucks* section. The first prototype of the vehicle was completed in 1972 with first production models following in 1974. The Italian Army designation for the vehicle is the Autogru AG 70-5 t (6 × 6).

The chassis is the ladder type with two longitudinal pressed steel channels, to which are riveted the cross-members, brackets and spring supports. The forward control cab is all-steel and has a removable canvas top and side screens and a windscreen which can be folded flat against the bonnet. Standard equipment includes a cab heater and ventilator.

Mounted at the rear of the vehicle is a hydraulically operated crane with an extensible jib which can lift a maximum load of 5000 kg. Before the crane is used two stabilisers are extended either side and lowered to the ground. The FIAT 6605 AG has two winches, one front-mounted with a capacity of 9200 kg and one rear-mounted with a capacity of 20 000 kg.

The transmission consists of a set of gears mounted on four shafts (input, primary, layshaft and reverse). Shifting from each gear is controlled by a lever through a pneumatic servo. Shifting from the high to the low range, or vice versa, is by electro-pneumatic control with a pre-selector switch, interlocked with the clutch pedal. The transfer box is mechanical and consists of helical constant mesh gears mounted on three shafts (input, intermediate and output) of which the input one carries the dog clutch with a lockable divider differential distributing power to the front and rear axles.

IVECO FIAT 6605 AG (6 × 6) recovery vehicle showing front-mounted winch

Specifications
Cab seating: 1 + 1
Configuration: 6 × 6
Weight:
(empty) 19 000 kg
(loaded) 25 000 kg
Max load: 5000 kg
Towed load: 15 000 kg
Length: 8.32 m
Width: 2.5 m
Height:
(cab) 2.74 m
(top of crane in travelling position) 3.01 m
Ground clearance: 0.363 m
Track: 2.072 m
Wheelbase: 3.217 m + 1.365 m
Angle of approach/departure: 45°/40°
Max speed: (road) 80 km/h
Range: 700 km
Fuel capacity: 360 l
Max gradient: 60%
Max side slope: 20%
Fording: 1.5 m
Engine: Model 8212.02 6-cylinder in-line water-cooled diesel developing 260 hp at 2200 rpm
Gearbox: manual with 8 forward and 2 reverse gears
Clutch: dual dry plate
Transfer box: 2-speed
Steering: ZF hydraulic-assisted
Turning radius: 8 m
Suspension:
(front) 2 semi-elliptical constant rate leaf springs with double-acting hydraulic shock absorbers
(rear) rocker and torque arms with 2 constant rate leaf springs
Tyres: 14.00 × 20
Brakes:
(main) drum air-operated on all wheels, dual circuit with connections for trailer braking
(parking) drum, hand-operated, mounted on transfer rear output shaft
Electrical system: 24 V
Batteries: 4 × 12 V, 90 Ah

Status
In service with the Italian Army.

Manufacturer
IVECO FIAT SpA, Defence Vehicle Division, Via Volta 6, I-39100 Bolzano, Italy.
Tel: 471 905111. Telex: 400541.
Fax: 471 905444.

IVECO FIAT 90 PM 16 (4 × 4)
Wrecker with 5-tonne Crane

Description

The IVECO FIAT 90 PM 16 (4 × 4) truck chassis was developed to mount a 5000 kg capacity FARID crane boom. The crane is mounted behind the vehicle cab on a sheet steel subframe connected to the chassis by brackets. Onto this subframe are mounted the super-structure, crane and outriggers and when the crane is in use the entire vehicle is raised onto the outriggers for overall stabilisation. The crane is a FARID model F 5 which is hydraulically operated. The maximum boom length is 5.7 m, the maximum boom elevation 75° and the traverse is a full 360°. The crane has a maximum pull to the rear of 5000 kg but extra pull capacity is provided by a rear-mounted auxiliary winch with a 4000 kg capacity. A self-recovery winch is mounted at the front and this has a capacity of 3000 kg. The four outriggers, one at each corner of the subframe, are hydraulically operated from a panel at the side of the vehicle; the crane controls are on a panel by the operator's seat.

Accessories include a draw bar, collapsible snatch blocks, a set of chains with hooks, a spare wheel holder and tool boxes. The deck of the subframe, which is covered with a non-slip steel plate, measures 3.4 m long and 2.3 m wide, and may be used for carrying extra equipment or cargo.

Specifications

Cab seating: 1 + 1
Configuration: 4 × 4
Weight:
 (gross) 9700 kg
 (curb) 8200 kg
Payload: (load hang to hook) 1500 kg
Towing capacity: 4000 kg
Length: (inc crane overhang) 7.042 m
Width: 2.476 m
Height: (cab) 2.627 m
Ground clearance: 0.47 m
Track: 1.851 m

IVECO FIAT 90 PM 16 (4 × 4) wrecker with 5-tonne crane

Wheelbase: 3.7 m
Angle of approach/departure: 42°/42°
Max speed: 80 km/h
Range: 700 km
Power-to-weight ratio: 16.5 hp/t
Max gradient: 60%
Side slope: 30%
Fording: 0.7 m
Engine: Model 8062.24 6-cylinder supercharged direct injection water-cooled diesel developing 160 hp at 3200 rpm
Gearbox: manual with 5 forward and 1 reverse gears
Clutch: single dry plate
Transfer box: 2-speed
Steering: recirculating ball with hydraulic servo

Turning radius: 7.5 m
Suspension: leaf springs (dual at rear) with hydraulic shock absorbers (telescopic)
Tyres: 12.5 R20 PR22

Status

Production complete. In service with Venezuela (60).

Manufacturers

Chassis: IVECO FIAT SpA, Defence Vehicle Division, Via Volta 6, I-39100 Bolzano, Italy.
Tel: 471 905111. Telex: 400541. Fax: 471 905444.
 Crane: FARID SpA, Corso Savona 39 bis, I-10024 Moncalieri, Italy.
Tel: 011 645454. Telex: 220348.

IVECO FIAT 90.17 WM (4 × 4)
Wrecker

Description

The IVECO FIAT 90.17 WM (4 × 4) wrecker replaced the IVECO FIAT 90 PM 16 wrecker (see previous entry) in production and is based on the chassis of the IVECO FIAT 90.17 WM (4 × 4) truck fitted with a 6000 kg capacity crane. The hydraulic crane is mounted behind the vehicle on a sheet steel subframe connected to the chassis by brackets. Onto this subframe are mounted the superstructure, crane and outriggers and when the crane is in use the entire vehicle is raised onto the outriggers for overall stabilisation. The crane maximum boom length is 5.1 m, the maximum boom elevation 60° and traverse is 220°. The crane has a maximum pull to the rear of 6000 kg but extra pull capacity is provided by a rear-mounted auxiliary winch, also with a 6000 kg capacity. A self-recovery winch is mounted at the front and this has a capacity of 3000 kg. The four outriggers, one at each corner of the subframe, are hydraulically operated while the crane controls are in the crane turret cab.

Accessories include a spare wheel holder and tool boxes. The deck of the subframe is covered with a non-slip steel plate and may be used for carrying extra equipment or stores.

Specifications

Cab seating: 1 + 1
Configuration: 4 × 4
Weight: (gross) 9080 kg
Payload: (load hang to hook) 2000 kg
Towing capacity: 4000 kg
Length: (inc crane overhang) 6.76 m
Width: 2.3 m
Height: (cab) 2.75 m
Ground clearance: 0.47 m
Track: 1.852 m

IVECO FIAT 90.17 WM (4 × 4) wrecker with 6-tonne crane

Wheelbase: 3.7 m
Angle of approach/departure: 45°/30°
Max speed: 80 km/h
Range: over 500 km
Max gradient: 60%
Side slope: 30%
Fording: 0.7 m
Engine: Model 8060.25 6-cylinder supercharged direct injection water-cooled diesel developing 170 hp at 3000 rpm
Gearbox: manual with 5 forward and 1 reverse gears
Clutch: single dry plate
Transfer box: 2-speed
Steering: recirculating ball with hydraulic servo

Turning radius: 7.5 m
Suspension: leaf springs (dual at rear) with telescopic hydraulic shock absorbers
Tyres: 14.5 × 20

Status

In production.

Manufacturer

IVECO FIAT SpA, Defence Vehicle Division, Via Volta 6, I-39100 Bolzano, Italy.
Tel: 471 905111. Telex: 400541.
Fax: 471 905444.

IVECO FIAT 230.35 WM (6 × 6) Recovery Vehicle

Description
The IVECO FIAT 230.35 WM (6 × 6) recovery vehicle is a variant of the IVECO FIAT 230.35 WM (6 × 6) 10 000 kg truck fitted with a 14 000 kg crane. The recovery equipment is mounted on a welded steel subframe that is linked by brackets to the vehicle chassis, crane, winch outriggers and related control units. The upper part of the subframe carries the 360° rotating platform for the crane which is an Isoli Model M 140 — 49.8 t/m with a maximum lifting capacity of 14 000 kg. The crane hydraulics are powered from the main engine with the crane using a telescopic boom. The crane has a hook-lifting speed of 8 m/min and maximum elevation is 55°. The maximum boom length is 6.35 m and the minimum 3.55 m.

The four outriggers are operated independently of each other and have independent controls for all movements. A hydraulic recovery winch is fitted to the side of the vehicle for front and rear operations. It has a maximum pulling capacity (on the first layer) of 15 000 kg.

The IVECO FIAT 230.35 WM (6 × 6) recovery vehicle is fitted with a torque converter to obtain the maximum tractive effort in any gear.

Specifications
Cab seating: 1 + 2
Configuration: 6 × 6
Weight:
(kerb) 19 000 kg
(GVW) 25 000 kg
Load: (load hang to hook) 5000 kg
Towed load: (off road) 15 000 kg
Length: (overall) 8.48 m
Width:
(overall) 2.5 m
(cab) 2.494 m
Height:
(overall) 3.06 m
(cab) 3 m

Ground clearance: 0.35 m
Track:
(front) 2.027 m
(rear) 2.032 m
Wheelbase: 3.3 m + 1.38 m
Angle of approach/departure: 45°/30°
Max speed: 83 km/h
Range: 600 km
Fuel capacity: 300 l
Max gradient: 60%
Side slope: 30%
Fording: 0.85 m
Engine: FIAT 8280.02 V-8 17.2 l water-cooled diesel developing 352 hp at 2400 rpm
Transmission: Type ZF 4 S 150 GPA with 8 forward and 1 reverse gears, with torque converter
Transfer box: electro-pneumatically lockable
Steering: power-assist, recirculatory ball
Turning radius: 9.5 m
Suspension:
(front) single flexibility leaf springs with hydraulic telescopic shock absorbers
(rear) single flexibility leaf springs, reversed, fully articulated
Tyres: 14.00 × 20
Brakes:
(main) drum, air on all wheels
(parking) mechanical on rear wheels
(exhaust) pneumatic, pedal control
Electrical system: 24 V
Batteries: 4 × 12 V, 143 Ah
Generator: 650 W

Status
In production.

Manufacturer
IVECO FIAT SpA, Defence Vehicle Division, Via Volta 6, I-39100 Bolzano, Italy.
Tel: 471 905111. Telex: 400541.
Fax: 471 905444.

IVECO FIAT 230.35 WM (6 × 6) recovery vehicle

IVECO FIAT 260.35 WM (6 × 6) Recovery Vehicle

Description
The IVECO FIAT 260.35 WM (6 × 6) recovery vehicle is a variant of the IVECO FIAT 260.35 WM (6 × 6) 10 000 kg truck fitted with a 12 000 kg hydraulic crane. The recovery equipment is mounted on a welded steel subframe, linked by brackets to the vehicle chassis, crane, winch, outriggers and related control units. The upper part of the subframe carries the 360° rotating platform for the crane, an Isoli Model M 120 — 42.8 t/m with a maximum lifting capacity of 12 000 kg. The hydraulic system uses three pumps driven from the vehicle main engine with the crane having a telescopic extendible boom. The crane has a hook-lifting speed of 10 m/min with the maximum elevation angle being 50°. The maximum boom length is approximately 6.4 m and the minimum approximately 3.6 m.

The four hydraulic outriggers are operated independently of each other and have independent controls for all movements. An axle lock can lock the rear bogie, raising it off the ground for increased stability during crane operations. A hydraulic recovery winch is fitted to the side of the vehicle cab for front and rear operations. It has a maximum pulling capacity (on the first layer) of 15 000 kg.

The IVECO FIAT 260.35 WM (6 × 6) recovery vehicle is fitted with a torque converter to obtain the maximum tractive effort in any gear.

Specifications
Cab seating: 1 + 1
Configuration: 6 × 6
Weight:
(kerb) 20 600 kg
(GVW) 25 600 kg
Load: (load hang to hook) 5000 kg
Towed load: (off road) 15 000 kg
Length: (overall) 8.86 m
Width: (overall) 2.5 m

IVECO FIAT 260.35 (6 × 6) recovery vehicle with 12-tonne crane

Height:
(overall) 3.03 m
(exhaust over cab) 3.123 m
Ground clearance: 0.312 m
Track:
(front) 1.927 m
(rear) 1.809 m
Wheelbase: 3.85 m + 1.38 m
Angle of approach/departure: 33°/27°
Max speed: 94 km/h
Range: 600 km
Fuel capacity: 300 l
Max gradient: 60%
Side slope: 30%
Fording: 0.65 m
Engine: FIAT 8280.02 V-8 17.2 l water-cooled diesel developing 352 hp at 2400 rpm
Transmission: Type ZF 4 S 150 GPA with 8 forward and 1 reverse gears, with torque converter
Transfer box: electro-pneumatically operated
Steering: power-assist, recirculatory ball
Turning radius: 9.5 m

Suspension:
(front) single flexibility leaf springs with hydraulic telescopic shock absorbers
(rear) single flexibility leaf springs, reversed, fully articulated
Tyres: 12.00 × 20
Brakes:
(main) drum, air on all wheels
(parking) mechanical on rear wheels
(exhaust) pneumatic, pedal control
Electrical system: 24 V
Batteries: 2 × 12 V, 143 Ah
Generator: 650 W

Status
In production.

Manufacturer
IVECO FIAT SpA, Defence Vehicle Division, Via Volta 6, I-39100 Bolzano, Italy.
Tel: 471 905111. Telex: 400541.
Fax: 471 905444.

Astra BM 20MR1 (6 × 6) Recovery Vehicle

Description

The Astra BM 20MR1 (6 × 6) recovery vehicle uses the chassis of the Astra BM 20M series of vehicles which includes the Astra BM 20MT dump truck. The fully enclosed forward cab, which is common to the BM 20M series, is made of glass fibre with a metallic frame. In addition to the driver and passenger seats, there are two folding seats in the rear of the cab for emergency use. The chassis is made of high-strength steel and the frame consists of two double C-shaped side-members connected through rigid cross-members.

Mounted on the rear is a 7500 kg crane with a single boom extension. The crane is mounted on a 360° turntable and has a lifting capacity of 7500 kg at a distance of 2.5 m; this decreases to 3600 kg at 5.7 m, the maximum extension of the jib. Hydraulic power for the crane is also used to raise and lower the four outriggers which are connected directly to the platform. The crane operator's cab rotates with the crane and is open.

Mounted just behind the driver's cab is an auxiliary winch with a capacity of 15 000 kg. The winch is provided with 75 m of cable.

Variants

There are two further variants of the Astra BM 20MR1. One is the Astra BM 20MR2 which is equipped with a 16 000 kg extending jib crane which is intended for use with engineer equipments. Fully loaded this variant weighs 23 500 kg and is 10.12 m long.

A further variant is the Astra BM 20NR2 with a 20 000 kg crane.

Specifications

Cab seating: 1 + 3
Configuration: 6 × 6
Weight:
 (chassis and accessories) 9700 kg
 (chassis, accessories and crane) 17 820 kg
Towed load: 28 000 kg
Length: (overall) 8.59 m
Width: 2.5 m
Height:
 (cab) 2.75 m
 (top of crane in travelling position) 3.3 m
Ground clearance: 0.365 m
Track:
 (front) 2 m
 (rear) 1.85 m
Wheelbase: 3.485 m + 1.3 m
Max speed: (road) 67.2 km/h
Range: 1000 km
Fuel capacity: 280 l
Max gradient: 70%
Engine: FIAT Model 8210.02 6-cylinder in-line diesel developing 260 hp at 2200 rpm
Gearbox: ZF manual, 6 forward and 1 reverse gears
Clutch: single dry plate
Transfer box: 2-speed
Steering: hydraulic assisted
Suspension:
 (front) semi-elliptical springs with 4 rubber bumpers and hydraulic shock absorbers
 (rear) oscillating semi-elliptical type springs with rocker arm system
Tyres: 12.00 × 20
Brakes:
 (main) air
 (parking) mechanical
Electrical system: 24 V
Batteries: 4 × 12 V

Status

In production.

Manufacturer

Astra Veicoli Industriali SpA, Via Caorsana 79, I-29100 Piacenza, Italy.
Tel: 0523 5431. Telex: 530148.
Fax: 0523 69293.
Astra Veicoli is part of the IVECO organisation.

Astra BM 20MR1 (6 × 6) recovery vehicle

JAPAN

Mitsubishi Model FW415M1 (6 × 6) Recovery Vehicle

Description

This recovery vehicle uses the same chassis as the Type 74 (6 × 6) 10 000 kg cargo truck used by the Japanese Self-Defence Force. The two-door all-steel control cab can be tilted forward to allow access to the engine for maintenance.

Mounted to the rear of the cab is a hydraulically operated crane with a telescopic jib. When the recovery equipment is being used, two stabilisers are lowered each side of the recovery equipment. Winches are provided front and rear and earth anchors can be fitted to the rear of the vehicle if required.

Specifications

Cab seating: 1 + 2
Configuration: 6 × 6
Weight:
 (unladen) 18 100 kg
 (laden) 18 340 kg
Length: 9.32 m
Width: 2.49 m
Height: 3.23 m
Wheelbase: 4.15 m + 1.3 m
Track:
 (front) 1.915 m
 (rear) 1.865 m
Max speed: (road) 101 km/h
Engine: 8-cylinder diesel developing 300 hp at 2500 rpm
Turning radius: 10.5 m
Tyres: 10.00 × 20

Status

In production. In service with the Japanese Ground Self-Defence Force.

Mitsubishi Model FW415M1 (6 × 6) recovery vehicle

Manufacturer

Mitsubishi Motors Corporation, 33-8, Shiba 5-chome, Minato-ku, Tokyo, Japan.
Tel: 456 1111. Telex: 26639 bisijiko j.

Type 73 (6 × 6) Light Wrecker

Description

The Type 73 (6 × 6) light wrecker is based on the chassis of the Type 73 (6 × 6) 3500 kg truck which was introduced into Japanese Self-Defence Force service in 1973 — for full details of this vehicle refer to entry in the *Trucks* section. The latest version of the Type 73 light wrecker (manufacturer's designation was SKW440MR but is now SKW463MR) has improvements to the engine, axles, cab, and so on. It has a two-man forward control cab with a canvas roof and a windscreen that can be folded forward onto the bonnet. The load-carrying area behind the cab carries a hydraulic crane with a maximum lifting capacity of 4800 kg. Stabilising jacks are lowered when the crane, which has a full 360° traverse, is in use. There is also a recovery winch with a capacity of 4500 kg.

Specifications

Cab seating: 1 + 1
Configuration: 6 × 6
Weight:
  (unladen) 14 200 kg
  (laden) 19 160 kg
Towed load: (road) 6000 kg
Length: 7.81 m
Width: 2.49 m
Height: 3.06 m
Ground clearance: 0.33 m
Wheelbase: 3.295 m + 1.31 m
Track:
  (front) 1.97 m
  (rear) 1.84 m
Angle of approach/departure: 44°/46°
Max road speed: 95 km/h
Range: 500 km

Fuel capacity: 170 l
Fording: 0.8 m
Engine: Isuzu 8PD1 V-8 liquid-cooled diesel developing 240 hp at 2300 rpm
Transmission: manual with 5 forward and 1 reverse gears
Clutch: single dry plate
Transfer box: 2-speed
Steering: power
Turning radius: 9.4 m
Suspension:
  (front) elliptical springs and hydraulic shock absorbers
  (rear) semi-elliptical springs
Brakes:
  (main) air/hydraulic
  (parking) mechanical

Tyres: 11.00 × 20
Electrical system: 24 V
Winch capacity: 4500 kg

Status
In production. In service with the Japanese Ground Self-Defence Force.

Manufacturer
Isuzu Motors Limited, 22-10 Minamioi 6-chome, Shinagawa-Ku, Tokyo, Japan.
Tel: 03 762 1111. Telex: 0246 6689.

KOREA, SOUTH

KM502 5-tonne (6 × 6) Wrecker

Description

The KM502 5-tonne (6 × 6) wrecker is part of the Asia Motors KM50 series of 5-tonne vehicles. It is fitted with a MAN diesel engine and a locally produced power train. (For details of the other vehicles in the KM50 series refer to entry in the *Trucks* section.)

The KM502 is equipped with a mechanical 9070 kg capacity winch fitted with 81 m of cable.

Specifications

Cab seating: 1 + 2
Configuration: 6 × 6
Weight:
  (kerb, front axle) 4728 kg
  (kerb, rear axle) 11 404 kg
  (kerb, total) 16 132 kg
  (gross, front axle) 11 329 kg
  (gross, rear axle) 20 244 kg
  (gross, total) 21 537 kg
Payload: 5441 kg
Length: (overall) 9.048 m
Width: 2.477 m
Height:
  (top of cab) 2.689 m
  (top of crane) 2.692 m
Ground clearance: 0.27 m
Track:
  (front) 1.88 m
  (rear) 1.829 m
Wheelbase: 4.547 m
Angle of approach/departure: 34°/43°
Max speed: 85 km/h
Range: (cruising) 805 km
Fuel capacity: 500 l
Gradient: 68%
Fording: (without kit) 0.762 m
Engine: MAN D2156HM 10.35 l 6-cylinder water-

KM502 5-tonne (6 × 6) wrecker

cooled diesel developing 236 hp at 2200 rpm
Gearbox: manual with 5 forward and 1 reverse gears
Clutch: single dry disc
Transfer box: 2-speed
Steering: power-assist
Turning radius: 14.58 m
Suspension:
  (front) semi-elliptical leaf springs with shock absorbers
  (rear) semi-elliptical inverted leaf springs
Tyres: 11.00 × 20
Brakes: air over hydraulic
Electrical system: 24 V

Batteries: 4 × 12V, 100 Ah
Alternator: 60 A

Status
In production. In service with the Republic of Korea armed forces.

Manufacturer
Asia Motors Co Inc, 15 Yoido-dong, Yungdeungpo-Ku, Seoul, Republic of Korea.
Tel: 783 1501/9. Telex: 24374 asiamco k.

NETHERLANDS

DAF YBZ 3300 DKX 500 (6 × 6) Heavy Recovery Vehicle

Description

During early 1990 the DAF YBZ 3300 DKX 500 (6 × 6) heavy recovery vehicle was chosen by the Dutch Ministry of Defence as the replacement for the DAF YB 616/626 recovery vehicles. The new vehicle is equipped with a Hägglunds Moelv recovery crane which uses hydraulically operated outrigger arms and a large hoist arm at the rear. Three Rotzler winches are provided.

Production started 1991 with deliveries made during 1992 and 1993. In total, 255 units have been ordered with an option for a further 30 units. The Moelv crane is built under licence by DAF Special Products.

Specifications

Cab seating: 1 + 1 or 2
Configuration: 6 × 6
Weight:
  (empty) approx 11 000 kg
  (GVW) 27 500 kg
Towed load: (suspended) 6000 kg
Length: 8.35 m
Width: 2.5 m
Height: (overall) 3.6 m
Ground clearance:
  (front) 0.36 m
  (rear) 0.9 m
Track:
  (front) 1.97 m
  (rear) 1.82 m
Wheelbase: 5 m
Angle of approach/departure: 30°/37°
Max speed: 88 km/h
Range: 500 km
Max gradient: 50%

DAF YBZ 3300 DKX 500 (6 × 6) heavy recovery vehicle

Side slope: 30%
Fording: 0.9 m
Engine: DAF DKX 1160 ATi 11.6 l 6-cylinder turbo-charged diesel developing 325 hp at 2200 rpm
Gearbox: ZF 16 S-160 A with 8 forward and 1 reverse gears with splitter on each gear
Dropbox: ZF A 800
Steering: ZF 8098 hydraulic, power-assist
Turning radius: 12 m
Suspension: DAF semi-elliptic with Koni hydraulic shock absorbers on front
Tyres: 12.00 R 24 XL
Brakes:
  (main) air mechanical, dual line
  (parking) spring cylinders on front and 2nd axle

Electrical system: 24 V
Batteries: 2 × 12 V, 125 Ah
Alternator: 55 A

Status

Production commenced in 1991 for the Dutch armed forces.

Manufacturer

DAF International Military Co-ordination, Hugo van der Goeslaan 1, NL-5643 TW Eindhoven, Netherlands. Tel: 040 142872. Telex: 51980 DAF BP NL. Fax: 040 115456.

DAF YB 616 and YB 626 (6 × 6) Recovery Vehicles

Description

The YB 616 and the later YB 626 (6 × 6) recovery vehicles are both based on the chassis of the YA 616 (6 × 6) 6-tonne cargo truck which was in production for the Netherlands Army from 1957 to 1958. Over 260 of these vehicles were supplied to the Netherlands Army and a smaller number to the Netherlands Air Force. The first model, the YB 616, had dual rear wheels while the later YB 626 has single rear wheels.

The cab is of all-steel construction and if required the sides and roof can be removed and the windscreen folded down. Mounted at the rear is an Austin-Western hydraulically operated crane built under licence in the Netherlands by DAF. The hydraulic system is powered by the truck engine through a transfer PTO to a hydraulic pump assembly mounted underneath the oil reservoir; this is located in the centre of the tool box.

Two stabiliser jacks each side of the vehicle are lowered when the crane is being used. The front-mounted winch has a capacity of 9072 kg and the rear winch has a capacity of 20 412 kg.

Specifications

(YB 616; data in square brackets relate to YB 626 where different)
Cab seating: 1 + 1
Configuration: 6 × 6
Weight:
  (total) 15 670 [17 270] kg
  (on front axle) 4960 [6700] kg
  (on rear bogie) 10 710 [10 575] kg
Length: (overall) 8.85 m
Width: 2.5 m
Height: 3 m
Ground clearance: 0.31 m
Track:
  (front) 1.885 m

DAF YB 616 (6 × 6) recovery vehicle

  (rear) 1.83 [1.828] m
Wheelbase: 3.475 m + 1.37 m
Angle of approach/departure: 28°/32°
Max speed: (road) 80 km/h
Range: 400 km
Fuel capacity: 400 l
Gradient: 59%
Fording: 0.75 m
Engine: Continental R6602 6-cylinder water-cooled petrol developing 232 hp at 2800 rpm
Transmission: 5 forward and 1 reverse gears and 2-speed transfer case
Turning radius: 11 m
Tyre size: 14.00 × 20
Electrical system: 24 V

Batteries: 2 × 12 V
Generator: 900 W

Status

Production complete. In service with the Netherlands Army and Air Force. Due to be replaced by the DAF YBZ 3300 DKX 500 (6 × 6) heavy recovery vehicle by end of 1993.

Manufacturer

DAF International Military Co-ordination, Hugo van der Goeslaan 1, NL-5643 TW Eindhoven, Netherlands. Tel: 040 142872. Telex: 51980 DAF BP NL. Fax: 040 115456.

SOUTH AFRICA

SAMIL Recovery Vehicles

SAMIL produced two types of recovery vehicle, one based on the chassis of the SAMIL 50 and the other based on the chassis of the SAMIL 100. Full details of the SAMIL 50 and SAMIL 100 can be found under the SAMIL entry in the *Trucks* section but information relevant to the two recovery vehicles is provided below. Chassis specifications are given under the SAMIL trucks entries.

SAMIL 50 recovery vehicle

The SAMIL 50 recovery vehicle may be provided with a fully protected cab for use against land mine fragments

or small arms fire. It has two winches driven by a power take-off from the main gearbox with a combined pull of 20 000 kg and two booms which extend to the rear for a suspended tow. The combined lifting capacity of the booms is 7250 kg when retracted and 2500 kg when fully extended. The rear platform is used for recovery equipment stowage and self-recovery rollers are fitted to each corner of the superstructure. The protected cab, when fitted, has seating for four men.

SAMIL 100 recovery vehicle

The SAMIL 100 recovery vehicle is normally fitted with the standard cab of the SAMIL 100 truck and not with a mineproof cab. However, the cab can be enlarged to carry a crew of five men. The recovery hamper is

carried to the rear of the vehicle and consists of a twin jib structure on a flat bed heavy duty body. The main winch is mounted centrally and much of the space at the rear is taken up with recovery equipment stowage.

Status

Production complete. In service with the South African Defence Forces.

Manufacturer

Enquiries to: Armscor, Private Bag X337, Pretoria 0001, South Africa.
Tel: (012) 428 1911. Telex: 320217.
Fax: (012) 428 5635.

SAMIL 100 (6 × 6) recovery vehicle

SAMIL 50 recovery vehicle with mineproof cab

Withings MK 1A (6 × 6) Recovery Vehicle

Description

The Withings MK 1A (6 × 6) recovery vehicle is based on the chassis of the SAMIL 100 (6 × 6) 10 000 kg truck suitably modified for the recovery role. The vehicle is normally fitted with a mineproof cab.

The main recovery equipment is a centrally located heavy duty winch which is used to pull disabled

vehicles and power a towing arm system which can lift a mass of 8000 kg from 0.75 m to 1.6 m above ground level and lock it there for towing. The main winch can also be utilised for forward self-recovery and may also be used to provide lifting power for two demountable crane arms. These are normally stowed on top of the operating deck area and in use extend to a maximum of 4.5 m behind the vehicle; maximum lift height is 4 m. Other recovery equipment carried includes four skid pans with chains, tools, sheaves, a cable guard and two adjustable spotlights.

Specifications
Crew: up to 4
Configuration: 6 × 6
Axle rating:
  (front) 7500 kg
  (rear) 10 000 kg/13 000 kg
Length: 9.77 m
Width: 2.495 m
Height: 3.35 m
Ground clearance: 0.355 m
Track:
  (front) 2.002 m
  (rear) 2.048 m
Wheelbase: 5.94 m
Angle of approach/departure: 30°/35°
Engine: Deutz Diesel Type F 10 L 413F
Gearbox: Fuller RT 14609
Clutch: Fichtel & Sachs 42 mm
Transfer box: Getrag Z90
Steering: ZF 8043 ball and nut
Suspension: semi-elliptic leaf springs
Brakes: drum front and rear
Tyres: 16.00 R 20
Electrical system: 24 V
Batteries: 2 × 12 V, 118 Ah
Alternator: 28 V, 55 A

Status
In production.

Manufacturer
TFM (Pty) Limited, PO Box 46131, Orange Grove, Transvaal, South Africa.
Tel: 316 2106. Fax: 316 1462.

Withings MK 1A (6 × 6) recovery vehicle

SWEDEN

Scania P113 HK (6 × 6) Recovery Vehicle

Description

The Scania P113 HK recovery vehicle is based on the Scania P1123 HK LS 43 truck chassis. The vehicle is equipped with a forward control CP19 cab with seating for the driver, a tilting passenger seat and a bench seat for three further passengers at the rear. The cab may be tilted forward hydraulically 60° for maintenance.

The recovery rig is a Hägglunds Moelv BV 730 which consists of a hydraulic crane with a maximum lifting moment of 28 t/m. The maximum lifting capacity is 8400 kg. The vehicle is also provided with a towing lift boom with a maximum lift capacity of 7000 kg and a recovery winch with a maximum single cable pulling force of 20 000 kg. The winch is provided with 85 m of cable and can be slewed through 300°. When the recovery rig is in use four hydraulic outriggers are deployed for stability. The vehicle is also provided with a self-recovery winch with a maximum pulling force of

10 000 kg equipped with 50 m of cable.

Ancillary equipment includes a rotating beacon, two working lights, an auxiliary heater for the cab and engine, an electrical engine heater, a 24 V emergency outlet and a spare wheel carrier.

Specifications
Cab seating: 1 + 4
Configuration: 6 × 6
Weight:
  (kerb) 21 000 kg

(GVW) 28 000 kg
Length: 8.65 m
Height: (overall) 3.2 m
Wheelbase: 4.25 m + 1.45 m
Max speed: 100 km/h
Fuel capacity: 300 l
Engine: DS11 75 11 l 6-cylinder liquid-cooled turbo-charged direct injection diesel developing 310 hp at 2000 rpm
Gearbox: GRH871 10-speed full synchromesh with hydraulic torque converter acting in low range
Clutch: K432 single dry plate
Transfer box: GT811 2-speed
Steering: hydraulic power-assist
Suspension: semi-elliptic steel leaf springs
Tyres: 14.00 × R20
Brakes:
(main) dual circuit air
(parking) spring
Electrical system: 24 V

Status
In production. In service with the Norwegian Army.

Manufacturer
SAAB-Scania, Scania Division, S-151 87 Södertäljie, Sweden.
Tel: 46 8 553 810 00. Telex: 10200 scania s.

Scania P113 HK (6 × 6) recovery vehicle in action

Volvo F10 (4 × 4) Recovery Vehicle

Description
The Volvo F10 (4 × 4) recovery vehicle is basically the 4 × 2 model with a slightly lower front axle capacity. The forward control cab is spring-mounted on the chassis and can be hydraulically tilted forward 60° to give access to the engine for maintenance. The cab has a roof hatch and a heater/fresh air system and can be fitted with an air-conditioning system if required. The F10 can also be supplied with a sleeper cab with single or twin bunks.

Mounted to the rear of the cab is the Bärgningsbilar EKA D2030 recovery equipment which can be used for three main roles: recovering disabled vehicles; towing disabled vehicles once they have been recovered; and changing components in the field.

The lifting device centres around the main lift boom which is raised by a telescopic ram. The folding boom, which stems from the main boom, houses the hydraulically operated extensible boom which is used for reaching under vehicles. A variety of lifting and towing attachments connect to the extensible boom for direct recovery. The main boom is positioned on the centre line of the vehicle and is extended and retracted by a hydraulic ram and can be mechanically locked in three different positions.

The folding boom houses the extensible boom vertically when not in use, and is locked in the stowed position by an automatic mechanical lock. Two extensible legs behind the rear axle provide anchorage and stability when winching or craning. The anchor legs are individually extended and retracted by hydraulic rams and each leg has a wide spade with profiled teeth.

A hydraulic winch on the top of the main boom has a hydraulically released spring-loaded brake, free spool and reversing facilities. The cable runs through the main boom and out via guide rollers fitted in the end of the main boom. The cable tensioner provides tension when winding in without load on the cable. Power is provided by a hydraulic piston pump driven by the vehicle's PTO which has an in-built strainer and return filter fitted. The hydraulic oil reservoir is an integral part of the main boom and the direction control valve with six operating levers is on the offside rear locker. Pressure relief valves are fitted to prevent overloading of the various hydraulic systems and a pressure gauge shows the working pressure and how much lifting or pulling power is being used.

Optional equipment includes an auxiliary 10 000 kg capacity winch mounted on the main boom, 5000 or 7000 kg front winch with ballasted front bumper, second telescopic ram to increase lifting power, extra hydraulic pump for faster winching speed, various towing and lifting equipment, illuminated signs and flashing lights, side leg for extra stability when side winching, second set of operating levers in opposite compartment and a remote-control unit which allows the operator to operate the controls of the recovery equipment from a distance of up to 100 m.

Specifications
Configuration: 4 × 4
Length: 6.3 m
Width: 2.489 m
Height:
(cab roof) 2.911 m
(air intake) 3.244 m
Track:
(front) 1.945 m
(rear) 1.82 m
Wheelbase: 4.6 m
Fuel capacity: 300 l

Engine: TD 100A diesel developing 250 hp at 2200 rpm
Gearbox: manual with 4 forward and 1 reverse gears, 2-speed transfer box
Clutch: twin dry plate
Steering: recirculating ball and nut with built-in servo unit
Turning radius: 7.6 m
Brakes:
(main) dual circuit air
(parking) air-operated spring on rear wheels exhaust brake
Electrical system: 24 V

Boom
Max lifting height: 4.5 m
Max lifting capacity:
(at horizontal level) 22 000 kg
(in crane position) 10 000 kg
Reach: 2.4 m

Winch
Max pulling power: (when stalling) 34 000 kg
Max rope speed:
(at low pulling power) approx 19 m/min
(at high pulling power) approx 1 m/min
Rope diameter: 26 mm
Rope length: 40 m

Status
In service with undisclosed countries including Malaysia (30).

Manufacturer
Volvo Truck Corporation, S-405 08 Göteborg, Sweden.
Tel: 46 31 666000. Telex: 27000 volvo s.
Fax: 46 31 510465.

Volvo F10 (4 × 4) recovery vehicle showing HIAB crane to cab rear

Volvo F10 (4 × 4) recovery vehicle from side

UNITED KINGDOM

Reynolds Boughton (4 × 4) 6000 kg Recovery Vehicle

Description

The Reynolds Boughton (4 × 4) 6000 kg recovery vehicle was developed as the replacement for the Recovery Vehicle, Wheeled Light, Bedford RL (4 × 4). It uses a Bedford MJP2BMO chassis with a 3.962 m wheelbase and a Bedford TK style cab. The recovery unit is mounted on the rear and is constructed on load-carrying longitudinal main channels with cross-channel

Reynolds Boughton (4 × 4) 6000 kg recovery vehicle with crane jib at maximum 1.727 m extension and with stabiliser legs in position

bearers gusseted at all intersections. Six stowage lockers are fitted, three to each side. The floor has a non-slip metal covering. Access steps are at the front and rear.

The recovery jib is mounted on a main turret tower. The jib has inner and outer rectangular box sections and a position stay is provided for use when carrying suspended loads. The winch is mounted on the hydraulically operated jib. The cable diameter is 14 mm, and the lifting capacity 6000 kg. Four hydraulically powered stabiliser legs are provided, one at each corner of the recovery unit, and each leg is indepen-

dently operated for levelling. The hydraulic pump is driven from a power take-off on the vehicle gearbox. All crane operations are carried out from the crane turret platform while stabiliser levelling is from the side of the vehicle. Most of the hydraulic piping is carried in flexible two-wire hose.

A recovery winch is mounted in the centre of the vehicle, having a capacity of 6096 kg. The 14 mm cable for this winch is 65 m long and there is also a heavy duty ground anchor centrally mounted between the axles. An overload safety device is linked to the crane hydraulics to operate when the hook load exceeds 105 per cent of the safe working load. The crane functions can then only be moved into a safe condition.

Specifications
Cab seating: 1 + 2
Configuration: 4 × 4
Length: 6.579 m
Width: 2.438 m
Height: 2.667 m
Wheelbase: 3.962 m
Jib radius retracted: 3.327 m
Jib extension: 1.727 m
Max rear lift:
  (0.482 m jib overhang from body rear) 6000 kg
Crane slewing speed: 270° in 40 s
Jib extension from retract to extension: 16 s

Status
In production. In service with the British Army (deliveries complete), Brunei and Oman.

Manufacturer
Reynolds Boughton Limited, Bell Lane, Amersham, Buckinghamshire HP6 6PE, UK.
Tel: 0494 764411. Telex: 83132.
Fax: 0494 765218.

Foden (6 × 6) Recovery Vehicle

Description

The Foden (6 × 6) recovery vehicle is a derivative of the Foden FH-70 gun tractor and limber vehicles described in the *Trucks* section although the recovery vehicle embodies many improvements to enhance overall performance. The British Army has 333 of these vehicles in service.

The Foden (6 × 6) recovery vehicle retains many of the features of the FH-70 gun tractor and limber medium mobility vehicles with attendant advantages in spares scalings. The Foden non-corrosive, fire-retardent glass-reinforced plastic tilting cab has seating for four men, bunk or stretcher facilities and is fully fitted for radio. A strengthened roof incorporates both observation hatches and machine gun mountings.

The vehicle has a maximum road speed of 97 km/h and is powered by a Perkins (Rolls-Royce) Eagle engine, a Fuller main gearbox and GKN hub reduction axles and transfer gearbox. When fully equipped with its full complement of recovery equipment it can climb, hold and restart on 33 per cent gradients.

A front-mounted 10-tonne winch provides a self-recovery capability. Recovery eyes and detachable NATO-pattern towing hooks are provided at both front and rear.

The vehicle is fitted with the Eka Limited hydraulically operated Compact recovery unit model AK 6500 EA12/1. With its drawbar, support/suspend towing and winching facilities, this unit can recover all of the British Army's in-service logistic support and armoured wheeled vehicles up to a gross vehicle weight of 30 000 kg. A Rotzler type 25000 HS/390 25 000 kg single line pull main winch is fitted and two rear anchor spades provide anchorage for the vehicle.

A slewing crane with 220° of slewing angle and a maximum lift capacity of 12 500 kg provides optimum lifting facilities and for vehicle stability two extensible hydraulically operated outriggers are fitted, one to each

side of the vehicle. The boom has a straight lift capacity of 12 500 kg at 2.5 m extension and 5800 kg at 7.7 m. Detachable load-bearing feet are also provided for the rear ground anchors when these are used as stabilisers.

All recovery and lifting functions are controlled from a locker-mounted console or from a remote-control unit with 30 m of wander lead.

Optional engines and transmissions are available.

Specifications
Cab seating: 1 + 3
Configuration: 6 × 6
Weight: (loaded) 25 338 kg
Length: 9.055 m
Width: 2.482 m

Height: (cab) 3.35 m
Ground clearance: 0.42 m
Track:
  (front) 2.029 m
  (rear) 2.06 m
Wheelbase: 3.97 m + 1.516 m
Angle of approach/departure: 28°/29°
Max road speed: 97 km/h
Fuel capacity: 360 l
Max gradient: 33%
Engine: Perkins Eagle 290 L 6-cylinder in-line turbocharged 4-stroke diesel developing 290 bhp at 1950 rpm
Gearbox: Fuller RTX 11609B 9-speed constant mesh
Clutch: Spicer twin plate hydraulically operated
Transfer box: GKN/Kirkstall AGB 7000 Mark 11

Foden (6 × 6) recovery vehicle (M Bell)

2-speed with optional integral PTO
Axles:
(front) Kirkstall SD66-11-1S 10 t with differential lock
(rear) Kirkstall D66-11-1SHF and D66-11-1S with differential locks on both axles, 6.64:1 overall axle ratio.
Third differential on foremost axle
Steering: recirculatory ball with integral power-assistance

Turning circle: (kerb to kerb) 25 m
Suspension: semi-elliptical laminated springs front, two-spring fully articulating rear spring
Brakes: air, split-circuit, trailer brake connection to front and rear of chassis
Wheels and tyres: 16.00 × 20 — 28 ply tyres, 11.25 rims
Electrical system: 24 V
Batteries: 2 × 12 V

Status
In service with the British Army (333).

Manufacturer
Foden Trucks, a division of PACCAR UK Limited, Moss Lane, Sandbach, Cheshire CW11 9YW, UK. Tel: 0270 763244. Fax: 0270 762758.

Scammell S24 (6 × 6) Recovery Vehicle

Description
The Scammell S24 (6 × 6) recovery vehicle was developed for military use from a range of heavy duty civilian trucks to ensure commonality with the large numbers of Scammell trucks in service worldwide. The S24 can operate under a wide range of climatic conditions and, if required, certain appliqué kits can be used to operate under extreme climates.

The recovery equipment used on the S24 recovery vehicle consists of a 15 000 kg capacity hydraulic crane and a 25 000 kg capacity hydraulic winch. The crane is produced by Reynolds Boughton Limited and can traverse through 270°. It is equipped with 16 mm wire rope and when in use is stabilised by four outrigger legs that are lowered hydraulically. The hydraulic power for the system is derived from the vehicle gearbox power take-off.

There is space on the vehicle rear deck for a spare wheel, towing bars and other recovery equipment. Optional equipment includes various floodlights and a flashing beacon for the roof.

The S24 is powered by a Cummins NTE 350 turbocharged and after-cooled in-line diesel engine developing 350 hp at 2100 rpm. Two cooling radiators are used. The transmission is a Fuller RTX 14 614 15-speed manual gearbox and 16.00 × 20 tyres are used throughout.

The S24 recovery vehicle can maintain a continuous

Scammell S24 (6 × 6) recovery vehicle

operational speed of 40 km/h climbing a 14 per cent gradient. As a solo unit it can travel at 74 km/h and will climb a 52 per cent gradient.

Status
In service with various nations.

Manufacturer
Unipower Vehicles Limited, 34 Greenhill Crescent, Watford Business Park, Watford, Hertfordshire WD1 8QU, UK.
Tel: 0923 816555. Telex: 261760 unitrk g.
Fax: 0923 228621.

Scammell Crusader (6 × 4) Recovery Vehicle

Description
In 1977 the British Army ordered 130 Scammell Crusader 6 × 4 recovery vehicles. They have the same chassis, cab, engine and transmission as the Scammell Crusader 35 000 kg tractors used by the Royal Engineers for hauling semi-trailers which are fully described in the *Trucks* section. The full designation of the vehicle is Recovery Vehicle, Wheeled, CL (Low Mobility Recovery Vehicle).

The vehicle can provide recovery support for wheeled vehicles up to the 16-tonne range and can support or suspend tow laden 8-tonne or unladen 16-tonne vehicles and straight tow vehicles up to 30 tonnes gross weight on gradients not exceeding one in five.

The main recovery equipment, of Swedish Eka design, consists of hydraulically operated earth anchors, main boom and a winch, which, together with stowage bins, are mounted on a subframe at the rear of the vehicle. The main boom is lifted by a hydraulic ram and incorporates a folding boom which houses an extending boom that carries a variety of attachments for support or suspend tow. When support or suspend towing, a rear bogie blocking system maintains sufficient front axle loading for safe steering.

A winch with a maximum pulling capacity of 7000 kg is mounted at the front behind the bumper. The main boom can lift 7500 kg at a maximum distance of 2.6 m from the rear bogie centre line and the main winch exerts a maximum pull of 20 000 kg. Both winches have fail-safe automatic brakes capable of holding the maximum winch loads. Using the main winch, with suitable attachments to the extending boom, there is a limited craning facility for loads up to 3000 kg. Apart from main controls for the recovery equipment housed at the right-hand rear side of the vehicle, a hand-held

Scammell Crusader (6 × 4) recovery vehicle

remote-control unit, usable up to 30 m away, can operate the main recovery functions.

Specifications
Cab seating: 1 + 3
Configuration: 6 × 4
Weight: 16 700 kg
Length: 8.37 m

Width: 2.98 m
Height: 3.28 m
Track:
(front) 2.05 m
(rear) 1.98 m
Wheelbase: (first axle to centre of rear bogie) 4.59 m
Max speed: 78 km/h
Range: 1150 km

Fuel capacity: 455 l
Max gradient: 33%
Engine: Rolls-Royce Eagle 305 Mk 111 turbocharged diesel developing 305 bhp at 2100 rpm
Transmission: manual with 15 forward and 3 reverse gears
Turning radius: 11 m
Steering: ball and nut, power-assisted
Suspension:
(front) longitudinal semi-elliptical springs pivoted front with slipper rear ends, and telescopic shock absorbers
(rear) fully articulated, inverted longitudinal semi-elliptical springs, trunnion-mounted at centre with slipper rear ends
Tyres: 11.00 × 20
Brakes:
(main) air
(parking) hand on all wheels
Electrical system: 24 V
Batteries: 4 × 12 V, 100 Ah

Status
Production complete. In service with the British Army

(130), and Royal Air Force (2).

Manufacturer
Unipower Vehicles Limited, 34 Greenhill Crescent, Watford Business Park, Watford, Hertfordshire WD1 8QU, UK.
Tel: 0923 816555. Telex: 261760 unitrk g.
Fax: 0923 228621.

UNITED STATES OF AMERICA

2½-ton (6 × 6) M60 and M108 Wreckers

Development
The M60 and M108 wreckers, or to give them their official US Army designations, Truck, Wrecker: Crane, 2½-ton, 6 × 6, M108 and Truck, Wrecker: Light, 2½-ton, 6 × 6, M60, are both members of the M35 series of 2½-ton (6 × 6) truck family and the reader is referred to this entry in the *Trucks* section for both the development history and technical description of the basic vehicle.

Description
The M60 uses the M45C chassis while the M108 uses the M45 chassis. The M45C chassis has a walking beam suspension on the rear axle. The crane on the rear of the M60 can be traversed through 270° and has a maximum elevation angle of 45°. Its jib can be extended from 2.438 m to a maximum of 4.876 m and can lift up to 3628 kg with the outriggers in position and the jib retracted, or 1814 kg with the jib fully extended and the outriggers in position. There are two outriggers mounted either side of the crane platform. A winch

mounted at the front of the vehicle has a maximum capacity of 4536 kg.
The M108 also has a front-mounted winch with a maximum capacity of 4536 kg, two stabilisers either side, and a hydraulically operated crane.

Specifications
(M60; data in square brackets relate to M108 where different)
Chassis designation: M45C [M45]
Configuration: 6 × 6
Weight: (empty) 10 900 [9000] kg
Length: 7.02 [7.7] m
Width: 2.36 [2.44] m
Height: 2.477 [2.515] m
Ground clearance: 0.33 m
Track:
(front) 1.72 m
(rear) 1.778 m
Wheelbase: 3.302 m + 1.219 m
Angle of approach/departure: 40°/40°
Max speed: (road) 93 km/h
Range: 480 km
Fuel capacity: 189 l
Max gradient: 63%

Fording:
(without preparation) 0.76 m
(with preparation) 1.828 m
Engine: Reo model OA-331 or Continental COA-331 6-cylinder developing 146 hp at 3400 rpm
Transmission: 5 forward and 1 reverse gears and 2-speed transfer box
Turning radius: 11.429 m
Tyres: 9.00 × 20
Brakes: air/hydraulic
Electrical system: 24 V
Batteries: 2 × 12 V

Status
Production complete. In service with the US Army and many other armed forces, including Austria.

Manufacturers
The basic chassis has been manufactured by many companies including Curtiss Wright, Kaiser Jeep, Reo, Studebaker and White. Last manufacturer was the AM General Corporation, 14250 Plymouth Road, Detroit, Michigan 48232, USA.

M62, Truck, Wrecker: Medium, 5-ton, (6 × 6)

M246, Truck, Tractor, Wrecker: 5-ton, (6 × 6)

M543, Truck, Wrecker: Medium, 5-ton, (6 × 6)

Description
These vehicles are all members of the M54 series of 5-ton (6 × 6) trucks which were developed after the end of the Second World War, and the reader is referred to this entry in the *Trucks* section for the development history and technical description of the basic vehicle.

M62
This has a hydraulically operated crane mounted at the rear which has a maximum lifting capacity of 9072 kg when used with the two stabilisers either side of the vehicle. A winch is mounted at the front with a maximum capacity of 9072 kg when being used to the front and 18 144 kg when being used to the rear. Later models of the M62 are the M62A1 and M62A2.

M246
This was designed for use as both a recovery vehicle and for towing semi-trailers. The Austin-Western crane at the rear has a jib which can be extended from 3.504 to 7.924 m. This crane can be slewed through 360° and its jib elevated to a maximum of 45°. Later models of the M246 are the M246A1 and the M246A2, which has a Continental LDS 465-1 or LDS 465-2 multi-fuel engine. The M246 was replaced in production by the similar M819 for which there is a separate entry.

Truck, Tractor, Wrecker: 5-ton (6 × 6) M246 with front-mounted winch (US Army)

Truck, Wrecker: Medium, 5-ton (6 × 6) M62 (US Army)

M543

This has a Gar Wood hydraulically operated crane at the rear which can lift a maximum of 4536 kg. Two stabilisers are provided each side and a winch is mounted at the front and rear. The M543A1 has a diesel engine. In 1963 the M543A2 was introduced. It has an LDS-465 multi-fuel engine which develops 180 hp at 2600 rpm and gives the vehicle a maximum road speed of 84 km/h and a range of 938 km. The M543A2 was replaced in production by the similar M816 for which there is a separate entry.

Status

Production complete. In service with US forces and many other armed forces including Australia (a few M543s and M543A1s are in service) and Spain (all re-engined with Spanish diesels).

Manufacturers

The basic chassis has been manufactured by various companies since the early 1950s including International Harvester, Kaiser Jeep (now AM General Corporation) and Mack Trucks. Last manufacturer was AM General Corporation, 14250 Plymouth Road, Detroit, Michigan 48232, USA.

Specifications

Designation	M62	M246	M543
Chassis designation	M40C	M63C	M40C
Configuration	6 × 6	6 × 6	6 × 6
Towed load			
(road)	13 608 kg	20 865 kg	13 608 kg
(cross-country)	9072 kg	17 010 kg	9072 kg
Weight (empty)	15 275 kg	14 829 kg	15 603 kg
Length	7.848 m	8.953 m	10.007 m
Width	2.463 m	2.489 m	2.444 m
Height	2.59 m	3.352 m	2.743 m
Ground clearance	0.279 m	0.279 m	0.279 m
Wheelbase	3.86 m + 1.371 m	4.775 m + 1.371 m	3.86 m + 1.371 m
Angle of approach/departure	37°/38°	35°/55°	37°/38°
Max speed (road)	84 km/h	84 km/h	84 km/h
Range	344 km	369 km	360 km
Fuel capacity	295 l	295 l	295 l (some have 504 l)
Max gradient	36%	47%	61.4%
Fording			
(without preparation)	0.762 m	0.762 m	0.762 m
(with preparation)	1.981 m	—	1.981 m
Engine	Continental 6-cylinder petrol developing 196 hp at 2800 rpm		
Transmission	5 forward and 1 reverse gears and 2-speed transfer case		
Turning radius	12.648 m	14.325 m	14.5 m
Tyres	11.00 × 20	11.00 × 20	11.00 × 20
Brakes	all have hydraulic brakes, air-actuated		
Electrical system	24 V	24 V	24 V
Batteries	2 × 12 V	2 × 12 V	2 × 12 V

M816, Truck, Wrecker, 5-ton, (6 × 6)

M819, Tractor, Wrecker, 5-ton, (6 × 6)

Description

Both these vehicles are members of the M809 series of 5-ton (6 × 6) trucks and the reader is referred to the entry in the *Trucks* section for the development history of the series.

The M816 is provided with a revolving hydraulic crane at the rear which has a self-supported extensible boom and boom to ground supports. Outriggers are provided to stabilise the vehicle when the crane is being used. Winches are supplied. The M819 also has a hydraulic crane mounted on the rear but has a longer wheelbase and can tow a trailer or vehicle weighing up to 13 608 kg on roads, or 9076 kg across country.

Optional kits for these vehicles include an air brake kit, closure hard top, deep water fording kit, slave receptacle, thermal barrier kit, winterisation personnel heater kit and a powerplant kit.

Status

M816 in service with the US Forces, Australia, South Korea, Philippines (36), Zaïre and many other forces. M819 production complete.

Manufacturer

LTV Missiles and Electronics Group, AM General Division, 105 N. Niles Avenue, PO Box 7025, South Bend, Indiana 46634-7025, USA.
Tel: (219) 237 6222. Telex: 258467.
Fax: (219) 237 6242/6050.

M816 5-ton (6 × 6) wrecker (C R Zwart)

Specifications

Designation	M816	M819
Chassis type	M809A1	M811A1
Cab seating	1 + 2	1 + 2
Configuration	6 × 6	6 × 6
Weight		
(unloaded)	16 385 kg	15 392 kg
(on front axle empty)	4966 kg	6304 kg
(on rear bogie empty)	11 418 kg	9251 kg
Length	9.042 m	9.124 m
Width	2.484 m	2.489 m
Height	2.69 m	3.352 m
Ground clearance	0.295 m	0.295 m
Track	1.88 m (front) and 1.829 m (rear)	
Wheelbase	4.547 m + 1.371 m	4.125 m + 1.371 m
Angle of approach/departure	35°/34°	36°/55°
Max speed (road)	84 km/h	83.6 km/h
Range	805 km	563 km
Fuel capacity	295 l	295 l
Max gradient	31%	31%
Fording		
(without preparation)	0.762 m	0.762 m
(with preparation)	1.879 m	1.879 m
Engine	Model NHC-250 6-cylinder in-line diesel developing 240 hp (gross) at 2100 rpm	
Transmission	5 forward and 1 reverse gears, 2-speed transfer box	
Tyres	11.00 × 20	12.00 × 20
Electrical system	24 V	24 V

M984A1 Recovery Vehicle 10-ton (8 × 8)

Description

The M984A1 Recovery Vehicle 10-ton (8 × 8) is the recovery component of the Oshkosh HEMTT family of vehicles. For full details of the HEMTT family refer to the entry in the *Trucks* section.

The M984A1 recovery vehicle follows the same general construction lines as the rest of the HEMTT family. The M984A1 recovery system consists of a main recovery winch, a self-recovery winch and ground spades. The main recovery winch has a capacity of 27 216 kg and is an automatic, two-speed, hydraulically operated winch drum with fully proportional controls. It has 56.4 m of usable wire rope. The winch automatically shifts to low speed when recovering heavy loads. The main recovery winch system, which includes a fairlead/tensioner device, provides the capability of recovering stranded vehicles at up to 32° to the left or right, or 23° below the vehicle. The fairlead/tensioner also provides proper winding on the wire rope of the drum winch by maintaining an even rope tension between the rear of the vehicle and the drum. The self-recovery winch is a standard HEMTT winch with forward deployment and a bare drum capacity of 9072 kg. The ground spades are emplaced manually. The main winch can be operated using a remote-control unit.

The M984A1 uses a lift and tow system that can be deployed and attached to a disabled vehicle in 2 to 3 minutes. The system consists of a crossbar that 'floats' on a 102 mm ball. The ball is supported by three hydraulic cylinders which provide precise positioning of the crossbar during connection to the disabled vehicle. The ball system provides articulation and stability when travelling over uneven terrain and when cornering.

The M984A1 is equipped with a material handling crane with a lift capacity of 6350 kg. The crane has the lift and reach capability to support the removal and replacement of powerpacks from a wide range of wheeled and tracked vehicles including the M1, M1A1, M2, M3, M109A2, M88A1 and M60A3. The crane can be operated using a remote-control unit.

The M984A1 has an equipment body with stowage provisions for support equipment including oxygen/acetylene welding equipment, tow adaptors, chain slings and snatch blocks. The stowage provisions include 10 lockable and watertight individual compartments. The entire body can be removed for air transport weight reduction in less than 10 minutes.

M984A1 (8 × 8) recovery vehicle

Specifications

Cab seating: 1 + 1
Configuration: 8 × 8
Weight:
　(chassis) 14 968 kg
　(kerb) 22 226 kg
　(GCW) 45 360 kg
Length: 9.957 m
Width: 2.438 m
Height:
　(travelling) 2.845 m
　(top of cab) 2.565 m
　(crane extended) 3.759 m
　(loading, flat bed) 1.6 m
Ground clearance: 0.33 m
Wheelbase: 4.85 m
Angle of approach/departure: 43°/45°
Max speed: 88 km/h
Range: 483 km
Fuel capacity: 589 l
Fording: 1.219 m
Engine: Detroit Diesel 8V-92TA V-8 developing 445 hp at 2100 rpm

Gearbox: Allison HT740D with torque converter, 4 forward, 1 reverse
Transfer box: Oshkosh 55000 2-speed
Steering: integral hydraulic main and booster gears
Suspension:
　(front) Hendrikson RT340
　(rear) Hendrikson RT500
Tyres: 16.00R × 20
Electrical system: 24 V
Batteries: 4 × 12 V

Status

Production for export continuing. In service with the US Army and Saudi Arabia.

Manufacturer

Oshkosh Truck Corporation, POB 2566, Oshkosh, Wisconsin 54903, USA.
Tel: (414) 235 9150. Telex: 54903-2566.
Fax: (414) 233 9540.

Freightliner (6 × 6) Wrecker

Description

The Freightliner (6 × 6) Wrecker is a member of the Freightliner Military Truck Family; for details of this family refer to the entry in the *Trucks* section.

The Freightliner Military Truck Family is based on the M915A2 and M916A1 series of long-haul trucks and utilises many components and other items carried over from commercial models. Many well-proven features of the Family are used with the Freightliner (6 × 6) wrecker, including an aluminium cab and an engine of advanced fuel-efficiency design.

The main recovery feature is a rotating hydraulic boom crane mounted on a turntable over the rear axle bogies. The boom has a capacity of 18 144 kg and can lift and tow loads of up to 7031 kg.

Specifications

Cab seating: 1 + 1
Configuration: 6 × 6
Weight:
　(kerb) 18 080 kg
　(front axle, loaded) 7258 kg
　(rear axles, loaded) 23 587 kg
Length: 9.32 m
Width: 2.49 m
Height:
　(overall) 3.24 m
　(cab) 2.97 m
Ground clearance: 0.23 m

Freightliner (6 × 6) Wrecker

Wheelbase: 5.79 m
Angle of approach: 26°
Max speed:
  (road) 85.3 km/h
  (3% gradient) 40.22 km/h
Fuel capacity: 379 l
Fording: 0.51 m
Engine: Detroit Diesel DDE 12.7 l 6-cylinder high torque rise diesel developing 400 hp at 2100 rpm

Transmission: Allison HT-740 AT with torque converter, 4 forward, 1 reverse speeds
Transfer box: Oshkosh Series 55,000, 2-speed
Steering: Ross integral power
Turning radius: 26.33 m
Brakes: air/mechanical; Eaton front, Rockwell rear
Tyres: 315/80 R 22.5
Electrical system: dual 12/24 V
Batteries: 4 × 12 V

Status
In production.

Manufacturer
Freightliner Corporation, 4747 N Channel Avenue, PO Box 3849, Portland, Oregon 97208, USA.
Tel: (503) 735 7183.

RECOVERY EQUIPMENT

GERMANY

Rotzler Winches

Description
The Rotzler company manufactures a wide range of hydraulic winches for both civil and military applications including winches with planetary gearboxes for lifting or for pulling and recovery, and Treibmatic winches. Brief specifications are given in the tables below.

Status
In production. In service with German and other armed forces.

Manufacturer
Rotzler GmbH and Company, Postfach 1165, D-7853 Steinen, Federal Republic of Germany.
Tel: 07627 701-0. Telex: 773716.
Fax: 07627 701-166.

Winches with Planetary Gearboxes for Pulling and Recovery

Type	Max pulling force	Cable diameter	Max cable	Drum diameter	Drum width	Reduction
HZ 010/1-8	15 kN	7 mm	19 m	205 mm	181 mm	8
HZ 051/2-58	50 kN	13 mm	15 m	208 mm	242 mm	58
HZ 051/2-58	70 kN	14 mm	14 m	208 mm	242 mm	58
HZ 070/2-58[1]	70 kN	14 mm	12 m	208 mm	195 mm	58
HZ 090/2-96	100 kN	16 mm	15 m	240 mm	242 mm	96
HZ 100/2-96[1]	100 kN	16 mm	11 m	240 mm	175 mm	96
HZ 180/3-367	150 kN	22 mm	13 m	300 mm	242 mm	367
HZ 180/3-367	200 kN	24 mm	18 m	300 mm	340 mm	367
HZ 250/3-367	250 kN	26 mm	16 m	290 mm	300 mm	367
HZ 250/3-390	250 kN	26 mm	16 m	390 mm	274 mm[2]	390
HZ 300/3-390	300 kN	28 mm	15 m	390 mm	274 mm[2]	390
HZ 350/3-390	350 kN	30 mm	13 m	390 mm	274 mm[2]	390
HZ 400/3-390	400 kN	30 mm	13 m	390 mm	274 mm[2]	390

[1] winch for side mounting   [2] 447 mm possible

Treibmatic Winches

Type	Pull force	Pressure	Speeds	Cable diameter	Usable cable length
TR 035	50 kN	165 bar	2	13 mm	60 m
TR 035	50 kN	235 bar	1	13 mm	60 m
TR 080	80 kN	145 bar	2	16 mm	60 m
TR 080	80 kN	265 bar	1	16 mm	60 m
TR 200	200 kN	200 bar	2	24 mm	75 m
TR 650/3	350 kN	290 bar	2	33 mm	120 m
TR 2000	500 kN	300 bar	2	35 mm	190 m

Winches with Planetary Gearboxes for Hoisting

Type	Hoisting force	Cable diameter	Max cable length	Drum diameter	Drum width	Reduction
HK 010-170-5.3	10 kN	8 mm	13 m	170 mm	178 mm	5.33
HK 016-200-6.5	14 kN	10 mm	11 m	200 mm	147 mm	6.5
HK 035-230-36	30.8 kN	10 mm	11 m	230 mm	140 mm	36
HK 050-252-49	50 kN	16 mm	21 m	252 mm	340 mm	49
HK 075-208-58	30 kN	13 mm	16 m	208 mm	270 mm	58
HK 075-400-42.8	43 kN	16 mm	40.7 m	400 mm	454 mm	42.8
HK 130-480-40.5	68.5 kN	20 mm	54 m	480 mm	630 mm	40.5
HK 130-434-44.2	70 kN	18 mm	54 m	432 mm	630 mm	44.2
HK 200-418-40.5	89 kN	20 mm	59 m	418 mm	799 mm	40.5
HK 450-575-65.5	102 kN	23 mm	69 m	575 mm	1111 mm	65.5

ITALY

FARID Recovery Equipment

Description
The Italian company of FARID has developed a range of heavy duty recovery equipment which can be installed on a variety of tracked and wheeled chassis. The equipment can be divided into three families; slewing cranes, fixed turret cranes and pick-up platforms; all of these are hydraulic but have different applications.

Slewing Cranes
Model F 25 cross-country
This model can be installed on a 6 × 6 chassis that has a recommended gross vehicle weight of not less than 28 000 kg. The hydraulic crane has a lifting capacity of 25 000 kg and can be slewed through 360°; it is stopped in the desired position by an automatic belt braking device.

The telescopic boom is provided with two hydraulic plus one mechanical extensions and can reach a height of 16 m, and horizontally 12.7 m from the rear and side boards. Before operations four outriggers are lowered to the ground, two each side, by means of hydraulic and independent control.

Two auxiliary hydraulic winches are fitted, one on the rear having a capacity of 10 000 kg with 75 m of 20 mm diameter steel cable, and a self-recovery unit with a capacity of 5000 kg and 75 m of 12 mm steel cable. Both winches are controlled from the driver's cab.

Power is provided by two hydraulic piston pumps driven by the vehicle's PTO which has an in-built strainer and return filter fitted. The crane is also provided with a pressure relief valve to prevent overloading of the various hydraulic systems, lock valves on the outrigger's cylinder, and a pressure gauge, showing the working pressure, in front of the operator's seat.

Standard equipment includes tow hitch, snatch block chains, tools, yellow flashes and rear spotlight for operations at night.

Fixed Turret Cranes
Model F 20 f
This wrecker crane consists of a fixed turret on which a telescopic boom is hinged. The boom is provided with hydraulic hoisting and two hydraulic extensions. This model can be installed on a chassis and cab that have a gross vehicle weight of not less than 19 000 kg. The two main hydraulic winches are fitted on the turret and are provided with independent control, 50 m of 16 mm diameter steel cable and have a capacity of 10 000 kg each.

The two main steel cables, after passing through their independent rocking heads, end with a steel hook. These two winches can be used both together, having a total capacity of 20 000 kg, or separately. For lateral strength one winch anchors while the other provides pull.

Before the crane is used, two rear stiff legs are lowered to the ground by means of hydraulic and independent controls. A third hydraulic winch, having a capacity of 15 000 kg and 100 m of 20 mm diameter steel cable, is mounted on the rear part of the vehicle so that a total pulling capacity of 35 000 kg can be obtained.

The front-mounted winch has a capacity of 5000 kg and is provided with 75 m of 16 mm steel cable and is controlled from the driver's cab.

The rear hydraulic lift-and-tow device is made by a

FARID F 25 (6 × 4) cross-country recovery vehicle

FARID F 12 f recovery vehicle

foldable boom and has a variety of lifting and towing attachments to permit towing of disabled vehicles once they have been recovered.

All the control levers are fitted on the rear part of the vehicle and the boom and winch controls are duplicated on a remote-control. Tow hitch, snatch block, chains, tools, yellow flashes and spotlights for night operations are fitted as standard.

Model F 12 f

This wrecker equipment has the same main features as the Model F 20 f but is a lighter version. It can be installed on a chassis/cab combination that has a gross vehicle weight of not less than 13 000 kg.

The two main hydraulic winches fitted on the turret have a capacity of 6000 kg each and are provided with 35 m of 16 mm diameter steel cable. The third hydraulic winch also has a capacity of 6000 kg but is provided with 75 m of 16 mm diameter steel cable. It is mounted on the rear of the vehicle so that a total pulling capacity of 18 000 kg can be obtained.

The front-mounted hydraulic winch has a capacity of 4000 kg and is provided with 46 m of 11 mm diameter steel cable and is controlled from the driver's cab. Standard equipment includes remote-control, tow hitch, snatch block, chains, standard tools, yellow flashes and rear lights for night operations.

Pick-up Platform

This equipment is to be installed on a chassis/cab combination having a gross vehicle weight of not less than 7500 kg and has been designed for the recovery of light trucks and Land Rover type vehicles. The pick-up platform truck is made up of three separate parts each of which has its own task: the boom crane is

Specifications

Model	F 25	F 20 f	F 12 f	Pick-up platform
Turret	360° slewing	fixed	fixed	none
Max lifting capacity	25 000 kg	20 000 kg	12 000 kg	2000 kg
(fully extended)	3000 kg	5000 kg	2700 kg	800 kg
Max pulling capacity	10 000 kg	35 000 kg	18 000 kg	3000 kg
Max boom height	17 m	12 m	10 m	5 m
Max horizontal extension				
(from rear end)	9 m	6 m	5 m	2 m
Main cable				
(diameter)	14 mm	16 mm	16 mm	12 mm
(length)	150 m	50 m	35 m	30 m
Max rear auxiliary winch capacity	10 000 kg	15 000 kg	6000 kg	n/app
Max front-mounted winch capacity	5000 kg	5000 kg	4000 kg	3000 kg
Rear auxiliary winch cable				
(diameter)	20 mm	20 mm	16 mm	n/app
(length)	70 m	100 m	75 m	n/app
Front auxiliary winch cable				
(diameter)	16 mm	16 mm	11 mm	12 mm
(length)	75 m	75 m	46 m	30 m

provided with hydraulic hoisting, hydraulic extension and a 3000 kg winch; it is for lifting or pulling broken down vehicles and after use it is stowed between the platform rails. The loading platform permits the transport of one vehicle which is loaded on it. It is hydraulically lifted and two rear loading ramps can be extended by means of a hydraulic and independent control. Before operations are carried out two rear-mounted hydraulic stiff legs are lowered to the ground. The rear hydraulic 'lift-and-tow' device is for towing a second vehicle, when the first one has already been loaded over the platform. Standard equipment includes

front winch remote-control, snatch block, chains, yellow flashes and rear lights for recovery operations at night.

Status

In production. In service with many armed forces in Africa and the Middle East.

Manufacturer

FARID SpA, Corso Savona 39 bis, I-10024 Moncalieri, Italy.
Tel: 011 645454. Telex: 220348.

NORWAY

Hägglunds Moelv Recovery Unit RV 730

The Hägglunds Moelv Recovery Unit RV 730 was designed for heavy recovery operations including winching, towing and hoisting. The unit can be mounted on various types of 6 × 6 vehicle chassis including Mercedes-Benz, IVECO, DAF, Scania and other types.

The unit has four hydraulically actuated outriggers that are separately controlled. With the outriggers extended the vehicle is lifted clear of the ground to provide stability in all directions and provide anchoring when using the recovery winch. The outrigger frame is separate from the vehicle chassis so no forces are imparted during operations.

The main recovery winch has a capacity of 20 tonnes single pull and is mounted in the crane slewing frame to provide the capability to pull a load towards the recovery vehicle without extra rigging. The winch speed is dependent on the actual pulling force. The unit can also be equipped with a side-mounted

hydraulic self-recovery winch with a capacity of 10 tonnes.

The unit is equipped with a hydraulic crane with arm elevation from horizontal to +70°. The arm has a hydraulic telescopic extension jib that can operate with a full load of 8400 kg. The crane traverse is symmetrical over the rear of the recovery vehicle; a full 360° traverse is optional. The crane can be operated from a seat to the right of the crane arm or from a remote position.

In addition to the crane, the unit is fitted with a lifting and towing boom mounted at the rear. The boom is hydraulically operated and has a telescopic extension and tilting support point for towing attachments. The boom capacity is variable according to customer requirements. A NATO towing hook is mounted on the boom.

The outriggers are dimensioned so that each can carry the full pulling force of 40 tonnes. This capacity can be used over a rear arc of 30° each side without extra anchoring. Side pulls are limited to 15 tonnes without extra anchoring. Anchor points are provided to

utilise the full 40-tonne capacity.

The unit can be provided with a carrying platform for spares and lockable tool cabinets are provided.

Specifications
Weight:
(total) approx 20 000 kg
(front axle) 8000 kg
(bogie axle) 12 000 kg
Length:
(travelling) 8.75 m
(between lowered outriggers) 5.7 m
Width:
(travelling) 2.5 m approx
(between lowered outriggers) 4.2 m
Height: 3.25 m
Crane max lift capacity: 8400 kg
Max winch capacity, single cable: 20 000 kg
Max anchoring on outriggers: 40 000 kg
Max crane outreach: 6.35 m
Max lift height: 8 m

Status
In production.

Manufacturer
Hägglunds Moelv A.S., POB 244, N-2391 Moelv,
Norway.
Tel: 47 6568500. Telex: 76350 hagmo n.
Fax: 47 6567056.

*Hägglunds Moelv RV 730 recovery unit fitted to
Scania P113 HK (6 × 6) recovery vehicle*

SOUTH AFRICA

TFM Model 15 and 26 Recovery Equipments

Description
The TFM Model 15 and 26 recovery equipments, of 15-tonne and 26-tonne capacity respectively, are of very rugged construction and have been optimised for military use. They can be mounted on any suitable single or double axle rear chassis. The main features include twin lockable and extendible booms with an individual service drum for each boom and a sturdy A-frame tow hitch at the rear.

Each equipment is powered by a slow speed, high torque, radial piston hydraulic motor close-coupled to the transmission. The transmission unit has a single impact, dual output capacity, giving the hydraulic circuit a dual range pressure system to ensure safe operation with either single or twin service cables.

Specifications

	Model 15	Model 26
Retracted boom	7500 kg	12 500 kg
Extended boom	3700 kg	6000 kg
Drum rating	7500 kg	12 500 kg
Single line safe load	3000 kg	4500 kg
Cable diameter	13 mm	16 mm

TFM Model 26 recovery equipment fitted to a crew-cabbed SAMIL 100 recovery vehicle

Status
In production.

Manufacturer
TFM (Pty) Limited, PO Box 46131, Orange Grove,
Transvaal, South Africa.
Tel: 316 2106. Fax: 316 1462.

TFM HW-30 Drag Winch

Description
The TFM HW-30 is a heavy duty drag winch for use in conjunction with recovery units or on its own, although it is not designed for use as a personnel hoist. It is powered by a radial piston hydraulic motor via a hydraulic dog clutch.

The clutch can be manually disengaged for manual cranking operation and a manually engaged winch brake is standard. The drum winch, hydraulic motor and all controls are coupled together as a compact unit and mounted on a transarm. Design features include high grade precision castings and a precision machined brass main worm wheel and gear.

Specifications
Unit weight: 630 kg
Rope length: 102 m
Rope diameter: 26 mm
Max rope pull:
  (1st layer) 25 000 kg
  (2nd layer) 21 500 kg
  (3rd layer) 18 700 kg
  (4th layer) 16 600 kg

Status
In production.

Manufacturer
TFM (Pty) Limited, PO Box 46131, Orange Grove,
Transvaal, South Africa.
Tel: 316 2106. Fax: 316 1462.

TFM HW-30 drag winch

TFM 25-tonne Recovery Winch

Description
This is a self-spooling, constant pull 25-tonne winch with a nominal rope speed of 9 m/min at rated load. The technology utilised is centred in a three-stage planetary reduction drive and hydraulic circuitry. All other components are fabricated in-house. The winch utilises a proprietary self-aligning platform which inherently assures correct spooling. The winch is intended mainly for the recovery role but could have other applications. It is claimed that the winch is available at a significant price reduction compared to other available winches.

Specifications
Weight: (fully installed) 2080 kg
Drum diameter: 495 mm (grooved)
Drum width: 600 mm
Rope length: 100 m (120 m optional)
Rope diameter: 26 mm
Max rope pull:
  (1st layer) 25 t
  (2nd layer) 23 t
  (3rd layer) 21 t

Status
In production.

Manufacturer
TFM (Pty) Limited, PO Box 46131, Orange Grove, Transvaal, South Africa.
Tel: 316 2106. Fax: 316 1462.

TFM 25-tonne recovery winch

UNITED KINGDOM

Reynolds Boughton Recovery Cranes

Description
Reynolds Boughton Limited has developed a range of hydraulic slewing recovery cranes with lifting capacities from 6 to 15 tonnes. These equipments can be installed on a variety of vehicles. The range comprises the following:

15/50 SHR
This is a 15-tonne lift capacity 270° slewing hydraulic recovery crane with a telescopic jib. It is available with a 25/50-tonne line pull winch. The crane is suitable for recovering heavy duty vehicles and MBTs from most situations by using the main winch and a ground anchor. Recovery is completed by using the suspended tow equipment provided. The main winch can be used for self-recovery.

10/50 SHR
This is a 10-tonne lift capacity 270° slewing hydraulic recovery crane with a telescopic jib. It is available with a 25/50-tonne line pull winch. Using the main winch and a ground anchor this equipment is suitable for recovering all wheeled vehicles, and can be adapted for general workshop and stores handling using four independent hydraulic stabilising legs. The main winch can be used for self-recovery.

6/16 SHR
This is a 6-tonne lift capacity 270° slewing hydraulic recovery crane with a telescopic jib that is available with a 6/8-tonne line pull winch. It is suitable for

Reynolds Boughton 15/50 SHR recovery equipment on Scammell S24 (6 × 6) recovery vehicle

recovering smaller vehicles in the 2/4-tonne range using the main winch and a ground anchor. A special A-frame at the chassis rear is fitted for suspended towing. Stores and equipment can also be handled. The main winch can be used for self-recovery.

10/50 UAL
This is a 15/10-tonne lift 270° slewing hydraulic recovery crane with a telescopic jib and an 8-tonne lift under-axle equipment. Using one-man operation it is suitable for all types of wheeled vehicles. It is available with a 25/50-tonne line pull recovery winch for heavy

duty, MBT and self-recovery.

Status
In production. In service with many armed forces in Africa, the Middle East and the Far East.

Manufacturer
Reynolds Boughton Limited, Engineering Division, Bell Lane, Amersham, Buckinghamshire HP6 6PE, UK.
Tel: 0494 764411. Telex: 83132.
Fax: 0494 765218.

Boughton Winches

Description
Reynolds Boughton Limited produce a range of mechanical and hydraulic freespool winches suitable for a wide range of applications. Many are used in conjunction with recovery equipments. Details of the

Boughton H10000 hydraulic winch on Case 721 Medium Wheeled Tractor

Mechanical drive winches

Type	Rated capacity	Transmission	Brake	Fairlead	Anchor
TTB100	6.8 t	forward/reverse	auto	option	—
1N	7 t	single speed	manual	option	option
VM16	8.2 t	forward/reverse	manual	option	—
20	10 t	two speed	manual	standard	standard
30	10 t	forward/reverse	manual	option	option
40	15 t	two speed or forward/reverse	manual	option	option
5	25 t	forward/reverse	manual[1]	option	option
80	35 t	forward/reverse	auto	option	—
120	55 t	forward/reverse	auto	option	—

Hydraulic drive winches

Type	Rated capacity	Transmission	Brake	Fairlead	Anchor
VH6	3 t	forward/reverse	auto[1]	option	—
VH8	3.8 t	forward/reverse	auto[1]	option	—
VH10	5 t	forward/reverse	auto[1]	option	option
H5000	5 t	forward/reverse	auto	option	option
H7500	7.5 t	forward/reverse	auto	option	option
H10000	10 t	forward/reverse	auto	option	option
H12500	12.5 t	forward/reverse	auto	option	option

Hydraulic drive winches continued

Type	Rated capacity	Transmission	Brake	Fairlead	Anchor
H15000	15 t	forward/reverse	auto	option	option
H20000	20 t	forward/reverse	auto	option	option
H25000	25 t	forward/reverse	auto	option	option
1NH	7 t	forward/reverse	manual	—	option
2H	12 t	forward/reverse	manual[1]	option	option
5H B200	19 t	forward/reverse	manual[1]	option	—
5H B270	26 t	forward/reverse	manual[1]	option	—
VH45	20 t	forward/reverse	auto	option	—
VH55	25 t	forward/reverse	auto	option	—

[1] Auto is optional

range are provided in the following table and it should be noted that in each case the rated performance is based on bare drum performance.

Recent winch contracts include the following:

H5000 to the US Marine Corps for new Ribbon Bridge launching equipment

H7500 for the UK Ministry of Defence's winch variant of the 4-tonne Leyland DAF truck

H10000 for the Case 721 Medium Wheeled Tractors for the British Army

H25000 for Royal Navy aircraft tugs

VH8 for the UK Ministry of Defence's 2-tonne TUH.

Status

In production and in widespread service – see text.

Manufacturer

Reynolds Boughton Limited, Engineering Division, Bell Lane, Amersham, Buckinghamshire HP6 6PE, UK. Tel: 0494 764411. Telex: 83132. Fax: 0494 765218.

Boughton Recovery Equipment

Description

A complete range of recovery equipment has been developed by Reynolds Boughton Limited. This equipment is suited for use with the Reynolds Boughton range of recovery cranes but is applicable to other vehicles. The range includes recovery chains, ground anchors, A-frames, tow poles, sand wedges, gun planks, pioneer kits, and so on.

Status

In production. In service with many armed forces.

Manufacturer

Reynolds Boughton Limited, Engineering Division, Bell Lane, Amersham, Buckinghamshire HP6 6PE, UK. Tel: 0494 764411. Telex: 83132. Fax: 0494 765218.

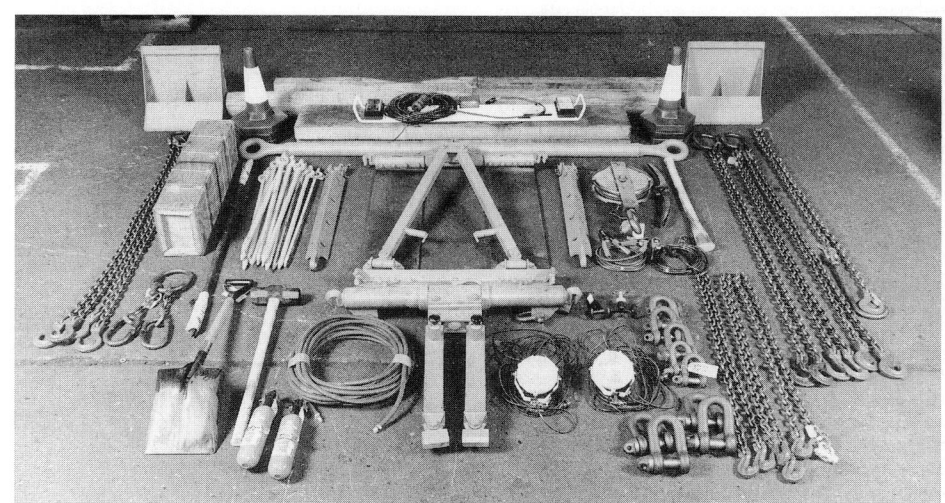

A selection of Boughton recovery equipment

Marlow Kinetic Energy Recovery Rope (KERR)

Description

The Marlow Kinetic Energy Recovery Rope (KERR) system was developed in conjunction with the British Army to provide a fast and effective recovery method and is particularly suited to armoured vehicles in tactical situations where wheeled or tracked recovery vehicles are not available. Using KERR it is possible for lighter vehicles to recover heavier vehicles; the rope sized for the recovering vehicles should be used (see under Specifications).

In use, the towing vehicle reverses as close as possible to the vehicle to be recovered. The rope is connected and snaked to allow tangle-free deployment. For situations where it is not possible to get close to the bogged vehicle, extension cables may be used. The KERR must be connected directly to the recovery or towing vehicle.

The towing vehicle then accelerates to the maximum speed possible and snatches the rope with its total energy at that maximum speed. The towing vehicle is slowed or halted and its kinetic energy is converted into the potential energy of a stretched rope. If the bogged vehicle has power to assist the transfers of energy by the KERR, a faster recovery can be accomplished. After a slight pause the bogged vehicle rises free. If the vehicle is not freed by the first attempt the process is repeated. Once free, continued towing by KERR is possible.

Marlow Ropes Limited also manufacture lightweight bridles which can be used in conjunction with the KERR. These bridles are described as ideal replacements for the heavy wire ropes used on many armoured vehicles and they can be made to suit any size of vehicle. They are available in Polyester, Kevlar/Twaron and the high modulus polyethylene fibres such as Spectra/Dyneema.

Typical recovery operation involving a Marlow Kinetic Energy Recovery Rope, with a British Army Spartan APC recovering a Scorpion reconnaissance vehicle

Specifications

Gross weight of vehicle	Rope size	Rope strength	Overall length of rope	Rope weight
Under 7000 kg	32 mm	20 000 kg	12.2 m	9.5 kg
7000 to 7990 kg	36 mm	24 800 kg	12.2 m	12.5 kg
8000 to 11 990 kg	40 mm	30 000 kg	13.7 m	17 kg
12 000 to 15 490 kg	48 mm	42 000 kg	13.7 m	25 kg
15 500 to 18 490 kg	52 mm	48 800 kg	13.7 m	29 kg
18 500 to 21 990 kg	56 mm	56 000 kg	13.7 m	34 kg
22 000 to 23 990 kg	60 mm	63 800 kg	13.7 m	39 kg
24 000 to 30 990 kg	64 mm	72 000 kg	15 m	49 kg
31 000 to 43 990 kg	68 mm	79 500 kg	19 m	67 kg
44 000 to 54 990 kg	72 mm	90 000 kg	21 m	84 kg
55 000 to 65 000 kg	80 mm	110 000 kg	21 m	103 kg

Status

In production. In service with the British Army and more than 20 other armed forces, including Canada and the US Army.

Manufacturer

Marlow Ropes Limited, Diplocks Way, Hailsham, East Sussex BN27 3JS, UK.
Tel: 0323 847234. Telex: 87676.
Fax: 0323 440093.

Tirfor Recovery Equipment

Description

The Tirfor models T-7, TU-16 and T-35 are all portable hand-operated machines which can be used for a wide range of loading, lifting, hauling and lowering operations. They are reversible and are available with a range of accessories which includes slings, shackles, snatch blocks, ground anchors, automatic wire rope reeling devices, wire rope grips and girder clamps. The latest model is the TU-16H, which is a hydraulically operated strengthened TU-16. Hydraulic pump units allow the operation of one, two or four TU-16Hs and the system can work both forwards (pulling or lifting) or reverse (lowering). The hydraulic power system gives the TU-16H a normal capacity of 1600 kg. This model can be operated from a unit with the following capability:

    Flow: 8 - 13 l/min maximum
    Pressure: 120 - 140 bars
    Hydraulic oil: 2° to 5° Engler viscosity at 50° C
    Viscosity index: over 100
    Filter: 40 microns

For light recovery operations the company offers the Jockey, which weighs less than 1.8 kg and can lift 300 kg, and pull up to 500 kg. The handle has been designed to bend when the rated pulling capacity is exceeded by 50 per cent.

Tirfor T-35 being used with Williams Fairey Medium Girder Bridge

Other hand-operated Tirfor machines:

Model	J5 Junior	T508	T-30
Pulling capacity	800 kg	1200 kg	5000 kg
Lifting capacity	500 kg	800 kg	3000 kg
Weight	4 kg	6.6 kg	27 kg
Breaking strength	3000 kg	4800 kg	16 800 kg
Diameter of wire rope	6.5 mm	8.2 mm	16.3 mm

Status

All this equipment is in production. The T-7, TU-16 and T-35 are used by many armed forces around the world.

Manufacturer

Tirfor Limited, Old Lane, Halfway, Sheffield S19 5GZ, UK.
Tel: 0742 482266. Fax: 0742 475649.

Specifications

Model	T-7	TU-16	T-35
Safe working load for lifting operations	750 kg	16 kg 2500 kg (pulling)	3000 kg 5000 kg (pulling)
Effort	27 kg	46 kg	43.2 kg (slow speed) 68.1 kg (fast speed)
Distance of rope travel for one complete cycle of operating lever	64 mm	70 mm	38 mm (slow speed) 48 mm (fast speed)
Mechanical advantage	28:1	38:1	70:1 (slow speed) 45:1 (fast speed)
Weight of machine only	5.9 kg	18 kg	26.8 kg
Overall dimensions (without handle)	510 × 10 × 204 mm	660 × 356 × 152 mm	718 × 140 × 318 mm
Length of operating handle (fully extended)	0.731 m	1.13 m	1.157 m
Standard length of wire rope	9.15 m	18.3 m	9.15 m
Rope diameter	8.2 mm	11.3 mm	16.3 mm
Rope end fitting	safety hook	safety hook	shackle

Trailer, Dummy Axle, Recovery, 1–5-tonne (FV2692)

Description

The trailer is capable of performing a suspended tow of wheeled armoured and unarmoured vehicle casualties up to a gross vehicle weight of 6250 kg. The trailer has an unsprung twin-wheeled axle carrying the integrally constructed chassis frame and jib. The recovery is not effected by the dummy axle trailer but lifting onto the trailer for towing may be carried out by means of a hand winch and four-fall pulley system. A system of spreader bars and chains allows the winch unit to be relieved of all load once the casualty is attached to the dummy axle. High- and low-level floodlights are fitted to facilitate night-time operations. An emergency lighting kit is carried to fit the rear of the disabled vehicle.

Specifications

Weight: (unladen) 1883 kg
Length: 3.47 m
Width: 2.362 m
Height: 2.31 m
Wheelbase: (axle to towing eye) 2.76 m
Track: 1.816 m
Tyres: 8.25 × 15 (radial ply)

Trailer, Dummy Axle, Recovery, 1–5-tonne (FV2692)

Brakes: 312 × 190 mm S cam units, overrun operated when unladen and air-operated when laden
Handbrake: mechanical operating via overrun system

Status

In service with the British Army.

Manufacturer

Defence Equipment Division, Rubery Owen Group Services Limited, Darlaston, PO Box 10, Wednesbury, West Midlands WS10 8JD, UK.
Tel: 021 526 3131. Telex: 338236/7.

Superwinch 10-ton Winch FF 10/12

Description
When the ranges of Foden Low and Medium Mobility vehicles were undergoing initial acceptance trials, the

Superwinch FF 10/12 winch fitted to Foden (6 × 6) recovery vehicle

Ministry of Defence issued a specification for a forward-mounted hydraulic recovery winch, with a minimum line pull of 10 tons, to provide a bare drum capacity of 12.5 tons at 140.6 kg/cm^2 (2000 psi). Superwinch Limited was awarded the contract for its model FF 10/12 winch.

The FF 10/12 uses aluminium castings and has a drum capacity of 50 m of 18 mm cable although it is recommended that only 40 m should be used. In use the FF 10/12 has overload protection provided by pressure relief through an adjustable valve. Free spool is obtained by a hand-operated involute splined clutch. The spiroid gear ratio is 1:25.33.

The FF 10/12 is in British Army service on Foden Low Mobility 6 × 4 and 8 × 4 vehicles and on the Foden Medium Mobility 6 × 6 FH-70 Tractor and Limber vehicles. It is also fitted to the Foden (6 × 6) recovery vehicle.

Specifications
Line pull: 10.7 t
Line speed: (2nd layer rope)
(flow rate 60 l/min) 4.9 m/min
(flow rate 99 l/min) 7.6 m/min
(flow rate 150 l/min) 11.6 m/min
Bare drum line pull: 12.5 t
Capacity of 18 mm cable:
(maximum) 50 m
(recommended) 40 m
Drum:
(barrel diameter) 270 mm
(flange diameter) 435 mm
(width) 258 mm
Operating pressure: 140.6 kg/cm^2
Height: 817 mm
Width: 946 mm
Depth: 670 mm

Status
In production. In service with the British Army.

Manufacturer
Superwinch Limited, Whitchurch Road, Tavistock, Devon PL19 9DR, UK.
Tel: 0822 614101. Telex: 45324.
Fax: 0822 615204.

Superwinch Light Recovery Equipment

Description
Superwinch Limited produces a range of recovery equipment suitable for fitting to light vehicles. This

Land Rover fitted with Superwinch drum winch and ground anchors

range includes capstan and drum winches, power take-offs and accessories.

There are two types of capstan winch; the Capstan 99 and the Capstan 199. The Capstan 99 is produced for use with all models of Land Rover and is in service with the British Army. It is driven from the front of the crankshaft and has a recommended line pull of 1400 kg, although it is overload tested to 2500 kg. It is recommended that 5.8 mm rope is used. The winch is supplied in kit form and can be fitted in approximately 3 h. Overload protection is provided by a shear pin in the driveline, a feature shared by all the light Superwinch units. The Capstan 199 is a version for the Range Rover or six-cylinder Toyota Land Cruiser and is similar except for the weight which is 33 kg, 3 kg more than the Capstan 99.

The Superwinch drum winch can be fitted to the Land Rover. It has a line pull of 2270 kg and can be provided with 9 mm or 11 mm cable. Weight is 65.3 kg, less cable. It is provided in kit form and can be fitted by one man in 8 to 10 hours. Control can be from inside or outside the cab.

A drum winch is produced for use with the Land Rover Defender One Ten and is suitable for fitting to the four-cylinder models. It uses a mechanical drive from a power take-off fitted to the rear of the gearbox transfer case. It has an automatic overload protection adjustable to suit the maximum line pull permitted. To

fit the winch to the Defender One Ten takes approximately 6 h. In use it can be controlled from inside or outside the cab. Either 9 mm or 11 mm cable can be used, 77 m of the 9 mm and 46 m of the 11 mm. The maximum line speed in fifth gear is 11.73 m/min and the total weight of the winch and accessories (less cable) is 92.76 kg.

When using Superwinch units on a Land Rover it is recommended that a special heavy duty bumper is fitted to the vehicle. Other accessories include ground anchors which are provided with reversible plates to provide straight edges for use on hard ground and splines for use on earth surfaces. A chain secures the anchor to the bumper. When not in use the anchors fold flat, measuring 610 × 311 × 76.2 mm. Weight per pair is 45 kg.

Status
In production. Capstan 99, heavy duty bumper and ground anchors in service with the British Army.

Manufacturer
Superwinch Limited, Whitchurch Road, Tavistock, Devon PL19 9DR, UK.
Tel: 0822 614101. Telex: 45324.
Fax: 0822 615204.

Rubery Owen Recovery Equipment

Description
A special range of lightweight recovery equipment has been designed by Rubery Owen, using safety factors as low as 1.5 times the working load limit. Meeting the needs of skilled recovery personnel, all the equipment has been subjected to rigorous field and destruction test programmes.

Status
Manufactured as required. In service with the British Army.

Manufacturer
Defence Equipment Division, Rubery Owen Group Services Limited, Darlaston, PC Box 10, Wednesbury, West Midlands WS10 8JD, UK.
Tel: 021 526 3131. Telex: 338236/7.

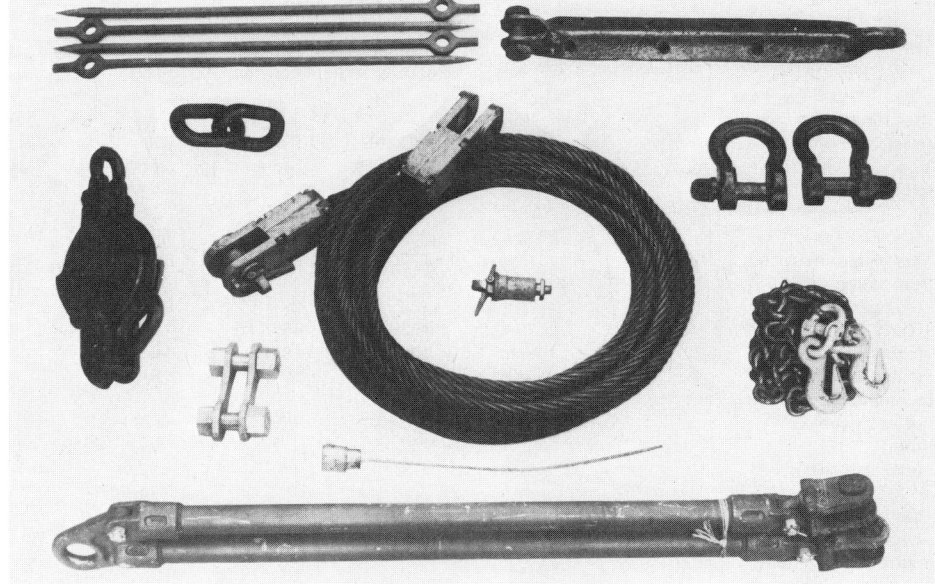

Selection illustrated is typical of recovery equipment supplied by Rubery Owen

UNITED STATES OF AMERICA

Holmes International Recovery Equipment

Development
Ernest Holmes built its first recovery vehicle before the First World War. From 1973 to 1987 Holmes International was a division of the Dover Corporation. In 1987 Holmes International Inc became a privately owned company. Since 1914 it has developed a wide range of twin-boom equipment which can be mounted on a variety of wheeled and tracked chassis, including chassis available from Kenworth, Navistar, Chevrolet, GMC, Ford, Dodge, AWD Bedford, Foden and Mercedes-Benz. A complete line of single boom hydraulic wreckers from 2 to 45 tonnes is also available. Steel and aluminium deck tilt bed carriers are also manufactured.

The main advantage of the twin-boom recovery equipment is that the vehicle can recover disabled vehicles from the side as well as the rear because the booms can be swung to the left and right of the vehicle. By securing the cable from one of the booms to a suitable anchorage point, the second boom can handle vehicles equalling the weight of the recovery vehicle itself.

Descriptions
Holmes FW-35 Towing Unit
The Holmes FW-35 towing unit is designed to be fitted over the 'fifth wheel' turntable unit of heavy tractors for extreme heavy duty lift and towing of tactical vehicles, such as tank recovery vehicles and missile carriers. When fitted the FW-35 is capable of taking a gross cargo weight of up to 38 555 kg, and it can lift up to 15 875 kg. Once lifted the towed vehicle travels on its rear axle(s). These units are in use by US armed forces in Europe.

Holmes ProStar Wheel Lift
This is an all hydraulic add-on wheel lift with 1360 kg lifting capacity and 3400 kg towing capacity. It can be mounted on most light chassis wreckers and has combined lift and tilt functions. Power is derived from an electric/hydraulic powerpack or directly from a hydraulic system.

Holmes Protech PT1102
This equipment includes a hydraulic wheel lift (1360 kg lifting capacity and 3400 kg towing capacity) with independently controlled lift, tilt and extension functions plus a special boom wrecker. The wrecker has a fixed boom angle and a manual extension. This equipment can be installed on a two-axle chassis with dual rear wheels and a gross vehicle weight of not less than 4536 kg.

Holmes Protech PT3105 and PT3210
These equipments can be installed on a two-axle

Holmes 750 equipment installed on Mack R (6 × 6) truck chassis for the Australian Army

chassis with dual rear wheels and a gross vehicle weight of not less than 4536 kg. The equipment includes a hydraulic wheel lift (1360 kg lifting capacity and 3400 kg towing capacity) with independently controlled lift, tilt and extension functions and a single boom hydraulic powered wrecker. There are dual hydraulic cylinders to raise and lower the boom. The main difference between the two models is that the PT3105 has a single winch while the PT3210 has two.

Holmes 750 Wrecker
This equipment can be installed on a two- or three-axle chassis that has a gross vehicle weight of not less than 14 514 kg. Equipment which can be fitted (including optional equipment) includes two stiff legs and a bolster, chain and pinion guards, extensible or non-extensible booms, controls recessed into the body, towing chains, rear jacks to increase lifting stability, dual power unit with a gear reduction of 214 to 1, 14 anchor points, backlash brakes, telescoping outboard legs, cable drums with guards, and two snatch blocks. In service in Australia.

Holmes 1601 Python Hydraulic Wrecker
The Holmes 1601 is a single boom wrecker with a hydraulic extension of 1.64 m. Its structural capacity is

Specifications

Model	1701 Lancer	1801 Victor
Basic wrecker rating	31 750 kg	40 823 kg
Boom rating		
(retracted)	31 750 kg	40 823 kg
(fully extended)	10 886 kg	13 608 kg
Winch characteristics (each drum)		
(load rating, first cable layer)	18 144 kg	23 587 kg
(drum diameter)	381 mm	508 mm
(line speed)	5.79 m/min	6.096 m/min
(cable length, max)	86.87 m	94.5 m
(gearbox/cable drum gear reduction)	214 to 1	485 to 1
Winch type	worm drive	worm drive
Winch cable diameter	15.875 mm	19 mm
Cable length (each drum)	76.2 m	91.44 m
Working load limit (single line)	5883 kg	8373 kg
Breaking strength (single line)	20 593 kg	29 302 kg
Wrecker height above truck frame	1.963 m	2.083 m
Wrecker body width	2.438 m	2.438 m
Weight		
(wrecker with body approx)	5693 kg	7824.5 kg
(wrecker without body approx)	4241 kg	6373 kg

Specifications

Model	PT1102	PT3105	PT3210	750	1601	1625	1701	1801
Type	mechanical	hydraulic	hydraulic	mechanical	hydraulic	hydraulic	hydraulic	hydraulic
Rating								
(both booms)	n/a	n/a	n/a	22 680 kg	n/a	n/a	n/a	n/a
(each boom)	3630 kg	9090 kg	9090 kg	11 340 kg	19 958 kg	22 680 kg	31 750 kg	40 823 kg
(boom fully extended)	1815 kg	2720 kg	2720 kg	5443 kg	6450 kg	9072 kg	10 886 kg	13 608 kg
Drum rating								
(number of winches)	1	1	2	2	2	2	2	2
(each drum)	2630 kg	4536 kg	4536 kg	11 340 kg	9979 kg	15 876 kg	23 452 kg	30 535 kg
(cable diameter)	10 mm	10 mm	10 mm	14.3 mm	14.3 mm	16 mm	16 mm	19 mm
(cable length)	23 m	30 m	30 m	61 m	61 m	61 m	76.2 m	94.5 m
Recommended working limit								
of each cable	1585 kg	1585 kg	1585 kg	4309 kg	3493 kg	4990 kg	5883 kg	8373 kg
Boom								
(max extension)	0.75 m	1.53 m	1.53 m	1.93 m[1] / 2.44 m*	1.64 m	1.64 m[1] / 2.44 m*	2.44 m	2.54 m
(horizontal swing)	n/a	n/a	n/a	90°	n/a	n/a	n/a	n/a
(vertical swing)	fixed	60°	60°	60°	60°	60°	60°	60°
Height of equipment								
above truck chassis	varies with chassis	varies with chassis	varies with chassis	1.99 m	1.52 m	1.4 m	1.96 m	2.08 m

[1] single axle
* tandem axle

19 954 kg retracted and 6350 kg at full extension. The structure incorporates the Holmes mast which allows for greater recovery capability during side pulls. Optional outboard legs increase the performance capacity during side pulls. A minimum front axle rating of 3175 kg and 10 433 kg for the rear axle are required.

Holmes 1625 Hydraulic Wrecker

The Holmes 1625 incorporates many well-proven Holmes features plus some new technological features. It has a long or short boom configuration to suit the chassis and to suit single or tandem axles. The single boom extends 1.6 m with a retracted capacity of 22 680 kg while the fully extended capacity is 9072 kg. Height above the truck frame is 1.4 m. Optional side legs can increase the side pull of the unit. Minimum gross vehicle weight required is 12 777 kg.

Holmes Model 1701 Lancer Wrecker

The Holmes Model 1701 uses a single, non-traversable boom. The type is described as a 35-tonne power wrecker and uses a system of stabilising jacks and stays for lifting heavy loads. The single boom has a single stage maximum extension of 2.438 m and has a maximum lift of 31 750 kg retracted and 10 886 kg

extended. The boom is located on a steel mast structure which also carries a single adjustable extending stabiliser leg on each side. The mast can also be used as the main load-carrying structure when side pulls are used as the Model 1701 uses a twin-winch system. The twin winches can be used either over twin cable pulleys at the end of the boom or over the sides of the central mast. Twin hydraulic cylinders raise and lower the boom. With side pulls it is possible to use one winch cable as an anchor for improved stability. The winches, which are similar to those used on the Model 750, are specially produced for wrecker use and have such features as manual rewind and nylon bearings. The winch gear reduction is 459 to 1.

Holmes Model 1801 Victor Wrecker

The Holmes Model 1801 Victor wrecker follows the same general lines as the Model 1701 but the lifting capacity is much greater. The single non-traversable boom of the Model 1801 has a maximum extension of 2.54 m. Retracted it has a maximum lift capacity of 40 823 kg and fully extended it can lift 13 608 kg. This lift capacity enables the vehicle to assist disabled AFVs using other vehicles as anchors to assist in side pulls. The Model 1801 boom has the lifting capacity to enable

it to be used as a heavy repair vehicle, lifting tank turrets and engine packs when necessary. The Model 1801 has a three-stage hydraulic motor. One 321.7 l/min stage drives one winch and the boom extension cylinder. Another 321.7 l/min stage drives the other winch and the boom lift cylinders. A third 56.8 l/min stage drives the outboard legs and rear jacks. Each stage can be operated independently.

Holmes TH395 Super Heavy Duty Truck Hitch

The TH395 super heavy duty truck hitch is rated at 11 340 kg lift capacity and 38 102 kg towing capacity and uses 15.8 mm alloy chains. A full contact anchor bar reduces towed vehicle bumper damage and 10 grease fittings provide adequate lubrication to maintain operational life.

Status

In production. In service with many armed forces throughout the world.

Manufacturer

Holmes International Inc, 2505 East 43rd Street, Chattanooga, Tennessee 37407, USA.
Tel: (615) 867 2142. Telex: 558409.

Paratech MAXIFORCE Air Lifting Bags

Description

The Paratech MAXIFORCE air lifting bag is a thin, strong, moulded envelope made from neoprene embedded with three full layers of Kevlar aramid reinforcement on each side. Each lifting bag has a single inlet/outlet used to inflate and deflate the bag; the usual inflation agent is compressed air. The bags have a wide range of applications and can be used on soft ground, under water or when it is not possible to use jacks or other lifting devices. They can also be used for odd-shaped or cylindrical loads and for many other load-lifting applications.

A MAXIFORCE system can be quickly set up as even the largest bag can be fully inflated in less than 60 seconds. It is also completely silent in use. All that is required to operate the system is positioning a MAXIFORCE bag under the load involved and inflating the bag. Using the energy of compressed air a load is moved within seconds. The bags require only 25 mm of insertion space and operate on air pressure up to 8 bar (118 psi) so air sources such as air cylinders, truck air brake systems, compressors and foot pumps can be used for inflation. Inflation and deflation is operator controlled by use of a safety control valve which can control two bags independently.

All MAXIFORCE bags have a positive grip surface designed for maximum friction and hold. As an

additional safety precaution during lifting operations a bright yellow 'X' is moulded into both sides of each bag. This ensures high visibility and exact centering of the bag under a load for maximum lift heights and stability.

The weight of a MAXIFORCE air lifting bag is 4.2 to 20 kg depending on size and type.

Status

In production.

Manufacturer

Paratech Incorporated, 1025 Lambrecht Road, Frankfort, Illinois 60423, USA.
Tel: (815) 469 3911. Fax: (815) 469 7748.

A Paratech MAXIFORCE air lifting bag being used to lift a tracked construction vehicle

A selection of Paratech MAXIFORCE air lifting bags and accessories

BRIDGING SYSTEMS

Mechanised bridges
Tactical floating bridges and ferries
Tactical (non-floating) and line of communication bridges
Bridging boats

MECHANISED BRIDGES

CHINA, PEOPLE'S REPUBLIC

Type 84 Armoured Bridgelayer

Description

The Type 84 armoured bridgelayer uses the hull and suspension of the Type 69 MBT. The vehicle has a crew of three with the driver in the normal position at the hull front. The other two are seated inside the hull with a small observation hatch provided for the commander. This is fitted with a periscope and an infra-red night vision device. The vehicle is equipped with a Type 899 radio set and a Type 803 set is used for crew inter-communications. Also carried is a single 7.62 mm machine gun.

A hydraulically operated stabiliser blade, used during the final stages of bridgelaying, is mounted under the front of the hull and may also be used for obstacle clearing and dozing operations.

The bridge is of the Biber type with some alterations to the laying system. The bridge is constructed of light steel and is in two halves, one half carried on top of the other. Total length is 18 m of which 16 m can normally be used and the maximum weight carried on the main trackways is 40 000 kg. A narrower internal auxiliary trackway is limited to 8000 kg. The bridgelaying mechanism is driven using hydraulic actuators and rams carried on forward and rear operating assemblies and a rail framework is used to carry and move the bridge into position.

The laying sequence commences with the positioning of the carrier vehicle close to the obstacle to be bridged. Operations commence with both halves of the bridge being moved backwards along the carrier frame. As this is carried out the rear of the upper half is raised slightly, followed by the front. This upper bridge half lifts clear of the lower half, allowing the hydraulic system to move the latter forwards along the carrier frame as far as it will go on the forward positioning assembly. At this point the hydraulic ram system at the rear of the vehicle is swung downwards to the rear after which the lower half is moved forward yet again by a ram on the forward assembly. This allows both halves to be lowered to the same level and they can then be joined. The ram system at the rear is then disconnected to allow the forward assembly to push the entire bridge forwards to its maximum extent. Before this operation is completed the stabiliser blade at the front is lowered to the ground to provide support for the vehicle as the bridge is extended. At the full extension point the carrier frame is tilted forward by the forward hydraulic assembly until the far end of the bridge touches the ground. The carrier vehicle is then reversed slowly as the near end of the bridge is lowered, after which the carrier frame is disconnected to complete the operation. Recovery is carried out in the opposite sequence.

The bridge can be assembled and carried to the

Type 84 armoured bridgelayer in travelling configuration

laying point positioned centrally on the carrier frame in order to save time at the actual bridging position. The time required for a complete bridge launch operation is between 3-5 minutes and between 3-6 minutes for recovery. A height difference between banks of 4 m is possible with the slope limit for the carrier vehicle being 10° under such conditions. The bridge can be launched with the carrier vehicle positioned on a side slope of between 8 and 10°.

Specifications
Crew: 3
Weight: (combat) 38 500 kg
Length: (with bridge) 9.879 m
Width: (overall) 3.27 m
Height: (with bridge) 2.978 m
Ground clearance: 0.35 m
Track: 2.64 m
Length of track on ground: 3.845 m
Ground pressure: 0.852 kg/cm^2
Max speed: (road) 50 km/h
Range: 365 km
Fuel capacity: 930 l
Fording: 1.1 m
Gradient: 25°
Side slope:
(travelling) 15°
(launching bridge) 8-10°
Engine: Model 12150 L-7BW V-12 water-cooled diesel

developing 580 hp at 2000 rpm
Transmission: manual, 5 forward and 1 reverse gears
Electrical system: 24 V
Batteries: 4 × Type 65
Armament: 1 × 7.62 mm MG
Ammunition carried: 1500 rounds

Bridge
Weight: 8000 kg
Load capacity:
(main bridge) 40 000 kg
(auxiliary bridge) 8000 kg
Length:
(complete) 18 m
(usable) 16 m
Width: 3.2 m
Track width:
(main bridge) 0.6 m
(auxiliary bridge) 0.55 m

Status
In production. In service with the Chinese Army and Thailand.

Manufacturer
China North Industries Corporation, 7A Yue Tan Nan Jie, PO Box 2137 Beijing, Beijing, China.
Tel: 867570. Telex: 22339 cnic cn.
Fax: 867840.

Heavy Mechanised Bridge Type 84A

Description

The Heavy Mechanised Bridge Type 84A is a close derivative of the TMM truck-mounted treadway bridge (see separate entry in this section) and can be used by tracked vehicles up to a maximum weight of 50 tonnes and by wheeled vehicles with a maximum axle load of 13 tonnes. The bridge sections are carried and placed into position by an 8 × 8 truck and the general laying

sequence and operation are much the same as those for the TMM (qv).

Specifications
Weight of bridgelayer: (total) approx 20 t
Length of single span: 10.5 m
Roadway width: 3.8 m
Total length of bridge: 50 m
Bridge height:
(max) 3.8 m
(min) 2.2 m
Capacity: (tracks) 50 000 kg

Status
In production.

Manufacturer
China Shipbuilding Trading Company Limited, 10 Yuetan Beixiaojie, Beijing, China.
Tel: 893086. Telex: 22335 cssc cn.

COMMONWEALTH OF INDEPENDENT STATES

PMM-2 Amphibious Bridging and Ferry System

Description
The floating bridging and ferry system originally known in the West as the Amphibious Bridging System (Tracked), or ABS(T), is now known to be the PMM-2, or *Paromno-Mostovaya Maschina-2*. This vehicle has a tracked suspension based on the use of T-64 track and road wheel components and uses a chassis similar to that employed with the PTS-2 amphibious carrier, the MDK-3 trench digging machine and what is probably the base vehicle for the series, the MT-T heavy tracked transporter. It is thus extremely likely that the engine used to power the PMM-2 is the V-64-4 diesel.

The PMM-2 is the replacement vehicle for the GSP heavy amphibious ferry (see entry in *Floating bridges and ferries* section) and uses a similar chassis and float layout but with the PMM-2 the float units unfold for use and can be folded back for road transport. The PMM-2 is able to ferry loads of up to around 50 tonnes.

In use the PMM-2 follows the same general lines as the GSP but the float units are mechanically unfolded using hydraulic mechanisms just before or as the vehicle enters the water. The top float unfolds to the right and the second section, which is slightly shorter than the top section as it is located behind the cab, to the left. Also unfolded mechanically are two two-section loading ramps each side. Once in the water, propulsion is provided by two propeller units at the rear. These are lowered once the vehicle is in the water and the drive is taken from the main engine. The propellers are concealed within prominent cowls to prevent damage; the cowls also support small steering rudders.

PMM-2 units can be connected together to form floating bridges by using latching mechanisms on the outer edges of the float units. Bridges up to 10 units wide have been reported and no bridging boats are apparently involved in the formation of such bridges.

Individual PMM-2 units can also be used to bridge

A PMM-2 bridging and ferry unit

small water gaps. The overall width of the PMM-2 on the road is about 3.3 m so once the side floats are lowered the overall width is 9.9 m. The loading ramps each have a usable length of at least 5 m so a single PMM-2 can probably be used to bridge water gaps almost 20 m wide. In practice this width is probably reduced to around 17 m.

It has been reported that the PMM-2 has a crew of five but the cab appears to be too small to accommodate this number and the number of men required to actually operate the vehicle as a ferry would probably be limited to three. The PMM-2 probably has a

collective NBC protection system for the cab, in common with other vehicles using the same or similar chassis.

Estimates of the PMM-2's dimensions are that it has an overall length of 12.8 m, a width of 3.3 m and an overall height of around 3.5 m.

Status
In service with the CIS.

Manufacturer
State factories.

MTU-72 Armoured Bridgelayer

Description
A number of T-72B MBTs have been converted to the MTU-72 armoured bridgelayer configuration by removing the turret and replacing it with a bridge-launching system and bridge having an overall length, when laid, of 20 m. The bridge has a maximum capacity of 50 000 kg, is 3.3 m wide, and can span a gap of 18 m. By itself the bridge weighs 6400 kg.

The overall layout and operating method of the resultant MTU-72 are similar to those of the MTU-20 and MTU bridgelayers (see following entries). The time required to lay a bridge is 3 minutes, and 8 minutes for retrieval.

The vehicle may be fitted with an add-on front-mounted dozer blade.

A similar vehicle based on the chassis of the T-72 MBT, known as the BLP-72, was developed to the prototype stage by the former East German Army. No details are available but it is believed to be generally similar to the MTU-72.

Specifications
Crew: 2
Weight: 40 000 kg
Power-to-weight ratio: 21 hp/t
Length: (with bridge) 11.64 m
Width: 3.46 m
Height: (with bridge) 3.38 m
Ground clearance: 0.492 m
Max speed: (road) 60 km/h
Range: (road) 500 km
Fording:
  (normal) 1.2 m
  (with preparation) 4.5 m
Engine: diesel developing 840 hp

Prototype of BLP-72 armoured bridgelayer produced by the former East Germany and based on the T-72 MBT (Michael Jerchel)

MTU-72 armoured bridgelayer in travelling configuration

Bridge capacity: 50 000 kg
Bridge weight: 6400 kg
Bridge length: 20 m
Bridge width: 3.3 m

Gap spanned: 18 m

Status
In service with the CIS in limited numbers.

Manufacturer
State factories.

MTU-20 Armoured Bridgelayer

Development/Description
The MTU-20 was introduced into the former Soviet Army in 1967 as the replacement for the older MTU bridgelayer and is based on the T-55 tank chassis rather than the T-54 tank chassis used for the MTU.

The method of laying the bridge is almost identical to that of the MTU bridgelayer and the reader is referred to this entry for the method of launching and for a description of the chassis (see following entry). Stabilisers at the nose of the tank are lowered into position before the bridge is launched.

The bridge weighs 7000 kg and is of the box construction type. It has a maximum length of 20 m and can span a gap of up to 18 m. It is 3.3 m wide, 1 m high and has a maximum capacity of 60 000 kg. When travelling the ends of the bridge are folded back through 180° so that they lie on top of the bridge. They are lowered and locked in position before the bridge is launched. The bridge takes 5 minutes to lay in position and between 5-7 minutes to recover.

As the MTU-20 is based on a T-55 chassis it is thought likely that an NBC system is installed.

Specifications
Crew: 2
Weight: (with bridge) 37 000 kg
Length: (with bridge) 11.64 m
Width: (with bridge) 3.3 m
Height: (with bridge) 3.4 m
Ground clearance: 0.425 m
Track: 2.64 m
Track width: 580 mm
Length of track on ground: 3.84 m
Ground pressure: 0.83 kg/cm^2
Max speed: (road) 50 km/h
Range: 500 km
Fuel capacity: 960 l
Fording: 1.4 m

Nigerian Army MTU-20 armoured bridgelayer (Henry Dodds)

Gradient: 40%
Vertical obstacle: 0.8 m
Trench: 2.7 m
Engine: V-55, V-12, water-cooled diesel developing 580 hp at 2000 rpm
Transmission: manual with 5 forward and 1 reverse gears
Electrical system: 24 V
Batteries: 4, 280 Ah
Armament: nil
Armour
glacis plate: 100 mm at 60°

upper hull sides: 70 mm at 0°
hull rear: 60 mm
hull floor: 20 mm
hull roof: 30 mm

Status
Production complete. The MTU-20 is known to be in service with Afghanistan, Egypt, Finland, Germany, India, Israel, Nigeria, Syria and the CIS.

Manufacturer
State factories.

MTU Armoured Bridgelayer

Development
The MTU bridgelayer (MTU - *Mostoykladchik tankoviy ustroystvo*) entered service in 1958 as the replacement for an older bridgelayer based on a T-34 MBT chassis. Since 1967 the MTU has been replaced in many units by the MTU-20 (see previous entry), which has the ability to span a gap of up to 18 m compared with the 11 m of the MTU. The MTU is also sometimes referred to as the MTU-1 and late production models use a T-55 chassis rather than the T-54 chassis.

Description
The MTU is based on the chassis of the T-54 MBT with its turret removed. The driver is seated at the front of the hull on the left side and is provided with two periscopes for observation and a single-piece hatch cover. The commander is seated in the crew compartment to the rear of the driver with the engine and transmission at the rear of the hull. The suspension is of the torsion bar type and consists of five road wheels with the idler at the front and the drive sprocket at the rear. There are no track return rollers.

A 12.7 mm DShKM machine gun mounted in the centre of the hull between the two treadways has to be removed before the bridge can be laid in position.

The MTU does not have an NBC system and has no deep fording capability. Auxiliary fuel drums and an unditching beam are often carried at the rear of the hull.

The bridge itself is 12.3 m long, 3.27 m wide and 1 m high, and will span a gap of 11 m. It has a maximum loading capacity of 50 000 kg.

The bridge consists of four box-truss panels. The

MTU armoured bridgelayer in travelling configuration

outer treadways are used by tracked vehicles and the inner treadways by smaller vehicles. When travelling the ramp sections of the inner treadways are folded on top of the main treadways.

The bridge is positioned as follows: a chain drive mechanism moves the bridge over the cantilever launching girder until the far bank is reached, the cantilever launching girder is depressed and lowers the span onto the near bank. The bridge takes between 3 to 5 minutes to launch and can be retrieved from either end.

Specifications
Crew: 2
Weight: (with bridge) 34 000 kg
Length: (with bridge) 12.3 m
Width: (with bridge) 3.27 m

Height: (with bridge) 2.87 m
Ground clearance: 0.425 m
Track: 2.64 m
Track width: 580 mm
Length of track on ground: 3.84 m
Ground pressure: 0.76 kg/cm^2
Max speed: (road) 48 km/h
Range: 400 km
Fuel capacity: 812 l
Fording: 1.4 m
Gradient: 60%
Vertical obstacle: 0.8 m
Trench: 2.7 m
Engine: V-54, V-12, water-cooled diesel developing 520 hp at 2000 rpm
Transmission: manual with 5 forward and 1 reverse gears

Electrical system: 24 V
Batteries: 4, 280 Ah
Armament: 1 × 12.7 mm DShKM MG
Armour
glacis plate: 100 mm at 60°
upper hull sides: 70 mm at 0°
hull rear: 60 mm
hull floor: 20 mm
hull roof: 30 mm

Status
Production complete. The T-54 is used by the following countries, some of which also use the MTU bridgelayer: Afghanistan (confirmed), Albania, Algeria, Angola, Bangladesh, Bulgaria, China, CIS (confirmed), Congo, Cuba, Cyprus, Czechoslovakia (does not use the MTU), Egypt (confirmed), Equatorial Guinea, Ethiopia, Finland (confirmed), Germany (confirmed), Guinea, Guinea-Bissau, Hungary, India, Iraq, Israel (confirmed),

North Korea, Libya, Mali, Mongolia, Morocco, Mozambique, Nigeria, Pakistan, Peru, Poland, Romania, Somalia, Sudan, Syria (confirmed), Vietnam, Yemen, the former Yugoslavia and Zimbabwe.

Manufacturer
State factories.

TMM Truck-mounted Treadway Bridge

Description
The TMM (heavy mechanised bridge) consists of four 10.5 m spans, each of which is carried and launched from the rear of a modified KrAZ-214 (6 × 6) 7000 kg truck or the more recent KrAZ-255B (6 × 6) 7500 kg truck. The latter model has improvements in the bridgelaying mechanism and is recognisable by the spare tyre, which is carried on the roof of the cab, rather than at the rear of the cab as on the KrAZ-214. The model carried on the KrAZ-255B (6 × 6) truck is designated the TMM-3. Three of the spans have integral mounted adjustable trestle legs; the fourth (or far-shore) span does not as it is the link between the third span and the far bank.

The system operates as follows: before launching the treadway the trestle legs must be adjusted to the correct height, so the roadway is level when the bridge has been positioned. During transit they are folded and stored beneath the folded scissors span. The treadways are then spread to the full roadway width of 3.8 m. The truck backs up to the river and the hydraulic launching girder raises the folded span to the vertical position, the span is straightened by a cable and winch system and then lowered. As it is lowered into position, the integral trestle legs swing into place. Once in position the cables are disconnected, the launching

girder is brought back into the travelling position and the truck moves off. This procedure is repeated until the bridge is complete. If required the bridge can be extended past the basic four spans by further additions. The launched spans can be recovered from either end and recovery takes about the same time as launching.

A complete TMM with four spans can cross a gap of up to 40 m in 45-60 minutes in daylight or 60-80 minutes at night. These times are for an average crew and can be halved by a well-trained crew. To reduce the possibility of detection, the TMM can also be laid under the surface of the water, which takes 50 per cent longer than the normal method. Log and metal plate supports can be used to support the trestle legs when obstacles up to 5 m deep are encountered or when the slope is too great.

A Chinese-produced version of the TMM is known as the Heavy Mechanised Bridge Type 84A. See separate entry in this section for known details.

Specifications
Vehicle with bridge
(full technical characteristics of the KrAZ-214 will be found in the *Trucks* section)
Cab seating: 1 + 2
Configuration: 6 × 6
Weight: 19 500 kg
Length: 9.3 m
Width: 3.2 m

Height: 3.15 m
Ground clearance: 0.36 m
Track: 2.03 m
Wheelbase: 4.6 m + 1.4 m
Max speed: (road) 55 km/h
Range: 530 km
Fuel capacity: 450 l
Fording: 1 m
Engine: YaMZ M206B, 6-cylinder water-cooled diesel developing 205 bhp at 2000 rpm
Transmission: manual with 5 forward and 1 reverse gears and 2-speed transfer box
Tyres: 15.00 × 20

Bridge
Weight: 7000 kg
Length: 10.5 m
Width: 3.8 m
Trestle leg length: adjustable between 1.7-3.2 m
Capacity: 60 000 kg

Status
Production complete. In service with Bulgaria, Hungary and other armed forces including China, Germany and the former Yugoslavia. The Bulgarian Army developed a modified bridge using tubular section metal parts. It is not known if it was adopted or produced in quantity.

Manufacturer
State factories.

TMM-3 truck-mounted scissors bridge being lowered into position, showing front wheels of KrAZ-255B 7500 kg (6 × 6) truck off ground as centre of gravity is well to rear when bridge is being lowered into position

KMM Truck-mounted Treadway Bridge

Description
The KMM (mechanised treadway bridge) consists of five 7 m spans, each of which is carried and launched from the rear of a modified ZIL-157 (6 × 6) 2500 kg truck. Four of these spans have integral-mounted adjustable trestles while the fifth (or far-shore) span does not as it is the link between the fourth span and the far bank.

Each trestle has a pair of octagonal shoes with a tip that protrudes about 0.6 m below the shoe. When buried in the soil the tip provides additional stabilising

strength to the bridge support. When travelling the trestle shoes are detached from the trestle columns.

The system works as follows: before launching the treadway, the trestle legs must be adjusted to the correct height, so the treadway is level when the bridge has been positioned, and the treadway is spread to the full roadway width of 2.95 m. Each clear span can bridge a gap of 6 m and a set of five spans can bridge 34 m. Bridge capacity is reported to be 12 000 kg. The truck then backs up to the river, and the span is raised hydraulically to the vertical with the launching girder. Once in this position, the launching girder serves as a brace for the cables which support the downward movement of the span. Once the launch has been

completed, the launching girder is lowered back to the travel position. The procedure is repeated with more spans until the far bank has been reached. The launched spans can be recovered from either end with recovery taking about the same time as launching.

A single KMM can span a gap of up to 9.5 m and can be launched in about 15 minutes. A complete five-span KMM bridge can span a gap of up to 34 m in 45-60 minutes in daylight, or 60-80 minutes at night. These times are for an average crew and can be halved by a well-trained crew. If required the KMM can also be laid under water to reduce the possibility of detection, which takes approximately 50 per cent longer than the normal method.

KMM truck-mounted treadway bridge on ZIL-157 (6 × 6) 2500 kg truck with TMM truck-mounted treadway bridge on KrAZ-255B (6 × 6) 7500 kg truck behind (Egyptian Ministry of Defence)

Specifications
Vehicle with bridge
Cab seating: 1 + 2
Configuration: 6 × 6
Weight: 8800 kg
Length: 8.3 m
Width: 3.15 m
Height: 3.36 m

Ground clearance: 0.31 m
Track:
  (front) 1.755 m
  (rear) 1.75 m
Wheelbase: 3.665 m + 1.12 m
Max speed: (road) 40 km/h
Range: 430 km
Fuel capacity: 215 l

Max gradient: 28%
Fording: 0.8 m
Engine: ZIL-157K 6-cylinder water-cooled petrol developing 109 hp at 2800 rpm
Transmission: manual with 5 forward and 1 reverse gears and 2-speed transfer box
Tyres: 12.00 × 18

Bridge
Weight: 1420 kg
Length: 7 m
Width:
  (without trestle leg) 2.95 m
  (with trestle leg) 3.95 m
Trestle leg height: 1-3 m (adjustable)
Capacity: 15 000 kg
Crossing speed:
  (tracked vehicles) 1 km/h
  (wheeled vehicles) 15-20 km/h
Minimum distance between crossing vehicles: 15 m

Status
Production complete; replaced in many front-line units by the TMM truck-mounted treadway bridge. In service with members of the former Warsaw Pact and other armed forces including China and Egypt.

Manufacturer
State factories.

CZECHOSLOVAKIA

MT-55A Armoured Bridgelayer

Development/Description
The MT-55A armoured bridgelayer was the replacement for the earlier MT-34 and was adopted by Czechoslovakia, the former Soviet Union and other countries. It is based on a T-55A tank chassis with the turret removed. The basic chassis is similar to that used for the T-54/T-55 ARVs and, as many vehicles are converted MBTs rather than 'new' vehicles, the reader is referred to this entry in the *Armoured recovery vehicles* section for a description.

There are two types of scissors bridge. The first model has circular holes in the sides of the bridge, similar to those on the bridge carried by the earlier MT-34 bridgelayer, while the more recent model has solid panels. It is possible to mistake the latter for the German BLG-60 armoured bridgelayer. The main distinguishing feature between the two is that the bridge surface of the MT-55A has a pattern whereas the BLG-60's is smooth with a plastic covering.

The bridge is launched over the front of the vehicle hydraulically by an electro-hydraulic control system. In an emergency the hydraulic system can be operated with the aid of three mechanical levers and, if the engine fails, the tank's batteries can provide sufficient power to launch the bridge.

The launching procedure is as follows: the MT-55A stops short of the gap and raises the bridge slightly from its horizontal travelling position, the launching girder foot is lowered to the ground and the span is raised to the vertical. The bridge is then unfolded and lowered across the gap. The bridge takes between 2-3 minutes to lay in position and 5-6 minutes to retrieve. The bridge itself weighs 6500 kg and when opened out is 18 m long, 3.34 m wide and 0.9 m high. It has a maximum clear span of 16 m and a maximum capacity of 50 000 kg.

Standard equipment on the MT-55A includes an NBC system, snorkel, inclinometer and other equipment for determining the width of the gap before the bridge is laid in position.

Specifications
Crew: 2

MT-55A armoured bridgelayer in travelling configuration

Weight: (with bridge) 36 000 kg
Length: (with bridge) 9.88 m
Width: (with bridge) 3.34 m
Height: (with bridge) 3.35 m
Ground clearance: 0.425 m
Track: 2.64 m
Track width: 580 mm
Length of track on ground: 3.84 m
Ground pressure: 0.81 kg/cm^2
Max speed:
  (road) 30-32 km/h
  (cross-country) 16-20 km/h
Range: 400 km
Fuel capacity: 960 l
Fording:
  (normal) 1.4 m
  (with preparation) 4 m
Gradient: 60%
Vertical obstacle: 0.8 m
Trench: 2.7 m
Engine: V-55, V-12, water-cooled diesel developing 580 hp at 2000 rpm

Transmission: manual with 5 forward and 1 reverse gears
Electrical system: 24 V
Batteries: 4, 280 Ah

Armour
glacis plate: 100 mm at 60°
upper hull side: 70 mm at 0°
hull rear: 60 mm
hull floor: 20 mm
hull roof: 30 mm

Status
Conversions from T-55 MBTs available. In service with the CIS, Czechoslovakia, India, Iraq, the former Yugoslavia and some countries in the Middle East.

Manufacturer
VOP 025 N.Jičín, sp, Dukelská 105, 742 42 Nový Jičín, Czechoslovakia.
Tel: 0656 22919. Telex: 52196.
Fax: 0656 22961.

AM-50A and AM-50B Truck-mounted Scissors Bridges

Description

In 1972 Czechoslovakia introduced a scissors bridge launched over the rear of a Tatra 813 (8 × 8) truck and known as the AM-50A (Automobilni Most 50A). It is launched in a similar fashion to the TMM treadway bridge but the Czechoslovak system has the added advantage that the trestle columns have hydraulic rather than manual adjustment. Another feature is that the bridge has a full width roadway rather than the two single tracks of the TMM system.

The AM-50B is an essentially similar bridge carried on the Tatra 815 (8 × 8) truck; this was introduced in 1989.

A single AM-50B bridge weighs 5700 kg and has a load capacity of 50 tonnes. Using a crew of two or three, each bridge can span a 12.5 m gap, with the width with the bridge rims unfolded being 4 m. As the bridge can be laid onto hydraulic trestle columns extra bridges can be added to span large gaps. For instance, up to eight AM-50B bridges can be used to cross a water obstacle 107 m wide and 6 m deep. The time to lay a single AM-50B bridge is up to 7 minutes and up to four can be laid in line in about 30 minutes. Each telescopic trestle leg can be varied in height from 2 to 6.05 m; each leg weighs 1750 kg.

Once the bridge is in position wheeled vehicles can cross at a speed of up to 40 km/h; the speed for tracked vehicles is 20 km/h.

Truck-mounted AM-50A scissors bridge on Tatra 813 (8 × 8) truck in Indian Army service

Specifications (AM-50B)
Crew: 2 or 3
Weight:
  (vehicle and bridge) 26 500 kg
  (bridge) 5700 kg
  (trestle leg) 1750 kg
Bridge capacity: 50 000 kg
Bridge span: 13.5 m
Bridge width: (rims unfolded) 4 m
Length of bridge travelling: 11.6 m
Width of bridge travelling: 3.15 m
Height of bridge travelling: 3.8 m
Length of trestle legs: 2 to 6.05 m
Time to lay one bridge: up to 7 min

Status
AM-50B in production. In service with the Czechoslovak Army and India.

Manufacturer
Czechoslovak state factories.

FRANCE

AMX-30 Armoured Bridgelayer

Development/Description
The prototype of the AMX-30 bridgelayer was built in 1966/67, but there were initial technical problems and CODER-Industries was formed to take over the manufacturing activities for the bridge.

This bridgelayer was produced only for Saudi Arabia.

The Class 50 bridge is composed of two hinged elements with removable widening panels and wheel guides. When opened out it is 22 m long and will span a gap of up to 20 m. The bridge is 3.1 m wide without the widening panels and 3.92 m wide with them. The bridge is launched hydraulically over the rear of the vehicle and takes about 5 minutes to lay into position. It can be recovered from either end. The bridge can be launched on relative slopes of 30 per cent with a relative slant reaching 15 per cent.

The basic chassis is almost identical to that of the standard AMX-30 MBT. The hull provides the crew with protection against small arms fire and artillery splinters, and is fitted with the same NBC system as the MBT.

The driver is seated at the front of the vehicle on the left side and is provided with a single-piece hatch cover and three periscopes for observation. One of these can be replaced by a night periscope of the infra-red or image intensification type. The commander and bridge operator are seated to the rear of the driver. The engine and transmission are at the rear of the tank and are separated from the crew compartment by a fireproof bulkhead.

The suspension is of the torsion bar type and consists of five road wheels with the drive sprocket at the rear and the idler at the front. There are five track support rollers which support the inside of the track only. The first two and last two road wheels are mounted on bogies and are provided with hydraulic shock absorbers.

AMX-30 bridgelayer with bridge folded for travelling (ECP Armées)

Specifications
Crew: 3
Weight:
  (with bridge) 42 500 kg
  (without bridge) 34 000 kg
Length:
  (with bridge) 11.4 m
  (hull only) 6.7 m
Width:
  (with bridge) 3.95 m
  (without bridge) 3.15 m
Height: (with bridge) 4.29 m
Ground clearance: 0.4 m
Track: 2.53 m
Track width: 570 mm
Length of track on ground: 4.12 m
Ground pressure: (with bridge) 0.93 kg/cm^2
Max road speed:
  (with bridge) 50 km/h
  (without bridge) 60 km/h
Range: 600 km
Fuel capacity: 1100 l
Fording: 1 m
Gradient: 50%
Side slope: 25%
Vertical obstacle: 0.93 m

Trench: 2.9 m
Engine: Hispano-Suiza HS-110, 12-cylinder, water-cooled, multi-fuel diesel developing 700 hp at 2400 rpm
Transmission: automatic with 5 forward gears; a reverse gear gives the same speeds in reverse
Electrical system: 28 V
Batteries: 8 × 12 V, 100 Ah in 2 groups of 4
Armament: nil

Status
Production complete. In service with Saudi Arabia.

Manufacturers
Bridge: CODER-Industries, BP 4, F-13367 Marseilles Cedex 11, France.
Chassis: Centre de Roanne.
Enquiries to Giat Industries, 13 route de la Minière, F-78034 Versailles Cedex, France.
Tel: (1) 30 97 37 37. Fax: (1) 30 97 39 00.

AMX-13 Armoured Bridgelayer

Description

The AMX-13 bridgelayer, or *Char Poseur de Pont AMX-13*, entered service with the French Army in the 1960s but was not produced in large numbers. The bridge was designed and built by Société Nouvelle de Gestion des Etablissements CODER.

The basic chassis is similar to that of other members of the AMX-13 light tank family. The driver is seated at the front on the left side and is provided with three periscopes for observation and a single-piece hatch cover. The engine is to the right of the driver. The other two crew members, the commander and the operator, are seated in the crew compartment to the rear of the driver's position. The suspension is of the torsion bar type and consists of five road wheels with the drive sprocket at the front and the idler at the rear. There are four track return rollers. Hydraulic shock absorbers are provided for the first and fifth road wheel stations.

The bridge is laid hydraulically over the rear of the vehicle and can be picked up again from either end. It is in two halves connected by a hinge. The bridge is 14.3 m long when unfolded and 7.15 m long folded. Overall width is 3.16 m, height unfolded 1.12 m and height folded 1.8 m. Weight is 4630 kg. The bridge is provided with widening panels and wheel guides. When the bridge has been laid in position, vehicles up to Class 25 can cross. Two bridges laid side by side will take vehicles up to Class 50.

Singapore Shipbuilding and Engineering Limited produces an armoured bridgelayer based on the AMX-13 and known as the Light Assault Bridge LAB 30. For details refer to the entry under Singapore in this section.

Specifications

Crew: 3
Weight:
  (with bridge) 19 200 kg
  (without bridge) 15 100 kg
  (bridge) 4630 kg
Length:
  (with bridge) 8.02 m
  (without bridge) 6.44 m
  (hull) 4.88 m
Width:
  (with bridge) 3.16 m
  (without bridge) 2.51 m
Height:
  (with bridge) 4.05 m
  (without bridge) 2.72 m
Ground clearance:
  (with bridge) front 0.43 m; rear 0.36 m
  (without bridge) 0.48 m
Track: 2.16 m
Track width: 350 mm

Length of track on ground: 2.8 m
Ground pressure:
  (with bridge) 0.905 kg/cm^2
  (without bridge) 0.755 kg/cm^2
Max road speed:
  (with bridge) 40 km/h
  (without bridge) 60 km/h
Range: (road) 350 km
Fuel capacity: 480 l
Fording: 1 m
Gradient:
  (with bridge) 30%
  (without bridge) 60%
Side slope:
  (with bridge) 20%
  (without bridge) 50%
Vertical obstacle:
  (forward) 0.65 m
  (reverse) 0.45 m
Trench:
  (with bridge) 1.3 m
  (without bridge) 1.6 m
Engine: SOFAM Model 8 GXb 8-cylinder water-cooled petrol developing 250 hp at 3200 rpm
Transmission: manual with 5 forward and 1 reverse gears (2nd, 3rd, 4th and 5th gears synchromesh)
Electrical system: 24 V
Batteries: 4 × 12 V, 95 Ah
Armament: nil
Armour
crew compartment front: 30 mm
crew compartment sides and rear: 20 mm
crew compartment roof: 10 mm
hull rear: 15 mm
hull glacis: 15 mm
floor forward: 20 mm
floor rear: 10 mm

Status

Production complete. In service with Argentina, France and Indonesia.

Manufacturer

Creusot-Loire Industrie, Division Mécanique Spécialisée, Immeuble Ile de France, Cedex 33, F-92070 Paris La Défense, France.
Tel: (1) 49 00 60 50. Telex: MOTOY 615 638 F.
Fax: (1) 49 00 58 99.

AMX-13 bridgelayer opening out bridge. Note stabilisers at rear of hull (ECP Armées)

Assault Treadway Bridge MLC 65

Description

The Assault Treadway Bridge (*Travure Courte Portée – TCP*) was developed by CNIM under contract to the Direction Technique des Armements Terrestres to support crossings of 12 m gaps (that is, 80 per cent of gaps in the European theatre) by armoured units. A feature of this bridge is that it does not require a dedicated armoured vehicle for launching. The first prototype was shown in June 1990.

The bridge is of the scissors type with a military load classification (MLC) of 65. It is transported on a single-axle trailer towed by a light truck. The bridge is towed to near the launching site and, after unfolding and arranging the trackways, is lifted from the trailer by an armoured vehicle equipped with a dozer blade, a winch and a crane jib. The French Army intends to use the AMX-30 combat engineer vehicle (EBG) for the launching role but other suitably equipped armoured vehicles weighing around 40 tonnes can be used. An accessory kit is used to adapt the launching vehicle. Once lifted from the trailer the bridge is carried to the launch point and the entire launching operation is carried out with the vehicle crew under their armoured cover. During the launch operation the crane jib and winch are used to lift the folded bridge to an upright position, after which the bridge opens and is deployed without any external power.

The time taken to prepare and take the bridge from its trailer is about 10 minutes while the actual launch operation takes approximately 3 minutes.

Specifications

Bridge
Weight: 4800 kg
Length:
  (folded) 8 m
  (unfolded) 14 m
Width:
  (folded) 2.14 m
  (roadway) 4 m
Height: (folded) 2.9 m

Trailer, loaded
Weight: 6000 kg

Assault Treadway Bridge being carried towards its launch point by an AMX-30 combat engineer vehicle (EBG)

Length: 9.45 m
Width: 2.5 m
Height: 3.7 m

Status
Prototype.

Manufacturer
Constructions Industrielles de la Méditerrannée (CNIM), Zone Industrielle de Brégaillon, BP 208, F-83507 La-Seyne-sur-Mer Cedex, France.
Enquiries to CNIM Head Office, 35 rue de Bassano, F-75008 Paris, France.
Tel: (1) 47 23 55 24. Telex: 642 869 f.
Fax: (1) 47 23 49 23.

PAA Self-propelled Bridge System

Development
The PAA (*Pont Automoteur d'Accompagnement*) was developed as a bridging system to support assault units, pending the arrival of engineer units with permanent bridges.

Development can be traced back to the late 1950s when the German company Eisenwerke, under contract to the Service du Matériel du Genie, built three prototype vehicles. Between 1963 and 1968 the Direction des Constructions et Armes Navales (DCAN) at Lorient and the Etablissement d'Expériences Techniques d'Angers completely redesigned the vehicle. Two prototypes were built, the first of which was completed in 1968 and the second in 1970. After extensive trials, the PAA was adopted by the French Army in 1972 and production began at Lorient in 1973. First production vehicles were delivered to the French Army in 1974, and by early 1978, 51 had been delivered. Production was completed the same year.

Description
The PAA consists of a rigid and watertight hull of light alloy (AZ5G) construction with a removable span in two sections on the front and an access ramp at the rear. The hull is divided into three compartments, front, centre and rear. The front section is the crew compartment with the driver seated on the left and the operator on the right. This compartment is provided with an NBC and air-conditioning system. The engine compartment is in the centre and is provided with an electric pump which automatically operates as soon as water reaches a certain level. The rear compartment contains the fuel tanks.

Power is transmitted by the engine to the four road wheels through a Guinard-Clark hydrokinetic torque converter, a power-assisted Clark-Genemat gearbox and a sliding joint transmission shaft. Steering is power-assisted.

The hydraulic system operates the following: retraction and extension, and locking and unlocking of the forward and rear sets of wheels, tilting of the prismatic boom supporting the span, opening and closing of the two access ramp hinged links, locking and unlocking of the span on the prismatic boom, and the hoisting and lowering of the span.

The PAA can be used in two basic roles: first by laying its bridge and then leaving the bridge in place, and second by laying the span and remaining in position, with the vehicle acting as the ramp of the bridge.

When deployed, the four wheels of the PAA are raised off the ground and the hull is supported on shoes. The bridge and ramp have a normal width of 3.05 m but this can be increased to 3.55 m with widening panels. These are normally carried in a Berliet GBC 8 KT (6 × 6) truck which also carries the wheel guide sections, hand-rope posts and ropes. The widening panels can be left on the vehicle for travelling, but are normally removed to reduce the overall width of the vehicle.

The removable span has a total length of 21.72 m and consists of two symmetrical sections coupled by a hinge. The access ramp also consists of two symmetrical hinge-coupled sections which permit the access ramp to be folded on the body of the bridge when not in use. The prismatic boom is hinged at the front part of the body by a rugged hinge, and houses the hydraulically operated hoisting, gripping and locking devices.

With the vehicle remaining in position the PAA can be used to span a gap, with soft banks, up to 17.4 m wide, or a gap of up to 22.4 m with hard banks. The bridge itself can span a gap, with soft banks, of up to 15.63 m, or, with hard banks, up to 20.63 m. This bridge can be used by vehicles up to Class 40 or, with precautions, Class 45. By using two PAA vehicles and a special jointing section, it is possible to bridge a gap of up to 40 m. A triangular support boom has also been developed which has an adjustable leg and is used to span 40 m gaps.

Specifications
Weight:
(loaded) 34 500 kg
(without span but including 18 widening panels) 25 620 kg
Length:
(travelling) 13.15 m
(bridge unfolded) 38.25 m
Width:
(without widening panels) 3.05 m
(with widening panels) 3.55 m
Height: 3.99 m
Max speed: (road) 60 km/h
Range: (road) 800 km
Fording: 1.5 m
Gradient: 50%
Side slope: 20%
Turning radius: 20.5 m
Engine: Deutz V-12 diesel developing 300 hp
Brakes: air/oil, 2 independent front and rear systems, disc brakes on all axles
Electrical system: 24 V
Batteries: 4

Status
Production complete. In service with the French Army.

Manufacturer
DCAN Lorient. Enquiries to Direction Techniques des Constructions Navales, 2 rue Royale, BP 1, F-75200 Paris Naval, France.
Tel: (1) 260 33 30. Telex: 650 421.

PAA bridge in travelling configuration (P Touzin)

AMX-30 MBT crossing PAA bridge

Gillois Series 2 Ferry System

Development
The Gillois Series 2 is a development of the Gillois Bridge and Ferry System, details of which can be found in this section under International. The Gillois Series 2 is intended primarily as a ferry system and differs from the original version mainly in having an increased load capacity (to 45 000 kg) and in being fully powered in all aspects so that preparation time for use is reduced to 5 minutes. The French Army ordered 60 units.

Description
The layout and general description of the Gillois Series 2 is similar to that of the ramp unit of the original Gillois system. When travelling the vehicle has a front-mounted cab for the crew of four. The main hull is steel but the top-mounted ramp and the side walls are aluminium. All the preparation stages are powered, including raising the side walls for inflation of the main flotation cells. Raising and lowering the ramp is also powered. For use the ramp may be placed at an angle of up to 26.5° above the horizontal or 15° below. This enables the ramp to be used at a height of 3.4 m above the horizontal or 2 m below. The ramp and main ferry vehicle have a load capacity of up to 45 000 kg and as the 50 m² loading area has a width of 3.3 m it can carry French Army armoured vehicles such as the AMX-30 MBT or the 155 mm GCT self-propelled gun. In the water the Gillois Series 2 is propelled by a propeller that can be swivelled through 360° for manoeuvring.

Although the Gillois Series 2 has a normal crew of

four, only two are needed to operate the system.

Specifications
Crew: 4
Configuration: 4 × 4
Weight:
  (total) approx 28 300 kg
  (front axle) approx 13 600 kg
  (rear axle) approx 14 700 kg
Length:
  (travelling) 11.28 m
  (floating, ramp extended) 19.6 m
  (ramp section) 7.753 m
Width:
  (travelling) 3.7 m
  (floating) 6.94 m
  (load area) 3.3 m
Height: 3.59 m
Loading area: 50 m²
Wheelbase: 6.2 m
Track:
  (front) 1.79 m
  (rear) 2 m
Max speed:
  (road) 60 km/h
  (water, empty) approx 12 km/h
  (water, loaded) approx 11 km/h
Range:
  (road) approx 800 km
  (water) approx 12 h
Gradient: 50%
Engine: Deutz air-cooled diesel developing 250 hp at

Gillois Series 2 ferry unit

2100 rpm
Tyres: 21 × 25 tubeless

Status
In production. Ordered for the French Army (60).

Manufacturer
Chaudronnerie et Forges d'Alsace (CEFA), BP 11, Route de Woerth, F-67250 Soultz-sous-Forêts, France. Tel: 88 80 49 47. Telex: 870 030 f. Fax: 88 80 50 05.

Engin de Franchissement de l'Avant (EFA)

Development
The *Engin de Franchissement de l'Avant* (EFA) was originally known as the *Matériel Amphibie de Franchissement* (MAF) which was under competitive development as the replacement for the Gillois system currently used by the French Army. The Etablissement Technique d'Angers was in charge of the study and evaluation of two prototypes and overall project management was under the Direction Technique des Armements Terrestres. Two prototypes were built and evaluated, the petrol-engined MAF 1 is under direction of the Lorient Board for the Construction of Naval Weapons (Direction des Constructions et Armes Navales de Lorient) and the MAF 2 under the direction of the Alsace Metals and Steel Company (Chaudronnerie et Forges d'Alsace) and Eisenwerke Kaiser-

slautern Göppner of Germany.

The French Army decided to provide funds for further testing of the MAF 2 after the first prototype had been completed. These trials were completed in 1987 and the French Army ordered 80 units to replace the Gillois bridge and ferry system (see entry under International in this section).

Description
The hull of the EFA is made of welded light alloy. On the top of the vehicle, at each end, is a 12 m jointed ramp also of welded light alloy. Before the unit enters the water, airbags are positioned under hinged flaps on either side of the hull and inflated. The unit has four large wheels with low-pressure tyres and is driven in the water by two pump-jets, one each end of the hull, which can be rotated through 360°.

The EFA can be used both as a bridge and a ferry. As a bridge it has a 23.5 m span, can take loads of up to MLC 70, and be used in rivers flowing at up to 3 m/s.

As a ferry the EFA can carry loads of up to 95 000 kg provided the load is distributed over the loading surface.

Specifications
Crew: 4
Weight:
  (total) 41 000 kg
  (front axle loading) approx 20 500 kg
  (rear axle loading) approx 20 500 kg
Length:
  (travelling) 12.35 m
  (as bridge) 23.54 m
  (as ferry) 34.8 m
Width:
  (travelling) 3.6 m
  (airbags in position) 6.814 m
Height: (travelling) 3.9 m
Track: 2.17 m
Wheelbase: 6.6 m
Max speed:
  (road) 70 km/h
  (water, loaded) 12 km/h
  (water, empty) 14 km/h
Range:
  (road) approx 700 km
  (in water) approx 12 h
Fording: (without preparation) 0.8 m
Gradient: 50%
Side slope: 30%
Engine: Badouin 12 F 120 SR water-cooled diesel developing 750 hp at 2700 rpm
Suspension: hydropneumatic with level correction
Tyres: 26.5 × 25 XL
Electrical system: 24 V

Status
Ordered for the French Army (80). First deliveries during 1992.

Manufacturer
Chaudronnerie et Forges d'Alsace (CEFA), BP 11, Route de Woerth, F-67250 Soultz-sous-Forêts, France. Tel: 88 80 49 47. Telex: 870 030 f. Fax: 88 80 50 05.

Engin de Franchissement de l'Avant (EFA)

GERMANY

BLG-60, BLG-67 and BLG-67M2 Armoured Bridgelayers

Development/Description
The BLG-60 was a joint development between what was then East Germany and Poland and is used by their armies in place of the Czechoslovak MT-55 scissors bridgelayer. The bridge is launched in a similar fashion to the MT-55 and the reader is referred to this entry for the method of launching the bridge.

In position the bridge has a total length of 21.6 m, a width of 3.2 m and a height of 0.8 m. It can span a maximum gap of 20 m compared with the maximum span of 16 m of the MT-55, and has a maximum capacity of 50 000 kg.

The main external differences between the MT-55 and the BLG-60 are that the surface of the BLG-60's bridge is smooth and covered in plastic (the MT-55 has a patterned surface), the bridge girder ends are closed (on the MT-55 they are open), and the pulley wheels for the scissors action operating gears are solid. The BLG-60 is provided with an NBC system and a snorkel.

Reference has been found to a BLG-67 bridgelayer and it is assumed that this is an improved version of the basic BLG-60. The BLG-67M2 is a special variant designed to lay two- and three-span bridges. All its main assemblies (chassis, track bridge, span-laying gear, span fastening system, hydraulics, electrical control system, and so on) have been modified. The base of the extendable arm of the span-laying gear has been lengthened and the surface on which this arm rests is lined with rubber. The edges of the roadway have been widened to provide a width of 3.47 m. Anchorages are provided on the left- and right-hand side of the base span while the bridge is being laid.

When two- or three-span bridges are laid in water with a current speed above 0.2 m/s, a bridge anchorage system is employed. This uses a tie, reel and hoist with the reel holding 40 m of steel cable. One end of the cable is attached to the front of a bridge while the other is passed through the hoist affixed to a tie driven into the ground. The hoist draws and grips the cable with two pairs of jaws operated by a hand lever. Each BLG-67M2 carries two anti-current anchors.

Multi-span bridges are formed by laying the first span with one end on a bank and the other at the bottom of the gap to be bridged. A second span is then laid from the first and if necessary, a third span is then

BLG-60 armoured bridgelayer on GSP heavy amphibious ferry

emplaced to either extend the span or to accommodate a difference in height on the far bank. The span support points should be situated not more than 2.5 m from the span ends on which the next span rests. Once emplaced the spans are connected and anchored by three grab links, two further links, a block and the hoist and line from the anti-current anchor system. A suitable track bridge or pontoons can be used as intermediate supports.

Multi-span bridges have to be monitored for alignment after 10 vehicles have crossed (two spans) or in the case of three spans, every three vehicles. Vehicles have to cross the multi-span bridges in low gear at a constant speed.

A special training version of the BLG-67M2 was introduced for trainee drivers. The vehicle is used for training in laying bridges, vehicle maintenance and repair.

Specifications (BLG-60)
Crew: 2-3
Weight:
(with bridge) 37 000 kg
(without bridge) 31 000 kg
Length: (with bridge) 10.57 m
Width: (with bridge) 3.48 m
Height: (with bridge) 3.4 m
Ground clearance: 0.425 m
Track: 2.64 m
Track width: 580 mm
Length of track on ground: 3.84 m

Ground pressure: 0.83 kg/cm²
Max speed: (road) 50 km/h
Range: 500 km
Fuel capacity: 960 l
Fording: 1.4 m
Gradient: 58%
Vertical obstacle: 0.8 m
Trench: 2.7 m
Engine: V-55, V-12, water-cooled diesel developing 580 hp at 2000 rpm
Transmission: manual with 5 forward and 1 reverse gears
Electrical system: 24 V
Batteries: 4, 280 Ah
Armament: nil

Armour
glacis plate: 100 mm at 60°
upper hull side: 70 mm at 0°
hull rear: 60 mm
hull floor: 20 mm
hull roof: 30 mm

Status
Production complete. In service with the German, Indian, Iraqi (at least 24 BLG-60s) and Polish armies. Bulgaria uses the BLG-67.

Manufacturers
Chassis: Polish state factories.
Bridge and conversion work: Germany.

Krupp-MAN Leguan Bridgelayer

Development
The mobile bridgelayer known as the Leguan was originally known as the Iguana but development and the adoption of the MAN-ÖAF 36.365 VFA 8 × 8 truck as the launch vehicle led to a change of designation. The bridge employed is a 26 m bridge with a bridging classification of Class 60. This bridge has an effective span of 25 m and Krupp-MAN states that it is able to span over 85 per cent of all natural obstacles likely to be encountered.

During early 1987 it was announced that MAN GHH had been awarded a contract by the Norwegian Ministry of Defence for the supply of 14 Leguan bridgelayers plus 14 additional bridges, with an option for another 12 of each. The total contract value amounted to more than DM 100 million.

Description
The carrying vehicle is a modified MAN-ÖAF 36.365 VFA 8 × 8 truck with a low-slung forward control cab (other vehicles can be used), with a good cross-country performance and a reinforced chassis, on which a frame is supported which can be shifted along its length and which carries the entire bridgelaying equipment. The bridge consists of four interchangeable wheel tread girders 13 m long, 2 m wide and weighing 2500 kg each. Bolt connections join the bridge girders and when travelling the bridge halves lie one on top of the other. The laying equipment consists

Krupp-MAN Leguan bridgelayer in travelling configuration

of the laying arm at the rear end of the shifting frame, which moves the bridge longitudinally by means of a roller guide, and a geared drive. The top bridge half is taken up by an arm at the front end and is supported by

an auxiliary arm at the rear. The bridge can be laid with a traverse and longitudinal inclination of up to 10 per cent. Laying is carried out automatically with the two-man crew monitoring the sequence.

The laying sequence commences with the vehicle reversing to the bank until the end of the shifting frame is approximately 7.5 m from the edge. After raising the top bridge half, which is suspended at the front in the slewing supporting arm, and with the roller at its rear end resting on the top chord of the lower wheel tread girder, the lower bridge half is advanced and then lowered by 10 per cent. It is held at the front by the slewing supporting arm and at the rear by the coupling support arm. The bridge halves are then coupled automatically by lowering the coupling supporting arm. The bridge is then pushed back until its centre of gravity is over the two rear axles of the carrying vehicle, where it is held until the shifting frame has been moved under the bridge and the hydraulic supports have been lowered. The next stage is for the bridge to be fully advanced when it is clamped in the laying arm by the roller carriage. At this stage the ramp tip is placed on the far bank. This removes the load from the rollers and the laying arm can be removed to lower the bridge. For the final stage the supports are retracted and the shifting frame is moved back. The bridge is then ready for use. The entire laying process takes approximately 8 minutes. Reloading the bridge is carried out in the reverse order and can be carried out from either bank.

The bridge is constructed of standard commercial aluminium alloy, grade Al Zn 4.5 Mg 1 and has a flat ramp design. The estimated bridge life is 10 000 Class 60 crossings. Preparation of crossings is not normally necessary.

Variants

The Leguan bridgelayer can be used to create ferries. For details refer to entry in the *Tactical floating bridges and ferries* section.

An Improved Leguan Bridgelayer system capable of laying bridges up to 42 m long has been developed.

For details see following entry.

Leguan bridges have been adapted to be carried and launched by M47/M48 MBT chassis. For details see separate entry in this section.

In association with General Dynamics of the United States a MAN Leguan bridge was entered for the US Army Heavy Assault Bridge (HAB) programme. For details see under United States in this section.

Specifications

Crew: 2
Weight:
(vehicle) 25 000 kg
(bridge) approx 10 000 kg
(total) approx 36 000 kg
Length:
(overall, with bridge) 13.4 m
Width:
(overall, with bridge) 4.01 m
(without bridge) 3.1 m
Height:
(overall with bridge) 3.922 m
(overall without bridge) 2.73 m
(top of cab) 2.1 m
Ground clearance: 0.4 m
Wheelbase: 1.5 m + 3.225 m + 1.45 m
Angle of approach/departure: 20°/25°
Max road speed: 73 km/h
Range: 600-700 km
Fuel capacity: 400 l
Max gradient: 100%
Engine: MAN D 2840 water-cooled diesel developing 350 hp at 2300 rpm
Transmission: manual, converter-and-clutch unit Type 400 + 4S
Transfer box: 2-speed G 0801
Steering: ball and nut, ZF Model 8046
Turning circle: 33 m

Suspension:
(front) semi-elliptical leaf springs with progressively acting hollow rubber springs and stabilisers
(rear) semi-elliptical springs with stabilisers
Brakes:
(main) dual circuit air
(parking) mechanical on rear wheels
(engine) pneumatically actuated on exhaust
Tyres: 16.00 × 20
Electrical system: 24 V
Batteries: 2 × 12 V, 173 Ah each

Bridge
Classification: Class 60/70
Weight: approx 10 000 kg
Length: 26 m
Width:
(bridge) 4.02 m
(wheel tread girder) 1.555 m
Height:
(bridge centre) 1.1 m
(ramp tip) 0.075 m

Status

In production. In service with Norway.

Manufacturers

Krupp Industrietechnik GmbH, Sub-Division Structural Engineering, Postfach 141960, Franz-Schubert-Strasse 1-3, D-4100 Duisburg 14, Federal Republic of Germany.
Tel: 021 35 781. Telex: 0855486.
MAN GHH, PO Box 1253, D-6095 Ginsheim-Gustavsburg 1, Federal Republic of Germany.
Tel: 061 34 55-1. Telex: 4182 058 man d.
Fax: 06134 55-202.

Krupp-MAN Improved Leguan 42 m Bridgelayer

Description

The Improved Leguan 42 m Bridgelayer can be used to lay bridges up to 42 m long and closes the gap between the short Leguan bridges up to 26 m long and floating bridges which are normally used above a length of approximately 40 m.

The Improved Leguan system is based on the standard Leguan all-terrain 8 × 8 wheeled carrier and launch vehicle (see previous entry) which is modified so that it can lay a 42 m bridge as well as the original 26 m version. With the Improved Leguan system the following bridge lengths can be built:

26 m; 2 ramps
34 m; 2 ramps, 1 centre section
42 m; 2 ramps, 2 centre sections.

The bridge is designed for a normal loading of MLC 70 tracked vehicles and MLC 96 wheeled vehicles 'with caution'.

With the basic Improved Leguan 42 m bridge set the Leguan vehicle (the prototype uses a MAN-OÄF 42.365 8 × 8 with a 365 hp engine) carries two 13 m ramp sections ready to be launched as a normal 26 m Leguan bridge if required (for details see previous entry). Carried on a separate all-terrain support vehicle are two extra centre sections, each 8 m long. The support vehicle (typically a MAN-OÄF 34.370 8 × 8) carries handling equipment to allow the centre sections to be inserted between the two ramp halves to form a 34 or 42 m bridge as required.

Once the launch vehicle has arrived at the launch site it is aligned and a shifting frame is extended towards the gap to be crossed. Supporting arms are extended and the two ramp halves are separated. An extra bridge section, or sections, can then be inserted and connected between the ramp halves by the support vehicle using its crane-type handling equipment. A launching girder is then extended over the gap and once the bridge has come to rest on the far bank the bridge is lowered. The launch vehicle

separates from the bridge and the bridge is ready for use.

The advantages of this laying method are that the bridge sections remain coupled to the launch girder and that the bridge sections are connected to each other at exactly defined positions on the launch vehicle. Thus, using the handling equipment, the centre sections need only be roughly aligned on the launch vehicle. Guides on the vehicle allow the bridge sections to be aligned exactly so that they can be coupled. All coupling procedures are fully automatic and require no manual intervention. Laying and loading the bridge are controlled step-by-step by an electronic control system that eliminates operating errors and allows the bridge to be laid at night.

The laying operation for a 42 m bridge requires a space measuring approximately 25 × 10 m and involves only four men (the crews of the laying and support vehicles). The laying time for a 42 m bridge is approximately 25 minutes.

Leguan 42 m bridge in fully extended form

Leguan 42 m bridge launch vehicle carrying ramp sections

Leguan 42 m bridge carrier carrying two centre sections

Specifications

Weight:
(laying vehicle with laying equipment) 26 t
(2 ramp sections) 13 t
(total) 42 t
Length: (laying vehicle with bridge, overall) 15.226 m
Width:
(with bridge) 4.02 m
(without bridge) 3.15 m
Height: (overall) 4 m

Bridge lengths: 26, 34 or 42 m
Bridge width: 4.01 m
Bridge height: 1.185 m
Weight:
(ramp section, complete) 6900 kg
(centre section, complete) 6500 kg

Status

Prototype completed.

Manufacturers

Krupp Industrietechnik GmbH, Sub-Division Structural Engineering, Postfach 141960, Franz-Schubert-Strasse 1-3, D-4100 Duisburg 14, Federal Republic of Germany.
Tel: 021 35 781. Telex: 0855486.
MAN GHH, PO Box 1253, D-6095 Ginsheim-Gustavsburg 1, Federal Republic of Germany.
Tel: 061 34 55-1. Telex: 4182 058 man d.
Fax: 06134 55-202.

MAN M47/M48 Leguan Armoured Bridgelayer

Description

The MAN M47/M48 Leguan armoured bridgelayer is an adaptation of a M47 or M48 MBT chassis to carry and launch the standard MLC 70 26 m Leguan bridge (see entry in this section). One trial M47 conversion for tests has been successfully conducted in Spain in co-operation with Peugeot Talbot España SA. It is based on an M47 chassis and known as the VLPD-26/70 E 'Lanzador'. The conversion can be carried out on MBTs such as the Centurion, Leopard 1/2, M1, and so on.

The M47/M48 Leguan conversion utilises as many standard Leguan components as possible but the overall bridge launch position is forward instead of to the rear as it is on the wheeled Leguan vehicle. This entails displacing the normal launch components through 180° but the basic Leguan launch procedures are maintained.

The bridgelaying M47/M48 tank chassis has to undergo some modifications in addition to the removal of the turret. The laying components include a traversing laying arm on the hull roof, roller carriages, a bridge advance unit, auxiliary arms and a hydraulic cylinder supported by the hull. A rear arm is used for coupling the bridge halves and there are hydraulic and electrical switching and control components inside the hull.

Modification to the tank hull includes removing the top frontal armour plate and front roof plate together with the turret ring. New armour and roof plates with hatches are welded into place and extra plates are added along the side walls and engine cover. A new forward support blade, described as an outrigger system, is added to the front hull. Once lowered, by two hydraulic cylinders, the support blade levels the laying vehicle on adverse slopes and provides support during the bridge laying operations.

The Leguan laying arm rests in a bearing welded to the hull roof with its traversing cylinder pivoting on girders welded inside the hull. A line and cable bushing close to the bearing provides protection for the electrical cables and hydraulic lines connecting the control unit inside the hull and the switches and actuators in the laying arm. Extra welded stiffening webs transmit loads from the bearing to the rear roof plate and the area around the traversing cylinder is kept watertight by a plastic cover.

A rear arm assembly is secured to base plates welded to the top rear corners of the side walls. The laying arm is supported by the hull roof and controlled by a hydraulic cylinder inside the hull. The laying arm accommodates the roller carriages for the bridge as well as the bridge advance unit as well as auxiliary arms for use during the coupling of the bridge halves. A two-element outrigger arm is provided at the hull rear to assist the coupling of the bridge sections; this arm can be lowered to a travelling position when a bridge is not being carried. The rear arm base also supports the bridge.

On arrival at a bridge launch site the bridgelayer is driven to the point to be bridged and the support blade is lowered and extended to ensure the bridge is in a horizontal position. Forward slopes up to 20 per cent up and down can be accommodated, as can transverse slopes of up to 10 per cent – the maximum downwards laying step is 0.8 m.

To commence the laying operation the rear end outrigger arm is swung vertically to lift the bridge upper section. The bridge advance unit moves the lower bridge section forward towards the coupling position as the auxiliary arms move upwards to lift the upper section. At that point the rear end outrigger arm is lowered and the laying arm swings the front section ready for coupling. Claw couplings then slide into each other and the rear end outrigger is disengaged. The laying arm swings upwards and coupling is complete. The bridge advance unit can then move the complete bridge forward into position. Once fully extended the laying arm lowers first the far end and then the near end, ready for the support blade to be raised and the laying arm disengaged from the bridge. The bridgelayer can then withdraw. Only two men, the driver and commander, are involved in the laying operation which takes between 3.5 and 4 minutes.

Specifications (VLPD-26/70 E 'Lanzador')

Crew: 2
Weight: (with bridge) 50 370 kg
(without bridge) 43 000 kg
(bridge) 10 000 kg
Ground pressure:
(with bridge) 1.15 kg/cm^2
(without bridge) 0.93 kg/cm^2
Length: (with bridge) 13.5 m
(without bridge) 11.73 m
Width: (with bridge) 4.1 m
(without bridge) 3.56 m
Height: (with bridge) 3.9 m
(without bridge) 2.81 m
Ground clearance: 0.47 m
Angle of approach/departure:
(with bridge) 24°/30°
(without bridge) 26°/30°
Max speed: (with bridge) 50 km/h
Range: 600 km
Gradient: (with bridge) 45%
Side slope: 30%
Vertical obstacle: 0.48 m
Trench: 2.45 m
Engine: Teledyne Continental AVDS-1790-2D turbocharged diesel developing 760 hp at 2400 rpm
Transmission: GMC-Allison CD-850-6A

MAN M47 Leguan armoured bridgelayer

MAN M47 Leguan armoured bridgelayer

Bridge weight: 10 000 kg
Load classification: MLC 70
Bridge length:
(extended) 26 m
(folded) 13.5 m
Gap spanned: 24 m
Bridge width: 4.01 m
Roadway width: (each) 1.555 m
Bridge height: (max) 0.9 m

Status
Prototype conversion and tests successfully completed in Spain.

Manufacturers
MAN GHH, PO Box 1253, D-6095 Ginsheim-Gustavsburg 1, Federal Republic of Germany. Tel: 061 34 55-1. Telex: 4182 058 man d. Fax: 06134 55-202.

Peugeot Talbot España SA, Productos Especiales, Departmento Ventas/Marketing, Apartado no 140, Madrid, Spain.
Tel: 347 23 70. Telex: 27590.
Fax: 347 22 43.

Brückenlegepanzer Biber Armoured Bridgelayer

Development

Development of an armoured bridgelayer based on the Leopard 1 MBT commenced during 1965. In 1969 prototypes of two different types of bridgelayer based on the chassis of the Leopard 1 MBT were built, known as Type A and Type B. The Type A had a telescopic boom which was extended to the far bank; the bridge was then slid across and the telescopic boom removed. The Type B was of the cantilever type. The bridge was designed by Klöckner-Humboldt-Deutz, with Porsche in charge of overall development. After comparative trials, the Type B was selected for production by MaK of Kiel and the first production bridgelayers, known as the Biber, were completed in 1975. The official German Army designation is *Brückenlegepanzer Biber* or BRP-1.

Description

The hull of the Biber (Beaver) is almost identical to that of the Leopard 1 MBT with the driver seated at the front of the hull on the right side and the commander in the centre, and the engine and transmission at the rear. The torsion bar suspension consists of seven road wheels with the drive sprocket at the rear and the idler at the front. There are four track return rollers. The first, second, third, sixth and seventh road wheel stations are provided with a hydraulic shock absorber. The tracks are of the double-pin type and have rubber pads. Standard equipment includes an NBC system.

The bridge is of aluminium construction and has a total span of 22 m, which allows a gap of up to 20 m to be breached. The main advantage of the Biber is that its bridge is extended horizontally rather than vertically as with the majority of bridgelayers. When travelling the bridge is carried in two 11 m halves, one above the other. The bridge may be taken up from either end and, according to MaK, allows some 60 per cent of all watercourses and most of the soil cuttings in Germany to be crossed.

The bridge was designed to take AFVs and other vehicles up to MLC 60. The bridge can be laid on longitudinal and lateral slopes of 10 per cent; the opposite bank can be 2 m higher or lower, or have a difference in inclination of 10 per cent towards the bank on the laying vehicle's side.

When the Biber arrives at a gap or river, the vehicle first lowers the support blade (which can also be used for dozing operations such as preparing a river bank) at the front of the hull. The lower half of the bridge slides forward until its end is lined up with the end of the upper half and the two sections are then locked together and extended over the gap. The bridge is lowered into position and the cantilever arm withdrawn.

Biber armoured bridgelayer in the process of laying a bridge

The Biber then raises the support blade and pulls away. The bridge can be retrieved from either end by performing the laying operations in the reverse order. Power for the bridgelaying operation comes from a central hydraulic system consisting of hydraulic pumps, an oil tank, valve blocks, control valves, and hydraulic cylinders. All operations are controlled by electrical non-contact limit switches, using a sequence control system.

Specifications
Crew: 2
Weight:
(with bridge) 45 300 kg
(without bridge) 35 100 kg
Length:
(with bridge) 11.82 m
(without bridge) 10.56 m
Width:
(with bridge) 4 m
(without bridge) 3.25 m
Height:
(with bridge) 3.55 m
(without bridge) 2.56 m
Ground clearance: 0.42 m
Track: 2.7 m
Track width: 550 mm
Length of track on ground: 4.236 m
Ground pressure: 0.97 kg/cm^2
Max speed: (road) 62 km/h
Range:
(road) approx 450 km
(cross-country) 300 km
Fuel capacity: 995 l
Fording:
(without preparation) 1.2 m
(with preparation) 1.65 m
Gradient: 60%
Side slope: 30%
Vertical obstacle: 0.7 m

Trench: 2.5 m
Engine: MTU MB 838 Ca M-500 10-cylinder multi-fuel developing 830 hp at 2300 rpm
Transmission: ZF HP 250 with 4 forward and 2 reverse gears
Electrical system: 24 V
Batteries: 6, 300 Ah, charged by 3-phase generator driven from main engine
Armament: 8 smoke dischargers

Armour
nose: 70 mm at 55°
glacis: 70 mm at 60°
glacis top: 25 mm at 83°
sides upper: 35 mm at 50°
sides lower: 25 mm at 90°
hull rear: 25 mm at 88°
hull roof: 10 mm
hull floor: 15 mm

Bridge
Weight: 9940 kg
Length:
(total) 22 m
(effective) 20 m
Width: 4 m
Width of one track: 1.55 m
Classification: MLC 50

Status
Production complete. In service with Australia (5), Canada (6), Germany (105) and the Netherlands (25). Production in Italy by OTO Melara for the Italian Army (64) is complete.

Manufacturer
MaK System Gesellschaft mbH, Falckensteiner Strasse 2, PO Box 9333, D-2300 Kiel 17, Federal Republic of Germany.
Tel: 431 3995-02. Fax: 431 3995 446.

Jung-Jungenthal M47/M48 Armoured Bridgelayer Conversions

Description

In addition to their involvement in M47/M48 armoured recovery vehicle conversions (see entry under *Armoured recovery vehicles*) Jung-Jungenthal GmbH also carry out armoured bridgelayer conversions based on the same vehicles.

The bridgelaying system involved was developed by the Swiss Eidgenössiche Konstruktions-Werkstätte in Thun (K + W – Thun) in co-operation with several Swiss companies. The system was originally developed in Switzerland for the Swiss BrüPz 68 (see entry in this section).

As fitted to the M47/M48 chassis the bridge consists of two four-part rails connected by two girders. The laying process is hydraulically operated as the bridge is advanced and laid by a guide frame and tracer. The bridge can be laid within 2 minutes and recovered in 3 minutes.

The bridge has a normal load capacity of 50 tonnes which can be increased to 60 tonnes for exceptional loads. The bridge itself is 18.2 m long and 3.79 m wide. It is possible to use the bridge in multiples of two or three to cross wide gaps.

Specifications
Bridge weight: 6800 kg
Bridge length: 18.2 m
Bridge width: 3.79 m
Width of guide rails: 1.48 m
Load capacity:
(normal load) 50 000 kg
(exceptional load) 60 000 kg

Status
Prototypes.

Manufacturer
Jung-Jungenthal GmbH, PO Box 20, D-5242 Kirchen, Federal Republic of Germany.
Tel: 02741 683-0. Telex: 875319.
Fax: 02741 683 246.

Jung-Jungenthal M47/M48 armoured bridgelayer conversion

M3 Amphibious Bridging and Ferry System

Development/Description
The M3 amphibious bridging and ferry system is under development to be in service by 1995-96 as the replacement for the earlier M2 system (see following entry). Four German Army M3 prototypes have been produced plus three for the British Army. The prototypes will undergo trials with the German and British armies before production commences. Four additional units as pre-series models were in production for delivery in 1990-91.

Total requirements were understood to be 130 units for the German Army and 70 for the British Army.

The M3 incorporates several improvements over the existing M2 versions, including the ability to be driven on land and water from the same end (when the M2 is in the water the cab is at the rear). Three bridging ramps are carried in place of the M2's four and each bridge module has a length increase of 2.3 m. Extra flotation is provided by flotation bags inside the wheel arches. In general terms the M3 operates in much the same manner as the M2 (see following entry). All-wheel steering is possible and a tyre pressure adjusting system is fitted. The M3 has a load classification of MLC 70.

For standard configurations with an M3 bridge, the bridge length (L) is calculated based on the number (N) of units by using the formula:
$$L = N \times 11.5 + 8.35 \text{ m}.$$

Specifications
Crew: 2 or 3
Configuration: 4 × 4
Weight: (total) approx 25 300 kg
Front axle load: 12 300 kg
Rear axle load: 13 000 kg
Length: 12.882 m
Width:
  (side floats folded) 3.35 m
  (side floats unfolded) 6.57 m

M3 amphibious bridging and ferry system unit in travelling configuration

Height: (wheels in normal position) 3.93 m
Ground clearance: (wheels in normal position) 0.7 m
Track: (front and rear) 2.4 m
Wheelbase: 6.5 m
Max speed: (road) approx 80 km/h
Range:
  (land) 725 km
  (as ferry) 6.25 h
Max gradient: 60%
Fording: amphibious
Engine: Deutz (KHD) BF 8 L 513 C diesel developing 347 hp at 2300 rpm
Turning circle diameter: (all wheel steering) 25.4 m

Performance (with/without wheel arch inflation)
Immersion:
  (one-bay ferry, without payload) 0.53/0.49 m
  (two-bay ferry, with MLC 70 payload) 0.99/0.92 m
  (bridge with MLC 70 payload) 0.84/0.77 m

Useful bridge roadway width: 4.76 m
Water travelling speed:
  (one-bay ferry, without payload) approx 14 km/h
  (one-bay ferry with 12 t payload) approx 13 km/h
  (two-bay ferry with MLC 70 payload) approx 11 km/h
Average fuel consumption:
  (land) 55 l/100 km
  (water) 64 l/h

Status
7 units undergoing trials, 4 units in pre-production stage.

Manufacturer
Eisenwerke Kaiserslautern GmbH, Barbarossastrasse 30, D-6750 Kaiserslautern, Federal Republic of Germany.
Tel: 06 31 857 339. Telex: 45810.
Fax: 06 31 857 300.

M2 Amphibious Bridging and Ferry System

Development
The M2 amphibious bridging and ferry system was developed by Eisenwerke Kaiserslautern (EWK) and Klöckner-Humboldt-Deutz (KHD). First production units were delivered to German Army Pioneer battalions early in 1968.

There have been five versions of the M2, as follows:
M2A; used for trials only
M2B; production version for British and German armies, now modified to M2D (see below)
M2C; version for Singapore with Deutz Model F 8 L 413 F diesel engines
M2D; conversion of M2B to accommodate Class 70 (tracked) and Class 92 wheeled vehicles following the introduction of the Challenger 1 MBT into British Army service. The extra load is accommodated by the use of engine-inflatable bags at the centre, front and rear

sides along with some other modifications
M2E; proposed interim updated version with a hydraulic crane and a more powerful engine, but although one vehicle was fitted with a new engine this version was not proceeded with.

For details of the M3 version see previous entry.

Description
The M2 has a chassis of high alloy construction with the four-man crew seated in the cab at the front of the vehicle. All four wheels can be steered and the suspension is adjustable.

Before entering the water the hydraulically operated hinged buoyancy tanks, which when travelling are on the top of the vehicle to reduce the overall width, are swung through 180° into position. The decking is positioned in a few minutes by a light alloy crane which when travelling is on the centreline of the vehicle. When assembled the roadway is 7.62 m long and 5.486 m wide. When the roadway has been positioned the crane is traversed 90° to the centre of the unit.

Once in the water, the units are coupled together to form a Class 50 bridge or ferry. For the latter, three M2s are required.

The M2 is fully amphibious: one of the main engines drives two 600 mm propellers for sideways propulsion while the second engine powers the 650 mm diameter steering propeller. One of the two side propellers can also be used for steering. When swimming, the cab of the M2 is to the rear and the wheels are raised to reduce drag.

Specifications
Crew: 4
Configuration: 4 × 4
Weight: 22 000 kg
Length: (travelling) 11.315 m
Width: (travelling) 3.579 m
Overall width: (with ramps and buoyancy tanks in position) 14.16 m
Height: (travelling) 3.579 m
Ground clearance: 0.6-0.84 m

Track:
(front) 2.13 m
(rear) 2.161 m
Wheelbase: 5.35 m
Max speed:
(road) 60 km/h
(water, single unit) 14 km/h
Range:
(road) 1000 km
(water) 6 h
Max gradient: 60%
Engines: Deutz Model F 8 L 714a V-8 diesels developing 178 hp at 2300 rpm each (Singapore vehicles have Deutz model F 8 L 413 F diesels developing 180 hp at 2300 rpm)
Turning circle: 25.4 m
Tyres: 16.00 × 20

Status
Production complete. In service with Germany, Singapore (36) and the United Kingdom. The British Army M2D unit is 28 Amphibious Engineer Regiment, Royal Engineers.

Manufacturer
Eisenwerke Kaiserslautern GmbH, Barbarossastrasse 30, D-6750 Kaiserslautern, Federal Republic of Germany.
Tel: 06 31 857 339. Telex: 45810.
Fax: 06 31 857 300.

M548 crossing bridge formed by M2Ds of 28 Amphibious Engineer Regiment, Royal Engineers (Tom Foulkes)

INDIA

Kartik Armoured Bridgelayer

Description
During the 1989 Republic Day parade held in New Delhi, the Indian Army displayed the prototype of an armoured bridgelayer known as the Kartik. The Kartik is based on the chassis of the Vijayanta MBT, the Indian-produced version of the Vickers Mk 1 MBT, lengthened by the addition of an extra road wheel each side. The vehicle has a crew of three.

The Kartik uses a hydraulically operated scissors-type bridge similar to that used on the German BLG-60 AVLB, also in service with India. If this is correct the bridge has a total length of 21.6 m and a maximum capacity of 50 000 kg.

Status
Prototype.

The Kartik armoured bridgelayer

INTERNATIONAL

Gillois Bridge and Ferry System

Development
The Gillois bridge and ferry system was designed by General J Gillois of the French Army with production being undertaken by the German company EWK. Further development by the company resulted in the M2 amphibious bridge and ferry system which was adopted by the British, German and Singapore armies. The US Army had a number of Gillois units which it called the Amphibious River Crossing Equipment (or ARCE). In the late 1950s the Americans developed their own amphibious bridge and ferry system called the Mobile Assault Bridge (MAB).

This system is scheduled to be replaced in the French Army by the EFA (see entry in this section).

Description
The Gillois bridge and ferry system consists of two major units, the bridge unit and the ramp unit. Each unit has a hull of all-welded construction with five compartments. The four-man crew compartment is at the front of the hull and is fully enclosed. Two compartments hold the wheels, which are retracted once the unit is afloat. The centre compartment houses the engine and air compressor units, while the fifth compartment forms the bow of the unit when waterborne, or the rear when travelling on land.

Each unit has a pneumatic float on each side of the hull which is inflated before the vehicle enters the water. When inflated each float is 10.972 m long and 1.371 m in diameter. These floats provide stability and additional buoyancy when afloat. In daylight, with a trained crew, it takes about 25 minutes to prepare the unit for use. When in the water the vehicle is propelled by a propeller unit at the front of the hull, in the crew compartment. This propeller rests on the top of the hull when travelling on land.

Bridge unit
The bridge superstructure consists of two steel treadways with an aluminium filler panel, and has an effective length of 8 m. When travelling on land the superstructure is carried in the longitudinal position and on entering the water it is rotated through 90° and widened to provide a roadway 4 m wide. The filler panel is lowered hydraulically. Each treadway is equipped with a male plug at one end and a female receiver at the other end. When two superstructure units are brought together, a hydraulic lock pin cylinder mounted beneath the male plug is actuated and the pin connects the lower chord on the two adjacent treadways of the bridge units.

Ramp unit
The ramp superstructure consists of two treadway sections with an effective length of 4 m. Each treadway section consists of four major components: a welded aluminium tapered ramp, a short steel deck section, two hydraulic articulator cylinders and hinged filler panels. The ramp superstructure is transported in a longitudinal position and on entering the water the ramp is rotated through 90° and then widened to provide a roadway 4 m wide. The ends of the short deck section are identical to the bridge unit superstructure and the two can be connected. The centre gap between the two aluminium ramp treadway sections is filled by a system of hinged panels, connected to the upper chord of the short steel deck section and the aluminium ramp sections. Once the units have been joined up in the water, the hydraulic lines of the four hydraulic articulator cylinders are transferred from the ramp unit hydraulic system to the bridge unit. Once sufficient bridge units are connected to the ramp unit,

Gillois vehicle carrying an AMX-30 MBT; this vehicle is a ramp unit (P Touzin)

Gillois bridge unit with pneumatic floats inflated (P Touzin)

the ramp is hydraulically raised and the ramp hull is removed from beneath the ramp superstructure.

When being used as a bridge, the Gillois bridge can take vehicles up to Class 60 in currents of up to 2.98 m/s. The following rafts can be constructed:

One-bay raft using the ramp unit which can carry two AMX-13 light tanks with care
Two-bay raft which can carry between 29 900 and 49 896 kg with care
Three-bay raft which can carry between 64 870 and 79 834 kg
Four-bay raft which can carry between 89 810 and 109 771 kg

Specifications

	Bridge vehicle	Ramp vehicle
Crew	4	4
Configuration	4 × 4	4 × 4
Weight	26 950 kg	27 400 kg
Length (travelling)	11.861 m	11.861 m
Width (travelling)	3.2 m	3.2 m
Width (deployed)	5.994 m	5.994 m
Ground clearance	0.715 m	0.715 m
Height	3.991 m	3.991 m
Track		
(front)	1.79 m	1.79 m
(rear)	1.79 m	1.79 m
Wheelbase	6.197 m	6.197 m
Max speed		
(road)	64 km/h	64 km/h
(water)	12 km/h	2 km/h
Range	780 km	780 km

	Bridge vehicle	Ramp vehicle
Fuel capacity	547 l	547 l
Gradient	50%	50%
Fording	amphibious	amphibious
Engine	Deutz, V-12, 4-cycle air-cooled diesel developing 220 hp at 2000 rpm	
Tyres	18 × 25	18 × 25

Status

Production complete. In service with the French Army.

Manufacturer

Eisenwerke Kaiserslautern Göppner GmbH, Barbarossastrasse 30, D-6750 Kaiserslautern, Federal Republic of Germany.
Tel: 06 31 857 339. Telex: 45810.
Fax: 06 31 857 300.

ISRAEL

Alligator Armoured Bridgelaying System

Description

The Alligator armoured bridgelaying system consists of three main components. One is the bridge set of two

bridges, one 22 m long and the other 15 m long. The second component is the launching mechanism which is mounted on an AMX-13 light tank chassis. The system is completed by the control system.

The lightweight bridges are made of high strength aluminium alloy having a load capacity of MLC 30. The bridges are constructed with two symmetric treadways

transversely connected by beams. There is also a folding and locking mechanism. Each trackway has a centre section and two ramps. There is no hydraulic system in the bridge.

The launch mechanism is carried on a modified AMX-13 light tank chassis with the gun turret removed. An armoured superstructure protects the launch mech-

An Alligator bridge in position

Specifications

System					
Bridge length	22 m	15 m			
Weight					
(complete system)	20 300 kg	18 500 kg			
(vehicle with system)	16 000 kg	15 000 kg			
(bridge)	4300 kg	3500 kg			
Length					
(overall)	9 m	9 m			
(vehicle with system)	7.6 m	7.6 m			
Width					
(complete system)	3.2 m	3.2 m			
(vehicle with system)	2.6 m	2.6 m			
(bridge)	3.2 m	3.2 m			
Height					
(overall)	3.6 m	3.4 m			
(vehicle with system)	3 m	3 m			
Ground clearance	0.4 m	0.4 m			
Max speed					
(road)	51 km/h	51 km/h			
(cross-country)	30 km/h	30 km/h			
Range (road)	350 km	350 km			
Fording	0.8 m	0.8 m			
Gradient	50%	50%			
Side slope	30%	30%			
Vertical obstacle					
(forward)	0.65 m	0.65 m			
(to rear)	0.45 m	0.45 m			
Trench	1.6 m	1.6 m			
Bridge					
Bridge length	22 m	15 m			
Load capacity	MLC 30	MLC 30			
Max gap capability	20 m	14 m			
Folded length	9 m	9 m			
Width					
(overall)	3.2 m	3.2 m			
(roadway)	3 m	3 m			
(trackway)	1.2 m	1.2 m			
Height					
(folded)	1.47 m	1.24 m			
(deployed)	0.735 m	0.735 m			
Centre gap	0.6 m	0.6 m			
Ramp slope	8%	12%			
Max twist angle	10%	10%			
Transverse slope	15%	15%			
Uphill slope	25%	25%			
Downhill slope	15%	15%			

anism and has a position for the commander. Launching is carried out using a launcher and outriggers which are hydraulically operated to move and position the bridge using a flip cantilever mode. Launch and retrieval can be carried out from either end. Launching takes 3 to 4 minutes and retrieval takes 4.5 to 5.5 minutes.

The control system controls the hydraulics in either an automatic or manual mode. The system can be operated by either member of the two-man crew (driver and commander) or from outside the system vehicle.

If required, two identical bridges can be used in a tandem combination to increase the gap crossing capability. Two 15 m bridges can then be used to cross a 21 m gap while two 22 m bridges can cross a 32 m gap.

A bridge can be crossed even when one main structural chord is damaged. Vehicles crossing a bridge can do so at speeds of up to 25 km/h in crosswinds of less than 20 km/h.

Status
In production.

Manufacturer
TAAS – Israel Industries Ltd, POB 1044, Ramat Hasharon, 47100 Israel.
Tel: (3) 542 52 22. Telex: 33 719 misbit il
Fax: (3) 48 96 39.

Deploying an Alligator armoured bridgelaying system

JAPAN

Type 67 Armoured Vehicle Launched Bridge

Development/Description
The Type 67 AVLB is basically a turretless Type 61 MBT carrying a scissors bridge and launching mechanism. This AVLB was preceded by a trials vehicle based on a Sherman M4A3E8 tank with its turret replaced by a scissors bridge.

The bridge is similar in design and construction to the American M48 AVLB bridge but is much shorter. When opened out it is 12 m long, compared with the M48's bridge which is 19.202 m long; it will span a gap of up to 10 m. The bridge is opened out over the front of the Type 67 and can be picked up from either end. Launching time is between 3-5 minutes. The bridge has a maximum loading capacity of 40 000 kg.

The chassis is almost identical to that of the Type 61 MBT, with the driver seated at the front of the hull on the right side with three periscopes for observation and a single-piece hatch cover. The other two crew members are positioned in the centre of the hull with the engine and transmission at the rear. The suspension is of the torsion bar type and consists of six road wheels, with the drive sprocket at the front and the idler at the rear, and three track return rollers per side. Hydraulic shock absorbers are provided for the first, second, fifth and sixth road wheel stations.

Specifications
Crew: 3
Weight: 35 000 kg

Type 67 AVLB commencing its bridgelaying sequence (K Nogi)

Length:
(with bridge) 7.27 m
(hull) 6.32 m
Width:
(with bridge) 3.5 m
(without bridge) 2.95 m
Height: (with bridge) 3.5 m
Ground clearance: 0.4 m
Track: 2.45 m

Track width: 500 mm
Length of track on ground: 3.7 m
Ground pressure: 0.95 kg/cm²
Max speed: (road) 45 km/h
Range: 200 km
Fording: 1 m
Gradient: 60%
Vertical obstacle: 0.8 m
Trench: 2.7 m
Engine: Mitsubishi Type 12 HM 21 WT V-12 turbocharged air-cooled diesel developing 650 hp at 2100 rpm
Transmission: mechanical with 5 forward and 1 reverse gears, with 2-speed auxiliary reduction unit
Electrical system: 24 V
Batteries: 4 × 12 V, 200 Ah
Armament: 1 × 7.62 mm MG
Armour
hull front: 46 mm
hull sides: 25 mm
hull rear: 15 mm

Status
Production complete. In service only with the Japanese Ground Self-Defence Force.

Manufacturer
Production was undertaken at the Maruko, Tokyo, plant of Mitsubishi Heavy Industries, but AFV production is undertaken at the Sagamihara Plant, near Tokyo. Mitsubishi Heavy Industries, 5-1, Marunouchi 2-chome, Chiyoda-ku, Tokyo, Japan.
Tel: 212 3311. Telex: 22282.

Type 70 Self-propelled Pontoon Bridge

Development/Description

During the early 1960s the Japanese Ground Self-Defence Force issued a requirement for a self-propelled pontoon bridge system which could also be used as a ferry. Development by the Hitachi Manufacturing Company began in 1965 and the first prototype bridge was completed the following year. After further trials it was standardised as the Type 70 Self-propelled Pontoon Bridge.

In concept the Type 70 is similar to the German M2. Before entering the water a hydraulic mechanism rotates the floats from the deck through 180° so that they lie along the sides of the vehicle and provide extra flotation. When afloat, the wheels which have large low-pressure tyres, are retracted into the hull to reduce water resistance. To provide additional buoyancy the wheel wells are pressurised. The vehicle is fitted with a central tyre pressure regulation system which allows the tyre pressure to be adjusted to suit the type of ground being crossed.

Once afloat a built-in crane emplaces the three treadways and the units are joined to form a ferry bridge. The crane is also used to emplace drive-on ramps. Three Type 70 units coupled together have a capacity of 40 000 kg and a roadway width of 3.9 m.

Type 70 self-propelled pontoon bridge units in travelling order (Kensuke Ebata)

Specifications
Configuration: 4 × 4
Weight: 26 000 kg
Length: 11.4 m
Width:
(without floats) 2.8 m
(floats extended) 5.4 m
Height: 3.4 m
Superstructure length: 8.5 m
Superstructure width: 3.8 m

Engine: Nissan V-8 diesel developing 330 hp at 2200 rpm
Max speed:
(road) 56 km/h
(water)12 km/h
Gradient: 47%

Status
In service with Japanese Ground Self-Defence Force.

Type 81 Bridgelayer

Description

The Type 81 bridgelayer is a Type 74 (6 × 6) 10 000 kg truck chassis with a hydraulically launched bridge mounted to the rear and laid from the rear of the cab.

To lay a bridge which can take armoured vehicles weighing up to 42 000 kg, two vehicles are required. Each vehicle carries a bridge span with one also carrying two telescopic pier legs. The latter vehicle approaches the gap to be bridged tail first and the telescopic pier legs are attached to the end of the bottom pier half. The bottom pier half is then hydraulically driven by rams out across the gap. As the bridge half is driven across the gap the two pier legs fall downwards and when the full length of the first bridge half is reached, the top half is attached and the hydraulic rams then push the second half out to the full extent. When the full extent of the bridge half is reached the two are lowered with the telescopic pier legs resting on the ground. The legs can accommodate slight variations in level and the full weight of the two connected bridge halves is taken up by lowering the bridge to the ground at the truck end. The weight of the span in the centre is then taken onto foot pads, each about 1 m², and a ramp is fitted to the truck end, ready for the second truck to approach backwards onto the bridge to lower the second half of the bridge span. This is carried out in exactly the same way as the first except that there are no pier legs. Once the second bridge section has been laid, a further drive-on ramp

Type 81 mechanised bridge in travelling configuration (K Nogi)

can be fitted to the far end and the bridge is ready for use. Some additional levelling may be required before heavy vehicles use the bridge.

The above relates to a two-section bridge but extra sections along with extra pier legs may be employed to build longer bridges when necessary. The maximum bridging length is 60 m which requires 10 bridging sets.

Specifications
Crew: 2
Configuration: 6 × 6
Weight: 21 800 kg
Length: 9.6 m
Width: 2.85 m

Height: 3.4 m
Max road speed: 85 km/h
Vertical obstacle: 0.8 m

Bridge
Capacity: MLC 42
Length: 10 m
Width: 3.75 m
Max bridging height: 4 m
Bridging height variation: 2 m
Max bridging length: 60 m (10 sets)

Status
In service with Japanese Ground Self-Defence Force.

KOREA, SOUTH

K-1 Armoured Vehicle Launched Bridge

Description

The K-1 armoured vehicle launched bridge (K-1 AVLB) is a derivative of the K-1 MBT, also known as the Type 88 MBT (for details of the Type 88 refer to *Jane's Armour and Artillery 1992-93* pages 101 to 103). The K-1 AVLB was developed in co-operation with Vickers Defence Systems of the UK which was awarded a contract to design and build the bridge and launch system in early 1989. The bridge and launch system

was built in the UK and in 1990 was shipped to South Korea where it was integrated with the K-1 chassis.

The K-1 AVLB is based on the chassis and running gear of the Type 88/K-1 MBT which was developed by the Land Systems Division of General Dynamics in the United States. It is powered by a 1200 hp water-cooled, multi-fuel MTU 871 Ka-501 diesel coupled to an electronically controlled transmission.

The crew is two men, the commander and driver. The commander is located under a cupola in the hull roof. An integral crew heating system is provided but NBC protection is restricted to individual systems.

Automatic fire detection and suppression systems are provided in the engine and crew compartments.

The bridge is of the scissors type and can bridge a gap with a clear span of 20.5 m; the load classification is MLC 66 and the bridge alone weighs 12 900 kg. The anticipated service life is over 8000 crossings. Launch time is 3 minutes and retrieval time 10 minutes. The bridge can be launched with a side slope of 3° and a longitudinal slope of ±10°; bank height difference is 2.4 m.

A pintle for a 7.62 mm machine gun is mounted over the commander's cupola on the hull roof and a smoke grenade discharger is mounted on the hull front.

K-1 armoured vehicle launched bridge

K-1 armoured vehicle launched bridge

Specifications
Crew: 2
Weight:
  (vehicle and bridge) 53 000 kg
  (bridge) 12 900 kg
Length overall: 12.5 m
Width overall: 4 m
Height overall: 4 m
Max speed: (road) 65 km/h
Fording: 1.2 m

Gradient: 60%
Side slope: 30%
Vertical obstacle: 0.8 m
Trench: 2.7 m
Engine: MTU MB 871 Ka-501 diesel developing 1200 hp at 2600 rpm
Transmission: ZF LSG3000 automatic with 4 forward and 2 reverse gears
Suspension: hydro-pneumatic and torsion bar
Electrical system: 24 V

Armament: 1 × 7.62 mm MG

Status
Prototype.

Manufacturer
Hyundai Precision & Ind Co Ltd, 140-2, Gye-Dong, Chongro-Ku, Seoul, South Korea.
Tel: (82-2) 746 4010. Telex: HDPIC K23238.
Fax: (82-2) 741 2248.

PAKISTAN

M47M Armoured Vehicle Launched Bridge

Description
The Military Vehicle Research and Development Establishment at Rawalpindi has developed an armoured vehicle launched bridge (AVLB) based on the turretless chassis of an M47M tank for the Pakistan Ministry of Defence. The project has been described as a step towards indigenous development and self-reliance. For details of the original M47M tank refer to *Jane's Armour and Artillery 1992-93* pages 156 and 157.

The bridge launching mechanism is installed on the hull of the turretless M47M and is used to launch an aluminium alloy folding scissors bridge with a maximum span of 21.4 m. The bridge has a maximum clear span of 20.3 m. The vehicle has a crew of two, a driver and a commander/operator who uses 13 hydraulic cylinders to launch the bridge in about 3 minutes. Power for the hydraulic system is provided by the M47M launch vehicle's main engine.

The bridge launching sequence commences with the main launching cylinder lifting the main launching beam from its transport position. When the bridge reaches an angle of 45° the bridge unloading cylinder is operated and starts to retract. As it retracts it pulls a set of two steel ropes passing over a system of pulleys and joined to the further part of the bridge. This initiates the bridge unfolding sequence. The travel of the main launching cylinder and the bridge operating cylinder continues until the nearest part of the bridge rests on the ground in front of the launcher. In this position the launching cylinders block the movement of the launching frame and the bridge is pushed further by auxiliary cylinders. The fulcrum of operation shifts and the operation of the bridge-opening cylinders continues until the bridge is fully open. The bridge is then lowered into position by the main operating cylinder. At this

M47M armoured vehicle launched bridge with 21.4 m bridge in transport position

point the operator actuates three unlocking cylinders which disengage the launching beam from the bridge. A mechanical lock is opened at the same time to allow the launching vehicle to move away from the bridge. The bridge is recovered in the reverse sequence. If the launch vehicle engine or the hydraulic pumps fail there is provision for manual launching of the bridge.

The M47M launcher can also be used to lay a short single span bridge. This bridge is one half of the folding 21.4 m bridge fitted with an extra set of folding ramps. No details are available regarding this variant but it is assumed that it is launched in the same manner and sequence as the full-size folding bridge.

Specifications
AVLB
Crew: 2
Weight: 54 000 kg
Width: 4 m

Height: 3.83 m

Bridge
Weight: 9800 kg
Max span of bridge: 21.4 m
Max clear span: 20.3 m
Bridge width: 4 m
Distance between treadways: 0.96 m

Status
Prototype.

Manufacturer
Military Vehicle Research and Development Establishment, PO Box 240, Abid Majid Road, Rawalpindi, Pakistan.
Tel: 67911-15.

POLAND

SMT-1 Truck-mounted Treadway Bridge

Description

The SMT-1 consists of four 11 m spans each of which is carried on the rear of a Star 66 2500 kg (6 × 6) truck (or the later Star 660 M1 or Star 660 M2). They are launched over the front of the vehicle, unlike the TMM and KMM treadway bridges which are launched over the rear.

Unlike the TMM and KMM treadways, the SMT-1 treadways do not have to be spread before launching, as they are fixed. Each treadway consists of tubular steel trusses welded together by struts, crosspieces and diagonal stiffeners with steel mesh panels mounted on the top of the trusses to form the treadway. The SMT-1 is much lighter than the TMM treadway: the TMM weighs 666 kg and the SMT-1 210 kg/m.

Each span is launched in 3-5 minutes with the launching controlled from the cab. Individual spans of the SMT are used for other purposes, for example as ramps on pontoon bridges. The SMT-1 is often used as a single-span bridge without the trestle legs. Additional spans are carried on a single-axle trailer which has dual tyres.

The SMT-1 truck-mounted treadway bridge is used in conjunction with the PSMT-1 intermediate support which is also used with other bridges such as the German BLG-60 AVLB. The PSMT-1 is positioned by crane or floated into position. It consists of a platform and four trestles which are adjustable in height. The trestles are 5 m long and can be folded for travel. The PSMT-1 is capable of floating, primarily because of the plastic foam material used in its construction. It is transported on a single-axle trailer and can be floated directly by reversing the prime mover into the water.

Specifications
Bridge
Weight: 2300 kg
Length: 11 m
Width: 3 m
Trestle leg height: adjustable to 3.5 m
Capacity: 40 000 kg

Status
Production complete. In service with the Polish Army.

Manufacturer
Polish state factories.

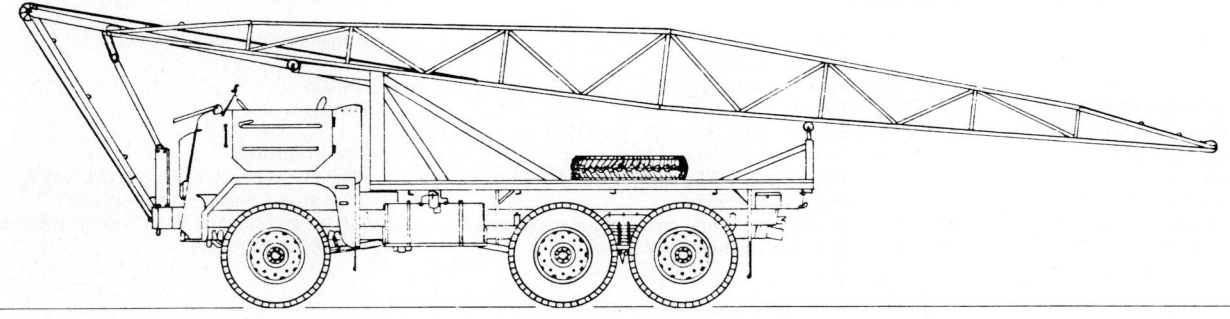

SMT-1 bridgelayer carried on Star 66 (6 × 6) truck chassis

SERBIA

Truck-mounted Scissors Treadway Bridge

Description

This truck-mounted scissors bridge consists of three 13 m spans carried and launched from the rear of a modified FAP 2220BDS (6 × 4) truck.

The system is laid in a similar manner to the TMM truck-mounted scissors treadway bridge and has similar capabilities. The trestle legs can be extended to a maximum of 4 m, whereas the TMM's trestle legs can be extended to only 3 m, enabling the bridge to be used for deeper crossings.

The treadway bridge is laid as follows: before launching the treadway, the trestle legs are adjusted to the correct height so that the roadway is level when the bridge is in position; the truck then backs up to the river and the treadway is raised to the vertical position. The span is then straightened and lowered into position and at the same time the trestle legs swing into place. Once this is complete, the truck drives off and the procedure is repeated until the bridge is complete. Each individual span takes 5-6 minutes to lay in position and can be recovered from either end. Recovery takes about the same time as launching. A complete three-span bridge will span a river up to 36 m wide.

Specifications
Vehicle with bridge
(full technical characteristics of the FAP 2220BDS will be found in the *Trucks* section)
Cab seating: 1 + 1
Configuration: 6 × 4

Truck-mounted scissors treadway bridge in travelling position on FAP 2220BDS (6 × 4) truck

Weight: 20 000 kg
Length: 8.2 m
Width: 2.5 m
Height: 2.56 m
Track:
   (front) 1.97 m
   (rear) 1.745 m
Wheelbase: 3.12 m + 1.2 m
Max road speed: 60 km/h
Range: 300 km (estimate)
Fuel capacity: 200 l
Engine: Famos 2F/002A 6-cylinder water-cooled diesel developing 200 hp

Tyres: 11.00 × 20

Bridge
Length: 13 m
Width: 2.5 m
Trestle leg length: 4 m

Status
In service with the former Yugoslav Army.

Manufacturer
State factories.

SINGAPORE

Light Assault Bridge LAB 30

Description
The Light Assault Bridge LAB 30 is very similar to the French AMX-13 armoured bridgelayer (qv) and is based on an AMX-13 light tank chassis. The bridgelayer is produced by removing the AMX-13 tank turret and replacing it with the mechanism to lay a folding or sliding assault bridge. The hydraulically operated mechanism is incorporated on the front and rear of the

tank chassis and operates in a manner very similar to that of the French AMX-13 system.

The folding bridge employed is manufactured entirely from aluminium alloy and weighs 3200 kg. Length is 14 m and width 2.9 m. The bridge can be launched within 3-4 minutes and will take loads up to Class 30. The bridge can cross a gap of 12 m (on soft ground) or 13 m (on hard ground). With two bridges placed side-by-side the load class can be increased to Class 60.

When travelling complete with its bridge the LAB 30 is 7.38 m long and 3.2 m high.

Status
In production.

Manufacturer
Singapore Shipbuilding and Engineering Limited, 7 Benoi Road, Singapore 2262.
Tel: 65 861 2244. Telex: 21206 singa rs.
Fax: 65 861 3028.

SWEDEN

Brobandvagn 941 Armoured Bridgelayer

Development/Description
The first prototype of the *Brobandvagn* 941 (or Brobv 941) was completed by Hägglunds in 1968. It entered production late in 1972 and 17 vehicles were delivered to the Swedish Army the following year.

The chassis and hull of the Brobv 941 are almost identical to those of the Bgbv 82 armoured recovery vehicle, and the reader is referred to this entry in the *Armoured recovery vehicles* section for a full description of the chassis. The main difference between the two vehicles, apart from the bridge, is that the Brobv 941 does not have a 20 mm gun turret mounted on the left side of the crew compartment.

The gunner can fire his 7.62 mm machine gun from either his open hatch or from an alternative position on top of the bridgelaying mechanism when engaging aircraft. In addition, provision was made for mounting a 7.62 mm machine gun in the loading platform at the rear, and on the commander's hatch. The crew of four consists of the commander, driver, gunner and operator, all seated in the front compartment.

At the front of the vehicle is a hydraulically operated bulldozer blade, which can be used for levelling operations as well as stabilising the vehicle when the bridge is being laid. On arriving at the river or ditch, the dozer blade is first lowered into position, a telescopic beam is extended until the point of the beam reaches the other bridge abutment, the aluminium bridge is slid across the beam which is then withdrawn so that the bridge is horizontal. The laying mechanism then returns to the travelling position, the dozer blade is raised, and the vehicle can cross the bridge. This complete operation takes less than 5 minutes with all the crew under armour protection. If required, one of the crew can be outside the vehicle directing the laying of the bridge via a communications link with the vehicle. The bridge itself is 15 m long and has a maximum load capacity of 50 000 kg.

The Brobv 941 is fully amphibious, being propelled in the water by its tracks. Before entering the water a trim vane is erected at the front of the vehicle and the electric bilge pumps switched on. When the Brobv 941 is afloat, the bridge, which is buoyant, is towed behind the vehicle.

Infra-red night vision equipment is provided but the

Brobv 941 in travelling order

vehicle does not have an NBC system, although provision was made for one in the design of the vehicle.

Specifications
Crew: 4
Weight:
 (with bridge) 28 400 kg
 (without bridge) 21 400 kg
Length:
 (with bridge) 17 m
 (without bridge) 6.7 m
Width:
 (with bridge) 4 m
 (without bridge) 3.25 m
Height:
 (with bridge) 3.24 m
 (without bridge) 2.9 m
Ground clearance: 0.41 m
Track width: 450 mm
Length of track on ground: 3.6 m
Ground pressure: 0.84 kg/cm^2
Max speed:
 (road) 56 km/h
 (water) 8 km/h
Range: 400 km

Fuel capacity: 550 l
Fording: amphibious
Gradient: 60%
Side slope: 30%
Vertical obstacle: 0.6 m
Trench: 2.5 m
Engine: Volvo-Penta THD 100C 6-cylinder in-line turbocharged diesel developing 310 bhp at 2200 rpm
Transmission: Volvo-Penta R61 with 8 forward and 2 reverse gears
Electrical system: 24 V
Batteries: 2 × 12 V, 152 Ah
Armament:
 1 × 7.62 mm MG
 12 smoke dischargers

Status
Production complete. In service with the Swedish Army.

Manufacturer
Hägglunds Vehicle AB, S-891 02 Örnsköldsvik, Sweden.
Tel: 46 660 800 00. Telex: 6051 haegg s.
Fax: 46 660 826 12.

SWITZERLAND

Brückenlegepanzer 68/88

Development
The first prototype of the *Brückenlegepanzer* 68 (BrüPz 68) was based on the chassis of the Pz 61 MBT but production vehicles were based on the chassis of the later Pz 68 MBT. The prototype vehicles carried a steel bridge which was replaced on production vehicles by an aluminium bridge. Production was completed in June 1977. Since then several modifications have

been introduced, including a fully automatic hydraulic bridgelaying system, resulting in a change of designation to BrüPz 68/88.

The bridgelaying system was developed by the Eidgenössische Kinstruktions-Werkstätte in Thun (K + W – Thun) in co-operation with several other Swiss companies.

The bridge and bridgelaying system used with this vehicle have also been utilised by Jung-Jungenthal GmbH of Germany for conversions of M47 and M48 MBTs to the armoured bridgelayer role. See entry

under Germany in this section.

Description
The hull of the *Brückenlegepanzer* 68/88 (BrüPz 68/88) is almost identical to that of the Pz 68 MBT. The driver is seated at the front of the hull and is provided with three periscopes for observation and a single-piece hatch cover. The commander and the bridge operator are seated in the centre of the vehicle with the engine and transmission at the rear.

The suspension of the BrüPz 68 is the Belleville type

BrüPz 68/88 laying a bridge

BrüPz 68/88 crossing a laid bridge

and consists of six road wheels with the drive sprocket at the rear and the idler at the front. There are three track return rollers. Each road wheel is independently sprung by layers of Belleville washers.

The bridge itself has an overall length of 18.23 m and a width of 3.79 m, maximum trackway width being 3.55 m. Its maximum capacity is 60 000 kg but it is normally limited to a maximum load of 50 000 kg. The bridge is launched as follows: the bridgelayer approaches the obstacle and halts, the bridge is tilted forwards and a beam slid across to the far bank, the bridge is slid across the beam until it reaches the far bank and the beam is then withdrawn back into the horizontal position. The laying sequence is fully automatic once initiated. A bridge takes between 2 minutes to lay and under 5 minutes to recover.

Specifications
Crew: 3
Weight:
  (with bridge) 47 000 kg
  (without bridge) 37 200 kg
Length: (with bridge) 20.1 m
Width: (with bridge) 4 m
Height: (with bridge) 3.3 m
Ground clearance: 0.4 m
Track: 2.59 m
Track width: 520 mm
Length of track on ground: 4.22 m
Ground pressure: 0.98 kg/cm^2
Max speed: (road) 55 km/h
Range:
  (road) 300 km
  (cross-country) 160 km
Fuel capacity: 855 l
Fording: 1.1 m
Gradient: 70%

Vertical obstacle: 0.7 m
Trench: 2 m
Engine: MTU MB 837 8-cylinder diesel developing 660 hp at 2200 rpm
Transmission: semi-automatic with 6 forward and 6 reverse gears
Electrical system: 24 V
Batteries: 4 × 6 V, 360 Ah
Armament: 8 × smoke dischargers
Armour: 20-60 mm

Status
Production complete. In service with the Swiss Army.

Manufacturer
Swiss Federal Armament Works, CH-3602 Thun, Switzerland.
Tel: 41 33 281111. Telex: 921256.
Fax: 41 33 282047.

UNITED KINGDOM

Thompson Modular Bridge – Tank Launched Bridges

Description
The Thompson Modular Bridge (TMB), being developed by Thompson Defence Projects (part of the Industrial Power Group of Rolls-Royce plc) for the British Army's Bridging for the 1990s programme, is a comprehensive bridging system covering Tank Launched or Close Support Bridges (mechanised bridges) and Line of Communication or Dry Support Bridges, together with dedicated logistic support vehicles. (See also entry under *Tactical (non-floating) and line of communication bridges*.)

All the bridges are built from a range of seven modular panels of advanced aluminium alloy fabrication which are interchangeable through the various bridge types (with the exception of the 6.75 m ramp) to form two interconnecting trackways, with a 4 m overall bridge width and a 1 m girder depth.

There are three basic Tank Launched Bridges (also known as Close Support or Assault Bridges): the No 10, No 11 and No 12. The No 10 bridge is a single fold scissoring bridge 26 m long and capable of spanning 24.5 m. A shorter bridge length can be achieved by the removal of two 4 m panels, reducing to a 22 m bridge. It can also be fitted with an Assault Trestle to provide a 21 m trestle bridge. The No 10 bridge is constructed from 8 m ramp panels, 4 m panels and 2 m hinge panels. The folding mechanism uses scissoring parts which eliminate the need for hydraulics on the bridge, and allow the bridge to be launched on sites where longitudinal slopes would defeat horizontally launched bridges.

The No 11 bridge is built from four 8 m ramp panels and is a 16 m long, 14.5 m span up-and-over launched bridge.

The No 12, shortest of the Tank Launched Bridges, consists of four 6.75 m ramp panels (the only panels

not fully interchangeable with the rest of the TMB system) and is an up-and-over launched bridge, 13.5 m long and capable of spanning 12 m. Its girder depth of 0.71 m enables two bridges to be conveyed and launched by the Chieftain AVLB. The two No 12 bridges with a unique launching system allow the AVLB to construct two bridges without having to be resupplied, for the crossing of two short gaps, or in combination to cross a wider single gap, all without crew exposure.

A small modification kit enables the existing Chieftain AVLB to convey and launch the new range of bridges to be carried and launched from under armour while still allowing existing in-service bridges to be carried and launched. Alternatively, any suitable armoured tracked or wheeled vehicle could be modified as a suitable launch platform.

All the bridges are designed and tested in accordance with the UK/US/GE Trilateral Design and Test Code and are classified MLC 70 for both wheeled and tracked vehicles. They can all be crossed by fully laden tank transporters at MLC 105. Launching without crew exposure is possible with all bridges in 3 minutes, and they can all be recovered in 5 minutes from either end (except those fitted with a trestle).

To increase the length capability, combination bridges may be built using two or three of the above bridges, the first bridge being launched from the home bank with the far end supported on the base of the gap, a floating pier, or a trestle. Gaps up to a nominal 60 m span and 5 m depth can be bridged in this way. Combination bridges are classified as MLC 70 for tracked vehicles.

A wheeled Tank Bridge Transporter (TBT), an 8 × 8 improved medium mobility vehicle, forms part of the TMB system, its primary use being the rapid resupply of the AVLB. The TBT can carry all variants of the tank launched bridges and is equipped with mechanisms to load and offload them. An excellent cross-country performance and flexibility allow it to travel virtually

anywhere tracked vehicles can go. The TBT has a high degree of commonality with the vehicles used to launch and transport Dry Support Vehicles (see also entry under *Tactical (non-floating) and line of communication bridges*) and is manufactured by Unipower plc (see entry in *Trucks* section).

It August 1992 in was announced that the TLB was to be evaluated in connection with the American HAB programme (see separate entry in this section for details). Southwest Mobile Systems of St Louis, Missouri, acting in co-operation with Thompson Defence Projects, had been awarded a $5 383 481 firm fixed price contract to deliver and support two Chieftain AVLBs and two No 10 tank bridges for testing as part of the HAB programme.

Specifications
No 10 Tank Bridge
Length overall: 26 m
Ramp length: 6 m
Width overall: 4 m
Depth of section: 1 m
Max span: 24.5 m
Weight: 13 000 kg
Panels: 4 × 8 m ramp panels, 4 × 4 m panels, 2 × 2 m hinge panels

No 10 Trestle Bridge
Length overall: 21 m
Ramp length: 6 m
Width overall: 4 m
Depth of section: 1 m
Max span: 18 m usable for combination bridge
Weight: 13 000 kg with trestles
Panels: 2 × 8 m ramp panels, 4 × 4 m panels, 2 × 2 m hinge panels, 2 × trestle adaptor panels, 2 × assault trestles

No 11 Tank Bridge
Length overall: 16 m

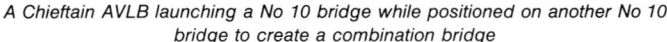

A Chieftain AVLB launching a No 10 bridge while positioned on another No 10 bridge to create a combination bridge

A Chieftain AVLB in the process of launching one of two No 12 bridges

Ramp length: 6 m
Width overall: 4 m
Depth of section: 1 m
Max span: 14.5 m
Weight: 7000 kg
Panels: 4 × 8 m ramp panels

No 12 Tank Bridge
Length overall: 13.5 m
Ramp length: 5.25 m
Width overall: 4 m

Depth of section: 0.71 m
Max span: 12 m
Weight: 5700 kg
Panels: 4 × 6.75 m ramp panels

Combination Bridge
Bridges: No 10 and trestle bridge, No 11 and No 12 bridges
Quantity: 2 or 3 bridges
Max span: 60 m
Max gap depth: 5 m

Status
Under development for the British Army. Under evaluation for the US Army Heavy Assault Bridge (HAB) programme.

Manufacturer
Thompson Defence Projects Limited, PO Box 100, Spring Road, Ettingshall, Wolverhampton WV4 6JY, UK.
Tel: 0902 353353. Telex: 337412 NEITOM G.
Fax: 0902 405500.

Chieftain AVLB

Development
The Chieftain AVLB (FV4205) was developed as the replacement for the Centurion AVLB (FV4002) and the Centurion ARK (FV4016). Development of the Chieftain bridgelayer began in 1962, but owing to some necessary redesign, the first production vehicles were not delivered to the Army until 1974. Design work on the AVLB was carried out by the then Military Vehicles and Engineering Establishment, AP Precision Hydraulics and the Hydraulic Controls Department of Tubes (Birmingham).

The Chieftain AVLB is used by only one regiment of the British Army: 32 Armoured Engineer Regiment, Royal Engineers. Within the British Army each Chieftain AVLB is part of a system that includes the bridgelayer carrying a No 8 tank bridge and another No 9 tank bridge carried on a Crusader tractor and semi-trailer. Under certain circumstances the No 9 bridge can be laid directly from the semi-trailer.

The production total of Chieftain AVLBs for the British Army was 37, with a further 14 produced for Iran.

In order to increase the number of Chieftain AVLBs available to the British Army, eleven Mark 1/4 Chieftain MBTs were converted by Vickers Defence Systems of Newcastle to the bridgelayer role. These are known as the Mark 6 and are some 3000 kg heavier than earlier AVLBs. They have a more powerful hydraulic pump and system and have other modifications such as a toe plate for fitting mine ploughs and an intercom system built into the bridge boom. The first Mark 6 AVLB was completed in 1985 with first deliveries later the same year. Deliveries were completed by the end of 1986.

Description
The hull of the AVLB is similar to that of the basic Chieftain MBT. The driver is seated at the front of the hull and is provided with a single-piece hatch cover and a periscope. The commander and radio operator are behind the driver. The engine and transmission are at the rear of the hull. The suspension is of the Horstmann type and consists of three bogies per side, each bogie with two sets of road wheels and a set of three horizontal springs. The first and last road wheel stations have a hydraulic shock absorber. The drive sprocket is at the rear and the idler at the front, with three track return rollers. The top half of the track is covered by armoured skirts which are removable for maintenance. The Chieftain AVLB has an NBC system.

The Chieftain AVLB can have either a No 8 or a No 9 Tank Bridge, the latter manufactured by Laird.

The No 8 bridge is carried folded and is launched over the front of the vehicle. The hull-mounted hydraulic pump, which is driven from a PTO on the main engine, operates five cylinders arranged to launch the bridge in three manually sequenced stages. Once the clamps have been removed the launching can begin. The Stage 1 cylinders pivot the folded bridge about the forward part of the glacis casting. This operation is continued until the launching pad meets the ground or Stage 1 cylinders reach the end of their stroke, when the folded bridge will be at an angle of about 30° to the horizontal. The Stage 2 cylinders then tilt the launching pad on the ground until approximately level. At this point the bridge is partly scissored by the rods connecting the central quadrant to the launching frame and is approximately vertical. Once the Stage 2 cylinders have reached the end of their strokes, the single Stage 3 cylinder is actuated causing the bridge to scissor further until the far end reaches the required bank height. At this point the rods slacken and on further lowering the bridge becomes a rigid connection at its centre point. The rods are then free and can be detached using the remotely operated release mechanism, thus separating the rods from the launching structure. The tank then reverses and the launching structure is removed from the bridge. The tank retracts all its cylinders and then either moves to the rear to pick up another bridge or crosses the bridge and picks up the bridge from the other end. The launch normally takes between 3-5 minutes, with recovery of the bridge taking about 10 minutes.

The bridge girders and launching structure are made of high-strength nickel-alloy maraging steel developed by the International Nickel Company. The deck and kerbing are of weldable aluminium alloy. The bridge is made up of two tracks, each 1.62 m wide, with a 0.76 m centre gap between. Each track is divided into four parts, two toe pieces each 4.55 m long and two centre pieces each 7.6 m long. A hinge is provided at each joint. The bridge has a maximum capacity of Class 60; Land Rovers and similar small vehicles can cross on a single track, allowing two-way traffic with vehicles of this size. By hinging the 4.55 m long toes of the bridge and dropping them at will, it is possible to cater for a range of bank conditions. A bank-sensing device is incorporated in the ramp sections.

In order to permit crossing gaps that are wider than the standard No 8 bridge an extension trestle has been introduced. This trestle is fitted in place of the far bank end ramps on a standard No 8 bridge in such a fashion that the trestle is allowed to unfold and swing downwards as the bridge is fully extended. The trestle then supports the No 8 bridge to allow another AVLB to cross, in order to lay a further bridge.

The No 9 bridge consists of two interconnected trackways 13.411 m long and 1.62 m wide, with a gap between them of 0.76 m. Total effective roadway width is 4.01 m. The bridge takes between 3-5 minutes to launch and can be recovered from either end. It is launched in three stages: Stage 1 raises the bridge from the horizontal to an angle of 45°, Stage 2 raises it to the vertical and Stage 3 lowers it to the horizontal. The launching arm is then disengaged, the vehicle is reversed away and the launching structure retracted.

Each Chieftain bridgelayer normally has one No 8 and one No 9 tank bridge, one carried on the vehicle and the other on a specially adapted Scammell Crusader prime mover towing a semi-trailer.

Chieftain AVLB carrying No 9 tank bridge

Chieftain AVLB operating in the Gulf region without a bridge and using mine ploughs; extra armour is fitted

Following a small modification, Chieftain AVLBs can also carry No 10, No 11 and No 12 tank-launched bridges. These are under development by Thompson Defence Projects (see previous entry).

Some Chieftain bridgelayers have been converted to carry the same type of mine plough as that fitted to the Centurion AVRE 105. Vehicles operating in the Gulf region during Desert Shield/Storm were fitted with extra armour and other protection measures.

Specifications (with No 8 bridge)
Crew: 3
Weight: 53 300 kg
Length: 13.741 m
Width: 4.165 m
Height: 3.923 m
Ground clearance: 0.5 m
Track width: 610 mm
Length of track on ground: 4.8 m
Ground pressure: 0.9 kg/cm^2
Max speed: (road) 48 km/h
Range: 400 km
Fuel capacity: 950 l
Fording: 1.066 m

Gradient: 60%
Vertical obstacle: 0.9 m
Trench: 3 m
Engine: Leyland L60, 2-stroke, compression ignition, 12-cylinder vertically opposed multi-fuel developing 730 hp at 2100 rpm
Transmission: TN12 with 6 forward and 2 reverse gears, plus emergency mechanical selection for second gear forward and low reverse
Electrical system: 28.5 V (24 V nominal)
Batteries: 4 × 12 V, 200 Ah
Armament: 2 × 7.62 mm GPMGs

No 8 Tank Bridge
Overall length: 24.384 m
Centre section length: 7.62 m
Ramp end length: 4.572 m
Overall width: 4.165 m
Roadway width: 4.012 m
Centre gap: 0.762 m
Depth of centre section: 0.914 m
Max span:
  (firm banks) 22.86 m
  (soft banks) 22.25 m

Weight: 12 200 kg

No 9 Tank Bridge
Overall length: 13.411 m
Overall depth: 0.914 m
Overall width: 4.165 m
Max clear span: (firm bank) 12.192 m
Weight: 9144 kg

Status
In service with the British Army and the Iranian Army.

Manufacturer
Chassis: Royal Ordnance Leeds built all production AVLB chassis but in late 1986 this facility was taken over by Vickers Defence Systems.
Enquiries to Vickers Defence Systems, Scotswood Road, Newcastle upon Tyne NE99 1BX, UK.
Tel: 091 273 8888. Telex: 53104.
Fax: 091 273 2324.

Vickers Armoured Bridgelayer

Development
Preliminary design work on the Vickers Armoured Bridgelayer (VAB) started during the late 1970s to meet the requirement for a family of support vehicles for the Vickers MBT which was being ordered in increasing numbers. The first order for six VABs was placed by Nigeria in 1981. A further six were ordered in 1985.

Description
The hull, automotive and running gear components of the VAB are based on the Vickers MBT with the hull structure divided into three main compartments. There is accommodation for a crew of three; the driver, radio operator and commander. The forward compartment is divided into two sections by a panel on the right of the driver who is seated on the centre line of the compartment. The panel provides a mounting face for some vehicle control units and behind it are the batteries and a stowage space. The vehicle controls and the bridge control units are located within the driver's compartment. Three wide angle periscopes are provided for driving with the hatch closed. The driver's seat has provision for vertical and fore and aft adjustments. The maximum possible opening is provided between the centre and forward compartments. The driver, by dropping his seat backrest, can enter or leave his position through the centre compartment, thus making a change of crew possible without opening up the vehicle.

The centre or crew compartment has seating for the commander and radio operator. The commander's seat is positioned directly under a rotating cupola fitted to the centre of the roof plate. Behind the commander

and to his right is the radio operator and radio sets. Beneath the radio equipment are two batteries and space for personnel kit in the left-hand pannier space. The crew ventilation system is in the right-hand pannier space. To the centre and left rear of the commander's seat are hydraulic pumps, filters, tank, valves and other

components for operating the bridge launch equipment.

The rear compartment accommodates the 800E powerpack and transmission unit. In common with the other Vickers MBT series the VAB may be fitted with a Perkins CV12 800E or a General Motors 12V-71T

Vickers armoured bridgelayer (VAB)

diesel. Panniers above each track contain bag-type fuel tanks. Lifting and towing eyes are welded to the hull front and rear.

Both batches of VABs for Nigeria are fitted with a conventional tank bridge. This bridge is 13.41 m long with a military load classification of 60/70. The bridge launching equipment is hydraulically operated with the power provided by a pump driven from a power take-off from the main engine. The launching operation is in four stages:

1) bridge securing and clamping devices released
2) bridge launched hydraulically
3) release of bridge from launching structure
4) vehicle reverses to withdraw clear of bridge.

To recover the bridge after use, the bridgelayer vehicle is aligned with the bridge so that the launching arm engages with the bridge lifting brackets. The hydraulic lifting mechanism then recovers the complete bridge onto the roof of the vehicle for re-use.

Specifications
Crew: 3
Weight: (with bridge) 43 910 kg
Length: (with bridge) 13.7 m
Width: (with bridge) 4.16 m
Height: (with bridge) 3.25 m
Ground clearance: 0.432 m
Max range: 600 km
Fuel capacity: 1000 l
Fording: 1.1 m
Gradient: 60%
Side slope: 30%
Vertical obstacle: 0.914 m
Trench: 3 m
Engine: Perkins CV12 800E V-12 diesel developing 800 bhp at 2300 rpm
or General Motors 12V-71T V-12 diesel developing 720 bhp at 2500 rpm
Transmission: TN12 automatic

Clutch: centrifugal
Steering: Merritt regenerative
Electrical system: 24 V
Armament: 1 × 7.62 mm MG

Bridge
Length: (overall) 13.4 m
Width: 4.16 m
Classification: MLC 60/70

Status
In service with the Nigerian Army (12).

Manufacturer
Vickers Defence Systems, Scotswood Road, Newcastle upon Tyne NE99 1BX, UK. Tel: 091 273 8888. Telex: 53104. Fax: 091 273 2324.

UNITED STATES OF AMERICA

M48 and M60 Armoured Vehicle Launched Bridges

Development
In the 1950s the standard AVLB of the US Army was the M48A2 AVLB. This was an M48 MBT chassis fitted with a scissors bridge designed by the US Army Engineer Research and Development Laboratories (now the Belvoir Research, Development and Engineering Center) at Fort Belvoir, Virginia. Production of the M48 was completed in 1959 and from 1963 the chassis of the M60 MBT was used. The chassis of these two vehicles is almost identical, the major difference being the type of engine. The M48, M48A1 and M48A2 were all powered by a 12-cylinder petrol engine which developed between 810 and 825 hp at 2800 rpm, while the M48A3 was powered by a 12-cylinder diesel (AVDS-1790-2A) engine which developed 750 hp at 2400 rpm, giving the vehicle an increased operational range. In FY78 the US Army requested $20.9 million to convert 136 M48A1 and M48A2 tanks into M48A5 AVLBs. (These vehicles now have M60 AVLB launcher components and the AVDS-1790-2D engine).

The US Army had plans to convert a further 50 M48A5 and 400 M60 gun tanks to the bridgelaying role for use by Engineer formations, although there are now no current plans for the M60. It was planned that the US Army would have 1100 AVLBs of all kinds by FY89.

Description
The basic chassis of the M60 AVLB is almost identical to that of the M60 MBT, except that the driver is located aft of his MBT location and accommodation is made in the same area for the commander, since the MBT turret is removed for the AVLB configuration. The engine and transmission are at the rear. Early M48 AVLBs had two turrets, each with a 0.50/12.7 mm Browning M2 machine gun, but they were later removed and replaced by two conventional hatch covers. The crew of two consists of the driver and commander.

The suspension is of the torsion bar type and consists of six road wheels with the idler at the front and the drive sprocket at the rear, with three track return rollers. Hydraulic shock absorbers are fitted at the first, second and sixth road wheel stations.

The bridge weighs 13 380 kg and is made of aluminium. It is carried folded and launched over the front of the vehicle hydraulically as follows: the AVLB is driven up to the obstacle and halted, the bridge is raised hydraulically into the vertical, unfolded and lowered into place and the launcher detached. The bridge takes 3 minutes to launch and can be recovered from either end. Recovery time is between 10-60

M48 AVLB with bridge about to reach fully laid position

minutes depending on the ground conditions. The bridge has an overall length of 19.202 m and can span a gap of up to 18.288 m. Its maximum capacity is 54 431 kg.

Specifications (M60 AVLB)
Crew: 2
Weight:
(with bridge) 55 205 kg
(without bridge) 41 730 kg
Length:
(with bridge) 11.28 m
(chassis) 8.648 m
Width:
(with bridge) 4.002 m
(chassis) 3.64 m
Height:
(with bridge) 3.9 m
(without bridge) 3.04 m
Ground clearance: 0.36 m
Track: 2.921 m
Track width: 711 mm
Length of track on ground: 4.235 m
Ground pressure: 0.92 kg/cm²
Max speed: (road) 48.28 km/h
Range: 500 km
Fuel capacity: 1420 l
Fording: 1.219 m
Gradient: 30%

Vertical obstacle: 0.914 m
Trench: 2.59 m
Engine: Continental AVDS-1790-2A or AVDS-1790-2D 12-cylinder diesel developing 750 bhp at 2400 rpm
Transmission: Allison CD-850-6 with 2 forward and 1 reverse ranges
Electrical system: 24 V
Batteries: 6 × 12 V, 100 Ah
Armament: nil
Armour
hull front: 101-120 mm
hull sides front: 76 mm
hull sides and rear: 51 mm
hull top: 57 mm
hull floor: 12.7-63 mm
hull rear: 44 mm

Status
Current users are known to include Germany, Israel, Pakistan (M48), Singapore (12 M60), Spain and the US Army and Marine Corps.

Manufacturers
M48 chassis support: General Dynamics, Land Systems Division, 38500 Mound Road, Sterling Heights, Michigan 48310-3200, USA.
Bridge: Southwest Mobile Systems Corporation, 200 Sidney Street, St Louis, Missouri 63104, USA. Tel: (314) 771 3950. Fax: (314) 771 1169.

Mobile Assault Bridge/Ferry

Development

The Mobile Assault Bridge (MAB) was developed from 1959 by the US Army Engineer Research and Development Laboratories at Fort Belvoir, Virginia (now the Belvoir Research, Development and Engineering Center). The first production batch had hulls of riveted construction. Totals of 32 end bays and 66 interior bays were delivered to the US Army between April 1963 and December 1967. The basic vehicle was manufactured by the FMC Corporation of San Jose, California, with the interior and end bridge bays being built by the Consolidated Diesel Electric Corporation of Schenectady, New York.

After the initial batch of MABs was built, a product improvement programme was initiated which was completed in September 1970. This version has an all-welded hull and an improved electrical and hydraulic system. A total of 220 MABs of the improved design was built for the US Army between 1973 and 1976.

The MAB is issued on the scale of 24 units for each division and non-divisional bridge units. The total requirement, for 298 units to equip NATO earmarked units, was completed with FY74 funding. It was for 44 MAB end bays at a cost of $1.5 million, 88 interior bays at $1.6 million and 132 MAB transporters at $18.4 million.

Description

The MAB consists of a 4 × 4 transporter which is fitted with either an interior bay or an end bay superstructure. These two types of superstructure can be interchanged, with the aid of a crane, in approximately 15 minutes. The hull is of all-aluminium construction which is either welded or riveted together. The sides and deck are 3.175 mm thick while the bottom, bow and stern are 4.7 mm thick. Reinforcing ribs provide additional strength to the sides and bottom of the transporter.

The crew consists of three: a driver who is also the bridge crew chief, an assistant driver who is also the bridge pilot, and a crewman. The three-man watertight cab is mounted at the front of the hull and can be removed for transportation if required. Entrance to the cab is by two hatches in the roof and rear of the cab.

The air compressor provides power for the windscreen wiper, tyre inflation and brake system. The MAB has two hydraulic systems. The high pressure system provides power for positioning the superstructure, raising and lowering the wheels and operating the capstans. The low pressure system operates the power steering (all four wheels can be steered), marine drive functions and the air blower for the wheel-well pressurisation. Each MAB has four electrically operated bilge pumps, which are located at the four corners of the engine compartment and have a combined capacity of 509 l/min.

Two hydraulically operated capstans are provided, one on the forward and one on the aft deck, to pull units together for pinning during superstructure connection. The capstans have a capacity of 2268 kg at 15.24 m/min. An anchor with 60.96 m of line is stowed on the top of the cab.

The MAB is propelled in water by a single 711 mm propeller which is mounted at the rear of the hull. This has a maximum thrust of 2272 kg and when in the

Mobile Assault Bridge in travelling configuration

travelling position is swung up horizontally. The propeller system can be rotated 360° for steering and reversing. Once in the water, the wheels are raised and the propeller lowered into position. Draught when loaded is 1.066 m.

The interior bay superstructure is constructed of welded steel girders and an extruded aluminium decking. It is carried parallel to the axis of the hull for road travel and is rotated 90° for use during water operations. When extended it has an effective length of 7.924 m and is 3.657 m wide. After the 228 mm kerbs are raised, the bridge deck has an overall width of 4.224 m.

The end bay superstructure is constructed of aluminium girders with aluminium decking and consists of two sections hinged together. The end bay superstructure section is 7.315 m long and 3.657 m wide with the kerbs down. The combined ramp and deck section is 10.972 m long. The superstructure can be rigged before entering the water and can be rotated either to the left or the right. The ramp can be articulated to reach different bank heights down to and including 0.914 m below water level.

The MAB can be used for two basic roles, either as a ferry unit, or as a floating bridge. Ferries and bridges are assembled by joining successive MAB units. In ferry assembly an end bay and an interior bay are jointed to form a double bay, two of which are then joined to form a four-unit ferry which can be used to carry a 60 tonne load at 12.875 km/h.

Bridges are constructed by connecting units and then lowering the ramps from the end bays to the shore. The combined crews can assemble a four-unit ferry in about 6 minutes, and dismantle it in about 4 minutes.

In a stream, bridges can be assembled at the rate of 4.572 to 6.096 m/min and dismantled at the rate of 4.572 to 7.62 m/min. When assembled the bridge has a maximum capacity of 60 tonnes with a gap of at least 30.48 m between MBTs and other heavy vehicles crossing.

Specifications

Crew: 3
Configuration: 4 × 4
Weight:
　(basic vehicle) 15 386 kg
　(vehicle with interior bay) 21 850 kg
　(vehicle with end bay) 24 599 kg
Length: 13.03 m
Width:
　(travelling) 3.657 m
　(over wheels) 2.844 m
Height:
　(travelling, interior bay) 3.3 m
　(travelling, end bay) 3.568 m
Ground clearance: 0.457 m
Track: 2.336 m
Wheelbase: 5.943 m
Angle of approach/departure: 22°/20°
Max speed:
　(road) 64 km/h
　(water) 16.126 km/h
Range:
　(land) 596 km
　(water) 185 km
Fuel capacity: 380 l
Gradient: 60%
Side slope: 20%
Fording: amphibious
Engine: 336 hp diesel
Electrical system: 24 V
Batteries: 4 × 12 V

Status

Production complete. In service with Belgium, Israel and the USA.

Manufacturer

ConDiesel Mobile Equipment Division, CONDEC Corporation, 84 Progress Lane, Waterbury, Connecticut 06705, USA.

Heavy Assault Bridge (HAB)

Development

The Heavy Assault Bridge (HAB) is the outcome of concept evaluation work by the US Army that followed on from the cancellation of the 'Bridging in the 1980s' programme in 1981. The result of the evaluation was that a new heavy assault bridge with a Class 70 load classification would be required. A minimum gap-crossing capability of 30 m was initially specified. A request for quotations was issued to industry and from the resultant designs the US Army selected the submission from BMY with Israel Military Industries, Haifa Division, as a major subcontractor. BMY was awarded a contract for the design and manufacture of

one prototype HAB system in April 1983 and design approval was given in November 1984. Additional systems were added to the contract later; three were produced and system testing was completed on one of them.

Testing by the US Government commenced in late 1988 and was scheduled to continue until July 1990. However during 1989 the US Army requested that all work on the project was to be stopped.

The HAB system was planned for fielding during the second quarter of FY94 and the HAB was to be used primarily with the US Army's M1 and M1A1 Abrams MBT fleet. Basis of issue was planned as 24 per Engineer Battalion in a Heavy Division and six per Engineer Company in a Heavy Brigade.

During late 1989 a US Army requirement for a new

version of the HAB was issued. This HAB is to have a three-part bridge with a total length of 26 m and will be able to span a gap of up to 24 m. It will use some components of the original HAB and will be similar in appearance apart from the length. The bridge will be manufactured using aluminium components in place of the original composite materials. The bridge will be so constructed that infantry will be able to walk across each deck.

BMY Combat Systems was awarded a contract to design and construct a new 26 m MLC 70 HAB, with Israel Military Industries as a major subcontractor. Their HAB will be carried and launched from a M1 Abrams MBT chassis. By late 1990 two launcher systems had been completed with two bridges under construction. Contractor testing was expected to begin by the end of 1990, with Government testing to commence in 1991.

In March 1990, General Dynamics, Land Systems Division, was also awarded a contract for a complete M1-based HAB. Its version uses the German MAN Leguan bridge system (see separate entry in this section) with its launching system modified for the M1 chassis. MAN GHH is a sub-contractor to General Dynamics, Land Systems Division.

The General Dynamics/MAN HAB contract involves two prototype demonstrators for the Fort Belvoir Research, Development and Engineering Center and is worth $12.459 million. The prototypes use the M1 Abrams chassis while the Leguan bridge involved has a length of 26 m and a load classification of MLC 70. Power for the Leguan hydraulics is provided by a 65 hp auxiliary power unit designed by Stewart and Stevenson of Houston, Texas. Weight is 64.6 tonnes, length overall 13.4 m and height (with bridge) 3.9 m. The M1 bridgelayer vehicle has a crew of two. The contract called for the complete assembly and testing sequence to be completed by the end of October 1992.

It August 1992 in was announced that a third system was to be evaluated in connection with the HAB programme. Southwest Mobile Systems of St Louis, Missouri, had been awarded a $5 383 481 firm fixed price contract to deliver and support two Chieftain AVLBs and two No 10 tank bridges (see entry under United Kingdom in this section for details of these equipments).

Specifications (General Dynamics/MAN version)
Crew: 2
Weight: 64.6 t
Length:
(overall, with bridge) 13.4 m
(hull) 7.636 m
Width: (with bridge) 4.01 m
Height:
(with bridge) 3.9 m
(without bridge, reduced) 2.45 m
Ground clearance: 0.482 m
Track width: 635 mm
Max speed: (governed) 72.4 km/h

General Dynamics/MAN Leguan bridge version of Heavy Assault Bridge (HAB) mounted on M1 Abrams chassis

Range: 418 km
Fording: (without kit) 1.219 m
Gradient: 60%
Vertical obstacle: 1.07 m
Trench: 2.69 m
Engine: Lycoming Textron AGT 1500 gas turbine developing 1500 hp at 30 000 rpm
Transmission: Allison Transmission Division of General Motors X-1100-3B automatic with 4 forward and 2 reverse gears
Electrical system: 24 V

Status
Prototypes – see text.

Contractors
BMY Division of HARSCO, PO Box 15512 Pennsylvania 17405-1512, USA.
Tel: (717) 225 4781. Telex: 510 657 4212.

General Dynamics, Land Systems Division, 38500 Mound Road, Sterling Heights, Michigan 48310-3200, USA.
TAAS – Israel Industries Ltd, POB 1044, Ramat Hasharon 47100, Israel.
Tel: (3) 542 52 22. Telex: 33 719 misbit il.
MAN GHH, PO Box 1253, D-6095 Ginsheim-Gustavsburg 1, Federal Republic of Germany.
Tel: 061 34 551. Telex: 4182058 man d.
Fax: 061 34 55202.
Southwest Mobile Systems Corporation, 200 Sidney Street, St Louis, Missouri 63104, USA.
Tel: (314) 771 3950. Fax: (314) 771 1169.
Thompson Defence Projects Limited, PO Box 100, Spring Road, Ettingshall, Wolverhampton WV4 6JY, UK.
Tel: 0902 353353. Telex: 337412 NEITOM G.
Fax: 0902 405500.

Light Assault Bridge (LAB)

Development
In early 1983 the US Army Mobility Equipment Research and Development Command (MERADCOM, now the Belvoir Research, Development and Engineering Center, Fort Belvoir, Virginia) awarded Foster-Miller Associates of Waltham, Massachusetts, a contract for the design of a new bridge for the US Army's Light Infantry Divisions. The MLC 30 bridge is to be used during combat assaults by and for logistics support of light combat forces. Three prototypes were constructed by Southwest Mobile Systems Corporation for US Army testing.

Description
The Light Assault Bridge (LAB) is a self-contained three-section bridge mounted on its own launcher. It is capable of spanning a 23 m gap with a military load classification of MLC 30. The launcher/trailer is an integral part of the bridge system and is used during the launch, recovery and transport of the bridge.

The LAB was designed and constructed using aircraft construction techniques to combine lightness with strength. It can be towed by a variety of vehicles including the M9 ACE, the M2/M3 Bradley, the M985 HEMTT truck and the AAV7A1. It is air-transportable in a C-141 or larger transport aircraft.

The LAB uses its own diesel/hydraulic power unit to raise and lower the bridge. Launching takes up to 5 minutes and recovery up to 15 minutes, using a two-man crew. Control of launch and recovery can be carried out from a position on the launch trailer or using a remote-control unit. Launch and recovery can be carried out using either end of the bridge. The trailer is fitted with run-flat tyres.

Specifications
Crossing length: 23 m

Launching Light Assault Bridge

Width of bridge: 3.3 m
Transport width: 2.8 m
Weight: 8160 kg
Load capacity: MLC 30

Status
Undergoing operational and technical evaluation for the US Army.

Manufacturer
Southwest Mobile Systems Corporation, 200 Sidney Street, St Louis, Missouri 63104, USA.
Tel: (314) 771 3950. Fax: (314) 771 1169.

TLB Trailer Launched Bridge

TLB Trailer Launched Bridge on tow by M60 MBT

Development

The TLB Trailer Launched Bridge had its origins in a US Marine Corps requirement for a Light Assault Bridge (LAB). The eventual contract was placed with a consortium of TAAS – Israel Industries Ltd, and BMY Inc of York, Pennsylvania. TAAS – Israel Industries Ltd, is the prime contractor with responsibility for the design and manufacture of the TLB with BMY designing and manufacturing the launcher and trailer. The programme commenced in May 1984 with the first two prototypes delivered in September 1987 and January 1988. Both were tested by the US Army Test and Evaluation Command (TECOM) and the US Marine Corps. TLBs will be able to carry and lay the existing AVLB.

The US Marine Corps was expected to 'authorise for service' the TLB during 1990 with procurement being included in the FY92 budget. There was no programme activity at the end of 1990.

TAAS – Israel Industries Ltd, has marketed this bridge as the TLB 24 24 m Trailer Launched Bridge.

Description

The TLB 24 is a three-section bridge mounted on, carried on and deployed from a tilt-frame trailer. The bridge is 24 m long with an active span of 22 m and a load classification of MLC 70. The bridge and trailer are constructed of high strength aluminium alloy (AL7005 and AL7075) while the deploying mechanism is constructed from high strength steel and aluminium alloys. The trailer, which carries two 34 hp diesel engines, either of which can power the system hydraulics and electrics, and will also be capable of launching the Armoured Vehicle Launched Bridge (AVLB) and the HAB. The TLB can be folded down to a width of 2.9 m allowing it to be carried in a C-130 transport aircraft. When in use the trailer is carried on a four wheel suspension system.

On operations the TLB 24 is towed or pushed into position by an M1 Abrams, M60 or other type of MBT, an M88-series ARV or an Oshkosh MK 48/14 (8 × 8) truck. Once at the site, the diesel-electric mechanism on the trailer is then controlled from within the towing vehicle, or from the trailer itself if required. The deploying mechanism is activated to elevate the bridge until the trailer footplate engages the ground, when the bridge is partially opened from the near hinge. The rear section is then raised and the centre and far sections are lowered and advanced. The far end is then opened and the entire bridge is cantilevered to its full 24 m length and emplaced. The deploying operation takes less than 5 minutes and retrieval from either end takes less than 10 minutes. Once the bridge is in position the trailer can be towed away.

TLB Trailer Launched Bridge prototype undergoing tests

Specifications (provisional)
Weight:
(total) 17 183 kg
(bridge) 8273 kg
(trailer) 8910 kg
Length:
(overall, bridge and trailer) 11.91 m
(trailer) 11.43 m
(folded bridge) 10.54 m
Width:
(overall, trailer) 1.371 m
(bridge) 3.81 m
(launcher frame) 2.67 m
(wide bridge treadway) 2.2 m
(narrow bridge treadway) 1.61 m
(folded bridge) 2.92 m
Height:
(bridge and trailer) 3.48 m
(folded bridge) 2.03 m
(girder) 1.02 m
(trailer) 1.5 m
Bridge length: 24 m
Max span: (hard banks) 23 m

Bridge classification: MLC 70

Status
Prototypes under test for the US Marine Corps. No programme activity at the end of 1990.

Manufacturers
Trailer and launcher: BMY Division of HARSCO, PO Box 15512, York, Pennsylvania 17405-1512, USA. Tel: (717) 225 4781. Telex: 510 657 4212.
Bridge: TAAS – Israel Industries Ltd, POB 1044, Ramat Hasharon 47100, Israel.
Tel: (3) 542 52 22. Telex: 33 719 misbit il. Fax: (3) 48 96 39.

TACTICAL FLOATING BRIDGES AND FERRIES

AUSTRIA

4-tonne Ferry Boat

Description
Designed to replace existing ferry equipments, the 4-tonne ferry boat was produced by a Linz shipyard and was first used for trials by Austrian Army engineer units in early 1985. The basis of the ferry is an aluminium boat designed specifically for combat engineer purposes that can be joined together in units of three by a ferry bridge equipped with hydraulic ramps.

The stackable ferry boat uses an aluminium welded structure of cross-rib design and fitted with a seal-welded double bottom. Each ferry boat has a payload of 4000 kg and is unsinkable. The ferry superstructure connects three of the ferry boats side-by-side and is formed of two aluminium trackways that are themselves buoyant. Four spacers between the hulls of the boats serve as an assembly aid and as treadboards when the ferry is in use.

The ferry is driven by three 40 hp outboard motors. The full crew is a ferry commander, three outboard motor controllers and eight sappers. The same crew is sufficient to construct the ferry.

Specifications
Boat
Weight: approx 500 kg
Length: 7.37 m
Width: 1.97 m
Height: (front/rear) 0.82 m/0.67 m

Ferry
Weight: (fully equipped) approx 3000 kg
Length of trackways: 7.5 m
Overall width: 14.5 m
Draught: between 0.2 to 0.4 m
Minimum navigable depth: approx 0.7 m

Status
In service with the Austrian Army.

Aluminium Footbridge

Description
This consists of a string of aluminium hollow-plate floats connected to form a flush deck walkway without any additional superstructure. Each float is reinforced internally with truss stiffeners and can support a load of 136 kg in the water. The deck surface is covered with a plastic material.

The footbridge is assembled by joining the floats end-to-end with pot-shaped connecting devices attached to the adjoining corners, which also float. In a strong current an additional float is added either side of the bridge at intervals. Guy ropes extending from the eyelets on the connectors to the shore anchor the bridge.

Specifications
Float
Weight: 81 kg
Length: 5 m
Width: 1.2 m
Depth: 0.13 m

Status
Believed to be in service with the Austrian Army.

CHINA, PEOPLE'S REPUBLIC

Type 79 and Type 79-A Ribbon Bridge

Description
The Type 79 Ribbon Bridge was developed from the CIS PMP Heavy Folding Pontoon Bridge and the American Ribbon Bridge. The construction, operating and other details are similar to those for the PMP and reference can be made to the PMP entry in this section.

Figures supplied for the Type 79 state that when a pontoon bridge is constructed across a river flowing at a velocity of 2.5 m/s, a 50-tonne capacity bridge 6.5 m wide and 312 m long can be produced. Figures for a 20-tonne capacity bridge under similar circumstances produce a bridge 3.2 m wide and 527 m long. Construction of a floating bridge with a capacity of up to 110 tonnes takes only 15 minutes.

A later version is known as the Type 79-A Ribbon Bridge. This appears to differ only in dimensions from the original version and is launched from a 6 × 6 truck. The details of a single Type 79-A pontoon unit are as follows:

Weight: 7200 kg
Length: 6.9 m
Width: 8.092 m
Height: 1.1 m

Assembled Type 79 Ribbon Bridge in position

Status
In production. In service with the Chinese armed forces and offered for export.

Manufacturer
China Shipbuilding Trading Company Limited, 10 Yuetan Beixiaojie, Beijing, China.
Tel: 893086. Telex: 22335 cssc cn.

COMMONWEALTH OF INDEPENDENT STATES

DPP-40 Floating Bridge Equipment

Description
Reports have been noted of a new floating bridge equipment known as the DPP-40. The DPP-40 uses inflatable pontoon supports and is capable of carrying light armoured vehicles. From what little information is available it would appear that the DPP-40 is used mainly by airborne formations and could be the replacement for the PVD-20 airportable bridge.

Status
In service with the CIS armed forces.

GSP Heavy Amphibious Ferry

Description

The GSP (*Gusenichniy Samokhodniy Parom*), introduced in 1959, was the standard heavy amphibious ferry of the former Warsaw Pact armed forces. Numbers were used by the Egyptian Army during the crossing of the Suez Canal in October 1973.

A complete GSP ferry consists of two units, left and right, which are not interchangeable and which enter the water separately and are then linked up. Once linked together the pontoon, which when travelling on land is in the inverted position, is swung through 180° into the floating position. Each unit carries retractable trackways which enable vehicles to be loaded or unloaded either side. The GSP can carry a maximum load of 52 000 kg. According to US reports, under favourable circumstances a tank is able to fire its main armament when loaded on the GSP.

The track suspension of the GSP is similar to that used on members of the PT-76 light amphibious tank family and consists of seven road wheels with the idler at the front and the drive sprocket at the rear. There are no track return rollers. The hull of the GSP is of lightweight welded steel filled with plastic foam, both to increase its buoyancy and to reduce its vulnerability to damage by enemy fire. Before entering the water a trim vane is erected at the front of the hull, although this was not fitted to early units. Each unit is propelled in the water by two propellers which are mounted in separate tunnels under the hull. As a direct result of user experience the GSP has been modified in recent years. These modifications include an improved suspension which has given the unit a higher ground clearance, a stronger hull and an improved cab for the crew at the front of the hull.

The GSP has two major disadvantages: GSPs cannot be joined together to form a floating bridge and the bank where the GSP unloads must be no higher than 0.5 m and must have a minimum water depth of 1.2 m, otherwise the GSP will be damaged.

Specifications
Half-ferry unit
Crew: 3
Weight: 17 000 kg
Length: 12 m

Width: 3.24 m
Height: 3.2 m
Ground clearance: 0.35 m
Track: 2.62 m
Track width: 360 mm
Length of track on ground: 4.83 m
Ground pressure: 0.52 kg/cm^2
Max speed: (road) 40 km/h
Range: (road) 300 km (estimate)
Fuel capacity: 370 l
Fording: amphibious
Gradient: 45%
Vertical obstacle: 0.8 m (estimate)
Trench: 3 m (estimate)
Engine: Model 8D6 6-cylinder water-cooled diesel developing 240 hp at 1800 rpm

Full-ferry
Weight: 34 000 kg
Length: 12 m
Width: 12.63 m
Draught:
  (unloaded) 0.97 m
  (loaded) 1.5 m
Max water speed:
  (unloaded) 10.8 km/h
  (loaded) 7.7 km/h
Roadway width: 3.54 m
Roadway track: 1.66 m
Max payload: 52 000 kg

Status
Production complete. In service with Afghanistan (6), Egypt, India (18), Iraq, Israel, Nicaragua, Uganda, the former Yugoslavia and members of the former Warsaw Pact. Known as the GSP-55 in Germany.

Manufacturer
State factories.

GSP heavy amphibious ferry

PVD-20 Airportable Bridge

Description

The PVD-20 was designed for use by the airborne units of the former Warsaw Pact and if required can be dropped by parachute. On the ground the bridge is transported in 10 GAZ-63 (4 × 4) 2000 kg trucks or six ZIL-157 (6 × 6) 2500 kg trucks. The PVD-20 can be used as a bridge or as a raft.

The basic bridge consists of 10 units, each unit with two NDL-20 pneumatic boats and treadways weighing 100 kg each and made of duralumin to save weight, plus ancillary equipment. A complete PVD-20 bridge system consists of 20 NDL-20 pneumatic boats and 60 treadways. Using one set, ten 4-tonne, six 6-tonne or four 8-tonne rafts can be assembled.

Specifications
NDL-20 pneumatic boat
Weight: 150 kg
Length: 6 m
Width: 2.2 m
Depth: 0.55 m

Bridge construction

Type	4 t	6 t	8 t
Length	88.2 m	88.2 m	64.6 m
Assembly time	50 mins	50 mins	50 mins

PVD-20 airportable bridge being used as a ferry carrying Czechoslovak Praga V3S (6 × 6) 3000 kg truck

Raft construction

Type	4 t	6 t	8 t
Length	5.85 m	8.8 m	11.75 m
Rafts per set	10	6	4
NDL-20s per raft	2	3	5
Assembly time	15 mins	20 mins	25 mins

Status
In service with members of the former Warsaw Pact including Poland and the CIS.

Manufacturer
State factories.

PMP Heavy Folding Pontoon Bridge

Description

The PMP (*Pomtommo Mostovoy Park*, or pontoon bridge set) was considered to be a major breakthrough in the design of floating bridges. It was used successfully by the Egyptian Forces during the crossing of the Suez Canal in October 1973. Since the introduction of the PMP (or Ribbon Bridge as it is also known) the US Army developed and put into production a similar bridge system called the Ribbon Bridge. The pontoons on the American bridge are made of aluminium rather than steel and are therefore much lighter: the American river pontoon weighs 5440 kg while the CIS one weighs 6676 kg, and the American shore pontoon weighs 5310 kg while the CIS one weighs 7252 kg.

Each pontoon of the PMP is constructed of SKhL-4 steel and is in four major sections which are hinged together. They are carried in the folded position on the rear of a 6 × 6 or 8 × 8 truck. Initially the CIS used the KrAZ-214 (6 × 6) 7000 kg truck chassis but this was later supplemented by the more powerful KrAZ-255B

(6 × 6) 7500 kg truck.

The pontoon is launched as follows: the travel locks on the pontoon are disengaged and the truck backs to the edge of the water; it brakes sharply and the pontoon slides over a roller system into the water where it almost immediately unfolds; six locking devices are activated stiffening the pontoon, and the pontoons are then normally connected together on the near shore to form a continuous roadway which is swung into position by bridging boats. Once in position the bridge is ready for immediate use. The surface of the roadway is ribbed to prevent vehicles from skidding

Tanks crossing PMP pontoon bridge during exercise

Raft construction

Type	40 t	60 t	80 t	110 t	150 t	170 t
Length	13.5 m	20.25 m	27 m	39.25 m	52.75 m	59.6 m
Rafts per set	16	10	8	4	4	4
Pontoons per raft	2	3	4	5 + 1 shore	7 + 1 shore	8 + 1 shore
Assembly time	8 min	10 min	12 min	15 min	20 min	20 min

when they cross the bridge.

The pontoon is recovered as follows: the pontoon truck backs up to the water's edge and an integral jib is unfolded from the truck bed, two cables are strung from the winch, which is to the rear of the cab, through the jib pulley, around the pontoon retrieval guides, and secured to the pontoon retrieval studs. The winch then simultaneously folds and lifts the pontoon on to the truck bed. The jib is folded back into the truck bed, and the pontoon winched over the roller and secured.

The basic bridge has a capacity of 60-tonnes but it is also possible to build a half-width bridge of 20-tonne capacity and of greater length. This is achieved by splitting the pontoons lengthwise once they are launched. Full length pontoons are placed at intervals to give greater stability.

The PMP can also be used to construct rafts of varying sizes, the maximum having a capacity of 170-tonnes.

The Czechoslovak Army uses a Tatra 813 (8 × 8) 8000 kg roadway truck in conjunction with the PMP; details will be found in the *Portable roadways* section. They also have some of their Tatra 813 (8 × 8) 8000 kg trucks fitted with a dozer blade, which are used to prepare river banks before launching the pontoons. The PMP has also been used by German forces to assist in the unloading of landing ships.

A complete PMP pontoon set consists of 32 river pontoons, four shore pontoons and 12 BMK-T (or BMK-130/BMK-130M or BMK-150/BMK-150M) bridg-

ing boats. A half set has 16 river and two shore pontoons.

A variant of the PMP is produced in China as the Type 79 Ribbon Bridge. Refer to the relevant entry in this section for details.

The Serbian Floating Bridge Set M71 (KPM-M71) is based on the PMP but differs in some details and dimensions. For details see entry in this section.

In Germany, EWK produces an all-steel version of the American Ribbon Bridge which is very similar to the original PMP. See entry in this section for details.

Specifications

	River pontoon (open)	Shore pontoon (open)
Weight	6676 kg	7252 kg
Length	6.75 m	5.58 m
Width	7.1 (3.21 m)*	7.02-7.32 m (3.3 m)*
Depth	0.915 m	0.73 m

* Folded dimensions are in brackets

Bridge construction

Type	20 t	60 t
Roadway width	3.27 m	6.5 m
Length of bridge		
(whole set)	389 m	227 m
(half set)	281 m	119 m
Working party	82 men*	82 men*
Assembly time	50 min*	30 min*
Number of whole pontoons including shore		
(whole set)	34	34
(half set)	18	18

* Data are for whole set

Two additional shore pontoons are held in bridge set

The bridge can be constructed in streams with a maximum velocity of 2 m/s

Status

In production. In service with members of the former Warsaw Pact (except Poland which uses the Polish designed PP-64 and Romania which uses the Romanian design PR-60). It is also used by Afghanistan (15), China (Type 79), Egypt (some carried on German Magirus-Deutz 6 × 6 chassis), India (156), Iraq, Israel and Serbia. The PMP is known as the PMS in Czechoslovakia.

Manufacturer

State factories.

PMP pontoon bridge unit carried by KrAZ-255B (6 × 6) 7500 kg truck (Stefan Marx)

FAP 2220BDS (6 × 4) 8000 kg truck recovering PMP pontoon

PPS Heavy Girder Floating Bridge

Description
The PPS heavy girder floating bridge, first observed in 1962, consists of large sectional pontoons, Warren-type truss girders with a full flushdeck roadway mounted on top. Each pontoon consists of a bow

section, two centre sections, and a stern power unit. Each section is carried on the rear of a ZIL-151 (6 × 6) 2500 kg truck. The pontoon is approximately 23 m long when assembled. The deck is about 0.38 m below the gunwales, which support six rows of truss girders, with the top chords carrying I-beam stringers. Decking is laid on these I-beams to form a roadway about 6 m wide. The bridge has a maximum capacity of at least

60-tonnes.

Status
In service with the CIS.

Manufacturer
State factories.

CZECHOSLOVAKIA

LMS Light Pontoon Bridge

Description
The LMS light pontoon bridge is similar in design to the larger Czechoslovak SMS medium/heavy pontoon bridge. Both the centre and bow pontoons are aluminium. The centre pontoon is fully enclosed while the bow pontoon has an open deck. Once the pontoons are in the water they are assembled, balks added and bolted together, and then the trackway is added, which can be of the full width roadway type, or a dual trackway, the latter being more common. The LMS can also be used as a raft with the following types being constructed: 10-tonne, 15-tonne, 20-tonne and 24-

tonne. The rafts are propelled by a 22 hp outboard motor and can attain a maximum speed in water of 11 km/h.

A complete LMS light pontoon bridge set consists of 48 bow and 24 centre sections, which are carried in Praga V3S (6 × 6) 3000 kg trucks.

Specifications

	Bow pontoon	Centre pontoon
Weight	470 kg	450 kg
Length	5.43 m	4 m
Width	2.02 m	2.02 m
Depth	0.8 m	0.8 m

Bridge construction

Bridge type	15 t	20 t
Roadway width	3 m	3 m
Pontoon sections per support	3	3
Assembly time	40 mins	n/a

Status
Production complete. In service with the Czechoslovak Army.

Manufacturer
Czechoslovak state factories.

FRANCE

Light Infantry Bridge Type 1949

Description
The light infantry bridge type 1949, introduced in 1949 and modified in 1962, can be used as either a footbridge or a light raft. In the former role, the pneumatic floats, which are also used for reconnaissance, are fixed under the spans of the bridge. A complete bridge set contains sufficient equipment to span a river up to 50 m wide when the current is slower

than 3 m/s, or a maximum gap of 100 m when the current is 1.5 m/s or slower.

The bridge set can also be used for the assembly of two rafts, each of which can support a maximum load of 2 tonnes. When the current is up to 2.5 m/s the raft can be pulled across the river by cables, but if the current is faster than 2.5 m/s two pneumatic boats with outboard motors are used to push the raft across the river. The raft has two trackways and two ramps at each end which are lowered manually for loading and unloading.

The complete bridge set weighs about 2800 kg, consists of 20 floats and 18 duckboards, and the individual components are light enough to be carried by hand.

Specifications
Floats
Weight: 49 kg
Length: 3.7 m
Width: 1.4 m
Depth: 0.5 m

Duckboards
Weight: 38 kg

Length: 3 m
Width: 0.6 m
Depth: 0.1 m

Assembled bridge
Total length: 51 m
Width of walkway: 0.6 m
Assembly time:
(day) 34 mins
(night) 51 mins
Carrying capacity:
(day) 75 men/min
(night) 40 men/min

Status
Production complete. In service with the French Army.

Manufacturers
Spans: Atelier de Construction de Tarbes, 2 rue Alsace-Lorraine, BP 313, F-065013 Tarbes, France. Floats: Société Industrielle Angevinière et Joué-les-Tours and the Société Zodiac.

Light infantry bridge type 1949 being used as footbridge

MLF Light River Crossing Equipment

Description
The MLF light river crossing equipment (*Matériel Léger de Franchissement*), also known as the CASTOR light spanning equipment Type F2, was developed by the Etablissement Technique d'Angers and was adopted by the French Army in 1976.

The MLF can be used as a floating bridge; a raft or an individual flotation unit can be used as an assault or river boat. When being used as the latter it can carry 32 men, and is propelled in the water by paddles or an outboard motor.

The flotation units, which are of light alloy construction, are made up of two flat-bottom boats assembled stern to stern by pins, and have an assembled length of 9.8 m. The gunwales are capped by stiffeners which are attached to the boat by four locking pins. Each unit is also provided with handrails, outboard motor attachment and a floor.

The bridge deck comprises two tracks made up of

deck components, steel assemblies, articulation units and ramp units. The central deck units fill the space between the tracks and are of reinforced plastic. The bridge decks are secured to the flotation units by the sets of tiltable pegs on the gunwale stiffeners. The bridge deck components are made of light-alloy sections welded together and are provided with anti-skid strips. The deck bridge components are arranged in pairs, end to end, and spaced 0.7 m apart.

The articulated joints provide the connection between the bridge deck components located on the floating support and those acting on the ramp. Each articulation joint weighs 165 kg and is adjusted manually. The ramp units are of welded light alloy construction and assembled by means of pins. Each ramp weighs 50 kg and is provided with a steel contact edge. Each bridge deck unit can be fitted with a track guide in tubular light alloy, which is articulated on bosses welded to the outside of the bridge deck. The track guide can be retracted into a free space on the side of the bridge deck.

The French Army version of this equipment consists of four flotation units and three deck sections forming a

loading length of 10.5 m with two ramp sections on each side. The resultant raft has a capacity of Class 16 in a river flow rate of 1.5 m/s. Propulsion is by two 40 hp outboard motors.

Rafts
Various types of raft of two, three, four, five or six flotation units can be assembled. A 4/3 type basic raft can be assembled by three teams of eight men in about 40 minutes. This raft can be carried on a Renault 4000 (4 × 4) 4000 kg truck towing an SKD 3536 trailer carrying the eight flotation unit halves stacked one inside the other. The raft is either propelled in the water by outboard motors or pushed by a bridging boat. For example, a 4/3 raft would be propelled by two 40 hp outboard motors on the first and fourth flotation units.

Bridges
Two types of bridge can be built using the MLF system: the medium bridge composed of bridge deck units with flotation units under them, and the heavy duty bridge with the flotation units positioned one alongside the other. The medium bridge (1/1) is 8.07 m long and will

Assembling a bridge using MLF light river crossing equipment

A Renault TRM 2000 (4 × 4) 2000 kg truck crossing a bridge built from MLF light river crossing equipment

span a river 7 m wide, while the heavy duty bridge has an overall length of 16.13 m and will span a river of 15 m.

Specifications
Individual flotation unit
Length: 4.9 m
Width: 1.75 m
Height: 0.75 m
Weight:
(without equipment) 160 kg
(with floor and superstructure) 235 kg
(with floor, superstructure and gunwale stiffeners) 250 kg

Bridge decks
Length: 3.44 m

Width: 1 m
Depth: 0.26 m
Weight: 205 kg

Raft and bridge load capacities in tonnes

Type of raft or bridge	Current speed		
	1.5 m/s	2 m/s	2.5 m/s
2/2 raft	6	—	—
3/3 raft	10	8	6
4/3 (basic) raft	16	13	10
6/4 raft	22	20	15
Medium duty bridge	15	13	8
Heavy duty bridge	22	20	16

Status
In production. In service with the French Army and one overseas army.

Manufacturer
Atelier de Construction de Tarbes, 2 rue Alsace-Lorraine, BP 313, F-65013 Tarbes, France.
Tel: (62) 37 62 62. Telex: ARSEN 531 581 F.
Enquiries to Giat Industries, 13 route de la Minière, F-78034 Versailles Cedex, France.
Tel: 30 97 37 37. Fax: 30 97 39 00.

CNIM Pont Flottant Motorisé Mle F1

Development
The *Pont Flottant Motorisé Modèle* F1 (PFM Mle F1) was developed by Constructions Navales et Industri-elles de la Méditerranée (CNIM) under contract to the Direction Technique des Armements Terrestres. It was tested in competition with a similar system developed by Creusot-Loire and compared to other equipment available in western nations during 1979-80. It was adopted by the French Army in early 1981. French Army engineer units will take delivery of 3600 m of PFM bridging.

Production of the French Army PFM units commenced during February 1984 with the first deliveries to operational units starting at the end of 1985. The first unit concerned was the First Army Engineers based at Strasbourg. In service the PFM is used in the forward area for tactical river crossing and in the rear areas can be used to form line of communications bridges.

Description
The PFM Mle F1 may be employed as either a bridge or a raft, and can be used in rivers with a current of up to 3 m/s as an MLC 70 raft, and with a current of up to 3.5 m/s as an MLC 70 bridge (MLC 80 with restrictions). The equipment can be launched from banks up to 4 m high, used as a raft or bridge from banks 3 m high and recovered from banks 2 m high. The main advantages claimed for the PFM Mle F1 are that floating bridges and rafts can be assembled rapidly with minimum manpower, and the main elements can be launched and recovered without cranes, bridging boats or other ancillary equipment. Section assembly is eased by the use of pre-locking devices. The PFM Mle F1 is practically unsinkable as the various elements are filled with polyurethane foam or are partitioned. The equipment is claimed to be easy to use and maintain.

The PFM Mle F1 consists of two major components, the centre section and the approach ramp. The centre section has locking elements at both ends, two wing

tanks and two ballast tanks. The centre and wing units are constructed from light alloy, the ballast tanks from laminated GRP. Included in the centre section is a light alloy framework which contains the outboard motor (55 or 75 hp). The approach ramps are also light alloy and their ends can be set hydraulically into various positions to suit the river bank height. The centre section and ramp are transported folded on a special semi-trailer towed by a 6 × 6 tractor. The resultant articulated unit normally has a 10 × 6 configuration but the trailer wheels can be hydraulically driven to create a 10 × 10 unit when crossing rough terrain. The semi-trailer is provided with power for unfolding, launching,

recovery and refolding the section. The components are launched as follows: the tractor reverses to the water's edge and the section is unfolded, the sliding frame is set back, hydraulic rams push up the forward end of the tilting frame and the section slides down into the water. A number of 10 m long sections are assembled in the water and the bridge is completed by adding the approach ramps. Each section of the bridge is propelled in the water by two outboard motors.

A team of 21 men can assemble a Class 70 raft in 20 minutes. Each such raft would consist of three centre sections and two approach ramps. A team of 45 men can build a 100 m bridge in 45 minutes.

155 mm GCT self-propelled guns crossing a PFM Mle F1 bridge (P Touzin)

Specifications

Main section
Weight: 10 500 kg
Length: 10 m
Width:
(folded) 3.6 m
(unfolded) 9.8 m
Track width: 4 m
Height:
(folded) 2.1 m
(unfolded) 0.73 m
Draught: (unloaded) 0.18 m
Positive buoyancy: 42 t

Approach ramp
Weight: 7500 kg
Length: 12 m
Track width: 4 m

Trailer and section with TRM 10 000 tractor
Weight: 31 000 kg
Length: 18 m
Width: 3.6 m
Height: 4 m
Ground clearance: 0.3 m
Max road speed: 80 km/h
Max off road speed: 10 km/h
Fording: 1.2 m

Status

In production. In service with the French Army and ordered by two European armies.

Manufacturer

Constructions Navales et Industrielles de la Méditerranée (CNIM), Zone Industrielle de Brégaillon, BP 208, F-83507 La-Seyne-sur-Mer Cedex, France.
Tel: 94 30 30 00. Telex: 401 235 f cnim f.
Fax: 94 30 31 00.
Enquiries to CNIM Head Office, 35 rue de Bassano, F-75008 Paris, France.
Tel: (1) 47 23 55 24. Telex: 642869 f.
Fax: (1) 47 23 49 23.

BAC 20 and BAC 60 Autonomous Ferries

Description

The BAC 20 and BAC 60 autonomous ferries are intended for use in assault crossings by engineer units in infantry and armoured divisions. Both can carry wheeled or tracked vehicles, the BAC 20 up to MLC 20 or 30, and the BAC 60 up to MLC 50 or 60.

The BAC 20 ferry is derived directly from the *Pont Flottant Motorisé* (PFM – see previous entry) and consists of a single PFM centre section with folding ramps fitted. The ferry is launched in the same way as the normal PFM sections and is ready to operate immediately after launching. Ready-to-use time from arrival on site is thus less than 5 minutes. When in the water propulsion is provided by two 75 hp outboard engines.

The BAC 60 consists of two PFM centre sections each permanently fitted at one end with a folding ramp. The two 'half BAC 60' units can be assembled when on the water and ready-to-use time can be around 7 minutes.

BAC 20 and the half BAC 60 units are carried, launched and retrieved by the PFM transport vehicle. Both equipments can carry their own transport vehicle.

Specifications

Model	BAC 20	BAC 60
Crew	4	8
Weight	11 000 kg	22 500 kg
Length		
(ramps folded)	11.6 m	21.6 m
(ramps unfolded)	17.4 m	27.4 m
Width		
(folded)	3.6 m	3.6 m
(unfolded)	9.8 m	9.8 m
Max useful length	15 m	25 m
Height		
(folded)	2.1 m	2.1 m
(unfolded)	0.7 m	0.7 m
Assembly time	5 min	7 min
Special semi-trailer		
Weight loaded	20 500 kg	20 500 kg
Length with TRM 10 000		
tractor	18 m	18 m
Width		
(loaded)	3.6 m	3.6 m
(unloaded)	2.5 m	2.5 m
Height	4 m	4 m
Speed		
(road)	80 km/h	80 km/h
(off road)	10 km/h	10 km/h

Status

Prototypes.

Manufacturer

Constructions Navales et Industrielles de la Méditerranée (CNIM), Zone Industrielle de Brégaillon, BP 208, F-83507 La-Seyne-sur-Mer Cedex, France.
Tel: 94 30 30 00. Telex: 401 235 f cnim f.
Fax: 94 30 31 00.
Enquiries to CNIM Head Office, 35 rue de Bassano, F-75008 Paris, France.
Tel: (1) 47 23 55 24. Telex: 642869 f.
Fax: (1) 47 23 49 23.

BAC 20 autonomous ferry carrying engineer equipment

BAC 60 autonomous ferry carrying PFM bridging unit

GERMANY

Infantry Bridge

This consists of small rubber dinghies, footboards, handrails and ropes, and retaining ropes, and is used by infantry to cross rivers and streams.

Status

In service with the German Army.

German infantry crossing lightweight bridge of rubber dinghies and footboards (Federal German Ministry of Defence)

Light-Metal Floating Bridge

Description

This is called the *Schlauchbootbrücke* MLC 12-60 by the German Army and has been supplemented by the German version of the American-designed Ribbon Bridge.

It consists of an aluminium deck superstructure supported on pneumatic floats or aluminium boats. The floats are made of rubberised fabric and are inflated by an air compressor. One end of each float is upturned and the other is fitted with a stern mount on which an outboard motor can be mounted.

The deck balk is made of aluminium alloy covered in non-skid plastic, the saddle beam assembly is also of aluminium alloy and the connectors are steel.

Unlike the American M4T6 bridge the deck balk is not laid in a staggered pattern, but in parallel rows with individual balks joined end-to-end by H-shaped balk connectors.

The roadway can be either a flush deck or a treadway type. The overall width of the flush deck roadway is 4.2 m and the width of the treadway bridge

Bridge, pneumatic float, Class 12-60 in position (German Army)

can be varied from 3 to 4.9 m, depending on the number of balks used in each treadway.

The last floating bay is provided with an articulated balk connector which allows the roadway of the shore span to fluctuate between 30°.

A complete bridge set, which is carried on six 7000 kg trucks and three 1500 kg trailers, includes 10 floats which is sufficient to make an MLC 12, 30 or 60 floating bridge, a Class 12, 24, 30 or 60 ferry or a short dry-gap bridge of MLC 24, 30 or 60.

Specifications

	Pneumatic float	Deck balk
Weight	329 kg	146 kg
Length	10.8 m	4.8 m
Width	2.3 m	0.34 m
Depth	0.8 m	0.27 m

Bridge assembled

Class	16	30	50
Length	86 m	43 m	28 m
Width of roadway	4.2 m	4.2 m	4.2 m
Centre-to-centre of floats	9.6 m	4.8 m	3.3 m

Status

Production complete. In service with the German Army and Indonesia.

Manufacturer

MAN GHH, PO Box 1253, D-6095 Ginsheim-Gustavsburg 1, Federal Republic of Germany. Tel: 061 34 55-1. Telex: 4182 058 man d. Fax: 061 34 55-202.

Hollow Plate Assembly Bridge

Description

This heavy floating bridge, called the *Hohplattenbrücke* MLC 50/100 by the German Army, consists of hollow rectangular St 52 steel pontoon sections joined end to end and side by side to form a bridge. Two types of pontoon are used, bow and centre, connected by upper and lower coupling devices to form a bridge. The pontoon deck, which is covered with non-skid plastic, serves as a roadway. A complete bridge set consists of 60 bow and 40 centre pontoons. A long ramp to accommodate extreme bank heights is also available.

A 10 000 kg truck carries three pontoon sections and tows a trailer carrying a further two. The pontoons are launched hydraulically by tilting the truck bed, or in the case of the trailer, by tilting manually, so that they slide into the water. They can also be lifted off the truck or trailer by a crane. Once in the water the pontoons are assembled into a bridge with the aid of bridging boats.

A Class 50 bridge consists of two rows of pontoons and can be assembled by an engineer company in 5 hours. The completed bridge is 115 m long, including ramps, and has a roadway width of 4.2 m.

A Class 80 bridge consists of three rows of pontoons and can be assembled by an engineer company in 6 hours. The completed bridge is 80 m long, including ramps, and has a roadway width of 6.4 m.

A Class 50 ferry can also be constructed with 12 bow and eight centre pontoons.

Mobile crane lowering bow section of floating bridge Class 50/80 into position (Federal German Ministry of Defence)

Specifications

	Bow pontoon	Centre pontoon
Weight	1207 kg	1153 kg
Length	4.7 m	4.2 m
Width	2.1 m	2.1 m
Depth	0.8 m	0.8 m

Status

Production complete. In service with Germany, Iraq, the Netherlands and Pakistan.

Manufacturer

MAN GHH, PO box 1253, D-6095 Ginsheim-Gustavsburg 1, Federal Republic of Germany. Tel: 061 34 55-1. Telex: 4182 058 man d. Fax: 061 34 55-202.

Krupp Festbrücke Floating Bridges

Description

The Krupp Festbrücke system, also known as the Light-Metal S bridge, can be adapted to become a floating bridge or ferry by the addition of extra modular components. Main components are still the twin-triangular, cross-section, wheel tread girders but to this are added a hydraulic ramp adjusting section, pontoons with load-bearing saddles and anchoring and drive units. These floating bridges and ferries can carry loads up to Class 60.

The floating bridge can be adapted to almost all shore conditions by using the ramp adjusting section. One side of this section is joined to the floating bridge and the height and angle of the outer section can be raised or lowered 20° by means of a hand-operated hydraulic pump acting on a pressure cylinder. This angle corresponds to a difference in height of approximately 7.6 m with a ramp length of 19.3 m. The time required for raising and lowering the ramp from the highest to the lowest point is 5 min. A special pressure compensating unit between pressure cylinders positioned close to each other in the bridge cross-section prevents tilting or jamming during raising or lowering. These adjusting sections can also be used as part of the floating bridge itself so that the bridge can be assembled from one shore and can assume angles to suit the required conditions.

The Festbrücke pontoons are light metal components each 8.8 m long, 2.25 m wide and 1.23 m high. Each has a carrying capacity of 11 400 kg at which weight each will have a freeboard of 300 mm. For supporting a bridge two single pontoons are joined stern-to-stern using twin pins inserted vertically over the full height. Each pontoon has a foam-filled decking covered by metal plating and each weighs 830 kg. The pontoons can be powered by 115 hp outboard engines and various accessories are available including mooring posts, trimming tanks, an anchor, a winch with 100 m of cable, and so on. Normally these pontoons are carried on special trailers 9.4 m long onto which the

Krupp Festbrücke in use as floating bridge

pontoons can be stacked five high to a height above the trailer carrying area of 2.43 m.

The bridge and pontoon are connected by longitudinal saddle girders set on each pontoon wall and joined by crossbeams. The lower chords of the Festbrücke are engaged by clamping jaws. For launching from a shore each pontoon is set afloat using at least three inflatable load rollers each with a diameter of 0.5 m and a length of 3 m.

The floating Festbrücke is anchored with winches on each pontoon. If this system cannot be used each pontoon uses its outboard engine. When used as a floating bridge the load capability can be altered by changing the pontoon spacing.

It is anticipated that most floating bridges will be between 60 and 200 m long. These bridges can be used in water velocities of up to 3 m/s. Normal crossing speeds should not exceed 10 km/h.

When used as a ferry, the Festbrücke is powered by the pontoon outboard engines alone, and can reach speeds of up to 20 km/h on smooth water.

Status

In production. In service with European and other armies.

Manufacturers

Krupp Industrietechnik GmbH, Sub-Division Structural Engineering, Postfach 14 19 60, Franz-Schubert Strasse 1-3, D-4100 Duisburg 14, Federal Republic of Germany.
Tel: 021 35 781. Telex: 0855486.
MAN GHH, PO Box 1253, D-6095 Ginsheim-Gustavsburg 1, Federal Republic of Germany.
Tel: 061 34 55-1. Telex: 4182 058 man d.
Fax: 061 34 55-202.

Folding Float Bridge 2000 (FSB 2000)

Development

The Folding Float Bridge 2000, or Faltschwimmbrücke 2000 (FSB 2000) was developed jointly by Krupp Industrietechnik and MAN Gutehoffnungshütte GmbH as a result of experience gained in the manufacture and use of the German version of the US Ribbon Bridge. The construction of the FSB 2000 followed extensive testing with models in the Research Institute for Inland Waterway Shipbuilding at Duisburg. The FSB 2000 has been selected as a candidate for the US Army's Improved Ribbon Bridge (IRB – see separate entry in this section).

Folding Float Bridge 2000 (FSB 2000) ramp section being launched from its carrier vehicle

Description

The FSB 2000 can be used in water with stream velocities of up to 3.5 m/s with a load of MLC 70 and up to MLC 80 in exceptional cases. It can be used in a similar fashion to the existing Ribbon Bridge and can be used for the construction of ferries and floating bridges. It is completely compatible with existing American and German Ribbon Bridges.

The FSB 2000 consists of inner and ramp sections with a new streamlined cross-section with 30° bows. Each inner and ramp section is folded into a 'W' shape for transport on an all-terrain 7000 kg capacity truck. The sections unfold automatically as they are launched from the carrier truck. Once in the water the sections can be assembled by a bridging boat into ferries or bridges. A ferry can be assembled in a modular fashion from two ramp sections and the necessary number of inner sections. The effective roadway width is 4.1 m with footpaths 2.2 m wide on either side of the road. The assembly time for a 100 m bridge can be as low as approximately 60 minutes, and up to 200 MLC 80 vehicles can cross the bridge every hour. A ferry consisting of two inner sections and two ramp sections can carry vehicles up to MLC 70 in stream velocities of

up to 3.5 m/s. To accommodate various bank conditions and heights the ramp sections can be adjusted hydraulically to a height of approximately 2.2 m above water level. Minimum water depth for operations is 1.2 m. Each section has four crane lifting points for handling.

Advantages claimed for the FSB 2000 over similar equipments include improved floating stability due to the new cross-sectional shape, a higher ferry capacity, the ability to cope with greater bank heights, a flatter approach slope onto the bridge, an improved bridge-crossing performance, a continuous road panel, no heavy ramp plates, a stronger overall construction and improved handling in the water and at launch.

Specifications (inner and ramp sections)
Weight:
(inner section) 4800 kg
(ramp section) 5200 kg
Effective length: 6.7 m
Width:
(folded) 3.03 m
(unfolded) 8.85 m

(roadway) 4.1 m
(walkways) 2 × 2.22 m
Height:
(unfolded, bow) 1.27 m
(unfolded, deck) 0.737 m
(folded) 2.35 m
(road transport) 3.95 m
Material: AlMgSil

Status

In production. Ordered by Switzerland.

Manufacturers

Krupp Industrietechnik GmbH, Sub-Division Structural Engineering, Postfach 14 19 60, Franz-Schubert Strasse 1-3, D-4100 Duisburg 14, Federal Republic of Germany.
Tel: 021 35 781. Telex: 0855486.
MAN GHH, PO Box 1253, D-6095 Ginsheim-Gustavsburg 1, Federal Republic of Germany.
Tel: 061 34 55-1. Telex: 4182 058 man d.
Fax: 061 34 55-202.

Bundeswehr Faltschwimmbrücke (FSB)

Development/Description

In 1976 the then West German Army decided to participate in the US Army's test and evaluation programme of the first production Ribbon Bridge which is fully described in the USA section. The trials were carried out in West Germany between September 1976 and March 1977. Early in 1977 the West German Army decided to adopt the Ribbon Bridge System and subsequently undertook the redesign to meet European requirements allowing production in Germany. Production by EWK began in 1978 with first deliveries being made to the German Army in December 1978. Each of the German Army's 12 Division Combat Engineer Companies has one complete set of 26 segments; 18 bridge segments and eight ramp elements. In Germany the system is known as the Faltschwimmbrücke, or FSB.

The German version of the Ribbon Bridge, unlike the US model, is built to metric standards as well as incorporating a number of improvements to suit German requirements, none of which affect its compatibility with the original US version.

The hydraulic system for raising the ramp bay to adjust to varying bank conditions has been modified and non-polluting hydraulic fluid introduced; on the original model, oil sometimes leaked out and water got in. Other improvements include winch-operated approach ramps, changes made to interior bays to prevent the cables from getting crushed as the section folds, non-skid coating on roadways and walkways and stops on the bridge sections to keep the bridging boats in place when the bridge is being used as a raft.

The Faltschwimmbrücke is carried on the rear of the MAN (6 × 6) 7000 kg truck, designated the Lkw 7t gl Brückentransporter. Bridges used by the Egyptian, Nigerian and Turkish armies are carried on IVECO 6 × 6 trucks. Full specifications of these trucks are given in the Trucks section.

EWK also produces an all-steel version of the system which is compatible with the original PMP system. This version was originally developed for Egypt. The main differences between the steel and the aluminium versions are given in the specification tables below. The all-steel version is in service with Egypt.

Specifications

Vehicle with folded unit
Cab seating: 1 + 2
Configuration: 6 × 6
Weight: (loaded) 18 800 kg
Length: (overall) 10.4 m
Width: (overall) 3.31 m
Height: (overall) 3.93 m
Ground clearance: 0.415 m
Wheelbase: 5.4 m
Angle of approach/departure: 45°/31°
Max speed: 90 km/h
Range: 700 km
Max gradient: 60%
Fording: 1.2 m

Bridge section	Aluminium	Steel
Weight	5400 kg	7700 kg
Length	6.7 m	6.7 m
Width unfolded	8.12 m	8.02 m
Road width	4.1 m	6.6 m

Ramp section	Aluminium	Steel
Weight	5500 kg	7500 kg
Length	5.6 m	5.5 m
(with unfolded plate)	7.6 m	7.5 m
Road width	4.1 m	6.6 m

Status

In production. In service with the Australian, Belgian, Canadian, Egyptian, German, Nigerian, Portuguese, Swedish and Turkish armies.

Manufacturer

Eisenwerke Kaiserslautern GmbH, Barbarossastrasse 30, D-6750 Kaiserslautern, Federal Republic of Germany.
Tel: 06 31 857 339. Telex: 45810.
Fax: 06 31 857 300.

Faltschwimmbrücke (FSB) in use as a raft

Leguan Floating Ferry

Description

The Leguan bridgelayer can be used to launch floating ferries up to load class MLC 70. For this the Leguan requires additional pontoons and hydraulically operated ramp aprons fixed to the bridge tips. For details of the Leguan bridgelayer and its normal operating sequence refer to the entry in the Mechanised bridges section.

The complete Leguan floating ferry consists of a modified Leguan bridge with ramps, a hydraulic system and pontoons with bridge saddles. To connect the ramp girder to a bridge, use is made of two openings in each Leguan bridge wheel tread girder. Normally these openings are closed by adaptors held in place by plug-in strips and an interlocking system. Each adaptor weighs 23 kg. When the bridge is used as a ferry the openings are closed by the ramp connection systems that form the connection between the bridge on one side and the ramp girder and hydraulic system on the other. The units are 1.4 m wide and the ramp connection systems weigh 137 kg for each tread girder. All are coated with the same anti-slip covering as the Leguan bridge.

Each ramp girder is 4.8 m long and can accommodate a difference in levels of approximately 1.32 m; this is a maximum gradient of 29 per cent (16°). One ramp girder weighs 620 kg. The hydraulic system is used as an adjusting element. The total weight of the hydraulic system for one ramp is 600 kg.

The pontoons used with the ferry are unsinkable aluminium boats coupled at their bluff sterns to form a pontoon. The pontoons are connected to the Leguan bridge and are fixed to the lower chord sections of the outer sides of the wheel tread girders. Two sets of three pontoons are required for MLC 60 loads and three pontoons for loads up to MLC 27. Each pontoon, that is, two connected boats, is 17.6 m long, 2.25 m wide and 1.225 m high.

To lay the Leguan bridge across the pontoons the laying procedure is much the same as for a normal Leguan bridge.

It is claimed that the Leguan ferry has good manoeuvrability and is well suited for use in shallow water.

MLC 27 Leguan floating ferry in use

Status

In service with Norway.

Manufacturer

Krupp Industrietechnik GmbH, Sub-Division Structural Engineering, Postfach 14 19 60, Franz-Schubert Strasse 1-3, D-4100 Duisburg 14, Federal Republic of Germany.
Tel: 021 35 781. Telex: 0855486.
MAN GHH, PO Box 1253, D-6095 Ginsheim-Gustavsburg 1, Federal Republic of Germany.
Tel: 061 34 55-1. Telex: 4182 058 man d.
Fax: 061 34 55-202.

Heavy Ferry

Description

The *Pionier Fahre*, or heavy ferry, was designed and built by the Boden-Werft shipyards at Kressbronn. It consists of 12 pontoons, each of which weighs 10 300 kg and can be transported on a railway flatcar with a loading space of at least 8.8 m, or on truck trailers. On arrival at the launch site the pontoons are joined side-by-side in three rows, with four pontoons in each row. When assembled the ferry is 36.6 m long and 7.6 m wide with the deck of the pontoons serving as the roadway, which has a usable width of 5.2 m.

The 120-tonne heavy ferry is powered by four 125 hp diesel engines, one at each corner pontoon, each of which powers a propeller which can be raised or lowered hydraulically and can be traversed through 360°. Maximum water speed is 16 km/h.

A feature of the heavy ferry is that the bridge, on the right side, can be raised or lowered to permit the ferry to pass under bridges and other river obstacles. There are ramps fore and aft for loading and unloading and a 20 mm cannon can be mounted on each side for air defence.

Specifications
Pontoons
Length: 9.1 m
Width: 2.59 m
Depth: 1.9 m

Assembled ferry
Length: 36.6 m
Width: 7.6 m
Capacity: 120 000 kg

Status
Production complete. In service with the German Army.

Heavy ferry carrying British soldiers and equipment across the Rhine (Ministry of Defence)

GREECE

Aluminium Floating Footbridge

Description
The aluminium floating footbridge, as produced by TEMAK SA, is a licence-produced version of the US Aluminium Floating Footbridge; for details and specifications see the relevant entry in the United States of America section.

Status
In production. In service with the Greek Army.

Manufacturer
TEMAK SA, 21 K Varnali Street, 121 34 Peristeri, Athens, Greece.
Tel: 51 35 886. Telex: 224268 tema gr.

TEMAK aluminium floating footbridge

Light Tactical Bridge and Raft

Description
This equipment is a licence-built version of the US Bridge Floating: Raft Section, Light Tactical. For a full description and specifications see the relevant entry in the United States of America section.

Status
In production. In service with the Greek Army.

Manufacturer
TEMAK SA, 21 K Varnali Street, 121 34 Peristeri, Athens, Greece.
Tel: 51 35 886. Telex: 224268 tema gr.

TEMAK light tactical bridge and raft

ISRAEL

Two-Tank Ferry Raft (2TFR)

Description

The Two-Tank Ferry Raft (2TFR) is intended for use as a ferry raft carrying one or two MBTs or for connecting with one or more 2TFRs to form a floating bridge. On land the 2TFR is sufficiently mobile to allow it to be towed into position by the tanks that will use it to cross water obstacles, and on roads the 2TFR may be towed by heavy trucks. Each 2TFR is an independent unit handled by a crew of three. A 33-man force with 11 2TFRs can bridge 300 m of water. Linking time for two 2TFR units is about 5 minutes.

The 2TFR consists of a floating loading platform, 21 m long and 5 m wide, with two side floats, each 21 m long and 1.6 m wide. The side floats are folded onto the loading platform during transit and are usually opened before reaching the operational area. At each end of the platform is a hinged loading ramp, 7.5 m long and 5 m wide, which is folded up onto the platform until the unit is launched. Both side floats and platform are filled with rigid polyurethane foam to ensure buoyancy in the event of battle damage.

The 2TFR is propelled by two identical power units which may be produced by Schottel (Germany) or Stewart and Stevenson (USA). The two power units may be controlled from either of two control units, or from a remote-control unit which may be mounted anywhere on the 2TFR. The power units propel the raft in the water and raise and lower the side floats and loading ramps. Each power unit is connected to the propulsion unit by a 270° pivot for steering. The propeller shaft can be raised and lowered to suit varying water depths and in transit the whole propulsion unit can be angled upward and over for road clearance. On land the raft travels on a wheeled undercarriage with four pairs of wheels, each pair with its own suspension. The wheels are low pressure and specially designed. Once waterborne the entire undercarriage can be uncoupled and dropped. A hydraulically operated tow boom, powered by either of the power units, is located on the stern of the raft, and is self-uncoupling.

In use the 2TFR is towed by a heavy truck, semi-trailer or wheeled tractor to the nearest possible point by road. When the road is left the 2TFR is hitched to a tank by the hydraulic boom on the stern of the raft, and towed to the edge of the water obstacle. The tank then pulls the raft round and pushes it into the water. The tow boom is uncoupled from the raft and drops off the tank. The 2TFR can then proceed under its own power

2TFR carrying Centurion and M48 tanks

and the undercarriage can be separated from the raft. The loading ramps are extended and once lowered the raft can take on its load of two MBTs. The entire sequence, once the raft is in the water, takes under 5 minutes.

The wheels on the undercarriage may be fitted with high speed brakes, and for road towing the width of the 2TFR may be reduced to 4.25 m. For water use the undercarriage can be supplied in a retractable form, in which state the wheels will extend only 0.5 m. Propulsion hydrojets may be used in place of the normal propulsion units, and another option is that the 2TFR can be fitted with only one loading ramp allowing the raft to be used as a one-direction raft with both propulsion units at the rear. A smaller version of the 2TFR can be produced which will carry only one tank. This unit will have a transit length of 17 m and a width of 4.45 m.

For maintenance, the power units can be removed and stored separately from the rest of the raft. Tank drivers need no special training to tow the 2TFR.

Specifications
Crew: 3
Length:
(transit) 21 m
(water) 31 m
(bridging formation) 27.5 m
Width:
(road) 5.25 m
(water, side floats down) 8.25 m
Height:
(road) 5.1 m
(water) 3.5 m

Loading platform width: 5 m
Weight:
(transit, less power units) 46 000 kg
(ready for launch) 54 000 kg
(waterborne) 48 000 kg
Towing speed:
(road) 60 km/h
(tank-towed, off road) 25 km/h
Uphill inclination angle: (tank-towed) 11°
Lateral inclination angle: (tank-towed) 15°
Turn radius: 20 m
Speed in water:
(unloaded) 14 km/h
(one tank) 11 km/h
(two tanks) 9 km/h
Draught:
(unloaded) 0.35 m
(one tank) 0.74 m
(two tanks) 1.2 m
Manoeuvrability: 360°
Operational time before refuelling: 12 h
Sea-going capability: to sea scale 3
Bridging capability:
(resistance to current) velocities up to 2.5 m/s
(length) unlimited

Status
In service with the Israeli Army.

Manufacturer
TAAS – Israel Industries Ltd, POB 1044, Ramat Hasharon 47100, Israel.
Tel: (3) 542 52 22. Telex: 33719 misbit il.
Fax: (3) 48 96 39.

JAPAN

Aluminium Floating Footbridge

Description

The Japanese aluminium floating footbridge is very similar to the old US M1938 footbridge. Major differences are that aluminium alloy is used instead of white pine for the float body and the duckboard stringer and cedar wood is substituted for pine in the transverse slats of the duckboard. The floats are filled with foam

rubber to give increased buoyancy.

A bridge set, which is carried on two 2500 kg trucks, consists of 21 duckboards and 42 floats which is sufficient to provide 76 m of walkway 0.55 m wide and has a carrying capacity of 75 men/min in single column. It can be assembled in 11 minutes by a working party of 45 men. Alternatively, a reinforced footbridge 25.2 m long and 1.65 m wide with a capacity of 150 men/min in two columns can be assembled by 45 men in 18 minutes.

Specifications

	Floats	Duckboards
Weight	43 kg	37 kg
Length	3 m	3.6 m
Width	0.25 m	0.55 m
Depth	0.4 m	0.15 m

Status

Production complete. In service with the Japanese Ground Self-Defence Force.

Japanese floating bridge ready to receive vehicle (K Ebata)

Japanese floating bridge with Type 70 SPRR being carried (K Ebata)

Light Tactical Raft

Description

This is similar to the US Bridge Floating: Raft Section, Light Tactical and is transported on 2500 kg (6 × 6) trucks. It consists of Japanese folding assault boats which are joined stern-to-stern to form a pontoon. Either two bow sections or one bow and one stern section may be joined. Attached to the gunwales of the pontoons are dual plywood treadways which form the raft deck. Siderails are then placed along the inside edge of the treadways to stop vehicles being driven off.

Rafts of 9, 10 and 13-tonne capacity can be assembled with three, four or five pontoons respectively. A three-pontoon raft is normally propelled by one 25 hp outboard motor and the four- and five-pontoon rafts are propelled by two outboard motors. Maximum speed of a loaded three-pontoon raft is 6.5 km/h.

Specifications

	Pontoon	Treadway
Weight	269 kg	100 kg
Length	7.7 m	2.5 m
Width	1.5 m	0.9 m
Depth	0.65 m	0.18 m

Assembled raft

Raft Class	9 t	10 t	13 t
Number of pontoons	3	4	5
Number of treadways	8	10	12
Overall length of deck	9 m	12 m	15 m
Distance between pontoon centres	2.5 m	2.5 m	2.5 m

Status

Production complete. In service with the Japanese Ground Self-Defence Force.

NETHERLANDS

Damen FAC 540 Floating Bridges and Ferries

Description

The Damen FAC 540 fast assault craft can be used in the construction of a floating footbridge or light ferries for loads up to MLC 8. All the bridges and ferries are based on the use of the aluminium-hulled FAC 540, designed to carry a fully equipped infantry section of 12 men plus two crew.

A tactical ferry raft for loads up to MLC 8 can be assembled using four FAC 540 boats joined stern-to-stern in a catamaran configuration. The same configuration can be used as a light tactical bridge. Each set of four FAC 540 boats is supplemented by a set comprising eight aluminium track units with a width of 762 mm for vehicles with single or dual rear tyres. The set also contains four aluminium track couplings and accessories, eight aluminium gunwale saddles to support the tracks, 12 nylon track fasteners to secure the tracks to the boats, six stainless steel pins to couple the tracks and four nylon rigging lines to raise and lower the hinged tracks. This type of raft can carry a 3-tonne truck at speeds of 7 to 10 knots.

The same set can be used to assemble a trimaran ferry raft with a total of six FAC 540 boats joined stern-to-stern. This type of raft has a load capacity of MLC 8 'plus' and can carry vehicles up to 7.3 m long. A raft created using racks laid directly across three FAC 540 boats can have a capability of MLC 2. Both types of raft can travel at 10 to 15 knots.

Light tactical footbridges can be assembled using the same components as the ferry rafts but with special end ramps, anchor winches, heavy anchors and steel cables and shore anchors. The FAC 540 boats may be joined stern-to-stern for MLC 8 bridges or used as single units to carry the single trackway.

When the FAC 540 boats are used as ferry rafts they can be powered by either a Johnson Workhorse 25 hp longshaft outboard motor with 22.7 l of fuel or a Yamaha 40 hp longshaft model with 24 l of fuel. The number of engines depends on the raft capacity; a MLC 8 raft requires two motors.

Specifications (FAC 540)

Weight: 235 kg
Payload: 2200 kg
Length: 5.4 m
Beam: 1.83 m
Draught: 0.62 m
Max speed:
(with 4 men) 25-30 knots
(1200 kg payload) 10-12 knots

Status

In production. In service with the Corps of Engineers in Brunei and Malaysia and with the Royal Netherlands Marine Corps.

Manufacturer

Damen Shipyards, Industrieterrein Avelingen West 20, PO Box 1, NL-4200 AA Gorinchem, Netherlands. Tel: 01830 39911. Telex: 25335 dame nl. Fax: 01830 32189.

A tactical raft using four FAC 540 fast assault craft carrying a Volvo 4140 (6 × 6) truck

Loading a Volvo 4140 (6 × 6) truck onto a tactical raft based on four FAC 540 fast assault craft

POLAND

PP-64 Heavy Folding Pontoon Bridge

Description

In 1964, following the success of the PMP heavy folding pontoon bridge, Poland started design work on a folding pontoon bridge. The initial prototype was finished in 1965 with first production units being completed the following year.

In design the PP-64 is different from the PMP and has a much faster construction rate. According to some sources this is over 25 m/min. The basic bridge has a capacity of 40 tonnes whereas the PMP has a capacity of 60 tonnes, which is not a great tactical disadvantage as the PP-64 can still handle the T-54/T-55 and T-62 MBTs. The PP-64 can probably handle MBTs such as the T-64 and T-72.

A PP-64 set consists of 48 river pontoons carried on trucks, six shore pontoons carried on trucks, 12 ramps for ferries carried on trucks which also tow the KH-200 bridging boats, six KH-200 bridging boats and one special connecting piece for use in joining PP-64 with PMP bridges.

Three types of bridge can be built: 40-tonne (A), 40-tonne (B) and 80-tonne. The 40-tonne (A) is the single roadway type and is 186 m long, 4.35 m wide roadway width, can take a 12-tonne axle load and be constructed in rivers with a maximum velocity of 1.2 m/s. A working party consists of 60 pontoon workers, 60 drivers, six powerboat operators and 10 NCOs. The 40-tonne (B) is also the single roadway type and is 145 m long, 4.35 m wide, can take a 12-tonne axle load and be constructed in rivers with a maximum velocity of 2 m/s. A working party consists of 54 pontoon workers, 60 drivers, six powerboat operators and 10 NCOs. The 80-tonne bridge is double width, 97 m long, has a roadway width of 8.7 m, can take a 12-tonne axle load and be constructed in rivers with a maximum velocity of 3 m/s. The working party consists of 54 pontoon workers, 60 drivers, six powerboat operators and 10 NCOs.

The following ferries can be constructed with the basic PP-64 set: six 40-tonne ferries 14.8 m long and 12.8 m wide each with eight river pontoons, one shore pontoon and two ramps, a working party of 20 pontoon workers and three NCOs, and two powerboats per ferry; or two large ferries 37 m long and 12.5 m wide each with 20 river pontoons, two shore pontoons and four ramps, a working party of 30 pontoon workers and four NCOs and three powerboats per ferry.

The bridge is launched as follows: the truck backs up to the river and the pontoon, which is in two parts hinged in the middle, is unfolded and then launched. The pontoons are carried on the rear of a Star 660 M2 (6 × 6) 2500 kg truck. PMP pontoons are much heavier and therefore have to be carried on a 7000 or 7500 kg (6 × 6) truck chassis. Bridging boats used with the PP-64 are the CIS BMK-130 and the Polish KH-200.

Specifications
Pontoon
Weight: 1000 kg
Length: 3.7 m
Width: 6.2 m
Depth: 0.85 m

Status
In service with the Polish Army.

Manufacturer
Polish state factories.

PP-64 heavy folding pontoon bridge in travelling position on rear of Star 660 (6 × 6) 2500 kg truck

ROMANIA

PR-60 Heavy Pontoon Bridge

Description
The PR-60 was developed by the Romanians as the replacement for the old Soviet-supplied TMP heavy pontoon bridge and it can also be used as a raft. The PR-60 is not of the folding type like the CIS PMP and Polish PP-64 and is therefore slower to construct.

The PR-60 consists of enclosed shore and river pontoons, which are launched from the rear of the Bucegi SR-114 (4 × 4) 4000 kg truck by gravity and are recovered by being lifted out of the water by a crane as the truck has no recovery capability. Once launched the pontoons are connected to form a continuous roadway. Both single- and double-lane bridges can be constructed, the latter with double pontoons.

A complete PR-60 pontoon set consists of 56 river pontoons and four shore pontoons. Each Bucegi SR-114 (4 × 4) truck carries either one shore pontoon or two river pontoons resting on top of each other.

Specifications
	River pontoon	Shore pontoon
Weight	1200 kg	1350 kg
Length	6 m	6.2 m
Width	2.4 m	4.2 m
Height/depth	0.7 m	0.7 m

Bridge construction
Bridge type	40 t	60 t
Roadway width	3.8 m	7.6 m
Bridge length	142.8 m	80.4 m
Assembly time	1 h	1.5 h
Number of pontoons*	50	60

* Including shore pontoons

Status
In service with the Romanian Army.

Manufacturer
Romanian state factories.

SERBIA

Floating Bridge Set M71 (KPM-M71)

Description
The design of the Floating Bridge Set M71, or KPM-M71, is based on the CIS PMP heavy folding pontoon bridge. Each set is composed of 32 floating sections and four shore sections loaded onto 36 FAP 2026 BDS/AV-PMP (6 × 4) trucks equipped with special carrying platforms. A further two FAP 2026 BDS/AV-PMP trucks carry a set of bridge surfacing and anchor posts. The set is completed by up to 12 R-M88 bridging boats towed by FAP 2026 BDS/AVG trucks, and 12 C(H)A 70 aluminium boats with 40 hp outboard engines.

The KPM-M71 can be used to bridge water with a minimum depth of 0.4 m at the shore and 0.4 to 0.8 m under the floating sections if the bottom is flat. The maximum water velocity possible during use is 2 m/s. Vehicles driving over the bridge can attain a maximum speed of 20 km/h.

The KPM-M71 bridging set can be assembled to build a pontoon bridge with a 20-tonne or 60-tonne capacity. Ferries with payloads of 40, 60, 80, 110 or 150 tonnes can also be assembled. Bridge assembly time is given as 50 minutes while a ferry can be assembled in 8-20 minutes, depending on the size.

When being driven on good roads a complete KPM-M71 set can reach speeds of up to 60 km/h.

All bridge unit maintenance and minor repairs can be carried out using a set of tools, spare parts and materials supplied with the KPM-M71 set.

Launching a floating section from a Floating Bridge Set M71 (KPM-M71)

Specifications

Section	Floating	Shore
Length	6.62 m	5.5 m
Width		
(transport)	3.15 m	3.192 m
(floating)	8.03 m	7.186 m
(roadway)	6.5 m	6.5 m

Height		
(transport)	2.22 m	2.2 m
(floating)	1.1 m	1.019 m
Weight of unit	8380 kg	8730 kg
Weight with truck	20 540 kg	20 890 kg

Status
In service with the former Yugoslav Army.

Contractor
Federal Directorate of Supply and Procurement (SDPR), YU-11105 Beograd, 9 Nemanjina Street, Serbia.
Tel: 621 522. Telex: 71000/72566 SDPR YU.
Fax: 38 11 631588/630621.

M-70 Light Pontoon Bridge

Description
The M-70 is of local design and construction and can be used both as a light pontoon bridge and as a raft. Each pontoon consists of two aluminium half-pontoons joined together. The balk and decking are also of aluminium construction. The load of the bridge depends on the velocity of the stream. For example a 12-tonne bridge can be constructed in a stream with a maximum velocity of 2.5 m/s, and a 16-tonne bridge can be constructed in a stream with a maximum velocity of 2.1 m/s.

A raft normally consists of four complete pontoons (eight half-pontoons) and the balk from three bridge bays, with or without articulators. Again, the load depends on the velocity of the stream. Twelve-tonne rafts can be constructed for use in streams with a maximum velocity of 2.5 m/s and 16-tonne rafts can be constructed for use in streams with a maximum

velocity of 2.1 m/s.

A complete M-70 light pontoon bridge set has a total of 60 half-pontoons plus deck balk and other ancillary equipment; the deck balk is carried in the rear of a TAM 4500 (4 × 4) 4500 kg truck, which also tows a single-axle pole-type trailer carrying six half-pontoons inverted on top of each other.

Specifications
Pontoon
Weight: 295 kg
Length: 5.64 m
Width: 2.04 m
Depth: 0.86 m

Bridge construction

Type	12 t and 16 t
Roadway width	2.8 m
Length	120 m
Half-pontoons per support	2

Assembly time	45-60 minutes

Raft construction

Type	12 t and 16 t
Length	9 m
Rafts per set	7
Half-pontoons per raft	8
Working party	30 men
Assembly time	15 minutes

Status
Available. In service with the former Yugoslav Army.

Contractor
Federal Directorate of Supply and Procurement (SDPR), YU-11105 Beograd, 9 Nemanjina Street, Serbia.
Tel: 621 522. Telex: 71000/72566 SDPR YU.
Fax: 38 11 631588/630621.

SINGAPORE

Floating Bridge System FBS 60

Description
The Floating Bridge System FBS 60 is intended for the construction of floating bridges and ferries and for ease of erection and speed of recovery. The complete FBS 60 consists of bridge sections, a bridge transporter, a bridging boat (described as a push-pull tug boat) and a boat trailer or boat carriage. For details of the associated bridging boat and its trailer or carriage refer to the entry in the *Bridging boats* section.

An FBS 60 floating bridge consists of two types of section, inner and ramp. Both can be folded for transport and will unfold automatically when launched into the water. The inner and ramp sections are made of aluminium and can be coupled together using pins to form floating bridges or rafts capable of carrying Class 60 loads. Each section has four main assemblies, two outer pontoons and two inner pontoons with the inner pontoons forming the roadway.

A typical FBS 60 floating raft consisting of two inner sections with a ramp section at each end is 27.2 m long and can be constructed by a team of 16 men. A normal set of FBS 60 consists of nine inner sections and four ramp sections. Using the nine inner sections and two of the ramp sections a floating bridge 74.1 m long can be constructed. If all the inner sections of two FBS 60 sets (that is, 18 inner sections) are combined with two ramp sections a floating bridge 134.4 m long is formed.

The FBS 60 sections are normally carried on 6 × 6 7000 kg trucks. These are carried on bridge transporters that are also used for the launching and retrieval of the sections. The complete length of a typical loaded bridge transporter is of the order of 10.8 m and height is around 4 m. Width overall is 3.4 m.

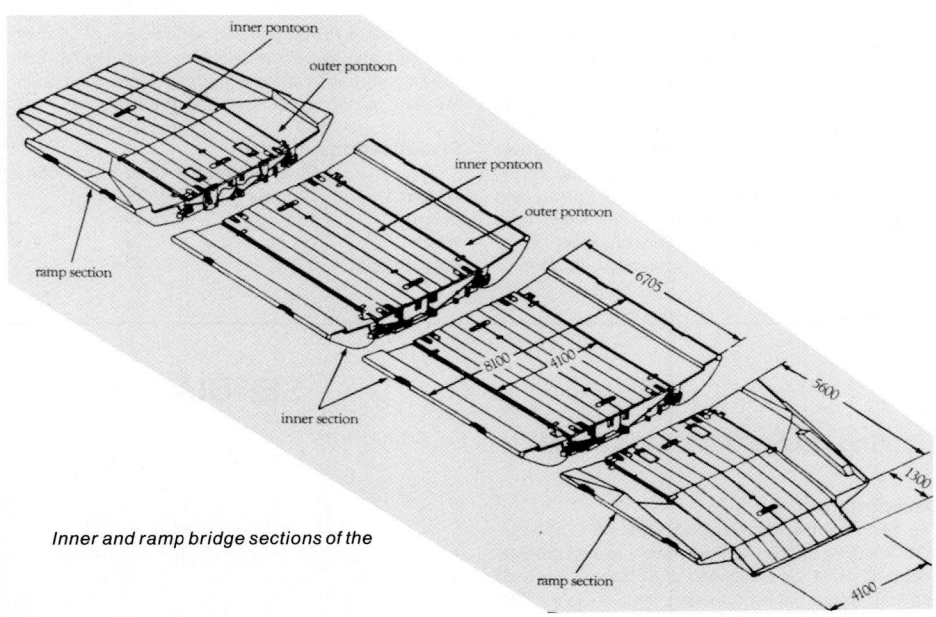

Inner and ramp bridge sections of the

Inner and ramp bridge sections of the Floating Bridge System FBS 60

Specifications (inner and ramp sections)
Weight: 5500 kg
Width:
(folded) 3.2 m
(unfolded) 8.1 m
Height: (unfolded) 1.1 m
Roadway width: 4.1 m

Status
In production.

Manufacturer
Singapore Shipbuilding and Engineering Limited, 7 Benoi Road, Singapore 2262.
Tel: 8612244. Telex: singa rs 21206.
Fax: 8613028.

SWITZERLAND

Bridge, Pneumatic Float, Model 1961

Description
This bridge, designated the *Schlauchbootbrücke* Model 1961, was designed by Krupp and MAN of Germany to meet the requirements of the Swiss Army.

It entered service in 1961 as the replacement for the Model 1935 pontoon bridge.

The Model 1961 uses the same aluminium deck balk as the German Class 16/30/50 pneumatic floating bridge, from which it differs in having turned ends. The floats each have 12 air compartments and can support a normal load even with four compartments punctured. It is claimed that even with one float destroyed the

floating bridge will carry its normal load.

A Class 50 bridge is 100 m long with a distance between the floats of 4.8 m, and can be assembled, in currents with a velocity of up to 3.5 m/s, in 3 hours by a 132-man team. The bridge is assembled by the successive raft method with each raft being assembled along the river bank and then brought into the line of the bridge by two or three assault boats powered by an

85 hp outboard motor. The basic bridge has a roadway width of 4.2 m, but a two-lane roadway, 5.6 m wide, can also be constructed. The Model 1961 bridge can also be used to assemble ferries with capacities of 16, 30 and 50 tonnes.

Specifications
Pneumatic float
Weight: 45 kg

Deck balk
Weight: 145 kg
Length: 4.8 m
Width: 0.35 m
Depth: 0.25 m

Raft class	16 t	30 t	50 t
Number of floats	2	3	4
Overall length of deck	9.6 m	14.4 m	19.1 m
Assembly time	1.5 h	1.5 h	2 h
Working party	33 men	33 men	33 men

Swiss bridge, pneumatic float, Model 1961 being assembled

Status
Production complete. In service with the Swiss Army.

UNITED KINGDOM

Class 16 Airportable Bridge

Description
The Class 16 airportable bridge was designed by the Military Engineering Establishment at Christchurch (now Royal Armament and Research Development Centre, Christchurch). Production and marketing of the bridge are undertaken by Laird (Anglesey) Limited.

The bridge is constructed of a high strength aluminium zinc-magnesium alloy and can be used either as a clear span bridge of up to 15.2 m in length, as a floating bridge of any length or as a powered raft with a maximum speed of 6 knots. All have a non-skid roadway 3.3 m wide when assembled.

The basic components of the Class 16 bridge are the deck boxes, ramps, articulator boxes, floats and the sponsons. These components are normally carried by Land Rovers which also tow a single-axle trailer. A Puma helicopter can carry any component of the Class 16 bridge and a C-130 transport aircraft can carry all the components required to build a ferry.

The deck box combines the functions of bridge girders and cross girders, and contributes buoyancy in floating applications. The top of the box forms the deck of the bridge. At either end of the bridge tapered ramps provide access. When being used as a floating bridge or raft, hydraulically operated articulator boxes are fitted between the deck boxes and the ramps to allow adjustment for varying heights. For floating bridges and rafts, pneumatic floats are fitted to give additional buoyancy and stability. When being used as a floating raft for powered raft operations, sponsons with integral turntable brackets are fitted at each corner of the raft, each sponson having a 40 hp outboard motor.

Clearspan bridge
A 15.2 m clearspan bridge is assembled from seven deck boxes and two pairs of ramps. Three Land Rovers and trailers carry all the components for one 15.2 m clearspan bridge. The bridge can be constructed and positioned by 16 men in approximately 20 minutes using a special launching nose and rollers. A launching nose and three pairs of rollers are used for building and launching the bridge. One pair of rollers is subsequently used as a landing roller on the far bank. The angle of the launching nose can be altered by means of its built-in jack to allow for varying heights of the far bank. The far end of the bridge is lowered to the ground by operating a jack.

Floating bridge
A floating bridge 58 m long can be assembled from 40

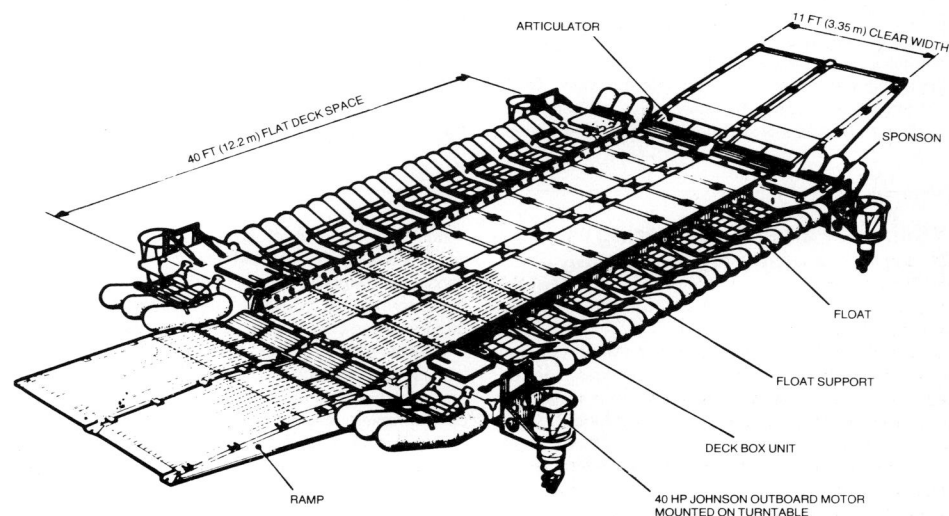
Class 16 airportable bridge being used as raft

Specifications
	Deck box	Ramp	Articulator box	Float and support frame	Sponson (with motor and accessories)
Length	3.6 m	3.6 m	1.8 m	2 m	2 m
Width	1.2 m	1.8 m	1.2 m	1.2 m	1.2 m
Height	0.38 m	0.38 m	0.38 m	0.75 m	0.75 m
Weight	305 kg	346 kg	279 kg	23 kg	281 kg

deck boxes, two pairs of articulator boxes and two pairs of ramps and floats using a standard bridge set. Five Land Rovers and trailers carry all the necessary components for a floating bridge. A team of 24 men takes 45 minutes to build the 58 m bridge and there is no limit to the length of floating bridge that can be built. The floating bridge is assembled in the same manner as the raft but the sponsons are omitted and floats fitted in their place.

Powered raft
The standard raft has a 12.2 m level deck and is 22 m overall. It is assembled from 10 deck boxes, two pairs of articulator boxes, two pairs of ramps, floats and four sponsons with outboard motors. Twenty Land Rovers and trailers carry all the components necessary to build one standard powered raft. Building time is approximately 40 minutes with 24 men. The raft is constructed as follows: the ramps and articulators are assembled and launched in the water, deck boxes added, then the rear articulator and finally the rear ramps, the sponsons and outboard motors are fitted to the raft and the floats are fitted to the boxes. The floats are inflated from the Land Rovers' exhaust gases. Longer rafts may be built up to a maximum length of 28 m overall, with an 18.3 m level deck. These are powered by six outboard motors and have a total distributed load of 24 tonnes.

Status
Production as required. In service with Australia, Canada, Nigeria and the United Kingdom.

Manufacturer
Laird (Anglesey) Limited, Beaumaris, Gwynedd LL58 8HY, UK.
Tel: 0248 810431. Fax: 0248 810300.

Class 80 Heavy Ferry

Description

The Class 80 heavy ferry, introduced in the 1950s, was designed for rapid crossing of wide water obstacles by all tracked and wheeled vehicles up to Class 80.

The ferry consists of four main pontoon sections, four bow pontoon sections, four buoyancy sections and four hydraulically operated ramps. All pontoon sections and ramp sections are made of aluminium alloy.

The four main pontoon sections are in the centre with buoyancy sections on either side and the bow pontoon and ramps at either end. Loads are carried only on the four main pontoon sections.

Built into each bow pontoon section are four Gill hydrojet propulsion units, each powered by a 120 hp Rolls-Royce petrol engine. The powerpack, consisting of the engine, clutch and gearbox, is bolted onto the deck of each bow pontoon section. The Gill propulsion unit is basically an axial-flow pump that takes in and ejects water at the base of the pontoon. For steering the jet can be traversed through a full 360°.

A complete Class 80 heavy ferry is carried on four 10- or 14-tonne trucks, each of which tows a special four-wheeled trailer, and two 4-tonne trucks each towing a 1-tonne trailer. Each 10-tonne truck carries one bow pontoon and one buoyancy section with the trailer carrying one main pontoon section and one ramp unit.

For assembly, two cranes and two dozers are normally used: the cranes lift the pontoons from the truck and the dozers push them into the water. Once assembled the Class 80 heavy ferry can carry one MBT, or three APCs or six wheeled vehicles. Maximum

Class 80 heavy ferry carrying Chieftain MBT (Ministry of Defence)

speed without a load is 14 km/h and with a load is 11 km/h.

Assembled Class 80 Heavy Ferry
Assembled time with 30 man team: 30 mins
Assembled length:
  (without ramps) 19.5 m
  (with ramps) 31.7 m

Width:
  (overall) 8.7 m
  (usable) 4.6 m

Status
Production complete. In service with Australia and the British Army.

Specifications

	Main pontoon section	Bow pontoon section	Buoyancy section	Ramp
Weight	4830 kg	2030 kg	760 kg	1270 kg
Length	9.8 m	5.5 m	4.3 m	6.1 m
Width	2.3 m	2.1 m	2.1 m	2.1 m
Depth	1.2 m	1.2 m	1.2 m	n/app

Williams Fairey Engineering Floating Medium Girder Bridge

Description

By use of the Medium Girder Bridge (MGB) pontoon (powered or unpowered), floating bridges can be constructed using MGB system components (for full details of the MGB refer to entry under *Tactical (non-floating) and line of communications bridges*). Single or double storey configurations can be constructed.

For bank heights of 2 m or less, single storey construction can be adopted. This is the fastest time of construction where 100 m of bridge can be constructed on a normal site in under 1 hour. This configuration requires more pontoons than double storey bridges.

Double storey floating construction allows long landing bays of up to 26.5 m and is suitable for higher bank heights, difficult shore lines or where there is a considerable rise and fall in the water level.

The aluminium pontoons used for floating MGBs are the same as those used for the MGB ferry – see

following entry.

Status

In production and widespread service.

Manufacturer

Williams Fairey Engineering Limited, PO Box 41, Crossley Road, Heaton Chapel, Stockport, Cheshire SK4 5BD, UK.
Tel: 061 432 0281. Telex: 667866.
Fax: 061 431 3575.

A Class 60 single storey floating MGB

A continuous double storey 110 m floating MGB

A double storey floating MGB under construction

Williams Fairey Engineering Medium Girder Bridge Powered Pontoon and Ferry

Description

The Williams Fairey Engineering Medium Girder Bridge (MGB) pontoon can be powered by means of a Schottel water jet driven by a Deutz air-cooled diesel engine. The engine assembly is mounted in a lightweight frame which is secured to the floor by four clamps and can be rapidly removed for either maintenance or complete in-field replacement. The Schottel pump jet is mounted by clamps in the floor of the pontoon and can also be rapidly removed for servicing.

There are no protrusions on the underside of the pontoons thus enabling the unit to operate in shallow or heavily obstructed water without problems of fouling. Steering is effected by rotating the jet outlet which, with its 360° movement, provides the pontoon with a high level of manoeuvrability.

The powered pontoon is primarily intended for use on MGB ferries with four units on a Class 70 and two each on Class 27 and Class 20 ferries. However, they can also be effectively used during the construction of floating bridges providing a rapid means of placing piers.

Each pontoon is of open-top construction which allows stacking (less powerpack) for transport and storage. The aluminium pontoons have sealed in-built buoyancy which alone provides adequate flotation for the ferry or bridge structure. They are self-draining and anchor winches are fitted as standard. Each pontoon has a (net) buoyancy of 12 000 kg at 300 mm freeboard. They can be stacked with four pontoons one inside the other to form a load 2.7 m high. Such a stack can be carried on a non-dedicated truck of the DROPS type which can be used to launch and recover the pontoons.

The MGB ferry is essentially a single storey bridge connected to MGB pontoons to provide a range of ferries from MLC 20 upwards. The pontoons may be connected to form rafts by the use of raft saddles which are constructed in three sections: a centre section and two arms. They pivot to allow the assembly to be stowed within the pontoon during transportation. The construction sequence is similar to that of a long single storey MGB. The end of the bridge is supported on a roller beam and the first landing bay is completed by adding top panel bays followed by hinge panels. Further top panels are fitted and the girder boomed out to allow connection between the piers or rafts at the saddle or hinge panel position. The construction continues with further top panels up to the second pair of hinge panels and then completion of the second landing bay.

Williams Fairey Engineering Limited markets a standard range of three ferries: MLC 20, 27 and 70. Other options up to MLC 90 are possible.

Specifications (MGB pontoon)

Weight: (less powerpack) 1100 kg approx
Length: 7.96 m
Width: 2.6 m
Height: 1.17 m
Max current speed: (laden) in excess of 3 m/s
Available buoyancy: (net) 12 000 kg at 300 mm freeboard
Powerpack: Deutz air-cooled diesel
Water jet: Schottel pump jet providing thrust through 360°

Status

In production. In service with three countries.

Manufacturer

Williams Fairey Engineering Limited, PO Box 41, Crossley Road, Heaton Chapel, Stockport, Cheshire SK4 5BD, UK.
Tel: 061 432 0281. Telex: 667866.
Fax: 061 431 3575.

MGB Class 60 ferry carrying Chieftain MBT

Unloading stack of four MGB pontoons using Boughton DROPS/PLS system fitted to Foden 8 × 4 Low Mobility truck

MEXEFLOTE – Multi-purpose Pontoon and Harbour Equipment

Description

MEXEFLOTE is a multi-purpose pontoon equipment designed specifically for marine applications. It is of MLC 60 and can be rapidly constructed as lighterage rafts, for use at sea and in harbours, and can also be assembled as causeways, jetties and other floating structures. The equipment can be used in the following wave conditions: pontoons connected into rafts, causeways and jetties in 0.61 m waves; operation of rafts, causeways and jetties in 1.22 to 1.52 m waves; survival of causeway, raft or jetty (unladen) at moorings in 2.74 to 3.05 m waves; survival of causeways or rafts (unladen) in tow in 3.66 m waves.

The system is based on the use of three steel pontoons: bow, centre and stern. These can be connected end to end and side to side to form rafts, causeways, jetties and floating platforms of any shape. The pontoons are of welded steel construction with flush sides. Built into the sides and ends of the pontoons are recessed slots into which the connectors are fitted. There is a 50 mm gap between pontoons.

The bow pontoon consists of a forward section, an aft section and a ramp. The forward section is hinged to the bottom edge of the box-shaped aft section and can articulate vertically to a maximum of 457 mm above the deck level and lowered to a maximum of 380 mm below the surface of the aft section. The manually operated, demountable articulator is mounted in a recess in the aft section and is connected to the forward section by an articulator ram. The articulator has a safe working load of 81 280 kg. The pontoon ramp is hinged to the forward section and slides over the forward end of the aft section to bridge the gap between the sections.

The centre pontoon is a box-shaped unit with an

90-tonne MEXEFLOTE being used as general lighterage raft at Marchwood Military Port

internal lateral bulkhead dividing the interior into two watertight compartments. Each compartment has a hatch cover, air-line connector and a bilge discharge outlet fitted with nylon plugs set flush with the deck surface.

The stern pontoon is also a box-shaped unit with an internal lateral bulkhead dividing the interior into two watertight compartments. Each compartment has a hatch cover, air-line connector and a bilge discharge outlet fitted with nylon plugs set flush with the deck surface. The bottom edge of the stern pontoon is chamfered to allow the propeller and skeg of the propelling unit to be rotated through 360° when the unit

is mounted at the stern of the pontoon.

The pontoon connector is a rectangular unit weighing 73.94 kg and fits into any full length connector slot of a pontoon and is used to join together pontoons side by side and end to end. Each connector has one fixed pin and one movable pin at the bottom which can be raised or lowered by a handle in the top of the connector to make the bottom connection of adjoining pontoons. The top connection is made by passing a short bolt of each adjoining pontoon through a hole in the connector.

The pontoon link is a triangular box-shaped unit which weighs 20.87 kg. This has short bolt holes through the top and a fixed pin at the bottom which fits through a hole in a jaw at the bottom of the short slot in the side of the bow pontoon forward section and in the end of the stern section.

Rafts
The most common types of raft are:
20.22 × 7.42 m which can carry one Class 60 tank or three 4000 kg trucks.
38.4 × 7.42 m which can carry two Class 60 tanks or six 4000 kg trucks.
38.4 × 12.9 m (Maxi-MEXEFLOTE) which has a maximum capacity of 198 000 kg and can carry three Class 60 tanks or equivalent vehicles.

A Landing Ship Logistic, or similar ship, is capable of carrying one 38.4 × 7.42 m raft on each side or two 20.22 × 7.42 m rafts on each side. When approaching the beach these are released and can be used as rafts

(with the addition of propulsion units) or connected end to end to form a causeway to the beach.

The MEXEFLOTE pontoons can easily be handled as they are compatible with ISO container storage and handling systems: the centre and bow pontoons conform to the 6.1 × 2.4 m container dimensions.

Status
Placed back into production for British Army. Production was originally undertaken by the Gloster

Railway Carriage and Wagon Company (a member of the Wingate Group). In service with the British Army and other armed forces.

Manufacturer
GEC Engineering (Accrington) Limited, Blackburn Road, Clayton-le-Moors, Accrington, Lancashire BB5 5JW, UK.
Tel: 0254 382 151. Telex: 63124.

Specifications
MEXEFLOTE

	Bow pontoon	Centre pontoon	Stern pontoon
Weight	5909 kg	4654 kg	4418 kg
Length	7.92 m	6.1 m	6.1 m
Width	2.44 m	2.44 m	2.44 m
Depth	1.45 m	1.45 m	1.45 m

Acrow Uniflote System

Description
The Acrow Uniflote was conceived in the late 1950s as a flotation system based on unit construction principles in which identical flotation units can be assembled together to form rafts of various load-carrying capacities, as well as pontoon bridges.

Uniflote is used by military forces throughout the world for line of communication bridges, floating bridges, ship-to-shore causeways and as vehicle and personnel rafts. It is also widely used for civil purposes such as landing stages, Ro-Ro terminals, and temporary applications to carry land-based plant such as cranes, excavators and pile driving equipment for marine works.

All Uniflote equipment can be carried on standard commercial vehicles and if necessary can be skidded into the water. Assembly in the water is accomplished by a maximum of four men, and the units are held together by locking pins inserted in the couplers.

The standard Uniflote is 5.283 m long, 2.438 m wide and 1.219 m deep. It is a structural steel-framed unit of all welded construction with 4 mm skin-plates welded to the frame. Two internal watertight bulkheads are incorporated to provide three watertight compartments, each with a watertight hatch. Individual compartments in the flotation units can be flooded or emptied by compressed air. Under a load of 10 000 kg, each Uniflote maintains a freeboard in the region of 0.23 m. Couplers are placed so that Uniflotes can be joined end to end, side to side and end to side. Steel gunwales are provided along the side of the Uniflote and are drilled to allow simple saddles to be fitted. The couplers allow for the transmission of loads throughout a Uniflote raft. Concentrated loads can be applied to the gunwales through saddle attachments. Runners are attached to the bottom to assist in skidding operations on shore, and four lifting shackles are fitted. The Uniflote is also available in a 1.828 m deep version.

The standard Uniflote has the deck set approximately 80 mm below gunwale level so that a replaceable timber deck may be fitted if required. This is fitted in the form of three pre-assembled mats (one centre and two outer sections) to each Uniflote. Each mat is designed so that it is retained laterally by the gunwales and is of such a thickness that it stands 50 mm above the gunwale level. Side rings enable Uniflotes to be craned from the shore to the water. Cross junction and side junction mats are also available. The special military version has an integral steel deck set level with the top of the gunwales over which traffic may drive direct.

50-tonne Uniflote ferry carrying Grove Coles 315M crane truck

Scow ends are designed to be attached to either end or side of the Uniflote and have identical end sections. They also have short lengths of gunwale to correspond with the gunwales in the Uniflote. The bottom plate slopes up at an angle of 30° and terminates in a reinforced nosing plate on which a bollard is mounted.

The ramp unit can be connected to the end or sides of the basic Uniflote by ramp connectors which allows the ramp to articulate and gives access for shore loading over a wide variation in bank heights.

The various Interflote connectors available allow Uniflotes to be spaced apart, giving greater stability to floating platforms where required without the need for additional buoyancy.

A range of saddles is available to allow the secure fixing of winches and propulsion units. These saddles can be fitted over a bow or stern unit, over the junction between a bow or stern unit and a Uniflote, over a Uniflote, over the junction between two Uniflotes, or an outrigger (fitted to the side of a Uniflote). Other saddles are available for fixing Acrow Panel or Bailey bridging, and other ancillary equipment.

Details of the Thos Storey Motorflote are given in the *Bridging boats* section.

Specifications
Standard Uniflote (U4/1A)
Weight: 2895 kg

Length: 5.283 m
(coupler to coupler) 5.41 m
Width: 2.438 m
Height: (without gunwale) 1.219 m
Gunwale size: 76.2 × 76.2 mm

Bow Unit (female U4/3A, male U4/2A)
Weight: 843 kg
Length: 1.82 m
Width: 2.438 m
Height: 1.219 m

Ramp Unit (U4/6A)
Weight: 1879 kg
Length: 3.658 m
Height: 1.219 m

Status
In production. In service with many armed forces all over the world including Belgium and Brazil.

Manufacturer
Thos Storey (Engineers) Limited, 52 Queens Road, Weybridge, Surrey KT13 0AN, UK.
Tel: 0932 858133. Telex: 21868.
Fax: 0932 855588.

FBM Marine Mexecell Modular Logistics System

Development
The Mexecell modular logistics system was developed by FBM Marine Limited using experience gained during the production of a similar pontoon system for

the British Army's Military Port at Marchwood, near Southampton. FBM Marine Limited won a contract to design and project manage the construction of a Diving Platform for the US Navy's Underwater Construction Teams (UCTs). FBM's US partner for the Diving Platform is the Marinette Marine Corp, Marinette, Wisconsin.

The contract was to design and construct a modular

floating platform for use in diving operations. The UCTs are responsible for the repair and maintenance of various types of US Navy fleet systems such as moorings and cables; and harbours during a contingency or active service. The current platform is being phased out and this contract provides the prototype platform, the first of six to be delivered. The 60 × 32 ft platform is constructed from the FBM Mexecell ISO compatible steel pontoon units.

The Mexecell modular concept provides natural building blocks which together with a simple but effective connector system offers total versatility, rugged construction, and allows the cell units to be assembled on site without the need for specially trained personnel. The ISO compatible cells based on the 20 × 8 × 4.5 ft half height container module enables the component parts of the platform, or any other Mexecell based structure, to be transported to the operational area using conventional containerised shipping, road or rail systems.

Description

The Mexecell is an ISO-compatible steel cell capable of being used in multiple configurations for logistical support and maritime related applications. The system consists of four basic units; bow, centre, stern and jet cell modules. They can be connected together end to end and side to side to form any desired configuration. To increase flexibility the Mexecell bow module can be raised above deck level to give a raked end or lowered below the bottom of the module to provide a loading ramp.

Applications for the Mexecell system include floating causeways, beach landing ferries, Ro-Ro discharge platforms, underwater construction platforms, drilling platforms, offshore elevated platforms, barge trains, diving support platforms, elevated structures and offshore wave breaks.

Mexecell is designed for total integration for transport by container ships, container road vehicles and ISO container handling equipment. The deck loading capability can cope with wheeled vehicles up to MLC 60 and tracked vehicles up to MLC 70. The Mexecell design features an open cell structure free of any internal bracing which allows the interior to be used for the carrying of cargo such as fuel or water in flexible bags for bulk liquid transfer, general stores and system components. The cell has flush sides and decks to minimise the risk of damage during assembly.

Mexecell can be clipped and unclipped afloat in conditions up to Sea State 3 and assemblies can survive in conditions up to Sea State 6.

The Mexecell uses high precision jaw units that form the key to the fabrication concept. The jaws can be replaced in the field with the minimum of support equipment. Assemblies are not compromised when individual modules are removed for repair or replacement.

Mexecell modules are available in two lengths, 6.096 and 12.19 m. Accessories for the system include a range of 'quick fit' items including bitts, cleats, fender attachments, navigation lighting, beach ramps, spud

Artist's impression of offshore offloading facility and ferry raft constructed using FBM Marine Mexecell modular logistics system

wells (for external pile fixing) and spud cells (for internal pile fixing) both for fixing up to 0.609 m piles.

Also available is a self-contained propulsion unit which consists of a 360° steerable water jet. The unit has a flush bottom profile for shallow water operations with a 210 hp marine diesel powering the water jet. The engine, pump jet, fuel tank and all ancillary equipment are contained in a Mexecell stern module. All manoeuvring controls are remotely led via an umbilical cord to a driver's harness pack to allow complete control and give the driver mobility across the deck. For very large Mexecell structures propulsion can be provided by propulsion units connected as bow thrusters with all controls grouped together in one pack. A fixed console can also be fitted.

For use in the elevated causeway (ELCAS) application Mexecell is connected using a cantilevered construction technique above the surf zone. An offloading shore facility can be fully operational within seven days from the arrival of its transporting vessel at the erection site. ELCAS represents an entire system of cranes,

pile drivers, pile extractors, lighting, generators, turntables, vehicle handling equipment and Mexecell modules. All the equipment is transported from a seaward discharging location by Mexecell floating causeways.

Specifications (Individual Mexecell)
Length:
(bow pontoon) 7.92 m
(centre and stern pontoons) 6.1 m
Width: (all pontoons) 2.44 m
Height: (all pontoons) 1.45 m

Status
In service with US Department of Defense.

Manufacturer
FBM Marine Limited, Cowes Shipyard, Cowes, Isle of Wight PO31 7DL, UK.
Tel: 0983 297111. Telex: 86466 fambro g.
Fax: 0983 299642.

UNITED STATES OF AMERICA

Aluminium Floating Footbridge

Description
The aluminium floating footbridge consists of treadways, pontoons, handrail posts, ropes, holdfasts and approach posts. One bridge set contains 144 m of bridge in normal type of assembly and is allocated on the scale of one bridge set per corps/army engineer float bridge company. Half the bridge set is carried on a 2½-tonne (6 × 6) truck which tows a 2½-tonne utility pole-type trailer. The complete bridge can be carried in a C-130 Hercules transport aircraft and one half set of the footbridge can be delivered by parachute from a C-130 using two 2721 kg bearing platforms.

The treadways are made of aluminium and consist of two I-beams carrying traverse channels which support a corrugated aluminium sheet tread. The ends of the I-beam are fitted with spring-loaded connectors, male at one end and female at the other to provide connection between the treadways.

The pontoons are of sheet aluminium reinforced with light aluminium members. The pontoon has a false bottom 171 mm above its true bottom which provides a compartment filled with a light cellular plastic material. Each gunwale is fitted with two hooks which grip the outer bottom flanges of a treadway I-beam. Each

pontoon has a hole 25 × 51 mm in the bow and stern just above the false bottom to make the pontoon self-bailing.

The handrail post is of aluminium 32 mm in diameter and is mounted on a base of aluminium bar. This is installed by inserting the base in a socket in the treadway and rotating the post 180° to lock it in position. Each bridge set contains 12.7 mm diameter manila rope which is cut as required for handrail line, guy lines and bridle ties. Two 182.88 m reels of 9.5 mm galvanised wire rope for use as anchor cables and guys for improvised cable towers are provided together with 20 wire rope clips, four holdfasts (each complete with nine pickets) and 16 approach posts.

The bridge is normally assembled using the successive bay method but if the water is too deep for this method the bridge is assembled in sections, which takes twice as long. The bridge can also be assembled on the shore, which requires a shore assembly area as long as the bridge, straight, and cleared to a width of 6.096 m. Finally the bridge can be assembled in the water or on steep banks. In this case two skids are set in the water and inclined against the bank. This allows the bays or bridge sections to be launched into the water. In currents up to 2.438 m/s the number of troops who can cross single file at two-pace intervals is as follows:

Daylight: 75 men/min, single file, double time
Moonlight: 40 men/min, single file, quick time
Blackout: 25 men/min, single file, quick time
If the current velocity is between 2.743 and 3.352 m/s, the crossing rates should be reduced by 20 per cent.

If required the pontoons can also be used as rafts. An expedient two-pontoon raft is formed by lashing two pontoons side by side with one treadway across them. This will carry one wounded man and two paddle men, one in the bow and one in the stern. A three-pontoon expedient raft is formed by lashing three pontoons side by side with one treadway across them and an additional treadway along each side of the centre treadway. This can carry four wounded men and four paddle men, two in the bow and two in the stern.

An expedient bridge 30.48 m long, which will take a Jeep-type vehicle and trailer, can be constructed from the components of the aluminium footbridge set. This may not be used where the current exceeds 1.524 m/s.

Specifications
Assembly time
Daylight: 15 mins plus 1 min/4.572 m of bridge
Night-time: (with illumination or moonlight) 20 mins plus 1¼ min/4.572 m of bridge
Blackout: 30 mins plus 2 mins/4.572 m of bridge

Maximum safe allowable deflection

Number of bays	Effective length of bridge	Max allowable deflection
4	13.716 m	0.05 m
6	20.57 m	0.1 m
8	27.43 m	0.152 m
10	34.29 m	0.254 m
12	41.148 m	0.381 m
18	61.72 m	0.863 m
24	82.29 m	1.549 m
36	123.44 m	3.479 m

Treadway
Weight: 38.1 kg
Length:
 (overall) 3.555 m
 (effective) 3.428 m
Width:
 (overall) 0.711 m
 (walkway) 0.527 m
Depth: 0.133 m

Pontoon
Weight: 45.36 kg
Length: 4.267 m
Width: 0.609 m
Depth: 0.367 m (gunwale)

Post
Weight: 1.02 kg
Length: 1.092 m

Weight of complete bridge set: 4105 kg

Colombian Army bridging truck loaded with aluminium floating footbridge pontoons

Status
In service with the US Army and other countries including Australia, Colombia and South Korea. Licence-produced in Greece (qv).

Bridge Floating: Raft Section, Light Tactical

Description

This bridge set has sufficient components for one four-pontoon reinforced raft, or 13.41 m of normal bridge. The same set is used in assembling a combination of floating bridges or rafts of various classes. One bridge set is carried by two 2½-ton (6 × 6) trucks, one of which tows a 2½-ton pole-type trailer which carries the eight half-pontoons stacked one on top of the other.

Two aluminium half-pontoons are joined stern to stern to form a complete pontoon. The deck panel is positioned and retained laterally by four retainer lugs on the pontoons. One end of each deck panel is male and the other female. Two deck filler panels are used to fill the space between one set of deck panels. These are normally retained in position by pintles, but provision is made for bolting the filler panels to the deck panels. Two types of ramp panel are provided, one to mate with the male end of a deck section and one with the female end. The articulating assembly is provided to permit variations in the end span abutment elevations in bridges and rafts from 1.041 m above the horizontal position of the deck to 0.482 m below. It consists of male and female sections. A connecting pin and adjusting bar are used to join the two sections.

There are two sizes of kerb. The deck panel kerb is used on the normal bay of the superstructure and the short ramp kerb is used on the ramp and articulator

panels. These are held in position by holding lugs that extend from the bottom of the kerb and bear directly on the underside of the top flange of the deck panel.

A raft normally consists of three bays of decking with ramps at each end on four complete pontoons. The loading space from kerb to kerb is 2.743 m and loading length is 8.992 m.

The bridge is rated as Class 11 in a current of 2.438 m/s and the four-pontoon three-bay raft as Class 12 in a current of up to 2.438 m/s. The light tactical bridge has loading space kerb to kerb of 2.743 m with the pontoons normally being spaced at 3.352 m centres. Reinforced bridges have the pontoons spaced at 2.438 m centres.

Each pontoon is provided with a fluked marine anchor and each raft set is issued with four outboard motor brackets. The outboard motors normally used are rated at 25 hp.

A six-pontoon, four-bay reinforced raft has a length of 21.336 m, a loading length of 12.192 m and a roadway width (kerb to kerb) of 3.352 m.

Ferry conversion set
Trail ferry method
A bicycle traveller allows the raft to move smoothly along a ferry cable. The ferry cable is stretched across the river and made fast. The bicycle traveller is attached to the cable so that its sheaves roll smoothly. The hauling line is attached to the grommet in the bicycle traveller and the manoeuvre lines to the snatch blocks which are attached to the sheave housings of

the traveller. On the raft, the hauling line is attached to the upstream end of the centre pontoon. The manoeuvre lines are attached to the gunwales of the outside pontoons. The ferry is operated by adjusting the manoeuvre lines so that the raft is at an angle to the stream current. The upstream end of the pontoon inclines towards the opposite shore. The current pushes against the upstream side of the pontoon and forces the raft across the river. As the pontoons are pushed into the current, the speed of the raft increases. This method may be used when the current exceeds 0.914 m/s.

The Flying Ferry works on a similar principle to the trail ferry except that the raft is held in the stream by an anchor well upstream from the crossing site. As the raft moves from shore to shore, it swings in an arc of a circle centred on the anchor. This ferry requires a maximum stream or river velocity of 1.219 m/s.

Specifications
Half-pontoon
Weight: 295 kg
Length: 5.638 m
Width: 2.044 m
Depth: 0.863 m

Deck Panel
Weight: 256.28 kg
Length: 3.701 m
 (effective) 3.352 m
Width: 1.066 m
Depth: 0.323 m

Deck filler panel
Weight: 43 kg
Length: 1.647 m
Width: 0.787 m
Height: 0.161 m

Ramp panel
Weight:
 (male) 149.9 kg
 (female) 181 kg
Length:
 (male) 2.438 m
 (female) 2.136 m
Width: 1.066 m
Height: 0.323 m

Articulating assembly
Weight: 290 kg

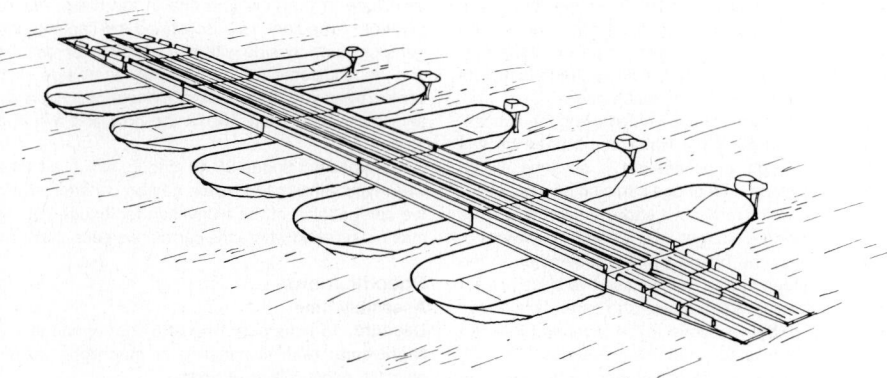

Bridge Floating: Raft section, Light Tactical (five-bay normal raft)

Length: 2.2 m
Width: 1.066 m
Height: 0.514 m

Kerb
Weight:
(normal) 49.9 kg

(short) 9.07 kg
Length:
(normal) 3.295 m
(short) 0.865 m

Construction time
4-pontoon, 3-bay raft: 30 min

5-pontoon, 5-bay raft: 35 min
6-pontoon, 4-bay raft: 45 min

Status
In service with the US Army and other armed forces including South Korea. Licence-produced in Greece (qv).

Ribbon Bridge

Development
The Ribbon Bridge was developed by the Pacific Car and Foundry Company of Renton, Washington, and the US Army Mobility Equipment Research and Development (MERADCOM) Center (now the Belvoir Research, Development and Engineering Center) at Fort Belvoir, Virginia, and is based on the design of the CIS PMP Ribbon Bridge. The Ribbon Bridge has two main differences from the PMP: it is aluminium rather than steel and so weighs about a third less, and the PMP uses torsion bars to help unfold the pontoons, which is effective in launching but means that the torsion force must be overcome during retrieval, which results in longer retrieval times. Development of the American bridge began in 1969 and the bridge was type classified as standard A in June 1972, less than three years after development started. The first production contract, worth $10 million, was awarded to the Consolidated Diesel Electric Division of the CONDEC Corporation at Old Greenwich, Connecticut (later ConDiesel Mobile Equipment of Waterbury, Connecticut), and was for 250 interior bays, 50 ramp bays and 300 transporter trucks. The Ribbon Bridge will augment and replace the mobile assault bridging emplaced by the forward elements. It can be placed in use 10 times faster with a fifth of the personnel required to emplace standard floating bridges. The bridge can support 80-tonne loads in currents of up to 2.438 m/s and up to 110-tonnes when conditions are ideal.

The Ribbon Bridge system was first fielded by the US Army in Germany and South Korea in 1976. A normal US Army bridge company has 18 interior bays and 12 ramps.

A FY84 request was for 585 interior bays and 257 ramp bays. The resultant contract was awarded to ConDiesel Mobile Equipment.

Southwest Mobile Systems has been the only producer of the Ribbon Bridge Transporter since 1984 and has two multi-year contracts with the US Army for over 500 systems.

Description
The Ribbon Bridge consists of integral float-deck elements connected longitudinally to form a continuous floating roadway. There are two basic bridge elements, the interior bay and the ramp bay. The interior bay consists of the roadway pontoons and two bay pontoons joined by hinges and pins. During deployment,

the bow and roadway pontoons automatically unfold in the water. The ramp bay unfolds in the same manner as the interior bay. Ramp bays also have the capability to adjust to river bank slopes of up to 20° through the use of hydraulic cylinders.

The bays are carried folded on the rear of specially modified M812 5-ton (6 × 6) trucks (or other 6 × 6 trucks having the same capacity). Launching of bridge bays may be accomplished by one of three modes; free, controlled or high bank. In the free launch mode the truck is backed into the water. A minimum depth of 0.914 m is required to free launch an interior bay (1.125 m for ramp bay) with a 10 per cent river bank slope. Water pressure and the pontoon hinging arrangement permit the bay to automatically unfold. The bridge assembly crew then lock the bay sections using a series of latches. Bays are joined together using a lock pin mechanism and a special T-wrench.

The bridge is normally assembled along the shore and the complete bridge is then swung across the river using bridge erection boats. Bridging boats are used to hold the bridge in position and in a current with a velocity of 2.5 m/s are normally positioned every 20 m. If the bridge is to remain in place for extended periods overhead anchor cables may be employed. It can also be constructed using the method of successive bays or rafts. If required, individual bays can be emplaced by helicopter. The Ribbon Bridge can be constructed at the rate of 6.705 m/min over rivers with a current of up to 2.438 m/s. The roadway itself is 4.089 m wide and there is a 1.219 m walkway on either side.

To retrieve a bridge bay the transporter is backed into the water and the boom is raised to the vertical. The lifting cable runs from the winch over a sheave at the top of the boom and down to the bridge bay. The cable hook is attached to the roadway hinge pin and when the cable is reeled in, one end of the bay is lifted out of the water until water pressure acting on the other end causes the bay to fold up. At this time, a series of latches automatically lock the bay in the folded position. The bay is then lowered into the aft tiedown locks at the back of the transporter, the boom is lowered, and the bay is winched onto the transporter. The front locking pin is engaged and the vehicle is ready to drive away. Bridge sections can be launched or retrieved by one man but each transporter carries an assistant to speed up operations, especially during retrieval, and to assist in assembling the bridge.

The bridge transporter was originally a dedicated vehicle with little use when not carrying bridge equipment. In order to overcome this shortcoming, a special

pallet has been developed which permits the transporter to haul up to 9000 kg of cargo (4500 kg across country). The pallet can be self-loaded or off-loaded while carrying up to 4500 kg, a feature which lends itself to pre-palletised loads.

Specifications
Interior bay
Weight: 5443 kg
Length:
(folded) 6.93 m
(unfolded) 6.93 m
Width:
(folded) 3.22 m
(unfolded) 8.13 m
Height:
(folded) 2.31 m
(at bow, unfolded) 1.12 m
(at roadway, unfolded) 1.09 m

Ramp bay
Weight: 5307 kg
Length:
(folded) 5.79 m
(unfolded) 7.79 m
Width:
(folded) 3.2 m
(unfolded) 8.13 m
Height:
(folded) 2.31 m
(of roadway, unfolded) 0.736 m
(of shore end, unfolded) 0.381 m

Transporter loaded
Weight: 17 931 kg
Length: 9.6 m
Width: 3.43
Height: 3.91 m

Status
In service with the US Army and some other armed forces. It has been adopted by the German Army for which model there is a separate entry, South Korea and the Netherlands.

Manufacturer
Ribbon Bridge Transporter
Southwest Mobile Systems Corporation, 200 Sidney Street, St Louis, Missouri 63104, USA.
Tel: (314) 771 3950. Fax: (314) 771 1169.

Interior bays of Ribbon Bridge at intermediate retrieval on back of M812 (6 × 6) truck with CSB (RBEB) in background

US Army Ribbon Bridge assembled during exercise in Holland (C R Zwart)

Improved Ribbon Bridge

Development/Description

The US Army has a requirement for an Improved Ribbon Bridge (IRB) with a number of significant improvements over the existing Ribbon Bridge already in service (see previous entry).

BMY Combat Systems has completed an IRB design with a 40 per cent improvement in fast water performance due to a new bow profile. The BMY IRB is to MLC 70 standard and can be transported, launched and recovered by a modified version of the M985 HEMTT (8 × 8) truck currently in service with the US Army; the truck will be a dedicated carrier. The new IRB interior and ramp bays are filled with foam for improved survivability and buoyancy and can be used in rivers with a water speed of up to 3.2 m/s; the current Ribbon Bridge can be used at water speeds of up to 2.438 m/s. The IRB will be interconnectable with existing Ribbon Bridge units and can be used with banks up to 2 m high. Vertical extensions are added to either side of the bridge to prevent water flowing over the upper surfaces when the bridge is under maximum load.

BMY built two ramp and six interior bays for US Army trials.

In competition, Southwest Mobile Systems Corporation was awarded a $7.488 million contract for a folding float bridge. The bridge involved is the German MAN Folding Float Bridge 2000 (FSB 2000 – see separate entry in this section) carried on and launched from a US-designed chassis.

Status

Development – see text.

Contractors

BMY Division of HARSCO, PO Box 15512, York, Pennsylvania 17405-1512, USA.
Tel: (717) 225 4781. Fax: (717) 225 4615.
Southwest Mobile Systems Corporation, 200 Sidney Street, St Louis, Missouri 63104, USA.
Tel: (314) 771 3950. Telex: 3950.
MAN GHH, PO Box 1253, D-6095 Ginsheim-Gustavsburg 1, Federal Republic of Germany.
Tel: 061 34 55-1. Telex: 4182 058 man d.
Fax: 061 34 55-202.

Bridge, Floating Aluminium, Highway Type, Deck Balk Superstructure on Pneumatic Floats (M4T6)

Raft constructed from several M4T6 float sections ferrying M728 Combat Engineer Vehicle (US Army)

Description

The M4T6 floating bridge combines the best features of the Class 60 and M4 bridges. It consists of the substructure of the Class 60 bridge (24-tonne pneumatic float with saddle assembly) adapted to the superstructure (aluminium balk) of the M4 bridge. It is hand-erectable and airportable, and like the Class 60 bridge can carry all vehicles in the armoured and infantry division. The bridge is issued on the scale of division (armour, infantry and mechanised) engineer battalion: four sets, and corps/army float bridge company: five sets.

The M4T6 floating bridges, rafts and ferries consist of a deck built of square, hollow aluminium sections (balk), supported on pneumatic floats. The pneumatic float consists of two half-floats assembled stern to stern. The saddle panels rest on the float and are attached to it with straps through the D-rings. The saddle beams rest on the saddle panels with the carrying handles of the saddle beams in line with the D-rings on the saddle panels. The straps on the floats are run through the D-rings on the saddle panels, and then through the carrying handles of the beam. The spring-actuated catches of the saddle panels are then placed over the flanges of the saddle beams. The saddle adaptors rest on the saddle beams and are connected using sliding retainer lugs. The balk-connecting stiffeners rest on the saddle adaptors and are connected to them by four connecting pins. The balk-connecting stiffeners support the balk. Each of the latter has lugs which fit into recesses in the balk-connecting stiffener and are secured by balk-connecting pins. Kerb adaptors inserted between the balk and the balk-connecting stiffener are used to raise the balk to form a kerb.

The M4T6 bridge is normally assembled using the successive bay or successive raft method. Reinforced floating sections are constructed by placing the floats closer together than normal. Minimum float spacing is 3.048 m centre to centre. The bridge set can also be used to assemble bridges with a reduced capacity. A full width bridge with floats spaced at intervals of 9.144, 13.716 or 18.288 m can be constructed for light loads, and when heavier loads are required, the capacity of the bridge can be increased by adding floats and/or deck balk without the necessity of breaking the bridge. A half-width bridge using the 12-tonne half-float spaced on 4.572 m centres can also be constructed, but its capacity cannot be increased without dismantling the bridge.

Specifications
Pneumatic half-float
Weight: 340 kg
Length: 6.705 m
Width: 2.743 m

Float connections
Length of bar: 2.2 m

Saddle
Weight:
 (interior saddle panel) 74.84 kg
 (end panel) 81.64 kg
 (centre beam) 211 kg
 (end beam) 125.74 kg
 (outriggers) 3 kg
 (saddle adaptor normal) 118 kg
 (saddle adaptor offset) 125 kg

Normal deck balk (22 per floating bay)
Weight: 102 kg
Length: 4.572 m
Width and height: 222 mm × 234 mm

Short deck balk
Weight: 55.33 kg

Length: 2.54 m
Width and height: 222 mm × 234 mm

Tapered deck balk
Weight: 453 kg

Kerb adaptor
Weight: 6.804 kg

Abutment plates
Bearing plate
Weight: 74.84 kg
Length: 1.771 m
Width: 0.304 m
Height: 95 mm
Cover plate
Weight:
 (short cover plate) 12.7 kg
 (long cover plate) 43.99 kg
Length:
 (short cover plate) 0.457 m
 (long cover plate) 1.625 m

Ramps (4 required each end)
Weight: 107 kg

Other equipment includes universal trestle, trestle bracing and accessories, handrail posts and ropes, bicycle traveller, anchors and holdfasts. All components are normally carried in 5-tonne (6 × 6) trucks.

Status
In service with the US Army and other armed forces.

Light Assault Ferry (LAF)

Description

The Light Assault Ferry has been proposed as an item of engineering equipment for the US Army Light Infantry Divisions. As yet it appears to be more of a development concept that an operational requirement. A sum of $750 000 per unit was proposed for budgetary forecasts.

The Light Assault Ferry will be towed into action on trailers by the vehicles that will use it to cross water obstacles. It may be used as a ferry or be built up to form a float bridge and in both cases it will be propelled or anchored by self-contained power units. Once the ferry has been placed in position by the water obstacle it will be assembled so that the central deck area is surrounded by hydraulically operated ramps front and rear and two side floats. Power from the self-contained power units is used to drive the hydraulic system. Each ferry will have a crew of two but a further two men will be required for assembly. A floating bridge 150 m long can then be assembled in 40 minutes using 44 men. The time taken to assemble a ferry is about 5 minutes. The Light Assault Ferry will be capable of air transport in a C-130 transport aircraft.

Status
Development concept.

TACTICAL (NON-FLOATING) AND LINE OF COMMUNICATION BRIDGES

AUSTRALIA

Transfield-MBK Line of Communication Bridging System

Development/Description
The Australian Company Transfield Construction, in association with design consultants McMillan, Britton and Kell of Sydney, New South Wales, designed a new line of communication bridge system for the Australian Army. The bridge, built at Transfield Construction's manufacturing plant at Seven Hills, Sydney, New South Wales, is constructed using steel and with bridge construction and launching principles similar to those of the Bailey Bridge. By using material handling equipment, component size and weight can be increased without jeopardising the speed and ease with which construction, launch and recovery can be accomplished. Thus individual sections can be heavier and are simpler and faster to put together than the equivalent Bailey-type bridge.

The bridge is two lanes wide with steel decking. The main load-carrying components comprise through-trusses each side which are assembled from standard 5 m long steel panels and chord reinforcements connected by pins. The arrangement of panels and reinforcement depends on the span and loading. Universal jackable end posts enable construction time to be shortened and launching rollers are adjustable for level and tilt. Each Universal end post assembly incorporates a 1.5 m range jacking system. The deck units incorporate huck bolts to avoid distortion problems. The design loading is MLC 80 (single lane) or

Transfield-MBK Line of Communication bridging system in use

MLC 35 (twin lane).

Testing was conducted by the School of Civil and Mining Engineering at the University of Sydney and full-scale user trials were conducted by the Australian Army School of Military Engineering. The Australian Army issued a contract for 32 bridging sets worth A$7.5 million; production was completed during 1988. Pier sets and floating pontoons compatible with the system are under development.

Status
In service with the Australian Army (32 sets).

Manufacturer
Transfield Construction Pty Limited, 100 Arthur Street, North Sydney, New South Wales 2060, Australia. Tel: 02 929 8600. Telex: AA21396. Fax: 02 929 7187.

COMMONWEALTH OF INDEPENDENT STATES

PVM Foot Suspension Bridge
LVM Light Suspension Bridge
TVM Heavy Suspension Bridge

Description
These suspension bridges were designed primarily for use in mountainous country and are normally transported by pack animals, or if the terrain is suitable, by motor transport.

The PVM (pedestrian suspension footbridge) set contains sufficient components to construct either two bridges 60 m long and 0.7 m wide, or a single bridge 120 m long and 0.7 m wide. A team of 18 men can erect the former in 2 hours or the latter in 3 hours. The complete PVM bridge set weighs 4360 kg and can be transported by 46 pack animals.

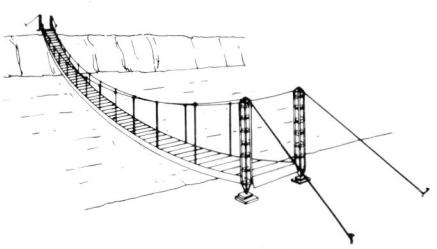

PVM foot suspension bridge

The LVM (light suspension bridge) set contains sufficient components to construct either two bridges 40 m long and 2 m wide or a single bridge 80 m long

and 2 m wide. With a team of 27 men, the former can be erected in 4 hours and the latter in 2 hours. The complete LVM bridge set weighs 13 500 kg and can be transported by 160 pack animals, the maximum weight of each individual component not exceeding 50 kg. The LVM has a maximum rated capacity of 2000 kg but the maximum axle load of any vehicle must not exceed 635 kg.

The TVM (heavy suspension bridge) is 60 m long and has a maximum rated capacity of 10 000 kg.

Status
In service with the CIS armed forces.

Manufacturer
State factories.

Underwater Bridge Set

Description
This set consists of hollow pontoons carried on specially modified ZIL-131 (6 × 6) 3500 kg trucks. These pontoons are estimated to be 8 to 8.5 m long and 3 to 3.5 m wide, and are offloaded from the trucks by gravity (similar to the TPP and PMP pontoons). They are then assembled on the shoreline to form a ribbon bridge and brought into position by powerboats. Bridge piers or pilings are then placed, after which the bridge is sunk into position by flooding the pontoons.

Status
In service with the CIS armed forces.

Manufacturer
State factories.

Underwater bridge set in use with ZIL-131 (6 × 6) 3500 kg truck crossing

MARM Sectional Arch Bridge

Description
The MARM is a sectional bridge which is used for bridging dry gaps and rivers, and is often used as a road overpass. The spans are approximately 6 m long and are supported by integral folding trestles which are adjustable in height. These trestles are normally assembled by a truck-mounted crane such as the K-162 and are laid side by side to permit wide vehicles, such as tanks, to use the bridge. Once the trestles are positioned, bracing is normally added. The bridge has a maximum capacity of 50 tonnes.

The spans are transported two at a time by ZIL-130V1 (4 × 2) 5000 kg tractor trucks which tow a single-axle, four-wheeled, pole-type trailer.

Status
In service with former Warsaw Pact countries.

Manufacturer
State factories.

T-54 MBTs crossing MARM sectional arch bridge used as overpass

Construction of MARM bridge over waterway in combination with heavy barge bridge elements

RMM-4 Portable Steel Fixed Bridge

Description
The RMM-4 portable steel fixed bridge was developed in the 1940s but is no longer in front line use with the CIS; it is most probably held in reserve. The bridge is used in forward areas to replace destroyed bridges, and in addition to being used as a clear-span bridge can, with the aid of intermediate supports, be used for the construction of longer bridges.

A complete RMM-4 bridge set consists of 24 intermediate and 8 end sections which are carried in 12 GAZ-63 (4 × 4) 2000 kg trucks. The bridge consists of a timber deck which is supported by two to four deck-type steel trusses. These are assembled by bolting sections together. The number of trusses depends on the required capacity and the length of the bridge required. The assembled trusses form girders which are pushed across the gap manually or mechanically by using a launching nose and rollers, which are removed after the span is emplaced. The bridge is completed by adding the approach ramps.

Specifications

	Intermediate truss section	End truss section
Weight	500 kg	500 kg
Length	3 m	3.5 m
Width	0.8 m	0.8 m
Height	1.85 m	1.85 m

Bridge construction

Type	16 t	30 t	60 t
Roadway width	3 m	4 m	4 m
Length	25 or 34 m	25 m	16 m
Number of trusses	2 or 3	4	4
Working party	n/a	40 men	40 men
Assembly time	n/a	150 mins	120 mins

Status
No longer in front line service with the CIS armed forces but probably held in reserve. May still be in service with other countries.

Manufacturer
State factories.

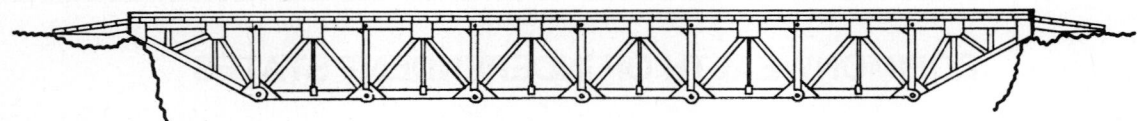

Side elevation of RMM-4 portable steel fixed bridge

SARM Sectional Deck Truss Bridge

Description
The SARM is a sectional deck truss bridge made up of triangular and rectangular sections bolted together to support a roadway of steel deck panels. A single roadway is 4.2 m wide and has a capacity of 40 tonnes and a dual roadway has a capacity of 60 tonnes and is 7.2 m wide. The bridge is carried on single-axle semi-trailers which are towed by MAZ-504 or ZIL-130V (4 × 2) 5000 kg tractor trucks.

Deck truss is made of welded steel sections, roadway panels with kerbing sections welded together. Clear spans of 18.6, 25.6 and 32.6 m are feasible.

Where possible, existing piers are used in the construction of the SARM bridge but where none is available and the span required is greater than 32.6 m, piers have to be provided. For low-level bridges, either pile bents or trestle bents are used, while for high-level bridges panel-type crib piers are used. Steel towers can be used on existing bridge supports, piles or floating supports. Tower supports are adjustable at 2 m intervals, the maximum height being 8.8 m.

The SARM takes a relatively long time to build compared with more recent tactical bridges. For example a 158 m bridge takes about 24 hours to construct. As the maximum weight of any individual component is only 4400 kg, a 5000 kg capacity crane is sufficient in the construction of the SARM. Other elements in the SARM bridge system include pile drivers, crane trucks, gang saws and powerboats.

Status
In service with the CIS armed forces.

Manufacturer
State factories.

REM-500 Railway and Road Section Bridge

Description

The REM-500 is a sectional railway bridge which can also be used as a road bridge with the addition of a wooden floor. It is employed over wide and shallow water barriers, closing breaches in railway lines and as approaches for floating bridges.

The bridge is composed of individual steel spans, 12.51 m long and weighing 10 700 kg, which rest on trestles that can be adjusted in height from 3-12.7 m and weigh between 5000 and 7000 kg. The trestles' feet are provided with large circular baseplates so that they will not sink into soft ground. The footers have an area of 7 m^2 and a ground pressure of 1.2 kg/cm^2. Both longitudinal and transverse bracing is provided where necessary. The bridge can be built across rivers with maximum water depth of 7 m and maximum water velocity of 1.2 m/s.

The bridge can have a single track of either European (1.435 m) or CIS (1.524 m) standard gauge. The speed of a train crossing the bridge must not exceed 30 km/h, with a maximum axle load of 20 tonnes. The REM-500 can also be used in combination

REM-500 section bridge being built

with floating railway bridges which use river barges as their floating supports. The bridge is constructed a span at a time with each span and trestle being positioned at once by an overhead gantry (called the SRK-2D) which travels along the completed spans.

Status

In service with the Polish and CIS armed forces.

Manufacturer

State factories.

NZhM-56 Heavy Floating Railway and Road Bridge

Description

The NZhM-56 was developed after 1945 as the replacement for the wartime SP-19 bridge which could be used as either a road bridge or railway bridge. The NZhM-56 bridge can carry road and rail traffic at the same time.

The pontoons which support the bridge are made up of three sections, bow (coded H), centre (coded C) and stern (coded K). Each of these sections is carried on the rear of a modified ZIL-131 (6 × 6) 3500 kg truck or a ZIL-157 (6 × 6) 2500 kg truck, which also tows a single-axle four-wheeled trailer to support the end of the pontoons. Unloaded, these vehicles are very similar in appearance to a timber truck and trailer combination. Other equipment includes truck-mounted cranes, adjustable height piers for the construction of the shore connecting span, superstructure, and both conventional and special bridging boats. The latter are carried on special four-wheeled trailers and towed by KrAZ-214 (6 × 6) 7000 kg trucks.

The pontoons are unloaded from the vehicles at the water's edge by truck-mounted cranes. They are then joined up into rafts, and the superstructure is added and positioned by special powerboats. These are very short and have a square-cut bow which allows them to push the pontoons into position. When the bridge is in position, one of the special powerboats is normally positioned at every second or third pontoon. A more recent modification to the pontoon trucks allows the pontoons to be launched by gravity, thus speeding up the construction of the rafts and reducing the reliance on truck-mounted cranes.

NZhM-56 heavy floating railway and road bridge with train carrying PT-76 and T-54 tanks on railway flat wagons

The superstructure carries both the road and railway sections, the latter at the higher level. The railway section is made up of a large I-beam laid on its side carrying a steel deck with either the CIS gauge (1.524 m track) or the European gauge (1.435 m track). This superstructure rests on a steel trestle which is fitted to the deck of the centre pontoon section. The roadway section is mounted across the centre and stern sections of the pontoon and consists of I-beam stringers supporting a wooden deck with a capacity of at least 40 tonnes.

Specifications (estimated)
Pontoon (less power unit)
Length: (overall) 25.7 m
Width: (overall) 2.4 m
Height: (overall) 1.4 m

Sections

Type	H	C	K
Length	8.6 m	8.4 m	8.6 m
Width	2.4 m	2.4 m	2.4 m
Height	1.4 m	1.4 m	1.4 m

Power unit
Length: 5.2 m
Width: 2.4 m
Height: 1.5 m

Status
In service with members of the former Warsaw Pact.

Manufacturer
State factories.

Heavy Barge Bridges

Description

Armies which were once members of the Warsaw Pact make wide use of heavy floating road and railway bridges constructed from standard inland waterway barges of various capacities. CIS forces normally use standard 600-tonne and 1000-tonne barges suitably modified. These can be used to bridge a river in three different ways. The most common method is by placing the barges end to end with the vehicles crossing from one barge to another over the bows of the barge. A river 400 m wide would require seven 600-tonne

standard barges which would take about 24 hours to position. Equipment required to position this bridge would include truck-mounted cranes, bulldozers, bracing equipment and three river tugboats, one with a 300 hp engine and two with 475 hp engines.

The second method is connecting the barges side by side with the barges resting in the direction of the current. Some of the barges used for this method have been provided with special supports which can carry an integral roadway. The third method is to connect the barges side by side, but aligning them on a slant towards the current, with the vehicles crossing from one barge to another via the sides of the barges. The main disadvantages of these bridges are the length of

time required to position the barges and the delay to other river traffic when the barges are in position.

These barges are also used for railway bridges, where the barges are used as pontoons. Finally, river barges have been used to construct heavy ferries which are pulled by tugboats.

Status

Produced in most former Warsaw Pact countries using locally produced components. They are known to be used in Hungary and the CIS.

Manufacturer

State factories.

CZECHOSLOVAKIA

MS-1 (SM-60) Heavy Panel Bridge

Description

The MS-1 (SM-60) is a single-storey through-truss type bridge which in some respects resembles the Bailey Bridge. The MS-1, however, has truss members made of triangles placed back to back to form verticals while the Bailey bridges are of the diamond-shaped pattern.

The bridge has a maximum capacity of 60 tonnes and a maximum clear span of 21 m. Its roadway is 4 m wide. Multi-span bridges can be constructed with the aid of trestles. These have circular base plates and can be adjusted for heights of between 1.5 and 7 m. The bridge is assembled with the aid of cranes and is launched by the cantilever method. The heaviest part of the bridge weighs 3150 kg. The bridge components are carried on standard Tatra 111 (6 × 6) 10 000 kg trucks or similar vehicles.

Status

In service with the Czechoslovak Army and Pakistan.

Manufacturer

Czechoslovak state factories.

MS-1 (SM-60) heavy panel bridge showing trestles

GERMANY

Dornier Foldable Dry Support Bridge

Development

During 1984 the Federal Procurement Office of the German Armed Forces awarded a contract to Dornier System GmbH for the final development and production of an operational prototype of a foldable dry support bridge with a span of 40 m. The first Foldable Bridge set was handed over to the German Ministry of Defence proving ground at Koblenz in May 1987 for intensive tests. The German Army certified the bridge in early 1991 and approved a modified version in July.

A 45.9 m pre-series type bridge has been built for company use and has been demonstrated following a short Ministry of Defence test starting in August 1990.

In June 1992 it was announced that Dornier GmbH and CNIM of France had founded a joint 'Eurobridge' corporation for the production and marketing of the Dornier Foldable Bridge and for the joint development of future bridges.

The US Army selected the Foldable Dry Support Bridge as their candidate for their Heavy Dry Support Bridge (HDSB) programme. A contract was awarded to Dornier GmbH to reinforce the traversing beam to meet the slightly higher requirements of the HDSB.

Description

The main advantages claimed for the Dornier Foldable Bridge (*Faltfestbrücke*) are high mobility, easy transport due to compact bridge units during transport, limited bank space requirements (15 to 20 m), assembly without preparation and physical strain, long automatically foldable bridge units, a closed road surface over the entire width of 4.4 m, a high crossing capacity, ease of driving even small vehicles and motor cycles when crossing the bridge, high transverse stiffness, and flexible spans from 14 up to 39.5 m. (A company-owned bridge has a span of 45.9 m.)

The Dornier Foldable Bridge is a fixed aluminium structure which is transported on trucks with suitable rigs so that during transport the bridge bays do not exceed 2.75 m in width and 4 m in height. The bridge deck consists of sections folded parallel to the bridge axis and a supporting traversing beam with bank beams. The bridge has been designed for a nominal load of MLC 70 and a crossing speed of 25 km/h. It has been exceptional load tested with a 110-tonne load of two Leopard 2 MBTs in a tractor-trailer combination.

The 39.5 m bridge can be assembled by a five-man crew in less than 60 minutes without physical strain. The launching vehicle is equipped with a crane,

Leopard 2 MBT crossing a 40 m Dornier Foldable Bridge

a fulcrum system and launching equipment. The hydraulic crane has a load-carrying capacity of 4800 kg for a working radius of 7.7 m. It is equipped with a hoisting device for carrying the bridge bays and traversing beam. The bridge bays are so arranged that using the hoisting device the bays will automatically unfold to full 4.4 m road width as they are lifted.

On arrival at the bridging site the fulcrum system of the launching vehicle is extended, the launching beam is placed into the launching position and after placing a traversing beam ramp section into position on the launching beam, a bank beam is attached. The traversing beam ramp with the bank beam attached is moved outwards. The first traversing beam inner section is positioned on the launching vehicle and coupled. The traversing beam sections are gradually moved outwards as more beam sections are coupled until the second traversing beam ramp is placed onto the launching vehicle and coupled. The traversing beam is then completely extended and the first bank beam is lowered onto the opposite bank. After fitting a

second bank beam at the launch end the traversing beam is ready for the bridge assembly.

Bridge assembly commences with the first bridge ramp bay being placed onto the traversing beam. A set of access (climbing) ramps is placed on the ramp bay and the launching beam is used to move the ramp bay along the traversing beam and outwards over the gap. The hydraulic drive for the bridge is then connected to the traversing beam via a power take-off on the launching vehicle. This is used to drive the ramp bay further along the traversing beam to allow the first of the bridge interior bays to be placed into position and coupled using a snap ring mechanism on the top chord and a pin-joint mechanism at the lower chord (the latter can be operated manually or using a power tool). The coupled bridge bays are then driven along the traversing beam and the process is repeated until the last interior bay is in position and the second ramp bay is coupled. The traversing beam on both sides of the gap can then be lowered into the bank beams, until the bridge ramp bays rest on to the bank beams and the access ramps are attached. The bridge is then ready for use.

The bridge is recovered in the reverse order. As the bridge bays are lifted by the crane hoisting device they fold automatically to transport width of 2.75 m.

An operational bridge set for a 39.5 m Foldable Bridge consists of the launching vehicle and five trucks. The Bundeswehr uses 8 × 8 trucks for launch and logistic purposes but 6 × 6 trucks can be used to carry the bridge components. A typical 39.5 m bridge set could be transported as follows:

launching vehicle (8 × 8) carrying one traversing beam ramp

one truck carrying one traversing beam ramp and two bank beams

one truck carrying four traversing beam sections and 40 access ramps

one truck carrying one bridge ramp bay and one bridge interior bay

one truck carrying two bridge interior bays

one truck carrying one bridge interior bay and one bridge ramp bay.

Bridge lengths that can be built include 13.9 m (two bays), 20.3 m (three bays), 26.7 m (four bays), 33.1 m (five bays), and 39.5 m (six bays). All bridges are constructed by the truck crews only.

A company-owned bridge set has a span of 45.9 m (MLC 60) and an overall length of 54 m.

Specifications
Max bridge span: 39.5 m (or 45.9 m)
Max gap: 38.8 m (or 45.2 m)
Length overall: 47.6 m (or 54 m)
Road width: 4.4 m
Height: 1.26 m
Ramp length: 9.7 m

Weight:
(bridge interior bay) 4000 kg
(bridge ramp bay) 4000 kg
(bridge access ramps) 70 kg
(traversing beam inner section) 525 kg
(traversing beam ramp section) 680 kg
(bank beam) 600 kg

Status
Testing completed during 1991. German Army deployment expected to start in 1993 (six-bay 39.5 m version).

Manufacturer
Dornier GmbH, Postfach 1420, D-7990 Friedrichshafen 1, Federal Republic of Germany.
Tel: 075 45/81. Telex: 0734209-0.
Fax: 075 45 844 11.

Krupp Festbrücke System

Description
The Krupp Festbrücke is a single-lane road bridge of wheel-tread girder design which can be used by tracked and wheeled vehicles of all types up to Class 60 for normal loading and Class 70 in special load cases.

The main load-bearing elements are the two triangular, torsion-resistant, wheel tread girders in between which are suspended intermediate plates. The roadway width is 4.026 m and the structural height 1.5 m with a ramp inclination of approximately 13 per cent. The commercially available construction material is a weldable, cold-hardened aluminium alloy, Al Zn 4.5 Mg 1. Weight of the bridge is 435 kg/m and the heaviest single component is the 260 kg wheel tread girder plate.

The bridge is assembled by hand and is pushed over an obstacle using a special erection platform. It is possible to assemble the bridge from a helicopter.

After training, a 34.4 m bridge can be assembled in 25 minutes, a 47 m bridge in 100 minutes and a 60 m bridge in 2 hours (all times approximate).

For obstacles of up to 60 m the Festbrücke can be constructed as a single-field girder with or without a reinforcement kit or as a two-field girder with pendulum support. Obstacles over 60 m in width can be crossed using the Festbrücke as a continuous girder bridge supported on trestles. Use of the Festbrücke as a floating bridge or ferry is covered in the appropriate section.

Specifications
Bridge length, single-span girder: 17.6-59.6 m
Roadway width: 4.026 m
Height: 1.5 m

Ramp inclination: 13%
Bridge weight: 435 kg/m
Heaviest component: 260 kg

Status
In production. In service with European and other armies, including Argentina.

Manufacturers
Krupp Industrietechnik GmbH, Sub-Division Structural Engineering, Postfach 14 19 60, Franz-Schubert Strasse 1-3, D-4100 Duisburg 14, Federal Republic of Germany.
Tel: 021 35 781. Telex: 0855486.
MAN GHH, PO Box 1253, D-6095 Ginsheim-Gustavsburg 1, Federal Republic of Germany.
Tel: 061 34 55-1. Telex: 4182 058 man d.
Fax: 061 34 55-202.

Krupp Festbrücke bridge with pendulum support

Krupp Festbrücke bridge with reinforcement kit

SE Road and Railway Bridge

Description
The MAN Gustavsburg SE method of bridge assembly is suitable for the following types of construction:

1. road bridges, both single- and double-lane and in special cases three-lane
2. railway bridges, single-track and in special cases double-track with three main girders
3. combined bridges with steel roadways for use by both road and rail traffic without any modifications
4. narrow bridges for erection by launching within the railway clearance gauge
5. floating bridges, single- and double-lane
6. heavy duty ferries
7. heavy duty landing stages for ships and ferries
8. rocker posts and piers
9. erection equipment
10. framework for gantry cranes.

The roadway may be of steel, wood or reinforced concrete and can be installed between the main girders at different heights rising respectively by 1.05 m from the bottom to top position. The height of the roadway can therefore be adapted to suit any existing abutment.

Single-lane steel roadways are 4.4 m wide with double-lane versions 6.1 m wide. Single-lane concrete roadways have a width of 4.3 m, double-lane 6 m and three-lane 9 m. Other roadway widths can be built. Brackets for footways can be bolted onto the outer sides of the main girders.

As a railway bridge the SE bridge is designed to carry the German load train 0.85 S (1950). As a road bridge it corresponds to Class 80 of military loads. The spans can be adapted to other load conditions. Should the bridge be used as a road bridge only a lighter construction can be used.

The assembly consists almost entirely of high grade structural steel St 52-3 with a few auxiliary parts of structural steel St 37-2. Connecting bolts are of tempered steel.

The superstructure of the SE bridge consists of truss-type main girders with parallel chords, crossbeams and the necessary bracings. These parts are identical for both the road and railway bridge. Decking plates and kerbs are provided for the road bridge whereas the through-type railway bridge is equipped with stringers, sleepers and rails which are placed on the crossbeams and bolted. The narrow deck-type railway bridge has sleepers fixed to the main girders direct by means of special sleeper angles. The standard distance between the crossbeams is 2.1 m.

The main girder truss consists of the chord, rhombic member, and post. The rhombic member is 2.1 m high and wide. The main girder height can be increased by 1.05 m in each case, 2.1 m being taken as a starting basis. The standard height of 2.1 m is a storey. It is thus possible to construct main girders up to six storeys at half-storey intervals. The main girders can

MAN SE bridge for railway use

be single-truss as well as multiple-truss.

The SE bridge can also be used as a road bridge on floating supports, particularly across wide rivers. These bridges are supported on approved types of pontoons which can be coupled on all sides and combined into floating supports of any shape. Suitable barges can also be used for this purpose. It is advisable to construct a floating bridge from ferries approximately 20 m in length. The pontoons can be provided with outboard engines to enable the parts of the bridge to be floated into position. Similar ferries with ramps can also be used as transport ferries for all loads. Supports and piers can be constructed from SE assembly units

with a few additional parts for the head and base structures.

As a rule a mobile crane will be used for assembly but if the spans are small manual assembly is possible. The heaviest standard unit is the cross-girder which weighs 692 kg. Other heavy parts are the crossbeam (553 kg), the long chord section (494 kg) and the rhomboid truss unit (209 kg) with all other units being lighter in weight. The heaviest piece of the crossbeams to be assembled in the lightweight construction weighs 379 kg. The units are connected by means of fitted bolts.

Only 39 standard units are required for the SE

bridges. The assembly units are supplemented by three types of bolt and five bearing parts. For large spans, flange plates, two longer types of screw and heavy bearings are also required. Roadway panels with embedded railway lines are supplied for bridges designed to carry both road and rail traffic.

The SE bridge erection process involves erecting the assembly in front of the bridge entry and subsequently shifting it into its final position. Bridge spans in excess of 100 m are usually constructed by the cantilever method with the aid of a mobile crane. The cross-section of the narrow deck type does not exceed the railway clearance gauge so the span can be shifted forwards from tunnels or existing superstructures. The bridge is mounted on roller trestles, moved forward and lowered into the bearings by hydraulic jacks.

All units can be carried by ordinary trucks. The 5 m crossbeams and wind braces are the longest units. Special equipment and tools are provided for assembly of the SE bridge and when the bridge components are stored in the open they should be kept covered and raised free of the ground level.

Status
In production. In service with Egypt, Germany, Iraq, Italy, Spain and Sweden.

Manufacturer
MAN GHH, PO Box 1253, D-6095 Ginsheim-Gustavsburg 1, Federal Republic of Germany.
Tel: 061 34 55-1. Telex: 4182 058 man d.
Fax: 061 34 55-202.

MAN Short-Span Bridge

Description
The MAN Short-Span bridge is a light bridge intended for the rapid crossing of anti-tank ditches, ravines, canals and small streams and rivers. Formed by resting beams on two supports, the bridge length can be varied by units 2.2 m long, with a maximum length of 41.8 m. The width of the bridge depends on the number of beams placed side by side, with the usual width being 4.2 m with five beams in use. Longitudinally

the beams are joined together by connecting bolts in the top and bottom chords. Crosswise they are held in place by yokes fitted from above.

Depending on the ground conditions the bridge can be built with or without ramps with the inclination of the ramps being 10 or 25 per cent. The deck is coated with a plastic compound to provide a skid-free surface.

The weights of the various bridge components are such that the bridge can be erected manually. Two beams are usually erected at the same time with all parts being carried for assembly by handles. As assembly progresses the completed bridge sections

are pushed forward using roller-bearing assemblies and a forward horn to reach the far side of the obstacle. It is also possible to erect a bridge using an assembly carriage. A hydraulic jack may be used to assist in assembly and to push forward the completed sections and for assembly of maximum length bridges a framework is used to act as a counterbalance ballasted by extra bridge sections.

The three main construction components can be folded for stowage and transport and are most frequently carried in transport racks fitted with suspension lugs for helicopter transport. A 7000 kg (6 × 6) truck is normally employed for transport.

The bridge weight is 0.13 t/m of beam length or 0.155 t/m^2. Total weights are provided in the table.

A construction team comprises 30 men and construction times are calculated from the arrival of loaded trucks to the opening of the bridge to traffic. These are as follows:

Bridge type	Length	Time*
4-beam, open deck	19.8 m	33 min
4-beam, open deck	22 m	36 min
4-beam, open deck	24.2 m	39 min
5-beam, closed deck	22 m	44 min
5-beam, closed deck	24.2 m	48 min
5-beam, closed deck	26.4 m	52 min

* plus 7 min for removing transport racks from trucks and lowering them to ground

Status
In production. In service in Spain and Switzerland.

Manufacturer
MAN GHH, PO Box 1253, D-6095 Ginsheim-Gustavsburg 1, Federal Republic of Germany.
Tel: 061 34 55-1. Telex: 4182 058 man d.
Fax: 061 34 55-202.

MAN Short-Span bridge

MAN F Bridge

Description
The MAN F bridge (F – framework) is a bridge system consisting of standardised components for building

MAN F bridge erected in Ghana

single- or two-lane bridges with a maximum span of 70 m in 3 m graduations. The bridges can be installed temporarily or permanently.

The F bridge components are constructed of St 52 grade steel and are joined together by high-strength bolts. Steel or wood can be used for the deck

materials. Constructed bridges can be dismantled at any time to be set up elsewhere in similar or different combinations. The usual method of installation is to roll the bridge into position using a launching nose and a short cantilever section at the rear to carry ballast. The launching nose and the cantilever section use the same type of components as the rest of the bridge. All elements of the F bridge system are of such a size that they can be handled by standard lifting tackle and carried on standard trucks.

A reinforced version, known as the FT bridge, is available for use as a railway bridge.

Specifications

Bridge type	Single-lane	Two-lane
Deck width	4 m	6.5 m
Free span		
single-storey	44 m	30 m
double-storey	61 m	47 m
three-storey	70 m	58 m

Status
In production. In service in Burma and Ghana.

Manufacturer
MAN GHH, PO Box 1253, D-6095 Ginsheim-Gustavsburg 1, Federal Republic of Germany. Tel: 061 34 55-1. Telex: 4182 058 man d. Fax: 061 34 55-202.

MAN Short Trackway Bridge

Description
The MAN Short Trackway Bridge (STB) was designed to cross small gaps, ditches and gullies. It consists of identical trackways which are laid separately and then connected by detachable braces. Each trackway consists of one trackway girder with a fixed ramp, one hinged ramp and one connection bolt. The complete structure is constructed using extruded sections and sheets of a high tensile aluminium alloy.

The Standard Bridge consists of one pair of trackways. It is 5.21 m long, can span gaps of up to 4 m and can carry MLC 24 loads.

The Extended Bridge is 9.21 m long and can span gaps of up to 8 m. This bridge is formed from two pairs of trackways joined by a connecting bolt and without any further reinforcement. This bridge can carry loads up to MLC 18 with a maximum crossing speed of 25 km/h.

On both bridges the distances between the trackways can be adjusted to intervals of 1, 1.2 or 1.4 m.

Standard and Extended Bridges can be vehicle-launched and retrieved using a launching frame and a vehicle winch. The Standard Bridge can also be launched manually if bank conditions are suitable. Retrieval can be from either end of the bridge.

A single trackway weighs 180 kg and can be carried by six men using integral carrying handles. Bridges can be transported on truck cargo areas or laterally attached to armoured vehicles such as M113 APCs.

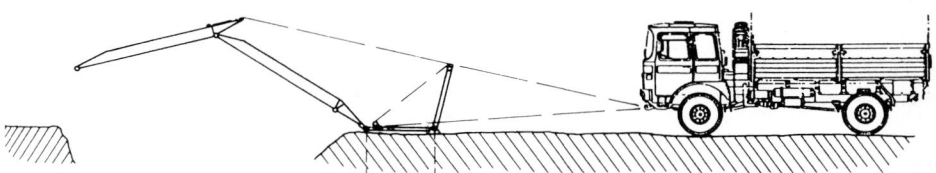

Truck using a launching frame to lay a lengthened Short Trackway Bridge

AMX-13 light tank crossing emplaced Short Trackway Bridge

Specifications

Unit	Trackway	Standard Bridge	Extended Bridge
Weight	180 kg	365 kg	730 kg
Length	5.21 m	5.21 m	9.21 m
Max span	4 m	4 m	8 m
Track width	0.6 m	0.6 m	0.6 m
Width overall	0.7 m	0.7 m	0.7 m
Trackway height	0.28 m	0.28 m	0.28 m
Ramp slope	1:4.5	1:4.5	1:4.5
Laying slope	10%	10%	10%
Load class	—	MLC 24	MLC 18

Status
In production. Order for more than 200 bridges placed.

Manufacturer
MAN GHH, PO Box 1253, D-6095 Ginsheim-Gustavsburg 1, Federal Republic of Germany. Tel: 061 34 55-1. Telex: 4182 058 man d. Fax: 061 34 55-202.

HUNGARY

Hungarian Barge Bridge

Description
Hungary uses a standard nose-to-stern barge bridge using standard inland waterway barges. Each barge is 80.4 m long and 10 m wide and can be used for road or rail traffic, but not both together. Modified barges can be used normally in peacetime and then quickly converted when needed.

Each barge has a payload of 1600 tonnes, and the draught, depending on the weight carried, may be from 0.4 to 2.5 m. Normal deck loading for an evenly distributed load is 3000 kg/m^2, but an individual load can produce a deck loading as high as 10 000 kg/m^2.

Status
In service with Hungarian forces.

Manufacturer
Hungarian state factories.

Hungarian barge bridge for railway traffic being assembled

Hungarian barge bridge in position being used for railway traffic

ISRAEL

RDB-62 Rapid Deployment Bridge

Description
TAAS – Israel Industries Ltd has developed a concept for a 62 m modular rapid deployment bridge (RDB) which can be transported by a fleet of ten trucks, mechanically launched by a team of 12 men within 100 minutes, and capable of carrying MLC 70 loads. The launching configuration uses the auxiliary bridge method. All launching operations are effected from the near side to the far bank. The RDB-62 can bridge gaps of up to 60 m and has two trackways. Extensive use is made of lightweight thin-wall structures utilising sophisticated technologies, materials and alloys.

Status
Development prototypes.

Manufacturer
TAAS – Israel Industries Ltd, POB 1044, Ramat Hasharon 47100, Israel.
Tel: (3) 542 52 22. Telex: 33 719 misbit il.
Fax: (3) 48 96 39.

Merkava MBT crossing an early example of a RDB-62 rapid deployment bridge

SPB36 Sectional Personnel Bridge

Description
Intended for infantry use, the SPB36 sectional footbridge is transported in nine 4 m sections and assembled on site by three men in 10 minutes. An earlier version was known as the SPB24 and used six 4 m sections.

Each SPB36 section weighs 40 kg and is carried by two men using its retractable handles. When assembled the bridge is 36 m long and can be launched across a gap by one man who uses a roller mounted on a small frame. The bridge has a handrail on each side and is only 0.98 m wide. Stretchers can be carried across the bridge by placing them on a two-wheel bogie mounted on the handrails; the stretcher can then be pushed across the bridge by one man. When launching the bridge across water obstacles a small pontoon can be fitted to the leading edge. The SPB36 has been tested by the US Army.

SPB36 stands for Sectional Personnel Bridge 36 m.

Specifications
Weight: (each section) 40 kg
Length:
   (complete bridge) 36 m
   (section) 3.986 m
Width:
   (overall) 0.98 m
   (walkway) 0.378 m
Height: 0.75 m
Dimensions packed
Length: 3.986 m
Width: 2.1 m
Height: 1.56 m

Troops crossing an SPB24 sectional personnel bridge

Crossing capacity:

Span	Men	Interval
36 m	3	17 m
32 m	3	17 m
28 m	4	11 m
24 m	6	4 m
20 m	9	2 m
16 m	10	1.5 m
8 m	close order formation	

It is possible to pack up to six bridge sections together with a launching pontoon for transport by truck or other vehicle including a Jeep-towed two-wheel trailer platform.

Status

In production.

Manufacturer

TAAS – Israel Industries Ltd, POB 1044, Ramat Hasharon 47100, Israel.
Tel: (3) 542 52 22. Telex: 33 719 misbit il.
Fax: (3) 48 96 39.

TAB 12 AT 12 m, Air-Transportable Towed Assault Bridge

Description

The TAB 12 AT 12 m, air-transportable towed assault bridge is intended for bridging anti-tank ditches or other obstacles up to 10 m wide and can carry vehicles weighing up to 70 tonnes. The bridge was designed to be easily separated into two sections along its longitudinal axis for transport in a C-130 transport aircraft, and it was also designed to absorb the loss of up to 50 per cent of its structural beams as well as its complete wheel and suspension system from mines or direct fire and still fulfil its MLC 70 mission.

The main body is constructed of four pre-stressed beams made of 2.2 mm steel plates. The upper surface consists of formed steel plates with anti-sliding

elements. The front section is manufactured from steel bars which are extended to enable the bridge to reach the opposite bank of the obstacle when deployed for use. The front section can be folded by operating a simple mechanism which is activated by the tank crew using the tank's main gun if necessary. Normally the bridge is towed into action by an M60 or Centurion tank but many other tank types can be used with the TAB 12 AT. The bridge is towed on four wheels on a single axle in the centre of the bridge. A coupling hook is also fitted for either towing the bridge or deploying when it is pushed across an obstacle.

In use the bridge is towed to the obstacle with the bridge coupled to the rear of the tank. At the obstacle the tank and bridge make a 180° turn ready for the bridge to be deployed in one of two possible ways. One is for the tank to reverse and push the bridge across the obstacle or the bridge can be uncoupled for the

tank to make a further 180° turn and recouple the bridge to the front of the tank. The bridge is then pushed across the obstacle; this latter operation is normally carried out some distance before the obstacle is reached. The bridge hitch is then disconnected from the tank using a mechanical device; early versions used a pyrotechnic disconnect.

The bridge is supplied with an adaptor which is bolted onto the tank's forward section to permit connection with the bridge by means of the coupling hook.

Specifications

Weight: (total) 9840 kg
Length:
(including coupling hook and extensible front section) 19 m
(bridge) 12 m
Width:
(with siderails) 5 m
(crossing) 4.2 m
Effective maximum height of obstacle: 2.5 m
Bridge classification: MLC 70

Status

In production. In service with Israeli defence forces. Has been tested by US Marine Corps.

Manufacturer

TAAS – Israel Industries Ltd, POB 1044, Ramat Hasharon 47100, Israel.
Tel: (3) 542 52 22. Telex: 33 719 misbit il.
Fax: (3) 48 96 39.

TAB 12 AT 12 m, air-transportable towed assault bridge being pushed into position over dry obstacle with front horns erected and pusher bar still connected to MBT

ITALY

Drago Modular Mountain Bridge

Description

Drago Engineering SpA has been involved in the construction of light structures for over 40 years and is currently producing a range of products including light modular bridges for use in mountain areas. The materials used for its modular mountain bridges are mainly light magnesium and aluminium alloys.

The Modular Mountain Bridge can be constructed to accommodate three weight classes, Class 5, 8 and 12. The bridges are built up from a number of 2.5 m span bays using tubular alloy components as the main structural elements. Deck baulks are added when the bridge structure is complete. The bridges can be constructed without recourse to special tools or equipment and it is possible to bring all the bridge components to the site using pack transport by animals or light vehicles. It is possible to use many of the bridge components for other purposes such as the construction of aerial ropeway towers or observation towers, and for the internal bracing of underground shelters and observation posts.

Status

In production.

Manufacturer

Drago Engineering SpA, Viale Trieste 24, I-39100 Bolzano, Italy.
Tel: 471 916339. Telex: 500 198.
Fax: 471 935604.

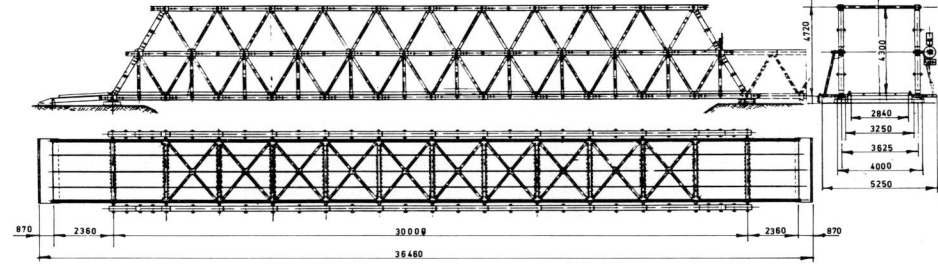

General layout drawing of Drago Class 12 modular mountain bridge

Specifications

Bridge class	5	8	12
Span of one bay	2.5 m	2.5 m	2.5 m
Max span	37.5 m	35 m	30 m
Useful width	3.05 m	3.05 m	3.05 m
Useful height	4.15 m	4.15 m	4.15 m
Length of longest element	3.25 m	3.25 m	3.25 m
Weight of heaviest element	125 kg	125 kg	125 kg
Average weight/m	470 kg	470 kg	470 kg
Bridge total weight/m	19 700 kg	16 920 kg	14 000 kg
Useful deck surface	114.37 m²	106.75 m²	91.5 m²

JAPAN

Bridge, Panel, Class 30

Description
The Bridge, Panel, Class 30, a modified version of the American M2 Bailey Bridge, was introduced in 1960. The main difference between the American and Japanese versions is that the Japanese components are smaller and lighter, facilitating handling and reducing transport requirements.

Typical examples are the truss of the Japanese model which is 2.5 m long, 1.3 m high and weighs 222 kg compared with the American model which is 3.3 m long, 1.5 m high and weighs 262 kg. The Japanese bridge does however have a narrower

roadway (3.4 m) and a smaller carrying capacity than the American M2 bridge. A Class 30 bridge, which is assembled with a 40-man team, is 25 m long and has a roadway width of 3.4 m.

Specifications
Truss panel
Weight: 222 kg
Length: 2.5 m
Width: 0.2 m
Height: 1.3 m

Transoms
Weight: 241 kg
Length: 5 m

Width: 0.2 m
Height: 0.25 m

Stringers
Weight: 88 kg
Length: 2.5 m
Width: 0.6 m
Height: 0.1 m

Status
Production complete. In service with the Japanese Ground Self-Defence Force.

Manufacturer
Kisha Seizo Kaisha Limited, Tokyo, Japan.

POLAND

DMS-65 Heavy Girder Bridge

Description
The DMS-65 is basically a modern development of the well-known Bailey panel bridge. It is normally built as a single-storey, through-truss road bridge, but can also be constructed as a deck-truss railway bridge. There are only five basic elements of the bridge which are carried in Star 66M (6 × 6) 2500 kg cargo trucks. The DMS-65 can be assembled by manpower or with the aid of cranes, and bridges of different lengths, with either single or multiple spans, can be built. The roadway consists of metal plates which are covered with crushed stone.

Status
In service with the Polish Army.

Manufacturer
Polish state factories.

Star 660 (6 × 6) 2500 kg truck carrying DMS-65 components

Bailey Type Panel Bridges

Description
The British-designed Bailey Bridge was adopted by the US Army during the Second World War, and the old Soviet Union obtained some of these under Lend-Lease. Some of these bridges may still be in service

with countries of the former Warsaw Pact, together with local copies of the bridge. Poland is one of the countries which copied the Bailey Bridge with some minor modifications. This is distinguishable from the standard Bailey Bridge by the increased number of holes in the transom.

There are separate entries in this section for the Czechoslovak MS-1 (SM-60) and the Polish DMS-65

panel bridges, both of which resemble the Bailey Bridge in some respects.

Status
In service with the Polish Army.

Manufacturer
Polish state factories.

SINGAPORE

Portable Assault Bridge PAB 15

Description
The Portable Assault Bridge PAB 15 was designed to be manportable and can be carried by wheeled or tracked vehicles to bridge small gaps or other obstacles. It can carry loads of up to 15 tonnes in any configuration.

The PAB 15 consists of two standard 4 m panels and one 2 m panel connector which can be coupled together to bridge gaps up to 10 m wide. For a complete PAB 15 the 2 m panel connector is placed in the centre of the two 4 m panels and a supporter unit is placed underneath. A 4 m panel can be used by itself to bridge small gaps. Two PAB 15 bridges are placed side by side to carry vehicles.

A complete PAB 15 bridge can be constructed by four men within 10 minutes.

Specifications
Panel	4 m	2 m
Weight	135 kg	62 kg
Length	4.06 m	2.07 m
Width	0.76 m	0.76 m
Height	0.21 m	0.21 m

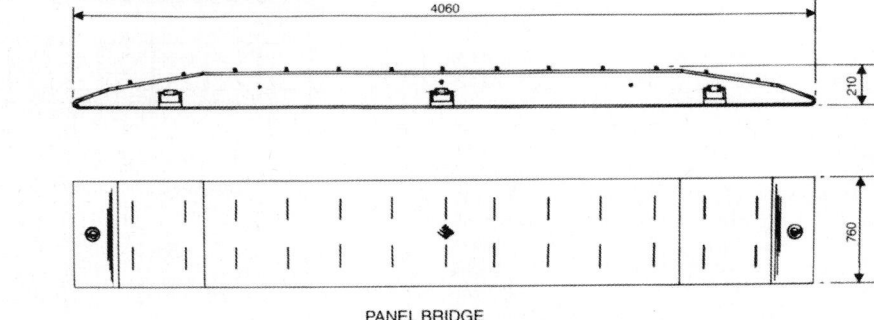

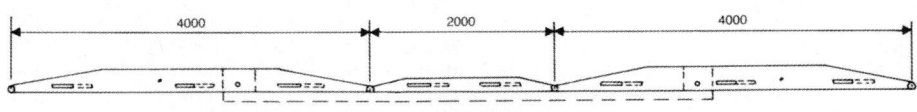

Main components of Portable Assault Bridge PAB 15 with supporter unit below

Status
In production.

Manufacturer
Singapore Shipbuilding and Engineering Limited, 7 Benoi Road, Singapore 2262.

Tel: 8612244. Telex: singa rs 21206.
Fax: 8613028.

SWITZERLAND

Bridge, Steel Truss, Model 52

Description
This bridge was designed in the early 1950s to meet the requirements of the Swiss Army. It is a through-deck type Warren truss bridge that can be erected by the cantilever method using a crane and derrick. It can also be assembled on the river bank and pushed across the gap with the aid of a launching nose.

The truss members are square or rectangular, box-shaped and airtight. The hollow beams are made of either lightweight or heavyweight steel sections, light sections for the diagonals and heavy sections for the top and bottom chords. The truss members have the same external dimensions but not the same weight. Stringers are made of two I-beams welded together, similar to the Bailey stringers. The transoms which carry the floor can be placed on either the top or the bottom of the trusses. The basic bridge is Class 20, but a Class 55 can be built by adding a second truss to the existing structure.

Specifications
Chord members (truss)
Weight: 117 kg
Length: 3 m
Width: 0.15 m
Depth: 0.15 m

Diagonals (truss)
Weight: 89 kg
Length: 3 m
Width: 0.15 m
Depth: 0.15 m

Transoms
Weight: 443 kg

Stringers
Weight: 112 kg
Length: 3 m
Depth: 0.15 m

Assembled Bridge

	20 t	55 t
Class	**20 t**	**55 t**
Roadway width	4.2 m	4.2 m
Assembly time	5.5 to 6 h	8 to 8.5 h
Working party	77 men	77 men

Status
In service with the Swiss Army.

UNITED KINGDOM

Thompson Modular Bridge (TMB)

Description
The Thompson Modular Bridge (TMB), under development by Thompson Defence Projects for the British Army's Bridging for the 1990s programme, is a comprehensive bridging system covering line of communications bridges (also known as dry support bridges) and tank-launched bridges (see separate entry in the *Mechanised bridges* section for that aspect of the system). All bridges are built from a range of seven modular panels which are interchangeable through the various bridge types. Dry support bridges are used for longer spans and where AVLBs are not available.

All the bridges are launched by the Automotive Bridge Launching Equipment (ABLE), with components transported to the bridging site on Bridging Vehicles. The ABLE consists of a truck-mounted crane and a launch mechanism. The launch is achieved by deploying a launch rail across the gap and lowering it onto the far bank. The bridge is assembled beneath the launch rail and winched across the gap. The launch rails, which are carried on the ABLE, are recovered, thus allowing the ABLE to proceed to other bridge sites to carry out further launches. Recovery by ABLE can be carried out from either end of the bridge and ABLE can be used to recover any of the tank-launched bridges in the TMB system. The Bridging Vehicles carry all the bridge components to the bridging site. They are fitted with truck-mounted cranes which facilitate loading/unloading and assist in the launch of the bridge. The launch can be completed with only one crane operable while the Bridging Vehicles can be used for carrying general cargo when not required for bridging purposes.

A Bridge Set consists of 8 m ramp panels, 8 m panels, 4 m panels and 2 m panels to enable a bridge to be constructed from a minimum length of 16 m in 2 m increments up to 32 m. The bridge is 4 m wide and, with in-fill deck units fitted, provides a continuous trackway over the width. A Bridge Set is carried on two Bridging Vehicles.

To enable longer bridges to be built, Long Span Equipment is added to the 32 m bridge set. This allows bridges up to 56 m to be built in 2 m increments, using reinforcement links and a king post system.

Two Span Equipment provides the flexibility for the bridge to be supported mid span by an intermediate floating or fixed pier. An articulator panel and a rocking roller set provide both the support and change of angle at that support. The Long Span Equipment can also be used to reinforce one span of a two span bridge. The maximum Two Span Bridge length is 60 m with a fixed pier, and 62 m with a floating pier. Two Span Equipment, including the necessary trackway to extend the bridge to 62 m, is carried on two extra Bridging Vehicles.

A 32 m bridge can be launched in approximately 30 minutes and dressed with in-fill decks and kerbs, and so on, in an additional 10 minutes by a crew of 10.

Classification of the bridges is MLC 70 wheeled and tracked for all spans, including the 56 m Long Span

Thompson ABLE placing launch rail over 32 m gap to be bridged

Bridges. Many of the bridges can be crossed by some specific fully laden tank transporters, albeit at slightly reduced spans. The bridges were designed using the US/UK/GE Trilateral Design and Test Code.

The ABLE and Bridging Vehicles are Improved Medium Mobility Load Carriers (IMMLC) giving a good cross-country capability with 8 × 8 configuration, enabling them to reach most bridging sites accessed by AFVs. The vehicles have a high degree of commonality with each other and with the TBT used as part of the Tank Launched Bridge system (see separate entry under *Mechanised bridges*), although other vehicles could be used.

Specifications
32 m Bridge Set
Length overall: 32 m
Panels: 4 × 8 m ramp panels; 2 × 8 m panels; 3 × 4 m panels; 2 × 2 m panels
Ramp length: 6 m
Width overall: 4 m
Depth of section: 1 m
Max span: 30 m
Weight: 18 900 kg
Launch/recovery times: 30 min/40 min
Dressing time: 10 min
Crew: 10

Long Span Equipment (current system capability)
Length overall: 44 m (with 32 m Bridge Set)

Extra panels: 16 m of panels; 2 × 4 m reinforcement panels; reinforcement anchorages; 2 additional launch rail panels
Width overall: 4 m
Depth of section: 1 m
Max span: 42 m
Weight: (total, 44 m bridge) 31 093 kg
Launch/recovery times: 45 min/60 min
Dressing time: 15 min
Crew: 11

Two Span Equipment
Length overall:
  (fixed pier) 60 m
  (floating pier) 62 m
Extra panels: extra 28 m of panels; 2 × 2 m articulator panels; 2 × rocking rollers
Width overall: 4 m
Depth of section: 1 m

Max span:
  (fixed pier) 58 m
  (floating pier) 60 m
Launch/recovery times: 60 min/90 min
Dressing time: 20 min
Crew: to be defined

Status
Development. Undergoing Contractor Field Trials and User Trials with the British Army.

Manufacturer
Thompson Defence Projects Limited, PO Box 100, Spring Road, Ettingshall, Wolverhampton WV4 6JY, UK.
Tel: 0902 353353. Telex: 337412 NEITOM G.
Fax: 0902 405500.

Thos Storey Bailey Bridge

Development/Description
The Bailey Bridge was originally developed by Sir Donald Bailey at the Military Engineering Experimental Establishment at Christchurch and was widely used during the Second World War. In 1948, Thos Storey (Engineers) gained a licence from the National Research Development Corporation to manufacture and sell Bailey bridging components and equipment. In 1950 this licence was extended granting exclusive rights to the patent, production and selling of the Bailey Bridge system. Since then the company has been continually improving the system which remains in production to meet a continuing demand.

The Bailey Bridge was designed as a universal unit-construction military bridging system, with the Bailey panel as its basic component. The great advantage of the system lies in its use of these standard interchangeable components, which, combined with the simplicity of design, enables it to be erected in a short time by unskilled labour under limited specialist supervision.

The Bailey panel, the basic component, is made of high tensile steel. Panels can be connected together to form beams or columns. They are connected by panel pins and chord bolts to give a series of composite girders with varying strengths to meet loading conditions.

Using basic equipment, the maximum span is 61 m and the maximum military load is Class 80. The bridge can be constructed in three widths, 3.28, 3.81 and 4.19 m. The bridge is normally constructed on rollers on one side of the gap and then launched into position using a skeleton, cantilever nose, which is detached after the bridge has crossed the gap.

Over the years, Thos Storey has improved the original design. These improvements include a new steel decking which is quick and easy to erect, provides an anti-skid surface and unlike the wooden deck has a long life. This can be used with the

Through-type Bailey Bridge with decking system carried between two side girders formed from Bailey panels

standard, standard widened, extra wide or double width Bailey Bridges. Another development is the Thos Storey Bailey panel, which provides an extra 40 per cent safe working shear load plus increased bending capacity and is completely interchangeable with the standard Bailey panel. Finally a double width Bailey 7.23 m wide was developed to permit two-way traffic.

In 1991 Thos Storey (Engineers) Limited introduced a new decking system comprising a main deck element, kerb units, transoms and fixings. The decking was designed in three weights; light, medium and heavy. Road widths are: standard, 3.285 m; single carriageway, 3.685 m; extra wide, 4.422 m; double wide, 7.37 m; and triple wide 11.055 m. New fixing systems make the decks easier and quicker to handle and install. The clamp design utilises a 'Halfen'-type channel system which allows deck elements to be placed in position with the hold-down bolts introduced afterwards. Normal installations require one bolt and clamp to hold down four deck units at the corners with

outer edge corners needing only a single bolt and clamp. The units weigh between 309 and 339 kg and are also compatible with Thos Storey Acrow Panel bridging systems.

In addition to being used as a road bridge, the Bailey bridge has been widely used for other applications including rail and foot bridges, retractable lift bridges, derrick supports and mobile gantries. It can also be used in conjunction with the Acrow Uniflote for floating bridges.

Status
In production. In service with many armed forces all over the world.

Manufacturer
Thos Storey (Engineers) Limited, 52 Queens Road, Weybridge, Surrey KT13 0AN, UK.
Tel: 0932 858133. Telex: 21868.
Fax: 0932 855588.

Acrow Panel Bridge

Description
The Bailey Bridge was designed to take military traffic up to Class 80 standard and to cope with the maximum single-axle loadings of 20 tonnes. Today a bridge may have to be Class 150 and cope with single-axle loadings of 60 tonnes or more, particularly where heavy earthmoving equipment is using the bridge. Such capacities could be achieved only by making extensive modifications to the standard Bailey design.

Thos Storey decided that a new design was required, based on the Bailey system and principles, but taking advantage of modern developments in bridge design and steel technology. The result is the Acrow panel bridge which uses the Bailey unit construction system with its ease of assembly, but employs higher tensile steels and advanced design to give enhanced load-

carrying capacity, and in particular, a fatigue life many times that of the Bailey system at less cost.

Like the Bailey Bridge, the decking can be either steel or timber. Varying strengths of decking can be provided depending on the axle load the bridge is required to carry. The Acrow Panel Bridge can have roadway widths of 3.43, 4.13, 4.84 and 7.23 m to give two-lane traffic using standard equipment. Again, as with the Bailey, the Acrow panel bridge can be launched on rollers and constructed using unskilled labour without a crane if necessary.

Acrow panel equipment can be used even more successfully than Bailey equipment to produce structures other than road bridges, for example rail bridges and gantries. All components of the bridge have been designed to be carried in standard military transport vehicles. Bridges can be installed either for permanent use, or subsequently dismantled and stored for re-use when required.

The major advantages of the Acrow panel bridge can be summarised as follows: improved bending-moment capacity, improved shear capacity, improved stability against buckling under load, increased efficiency of stress transfer, greater rigidity and stability overall and a fatigue life approximately four times that of the standard Bailey Bridge.

The Acrow panel bridge is constructed on rollers on one side of the gap to be bridged and an additional temporary structure, utilising standard components, is built on the leading end. The length of the nose is so judged that when the construction is moved across the gap, the nose tip engages on rollers on the opposite bank before the point of balance is reached. With the bridge positioned across the gap, the launching nose is removed and dismantled. The bridge is then jacked up off the rollers and lowered on to permanent bearings on the abutments on either bank.

Basic Components

The Acrow panel is the basic truss component. This has a shear capacity in a single storey of 25 tonnes, 67 per cent more than the standard Bailey panel, and a shear capacity in a double storey of 41 tonnes, again 67 per cent more than the standard Bailey Bridge.

Panel pins with circlips are used to connect panels end to end. These provide a locking feature which is also a useful precaution against tampering.

Chord reinforcements can be bolted to top and bottom panels for additional bending movement capacity and are staggered over panel joints in the compression chord to provide greater stability under load. Four bolts are used to connect panels to chord reinforcements to increase the efficiency of stress transfer.

Chord bolts are used to connect panels one on top of another in the case of two or more panel heights or to connect chord reinforcements to panels.

Transoms of different lengths give four roadway widths; there are two basic profiles and light, heavy and super heavy versions. Transoms are located by dowels and bolted down to the transom seatings at intersections between diagonals and the bottom chord of panels at exactly 1.52 m centres.

The steel decking is available in different versions for different load requirements. Deck units, consisting of chequer plate decking welded to the stringers, are clamped at each transom. Decking can terminate 0.762 m inside the ends of the bridge or may be extended 0.762 m onto abutments. Sloping ramps can be provided.

In the timber decking, deck chesses are held in position by steel kerb units which are bolted down to the outer stringers.

An Acrow four-panel type pier can be constructed for use as a supporting member for the bridge. This form of construction is very rigid and will carry an axial load of 400 tonnes on a pier as high as 41 m. Two panel adjustable towers, capable of carrying axial loads of up to 200 tonnes (dependent on height) can also be provided.

The Acrow panel bridge can also be used in conjunction with the Acrow Uniflote system, for floating bridges, jetties and Ro-Ro terminals.

In 1978 Thos Storey (Engineers) introduced the

Heavy earthmoving equipment crossing Ultra Wide Acrow Panel Bridge

AB1X hybrid panel for use with either Bailey or Acrow panel bridging. It is manufactured from the same materials as the AB1 Acrow panel, which has better shear capacity, bending-movement capacity and fatigue life than the Bailey. Used one way up the hybrid panel accepts the Acrow Panel decking system at standard 5-foot centres in the normal way and the other way up reverts to a Bailey panel and can be used with standard Bailey decking and other components to form Bailey bridging, with the added advantage that the shear capacity is increased by the full 67 per cent of an Acrow Panel.

In 1991 Thos Storey (Engineers) Limited introduced a new decking system comprising a main deck element, kerb units, transoms and fixings. The decking was designed in three weights; light, medium and heavy. Road widths are: standard, 3.285 m; single carriageway, 3.685 m; extra wide, 4.422 m; double wide, 7.37 m; and triple wide 11.055 m. New fixing systems make the decks easier and quicker to handle and install. The clamp design utilises a 'Halfen'-type channel system which allows deck elements to be placed in position with the hold-down bolts introduced afterwards. Normal installations require one bolt and clamp to hold down four deck units at the corners with outer edge corners needing only a single bolt and

clamp. The units weigh between 309 and 339 kg and are also compatible with Thos Storey Bailey bridging systems.

Bridge widths

	Single Traffic Lane Bridges	
Roadway width		Clearance between inner trusses
	Type of Bridge	
3.43 m	Standard Acrow Panel Bridge	3.76 m
4.13 m	Extra Wide Acrow Panel Bridge	4.78 m
4.85 m	Ultra Wide Acrow Panel Bridge	5.48 m
	Two Traffic Lane Bridges	
7.23 m	Double Width Acrow Panel Bridge	7.6 m

Status

In production. In service with many armed forces around the world.

Manufacturer

Thos Storey (Engineers) Limited, 52 Queens Road, Weybridge, Surrey KT13 0AN, UK.
Tel: 0932 858133. Telex: 21868.
Fax: 0932 855588.

Acrow Heavy Bridge

Description

Acrow panel bridges, like the Bailey, are normally limited to a clear span of 61 m. But there are occasions when a longer span is required and to meet this requirement Thos Storey developed the Acrow heavy bridge. The bridge is of the Warren truss type and has all the advantages of unit construction based on the uniformity of similar components produced by a strict jig control during the manufacturing process. The bridge has been designed for two-lane traffic on single spans of up to 100 m in length, or for single line railway bridges. The maximum span depends on the loading required.

The Acrow heavy bridge was designed to be launched in the same way as the Bailey, with a cantilever nose on the front. Although it has been designed primarily for use as a permanent bridge, it is quick and easy to erect and can, if necessary, be dismantled and re-used elsewhere. A crane is required to assist erection of the bridge but because of the simplicity of the design and the method of assembly no skilled labour is required.

Alternative *in situ* reinforced concrete, with or without asphalt wearing surface, steel, or timber decking systems are available. In each case the decking is rigidly connected to the bridge structure, forming an integral part of the bridge. Footwalks can be cantilevered on either side of the bridge structure outside the main trusses.

Each component of the bridge is an all-welded

82.3 m Acrow heavy bridge for two-lane traffic

fabrication designed not only for its structural purpose but also for ease of handling, transportability and for rapid and simple construction on site.

Status

In production. In service in many parts of the world.

Manufacturer

Thos Storey (Engineers) Limited, 52 Queens Road, Weybridge, Surrey KT13 0AN, UK.
Tel: 0932 858133. Telex: 21868.
Fax: 0932 855588.

Mabey and Johnson Military Bridging System

Description

In October 1989 Mabey and Johnson Limited first presented their new Military Bridging System which was based on their Compact 200 system but upgraded to meet military requirements. The concept of the bridge has its roots in the Bailey design but the application of high grade steels and advanced computer design and analysis techniques has led to more effective structures for system economy and applications.

The design of the system is modular, allowing full spans of up to 61 m to be built. Floating bridges or multi-pier systems can be used to bridge any width of river. Loads up to MLC 100 have been proven during extensive testing. A typical MLC 70 30 m bridge can be built by 30 men within 2-3 hours. Erection times are considerably shortened by the use of special Quick Action Bolts which can be replaced later by conventional nuts and bolts, if required.

The system's main structural components are fabricated from high tensile steel which is then hot-dip galvanised to prevent corrosion, thus minimising the maintenance requirement. The structures are designed and tested to have a very long fatigue life. No component weighs more than 400 kg and a complete bridge set weighs less than 40 000 kg.

The Military Bridging System can be built using unskilled labour. For transport a 30 m bridge can be carried in nine 4-tonne trucks, four 6.096 m ISO containers, or four DROPS flatracks. Following the usual site survey, bridge bearing rollers are set up to line up with the far bank. A launching nose constructed from four 5 m nose bays is assembled using light-

Mabey and Johnson Military Bridging System MLC 70 bridge

weight composite aluminium/steel components and the bridge is constructed behind the nose. The launching nose is removed once the bridge has been launched across the gap and an integral hydraulic jacking system then lowers the bridge onto its bearings and toe-of-ramp units are fitted to the inboard ramps. The bridge is then ready for use.

When assembled, all Mabey and Johnson Military Bridging Systems have a steel deck roadway width of 4.2 m; each deck unit is 3.05 m long. Inboard ramps are 6.1 m long and have a slope of less than 1 in 10. Simple bridges are produced using single side panels only. By introducing double or triple side panels and adding reinforcing elements or heavy chord reinforcements and high shear panels, heavier loads and longer bridge lengths can be produced. For instance, a 30.5 m MLC 70 bridge can be built using single side

panels only. By contrast a 48.8 m MLC 100 bridge can be built using triple side panels reinforced on the inner, centre and outer panels lines, plus heavy chord reinforcements.

The standard Military Bridging System lengths are 9.144, 12.192, 15.248, 18.3, 21.288, 24.384, 27.432, 30.48, 33.528, 36.576, 39.624, 42.672, 45.728, 48.758, 51.816, 54.912, 57.912 and 60.96 m.

Status

Ready for production.

Manufacturer

Mabey and Johnson Limited, Floral Mile, Twyford, Reading, Berkshire RG10 9SQ, UK.
Tel: 0734 403921. Telex: 848649 mabeyt g.
Fax: 0734 404756.

Mabey Bailey Bridging

Development

The Mabey Group has fabricated and erected bridges for over a century, and supplies a complete range of unit construction and modular bridges worldwide. Mabey and Johnson is a British Government authorised manufacturer of Bailey bridging, which it has supplied to the British Army and armies overseas. It is bridging consultant to NATO.

Description

Bailey is a through-type bridge in which the roadway is carried between the main girders. It has been designed on the unit construction principle; the basic unit is a bay of 3.05 m which means that bridges of varying spans and load capacities can be built from a stock of standard parts. The Bailey system has been devised for construction by unskilled labour under the supervision of an engineer. The heaviest component can be carried by six men and all components can be carried to the site in standard 3000 kg trucks.

Various decking systems have been developed to cater not only for the usual military loadings, but also for civilian loading and roadway width requirements. Decks can be supplied in timber or stiffened steel plate in 3.28, 3.81 and 4.19 m widths or combined in a three-

Mabey and Johnson Bailey bridging in position

truss dual carriageway configuration. Special timber decks are also available for abnormal heavy-axled vehicles.

The latest development, marketed as 'Mabey Compact Bailey', incorporates grade 55 steel and improvements to panel, bracing and deck system giving greater strength and enhanced fatigue life. It is the result of extensive research and development and was proved in full-scale tests at the Military Vehicles and Engineering Establishment, Christchurch (now the RARDE Christchurch).

All these equipments can be erected by launching

from one side of the gap to be bridged, and equipment and detailed instructions for these operations are supplied.

Status

In production. In service.

Manufacturer

Mabey and Johnson Limited, Floral Mile, Twyford, Reading, Berkshire RG10 9SQ, UK.
Tel: 0734 403921. Telex: 848649 mabeyt g.
Fax: 0734 404756.

Mabey Universal Bridging

Description

Mabey and Johnson used its wide experience of the Bailey Bridge to develop the Universal bridge, which entered production and service in 1975.

The equipment extends the capability of speedily erected panel bridging as it is available in no fewer than six carriageway widths and for long spans up to 100 m. The road widths are 3.28 m (standard) and 4.19 m (extra wide) for single-lane traffic, two-lane roadways of 6.1 and 7.5 m, and three-lane of 9.1 and 10.9 m. For special vehicles, decks to carry 40- and 60-tonne axles can be provided.

As with Bailey, the construction strength can be varied to suit the loading, and bridge construction is

Mabey Universal Bridging in position

chosen by reference to load tables. The equipment is intended as a military line of communication bridge and for long-term and permanent civilian use. To this end, load factors are a minimum of 1.7 in accordance with British Standards, and low maintenance is a significant factor in the detailing of parts. If required, the bridges can be completely galvanised. The roadway comprises steel panel decking which will accept an asphalt wearing course if required, or can be supplied with an epoxy anti-skid wearing course.

The deeper Universal panel (4.5 × 2.36 m) has more than twice the bending resistance of Bailey, resulting in simpler and lighter truss formations. The deeper panel also makes single-storey spans possible up to 54 m, thus extending economical single-storey bridging through all the spans normally encountered in practice. With double-storey, spans up to 100 m are possible.

The bridges can be launched by the standard cantilever method, thus combining most of the benefits of Bailey, including ease of erection, multiple use, and guaranteed load-carrying capacities with permanent bridge capability.

Status
In production and service.

Manufacturer
Mabey and Johnson Limited, Floral Mile, Twyford, Reading, Berkshire RG10 9SQ, UK.
Tel: 0734 403921. Telex: 848649 mabeyt g.
Fax: 0734 404756.

Williams Fairey Engineering Medium Girder Bridge

Development
The Medium Girder Bridge (MGB) was designed and developed by the Military Vehicles and Engineering Establishment at Christchurch (MVEE(C)), now the Royal Armament Research and Development Establishment Christchurch (RARDE(C)), with production, marketing and further development undertaken by Williams Fairey Engineering Limited. The MGB entered service with the British Army in 1971 and since then has been adopted by 35 countries.

The main advantages of the MGB can be summarised as follows: it is quickly and easily built by hand, little training is required, no site preparation or grillages are required, it is easily transported by road or air as palletised loads, is of light and sturdy construction, it has a multi-span capability with span junction set, a portable pier set is available, it can also be used as a ferry or floating bridge of unlimited length, it has a load capacity of up to MLC 70 (tracked) or MLC 100 (wheeled) and little or no maintenance is required.

Description
The MGB is a lightweight, easily transported bridging system which can be quickly erected by hand to provide a flexible and manoeuvrable bridging system covering the full range of military bridging requirements. The MGB has also been adopted by a number of governments for emergency bridging operations.

Much of the success of the MGB lies in the material from which the components are manufactured. The RARDE(C) developed a weldable alloy of aluminium, zinc and magnesium (DGFVE 232B) necessary to ensure both the strength and the lightness of the bridge. Seven major components are used in the basic bridge construction, and all except two weigh under 200 kg, and can be easily handled by a team of four men. The two heavier components are handled by six-man teams.

The MGB is a two-girder deck-type bridge in which the longitudinal girders with the deck units between produce a 4 m wide roadway. Girders of top panels joined at each end by a bankseat form a shallow single-storey construction for heavy loads at short spans and lighter loads at longer spans up to 22.4 m. A double-storey configuration using deeper girders of top and bottom panels, together with additional end of bridge components, can be constructed for heavier loads over longer spans.

The MGB can be supported on unprepared and uneven ground without foundations. It is constructed on one roller beam for single-storey construction and on two roller beams 4.6 m apart in a building frame for double-storey construction. The ends of the roller beam can be adjusted in height within the building frame so that no levelling or other preparation of the ground is required.

All components of the MGB are transported in standard loads of up to 3500 kg on a special pallet. The British Army uses the Bedford TM 4-4 or MK (4 × 4) which also tows a two-wheeled trailer carrying another pallet. There is a separate entry for the MGB trailer (FV2842) in the *Trailers* section. When the vehicle and trailer arrive at the bridge-building area the pallet is attached to a stationary vehicle, or an alternative anchorage point, and the towing vehicle is driven away pulling off the pallet, which falls onto the ground. Rubber buffers cushion the fall. A single 9.8 m bridge is transported on two pallet loads while a 31 m double-storey bridge is transported on 10 pallet loads. Any

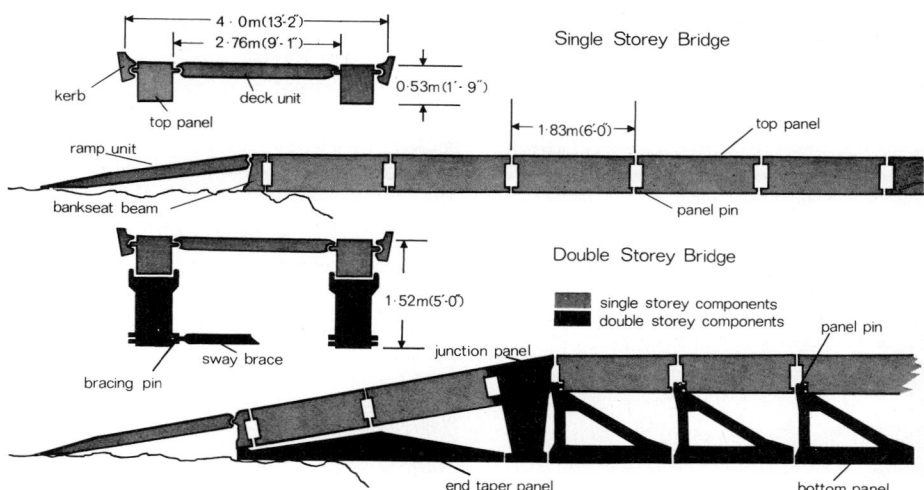

Main components of MGB

49 m link reinforced MGB being crossed by a Chieftain MBT

Link reinforced 49 m MGB

vehicle of suitable capacity may be used and special pallets for specific vehicles have been introduced.

Single-span bridging

The MGB can be built either in the single- or double-storey configuration. Single-span single-storey bridges can be used by Class 70 vehicles at a length of 9.8 m and by lighter vehicles up to a maximum length of 22 m at Class 16. Single-span double-storey bridges can be used by Class 70 vehicles at lengths of up to 31 m and at increasing lengths for lower load classes, to a maximum length of 49 m at Military Load Class 16.

The single-storey bridge is constructed using top panels pinned together forming two girders and joined at each end by a bankseat beam. In the double-storey configuration, the girders consist of top and bottom panels with junction panels, and end taper panels forming the sloping end of the bridge. In both cases, ramp, deck and kerb units complete the construction.

Single-span bridges are launched using a centrally mounted launching nose made up of 3 m sections. During launching, the bridge is supported on roller beams at the home bank and a roller at the far bank. Single-storey bridges are launched over one roller beam, supported on baseplates. Double-storey bridges are launched over two such roller beams supported 4.6 m apart in a building frame. To adjust the height and levels of the roller beams, a hydraulic jack (with a lift of 300 mm) can be mounted at each corner of the building frame. These jacks are also used to lower the bridge on both banks after construction.

Reinforcement set

This extends the single-span capability of the MGB to MLC 60 at 49.4 m and MLC 70 at 45.8 m. It complements the capability of the MGB pier and span junction equipment as it can be used in terrain where deep valleys make it impracticable to use piers. The kit contains all the additional components required for use with normal double-storey bridge sets to construct a length of reinforced Class 60 MGB from 32.9 to 49.4 m. The latest reinforcement sets provide a capability of MLC 70 at a span of 45.8 m. The kit consists of reinforcing links 3.66 m long (with one pair of links 1.83 m long to provide the greatest range of spans), which are connected to form a pair of chains, one beneath each bridge girder. Links are connected to bottom panels at the ends of the bridge by an anchorage assembly. The links are positioned 2 m below the bridge by reinforcing posts which enable the system to be tensioned towards a vertical position by Tirfor cable jacks (details of these will be found in the *Recovery equipment* section). The reinforcing is added by an extra party of eight men while the bridge is being constructed by the normal 24-man team.

The reinforcement set is in service with the British Army, US Army and Marine Corps and 16 other countries.

Reduced slope End of Bridge

The standard slope of a double-storey MGB End of Bridge is 1:5. A reduced slope can be desirable when a bridge is being used in a line of communications role and thus by second echelon vehicles with longer wheelbases and lower ground clearances. For this

Close-up of Universal light pier in position

purpose an End of Bridge with a slope of 1:10 is available with an overall length of 4.267 m, as opposed to the normal 3.086 m.

Span junction set

The basic single span MGB can be given a multi-span capability by the use of the MGB span junction set. This equipment enables bridges of any length up to Class 60 load capacity to be hand-built over any fixed or floating supports, existing or improvised.

The span junction set consists of span junction posts pinned to top and bottom panels. The span junction posts are themselves pinned together at the top and hinged by an articulator connected to the lower half of the span junction posts. A span junction link is fitted to join the bottom chords of the junction post to permit movement over rollers during launching. After launching the junction link is removed to allow articulation of the junction posts. The other main component is the capsill. This is a beam to which rocking rollers which incorporate bridge bearings can be pinned. The capsill fitted with rocking rollers can be used on top of a pier to carry the bridge during launching or in the MGB adjustable roller beam support to form the heavy duty capsill roller beam (CRB) required when launching most multi-span bridges.

Portable pier set

The portable pier set provides the MGB with its own two-legged pier which can be assembled during the building of the bridge. Two legs pass through housing at each end of a pier beam. The legs are constructed in 3 m sections and piers up to 6 m in height can be used in water gaps with current speeds of up to 5.5 m/s. In dry gaps, legs up to 12 m can be used.

The pier beam with housing, leg base section and one standard leg section at each end is pre-assembled

and then pinned to the span junction post on the home bank and launched with the bridge. Once the bridge is in position, the adjustable braces are used to set the pier beam vertical before the legs are lowered and any additional leg sections are added. The pier components are also transportable on the standard MGB pallet and the heaviest component weighs 408 kg.

Multi-span

Using the MGB portable pier set for multi-span bridges, the piers can be launched with the bridge by temporarily placing the first pier in position as the next is brought up, then moving the piers successively by booming the bridge back and forward.

The span junction components allow double-storey floating bridges of any length to be constructed on virtually any type of floating support which has sufficient buoyancy.

The articulation provided by the span junction bay and the use of long landing bays means that the MGB is the only modern military bridge equipment which can be used in a situation where bank heights range from 0 to 5 m. Even this range can be extended to 6 m if the MGB portable pier is used to form trestle bays.

Floating MGB/MGB Ferry/MGB Pontoon

See entry in the *Tactical floating bridges and ferries* section.

MACH MGB

MACH (Mechanically Aided Construction by Hand) was introduced to meet the reduced manning requirements of modern armed forces. With a minimal purchase of additional components the normal MGB set can be held as part-assembled modules and constructed using a suitable crane or Crane Attachment Lorry-Mounted (CALM). The normal MGB team on an operational site can be reduced from 1 + 24 to 1 + 14 (optimum) or a minimum of 1 + 8.

Universal Light Pier

The Universal Light Pier was developed to meet the needs of the Swiss Army for a rapidly built pier for use with the MGB in mountain terrain. It is of modular construction and was designed to be independently erected from the bottom of a gap by a team of 12 men in 1 hour. The pier enables long two-span bridges to be built, for example 60 m at MLC 60 and 90 m at MLC 20. The pier legs can be up to 20 m long and can take loads of up to 120 tonnes.

Ski jump for V/STOL

The components of the MGB readily adapt to the Ski jump profile when raised at one end. The ramp surface comprises three MGB single-storey girders supporting MGB deck units between them. Outrigger units provide a total ramp width of 10 m.

Container ship flight deck

The MGB will provide a rapid easily erected flight deck on a wide range of commercial container ships. An MGB deck structure is supported on beams mounted on ISO containers which creates a hangar space underneath and/or side dispersal.

A MACH MGB with reduced slope End of Bridge being crossed by engineer equipment

A MACH MGB under construction

Specifications

NATO stock number	Service designation	Unit weight
8714	Top panel	175 kg
8710	Bottom panel	197 kg
8713	Junction panel	182 kg
8611	End taper panel	272 kg
8687	Bankseat beam	258 kg
8723	Ramp unit	120 kg
8698	Deck unit	74 kg

Bridge lengths and load classification

Load Class	Single-storey		Double-storey	
	Bays	Span	2 ends +bays	Span
100	5	9.8 m	10	27.4 m
70	5	9.8 m	12	31.1 m
60	5	9.8 m	13	33.0 m
50	5	9.8 m	14	34.8 m
40	6	11.6 m	16	38.5 m
30	8	15.2 m	18	42.0 m
24	9	17.1 m	20	45.8 m
20	10	19.0 m	21	47.6 m
16	12	22.5 m	22	49.4 m

The load class equates to a multi-axled wheeled vehicle of about the same weight in tonnes as the load class, and to a tracked vehicle of weight less than the load class (about 6 tonnes less for MLC 60). The exact load class of a vehicle depends on axle spacing, wheel loadings and track length and so on.

Span junction set

NATO stock number	Service designation	Unit weight
8159	Post span junction	260 kg
8157	Articulator, hydraulic	172 kg
8153	Capsill bridging	160 kg
8154	Roller assembly, rocker bearing	111 kg
8125	Beam, pier, half-section	445 kg
8123	Housing, pier leg	272 kg
8122	Pier leg, base section	162 kg
8121	Pier leg, standard section	208 kg
8119	Beam, grillage, pier	82 kg
8118	Sleeper pier	64 kg

Approximate weight of portable pier in bridge with length 12.2 m is 4026 kg.

MGB configurations

Type	Length	Class	Building party	Building time	Transport in 4000 kg pallet loads
Single-storey	9 m	70	9	15 mins	2
	22 m	16	17	30 mins	5
Double-storey	30 m	70	25	45 mins	10
	49 m	16	25	1 h 20 mins	16
2-span + pier	51 m	60	40	3 h	20
3-span + piers	76 m	60	40	6 h	27
Reinforcing kit	45.8 m	70	32	2 h	18
	49 m	60	32	2 h	18
Single-storey floating bridge	any	60	n/a	dependent on length	dependent on length
Double-storey floating bridge	any	60	40+	dependent on length	dependent on length

Status

In production. Up to July 1992, 36 countries had purchased the Medium Girder Bridge including Australia, Brunei, Canada, Denmark, Germany, Ghana, India, Iraq, Ireland, Italy, Jordan, Kenya, South Korea, Malaysia, Morocco, Netherlands, New Zealand, Nigeria, Pakistan, Peru, Philippines, Singapore, South Africa, Sweden, Switzerland (Festbrücke 69), Tanzania, Thailand, United Kingdom, USA (over 100 sets delivered to the US Army and Marine Corps), Venezuela and Zambia.

Manufacturer

Williams Fairey Engineering Limited, PO Box 41, Crossley Road, Heaton Chapel, Stockport, Cheshire SK4 5BD, UK.
Tel: 061 432 0281. Telex: 667866.
Fax: 061 431 3575.

Williams Fairey Engineering Axial Folding Bridge

Development

The Williams Fairey Engineering Axial Folding Bridge was developed using background knowledge gained from the Medium Girder Bridge and is a dry support bridge capable of forming a span up to 60.96 m long. The Axial Folding Bridge was designed for ease of transportation, rapid assembly with minimum labour and operational simplicity.

An Axial Folding Bridge was supplied to the US Navy for use as a Lightweight Modular Multi-purpose Spanning Assembly (LMMSA). This is used in association with the ELCAS (Elevated Causeway) programme carried out at the National Civil Engineering Laboratory at Port Hueneme in the USA. The LMMSA will be used as part of the ELCAS RESTORE programme to cross damaged sections of ELCAS, and make rapid connections between ships and ELCAS and ELCAS and shore.

Description

The Axial Folding Bridge is formed from three main modules; a parallel module (forming the main part of the bridge), a ramp module and a reinforcement module. Using only the parallel and ramp modules,

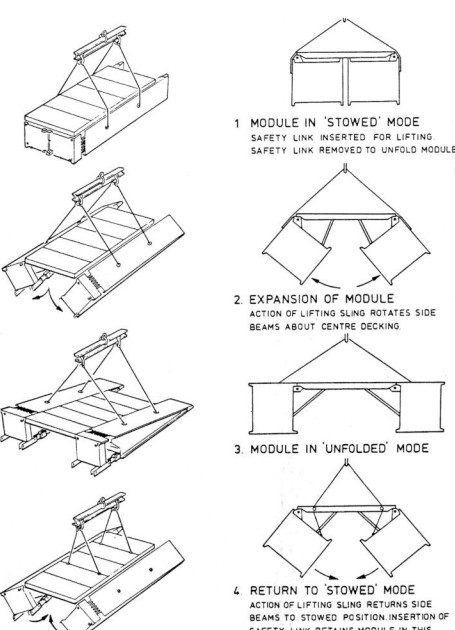

Sequence of folding and unfolding used for Axial Folding Bridge

US Army truck crossing a 41 m Axial Folding Bridge

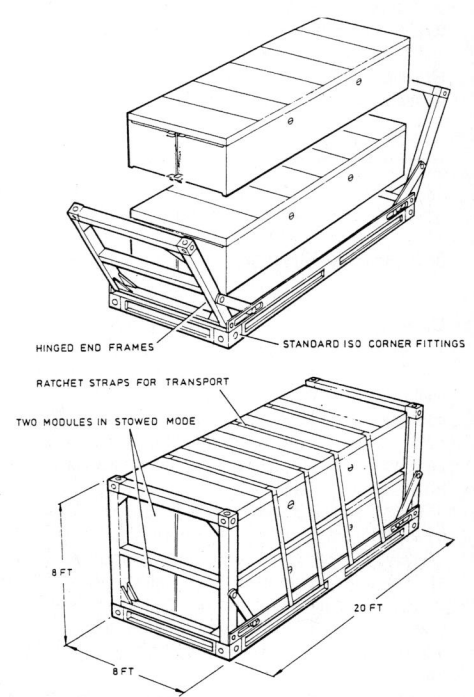

ISO modular packing for Axial Folding Bridge modules

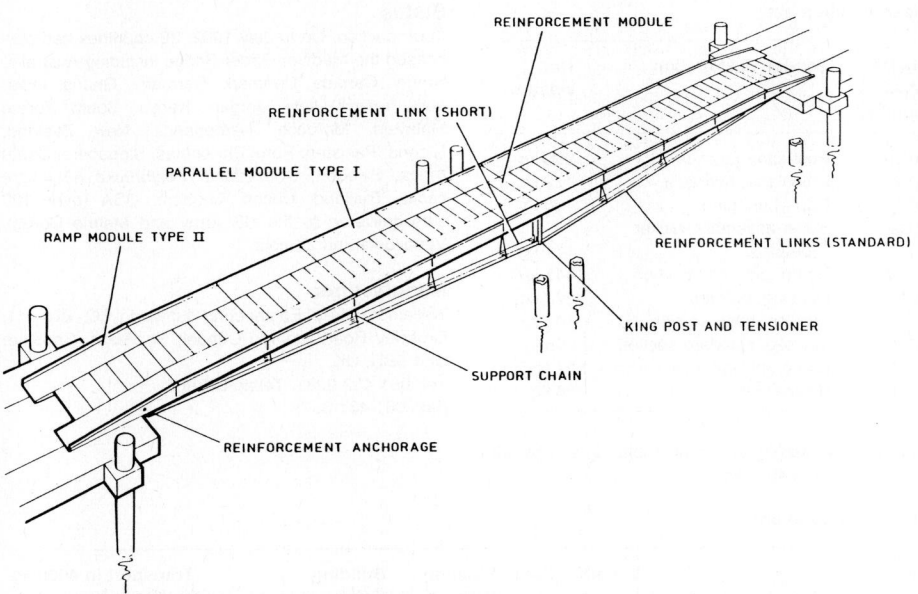

Outline drawing showing the main components of a 60.96 m Axial Folding Bridge

and a launching nose. The crane is used to lift the modules from their packs, with the crane attachment arranged such that as the modules are lifted they automatically open outwards, that is, the sidebeams rotate about the centre decking with its integral roadway. Once opened the module is 4.038 m wide (each sidebeam is 0.99 m wide and 1.03 m deep). The crane then lifts each module onto a building frame where it is connected to the previous module and pushed towards and across the gap to be bridged. The first module to be used is a ramp module which also carries a forward pylon and rear attachment to hold the launching nose in place. Extra parallel modules are added until the launching nose reaches the far bank. By that time the full bridge length should have been assembled and the entire bridge can be launched across the gap. The reinforcement system consists of a centre module containing a king post and tensioner and reinforcement links. The reinforcement links are connected to the bridge by support chains.

Retrieval is the reverse of the build procedure and can be carried out from either bank.

Timings have indicated that a 36.57 m bridge can be trestle-launched by eight men in 40 minutes.

Status
In production for the US Navy.

Manufacturer
Williams Fairey Engineering Limited, PO Box 41, Crossley Road, Heaton Chapel, Stockport, Cheshire SK4 5BD, UK.
Tel: 061 432 0281. Telex: 667866.
Fax: 061 431 3575.

bridges from 43 m at MLC 70 to 61 m can be constructed. Adding the reinforcement set increases the load classification of the longest bridge to MLC 70.

The modules are transported in pairs on ISO, DROPS or PLS flatracks or, alternatively, transport can be by standard 10-tonne capacity trucks. The flatracks can be handled by standard ISO material handling equipments.

The Axial Folding Bridge is constructed and launched by conventional mobile cranes, using a roller frame

---

PML Assault Bridge

Description
The PML assault bridge was designed in answer to a British Army requirement for a bridging system to carry troops across narrow to medium gaps. The bridge is simple and lightweight, and is transportable on standard 4-tonne trucks.

A bridge set consists of 18 identical open trapezoidal modules, each approximately 2 m long, and 34 handrail members for linking adjacent modules. A system of outriggers can be easily attached at the first module to aid stability. The modules are assembled and launched using a launch frame which can be anchored in place using cables and ground anchors. The total length of the bridge is variable in 2 m increments up to 36 m. All components, including the bridge flooring and connectors, are fabricated from aluminium alloy.

Status
Available.

Troops crossing an emplaced PML assault bridge

Manufacturer
PML, Stanelaw Way, Tanfield Lea Industrial Estate, Stanley, Co Durham DH9 9XG, UK.

Tel: 0207 231241. Telex: 53231.
Fax: 0207 284244.

UNITED STATES OF AMERICA

M2 Bailey Bridge

Description
The M2 Bailey Bridge was developed by the US Army Research and Development Laboratories. It has been well-proven both as a tactical and as a line of communication bridge and is capable of carrying heavy traffic loads. It is used for both temporary and permanent service. In emergencies it can be open to traffic in 1 to 3 days.

The M2 Bailey Bridge is an all-purpose prefabricated steel panel bridge designed for portability and speed of erection under adverse conditions. Optimum spans are 12.2 to 61 m. Width is 3.809 m between steel kerbs and 4.343 m between trusses. The components are manufactured in fixtures to ensure accuracy and interchangeability. The heaviest component weighs 281 kg.

The Bailey roadway is supported between two trusses or multiple-truss girders. It consists of longitudinal runner planks over transverse planks (chess)

M2 Bailey Bridge being launched (top) and completed (bottom)

laid over steel stringers supported by floorbeams (transoms) which rest on and are clamped to truss bottom chords. Steel kerbs secure the chess to the stringers. The basic truss element is the panel which is 3.048 m long, 1.448 m deep and 165.1 mm wide. Pin-connected end to end, trusses of any length are formed. Where strength exceeding that of single trusses is needed, multiple-truss girders can be assembled with either two or three panels side by side in single-, double- or triple-storey heights. End ramps extend the deck 3.048 m onto the approach runway.

Bailey truss panels, end posts, transoms and ramps are of low-alloy high tensile steel having a yield point of 3515 kg/cm^2 and an ultimate strength of 4921.7 kg/cm^2.

The cantilever method of erection is accomplished without falsework. The bridge is assembled on stationary rollers and then pushed or pulled across the gap. A skeleton launching nose is assembled from standard bridge components and fixed to the leading end of the bridge. The nose precedes the leading end of the bridge while the bridge proper, acting as a counterweight, enables the nose to reach and land on rollers on the far bank. The bridge is then rolled into position, the nose is removed and the span is lowered onto its bearings. A 24.4 m double-truss bridge has been completed in less than 40 minutes in competitive trials.

There are approximately 15 major components in an average Bailey Bridge and about 50 components, fittings, accessories, special items and tools are available.

Specifications
Length of single span:
(minimum) 9.144 m
(maximum) 61 m
Width of roadway: 3.809 m

Status
Production complete. In service with the US Army and other armed forces.

Supplier
Bailey Bridges Inc, PO Box 1186, San Luis Obispo, California 93406, USA.
Tel: (805) 543 8083. Fax: (805) 543 8983.

Line of Communication Bridges

Listed below is a *résumé* of the various types of line of communication bridging available to the US Army. All the types listed are standard but their scales of issue are not determined and thus they may be issued as required.

Bridge Fixed: Highway, 27 to 36 in Beam, Wide Flange Stringers, 51 in Plate
This type of beam and girder bridge may be used as a single span bridge or can be combined into a multiple-span bridge with intermediate supports. The number and types of stringers are determined by span length. Three depths of stringer are available: 686, 914 and 1295 mm. Using the basic components a two-way traffic bridge with a Class 60 capacity, or a single track Class 100 capacity bridge, with open lengths of up to 39 m, can be constructed. Standard components consist of abutments, bents, piers, towers and pier and tower foundations.

A double-lane bridge 39 m long with square ends weighs 194 tonnes when constructed. A double-lane bridge 11.94 m long with square ends will weigh 22 tonnes.

Bridge Fixed: Highway, Semi-permanent
Produced in lengths of 9.14, 18.29 and 27.43 m this type of bridge can take loads up to Class 50. The bridges are issued in sets of components including girders, bearing plates and assorted clips and bolts.

The timber decking used for the roadway is not issued in the set and has to be obtained locally. The sets are normally carried on rail cars but can be road transported on 8-or 16-tonne flatbed trailers. When assembled the bridge is 4.724 m wide. A 9.14 m long bridge weighs 5860 kg; an 18.29 m long bridge weighs 20 774 kg; and a 27.43 m long bridge weighs 27 941 kg.

Bridge Fixed: Railway, Through-truss, 70 ft Long Span
Although intended primarily for railway use, this type of bridge can also be used for road traffic when wide gaps must be bridged without intermediate piers. It can be erected in the field by unskilled labour under the direction of a skilled engineer. The bridge is composed of a launching nose, a tail frame, trolleys, receiving and lowering equipment, and erection gantries and travellers. This type of bridge is always constructed as a through-type structure. It uses a conventional floor system with ties fastened directly to the stringers by hook bolts.

When fully assembled this type of bridge is 21.34 m long, 59.9 m wide and 41.53 m high. Weight is 44 162 kg.

Bridge Fixed: Railway, I-Beam
Intended primarily for railway use, this type of bridge is constructed in spans of 5.18, 6.4, 8.23 and 10.67 m with the smallest three spans being the more usual. The bridge spans are issued as standard rolled, wide-flange I-beams which can be assembled by unskilled

labour. Intermediate piers and supports are constructed from standard parts. The two smallest spans are 457 mm high; the two largest 610 mm high. A 5.18 m span weighs 2315 kg; a 6.4 m span weighs 3926 kg; and an 8.23 m span weighs 5225 kg.

Bridge Fixed: Railway, 27 to 36 in Beam, Wide Flange Stringers, 51 in Plate G
This type of bridge follows the same general lines as the corresponding Highway bridge and uses the same sizes of stringers. As with the Highway bridge, the number and depth of stringers are determined by the span length. The shortest span that is normally constructed with the associated substructures of abutments, bents, piers, towers and pier and tower foundations is 6.1 m; construction time is about 80 man hours. The longest bridge length available is 30.5 m for which the construction time is 1300 man hours. The bridge can be built in varying widths to suit the rail gauge. A typical narrow gauge rail bridge would be 1.38 m wide. A wide gauge bridge would be 1.84 m wide. The weight of materials for the smallest type of bridge is about 3630 kg; for the largest 112 490 kg.

Bridge Fixed: Railway, Deck, 70 ft Long Span
Designed to take a single track railway, this truss girder, deck-type bridge is issued in crated form weighing 65 924 kg. Included in the kit are angle bracing, bedplates, chords, diagonal and vertical webs, splice plates and vertical end posts. When constructed the bridge is 21.34 m long.

BRIDGING BOATS
BELGIUM

Advanced Bridge Erection Boat

Description
In mid-1986 it was announced that a contract to supply FSB erection boats for the Belgian Army had been won by Meuse et Sambre SA, a member of the Belgian Shipbuilders Corporation NV. The boat involved is the Advanced Bridge Erection Boat, or ABEB.

The ABEB hull form has a moderate deep vee, a hard chine and spray deflection rails. The 7.76 m long hull form offers a high planing speed coupled with stability. The craft is configured such that flooding any one compartment will not affect the boat's ability to stay afloat and upright. A large working deck is provided aft and projects over the propulsion nozzles to provide them with protection. Draught is 0.53 m.

The propulsion systems are placed amidships in two separate compartments. Should either one of these compartments flood, enforcing an engine shutdown, the craft will still be able to operate at reduced power. The main engines are two Deutz BF 6 L 913 C air-cooled diesels with each engine coupled to a resiliently mounted Twin Disc MG 506 reverse/reduction gearbox unit. Two KaWeMa 32 S62/6 water jet units are driven by a shaft from each gearbox unit via an SKF gear type coupling. The water jets were specially developed for the ABEB and are fitted with a six-bladed NAB impeller.

The twin waterjet units are widely spaced and are controlled by a single crew member using single

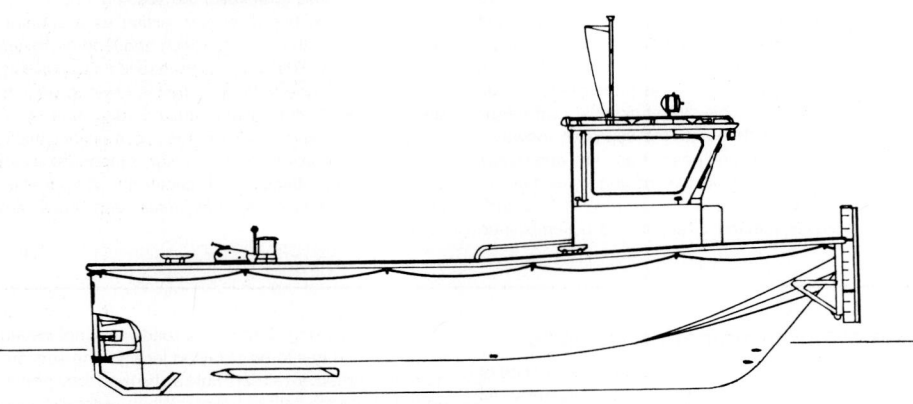
Advanced Bridge Erection Boat (ABEB)

levers. A hand hydraulic steering system is also incorporated for the nozzle direction control.

The ABEB can be carried on a special trailer but was designed to be carried on a MAN FSB carrier truck or a similarly equipped vehicle.

Specifications
Length: 7.76 m
Beam: 3.23 m
Draught: 0.53 m
Max speed: 52 km/h
Engines: 2 × Deutz BF 6 L 913 C air-cooled diesels,

each developing 191 hp at 2500 rpm
Fuel capacity: 400 l
Endurance at full power: 5 h

Status
In production for the Belgian Army.

Manufacturer
Meuse et Sambre SA, a member of the Belgian Shipbuilders Corporation NV, Suikerrui 5, PO Box 12, B-2000 Antwerp, Belgium.

CANADA

Versatech Model 27/4 Combat Support and Bridge Erection Boat

Development
Versatech Products Inc of Burnaby, British Columbia, has been producing its Sealander work boats since 1972. Thus, when the Canadian Armed Forces issued a requirement for a bridge boat erection (BBE), Versatech was able to meet the Army's specification and the prototype was used in joint Canadian/US Army exercises. As a result of these trials the Canadian Armed Forces ordered five Model 27/4 BBEs and a further 15 units were delivered during 1984.

Description
The Model 27/4 may be regarded as a combat support boat in addition to its role as a bridge erection boat. The vessel has enough foredeck space to carry a Jeep-sized vehicle and/or personnel and cargo. A vehicle loading ramp is fitted to the bluff bow which mounts two bridge erection push bars which can also be used to nudge pontoons. A towing bollard is also fitted and there is provision for a removable davit and winch. The Model 27/4 has a glass fibre hull with extra thickness in all stress areas. A balsa core stiffening is applied to the bow area and bottom. Buoyancy is increased by the use of polyurethane foam making the vessel virtually unsinkable. Full length Kevlar sponson protection shoes are fitted and the jet pan is a patented design made from aluminium. Marine grade aluminium is used for the superstructure and there is an open-rear cabin located amidships. Power comes from the twin Mercury M1E-340s driving twin Jacuzzi 20 YS water-jets that can provide a top speed in excess of 32 km/h, even when fully loaded.

Additional features include a vessel lifting rig, remov-able push bars, a sternguard/swim grid, removable full length safety rails, a demountable cabin top, an exhaust muffler to reduce heat signature radiation, a Halon fire suppression system, four automatic and two manual bilge pumps, screen wipers, and vehicle loading tracks. The instrument panel is a plug in/plug out component used to disable the vessel if required. The Model 27/4 can be operated by a single crew member. Under routine bridging operations the vessel

Versatech Model 27/4 loading Jeep

has an endurance of 8 hours.

Specifications
Weight:
  (bare hull) 1820 kg
  (full fuel and crew) 7315 kg
Payload:
  (sheltered waters) 3360 kg
  (sea conditions) 2270 kg
Length:
  (overall) 9.34 m
  (waterline) 8.33 m
Beam: 3.02 m
Draught:
  (unladen) 0.229 m
  (laden) 0.406 m
Max speed:
  (full fuel and crew) 40 km/h plus

  (laden) 32 km/h plus
Fuel capacity: 946 l
Endurance: 8 h
Engine: twin Mercury M1E-340 with 2.5:1 transmissions
Max static thrust:
  (forward) 2497 kg
  (reverse) 1135 kg

Status
In service with the Canadian Armed Forces.

Manufacturer
Versatech Products Inc, 2479 Bellevue Avenue, Burnaby, West Vancouver, British Columbia V7V 1E1, Canada.

COMMONWEALTH OF INDEPENDENT STATES

BMK-T Bridging Boat

Description
The BMK-T is the most powerful bridging boat in the CIS inventory and is used with pontoon bridges such as the PMP. The boat is carried on the rear of a KrAZ-214 (6 × 6) 7000 kg or KrAZ-255 (6 × 6) 7500 kg truck chassis and is launched by gravity, often with its engine running ready for immediate use. The recovery technique is as follows: the truck is reversed into the water and a cable from the truck's winch is connected to the stern of the BMK-T and the boat is then pulled out of the water over runners at the rear of the truck until it is back in the travelling position.

The hull of the BMK-T is of the 'sled' design for greater stability and has four enclosed compartments. Even if two non-adjacent compartments are flooded, the boat will not sink. The crew cabin is towards the front of the boat and is fully enclosed. The engine compartment is to the rear of the crew cabin and is also fully enclosed, allowing the boat to operate in very rough water. It is propelled in the water by two propellers at the stern which have a maximum speed of 945 rpm. On encountering an obstacle during forward travel the two propellers are lifted out of the water automatically by hinges at the stern. When in the travelling position, the propellers are swung through 180° so that they are on top of the boat. The BMK-T is highly manoeuvrable in the water and can be steered equally well in reverse. All controls are electrical and if required the boat can be remote-controlled by a cable

BMK-T bridging boat in water

from a maximum distance of 30 m. A pusher knee is mounted at the bow, although the boat is also used for towing pontoons.

Specifications
Crew: 2
Weight: 6000 kg
Length: 8.6 m
Beam: 2.7 m
Depth: 2.2 m
Draught: 0.75 m
Max speed: 17 km/h
Fuel capacity: 300 l
Fuel consumption: 20 l/h
Endurance: 15-17 h
Towing power:
  (forward) 2000 kg
  (reverse) 750 kg

Engine: YaMZ-236, SP4 V-6, water-cooled diesel developing 180 hp at 2100 rpm

KrAZ-255B with BMK-T Boat
Weight: 19 100 kg
Length: 10.6 m
Width: 2.8 m
Height: 3.76 m

Status
In service with Germany and countries of the former Warsaw Pact.

Manufacturer
State factories.

BMK-130 and BMK-150 Bridging Boats

Description
BMK-130/BMK-130M
The hull of the BMK-130 is of steel construction and is divided into individual watertight compartments. Mounted each side of the hull is a strut and a wheel which assist in the launching and recovery of the boat. Once afloat, the wheels are folded up alongside the hull. The BMK-130M, introduced in the mid-1960s, has a modified hull and when afloat the wheels are swung forward and stowed in wells on either side of the hull. This reduces not only drag but also the chances of damage to the wheels when afloat. The launching sequence is as follows: the bow attachment is connected to the front bumper of the truck, the boat is pushed into the water stern first and once the boat is afloat it is disconnected from the truck and the wheels of the boat are swung forward and stowed in the wells.

The former Yugoslavia produced a bridging boat based on the BMK-130M known as the RPR M68. For details see entry under Serbia in this section.

BMK-150/BMK-150M
Until the introduction of the BMK-T this was the most powerful bridging boat used in the former Warsaw Pact. It has a hull of aluminium construction and is much lighter than the BMK-130, and has two engines with separately controlled twin screws. Unlike the BMK-130, this boat is provided with a windscreen and a cover that can be erected in bad weather. The basic BMK-150 has wheels which fold up on the outside of the hull, while the later BMK-150M has wheel wells.

Status
Production complete. In service with members of the former Warsaw Pact.

Manufacturer
State factories.

BMK-150M bridging boat (Jane's Intelligence Review)

Specifications

Type	BMK-130M	BMK-150	BMK-150M
Crew	2	2	2
Weight	3450 kg	2500 kg	3800 kg
Length	7.85 m	8.2 m	7.4 m
Beam	2.1 m	2.55 m	2.55 m
Depth	1.5 m	2 m	n/a
Draught	0.622 m	0.66 m	0.75 m
Max speed	21 km/h	22 km/h	22 km/h
Fuel capacity	n/a	300 l	150 l
Endurance	12 h	7 h	6 h
Engine model	YaAZ-M204VKr-2, 5	M51-SPE-3, 5(2)	M70 SPA 3.5
Engine type	diesel	petrol	diesel
Number of cylinders	4	6	4
Hp	120	62 × 2	119 × 2
Cooling	water	water	water
Towing power			
(forward)	1450 kg	1500 kg	n/a
(reverse)	800 kg	n/a	n/a

BMK-70 and BMK-90 Bridging Boats

Description
BMK-70
The BMK-70 was widely used by the old Red Army during the Second World War for a wide variety of roles including the assembly of pontoon bridges, towing barges and rafts and for general ferrying work. It is no longer in front-line service but is probably held in reserve. The hull of the BMK-70 is of steel construction. It is normally carried on a trailer of the single-axle pole-type or on a two-axle trailer.

BMK-90
This was developed in the 1950s and has a more powerful engine than the BMK-70. The BMK-90 has a

hull of corrugated steel whereas the later BMK-90M has a hull of duralumin as well as a redesigned propeller shaft. The boat is provided with a wheel and strut on each side of the hull to assist in the launching and recovery of the boat. When waterborne these can be folded up alongside the boat or removed. This feature was subsequently adopted by the later BMK-130 and BMK-150 bridging boats. The BMK-90 is transported on the PBMK-90 single-axle trailer which weighs 2100 kg.

The Germans produced a boat known as the BB-120 based on the BMK-90 bridging boat and the Chinese also produce a copy of the BMK-90 which can be fitted with a canvas cover over the cockpit area. The designation of the Chinese boat, which is used in conjunction with the Type 79 Ribbon Bridge, is not known.

Specifications

Type	BMK-70	BMK-90	BMK-90M
Crew	2	2	2
Weight			
(without fuel)	2450 kg	2450 kg	2200 kg
Length	7.83 m	7.83 m	7.85 m
Beam	2.1 m	2.1 m	2.1 m
Depth	1.5 m	1.5 m	1.5 m
Draught	0.64 m	0.53 m	0.52 m
Max speed			
(unloaded)	20.5 km/h	20.5 km/h	20.5 km/h
(loaded)	n/a	8 km/h	8 km/h
Fuel capacity	n/a	340	340
Endurance	n/a	14 h	14 h
Engine model	ZIL-20S	ZIL-120	ZIL-120
Engine type	petrol	petrol	petrol
Number of			
cylinders	6	6	6
Hp	75	90	90
Cooling	water	water	water
Towing power			
(forward)	681 kg	1100 kg	1100 kg
(reverse)	n/a	1400 kg	1400 kg

Status
Production complete. The BMK-70 is held in reserve while the BMK-90 and BMK-90M are still in service with some countries of the former Warsaw Pact.

Manufacturer
State factories.

BMK-90 bridging boat with wheels lowered

CZECHOSLOVAKIA

Mo-108, Mo-111 and Mo-930 Bridging Boats

Mo-108
This is identical to the Mo-111 but is powered by a T-108, V-8 air-cooled diesel which develops 105 hp, giving the boat a lower performance than the Mo-111.

Mo-111
This is basically a modification of a Second World War German bridging boat and retains the German design of three rudders and a Kort nozzle, a metal ring-guard which houses the screw. The Mo-111 is transported on a large two-wheeled trailer called the MP-4. It is also known as the M-111 and the Tatra 111. The Mo-111 was introduced in the 1950s and built at the CXD plant at Decin.

Mo-930
This is the latest Czechoslovak bridging boat and uses the same engine as the Tatra 813 (8 × 8) truck to power a single screw. The Mo-930 is transported on a single-axle trailer weighing 2500 kg.

Specifications

Type	Mo-111	Mo-930
Crew	2	2
Weight	3200 kg	4000 kg
Length	7.5 m	7.68 m
Beam	2.2 m	2.2 m
Depth	1.2 m	n/a
Draught	0.85 m	0.85 m
Max speed	24 km/h	20 km/h
Fuel capacity	178 l	n/a
Endurance	n/a	7 h

Type	Mo-111	Mo-930
Engine model	T-111A-4	T-930-53
Engine type	diesel	petrol
Cylinders	V-12	V-12
Hp	170	200
Cooling	air	air
Towing power		
(forward)	n/a	2275 kg
(reverse)	n/a	1200 kg

Status
Production complete. In service with the Czechoslovak Army.

Manufacturer
Czechoslovak state factories.

FRANCE

F1 Pontoon Boat

Development
The F1 pontoon boat was designed to meet the requirements of the Corps of Engineers by the Etablissement Technique d'Angers (ETAS) with production being undertaken by the Atelier de Construction de Tarbes (ATS). The first prototype was built by the ETAS with the second being built with the assistance of the ATS. The two prototypes were followed by five pre-production boats which were completed in 1971. A total of 135 production model F1 pontoon boats were built for the French Army between 1972 and 1975.

The boat was designed to undertake a wide range of roles including the pushing and pulling of pontoons, installation of protective nets, transport of personnel and cargo, a platform for divers, and other bridging and mooring roles.

Description
The hull of the F1 pontoon boat is made of all-welded alloy (AG4MC) with 4.1 m³ of the boat filled with polyurethane foam to make it virtually unsinkable. The boat consists of two sections, fore and aft. The fore

section contains the engine and crew compartment while the aft section contains the two propellers, their protective frames and steering motor. This is hinged to the main hull and can be swung upwards by two hydraulic joints to enable the boat to be operated very close inshore.

The engine is mounted forward of the crew compartment, and transmits power to a reduction gearbox with twin output shafts coupled via electromagnetic clutches to two variable displacement hydraulic pumps. Each

pump feeds oil under pressure to a hydraulic motor mounted in a submerged nacelle directly behind the propeller. Each propeller has four blades and is 0.9 m in diameter. The boat has no rudder, as the propellers, which are pod-mounted, can be traversed through 360°. The boat has an exceptional acceleration and deceleration performance.

The boat is provided with three bilge pumps with a capacity of 1200 l/h each. Hand-operated capstan winches with a 3500 kg capacity are mounted on either

F1 pontoon boat

side of the hull and there is a towing post at the front of the hull and a second towing post at the rear of the crew compartment. The height of the rubber clad bow fender post can be adjusted. Two white light searchlights (one movable and one fixed) with a range of 100 m are provided together with two infra-red lights with a range of 50 m (one fixed and one movable).

The F1 pontoon boat is normally carried in two sections, with the bow section being carried on the rear of a Berliet GBC 8 KT (6 × 6) 4000 kg truck, which also tows a single-pole 2500 kg trailer carrying the rear half of the boat. These are offloaded by a crane and assembled in the water. It takes only 3 minutes to assemble the two units.

Specifications
Crew: 2-3
Weight:
  (forward section) 3000 kg
  (aft section) 1800 kg
Length: 8.3 m
Beam: 2.49 m
Height above waterline, excluding lights: 1.3 m
Draught:
  (max) 1.15 m
  (minimum) 0.45 m
Max speed: 25 km/h
  (carrying 3 men plus 400 kg of cargo) 24.4 km/h
  (pushing 4-pontoon floating bridge with a 40 t load) 9.36 km/h

Engine: Deutz F 10 L 413 V-10 air-cooled diesel developing 237 hp at 2400 rpm
Electrical system: 24 V
Batteries: 4 × 6 V

Status
Production complete. In service with the French Army.

Manufacturer
Atelier de Construction de Tarbes, 2 rue Alsace-Lorraine, BP 313, F-65013 Tarbes, France.
Enquiries to Giat Industries, 13 route de la Minière, F-78034 Versailles Cedex, France.
Tel: 30 97 37 37. Fax: 30 97 39 00.

GERMANY

Bridging Boat

Description
This bridging boat, known as the Bugsierboot, is used in the construction of floating bridges (including the German version of the Ribbon Bridge) and ferries. It has two adjustable pushing knees at the front, a windscreen that can be fitted with a removable canvas cover to give some degree of protection to the crew, and is propelled in water by two propellers. The hull is aluminium and the built-in air compartments make it very difficult to sink. The boat is carried on and launched from a two-wheeled single-axle trailer.

Specifications
Crew: 2
Weight: 4600 kg
Length: 7.45 m
Beam: 2.48 m
Depth: (overall) 1.85 m
Max speed: 22.5 km/h
Engine: air-cooled diesel developing 250 hp

German bridging boat as used by the Belgian Army (C R Zwart)

Trailer plus boat
Weight: 8100 kg
Length: 9.75 m
Width: 2.48 m

Height: 3.36 m

Status
In service with the Belgian and German armies.

ITALY

SAI Ambrosini Bridging Boat

Description
This bridging boat was designed by SAI Ambrosini to meet the requirements of the Italian Army and entered service in 1974. The stainless steel hull is divided into six watertight compartments to guarantee buoyancy. The inboard-mounted engine is towards the front and the semi-enclosed cabin towards the rear.

Specifications
Crew: 2-3
Weight: 3800 kg
Length: 7.5 m
Beam: 2.45 m
Height:
  (without cabin) 1.8 m
  (with cabin) 2.3 m
Draught: 0.7 m
Max speed:
  (pushing or towing half MLC 60 raft in 1.75 m/s current) 3 km/h
  (in calm water without load) 25 km/h
Endurance: 6 h
Turning radius: 8.5 m
Engine: Deutz model SF12L413 12-cylinder 16.96 l air-cooled diesel developing 260 hp

Status
Production complete. In service with the Italian Army.

SAI Ambrosini bridging boat being lowered into water by Astra BM 20MB1 crane truck. Boat has cockpit/cabin housing removed

Manufacturer
SAI Ambrosini – Società Aeronautica Italiana SpA, Viale Roma 25, I-06065 Passignano sul Trasimeno (PG), Italy.
Tel: 075 827 592. Telex: 660140 sai i.
Fax: 075 827 650.

SAI Ambrosini 121 Thruster Bridging Boat

Description

The SAI Ambrosini 121 Thruster bridging boat was designed to cope with loads involved in the assembly of Class 60 floating bridges on rivers and inland water obstacles. It can be used with several types of floating bridge and can be used in the assembly of non-floating bridging such as the Bailey Bridge. The hull is constructed from stainless steel with light alloy components. The layout is conventional with the engine compartment at the rear, the main crew compartment amidships and a bluff bow. On the bow is an angled assembly for nudging bridging components into place and behind this there is a small working area for assemblers. The crew compartment can be covered with a canvas tilt for extra shelter. The cockpit area can accomodate four persons or a load of 500 kg.

Specifications

Weight: (fully equipped) 4450 kg
Length: 7.45 m
Beam: 2.44 m
Max draught: 0.78 m

SAI Ambrosini 121 Thruster bridging boat

Max speed: 20 km/h
Endurance: 9 h
Turning radius: 4 m
Fuel capacity: 274 l
Engines: 2 × AIFO 8061 SM 5.5 l 6-cylinder water-cooled (closed-circuit) turbo diesels developing 173 hp each at 2950 rpm
Propulsion: Schottel SRP 50/50 steering traction screws traversing through 360°
Tow and thrust values:
  (forward) 2400 kg
  (reverse) 1200 kg

Status

In production. In service with the Italian Army.

Manufacturer

SAI Ambrosini – Società Aeronautica Italiana SpA, Viale Roma 25, I-06065 Passignano sul Trasimeno (PG), Italy.
Tel: 075 827 592. Telex: 660140 sai i.
Fax: 075 827 650.

SAI Ambrosini 126 Multi-purpose Boat

Description

The SAI Ambrosini 126 multi-purpose boat is intended for a variety of military purposes but is equipped with a bluff bow to enable it to push heavy floating structures such as bridging components in shallow waters. It is also suitable for towing similar equipments. The SAI Ambrosini 126 is powered by two inboard FIAT diesel engines each driving a Castoldi TD 318 hydrojet that can be traversed for a high level of manoeuvrability.

The hull of the SAI Ambrosini 126 can be manufactured either in steel or in 5083 light alloy and is designed to render the vessel unsinkable. The cockpit is located well forward although other configurations are possible and it is possible to fit either a diving platform over the stern or carry stores or pallets behind the cockpit.

Specifications

Weight: 2250 kg
Length: 7.5 m
Total width: 2.58 m
Draught: 0.45 m
Max speed: 35 knots

SAI Ambrosini 126 multi-purpose boat

Endurance: 7 h at 20 knots
Engines: 2 × FIAT AIFO 8061 SM06 diesels developing 170 hp each
Hydrojets: 2 × Castoldi TD 318

Status

Production.

Manufacturer

SAI Ambrosini – Società Aeronautica Italiana SpA, Viale Roma 25, I-06065 Passignano sul Trasimeno (PG), Italy.
Tel: 075 827 592. Telex: 660140 sai i.
Fax: 075 827 650.

NETHERLANDS

Damen Bridge Support Boat 700

Description

The Damen Bridge Support Boat 700 (BSB 700) was designed specifically to operate with the Ribbon Bridge system. It has a high tensile steel hull and one partly elevated deck with the engine located forward. The hull is divided into four watertight compartments accessible via flush deck-mounted hatches. All hatches and the mast are made of aluminium. Just aft of midships is an open cockpit with seating for a helmsman and all the controls.

Power is derived from a single 246 hp air-cooled diesel engine which provides power for two hydraulic pumps driving two four-bladed propellers. The swivelling hydraulic propellers are also used for steering through 360°. The engine provides a static bollard pull of 2.6 tonnes and for positioning bridge components in a water flow of around 5 knots the boat develops a thrust of 2.1 tonnes.

Standard equipment includes a helmsman seat in

Two Damen BSB 700s in action with Ribbon Bridge ferry

the cockpit, an aluminium sun awning over the cockpit, a polyethelene fender around the vessel (except the stern), two hand winches, two hoisting eyes, a dismountable mast, a hand bilge pump and an anchor and line.

For transport and launching the Damen Bridge Support Boat 700 is carried on the DAF YGZ 2300 (6 × 6) 10 000 kg Ribbon Bridge launcher.

Specifications
Weight: 6000 kg
Length overall: 7 m
Beam: 2.9 m
Depth: 1.35 m
Draught: 0.75 m

Max speed: 16 km/h
Engine: Deutz BF 8L 513 air-cooled diesel
developing 246 hp at 2300 rpm

Status
In service with the Royal Netherlands Army (58).

Manufacturer
Damen Shipyards, Industrieterrein Avelingen West 20,
PO Box 1, NL-4200 AA Gorinchem, Netherlands.
Tel: 01830 39911. Telex: 25335 dame nl.
Fax: 01830 32189.

POLAND

KH-200 Bridging Boat

Description
The KH-200 was developed in the late 1960s and after
four years of trials was approved for production in
1971. It has a hull of all-steel construction and a pusher
knee mounted at the bow, similar to that mounted on
the CIS BMK-T bridging boat. The crew are seated in a
cabin towards the bow which has an open back. The
engine is mounted to the rear of the crew and drives a
single propeller at the rear. The KH-200 is used with
the PP-64 heavy folding pontoon bridge and can also
be used as a transporter carrying up to 15 troops. The
boat is transported on a large two-axle trailer which
weighs 2800 kg unladen.

Specifications
Crew: 2-3
Weight: 3865 kg
Length: 8.14 m
Beam: 2.3 m
Draught: 0.72 m
Max speed: 25 km/h
Endurance: 12.1 h
Towing power:
  (forward) 2500 kg
  (reverse) 1200 kg
Engine: Leyland UE 680 6-cylinder water-cooled
diesel developing 169 hp

Polish KH-200 bridging boat

Status
In service with the Polish Army.

Manufacturer
Polish state factories.

SERBIA

RPR M68 Bridging Boat

Description
Described as a tug vessel, the RPR M68 bridging boat
is based on the CIS BMK-130M (see separate entry in
this section) and is intended for pushing and towing
floating bridges and ferries. It can also be used to carry
personnel and cargo.

The overall design of the RPR M68 closely follows
that of the BMK-130M. It has an all-steel hull and is
equipped with travelling wheels that fold upwards into
wheel wells when the boat is in the water; when the
wheels are lowered the boat can be towed by a truck.
Power is supplied by a diesel engine located amidships

and developing approximately 140 hp.
A small cabin can be erected for the helmsman and
a small mast carrying a floodlamp can also be
provided.

Specifications
Crew: 2
Weight:
  (standard) 3940 kg
  (full load) 4220 kg
  (transport) 4300 kg
Length: 7.88 m
Beam: 2.1 m
Draught: (mean) 0.64 m
Max speed: (full load) 15.55 km/h

Tractive force:
  (forward) 16.5 kN
  (astern) 8.25 kN

Status
In service with the former Yugoslav armed forces.

Contractor
Federal Directorate of Supply and Procurement
(SDPR), YU-11005 Beograd, 9 Nemanjina Street,
Serbia.
Tel: 621 522. Telex: 71000/72566 SDPR YU.
Fax: 38 11 631588/630621.

RPR M68 bridging boat

RPR M68 bridging boat

SINGAPORE

FBS 60 Bridging Boat

Description
The FBS 60 bridging boat is an integral part of the Floating Bridge System FBS 60 (for details of this system refer to entry in the *Tactical floating bridges and ferries* section) and is intended for manoeuvring FBS 60 bridge sections.

The craft is referred to as a push-pull tug boat and uses a single conventional screw propulsion system powered by a 250 hp engine. The boat is constructed of steel and is conventional in layout with the control position well forward and the engine located amidships. A pushing knee is fitted over the squared-off bows.

For road transport the awning over the control position can be lowered or removed. The boat can be carried on a special trailer towed behind a 6 × 6 7000 kg bridge transporter vehicle. The trailer is 9.7 m long overall. As an alternative the boat may be carried on a special boat carriage carried by a bridge transporter vehicle. Using the boat carriage, launching and retrieval times are quicker than using the trailer. The boat carriage is 7 m long, 2.9 m wide and 2 m high. Weight is 1400 kg.

Specifications
Length overall: 7.45 m
Length at waterline: 7 m
Beam: (moulded) 2.4 m
Depth: (moulded) 1.3 m

Max draught: (aft) 0.6 m
Weight: 4600 kg
Engine output: 250 hp
Bollard pull: 1900 kg
Free running speed: 21.3 km/h (11.5 knots)

Status
In production.

Manufacturer
Singapore Shipbuilding and Engineering Limited, 7 Benoi Road, Singapore 2262.
Tel: 8612244. Telex: singa rs 21206.
Fax: 8613028.

UNITED KINGDOM

FBM Marine CSB Bridge Erection Boat

Development
Based on a requirement issued by the United Kingdom Military Vehicles and Engineering Establishment at Christchurch (now the Royal Armament Research and Development Establishment, Christchurch), the Fairey company (now FBM Marine Limited) started development of the 8 m CSB in the Autumn of 1975 with the first prototype being delivered to the British Army for trials early in 1977. As a result of extensive trials by the British Army both in the United Kingdom and on the Rhine in Germany, a pre-production boat was ordered by the British Army for further trials. It was delivered in May 1978. The boat was accepted for service with the British Army in February 1979, and an order placed for 56 boats the following year. In 1983 the Ministry of Defence ordered a further 12 CSBs for the British Army to replace those lost on the *Atlantic Conveyor* during the Falkland Islands campaign. After extensive evaluation by the US Army MERADCOM (now the Belvoir Research, Development and Engineering Center, Fort Belvoir, Virginia) the CSB was accepted under NATO Standardisation and Rationalisation arrangements, and 280 are in service with the US Army.

The Stealth version of the CSB (see under Variant for details) is in full licenced production in South East Asia. In 1992 there were over 1200 CSBs in operation.

Description
Based on the Allday 8 m hull, the boat features a pusher bow and an aft-mounted capstan/tow hook. The mast and cabin top are both removable for low profile operations, and transport/stowage. The two self-draining cockpits are each designed to accommodate a standard 1000 kg NATO pallet.

The CSB bridge erection boat is made of welded marine grade aluminium alloy for a lightweight, yet extremely strong boat. Based on a well-tried hull, the craft was designed to meet the requirements of the British Army for a boat to assist with bridging operations and other river and estuary support and assault duties. Ultra Hydraulics waterjets enable the boat to be used in shallow water with twin 212 shp turbocharged marine diesels providing the power. Transport, launching and recovery is by special cradle on a Ribbon Bridge Transporter Truck or by a towed off-road trailer.

Standard equipment includes navigation and towing lights and a searchlight, fire extinguishers, windscreen wipers, bilge pumping system, heavy duty fendering, Explosafe filled fuel tank and built-in buoyancy to float craft in an upright position.

The batch of 12 ordered by the Ministry of Defence during 1983 all have 'winterisation' kits for operations at low temperatures. This includes extra cable insulation, more powerful screen wipers, pump and engine heaters, defrosting equipment and personnel heaters. Current production craft incorporate 'keel' or 'remote' engine cooling depending on the operating environment.

US Army Ribbon Bridge Erection Boats in action during the construction of a Ribbon Bridge

The US Army refers to the CSB as the Ribbon Bridge Erection Boat (RBEB). CSBs for the US Army are produced by the Advanced Technology Corporation of Charleston, South Carolina.

In September 1992 FBM Support Services completed a two-year $10 million modification programme on the 248 CSBs in service with the US Army at locations in Europe and the United States. The modifications updated the cooling system and associated electrical circuitry and enable the engines to be started prior to launch.

Variant
In response to a requirement from a Far Eastern customer (South Korea) FBM Marine developed a version of its CSB bridge erection boat offering a drastic reduction in noise levels. The noise level in the cab is reduced from 101 dBA to 84 dBA and the optimum speed for this reduced noise level is 7 knots. At this speed the boat is inaudible at approximately 285 m with a background noise of 42 dBA approaching the listener and at 530 m when departing.

The twin Sabre Marine 212 diesel engine installation is enclosed by adding a glass fibre hood and transverse bulkheads, all lined with 32 mm black PVC-faced foam with a heavy polymeric barrier. Entry points for services through the bulkheads are sealed. Hull side panels and hatch covers are lined with 3 mm bitumen foil vibration damping material.

Burgess 100 mm ADS through-adsorption type exhausts have replaced the side-shell water injected units. The engines are installed on Metzeler Fluidastic rubber hydraulic resilient mounts. Extra cooling for the enclosed engine compartment is provided by two Jabsco 24 V electric fans.

Other changes introduced with the Stealth CSB involve the replacing of the original goal-post mast by a simple pole mast in front of the wheelhouse. The Stealth CSB prototype had rotatable nozzles fitted to the Dowty waterjets. These improve reversing and obviate icing problems.

The Stealth CSB has been in licenced production in South Korea by sub-contractors Korea Tacoma Marine Industries (KTMI) since 1985. During 1992 FBM Support Services Limited were awarded a contract worth more than $7 million for the supply of materials and technology transfer to KTMI. The contract involved the materials for 55 craft and it is anticipated that further contracts will result in the same number of sets being supplied each year until 1997.

Specifications
Length:
  (with pushing knee) 8.38 m
  (waterline) 6.98 m
Beam over fenders: 2.49 m
Height:
  (without cab) 1.98 m
  (with cab) 2.79 m
Weight:
  (fully fitted out and fuelled) 4080 kg
Maximum payload: 2000 kg
Draught:
  (fully fitted out and fuelled) 0.56 m
  (fully laden) 0.66 m
Engines: twin Sabre 212 turbocharged marine diesels

each continuously rated at 212 shp at 2450 rpm
Propulsion units: twin Dowty 300 mm two-stage waterjets coupled to engines through Borg Warner 72C hydraulic direct drive reverse gearbox
Max static forward thrust: 2000 kg
Max static reverse thrust: 1000 kg
Max speed:
(unladen) 44 km/h

(fully laden) 31 km/h
Fuel tank capacity: 227 l

Status

In production. In service with the engineer units of five armies including Greece (18), Turkey, the United Kingdom and the USA (280). The Stealth CSB is in licenced production in South Korea.

Manufacturer

FBM Marine Limited, Cowes Shipyard, Cowes, Isle of Wight PO31 7DL, UK.
Tel: 0983 297111. Telex: 86466 fambro g.
Fax: 0983 299642.

RTK Combat Support Boat Type CSB 508

Description

The CSB 508 was designed to undertake a wide range of duties including bridging, tug boat, supply and diving. The boat is capable of static thrusts of up to 1700 kg for tugging purposes and can transport 3050 kg of cargo. The wide deck and bow ramp permit the loading of men and equipment from either beach or quay and with the jet propulsion system the boat has a draught of 0.42 m, allowing the boat to operate in very shallow water.

The hull of the CSB 508 is made of glass fibre reinforced plastic and has a built-in foam buoyancy in excess of the craft's gross displacement, making the boat unsinkable. The hull requires the minimum of maintenance and can easily be repaired in operation.

The deck has a non-slip bonded grit surface applied. The gunwales are of stainless steel rolled section and full peripheral fendering is provided at the gunwale with a solid nylon rubbing strake installed at the waterline. The winch-operated ramp is reinforced and has a non-slip surface. Scuppers for the removal of water from the deck are located at the transom.

Two pushing knees are mounted at the bow and a towing post is mounted aft of the helmsman's seat.

Standard equipment includes six warping bollards and four lifting points mounted on the gunwale rail, navigation lights, floodlight, klaxon and a rechargeable fire extinguisher.

Optional equipment includes an illuminated helmsman's compass, deck gear, cargo/vehicle lashing kit, demountable jib crane with a capacity of 250 kg and a four-wheel close-coupled boat trailer.

Specifications

Length: (overall) 8.23 m
Beam: (overall) 2.9 m
Height:
(overall) 1.88 m
(of gunwales above deck) 0.75 m
Deck area: 15.1 m^2
Fuel capacity: 2 × 135 l pannier tanks

Status

In production. In service with several countries.

Manufacturer

RTK Marine Limited, Lake Avenue, Hamworthy, Poole, Dorset BH15 4NY, UK.
Tel: 0202 685581. Telex: 418281 romarp g.
Fax: 0202 683347.

RTK combat support boat Type CSB 508

Thos Storey Motorflote

Description

The Thos Storey Motorflote was designed for use with the Thos Storey Uniflote System and consists of a modified Uniflote box-section pontoon powered by an internal marine diesel engine. The engine drives a propeller situated in a protected area underneath the rear of the Motorflote. Steering is carried out by a rudder operated from a wheel in the control cabin in the centre of the Motorflote pontoon. Having a simple box-section the Motorflote can be readily secured to any Uniflote pontoon combination such as a raft or ferry. The advantages of using the Motorflote in place of orthodox outboard engines on a Uniflote raft or float are said to be that the Motorflote can be easily connected and disconnected to any Uniflote System

construction, the propeller is less vulnerable to damage as it is contained within a protected area, and the Motorflote is quieter and cheaper.

The control cabin may be fully open or enclosed, and handrails can be fitted if required. Two Motorflotes have operated in the Falkland Islands propelling a 12-Uniflote ferry with a capacity of over 100 tonnes.

Specifications

Length: 3.05 m
Width: 2.44 m
Depth:
(deck to skids) 1.71 m
(deck to cabin top) 2.14 m
(total) 3.85 m
Draught: 1.1 m
Freeboard: 0.61 m
Weight: approx 4500 kg

Fuel capacity: 226 l
Engine: Mermaid Mariner 6-cylinder 6.227 l diesel developing 115 bhp at 2600 rpm continuous
Propeller diameter: (4 blades) 0.7 m
Static bollard pull: 13.9 kN
Speed in still water:
(unladen pushing) 2.4 m/s
(unladen towing) 1.8 m/s
(loaded pushing 150 t) 1.7 m/s

Status

In production.

Manufacturer

Thos Storey (Engineers) Limited, 52 Queens Road, Weybridge, Surrey KT13 0AN, UK.
Tel: 0932 858133. Telex: 21868.
Fax: 0932 855588.

Uniflote raft being propelled by Motorflote

Motorflote with auxiliary bow fitted for use when not pushing Uniflote ferry

MINE WARFARE EQUIPMENT

Mines
Minelaying equipment
Mine detection equipment
Mineclearing equipment
Minefield marking equipment

MINES

ARGENTINA

FMK-1 Non-metallic Anti-personnel Mine

Description
The FMK-1 is a small circular non-metallic anti-personnel mine 82 mm in diameter and 43 mm deep. In its storage and transport form it is carried with two safety and arming pins held in place by a length of yellow tape. The same tape also holds in place a steel washer and a small shaped collar. When the tape is removed the washer can fall away or be kept in place manually for later detection. In practice the washers are not retained. The shaped collar is placed in position in the pressure detonator train in such a way that the mine can be used either as an anti-personnel mine or as the igniter for the FMK-3 anti-tank mine (see below). These mines were encountered in the Falkland Islands.

Status
In service with the Argentine armed forces.

FMK-1 non-metallic anti-personnel mine

FMK-3 Non-metallic Anti-tank Mine

Description
The FMK-3 non-metallic anti-tank mine is basically a block of explosive contained in a plastic-coated case 240 mm square and 90 mm deep. A central well on the top of the explosive block will accommodate an FMK-1 anti-personnel mine with a shaped collar in the base arranged to suit the heavier pressures involved with a tank target. A rope handle is mounted on one side. These mines were encountered in the Falkland Islands and as they contain virtually no metal components they are difficult to detect.

Status
In service with the Argentine armed forces.

FMK-3 non-metallic anti-tank mine

AUSTRIA

DNW HM 1000 Anti-personnel Mine

Description
The Dynamit Nobel Wien (DNW) HM 1000 is a Claymore-type anti-personnel mine encased in a moulded plastic body containing the high explosive charge and 1500 steel spheres. Two pairs of scissor legs are used to emplace the mine and a sight is located on top of the body for laying. A non-removable cap is equipped with two detonator wells for firing either by a pull or tripwire system or by electrical means.

The effects of the HM 1000 are such that on a 20 mm thick wooden wall measuring 50 × 2 m there will be four complete penetrations/m². The ball splinters are lethal for up to 30 m and can cause serious wounding for up to 50 m. The lethal area behind the mine is 6 m.

Specifications
Weight: 2.4 kg
Length: 290 mm
Height: 130 mm
Width: 30 mm
Weight of ball splinters: 0.85 kg
Number of ball splinters: 1500

Status
In production.

DNW HM 1000 anti-personnel mine

Manufacturer
Dynamit Nobel Wien GmbH, A-8430 Leibnitz, Austria.
Tel: 0 34 52 21 01. Telex: 034 405 assma a.
Fax: 0 34 52 22 97.

DNW PM 3000 Anti-tank Mine

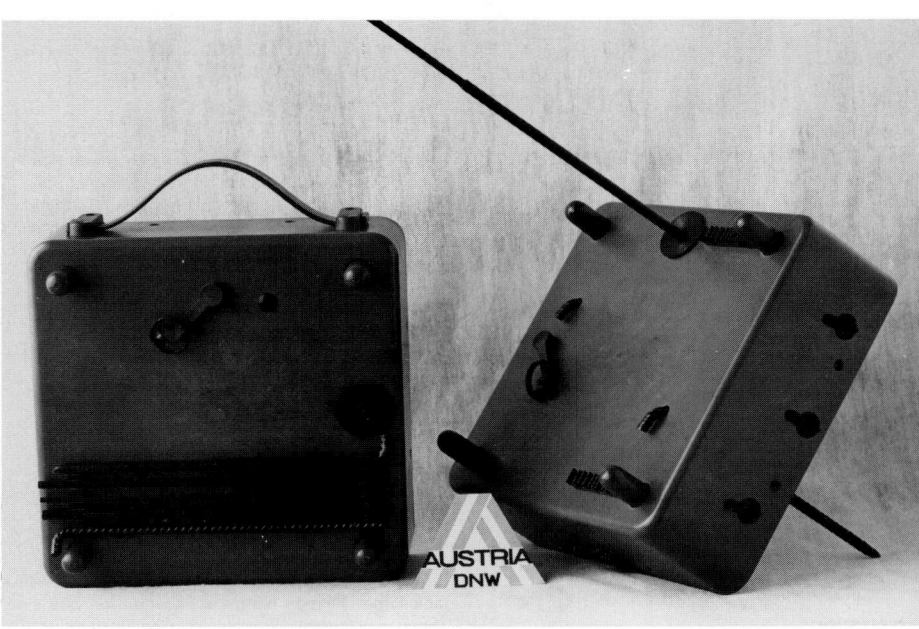

DNW PM 3000 anti-tank mine

Description

The DNW PM 3000 anti-tank mine is a variable-function mine using either pressure or electrical detonation. The pressure method employs a tilt-rod detonation system. Alternatively, four pressure trigger devices on each corner, on the bottom of the mine, will cause it to detonate even if a target tank rolls over only one corner or edge of the mine. The electrical detonator is used to neutralise the mine either by detonation or deactivation after a fixed period of time. This electrical system can also be used to deactivate the mine for storage and handling. If required each particular detonation system can be deactivated leaving the others active, for example the tilt-rod alone can be activated, leaving the pressure triggers and electrical system inert.

The PM 3000 body is constructed from corrosion-free and fireproof materials. When laid the mine may be fixed in place by a picket stake and an anti-handling device is fitted. The pressure-fuze system cannot be detonated by blast from clearing explosions or artillery fire. If required the PM 3000 can be laid mechanically when the pressure system will activate automatically. If required the PM 3000 can be fired electrically by remote or radio control.

Specifications
Weight: (approx) 8 kg
Length: 280 mm
Width: 280 mm
Height: 100 mm
Tilt-rod height: 500 mm

Operating pressure: 250 kg
Armour piercing capability: approx 180 mm at 500 mm

Status
In production.

Manufacturer
Dynamit Nobel Wien GmbH, A-8430 Leibnitz, Austria. Tel: 0 34 52 21 01. Telex: 034 405 assma a. Fax: 0 34 52 22 97.

ATM 2000E Anti-tank Mine

Intertechnik ATM 2000E anti-tank mine

Description

The ATM 2000E (Anti-Tank Mine 2000 Electronic), also known as the PzMi 88, is an advanced plastic-bodied mine utilising the latest available electronic technology and containing a minimum of metal components. A microprocessor-based sensor system inside the mine is able to carry out a number of independent sensor checks together with a number of manual controls for a very flexible range of operational sequences.

Commencing with the method of laying, either hand or mechanical methods may be used. For the latter the ATM 2000E can be mechanically laid using the Intertechnik AID 2000 minelayer (see entry in the *Minelaying equipment* section). In either case the mine circuits will not auto-activate for 10 minutes after laying. The circuits can be manually deactivated at any time and at no risk to the operator. After deactivation the mine can be lifted and is then ready for immediate re-use if required. An automatic deactivation facility is included in the circuitry and the timing may be varied in accordance with customer preference.

The mine may be laid either on or below the surface. Once activated the sensor uses a combination of acoustic and magnetic sensors to locate a target, and the microprocessor system can discriminate between types of target. The normal pressure plate facility is retained. When called upon to detonate, a small clearing charge removes earth or other covering from the main warhead. The fuzing circuits allow the mine to be used against targets travelling at speeds between 0.5 and 60 km/h and the self-forging fragment warhead can penetrate up to 300 mm of monobloc armour or 100 mm of armour-plated steel plus six 10 mm witness plates.

In addition to the above features the ATM 2000E can be detonated remotely by a conventional exploder device and there is a manual switch that can be used to engage an anti-handling device if required.

Inert training versions are available while another training variant can be supplied with only the electronic components in an operable state.

Associated with the ATM 2000E is the DEAK 2000 deactivation device. This can be used to locate buried ATM 2000E mines and can indicate the position and operating condition of the buried mine. It can also be used to deactivate the mine electronics.

Specifications
Weight: 6.5 kg
Weight of explosive: 1.5 kg
Dimensions: 251 × 251 × 130 mm
Penetration:
(monobloc steel) 300 mm
(armour-plated steel) 100 mm plus 6 × 10 mm witness plates

Status

In production. In service with the Austrian Army.

Manufacturer

Intertechnik Techn. Produktionen-GmbH, A-4040 Linz, Industrielle 56, PO Box 100, Austria. Tel: (0732) 78 92-0. Telex: 221522. Fax: (0732) 78 92-13.

SMI 17/4C Giant Shotgun

Description
The SMI 17/4C is a novel weapon concept in that it is intended for clearing barbed wire and similar obstacles, yet it has considerable potential as an anti-personnel or anti-vehicle mine. It consists of a dished plate some 300 mm across that is intended to fire a matrix of steel balls, each some 8 to 9 mm in diameter, in a narrow-dispersion cone out to a range of 50 m or more. At 50 m the closely controlled steel ball cone is powerful enough to clear a way through a five-coil barbed wire obstacle with three coils underneath and two on top. The steel ball cone diameter at 50 m is only 2 m across and at that range each ball can penetrate 8 mm of armour plating. It can also be used to clear dense jungle foliage. Before firing the SMI 17/4C Giant Shotgun is supported on a simple steel frame and the dished plate can be swivelled vertically and locked in position by simple thumbscrews.

Specifications
Weight: 8 kg
Diameter of mine face: 302 mm
Depth: 150 mm
Height to centre of face axis: 240 mm
Weight of charge: 5 kg
Type of charge: Composition B

Status
Development complete.

Manufacturer
SMI, Military Defence Products, Südsteirische Metall-industrie GmbH, A-8430 Leibnitz, Austria.
Tel: 03452 2101. Telex: 034405 assmann a.
Fax: 03452 2297.

SMI 17/4C Giant Shotgun

SMI Directional Fragmentation Mines

Description
A new range of SMI directional fragmentation mines replaced the former SMI 20/1C, 21/3C and 21/11C – for details of these mines refer to *Jane's Military Logistics 1990−91* page 194.

The new range involves the APM 19 and APM 29 anti-personnel mines and the AVM 100 and AVM 195 anti-vehicle mines. All were designed to ensure accuracy and high fragment density in the required target area plus optimum penetration. On all four mines the body is made of reinforced plastic. The APM 19 and APM 29 are each mounted on two pairs of scissor legs while the AVM 100 and AVM 195 are mounted on tripods. Each mine is equipped with a sight and two fuze wells. They can be detonated by an electrical detonator, a detonating cord, a tripwire, a pull-type igniter, a shock tube or a passive sensor system. If required several mines can be detonated simul-taneously. A two-phase infra-red sensor system is under development for the AVM 100 and AVM 195 – the first phase selects a worthwhile target and the second determines the detonation time in relation to target speed and range. The sensor can be preset to remain effective from 3 to 60 days and can also select a target vehicle in a column (from 1 to 8).

As an indication of penetrating power the APM 19 can penetrate 20 mm of pinewood at a range of 50 m. The AVM 100 and AVM 195 can both penetrate 6 mm of armoured steel at 50 m and 2 mm of mild steel at 150 m.

Specifications
Model	APM 19	APM 29	AVM 100	AVM 195
Weight	1.9 kg	2.9 kg	10 kg	19.5 kg
Length	230 mm	265 mm	410 mm	620 mm
Width	35 mm	45 mm	65 mm	70 mm
Height	95 mm	120 mm	195 mm	230 mm
Weight of main charge	0.9 kg	1.45 kg	5.4 kg	10.3 kg
Number of fragments	923	923	843	1340
Fragment diameter	4.7 mm	5.6 mm	9.5 mm	10.3 mm
Effective range	50 m	50 m	100 m	150 m

Status
In production.

Manufacturer
SMI, Military Defence Products, Südsteirische Metall-industrie GmbH, A-8430 Leibnitz, Austria.
Tel: 03452 2101. Telex: 034405 assmann a.
Fax: 03452 2297.

SMI 22/7C Off-route Anti-tank Mine

Description
The SMI 22/7C off-route anti-tank mine is aimed by the integral sight along a predetermined line across an important road or passage and the sensor is placed as required and then connected to the mine. The mine can be fitted with a self-neutralisation device if required.

The main charge when detonated forms a projectile with a very high penetrating power. The mine also has an integral electronics unit with two sensors that can differentiate between various types of vehicle. The maximum distance that the mine can be positioned off the route is 50 m. It is also fitted with a self-deactivation device which operates after a predetermined time.

Inert training mines are available.

Specifications
Weight: 13.5 kg
Length: 290 mm
Diameter: 180 mm
Weight of main charge: 7 kg
Type of main charge: Composition B
Maximum effective range: 50 m
Armour penetration:
  (30 m) 80 mm steel
  (50 m) 70 mm steel
Penetration diameter: 80 mm
Deviation from flight path: 0.5°
Battery life: (operational) 3 months

Status
Trials.

Manufacturer
SMI, Military Defence Products, Südsteirische Metall-industrie GmbH, A-8430 Leibnitz, Austria.
Tel: 03452 2101. Telex: 034405 assmann a.
Fax: 03452 2297.

SMI 22/7C off-route anti-tank mine complete with stand

Hirtenberger APM-1 Horizontal Anti-personnel Mine

Description
The APM-1 horizontal anti-personnel mine is of the Claymore type but is mounted on a small tripod with a pan and tilt head to enable it to be aimed in any direction. The convex face of the mine can project approximately 290 spherical steel projectiles in a 60° arc in such a way that 10 m from the mine there are 10 or 11 effective projectiles/m². In a lateral dispersion range of 40° at 25 m there are 4 or 5 effective projectiles/m². Each projectile weighs approximately 0.5 g and has a diameter of 5 mm. Projectiles are considered effective when penetrating 20 mm of pine or 4 mm of aluminium sheet. The explosive charge is Composition B.

Specifications (approximate)
Weight: 1 kg
Length: (mine body) 140 mm
Height: (mine body) 80 mm
Width: (mine body) 40 mm
Height with tripod: 280 mm
Weight of explosive charge: 0.36 kg
Fragment velocity: 1460 m/s
Number of fragments: 290
Fragment weight: 0.51 g
Fragment diameter: 5 mm

Status
In production.

Manufacturer
Hirtenberger AG, A-2552 Hirtenberg, Austria.
Tel: 02256 81184. Telex: 14447.
Fax: 02256 81807.

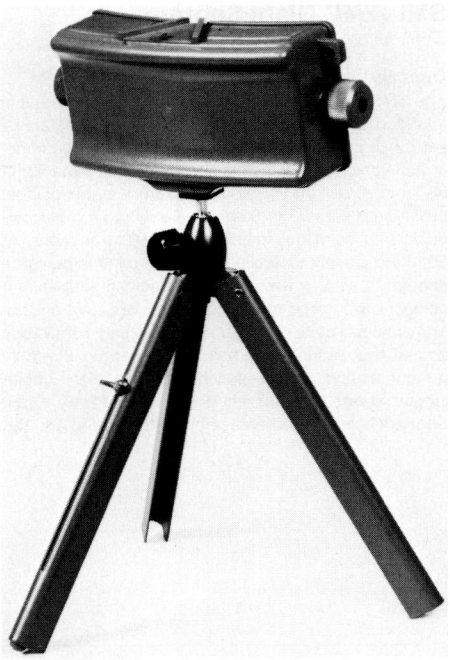

Hirtenberger APM-1 horizontal anti-personnel mine

Hirtenberger APM-2 Anti-personnel Mine

Description
The Hirtenberger APM-2 anti-personnel mine replaced the APM-3 in the Hirtenberger range (for details of this mine see *Jane's Military Vehicles and Ground Support Equipment 1985*, page 168), but is of the same controlled fragmentation (Claymore) type for operations against personnel and light vehicles.

In use the APM-2 can be placed against a tree or other object but is usually placed on the ground mounted on two pairs of scissor-type legs that can be screwed into the body. The mine body is double curved and made of plastic. The front of the body holds a fragmentation face containing approximately 1450 0.5 g steel balls embedded in a plastic matrix. The fragmentation face is formed horizontally convex and vertically concave to direct the splinters in a 60° arc and to control the vertical dispersion of them. The body contains a 1.3 kg charge of Composition B. On the back of the mine body are two protruding filling holes to provide tactile recognition of the rear of the mine in the dark.

The APM-2 has two detonator wells on both sides of the body to permit electrical or detonation cord firing from two sources. Detonating cord may also be used to fire a number of mines in series. For nuisance raids or similar purposes the APM-2 can be fitted with a time fuze with a delay range of 1 min up to 24 hours. The minimum safety distance for personnel firing the APM-2 is 15 m in a foxhole and 80 m under cover.

On firing there are 7 to 10 effective splinters/m² on 2 m high tables placed at a distance of 50 m from the mine – an effective splinter is taken as one penetrating 20 mm of pine or 4 mm of aluminium.

Training versions are available.

Specifications (approximate)
Weight:
(total) 2.95 kg
(charge) 1.3 kg
Length: (mine body) 315 mm
Height:
(mine body) 155 mm
(with mounting) 455 mm
Depth: (mine body) 40 mm
Type of charge: Composition B
Number of splinters: 1450
Weight of splinter: 0.5 g
Diameter of splinter: 5 mm
Initial velocity of splinters: 1660 m/s

Status
In production.

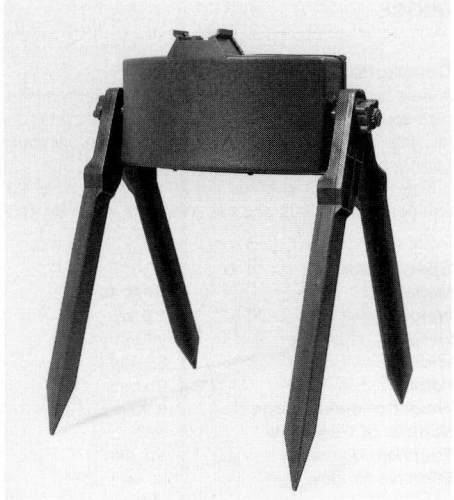

Hirtenberger APM-2 anti-personnel mine from front

Manufacturer
Hirtenberger AG, A-2552 Hirtenberg, Austria.
Tel: 02256 81184. Telex: 14447.
Fax: 02256 81807.

DRAGON Electronic Fuze System for Off-route Anti-tank Mines

Description
The DRAGON electronic fuze system is an autonomous passive sensor system designed for use with anti-tank or anti-vehicle mines. The system can be used to cover a pre-selected area for a pre-determined time selected by the user and at the end of that time, if the system and mine have not been activated, the system can be returned to a safe condition with that safe condition indicated. The system and mine can then be re-used.

The DRAGON fuze system is contained inside a single casing which can be adapted to fit a number of designs and types of mine. The system has two acoustic microphone sensors, one each side of the casing, and one infra-red sensor, the latter combining a sensitive detector and an optical system focusing incoming infra-red radiation onto the detector.

A control circuit features battery voltage monitoring, an operational period control and a motion sensor. If the battery voltage falls below an operational level the mine will be returned to a safe condition and the condition is indicated. As the user deploys the mine he

The DRAGON electronic fuze system for off-route anti-tank mines in position

has the choice of eight pre-determined operational periods which can be set from one day to 60 days. After that period the mine is returned to a safe condition and the condition is indicated. The user can also select the number of targets that can pass before the mine is initiated. A mechanical safety device is incorporated in the fuze to allow the mine to be deployed and collected without danger to the user. Countermeasure and anti-handling protection circuits involving four position sensors can be added if required.

In operation the system commences with an activation period under the control of a safety and arming device. Once initiated after a safety delay, the system enters a stand-by mode involving the minimum current consumption. Only the operational period countdown timer and one microphone sensor are maintained in an activated state and they remain so until a potential target approaches. Once sensed, the target's sound signature causes the second microphone and the infra-red sensors to be activated. The two acoustic sensors are then combined and analysed to determine target range while the infra-red sensor is used to actually initiate the mine, all under the control of a 16-bit single chip micro-controller. Only when the acoustic and infra-red sensor signals combine to indicate the optimum firing conditions will be the mine be initiated. If the target line is not crossed or the infra-red sensor cannot locate the target, the system will return to the standby mode and the operational period countdown will continue.

The DRAGON electronic fuze system has an effective range of from 3 to 80 m and can be triggered by target speeds of from 3 to 60 km/h. It can be used over an operational temperature range of from −35 to +63°C.

Status
In production.

Manufacturer
Hirtenberger AG, A-2552 Hirtenberg, Austria.
Tel: 02256 81184. Telex: 14447.
Fax: 02256 81807.

HELKIR Electronic Fuze System for Anti-helicopter Mines

Description
The HELKIR electronic fuze system is intended for use against low flying helicopters within a range of 150 m and was designed to be adapted to a range of heavy fragmentation mines. The system can be used to cover a pre-selected area for a pre-determined time selected by the user and at the end of that time, if the system and mine have not been activated, the system can be returned to a safe condition with that safe condition indicated. The fuze system and mine can then be re-used.

The HELKIR fuze system is contained inside a single casing housing an acoustic microphone sensor and an infra-red sensor, the latter combining a sensitive detector and an optical system focusing incoming infra-red radiation onto the detector.

A control circuit features battery voltage monitoring, an operational period control and a motion sensor. If the battery voltage falls below an operational level the mine will be returned to a safe condition and the condition is indicated. As the user deploys the mine he has the choice of eight pre-determined operational periods which can be set from one day to 120 days. After that period the mine is returned to a safe condition and the condition is indicated. A mechanical safety device is incorporated in the fuze to allow the mine to be deployed and collected without danger to the user. Countermeasure and anti-handling protection circuits involving three position sensors can be added if required.

In operation the system commences with an activation period under the control of a safety and arming device. Once initiated after a 15 minute safety delay, the system enters a standby mode involving the minimum current consumption. Only the operational period, activation circuits, crystal oscillator countdown timer and the microphone sensor are maintained in an activated state and they remain so until a potential target approaches. Once sensed, the target's sound signature is analysed. If the correct characteristics and sound level of the target's sound signature is detected (that is, the distinct sound produced by helicopter rotors) the infra-red sensor is activated. The infra-red sensor scans the area covered by the fragment spread of the mine involved so if a target appears in that area the mine is initiated. If the infra-red sensor cannot locate the target, the system will return to the standby mode and the operational period countdown will continue.

The HELKIR electronic fuze system has an effective range of from 5 to 150 m and can be triggered by target speeds up to 250 km/h. It can be used over an operational temperature range of from −35 to +63°C.

Status
In production.

Manufacturer
Hirtenberger AG, A-2552 Hirtenberg, Austria.
Tel: 02256 81184. Telex: 14447.
Fax: 02256 81807.

The HELKIR electronic fuze system for anti-helicopter mines in position on a heavy fragmentation mine

BRAZIL

Anti-personnel Mine Min AP NM AE T1

Description
The Min AP NM AE T1 (*Mina Anti-Pessoal Não-Magnética Alto Explosiva modelo T1*) is a non-metallic anti-personnel mine undetectable by conventional mine detectors. It has a main charge of Pentolite 50:50 and a secondary (booster) charge of Nitropenta.

Specifications
Weight of complete mine: 420 g
Diameter: 85 mm
Height: (including fuze) 95 mm
Activation pressure: 17 kg
Effective range: 0.5 m

Status
In production. In service.

Manufacturer
Química Tupan SA, Avda Rio Branco 26, 4° Andar, 20090 Rio de Janeiro, RJ – Brazil.
Tel: 21 263 1057. Telex: 23904.

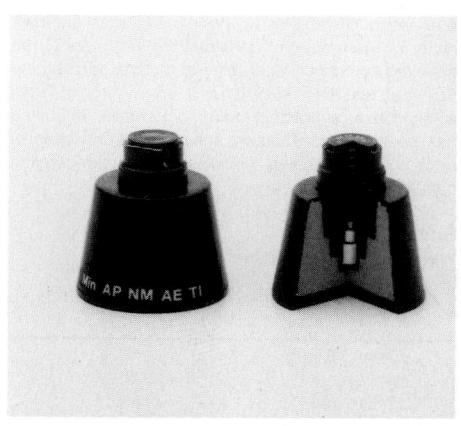

Anti-personnel mine Min AP NM AE T1

Anti-personnel Mine T-AB-1

Description

The anti-personnel mine T-AB-1 is a small cylindrical mine manufactured almost entirely from plastic. Coloured olive green, it contains 62 g of 50:50 Pentolite and uses an AC Min NM AE T-AB-1 pressure fuze. The fuze will detonate when subjected to a weight of 18 kg causing a minimum displacement of 5 mm. The fuze has what is described as a 'safety enclosure' system which has to be removed before the fuze is screwed into a well in the centre of the mine body.

The T-AB-1 anti-personnel mine is fully waterproof and can be laid under water. It is proof against sympathetic detonation from a distance of 0.5 m and is resistant to handling and other shocks.

The T-AB-1 anti-personnel mine is used as the booster for the anti-tank mine T-AB-1 (see following

entry). A practice version is available. This is made of grey plastic and produces a puff of non-toxic smoke when actuated. Weight of the practice version is 70 g.

Specifications

Weight: 125 g
Diameter: 60 mm
Height: 61 mm
Weight of main charge: 62 g
Type of main charge: 50:50 Pentolite
Activation pressure: 18 kg

Status

In production.

Manufacturer

Britanite Indústrias Químicas Ltda, Rodovia BR-116, km 71, Brazil.
Tel: 041 772 1211. Telex: 041 5513.

Anti-personnel mine T-AB-1

Anti-tank Mine T-AB-1

Description

The anti-tank mine T-AB-1 is a rectangular plastic mine that employs the anti-personnel mine T-AB-1 (see previous entry) as a booster. When being prepared for laying the circular pressure plate is removed to reveal a central well. An anti-personnel mine T-AB-1 is then prepared by removing its fuze 'safety enclosure' and screwing the fuze into the body of the anti-personnel mine. The anti-personnel mine is inserted into the well of the anti-tank mine and its pressure plate screwed into place.

The pressure plate is an olive green plastic material fastened to the booster compartment by shear pins. The shear pins will rupture when subjected to a minimum weight of 200 kg on the pressure plate and displaced 5 mm. This will then actuate the anti-personnel mine booster to detonate the main charge of TNT.

The anti-tank mine T-AB-1 is proof against sympathetic detonation when emplaced 2 m from each other and is proof against handling and other shocks.

The olive green plastic body, which has an integral carrying handle, is completely waterproof so the mine can be laid under water.

A practice version with a grey plastic body is available. When actuated it produces a puff of non-toxic smoke. Weight of the practice version is 6 kg.

Specifications

Weight: 5.9 kg
Length: 243 mm
Width: 243 mm
Height: 138 mm
Weight of main charge: 5.2 kg
Type of main charge: TNT
Activation pressure: 200 kg

Status

In production.

Manufacturer

Britanite Indústrias Químicas Ltda, Rodovia BR-116, km 71, Brazil.
Tel: 041 772 1211. Telex: 041 5513.

Anti-tank mine T-AB-1 with pressure plate removed to reveal well with anti-personnel mine T-AB-1 booster in place

Anti-tank Mine Min AC NM AE T1

Description

The Min AC NM AE T1 *(Mina Anti-Carro Não-Magnética Alto Explosiva modelo T1)* is an anti-tank mine of non-metallic construction that cannot be detected by conventional mine detectors, such as the SCR-625 and AN/PRS-5. It has a main charge of Trotil, a secondary (reinforcing) charge of Pentolite 50:50 and has been proved effective against different types of tracked and wheeled vehicles. A plastic carrying handle is incorporated.

Specifications

Weight of complete mine: 8 kg

Weight of Trotil charge: 7 kg
Length: 225 mm
Width: 255 mm
Height: 155 mm
Activation pressure: 60 to 140 kg
Effective range: (max) 2 m

Status

In production. In service.

Manufacturer

Química Tupan SA, Avda Rio Branco 26, 4° Andar, 20090 Rio de Janeiro, RJ – Brazil.
Tel: 21 263 1057. Telex: 23904.

Anti-tank mine Min AC NM AE T1

BULGARIA

PM-79 Anti-personnel Mine

Description
The PM-79 anti-personnel may be regarded as being in the same group of mines as the CIS PMN, although it is generally smaller overall.

The PM-79 uses the same arming principle as the PMN in that a side-mounted firing pin is held in the safe position by a safety pin. When the safety pin is removed as the mine is emplaced a wire is left free to cut its way through a lead strip. This provides an arming safety of about 20 minutes. At the end of that period the firing pin is allowed to move forward under spring pressure until it strikes a centrally located post. This post will hold the firing pin away from the detonator until a pressure of between 50 and 250 kg is applied to a metal plate on top of the mine body; the plate is covered by a thin metal cap. Pressure will distort the plate and lift the central post out of the path of the firing pin. The remaining firing pin spring pressure will then force the firing pin into the detonator to ignite the 70 g main charge.

The PM-79 may be emplaced on the surface by mechanical means and has a plastic body. It is stated to be resistant to explosive mineclearing methods.

Specifications
Weight: from 255 to 323 g
Diameter: 87.2-88.2 mm
Height: 47-49.6 mm

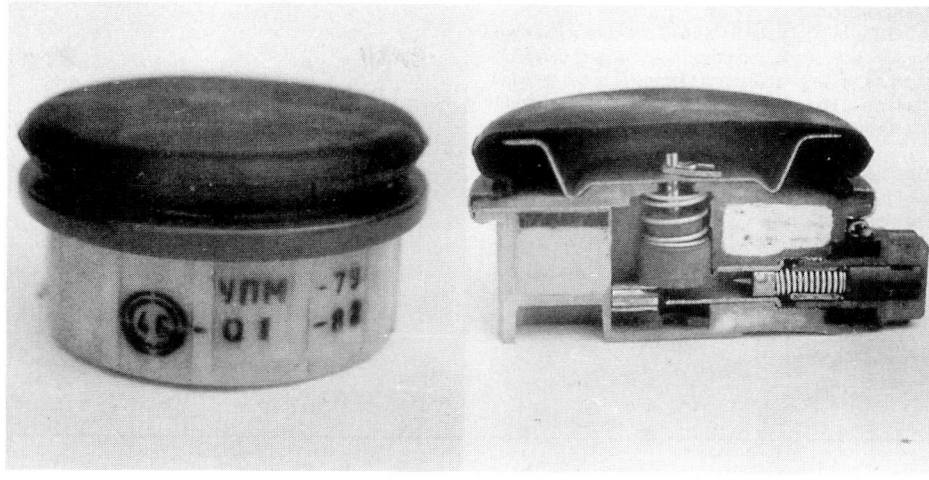

PM-79 anti-personnel mine with cutaway example on right

Weight of main charge: 70 g
Operating pressure: 50-250 kg

Status
In production. In service with the Bulgarian armed forces. Has been offered for export and has been encountered in the Far East.

Agency
KINTEX, POB 209, 66 Anton Ivanov Boulevard, Sofia, Bulgaria.
Tel: 66 23 11. Telex: 22471.

PSM-1 Bounding Anti-personnel Mine

Description
The PSM-1 is a bounding anti-personnel mine of conventional design and operation. The mine may be used with two MVN-2M pressure igniters plus a plastic MUV-2 tripwire igniter. Activation of any of the igniters will cause the mine warhead to be ejected from the buried mine body up to a height of between 0.5 and 1.5 m, where it will explode. The explosion will scatter fragments to create a lethal radius of 20 m and a wounding radius of up to 40 m. The mine may also be command activated by an EVU-3 electrical fuze.

Specifications
Weight:
(fuzed) 3 kg
(unfuzed) 2.7 kg
Diameter: 75 mm
Height:
(fuzed) 249 mm
(unfuzed) 112 mm
Weight of explosive: 170 g

Status
In production. In service with the Bulgarian armed forces. Has been offered for export and has been encountered in the Far East.

Agency
KINTEX, POB 209, 66 Anton Ivanov Boulevard, Sofia, Bulgaria.
Tel: 66 23 11. Telex: 22471.

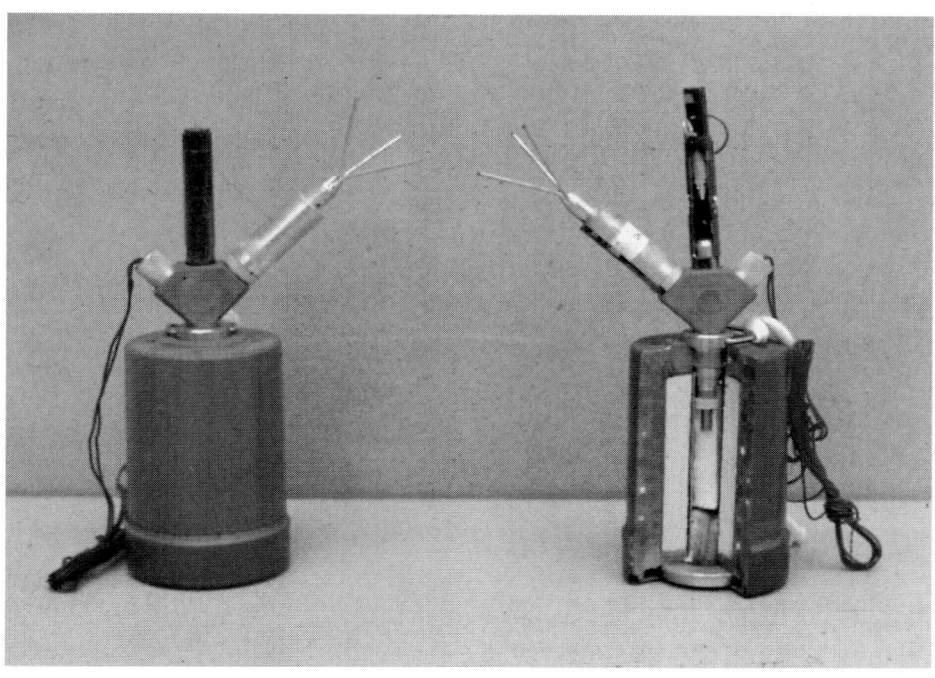

PSM-1 bounding anti-personnel mine with cutaway example on right

PTM-80P Anti-tank Mine

Description
The PTM-80P is a plastic-bodied anti-tank mine which can be used under damp or waterlogged conditions such as those encountered in coastal areas or water obstacles. The mine is conventional in design and is fitted with a VPTM-80P clockwork delay pressure fuze.

Specifications
Weight: 9 kg
Diameter: 320 mm
Height: 90 mm
Weight of explosive: 7.6 kg

Status
In production. In service with the Bulgarian armed forces. Offered for export.

PTM-80P anti-tank mine with cutaway example on right

Agency
KINTEX, POB 209, 66 Anton Ivanov Boulevard, Sofia, Bulgaria.
Tel: 66 23 11. Telex: 22471.

CANADA

C3A2 Non-metallic Anti-personnel Mine (Elsie)

Description
This groundburst plastic anti-personnel mine was developed by the Canadian Army. It was accepted as standard by the ABC countries and is produced in Canada for the British Army.

The mine consists of two assemblies, a body and a charge. The body assembly is 51 mm in diameter, 76 mm long and weighs 76 g. The charge assembly is 38 mm long, 57 mm wide (with safety clip) and weighs 28 g. Total weight of explosive is 7.8 g of Composition A5 initiated by a 6 g aluminium steel detonator.

The body assembly has a transit plug which is removed after the body assembly has been emplaced and replaced by the charge assembly fitted with a safety clip. When the safety clip is removed the mine will operate when a force of 7.25 to 11.8 kg is applied.

The mine is olive-coloured or sand beige and was designed with integral camouflage material. It is undetectable with conventional electromagnetic equipment but if required a detector ring can be fitted to enable the mine to be detected.

The practice version is designated the C4A1 and is emplaced in the same manner as the C3A2 and functions in the same way except it produces a blue smoke charge when actuated. The C4A1 is reusable at least five times by the replacement of the spotting charge and re-cocking of the body assembly. Inert and dummy versions of the mine are also produced.

Status
In production. In service with the Canadian Armed Forces and the British Army.

Manufacturer
SNC Industrial Technologies Inc, 5 Montée des Arsenaux, Le Gardeur, Québec, Canada J5Z 2P4. Tel: (514) 581 3080. Fax: (514) 581 0231.

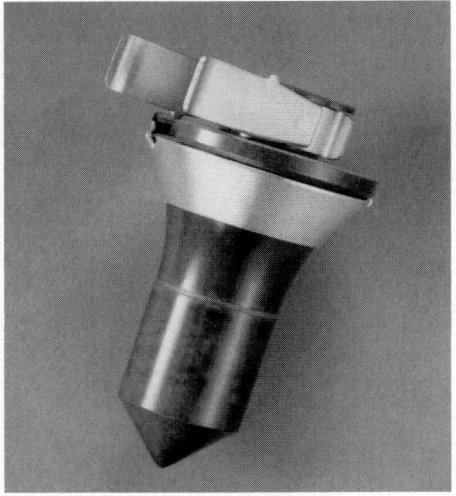

C3A2 non-metallic anti-personnel mine complete with safety clip

CHILE

FAMAE Anti-personnel Mines

Description
FAMAE is part of the Chilean armed forces and runs an ammunition and weapons manufacturing organisation. Among its many products are two anti-personnel mines, both of which use the high impact plastic body of the FAMAE GM 78-F7 hand grenade. The two anti-personnel mines are the pressure-activated MAPP 78-F2 (*mina anti-personal de presión*) and the other the pull-activated MAPT 78-F2 (*mina anti-personal de tracción*).

The MAPP 78-F2 is activated by a small pressure plate on top of the mine while the MAPT 78-F2 is activated by a tripwire mechanism. Both rely upon blast for their effects and are stated to be effective over a radius of 2 m. Both contain 87 g of TNT. The MAPP 78-F2 weighs 222 g while the MAPT 78-F2 weighs 205 g. For handling and transport safety the MAPP 78-F2 uses a sprung plastic collar under the pressure plate; the collar is removed as the mine is laid. The MAPT 78-F2 uses a conventional safety pin with an operation similar to that of a hand grenade. There are two tripwire attachment points on the fuze mechanism of this mine.

Status
In production. In service with the Chilean Army.

Manufacturer
FAMAE Fabricaciones Militares, Avenida Pedro Montt 1568/1606, Santiago, Chile.
Tel: 5561011. Telex: 242 346 famae cl.

FAMAE MAPP 78-F2 pressure-activated anti-personnel mines

FAMAE MP-APVL 83-F4 Anti-tank Mine

Description
The FAMAE MP-APVL 83-F4 (*mina anticarros livianos y vehiculos*) appears to be based on the American Second World War M1A1 and M4 anti-tank mines but has a plastic body with a laminated steel base plate. The main charge is mainly TNT and weighs 2 kg but the body also contains a number of steel balls weighing 3.5 kg to add to the mine's destructive effects against lightly armoured vehicles. The main charge is initiated by 0.2 kg of Pentolite.
The mine weighs 6.75 kg complete.

Status
In production. In service with the Chilean Army.

Manufacturer
FAMAE Fabricaciones Militares, Avenida Pedro Montt 1568/1606, Santiago, Chile.
Tel: 5561011. Telex: 242 346 famae cl.

FAMAE MP-APVL 83-F4 anti-tank mine

FAMAE MAT.84-F5 Anti-tank Mine

Description
The FAMAE MAT.84-F5 anti-tank mine (*mina anti-tanque*) is a circular plastic-bodied anti-tank mine containing a main charge of Pentolite weighing 9.3 kg. The mine body is made of high impact plastic 3 mm thick with a circular pressure plate on the top. The mine is armed by unscrewing a safety plug from the side-mounted fuzing system before laying.
The mine weighs 10.3 kg complete.

Status
In production. In service with the Chilean Army.

Manufacturer
FAMAE Fabricaciones Militares, Avenida Pedro Montt 1568/1606, Santiago, Chile.
Tel: 5561011. Telex: 242 346 famae cl.

FAMAE MAT.84-F5 anti-tank mine

CHINA, PEOPLE'S REPUBLIC

Type 72 Anti-personnel Mine Series

Description
All the Type 72 anti-personnel mines are visually identical, being small low metallic content cylindrical mines with a slightly domed upper surface. Each mine is only 78 mm in diameter and 37 mm high. The weight is 150 g of which 34 g is explosive.

The mines are pressure-activated by a pressure of between 3 and 7 kg. However, the Type 72B and 72C use electronic circuitry on a printed circuit board to delay arming and also have an anti-handling device which detonates the mine if the body is tilted more than 10°. The Type 72C also has a self-destruct capability. Externally all three are visually identical, having a light green top cover and a green body.

Once emplaced all three mines are outwardly identical. However, the Type 72A has a safety pin with a round end. On the Type 72B it is triangular while the end of the safety pin for the Type C is reported to be rectangular.

With the Type 72A, removal of the safety pin will permit the pressure plate under the sealed rubber top cover to descend to activate the mine when pressure is applied. When the safety pin is in place three spring-loaded detents block any pressure plate movement. Once the pin has been removed the pressure plate is free to move down against a domed fibre-reinforced plastic plate which, once enough pressure has been applied, will flip downwards to permit a striker pin in its centre to contact the detonator.

On the Type 72B removal of the safety pin will not only release the pressure plate to move downwards when pressure is applied but it will also permit an internal switch plate to turn and switch on the electronic circuitry. After a short delay the electronics will assume that the position assumed by the mine is a fixed datum point. Thereafter any movement of 10-12° from that datum will cause the mine to detonate. Pressure on the pressure plate will also detonate the mine.

Status
In service with the Chinese armed forces. Encountered throughout South-east Asia.

Manufacturer
State factories.

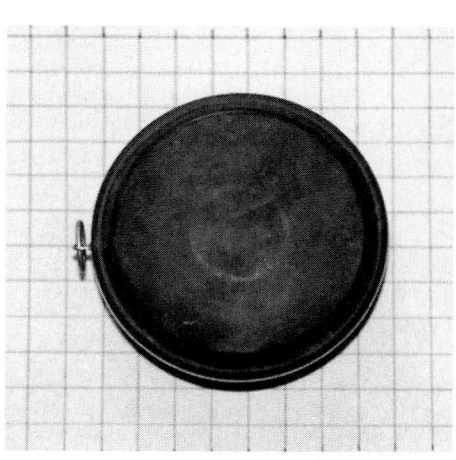

Top view of Type 72 anti-personnel mine

Anti-personnel Shrapnel Mine

Description
This is the Chinese version of the CIS POMZ-2 anti-personnel mine but it is lighter and requires a greater operating force. The mine consists of a wooden stake, serrated cast-iron body, cylinder of cast TNT and a pull-actuated fuze. It has an effective radius of 20 m. The mine operates as follows: a pull on the tripwire removes the pull pin in the fuze, which releases the striker to hit the percussion cap and detonate the mine.

Specifications
Weight: 1.4 kg
Diameter: 60 mm
Height: (without stake) 105 mm
Main charge type: TNT
Weight of main charge: 1.17 kg
Operating force: 9-18 kg

Fuze: MUV or UPF

Status
In service with the Chinese Army and probably supplied to countries which have received Chinese military aid.

Manufacturer
Chinese state arsenals.

Type 69 Anti-personnel Bounding Mine

Description
The Type 69 anti-personnel bounding mine is very similar to those in the CIS OZM series. The mine can be operated by a pressure or tripwire fuze and when this is activated the mine body projects the main charge up to a height of 1.5 m. It then bursts to produce, on average, 240 fragments each weighing 0.7 g.

Specifications
Weight:
(total) 1.35 kg
(main charge) 0.105 kg
Height:
(total) 168 mm
(body) 114 mm
Diameter: 61 mm
Main charge type: TNT
Number of fragments: approx 240
Operating force:
(pull-release) 1.5-4 kg
(pressure) 7-20 kg
Lethal radius: approx 11 m
Height of burst: 1-1.5 m

Status
In production. In service with Chinese armed forces and other nations.

Manufacturer
China North Industries Corporation, 7A Yue Tan Nan Jie, PO Box 2137 Beijing, Beijing, China. Tel: 867570. Telex: 22339 cnin cn.

Type 69 anti-personnel bounding mine

Portable Bounding Anti-personnel Mine

Description
Intended for use as an ambush-type weapon, this portable bounding anti-personnel mine is contained in a small pot-type container which is emplaced as required. The mine is detonated using either a pressure system, with an operating pressure of 7 to 20 kg, or a tripwire system with a pull tension of between 1.5 to 4 kg. As the mine is detonated four minelets are ejected outwards to explode about 15 m away from the mine position and at a height of between 0.2 and 0.5 m. As the minelets explode they release 6000 steel balls to create a lethal radius of not less than 25 m. The minimum safety distance for this mine is stated to be 300 m.

Specifications
Weight: 2.8 kg
Diameter: 135 mm
Height: 109 mm
Weight of charge: 0.46 kg
Contents of minelets: 6000 steel balls

Status
In production.

Manufacturer
China North Industries Corporation, 7A Yue Tan Nan Jie, PO Box 2137 Beijing, Beijing, China. Tel: 867570. Telex: 22339 cnin cn.

Chinese Portable Bounding Anti-personnel Mine (C F Foss)

Type 72 Anti-tank Mine

Description
The Type 72 anti-tank mine is a Chinese copy of the CIS TM-46 and differs from the original in few details. The Type 72 uses a Type 72-A blast resistant fuze but a double impulse fuze may be used as an alternative. The main charge is 50:50 RDX:TNT and the metallic mine case is sealed to allow for use under water to a depth of 1.2 m.

Specifications
Diameter: 279 mm
Height: 93 mm
Weight:
(total) 8.13 kg
(main change) 5 kg
Type of charge: RDX/TNT 50/50
Operating pressure: 300-700 kg

Status
In production. In service with the Chinese Army and may be used by other nations.

Manufacturer
China North Industries Corporation, 7A Yue Tan Nan Jie, PO Box 2137 Beijing, Beijing, China. Tel: 867570. Telex: 22339 cnin cn.

Type 72 anti-tank mine

Type 72 Non-metallic Anti-tank Mine

Description
The Type 72 non-metallic anti-tank mine is circular with a slightly domed pressure plate on top. This plate is slightly elastic and requires a pressure of between 300 and 800 kg before it moves downwards far enough to contact the Type 72 blast resistant fuze or Type 69 double impulse fuze. This operating pressure causes the pressure plate to move downwards about 9.5 mm (±0.9 mm) before the fuze actuates. The fuze sets off a booster charge which in turn detonates the main charge of 50:50 RDX:TNT. The body is all-plastic and a handle that folds inwards into the base is provided. Just above this handle is a plug that covers either an anti-lift device well or a well for a remote-control detonator.

Type 72 non-metallic anti-tank mine

The Type 72 may be emplaced manually, or mechanically by a truck-towed minelayer similar in overall appearance to the CIS PMR series.

Specifications
Diameter: 270 mm
Height: 100 mm
Weight:
    (total) 6.5 kg
    (main charge) 5.4 kg
Type of charge: RDX:TNT 50:50
Operating pressure: 300-800 kg

Status
In production. In service with the Chinese Army and offered for export.

Manufacturer
China North Industries Corporation, 7A Yue Tan Nan Jie, PO Box 2137 Beijing, Beijing, China. Tel: 867570. Telex: 22339 cnin cn.

COMMONWEALTH OF INDEPENDENT STATES

PMN Anti-personnel Mine

Description
The PMN anti-personnel mine was introduced into service around 1960 and was deployed along the old East German border, as well as in Vietnam. It has also been encountered in southern Africa. Another version of this mine is the PMN-6.

The case is made of duroplastic and has a side hole for the firing mechanism and primer charge, opposite which is the initiator adaptor plug. The top half of the mine has a rubber cover for the pressure plate, which is secured to the case by a thin metal band.

After the mine has been laid and the safety pin removed, there is a 15 to 20 minute delay in arming. This is because the firing pin moves forward under pressure of the firing pin spring until a wire in the after end of the firing pin spindle contacts a lead strip in the arming delay assembly. After the 15 to 20 minute period the wire cuts through the lead strip and releases the pin, which moves forward into a cavity of the pressure cylinder. This is held in place by a step in the cylinder and remains in this position until the mine is set off. When pressure is applied to the top of the case,

PMN non-metallic anti-personnel mine with safety pin in position but with safety cap removed to show lead bar and steel cutting wire that provide a 20 minute arming delay once the safety pin has been removed

the spring-loaded striker is released which in turn hits a percussion cap capsule, which sets off the main charge.

A PMN-2 anti-personnel mine also exists about which little is known. It is about the same size as the standard PMN but uses a one-piece pressure plate with raised ribs radiating from a central raised area. It appears to use some form of electrical or electronic fuze.

Specifications
Weight: 600 g
Diameter: 112 mm
Height: 56 mm
Main charge: TNT
Main charge weight: 240 g
Booster charge: Tetryl
Booster charge weight: 9 g
Operating force: 0.23 kg

Status
In service with members of the former Warsaw Pact. The mine has also been encountered in the Far East and Africa. In service with Afghanistan (est 25 000 to 30 000), China, Iraq and Vietnam.

Manufacturer
State factories.

POMZ-2 and POMZ-2M Anti-personnel Stake Mines

Description
The POMZ-2 anti-personnel stake mine was developed during the Second World War and consists of a wooden stake with a cast iron fragmentation body with six rows of fragmentation, rather like that of a hand grenade, and a cylinder of cast TNT.

These mines are normally laid in clusters of four or more and are equipped with tripwires. When fitted with the MUV fuze, a pull on the tripwire removes the striker-retaining pin, which releases the spring-driven striker against the percussion cap and detonates the mine. If fitted with the VPF fuze, when the tripwire is pulled it removes the pullring from round the head of the striker bolt, releasing the spring-loaded striker against the percussion cap and detonating the mine. Late models are designated the POMZ-2M. These

have a threaded fuze well and five rows of fragmentation whereas the POMZ-2 has six.

Specifications
Model	POMZ-2	POMZ-2M
Weight	2 kg	1.7 kg
Diameter	64 mm	64 mm
Height (with fuze but without stake)	135 mm	111 mm
Main charge type	TNT	TNT
Weight of main charge	75 g	75 g
Operating pressure	1 kg	1 kg
Fuze	MUV or VPF	MUV or VPF

Status
In service with members of the former Warsaw Pact. A similar mine is made in China, which is lighter and requires a greater operating force (9 to 18 kg). The North Koreans also make a mine similar to the POMZ-2. Also in service with Afghanistan, Angola, the former

POMZ-2 anti-personnel stake mine

Yugoslavia and Vietnam.

Manufacturer
State factories.

Wooden Anti-personnel Mines PMD-6, PMD-6M, PMD-7, PMD-7ts and PMD-57

Description
The PMD-6 wooden anti-personnel mine was developed before the Second World War and was first used operationally in the Russo/Finnish Winter War of 1939/40. The mine consists of a wooden box with a hinged lid that overlaps the sides. A deep groove is cut in the front end of the lid so that it may fit over the fuze and rest on the striker retaining pin. Some mines have a safety device which consists of a safety rod which prevents the lid from actuating the fuze prematurely. The mine operates as follows: pressure on the lid forces the winged retaining pin from the striker and this detonates the mine.

The PMD-6M is the post-war model of the PMD-6 and has the MUV-2 pull fuze.

The PMD-7 followed the PMD-6 and is a smaller mine and therefore has less explosive. The PMD-7ts has a mine body made of a single block of wood hollowed out for the charge which is the same as that used on the POMZ-2 anti-personnel stake mine. The PMD-57 is a post-war wooden anti-personnel mine.

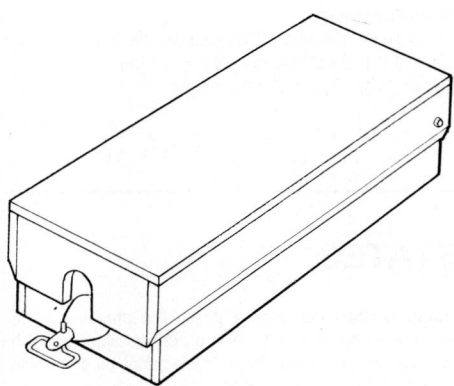

Wooden anti-personnel mine model PMD-6

PMD-57 wooden anti-personnel mine

Specifications

Model	PMD-6	PMD-7	PMD-7ts
Weight	0.4 kg	0.3 kg	0.3 kg
Length	200 mm	152 mm	152 mm
Width	89 mm	76 mm	76 mm
Height	64 mm	51 mm	51 mm
Main charge type	TNT	TNT	TNT
Weight of main charge	200 g	75 g	75 g
Operating force	1-9 kg	1-9 kg	1-9 kg
Fuze	MUV	MUV	MUV

Status
These mines are still held by countries of the former Warsaw Pact. The PMD-6 is known to be manufactured in China and is in service with Afghanistan (PMD-6M), North Korea and Vietnam.

Manufacturer
State factories. Can be easily produced by unskilled labour.

MON-50, MON-100 and MON-200 Directional Anti-personnel Mines

Description
The MON-50, MON-100 and MON-200 are directional anti-personnel mines with the numerals in their designation intended to reflect their effective range in metres. All three models can be detonated by tripwires or similar means, or by a seismic remote-control device known as the UMK (*upravlyaemoye minnoye kompleks*). The UMK is the central processing unit of a system that has four remote sensor units connected to it by wires; it is possible that the wires also have a sensor function. The cylindrical central processing unit is connected to a series of directional fragmentation mines, either ground emplaced or secured to trees or other supports. The processing unit can sense exactly what sector is being actuated and fire only the mine(s) in that sector.

MON stands for *minnoye oskolochonym napravleniem* – anti-personnel mine with directional fragments. The smallest of the MON series is the MON-50, a copy of the American M18A1 Claymore mine with some changes made to the internal fragmentation resin matrix which may contain steel balls or short steel cylinders. The blast from the MON-50 covers an arc of 60°; the maximum effective range is 50 m. This mine, normally mounted on four scissor-type folding legs, is usually tripwire or manually activated from a remote position rather than by the UMK device. The MON-50 may also be mounted on a special adjustable rotary head device which may be either screwed into a tree or timber support or clamped in a vice system to a railway line or other location.

The MON-100 is a cylindrical-dished plate mine with a sheet steel body which can be mounted on a fixing bracket or attached to a tree, with the concave face mounted towards the target. The mine is 236 mm in diameter, 82.6 mm deep and with a 1.89 kg main charge of TNT containing approximately 400 steel fragments. Total weight is 7.53 kg. The fuze is the MD-5M. At 100 m the width of the area covered by lethal fragments is from 6.5 to 9.5 m wide. The MON-100 is also manufactured in Poland.

MON-50 (left) and MON-100 (right) directional anti-personnel mines; the MON-50 is fitted with an adaptor for use with the UMK device while the MON-100 is on a demonstration stand

The MON-200 is an enlarged MON-100, 434 mm in diameter and 130 mm deep. It weighs 25 kg of which 12 kg is the main charge of TNT. At 200 m the area covered by approximately 900 lethal fragments is from 10.5 to 14.5 m wide.

A MON-500 is known to exist.

Specifications (MON-50)
Weight:
(with steel balls) 1.9 kg
(with steel cylinders) 2.1 kg
Weight of explosive: 0.7 kg
Length of body: 225 mm
Height of body: 155 mm
Depth of body: 64 mm

Status
In service with CIS armed forces.

Agency
ELECTRONINTORG Limited, 24/2, ul. Usievicha, 125315 Moscow, Russia.
Tel: 151 06 40/155 49 12. Telex: 411326.
Fax: 151 54 41/151 74 11.

MON-90 Directional Anti-personnel Mine

Description
The MON-90 is a larger version of the MON-50 (see previous entry) intended for the anti-landing or ambush role. It weighs 12.4 kg of which 6.45 kg is formed by the explosive filling. When detonated the mine scatters short steel cylinder fragments set in a matrix into the explosive over an arc of 54° out to an assured casualty range of 90 m. At that range the width of the fragmentation arc is 85 m.

The MON-90 is issued with a fixing clamp; there are no legs. One configuration seen features the mine set on a flat mounting board with a front-facing pointer being used to align the mine with the intended target area. A multi-directional clamping device has also been reported. For fine directional adjustment there is a simple sight system set into the top of the body. It takes one man about 5 minutes to set up the mine. A webbing carrying handle is located under the mine body.

Fuzes which can be used with the MON-90 include the EDPr electrical detonator, the VZD-6CH, VZD-144, and the NM with either the MVE-72, VP-12/VP-13 series or the MUV-4 series.

Specifications
Weight:
(mine body) 12.4 kg
(packaged, complete set) 23 kg
(explosive) 6.45 kg (±0.1 kg)
Length of body: 455 mm

Cutaway demonstration model of MON-90 directional anti-personnel mine

Height of body: 377 mm
Depth of body: 291 mm

Status
In production. In service with the CIS armed forces and offered for export.

Agency
ELECTRONINTORG Limited, 24/2, ul. Usievicha, 125315 Moscow, Russia.
Tel: 151 06 40/155 49 12. Telex: 411326.
Fax: 151 54 41/151 74 11.

PFM-1 Anti-personnel Mine/Bomblet

Description
The PFM-1 anti-personnel mine/bomblet was first used during the Israeli-Syrian conflict in October 1973 and was employed in large numbers in Afghanistan. It has been marked as the PFM-1 (anti-personnel high explosive mine) or PMZ (area denial mine).

The PFM-1 is a small air-delivered plastic weapon with a low metallic signature containing 35 to 40 g of liquid explosive. The liquid explosive has four components and has a density of 1.57 g/ml. The device is designed to maim rather than kill and has no self-destruct or neutralising capability.

The PFM-1 has an irregularly shaped bulbous body containing the liquid explosive in its lower part which is flexible to a limited degree. The casing, which weighs approximately 12 g, is manufactured from a high density polyethylene. In the firmer centre are the delayed arming and initiation systems. The rest of the body is a flat section that acts as a form of stabiliser while the weapon is dropped from an aircraft. The material used for the body is very low density polythene and may be coloured green, sand or white.

In Afghanistan PFM-1 mines were sown by Mi-8 Hip or similar helicopters with each helicopter usually carrying two 144-mine scattering units. Each unit comprises six 12-mine packets and the units are suspended from the helicopter's load-carrying points with one portion remaining on the hard point after launch. For launching the two solid side-covers of the unit are pushed apart mechanically by piston-like levers operated by springs and hydraulic pressure. When each of the six 12-mine packets is released the mines are scattered randomly by the airflow or on impact with the ground. The packets are made of a very thin foil and have dimensions of approximately 250 × 250 × 250 mm.

The PFM-1 mines can also be scattered from 240 mm mortar bombs fired to a range of between 12 000 to 15 000 m. With this system the mines are packed into units that look like green plastic bags, each

Helicopter-dispensed PFM-1 anti-personnel mines

containing about 20 mines. Each unit measures approximately 200 × 200 × 100 mm, and the unit scatters the mines by exploding an internal charge in the middle of the bag upon impact with the ground. The mines are then scattered over a radius of between 100 and 200 m.

When released from fixed or aimable containers carried on fixed-wing aircraft or helicopters a safety/arming plug is released from one side of the central part of the body. As the mine falls to the ground a piston is then allowed to travel under spring pressure through a silicon-based viscous liquid. This provides an arming delay that does not arm the weapon until after it is on the ground. Thereafter any distortion of the plastic body will cause the striker to hit the detonator. This distortion may be from a single movement produced by stepping on or kicking the mine but the mine may also be detonated by an accumulation of light pressures such as those produced by handling. The fuze employed is the MVDM although it is sometimes marked as the VGM-572.

The PFM-1 was named the 'Green Parrot' by Afghan tribesmen and this name has been used in some Western references.

The PFM-1S is a variant with a self-destruct feature.

Specifications
Weight: 70 g
Width over wings: 112 mm
Height central body: 60 mm
Thickness of body: 15 mm
Weight of charge: 35-40 g
Type of charge: liquid explosive

Status
In service with CIS armed forces.

Manufacturer
State factories.

OZM, OZM-3 and OZM-4 Bounding Anti-personnel Mines

Description

During the Second World War, the Soviets used the improvised OZM (fragmentation obstacle mines). These consisted of an artillery shell (122 or 152 mm) or a mortar (120 mm) bomb buried in the ground, nose down. Under the nose was a UVK-1 propellant assembly and a flash tube running to the surface. These mines are detonated by either a remote electrical firing capability, pressure on a fuze or by pulling a wire attached to the fuze. This sets off the propellant which forces the mine out of the ground and ignites the delay element. The delay unit burns until it explodes the detonator. The mines explode 1.5 to 2.4 m above the ground. Guidance of the mine upwards is achieved by earth piled around its body during emplacement. Although intended primarily for anti-personnel use, these mines were capable of disabling an armoured vehicle.

The cylindrical OZM-3 bounding anti-personnel mine was introduced post-war and can be set off by electrical or other remote-control, pull fuze, pressure fuze or a pull-tension fuze. When set off, the base of the mine blows through with the rest of the mine bounding. The height of the explosive (1.5 to 2.4 m) is determined by a tethering wire. This mine has an effective radius of 25 m.

The OZM-4 is a further development of the OZM-3 that cannot be fired electrically. The mine body is made of cast iron without pre-fragmentation. Detonation height is controlled by a tethering wire and is approximately 0.8 m. Height without a fuze is 140 mm and diameter 91 mm. The OZM-4 is intended for use with the MUV, MUV-2 or similar pull fuzes but has been encountered fitted with a Ro-8 pressure fuze.

Specifications (OZM-3)

Weight: 3 kg
Diameter: 75 mm
Height: 120 mm
Main charge type: TNT
Weight of main charge: 75 g

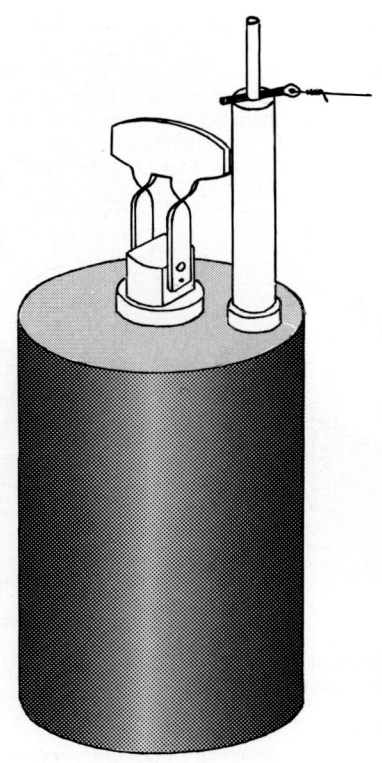

OZM-3 bounding anti-personnel mine

Status

The OZM-3 is in service with countries of the former Warsaw Pact and has been used in Afghanistan. The OZM-4 is in service with former Warsaw Pact nations and has been encountered in southern Africa.

Manufacturer

State factories (also field assembly for OZM mines).

OZM-4 bounding mine fitted with Ro-8 pressure fuze

OZM-72 Bounding Anti-personnel Mine

Description

The OZM-72 bounding anti-personnel mine is a derivative of the OZM mine series (see previous entry). The OZM-72 follows the same general lines as the earlier OZM mines and operates in a similar manner but the OZM-72 has a larger diameter (108 mm as opposed to 75 mm) and the height overall is 173 mm high as opposed to 120 mm. The top of the mine has a different layout with two plugs. It would also appear that the manufacturing method used for the mine body has been changed as the bottom of the body has a crimped base. It is understood that the fuze is similar to, or the same as, the fuze used on the OZM-4.

The mine is fired by either electrical remote-control or a pull or pressure fuze. As the mine is fired a propellant charge blows the mine upwards until a tethering wire is drawn taut to detonate the mine fuze at a height of about 1 m above the ground surface. The lethal radius of the resultant fragments is approximately 25 to 30 m.

Specifications

Weight: 5 kg
Weight of explosive: 0.7 kg
Height overall: 173 mm
Diameter: 108 mm

Status

In production. In service with former Warsaw Pact armed forces.

Agency

ELECTRONINTORG Limited, 24/2, ul. Usievicha, 125315 Moscow, Russia.
Tel: 151 06 40/155 49 12. Telex: 411326.
Fax: 151 54 41/151 74 11.

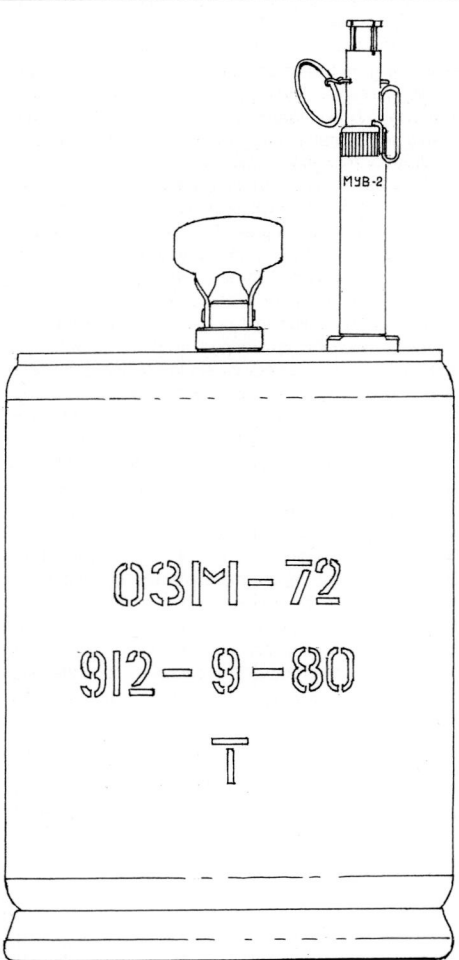

Side view of the OZM-72 bounding anti-personnel mine

OZM-160 Bounding Anti-personnel Mine

Description
The OZM-160 bounding anti-personnel mine is a large and bulky device that also has applications in the anti-vehicle and possibly anti-helicopter roles. It consists of a mine body that ejects a converted 203 mm artillery projectile vertically upwards to detonate and scatter fragments over a lethal radius of some 40 m.

The OZM-160 mine is installed by digging a hole over 1 m deep, into which the mine is placed – hooks are provided on the mine body to assist when lowering the mine into position. The mine body, which resembles a mortar tube, is 1.03 m long and has a closed base while a cover at the top of the mine is removed before use. The mine is normally fired remotely (although other firing methods could be employed) and a propelling charge at the base of the mine ejects the projectile vertically upwards. The projectile is tethered to the base of the mine by a cable so at a height of approximately 1.5 m the cable pulls a pin from the base of the projectile and the main charge detonates.

The OZM-160 weighs 85 kg and the projectile main charge weighs 4.5 kg. Diameter of the mine body is 245 mm.

Status
In service with CIS armed forces. Has been encountered in Afghanistan.

Manufacturer
State factories.

PGMDM Scatterable Anti-tank Mine

Description
The PGMDM scatterable anti-tank mine may be dispensed from aircraft or helicopters and has the same triangular bar-mine shape and appearance as the German AT-1 (which did not enter service) and the French Mitral (qv) scatterable anti-tank mines. The PGMDM differs in that it uses a liquid explosive charge contained in a thin flexible plastic cover.

The PGMDM uses the same MVDM pressure-operated fuze employed on the PFM-1 anti-personnel mine. This fuze may be operated by a single pressure or an accumulation of slight pressures, for example by handling, and is electrically activated on release – after a 30 second delay all operations are mechanical. The mine is reported to be spongy to the touch as the plastic casing is very thin.

The mine has an overall length of 300 mm and a height of 75 mm; the base measures 65 mm. The circular metal fuze is set at one end of the body and has a diameter of approximately 55 mm; the fuze protrudes 20 mm from the mine body. These dimensions put the weight between 1.4 kg and 2 kg. Since most of the weight is made up of the liquid explosive

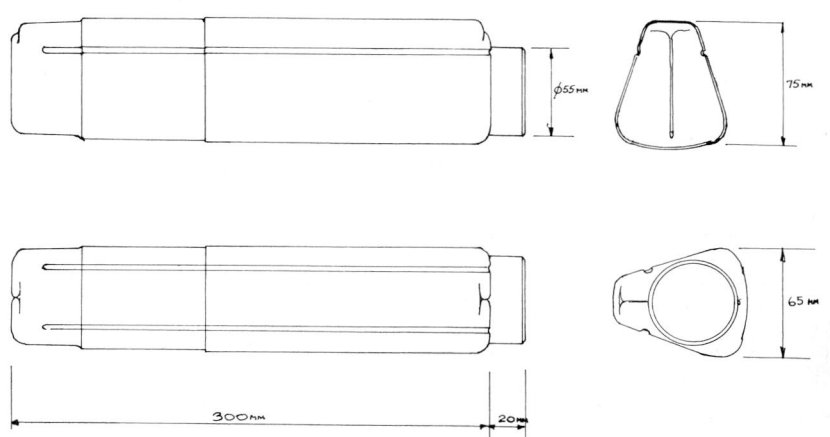

Drawing of PGMDM scatterable anti-tank mine showing main dimensions

filling this is enough to damage a tank track or vehicle wheel.

The PGMDM has a clockwork self-destruct timer that can be preset to any one of 12 settings, with the maximum setting understood to be 20 hours.

Status
In production. In service with CIS armed forces.

Manufacturer
State factories.

TM-72 Anti-tank Mine

Description
Little information is available regarding the TM-72 anti-tank mine. At first sight it appears to resemble the TM-62M but with a deeper body containing more explosive. However, calculations using the one available illustration reveal that its approximate diameter of 250 mm is less than that for the TM-62M (315 mm). As the TM-72 body depth is approximately 97 mm its internal volume is approximately the same as that of the TM-62M. From this it follows that the weight of the explosive charge must be roughly comparable for both mines. This gives rise to the possibility that the TM-72 uses some form of explosively formed fragment or a similar type of anti-armour warhead.

The TM-72 uses the MVCh-62 clockwork delay fuze.

Status
In service with CIS armed forces.

Manufacturer
State factories.

TM-72 anti-tank mine

TM-62 Anti-tank Mine

Description

In its metallic form the TM-62 anti-tank mine is a progressive development of the TM-57 but is also used as the 'family' name for a group of anti-tank mines that differ in their construction. These are:

    TM-62M metal casing
    TM-62 P2 plastic casing
    TM-62 P3 plastic casing
    TM-62D rectangular wooden case
    TM-62B waterproof cardboard casing.

These mines all appear to have a built-in firing delay of approximately 2 seconds to ensure that the tank is well over the mine before it detonates.

The TM-62M uses a sheet steel casing, is similar in appearance to the TM-57 and has provision for a tilt-rod detonator. The central fuze well of the TM-62 has a diameter of 122 mm and a depth of 80 mm. Fuzes that can be used with the TM-62 series include the MVN-72 magnetic influence fuze and the MVCh-62. The TM-62M is also produced in Poland.

The plastic-bodied TM-62 P2 and P3 both have a body diameter of 308 mm. The TM-62 P2 has a height of 82 mm unfuzed while the TM-62 P3 has a height of 84 mm, also unfuzed.

Specifications (TM-62M)
Weight:
    (complete with detonator) 11.12 kg
    (without detonator) 10.32 kg
Diameter: 317.5 mm
Height:
    (overall) 115 mm
    (without fuze) 83 mm
Main charge weight: approx 7 kg
Operating pressure: 175-600 kg
Fuze: MVCh-62 mechanical time

Status
In production. In service with former Warsaw Pact armed forces.

Manufacturer
State factories.

TM-62M anti-tank mine fitted with MVN-72 magnetic influence fuze; the fuze is actually a UMVN-72 training fuze

TM-62D anti-tank mine without its fuze (Jane's Intelligence Review)

Base of a TM-62B anti-tank mine showing the carrying handle

TM-57 Anti-tank Mine

Description

In appearance, the TM-57 metallic anti-tank mine is very similar to the TM-46 and TMN-46 anti-tank mines. The TM-57 has a larger charge and improved fuzing, and can be laid by hand or mechanically. It can be recognised as it has no well in the bottom for an anti-lift device (although it does have one in the side) and has seven ribs underneath (the TMN-46 has five ribs) along with a carrying handle. Some TM-57 mines have two filling plugs in the base.

The TM-57 can be fitted with the MVZ-57 fuze. This has a clockwork delay mechanism that is prepared by removing a spring clip as the mine is emplaced by hand. A button on the fuze is then pressed and 45 seconds later the detonator tilts upright into the operating position. The MVSh-57 tilt-rod fuze may be used with the TM-57.

Specifications
Weight: 9.5 kg
Diameter: 315 mm
Height:
    (overall, with MVZ-57 fuze) 115 mm
    (without fuze) 95 mm
Main charge type: cast TNT
Main charge weight: 7 kg
Operating force: 200-300 kg
Fuze model: MVZ-57p or MVSh-5

Status
In production. In service with countries of the former Warsaw Pact.

Manufacturer
State factories.

TM-57 anti-tank mine fitted with MVZ-57 fuze

TM-46 Anti-tank Mine

Description
The TM-46 is metallic and can be laid either by hand or mechanically. The MVM pressure fuze is used for mechanical laying, or the MV-5 fuze for hand laying. The mine is detonated as follows (MV-5): pressure applied to the pressure plate compresses the striker spring in the fuze until the striker-retaining ball escapes into a recess in the pressure cap, releasing the spring-loaded striker which detonates the mine. In appearance the TM-46 is almost identical to the TMN-46, which however has a fuze well in the bottom of the mine for booby-trapping.

The Israeli No 6 anti-tank mine is an exact copy of the TM-46. A version produced in China is known as the Type 72 and one produced in Egypt is known as the M/71. The TM-46 has also been produced in Bulgaria.

Specifications
Weight: 8.4 kg
Diameter: 304 mm
Height: 91 mm
Main charge type: TNT
Main charge weight: 5.3 kg
Booster charge: TNT
Booster charge weight: 198.45 g
Operating force: approx 210 kg
Fuze model: MV-5 or MVM (angled tilt-rod) MVSh-46

Status
In service with former Warsaw Pact countries and has been exported to the Middle and Far East and Africa.

Manufacturer
State factories.

TM-46 metallic anti-tank mine

TMN-46 (Anti-lift) Anti-tank Mine

Description
The TMN-46 is metallic and can be laid either by hand or mechanically. The MVM pressure fuze is used for mechanical laying, or the MV-5 fuze for hand laying. There is a fuze well in the bottom of the mine for booby-trapping. The mine is detonated as follows (MV-5 fuze): pressure forces the pressure cap down on the head of the fuze, depressing it and releasing the striker to detonate the mine. In appearance, the TMN-46 is almost identical to the TM-46, which does not have the fuze well in the bottom of the mine for booby-trapping.

Specifications
Weight: 8.98 kg

Diameter: 304 mm
Height: 110 mm
Main charge type: TNT
Main charge weight: 5.95 kg
Booster charge: Tetryl
Booster charge weight: 76.54 g
Operating force: 210 kg
Fuze model: MV-5 (hand laying) or MVM MVSh-46 angled tilt-rod

Status
In service with countries of the former Warsaw Pact.

Manufacturer
State factories.

TMN-46 (anti-lift) anti-tank mine showing filler plug

TMD-B and TMD-44 Anti-tank Mines

Description
The TMD-B wooden anti-tank mine entered service with the Red Army in 1943 and was also used in Korea. The wooden box is of simple construction with the boards being either nailed together or fastened by tongue-and-groove joints. On the top of the mine are three pressure boards. The centre board is hinged and held in place by a wooden locking bar approximately 63 mm thick. An MV-5 pressure fuze is inserted when the board is in the raised position. When the weight of a vehicle is applied to the top of the mine the centre pressure board presses down on the thin wooden locking bar until the latter breaks. Immediately this happens the centre pressure board presses down directly onto the MV-5 pressure fuze and the mine is detonated. The main charge normally consists of two waterproof paper-wrapped blocks of pressed amatol, ammonite or dynammon.

The TMD-44 is similar to the TMD-B but has a centrally located plastic fuze well cover and only two pressure boards. Like the TMD-B, it uses the MV-5 pressure fuze.

Specifications

Model	TMD-B	TMD-44
Weight	7.7 kg	10 kg
Length	318 mm	315 mm
Width	279 mm	280 mm
Height	140 mm	158 mm
Main charge type	varies	varies
Weight of main charge	5-6.8 kg	6 kg
Booster charge	TNT	n/a
Weight of booster charge	199 g	n/a
Operating force	200 kg	200 kg
Fuze model	MV-5 (pressure)	MV-5 (pressure)
Detonator	MD-2	MD-2

Status
The TMD-B is in service with members of the former Warsaw Pact and is known to be used by North Korea and Vietnam. It has been encountered in southern Africa.

The TMD-44 is not currently in service but is thought to be held in reserve with CIS forces. Cuba produced a variant with a bakelite fuze well, an MV-5 fuze and an MD-2 detonator.

The TMD-B is sometimes converted for anti-

TMD-B wooden anti-tank mine

personnel use. The Yugoslav (now Serbian) version of the TMD-B is known as the TMD-1.

Manufacturer
State factories.

TMK-2 Anti-tank Mine

Description
The TMK-2 anti-tank mine was introduced into service around 1955 and consists of a sheet steel, double-truncated, conical mine body with the shaped charge in the lower half. The mine is fitted with an adjustable-length, tilt-rod fuze which is fitted into a holder attached to the side of the mine at the point of its greatest diameter. The mine is normally buried in the ground with only the tilt-rod fuze showing. The shaped charge

has sufficient power to penetrate the belly armour of a tank. The mine itself is 350 mm high, 300 mm in diameter at the widest point, and weighs 8.5 kg. Total weight of the assembly is 12.5 kg. Most examples appear to be olive green in colour.

Status
In service with the CIS armed forces.

Manufacturer
State factories.

Troops receiving instruction in use of TMK-2 anti-tank mine

PDM-1, PDM-1M, PDM-2 and PDM-6 River-bottom Mines

Description
The PDM anti-landing mines were designed to disable and damage landing craft and amphibious vehicles and would be used in rivers or lakes with a maximum velocity of 1.5 m/s. They can also be used on the sea

shore in depths of water ranging from 1 to 5 m.

PDM-1
This is similar to the PDM-1M but lacks a booster in the firing chain.

PDM-1M
This consists of a hemispherical case resting on a steel and concrete base and is normally used in water 1 to

2 m deep. The mine is detonated when the VPDM-1M tilt-rod fuze is struck. Two men can lay and arm the mine in 10 to 20 minutes.

PDM-2
This mine is also spherical and rests on a concrete base. It has a VPDM-2 tilt-rod fuze and is normally used in water from 2.4 to 3.8 m deep.

PDM-6
This is similar to the PDM-1M but has four fuze wells, one of which is in the bottom of the mine and is used as an anti-disturbance device. Each of the three fuze wells in the top of the mine has a tilt-rod fuze which can be adjusted so that the mine will detonate immediately on contact, or so that a rod deflection will trigger the mine.

Inert training version of PDM-1M river-bottom mine

Specifications

Model	PDM-1M	PDM-2	PDM-6
Weight	21 kg(1)	100 kg(2)	47.5 kg(4)
Height	1 m	1.4 m(3)	2.5 m(5)
Diameter	—	270 mm	500 mm
Base diameter	—	—	1 m
Main charge type	TNT	TNT or Ammonite	TNT or PETN
Weight of main charge	10 kg	15 kg	28 kg
Operating force	18-26 kg	40-50 kg	n/a

(1) Without concrete base which weighs 24-29 kg
(2) On low stand, 135 kg on high stand
(3) Range from 1.1-2.7 m depending on type of stand
(4) With base plate
(5) Mine body only, between 550-1050 mm with fuze

Status
In service with former Warsaw Pact countries.

Manufacturer
State factories.

PMK-1 Railway Mine

Description
The PMK-1 is one of a series of similar mines intended to be buried under railway lines and detonated by the weight of trains passing over the lines above the mine. With the PMK-1 the fuze involved is an MD-5M which actuates the ZK-1 striking mechanism when the rail is bent either 3.2 mm downwards or 3.3 mm upwards. The mine may also be command detonated using an electrical fuze. The mine itself is a sheet metal casing containing 7.1 kg of TNT.

Although this mine originated in the CIS it is also produced in Poland and is in service with other countries of the former Warsaw Pact.

Specifications
Weight: 8.5 kg
Mine body dimensions: 330 × 141 × 115 mm
Height, with detonator: 195 mm
Weight of main charge: 7.1 kg
Type of main charge: TNT

Status
In service with former Warsaw Pact countries.

Manufacturer
State factories.
Also available from Cenzin Foreign Trade Enterprise, ul. Frascati 2, 00-489 Warsaw, Poland.
Tel: 29 67 38. Telex: 814 505 czi Pl.
Fax: 628 63 56.

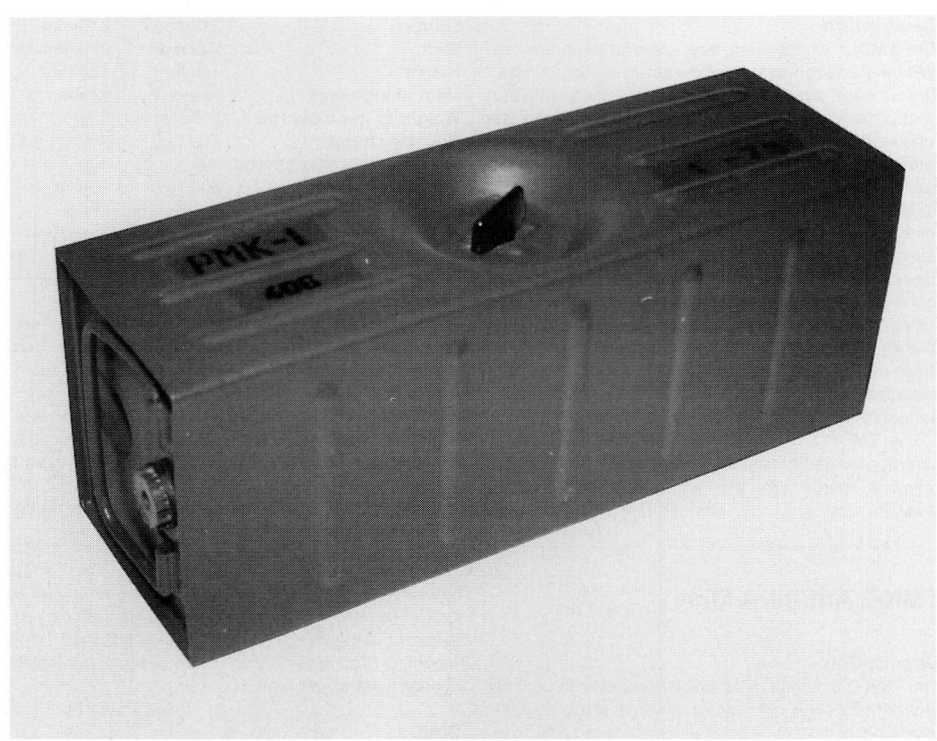

PMK-1 railway mine

CZECHOSLOVAKIA

PP-Mi-Ba Anti-personnel Mine

Description
This is a circular anti-personnel plastic mine.

Specifications
Weight: 340 g

Diameter: 150 mm
Height: 60 mm
Main charge: TNT
Weight of main charge: 200 g
Operating force: 0.5-1 kg

Status
In service with the Czechoslovak Army.

Manufacturer
Czechoslovak state factories.

PP-Mi-D Anti-personnel Mine

Description
The PP-Mi-D wooden anti-personnel mine is almost identical to the CIS PMD-7 mine except that it uses the Ro-1 fuze.

Specifications
Weight: 0.5 kg
Length: 135 mm
Width: 105 mm
Height: 55 mm
Main charge: TNT
Weight of main charge: 200 g
Operating force: 4 kg

Status
In service with the Czechoslovak Army.

Manufacturer
Czechoslovak state factories.

PP-Mi-Sb and PP-Mi-Sk Anti-personnel Stake Mines

Description
The PP-Mi-Sb anti-personnel stake mine is very similar in appearance to the German Second World War concrete ball mine, and also has a body of concrete with steel scrap fragments. It uses the UPM-1 pull fuze. Its external recognition feature is its smooth surface. The mine can also be taken off the stake and buried. In this case an Ro-2 pressure fuze is used.

The PP-Mi-Sk is almost identical to the CIS POMZ-2M stake mine but uses the Ro-2 pull fuze. This mine has six rows of fragments, the same as the CIS POMZ-2.

These mines operate as follows: when the striker-retaining pin is removed, the spring-loaded striker falls on and fires the percussion cap and detonator that set off the main charge.

Specifications

Model	PP-Mi-Sk	PP-Mi-Sb
Weight	1.6 kg	2.1 kg
Diameter	60 mm	75 mm
Height (with fuze but excluding stake)	137 mm	140 mm
Main charge type	TNT	TNT
Weight of main charge	75 g	75 g
Operating force	n/a	1 kg

Status
In service with countries of the former Warsaw Pact.

Manufacturer
Czechoslovak state factories.

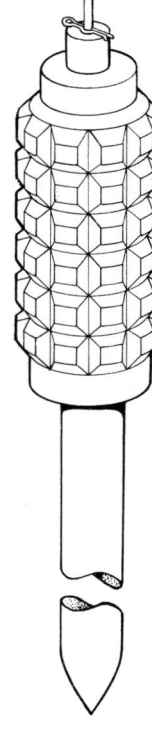

PP-Mi-Sk anti-personnel stake mine

PP-Mi-Sr Bounding Anti-personnel Mine

Description
The PP-Mi-Sr metallic bounding anti-personnel mine has a central fuze well with a transit cap. On opposite sides of the fuze well are the filler and the detonator well plugs. The body of the mine fits into an outer casing that also contains the propelling charge. The space between the inner and outer walls of the mine body is filled with shrapnel made of short pieces of steel rod. The mine has an effective fragmentation radius of 20 m.

The mine can be fitted with the Ro-8 pressure fuze or the Ro-1 pull fuze: in both cases the fuze ignites a delay train. After 3 to 5 seconds the propellant charge ejects the body of the mine from the container taking with it the wire attached to the bottom of the container. When the wire becomes taut at a height of approximately 1 m it activates the integral fuze, which fires the detonator and then the mine.

There are three other ways of employing this mine:
1. By inserting the Ro-1 pull fuze into the detonator well with the detonator upside down which converts the mine into a non-bounding anti-personnel mine.
2. Using the Ro-1 pull fuze in the normal fuze well and retaining the bounding feature.

PP-Mi-Sr bounding anti-personnel mines fitted with (left) Ro-8 pressure fuze and (right) Ro-1 pull fuze

3. Using the P-1 or P-2 electric squibs for remote-control.

Specifications
Weight: (without fuze) 3.2 kg
Diameter: 102 mm
Height: 152 mm

Main charge: TNT
Weight of main charge: 325 g
Booster charge: black powder
Booster charge weight: 37 g
Operating force:
  3-6 kg with Ro-8 pressure fuze
  4-8 kg with Ro-1 pull fuze

Status
In service with the Czechoslovak Army and some Near Eastern armies.

Manufacturer
Czechoslovak state factories.

PT-Mi-Ba Anti-tank Mine

Description
The PT-Mi-Ba circular non-metallic anti-tank mine introduced into the Czechoslovak Army in the 1950s is also known as the PT-Mi-Ba-53. It is similar in physical appearance to the German Second World War Teller-mines 42 and 43. It consists of two bakelite mouldings cemented together, and can be laid by hand or mechanically. The fuze well is in the bottom of the mine and is closed by a threaded cover plate. The two filler holes are also in the bottom of the mine and are closed by lugs. These lugs also hold either end of the carrying handle. The mine operates as follows: force on the pressure plate ruptures the shear groove, puts pressure on the fuze, which activates the detonator and starts the firing chain. The fuze contains some metallic components. No provision is made for booby-trapping.

Specifications
Weight: 7.83 kg
Diameter: 324 mm
Height: 115 mm
Main charge: TNT
Weight of main charge: 6 kg
Booster charge: TNT
Weight of booster: 208 g
Operating force: 200-400 kg
Fuze model: Ro-7-11 (pressure)

Status
In service with the Czechoslovak Army and some Middle Eastern armies.

Manufacturer
Czechoslovak state factories.

PT-Mi-Ba anti-tank mine

PT-Mi-Ba-II Anti-tank Mine

Description
The PT-Mi-Ba-II anti-tank mine is a rectangular non-metallic mine made almost entirely from a bakelite-type plastic. The mine is transported inside a wooden case in such a way that an internal plastic lid covers two Ro-7-11 fuzes inserted in the varnished main charge and two pressure switch extension rods. For laying, the lid of the wooden carrying case is removed and discarded and the plastic lid is removed and replaced upside down onto the mine. Internal cross supports hold the lid in position above the main charge and the fuzes. The two pressure switch extension rods are then placed into wells in the lid and the mine is ready for laying, often complete with the base and sides of the wooden carrying case. When a vehicle travels over the mine, pressure is exerted on the two protruding extension rods, which then shear off downwards to apply pressure to the tops of the two Ro-7-11 pressure fuzes.

Specifications
Weight: 9.6 kg
Length: 395 mm
Width: 230 mm
Height: 135 mm
Main charge: TNT
Weight of main charge: 6 kg
Operating force: 200-450 kg
Fuze: 2 × Ro-7-11 (pressure)

Status
In service with the Czechoslovak Army.

Manufacturer
Czechoslovak state factories.

Side view of PT-Mi-Ba-II anti-tank mine prepared for laying and still in its wooden carrying case

---

PT-Mi-Ba-III Anti-tank Mine

Description
The PT-Mi-Ba-III bakelite non-metallic anti-tank mine is circular and can be laid by hand or mechanically. A carrying handle slides into the mine for storage purposes. The mine operates as follows: force on the pressure plate ruptures the shear groove, puts pressure on the fuze, which activates the detonator and starts the firing chain. The fuze contains some metallic components. No provision is made for booby-trapping. This mine is resistant to short duration clearing methods. A training version is available.

This mine is also produced in Bulgaria where it is known as the PTM-BA-III.

Specifications
Weight: (without fuze) 9.65 kg
Diameter: 320 mm
Height: 109 mm
Main charge: TNT
Weight of main charge: 7.25 kg
Operating force: 200 kg
Fuze model: Ro-7-11 (pressure)

Status
In service with the Czechoslovak Army.

Manufacturer
Czechoslovak state factories.

Czechoslovak PT-Mi-Ba-III anti-tank mine

PT-Mi-K Anti-tank Mine

Description
This metallic anti-tank mine can be laid mechanically or by hand. Before laying a collapsible pressure ring is removed from the mine to insert the Ro-5 or Ro-9 fuze and primary charge (both held in a tubular container) into the central well and the pressure ring is then replaced. When pressure is exerted from above onto the collapsible pressure ring the corrugations of the ring collapse. This allows the pressure plate to press down onto the firing pin in the fuze via two spring plates. When sufficient pressure has been exerted a shear pin on the fuze breaks to release the firing pin and the detonation sequence commences. This system is proof against most explosive clearance methods. An anti-lift device can be incorporated by removing a screw cap from the bottom of the tubular fuze and

primary charge container and introducing an anti-lift detonator.

Specifications
Weight: 7.2 kg
Diameter: 300 mm
Height: 102 mm
Main charge: TNT
Main charge weight: 4.9 kg
Booster charge: 99 g
Operating force: 300-450 kg
Fuze model: Ro-5 or Ro-9

Status
In service with the Czechoslovak Army and some Middle Eastern armies.

Manufacturer
Czechoslovak state factories.

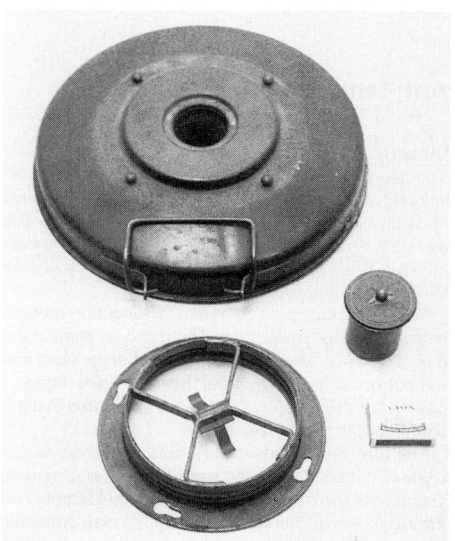

PT-Mi-K anti-tank mine with tubular fuze and primary charge container and collapsible pressure plate removed

---

PT-Mi-D, PT-Mi-D-I and PT-Mi-D-II Anti-tank Mines

Description
The PT-Mi-D wooden anti-tank mine resembles a rectangular wooden box. To prepare the mine for use a central wooden cross-piece on top of the mine is removed and replaced upside down. The cross-piece is shaped so that the upper portion protrudes above the surface by about 30 mm. Pressure on this cross-piece exerts pressure on two wooden blocks (one each side inside the box) held in position by thin shear dowels. The dowels break and the blocks remove the safety pins from two Ro-1 pull fuzes. The Ro-1 fuzes are each connected to a 200 g TNT block, each of which acts as a primary charge for its own 2.5 kg main charge. The mine can be booby-trapped by passing an anchor wire through one of two holes in the bottom of the box container to one of the Ro-1 fuzes.

The PT-Mi-D-I and PT-Mi-D-II are similar to the PT-Mi-D but have different dimensions and weights.

Specifications (PT-Mi-D)
Weight: 7.8 kg
Length: 320 mm
Width: 230 mm
Height: 140 mm
Main charge: TNT
Weight of main charge: 5 kg
Booster charge: two 200 g TNT blocks
Operating force: 200-450 kg
Fuze model: Ro-1

Status
In service with the Czechoslovak Army.

Manufacturer
Czechoslovak state factories.

PT-Mi-D anti-tank mine ready for use

PT-Mi-P Anti-tank Mine

Description
This is the Czechoslovak equivalent of the CIS TMK-2 anti-tank mine and is hemispherical in shape. The TNT explosive charge is concave at the top and a 5 mm thick steel plate with the same configuration is fitted on top. This gives the mine a shaped charge effect. The

mine is fitted with an adjustable length, tilt-rod activated Ro-9 fuze which is mounted on the side of the mine.

Specifications
Weight: (with fuze) 10 kg
Diameter: 238 mm
Height of body: 234 mm
Height with tilt mast: 745 mm
Weight of main charge: 5.8 kg

Main charge type: TNT
Operating force: 5.7 kg

Status
In service with the Czechoslovak Army.

Manufacturer
Czechoslovak state factories.

Na-Mi-Ba Anti-tank Mine

Description
This is a non-metallic circular anti-tank mine which can be laid either mechanically or by hand. It is believed to have a mechanical chemical fuze rather than the Ro-7-II pressure fuze used on the other Czechoslovak

non-metallic anti-tank mines.

Specifications
Diameter: 200 mm
Height: 250 mm
Main charge: Tritol
Weight of main charge: 2.4 kg
Operating force: 2.2 kg

Status
In service with the Czechoslovak Army.

Manufacturer
Czechoslovak state factories.

Anti-tank Mine TQ-Mi

Description
This circular anti-tank mine has a pressed cardboard case with a fuze body and glass cap. The fuze is of the pressure/chemical type.

Specifications
Weight: 10 kg
Diameter: 560 mm
Height: 150 mm
Main charge type: TNT
Weight of main charge: 5.21 kg
Booster type: Toul
Weight of booster: 100 g

Operating force: 320 kg

Status
In service with the Czechoslovak Army.

Manufacturer
Czechoslovak state factories.

DENMARK

Anti-tank Mine Fuze M/88

Description

The electronic Anti-tank Mine Fuze M/88 was developed in co-operation with the Royal Danish Army Material Command. It is offered as a cost-effective alternative retrofit solution for existing non-metallic mines. This fuze is licence-produced by Royal Ordnance as the RO 150.

The M/88 can provide most existing non-metallic mines with a full width capability. It can be fitted to the Bar Mine using two plastic straps with snap locks and without using tools. On other types of mine fitting is carried out using various interfaces integrated into the bottom of the mine fuze.

The fuze has an advanced electronic sensor which ensures correct functioning regardless of target speed. The sensor can be preset to disregard light targets and the fuze has a built-in anti-tilt device. It is also protected against electronic mineclearing measures.

The 7.8 g transfer charge of TNT/RDX 45:55 is integrated into the fuze bottom and can be fitted without having to open the fuze. The fuze case is waterproof to a depth of 2 m in salt and fresh water and is manufactured using modified polycarbonate materials in a green colour although various shades of brown can be produced.

The M/88 has a 15 minute arming delay and will self-neutralise after 90 days. Burying depth is up to 150 mm in earth. It can be used with mechanical minelayers. Minimum shelf life is 10 years although the battery may have to be changed after 5 years.

Weight of the M/88 is 835 g including the battery. Dimensions are 218 × 97 × 54 mm. The operating temperature range is from −33 to +58°C.

Status

In production. In service with the Royal Danish Army. Licence-produced in the United Kingdom by Royal Ordnance.

Manufacturer

Nea-Lindberg A/S, Industriparken 39-43, PO Box 226,

M19 anti-tank mine fitted with M/88 fuze

DK-2750 Ballerup, Denmark.
Tel: 42 97 22 00. Telex: 35 338 nealin dk.
Fax: 42 65 61 38.

EGYPT

Egyptian Anti-personnel Mines

Description

Few details of the three anti-personnel mines produced by the Maasara Company for Engineering Industries are available other than illustrations. A mine described as the A/P Plastic Mine appears to be a close copy of the Israeli No 4 anti-personnel mine while the Anti-Personnel Fragmentation Directional Mine is based on the American M18 Claymore. The Anti-Personnel Jumping Mine is a small pot-type mine actuated by a tripwire.

Status

In production.

Manufacturer

Maasara Company for Engineering Industries, PO Box Maasara, Cairo, Egypt.

A/P Plastic Mine

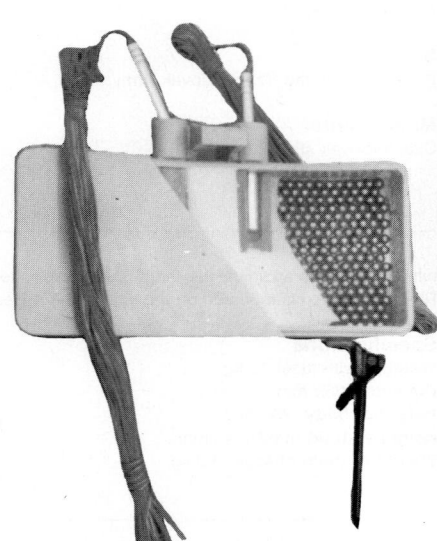

Anti-Personnel Fragmentation Directional Mine

Anti-Personnel Jumping Mine

T/78 Anti-personnel Mine

Description

The T/78 is described as an anti-personnel plastic mine and is a small booby-trap type mine detonated by a tripwire or some form of pull-action device. The detonator train protrudes some distance from the mine body and is held in a rigid frame. It seems very likely that some form of fragmentation sleeve or cover can be fitted to these mines to add to their anti-personnel effect.

Specifications
Weight:
  (total) 270 g
  (charge) 190 g
Height: 135 mm
Width: 67.5 mm
Depth: 40.6 mm
Type of charge: TNT

Status

In production. In service with the Egyptian armed forces and possibly some other Middle Eastern armed forces.

Manufacturer

Heliopolis Company for Chemical Industries, Haikstep, Heliopolis, Egypt.
Tel: 665314. Telex: 92708 hcico.

Anti-personnel Bounding Mine

Description
Described as a jumping mine, this anti-personnel bounding mine is emplaced on a wooden stake. On top of the stake is a steel cup containing the mine body which contains a tripwire-activated fuze. As the fuze is operated, a striker pin fires a primer cap and a propelling charge to project the mine vertically upwards. The striker pin also initiates a one second delay for the TNT/Hexogen charge inside the mine body. The mine thus explodes about 1 m from the ground surface and scatters steel balls and fragments in all directions out to a range of 30 m. The lethal radius is stated to be 15 m.

Specifications
Mine body diameter: 53.5 mm
Height: 165 mm
Type of charge: TNT/Hexogen
Number of fragments: at least 5000

Status
In production.

Manufacturer
Kaha Company for Chemical Industries, PO Box 2332, Cairo, Egypt.

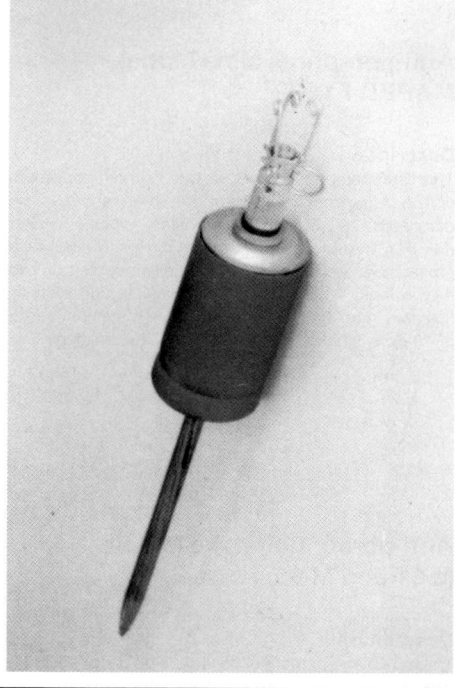

Egyptian anti-personnel bounding mine

M/71 Anti-tank Mine

Description
The M/71 metallic anti-tank mine is a direct copy of the CIS TM-46 produced in Egypt. It differs from the original in minor details only and the data provided are from Egyptian sources.

Specifications
Weight:
(total) 9.8 kg
(charge) 6.25 kg

Diameter: 315 mm
Height: 100 mm
Type of charge: TNT

Status
In production. In service with the Egyptian armed forces and possibly some other Middle Eastern armed forces.

Manufacturer
Heliopolis Company for Chemical Industries, Haikstep, Heliopolis, Egypt.
Tel: 665314. Telex: 92708 hcico.

Egyptian M/71 anti-tank mine

M/80 Anti-tank Mine

Description
The M/80 anti-tank mine is a circular mine with a ribbed plastic body and a pressure plate covering most of the area on top of the mine. It has the appearance of being designed to be mechanically laid or scattered but a plastic handle is provided at the side. The pressure plate has a mottled appearance to allow it to blend with the surrounding terrain and for desert use the body is a sand colour. No other details are available.

Specifications
Weight:
(total) 3.5 kg
(charge) 2.4 kg
Diameter: 204 mm
Height: 108 mm
Type of charge: TNT/Hexogen

Status
In production. In service with the Egyptian armed forces and possibly some other Middle Eastern armed forces.

Manufacturer
Heliopolis Company for Chemical Industries, Haikstep, Heliopolis, Egypt.
Tel: 665314. Telex: 92708 hcico.

Anti-tank Mine

Description
This circular anti-tank mine is a copy of the Italian SACI mine. It has a case of plastic with the three fuzes in the top of the mine. These are covered by a pressure plate 190 mm in diameter. The only metallic parts in the mine are the fuze striker and the detonator. The mine is detonated as follows: pressure on the top of the mine crushes the pressure plate, which ruptures the shear mechanism and detonates the mine.

Specifications
Diameter: 280 mm
Height: 205 mm

Main charge type: TNT
Weight of main charge: 7 kg
Booster charge: 2 RDX pellets
Operating force: 63.5-362 kg

Status
In service with the Egyptian Army.

FRANCE

Anti-personnel Mine Model MAPED F1

Description

This anti-personnel mine is the French equivalent of the American M18 Claymore mine and can be detonated by a remote-controlled electric igniter (Mk F1), wire-breaking electronic igniter (Mk F2) or a pressure igniter. The mine is normally mounted on two A-type legs. When detonated it projects 500 metallic splinters in an arc 60° to the front to a maximum range of 40 m. A smoke model is available for training.

Specifications
Weight: 1 kg
Length: 180 mm
Width: 60 mm
Height: (with legs) 220 mm
Main charge type: plastic explosive

Status
In production. In service with the French Army and other armies.

Manufacturer
ALSETEX SAE, 35 rue Tronchet, F-75009 Paris, France.
Tel: (1) 42 65 50 16. Telex: 280 384 f alexplo.
Fax: (1) 42 65 24 87.

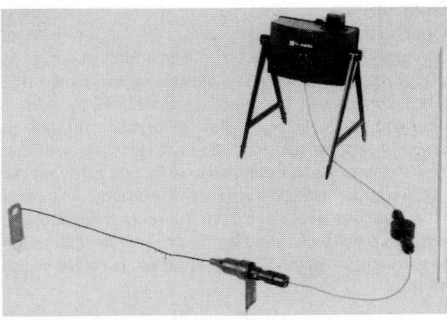

Anti-personnel mine Model MAPED F1 with legs in position

Anti-personnel Stake Mines M 61 and M 63

Description

These two anti-personnel mines are both staked to the ground using an integral stake. Both mines have sealed plastic cases and can be detonated by pressure or a tripwire. The M 63 has an anti-lifting device as a standard fitting. This is made of a traction trapping igniter. Both mines are fitted with a rigid removable cap for safe transport handling and installation. It contains an undetectable pressure igniter. These mines detonate under a minimum force of approximately 15 kg applied to the head of the igniter.

For training, a smoke model is available.

Specifications

Model	M 61	M 63
Weight	125 g	100 g
Diameter	35 mm	35 mm
Height	270 mm	270 mm
Main charge type	TNT	Tetryl
Weight of explosive	57 g	30 g

Status
In production. In service with the French Army and other armies.

Manufacturer
ALSETEX SAE, 35 rue Tronchet, F-75009 Paris, France.
Tel: (1) 42 65 50 16. Telex: 280 384 f alexplo.
Fax: (1) 42 65 24 87.

Anti-personnel stake mine M 61

Anti-personnel Mine M 59 (Mi APDV 59)

Description

The M 59 (Mi APDV 59), or Inkstand mine as it is also known, was developed as the replacement for the earlier Model 1951 anti-personnel mine. The case is made of plastic with the undetectable M 59 pressure friction fuze being inserted in the top of the mine. Attached to the mine is a metal detection plate which is removed before the mine is emplaced. A smoke model of this mine is available for training.

Specifications
Weight: 130 g
Diameter: 62 mm
Height: (with fuze) 55 mm
Main charge type: TNT
Weight of main charge: 56.7 g
Booster charge: Tetryl
Weight of booster charge: 17 g

Status
In production. In service with the French Army and other armies.

Manufacturer
ALSETEX SAE, 35 rue Tronchet, F-75009 Paris, France.
Tel: (1) 42 65 50 16. Telex: 280 384 f alexplo.
Fax: (1) 42 65 24 87.

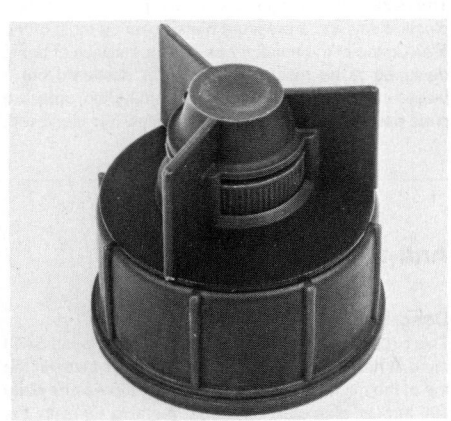

Anti-personnel mine M 59 (Mi APDV 59)

Anti-personnel Bounding Mine Model 1951/1955

Description
This mine consists of a cylindrical metal case which acts as a mortar, and a canister which contains the main charge, integral fuze, steel shrapnel, and is closed by a cap which contains the main, central and self-destruction fuze well plug.

The mine can be activated by a tilt of the rod or downward pressure on the rod when the mine is fitted with a tilt-rod fuze, or a pull on the tripwire when the mine is fitted with a pull fuze. This initiates the fuze and fires the delay train and the propelling charge. The expanding gases project the canister into the air. The canister has a cord attached to its lower end and when it reaches a height of 1.5 m (the full length of the cord),

it pulls out the retaining pin of the canister fuze. This releases the striker-retaining balls which escape and free the spring-driven striker. This initiates the firing chain which consists of a percussion cap, detonator and the main charge which hurls shrapnel in all directions up to a radius of 45 m.

Specifications
Weight: 4.49 kg
Diameter: 97 mm
Height: 158 mm
Main charge type: picric acid
Weight of main charge: 408 g
Operating force: 3 kg
Fuze: Model 1952 tilt-rod

Status
In service with the French Army.

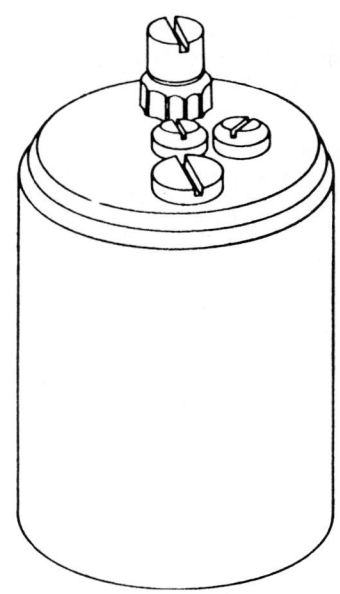

Anti-personnel bounding mine Model 1951/1955

Anti-personnel Mine Model 1951

Description
This non-metallic anti-personnel mine consists of a ribbed plastic case with an integral pressure-friction fuze mounted in the centre. The mine operates as follows: when pressure is applied to the top of the mine, the shear collar holding the firing pin fails. This pin is coated when with a friction compound and when its tapered end slides against the mating sleeve, a flame is produced. This ignites the detonator which sets off the main charge.

Specifications
Weight: 85 g
Diameter: 69 mm
Height: 50 mm
Main charge type: PETN
Weight of main charge: 51 g
Operating force: 14-24 kg

Status
In service with the French Army.

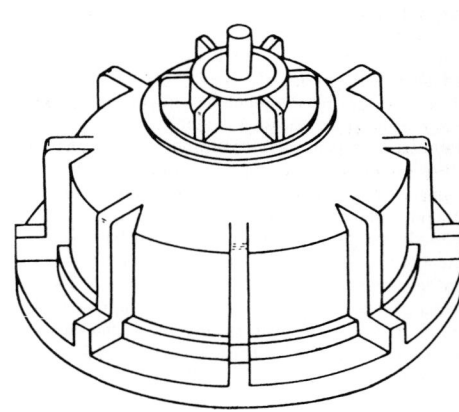

Anti-personnel mine Model 1951

Horizontal Action Anti-tank Mine Mle F1

Description
The Horizontal Action Anti-tank Mine (*mine antichar à action horizontale:* MIACAH F1) consists of a cylindrical drum pivot mounted on a circular frame. The drum, which has a carrying handle, contains a shaped charge which can penetrate 50 mm of armour at a range of 80 m with an angle of impact of 0°, or at a range of 40 m with a 30° angle of impact and can penetrate 70 mm of armour at a range of 40 m, with an angle of impact of 0°.

The mine is normally anchored to the ground, camouflaged and pointed across the tank's expected route. A wire is stretched out in line with the mine. When a tracked vehicle crosses this wire the mine operates and the shaped charge penetrates the side armour of the tank.

The mine can be initiated by sensor devices such as the IRMAH Mle F1 (see following entry) or the

ALSETEX SAE Programmable Igniter (see separate entry).

A training model of the mine is available. It is called the MIACAH d'Exercice Mle F1 (MIACAH X F1) and has the shaped charge replaced by an Alsetex MMI 30699 marking cartridge which has an effective range of 50 m. This is positioned in a similar manner to the real mine and when the tracked vehicle crosses the wire the cartridge marks the point of impact on the tank by the use of a marking sponge.

Specifications
Weight: 12 kg
Length: 260 mm
Diameter: 200 mm

Status
In production. In service with the British (the British mines were filled in the United Kingdom), French and other armed forces. The training mine MIACAH d'Exercice is in service with the British, French and other armies.

Horizontal action anti-tank exercise mine Mle F1

Manufacturer
Enquiries to Giat Industries, 13 route de la Minière, F-78034 Versailles Cedex, France.
Tel: 30 97 37 37. Fax: 30 97 39 00.

Horizontal Action Anti-tank Mine F1 with Infra-red Radiation Sensor IRMAH Mle F1

Description

This is a standard action anti-tank mine Mle F1 (MIACAH F1) fitted with an infra-red and acoustic sensor type IRMAH Mle F1 to improve the mine's performance in difficult terrain such as marsh, rocky ground and snow.

The sensor is attached to the main body of the mine and utilises the infra-red and acoustic emissions from the target vehicle to trigger the mine. It is capable of detecting targets up to 80 m away when travelling at speeds of between 5 and 60 km/h. A built-in programmer enables the mine to engage either the first, second or third target detected. It also has built-in immunity to countermeasures.

Specifications (IRMAH Type F1 sensor unit)

Weight: 1.35 kg
Length: 250 mm
Diameter: 80 mm
Power supply: from MIACAH mine
Detection range: 0-80 m for target moving at 5-60 km/h

Status

In production. In service with the French Army.

Manufacturer

Enquiries to Giat Industries, 13 route de la Minière, F-78034 Versailles Cedex, France.
Tel: 30 97 37 37. Fax: 30 97 39 00.

Horizontal action anti-tank mine Mle F1 with IRMAH infra-red radiation sensor

ALSETEX Mitral Scatterable Anti-tank Mine

Description

The ALSETEX Mitral scatterable anti-tank mine was designed to be distributed in a number of ways and is intended as a tank track destruction mine. It can be scattered from an aircraft or helicopter munitions dispenser, by a rocket or similar vehicle, or from a ground-based launcher.

The Mitral anti-tank mine is of the small bar type and has three sides so that at any one instant one face of the mine with its centrally located fuze is always pointing upwards. It has a clockwork igniter delay device that starts to operate as soon as the mine is released or fired. This device completes the alignment of the pyrotechnical chain after a given time, and the same device also self-destructs after a pre-arranged period.

The edges of the mine are provided with flexible shock dampers to soften the shock of landing. The mines can be scattered from an aircraft or helicopter munitions dispenser in clusters, and may even be dispensed individually from helicopters. Rockets could carry from 6 to 12 mines and ground-based launchers could fire the mines using a small explosive charge – these ground-based launchers could be static or mounted on a vehicle.

Specifications

Weight: 2.6 kg
Length: 300 mm
Edge: 100 mm

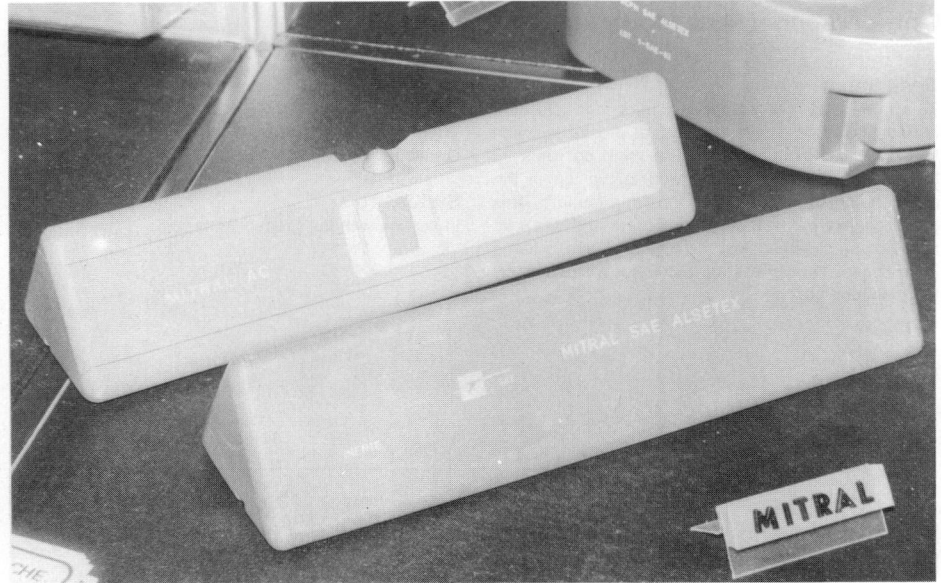

ALSETEX Mitral scatterable anti-tank mines

Type of charge: RDX based

Status

Development.

Manufacturer

ALSETEX SAE, 35 rue Tronchet, F-75009 Paris, France.
Tel: (1) 42 65 50 16. Telex: 280 384 f alexplo.
Fax: (1) 42 65 24 87.

HPD 1 Anti-tank Mine

Description

The HPD 1 anti-tank mine may be laid or buried manually or automatically by the Matenin mine burying system, details of which will be found in the *Minelaying equipment* section. The mine employs a modular design with the power supply in one section and the clearing and main charges in the other. A magnetic igniter activates the mine fuze when a tank passes overhead, that is under the belly or tracks of the tank. During trials the mine perforated 100 mm of belly armour and broke the tracks of a tank. The mine is normally buried so the first charge removes the earth covering the mine while the second charge, which is of the shaped type, ignites to inflict the main damage to the target.

The mine conforms to US specification MIL-STD-331.

Specifications

Weight: 7 kg
Length: 280 mm
Width: 185 mm
Height: 105 mm

Status

In production. In service with France and one NATO country.

Manufacturer

Thomson-TRT Défense, Ammunition Electronics Activity, 533 avenue du Général de Gaulle, F-92140 Clamart, France.
Tel: (1) 46 01 25 00. Fax: (1) 46 30 35 42.

HPD 1 anti-tank mine

HPD 2 Anti-tank Mine

Description

The HPD 2 anti-tank mine has been referred to as the HPD F2 and is a development of the original HPD. It is described as a second-generation high-power mine which can produce explosively formed fragments to penetrate tank belly armour up to 100 mm thick across the width of a tank.

The HPD 2 has been ordered by the French Army plus Belgium (contract worth $53 million), Norway and Switzerland. The Swiss contract is worth SF 342 million, with deliveries scheduled between 1991 and 1994.

Designed to be used with existing minelaying systems the HPD 2 consists of two modular sub-assemblies. One is the fuze section which contains the magnetic induction sensors, the laying safety, the self-neutralising system, the power supplies, a pyrotechnic safety, and the arming devices. The other section contains the clearing charge to blow away any covering earth or snow and the main shaped charge. It can be laid in up to 1.5 m of water and is highly resistant to mechanical, explosive and magnetic countermeasures. The self-neutralisation system is such that if the mine is not used during a preset length of time it can be lifted and re-used. The mine is provided with a visual self-neutralising indicator.

Specifications

Weight: 7 kg
Length: 280 mm
Width: 185 mm
Height: 105 mm
Temperature range: −35 to +63°C

Status

In production for Belgium, France, Norway and Switzerland.

Manufacturer

Thomson-TRT Défense, Ammunition Electronics Activity, 533 avenue du Général de Gaulle, F-92140 Clamart, France.
Tel: (1) 46 01 25 00. Fax: (1) 46 30 35 42.

HPD 2 anti-tank mine

Anti-tank Mine HPD-1A

Description

This mine was designed to be laid or buried by the mechanical laying devices of the HPD family. It is fitted with an influence fuze capable of operating across the width of vehicles weighing 8000 kg and above. When laid on the surface the mine is capable of penetrating 200 mm of armoured vehicle belly plate from a stand-off distance of 0.5 m. If it is buried under 150 mm of earth it can penetrate 50 mm of belly armour from the same stand-off distance. The HPD-1A can be fitted with an earth-clearing blasting charge which allows a buried mine to have the same perforating performance as a mine laid on the surface. It will also destroy tank tracks. Arming is initiated after a 10 minute delay and the mine can be set for self-neutralisation after one month.

Specifications

Weight: 7 kg
Length: 280 mm
Height: 103 mm
Width: 187 mm
Weight of main charge: 3.3 kg
Power supply: 2 rechargeable lithium batteries

Status

Development.

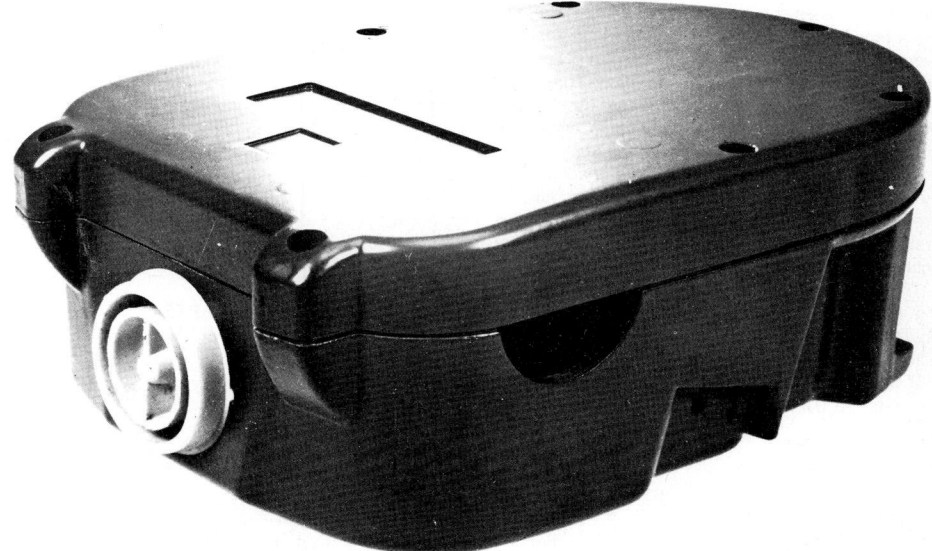

Anti-tank mine HPD-1A

Manufacturer

Centre de Bourges.
Enquiries to Giat Industries, 13 route de la Minière, F-78034 Versailles Cedex, France.
Tel: 30 97 37 37. Fax: 30 97 39 00.

ACPR Anti-tank Mine Type F2

Description

The ACPR (*antichar à pose rapide*) anti-tank mine Type F2 was designed to break the tracks or destroy the wheels of AFVs to obtain a mobility kill. The mine body is made from two resin-based half-casings and is fitted with a pressure plate that detonates the mine only when a tank, APC or heavy wheeled combat vehicle passes over it. The mine is undetectable and can be laid by a minelayer or buried manually. It is provided with a safety double fuze-train interrupter that remains active for 15 minutes after laying. It can be raised and re-used if necessary. A secondary fuze well is provided for an extra igniter or booby-trap system.

Specifications

Weight: 5.8 kg
Length: 280 mm
Height: 103 mm
Width: 188 mm
Weight of main charge: 5.8 kg

Status

In production.

Manufacturer

Société E Lacroix, BP 213, F-31601 Muret Cedex, France.
Tel: (33) 61 56 65 00. Telex: 531 478 f lacart.
Fax: (33) 61 51 42 77.

ACPR anti-tank mine Type F2

Anti-tank Pressure Mine ACPR

Description
The ACPR is a non-metallic thermoplastic anti-tank track mine designed for mechanical or manual laying. When the Matenin minelaying system is used this mine can be laid at a rate of up to 500 mines/hour. The mine is fitted with a safety arming timer which enables the mine to be laid or buried while it is inert. The device is two-way and allows the mine to be recovered for relaying if it is disarmed correctly. Detonation is by the application of pressure to the pressure plate on the upper face of the mine. This activates a percussion igniter which initiates the firing chain and detonates the main charge. A booby-trap well is also fitted.

It is claimed that the mine is virtually undetectable and can resist explosive mineclearing due to its anti-blast pressure plate. The mine has a dual security

Anti-tank track mine ACPR

delay for storage and emplacement (from 0 to 9 minutes), and the mine is recoverable and reusable due to the complete reversibility of the arming mechanism. No maintenance is necessary during the normal shelf life of the mine.

Specifications
Weight: 5.8 kg
Length: 280 mm
Width: 185 mm
Height: 105 mm
Weight of main charge: approx 4 kg

Status
In production. In service with the French Army and other armies.

Manufacturer
ALSETEX SAE, 35 rue Tronchet, F-75009 Paris, France.
Tel: (1) 42 65 50 16. Telex: 280 384 f alexplo.
Fax: (1) 42 65 24 87.

Anti-tank Shaped Charge Mine Models 1953 and 1954

Description
Both these mines consist of a light alloy tube containing a modified 73 mm Strim shaped charge anti-tank grenade. The mines are normally buried in the ground with the aid of a special boring tool. When buried in a hole 330 mm deep, with the mine covered by 50 mm of earth, and the belly of the tank 600 mm above the ground, the mine will penetrate 100 mm of armour.

The Model 1953 consists of a pair of grenades joined by a detonating cord and is operated as follows: pressure on the trigger mine or offset fuzing device fires the fuze and the detonating cord continues the firing chain to the two shaped charge grenades.

The Model 1954 consists of a single grenade with the tilt-rod mounted alongside the mine. The mine operates as follows: lateral pressure on the tilt-rod actuates the fuze which detonates the mine. To ensure that the tank is completely over the mine before it detonates, a 0.5 second delay is built into the firing chain.

Specifications
Model	1953	1954
Weight	1.9 kg	1.2 kg
Diameter of charge	73 mm	73 mm
Height	280 mm	280 mm
Weight of main charge	300 g	300 g

Status
Production complete. In service with the French Army.

Manufacturer
Luchaire Défense, 180 boulevard Haussmann, F-75008 Paris, France.
Tel: (1) 45 62 40 22. Telex: 650 312 f.

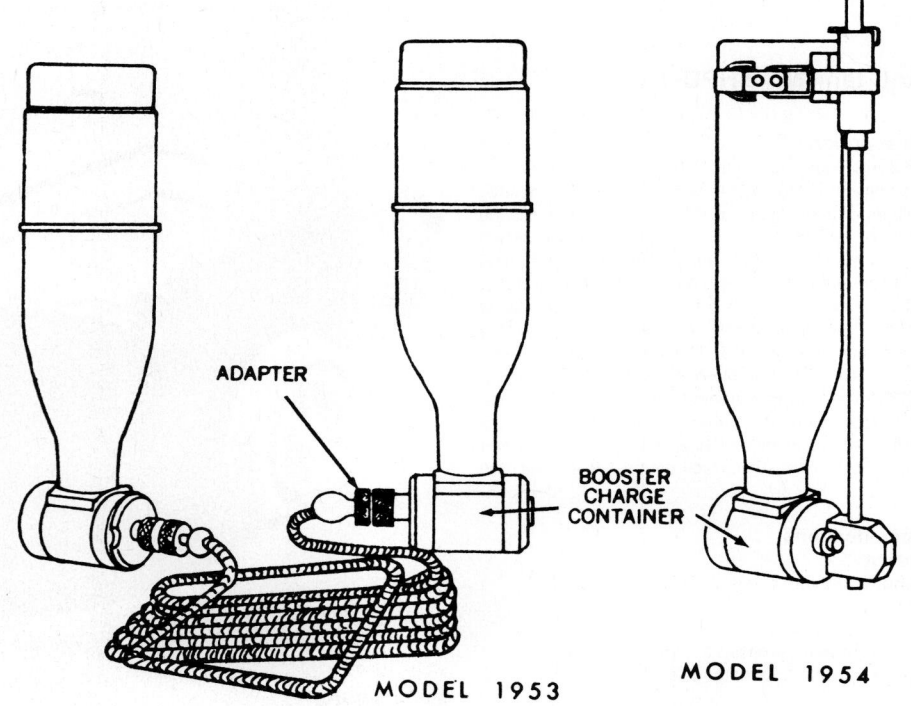

Anti-tank shaped charge mine Model 1953 complete with detonating cord and anti-tank shaped charge mine Model 1954

M 51 and M 52 MACI Anti-tank Mines

Description
The M 51 MACI (*mine antichar indétectable*) consists of three sections of cast TNT reinforced with glass wool, the pressure-plate section, the central core that holds the fuze and detonator, and an outer clamping ring which holds the first two sections together. The latter also contains the anti-lifting well and the carrying handle. There is a second anti-lifting well in the bottom of the mine. The mine can either be used to damage tank tracks or attack belly armour according to three selectable ignition modes:

1) When fitted with the M 61 pressure-friction fuze, housed in the fuze recess, the mine operates as follows: pressure on the top of the mine shears away the pressure plate and the plastic fuze collar fails; a plastic cone coated with a glass and phosphorous mixture is pressed into a plastic mating sleeve causing friction and flashes, thus initiating the firing chain to

ALSETEX anti-tank mines, from right, (A) M 51 MACI, (B) M 52 MACI, (C) M 51 MACI fitted with tentacle (or spider) lateral pressure fuze

detonate the mine.

2) The mine will detonate under belly armour when it is fitted with a tentacle, or spider, fuze. This is an electronic fuze that operates when two opposed tentacles are simultaneously squeezed or when direct pressure is applied to the fuze. This fuze has a delayed arming safety device for laying.

3) The mine may be used with a tilt-rod fuze which is activated by vertical or lateral pressure.

The M 52 MACI (*mine antichar indétectable*) consists of three sections of cast TNT reinforced with glass wool, with a carrying handle. The basic mine is similar in appearance to the M 51 MACI anti-tank mine and is detonated either by an M 61 pressure-friction fuze, a tentacle (spider) fuze, or a tilt-rod fuze.

For training purposes, smoke-producing models are available.

Specifications
Weight:
(M 51 MACI) 7 kg
(M 52 MACI) 9 kg
Diameter: 300 mm
Height:
(M 51 MACI) 95 mm
(M 52 MACI, less tilt-rod) 120 mm

Main charge type: cast TNT
Weight of main charge: 6.486 kg
Booster type charge: RDX
Weight of booster: 498 g
Operating force: 300 kg

Status
In production. In service with the French Army and other armies.

Manufacturer
ALSETEX SAE, 35 rue Tronchet, F-75009 Paris, France.
Tel: (1) 42 65 50 16. Telex: 280 384 f alexplo.
Fax: (1) 42 65 24 87.

APILAS Autonomous Off-route Mine

Description
The APILAS autonomous off-route mine can be produced in a range of anti-tank systems, all based on the use of a 112 mm shaped charge rocket. The rocket weighs 4.3 kg (of which 1.5 kg is explosive), is fired from a tube at 293 m/s and can penetrate over 720 mm of rolled homogenous armour.

APILAS is mounted on a three-legged tubular steel stand and, when folded, is manportable. It may be deployed in any terrain by one man in less than 5 minutes and can destroy all known armoured vehicle targets travelling at speeds up to 80 km/h.

APILAS may employ a range of four different target detection and firing systems. They are:

the British Aerospace Ajax sensor. For full details of this system refer to the Apajax entry in the International section

the PIAF (*piège à fibre optique*) ground-based optical fibre detection sensor from Luchaire. This system is alerted by an acoustic detector which can recognise the type of target to be attacked. PIAF can be pre-programmed to remain active for periods of 3, 6, 12, 24, 48, 72 or 96 hours

the 120 A sensor from ITS. This system uses one, two or three breakwires laid on the ground to form a barrier. The system can be programmed to remain active in one hour steps from 1 to 99 hours or 40 days

the APA sensor from ALSETEX/SERAT, using a single breakwire laid on the ground to fire the rocket. The APA system has variable active operational period options from 1 minute to 40 days.

All systems have engagement distances from 3 to 40 m, apart from the Ajax system which can engage

The range of APILAS autonomous off-route mines showing the four target detection and firing systems possible

targets from 3 to 150 m.

The APILAS mine is 1.1 m long and weighs between 12 and 15 kg, depending on the sensor system involved.

For training the rocket can be replaced by a sub-calibre barrel firing a 7.5 mm bullet with a trajectory similar to that of the rocket.

Status
Prototypes.

Manufacturer
Manurhin Défense, 13 route de la Minière, F-78034 Versailles Cedex, France.
Tel: 30 97 37 37. Fax: 30 97 39 00.

ALSETEX Programmable Igniter

Description
The ALSETEX Programmable Igniter is used for the electrical and mechanical ignition of various explosive devices, including mines. The igniter will actuate the device on receipt of signals from a range of sensor devices which can include tripwires, infra-red sensors, acoustic devices, and so on, or in a time programmed mode. The time programmes can be set in periods of from 0 to 96 hours, in one hour increments, or from 0 to 30 days, in one day increments. At the end of the pre-programmed period the igniter will either cause the explosive device to self-destruct or return to a safe condition; in the latter case the igniter and device can be recovered and re-used.

The igniter is contained inside a hermetically sealed case and can be used over a temperature range of from −40 to +63°C. Power is supplied by two lithium cells. The igniter may be used with tripwires up to 100 m long. An anti-lifting device is incorporated.

A version of this igniter intended for use with the off-route MIACAH F1 weighs 1 kg, is 70 mm high and has a diameter of 185 mm.

Status
Under evaluation by the French Army.

Manufacturer
ALSETEX SAE, 36 rue Tronchet, F-75009 Paris, France.
Tel: (1) 42 65 50 16. Telex: 280 384 f alexplo.
Fax: (1) 42 65 24 87.

The ALSETEX Programmable Igniter intended for use with the MIACAH F1 off-route mine

SISMA Detector

Description
The SISMA (*l'allumeur autonome à influences*) is a self-contained proximity detector used for detonating hollow charges, mines and adapted charges. The simultaneous presence of a seismic and magnetic influence causes the detonator to fire. It is effective against both tracked and wheeled vehicles weighing over 8000 kg and within a speed range of 2 to 90 km/h. The vehicle does not have to come into contact with the mine to ensure detonation.

A self-neutralising device is fitted which is programmable to 3, 8 or 15 days. When it is activated the pyrotechnic actuator, attached to the detonator body by a red and white cord, is ejected.

Specifications
Weight: 350 g
Dimensions: 110 × 83 × 25 mm
Arming delay: 5 min

Status
Under evaluation.

Manufacturer
Giat Industries, 13 route de la Minière, F-78034 Versailles Cedex, France.
Tel: 30 97 37 37. Fax: 30 97 39 00.

SISMA detector

GERMANY

PPM-2 Anti-personnel Mine

Description
The PPM-2 anti-personnel mine has a circular plastic body and uses a piezoelectric fuzing system. The mine can be carried slung from a belt by an integral clip. The safety is a steel pin inserted through the sealing ring which separates the upper and lower halves of the mine body and the pin also holds out a spring-loaded plate while at the same time mechanically holding a connector strip from a connector block. Only when the spring is withdrawn can an electrical path be formed from a piezoelectric plunger to the igniter.

Normally pressure on the top of the mine will shear a thin plastic collar and depress a plunger, creating a piezoelectric voltage to ignite the mine via a nitropenta and trinitrotuol igniter chain. If the safety pin is still inserted and the connecter strip somehow makes contact with the connector block and a voltage is produced, that voltage will pass harmlessly through the low resistance steel pin rather than through the connector strip which is made of metal-impregnated plastic with a relatively high resistance. Only when the pin is withdrawn and pressure on the mine plate creates the piezoelectric effect will the resultant voltage pass through the metal-impregnated strip as there is no other path for it to follow.

Specifications
Weight: 371 g
Body diameter: 124.5 mm
Max width: 140.8 mm
Height: 62 mm
Type of main charge: TNT
Weight of main charge: 110 g
Weight of primer and secondary charge: 0.65 g
Main charge diameter: 76.5 mm
Main charge height: 20.5 mm

Status
In service with the German Army and some other nations. Has been encountered in South Africa.

Manufacturer
Former East German state factories.

PPM-2 anti-personnel mine with safety pin in place

PM-60 (or K-1) Anti-tank Mine

Description
Developed in 1958, the PM-60 (or K-1) plastic anti-tank mine has a two-part circular body with two fuze wells. The body contains the pressure plate (on top), filler shield, filler seal, spacer, booster assembly, detonator and fuze. The fuze is threaded into the booster assembly. The detonator is installed in the booster well cap, below the fuze, and is contained by a closing plug. Two models of the PM-60 are known to be in service, one with a mechanical fuze which has a small number of metal components, and a second with a chemical fuze. Both have a bottom fuze for booby-trapping and can be laid by hand or mechanically. The mine is operated as follows: pressure applied to the pressure plate is transmitted to the fuze, driving the firing pin into

PM-60 anti-tank mine

the primer which initiates the detonator-booster main charge firing chain and ignites the mine. If required, a blasting cap and firing device may be installed in the booby-trap well in the base of the mine, which initiates the secondary booster and main charge.

Specifications
Weight: 11.35 kg
Diameter: 320 mm
Height: 117 mm
Main charge type: TNT
Weight of main charge: 7.5 kg
Booster charge: Tetrol
Weight of booster: 499 g
Operating force: 200-500 kg

Status
In service with numerous armed forces.

Manufacturer
Former East German state factories.

Dynamit Nobel DYNAMINE Family of Mines

Development
The DYNAMINE family of mines is a private development by Dynamit Nobel AG to produce a range of mines based on the technology used for the AT2 anti-tank mine described in a separate entry in this section. In addition to the basic AT2, which is part of the family, there are a further four mines as described later.

All variants in the DYNAMINE family are capable of being laid or scattered by the MLRS or LARS rocket systems, the Skorpion minelaying system, helicopters or manually.

Description
The DYNAMINE family of mines is based on, and includes, the AT2 anti-tank mine (for full details see separate entry in this section) and shares the same handling, shipping and storage safeties and a 10-year shelf life. All the mines have a body diameter of 103.5 mm and weigh between 2.2 and 2.7 kg. Details of the different mines are as follows:

Anti-personnel Mine AP2
The warhead of the AP2 consists of a fragmentation casing lined internally with heavy metal balls. After emplacement and orientation the mine ejects three tripwires, each with a length of approximately 13 m, which will activate the mine on tension. The radius of penetration of 1.5 mm steel with more than 2 fragments/m² is more than 20 m.

Anti-materiel (AM) mine
The warhead of this mine is basically the same as the AP2 anti-personnel mine but the casing forms larger projectiles that are explosively formed to spread laterally at high velocity to produce a high degree of penetration against light armour to a range of approximately 100 m (where projectile fragments are able to penetrate 20 mm of mild steel). The AT2 shaped charge is retained and detonation will also result in a large number of fragments with anti-personnel effects. The mine is activated by the S3 sensor of the AT2 mine.

Signal mine (S-mine)
These mines may be emplaced either individually or in a mix with other types. When the noise of approaching enemy units is detected and filtered by acoustic sensors the mine is activated. A rocket motor then lifts

AP2 anti-personnel mine variant of DYNAMINE

the mine vertically to release the transmission antenna and transmit coded signals on a pre-programmed frequency.

Shallow water mine (SW-mine)
Intended for the protection of shore lines and shallow water, the shallow water mine has a flotation air bag which replaces the shaped charge cover and parachute of the basic AT2 mine and there is no erection mechanism. The shaped charge is retained to make the mine effective against landing craft and amphibious vehicles.

Status
All versions at various development stages.

Manufacturer
Dynamit Nobel AG, Defence Technology Division, D-5210 Troisdorf, Federal Republic of Germany. Tel: 2241 89-0. Telex: 885 666 dn d. Fax: 2241 89 1669.

Anti-personnel Mine DM 11

Description
The only information available on this mine is that it is circular and has a pressure fuze. A practice version of the mine, designated anti-personnel DM 18 practice mine, is also available.

Specifications
Weight: 200 g
Diameter: 81 mm
Height: 37 mm

Type of main charge: RDX/TNT
Weight of main charge: 114 g
Operating force: 5-10 kg

Status
Production complete. In service with the German Army.

Manufacturer
DIEHL Ordnance Division, Fischbachstrasse 16, D-8505 Röthenbach, Federal Republic of Germany. Tel: 911 509 2948. Telex: 622591-44. Fax: 911 509 2870.

Anti-personnel mine DM 11 with transport cover removed

Anti-tank Mine DM 11

Description
This circular anti-tank mine is very similar in appearance to the French M 51 MACI anti-tank mine and is made entirely of explosives mixed with five per cent polyester resin for added strength. The DM 46 plastic fuze is in the centre of the mine and is of the pressure friction type. There is also an anti-lifting well in the side of the mine.

The training version of the DM 11 is known as the DM 30 with a smoke charge practice version known as the DM 18A1.

Specifications
Weight: 7.4 kg
Diameter: 300 mm
Height: 95 mm
Main charge type: TNT
Weight of main charge: 7 kg
Booster charge type: RDX
Booster charge weight: 500 g
Operating force: 150-400 kg

Status
Production complete. In service with the German Army.

Anti-tank mine DM 11

Anti-tank Mine DM 21

Description
The anti-tank mine DM 21 is a circular metallic mine that can be laid manually and is effective against tracked and wheeled vehicles. The mine is equipped with a webbing carrying strap on one side and the main fuze well is central, containing a DM 1001 mechanical pressure fuze. The main body is sealed to the extent that the mine can remain under water for up to three months. After arming the mine is actuated only after a delay of 5 minutes.

Specifications
Weight: 9.2 kg
Diameter: 300 mm
Height: 100 mm
Weight of main charge: 4.8 kg

Status
Production complete. In service with the German Army.

Manufacturer
DIEHL Ordnance Division, Fischbachstrasse 16, D-8505 Röthenbach, Federal Republic of Germany. Tel: 911 509 2948. Telex: 622591-44. Fax: 911 509 2870.

Anti-tank mine DM 21

PARM DM 12 Off-route Anti-tank Mine

Description
The PARM (*Panzerabwehr-Richtmine*) is primarily intended for use as an off-route anti-tank mine. It was developed and qualified in accordance with US MIL-STD-331A. The mine body is situated on a small tripod allowing the warhead to be aimed through 360° and to an elevation of +90 and -45°. The main components

include a fin-guided warhead with a highly sophisticated shaped charge, a launching system and a fibre optic sensor cable connected to electronic logic circuitry. The weapon is effective at ranges from 2 to 40 m and laying and aiming of the mine are manual. Initial velocity of the warhead is 120 m/s and its penetration capability is more than 600 mm of armoured steel.

The PARM is armed after a delay of 5 minutes and can remain operational for up to 40 days. Power for the circuitry is provided by a lithium battery with a shelf life

of 10 years.

As an alternative to the fibre optic sensor cable, the PARM may be used with an active infra-red sensor known as the Active Relief Sensor (ARES) – when this sensor is used the effective range of PARM is increased to 100 m. The ARES operates in two modes, rest and wake. An acoustic warning sensor activates the transition from rest to wake after which a four-channel infra-red and optical firing sensor locks onto the target. Data signals are then processed and the mine is fired at the optimum instant. The mine may be

PARM off-route anti-tank mine in firing position

fired remotely if required.

Service testing and service qualification occupied from March 1983 to March 1988. The PARM was authorised for introduction into the German Army in June 1988. In October 1990 it was announced that the German Army is to receive 50 000 PARMs with delivery of the first batch of 25 000 taking place between 1991 and 1994. The second batch involves an option to be executed not later than March 31, 1993. The batches were worth DM 104.4 million and DM 101.9 million respectively.

The PARM is marketed in the United States as the Sensored Tactical Off-Road Mine (STORM) by Conventional Munitions Systems Incorporated, of Tampa, Florida.

Specifications
Warhead diameter: 132 mm
Warhead calibre: 128 mm
Weight: (total) 10 kg
Weight of charge: 1.4 kg
Length: 640 mm
Height: (armed in firing position) 391 mm
Elevation: −45 to +90°
Traverse: 360°
Range:
   (optical tape sensor) 2-40 m
   (ARES sensor) 5-100 m
Operational life: 40 days
Operating temperature: −40 to +65°C

Status
In production for German Army − see text.

Manufacturer
Messerschmitt-Bölkow-Blohm   GmbH,   Defence Systems Group, PO Box 801149, D-8000 Munich 80, Federal Republic of Germany.
Tel: 49 89 607 28451. Fax: 49 89 607 28727.

Panzerfaust 3 Off-route Mine with SIRA

Description
By placing a standard Panzerfaust 3 shoulder-launched anti-tank rocket launcher onto a tripod and coupling it to a SIRA sensor system the weapon can be converted into an unattended off-route anti-tank mine. The SIRA is fitted to the weapon by means of the dovetail which normally accepts the Panzerfaust firing device.

The SIRA (sensor infra-red acoustic), produced by Alliant Techsystems, automatically fires the 110 mm Panzerfaust 3 warhead with accuracy. Targets approaching the surveillance area of the off-route mine will cause acoustic activation of the infra-red sensor. Once activated the infra-red sensor is used to precisely determine the target position by evaluation of the speed, direction of motion, temperature and distance parameters. Evaluation of the signals and system control is performed by a microprocessor. The Panzerfaust 3 110 mm warhead can penetrate over 700 mm of rolled homogenous armour. Effective range is up to 150 m.

The sensor system has all-weather and day and night capability. The multi-sensor principle provides for a high degree of functional reliability. Background noise and countermeasures such as decoys or flares will be rejected by a sophisticated algorithm especially developed for these purposes. Special processor functions include programmable target counting and direction of motion discrimination.

Specifications
Target speed range: 30 to 60 km/h
Effective range: up to 150 m
Sensor dimensions: 100 × 150 mm
Operational life: up to 40 days
Power supply: 2 × 3.4 V lithium cells
IR sensor: passive, two-colour sensitive
IR optics: double parabolic off axis
Acoustics sensor: capacitive microphone
Processor: 8-bit CMOS

Status
Advanced development.

Manufacturer
Dynamit Nobel AG, Defence Technology Division, D-5210 Troisdorf, Federal Republic of Germany.
Tel: 2241 89-0. Telex: 885 666 dn d.
Fax: 2241 89 1669.

SIRA sensor fitted to Panzerfaust 3

AT2 Anti-tank Mine

Development
The AT2 (DM 1233) anti-tank mine has been in production since 1980, originally for use with the German 110 mm Light Artillery Rocket System (LARS − for full details see *Jane's Armour and Artillery 1992-93* pages 722 and 723). The AT2 was further developed for use in the scatterable anti-tank mine rockets fired by the LTV 227 mm Multiple Launch Rocket System (MLRS − *Jane's Armour and Artillery 1992-93* pages 723 to 727). The mine is also used with the German Skorpion minelaying system (see entry in *Minelaying equipment* section). In addition the AT2 is used as the basis for the private venture DYNAMINE family of mines by Dynamit Nobel AG.

With LARS the AT2 has been known as the AT2 Medusa. Production of AT2 for LARS ceased during 1985 after 300 000 DM 1233 mines had been produced.

Production of 640 000 AT2s (DM 1274), packed into 20-round magazines (with four tubes of five mines each) for the Skorpion minelaying system, is continuing. During 1992 production commenced of approximately 350 000 AT2 mines (DM 1399) for MLRS (for Germany and the United Kingdom).

Description
The AT2 has two main subassemblies, the warhead and the safe and arm assembly.

The warhead comprises a parachute that is used when the mine is used with LARS or MLRS and reduces impact with the ground; a warhead case to protect the shaped charge against damage; a cover to protect the stand-off above the shaped charge; the S3 target sensor which causes the mine to detonate with an appropriate delay when any part of a target vehicle contacts it; and the shaped charge which produces an optimised behind armour effect.

The safe and arm (S & A) assembly housing accommodates and protects the complete assembly comprising the electronic elements, the mechanical elements and the power supply. There is also an erection mechanism that orientates the mine in its operational position, an electronic fuze assembly to control the functional process and evaluate the sensor signals, and the mechanical fuze assembly. The sensors pass on signals to the electronic fuze assembly if there is an attempt to handle or move the mine or if a vehicle passes over the mine. Power is derived from a battery which is activated by a pyrotechnic element just before the mine is emplaced.

The AT2 is effective across the full width of a target vehicle and can be set for six different self-destruct times. An anti-handling device prevents the mine from being lifted and it is resistant to rapid clearing means such as line charges or other explosives. The mine is not affected by electromagnetic radiation or pulses.

For manual laying AT2 mines can be delivered packed in shipping containers each holding five mines and weighing 12 kg. The five mines can be emplaced manually in 1 minute.

The AT2 has a shelf life of 10 years.

Specifications
Weight: 2.22 to 2.25 kg, depending on version
Diameter: 103.5 mm
Height: (without sensor) 128 mm
Penetration: (against rolled homogenous armour) up to 140 mm

Status
In production. In service with the German Army and under consideration by several NATO nations.

Manufacturer
Dynamit Nobel AG, Defence Technology Division, D-5210 Troisdorf, Federal Republic of Germany.
Tel: 2241 89-0. Telex: 885 666 dn d.
Fax: 2241 89 1669.

AT2 anti-tank mine as used in Light Artillery Rocket System (LARS) and (without the parachute) Skorpion

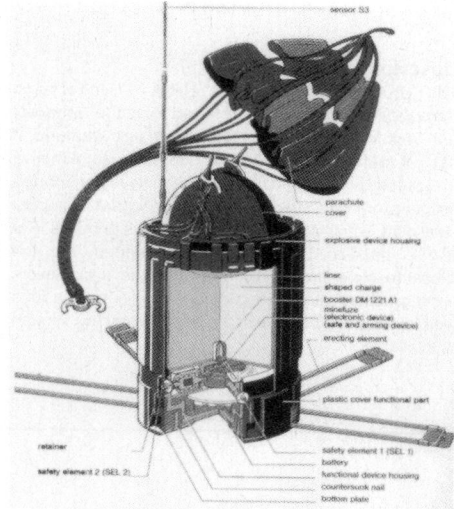

AT2 anti-tank mine (DM 1399) for Multiple Launch Rocket System (MLRS) showing main components

HUNGARY

Gyata-64 Anti-personnel Mine

Description
The Gyata-64 is a small, non-metallic, anti-personnel mine which uses approximately 0.4 kg of explosive packed into a dark brown phenolic moulding covered with a black rubber shroud. The main charge is two blocks of cast TNT.

Specifications
Weight: 0.45 kg
Diameter: 106 mm
Height: 61 mm
Type of charge: cast TNT

Status
In service with the Hungarian Army.

Manufacturer
Hungarian state factories.

Gyata-64 anti-personnel mine

M62 Anti-personnel Mine

Description
The M62 plastic anti-personnel mine is similar in size to the Hungarian M49 wooden anti-personnel mine and has the same amount of explosive. The mine has the following metal components: pivot pin, safety pin, fuze and striker pin, striker spring and detent. The mine operates as follows: when pressure is applied, the lid pivots about the hinged end and the free end of the lid pushes the winged pin down, out of the firing pin. When the winged pin is removed, the firing pin is driven forwards, striking the primer and detonating the mine.

Specifications
Weight: 318 g
Length: 187 mm
Width: 50 mm
Height: 65 mm
Main charge type: TNT
Weight of main charge: 75 g
Operating force: 1.5-4.5 kg

Status
In service with the Hungarian Army.

Manufacturer
Hungarian state factories.

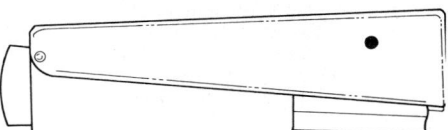

M62 plastic anti-personnel mine

M49 Wooden Anti-personnel Mine

Description
The M49 wooden anti-personnel mine is similar to the CIS PMD-7ts anti-tank mine, but is longer and made in two halves with the top half fitting over the lower and the fuze projecting through at one end. Activation is by a tripwire that triggers a pull fuze. The pull required is only 1 kg.

Specifications
Weight: 0.33 kg
Length: 185 mm
Width: 50 mm
Height: 58 mm
Main charge type: TNT
Weight of main charge: 75 g
Operating force: 1 kg

Status
In service with the Hungarian Army.

Manufacturer
Hungarian state factories.

UKA-63 Anti-tank Mine

Description

The UKA-63 anti-tank mine (UKA – *Universzalis Kumulativ Akna*) has been referred to as the Universal anti-tank mine and uses a shaped charge warhead. It has a metal body and can operate with either a pressure fuze or a tilt-rod fuze. The mine is transported with a protective steel band secured under the pressure plate which operates on the bellows principle. For use a bakelite EBG-68 fuze is inserted into the pressure plate fuze well. This fuze has a clockwork arming action with a tilting detonator. There is a fuze well for an anti-lift device in the base. A training version is available.

Specifications
Diameter: 298 mm
Overall height: 120 mm
Height without fuze: 105 mm
Fuze: EBG-68

Status
Production probably complete. In service with the Hungarian Army and has been encountered in southern Africa.

Manufacturer
Hungarian state factories.

UKA-63 anti-tank mine

INDIA

Indian Anti-personnel Mines

Description
The Indian Ordnance Factories produce two types of anti-personnel mine, both based on US designs. One is the Mine Anti-personnel Non-metallic M14 (AP NM M14), a pressure mine, and the other the Mine AP M16A1, a bounding mine. The latter is fitted with the Fuze Mine Combination M605 while the M14 has an integral fuze. Both mines differ from the US originals only in detail but the data taken from Indian sources and provided in the table below do differ from US data in some respects.

Specifications

Model	M16A1	M14
Weight	3.57 kg	100 g
Diameter	103 mm	50 mm
Height	203 mm	43 mm
Weight of charge	n/a	28.4 g
Type of charge	TNT	tetryl

Status
In production. In service with the Indian armed forces.

Manufacturer
Ordnance Factory Board, 10-A Auckland Road, Calcutta 700 001, India.
Enquiries to Director (Exports), Department of Defence Production & Supplies, Ministry of Defence, New Delhi 110 011, India.
Tel: 011 3012703. Telex: 031 2379 MOD IN.

Indian Ordnance Factories Mine AP M16A1

Indian Ordnance Factories Mine Anti-personnel Non-metallic M14

Mine Anti-tank Non-detectable 1A

Description
The Mine Anti-tank Non-detectable 1A is made of plastic apart from the striker pin, striker spring, safety clip and detonator holder. The striker pin is made of stainless steel and the detonator holder of brass but the amounts used are stated to be insufficient to be detected by conventional mine detectors. The main charge is TNT and the fuze can be fitted either in the crown of the mine or under the base. Rotating the pressure plate on the crown arms the mine. If the mine is not armed the mine will not detonate even when a heavy tank passes over the mine. The fuze is stated to be blastproof and will not be actuated by explosive clearing systems or artillery fire. The fuze is actuated by a pressure of between 172 and 244 kg.

The mine has a shelf life of 30 years while the fuze has a shelf life of 10 years.

A training version is available.

Specifications
Weight: 7.3 kg
Diameter: 280 mm
Height: 152 mm
Main charge type: TNT

Indian Ordnance Factories Mine Anti-tank Non-detectable 1A

Weight of main charge: 6.75 kg
Operating force: 172-244kg

Status
In production. In service with the Indian armed forces.

Manufacturer
Ordnance Factory Board, 10-A Auckland Road, Calcutta 700 001, India.
Enquiries to Director (Exports), Department of Defence Production & Supplies, Ministry of Defence, New Delhi

110 011, India.
Tel: 011 3012703. Telex: 031 2379 MOD IN.

Mine Anti-tank Non-detectable 3A

Description
The Mine Anti-tank 3A Non-detectable (ND) is a copy of the British Bar Mine (see separate entry in this section) and differs from it in few respects although the details provided in the Specifications table do differ in detail. The mine operates in exactly the same way as the Bar Mine and is laid using a very similar mechanical minelaying system.

Specifications
Weight with fuze: 11 kg
Length overall: 1.21 m
Height: 80 mm
Weight of main charge: 8 kg

Status
In production. Understood to be in service with the Indian Army.

Manufacturer
Ordnance Factory Board, 10-A Auckland Road, Calcutta 700 001, India.
Enquiries to Director (Exports), Department of Defence Production & Supplies, Ministry of Defence, New Delhi 110 011, India.
Tel: 011 3012703. Telex: 031 2379 MOD IN.

INTERNATIONAL

ARGES

Development/Description
ARGES (Automatic Rocket Guardian with Electronic Sensor) is being developed by an international consortium to meet an Anglo/French/German requirement for an Aimed Controlled Effect Anti-tank Mine (ACEATM) or, in French, Mine Antichar Pointable à Effet Dirige (MACPED). ARGES is an autonomous off-route mine capable of defeating enemy armour out to a range of 100 m under any weather conditions.

The ARGES mine consists of a target detection and firing system, an anti-tank rocket and a tripod-mounted launch tube. The system is activated by an acoustic alerter and a target selection system. Firing is triggered by passive and active infra-red detection. The rocket is fitted with a tandem warhead capable of penetrating the sides of and destroying all main battle tanks. ARGES is programmable with an active period of between 3 hours and 40 days, a target counter from 1 to 3, and a secure access code. The mine is redeployable and can be re-programmed and relaid up to five times. The mine weighs 15 kg, is 1.02 m long and can be set up by one man within 5 minutes. The mine is being designed to allow the later addition of a remote-control unit.

A fixed-price development contract worth $25.8 million was awarded by the Direction des Armement Terrestres (DAT) in February 1991. The winning consortium is led by Giat Industries of France and includes Hunting Engineering Limited of the United Kingdom and Dynamit Nobel and Honeywell Regel-systeme of Germany. Project definition has been completed and full scale development began in May 1992 with planned completion in 1994. The eventual production contract could be worth more than $400 million.

Giat Industries is responsible for project management and overall integration of the system. The main rear warhead is believed to be a development of the

The ARGES off-route mine selected for further development for the ACEATM programme

Panzerfaust 3 warhead and is being designed by Dynamit Nobel. The front warhead and the tandem warhead integration are the responsibility of Hunting Engineering Limited who is also developing the launch tube and the tripod. The projectile's rocket motor is believed to derive from that developed by Royal

Ordnance for Hunting Engineering Limited's LAW 80 anti-tank weapon. Honeywell Regelsysteme is responsible for the sensor.

Status
Full scale development.

Apajax Aimed Controlled Effect Anti-tank System
Ajax Off-route Anti-tank Mine Sensor System

Development
The Ajax off-route anti-tank mine sensor system was developed by British Aerospace Systems and Equipment (Plymouth), using sensor experience amassed since 1972. An early version of Ajax was used with the LAWMINE off-route anti-tank mine project, cancelled in 1986.

During 1987 Ajax was demonstrated with the French APILAS anti-tank weapon system in a combination known as Apajax. British Aerospace combined with French and German concerns to produce Apajax, a submission for the NATO requirement for an Aimed

Controlled Effect Anti-tank Mine (ACEATM). British Aerospace produces the Ajax sensor, Manurhin Défense produces the rocket, launcher and mounting, Rheinmetall produces the warhead while SERAT remains the APILAS design authority.

Development began in 1979 and the first development stage was completed during 1987. By November 1988 Apajax was in the final development stage.

Ajax has been demonstrated coupled to an AT4 anti-tank rocket launcher and with the LAW 80.

Description
The Ajax sensor is a passive infra-red system consisting of an acoustic and seismic alerting system, an array of passive infra-red sensors and a microprocessor. The single power source is a battery which is installed as the weapon is deployed. The system is intended for use against MBTs and heavily armoured vehicles when moving at speeds of between 3 and

80 km/h across the line of fire.

The Ajax system engages targets travelling at any angle between 45 and 135° from the line of fire. Minimum target engagement distance is 5 m and the maximum 200 m. The active life of the sensor is up to 40 days and may be programmed by the operator at the time of emplacement.

On deployment the following options can be programmed into the sensor: target distance (if known); target selection in a column of vehicles; anti-handling system (if required); and choice of attack direction – right, left or both.

Setting up time for the Apajax takes 5 minutes during daylight and 10 minutes at night. The full deployment sequence includes unfolding the tripod support legs, adjusting the rear legs for slope and elevation, installing the battery and choosing the programmable functions using the sensor keypad. The system will then arm after 10 minutes.

The APILAS weapon used with Apajax has a calibre of 112 mm and the rocket weighs 4.3 kg, of which 1.5 kg is explosive. At 21°C the muzzle velocity is 293 m/s and the warhead penetration is in excess of 720 mm of rolled homogenous armour.

The complete weight of Apajax is 12 kg and it is 1.1 m long. There are three main subassemblies; the firing unit, the rocket and the Ajax sensor system. The firing unit is mounted on a tripod with the folding front leg designed to protect the sensor unit when folded. The two rear legs can be swivelled and adjusted in height for correction of elevation and slope. A sight is fitted. The firing unit is connected to the Ajax sensor system by wires housed in the tube.

A special training launcher is available. This is a standard Apajax except for the rocket which is replaced by a laser projector fitted inside the tube.

Status
Pre-production.

Manufacturers
Ajax
British Aerospace, Systems and Equipment, Clittaford Road, Southway, Plymouth, Devon PL6 6DE, UK.
Tel: 0752 707951. Telex: 45564.
Fax: 0752 707951.
APILAS
Manurhin Défense, 13 route de la Minière, F-78034 Versailles Cedex, France.
Tel: 30 97 37 37. Fax: 30 97 39 00.

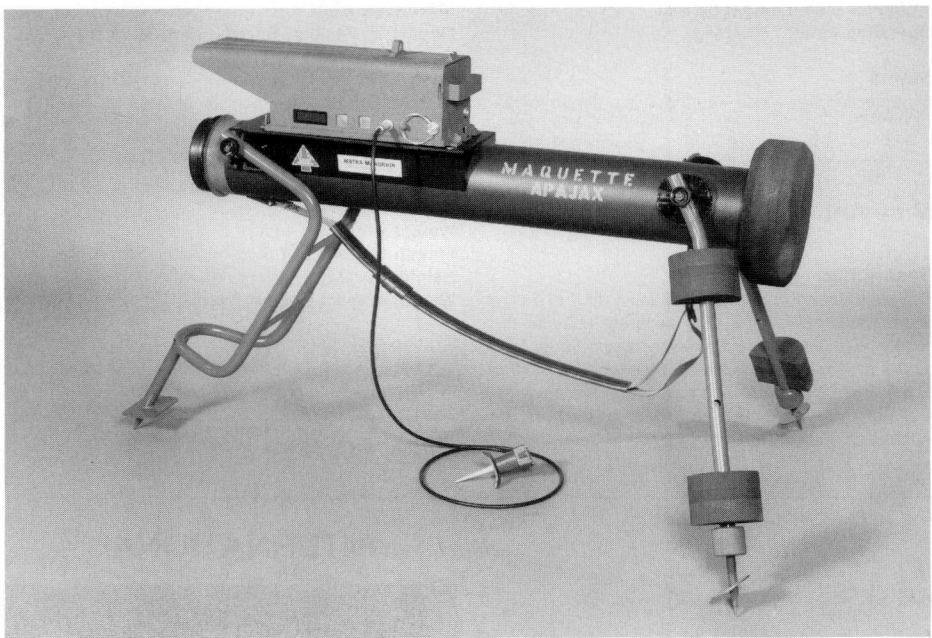

Ajax sensor mounted on Apajax off-route anti-tank mine

ATIS Anti-tank Mine

Description
The Italian Army has a requirement for a new generation buried anti-tank mine. In response to this requirement Ferranti Instrumentation Limited and Tecnovar Italiana SpA are proposing the Anti-Tank Influence Sensor (ATIS).

The ATIS uses Ferranti 'I2F' intelligent influence fuze technology and may be surface-laid or buried. After being alerted by an acoustic sensor, the ATIS fuze uses electronic intelligence to determine the speed of an approaching tank target. Advanced signal processing of the received sensor information establishes the vehicle's front edge, and with the known target speed, the firing command is initiated to detonate the mine under the centre portion of the target. The mine uses a dual shaped charge warhead capable of penetrating 150 mm of armour. Anti-handling devices are incorporated and a short-range remote-control can be fitted. Mine weight is 5.5 kg.

Status
Development.

Manufacturers
Tecnovar Italiana SpA, 95 Via Argiro, I-70121 Bari, Italy.
Tel: 080 5211744. Telex: 810345 tecvar i.
Fax: 370400.
Ferranti Instrumentation Limited, Weapons Equipment Division, St Mary's Road, Moston, Manchester M10 0BE, UK.
Tel: 061 681 2071. Telex: 667857.
Fax: 061 682 2500.

ATIS anti-tank mine

ISRAEL

No 4 Anti-personnel Mine

Description
This is a rectangular plastic anti-personnel 'shoe' mine fitted with a hinged cover. It is activated by an 8 kg force on a pressure plate. The mine's firing device is produced with a delayed arming device to prevent accidental actuation.

Specifications
Weight: 350 g
Length:
  (armed) 160 mm
  (unarmed) 135 mm
Width: 70 mm
Height: 55 mm
Main charge type: TNT
Weight of main charge: 180 g
Weight of booster charge: 22 g
Operating force: (nominal) 8 kg

Status
In service with the Israeli Army and some other countries, including Argentina.

Manufacturer
Explosive Industries Limited, PO Box 1363, Tel Aviv, Israel.
Tel: 03 5243077. Fax: 03 5243051.

No 4 anti-personnel mine

No 10 Anti-personnel Mine

Description
This is a circular plastic anti-personnel mine that can be laid on the ground or easily buried. It is armed by removing a safety cap and fitting a pressure fuze assembly, which is activated by a 15 to 35 kg force being applied to a pressure plate.

Specifications
Weight: 120 g
Diameter: 70 mm
Height: 75 mm
Main charge type: TNT
Weight of main charge: 50 g
Fuze type: pressure
Operating force: 15-35 kg

Status
Production complete. In service with the Israeli Army.

Manufacturer
TAAS – Israel Industries Ltd, POB 1044, Ramat Hasharon 47100, Israel.
Tel: (3) 542 52 22. Telex: 33 719 misbit il.
Fax: (3) 48 96 39.

No 12 (or M12A1) Anti-personnel Mine

Description
This is a picket-mounted tripwire-actuated bounding anti-personnel mine made of metal. The ignition assembly is a three-anchor pull, pressure or push unit with a built-in 4.5 second delay. Once triggered a small propellant charge causes the main mine body to bound about 1 m into the air where it explodes. The filling is 260 g of TNT and a number of cast-steel ball-bearings to cause fragmentation, the effective radius of which is about 40 m.

Specifications
Weight: 3.5 kg
Diameter: 102 mm
Height:
  (fuzed) 240 mm
  (packed) 159 mm
Main charge type: TNT
Weight of main charge: 260 g

Status
In service with the Israeli Army.

Manufacturer
TAAS – Israel Industries Ltd, POB 1044, Ramat Hasharon 47100, Israel.
Tel: (3) 542 52 22. Telex: 33 719 misbit il.
Fax: (3) 48 96 39.

No 12 (or M12A1) anti-personnel mine

No 6 Anti-tank Mine

Description
During the various Middle East conflicts the Israeli armed forces captured so many ex-Soviet TM-46 anti-tank mines that the type was taken into Israeli service as standard. The TM-46 was copied direct to produce the Israeli No 6 anti-tank mine. The No 6 has also been exported. It was one of the anti-tank mines encountered by the British armed forces in the Falkland Islands.

The No 6 mine may be fitted with the mechanical pressure fuze No 61 or the tilt-rod fuze No 62A. The latter is proof against demolition charge shockwaves and has a well-thread matched to that of the American M15 mine series. The No 62A fuze weighs 0.5 kg and is 200 mm high; activating force is 180-200 kg.

Specifications
Weight: 9 kg
Diameter: 305 mm
Height: 110 mm
Main charge type: TNT
Weight of main charge: 6 kg
Weight of booster charge: 45 g
Operating force: approx 300 kg

Status
In service with the Israeli Army, Argentina, and some other nations.

Manufacturer
Explosive Industries Limited, PO Box 1363, Tel Aviv, Israel.
Tel: 03 5243077. Fax: 03 5243051.

No 6 anti-tank mine

ITALY

Valsella VS-50 Anti-personnel Scatter Drop Mine

Description
The VS-50 anti-personnel mine is an all-plastic mine fitted with a pressure fuze and is suitable both for conventional laying and for scattering from ground vehicles, helicopters or low-flying aircraft.

The mine is provided with a double anti-shock device operating mechanically and pneumatically. The anti-shock device prevents the mine from being triggered when an impulsive load is applied onto the pressure plate caused by an accidental drop, when scattered by helicopter dispenser, by the explosion of a nearby or suspended charge, or by the action of fuel-air explosive mineclearing systems.

The VS-50 mine is non-magnetic, waterproof and has a long storage and field life. It was developed according to NATO and FINABEL standards and has been approved by the Italian Army.

A training model which gives off smoke when actuated is available.

This mine has been produced by Chartered Industries of Singapore and has been referred to by them as the SPM-1.

Specifications
Weight: approx 185 g
Max diameter: 90 mm
Height: 45 mm
Main charge type: RDX
Weight of main charge: 43 g
Operating force: about 10 kg
Operating temperature range: −32 to +60°C
Storage temperature: −40 to +70°C

Status
In production. In service with undisclosed countries.

Manufacturer
Valsella Meccanotecnica SpA, I-25014 Castenedolo, Brescia, Italy.
Tel: 30 273 2621. Telex: 300495 emmeti i.
Fax: 30 273 1687.

Valsella VS-50 anti-personnel scatter drop mine without safety device

Valsella VS-Mk 2 Anti-personnel Scatter Drop Mine

Description
The VS-Mk 2 non-metallic mine was designed for scatter-laying from helicopters using the Valsella helicopter-mounted mine-dropping system. It can also be scattered from vehicles or by hand. It is non-magnetic and fully waterproof.

The VS-Mk 2 has a disc-shaped resin-based plastic case available in various camouflage colours. It is activated by pressure applied to both the pressure plate on the mine's top face and on its bottom face.

The mine is provided with a double anti-shock device operating mechanically and pneumatically. The anti-shock device prevents the mine from being triggered when an impulsive load is applied onto the pressure plate caused by an accidental drop, when scattered by helicopter dispenser, by the explosion of a nearby or suspended charge, or by the action of fuel-air explosive mineclearing systems.

A model fitted with an electrical anti-lift device is known as the VS-Mk 2-E.

Specifications
Weight: approx 135 g
Diameter: 90 mm
Height: 32 mm
Main charge type: RDX
Main charge weight: 33 g (22 g for VS-Mk 2-E)
Operating force: 10 kg
Operating temperature range: −32 to +60°C
Storage temperature range: −40 to +70°C

Status
In service with the Italian Army and other undisclosed armies.

Manufacturer
Valsella Meccanotecnica SpA, I-25014 Castenedolo, Brescia, Italy.

Valsella VS-Mk 2 anti-personnel scatter drop mine with safety device

Tel: 30 273 2621. Telex: 300495 emmeti i.
Fax: 30 273 1687.

Valsella VS-Mk 2-EL Anti-personnel Scatter Drop Mine

Description
The VS-Mk 2-EL is an anti-personnel, blast effect, electronic programmable mine with a pressure sensitive fuze and an anti-lift device.

The VS-Mk 2-EL is a general purpose mine which can be laid manually both on the surface and buried, scattered by the Istrice land mine scattering system or the manportable GRILLO 90 system, or dropped by the VS-MDH helicopter dispenser.

The mine is disc-shaped and is provided with a microprocessor for the identification, discrimination and selection of signals received by the pressure-sensitive fuze. The microprocessor also controls and governs all mine functions in all possible modes, neutralising the mine when any malfunction occurs. The mine is provided with a safety and arming device which renders the mine safe under all conditions, thereby allowing its 'ready for use' state during storage and transport.

After arming the mine goes through the programmed modes, including self-neutralising or self-destruct, according to choice, at the end of the programmed life. The active life and anti-lift times for the mine are separately programmable in intervals of one hour up to one year.

The mine detonates when a valid pressure is applied to the pressure-sensitive fuze during the active life period or when an attempt is made to lift the mine during the anti-lift period. The mine can cause serious injuries to personnel and can damage the wheels of

Valsella VS-Mk 2-EL anti-personnel scatter drop mine

light vehicles. It can operate even when laid upside down or below 1 m of water, and is difficult to detect by sight or by metal detectors. The mine has a high immunity to clearance measures such as suspended charges, bangalore torpedoes or fuel-air devices. It will not respond to the detonation of another mine nearby.

The VS-Mk 2-EL is provided with a complete set of electronic accessories. These include a VS-MP1 main programmer intended for officer-level use; a pocket-sized VS-SP1 secondary programmer intended for use by sappers; a bench-size VS-SP-2 secondary programmer for the mass programming of complete tubes or boxes of mines; and a manportable VS-DS-1 status detector for the detection and interrogation of deployed mines.

The VS-Mk 2-EL complies with all the latest NATO and FINABEL standards.

Practice and training versions are available.

Specifications
Weight: 200 g
Max diameter: 89.5 mm
Height: 35 mm
Main charge type: HE
Main charge weight: 15 g
Active life time: 0 to 365 days in 1 h increments
Anti-lift time: 0 to 365 days in 1 h increments
Arming delay: 10 min
Operating temperature range: −32 to +60°C
Storage temperature range: −40 to +70°C

Status
In production.

Manufacturer
Valsella Meccanotecnica SpA, I-25014 Castenedolo, Brescia, Italy.
Tel: 30 273 2621. Telex: 300495 emmeti i.
Fax: 30 273 1687.

Tecnovar TS-50 Anti-personnel Scatter Mine

Description
The TS-50 is a circular plastic anti-personnel mine which is fully waterproof and non-buoyant. It can be laid by hand, to a maximum depth of 30 mm, or by the Tecnovar DAT minelaying system for helicopters flying at a maximum speed of 200 km/h and at altitudes of up to 100 m. Actuation is by application of a 12.5 kg force to a pressure plate. A training version is also available.

This mine is produced in Egypt as the Anti-personnel Plastic Mine T/79, and has also been produced by Chartered Industries of Singapore.

Specifications
Weight: 186 g
Diameter: 90 mm
Height: 45 mm
Main charge type: T4
Weight of main charge: 50 g
Operating force: 12.5 kg
Operating temperature range: −40 to +70°C

Status
In production. In service with the Egyptian armed forces and the Italian Army.

Manufacturer
Tecnovar Italiana SpA, 95 Via Argiro, I-70121 Bari, Italy.
Tel: 080 5211744. Telex: 810345 tecvar i.
Fax: 3470400.

Tecnovar TS-50 anti-personnel scatter mine with safety device removed

BPD SB-33 Scatterable Anti-personnel Mine

Description
The SB-33 scatterable anti-personnel mine was developed from early 1977 and entered production in October 1977. The main features of the mine can be summarised as follows: irregular shape and small size that make it difficult to locate on the ground; low weight which increases the quantity of mines that can be carried by a helicopter; wide pressure plate which allows the mine to function either upright or upside down; an anti-shock device which makes it insensitive to countermeasures such as fuel-air explosives, and the mine can be scattered from helicopters with the BPD SY-AT system or laid by hand. It can also be buried just under the surface of the ground.

The mine is circular and has a plastic case which is available in any colour. If required it can also be delivered coated with a special paint that makes it undetectable by infra-red equipment.

When the mine is scattered with the SY-AT system its safety pin remains in position until the mine leaves the magazine. The mine is maintenance-free and has a shelf life of 10 years, it is waterproof and will not float. It is available with an electronic anti-removal device and a training version is produced.

The magazine is used for carrying and storing the mines as well as being used in the SY-AT system. The detonator can be inserted into the mine when the mine is still in its magazine.

BPD SB-33 scatterable anti-personnel mines

The SB-33 is also produced in Spain for the Spanish Army and in Greece, where it is known as the EM-20 anti-personnel mine. It is also produced in Portugal.

Specifications
Weight: 140 g
Diameter: 88 mm
Height: 32 mm
Main charge type: HE
Weight of main charge: 35 g
Operating force: 5-20 kg

Status
In production. In service with some NATO and other countries including Spain and Argentina. The SB-33 is also produced in Portugal, Spain and Greece.

Manufacturers
BPD Difesa e Spazio srl, Corso Garibaldi 20-22, I-00034 Colleferro (Rome), Italy.
Tel: 06 97891. Telex: 611434 bpd cf 1.
Explosivos Alaveses SA, Orense 68, 10 Floor, E-28020 Madrid, Spain.
Tel: 571 55 59. Telex: 43 484 xpal e.
Fax: 279 79 14.
ELVIEMEK SA, Atrina Centre, 32 Kifissias Av, G-15125 Paradissos Amarousiou, Athens, Greece.
Tel: 6828601. Telex: 214258 elv gr.
Fax: 6841524.
Sociedade Portuguesa de Explosivos SARL, Avenida Infante Santo 76, 5°, P-1300 Lisbon, Portugal.
Tel: 60 30 80. Telex: 12398 spelex p.

Anti-personnel Mine, Air-droppable, Maus-1

Description
This circular anti-personnel mine has a resin-based plastic and metal case. It was designed to be dropped from aircraft and helicopters at speeds up to 100 km/h and from a height of 100 m. There is a safety pin in the side of the mine, which keeps open the valve connecting the space under the rubber diaphragm to the outside and allows air to enter and leave. The mine is operated as follows: when pressure is applied to the top of the mine, the rubber diaphragm is compressed, pushing down the integral igniter which triggers the M41 detonator that fires the mine.

Specifications
Weight: 267 g
Diameter: 89 mm
Height: 46 mm
Main charge type: T4
Weight of main charge: 15.5 g
Operating force: 8.9-11.8 kg

Status
In service with the Italian Army.

Maus anti-personnel air-droppable mine

Tecnovar VAR/40 Anti-personnel Mine

Description
The VAR/40 is a cylindrical button-head type of mine made of a resin-based plastic. It is a small and compact mine that can be carried by soldiers in pockets or knapsacks. The mine is buried so that only the button-head is jutting out of the ground and the safety cap is then removed from the head. A 12 to 13 kg load on the button-head activates the mine, which is capable of damaging light vehicles. The VAR/40 is fully waterproof and non-floating. A training version is available.

Specifications
Weight: 105 g
Diameter: 78 mm
Height: 45 mm
Main charge type: T4 or Composition B
Weight of main charge: 40 g
Operating force: 12-13 kg
Operating temperature range: −41 to +70°C

Status
In production.

Manufacturer
Tecnovar Italiana SpA, 95 Via Argiro, I-70121 Bari, Italy.
Tel: 080 5211744. Telex: 810345 tecvar i.
Fax: 370400.

Tecnovar VAR/40 anti-personnel mine

Tecnovar VAR/100 Anti-personnel Mine

Description
The VAR/100 is a cylindrical button-head type of mine made of resin-based plastic. It is a small and compact anti-personnel and sabotage mine that can be carried by soldiers in their pockets and knapsacks. It is fully waterproof and non-buoyant. The mine is buried with only the button-head jutting out of the ground, and the safety cap is then removed from the head. A 12 to 13 kg force on the button-head activates the mine, which is capable of severely damaging light vehicles. A training version is available.

Specifications
Weight: 170 g
Diameter: 78 mm

Height: 57 mm
Main charge type: T4 or Composition B
Weight of main charge: 100 g
Operating force: 12-13 kg
Operating temperature range: −41 to +70°C

Status
In production.

Manufacturer
Tecnovar Italiana SpA, 95 Via Argiro, I-70121 Bari, Italy.
Tel: 080 5211744. Telex: 810345 tecvar i.
Fax: 370400.

Tecnovar VAR/100 anti-personnel mine with safety cap in position

Tecnovar VAR/100/SP Anti-personnel Mine

Description
The VAR/100/SP is a cylindrical cast-iron button-type mine fitted with a splinter casing and a three-prong actuator assembly. It is fully waterproof and non-buoyant. It can be buried, so that only the button-head with its three-pronged pressure actuator unit is jutting out of the ground, or mounted on a metal pile some 800 mm above ground. Actuation may be either by the application of a 12 to 13 kg force to the three prongs or by a pull from a 6 kg force on one or both tripwires that can be attached to the mine. The pull causes a jerk-igniter attached to the button-head to detonate the main charge which splinters the 1.6 kg cast-iron casing into about 500 pieces, the lethal radius of which extends to some 25 m from the point of detonation. The mine is also capable of damaging light vehicles. A training version is available.

Specifications
Weight: 1.77 kg
Diameter: 120 mm

Tecnovar VAR/100/SP anti-personnel mine with latch and wire spools for trap device

Height: 138 mm
Main charge type: HE
Weight of main charge: 100 g
Effective radius: 25 m
Operating force:
  (pressure) 12-13 kg
  (pull) 6 kg
Operating temperature range: −41 to +70°C

Status
In production.

Manufacturer
Tecnovar Italiana SpA, 95 Via Argiro, I-70121 Bari, Italy.
Tel: 080 5211744. Telex: 810345 tecvar i.
Fax: 370400.

Tecnovar BM/85 Bounding Anti-personnel Mine

Description
The cylindrical BM/85 bounding anti-personnel mine uses the latest plastic materials and can be actuated by pressure, tripwire or electrical means. Once the mine has been emplaced and the safety ring removed from the fuze any actuation of the mine will cause the mine to be fired upwards to a height of approximately 0.45 m where the resultant explosion will scatter around 1000 fragments over a lethal radius of 25 m.

Specifications
Weight: 2 kg
Diameter: 120 mm
Height: 200 mm
Main charge type: Composition B
Weight of main charge: 450 g
Number of fragments: approx 1000

Status
In production.

Manufacturer
Tecnovar Italiana SpA, 95 Via Argiro, I-70121 Bari, Italy.
Tel: 080 5211744. Telex: 810345 tecvar i.
Fax: 370400.

Tecnovar BM/85 bounding anti-personnel mine

Valsella Anti-personnel Bounding Mine Valmara 69

Description
This cylindrical anti-personnel bounding mine has a plastic case with a removable fuze mounted on the top. To obtain a more effective fragmentation pattern the main charge, surrounded by more than 1000 metal splinters, is projected about 0.45 m into the air by a propelling charge before detonation. The lethal casualty radius is at least 25 m. The explosive train of the mine consists of a percussion igniter cap, a propelling charge, a percussion detonator, a booster detonating charge and a main explosive charge.

The mine is fitted with a tripwire fuze. The traction load on the tripwire required to activate the fuze is 6 to 8 kg. The fuze can also be activated by direct pressure on one or more of the fuze prongs. When activated the fuze primes the igniter cap which fires the propelling charge. The internal body of the mine is then projected into the air and successively exploded. The striker mechanism cannot strike the detonator until the the body is ejected. The mine is fully waterproofed.

Practice and training versions are available.

This mine has also been produced by Chartered Industries of Singapore.

Specifications
Weight: approx 3.2 kg
Diameter: 130 mm
Height: (with fuze) 205 mm
Main charge type: Composition B
Weight of main charge: approx 420 g
Type of booster charge: RDX
Weight of booster charge: 13 g
Operating force:
(pressure) 10.8 kg
(pull) 6 kg
Operating temperature range: −32 to +60°C
Storage temperature range: −40 to +70°C

Status
In production. In service with the Italian Army and other armies, including Iraq.

Manufacturer
Valsella Meccanotecnica SpA, I-25014 Castenedolo,

Anti-personnel bounding mine Valmara 69

Brescia, Italy.
Tel: 30 2732621. Telex: 300495 emmeti i.
Fax: 30 2731687.

Valsella VS-JAP Anti-personnel Bounding Mine

Description
The Valsella VS-JAP is an anti-personnel bounding mine. To obtain a more effective fragmentation pattern the Composition B main charge, surrounded by splinters, is projected into the air by a propelling charge prior to exploding. The casualty radius is at least 25 m and within this radius the mine is lethal.

The VS-JAP is fitted with a tripwire fuze. The traction load on the tripwire required to activate the fuze ranges between 4 and 6 kg. The fuze can also be activated by direct pressure on the fuze prongs. When activated, the fuze fires the igniter cap which, in turn, fires the propelling charge. The internal body of the mine is then projected into the air and successively exploded. The striker mechanism cannot strike the detonator until the body is ejected. The mine is completely waterproof.

Practice and training versions are available.

Specifications
Weight: approx 2.8 kg
Diameter: 130 mm
Height: (with fuze) 190 mm

Main charge type: Composition B
Weight of main charge: approx 500 g
Booster charge type: RDX
Weight of booster charge: 9 g
Operating force:
(pressure) 10 kg
(pull) 4-6 kg
Operating temperature range: −32 to +60°C
Storage temperature range: −40 to +70°C

Status
In service with an undisclosed country.

Manufacturer
Valsella Meccanotecnica SpA, I-25014 Castenedolo, Brescia, Italy.
Tel: 30 2732621. Telex: 300495 emmeti i.
Fax: 30 2731687.

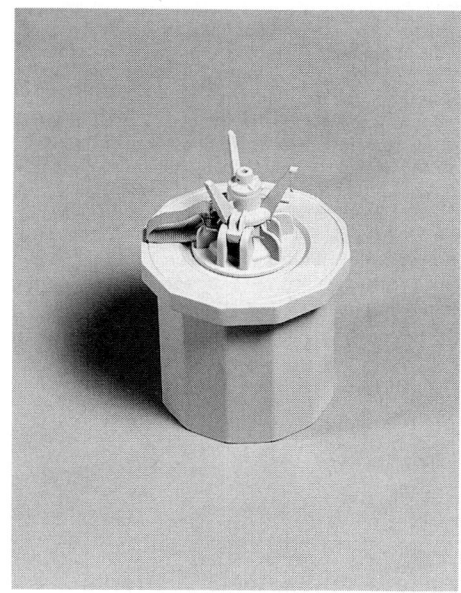

Valsella VS-JAP anti-personnel bounding mine

Valsella VS-APFM1 Anti-personnel Bounding Mine

Description
The Valsella VS-APFM1 anti-personnel bounding mine is an improved version of the Valmara 69 anti-personnel bounding mine (see entry in this section) with an advanced electronic fuze. The warhead is derived from the Valmara 69 model and includes some modifications to increase effectiveness.

The mine is armed by the combined movement of an arming lever and a release button. After a safety delay of 10 min from arming, three tripwires are automatically ejected by the fuze. A traction load of about 500 g on one tripwire activates the fuze. The priming train is first aligned and then the ejection sequence of the warhead is initiated, terminating in the warhead activation.

Both the primer in the fuze and the detonator in the warhead are kept in the SAFE position until activation. The fuze includes a self-neutralisation feature which can be electrically set in the field using a pocket-sized electronic programmer.

Practice and training versions are available.

Specifications
Weight: approx 3.5 kg
Diameter: 130 mm
Height: 190 mm
Weight of main charge: 500 g
Activation: by automatically extended tripwires
Activation load: approx 500 g
Arming delay: 10 min
Self-neutralising delay: 0 to 365 days in increments of 1 h
Operating temperature range: −32 to +60°C
Storage temperature range: −40 to +70°C

Status
Development complete.

Manufacturer
Valsella Meccanotecnica SpA, I-25014 Castenedolo, Brescia, Italy.
Tel: 30 2732621. Telex: 300495 emmeti i.
Fax: 30 2731687.

Valsella VS-APFM1 anti-personnel bounding mine with electronic fuze

BPD P-25 Anti-personnel Mine

Description
The BPD P-25 anti-personnel mine was developed from early 1977 and entered production in 1978. It consists of a cylindrical plastic casing which can be delivered in any colour, with the fuze mounted on top. The mine can be buried but for maximum effect should be staked to the ground. The mine is activated by two tripwires which can extend up to 15 m away from the mine. When activated the charge explodes and splinters are scattered in a radial path. The effective range of the P-25 mine is 15 m.

The mine is waterproof, will not float and has a maintenance-free life of at least 10 years. Smoke-producing and inert models are available for training.

Specifications
Weight: 0.7 kg
Diameter: 75 mm
Overall height: 180 mm
Weight of main charge: 180 g
Main charge type: TNT or T4
Operating force: 2-10 kg

Status
In production.

Manufacturer
BPD Difesa e Spazio srl, Corso Garibaldi 20-22, I-00034 Colleferro (Rome), Italy.
Tel: 06 97891. Telex: 611434 bpd cf 1.

BPD P-25 anti-personnel mine

BPD P-40 Anti-personnel Jumping Mine

Description
The BPD P-40 anti-personnel jumping mine was developed from early 1977 and entered production in 1978. It consists of a cylindrical casing, which can be made in any colour, inside which is another container holding the high explosive and fragments. The mine is buried with just the fuze showing above the ground. The fuze is attached to the two tripwires which can be up to 15 m from the mine. The mine operates as follows: when the tripwire is pulled the inside container is ejected into the air and when it reaches a pre-determined height it explodes and scatters the fragments in a radial path. Trials conducted by BPD have shown that this mine will cause injury to at least 55 per cent of men standing within a radius of 15 m of the mine when it is ignited.

The mine is waterproof, will not float and has a minimum maintenance-free life of 10 years. Smoke-producing and inert training models are available.

Specifications
Weight: 1.5 kg
Diameter: 90 mm
Height with fuze: 200 mm
Height of casing: 120 mm
Main charge type: TNT
Weight of main charge: 0.48 kg
Operating force: 2-10 kg

Status
In production.

Manufacturer
BPD Difesa e Spazio srl, Corso Garibaldi 20-22, I-00034 Colleferro (Rome), Italy.
Tel: 06 97891. Telex: 611434 bpd cf 1.

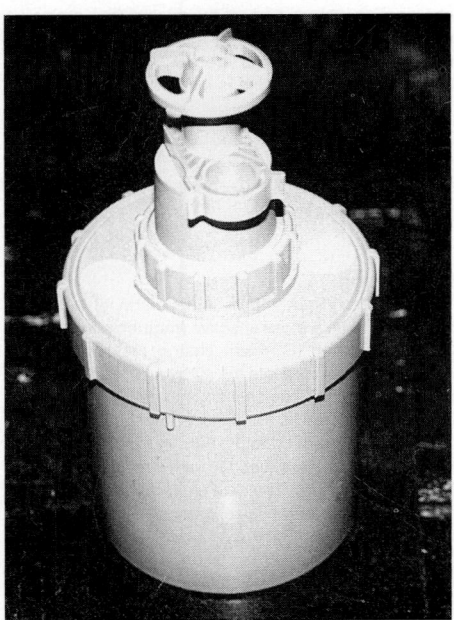

BPD P-40 anti-personnel mine with safety clip in position

Valsella VS-SAPFM3 Scatterable Anti-personnel Bounding Mine

Description
The Valsella VS-SAPFM3 is one of the munitions used with the Istrice mine scattering system (see entry in the *Minelaying equipment* section) and is a scatterable, anti-personnel bounding fragmentation mine provided with an electronic fuze with an active life program-mable in the field.

The VS-SAPFM3 is visually identical to the Valsella VS-SATM1 scatterable anti-tank mine (see separate entry in this section). It has a cylindrical shape with the body surrounded by lateral springs and closed by a cover. The body contains the main charge, the splinters, the ejection charge, and the cover locking mechanism. In the upper part of the body are the electronics, the safety and arming device, and the tripwire assemblies. The mine is watertight and complies with the latest standards and STANAGs.

When the mine is stored in an Istrice launching tube the detonator and the igniter for the mine are misaligned with the pyrotechnic trains. The safety and arming device will keep the priming train misaligned for an arming delay of at least 10 minutes after ejection from the launch tube. The arming delay commences once

Valsella VS-SAPFM3 scatterable anti-personnel bounding mine

the mine has left the launch tube. On landing the lateral springs around the body will maintain the mine in an upright position. Once the delay has expired tripwires are deployed so that any traction on one of the tripwires will activate the fuze. The fuze will initiate the

upwards propulsion of the mine charge body with its subsequent detonation, producing approximately 1600 splinters. At 15 m the splinters will have a residual kinetic energy of 30 kg/m while the saturation level at 25 m will be 2 splinters each square metre.

Specifications
Weight: 2.3 kg
Height: 105 mm
Diameter: 128 mm
Weight of main charge: 450 g
Main charge type: Composition B
Arming delay: 10 min
Active life: programmable between 0 and 365 days in increments of 1 h
Number of splinters: approx 1600
Operating temperature range: −32 to +60°C
Storage temperature range: −40 to +70°C

Status
Development.

Manufacturer
Valsella Meccanotecnica SpA, I-25014 Castenedolo, Brescia, Italy.
Tel: 30 2732621. Telex: 300495 emmeti i.
Fax: 30 2731687.

Valsella VS-DAFM 1 Directional Anti-personnel Mine

Description
The VS-DAFM 1 is a fixed directional fragmentation anti-personnel mine of the Claymore type used for tactical applications such as the defence of military installations, reaction against an airborne landing or enemy infiltration, and ambushes. The mine is effective against non-armoured vehicles and can penetrate unarmoured vehicle bodies, fuel tanks and engine components.

The VS-DAFM 1 mine projects a fan-shaped pattern of steel balls over a 60° horizontal arc covering a casualty range of at least 50 m to a height of about 3 m. The mine can be coupled to two independent firing systems through two priming wells. It is possible to fire two or more mines simultaneously.

The mine is issued as a kit which includes the mine itself plus a set of accessories for firing in different modes to suit the tactical situation.

Specifications
Weight: (with accessories) 3.6 kg
Width: 342 mm
Height: (feet folded) 168 mm
Actuating load: 3-6 kg
Coverage: 2 splinters/m² at 50 m
Penetration: 2 mm mild steel plate at 50 m
Max height of arc: approx 3 m
Operating temperature range: −32 to +60°C
Storage temperature range: −40 to +70°C

Status
In service with an undisclosed country.

Manufacturer
Valsella Meccanotecnica SpA, I-25014 Castenedolo, Brescia, Italy.
Tel: 30 2732621. Telex: 300495 emmeti i.
Fax: 30 2731687.

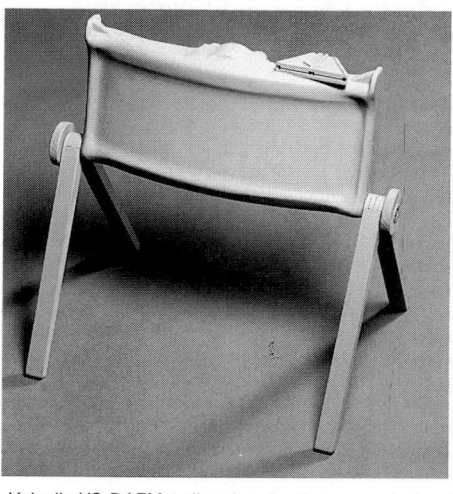

Valsella VS-DAFM 1 directional anti-personnel mine

Valsella VS-DAFM 6 and VS-DAFM 7 Directional Anti-materiel Mines

Description
These mines are fixed directional fragmentation anti-materiel (anti-personnel and anti-armour) mines used primarily for the defence of tactically important areas such as airfields and landing zones. They may also be used for the defence of fixed installations and tactical areas, for covering areas during withdrawals or for covering the movement of troops.

Both mines project a fan-shaped pattern of metal balls in a 38° horizontal arc, covering an effective area with a radius of 100 to 150 m to a height of about 4 m. Both models can penetrate 6 mm of rolled homogenous armour at a range of 50 m.

Both mines are issued as a kit which includes the mine itself plus a set of accessories for firing in different modes to suit the tactical situation.

Status
Development complete.

Manufacturer
Valsella Meccanotecnica SpA, I-25014 Castenedolo, Brescia, Italy.
Tel: 30 2732621. Telex: 300495 emmeti i.
Fax: 30 2731687.

Specifications

Model	VS-DAFM 6	VS-DAFM 7
Weight	18.2 kg	10.7 kg
Height (less support)	270 mm	170 mm
Width (less support)	530 mm	190 mm
Actuation load	3-6 kg	3-6 kg
Coverage	2 splinters/m² at 100 m (both models)	
Penetration	6 mm RHA at 50 m (both models)	
Height of arc	approx 4 m	approx 4 m
Temperature limits		
(firing)	−32 to +60° (both models)	
(storage)	−40 to +70° (both models)	

Valsella VS-DAFM 6 anti-materiel mine

Valsella SATM Scatterable Anti-tank Mine

Description
The SATM scatterable anti-tank mine is provided with a single liner shaped charge and an influence fuze. It can be launched from the Valsella Istrice land mine scattering system.

The SATM has a cylindrical body and is fitted with deployable fins which provide stabilisation during flight and maintain the correct orientation for landing. Once in position the SATM can use its shaped charge to attack the belly armour of a target MBT. There is a dual-action inertial safety arming device.

The SATM dual-sensor integral fuze features target discrimination combined with a high immunity to mineclearing countermeasures. The mine also has a self-destruct capability which is electrically programmed at launch.

Specifications
Weight: 1.4 kg
Diameter:
  (maximum) 114 mm
  (minimum) 96 mm
Height: (total) 106 mm
Weight of main charge: 0.4 kg
Operating temperature range: −32 to +60°C
Storage temperature range: −40 to +70°C

Status
In production.

Manufacturer
Valsella Meccanotecnica SpA, I-25014 Castenedolo, Brescia, Italy.
Tel: 30 2732621. Telex: 300495 emmeti i.
Fax: 30 2731687.

Valsella SATM scatterable anti-tank mine

Valsella VS-SATM1 Scatterable Anti-tank Mine

Description

The Valsella VS-SATM1 is a scatterable, full width, anti-tank mine provided with a dual sensor influence electronic fuze with an active life programmable in the field prior to scattering. The VS-SATM1 is intended for use with the Istrice mine scattering system, the manportable GRILLO 128 single-tube launcher and the VS-MDH helicopter system. It may also be hand emplaced.

The VS-SATM1 uses an explosively formed projectile which is effective against MBTs and APCs, both wheeled and tracked. The mine can produced a complete kill when fired against belly armour or a mobility kill when fired under tracks or wheels. Advantages claimed for the mine include good target discrimination, virtually independent of target speed; zero false activations; high warhead effectiveness against current and future MBTs; and a self-destruct or self-neutralisation capability at the end of the electronically preset active life period. The choice between the two latter alternatives is made prior to manufacture.

The VS-SATM1 is visually identical to the VS-SAPFM3 scatterable anti-personnel mine (see separate entry in this section), and thus has a cylindrical body surrounded by lateral support springs and with a closed cover. The mine is provided with a safety and arming device which renders the mine safe under all conditions, allowing its 'ready for use' state during transport and storage. The mine is resistant to countermeasures, and is capable of selecting only the correct firing stimuli.

The warhead can penetrate 100 mm of rolled homogeneous armour (RHA) and is designed to obtain the maximum behind-armour effects by using spall fragment projection and the generation of an over-pressure inside the target. It is effective even when submerged under water.

The VS-SATM1 is provided with a complete set of electronic accessories. These include a VS-MP1 main programmer intended for officer-level use; a pocket-sized VS-SP1 secondary programmer intended for use by sappers; a bench-size VS-SP-2 secondary programmer for the mass programming of complete tubes or boxes of mines; and a manportable VS-DS-1 status detector for the detection and interrogation of deployed mines.

The VS-SATM1 complies with the latest NATO STANAGs and MIL-STDs.

Practice and training versions are available.

Specifications
Weight: 2.5 kg
Height: 105 mm
Diameter: 128 mm
Weight of explosive charge: 800 g
Arming delay: 10 min
Active life: programmable between 0 and 365 days in increments of 1 h
Operating temperature range: −32 to +60°C
Storage temperature range: −40 to +70°C

Status
Production.

Manufacturer
Valsella Meccanotecnica SpA, I-25014 Castenedolo, Brescia, Italy.
Tel: 30 2732621. Telex: 300495 emmeti i.
Fax: 30 2731687.

Valsella VS-1.6 Anti-tank Scatter Mine

Description

The Valsella VS-1.6 anti-tank scatter mine is a pressure-activated, anti-track, all-plastic mine which is undetectable by standard metal detectors. It can be scattered from ground vehicles, helicopters and low-flying aircraft, or can be manually buried. The mine is waterproof and can be operated to a depth of 1 m.

The mine is provided with a double anti-shock device operating mechanically and pneumatically. This device prevents the mine from being triggered when an impulsive load is applied onto the pressure plate, caused either by an accidental drop, when scattered by a helicopter dispenser, by the detonation of a nearby or suspended explosive charge, or by the action of fuel-air explosive mineclearing systems.

The bottom cover of the mine is provided with a plug housing the detonator. During transport and storage this plug is replaced by a dummy plug, coloured blue, for extra safety.

Either surface-laid or buried down to 70 mm below

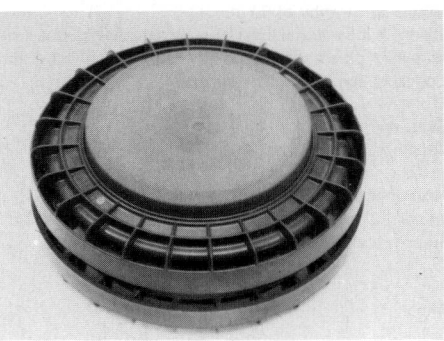

Valsella VS-1.6 anti-tank scatter mine

the ground surface, the VS-1.6 can cause an immobilising 'kill' by cutting tank tracks or causing major damage to MBT suspensions.

The VS-1.6 was developed according to NATO and FINABEL standards and has been type classified by the Italian Army.

An electronic model with anti-lift and independently

programmed active life times is also available. This model, known as the VS-1.6-EL, has a detonating train which is kept out of alignment until firing.

Practice and drill versions are available.

Specifications
Weight: 3 kg
Diameter: 222 mm
Height: 92 mm
Main charge type: HE
Weight of main charge: 1.85 kg
Operating force: 180-220 kg
Operating temperature range: −32 to +60°C
Storage temperature range: −40 to +70°C

Status
In production. Type classified by the Italian Army and in service with several countries.

Manufacturer
Valsella Meccanotecnica SpA, I-25014 Castenedolo, Brescia, Italy.
Tel: 30 2732621. Telex: 300495 emmeti i.
Fax: 30 2731687.

BPD SB-81 Scatterable Anti-tank Mine

Description

The BPD SB-81 can be scattered from helicopters with the BPD SY-AT system, or laid manually. It can be buried in the ground to a maximum depth of 100 mm. Air-dropping does not impede its ability to destroy tank tracks or irreparably damage tank running gear.

The mine is circular and has a plastic case available in any colour. It is pressure-activated and will function whether it lands on its top or its bottom.

The SB-81 is waterproof, will not float, is maintenance-free and has a shelf life of ten years. The explosive content of the mine can be removed and stored separately. The magazine is used for carrying and storing the mine as well as being used in conjunction with the SY-AT scattering system. The detonator can be inserted into the mine even when it is stored in the magazine.

Other versions of the mine are available including a model with an electronic anti-removal and self-neutralising device, and another with an electronic anti-

removal device and a self-destruction device, which both operate at pre-determined times. In appearance these are identical to the standard mines. Smoke and inert models are available for training purposes.

The SB-81 is produced in Spain (as the EXPAL SB-81) and in Portugal.

Specifications
Weight: 3.2 kg
Diameter: 232 mm
Height: 90 mm
Main charge type: HE
Weight of main charge: 2 kg
Operating force: 150-310 kg
Packaging: magazine containing 5 weighs 19.5 kg

Status
In production. In service in Argentina, Italy and Spain (for Spanish Army).

Manufacturers
BPD Difesa e Spazio srl, Corso Garibaldi 20-22, I-00034 Colleferro (Rome), Italy.
Tel: 06 97891. Telex: 611434 bpd cf 1.

BPD SB-81 scatterable anti-tank mine

Explosivos Alaveses SA, Orense 68, 10th Floor, E-28020 Madrid, Spain.
Tel: 5715599. Telex: 43 484 xpal e.
Fax: 2797914.
Sociedade Portuguesa de Explosivos SARL, Avenida Infante Santo 76, 5°, P-1300 Lisbon, Portugal.
Tel: 60 30 80. Telex: 12398 spelex p.

Valsella VS-3.6 Anti-tank Mine

Description

The Valsella VS-3.6 anti-tank mine is an all-plastic pressure-activated mine formed by the combination of the detachable pressure fuze model VS-N with a mine body filled with a Composition B main charge. Although reduced in size and weight compared to some other mines, the VS-3.6 is highly effective against MBT tracks and suspensions.

The VS-N fuze is provided with a pneumatic anti-shock device. This device prevents the mine from being triggered when an impulsive load is applied onto the pressure plate, caused either by an accidental drop, by the detonation of a nearby or suspended explosive charge, or by the action of fuel-air explosive mineclearing systems.

The fuze and mine body are made of high performance plastics and are watertight and shock resistant under the most severe operational conditions. The mine can be employed in flooded areas and being all-plastic, apart from a few small metal components, is

Valsella VS-3.6 anti-tank mine

undetectable by standard metal detectors. A typical planting depth is from 50 to 70 mm below ground surface.

The VS-3.6 was developed according to NATO and FINABEL standards and has been type classified by the Italian Army. The VS-N fuze is in service with the Italian Army.

Practice and drill versions are available.

Specifications
Weight: 5 kg
Diameter: 248 mm
Height: 115 mm
Main charge type: Composition B
Weight of main charge: 4 kg
Operating force: 180-220 kg
Operating temperature range: −32 to +60°C
Storage temperature range: −40 to +70°C

Status
In production. Approved by the Italian Army. VS-N fuze in service with the Italian Army.

Manufacturer
Valsella Meccanotecnica SpA, I-25014 Castenedolo, Brescia, Italy.
Tel: 30 2732621. Telex: 300495 emmeti i.
Fax: 30 2731687.

Valsella VS-2.2 Anti-tank Mine

Description

The Valsella VS-2.2 anti-tank mine is an all-plastic pressure-activated mine formed by the combination of the detachable pressure fuze model VS-N with a mine body filled with a Composition B main charge. Although

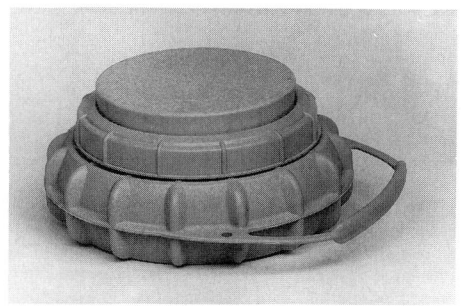

Latest body configuration for Valsella VS-2.2 anti-tank mine

reduced in size and weight compared to some other mines, the VS-2.2 is highly effective against MBT tracks and suspensions.

The VS-N fuze is provided with a pneumatic anti-shock device. This device prevents the mine from being triggered when an impulsive load is applied onto the pressure plate, caused either by an accidental drop, by the detonation of a nearby or suspended explosive charge, or by the action of fuel-air explosive mineclearing systems.

The fuze and mine body are made of high performance plastics and are watertight and shock resistant under the most severe operational conditions. The mine can be employed in flooded areas and being all-plastic, apart from a few small metal components, is undetectable by standard metal detectors. A typical planting depth is from 50 to 70 mm below ground surface.

The VS-2.2 was developed according to NATO and FINABEL standards and has been type classified by the Italian Army. The VS-N fuze is in service with the Italian Army.

Practice and drill versions are available.

This mine has also been produced by Chartered Industries of Singapore.

Specifications
Weight: 3.8 kg
Diameter: 230 mm
Height: 115 mm
Weight of main charge: 2.7 kg
Charge type:
 (main) Composition B
 (booster) RDX
Operating force: 180-220 kg
Operating temperature range: −32 to +60°C
Storage temperature range: −40 to +70°C

Status
In production. Type classified by the Italian Army and in service with Singapore and with several other undisclosed countries. The VS-N fuze is in service with the Italian Army.

Manufacturer
Valsella Meccanotecnica SpA, I-25014 Castenedolo, Brescia, Italy.
Tel: 30 2732621. Telex: 300495 emmeti i.
Fax: 30 2731687.

Valsella VS-AT4-EL Anti-tank Mine

Description

The Valsella VS-AT4-EL anti-tank mine is a general purpose, electronic mine with a pressure sensitive fuze which can be electronically programmed in the field. It is provided with an anti-lift device and a target counting capability enabling it to select an individual target in a column of vehicles. The mine is effective against the wheels and tracks of modern armoured vehicles and is capable of producing a mobility kill. It may be used with mechanised minelaying equipments but may be surface-laid or emplaced manually.

The anti-lift and active life times of the VS-AT4-EL are programmable in the field between 0 and 365 days in increments of one hour. At the end of its active life the mine will either self-neutralise or self-destruct; this feature is selected prior to manufacture. The fuze contains a safety and arming device which conforms to the latest NATO and FINABEL standards, allowing a 'ready to use' state for storage and transport.

The fuze can discriminate the correct firing stimuli among other influences such as battlefield disturbances, electromagnetic radiations and mechanical or explosive clearing systems.

The VS-AT4-EL is provided with a complete set of electronic accessories. These include a VS-MP1 main programmer intended for officer-level use; a pocket-sized VS-SP1 secondary programmer intended for use by sappers; a bench-size VS-SP-2 secondary programmer for the mass programming of complete tubes or boxes of mines; and a manportable VS-DS-1 status

Valsella VS-AT4-EL anti-tank mine

detector for the detection and interrogation of deployed mines.

The VS-AT4-EL complies with the latest NATO STANAGs and MIL-STDs.

Practice and training versions are available.

Specifications
Weight: approx 6 kg
Length: 280 mm

Height: 188 mm
Width: 104 mm
Weight of main charge: 4.5 kg
Active life: programmable between 1 h and 365 days in increments of 1 h
Anti-lift feature: programmable between 0 and 365 days in increments of 1 h
Operating temperature range: −32 to +60°C
Storage temperature range: −40 to +70°C

Status
In production.

Manufacturer
Valsella Meccanotecnica SpA, I-25014 Castenedolo, Brescia, Italy.
Tel: 30 2732621. Telex: 300495 emmeti i.
Fax: 30 2731687.

Valsella VS-HCT Anti-tank Mine

Description
The Valsella VS-HCT anti-tank mine was developed to meet a specification issued for a full width mine by the Italian Army and entered series production in 1979. The VS-HCT anti-tank mine is fitted with a high-performance shaped charge and a dual-sensor electronic influence fuze that is effective across the full width of an armoured vehicle. The blast effect is used to damage the tracks and the shaped charge can penetrate the belly armour to a depth of more than 175 mm.

The VS-HCT can be laid manually or mechanically to a maximum depth of 100 mm. A number of safety features are incorporated for use during storage, transporting and laying. These include a removable composite detonator and interruption of the detonating train when in the safe, mechanical and electronic arming delay states.

The VS-HCT is cylindrical and has a plastic water-tight casing. The fuze is powered by a replaceable military-grade lithium battery pack.

In operation a magnetic sensor inside the VS-HCT detects the change in the local magnetic field when a tank approaches. The sensor's signal is processed by an electronic circuit for optimum discrimination of

Valsella VS-HCT anti-tank mine

the target and for correct timing of the firing pulse. The explosive train is primed by an electrical device which initiates a composite percussion detonator. The detonator includes a first stage to ignite the clearing charge and a delayed detonator, the delay being determined by the degree to which uncovering is required.

It is claimed that the effectiveness of the VS-HCT is such that one mine can be as effective as three normal pressure mines but with a much greater chance of obtaining a tank 'kill' rather than merely disabling the target. The mine is provided with a built-in timer for self-neutralisation and 10 self-neutralising time periods can be selected at the moment of laying – these vary from 1 to 128 days. The VS-HCT can also be fitted with an anti-lift device and a status indicator that can be checked remotely with a special detector device.

Specifications
Weight: approx 4 kg
Diameter: 222 mm
Height: 110 mm
Weight of main charge: approx 2.05 kg
Operating temperature range: −32 to +60°C
Storage temperature range: −40 to +70°C

Status
In production.

Manufacturer
Valsella Meccanotecnica SpA, I-25014 Castenedolo, Brescia, Italy.
Tel: 30 2732621. Telex: 300495 emmeti i.
Fax: 30 2731687.

Valsella VS-HCT2 Full width Anti-tank Mine

Description
The Valsella VS-HCT2 anti-tank mine is fitted with electronic combined dual-sensors, and a shaped charge providing a full width 'kill' capability against any type of MBT or APC. When fired under the tracks of a target the mine cuts the tracks and causes severe damage to the suspension. When fired between the tracks the mine perforates the belly armour and internal plates and creates a peak increase of the internal pressure which is well above the crew survival level.

The main features of the VS-HCT2 are optimised full width effectiveness, good target discrimination (independent of speed), a dual-safety arming device which interrupts the pyrotechnic and detonating trains, self-neutralising (or self-destruct) and anti-lift capabilities which are electrically programmable in the field, and a high immunity against mineclearing countermeasures. The mine is also provided with a target counting feature for the selection of an individual target in a column of vehicles.

The VS-HCT2 can be buried either manually or mechanically using a chute minelayer. The self-neutralisation time is accurately preset just before laying using a portable electronic programmer. The

Valsella VS-HCT2 full width anti-tank mine

programmed value may be altered any number of times. For extra safety the exact status of a mine can be checked using a special stand-off detector before a self-neutralised mine is recovered.

The VS-HCT2 was developed according to Italian Army specifications and meets NATO and FINABEL requirements.

In tests the VS-HCT2 has penetrated a 50 mm plate set 500 mm above the mine and a further five 25 mm thick witness plates.

The fuze can be supplied either with a self-neutralising or self-destruct capability. A practice version (with smoke effect) and a training model are available. The training model can be stripped down into the main component parts.

Specifications
Weight: 6.8 kg
Length: 260 mm
Width: 260 mm
Height: 128 mm
Weight of main charge: 2.3 kg
Type of main charge: Composition B
Arming delay: 15 mins, mechanical and electronic
Self-neutralisation and anti-lift delay: electrically programmable in steps of 1 h up to 365 days
Waterproofing: tested under 0.1 kg/cm²
Operating temperature range: −32 to +60°C
Storage temperature range: −40 to +70°C

Status
In production.

Manufacturer
Valsella Meccanotecnica SpA, I-25014 Castenedolo, Brescia, Italy.
Tel: 30 2732621. Telex: 300495 emmeti i.
Fax: 30 2731687.

Valsella VS-HCT4 Full width Anti-tank Mine

Description
The Valsella VS-HCT4 anti-tank mine is fitted with an electronic combined magnetic and seismic influence fuze, and a shaped charge providing a full width 'kill' capability against any type of MBT or APC. When fired under the tracks of a target the mine cuts the tracks and causes severe damage to the suspension. When

fired between the tracks the mine perforates the belly armour and internal plates and creates a peak increase of the internal pressure which is well above the crew survival level.

The main features of the VS-HCT4 are optimised full width effectiveness, good target discrimination (independent of speed), a dual-safety arming device which interrupts the pyrotechnic and detonating trains, self-neutralising (or self-destruct) and anti-lifting capabilities which are electrically programmable in the field, and a high immunity against mineclearing counter-

measures.

The VS-HCT4 can be buried either manually or mechanically using a fully automatic mine burier. The self-neutralisation time is accurately preset just before laying using a portable electronic programmer; this operation is performed automatically on the mechanical minelayer. The programmed value may be altered any number of times.

The VS-HCT4 was developed according to Italian Army specifications and meets NATO and FINABEL requirements.

In tests the VS-HCT4 has penetrated a 50 mm plate set 500 mm above the mine and a further five 25 mm thick witness plates.

The fuze can be supplied either with a self-neutralising or self-destruct capability. A practice version (with smoke effect) and a training model are available. The training model can be stripped down into the main component parts.

Specifications
Weight: 6.5 kg
Length: 280 mm
Width: 188 mm
Height: 104 mm
Weight of main charge: 2.3 kg
Type of main charge: Composition B
Target speed range: 1 to 70 km/h

Arming delay: 10 min
Self-neutralisation and anti-lift delay: programmable in increments of 1 h up to 365 days
Waterproofing: tested under 0.1 kg/cm^2
Operating temperature range: −32 to +60°C
Storage temperature range: −40 to +70°C

Status
In production.

Manufacturer
Valsella Meccanotecnica SpA, I-25014 Castenedolo, Brescia, Italy.
Tel: 30 2732621. Telex: 300495 emmeti i.
Fax: 30 2731687.

Valsella VS-HCT4 full width anti-tank mine

BPD SB-MV/1 Anti-tank Mine

Description
The SB-MV/1 anti-tank mine is a development of the SB-MV/T anti-tank mine that entered series production in early 1979.

The SB-MV/1 is circular and has a plastic casing which is available in a variety of colours. It is of the hollow charge type and has an influence fuze. BPD claims that it is three times more effective than conventional anti-tank mines as it acts against the belly armour of the tank as well as its tracks. The mine will penetrate up to 150 mm of steel armour and cause serious damage to the interior of the tank, immobilising it.

The mine can be laid by hand or mechanically and is normally buried to a maximum depth of 100 mm. If the arming lever is rotated and the detonator inserted after the lever has passed the arming delay, a safety circuit that stops the mine igniting comes into operation. When in its packing case, the mine cannot be activated as the arming lever cannot be moved from its safety position. A delayed mechanical arming is incorporated in the mine so that it does not become fully active until after the external arming lever has been operated.

The mine operates as follows: the approach of a tank towards the mine is accompanied by vibrations in the ground which are detected by the seismic transducer and the electronic amplification and discrimination circuit of the fuzing system. This alerts the magnetic

BPD SB-MV/1 anti-tank mine

sensor part of the system which locates the tank by detecting the change in the magnetic field of the earth caused by the metallic mass of the tank and, when it is over the mine, transmits a signal to the firing circuit. This operates both the ignition cap of the uncovering charge — which blows off the upper part of the mine and any camouflage over it to leave the liner of the bursting charge unobstructed — and the detonator. The detonator has a time-lag built-in to delay the firing of the booster charge and the main charge. The delay is determined by the uncovering time.

Only two-thirds the number of SB-MV/1 anti-tank mines are needed to provide the same obstructive capability as Second World War type mines. They also

require a third of the time and need fewer personnel to lay.

The mines are packed in magazines of five, and the detonators can be inserted into the mines without removing the mines from the magazine. The mines can be quickly removed from the magazine for manual laying and the magazine is also used when the mines are being laid mechanically.

The mine is fitted with an anti-lifting device designed to operate the detonator if any change in trim of the mine is detected and a self-neutralisation device which is programmed to operate after a preset period.

Specifications
Weight: 5 kg
Diameter: 236 mm
Height: 113 mm
Main charge type: melted CB
Weight of main charge: 2.4 kg
Booster charge type: compressed RDX
Uncovering charge type: propelling powder
Power supply: replaceable lithium batteries

Status
In production. Ordered by Australia.

Manufacturer
BPD Difesa e Spazio srl, Corso Garibaldi 20-22, I-00034 Colleferro (Rome), Italy.
Tel: 06 97891. Telex: 611434 bpd cf 1.

Tecnovar TC/2.4 Anti-tank Mine

Description
The Tecnovar TC/2.4 anti-tank mine is a non-metallic mine that may be emplaced manually or mechanically. The circular body of the mine is completely waterproof and non-buoyant and is designed for laying in fresh or sea water or in marshy ground. It will operate even if laid under snow up to 1 m deep. For normal use the mine is emplaced with the pressure plate 75 to 150 mm below ground level. The mine will operate at a pressure of between 180 and 310 kg and the Composition B main charge (other types of explosive may be used) is sufficient to wreck the track and running gear of any tank. The TC/2.4 is stated to be proof against mine countermeasures such as mine rollers, blast devices, and fuel-air explosives. The mine is not detectable by magnetic mine detectors. An anti-lift device may be fitted.

Inert training versions of this mine are available.

Specifications
Weight: 3.3 kg
Diameter: 204 mm
Height: 108 mm
Main charge type: Composition B
Weight of main charge: approx 2.4 kg
Operating force: 180-310 kg
Operating temperature range: −31 to +70°C

Status
In production.

Manufacturer
Tecnovar Italiana SpA, 95 Via Argiro, I-70121 Bari, Italy.
Tel: 080 5211744. Telex: 810345 tecvar i.
Fax: 370400.

Tecnovar TC/2.4 anti-tank mine

Tecnovar MATS/2.6 Anti-tank Scatter Drop Mine

Description
The Tecnovar MATS/2.6 is a circular plastic anti-tank mine. It is fully waterproof and has been designed for rapid laying from helicopters flying at speeds of up to 200 km/h and altitudes up to 100 m. The system used to dispense the mines is the Tecnovar DAT mine dispenser. The mine may also be laid by vehicles or buried by hand at depths down to 75 mm. The MATS/2.6 is pressure activated and is capable of destroying any armoured vehicle tracks. Two versions of the mine are available together with inert training versions.

Specifications
Weight:
   (version 1) 3.6 kg
   (version 2) 5 kg
Diameter:
   (version 1) 220 mm
   (version 2) 260 mm
Height: 90 mm
Main charge type: T4 or Composition B
Weight of main charge:
   (version 1) 1.5 kg
   (version 2) 2.4 kg
Operating force:
   (average) 180 kg
   (max) 310 kg
Operating temperature range: −31 to +70°C

Status
In production. In service with the Italian Army.

Manufacturer
Tecnovar Italiana SpA, 95 Via Argiro, I-70121 Bari, Italy.

Tecnovar MATS/2.6 anti-tank scatter mine

Tel: 080 5211744. Telex: 810345 tecvar i. Fax: 370400.

Tecnovar TC/3.6 and TCE/3.6 Anti-tank Mines

Description
The TC/3.6 is a circular plastic anti-tank mine that is fully waterproof and non-buoyant. It can be laid by hand, to a depth of between 75 and 150 mm in soil and up to 1 m in snow, or mechanically from a vehicle.

The TCE/3.6 anti-tank mine is physically similar to the TC/3.6 but is fitted with an electronic arming and disarming device that can be used to activate or deactivate a minefield sector composed of these mines on receipt of a command signal.

Actuation of both mines is by the application of a load of 180 kg to a pressure plate. Each type of mine is capable of destroying the tracks and severely damaging the suspension of armoured vehicles. Training versions are available.

The TC/3.6 is produced in Portugal by Explosivos da Trafaria SARL of Lisbon.

Tecnovar TC/3.6 anti-tank mine; the TCE/3.6 is visually identical

Specifications
Weight: 6.8 kg
Diameter: 270 mm
Height: 145 mm

Main charge type: Composition B
Weight of main charge: 3.6 kg
Operating force:
   (average) 180 kg
   (max) 310 kg
Operating temperature range: −31 to +70°C

Status
In production.

Manufacturers
Tecnovar Italiana SpA, 95 Via Argiro, I-70121 Bari, Italy.
Tel: 080 5211744. Telex: 810345 tecvar i.
Fax: 370400.
Explosivos da Trafaria, SARL, Rua Joaquim António de Aguiar, 66-4°, P-1092 Lisboa Codex, Portugal.
Tel: 691390. Telex: 64053 extral p.
Fax: 691461.

Tecnovar MAT/5 Anti-tank Mine

Description
The Tecnovar MAT/5 anti-tank mine is of the non-metallic type and is stated to be undetectable by magnetic mine detectors. It is also stated to be proof against mine rollers and flails, together with blast and fuel-air explosive mineclearing methods.

The MAT/5 is waterproof and may be laid in fresh or sea water (the mine is non-buoyant), in marshy ground and under up to 1 m of snow. The normal emplacement depth under soil is with the pressure plate between 75 to 150 mm below the ground surface. Laying may be mechanical or manual. Operating pressure is between 180 to 310 kg and on detonating the main charge of Composition B (other explosives may be used) can wreck a tank track and cause extensive damage to the running gear and suspension.

The MAT/5 is fitted with a storage and handling safety device which prevents accidental detonation

even if the detonator explodes accidentally. An anti-lift device may be fitted.

Inert training versions are available.

Specifications
Weight: 7 kg
Diameter: 290 mm
Height: 108 mm
Main charge type: Composition B
Weight of main charge: approx 5 kg
Operating force: 180 to 310 kg
Operating temperature range: −31 to +70°C

Status
In production.

Manufacturer
Tecnovar Italiana SpA, 95 Via Argiro, I-70121 Bari, Italy.
Tel: 080 5211744. Telex: 810345 tecvar i.
Fax: 370400.

Tecnovar MAT/5 anti-tank mine

Tecnovar MAT/6 Anti-tank Mine

Description
The Tecnovar MAT/6 is a non-metallic anti-tank mine that is undetectable by magnetic mine detectors. The body is made from synthetic resins, is non-buoyant and waterproof and can be laid under salt or fresh water and in marshy ground. Manual or mechanical laying methods can be employed with the usual planting depth being with the pressure plate between 75 and 150 mm below the surface of the ground. When detonated the mine can destroy any tank track and cause extensive damage to road wheels and to the tank's suspension.

The MAT/6 has a built-in safety system to prevent accidental explosions during storage or handling. Anti-lift devices can be fitted.

Inert training versions are available.

Specifications
Weight: 7.1 kg
Diameter: 270 mm
Height: 142 mm
Weight of main charge: approx 6.3 kg
Operating force: 180 to 310 kg
Operating temperature range: −31 to +70°C

Status
In production.

Manufacturer
Tecnovar Italiana SpA, 95 Via Argiro, I-70121 Bari, Italy.
Tel: 080 5211744. Telex: 810345 tecvar i.
Fax: 370400.

Tecnovar MAT/6 anti-tank mine

Tecnovar TC/6 and TCE/6 Anti-tank Mines

Description
The Tecnovar TC/6 is a circular resin-based plastic anti-tank mine that is fully waterproof and non-buoyant. It can be laid by hand, to a depth of between 75 and 150 mm in soil and up to 1 m in snow, or laid mechanically from a vehicle.

The TCE/6 is physically similar to the TC/6 mine and is fitted with an electronic arming/disarming device, that can be used to activate or deactivate a minefield or minefield sector composed of these mines on receipt of a command signal.

Actuation of both mines is by the application of force to a pressure plate. Both mines are capable of destroying the tracks and severely damaging the suspension of armoured vehicles. Training versions are available.

The TC/6 is produced in Egypt as the Anti-tank Plastic Mine T.C.6. It is also produced in Portugal by Explosivos da Trafaria SARL.

Specifications
Weight: 9.6 kg
Diameter: 270 mm
Height: 185 mm
Main charge type: Composition B
Weight of main charge: 6 kg
Operating force:
(average) 180 kg
(max) 310 kg
Operating temperature range: −31 to +70°C

Status
In production.

Manufacturers
Tecnovar Italiana SpA, 95 Via Argiro, I-70121 Bari, Italy.
Tel: 080 5211744. Telex: 810345 tecvar i.
Fax: 370400.
Explosivos da Trafaria, SARL, Rua Joaquim António de Aguiar, 66-4°, P-1092 Lisboa Codex, Portugal.
Tel: 691390. Telex: 64053 extral p.
Fax: 691461.

Tecnovar TC/6 anti-tank mine; the TCE/6 is visually similar

Tecnovar BAT/7 Anti-tank Mine

Description
Described as a belly attack anti-tank mine the Tecnovar BAT/7 appears to be of the self-forged fragment warhead type. The mine is completely waterproof and can be emplaced under fresh or salt water and in marshy ground. It is non-buoyant. Operational life is six months.

The BAT/7 uses an electronic magnetic-acoustic sensor to detonate the mine. On detonation the mine is stated to be able to destroy tank tracks and penetrate up to 150 mm of tank belly armour. Tests against armour plates have demonstrated penetrations of 200 mm.

Inert training versions are available.

Specifications
Weight: approx 5.6 kg
Diameter: 270 mm
Height: 160 mm
Weight of main charge: 3.6 kg
Operational life: 6 months
Operating temperature range: −30 to +70°C

Status
In production.

Manufacturer
Tecnovar Italiana SpA, 95 Via Argiro, I-70121 Bari, Italy.
Tel: 080 5211744. Telex: 810345 tecvar i.
Fax: 370400.

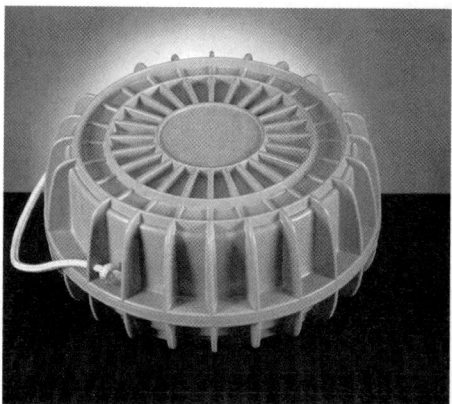

Tecnovar BAT/7 anti-tank mine

BPD SBP-04 and SBP-07 Anti-tank Mines

Description
Both these mines were designed for hand laying and are identical in design and operating characteristics, differing only in their dimensions and weight of high explosive. The mines have the same firing pressure type device which can easily be removed for arming. When activated the mines have sufficient explosive to break the tracks of a tank or damage its suspension.

The mines are non-magnetic and have a plastic case which is available in any colour. They are also waterproof, will not float, are maintenance-free and have a shelf life of 10 years. A smoke-producing model is available for training.

The SBP-04 and SBP-07 mines can be fitted with a SAT igniter that has countermeasures against fuel-air explosive sweeping techniques. A version known as the SAT-TL is externally identical to the basic SAT but can be programmable and remote-controlled. A version fitted with an anti-lift and programmable self-neutralisation device is designated SAT/QZ. It is also physically identical to the basic SAT. The SAT can be retrofitted to numerous older models of anti-tank mine.

SAT/QZ igniter, top (left) and bottom (right)

Status
In production. All three igniter types are in production.

Manufacturer
BPD Difesa e Spazio srl, Corso Garibaldi 20-22, I-00034 Colleferro (Rome), Italy.
Tel: 06 97891. Telex: 611434 bpd cf 1.

Specifications

Mine	SBP-04	SBP-07
Weight	5 kg	8.2 kg
Diameter	250 mm	300 mm
Height	110 mm	130 mm
Main charge type	HE	HE
Weight of main charge	4 kg	7 kg
Operating force	150-310 kg	150-310 kg

Igniter	SAT	SAT/TL	SAT/QZ
Weight	700 g	950 g	1 kg
Diameter	182 mm	182 mm	182 mm
Height	76 mm	76 mm	76 mm

JAPAN

Anti-tank Mine Type 63

Description
The Type 63 anti-tank mine is circular and non-metallic. It is waterproof and can therefore be used for underwater operations, for example buried in the beds of streams which may be forded by tanks and other vehicles. The mine is activated as follows: pressure is applied to the pressure plate and this compresses a hard rubber collar, the pressure forces the firing pin past steel balls to initiate the booster which sets off the main charge.

Specifications
Weight: 14.515 kg
Diameter: 305 mm
Height: 216 mm
Main charge type: Composition B
Weight of main charge: 11 kg
Operating force: 181 kg

Status
In service with the Japanese Ground Self-Defence Force.

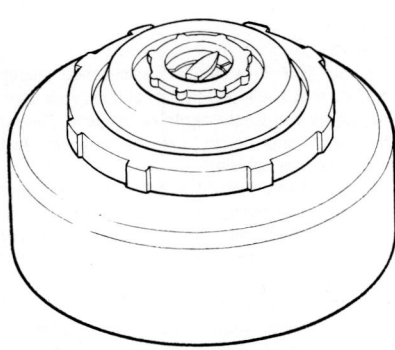

Anti-tank mine Type 63

KOREA, NORTH

Anti-personnel Mine Model 15

Description
This anti-personnel mine is an adaptation of the CIS POMZ-2M mine. The cast-iron body has five rows of serrations with the fuze at the top. The fuze is a copy of the CIS MUV pressure fuze or the UPF pull fuze. The TNT charge is in the centre of the body which is closed at its lower end by the wooden picket which is used to emplace the mine in the ground.

Specifications
Weight: (without stake) 2.6 kg
Length: (without stake) 107 mm
Diameter: 60 mm
Main charge type: TNT
Weight of main charge: 75 g
Operating force: 1 kg

Status
In service with the North Korean Army.

Manufacturer
North Korean state arsenals.

KOREA, SOUTH

Anti-personnel Mine M18A1

Description
The South Korean anti-personnel mine M18A1 is a licence-produced version of the US M18A1 for which there is an entry in this section. Data relating to the South Korean mine are the same as that for the US M18A1.

Status
In production. In service with the South Korean armed forces.

Manufacturer
Korea Explosives Company Limited, 34 Seosomoon-Dong, Chung-Ku, Seoul, Republic of Korea. Tel: 752 6679. Telex: k23684 komite.

South Korean-produced M18A1 anti-personnel mine showing fragment matrix

Anti-personnel Mine K440

Description
The anti-personnel mine K440 is a close copy of the American M18A1 Claymore mine but with the lettering on the body in Korean characters. It is used in exactly the same way as the American mine and the general appearance and characteristics are the same. Data provided by the manufacturer differ in some respects from the M18A1 so they are provided in the Specifications.

The firing device for the K440 is the Firing Device K1, the test set is the K2 and the electrical blasting cap assembly is the K3. A single K440 mine and its K2 test set are carried in an M7 bandolier.

Specifications
Length: 178 mm
Width: 40 mm
Height: 104 mm
Weight of main charge: 0.682 kg
Type of main charge: Comp C4
Number of steel ball fragments: 770
Dispersion:
  (horizontal) 60°
  (vertical) up to 2 m
Lethal range: 50 m
Effective range: 100 m
Operating temperature range: −40 to +51.5°C

Status
In production.

Manufacturer
Daewoo Corporation, 541 Namdaemoon-Ro 5-Ga, Chung-Gu, Seoul, Republic of Korea. Tel: (2) 77191. Telex: 233415 daewoo k. Fax: (2) 7561225.

Anti-tank Mine M19

Description
The South Korean M19 anti-tank mine is a licence-produced version of the American M19 anti-tank mine for which there is a separate entry in this section. Data relating to the South Korean M19 is exactly the same as for the US M19.

Status
In production. In service with the South Korean armed forces.

Manufacturers
Korea Explosives Company Limited, 34 Seosomoon-Dong, Chung-Ku, Seoul, Republic of Korea.
Tel: 752 6679. Telex: k23684 komite.
Daewoo Corporation, 541 Namdaemoon-Ro 5-Ga, Chung-Gu, Seoul, Republic of Korea.
Tel: (2) 77191. Telex: 233415 daewoo k.
Fax: (2) 7561225.

South Korean-produced M19 anti-tank mine

NETHERLANDS

Anti-personnel Mine Model 15

Description
The non-metallic anti-personnel mine Model 15 consists of a plastic box with a hinged lid with the fuze well on the opposite side of the hinge. This mine has no safety device and is detonated as follows: pressure on the lid of the mine pushes down on top of the No 15 pressure fuze, which crushes the ampoule. The acid and powder then ignite and in turn ignite the primer which detonates the mine.

Specifications
Weight: 0.79 kg
Length: 113 mm
Width: 100 mm
Height: 67 mm
Main charge type: TNT
Weight of main charge: 176 g
Operating force: 6-25 kg

Status
In service with the Netherlands Army.

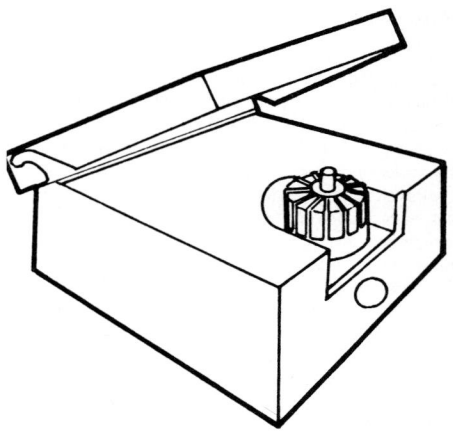

Anti-personnel mine Model 15

Anti-personnel Mine Model 22

Description
This circular anti-personnel mine consists of four main components: plastic case, integral fuze, main charge and the detonator. The plastic case is provided with external strengthening ribs. The Model 22 pressure-friction fuze is in the centre of the mine with the striker showing above the top of the mine. The mine is detonated as follows: pressure on the striker causes the shear collar to fail, which fires the striker which is charged with a friction compound into a mating sleeve where abrasion causes the friction compound to flash, setting off the detonator and then the main charge.

Specifications
Weight: 85 g
Diameter: 72 mm
Height: 50 mm
Main charge type: TNT
Weight of main charge: 40 g
Operating force: 5-25 kg

Status
In service with the Netherlands Army.

26C1 Non-metallic Anti-tank Mine

Description
The 26C1 non-metallic anti-tank mine consists of a cast TNT charge contained within a glass fibre case. Most of the weight of the mine consists of the cast TNT charge which relies upon blast effects alone to damage tank tracks and suspensions. The mine has a pressure friction fuze that operates when a pressure of 350 kg is applied to the pressure plate. A safety handle is used to arm the mine once the detonator and fuze have been placed in a central well and there are two secondary fuze wells, one on the side and one on the bottom.

For training purposes there is a cast-iron inert version of the 26C1 known as the NR-26.

Specifications
Weight: (explosive) 9 kg
Diameter: 300 mm
Height: 120 mm
Operating force: 350 kg

Status
In service with the Netherlands Army.

Cast-iron training version of 26C1 non-metallic anti-tank mine known as NR-26

Anti-tank Mine Type 2, T40

Description
This metallic anti-tank mine consists of two dished pressings joined by a watertight seal. A carrying handle is provided. The two filler plugs are on top of the mine, either side of the central socket, which contains the pressure fuze. The mine is waterproof and operates as follows: pressure applied to the top of the mine crushes the fuze cover, which depresses the plunger and plunger housing, and compresses the striker spring. The plunger has a recess which, when opposite the striker-release balls, lets them escape into it, releasing the spring-loaded striker. This fires the percussion cap which ignites the detonator, which in turn fires the booster which sets off the main charge.

Specifications
Weight: 6 kg
Diameter: 280 mm
Height: 90 mm
Main charge type: TNT
Weight of main charge: 4.08 kg
Operating force: 45 kg

Status
In service with the Netherlands Army.

Anti-tank Mine Model 25

Description
The Model 25 anti-tank mine is circular and has a steel case. There are two anti-lifting fuze wells, one in the side and the other in the bottom of the mine. The mine has three booster charges, one surrounding the main fuze well in the centre of the mine and the other two around each of the two anti-lifting fuze wells.

The mine is detonated as follows: pressure on the top of the mine forces down the pressure plate onto the fuze (the Model 29). This shears the shear pin, releasing the spring-loaded striker, which hits the percussion cap, ignites the detonator and sets off the mine.

Specifications
Weight: 12.97 kg
Diameter: 305 mm
Height: 128 mm
Main charge type: TNT
Weight of main charge: 9 kg
Booster charges: 3
Operating force: 250-350 kg

Status
In service with the Netherlands Army as the NR-25.

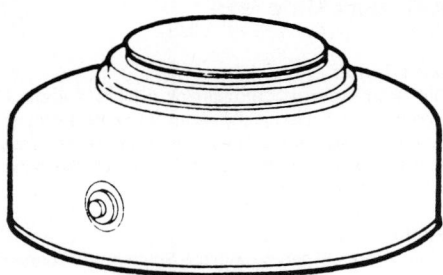

Anti-tank mine Model 25

PAKISTAN

Pakistan Ordnance Factories Anti-personnel Mine

Description
This small anti-personnel mine has a plastic body with minimal metal content. The main charge is tetryl. For transport the mine and detonator holder are packed separately together with a transit plug. For preparation the transit plug and safety covers are removed and the detonator holder is screwed into the base to arm the mine before laying. A length of nylon cord is supplied to allow the mine to be fixed to a picket if required. A metal detection disc can be fitted. It is waterproof.

This mine produces few fragments and relies on blast for its anti-personnel effects. The casualty radius is given as 3 m with a 'damage' zone extending to 10 m. Safety radius is 50 m.

This mine is used as the detonator for the Pakistan Ordnance Factories anti-tank mine (qv).

Specifications
Weight: 95 g
Diameter: 72 mm
Height: approx 44.6 mm
Main charge type: tetryl
Weight of main charge: 30 g

Pakistan Ordnance Factories anti-personnel mines

Status
In production. In service with the Pakistan armed forces.

Manufacturer
Pakistan Ordnance Factories, Wah Cantt, Pakistan.
Tel: 596 82019. Telex: 5840 pofac pk.
Fax: 51 584175.

Pakistan Ordnance Factories Bounding Anti-personnel Mine

Description
This bounding anti-personnel mine has a cast steel body with two actuating modes, pressure or pull firing. The mine is supplied with a spool of tripwire for laying. When the firing mechanism is activated the propelling charge in the base of the mine body is ignited to propel an inverted ARGES-69 hand grenade (also produced in Pakistan) to a height of between 1.25 and 2 m where it detonates to disperse steel fragments over a lethal radius of approximately 25 m. The normal weight of an ARGES-69 grenade is 0.485 kg.

This mine has been referred to as the P-3 but the latest version is known as the P-7.

Status
In production. In service with the Pakistan armed forces.

Manufacturer
Pakistan Ordnance Factories, Wah Cantt, Pakistan.
Tel: 596 82019. Telex: 5840 pofac pk.
Fax: 51 584175.

Pakistan Ordnance Factories P-3 bounding anti-personnel mine

Pakistan Ordnance Factories Directional Mine P5 Mark 1

Description
The P5 Mark 1 directional fragmentation mine is of the Claymore type and uses a melamine plastic body secured to a simple scissor-leg support frame by screws. The main body of the mine contains a matrix of 760 steel balls embedded in polystyrene. The mine can be fired either by a tripwire or by electrical means from a remote position. Two detonator wells are provided on top of the mine body and between them a rudimentary sight for aiming purposes is provided. The height and direction of the mine arc can be varied by using two thumbscrews on the metal support frame. The convex face of the mine body is placed towards the target area; the rear face can be determined by touch as the side where the bolts securing the body halves protrude.

Late production versions of this mine closely resemble the American M18A1 mine (qv).

The complete mine weighs 1.6 kg.

Status
In production. In service with the Pakistan armed forces.

Manufacturer
Pakistan Ordnance Factories, Wah Cantt, Pakistan. Tel: 596 82019. Telex: 5840 pofac pk. Fax: 51 584175.

Pakistan Ordnance Factories Non-metallic Anti-tank Mines P2 and P3

Description
The P3 non-metallic anti-tank mine uses a very simple detonating method. On top of the circular body is a raised pressure plate made from a strong but flexible plastic. When pressure is applied to the plate it will bend only after a certain weight limit (more than 200 kg) has been exceeded. The pressure plate will then break or bend downwards onto a centrally placed anti-personnel mine to detonate the main charge of TNT or Composition B. No anti-lift device well appears to be incorporated although this could be easily introduced. A canvas carrying strap is provided at one side.

The P2 Mark 3 mine is similar to the P3 but uses a squared-off housing to surround the basic circular mine and facilitate mechanical laying and handling. The surround has a canvas carrying strap. Weight of the P2 is approximately 6.6 kg.

If required, both mines can be supplied with a steel disc to assist detection.

Status
In production. In service with the Pakistan armed forces.

Manufacturer
Pakistan Ordnance Factories, Wah Cantt, Pakistan. Tel: 596 82019. Telex: 5840 pofac pk. Fax: 51 584175.

Pakistan Ordnance Factories P2 non-metallic anti-tank mine

PERU

Anti-personnel Mine MGP-30

Description
The MGP-30 anti-personnel mine is a small circular non-metallic mine of conventional design that can be laid manually or scattered from aerial platforms or land vehicles. It is completely waterproof and is armed following the removal of a pin on the side of the mine body. The body colour may be altered to suit customer requirements.

An inert training version is available.

Specifications
Weight: 80-125 g
Diameter: 90 mm
Height: 40 mm
Weight of main charge: 35-80 g
Operating force: 15 kg

Status
Available.

Manufacturer
SIMA-CEFAR, Avenida Contralmirante Mora 1102, Base Naval, Callao, Peru. Tel: 657183. Telex: 26128 PE. Fax: 657183.

Anti-personnel mine MGP-30 (right) with training version (left)

POLAND

MPP-B 'Wierzba' Anti-tank Mine

Description
The MPP-B 'Wierzba' anti-tank mine resembles some of the mines in the CIS TM-62 series but appears to have a non-metallic body and differs in detail. It was designed to be laid either mechanically or manually and is provided with a webbing carrier strap. The main charge is 8.1 kg of TNT.

The pressure fuze is known as the MWCz-62, a direct copy of the CIS clockwork delay MVCh-62. The MPP-B has provision for a booby-trap device set in a well in the base of the mine. The well can also be occupied by an Erg electrical detonator for command detonations.

Specifications
Weight:
(with fuze) 9.7 kg ±0.3 kg
(without fuze) 8.9 kg ±0.3 kg
Diameter: (max) 320 mm
Height:
(with fuze, max) 128 mm
(without fuze, max) 85.9 mm
Weight of main charge: 8.1 kg
Type of main charge: TNT

Status
In production. In service with the Polish armed forces.

Agency
Cenzin Foreign Trade Enterprise, ul. Frascati 2, 00-489 Warsaw, Poland. Tel: 29 67 38. Telex: 814 505 czi Pl. Fax: 628 63 56.

MPP-B 'Wierzba' anti-tank mine

PORTUGAL

MAPS Anti-personnel Mine

Description
The design of the MAPS (*mina anti-pessoal de plástico*) anti-personnel mine appears to be based on that of the Belgian PRB anti-personnel mine NR 409 but it differs in some respects. It is a small, circular and waterproof mine manufactured almost entirely from non-metallic materials – out of the total weight of 180 g only 1 g is metallic.

The MAPS is issued packed in cardboard tubes each containing five mines, and with a clear plastic safety disc covering the entire upper surface of each mine. The safety disc is held in place by a pin. Once the pin and safety disc have been removed the mine is armed and will be detonated by a slight pressure on the fuze membrane.

The MAPS is normally coloured olive green and the main charge may be either TNT or Composition B.

Specifications
Weight: 180 g
Diameter: 88 mm
Height: 35 mm
Main charge type: TNT or Composition B

Weight of main charge: 85 g

Status
In production. In service with the Portuguese armed forces.

Manufacturer
Explosivos da Trafaria, SARL, Rua Joaquim António de Aguiar, 66-4°, P-1092 Lisboa Codex, Portugal. Tel: 691390. Telex: 64053 extral p. Fax: 691461.

Anti-personnel Mine m/966

Description
This small rectangular anti-personnel mine of the fragmentation type is fitted with a pull fuze inserted into the upper surface. Pressure on a tripwire detonates the mine to produce fragments from the metallic body of the mine.

Status
Production complete. Has been encountered in parts of southern Africa.

Anti-personnel mine m/966

Anti-personnel Bounding Mine M432

Description
The M432 anti-personnel bounding mine is a standard pot-type mine that projects a prefragmented projectile upwards when actuated. The projectile then explodes to scatter its anti-personnel fragments. The mine is claimed to be effective against soft-skin vehicle tyres.

The M432 is a vertical cylinder with a T253 trip or pull-actuated fuze assembly placed off-set from the centre on top of the mine body. Actuating the fuze will cause a propelling charge under the fuze to propel an inner body containing the main charge and fragmentation sleeve upwards, together with the fuze assembly. A wire cable remains attached to the mine body and when the inner body has reached a height of about 1 m the cable operates a striker in the main charge. This will ignite a detonator to fire the main charge via a booster charge and spread 1240 effective fragments from the prefragmented sleeve over a lethal radius of 25 m.

Specifications
Weight: 3.9 kg
Diameter: 105 mm
Height with fuze: 268 mm

Height of mine body: 131 mm
Weight of main charge: 0.8 kg
Main charge type: TNT
Number of effective fragments: 1240
Lethal radius: 25 m
Safety radius: 400 m

Status
In production.

Manufacturer
Sociedade Portuguesa de Explosivos SARL, Avenida Infante Santo 76, 5°, P-1300 Lisbon, Portugal. Tel: 60 30 80. Telex: 12398 spelex p.

Anti-personnel Fragmentation Mine m/966

Description
The Anti-personnel Fragmentation Mine m/966 is of the bounding type fitted with a pressure fuze. Pressure on the fuze sets off a small charge in the mine body to propel a 60 mm m/964 mortar bomb body upwards to a height of approximately 1 m before bursting to scatter fragments.

The design of the m/966 appears to be based on that of the American M2A4 bounding mine (qv).

Status
Production complete. Has been encountered in parts of southern Africa.

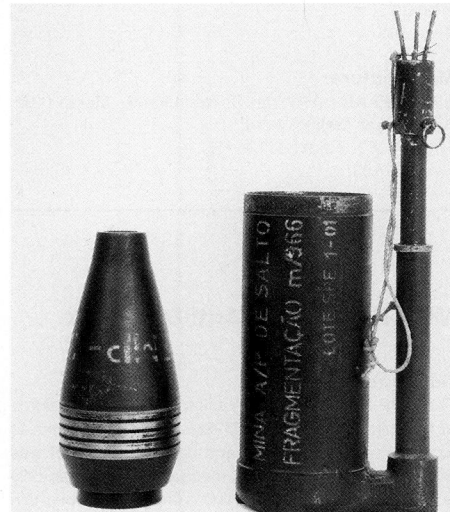

Anti-personnel fragmentation mine m/966 showing body of 60 mm m/964 mortar bomb used by mine

ROMANIA

Lightweight Anti-personnel Mine

Description
The Romanian Lightweight Anti-personnel Mine, described as an anti-infantry mine, is a small circular plastic mine containing a 50 g charge of TNT or RDX. It may be laid mechanically or manually and operates when pressure is applied to either surface. A mechanical security device is provided. No further information is available.

Specifications
Weight: 110 g
Diameter: 70 mm
Height: 45 mm
Weight of charge: 50 g
Type of charge: TNT or RDX

Status
In service with the Romanian armed forces.

Manufacturer
Romanian state factories.

Romanian Lightweight Anti-personnel Mine

MS-3 Ambush Mine

Description
The MS-3 Ambush Mine is a small anti-personnel device that can be employed as an anti-lift device for anti-tank mines or as a booby-trap mine operated by a device that relies on a pressure-release principle. In appearance the circular MS-3 resembles the CIS PMN anti-personnel mine (see entry in this section) and is about the same size, but the MS-3 uses a different rotary switch arming device. The MS-3 operates following a pressure decrease of approximately 6 kg on a pressure button.

Specifications
Weight: 0.63 kg
Diameter: 110 mm
Height: 65 mm
Weight of main charge: 0.31 kg
Pressure load: 6 kg minimum

Status
In service with the Romanian armed forces.

Manufacturer
Romanian state factories.

Romanian MS-3 Ambush Mine

Directional Anti-personnel Mine

Description
This directional anti-personnel mine has a box-shaped body containing a matrix of 1450 fragments embedded in a main charge of cast TNT; each fragment weighs 3 g and has an approximate diameter of 9 mm. The mine body is located on a small tripod and can be arranged to point in any direction using a pan and tilt head.

The mine is fired electrically, probably by remote-control, via an EMP-200 or pressed TNT igniter. As the mine is fired the fragments are spread over an arc 4 m high and up to 60 m wide, out to a minimum effective range of 100 m.

Specifications
Weight:
  (mine) 19 kg
  (tripod) 3.8 kg
  (packed) 34 kg
Width: (mine body) 400 mm
Height: (mine body) 260 mm
Depth: (mine body) 100 mm
Weight of main charge: 12 kg
Type of main charge: cast TNT
Weight of igniter: 50 g
Type of igniter: EMP-200 or pressed TNT
Number of fragments: 1450
Diameter of fragment: 9 mm
Weight of fragment: 3 g

Status
In service with the Romanian armed forces.

Manufacturer
Romanian state factories.

Romanian directional anti-personnel mine

MAT-62B Anti-tank Mine

Description
The MAT-62B anti-tank mine is of the non-metallic type. It has a circular body made up of the main cast TNT charge in a thin plastic container with a pressure fuze located in the upper centre. An integral fabric carrying handle is supplied.

The mine is detonated by a minimum force of 200 kg being applied to the pressure force. The fuze uses a CD-11R igniter to fire the main charge which is sufficient to break a tank track or destroy an armoured vehicle wheel.

Specifications
Weight: 9.8 kg
Diameter: 340 mm
Height: 133.5 mm
Weight of main charge: 7.2 kg
Type of main charge: cast TNT

Status
In service with the Romanian armed forces.

Manufacturer
Romanian state factories.

MAT-62B anti-tank mine

MC-71 Anti-tank Mine

Description
The MC-71 anti-tank mine is a shaped charge device triggered from a tilt-rod mast fuze arrangement located on a separate circular base. The main mine body is made up of the shaped charge covered by a cone-shaped upper section that is supplied with a carrying handle. The mine is buried before use with the mast fuze assembly placed either next to or close to the main mine body so that the mine can be made to detonate under a tank track or belly; it is possible that one mast fuze can be used to detonate more than one mine. In both cases a 0.2 to 0.4 second delay is introduced to ensure the mine detonates under the tank. The mast fuze requires a pressure of from 10 to 20 kg to operate; the mast is 800 mm high and weighs 120 g.

Specifications
Weight complete: 8.2 kg
Mine body diameter: 350 mm
Mine body height: 260 mm
Weight of shaped charge: 5.1 kg
Type of shaped charge: cast TNT

Status
In service with the Romanian armed forces.

Manufacturer
Romanian state factories.

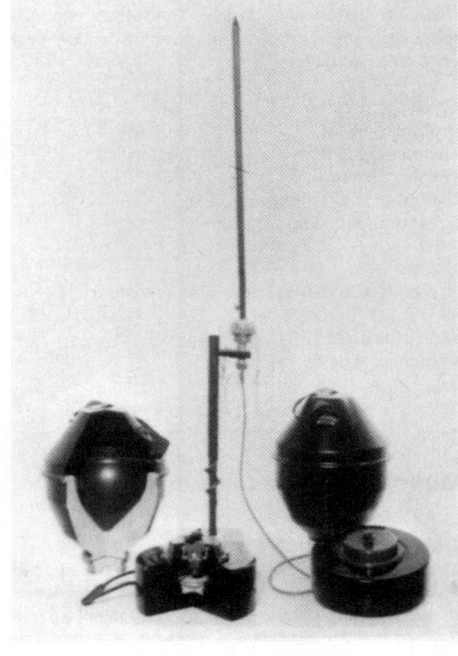

MC-71 anti-tank mine showing fuze mast assembly and main mine body

SERBIA

UDAR Fuel-Air Explosive Anti-personnel Mine

Description
The UDAR fuel-air explosive anti-personnel mine is effective against personnel and lightly armoured vehicles as it is capable of producing a direct blast wave pressure of 20 bars and a reflected blast wave pressure of 40 bars. This pressure is effective against personnel over a radius of up to 40 m.

The UDAR mine is laid in a prepared location below the ground surface and is activated remotely. The mine is in two main parts, the base assembly and the drum-shaped mine body. On activation a charge in the base assembly projects the mine body vertically upwards. The mine body is connected to the base assembly by two wires, both bearing detonators. At a preset height the mine body is disrupted by a small internal charge to release the fuel-air explosive cloud into the surrounding atmosphere. The two detonator assemblies are then ignited to detonate the explosive cloud.

The standard UDAR mine has a total weight of 40 kg, of which approximately 20 kg is the fuel-air explosive. A smaller version exists with a total weight of 20 kg and a charge weight of approximately 10 kg; this is effective over a radius of up to 25 m.

UDAR mines may be employed as individual mines or in groups. It has been stated that when a group of more than 500 UDAR units is activated, the result in blast terms is equivalent to detonating 1 kT of TNT.

Status
Available.

Contractor
Federal Directorate of Supply and Procurement (SDPR), YU-11005 Beograd, 9 Nemanjina Street, Serbia.
Tel: 621522. Telex: 71000/72566 SDPR YU.
Fax: 38 11 631588/630621.

PMA-3 Anti-personnel Mine

Description

The PMA-3 anti-personnel mine is constructed entirely of polystyrene and phenoplast and is thus proof against metal detection devices. It is a small circular mine resistant to high air pressures, including the blast from a 20 kT nuclear weapon detonated at an altitude of 600 m and 500 m from the ground zero. In effect the PMA-3 consists of two plates, one fixed and carrying the fuze and the other pivoting about the fuze and containing the main 35 g tetryl charge.

For transport the PMA-3 is carried with the fuze separate from the mine and the fuze is not fitted into the fuze well until it is ready for laying. Once the fuze has been inserted a length of adhesive tape is removed from the perimeter of the mine body to free a length of string which is then pulled to remove the safety element connecting pin. The mine is then ready for use and any weight from 8 to 20 kg and above will

PMA-3 anti-personnel mine

cause the top pressure plate to pivot about the fuze. Once this displacement exceeds 6 mm a pellet of an incendiary composition in the fuze is broken and the resultant flash ignites an M-17 P2 detonator to set off the main charge.

The PMA-3 service life is six months. The mine is encased in a rubber lining that renders it airtight and, to

a limited extent, watertight. The normal laying depth is recommended to be between 20 and 40 mm depending on soil conditions.

Specifications
Weight: 183 g
Diameter: 111 mm
Height: 40 mm
Main charge type: tetryl
Weight of main charge: 35 g
Operating pressure: 8-20 kg

Status
In service with the former Yugoslav Army.

Contractor
Federal Directorate of Supply and Procurement (SDPR), YU-11005 Beograd, 9 Nemanjina Street, Serbia.
Tel: 621522. Telex: 71000/72566 SDPR YU.
Fax: 38 11 631588/630621.

PMA-2 Anti-personnel Mine

Description

The PMA-2 is a cylindrical anti-personnel mine with a ceramic body. The mechanical pressure fuze, which is operated by a pressure of 7 to 15 kg, is inserted into the fuze well on top of the mine.

A practice mine, the VPMA-2, is identical to the PMA-2 in all respects other than detonation and produces a grey smoke cloud which lasts for a minimum of 5 seconds. The complete VPMA-2 can be used only once; only the body is reusable.

Specifications
Weight: 135 g
Diameter: 68 mm
Height: 61 mm
Main charge type: TNT
Main charge weight: 100 g

Status
In service with the former Yugoslav Army.

Contractor
Federal Directorate of Supply and Procurement (SDPR), YU-11005 Beograd, 9 Nemanjina Street, Serbia.
Tel: 621522. Telex: 71000/72566 SDPR YU.
Fax: 38 11 631588/630621.

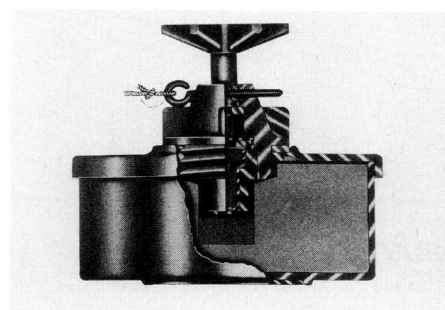

Cross-section of PMA-2 anti-personnel mine with safety pin in place

PMA-1 and PMA-1A Anti-personnel Mines

Description

The PMA-1 plastic non-metallic anti-personnel mine consists of a box with a hinged cover containing a fuze, detonator and the explosive charge. In the bottom of the mine case are two drain holes for use in wet terrain.

The mine operates as follows: when pressure of 3 to 15 kg is applied to the lid, the projection on the lid crushes the capsule and ignites the contents, which actuates the No 8 detonator and initiates the explosive charge.

There is a PMA-1A which differs from the basic PMA-1 only in detail.

The practice version of the PMA-1A is the VPMA-1A made up of a mine body, mine cover, an explosive

charge simulator, a practice fuze, a smoke container, a safety 'element' and a practice detonator. The smoke container, fuze and practice detonator can each be used only once and the entire practice mine has a minimum life of five actuations. Each actuation produces a grey smoke cloud lasting 5 seconds.

Specifications
Weight: 400 g
Length: 140 mm
Width: 70 mm
Height: 30 mm
Main charge type: TNT
Weight of main charge: 200 g
Fuze: UPMAH-1 chemical pressure fuze

Status
In service with the former Yugoslav Army.

Contractor
Federal Directorate of Supply and Procurement (SDPR), YU-11005 Beograd, 9 Nemanjina Street, Serbia.
Tel: 621522. Telex: 71000/72566 SDPR YU.
Fax: 38 11 631588/630621.

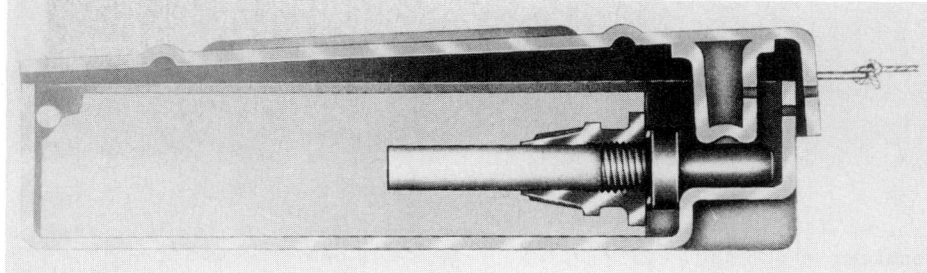

Cross-section of PMA-1A anti-personnel mine showing location of fuze and detonator and with safety pin in place

PROM-1 Bouncing Anti-personnel Mine

Description

This cylindrical bouncing anti-personnel mine has an UPROM-1 fuze which can be activated by pressure or a pull release (that is, attached to a tripwire). In the former case, the pressure pushes the cylinder down, freeing the retaining balls and allowing the striker to hit the percussion cap which explodes, igniting the bouncing charge and ejecting the mine 0.7 to 0.8 m above the ground. The main charge then explodes and

causes fragmentation which is lethal to a radius of 50 m and dangerous to a radius of 100 m. The training version is designated VPROM-1.

Specifications
Weight: 3 kg
Diameter: 75 mm
Height: (with fuze) 470 mm
Main charge type: TNT
Weight of main charge: 425 g
Operating force:
  (pull) 3-5.5 kg
  (pressure) 9-16 kg

VPROM-1, training version of PROM-1 bouncing anti-personnel mine

Status
Production complete. In service with the former Yugoslav Army.

Contractor
Federal Directorate of Supply and Procurement (SDPR), YU-11005 Beograd, 9 Nemanjina Street, Serbia.
Tel: 621522. Telex: 71000/72566 SDPR YU.
Fax: 38 11 631588/630621.

PMR-2A Anti-personnel Mine

Description
The PMR-2A anti-personnel mine is the equivalent of the CIS POMZ-2 and the Czech PP-Mi-Sb stake lines. The mine, which is secured to the top of a wooden stake driven into the ground, is actuated by a tripwire. The mine has a cast steel fragmentation body containing a charge of 100 g of pressed TNT. Operation of this mine is entirely conventional. A pull of more than 3 kg on a thin tripwire will extract a pin from the fuze at the top of the mine. This will release a spring-loaded pin to ignite a percussion cap which in turn fires a No 8 detonator cap to ignite the main charge. The resultant splinters are lethal within a radius of 30 m and can cause serious wounding at up to 40 m.

A version known as the PMR-2AS contains an element mounted above the fuze which illuminates when the mine is fired.

Practice versions of these mines are known as the VPMR-2A and VPMR-2AS.

Specifications (PMR-2A)
Weight: 1.7 kg approx
Diameter: 66 mm
Height: 132 mm
Weight of charge: 100 g
Lethal radius: 30 m

Status
In service with the former Yugoslav Army.

Contractor
Federal Directorate of Supply and Procurement (SDPR), YU-11005 Beograd, 9 Nemanjina Street, Serbia.
Tel: 621522. Telex: 71000/72566 SDPR YU.
Fax: 38 11 631588/630621.

Practice versions of PMR-2A anti-personnel mine; (left) VPMR-2A, (right) VPMR-2AS

MRUD Anti-personnel Mine

Description
The MRUD anti-personnel mine is of the Claymore type and fires a lethal band of steel spheres over an area to its front when ignited. The body of the mine is plastic and contains a mass of plastic explosive weighing 0.9 kg into which are cast 650 steel balls, each 5.5 mm in diameter. On firing, the balls are propelled in a fan 60° horizontally and 3° vertically, and are lethal to a range of 50 m.

The mine is emplaced using two pairs of scissor legs under the mine body. Firing is carried out electrically from a range of at least 30 m and several mines can be fired at once using a manual inductor. Circuits may be tested using a simple circuit test unit. The mine can be used for up to 24 hours under water.

Specifications
Weight: 1.5 kg
Length: 231 mm
Height:
　(legs closed) 318 mm
　(body) 89 mm
Depth: 46 mm
Weight of main charge: 0.9 kg
Type of main charge: plastic explosive
Number of steel balls: 650
Diameter of steel balls: 5.5 mm
Lethal range: 50 m

Status
In service with the former Yugoslav Army.

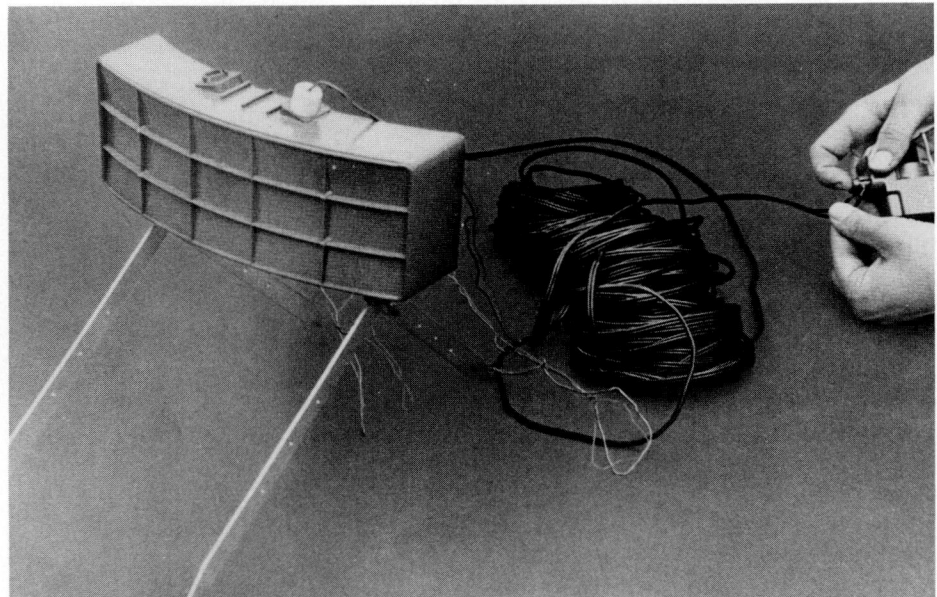

MRUD anti-personnel mine with manual inductor on right

Contractor
Federal Directorate of Supply and Procurement (SDPR), YU-11005 Beograd, 9 Nemanjina Street, Serbia.

Tel: 621522. Telex: 71000/72566 SDPR YU.
Fax: 38 11 631588/630621.

PMR-1 and PMR-2 Anti-personnel Stake Mines

Description
The PMR-1 anti-personnel mine is very similar to the CIS POMZ-2M mine but has nine instead of five rows of fragments. The PMR-2 mine has a concrete and scrap metal fragmentation body and is similar to the Czechoslovak PP-Mi-Sb. This mine uses the UPM-1 pull fuze. A training model is designated the VPMR-3.

Specifications

Model	PMR-1	PMR-2
Weight	2 kg	2.2 kg
Diameter	80 mm	80 mm
Height (with fuze)	120 mm*	120 mm
Main charge type	TNT	TNT
Weight of main charge	75 g	75 g

* Excluding stake

Status
In service with the former Yugoslav Army.

Contractor
Federal Directorate of Supply and Procurement (SDPR), YU-11005 Beograd, 9 Nemanjina Street, Serbia.
Tel: 621522. Telex: 71000/72566 SDPR YU.
Fax: 38 11 631588/630621.

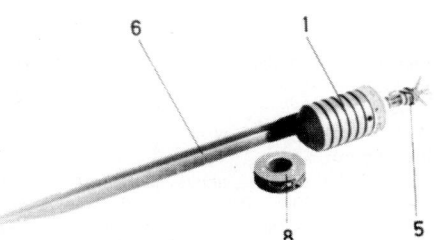

VPMR-3, training version of PMR-1 and PMR-2 anti-personnel stake mines with (1) mine body, (5) practice fuze, (6) stake/carrier and (8) tripwire on bobbin

TMA-5 and TMA-5A Anti-tank Mines

Description
The TMA-5 is a square plastic-bodied anti-tank mine with a central fuze well. The four corners of the plastic outer casing have been reinforced and elongated to allow several mines to be stacked on top of each other. A carrying handle is included as an integral part of the body. The mine may be laid in any type of round within a 600 × 600 × 600 mm space which must be clear to ensure the correct functioning of the UANU-1 fuze, which requires a pressure of 100 to 300 kg to operate. There are four holes in the base of the mine to which drawstrings for various anti-lift devices can be secured. A small cord carrying handle is also fixed to the base.

The TMA-5A differs only in detail from the TMA-5.

The practice version of the TMA-5 is the VTMA-5 which has a hard rubber body. It consists of the hard rubber mine body, a protective cover for the smoke container, the smoke container, a practice fuze and a cover for the fuze well. The VTMA-5 may be used at least 30 times but for each detonation new covers, practice fuzes and smoke containers are required. When detonated the VTMA-5 produces yellow smoke for at least 5 seconds.

Specifications (TMA-5A)
Weight: 6.6 kg
Length: 312 mm
Width: 275 mm
Height: 113 mm
Weight of main charge: 5.5 kg
Weight of booster: 150 g
Type of main charge: cast TNT
Operating pressure: 100-300 kg

Status
In service with the former Yugoslav Army.

Contractor
Federal Directorate of Supply and Procurement (SDPR), YU-11005 Beograd, 9 Nemanjina Street, Serbia.
Tel: 621522. Telex: 71000/72566 SDPR YU.
Fax: 38 11 631588/630621.

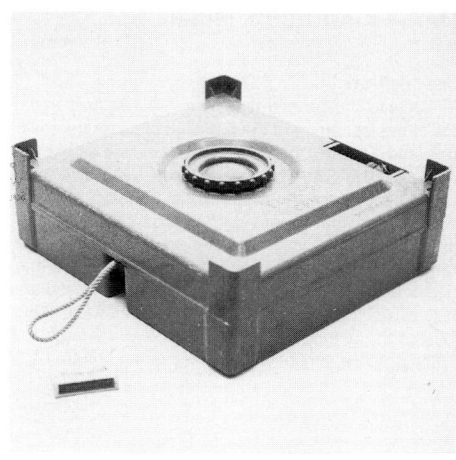

TMA-5 anti-tank mine

TMA-4 Anti-tank Mine

Description
The TMA-4 is a circular plastic anti-tank mine which is larger than the TMA-3, and also has multiple fuze wells. The top three wells take the UTMAH-4 fuze and the bottom well is used for a booby-trapping device. The mine is fitted with a canvas carrying handle on the side.

The practice version of this mine is the VTMA-4.

Specifications
Weight: 6.3 kg
Diameter: 285 mm

Height: 110 mm
Weight of explosive: 5.5 kg
Type of main charge: cast TNT
Operating pressure: approx 200 kg

Status
In service with the former Yugoslav Army.

Contractor
Federal Directorate of Supply and Procurement (SDPR), YU-11005 Beograd, 9 Nemanjina Street, Serbia.
Tel: 621522. Telex: 71000/72566 SDPR YU.
Fax: 38 11 631588/630621.

TMA-4 anti-tank mine

TMA-3 Anti-tank Mine

Description
The TMA-3 circular plastic anti-tank mine is blast- and water-resistant. All parts of the mine are non-metallic and the canvas carrying handle is embedded in the cast explosive of the mine. The three fuze wells in the top of the mine casing each accept a UTMAH-1 fuze, which are left exposed after they have been screwed into position. The bottom fuze well is used for an anti-handling device.

The practice version of this mine is the hard rubber VTMA-3.

Specifications
Weight: 6.6 kg
Diameter: 265 mm
Height: 80 mm
Main charge type: Trotyl or TNT
Weight of main charge: 6.5 kg
Operating force: 180-350 kg
Fuze model: UTMAH-1

Status
In service with the former Yugoslav Army.

Contractor
Federal Directorate of Supply and Procurement (SDPR), YU-11005 Beograd, 9 Nemanjina Street, Serbia.
Tel: 621522. Telex: 71000/72566 SDPR YU.
Fax: 38 11 631588/630621.

Unfuzed TMA-3 anti-tank mine with wooden carrier box for associated UTMAH-1 fuzes

TMA-2 Anti-tank Mine

Description
This plastic anti-tank mine is rectangular and has two fuze wells each of which covers a pressure fuze. When pressure is applied to any part of the mine's upper surface the flexible top of the mine moves downwards until one or both of the fuze well caps come into contact with the pressure fuzes and detonate the mine. The base of the mine has a small hole to which a drawstring for an anti-lift device can be attached.

The practice version of the TMA-2 is the VTMA-2A.

Specifications
Weight: 7.5 kg
Length: 260 mm

Width: 200 mm
Height: 140 mm
Main charge type: TNT
Weight of main charge: 6.5 kg
Operating force: 120-320 kg
Fuze model: UTMAH-1

Status
In service with the former Yugoslav Army.

Contractor
Federal Directorate of Supply and Procurement (SDPR), YU-11005 Beograd, 9 Nemanjina Street, Serbia.
Tel: 621522. Telex: 71000/72566 SDPR YU.
Fax: 38 11 631588/630621.

TMA-2 anti-tank mine

TMA-1A Anti-tank Mine

Description
This plastic circular anti-tank mine has two fuze wells, one in the top centre of the pressure plate for the main fuze, and a second in the bottom of the mine for booby-trapping. The TMA-1A has a very distinctive corrugated top pressure plate. Along the body circumference are four openings set crosswise for the insertion of joints which are designed to regulate the treading force. The downward pressure breaks the fuze cap, which causes friction to ignite the incendiary mixture which in turn ignites the No 8 detonator. This initiates the primer and the main explosive charge.

The practice version of this mine is the VTMA-1A.

Specifications
Weight: 6.5 kg
Diameter: 315 mm
Height: 100 mm
Main charge type: TNT
Weight of main charge: 5.4 kg
Operating force: 100 kg
Fuze model: UTMAH-1

Status
In service with the Yugoslav Army. Being replaced by more modern TMA-type mines.

Contractor
Federal Directorate of Supply and Procurement (SDPR), YU-11005 Beograd, 9 Nemanjina Street, Serbia.
Tel: 621522. Telex: 71000/72566 SDPR YU.
Fax: 38 11 631588/630621.

VTMA-1A, training version of TMA-1A anti-tank mine with (1) mine body, (2) mine cover, (4) smoke container and fuze stopper and (6) safety pins

TMM-1 Anti-tank Mine

Description
The TMM-1 metallic anti-tank mine is a copy of the German Second World War Tellermine 43 (also called the Mushroom mine). The mine can be laid by hand or mechanically, for example by a PMR-3 minelayer. The TMM-1 has two anti-lifting wells, one in the bottom and one in the side. The mine is operated as follows: downward pressure on the mushroom crushes the walls and forces the head of the striker down, igniting the mine.

The practice version of the TMM-1 is the VTMM-1 which has a hard rubber body and a useful life of at least 30 operations. It is identical to the TMM-1 and uses the VUTMM-1 practice fuze which can be used at least 10 times provided the practice detonator, percussion primer and element are replaced after every

VTMM-1, training version of TMM-1 anti-tank mine with (1) mine body and (2) mine cover

activation. When activated the VTMM-1 produces a yellow smoke cloud that lasts at least 5 seconds.

Specifications
Weight: 8.6 kg
Diameter: 310 mm
Height: 100 mm
Main charge type: Trotyl
Weight of main charge: 5.6 kg
Operating force: 130-420 kg
Fuze model: UTMM (pressure)

Status
In limited service with former Yugoslav Army reserve units.

Contractor
Federal Directorate of Supply and Procurement (SDPR), YU-11005 Beograd, 9 Nemanjina Street, Serbia.
Tel: 621522. Telex: 71000/72566 SDPR YU.
Fax: 38 11 631588/630621.

TMRP-6 Anti-tank Mine

Description
The TMRP-6 anti-tank mine is described as being highly destructive as it uses the twin explosion principle; the first explosion clears the area of soil above the mine ready for the second explosion which propels a convex steel sheet upwards to form a rudimentary self-forging fragment. The mine is said to be able to penetrate up to 40 mm of armour at distances of up to 800 mm.

The TMRP-6 may use either a pressure ignition system or a tilt-rod system. Both are used with the UTMRP-6 fuze which has several transport safeties incorporated. To arm the mine a plastic safety element has to be removed, a small key wrench is inserted into the fuze body to align the initiation train, and the tilt-rod has to be inserted into the fuze itself. The mine then arms itself using a simple clockwork mechanism after a delay of 1 or 4 minutes. When the fuze is actuated by pressure in excess of 150 kg (1.3 to 1.7 kg on the tilt-rod) it detonates a small charge of black powder that blows off the top part of the mine to expose the main

Insertion of tilt-rod into fuze of TMRP-6 anti-tank mine

charge and the convex steel sheet. The main charge is 5.1 kg of cast TNT and the detonator is tetryl.

The TMRP-6 may be laid manually or direct from a helicopter. It may also be laid mechanically using a locally produced version of the CIS PMR-3 towed minelayer (see *Minelaying equipment* section for both entries). The mine may be laid in swampy ground. It is possible to fit an anti-lift device, and the same fuze well

under the body may be used to fit an electrical connector for remote electrical firing.

Specifications
Weight: 7.2 kg
Diameter: 290 mm
Height: 132 mm
Weight of main charge: 5.1 kg
Type of main charge: cast TNT
Operating force:
(pressure) 150 kg
(tilt-rod) 1.3-1.7 kg
Fuze: UTMRP-6

Status
In service with the former Yugoslav Army.

Contractor
Federal Directorate of Supply and Procurement (SDPR), YU-11005 Beograd, 9 Nemanjina Street, Serbia.
Tel: 621522. Telex: 71000/72566 SDPR YU.
Fax: 38 11 631588/630621.

SOUTH AFRICA

High-explosive Anti-personnel Mine

Description

Known as the Mine A/P HE or R2M1, this small anti-personnel mine has a circular moulded plastic body filled with 58 g of RDX/WAX 88:12. It has an operating pressure of between 3 and 7 kg and it can be laid in streams and rivers up to a depth of 1 m. Before use, a waterproof booster is inserted into the waterproof detonator and the mine is armed by removing a cord attached to a safety pin and clip.

A practice mine is available which is coloured light blue instead of the normal brown. This practice mine fires a small smoke pellet in place of the operational charge but is otherwise identical. It weighs 126 g.

Specifications
Weight: 128 g
Weight of main charge: 58 g
Weight of firing mechanism: 6.5 g

Status

In production. In service with South African armed forces.

Manufacturer

Enquiries to: Armscor, Private Bag X337, Pretoria 0001, South Africa.
Tel: (12) 428 1911. Telex: 320 217.
Fax: (12) 428 5635.

Mine A/P HE

Shrapnel Mine No 2

Description

The Shrapnel Mine No 2 is a copy of the American M18A1 Claymore mine and differs from it in only a few details. The body is moulded polystyrene and contains 680 g of plastic explosive which forms the main propellant charge for the matrix of steel fragments. Optimum range is given as 15 m with a maximum of 50 m. The mine can produce a fan-like pattern of projectiles 2 m high and 50 m wide at 50 m. As with the M18A1, two detonator points are provided on top of the mine body, between which is a simple sight. Two pairs of folding legs support the mine in position.

Each mine weighs 1.58 kg.

Status

In production. In service with South African armed forces.

Manufacturer

Enquiries to: Armscor, Private Bag X337, Pretoria 0001, South Africa.
Tel: (12) 428 1911. Telex: 320 217.
Fax: (12) 428 5635.

Shrapnel Mine No 2

Anti-tank Mine No 8

Description

Known generally as the High Explosive Anti-tank Mine, the No 8 has an injection-moulded thermo-plastic body with a main charge of 7 kg RDX/TNT 60:40. The only metal used in construction is the striker mechanism of the initiator. During transit or storage, the mine is fitted with a transit plug which is not removed until the mine is being prepared for laying. A cord carrying handle is provided. An impact load of from 150 to 220 kg is required to detonate the mine and a two-position safety lever is provided. The top of the detonator plate is moulded in an irregular pattern to aid concealment and the normal body colour is neutria.

Specifications
Weight: 7.4 kg
Weight of main charge: 7 kg
Weight of firing mechanism:
  (LZY waterproof detonator) 6.5 g
  (tetryl booster) 3 g
  (RDX/WAX 88:12 charge) 58 g

Status

In production. In service with South African armed forces.

Manufacturer

Enquiries to: Armscor, Private Bag X337, Pretoria 0001, South Africa.
Tel: (12) 428 1911. Telex: 320 217.
Fax: (12) 428 5635.

Anti-tank mine No 8

SPAIN

Anti-personnel Mine Model FAMA

Description

This anti-personnel mine consists of an upper and lower case, both plastic, joined and sealed by a sealing ring. The fuze is in the top of the mine and is protected by a circular cover. The mine is detonated as follows: pressure is applied to the top of the mine, which causes the upper cover to break along the shear groove; the inner portion then moves downwards until it contacts the firing pin plunger, which shears at a shear collar and drives the firing pin into the primer, igniting the detonator which sets off the mine. A practice version has also been produced with slightly different dimensions (diameter: 73 mm, height: 33 mm).

Specifications
Weight: 86 g
Diameter: 71 mm
Height: 38 mm
Main charge type: TNT or Tetryl
Weight of main charge: 50 g
Operating force: 30 kg

Status

In service with the Spanish Army.

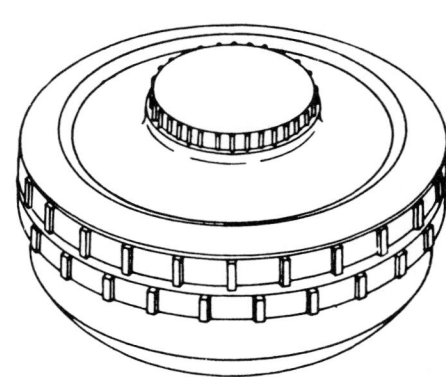

Anti-personnel mine model FAMA

Anti-personnel Mine P-S-1

Description
The P-S-1 is a cylindrical steel case anti-personnel bounding mine with a top-mounted fuze assembly. Actuation is by a pull on a tripwire connected to the fuze unit which fires the main body propelling charge to a height of approximately 1.2 m where it explodes into small fragments. The effective radius against personnel is 20 m. Training and practice versions are available.

Specifications
Weight: 3.78 kg
Diameter: 98 mm

Height:
(mine plus fuze) 189 mm
(mine only) 127 mm
Main charge type: TNT
Weight of main charge: 450 g
Weight of shrapnel: 2.6 kg
Effective radius: 20 m

Status
In service with the Spanish Army.

Manufacturer
Explosivos Alaveses SA, Orense 68, 10th Floor, E-28020 Madrid, Spain.
Tel: 5715559. Telex: 43484.
Fax: 2797914.

P-S-1 anti-personnel mine complete with fuze and detonator

Anti-tank Mine C-3-A

Description
The C-3-A is a circular anti-tank mine consisting of a plastic mine body and a central plastic fuze and pressure plate assembly. Actuation is by means of a heavy load to the top-mounted pressure plate. A C-3-B version is essentially similar.

Instruction, training and practice versions are available.

Specifications
Weight: 5.9 kg

Diameter: 285 mm
Height: 115 mm
Type of main charge: TNT
Weight of main charge: 5 kg

Status
In service with the Spanish Army and with Argentina.

Manufacturer
Explosivos Alaveses SA, Orense 68, 10th Floor, E-28020 Madrid, Spain.
Tel: 5715559. Telex: 43484 xpal e.
Fax: 2797914.

C-3-A anti-tank mine with travelling cap fitted

SWEDEN

Anti-personnel Mine Type LI-11

Description
The anti-personnel mine LI-11 consists of a fixed lower

Cross-section of LI-11 anti-personnel mine

part and a movable upper part, both made of rubber and held together by a moisture-proof rubber casing. The mine incorporates a humidity shield allowing it to be used in marshy ground.

The mine has a pressure fuze and is detonated when pressure is applied to the centre or edge. It cannot be detonated by the shock waves from other detonating mines.

When being carried a safety ring is fitted in place of the detonator. A practice mine which emits orange smoke is also in service.

Specifications
Weight: 200 g
Diameter: 80 mm

Height: 35 mm
Main charge type: TNT
Weight of main charge: 110 g
Operating force: 5-10 kg
Operating temperature: −40 to +65°C

Status
Production complete. In service with the Swedish Army as *Truppmina 10*.

Manufacturer
Lindesbergs Industri AB (LIAB), Box 154, S-711 00 Lindesberg, Sweden.
Tel: 46 581 125 70. Telex: 73202.
LIAB is now part of Bofors AB.

Area Defence Mine FFV 013

Description
Development of the FFV 013 area defence mine began in the early 1970s. The Swedish Army carried out troop trials with the mine in 1978 and orders for the mine have since been placed by the Swedish armed forces, Switzerland, Norway and Ireland. In September 1990 it was announced that the FFV 013 will be licence-produced in Japan by Ishikawa Seisakusho Limited from the beginning of 1991 onwards. An initial order worth SEK 30 million was delivered direct to Japan by FFV in late 1990.

The FFV 013 mine, known as the *Fordonsmina* 13 by the Swedish Army, is intended for use in tactical situations where quick reaction and instantaneous firepower are required, such as defence against airborne and heliborne landings, airfield defence, defence of vulnerable points and ambushes.

The mine consists of a prefragmented plate behind which an explosive charge is contained in a glass fibre housing. On detonation, the explosive charge accelerates the prefragmented plate to a high velocity. The plate, which consists of balls with a hexagonal cross-section, will then disintegrate and the balls will continue in their trajectories in an unchanged pattern. At a range of 150 m, the balls cover an area 100 m wide and 3 to 4 m high.

The mine is normally mounted on a tripod or on a permanent emplacement. The mine is ignited by a special shock tube system which is non-electric and is thus insensitive to electrical radiations or pulses from thunderstorms.

Variant
FFV 013R
The FFV 013R is an area defence mine half the weight of the FFV 013 but exactly the same in construction and tactical use. It weighs 10 kg and has an effective range of 100 m where it will cover an arc 70 m wide and 2 to 3 m high. When fired the FFV 013R projects 840 ball fragments, each approximately 3 g in weight,

Area defence mine FFV 013 on left with FFV 013R on right

at a fragment density of 2 fragments/m². The FFV 013R is under evaluation by several countries.

Specifications (FFV 013)
Weight:
(mine body) 20 kg
(container with mine, tripod and firing device) 35 kg
Width: (mine body) 420 mm
Height: (mine body) 250 mm
Number of ball fragments: approx 1200
Fragment density: (within 150 m) approx 2 fragments/m²

Weight of ball fragment: approx 6 g
Impact energy: 150 J at 150 m

Status (FFV 013)
In production. Ordered for the Swedish, Swiss and Norwegian armed forces, Ireland and Japan. Licence-produced in Japan from 1991 onwards.

Manufacturer
Bofors AB, S-69 180 Karlskoga, Sweden.
Tel: 46 586 81 000. Telex: 73210.
Fax: 46 586 58 145.

Light Off-route Mine FFV 016

Description
The FFV 016 light off-route mine was designed to create an explosively formed projectile (EFP) and is intended for use in an off-route mode against armoured personnel carriers. The mine produces a projectile with an initial velocity of approximately 2000 m/s. At a range of 30 m the projectile will penetrate 60 mm of armour and produce a hole 80 mm in diameter.

The mine weighs 2.6 kg, is easy to handle and can be attached to a tree, pole or similar structure, and is manually triggered. Tactically it can be used for ambushes on roads, tracks and in urban areas, and for covering minefields.

Status
In production.

Manufacturer
Bofors AB, S-69 180 Karlskoga, Sweden.
Tel: 46 586 81 000. Telex: 73210.
Fax: 46 586 58 145.

Light off-route mine FFV 016

Anti-tank Mine FFV 028

Development
In the second half of the 1960s studies were made in Sweden to find new and more effective anti-tank mines. The main requirements were the ability to kill the tank, rather than immobilise it temporarily, and that the mine should permit a reduction of the mine density in the minefield without reducing the probability of a mine being activated. Full scale development of the mine began in the early 1970s and in early 1978 the mine was at the pre-production stage. The FFV 028 was ordered by the Swedish armed forces in 1982, and by the German armed forces in 1985.

The 1985 contract was placed by the then West German Ministry for Armament and Procurement and was initiated by the delivery of a trials batch of 200 mines. The full contract was for 125 200 FFV 028 SN D-31 mines at a cost of DM 141.2 million with German participation in production expected to reach a level of 35 per cent.

In December 1985 the Netherlands Ministry of Defence placed an order worth SKr 365 million for FFV 028 mines and their associated minelayers. A further order worth SKr 200 million was placed during September 1989.

Description
The mine, known as the *Stridsvagnsmina* 6 by the Swedish armed forces, consists of two main components, the body and the fuze. The body contains the hollow charge with the liner and the battery housing. The battery is a standard single-cell type and maintains its performance even at low temperatures. It has a shelf life of more than 10 years and can be replaced from the outside of the mine. The hollow charge of the mine is contained in a non-magnetic housing.

The FFV 028 can be laid by hand or by the FFV mechanical minelayer which was developed specifically for use with this mine. Details will be found in the *Minelaying equipment* section.

When laying the mine, the transport safety is removed and the arming lever is pressed down and turned 90°. This connects the battery and the electric time circuit starts. The shutter is released and its time mechanism starts. When the time delay has expired, the shutter turns to the armed position, the explosive train is aligned and the electric detonator is connected to the electronic unit. At this time the electronic safety also ceases and the mine is armed.

The mine is effective against the whole width of the tank and operates as follows: when a vehicle passes over the mine its fuze senses the disturbances in the terrestial magnetic field, the electronic unit processes the signal and, when the conditions for initiation have been met, it emits an initiation pulse to the electric detonator. The uncovering charge blows off the upper part of the fuze and any camouflage over the mine. Thus the hollow charge jet is unobstructed when the bursting charge detonates after a certain delay. The mine will penetrate the belly armour of any tank and causes considerable damage by blast and fragments. As there is a trend to stow all ammunition in a tank below the turret ring, it is highly probable that the ammunition of the tank will explode. The mine is insensitive to shock waves caused by artillery fire or nuclear explosions.

The FFV 028 has a considerably higher probability of being actuated than a conventional mine: 2.5 to 3 times as many conventional mines as FFV 028 mines are required to attain the same probability of a mine being actuated in a minefield.

The FFV 028 SN has a self-neutralisation mechanism that operates after a selected period of between 30 and 180 days. The mine can be manufactured with an arming delay of up to 60 minutes.

Specifications
Weight: 8.4 kg
Diameter: 250 mm
Height: 120 mm
Main charge type: RDX/TNT
Weight of main charge: 4 kg
Operational life: preselected, from 30 to 180 days
Self-destruct/neutralisation: yes
Anti-lift device: yes

Status
In production. In service with the Dutch, Swedish and German armed forces.

Manufacturer
Bofors AB, S-69 180 Karlskoga, Sweden.
Tel: 46 586 81 000. Telex: 73210.
Fax: 46 586 58 145.

Anti-tank mine FFV 028

Anti-tank Mines Models 41-47 and 47

Description
These anti-tank mines (*Stridsvagnsminor*) are circular and have a metal case and a carrying handle. They differ only in their size and weight. The five-armed pressure spider is supported by a metallic band attached to a collar that screws into the fuze well which is in the centre of the mine with the booster charge under the fuze. The mine functions as follows: pressure on the top of the spider forces this down until it pushes on the fuze, the shear pin of the fuze fails and the plunger moves downwards, compressing the striker spring and allowing the retaining balls to escape, the striker is driven downwards and hits the percussion cap, which fires the detonator, then the booster, and the mine explodes.

There is also an anti-tank mine Model 47-52 B

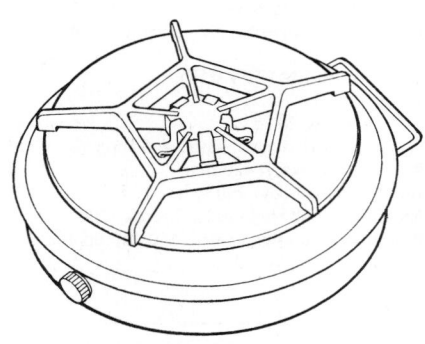

Anti-tank mine Model 41-47

(*Stridsvagnsmina* m/47-52 B). This is a Model 47 anti-tank mine body with the same pressure adaptor m/49 with optional three-pronged sensor or tilt-rod as that

used on the anti-tank mine Model 52 B (see following entry). As with the Model 52 B, the three-pronged sensor will operate at a pressure of 100 to 200 kg or 15 kg applied to the tilt-rod.

Specifications
Weight:
  (Model 41-47) 8 kg
  (Model 47) 9.5 kg
Diameter: 270 mm
Height with spider: 125 mm
Main charge type: TNT
Weight of main charge: 5 kg
Type of booster: pressed TNT
Operating force:
  (centre of spider) 200 kg
  (edge of spider) 400 kg

Status
In service with the Swedish Army.

Anti-tank Mines Models 52 and 52 B

Description
These circular anti-tank mines have moulded plywood cases covered with waterproof fabric. A carrying handle is provided on the side of the mine. The single fuze well is in the top of the mine and a Model 47 pressure fuze is installed. Three types of pressure piece may be used with the mine: a pentagonal spider, a small three-pronged pressure piece or a tilt-rod.

The Model 52 operates as follows: pressure on the pressure piece crushes the head of the fuze, causing

the shear pin to fail, the fuze plunger moves downward allowing the striker-retaining balls to escape, the striker then hits the percussion cap, which fires the detonator and the mine explodes.

There is also a Model 52 B which may be fitted with either a three-pronged pressure sensor or a tilt-rod fitted to a pressure adaptor m/49 (*Brytutlösare* m/49). The mine operates when a pressure of 100 to 200 kg is applied to the three-pronged sensor or 15 kg to the tilt-rod. Both applications use a fuze model m/47 (F) (*Mintändare* m/47 (F)). The Model 52 B (*Stridsvagns-mina* m/52 B) weighs 9.5 kg.

These mines can also accommodate the Mine Fuze

15 and 16 (see following entries).

Specifications
Weight: 8.98 kg
Diameter: 345 mm
Height: 77 mm
Main charge type: TNT
Weight of main charge: 7.48 kg
Operating force: 250 g (with tilt-rod fuze) 14.5 kg

Status
In service with the Swedish Army.

Mine Fuze 15

Description
The Mine Fuze 15, at one time known as the ATF-1, was developed by Bofors Electronics AB (now Nobel-Tech Electronics AB) to upgrade pressure-operated anti-tank mines by giving them a full width attack capability. The fuze has a tilting rod sensor that controls arming and initiates the mine after a customer-defined delay. With the arming lever at safe the

explosive chain is blocked. The mine's status is indicated by the position of the arming lever and the inspection window. The fuze can be made safe after arming to allow the mine or fuze to be used elsewhere.

The Mine Fuze 15 is made from plastic and contains a minimum of components. It was designed for mass production and can be fitted to many mines by using adaptors or by minor design changes.

The height of the fuze without the tilt-rod is 125 mm and 760 mm with the tilt-rod fitted. Diameter is 64 mm and weight 400 g.

Status
In series production for the Swedish Army.

Manufacturers
NobelTech Electronics AB, S-175 88 Järfälla, Sweden.
Tel: 46 8 580 85388. Telex: 126 88 nobelte s.
Fax: 46 8 580 322 44.
Bofors AB, S-69 180 Karlskoga, Sweden.
Tel: 46 586 81 000. Telex: 73210.
Fax: 46 586 58 145.

Mine Fuze 16

Description
The Mine Fuze 16 is an electronic fuze developed for the Swedish Army. It may be used to upgrade numerous types of pressure-operated anti-tank mines to a full width attack capability. It is provided with a sensor which senses any changes in the local terrestial magnetic field, such as those produced when a vehicle passes over the fuze. The fuze can be adapted to most non-metallic mines and is resistant against manual clearance, magnetic signature duplicators and mine rollers.

For use the fuze is fitted to the mine, the transport safety cover is removed, pressure is applied to a shutter detent bolt and an arming lever is then turned. The fuze will become active after a 5 minute delay.

The fuze will operate to a depth of 200 mm. Active life is six months and shelf life 20 years (minimum). The fuze weighs 600 g, has an overall height of 127 mm (66 mm above the mine) and a diameter of 125 mm.

Status
In series production for the Swedish Army.

Manufacturers
NobelTech Electronics AB, S-175 88 Järfälla, Sweden.
Tel: 46 8 580 85388. Telex: 126 88 nobelte s.
Fax: 46 8 580 322 44.
Bofors AB, S-69 180 Karlskoga, Sweden.
Tel: 46 586 81 000. Telex: 73210.
Fax: 46 586 58 145.

Mine Fuze 16 fitted to anti-tank mine Model 52 with tilt-rod Mine Fuze 15 on right

SWITZERLAND

Anti-personnel Mine P59

Description
The P59 is circular and consists of a waterproof cover, plastic nylon body, firing mechanism and the explosive charge. When pressure is applied to the top of the mine, the striker is depressed, which breaks the glass, strikes the detonator and initiates the mine.

Specifications
Diameter: 72 mm
Height: 54 mm
Main charge type: pressed TNT
Weight of main charge: 48-59 g
Operating force: 5 kg

Status
In service with the Swiss Army.

Anti-personnel Mine Model 49

Description
This mine is cylindrical with a carrying handle and is normally staked to the ground. Its concrete fragmentation jacket contains embedded steel shrapnel. This mine uses the Model ZDZ-49 combination fuze which can be activated by pull, tension-release or pressure. The fuze well is in the top of the mine.

Specifications
Weight: 8.618 kg
Diameter: 150 mm
Height: 224 mm
Main charge type: TNT
Weight of main charge: 0.49 kg
Operating force: 8 kg

Status
In service with the Swiss Army.

UNITED KINGDOM

Mines In The New Century (MINX)

Description
In early 1991 requests for proposals were issued for the Ministry of Defence's Mines In The New Century (MINX) Programme which is intended to replace the Royal Ordnance Bar Mine system (see entry in this section). The MINX programme will take a systems approach comprising command and control (including the remote-control of minefields) and logistics as well as the mines and the minelayer. Training and maintenance systems are included.

Industry will be invited to submit a feasibility study as well as a supporting proposal for project definition and full development. At the end of the first project definition phase the number of contractors will be reduced to two for the second phase. If approval to proceed is given, one will be selected to carry out full development and initial production.

To compete for the MINX programme Royal Ordnance has formed a team including Nea Lindberg of Denmark, Marine Air Systems of New Zealand, Faber Design Consultancy and HVR Consulting Services Limited.

Hunting Engineering Limited has teamed with Bofors AB and Texas Instruments (Bedford).

Ferranti International are known to be interested in bidding for the MINX programme but no details regarding their entry team have been released.

By late 1992 the entire MINX programme was understood to be on hold with further activity being suspended.

Status
Early project proposals – see text.

THORN EMI Ranger Barrier Defence System

Description
The THORN EMI Ranger scatterable mine system was developed by the Royal Armament Research and Development Establishment at Fort Halstead and THORN EMI Electronics Limited.

It has a variety of applications including covering rows of anti-tank mines as they are being laid, covering an existing anti-tank minefield by firing anti-personnel mines from outside the field, delaying the repair of demolitions, rapid infesting of woods, roadsides and tracks to impede and canalise enemy movement, infesting the far bank of a canal or river to impede enemy movement.

The system consists of 72 disposable tubes loaded in a discharger which can be mounted on any medium or heavy vehicle. The British Army uses the FV432 armoured personnel carrier with the Ranger system mounted on the top of the hull and the vehicle towing the Bar minelaying system. Each tube contains 18 anti-personnel mines which are ejected by means of a cartridge. The firing is controlled manually and each tube can be fired independently. The mines disperse in flight and form a random pattern on the ground. This pattern can be varied by traversing, elevating and by selecting the number of tubes to be fired. The launcher can travel safely fully loaded, as the mines are not armed until 20 seconds after firing. Palletised resupply mines, already in tubes, enable the complete system of 1296 mines to be reloaded in under 6 minutes. The system comprises four main units, dischargers, filled magazine, firing control unit and the mine.

Discharger

The discharger is mounted on pivots and is adjustable in both elevation and azimuth. An adaptation frame can be designed and produced to enable the discharger to be installed on most vehicles. A power supply of 24 V DC is required. The magazines are locked into position in the dischargers which incorporate a safety system making all mines inoperative until ready to be fired. This is the first of three safety devices to be operated before the mine is fuzed for operation.

Magazine

The disposable magazine consists of an aluminium breech assembly attached to a disposable tube of paper/polythene/paper layered material. The cartridge fits into the breech assembly and makes contact with the electrical firing circuit when the magazine is loaded into the discharger. The 18 mines are held firmly in the tube by an end cap which prevents accidental ejection and also provides an environmental seal. The tubes are mounted in sets of four, with a suitable carrying handle, to enable rapid loading of the discharger. The electrically initiated cartridge propels the mines at distances of up to 100 m, depending on ground and wind conditions.

Firing control unit

The firing control unit produces firing impulses and is controlled by a hand-held unit on a wander-lead which

Inert Ranger practice mines, from left: underside primed and ready to fire; top side; after firing and cocked for use

incorporates a push-button. As one cartridge is fired, the unit sets the system so that the next cartridge is fired when the push-button is pressed again. This sequence continues until all 72 tubes have been discharged.

The mine

The mine is cylindrical and measures 32 mm deep and 62 mm in diameter. It is moulded from polycarbonate plastic and is assembled on either side of a central bulkhead and includes a safety system, arming system and a main charge. The charge consists of approximately 10 g of RDX/Wax encased in a metal container with a CE pellet to ensure reliable take-over from the detonator. The mine is pressure-actuated and has been designed to immobilise personnel without inflicting a fatal wound.

Three safety devices are incorporated into the mine to ensure that the mine does not arm until 20 seconds after leaving the discharger. As the time of flight is less than 5 seconds, the mine can be on the ground, having come to rest, for some 15 seconds before automatic arming occurs. The mine is camouflaged green but can be provided in alternative colours. The mine is waterproof and operates under water.

For training and drill purposes, a low-cost compressed peat drill mine for use with a special drill

magazine is employed. This obviates the time-consuming clearance of training areas.

Specifications
Payload: 1296 mines
Weight:
  (of discharger fully loaded) 630 kg
  (of operational magazine loaded) 14 kg
Azimuth: adjustable through 180°
Elevation: adjustable over +5° to +35°
Loading time: (with 2 men) under 6 min
Range: 100 m
Firing rate: 1 tube of 18 mines/s (max)
Height: (above vehicle platform) 1.3 m
Width: 2.2 m
Length: 1.5 m

Status
Production complete. In service with the British Army.

Manufacturer
THORN EMI Electronics Limited, Defence Systems Division, Victoria Road, Feltham, Middlesex TW7 7JS, UK.
Tel: 081 890 3600. Telex: 24325 emifel g.
Fax: 081 890 4729.

Bar Mine System and FWAM

Description
The Bar mine system was developed by the Royal Armament Research and Development Establishment at Fort Halstead, Kent, as the replacement for the Mark 7 anti-tank mine. The system consists of two major components, the mine and the minelayer.

The L9 Bar mine is plastic with only a few metal components in the fuze and is difficult to detect using current electromagnetic mine detectors. The mine is stored complete with its fuze, which saves time and manpower in fitting the fuze before the mine can be laid.

The long shape of the Bar mine doubles the chance of it being actuated by a tank and dramatically reduces the number of mines required to lay a minefield. Trials have confirmed that the Bar mine is completely effective against any tank track when the tank has a part of the mine inboard of the tracks. The explosive effect is sufficient to break the tracks and damage the belly armour of the tank.

Fuzes currently employed with the Bar mine are pressure-operated single-impulse and double-impulse types (the latter counteracts mine roller clearance). To further enhance the Bar mine three additional fuzes are available offering anti-disturbance and Full Width Attack Mine (FWAM) capability. The FWAM fuzes were developed by Marconi Radar and Control Systems. Over 100 000 FWAM fuzes were produced by the

Marconi facility at Hillend, Fife. The range of fuzes was expanded during 1990 by the introduction of the RO 150 electronic fuze; this is the Danish Nea-Lindberg M/88 fuze produced under licence by Royal Ordnance.

All types of fuze are armed by initially pulling out lanyards as the mine is loaded into the minelayer and then by an arming mechanism mounted near the end of the minelayer conveyor belt. FWAM and anti-disturbance fuzes are fitted with timers to delay arming by between 10 and 30 minutes after laying. The anti-disturbance fuze employs a mercury switch system and counteracts mine plough clearance and other methods of mine removal.

The FWAM mechanical fuze has a sensor mast which is raised into position by a spring when the fuze is armed. The mast sensor is activated by contact with the underbelly of a moving tank. The FWAM electronic fuze is activated by seismic disturbance coupled with electromagnetic signature recognition. The thin film electronics are powered by a lithium copper oxide battery which gives a six-month laid life and a five-year shelf life. FWAM fuzes employ timer delays to ensure the most vulnerable area of a target tank's underbelly is above the mine at the point of detonation. It is intended that all three option fuzes will be used in a 'mix' when laying minefields.

The Bar mine has been designed for use with the Bar minelayer but can also be laid by hand; a manportable pack of four mines is available. The Bar mine is normally packed in pallets of 72 mines which can be handled by a fork lift truck. The pack of 72 mines weighs 919 kg of which 88 per cent are Bar mines and the remainder packing. Practice and drill versions of the Bar mine are also available, including the L11A2 and L20A1 Rottable Drill Barmines. These are biodegradable rectangular cardboard tubes filled with dried sand and having external fitments representative of their operational counterparts.

The Bar minelayer is simple in design and has no

Bar minelayer in action towed by an FV432 APC

Mast sensor for mechanical fuzed Full Width Attack Mine (FWAM)

complicated hydraulic or electrical components. The crew place the Bar mines on to the loading chute and pull out the arming lanyards. The mines are armed automatically as they pass through the layer into the ground. The laying depth and mine spacing are adjustable, and wearing parts such as the plough point can be replaced quickly and easily. A chain towed behind the minelayer levels the earth again.

To provide additional stability for fast towing and very rough terrain, cage wheels can be attached either side of the layer. The British Army uses the FV432 APC to tow the Bar minelayer, but the equipment can also be towed by other vehicles such as the M113, TM 4-4 8-tonne truck, any 4-tonne truck or the LWB Land Rover. The tow bar and mine conveyor belt can be adjusted for height.

The Bar minelayer can lay between 600 and 700 mines/hour with one towing vehicle and a three-man crew. To maintain this high rate of laying over long periods additional crews and vehicles are required.

The main advantages of the Bar mine system can be summarised as follows: high rate of laying mines, simplicity of operation, reduced manpower requirements, reduced number of mines to cover a given area and simplified storage and logistics.

A copy of the Bar Mine is produced in India; see separate entry in this section.

Specifications
Bar Mine
Weight: 11 kg
Length: 1.2 m
Width: 108 mm
Height: 81 mm
Weight of explosive: 7.2 kg

Bar Mine Pack
Weight: 919 kg
Length: 1.26 m
Width: 1.02 m

Height: 0.84 m
Quantity of mines: 72

Bar Minelayer
Weight: 1240 kg
Length: 4.19 m
Width: (with wheel cages) 1.6 m
Height: 1.27 m

Status
In service with the British Army, Danish Army (Pansermine M/75), Egypt, India and some other countries.

Manufacturer
British Aerospace Defence Limited, Royal Ordnance Division, Euxton Lane, Chorley, Lancashire PR7 6AD, UK.
Tel: 0257 65511. Fax: 0257 242199.

Adder, Addermine and Addermine/Ajax

Description
Adder, Addermine and Addermine/Ajax are all off-route anti-armour weapons based on a standard LAW 80 anti-tank rocket launcher. The same tripod and firing unit are used for each version.

Adder is a Hunting Engineering private venture which enables a soldier to fire LAW 80 remotely using a standard Shrike initiator unit up to 200 m away.

Addermine is suitable for use as an off-route mine and is fired when a trip or breakwire is actuated.

Addermine/Ajax is a fully autonomous off-route mine system employing the Ajax sensor system. (For details of Ajax refer to the entry under International in this section).

LAW 80 fires a 94 mm rocket with an effective range of from 20 to 500 m. When extended the LAW 80 is 1.5 m long and weighs 9 kg. It can penetrate armour in excess of 650 mm thick.

Status
Development complete.

Addermine/Ajax autonomous off-route mine

Manufacturer
Hunting Engineering Limited, Reddings Wood, Ampthill, Bedford MK45 2HD, UK.

Tel: 0525 841000. Telex: 82105 huneng g.
Fax: 0525 405861.

Anti-tank Mine Mark 7

Description
The Mark 7 anti-tank mine was the replacement for the Mark 5 anti-tank mine and has been partially replaced in the British Army by the Bar mine.

The Mark 7 is circular with a carrying handle on the side of the mine. The waterproof pressure plate, which also contains the fuze well cover, is in the centre of the top of the mine. There is a second anti-lifting fuze well in the base of the mine.

The mine operates as follows: when sufficient pressure is applied to the top of the mine, the pressure plate is forced down on to the top of the pressure fuze, and the striker, which is held by a Belleville spring, is forced down until the spring returns, driving the striker against the percussion cap, firing the detonator, and the mine explodes.

A tilt fuze kit (L93A1) has been introduced for use with the Mark 7. This consists of a number of frangible

carbon rods each containing a pre-stressed spring mechanism which operates the mine detonator once the rod is broken. The rods are of variable lengths with the longest being 850 mm. The operation is such that the mine will detonate 0.7 second after the rod is broken.

Specifications
Weight: 13.6 kg
Diameter: 325 mm
Height: 130 mm
Main charge type: TNT
Weight of main charge: 8.89 kg
Booster type: Tetryl
Weight of booster: 850 g
Operating force: 275 kg

Status
Production complete. In service with the British Army and many other armed forces.

Mark 7 anti-tank mine with tilt-rod detonator

Manufacturer
British Aerospace Defence Limited, Royal Ordnance Division, Euxton Lane, Chorley, Lancashire PR7 6AD, UK.
Tel: 0257 65511. Fax: 0257 242199.

Mine, Anti-tank, Non-metallic

Description

The Mine, Anti-tank, Non-metallic was first placed in production in 1961 and since then has been used mainly for training and as a reserve item. It is not normally used as a front line anti-tank mine. The current designation is Mine, Anti-tank, L3A1 (Non-metallic).

This anti-tank mine is constructed using two polythene mouldings joined together and filled with TNT. The pressure fuze on the top is armed by rotating a metal key through 180° which is then removed; the key can be replaced and turned to render the mine safe if required. The mine is covered with a thin black rubber coating and a handle is provided for carrying. The pressure fuze used is the L39.

Specifications
Weight: 7.7 kg
Diameter: 266 mm
Height: 145 mm
Weight of explosive: 6 kg
Type of explosive: TNT
Operating pressure: 120-200 kg

Status
Reserve use with the British Army.

Mine, Anti-tank, Non-metallic

Marconi Full Width Attack Fuzes

Description

Marconi Radar and Control Systems has developed four types of anti-tank mine fuze designed to be adapted to suit a wide range of existing mine designs. By using these fuzes existing stocks of mines can be modernised to suit them for current operational conditions at a relatively low cost.

There are four types of fuze, two full width attack fuzes and two simpler and lower cost fuzes. They can be fitted to mines using simple adaptors and for each type of mine the adaptors ensure correct physical and explosive interfaces between the fuze and the mine.

Options for all fuzes include anti-handling protection, self-sterilisation and self-destruction.

The four fuzes are as follows:

MM/E
An electronic full width attack fuze using a special sensor and algorithm system.

MM/MP
A combination of belly and track pressure sensors, the latter using pressure processing for maximum effectiveness, giving full width attack capability.

MM/M
Provides effective belly attack under the most vulnerable part of a target vehicle.

MM/P
The Marconi Pressure Fuze with a pressure processing sensor.

Status
Ready for production.

Manufacturer
Marconi Radar and Control Systems, Chobham Road, Frimley, Camberley, Surrey GU16 5PE, UK.

Marconi MM/E full width attack electronic fuze fitted to Mark 7 anti-tank mine

Tel: 0276 63311. Telex: 858202 mccsl g.
Fax: 0276 29784.

UNITED STATES OF AMERICA

Area Denial Artillery Munition (ADAM)

Description

The Area Denial Artillery Munition (ADAM) consists of a projectile fired from 155 mm howitzers; it is a member of the Family of Scatterable Mines (FASCAM). There are two types of projectile: the M692 projectile carries 36 mines with a long (more than a day) self-destruct time and the M731 projectile carries 36 mines which have a factory-set short (less than a day) self-destruct time.

After ground impact the M74 wedge shaped mines expel seven tripwires and the detonator unit is armed so that if any disturbance is detected the mine will explode. It also detonates if the battery voltage drops to a level which impairs the mine's function or at the set self-destruct time. On detonation the wedge body breaks up and the fragmentation sphere unit, containing 21.25 g of Composition A5 explosive, is propelled upwards to a predetermined height by 51 g of M10 liquid propellant surrounding the unit and explodes. A spherical fragmentation pattern is produced with hundreds of fragments moving at velocities in the order of 900 m/s.

The M74 mine is used as the basis for the M86 Pursuit Deterrent Mine (PDM – see entry in this section).

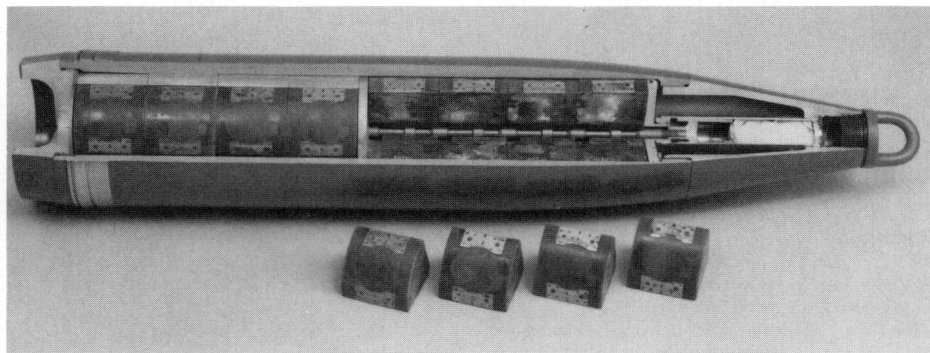

Cutaway model of Projectile, 155 mm, HE, M692/M731 ADAM (Area Denial Artillery Munition) with ADAM mines in front

The projectile is of the separate-loading type and is handled in the same way as a conventional artillery projectile. It has an M762 fuze which is set to function at a predetermined time in flight. This initiates the explosive charge which projects the mines from the rear of the projectile. Centrifugal force dispenses the mines radially from the projectile.

These mine projectiles can be fired to a maximum range of 17 740 m and would normally be used in conjunction with the RAAMS mines to provide a mine-field with both anti-tank and anti-personnel mines.

Status
In production. In service with the US Army and Marine Corps.

Manufacturer
Alliant Techsystems Inc, 5901 Lincoln Drive, Edina, Minnesota 55436, USA.
Tel: (612) 939 2440. Fax: (612) 939 2749.

Anti-personnel Mine M18A1

Description

The M18A1, or Claymore as it is usually known, is a directional, fixed fragmentation mine which is used for defensive and ambush purposes. The original model was designated the M18 and was slightly lighter than the M18A1 model.

The M18A1 consists of a curved rectangular moulded case of glass fibre-filled polystyrene plastic. In the front part are 700 steel spheres embedded in a plastic matrix, with C-4 plastic explosive behind the spheres. The fragmentation face is convex horizontally to direct the fragments and concave vertically to control the vertical dispersion of the fragments. A moulded peep-sight is provided on the top of the mine for sighting. The two detonator wells are in the top of the mine. The mine is mounted on two pairs of scissors-type folding legs.

The mine is normally fired from a distance by an M57 firing device. This is a hand-held pulse generator which by a single actuation of the handle produces a double electrical pulse. The M57 is attached to 30 m of wire which is connected to an M4 blasting cap in the mine.

The Claymore can also be activated by a pull wire or a tripwire.

When detonated, a fan-shaped sheaf pattern of spherical steel fragments is projected in a 60° horizontal arc covering a casualty area of 50 m to a height of 2 m. There is a danger area of 16 m to the rear of the mine.

The M7 bandolier contains the mine, firing device, M40 test set and electric blasting cap assembly M4.

There is a practice version of the M18A1 designated the M68.

The M18A1 is widely licence-produced, for example in Chile and South Korea (qv). The design has also been copied direct as with the South African Shrapnel Mine No 2 (qv) and the South Korean K440 (qv), while the CIS MON-50 is visually very similar. The latest form of the Pakistan Ordnance Factories Direction Mine P5 Mark 1 (qv) is based on the M18A1.

Specifications
Weight: 1.58 kg
Length: 216 mm
Width: 35 mm
Height: 83 mm
Main charge type: Composition C-4
Weight of main charge: 682 g
Operating temperature range: −40 to +51.5°C

Status
In service with Australia, Chile, Ecuador, South Korea, Malaysia, Oman, Thailand, United Kingdom and the US Army.

Manufacturer
Morton Thiokol Inc, Ordnance Marketing, 401 Market Street, Suite 1120, Shreveport, Louisiana 71101, USA. Tel: (318) 222 7675. Telex: 22101.

M18A1 anti-personnel mine in position

Anti-personnel Mine M26

Description
The M26 mine is a small integrally fuzed anti-personnel bounding mine. The main body is made of die-cast aluminium and is cylindrical, tapering towards the bottom where there are four vertical ribs on the outside of the mine body. Inside the body is the fragmentation ball assembly which consists of a steel ball containing an explosive charge and a delay and booster unit recessed within the charge. At the base of the ball is the propelling charge.

Actuation may be either by directly applying a force to the mine top or by a pull on one or more of four 6.1 m long tripwires that may be attached to the mine top via a trip lever. The propelling charge then ejects the fragmenting steel ball assembly to a height of about 2 m where the delay and booster charge detonates the main charge to shatter the steel ball.

The training version of this mine is the M35 which is reloadable and uses a blank 0.32 pistol cartridge to fire a capsule of blue dye.

Specifications
Weight: 1 kg

Diameter: 79 mm
Height: 145 mm
Main charge type: Composition B
Weight of main charge: 170 g
Booster charge type: Tetryl
Weight of booster charge: 1.5 g
Operating temperature range: −40 to +51.5°C
Operating force: 6.4-12.7 kg

Status
In service with the US Army.

Anti-personnel Bounding Mines, M16, M16A1 and M16A2

Description
The anti-personnel bounding mine M16A1 (an earlier model was the M16) consists of a sheet steel case which contains the projectile and the propelling charge, and an M605 combination fuze which is screwed into the top of the mine and extends through the centre of the projectile to the bottom of the case where the propelling charge is located.

The mine operates as follows: pressure applied to

one of the three prongs or the fuze compresses the pressure spring and forces the trigger downwards, forcing the release pin outwards and the firing pin is released. This initiates the firing chain and the cast-iron projectile is propelled into the air. When this reaches a height of 1 m the main charge detonates and metal fragments are scattered in all directions. The mine can also be fitted with a tripwire and in this case operates as follows: when a pull is applied to the tripwire the release pin ring of the fuze pulls the release pin outwards to a position where the firing pin is released and the mine then operates as above. There is an inert training version of this mine. The M16A2 is an advanced version of the M16 series and incorporates

only one booster detonator and delay instead of two of each. This allows for a greater explosive charge.

An inert version of the M16 series is known as the M16A1, inert with fuze, M605 inert.

M16 series mines are known to be in production in Greece (by Hellenic Arms Industry SA, M16A2) and India (Indian Ordnance Factories, M16A1, see entry in this section). South Korea produces the M16A2 as the KM16A2.

Status
In service with the US Army and other countries including Greece and India.

Anti-personnel bounding mine M16A2

Specifications

Model	M16	M16A1	M16A2
Weight	3.74 kg	3.74 kg	2.83 kg
Height	199 mm	199 mm	199 mm
Diameter	103 mm	103 mm	103 mm
Main charge type	TNT	TNT	TNT
Weight of main charge	521 g	513 g	590 g
Type of booster	Tetryl	Tetryl	Composition A5
Weight of booster	54 g	33 g	11 g
Weight of propelling charge	70 g	70 g	70 g
Type of propelling charge	black powder	black powder	black powder
Operating force			
(pressure)	3.6-20 kg	3.6-20 kg	3.6-20 kg
(tripwire)	1.6-3.8 kg	1.6-3.8 kg	1.6-3.8 kg
Operating temperature range	−40 to +51.5°C	−40 to +51.5°C	−40 to +51.5°C

Selectable Lightweight Attack Munition (SLAM)

Description
The Selectable Lightweight Attack Munition, or SLAM, is intended for use by US Army (and other) Special Forces and can be used as an anti-armour mine or as a lightweight demolition charge. The Project Manager for the SLAM programme is Picatinny Arsenal, New Jersey, and the Combat Developer is the US Army's JFK Special Warfare Center and School at Fort Bragg, North Carolina.

A full scale development contract was awarded to Alliant Techsystems Inc. Their SLAM uses one eight-position selector switch to provide all required delay and option settings and a colour-coded pictograph is provided on the body of the unit to assist the user; the body has a dull non-reflective finish to enhance

camouflage.

The SLAM has four main modes. In the first a magnetic fuze enables the unit to be used as an anti-armour mine to defeat target belly armour. An alternative anti-armour mode is performed when the SLAM is used as an off-route mine in a trip-line mode to defeat armoured targets up to 7.5 m away. The SLAM may also be used as a timed demolition device or as a command detonation device when used in conjunction with a standard blasting cap.

In use the selector switch is set to the required function, the battery is activated by moving a locking lever, a self-check sequence is conducted and indicated if the unit is functioning correctly, and a safety pin is removed. The SLAM is then placed in position. In the trip-line mode the SLAM's explosively formed penetrator (EFP) can defeat armoured targets up to a distance of approximately 7.5 m. The SLAM self-neutralises quietly in the mine and trip-line modes to

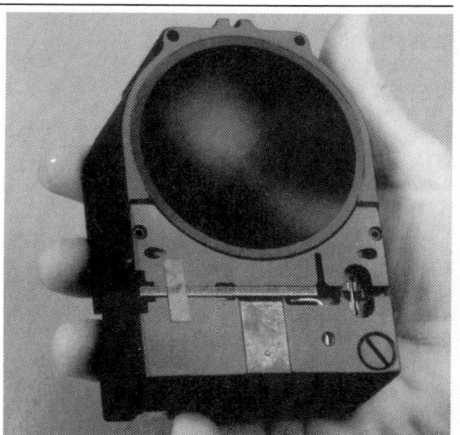

Alliant Techsystem's Selectable Lightweight Attack Munition (SLAM)

maintain its covert operation. The unit is usable after self-neutralisation.

The SLAM may be carried in a uniform pocket or slung from the shoulder using an attached carrying strap. No maintenance is required.

Specifications
Weight: 1 kg
Volume: 573 cm^3
Length: 127 mm
Width: 89 mm
Depth: 54.6 mm

Status
Full scale development.

System Contractor
Alliant Techsystems Inc, 5901 Lincoln Drive, Edina, Minnesota 55436, USA.
Tel: (612) 536 4557. Fax: (612) 536 4545.

M86 Pursuit Deterrent Munition (PDM)

Description
The M86 Pursuit Deterrent Munition (PDM), also known as the Pursuit Deterrent Mine, was developed by Honeywell Defense Systems (now Alliant Techsystems Inc) sponsored by Picatinny Arsenal. The PDM is intended for use by special forces who require a small mine that can be laid rapidly in the path of pursuing enemy forces and is basically a single 'wedge' from an Area Denial Artillery Munition (ADAM) allied to a hand-grenade type fuzing system, complete with safety pin and arming lever.

In use the safety pin is withdrawn and the arming lever released prior to the PDM being placed or thrown into position. After a 60 second delay the munition/mine releases seven tripwires, each to a maximum distance of 6 m, to sense any disturbance in the vicinity. The PDM performs an electronic self-check programme and is fully armed 65 seconds after the battery is activated. Upon sensing any disturbance the device will detonate, hurling a spherical M43 warhead 1 to 2 m upwards to explode and scatter fragments. If not detonated the munition/mine has a preset self-destruct time but if that fails the mine will detonate when the internal battery level falls below a certain

point.

The PDM is 82.5 mm high, 57 mm wide (on each side) and weighs 0.54 kg. Explosive weight is 21.9 g. PDMs are issued in sets of two carried in a bandolier.

In May 1988 Honeywell Defense Systems (now Alliant Techsystems Inc) was awarded a contract worth $11 170 598 for the production of 42 919 M86 PDMs. The mines were produced in New Brighton, Minnesota, and the contract was completed by late September 1989.

Production of a further 9500 PDMs was undertaken by the Thiokol Corporation at the Louisiana Army Ammunition Plant from January 1991 onwards.

As a private venture, Alliant Techsystems has developed a one-man portable dispenser capable of projecting a number of ADAM/PDM type munitions over an area of 80 × 80 m.

Status
In service with US Army.

Manufacturer
Alliant Techsystems Inc, 5901 Lincoln Drive, Edina, Minnesota 55436, USA.
Tel: (612) 939 2440. Fax: (612) 939 2749.

M86 Pursuit Deterrent Munition (PDM)

Anti-personnel Mine M14

Description
This small circular blast type anti-personnel mine consists of a waterproof all-plastic body with an integral plastic fuze which has a steel firing pin, and a main charge. The plug-type plastic detonator holder with the M46 detonator is packaged separately and is installed in the base of the mine when required.

The mine operates as follows: pressure applied to the top of the mine depresses the pressure plate and this depresses the lock key, forcing the lock ring to slide through notches in the inner ring of the spider and depress the Belleville spring. This snaps into reverse and drives the firing pin into the detonator and this explodes the Tetryl or Composition B main charge.

The pressure plate on the top of the mine has a yellow indicating arrow which points to the letter S for safe or A for armed. Slots are provided in the pressure

plate for the insertion of a steel, U-shaped safety clip which is removed by pulling the pull cord.

There is also a training version called the Mine, Anti-Personnel Practice: NM, M17, which emits a smoke charge when activated.

Specifications
Weight: 93.2 g
Diameter: 56.13 mm
Height: (max) 43.18 mm
Main charge type: Tetryl or Composition B
Weight of main charge: 28.4 g
Operating force: 9-16 kg
Operating temperature range: −40 to +51.5°C

Status
In service with the US Army and the Danish Army (Fodfolksmine M/56). Also produced in India (qv) and in Turkey (by MKEK).

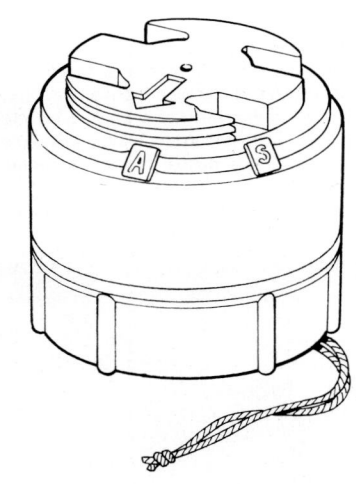

Anti-personnel mine M14

Anti-personnel Bounding Mine M2A4

Description
The anti-personnel bounding mine M2A4 (earlier models were designated the M2, M2A1 and M2A3) consists of a baseplate on which is mounted the M6A1 combination fuze and a projector tube which contains the projectile and a propelling charge. The projectile is a modified 60 mm mortar bomb.

The mine is normally buried in the ground with the fuze prongs extending above the ground by 6 to 19 mm. No provision is made in the design of the mine for the installation of an anti-lifting device.

The mine is operated as follows: pressure on one or more of the three prongs or a pull on the tripwire attached to the release pin ring of the fuze releases the firing pin which strikes the percussion cap and initiates the firing chain. The propelling charge projects the shell from the mine and at a height of 2 to 3 m it explodes.

An inert version of this mine is available for training and a practice version is designated the mine, anti-

personnel practice M8 with fuze combination, practice M10 or M10A1. The M8 has the mortar bomb replaced by a cardboard tube that contains a spotting charge assembly, which gives off a bang. The M8A1 uses smoke pellets.

The M2A4 is licence-produced in Taiwan (qv), while the Portuguese m/966 (qv) is a close copy.

Specifications
Weight: 2.948 kg
Diameter: 104 mm
Height: (including fuze) 244 mm
Main charge type: TNT
Weight of main charge: 154 g
Booster type: Tetryl
Weight of booster charge: 16 g
Operating force:
  (pressure) 3.6-9 kg
  (pull) 1.36-4.5 kg
Operating temperature range: −40 to +51.5°C

Status
In service with the US Army and Danish Army (Fodfolksmine M/51) and Taiwan.

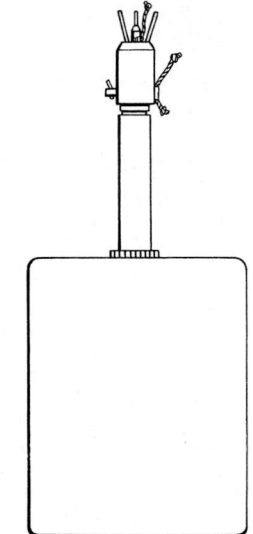

Anti-personnel bounding mine M2A4 with fuze mine combination M6A1

Anti-helicopter Mine (AHM)

Development

The US Army has a requirement for an anti-helicopter mine (AHM) that will be both scatterable or manually laid. The intention is that the AHM will be able to detect and attack low-flying helicopters, forcing them to fly at higher altitudes where other air defence weapons can engage them. It is intended that the mine will incorporate a passive identification system to distinguish friendly helicopters from those of an enemy. It is understood that the various options studied included an autonomous air defence weapon based on a ground-to-air missile such as Stinger, and 'smart' munitions that would scatter terminally guided bomblets or wire entanglements as a helicopter approached.

Following a six-month concept definition study, seven companies made submissions to the US Army Armament Research, Development and Engineering Center at Picatinny Arsenal, New Jersey. The seven companies were Ferranti International, Textron, Honeywell, Lockheed, Hughes, Texas Instruments and General Dynamics. From these, three companies were selected for further development contracts awarded in June 1989. The contracts were awarded by the US Armament Research and Development Command, also based at Picatinny Arsenal.

Textron Defense Systems of Wilmington, Massachusetts, was awarded a $1 million increment as part of a $16 202 030 cost-plus-fixed-fee contract. Their submission weighs 18.1 kg, can be turned on and off by secure communication links and provides a full 360° azimuth coverage. The general configuration of the Textron AHM follows that of the Wide Area Mine (WAM – qv).

Texas Instruments, Defense Systems and Electronics Group of Dallas, Texas, was also awarded a $1 million increment as part of an $8 362 486 cost-plus-fixed-fee contract.

The third contract was awarded to Ferranti International of the United Kingdom and was worth $8 380 421. Work on the advanced munition, which incorporates state-of-the-art sensor and warhead technologies, together with non co-operative IFF, was carried out by Ferranti Aerospace Components based at Moston, Manchester. Their development and (if successful) production stages will be bid in conjunction with Alliant Techsystems. The Ferranti/Alliant Techsystems AHM is compatible with scattering and remote deployment systems and once deployed is autonomous in operation. It employs a multiple explosively formed projectile (EFP) warhead and may incorporate a command and control module to facilitate remote arming and disarming.

The first part of these contracts, which resulted in brassboard models of the AHM to prove the concepts and technologies involved, was completed in July 1991 following a series of 'shoot-off' trials. These resulted in the selection of two contractors, Ferranti and Textron, to continue into the second phase. The second phase,

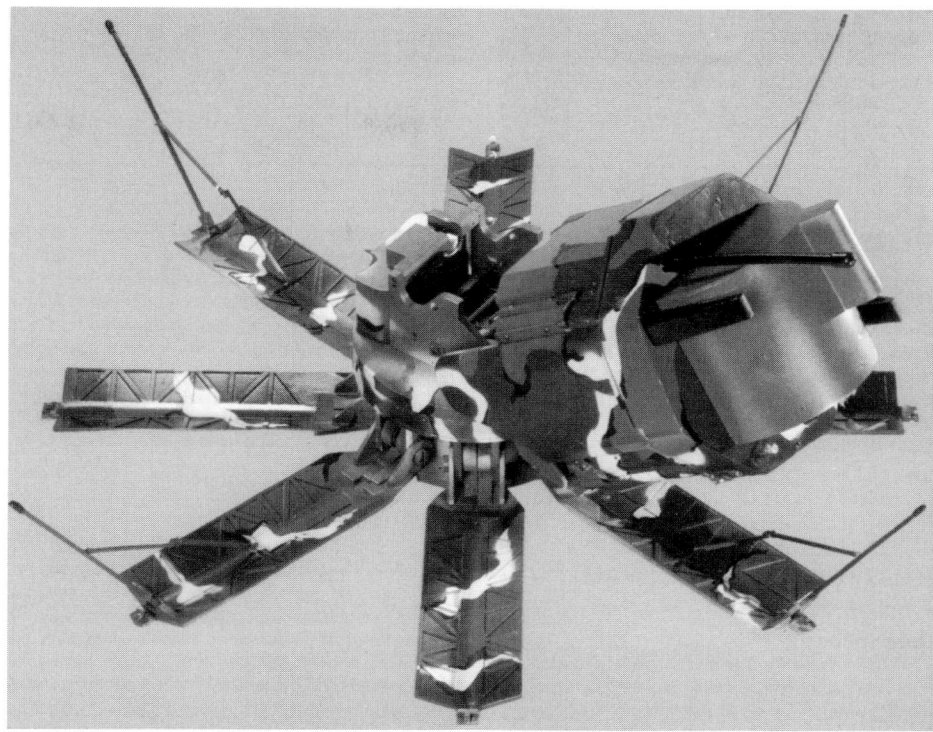
Model of the Textron submission for the Anti-helicopter Mine (AHM) programme

due to be completed by 1st September 1993, will be the development of a form, fit and function version for field demonstration.

The outline specifications provided relate to the Ferranti/Alliant Techsystems AHM.

Outline Specifications (Ferranti/Alliant Techsystems)

Weight: 10 kg
Diameter: 180 mm
Length: 335 mm
Target speed: 0-350 km/h
Target altitude: 0-100 m plus
Coverage: 360° azimuth
IFF: non-cooperative
Sensors: passive acoustic and infra-red
Warhead: multiple EFP

Status

Development – see text.

Contractors

Ferranti Aerospace Components, St Mary's Road, Moston, Manchester M10 0BE, UK.
Tel: 061 681 2071. Fax: 061 682 2500.
Textron Defense Systems, 201 Lowell Street, Wilmington, Massachusetts 01887, USA.

Model of the Alliant Techsystems/Ferranti submission for the Anti-helicopter Mine (AHM) programme

Tel: (617) 657 5111. Telex: 947488.
Fax: (617) 657 2138.

GATOR Anti-armour System

Description

The GATOR anti-armour system was developed over several years. It was designed for laying from high-speed aircraft of the US Air Force, Navy and Marine Corps for interdiction of second echelon enemy forces in assembly areas and on the march. Standardisation was in late 1981.

The mines developed for the system are the Honeywell BLU-91/B anti-tank mine and the Aerojet BLU-92/B anti-personnel mine. They have three selectable self-destruct times which can be set at the dispenser. The BLU-91/B uses micro-electronic circuitry to detect targets, discriminate armoured vehicles and detonate the mine when the target reaches the most vulnerable approach point. The mine uses a Misznay-Schardin explosive charge to defeat the belly armour of most vehicles. Weight of a BLU-91/B is 1.95 kg. The BLU-92/B produces fragments for its anti-personnel effects and is intended to discourage minefield clearing. Weight is 1.678 kg. Both mines have

dimensions of 146 × 127 × 66 mm.

The minimum dispensing altitude is approximately 60 m at speeds up to 700-800 knots. A single aircraft can deliver some 600 mines over an area of 200 × 300 m by varying the number of dispensers dropped, the rate of release of the dispensers and the aircraft release parameters. The following cluster bomb units have been identified with the GATOR system:

CBU-78/B: SUU-58/B (Mark 7 Rockeye) dispenser with 45 BLU-91/B and 15 BLU-92/B. Weight is 222.2 kg, length 2.16 m and diameter 330 mm. Used by US Navy.
CBU-82/B: SUU-58/B dispenser with BLU-91/B
CBU-83/B: SUU-58/B dispenser with BLU-92/B
CBU-84/B: SUU-54A/B dispenser with BLU-91/B and BLU-92/B
CBU-85/B: SUU-54A/B dispenser with BLU-91/B
CBU-86/B: SUU-54A/B dispenser with BLU-92/B
CBU-89/B: SUU-64/B Tactical Munitions Dispenser (TMD) with 72 BLU-91/B and 22 BLU-92/B. Weight is 322 kg, length 2.337 m and diameter 406 mm. Used by US Air Force.

BLU-92/B GATOR anti-personnel mine

The GATOR mine system is now centred around the CBU-78/B and the CBU-89/B dispensers.

GATOR mines are also used with the Volcano multiple delivery mine system (see entry in the *Minelaying equipment* section).

Status
In production. In service with the US Air Force, Navy and Marine Corps.

Manufacturer
Aerojet Ordnance, 9236 E Hall Road, Downey, California 90241, USA.
Tel: (213) 923 7511. Telex: 673599.

GEMSS Mines

Description
Two mines are used with the Ground Emplaced Mine Scattering System (GEMSS) M128 vehicle-towed mine dispenser (the Frisbee Flinger) and the M138 Flipper portable minelaying device; the M74 anti-personnel mine and the M75 anti-tank mine. Both mines have the same dimensions but the M74 is a fragmenting blast mine actuated by automatically deployed tripwires while the M75 is intended to attack tank belly armour and tracks using a magnetic influence fuze. The M75 is also used with the Remote Anti-Armor Mine System (RAAMS). Both types of mine are delivered for M128 use packed in shipping containers each holding 40 mines packed in sleeves of five. A shipping container holding M74 anti-personnel mines weighs 88.45 kg and a container holding M75 anti-tank mines weighs 97.5 kg. An inert practice mine is known as the M79.

Specifications

Model	M74	M75
Employment	anti-personnel	anti-tank
Weight	1.4 kg	1.678 kg
Diameter	119 mm	119 mm
Height	66 mm	66 mm

Status
In production. In service with the US Army and some other armies.

XM93 Wide Area Mine (WAM)

Description
The XM93 Wide Area Mine (WAM) was designed to meet a US Army requirement for an improved countermobility weapon. Unlike conventional mines that require a target vehicle to run directly over them for warhead activation, the WAM is capable of attacking and destroying any tank, tracked vehicle or heavy truck that moves within a 360°, 100 m radius.

Each WAM consists of a ground launcher, erected and supported by spring-loaded legs, and a sublet (similar to the Skeet munition employed by the US Air Force SFW cluster bomb) which is launched by a gas generator in a rapidly spinning and coning motion over the target. The ground launcher contains seismic and acoustic sensors that detect, classify, track and engage targets as they move in the mine's vicinity. If all attack criteria are satisfied, the launcher swivels in azimuth and tilts in elevation to aim the sublet's trajectory.

An infra-red sensor on the sublet searches the ground in a near circular pattern looking for the target. When pre-established target detection and aimpoint criteria have been satisfied, the sublet's microcomputer initiates the explosively formed penetrator warhead which fires a high velocity, heavy metal slug (450 g of tantalum) at the target; it is capable of defeating a target's top armour.

In August 1987, competitive Proof-of-Principle programme awards were made to Honeywell Defense Systems (now Alliant Techsystems) and Textron Defense Systems, a division of Textron Inc, for the advanced development of a WAM. Both contractors conducted extensive component, subsystem and system tests until mid-1989. In April 1990, Textron was awarded a $69.4 million full scale development for a Hand Emplaced Wide Area Mine. Textron were also awarded a contract modification to incorporate an improved secure, two-way mine communication system to permit on/off control and recovery of minefield activity data. Initial issue is scheduled to be during the fourth quarter of FY94.

The mine under current development is handemplaced, and can be activated remotely over a oneway data link by the M131 Modular Mine Pack System (MOPMS – see entry under *Minelaying equipment*) remote-control unit. Future delivery variants include the M139 Volcano multiple mine delivery system (*ibid*), the Multiple Launch Rocket System (MLRS), and the Army Tactical Missile System (ATACMS).

Status
Full scale development of hand-emplaced version.

Contractor
Textron Defense Systems, 201 Lowell Street, Wilmington, Massachusetts 01887, USA.
Tel: (617) 657 5111. Telex: 947488.
Fax: (617) 657 2138.

Model of Textron Defense Systems' Wide Area Mine (WAM)

Model of Wide Area Mine (WAM) showing mine launcher aimed and tilting towards its target and propelling an anti-armour sublet

M21 Heavy Anti-tank Mine

Description

The M21 metallic anti-tank mine is circular and has a sheet steel case. An adjustable carrying strap attached to the side of the mine can also be used for lifting the mine into position.

The top cover of the mine contains a charge cap assembly which has a threaded hole in the centre into which the fuze is screwed. For travelling this is covered by a plug assembly. Under the charge cap assembly is the black powder expelling charge and under this is the concave steel plate, beneath which is the high explosive charge.

The M21 mine has an M607 fuze which can be fitted with an extension rod adaptor and an extension rod which is actuated when it comes into contact with the tracks or belly of the tank. With the extension rod and adaptor removed, the fuze may be used as a pressure-type fuze.

When fitted with the extension rod the mine is operated as follows: when the rod is tilted with a minimum horizontal force of 1.7 kg through an angle of 20° or more the plastic collar in the fuze is broken. When used with the rod, a minimum force of 132 kg applied to the top of the mine will shatter or break the plastic collar. Once this plastic collar is shattered or broken, the tilt-rod in the fuze presses against the

bearing cap, forcing it downward causing the Belleville spring to snap into the reverse position, driving the firing pin assembly into the M46 detonator which fires the black powder charge. This blows off the top cover of the mine and the pressure created by this explosion drives a firing pin into the M42 primer, initiating the main firing chain. The main charge detonates and blows the body of the mine apart and causes the steel plate to be ejected upwards at a high velocity into the belly of the tank.

The M21 can also use the M612 pneumatic fuze and the M609 influence fuze.

Specifications

Weight: 7.9 kg
Diameter: 230 mm
Height:
 (with tilt-rod) 813 mm
 (with fuze) 206 mm
Main charge type: Composition H6
Weight of main charge: 4.9 kg
Type of booster: RDX
Weight of booster: 11 g
Operating force: 132 kg
Operating temperature range: −40 to +51.5°C

Status

In service with the US Army.

M21 heavy anti-tank mine

M24 and M66 Off-route Anti-tank Mines

Description

Picatinny Arsenal started development of the M24 off-route (or off-the-road) anti-tank mine in December 1961. Between September and November 1968 Picatinny delivered 50 000 of these mines to the US Army. They are issued at the rate of 15 per company to armour, airborne, infantry, mechanised and engineer combat battalions.

The mine consists of a discriminating pressure-actuated vehicle detector tapeswitch (designated the M2), a battery-powered M61 demolition firing device, and an M143 plastic dispenser tube for launching the M28A1 or M28A2 HEAT rocket. The latter is fin-stabilised and is the same as that used for the 3.5-inch M20 rocket launcher. The launcher is located up to 30 m off-the-route and is sighted along the tapeswitch vehicle detector. When the target traverses the tape-switch the circuit is completed and the rocket is launched. The HEAT warhead of the M28 rocket will penetrate all known conventional armour.

The M66 anti-tank mine is similar to the M24 but uses a seismic alerter.

Specifications

Weight: (loaded) 8.164 kg
Length: 609 mm
Height: 89 mm
Main charge type: Composition B
Weight of main charge: 853 g
Weight of rocket: 4 kg
Operating temperature range: −40 to +51.5°C

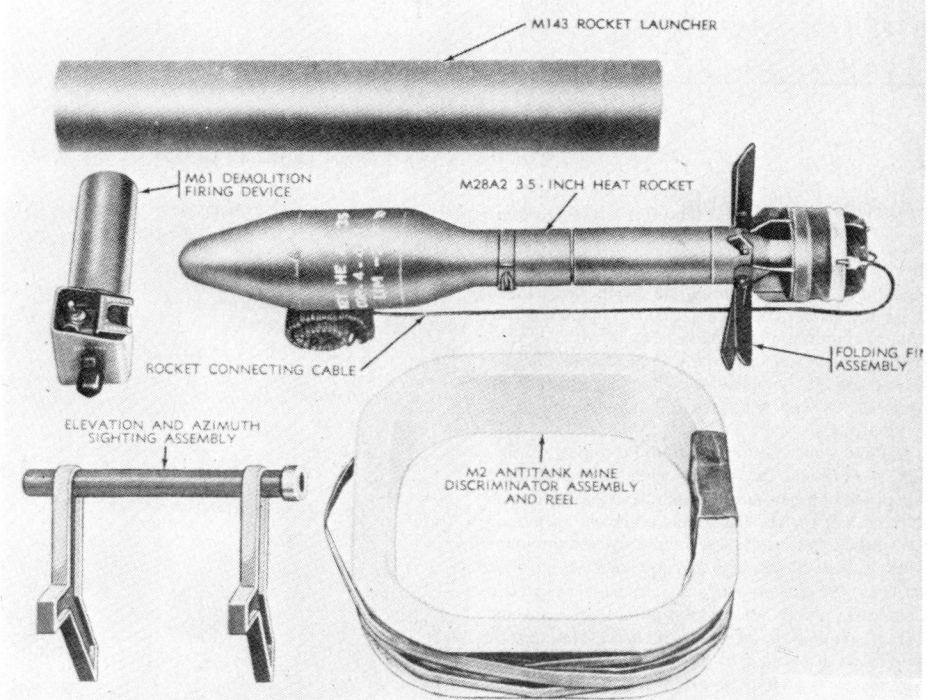

Main components of M24 off-route anti-tank mine (US Army)

Status

Production complete. In service with the US Army.

Manufacturer

Picatinny Arsenal, Dover, New Jersey, USA.

M19 Anti-tank Mine

Description

The M19 non-metallic anti-tank mine is square and has an all-plastic case. A carrying handle is provided on one side of the mine. The main fuze well is in the centre of the mine and there are also two anti-lifting fuze wells, one in the side of the mine and the second in its base.

The mine has an M606 fuze which is of the mechanical pressure type and is also plastic. The mine operates as follows: when sufficient pressure is applied to the top of the mine, the pressure plate is depressed and this depresses the Belleville spring of the fuze,

Mine: AT: Training, M80, inert practice version of M19 anti-tank mine

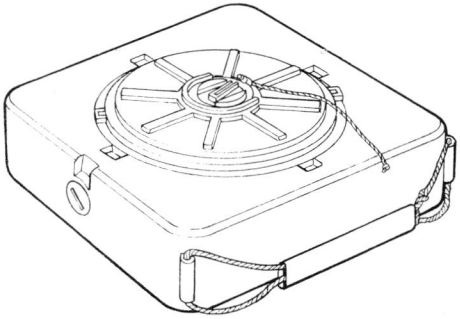

M19 anti-tank mine

which snaps into reverse, driving the firing pin into the detonator. This explodes and sets off the booster, which then sets off the main charge.

Sympathetic detonation can be avoided if the mine is buried 38 mm deep, with a 45° slope of holes and 5.5 m centre-to-centre between adjacent mines. The M19 is waterproof and can be laid on river beds.

An inert training version of this mine is available, designated the Mine: AT: Training, M80.

The M19 is licence-produced in South Korea by the Korea Explosives Company (qv) and the Daewoo Corporation, and in Chile (Industrias Cardoen).

Specifications
Weight: 12.56 kg
Length: 332 mm
Width: 332 mm
Height: 94 mm
Main charge type: Composition B
Weight of main charge: 9.53 kg
Type of booster: RDX
Weight of booster: 52 g
Operating force: 136-227 kg
Operating temperature range: −40 to +51.5°C

Status
In service with the US Army and some other nations. Licence-produced in Turkey.

M15 Anti-tank Mine

Description
This heavy metallic anti-tank mine is circular and has a carrying handle. The main fuze well is in the centre of the mine and there are also two anti-lifting fuze wells, one in the side and the other in the bottom of the mine. The M15 is fitted with the M603 or M608 mechanical pressure fuze and operates as follows: when sufficient pressure is applied to the top of the mine the pressure plate is depressed, which depresses the Belleville spring which snaps into reverse, driving the firing pin into the detonator. This explodes the booster which in turn ignites the main charge.

A practice version of this mine is designated the M12 (or M12A1) and has the M604 fuze, with a smoke charge in the main fuze well. Another practice mine is designated the M20.

In order to extend the service life of the M15 mine a tilt-rod fuze system was developed for introduction into service during 1988.

The US Army is undertaking a M15 product-improvement programme which would enable the M15 to have a full width attack capability, involving electronic sensor-equipped fuzes. Several companies have submitted proposals.

Specifications
Weight: 14.27 kg
Diameter: 337 mm
Height: 125 mm
Main charge type: Composition B
Weight of main charge: 10.33 kg
Type of booster: RDX
Weight of booster: 11 g
Operating force: 159-340 kg
Operating temperature range: −40 to +51.5°C

Status
In service with Belgium, Canada and the US Army.

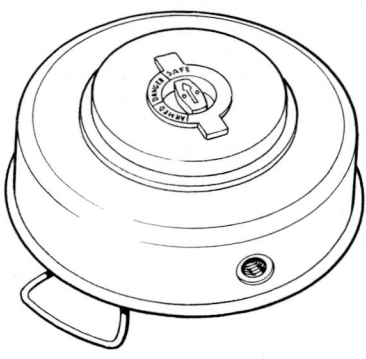

M15 anti-tank mine

VIETNAM

Anti-personnel Mine

Description
During the Vietnam conflict the North Vietnamese armed forces were adept at producing numerous patterns of improvised land mines, few of which (if any) remain in service. During early 1989 reports of a new Vietnamese anti-personnel mine began to appear from Cambodia. These mines have been referred to as Apple Mines.

The mine involved turned out to be a local conversion of American BLU-24 bomblets recovered from various air-dropped area denial munitions left behind after the Vietnam conflict. These bomblets have been converted to both land mines and projected grenades with tails. In their land mine form the bomblets are fitted with a tripwire-activated fuze and are usually placed in a pronged steel rod post; a weight of between 3 and 5 kg is required to activate the fuze. The fuze is understood to be easy to remove and its standard of manufacture is poor to the extent that the fuze body is pressed steel with a lapped junction that can allow moisture to penetrate. The latter features necessitates the use of a polythene cover to protect the fuze against rain after the mine is emplaced.

The internally serrated steel-bodied bomblet has a maximum diameter of 69 mm and a height of 62.5 mm; height overall is approximately 140 mm.

Status
In service with the People's Army of Vietnam.

Manufacturer
State factories.

Vietnamese anti-personnel mine based on American BLU-24 bomblet

MINELAYING EQUIPMENT

AUSTRIA

AID 2000 Minelaying System

Description
The AID 2000 (Austrian Intermittent Digger 2000) is a trailer-mounted minelaying system intended for use with the Intertechnik ATM 2000E anti-tank mine (qv), although the system can be adapted to handle other mines. The AID 2000 can lay up to 250 mines/hour (at a laying distance of 2 m in normal soil) at depths of from 50 to 300 mm in 50 mm increments and at intervals of from 1.5 to 12 m, as required.

The self-contained AID 2000 is operated by one man and utilises a 54 hp air-cooled diesel engine to power the system. The trailer carrying the system can be towed by virtually any in-service truck, with mines being fed into the system via rails protruding over the truck cargo area. Once the system has been started the laying process is virtually automatic and soil disturbance after laying is minimal.

Specifications
Crew: 1
Weight: approx 6500 kg
Length: approx 6 m
Width: approx 2.5 m
Height: approx 2.7 m
Towing speed: (road) up to 100 km/h
Fording: 0.8 m
Engine: air-cooled diesel developing 54 hp

AID 2000 minelaying system in operation

Laying capacity: up to 250 mines/h
Laying interval: 1.5-12 m
Laying depth: 50, 100, 150, 200, 250 or 300 mm

Status
In production.

Manufacturer
Intertechnik Techn. Produktionen-GmbH, Industriezeile 56, Postfach 100, A-4040 Linz, Austria. Tel: (0 732) 78 92-0. Telex: 221522. Fax: (0 732) 78 92-13.

Minelaying Chute

Description
The Austrian Army uses a vehicle-mounted minelaying chute to dispense anti-tank mines rapidly onto the ground. The mines are fed onto the chute by hand and then slide to the ground by gravity. The system can lay 380 mines in 15 minutes over a distance of 1600 m. Several vehicles operating in parallel can lay a minefield sufficiently dense to hinder or stop an armoured attack temporarily.

Status
In service with the Austrian Army.

Truck towing minelaying chute with Panzermine 75 anti-tank mines sliding to the ground

CHINA, PEOPLE'S REPUBLIC

Type 74 Minelaying Rocket System

Description
The Type 74 minelaying rocket system is used by engineer units of the People's Liberation Army for the rapid laying of anti-tank minefields in forward areas. The Type 74 units are organised into batteries of four launchers carried on Jiefang CA-30A (6 × 6) trucks and each battery can lay a 400 × 400 m minefield to a maximum range of 1500 m.

Each CA-30A truck carries on the rear a set of 10 launcher rails 4 m long. On the road each truck can carry some of the launcher crew seated behind the cab on an open bench seat. Before firing the crew has to take cover and the cab windows are covered by steel shutters. The rockets are loaded onto the rails manually with five rockets above and five below the launcher rails. The rails may be elevated between +7 and +48° and traverse is 90° left and 45° right; when on the move the rails point forward. A salvo of 10 rockets can be fired in 15 seconds.

The Type 74 minelaying rockets each weigh 127 kg and contain 10 Type 69 or Type 70 plastic-cased

8-round rocket minelaying system mounted on CA-30A (6 × 6) trucks

Type 74 minelaying rockets on Type 74 launcher

anti-tank mines. The diameter of the rocket head is 284 mm. The rockets are delivered to the launcher in one- or two-rocket wooden boxes. The rocket motor body has an estimated diameter of 160 mm, and four tail fins are used for stabilisation. Each rocket is 2.47 m long.

Variant
8-round minelaying rocket system
An 8-round minelaying rocket system is in production for the Chinese armed forces. This is carried by the same CA-30A truck as the Type 74 system but the rockets are larger overall and have ring stabilisers at the tail. The launchers use frames instead of rails and are constructed from tubular steel welded into two banks of four cells. No other details are available.

Specifications (Type 74)
Launcher
Weight:
 (complete with rockets and crew) approx 8780 kg
 (empty) 6954 kg
Length: (complete, travelling) 6.44 m
Width: 2.27 m
Height: 2.93 m
Max speed: 40 km/h
Length of launcher rail: 4 m
Traverse: 90° left/45° right
Elevation: +7° to +48°
Max range: 1500 m

Rocket
Head diameter: 284 mm
Length: 2.47 m
Weight: 127 kg
Number of mines carried: 10

Status
In production. In service with the Chinese armed forces.

Manufacturer
China North Industries Corporation, 7A Yue Tan Nan Jie, PO Box 2137 Beijing, Beijing, China. Tel: 867570. Telex: 22339 cnin cn.

COMMONWEALTH OF INDEPENDENT STATES

GMZ-3 Tracked Minelayer

Description
The GMZ-3 (*gusenichniy minniy zagraditel-3*) tracked minelayer is based on the chassis of the SA-4 (Ganef) surface-to-air missile system. The driver is seated at the front of the vehicle on the left side with the engine to his right. This leaves the rear of the vehicle clear for the mounting of the minelaying equipment and the stowage of mines. The suspension of the GMZ consists of seven road wheels with the drive sprocket mounted at the front and the idler at the rear. There are four track return rollers. The minelayer is of the plough type and resembles the CIS PMR-3 and the German MLG-60 mechanical minelaying systems but is more advanced than both. Mines are fed into the minelayer via two chutes, one either side.

The GMZ can carry 208 anti-tank mines which are loaded into the rear armoured compartment through two large roof hatches. The laying system spaces the mines at intervals of between 4 and 5.5 m at a speed of 2 to 3 km/h and a rate of 4 mines/min. When laying mines on the surface the rate is 8 mines/min at a road speed of between 6 and 16 km/h. Mines may be laid under either manual or automatic control and can be buried in up to 120 mm of soil or up to 500 mm of snow. Mines weighing up to 12 kg can be handled by the system.

A land navigation system is carried by the GMZ-3. Infra-red vision equipment enables the GMZ to carry out minelaying operations during darkness. A platoon of three GMZ-3s is attached to the engineer battalion of each motorised rifle or tank division, replacing the PMR-3.

The armament of the GMZ-3 is a single 14.5 mm machine gun on a mounting over the commander's position. Smoke grenade launchers are provided and there is a smoke production system incorporated into the vehicle's exhaust system.

GMZ-3 tracked minelayer

Specifications
Crew: 3
Weight: 28 500 kg
Power-to-weight ratio: 18.42 hp/t
Length: (travelling) 8.62 m
Width: 3.25 m
Height: (travelling) 2.7 m
Ground clearance: 430-470 mm
Max speed:
 (road) 60 km/h
 (road, cruising) 40-45 km/h
 (dirt roads) 25-30 km/h
Range: (road) 500 km
Gradient: 57.7%
Side slope: 46.7%
Vertical obstacle: 0.7 m
Trench: 2.5 m
Engine: water-cooled diesel developing 513 hp

Armament: 14.5 mm KPVT MG

Mine capacity: 208
Work speed:
 (surface laying) 6-16 km/h
 (burying) 2-3 km/h
Minelaying rate:
 (surface laying) 8 mines/min
 (burying) 4 mines/min
Mine spacing: 4-5.5 m apart
Reload time: 12-15 min

Status
In service with the CIS. Offered for export.

Manufacturer
State factories.

PMR-2, PMR-3 and PMZ-4 Towed Minelayers

Description
The PMR-2 (*pritsepniy minniy zagraditel-2*) is a two-wheeled trailer with two chutes. The upper part of the chute has a wide mouth into which the anti-tank mines are loaded. They then slide down a double roller conveyor into the distributing mechanism, which spaces them at intervals of 2 or 4 m. The chain drive distribution mechanism is controlled by a three-position lever mounted on the control box. The mines are laid on the surface and buried by a follow-up team if required. The trailer is normally towed by a 6 × 6 truck or a BTR-152 (6 × 6) armoured personnel carrier, with a crew of seven. The work speed of the PMR-2 is 3 to 5 km/h and mine load is 120 mines.

The PMR-3 (*pritsepniy minniy zagraditel-3*) has a single chute and the operator, who is seated on the two-wheeled trailer, can select either surface or buried laying, to 300 or 400 mm depth, and also controls the spacing of the mines. The PMR-3 is normally towed by a specially modified BTR-152 (6 × 6) armoured personnel carrier which carries 120 TM-46 or similar anti-tank mines. A fully loaded BTR-152, carrying 120 mines, can lay a minefield 500 m long (when the mines are spaced at 4 m intervals) in 5 minutes.

For both systems the capacity varies if the tow vehicle is other than the BTR-152, as follows: ZIL-157, 200; BTR-60, 100 to 130; Ural-375, 350. The PMZ-4 towed minelayer is the same as the PMR-3 but with a 200-mine capacity.

PMR-2 minelayer in travelling position

Specifications (PMR-3)
Crew: 4 or 5
Length: 3 m
Width: 2 m
Height: 2.5 m
Tyres: 7.50 × 20
Mine spacing: 4-5.5 m apart
Burial depth: (soft soil) 300-400 mm
Work speed:
  (surface laying) 4-10 km/h
  (burying) 2-3 km/h
Minelaying rate: 10-12 mines/min
Reload time: 10-12 min

Status
In service with former Warsaw Pact countries and other countries that have received CIS aid including Afghanistan (PMR-3).

PMR-3 towed minelayer with towing eye nearest camera (C F Foss)

Manufacturer
State factories.

Minelaying Chutes

Description
Before the introduction of mechanical minelaying equipment such as the PMR-2 and the PMR-3 the former Warsaw Pact armies made wide use of simple minelaying chutes for laying anti-tank mines. They were attached to the sides or rear of 6 × 6 trucks or the BTR-152 (6 × 6) armoured personnel carrier. The mines were fed onto the chute by hand and then slid to the ground by gravity. They were normally left on the surface but were sometimes buried by follow-up teams.

This method of laying mines is still used when a minefield has to be laid rapidly. The Polish Army uses the chute method to lay T-62 mines from the rear hatches of OT-64 (8 × 8) armoured personnel carriers. The method's major disadvantage is that the surface-laid mines can be easily detected.

Specifications (anti-tank chute)
Length: 4.8 m
Width: 0.406 m
Height: 1.27 m
Laying rate: 4 mines/min

Status
Still used as an emergency minelaying method by former Warsaw Pact units.

Minelaying chute in use on BTR-152 (6 × 6) APC

Manufacturer
Eastern Bloc state factories.

Anti-tank Minelaying Helicopter

Description
Reports in CIS military periodicals have indicated that they use a helicopter-borne anti-tank minelaying system to protect the flanks of armoured spearhead units. The system is basically a chute (4.8 m long, 0.406 m wide and 0.127 m high) attached to the side of the helicopter down which mines slide to the ground. Although this method has the disadvantage of the mines being conspicuous it does allow the tactical

commander a quick reaction and long-range capability for laying anti-tank mines.

Helicopters seen with this system are the Mil Mi-4 Hound (estimated carrying capacity 200 metallic anti-tank mines such as the TM-46 with MVM fuze) and the Mil Mi-8 Hip C (estimated carrying capacity 400 metallic anti-tank mines).

Status
In service with the CIS and other former Warsaw Pact forces, including Poland.

Mil Mi-8 Hip C laying anti-tank minefield

EGYPT

Mine Dispensing System

Description
This Egyptian mine dispensing system consists of six

mine scattering modules mounted on a Fahd (4 × 4) armoured personnel carrier or a similar vehicle. Each of the six modules contains 20 tubes from which mines are fired to create an anti-armour minefield with a density and coverage dependent on the speed of the

carrier vehicle and other factors such as the rate of firing and the number of tubes involved.

Each tube contains five mines, each with a diameter of 110 mm and weighing 2 kg. Each mine is fitted with an electromagnetic sensor unit that can detect approaching armour and detonate the mine to penetrate 120 mm of armour at a distance of 0.5 m. The mines also have anti-clearing and self-destruct features. The system can carry and dispense a total of 600 mines.

The same anti-armour mine can also be carried and scattered by the Egyptian 210 mm SAKR 80 artillery rocket system. A SAKR 80 warhead can carry 65 anti-armour mines. For details of the SAKR 80 system refer to *Jane's Armour and Artillery 1992-93* pages 718 and 719.

Status
Believed to be ready for production.

Manufacturer
SAKR Factory for Developed Industries, PO Box 33, Heliopolis, Cairo, Arab Republic of Egypt.
Tel: 660250. Telex: 92175 cerva un.
Fax: 2901978.

Artist's impression of the Egyptian mine dispensing system carried on a Fahd (4 × 4) armoured personnel carrier

FRANCE

Minotaur Scatterable Minelaying System

Description
The Minotaur scatterable minelaying system consists of a series of modules carried on a tracked or other vehicle. The system may also be mounted on a light towed carriage or carried by infantry in a man-transportable backpack form. The system is designed to create rapid minefields to act as a barrier to enemy movement and as a counter to a surprise attack.

The system can be used to create minefields on either side of the moving carrier vehicle, to one side only, or to the rear. A carrier vehicle could carry up to six or eight modules. Each module contains 20 launching tubes and each module is mounted on a traversing base that can be traversed 40° right and left of centre. Mines can be dispensed to a maximum range of 300 m to each side and 90 m to the rear.

Each launch tube contains five anti-tank mines or 10 anti-personnel mines. The anti-tank mines used with

the system are the same as those used with the mine launching tubes mounted on the AMX-30 combat engineer tractor, or EBG (see entry under *Armoured engineer vehicles* for details) and the Giat 155 mm OMI 155 H1 artillery projectile (for details refer to *Jane's AFV Retrofit Systems 1991-92* page 84).

The anti-tank mines, known as the AC DISP F1, are 139 mm in diameter, weigh 2.6 kg and contain 0.7 kg of explosive. The launcher discharges the mines to a distance of up to 300 m and the mines are then triggered by any vehicle weighing over 1500 kg. According to Giat Industries, the mines will penetrate a tank floor equivalent to 50 mm of armour plate at 500 mm stand-off distance and 60° incidence, or break up a tank's track if the mine is run over. Self-destruction of the mines is automatic after a preset time.

The overall weight of a container of five anti-tank mines is 16 kg and a loaded module weighs 690 kg. The space requirement for a single 20-container module measures 1 × 1 m.

To date the Minotaur system has been mounted on

tracked Alvis Sapper and Stormer flat bed systems carriers and ACMAT (6 × 6) trucks. It is understood that the French Army is interested in mounting the system on tracked AMX VCI infantry combat vehicles converted to armoured flat bed carriers as they are phased out of service from their original role.

The Minotaur system is one of the contestants for the United Kingdom Vehicle Launched Scatterable Mine System (VLSMS) and a number of Minotaur systems mounted on Stormer tracked carriers were fielded by the British Army during Desert Shield/Storm. The Stormer carries six 20-container Minotaur modules.

Status
Production as required. Purchased by British Army.

Manufacturer
Giat Industries, 13 route de la Minière, F-78034 Versailles Cedex, France.
Tel: 30 97 37 37. Fax: 30 97 39 00.

Minotaur scatterable minelaying system mounted on Alvis Stormer flat bed systems carrier

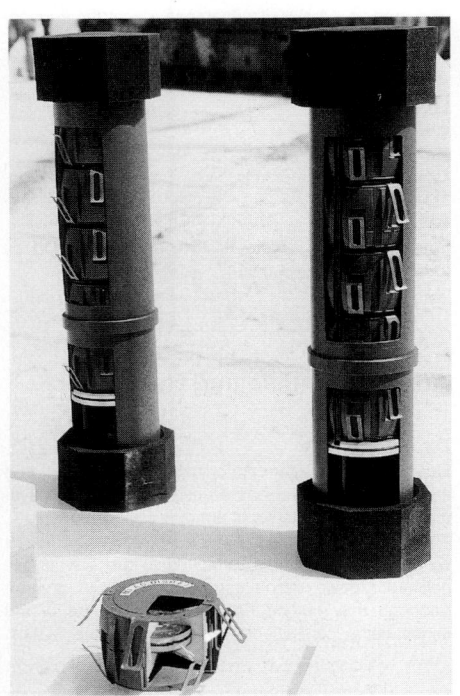

Cutaway launch containers and an AC DISP F1 mine used with the Minotaur scatterable minelaying system

ARE Type SOC Plough-type Minelayer

Description

The ARE plough-type minelayer was developed specifically for use with the HPD anti-tank mine which is in production for the French Army by TRT Défense, although it can be adapted for use with other mines. The minelayer is towed behind a 4-tonne truck or tracked vehicle, which also carries the crew and mines. A crew of four is required to operate the complete system: commander, two loaders and the driver. A canvas top can be fitted for weather protection.

The minelayer opens up a furrow in the ground, lays the mines and then replaces the top soil. If required the mines can be laid on the surface. The HPD mines can be buried to a maximum depth of 250 mm and can be spaced 2.5, 3.3 or 5 m apart. Maximum laying rate is between 900 and 1500 mines/hour.

Specifications

Crew: 4
Weight: 2500 kg
Length:
(travelling) 4.86 m
(operating) 5.685 m
Width: 2.335 m

ARE Type SOC plough-type minelayer

Height:
(travelling) 2.245 m
(working, canvas hood up) 2.07 m
(working, canvas hood down) 2 m
Max towing speed:
(on roads) 80 km/h
(operating) 4.5-10 km/h
Towing effort: 40 kN
Laying rate: 900 to 1500 mines/h
Burying depth: 0-250 mm

Status
In service with one non-French army.

Manufacturer
Giat Industries, 13 route de la Minière, F-78034 Versailles Cedex, France.
Tel: 30 97 37 37. Fax: 30 97 39 00.

Matenin Mine Distributor

Description

To meet the French Army's requirement for at least 150 systems of this type and in competition with Creusot-Loire, Etablissements Matenin designed and built a mine distributor for the HPD anti-tank mine. Following trials held in 1982 the Matenin system was chosen as the model for the French Army.

Towed by a truck carrying the mines, the mines are manually placed into the layer to slide down the chute under gravity. They are automatically armed in the process. The laying distance between mines is adjustable. Weight of the minelayer is 150 kg and it can be broken down into three parts for transport purposes. The maximum laying speed is approximately 1800 mines/hour.

Status

In production. In service with the French Army.

Manufacturer

Etablissements Matenin, 34 avenue des Champs Elysées, F-75008 Paris, France.
Tel: (1) 43 59 22 00. Telex: 801 622.

Matenin mine distributor

Matenin Mine Burier

Description

The Matenin mine burier is a self-propelled 4 × 4 vehicle based on components used in the Matenin trench digger. Development began in 1971. It is capable of cross-country operations and can lay or bury mines on any ground which can be negotiated by armoured fighting vehicles. It can also lay mines in river and stream beds not more than 1.2 m deep.

The mines are buried by a hydromechanical push tool that enters and leaves the soil by the same route. There is no exterior change in vegetation as the entry point is automatically closed by a roller which stamps down the vegetation after the mine is buried. The stopping, deceleration and acceleration of the vehicle after each burial are fully automatic due to its hydrostatic transmission.

The vehicle carries four containers each loaded with 112 mines. The mines may be laid in straight lines, curves (with diameters under 20 m) and zig zags. The distance between mines can be varied between 2.5 and 10 m during laying. The average burying speed is 400 mines/hour but with a 3 m interval between mines this can be increased to 500 mines/hour. The vehicle is used by the French Army to lay HPD anti-tank mines.

Variant

Mine Burier on MAN Truck
The Matenin mine burier system has been adapted to be carried on a MAN (6 × 6) truck. In this mode, handling the mines is carried out manually and involves a crew of four (including the vehicle driver) but the operating system is otherwise similar to the standard mine burier. The mine capacity of the truck system is increased to 560 anti-tank mines; eight containers with 70 mines each.

This variant is in production for the Belgian Army. The first batch of 25 units out of a total of 274 was ordered in early 1988. In Belgian service the truck-mounted system will be used to bury HPD F2 anti-tank mines.

Specifications (Matenin vehicle)

Crew: 1 + 2
Configuration: 4 × 4 or 4 × 2
Weight:
(empty) 12 700 kg
(loaded) 16 000 kg
Length: 7.3 m
Width: 2.5 m
Height: 2.8 m
Ground clearance: 0.5 m
Wheelbase: 3 m
Max speed: (road) 70 km/h
Average speed: (road) 50 km/h
Speed with hydrostatic transmission: 3.6 km/h
Range: (road) 600 km
Endurance while laying: 11 h
Max gradient: 50%
Max side slope: 25%
Vertical obstacle: 0.45 m
Trench: 0.65 m
Fording: 1.2 m

Matenin mine burier in operational mode

Matenin mine burying system on MAN (6 × 6) truck (C R Zwart)

Engine: MAN type D2156 HM 6-cylinder water-cooled diesel developing 225 hp at 2400 rpm
Transmission: power-shift hydromechanical unit with torque converter, 6 forward and 3 reverse gears
Steering: power-assisted
Turning radius: 11 m
Tyres: 16.00 × 25 low pressure

Brakes: air
Winch capacity: 5000 kg (10 000 kg when tackle is used)
Electrical system: 24 V

Status
In production. In service with the French Army. Truck-mounted system in production for Belgium (total requirement 274).

Manufacturer
Etablissements Matenin, 34 avenue des Champs Elysées, F-75008 Paris, France.
Tel: (1) 43 59 22 00. Telex: 801 622.

GERMANY

MLG-60 Mechanical Minelayer

Description
In appearance the MLG-60 is very similar to the CIS PMR-3, its main difference being the large twin follow-up scraper mounted high on the rear of the two-wheeled trailer and the absence of a seat for the operator as he is seated in the towing vehicle. The MLG-60 can lay the mines on the surface or bury them. Mine spacing is between 4 and 6 m. The unit is normally towed by a 6 × 6 truck or a BTR-152 (6 × 6) armoured personnel carrier.
    The MLG-60M is a slightly improved model.

Specifications (MLG-60M)
Crew: 2
Weight: 800 kg
Length:
    (travelling order) 4.9 m
    (operating order) 5.9 m
Width: 1.87 m
Height:
    (travelling order) 1.95 m
    (operating order) 2.1 m
Operating speed: 3-5 km/h
Tyres: 10-20 extra

Status
In service with the German Army.

MLG-60 minelayer being towed by BTR-152 APC

Manufacturer
Former East German state factories.

Mine Launching System (MiWS) Skorpion

Development
The Dynamit Nobel Mine Launching system (*Minenwurf* system) has been under active development since 1978 and the first deliveries of the system (including training ammunition) were made to the German Army in 1986. The system was originally known as the *Minenstreumittel* (MSM) system and encompassed the MSM-Fz vehicle-launching system (now known as Skorpion – see below) and the MSM-Hs helicopter-launching system which has been flight tested. The vehicle-mounted version is marketed as the Vehicle Launched Scatterable Mines System (VLSMS) Skorpion.
    Contracts called for the delivery of 301 M548GA1 tracked carriers (conversions carried out by Krauss-Maffei with last deliveries during 1989), 2030 training magazines and 32 000 loaded mine magazines (until 1992). Production of the latter is at a rate of 450 magazines (9000 mines) a month.

Description
The MiWS (Skorpion) consists of a modified M584GA1 tracked carrier on the rear of which is mounted the mine launching assembly with six mine launcher units, each mounted on a turntable. Each mine launcher unit has five pre-loaded magazines, each of which holds 20 AT2 anti-tank mines (for details of the AT2 refer to entry in the *Mines* section). The magazines have a metal body with foam filling and contain four ejection units with glass-reinforced plastic tubes. Each unit holds five AT2 anti-tank mines, all of which are ejected

MiWS Skorpion with M548GA1

from the unit at once. Each magazine unit has an external cable which is connected to the launcher system after loading. Magazine units are delivered packed 10 to a standard NATO pallet and are discarded after use.
    Carried inside the vehicle cab is the EPAG timing, testing and firing device which acts as the main control unit for the system. The unit can be used to pre-select the resultant mine barrier data and can be placed into

an automatic mode. Data that can be keyed into the unit prior to operations include six mine self-destruct times, six mine densities of from 0.1 to 0.6 mines/m, automatic or single launching, and alternate launching on both sides or from one side only. The EPAG unit also has a self-test mode with module fault display, testing modes for the launcher electrical system, a mode for monitoring operational conditions and a display showing ammunition ready to launch.

MiWS Skorpion-AB with Bv 206 all-terrain carrier

Depending on the settings entered into the EPAG the Skorpion MiWS will eject the groups of five AT2 anti-tank mines as the vehicle moves forwards independent of its speed. Mines are ejected obliquely to the rear. The resultant mine barrier density will depend on the EPAG settings but a typical example is that a single combat load of 600 mines can form a mine barrier strip 1500 m long with a density of 0.4 mines/m of front in approximately 5 minutes, travelling at a speed of 20 km/h. A typical mine barrier strip is 50 m wide. A typical Skorpion mine barrier has two or more parallel strips.

Various training aids, including reusable training ammunition, are available for the system.

A helicopter-carried system based on the Bell UH-1D (other helicopter types can be used) has been developed and has undergone flight tests. This system uses two magazine frames and the EPAG. The frames are held on a transverse support with damping and suspension facilities. Assembly time for the system is about 15 minutes. The mines are dispensed from an altitude of between 5 and 15 m. A typical combat load of 2 × 5 mine magazines (200 AT2 anti-tank mines) can produce a 500 m long mine barrier strip (typical example) with a density of 0.4 mines/m of front in 20 seconds (flying at a speed of 50 knots).

A third member of the Skorpion family involves an on-going programme for the Swedish Army to mount the system on the Bv 206 tracked all-terrain carrier. The launching assembly with four magazine frames (400 AT2 DM1274 anti-tank mines) is mounted on the rear unit of the Bv 206. In March 1991 Skorpion-AB (airborne) was tested by Swedish Army engineers in 1 m deep soft snow; it can be carried inside a CH-53 helicopter. A light armoured version of the Bv 206 is available. Skorpion-AB is in the final stages of adoption.

During Operation Desert Shield/Storm four M548GA1 Skorpion tracked carriers fitted with armoured cabs were deployed by the British Army.

Specifications
Mine launcher
Crew: 2
Combat weight: 12 000 kg
Length: 5.87 m
Width:
(loading and transport) 2.68 m
(laying position, loaded) 2.87 m
Height: (top of machine gun) 3.52 m
Max speed: 40 km/h (FRG limit)
Range: (cruising) 500 km
Engine: diesel developing 210 hp
Armament: 1 × 7.62 mm MG

Mine launching assembly
Weight:
(combat, loaded) approx 4000 kg
(empty) approx 1900 kg
Length: 3.347 m
Width: (platform) 2.285 m

Mine magazine
Weight: 70 kg
Length: 728 mm
Width: 130 mm
Height: 520 mm
Contents: 20 mines

Status
In service with the German Army and under consideration by several other countries.

Prime Contractor
Dynamit Nobel AG, Defence Division, PO Box 1261, D-5210 Troisdorf, Federal Republic of Germany. Tel: 0 22 41 89-0. Telex: 885 666 dn d. Fax: 0 22 41 89 1669.

ITALY

BPD ST-AT/V Anti-tank Minelayer

Description
The BPD ST-AT/V anti-tank minelayer was designed for use with the BPD SB-MV/1, SB-81 and SB-81/AR anti-tank mines. The system is of the towed type and can be hitched to any standard vehicle towing hook.

The ST-AT/V is constructed onto a welded steel frame fitted with a single axle carrying large diameter low-pressure tyres for cross-country travel. The system is provided with a hydraulic circuit to carry out all the mechanical operations under the control of a single crewman operating an electronic switching control unit; another crewman loads the mine conveyor from the towing vehicle. As an alternative the system can be connected to the towing vehicle electrical supply. The hydraulic power is supplied by a pump driven from the wheels via a gearbox on the axle's self-locking differential unit.

The electronic control unit is based on a low energy consumption microprocessor and controls all the laying operations from a remote switch panel. The panel is located close to the mine conveyor to the front of the towed unit. The position is provided with an intercom for communication with the towing vehicle driver.

Mines are placed on the mine conveyor by a loader in the rear of the towing vehicle. The mine safety devices are removed as the mine is loaded and the mine is conveyed to the unit plough share under the control of the electronic control unit. The spacing intervals can be varied from 2 to 99.9 m, and the laying depth is from 150 to 200 mm; the mine arming safety device is removed as the mine is emplaced in the furrow. Various types of plough can be used and there is a safety device that raises the share if an under-

BPD ST-AT/V anti-tank minelayer in operation behind Australian Army M113 APC

ground obstacle is encountered. Scraper devices behind the plough smooth off the ground surface after laying for added mine concealment.

For road transport the plough is raised from its operational position and locked. A canvas cover is fitted when the unit is not in operation and lifting eyes are provided for handling and for slinging under helicopters.

This minelayer is also produced in Spain by Explosivos Alaveses SA (EXPAL).

Specifications
Crew: (on unit) 1
Weight: approx 2400 kg
Length:
(operational) 5.4 m
(on tow) 4.4 m
Width: 2.2 m
Height: 2.2 m
Max towing speed: 80 km/h
Laying speed: 2-8 km/h
Laying depth: 150 to 200 mm
Mine interval programming: 2 to 99.9 m
Interval accuracy: 0.1 m
Electrical system: 24 V
Batteries: 2 × 12 V, 80 Ah

Status
In production. Ordered by Australia (8).

Manufacturers
BPD Difesa e Spazio srl, Corso Garibaldi 20-22, I-00034 Colleferro (Rome), Italy. Tel: 06 97891. Telex: 611434 bpd cf 1. Explosivos Alaveses SA, Apdo 198, E-01080 Vitoria, Spain. Telephone: 45 22 23 50. Telex: 35508.

GRILLO 90 Manportable Mine Launcher

Description

The GRILLO 90 is a portable, disposable, single-tube mine launcher intended to create small rapidly emplaced anti-personnel minefields. It launches the mines without generating noise or flash by using a gas generator. A single launcher can launch a set of 15 anti-personnel mines of the VS-Mk 2 type.

The GRILLO 90 is a mortar-type launcher using mainly reinforced plastic components and is operated by a firing lever. It is provided with a carrying sling on which are two metal labels to be used as references for setting the angle of elevation. After having positioned the GRILLO 90 on the ground and setting the elevation angle to either 45 or 60° by placing one foot on the relevant metal label and elevating the barrel until the sling is tensioned, the launcher is fired by removing the safety and actuating the firing lever. The GRILLO 90 is stated to be completely safe in functioning, handling and storage, even in the case of a misfire.

The launcher is available in two versions; Short Range and Long Range. Practice versions with re-usable barrels and percussion devices are available for training purposes.

Status
In production.

Manufacturer
Valsella Meccanotecnica SpA, I-25014 Castenedolo, Brescia, Italy.
Tel: 30 2732621. Telex: 300495 emmeti i.
Fax: 30 2731687.

GRILLO 90 manportable mine launcher in operation

Specifications

Model	Short Range	Long Range
Weight, ready to fire	5.6 kg	8 kg
Length, transport	750 mm	970 mm
Base plate dimensions	120 × 125 mm	140 × 140 mm
Launch tube diameter		
(external)	95 mm	95 mm
(internal)	90 mm	90 mm
Range		
(45°)	60 m	160 m
(60°)	50 m	130 m
Standard deviation	approx 4 m	approx 4 m
Noise at 30 m	56 dBA	65 dBA
Temperature range		
(operating)	−32 to +60°C	−32 to +60°C
(storage)	−32 to +70°C	−32 to +70°C

GRILLO 128 Manportable Mine Launcher

Description

The GRILLO 128 is a portable, disposable, single-tube mine launcher intended to create small rapidly emplaced anti-tank minefields. It launches the mines without generating noise or flash by using a gas generator. A single launcher can launch a set of 5 anti-tank mines of the VS-SATM1 type.

The GRILLO 128 is a mortar-type launcher using mainly reinforced plastic components and is operated by a firing lever. It is provided with a carrying sling on which are two metal labels to be used as references for setting the angle of elevation. After having positioned the GRILLO 128 on the ground and setting the elevation angle to either +45 or +60° by placing one foot on the relevant metal label and elevating the barrel until the sling is tensioned, the launcher is fired by removing the safety and actuating the firing lever. The GRILLO 128 is stated to be completely safe in functioning, handling and storage, even in the case of a misfire.

Practice versions with reusable barrels and percussion devices are available for training purposes.

Specifications
Weight, ready to fire: 14.5 kg
Length, transport: 920 mm
Base plate dimensions: 140 × 140 mm
Launch tube diameter:
(external) 134 mm
(internal) 128 mm
Range:
(45°) 60 m
(60°) 50 m
Standard deviation: approx 4 m
Noise at 30 m: 120 dBA
Temperature range:
(operating) −32 to +60°C
(storage) −32 to +70°C

Status
In production.

Manufacturer
Valsella Meccanotecnica SpA, I-25014 Castenedolo, Brescia, Italy.
Tel: 30 2732621. Telex: 300495 emmeti i.
Fax: 30 2731687.

GRILLO 128 manportable mine launcher in operation

Valsella Istrice Land Mine Scattering System

Description

The Istrice land mine scattering system was designed to deploy minefields with fast and safe operation, high flexibility in the pattern and density of the resultant minefield and a short preparation time.

The Istrice system consists of the following components:

    a launcher which can be installed on several types of military vehicle
    a fire control unit
    canisters and magazines
    the carrier vehicle
    the mines.

The mines are stored in launch tubes and are ejected by an electrically fired gas generator. Arrays of tubes are assembled in modular canisters.

The launcher consists of up to eight launch units arranged in pairs with each pair on a single frame. The units, mounted on a trunnion bearing, are adjustable in traverse by hand while the angle of elevation is fixed.

The system is controlled by a fire control unit installed in the carrier vehicle cab. Using this unit the status of the launcher can be monitored, launch parameters can be set and data relevant to the launch operation are displayed in real time. A log of the deployed minefield is automatically provided.

The mines are stored in sealed launch tubes which also act as magazines for storage and transport. The magazines are assembled into canisters fitted with mechanical and electrical connections to the magazines and to the launch units. The launcher can be loaded using either magazines or full canisters.

The launcher is installed on the carrier vehicle in minutes using an interface frame. No mechanical or electrical modification of the vehicle is required. The minimum width of the vehicle platform required for installation is 2.2 m. Depending on the platform length, two, three or four pairs of launch units can be installed. The minimum loading capacity required for the vehicle is 3.9, 5.9 or 7.9 tonnes respectively. Istrice has been field tested on the IVECO FIAT 90 PM 16 (4 × 4) 4000 kg truck (three pairs of launch units) and the IVECO FIAT 230 PM 35 (6 × 6) 10 000 kg truck (four pairs of launch units). The launcher can also be installed on several models of tracked cargo vehicle such as the OTO Melara OTO C14, the FMC M548, and the ARIS-converted M113 APC.

Istrice can scatter several types of anti-personnel and anti-tank mine including the VS-SATM1 full width electronic anti-tank mine, the VS-Mk2-EL electronic

Four-unit Istrice land mine scattering system on an IVECO FIAT 90 PM 16 (4 × 4) truck

Four-unit Istrice land mine scattering system on an ARIS-converted M113 APC

anti-personnel mine, and the VS-SAPFM3 electronic bounding anti-personnel mine.

The Istrice is available in two versions; Short Range (50 m) and Long Range (250 m).

Specifications
Mine payload:
(anti-tank only) 720 mines
(anti-personnel only) 3840 mines
Weight:
(launcher, loaded with a/t mines) 3900 or 4100 kg
(launcher, loaded with a/p mines) 3100 or 3400 kg
(launcher without canisters) 1000 kg
Width: 2.2 m
Height over platform: 1.4 m
Traverse: 90°
Elevation: +60° or +45°, both fixed
Scatter rate:
(a/t mines) max 500 mines/min
(a/p mines) max 4200 mines/min
Launch distance: 50 or 250 m
Power requirements: 24 V DC, 4 A

Status
In production.

Manufacturer
Valsella Meccanotecnica SpA, I-25014 Castenedolo, Brescia, Italy.
Tel: 30 2732621. Telex: 300495 emmeti i.
Fax: 30 2731687.

Valsella VS-MDH Scatter-dropping Mine System

Description
The VS-MDH scatter-dropping mine system (at one time known as the VS/MD system) was designed to allow the scatter-dropping of 2080 anti-personnel (VS-50 or VS-Mk 2 or VS-Mk 2-EL) or 200 anti-tank mines (VS-1.6 or VS-1.6-EL) in mixed loads and varying ratios. The complete system consists of two main components; the control panel in the helicopter and the mine dispenser. This consists of a metal rack designed to accept 40 modular disposable magazines. On the bottom of each magazine is a stop which keeps the mines in place during storage, shipment and while inserting the magazines into the rack of the dispenser. Once in the dispenser the stop is removed.

The anti-personnel mines are dropped in groups of 52 and anti-tank mines in groups of five. They are dispensed through doors in the bottom of each magazine. The door-opening sequence has been designed to prevent any change in the centre of gravity of the dispenser. At the end of the scatter-dropping programme, a safety device actuated by a push-button closes all the doors.

The dispenser is attached to the centre-of-gravity hook of the helicopter by a special ring connector. The system's remote controls are connected to the control panel in the helicopter via a cable fitted with a multi-pole slip ring connector. This has been designed for quick release both on the ground and in the air in case of an emergency.

The compact control panel can be mounted on the console of the helicopter, or in any other suitable position. The system has been designed for both manual and automatic scatter-dropping and consists of an electronic control unit which can open the doors at intervals of 0.1 to 0.6 second. This, together with the speed of the helicopter, allows the mines to be dispersed according to the tactical requirement.

A readout on the control console indicates when each door of the dispenser is opened and the operator can also monitor, at a glance, how many mines have been dispensed and how many are left. When

UH-1 helicopter carrying Valsella VS-MDH scatter-dropping mine system laying minefield

operated manually, one door opens every time the button is depressed. There is also an emergency device which, when operated, causes the complete dispenser to be emptied at once. The system requires a 28 V DC electrical supply.

Specifications
Weight:
(dispenser) 310 kg
(loaded with anti-tank mines) 1160 kg
(control unit) 1.2 kg
Dispenser:
(length) 1.75 m
(width) 1.55 m
(height) 1.6 m
Control unit:
(length) 180 mm
(width) 120 mm
(height) 100 mm
Number of mines carried:
(anti-personnel) 2080
(anti-tank) 200
Power supply: 28 V DC
Max power load: 8 A

Status
In service with various undisclosed countries.

Manufacturer
Valsella Meccanotecnica SpA, I-25014 Castenedolo, Brescia, Italy.
Tel: 30 2732621. Telex: 300495 emmeti i.
Fax: 30 2731687.

BPD SY-AT Helicopter Anti-tank and Anti-personnel Mine-scattering System

Description
The BPD SY-AT helicopter-carried scattering system was designed for use with the BPD SB-81 anti-tank and BPD SB-33 anti-personnel mines. The first production SY-AT system was completed in April 1978.

BPD SY-AT helicopter anti-tank and anti-personnel mine-scattering system slung under Lama helicopter

The system is composed of a basic distributor module and two ancillary modules. The former is connected to the baricentric hook of the helicopter by a special suspension sling and connector hook which also contains the electrical connection. The unit can be carried slung under standard helicopter types.

The mines are dispensed through hatches in the bottom of the distributors. The hatches can be opened at a programmed frequency, or manually by pushing a button on the control console mounted in the helicopter. Safety blocks ensure that the hatches do not open until the helicopter reaches the target area. The scattering ratio of anti-tank to anti-personnel mines is variable according to mission requirements and is controlled from the control panel. Indicators on the panel advise the operator when the magazines are empty as well as how many full magazines remain. Safety pins are removed from the mines as they leave the plastic magazines. In an emergency it is possible to discharge all the mines in the distributor simultaneously.

The basic module contains 32 magazines which contain 2496 anti-personnel or 160 anti-tank mines. The ancillary distributors are hooked on each side of the basic module, each with eight magazines for 624 anti-personnel or 40 anti-tank mines, or a combination. The complete system, basic module and two ancillary modules, has a total of 3744 anti-personnel mines or 240 anti-tank mines, or a combination of both types.

Specifications
Magazine of anti-tank mines
Weight:
(empty) 3.5 kg
(loaded) 19.5 kg
Number of SB-81 mines: 5
Dimensions: 246 × 110 × 1142 mm

Magazine of anti-personnel mines
Weight:
(empty) 3.6 kg
(loaded) 15 kg
Number of SB-33 mines: 78
Dimensions: 246 × 110 × 1142 mm

Basic distributor module
Empty weight: 150 kg
Loaded weight:
(with anti-tank mines) 774 kg
(with anti-personnel mines) 630 kg
Capacity: 32 magazines containing 5 anti-tank or 78 anti-personnel mines each
Dimensions: 1545 × 1320 × 1380 mm

Ancillary distributor module
Weight empty: 35 kg
Loaded weight:
(with anti-tank mines) 191 kg
(with anti-personnel mines) 155 kg
Capacity: 8 magazines containing 5 anti-tank or 78 anti-personnel mines each
Dimensions: 1545 × 399 mm

Complete unit
Weight: (empty) 220 kg
Weight loaded:
(with anti-tank mines) 1156 kg
(with anti-personnel mines) 940 kg
Capacity: 48 magazines each holding 5 anti-tank or 78 anti-personnel mines each
Dimensions: 1545 × 2119 × 1380 mm
Voltage requirements: 24-28 V DC

Status
In production. In service with various countries.

Manufacturer
BPD Difesa e Spazio srl, Corso Garibaldi 20-22, I-00034 Colleferro (Rome), Italy.
Tel: 06 97891. Telex: 611434 bpd cf 1.

Tecnovar DAT Scatter-dropping Mine System

Description
The DAT scatter-dropping mine system provides for automatic or manual dropping of loads of either TS-50 anti-personnel or MATS anti-tank mines, or a combination of both. The complete system consists of two main components, the electronic programmer fitted to the instrument panel of the carrier helicopter and the automatic dispenser system. There are two versions of

Tecnovar DAT scatter-dropping mine system in use slung under Lynx helicopter

the dispenser: model A, which can carry 128 anti-tank or 1280 anti-personnel mines, and model B, which can carry 64 anti-tank, 640 anti-personnel or 32 anti-tank and 320 anti-personnel. The mines are carried in preloaded magazines slotted into the dispenser. The anti-tank magazine carries eight mines and the anti-personnel magazine 40 mines. The two models can be coupled together to form combinations, such as A + A, A + B and A + A + B. The type of combination used depends on the underslung cargo capacity of the helicopter and the type of minefield to be laid.

The dispenser system is attached to the helicopter on the end of a sling fitted with a rotary hook. The distributor doors are opened only after the correct signal is received from the electronic programmer unit, which controls the interval between door openings. The interval may be set between 0.1 and 9.9 second in increments of 0.1 second.

For an anti-personnel minefield the mines are dropped in groups of 80, for an anti-tank minefield in groups of eight and for a mixed minefield in groups of four anti-tank mines and 40 anti-personnel mines. The typical flight altitude for laying is up to 100 m at speeds of up to 200 km/h.

Specifications
Anti-personnel mine magazine
Construction: steel
Length: 280 mm
Width: 145 mm
Height: 910 mm
Weight: (empty) 8 kg
Capacity: 40 TS-50 anti-personnel mines

Anti-tank mine magazine
Construction: steel
Length: 290 mm
Width: 200 mm
Height: 910 mm
Weight: (empty) 11.5 kg
Capacity: 8 MATS anti-tank mines

Model A dispenser unit
Length: 1214 mm
Width: 1224 mm
Height: 1244 mm
Weight:
(empty, including sling, cables and hook) 170 kg
(filled with 128 anti-tank mines) 800 kg
(filled with 1280 anti-personnel mines) 740 kg

Model B dispenser unit
Length: 622 mm
Width: 1224 mm
Height: 1244 mm
Weight:
(empty, including sling, cables and hook) 100 kg
(filled with 64 anti-tank mines) 425 kg
(filled with 640 anti-personnel mines) 355 kg
(filled with 32 anti-tank and 320 anti-personnel mines) 385 kg

Typical combinations of Models A and B dispenser units

	A + A	A + B	A + A + B
Length	2.428 m	1.836 m	3.050 m
Height	1.244 m	1.244 m	1.244 m
Width	1.224 m	1.224 m	1.224 m

Power requirement for electronic programmer: 28 V DC

Status
Models A and B in production and service.

Manufacturer
Tecnovar Italiana SpA, 95 Via Argiro, I-70121 Bari, Italy.
Tel: 080 5211744. Telex: 810345 tecvar i.
Fax: 370400.

JAPAN

Japanese minelayer being towed by Type 60 armoured personnel carrier and showing onboard operator position (Kensuke Ebata)

Japanese minelayer being towed by Type 60 armoured personnel carrier (Kensuke Ebata)

POLAND

SUM-OF Tracked Minelayer

Description

The SUM-OF tracked minelayer was designed specifically for the rapid laying of surface and buried anti-tank mines. The minelayer has a crew of two and is carried on a special tracked chassis with six road wheels and a torsion bar suspension.

The minelaying system is carried at the rear of the vehicle with mines being automatically fed into the system from two magazines carried within the armoured superstructure. The mine magazines are replenished using a K10 crane mounted at the rear of the vehicle; the crane has a lifting capacity of 2800 kg. Supervision of the laying process can be carried out using a rear-mounted video camera connected to a monitoring screen inside the vehicle. The monitoring screen is located over a control panel used to control the minelaying operations. Provision is made for operations under NBC conditions by an air filtration system and a GO-27 detection device.

When burying mines the vehicle can travel at a speed of between 6 and 10 km/h. When laying surface mines the speed range is from 6 to 20 km/h. It is possible to lay mines in water up to 0.9 m deep at a speed of 6 km/h.

The vehicle is armed with a 12.7 mm NSW machine gun. 902A smoke grenade launchers are also provided.

Specifications
Crew: 2
Weight: approx 32 000 kg
Length: (travelling) 10.41 m
Width: (travelling) 3.354 m
Height: (travelling) 2.87 m
Max speed: 65 km/h
Range: 500 km
Gradient:
　(travelling) 25°
　(operating) 19°
Fording:
　(normal) 0.9 m
　(with preparation) 1.5 m
Engine: diesel developing 700 hp
Armament: 1 × 12.7 mm NSW MG
Laying speeds:
　(buried mines) 6-10 km/h
　(surface mines) 6-20 km/h
　(under water) 6 km/h

Status
Available. Offered for export.

Manufacturer
Research and Development Centre of Mechanical Appliances, 44-101 Gliwice, ul. Toszecka 102, Poland. Tel: (48) (032) 31 72 41. Telex: 036 197. Fax: (48) (032) 31 58 87.

SUM-OF tracked minelayer in travelling position and with handling crane partially raised

SERBIA

Yugoslav Towed Minelayer

Description
The former Yugoslav state factories produced a towed minelayer which resembles the PMR-3 in layout and operation but which is used to emplace the TMRP-6 anti-tank mine. The minelayer is towed behind a suitable 4 × 4 or 6 × 6 wheeled vehicle and mines are fed into the dispenser chute direct from the vehicle's rear cargo area. At the end of the dispenser chute two sets of ploughs open up the soil to bury the mine and then push back the soil to disguise the mine's position.

No details regarding performance or dimensions are available.

Status
In service with the former Yugoslav Army.

Towed minelayer laying TMRP-6 anti-tank mines

SWEDEN

FFV Minelayer

Description
This mechanical minelayer was developed by FFV (now part of Bofors AB) and was designed specifically for use with the FFV 028 anti-tank mine. Development began in 1976.

During 1985 the German army placed an order worth DM 43 million for 300 of these minelayers. The Netherlands placed an order in late 1985 and a further order was placed by them in September 1989.

The FFV minelayer can lay the mines either on the surface or buried to a depth of 0.2 m. The distance between the mines can be varied between 1 and 99 m and maximum laying capacity is 20 mines/minute at a speed of 7 km/h. All the crew has to do is remove the transport safety tab and place the mine on the chute. The minelayer then buries the mine and replaces the soil. The system can be towed behind most types of vehicle.

Specifications
Crew: 1 + 3
Weight: 2800 kg
Length: 5.3 m
Width: 2.5 m

Status
In production. In service with the Dutch and German armies.

Manufacturer
Bofors AB, S-631 87 Eskilstuna, Sweden.
Tel: 46 16 15 50 00. Telex: 46075 ffvhk s.
Fax: 46 16 12 43 10.

FFV minelayer

UNITED STATES OF AMERICA

M128 Vehicle-towed Mine Dispenser

Development
The Ground Emplaced Mine Scattering System (GEMSS) M128 (or Frisbee Flinger as it is more popularly known) was developed by Picatinny Arsenal and the Ordnance Division of the FMC Corporation of San Jose, California. The M128 was type classified for US Army service in 1980 but introduction into service was delayed. During FY82 and FY83 59 and 52 units respectively were purchased. None were purchased in FY84 but in FY85 81 units at a cost of $30.1 million were scheduled. The first unit was equipped in the first quarter of FY86. The final equipment buy was completed during the first quarter of FY88. The M128 is issued on the basis of one to selected engineer companies.

Description
The M128 is mounted on a modified M794 flat bed trailer designated the M979, and can be towed behind a truck or tracked vehicle such as an M113 APC, over both roads and cross-country. Anti-tank and anti-personnel mines of the same dimensions are carried in the drum-type magazine and can be dispensed concurrently or separately to pre-selected patterns and minefield densities. Weight of the M128 empty is 4773 kg and loaded 6364 kg.

The M128 feeds mines out of a hydraulic drum-type magazine, flips them through a directional tunnel and sends them spinning to the ground. The mines are left on the surface and a percentage of mines in each batch are fitted with an anti-disturbance mechanism.

The system uses the M74 anti-personnel and M75 anti-tank mines. It can carry up to 800 mines in its storage drums and dispense 2 mines/second. The mines have a factory-set long (more than a day) self-destruct time, which can be changed to a still longer time by the M128 while the mines are being dispensed. The anti-personnel mine is tripwire-activated and has a blast kill mechanism. The anti-tank mine is very similar to the mine used in the Remote Anti-Armor Mine System (RAAMS). Both types of mine have anti-disturbance features fitted. For further details of these mines refer to the entry in the *Mines* section.

Inside their crates the mines are packed in tubular sleeves each carrying five mines. Loading the M128 dispenser takes from three to five men up to 20 minutes with the normal mine mix being five anti-tank to one anti-personnel.

Status
In service with US Army.

M128 vehicle-towed mine dispenser with jacks lowered

M139 Volcano Multiple Delivery Mine System

Development
Volcano was originally an Aerojet Ordnance Company programme but was later passed to Honeywell Defense Systems Division (now Alliant Techsystems) which was awarded an initial $10.5 million contract for the advanced development of the system. The material developing agency is the Project Manager, Mine Countermine Demolition at Picatinny Arsenal. The US Army Engineer School and Center at Fort Leonard Wood is in charge of combat development.

The M139 Volcano system was expected to be type classified during 1987 but this was delayed by extended testing. In late September 1987 a firm-fixed-price contract was awarded to Honeywell's Defense Systems Division (now Alliant Techsystems Inc). The contract was worth $19 592 590 and was for six units. The US Army's FY88 request was for 23 000 M87 canisters at a cost of $34.5 million. Also involved in the programme was Day and Zimmerman Inc of Texarkana, Texas.

By October 1990 the 5-tonne truck system was type classified and in production by Brunswick Defense; they were awarded a $4 million contract to produce 24 launch systems for delivery during 1991. The UH-60A and M548A1 systems were type classified during June 1991.

Description
The M139 Volcano multiple delivery mine system can rapidly dispense up to 960 GATOR anti-tank mines and anti-personnel mines from expendable canisters mounted on as many as four launcher racks. The system is designed to be carried by either the M817 engineer dump-truck, the M814 5-tonne cargo truck, the M548A1 tracked carrier, or the UH-60 Black Hawk helicopter, although other vehicles or helicopters could be used.

The main system components are the expendable M87 Mine Canister which holds six mines; five GATOR BLU-91/B anti-tank mines and one BLU-92/B anti-personnel mine. The other component is the M139 Dispenser, a reusable item consisting of the launcher rack, the dispenser control unit (DCU) and mounting hardware. Each launcher rack can hold up to 40 canisters and is connected to the mounting hardware which is an angled mounting bracket holding up to four launcher racks. Only one DCU is used for each system to provide fire signals, both for testing the system and for setting the arming and one of three self-destruct times.

After the Volcano system has been mounted in the carrier vehicle or helicopter and the DCU has been

Volcano fitted to M929 dump truck

programmed for the carrier vehicle speed and the minefield length, the firing sequence can be initiated by the operator. Upon receiving the initial firing command, the DCU begins to fire canisters on alternating sides of the carrier vehicle in the sequence prescribed for uniform minefield density. The propellant charge at the base of the canister expels the mine stack and, as it leaves the end of the canister, the mines receive electrical impulses through a strap interlaced between them. These electrical impulses arm the mine and set its self-destruct time. As the mine stack reaches the slack limit of the strap the mines are dispersed by the increasing tautness of the interlaced strap.

A Volcano minefield can have a nominal density of 0.9 mines/m along a 1 km front, although this can be varied. The mine delivery speed is from 8 to 88 km/h for ground vehicles and from 20 to 120 knots for helicopters. At a ground speed of 88 km/h 960 mines can be dispensed in 43 seconds. A helicopter flying at 120 knots can dispense 960 mines in 17 seconds. A typical Volcano-dispensed minefield strip is 125 m wide and 1150 m long.

The 5-ton truck version of Volcano weighs 3255 kg.

The UH-60A version weighs 2940 kg and the M548A1 version 3325 kg.

For training there are two Volcano training canisters: the M88 practice canister holding six dummy mines and the M89 canister with an electronic dummy load.

As a private venture Alliant Techsystems have developed a lightweight Volcano system known as Volcano Light. This consists of a 20-canister dispenser assembly carried on the rear of a M998 HMMWV. The assembly can carry 120 anti-armour or 300 anti-personnel mines and can be fixed on a swivel mount in one of five positions for dispensing.

Status
In production for US Army.

System Contractors
Alliant Techsystems Inc, 5901 Lincoln Drive, Edina, Minnesota 55436, USA.
Tel: (612) 939 2440. Fax: (612) 939 2749.
Brunswick Defense, One Brunswick Plaza, Skokie, Illinois 60077, USA.
Tel: (312) 470 4700. Telex: 190127.

M131 Modular Pack Mine System (MOPMS)

Description

The M131 Modular Pack Mine System (MOPMS) is a member of the Family of Scatterable Mines (FAS-CAM). It is a portable system for selective protection and small area coverage for withdrawing friendly forces. Type classification was in June 1986.

The MOPMS modules, weighing 68 kg each, are taken to the operation site by truck and carried by two men to the required position. If unused they can be retrieved and reused. Firing of modules is by a M71 coded remote-control unit (RCU) or by a signal sent through a cable connected to a standard US Army blasting device on the dispenser module. Each MOPMS unit contains 17 M131 anti-tank/anti-vehicle and four M132 anti-personnel mines.

The mines contain three Large Scale Integrated (LSI) micro-electronic chips in the electronics package, which also includes a command destruct/recycle receiver and a sensor circuit. The package fits within 95 cm³. Ammonium/lithium batteries are fitted that remain passive until the command to scatter the mines is received. On landing the magnetic field sensor orientates the anti-tank/anti-vehicle mine towards the target vehicle and enables the entire belly of the target

M131 Modular Pack Mine System dismantled to show major components and 21 mines carried

vehicle to be attacked by the warhead, in addition to tank tracks or wheels.

The mines are supplied with preset self-destruction devices or can be detonated by remote-control. The built-in timers can be recycled, extending the life of the minefield. If the mines are not dispensed the sealed dispenser can be moved intact to a new location.

The M132 anti-personnel mine is activated by four tripwires. These are automatically deployed on landing and, when disturbed, initiate a fragmenting kill mechanism.

For training the M136 dispenser is used. This is an inert dispenser identical to the M131 but with a light to indicate the receipt of a firing signal.

In October 1987 Hughes Aircraft Company was awarded a $18.9 million contract for the low rate initial production of electronics for over 32 000 MOPMS mines, 1600 module control units and 580 remote-control systems. In FY88 the US Army requested $62.5 million for 6498 MOPMS dispensers with production scheduled to commence in January 1989 and to be completed in September 1990. In July 1989 the Acudyne Corporation of Janesville, Wisconsin, was awarded a $34 153 592 firm-fixed-price contract for the production of MOPMS electronic assemblies. Planned procurement was scheduled for about 3600 units in FY90 and 4600 units in FY91.

Status

In production for the US Army.

Manufacturers

Engineering development of the command destruct/recycle electronics was undertaken by Hughes Aircraft Company Ground Systems Group, Fullerton, California, USA.

Aerojet is responsible for the dispenser and Alliant Techsystems Inc is systems integrator with responsibility for the mines.

M57 Anti-Tank Mine Dispensing System (ATMDS)

Description

The M57 Anti-Tank Mine Dispensing System is a sidelift plough with a side-insertion mine chute mounted on a two-wheeled trailer towed by a 2½-ton (6 × 6) truck which carries the crew and a supply of mines. The M57 can lay M15 anti-tank mines on the surface, or buried below the ground at a sustained rate of 375 mines/hour. The mines can be buried to a maximum depth of 152 mm. The system is not suited to use in very hard soil or on side slopes. It is issued on the scale of one per combat engineer company in Europe.

Status

In service with the US Army.

Complete M57 ATMDS from mine pallets on left to dispenser on right (US Army)   *Sidelift plough of M57 ATMDS with mine dispenser chute above (US Army)*

Remote Anti-Armor Mine System (RAAMS)

Description

The Remote Anti-Armor Mine System (RAAMS) consists of a 155 mm projectile carrying anti-armour mines which are fired from M109 series self-propelled howitzers. It is a member of the Family of Scatterable Mines (FASCAM). Initial production commenced during 1978.

There are two types of projectile: the M741 projectile carries nine mines with a factory-set short self-destruct time of under 24 hours and the M718 carries nine mines with a factory-set long self-destruct time of over 24 hours.

Each circular M75 anti-tank mine weighs about 2.26 kg. Arming is automatic on landing. Actuation is by a magnetic influence fuze that operates against the width of the tank. The detonation then occurs in two stages: the first when a clearing charge blows off the mine cover and removes any ground debris and the second 30 ms later when the main charge, which consists of 572 g of PBX 0280 (95:5 RDX:Estane) and two plate charges so as to make the ground orientation

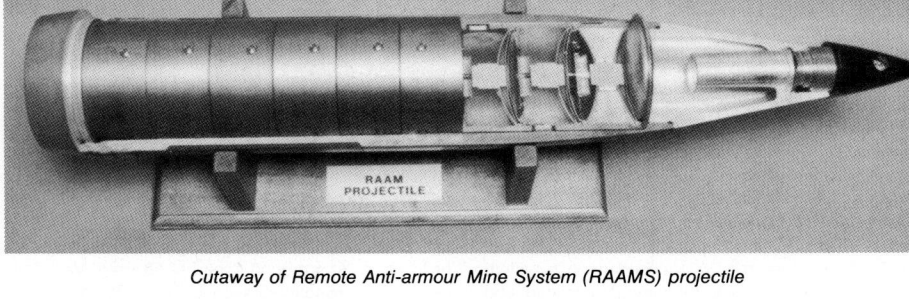

Cutaway of Remote Anti-armour Mine System (RAAMS) projectile

of the mine non-critical, is detonated. The mine is capable of destroying any tank passing over it and is said to cause a spalling effect when it penetrates tank belly armour. The projectile is fired to a maximum range of 17 000 m and a single battery of six 155 mm self-propelled howitzers can lay a minefield 300 m long and 250 m deep with two salvos. The 12 projectiles fired, each weighing 46.7 kg, provide a density of 0.001 mine/m² for the minefield. The density can be changed to meet the tactical situation by varying the lay of the guns and the number of rounds fired.

Status

In production for the US Army and Marine Corps.

Manufacturer

Alliant Techsystems Inc, 5901 Lincoln Drive, Edina, Minnesota 55436, USA.
Tel: (612) 939 2440. Fax: (612) 939 2749.

M56 Helicopter-delivered Scatterable Mine System

Development

The M56 offensive/defensive scatterable mine system was the first member of the Family of Scatterable Mines (FASCAM) to enter service with the US Army. It originated in the early 1960s as a design concept that became a weapons requirement during the Vietnam War and was developed as the XM56 system by the US Army's Picatinny Arsenal in the early 1970s under the direction of the Armament Research and Development Command. The system was type classified in FY74 and was in production from 1975 to 1977. It entered service in the European theatre of operations in 1977.

Description

The system's basic components are two SUU-13/A bomb dispensers, a control panel inside the carrying aircraft, normally a Bell UH-1D helicopter, and an interconnecting wiring harness. The dispenser holds 40 canisters, each of which contains two mines. The dispensers are suspended on the standard weapons pylons of the carrier helicopter, on either side of the fuselage. The control panel for the system is in the cockpit and allows the pilot to control the modes, patterns and density of the minefield to be laid. It can also be used to drop the dispensers simultaneously if necessary. The wiring harness is removable, which eliminates any modification to the helicopter's electrical system and greatly simplifies the transference of the M56 system between aircraft.

The commander who issues the initial order for an aircraft emplacement of scatterable mines determines the location, length, width and mine density/m² of the required minefield. One aircraft on a contour flight sortie can lay a minefield 100 m long and 40 m wide with a mine density of 0.04 mine/m², and 30 sorties can provide a minefield strip 2000 m long and 40 m wide with a density of 0.06 mine/m².

The M56 mine is 254 mm long with a 114 mm diameter half-round body and weighs approximately 2.7 kg. The explosive filling, Composition H6, weighs 1.4 kg. Once the mine is launched by a small propellant cartridge downwards from the dispenser at 4.6 m/s, the initial arming is achieved and four spring-folded fins open to increase the frictional drag of the mine and slow it down to minimise the impact force. They also orientate the mine in flight so that it strikes the ground with the flat face uppermost so as to

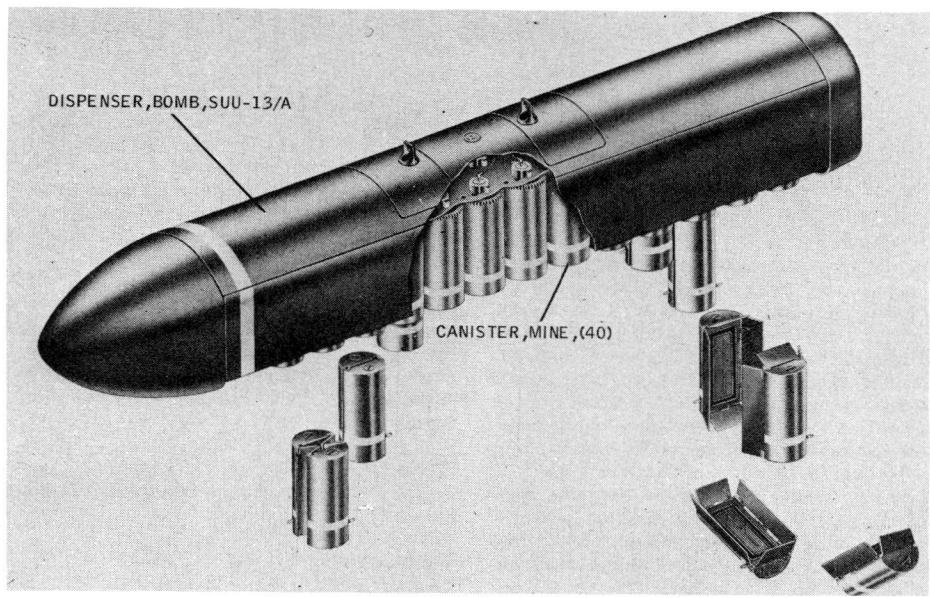

DISPENSER,BOMB,SUU-13/A

CANISTER,MINE,(40)

SUU-13/A dispenser

activate the final arming device some 1 to 2 minutes after impact. The dispenser contains a mixture of the three variants of the M56 mine, all superficially identical, which prevents detection of the type or its capabilities by simple inspection. The basic version is the anti-tank/anti-vehicular mine that is activated when a pressure plate on the flat side of the mine is depressed and sends a firing signal to the electro-mechanical fuze. The anti-tank/anti-roller version is designed to defeat minefield roller-clearing operations by allowing the rollers to pass over the mine without detonation and then exploding on contact with the following tank tracks. The last version is the anti-disturbance mine which is designed to explode when it is picked up, jarred, rolled or tampered with by any physical means (including, under certain circumstances, the rotor wash of a helicopter) thus discouraging manual clearance parties. All three versions can also be used to mine shallow water fording areas as submergence does not decrease their capabilities or operational efficiency. The variants are also fitted with factory-set (longer than one day) self-destruct timers.

The M56 system has two major disadvantages: the vulnerability of the carrier aircraft to groundfire, as the

mines must be dropped from at least 30.5 m above ground level to ensure correct orientation and arming on impact, and the total system weight of 580 kg which necessitates some external structural modifications to the aircraft.

The system is issued to assault helicopter companies and air cavalry troops on the scale of one system per three UH-1 helicopters. The complete system comprises one fully loaded M56 dispenser and four refill kits.

Status
In service with the US Army.

Specifications
Mine
Weight: 2.7 kg
Length: 254 mm
Diameter: 114 mm
Main charge type: Composition H6
Weight of main charge: 1.4 kg
Fuze type: electromechanical

M138 Flipper Portable Minelaying Device

Description

The portable minelaying device known as Flipper was developed by the US Army Armament, Research, Development and Engineering Center at Picatinny Arsenal, New Jersey, as an in-house programme. Production was carried out by the Peerless Instrument Company of Queens, New York, and the first units were produced during 1990.

The M138 Flipper is intended to augment the M128 vehicle-towed mine dispenser in scattering M74 anti-personnel and M75 anti-tank mines. The intention is to provide field commanders with the ability to emplace minefields at short notice and under varying field conditions.

The unit is transported contained in a packing box

which can be air-dropped. Two men can install a Flipper on the rear of a vehicle such as a 2½-ton or larger truck in about 10 minutes using a clamp assembly and a power lead to connect the unit to the vehicle's electrical system. As the truck is driven along, a soldier manually feeds mines into the launcher which uses a spinning tyre encased in a metal frame. After it is fed, the mine is armed, spun and launched at the rate of one every 10 seconds.

Status
In service with the US Army.

Development Agency
US Army Armament Research, Development and Engineering Center, Picatinny Arsenal, Dover, New Jersey 07806, USA.
Tel: (201) 724 4021.

Soldier loading the M138 Flipper portable minelaying system

MINE DETECTION EQUIPMENT

AUSTRALIA

TM-4 Image Processing Magnetometer System

Description
The TM-4 is a self-contained digital magnetometer system for the computer-aided location of ferrous ordnance. Fully positioned magnetic field measurements to 0.01 nT resolution may be digitally recorded at up to 200 per second. An in-built odometer eliminates the pre-marking of search lanes. On-site image processing and computer-aided unexploded object anomaly recognition and identification enable assurance confidence levels to be specified for each search environment and provide a verifiable record of an EOD operation. Typically, the detection assurance depth equals or exceeds the maximum expected penetration depth for all ferrous ordnance. Explosive ordnance disposal (EOD) insurance underwriting has been obtained by users of the system.

Up to 2 hectares/day may be searched on foot, providing 100 000 positioned magnetic field measurements. The system may also be vehicle-mounted on request, with multiple, optically pumped, atomic resonance type magnetic sensors. A real-time digital filter suppresses interference from mains electricity.

Power is supplied by 30 V rechargeable batteries with a life of 7 hours per pack.

Specifications
Resolution: 0.01 nT
Position accuracy: 0.1% of distance between controls
Survey rate: up to 400 positioned measurements/s
Power supplies: 30 V rechargeable batteries
Battery pack life: 7 h

Status
In service with the Australian Department of Defence and others.

Manufacturer
Geophysical Technology Pty Ltd, PO Box AU9, Armidale, New South Wales 2351, Australia. Tel: 61 67 73 2617. Fax: 61 67 71 1661.

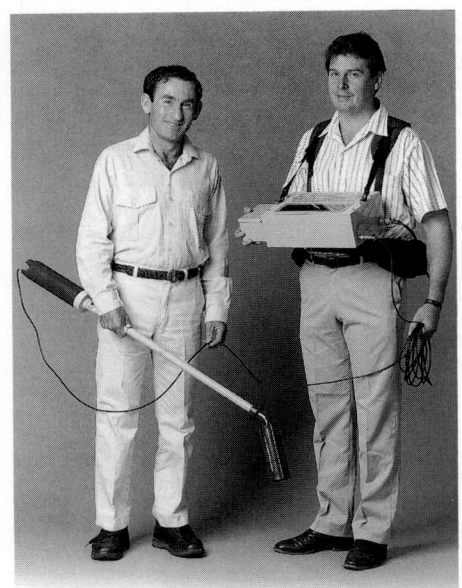

TM-4 magnetometer as used for hand-held operations

AUSTRIA

AN-19/2 Mine Detector

Development
The AN-19/2 was originally developed by co-operation between the Dipl.Ing. Hans Schiebel Elektronische Geräte GmbH of Vienna and NobelTech Electronics AB of Sweden. It is a design derivative of the AN-17/1 originally developed by Hans Schiebel. NobelTech Electronics (then the Defence Electronics Group of Philips Elektronikindustrier AB) delivered a large quantity of AN-19/2s to the Swedish Army during 1986 and 1987. Since then this instrument has been marketed by Schiebel Elektronische Geräte GmbH of Vienna, one result being the sale of over 10 000 units to the US Army where the equipment is known as the AN/PPS-12. The AN-19/2 is also used by the United Nations.

The AN-19/2 has been approved for procurement by NATO and some other countries. The German armed forces procured quantities of this instrument with deliveries extending from late 1989 to 1994. The United Kingdom ordered 700 units for use in the Gulf region during 1991.

Description
The AN-19/2 was designed to detect very small metallic objects such as plastic mines with a small metal content and uses a detector system with minimum mutual interference between adjacent detectors. The system produces a high degree of discrimination independent of ambient temperature and battery condition. Also inherent in the system is the ability to maintain search sensitivity independent of search head speed, from standstill to normal speed. The lightweight search head can detect metallic objects in a limited depth of fresh or sea water.

The main components of the AN-19/2 are the electronics unit, the search head with its telescopic pole and cable, the headphone and the carrying bag. An aluminium transport case is available.

The electronics unit contains the control panel, the internal printed circuit board and the battery container. There are sockets on the control panel for the headphone cable plug and the search head cable plug. When the plugs are removed the sockets are protected by rubber caps. The control panel contains the power switch, headphone volume control, sensitivity control knob and the failure warning lamp. The printed circuit board is sealed within the case and the waterproof and leakproof battery container holds four 1.5 V R20 batteries. There is a built-in test circuit for function and battery condition checks.

The search head consists of concentric transmitter and receiver coils embedded in a plastic head. This low-weight head permits visual inspection of the ground when searching. The coils are connected to the electronics unit via a cable and plug. The cable is of special rubber material that remains flexible down to −40°C. The cable is secured to the telescopic pole with cable clamps allowing the search head to be changed in the field. The telescopic pole consists of an inner and outer tube, an arm support cup and adjustable handle. The inner tube is made of GRP and the joint between the search head and the pole has a plastic shear bolt that will break if excessive force is applied to the pole. A spare bolt is supplied in the carrying bag.

The headphone has a single side speaker so the operator can also hear surrounding noises. It can be worn under a helmet.

The carrying bag can be adjusted as a backpack and contains all the parts of the AN-19/2 plus spare batteries.

In operation the transmitting coil in the search head is energised by electrical pulses to build up a magnetic field. The field induces eddy currents in metal objects in the vicinity which give rise to a secondary field to be detected by the receiving coil. The signal from this coil is processed in the electronics unit to create a sound in the headphone. Approximately 3 minutes are required to prepare the equipment for operation. An operator can be fully qualified to use and maintain the equipment after 8 hours of training.

Specifications
Weight:
(set with bag and batteries) 6.2 kg
(search head with telescopic pole) 1.3 kg
(electronics unit) 1.1 kg
(headphone) 0.15 kg
(carry bag) 1.2 kg
(transport case) 2.35 kg

AN-19/2 mine detector in use

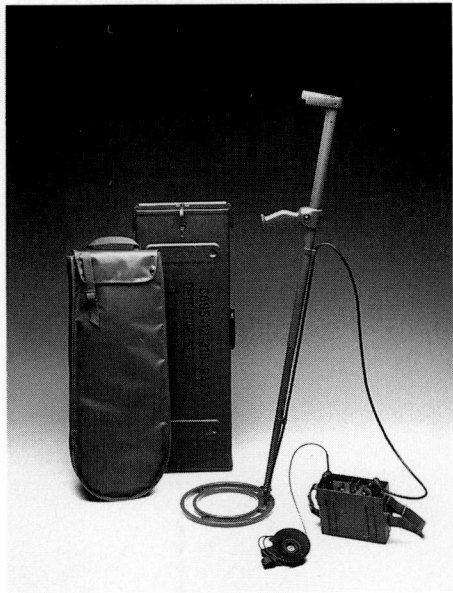

AN-19/2 mine detector

Dimensions:
(transport case) 800 × 300 × 130 mm
(electronics unit) 185 × 80 × 150 mm
(search head diameter) 270 mm
(telescopic pole length) 770 to 1620 mm
Battery voltage: 6 V
Battery life: 70 h
Operating temperature: −40 to +55°C

Detection range:
(mine with 0.15 g metal content) up to 100 mm
(typical anti-tank mine) up to 500 mm

Status
In production. In service with Austria, Canada, Germany, some Gulf states, Netherlands, Sweden, United Kingdom (700), US Army (over 10 000 units)

and United Nations forces operating in Afghanistan, Cambodia and Lebanon.

Manufacturer
Dipl.Ing. Hans Schiebel Elektronische Geräte GmbH, Margaretenstrasse 112, A-1050 Wien, Austria.
Tel: 546 26 0. Fax: 545 23 39.

BULGARIA

M62 Mine Detector

Description
This Bulgarian mine detector can detect metallic mines or plastic mines with some metallic components such as metallic fuzes.

The detector head assembly is rectangular and is mounted on a search handle which also contains the power source and operating controls. It is of the

induction-coil low-frequency type and can detect a metallic object 300 mm in diameter at a range of 500 mm. Weight of the complete equipment is 2.5 kg.

Status
In service with the Bulgarian Army.

Manufacturer
Bulgarian state factories.

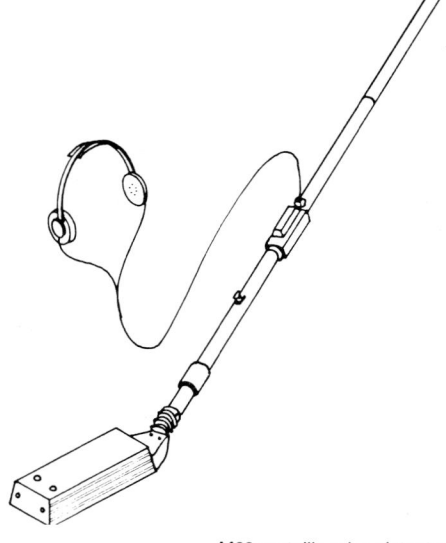

M62 metallic mine detector

CHINA, PEOPLE'S REPUBLIC

Model 82 Portable Mine Detector Set

Description
The Model 82 portable mine detector set contains two separate detectors, the main set being used for detecting non-metallic mines and the auxiliary set being used for detecting metallic mines. Both are contained in a sealed metal carrying case that is water and vibration-proof and the entire equipment is claimed to be waterproof to the extent that the main set can be immersed in water for 24 hours and still remain operational.

Both types of detector can be carried on a telescopic aluminium pole. The detector head is shrouded in rubber and is capable of absorbing impacts such as being dropped 1 m. The entire equipment is also corrosion-proofed. All cables used with the set can be used in temperatures as low as −40°C (upper temperature limit +50°C).

Power for the set is derived from a single non-rechargeable 12 V zinc-mercury battery and 1.5 V R20 and R14 batteries.

It is claimed that an operator can use the Model 82 after only one hour of training using the instruction manual supplied with each set.

The main set weighs 3.5 kg and the auxiliary set 1.5 kg.

Status
In production. In service with the Chinese armed forces.

Manufacturer
China National Electronics Import and Export Corporation, A23 Fuxing Road, Beijing 100036, China.
Tel: 8219534. Telex: 22475 ceiec cn.

Shanghai Research Institute Mine Detectors

Description
The Shanghai Research Institute of Microwave Technology has designed three models of portable mine detector, the Models 82-G, 120 and 85-S.

The Model 82-G is designed to detect metallic and non-metallic mines or packed explosives buried in the earth's subsurface. It is powered by an R6 battery and can remain operational for up to 20 hours of continuous use. The detector has a rectangular search head and has its electronics unit mounted over the carrying handle. The headphones are worn inside a flying-type helmet.

The Model 120 can detect mines with small metal components and has a ground rejection function for use when operating over soil with a magnetic content. The detector is powered by an R6 battery and can be used continuously for up to 30 hours. The search head is circular and the electronic unit is mounted to the side of the carrying handle. Headphones are worn inside a flying-type helmet.

The Model 85-S is a special purposes mine detector with a small and narrow search head and is suitable for detecting mines with minimal metal content. It is characterised by its small size, light weight and high reliability. It has a ground rejection function for use under conditions of differing types of soils.

Specifications
Model 82-G
Weight: less than 3 kg
Detecting head dimensions: 225 × 225 mm
Length of handle: 750 to 1524 mm
Range of detecting head above ground: 20 to 80 mm
Maximum detection depth with head 50 mm over ground:
(anti-tank mines with 275 mm diameter) not less than 100 mm
(anti-personnel mines with 78 mm diameter) not less than 30 mm

Model 120
Weight: less than 3.7 kg
Detecting head diameter: 220 mm
Length of handle: 700 to 1524 mm
Detection sensitivity: max detection distance for M25 a/p mines (distance of detection head above mine) not less than 140 mm

Model 85-S
Weight: less than 2 kg
Detecting head dimensions: 54 × 220 mm
Detection sensitivity: (M25 anti-personnel mines) not less than 80 mm
Operating temperature range: (all models) −40 to +55°C

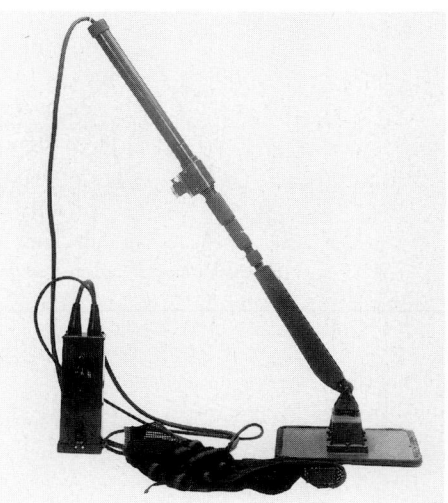

Model 82-G mine detector

Status
In production.

Manufacturer
Shanghai Research Institute of Microwave Technology, PO Box 5321, Shanghai, China.
Tel: 549667.

COMMONWEALTH OF INDEPENDENT STATES

IMP and IMP-2 Mine Detectors

Description
The IMP and IMP-2 can detect metallic mines, or plastic mines which contain some metallic components.

The IMP mine detector consists of the detector head assembly, a four-piece search handle, tuning box which is combined with the battery pack, power supply which consists of four 1.6 V batteries and the head-phones.

When dismantled all the components are carried in a lightweight rectangular metal box. The detector head assembly consists of two transmitting antennas and a receiving antenna, all encased in a bakelite cylinder (417 mm long × 38 mm diameter). The handle consists of four aluminium sections which when joined together are 1.58 m long. One or more of these sections can be removed to reduce the length of the equipment for use in confined areas. The tuning box, or amplifier, consists of five transistors and associated components which are mounted in a lightweight metal box, with the tone regulator on top of the tuning box.

An added advantage of the IMP over earlier CIS mine detectors is that the equipment can be used under water to a maximum depth of 1 m.

The IMP-2 is similar overall to the IMP but is much lighter and may be powered by several types of battery or accumulator. It also has a longer telescopic probe handle and is generally more sensitive.

Specifications (IMP-2)
Weight of detector head: 2 kg
Probe handle length: 830-1500 mm
Processor unit dimensions: 195 × 130 × 45 mm

Detection ranges
Copper coin (1 g): 80-100 mm
Gold wedding ring: 200 mm
Steel nail (70 × 3 mm): 120 mm
Steel needle: 90-100 mm
7.62 mm pistol: 400 mm
Steel disc (300 mm diameter): 400-600 mm

Status
In service with the CIS and some other nations, including Bangladesh (60 IMP).

Manufacturer
KB Proekt, Tomsk, CIS.
Tel: 44 40 65.

Marketing Agency
V/O Mashproborintorg 6, 2nd Spasonalivkovky Per., 11909 Moscow, Russia.
Tel: 2301652-2380687. Telex: 411236.
Fax: 2302126.

IMP mine detector being used in snow

Helicopter-mounted Mine Detectors

Description
A number of former Warsaw Pact countries, including Poland, have fitted helicopters with a search head which is suspended from a cable under the helicopter. This flies over the suspected area and if a minefield is located the pilot radios the units on the ground and a more complete search, using conventional mine detectors, is carried out. This system allows a commander to carry out area searches ahead of the main units.

Status
Limited service.

Manufacturer
Eastern Bloc state factories.

DIM Vehicle-mounted Mine Detector

Description
The DIM vehicle-mounted mine detector consists of a UAZ-69 (4 × 4) light vehicle, or the more recent UAZ-469 (4 × 4) light vehicle, modified to carry a frame on which is mounted a non-magnetic sensing head. This is supported by a frame attached to the front bumper. When travelling the equipment is swung upwards through 180° and rests on top of the cab. When required for use, the equipment is swung forward and rests on two rubber-tyred wheels which are in contact with the surface of the road. The sensing head is mounted in front of the two wheels and is provided with three sets of dual wheels.

The DIM system will detect mines to a maximum depth of 250 mm, or when fording to a depth of 700 mm with a sweep width of 2.2 m. The vehicle is normally driven at a maximum speed of 10 km/h during mine detection operations and once a mine or metallic object has been detected an audio alarm sounds and the vehicle stops automatically. Once the vehicle comes to a halt its operator can adjust the search coils to pinpoint the exact location of the metal object. No provision is made for remote-control of the vehicle.

As the equipment lacks mobility, it is normally used only for clearing roads and airfields. The system was mounted on T-62 MBTs in Afghanistan.

Status
In service with former Warsaw Pact members and some countries in the Middle East.

Manufacturer
State factories.

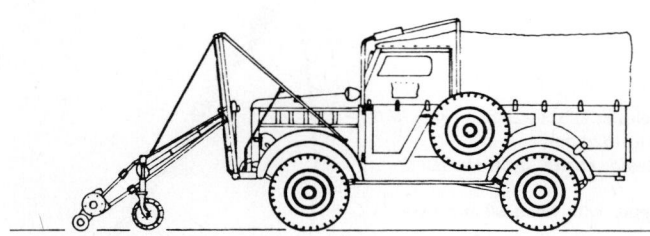 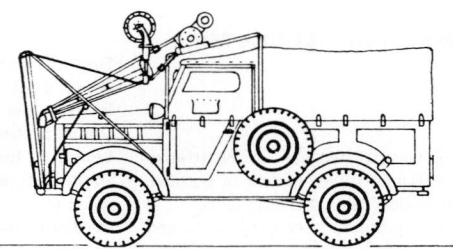

DIM mine detector mounted on front of UAZ-69 (4 × 4) vehicle. Left: equipment in operating position; right: in travelling position

CZECHOSLOVAKIA

M-10 and M-11 Metallic Mine Detectors

Description
Both these mine detectors operate on the beat-frequency oscillation principle, the only difference between the two models being the construction of their search head. The M-10's search head consists of two detachable plates 300 mm in diameter which overlap by 100 mm while the M-11 has a single plate of the same effective area.

The equipment consists of the search head assembly, search handle consisting of four jointed aluminium sections each 500 mm long, tuning box with tone regulator, power supply of three dry cells (25 V), and the headphones. The tuning-box tone regulator and the batteries are carried in a canvas pack on the operator's back. The batteries, when not in use, are kept in a small pouch on the side of the pack.

The complete equipment weighs 12 kg.

Status
In service with the Czechoslovak Army and Indonesia (50).

Manufacturer
Czechoslovak state factories.

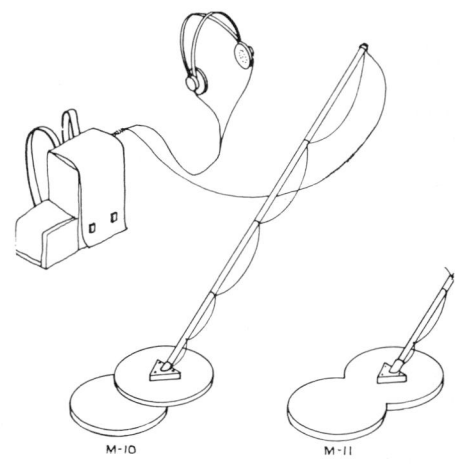

M-10 and M-11 mine detectors showing different heads

FRANCE

Metallic Mine Detector Model F1

Description
The electromagnetic metallic mine detector Model F1 (*Le Détecteur Electromagnétique de Mines*) was designed for detecting anti-tank and anti-personnel mines that contain at least one metal component.

The complete detector is packed into a case 655 mm long, 320 mm wide and 160 mm high, which has two foam packing pieces to protect the equipment from vibration. The complete equipment can be assembled for use in less than 5 minutes.

The mine detector consists of five major components: the detecting head, telescopic handle, electronics box, connecting cable and a set of standard dry batteries. The batteries provide sufficient power for up to 30 hours of continuous use. The accessories are the flexible cover for the detection head and headset with cable and connector. The former is fitted to the detection head when the terrain has fluctuating temperatures, for example shade and sunshine areas.

There are two methods of using this mine detector, upright and prone. For the upright method, the telescopic handle is extended and the angle of the search head on the handle is adjusted to enable the operator to sweep the head in front of him from side to side as he proceeds forward. For the prone position, the sweep motion is similar but the operator lies on the ground with the handle and the head parallel to the ground.

Specifications
Weight ready for use: 3.5 kg
Dimensions: 650 × 300 × 155 mm
Operational life of batteries: 30 h (continuous)
Operating temperature range: −31.5 to +51°C

Detection capability	Detection range
1 g of steel	100 mm
20 g of aluminium	300 mm
100 g of aluminium	450 mm

Status
Production complete. In service with the French Army, under designation DHPM-1A.

Manufacturer
Giat Industries, 13 route de la Minière, F-78034 Versailles Cedex, France.
Tel: 30 97 37 37. Fax: 30 97 39 00.

Metallic mine detector Model F1

GERMANY

MSG 64 Metallic Mine Detector

Description
This equipment consists of an oval head assembly which can be adjusted to various angles, three-piece search handle, tuning box in the second handle, tone regulator on the lower portion of the second handle, power supply of four 1.2 V dry batteries in the lower portion of the second handle and the headphones.

The detector head is waterproof and can detect metallic shaped objects 50 mm in diameter at a range of 180 mm. When disassembled the complete equipment is carried in a camouflaged water-repellent canvas case.

Specifications
Weight:
(complete equipment) 4.4 kg
(detector) 2.35 kg
Length of search handle: 2.4 m

Status
In service with the German Army.

Manufacturer
Former East German state factories.

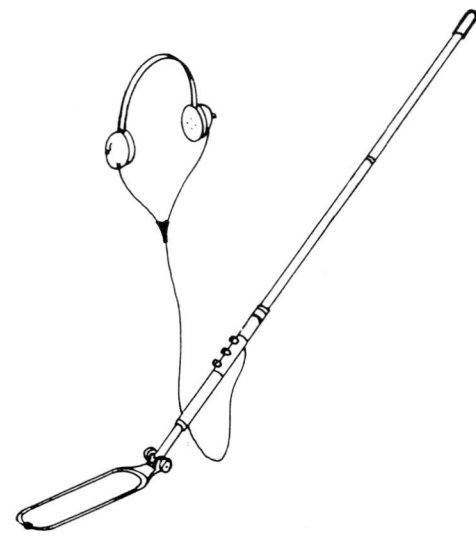

MSG 64 metallic mine detector

Vallon CAMAD Detection System

Description

CAMAD stands for Computer-Aided Magnetic Anomaly Detection for underground surveillance. It is a computer-based system for the location and identification of buried ferrous objects and comprises both software and hardware. The complete CAMAD system consists of the EL 1302B or ET 1340B detectors (see entries in this section for information), a data acquisition unit (DAU), an IBM-compatible personal computer and the CAMAD software. After the data acquisition unit used with the detectors has stored magnetic flux readings from a survey the data are transferred to a personal computer via an RS232 interface. The CAMAD software then evaluates and stores the resultant data and can produce visual and/or printed indications of magnetic flux variations together with matrices of locations.

Status

In production. In service with various undisclosed countries.

Manufacturer

Vallon GmbH, Im Grund 3, D-7412 Eningen, Federal Republic of Germany.
Tel: 7121 82187. Telex: 7 29924 valon d.
Fax: 7121 83643.

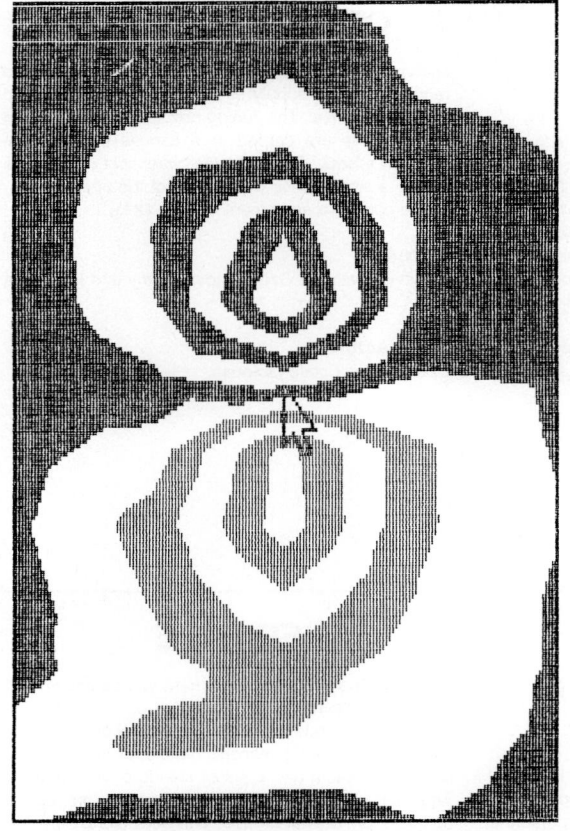

Example of types of graphic presentation produced by Vallon CAMAD computer-based detection system

Vallon Micro-CAMAD Detection System

Description

The Vallon Micro-CAMAD Detection System is a computer-aided system specifically designed for the operating conditions encountered by explosive ordnance disposal personnel. It consists of a microcomputer and the corresponding self-contained software to support detection work. For location of objects the course of magnetic field change is graphically indicated on a display indicating the course of the previously passed 5 m of the measuring track. Object depth and position can then be calculated on site.

The micro-computer is connected to the metal detector only and is thus independent of any other power supplies. In its standard version the Micro-CAMAD includes a battery-operated portable graphics printer. The integral software leads the operator using menu techniques. Software modules for land and borehole detection are included.

Status

In production.

Manufacturer

Vallon GmbH, Im Grund 3, D-7412 Eningen, Federal Republic of Germany.
Tel: 7121 82187. Telex: 7 29924 valon d.
Fax: 7121 83643.

A typical Vallon Micro-CAMAD Detection System display

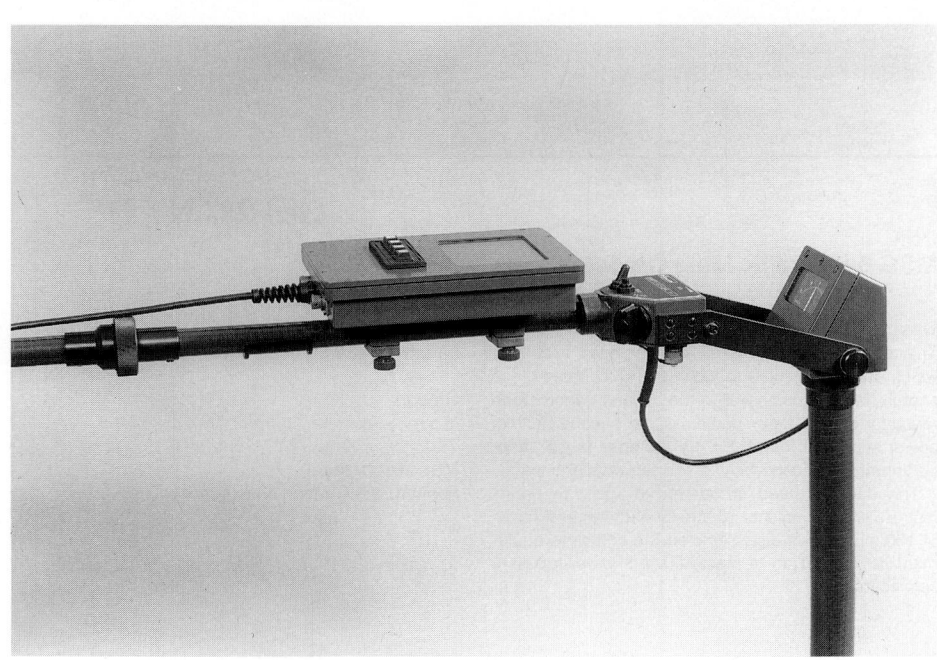

Vallon Micro-CAMAD Detection System

Vallon Micro-CAMAD Software MC1-EVA

Description
Development of the Micro-CAMAD system for large-scale detection work led to the MC1-EVA software package. This is based on survey data transferred from the MC1 micro-computer used with the Micro-CAMAD system to a personal computer. These data are not computed but are displayed directly in graph form.

MC1-EVA (EVA – evaluation and analysis) enables the operator to combine the graphs in any way required (for example placing them side-by-side or one on the other, or extending or scaling down sizes). The operator can enter individual comments and print out the graphs in hard copy form.

Status
In production.

Manufacturer
Vallon GmbH, Im Grund 3, D-7412 Eningen, Federal Republic of Germany.
Tel: 7121 82187. Telex: 7 29924 valon d.
Fax: 7121 83643.

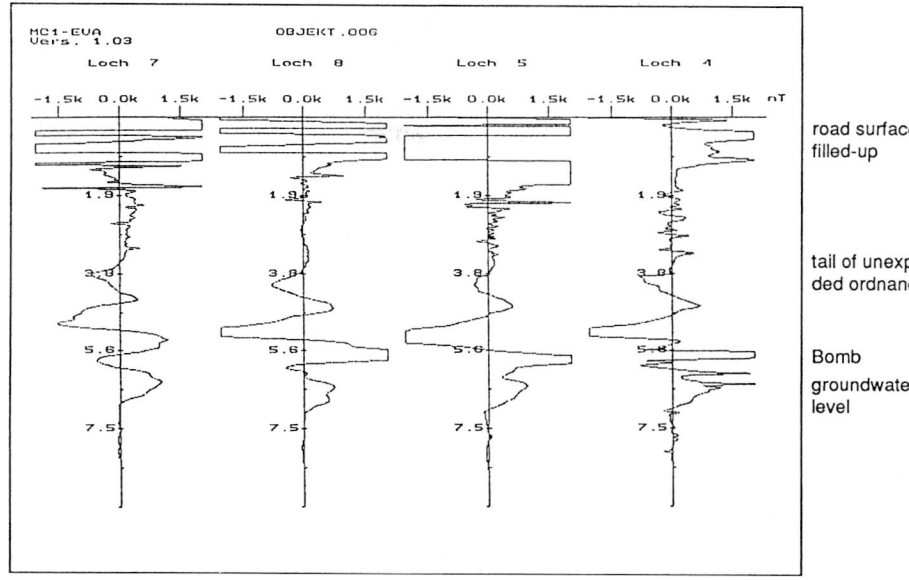

Printout of a typical set of MC1-EVA detection graphs

Vallon Iron Detector EL 1302A1

Description
The Vallon EL 1302A1 senses the earth's magnetic field and indicates any disturbance caused in the field by buried objects such as mines, bombs and artillery projectiles. Indications are provided both acoustically and visually. This equipment is intended for land-based detection and the detector has an interface for the MC1 micro-computer.

For computer-aided magnetic anomaly detection (CAMAD – see entry in this section), the EL 1302A1 is modified to the EL 1302B version by means of a digitiser and an RS232 interface.

Specifications
Weight of instrument: 4 kg
Weight of instrument in case: 10 kg
Dimensions of case: 785 × 285 × 140 mm
Power supply: 6 × 1.5 V monocell type IEC R 14
Detection depth: 6 m

Status
In production. In service with various undisclosed countries.

Manufacturer
Vallon GmbH, Im Grund 3, D-7412 Eningen, Federal Republic of Germany.
Tel: 7121 82187. Telex: 7 29924 valon d.
Fax: 7121 83643.

Vallon iron detector EL 1302A1 in use

Vallon Iron Detector ET 1340

Description
The Vallon Iron Detector ET 1340 is used for defined area examination of various forms of ordnance as well as buried pipes, cables and covers to a depth up to 15 m. The instrument monitors the earth's magnetic field and signals any disturbance of the field by a buried object by visual or acoustic means.

For computer-aided magnetic anomaly detection (CAMAD – see entry in this section), the ET 1340 is modified into the ET 1340B by means of a digitiser and an RS232 interface.

Specifications
Weight of set: 15 kg
Weight in case complete: 37 kg
Dimensions of case: 2040 × 340 × 230 mm
Power supply: 5 × 1.5 V cells
Detection depth: up to 15 m

Status
In production. In service with various undisclosed countries.

Manufacturer
Vallon GmbH, Im Grund 3, D-7412 Eningen, Federal Republic of Germany.
Tel: 7121 82187. Telex: 7 29924 valon d.
Fax: 7121 83643.

Vallon iron detector ET 1340 in use

Vallon Metal Detector Model ML 1612B

Description

The Vallon Metal Detector ML 1612B was designed to detect all kinds of ferrous and non-ferrous metals buried underground. The detecting system is water-tight and the electronics housing involved is splashproof with the detector head being carried on an adjustable glass fibre telescopic carrying bar.

The design of the search coil is computer-optimised for pinpointing. This ensures a very precise localisation of small metallic objects without loss of detection speed compared to large ring-shaped coils. An optional stick probe with a solid tip can be used for the detection of objects in undergrowth, hay and other loose material. It can be used with or without an extension tube.

The electronics unit has an automatic battery test facility, a volume control and continuously adjustable sensitivity.

Specifications

Weight of set: 3 kg
Shipping weight complete: 16 kg
Dimensions of case: 782 × 300 × 142 mm
Carrying bar length: adjustable 0.96 to 1.9 m
Power supply: 4 × 1.5 V monocell type IEC R 20 or rechargeable Ni/Cd accumulators KR 35/62

Status

In production. In service with various undisclosed countries.

Manufacturer

Vallon GmbH, Im Grund 3, D-7412 Eningen, Federal Republic of Germany.
Tel: 7121 82187. Telex: 7 29924 valon d.
Fax: 7121 83643.

Vallon ML 1612B metal detector

Vallon Underwater Metal Detector MW 1630

Description

The Vallon Underwater Metal Detector MW 1630 was designed for use by divers, is watertight up to a depth of 60 m and is balanced for use under water. The electronics were designed specifically for underwater use and provide a high level of detection sensitivity under all environmental conditions (for example, fresh or salt water, mineralised terrain, and so on). Standard equipment includes accessories required for detection work along river banks and in shallow water.

Status

In production. In service with various undisclosed countries.

Manufacturer

Vallon GmbH, Im Grund 3, D-7412 Eningen, Federal Republic of Germany.
Tel: 7121 82187. Telex: 7 29924 valon d.
Fax: 7121 83643.

Vallon Underwater Metal Detector MW 1630

FÖRSTER Search Instrument FEREX 4.021

Description

The FÖRSTER search instrument FEREX 4.021 was developed to replace the earlier models 4.015 and 4.016 detectors. It may be regarded as a search instrument for ferro-magnetic objects, that is for the detection and exact location of unexploded bombs, pipes, cables and so on. Depending on the size and position of these parts they can be detected to a depth of 6 m.

The FEREX 4.021 meets military standards of construction and operation and uses lightweight and splashproof components. The probe is watertight to a depth of 100 m. The instrument uses 1.5 V standard cells for the power supply and it also has built-in functional test and auto-zero compensation.

The FEREX 4.021 has three basic components: control unit, power supply and probe. Depending on the application, three versions of the FEREX 4.021 can be supplied by using the basic components with additional accessories. These are:

FEREX K. This is the complete equipment for land, underwater and borehole applications

FEREX L. For searching, locating and measuring on land

FEREX W. For underwater and borehole use

The complete FEREX K can be supplied packed in a shockproof aluminium transit case. The FEREX L can be packed into a special rucksack, as can the FEREX W.

Specifications

Weight of L version complete: 5.5 kg
Weight of basic components: 3.8 kg
Dimensions of transit case: 1.12 × 0.175 × 0.31 m
Operating voltage: 6-12 V
Batteries: 6 monocells each 1.5 V (IEC R 20)
Sensitivity range: 0.3-10 000 nT (8 steps)
Operating temperature range: −30 to +65°C
Probe underwater limit: 100 m

Status

In production. In service with the US Navy, British Army, Canadian, Danish and other NATO armed forces, the Australian and Singapore armies, and many other undisclosed countries.

Manufacturer

Institut Dr Förster GmbH and Co KG, In Laisen 70, PO Box 1564, D-7410 Reutlingen, Federal Republic of Germany.
Tel: 7121 140-0. Telex: 729 781 ifr d.
Fax: 7121 140488.

FEREX 4.021 Model L in use

FÖRSTER FEREX CAST 4.021.06 Data Acquisition System

Description
The FÖRSTER FEREX CAST (computer-aided search technique) is a data acquisition system for the interpretation of magnetometer search data. It provides a faster and more accurate localisation of ferro-magnetic objects compared to more conventional search techniques and may be used to search for buried unexploded ordnance, pipes, wrecks, and so on.

The search system consists of a FEREX search instrument, a data acquisition module and an IBM-compatible personal computer. The system automatically collects and stores the measured magnetometer data. The data are then evaluated and the resultant calculations are filed and/or displayed by the computer in graphic form. After minimal operator training time the system can detect and display the position of buried objects.

Status
In production.

Manufacturer
Institut Dr Förster GmbH and Co KG, In Laisen 70, PO Box 1564, D-7410 Reutlingen, Federal Republic of Germany.
Tel: 7121 140-0. Telex: 729 781 ifr d.
Fax: 7121 140488.

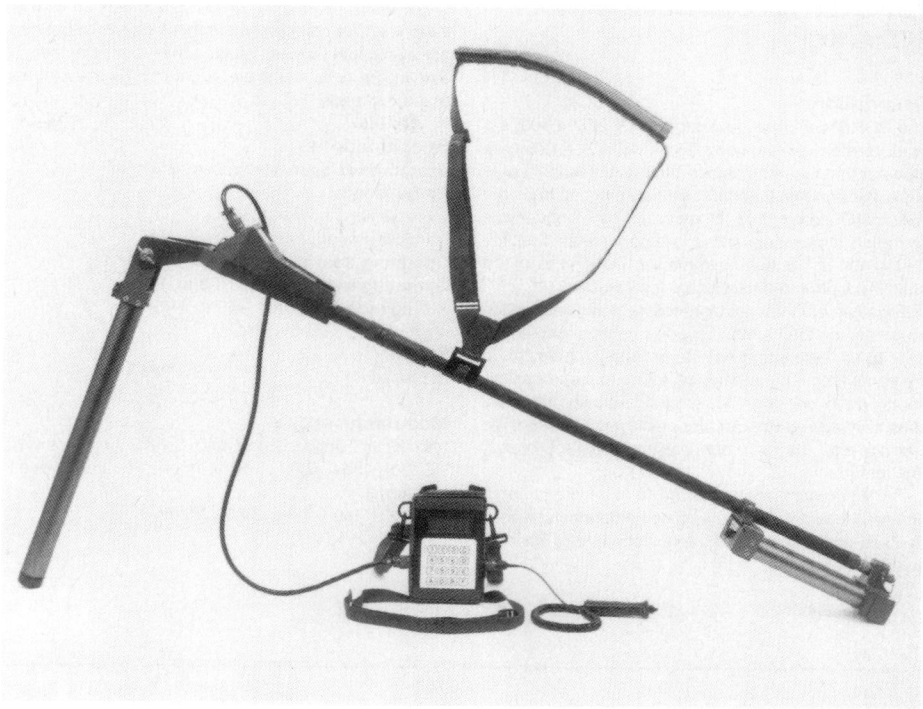

Complete FEREX CAST data acquisition system

FÖRSTER Mine Detector METEX 4.125

Description
The FÖRSTER Mine Detector METEX 4.125 has replaced the earlier METEX 4.122. It may be used to detect ferrous and non-ferrous metal objects but its primary use is in the detection of mines underground and in shallow water. Metallic anti-tank mines can be detected to a depth of approximately 700 mm and it is also possible to detect plastic mines with a small metal content.

The METEX 4.125 is constructed to military standards of design and operation and uses light and splashproof components; the search coil may be used completely under water. Standard 1.5 V batteries are used for the power supply and the instrument has built-in functional and battery test features.

The METEX 4.125 has three basic components: a search coil with telescopic handle, a control unit with power supply, and headphones. The complete equipment can be supplied in an aluminium transit case which also contains a carrying bag with strap, test piece, handgrip, armrest and rucksack.

For searches under difficult environmental conditions the METEX 4.125 may be equipped with a truncheon probe approximately 400 to 1100 mm in length.

METEX 4.125 in use

Specifications
Weight of components: 3.5 kg
Weight with transit case: 15 kg
Dimensions of transit case: 0.74 × 0.4 × 0.16 m
Length of search coil with handle:
(minimum) 0.94 m
(max) 2 m
Search coil diameter: 0.26 m
Truncheon probe diameter: approx 30 mm
Truncheon probe length: 400 to 1100 mm
Batteries: 6 × 1.5 V (IEC R 14)
Battery life: 80 h approx

Status
In production. In service with undisclosed countries.

Manufacturer
Institut Dr Förster GmbH and Co KG, In Laisen 70, PO Box 1564, D-7410 Reutlingen, Federal Republic of Germany.
Tel: 7121 140-0. Telex: 729 781 ifr d.
Fax: 7121 140488.

FÖRSTER Mine Detector MINEX 2FD 4.400

Description

The FÖRSTER mine detector MINEX 2FD 4.400 is a product-improved version of the METEX 4.125 (see previous entry) and includes the latest technology in electronics, material and design. It is claimed to be the first metal detector to incorporate two frequencies operating simultaneously. It is also claimed that the 2FD 4.400 is the first instrument of its kind to use a multi-layer printed circuit board 'coil system'.

Together with its microprocessor-controlled phase selection, the 2FD 4.400 can achieve maximum sensitivity to all metals and optimal ground suppression at the same time. The instrument is also microprocessor-controlled in operation for ground exclusion balance, sensitivity adjustment, and for displayed detection and fault signals – the instrument has functional and battery test features.

The instrument is constructed to full military standards and uses strong waterproof components; it may be used under any climatic conditions and under both fresh and sea water.

Power is provided by three 1.5 V IEC R 20 alkaline batteries. The complete equipment can be supplied in an aluminium transit case which also contains a carrying harness, a test piece, a handgrip and armrest, and a rucksack.

Specifications
Search head diameter: approx 257 mm
Probe length:
(maximum) approx 1.85 m
(minimum) approx 0.8 m
Operating time at ambient 20°C: 30 h
Operating temperature: −32 to +60°C
Storage temperature: −55 to +75°C

Status
In production.

Manufacturer
Institut Dr Förster GmbH and Co KG, In Laisen 70, PO Box 1564, D-7410 Reutlingen, Federal Republic of Germany.
Tel: 7121 140-0. Telex: 729 781 ifr d.
Fax: 7121 140488.

MINEX 2FD 4.400 in use

INTERNATIONAL

AN-19/2 Mine Detector

Development

The AN-19/2 was developed by co-operation between the Dipl.Ing. Hans Schiebel Elektronische Geräte GmbH of Vienna and NobelTech Electronics AB of Sweden. It is a design derivative of the AN-17/1 originally developed by Hans Schiebel. NobelTech Electronics (then the Defence Electronics Group of Philips Elektronikindustrier AB) delivered a large quantity of AN-19/2s to the Swedish Army during 1986 and 1987.

The AN-19/2 has been approved for procurement by NATO and some other countries. The German armed forces procured quantities of this instrument with deliveries extending from late 1989 to 1994. The United Kingdom ordered 700 units for use in the Gulf region during 1991.

Description

The AN-19/2 was designed to detect very small metallic objects such as plastic mines with a small metal content and uses a detector system with minimum mutual interference between adjacent detectors. The system produces a high degree of discrimination independent of ambient temperature and battery condition. Also inherent in the system is the ability to maintain search sensitivity independent of search head speed, from standstill to normal speed. The lightweight search head can detect metallic objects in a limited depth of fresh or sea water.

The main components of the AN-19/2 are the electronics unit, the search head with its telescopic pole and cable, the headphone and the carrying bag. An aluminium transport case is available.

The electronics unit contains the control panel, the internal printed circuit board and the battery container. There are sockets on the control panel for the headphone cable plug and the search head cable plug. When the plugs are removed the sockets are protected by rubber caps. The control panel contains the power switch, headphone volume control, sensitivity control knob and the failure warning lamp. The printed circuit board is sealed within the case and the waterproof and leakproof battery container holds four 1.5 V R20 batteries. There is a built-in test circuit for function and

AN-19/2 mine detector in use

battery condition checks.

The search head consists of concentric transmitter and receiver coils embedded in a plastic head. This low-weight head permits visual inspection of the ground when searching. The coils are connected to the electronics unit via a cable and plug. The cable is of special rubber material that remains flexible down to −40°C. The cable is secured to the telescopic pole with cable clamps allowing the search head to be changed in the field. The telescopic pole consists of an inner and outer tube, an arm support cup and adjustable handle. The inner tube is made of GRP and the joint between the search head and the pole has a plastic shear bolt that will break if excessive force is applied to the pole. A spare bolt is supplied in the carrying bag.

The headphone has a single side speaker so the operator can also hear surrounding noises. It can be worn under a helmet.

The carrying bag can be adjusted as a backpack and contains all the parts of the AN-19/2 plus spare batteries.

In operation the transmitting coil in the search head is energised by electrical pulses to build up a magnetic field. The field induces eddy currents in metal objects in the vicinity which give rise to a secondary field to be detected by the receiving coil. The signal from this coil is processed in the electronics unit to create a sound in the headphone. Approximately 3 minutes are required to prepare the equipment for operation. An operator can be fully qualified to use and maintain the equipment after 8 hours of training.

Specifications
Weight:
(set with bag and batteries) 6.2 kg
(search head with telescopic pole) 1.3 kg
(electronics unit) 1.1 kg
(headphone) 0.15 kg
(carry bag) 1.2 kg
(transport case) 2.35 kg
Dimensions:
(transport case) 800 × 300 × 130 mm
(electronics unit) 185 × 80 × 150 mm
(search head diameter) 270 mm
(telescopic pole length) 770 to 1620 mm
Battery voltage: 6 V
Battery life: 70 h
Operating temperature: −40 to +55°C
Detection range:
(mine with 0.15 g metal content) up to 100 mm
(typical anti-tank mine) up to 500 mm

Status
In production. In service with Austria, Canada, Germany, Netherlands, Sweden, United Kingdom (700) and United Nations forces operating in Afghanistan and Lebanon.

Manufacturers
NobelTech Electronics AB, S-175 88 Järfälla, Sweden.
Tel: 46 8 580 85388. Telex: 126 88 nobelte s.
Fax: 46 8 580 322 44.
Dipl.Ing. Hans Schiebel Elektronische Geräte GmbH, Margaretenstrasse 112, A-1050 Wien, Austria.
Tel: 546 26 0. Fax: 545 23 39.

IRAQ

Mansour-7 Mine Detector

Description
The Mansour-7 mine detector was designed to detect buried metallic mines and the metal components of plastic-bodied mines at depths between 50 and 400 mm below the ground surface. No further details are available.

Status
In service with the Iraqi armed forces.

Manufacturer
State factories.

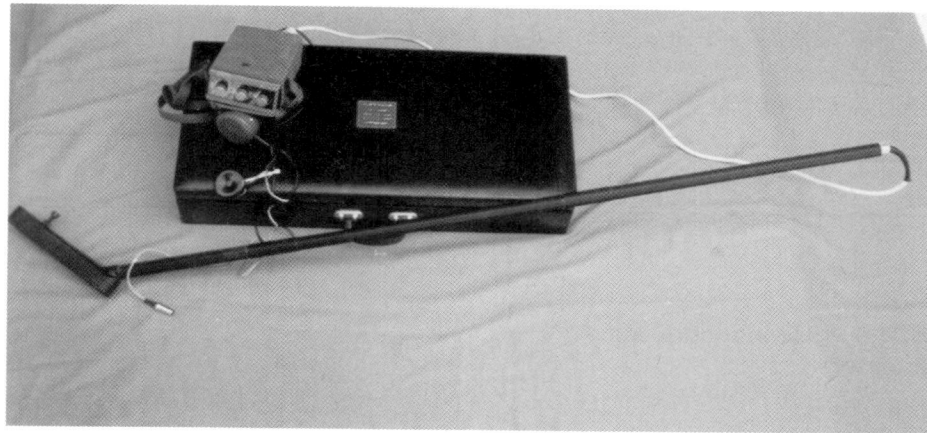

Mansour-7 mine detector showing main components

ISRAEL

BETA BMD-34 Metallic Mine Detector

Description
The BETA metallic solid-state mine detector type BMD-34 is a sensitive, sophisticated, miniature detector which can be used to detect metallic anti-tank or anti-personnel mines in both magnetic or non-magnetic soils. The instrument detects any conductive material, ferrous or non-ferrous, in any type of soil.

The instrument comprises a search head mounted on the end of a telescopic handle, a belt-carried electronic control unit, and a headset for the audible output signal. As an optional extra, a visual display can be clamped on the telescopic handle. The visual display consists of a 40 mm diameter meter with a central zero and a self-illuminated scale.

The controls consist of an on/off control, search head balance knob and the battery check toggle switch. The mine detector is human-engineered for the minimum of adjustments during operation and features an automatic compensation for variables such as search head characteristics, amount of magnetic material in the soil and temperature variations.

The mine detector has been designed for military use under severe environmental conditions. It is immersion-proof in 2 m of water, shock and vibration-proof and has electromagnetic interference protection.

Specifications
Weight of equipment ready for use: 2.9 kg
Detection capability: metallic anti-tank mine 300 mm deep
Operating temperature range: -15 to $+72°C$

Status
In production since 1976. In service with undisclosed countries.

Manufacturer
BETA Engineering and Development Limited, PO Box 98, Beer-Sheva 84100, Israel.
Tel: 057 34341. Telex: 5388 beta il.

BETA BMD-34 metallic mine detector in use

KOREA, SOUTH

NMD-9 and GDS-17 Mine Detection Sets

Description
Developed by the Agency for Defence Development of Korea, the NMD-9 is a rugged, solid-state portable device capable of detecting metallic and non-metallic mines. The GDS-17 is used for the detection of metal objects only.

The search head of the NMD-9 generates and radiates a continuous wave RF signal and receives and demodulates the resultant signal for aural presentation in a headset. The GDS-17 uses a pulse induction detection system.

The search head is encased in a rubber cover and is mounted on the end of a long telescopic carrying handle which also mounts the control box. The control box contains the system electronics on a single board

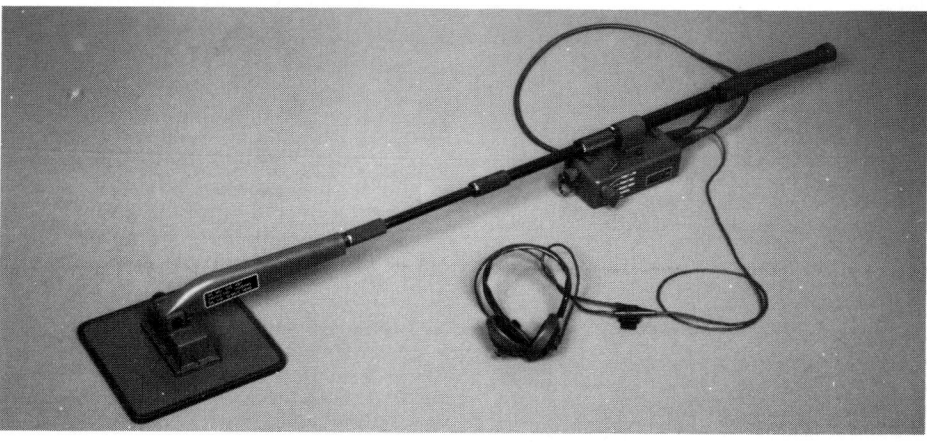

NMD-9 mine detection set

and the battery which has an operating life of 15 hours (NMD-9) in continuous use (GDS-17, 28 hours). The control box also has a 'search' switch used to locate the general presence of a mine when a 'point' mode with three varying degrees of sensitivity may be selected.

Specifications (NMD-9)
Weight:
  (in use) 4 kg

  (in carrying case) 10.8 kg
Length of telescopic handle: 540 to 1460 mm
Battery voltage:
  (NMD-9) +15 V/−15 V
  (GDS-17) +12 V
Dimensions of carrying case: 600 × 380 × 200 mm

Status
In production.

Manufacturers
Gold Star Electric Company Limited, 27-2, Yeoeuido-dong, Youngdungpo-ku, Seoul 150, Republic of Korea. Tel: 783 9311. Telex: 28295 gswave k. Fax: 784 3549.
Daewoo Corporation, 541, 5-Ga, Namdaemoon-Ro, Jung-Gu, Seoul, Republic of Korea. Tel: 7 7191. Telex: 233415 daewoo k. Fax: 756 1225.

SOUTH AFRICA

MIDAS Pulse Induction Mine Detector

Description
The MIDAS pulse induction mine detector is a self-contained, lightweight equipment with self-nulling and confidence-tone features. It uses a three-part modular construction to minimise maintenance and has three selective sensitivity levels to ensure early and accurate target acquisition. MIDAS can work continuously for up to 28 hours powered by a 15 V battery; an alarm is given once the battery has discharged.

The foam-filled Kevlar search head is rectangular or round. The dimensions of the rectangular head are 616 × 270 mm and a diameter of 350 mm for the round head; these provide instantaneous search areas of 166 320 mm² and 70 686 mm² respectively. The heads can be made to a size or shape to suit customer requirements.

The head is mounted on a telescopic handle that can be extended to a maximum length of 2.2 m; fully closed the length is 1.74 m. The most commonly used operating length is 2 m. The system electronic unit and battery holder is at the top end of the handle secured in such a way that it counterbalances the weight of the search head and handle.

Weight of the complete equipment, with battery, is 3.5 kg.

Status
In production.

Manufacturer
Enquiries to Armscor, Private Bag X337, Pretoria 0001, South Africa. Tel: (12) 428 1911. Telex: 320217. Fax: (12) 428 5635.

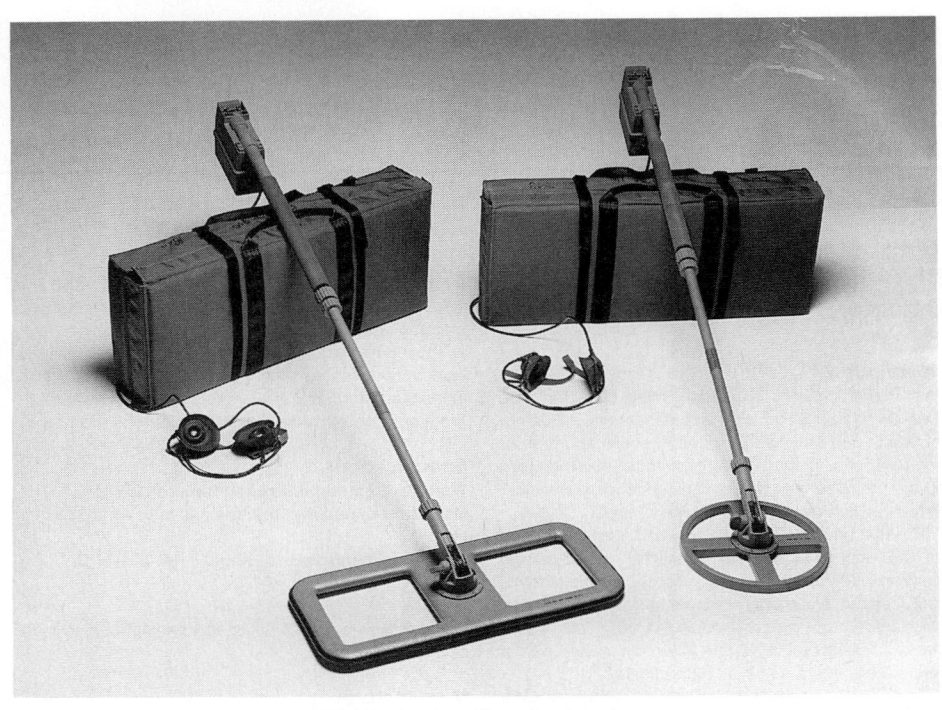

MIDAS pulse induction mine detectors

UNITED KINGDOM

Mine Detector No 4C

Description
The United Scientific Instruments Mine Detector No 4C has been the standard mine detector of the British Army since 1968. Earlier models were the No 4 and No 4A. It comprises a search head mounted on a telescopic handle, an amplifier unit, headphones and connecting cables. For transport, the equipment is disassembled and carried in a wooden transport case which also contains the spare battery, test boxes, extension cables and other accessories.

The search head contains two mutually reacting inductance coils. Inductance is adjustable by means of a dust core trimmer assembly, and when adjusted the mutual inductance of the two coils is in balance. When any metal component is brought within the field of the coils, the balance is distorted, resulting in an oscillating difference potential. This is then amplified by the amplifier unit and fed to the earphone as a distinctly audible signal.

There are two modes of operation, normal and in ferrite-bearing soil (pavé). The former is used for detecting metallic mines in normal soil while the latter is used for detecting metallic mines in ground pavé, or if there are likely to be any metallic splinters on the surface. The preferred mode of operation is selected by a selector switch on the amplifier unit.

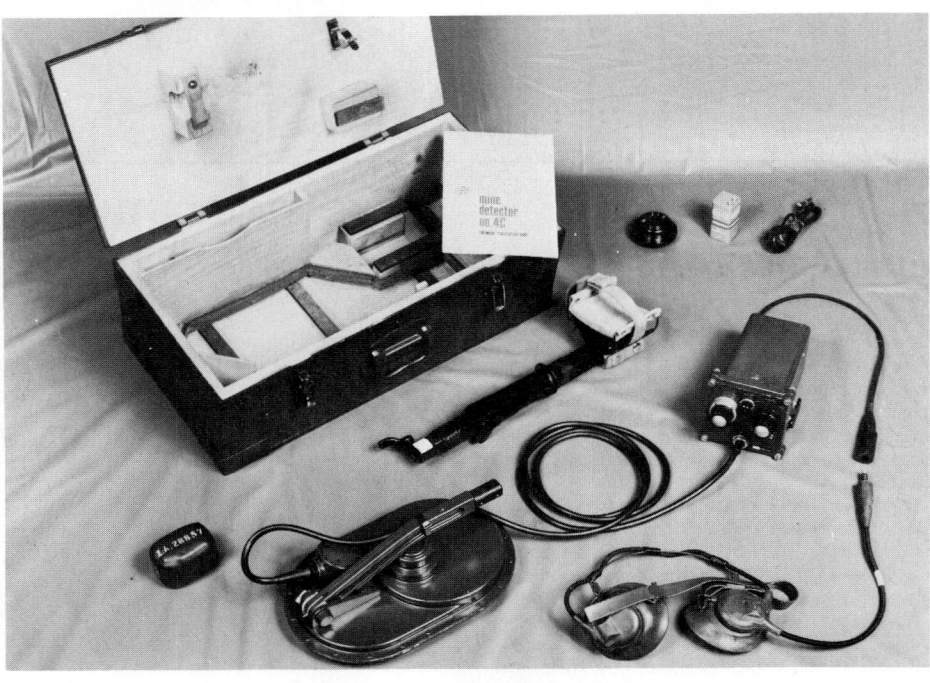

Component parts of Mine Detector No 4C

For use, the telescopic pole is extended, one end strapped to the forearm and the other attached to the search head. The amplifier unit, which also contains the batteries, is clipped to the operator's belt and the cable from the search head is plugged into the unit. The lead of the earphones is connected to the amplifier unit and the equipment is then ready for immediate use.

There are two methods of searching for mines, upright and prone. For the upright method, the telescopic handle is extended and the angle of the search head on the handle is adjusted to enable the operator to sweep the head in front of him from side to side as he proceeds forward. For the prone position the sweep motion is similar but the operator lies on the ground, the handle is not extended and the head is parallel to the ground.

Specifications
Weight of detector in transit case: 14.4 kg

Transit case
Length: 533 mm

Width: 254 mm
Height: 203 mm

Search head
Weight: 1.8 kg
Length: 285 mm
Width: 185 mm
Height: 108 mm

Telescopic handle
Weight: 1.15 kg
Length:
(collapsed) 380 mm
(fully extended) 1.28 m

Amplifier unit
Weight with battery: 1.8 kg
Length: 216 mm
Width: 108 mm
Height: 108 mm

Battery type: 9 V dry cell PP6 or equivalent
Current consumption: 3.3-3.6 mA

Operational life of battery: 300 h of intermittent use

Detection capacity	Detection range
British Mk 7 anti-tank mine normal ground	510 mm
British Mk 7 anti-tank mine pavé ground	320 mm

Status
Production complete. In service with the British Army and several overseas nations.

Manufacturer
United Scientific Instruments plc, Unit 5, Quinn Close, Manor Park, Whitley, Coventry CV3 4LH, UK. Tel: 0203 539299. Telex: 31332. Fax: 0203 539281.

MD2000 Metallic Mine Detector

Description
The MD2000 metallic mine detector is a multi-role, manportable instrument for the detection of ferrous and non-ferrous objects. The equipment operates on the pulse induction principle and may be used with probe heads in addition to the normal halo search heads. Upgrades have improved sensitivity, particularly to minimum metal targets. The MD2000 is easy to operate, being completely automatic in operation and requiring no tuning for different ground conditions. The search heads may be operated immersed in water with no adjustments.

The full field pack is supplied equipped with two search probes, a search halo head, a loudspeaker and earpiece audio devices, and the control unit which houses the batteries packed into a weather-resistant soft carry case. A short pack may be specified for mine detection operations only, and lacks the search probes.

The MD2000 may be operated using dry cells or rechargeable batteries. It is NATO codified.

Detection ranges
Item	Search loop	Probe
7.62 mm cartridge case	400 mm	190 mm
Parkray timer	410 mm	200 mm
Walther pistol	590 mm	300 mm
0.22 rifle	700 mm	430 mm
Pressure pad (large)	1100 mm	710 mm
Bar mine fuze	330 mm	150 mm
Mark 7 a/t mine	1200 mm	580 mm
PMN a/p mine	570 mm	260 mm

Specifications
	Dimensions	Weight
Field pack complete	1030 × 400 × 80 mm	6 kg
Electronics less batteries	248 × 172 × 42 mm	1.42 kg
300 mm search loop (handle extended)	1300 × 318 × 59 mm	0.9 kg
1 m search probe	980 × 42 mm	0.695 kg
400 mm search probe	457 × 42 mm	0.485 kg

Status
In production. In service with the British Army and police forces and with similar organisations worldwide.

Manufacturer
Guartel Limited, 32 St Mary's Road, London W5 5EU, UK.
Tel: 081 567 0702. Fax: 081 579 2158.

MD2000 in use with search probe

MD2000 metallic mine detector with 300 mm loop in use

MD4 Metal Detector

Description

The MD4 metal detector was developed in collaboration with the United Kingdom Ministry of Defence and was specifically designed for improvised ordnance disposal (IOD) and explosive ordnance disposal (EOD) operations, although it may be used for mine detection and clearance. It is in service with the British Army for the above-mentioned applications.

The construction of the MD4 is such that all electronics, controls, detection head and batteries are contained within a hand-held probe. There are only two operating controls, ON/ZERO and OFF. Sensitivity is stated to be high. The operating principle is multi-sampling pulse induction and detection indication is by a built-in speaker or earphone. The equipment is fully ruggedised, waterproof and ECM compatible.

The MD4 is NATO codified and supplied packed into a shockproof aluminium transit case with a soft carry case, an earpiece attachment and a spare battery cassette.

Specifications
Weight: 2 kg
Length: 1.231 m
Diameter: 39 mm
Battery life: 12-14 h

Status
In production and in service with the British Army and other undisclosed organisations.

Manufacturer
Guartel Limited, 32 St Mary's Road, London W5 5EU
UK.
Tel: 081 567 0702. Fax: 081 579 2158.

MD4 metal detector

White's Electronics Military Mine Detector

Description

White's Electronics (UK) Limited is a subsidiary of an American electronics company and, with the co-operation of several governments and military advisers, has produced a modern concept military mine and bomb detector. The unit is extremely sensitive to both very small objects such as firing pins, and large objects such as bombs. This sensitivity will remain constant until the batteries are discharged. Mineralised soil and salt water will have little or no effect on sensitivity levels as the unit was designed to automatically compensate for these conditions. The equipment produces virtually no DC magnetic field. Visual and aural indications of metal are provided (the visual element can be on the search head if required).

The aluminium control box is waterproof, resilient and weighs 1 kg. There are only three controls; on, push auto-tune and a lockable audio threshold control. Three LEDs are used to indicate unit faults, when batteries need replacing and when batteries are approaching the end of their operational life. There is also an audio alert system which operates in conjunction with the LEDs. The box is carried in a weatherproof canvas bag on a shoulder strap or belt loops.

An aluminium battery box contains four 1.5 V D-sized alkaline manganese batteries with an operational life at 20°C of approximately 20 hours. Normally the battery box is used next to the control box but an extension lead allows the box to be kept under clothing in cold conditions. Battery box weight empty is 0.53 kg.

The three-piece rod set carries a 280 mm search coil which can operate when submerged. The rod length can be varied from 1.6 m down to 596 mm and has a handgrip and armrest, both of which are adjustable.

The equipment is completed by a waterproof headset which can be worn over or under a helmet. All the components can be carried in a special shoulder bag which also carries an extra battery box and spares.

Two probes are available as accessories to this equipment. One is 1 m long and the other 400 mm. Both may be used under water.

Total weight of the equipment when in use is 4.61 kg. Total weight complete with spares, tools and eight batteries packed into an optional aluminium carry case is 11.42 kg. Operating temperature range is from −40° to +85°C.

Detection sensitivity
Steel strip: (50 × 12.5 × 1 mm) 350 mm
Aluminium sheet: (20 × 40 mm) 320 mm
20 mm anti-personnel projectile: 450 mm
Metal anti-tank mine: (diameter 200 mm) 800 mm
Coil spring: (23 mm long, diameter 7.1 mm) 90 mm
Ball bearing: (diameter 4.7 mm) 80 mm
Aluminium cap: (6.5 mm long, diameter 5.9 mm) 120 mm
Steel pin: (10 mm long, diameter 1.5 mm) 140 mm

Status
In production. In service with Chile, Malawi, Norway, Tunisia, US Marine Corps, United Nations forces and some other nations.

Manufacturer
White's Electronics (UK) Limited, 13 Harbour Road, Inverness IV1 1RY, UK.
Tel: 0463 223456. Fax: 0463 224048.

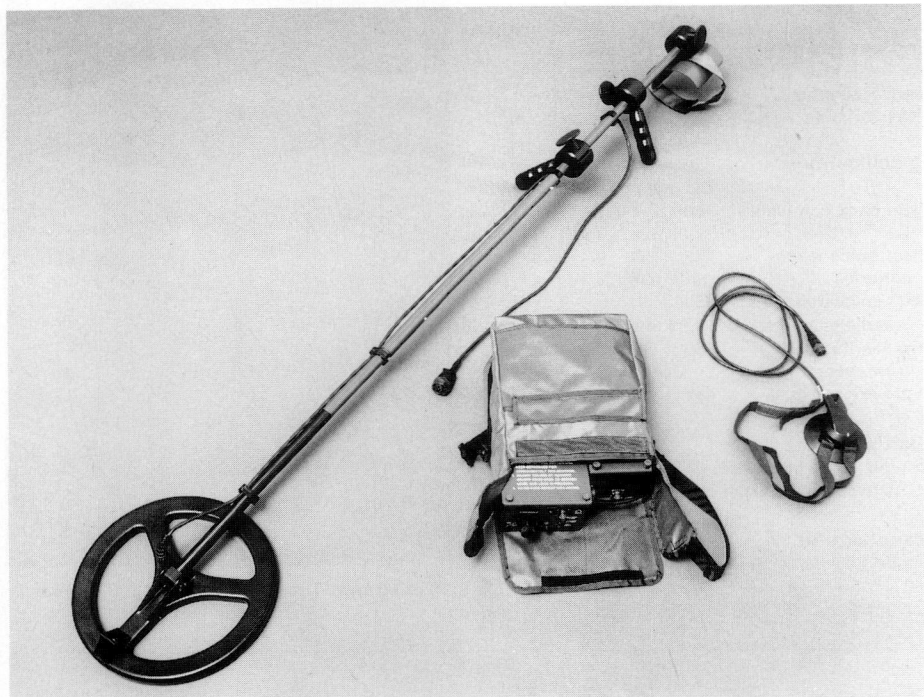

White's Electronics military mine detector

Computer Aided Munition Identification System (CAMIS)

Description

The Computer Aided Munition Identification System (CAMIS) was developed by Negretti Aviation Limited as a purpose-designed computer-based system providing explosive ordnance disposal (EOD) departments and teams with rapid access to detailed munitions data. The data provide the operator with neutralisation, render safe and counter-mining procedures. The system is supplied complete and ready to use with all software installed. A basic set of data is available for the database while further data may be readily added by the user or by the supplier.

The system may be used on-site and includes a video camera which may be used to provide direct on-screen comparisons for identification purposes or for the insertion of a new record into the database. If required the system can be security protected and it may also be used for simulation and training.

Status
Available. In service with an undisclosed organisation.

Manufacturer
Negretti Aviation Limited, 6 Manor Court, Barnes Wallis Road, Fareham, Hampshire PO15 5TH, UK.
Tel: 0489 579090. Telex: 47671.
Fax: 0489 579013.

UNITED STATES OF AMERICA

Minefield Reconnaissance and Detector System (MIRADOR)

Development/Description
In May 1986 the Belvoir Research, Development and Engineering Center announced contract awards for the Minefield Reconnaissance and Detector System (MIRADOR). MIRADOR will be a multi-sensor system designed to detect metallic and non-metallic mines,

both on and off roads. Operationally it will be employed in high-risk areas as a self-propelled system remotely operated from a parent vehicle or mounted on a remotely controlled tactical vehicle. The system could also be manually operated in low-risk areas during routine operations. In both cases MIRADOR will be used in advance of other operational forces.

The eventual system will be employed in support of combat engineer, infantry and armoured units. During offensive operations, MIRADOR will be used to search

known or suspected areas to detect mines and minefields. For counterattacks it will be used to detect rapidly emplaced minefields.

Contracts for the MIRADOR prototypes were issued to Gould Electronics of Glen Burnie, Maryland ($4.8 million), and Foster and Miller Inc of Waltham, Massachusetts ($4.3 million).

Status
Development.

GDE Non-metallic Mine Detectors

Description
The US Army has a requirement for a system capable of detecting non-metallic mines with a minimal or non-existent metal content. General Dynamics, Electronics Division, was awarded a contract by the Defense Advanced Research Projects Agency (DARPA) to develop such a system and, following investigation into the various technologies possible, decided to concentrate on the use of radio frequencies (RF) to provide aural and visual methods of buried object display. The use of RF means that any buried objects can be detected while nearly all existing systems rely upon the presence of metals and thence magnetic anomaly or similar detection methods.

The first GDE unit involving the use of RF is a hand-held detector with a search head containing a four-element antenna. Using the antenna a low-powered RF source operating on three sequenced frequencies electronically illuminates the ground and any targets while backscattered radiation is measured for target presence and location. A pre-programmed micro-

processor switches the transmit and receive ports of the antenna to collect both phase and amplitude reflected data from a buried target. After data acquisition, special algorithms operate on the data for the extraction of information which signifies the presence of a target. With the first hand-held detector model, evidence of a target is provided aurally as a 300 to 3000 Hz tone in a headset and visually on a small LCD display mounted on the detector handle. System electronics are carried in a backpack.

The first hand-held detector using RF principles was produced by late 1991. A second and more advanced model employs a search head with 40 micro antennas. The dimensions of the search head and the antennas are optimised for search and detection sensitivity while the operator's backpack is used to contain and carry the circuitry necessary for the system to provide a graphic display of targets on a colour screen carried on the detector handle. The antennas' sweeps and responses provide sufficient data for the system to provide a graphic indication of the shape and location of buried objects, whatever their material composition.

The hand-held detector makes use of lightweight materials and has a length (with handle) of about

1.524 m. On the first model the search head measures 356 × 356 mm and total weight is 5.4 kg. The batteries used are of the BA-3090/U and BA-3030/U type, providing a life of 8 hours in continuous use at 22°C.

Detection capabilities for plastic objects are as follows:

Small – 0 to 51 mm
Medium – 0 to 152 mm
Large – 0 to 305 mm

It is anticipated that, using the system, there will be an 80 per cent detection probability during development tests and a 90 to 95 per cent detection probability with production versions.

A vehicle-mounted detection system is also under development, using similar RF principles to the hand-held detectors.

Status
Prototypes.

Manufacturer
General Dynamics, Electronics Division, PO Box 85227, San Diego, California 92138, USA. Tel: (619) 573 6111.

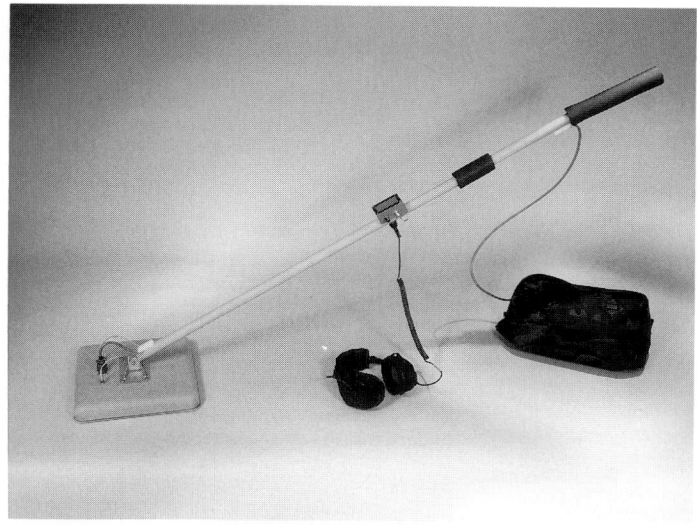

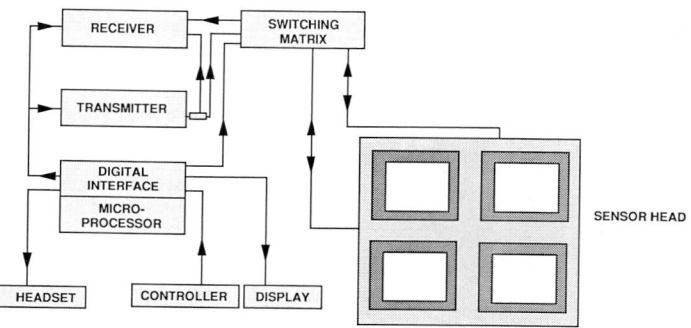

Schematic layout of GDE non-metallic mine detection system

Prototype of GDE hand-held non-metallic mine detector showing electronics unit backpack and LCD display on handle

---

AN/PRS-7 Non-metallic Mine Detector

Description
The AN/PRS-7 (company designation is the 4D6) was developed by the US Army with production being undertaken by Fourdee Inc. It is a simple, rugged solid-state equipment capable of detecting non-metallic anti-tank and anti-personnel mines.

The AN/PRS-7 consists of four major components: search head, handle, control box and headset.

The mine is detected by the field of the square search head assembly, which consists of two transmitting antennas, one receiving antenna and transmission wires which run inside the handle to the control box. The search head generates and radiates a continuous

wave RF signal and receives and demodulates this signal. A rubber bumper is mounted around the search head as a protective measure.

The telescopic handle, which is detachable from the search head, can be extended from 0.482 to 1.752 m. The handle is normally used in the walking position with the search head about 1.219 m away from the operator's body. The detector head can also be swivelled to allow the operator to use the equipment while prone.

The control box, which is mounted on the handle, consists of the signal processing board with its associated electronic components, the battery and the controls. The latter features a 'search' mode that is used to locate the presence and general position of the mine. The exact position of the mine is determined in

the 'point' mode, using any of the sensitivity levels. By control sensitivity selection, the mine detector will discriminate and work effectively on both magnetic and non-magnetic soil, and terrain covered with other debris. The AN/PRS-7 performed well in the Far East, Europe and the USA but when confronted with non-metallic mines in desert soils, as found in the Middle East, the response was poor.

The presence of a mine is indicated audibly to the operator through the headset assembly, which consists of two headphones which produce a 1000 Hz signal.

One complete AN/PRS-7 system comprises the mine detector, replacement mode, spare battery and bolt, arctic warming case for battery, carrying case, and operating and maintenance handbooks.

Specifications
Weight:
(mine detector) 4.082 kg
(complete equipment in case) 10.886 kg
Case:
(length) 615 mm
(width) 406 mm
(height) 184 mm
Audio frequency of headset: 1000 Hz
Battery voltage: 16.2 V
Battery type: mercury
Battery life: 28 h continuous operation
Battery capacity:
(+ section) 0.5 Ah
(− section) 1.8 Ah
Operating temperature range: −31.7 to +51.7°C
Storage temperature range: −53.9 to +68.3°C
Relative humidity operational: 95%
Relative humidity storage: 100%

Status
Production complete. In service with the US Army and many other armed forces. By 1979, Fourdee had delivered over 30 000 mine detectors to various countries. The AN/PRS-7 is being replaced by a product-improved version, the AN/PRS-8.

Left: AN/PSS-11 metallic mine detector; right: AN/PRS-7 non-metallic mine detector (US Army)

AN/PRS-8 Metallic and Non-metallic Mine Detector

Description
In FY76 the US Army Mobility Equipment Research and Development Command (MERADCOM) initiated an AN/PRS-7 Product Improvement Program (PIP) with the Cubic Corporation Defense Systems Division. Under this the detector was improved using new solid-state electronics and signal processing equipment for better mine detection in any type of soil, the designation AN/PRS-8 being assigned to the detector. The new solid-state transmitter and receiver sweeps over a wide radio frequency band instead of the single frequency of the earlier AN/PRS-7 and provides an

AN/PRS-8 hand-held mine detector

order of magnitude increase in the search head data gathered. This is then processed by a single board processor module fitted with a 16-bit microprocessor and memory on a single chip. The algorithm used is one developed from that used on the AN/VRS-5 vehicle-mounted road mine detector system (now cancelled) and results in a vastly increased performance over the AN/PRS-7, specifically in a higher detection rate and fewer false alarms.

The detector adapts its threshold sensitivity to various soils automatically. Handling characteristics have been improved with end-point blanking to eliminate false alarms produced by the operator's tendency to tilt the search head at the ends of the swing, a metronome pacing signal to set the optimum search sweep rate, and more distinctive audio signals. An automatic switch from 'search' to 'point' is also included.

In late 1981 a $7.3 million contract was placed for 1461 AN/PRS-8 detectors. This contract included retrofit kits to update the 9500 AN/PRS-7 detectors in service to AN/PRS-8 standard.

Specifications
Search head assembly
Weight: 0.77 kg
Length: 221 mm
Width: 221 mm
Height: 56 mm

Control box (without battery)
Weight: 0.857 kg
Length: 180 mm
Width: 64 mm
Height: 78 mm

Battery
Weight: 0.25 kg
Length: 95 mm
Width: 38 mm
Height: 65 mm

Long handle
Weight: 0.62 kg
Length: 0.48 m
Height:
(nested) 35 mm
(extended) 1.46 m

Short handle
Weight: 0.11 kg
Length: 0.3 m
Width: 30 mm
Height: 56 mm

Miscellaneous (headset, cables, straps, and so on)
Weight: 1.2 kg

Carrying case
Weight:
(without unit) 6.2 kg
(with unit) 10 kg
Length: 0.6 m
Width: 0.4 m
Height: 0.19 m

RF frequency range: 300-600 MHz
Audio frequency:
(search mode) 1 click/2.5 s
(point mode) 3-150 clicks/s
Temperature range:
(operating) −32 to +52°C
(storage) −55 to +70°C
Battery complement: Type BA-5847 (Lithium)/U
Battery voltage: +5.6 V nominal
Battery life: 20 h at ambient room temperatures

Status
In service with the US Army. A total of 9500 AN/PRS-7 detectors underwent product improvement.

AN/PSS-11 Metallic Mine Detector

Description
The AN/PSS-11 was developed by the US Army with production being undertaken by Cubic Corporation's Defense Systems Division. The work involved was carried out by Cubic Corporation's Defense Systems Division under contract to the US Army Mobility Equipment Research and Development Command (MERADCOM), now the Belvoir Research, Development and Engineering Center.

The AN/PSS-11 is a simple, rugged, solid-state equipment which can detect metallic anti-tank and anti-personnel mines of ferrous and non-ferrous materials.

The equipment consists of five major components: detection head, telescopic handle, control box, receiver/transmitter and headset.

The detection head is square and contains four coils which are electrically balanced. These transmitter coils send out electromagnetic waves which set up a magnetic field with a radius of 0.914 to 1.219 m. When a metallic object is encountered, the magnetic field is distorted, which results in an imbalance in the mutual inductance bridge.

The receiver/transmitter, which is carried in a pouch on the operator's belt, amplifies the imbalance and causes a signal increase in the headset, and indicates the presence of the metallic object. A phase discriminating circuit cancels false signals caused by salt

water or magnetic soils and only signals caused by metallic objects are transmitted to the headset.

The control box is on the handle and nulls the signal to the headset to establish initial balance condition and has low, intermediate and high sensitivity selections to locate metallic objects and pinpoint their exact positions.

The telescopic handle, which is detachable from the detector head, can be extended from 0.482 to 1.752 m. It is identical to the handle on the AN/PRS-8. The handle is normally used in the walking position with the search head about 1.219 m from the body. The detector head can also swivel to allow the operator to use the equipment while prone.

The headset consists of two headphones which

produce a 625 Hz audible sound.

A complete AN/PSS-11 set consists of a carrying case, mine detector, spare modules, spare batteries, arctic kit, and operations and maintenance handbook.

Specifications

Weight: 10 kg
Case:
  (length) 600 mm
  (width) 400 mm
  (height) 180 mm
Audio frequency of headset: 625 Hz
Battery voltage: 10.7 to 14 V
Battery type: BA-1568/U

Battery life: 70 h continuous operation
Detection capability:
  (small metal object) 304-355 mm
  (large metal object) 1.219-1.828 m
Operating temperature range: −32 to +52°C
Storage temperature range: −55 to +70°C
Relative humidity operational: 100%
Relative humidity storage: 100%

Status

In production. $10 million contract placed for US Army use, April 1983. Also ordered by Egypt ($4.5 million contract 1983). Known to be in service in Brazil.

AN/PSS-11 hand-held mine detector in use

MINECLEARING EQUIPMENT

CANADA

MREL LEXFOAM Liquid Explosive Foam Mine Clearing Systems

MREL (Mining Resource Engineering Limited) LEX-FOAM liquid explosive foam is a patented explosive based on nitromethane which may be used for clearing minefields of unexploded ordnance. Other applications include the breaching of walls and vehicles for access and the explosive welding of metals.

LEXFOAM stock solution is transported in 45 gallon (204.5 l) drums as a flammable liquid and its explosive properties can be tailored to suit the application. The detonation velocity and resultant pressure vary with the foam density and layer thickness. A typical density and layer thickness capable of clearing hardened fuzed and unfuzed anti-tank and anti-personnel mines buried in sand is 0.25 g/cc and 25 mm respectively. Detonation pressures and impulses can range between 5 and 20 kbar and 100 and 1500 bar/ms for foam densities between 0.1 and 0.6 g/cc respectively.

In use, drums containing the LEXFOAM concentrate are taken close to the operational area and thoroughly mixed with liquid propane in a dispersal tank prior to being over-pressurised with nitrogen. The mixture is prepared in 10 kg capacity backpack units or 200 kg capacity palletised or truck-mounted units. For large scale area coverage LEXFOAM can be dispensed from 2200 kg capacity towable units. For small scale use LEXFOAM can be dispensed from hand-held aerosol-type canisters. If required, LEXFOAM can be prepared at a central depot.

In a typical mineclearing operation using the 10 kg capacity backpack unit, the LEXFOAM is sprayed using a spray wand 3 m long. The foam may be sprayed generally in large patches or in more defined patches over detected mines which may then be explosively linked to each other by thin strips of LEXFOAM or detonating cord to allow all the patches to be detonated from a single detonator source. Once deployed LEXFOAM can be detonated by standard military or industrial blasting caps. The foam is cap sensitive above a density of 0.2 g/cc.

Other MREL explosive systems include the following: BREACHCASE, a wall-breaching device; R-SEF rigid solid explosive foam; F-SEF flexible solid explosive foam; DRESTRUCTOR, a bulk explosives container shaped for demolition; DRESCAVATOR, a bulk explosives container shaped for cratering; and L-PWG, a liquid plane wave generator.

Status
In production. Under test with the Canadian Department of National Defence and the US Marine Corps.

Spraying LEXFOAM from a 10 kg capacity backpack

Manufacturer
Mining Resource Engineering Limited, 1555 Sydenham Road, R.R.8 Kingston, Ontario, Canada K7L 4V4. Tel: (613) 545 0466. Fax: (613) 542 8029.

FALCON Mineclearing System

Description
The FALCON (Fuel/Air Line Charge Ordnance Neutraliser) mineclearing system was developed by Thomson-CSF Systems Canada in association with Brome Laboratories of Québec and TES Limited of Ottawa. The system underwent trials for the Canadian Armed Forces at the Defence Research Establishment at Suffield, Alberta, until the end of 1989.

FALCON uses a finned rocket powered by four 2.75-inch/70 mm CRV-7 rocket motors to tow a 300 m hose across a minefield. The hose is packed inside a large crate and is connected to the rocket by cable before launch. The rocket is launched along a ramp carried alongside the crate. After launch the hose is filled with propylene oxide to create an explosive fuel-air cloud which is produced by a detonating cord inside the hose. After a 400 μs delay the fuel-air cloud is ignited by secondary charges spaced every 15.24 m along the hose.

The blast created by FALCON can clear single impulse anti-tank and anti-personnel mines from a well defined path 200 m long and 10 m wide. A 100 m safety stand-off is produced by filling the portion of the hose closest to the firing point with water. The entire launching and firing sequence takes less than 3 minutes.

The prototype FALCON system is mounted on a twin-axle trailer towed into position by an M113 APC or a 5-tonne truck. The intention is that the production

The FALCON mineclearing system

system will feature the expendable portion of the system transported as a palletised load. The rest of the system may be trailer-, truck- or skid-mounted, as required by the customer.

Status
Development.

Manufacturer
Thomson-CSF Systems Canada Inc, 18 Auriga Drive, Nepean, Ontario, Canada K2E 7T9.
Tel: (613) 723 7000. Telex: (613) 053 3769.
Fax: (613) 723 5600.

CHILE

Cardoen Bangalore Torpedo

Description
This is used for clearing minefields and obstacles such as barbed wire. It consists of 1.5 m lengths of 65 mm diameter light aluminium or steel pipes filled with high explosive. A complete issue unit consists of four main pipe charge sections, four sleeve connectors and two heads.

Each pipe charge weighs 7.5 kg and is filled with 5 kg of cast Pentolite and Mexal 1500 explosive. The torpedo assembly is detonated by a standard No 8 blasting cap. Total assembled weight is approximately 31 kg and the torpedo is capable of clearing paths 4 to 5 m wide.

Status
In production. In service with the Chilean armed forces.

Manufacturer
Industrias Cardoen Ltda, Avenida Los Conquistadores 1700, Piso 28, Santiago, Chile.
Tel: 2313420. Telex: 341630 incar cl.

Cardoen Bangalore torpedo

FAMAE Bangalore Torpedo

Description

The FAMAE Bangalore torpedo is delivered packed in wooden cases each holding six torpedoes ready for individual use or to be assembled into lengths to suit any minecIearing or demolition task. Each section of the torpedo is 1.578 m long and consists of a tubular body with an ogive and coupling devices. Diameter is 60.3 mm and the weight of each unit is 9 kg. Standard No 8 detonators are used to fire the assembled torpedoes. A complete wooden box weighs approximately 65 kg.

Status

In production. In service with the Chilean armed forces.

Manufacturer

FAMAE Fabricaciones Militares, Avenida Pedro Montt 1568/1606, Santiago, Chile.
Tel: 561011. Telex: 242 346 famae cl.

CHINA, PEOPLE'S REPUBLIC

425 mm Type 762 Minecfearing Rocket and Launcher

Description

The 425 mm Type 762 minecIearing rocket is launched from the 425 mm minecIearing rocket launcher based on the hull and chassis of the Type 83 152 mm self-propelled gun-howitzer (for details refer to *Jane's Armour and Artillery 1992-93* pages 544 and 545). This launcher vehicle follows the same general lines as the Type 83 and carries two 425 mm Type 762 rockets on two rails mounted on a low turret at the hull rear which can be traversed 90° right and left. The launcher rails can be elevated hydraulically from +5 to +45° and when fired the rockets have a maximum range of between 800 and 1000 m. Each rocket can clear a path through a minefield 130 m long and 12 to 22 m wide.

The launcher turret mounts a 7.62 mm machine gun provided with 500 rounds for anti-aircraft, ground target or dismounted use. Firing ports for crew weapons are provided on each side and to the rear of the turret for self-defence. The hull armour is stated to be proof against 7.62 mm projectiles and shell splinters. A door is provided at the rear of the hull. Equipment provided includes a Type WG002 panoramic telescope, a 0.5 m stereo-optical rangefinder, a Type TYG-1 night vision device for the driver, a Type 889 radio set and a Type 803 intercom set.

Specifications

Launch vehicle
Crew: 4
Weight: (combat) 27 000 kg
Length:
  (overall) 7.162 m
  (hull) 6.405 m
Width: 3.236 m
Height: 3.2 m
Ground clearance: 0.45 m
Track: 2.62 m
Track width: 480 mm
Length of track on ground: 4.601 m
Ground pressure: 0.62 kg/cm^2
Max speed: (road) 55 km/h
Average speed:
  (on highway) 40-42 km/h

425 mm Type 762 minecIearing rocket launcher with launcher rails elevated

  (on country road) 30-32 km/h
Range: (highway) 450 km
Fording: 1.3 m
Gradient: 31°
Side slope: 25°
Vertical obstacle: 0.7 m
Trench: 2.6 m
Engine: Type 12150L diesel developing 520 hp
Armament: 1 × 7.62 mm MG
Ammunition carried: (7.62 mm) 500 rds

Type 762 rocket
Rocket diameter: 425 mm
Total length: 4.7 m
Total weight: 7605 kg
Warhead weight: 600 kg
Rocket section weight: (with fins) 150 kg
Temperature range: −40° to +50°C

Max speed under standard conditions: 100 m/s
Max range: 800-1000 m
Cleared path: (1 rocket)
  (length) 130 m
  (width) 12-22 m

Status

In production. In service with the Chinese Army.

Manufacturer

China North Industries Corporation, 7A Yue Tan Nan Jie, PO Box 2137 Beijing, Beijing, People's Republic of China.
Tel: 86 6848. Telex: 22339 cnic cn.

Type 84 Portable MinecIearing Device

Description

The Type 84 portable minecIearing device is a rocket-based system that is normally carried into action as a backpack although handles are provided on the case. The complete system is contained in a light steel case fitted with shoulder straps and when in position the case is opened so that the lid acts as a firing support. The rocket is then fired from a safe distance and as it travels forward the rocket pulls an explosive-filled hose from the case. The hose has a length of about 20 m and once it is on the ground the explosive is detonated to clear mines from a path approximately 20 m long and 1 m wide.

Status

In production. In service with the Chinese armed forces and offered for export.

Manufacturer

China North Industries Corporation, 7A Yue Tan Nan Jie, PO Box 2137 Beijing, Beijing, People's Republic of China.
Tel: 86 6848. Telex: 22339 cnic cn.

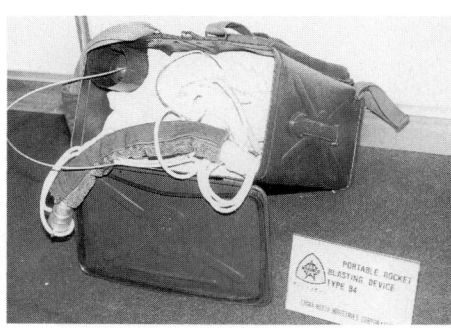

Type 84 portable minecIearing device

Bangalore Torpedoes

Description
The armed forces of the People's Republic of China employ at least four types of Bangalore torpedo for clearing minefields and other obstacles. Three types use a heavy steel body and the other a lightweight metal body, but all four employ pull friction igniters that allow them to be used as extemporised land mines with tripwires if required. The torpedoes have conventional rounded noses, although simple plugs may be fitted at both ends. Booster charges may be used but are not always fitted. As with other such devices, lengths of torpedo can be joined to make up any length as required.

Specifications
Type	Type 1	Type 2	Type 3	Lightweight
Length	0.998 m	0.99 m	1.187 m	0.99 m
Diameter	33 mm	45.7 mm	35.5 mm	54 mm

Status
In service with the Chinese Army and exported to some other countries.

Manufacturer
Chinese state arsenals.

COMMONWEALTH OF INDEPENDENT STATES

Tank-mounted Mineclearing Rollers and Ploughs

Description
PT-54
The PT-54 was introduced into service in the 1950s as the replacement for the earlier PT-3 system. The equipment consists of two independent roller sets which are mounted on arms in front of each track. Each roller set has six rollers, and provision is made for clearing mines fitted with tilt-rod fuzes before they can detonate under the hull. To enable following tanks to see which ground has been cleared the equipment leaves a furrow in the ground 80 mm deep and 100 mm wide. As the tank moves forward the rollers should detonate any mines in its path. The area between the tracks remains uncleared. To widen the lane, additional tanks fitted with mineclearing rollers are used. Normally three tanks work in a wedge pattern to clear a minefield. The PT-54 system weighs 8800 kg and clears two paths, each 1.3 m wide, with a gap 1.2 m wide between them.

PT-54M
This is a modified PT-54 system with five rollers in each section in place of the six of the original. Weight is 7000 kg and the cleared path is reduced to 0.89 m each side.

PT-55
This is similar to the PT-54 but has only four rollers in each section and clears a narrower path (0.83 m wide each side with a central 1.7 m gap), but at a higher speed than the PT-54. The PT-54/55 series takes 3 to 5 minutes to detach and can survive the explosions of 10 swept anti-tank mines. Weight of the PT-55 is 6700 kg.

KMT-4
This was introduced into service in the 1960s and consists of a 600 mm wide cutting device with five cutting tines mounted at an angle in front of each track. Each cutting device is lowered to the ground by a hydraulic ram. This equipment has a number of advantages over the roller-type mineclearing equipment which can be summarised as follows: reduced weight of equipment, retention of tank's cross-country mobility, and the removal of mines from a path instead of their detonation. The KMT-4 is normally allotted at the rate of three sets to each tank company.

KMT-4M
The KMT-4M was introduced during the late 1960s and is basically the KMT-4 with improvements to the blade attachment system.

KMT-5
The KMT-5 was introduced into service to combine the plough and roller mineclearing equipment. The plough system used is the KMT-4 but the roller design is new, lighter, and has only three rollers per section. Each KMT-5 roller sweeps approximately 800 mm. When not in use the system is carried on a KrAZ-214 (6 × 6) truck fitted with a special KM-61 auxiliary crane.

The roller and plough cannot be used simultaneously other than on good, flat ground. The choice of using the rollers or ploughs depends on the type of terrain, soil or minefield to be breached. The system is fitted with a quick-release disconnect unit to allow the tank driver to release both systems rapidly. The KMT-5 system can survive eight to ten 5 to 6 kg explosions but cannot be used in snow thicker than 200 mm or over loose, ploughed land. Weight is approximately 7300 kg.

KMT-5M
The KMT-5M is an improved version of the KMT-5 that incorporates a lane marking plough and the PSK

KMT-4 tank-mounted mineclearing plough mounted on T-62 MBT

Modified Iraqi T-55 MBT fitted with KMT-5 plough and roller mineclearing equipment (Christopher F Foss)

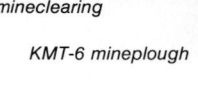
KMT-6 mineplough

T-55 MBT fitted with PT-55 mineclearing rollers clearing minefield

equipment which marks the clear lane at night with a luminous substance. For details of the PSK refer to entry in the *Minefield marking equipment* section.

The Romanian D-5M mineclearing system is a virtual copy of the KMT-5M – see separate entry in this section.

KMT-6

The KMT-6 mineplough was introduced during the late 1960s and is an improved KMT-4M developed for the T-64 MBT. It has also been fitted to the T-72 MBT. The KMT-6 can be fitted with a hard surface attachment for clearing scatterable mines. Each plough can clear a path 0.75 m wide, leaving an intermediate space of 1.9 m.

KMT-6 M2

The KMT-6 M2 is a modified KMT-6. One of the modifications involves three holes in the equipment drawbar in place of the original one to simplify procedures when moving the plough to the travelling position. Some components on the blade sections have been reinforced and the device for triggering tilt-rod fuzes has been modified to allow it to remain attached when travelling; leather straps secure the device in the travelling position. For handling, a

BRANO Type 11-10 0.8-tonne capacity ratchet lift is used in place of the usual hand winch. Some extra tools are also provided.

KMT-7

The KMT-7 roller is similar to the KMT-5 but utilises a box channel frame and the rollers are less 'cleated'. The ploughs used with the KMT-7 are similar to those used with the KMT-6. The supporting frames for the rollers are L-shaped to allow the rollers to swing past the frame when a mine is detonated. Chains are fitted between the rollers to detonate tilt-mast fuzes. As with previous models the rollers are carried on a separate vehicle and are fitted using a crane. The KMT-7 can clear tracks 1.65 m wide with an intermediate space 2.16 m wide.

KMT-1990

This mineplough may be known as the KMT-8 and is a modified KMT-6 with a modified operating mechanism which may allow the simultaneous fitting of a roller mechanism while also enhancing the clearance depth. The KMT-1990 can be used as part of the KMT-7 combination.

Associated equipment

The KM-61 crane on the KrAZ-214 (6 × 6) chassis was designed specifically for use with the plough and roller type mineclearing equipment and is used to position and remove the equipment. The crane has a maximum capacity of 3200 kg with boom at a reach of 2 m. It can be rotated a maximum of 80° from the forward axis of the truck and may be used on slopes up to a maximum of 4° in any direction.

Specifications

Type	PT-54	PT-54M	PT-55	KMT-5
Weight (equipment)	8808 kg	70 kg	6700 kg	7500 kg
(section)	3752 kg	2700 kg	n/a	2265 kg
(roller)	500 kg	500 kg	500 kg	n/a
(plough)	—	—	—	420 kg
Assembly (length)	n/a	2.64 m	n/a	3.18 m
(width)	3.9 m	3.8 m	n/a	4 m
Lane swept (each)	1.3 m	0.89 m	0.83 m	0.73-0.81 m
Width unswept	1.2 m	n/a	1.7 m	2.1 m
Operating speed	6-10 km/h	n/a	8-12 km/h	n/a
Safe turning radius	40 m	n/a	85 m	65 m
Ditch crossing ability	3 m	n/a	n/a	2.5 m
Attachment time	10-15 min	10-25 min	10-15 min	n/a

Status

In service with former Warsaw Pact countries. Tank-mounted mineclearing rollers are also known to be in service with India (mounted on T-72), the former Yugoslavia and a number of countries in the Middle East including Egypt, Iraq and Syria. The equipment is usually mounted on a T-54/T-55 MBT but some T-62s and the more recent T-72, T-74 and T-80 MBTs have provision for installing mineclearing equipment of the roller or plough type.

Manufacturer

State factories.

Mineclearing Plough for BMP

Description

The mineclearing plough used on the BMP-1 and BMP-2 has also been referred to as the KMT-10 and is much smaller than the rest of the CIS mineclearing plough equipments. The BMP mineclearing ploughs are narrow and have only two digging tines which probably limits them to clearing surface-laid or shallow-buried mines; the intention is probably to clear scatterable mines. To reduce the travelling width the outer section of each plough can be folded inwards and held in place by a spring lock. Despite the small size of the ploughs they apparently affect the carrier vehicle's amphibious abilities so an extra flotation device is secured to the lower front of the hull. It is possible that this device could be a layer of extra composite or other armour to provide extra protection when clearing mines.

Status

In production. In service with the CIS and probably some other former Warsaw Pact armies.

Manufacturer

State factories.

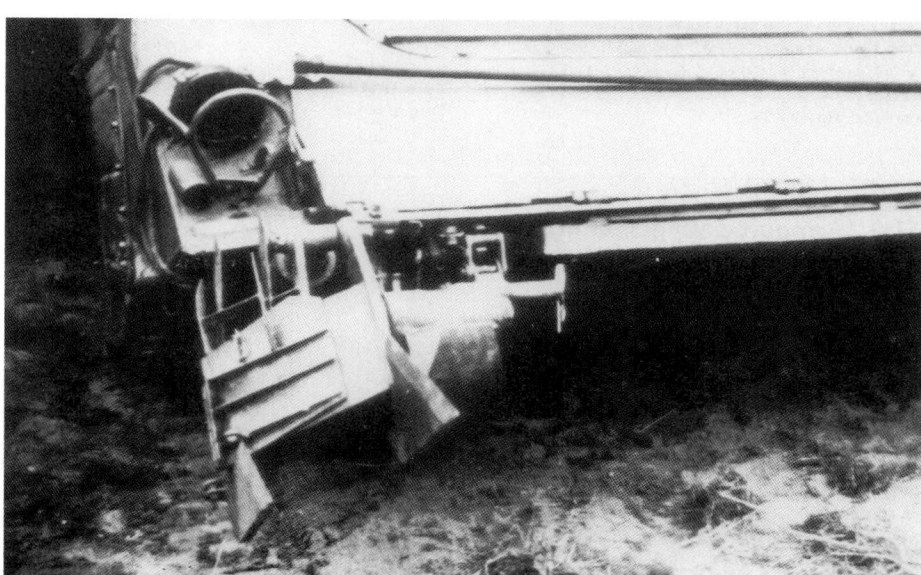

Mineclearing plough fitted to BMP IFV

M1977 Armoured Mineclearing Vehicle

Description

During 1986 reports from Afghanistan mentioned a new armoured mineclearing vehicle. This emerged as a variant of the M1977 armoured recovery vehicle (for details refer to the entry in the *Armoured recovery vehicles* section) converted to use the tank-mounted mineclearing plough and roller KMT-5 (see penultimate entry).

On the M1977 mineclearing vehicle the driver is seated at the front right with a circular turret to his left which appears to be armed with a 14.5 mm KPVT heavy machine gun. The KMT-5 system is mounted on the front hull. Vehicles operating in Afghanistan mainly limit the KMT-5 system to the mineclearing rollers only to avoid the mineploughs damaging tracks and roads to the extent that wheeled vehicles cannot follow the cleared path. M1977 mineclearing vehicles observed elsewhere carry the full KMT-5 array.

As the M1977 ARV was based on the T-55 MBT many of the hull and running gear features of the MBT are carried over to the mineclearing vehicle, including

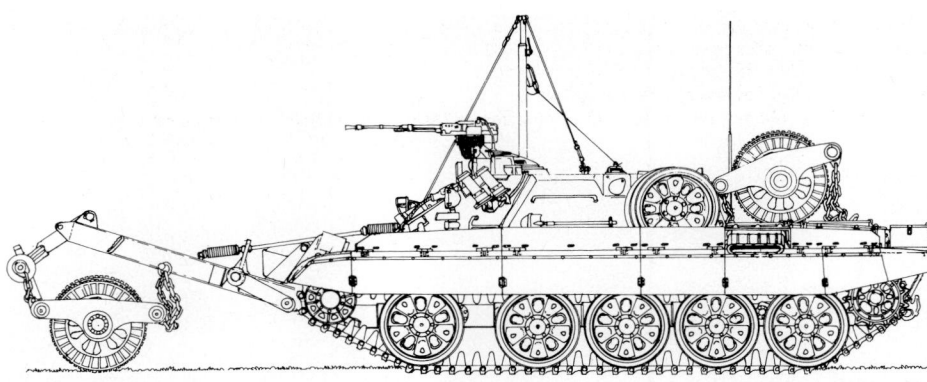

Side-view drawing of M1977 armoured mineclearing vehicle fitted with mineclearing rollers from KMT-5 set (not to 1/76th scale)

the ability to produce smoke screens by injecting diesel fuel into the exhaust outlet above the fourth and fifth left road wheel stations.

Status

In service with the CIS.

Manufacturer

State factories.

MTK Armoured Mineclearing Vehicle

Description

The MTK armoured mineclearing vehicle is a derivative of the BTR-50PK tracked armoured personnel carrier carrying a UR-67 rocket launcher system using a length of UZR-3 high explosive line charge 170 m long. The UZR-3 charge is carried in a fabric tube container carried inside the hull of the vehicle. In use the MTK vehicle is driven to the edge of a minefield and aligned before the rocket is fired from its elevated launcher at the rear of the hull. As the rocket travels it tows the line charge, which is secured by a line to the launch vehicle, across the minefield. The line charge is then positioned by the vehicle crew using the securing line and detonated to clear any mines in its vicinity. The MTK carries three UR-67 rocket and line charge systems.

The MTK weighs just over 14 tonnes and is 7.1 m long.

For details of the BTR-50PK APC refer to *Jane's Armour and Artillery 1992-93 pages 325 and 326.*

Status

In service with the CIS.

Manufacturer

State arsenals.

MTK armoured mineclearing vehicle with UR-67 launcher elevated for firing

MTK-2 Armoured Mineclearing Vehicle

Description

An armoured mineclearing vehicle based on the chassis of the amphibious 122 mm 2S1 self-propelled howitzer was known in the West as the M-1979 but is now understood to be the MTK-2 which has a low turret-like superstructure that contains three UR-77 rockets on launch ramps. These, together with the upper part of the superstructure, are hydraulically elevated for firing. Range of the rockets is estimated to be between 200 and 400 m with each rocket connected, via a towing line, to two 170 m lengths of UZR-3 mine clearance hose that are stowed folded in the uncovered base of the turret on the vehicle roof.

The hoses are connected by a cable to the vehicle which, by using guide rails and reversing the vehicle, allows the vehicle crew to position the hoses in the optimum breaching position once the launching has been carried out. The hoses are then command detonated to clear a path up to 140 m long and 2 m wide through minefields provided with pressure fuzes. When tilt-mast fuzes are involved the cleared path can be as much as 8 m.

The MTK-2 is capable of operating in an NBC

MTK-2 armoured mineclearing vehicle

environment, is amphibious, and has a good cross-country performance. It has a crew of two, weighs approximately 15 tonnes and is 7.07 m long; the width is 3.14 m and height overall approximately 2.45 m.

Details of the 122 mm 2S1 self-propelled howitzer

are given in *Jane's Armour and Artillery 1992-93*, pages 553 to 557.

Status
Trials during 1979/80. Thought to have entered service

in 1981/82.

Manufacturer
State factories.

ITB-2, SPZ-2 and SPZ-4 Mine Clearance Charges

Description
ITB-2
A rocket-launched anchor and cable is propelled across the minefield and then a winch, or other source of motive force, is used to draw more cable with explosive charges toward the anchor and onto the minefield. Once in position the charge is detonated.

SPZ-2
The SPZ-2 uses a metal-framed anchor guide, placed

at the forward edge of the minefield, to draw by winch, at a rate of 200 m/h, a cable, with explosive charges attached, across the minefield. The charges may be either single, double or triple and, depending on type, may clear a path 300 to 500 m long and up to 6 m wide.

SPZ-4
This consists of a double or triple charge which can either be pushed into the minefield by a tank at a rate of 100 m/h, or, if the tank is equipped with roller or plough type mineclearing equipment, laid behind the tank in the gap between the cleared paths left across the minefield by the mineclearing equipment. In the former case, the charge is detonated after it has been

positioned by the tank while in the latter case the charge is detonated by the tank crew.

Status
In service with the CIS.

Manufacturer
State factories.

BDT Mineclearing Charge

Description
The BDT mine clearance charge consists of three separate linear charges which are connected in parallel to form a triple charge. The BDT can also be disassembled to form a single or double charge. Each charge consists of a light metal tube 50 mm in diameter filled with 8.62 kg of cast TNT per linear 305 mm. Lengths of charges can be coupled together to form any desired length. Maximum practical length is 500 m

and a squad of men can assemble a 500 m triple charge in between 1 and 1.5 hours.

Once the charge has been assembled to the desired length, the nose and detonator are added, and a roller is fitted to the forward end of the charge with a shield mounted above to ensure that there is no premature detonation by enemy small arms fire. The BDT is normally assembled to the rear and towed by a tracked vehicle to the minefield at a maximum speed of 10 km/h. The tank then pushes the BDT into the minefield where it is detonated by either an electric blasting cap which is initiated by a firing cable

connected to the batteries of the pushing tank or by the detonation box. This contains a number of percussion detonators, connected by a booster charge, which are detonated by machine-gun fire from the pushing tank. When detonated, a triple BDT line charge will clear a path 6 m wide.

Status
In service with the CIS and others.

Manufacturer
State factories.

UZ-1 and UZ-2 Bangalore Torpedoes

Description
The UZ-1 and UZ-2 Bangalore torpedoes are used for clearing a path through minefields and barbed wire. Each section of a UZ-1 Bangalore torpedo consists of a metal tube 1 m long and 53 mm in diameter containing 5.3 kg of explosive. Each section of a UZ-2 Bangalore torpedo is 2 m long, 53 mm in diameter, weighs 10 kg,

and contains 3 kg of explosive. Collars are provided for connecting sections together for the required length.

When assembled, the Bangalore torpedo is pushed across the minefield and detonated, which clears a path between 2.5 and 3 m wide. If a wider path is required, double or triple charges may be assembled with special collars. These charges may also be placed on carts, sleds or rollers, not only for ease of movement and employment but also for maintaining a more favourable detonation height. A metal shield is sometimes positioned on the forward end of the

torpedo to ensure that there is no premature detonation by enemy small arms fire. Fuzes used with the UZ-2 include the MD-5M and the EDP-R.

The UZ-2 is produced in Bulgaria and is probably manufactured by other former Warsaw Pact countries.

Status
In service with former Warsaw Pact countries.

Manufacturer
State factories.

Electromagnetic Countermine System

Description
Reports have been made of an electromagnetic countermine system fitted to some CIS MBTs. The system involves the installation of a flat assembly on the front glacis of the tank hull, an installation which

involves the relocation of some equipment such as the driving lights. Cables connect the assembly to internal junction boxes so it is assumed that the system is powered by the host vehicle's electrical system.

It is also assumed that this system operates in much the same manner as the American VEMASID (qv) in that the assembly houses an electrical coil which creates and projects an electromagnetic field forward of the host vehicle. The field will then detonate any

mines with electromagnetic fuzes before the host vehicle reaches them.

Status
In service with the CIS armed forces.

Manufacturer
State factories.

CZECHOSLOVAKIA

Tank-mounted Mineclearing Roller Tank-mounted Mineclearing Plough

Description

The Czechoslovak Army uses tank-mounted mine-clearing rollers and ploughs of its own design. The former consists of three to five rollers of varying thickness mounted on an arm in front of each track in a manner similar to the CIS equipment. The Czechoslovak rollers are bigger than their CIS counterparts and also have a different type of serrated edge. Between and in front of the two sets of rollers is a frame for detonating the tilt-rod fuzes of any mines before the tank passes over them.

The plough type equipment is similar in concept to the CIS equipment but uses a larger plough and also has a frame for detonating mines with tilt-rod fuzes.

Status

In service with the Czechoslovak Army.

Manufacturer

Czechoslovak state factories.

T-55 MBT fitted with Czechoslovak mineclearing rollers

Mineclearing Charges

Description

The Czechoslovak Army has a two-wheeled trailer which is towed behind a T-54/T-55 MBT fitted with mineclearing equipment of the roller or plough type. The trailer lays a series of explosive cords behind the tank on those parts of the ground which have not been cleared by the mineclearing equipment installed on the front of the tank. The cords are detonated from inside the tank and clear any remaining mines.

The Czechoslovak Army also has a trailer-mounted mine clearance system. This is an armoured four-wheeled trailer towed behind an OT-64 (8 × 8) APC or similar vehicle, and contains rockets to which a number of flexible mineclearing explosive lines are attached. This is fired over the minefield and then detonated.

Status

In service with the Czechoslovak Army.

Manufacturer

Czechoslovak state factories.

EGYPT

Fateh-1 Anti-personnel Mineclearing System

Description

The Fateh-1 anti-personnel mineclearing system is manportable by two men and is transported in a carrying box containing a line charge, a rocket motor and a rocket launching rail frame. In use the system is carried in its camouflaged box to the launching point and the launching frame is erected on one side of the box. The rocket is then placed on the launch rail and launched electrically to pull the line charge across the anti-personnel minefield to be breached. The line charge is then detonated to clear a path up to 120 m long and up to 0.6 m wide. The furthest point of clearance from the launching point is 140 m.

Inert drill and practice versions are available.

Specifications

Weight: 72 kg
Dimensions: 900 × 500 × 300 mm
Weight of line charge: 50 kg
Length of line charge: 120 m

Manufacturer

SAKR Factory for Developed Industries, PO Box 33, Heliopolis, Cairo, Arab Republic of Egypt.
Tel: 660250. Telex: 92175 cerva un.
Fax: 202-2901978.

Fateh-1 anti-personnel mineclearing system ready for launch

Gehad-1 Anti-tank Mineclearing System

Description
The Gehad-1 anti-tank mineclearing system is towed into action on a single-axle trailer by a tank or other armoured vehicle. Once at a launch position the trailer is disconnected from the towing vehicle and stabilised by four jacks, one at each corner. A pallet containing the line charge is pulled from the trailer to a position just in front of the towing arm and on the ground. A rocket launching frame on the trailer is prepared and a two-stage rocket motor is then placed on the launch rail.

After the rocket has been fired it pulls a line charge from its pallet and across the anti-tank minefield to be breached. The exact distance to which the line charge will be pulled is dependent on the burn time of the two-stage rocket motor but the furthest point of detonation from the launch point will be 200 m. The charge is 120 m long and weighs 6 kg/m. When detonated electrically, the line charge will clear anti-tank mines from a path 120 m long and 4 m wide.

Inert drill and practice versions are available.

Gehad-1 anti-tank mineclearing system ready for launch

Specifications
Trailer capacity: 2000 kg
Trailer flatbed dimensions: 3 × 1.5 × 0.5 m
Weight of line charge: 6 kg/m
Length of line charge: 120 m

Manufacturer
SAKR Factory for Developed Industries, PO Box 33, Heliopolis, Cairo, Arab Republic of Egypt.
Tel: 660250. Telex: 92175 cerva un.
Fax: 202-2901978.

GERMANY

MIPAG Scatterable Mineclearing System

Description
Krauss-Maffei has developed a scatterable mineclearing system known as MIPAG which can be attached to armoured tracked and wheeled vehicles.

MIPAG is mechanical in operation and operates on a pulsating principle. It is pushed in front of the carrier and can clear scatterable mines from roads, paths and light terrain. The attachment can be fitted to any suitably equipped armoured vehicle in about 10 minutes and weighs 120 kg. It extends 4 m in front of the carrier vehicle and clears a lane 4.7 m wide. Maximum clearing speed on paved roads is 30 km/h.

Status
Development.

Manufacturer
Krauss-Maffei Wehrtechnik GmbH, Krauss-Maffei Strasse 2, D-8000 Munich 50, Federal Republic of Germany.
Tel: 89 8899 0. Telex: 523163 31.
Fax: 89 81201 90.

MIPAG scatterable mineclearing system fitted to Leopard 2 MBT

Keiler Armoured Mineclearing Vehicle

Development
In 1973 the Federal German Defence Ministry and the Procurement Office issued a request for proposals for a rapid land mine clearance system (*Landminen-Schnellräummittel*). A number of companies, including Krupp MaK (now MaK System Gesellschaft mbH), AEG/Telefunken, Dynamit Nobel, Industriewerke Karlsruhe and Rheinstahl (now Thyssen-Henschel) submitted proposals for the system.

During 1982 it was revealed that the then West Germany, in a co-operative venture with the French Government, had produced a test bed flail tank based on the chassis of the M48. This vehicle was the end product of a definition phase of development and in 1983 MaK became the general contractor for further development of the vehicle, named Keiler, and was responsible for the manufacture of two further prototypes in 1985.

Preliminary and final company testing was carried out with the two prototypes and troop tests by the Federal German Army commenced during the second half of 1990. A contract award was placed in mid-1992

for 72 units (since reduced to 24) with series production commencing during 1993. The first units will be handed over to the Bundeswehr during 1995.

Description
The Keiler (Wild Boar) armoured mineclearing vehicle is based on a modified M48A2 MBT hull and unmodified M48 running gear and carries a flail-type mineclearing system at the front. The vehicle has a crew of two (commander and driver). Power is provided by a powerpack consisting of an improved MTU MB 871 Ka-501 diesel engine and a Renk HSWL 284 M transmission.

The mineclearing system is powered by hydraulic motors on a pump distribution gearbox. In order to suppress low frequency vibrations which would make the clearing process impossible, the mineclearing vehicle was supplied with a front support. With the front support in position the vehicle can reach speeds of up to 25 km/h. The elevation cylinders for the front support are integral with the front part of the vehicle.

The mineclearing system uses a cantilever arm which operates the system from the travelling position to the 20° clearing position. There is a tilt and elevation system for terrain adjustment and a carrier arm and clearing shaft frame carrying hydraulic motors. The

system is completed by two clearing shafts carrying 24 flails, and a height measuring device.

There are three operating modes: driving; clearing standby; and clearing. During the clearing mode it is possible to select either an automatic mode or a manual mode; the latter is also used as an emergency mode when the automatic mode is inoperable. In either mode paths up to 4.7 m wide can be cleared and a clearing depth of +50, −50 or −250 mm can be pre-selected. The height measuring device located on one side operates the clearing depth mechanically. Variations in terrain level are catered for by a self-regulating device.

The rotating flails can either destroy mines in their path, throw them to one side or detonate them before they pass under the clearing system. It is claimed that the system will clear 98 per cent of mines in its path. A typical clearing speed in medium-heavy soil is 120 m in 10 minutes at a 250 mm clearing depth. During clearing operations it is not normally necessary to replace flail heads until a path 3000 m long has been cleared. Remote-control during clearing operations is possible.

An automatic cleared path lane-marking system is carried on the rear of the hull. When the mineclearing system is not in use it is carried on racks over the hull.

The only armament carried is smoke dischargers.

Keiler armoured mineclearing vehicle in clearing mode with front support lowered

Keiler armoured mineclearing vehicle in driving configuration

Specifications
Crew: 2
Combat weight: 53 000 kg
Power-to-weight ratio: 14.1 kW/t
Length:
  (driving) 7.83 m
  (clearing) 10.7 m
Width:
  (driving) 3.76 m
  (clearing) 6.35 m
Height:
  (driving) 3.75 m
  (clearing) 2.76 m

  (hull deck) 1.99 m
Ground clearance:
  (overall) 390 mm
  (front support) 260 mm
Max cruising speed: 50 km/h
Fording: (without preparation) 1.2 m
Gradient: 60%
Range: (cruising, driving only) approx 325 km
Trench: 2.6 m
Engine: MTU MB 871 Ka-501 diesel developing 1100 hp at 2200 rpm
Transmission: Renk HSWL 284 M
Armament: smoke dischargers

Clearing speed: 0.1-4 km/h
Clearing width: 4.7 m
Max clearing depth: 250 mm

Status
24 units ordered during 1992. First units to be handed over during 1995.

Manufacturer
MaK System Gesellschaft mbH, Falkensteiner Strasse 2, PO Box 9333, D-2300 Kiel 17, Federal Republic of Germany.
Tel: 431 3995-02. Fax: 431 3995 446.

Comet No 3001 One-man Minesweeping Line Device

Description
The basic system consists of an 18 kg box containing an 82 m long detonating cord with 75 × 100 g plastic explosive charges placed along it at 1 m intervals. A smokeless solid propellant rocket with a launching projector is fitted with a foot-plate and ground spike. The rocket is equipped with a propellant fuze which has a 6 second delay and the detonating cord has a fuze, also with an 8 second delay. The rocket's towing gear consists of two 2.6 m long steel wire ropes fitted with thimbles.

The mode of operation is that the elements of the system are assembled by one man approximately 20 m in front of the minefield to be breached. The rocket is fired using the fuze and the minesweeping line is extended to its full length. The line is then detonated either automatically by the fuze or electrically by hand. As detonation takes place all the mines lying under the explosives will be detonated as well. The consecutive craters thus created result in a narrow mine-free path approximately 74 m long. If a longer path is required then the procedure is repeated with a second unit. A training system No 3002 is available and can be used for repeated firings.

Status
Development complete.

Manufacturer
Comet GmbH Pyrotechnik-Apparatebau, Postfach 10

Comet No 3001 one-man minesweeping line device with packing case

02 67, D-2850 Bremerhaven-1, Federal Republic of Germany.
Tel: 0471 393-0. Telex: 0238731.
Fax: 0471 393-94.

Comet No 3030 Minesweeping System MRL-80

Description
The Comet No 3030 mine sweeping system MRL-80 consists of two transport units, each with two carrying bars. The units can be either carried by two men or dragged along on integral skids.

One transport unit contains the rear blasting unit, the ignition system with the blasting cap fuzes and the retardation system. The second unit contains the front

blasting unit, the rocket, a shock absorber and one rocket igniter with a 40 second delay. The ladder-type blasting units consist of 281 blasting tubes, each with 285 g of explosive, connected at both ends by a steel rope. Parallel to the steel ropes is a detonating cord to initiate the blasting tubes.

In use, both transport units and their blasting units are linked in front of the minefield to be breached. As the rocket is fired it pulls out the blasting units to their maximum length and after 6 seconds the system is ignited automatically. This leaves a clearly visible cleared path approximately 70 m long and 0.6 m wide.

A training version which can be re-used is available.

Status
Development complete.

Manufacturer
Comet GmbH Pyrotechnik-Apparatebau, Postfach 10 02 67, D-2850 Bremerhaven-1, Federal Republic of Germany.
Tel: 0471 393-0. Telex: 0238731.
Fax: 0471 393-94.

ISRAEL

Full Width Mine Plough

Description
The Full Width Mine Plough is used for the mechanical clearing of a 5 m wide path through anti-tank minefields to open safety lanes for tanks, APCs and other vehicles. The plough can be used in most soil types other than rocky ground and can also be used to clear scatterable mines.

The plough, designed as an 'add-on' kit for Caterpillar D9H bulldozers, has a V-shaped blade with hardened teeth. It is mounted on three points of the bulldozer blade and clamped in place. Two hinged feeler arms with electric sensors travel in front of the plough to assess the terrain level and transmit information to an electro-hydraulic control system which raises or lowers the plough accordingly. The tractor's hydraulic actuators are used for elevation and tilt. This automatic depth control enables operations at night and in poor visibility.

The Full Width Mine Plough can be adapted to fit onto other models of bulldozer apart from the D9H.

Specifications
Weight of plough: 5.5 t
Width:
(plough) 6 m
(cleared path) 5 m

Full Width Mine Plough fitted to D9H bulldozer

Depth of clearing: up to 400 mm
Diameter of cleared mines: 200 mm and more
Clearing speed: up to 8 km/h depending on soil conditions

Status
Development complete.

Manufacturer
TAAS – Israel Industries Ltd, POB 1044, Ramat Hasharon 47100, Israel.
Tel: (3) 542 52 22. Telex: 33 719 misbit il.
Fax: (3) 48 96 39.

Ramta Track Width Mine Plough (TWMP)

Description
The Ramta Track Width Mine Plough (TWMP) can be fitted to all types of modern MBT in use. No alterations to the tank are needed as the plough is attached to the towing lugs on the tank front hull. Transferring the TWMP from one tank to another takes less than 1 h using the tool kit supplied. It consists of two plough units with separate lifting mechanisms and depth control systems.

The TWMP is operated by the tank driver. When travelling the ploughs are raised and secured by a locking device. For operations the driver releases the locking devices and the ploughs drop freely for the teeth to dig into the ground and dislodge buried mines which are then pushed aside. Any tilt-rod mines in the central unploughed area between the ploughs will be detonated by a chain suspended between the ploughs. Each plough unit operates independently and follows the natural terrain contours, clearing a path wider than the tank tracks.

After use the TWMP can be lifted back to the travelling position by a mechanical device connected to the track tension wheel or by 24 V DC electrical motors.

The TWMP has been fitted to Centurion, M48, M60, M1 Abrams, Leopard I, Leopard II and Merkava tanks.

Israel Aircraft Industries has developed a remote-control system for mineclearing tanks equipped with the TWMP or other mineclearing systems. The system is known as Pele and can control mineclearing tanks from distances of up to 3 km.

Other items that can be used with the TWMP include a version of the Scatterable Mine Clearing Device (SMCD – see following entry) and the Anti-magnetic Mines Actuating Device (AMMAD). The AMMAD actuates magnetic mines before the arrival of the host tank and is an add-on kit also known as the Improved Dogbone Assembly (IDA). It can be fitted to TWMP/MCBS or mine roller systems without any special adaptation and does not affect the host vehicle's mobility or firepower. A special onboard AMMAD can be fitted to virtually any tracked or wheeled vehicle. Approximately 1000 AMMADs have been supplied to the US Army and Marine Corps and were used by the

Ramta Track Width Mine Plough (TWMP) fitted to M60 MBT

US Army during Operation Desert Shield/Storm.

In January 1989 it was announced that the US Army would receive more than 400 versions of the Ramta TWMP, known to the US Army as the Mine Clearance Blade System (MCBS). The MCBS was operated by the Allied forces during the Desert Storm operations in the Persian Gulf.

Specifications (as fitted on M60 tank)
Max lifted height above ground: 1.6 m
Ploughing depth: 300 mm
Ploughed width each side: 1.154 m
Unploughed width between tracks: 1.612 m
Skidshoe track each side: 0.45 m
Chain track in centre: 0.712 m
Clearing speed:
(loess) 6.5 km/h
(sand and clay) 9.5 km/h
(stony) 6.5 km/h

Status
In production. In service with Israeli armed forces and the US Army (more than 400).

Manufacturer
Ramta Structures and Systems, Israel Aircraft Industries Limited, PO Box 323, Be'er Sheva 84102, Israel.
Tel: 972 57 72231. Telex: 5298 iabs il.
Fax: 972 57 276770.

Scatterable Mine Clearing Device (SMCD)

Description

The Scatterable Mine Clearing Device (SMCD) is an add-on device which can allow any vehicle to have a capability to create a safe path through rapidly deployed scatterable mines on roads and other hard surfaces.

The SMCD can be adapted to fit wheeled or tracked vehicles by using a specifically designed mounting frame. No alterations to the vehicle are needed as the SMCD is attached to existing towing lugs on the front of the vehicle. The system consists of two independently operated minesweeping pushbeams capable of following the grade line of a road both in pitch and roll directions simultaneously. Separate electrically operated lifting and locking devices are provided for each pushbeam. The SMCD is operated by the driver using a control box within the host vehicle. Power is taken from the vehicle's 24 V DC electrical system. When travelling the pushbeams are raised and secured by locking devices. For operations the driver releases the locking devices and the pushbeams drop freely until they rest and adjust themselves automatically to the road grade and level.

The pushbeam is based on a four bar principle with one end pinned to the main frame. The main frame is specifically designed to adapt to the host vehicle. The other (front) end is connected by a sweptback traverse beam which incorporates rows of highly tensioned wires.

With the host vehicle travelling on a hard flat surface at speeds ranging from 12 to 30 km/h, the lowered SMCD sweeps by dispersing away and to the side any scatterable mines lying the in the path of the vehicle. On impact with the tensioned wires mounted in front of a pushbeam, the mines cause an instantaneous spring back of the wires, thus shoving away the mines rapidly. In effect the tensioned wires use their strength and size to act as a catapult. Any detonation of a mine will thus occur at a safe stand-off distance from the host vehicle.

A generally similar SMCD has also been developed for use with track width mineploughs (see previous entry), using the same tensioned wire concept.

A standard SMCD weighs approximately 700 kg and is 1.5 m long in the mounted lowered operational position. The width is approximately 4 m.

Status
In production.

Manufacturer
Ramta Structures and Systems, Israel Aircraft Industries Limited, PO Box 323, Be'er Sheva 84102, Israel.
Tel: 972 57 72231. Telex: 5298 iabs il.
Fax: 972 57 276770.

Scatterable Mine Clearing Device (SMCD) mounted on M60A1 MBT

RKM Mineclearing Rollers

Description

The RKM mineclearing rollers can be used on M47, M48, M60, M60A1, M1, Centurion, Chieftain, AMX-30 and all types of Leopard MBTs.

The RKM mineclearing rollers are track width rollers mounted in two banks in front of the carrier tank pushed and suspended from two pusher arms. The weight and suspension of the rollers is used to detonate any mine over which they travel and a weighted chain between the two roller banks is used to detonate any tilt-rod actuated mines that might explode under the tank's belly. As the rollers detonate a mine, the force of the explosion causes the roller to be lifted upwards on its suspension arm thus reducing the force of the blast which is distributed in the mass of the roller and arm and in the mass of the carrier vehicle attachment point.

The two sets of rollers can articulate independently with each set being able to move upwards 152 mm and downwards 254 mm to take account of ground surface irregularities. The entire roller banks can caster up to 30° either side when the carrier tank makes a turn. No modification is necessary to couple the mineclearing roller system to a tank as special adaptors shaped to the front glacis of each MBT are provided. The rollers are connected to the tank by a standard 5-tonne lifting device which is available in any tank unit for maintenance purposes. Using such a device two soldiers can fit the system in about 15 minutes. In an emergency the system can be disconnected from the tank from within the carrier tank without the crew having to

RKM mineclearing rollers fitted to Leopard 1 MBT

leave the interior. This manual release facility can be completed in 30 seconds.

Status
In production. In service with Israeli armed forces and exported to several countries.

Manufacturer
Urdan Industries Limited, Industrial Zone, Netanya 42378, Israel.
Tel: 972 53 338074. Telex: 341822 uasf il.
Fax: 972 53 610246.

TAAS – Israel Industries POMINS II Portable Mine Neutralisation System

Description

Developed and proved by the Israel Defence Force, POMINS II is described as a second-generation portable mine neutralisation system that can be carried by two men. Designed for infantry use it can be set up and used in less than 1 minute to clear a path through anti-personnel minefields, barbed wire or both. No details have yet been released referring to the cleared path width or length.

POMINS II consists of two subsystems each carried by one man using a special backpack harness that is an integral part of the system. The two subsystems are the launcher, comprising a rocket motor and the forward part of a line charge, and the container with the rear part of the line charge. In use the two subsystems are set approximately 1 m from the starting point of the path to be cleared. The covers are removed from both subsystems and the line charges are connected by a quick-connector. The system is then ready for use and

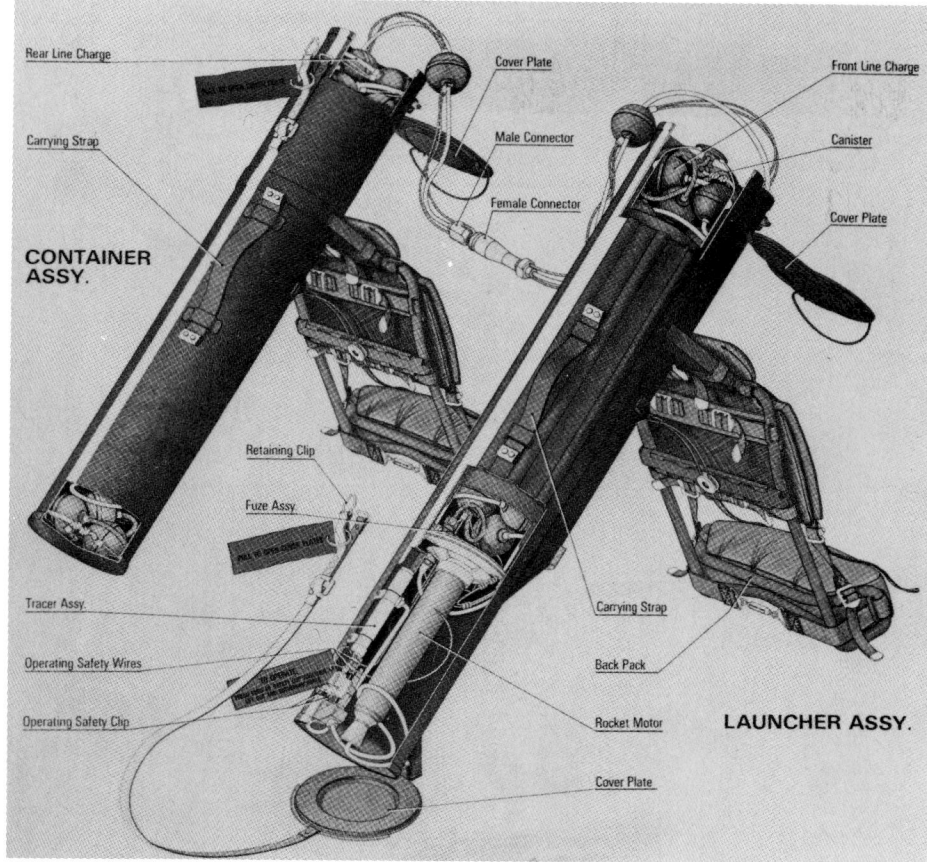

Main components of POMINS II portable mine neutralisation system

5 seconds the fuze ignites the line charge to clear a path. At night a marker indicates the beginning of the cleared path.

Safety features incorporated into POMINS II are such that the launch pin cannot be removed until the covers of the sections have been removed. Even then two actions are required to withdraw the launch pin. These are that the arms of a safety catch have to be pressed together to release a pull ring and only then can the launch pin be pulled. Another safety feature is the delay period that allows troops to take cover before the launch, and the system is trajectory-safe as only deployment of the front line charge completes the arming of the fuze. The fuze meets the safety requirements of MIL-STD-1316B.

POMINS II can withstand submersion in 1 m of water, a 5 m drop onto concrete (simulating a parachute drop) and loose cargo transportation. Both subsystems are watertight and dustproof. For transport both subsystems are wrapped in clear, heat-sealed polyethylene bags and packed in a foamed polyurethane case. The packed case weighs approximately 70 kg.

See also the entry on APOBS in the United States of America section.

Specifications

Subsystem	Launcher	Container
Material	aluminium	aluminium
Length	1.1 m	0.84 m
Diameter	170 mm	155 mm
Weight with		
backpack harness	25 kg	22 kg

Status
In production. In service with Israeli armed forces.

Manufacturer
TAAS – Israel Industries Ltd, POB 1044, Ramat Hasharon 47100, Israel.
Tel: (3) 542 52 22. Telex: 33 719 misbit il.
Fax: (3) 48 96 39.

when the launch pin is withdrawn a delay unit is activated to allow time (17 seconds) for nearby troops to take cover. A canister, propelled by the rocket motor, then leaves the launcher which draws out the forward and rear interconnected line charges. When the entire line charge is extended it falls to the ground and after

---

Cleared Lane Explosive Widening and Proofing Charge (CLEWP)

Description
The Cleared Lane Explosive Widening and Proofing Charge (CLEWP), an explosive line charge, is used to clear a 150 m long path through a minefield thereby allowing the safe passage of tanks and other vehicles. It is commonly used in conjunction with a tank carrying a mineplough or rollers to ensure that the cleared path is free of anti-personnel mines and other mines that may have escaped the mechanical clearing method.

CLEWP is carried in an armoured container on the back of the clearing tank. As the carrier tank moves into the minefield a pyrotechnic device blows the spring-loaded lid off the container and onto the ground where it acts as an anchor for the charge. As the tank moves forward the charge is laid along the path behind it. The charge has 6 kg of explosive per metre and the charge string is 150 m long. When the end is reached the armoured container is dropped from the vehicle which then moves forward at least 20 m. The charge is then fired by remote-control from within the carrier

Lid of Cleared Lane Explosive Widening and Proofing Charge (CLEWP) resting on ground as charge is pulled from container

tank. The resultant explosion removes any mines or other explosive devices from the cleared path. A fail-safe protection circuit is used to prevent the possibility of an explosion within the container. It is possible to activate only part of the charge.

Status
Development.

Manufacturer
TAAS – Israel Industries Ltd, POB 1044, Ramat Hasharon 47100, Israel.
Tel: (3) 542 52 22. Telex: 33 719 misbit il.
Fax: (3) 48 96 39.

No 21 Demolition Bangalore Torpedo Charge

Description
Although this charge is used primarily to breach barbed wire fences it may also be employed against minefields. The assembly consists of four sections of aluminium

pipe charge, four sleeve couplings and two head units. The charge is actuated by a No 41 firing device with an 18 second delay.

The 1.1 m long charge sections are assembled into the charge unit and pushed into the minefield. Detonation is then accomplished by use of the No 41 firing unit and the resultant explosion clears a narrow path by detonating the mines underneath it.

Specifications
Total charge assembly weight: 19.35 kg
Single charge section
Length: 1.1 m
Diameter: 57 mm
Weight: 4 kg
Charge type: cast TNT
Charge weight: 3.3 kg

Status
In service with the Israeli Army.

Manufacturer
TAAS – Israel Industries Ltd, POB 1044, Ramat Hasharon 47100, Israel.
Tel: (3) 542 52 22. Telex: 33 719 misbit il.
Fax: (3) 48 96 39.

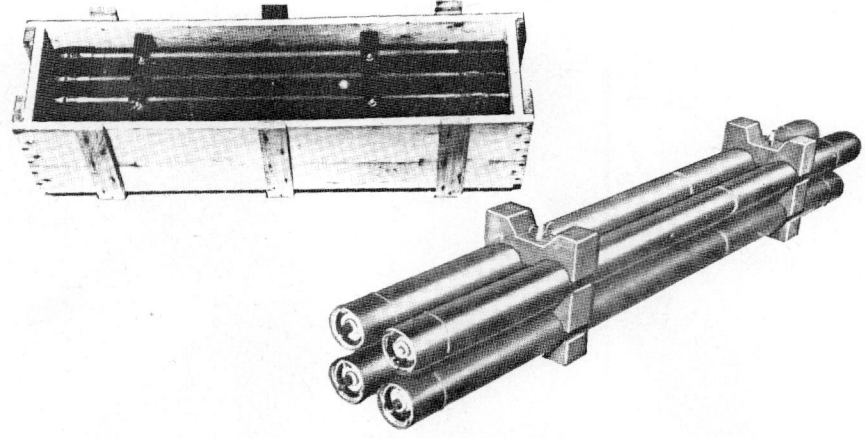

No 21 demolition Bangalore torpedo charge

No 30 Demolition Pipe Charge

Description
The pipe charge assembly consists of 26 steel pipe charge sections, two front skids fitted with obstacle clearing wheels and four detonating units fitted with No 41 firing devices that have 18 second delays.

The pipe charge is used for breaching barbed wire fences and minefields. The 2.162 m long sections are assembled into a unit of the required length and an obstacle-clearing skid unit is fixed to the front to facilitate pushing the charge into position. Detonation is accomplished by the 380 mm long detonating unit fitted with a No 41 firing device. The wide path cleared by the resulting explosion is some 50 m long.

Specifications
Pipe charge section
Length: 2.162 m
Diameter: 55 mm
Weight: 8.5 kg
Charge type: Composition B
Charge weight: 3 kg

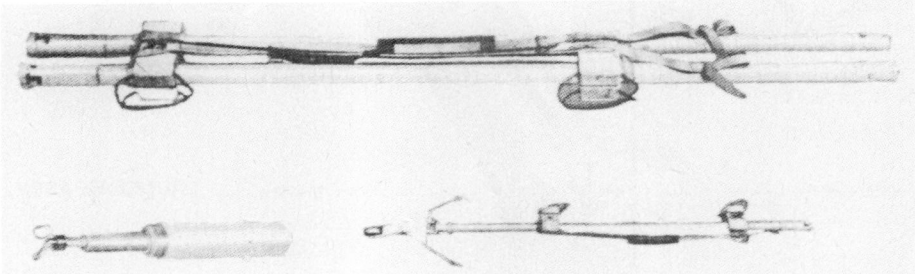

No 30 demolition pipe charge

Pipe skid unit
Length: 2.7 m (with pipe section)
Weight: 17 kg

Detonating unit
Length: 380 mm (with No 41 firing device)
Weight: 1.5 kg (with No 41 firing device)
Charge type: Composition B
Charge weight: 0.5 kg

Status
In service with the Israeli Army.

Manufacturer
TAAS – Israel Industries Ltd, POB 1044, Ramat Hasharon 47100, Israel.
Tel: (3) 542 52 22. Telex: 33 719 misbit il.
Fax: (3) 48 96 39.

Israeli Mineclearing Equipments

Description
In addition to the Israeli mineclearing equipments mentioned elsewhere in this section the Israeli defence forces also operate two further items.

One is a special turretless Centurion mineclearing tank. This vehicle has its turret replaced by an armoured enclosed superstructure provided with roof hatches and mountings for at least three machine guns. The tank pushes a set of RKM mineclearing rollers and more combat engineering and mineclearing equipment is stowed along each side of the vehicle and superstructure. Some of these vehicles have been observed fitted with Blazer reactive armour.

The second item of equipment is a towed minefield clearance system based on a single-axle trailer. The system uses a rocket and explosive-filled hose which are fired electronically from a towing vehicle.

Status
In service with the Israeli defence forces.

Centurion tank converted to mineclearing role and fitted with RKM mineclearing rollers

Israeli towed mineclearing system

JAPAN

Japanese Mineclearing Equipment

Description
Japan is known to have developed at least two items of mineclearing equipment. The first is a tank-mounted mineclearing roller system on which no information is available, and the second a rocket-propelled explosive-filled mineclearing charge, known as the Type 70 flexible detonating cable, designed for clearing anti-personnel minefields. The equipment consists of a rocket launcher frame and a rocket with a wire rope attached to its end. The rope is attached to eight coils of flexible detonating cable. The end of this cable is attached to a nylon rope which is anchored to the ground. The rocket is fired across the minefield and brought to a halt by the anchored cable. It falls to the ground and the detonating cable is ignited, clearing a path about 130 m long through the anti-personnel minefield.

Status
In service with the Japanese Self-Defence Force (Army).

Manufacturer
Type 70 flexible detonating cable: Aeronautical and

Type 70 flexible detonating cable ready for launch. On left is anchor and nylon rope, in centre coil of flexible detonating cable, and on right rocket launcher and rocket

Space Division, Nissan Motor Company Limited, 5-1 3-chome, Momoi, Suginami-ku, Tokyo, Japan. Tel: (3) 390 1111. Fax: (3) 399 9100.

PAKISTAN

Pakistan Ordnance Factories Bangalore Torpedo

Description
The Bangalore Torpedo produced by the Pakistan Ordnance Factories is orthodox in design and uses a steel tube filled with Amatol 50:50. It can be fired from a distance using a variety of standard detonators and may be used for demolition purposes as well as mineclearing. Each unit is fitted with connecting lugs to allow units to be connected in line to create longer minefield breaches.

Specifications
Weight: 6.6 kg
Length: 1.83 m
Diameter: 41.3 mm

Filling: Amatol 50:50

Status
In production.

Manufacturer
Pakistan Ordnance Factories, Wah Cantt, Pakistan. Tel: 0596 82019. Telex: 5840 pofac pk. Fax: 51 584175.

POLAND

PW-LWD Tank-mounted Rocket-propelled Equipment

Description
This equipment consists of a rocket (probably an AT-1 Snapper ATGW) with a 170 m explosive-filled hose attached and is mounted in a boat-shaped container on the left and/or right rear of a T-55A MBT which may also be fitted with the KMT-4 mineclearing plough. This equipment model is known to be in service with the Polish Army and has the designation PW-LWD. It has also been observed mounted on Polish Army T-72 MBTs.

The PTS tracked amphibian has also been observed carrying a modified S-60 57 mm anti-aircraft gun carriage fitted with two launcher bins for a 170 m long rocket-propelled explosive hose which is essentially similar to the PW-LWD. The carriage allows a full 360° traverse and the system is used to clear gaps in mined coastal waters and rivers.

Status
In service with the Polish Army.

Manufacturer
State factories.

Polish Army PW-LWD carried on a T-55A MBT fitted with KMT-4 plough-type mineclearing equipment, provision for mounting roller-type mineclearing equipment, and launcher bins for rocket-propelled explosive hose for mineclearing

ROMANIA

D-5M Mineclearing System

Description
The Romanian D-5M mineclearing system is essentially a copy of the KMT-5M mineclearing plough and roller system (see entry in this section) and is normally mounted on a T-55 tank.

The system can be mounted on the tank by a four-man team in 45 minutes and can be dismounted in an emergency in 1 second, without any crew member having to leave the vehicle. The driver can select to use either the roller or plough mode; as with the KMT-5 and KMT-5M they cannot be used together.

The mineclearing speed will vary according to a number of factors but is typically between 6 and 12 km/h. Each block of rollers clears a path 730 to 810 mm wide.

Specifications
Weight: between 7300 and 7500 kg
Width: 3.8 m
Length: 3.16 m
Length with carrier tank: 10.05 m

Status
In production. In service with the Romanian Army.

Manufacturer
Romanian state factories.

Romanian Army T-55 MBT fitted with D-5M mineclearing system

SINGAPORE

CIS Bangalore Torpedo

Description
The Bangalore Torpedo produced by Chartered Industries of Singapore is virtually identical to the US M1A1. It is issued in four-section tubes made from aluminium. Each section weighs 4.5 kg and is loaded with 3.25 kg of cast TNT grade 1. Each section is 1.1 m long and has a diameter of 55 mm. The sections are joined by connecting sleeves. Four compressed PETN boosters are used. Standard non-electric detonators can be employed to detonate the charges.

Status
Available.

Manufacturer
Chartered Industries of Singapore (PTE) Limited, 249

CIS Bangalore Torpedo

Jalan Boon Lay, Singapore 2261.
Tel: 2651066. Telex: 21419 cis rs.
Fax: 2610766.

Charge, Mineclearing, 50 m

Description
This mineclearing pipe charge is issued as a kit consisting of 24 main sections, two front skid units and four detonating units. The 24 main sections can be joined together to clear a path through a minefield 50 m long and 0.5 m wide, but the set may be used to form shorter charge lengths as required.

The front skid unit contains no explosive, is 2.6 m long and weighs 12 kg. The main function of this unit is to carry the remainder of the charge across the gap to be breached. It has on its nose a hinged carrier assembly with three small plastic wheels which enable the charge to be pushed manually across the ground from the rear. The charge may be pushed into place either fully assembled or assembly can be gradually carried out as the charge is emplaced.

Each main section is 2.14 m long and has a diameter

of 51 mm. Weight is 10 kg and the explosive filling is 3 kg of Composition B. Each unit has push-on connectors to join it to other sections, the front skid unit or a detonator unit.

A detonator unit is 210 mm long, 51 mm in diameter and weighs 1 kg, of which 0.5 kg is the Composition B filling. It is the last unit to be added to the pipe charge although on long charges an extra detonator unit may be added in the centre. The detonator unit, and thus the charge, may be detonated electrically or by a blasting cap.

Status
In production.

Manufacturer
Chartered Industries of Singapore (PTE) Limited, 249
Jalan Boon Lay, Singapore 2261.
Tel: 2651066. Telex: 21419 cis rs.
Fax: 2610766.

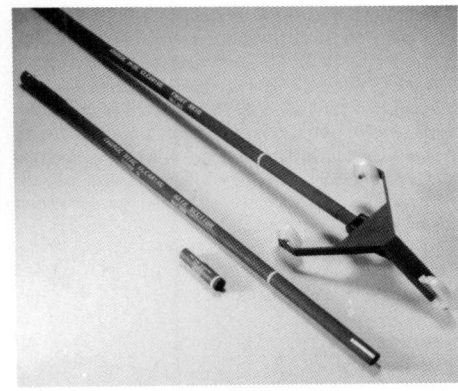

Charge, Mineclearing, 50 m

SOUTH AFRICA

Plofadder 160 Mineclearing System

Description

The Plofadder 160 (Puff Adder) mineclearing system was developed and placed in production by SOMCHEM, a subsidiary of Armscor. Development commenced in mid-1984 and was completed by late 1989. Service acceptance was in mid-1990 with the first production system completed later the same year. Plofadder was first used operationally in Angola during 1987 and 1988.

Plofadder 160 consists of a container which can be carried on the rear of a truck, armoured vehicle or trailer. Inside the container is a 100 mm diameter solid propellant rocket, 170 m of coiled explosive woven like a rope, and a retarding system.

The system is deployed 50 m from the edge of the minefield to be cleared and the safe and arm unit which couples the rocket to the line is activated. The total time taken to prepare the system for operation is less than 3 minutes. The operator, typically seated under cover in an armoured carrier or towing vehicle, then presses a firing button to activate the system. The rocket breaks through the roof of the container, taking the explosive line with it. For retardation the Plofadder uses a drum-type hydraulic brake which is less susceptible to wind influence than parachutes.

Once the line falls to the ground it is automatically detonated after a delay of approximately 20 seconds. Typically, the system can clear a path through single-impulse anti-tank mines from 120 to 160 m long and 4.5 to 4.8 m wide, depending on the type of soil and the mines involved. Accuracy of line charge fall to line of aim tolerance is an angle of 10° and the tolerance accuracy of breach length is 10 m.

Plofadder 160 can be used in tandem to clear minefields in depth. It can be used operationally over a temperature range of from −15 to +65°C while the shelf life is more than 5 years over a temperature range of +5 to +35°C.

A launch pack weighs 1550 kg and measures 2509 × 1012 × 1320 mm.

SOMCHEM is also developing two portable mine-clearing systems to meet South African Army require-ments. The Plofadder 38 is a one-man system intended to clear a path 38 m long and 0.9 m wide. The Plofadder 150 is a four-man system capable of clearing a path 150 m long and 0.9 m wide.

Status

In production. In service with the South African Defence Forces.

Manufacturer

SOMCHEM, PO Box 187, Somerset West 7129, South Africa.
Tel: 27 24 429 2911. Fax: 27 24 42 2111.

Looking along the line of a Plofadder mineclearing system detonation

A Plofadder 160 mineclearing system loaded onto a Büffel APC

Loading a Plofadder 160 launch pack onto a vehicle

SPAIN

EXPAL Bangalore Torpedo

Description

The EXPAL Bangalore Torpedo follows conventional lines and is issued in six units. The first unit is a sheet steel ogival head and the other five are steel tubes each filled with 2.7 kg of Amatol 80:20. The units are joined together by sleeves and the weight of the complete torpedo is 28 kg. Detonation can be carried out by electrical means or by a blasting cap.

Status

In production.

Manufacturer

Explosivos Alaveses SA, Orense 68, 10th Floor, E-28020 Madrid, Spain.
Tel: (1) 571 5559. Telex: 43484 xpal e.
Fax: (1) 279 7914.

SWEDEN

Minvält 1

Description

Development of a mine roller system to equip the Swedish Army's tank divisions began at the Tank Warfare School at Skövde in 1979-80. Production of the *Minvält 1* (Mine Roller 1 – also known as the NMH 1K) system began during late 1987 and deliveries began to all combat vehicle divisions in February 1989.

The *Minvält 1* system uses two sets of three heavy steel discs suspended from a coupling pushed in front of the carrier vehicle's tank tracks. Two types of coupling have been produced, Coupling 1 (*kopplingsfäste 1*) for use with variants of Centurion tank (*stridsvagn 101, 102, 104*) and Coupling 2 for use with the S-tank (*stridsvagn 103*). The mine rollers are intended to detonate pressure-activated anti-tank mines. Tilt-rod activated anti-tank mines located between the rollers are activated by a chain slung between each set of rollers. Each set of rollers is able to withstand the detonation of 15 to 20 heavy anti-tank mines and still continue to detonate mines across the full roller width.

The overall weight of the mine rollers is 6000 kg with the coupling weighing a further 1000 kg. The mine roller, complete with the couplings, can be transported in sections on trucks fitted with cranes. A tank crew can fix the mine roller to a vehicle in between 30 to 40 minutes and minefield clearing can then commence immediately. The minefield breaching speed is between 8 and 15 km/h, depending on the terrain. Short distances can be cleared at a maximum speed of 25 km/h.

The mine rollers can be removed by the crew in 20 minutes but for emergency release the mine roller is removed in 5 seconds by releasing four explosive

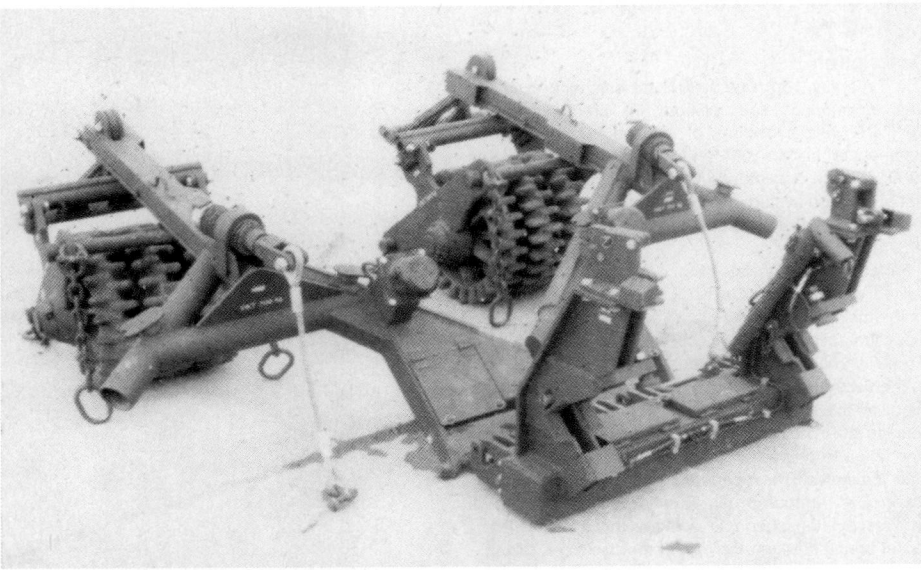

Swedish Minvält 1 mine rollers with Coupling 1 for attachment to Centurion-type MBTs

spring bolts in the coupling assembly. The emergency release system is controlled by the driver using a TA 11 igniter system (*tändapparat TA 11*) connected to a 24 V supply.

The mine roller system is intended to be used in conjunction with a cleared lane marking system which is still under development. One system under examination involves a central spray device mounted on the rear of the mine roller carrier tank.

Status

In production for the Swedish Army.

Manufacturer

Norbergs Maskin & Hydraulik AB, Box 69, S-77801 Norberg, Sweden.
Tel: 46 223 231 50. Telex: 7524 norberg s.
Fax: 46 223 204 32.

Mineclearing Device m/60

Description

The Mineclearing Device m/60 (referred to as a mineclearing snake) consists of a rocket which is fired from a simple launching device and to which a hose filled with explosive is connected. At the rear end of the hose a 3.6 m diameter parachute is fastened to stretch the hose so that, when it falls to the ground, the hose is practically straight. There are igniters in the front and rear ends of the hose which ignite delay compositions when the rocket is fired and which, after 15 seconds, initiate the explosive in the hose via primers.

At detonation all anti-personnel mines within a distance varying between 150 mm and 1 m, depending on the sensitivity of the mines, are exploded. Anti-tank mines with normal sensitivity are also exploded while more shockproof mines are thrown aside or uncovered. The device produces a clearly defined path with a

width of 300 mm to 2 m and a length of up to 150 m. The rocket has a range of 200 to 225 m.

The device can be prepared for firing in less than 1 minute. It is carried by a section of seven men supervised by a section commander. One man carries the rocket with the launching device (which also serves as a carrying rack) and the detonator. The other six men each carry 25 m of hose and one of them also carries the parachute. The rocket pack weighs 18 kg, the hose pack with parachute 15.5 kg, and the other hose packs 14 kg.

Specifications
Rocket
Calibre: 103 mm
Weight:
    (complete) 9.5 kg
    (connection extras) 1.7 kg
    (propellant) 4.3 kg
Velocity: 50 m/s

Range: 200 to 225 m

Explosive hose
Material: terylene
Total length: 150 m (6 × 25 m sections)
Diameter: 32 mm
Weight per 25 m length: 12.5 kg
Weight of filling: 0.4 kg/m
Type of filling: desensitised PETN

Status

Production complete. In service with the Swedish Army.

Manufacturer

Bofors AB, S-691 80 Bofors, Sweden.
Tel: 46 586 81000. Telex: 73210.
Fax: 46 586 58142.

UNITED KINGDOM

Giant Viper Anti-tank Mineclearing Equipment

Description

The Giant Viper (L5) mine clearance system consists of a 230 m long, 67 mm diameter hose filled with plastic explosive. This is packed coiled in a wooden box which is mounted on a two-wheeled trailer, which can be towed by a variety of tracked vehicles (for a photograph of this trailer refer to entry in the *Trailers* section). The British Army uses the Chieftain AVRE, Centurion AVRE, FV432 APC or the Combat Engineer Tractor to tow the trailer. The hose is fired across the minefield by a cluster of eight rocket motors. The tail end of the hose is fitted with arrester gear in the form of three parachutes which straighten the hose during flight and operate the striker mechanism, which

detonates the charge after the hose has landed.

The equipment is used as follows: the Giant Viper is towed to the firing point between 115 and 140 m from the edge of the minefield and the trailer, which remains attached to the towing vehicle during the operation, is lined up on the proposed line of flight, taking into account any factors which will alter the trajectory, such as wind. Giant Viper is then fired electrically from the towing vehicle. Giant Viper was designed to blast a passage for vehicles through a minefield up to 183 m long and 7.3 m wide. During trials, up to 90 per cent of anti-tank mines were cleared, provided that they were not blast-proofed or multi-impulse fuzed.

An extension of the Giant Viper system known as the Tandem Firing Concept was developed for use with various towing vehicles, including MBTs. The vehicle tows two Giant Viper trailers, one behind the other. The rear Giant Viper is fired outside the minefield as normal

and the trailer is jettisoned. The vehicle and the remaining Giant Viper trailer then proceed into the minefield to the second firing point where the process is repeated. This allows minefields up to 400 m deep to be breached.

Each Giant Viper system requires the support of a 4000 kg truck. The expendable stores are packed in containers which can be manhandled, except the box containing the hose which weighs 2136 kg and is handled by a forklift truck or crane.

For training purposes, practice equipment is available which is identical to the live system in all respects except that the line charge contains an inert filling. The training version is supplied with sufficient components to enable a maximum of six projections to be made. This equipment is in service with the British Army.

In mid-1992 the Ammunition Division of Royal Ordnance was awarded a contract worth $16.9 million to carry out a mid-life improvement programme to the Giant Viper mineclearing system. The contract involves development over a two-year period with the production phase taking a further 30 months.

The main improvements involve the replacement of the eight-rocket cluster by a single new rocket using a new launch tube and having a slightly increased impulse to provide an improved lay of the hose. Other changes include a new safety, arming and firing unit, an advanced electrical system to allow all pre-firing checks to be carried out from within the towing vehicle, replacing the drogue chutes with Velcro-type tear webbing, and replacing the practice hose with a new ballistically matched rope with a heavy central steel wire for training purposes over a life of at least 100 firings.

The improved Giant Viper will provide a user with reduced life cycle costs, quicker into-action times, improved reliability and safety, and a reduction in training times.

Specifications
Hose box
Weight: 2136 kg
Length: 3.15 m
Width: 1.74 m
Height: 1.18 m

Hose
Length: 230 m
Diameter: 67 mm
Filling: aluminised plastic explosive PE6/Al

Head range: (average) 300-350 m
Tail range: (average) 110-120 m

The detonation of Giant Viper anti-tank mineclearing equipment during an exercise in the Gulf region

Accuracy: 10° either side of aim
Cleared zone: 183 m (minimum) × 7.3 m wide

Status
In production. In service with the British Army and Jordan (100 units).

Manufacturer
British Aerospace Defence Limited, Royal Ordnance Division, Euxton Lane, Chorley, Lancashire PR7 6AD, UK.
Tel: 0257 65511. Fax: 0257 242199.

Rapid Operational Minefield Attack and Neutralisation System (ROMANS)

Description
The Rapid Operational Minefield Attack and Neutralisation System (ROMANS) has been developed jointly by

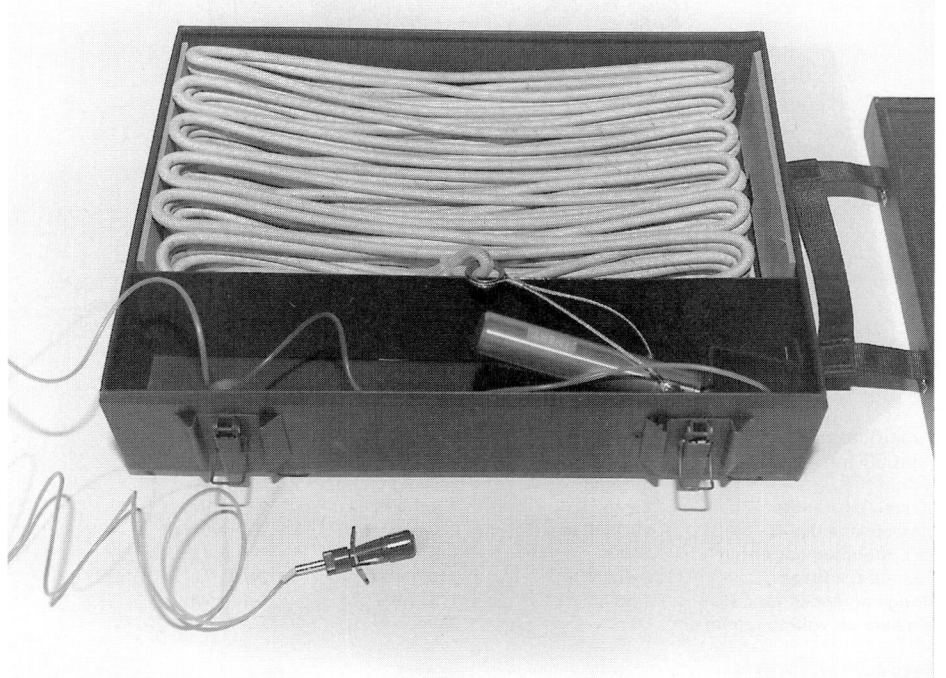

Rapid Operational Minefield Attack and Neutralisation System (ROMANS)

Royal Ordnance Ammunition Division (Chorley) and North American Explosives (Graham, Kentucky) – North American Explosives is a joint venture between Royal Ordnance and The Ensign-Bickford Company of Simsbury, Connecticut. The system was developed in response to a US Army requirement for a Small Arms Projected Line Charge (SAPLIC).

SAPLIC calls for an anti-personnel mineclearing

system which can be carried and operated by one man and produces a minefield breach 50 m long and 0.6 m wide. The system has to weigh no more than 9 kg. (The small arms projection requirement was later dropped.)

The essential features of ROMANS are a carrying case/launcher; a ready-to-fire rocket; a line charge containing Demex 200 explosive (which is insensitive to bullet strike); a shock tube for rocket and charge initiation; and a retardation system. All these components are contained within the carrying case.

In use the system is carried to a point close to the minefield to be breached. The lid is opened and the light metal spacer removed. The lid can be weighted with rocks or similar materials to provide extra anchoring. The shock tubes are deployed to a point about 20 m behind the unit and the rocket is fired. The rocket travels in a low trajectory, towing out the line charge. A tear webbing system is used to provide as straight a lay as possible. The line charge is then detonated, producing a path 50 m long and 0.6 m wide. Computer modelling and live firings have produced a minimum 95 per cent clearance possibility.

By the end of 1991, prototypes were produced for user evaluation in the United States and cord evaluation studies have been undertaken by Sandia Laboratories. A study on an automatic detonation system has been completed.

Status
Development.

Manufacturers
British Aerospace Defence Limited, Royal Ordnance Division, Euxton Lane, Chorley, Lancashire PR7 6AD, UK.
Tel: 0257 65511. Fax: 0257 242199.
North American Explosives, Highway 175, PO Box 146, Graham, Kentucky 42344, USA.
Tel: (502) 338 1988. Fax: (502) 338 4910.

Schermuly Rapid Anti-personnel Minefield Breaching System Mark 3 (RAMBS 3)

Description

The Rapid Anti-personnel Minefield Breaching System Mark 3 (RAMBS 3) is a self-contained, lightweight (7 kg), one-shot method of quickly clearing safe lanes through surface-laid anti-personnel minefields. RAMBS 3 uses a rocket-assisted Line Carrying Projectile (LCP) fired from a standard assault rifle to propel an explosive line 60 m across a minefield. Detonation of the line charge enables the breaching of the minefield (including tripwires) by secondary detonation, disruption or dispersal of the mines.

The breach is based on the use of 60 m of explosive line which is coiled ready for use in the bottom tray of a camouflaged haversack. Before launching the kit is secured by a restraining strap and the LCP, which is attached to the explosive line by a bridle, is fitted over the rifle muzzle. Using a standard rifle round and bullet, the LCP is propelled across the minefield, towing the explosive line in the direction in which the breach is to be made. The explosive line is then command detonated using a simple percussion firing device. The resultant explosion clears a path approximately 60 m long and 0.6 m wide. With training, the entire operation can take less than 60 seconds. Lightsticks are provided as breach markers.

RAMBS 3 uses an RDX plastic bonded (PBX) explosive line which provides an improved blast overpressure in the mine killing zone. It is insensitive to

A Rapid Anti-personnel Minefield Breaching System Mark 3 (RAMBS 3) about to be fired

bullet attack and provides an improved discernible pathway in day, night or low visibility.

Status

In production for an undisclosed NATO customer.

Manufacturer

Pains-Wessex (Schermuly) Limited, High Post, Salisbury, Wiltshire SP4 6AS, UK.
Tel: 0722 411611. Telex: 47486 pw sch g.
Fax: 0722 412121.

Pearson Mine Ploughs

Development

The Pearson Mine Plough is available in three versions: the Track Width Mine Plough (TWMP); the Engineer Mine Plough (EMP) and the Full Width Mine Plough (FWMP). The TWMP has five tines per side, the EMP has seven, while the FWMP clears the whole width of the vehicle. The only difference between the TWMP and the EMP is the number of blades, and they are interchangeable.

The EMP comprises two independent ploughs, left and right, pivoted from a common mounting plate. Unlike ploughs which have a single pivot, the Pearson plough is mounted on a sophisticated linkage which provides maximum ploughing stability throughout the range of movement. The top link is a hydraulic cylinder which lowers and raises the plough from the control box operated by the driver.

The FWMP is the EMP with the addition of a third plough in the centre and two arms which locate the depth control skids in front of the ploughs. An EMP can be converted into an FWMP in about 20 minutes.

The only modifications to the vehicles required to fit the plough are two wedge blocks welded to the toe plate, an entry point for the single electrical harness, and a mounting bracket next to the driver for the control box. On most tanks the existing eyes at the top of the toe plate are used to pin the plough in place, enabling the plough to be fitted or removed within minutes. In an emergency the plough can be jettisoned using explosive pins.

The mounting system, harnesses and control box are identical to those used by the Pearson Combat Dozer (see entry under *Armoured engineer vehicles*).

Jacklift Pallet

The Pearson Jacklift Pallet enables front end attachments to be fitted and removed from fighting vehicles without the need for cranes or other lifting equipment. The hydraulic pallet enables two men to install a mine plough or bulldozer unit on any MBT in 10 to 15 minutes.

The Jacklift consists of a pallet with three independently operated hydraulic legs mounted on a demounting sledge. Unloading the pallet and sledge from a vehicle or container is achieved by towing the entire configuration down two ramps until it lays on the ground. The pallet, sledge and equipment may then be

Pearson Full Width Mine Plough (FWMP) fitted to Chieftain AVRE

Specifications

Type	FWMP	EMP	TWMP
Weight	2950 kg	2400 kg	2300 kg
Cleared lane width	3.8 m	2 × 1.4 m	2 × 1.1 m
Cleared lane depth	200-400 mm	200-400 mm	200-400 mm
Max operating current	240 A	240 A	240 A
Operating voltage	24/28 V	24/28 V	24/28 V
Ploughing speed range	1-10 km/h	1-10 km/h	1-10 km/h
Min safe ploughing radius	50 m	50 m	50 m

towed any distance into the required position.

The mine plough or bulldozer can then be raised to the required height for fitting to the vehicle by manually jacking the three hydraulic legs. This takes about 2 minutes. Each hydraulic leg incorporates an individual pump and ram unit which allows for precise control of height and pitch of the equipment to be fitted.

The Jacklift Pallet weighs 480 kg, is 4.1 m wide and 2.27 m long. Maximum lift is 555 mm and load capacity 5500 kg. Deck height is 190 mm.

Status

Production as required. In service with the British Army and in the Middle East, including Jordan.

Manufacturer

Pearson Engineering, Wincomblee Road, Walker, Newcastle upon Tyne NE6 3QS, UK.
Tel: 091 234 0001. Telex: 538253.
Fax: 091 262 0402.

Pearson Surface Mine Plough (SMP)

Description

The Pearson Surface Mine Plough (SMP) was designed to meet the requirements of the United Kingdom Ministry of Defence Staff Target 3916, and was selected by them after a programme of competitive evaluation.

The SMP is a multi-section, multi-bladed V-plough which physically removes mines from the path of a vehicle. The combination of the articulated blades and the in-built hydraulic system enables the plough to conform to the local topography, maintaining blade contact with the ground across its width. The blades are articulated in such a way that they are able to ride up and over small obstacles without damage, even at speed. The SMP has been demonstrated working with 100 per cent efficiency on forest tracks at speeds up to 25 km/h.

The SMP has been extensively tested on all types of terrain including hard surfaces, rutted tracks, grassland, moorland, sand and stony desert, all under wet and dry conditions. The tests were carried out using both a tracked APC and a 4 × 4 truck.

The SMP is light enough to be carried by vehicles from a 4 × 4 truck (heavier than 4 tonnes) to an MBT and is robust enough to pass blast trials and remain operational. It uses the Pearson Wedge Block Mounting System which enables it to be fitted to or removed from vehicles within a few minutes. The only vehicle modifications required are two wedge blocks welded to the toe plate (or a small adaptor bracket fitted), an entry point for the control/power harness, and an internal mounting bracket for the control box.

Variant

Airfield Clearance Plough (ACP)
The Airfield Clearance Plough (ACP) is a development of the SMP with the major difference being that the

Pearson Surface Mine Plough (SMP) fitted to FV432 APC fitted with Pearson Pathfinder Marking Device

ACP uses a straight angled blade. It is also heavier and stronger. Mines and other surface debris are cleared to one side so that by repeated passages a large area can be rapidly cleared. As with the SMP, the ACP requires no power while operating and can be fitted to a wide range of vehicles with little modification.

The ACP is being developed in co-operation with several European nations and a prototype has been demonstrated.

Specifications (SMP)

Weight: 1150 kg
Width overall: 4.6 m (18 blade version with deflectors)

Width of cleared path: 3.4 m (min, 18 blade version)
Max operating current: 140 A (intermittent)
Operating voltage: 24/28 V

Status

SMP in service with the British Army.
ACP under development.

Manufacturer

Pearson Engineering, Wincomblee Road, Walker, Newcastle upon Tyne NE6 3QS, UK.
Tel: 091 234 0001. Telex: 538253.
Fax: 091 262 0402.

COMIRO Full Width Mineclearing Roller

Description

The COMIRO full width mineclearing roller was designed to detonate anti-disturbance fuzed mines in the path of the host vehicle. It uses a single roller in the form of a helical coil which provides full width protection and can operate at speeds of up to 50 km/h. The system is fitted to the host vehicle with blow-out pins and is interchangeable with the SCAMBA full width mineclearing plough (see following entry). The unit has an overall width of 3 m and weighs 1450 kg. Power requirements are 24 V DC at 180 A (intermittent). The system is airportable.

Status

Prototypes.

Manufacturer

Firth Defence Systems Limited, Aston Works, Bramley, Leeds LS13 2BY, UK.
Tel: 0532 393293. Telex: 557571 frthds g.
Fax: 0532 590867.

COMIRO full width mineclearing roller fitted to FV432 APC

SCAMBA Full Width Mineclearing Plough

Description

The SCAMBA (Scatterable Minefield Breaching Apparatus) full width mineclearing plough can be used with a wide range of suitably adapted armoured vehicles from armoured personnel carriers upwards. It has been under development as a private venture since early 1987 and several prototypes have been built. The system was developed to provide a reliable high speed countermeasure to the threat posed by the

use of scatterable mines delivered by a variety of weapon systems.

The SCAMBA weighs 1200 kg so the carrier vehicle's mobility is not impaired. The system was designed for off-road conditions and mineclearing speeds of up to 20 km/h are typical; a variety of different terrains can be negotiated.

Blast-resistant materials are incorporated into the structure. A fragmentation deflection cone and a blast protection block mounted onto the vehicle toe plate combine to give a high degree of protection for the vehicle and crew. SCAMBA is attached to the carrier vehicle by three high tensile locating pins. Explosive

'blow-out' pins which enable the plough to be quickly jettisoned are also available. The mineclearing blades are raised and lowered using a winch controlled by the vehicle driver from under cover. Power for the winch is supplied from the carrier vehicle's inter-vehicle starting socket. Once the blades have been lowered operation is fully automatic.

The standard SCAMBA system clears a path 3.1 m wide. Plough blade extensions are an option to enable the cleared path to be widened. Other options include a mine detection coil and an electro-hydraulic mounting frame.

Specifications
Weight: 1200 kg
Cleared path width: 3.1 m
Operating speed: up to 20 km/h
Power requirements: 24 V DC, 180 A (intermittent)

Status
Prototypes. Has been tested by the British Army.

Manufacturer
Firth Defence Systems Limited, Aston Works, Bramley,
Leeds LS13 2BY, UK.
Tel: 0532 393293. Telex: 557571 frthds g.
Fax: 0532 590867.

SCAMBA full width mineclearing plough fitted to FV432 APC

Aardvark Rapid Area Clearance Equipment (RACE)

Description
The Aardvark Rapid Area Clearance Equipment
(RACE) was developed to meet the British Army's
General Staff Target 3916 for a scatterable mine
clearance device.

RACE is similar in concept to the Aardvark Joint
Services Flail Unit (see entry in this section) and uses
the same type of striker heads. The system has two
1.524 m rotors that operate independently but in
unison. The two rotors have their own individual motors
and together clear a path approximately 3.048 m wide.
Chain heads can be varied to suit the operational
conditions and types of mine being cleared. The flail
chains are 0.609 m long and were designed to disrupt,
lift and throw mines to one side. The system was
designed to clear mines with an explosive content of up
to 2 kg. The direction of rotation of the flails can be
changed in 3 seconds. Mines can be cleared from
most surfaces including cultivated fields, front banks
and some types of ditch. Typical clearance speeds are
15 km/h on hard surfaces and from 8 to 15 km/h cross-
country, depending on the operating conditions.

The RACE system can be installed on cross-country
trucks and light armoured vehicles such as M113 and
FV432 APCs; the only modification to the latter is the
provision of four bolts to which RACE can be quickly
attached. The size of the system is such that it can be
left on the vehicle without degrading its operational
capabilities. Normally the system would run off the
prime mover's hydraulic power take-off although the
prototype uses an auxiliary power unit.

Status
Prototype.

Manufacturer
Aardvark Clear Mine Limited, Shevock Farm, Insch,
Aberdeenshire AB5 6XQ, UK.
Tel: 0464 20122. Telex: 73509 aard g.
Fax: 0464 20985.

Aardvark Rapid Area Clearance Equipment (RACE) undergoing trials

Vickers-Aardvark Tank Flail

Description
The Aardvark flail device (see following entry) has
been adapted for attachment to armoured fighting
vehicles and as such is manufactured and marketed by
Vickers Defence Systems.

The complete flail unit is a bolt-on system that can be
attached to existing towing and lifting points on the
carrier vehicle using simple adaptor brackets – no
additional drillings or welds are required. To fit the
system takes 1 hour using a 2000 kg lifting device.

The flail system can be fitted to many types of
armoured vehicle other than tanks but the lowest
practical vehicle weight is 10 000 kg. The main components are a powerpack, hydraulic and electrical
connections, the rotor and flail assembly and a control
unit. The overall weight is approximately 4000 kg, of
which 2000 kg is the powerpack. The 135 hp diesel-
hydraulic powerpack is self-contained and mounted at
the rear of the vehicle where its weight counterbalances the rotor and flail assembly.

Hydraulic and electrical connections between the
powerpack, the rotor and flail assembly and the control
panel are routed through an armoured conduit attached
to the carrier vehicle hull. Universal couplings and
isolating valves are provided and there are parallel
systems to minimise the effects of damage. There is a
PTO on the hydraulic unit.

Final drive to the rotor is by 'V' drive belts, five each
side. The rotor runs at a constant speed and has a
much smaller diameter than previous flail types to
minimise blast effects. The chain coupling incorporates
an interlock system which accelerates the chain to
increase the impact velocity, reduces the chance of
tangling and modifies the rotor geometry to give the
most effective apparent diameter. Chain tips are
replaceable and alternative types are available (a
hammerhead chain tip weighs 0.9 kg). The rotor
diameter is 165 mm and runs at approximately 250 rpm
with a power input of 120 hp. There are 72 chain flails,
each with an effective length of 1.22 m and fitted at
50 mm centres in adjacent rows; there are six rows of
chains.

The control unit has start and stop and rotor
height/flail depth controls. An automatic control system
ensures that the chain tips penetrate the surface to a
constant depth, regardless of ground conditions or
contours. Blast effects are partially counteracted by a
further automatic override.

The flail system can clear a path 3.66 to 4.66 m wide
to a maximum theoretical flailing depth of 915 mm. The
beat pattern at 2 km/h is 2.66 beats/cm^2 which can
neutralise all known production mines to a buried depth
of 75 mm.

The system can survive mine blasts equivalent to
10 kg of TNT. The life of a chain tip is between 30 and

Vickers-Aardvark flail on Centurion MBT

50 hours while a chain will last for approximately 300 hours. The drive belts and bearings have a life of 200 hours.

Status
Ready for production.

Manufacturer
Vickers Defence Systems, Scotswood Road, Newcastle upon Tyne NE99 1BX, UK.
Tel: 091 273 8888. Telex: 53104.
Fax: 091 273 2324.

Aardvark Joint Services Flail Unit (JSFU)

Description
The Aardvark Mark 3 Joint Services Flail Unit (JSFU) is a half-track vehicle designed to carry the Aardvark flail device in operational conditions. The flail assembly is attached to the rear chassis and controlled from a two- or three-man fully armoured crew cab. The power train, incorporating a 120 hp in-line diesel engine with an integrally mounted 16-speed transmission and lockable differential, is located between the crew cab and the flail assembly and is fully protected by an armour-plated compartment hood and a full length belly plate.

The flail assembly consists of a 3.05 m wide, 175 mm diameter, double-sleeved rotor carrying 72 chains along a triple helix design (seven chains per 305 mm). Each chain can be fitted with a choice of different striker heads (for example, disc, ball or T-head hammer).

Power to the rotor is supplied from a power train PTO via the assembly support arms. A resistant blast deflector plate is attached between the flail and the prime mover. The boom arms are raised and lowered hydraulically and incorporate automatic contouring and depth control features. The air force/hard surface version can accommodate an angle dozer plate and support wheel attachments.

Clearance speeds vary depending on the type and quantity of devices encountered. An optimum beat or sweep pattern should be maintained throughout active operations. Trials have shown that rough terrain/cross-country speeds average 3 km/h while the unit has cleared surface-laid objects on hard surfaces (for

Aardvark Joint Services Flail Unit (JSFU) Mark 3C in action in Kuwait

example, airfields) at 15 km/h.

Optional extras include a 7.62 mm machine-gun turret installation on the cab roof and side-mounted smoke dischargers.

Specifications
Crew: 1 + 1 or 2
Weight: approx 12 000 kg
Length: 8.08 m
Width: 3.55 m
Height: 2.67 m
Max road speed: 20 km/h
Max operating gradient: 33%

Beaten path: 3.05 m

Status
In production. Units have been sold to the United Kingdom, United States, countries in Africa, the Middle East (including Egypt and Saudi Arabia) and Sweden.

Manufacturer
Aardvark Clear Mine Limited, Shevock Farm, Insch, Aberdeenshire AB5 6XQ, UK.
Tel: 0464 20122. Telex: 73509 aard g.
Fax: 0464 20985.

UNITED STATES OF AMERICA

Project Remote
In response to an urgent request from the US Army and Marine Corps operating in Saudi Arabia during the run-up to Operation Desert Storm, the US Army Tank-Automotive Command (TACOM) Research, Development and Engineering Center assembled and outfitted 20 remote-control modification kits for M60A1/A3 tanks to allow them to be operate with track width mine ploughs (TWMPs) for remotely controlled mineclearing in forward areas. The programme was named Project Remote.

The Project Remote kits were based on target tank systems modified and supplemented with TACOM-supplied equipment, including an interface for the TWMP. The kits contained various safety override systems with duplication of some critical systems and mechanisms, including the communications systems.

The remotely controlled M60s with TWMPs were intended to operate in two-vehicle teams, the M60 breaching tank and a controlling M60 or M1 Abrams

tank. The operator in the control tank guides the breaching tank using the control tank's main gun optics or thermal imaging equipment.

The short duration of Operation Desert Storm did not allow any operational use of the Project Remote kits but they have since been fitted to tanks at several US Army locations in the United States.

Status
In service with the US Army.

Vehicle Magnetic Signature Duplicator (VEMASID)

Description
The Vehicle Magnetic Signature Duplicator (VEMASID) is a system designed to detonate magnetically fuzed mines before the carrier vehicle reaches them. The VEMASID system projects an electromagnetic field in front of the host vehicle. Any magnetically fuzed mines in the path of the carrier will then be detonated before the carrier reaches them.

VEMASID operates by using an electromagnetic coil mounted on the front of the carrier vehicle. Radiation from the coil induces the magnetically fuzed mines to detonate. It has been fitted onto the M1 and M60 tank series and M109-series self-propelled howitzers and can be adapted to a number of combat vehicles. On all vehicles the coil is carried over the front hull of the vehicle. The coil is usually held in place by tie-down straps, and can be fitted by four men within 60 minutes. VEMASID can be used in conjunction with other mineclearing devices such as mine rollers or ploughs

Arrow points to Vehicle Magnetic Signature Duplicator (VEMASID) coil on turret of M109A3 self-propelled howitzer

for breaching minefields with both pressure and magnetically fuzed mines.

The coil for the majority of vehicles weighs 129.7 kg. A typical assembly measures 1.625 × 0.86 × 0.305 m. The system operates off the vehicle's 28 V power supply and the weight of the electronics package carried internally is 12.7 kg. The full VEMASID kit consists of the coil, amplifier, control panel (placed near tank commander or driver) and cables.

During 1987 Honeywell Inc, Defense Systems Division (now Alliant Techsystems Inc) of Minnetonka, Minnesota, was awarded a \$4 402 000 increment as part of a \$20 900 537 contract for full-scale engineering development, fabrication, test and demonstration of VEMASID kits. The contract covered a total of 30 testbed units, six test sensors and 25 training mines. The work was completed by September 1992. The system was developed under contract to the US Army's Belvoir Research, Development and Engineering Center and Project Manager Mines, Countermine and Demolitions (PM-MCD) at Fort Belvoir, Virginia.

Status
Type classified for the M109 and M992 series of vehicles.

Manufacturer
Alliant Techsystems Inc, 5901 Lincoln Drive, Edina, Minnesota 55436, USA.
Tel: (612) 939 2467. Fax: (612) 939 2749.

Field-expedient Countermine System (FCS)

Description
The Field-expedient Countermine System (FCS) was developed by Alliant Techsystems in under 100 days in order to meet a US Marine Corps 'Desert Storm' requirement for a method of neutralising magnetically fuzed mines. The FCS was developed in co-operation with the Program Manager Engineer Systems at the US Marine Corps Research, Development and Acquisition Command in Quantico, Virginia and was tested under desert conditions at the Marine Corps Air-Ground Combat Center in Twenty Nine Palms, California. Using experience gained with the development of FCS, Alliant Techsystems is completing system development of a Magnetic Countermine System (MACS) for the US Marine Corps. The design of the FCS was based on the Required Operational Capability Document for a MACS.

The FCS operates by projecting an electromagnetic field ahead of the host vehicle to allow a magnetic mine fuze to sense the field and detonate prematurely. The system is self-contained and consists of an electronic controller which generates a magnetic signature through a flexible coil that is field-wound from two spools of wire and secured to the front of the host vehicle. A support kit contains tools and minimal mounting material. A remote status indicator detects faults in the system and allows the vehicle driver or commander to monitor system operation.

The system weighs less than 43 kg and has no effect on host vehicle performance. Externally mounted components and electrical connections are waterproofed and operable when submerged in salt water. No through-hull modifications are required and the system can be installed or removed by two men within 60 minutes without auxiliary support equipment. The coil is flexible and allows the normal operation of components such as an Assault Amphibian Vehicle (AAV) bowplane or a Light Armoured Vehicle (LAV) trim vane. The kit can be adapted to a variety of wheeled and tracked vehicles. No auxiliary power supply is required.

Status
In service with the US Marine Corps.

Manufacturer
Alliant Techsystems Inc, Ordnance Systems, 5901 Lincoln Drive, Edina, Minnesota 55436, USA.
Tel: (612) 939 2467. Fax: (612) 939 2749.

Caterpillar Track Width Mine Plough

Description
In response to a US Marine Corps requirement, Caterpillar Inc developed a Track Width Mine Plough (Plow) for use with the AAV7 series of amphibious assault vehicles. The plough is lightweight (2041 kg) for amphibious operations and uses six tines per blade; the tine depth is operator adjustable and they can be replaced. For transport the plough is carried stowed within the vehicle width and there are automatically positioned fold-out blade wings. The plough follows ground contours independent of vehicle attitude and can be released should a blade hit an immovable object. A skid plate is located behind each blade.

Specifications
Weight: 2041 kg
Overall plough width:
  (travelling) 3.276 m
  (deployed without wing) 3.632 m
  (deployed with wing) 4.75 m
Blade width: (each) 1.117 m

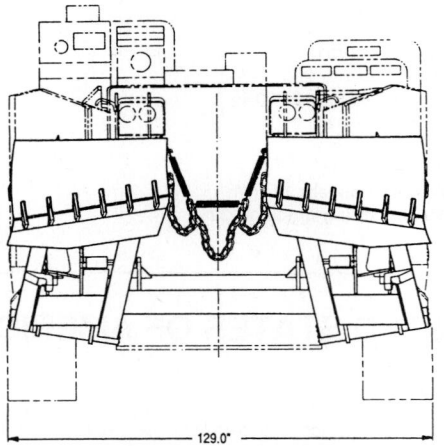

Drawings showing outline details of Caterpillar Track Width Mine Plough

Tines per blade: 6

Status
Prototype.

Manufacturer
Caterpillar Inc, Defense & Federal Products, 100 N E Adams Street, Peoria, Illinois 61629-8000, USA.
Tel: (309) 675 6938. Telex: 404435.

Mine Clearing/Armor Protection Kit

Description
Under an Urgent Procurement contract from the US Army Tank-Automotive Command, Caterpillar Inc manufactured Mine Clearing/Armor Protection (MCAP) kits for installation on Caterpillar T-9 Track Type Tractors to be used by US Army Engineers during Operation Desert Storm. MCAP kits are employed by US Army Engineer units for countermine training.

The kit consists mainly of an angled rake assembly fitted to the front of the T-9 tractor and an armoured enclosure for the operator. The angled rake assembly side-casts to the right all known varieties of surface-laid or buried land mines down to a depth of 305 mm (12 in) and can clear a path 3.576 m (12 ft) wide; clearing efficiency is stated to exceed 95 per cent. The assembly is provided with replaceable tines and is fitted with an automatic flotation device. It is used to widen existing breaches established in minefields by mineclearing line charges, track width mine ploughs and other similar devices. Subsequent passes by a T-9

Mine Clearing/Armour Protection (MCAP) kit fitted to T-9 Track Type Tractor

fitted with the MCAP can further widen a path and over a period of time entire minefields can be cleared. The rake assembly can be installed by two men in 10 minutes.

The armoured enclosure for the operator consists of a number of rolled homogeneous armour panels proof against 7.62 mm armour-piercing projectiles and land mine or artillery fragments. Panels are provided around the operator's compartment, engine, belly, fuel tank, and lift cylinders. The operator's station has two access doors and two fans for ventilation. Eight transparent armoured vision ports are provided and

there are service access panels for maintenance. The armour can be installed by two men.

Specifications
Weight:
(rake assembly) 1769 kg
(armour) 3084 kg
Length:
(rake assembly) 3.9 m
(T-9 tractor with rake fitted) 9.187 m
Width: (overall) 3.874 m
Height: (to top of operator's cab) 3.246 m

Cleared path width: 3.657 m
Raking depth: 305 mm

Status
In service with the US Army.

Manufacturer
Caterpillar Inc, Defense & Federal Products, 100 N E Adams Street, Peoria, Illinois 61629-8000, USA. Tel: (309) 675 6938. Telex: 404435.

Mine Clearance Kit (MCSK)

Description
The US Army and Marine Corps use a mine clearance kit (MCSK) that can be adapted to suit a variety of vehicles. It has been fitted to the AAVP7A1 armoured amphibious assault vehicle.

On the AAVP7A1 the mine clearance kit consists of three rockets launched from a frame carried on two arms over the vehicle hull. Each of the rockets carries a 107 m long line charge which is fired forward of the vehicle. The line charge is carried inside the vehicle hull but once the charge has been launched and is on the ground it can be detonated via electrical wires interwoven in the snubbing line. The charges can be used to clear wire and other obstacles as well as mines.

Status
Development.

Mine clearance kit fitted to AAVP7A1 armoured amphibious assault vehicle

M173 Mineclearing Equipment

Description
The M173 mineclearing equipment was developed by Picatinny Arsenal and the Martin Company of Baltimore. The equipment consists of a boat-shaped glass fibre sled which is divided up into three compartments. The front compartment contains an M95 JATO rocket attached to a 91.4 m length of M96 linear demolition charge coiled in the centre compartment. The rear compartment contains the accessories and towing cable when not being used.

The sled, which will float, can be towed behind a tracked vehicle such as an M113 APC or an M48 MBT. The sled is normally brought up to the edge of the minefield and the rocket is launched across the minefield trailing the M96 linear demolition charge. The rocket is halted by an arresting wire attached to the sled. The line then falls onto the minefield and detonates, exploding any mines in its path.

Specifications
Weight: 1406 kg
Length: 3.683 m
Width: 1.435 m

Height: 0.609 m
Type of explosive: Composition C4
Length of M96 charge: 91.4 m
Charge weight:
(total) 780 kg
(explosive) 680 kg
Number of charges on line: 1200 (600 pairs)
Electrical supply: 24 V

Status
In service with the US Army.

Mineclearing Line Charge M58/M59 (MICLIC)

Development
The Mineclearing Line Charge M58A1 (MICLIC) was originally a US Marine Corps equipment. It was type classified by the US Army in August 1985 and the first units were issued for training purposes at the beginning of October 1986. The equipment was modified to M58A3 standard and the M58A4 version is the main production model. The M59 is used by the US Marine Corps on their amphibious vehicles.

With the US Army, MICLIC is issued to US Army engineer units and towed by M113 APCs, M2/3 Bradley combat vehicles and the M9 ACE.

Description
The M58A4 Linear Demolition Charge is used to clear a path for tanks, vehicles and personnel through minefields.

The linear charge is approximately 106.7 m long and consists of approximately 816 kg of Composition C4 explosive distributed in unit charges assembled around a core of nylon rope and detonating cord. A steel pallet serves as a storage and transport container for the linear charge, an arresting cable and the M1134A1E1 electric fuze. For ground launch the pallet containing the linear charge is secured at a set location by driven steel posts. The launch may also be made from a pallet

Mineclearing Line Charge M58A4 (MICLIC) mounted on Caterpillar Combat Support Trailer being towed by M113 APC

mounted on an M353 (or similar) trailer equipped with an M155 launching system and towed behind an armoured vehicle. At the target area the pallet is aligned to the direction of intended flight. For ground launch the ground launcher assembly is attached to the pallet and an MK 22 MOD 4.5-inch/127 mm rocket motor is positioned on the launcher. The towed launcher has an integral launcher assembly. After fuzing the linear charge the charge rocket motor

harness is secured to the rocket motor. An M34 firing device is used to fire the rocket from a remote or protected position.

When fired, the rocket pulls the linear charge out of the pallet and over the target area. Forward travel of the charge is limited by the burn time of the rocket motor and the 62.48 m long arresting cable. After the charge is deployed an electrical pulse from the firing device detonates the charge via an M1134 fuze to clear a path approximately 12 m wide and 100 m long.

The M68A2 Inert Linear Demolition Charge is an inert version of the M58A3 used for practice and training. This inert charge uses moulded synthetic rubber pellets in place of high explosive pellets and an inert fuze, the M1147.

Specifications
Weight complete: (loaded) 1406 kg
Pallet:
    (length) 2.362 m
    (width) 1.346 m
    (height) 0.711 m

Charge weight: 926.25 kg
Length of linear charge: approx 106.7 m
Number of pellets: 1400
Pellet weight: 0.567 kg
Type of explosive: Composition C4
Weight of explosive: approx 826 kg
Arresting cable length: 62.48 m

Rocket motor
Weight:
    (ready to fire) 52.16 kg
    (motor propellant) 20.865 kg
    (packed) 84.37 kg

Length: 1.93 m
Diameter: 127 mm
Length of motor cable: 3.05 m

Status
In production. In service with the US Army and Marine Corps.

Manufacturer
Morton Thiokol Inc, Ordnance Marketing, 401 Edwards Street, Suite 1111, Shreveport, Louisiana 71101, USA. Tel: (318) 222 7725. Telex: 22101. Fax: (318) 222 8151.

Anti-personnel Mine Clearance Device M1 and M1A1

Description
This kit, officially designated Cable, Detonating, Anti-Personnel, Mineclearing, M1, consists of a circular aluminium storage and carrying case, a 52 m length of detonating cable, propulsion unit, launcher unit and the firing equipment.

The detonating cable consists of 19 strands of nylon-covered detonating cord, each of which contains 100 g of oil-soaked PETN per 305 mm. The launcher unit consists of a folding stand constructed of aluminium

angles with connected legs.

The propulsion unit consists of a rocket unit with a length of wire rope attached to the front of the detonating cable, length of time fuze and two M2 fuze lighters. The cable is detonated after a 15 second delay.

The equipment is used as follows: the complete equipment is positioned just outside the minefield and one end of the detonating cable is staked to the ground. The cord is projected by the launcher across the minefield by the jet propulsion system, falls to the ground and is detonated.

The M1 is supplemented by the M1A1 (formerly the M1E1) which follows the same general lines. It is

slightly larger and heavier (weight crated 64.4 kg with the explosive line weighing 28.5 kg). When detonated it can clear a path about 2.44 m wide of anti-personnel mines.

Specifications
Weight of complete equipment: 42 kg
Diameter of storage case: 420 mm
Type of explosive: PETN
Weight of explosive: 21 kg

Status
In service with the US Army.

Projected Charge M3A1

Description
The Projected Charge M3A1 consists of two parallel, linear, corrugated aluminium or steel plates bolted together to form a rigid assembly. This is flexible in the vertical plane to allow it to pass over rough ground and

rigid in the horizontal plane to maintain as straight a course as possible when being pushed.

When assembled it is 360 mm wide, 130 mm high and 122 m long. Aluminium models weigh 4082 kg and steel models between 5670 and 6800 kg. Both contain up to 2042 kg of high explosive. Once assembled, the charge is pushed by a tracked vehicle such as an M48 or M60 MBT across the minefield and then detonated

by the action of rifle or machine-gun fire. The complete charge then explodes along its entire length and the pressure waves created should detonate any mines in the immediate area.

Status
In service with the US Army.

Projected Charge M157

Description
The Projected Charge M157 is an updated version of the Projected Charge M3A1 and follows the same general lines. The M157 is issued in kit form and takes from 6 to 8 man hours to assemble. It is drawn from stocks only as and when required. Each M157 section is made up from 62 centre loading sections, each 1.524 m long and weighing 64.4 kg; 13 body sections which are inert, 1.524 m long and weighing 35.8 kg;

two impact fuze sections each 1.524 m long and weighing 69.4 kg with an M603 fuze; a single fuze; a single tail section weighing 70.3 kg. Each centre loading section and impact fuze section contains 20.4 kg of Composition B and 2.268 kg of Composition B4.

The M157 is assembled in a rear area and towed to the edge of the minefield where it is pushed across the area to be cleared. The M157 is detonated by firing at the impact plate on the impact fuze sections with either 7.62 mm or 0.50/12.7 mm ball ammunition. Once a hit is registered the charge explodes leaving a path 90 m

long, 4 to 5 m wide and 1 to 1.5 m deep.

Specifications
Length: 122.225 m
Width: 305 mm
Height: 178 mm
Weight: 4989 kg

Status
In service with the US Army.

Torpedo, Bangalore M1A1 and M1A2

Description
This is used for clearing minefields and other obstacles such as barbed wire. It consists of 1.524 m lengths of high-explosive steel tubes with connecting sleeves. A complete item of issue consists of 10 loaded assemblies, 10 connection sleeves and one nose sleeve. Each sleeve, which is 54 mm in diameter, is filled with Amatol, with 102 mm of TNT at each end. Total weight of explosive in each assembly is 4.09 kg.

Each end of the tube contains a threaded well to accommodate a firing device with a crimped-on non-electric blasting cap or a delay detonator. The firing device can consist of six turns of detonating cord wrapped around one end of a loading assembly, to which is attached an 8 to 15 second delay detonator. When one loading assembly is detonated, the entire series will be detonated. The connecting sleeve consists of a short tube into which the ends of the loading assemblies fit, held in position by spring clips. The nose sleeve has a round point to assist in pushing the torpedo through obstacles.

The lengths of tube are connected together for the

required length and then pushed across the minefield and detonated. The shock waves created by the explosive should detonate any mines in its path, although many modern mines have been designed to resist detonation by this method.

The M1A1 is supplemented by the M1A2 which follows the same general lines but each loading charge weighs 6.8 kg and total weight is 89.8 kg.

Status
In service with the US Army and Marine Corps.

Anti-personnel Obstacle Breaching System (APOBS)

Description
The US Marine Corps is developing a countermine system known as the Anti-personnel Obstacle Breaching System (APOBS). Development is being con-

ducted at the Naval Coastal Systems Center in Panama City, Florida.

APOBS is based on the Israeli POMINS II portable mine neutralisation system (see entry in this section for details) but with some operational and safety modifications. These include a command firing mode to allow the user to fire at will from a set back location.

It is anticipated that APOBS will be in service with

US Marine Corps engineer and infantry units by the end of FY93 or early FY94. It will replace the Bangalore Torpedo currently in use.

Status
Development.

Light Forces Countermine Projects

Description

As part of the US Army's Light Forces Countermine programme, the US Army Belvoir Research, Development and Engineering Center is carrying out a number of mineclearing development projects including those outlined below. Most of these projects are investigative only and only a few, if any, are expected to be recommended for further development.

Small Projected Line Charge

This is a small, self-contained, lightweight (less than 6.8 kg), manportable system that will allow soldiers to breach a path through buried and surface-laid anti-personnel minefields. The system will consist of 50 m of flexible explosive line charge carried across a minefield by either a bullet trap, using the standard M16 rifle, or a small rocket.

Chemical Neutralisation

This manportable, self-contained system will use a small amount of a reactive chemical to neutralise the main charge and/or detonator in a mine or booby trap. It will operate by chemically changing the characteristics of an explosive to a non-explosive compound. The dispenser will weigh less than 0.9 kg, fit into a standard M16 ammunition pouch, and contain enough chemical to neutralise one to three mines.

Foam Neutralisation

The Expedient Foam Neutralisation System is a lightweight, self-contained rigid foam dispenser that will safely encapsulate anti-personnel mines and booby traps, thereby disabling the fuze mechanism. It will work equally well on both tripwire and pressure-activated fuze mechanisms. The dispenser will weigh less than 0.9 kg, fit into a standard M16 ammunition pouch, and contain enough chemical to neutralise three to five mines.

Drag Mat

This non-dedicated light vehicle-mounted chain drag mat can be attached to an HMMWV or CUCV, with slight additional armour, to clear a path through surface-laid or scatterable mines on roadways. The drag mat can withstand repeated detonations and forms a footprint 3.05 m long in front of the carrier vehicle. The mat is 2.3 m wide and weighs 363 kg. The resultant clear path can be up to 2.9 m wide (according to the carrier vehicle width) and maximum clearance speed is 24 km/h. When not in use all components can be carried or stored on the vehicle ready to be assembled by the vehicle crew.

Mini-flail

This is an expendable, remotely controlled mini-flail system mounted on a small commercial 'skid steer' chassis and intended for the neutralisation of anti-personnel mines and booby traps. Control can be by radio or cable. Outlined dimensions are: weight less than 1134 kg; length less than 2.44 m; width less than 1.524 m; and height less than 1.22 m. The system can be sling deployed under a UH-1H helicopter.

Vehicle-mounted Mini-flail

This system is still in the concept stage and is carried on a low cost, petrol-engined carrier vehicle and intended for the clearance of anti-personnel minefields by radio control from a line-of-sight range of up to 137 m. The system weighs 590 kg, is 3.175 m long, 1.6 m wide and 1.22 m high. It can clear a path 1.22 m wide at a maximum clearance speed of 4.8 km/h.

Modular Trail Flail

The Modular Trail Flail consists of a specially designed four-wheel drive chassis powered by a standard two-cylinder 650 cc motorcycle engine. The vehicle is made up from 11 modules with the heaviest being the engine at 68 kg; assembly and breakdown are carried out using pins and a hammer only. Remote-control by a 15.24 m cable or line-of-sight radio is used with direction changes made using skid steering. The system weighs 850 kg, is 3.075 m long, 0.914 m wide and 1.12 m high. It can clear a path 0.686 m wide at a maximum clearance speed of 1.9 km/h.

Status

Developments.

Development Agency

US Army Belvoir Research, Development and Engineering Center, Fort Belvoir, Virginia 22060-5606, USA.
Tel: (703) 664 6873.

MINEFIELD MARKING EQUIPMENT
COMMONWEALTH OF INDEPENDENT STATES

PSK Clear Lane Marking System

Description
The PSK clear lane marking system is a flare dispenser for marking a cleared lane through minefields. The PSK can be fitted to virtually all T-54, T-55, T-62 and T-72 MBTs except the command tank variants. Suitable vehicles have a distinctive square panel with four bolts on the upper hull rear onto which the device is fitted. The PSK holds a number of cassettes each of which can dispense six phosphorous-based flares. The flares are dispensed downwards at 15 m intervals and each flare burns on the ground for about 20 minutes.

The PSK is usually used in conjunction with the KMT-5M mineclearing plough and roller equipment (see entry in the *Mineclearing equipment* section).

Status
In service with former Warsaw Pact armed forces and other armed forces that have received CIS military aid.

Manufacturer
State factories.

PSK clear lane marking system mounted on rear of Iraqi modified T-55 MBT

Close-up of top of PSK clear lane marking system dispenser showing four flare cassettes

FRANCE

Minefield Lane Marking Lamp F1

Description
This flashing lamp (French Army designation is *Lampe Clignotante pour lot léger de balisage de champ de mines modèle D1F1*) is used for marking cleared lanes through minefields, and can be seen from a distance of up to 100 m which can be reduced by a screen if necessary.

The lamp can be mounted on a pole or left on the ground, and a green filter can be fitted over the lamp if required.

Specifications
Weight: (without battery) 185 g
Height: 170 mm
Diameter: 50 mm
Power supply: 1 BA 30 battery
Operating period: 100 h
Operating temperature range: −31.5 to +51°C

Status
In service with the French Army.

Manufacturer
Giat Industries, 13 route de la Minière, F-78034 Versailles Cedex, France.
Tel: (1) 30 97 37 37. Fax: (1) 30 97 39 00.

GERMANY

German Army Minefield Marking Set

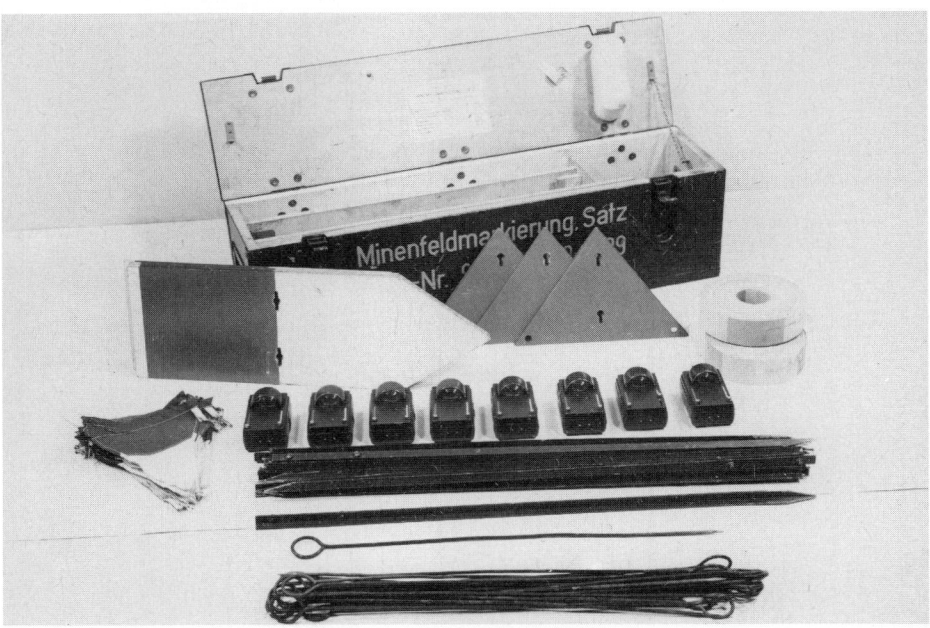

German Army minefield marking set

ISRAEL

Clear Lane Marking System (CLAMS)

Description

The Clear Lane Marking System (CLAMS) is a self-contained add-on system which can be mounted on the rear of an armoured vehicle (other types of vehicle can also use the system) to mark a cleared path through a minefield. Normally only one CLAMS dispenser is centrally mounted to a vehicle to indicate the centre of a cleared path but if two CLAMS units are mounted one each side of a vehicle they can indicate the boundaries of a cleared path.

CLAMS has two main components, a dispenser and the markers. The dispenser is a sheet metal box with a cover into which 150 markers can be loaded. It also has a release mechanism and a light stick activator. There is an accessory compartment for stowage of the control box, ground travel meter, electrical harness and the loading accessories when not in use. In use the dispenser may be fitted to the user vehicle by two men in about 10 minutes. An adaptor is mounted on the vehicle, which may incorporate a heat shield if required, and a cable harness connects the dispenser to the control box mounted in the driver's compartment. The system may be operated manually or automatically. In the automatic mode the interval for release of the markers may be set at 6, 12, 18, 24, 36 or 48 m with the intervals being measured by a ground travel meter attached to the vehicle's speedometer. Manual release is carried out by pressing a release button on the control unit.

The marker consists of a sheet metal base disc on

CLAMS marker in position

which is mounted a light stick and a flag. The light stick is automatically activated as it is released from the dispenser and glows for approximately 12 hours. For marking by day the flag alone may be used. The base is so designed that it will ensure the light stick is erect once dropped and is base-heavy to remain upright even in high winds. After use the markers may be retrieved and reused. Light sticks are available in green, blue and orange, the flags are red and the normal colour for the base is white, although other colours are available.

In addition to indicating cleared paths through minefields, CLAMS may be used to indicate passages through difficult terrain, indicate the periphery of chemical or nuclear fallout contamination, or marking emergency runways for aircraft.

In April 1987 a contract worth $2 185 000 was awarded to the BMY Corporation of York, Pennsylvania, for the production of CLAMS units for the US Army. With the US Army CLAMS is used by minefield-breaching tanks such as M1 and M60-series MBTs fitted with mine rollers.

Specifications
Markers
Light stick height: 127 mm
Base disc diameter: 155 mm
Weight: 300 g

Dispenser
Length: 860 mm
Width: 280 mm
Height: 970 mm
Weight:
(empty) 165 kg
(loaded) 210 kg
Operating voltage: 24 V DC (12 V optional)

Status
In production. In service with Israeli armed forces and the US Army.

Manufacturer
TAAS – Israel Industries Ltd, POB 1044, Ramat Hasharon 47100, Israel.
Tel: (3) 542 52 22. Telex: 33 719 misbit il.
Fax: (3) 48 96 39.

UNITED KINGDOM

Pearson Pathfinder Marking Device

Description

Pathfinder is a self-contained electro-pneumatic marking system. It is lightweight and compact and can be operated from under armour from any military vehicle. It places marker poles at preset intervals or distances to mark hazardous areas and minefield breach boundaries in particular. It is usually mounted on either side of a breaching vehicle to mark the edges of a cleared path.

Pathfinder may be arranged in a variety of ways depending on use and installation. The most common arrangement involves twin maker units, one either side of the vehicle. Systems involving single emplacement units may be used, for example, on a reconnaissance vehicle for the rapid defile marking role.

The Marker Unit holds 100 marker poles in a quick-change magazine. A full magazine weighs 32 kg and can be changed in 30 to 60 seconds. Marker poles are constructed from lightweight tube with a stainless steel tip at one end and a seal at the other. Standard marker poles are white with dayglo and reflective bands which ensure that the rod can be seen in poor visibility conditions. Poles containing a self-powered light source are an option.

A deployment frame moves the Marker Unit to its working position. This frame also retracts the Marker Unit to its stowed position within the confines of the vehicle where it is safe and does not restrict the vehicle's mobility.

The Compressor Unit provides the compressed air required to operate the system. The unit is driven by a 24 V DC motor which is particularly suited to heavy and continuous working. The compressed air is filtered and dried before delivery to the Marker Unit.

A control box provides all the control functions necessary to operate the equipment. The control box is usually located in the driver's compartment and operable from both the head-out and head-down positions.

Pathfinder has two modes of operation; manual and timed. In the manual mode, marker poles are fired only when the operator presses the manual fire buttons. This mode can select either the left- or right-hand Marker Units.

In the timed mode, marker poles are fired at preset time intervals which are changed by means of the time selector switch on the control box. The time interval required will be dictated by the speed of the vehicle on which the system is mounted. In this mode, discretional firing can still be achieved using the manual control buttons.

Marker pole firing is possible only when the Marker Unit is fully deployed and a system of limit switches ensures operator safety.

Specifications
Marker poles
Number per magazine: 100
Weight: (each) 125 g
Length: 1 m
Penetration: up to 200 mm

Marker Unit
Weight: 140 kg
Length: 1.3 m
Deployment time: 10 s

Status
In production. In service with the British Army and in Saudi Arabia. Under evaluation by the US Marine Corps and some European armies.

Pathfinder marking device deployed for use on Centurion AVRE 165

Manufacturer
Pearson Engineering, Wincomblee Road, Walker, Newcastle upon Tyne NE6 3QS, UK.
Tel: 091 234 0001. Telex: 538253.
Fax: 091 262 0402.

Hunting Engineering Lightweight Marking System (LIMAS)

Description

The Hunting Engineering Lightweight Marking System delineates minefields and other hazards, route and lane markings and similar operations. It utilises a lightweight picket post with one end slotted to hold tape, wire or light rope; a flanged interface unit secured by a steel pin which is hammered into the ground or tarmac surface; yellow and red tape 16 mm wide; and a simple hand-held dispenser. Minefield and other marking triangles and signs can be provided. Using this equipment a two-man team can mark perimeters faster than 1 km/h, and therefore it is compatible with mechanical minelaying systems.

Packaging can be arranged to suit customer requirements and satchels are available to enable one man to carry equipment sufficient for 250 m of fencing.

Status

In production.

Manufacturer

Hunting Engineering Limited, Reddings Wood, Ampthill, Bedford MK45 2HD, UK.
Tel: 0525 841000. Telex: 82105.
Fax: 0525 405861.

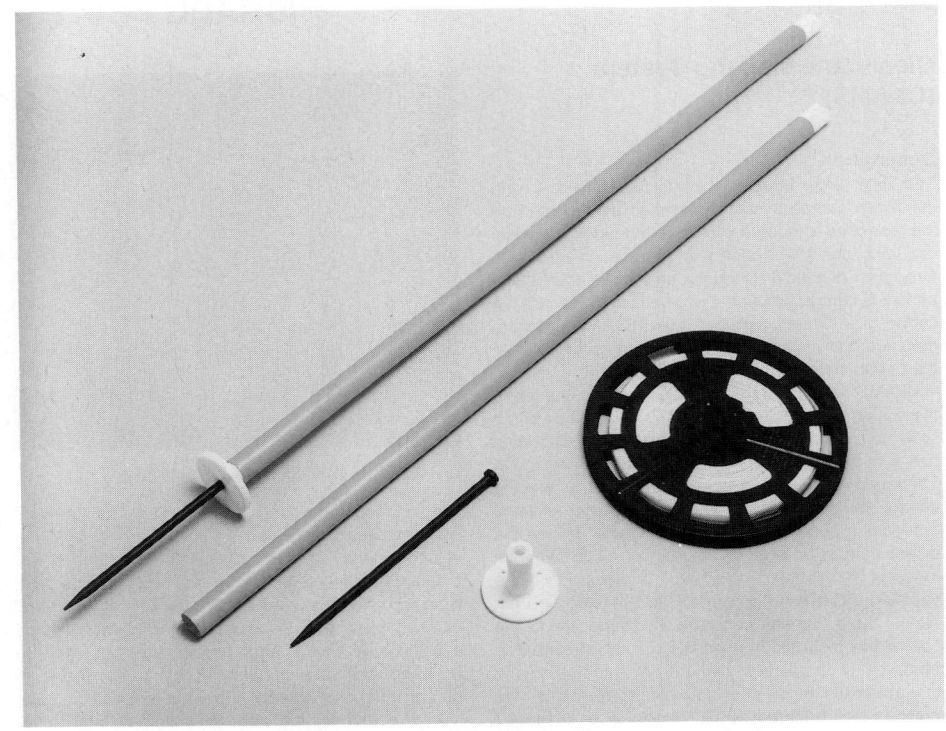

Components of Hunting Engineering lightweight marking system

Betalight Illuminated Defile Marker

Description

The Saunders-Roe Developments Limited Defile Marker was originally designed for use with the Medium Girder Bridge but has since undergone extensive trials by the British Army covering a wide range of other applications, including marking routes through minefields.

When being used for bridge marking, two inward facing Defile Markers show the commencement of the defile, upward facing ones guide through the defile and two outward facing ones indicate the end of the defile.

The Defile Marker consists of a white arrow on a black background with a Betalight illuminated head, fitted in a tough plastic housing. The arrow can be rotated to one of eight fixed positions, allowing position or other information to be indicated.

Illumination is provided by SRDL Betalight self-powered light sources which are borosilicate glass capsules internally coated with phosphor and filled with tritium gas which activates the phosphor to emit light. The arrow is clearly visible in both day and night conditions. They are perfectly safe for the user and have a long maintenance-free life of between 15 and 20 years. The marker is small, compact and soldier-proof. It will withstand normal army mechanical environmental requirements and can be used in all climatic conditions.

The marker can be attached to military police mounting poles, screwed or attached to mortar base

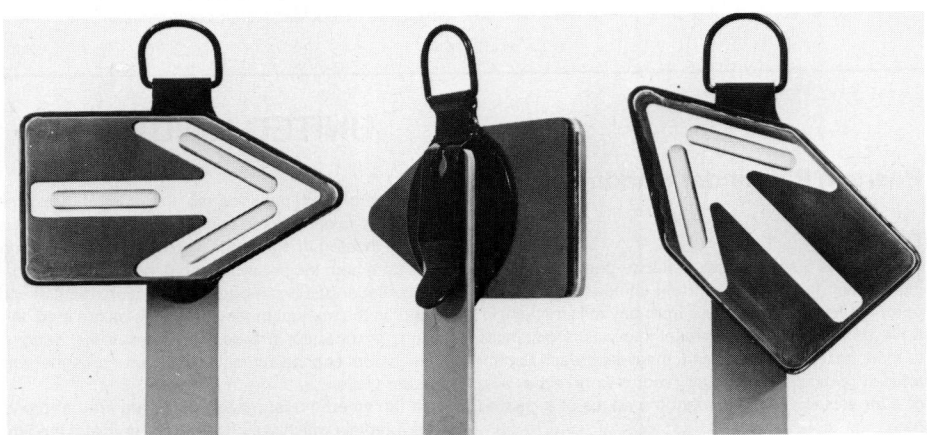

Saunders-Roe Developments Betalight illuminated defile marker in different positions

plates or to the entry flag of a bridging layout, or even to a bayonet. The ring allows the marker to be attached to a nail, tree or other available support. A total of 12 Defile Markers can be carried in a standard 7.62 mm ammunition box.

Specifications

Weight: 170 g
Length: 130 mm
Width: 70 mm
Height: (including backplate) 27 mm

Status

In production. In service with the British Army and other armed forces.

Manufacturer

Saunders-Roe Developments Limited, Millington Road, Hayes, Middlesex UB3 4NB, UK.
Tel: 081 573 3800. Fax: 081 561 3436.

UNITED STATES OF AMERICA

Hand-emplaceable Minefield Marker Set M133

Description

The Hand-emplaceable Minefield Marker Set M133 was developed by the US Army Mobility Equipment Research and Development Command (MERADCOM) (now the Belvoir Research, Development and Engineering Center at Fort Belvoir, Virginia), and is used for the temporary rapid marking of indefinite-life minefields by troops on foot. The major components of the equipment are a pole, orange fluorescent marking tape and an orange flashing light (152.4 mm long and 50.8 mm in diameter) which is mounted on top of the pole. The lamp is neon and initially flashes at about 82 times/minute. A shield inside the dome of the flasher prevents the light from being seen directly overhead. A reflector behind the neon lamp directs the light so that it can be seen from only one direction. The outside of the plastic case has a reflective surface to make it visible in light from vehicle headlights. Additional components are provided in the kit for emplacing and retrieving the poles. The poles are normally spaced at intervals of between 10 and 15 m except for those adjacent to corner poles which are then spaced 4 m from the corner pole; the marking tape is threaded through a holder on the side of the pole. The equipment was designed to mark a 700 to 1000 m perimeter minefield if the average pole spacing is not less than 10 m, for 15 days under intermediate cold temperature conditions and to be re-used between three and ten times.

Method of employing hand-emplaceable minefield marker set M133 (US Army)

Status

Entered US Army service late 1980.

Cyalume Lightsticks

Description

Cyalume lightsticks may be used for a variety of military purposes ranging from emergency lighting to marking the perimeters of minefields by simply placing them end-on into the ground. The lightsticks are activated by snapping the plastic body to allow two liquids to mix, thereby producing a phosphor-based chemical reaction which emits light. The lightsticks may be red, yellow, blue or green and are used in the CLAMS system (qv). Normal life is up to 12 hours.

Cyalume produces a holder for these lightsticks known as the Combat Light. This plastic container may be worn on a uniform and is so arranged that a simple shutter allows the light to be blocked off if required. The Combat Light holder may be used on a stake or pole to act as a route guide or denote a route through a minefield. For this purpose a keyhole clip is provided. The Combat Light holder is 70 mm long and can be re-used indefinitely.

The Combat Light and the Lightsticks are produced under licence in Israel by Rabintex.

Status

In production.

Manufacturer

American Cyanamid Company, Chemical Light Department, One Cyanamid Plaza, Wayne, New Jersey 07470, USA.
Tel: (201) 831 2000. Telex: 219136.

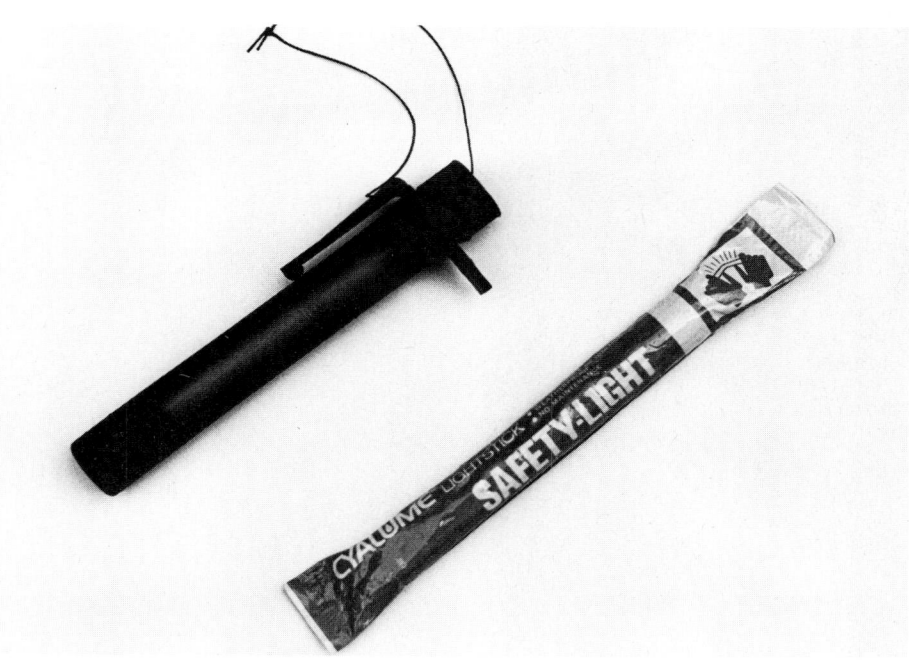

Cyanamid Combat Light on left with Lightstick in foil wrapper on right

Infantry and Sapper Minefield Breaching and Marking Set

Description

Intended to form part of the Light Forces Countermine programme, the Infantry and Sapper Minefield Breaching and Marking Set, also known as the Squad Sapper Set, is a proposal intended to provide dismounted engineer or infantry squads with the ability to conduct a clandestine minefield breach and mark the resultant clear path. The expendable set consists of an AN/PRS-11 mine detector carrier assembly plus a set of items including the following: a box of chemical lights plus 10 holders with stakes; two rolls of non-adhesive white tape; six non-metallic mine probes; a set of bolt cutters; 14 mine markers; a roll of minefield markers; a carrying bag; and a grapnel with a 30.5 m line.

Status

Project.

Development Agency

Belvoir Research, Development and Engineering Center, Fort Belvoir, Virginia 22060-5606, USA.
Tel: (703) 664 6873.

TRANSPORT EQUIPMENT

Lightweight vehicles (up to 1000 kg)
Special attack vehicles
Trucks (over 1000 kg)
Tank transporters
Amphibians
Tracked prime movers, cargo carriers and
    armoured logistic vehicles
Over-snow vehicles
Trailers
Materials handling equipment

LIGHTWEIGHT VEHICLES

AUSTRIA

Steyr-Puch 700 AP (4 × 4) 555 kg Haflinger Light Vehicle

Description

The Haflinger all-terrain light vehicle was designed by Erich Ledwinka in the 1950s and entered production in 1959. Production was completed in 1974.

Its layout is unusual with the driver and one passenger at the front, two seats in the centre and the cargo area at the rear. The two rear seats can be folded flat to increase the load-carrying area of the vehicle. The engine is mounted at the very rear, under the cargo area. The Haflinger has a windscreen that can be folded forward and removable canvas top and sides. A wide range of optional equipment included a PTO, extra low gear (until the model with a five-speed gearbox was introduced), tropical kit, snowplough and a 1500 kg capacity winch.

The Austrian Army uses the vehicle as a cargo carrier, command vehicle and a radio vehicle and some have been fitted with a 12.7 mm Browning machine gun or a recoilless rifle.

In 1962 a long wheelbase model was introduced, which was available with the Haflinger-type top or a fully enclosed cab. This model was 3.125 m long, 1.4 m wide, 1.74 m high, with a wheelbase of 1.8 m and unladen weight of 700 kg.

Swiss Army Steyr-Puch 700 AP (4 × 4) Haflinger

Specifications
Cab seating: 1 + 3
Configuration: 4 × 4
Weight:
  (empty) 645 kg
  (loaded) 1200 kg
Max load: 555 kg
Max weight:
  (on front axle, loaded) 620 kg
  (on rear axle, loaded) 700 kg
Load area: 1.54 × 1.275 m
Length: 2.85 m
Width: 1.4 m
Height:
  (overall) 1.74 m
  (reduced) 1.36 m

Ground clearance: 0.24 m
Track: 1.13 m
Wheelbase: 1.5 m
Max speed: 75 km/h
Range: 400 km
Fuel capacity: 31.5 l
Max gradient: 65%
Fording: 0.4 m
Engine: Model 700 AP 2-cylinder air-cooled petrol developing 24 hp at 4500 rpm. From 1967 production vehicles were fitted with engines that developed 27 hp at 4800 rpm
Gearbox: manual with 4 forward and 1 reverse gears Vehicles produced after 1966 had 5 forward and 1 reverse gears
Clutch: single dry plate
Suspension: independent with coil/rubber springs

Turning radius: 3.8 m
Tyres: 165 × 12
Brakes:
  (main) hydraulic
  (parking) mechanical
Electrical system: 12 V

Status
Production complete. In service with Austria, Indonesia (1000), Italy, Nigeria and Switzerland.

Manufacturer
Steyr-Daimler-Puch Fahrzeugtechnik GmbH, Werke Graz, Postfach 823, A-8011 Graz, Austria. Tel: 316 400 10. Telex: 311315 stdpwg a.

BRAZIL

ENGESA EE-12 (4 × 4) 500 kg Light Vehicle

Description

The EE-12 is a small four-seater vehicle of distinctive appearance. It has a conventional layout with the four-cylinder petrol or diesel engine at the front under a sloped bonnet and with separate seats for the driver and a passenger; a bench seat at the rear can accommodate a further two passengers. Normally the EE-12 is driven open with no weather protection for the occupants other than a forward-folding windscreen but it is possible to fit a canvas tilt with roll-down blinds. There are no side doors other than canvas covers. A spare wheel is carried at the rear along with a jerrican.

The overall construction of the EE-12 is very robust. The front and rear bumpers are equipped with towing shackles and a towing pintle is provided at the rear.

The EE-12 can be provided in a number of variations. One is as a carrier for a 7.62 or 12.7 mm machine gun or a 106 mm recoilless rifle. This carrier has an open rear with the jerrican and spare wheel moved to the vehicle sides, and the windscreen is split to allow the gun barrel to protrude over the bonnet. A hard-top version is available and has been exported to Angola. Other variants include an anti-tank missile carrier, a radio communications vehicle and a front line stretcher carrier.

ENGESA EE-12 (4 × 4) 500 kg light vehicle

Specifications
Seating: 1 + 3
Configuration: 4 × 4
Weight: (loaded) 2160 kg
Max load: 500 kg
Towed load: 250 kg
Length: 3.57 m
Width: 1.77 m
Height:
  (overall) 1.9 m
  (windscreen down) 1.5 m
Ground clearance: 0.23 m
Track: 1.454 m
Wheelbase: 2.16 m
Angle of approach/departure: 70°/50°
Max speed: (road) 110 km/h
Fuel capacity: 92 l

Max gradient: 70%
Side slope: 30%
Fording: 0.6 m
Engine: GM 151 2.47 l, 4-cylinder petrol developing
85 hp at 4400 rpm or
Perkins 2.8 l, 4-cylinder diesel developing 70 hp
Transmission: Clark 240 V manual with 5 forward and
1 reverse gears
Transfer box: single-speed for front axle engagement
Steering: mechanical

Turning radius: 6 m
Suspension: coil springs and telescopic shock absorbers, location by longitudinal and traverse control links;
250 mm wheel travel
Tyres: 7.50 × 16
Brakes: servo-assist dual circuit; disc front, drum rear
Electrical system: 24 V
Batteries: 2 × 12 V, 63 Ah
Alternator: 40 A

Status
In production. In service with Angola.

Manufacturer
ENGESA Engenheiros Especializados SA, Avenida
Tucunare 125/211, Caixa Postal 152/154, 06400
Barueri, SP, Brazil.
Tel: 11 421 4711. Telex: 1171 302 enes br.

Bernardini Xingu BT25 and BT50 (4 × 4) Light Vehicles

Description
The Bernardini Xingu BT25 and BT50 (4 × 4) light vehicles are basically Jeep-type vehicles. Both are described as ½-tonne vehicles. The main difference is that the BT50 has a longer wheelbase but in most other respects the two vehicles are similar.

Both vehicles are conventional in layout with the engine forward under a steel bonnet and seating for the driver and three passengers under an optional soft-top. Canvas screen doors are normally fitted. The BT50 could be used as a light pick-up truck with the rear passenger bench seat removed. A protective grill for the radiator is fitted across the front of the vehicle and a spare wheel is usually carried at the rear on a small tailgate. A towing hitch is fitted under the tailgate. Floating axles are used front and rear.

In July 1990 the previously fitted OM-314 diesel engine was replaced on the production lines by an OM-364 unit delivering the same horsepower.

Variants of these vehicles include a ¾-tonne pick-up truck version of the BT50 with a canvas tilt carried over bows and the spare wheel on the left-hand side in front of the cab door. A variant of the BT25 is used as a carrier for an M40A2 106 mm recoilless rifle – this version has a split front windscreen to accommodate the recoilless rifle barrel when travelling. Other variants of both models include communications vehicles with various radio fits.

Optional equipment on both models includes a front-mounted 2500 kg capacity winch, a folding aerial bracket and an extra spare wheel carrier. A light cargo trailer is available.

Specifications
Cab seating: 1 + 3
Configuration: 4 × 4
Weight:
(BT25) 1600 kg
(BT50) 1700 kg
Length:
(BT25) 3.93 m
(BT50) 4.4 m
Width: 1.8 m
Height: 1.965 m
Ground clearance: 0.23 m
Track:
(front) 1.415 m
(rear) 1.4 m
Wheelbase:
(BT25) 2.285 m
(BT50) 2.755 m
Max speed: 115 km/h

Range: 950 km
Max gradient: 60%
Side slope: 30%
Fording: 0.7 m
Engine: OM-364 4-cylinder water-cooled diesel developing 94 hp at 2800 rpm
Gearbox: manual, 4 forward and 1 reverse gears
Clutch: single dry plate
Transfer box: 2-speed
Steering: worm and roller
Turning radius:
(BT25) 5.3 m
(BT50) 6.3 m
Suspension: semi-elliptical leaf springs with double-action hydraulic shock absorbers
Tyres: 7.50 × 16
Brakes: dual circuit hydraulic with vacuum auxiliary
Electrical system: 24 V
Batteries: 2 × 12 V, 60 Ah
Alternator: 35 A

Status
In production.

Manufacturer
Bernardini SA Indústria e Comércio, Rua Hipólito Soares 79, São Paulo – SP – 04201, Brazil.
Tel: 011 273 8996. Telex: 011 21605 bsaibr.

Bernardini BT25 Xingu (4 × 4) light vehicle carrying 106 mm recoilless rifle

Bernardini BT50 Xingu (4 × 4) ¾-tonne pick-up truck

ENGESA EE-34 (4 × 4) 750 kg Light Vehicle

Description
The prototype ENGESA EE-34 (4 × 4) 750 kg light vehicle was completed in 1980 and production commenced in 1982.

The body of the EE-34 is made of pressed steel and the layout is conventional with a cargo area at the rear. The standard form is a pick-up truck for general-purpose load carrying with seating for the driver plus a bench seat for two passengers. Standard equipment includes a windscreen that folds downwards onto the bonnet when not in use, vinyl doors, a removable vinyl top and a drop tailgate for loading stores. The maximum payload across country is 750 kg and on roads 1000 kg.

Variants include a light truck version and an ambulance with a pressed steel body. This has space for four stretchers or two stretchers plus three seated casualties or six seated casualties. The ambulance body is entered by two large rear doors.

Specifications
Cab seating: 1 + 2
Configuration: 4 × 4
Weight:
(unladen) 2500 kg
(laden, road) 3580 kg
(laden, cross-country) 3330 kg
Max load:
(road) 1000 kg
(cross-country) 750 kg
Length: 5.32 m
Width: 2.04 m
Height:
(tarpaulin) 2.2 m
(cab top) 2 m
(windscreen down) 1.493 m
Ground clearance: 0.23 m

Track: 1.55 m
Wheelbase: 2.95 m
Angle of approach/departure: 42°/52°
Max speed: (road) 100 km/h
Range: 600 km
Max gradient: 60%
Max side slope: 30%
Engine: Perkins 4.236 4-cylinder diesel developing 82 hp at 2800 rpm
Gearbox: manual, 4 forward and 1 reverse gears
Clutch: single dry plate
Transfer box: mechanical, 2-speed
Steering: mechanical
Suspension: leaf springs and hydraulic shock absorbers
Tyres: 7.50 × 16
Brakes:
(main) hydraulic, disc front and drum rear
(parking) drum, operating on transmission output shaft
Electrical system: 24 V

ENGESA EE-34 (4 × 4) 750 kg pick-up truck

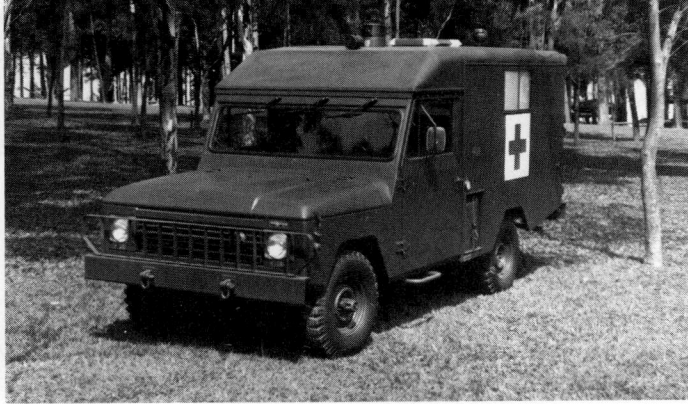

ENGESA EE-34 (4 × 4) ambulance

Status
In production. In service with the Brazilian armed forces.

Manufacturer
ENGESA Engenheiros Especializados SA, Avenida Tucunaré 125/211, Caixa Postal 152/154, 06400 Barueri, SP, Brazil.
Tel: 11 421 4711. Telex: 1171 302 enes br.

UAI M1-34 (4 × 4) 750 kg Light Vehicle

Description
The UAI M1-34 (4 × 4) 750 kg light vehicle was due to enter production during 1988. It is a conventional design powered by an 87 hp diesel engine through a five-speed mechanical transmission and dual reduction transfer box. The cargo capacity for cross-country use is 750 kg plus a 1000 kg trailer. On roads this can be increased to 1000 kg plus a towed load of 1800 kg.

Status
In production.

Manufacturer
Terex do Brasil SA, Rodovia BR-252, Anel Rodoviário – 31250 Belo Horizonte, MG – Brazil.
Tel: 31 441 3444.

UAI M1-34 (4 × 4) 750 kg light vehicle

CANADA

Bombardier Iltis (4 × 4) 500 kg Light Vehicle

Development
In October 1981 Volkswagen AG of Germany agreed to cede and transfer to Bombardier Inc of Canada the design and manufacturing technology of its Iltis (4 × 4) 500 kg light vehicle as used by the German Army. The agreement also granted to Bombardier the worldwide rights for the marketing, sale and distribution of the Iltis, as well as the rights to manufacture and market the civilian version of the vehicle. Bombardier also acquired the tooling equipment used in the manufacture of the Iltis.

Before this announcement the Canadian Department of National Defense asked the company to submit a proposal, based on the Iltis, for the replacement of the existing utility 4 × 4 vehicles of the Canadian Armed Forces. In November 1983 it was announced that the Canadian government had awarded a contract for 1900 (later increased to 2500) Iltis vehicles to the Logistic Equipment Division of Bombardier Inc. The contract included the supply of spare parts, manuals and training programmes for operators and maintainers and was valued at C$68 million. Production for this contract began at the end of Summer 1984, and was completed by the end of 1985. During 1984 an order for over 2500 was placed for the Belgian armed forces (2673 were delivered).
Production ceased in 1988.

Description
Originally a Volkswagen design, the Iltis uses components from the Volkswagen Polo and Audi Quattro vehicles. The all-steel body has a conventional layout with the engine at the front and the cargo area to the rear. The driver and front passenger have separate seats and there is seating for two more passengers to the rear. The rear seats can be folded down to increase the load-carrying area and the vehicle is provided with a folding hood, removable side flaps and a folding windscreen. The driver can select either a full 4 × 4 drive for cross-country or 4 × 2 for road drive in which case the front axle is disengaged. An integral roll bar is provided.

The Iltis can be lifted by the UH-60 Black Hawk helicopter and has been tested for low altitude parachute extraction from transport aircraft, and for parachute dropping.

Optional extras for the Iltis include a turbocharged diesel engine, an electric winch kit, a rear pintle hook, a three-door glass fibre hard-top, up to three radio equipment outlets and weapon mounting systems for 7.62 mm and 0.50/12.7 mm machine guns, the MK19 40 mm grenade launcher and anti-tank missile systems such as MILAN and TOW.

Variants of the basic Iltis include an ambulance, a command vehicle, a cable layer, a communications vehicle and a version carrying artillery sound ranging equipment.

Specifications
Cab seating: 1 + 3
Configuration: 4 × 4
Weight:
  (empty) 1550 kg
  (loaded) 2050 kg
Max load: 500 kg

Bombardier-produced Iltis in service with Belgian Army

Max towed load:
(with brakes) 2000 kg
(without brakes) 750 kg
Length: 3.887 m
Width: 1.52 m
Height: 1.837 m
Ground clearance: 0.225 m
Track:
(front) 1.23 m
(rear) 1.26 m
Wheelbase: 2.017 m
Angle of approach/departure: 41°/32°
Max speed: 130 km/h
Fuel capacity: 85 l
Range: 700 km

Max gradient: 77%
Fording: 0.6 m
Engine: VW 183 4-cylinder OHC petrol developing 75 hp at 5000 rpm
Gearbox: manual with 4 forward and 1 reverse gears plus a cross-country gear
Clutch: single dry plate
Steering: rack and pinion
Turning radius: 5.5 m
Suspension: overhead semi-elliptical leaf springs and double-acting shock absorbers
Tyres: 6.50 × R-16
Brakes:
(main) hydraulic, dual circuit, drum
(parking) mechanical

Electrical system: 24 V
Batteries: 2 × 12 V, 45 Ah

Status
Production complete. In service with Belgium (2673), Cameroon Armed Forces, Canadian Armed Forces (2500) and the Oman Royal Guard Brigade.

Manufacturer
Bombardier Inc, Logistic Equipment Division, Valcourt, Québec, Canada J0E 2L0.
Tel: (514) 532 2211. Telex: 5832 575.

CHINA, PEOPLE'S REPUBLIC

Beijing BJ-212, BJ-212A and BJ-212-E Light Vehicles

Description

Production of the basic BJ-212 began in 1965. These light vehicles are similar in appearance to the UAZ-469B, the BJ-212 seating five persons and the BJ-212A seating up to eight. The latter also has a slightly increased payload. The BJ-212A has no rear side door and has a conventional tilt (if fitted) as opposed to the raised 'convertible' cover of the BJ-212. The BJ-212LA has seating for up to eight persons but has a tailgate. There is a folding longitudinal seat to allow the BJ-212LA to be used as a light utility vehicle. The BJ-212LA weighs 1485 kg empty and has a payload of 600 kg.

All versions have an identical layout with the engine at the front and the passenger or cargo compartment to the rear. The driver's seat has a seat for one passenger by its side. On the BJ-212 a single bench seat accommodates three more passengers while on

the BJ-212A there are two bench seats along the sides for six passengers. The windscreen can be folded forward over the bonnet on both versions. The BJ-212A has a rear tailgate that can be folded down for access.

A version of the Beijing BJ-212 is used to carry the NORINCO Type 75 105 mm recoilless rifle. This version can be identified by the split windscreen provided to accommodate the length of the barrel.

Variant

BJ-212-E
Prototypes of the BJ-212-E were produced from 1986 onwards and underwent evaluation trials for the Chinese armed forces. The main change from the basic BJ-212 and BJ-212A is the provision of a new 2.46 litre four-cylinder in-line petrol engine of AMC design plus a new gearbox and transmission. The AMC engine produces 103 hp at 5000 rpm and provides a decrease in vehicle unloaded weight to 1460 kg. The maximum load capacity is unchanged but the towed load capacity has been increased to

900 kg. Maximum speed is also increased to 130 km/h. The BJ-212-E has been produced in two- and four-door versions. The overall dimensions of the BJ-212-E are unchanged from those of the BJ-212 and BJ-212A.

Model	BJ-212	BJ-212A
Seating	1 + 4	1 + 7
Configuration	4 × 4	4 × 4
Weight		
(unladen)	1530 kg	1520 kg
(laden)	1955 kg	2120 kg
Max load	425 kg	600 kg
Towed load	800 kg	800 kg
Length	3.86 m	3.86 m
Width	1.75 m	1.75 m
Height		
(unladen)	1.87 m	2.105 m
(laden)	1.83 m	1.97 m
Wheelbase	2.3 m	2.3 m
Track (front and rear)	1.44 m	1.44 m
Ground clearance	0.22 m	0.22 m
Max speed	98 km/h	98 km/h
Gradient		
(less trailer)	30°	30°
(with trailer)	22.5°	22.5°
Fording	0.5 m	0.5 m
Engine	2.445 l water-cooled 4-cylinder in-line 4-stroke petrol developing 75 hp at 3500-4000 rpm	
Gearbox	manual, 3 forward and 1 reverse, synchromesh on 2nd, 3rd	
Clutch	single dry plate	
Transfer box	2-speed	2-speed
Suspension	longitudinal semi-elliptical leaf springs with hydraulic double-acting telescopic shock absorbers	
Steering	recirculating ball	
Turning radius	6 m	6 m
Brakes	hydraulic drum	
Tyres	6.50 × 16	6.50 × 16
Electrical system	12 V	12 V
Battery	12 V, 54 Ah	12 V, 54 Ah

Status

BJ-212 and BJ-212A in production. In service with Chinese armed forces, Chad, Pakistan and some other nations. Over 400 000 units have been produced. BJ-212-E, only prototypes to date.

Manufacturer

Beijing Jeep Corporation Limited, Chuiyangliu Chaoyang District, Beijing, People's Republic of China.
Tel: 771 2233. Telex: 20039 bjc cn.

Pakistan Army BJ-212 (4 × 4) 425 kg light vehicle (China Motor Vehicle Documentation Centre)

Beijing Jeep Corporation XJ Cherokee

Development/Description
In May 1983 it was announced that a production agreement between the American Motors Corporation and the Chinese Beijing Automotive Works had been signed. The agreement established the Beijing Jeep Corporation to produce Jeeps on a new production line in China, initially using pre-packed kits delivered from an AMC plant in Ontario, Canada.

The model selected for initial production was the Jeep XJ Cherokee and the first models were produced in Beijing during September 1985. Details of the XJ Cherokee can be found under the Jeep entry in this section.

Initial production plans for 1986 envisaged a rate of 4000 vehicles a year but this was not achieved due to foreign exchange problems and the expected rate became 2100 vehicles a year with an eventual production total of at least 15 000 vehicles. The XJ Cherokee has been evaluated by the Chinese armed forces. Over 10 000 units have been produced. The

Chrysler Motor Corporation took over from AMC in 1986.

Status
In production. Under evaluation by the Chinese armed forces.

Manufacturer
Beijing Jeep Corporation Limited, Chuiyangliu Chaoyang District, Beijing, People's Republic of China. Tel: 771 2233. Telex: 20039 bjc cn.

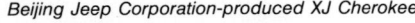

Beijing Jeep Corporation-produced XJ Cherokee

Beijing Jeep Corporation-produced XJ Cherokee

COMMONWEALTH OF INDEPENDENT STATES

LuAZ-967M Amphibious Battlefield Support Vehicle

Description
This vehicle was developed in the 1960s and was first seen during trials with troops based in East Germany in the latter part of that decade. It was generally deployed during 1976 and was originally used as a battlefield medical evacuation vehicle but is now also used as a general light support vehicle. The LuAZ-967M uses some components of the LuAZ-969 (4 × 4) light vehicle described in the following entry.

The body of the LuAZ-967M is made of all-welded steel with the engine at the front. The driver sits immediately behind the windscreen which folds forward to reduce the overall height. His seat is on the centre line of the vehicle and can be folded down so that he can drive lying flat. The steering column and steering wheel can also be lowered.

As a battlefield medical evacuation vehicle the LuAZ-967M has two folding seats for walking wounded as well as two stretchers, but its normal load is two patients plus the driver. It is fully amphibious, being

propelled in the water by its wheels. A treadway is carried on each side of the vehicle for crossing trenches and other obstacles. There is a winch with a capacity of 200 kg and 100 m of cable mounted at the front of the vehicle; this winch may be used to winch in wounded personnel on a canvas mat.

The LuAZ-967M is also used by airborne forces as a light support vehicle and as a weapon carrier; in the latter role it has been observed carrying an AGS-17 grenade launcher, the AT-4 'Spigot' anti-tank guided missile and an 82 mm B-10 recoilless rifle. An ammunition carrier version can carry up to 320 kg of small arms ammunition.

Specifications
Seating: 1 + 2 or 6
Configuration: 4 × 4
Weight:
 (empty) 930 kg
 (loaded) 1350 kg
Max load: 420 kg
Max towed load: 300 kg
Length: 3.682 m
Width: 1.712 m

Height: (including windscreen) 1.55 m
Ground clearance: 0.285 m
Angle of approach/departure: 34°/36°
Max road speed: 75 km/h
Max water speed: 5-6 km/h
Range: 411 km
Fuel capacity: 37 l
Fuel consumption: 9 l/100 km at 40 km/h
Gradient: 58%
Fording: amphibious
Engine: MeMZ-967A 4-cylinder air-cooled petrol developing 37 hp at 4200 rpm
Gearbox: manual, 4 forward and 1 reverse gears, plus cross-country gear
Turning radius: 5.8 m
Suspension: individual torsion bar
Electrical system: 12 V

Status
Production complete. In service with the CIS.

Manufacturer
Lutsk Motor Vehicle Plant, Ukraine.

LuAZ-967M amphibious battlefield medical evacuation vehicle (Michael Jerchel)

LuAZ-967M amphibious battlefield medical evacuation vehicle

LuAZ-969 (4 × 4) Light Vehicle

Description
In 1965 the Zaporozhe Motor Vehicle Plant developed a 250 kg vehicle, based on the ZAZ-966 passenger car, called the ZAZ-969, but it was not placed in production. In the late 1960s the project was transferred to the Lutsk Machine Building Plant and the designation was changed from the ZAZ-969 to the LuMZ-969. Production finally began in 1972 under the designation LuAZ-969 as the plant name was changed from the Lutsk Machine Building Plant to the Lutsk Motor Vehicle Plant. The vehicle is intended primarily for civilian use although it has military applications. The chassis of the LuAZ-969 light vehicle was also used as the basis for the LuAZ-967M amphibious battlefield medical evacuation vehicle described in the previous entry.

The vehicle has an all-steel body with the engine at the front and the crew compartment at the rear with two side doors, a windscreen which can be folded forward onto the bonnet and a removable canvas top. The driver can select either 4 × 4 or 4 × 2 drive, in which case the rear instead of the front axle is disengaged. A winch with a capacity of 200 kg and 100 m of cable can be fitted.

The latest model is the LuAZ-969M. This is powered by an engine developing 40 hp at 4200 rpm, giving the vehicle a maximum road speed of 85 km/h. Empty

LuAZ-969M (4 × 4) light vehicle

weight is 970 kg, overall length is 3.37 m and width is 1.64 m.

Specifications (LuAZ-969)
Cab seating: 1 + 1
Configuration: 4 × 4
Weight:
  (empty) 820 kg
  (loaded) 1200 kg
Weight on front axle: (empty) 510 kg
Weight on rear axle: (empty) 310 kg
Towed load: 300 kg

Length: 3.2 m
Width: 1.6 m
Height: 1.77 m
Ground clearance: 0.3 m
Track: 1.32 m
Wheelbase: 1.8 m
Max speed: 75 km/h
Range: 400 km
Fuel capacity: 32 l
Gradient: 58%
Fording: 0.45 m
Engine: MeMZ-946 V-4 air-cooled petrol developing 27 hp at 4000 rpm
Gearbox: manual with 4 forward and 1 reverse gears
Transfer box: 2-speed
Turning radius: 3 m
Suspension: torsion bar
Tyres: 5.90 × 13
Brakes:
  (main) hydraulic
  (parking) mechanical
Electrical system: 12 V

Status
In production.

Manufacturer
Lutsk Motor Vehicle Plant, Ukraine.

UAZ-469B (4 × 4) 600 kg Light Vehicle

Development
For many years the standard Jeep-type vehicle of the old Soviet Army was the UAZ-69 (or GAZ-69), but for a number of reasons it was never considered a satisfactory design. In 1960 a new 4 × 4 light vehicle called the UAZ-460B was tested. This used many components of the UAZ-450 truck, but was not placed in production. Further development of this vehicle resulted in the UAZ-469B which began production late in 1972 and entered service the following year. The UAZ-469B (also known as the UAZ-31512) uses many components, including the axles, brakes, engine, transmission and parts of the chassis of the UAZ-452 series of 4 × 4 light vehicles.

The latest model of the basic UAZ-469 is known as the UAZ-3151 (see under Variants in this entry). This model replaced all others on the production lines from 1990 onwards.

Description
The basic vehicle has an all-steel body with the engine at the front and the four-door crew compartment towards the rear, with a removable canvas top, and windscreen that can be folded down flat against the bonnet. The tops of the doors can also be removed. There are two individual seats at the front, a three-man seat in the centre and two men can sit facing each

other at the rear. Normal load is two men plus 600 kg of cargo or seven men and 100 kg of cargo. A hard-top can be fitted if required.

In 1973 the UAZ-469 was shown. This has a number of improvements including a portal axle which gives the vehicle both a higher ground clearance (300 mm) and improved cross-country capability, but the engine is identical to that in the standard UAZ-469B.

The UAZ-469 has been sold in the West as the Tundra.

Variants
Variants include the UAZ-469BG ambulance (latest designation UAZ-3152) which can carry a driver and four patients, van-type vehicles and a special version for dispensing lane marking pennants into the ground.

The UAZ-3151 is an improved version of the basic UAZ-469. The overall appearance of the new model is similar to that of the original vehicle but the independent front suspension uses coil springs and a more powerful UAZ four-cylinder engine developing 85 hp is fitted; petrol and diesel engines are available. Other changes include improved seating and heating. Extra shock absorbent panels have been fitted to the body. The maximum towed load is increased to 800 kg.

Iraqi Army UAZ-469s have been observed carrying four RPG-7 anti-tank rocket launchers on a post-type mounting in the rear area.

A radio communications version used by the former East German Army was known as the Funkstation R-1125F.

Specifications
Cab seating: 1 + 6
Configuration: 4 × 4
Weight:
  (empty) 1540 kg
  (loaded) 2290 kg
Weight on front axle: (loaded) 1000 kg
Weight on rear axle: (loaded) 1400 kg
Max load: 600 kg
Max towed load:
  (unbraked) 600 kg
  (braked) 2000 kg
Length: 4.025 m
Width: 1.785 m
Height: 2.015 m
Ground clearance: 0.22 m
Track: 1.422 m
Wheelbase: 2.38 m
Angle of approach/departure: 52°/42°
Max speed: 100 km/h
Range: 750 km
Fuel capacity: 78 l
Max gradient: 62%
  (towing trailer) 40%
Vertical obstacle: 0.45 m
Fording: 0.7 m
Engine: ZMZ-451M 4-cylinder water-cooled petrol developing 75 hp at 4000 rpm
Gearbox: manual with 4 forward and 1 reverse gears
Transfer box: 2-speed
Turning radius: 6.5 m

UAZ-469B (4 × 4) 600 kg light vehicle (Michael Jerchel)

UAZ-469B (4 × 4) 600 kg light vehicle (Stefan Marx)

Tyres: 8.40 × 15
Brakes:
  (main) hydraulic
  (parking) mechanical
Electrical system: 12 V

Status

Replaced in production from 1990 onwards by the UAZ-3151. The UAZ-469B is in service with former members of the Warsaw Pact including Hungary, Poland and the CIS. Also exported to other countries including Afghanistan, Cuba, Egypt, Iran, Iraq and Syria.

Manufacturer

Ul'yanovsk Motor Vehicle Plant, Ul'yanovsk, CIS.

GAZ-69 and GAZ-69A (4 × 4) Light Vehicles

Description

The GAZ-69 series of light 4 × 4 vehicles entered production at the Gor'kiy Plant in 1952 and continued in production there until 1956 when production was transferred to the Ul'yanovsk Plant. They were then also known as the UAZ-69 and UAZ-69A and production continued until the UAZ-469B was introduced. These vehicles used many components of the UAZ-450 range of civilian vehicles.

There are two basic models in service, the GAZ-69 and the GAZ-69A. The former has two doors and has been designed to carry 500 kg of cargo. Bench seats down each side in the rear seat two men on each side facing each other. The spare wheel is mounted externally on the left side of the body. This model is widely used as a command/radio vehicle and for towing recoilless rifles and light anti-aircraft guns such as the 23 mm ZU-23. The second model is the GAZ-69A, which has four doors and can carry five men plus 100 kg of cargo. The spare wheel is carried under the rear of the vehicle. Both models have a removable top, windscreen that can be folded forward onto the bonnet and removable door tops.

Late production models of the UAZ-69 were the UAZ-69M which has a 65 hp M-21 engine, and the UAZ-69-68. Late production models of the UAZ-69A were the UAZ-69AM which also has a 65 hp engine and the UAZ-69A-68.

Variants

Anti-tank (missile)
This is armed with four Snapper anti-tank missiles mounted at the back facing the rear. When travelling they are covered by a tarpaulin cover, which is folded downwards when they are deployed. These missiles can be launched from within the vehicle, an observation window being provided on the right side of the cab rear for this purpose, or away from the vehicle with the aid of a separation sight and controller. This version is no longer deployed by the former Warsaw Pact nations but may still be used by the former Yugoslavia and countries in the Middle East.

Anti-tank (recoilless rifle)
Some countries in the Middle East have mounted a recoilless rifle on the rear of the vehicle.

Aircraft starter
This is the GAZ-69 with a modified rear on which is mounted an aircraft starting unit.

Mine detector vehicle
The GAZ-69 can be fitted with the DIM mine detection system; there is a separate entry for this in the *Mine detection equipment* section.

North Korea
North Korea built a version of the GAZ-69A (4 × 4) vehicle with a revised front.

Romania
Romania produced the GAZ-69 under the designation M-461. This was almost identical to the original but had a four-speed gearbox.

UAZ-456
This is a tractor version for towing semi-trailers.

Specifications

Model	GAZ-69	GAZ-69A
Configuration	4 × 4	4 × 4
Weight (empty)	1525 kg	1535 kg
(loaded)	2175 kg	1960 kg
Weight on front axle		
(loaded)	940 kg	935 kg
Weight on rear axle		
(loaded)	1235 kg	1035 kg
Max load	500 kg	5 men
		+ 100 kg
Towed load	850 kg	850 kg
Length	3.85 m	3.85 m
Width	1.85 m	1.75 m
Height	2.03 m	1.92 m
Ground clearance	0.21 m	0.21 m

Model	GAZ-69	GAZ-69A
Track	1.44 m	1.44 m
Wheelbase	2.3 m	2.3 m
Angle of approach/ departure	45°/35°	45°/35°
Max speed	90 km/h	90 km/h
Range	530 km	420 km
Fuel capacity	75 l	60 l
Fuel consumption	14 l/100 km at 40 km/h	
Max gradient	60%	60%
Fording	0.55 m	0.55 m
Engine	M-20 4-cylinder water-cooled petrol developing 52 hp at 3600 rpm	
Gearbox	manual with 3 forward and 1 reverse gears	
Clutch	single disc, dry	single disc, dry
Transfer box	2-speed	2-speed
Steering	globoid worm with double collared cone	
Turning radius	6 m	6.5 m
Suspension	longitudinal semi-elliptical springs with double-acting hydraulic shock absorbers front and rear	
Tyres	6.50 × 16	6.50 × 16
Brakes (main)	hydraulic on all wheels	
(parking)	on transmission	
Electrical system	12 V	12 V
Batteries	2 × 6 V ST 54	2 × 6 V ST 54
Generator	250 W	250 W

Status

Production complete. In service with members of the former Warsaw Pact and most countries that have received Soviet aid, for example Cuba, Egypt, Finland, Syria and Vietnam.

Manufacturers

Gor'kiy Motor Vehicle Plant, Gor'kiy, Russia (1952-56) and Ul'yanovsk Motor Vehicle Plant, Ul'yanovsk (from 1956 onwards).

GAZ-69 (4 × 4) 500 kg light vehicle (Stefan Marx)

GAZ-69 (4 × 4) 500 kg light vehicle (Michael Green)

UAZ-452D (4 × 4) 800 kg Light Vehicle

Description

The UAZ-452D (4 × 4) light vehicle entered production at the Ul'yanovsk Motor Vehicle Plant in 1966. Although used primarily for civilian applications, the vehicle and its variants are used in some numbers by the armed forces, especially as ambulances and command vehicles.

The UAZ-452D has a two-door all-steel forward control type cab. The rear cargo area has drop sides and a drop tailgate.

Variants of the vehicle are the UAZ-452 (van), UAZ-452A (ambulance carrying three seated patients plus three stretcher patients), UAZ-452P (tractor truck), UAZ-452E (with shielded electrical system), UAZ-452DE (with shielded electrical system) and the UAZ-452V (10-seat bus).

The vehicle was preceded by the UAZ-450 series of 4 × 4 vehicles which were in production from 1958 to 1966 and included the UAZ-450 (van), UAZ-450A (ambulance), UAZ-450B (bus) and the UAZ-450D (cargo truck). These were all powered by a 65 hp four-cylinder petrol engine and had a gearbox with three forward and one reverse gears and a two-speed transfer case.

In 1962 a series of similar 4 × 2 vehicles, the UAZ-451 (van) and the UAZ-451D (cargo), entered production. These were replaced by the improved UAZ-451M in 1966. The UAZ-451DM is also a 4 × 2 vehicle which can carry 1000 kg of cargo.

The UAZ-452 series is being replaced in production by the UAZ-3251. This is a generally improved version of the earlier models and is produced with UAZ diesel or petrol engines developing 85 hp.

Specifications (UAZ-452D cargo truck)
Cab seating: 1 + 1
Weight:
 (empty) 1670 kg
 (loaded) 2620 kg
Weight on front axle: (loaded) 1190 kg
Weight on rear axle: (loaded) 1143 kg
Max load: 800 kg
Towed load: 850 kg
Load area: 2.6 × 1.87 m
Length: 4.46 m
Width: 2.004 m
Height:
 (cab) 2.07 m
 (load area) 1.04 m
Ground clearance: 0.22 m
Track: 1.442 m
Wheelbase: 2.3 m
Angle of approach/departure: 34°/33°
Max speed: 95 km/h
Range: 430 km
Fuel capacity: 56 l
Fuel consumption: 13 l/100 km
Gradient: 58%
Fording: 0.7 m
Engine: ZMZ-451E 4-cylinder water-cooled petrol developing 72 hp at 4000 rpm
Gearbox: manual with 4 forward and 1 reverse gears
Clutch: single dry disc
Transfer box: 2-speed

UAZ-452D (4 × 4) light vehicle (Henry Dodds)

Turning radius: 6 m
Suspension: longitudinal semi-elliptical springs with hydraulic double-acting shock absorbers on both axles
Tyres: 8.40 × 15
Brakes:
 (main) hydraulic
 (parking) mechanical
Electrical system: 12 V
Battery: 1 × STE-54EM

Generator: 250 W

Status
Being replaced in production by the UAZ-3251. In service with former Warsaw Pact countries and Egypt.

Manufacturer
Ul'yanovsk Motor Vehicle Plant, Ul'yanovsk, CIS.

EGYPT

Egyptian Jeep Production

Development
Egypt is manufacturing under licence from the Chrysler Corporation the YJ (4 × 4) Jeep. This agreement is part of the Arab Organisation of Industrialisation Plan passed to the Chrysler Corporation from the American Motors Corporation during their 1987 merger.

The first production Egyptian Jeeps (CJ-7) were completed in 1978 and 2500 vehicles were built in 1979, all of which were supplied to the Egyptian Army. Since then over 13 000 vehicles have been built, including the CJ-7, CJ-8 (both with an average of 30 per cent local content), J-20, AM-720 and Jeep Waggoneer.

The YJ-L entered production in 1989 with 800 units for the Egyptian Army and 350 for the Kuwait Military Forces. The YJ-L differs from its predecessor by having an improved severe use air flow system, larger 7.50 × 16 tyres, heavy duty shock absorbers and springs and a payload of 750 kg. Optional extras include a Ramsey 3630 kg winch and blackout lights.

Variants
Several variants of Egyptian-produced Jeeps are in Egyptian Army use. They include versions of the CJ-7 used as Swingfire anti-tank missile launch vehicles (carrying four missiles) or Swingfire missile resupply vehicles (carrying 13 missiles). Other missile-carrying CJ-7s include versions for the SA-7 SAM and its Egyptian-produced version, the Sakr Eye.

Variants of the CJ-8 in Egyptian Army service include 500 TOW anti-tank missile carriers delivered direct from the USA plus a number of TOW missile resupply vehicles, a refrigerated mobile blood bank with demountable electrical generators, an 80 mm multiple rocket launcher carrier (for details refer to *Jane's Armour and Artillery 1992-93* page 721), a mobile workshop, an NBC reconnaissance vehicle, an ambulance, a communications vehicle and a command vehicle.

A border patrol unit supplied to Kuwait was a YJ-L fitted with a 0.50/12.7 mm machine gun mount, a 24 V system, an electronic land navigation system and an auxiliary fuel tank providing a total fuel capacity of 100 litres.

Jeep Corporation YJ-L (4 × 4) light vehicle, long wheelbase version of YJ-S (Wrangler)

Egyptian-built Jeep YJ-L border patrol vehicle

Specifications (YJ)

Configuration: 4 × 4
Weight:
 (kerb) 1450 kg
 (GVW) 2200 kg
Max load: 750 kg
Length: 4.492 m
Width: 1.676 m
Height: (open body) 1.744 m
Wheelbase: 2.627 m
Angle of approach/departure: 45°/30°
Fuel capacity: 68.2 l (91 l optional)

Engine: 242 CID 4 l 6-cylinder MPI petrol developing 173 hp or 150 CID 2.5 l 4-cylinder MPI petrol
Gearbox: AX5 with 5 forward and 1 reverse gears
Transfer box: 2-speed
Suspension:
 (front) Dana Model 30 semi-floating axle with multi-leaf XHD springs mounted below plus track bar and stabiliser bar
 (rear) Dana Model 44 w/Trac-Loc semi-floating with multi-leaf XHD springs mounted below; a track bar is utilised
Turning circle: 10.5 m

Brakes: disc front, drum rear
Electrical system: 12 V (24 V optional)

Status

In production. In service with Egypt (CJ and YJ), Kuwait (YJ) and Oman (CJ).

Manufacturer

Arab American Vehicles Co (AAV), PO Box 2419, Horreia, Heliopolis, Cairo, Egypt.
Tel: 202 290 3503. Telex: 93791 aav un.
Fax: 202 290 3562.

FRANCE

LOHR Fardier FL 500 and FL 501 (4 × 4) 500 kg Light Vehicles

Description

These light airportable vehicles were developed by SOFRAMAG (now LOHR) for the use of airborne troops and 300 were delivered to the French Army. A C-130 or C-160 Transall transport aircraft can carry six FL 500s ready for air-dropping or 12 FL 500s for delivery as cargo. The SA 330 Puma helicopter can carry one FL 500 and one 120 mm mortar. The vehicle can carry a maximum load of 500 kg, including the driver, and tow a trailer or weapon such as a 120 mm Thomson Brandt mortar, weighing a maximum of 500 kg.

The FL 500 has a chassis of tubular steel welded construction with the load area covered by aluminium sheeting. The driver is seated at the front of the vehicle on the left side and if required, an inverted U-shaped safety bar can be fitted to the rear of the driver's position.

The engine is mounted crosswise in the centre of the vehicle and connected to the front and rear axles by two Cardan-driven central transmission units with shock-absorbing guides. The light alloy reinforced axles are mounted on cushioned rubber and the suspension arms consist of helicoidal springs placed horizontally on each side of the chassis, in two suspension boxes.

Brakes are hydraulic on all wheels, with an independent parking brake for each rear wheel. A complete lighting system is installed enabling the vehicle to be driven on roads.

The final production version was the FL 501 with an optional 36 hp engine fitted as standard. This allows loads of up to 600 kg to be towed. The FL 501 has been demonstrated carrying two MATRA SATCP surface-to-air missiles.

The FL 500 has been used for trials with the MILAN ATGW system and has been equipped with light machine guns. Alternative loads could include radios and the FL 500 and FL 501 can be used to tow 120 mm mortars.

Specifications

Cab seating: 1
Configuration: 4 × 4
Weight:
 (empty) 680 kg
 (loaded) 1180 kg
Max load: 500 kg
Towed load:
 (FL 500) 500 kg

LOHR Fardier FL 501 (4 × 4) 500 kg light vehicle

 (FL 501) 600 kg
Load area: 1.93 m²
Length:
 (laden) 2.41 m
 (unladen) 2.375 m
Width: 1.5 m
Height:
 (steering wheel) 1.18 m
 (load area) 0.92 m
Ground clearance:
 (unloaded) 0.25 m
 (loaded) 0.2 m
Track: 1.26 m
Wheelbase: 1.735 m
Angle of approach/departure: 90°/90°
Max speed: (road) 80 km/h
Range: (road) 200 km
Fuel capacity: 25 l
Max gradient: 60%
Max side slope: 30%
Vertical obstacle: 0.2 m
Fording: 0.4 m
Engine: Citroën AK 2 flat twin petrol developing 29 hp (DIN) at 6750 rpm or (FL 501) Citroën V06/630 flat twin, air-cooled petrol developing 36 hp at 5500 rpm

Gearbox: Citroën manual with 4 forward and 1 reverse gears
Steering: rack and pinion
Turning radius: 4.8 m
Suspension: independent, with helical spring and hydraulic shock absorber at each wheel station
Brakes:
 (main) hydraulic disc
 (parking) handbrake on each rear wheel
Electrical system: 12 V
Battery: 1 × 12 V, 30 Ah
Alternator: 390 W

Status

Production complete. In service with the French Army (300), Argentina, Spain (parachute brigade) and Tunisia.

Manufacturer

LOHR SA, F-67980 Hangenbieten, France.
Tel: 88 38 98 00. Telex: 870082 f.
Fax: 88 96 06 36.

LOHR VLA Light Airmobile Vehicle

Description

The LOHR VLA (Véhicule Léger Aéromobile) was developed in response to a requirement from the French Army for a light vehicle capable of being transported in or under an NH 90 helicopter. Three prototypes have been completed.

The VLA is a 4 × 4 multi-purpose light vehicle with a welded tube chassis and aluminium and polyester panel body; one or two roll bars can be incorporated. The engine is located in the centre of the chassis and is allied to an automatic transmission with an integral differential. The driver is seated far forward in a well with seating for one passenger on the right. Behind the well is a small load platform over the engine compartment with a further cargo/passenger well at the rear; this can accommodate three passengers. The cargo well may be used to mount various weapons, such as a MILAN or TOW ATGW, and a machine gun may be mounted in front of the passenger.

For air transport, a C-130 or C-160 transport aircraft can carry up to 10 VLAs stacked in twos one above another, or four vehicles on paradrop pallets. For transport slung under helicopters the VLA is provided with four lashing rings and stowage space for slings.

Optional equipment includes a winch, a tarpaulin to cover the load and rear areas and removable light modular armour. Proposed versions include an air defence variant carrying a light surface-to-air missile system, a fire support vehicle with a 12.7 mm machine gun, a field ambulance, a light recovery version, a light reconnaissance vehicle with radios, a 120 mm mortar tractor, a light load carrier towing a small trailer and a command version with an extendible canvas penthouse.

Specifications

Seating: 2 + 3
Configuration: 4 × 4
Weight empty: 1200 kg
Combat weight: 2000 kg
Max load: 800 kg
Towed load: 1200 kg
Length: (body) 3.2 m
Width: 1.75 m
Height:
  (body) 1.03 m
  (roll bar) 1.66 m
Ground clearance: 0.29 m
Wheelbase: 1.965 m
Max speed: 90 km/h
Range: 800 km
Max gradient: 60%
Max side slope: 30%
Fording: 0.8 m
Engine: Peugeot XUD 9A diesel developing 70 hp
Transmission: automatic with 4 forward and 1 reverse gears
Steering: rack bar
Suspension: MacPherson front; torsion bar at rear
Tyres: 7.00 R 16 Michelin XC type L

LOHR Véhicule Léger Aéromobile (VLA)

Status
Prototypes.

Tel: 88 38 98 00. Telex: 870082 f.
Fax: 88 96 06 36.

Manufacturer
LOHR SA, F-67980 Hangenbieten, France.

Auverland/SAMO (4 × 4) Light Vehicles

Description

The 4 × 4 SAMO light vehicle was produced in standard and long wheelbase versions. According to the manufacturer, the standard version has a road-carrying capacity of 1200 kg and the long wheelbase version a road-carrying capacity of 1800 kg. Their cross-country capacities have not been announced but have been estimated at 800 kg and 1200 kg respectively. The ladder-type chassis is made up of two rectangular box-section main members, 120 × 60 mm and 5 mm wall thickness, linked by six transverse crossmembers, three welded and three bolted (two of which constitute the bumpers). The body structure is 2 mm thick sheet steel welded onto the chassis giving exceptional rigidity overall.

The layout of both vehicles is similar with the engine at the front, driver and passenger seats in the centre and the cargo area at the rear with a bench seat down each side and a tailgate. The basic model is fitted with removable bows, canvas top and a windscreen that can be folded down onto the bonnet if required. A hard-top model is also offered.

Optional equipment includes a 24 V electrical system, different tyres (for example 9.00 × 16), 3500 kg capacity winch, PTO, cooling radiator for engine oil, water tank, power clutch, power brakes, searchlight, vertical exhaust, heater, right-hand drive, special equipment for operations in the desert, long-range fuel tanks, overdrive, power-assisted steering, heavy duty axles (front with capacity of 1250 kg, rear 2500 kg), additional fuel tank, folding windscreen, gearbox and axle protection plates and tropical ventilation.

Specifications

Model	Standard	LWB
Cab seating	2 + 4	2 + 8
Configuration	4 × 4	4 × 4
Weight (empty)	1400 kg	1600 kg
(loaded)	2600 kg	3400 kg
Max load	1200 kg	1800 kg
Towed load (road)	3000 kg	3000 kg
(cross-country)	800 kg	800 kg
Load area	1.1 × 1.4 m	1.67 × 1.41 m
Length	3.6 m	4.23 m
Width	1.592 m	1.592 m
Height (overall)	1.9 m	1.9 m
(reduced)	1.3 m	1.3 m
(load area)	0.7 m	0.7 m
Ground clearance	0.216 m	0.216 m
Track	1.36 m	1.36 m
Wheelbase	2.04 m	2.54 m
Angle of approach/departure	42°/35°	42°/30°
Max speed (road)	115 km/h	115 km/h
Range	900 km	900 km
Fuel capacity	55 l	55 l
Max gradient	65%	65%
Max side slope	30%	30%
Fording	0.6 m	0.6 m
Engine	Peugeot 4-cylinder diesel developing 67.4 hp at 4000 rpm or Renault 4-cylinder diesel developing 85 hp at 3000 rpm or Renault 4-cylinder petrol developing 80 hp at 5000 rpm	
Gearbox	manual with 4 forward and 1 reverse gears	
Clutch	single dry plate	single dry plate
Transfer box	2-speed	2-speed
Steering	recirculation and ball	recirculation and ball
Turning radius	5.3 m	6.4 m
Suspension	semi-elliptical springs and hydraulic shock absorbers	
Tyres	7.50 × 16	7.50 × 16
Brakes (main)	hydraulic	hydraulic
Electrical system	12 V (24 V optional)	12 V (24 V optional)

LWB SAMO (4 × 4) with box body

LWB SAMO (4 × 4) light vehicle

Variants

Both models can be modified for a wide range of roles including an ambulance, command vehicle and radio vehicle. The standard model can be armed with a 12.7 or 7.62 mm machine gun. The long wheelbase model can be armed with ATGWs, a 106 mm recoilless rifle or a 20 mm cannon.

Status

Production complete. In service with Burkina Faso, Burundi, Cameroon, Central African Republic, Chad, Congo, Ivory Coast, Madagascar, Zaïre and other countries.

Manufacturer

Auverland SA, BP 12, F-42260 Saint-Germain-Laval, France.
Tel: 77 65 54 44. Telex: 310663 f.
Fax: 77 65 49 18.

Auverland Type A3 (4 × 4) 500 kg Light Vehicle

Description

The Auverland Type A3 (4 × 4) light vehicles are produced in a range to meet various user requirements. The base vehicle, the Type A3, is available in one of two chassis lengths, and various diesel or petrol engines can be fitted.

The base model of the Type A3 is powered by a diesel engine. The Type A3MH is intended for transport by helicopter while the Type A3L has a longer wheelbase and can carry up to nine passengers or a payload of 800 kg. There is also a 4 × 2 version of the basic Type A3.

The Type A3 is a small Jeep-type vehicle available in various forms. The layout is conventional with the engine at the front and seating for the driver and two passengers. A small area at the rear can be used to carry 500 kg of payload or two extra passengers. The vehicle is constructed so that the body is isolated from the rectangular tube chassis.

There are two chassis lengths available (3.65 m and 3.85 m) and the vehicle can be supplied in soft- or hard-top versions with standard or comfort pick-up variants. A small winch can be fitted at the front, if required.

The standard engine is a Peugeot XUD 9 diesel. Engine options include the Peugeot XUD 11 diesel developing 84.5 hp (for the Type A3 SL) and the Peugeot XY 52C petrol developing 94 hp. A 24 V electrical system can be fitted.

Variants include the Type A3 MHCB light armoured vehicle, the Type A3 SL 4 × 2 armed with a 12.7 mm machine gun, the Type A3 'Gendarmerie' with a long wheelbase and hard-top, and a Type A3 produced for the French Air Force armed with a 7.62 mm AA 52 machine gun.

Specifications

Cab seating: 1 + 1 (up to 4 in rear)
Configuration: 4 × 4
Weight:
 (short chassis, empty) 1150 kg
 (long chassis, empty) 1170 kg

Auverland Type A3 (4 × 4) 500 kg light vehicle

 (loaded) 1670 kg
Max load: 500 kg
Length:
 (short chassis) 3.65 m
 (long chassis) 3.85 m
Width: 1.54 m
Height: 1.7 m
Ground clearance: 0.25 m
Track: 1.342 m
Wheelbase: 2.25 m
Angle of approach/departure: 50°/45°
Max speed: 115 km/h
Fuel capacity: 80 l
Gradient: 100%
Engine: Peugeot XUD 9 1.905 l diesel developing 64 hp (DIN) at 4600 rpm
Gearbox: Peugeot BA 7/4 with 4 forward and 1 reverse gears
Clutch: single dry plate

Transfer box: Auverland A80 2-speed
Turning radius: 5 m
Suspension: coil springs with telescopic shock absorbers
Brakes: disc front, drum rear, dual circuit
Tyres: 6.50 × 16
Electrical system: 12 V (24 V optional)
Battery: 1 × 12 V, 60 Ah

Status

In production. In service with the French Navy and Air Force and Ministry of Defence.

Manufacturer

Auverland SA, BP 12, F-42260 Saint-Germain-Laval, France.
Tel: 77 65 54 44. Telex: 310663 f.
Fax: 77 65 49 18.

Citroën Méhari Armée

Description

The Citroën Méhari Armée is a military version of the standard civilian Méhari vehicle. Its low weight enables it to be used for a variety of military applications such as traffic control, command/radio vehicle and light supplies carrier. Over 8000 of these vehicles were delivered to the French armed forces and police.

The vehicle has an all-steel chassis with a plastic body. The engine is mounted at the front with the driver's and passenger's seats in the centre and the cargo area at the rear.

There are two basic models of the Méhari, two plus two and two-seat utility. The first has two seats at the front, removable or foldaway back seat, fold-down windscreen, black cotton canopy, safety door chains and an anti-theft device. Optional equipment includes a complete hood with transparent side panels and doors. The two-seat utility model has the two seats at the front, flat load area at the rear, fold-down windscreen, black cotton canopy, safety door chains and an anti-theft device. Optional equipment includes a hood without transparent side panels and doors.

Trials confirmed that the Méhari Armée is suitable for dropping by parachute when strapped to a landing platform. The basic vehicle can be used for a variety of roles including ambulance, traffic control and radio vehicle.

Citroën Méhari Armée

Specifications
Cab seating: 1 + 1
Configuration: 4 × 2 (front wheel drive)
Weight:
(empty) 570 kg
(loaded) 955 kg
Max load: 385 kg
Load area: 1.34 × 1 m
Length: 3.52 m
Width: 1.53 m
Height:
(overall) 1.635 m
(load area) 0.65 m
Wheelbase: 2.37 m
Max speed: (road) 100 km/h

Range: 300 km
Fuel capacity: 25 l
Max gradient: 40%
Engine: AK 2 2-cylinder petrol, air-cooled developing 29 hp at 5500 rpm
Gearbox: manual with 4 forward and 1 reverse gears
Clutch: single dry plate
Steering: rack and bar
Turning radius: 5.35 m
Suspension: both axles suspended by arms with lateral interplay on spiral springs. Hydraulic shock absorbers front and rear
Brakes:
(main) hydraulic
(parking) mechanical

Electrical system: 12 V or 24 V
Batteries: 2 × 12 V

Status
Production complete. In service with Spain and the French Army, Air Force, Navy and Police.

Manufacturer
SA Automobiles Citroën, 62 boulevard Victor Hugo, F-92200 Neuilly-sur-Seine, France.
Tel: 47 48 41 41. Telex: citr 614830 f.

Citroën A FAF 400 kg (4 × 2) and 400 kg (4 × 4) Light Vehicles

Description
The Citroën A FAF is basically a standard civilian vehicle with the minimum of modifications for military use. Two models are currently in service, a 4 × 4 version and a 4 × 2 version, both with a 400 kg payload. For ease of maintenance and obtaining spare parts, all the automotive components are from Citroën A type vehicles of which well over seven million were built.

The chassis and body are all-steel and the windscreen can be folded forward onto the bonnet. The layout is conventional with the engine at the front, passenger and driver seats in the centre and the load area at the rear. A model is also available with an additional two-man bench seat behind the driver's and front passenger's seats, which folds forward to increase the cargo area. In wet weather a cover can be erected over the top of the vehicle.

The Citroën A FAF is suitable for a number of roles including cargo carrier, command/radio and reconnaissance and can be dropped by parachute. Optional equipment includes a 24 V electrical system and hydraulic shock absorbers.

Portuguese Army Citroën A FAF (4 × 4) 400 kg light vehicle

Specifications
(4 × 2 version; data in square brackets relate to 4 × 4 model where different)
Configuration: 4 × 2 [4 × 4]
Weight:
(empty) 690 [850] kg
(loaded) 1090 [1250] kg
Max payload: 400 kg
Length: 3.62 m
Width: 1.55 m
Height: 1.68 m
Wheelbase: 2.4 m
Track:
(front) 1.26 m
(rear) 1.28 m
Ground clearance: 0.238 m

Max speed: 100 [110] km/h
Gradient: 50%
Fuel capacity: 66 l
Fording: 0.35 m
Engine: air-cooled Citroën 4-stroke petrol developing 28.5 hp (DIN) at 6750 rpm [same engine or 4-cylinder petrol developing 34 hp (DIN) at 5500 rpm]
Gearbox: manual with 4 forward and 1 reverse gears (road, 4 forward and 1 reverse gears, cross-country, 3 forward and 1 reverse gears, rear differential)
Clutch: single dry plate
Steering: rack and pinion
Turning radius: 6 m
Brakes:
(main) (front) disc on gearbox
(main) (rear) disc on differential

(parking) acts on front wheels
Suspension: arms with lateral interaction, working with helicoidal springs and inertia stabilisers
Tyres: 155.14 × CM
Electrical system: 12 V, 48 Ah (24 V optional)

Status
Production complete. The 4 × 4 model is in service with Burundi and Portugal. Produced in Greece as the Namco Pony (qv).

Manufacturer
SA Automobiles Citroën, 82 boulevard Victor Hugo, F-92200 Neuilly-sur-Seine, France.
Tel: 47 48 41 41. Telex: citr 614830 f.

SMAI LWV (4 × 4) 800 kg Light Vehicle

Description
The SMAI LWV (4 × 4) 800 kg lightweight vehicle was designed for use by airborne and special forces with emphasis being placed on ease of maintenance and production, and economy.

The SMAI LWV (lightweight vehicle) is a Jeep-type vehicle of small overall dimensions. The design of the chassis is such that the sidemembers are reversible and the wheel housings are identical on each wheel station. The body side panels and the front and rear panels are also interchangeable.

The layout of the vehicle is conventional with the engine forward and seating for a driver and four passengers – it is possible to seat up to six passengers with a special layout. The construction of the body is such that above the front wheel housings and forward of the dashboard the body is fitted with a transverse

member passing across the width of the vehicle. This member, which can be removed to improve engine and electrical component access, carries the hinging points for the hood, the windshield, the steering column and the dashboard. All these elements can be released using catches.

The rigid axles are carried on the ends of longitudinal arms hinged to the chassis to ensure that the wheels remain permanently in contact with the ground. Transverse axle guidance is enhanced by the use of Panhard rods hinged to the chassis. The suspension proper consists of coil springs and hydraulic shock absorbers.

To ease production the choice of engine, gearbox, and so on, is left to the customer and the vehicle can accommodate a variety of commercially available four-, five- or six-cylinder in-line, V-6 or V-8 petrol or diesel engines with capacities of 2 to 4 litres. Similarly the choice of gearbox and transmission is also left to the customer.

The SMAI LWV was designed for air transport and

up to seven vehicles can be carried ready for use in a C-130H transport aircraft (nine in a C-130E). The vehicles can also be carried or stored stacked one on top of the other.

The LWV is considered suitable for a range of military roles including as a troop carrier (in its basic form), as an ambulance, as a missile team support vehicle, for anti-tank missile transport, forward reconnaissance, command and liaison and as an ultra-rapid intervention vehicle. It is possible to mount automatic weapons with calibres of up to 20 mm.

The SMAI Pick-Up (4 × 4) light vehicle is a larger version of the basic LWV (see following entry).

Specifications
Cab seating: 1 + 4
Configuration: 4 × 4
Weight:
(empty) approx 1650 kg
(loaded) approx 2650 kg
Max load: (road and cross-country) 1000 kg

SMAI LWV (4 × 4) 800 kg light vehicle

SMAI LWV (4 × 4) 800 kg light vehicle

Towed load: 2500 kg
Length: 3.5 m
Width: 1.7 m
Height: 1.73 m
Ground clearance: 0.37 m
Track: 1.5 m
Wheelbase: 2.4 m
Angle of approach/departure: 66°/37°
Max speed: 125 km/h
Range: up to 1000 km
Fuel capacity: 1, 2 or 3 × 50 l

Fording: 0.55 m
Engine: see text
Gearbox: see text
Clutch: single dry plate
Transfer box: SMAI 2-speed
Suspension: coil spring with hydraulic shock absorbers
Electrical system: 12 or 24 V

Status
Prototypes. Diesel-engined versions ready for production.

Manufacturer
SMAI – Soudure et Mécanique Appliquée Industrielles, 50 rue de la Fosse-aux-Loups, F-95100 Argenteuil, France.
Tel: (1) 39 82 65 96. Telex: smavarg 607298 f.
Fax: (1) 39 82 02 09.

SMAI Pick-Up (4 × 4) Light Vehicle

Description
The SMAI Pick-Up (4 × 4) light vehicle is an enlarged development of the smaller SMAI LWV (see previous entry) and uses the same overall layout, construction and appearance. The basic Pick-Up is a completely open vehicle that can be configured into a variety of forms with a total loaded weight of between 4500 and 5500 kg.

As with the SMAI LWV, the Pick-Up may be fitted with a variety of engines, both diesel and petrol, and drive chains according to role and customer requirements. The details provided in the Specifications are applicable to the prototype.

The Pick-Up body and/or cab can be configured into a number of vehicle types including a light tactical vehicle, ambulance, light fire tender, and so on.

Specifications
Cab seating: 1 + 1 or 2
Configuration: 4 × 4
Total weight: 4500 to 5500 kg
Length: 4.86 m
Width: 1.87 m
Height: 1.95 m
Ground clearance:
(under floor) 0.45 m
(under axle) 0.23 m
Track:
(front) 1.65 m
(rear) 1.62 m
Wheelbase: 3.2 m
Angle of approach/departure: 52°/35°
Max speed: 120 km/h
Range: more than 700 km
Fuel capacity: 2 × 50 l
Fording: more than 0.6 m
Engine: Renault SOFIM type 8140-IDS turbo diesel
Gearbox: Renault type 2 or ZF, both with 4 forward and 1 reverse gears
Clutch: single dry plate
Transfer box: SMA 2-speed
Suspension: coil spring with hydraulic shock absorbers
Electrical system: 12 or 24 V

Status
Prototypes – ready for production.

Manufacturer
SMAI – Soudure et Mécanique Appliquée Industrielles, 50 rue de la Fosse-aux-Loups, F-95100 Argenteuil, France.
Tel: (1) 39 82 65 96. Telex: smavarg 607298 f.
Fax: (1) 39 82 02 09.

SMAI Pick-Up (4 × 4) light vehicle configured as light fire tender

Peugeot P4 (4 × 4) 750 kg Light Vehicle

Development
The standard light vehicle of the French Army was the Hotchkiss M 201 (4 × 4) 400 kg, production of which was completed in 1969. To replace this fleet three manufacturers each submitted 12 vehicles for extensive trials; these were the Renault TRM 500 (4 × 4) 500 kg based on the Italian FIAT 1107 AD, the Citroën C 44 based on the German Iltis and the Peugeot P4 based on the Mercedes-Benz vehicle. Early in 1981 the French Army selected the Peugeot P4 and placed an order for 15 000 vehicles. Mass production, by Panhard, began in early 1983 with the first 2400 vehicles being fitted with petrol engines. The P4 is often referred to as the VLTT (*Véhicule de Liaison Tout Terrain*).

Description
The layout is conventional with the engine at the front, driver and passenger immediately behind the engine and the cargo area at the rear with a two-man bench seat down either side and an opening tailgate on which the spare wheel is mounted.

The front seats are adjustable and hinge forward to give access to the rear seats and the tool boxes beneath each of them. The driver and passengers are provided with seat belts with automatic rollers. The bench seats in the rear can be folded down to clear the load-carrying area.

The chassis is formed from two parallel longitudinal

Peugeot P4 (4 × 4) 750 kg light vehicle

Peugeot P4 (4 × 4) light vehicle armed with 106 mm recoilless rifle

Model	SWB	LWB
Configuration	4 × 4	4 × 4
Weight (empty) (petrol/diesel)	1815/1895 kg	1985/2065 kg
(loaded) (petrol/diesel)	2565/2645 kg	2985/3065 kg
Max load	750 kg	750 kg
Length	4.2 m	4.65 m
Width (with antenna mount)	1.83 m	1.83 m
(less antenna mount)	1.7 m	1.7 m
Height	1.9 m	1.9 m
Ground clearance	0.24 m	0.24 m
Track	1.4 m	1.4 m
Wheelbase	2.4 m	2.85 m
Angle of approach/departure	42°/37°	42°/37°
Fording	0.5 m	0.5 m
Gradient (loaded) (petrol/diesel)	73.5/55%	73.5/55%
Side slope (loaded)	30%	30%
Max speed (petrol/diesel)	118/108 km/h	118/108 km/h
Fuel capacity	75 l	75 l
Engine	Peugeot 1.971 l 4-cylinder petrol developing 79 hp at 4750 rpm or Peugeot 2.498 l 4-cylinder diesel developing 70.5 hp at 4500 rpm	
Gearbox	manual, 4 forward and 1 reverse gears	
Clutch	single dry disc with ball-bearing thrust mechanism	
Transfer box	2-speed	2-speed
Steering	rack and pinion with damper	
Turning radius	5.5 m	6.45 m
Suspension (front)	coil springs, anti-sway bar and double-acting telescopic hydraulic shock absorbers	
(rear)	coil springs and double-acting telescopic hydraulic shock absorbers	
Tyres	700 RC 16 x C type L	700 RC 16 x C type L
Brakes	hydraulic dual circuit, discs front and drum rear	
Electrical system	24 V	24 V
Generator	1200 W	1200 W

beams with rectangular sections connected by five round transverse members. The rear axle is fitted with a hydraulically controlled differential lock.

The sheet metal body is connected to the chassis with eight flexible mounts and has a removable roll-over bar and a folding windscreen of bonded safety glass. Fixtures, bumpers, inner bumper liners and the front portion are mounted to the body structure. For ease of replacement these are bolted on. The two cloth doors have translucent window panels and are removable. The rear troop/cargo area is covered by a tarpaulin of plastic-coated cloth, with translucent sides and rear windows, which folds to the rear and is easily removable.

The fuel tank is below the floor of the vehicle between the chassis beams. A fuel can is carried externally at the rear of the vehicle on the left side. The P4 is fitted with a towing eye at the front and a trailer hitch at the rear with an electric trailer plug. The electrical system includes a park plug, lantern plug and a connection box for a two-way radio.

Optional equipment includes power-assisted steering, front locking differential, PTO front and rear, front-mounted electric winch, 15 litres fuel can and various adaptors for mounting machine guns and other weapons.

The basic vehicle is used by the French Army for a variety of roles, including one armed with twin F1 machine guns for use by scout teams and traffic control squads while another is equipped with a MILAN ATGW launcher and four missiles and used by motorised infantry. The P4 has also been demonstrated carrying the Mygale air defence system and various forms of radar. An LWB model is also available with a drop tailgate, bows, tarpaulin cover and back-to-back seating for eight fully equipped soldiers at the rear. The P4 has been demonstrated carrying a 106 mm recoilless rifle. Both the SWB and LWB versions are fitted with radios for use in the command role and fully enclosed van-type versions of both the LWB and SWB models are available. There is also a fully equipped workshop vehicle version and an ambulance, both LWB. A fully enclosed SWB armoured variant has been demonstrated. The P4 has been demonstrated carrying NBC decontamination equipment.

Status
In production. In service with the French Army, Gabon and Togo.

Manufacturer
Automobiles Peugeot, 75 Avenue de la Grande-Armée, F-75116 Paris Cedex 16, France. Tel: (1) 40 66 55 11. Telex: 610700 f.

SOVAMAG TC10 (4 × 4) 1000 kg Multi-purpose Vehicle

Description
The SOVAMAG TC10 (4 × 4) 1000 kg multi-purpose vehicle has the general appearance of the American Jeep but is a larger vehicle and can carry a larger (1000 kg) payload. It has square military lines and is ruggedly constructed. Layout is conventional with the 2.498 litre diesel engine and radiator protected behind a sturdy front bumper and a grill guard. This grill guard can be hinged forward to provide extra front stowage capacity.

There are seats for the driver and a passenger while at the rear is the main cargo-carrying area. This has a reinforced floor and bench seats for four men along each side. These seats can be folded up for access to three stowage compartments each side. Access to the cargo area is via a small hatch that opens to the right and carries the spare wheel. In addition to carrying cargo or passengers, the area can be used to mount light weapons such as machine guns or a recoilless rifle. A canvas roof carried on a removable light tubular steel frame provides overhead and side weather protection.

Standard equipment includes two 40 litre drinking water tanks and a jerrican rack at the rear. A standard towing hook is also provided. There is provision for a radio aerial and the normal electrical system is 24 V. The forward-opening bonnet allows easy access to the engine and all maintenance and repairs can be carried out using normal tools.

Specifications

Cab seating: 1 + 1 (8 in rear)
Configuration: 4 × 4
Weight:
  (laden) 2860 kg
  (unladen) 1760 kg
Payload: (road) 1100 kg
Length: 4.45 m
Width: 1.72 m
Height: (unladen) 2 m
Ground clearance: 0.23 m
Wheelbase: 2.769 m
Max speed: 120 km/h
Fuel capacity: 105 l
Range: approx 1000 km
Gradient: 30%
Engine: Peugeot XD3-4X94 2.498 l water-cooled diesel developing 72.5 hp at 4000 rpm
Gearbox: Peugeot BA 7.5 manual, 5 forward and

1 reverse gears
Transfer box: Auverland A80 2-speed
Brakes: hydraulic, discs front, drums rear
Tyres: 7.50 × 16
Electrical system: 24 V
Batteries: 2 × 12 V, 55 A

Status

In production. In service with several countries.

Manufacturer

SOVAMAG, 74 rue du Docteur Bauer, F-93400 Saint-Ouen, France.
Tel: (1) 42 52 20 88. Telex: 642738 f.
Marketed by: Auverland SA, BP 12, F-42260 Saint-Germain-Laval, France.
Tel: 77 65 54 44. Telex: 310663 f.
Fax: 77 65 49 18.

SOVAMAG TC10 (4 × 4) 1000 kg multi-purpose vehicle armed with 7.62 and 12.7 mm machine guns

---

PONCIN (6 × 6) 1000 kg Light Vehicle

Description

First seen publicly in 1990, the PONCIN (6 × 6) 1000 kg light vehicle is a conventional design that incorporates independent suspension on all wheels to provide the vehicle with good traction over all types of terrain or roads.

The chassis uses a novel design with a steel body. The layout is conventional with the engine forward and the driver seated behind a flat folding windscreen. There is space for one passenger next to the driver and both are protected by a roll bar behind the seats. The cargo area at the rear is left open on the prototype but there is enough space to seat at least four passengers. It is possible that further development will increase the load-carrying capacity to 1500 kg.

Power may be provided by a Renault petrol or diesel engine. All wheels have disc brakes, with the front brakes being ventilated.

A 4 × 4 version resembling a Jeep is available.

Specifications

Seating: 1 + 1 (up to 4 in rear)
Configuration: 6 × 6
Weight:
  (unladen) 1600 kg
  (laden) 2600 kg
Max load: 1000 kg
Length: 4.48 m
Width: 1.75 m
Height: 1.87 m
Ground clearance: 0.26 m
Track:
  (front) 1.455 m
  (rear) 1.43 m
Wheelbase: 2.14 m + 0.83 m
Angle of approach/departure: 50°/40°
Max speed: 120 km/h
Fuel capacity: 70 l
Engine: Renault J8S 890 2.1 l 4-cylinder in-line turbo diesel developing 87 hp or
Renault J7T P780 2.165 l 4-cylinder in-line petrol developing 95 hp
Gearbox: manual, 4 forward and 1 reverse gears
Clutch: single dry disc
Transfer box: 2-speed
Suspension: independent coil springs on all wheels
Brakes: discs on all wheels, front wheels ventilated
Tyres: 6.50 × 16

Status

In production.

Manufacturer

PONCIN SA, ZI de Glaire, F-08200 Sedan, France.
Tel: (33) 24 27 15 27. Telex: V.PONCIN 840077 f.
Fax: (33) 24 27 64 72.

PONCIN (6 × 6) 1000 kg light vehicle with AMX-30 combat engineer tractor (EBG)

GERMANY

Kraka 640 (4 × 2) 870 kg Light Vehicle

Description

The Faun Kraka (an abbreviation for *Kraftkarren*, or power cart) was originally designed by Nicholas Straussler with the prototype being completed in the 1960s by the German company Zweirad Union, which was subsequently taken over by Faun. The first production vehicles were officially handed over to the Federal German Army in June 1974, and 762 were built for German Army airborne units.

The Kraka was designed specifically for airborne and airmobile forces and can be transported by aircraft or helicopter. The CH-53 helicopter can carry five folded Krakas and the C-160 Transall aircraft can carry 16 folded or 10 in the normal position. The driver is seated at the front of the vehicle with the flat cargo area to his rear. The engine and gearbox are mounted at the rear, just in front of the rear axle. Power is transmitted from the engine to the clutch and gearbox, to the final drives and then by chains to the rear road wheels.

The Kraka is made up of five major sections: the front axle with the two wheels and steering system; the front bodywork, with two boxes for stowing tools and kit, instrument panel, electric circuitry, handbrake system and the two suspension springs; the fuel tank; the rear section with the engine, gearbox and rear axle; and the front and rear platforms, with driver's seat, two retractable passenger seats and four side guard rails.

There were five different versions of the Kraka: the basic model 644, the 643, 642, 641 and finally the 640 which is the model used by the German Army. The basic 644 model can carry a maximum payload of 1000 kg and has no passenger seats or rear platform. The 643 has a rear platform and side flaps for load carrying. The 642 has additional front wheel covers, padded seats and foot rests for the passengers, and mud flaps. The 641 has additional stowage boxes on either side of the driver, large instrument panel and mudguards for the front wheels. The 640 is the 644 with all the optional accessories including a 45 Ah battery in place of the standard 25 Ah battery.

The German Army fitted many vehicles with the MILAN ATGW system and six missiles, which have replaced the previous 106 mm M40 recoilless rifles. The vehicle can also be armed with a 20 mm Rheinmetall cannon and adapted for a wide range of other applications including ambulance vehicle, cable layer, fire-fighting unit, generator, mortar-carrying vehicle (carrying a 120 mm mortar and 20 rounds of ammunition), NBC decontamination vehicle, radio, starter vehicle, towing vehicle for aircraft and helicopters, warm air vehicle and fitted with water purification equipment.

Faun Kraka (4 × 2) 870 kg light vehicle carrying Rheinmetall 20 mm cannon (Bob Morrison – Military Scene)

Faun Kraka (4 × 2) 870 kg light vehicle carrying 81 mm mortar

Specifications

Seating: 1 + 2
Configuration: 4 × 2
Weight:
(loaded) 1610 kg
(empty) 735 kg
Max load: 870 kg
Weight on front axle: (loaded) 610 kg
Weight on rear axle: (loaded) 1000 kg
Towed load:
(trailer with brakes) 960 kg
(trailer without brakes) 350 kg
Load area: 1.4 × 1.4 m
Length: 2.78 m
(folded) 1.85 m
Width: 1.51 m
Height: 1.19 m
(load area) 0.755 m
Ground clearance: 0.25 m

Track:
(front) 1.138 m
(rear) 1.13 m
Wheelbase: 2.058 m
Max speed: 55 km/h
Fuel capacity: 24.5 l
Max gradient: 55%
Fording: 0.5 m
Engine: BMW 427 2-cylinder 4-stroke petrol developing 26 hp at 4500 rpm
Gearbox: BMW 959 manual with 4 forward and 1 reverse gears
Clutch: single dry plate
Steering: rack and pinion
Turning radius: 4.375 m
Suspension:
(front) 2 semi-elliptical transverse springs with one parabolic spring with rubber hollow spring
(rear) engine suspension arm with rubber spring

Tyres: 22.00 × 12 (Lypsoid)
Brakes:
(main) hydraulic on all wheels
(parking) mechanical, rear wheels
Electrical system: 12 V
Battery: 1 × 12 V, 45 Ah
Generator: 130 W

Status
Production complete. In service with the German Army (762).

Manufacturer
Faun GmbH, Postfach 10 01 08, D-8560 Lauf a.d. Pegnitz, Federal Republic of Germany.
Tel: 091 23 185-0. Telex: 626093.
Fax: 091 23 753 20.

VW 181 (4 × 2) 400 kg Light Vehicle

Description
The VW 181 is basically the standard civilian Volkswagen 181 modified to meet military requirements. A total of 2000 was supplied to the Federal German Army between 1969 and 1970 under the designation Pkw 0.4t.

The chassis consists of a central tubular frame with the floor welded into position. The sheet steel body has four doors each with a removable plastic window, folding windscreen and a folding PVC top. The engine is mounted at the rear. Stowage space is provided under the bonnet and to the rear of the two rear seats which fold down individually. The rear cargo area and the backs of the rear seats are provided with C-profile rails for securing equipment such as radios. When being used as a radio vehicle an additional dynamo is fitted.

Standard equipment on the military version includes an axe, headlamp blackout covers, map light, radio suppression, reclining front seats, four rifle mounts, spade, starting handle, towing eye, towing hook and a wheel chock.

Specifications

Cab seating: 1 + 3
Configuration: 4 × 2
Weight:
(loaded) 1350 kg
(empty) 900 kg
Max load: 450 kg
Weight on front axle: (loaded) 550 kg
Weight on rear axle: (loaded) 800 kg
Towed load: 650 kg
Length: 3.78 m
Width: 1.64 m
Height: 1.62 m
Ground clearance: 0.205 m
Track:
(front) 1.354 m
(rear) 1.446 m

Danish Army VW 181 (4 × 2) 400 kg light vehicle

Wheelbase: 2.4 m
Angle of approach/departure: 36°/31°
Max speed: (road) 113 km/h
Range:
(road) 320 km
(cross-country) 260 km
Fuel capacity: 40 l
Max gradient: 48% (road, low gear)
Fording: 0.396 m
Engine: 4-cylinder petrol developing 44 bhp at 4000 rpm
Gearbox: manual with 4 forward and 1 reverse gears
Clutch: single plate, dry
Steering: worm and roller with hydraulic damper
Turning radius: 5.48 m
Suspension: torsion bar with shock absorbers
Brakes:
(main) hydraulic
(parking) mechanical

Electrical system: 12 V
Battery: 1 × 12 V, 36 Ah (45 Ah also produced)
Generator: 280 W

The above specifications relate to vehicles used by the German Army. Later models are powered by a petrol engine developing 48 bhp at 4000 rpm and have other detail differences.

Status
Production complete. In service with Austria, Denmark, France and the Netherlands. It is still produced in Mexico.

Manufacturer
Volkswagenwerk AG, D-3180 Wolfsburg 1, Federal Republic of Germany.
Tel: 5361 90. Telex: 95 860.
Fax: 5361 928282.

VW Iltis (4 × 4) 500 kg Light Vehicle

Development
In the 1960s France, West Germany and Italy started a joint project for a new 500 kg (4 × 4) amphibious vehicle which became known as the Europe Jeep. Prototypes were built by two consortia, FIAT/MAN/Saviem and Hotchkiss/Büssing/Lancia, but France subsequently withdrew and in 1976 the project was cancelled.

The Federal German Army then issued a new requirement for a 4 × 4 vehicle which could carry 500 kg of cargo both on roads and cross-country and this time the amphibious requirement was dropped. Both Daimler-Benz and Volkswagen built prototypes for trials and in 1977 the Volkswagen Iltis was selected for production as the Lkw 0.5 t tmil gl. Production of the Iltis continued until December 1981 when the last of 8800 vehicles was handed over to the German armed forces. Of this total 8470 went to the Army, 310 to the Luftwaffe and the remaining 20 to the Navy.

Production in Germany ceased in 1982 but in 1983 production of the Iltis was transferred to Bombardier of Canada. For a description and the specifications of this vehicle refer to the entry under Canada in this section.

Status
Production complete. In service with the German Army (approx 8800). In October 1981 the Canadian company Bombardier Inc obtained a licence to produce the Iltis. Further details are given in this section under Canada.

Volkswagen Iltis (4 × 4) 500 kg light vehicle configured as field ambulance (Bob Morrison – Military Scene)

Manufacturer
Volkswagenwerk AG, D-3180 Wolfsburg 1, Federal Republic of Germany.

Tel: 5361 90. Telex: 95 860.
Fax: 5361 928282.

Mercedes-Benz (4 × 4) 750 kg Light Vehicle

Development
The Mercedes-Benz (4 × 4) 750 kg light vehicle was entered by Peugeot in the French Army competition for a new light vehicle to replace the current Hotchkiss M 201. After comparative trials the P4 was selected by the French Army and entered service in 1982. There is a separate entry in this section for the Peugeot P4 (4 × 4) light vehicle and its variants.

Mercedes-Benz offers its vehicle for civil and military use with a standard wheelbase of 2.4 m or a long wheelbase of 2.85 m. The main components of the vehicle, with the exception of the specially designed transfer case, are from Mercedes-Benz passenger car and light truck series production. Four different engines and four different bodies are available: for example, a fully enclosed four-door model is offered on the long wheelbase chassis.

Gelaendewagenfahrzeug Gesellschaft (GFG) began production in 1980 with an initial target of 9000 vehicles a year. The Austrian-based GFG is owned jointly by Mercedes-Benz and Steyr-Daimler-Puch. Daimler-Benz supplies engines, transmissions and axles and Steyr-Daimler-Puch the chassis and body. In July 1981 it was announced that Steyr-Daimler-Puch was to buy out its German partner, Daimler-Benz, in the GFG company. The Austrian group continues to manufacture the vehicles on contract for Daimler-Benz at its works at Graz and remains responsible for sales in Austria, Switzerland and the former Yugoslavia, and COMECON countries under the name Puch. Daimler-Benz still hold the sales rights to all other markets under the Mercedes-Benz name.

This vehicle is licence-produced in Greece (5000 units) by Steyr Hellas SA and called the 240 GD.

Description
The layout of the vehicle is conventional with the engine at the front, driver and passenger immediately behind the engine, two passenger seats and a small cargo area at the back. The two passenger seats can be folded forward to give a load area of 1.23 × 1.52 m. The floor of the load area is made of sheet steel and is fitted with C-type rails, which allows communications equipment to be installed quickly. The vehicle has a folding hood, removable side flaps and a folding windscreen. A self-recovery front winch may be fitted.

Optional military equipment includes a radiator and engine guard, brush guards for the headlights, a weapons rack, a swivelling spare wheel carrier and a carrier in the rear for a 20 litre fuel container.

There are station vehicle and van variants of the basic vehicle and Binz produced a special body to form the Binz 2000 GS forward-area ambulance. There is also a light cable-laying version with an open rear and a side-mounted spare wheel on the right. Various seating arrangements are possible with the short wheelbase version having up to eight seats and the long wheelbase version up to ten. A radio/command variant, a cable-laying vehicle, an NBC decontamination variant and a variant carrying anti-tank missiles have been demonstrated.

Specifications
(Standard wheelbase version, data in square brackets relate to long wheelbase version)
Configuration: 4 × 4
Weight:
  (empty, including driver) 1670 [1780] kg
  (loaded) 2400 [2800] kg
Max load: 750 [1000] kg
Max towed load:
  (braked) 2500 kg
  (unbraked) 750 kg
Length: 4.145 [4.595] m
Width: 1.7 m
Height: (overall) 1.995 [1.975] m
Ground clearance: 0.24 m
Track: 1.425 m
Wheelbase: 2.4 [2.85] m
Angle of approach/departure: 39°/34°
Max road speed:
  (OM616 engine) 117 km/h
  (OM617 engine) 117 km/h
  (M115 engine) 137 km/h
Fuel capacity: 70 l
Max gradient: 80%
Side slope: (static) 25°
Fording: 0.6 m
Engine: OM616 4-cylinder diesel, 2404 cc, 72 hp (DIN) at 4200 rpm

Norwegian Army Mercedes-Benz (4 × 4) 750 kg light vehicle (Bob Morrison – Military Scene)

or OM617 5-cylinder diesel, 3005 cc, 88 hp (DIN) at 4200 rpm
or M115 4-cylinder petrol, 2307 cc, 90 hp (DIN) at 4800 rpm
Gearbox: manual, 4 forward and 1 reverse gears
Clutch: single dry plate
Transfer box: VG 080 for mechanical front-axle engagement and synchronised cross-country gear
Steering: recirculating ball, power-assisted
Turning radius: 5.5 [6.2] m
Suspension: front and rear, coil springs and telescopic shock absorbers. Both front and rear axles are located by 1 transverse and 2 longitudinal control links
Tyres: 20.5 R 16 (7.00 R 16 optional)

Brakes: (main) hydraulic, dual circuit with vacuum booster, disc front, drum rear
Electrical system: 24 V
Batteries: 2 × 12 V, 45 Ah
Alternator: 27 or 55 A

Status
In production. In service with Abu Dhabi (25), Algeria (90), Argentina (1200), Austria (1200), Denmark (1300), France (15 000, local production – see separate entry), Germany (12 000 plus 870 for Federal German Border Guard and 200 for Federal German foreign aid), Greece (5000, local production), Guatemala (50), Kuwait (400), Luxembourg (38), Netherlands (3195

ordered in mid-1990), Norway (3500), Oman, SHAPE (350), Singapore (311), Switzerland (4100), UNO (100), United Kingdom (captured Argentine vehicles used in Falkland Islands), US Army Europe (380), Yugoslavia (500), Zambia (50) and other undisclosed African countries (50).

Manufacturer
Daimler-Benz AG, Stuttgart-Untertürkheim, Federal Republic of Germany, but production is undertaken in Graz, Austria by Steyr-Daimler-Puch (GFG).
Tel: 0711 17-0. Telex: 725420 db d.
Fax: 0711 17 2244.

INDIA

VV501 Toofan (4 × 4) 500 kg Light Vehicle

Description
The VV501 Toofan (4 × 4) light vehicle was developed at the Indian Vehicle Research and Development Establishment (VRDE). Seven prototypes were completed and used for Indian Army trials.

The VV501 is a Jeep-type vehicle of conventional layout with the water-cooled petrol engine mounted forward under a prominent square bonnet. The radiator is large for a vehicle of its size and the headlamps are set into large square mudguards. The cab has seating for the driver and one passenger and the cargo area to the rear may be adapted for up to four passengers. The prototypes were fitted with a canvas top and sides but it is expected that more specialised body types will be fitted on production examples.

Specifications
Cab seating: 1 + 1
Configuration: 4 × 4
Weight: (gross) 2500 kg
Max load: 500 kg
Length: 4 m

Width: 1.72 m
Height: 1.95 m
Max speed: 120 km/h
Range: 500 km
Engine: 6-cylinder water-cooled 4 l petrol developing 110 bhp at 3200 rpm
Gearbox: manual, 3 forward and 1 reverse gears
Transfer box: 2-speed

Status
Prototypes. User trials completed.

Mahindra (4 × 4) Army Model Vehicles

Development
Mahindra and Mahindra Limited first assembled imported Jeep kits in 1947 in technical association with the Willys Overland Corporation of the USA. A phased local manufacture of the vehicle was undertaken from 1954 onwards and was completed in 1968. A wide range of petrol and diesel utiltity vehicles are manufactured and over 500 000 vehicles have been sold within India; Mahindra and Mahindra Limited is the chief supplier of light 4 × 4 vehicles to the Indian Defence Forces.

Exports commenced in 1968 and since then nearly 40 000 vehicles have been exported. From 1980, 25 000 units were delivered in knock-down form for assembly in Iran.

In 1979 the company entered into an agreement with Automobiles Peugeot of France to manufacture the XPD 4.90 diesel engine at its Igatpuri plant. The XD3 Peugeot Diesel engine was manufactured in the same plant from 1991 onwards.

Mahindra and Mahindra Limited has a joint venture company in Greece, Mahindra Hellas SA, engaged in the assembly of CJ series vehicles to European specifications and fitments.

Specifications

Model	CJ340	CJ540	MM540
Seating	1 + 2	1 + 2 (or 4)	1 + 2 (or 4)
Configuration	4 × 4	4 × 4	4 × 4
Gross vehicle weight	1760 kg	1810 kg	1810 kg
Towing capacity	1800 kg	1800 kg	1800 kg
Length	3.39 m	3.75 m	3.81 m
Width	1.6 m	1.6 m	1.78 m
Wheelbase	2.032 m	2.286 m	2.426
Track (with 7.00 × 15 tyres)	1.23 m	1.23 m	1.29 m
Max speed (2.1 litre diesel)	105 km/h	105 km/h	105 km/h
Fuel capacity	40 l	40 l	40 l
Engine (diesel)	2.1 or 2.5 l		
(petrol)	2.2, 2.3 EFI or 2.5 l		
Transmission	3-speed (1st gear non-synchromesh) or 4-speed (1st gear non-synchromesh) or 5-speed (all synchromesh)		
Transfer case	2-speed	2-speed	2-speed
Turning radius	5.3 m	5.86 m	6.34 m
Suspension	semi-elliptical underslung leaf springs with double-acting telescopic shock absorbers		
Tyres	6.00 × 16 or 7.00 × 15 or P235/75 R15		
Brakes (main)	hydraulic power assist		
(parking)	mechanical or transmission drum		
Electrical system	12 V	12 V	12 V
Battery (diesel)	90 Ah	90 Ah	Ah
(petrol)	60 Ah	60 Ah	60 Ah
Alternator	35 A	35 A	35 A

Mahindra CJ340 Army Model with 106 mm recoilless rifle

Mahindra MM540 (4 × 4) light vehicle

Description

Two series of 4 × 4 vehicles are in production, the CJ and MM series. The CJ series is available in 2.032 m and 2.286 m wheelbase versions, and the MM series with a 2.426 m wheelbase. Both series come with a variety of options for seating, body configurations and with diesel or petrol engines.

Standard military fittings include blackout lighting, a radio suppression kit (for petrol-engined vehicles), a starting crank assembly, a radiator chaff screen, a rifle bracket, shovel, pick and helve stowage, an oil can carrier, starting handle stowage, four grip handles, a dashlight switch, a fuel tank dipstick, sign plates, a speedometer seal, a fuel tank strainer and headlight brush guards.

The CJ combat vehicle version can carry a 106 mm recoilless gun. This version has a split windscreen through which the barrel of the recoilless gun protrudes when travelling and there are two squab seats for the gunners at the rear.

Status

In production. In service with the Indian armed forces and some other nations including Bangladesh (100 CJ) and Sri Lanka (175 CJ).

Manufacturer

Mahindra and Mahindra Limited, Overseas Operations, Gateway Building, Apollo Bunder, Bombay 400 039, India.
Tel: 20211031. Telex: 2361/5944.

Jonga (4 × 4) 400 kg Light Vehicle

Description

The Jonga is basically the Japanese Nissan Patrol (4 × 4) light vehicle built under licence at the Vehicle Factory at Jabalpur. It is used by the Indian Armed Forces and some have been fitted with SS-11 ATGWs for anti-tank use. In 1977 it was reported that the Indian Government had sold 200 to the Mozambique Army.

The Jonga has undergone some changes during its production life and is currently produced with a 145 hp 4 litre petrol engine in place of the earlier 125 bhp unit. It is also available with a Perkins P4(V) diesel engine. The Jonga has been offered for export and commercial sales as the Nissan Patrol D 60 N. The data in the Specifications table refer to this version.

Specifications

Cab seating: 1 + 2 (up to 4 in rear)
Configuration: 4 × 4
Weight:
 (empty) 1570 kg
 (loaded) 2075 kg
Max load: 400 kg
Length: 3.77 m
Width: 1.693 m
Height: 1.98 m
Ground clearance: 0.222 m
Track:
 (front) 1.386 m
 (rear) 1.404 m
Wheelbase: 2.2 m
Max speed: 117 km/h
Fuel capacity: 50 l
Max gradient: 60%

Jonga (4 × 4) light vehicle carrying SS-11 anti-tank missiles

Engine: Patrol 3.956 l 6-cylinder water-cooled petrol developing 145 bhp at 3800 rpm
Gearbox: synchromesh with 3 forward and 1 reverse gears
Clutch: single dry plate
Transfer box: 2-speed
Steering: worm and roller
Turning radius: 5.5 m
Suspension: semi-elliptical leaf springs (4 front, 5 rear) with double-acting telescopic shock absorbers
Tyres: 7.00 × 16
Brakes:
 (main) hydraulic drum on all four wheels

(parking) mechanical on transfer case shaft
Electrical system: 12 V
Batteries: 1 × 12 V, 60 Ah
Alternator: 35 A

Status

In service with the Indian Army and Mozambique.

Manufacturer

Vehicle Factory, Indian Ordnance Factories, Jabalpur 482009, Madhya Pradesh, India.
Tel: 21969/21970. Telex: 076219.

Carrier (4 × 4) 750 kg Light Truck

Description

The Carrier (4 × 4) 750 kg light truck is a Japanese Nissan D4W73 vehicle produced under licence in India. The first production units were completed at the Defence Unit (Ordnance Factory) at Jabalpur during 1961 and production continues.

The usual form of the Carrier is as a general-purpose light utility truck with a two-man hard-topped cab and a cargo area covered by a canvas tilt over removable bows. The cab windscreen can be folded forwards onto the bonnet and some vehicles feature a square roof hatch over the passenger seat. The cargo area has a drop tailgate and folding seats may be provided along the sides.

Some vehicles are fitted with a front-mounted winch. Variants include a desert operations vehicle with oversize sand tyres, a field ambulance and a light fire tender.

Specifications

Cab seating: 1 + 1
Configuration: 4 × 4
Weight:
 (empty) 2690 kg
 (loaded) 4190 kg
Max load:
 (road) 1500 kg
 (cross-country) 750 kg
Length: 4.73 m
Width: 2.045 m

Carrier (4 × 4) 750 kg light truck

Carrier (4 × 4) 750 kg light truck

Height: (overall) 2.355 m
Ground clearance: (axles) 0.26 m
Track: 1.6 m
Wheelbase: 2.8 m
Max speed: 95 km/h
Fuel capacity: 110 l
Engine: 3.956 l 6-cylinder water-cooled petrol developing 145 hp at 3800 rpm
Gearbox: manual, 4 forward and 1 reverse gears

Clutch: single dry plate
Transfer box: 2-speed
Suspension: semi-elliptic leaf springs
Brakes: hydraulic
Electrical system: 12 V

Status
In production. In widespread service with the Indian Army.

Manufacturer
Vehicle Factory, Indian Ordnance Factories, Jabalpur 482009, Madhya Pradesh, India.
Tel: 21969/21970. Telex: 076219.

ISRAEL

M-242 Storm (4 × 4) 800 kg Multi-Mission Vehicle (MMV)

Description
The M-242 Storm Multi-Mission Vehicle (MMV) was designed to fulfil several military functions including general utility, patrol and reconnaissance, command, and anti-tank weapons vehicle.

After decades of experience with 4 × 4 vehicles by the Israeli Defence Forces, the M-242 introduced innovations such as a reinforced body and frame, an updated drive train and a 175 hp petrol engine with a fuel injection system. An automatic transmission is an option.

The M-242 Storm is produced with two frame lengths, 4.5 m and 4.15 m. The layout of the vehicle is conventional with the engine at the front, the driver and one passenger seated behind the engine, and space for further passengers or other loads at the rear. The front axle is fully floating while the rear axle is semi-floating.

Apart from the main general-purpose utility vehicle version, which can be fitted with a soft-top, there are three main variants of the M-242. The short frame version may be used for the command vehicle variant which can fitted with machine gun mountings and other special equipment; it can be fitted with a soft-top to

protect the equipment carried. The long frame version is available with a hard-top and an air-conditioning system. The anti-tank weapon vehicle can carry a 106 mm recoilless rifle or a missile system.

One further vehicle is a police vehicle intended to handle riots in crowded urban areas or off-roads. This version is provided with transparent polycarbonate sheets which protect the occupants against stones, incendiary bombs and splinters. The side panels and doors have firing ports for riot control weapons.

Optional equipment for all models includes blackout lamps, a radio antenna base, a container mounting and a winch. The electrical system may be 12 or 24 V.

Specifications
Cab seating: 1 + 3 to 5
Configuration: 4 × 4
Gross vehicle weight: 2350 kg
Max load: (off-road) 540 kg (850 kg optional)
Length:
 (long frame) 4.5 m
 (short frame) 4.15 m
Width: 1.62 m
Height:
 (folded windscreen) 1.45 m
 (open windscreen) 1.8 m
 (closed cab) 1.95 m
Max speed: 145 km/h

Fuel capacity: 75 l
Max gradient: 75%
Engine: 4 l 6-cylinder in-line petrol with fuel injection developing 175 hp, fitted with Vortox 2-stage air cleaner
Transmission: Aisin AX15 with 5 forward and 1 reverse gears
Clutch: 266.7 mm hydraulic
Transfer box: NP 231 2-speed
Steering: recirculating ball
Turning radius: 5.73 m
Suspension: front and rear leaf springs with double-acting shock absorbers
Tyres: 7.00 × 15 8-ply
Brakes: dual hydraulic with rear drum self-aligning and disc front
Electrical system: 12 V (24 V optional)
Batteries: 1 or 2 × 12 V, 60 Ah
Alternator: 90 A

Status
In production. In service with the Israeli defence forces.

Manufacturer
Automotive Industries Limited, POB 535, Nazareth Illit, 17105 Israel.
Tel: 972 6 558111. Telex: 46217 ail il.
Fax: 972 6 558103.

M-242 Storm (4 × 4) Multi-Mission Vehicle (MMV)

M-242 Storm (4 × 4) Policing Vehicle

ITALY

Fresia F18 (4 × 4) 400 kg Mountain Power Truck

Description
The Fresia F18 (4 × 4) 400 kg mountain power truck was developed to meet the requirements of Italian mountain troops for a vehicle which could be used to transport equipment and stores over mountain roads and tracks. The prototype was completed in 1974 and following extensive trials a pre-production batch was delivered for operational trials with Italian mountain units in June 1978. The original vehicles were limited in load capacity to 200 kg but development increased the capacity to 400 kg.

The Fresia F18 is a small all-wheel drive vehicle with

an open platform for carrying up to 400 kg of cargo. The vehicle can be steered by the operator when seated on the platform or when walking behind. The engine is mounted in the centre of the vehicle under the load area which has a folding handrail on the sides and rear. The transmission is hydrostatic and steering is power-assisted on both axles. Each wheel has independent suspension.

Specifications
Configuration: 4 × 4
Weight:
 (empty) 390 kg
 (loaded) 790 kg
Max load: 400 kg
Length: (over load platform) 1.86 m

Width: 1.05 m
Height:
 (over steering wheel) 1.01 m
 (load platform) 0.74 m
Ground clearance: 0.21 m
Track: 0.71 m
Wheelbase: 1.2 m
Max speed: 20 km/h
Fuel capacity: 40 l
Max gradient: 60%
Max side slope: 30%
Engine: Briggs and Stratton Type 422400 694 cc 2-cylinder air-cooled petrol developing 18 hp at 3600 rpm
Gearbox: hydrostatic closed circuit with variable displacement radial piston primary pump and 2 fixed displacement orbital hydraulic motors

Steering: hydraulic, power-assisted on all 4 wheels
Turning radius: (internal) approx 2 m
Suspension: independent with transverse leaf springs for each axle and hydraulic shock absorbers
Brakes:
   (main) operating on hydrostatic transmission
   (parking) disc brakes on all 4 wheels
Tyres: 26 × 12.00
Electrical system: 12 V
Battery: 1 × 12 V, 45 Ah

Status

In service with Italian Army mountain units.

Manufacturer

Fresia SpA, Via Trento Trieste 30, I-17017 Millesimo (SV), Italy.
Tel: (19) 565065. Telex: 571254 fresof i.

Fresia F18 (4 × 4) 400 kg mountain power truck

FIAT Campagnola 1107 AD (4 × 4) 750 kg Light Vehicle

Description

The FIAT Campagnola 1107 AD (4 × 4) light vehicle entered production in 1974 as the replacement for the FIAT AR-59. The main improvements included a more powerful engine, increased load-carrying capability and the option of a hard-top.

The vehicle was produced in hard- and soft-top versions and there was also a longer model, with an overall length of 4.025 m and with the same wheel-base, also in hard- and soft-top models. The longer model has three-man bench seats down either side behind the front seat rather than two as in the basic model. FIAT also offered the FIAT Campagnola 2500 powered by a four-cylinder diesel engine developing 72 hp at 2400 rpm, with a maximum road speed of 120 km/h and a fuel consumption of 12.6 l/100 km. Empty weight of the canvas-top model is 1880 kg.

Special equipment for operation in dusty and tropical zones includes an air cleaner with centrifugal pre-cleaner, fuel filter between feed pump and carburettor, sealed type declutch thrust bearing, engine compartment front protection and a low octane number petrol engine with 7.5 compression ratio, developing 75 hp.

The body is of all-steel construction and has two side doors and a tailgate. Seating is provided for three including the driver at the front and four at the rear, two each side on bench-type seats. The canvas-top and side curtains can be removed and the windscreen folded forward flat against the bonnet.

Standard equipment includes a spare wheel, heater, ventilating and defrosting system, pintle towing hook at the rear, towing eyes at the front, fire extinguisher, pick and shovel and additional fuel cans.

The Italian Army uses the FIAT 1107 AD as a TOW anti-tank missile launcher carrier. The vehicle can easily be adapted for a wide variety of other roles such as an ambulance, and a command or radio vehicle.

Specifications

(canvas-top model; data in square brackets relate to hard-top where different)
Cab seating: 3 + 4 [3 + 6, LWB version]
Configuration: 4 × 4
Weight:
   (empty) 1670 [1740] kg
   (loaded) 2420 [2490] kg

FIAT Campagnola 1107 AD 750 kg light vehicle (Bob Morrison – Military Scene)

Max load: 750 kg
Towed load:
   (road) 1300 kg
   (off-road) 900 kg
Length: 3.775 [4.025] m
Width: 1.58 m
Height: 1.901 m
Ground clearance: 0.275 m
Track:
   (front) 1.365 m
   (rear) 1.404 m
Wheelbase: 2.3 m
Angle of approach/departure: 44°/45° [44°/28°]
Max speed: (road) 120 km/h
Range: 400 km
Fuel capacity: 57 l
Max gradient: (SWB) 100%
Max side slope: 40%
Fording: 0.7 m
Engine: FIAT 4-cylinder in-line petrol developing 80 hp (DIN) at 4600 rpm
Gearbox: manual with 5 forward and 1 reverse gears
Clutch: single dry plate

Transfer box: 2-speed
Steering: hourglass and roller
Turning radius: 5.4 m
Suspension: independent McPherson type with longitudinal torsion bar, single telescopic shock absorbers at front and twin at rear
Tyres: 7.00 × 16 C
Brakes:
   (main) drum, hydraulically operated on all 4 wheels, dual circuit
   (parking) operates on rear drums
Electrical system: 24 V
Batteries: 2 × 12 V, 45 Ah
Generator: 26 A

Status

Production complete. In service with Italy and Tunisia (400). Produced in Yugoslavia.

Manufacturer

FIAT, Direzione Mezzi Speciali, Corso G Marconi 10/20, Turin, Italy.

JAPAN

Mitsubishi (4 × 4) Light Vehicles

Description

In 1953 Mitsubishi obtained a licence from the American Willys (later Kaiser Jeep) company to manufacture the Jeep in Japan for both civil and military use. The first model was the CJ3B-JB and was followed by many

other models, all available with petrol or diesel engine, left- or right-hand drive, long or short wheelbase and with an open or enclosed passenger/cargo area.

For many years the standard ¼-tonne vehicle of the Japanese Self-Defence Force was the Mitsubishi J54A, powered by a four-cylinder petrol engine developing 75 hp at 3800 rpm, coupled to a manual gearbox with three forward and one reverse gears and

a two-speed transfer case. Basic details of the J54A are: 3.33 m length, 1.595 m width, 1.85 m height, 2.03 m wheelbase, 92 km/h maximum road speed and 6.00 × 16 tyres. Variants in service included an ambulance, anti-tank armed with a 106 mm Type 60 recoilless rifle, and anti-tank armed with two KAM-3D (Type 64) wire-guided anti-tank missiles.

The J54A was replaced by the J24A, designated the

Type 73 by the Japanese Ground Self-Defence Force (Army).

Specifications (J24A)
Seating: 1 + 5
Configuration: 4 × 4
Weight:
  (empty) 1470 kg
  (loaded) 1970 kg
Max load: 480 kg
Length: 3.75 m
Width: 1.665 m
Height: 1.95 m
Ground clearance: 0.21 m
Track: 1.296 m

Wheelbase: 2.225 m
Fuel capacity: 48 l
Max speed: 100 km/h
Engine: 4-cylinder diesel developing 80 bhp at 3500 rpm
Gearbox: manual with 4 forward and 1 reverse gears
Clutch: single dry plate
Transfer box: 2-speed
Steering: recirculating ball
Turning radius: 5.8 m
Suspension: semi-elliptical leaf springs with hydraulic shock absorbers
Tyres: 7.00 × 15

Brakes:
  (main) hydraulic
  (parking) mechanical
Electrical system: 24 V

Status
In service with the Japanese Self-Defence Force, Burma, Indonesia and Thailand.

Manufacturer
Mitsubishi Motors Corporation, 33-8, Shiba 5-chome, Minato-ku, Tokyo, Japan.
Tel: 212 3311. Telex: 26639 bisijiko j.

Mitsubishi (4 × 4) Jeep used by the Japanese Ground Self-Defence Force and fitted with Type 64 (KAM-3D) ATGWs (Kensuke Ebata)

Mitsubishi (4 × 4) Jeep used by the Japanese Ground Self-Defence Force (Kensuke Ebata)

Toyota Land Cruiser (4 × 4) Series Light Vehicle

Description
The Toyota Land Cruiser was developed in the 1950s primarily for the civilian market but has since been adopted by a number of armies in the Middle East and South America.

The basic model has a conventional layout with the engine at the front and the passenger and cargo areas at the rear. The windscreen can fold flat against the bonnet and the side doors and vinyl-top are removable. Six basic models of the Toyota Land Cruiser are currently in production; these are hard-top (regular wheelbase of 2.285 m and super long wheelbase of 2.95 m), vinyl-top series (regular wheelbase of 2.285 m, long wheelbase of 2.43 m and super long wheelbase of 2.95 m) and pick-up (super long wheelbase of 2.95 m). In addition there is a four-door station wagon version of the Land Cruiser.

Status
In production. In service with armed forces in the Middle East (including Egypt), South Africa and South America.

Manufacturer
Toyota Motor Corporation, 1 Toyota-cho, Toyota, Aichi Prefecture 471, Japan.
Tel: 0565 28 2121. Telex: 4528371 toyota j.
The vehicle is also built under licence in Australia and Brazil.

Specifications

Model	Regular wheelbase	Long wheelbase	Super long wheelbase
Configuration	4 × 4	4 × 4	4 × 4
Weight (empty)	1680 kg	1740 kg	1865 kg
(loaded)	2295 kg	2445 kg	3035 kg
Max load	615 kg	705 kg	1170 kg
Length	3.915 m	4.275 m	4.955 m
Width	1.665 m	1.665 m	1.665 m
Height	1.955 m	1.96 m	2.03 m
Ground clearance	0.21 m	0.21 m	0.225 m
Track (front)	1.415 m	1.415 m	1.415 m
(rear)	1.4 m	1.4 m	1.41 m
Wheelbase	2.285 m	2.43 m	2.95 m
Fuel capacity	85 l	85 l	85 l
Engine	6-cylinder in-line OHV petrol developing 135 hp (DIN) at 3600 rpm		
	6-cylinder in-line OHV diesel developing 103 hp (DIN) at 3500 rpm		
	4-cylinder in-line OHV petrol developing 90 hp (DIN) at 3500 rpm		
	4-cylinder in-line OHV diesel developing 80 hp (DIN) at 3600 rpm		
Gearbox	all have manual, 4 forward and 1 reverse gears		
Clutch	single dry plate	single dry plate	single dry plate
Transfer box	2-speed	2-speed	2-speed
Steering	recirculating ball	recirculating ball	recirculating ball
Turning radius	5.3 m	5.5 m	6.5 m
Suspension (front and rear)	semi-elliptical springs with hydraulic double-acting shock absorbers at each wheel station		
Tyres	7.00-15-6 PR	7.00-15-6 PR	7.50-16-8 PR
Brakes (main)	hydraulic, all wheels	hydraulic, all wheels	hydraulic, all wheels
(parking)	mechanical	mechanical	mechanical
Electrical system	12 V	12 V	12 V

Toyota Land Cruiser (4 × 4) light vehicle with hard-top

Toyota Land Cruiser (4 × 4) light vehicle in long wheelbase pick-up configuration

Nissan Q4W73 (4 × 4) 750 kg Truck

Description
This was developed in the 1950s for the Japanese Self-Defence Force and was based on the Second World War American Dodge T214 ¾-ton (4 × 4) truck. Early production vehicles used the same engine as the early Nissan Patrol vehicle. This truck is still built under licence in India at the Defence Unit (Ordnance Factory) at Jabalpur (qv).

The layout of the vehicle is conventional with the engine at the front, two-man cab with removable top in the centre and the cargo area at the rear with a drop tailgate, removable bows and a tarpaulin cover. Variants in service include an ambulance and a fire-fighting vehicle.

Specifications
Cab seating: 1 + 1
Configuration: 4 × 4
Weight:
 (empty) 2690 kg
 (loaded, road) 4190 kg
 (loaded, cross-country) 3440 kg
Max load:
 (road) 1500 kg
 (cross-country) 750 kg
Max towed load: 2000 kg
Length: 4.71 m
Width: 2.045 m
Height: 2.39 m
Wheelbase: 2.8 m
Max speed: 97 km/h
Max range: 319 km
Fuel capacity: 68 l
Gradient: 60%
Fording: 0.51 m
Engine: 6-cylinder water-cooled petrol developing 145 hp at 4000 rpm
Gearbox: manual with 4 forward and 1 reverse gears
Clutch: single dry plate
Transfer box: 2-speed
Suspension: semi-elliptical springs and hydraulic shock absorbers
Tyres: 7.50 × 20
Brakes:
 (main) hydraulic
 (parking) mechanical
Electrical system: 12 V

Status
Production complete in Japan. Production continues in India. In service with the Japanese Self-Defence Force. Quantities were also supplied to Indonesia (600), South Korea and South Vietnam.

Manufacturer
Nissan Motor Company Limited, 17-1, Ginza 6-chome, Chuo-ku, Tokyo, Japan.
Tel: (3) 543 5523. Telex: 22503 nismo j.

Nissan Q4W73 (4 × 4) 750 kg truck

Toyota 2FQ15L (4 × 4) 750 kg Truck

Description
This truck was developed in the 1950s for the Japanese Self-Defence Force and is a further development of the Second World War American T214(WC52) ¾-ton (4 × 4) truck. It is very similar in appearance to the Nissan Q4W73 (4 × 4) 750 kg truck which was developed at the same time. Other Toyota trucks of this type include the FQ10 and FQ15 which are almost identical in appearance to the T214(WC52).

Production of the basic model ceased during the mid-1960s but many vehicles remain in use.

The layout of the Toyota 2FQ15L is conventional with the engine at the front, the two-man cab with removable top in the centre and the cargo area at the rear with a drop tailgate, removable bows and a tarpaulin cover.

The ambulance model is designated the HQ15V, has a crew of two and can carry five stretcher patients or nine seated patients. Basic data are: loaded weight 4300 kg, length 5.165 m, width 2.13 m and height 2.815 m.

Specifications
Cab seating: 1 + 1
Configuration: 4 × 4
Weight:
 (empty) 2800 kg
 (loaded, road) 3867 kg
 (loaded, cross-country) 3640 kg
Max load:
 (road) 1067 kg
 (cross-country) 840 kg
Length: 5.08 m
Width: 2.02 m
Height: 2.32 m
Wheelbase: 3 m
Max speed: (road) 82 km/h
Engine: Toyota 6-cylinder water-cooled petrol developing 105 bhp at 3200 rpm
Gearbox: manual with 4 forward and 1 reverse gears
Tyres: 7.50 × 20
Brakes:
 (main) hydraulic
 (parking) mechanical

Status
Production complete. In service with the Japanese Self-Defence Force. Also used by the US Army (in Far East only) and South Korea.

Manufacturer
Toyota Motor Company Limited, 1 Toyota-cho, Toyotashi, Aichi-ken, Japan.
Tel: 0565 28 2121. Telex: 4528371 toyota j.

Toyota 2FQ15L (4 × 4) 750 kg truck (Kensuke Ebata)

Toyota HQ15V (4 × 4) ambulance (Kensuke Ebata)

KOREA, SOUTH

Asia Motors KM41 Series of Light Vehicles

Description

The Asia Motors KM41 series of light vehicles are the standard light vehicles of the Republic of Korea armed forces. They were developed in co-operation with the ADD (Agency of Defence Development) in Korea and although similar in appearance to the Jeep CJ series there are many locally introduced changes to the original design.

The layout of the vehicle is conventional with the engine at the front and the main driver and passenger/load-carrying area to the rear. The same engine is used throughout the series and is a KG2000 1.985 litre four-cylinder petrol engine developing 73 hp at 4000 rpm.

The vehicles in the KM41 series are as follows:
KM410 utility vehicle
KM410L long wheelbase version of KM410
KM411 ambulance
KM412 TOW anti-tank guided missile launcher carrier
KM413 TOW anti-tank missile carrier
KM414 106 mm recoilless rifle carrier
KM415 searchlight carrier

Status

In production. In service with the Republic of Korea armed forces.

Manufacturer

Asia Motors Company Inc, 15 Yoido-dong, Yung-deungpo-gu, Seoul, Republic of Korea.
Tel: 783 1501/9. Telex: 24374 asiamco k.

Specifications

Model	KM410	KM410L	KM411	KM412	KM413	KM414	KM415
Purpose	utility	long wheelbase utility	ambulance	TOW launcher carrier	TOW missile carrier	106 mm RR carrier	searchlight carrier
Cab seating	1 + 3	1 + 5	1 + 1	1 + 3	1 + 1	1 + 3	1 + 1
Configuration	4 × 4	4 × 4	4 × 4	4 × 4	4 × 4	4 × 4	4 × 4
Weight (kerb)	1180 kg	1286 kg	1380 kg	1293 kg	1290 kg	1320 kg	1290 kg
(GVW)	1720 kg	1786 kg	1860 kg	1880 kg	1660 kg	1969 kg	1660 kg
Max load	540 kg	620 kg	480 kg	587 kg	370 kg	649 kg	370 kg
Length	3.35 m	3.925 m	3.841 m	3.405 m	3.276 m	3.301 m	3.276 m
Width	1.475 m	1.675 m	1.68 m	1.85 m	1.85 m	1.734 m	1.85 m
Height	1.705 m	1.946 m	1.946 m	1.705 m	1.73 m	1.705 m	1.73 m
Ground clearance	0.21 m	0.21 m	0.233 m	0.21 m	0.21 m	0.21 m	0.21 m
Track	1.23 m	1.23 m	1.23 m	1.23 m	1.23 m	1.23 m	1.23 m
Wheelbase	2.032 m	2.41 m	2.032 m	2.032 m	2.032 m	2.032 m	2.032 m
Angle of approach	45°	45°	51°	45°	45°	45°	45°
Angle of departure	30°	23°	19°	26°	30°	30°	30°
Max speed	105 km/h	105 km/h	105 km/h	105 km/h	105 km/h	105 km/h	105 km/h
Range	340 km	340 km	340 km	340 km	340 km	340 km	340 km
Fuel capacity	45.5 l	45.5 l	45.5 l	45.5 l	45.5 l	45.5 l	45.5 l
Gradient	75%	75%	75%	75%	75%	75%	75%
Fording	0.51 m	0.51 m	0.51 m	0.51 m	0.51 m	0.51 m	0.51 m
Engine	KG2000 1.985 l 4-cylinder OHV petrol developing 73 hp at 4000 rpm						
Gearbox	manual with 4 forward and 1 reverse gears with synchromesh on all gears						
Clutch	all single dry plate						
Transfer box	all 2-speed						
Steering	all ball and nut						
Turning radius	5.06 m	6 m	5.06 m	5.06 m	5.06 m	5.06 m	5.06 m
Tyres	all 6.00 × 16						
Brakes	all dual circuit drum						
Suspension (front)	semi-elliptical leaf springs with hydraulic double-acting shock absorbers						
(rear)	progressive semi-elliptical leaf springs with hydraulic double-acting shock absorbers						
Electrical system	24 V	24 V	24 V	24 V	24 V	24 V	24 V
Batteries	2 × 12 V, 45 Ah	2 × 12 V, 45 Ah	2 × 12 V, 45 Ah	2 × 12 V, 45 Ah	2 × 12 V, 45 Ah	2 × 12 V, 45 Ah	2 × 12 V, 45 Ah
Alternator	25 A	25 A	25 A	25 A	25 A	25 A	180 A

KM410 (4 × 4) light vehicle with open top

KM410L (4 × 4) light vehicle, the long wheelbase (2.41 m) variant of the KM410

NETHERLANDS

DAF 66 YA (4 × 2) 400 kg Utility Vehicle

Description
This vehicle is based on commercial components and the first prototype, known as the DAF 55 YA, was completed in 1970. In total, 1200 vehicles were built for the Dutch Army between 1973 and mid-1977.

The layout of the DAF 66 YA is conventional with the engine at the front and the passenger/cargo area at the rear. The body is an all-welded unit with a chassis of box-section members. The two rear seats can be folded down to increase the cargo carrying area. The windscreen can be folded forward onto the bonnet if required and collapsible bows and a tarpaulin cover are provided at the rear of the cargo area. Both front and rear bumpers are interchangeable and are provided with towing eyes.

Power is transferred from the engine to the transmission via an automatic clutch and an aluminium propeller shaft. The transmission comprises an infinitely variable twin-belt Vario-matic, a differential unit and secondary drive shafts to the rear wheels. Cooling air for the transmission is obtained from the front of the vehicle and through longitudinal box-section girders. If required, the differential unit can be provided with a locking device.

Hydraulic brakes are provided for all wheels, with a separate circuit for front and rear wheels. The front brakes are of the disc type and the rear brakes are of the drum type. Division of braking effort between front and rear is 73:27. The parking brake, applied by a lever on the propeller shaft tunnel, operates mechanically on the rear wheels. A vacuum brake booster can be fitted as an optional extra.

Standard equipment includes a spare wheel carried under the bonnet, windscreen washers, heater, transmission low-ratio hold control, hazard warning lights, inspection lamp socket, map reading light and cable connectors for radio operations.

The basic vehicle can be adapted for a variety of roles including use as a military police vehicle, radio vehicle (it has a 24 V electrical system as standard), and an ambulance carrying two stretcher patients plus the driver and attendant.

Specifications
Cab seating: 1 + 3
Weight:
 (empty) 860 kg
 (loaded) 1295 kg
Weight on front axle: (loaded) 560 kg
Weight on rear axle: (loaded) 735 kg
Max load: 435 kg
Load area: (with rear seats folded) 1.4 × 1.25 m

DAF 66 YA (4 × 2) 400 kg utility vehicle with bows and cover erected

Length: 3.75 m
Width: 1.52 m
Height:
 (with bows and tarpaulin cover raised) 1.59 m
 (windscreen folded flat) 1.11 m
Ground clearance: 0.19 m
Track:
 (front) 1.31 m
 (rear) 1.24 m
Wheelbase: 2.255 m
Angle of approach/departure: 31°/37°
Max speed: (road) 115 km/h
Range: 500 km
Fuel capacity: 50 l
Max gradient: 20%
Fording: 0.2 m
Engine: B 110E, water-cooled 4-cylinder in-line petrol developing 47 hp (DIN) at 5000 rpm
Gearbox: Vario-matic (3 positions: forward, neutral and reverse)
Clutch: single dry plate
Steering: rack and pinion
Turning radius: 4.77 m
Suspension:
 (front) independent by means of longitudinal torsion bars with anti-roll bar and telescopic double-acting hydraulic shock absorbers
 (rear) De Dion axle with semi-elliptical leaf springs and telescopic double-acting hydraulic shock absorbers
Tyres: 14.5 × 14
Brakes:
 (main) hydraulic
 (parking) mechanical
Electrical system: 24 V
Batteries: 2 × 12 V

Status
Production complete. In limited service with the Dutch Army and Indonesia (150). Being replaced in Dutch service by the Land Rover (4 × 4) and Mercedes-Benz (4 × 4).

Manufacturer
DAF Military Sales, Hugo van der Goeslaan 1, NL-5643 TW Eindhoven, Netherlands.
Tel: 040 143440. Telex: 51085 daf nl.
Fax: 040 144318.

PAKISTAN

Nispak (4 × 4) 400 kg Light Vehicle

Description
The Nispak was designed under the direction of the Inspector of Vehicles and Engineering Equipment, Pakistan Army, and is patterned on a Japanese Nissan (4 × 4) light vehicle. At least 90 per cent of the components of the Nispak, including the engine, transmission, chassis and body, are manufactured in Pakistan.

The layout of the Nispak is conventional with the engine at the front, driver and passenger in the centre and the cargo area at the rear. The single-piece windscreen folds forward onto the bonnet and the canvas cover folds down to the rear.

Specifications
Configuration: 4 × 4
Weight:
 (empty) 1580 kg
 (loaded, road) 2180 kg
 (loaded, cross-country) 1980 kg
Weight on front axle: (empty) 853 kg
Weight on rear axle: (empty) 727 kg
Max load:
 (road) 600 kg
 (cross-country) 400 kg
Towed load:
 (road) 907 kg
 (cross-country) 680 kg
Length: 3.772 m
Width: 1.689 m
Height: 1.981 m
Ground clearance: 0.235 m
Track:
 (front) 1.382 m
 (rear) 1.4 m
Wheelbase: 2.2 m
Max speed: 125 km/h
Range: 290 km
Fuel capacity: 50 l
Gradient: 65%
Fording: 1.88 m
Engine: 6-cylinder petrol developing 145 hp at 3800 rpm
Gearbox: manual, 3 forward and 1 reverse gears
Clutch: single dry plate
Transfer box: 2-speed
Turning radius: 5.69 m
Suspension: semi-elliptical springs and hydraulic shock absorbers
Tyres: 7.00 × 16
Brakes:
 (main) hydraulic
 (parking) mechanical
Electrical system: 24 V

Status
In service with Pakistan armed forces.

Manufacturer
Facility at Chaklala, Pakistan.

PHILIPPINES

Delta Explorer (4 × 4) Light Vehicle

Description
The Delta Explorer (4 × 4) light vehicle, originally known as the Delta Mini-Cruiser, was developed from 1972 by the Delta Motor Corporation with the assis-

tance of the Research and Development Centre of the Philippines Armed Forces. It was the country's first major project called for by the Self-Reliance Defence Posture Program initiated by the then President Marcos.

Following trials with 40 pre-production models, the Philippine armed forces placed an order for an initial

batch of 500 vehicles under the designation RJ-2.

The left-hand drive model is designated the RJ-2BL, and the right-hand drive version the RJ-2BR. The more recent diesel model, the DJ-2, is powered by an Isuzu C-190 4-stroke vertical in-line OHV diesel developing 55 bhp at 4000 rpm.

The vehicle entered service with the Philippine Army in 1975 and all foreign-made light utility vehicles were planned to be phased out of service. The export of the vehicle to any friendly foreign country was approved in principle by the Ministry of National Defence in February 1980.

The Explorer is powered by the same 12RM OHV petrol engine as in the Toyota Corona car, also manufactured in the Philippines, where practically all the components of the vehicle are manufactured, and the remaining imported components, about 10 per cent, are limited to the relatively unimportant parts which will eventually be made by Delta Motor Corporation. The company has the capacity to produce about 300 Explorer vehicles a month for export.

The Explorer chassis is of the channel section girder type with five crossmembers. The main panels are made of 1.6 mm thick steel and other panels of steel 1.2 mm thick. The layout is conventional with the engine at the front, driver and passenger in the centre and two two-man seats down each side at the rear. The crew compartment is covered by a tarpaulin cover which folds down at the back and the windscreen can be folded forward onto the bonnet. Apart from the basic military model there are two other canvas-topped versions, one with canvas doors and the other with steel doors.

The basic vehicle can also be used as a command vehicle and weapons carrier. More specialised variants are the ambulance and police versions.

Specifications

Model	RJ-2B	DJ-2B
Configuration	4 × 4	4 × 4
Cab seating	1 + 5	1 + 5
Weight (empty)	1070 kg	1220 kg
(loaded)	1740 kg	1740 kg
Weight on front axle (empty)	600 kg	670 kg
Weight on rear axle (empty)	470 kg	550 kg
Length	3.575 m	3.575 m
Width	1.595 m	1.595 m
Height (overall)	1.925 m	1.925 m
(reduced)	1.505 m	1.505 m
Ground clearance	0.215 m	0.215 m
Track (front)	1.3155 m	1.3155 m
(rear)	1.2693 m	1.2693 m
Wheelbase	2.185 m	2.185 m
Angle of approach/departure	52°/39°	52°/39°
Fuel capacity	45 l	45 l
Engine	Toyota 12RM, 1.587 l 4-cylinder OHV petrol developing 90 bhp at 5400 rpm	Isuzu C-190 4-stroke vertical in-line OHV diesel developing 55 bhp at 4000 rpm
Gearbox	manual, 4 forward and 1 reverse gears	
Clutch	single dry plate	single dry plate
Transfer box	2-speed	2-speed
Steering	2-shaft with worm and recirculating ball sector	
Turning radius	4.75 m	4.75 m
Suspension	front and rear, semi-elliptical leaf springs front and rear with hydraulic telescopic shock absorbers	
Axles (front)	full-floating with steering knuckles and hub locks	
(rear)	semi-floating hypoid type	
Tyres	6.00 × 16	6.00 × 16
Brakes (main)	dual system hydraulic drum type	
(parking)	mechanical	mechanical
Electrical system	12 V	12 V
Battery	1 × 12 V	1 × 12 V

Status
In service with Philippines, Qatar and UAE. Sold to Australia, Colombia, Italy, Pakistan and Thailand.

Manufacturer
Delta Motor Corporation, PO Box 305, MCC, Makati, Metro Manila 3117, Philippines.
Tel: 865 061. Telex: 5009 delta pm.

Military version of Delta Explorer (4 × 4) light vehicle with soft-top

Delta Explorer (4 × 4) light ambulance

PORTUGAL

UMM (4 × 4) Light Vehicle

Description
The UMM (4 × 4) light vehicle is available with Peugeot 2.5 litre diesel engines, either naturally aspirated (76 hp) or turbo intercooled (110 hp). The vehicle has a chassis formed from 120 × 60 mm steel channel section 4 mm thick which is reinforced by three crossmembers. The body is formed from 2 mm steel plate welded to the chassis. The body layout is

conventional, with the engine forward and the driver's position central. The rear of the body is an open platform onto which various types of body can be built. These range from a hard-top to various forms of soft-top. The driver's cab portion can be fitted with a canvas roof but may also use a hard-top. The rear area may be configured for personnel seating in various layouts or it may be left open for cargo carrying or for mounting various forms of light weapon or missiles.

The standard military version is powered by a 2.498 litre diesel engine but a 110 bhp turbocharged

version of the same engine is available.

Variants include an ambulance with a box body, a mortar carrier, a 106 mm recoilless rifle carrier and 7.62 and 12.7 mm machine gun carriers. Special missile-carrying variants include a version with a hard-top cab and a three-missile launcher for SS-11 anti-tank missiles, a MILAN or TOW anti-tank guided weapon launcher version and a special version with racks in the rear for Blowpipe or Mistral surface-to-air missiles. Also produced are police versions and one variant carrying a hydraulic inspection platform.

There is also a long wheelbase (3.078 m) version of the UMM. This version has a maximum load capacity of 1700 kg or up to 10 men in the rear.

The chassis cab model can carry standard NATO shelters.

The UMM can be para-dropped.

Specifications
(data in square brackets refer to long wheelbase version)
Cab seating: 2 + 6 [2 + 10 or 3 + 10]
Configuration: 4 × 4
Weight:
(empty) 1630 [1770] kg
(loaded) 2720 [3470] kg
Max load: (road) 1110 [1700] kg
Towed load:
(trailer with brakes) 3500 kg
(trailer without brakes) 1000 kg

Length: 4.05 [4.77] m
Width: 1.57 m
Height: 1.955 m
Ground clearance: 0.23 m
Track: 1.342 m
Wheelbase: 2.56 [3.078] m
Angle of approach/departure: 48°/44° [48°/35°]
Max speed: 120 [140] km/h
Fuel capacity: 60 l (120 l optional)
Max gradient: 45°
Fording: 0.6 m
Engine: 2.498 l 4-cylinder in-line water-cooled diesel developing 76 hp at 4500 rpm or turbocharged version of same engine developing 110 hp at 4150 rpm
Gearbox: manual with 5 forward and 1 reverse gears
Clutch: single dry plate
Transfer box: 2-speed
Steering: worm and roller, assisted

Turning radius: 5.26 m
Suspension: semi-elliptical leaf springs with double-acting telescopic shock absorbers front and rear
Tyres: 7.00 × 16
Brakes: ventilated discs front and drums rear, servo-assisted, dual circuit
Electrical system: 12 or 24 V (FFR)
Battery: 1 × 12 V 63 Ah
Alternator: 1000 W

Status
In production. In service with the Portuguese armed forces.

Manufacturer
UMM – União Metalo Mecânica Limitada, Rua das Flores 71, 2°Dt°, P-1200 Lisbon, Portugal.
Tel: 347 37 81. Telex: 18 432 sogusa p.

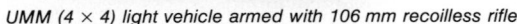

UMM (4 × 4) light vehicle armed with 106 mm recoilless rifle

UMM (4 × 4) light vehicle configured as hard-top personnel carrier

SOUTH AFRICA

Jakkals (4 × 4) Lightweight Airborne Vehicle

Description
The Jakkals (Jackal) lightweight airborne vehicle is a 4 × 4 utility vehicle designed for use by airborne forces. It resembles a small Jeep and is conventional in layout with the engine at the front and the driver and single passenger at the rear; space behind the seats is very limited. It is assembled using standard, commonly available vehicle components, including the engine. Production is carried out by Associated Automotive Distributors (Pty) Limited of Cape Town.

The Jakkals has an impact-resistant glass fibre body that can withstand an unlimited number of parachute drops. The vehicle is normally used together with a small single-axle trailer. Weight of the vehicle and trailer together is 1120 kg. Power is derived from a 1.6 litre petrol engine and a high- and low-range transmission with selectable 4 × 4 or 4 × 2 drive.

The vehicle carries a front-mounted hand-operated self-recovery winch, and a collapsible casualty evacuation stretcher, with securing straps, can be mounted over the passenger seat in less than 1 minute.

The dimensions of the Jakkals and its trailer are such that two vehicles with trailers will fit onto a standard 8 × 9-foot (2.438 × 2.74 m) air supply pallet. Thus a cargo aircraft such as a C-130 can carry 10 units. For para-dropping two 30.5 m or three 18.3 m parachutes are used for each pallet. The descent speed is typically 7 m/s. Once on the ground a vehicle can be unpacked from its pallet and prepared for use by two men in 10 minutes.

The Jakkals is produced in four basic versions: a general-purpose section vehicle carrying a 7.62 mm

Jakkals (4 x 4) lightweight airborne vehicle

machine gun; an attack vehicle with dual 0.50/12.7 mm machine guns; a mortar vehicle carrying an 81 or 120 mm mortar with ancillary equipment and first-line ammunition; and a stretcher vehicle for casualty evacuation. The Jakkals can also be used as a store-

carrier. Various adaptations of these basic variants are possible and any vehicle (other than the attack version) can be fitted with communications equipment and used as a command vehicle.

Specifications

Seating: 2
Configuration: 4 × 4
Weight:
(tractor) 940 kg
(trailer) 180 kg
Max load: (tractor) 350 kg
Towed load: 350 kg
Length: 2.408 m
Width:
(tractor) 1.211 m
(trailer) 1.191 m
Height:
(packed, tractor) 0.963 m

(packed, trailer) 0.91 m
(operational) 1.23 m
Ground clearance: 0.19 m
Track: 1.027 m
Wheelbase: 1.539 m
Angle of approach/departure: 45°/44°
Range: 200 km
Fuel capacity: 60 l
Engine: 1.6 l 4-cylinder petrol developing 63 hp at 5200 rpm
Gearbox: manual, synchromesh, with 4 forward and 1 reverse gears
Clutch: single dry plate
Transfer box: 2-speed

Turning circle: 9.74 m
Suspension: leaf springs front and rear with double-action shock absorbers
Tyres: 670 × 14 6 ply
Brakes: discs front, self-adjusting drums rear

Status

In production. In service with the South African Army.

Manufacturer

Enquiries to Armscor, Private Bag X337, Pretoria 0001, South Africa.
Tel: 012 428 1911. Telex: 30217.
Fax: 012 428 5635.

SPAIN

Santana Model 88 Militar (4 × 4) 500 kg Light Vehicle

Description

The first of these vehicles appeared during 1956 following an arrangement between Land Rover and Metalurgica de Santa Ana SA. In the years that followed the Land Rover holding in the concern was reduced to about 47 per cent and in early 1990 the association with Land Rover was terminated. The first Santana Model 88 was produced in 1970 and was produced in a variety of military and civilian forms.

The Santana Model 88 Militar closely resembles the British airportable 500 kg Land Rover. The chassis uses a stair-type construction with two parallel side-members with welded crossmembers. The chassis is painted and may be finished with a special galvanised anti-corrosion finish if the vehicle is used in a salt-water environment. A 2.286 litre petrol engine is fitted although a diesel engine is available if required. The front and rear axles both use the same differential while the front axle half shafts have universal joints; the rear axle is fully floating. Front and rear suspension uses semi-elliptical springs combined with double-action shock absorbers.

The driver's position is provided with a single seat for the driver and another seat for a passenger. Up to four men can be carried in the rear and a canvas- or hard-top may be fitted. A special deep wading version, capable of coping with water obstacles up to 1.9 m deep is available; this uses a depressurising system for the engine, gearbox and axles and all components are waterproofed.

Apart from the basic personnel and load (up to 500 kg) carried, the Model 88 Militar can be readily converted to a number of special purpose con-figurations and weapon carriers. The Model 88 Militar may also be para-dropped on a platform which, together with the parachute and fittings, weighs 2200 kg.

Variants

Communications version
This has a hard-top and the rear interior is fitted with a folding table for radio equipment or for use in a command role. The vehicle may be fitted with a 42 or 90 A alternator.

106 mm recoilless rifle
The 106 mm recoilless rifle is loaded into the rear of the vehicle via short ramps and once in position the barrel may be pointed through the centre of a split windscreen that can also be folded forwards over the bonnet. This version has a crew of four, the driver and three men, two of whom sit on squab seats at the rear on either side of the gun. Stowage is provided for eight rounds.

7.62 mm machine gun carrier
The 7.62 mm/0.30 Browning machine gun is mounted on a pivot secured to the rear area floor. This mounting allows a full 360° traverse and a maximum elevation of 36°. A similar arrangement which allows the mounting of a 0.50/12.7 mm Browning machine gun limits maximum elevation to 30°.

MILAN
The Model 88 Militar can be converted to carry a MILAN ATGM launcher on a special rear-mounted pivot. The pivot allows a full 360° traverse and elevation and depression of 10°. Up to four missiles may be carried, three of them in rear-mounted racks.

60 mm mortar
A 60 mm mortar is secured to the cargo area floor by a robust support plate. This allows firing through a full 360° arc.

Specifications

Cab seating: 1 + 1 (up to 4 in rear)
Configuration: 4 × 4
Weight:
(maximum) 2160 kg
(empty) 1660 kg
Load: 500 kg
Length: 3.725 m
Width: 1.574 m
Height: (with hood) 1.905 m
Track: 1.309 m
Wheelbase: 2.235 m
Fuel capacity: 97 l
Angle of approach/departure: 48°/32°
Engine: 2.286 l 4-cylinder in-line water-cooled petrol developing 61 hp at 4000 rpm or
2.286 l 4-cylinder in-line water-cooled diesel developing 59 hp at 4000 rpm
Gearbox: manual with 4 forward and 1 reverse gears
Clutch: hydraulic diaphragm and disc
Transfer box: 2-speed
Steering: worm and recirculating ball
Turning radius: 6.25 m
Suspension: semi-elliptical springs front and rear with double-action telescopic shock absorbers
Tyres: 6.00 × 16
Brakes:
(main) hydraulically operated drums front and rear
(parking) mechanical
Electrical system: 24 V
Batteries:
(petrol) 2 × 12 V, 57 Ah
(diesel) 2 × 12 V, 70 Ah
Alternator: 35 A (50 or 90 A optional)

Status

Production complete. In service with Spanish armed forces and some other nations including Egypt and Morocco.

Manufacturer

Land Rover Santana SA, Carretora de Vadollamas, S/N, 23.700 Linares, Spain.
Tel: 34 53 693051. Fax: 34 53 653201.

Land Rover Model 88 Militar carrying 0.50/12.7 mm Browning machine gun

Land Rover Model 88 Militar carrying MILAN anti-tank guided weapon launcher and three more missiles in containers at rear

Santana Model 109 Militar (4 × 4) Light Vehicle

Description
Metalurgica de Santa Ana SA was established in 1955 and in 1956 commenced production of the Land Rover in an agreement with Land Rover Limited. From that time Santana produced both military and civil versions of the Model 109 and introduced its own in-house modifications to production models. The association with Land Rover ceased during 1990.

The Santana Model 109 Militar bears a close resemblance to its British counterpart and is constructed along similar lines. Main differences occur with the engine which may be either a locally produced 2.286 litre petrol or diesel engine or a 3.429 litre six-cylinder petrol or diesel engine. The basic model is produced in several versions (see below) and can be configured to a wide variety of customer requirements.

A deep wading version of the Model 109 Militar was produced and is in service with the Spanish Marines. The Model 109 Militar can also be prepared for parachute drops by lashing it to a special platform in a stripped-down state. The complete load of prepared vehicle, fixtures and platform weighs 2800 kg.

Variants
Basic troop carrier
This is fitted with a soft-top but a hard-topped version is available. The vehicle carries the driver and nine men and the rear area holds cargo or supplies. It is also possible to mount various weapons in the cargo area including machine guns, a 60 mm mortar and a MILAN ATGM launcher.

Communications
This version usually has a hard-top and is specially produced for the communications role with extra screening of components and wiring looms, a 90 A alternator, extra internal racking and stowage and an engine oil cooler. Of the five versions that have been produced one has three long-range radios, another two ground-to-ground radio facilities, a further version acts as a 30-line telephone exchange, while a fourth version has three telex equipments. The fifth version is a special ground-to-ground communications station.

Light recovery vehicle
This variant carries a light electrical crane in the cargo area. The crane winch can lift loads of up to 1000 kg while the jib can tow loads of up to 750 kg if the towed vehicle uses only one axle, and 2040 kg if both axles are used.

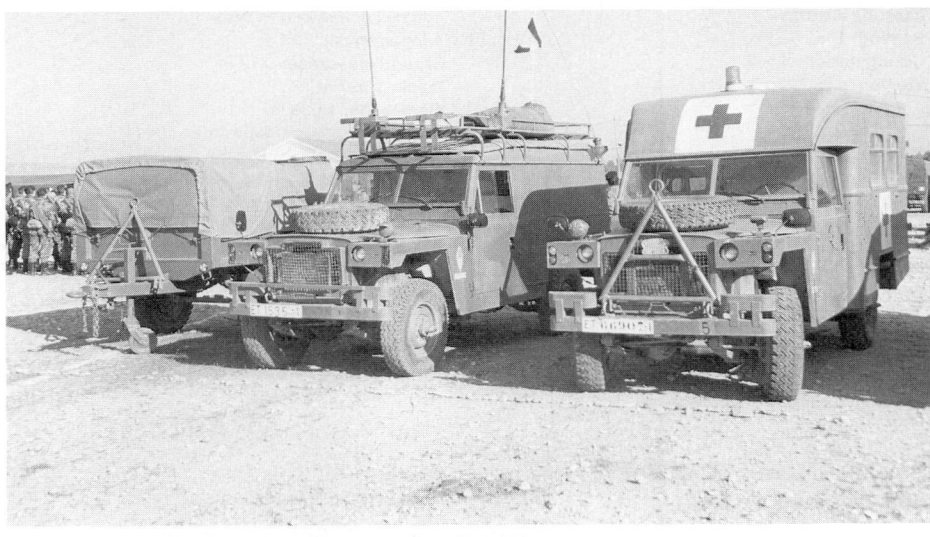

Basic troop-carrying version of Santana Model 109 Militar (left) with ambulance (right)
(Bob Morrison – Military Scene)

Ambulance
This variant has an insulated ambulance body capable of carrying either four stretcher cases or two stretcher cases and four seated casualties. Alternatively eight seated casualties can be accommodated. Two large access doors are provided at the rear and the interior is equipped with medical equipment stowage.

Specifications
Cab seating: 1 + 1 (plus 6 in rear)
Configuration: 4 × 4
Weight:
  (maximum) 3150 kg
  (empty) 1890 kg
Max load: 1000 kg
Length: 4.546 m
Width: 1.574 m
Height: (with hood) 2.008 m
Track: 1.309 m
Wheelbase: 2.768 m
Fuel capacity: 114 l
Angle of approach/departure: 52°/31°
Engine: 2.286 l 4-cylinder in-line water-cooled petrol developing 61 hp at 4000 rpm or
2.286 l 4-cylinder in-line water-cooled diesel developing 59 hp at 4000 rpm or
3.429 l 6-cylinder in-line, water-cooled petrol developing 95 hp at 4000 rpm or

3.429 l 6-cylinder in-line, water-cooled diesel developing 91.7 hp at 4000 rpm
Gearbox: manual with 4 forward and 1 reverse gears
Clutch: hydraulic diaphragm and disc
Transfer box: 2-speed
Steering: worm and recirculating ball
Turning radius: 6.25 m
Suspension: semi-elliptical springs front and rear with double-action telescopic shock absorbers
Tyres: 7.50 × 16
Brakes:
  (main) hydraulically operated drums front and rear
  (parking) mechanical
Electrical system: 24 V
Batteries:
  (petrol) 1 × 12 V, 57 Ah
  (diesel) 1 × 12 V, 70 Ah
Alternator: 35 A (50 or 90 A optional)

Status
Production complete. In service with the Spanish armed forces and some other nations including Egypt and Morocco.

Manufacturer
Land Rover Santana SA, Carretora de Vadollamas, S/N, 23.700 Linares, Spain.
Tel: 34 53 693051. Fax: 34 53 653201.

SWEDEN

Volvo L3314 (4 × 4) Laplander and Volvo C202 (4 × 4) Cross-country Vehicles

Development
The first prototype of the Volvo Laplander L3314 vehicle was completed in 1961 with production beginning the following year. Over 10 000 Laplanders were built for delivery to some 40 countries before production was completed. Two basic versions of the Laplander were built, a pick-up (designated PU) and a hard-top (designated HT). Both are used by the Swedish Army, the PU being known as the Pltgbil 903 and the hard-top as the Pltgbil 903B. Further development of the Laplander resulted in the C202.

Description
Volvo L3314 (4 × 4) Laplander
The chassis of the Laplander consists of an all-welded box-section frame of pressed and welded 3 mm sheet steel, two tubular crossmembers, one box-section crossmember and one U-section crossmember.

Both models have an all-welded steel body with a forward control two-door fully enclosed cab with a heater and defroster. The hard-top model has the same body as the pick-up but in addition has a fully

Volvo L3315 (4 × 4) Laplander with fully enclosed hard-top body

Specifications

Model	Laplander PU	C202 HT	C202 PU
Cab seating	1 + 1	1 + 7	1 + 1
Configuration	4 × 4	4 × 4	4 × 4
Weight (empty)	1520 kg	1795 kg	16 kg
(loaded)	2450 kg	2525 kg	2525 kg
Weight on front axle (empty)	935 kg	1020 kg	990 kg
Weight on rear axle (empty)	585 kg	775 kg	610 kg
Max load	900 kg	730 kg	925 kg
Towed load	1000 kg	1500 kg	1500 kg
Load area	2.3 × 1.535 m	2.27 × 1.4 m	2.27 × 1.53 m
Length	3.985 m	4.015 m	4.015 m
Width	1.66 m	1.68 m	1.68 m
Height	2.09 m	2.09 m	2.09 m
(load area)	0.665 m	0.665 m	0.665 m
Ground clearance	0.285 m	0.285 m	0.285 m
Track (front/rear)	1.338 m/1.338 m	1.348 m/1.338 m	1.348 m/1.338 m
Wheelbase	2.1 m	2.1 m	2.1 m
Angle of approach/departure	40°/40°	39°/48°	39°/48°
Max speed (road)	90 km/h	115 km/h	115 km/h
Range	330 km	330 km	330 km
Fuel capacity	46 l	51 l	51 l
Max gradient	60%	65%	65%
Max side slope	40%	40%	40%
Fording	0.8 m	0.45 m	0.45 m
Steering	cam and roller	cam and roller	cam and roller
Turning radius	5.4 m	5.4 m	5.4 m
Tyres	8.90 × 16	8.90 × 16	8.90 × 16
Brakes (main)	hydraulic	hydraulic	hydraulic
(parking)	mechanical	mechanical	mechanical
Electrical system	12 V	12 V	12 V

enclosed hard-top steel body built integrally with the cab containing six removable folding seats and a heater.

The vehicle is powered by a Volvo B18A four-cylinder petrol engine which develops 75 bhp (SAE) at 4500 rpm and is coupled to an M40 four-speed gearbox with four forward and one reverse gears. The transfer box has four gear positions: four-wheel drive in low ratio, neutral, four-wheel drive in high ratio and reverse drive in high ratio.

The suspension consists of semi-elliptical springs which have progressive springing with rubber bush-type helper springs and double-acting telescopic hydraulic shock absorbers at each wheel station. Brakes are hydraulic with the parking brake operating on the propeller shaft.

Optional fittings include Rockinger type towing hook, hitch plate, PTO (centre and rear), speed governor for PTO and side-mounted winch with a capacity of 2100 kg which can be used to the front or rear of the vehicle. Variants in use with the Swedish Army include an ambulance, fire-fighting and radio vehicles.

The L3315 is a 24 V version intended mainly for radio-equipped vehicles.

Volvo C202 (4 × 4)

The C202 was also manufactured in Hungary by Csepel. The vehicle was offered in three basic versions, a pick-up, a fully enclosed hard-top model and a canvas-top model. The pick-up model has a fully enclosed two-door all-steel cab and a single tailgate at the rear. The hard-top model has five doors, two each side and one at the rear. At the rear are two foldable seats, and two foldable bench seats. All versions have a heater and defroster for the front cab and the hard-top model also has a heater for the rear compartment. A wide range of specialised variants has been developed by Volvo including fire-fighting, ambulance, repair and rescue versions.

The C202 is powered by a Volvo B20A four-cylinder petrol engine which develops 82 bhp at 4700 rpm and is coupled to a manual Volvo M45 gearbox with four forward and one reverse gears. The transfer gearbox is a Volvo FD51. All wheel drive is engaged by a press button in the high range and automatically when low range is engaged.

Brakes are of the vacuum-hydraulic drum type. The parking brake is mechanical and operates off the propeller shaft. Suspension consists of semi-elliptical leaf springs, telescopic double-acting shock absorbers, and hollow-rubber springs to soften bottoming from extreme spring deflection. Optional equipment included an air-conditioning system, canvas top, electric engine heater, fire extinguisher, PTO, sand tyres, snow tyres, spotlight, tyre inflation pump, tropical radiator and a winch with a capacity of 2000 kg.

Status
The Volvo Laplander is no longer in production but remains in service with the Swedish Army and Civil Defence Corps, and with Norway (small numbers only). The Volvo C202 was manufactured in Hungary by Csepel.

Manufacturers
Volvo Truck Corporation, S-405 08 Göteborg, Sweden. Tel: 46 31 666000. Telex: 27000 volvo s. Fax: 46 31 510465.
Csepel, Hungary.

UNITED KINGDOM

Rolba Goblin (4 × 4) 410 kg Load Carrier

Development
During 1982 the British Army issued a requirement for a light load carrier capable of carrying 410 kg of explosive ordnance device (EOD) neutralisation equipment across country and with a maximum stipulated weight of 402 kg for helicopter transport. Rolba Limited produced a prototype in September 1983 by using as a basis an Austrian grass-cutting machine intended for use on mountains. This was the Rasant Bergtrak produced by Johann Nussmuller of Schwanberg, Austria. Once delivered, the prototype underwent trials at the MVEE Chertsey (now the RARDE Chertsey) during December 1983 and following these trials a batch of eight vehicles was delivered by June 1984.

Following experience gained with the 4 × 4 version of the Rolba Goblin, a 6 × 6 version was produced.

Description
The Rolba Goblin chassis is constructed in the form of a bathtub and welded from 3 mm aluminium sheet. This structure carries all brackets, attachment points, the load platform, operator controls, prime mover and auxiliaries, fuel tank and lifting lugs. The 1.21 × 1.665 m load platform is mounted across the rear and is detachable. The Goblin has a permanent 4 × 4 drive and is powered by a 602 cc Citroën AZ-KA air-cooled, twin-cylinder petrol engine. Integral with the engine and clutch unit is a four-speed gearbox and a built-in differential unit. As the Goblin is required operationally for short distances only, the fuel capacity is limited and

Rolba Goblin (4 × 4) 410 kg load carrier (right) with 6 × 6 version on the left

some of the fuel may be used to power a carried electrical generator. The front wheels are driven by Cardan shafts from each side of the gearbox then through reduction final drives. A roller chain on each side connects the front to the rear wheels to provide the full 4 × 4 drive. Skid-type steering is employed, using two control levers connected to a hydraulic brake system.

Specifications
Seating: 1
Configuration: 4 × 4
Weight: 390 kg
Payload: 410 kg
Load area: 1.21 × 1.665 m
Length: 2.502 m
Height:
(ground to platform) 0.65 m
(ground to steering levers) 1.26 m
Ground clearance: 0.2 m
Track: 1.41 m

Wheelbase: 1.5 m
Max road speed: 15.51 km/h
Fuel capacity: 25 l
Engine: Citroën AZ-KA air-cooled, 2-cylinder, 4-stroke petrol delivering 28 hp at 5750 rpm
Gearbox: manual with 4 forward and 1 reverse gears
Clutch: single disc
Steering: skid-type operating through hydraulically operated individual calliper brakes on each front drive shaft
Tyres: 21 × 11.00 – 8 terratrac rawhide

Brakes:
(main) hydraulic
(parking) mechanical
Electrical system: 24 V

Status
In service with the British Army.

Manufacturer
Rolba Limited, Charlwoods Road, East Grinstead, West Sussex RH19 2HU, UK.
Tel: 0342 313266. Telex: 95290.

SUPACAT (6 × 6) Light Vehicle

Development
The SUPACAT (6 × 6) light vehicle was designed as an all-terrain load carrier by SUPACAT Limited and ordered by many public service and other authorities. During 1984, 15 were ordered for the British Army and Royal Air Force in a variety of forms for range duties and other specialised tasks.

The SUPACAT was subsequently manufactured and marketed by Williams Fairey Engineering Limited and developed to the Mark 2 stage as an entrant for the British Army's All-Terrain Mobile Platform (ATMP) competition for the 5th Airborne Brigade. During 1987 it was announced that 38 SUPACAT Mark 2s had been ordered by the Army for the ATMP role and that a further two vehicles used for trials would be refurbished to full production standard.

Following the completion of the British Army's SUPACATs in early 1989, responsibility for marketing and production reverted to SUPACAT Limited.

Description
The SUPACAT is a 6 × 6 low ground pressure (0.21 to 0.35 kg/cm^2 on wheels according to load) vehicle running on 31 × 15.50 × 15 Avon Tredlite tyres. The vehicle uses a forward control driving position with accommodation for a passenger next to the driver and space for a further four men in the rear. The vehicle may be used in an all-flatbed form or with a fixed cab. A canvas tilt or a hard-top body may be used. The payload is up to 1400 kg (with resultant reduced mobility).

On roads, the SUPACAT can be driven at speeds up to 48 km/h and can ford water obstacles up to 0.863 m deep. It can be built with a limited amphibious capability. Tests have been carried out on sand and it can travel on snow up to 300 mm deep.

The original engine was a complete Citroën GS 1.3 litre unit that included the engine, torque converter, three-speed gearbox, transaxle and inboard brakes. This was replaced by a VW Audi 1.6 litre diesel engine coupled to a fully automatic gearbox (a turbocharged diesel engine is optional). A steering lever is provided, one mounting a grip-type throttle which operates the standard Citroën inboard disc brakes mounted on the transmission. From the brakes, shafts take the drive to the purpose-made gearboxes which transfer the drive to the centre axle shafts. The front and rear axles are driven mechanically from the centre axles.

Two SUPACATs can be driven directly into a CH-47D Chinook without preparation and the vehicle is compatible with the EH-101 helicopter. Four SUPACATs can be carried slung under a Chinook, two under a UH-60 Black Hawk and one under a Puma. For conventional air transport SUPACATs can be stacked one on another.

As well as being an all-terrain load carrier the SUPACAT can be used as an anti-tank or anti-aircraft missile carrier and launcher. A transporter trailer which tilts automatically for loading and off-loading can be supplied and can accommodate one SUPACAT. A load-carrying trailer known as the Fork Lift Pallet Trailer (FLPT) was developed for use with the SUPACAT – see entry under *Materials handling*

SUPACAT Mark 2 (6 × 6) light vehicle

equipment for details. The SUPACAT can tow a 105 mm Light Gun.

In British Army service SUPACATs have been fitted with anti-weather awnings and a casualty stretcher rack. Weapon applications have included acting as a MILAN ATGW carrier and firing point and as a 60 or 81 mm mortar carrier and firing platform. All British Army SUPACATs are fitted with machine gun mounts.

During Operation Granby all 40 of the British Army's SUPACATs were converted to enable them to be used as Rapier SAM support vehicles for 58 Battery, 12 Air Defence Regiment, RA. The conversion included the fitting of a heat resistant canopy, a revised cooling system and special fittings for Rapier equipment.

Following Desert Storm all SUPACATs were converted back to their normal configuration and 20 were handed over to the Royal Marines and Dutch Marines for Operation Safe Haven duties in Turkey and Kurdistan. One of the vehicles involved was fitted with a light crane for self-loading purposes. By mid-1991 all 20 SUPACATs involved had reverted to Army use.

Specifications (Mark 2)
Seating: 1 + 5
Configuration: 6 × 6
Weight:
(maximum) 2760 kg (3160 kg limited application)
(empty) 1760 kg
Payload: 1000 kg (up to 1400 kg with reduced mobility)
Ground pressure:
(tyres) 0.21 to 0.35 kg/cm^2 according to load
(tracks) 0.074 to 0.12 kg/cm^2 according to load
Load area: 1.445 × 1.87 m
Length: 3.335 m
Width: 2 m
Height:
(roll bar) 1.88 m
(cab) 2.085 m

(folded down) 1.21 m
(load platform) 0.94 m
Ground clearance: 0.215 m
Wheelbase: 0.923 m + 0.923 m
Angle of approach/departure: 57°/58°
Max speed: (road) 48 km/h
Fuel capacity: 50 l
Max gradient: 45°
Side slope: 40°
Vertical obstacle: 0.5 m
Fording: amphibious
Engine: VW Audi 068.D 1.588 l 4-cylinder OHC in-line water-cooled diesel developing 54 bhp at 4800 rpm (78 bhp at 5000 rpm) or
VW Audi 068.C turbocharged diesel developing 72 bhp at 4500 rpm
Gearbox: fully automatic 3-speed with park and reverse, manual override
Drive: twin helical reduction gearboxes to central axles and mechanical coupling to front and rear axles
Steering: combined power-assisted Ackermann (1st and 2nd axles) and skid steer (all axles) – lock-up facility for use with tracks
Brakes: hydraulic inboard disc
Electrical system: 12 V
Battery: 1 × 12 V, 66 Ah
Tyres: 31 × 15.5 × 15 Avon Tredlite

Status
In service with the British Army (50) and Royal Air Force (5).

Manufacturer
SUPACAT Limited, The Airfield, Dunkeswell, Honiton, Devon EX14 0RA, UK.
Tel: 0404 891777. Fax: 0404 891776.

Octad T8 × 8 1000 kg All-Terrain Vehicle

Description

The Octad T8 × 8 was completed in early 1986 after five years of development. It uses hydraulic transmission, with the option of adding tracks and a variety of ancillary functions including remote-control and hydraulic power take-off for winches and power tools.

The main body is steel and carries the engine and twin hydraulic swash-plate pumps on a subframe. It also houses the hydraulic transmission, oil reservoir, axles and axle drives. One pump drives each side. From the pumps the axle drive is by a closed loop system via fixed displacement hydraulic motors to sprockets and chains giving a full 8 × 8 drive. The hydraulic drive provides an inherent braking facility in addition to multi-disc brakes within the motor frames. The independent joystick control of each set of four wheels allows neutral turns and fine control. The hydraulic transmission provides high torque at low speeds. The vehicle can be supplied with customer-specified superstructures and in its standard form carries a payload of 1000 kg in addition to two crew. It is readily adaptable to remote-control.

Specifications
Cab seating: 1 + 1
Configuration: 8 × 8
Weight: (empty) 1450 kg
Max load: 1250 kg
Length: 3.4 m
Width: 1.8 m
Height: 2.005 m
Ground clearance: 0.314 m
Max speed: (over rough terrain) 30 km/h
Fuel range: 6 h
Fuel consumption: (nominal) 5.68 l/h
Max gradient: 100%
Engine: Ford 1.4 l lean burn petrol developing 74 hp at 4800 rpm or
Ford XLD 1.6 l diesel developing 52 hp at 4800 rpm
Transmission: hydraulic closed loop
Steering: hydrostatic
Suspension: tyres
Tyres: 26 × 12 × 12
Tracks: multi-segment steel/rubber composite
Brakes: hydraulic with disc brakes inside hydraulic motors
Electrical system: 12 V

Status
In production.

Manufacturer
Octad Limited, Unit 10, Holton Heath Trading Park, Poole, Dorset BH16 6LG, UK.
Tel: 0202 624284. Fax: 0202 624861.

Octad T8 × 8 1000 kg all-terrain vehicle fitted with optional tracks over wheels

---

Land Rover Defender 90 (4 × 4) Light Vehicle

Development

In 1990 the Land Rover range of vehicles was given the name 'Defender' so the Land Rover Ninety was renamed the Land Rover Defender 90. The original Land Rover Ninety was introduced in early 1984 with a 2.36 m wheelbase. Like the Land Rover One Ten (now the Defender 110), the Ninety was fitted with long travel coil spring suspension and front disc brakes. Both vehicles share a number of common components, in particular engines, transmissions and front end body panels.

At the same time as the adoption of the Defender name a significant package of product improvements was introduced, including the introduction of the 200 Tdi 2.5 litre direct injection turbocharged intercooled diesel engine with improvements in power, torque and economy over the previous direct injection unit. Other improvements concerned the cab ergonomics and electrical system.

The Land Rover Defender 90 is part of the Land Rover family of military vehicles which includes the Land Rover Defender 110, Land Rover Defender 130 and the Land Rover 6 × 6. The Defender 90 is in service with the British Armed Forces as the Truck, Utility, Light (TUL).

Description

The Land Rover Defender 90 is based on a boxed section steel chassis with the centre section approximately 190 mm deep. A crossmember is bolted in place to facilitate removal of the gearbox and transfer box, and wiring looms are routed along the insides of the box sections for maximum protection. The Defender 90 uses long travel coil springs all round to provide outstanding traction, ride and handling. Suspension movement is controlled at the front and the rear by long stroke hydraulic dampers. The Land Rover front beam axle is located by radius arms with Panhard rods providing lateral location. The rear axle is located by tubular trailing links with a centrally mounted 'A' frame.

Four engines are available for the Defender 90, including a 2.5 litre petrol, a 3.5 litre V-8 petrol, a 2.5 litre naturally aspirated diesel and a 2.5 litre direct injection turbocharged intercooled diesel. The Defender 90 uses the same gearbox and transfer box as the Defender 110 and has permanent four-wheel drive with a lockable centre differential.

Options include a truck cab; open-top with folding windscreen and detachable door tops; a roll-over bar; NATO standard towing jaw and 12-pin trailer socket; blackout lighting systems; air-conditioning; small arms clips; hand throttle; wire mesh lamp guards; disruptive pattern camouflage paint; raised air intake; waterproof screw-lens lamps; various front and rear seating options; external pick and shovel stowage; power take-offs.

The Land Rover Defender 90 has been developed for a variety of weapon system mounts, including an M40 106 mm recoilless rifle, machine guns, and the MILAN ATGW.

Specifications
Cab seating: 1 + 2 (4 in rear)
Configuration: 4 × 4
Weight (GVW):
(standard suspension) 2400 kg
(high load suspension) 2550 kg
Max load: between 920 and 1036 kg depending on model
Towed load:
(off road) 500 kg
(on road) 4000 kg
Length: 3.722 m
Width: 1.79 m

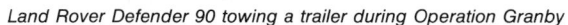

Land Rover Defender 90 towing a trailer during Operation Granby

Land Rover Defender 90 FFR with hard-top

Land Rover Defender 90 armed with twin 7.62 mm machine guns

Height: 1.993 m
Ground clearance: (7.50 × 16 tyres) 0.229 m
Track: 1.486 m
Wheelbase: 2.36 m

Angle of approach/departure: 51°/52°
Fuel capacity: 54.5 l
Engine: 2.495 l 4-cylinder in-line water-cooled petrol developing 83 bhp at 4000 rpm or

3.528 l V-8 water-cooled petrol developing 134 bhp at 5000 rpm or
2.495 l in-line water-cooled indirect injection naturally aspirated diesel developing 68 bhp at 4000 rpm or
2.495 l in-line water-cooled direct injection turbocharged intercooled diesel developing 107 hp at 3800 rpm
Gearbox: manual with 5 forward and 1 reverse gears
Clutch: diaphragm spring
Transfer box: 2-speed
Steering: manual, recirculating ball (power-assist optional)
Turning radius: 5.75 m
Suspension: beam axles front and rear with coil springs controlled by telescopic dampers
Tyres: 7.50 × 16, 6.00 × 16 or 20.5 × 16
Brakes: dual servo-assisted, discs front, drums rear
Electrical system: 12 V, 24 V or 12/24 V

Status
In production. In service with the British and other armed forces.

Manufacturer
Land Rover, Lode Lane, Solihull, West Midlands B92 8NW, UK.
Tel: 021 722 2424. Telex: 338641 lanrov g.
Fax: 021 742 1927.
Land Rovers are also assembled or manufactured in Australia, Kenya, Malaysia, Morocco, Turkey, Zaïre, Zambia and Zimbabwe.

Land Rover (4 × 4) 564 kg Airportable Light Vehicle

Development
This vehicle was designed and developed by Rover in conjunction with the Military Vehicles and Engineering Establishment to meet the special airportable requirements of the British Army, Royal Air Force and Royal Marines. It was shown for the first time at the Commercial Motor Show at Earls Court in September 1968. The vehicle is in service as a light 4 × 4 vehicle by the British forces but is progressively being replaced by the Land Rover Defender 90 (see previous entry). The engine, transmission, axles, suspension and brakes were from the commercial 88-in (2.23 m) Land Rover modified for military use.
Production was phased out during 1985.

Description
The layout of the vehicle is similar to other Land Rovers with the engine at the front, driver and two passengers in the centre and cargo area at the rear with a drop tailgate and a bench seat down either side.
The main feature of this vehicle is that the hood, body sides, doors, windscreen, bumpers and spare wheel can easily be removed to facilitate transport by aircraft or helicopter.

The basic model has a 12 V electrical system but a 24 V fitted-for-radio version is available with the two batteries installed between the front seats in place of the third seat in the 12 V model. This model features a unitary radio kit containing radio, batteries, operator's seat and radio mounting equipment installed in the rear of the vehicle.
Land Rover developed special models of the ½-tonne Land Rover to meet specific overseas requirements, a vehicle developed for the Netherlands Army, with a diesel engine (56 bhp at 4000 rpm) and 24 V 60 A electrical system, being typical.

Ambulance
This version can carry two stretchers in an emergency.

Anti-tank
To meet the requirements of a foreign army, Marshall of Cambridge (Engineering) Ltd designed a 106 mm Land Rover gun vehicle which entered service in 1977. This is the standard vehicle modified to mount a 106 mm M40 recoilless rifle in the rear of the vehicle. The design permits an arc of fire of 180° forwards. Seats for the crew of the weapon and stowage of 106 mm and 12.7 mm/0.50 in ranging machine gun ammunition are provided. A blast shield is fitted to the bonnet and a barrel clamp is fitted to the dashboard. Known users of this model include Saudi Arabia and

Sudan. A prototype of the airportable Land Rover with a 120 mm Wombat recoilless anti-tank weapon was built but was not proceeded with.

Specifications
Cab seating: 1 + 2
Configuration: 4 × 4
Weight:
(empty) 1386 kg
(stripped down) 1206 kg
(loaded) 2020 kg
Max load: 564 kg
Towed load: 1130 kg
Load area: 1.14 × 1.4 m
Length: 3.65 m
Width: 1.52 m
Height:
(overall) 1.95 m
(reduced) 1.47 m
(load area) 0.71 m
Ground clearance: 0.21 m
Track: 1.31 m
Wheelbase: 2.23 m
Angle of approach/departure: 49°/36° (58°/38° in stripped down form)
Max speed: (road) 105 km/h
Range: 600 km
Fuel capacity: 90 l

Airportable (4 × 4) 564 kg Land Rover (Bob Morrison – Military Scene)

Royal Air Force Airportable (4 × 4) 564 kg Land Rover with hard-top body (Bob Morrison – Military Scene)

Max gradient:
(high) 39%
(low) 115%
Fording: 0.5 m
Engine: 4-cylinder 2.286 l in-line OHV petrol developing 70 bhp at 4000 rpm or 4-cylinder 2.286 l in-line diesel developing 60 bhp at 4000 rpm
Gearbox: manual with 4 forward and 1 reverse gears
Clutch: single dry plate
Transfer box: 2-speed
Steering: recirculating ball
Turning radius: 6.4 m

Suspension: semi-elliptical springs with hydraulic shock absorbers
Tyres: 6.50 × 16 or 7.50 × 16
Brakes:
(main) drum, hydraulic oval line, servo-assisted
(parking) drum, mechanical on transmission
Electrical system: 12 V (24 V optional)
Battery: 1 × 12 V

Status
Production complete. In service with Belgium, Brunei, Guyana, Hong Kong, Indonesia (812), Jamaica, Libya,

Netherlands (24 V and a diesel engine), Saudi Arabia, Sudan and the United Kingdom.

Manufacturer
Land Rover, Lode Lane, Solihull, West Midlands B92 8NW, UK.
Tel: 021 722 2424. Telex: 338641 lanrov g.
Fax: 021 742 1927.

Land Rover Defender 110 (4 × 4) Light Vehicle

Development
In 1990 the Land Rover range of vehicles was given the name 'Defender' so the Land Rover One Ten was redesignated the Land Rover Defender 110. The original Land Rover One Ten was first shown publicly in early 1983 with a 110-in (2.794 m) wheelbase and combining a revised body style with a new chassis and coil sprung suspension. Early production in 1983 was mainly for the commercial market but since 1984 a large number of vehicles has been supplied for military contracts. In June 1984 it was announced that the first military order had been placed by an unspecified customer in the Far East. That order was for 900 vehicles and many similar orders have followed.

The United Kingdom Ministry of Defence has taken into service a large number of Defender 110s for use by the British armed forces, in General Service Cargo (GSC) and Fitted For Radio (FFR) variants. It is known to the British Armed Forces as the Truck, Utility, Medium (TUM).

At the same time as the adoption of the Defender name a significant package of product improvements was introduced, including the introduction of the 200 Tdi 2.5 litre direct injection turbocharged intercooled diesel engine with improvements in power, torque and economy over the previous direct injection unit. Other improvements concerned the cab ergonomics and electrical system.

The Land Rover Defender 110 is part of the Land Rover family of military vehicles which includes the Land Rover Defender 90, Land Rover Defender 130 and the Land Rover 6 × 6.

Description
In appearance the Land Rover Defender 110 is similar to earlier Land Rover models but can be identified by the new moulded injection grille and one-piece windscreen. The Defender 110 is available with either the integral Pick-Up body in soft- or hard-top versions, the High Capacity Pick-Up body with soft-top, or as a Station Wagon. The increased track involved the introduction of GRP deformable 'eyebrows' over the wheels which are held in place by frangible pins.

The Defender 110 is based on a box-section steel chassis used on the Range Rover but considerably strengthened. The chassis is robot welded and the centre-section is over 190 mm deep. The overall

strength is said to withstand the most demanding off-road conditions. Detail design of the chassis is such that the fuel tank has added protection. A bolt-in crossmember facilitates removal of the gearbox and transfer box, and the wiring looms are routed inside the chassis members for maximum protection.

The Defender 110 suspension uses coil springs in place of the earlier leaf springs. The coil springs are reinforced and provide 180 mm of wheel travel at the front and 210 mm at the rear. Minimum ground clearance is 0.21 m. Suspension movement at the front and rear is controlled by long-stroke hydraulic dampers. The Land Rover beam front axle is located by radius arms with a Panhard rod providing lateral location. A Salisbury axle is used on the rear, with 300 mm disc brakes being fitted on the front wheels with drum brakes fitted to the rear.

The increased track of the Defender 110 led to a redesigned steering linkage that provides a turning radius of 6.4 m. Factory-fitted power-assisted steering is optional.

Four engines are available for the Defender 90, including a 2.5 litre petrol, a 3.5 litre V-8 petrol, a 2.5 litre naturally aspirated diesel and a 2.5 litre direct injection turbocharged intercooled diesel.

The transmission is permanent four-wheel drive with a five-speed gearbox matched to a two-speed transfer box. This arrangement provides 10 forward and two reverse gears and the transfer box incorporates a lockable differential.

Factory-fitted options include: truck cab; open top with folding windscreen and detachable door tops; roll-over bar; NATO standard towing jaw and 12-pin trailer socket; blackout lighting systems; additional 68 litre fuel tank; air-conditioning; small arms clips; hand throttle; wire mesh lamp guards; raised air intake; disruptive pattern camouflage paint; waterproof screw-lens lamps; various front and rear seating options; cabinets in the body sides for stowing up to four jerricans; external pick and shovel stowage; and power take-offs.

A variety of weapon system mounts for the Defender 110 have been developed with weapon system manufacturers, including the MILAN ATGW and the LAU-97 70 mm multiple launch rocket system.

A wide range of conversions has been developed for the Defender 110, including a special forces patrol vehicle, an armoured patrol vehicle, a remotely piloted vehicle launcher system, mobile workshops, shelter vehicles, ambulances, a back hoe, fire tenders,

armoured and discreetly armoured personnel carriers, towlift recovery vehicles and a hydraulically operated multi-loader.

Variants
Australian Land Rover 110
Land Rover 110s are produced in Australia by Land Rover Australia at their facility in Moorebank, New South Wales. An initial order for 2500 vehicles for the Australian Army was placed and the first was handed over in August 1987. The 1000th vehicle was handed over in December 1988.

Australian 110s are powered by an Isuzu 4BD1T 3.9 litre turbocharged diesel engine developing 121 hp at 3000 rpm. The same engine is used to power the Australian Land Rover 110 Heavy Duty (6 × 6) truck – see separate entry in the *Trucks* section for details of this vehicle.

Special Operations Vehicle (SOV)
See entry in *Special attack vehicles* section.

Specifications
Cab seating: 1 + 2 in front (4 to 10 in rear)
Configuration: 4 × 4
Weight:
(standard suspension) 3050 kg
(levelled suspension) 2950 kg
Max load: 1486 kg
Towed load:
(on road) up to 4000 kg
(off road) 500 kg
Length: 4.631 m
Width: 1.79 m
Height: 2.035 m
Cargo bed length: 2.01 m
Ground clearance: 0.216 m
Track: 1.486 m
Wheelbase: 2.794 m
Angle of approach/departure: 50°/35°
Fuel capacity: 79.5 l
Engine: 3.528 l V-8 water-cooled petrol developing 134 bhp at 5000 rpm or
2.495 l 4-cylinder water-cooled in-line petrol developing 83 bhp at 4000 rpm or
2.495 l in-line water-cooled indirect injection naturally aspirated diesel developing 68 bhp at 4000 rpm or
2.495 l in-line water-cooled direct injection turbocharged intercooled diesel developing 107 hp at 3800 rpm

British Army Land Rover Defender 110 FFR (Bob Morrison – Military Scene)

Land Rover Defender 110 belonging to Belgian armed forces EOD unit (Bob Morrison – Military Scene)

Gearbox: manual with 5 forward and 1 reverse gears
Clutch: diaphragm spring
Transfer box: LT230T, 2-speed
Steering: manual, recirculating ball (power-assist optional)
Turning radius: 6.4 m
Suspension: beam axles front and rear with coil springs controlled by hydraulic telescopic dampers
Tyres: 7.50 × 16
Brakes: dual servo-assisted, discs front, drums rear
Electrical system: 12 V, 24 V or 12/24 V

Status

In production. In service with the British Armed Forces and some other nations including Australia, Belgium, Ireland, Netherlands and Turkey.

Manufacturers

Land Rover, Lode Lane, Solihull, West Midlands B92 8NW, UK.
Tel: 021 722 2424. Telex: 338641 lanrov g.
Fax: 021 742 1927.
Land Rover Australia, PO Box 59, Liverpool, New South Wales 2170, Australia.
Tel: 61 2 600 1333. Telex: AA 120222.
Fax: 61 2 600 8935.
Land Rovers are also assembled or manufactured in Kenya, Malaysia, Morocco, Turkey (by Otokar), Zaïre, Zambia and Zimbabwe.

Land Rover Defender 110 armed with 7.62 mm machine gun during Operation Granby
(Bob Morrison – Military Scene)

Land Rover (4 × 4) Vehicles

Development

After the end of the Second World War the British government was compelled to ration steel to the motor industry in proportion to the value of its exports. This created serious difficulties for the Rover company since its luxury cars were not proving to be exportable. It became obvious that the company would have to produce something which would have a world appeal and be outside the luxury class, a working vehicle which would attract buyers from agricultural and industrial markets of the world.

Early in 1947 a decision was made to build a new all-purpose cross-country vehicle and by late 1947 prototypes of a 4 × 4 vehicle suitable for both agricultural and industrial applications had been built. Trials proved the concept and Rover introduced the Land Rover at the Amsterdam Motor Show in April 1948. Quantity production began at Solihull in July 1948. The first model had an 80-in (2.032 m) wheelbase and was powered by a 1.6 litre petrol engine, which used many components, including the engine, of the Rover P3 '60' car. The basic model was fitted with a canvas hood and was followed late in 1948 by a fully enclosed estate model which could seat six plus the driver. The British government placed its first order for the Land Rover in 1949.

By 1950 over 24 000 Land Rovers had been built and in 1952 the 1.6 litre petrol engine was replaced by a 2 litre petrol engine. In 1954 the original 80-in (2.032 m) wheelbase model was replaced in production by an 86-in (2.184 m) model. In the same year the first long wheelbase model with a wheelbase of 107 in (2.717 m) and which could carry 750 kg of cargo, was introduced.

In 1956 the 86-in (2.184 m) model gave way to the 88-in (2.23 m) and the 107-in (2.717 m) was replaced by the 109-in (2.768 m) model. The same year the British Army adopted the Land Rover as its standard ¼-tonne (4 × 4) vehicle. In 1957 Land Rover offered a diesel engine in place of the standard petrol engine.

In February 1958 the Series II Land Rover was introduced in both 88-in (2.23 m) and 107-in (2.717 m) configurations with a 2¼ litre petrol engine. Late in 1958 production of the 107-in (2.717 m) was discontinued.

In September 1961 the Series IIA was introduced and the 2¼ litre engine replaced the 2 litre engine and in 1962 the 109-in (2.768 m) 12-seater station wagon and a new 1000 kg forward control Land Rover were introduced.

By April 1966 half a million Land Rovers had been completed and late in 1966 a 110-in (2.794 m) model

of the forward control Land Rover was introduced, powered by a six-cylinder petrol engine and capable of carrying 1500 kg of cargo.

From early 1967 a 2.6 litre six-cylinder petrol engine was offered for the 109-in (2.768 m) Land Rover. This was subsequently deleted in 1980 with the introduction of the 3.5 litre V-8 version.

Early in 1968, to comply with new legal requirements governing vehicle lighting in the Netherlands, Belgium and Luxembourg, a new headlight modification was made and for the first time the headlights were incorporated in the wings instead of the grille panel.

In September 1968 two new Land Rovers specifically for military use were introduced, the ½-tonne and 1000 kg, for which there are separate entries in this section. In 1970 the Range Rover, for which there is a separate entry in this section, was introduced.

By July 1971 half a million Land Rovers for export had been completed. The following year production of the forward control model ceased.

In October 1971 the Series III Land Rover was introduced with a restyled grille, redesigned safety facia, improved gearbox and other detailed modifications.

The millionth Land Rover was completed in June 1976 and in early 1979 production of the standard Land Rover was running at 1600 units a week, increased to 2700 units a week by 1981. About 70 per cent of Land Rovers are exported and according to the company, Vietnam is the only country not to have ordered the vehicle.

In 1979 Land Rover Limited, a new and autonomous company was formed to manufacture, develop and market Land Rovers and Range Rovers.

In March 1982, a 'High Capacity' version of the 109-in long wheelbase vehicle was introduced which was available in both full length hood and pick-up forms and in both cases provided greater passenger or cargo carrying ability than the standard body and was available in both 12 V and 24 V configurations. In its standard form the High Capacity 109-in had a gross vehicle weight of 3020 kg and a payload of up to 1450 kg, or seating for up to 13 including the driver.

Production of the 109-in and 88-in models was phased out during 1985.

A new range of Land Rover models was introduced in 1983, the long wheelbase version with a 110-inch (2.794 m) wheelbase and a short wheelbase version (introduced in 1984) with a nominal wheelbase length of 90 inches (actually 2.36 m). An extended wheelbase version with a 127-inch (3.226 m) wheelbase was also made available in crew cab and chassis cab form. In 1990, to distinguish the vehicles from other models manufactured by Land Rover, the range was given the name 'Defender'. The Defender family consists of the

short wheelbase Defender 90, the long wheelbase Defender 110 and the extended wheelbase Defender 130. All these vehicles have their own entries in this section.

Description
88-in (2.23 m)

No 88-in military model is now offered as it was initially replaced by the ½-tonne airportable vehicle and now the Land Rover Defender 90 is in production, but quantities of the civilian version were sold for military applications.

The Land Rover has an all-welded box-section ladder-type chassis. The body is of aluminium panels with the steel bumpers, cappings and other vital components galvanised. The layout is conventional with the engine at the front, driver and two passengers in the centre and the cargo area at the rear with a drop tailgate. The basic model has a galvanised steel hood frame and a full length hood.

Optional equipment for the standard and the long wheelbase model includes a front-mounted 2270 kg capacity mechanical drum winch controlled from the driver's seat, capstan winch with a 1360 kg capacity, overdrive, rubber helper springs, lamp guards and a fire extinguisher.

Land Rover developed special models of the 88-in Land Rover to meet special overseas requirements. In 1977 the Danish Army ordered a version based on the commercial model with a 2.25 litre diesel engine, and a 12 V and supplementary 24 V electrical system which entered service in 1978. Many armies adapted the vehicle to their own specific requirements, for example the Australians had some armed with a 106 mm M40 series recoilless rifle.

109-in (2.768 m)

This has a similar layout to the 88-in (2.23 m) model and was the standard vehicle in its load class in the British Army and many other armed forces but is being progressively replaced by the Defender 110. Standard equipment on the military version includes an FV design towing hook, twin fuel tanks, vehicle lashing eyes at front and rear, freight lashing points in the rear, oil cooler, FV pattern lights, stowage for shovel, pick and axe on tailboard, water jerrican at the bulkhead and provision for stowing a rifle on the dashboard. The fitted-for-radio version has a 90 A rectified electrical system with provision for charging radio batteries, full suppression of electrical equipment, radio table battery carrier, two 100 A batteries, coaxial leads and operator's seat.

There were many variants of the long wheelbase Land Rover in service including an anti-tank version armed with 120 mm Wombat recoilless rifle (now

British Army Series III Land Rovers (Bob Morrison – Military Scene)

British Army Land Rover ambulance (Bob Morrison – Military Scene)

withdrawn from use) or American 106 mm M40 recoil-less rifle, ambulance, command, fire control and numerous other roles. It is also used for towing artillery such as the Italian 105 mm Pack Howitzer, carrying or towing missiles such as the Bofors RBS 70 or Rapier and towing radars such as the THORN EMI Cymbeline. The chassis was also used as a basis for the Shorland armoured patrol vehicle and the SB.401 armoured personnel carrier.

Land Rover built modified versions of the long wheelbase model to meet specific overseas countries' requirements. In 1973 the Norwegian Army ordered the vehicle with a 24 V electrical system and fitted with lifting and towing facilities, petrol-burning heater, radio and aerial mountings and intervehicle starting capability. In 1976 the Dutch Army ordered a version based on the commercial long wheelbase Land Rover with a four-cylinder OHV diesel engine, 24 V electrical system, fresh air heater, sun visors, shovel and axe stowage, radio and aerial mountings and radio battery stowage.

In February 1979 Land Rover launched the 3.5 litre V-8 Land Rover which is in service with the Iraqi Army. The vehicle was developed for FFR and as a half-track (by Laird, but development was discontinued) and a 6 × 6 version was developed in conjunction with Hotspur Limited (details of which are given in the following section). This model was available in 3.175 m (standard body and armoured versions) and 3.529 m (standard) wheelbases.

The Range Rover's 3.5 litre engine was modified to give maximum torque for the Land Rover V-8 at a lower engine speed. Maximum 187 lb/ft at 2500 rpm compares with the Range Rover figure of 207 lb/ft at 3200 rpm and the 122 lb/ft at 2000 rpm produced by the six-cylinder engined Land Rover, which considerably improved the vehicle's off-road performance.

The Land Rover V-8 has permanent four-wheel drive, with high and low ratio gears and a differential lock, as on the Range Rover. Modification of the bodywork in the engine compartment provided plenty of room for the larger engine and allows easy access for servicing.

Military equipment for the V-8 Land Rover included an FV design towing hook, twin fuel tanks, front and rear lifting and towing rings, stowage for shovel, pick and axe on rear tailboard, rifle clips, bumperettes, wire lamp guard, oil cooler, split charge facility, hand throttle, bonnet-mounted spare wheel and raised air intake. To meet military requirements, 24 V electrics

were developed and are in service with Middle East defence forces. The 2.23 m (109 in) V-8 Land-Rover is no longer in production.

Specifications

88-in (2.23 m)
Cab seating: 1 + 2 in front (4 in rear)
Configuration: 4 × 4
Weight:
(empty) 1430 kg
(loaded) 2120 kg
Weight on front axle: (loaded) 930 kg
Weight on rear axle: (loaded) 1190 kg
Max load: 690 kg
Length: 3.65 m
Width: 1.68 m
Height: 1.97 m
Ground clearance: 0.2 m
Track: 1.33 m
Wheelbase: 2.23 m
Angle of approach/departure: 46°/30°
Max speed: (road) 105 km/h
Range: 560 km
Fuel capacity: 45 l
Max gradient:
(high) 39%
(low) 115%
Fording: 0.5 m
Engine: 4-cylinder OHV diesel developing 51 bhp at 4000 rpm or 4-cylinder OHV petrol engine developing 69 bhp at 4000 rpm
Gearbox: manual with 4 forward and 1 reverse gears
Clutch: single dry plate
Transfer box: 2-speed
Steering: recirculating ball
Turning radius: 5.79 m
Suspension: semi-elliptical springs front and rear with double-acting telescopic shock absorbers
Tyres: 7.50 × 16
Brakes:
(main) drum, hydraulic, tandem braking system
(parking) drum, mechanical on transmission
Electrical system: 12 V (24 V optional)

109-in (2.768 m) LWB
Cab seating: 1 + 2 in front (optional seating for 8 in rear)
Configuration: 4 × 4
Weight:
(empty) 1750 kg

(loaded) 2600 kg
Max load: 850 kg
Load area: 1.85 × 1.619 m
Length: 4.56 m
Width: 1.68 m
Height:
(overall) 1.98 m
(reduced) 1.52 m
Ground clearance: 0.2 m
Track: 1.33 m
Wheelbase: 2.768 m
Angle of approach/departure: 45°/29°
Max speed: 90 km/h
Range: 600 km
Fuel capacity: 90 l
Gradient:
(high) 25%
(low) 58%
Fording: 0.7 m
Engine: 4-cylinder in-line OHV petrol developing 69 bhp at 4000 rpm
Gearbox: manual with 4 forward and 1 reverse gears
Clutch: single dry plate
Transfer box: 2-speed
Steering: recirculating ball
Turning radius: 7.5 m
Suspension: semi-elliptical springs front and rear with hydraulic double-acting shock absorbers
Tyres: 7.50 × 16
Brakes:
(main) hydraulic, tandem braking system, servo-assisted
(parking) drum, mechanical on transmission
Electrical system: 12 V (24 V optional)

Status

Production complete. In service with over 140 armed forces.

Manufacturer

Land Rover, Lode Lane, Solihull, West Midlands B92 8NW, UK.
Tel: 021 722 2424. Telex: 338641 lanrov g.
Fax: 021 742 1927.
Land Rovers have also been assembled or manufactured in Australia, Kenya, Malaysia, Morocco, New Zealand, Nigeria, Trinidad, Turkey, Zaïre, Zambia and Zimbabwe.

Range Rover (4 × 4) 750 kg Vehicle

Development

The Range Rover, first announced in June 1970, combines a formidable cross-country capability with the comfort and road performance of a high-speed saloon car and is ideally suited to a variety of military applications including use as an ambulance, command/radio vehicle, fire tender, personnel carrier and border patrol vehicle. A number of factory approved conversions are available including 6 × 4 configurations equipped for use as fast response emergency units.

The four-door variant extends the vehicle's versatility still further, particularly for personnel carrier or security duties where ease of access for all passengers is important.

Description

The Range Rover is based on a rigid box-section steel chassis. The rubber-mounted steel body frame is clad in separate body panels, most of which are formed in lightweight, corrosion-resistant aluminium alloy.

From 1990 power was provided by a 3.9 litre V-8 petrol engine with fuel injection developing up to 185 bhp in high compression form. Power is trans-

mitted via a five-speed manual or four-speed automatic gearbox. A turbocharged 2.5 litre diesel engine developing 119 bhp is also available. The chain-driven two-speed transfer box features a viscous control unit for the permanent four-wheel drive system to automatically transfer torque away from a slipping axle to the one with more grip. This provides better off-road traction without the need for driver intervention.

The suspension features long travel coil springs to give maximum on-road comfort and good off-road performance. A ride-levelling device provides a good towing capability. A new suspension system was introduced on Vogue and Vogue SE models in 1991.

Discreetly armoured Range Rover

Range Rover Vogue SE

This features front and rear anti-roll bars and revised damper and spring rates to minimise body sway when cornering and preserve off-road abilities and good on-road ride. This suspension is available as an option on other models in the range.

The 1991 Range Rovers also featured a fuel system with an increase in capacity up to 81.8 litres. A modified filler system gives faster fill with reduced splashback.

To reflect the increased emphasis on long distance cruising, a cruise control system was introduced in 1991. This was standard on Vogue SE automatic vehicles and optional on Vogue automatic.

Disc brakes (ventilated at the front) with asbestos-free pads are fitted all round and an anti-lock braking system (ABS) with brake power booster is available as an option (it is standard on Vogue SE models).

Luxury-standard accommodation is provided for up to five persons, entry being gained through two or four doors. Central door locking is provided. The rear load area is accessed through a two-piece tailgate and may be extended by folding the rear seat squab which is asymmetrically split on four-door models.

Late models featured an improved heating and ventilation system with a heated front window being available. From 1991 a glass sunroof became avail-able to replace the steel version fitted to earlier vehicles; a blind provides screening when necessary. This feature was standard on the Vogue SE and optional on other models. Other improvements intro-duced in 1991 included an automatic dipping rear mirror on Vogue SE models, heated door locks, improved sound insulation and an uprated stereo system. A range of optional equipment includes a heavy duty suspension, air-conditioning (standard on some models), winches and towing equipment.

In 1993 the extended wheelbase Vogue LSE was introduced, powered by a 4.2 litre, catalyst-equipped V-8 engine and offering additional legroom and ride/handling refinements. This model features Electronic Air Suspension (EAS) which provides five alternative ride heights for easy access, reduced road noise within

the vehicle and improved off-road capability. EAS is standard on the Vogue SE and Vogue LSE (it is optional on the Vogue). Other models have long travel coil springs and all vehicles are fitted with anti-roll bars front and rear. For long distance cruising a cruise control system is standard on the Vogue LSE and SE and optional on Vogue petrol variants with both manual and automatic transmission.

Disc brakes (ventilated at the front) are fitted all round and an anti-lock brake system (ABS) with power brake booster is available as an option (it is standard on Vogue LSE and SE models). Electronic traction control (ETC), which offers enhanced traction in severe and off-road conditions is available on ABS-equipped vehicles (standard on Vogue LSE and SE and optional on others).

Luxury standard accommodation is provided for up to five persons. Central door locking is provided and the latest models are available with a security alarm system and remote locking. The rear load area is accessed through a two-piece tailgate and may be extended by folding the rear seat squab which is assymetrically split.

Land Rover's Special Vehicles division produces a number of Range Rover conversions including police and rapid assault vehicles and discreetly armoured specifications for the transport of VIPs and personnel. The discreetly armoured specification features Level 1 ballistic protection, a specially developed heavy duty suspension, and a full range of security options.

Specifications
Cab seating: 1 + 4
Configuration: 4 × 4
Weight: (2-door/4-door)
(empty) 1760 kg/1792 kg
(loaded) 2510 kg/2510 kg
Weight on front axle: (loaded, petrol) 1100 kg
Weight on rear axle: (loaded) 1510 kg
Max load:
(2-door) 750 kg
(4-door, petrol) 718 kg

(4-door, diesel) 636 kg
Length: 4.447 m
Width: 1.813 m
Height: 1.792 m
Ground clearance: 0.19 m
Track: 1.486 m
Wheelbase: 2.54 m
Angle of approach/departure: 45°/30°
Max speed: 171.2 km/h
Fuel capacity: 81.8 l
Engine: Rover V-8 3.528 l petrol with fuel injection developing 185 bhp at 4750 rpm or
VM 2.5 l 4-cylinder turbocharged IDI diesel developing 119 bhp at 4200 rpm
Gearbox:
(manual) 5 forward and 1 reverse gears
(automatic) 4 forward and 1 reverse gears
Clutch: (manual) single dry plate
Transfer box: 2-speed chain-driven with viscous control unit
Steering: recirculating ball with steering damper and power-assistance
Turning radius: 5.65 m
Suspension: coil springs, long-stroke hydraulic telescopic dampers, axles located by radius arms, self-energising ride-level unit on rear suspension
Brakes:
(main) hydraulic disc on all wheels, ventilated disc on front; ABS with brake power booster optional
(parking) mechanical on transmission
Electrical system: 12 V

Status
In production.

Manufacturer
Land Rover, Lode Lane, Solihull, West Midlands B92 8NW, UK.
Tel: 021 722 2424. Telex: 338641 lanrov g.
Fax: 021 742 1927.

Land Rover Discovery (4 × 4) Light Vehicle

Development
The Land Rover Discovery (4 × 4) light vehicle was first announced in November 1989 and is an all-terrain four-wheel drive vehicle designed to meet the require-ments of customers requiring the ability to traverse the most difficult off-road conditions yet retain a degree of style for driving on roads. The vehicle retains all the strength of the other models in the Land Rover range, including the ability to tow fully braked trailers weighing up to 4000 kg.

Discovery was launched as a three-door estate; a five-door version was introduced during 1990. The vehicle features the long travel coil spring suspension used on the Range Rover and Defender vehicles and has an all-disc braking system, beam axles and power steering as standard.

The Discovery is suitable for a variety of military and security tasks such as escort vehicle, police patrol vehicle and staff car.

Description
The Land Rover Discovery (4 × 4) light vehicle is based on a box-section chassis designed to minimise mud traps and which is treated with an electrophoretic anti-corrosion process. Exterior body panels are of aluminium alloy to provide a corrosion-resistant finish combined with low weight, enhancing the vehicle's low centre of gravity.

Power is provided by an all-alloy 3.5 litre V-8i fuel injected petrol engine or the 2.5 litre 200 Tdi direct injection turbocharged intercooled diesel engine. Transmission is via a five-speed manual or, on V-8i models, a four-speed automatic gearbox, and a two-speed transfer box with permanent four-wheel drive and a lockable centre differential. Beam axles are coupled to a long travel coil spring suspension all

round and the steering has power assistance as standard. Brakes are disc all round with dual circuit and servo-assistance.

The interior, with seating for up to seven, was designed to combine durability, practicality and style. There is internal stowage for maps and documents while entry is by either three or five doors with central locking standard on the five-door version (optional on the three-door). The rear compartment has a large capacity for kit or stores and this may be augmented by lowering the asymmetrically split rear seat. Folding seats in the rear compartment are available on all models.

A range of conversions is available from Land Rover's Special Vehicles division. Conversions include vehicles for police and paramilitary applications. A range of Discovery paramedic ambulances is also available in standard and extended wheelbase versions with medical and rescue equipment options.

Land Rover Discovery operating in Saudi Arabia during Operation Granby
(Bob Morrison – Military Scene)

Land Rover Discovery (4 × 4) light vehicle with five doors and 200 Tdi diesel
engine

Specifications

Cab seating: 1 + 4 (2 extra seats available)
Configuration: 4 × 4
Weight: (3-door/5-door)
(unladen, V-8i petrol) 1919/1986 kg
(unladen, 200 Tdi petrol) 2008/2053 kg
(laden, all models) 2720 kg
Towed load: (braked) up to 4000 kg
Length: 4.521 m
Width: 1.793 m
Height: 1.928 m
Ground clearance: 0.241 m
Track: 1.486 m
Wheelbase: 2.54 m
Angle of approach/departure: 41°/32°

Max speed:
(V-8i) 171.4 km/h
(200 Tdi) 147.4 km/h
Fuel capacity: 81.7 l
Engine: 3.528 l V-8 diesel with fuel injection developing 164 bhp at 4750 rpm (152 bhp with catalyst) or 200 Tdi 2.495 l direct injection turbocharged diesel with intercooler developing 111 bhp at 4000 rpm
Gearbox: manual, 5 forward and 1 reverse gears
Transfer box: 2-speed giving permanent 4-wheel drive with lockable centre differential
Steering: recirculating ball with steering damper and power-assistance
Turning radius: 5.95 m
Suspension: coil springs, hydraulic dampers; axle location by radius arms

Brakes:
(main) hydraulic, disc all round, dual circuit with servo-assistance
(parking) mechanical drum on transmission
Electrical system: 12 V

Status

In production. Ordered for supply to United Kingdom Ministry of Defence organisations.

Manufacturer

Land Rover, Lode Lane, Solihull, West Midlands B92 8NW, UK.
Tel: 021 722 2424. Telex: 338641 lanrov g.
Fax: 021 742 1927.

Land Rover Defender 130 (4 × 4) Light Vehicle

Development

In 1990 the Land Rover range of vehicles was given the name 'Defender'. Thus the Land Rover 127 was designated the Land Rover Defender 130. As the Land Rover 127 (4 × 4) light vehicle, the Defender 130 was first shown early in 1983 when it was displayed to potential customers as a concept vehicle in crew cab form. Production started during 1984 to supply vehicles to the commercial market but since 1987 the Defender 130 has entered service with a number of military customers. In August 1989 it was announced that 214 Land Rover 127s (now Defender 130s) were to be supplied to the Royal Air Force to support RAF Regiment Rapier surface-to-air missile squadrons.

As with the Land Rover Defender 90 and Defender 110 models (see entries in this section) the Defender 130 is fitted with long travel coil spring suspension and front disc brakes and has a high degree of commonality with other Land Rover models, including engines, transmissions, brakes, steering, electrical systems and front end body panels.

At the same time as the adoption of the Defender name a significant package of product improvements was introduced. This included the introduction of the 200 Tdi 2.5 litre direct inject turbocharged intercooled diesel engine with improvements in power, torque and economy over the previous direct injection unit. Other improvements concerned the cab ergonomics and electrical system.

Although designated the Defender 130, this vehicle retains the 127-in (3.226 m) wheelbase.

Description

The Land Rover Defender 130 is an extended chassis variant of the Land Rover Defender 110 with a payload capacity of up to 1600 kg dependent upon the type of body fitted. It is available either with a crew cab and pick-up rear body or with a chassis cab to which any one of a number of different body styles can be fitted.

The suspension uses long travel coil springs front and rear with suspension movement controlled by telescopic hydraulic dampers. The front and rear beam axles are located by front radius arms and rear trailing links, and lateral location is provided by a Panhard rod at the front of the vehicle and a centrally mounted 'A'

bracket at the rear.

Two engine options are available for the Defender 130; the 3.5 litre V-8 petrol engine and 2.5 litre direct injection turbocharged intercooled diesel. The Defender 130 uses the same transfer box, five-speed gearbox and permanent four-wheel drive system as the Land Rover Defender 90 and 110.

Among the factory-fitted options available on Military versions of the Defender 130 are: air-conditioning; a raised air intake; an open-top with folding windscreen and detachable door tops; power steering; a range of winches and power take-offs; a NATO towing jaw with 12-pin trailer socket; blackout lighting systems; 12, 24 or 12/24 V electrical systems; an additional fuel tank; wire mesh lamp guards; a disruptive pattern camouflage paint finish; various rear seating options; small arms clips; and external pick and shovel stowage.

The crew cab configuration is suitable for use as a light artillery tractor, housing both crew and equipment. The extra body length enables bulky cargo or missiles to be carried.

A number of variants of the Defender 130 have been developed including mobile workshops, shelter-carrying vehicles and ambulances.

Land Rover Defender 130 (4 × 4) ambulance during Operation Granby
(Bob Morrison – Military Scene)

Land Rover Defender 130 (4 × 4) Rapier missile support vehicles

Specifications
Cab seating: 1 + 2 (1 + 5 in crew cab)
Configuration: 4 × 4
Weight: (GVW) 3400 kg
Max load: up to 1600 kg (dependent upon type of body fitted)
Towed load:
  (off road) 750 kg
  (on road) 4000 kg
Length: 5.132 m
Width: 1.79 m
Height: (cab roof) 2.073 m
Ground clearance: 0.215 m
Track: 1.486 m
Wheelbase: 3.226 m

Angle of approach/departure: 50°/31°
Engine: 3.528 l V-8 water-cooled developing 134 hp at 5000 rpm or
2.495 l in-line water-cooled direct injection turbocharged intercooled diesel developing 107 hp at 3800 rpm
Gearbox: manual with 5 forward and 1 reverse gears
Clutch: diaphragm spring
Transfer box: LT230T, 2-speed
Steering: manual, recirculating ball (power-assisted optional)
Turning radius: 7.54 m
Suspension: beam axles front and rear with coil springs controlled by hydraulic telescopic dampers
Tyres: 7.50 × 16

Brakes: dual line servo-assisted, disc front, drums rear
Electrical systems: 12 V, 45/65 A; 24 V with outputs of up to 90 A; or 12/24 V

Status
In production. In service with the Royal Air Force and other armed forces. Licence-produced in Turkey by Otokar.

Manufacturer
Land Rover, Lode Lane, Solihull, West Midlands B92 8NW, UK.
Tel: 021 722 2424. Telex: 338641 lanrov g.
Fax: 021 742 1927.

Land Rover (4 × 4) 1000 kg Truck

Development
The 101-in (2.57 m) wheelbase forward control Land Rover was developed by the Rover Company in co-operation with the Military Vehicles and Engineering Establishment to meet a British Army requirement for a 1000 kg payload 4 × 4 vehicle with the added capacity of towing a 1500 kg powered axle trailer. The vehicle was first shown to the public in September 1968. A pre-production run of vehicles was completed in 1972 and the vehicle entered service with the British Army in 1975. Production is complete.

Description
The vehicle is of the forward control type with the engine at the front and the cargo area at the rear. The chassis is of steel frame construction with two U-sections overlapped and welded on the vertical faces, full length flat-topped sidemembers and intermediate support bearing for rear PTO on bolt-in crossmembers between the third and fourth crossmembers.

The 1000 kg Land Rover is powered by a military version of the successful lightweight aluminium Rover 3.5 litre V-8 engine, which is basically the same as the car engine but with a reduced compression ratio of 8.5:1 to enable it to operate on low octane fuels.

The four-speed all-synchromesh Range Rover type transmission with a high and low transfer box provides eight forward and two reverse gears. A third differential between the front and rear axles obviates transmission wind-up associated with four-wheel drive transmission. This differential can be locked by a vacuum-actuated control to provide maximum traction through both axles. The front axle drive provides a 35° steering lock through constant velocity joints.

The complete hood, body sides, windscreen, bumpers and spare wheel can be removed from the vehicle for air transport. The vehicle can be lifted by medium lift helicopters such as the Wessex and Puma.

Tool lockers are provided in the rear body behind the wheel arches. As a result of trials with the pre-production run, production vehicles have an anti-roll bar at the front, mud flaps and a folding rear entry step.

Standard equipment includes rear bumperettes, helicopter lifting rings front and rear, rotating towing hooks front and rear, trailer brakes operated from the towing vehicle using single line vacuum system on foot and handbrake.

The British Army uses this vehicle for a wide range of roles including towing the 105 mm Light Gun and for carrying MILAN ATGW firing posts and 81 mm mortars. The Australian and British armies have used the vehicle to tow the Rapier SAM system.

In 1975 the Royal Luxembourg Army ordered a number of vehicles with a 24 V electrical system (FFR), cable drum winch with front or rear pull and a fresh air heater to cab and rear body.

Variants
Ambulance
In July 1976 Marshall of Cambridge (Engineering) Limited received a contract from the Ministry of Defence for a two- to four-stretcher ambulance version of the Land Rover. This was built and designed to meet an MoD requirement for an improved pattern lightweight ambulance for casualty evacuation from

British Army Land Rover (4 × 4) 1000 kg truck (Bob Morrison – Military Scene)

forward areas to carry four stretcher or six sitting patients. The aluminium alloy thermally insulated body provides a high standard of patient comfort while a new pattern stretcher gear simplifies loading and unloading in the upper position. Additional equipment which may be fitted includes an Eberspacher heater, an air-conditioner, and automatic resuscitation equipment. This model is in service with the British Army.

MILAN carrier
The British Army uses this vehicle to carry MILAN ATGW teams. Each vehicle carries six men, two MILAN firing posts plus 14 missiles.

Communications vehicle
The British Army has a number of these vehicles fitted with a hard-top and carrying various forms of communications and electronic warfare equipment.

Anti-tank
The Egyptian Army uses this vehicle fitted with the British Aerospace Swingfire ATGW system. Four missiles carried in the rear of the vehicle can be launched away from the vehicle with the aid of a separation sight and controller.

Specifications
Cab seating: 1 + 1 (up to 8 in the rear)
Configuration: 4 × 4
Weight:
  (empty) 1924 kg
  (loaded) 3120 kg
  (stripped) 1580 kg
Weight on front axle: (loaded) 1608 kg
Weight on rear axle: (loaded) 1512 kg
Max load: 1000 kg
Load area: 2.49 × 1.727 m
Length: 4.127 m

Width: 1.842 m
Height: 2.138 m
Ground clearance: 0.254 m
Track:
  (front) 1.524 m
  (rear) 1.549 m
Wheelbase: 2.565 m
Angle of approach/departure: 50°/46°
Max speed: 120 km/h
Range: 560 km
Fuel capacity: 109 l
Max gradient: 60%
Engine: Rover V-8 petrol developing 128 bhp at 5000 rpm
Gearbox: manual with 4 forward and 1 reverse gears
Clutch: single dry plate
Transfer box: 2-speed with permanent 4-wheel drive
Steering: recirculating ball with steering damper
Turning radius: 5.14 m
Suspension: semi-elliptical taper leaf springs with telescopic hydraulic dampers, anti-roll bar at front
Tyres: 9.00 × 16
Brakes:
  (main) hydraulic, split system, servo-assisted
  (parking) drum, mechanical on transmission
Electrical system: 12 V (24 V optional)

Status
Production complete. In service with Australia, British Army (2500), Royal Air Force (being replaced by Land Rover Defender 130), Egypt, Iran and Luxembourg (57).

Manufacturer
Land Rover, Lode Lane, Solihull, West Midlands B92 8NW, UK.
Tel: 021 722 2424. Telex: 338641 lanrov g.
Fax: 021 742 1927.

UNITED STATES OF AMERICA

M151 (4 × 4) 362 kg Light Vehicle and Variants

Development

In 1950 the Continental Army Command placed a requirement with the Ordnance Corps for a new ¼-ton vehicle. Research and development began that year at the Ordnance Tank-Automotive Command. In 1951 the Ford Motor Company was awarded a development contract for the new vehicle and the first prototypes were completed in 1952. A further batch was completed in 1954 under the designation XM151 and in 1956 the XM151E1 (of conventional steel construction) and the XM151E2 (of aluminium construction) were built and tested. The former was selected for production in 1959; Ford was awarded the first production contract and first production vehicles were completed in 1960 at Ford's Highland Park Plant. The M151 replaced the M38 (4 × 4) ¼-ton vehicle in the US armed forces. Later production contracts were awarded to the AM General Corporation. The FY78 request was for only 3880 vehicles at a cost of $29.1 million. It was then stated that the engine of the vehicle no longer met emission standards and that this procurement would be the last for several years. Production ceased in 1985 only to re-start again in 1988 to supply vehicles for overseas sales to Pakistan and other nations. Production has now ceased.

Description

The body and chassis of the M151 are integral and are of all-welded construction. The layout of the vehicle is conventional with the engine at the front and the crew area at the rear with a removable canvas top and side curtains, and a windscreen that can be folded forward flat on the bonnet.

In 1964 the M151 was replaced in production by the M151A1 which had improved suspension as the earlier model had a tendency to oversteer. The M151A2 followed in 1970 with modifications to the rear suspension, dual brake system, collapsible steering wheel, two-speed wipers and modified lighting. The M151A2LC has a gearbox with three forward and one reverse gears (other vehicles have four forward and one reverse gears) and two-speed transfer case (other vehicles have a single-speed transfer case). The vehicle also has a different suspension which consists of semi-elliptical springs and shock absorbers instead of the coil springs and telescopic shock absorbers fitted to other versions.

The basic vehicle can also be armed with a pintle-mounted 7.62 mm M60 or a 0.50/12.7 mm M2 Browning machine gun and many have been fitted with the Hughes TOW ATGW system which replaced the 106 mm recoilless rifle.

Many kits are available including a front-mounted winch, heater, hard-top, 100 A alternator and a Xenon searchlight. The vehicle can ford to a depth of 0.533 m without preparation and 1.524 m with the aid of a kit.

From October 1986 a programme was initiated to retrofit roll-bars to about 11 000 M151-series vehicles. Most of the vehicles involved belong to National Guard and Army Reserve units. A contract to provide kits for 6000 vehicles was awarded to the Wright Automotive Corporation of Colorado Springs, Colorado in August 1987. The contract was worth just over $4 million.

Variants

M107 and M108 are communications vehicles with the radios installed in the rear of the vehicle. The passenger seat faces the rear to enable the radio operator to work his equipment.

M718 and M718A1 are ambulance versions and have a crew of two, a driver and a medical attendant. This version can carry a stretcher and three seated patients, two stretchers and two seated patients or three stretcher patients.

M825 is fitted with the M40 106 mm recoilless rifle mounted in the rear. This model has been replaced in US Army service by the Hughes TOW ATGW and kits are available to convert the M825 to the M151A2 standard. However, during mid-1987 25 M151A2s were converted to M825 standard by TACOM in order to meet a requirement from Somalia.

The UK company, A F Budge (Sales) Limited of Retford, Nottinghamshire, has proposed a diesel engine retrofit package for the M151A1/A2 series in which the original engine is replaced by a Perkins Prima 80T turbocharged 2 litre diesel unit developing 80 hp at 4500 rpm. This would result in an increase in range, reduced fuel consumption and improved reliability.

In the United States, Cummins Military Systems has proposed a retrofit programme for M151 series vehicles in which the engine would be replaced by a Cummins B3.9-105 diesel engine developing 105 hp at 2500 rpm. This would be coupled to a Chrysler A 727 automatic transmission to provide improved fuel economy, increased range and ease of maintenance.

Status

Production complete. In service with the US Army, Air Force and Marines and over 100 other countries including Ecuador (including M825), Egypt, Gambia,

Specifications

Model	M151	M151A1	M151A2	M718A1	M825
Cab seating	1 + 3	1 + 3	1 + 3	1 + 1	1 + 3
Configuration	4 × 4	4 × 4	4 × 4	4 × 4	4 × 4
Weight (empty)	1012 kg	1088 kg	1107 kg	1247 kg	1174 kg
(loaded)	1575 kg	1633 kg	1652 kg	1656 kg	1959 kg
Weight on front axle (empty)	574 kg	607 kg	618 kg	620 kg	655 kg
Weight on rear axle (loaded)	448 kg	481 kg	490 kg	626 kg	519 kg
Max load (road)	554 kg	544 kg	545 kg	409 kg	785 kg
(cross-country)	362 kg	362 kg	363 kg	409 kg	785 kg
Towed load (road)	970 kg	970 kg	970 kg	not authorised	not authorised
(cross-country)	680 kg	680 kg	680 kg	not authorised	not authorised
Length	3.352 m	3.371 m	3.371 m	3.631 m	3.645 m
Width	1.58 m	1.634 m	1.633 m	1.819 m	1.943 m
Height (overall)	1.803 m	1.803 m	1.803 m	1.94 m	1.621 m
(reduced)	1.332 m	1.332 m	1.333 m	1.313 m	1.346 m
Ground clearance	0.26 m	0.24 m	0.24 m	0.23 m	0.21 m
Track	1.346 m	1.346 m	1.346 m	1.346 m	1.346 m
Wheelbase	2.159 m	2.159 m	2.159 m	2.159 m	2.159 m
Angle of approach/departure	66°/37°	65°/37°	66°/37°	67°/36°	62°/33°
Max speed	106 km/h	104 km/h	90 km/h	90 km/h	80 km/h
Range	482 km	482 km	482 km	442 km	483 km
Fuel capacity	56 l	56 l	59.8 l	59.8 l	59.8 l
Max gradient	60%	60%	60%	60%	50%
Max side slope	40%	40%	40%	40%	30%
Fording (without preparation)	0.533 m	0.533 m	0.533 m	0.533 m	0.533 m
(with preparation)	1.524 m	1.524 m	1.524 m	1.524 m	1.524 m
Engine	L-142 4-cylinder liquid-cooled OHV petrol developing 72 hp at 4000 rpm				
Gearbox	manual with 4 forward and 1 reverse gears				
Clutch	single dry disc				
Transfer box	single-speed, integral with transmission. Driver can select either 4 × 4 or 4 × 2 drive				
Steering	worm and double roller				
Turning radius	5.486 m	5.638 m	5.638 m	5.638 m	5.638 m
Suspension	coil springs with hydraulic shock absorbers				
Tyres	7.00 × 16	7.00 × 16	7.00 × 16	7.00 × 16	7.00 × 16
Brakes (main)	hydraulic	hydraulic	hydraulic	hydraulic	hydraulic
(parking)	mechanical	mechanical	mechanical	mechanical	mechanical
Electrical system	24 V	24 V	24 V	24 V	24 V
Battery	1 × 2 HN	1 × 2 HN	1 × 2 HN	1 × 2 HN	1 × 2 HN

Portuguese Army M151A1 (4 × 4) ¼-ton light vehicle
(Bob Morrison – Military Scene)

M718A1 (4 × 4) ambulance

Greece, Indonesia, South Korea (141), Netherlands, Pakistan, Peru, Philippines, Portugal, Saudi Arabia, Senegal, Singapore (including M825), Somalia (M151 and M825), Spain (marines only), Thailand, Venezuela (including M825) and Zaïre. By early 1980 AMG had built 95 000 M151 series. The company held the production contract to supply M151A2 series vehicles on a 'requirement' basis.

Manufacturer
AM General Corporation, 14250 Plymouth Road, Detroit, Michigan 48232, USA.
Tel: (313) 493 3300. Telex: 023 5652.

M151A2 (4 × 4) ¼-ton light vehicle

Jeep (4 × 4) Light Vehicle

Development
The original Jeep (general purpose) vehicle was developed and manufactured for the US Army by Willys Overland. In 1963 Willys Overland became Kaiser Jeep which, in 1970, became the Jeep Corporation, a subsidiary of American Motors Corporation. Today Jeep Corporation manufactures the XJ range of compact 4 × 4 utility vehicles (see next entry) and the YJ range of small 4 × 4 utility vehicles, replacing the CJ range.

The CJ-5, CJ-6, CJ-7 and CJ-8 are no longer in production by Jeep Corporation but are in widespread use around the world. The latest model is the YJ, commercial name Wrangler, a successor to the CJ series. Militarised versions of the long wheelbase version (YJ-L) were due to commence production in Egypt during early 1988.

Jeep Corporation has manufacturing or assembly licensees in Australia, China (Beijing Jeep Corporation), Egypt (see separate entry), India (by Mahindra and Mahindra, see separate entry), Indonesia, Mexico, Pakistan and Venezuela.

Description
The layout of the YJ series is conventional with the engine at the front, individual seats for the driver and one passenger and folding transverse benches or two longitudinal seats in the rear. A vertically hinged tailgate provides access to the cargo area.

Automatic and manual four-speed and five-speed transmissions are available for the YJ series with a four-wheel drive system. A four-cylinder petrol engine is standard with a six-cylinder petrol engine as an available option.

A wide range of optional and heavy duty equipment is available including air-conditioning, soft- or hard-tops, heavy duty cooling, battery, tyres and suspension, and power steering. The military versions of the YJ are available with additional equipment including military wrap springs, lifting eyes, tow hooks and pintle hook, a blackout lighting system, 24 V auxiliary power and severe-use oil, air and fuel filtration systems.

In the United States, Cummins Military Systems has proposed a retrofit programme for Jeep series vehicles in which the engine would be replaced by a Cummins B3.9-105 diesel engine developing 105 hp at 2500 rpm.

This would be coupled to a Chrysler A 727 automatic transmission to provide improved fuel economy, increased range and ease of maintenance.

Specifications

Model	YJ regular wheelbase	YJ long wheelbase
Cab seating	1 + 5	1 + 5
Configuration	4 × 4	4 × 4
Weight (empty)	1316 kg	1471 kg
(loaded)	1882 kg	2200 kg
Max load	566 kg	729 kg
Towed load	907 kg	907 kg
Length	3.862 m	4.49 m
Width	1.676 m	1.676 m
Height (overall)		
(open body)	1.744 m	1.744 m
(soft-top)	1.828 m	1.828 m
(hard-top)	1.76 m	1.785 m
Ground clearance	0.207 m	0.207 m
Track	1.473 m	1.473 m
Wheelbase	2.373 m	2.627 m
Angle of approach/ departure	31°/32°	32°/22°
Fuel capacity	76 l	76 l
Engine	2.5 l 4-cylinder petrol developing 104 hp at 5000 rpm or 4.2 l 6-cylinder petrol developing 112 hp at 3000 rpm	

Model	YJ regular wheelbase	YJ long wheelbase
Gearbox	manual with 4 forward and 1 reverse gears	
Transfer box	2-speed	2-speed
Clutch	single dry plate	single dry plate
Steering	recirculating ball — power steering optional	
Turning radius	10.3 m	10.9 m
Suspension	semi-elliptical leaf springs with hydraulic shock absorbers	
Brakes	hydraulic dual circuit disc, front; drum rear (both power-assisted)	
Electrical system	12 V (24 V optional)	

Status
Production of commercial YJ-S (Wrangler) began in February 1986. Prototypes of YJ-L under test in Egypt; production in Egypt from early 1988. The YJ series is under evaluation by China and Pakistan.

Manufacturer
Jeep Corporation, International Operations, 27777 Franklin Road, Southfield, Michigan 48034, USA. Telex: 023 1255.

YJ-L long wheelbase version of YJ (4 × 4) series

Jeep XJ (4 × 4) Light Truck/Wagon Series

Description

The XJ Utility/Truck series (Cherokee, Wagoneer and Comanche Pick-up Truck) was introduced by Jeep Corporation in 1984 (wagon) and 1986 (truck). The Cherokee and Wagoneer are five-passenger wagons, capable of towing up to 2268 kg. The Commanche is a 1000 kg payload pick-up truck with a seating capacity for up to 13 when equipped with longitudinal rear seats in a rear cabin.

Automatic and manual four-speed and five-speed transmissions are available with a choice of 4 × 4 or 4 × 2 drive or permanent 4 × 4 (Cherokee only). Engines include a 2.5 litre or 4 litre petrol or a 2.1 litre turbocharged diesel.

The Cherokee is produced in China by the Beijing Jeep Corporation. For details see separate entry under China in this section.

Specifications

Model	XJ Wagon (Cherokee)	XJ Truck (Comanche)
Cab seating	1 + 4	1 + 2
Configuration	4 × 4	4 × 4
Weight (empty)	1363 kg	1464 kg
(loaded)	2213 kg	2464 kg
Max load	750 kg	1000 kg
Towed load	2268 kg	2268 kg
Length	4.2 m	4.928 m
Width	1.79 m	1.822 m
Height (hard-top)	1.63 m	1.666 m
Ground clearance	0.21 m	0.213 m
Track	1.473 m	1.473 m
Wheelbase	2.576 m	3.033 m
Angle of approach/ departure	42°/32°	44°/27°
Fuel capacity	76 l	76 l
Engine	2.5 l 4-cylinder petrol developing 104 hp at 5000 rpm or 4 l 6-cylinder petrol developing 173 hp at 4500 rpm or 2.1 l 4-cylinder turbocharged diesel developing 85 hp at 3750 rpm	

Model	XJ Wagon (Cherokee)	XJ Truck (Comanche)
Gearbox	manual with 4 forward and 1 reverse gears	
Transfer box	2-speed	2-speed
Clutch	single dry plate	single dry plate
Steering	recirculating ball — power steering optional	
Turning radius	10.9 m	12 m
Suspension	coil springs, front, semi-elliptical leaf springs rear, all with hydraulic shock absorbers	
Brakes	hydraulic dual circuit disc, front; drum rear (both power-assisted)	
Electrical system	12 V	12 V

Status

In production. Military versions under evaluation by Chinese Army.

Manufacturer

Jeep Corporation, International Operations, 27777 Franklin Road, Southfield, Michigan 48034, USA. Telex: 023 1255.

Jeep Corporation XJ (Cherokee) utility truck

Jeep Corporation XJ (Comanche) pick-up truck

M38 Series (4 × 4) 363 kg Light Vehicle

Development

The M38 was developed by Willys from 1950 to meet an urgent US Army requirement for a light 4 × 4 vehicle to replace the large number of Second World War Jeeps still in service. The M38 was basically the standard CJ-3A civilian vehicle with a deep fording kit, a 24 V electrical system and a semi-floating rear axle, and in appearance was similar to the wartime vehicle. The M38 was in production from 1950 to 1952 when it was replaced by the M38A1. The M38A1 is different in appearance from the M38 and has a more powerful engine and a slightly longer wheelbase. From the early 1960s the M38 and M38A1 were replaced in US Army service by the M151 (4 × 4) series of light vehicles.

Description

M38

The layout of the M38 is conventional with the engine at the front and the passenger/cargo area at the rear. Individual seats are provided for the driver and one passenger at the front with a bench seat for two passengers at the rear. The top of the vehicle can be covered by a canvas cover and when not in use the bows fold down at the rear of the vehicle. Both the M38 and M38A1 can be fitted with a front-mounted winch.

M38A1

The layout of the M38A1 is identical to the M38. The front axle is a full-floating, single reduction type fitted with a conventional differential with hypoid drive gears. The rear axle is a semi-floating single reduction type equipped with a conventional differential with hypoid drive gears. The M38A1C has a split windscreen to provide stowage space for the barrel when the vehicle is fitted with a 106 mm M40 series recoilless rifle. The

Specifications

Model	M38	M38A1	M170
Cab seating	1 + 3	1 + 3	1 + 1
Configuration	4 × 4	4 × 4	4 × 4
Weight (empty)	1247 kg	1209 kg	1344 kg
(loaded, road)	1791 kg	1753 kg	1706 kg
Max load (road)	544 kg	544 kg	n/app
(cross-country)	363 kg	363 kg	n/app
Towed load (road)	907 kg	907 kg	n/app
(cross-country)	680 kg	680 kg	n/app
Length	3.377 m	3.517 m	3.936 m
Width	1.574 m	1.539 m	1.536 m
Height	1.879 m	1.85 m	2.032 m
(reduced)	1.379 m	1.428 m	n/app
Ground clearance	0.234 m	0.234 m	0.23 m
Track	1.247 m	1.247 m	1.247 m
Wheelbase	2.032 m	2.057 m	2.565 m
Angle of approach/departure	55°/35°	55°/35°	46°/34°
Max speed (road)	88.5 km/h	88.5 km/h	88.5 km/h
Range	362 km	450 km	482 km
Fuel capacity	49 l	64.3 l	75.7 l
Max gradient	65%	69%	71%
Fording (without preparation)	0.939 m	0.939 m	0.381 m
(with preparation)	1.879 m	1.778 m	n/app
Engine model	Willys MC	Willys	Willys MD
Engine type	4-cylinder petrol	4-cylinder petrol	4-cylinder petrol
Output	60 bhp at 4000 rpm	72 bhp at 4000 rpm	68 bhp at 4000 rpm
Gearbox	manual with 4 forward and 1 reverse gears		
Clutch	single dry plate	single dry plate	single dry plate
Transfer box	2-speed	2-speed	2-speed
Turning radius	6.096 m	5.892 m	7.467 m
Suspension	semi-elliptical springs front and rear with hydraulic telescopic shock absorbers		
Tyres	7.00 × 16	7.00 × 16	7.00 × 16
Brakes (main)	hydraulic	hydraulic	hydraulic
(parking)	mechanical	mechanical	mechanical
Electrical system	24 V	24 V	24 V
Batteries	2 × 12 V	2 × 12 V	2 × 12 V

vehicle also has its rear bench seat removed to make space for the mount. Racks for ammunition under the mount are reached by a rear tailgate. The spare wheel on the M38 is mounted at the rear and on the M38A1C on the right side of the vehicle.

M170 Ambulance
The full designation of the vehicle is Truck, Ambulance: ¼-Ton, 4 × 4, M170, Front Line. It is a long wheelbase version of the M38A1 and can carry three patients on stretchers or six seated. The spare wheel is carried inside at the right of the front passenger seat and the handbrake has been modified to avoid interference with the left lower stretcher. Additional facilities include crash pads and an interior emergency light.

Status
Production complete. No longer in service with the US Army but still widely used by other countries, including the Netherlands. The M38 was built in Canada as the M38CDN while the M38A1 was built as the M38A1CDN.

Manufacturer
AM General Corporation, 14250 Plymouth Road, Detroit, Michigan 48232, USA.
Tel: (313) 493 3300. Telex: 023 5652.

M38A1 (4 × 4) 363 kg light vehicle in use by the Netherlands Army

M37 (4 × 4) 680 kg Cargo Truck and Variants M42, M43 and M201

Development
Immediately after the Second World War the standard 680 kg vehicle in the US Army was the wartime T214 (or Beep as it was more commonly known). This was replaced by another Dodge called the M37 (maker's designation T245). More than 136 000 M37 trucks were built between 1950 and 1970. From the late 1960s the M37 series was supplemented by the M715 series of 1¼-tonne trucks, but some M37s still remain in reserve service with the US Army.

Description
The basic cargo truck is designated the M37 (official designation Truck, Cargo: ¾-Ton, 4 × 4, M37) and can carry 907 kg of cargo on roads or 680 kg of cargo across country. Towed allowance is 2722 kg on roads and 1815 kg across country.

The engine is mounted at the front of the vehicle with the three-man cab in the centre and the cargo area at the rear. The cab has a windscreen which can be folded forward onto the bonnet, removable canvas roof and a door either side. The tops of the doors can be removed. The rear all-steel cargo area has a drop tailgate, removable bows and a tarpaulin cover, folding troop seats, removable front rack, seat backs and supports.

Power is taken from the engine through the clutch to the transmission; a short propeller shaft connects the transmission to the two-stage transfer case and power is then transmitted to the front and rear axles by a propeller shaft.

The basic chassis is designated the M56 (with or without a front-mounted winch with a capacity of 3402 kg) and other chassis are the M56C which has an improved rear suspension and the M56B1 which has a greater interchangeability of components with other vehicles.

Variants
Many countries have adopted the vehicle to mount light weapons such as machine guns, and in El Salvador some vehicles have been converted into lightly armoured patrol vehicles known as the VAL; for details refer to *Jane's Armour and Artillery 1992-93* page 348. The M37 was also built in Canada in the 1950s.

M42 Command Post
This differs from the cargo model in that it has side curtains with windows and a split-type rear curtain, map light, folding table and provision for the installation of communications equipment.

Specifications

Model	M37	M43	M201
Cab seating	1 + 2	1 + 2	1 + 2
Configuration	4 × 4	4 × 4	4 × 4
Weight (empty)	2585 kg	3952 kg	4218 kg
(loaded)	3493 kg	4617 kg	4218 kg
Length	4.81 m	5.004 m	5.174 m
Width	1.784 m	1.866 m	2.235 m
Height	2.279 m	2.333 m	2.323 m
Track	1.574 m	1.574 m	1.574 m
Wheelbase	2.844 m	3.2 m	3.2 m
Angle of approach/departure	38°/32°	32°/47°	44°/32°
Max speed	88.5 km/h	88.5 km/h	88.5 km/h
Range	362 km	362 km	362 km
Fuel capacity	91 l	91 l	91 l
Max gradient	68%	68%	68%
Fording (without preparation)	1.066 m	1.066 m	1.066 m
(with preparation)	2.133 m	2.082 m	2.082 m
Engine	Dodge T245 6-cylinder in-line petrol developing 78 bhp at 2300 rpm		
Gearbox	manual with 4 forward and 1 reverse gears		
Clutch	single dry plate	single dry plate	single dry plate
Transfer box	2-speed	2-speed	2-speed
Steering	worm and sector	worm and sector	worm and sector
Turning radius	7.01 m	7.62 m	8.229 m
Suspension	semi-elliptical springs with hydraulic shock absorbers front and rear		
Tyres	9.00 × 16	9.00 × 16	9.00 × 16
Brakes (main)	hydraulic	hydraulic	hydraulic
(parking)	mechanical	mechanical	mechanical
Electrical system	24 V	24 V	24 V
Batteries	2 × 12 V	2 × 12 V	2 × 12 V

M37 (4 × 4) without front-mounted winch and with tarpaulin cover folded

M43 Ambulance

This model has a fully enclosed steel body consisting of driver's and patients' compartments with a connecting door. It can carry four stretcher patients plus an attendant or eight seated patients and an attendant. A winch with a capacity of 3500 kg is mounted at the front of the vehicle. The M43B1 has an aluminium rather than a steel body and does not have the winch. An adjustable spotlight is mounted on top of the cab and this can be controlled from within the cab. A personnel heater and surgical light are provided for the rear compartment.

M201 Maintenance Truck

This has an all-steel body with compartments for stowing tools and supplies. It is used for telephone installation and maintenance.

Status

Production complete. In service with many armed forces including Greece, El Salvador, Spain, Thailand and Turkey. Dodge also exported large numbers of its Power Wagon vehicles for military use including the M611 (cargo) and M615 (ambulance).

Manufacturer

Dodge Division of Chrysler Corporation, Detroit, Michigan, USA.

SPECIAL ATTACK VEHICLES
BRAZIL

ENGESA EE-VAR (4 × 2) Light Vehicle

Description

The ENGESA EE-VAR (4 × 2) light vehicle is of the high speed and mobility 'dune buggy' type and was developed to carry out a variety of military cross-country roles such as reconnaissance and forward observation and as a light weapon carrier. It is air-transportable.

The ENGESA EE-VAR has left-hand seating for a driver and a passenger in side-by-side bucket seats behind a shallow sloping bonnet, with space for a further seat centrally behind them. The light chassis is protected by a 14 kg/m² Kevlar floor plate and 20 kg/m² Kevlar is used for a front deflector plate and further protection in front of the seats. A curved sheet of 8 kg/m² Kevlar is used to protect the engine mounting at the rear and an 8 mm thick polycarbonate semi-windshield may be fitted. The entire passenger area is protected by a tubular roll-over frame.

The air-cooled Volkswagen petrol engine is mounted at the rear. Much of the engine area and front and rear suspension is left open to improve cooling, reduce weight and provide access for repair and maintenance.

The vehicle can be used to mount a variety of weapons such as 5.56, 7.62 or 12.7 mm machine guns, 40 mm grenade launchers and TOW anti-tank missiles. Stowage is provided for personal equipment, ammunition, a camouflage cover for the vehicle, a map holder, communications equipment (when the optional 24 V electrical system is fitted), a first aid box, a spare tyre and a fuel container. There is also stowage for combat tools, a jack and a wheel wrench.

Specifications
Seating: 1 + 1 or 2
Configuration: 4 × 2
Weight:
(empty) 620 kg
(combat) 920 kg
Length: 3.5 m
Width: 1.82 m
Height: 1.3 m
Ground clearance: 0.35 m
Track:
(front) 1.4 m
(rear) 1.53 m
Wheelbase: 2.5 m
Angle of approach/departure: 70°/35°
Max speed: 138 km/h
Fuel consumption: (road) 10 km/l
Fuel capacity: 46 l
Max gradient: 80%
Side slope: 65%
Vertical obstacle: 0.34 m
Engine: Volkswagen 1.583 l flat 4-stroke air-cooled petrol developing 70 hp at 4200 rpm
Gearbox: Volkswagen manual with 4 forward and 1 reverse gears
Clutch: single dry plate
Steering: Gemmer worm and roller with hydraulic shock absorber
Suspension:
(front) torsion bars with 2 double-action shock absorbers
(rear) torsion bars with 4 double-action shock absorbers
Tyres:
(front) 8.25 × 15
(rear) 10.00 × 15
Brakes: disc front, drum rear
Electrical system: 12 V (24 V optional)
Battery: 1 × 12 V, 48 Ah
Alternator: 35 A

Status
In production. Has been trialled in the Middle East.

Manufacturer
ENGESA Engenheiros Especializados SA, Avenida Tucunare 125/211, Caixa Postale 152/154, 06400 Barueri, SP, Brazil.
Tel: 11 421 4711. Telex: 1171 302 enes br.

ENGESA EE-VAR (4 × 2) light vehicle

UNITED KINGDOM

Wessex Saker (4 × 2) Light Strike Vehicle

Description

The Wessex Saker (4 × 2) light strike vehicle is a high mobility vehicle intended for a number of tactical roles such as long-range incursion, reconnaissance, airfield security and installation defence. It has a low profile combined with good ground clearance, and produces a low thermal signature.

The Saker is based on a monocoque space frame chassis that can be readily adapted to a number of forms to suit role and customer requirements. The basic form is a two-seat vehicle with a rear-mounted diesel engine (a 2 litre air-cooled VW petrol engine is optional) with the two-man crew seated in the centre of the vehicle; three and four-seat versions are available. The area over the engine can be used for stowage and the crew position is protected by a roll-bar. Further stowage panniers or racks can be located along both sides of the vehicle.

The vehicle can be used to carry a number of types of weapon including 7.62 and 12.7 mm machine guns, the 30 mm ASP-30 cannon, anti-tank missiles (including Hellfire) and grenade launchers. Total payload is 700 kg and the Saker can tow trailers or weapons such as 120 mm mortars.

Numerous options are available including bush guards, extra fuel tanks, communications and navigation equipment, run-flat tyres, and so on. Kevlar armour can be used to provide extra protection for the crew.

The Saker is built by DML at Devonport Royal Dockyard.

In July 1991 Wessex (UK) plc concluded a licensing agreement with Manufacturing Assembly Inc (MAI) of Hunt Valley, Maryland, whereby MAI has the right to manufacture and market the Saker in the United States.

Specifications
Seating: 2, 3 or 4
Configuration: 4 × 2
Weight: (kerb) 1100 kg
Max load: 700 kg
Length: 3.9 m
Width: 1.86 m
Height: 1.73 m
Ground clearance: 0.35 m
Angle of approach/departure: 80°/65°
Side slope: 48°
Engine: Perkins Prima 80T 1.993 l 4-cylinder water-cooled turbocharged diesel developing 80 hp at 4500 rpm
Gearbox: 4 forward and 1 reverse gears incorporating limited slip differential
Clutch: single dry plate operated by hydraulic sealed split system
Steering: rack and pinion, power-assisted
Turning circle: 12.3 m
Suspension:
(front) torsion bar and single shock absorber with spring coil over
(rear) torsion bar and double shock absorber, one with single coil over
Tyres: 30 9.5 R 15LT
Brakes: discs front and rear operated by hydraulic sealed split system
Electrical system: 12 V (24 V optional)
Batteries: 2 × 12 V, 60 Ah

Status
In production.

Manufacturer
Wessex (UK) plc, Woolhampton Court, Woolhampton, nr Reading, Berkshire RG7 5ST, UK.
Tel: 0734 712663. Fax: 0734 713110.

Wessex Saker (4 × 2) 400 kg light strike vehicle   *Wessex Saker (4 × 2) 400 kg light strike vehicle*

Longline Light Strike Vehicle (LSV)

Description

The Longline Light Strike Vehicle (LSV) was developed to be a highly mobile vehicle for military use in hostile environments. It was designed as a weapon platform and for military missions such as reconnaissance and airborne operations. Commercially available major components and assemblies are used in its construction where possible.

The LSV is based on a high tensile tubular steel space frame with a Volkswagen 1.9 litre water-cooled engine located at the rear, together with the gearbox. Engine cooling is through a ducted radiator with two independently operated thermostatically controlled electric pans. A separate oil cooler is provided for the engine lubricant. The drive configuration may be 4 × 2 or 4 × 4 with lockable differentials or viscous couplings as required. The frame incorporates a full roll-over

cage and an integral weapon mounting base plate. A full length Makralon skid plate extends the full length of the underside and side panniers are provided for equipment or additional fuel tanks. The low sloping bonnet plate is aluminium and may be used for equipment stowage.

The driver is seated on the left with a separate seat for the navigator/gunner on the right; both seats are provided with safety harnesses. Two fuel tanks are located just behind the seats and may be provided with an optional ignition retardent system. A dual 12 V electrical system is provided. The exhaust system was designed to have a low aural and thermal signature.

Weapons that can be mounted on the LSV's UMI (Universal Mount Interface) include 7.62 and 12.7 mm machine guns (including the 12.7 mm GECAL Gatling gun), a 40 mm grenade launcher, a 30 mm ASP-30 cannon, or six MILAN anti-tank missiles and their launcher; a 60 mm mortar may be carried for dismounted use.

The LSV can be transported inside a standard ISO container and may be slung under CH-47D, Puma and Sea King helicopters. It has been para-dropped from a C-130 transport aircraft.

Specifications

Seating: 1 + 1
Configuration: 4 × 4 (or 4 × 2 with drive on rear wheels)
Weight:
 (unladen) 1220 kg
 (fully laden) 1850 kg
Load capacity: 454 kg
Length: 4.015 m
Width: 1.83 m
Height: (top of roll cage) 1.625 m
Ground clearance: 0.356 m
Wheelbase: 2.52 m
Max speed: (rough tracks) 100 km/h
Range: over 400 km
Fuel capacity: 70 l
Gradient: 50%
Side slope: (with weapons fitted) 50°
Fording: (unprepared) 0.5 m
Trench: 1 m
Engine: VW 1.9 l flat four water-cooled petrol developing 76 hp
Gearbox: VW manual with 5 forward (including a cross-country gear) and 1 reverse gears
Transmission: viscous permanent 4 × 4 with differential locks front and rear
Steering: rack and pinion
Turning radius: 6 m
Suspension: independent torsion bar front and rear, coil spring over shock absorbers
Tyres: 30 × 9.50 R15LT
Brakes: disc front, drum rear
Electrical system: dual 12 V
Batteries: 2 × 12 V
Alternators: 2 × 12 V, 60 A

Status
In production for British Army special forces.

Manufacturer
Longline Limited, 9 The Grange Industrial Estate, Albion Street, Southwick, Brighton, West Sussex BN42 4EN, UK.
Tel: 0273 870888. Fax: 0273 870808.

Longline Light Strike Vehicle (LSV) armed with a 12.7 mm GECAL Gatling gun

Land Rover Defender Special Operations Vehicle

Description

The Land Rover Defender Special Operations Vehicle (SOV) was introduced during 1992 and was specifically

designed to meet a requirement for a rapid reaction, air-portable, all-terrain weapons platform. An initial order for 60 units was placed by the US Army for use by their Special Forces (Rangers) during late 1992.

The SOV is based on the Defender 110 chassis and retains a high level of commonality with other Defender models in terms of permanent four-wheel drive, long

travel coil spring suspension, transfer box and the latest generation of gearbox, steering and braking systems.

The SOV is configured as a long wheelbase all-terrain weapons platform. The suspension uses long travel coil springs front and rear combined with telescopic dampers, rear trailing links, a Panhard rod at

Land Rover Defender Special Operations Vehicle (SOV)

the front and a centrally mounted 'A' bracket at the rear. The SOV is available with either the 200 Tdi direct injection turbocharged intercooled diesel or the 3.5 litre V-8 petrol engine.

The SOV can carry a wide range of weapons. The frame roll-bar mounted over the rear can carry one or two machine guns, including the 30 mm ASP-30 cannon, or a 40 mm grenade launcher, plus a further machine gun next to the driver. Racks and stowage bins located around the vehicle can be used to carry a 50 or 81 mm mortar and mounting and/or an anti-tank missile launcher. Further stowage bins can carry mines or demolition equipment in addition to the crew's personal kit.

The SOV may be carried inside a C-130 transport aircraft or the CH-47 and EH 101 helicopters and may be carried slung under medium and heavy lift helicopters. The SOV may be para-dropped.

Specifications
Crew: up to 6
Configuration: 4 × 4
Weight: (GVW) 3400 kg
Towed load:
  (off road) 1000 kg
  (on road, full trailer brakes) 4000 kg
Length: 4.445 m
Width: 1.89 m
Height: (gun ring) 1.93 m
Ground clearance: 0.216 m
Track: 1.486 m
Wheelbase: 2.794 m
Engine: 3.528 l V-8 water-cooled diesel developing 134 bhp at 5000 rpm or
2.491 l water-cooled direct injection turbocharged intercooled diesel developing 107 bhp at 3800 rpm
Gearbox: manual, 5 forward and 1 reverse gears
Clutch: diaphragm spring
Transfer box: LT 230T, 2-speed
Steering: manual, recirculating ball
Turning radius: 6.4 m
Suspension: beam axles front and rear controlled by hydraulic telescopic dampers
Brakes: dual servo-assisted; discs front, drums rear
Tyres: 7.50 × 16
Electrical system: 12 V
Alternator: 45 A

Status
In production. Order by US Army (60).

Manufacturer
Land Rover, Lode Lane, Solihull, West Midlands B92 8NW, UK.
Tel: 021 722 2424. Telex: 338641 lanrov g.
Fax: 021 742 5012.

UNITED STATES OF AMERICA

Chenowth Fast Attack Vehicle/Light Strike Vehicle (FAV/LSV)

Description
The Fast Attack Vehicle/Light Strike Vehicle (FAV/LSV) is an armed derivative of Chenowth's off-road racing vehicle which combines light weight, high speed and good cross-country mobility and manoeuvrability. The vehicle's low centre of gravity and rapid response rear-wheel drive provides a high cross-country speed.

The chassis is an open high strength 4130 chromoly tubular frame with an integral chromoly steel roll cage. Other safety features include a racing-type fuel cell which is explosion-resistant and run-flat capable rims on all four tyres. The standard engine, a 94 hp STD petrol unit, is air-cooled and rear-mounted. A diesel engine will become available in the near future.

Just forward and above the engine, the gunner/vehicle commander has the capability to fire forward and to the rear on a swivel seat. The assistant driver, the lower gunner, rides in the right-hand seat. All positions have suspension-type bucket seats fitted with retaining straps.

During Operation Desert Shield/Storm the FAV/LSV was operated by US and UK Special Forces and by the US Marines. Weapons can include two 7.62 mm machine guns, mounted fore and aft, together with one 0.50/12.7 mm M2 machine gun or a 40 mm MK 19 automatic grenade launcher. The FAV/LSV can also carry a TOW 2 anti-tank missile launcher, a 30 mm ASP-30 cannon, an AT-4 anti-tank rocket launcher or the Stinger SAM.

A two-man variant is also available.

Specifications
Seating: 3
Configuration: 4 × 2
Weight: (kerb) 950 kg
Payload: 680 kg

Chenowth 3-man Fast Attack Vehicle/Light Strike Vehicle (FAV/LSV) armed with 0.50/12.7 mm machine gun

Length: 4.14 m
Width: 2.1 m
Height: 2.03 m
Ground clearance: 0.406 m
Wheelbase: 2.87 m
Angle of approach/departure: 81°/48°
Max speed:
  (road) 135 km/h
  (off road) 60-120 km/h
Range: 515 km
  (with auxiliary tank) 965 km
Gradient: 75%
Side slope: 50%
Engine: STD 2 l air-cooled petrol delivering 94 hp at 4400 rpm
Gearbox: manual, 4 forward and 1 reverse gears
Suspension: independent
Steering: rack and pinion
Electrical system: 12 V (24 V optional)

Status
In production. In the inventory of US Navy, Marine Corps and Army (two-man version).

Manufacturer
Chenowth Racing Products Inc, 943 Vernon Way, El Cajon, San Diego, California 92020, USA.
Tel: (619) 449 7100. Fax: (619) 449 7103.

Warrior NMC-40 Long-range Fast Attack Vehicle

Description
The Warrior NMC-40 fast attack vehicle was designed and developed as part of the Fast Attack Vehicle (FAV) programme initiated by the US Army Tank-Automotive Command (TACOM). It was first shown publicly in July 1983 and is offered for sale and export.

The Warrior NMC-40 is a four-wheeled light vehicle with a high strength tubular steel roll-cage frame. Seating is provided for three men, two facing forward and one facing the rear. The air-cooled engine is a German-manufactured rear-mounted unit capable of generating land speeds in excess of 161 km/h. Provision has been made for mounting two weapons, usually two M60 machine guns or one M60 and an automatic 40 mm grenade launcher, one at the front and the other at the rear.

The Warrior NMC-40 is supplied complete with equipment ranging from personal body armour to radios and special tools. Also included are map cases, grenades in racks and a neoprene vehicle cover.

Specifications
Cab seating: 1 + 2
Configuration: 4 × 2
Weight: (less crew and armament) 748 kg
Ground clearance: 0.355 m
Range: (cross-country) 483-644 km
Gradient: 75%
Side slope: 40%
Max speed: 153-161 km/h
Engine: air-cooled 4-cylinder petrol developing 80 hp

Warrior NMC-40 long-range fast attack vehicle

Gearbox: manual with 4 forward and 1 reverse gears
Suspension: torsion bars and shock absorbers providing 0.355 m wheel travel front and rear
Steering: rack and pinion with dampers
Brakes: drums front and discs rear with hydraulic steering brake
Electrical system: dual 12 V, 100 A

Status
Ready for production.

Manufacturer
Nordac Manufacturing Corporation, Route 12, Box 124, Fredericksburg, Virginia 22405, USA. Tel: (703) 752 2552. Telex: 89 7440.

Teledyne (4 × 4) 725 kg Light Forces Vehicle (LFV)

Description
The Teledyne (4 × 4) 725 kg Light Forces Vehicle (LFV) was designed for a number of roles requiring a high degree of cross-country mobility, such as light reconnaissance, and as a light weapons carrier.

The LFV has a permanent 4 × 4 configuration and has seating for the driver and two passengers. Deep bolster configured seats are provided for the driver and the front passenger with similar seating for the passenger behind them. The turbocharged diesel engine is at the rear. An automatic transmission is provided and the accelerator pedal is oversized for better control under all conditions. Power steering is fitted and disc brakes are provided front and rear. The vehicle uses a pneumatic independent suspension, with load compensation, that can be controlled from the driver's position to lower the overall height of the vehicle for concealment or air transport. A tubular frame is provided for roll-over protection for the crew and the same frame can be used as the basis for mounting various weapons such as 7.62 or 12.7 mm machine guns, 30 mm light cannon and 40 mm grenade launchers. The LFV can also carry the TOW anti-tank missile system.

The LFV has considerable cross-country mobility and performance is such that it can achieve an acceleration of from 0 to 48 km/h in 4.5 seconds. For air transport seven LFVs can be carried in a C-130 aircraft and up to 15 in a C-141B Starlifter.

Specifications
Seating: 1 + 2
Configuration: 4 × 4
Weight: (kerb) 1134 kg
Max load: 725 kg
Length: 3.988 m
Width: 2 m
Height:
(operational) 1.575 m
(reduced) 1.346 m

Teledyne (4 × 4) 725 kg Light Forces Vehicle (LFV)

Ground clearance: 0.33 m
Wheelbase: 2.92 m
Angle of approach/departure: 66.5°/53.5°
Max speed: 113 km/h
Side slope: 60%
Vertical obstacle: 0.305 m
Fording: 0.76 m
Engine: turbocharged diesel developing 115 hp at 4800 rpm
Transmission: automatic with 3 forward gears and 1 reverse
Steering: power-assist
Suspension: pneumatic, independent

Tyres: 7.50 × 16 XS
Brakes: discs front and rear
Electrical system: 12 or 24 V
Alternator: 60 A

Status
Ready for production.

Manufacturer
Teledyne Continental Motors, General Products, 76 Getty Street, Muskegon, Michigan 49442, USA. Tel: (616) 724 2151. Telex: 22 8426. Fax: (616) 724 2928.

TPC RAMP-V (4 × 4) 909 kg Rapid Multi-purpose Vehicle

Description

The RAMP-V (4 × 4) 909 kg rapid multi-purpose vehicle was designed and developed by TPC Logistics Services Inc as a highly mobile vehicle for operations in desert and rough terrain environments. It was tested by the US Army Special Forces who procured a small number.

The RAMP-V can carry a cargo payload of 909 kg under normal conditions but in an emergency this can be increased to 1364 kg. When in use as a personnel carrier, the vehicle carries the driver and a passenger in the front seats and a further six combat troops in the rear, seated on cross-benches with three facing to the rear, just behind the driver and three facing forward at the rear. The RAMP-V is powered by a rear-mounted V-6 petrol engine using a cross-drive transaxle transmission. A forward-mounted radiator is used for cooling. The main frame of the chassis consists of 4130 chromoly steel tubing with roll-bars that can be used as weapon mountings and for crew and passenger protection. All components have been designed for operations over extended periods with a minimum of maintenance. The vehicle is also stated to have a low dust signature even when travelling at speed.

The RAMP-V is para-droppable and may be carried by most transport aircraft or alternatively under a helicopter. Apart from use as a logistics cargo carrier or a personnel carrier the vehicle may be used to mount various anti-tank, anti-aircraft or other weapons and may be used for medical evacuation. A command/control post is another option.

Specifications

Seating: 1 + 1 (up to 6 in rear)
Configuration: 4 × 4

RAMP-V (4 × 4) 909 kg rapid multi-purpose vehicle

Weight: (kerb) 997.9 kg
Payload:
  (normal) 909 kg
  (emergency) 1364 kg
Length: 4.37 m
Width: 1.93 m
Height: 1.78 m
Ground clearance: 0.406 m
Wheelbase: 2.74 m
Track:
  (front) 1.73 m
  (rear) 1.63 m
Max speed: 136 km/h
Range:
  (unimproved roads) 800 km
  (cross-country) 480 km

Gradient:
  (hard surface) 55°
  (sand) 45°
Side slope: 45°
Engine: 2.8 l V-6 petrol
Transmission: cross-drive transaxle
Suspension: independent torsion bar

Status

Procured by US Army Special Forces.

Manufacturer

TPC Logistics Services Inc, 1750 New Highway, Farmingdale, New York 11735, USA.
Tel: (516) 694 2010. Telex: 510 222 0894.

TRUCKS (over 1000 kg)

AUSTRALIA

Land Rover 110 Heavy Duty (6 × 6) Truck

Development
During 1981 Jaguar Rover Australia (JRA) (now Land Rover Australia) carried out market research that indicated a requirement for a heavy duty (6 × 6) derivative of the Land Rover 110 (now the Defender 110) with a payload of up to 3000 kg and a rear chassis length of up to 3.3 m. Several alternatives were investigated before a 6 × 6 version of the 110 was selected based on a trials vehicle produced by SMC Engineering (Bristol) Limited in the United Kingdom. Once in Australia this vehicle was fitted with an Isuzu 3.9 litre diesel engine and the original coil springs at the rear were replaced by semi-elliptical leaf springs. The resultant vehicles were involved in the Australian Army's Project Perentie. The first of 400 production vehicles was handed over to the Australian Army in March 1989.

Some of these vehicles have been fitted with Rover 3.5 litre V-8 petrol engines and are marketed as part of the Land Rover range in the United Kingdom.

Description
The Land Rover 110 Heavy Duty (6 × 6) truck maintains a great deal of commonality with the basic 4 × 4 Land Rover Defender 110 although the body of the Australian vehicle is wider. The basic engine is an Isuzu 3.9 litre diesel but the standard Rover 3.5 litre V-8 petrol engine may be fitted if required. The cab and front end of the JRA vehicle are the same as the Defender 110 but the spiral bevel front axle is uprated. The chassis is a heavy duty rigid chassis frame fabricated from steel tubing and steel pressings with special anti-corrosion treatment on all surfaces. The twin rear axles are Salisbury 8HA fully floating hypoid bevel gear axles with the centre axle differential offset to the right of the centre line and the rear axle differential offset to the left.

The rear tray on the basic vehicle carries a cargo/personnel carrier 3.2 m long and 2.082 m wide. It is normally covered by a heavy duty canvas canopy and inward or outward-facing seats can be provided for up to six men each side. Various options are on offer including a front-mounted Thomas T9000 M 4000 kg recovery winch, a brush guard, a towing pintle, various stowage racks and tie-down points.

The standard electrical system is 12 V. Fitted-for-radio (FFR) vehicles have a 24 V system with two 12 V batteries in a slide-out carrier under the left-hand front corner of the rear body.

The initial contract covers seven derivatives: cargo; cargo with winch; air defence FFR with winch; ambulance FFR with winch; general repair with winch; electronics repair; and an armed long-range patrol vehicle for the Australian SAS which carries on the rear a frame for a motor cycle. Other derivatives planned

Long-range patrol version Land Rover 110 Heavy Duty (6 × 6) truck armed with twin 7.62 mm machine guns and a 30 mm ASP-30 cannon

include a communications centre, a command post and a firefighting vehicle. A crew cab version has been developed.

Modular rear bodies, such as those used for the electronics and general repair vehicles, can be unloaded and used as free-standing units if required. The sides of some shelters can expand to increase working space and shelters can be clipped together when off the vehicle.

Specifications
Cab seating: 1 + 1 (up to 12 in rear)
Configuration: 6 × 6
Weight: (cargo/personnel FFR with winch)
(empty) 3600 kg
(loaded) 5600 kg
(gross combination mass) 7100 kg
Load area: 3.2 × 2.082 m
Length overall: 6.001 m
Width:
(overall) 2.2 m
(over mirrors) 2.43 m
Height:
(cab, unladen) 2.08 m
(cab, laden) 2.05 m
Ground clearance:
(front) 0.235 m
(rear) 0.215 m
Track: 1.698 m
Wheelbase: 3.04 m + 0.9 m
Angle of approach/departure:
(unladen) 45°/33°
(laden) 41°/30°

Max speed: 100 km/h
Range: (roads) 600 km
Fuel capacity: 2 × 65 l
Max gradient: 60%
Engine: Isuzu 4BD1 T 4-cylinder 3.856 l turbocharged diesel developing 121 hp at 3000 rpm
Gearbox: Land Rover LR95A with 4 forward and 1 reverse gears
Transfer box: 2-speed
Steering: Adwest power-assisted variable ratio worm and peg with power-assist
Suspension:
(front) long travel coil springs with telescopic dampers
(rear) dual rate semi-elliptical leaf springs linked via shackles to rubber-bushed load sharing rocker beam
Tyres: 7.50 × 16, 10 ply
Brakes: dual vacuum/hydraulic
Electrical system: 12 V (24 V optional)
Battery:
(standard) 1 × 12 V, 98 Ah
(FFR) 2 × 12 V, 95 Ah
Alternator: 70 A

Status
In production. In service with the Australian Army (400 ordered). Ordered by a Middle East country.

Manufacturer
Land Rover Australia, PO Box 59, Liverpool, New South Wales 2170, Australia.
Tel: 02 600 1333. Telex: 120222.
Fax: 02 600 8935.

Land Rover 110 Heavy Duty (6 × 6) ambulance

Land Rover 110 Heavy Duty (6 × 6) truck showing seating for 12 troops in rear

Mack Model RM6866RS (6 × 6) Truck

Truck, Cargo, Heavy, MC3 with spare wheel lowered

Description

The Mack Model RM6866RS (6 × 6) truck is produced in Australia by Mack Trucks Australia Pty Limited as the Truck, Cargo, Heavy, MC3. It is a version of the basic American Mack 'R' series. Three prototypes were produced (in Australia) in 1979. After evaluation an order was placed in 1981 for 906 units.

The basic vehicle is the Truck, Cargo, Heavy, MC3 which may be fitted with a winch. It is classified as an MLC 22 8 tonne capacity vehicle and many components and subassemblies are produced in Australia. The cargo body is a Mack design built by Walsh Engineering of Toowoomba, Queensland, and the EDE alternator is produced by the Ordnance Factory at Maribyrnong, Victoria.

The layout of the vehicle is conventional with the engine located at the front under a prominent bonneted cab and the cargo area to the rear. The front axle is a Kelsey Hayes SDA 18B (Fabco) rated at 8165 kg. The tandem rear axle unit is a Mack SS441W bogie rated at 20 000 kg.

The cab has seating for the driver and one or two passengers while the cargo area can have seating for 26 fully equipped troops.

Power is provided by an 11 litre Mack EM6-285 Maxidyne turbocharged diesel and a Maxitorque gearbox.

The standard winch carried is an Ateco 24L with a maximum pull of 10 575 kg and 60 m of cable.

The data in the Specifications table refer to the basic cargo vehicle.

Variants

Truck, Cargo, Heavy, With Crane, MC3
On this variant, an Abbey CTM 3000-1 hydraulic crane is mounted directly behind the cab. The crane has a maximum lift capacity of 3400 kg at 1.8 m. Power for the crane's hydraulic system is provided by a Powauto AH23BR11 power take-off on the transfer case. The cargo area is 5.016 m long and 2.39 m wide with seating reduced to 22 fully equipped troops. This variant weighs 12 810 kg unladen.

Truck, Wrecker, Heavy, MC3
On this variant the cargo area is replaced by a Holmes A750 recovery rig with a maximum towing lift of 7800 kg (for more details refer to entry under United States in *Recovery equipment* section). The vehicle also has a 10 500 kg recovery winch provided with 100 m of cable. This variant weighs 23 100 kg unladen.

Truck, Cargo, Arty Tractor/Medium Gun, Heavy, MC3 Ammunition
This variant is used to tow the Australian Army's 155 mm M198 howitzers and may also be used to carry ammunition. A collapsible crew shelter for the gun crew is provided behind the driving cab; it may be removed to provide more ammunition-carrying capacity. The cargo area is replaced by a flat bed platform divided by an Abbey CTM 3000-2 ammunition-handling hydraulic crane. The crane has a maximum lift capacity of 2000 kg at 3.053 m and a full 360° traverse. Power for the hydraulic system is provided by a Powauto AH23BR11 on the transfer case. A winch is fitted. This variant weighs 13 180 kg unladen.

Mixer, Concrete, Truck-Mounted, Heavy, MC3
This variant carries a Fowlerex Rheem Model 5 KH produced at Bulimba in Queensland. The hydraulically driven mixer has a capacity of 5.5 m³, and is used in association with a 204 litre water tank. This variant uses a ZF Model PK1400 gearbox and has an unladen weight of 13 700 kg.

Truck, Dump, Heavy, MC3
On this variant the cargo area is replaced by an 8 m³ capacity dump body produced by Hockney Alcan at Rocklea, Queensland. It is possible to arrange troop seating inside the dump body and up to 18 fully equipped troops can be carried. A winch may be fitted. This variant weighs 11 520 kg unladen.

Truck, Tank, Fuel, Heavy, MC3
For the refuelling role this variant carries a three-compartment tank produced by Holmwood Industries of Rochedale, Queensland. The tank has a capacity of 11 380 litres and the vehicle also carries the associated electrical and refuelling equipment such as four hose reels. This variant is 9.475 m long and weighs 12 160 kg unladen.

Truck, Tank, Water, Heavy, MC3
Carrying an aluminium three-compartment water tank with a highway operation capacity of 9240 litres, this variant also carries a spray bar, two hose reels, a 60 m hose and three dispensing cocks. This variant is 9.474 m long and weighs 11 800 kg unladen.

Distributor, Bituminous Substance, Tank Type, Truck-Mounted, Heavy, MC3
This variant differs from the others in the Australian Mack range by using a 6 × 4 drive configuration. The steel tank has aluminium lagging and a highway operations capacity of 7740 litres. A spray bar is provided along with two tar burner tubes. This variant is 10.194 m long and weighs 13 960 kg unladen.

Truck, Bridge Recovery, Heavy, MC3
This variant is equipped to launch and recover Ribbon Bridge sections and carries a Techlaunch ARK221 roll-on hook loader that can also be used to load a cargo tray when the Ribbon Bridge is not required. The loader is produced by Techmark Australia and manufactured in Melbourne, Victoria. It has a capacity of 6000 kg. The cargo tray is 5.8 m long and 2.5 m wide.

When carrying a Ribbon Bridge section this variant is 10.3 m long. When carrying the cargo tray the length is 10.5 m. The unladen weight is 14 800 kg.

Specifications (Truck, Cargo, Heavy, MC3)
Cab seating: 1 + 1 or 2
Configuration: 6 × 6
Weight: (unladen)
  (front axle) 5070 kg
  (rear axle) 6510 kg
  (total) 11 570 kg
Load area: 5.714 × 2.39 m
Length: 9.6 m
Width: 2.5 m
Height:
  (unladen) 3.155 m
  (laden) 3.125 m
Ground clearance:
  (unladen) 0.318 m
  (laden) 0.28 m
Track:
  (front) 1.911 m
  (rear) 1.81 m
Wheelbase: 4.765 m + 1.4 m
Angle of approach/departure: (laden) 31.5°/30.5°
Range: (first class roads) 550 to 590 km
Fuel capacity: 265 l
Max gradient: 50%
Side slope: 22.5°
Fording: 0.8 m
Engine: Mack EM6-285 Maxidyne 11 l intercooled 6-cylinder in-line turbocharged diesel developing 283 hp at 2100 rpm
Gearbox: Maxitorque with 5 forward and 1 reverse gears
Clutch: Spicer twin dry plate
Transfer box: 2-speed
Steering: Sheppard Model 592 integrated power-assist
Turning radius: 12.1 m
Suspension: multileaf springs
Tyres: 12.00 × 20
Brakes:
  (main) dual circuit, air
  (parking) spring on rear axles
  (trailer) dual circuit, air
Electrical system: 24 V
Batteries: 2 × 12 V, 61 Ah
Alternator: 140 A

Status

In service with the Australian Army (906).

Manufacturer

Mack Trucks Australia Pty Limited, 616 Boundary Road, Richlands 4077, Queensland, Australia. Tel: 07 375 3333. Fax: 07 375 3469.

AUSTRIA

Steyr-Daimler-Puch Pinzgauer Turbo D (4 × 4) 1500 kg and (6 × 6) 2000 kg Vehicles

Description

The Pinzgauer Turbo D (4 × 4) and (6 × 6) diesel-engined versions of the Pinzgauer range were developed from 1983 onwards and were first shown during 1985. Although the Turbo D resembles many of the earlier models it has many innovations apart from the six-cylinder diesel engine.

In appearance and general layout the 4 × 4 and 6 × 6 versions of the Turbo D resemble the earlier Pinzgauer models. The main change is to a water-cooled and turbocharged six-cylinder diesel engine. The wheelbases are lengthened on both the 4 × 4 and 6 × 6 and the track is wider. Changes were made to the driver's position instrument layout, disc brakes introduced and a larger fuel tank fitted to improve range. An automatic locking system is incorporated.

The 4 × 4 version has an automatic level control system acting on the rear axle. A pneumatic system is controlled by sensors that raise and lower the vehicle superstructure to suit the load being carried. This enables the centre of gravity to remain constant.

The Pinzgauer Turbo D is produced in a number of versions as follows:

Pinzgauer 716 M 4 × 4; personnel carrier with canvas top carrying the driver and up to nine passengers

Pinzgauer 716 MK 4 × 4; cargo or personnel carrier with closed body carrying the driver and one front passenger plus approximately 1250 kg of payload or eight passengers in the rear compartment

Pinzgauer 716 K 4 × 4; command vehicle carrying the driver and one front passenger plus three seats in the rear compartment (seating for a further five passengers is an option)

Pinzgauer 716 T 4 × 4; carrier for shelters and weapon systems carrying the driver, one passenger and approximately 1300 kg of payload

Pinzgauer 718 M 6 × 6; personnel carrier with canvas top carrying the driver and up to 13 passengers

Pinzgauer 718 MK 6 × 6; cargo or personnel carrier with closed body carrying the driver and one front passenger plus approximately 1700 kg of payload or 12 passengers in the rear compartment

Pinzgauer 718 K 6 × 6; command vehicle carrying the driver, one front passenger and three seats in the rear compartment (seating for seven more passengers is an option)

Pinzgauer 718 T 6 × 6; carrier vehicle for shelters and weapon systems carrying the driver, one passenger and approximately 1800 kg of payload.

The data in the Specifications table refer to the Pinzgauer 716 M 4 × 4 and the Pinzgauer 718 M 6 × 6.

Status

In production.

Steyr-Daimler-Puch Pinzgauer (4 × 4) Turbo D

Specifications

Model	Pinzgauer 716 M	Pinzgauer 718 M
Configuration	4 × 4	6 × 6
Weight empty	2200 kg	2650 kg
Weight loaded	3500 kg	4500 kg
Max load	1300 kg	1850 kg
Towed load	1500 kg	1800 kg
Length	4.48 m	5.26 m
Width	1.8 m	1.8 m
Height	2.045 m	2.045 m
Ground clearance	0.335 m	0.335 m
Track	1.52 m	1.52 m
Wheelbase	2.4 m	2.2 m + 0.98 m
Angle of approach/departure	40°/45°	40°/45°
Max speed	122 km/h	112 km/h
Fuel capacity	145 l	145 l
Gradient	100%	84%
Fording	0.7 m	0.7 m
Engine	2.383 l 6-cylinder in-line water-cooled turbocharged diesel developing 105 hp at 4350 rpm	
Transmission	ZF S 5-18/3 manual with 5 forward and 1 reverse gears or ZF automatic with 4 forward and 1 reverse gears	
Transfer box	2-speed	2-speed
Turning circle	11.5 m	13 m
Suspension	helical springs front and rear	helical springs front and rear with leaf springs at rear
Brakes	dual circuit power-assisted discs	
Electrical system	24 V	24 V

Manufacturer

Steyr-Daimler-Puch Fahrzeugtechnik GmbH, Postfach 823, Liebenauer Hauptstrasse 317, A-8011 Graz-Thondorf, Austria.
Tel: 316 41-951. Telex: 311315 stdpg a. Fax: 316 4001-469.

Steyr-Daimler-Puch Pinzgauer (4 × 4) 1000 kg and (6 × 6) 1500 kg Vehicles

Development

The Pinzgauer range of all-terrain vehicles was developed by Steyr-Daimler-Puch as the successor to the 700 AP Haflinger range of 4 × 4 vehicles. The first prototype of the 4 × 4 Pinzgauer was completed in 1965 with first production models being completed in 1971. The vehicle was adopted by the Austrian Army in 1973. The 6 × 6 model was first shown in 1968 and entered production in 1971/72.

Description

Both the 4 × 4 and 6 × 6 models are available with two basic types of body, fully enclosed or with a military-type cargo body. The former has an all-steel fully enclosed body with two doors in each side and a single door at the rear and the military-type body has a single door each side for the driver and one passenger. The tops of the doors are removable and the windscreen can be folded forward onto the bonnet. The rear cargo area has removable bows and a tarpaulin cover and there are bench seats down each side of the rear body for eight men in the 4 × 4 model and twelve in the 6 × 6 model.

The chassis consists of a torsion-resistant central tube with independent swing axles incorporating the transfer case and axle drive. The engine is mounted towards the front of the vehicle and is coupled to a ZF manual gearbox which transmits power via a propeller shaft to the transfer case, which also supports the hydraulically operated shifting clutch for the power transmission to the front axle. The drive shaft is to the front and rear differentials are within the central tube

chassis. The differentials have a hydraulically operated mechanical lock.

Optional equipment for the Pinzgauer includes antenna holder (middle and side), camouflage net holders, convoy lights, blackout blinds, divided windscreen, foldable table, jerrican holders, rear mounting trays, rifle racks, mounting points for shovels, split battery system, rear tow hook and a 125 litre petrol tank.

Variants

Pinzgauer Turbo D
See previous entry.

Ambulance
Versions of both the 4 × 4 and 6 × 6 Pinzgauer were available with a fully enclosed rear body which can be fitted with air-conditioning.

The Swiss Army ordered 310 Pinzgauer 6 × 6

Specifications

Configuration	4 × 4	6 × 6
Weight (empty, soft-top/hard-top)	1950/2100 kg	2350/2600 kg
(loaded, soft-top/hard-top)	3050/3100 kg	3900/4100 kg
Max weight on front axle (loaded)	1500 kg	1450 kg
Max weight on rear axle (loaded)	1550 kg	2600 kg (axles)
Max load	1000 kg	1500 kg
Towed load (road)	5000 kg	5000 kg
(cross-country)	1500 kg	1800 kg
Load area	2.25 × 1.592 m	3.03 × 1.592 m
Length	4.175 m	4.955 m
Width	1.76 m	1.76 m
Height	2.045 m	2.045 m
(load area)	0.94 m	0.94 m
Ground clearance	0.335 m	0.335 m
Track	1.44 m	1.44 m
Wheelbase	2.2 m	2 m + 0.98 m
Angle of approach/departure	45°/45°	45°/45°
Max speed	110 km/h	100 km/h
Fuel capacity	75 l	75 l
	(125 l optional)	(125 l optional)
Fuel consumption (road)	17 l/100 km	19 l/100 km
(cross-country)	6-10 l/h	7-11 l/h
Gradient	100%	100%
Side slope	40%	40%
Fording	0.7 m	0.7 m
Engine	Steyr 4-cylinder in-line air-cooled petrol developing 87 hp at 4000 rpm	
Gearbox	manual with 5 forward and 1 reverse gears	
Clutch	single dry plate	single dry plate
Transfer box	2-speed	2-speed
Steering	worm with roller	worm with roller
Turning circle	10.37 m	12.28 m
Suspension	independent. 4 × 4: coil springs at all wheel stations. 6 × 6: coil springs at front wheel stations; leaf springs and hydraulic shock absorbers rear suspension	
Tyres	7.50 × 16	7.50 × 16
Brakes	hydraulic drum	hydraulic drum
Electrical system	24 V	24 V
Batteries	2 × 12 V, 66 Ah	2 × 12 V, 66 Ah

ambulances in addition to the 1000-plus 4 × 4 and 6 × 6 cargo versions in service. As well as the driver and one medical assistant, the vehicle can carry four stretcher patients, or two stretcher and four seated patients, or six seated patients.

Anti-aircraft
The Austrian Army fitted a number of 6 × 6 Pinzgauers with 20 mm Oerlikon anti-aircraft cannon at the rear, with spare drum magazines stowed to the immediate rear of the driver's position.

Others
The basic military-type vehicles with cargo-type body are designated the 710 M (4 × 4) and 712 M (6 × 6), the radio vehicles the 710 K (4 × 4) and 712 K (6 × 6), the 6 × 6 firefighting vehicle the 712 FW, the 6 × 6 workshop vehicle the 712 W and the flat bed version, used to carry the 20 mm cannon is designated the 712 T.

In 1981 the 712 DK (6 × 6) was introduced; this has an enlarged four-door cab which extends to just over the second axle but still has a payload of 1500 kg.

Status

In production. In service with Austria, Ghana, Nigeria, Oman, Sudan, Switzerland, Tunisia and the former Yugoslavia. Also in service with various nations in the Middle East and South America.

Manufacturer

Steyr-Daimler-Puch Fahrzeugtechnik GmbH, Postfach 823, Liebenauer Hauptstrasse 317, A-8011 Graz-Thondorf, Austria.
Tel: 316 4001-951. Telex: 311315 stdpg a.
Fax: 316 4001-469.

Steyr-Daimler-Puch Pinzgauer (6 × 6) 1500 kg vehicle with open cargo body

---

Steyr 680 M (4 × 4) 4500 kg Truck

Description

The Steyr 680 M is a 4 × 4 cargo truck designed to carry a maximum of 4170 kg of cargo (when fitted with a winch) across country, although for practical purposes it is normally 4570 kg, or 6570 kg on roads.

The all-steel cab is of the forward type and has two doors, observation hatch in the roof, heater and fresh air ventilator. The rear cargo area is provided with removable bows, tarpaulin cover, collapsible seats for up to 20 men and a drop tailgate. A winch with 90 m of 13 mm diameter cable is fitted as standard.

The Steyr 680 M is being replaced in Austrian Army service by the Steyr 12 M 18 and 12 M 21 (see entry in this section).

The Steyr 680 M was produced by Steyr Hellas (now ELBO SA) in Greece as the 680 MH. It was produced for use by the Greek armed forces and for export.

A fuel tanker version is in service. The Steyr 680 M3 (6 × 6) 3500 kg truck is a development of the Steyr 680 M (4 × 4) truck (see following entry).

Specifications

Cab seating: 1 + 1
Configuration: 4 × 4
Weight:
  (empty, with winch) 5830 kg
  (road, loaded) 11 000 kg
  (cross-country, loaded) 8500 kg
Weight on front axle: (empty) 3260 kg
Weight on rear axle: (empty) 2570 kg
Max load:
  (road) 6500 kg
  (cross-country) 4500 kg

Towed load:
  (road) 8000 kg
  (cross-country) 4000 kg
Load area: 4.06 × 2.2 m
Length: 6.57 m
Width: 2.4 m
Height:
  (cab) 2.63 m
  (tarpaulin) 2.85 m
  (load area) 1.16 m
Ground clearance: 0.3 m
Track:
  (front) 1.81 m
  (rear) 1.67 m
Wheelbase: 3.7 m
Angle of approach/departure: 28°/28°
Max speed: (road) 80 km/h
Range: 450 km

Steyr 680 M (4 × 4) 4500 kg truck

Fuel capacity: 160 l
Max gradient: (in low-range at weight of 10 000 kg) 62%
Fording: 0.8 m

Engine: Steyr WD 610.23 6-cylinder direct injection water-cooled diesel developing 132 hp (SAE) at 2800 rpm
Gearbox: manual with 5 forward and 1 reverse gears

Clutch: single dry plate
Transfer box: 2-speed
Steering: ZF hydraulic
Turning radius: 7.25 m
Suspension: semi-elliptical springs front and rear
Tyres: 9.00 × 20
Brakes:
 (main) hydraulic, air-assisted
 (parking) mechanical
Electrical system: 24 V
Batteries: 2 × 12 V, 110 Ah

Status
Production complete. In service with Austria, Greece, Indonesia (750), Nigeria and Switzerland.

Manufacturers
Steyr Nutzfahrzeuge AG, Schönauerstrasse 5, A-4400 Steyr, Austria.
Tel: 7252/585-0. Telex: 28200.
Fax: 7252/26746, 28650.
Steyr Hellas SA (now ELBO SA), Industrial Area Sindos, 541 10 Thessaloniki, PO Box 10239, Greece.
Tel: 031 798502. Telex: 412586 elbo gr.
Fax: 031 798426.

Steyr 680 M3 (6 × 6) 3500 kg Truck

Description
The Steyr 680 M3 is a 6 × 6 cargo truck designed to carry a maximum of 3500 kg of cargo cross-country or 6500 kg of cargo on roads. It is a direct development of the Steyr 680 M (4 × 4) 4500 kg truck (see previous entry) and shares many common components with this vehicle.

The all-steel cab is of the forward control type and has two doors, observation hatch in the roof, heater and fresh air ventilator. The rear cargo area is provided with removable bows, tarpaulin cover, drop tailgate and collapsible seats down the centre. Most models have a 4500 kg capacity winch with 90 m of 13 mm diameter cable. Some vehicles have a hydraulic crane for unloading mounted to the rear of the cab.

Variants
Dump Truck
This is known as the Dreiseitenkipper and can tip to either side or the rear. Its loaded weight for road use is 13 000 kg and for cross-country use is 10 000 kg.

Rocket Launcher
In the 1960s the Austrian Army received a number of Czechoslovak 130 mm (32 round) M51 multiple rocket launchers mounted on the Czechoslovak Praga V3S (6 × 6) truck. They have now been mounted on a Steyr 680 M3 truck which has a larger four-door cab than the normal version. Details of the M51 are given in *Jane's Armour and Artillery 1992-93*, page 694.

Tanker
This is known as the Einheitstankwagen (or ETW for short) and carries 8000 litres of fuel.

680 MH 3
The 680 MH 3 is a licence-built version at one time produced by Steyr Hellas in Greece for the Greek Army. It was also offered for export. Some 55 per cent of this vehicle was produced in Greece.

Specifications
Cab seating: 1 + 1
Configuration: 6 × 6
Weight:
 (empty) 6500 kg
 (loaded, road) 12 000 kg
 (loaded, cross-country) 10 000 kg
Weight on front axle: (empty) 3200 kg

Steyr 680 M3 (6 × 6) 3500 kg truck

Weight on rear bogie: (empty) 3300 kg
Towed load:
 (road) 8000 kg
 (cross-country) 4000 kg
Load area: 4.06 × 2.198 m
Length: 6.73 m
Width: 2.4 m
Height:
 (cab) 2.63 m
 (tarpaulin) 2.85 m
 (load area) 1.21 m
Ground clearance: 0.3 m
Track:
 (front) 1.81 m
 (rear) 1.72 m
Wheelbase: 2.76 m + 1.2 m
Angle of approach/departure: 28°/32°
Max speed: (road) 79.7 km/h
Range: 500 km
Fuel capacity: 180 l
Max gradient: (low-range at weight of 10 500 kg) 99%
Fording: 0.8 m
Engine: Steyr model WD 610.74 6-cylinder direct injection supercharged diesel developing 165 hp (SAE) at 2800 rpm
Gearbox: manual with 5 forward and 1 reverse gears
Clutch: single dry plate
Transfer box: 2-speed

Steering: ZF hydraulic
Turning radius: 7.25 m
Suspension:
 (front) semi-elliptical springs with telescopic shock absorbers
 (rear) semi-elliptical springs, reverse mounted with reversible spring hangers positioned in middle of rear axles
Tyres: 9.00 × 20
Brakes:
 (main) hydraulic, air-assisted
 (parking) mechanical
Electrical system: 24 V
Batteries: 2 × 12 V, 110 Ah

Status
In production. In service with the Austrian Army. It was built by Steyr Hellas in Greece for the Greek Army.

Manufacturers
Steyr Nutzfahrzeuge AG, Schönauerstrasse 5, A-4400 Steyr, Austria.
Tel: 7252/585-0. Telex: 28200.
Fax: 7252/26746, 28650.
Steyr Hellas SA (now ELBO SA), Industrial Area Sindos, 541 10 Thessaloniki, PO Box 10239, Greece.
Tel: 031 798502. Telex: 412586 elbo gr.
Fax: 031 798426.

Steyr 10 M 14 and 10 M 18 (4 × 4) 4000 kg Trucks

Description

The Steyr 10 M 14 (4 × 4) 4000 kg truck was intro-duced in December 1990 and is a derivative of the Steyr 14 M 14 (4 × 4) 8000 kg truck but fitted with single-tyred rear wheels and with a lockable front axle differential for increased mobility. The Steyr 10 M 18 is essentially the same vehicle but fitted with a more powerful (177 hp) engine.

The layout uses a cab-over-engine forward control cab with seating for the driver and two passengers. The cab is the Steyr 152 (short version) with a hydraulic tilting mechanism. Left- and right-hand drive can be provided. The chassis has a low torsion ladder-type frame with riveted tubular crossmembers. The 140 hp diesel engine used on the 10 M 14 is turbo-charged and powers a synchromesh five-speed gear-box (six-speed on 10 M 18). Using a Steyr VG 450 two-speed transfer box, front wheel drive can be engaged. There are differential locks on both axles.

The cargo body has drop sides and is provided with a spare wheel at the front. The body can be covered by a tarpaulin over a frame. Seating for passengers in the rear can be along mid- or side-positioned bench seats. An optional 5000 kg capacity winch can be used to the front or rear.

These vehicles are also available as water or fuel bowsers, ambulances, fire tenders, shelter carriers and in other configurations.

Specifications

Cab seating: 1 + 2
Configuration: 4 × 4
Weight: (with winch)
  (empty) 6500 kg
  (loaded) 11 000 kg
Max front axle load: 5000 kg
Max rear axle load: 6000 kg
Max load: 4500 kg
Towed load: 6000 kg
Load area: 4.1 × 2.4 m
Length: 6.62 m
Width: 2.5 m
Height: 3.05 m
Ground clearance: 0.295 m
Track:
  (front) 1.907 m

Steyr 10 M 14 (4 × 4) truck

  (rear) 1.9 m
Wheelbase: 3.7 m
Angle of approach/departure: 41°/40°
Max speed: 100 km/h
Range: 800 km
Fuel capacity: 200 l
Gradient:
  (without trailer) 60%
  (with trailer) 40%
Side slope: 30%
Fording: 0.8 m
Engine: (10 M 14) Steyr WD 612.91 6.6 l 6-cylinder direct injection water-cooled diesel with turbocharger developing 140 hp (ISO) at 1300 rpm
(10 M 18) Steyr WD 612.73 6.6 l 6-cylinder water-cooled diesel with turbocharger developing 177 hp at 2200 rpm
Gearbox: (10 M 14) Steyr S51/5 synchromesh with 5 forward and 1 reverse gears
(10 M 18) ZF S6-36 synchromesh with 6 forward and 1 reverse gears

Clutch: single dry disc, hydraulic actuation
Transfer box: Steyr VG 450, 2-speed
Steering: ZF 8043, power-assist
Turning radius: 7.6 m
Suspension: semi-elliptical springs with telescopic shock absorbers
Tyres: 12.5 R 20 or 10.00 R 20
Brakes:
  (main) dual circuit hydro-pneumatic
  (parking) spring actuated, air
Electrical system: 24 V
Batteries: 2 × 12 V, 135 Ah

Status

In production.

Manufacturer

Steyr Nutzfahrzeuge AG, Schönauerstrasse 5, A-4400 Steyr, Austria.
Tel: 7252/585-0. Telex: 28200.
Fax: 7252/26746, 28650.

Steyr 12 M 18 and 12 M 21 (4 × 4) 5000 kg Trucks

Development/Description

In December 1985 the Austrian Ministry of Defence placed an order for 1000 12 M 18 and 12 M 21 (4 × 4) trucks to replace existing Steyr 680 trucks. The 12 M 18 was used as the basis for the American Stewart and Stevenson FMTV (Family of Medium Tactical Vehicles – see entry under United States in this section).

The Steyr 12 M 18 and 12 M 21 (4 × 4) 5000 kg trucks are described as a new generation of medium military trucks and are designed to carry a payload of 5350 kg both on and off roads. The main differences between the two models involve the type and power of the engine fitted and the gearboxes involved.

Both use a chassis consisting of a low-torsion ladder-type frame with bolted tubular crossmembers. The forward control cab is of all-steel construction and can be tilted forward up to an angle of 70° for access to the engine and transmission. The two-door cab has seats for the driver and up to three passengers. It is equipped with a roof observation hatch, a heater and a fresh air blower.

The front and rear axle differentials, as well as the inter-axle differential in the transfer box are all lockable.

The drop-side body has a tarpaulin frame which can be lowered for rail transport and mid-positioned bench seats for up to 18 men can be fitted. Alternative bodies could include fuel and water tankers, fire tenders, ambulances and other options. A driver training version is available.

Optional equipment includes a blackout lighting

Steyr 12 M 21 (4 × 4) 5000 kg truck with winch

system, a 5000 kg capacity hydro-winch with 50 m of cable, a machine gun mounting over the cab, air-conditioning, an electro-hydraulic tailgate (the Steyr LBW 1500 electro-hydraulic tailgate – see entry under *Materials handling equipment*) and a loading crane

fitted behind the driver's cab.

Variants include ambulances, recovery vehicles, firefighting vehicles, communication shelter carriers, mobile workshops and generators, tankers, light artillery tractors and weapon carriers.

Specifications
Cab seating: 1 + 1 with up to 18 in rear
Configuration: 4 × 4
Weight:
  (unladen) 6300 kg
  (laden) 11 500 kg
Weight on front axle: 5000 kg
Weight on rear axle: 6500 kg
Max load: 5200 kg
Towed load:
  (road) 10 000 kg
  (cross-country) 8500 kg
Platform dimensions: 4.1 × 2.43 m
Length overall: 6.36 m
Width: 2.5 m
Height:
  (cab) 2.93 m
  (top of tilt) 3.24 m
  (load area) 1.46 m
Ground clearance: 0.3 m
Track:
  (front) 2.061 m
  (rear) 2.005 m

Wheelbase: 3.5 m
Angle of approach/departure: 41°/44°
Max speed: (road) 100 km/h
Range: approx 700 km
Fuel capacity: 180 l
Gradient: approx 80%
Side slope: 30°
Fording: 0.8 m
Engine: (12 M 18) Steyr Model WD 612.74 6.6 l 6-cylinder direct injection turbocharged water-cooled diesel developing 182 hp at 2400 rpm
(12 M 21) Steyr Model WD 612.76 6.6 l 6-cylinder direct injection turbocharged (with boost air cooler) water-cooled diesel developing 215 hp at 2400 rpm
Clutch: single dry plate, hydraulically actuated
Gearbox: ZF 9 S 109 with 9 forward (8 + crawler) and 1 reverse gears
Transfer box: Steyr VG 1200, 2-stage
Steering: ZF Model 8043 power
Turning radius: 7.3 m
Suspension:
  (front) parabolic leaf springs with telescopic shock absorbers

(rear) parabolic leaf springs with telescopic shock absorbers and stabiliser bar
Tyres: 14.5 R 20 MPT
Brakes:
  (main) drum, dual circuit hydro-pneumatic
  (parking) spring actuated, air-operated
Electrical system: 24 V
Batteries: 2 × 12 V, 135 Ah

Status
In production. In service with the Austrian Army (over 1000), Kuwait, Pakistan, Thailand and United Nations forces. Used by Canadian Armed Forces for rapid airfield repair.

Manufacturer
Steyr Nutzfahrzeuge AG, Schönauerstrasse 5, A-4400 Steyr, Austria.
Tel: 7252/585-0. Telex: 28200.
Fax: 7252/26746, 28650.

Steyr 17 M 29 (4 × 4) 7000 kg Truck

Description
The Steyr 17 M 29 (formerly the 1291.280.4 × 4 M) is a 4 × 4 cargo truck designed to carry a maximum load of 7000 kg on both roads and cross-country, and to share many common components with the Steyr 24 M (6 × 6) 12 000 kg truck series.

The chassis consists of a low distortion parallel ladder frame with bolted tubular crossmembers. The forward control cab is of all-steel construction and can be tilted forwards at an angle of 70° to allow access to the engine and transmission for maintenance purposes. The driver's suspension seat is adjustable and the cab can be fitted with a single or twin passenger seat. The cab has two doors, observation/machine gun hatch in the roof, heater and a fresh air ventilator.

The rear cargo area is provided with removable bows, tarpaulin cover, drop tailgate and, down the centre, collapsible seats for 20 fully equipped troops. Seat benches, bows and the tarpaulin cover can be stowed behind the headboard.

Optional equipment includes a winch with a capacity of 10 000 kg and 60 m of cable; alternative engines and transmissions are also available.

The Steyr 17 M 29 has been produced in airfield crash tender form.

Various versions in 4 × 4 and 4 × 2 are licence-produced in China as part of the Hongyan heavy duty truck range manufactured at the Sichuan Truck Plant, Chongqing.

Specifications
Cab seating: 1 + 1
Configuration: 4 × 4
Weight:
  (empty) approx 10 000 kg
  (loaded) 17 000 kg
Weight on front axle: (loaded) 7000 kg
Weight on rear axle: (loaded) 10 000 kg
Max load: (road and cross-country) 7000 kg
Towed load:
  (cross-country) 10 000 kg
  (road) up to 11 500 kg
Load area: 5 × 2.43 m
Length: 7.73 m
Width: 2.5 m
Height: (cab platform) 3.246 m
Ground clearance: 0.37 m
Track: 2.072 m
Wheelbase: 4.2 m
Angle of approach/departure: 31°/36°
Max speed: (road) 95 km/h
Range: 700 km
Fuel capacity: 320 l (400 l optional)
Gradient: 100% (low range)
Fording: 0.8 m (1 m optional)
Engine: Steyr model WD 615.73, 9.726 l 6-cylinder, direct injection, turbocharged, intercooled, water-cooled diesel, developing 287 hp (SAE) at 2200 rpm
Gearbox: ZF 9 S 109 GP manual with 9 (8 + crawler) forward and 1 reverse gears
Clutch: single dry plate (or optional ZF hydraulic torque converter in combination with synchromesh gearbox or Allison automatic)
Transfer box: Steyr VG 1200 2-speed
Steering: ZF hydraulic
Turning radius: 9.8 m
Suspension:
  (front) semi-elliptical springs with telescopic shock absorbers
  (rear) semi-elliptical springs with telescopic shock absorbers
Tyres: 14.00 × 20
Brakes:
  (main) two circuit compressed air
  (parking) spring energy, air-operated
Electrical system: 24 V
Batteries: 2 × 12 V, 135 Ah

Status
In production. In service with Egypt, Ghana and Indonesia (200 plus). In licenced production in China.

Manufacturer
Steyr Nutzfahrzeuge AG, Schönauerstrasse 5, A-4400 Steyr, Austria.
Tel: 7252/585-0. Telex: 28200.
Fax: 7252/26746, 28650.

Steyr 17 M 29 7000 kg truck with brush guard

Steyr 17 M 29 7000 kg truck with bows and tarpaulin cover

Steyr 14 M 14 and 14 M 18 (4 × 4) 8000 kg Trucks

Description

The Steyr 14 M 14 (4 × 4) 8000 kg truck was originally designed as a 4 × 2 truck for Nigeria. It was converted to 4 × 4 by installing the transfer case from the Steyr 680 M and the front axle of the 12 M 18/21 (see entries in this section for details of both vehicles). This vehicle is licence-produced in Greece by the Hellenic Vehicle Industry SA (ELBO). The 14 M 18 is an essentially similar vehicle with a more powerful (177 hp) engine.

The layout of the 14 M 14 is conventional with a forward control cab and a cargo area to the rear. The cab has seating for the driver and two passengers and the cargo area has steel drop sides and a tailgate all covered by a tilt over bows. The cargo area has folding back-to-back benches for carrying troops.

Options include a right-hand drive version, a 5000 kg capacity rear winch, a driver training version, an electro-hydraulic tailgate, a blackout lighting system, a machine gun mount over the cab, air-conditioning, and a 24 V electrical system.

Specifications

Cab seating: 1 + 2
Configuration: 4 × 4
Weight:
  (empty) 6000 kg
  (loaded) 14 000 kg
Max front axle load: 5000 kg
Max rear axle load: 9500 kg
Max load: 8000 kg
Towed load: 6000 kg
Load area: 4.1 × 2.42 m
Length: 6.62 m
Width: 2.5 m
Height: 3.025 m
Ground clearance: 0.275 m
Track:
  (front) 1.872 m
  (rear) 1.721 m
Wheelbase: 3.7 m
Angle of approach/departure: 39°/53°

Steyr 14 M 14 (4 × 4) 8000 kg truck

Max speed: 80 km/h
Range: 700 km
Fuel capacity: 160 l
Max gradient:
  (without trailer) 60%
  (with trailer) 40%
Side slope: 30%
Fording: 0.8 m
Engine: (14 M 14) Steyr WD 612.22 6.6 l 6-cylinder direct injection water-cooled diesel developing 136 hp (DIN) at 2400 rpm
(14 M 18) Steyr WD 612.73 6.6 l 6-cylinder water-cooled turbocharged diesel developing 177 hp at 2200 rpm
Gearbox: ZF S6-36 synchromesh with 6 forward and 1 reverse gears
Clutch: single dry plate
Transfer box: Steyr VG 450, 2-speed
Steering: ZF 8043, power-assist
Turning radius: 7.6 m
Suspension: semi-elliptic leaf springs with telescopic shock absorbers front and rear

Tyres: 9.00 × 20
Brakes:
  (main) single circuit hydro-pneumatic (dual circuit optional)
  (parking) spring-actuated, air-operated
Electrical system: 12 V (24 V optional)
Batteries: 1 × 12 V, 165 Ah (2 × 12 V, 88 Ah optional)

Status

In production. In service with Canadian Forces Europe, Cyprus, Ghana, Greece, Nigeria, Thailand and Uganda. Licence-produced in Greece.

Manufacturers

Steyr Nutzfahrzeuge AG, Schönauerstrasse 5, A-4400 Steyr, Austria.
Tel: 7252/585-0. Telex: 28200.
Fax: 7252/26746, 28650.
ELBO SA, Industrial Area Sindos, 541 10 Thessaloniki, PO Box 10239, Greece.
Tel: 031 798502. Telex: 412586 elbo gr.
Fax: 031 798426.

ÖAF Type 20.320 (6 × 6) 10 000 kg Truck

Development

The ÖAF Type 20.320 (6 × 6) 10 000 kg truck is essentially a modified version of the German Army MAN 7000 kg truck built in Austria. Modifications have included the replacement of the Klockner-Humbolt-Deutz engine by a MAN unit, installation of a hydraulic crane and provision for mounting a machine gun on the roof of the cab. The initial order was for 350 trucks, the first of which was handed over in 1975.

Description

The chassis is constructed from welded box-section longitudinal girders strengthened by tubular cross-members. An auxiliary frame to the rear of the cab carries the loading crane.

The cab is made of welded sheet steel and is mounted on rubber supports on the chassis. It is divided into two compartments, crew at the front and engine at the rear. Forward-opening doors are fitted left and right and there are seats for three people which can be arranged to provide two couchettes. The centre seat has a 180° vertical movement and serves as a step for the machine gun slewing ring mounted on the roof. The roof has a sliding hatch. The spare wheel is housed in the upper part of the engine compartment and there is a small hoist provided to raise and lower it. The battery box is on the right side of the engine compartment.

The base for the body comprises seven sheet steel crossmembers bolted firmly to the chassis, the floor of which is 40 mm tongue-and-groove pine. The side and

ÖAF Type 20.320 (6 × 6) 10 000 kg truck

tailboards consist of 25 mm hollow-section aluminium. The front is 1.5 m high and the sides and rear boards 700 mm high. The sideboards are divided and removable seats for eight men are fitted to the floor either to the front or rear. If required a second similar seat-group can be fitted. With only one eight-seater in place there is a load area for 72 ammunition boxes on the floor. The three adjustable bows support the canvas tarpaulin which has windows towards the top.

The vehicle is radio-suppressed and a junction for an external current supply is provided. An Eberspeicher independent diesel-driven warm air heating unit is fitted as standard. Mounted to the rear of the cab is a Palfinger PK 7500 loading crane with a capacity of 7000 kg.

The last production version was the Type 20.320/G2 which has a centrally mounted winch with a 7500 kg capacity front and rear.

Specifications
Cab seating: 1 + 2
Configuration: 6 × 6
Weight:
(empty with crane and winch) 12 500 kg
(loaded, cross-country) 22 000 kg
Max load: (cross-country) 10 000 kg
Length: 8.85 m
Width: 2.5 m
Height:
(tarpaulin cover) 3.34 m
(cab) 3 m
Ground clearance: 0.415 m
Track: 2.07 m
Wheelbase: 3.8 m + 1.4 m

Angle of approach/departure: 42°/38°
Max road speed: 84 km/h
Max range: 700 km
Fuel capacity: 500 l
Gradient: 60%
Fording: 0.8 m
Engine: MAN D 2538 MTX V-8 diesel developing 320 bhp at 2500 rpm
Gearbox: hydraulic torque converter with lock-up clutch (foot-operated), 6-speed gearbox (6 forward and 1 reverse gears) and 3-axle transfer case with differential lock between front and rear axle drive
Steering: recirculating ball with hydraulic assistance
Turning circle: 19.5 m
Suspension: progressively acting helical springs and

hydraulic shock absorbers
Tyres: 14.00 × 20
Brakes:
(main) air/hydraulic
(parking) mechanical
Electrical system: 24 V

Status
Production complete. In service with the Austrian Army.

Manufacturer
Österreichische Automobilfabrik ÖAF-Gräf und Stift AG, Brünner Strasse 72, A-1211 Vienna, Austria.

Steyr 24 M (6 × 6) 12 000 kg Truck Series

Description
The base vehicle in the Steyr 24 M series (formerly the 1491.6 × 6 M) is a 6 × 6 cargo truck designed to carry a maximum load of 12 000 kg on both roads and cross-country, and to share many common components with the Steyr 17 M (4 × 4) 7000 kg trucks.

The chassis consists of a low distortion parallel ladder frame with bolted tubular crossmembers. The forward control cab is of all-steel construction and can be tilted forwards at an angle of 70° to allow access to the engine and transmission for maintenance purposes. The driver's suspension seat is adjustable and the cab can be fitted with a single or twin passenger seat. The fully enclosed cab has two doors, observation/machine gun hatch in the roof, heater and a fresh air ventilator.

There is a lockable differential lock between the two rear axles and a lockable differential on each of the rear two axles.

The rear cargo area is provided with removable bows, tarpaulin cover, drop tailgate and collapsible seats for troops down the centre. Seat benches, bows and the tarpaulin cover can be stowed behind the headboard.

Optional equipment includes a winch with a capacity of 10 000 kg and 60 m of cable.

Various versions in 6 × 4 and 6 × 6 are licence-produced in China as part of the Hongyan heavy duty truck range manufactured at the Sichuan Truck Plant, Chongqing.

Variants
Steyr 1491.260.K34/6 × 6 recovery vehicle
This variant mounts a lifting crane in place of the cargo area. Four telescopic stabiliser legs are provided for use when the crane is in operation and extra stowage is provided for tools and equipment. The crane has a lifting capacity of 13 000 kg.

Steyr 24 M 32 040/6 × 6 M
This vehicle was produced to participate in the Canadian Heavy Load Vehicle Wheeled (HLVW) contest. During 1988 the Canadian Department of National Defence ordered 1200 units to be assembled in Canada by UTDC Inc of Kingston, Ontario. For further details of these vehicles refer to separate entry under International in this section.

A military firefighting version of this vehicle is produced by Hellenic Vehicle Industry SA in Greece. It carries a 5500 litre water tank and a 700 litre foam tank.

Steyr 24 M 34 (6 × 6)
This version is used as a heavy artillery tractor and is equipped with an ammunition handling crane. Part of the cargo area is covered by a tarpaulin and is used as a crew compartment for the gun crew.

Steyr 24 M 32 12 000 kg truck

Steyr 24 M 34 S40/6 × 6 truck tractor
This variant is used as the prime mover for a tank transporter. For further details refer to the entry in the *Tank transporters* section.

Specifications (Steyr 24 M 34)
Cab seating: 1 + 1 (or 1 + 2)
Configuration: 6 × 6
Weight:
(empty) 12 000 kg
(loaded) 22 500 kg
Weight on front axle: (loaded) 7500 kg
Weight on each rear axle: (loaded) 10 000 kg
Max load: 12 000 kg
Towed load:
(cross-country) 15 000 kg
(road, up to) 40 000 kg
Load area: 6.2 × 2.43 m
Length: 8.92 m
Width: 2.5 m
Height: (cab platform) 3.246 m
Ground clearance: 0.37 m
Track: 2.072 m
Wheelbase: 4 m + 1.4 m
Angle of approach/departure: 31°/36°
Max speed: (road) 95 km/h
Range: (approx) 700 km
Fuel capacity: 400 l
Max gradient: 100% (low-range at weight of 22 500 kg)
Fording: 0.8 m (1 m optional)
Engine: Steyr model WD 815.74, 11.97 l V-8 direct injection, turbocharged, water-cooled diesel,

developing 342 hp at 2200 rpm
Gearbox: ZF 5 S 111 GP manual with 9 forward (8 + 1 crawler) and 1 reverse gears or optional ZF hydraulic torque converter in combination with synchromesh gearbox or Allison automatic
Clutch: single dry plate (mechanically operated with assistance of compressed air)
Transfer box: Steyr VG 1200 2-speed
Steering: ZF 8046 hydraulic
Turning radius: 10.45 m
Suspension: semi-elliptical springs with telescopic shock absorbers front and rear
Tyres: 14.00 × 20
Brakes:
(main) dual circuit compressed air
(parking) spring energy, air-operated
Electrical system: 24 V
Batteries: 2 × 12 V, 135 Ah

Status
In production. In service with Canada, Cyprus and Egypt. Licence-produced in China. Produced in Canada for the Canadian Department of Defence.

Manufacturer
Steyr Nutzfahrzeuge AG, Schönauerstrasse 5, A-4400 Steyr, Austria.
Tel: 7252/585-0. Telex: 28200.
Fax: 7252/26746, 28650.

Steyr 26 M 39 (6 × 6) 12 000 kg Truck

Description
The Steyr 26 M 39 (6 × 6) 12 000 kg truck is an improved version of the 24 M series cargo truck (see previous entry) developed to carry a 12 000 kg payload and tow a similar or heavier load. It is fitted with a 10 t/m material handling crane and a 10-tonne self-recovery winch. A central tyre inflation system is available.

Specifications
Cab seating: 1 + 1 or 1 + 2
Configuration: 6 × 6
Weight:
  (empty) 19 000 kg
  (loaded) 26 000 kg
Weight on front axle: 7500 kg
Weight on rear axles: 2 × 9500 kg
Max load: 12 000 kg
Towed load: (cross country) 15 000 kg
Load area: 5.2 × 2.4 m
Length: 8.4 m
Width: 2.55 m
Height: 3.1 m
Ground clearance: 0.42 m
Track: 2.1 m
Wheelbase: 4 m + 1.4 m
Angle of approach/departure: 35°/40°
Max speed: 95 km/h
Range: 700 km
Fuel capacity: 400 l
Gradient: 100%
Fording: 1 m
Engine: Steyr WD 815.76 12 l V-8 direct injection water-cooled turbocharged intercooled diesel developing 390 hp at 2200 rpm

Steyr 26 M 39 (6 × 6) 12 000 kg truck during desert trials

Gearbox: ZF 4 S 150 GP 8-speed synchromesh
Transfer box: Steyr VG 2000, 2-speed
Steering: ZF 8046 power-assist
Turning radius: 10.5 m
Suspension: semi-elliptical springs with shock absorbers front and rear
Tyres: 16.00 R 20
Brakes: dual circuit air
Electrical system: 24 V
Batteries: 2 × 12 V, 165 Ah each
Alternator: 28 V, 55 A

Status
In production.

Manufacturer
Steyr Nutzfahrzeuge AG, Schönauerstrasse 5, A-4400 Steyr, Austria.
Tel: 7252/585-0. Telex: 28200.
Fax: 7252/26746, 28650.

BRAZIL

ENGESA EE-15 (4 × 4) 1500 kg Truck

Description
The EE-15 (4 × 4) 1500 kg truck was designed by ENGESA for both civil and military use. Its chassis is of high tensile steel with crossmembers riveted into position. A rear towing hook and four lifting eyes are fitted. The cab has a vinyl top and doors, folding down windscreen with wipers, adjustable seat for the driver and a seat for the two passengers. The standard all-steel cargo body has a tailgate, bows and a tarpaulin cover.

A wide range of optional equipment is available including a body with tilting troop seats, a power take-off and engine starting pilot for cold areas.

ENGESA can supply the EE-15 with other types of body including ambulance, crash tender and van.

Specifications
Cab seating: 1 + 2
Configuration: 4 × 4
Weight:
  (empty) 4050 kg
  (loaded, road) 7050 kg
  (loaded, cross-country) 5550 kg
Max load:
  (road) 3000 kg
  (cross-country) 1500 kg
Max towed load: 1500 kg
Length: 5.65 m
Width: 2.25 m
Height:
  (cab) 2.4 m
  (tarpaulin) 2.5 m
Ground clearance: 0.27 m
Track: 1.71 m
Wheelbase: 3.3 m

Angle of approach/departure: 42°/35°
Max speed: (road) 80 km/h
Range: 600 km
Fuel capacity: 136 l
Max gradient: (loaded, cross-country) 60%
Max side slope: 30%
Fording: 0.9 m
Vertical obstacle: 0.4 m
Engine: Mercedes-Benz OM-352 6-cylinder in-line water-cooled diesel developing 130 hp at 2800 rpm
Gearbox: Mercedes-Benz G-3-60 manual with 5 forward and 1 reverse gears
Clutch: single dry disc
Transfer box: mechanical ENGESA, 2-speed with constant mesh helical gears, optional front or rear left side PTO
Suspension:
  (front) semi-elliptical springs and double-acting hydraulic shock absorbers

ENGESA EE-15 (4 × 4) 1500 kg truck fitted with van-type body

ENGESA EE-15 (4 × 4) 1500 kg truck

(rear) 2 semi-elliptical springs and double-acting hydraulic shock absorbers
Steering: mechanical
Turning radius: 8 m
Tyres: 9.00 × 20-12 PR
Brakes:
  (main) drum type, air/hydraulic

(parking) mechanical acting on transfer case
Electrical system: 24 V
Batteries: 2 × 12 V, 95 Ah

Status
In production. In service with Angola, Brazil, Chile, Colombia, Gabon and other undisclosed countries.

Manufacturer
ENGESA Engenheiros Especializados SA, Avenida Tucunaré 125/211, Caixa Postal 152/154, 06400 Barueri, SP, Brazil.
Tel: 11 421 4711. Telex: 1171 302 enes br.

ENGESA EE-25 (6 × 6) 2500 kg Truck

Description
The EE-25 (6 × 6) truck was developed by ENGESA for both civil and military applications. Its chassis is of high tensile steel with crossmembers riveted into position. A rear tow hook is provided. The layout of the vehicle is conventional with the engine at the front, cab in the centre and the cargo area at the rear. The cab has a vinyl top and doors, folding down windscreen with wipers, adjustable seat for the driver, and a single seat for the two passengers. The all-steel body has a tailgate, bows and a tarpaulin cover.

With the award of a contract to supply EE-25 trucks to Angola some modifications to the vehicle were introduced. The main changes were a strengthened chassis and a new body and cab. The engine and transmission remain the same but an air cleaner is introduced to the right-hand side of the bonnet. A 24 V electrical system was incorporated. Vehicles delivered to Angola have a brush guard over the front.

Optional equipment includes a 6 t/m capacity hydraulic crane, a centre or rear winch with a 7500 kg capacity and two drums with 80 m of 16 mm diameter cable, a power take-off, and an engine start pilot for cold areas. A 4 × 4 model of the EE-25 is also available.

The basic chassis can be used for a variety of roles including ambulance, crash tender, dump truck (4 × 4), recovery, tanker (fuel or water), lubrication vehicle, van (for example command or workshop) and NBC decontamination truck (4 × 4).

Specifications (6 × 6 model)
Cab seating: 1 + 2
Configuration: 6 × 6
Weight:
  (empty) 7100 kg
  (loaded, road) 12 100 kg
  (loaded, cross-country) 9600 kg
Max load:
  (road) 5000 kg
  (cross-country) 2500 kg
Length: 6.99 m
Width: 2.25 m
Height:
  (cab) 2.5 m

ENGESA EE-25 (6 × 6) 2500 kg truck

  (tarpaulin) 3.1 m
Ground clearance: (axles) 0.27 m
Track: 1.78 m
Wheelbase: (front axle to centre of rear axle) 4.2 m
Angle of approach/departure: 46°/50°
Max speed: (road) 80 km/h
Range: 700 km
Fuel capacity: 200 l
Max gradient: 60%
Max side slope: 30%
Fording: 0.9 m
Vertical obstacle: 0.6 m
Engine: Mercedes-Benz OM-352A 6-cylinder in-line diesel developing 156 hp at 2800 rpm
Gearbox: manual with 5 forward and 1 reverse gears
Clutch: single dry disc
Transfer box: ENGESA 2-speed
Steering: hydraulic
Turning radius: 9.5 m
Suspension:
  (front) semi-elliptical springs with double-acting

hydraulic shock absorbers
  (rear) semi-elliptical springs; rear axle is ENGESA Boomerang type with walking beams
Tyres: 11.00 × 20-14 PR
Brakes:
  (main) air/hydraulic drum
  (parking) mechanical acting on transfer case
Electrical system: 24 V

Status
In production. In service with Angola, Bolivia, Brazil, Chile, Colombia, Gabon, Libya and other undisclosed countries.

Manufacturer
ENGESA Engenheiros Especializados SA, Avenida Tucunaré 125/211, Caixa Postal 152/154, 06400 Barueri, SP, Brazil.
Tel: 11 421 4711. Telex: 1171 302 enes br.

ENGESA EE-50 (6 × 6) 5000 kg Truck

Description
The ENGESA EE-50 (6 × 6) 5000 kg truck was designed to meet the requirements of the Brazilian Army. Following trials with prototypes it was selected to become the standard 5000 kg truck of the Brazilian Army in the 1980s. First production vehicles were completed during late 1980.

The EE-50 chassis is made of riveted steel rails and crossmembers. The all-steel forward control cab can be tilted forward to allow access to the engine. The windscreen is in two parts, left and right, both hinged at the top and with a windscreen wiper.

The all-steel rear cargo area is provided with lateral tilting troop seats, drop tailgate, removable bows and a tarpaulin cover. Optional equipment includes an engine-starting pilot for cold weather and a fire detection and extinguishing system.

The EE-50 could be supplied with a number of types of body including an ambulance, van, fuel tanker, light recovery, water tanker, fire tender and mobile workshop.

ENGESA EE-50 (6 × 6) 5000 kg truck

Specifications

Cab seating: 1 + 1
Configuration: 6 × 6
Weight:
 (empty) 12 000 kg
 (loaded, road) 22 000 kg
 (loaded, cross-country) 17 000 kg
Max load:
 (road) 10 000 kg
 (cross-country) 5000 kg
Max towed load: 6000 kg
Length: 7.85 m
Width: 2.6 m
Height:
 (cab hatch) 3.025 m
 (tarpaulin cover) 3.5 m
Ground clearance: 0.35 m
Track: 2.1 m
Wheelbase: (first axle to centre of rear bogie) 4.5 m

Angle of approach/departure: 40°/50°
Max speed: 80 km/h
Range: 700 km
Fuel capacity: 300 l
Max gradient: 60%
Max side slope: 30%
Fording: 1.4 m
Vertical obstacle: 0.6 m
Engine: Scania D11 6-cylinder water-cooled diesel developing 202 hp (SAE) at 2100 rpm
Gearbox: manual, 5 forward and 1 reverse gears
Clutch: single dry plate
Transfer box: mechanical, 2-speed
Suspension:
 (front) leaf springs, front wheels driven by hypoid angular transmission and bevel differential gears
 (rear) leaf springs, ENGESA Boomerang articulated axle with hypoid angular transmission, bevel differential gears and side walking beams with

helical gears
Steering: integral hydraulic
Tyres: 14.00 × 20-18 PR
Brakes:
 (main) air
 (parking) air, on transfer case output shaft
Electrical system: 24 V

Status

Production complete. In service with Angola, the Brazilian Army and at least one other country.

Manufacturer

ENGESA Engenheiros Especializados SA, Avenida Tuncunaré 125/211, Caixa Postal 152/154, 06400 Barueri, SP, Brazil.
Tel: 11 421 4711. Telex: 1171 302 enes br.

Terex UAI M1-50 (6 × 6) 5000 kg Truck

Description

During 1987 Terex do Brasil SA produced the first examples of the UAI M1-50 (6 × 6) 5000 kg truck. It is powered by a locally produced 238 hp six-cylinder diesel engine coupled to a six-speed transmission produced by ZF do Brasil. A Terex dual reduction transfer box is used. A flexible steel chassis is used while the cab has a removable canvas top and a forward-folding windscreen. The rear cargo area has bench seating along the sides and a drop tailgate. A canvas cover on bows is provided.

The maximum load for cross-country operations is 5000 kg, plus a towed load of 6800 kg. For road operations the load can be increased to 16 000 kg, plus a towed load of 13 000 kg.

Status

In production for the Brazilian Army and Marine Corps.

Manufacturer

Terex do Brasil SA, Rodovia BR-252, Anel Rodoviário – 31250 Belo Horizonte, MG – Brazil.
Tel: 31 441 3444.

Terex UAI M1-50 (6 × 6) 5000 kg truck

TECTRAN Military Trucks

Description

TECTRAN is producing a range of military trucks with payloads of 2.5, 5 and 10 tonnes. The trucks share a common cab and many other components, the 2.5-tonne model having a 4 × 4 configuration while the others are 6 × 6.

The cab is of the normal control type and may have a hard or canvas top. An armoured cabin weighing 2100 kg is optional for the heavier models. Internal equipment can include air-conditioning and a radio installation.

A family of body types is also produced and it is possible for all chassis types to have an auxiliary frame for the installation of a torsion-free platform. Standard body types include a general cargo platform, a cargo/personnel body, a liquid load transporter, a dumper body, mechanical and electrical mobile workshops, command, control and communication posts, and a mobile satellite communications post body. By the addition of a fifth wheel over the rear axle(s) the vehicles can tow various semi-trailers.

The data in the Specifications table refer to the basic chassis only.

Status

Ready for production.

Manufacturer

TECTRAN Enginharia, Indústria e Comércio SA, Rodovia Presidente Dutra, Km 155/156, Caixa Postal 165, 12200 São José dos Campos, São Paulo, Brazil.
Tel: 123 31 8200. Telex: 123 3519.
Fax: 123 31 8775.

Specifications

Model	2.5 tonne	5 tonne	10 tonne
Cab seating	1+1	1+1	1+1
Configuration	4 × 4	6 × 6	6 × 6
Weight (chassis)	4800 kg	6700 kg	8500 kg
(payload and body)	3200 kg	6300 kg	11 500 kg
(GVW)	8000 kg	13 000 kg	20 000 kg
Length	6.7 m	7 m	7.85 m
Width	2.36 m	2.36 m	2.36 m
Height (cab)	3 m	3.05 m	3.05 m
Wheelbase	4.2 m	3.6 m + 1.3 m	3.8 m + 1.45 m
Track	2.053 m	1.943 m	2.07 m
Max speed (road)	80 km/h	85 km/h	90 km/h
Fuel capacity	210 l	300 l	300 l
Max gradient	60%	60%	60%
Fording	0.9 m	1 m	1 m
Engine	diesel, water-cooled, turbocharged		
Power	180 hp	200 hp	280 hp
Rpm	2600	2200	2300
Transmission	mechanical, fully synchronised		
Gears	5 f, 1 r	6 f, 1 r	6 f, 1 r
Clutch	single dry disc	single dry disc	single dry disc
Transfer box	2-speed	2-speed	2-speed
Steering	worm and gear, power-assisted		
Turning radius	8 m	8.7 m	10.2 m
Tyres	11.00 × 20	12.00 × 20	14.00 × 20
Brakes	drum, air	drum, air	drum, air
Electrical system	24 V	24 V	24 V

CANADA

Chevrolet 1¼-ton (4 × 4) Series

Description

In 1976 the Canadian Armed Forces selected a Chevrolet (4 × 4) 1¼-ton vehicle to replace the M37CDN (4 × 4) ¾-ton vehicle which entered service in the early 1950s. The first order was for about 600 vehicles, followed later in 1976 by a second order for 2848 vehicles at a total cost of $20.8 million.

The Chevrolet is a standard commercial vehicle with the minimum of modifications to suit it for military use. It has a 150 hp engine, automatic transmission, power steering and power brakes.

The layout of the vehicle is conventional with the engine at the front, two-door fully enclosed cab in the centre and the cargo area at the rear with a drop tailgate, troop seats, removable bows and a tarpaulin cover.

Variants include an ambulance, cable-layer, communications vehicle and a light repair vehicle.

Status

In service with the Canadian Armed Forces.

Manufacturer

Chevrolet Division, General Motors Corporation, now General Motors of Canada Limited, PO Box 5160, London, Ontario, Canada N6A 4N5.
Tel: (519) 452 5184. Telex: 645643.
Fax: (519) 452 5688.

Canadian Armed Forces Chevrolet 1¼-ton (4 × 4) truck (C R Zwart)

CHINA, PEOPLE'S REPUBLIC

Dong Feng EQ2080E4DY (6 × 6) 2500 kg Truck

Description

The Dong Feng (export name Aeolus) EQ2080E4DY (6 × 6) 2500 kg truck is the latest version of the EQ2080E range (formerly the EQ240 range) and is fitted with a Cummins 6B5.9 diesel engine; earlier models were powered by an EQ6100 5.417 litre petrol engine. It is a right-hand drive vehicle intended for operations in mountainous areas and over rough roads and tracks.

Layout is conventional with the engine forward, the steel cab having seating for the driver and two passengers, and the load area to the rear. The cargo body has a steel and wood floor, steel side racks and a tailgate. Optional extras include a power take-off and a 4500 kg winch mounted behind the front bumper. A left-hand drive version (the EQ2080E4D) is available.

Specifications

Cab seating: 1 + 2
Configuration: 6 × 6
Weight:
(laden, road) 9300 kg
(laden, cross-country) 7800 kg
Max load:
(road) 4000 kg
(cross-country) 2500 kg
Towed load: 2500 kg
Length: 6.34 m
Width: 2.4 m
Height: (cab, unladen) 2.4 m
Track: 1.774 m

Dong Feng EQ2080E4DY (6 × 6) 2500 kg truck

Wheelbase:
(front axle to centre of rear bogie) 3.74 m
(between rear axles) 1.1 m
Angle of approach/departure: 45°/44°
Max speed: 77 km/h
Fording: 0.85 m
Engine: Cummins 6B5.9 6-cylinder 4-stroke in-line water-cooled diesel developing 130 hp at 2800 rpm
Gearbox: manual with 5 forward and 1 reverse gears
Clutch: single dry disc
Transfer box: 2-speed
Turning radius: 8.2 m

Tyres: 11.00 × 18
Brakes: air

Status

In production. In service with Thailand (235).

Manufacturer

The Second Automobile Works, Shiyan, Hubei Province, People's Republic of China.
Tel: 24249. Telex: 40104 hb saw cn.

CA-30 (6 × 6) 2500 kg Truck

Description

The CA-30 (6 × 6) 2500 kg truck entered production at the First Automobile Works, Changchun, in 1959 and is the standard vehicle in its class in the Chinese Army. Production ceased in 1986.

The CA-30 is very similar to the ZIL-157 (6 × 6) 2500 kg truck but has a different cab with the headlamps sometimes in the mudguards rather than mounted externally as on the ZIL-157.

The layout of the vehicle is conventional with the engine at the front, two-door fully enclosed cab in the centre and at the rear the cargo area which consists of a wooden platform with sides, bench seats down each side which can be folded up when the vehicle is carrying cargo, and a drop tailgate. If required, the vehicle can be fitted with bows and a tarpaulin cover.

The CA-30 has been used for a number of military roles including that of artillery tractor and for carrying multiple 122 mm rocket launchers, including the Type 74 Minelaying Rocket System (see entry in *Minelaying equipment* section).

CA-30 (6 × 6) 2500 kg truck with winch and with box body for use in command post role (C F Foss)

Towed load: (cross-country) 3600 kg
Load area: 3.57 × 1.8 m
Length: 6.684 m
Width: 2.315 m
Height: (cab) 2.36 m
Ground clearance: 0.305 m
Track: (front and rear) 1.752 m
Wheelbase: (first axle to centre of rear bogie) 4.785 m
Max speed: (road) 65 km/h
Range: 680 km
Fuel capacity: 150 l
Max gradient: 30%
Fording: 0.85 m
Engine: Chieh'Fang 120 6-cylinder liquid-cooled petrol developing 95 hp at 2800 rpm
Gearbox: manual, 5 forward and 1 reverse gears
Clutch: single dry plate
Transfer box: 2-speed
Turning radius: 12.1 m
Suspension: (front and rear) semi-elliptical leaf springs
Tyres: 12.00 × 18
Brakes:
  (main) air
  (parking) mechanical
Electrical system: 12 V

Status
Production on request. In service with the Chinese Army and has been exported.

Manufacturer
First Automobile Works, Dong Feng Street, Changchun, Jilin, People's Republic of China.
Tel: 504051. Telex: 83009 jffaw cn.
Fax: 86 0431 867780.

Specifications
Cab seating: 1 + 2
Configuration: 6 × 6
Weight:
  (empty) 5450 kg
  (loaded, road) 9950 kg
  (loaded, cross-country) 7950 kg
  (on front axle, empty) 2360 kg
  (on rear bogie, empty) 3090 kg
Max load:
  (road) 4500 kg
  (cross-country) 2500 kg

Jiefang CA-10 (4 × 2) Liberation 3540 kg Truck

Development/Description
The CA-10 (4 × 2) Liberation 3540 kg truck entered production at the First Automobile Works at Changchun in July 1956. It is a modified ZIL-150 (4 × 2) 3500 kg truck. Although it has a very limited cross-country capability and was primarily produced for commercial purposes, it is used in some numbers as a cargo carrier and as a prime mover for light artillery. Compared with the original it has a less efficient engine and a lack of climbing power.

Over one million CA-10s of all types had been produced by the beginning of 1983.

The initial CA-10 was followed by the CA-10B in 1960. The CA-10BX with a higher compression ratio, maximum speed and power output appeared in September 1980. It also had changes to the camshaft, carburettor, fuel pump, oil sump, radiator, clutch, starter motor and electrical system, all of which went some way to overcoming earlier technical drawbacks.

The CA-10C appeared in January 1982 and is rated at 4500 kg. The CA-10CJ is fitted with a 100 hp engine and the CA-10CT with a 110 hp engine. The CA-15 has a 5.55 litre 115 hp engine.

The layout of the vehicle is conventional with the engine at the front, two-door fully enclosed cab in the centre and the cargo area at the rear with drop sides and a drop tailgate. Both left- and right-hand drive models are in service.

Variants are known to include a tractor truck, firefighting vehicles, tankers, crane carriers and dump trucks. Various wheelbase lengths have been produced.

The QH-140 truck, produced at the Qinghai plant, is a special variant for use at high altitudes. It was produced in petrol- and diesel-engined forms.

Specifications
Cab seating: 1 + 1
Configuration: 4 × 2
Weight:
  (empty) 3840 kg
  (loaded, road) 7375 kg
  (on front axle, empty) 1735 kg

Jiefang CA-10B (4 × 2) Liberation 3540 kg truck

  (on rear axle, empty) 2100 kg
Max load: (road) 3540 kg
Load area: 3.54 × 2.26 m
Length: 6.502 m
Width: 2.29 m
Height: 2.33 m
Ground clearance: 0.27 m
Track:
  (front) 1.69 m
  (rear) 1.74 m
Wheelbase: 3.98 m
Angle of approach/departure: 40°/24°
Max speed: 80 km/h
Range: 415 km
Fuel capacity: 158 l
Max gradient: 37%
Engine: CA-10 6-cylinder in-line liquid-cooled petrol developing 95 hp at 2800 rpm
Gearbox: manual, 5 forward and 1 reverse gears
Clutch: single dry plate
Turning radius: 9 m

Suspension:
  (front) semi-elliptical leaf springs and hydraulic shock absorbers
  (rear) semi-elliptical springs with overload springs
Tyres: 9.00 × 20
Brakes:
  (main) air
  (parking) mechanical
Electrical system: 12 V
Batteries: 2 × 6 V

Status
Production complete. In service with the Chinese Army. Replaced from 1987 onwards by the CA-1091 and CA-141 series of trucks (qv).

Manufacturer
First Automobile Works, Dong Feng Street, Changchun, Jilin, People's Republic of China.
Tel: 504051. Telex: 83009 jffaw cn.
Fax: 86 0431 867780.

Jiefang CA-1091 (4 × 4) 5000 kg Trucks

Description

The Jiefang CA-1091 series of 4 × 4 trucks are the military purpose successors to the Jiefang CA-10 truck series (see previous entry) and share many components with the Jiefang CA-141 series of 4 × 2 trucks (see next entry).

There are three basic models in the series. The CA-1091E2 uses a petrol engine and has a 12 V electrical system. The CA-1091K2E2 and CA-1091K3E2 have diesel engines and a 24 V system. All three models share the same drive train, chassis and cargo body.

The chassis uses a side girder type structure with riveted pressed longitudinal beams and eight crossmembers. Towing hooks are provided at the front and rear.

The cab has seating for the driver and two passengers. The one-piece hood can be tilted forward 50° for engine access. Optional equipment for the cab includes a heater and defrosting equipment. The cargo body uses mixed steel and timber construction and is fitted with side racks. A tailboard is provided along with a ladder for access and a rainproof tarpaulin.

Specifications

Cab seating: 1 + 2
Configuration: 4 × 4
Weight: (kerb)
 (CA-1091E2) 4700 kg
 (CA-1091K2E2) 4350 kg
 (CA-1091K3E2) 4195 kg
Max load: 5000 kg
Load area: 4.2 × 2.3 m
Length: 7.205 m
Width: 2.484 m
Height: 3.09 m
Ground clearance: (rear axle) 0.262 m
Track:
 (front) 1.8 m
 (rear) 1.74 m
Wheelbase: 4.05 m
Angle of approach/departure: (loaded) 28°/19°
Max speed: 90 km/h
Gradient: 28%
Engine:
 (CA-1091E2) Model CA-6102 5.56 l 6-cylinder water-cooled petrol developing 132 hp at 3000 rpm
 (CA-1091K2E2) Model CA-6110A 6.842 l 6-cylinder water-cooled direct injection diesel developing 157 hp at 2900 rpm
 (CA-1091K3E2) Model CY-6102BQ-6 5.785 l 6-cylinder water-cooled direct injection diesel developing 138 hp at 3000 rpm
Gearbox: Model LFO6S-CB with 6 forward and 1 reverse gears
Transfer box: 2-speed
Steering: circulating ball
Turning radius: 8 m
Suspension: leaf springs with double-acting hydraulic shock absorbers
Tyres: 9.00 × 20 or 9.00 R 20
Brakes:
 (main) air, drum type
 (parking) mechanical
Electrical system:
 (petrol) 12 V
 (diesel) 24 V

Status

In production.

Manufacturer

First Automobile Works, Dong Feng Street, Changchun, Jilin, People's Republic of China.
Tel: 504051. Telex: 83009 jffaw cn.
Fax: 86 0431 867780.

Jiefang CA-1091 series (4 × 4) 5000 kg truck

Jiefang CA-141 (4 × 2) 5000 kg Trucks

Description

The Jiefang CA-141 (4 × 2) 5000 kg truck entered trial production during 1983 in its original forward control cab form. A more orthodox model with a conventional bonnet entered production during 1987 and replaced the earlier CA-10 (qv). The CA-141 shares many components and the same general layout as the CA-1091 series of 4 × 4 trucks (see previous entry).

The CA-141 may be regarded as a fully updated version of the earlier CA-10 series and retains the same general layout of a bonneted cab with the cargo area open to the rear. The bonnet can be tipped forward to an angle of 50° for maintenance access and the cab has an adjustable seat for the driver and a dual seat for two passengers. The driver is provided with a comprehensive instrument panel, cabin and windscreen ventilation and large wide-vision windows.

The CA-141 is produced in a range of nine models, primarily for commercial purposes but some are used by the Chinese armed forces for a variety of roles. There is a choice of a petrol or diesel engine.

The CA-141K series of trucks have Model 6110 6.842 litre diesel engines. Included in this range are the CA-141K2Y and longer wheelbase CA-141K2YL trucks, both with a 6000 kg load capacity, and the CA-341K2Y dump truck with a 4.3 m³ capacity.

Specifications (CA-141K2Y)

Cab seating: 1 + 2
Configuration: 4 × 2
Weight:
 (kerb) 4350 kg
 (loaded) 10 350 kg
Max load: 6000 kg
Towed load: 6000 kg
Length: 7.205 m
Width: 2.476 m
Height: 2.425 m
Load area: 4.2 × 2.3 m
Ground clearance: 0.262 m
Track:
 (front) 1.8 m
 (rear) 1.74 m
Wheelbase: 4.05 m
Max speed: 110 km/h
Max gradient: 28%
Engine: Model 6110 6.842 l 6-cylinder in-line diesel developing 157 hp at 2900 rpm
Gearbox: manual with 6 forward and 1 reverse gears
Clutch: single dry plate
Steering: recirculating ball
Turning radius: 8.2 m
Suspension:
 (front) leaf springs with shock absorbers
 (rear) torsion bar
Brakes: dual circuit
Electrical system: 24 V
Battery: 6-QA-100
Alternator: 700 W

Status

In production at a rate of up to 100 000 units per year.

Manufacturer

First Automobile Works, Dong Feng Street, Changchun, Jilin, People's Republic of China.
Tel: 504051. Telex: 83009 jffaw cn.
Fax: 86 0431 867780.

Jiefang CA-141 (4 × 2) 5000 kg truck

Dong Feng EQ2100E (6 × 6) 3500 kg Truck

Description

The Dong Feng (export name Aeolus) EQ2100E (6 × 6) 3500 kg truck (formerly the EQ245) is a high mobility vehicle powered by an EQ6105-1 petrol engine. Layout is conventional with the engine forward, the steel cab having seating for the driver and two passengers, and the load area to the rear. The cargo body has a steel and wood floor and steel side racks. There is provision to tow a trailer weighing up to 4500 kg. A self-recovery winch may be fitted.

This vehicle is also used for commercial purposes such as geological and oil exploration and may also carry various forms of technical service vehicle bodies.

Dong Feng EQ2100E (6 × 6) 3500 kg truck

Specifications

Cab seating: 1 + 2
Configuration: 6 × 6
Weight: (without winch)
  (laden, road) 11 290 kg
  (laden, cross-country) 9790 kg
Max load:
  (road) 5000 kg
  (cross-country) 3500 kg
Towed load: 4500 kg
Length: 6.844 m
Width: 2.4 m
Height: (cab, unladen) 2.484 m
Track:
  (front) 1.876 m
  (rear) 1.87 m

Wheelbase:
  (front axle to centre of rear bogies) 4.025 m
  (between rear axles) 1.25 m
Angle of approach/departure: 44.5°/45°
Max speed: 82 km/h
Fording: 0.9 m
Engine: EQ6105-1 petrol
Gearbox: manual with 5 forward and 1 reverse gears
Clutch: double dry disc, 300 mm
Transfer box: 2-speed
Turning radius: 9.3 m

Tyres: 12.00 R 20
Brakes: air

Status
In production. In service with the Chinese armed forces and offered for export.

Manufacturer
The Second Automobile Works, Shiyan, Hubei Province, People's Republic of China.
Tel: 24249. Telex: 40104 hb saw cn.

EQ1110F4D (4 × 2) Truck

Description

The Second Automobile Works at Shiyan in Hubei Province manufactures 140 000 medium-weight trucks annually and is the largest truck manufacturer in China. One of its main products is the Dong Feng EQ1110, fitted with an EQ6100 5.4 litre six-cylinder 135 hp petrol engine. Under the export name Aeolus they have been exported to more than 10 nations in Asia, Africa (including Cameroon) and South America.

The EQ1110F4D (formerly the EQ4D142) is only one vehicle in the EQ1110 range and is a conventional design in the 11-tonne gross weight class. It is powered by a Cummins diesel but other models have been powered by a Renault 133 hp petrol engine. The drive configuration is 4 × 2 with the engine at the front and a conventional steel cab. The usual cargo body is steel with a raised 'ladder' grill to protect the cab rear. Twin tyres are fitted on the rear axle.

A similar vehicle with right-hand drive, the EQ1110F4DY, was also produced. The EQ1090 series is available for both military and commercial users.

EQ1110F4D (4 × 2) truck

Specifications

Cab seating: 1 + 2
Configuration: 4 × 2
Weight: (kerb) 4380 kg
Max load: 6400 kg
Length: 6.91 m
Width: 2.47 m
Height: 2.475 m
Track:
  (front) 1.81 m
  (rear) 1.8 m

Wheelbase: 3.95 m
Angle of approach/departure: 39.5°/21°
Max speed: 83 km/h
Gradient: 16°
Engine: Cummins 6B5.9 4-stroke in-line water-cooled diesel developing 130 bhp at 2800 rpm
Gearbox: manual with 5 forward and 1 reverse gears
Clutch: single dry disc
Turning radius: 8 m
Tyres: 9.00 × 20
Brakes: air

Status
Production of EQ4D142 complete but other similar models available.

Manufacturer
The Second Automobile Works, Shiyan, Hubei Province, People's Republic of China.
Tel: 24249. Telex: 40104 hb saw cn.

Dong Feng EQ1141G (4 × 2) 8000 kg Truck

Description
The Dong Feng (export name Aeolus) EQ1141G (4 × 2) 8000 kg truck is described as a high performance logistics vehicle. It has a forward control cab that can be tilted forward 43° to gain access to the Cummins 6BT5.9 diesel engine and features a conventional load area.

Specifications
Cab seating: 1 + 2
Configuration: 4 × 2
Weight:
  (empty) 14 100 kg
  (GCW) 22 100 kg
Max load: 8000 kg
Length: 7.73 m
Width: 2.47 m
Height: 2.71 m
Track:
  (front) 1.94 m
  (rear) 1.86 m
Wheelbase: 4.5 m
Angle of approach/departure: 34°/18°
Max speed: 88 km/h
Gradient: 14°
Engine: Cummins 6BT5.9 in-line water-cooled diesel developing 158 hp at 2600 rpm
Gearbox: manual with 5 forward and 1 reverse gears
Clutch: single dry disc
Turning radius: 8 m

Dong Feng EQ1141G (4 × 2) truck

Suspension: semi-elliptical springs with double-acting hydraulic shock absorbers
Tyres: 10.00 R 20, 16PR
Brakes: air

Status
In production.

Manufacturer
The Second Automobile Works, Shiyan, Hubei Province, People's Republic of China.
Tel: 24249. Telex: 40104 hb saw cn.

Hongyan CQ 261 (6 × 6) 8250 kg Truck

Description
The CQ 261 (6 × 6) 8250 kg truck can trace its design origins back to the early 1960s when Berliet GBU and GCH trucks were imported into China. Licence production in China followed and in 1977 the CQ 261 appeared.

The CQ 261 bears an overall resemblance to the Berliet original but has many changes to suit local production methods. The large forward control cab has a distinctive radiator grille and seating for at least two passengers in addition to the driver, and some cabs are fitted with a roof hatch. At least two forms of passenger door have been seen with later models having 'straight line' doors in place of the earlier sloping rear edge. The cargo area to the rear has steel drop sides and a tailgate and a towing hook is provided. Bench seats can be fitted along each side of the cargo area. A canvas tilt can be fitted.

A tractor version of this vehicle is known as the CQ 261Q25 and is fitted with a Model 614OZ engine developing 250 hp. There is also a long wheelbase tractor truck known as the CQ 261C25 and an 8 × 4 crane truck is known as the CQ 40D.

An 8 × 8 version is used to carry the components of the Type 79 Ribbon Bridge.

Similar vehicles are the Yan'An SX 250 (6 × 6) truck and the SX 161 (6 × 4) truck. The Yan'An QD 360 is a 6 × 4 dump truck variant of the SX 161.

CQ 261 (6 × 6) truck towing Type 66 152 mm gun-howitzer

Specifications
Cab seating: 1 + 2 or 3
Configuration: 6 × 6
Weight loaded:
  (roads) 26 460 kg
  (cross-country) 22 460 kg
Max load:
  (roads) 12 260 kg
  (cross-country) 8266 kg
Length: 7.947 m
Width: 2.5 m
Height: (top of cab) 3 m
Wheelbase: 4.93 m
Max speed: 61 km/h
Engine: Chongfa Model 6150 14.78 l 6-cylinder diesel

developing 200 hp
Gearbox: 5 forward and 1 reverse gears
Clutch: single dry plate
Transfer box: 2-speed
Brakes: dual circuit air

Status
In production. In service with the Chinese armed forces.

Manufacturer
Sichuan Automobile Factory, Dazu, Sichuan Province, People's Republic of China.

Other Chinese Military Vehicles

The Chinese Army still uses large numbers of vehicles supplied by the USSR in the 1950s including the GAZ-63, GAZ-51, ZIL-150 (Chinese model CA-10), ZIL-164, ZIL-151 and the ZIL-157 (Chinese model the CA-30, with workshop versions known as the QD402, X01000 and X8000). Chinese-designed vehicles include the 7000 kg capacity JN-150 Huang Ho dump truck and the CN-130 truck for towing semi-trailers.

In the 1950s vehicles were also obtained from other Eastern bloc countries including Czechoslovakia, the former East Germany, Romania and Hungary. In recent years China has obtained vehicles from a number of Western countries including Austria (Steyr trucks), France (Berliet trucks) and Sweden (Volvo trucks). The Berliet trucks were the 6 × 6 GBC 8MT and the heavier GBU (the Chinese model was known as the GCH).

COMMONWEALTH OF INDEPENDENT STATES

GAZ-66 (4 × 4) 2000 kg Truck

Description

The GAZ-66 (4 × 4) 2000 kg truck was the replacement for the GAZ-63 and entered production at the Gor'kiy Automobile Plant in 1964. All vehicles built since 1968 have a central tyre pressure regulation system fitted as standard. The GAZ-66 is widely used by the CIS armed forces and is also used for a variety of civilian roles.

The two-door all-steel forward control cab hinges forward to allow access to the engine for maintenance. The all-steel rear cargo body has fixed sides and a drop tailgate. The vehicle can be fitted with five bows and a tarpaulin cover if required. Standard equipment includes a cab heater and an engine pre-heater and many vehicles have a winch.

Variants

GAZ-66-02: with crane
GAZ-66-04: with shielded electrical system
GAZ-66-05: with shielded electrical system and crane
GAZ-66-01: with tyre pressure regulation system (also known as GAZ-66-51)
GAZ-66-02: with tyre pressure regulation system and winch
GAZ-66-03: with shielded electrical system
GAZ-66-04: with shielded electrical system and tyre pressure regulation system
GAZ-66-05: with shielded electrical system, tyre pressure regulation system and winch
GAZ-66-51: with tyre pressure regulation system and tropical equipment
GAZ-66-52: with winch and tropical equipment
GAZ-66-54: with shielded electrical system and tropical equipment

GAZ-66-55: with shielded electrical system, winch and tropical equipment
GAZ-66A: with tyre pressure regulation system and winch
GAZ-66E: with shielded electrical system
GAZ-66P: tractor truck, not placed in production
GAZ-66B: for airborne forces with collapsible canvas cab, removable doors and windscreen, telescopic steering wheel and tie-down points for parachute dropping
DDA-53C: NBC decontamination vehicle
AVTs-1.7: 1700 litre water tanker, built at Dalmatovo Molmashstroy plant
MZ-66: motor oil supply vehicle (820 litres)
Shop/van for command, communications and other roles
Multiple Rocket Launcher: the GAZ-66B is used as a carrier for a lightweight 12-tube version of the BM-21 known as the BM-21V Grad-P. For details of the BM-21 system refer to *Jane's Armour and Artillery 1992-93* pages 715 to 717.

Specifications (GAZ-66)

Cab seating: 1 + 1
Configuration: 4 × 4
Weight:
(empty) 3440 kg
(loaded) 5800 kg
Max load: 2000 kg
Towed load: 2000 kg
Load area: 3.33 × 2.05 m
Length: 5.655 m
Width: 2.342 m
Height:
(cab) 2.44 m
(load area) 1.11 m
Ground clearance: (axles) 0.315 m

Track:
(front) 1.8 m
(rear) 1.75 m
Wheelbase: 3.3 m
Angle of approach/departure: 42°/32°
Max speed: (road) 95 km/h
Range: 875 km
Fuel capacity: 210 l (2 × 105 l tanks)
Max gradient: 60%
Fording: 0.8 m
Engine: ZMZ-66 V-8 4.254 l water-cooled petrol developing 115 hp at 3200 rpm
Gearbox: manual with 4 forward and 1 reverse gears
Clutch: single dry plate
Transfer box: 2-speed
Steering: globoid worm with 3-collar roller and hydraulic booster
Turning radius: 10 m
Suspension: longitudinal semi-elliptical springs and hydraulic double-acting shock absorbers
Tyres: 12.00 × 18
Brakes:
(main) hydraulic
(parking) mechanical operating on transmission
Electrical system: 12 V
Battery: 1 × 6-ST-68

Status

Production of a replacement design anticipated. In service with former Warsaw Pact countries. Also exported to other countries, including Angola, Cuba, Egypt, Finland and Iran.

Manufacturer

Gor'kiy Motor Vehicle Plant, Gor'kiy, Russia.

GAZ-66 (4 × 4) 2000 kg truck with office body

GAZ-66 (4 × 4) 2000 kg truck towing a trailer as part of SA-13 'Gopher' SAM maintenance equipment

ZIL-157 (6 × 6) 2500 kg Truck

Description

The ZIL-157 (6 × 6) truck replaced the ZIL-151 (6 × 6) truck in production from 1958, and in 1961 the improved ZIL-157K entered production to be replaced in 1966 by the more powerful ZIL-131 (6 × 6) 3500 kg truck. In appearance the ZIL-157 is very similar to the ZIL-151 but has a slightly different cab (which was also fitted to late production ZIL-151s), and single instead of dual rear wheels.

The layout of the vehicle is conventional with the engine at the front, two-door fully enclosed cab in the centre, and the cargo area at the rear which consists of a wooden platform with sides, bench seats down each side which can be folded up when the vehicle is carrying cargo, and a drop tailgate. If required the vehicle can be fitted with bows and a tarpaulin cover. Standard equipment includes a cab heater and an engine pre-heater and many vehicles also have a winch.

Variants

ZIL-157V and ZIL-157KV: tractor trucks for towing semi-trailers (for example carrying SA-2, FROG-3, FROG-4 or FROG-5 missiles)
ZIL-157KG: with shielded electrical system
ZIL-157KE: temperate climate export model of ZIL-157K
ZIL-157KYu: tropical climate export model of ZIL-157K
ZIL-157GT: tropical climate export model of ZIL-157K with shielded electrical system
ZIL-157KYe: ZIL-157K chassis for special bodies
ZIL-157KYel: ZIL-157KYe chassis with high output generator
ZIL-157KYeG: ZIL-157KG chassis with shielded electrical system
ZIL-157YeT: ZIL-157KYe chassis, tropical climate export model
ZIL-157YeGT: ZIL-157KYeG chassis, tropical climate export model
ZIL-157KYeGT: ZIL-157KYeG chassis, tropical climate export model (chassis has features of the ZIL-157KYu)
ZIL-157YeT: ZIL-157KYe chassis, tropical climate

export model (chassis contains features of ZIL-157KYu)
ARS-12U: decontamination vehicle
AGV-3M and AGW-3M: decontamination stations
ATsM-4-157K: 4000 litre fuel truck (also on ZIL-157 chassis)
ATZ-3-157K and ATZ-3, 8-157K: fuel service trucks
ATsMM-4-157K: 4000 litre oil tank truck
AVTs 28-157: 2800 litre water tanker
CAS 16: Czech fire engine
Carrying pontoons and other bridging equipment
Crane truck
Carrying KMM treadway bridge system (details of this version are given in the *Mechanised bridges* section)
Multiple rocket system: 200 mm BMD-20 (4-round) (*Jane's Armour and Artillery 1987-88* page 785), 240 mm BM-24 (12-round) (*Jane's Armour and Artillery 1990-91* pages 738 and 739) and 140 mm (16-round) BM-14-16 (*Jane's Armour and Artillery 1992-93* pages 713 and 714)
VMZ-ZIL-157K: water and oil service truck which carries 1400 litres of water and 700 litres of oil and is equipped with a heater system which maintains the

temperature of the water at between +15 and +90°C and the oil at +80°C.

Specifications

Cab seating: 1 + 1
Configuration: 6 × 6
Weight:
  (empty, with winch) 5800 kg
  (loaded, with winch) 8450 kg
Max load: (road) 4500 kg
  (cross-country) 2500 kg
Towed load:
  (dirt road) 3600 kg
  (cross-country) 2500 kg
  (roads) 3600 kg
Load area: 3.57 × 2.09 m
Length: 6.922 m (with winch)
Width: 2.315 m
Height:
  (cab) 2.36 m
  (tarpaulin) 2.915 m
  (load area) 1.388 m
Ground clearance: 0.31 m
Track:
  (front) 1.755 m
  (rear) 1.75 m
Wheelbase: 3.655 m + 1.12 m
Angle of approach/departure: 35°/43°
Max speed: (road) 65 km/h
Range: 510 km
Fuel capacity: 215 l
Max gradient: 53%
Fording: 0.85 m
Engine: ZIL-157K 5.555 l 6-cylinder water-cooled petrol developing 109 hp at 2800 rpm
Gearbox: manual with 5 forward and 1 reverse gears
Clutch: single dry plate

ZIL-157 (6 × 6) 2500 kg trucks with box bodies housing AT-3 anti-tank missile simulators

Transfer box: 2-speed
Steering: cone worm with 3-ridge roller
Turning radius: 11.2 m
Suspension:
  (front) longitudinal semi-elliptical springs with hydraulic double-acting shock absorbers
  (rear) bogie with semi-elliptical springs
Tyres: 12.00 × 18
Brakes:
  (main) air
  (parking) mechanical

Electrical system: 12 V
Batteries: 2 × ST-84

Status
Production complete. In service in declining numbers with former Warsaw Pact countries and other armed forces.

Manufacturer
Likhachev Motor Vehicle Plant, Moscow, Russia.

ZIL-131 (6 × 6) 3500 kg Truck

Description

The ZIL-131 (6 × 6) truck entered production in December 1966 as the replacement for the earlier ZIL-157 (6 × 6) 2500 kg truck and uses many components of the ZIL-133 (6 × 4) truck. Main improvements over the ZIL-157 can be summarised as increased load-carrying capacity, more powerful engine, power steering, shorter wheelbase, waterproof ignition and the central tyre-pressure regulation system. The front axle is engaged automatically when the driver selects first gear and the driver can also engage the front axle manually when in second gear. The vehicle is used for transporting cargo, personnel and as a prime mover for towing artillery such as the 122 mm D-30 howitzer.

The layout of the vehicle is conventional with the engine at the front, fully enclosed two-door all-steel cab in the centre and the cargo area at the rear, consisting of a wooden platform with metal fittings and a hinged tailgate. The platform has recesses for the bows and hinged bench seats are provided down either side of the platform.

The ZIL-131 has a central tyre pressure regulation system and a 4500 kg capacity winch. Standard

equipment includes a cab heater and an engine pre-heater.

Variants

ZIL-131A: this is a truck with a standard ignition system rather than the shielded ignition system as fitted on the standard ZIL-131
ZIL-131D: dump truck
ZIL-131V: for towing semi-trailers
ZIL-131PM: fire engine
ZIL-137: tractor truck for towing a two-axle powered trailer (the complete unit then becomes a 10 × 10); also used to tow SA-6 'Gainful' SAMs on a single-axle trailer
ARS-14: decontamination vehicle
ATs 4, 2-131: 4200 litre fuel tank truck
ATs 4, 2-131: 4100 litre fuel tank truck
ATs 4, 3-131: 4400 litre fuel tank truck
ATZ 3, 8-131: 4300 litre fuel service truck
ATZ 4, 3-131: 4300 litre fuel service truck
AVTs 28-131: 2800 litre water tanker
PBU 50M: German well drilling plant

Shop/van
Various models are in service including bakery, maintenance and a field kitchen.

MA-41
This is a combined fuel, lubricant and water service vehicle. It carries 1700 litres of diesel, 340 litres of petrol, two 170 litre tanks of oil and 700 litres of water. Both the diesel and water tanks are heated as this unit is used in very cold climates.

SA-6 'Gainful' SAM Resupply Vehicle
Three missiles are carried in a triangular formation with the warhead sections projecting over the roof of the cab. A foldable crane is mounted at the rear of the truck to facilitate reloading of the SA-6 tracked launcher vehicle.

SA-3 'Goa' SAM Resupply Vehicle
Two missiles are carried adjacent to each other on a rail system with the warhead sections projecting over the roof of the cab. The SA-3 launcher is reloaded by backing the vehicle in line with the twin launcher rails, connecting up the resupply rails and then winching the missiles onto the launcher rails.

Multiple Rocket Launcher
A number of ZIL-131 trucks have been fitted with the 140 mm BM-14-16 multiple rocket system normally carried on the rear of a ZIL-151 (6 × 6) truck chassis

ZIL-131 (6 × 6) 3500 kg truck with tanker body (Antonio Moreno)

ZIL-131 (6 × 6) 3500 kg truck with command post body (Michael Jerchel)

(*Jane's Armour and Artillery 1992-93*, pages 713 to 714) and the 122 mm BM-21 multiple rocket system (*ibid* pages 715 to 717).

Specifications
Cab seating: 1 + 2
Configuration: 6 × 6
Weight:
(empty, with winch) 6700 kg
(loaded, cross-country) 10 425 kg
Max load:
(road) 5000 kg
(cross-country) 3500 kg
Towed load:
(road) 6500 kg
(dirt road) 4000 kg
Load area: 3.6 × 2.32 m
Length:
(without winch) 6.9 m
(with winch) 7.04 m

Width: 2.5 m
Height:
(cab) 2.48 m
(tarpaulin) 2.975 m
(load area) 1.43 m
Ground clearance: 0.33 m
Track: 1.82 m
Wheelbase: 3.35 m + 1.25 m
Angle of approach/departure: 36°/40°
Max speed: (road) 80 km/h
Range: 850 km
Fuel capacity: 340 l
Max gradient: 60%
Fording: 1.4 m
Engine: ZIL-131 6 l V-8 water-cooled petrol developing 150 hp at 3200 rpm
Gearbox: manual with 5 forward and 1 reverse gears
Clutch: single dry plate
Transfer box: 2-speed
Steering: screw and nut with hydraulic booster

Turning radius: 10.2 m
Suspension:
(front) longitudinal semi-elliptical springs with double-acting hydraulic shock absorbers
(rear) equaliser arm on longitudinal semi-elliptical springs
Tyres: 12.00 × 20
Brakes:
(main) air
(parking) mechanical
Electrical system: 12 V
Battery: 1 × 6 ST 78

Status
In production. In service with the CIS and other armed forces.

Manufacturer
Likhachev Motor Vehicle Plant, Moscow, Russia.

Ural-375 (6 × 6) 4000 kg Truck

Description
The first model of the Ural-375 entered production in 1961. It had an open cab with a canvas top and a stake-type rear cargo body. The second model was the Ural-375A, which had a number of automotive improvements as well as a fully enclosed all-steel cab. The Ural-375A was standardised as the Ural-375D; those with a winch (capacity of 7000 kg) are designated Ural-375T. The vehicle is fitted with a central tyre-pressure regulation system. The Ural-377 (6 × 4) truck uses many components of the Ural-375 truck.

The layout of the vehicle is conventional with the engine at the front, fully enclosed two-door all-steel cab in the centre and the cargo area at the rear with hinged bench-type seats, removable bows and a tarpaulin cover, and a drop tailgate. Standard equipment includes a cab heater and an engine pre-heater.

In 1973 a Ural-375D was tested with a YaMZ-740 V-8 water-cooled diesel engine, which develops 210 hp and is used in the KamAZ range of 6 × 4 trucks. It is now in production as the Ural-4320 (6 × 6) 4500 kg truck (see following entry).

Variants
Ural-375DK-1: Ural-375 adapted for operations in northern CIS
Ural-375K: Ural-375 adapted for operations in northern CIS
Ural-375L: timber truck
Ural-375N: cargo truck with drop sides
Ural-375S: tractor truck for towing semi-trailers
Ural-375Yu: designed for use in the tropics
ATs 5-375: 5000 litre fuel tank truck
ATsM 4-375: fuel tank truck
TZ 5-375: 5000 litre fuel service truck which also tows a PTs 4-754 trailer with another 4200 litres of fuel. This unit is provided with three 3 m hoses, a 15 m dispensing hose and a 9 m pressure hose
TMS-65: truck-mounted decontamination apparatus used for the rapid decontamination of vehicles and equipment. For details refer to *Jane's NBC Protection Equipment 1992-93* page 89
ATsG-5-375: 5000 litre fuel tanker, equipped with four SRGS-70 3 m and four SRGS-32 3 m metal hoses
ATMZ-4.5-375: fuel lubricant truck (4500 litres), equipped with six dispensing hoses
AC-40: fire engine
Crane truck: the crane model is fitted with an 8 T 210 crane on the rear
Shop/van: the basic chassis is used to mount a wide range of van type bodies for command, communications and other roles
Recovery vehicle: designated the KET-L (see entry in *Recovery vehicles* section)
Multiple Rocket Launcher: the Ural-375D is used to mount the BM-21 (40-round) 122 mm multiple rocket system (*Jane's Armour and Artillery 1992-93*, pages 715 to 717)

TZ 5-375 5000 litre fuel service truck based on Ural-375D (6 × 6) 4000 kg truck (Michael Jerchel)

RMT-35M electrical testing laboratory
Pontoon carrying vehicle
SA-4 'Ganef' transporter-loader (TZM).

Specifications
Cab seating: 1 + 2
Configuration: 6 × 6
Weight:
(empty, with winch) 8400 kg
(loaded, road) 13 300 kg
Max load:
(road) 4500 kg
(cross-country) 4000 kg
Towed load:
(road) 10 000 kg
(dirt road) 5000 kg
Load area: 3.9 × 2.43 m
Length: 7.35 m
Width: 2.69 m
Height:
(cab) 2.68 m
(tarpaulin) 2.98 m
(load area) 1.42 m
Ground clearance: 0.41 m
Track: 2 m
Wheelbase: 3.5 m + 1.4 m
Angle of approach/departure: 44°/40°
Max speed: (road) 75 km/h
Range: 750 km
Fuel capacity: 360 l
Max gradient: 60%

Vertical obstacle: 0.8 m
Fording:
(without preparation) 1 m
(with preparation) 1.5 m
Engine: ZIL-375 7 l V-8 water-cooled petrol developing 180 hp at 3200 rpm
Gearbox: manual with 5 forward and 1 reverse gears
Clutch: twin dry discs
Transfer box: 2-speed
Steering: double-thread worm, hydraulic booster
Turning radius: 10.5 m
Suspension:
(front) longitudinal semi-elliptical springs with hydraulic shock absorbers (all interchangeable with same units on the MAZ-500)
(rear) bogie with longitudinal semi-elliptical springs
Tyres: 14.00 × 20
Brakes:
(main) air/hydraulic
(parking) mechanical
Electrical system: 12 V
Battery: 1 × 6-STEN-140M
Generator: G51

Status
In production. In service with the CIS and other former Warsaw Pact countries. Also used by some Middle East nations.

Manufacturer
Ural Motor Vehicle Plant, Miass, Russia.

Ural-4320 (6 × 6) 4500 kg Truck

Description

The Ural-4320 (6 × 6) 4500 kg truck is a diesel-engined development of the Ural-375D truck produced by the Ural Motor Vehicle Plant, Miass. Development of the Ural-375D with a new diesel engine started in 1972 and the first production examples were produced in 1978.

The diesel engine is the YaMZ-740, produced at the Kama Motor Vehicle Plant, Naberezhnye Chelny. It is a 10.85 litre, eight-cylinder engine developing 210 hp at 2600 rpm. Fitting the new engine enabled the payload to be increased by 500 kg to 4500 kg, and the maximum speed is increased to 85 km/h. Fuel consumption is decreased by 30 per cent and maintenance by 10.8 per cent. Using typical CIS figures the engine produces 16 per cent more power at 19 per cent fewer rpm. To use this extra power the transmission and rear-axle gear ratios were reduced from 8:9 to 7:32 and numerous other small changes were made.

The main outward appearance is that the radiator shell has been lengthened in front to accommodate the longer diesel engine, which is also some 280 kg heavier than the earlier ZIL-375 petrol engine, leading to some revision of the axle loading. The front axle now assumes 4350 kg of the total weight instead of 3865 kg; the rear axle assumes 9075 kg instead of 9335 kg. This revision improves the traction of the Ural-4320 over soft ground.

Other improvements on the Ural-4320 relate to the fuel, cooling, exhaust and electrical systems which were all redesigned. Modifications were made to the frame, clutch, front suspension and other assemblies. Safety alterations include individual brake control links, an auxiliary motor brake and some warning devices. Inside the cab, alterations were made to the instrument layout and to the driver's seat which is now fully adjustable. A more powerful heater was installed and changes were made to the layout of the steering wheel and other controls. The batteries were moved from the driving cab.

There are four main versions of the Ural-4320: the basic model, the Ural-4420 and Ural-44202 tractors, and the Ural-43202 truck. Differences occur in tyre size and the fact that the Ural-4320 and Ural-44202 have tyre pressure regulation systems while the other two do not. In addition, chassis without loading platforms, stretched chassis for box bodies and some other models are produced.

A winch with 65 m of 17.5 mm cable is an option on all versions.

A recovery version has been produced (see entry in the *Recovery vehicles* section).

Ural-4320 (6 × 6) 4500 kg truck (Antonio Moreno)

One variant of the Ural-4320 is known as the MTP-A1.1. This is a special Technical Assistance Vehicle intended to provide field repairs to broken-down vehicles. It is equipped with tools, repair kits, a 700 kg capacity traversable telescopic hoist jib for use when conducting repairs and has limited recovery and towing facilities.

Status

In production. In service with the CIS armed forces.

Manufacturer

Ural Motor Vehicle Plant, Miass, Russia.

Specifications

Model	Ural-4320	Ural-4420	Ural-43202	Ural-44202
Use	truck	tractor	truck	tractor
Cab seating	1 + 2	1 + 2	1 + 2	1 + 2
Configuration	6 × 6	6 × 6	6 × 6	6 × 6
Weight (empty)	8020 kg	7900 kg	7800 kg	7390 kg
Front axle loading (empty)	4020 kg	3830 kg	4040 kg	3950 kg
Rear axle loading (empty)	4000 kg	4070 kg	3760 kg	3440 kg
Payload/semi-trailer capacity				
(on road)	5000 kg	7000 kg	5500 kg	7500 kg
(off road)	—	5000 kg	—	5500 kg
Towed load/semi-trailer weight				
(on road)	7000 kg	11 500 kg	15 000 kg	18 500 kg
(off road)	—	7000 kg	—	12 500 kg
Length	7.366 m	7.611 m	7.1 m	6.836 m
Width	2.5 m	2.5 m	2.5 m	2.475 m
Height	2.87 m	2.6 m	2.68 m	2.6 m
Ground clearance	0.4 m	0.345 m	0.4 m	0.345 m
Track (front)	2 m	2.02 m	2 m	2.02 m
(rear)	2 m	2.02 m	2 m	2.02 m
Wheelbase	3.525 m + 1.4 m	3.525 m + 1.4 m	3.525 m + 1.4 m	3.525 m + 1.4 m
Max speed	85 km/h	80 km/h	72 km/h	72 km/h
Fuel capacity (main tank)	210 l	210 l	300 l	300 l
(auxiliary)	60 l	none	60 l	none
Gradient	58%	50%	28%	28%
Angle of approach/departure	45°/40°	42°/38°	44°/45°	42°/70°
Fording	1.5 m	0.8 m	1.5 m	0.8 m
Engine	KamAZ-740 V-8 10.85 l, 4-stroke diesel developing 210 hp at 2600 rpm			
Gearbox	manual with 5 forward and 1 reverse gears			
Clutch	single dry disc			
Steering	worm with gear quadrant			
Turning circle	22.8 m	22.8 m	22.8 m	22.8 m
Suspension				
(front)	longitudinal semi-elliptical springs with hydraulic shock absorbers			
(rear)	longitudinal semi-elliptical springs with check springs			
Tyres	14.00 × 20	1.110 × 400.533	14.00 × 20	1.110 × 400.533
Brakes	dual circuit air plus auxiliary engine brake			
Electrical system	24 V	24 V	24 V	24 V
Trailer/semi-trailer coupling				
(height)	0.75 m	0.81 m	1.67 m	1.39 m

Ural-377 (6 × 4) 7500 kg Truck

Description
The Ural-377 is a 6 × 4 version of the Ural-375 (6 × 6) truck and entered production in 1965. The layout of the vehicle is conventional with the engine at the front, fully enclosed all-steel two-door cab in the centre and the cargo area at the rear. It has a longer cargo area than the Ural-375D, as the spare wheel is stowed on the right side of the chassis instead of to the rear of the cab

as on the Ural-375D. The rear cargo area has a wooden platform with drop sides and a drop tailgate. Standard equipment includes a cab heater and an engine pre-heater.

Variants
Ural-377D: adapted for use in northern regions with an insulated cab, cold weather tyres, central tyre pressure regulation system and windows with double glass
Ural-377M: the military version of the basic vehicle with a central tyre pressure regulation system not found on

the basic vehicle
Ural-377S: the tractor truck version for towing semi-trailers
Ural-377V: side dump truck version

Status
In production. In service with former Warsaw Pact countries and also exported for military use.

Manufacturer
Ural Motor Vehicle Plant, Miass, Russia.

Specifications

Model	Ural-377	Ural-377M	Ural-377S
Cab seating	1 + 2	1 + 2	1 + 2
Configuration	6 × 4	6 × 4	6 × 4
Weight (empty)	7275 kg	6635 kg	6970 kg
(dirt road)	15 000 kg	14 635 kg	n/app
Weight on front axle (loaded)	4000 kg	n/app	n/app
Weight on rear bogie (loaded)	11 000 kg	n/app	n/app
Towed load (road)	10 500 kg	n/app	19 000 kg
(dirt road)	5600 kg	n/app	n/app
Load area	4.5 × 2.326 m	4.5 × 2.326 m	n/app
Length	7.6 m	7.86 m	6.9 m
Width	2.5 m	2.5 m	2.5 m
Height (cab)	2.62 m	2.535 m	2.62 m
(load area)	1.6 m	1.6 m	n/app
Ground clearance	0.4 m	0.4 m	0.32 m
Track	2 m	2 m	2 m
Wheelbase	3.5 m + 1.4 m	3.5 m + 1.4 m	3.5 m + 1.4 m
Angle of approach/departure	44°/42°	44°/42°	44°/65°
Max speed (road)	75 km/h	70 km/h (est)	65 km/h
Range	550 km	500 km	740 km
Fuel capacity	300 l	300 l	300 l
Fording	0.8 m	0.8 m	0.8 m
Engine	ZIL-375Ya V-8 petrol developing 175 hp at 3000 rpm		
Gearbox	manual with 5 forward and 1 reverse gears		
Clutch	twin dry disc	twin dry disc	twin dry disc
Transfer box	2-speed	2-speed	2-speed
Steering	double-thread worm with hydraulic booster		
Turning radius	10.5 m	10.5 m	10.5 m
Suspension (front)	semi-elliptical springs with hydraulic shock absorbers (interchangeable with MAZ-500)		
(rear)	bogie with semi-elliptical springs		
Tyres	14.00 × 20	14.00 × 20	14.00 × 20
Brakes	air/hydraulic	air/hydraulic	air/hydraulic
Electrical system	12 V	12 V	12 V
Battery	1 × 6-STEN-140M	1 × 6-STEN-140M	1 × 6-STEN-140M
Generator	G130	G130	G130

Ural-377 (6 × 4) 7500 kg truck

Ural-377S (6 × 4) tractor truck (A McKrill)

ZIL-133 (6 × 4) 8000 kg Truck

Description
The ZIL-133 is the 6 × 4 version of the ZIL-130 (4 × 2) truck and also incorporates components of the ZIL-131 (6 × 6) truck. The prototypes had a 220 hp engine but production versions of the truck use a V-8 150 hp engine as used in the ZIL-130. The layout of the vehicle is conventional with the engine at the front, two-door fully enclosed cab in the centre and the cargo area at the rear with drop sides and a drop tailgate.

Variants
ZIL-133G1: long wheelbase truck, production
ZIL-133G: long wheelbase truck, not in production
ZIL-133B: agricultural dump truck, not in production
ZIL-133D: construction dump truck, not in production
ZIL-133V: tractor truck, not in production

ZIL-133G (6 × 4) 8000 kg truck

Status

The ZIL-133G1 is reported to be the only model in production.

Manufacturer

Likhachev Motor Vehicle Plant, Moscow, Russia.

Specifications

Model	ZIL-133	ZIL-133G1	ZIL-133V
Cab seating	1 + 2	1 + 2	1 + 2
Configuration	6 × 4	6 × 4	6 × 4
Weight (empty)	6200 kg	6875 kg	6350 kg
(loaded)	14 200 kg	14 875 kg	n/app
Max load (road)	8000 kg	8000 kg	n/app
Towed load (road)	9500 kg	n/app	19 000 kg
Length	8.07 m	9 m	6.325 m
Width	2.5 m	2.5 m	2.48 m
Height (cab)	2.41 m	2.395 m	2.41 m
Ground clearance	0.275 m	0.25 m	0.275 m
Track (front/rear)	1.8 m/1.79 m	1.835 m/1.85 m	1.8 m/1.79 m
Wheelbase	4.02 m + 1.36 m	4.6 m + 1.4 m	3.42 m + 1.36 m
Max speed (road)	97.5 km/h	80 km/h	86 km/h
Fuel capacity	170 l	170 l	250 l
Vertical obstacle	0.32 m	0.32 m	0.32 m
Engine	ZIL-133 V-8 water-cooled petrol developing 220 hp at 3600 rpm	ZIL-133 V-8 water-cooled petrol developing 150 hp at 3100 rpm	ZIL-133 V-8 water-cooled petrol developing 220 hp at 3600 rpm
Tyres	9.00 × 20	9.00 × 20	9.00 × 20

YaAZ-214 and KrAZ-214 (6 × 6) 7000 kg Trucks

Description

Until the introduction of the ZIL-135 (8 × 8) and the MAZ-535/MAZ-537 (8 × 8) trucks, the KrAZ-214 was the largest all-wheel drive truck in service with the old Soviet Army. The YaAZ-214 was produced at the Yaroslavl Plant from 1956 to 1959, when production was transferred to the Kremenchug Plant and the vehicle was renamed the KrAZ-214. Production continued until 1967 when it was replaced by the much improved KrAZ-255B. Early models were known as the YaAZ-214A and had a 12 V electrical system; later production models are known as the YaAZ-214B. These vehicles are closely related to the KrAZ-219 and YaAZ-210 trucks.

The layout of the vehicle is conventional with the engine at the front, fully enclosed cab in the centre and cargo area at the rear with a hinged tailgate, removable bows and a tarpaulin cover. The vehicle is fitted with a tyre pressure regulation system and standard equipment on all vehicles includes an 8000 kg capacity winch, cab heater and engine pre-heater.

Variants

Crane/shovel (E-305V), BM-25 250 mm (six-barrelled) Multiple Rocket System (*Jane's Armour and Artillery 1987-88*, page 783), timber truck, tractor truck, and for carrying bridging equipment such as the PMP heavy floating pontoon bridge and the TMM treadway bridge. The KrAZ-255B is now carrying out most of these roles.

Specifications

Cab seating: 1 + 2
Configuration: 6 × 6
Weight:
(empty) 12 300 kg
(loaded) 19 300 kg
Max load: (road) 7000 kg
Towed load:
(road) 50 000 kg

KrAZ-214 (6 × 6) 7000 kg truck

(cross-country) 10 000 kg
Load area: 4.565 × 2.5 m
Length: 8.53 m
Width: 2.7 m
Height:
(cab) 2.88 m
(tarpaulin) 3.17 m
(load area) 1.65 m
Ground clearance: 0.36 m
Track: 2.03 m
Wheelbase: 4.6 m + 1.4 m
Angle of approach/departure: 48°/32°
Max speed: 55 km/h
Range: 530 km
Fuel capacity: 450 l
Fuel consumption: 70 l/100 km
Max gradient: 30°
Fording: 1 m
Engine: YaMZ-M206B 6-cylinder water-cooled diesel developing 205 hp at 2000 rpm
Gearbox: manual with 5 forward and 1 reverse gears
Clutch: single dry disc
Transfer box: 2-stage, transfer case with inter-axle differential and drive line to front axle

Steering: worm with lateral quadrant with pneumatic booster
Turning radius: 13 m
Suspension:
(front) longitudinal semi-elliptical springs with hydraulic shock absorbers
(rear) bogie, longitudinal semi-elliptical springs
Tyres: 15.00 × 20
Brakes:
(main) air
(parking) mechanical
Electrical system: 24 V (early vehicles had 12 V system)
Batteries: 4 × 6-STM-128
Generator: 400 W

Status

Production complete. In service with former Warsaw Pact countries.

Manufacturers

Yaroslavl Motor Vehicle Plant, Yaroslavl, and Kremenchug Motor Vehicle Plant, Kremenchug, Ukraine.

KrAZ-255B (6 × 6) 7500 kg Truck

Description

The KrAZ-255B replaced the KrAZ-214 (6 × 6) truck in production from 1967 until 1979. It is very similar to the earlier vehicle but has a more powerful engine and a central tyre pressure regulation system.

The layout of the vehicle is conventional with the engine at the front, a fully enclosed two-door cab in the centre and the cargo area at the rear with a hinged tailgate, removable bows and a tarpaulin cover. Standard equipment on all vehicles includes a cab heater, engine pre-heater, winch with 12 000 kg capacity and suspension locking mechanism.

Variants

There are at least three variants of the KrAZ-255B, including the KrAZ-255L timber truck and the KrAZ-255V tractor truck. The latter weighs 10 600 kg and can tow a semi-trailer weighing 26 000 kg on roads or 18 000 kg across country. Principal dimensions are length 7.685 m, width 2.75 m and height 2.94 m. The fuel service truck is designated the TZ 8-255B and carries 8000 litres of fuel.

Many roles previously undertaken by the KrAZ-214 are now being carried out by the KrAZ-255B including carrying and laying the TMM treadway bridge, carrying and launching the PMP heavy floating pontoon bridge, carrying and launching the BMK-T bridging boat, crane truck, E-305 BV crane shovel, excavator EDV-4421,

ATsM 7-255B 7000 litre fuel tanker towing the PTsM 8925 5800 litre trailer, and USM pile driving set.

Specifications

Cab seating: 1 + 2
Configuration: 6 × 6
Weight:
(empty) 11 950 kg
(loaded, cross-country) 19 450 kg
Max load: 7500 kg
Towed load:
(road) 30 000 kg
(cross-country) 10 000 kg
Load area: 4.56 × 2.5 m
Length: 8.645 m

Width: 2.75 m
Height:
(cab) 2.94 m
(tarpaulin) 3.17 m
(load area) 1.65 m
Ground clearance: 0.36 m
Track: 2.16 m
Wheelbase: 4.6 m + 1.6 m
Angle of approach/departure: 48°/32°
Max speed: 71 km/h
Range: 750 km
Fuel capacity: 450 l
Fuel consumption: 38 l/100 km
Max gradient: 60%
Fording: 0.85 m
Engine: YaMZ-238 14.86 l V-8 water-cooled diesel developing 240 hp at 2100 rpm
Gearbox: manual with 5 forward and 1 reverse gears
Clutch: dual dry disc
Transfer box: 2-speed with differential between axles
Steering: screw and nut with rolling ball, hydraulic booster
Turning radius: 13 m
Suspension:
(front) longitudinal semi-elliptical springs with telescopic double-acting shock absorbers
(rear) equaliser type on 2 longitudinal semi-elliptical springs
Tyres: 15.00 × 20
Brakes:
(main) air
(parking) mechanical
Electrical system: 24 V
Batteries: 2 × 6-TST-165EMS

KrAZ-255B (6 × 6) 7500 kg truck (Michael Jerchel)

Generator: 500 W

Status
Production completed in 1979. In service with the CIS and other former Warsaw Pact countries.

Manufacturer
Kremenchug Motor Vehicle Plant, Kremenchug, Ukraine.

KrAZ-206V (6 × 6) Tractor Truck

Description
This 6 × 6 tractor truck is produced at the Kremenchug Motor Vehicle Plant. It is used to tow the MAZ-938 semi-trailer which weighs 7500 kg unloaded or 22 500 kg loaded. Alternatively it can tow the ChMZAP-93861 semi-trailer.

The KrAZ-206V is the replacement for the KrAZ-255V (6 × 6) tractor truck which itself is a member of the KrAZ-255B (6 × 6) family of 7500 kg trucks.

The layout of the KrAZ-206V is similar to that of the earlier vehicle with the engine at the front, two-door fully enclosed cab in the centre and the fifth wheel at the rear. Maximum weight on the fifth wheel is 9500 kg and maximum towed load is 27 500 kg on paved roads and 23 000 kg on dirt roads. The major automotive difference is the installation of a turbocharged version of the YaMZ-238 engine designated the YaMZ-238L which develops 300 hp compared to the 240 hp of the KrAZ-255V. The engine provides power to all six road wheels via an eight-speed gearbox and two-speed transfer case. The lockable inter-wheel differential on the second and third axles is pneumatically operated.

Specifications
Configuration: 6 × 6
Weight: 10 900 kg
Length: 8.22 m

Width: 2.72 m
Height: 3.23 m
Ground clearance: 0.37 m
Track: 2.16 m
Wheelbase: 4.6 m + 1.4 m
Engine: YaMZ-238L turbocharged V-8 water-cooled diesel developing 300 hp at 2100 rpm

Status
In production. In service with the CIS.

Manufacturer
Kremenchug Motor Vehicle Plant, Kremenchug, Ukraine.

KamAZ-5320 (6 × 4) 8000 kg Truck

Description
This is the basic member of a complete family of trucks available in both 6 × 4 and 6 × 6 configurations. Originally intended for commercial use they are now widely used by the CIS armed forces for long haul logistics. All are powered by a V-type water-cooled diesel engine with the same bore and stroke (120 × 120 mm). Brief specifications of the various engines are:

Model	YaMZ-7401	YaMZ-740*	YaMZ-741
Type	V-8	V-8	V-10
Capacity	10.85 l	10.85 l	13.58 l
Output	180 hp	210 hp	260 hp

* The YaMZ-740 engine is also used in the Ural-4320, described earlier in this section.

It has been reported that the KamAZ-5510 dump truck is available fitted with a German KHD 413 four-stroke air-cooled eight-cylinder diesel developing 256 hp at 2650 rpm, but it is probably for export only.

The basic cargo model is the KamAZ-5320 (6 × 4) that has a fully enclosed all-steel forward control cab that can be tilted forward for maintenance purposes. The rear cargo area has drop sides, removable bows and a tarpaulin cover. Standard features include an air filter working from the exhaust gases, air intake above the cab roof on the left side, centrifugal oil cleaner, chemical- and heat-treated crankshaft, hydraulic power steering, pneumatic clutch control, pneumatic preselector (a two-stage gearbox fitted between the clutch and the conventional gearbox), heater, driver's seat with suspension, and a heat and sound-proofed cab. In

Specifications

Model	KamAZ-5320	KamAZ-53202	KamAZ-5410	KamAZ-54102	KamAZ-4310
Type	cargo truck	cargo truck	tractor truck	tractor truck	cargo truck
Configuration	6 × 4	6 × 4	6 × 4	6 × 4	6 × 6
Weight (empty)	7080 kg	7240 kg	6445 kg	n/a	8715 kg
Max load	8000 kg	8000 kg	n/a	n/a	6000 kg*
Max towed load	11 500 kg	11 500 kg	19 000 kg	n/a	7000 kg*
Length	7.435 m	8.295 m	6.14 m	6.43 m	7.65 m
Width	2.506 m	2.496 m	2.48 m	n/a	2.5 m
Height (cab)	2.83 m	2.63 m	2.63 m	2.63 m	3.09 m
Ground clearance	0.28 m	0.285 m	0.285 m	n/a	0.365 m
Track (front)	2.026 m	2 m	2.01 m	n/a	2.01 m
(rear)	1.856 m	1.85 m	1.85 m	n/a	2.01 m
Wheelbase	3.19 m + 1.32 m	3.69 m + 1.32 m	2.84 m + 1.32 m	3.14 m + 1.32 m**	3.34 m + 1.32 m***
Max speed (road)	85 km/h	85 km/h	85 km/h	85 km/h	85 km/h
Engine	YaMZ-740	YaMZ-740	YaMZ-740	YaMZ-741	YaMZ-740

* cross-country
** also quoted as 3.04 m + 1.32 m
*** also quoted as 3.39 m + 1.32 m

long distance versions a bunk is provided.

For travelling on rough or dirt roads the 5320 and 5410 have their rear axles rated at 5500 kg each. Models travelling on improved roads, such as the 53212 and 54112 have axle ratings of up to 10 000 kg. The KamAZ-5320 is powered by a YaMZ-740 V-8 diesel engine that develops 210 hp. This engine is also installed in the latest version of the Ural-375 (6 × 6) truck and the Ural-4320 (4 × 4) 4500 kg truck.

Variants include the KamAZ-5511 (6 × 4) rear tipper truck. This has a wheelbase of 2.84 m + 1.32 m, a length of 7.125 m, width of 2.5 m and height of 2.708 m. Front track is 2.01 m and rear 1.85 m.

The KamAZ-4310 is a 6 × 6 version with a cross-country payload of 6000 kg and a towed load of 7000 kg. It is fitted with a central tyre pressure regulation system.

Variants

(6 × 4)
KamAZ-53201: chassis based on KamAZ-5320, 180 hp engine
KamAZ-53202: long wheelbase cargo truck
KamAZ-53203: chassis based on KamAZ-53202, 180 hp engine
KamAZ-5410: tractor truck
KamAZ-5411: rear tipper truck
KamAZ-54101: tractor truck for dump semi-trailers
KamAZ-54102: tractor truck for heavier loads, 260 hp engine
KamAZ-5510: dump truck, 180 hp engine
KamAZ-5511: rear tipper truck
KamAZ-55102: agricultural dump truck with trailer

(6 × 6)
KamAZ-4310: cargo truck with fixed sideboards
KamAZ-43101: cargo truck with drop sides

KamAZ-5320 (6 × 4) 8000 kg truck (Michael Jerchel)

KamAZ-43102: same as KamAZ-43101, bunk in cab
KamAZ-43103: same as KamAZ-4310 with bunk in cab
KamAZ-43105: empty weight 8200 kg, load capacity 7000 kg
AA-40 (43105)-189: airfield fire tender based on KamAZ-43105
KamAZ-4410 tractor truck

Status
In production.

Manufacturer
Kama Motor Vehicle Plant, Naberezhnye Chelny, CIS.

KrAZ-260 (6 × 6) 9000 kg Truck

Description
The KrAZ-260 (6 × 6) 9000 kg truck replaced the earlier KrAZ-255B and has been in production since 1979. It was first seen in public in 1985 towing the 2A36 152 mm nuclear-capable gun. That version had an open body with forward-facing bench seats for the gun crew, although it is possible that this was purely a 'parade' arrangement. The normal cargo body of the KrAZ-260 has a hinged tailgate with the cargo area covered by tilt-over removable bows. The KrAZ-260 has an increased payload (9000 kg as opposed to 7500 kg) compared to the KrAZ-255B and uses the YaMZ-238L V-8 turbocharged diesel engine. The gearbox has eight forward speeds and one reverse, and the two-speed transfer box has a lockable differential.

The KrAZ-260 is fitted with a 120 kN capacity winch provided with 53 m of 22 mm cable.

A 6 × 6 tractor truck version with a fifth wheel for towing semi-trailers is known as the KrAZ-260V. It has replaced the earlier KrAZ-255V1 and KrAZ-258B1 tractors in production.

The KrAZ-240 is a 6 × 4 variant of the KrAZ-260 (6 × 6) with an on-road load capacity of 16 800 kg. Wheelbase is 4.88 m + 1.4 m.

Specifications
Cab seating: 1 + 2
Configuration: 6 × 6
Weight:
 (empty) 12 775 kg
 (loaded) 22 000 kg
Max load: 9000 kg
Towed load:
 (empty) 30 000 kg
 (loaded) 10 000 kg
Length: 10.13 m
Width: 2.722 m
Height: (top of cab) 2.985 m
Ground clearance: 0.37 m
Track: 2.16 m

Wheelbase: 4.6 m + 1.4 m
Angle of approach/departure: 40°/35°
Max speed: 80 km/h
Fuel capacity: 2 × 165 l
Max gradient: 58%
Fording: 1.2 m
Engine: YaMZ-238L 14.86 l V-8 water-cooled turbo-charged diesel developing 288 hp at 2100 rpm
Gearbox: manual with 8 forward and 1 reverse gears
Clutch: single dry plate
Transfer box: 2-speed
Turning radius: 13.5 m
Tyres: 1.300 × 530-533

Status
In production. In service with the CIS armed forces and possibly some other former Warsaw Pact armed forces.

Manufacturer
Kremenchug Motor Vehicle Plant, Kremenchug, Ukraine.

KrAZ-260 (6 × 6) 9000 kg truck

KrAZ-260V (6 × 6) tractor truck

Ural-5323 (8 × 8) 9000 kg Truck

Description

The Ural-5323 (8 × 8) 9000 kg truck is a high mobility vehicle produced using numerous components and systems taken from other Ural and KamAZ trucks. The vehicle can be used for transporting supplies or personnel and may be used as the basis for mounting weapons or various combat systems.

The Ural-5323 weighs 10 550 kg empty and can carry 9000 kg of payload. It has a forward control all-metal cab placed directly over the engine to provide the maximum cargo-carrying area length and to spread the load weight more evenly over the axles. The cab can be tilted forward for engine and transmission access and has seating for the driver and one passenger.

The metal cargo platform is an open, low-sided area with hinged side benches that can be removed. The front and side boards are corrugated for extra strength and a tarpaulin can be erected over bows.

The standard engine is a KamAZ-7403 10.85 litre V-8 water-cooled turbocharged diesel developing 260 hp although an air-cooled Ural-745 diesel

developing 290 hp may be used. A third engine option is the Ural-746 air-cooled diesel developing 320 hp. To simplify starting at low temperatures the engine is equipped with a PZhD-30A pre-heater and an electric glow plug.

The transmission is operated via a dual dry plate KamAZ-142 clutch with mechanical linkage provided with pneumatic assist. The gearbox is a three-range, five-speed KamAZ-141 unit. The two-speed transfer case has a cylindrical power splitter that symmetrically supplies power to the differentials. Differential and shifting speed locks are remotely controlled using pneumatics on the transfer case. The main transmission supplies power to the axles via a two-stage reduction mechanism with a pair of cylindrical helical gears matched to a pair of spiral gears.

The forward and rear axle suspensions are mounted on rockers units. Each pair of axles has two longitudinal semi-elliptic leaf springs with the front (steering) axles provided with four hydraulic shock absorbers.

The service brakes are of the drum type with a twin-chamber hydro-pneumatic assist mechanism. One of the chambers acts as a reserve mechanism while the parking brake is mounted on the transfer case and

operates on the output shafts. Power steering is provided.

The vehicle is equipped with a central tyre pressure regulation system. To enable the vehicle to drive over various types of terrain the truck is provided with OI-25 14.00 × 20 tyres having a directional tread pattern.

The vehicle uses a 24 V electrical system with two 6ST-190TR or 6ST-190TRN batteries and a 1 kW generator. For operations in extremely cold conditions the batteries can be provided with an automatic heating system.

A standard component is a mechanical drum winch with a 7000 kg capacity and 60 m of cable. Power for the winch is taken from an auxiliary power take-off mounted on the transfer case.

Status

In production.

Manufacturer

Ural Motor Vehicle Plant, Miass, Russia (not confirmed).

KrAZ-257 (6 × 4) 12 000 kg Truck

Description

The KrAZ-257 (6 × 4) truck replaced the KrAZ-219 in production at Kremenchug in 1965-66. In appearance it is almost identical to the earlier vehicle but has many detailed changes as well as a more powerful V-8 engine.

The layout of the vehicle is conventional with the engine at the front, fully enclosed two-door cab in the centre and the cargo area at the rear with a wooden platform with drop sides and a drop tailgate. Standard equipment includes a cab heater and an engine pre-heater.

Variants

KrAZ-254: dump truck, developed to prototype stage but not placed in production
KrAZ-256: hopper-type dump truck
KrAZ-256B: strengthened hopper dump truck
KrAZ-256BS: strengthened hopper-type dump truck for use in cold climates
KrAZ-258: tractor truck for towing semi-trailers
Various crane trucks.

Specifications

Cab seating: 1 + 2
Configuration: 6 × 4
Weight:
  (empty) 11 130 kg
  (loaded) 23 385 kg
Max load: (road) 12 000 kg
Towed load: (road) 16 600 kg
Load area: 5.77 × 2.48 m
Length: 9.66 m
Width: 2.65 m
Height:
  (cab) 2.62 m
  (load area) 1.52 m
Ground clearance: 0.29 m
Track: (front/rear) 1.95 m/1.92 m
Wheelbase: 5.05 m + 1.4 m

KrAZ-258 (6 × 4) tractor truck towing van semi-trailer

Angle of approach/departure: 42°/18°
Max speed: (road) 60 km/h
Range: 1000 km
Fuel capacity: 450 l
Max gradient: (loaded) 18°
Engine: YaMZ-238 V-8 water-cooled diesel developing 240 hp at 2100 rpm
Gearbox: manual with 5 forward and 1 reverse gears
Clutch: twin dry disc
Transfer box: 2-speed
Steering: worm with lateral gear quadrant, pneumatic booster
Suspension:
  (front) longitudinal semi-elliptical springs with hydraulic shock absorbers
  (rear) equalising, on longitudinal semi-elliptical

springs
Tyres: 12.00 × 20
Brakes:
  (main) air
  (parking) mechanical
Electrical system: 24 V
Batteries: 2 × 6-STM-128 or 6-TST-165 EMS
Generator: G270 (500 W)

Status

In production. In service with former Warsaw Pact countries and Nicaragua.

Manufacturer

Kremenchug Motor Vehicle Plant, Kremenchug, Ukraine.

ZIL-135 Series (8 × 8) Trucks

Description

The ZIL-135 series of 8 × 8 trucks was introduced during the 1960s. The original design and development was carried out at the Likhachev Motor Vehicle Plant near Moscow, but production was carried out at the Bryansk Automobile Works for which reason the range is sometimes known as the BAZ-135L4 (the cargo truck version is also known as the ZIL-135L4). These trucks are widely used by members of the former Warsaw Pact for both military and civil applications.

The vehicle is powered by two petrol engines, each

of which drives the four wheels on one side of the vehicle. Steering is by the front and rear wheels only and these wheels are carried on axles with a torsion bar suspension. The two central axles are fixed and a central tyre pressure regulation system is fitted. The fully enclosed forward control cab has two doors, one on each side. When being used for missile launching roles the windscreen is fitted with covers to protect it from blast when the missile is launched.

Variants

FROG-7 Transporter/Launcher Vehicle
This carries and launches the FROG-7 (Luna M R-75) surface-to-surface tactical missile system. Mounted on

the right side of the vehicle is a hydraulic crane for reloading purposes. Stabiliser jacks are lowered to the ground before the missile is launched to provide a more stable firing platform.

FROG-7 Resupply Vehicle
This carries three FROG-7 missiles.

Sepal Transporter/Launcher Vehicle
This has a large cylindrical container which acts as the launcher for the Sepal cruise missile. This version has a different cab from the other members of this series and two stabiliser jacks are lowered to the ground either side before the missile is launched.

BM-22 Multiple Rocket System
The ZIL-135 series chassis is also used for the BM-22 220 mm Uragan 16-round multiple rocket launcher and its associated resupply vehicle or transloader. For details see *Jane's Armour and Artillery 1992-93*, page 712.

ZIL-135 Convoy Escort Vehicle
Reports from Afghanistan mentioned the use of an improvised convoy escort vehicle formed by mounting a ZU-23 twin 23 mm cannon on the rear of a ZIL-135 truck. Some form of armour was provided for the gun crew.

BAZ-135L4 Cargo Truck
This is produced at the Bryansk Plant and is used for carrying cargo. The rear cargo area is provided with a drop tailgate. Also referred to as ZIL-135L4.

ZIL-135 Tractor Truck
As far as is known, this is only used for civilian roles, primarily for carrying long lengths of pipe used in constructing pipelines.

ZIL-E-167
This is an experimental 6 × 6 vehicle based on the chassis of the ZIL-135, designed specifically for operations in the desert and snow. Basic specifications are: unladen weight 7000 kg, payload 5000 kg, length 9.268 m, width 3.13 m, height 3.06 m and maximum

road speed 65 km/h. It has the same engines as the ZIL-135.

SAKR-80 Artillery Rocket System
The ZIL-135 series is used as the basis for the Egyptian 325 mm SAKR-80 artillery rocket system. For details refer to *Jane's Armour and Artillery 1992-93* pages 718 to 719.

Specifications (BAZ-135L4 cargo truck)
Cab seating: 1 + 2
Configuration: 8 × 8
Weight:
  (loaded) 19 000 kg
  (empty) 9000 kg
Max load: 10 000 kg
Towed load:
  (road) 20 000 kg
  (cross-country) 18 000 kg
Load area: (estimated) 4.57 × 2.65 m
Length: 9.27 m
Width: 2.8 m
Height: 2.53 m
Ground clearance: (axles) 0.58 m
Track: 2.3 m
Wheelbase: 2.415 m + 1.5 m + 2.415 m
Max speed: 70 km/h
Range: 500 km
Fuel capacity: 768 l
Fuel consumption: 160 l/100 km

Max gradient: 57%
Vertical obstacle: 0.685 m
Trench: 2.63 m
Fording: 0.58 m
Engines: 2 × ZIL-375 7 l V-8 water-cooled petrol developing 180 hp (each) at 3200 rpm
Gearbox: hydro-mechanical
Steering: power-assisted, 1st and 4th axles
Turning radius: 12.5 m
Suspension: 1st and 4th axles have torsion bars, 2nd and 3rd axles are fixed to chassis and have no suspension
Tyres: 16.00 × 20
Brakes:
  (main) hydraulic, air-assisted
Electrical system: 24 V

Status
In service with Algeria (FROG-7), Bulgaria (FROG-7), CIS, Cuba (FROG-7), Czechoslovakia, Egypt (FROG-7 and SAKR-80), Germany (FROG-7), Hungary (FROG-7), Iraq (FROG-7), North Korea (FROG-7), Kuwait (FROG-7), Libya (FROG-7), Poland (FROG-7), Romania (FROG-7), Syria (FROG-7), Yemen (FROG-7) and the former Yugoslavia.

Manufacturer
Bryansk Motor Vehicle Plant, Bryansk, Russia.

ZIL-135 (8 × 8) truck configured as transloader vehicle for BM-22 220 mm multiple rocket system

FROG-7 transporter/loader vehicle based on ZIL-135 (8 × 8) truck chassis

MAZ-543 (8 × 8) Truck

Description
The MAZ-543 (8 × 8) truck uses many automotive components of the MAZ-537 (8 × 8) truck including the same engine. It was seen in public for the first time in November 1965. The engine is mounted at the front of the vehicle with a two-man cab on each side which hinge forward to allow access to the engine. Standard equipment includes a heater, engine pre-heater, central tyre pressure regulation system and power steering on the front four wheels.

Variants
The MAZ-543 is used to carry and launch the 'Scud A' (SS-1b), 'Scud B' (SS-1c) and 'Scaleboard' (SS-12) surface-to-surface missiles. The Scud launchers are known as the MAZ-543LTM or MAZ-7310LTM Uragan (Hurricane), or Kashalot (Sperm Whale); the vehicle is 12 m long and with the missile it weighs 29 000 kg. A version with single forward cab is used to carry the SSC-3 coastal defence missile system. Other missile-related variants include the fire control vehicle and trailer-erector-launcher units for the SA-10 'Grumble' SAM system. The 300 mm Smerch 12-round multiple rocket system is based on the MAZ-543 and there is also an associated reload vehicle.

Other variants include an aircraft crash tender, tractor truck and a cargo truck with a drop tailgate and stake-type sides.

A trials vehicle fitted with a gas turbine developing the equivalent of 1100 hp has been produced.

MAZ-543 (8 × 8) chassis as used to carry and launch 'Scud B' surface-to-surface missile

Specifications
Cab seating: 1 + 3
Configuration: 8 × 8
Weight: (chassis only) 17 300 kg
Max load: 15 170 kg
Length: 11.7 m
Width: 2.98 m
Height: 2.925 m
Ground clearance: 0.45 m
Track: (front and rear) 2.375 m
Wheelbase: 2.2 m + 3.3 m + 2.2 m
Max speed: 60 km/h
Range: 1525 km
Max gradient: 57%
Vertical obstacle: 0.78 m

Trench: 3.38 m
Fording: 1 m
Engine: D12A-525 38.88 l V-12 water-cooled diesel developing 525 hp at 2100 rpm
Tyres: 15.00 × 25
Electrical system: 24 V
Batteries: 4 × 6 V

Status
In production. In service with former Warsaw Pact countries, Iraq and the former Yugoslavia.

Manufacturer
Minsk Motor Vehicle Plant, Minsk, Belarus.

BAZ-5937 and BAZ-5939 (6 × 6) Special Purpose Vehicles

Description

The BAZ-5937 and BAZ-5939 are basically similar 6 × 6 special purpose vehicles that are amphibious and highly mobile. The vehicles have many uses and are employed as the carriers for components of the SA-8a and SA-8b 'Gecko' surface-to-air missile systems and the SS-21 'Scarab' surface-to-surface missile system. The BAZ-5937 is used for the SA-8a and SA-8b 'Gecko' transporter/erector/launcher and radar systems and for the SA-8 transport and reloading vehicle; the BAZ-5939 is used as the basis for the SS-21 'Scarab' launcher and reloading vehicles. The BAZ-5937 has its engine located just in front of the rear wheels while the SS-21 versions of the BAZ-5939 have the engine located between the first and second set of wheels. Many components are interchangeable between the two vehicles.

Being essentially similar, the two vehicles are often referred to as the BAZ-5937/39. Both use a long boat-shaped hull with the driver/operators' cab set forward in front of the load-bearing area. The cab has room for three occupants with one occupant seated in a semi-prone position behind the driver. The cab is equipped with an NBC protection system with the air filtration unit inside the cab over the left front wheel. A diesel heater is provided, with the heater blower coupled to the air filtration system.

The load area is constructed from welded steel plating with supports for strength and stabilisation. A door is used for access to the engine and generator area. Both vehicles use a type 5020B six-cylinder, four-stroke, water-cooled diesel engine rated at 290 hp.

The air intake system uses a two-stage filter; the air can be heated in winter. The primary starter system uses air pressure with a backup electrical starter. Fuel is carried in a 320 litre tank mounted in front of the left rear wheel.

The five-speed automatic transmission can be operated manually during amphibious operations. There is a two-stage hydraulic system. Final drive is transmitted to all six road wheels independently. For lubrication there is a dry sump oil injection system with pumps, a centrifugal filter and a cooling system. The engine cooling system is similar to that used on the BMP ICV, using injection cooling. The pump involved is combined with the oil pump. A diesel pre-warmer for the engine is provided by routeing the exhaust pipe through the oil and hydraulic fluid reservoirs.

Both vehicles are provided with power steering and brakes. The brakes are a two-part system with the first part controlling the right front, left middle and right rear wheels; the second part controls the left front, right middle and left rear wheels. A two drum emergency brake system is provided.

A 24 V electrical system is provided and the lighting system is similar to that used on the Ural-4320 (6 × 6) 4500 kg truck. The BAZ-5937 carries a 50 kW generator driven by a gas turbine along with a backup 35 kW generator powered by the transmission. Both generators can be used to provide power for the various weapon systems carried. An R-123 radio and an R-124 intercom are carried.

For amphibious operations the BAZ-5937/39 is powered by two water jets located in the rear. Maximum speed in water is 8 km/h. In the water, steering is effected by a rudder and the cab is protected by a raised baffle plate; the driver and co-driver use special vision devices.

Specifications (provisional)

Cab seating: 1 + 2
Configuration: 6 × 6
Weight: (basic configuration) 10 650 kg
Length: 9.16 m
Width: 2.78 m
Height: 1.95 m
Ground clearance: 0.43 m
Max speed:
 (land) 70 km/h
 (water) 8 km/h
Fuel capacity: 320 l
Fuel consumption: 40 l/100 km
Gradient: 60%
Engine: 5D20B V-6 four-stroke diesel developing 295 hp
Gearbox: 5 forward and 1 reverse gears
Clutch: hydraulically operated double disc dry
Suspension: independent torsion bar with vibration damping
Turning radius: 7 m
Electrical system: 24 V

Status

In production. BAZ-5937 (SA-8) in service with Algeria, Angola, CIS, Czechoslovakia, Guinea-Bissau, Hungary, India, Iraq, Jordan, Kuwait, Libya, Poland, Syria and the former Yugoslavia.

BAZ-5939 (SA-21) in service with the CIS, Czechoslovakia, and Syria.

Manufacturer

Likhachev Motor Vehicle Plant, Moscow, Russia.

Czech Army BAZ-5939 special purpose vehicle

BAZ-5937 special purpose vehicle configured as SA-8b 'Gecko' SAM transporter/erector/launcher

CZECHOSLOVAKIA

Praga V3S (6 × 6) 3000 kg Truck

Description

The V3S was developed in the early 1950s. Initial production was undertaken by Praga but in 1964 it was transferred to Avia as Praga began to concentrate on automotive components. It has been replaced in many Czechoslovak units by the CIS ZIL-131 (6 × 6) 3500 kg truck.

The layout of the Praga V3S is conventional with the engine at the front, cab in the centre and cargo area at the rear. The two-door cab is of all-steel construction. There is a circular observation hatch in the right side of the roof. The windscreen is of the split type and both parts can be opened horizontally for increased vision. The rear cargo area has a tarpaulin cover and removable bows which can be stowed to the rear of the cab when not required. Some V3S trucks have a winch with a 3500 kg capacity.

Variants include a crane truck, hopper type dump truck (V3S-K), shop/van (including some with an

A-frame mounted at the front of the vehicle), tanker (special), 3000 litre capacity tanker (V3S-C) and tractor truck (V3S-A). The chassis is also used to mount the 130 mm (32-round) M51 multiple rocket system (*Jane's Armour and Artillery 1992-93*, page 717) and was used as a basis for the M53/59 twin 30 mm self-propelled anti-aircraft gun system.

A 4 × 2 model of the Praga V3S was built under the designation S5T.

Specifications

Cab seating: 1 + 1
Configuration: 6 × 6
Weight:
 (empty) 5350 kg
 (loaded, road) 10 650 kg
 (loaded, dirt road) 8650 kg
 (loaded, cross-country) 8350 kg
Max load:
 (road) 5300 kg
 (dirt road) 3300 kg
 (cross-country) 3000 kg

Towed load:
 (road) 5500 kg
 (cross-country) 3100 kg
Length: 6.91 m
Width: 2.31 m
Height:
 (cab) 2.51 m
 (tarpaulin) 2.92 m
Ground clearance: 0.4 m
Track:
 (front) 1.87 m
 (rear) 1.755 m
Wheelbase: 3.58 m + 1.12 m
Angle of approach/departure: 72°/32°
Max speed: 62 km/h
Range: 500 km
Fuel capacity: 120 l
Fuel consumption: 27 l/100 km
Max gradient: 60%
Fording: 0.8 m
Engine: T-912 in-line air-cooled diesel developing 98 hp at 2100 rpm (late production vehicles have

Praga V3S (6 × 6) 3000 kg truck with command post box body

Praga V3S (6 × 6) 3000 kg truck towing 122 mm D-30 howitzer

T-912-2 developing 110 hp at 2200 rpm, which is also installed in the Praga S5T2 truck)
Gearbox: manual with 4 forward and 2 reverse gears
Clutch: single dry plate
Transfer box: 2-speed
Turning radius: 10.5 m
Suspension: (front and rear) semi-elliptical springs
Tyres: 8.25 × 20

Brakes:
(main) hydraulic, air-assisted
(parking) mechanical
Electrical system: 12 V

Status
Production complete. In service with the former Warsaw Pact countries as well as some countries in

the Middle East.

Manufacturer
Avia Závody NP, Letnany, Czechoslovakia.

BAZ SNA (6 × 6) 4000 kg Truck

Development/Description
In 1984 Bratislavské Automobilové Závody (BAZ) commenced design work on the replacement for the Praga V3S (6 × 6) 3000 kg truck. By late 1984 two prototypes were completed under the designation BAZ SNA. In May 1985 the third and slightly modified prototype was completed and all three then commenced a series of trials. Production commenced during 1987 with 6000 vehicles a year being produced for internal use only – no export was contemplated.

The overall layout of the BAZ SNA is similar to that of the original V3S but it has a new two-door cab with improved vision for the driver. The rear part of the cab can be tilted forward to allow access to the engine and transmission. There is a rectangular observation hatch on the right-hand side of the cab roof. The SNA is powered by a ZTS Martin-produced six-cylinder diesel engine coupled to a 10-speed gearbox produced by CKD-Praga and a clutch supplied by TAZ Trnava.

The prototypes used a rear cargo body with drop sides and a drop tailgate although it is envisaged that a wide range of bodies will be developed for specific military and civil applications. On the prototypes the

rear four wheels were fitted with single tyres. A spare wheel and tyre is carried to the rear of the cab.

The payload of the BAZ SNA is 4000 kg cross-country and 8000 kg on roads.

Status
In production for internal use only.

Manufacturer
Bratislavské Automobilové Závody, Bratislava, Czechoslovakia.
Tel: 991 91. Telex: 211 184.
Fax: 93 274.

First prototype BAZ SNA (6 × 6) 4000 kg truck with cab tilted forward for engine and transmission access

Third prototype BAZ SNA (6 × 6) 4000 kg truck

Tatra 813 (6 × 6 and 8 × 8) Trucks

Description
The Tatra 813 series of trucks, which is also known as the Kolos series, was developed in Czechoslovakia in the early 1960s with the first 8 × 8 production vehicles being completed in 1968. The vehicle is related to the OT-64 (8 × 8) amphibious armoured personnel carrier.

The standard cargo truck version has an all-steel forward control type cab which usually has one or two circular observation hatches in the roof. The cab is pressurised and is provided with an effective ventilation system and individual masks for each member of the crew. The engine is in the centre of the cab at the front, with the transmission to the rear of the cab, under the

cargo area. The rear cargo area has all-steel drop sides and a drop tailgate, removable seats, and can be equipped with bows and a tarpaulin cover if required. All military versions are fitted with a central tyre pressure regulation system and a 22 000 kg capacity winch. The vehicle is sometimes fitted with the BZ-T hydraulically operated dozer blade at the front; a snow plough can also be fitted.

The Tatra 813 (8 × 8) is widely used by Czechoslovakia (and by the former East Germany) as a cargo/personnel carrier, for towing heavy artillery up to 152 mm in calibre, and for towing trailers carrying engineer equipment and MBTs.

A more recent model is the Tatra 813-12, which is powered by a 310 hp multi-fuel engine.

Variants
The basic chassis (8 × 8) is used for a variety of roles including carrying and launching PMP heavy floating pontoon bridge units (these vehicles are often fitted with the BZ-T hydraulically operated dozer blade) for carrying and laying the truck-mounted AM-50 scissors bridge, described in the *Mechanised bridges* section. There is also a special roadway-laying version which is used with the PMP system, details of which will be found in the *Portable roadways* section.

The Tatra 813 (road prime mover) is the basic truck with the rear cargo area replaced with ballast. There is also a 6 × 6 cargo truck version with a multi-fuel engine, designated the Tatra 813-8.

The Tatra 813 (8 × 8) chassis is also used as the

Tatra 813 (8 × 8) truck

basis for the RM-70 122 mm (40-round) multiple rocket system with a fully armoured cab with 40 rockets in the ready-to-launch position and another 40 rockets ready to reload the launcher. Details of this model are given in *Jane's Armour and Artillery 1992-93*, pages 717 and 718. These are often fitted with the BZ-T hydraulically operated dozer blade for clearing obstacles and preparing fire positions.

There are two prime movers for civil use, the Tatra 4-813 T-3 (6 × 6) and the Tatra 4-813 T-2 (4 × 4), which can tow a trailer weighing up to 65 000 kg.

These do not have the central tyre pressure regulation system as fitted to the military versions. There are at least three dump truck models in service, the Tatra 813 S1 (6 × 6), Tatra 813 S3 (6 × 6) and the Tatra 813 S1 (8 × 8), which also do not have the central tyre pressure regulation system. Crane versions are also in service for both civil and military use.

Specifications
Cab seating: 1 + 6
Configuration: 8 × 8

Weight:
  (empty) 14 100 kg
  (loaded) 22 000 kg
Max load: 7900 kg
Towed load: (road) 100 000 kg
Length: 8.75 m
Width: 2.5 m
Height:
  (cab) 2.69 m
  (tarpaulin) 3.34 m
Ground clearance: 0.4 m
Track: (front/rear) 2.03 m/2.03 m
Wheelbase: 1.65 m + 2.2 m + 1.45 m
Max speed: (road) 80 km/h
Range: (road) 1000 km
Fuel capacity: 520 l
Max gradient: 100%
Trench: 1.6 m
Vertical obstacle: 0.6 m
Fording: 1.4 m
Engine: Tatra T-930-3 12-cylinder air-cooled diesel developing 250 hp at 2000 rpm
Gearbox: dual range 5-speed plus overdrive providing a total of 20 forward and reverse gears
Steering: power-assisted
Tyres: 15.00 × 21
Brakes:
  (main) air
  (parking) mechanical
Electrical system: 24 V

Status
Production complete. In service with Czechoslovak, Indian and the former East German forces.

Manufacturer
Tatra, Národni Podnik, 742 21 Koprivnice, Czechoslovakia.

Tatra T 815 VVN 20 235 6 × 6.1R 8000 kg Truck

Tatra T 815 VT 26 265 8 × 8.1R 10 000 kg Truck

Tatra T 815 VVN 26 265 8 × 8.1R 12 000 kg Truck

Description
The Tatra T 815 series of trucks replaced the earlier Tatra 813 series in production in Czechoslovakia and for a while the name of Kolos was applied to both. The Tatra T 815 series is produced for both military and civil use in a variety of forms including dump trucks, platform trucks, semi-trailer and ballast tractors and

special versions outlined under Variants.

The Tatra T 815 series follows the same general lines as the earlier Tatra 813 but there are many overall improvements. The Tatra T 815 VVN 20 235 6 × 6.1R and T 815 VVN 26 265 8 × 8.1R are described as off-road trucks and have two-door cabs. The Tatra 815 VT 26 265 8 × 8.1R is described as a special heavy road tractor and has a four-door cab and a correspondingly smaller load area. Both types of cab are all-metal, have a roof hatch, and can be tilted forward for maintenance purposes. The two-door cab has seating for a driver and three passengers with provision for an occasional berth. The four-door cab has seating for the driver and five passengers with provision for an occasional berth slung above the front seats. Both types of cab have a multi-fuel heater. They are also equipped with a collective NBC protection system that connects to individual masks, in addition to an air filtering and ventilation system.

On all models the chassis uses a frameless construction with the load-bearing area consisting of the individual main assembly unit cases interconnected by load-bearing tubes. Mounted on the crossmembers is a through-frame to which the cab, engine and clutch, steering box, winch, truck platform and front and rear bumpers (together with the trailer coupling) are all fitted. The load-carrying platform is mounted on the frame behind the cab and is fitted with a fixed head, drop sides and a hinged tailgate. Sideboard extensions can be converted into benches for carrying troops. A tarpaulin over sliding bows can be used to cover the load-carrying area.

The swinging half-axles, with independent wheel suspension on the four-axle vehicles, are constantly driven. Front wheel drive on the three-axle vehicle can be selected by the driver. Reduction gears in the wheels reduce power train stress and increase the vehicle's tractive effort. For uniform driving torque

Tatra T 815 VT 26 265 8 × 8.1R 10 000 kg truck

Tatra T 815 VT 26 265 8 × 8.1R 10 000 kg truck

Specifications

Model	T 815 VVN 20 235 6 × 6.1R	T 815 VT 26 265 8 × 8.1R	T 815 VVN 26 265 8 × 8.1R
Cab type	2-door	4-door	2-door
Cab seating	1 + 3	1 + 5	1 + 3
Configuration	6 × 6	8 × 8	8 × 8
Weight (empty)	12 700 kg	15 700 kg	15 100 kg
(loaded)	20 700 kg	25 700 kg	27 100 kg
Max load	8000 kg	10 000 kg	12 000 kg
Towed load (off road)	10 000 kg	15 000 kg	15 000 kg
(on road)	45 000 kg	70 000 kg	45 000 kg
Load area	5.36 × 2.41 m	5.36 × 2.41 m	6.25 × 2.41 m
Length	8.35 m	9.34 m	9.36 m
Width	2.5 m	2.5 m	2.5 m
Height (overall)	3.65 m	3.65 m	3.65 m
(cab roof)	3.03 m	3.03 m	3.03 m
(rear tow hook)	0.91 m	0.91 m	0.91 m
Ground clearance	0.41 m	0.41 m	0.41 m
Track (front/rear)	2.044/1.988 m	2.044/1.988 m	2.044/1.988 m
Wheelbase	3.27 m + 1.45 m	1.65 m + 2.97 m + 1.45 m	1.65 m + 2.97 m + 1.45 m
Angle of approach/departure	32°/35°	32°/35°	32°/35°
Max speed (road)	80 km/h	80.6 km/h	80 km/h
Range	1000 km	1000 km	1000 km
Fuel capacity	2 × 230 l	2 × 230 l	2 × 230 l
Gradient	100%	100%	100%
Side slope	30°	30°	30°
Trench	0.9 m	0.9 m	0.9 m
Vertical obstacle	0.6 m	0.6 m	0.6 m
Fording	1.4 m	1.4 m	1.4 m
Engine type	3-930-31 19 l V-12 diesel	3-930-51 19 l V-12 diesel	3-930-50 19 l V-12 diesel
Engine power	308 hp at 2200 rpm	347 hp at 2200 rpm	347 hp at 2200 rpm
Gearbox	10 forward, 2 reverse	10 forward, 2 reverse	10 forward, 2 reverse
Clutch	single plate	single plate	single plate
Steering	worm and roller, power-assist	worm and roller, power-assist	worm and roller, power-assist
Suspension (front)	torsion bars, shock absorbers	leaf springs, shock absorbers	leaf springs, shock absorbers
(rear)	leaf springs	leaf springs	leaf springs
Tyres	15.00-21 TO3	15.00-21 TO3	15.00-21 TO3
Brakes	dual circuit	dual circuit	dual circuit
Electrical system	24 V	24 V	24 V
Batteries	2 × 12 V, 175 Ah	2 × 12 V, 175 Ah	2 × 12 V, 175 Ah
Alternator	28 V/60 A	28 V/60 A	28 V/60 A

division, between the individual axle pairs a torque divider is inserted in the power train. There is also a system of inter-axle and axle differential locks.

Suspension on the four-axle vehicles is by longitudinally located leaf springs. The front axle of the three-axle vehicle uses torsion bars and is equipped with hydraulic telescopic dampers.

The 10-speed gearbox employs constant mesh helical gears. With the exception of the first and reverse all gears are provided with block synchromesh. Engaging five of the gears is indirect with a pneumatic servo; two optional direct gears are engaged electropneumatically using a preselector on the gear lever. There is also an auxiliary two-speed gearbox directly coupled to the gearbox for winch drive.

The winch has a capacity of 12 000 kg on all models and is supplied with 85 m of cable.

All three models are equipped to carry the ŠSP 1000 arrow-type snow plough and the 8 × 8 models can accommodate the BZ-T 815 dozer blade.

Variants

The 8 × 8 Tatra T 815 chassis is used as the basis for the 152 mm Dana self-propelled howitzer. For details of this equipment see *Jane's Armour and Artillery 1992-93* pages 559 to 561.

The 8 × 8 version of the Tatra T 815 has been adapted to carry the Czech 122 mm RM-70 (40-round) multiple rocket system. For information on this system see *ibid* pages 717 and 718. Other roles that will no doubt be carried over from the Tatra 813 include those of carrier for the PMP and other bridging systems, tractor truck, and artillery tractor for calibres up to 152 mm and above.

Czech 122 mm RM-70 (40-round) multiple rocket system mounted on Tatra T 815 (8 × 8) chassis

The 8 × 8 chassis is used as the basis for the ST-T 815 NBC decontamination vehicle, produced in small numbers, and as the carrier for the AM-50B truck-mounted scissors bridge (see entry under *Mechanised bridges* for details). Other 8 × 8 variants include the UDS-114a mobile earthmoving shovel and the UP-82 drilling machine.

The 6 × 6 chassis of the Tatra T 815 is used for a refuelling tanker known as the CA 18 T 815.

The T 815 VVNC 20 235 6 × 6.1R is produced under licence in India by Bharat Earth Movers Limited (BEML).

Status

In production. In service with the Czechoslovak and Indian armed forces.

Manufacturers

Tatra, Národni Podnik, 742 21 Koprivnice, Czechoslovakia.

Bharat Earth Movers Limited, Sheriff Bhatia Towers, 40/1 M.G. Road, Bangalore 560 001, India. Tel: 574496. Telex: 845 8178.

Tatra 148 (4 × 4) and (6 × 6) Trucks

Description

The Tatra 148 range of trucks was introduced in 1972 as the replacement for the older Tatra 138 series. They are very similar in appearance to the earlier vehicles but have more powerful engines and increased payload. A further development of the Tatra 148, the Tatra 157, was built.

The basic cargo model is designated the Tatra 148. This has a conventional layout with the engine at the front, all-steel two-door cab and the cargo area at the rear with a drop tailgate, bows and a tarpaulin cover. Vehicles fitted with a winch have the suffix N, for example Tatra 148 N.

Variants

The TZ 74 decontamination vehicle is based on the chassis of the Tatra 148 (6 × 6) truck chassis.

The CAS 32 is a fire engine with one 6000 litre water tank and a 600 litre foam tank.

A hydraulic servicing/inspection platform carrier was in production between 1975 and 1979.

Dump trucks included the Tatra 148 S1 (6 × 6), Tatra

148 S3 (6 × 6), Tatra 148 S3 CH-HMH (6 × 6), Tatra JMH (6 × 6, single-seater cab on left side), Tatra TMCH (forward control type cab, 6 × 6) and the Tatra 148 S3 CH-JMH (4 × 4).

Tractor trucks included the Tatra 148 NTt (6 × 6), Tatra 148 NTPt (6 × 6), Tatra NTPst (6 × 6), Tatra NTt (4 × 4) and Tatra TTt (4 × 4).

Specifications (Tatra 148)
Cab seating: 1 + 2
Configuration: 6 × 6
Weight:
  (empty) 11 060 kg

(loaded) 25 640 kg
Max load: (road) 14 580 kg
Towed load: (road) 13 580 kg
Length: 9 m
Width: 2.5 m
Height: 2.44 m
Ground clearance: 0.29 m
Track: (front/rear) 1.966 m/1.77 m
Wheelbase: 4.8 m + 1.32 m
Max speed: 71 km/h
Fuel capacity: 200 l
Fording: 1.4 m
Engine: T 2-928-1 V-8 air-cooled diesel developing

212 hp at 2000 rpm
Tyres: 11.00 × 20

Status
Production complete. It is believed that this vehicle is used by the Czechoslovak Army as the previous Tatra 138 was used for a variety of roles.

Manufacturer
Tatra, Národni Podnik, 742 21 Koprivnice, Czechoslovakia.

EGYPT

Egyptian Truck Production

Truck production in Egypt is concentrated on three main types. The first is a licence-manufactured version of the Jeep AM 720 1135 kg light vehicle (see entry under USA in this section for details) which is produced by the Arab American Vehicles Company at Horreia, Heliopolis. About 40 to 45 per cent of the vehicle is local content and the AM 720 is produced in various forms such as a troop carrier, ambulance, mobile workshop (with a ¼-tonne trailer) and communications shelter carrier. Another locally produced Jeep product is the J-20 which is produced in pick-up form for a variety of civil and military roles. About 20 per cent of the J-20 is local content. The company also produces CJ-7 and CJ-8 Jeeps (see entry under *Lightweight vehicles*).

The third vehicle is a locally produced version of the Magirus-Deutz (now IVECO Magirus) Mercur, known as the NASR. This 4 × 4 vehicle, the German origins of which date back to the 1950s, is produced in several

forms including a basic troop and cargo carrier with a 3350 kg payload, a mobile surgery and at least two types of NBC decontamination vehicle. The mobile surgery has an air-conditioned office-type body with its own 4 kW electrical generator, a clean water supply system and carrying enough medical equipment and supplies (including a refrigerated blood bank) to remain in the field for 3.3 days. When in position two penthouse tents can be erected each side of the vehicle or separately to provide extra working space. Each tent measures 4 × 4 m on each side and is 2.4 m high. The NASR is produced under the auspices of the Egyptian Ministry of Defence Vehicles Department.

Specifications (NASR)
Cab seating: 1 + 1 or 2
Configuration: 4 × 4
Weight:
  (empty) 3800 kg
  (loaded) 7150 kg
Max load: 3350 kg
Length: 7.2 m

Width: 2.4 m
Ground clearance: 0.315 m
Wheelbase: 4.2 m
Fuel consumption: 18.7 l/100 km
Fuel capacity: 150 l
Engine: NASR 112 H6 air-cooled diesel developing 112 hp at 2300 rpm (licence-produced version of Deutz F 6 L 614)
Gearbox: ZF 35 AK5 manual with 5 forward and 1 reverse gears
Clutch: single dry plate
Transfer box: 2-speed
Turning radius: 9 m
Suspension: semi-elliptic leaf springs with auxiliary springs at rear and shock absorbers in front
Tyres: 20.00 × 10

Status
All the above are in production and in service with the Egyptian armed forces.

FINLAND

Sisu A-45 (4 × 4) 3000 kg Truck

Description
The Sisu A-45 (4 × 4) truck was designed to carry 3050 kg of cargo across country and 4050 kg of cargo on roads. Maximum towed load is 2000 kg cross-country and 4000 kg on roads. The vehicle is used by the Finnish Army both in Finland and overseas as part of United Nations Forces. The vehicle is also used for a variety of civil applications.

The cab has a steel lower half with a door in each side, with a detachable glass fibre upper half. The driver's seat is adjustable and the cab has a heater as a standard feature. The engine is mounted to the immediate rear of the cab and projects into the load area of the vehicle. The rear platform is of steel construction and attached to the chassis by rubber

mountings. The sideboards and tailgate can be folded down. The tailgate has access steps. The load area can be fitted with bows and a tarpaulin cover if required. A tow hook is mounted at the rear of the vehicle and a pulling jaw is mounted in the centre of the front bumper.

Optional equipment includes a hydraulic mechanism for the operation of Sisu hydraulic motors in the trailer (for example when a two-wheel trailer is being towed the wheels of the trailer are powered giving the truck/trailer combination full 6 × 6 drive), trailer air pressure brake system, cold starting equipment, blowlamp-operated coolant and oil sump heater and a Sisu 6500 kg capacity hydraulic winch, with 60 m of cable which can be used to the front or rear of the truck.

There are ambulance, fire, radio, command and workshop variants.

Specifications
Cab seating: 1 + 2
Configuration: 4 × 4
Weight:
  (empty) 5950 kg
  (loaded, road) 10 000 kg
  (loaded, cross-country) 9000 kg
Max load:
  (road) 4050 kg
  (cross-country) 3050 kg
Towed load: 9000 kg
Load area: 4.28 × 2.16 m
Length: 6 m
Width: 2.3 m
Height:
  (cab) 2.6 m
  (tarpaulin) 2.8 m
  (load area) 1.29 m

Sisu A-45 (4 × 4) 3000 kg truck

Sisu A-45 (4 × 4) 3000 kg truck

Ground clearance: (axles) 0.4 m
Track: 1.89 m
Wheelbase: 3.7 m
Angle of approach/departure: 38°/38°
Max speed: (road) 100 km/h
Range: 700 km
Fuel capacity: 210 l
Max gradient: 60%
Fording: 1 m
Engine: 6-cylinder direct injection diesel developing 130 hp (DIN) at 2600 rpm or turbocharged diesel developing 160 hp (DIN) at 2600 rpm

Gearbox: manual with 5 forward and 1 reverse gears
Transfer box: 2-speed (front and rear axles have differential lock, planetary gears in wheel hubs)
Steering: hydraulically assisted
Turning radius: 8.2 m
Suspension: leaf springs front and rear with shock absorbers on front axle only
Tyres: 14.00 × R 20
Brakes:
  (main) air
  (parking) mechanical
Electrical system: 24 V

Batteries: 2 × 12 V, 145 Ah

Status
Production complete. In service with the Finnish Army.

Manufacturer
Oy Sisu-Auto AB, Sisu Defence, PO Box 189, SF-13101 Hämeenlinna, Finland.
Tel: 358 17 5851. Telex: 2315.
Fax: 358 17 197 130.

Sisu SA-110 VS (4 × 4) 3500 kg Truck

Description
The Sisu SA-110 VS (4 × 4) 3500 kg truck is a high mobility off-road vehicle intended for a number of front line logistic tasks. It has a distinctive forward control cab of steel construction with seating for the driver and two passengers. A roof hatch is provided and the windscreen is a single flat sheet of glass. The engine is located over the front axle. Front and rear axles are Sisu type BEB with differential locks. The main chassis frame is steel and the rear platform can accommodate a number of load-carrying body types or superstructures for roles such as firefighting and rescue, and so on. A typical cargo-carrying body consists of steel drop sides and a tailgate with an optional tarpaulin cover stretched over bows; folding bench seats are provided along each side. Another rear body type has partial drop sides at the side centres with coil fenders provided underneath to absorb the weight of a falling panel on opening. A towing hitch is provided at the rear.

Optional extras include a 3500 kg capacity winch provided with 30 m of wire rope, light armour, and a variable tyre pressure system with the controls in the cab.

Specifications
Cab seating: 1 + 2
Configuration: 4 × 4
Weight:
  (empty) 5950 kg
  (loaded) 9500 kg
Max load: 3550 kg
Length: 6.5 m
Width: 2.34 m
Height:
  (top of bows) 2.84 m
  (load platform) 1.4 m
Ground clearance: 0.57 m
Wheelbase: 3.4 m

Sisu SA-110 VS (4 × 4) 3500 kg truck

Angle of approach/departure: 43°/43°
Max speed: 100 km/h
Range: 700 km
Fuel capacity: 165 l
Max gradient: 100%
Side slope: 30%
Fording: 0.9 m
Engine: Valmet 411 DSJ diesel developing 144 hp at 2500 rpm or
Deutz BF 6 L 913 6-cylinder diesel developing 160 hp at 2800 rpm
Gearbox: ZF S 5-35/2 manual with 5 forward and 1 reverse gears
Clutch: single dry plate
Transfer box: Sisu 2-speed with differential lock
Steering: hydraulic power-assist

Suspension:
  (front) coil springs and shock absorbers
  (rear) leaf springs and shock absorbers
Tyres: 14.00 × 20 or 14.00 R 20
Brakes: dual circuit air over hydraulic, discs
Electrical system: 24 V
Batteries: 2 × 12 V

Status
In production.

Manufacturer
Oy Sisu-Auto AB, Sisu Defence, PO Box 189, SF-13101 Hämeenlinna, Finland.
Tel: 358 17 5851. Telex: 2315.
Fax: 358 17 197 130.

Sisu SA-130 VK (4 × 4) 6500 kg Truck

Description
The design of the SA-130 VK (4 × 4) 6500 kg truck began during the second half of 1978 with the first prototype being completed in February 1980. Following successful trials the vehicle was adopted by the Finnish Army and first production vehicles were completed in October 1980. Although the vehicle was designed primarily to tow artillery it is suitable for a wide range of civilian and military applications.

The SA-130 VK has a well-balanced load distribution and a twisting chassis which ensures that all four wheels are in contact with the ground at all times. The cab and cargo body are attached to the chassis with elastic pads which prevent the frames from twisting.

The all-steel forward control cab has seats for the driver and two passengers with the driver's seat being adjustable for length and height. Standard equipment in the cab includes a heater with a two-speed fan, roof hatch, washers and a camouflage net support frame. A heavy machine gun can be mounted on the cab roof.

The rear cargo area has a steel frame construction with removable sides. Standard equipment includes an 8000 kg winch with 50 m of cable that can be used to the front or rear of the vehicle.

The Sisu XA-180 armoured personnel carrier uses

Sisu SA-130 VK (4 × 4) 6500 kg truck

many components of the SA-130 VK. For details refer to *Jane's Armour and Artillery 1992-93*, pages 349 to 351.

Specifications
Cab seating: 1 + 2
Configuration: 4 × 4
Weight:
   (empty) 7600 kg
   (loaded) 14 000 kg
Weight on front axle: (loaded) 7000 kg
Weight on rear axle: (loaded) 8000 kg
Max load: 6400 kg
Length: 6.76 m
Width: 2.58 m
Height:
   (cab) 2.9 m
   (tarpaulin) 3.1 m

(load area) 1.5 m
Ground clearance: (axles) 0.4 m
Wheelbase: 3.85 m
Track: 2 m
Angle of approach/departure: 42°/39°
Max speed: 100 km/h
Range: 800 km
Fuel capacity: 225 l
Fording: 1 m
Engine: Valmet 620 DS 6-cylinder (in-line), water-cooled turbocharged diesel developing 180 hp at 2500 rpm
Gearbox: ZF manual with 6 forward and 1 reverse gears
Clutch: single dry plate
Transfer box: 2-speed
Steering: power-assisted
Turning radius: 8.2 m

Suspension: leaf springs and hydraulic shock absorbers
Tyres: 14.00 R 20
Brakes:
   (main) dual circuit air-operated
   (parking) spring-operated, controlled by compressed air operating on rear wheels
Electrical system: 24 V
Batteries: 2 × 12 V, 150 Ah

Status
In production. In service with the Finnish Army.

Manufacturer
Oy Sisu-Auto AB, Sisu Defence, PO Box 189, SF-13101 Hämeenlinna, Finland.
Tel: 358 17 5851. Telex: 2315.
Fax: 358 17 197 130.

Sisu SA-241 (6 × 6) 12 000 kg Truck

Description
The Sisu SA-241 (6 × 6) 12 000 kg is a straightforward development of the Sisu SA-130 VK (see previous entry) and differs mainly in having an extra axle added at the rear, a more powerful Cummins engine and changes to the transmission involving a single-speed transfer box and a permanent 6 × 6 drive configuration. The two vehicles have many components in common, including the cab.

Specifications
Cab seating: 1 + 2
Configuration: 6 × 6
Weight:
   (empty) 10 000 kg
   (loaded) 22 000 kg
Weight on front axle:
   (empty) 4500 kg
   (loaded) 7500 kg
Weight on rear bogie:
   (empty) 5500 kg
   (loaded) 8000 kg + 8000 kg
Max load: 12 000 kg
Length: 7.8 m
Width: 2.58 m
Height:
   (overall) 3.13 m
   (top of cab) 2.13 m
Ground clearance: (axles) 0.4 m
Wheelbase: 3.74 m + 1.44 m
Track: 2.01 m
Angle of approach/departure: 38°/54°
Max speed: 95 km/h
Range: 600 km
Fuel capacity: 250 l
Gradient: 45°
Side slope: 40°

Sisu SA-241 (6 × 6) 12 000 kg truck

Fording: 1 m
Engine: Cummins L 10 330 turbocharged and inter-cooled diesel developing 340 hp at 2200 rpm
Gearbox: manual, 8 forward and 1 reverse gears
Clutch: hydraulic converter and single dry plate
Transfer box: single-speed
Steering: hydraulic power-assist
Suspension: leaf springs and hydraulic shock absorbers
Tyres: 14.00 R 20
Brakes: dual circuit pneumatic
Electrical system: 24 V

Batteries: 2 × 12 V, 160 Ah

Status
In production. In service with the Finnish Army.

Manufacturer
Oy Sisu-Auto AB, Sisu Defence, PO Box 189, SF-13101 Hämeenlinna, Finland.
Tel: 358 17 5851. Telex: 2315.
Fax: 358 17 197 130.

FRANCE

Renault B110 Turbo (4 × 4) Light Vehicle

Description
The Renault B110 Turbo (4 × 4) light vehicle is the military version of a Renault commercial vehicle that can be used for a variety of tactical purposes, ranging from a 2270 kg light truck to a military ambulance. Also included in the range is an enclosed van-bodied light vehicle.

There are two chassis versions, the B110-35D and B110-45D which differ in their gross vehicle weight capacities, with the B110-45D having the greater capacity.

The B110 Turbo uses a flat frame chassis with parallel channel sidemembers treated with anti-corrosion protection. The vehicle uses a steel monocoque semi-forward control cab with a rearwards-sloping laminated windscreen. Inside the cab there is

seating for the driver and a bench seat for two passengers. The bonnet can be raised for engine maintenance and repair and a rear engine hood can be removed for further engine access.

As a light tactical truck the cargo area can be covered by a fabric tilt on removable bows. There is also a tailgate. The van-bodied version can be supplied with or without side-opening doors. For the ambulance version the bodywork alterations are carried out by Sanicar Ambulances. The ambulance can carry six stretchers or six patients. Entrance to the ambulance section is normally through two large doors at the rear but there is a side door on the right-hand side of the body.

Optional equipment includes an airlift kit, making the vehicle suitable for transport in the C-130, C-160 or similar aircraft; a differential locking device for the front axle; a removable towing bracket for mounting front or rear; and a removable electric winch.

Specifications
Cab seating: 1 + 2
Configuration: 4 × 4
Weight:
   (chassis and cab) 2725 kg
   (GVW, B110-35D) 3500 kg
   (GVW, B110-45D) 4500 kg
Max load:
   (B110-35D) 725 kg
   (B110-45D) 1725 kg
Length:
   (cab and chassis, max) 6.197 m
   (cab and chassis, min) 5.317 m
   (van body) 5.65 m
Width: (over cab) 2 m
Height: 3.05 m
Ground clearance: 0.276 m
Track:
   (front) 1.7 m
   (rear) 1.65 m

Renault B110 (4 × 4) platform truck fitted with drop sides and tarpaulin

Renault B110 (4 × 4) ambulance

Wheelbase: 3.26 m
Angle of approach: 53°
Max speed: 98.6 km/h
Fuel capacity: 67 l
Engine: Type 8140.27 IDS 2.5 l 4-cylinder turbocharged diesel developing 106 hp at 3800 rpm
Gearbox: Type S 5.24 manual synchromesh with 5 forward and 1 reverse gears
Clutch: single dry plate
Transfer box: Type 100 2-speed
Steering: hourglass worm and screw with hydraulic

power-assist
Suspension: leaf springs front and rear with hydraulic shock absorbers and front and rear anti-roll bars
Tyres: 9.00R × 16 XS
Brakes:
    (main) discs front, drums rear, dual circuit, hydraulic vacuum-assist
    (parking) mechanical on rear axle
Electrical system: 12 V
Batteries: 1 × 12 V, 90 Ah
Alternator: 70 A

Status
In production.

Manufacturer
Enquiries to Renault Véhicules Industriels, 40 rue Pasteur, BP 302, F-92156 Suresnes Cedex, France. Tel: (1) 40 99 71 11. Telex: 620 567 f. Fax: (1) 40 99 71 08.

Peugeot 504 Dangel (4 × 4) 1110 kg Light Vehicle

Description
The Peugeot 504 is basically a standard civilian 4 × 2 vehicle modified to 4 × 4 configuration and fitted with seats, bows and a tarpaulin cover in the rear cargo area. It is also known as the Pick Up Armée.

The layout of the Peugeot 504 is conventional with the engine at the front, three-man fully enclosed cab in the centre and the load area at the rear. The load area has a drop tailgate, removable bows, tarpaulin cover and bench seats running down the centre facing outwards. In addition to the driver and two passengers in the cab, 10 fully equipped troops can be carried in the rear.

The front and rear axles have Peugeot limited slip differentials. The Dangel transfer case is mounted in the tunnel and is independent of the transmission due to a short universal joint shaft turning in a reaction tube.

It gives four road and four cross-country gears. Shifting from road gears to all-terrain gears is fully synchronised and can be carried out while the vehicle is travelling.

Mounted at the front of the vehicle is a winch. Special protection is provided for the underside of the vehicle.

An ambulance version can carry three stretcher patients in the fully enclosed rear body which is also provided with a dual seat. A 4 × 2 version is also available.

Specifications
Cab seating: 1 + 2
Configuration: 4 × 4
Max load: 1110 kg
Load area: 2 × 1.5 m
Length: 4.8 m
Width: 1.73 m
Height: (cab) 1.74 m
Max road speed:
    (petrol model, no tarpaulin) 135 km/h

    (petrol model, with tarpaulin) 125 km/h
    (diesel model, no tarpaulin) 120 km/h
    (diesel model, with tarpaulin) 115 km/h
Engine: XN-1 4-cylinder petrol developing 96 hp at 5200 rpm or XN-2 4-cylinder diesel developing 70 hp at 4500 rpm
Gearbox: manual with 4 forward and 1 reverse gears
Clutch: single dry plate
Transfer box: 2-speed

Status
In production for the French Navy and Marines.

Manufacturer
Automobiles Peugeot, 75 Avenue de la Grande-Armée, F-75016 Paris, France.
Tel: (1) 40 66 59 76. Telex: 649 237 f.

Peugeot 504 Pick Up Armée (4 × 4) truck

Peugeot 504 (4 × 4) ambulance

Renault TRM 1200 (4 × 4) 1200 kg Truck

Description

The Renault TRM 1200 was previously known as the Saviem TP3 and was in production at Renault's Blainville factory from 1969; by mid-1981 some 9200 had been produced, of which 4000 were for the French Army and 4000 for overseas military sales.

The Renault TRM 1200 is based on standard commercial components and can carry 12 fully equipped men or 1200 kg of cargo.

The chassis consists of cold-drawn steel side-members with the crossmembers welded into position. The vehicle can be delivered with a two-door all-steel fully enclosed cab, or a cab with a tarpaulin roof, removable door tops and a windscreen which folds forward onto the bonnet when not required. The rear cargo area is provided with removable drop sides, drop tailgate, removable bows and a tarpaulin cover. Removable seats can be installed down the centre of the vehicle (for example back to back) or along each side of the vehicle.

Optional equipment includes a 72 hp petrol engine, a winch with a capacity of 2000 kg, 120 litre fuel tank in place of the standard 70 litre fuel tank, 7- and 12-pin outlet sockets, 10.50 × 20 tyres and a fire extinguisher.

Variants include an ambulance capable of carrying six stretcher patients or 12 seated patients which is in service with the French Army, command post (in service with the French police), dump truck, firefighting vehicle, and a light recovery vehicle.

Specifications

Cab seating: 1 + 1
Configuration: 4 × 4
Weight:
  (empty) 2620 kg
  (loaded) 3950 kg
Max load: (cross-country) 1330 kg
Load area: 3.025 × 1.85 m
Max towed load: 1000 kg
Length: 5.005 m
Width: 1.996 m
Height:
  (cab) 2.4 m
  (tarpaulin) 2.594 m
  (load area) 1.094 m
Ground clearance: 0.27 m
Track: 1.641 m
Wheelbase: 2.64 m
Angle of approach/departure: 31°/40°
Max speed: 95.5 km/h
Range: 600 km
Fuel capacity: 70 l

Max gradient: 58.9%
Fording: 0.5 m
Engine: Renault 712 4-cylinder diesel developing 72 hp at 3200 rpm
Gearbox: Renault 321-4 manual with 4 forward and 1 reverse gears
Clutch: single dry disc
Transfer box: Renault 433 2-speed
Steering: cam and roller
Turning radius: 8.25 m
Suspension: leaf springs with Evidgom pads and hydraulic shock absorbers
Tyres: 9.00 × 16
Brakes:
  (main) hydraulic
  (parking) mechanical
Electrical system: 24 V
Batteries: 2 × 12 V, 96 Ah

Status

Production complete. In service with the French Army, Algeria, Morocco and other undisclosed countries.

Manufacturer

Enquiries to Renault Véhicules Industriels, 40 rue Pasteur, BP 302, F-92156 Suresnes Cedex, France. Tel: (1) 40 99 71 11. Telex: 620 567 f. Fax: (1) 40 99 71 08.

Saviem TP3/Renault TRM 1200 (4 × 4) 1200 kg truck with command post body

Renault TRM 1200 (4 × 4) 1200 kg truck with soft-top cab, bows and tarpaulin cover

SUMB (4 × 4) 1500 kg MH 600 BS and SUMB (4 × 4) 3000 kg Trucks

Description

The SUMB (Simca-Unic Marmon-Bocquet) 1500 kg model MH 600 BS truck was developed in the late 1950s by M Bocquet, who was president of Marmon-Herrington which subsequently became Marmon-Bocquet. Series production was undertaken from 1964 and although production has ceased, it remains one of the standard 1500 kg trucks of the French Army.

The engine and cab are at the front with the cargo area at the rear. The cab has two doors and a canvas top mounted on an articulated frame, which enables the top to be folded to the rear to reduce the vehicle's overall height. The windscreen can be folded forward onto the bonnet. The rear cargo area has a drop tailgate, bows and a removable tarpaulin cover. A bench seat can be fitted down the centre of the rear cargo area when the truck is carrying passengers. A locking differential is fitted to the rear axle. Some versions have a front-mounted winch with 60 m of cable.

A long wheelbase model of this vehicle, known as the SUMB (4 × 4) 3000 kg truck, was produced from 1971 with the same engine, transmission and cab as the 1500 kg version, but a longer wheelbase and cargo area.

Variants include a fuel servicing vehicle and a light digger with a Poclain light shovel mounted to the rear of the cab. The SUMB is also used to carry communication shelters.

Specifications

(data in square brackets apply to the 3000 kg truck where it differs from the 1500 kg model)
Cab seating: 1 + 1
Configuration: 4 × 4
Weight:
  (empty) 3670 [4220] kg
  (loaded) 5300 [7420] kg
Max load: 1500 [3000] kg
Towed load: 2000 kg
Load area: 2.95 × 1.97 [4.4 × 2.29] m
Length: 5.195 [6.55] m
Width: 2.305 [2.41] m
Height:
  (cab) 2.27 m

SUMB (4 × 4) 3000 kg truck

(tarpaulin) 2.88 [2.97] m
Ground clearance: 0.33 [0.38] m
Track: 1.704 m
Wheelbase: 2.9 [4.1] m
Angle of approach/departure: 43°/42°
Max speed: (road) 85 [82] km/h
Range: 550 km
Fuel capacity: 130 l
Fuel consumption: 30-32 l/100 km
Max gradient: 60 [50]%
Max side slope: 30%
Fording:
  (without preparation) 0.8 m
  (with preparation) 1.2 m

Engine: 8-cylinder petrol developing 100 bhp at 3000 rpm or 6-cylinder diesel developing 100 bhp at 3000 rpm [6-cylinder diesel developing 100 bhp at 3000 rpm]
Gearbox: manual with 4 forward and 1 reverse gears
Clutch: single dry plate
Transfer box: 2-speed
Turning radius: 7.5 [11.5] m
Suspension: coil springs and hydraulic shock absorbers
Tyres: 10.00 × 20 [12.50 × 20]
Brakes:
  (main) hydraulic
  (parking) mechanical

Electrical system: 24 V
Batteries: 2 × 12 V

Status
In service with the French Army.

Manufacturer
FFSA, 3 bis rue Salomon de Rothschild 92, Suresnes, France.

Renault TRM 2000 (4 × 4) 2000 kg Truck

Development
Following a competition for a new 2000 kg truck in which five European vehicles were tested by the French Army, it was announced in March 1981 that the high mobility version of the Renault TRM 2000 (4 × 4) 2000 kg truck had been selected. The French Army had a requirement for some 12 000 vehicles with first production vehicles completed at Renault's Blainville facility during 1983. The first 2000 examples were delivered to signal units in the three French Army corps and were used to carry RITA communications equipment.

Description
The Renault TRM 2000 is produced in two versions, Standard and High Mobility. The main difference between the two is that the Standard has a ground clearance under the axle of 0.302 m as opposed to the High Mobility's 0.425 m.

The chassis consists of U-beam sidemembers (180 mm × 70 mm × 4 mm) with the crossmembers riveted and bolted together. A towing bracket and a protective skid pad are provided at the front with a 5-tonne towing hook at the rear.

The forward control cab is of all-steel construction but may have a tarpaulin cover, and is mounted onto the chassis at three points with elastic pads and two shock absorbers at the rear. The cab tilts forward and is provided with a torsion bar tilting mechanism with double lock and warning indicator lamp, toughened glass windscreen, fully wind-down door windows, rear quarter lights, two-man passenger seat and an adjustable driver's seat. To the rear of the cab is the spare wheel rack. In the cab roof a Creusot-Loire Industrie STR TA rail-mounted rotary support is fitted to a hatch. This mounting can accommodate a 7.5 or 7.62 mm machine gun and is a standard fitting.

The cargo area is provided with drop sides and rear, bows and a tarpaulin cover. If required seats can be fitted down the centre of the vehicle to carry 12 fully equipped troops (for example six down each side facing outwards).

Optional equipment includes a front-mounted winch with a capacity of 2500 kg and a pioneer tool holder.

Variants include a fully enclosed ambulance, command post with shelter-mounted RITA system, forward air control, 2000 litre fuel tanker, missile carrier, prime mover for heavy mortars and the 20 mm Tarasque 53 T2 anti-aircraft cannon, recovery vehicle, water tanker, a field ambulance carrying six casualties, and a workshop vehicle. In 1990 LOHR SA announced its Mo.120 RA, a TRM 2000 carrying a 120 mm mortar which can be fired from a flat bed area in place of the normal cargo body. A hydraulic system at the rear can lower a recoil spade assembly to counter recoil forces or the mortar can be lowered to the ground for firing.

Specifications
Cab seating: 1 + 2 (up to 12 in rear)
Configuration: 4 × 4
Weight:
  (empty) 3980 kg
  (loaded) 6300 kg
Max load: 2320 kg
Towed load: 2000 kg
Length: 5.02 m
Width: 2.2 m
Height: (cab) 2.713 m
Ground clearance:
  (axles) 0.425 m
  (centre of vehicle) 0.604 m
Track: (front and rear) 1.8 m
Wheelbase: 2.7 m
Angle of approach/departure: 42°/48°
Maximum road speed: 89 km/h
Range: 1000 km
Fuel capacity: 130 l

Max gradient:
  (1st gear, high range) 35%
  (1st gear, low range) 50%
Max side slope: 30%
Fording: 0.9 m
Engine: Type 720S 4-stroke 4-cylinder in-line turbo-compressor supercharged diesel developing 115 hp at 3000 rpm
Gearbox: S 5-24/3, 5 forward and 1 reverse gears
Clutch: single dry plate
Transfer box: 2-speed
Axles:
  (front) axle nose with single, non-locking differential
  (rear) axle nose with single reduction differential lock, total reduction 6.37. Electro-pneumatic rear axle differential lock control
Steering: ball race, hydraulic
Turning radius: 7 m
Suspension: semi-elliptical leaf springs front and rear, with Evidgom pads, hydraulic telescopic shock absorbers, anti-roll bar on rear axle
Tyres: 12.50 × 20
Brakes:
  (main) air, dual circuit with load equaliser on rear circuit
  (parking) mechanical
Electrical system: 24 V
Batteries: 2 × 12 V, 6TN, 125 Ah

Status
In production. In service with the French Army and other armed forces including Morocco (190), Namibia (50), Qatar (10) and FINUL (85).

Manufacturer
Enquiries to Renault Véhicules Industriels, 40 rue Pasteur, BP 302, F-92156 Suresnes Cedex, France.
Tel: (1) 40 99 71 11. Telex: 620 567 f.
Fax: (1) 40 99 71 08.

Renault TRM 2000 (4 × 4) 2000 kg truck towing a generator

Renault TRM 2000 (4 × 4) 2000 kg truck (Pierre Touzin)

Brimont BRUTT (4 × 4) 2225 kg Truck

Description

The Brimont BRUTT (4 × 4) 2225 kg truck was developed to meet a number of military and commercial roles that vary from front line cargo carrier and ambulance to forestry and firefighting.

The BRUTT has a forward control cab with a horizontal wedge front profile. Seating is provided in the cab for the driver and one passenger and the cab can be tilted forward for maintenance. The cab may have a hard- or soft-top with the hard-top version having provision to fit a roof hatch for access to a light machine gun mounting. The cargo area to the rear can be provided with side bench seating to carry up to 10 men and is covered by a canvas tilt stretched over bows. The rear area can also be used to accommodate a light weapon such as a 12.7 mm machine gun in a ring mounting. The payload for the open-backed version is 2225 kg; if the full canvas cover and bows are installed this is reduced to 1770 kg.

The chassis frame is constructed from high stress steel with two box-sections and crossmembers, all pre-coated with a special anti-corrosion finish. The axles are of the Brimont rigid type with optional lockable differentials. Coil springs are used for the front suspension and spring leaves at the rear. Anti-roll bars are fitted front and rear.

Various forms of gearbox can be fitted. The standard manual gearbox is supplied by ZF but a Peugeot gearbox will permit higher speeds. If the vehicle is to be used for towing light weapons, such as a 105 mm howitzer or 120 mm mortar, it is recommended that a ZF automatic gearbox is fitted. A power take-off from the transfer case is planned for future models.

Optional extras for the BRUTT include an open canvas-topped cab, a six-seat crew cab, an electrical 4500 kg capacity front winch, a reinforced subframe for carrying special equipment, blackout lighting and various tyre sizes.

An ambulance version has been produced. This has a hard rear body capable of accommodating six stretchers or eight seated casualties. A firefighting version is in service with the French Army.

Specifications

Cab seating: 1 + 1 (up to 10 in rear)
Configuration: 4 × 4
Weight:
(empty) 2275 kg

Brimont BRUTT (4 × 4) 2225 kg truck carrying 12.7 mm machine gun

(loaded) 4500 kg
Max load: 2225 kg
Towed load:
(braked) 8000 kg
(unbraked) 5250 kg
Length: 5.275 m
Width: 1.95 m
Height: (top of cab) 2.48 m
Ground clearance: 0.275 m
Track: 1.5 m
Wheelbase: 2.78 m
Angle of approach/departure: 44°/43°
Max speed: 96.4 km/h
Range: 430 km
Fuel capacity: 90 l + 2 jerricans
Max gradient: 58%
Fording: up to 0.9 m
Engine: Peugeot XD 3 T 2.5 l 4-cylinder diesel developing 95 hp at 4150 rpm
Gearbox: ZF manual with 5 forward and 1 reverse gears
Clutch: single dry plate
Transfer box: 2-speed

Steering: worm and ball, power-assist
Turning radius: 6.4 m
Suspension:
(front) coil springs with shock absorbers and anti-roll bars
(rear) leaf springs with shock absorbers and anti-roll bars
Tyres: 10.5 × 20 MPT
Brakes:
(main) servo-assisted, disc front, drum rear
(parking) mechanical on transmission
Electrical system: 24 V
Batteries: 2 × 12 V, 100 Ah
Alternator: 70 A

Status
Prototypes.

Manufacturer
Brimont SA, BP 3 Sillery, F-51500 Rilly-la-Montagne, France.
Tel: 26 06 96 00. Telex: 830 651 f.

ACMAT/ALM VLRA 1500 kg and 2500 kg (4 × 4) and 4500 kg and 5500 kg (6 × 6) Vehicles

Description

The VLRA *(Véhicule de Liaison, de Reconnaissance et d'Appui)* was developed in the late 1950s specifically for operations in the Sahara. Since then it has been adopted by the French Army and many other countries throughout the world and is also used for a variety of civil applications, for example by oil companies.

The layout of the vehicle is conventional with the engine at the front, cab in the centre and cargo area at the rear. The cab has a windscreen which can be folded forward onto the bonnet and a removable nylon canvas roof and side doors. A European cab (metal door and fabric top) and an all-metal cab are available. The spare wheel is mounted to the left of the driver's position, or in the rear cargo space. The cargo area at the rear has a drop tailgate, removable bows and nylon canvas covers. Seats can be fitted down the sides or centre of the cargo area when the vehicle is carrying passengers.

Special equipment fitted as standard includes long-range fuel tanks, giving an autonomy of 1600 km or 34 hour cross-country operation, and a 200 litre water tank. These figures are reduced to 900 km and 100 litres for the TPK 4.15 SM3. Standard equipment also includes four jerricans, two sand channels, twin

VLRA (4 × 4) TPK 4.20 SM3 troop carrier, the base vehicle of the ACMAT range, carrying the Matra Mistral ATLAS low altitude surface-to-air missile system

Specifications

Model	TPK 4.15 SM3/STL truck	TPK 4.20 SM3 truck	TPK 4.35 SM3/4.36 CTL LWB truck	TPK 6.40 SM3/CTL truck	TPK 6.50 SM3/CTL truck
Cab seating	1 + 2	1 + 2	1 + 2	1 + 2	1 + 2
Configuration	4 × 4	4 × 4	4 × 4	6 × 6	6 × 6
Weight (empty)	4150 kg	4300 kg	5300 kg	5700 kg	5950 kg
(loaded)	5650 kg	6800 kg	8800 kg	10 000 kg	11 500 kg
Max load	1500 kg	2500 kg	3500 kg	4500 kg	5550 kg
Max towed load	3000 kg	3000 kg	3000 kg	6000 kg	6000 kg
Load area	2.6 × 1.94 m	2.8 × 1.94 m	4 × 1.94 m	3.9 × 2.15 m	4.8 × 2.15 m
Length	5.28 m	6 m	7.25 m	6.94 m	7.83 m
Width	2.07 m	2.07 m	2.07 m	2.25 m	2.25 m
Height (steering wheel)	1.83 m	1.83 m	1.83 m	1.9 m	1.9 m
(tarpaulin)	2.38 m	2.62 m	2.62 m	2.64 m	2.64 m
(load area)	0.92 m	1.096 m	0.99 m	1.12 m	1.12 m
Ground clearance	0.287 m	0.287 m	0.287 m	0.3 m	0.3 m
Track (front)	1.76 m	1.76 m	1.76 m	1.76 m	1.76 m
(rear)	1.66 m	1.66 m	1.66 m	1.8 m	1.8 m
Wheelbase	3.3 m	3.6 m	4.3 m	4.1 m	4.5 m
Angle of approach/departure	51°/41°	43°/41°	43°/26°	43°/41°	43°/30°
Max road speed	100 km/h	100 km/h	100 km/h	85 km/h	85 km/h
Range	900 km	1600 km	1600 km	1600 km	1600 km
Fuel capacity	2 × 120 l	2 × 180 l	2 × 180 l	2 × 210 l	2 × 210 l
Max gradient	65%	65%	65%	55%	55%
Fording	0.9 m	0.9 m	0.9 m	0.9 m	0.9 m
Engine (Perkins 6.354.4)	120 hp at 2800 rpm	120 hp at 2800 rpm	120 hp at 2800 rpm	138 hp at 2800 rpm	138 hp at 2800 rpm
Gearbox (manual)	4 + 1 speed	4 + 1 speed	4 + 1 speed	5 + 1 speed	5 + 1 speed
Clutch	single dry plate	single dry plate	single dry plate	single dry plate	single dry plate
Transfer box	2-speed	2-speed	2-speed	2-speed	2-speed
Steering	worm and nut	worm and nut	worm and nut	worm and nut	worm and nut
Turning radius	8.4 m	8.5 m	11 m	10.35 m	10.35 m
Suspension	all have leaf springs and double-action hydraulic shock absorbers				
Tyres	12.50 × 20 XL	12.5 × 20 XL	12.5 × 20 XL	12.5 × 20 XL	12.5 × 20 XL
Brakes (main)	air/hydraulic	air/hydraulic	air/hydraulic	air/hydraulic	air/hydraulic
(parking)	mechanical	mechanical	mechanical	mechanical	mechanical
Electrical system	24 V	24 V	24 V	24 V	24 V
Batteries	2 × 12 V, 100 Ah	2 × 12 V, 100 Ah	2 × 12 V, 100 Ah	2 × 12 V, 100 Ah	2 × 12 V, 100 Ah

dry and oil-based air filtration equipment, a six-bladed 500 mm fan driven by twin fan belts as well as a specially designed water radiator. A heavy duty chassis, gearbox and suspension are also employed. The reduction box and axles are of ACMAT design.

All vehicles are suppressed to second degree (NATO standard) and a 3000 kg winch can be fitted to the front of the vehicle, if required. A 6000 kg towing hook is standard and a multi-position version is also available for artillery-towing duties. Full EEC lighting equipment is available if required as is power-assisted steering. Finally, all VLRA vehicles can be produced in left- or right-hand drive form.

The basic vehicle can be armed with a 5.56 or 7.62 mm machine gun, which is pedestal-mounted, and a 12.7 mm machine gun circular-mounted above the passenger's seat if required. Thomson Brandt 60 or 81 mm mortars can be mounted in the cargo space over the rear axle. For anti-tank use the VLRA can be armed with a launcher for the Euromissile MILAN ATGW system.

It is important to note the high degree of commonality of wearing parts throughout the entire range of ACMAT vehicles. Not only is the same engine used in every ACMAT vehicle, but a commonality level of over 80 per cent exists across the entire range of chassis and cabs.

While detailed items are the subject of continued research and development, the overall dimensions of the major components do not change, thus ACMAT is able to guarantee the availability of exchange components for the life of the vehicle.

Variants

Troop/Cargo Carrier – TPK 4.15 SM3
This parachutable, airportable (4 × 4) troop/cargo carrier has a carrying capacity of 15 fully equipped soldiers or 1500 kg of cargo. An operating range of 900 km is available, and a 100 litre drinking water tank is standard. Virtually all wearing parts are identical to the 4.20 SM3. It can be delivered by the low altitude parachute extraction system (LAPES).
Dimensions are:
Length: (overall) 5.28 m
Width:
(overall) 2.07 m
(internal) 1.94 m
Height:
(overall) 2.38 m
(internal) 1.44 m

VLRA (6 × 6) 6.50 SM3 heavy reconnaissance and support vehicle

Wheelbase: 3.3 m
Track: 1.66 m

Long-range Patrol – TPK 4.15 FSP
This vehicle is a long-range patrol version of the existing TPK 4.15 SM3 and 4.15 STL (4 × 4) 1500 kg troop/cargo carrier. The mechanical details are the same and the TPK 4.15 FSP can be readily adapted as a weapon carrier for machine guns and anti-tank missile systems such as MILAN. Weight of a fully loaded vehicle is 5650 kg.

Command and Transmission Vehicle – TPK 4.20 VCT
This parachutable, airportable command vehicle has nine seats of which two are folding and used by the radio operators. Other equipment fitted as standard includes five stowage compartments, folding table, antenna mounting, two supports for identification flag on front wings, handrail on commander's position for use during parades and a fold-down hood. Basic specifications are overall length 5.035 m, overall width

2.07 m, height with windscreen and hood lowered 1.331 m, wheelbase 3.3 m and track 1.66 m.

Multiple Rocket Launching Vehicle – TPK 4.15 LRM
This vehicle mounts a 40-tube launcher for the Belgian 70 mm LAU97 multiple rocket system. The launcher is mounted on the cargo-carrying area and is aimed using a hydraulic system. All 40 rockets can be fired in 6 seconds to a maximum range of 8000 m. Weight of the vehicle and loaded launcher is 5650 kg.

Troop Carrier – TPK 4.20 SM3
This parachutable, airportable (4 × 4) troop carrying vehicle has the capacity for 17 fully equipped soldiers. It can be adapted to carry a wide range of weapons, as noted in the Description. It is the base vehicle of the ACMAT range.

Other adaptations on the identical chassis include:
Split Dropside Truck – TPK 4.25 STL
Dropside Truck – TPK 4.36 STL

These two vehicles have hinging removable sides and tailgate for carrying pallets or shelters. The rear suspension is modified to give a floor height of 1.04 m above ground level when unladen.

Ambulance Vehicle – TPK 4.20 SAM
An airportable vehicle with a fully enclosed rear body with lateral windows, two large rear access doors, four stretchers with swivelling frames for ease of access, a folding seat, wash basin, hand pump, 200 litre water tank, first aid kit and cabinet.
Dimensions are:
Length: (overall) 5.8 m
Width:
  (overall) 2.04 m
  (internal) 1.95 m
Height:
  (overall) 2.52 m
  (internal) 1.58 m
Wheelbase: 3.6 m
Track: 1.66 m

Radio Command Post – TPK 4.20 PCR
An airportable vehicle designed for command and listening-in duties. The internal design, which includes wiring for wireless transmitters, two desks to carry equipment, two cupboards, chairs, and so on, can be completed to customer's individual requirements. Leading dimensions are identical to those given above, including the internal dimensions.

  Also available are:
TPK 4.20 SL7 – Light Recovery Truck
TPK 4.20 SC – 2500 litre Bowser Vehicle (water, oil, petrol, and so on.)
TPK 4.20 VPL2 – Scout Car
TPK 4.20 VBL – 10-man Light Armoured Personnel Carrier
TPK 4.20 SM 2000 kg Shelter Carrier (2.96 × 2.07 m platform)
TPK 4.20 FFM Firefighting Vehicle
TPK 4.20 SPM Foam Firefighting Vehicle

Double Cabin Patrol Vehicle – TPK 4.21 SM3
This patrol vehicle introduced the ACMAT double cabin which has four doors and cab seating for the driver and five men. There is seating for a further 12 men in the rear which is identical to the rear cargo area of the ACMAT TPK 4.15 SM3. The all-metal cab has roll-over bars incorporated and a heavy duty air-conditioner is optional.
Dimensions are:
Length: 6.445 m
Width: 2.07 m
Height: (cab) 2.29 m
Wheelbase: 4.2 m
Weight:
  (unladen) 5300 kg
  (laden) 6900 kg

Airportable 4-man Ambulance – TPK 4.25 SAM
This ambulance has a steel body with glass fibre insulation with internal racks to accommodate four stretchers. The internal dimensions of the ambulance body are 3.307 m long, 1.956 m wide and 1.675 m high. The driver's cab, which can be fitted with air-conditioning, may be all-metal. This ambulance is in service with the French Army.
Dimensions are:
Length: 6.33 m
Width: 2.17 m
Height: (overall, laden) 2.625 m
Wheelbase: 3.9 m
Weight:
  (unladen) 5500 kg
  (total, all up) 7000 kg

RITA Shelter Carrier – TPK 4.25 SH/STL
This communications shelter carrier has a carrier platform 3.4 m long and 2.07 m wide – when loaded the platform is 1.025 m above the ground. The platform has various securing points and a spare wheel is carried between the cab and the carrier platform. A tool box is carried on the left-hand side.
Dimensions are:
Length: 6.33 m
Width: 2.07 m
Height: (platform, laden) 1.025 m

Wheelbase: 3.9 m
Weight:
  (unladen) 4600 kg
  (laden) 7000 kg

Troop Carrier – TPK 4.35 SM3
This airportable (4 × 4) vehicle has a troop carrying capacity of 21 fully equipped soldiers or 3000 kg of cargo.
Other adaptations on the same chassis, a 'stretched' version of the TPK 4.20 SM3 above, include:
Workshop Vehicle – TPK 4.30 FAM
This vehicle is supplied as a fully equipped workshop vehicle and the following items are included: 28 kVA generating set, engine and transmission oil tanks, large working surfaces, lubricating and so on, oil-lines, air compressor, battery charging equipment, portable welder, seven power points for hand tools, column drill,

two tool cabinets (one with 14, one with 28 drawers) and tyre galvanising equipment.
Dimensions are:
Length: (overall) 6.9 m
Width:
  (overall) 2.22 m
  (internal) 2.14 m
Height:
  (overall) 2.79 m
  (internal) 1.8 m
Wheelbase: 4.3 m
Track: 1.66 m

Off-Highway Bus – TPK 4.30 SB
This airportable, rough terrain bus can carry 28 passengers with their luggage in comfort. Pneumatic doors are fitted front and rear. Air-conditioning can be supplied, if required.

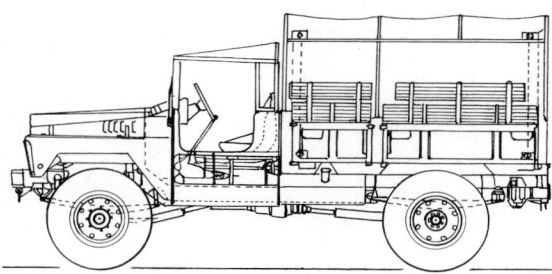

VLRA (4 × 4) ALM Type TPK 4.15 SM3 troop/cargo carrier

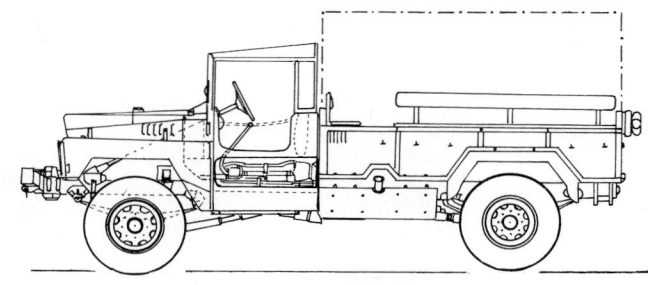

VLRA (4 × 4) ALM Type TPK 4.20 STL troop/cargo carrier

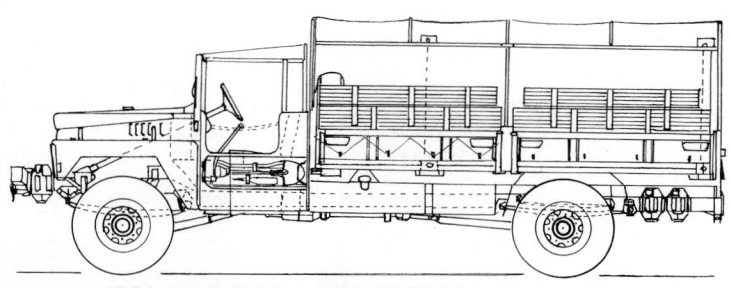

VLRA (4 × 4) ALM Type TPK 4.36 STL 21-seat troop carrier

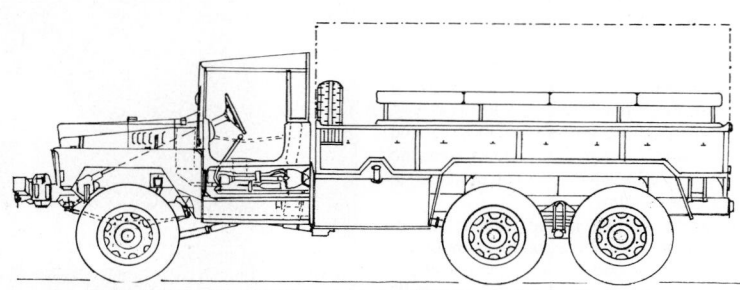

VLRA (6 × 6) 6.40 SM3 heavy reconnaissance and support vehicle

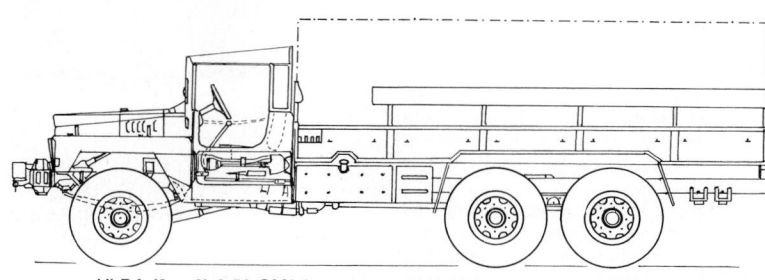

VLRA (6 × 6) 6.50 SM3 heavy reconnaissance and support vehicle

VLRA (4 × 4) TPK 4.15 FSP long-range patrol vehicle

VLRA (4 × 4) TPK 4.36 STL split drop side truck

Dimensions are:
Length:
(overall) 7.12 m
(internal) 4.3 m (driver excluded)
Width:
(overall) 2.2 m
(internal) 2.12 m
Height: 2.6 m
Wheelbase: 4.3 m
Track: 1.66 m

Other adaptations on the identical chassis include:
TPK 4.35 SCM – Mechanical Handling Vehicle, fitted with flat cargo area and telescopic hydraulic crane.
TPK 4.35 VPC – Convoy Protection Vehicle, fitted with 20 mm M693 Giat cannon.
TPK 4.30 FAE/FME, FMA1, FMA2 and FRA range of electrical and armament workshop vehicles.

Troop Carrier – TPK 6.40 SM3
This airportable 6 × 6 vehicle has a troop carrying capacity of 21 fully equipped soldiers or 4300 kg of cargo.

Reconnaissance and Support Vehicle – TPK 6.50 SM3
This 6 × 6 vehicle has an effective load of 5550 kg or 25 troops. Wheelbase from the front axle to the centre of the rear bogie is 4.5 m, and weight loaded is 11 500 kg.

Drop Side Truck – TPK 6.50 CTL
The ACMAT TPK 6.50 CTL is a drop-sided version of the TPK 6.50 SM3 (6 × 6) truck. The vehicle has a maximum effective load of 5550 kg and a cargo floor

height of 1.195 m to facilitate pallet loading. Standard ISO fixing points are incorporated in the body and shelters may be carried. Weight of the vehicle fully loaded is 11 800 kg.

Other adaptations on the same chassis, a 6 × 6 version of the TPK 4.20 SM3 above, include:
Shelter Carriers – TPK 6.40/50/60 SH
This vehicle is capable of carrying standard width and height shelters, up to a maximum length of 5.2 m. Corresponding sizes of refrigerating or plain shelters are available.
Dimensions are:
Length: (overall) 7.23 to 8.13 m
Width: (overall) 2.4 m
Height: (overall) 3.46 m
Wheelbase: 4.1 m-4.8 m
Track: 1.8 m

Bowser Vehicle – TPK 6.40 SC
An airportable 4000 litre bowser that is available for carrying water, oil or petrol.
Dimensions are:
Length: (overall) 6.94 m
Width: (overall) 2.25 m
Height: (overall) 2.13 m
Wheelbase: 4.1 m
Track: 1.8 m

NBC Decontamination Vehicle – TPK 6.40 CSD
This vehicle, also known as the CCSD 921, carries various NBC decontamination systems. For full details refer to *Jane's NBC Protection Equipment 1992-93* page 93.

Medium Recovery Vehicle – TPK 6.35 SL7
Uses a strengthened rear platform and a 3000 kg gantry crane plus a 9000 kg capacity winch at the front.

Heavy Duty Fire Tender – TPK 6.35 FFL
Carries a 3500 litre tank.

Tractor – TPK 6.35 TSR
This is based on a shortened chassis version of the TPK 6.40 SM3. It can tow a maximum load of 13 300 kg and is powered by a Perkins T6.354.4 engine rated at 180 hp. It is used in association with an ACMAT semi-trailer (see entry in *Trailers* section).

Also available are the TPK 6.40 SG – Tar Spreader, TPK 6.40 SB – 6000 kg Tipper and the TPK 6.40 WRT – 5000 kg Recovery Vehicle.

Status
In production. In service with French forces and many other countries including Benin, Burkina Faso, Cameroon, Chad, Gabon, Gambia, Ireland, Ivory Coast, Morocco, Senegal, Somalia, Togo and Zaïre. ACMAT vehicles are in service in 35 countries throughout the world.

Manufacturer
ACMAT (Ateliers de Construction Mécanique de l'Atlantique), Le Point du Jour, F-44600 Saint-Nazaire, France.
Tel: 40 22 33 71. Telex: 700 913 f.
Fax: 40 66 30 96.

ACMAT VLRA (4 × 4) ALM WPK 4.40 CTL 4000 kg Logistics Vehicle

Description
A prototype of the ACMAT VLRA (4 × 4) ALM WPK 4.40 CTL 4000 kg logistics vehicle was first shown in 1992. It may be regarded as a 4 × 4 version of the WPK 8.70 CTL (8 × 8) mentioned in the following entry and shares many components. The vehicle was produced as a private venture.

The WPK 4.40 CTL has a semi-forward control steel cab (the same as that used on the WPK 8.70 CTL) with a hard top and seats for the driver and one or two passengers. A 12.7 mm machine gun can be mounted on the roof over the passenger's seat and the one-piece windscreen can be folded forward or dismounted. To the rear of the cab is the multi-purpose cargo body with drop sides, drop tailgate, removable bows and a tarpaulin cover. The rear area can be configured to carry 20 troops, ammunition pallets or other stores. It can also be configured to carry a shelter or container. Standard equipment includes a 24 V electrical system and two fuel tanks to provide a range of 1300 km. A 150 litre water tank is placed between the body and the chassis.

ACMAT VLRA (4 × 4) ALM WPK 4.40 CTL 4000 kg logistics vehicle

Specifications

Cab seating: 1 + 1 or 2
Configuration: 4 × 4
Weight:
  (unloaded) 5800 kg
  (loaded) 9800 kg
  (front axle, loaded) 4200 kg
  (rear axle, loaded) 5600 kg
Max load: 4000 kg
Length: 6.645 m
Width: 2.4 m
Height: (overall, unloaded) 2.895 m
Ground clearance: 0.3 m
Wheelbase: 3.9 m
Track: 1.95 m

Angle of approach/departure: 35°/30°
Max speed: 100 km/h
Fuel capacity: 2 × 210 l
Range: 1300 km
Fording: 1 m
Gradient: (loaded) 65%
Side slope: 30%
Engine: Perkins 6-cylinder turbocharged diesel developing 165 hp at 2900 rpm
Transmission: Type CR 650 with 6 forward and 1 reverse gears
Transfer box: ALM ACMAT 2-speed
Steering: ACMAT Burman recirculating ball
Suspension: semi-elliptic springs with shock absorbers

Brakes: air/hydraulic
Tyres: 12.5 × 20 XS or 14.5 × 20 XS G 139
Electrical system: 24 V
Batteries: 2 × 12 V, 100 Ah

Status
Prototype.

Manufacturer
ACMAT, (Ateliers de Construction Mécanique de l'Atlantique), Le Point de Jour, F-44600 Saint-Nazaire, France.
Tel: 40 22 33 71. Telex: 700 913 f.
Fax: 40 66 30 96.

ACMAT VLRA (8 × 8) ALM WPK 8.70 CTL 6000 kg Logistic Vehicles

Description
The ACMAT VLRA (8 × 8) ALM WPK 8.70 CTL 6000 kg logistic vehicle was first shown in 1987 and was primarily designed to be a front line carrier for various forms of communications and radar shelters and containers. The ALM WPK 8.70 SH has the shelter carrier platform equipped to carry 15 ft/4.572 m ISO containers while the ALM WPK 8.75 is equipped to carry 20 ft/6.096 m ISO containers. The vehicle was designed to a French Army requirement and is air-transportable. The WPK 8.70 CTL 6000 kg logistic vehicle is a general purpose carrier but may be configured as a shelter carrier if required.

The vehicle has a full 8 × 8 drive configuration with both front axles being steerable. As with all other vehicles in the ACMAT range a high degree of component commonality has been maintained with many components of the 8 × 8 vehicle being the same as those used with other ACMAT 4 × 4 and 6 × 6 models. The main visible change on the 8 × 8, apart from the two twin-axle groupings, is to the cab which is a semi-forward control design. The cab may be either soft- or metal-topped with the windscreen folding forward on both types. The metal-topped version has provision for a 12.7 mm machine gun ring mounting over a roof hatch.

Under the rear carrier platform is provision for a spare wheel, side storage chests and a chest at the rear for a shelter access ladder housing. There is a side-mounted 210 litre fuel tank with another 210 litre tank under the platform that can be used for either fuel or water. Towing hooks are provided front and rear. A tool kit is provided.

It has been proposed that this vehicle could be used as an artillery rocket carrier and launch vehicle. A vehicle carrying a Bennes Marrel load handling system has been produced.

Specifications (WPK 8.70 CTL)
Cab seating: 1 + 2
Configuration: 8 × 8
Weight:
  (empty) 8000 kg
  (loaded) 14 000 kg
  (front bogie, loaded) 6050 kg
  (rear bogie, loaded) 7950 kg
Max load: 6000 kg
Length: 7.5 m
Width: 2.4 m
Height: (overall, unloaded) 2.725 m
Ground clearance: 0.3 m
Track: 1.95 m
Wheelbase: 1.22 m + 3.75 m + 1.22 m
Angle of approach/departure: 35°/33°
Max speed: 85 km/h
Range: 1000 km

Fuel capacity: 2 × 210 l
Max gradient: 55%
Side slope: 30%
Fording: 1 m
Engine: Perkins 6-cylinder turbocharged diesel developing 185 hp at 2900 rpm
Gearbox: Type CR 650 manual with 6 forward and 1 reverse gears
Clutch: single dry plate
Transfer box: ALM ACMAT type AL 450, 2-speed
Steering: ACMAT Burman recirculating ball
Suspension: slide-mounted inverted springs front and rear with radius arms mounted on silent blocks; telescopic shock absorbers on front
Tyres: 12.5 × 20
Brakes: air/hydraulic
Electrical system: 24 V
Batteries: 2 × 12 V, 100 Ah

Status
In production. In service with the French Army and Morocco.

Manufacturer
ACMAT, (Ateliers de Construction Mécanique de l'Atlantique), Le Point de Jour, F-44600 Saint-Nazaire, France.
Tel: 40 22 33 71. Telex: 700 913 f.
Fax: 40 66 30 96.

ACMAT VLRA (8 × 8) ALM WPK 8.75 SH logistic vehicle

ACMAT VLRA (8 × 8) ALM WPK 8.75 SH logistic vehicle in bare chassis form

---

Renault TRM 4000 (4 × 4) 4000 kg Truck

Description
The Renault TRM 4000 (4 × 4) 4000 kg truck was selected to be the standard vehicle in its class in the French Army which, in the early 1970s, stated that it had a requirement for 15 000 vehicles of this type. Production commenced at Renault's Blainville facility in 1973. At the end of 1987 the French Army had received 6300 TRM 4000 trucks out of an adjusted total requirement of 7500.

The vehicle is essentially a commercial vehicle (the Saviem SM8) modified to meet the requirements of the French Army and uses proven commercial components, including cab, engine, transmission, chassis and axles.

The basic model has single rear wheels and a payload of 4000 kg but there is also a model with dual rear wheels and a payload of 5800 kg. The chassis consists of longitudinal sidemembers with the cross-members welded into position. The two-door cab (type 812) is of all-steel construction and is of the forward control type. It can be tilted forward to an angle of 50° to allow access to the engine and can also be delivered with an observation hatch in the roof. The rear cargo area has drop sides, drop tailgate, removable bows

and a tarpaulin cover, and removable seats can be installed down the centre or sides of the vehicle.

Optional equipment includes long-range fuel tanks, different tyres, 4500 kg capacity winch, twin rear wheels, differential lock, additional seat in the cab, exhaust retarder, 24 V electrical system, blackout lights, 12-pin current outlet inspection socket on dashboard and a cab which can be split at door level to reduce overall height for air transport.

Variants include a Crotale missile carrier vehicle complete with hydraulic crane, a crane truck, a dump truck, firefighting vehicles, a light recovery vehicle, a 5000 litre tanker/refueller (Decauville), a van/command vehicle and a water tanker.

Specifications
Cab seating: 1 + 1
Configuration: 4 × 4
Weight:
  (empty) 5680 kg
  (loaded, road) 11 200 kg
  (loaded, cross-country) 10 000 kg
Weight on front axle: (loaded, cross-country) 3190 kg
Weight on rear axle: (loaded, cross-country) 2490 kg
Max load:
  (road) 5340 kg
  (cross-country) 4320 kg
Towed load: 6000 kg
Load area: 4.48 × 2.296 m
Length: 6.538 m
Width: 2.47 m
Height:
  (cab) 2.75 m
  (tarpaulin) 3.26 m
  (load area) 1.26 m
Ground clearance: 0.28 m
Track:
  (front) 1.836 m
  (rear) 2.018 m
Wheelbase: 3.85 m
Angle of approach/departure: 37°/39°
Max speed: (road) 87 km/h
Range: 700 km
Fuel capacity: 150 l
Max gradient: 50%
Max side slope: 30%
Fording: 0.9 m
Engine: Renault model 797 6-cylinder diesel developing 133 hp at 2900 rpm
Gearbox: ET 301 manual with 5 forward and 1 reverse gears
Clutch: single dry plate
Transfer box: G 300 2-speed
Steering: cam and roller with hydraulic power-

Renault TRM 4000 (4 × 4) 4000 kg truck

assistance
Turning radius: 10 m
Suspension: leaf springs with Evidgom pads, hydraulic shock absorbers
Tyres: 12.00 × 20
Brakes:
  (main) air, dual circuit
  (parking) mechanical
Electrical system: 24 V
Batteries: 2 × 12 V, 95 Ah
Alternator: 25/30 A

Status
Production complete. In service with the French Army and undisclosed countries.

Manufacturer
Enquiries to Renault Véhicules Industriels, 40 rue Pasteur, BP 302, F-92156 Suresnes Cedex, France. Tel: (1) 40 99 71 11. Telex: 620 567 f. Fax: (1) 40 99 71 08.

Berliet GBC 8 KT (6 × 6) 4000 kg Truck

Description
In the 1950s Berliet developed a 6 × 6 truck for use in North Africa called the Gazelle. With modifications it was subsequently adopted by the French Army in the late 1950s and by the time production had been completed over 18 000 trucks had been built.

The layout of the vehicle is conventional with the engine at the front, cab in the centre and cargo area at the rear. The two-door cab has a removable top, removable door tops and the windscreen can be folded forward onto the bonnet. The rear cargo area is provided with a drop tailgate with an integral step, removable sideboards, bows and a tarpaulin cover. The height of the bows can be adjusted for road or rail transport and bench-type seats can be fitted down the centre of the vehicle if required. Optional equipment included a Pan-Bonnier winch with a capacity of between 5000 and 7000 kg and drop sides for the rear cargo area. The KT series is powered by a multi-fuel engine while the MT series is powered by a diesel which develops 150 hp at 2100 rpm.

Variants
Long wheelbase
This is 8.32 m long, 2.4 m wide and 3.23 m high unladen; the wheelbase is 3.71 m + 1.28 m and empty weight of the vehicle is 9400 kg.

4 × 4 version
Small numbers of a 4 × 4 version were built for the Portuguese Army under the designation of GBC 8 (4 × 4).

Recovery vehicles
Details of these will be found in the entry for the Berliet TBC 8 KT (6 × 6) wrecker in the *Recovery vehicles* section.

Tipper
This can carry 4 m³ of soil. Unladen weight is 12 500 kg

and principal dimensions are: length 7.175 m, width 2.4 m, height 2.845 m, length inside tipper body 3.8 m and width inside tipper body 2.3 m.

Tractor truck
This has an overall length of 6.521 m, width of 2.4 m and a height (reduced) of 2 m.

Other variants include a firefighting vehicle, a 5000 litre fuel tanker, a mobile compressor, and a number of communications and command post vehicles carrying container/shelters.

Specifications
Cab seating: 1 + 2
Configuration: 6 × 6
Weight:
  (empty) 8370 kg
  (loaded) 12 370 kg
Weight on front axle: (empty) 4180 kg
Weight on rear bogie: (empty) 4190 kg
Max load: (cross-country) 4000 kg
Load area: 4.36 × 2.35 m
Length: 7.28 m
Width: 2.4 m
Height:
  (cab) 2.7 m
  (tarpaulin) 3.3 m
Ground clearance: (axles) 0.28 m
Track: 1.86 m
Wheelbase: 3.31 m + 1.28 m
Angle of approach/departure: 45°/45°
Max speed: 80 km/h
Range: 800 km
Fuel capacity: 200 l
Max gradient: 50%
Fording: 1.2 m
Engine: Berliet MK 520 5-cylinder OHV water-cooled multi-fuel developing 125 hp at 2100 rpm
Gearbox: Berliet BDSL 13 manual with 6 forward and 1 reverse gears
Clutch: single dry plate
Transfer box: 2-speed
Steering: worm gear and nut, servo-assisted

Turning radius: 10.5 m
Suspension:
  (front) semi-elliptical springs and hydraulic shock absorbers
  (rear) leaf springs on oscillating pivot
Tyres: 12.00 × 20
Brakes:
  (main) air
  (parking) mechanical
Electrical system: 24 V
Batteries: 4 × 12 V, 100 Ah

Berliet GBC 8 KT (6 × 6) 4000 kg truck carrying control and fire co-ordination post shelter for the SAMANTHA close-range air defence system

Status
Production complete. In service with Algeria, Austria, China, France, Iraq, Morocco and Portugal.

Manufacturer
Berliet is now part of Renault Véhicules Industriels, 40 rue Pasteur, BP 302, F-92156 Suresnes Cedex, France.
Tel: (1) 40 99 71 11. Telex: 620 567 f.
Fax: (1) 40 99 71 08.

Brimont ETR (4 × 4) Trucks

Description

Based on the company's experience in the development and production of agricultural tractors, forestry tractors and other cross-country vehicles, the Brimont group, which took over the activities of Latil in 1974, produced a 4 × 4 all-terrain vehicle called the ETR. This is suitable for a wide range of civil and military applications and has been adopted by the French Air Force.

The ETR (Engineered To Reliance) has a well-balanced load distribution and uses an articulating chassis with an oscillating device that ensures that all four wheels are in contact with the ground at all times. The arch-type axles with final planetary reduction in each wheel give a high ground clearance.

The all-steel forward control cab can be hinged forward to give access to the engine for maintenance. It is mounted on the chassis at three points with shock absorbers and variable suspension units. A special water-cooled system is fitted for the air-conditioning, heating and defrosting system.

Power is transmitted from the engine via the clutch to the hydromechanical reduction box and then by a short propeller shaft to a gear range multiplier which is coupled to the gearbox and transfer box. Power is then taken to the front and rear axles via propeller shafts.

The power train is a modular design and can be coupled with transfer boxes to give a wide range of speeds:
ETR-106, single ratio transfer box, 6 forward speeds (1.7 to 25 km/h) and 1 reverse speed (3 km/h).
ETR-112, single ratio transfer box plus double range, 12 forward speeds (1.4 to 25 km/h) and 2 reverse speeds (2.6 and 3 km/h).
ETR-206, double ratio transfer box, 6 road speeds (5.5 to 85 km/h), 6 working speeds (1.7 to 25 km/h) and 2 reverse speeds (1.5 to 10 km/h).
ETR-212, double ratio transfer box plus double range, 12 road speeds (4.8 to 85 km/h), 12 working speeds (1.4 to 25 km/h) and 4 reverse speeds (1.5 to 10 km/h).
ETR-406, double ratio transfer box plus hydromechanical reduction, 6 road speeds (5.5 to 85 km/h), 6 working speeds (1.7 to 25 km/h), 6 slow speeds (1 to 7.3 km/h), 6 extra-slow speeds (0.1 to 2.2 km/h) and 4 reverse speeds (0.1 to 10 km/h).
ETR-412, double ratio transfer box plus double range plus hydromechanical reduction, 12 road speeds (4.5 to 85 km/h), 12 working speeds (1.4 to 25 km/h), 12 slow speeds (0.9 to 7.3 km/h), 12 extra-slow speeds (0.1 to 2.2 km/h) and 8 reverse speeds (0.1 to 10 km/h).

A typical cargo model would have an all-steel rear cargo body with drop tailgate, troop seats, removable bows and a tarpaulin cover.

The ETR can be delivered with a rear steering axle driven by two double-acting hydraulic cylinders actuated by a hydraulic distributor or by a steering wheel in symmetrical or asymmetrical co-ordination. A combination of both front and rear steering allows crab-type driving. Turning radius with the front wheels only is 6.9 m and with the rear wheels as well, 4.37 m. The rear steering cannot be used at speeds of over 25 km/h and is automatically switched off when driving at over this speed.

Optional equipment includes a military-type cab with windscreen that folds forward and tarpaulin top, turbocharged Renault 798 engine developing 155 hp at 2900 rpm, different tyres, braking of the trailer with an electrical switch and a front-mounted winch with a capacity of 4500 kg.

Typical roles of the Brimont ETR (4 × 4) include use as an artillery (105 mm) or mortar (120 mm) prime mover, cargo carrier with or without a hydraulic crane, dump truck (side or rear tipping), engineer vehicles (those delivered to the French Air Force (designated the ETR 4 × 4 206 type VCUM) have a four-man cab, front loader, rear-mounted hydraulically operated shovel and rear cargo area with drop sides and four-man bench seat), firefighter fitted with 2500 litre water tank, 300 litre foam tank, 1000 l/min pump which can simultaneously project water and foam (used by the French Air Force under the designation of the ETR 4 × 4 206 S type VIFF), recovery vehicle (two-man cab, winch with a capacity of 4500 kg, chain pulley block moving on mobile gantry with a capacity of 2000 kg), shelter (for use in roles such as ambulance, command post and workshop), snow plough and tanker.

Specifications
Cab seating: 1 + 3
Configuration: 4 × 4
Weight empty: (average) 5400 kg
Weight on front axle: (empty) 3800 kg
Weight on rear axle: (empty) 1600 kg
Max load: (average) 5600 kg
Towed load: 8400 kg
Length: 4.965 m
Width: 2.27 m
Height: (cab) 2.66 m
Ground clearance: 0.465 m
Track: 1.8 m
Wheelbase: 2.955 m
Max road speed: 85 km/h (see text)
Range: 600 km
Fuel capacity: 200 l
Gradient: 70-100% depending on tyres and type of surface
Engine: Renault 797 6-cylinder diesel developing 132 hp at 2900 rpm
Gearbox: ZF, 6 forward and 1 reverse gears
Steering: power-assisted
Turning radius:
  (front wheels) 6.9 m
  (front and rear wheels) 4.37 m
Suspension: leaf springs with progressive flexible springs and hydraulic shock absorbers
Tyres: 14.5 × 20 E6
Brakes:
  (main) hydro-pneumatic
  (parking) disc brake on rear transmission
Electrical system: 24 V
Batteries: 2 × 12 V

Status
In production. In service with the French Air Force.

Manufacturer
Brimont SA, BP 3 Sillery, F-51500 Rilly-la-Montagne, France.
Tel: 26 06 96 00. Telex: 830 651 f.

Brimont ETR (4 × 4) dump truck

Brimont ETR (4 × 4) 5000 kg truck (P Touzin)

Renault TRM 160, TRM 180, TRM 200 and TRM 230 (4 × 4) Truck Series

Description

The Renault TRM 160, TRM 180, TRM 200 and TRM 230 (4 × 4) truck series was developed from the earlier Renault TRM 150.11 (4 × 4) truck (see *Jane's Military Vehicles and Logistics 1991-92* page 331 for details) to meet the military requirements of less technically advanced nations for a logistic vehicle with a degree of cross-country mobility. Many of the components used on the vehicles are of commercial origin or have been taken from models already in production.

The vehicles are equipped with a multi-purpose platform suitable for a variety of military roles including cargo or troop carrier, shelter carrier (3.05 or 4.57 m), recovery vehicle, water or fuel carrier, or weapon carrier.

The forward control cab is similar to that used on the Renault TRM 2000 (see entry in this section) but can have the headlights set into the radiator grille rather than into the front bumper. The all-steel cab can be tilted forward for engine and transmission access. The standard hard-topped cab may be fitted with a roof hatch for access to a light machine gun mounting. As an alternative the cab may be produced in 'torpedo' form with a canvas top and side screens in place of the steel doors. On the latter the windscreen can be folded forward onto the bonnet. With all cab types the driver

Specifications

Model	TRM 160.10	TRM 160.11	TRM 180.11	TRM 180.13	TRM 200.11	TRM 200.13	TRM 230.13
Cab seating	1 + 2	1 + 2	1 + 2	1 + 2	1 + 2	1 + 2	1 + 2
Configuration	4 × 4	4 × 4	4 × 4	4 × 4	4 × 4	4 × 4	4 × 4
Weight (cab and chassis)	4920 kg	5100 kg	5250 kg	5450 kg	5390 kg	5540 kg	5640 kg
(loaded)	10 000 kg	11 500 kg	11 500 kg	13 500 kg	11 500 kg	13 500 kg	13 500 kg
Load capacity	5080 kg	5400 kg	6250 kg	8050 kg	5110 kg	7850 kg	7860 kg
Towed load (road)	6000 kg	6000 kg	6000 kg	6000 kg	6000 kg	6000 kg	6000 kg
(off road)	4000 kg	4000 kg	4000 kg	4000 kg	4000 kg	4000 kg	4000 kg
Length	6.84 m	6.84 m	6.84 m	6.84 m	6.84 m	6.84 m	6.84 m
Width (cab)	2.19 m	2.19 m	2.19 m	2.19 m	2.19 m	2.19 m	2.19 m
(rear tyres)	2.28 m	2.322 m	2.322 m	2.368 m	2.368 m	2.368 m	2.368 m
Height, top of cab, empty	2.874 m	2.89 m	2.89 m	2.886 m	2.886 m	2.886 m	2.886 m
Ground clearance, rear axle, loaded	0.305 m	0.325 m	0.325 m	0.315 m	0.315 m	0.315 m	0.315 m
Track (front)	1.867 m	1.827 m	1.827 m	1.86 m	1.86 m	1.86 m	1.86 m
(rear)	1.919 m	1.954 m	1.954 m	2 m	2 m	2 m	2 m
Wheelbase	3.85 m	3.85 m	3.85 m	3.85 m	3.85 m	3.85 m	3.85 m
Angle of approach/departure	38°/40°	38°/40°	38°/40°	38°/40°	38°/40°	38°/40°	38°/40°
Max speed	91 km/h	95 km/h	92 km/h	92 km/h	94 km/h	94 km/h	92 km/h
Range	1000 km	1000 km	950 km	950 km	900 km	900 km	850 km
Fuel capacity	275 l	275 l	275 l	275 l	275 l	275 l	275 l
Gradient	50%	50%	50%	50%	50%	50%	50%
Max side slope	30%	30%	30%	30%	30%	30%	30%
Engine (type)	MIDS 06-02-26 U	MIDS 06-02-26 W	MIDR 06-02-26 V	MIDR 06-02-26 V	MIDR 06-02-26 W	MIDR 06-02-26 W	MIDR 06-02-26 X
(power)	159 hp/2600 rpm	159 hp/2600 rpm	182 hp/2800 rpm	182 hp/2600 rpm	196 hp/2500 rpm	196 hp/2500 rpm	226 hp/2350 rpm
Gearbox	S 5-25 manual	S 5-25 manual	S 6-36 manual	S 6-36 manual	S 6-36 manual	S 6-36 manual	S 6-36 manual
gears	5f/1r	5f/1r	6f/1r	6f/1r	6f/1r	6f/1r	6f/1r
Transfer box	2-speed	2-speed	2-speed	2-speed	2-speed	2-speed	2-speed
Electrical system	24 V	24 V	24 V	24 V	24 V	24 V	24 V
Alternator	50 A	50 A	50 A	50 A	50 A	50 A	50 A

has his own adjustable seat and a bench seat is provided for two passengers. Steering can be right- or left-handed.

The chassis is formed from beams measuring 234 × 70 × 7 mm.

Various options are available to customer request. They include: a spare wheel holder behind the cab; a power take-off from the gearbox; a fuel pre-heater; a hydraulic winch; and an automatic gearbox.

Status
In production.

Manufacturer
Enquiries to Renault Véhicules Industriels, 40 rue Pasteur, BP 302, F-92156 Suresnes Cedex, France. Tel: (1) 40 99 71 11. Telex: 620 567 f. Fax: (1) 40 99 71 08.

Renault TRM 200.13 (4 × 4) truck

Renault TRM 9000 (6 × 6) 9000 kg Truck

Development
The Renault TRM 9000 (6 × 6) (formerly known as the Berliet GBD) truck uses many components, such as the cab, gearbox, transfer case and steering, of the TRM 6000 (4 × 4) 6000 kg truck.

Production was undertaken at Vénissieux. First production vehicles were completed in 1975. The largest orders came from Algeria (500) and Morocco (1500). Production is complete.

Further development of the TRM 9000 resulted in the TRM 10 000 6 × 6 truck adopted by the French Army, for which there is a separate entry in this section.

Description
The two-door forward control cab has a removable canvas roof, removable side screens and a windscreen that can be folded forward against the bonnet if required. The rear cargo area is fitted with drop sides and a drop tailgate, removable bows and a canvas cover. If required seats can be fitted in the rear. Optional equipment includes a four-door six- or seven-seater cab, fully enclosed two- or four-door cab, winch with a capacity of 3500/4500 kg and 60 m of cable,

Renault TRM 9000 (6 × 6) 9000 kg truck

different tyres, dual wheels on the rear axles, additional 200 litre fuel tank, and an exhaust brake.

Variants include an artillery tractor able to tow

155 mm artillery weapons as well as carrying a gun crew and ammunition, a command/radio vehicle fitted with a container on the rear which could be fitted with

communications equipment, a 6000 litre water or fuel tanker, and a tipper with a two-man cab. The chassis has been used to mount Exocet or Otomat (for Egypt) anti-shipping missiles, as an RPV launching vehicle, and for supporting the Shahine anti-aircraft system supplied to Saudi Arabia; 38 vehicles were supplied to Saudi Arabia for this role. A recovery version known as the TRM 9000 CLD is fitted with a four-door cab. A tractor variant can tow a semi-trailer weighing a maximum of 27 000 kg; unladen weight is 15 000 kg.

Specifications
Cab seating: 1 + 1
Configuration: 6 × 6
Weight:
(empty) 11 000 kg
(loaded) 20 000 kg
Max load: (cross-country) 9000 kg
Max towed load: 10 000 kg
Length: 9.87 m
Width: 2.48 m
Height: (cab) 3.066 m

Ground clearance: 0.382 m
Track:
(front) 1.971 m
(rear) 1.886 m
Wheelbase: 3.8 m + 1.4 m
Angle of approach/departure: 45°/50°
Max speed: 82 km/h
Range: 800 km
Fuel capacity: 200 l
Max gradient: 45%
Max side slope: 30%
Fording: 1 m
Engine: Renault MIDS 06-20-30 6-cylinder turbocharged diesel developing 228 hp at 2200 rpm
Gearbox: BDS manual with 6 forward and 1 reverse gears
Clutch: air power-assistance
Transfer box: BT 20 2-speed
Steering: power-assisted
Turning radius: 11 m
Suspension:
(front) leaf springs with auxiliary springs and 2

mechanical buffer stops, telescopic shock absorbers (rear) balanced by leaf springs and 4 mechanical buffer stops
Tyres: 14.00 × 20
Brakes:
(main) air
(parking) mechanical
Electrical system: 24 V
Batteries: 4 × 6TN, 190 Ah

Status
Production complete. In service with armed forces including Algeria (500), Egypt (50), Morocco (1500) and Saudi Arabia (38). This vehicle is not used by the French Army.

Manufacturer
Enquiries to Renault Véhicules Industriels, 40 rue Pasteur, BP 302, F-92156 Suresnes Cedex, France. Tel: (1) 40 99 71 11. Telex: 620 567 f. Fax: (1) 40 99 71 08.

Berliet GBU 15 (6 × 6) 6000 kg Truck

Description
In the 1950s the Rochet-Schneider company developed a 6 × 6 truck called the T-6. This company was subsequently taken over by the Berliet Company and production of the vehicle, called the GBU 15, began in 1959. Production is complete and its replacement in the French Army is the Renault TRM 10 000 (6 × 6) 10 000 kg truck.

The forward control cab has four doors, removable canvas top and side screens, and its windscreen can be folded down onto the front of the cab if not required. The rear cargo area is provided with a drop tailgate, removable sides, removable bows and a canvas cover.

Mounted at the rear of the vehicle is a winch with a capacity of 8000 kg. The engine is the multi-fuel type and will run on a variety of fuels including petrol, paraffin, JP4, gas-oil, light fuel and mineral or vegetable oils in the lower power ranges. The rear wheel train consists of two tandem axles operating with a flexible progressive air-driven differential device. This ensures power even when two wheels on one side of the vehicle are not in contact with the ground.

Variants include an artillery tractor used to tow French Army 155 mm Model 1950 howitzers, and a tractor, designated the TBU 15, with an unladen weight of 13 500 kg; it can tow a semi-trailer carrying a light tank such as the AMX-13 to a maximum weight of 22 000 kg. A wrecker variant is called the TBU 15 CLD; full details are given in the *Recovery vehicles* section. There are also tanker and tipper variants.

Specifications
Cab seating: 1 + 3
Configuration: 6 × 6
Weight:
(empty) 14 500 kg
(loaded, road) 24 500 kg
(loaded, cross-country) 20 500 kg
Max load:
(road) 10 000 kg
(cross-country) 6000 kg

Berliet GBU 15 (6 × 6) 6000 kg truck (C R Zwart)

Max towed load: 15 000 kg
Length: 7.974 m
Width: 2.5 m
Height:
(cab) 3 m
(tarpaulin) 3.25 m
Track: 2.04 m
Wheelbase: 3.48 m + 1.45 m
Angle of approach/departure: 45°/45°
Max speed: 75 km/h
Range: 800 km
Fuel capacity: 400 l
Max gradient: 60%
Fording: 1 m
Engine: Berliet 6-cylinder multi-fuel, water-cooled developing 214 hp at 1800 rpm
Gearbox: manual with 5 forward and 1 reverse gears
Clutch: dry
Transfer box: 2-speed
Steering: screw and nut, power-assisted
Turning radius: 9.2 m

Suspension: longitudinal springs
Tyres: 14.00 × 20
Brakes:
(main) air, 3 circuits; front, rear and trailer
(parking) operates on rear wheels only
(emergency) pneumatic handbrake operates on rear wheels
Electrical system: 24 V

Status
Production complete. In service with Belgium, China, France and United Arab Emirates.

Manufacturer
Berliet is now part of Renault Véhicules Industriels, 40 rue Pasteur, BP 302, F-92156 Suresnes Cedex, France. Tel: (1) 40 99 71 11. Telex: 620 567 f. Fax: (1) 40 99 71 08.

Renault TRM 10 000 (6 × 6) 10 000 kg Truck

Development
The Renault TRM 10 000 (6 × 6) 10 000 kg truck was developed from the Renault TRM 9000 (6 × 6) 9000 kg truck. The main difference between the TRM 9000 and the TRM 10 000 is that the latter has a longer wheelbase, a more powerful engine and a different transmission.

The TRM 10 000 (6 × 6) 10 000 kg truck was selected by the French Army to be its standard truck in

this class; the initial requirement was 5000 vehicles. Pre-production manufacture commenced at Renault's Blainville factory in 1985. Production of the first full production batch of 178 commenced during mid-1987 and later the same year an order for a further 759 was placed. During 1988, 383 units were produced by which time the total requirements were 1500. By mid-1989 over 650 had been delivered.

Description
The chassis of the Renault TRM 10 000 consists of two U-shaped sidemembers (302 × 85 × 8 mm) with crossmembers bolted and riveted into position. The

front bumper is provided with a front towing shackle and impact buffers and shackles are provided front and rear.

The front axle is a Type PA 721 double reduction with bevel gear and reducers in the hubs. The rear tandem is a Type PMR 2021 with double reduction (taper gear and reducers in hubs) and inter-wheel and inter-differential locking.

The basic version has a forward control cab which can be tilted forwards for maintenance purposes and is provided with two doors, tarpaulin cover over removable roof bows, suspended adjustable driver's seat, adjustable passenger's seat, fold-down windscreen, heating, defrosting and ventilation equipment as standard.

The rear cargo area is provided with removable sides and tailgate, bows and a tarpaulin cover, and can be fitted with removable seats for 24 fully equipped troops. With the sides and rear removed the TRM 10 000 can carry standard 20 ft/6.096 m ISO containers.

Optional equipment includes an 8000 kg hydraulic winch which can be used to the front or rear, 10- to 40-tonne pivoting hook, rear impact buffers, fully enclosed four-door cab, hard-top on two-door cab, four seats in the two-door cab, one bunk in two-door cab, 12.7 mm anti-aircraft machine gun mount on top of two- or four-door cab, PTO on gearbox, automatic gearbox model 6 HP 500 with two gear VG 500 transfer box and torque distributor, trailer braking device, ISO coupling plugs (two circuits) and ISO front coupling plugs, class A anti-interference with 50 A alternator, 7- or 12-pin trailer plug, additional 250 litre fuel tank on left-hand side of chassis, tool box and boxes for wheel chains.

Variants include an artillery prime mover for 155 mm TR gun with four-door cab (adopted by the French Army), a dump truck, fuel or water tankers, hydraulic cranes of various types, a mine-carrying vehicle, a Tropomil aerial carrier, vehicles carrying multiple rocket launcher or various types of surface-to-surface missile, a missile resupply vehicle (for example Crotale or Shahine), a lubrication vehicle, a recovery vehicle or a tractor truck for various equipments, including PFM floating bridge components.

In 1990 Renault demonstrated a TRM 10 000 equipped with a Bennes Marrel load handling system capable of handling a 13 000 kg capacity flatrack. This version is powered by a 320 hp diesel engine and the wheelbase is lengthened to 4.3 m + 1.4 m. Loaded weight is 29 000 kg. This variant has been adopted by the French Army.

Specifications
Cab seating: 1 + 1 (up to 24 in rear)
Configuration: 6 × 6
Weight:
(cab and chassis) 10 290 kg
(loaded) 23 000 kg
Max load: 12 710 kg

Renault TRM 10 000 (6 × 6) 10 000 kg artillery tractors as used during Operation Desert Shield/Storm

Max towed load: 10 000 kg
Length: 9.246 m
Width: 2.5 m
Height: (cab roof) 3.11 m
Ground clearance: 0.382 m
Track:
(front) 2.004 m
(rear) 2.053 m
Wheelbase: 4.3 m + 1.4 m
Angle of approach/departure: 45°/30°
Max speed: (road) 89 km/h
Range: 1200 km
Fuel capacity: 250 + 250 l
Max gradient: 60%
Max side slope: 30%
Fording: 1.2 m
Engine: Renault MIDS 06-20-45 9.839 l 6-cylinder supercharged exhaust diesel developing 275 hp at 2200 rpm
Gearbox: Model B.9.150, 9 forward and 1 reverse gears
Clutch: hydro-pneumatic control
Transfer box: A 800 3D
Steering: Type 8046, hydraulic

Turning radius: 10.5 m
Suspension:
(front) semi-elliptical leaf springs (auxiliary and main springs), mechanical stops and telescopic shock absorbers
(rear) semi-elliptical leaf springs, mechanical stops
Tyres: 14.00 × 20
Brakes:
(main) air, dual circuit
(parking) locking on rear wheels
Electrical system: 24 V
Batteries: 4 × 12 V, 6TN, 125 Ah

Status
In production. In service with the French Army and Saudi Arabia (67). Ordered by some European armies.

Manufacturer
Enquiries to Renault Véhicules Industriels, 40 rue Pasteur, BP 302, F-92156 Suresnes Cedex, France. Tel: (1) 40 99 71 11. Telex: 620 567 f. Fax: (1) 40 99 71 08.

Renault TRM 10 000 (6 × 6) 10 000 kg truck

Renault TRM 10 000 (6 × 6) artillery tractor towing a 155 mm gun

---

Renault TRM 340.34 (6 × 6) 16 000 kg Truck

Description
The Renault TRM 340.34 (6 × 6) truck replaced the earlier TRM 12 000 (6 × 6) 12 000 kg truck in production. It was developed to meet a number of heavy engineer requirements and can be produced in a number of body forms.

The Renault TRM 340.34 has a semi-forward control cab with an adjustable seat for the driver and a bench seat for two passengers. The cab is constructed of high stress steel and is provided with air-conditioning and standard instruments. For maintenance the cab can be tilted forward to an angle of 70°.

The chassis is constructed from high strength

special steel U-members with section dimensions of 356 × 100 × 8 mm. Chassis crossmembers are bolted to the webs of the sidemembers while the integral front bumper is fitted with a towing block; various types of towing hook can be fitted. A Type PA 721 double reduction front axle is fitted while the rear axles are Type PMR 2032, also with double reduction. The rear axles are fitted with an inter-axle and inter-wheel differential locking device.

Optional equipment includes various spare wheel carriers, reinforced rear crossmembers for towing trailers weighing up to 75 000 kg, enlarged or extra fuel tanks, power take-offs from the gearbox, and accessories such as a fully sprung driving seat.

The TRM 340.34 has been produced in tipper form with an 11 m³ tipping body. Other body forms are available. Details of the TRM 340.34 T tractor truck can

be found in the *Tank transporters* section.

Specifications
Cab seating: 1 + 2
Configuration: 6 × 6
Weight:
(empty) 9580 kg
(loaded) 26 000 kg
Max load: 16 420 kg
Towed load: 12 000 kg
Length: 7.78 m
Width: 2.49 m
Height: (top of cab, empty) 3.003 m
Ground clearance: 0.312 m
Track:
(front) 1.91 m
(rear) 1.825 m

Renault TRM 340.34 (6 × 6) tipper truck

Wheelbase: 3.9 m + 1.35 m
Angle of approach/departure: 28°/48°
Max speed: (road) 87.8 km/h
Fuel capacity: 250 l
Max gradient: 50%

Side slope: 30%
Fording: 0.85 m
Engine: Type MIDR 06-35-40 12 l 6-cylinder water-cooled diesel supercharged by turbocompressor on exhaust and developing 335 hp at 1900 rpm

Gearbox: Type B9 with 8 synchronised forward and 1 reverse gears
Clutch: Type 430DTP2400 single dry plate
Transfer box: Type VG 1200 2-speed
Steering: worm and nut, power-assist
Turning radius: 12 m
Suspension:
  (front) semi-elliptical slide-mounted leaf springs with telescopic shock absorbers
  (rear) leaf springs flanged to oscillating pivots with compensator rods
Tyres: 12.00 × 20
Brakes:
  (main) air, independent front and rear circuits
  (parking) mechanical
Electrical system: 24 V
Batteries: 2 × 12 V, 143 Ah
Alternator: 55 A

Status
In production.

Manufacturer
Enquiries to Renault Véhicules Industriels, 40 rue Pasteur, BP 302, F-92156 Suresnes Cedex, France. Tel: (1) 40 99 71 11. Telex: 620 567 f. Fax: (1) 40 99 71 08.

GERMANY

L60 LA/PVB (4 × 4) 6200 kg Truck

Description
The L60 LA/PVB (4 × 4) 6200 kg truck is one of a series of trucks of East German origin that were placed in production to supersede the earlier W 50 series. The vehicle was produced for commercial as well as military purposes with the first examples appearing during 1986.

The L60 follows the same overall design layout as the W 50 but uses a new design of forward control cab (which can be tilted forward for engine access), a revised cab interior, a more powerful engine with improved fuel consumption, a new transmission and a revised chassis. The chassis uses a torsionally soft ladder frame and can accommodate a variety of types of body. The standard cargo body uses an all-steel platform covered by a tarpaulin stretched over bows with side benches along the sideboards to accommodate passengers.

Two forms of engine and transmission are fitted. A six-cylinder diesel engine, coupled to an eight-speed plus crawler ratio gearbox, provides power to carry a 6200 kg payload. A less powerful engine with a five-speed gearbox has a payload limitation of 5000 kg.

Specifications
Cab seating: 1 + 1 or 2
Configuration: 4 × 4
Weight:
  (empty) 6400 kg
  (loaded) 12 600 kg
Max load: (road) 6200 kg
Towed load: (road) 9000 kg
Length: 6.69 m
Width: 2.5 m
Height: 3.13 m
Track:
  (front) 1.9 m
  (rear) 1.775 m
Wheelbase: 3.2 m
Angle of approach/departure: 30°/19°

Max speed: 93 km/h
Fuel consumption: 26 l/100 km
Fuel capacity: 180 l
Max gradient:
  (towing) 42%
  (not towing) 50%
Engine: Model 6 VD 13.5/12 SRF 4-stroke diesel developing 173 hp at 2300 rpm or 4-cylinder diesel developing 120 hp at 2300 rpm
Gearbox: manual, synchronised, with 8 forward, 1 reverse and 1 crawling gears or manual with 5 forward and 1 reverse gears
Clutch: with hydro-pneumatic assist
Transfer box: 2-speed, lockable
Steering: hydraulic power-assist
Turning radius: 8 m
Brakes: combined air/hydraulic, dual circuit
Electrical system: 24 V
Alternator: 840 W

Status
Production complete. In service with the former East German armed forces and some other nations, including Iraq.

Manufacturer
VEB IFA-Automobilwerke, Ludwigsfelde, Bezirk Potsdam, Federal Republic of Germany.

L60 LA/PVB (4 × 4) truck

Mercedes-Benz Unimog (4 × 4) Series

Development
The Unimog (*Universal Motor Gerät*, or universal powerplant) was designed by Herr Friedrich in 1946 primarily for industrial and agricultural use. It was first shown in 1948 and initial production was undertaken by Gebr Boeringer at Goppingen in 1949. Two years later production was transferred back to Goppingen and since then large numbers of Unimogs have been manufactured for both civilian and military use, in many different models.

The number of Unimog models has grown considerably over the years, the largest 4 × 4 model being the U 1750 L with a maximum payload of 6000 kg. Only the later ranges of models are provided here. For the earlier models refer to *Jane's Military Logistics 1988* pages 410 to 413 and 418.

Unimogs are licence-produced in Australia and New Zealand.

Description
The layout of all vehicles in the series is basically the same with the engine and cab at the front and the cargo area at the rear. Most military models have a two-door cab with a hard- or soft-top and a windscreen which folds forward onto the bonnet, and a rear cargo area with a drop tailgate, drop sides, removable bows and a tarpaulin cover.

The Unimog vehicle is well known for its excellent cross-country capabilities and all vehicles are fitted with a differential lock on both the front and rear axles. For normal road use the vehicle is driven with only the rear wheels engaged while for cross-country use the front wheels are also engaged with the differential locks being used in very rough terrain.

A wide range of optional equipment is available for the vehicle including a fully enclosed two- or four-door cab, generator, front-mounted pump, snow ploughs and winches.

The Unimog is used for a variety of roles including use as an ambulance, command vehicle, firefighting vehicle, radio vehicle, workshop and as a prime mover for light artillery such as the Italian 105 mm Model 56 Pack Howitzer. Various specialised airfield vehicles have been produced. Unimogs are widely used for agricultural purposes.

In 1988 Mercedes-Benz rationalised their range of production models and devised new designations. The new range of models is as follows:

U 650 L. Powered by a 60 hp engine and with a wheelbase of 2.605 m. Payload is from 1200 to 2500 kg.

U 1150 L. Powered by 110 or 125 hp engines and with wheelbases of 2.9 or 3.4 m. Payload is from 2500 to 3000 kg.

U 1250 L. Powered by 125, 136 or 156 hp engines and with a 3.25 m wheelbase. Payload is from 3000 to 3500 kg.

U 1350 L. Powered by 136, 156 or 170 hp engines and with wheelbases of 3.25 or 3.7 m. Payload is from 3000 to 3500 kg.

U 1550 L. Powered by 156 or 170 hp engines and with wheelbases of 3.25 or 3.7 m. Payload is from 3000 to 3500 kg.

Specifications (all 4 × 4)

Model	U 600 L	U 800 L	U 1100 L (2.9 m WB)	U 1100 L (3.4 m WB)	U 1300 L	U 1700 L (3.25 m WB)	U 1700 L (3.85 m WB)
Cab seating	1 + 1	1 + 1	1 + 1	1 + 1	1 + 1	1 + 1	1 + 1
Weight (empty)	2250 kg	2860 kg	2860 kg	2980 kg	5250 kg	4900 kg	6900 kg
(loaded)	4200 kg	6000 kg	6000 kg	6000 kg	7500 kg	9000 kg	12 200 kg
(axle load, front/rear)	2600 kg	3600 kg	3700 kg	3700 kg	4000 kg	5300 kg	6500 kg
Max load	1250 kg	2500 kg	2800 kg	3000 kg	2250 kg	4000 kg	5000 kg
Load area	2.5 × 1.6 m	3 × 2 m	3 × 2 m	3.6 × 2 m	3.15 × 2.2 m	3.15 × 2.2 m	4.25 × 2.35 m
Length	4.74 m	5.1 m	5.1 m	5.7 m	5.54 m	5.58 m	6.7 m
Width	1.825 m	2.15 m	2.15 m	2.15 m	2.3 m	2.32 m	2.465 m
Height (cab)[1]	2.25 m	2.34 m	2.375 m	2.375 m	2.63 m	2.72 m	2.78 m
(canvas cover)[1]	2.365 m	2.665 m	2.7 m	2.7 m	2.83 m	3.02 m	3.14 m
Ground clearance[1]	0.39 m	0.405 m	0.44 m	0.44 m	0.44 m	0.5 m	0.5 m
Track	1.396 m	1.62 m	1.555 m	1.62 m	1.86 m	1.84 m	1.84 m
Wheelbase	2.605 m	2.9 m	2.9 m	3.4 m	3.25 m	3.25 m	3.85 m
Angle of approach/departure	45°/45°	45°/46°	45°/46°	45°/40°	46°/51°	48°/54°	45°/36°
Max speed	73 km/h	73 km/h	82 km/h	82 km/h	82 km/h	97 km/h	71.3 km/h
Fuel capacity	90 l	120 l	120 l	120 l	160 l	160 l	160 l
Gradient	70%	70%	70%	70%	70%	70%	70%
Max side slope	40°	40°	40°	40°	40°	40°	40°
Fording	0.8 m	0.8 m	0.8 m	0.8 m	1.2 m	1.2 m	1.2 m
Engine type	OM 616	OM 314	OM 352	OM 352	OM 352	OM 352 A	OM 352 A
Number of cylinders	4	4	6	6	6	6	6
Capacity	2.404 l	3.78 l	5.675 l	5.675 l	5.675 l	5.675 l	5.675 l
Hp/rpm	60/3500	75/2600	110/2800	110/2800	130/2800	168/2800	168/2800
Gears[2]	4 forward, 1 reverse	4 forward, 1 reverse	4 forward, 1 reverse	4 forward, 2 reverse	4 forward, 4 reverse	4 forward, 4 reverse	4 forward, 4 reverse
Clutch	single dry disc	single dry disc	single dry disc	single dry disc	single dry disc	single dry disc	single dry disc
Turning radius	5.6 m	6.25 m	6.25 m	6.9 m	6.9 m	7 m	7.9 m
Tyres	10.5 × 18	10.5 × 20	11.0 × 20	11.0 × 20	11.0 × 20	11.0 × 24	13.0 × 20
Electrical system	12 V	12 V	12 V	12 V	12 V or 24 V	12 V	12 V or 24 V

[1] Unloaded   [2] Transfer box fitted

Unimog U 600 L

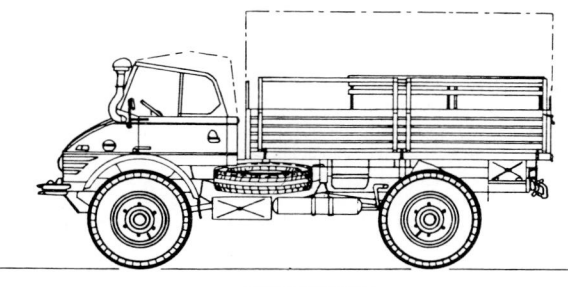

Unimog U 800 L

Unimog U 1100 L with 2.9 m wheelbase

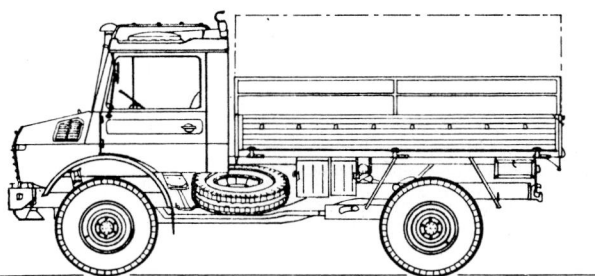

Unimog U 1300 L

Danish Army Unimog (4 × 4) with crew cab

Early production Unimog (4 × 4) with front-mounted winch in service with Portuguese Army

U 1650 L. Powered by 156 or 170 hp engines and with a 3.25 m wheelbase. Payload is from 3500 to 5000 kg. U 1750 L. Powered by a 170 hp engine and with a wheelbase of 3.25 or 3.85 m. Payload is from 5000 to 6000 kg.

During 1989 Mercedes-Benz introduced the 6 × 6 U 2150 L to the Unimog range. With a payload capacity of 8 tonnes, this model was produced to meet a requirement for a potential Far East customer. Powered by an OM 366 LA turbocharged diesel, the U 2150 L has a wheelbase of 3.25 m + 1.4 m and a gross vehicle weight of 16 000 kg. Length overall is 7.1 m. The UG 3/65 transmission features a fully synchromesh gearbox with eight forward and eight reverse gears. Maximum speed is 80 km/h.

The table includes the models produced prior to the 1988 designation changes.

Status
In service with Algeria, Angola, Australia, Belgium, Chile, Denmark, Egypt, France, Germany, Indonesia, Iraq, Kenya, Kuwait, Libya, Morocco, Mozambique, New Zealand, Nigeria, Pakistan, Peru, Portugal, Saudi Arabia, Singapore, South Africa, Syria, Tanzania, Tunisia, United Arab Emirates and United Kingdom (Army and Royal Air Force).

Manufacturer
Daimler-Benz AG, Gaggenau Plant, Germany.

Unimog U 1300 L with communications body (C R Zwart)

Enquiries to Daimler-Benz AG, Postfach 202, D-7000 Stuttgart-Untertürkheim, Federal Republic of Germany.   Tel: 0711 17 5 5186. Telex: 72524-0 db d. Fax: 0711 17 2244.

Mercedes-Benz L 508 DG MA (4 × 2) 2105 kg Truck

Description
The Mercedes-Benz L 508 DG MA (4 × 2) 2105 kg truck is used for transporting men and cargo in rear areas and has little cross-country mobility. It is a standard commercial vehicle with a minimum of modifications to suit it for military use. Final deliveries were made to the German Army during 1990.

The chassis is a bend-resistant parallel ladder frame with tubular crossmembers, except for the one at the rear. A coupling member is incorporated in the front crossmember suitable for a tow bar as used by the German armed forces.

The all-steel forward control cab is noise and temperature insulated. A heater is fitted as standard on all models and the L 508 D/35 van-type model, used as a command vehicle, has a heat exchanger and a special vent in the front part of the cab roof.

The rear cargo platform has a plywood floor with hinged steel side and tailboards, stowage boxes and support points for the centre bench and a tarpaulin frame as well as locating and lashing points for fitting a shelter or transporting pallets.

Swedish Army Mercedes-Benz L 508 DG MA (4 × 2) 2105 kg truck

Variants
L 508 D/35
This is the standard pick-up model with a wheelbase of 3.5 m, cargo area 4.06 m long and 2.26 m wide and maximum cargo capacity of 2460 kg.

L 608 D/41
This is a pick-up with a wheelbase of 4.1 m, cargo area 5.06 m long and 2.26 m wide and maximum cargo capacity of 3500 kg.

Specifications (L 508 DG MA)
Cab seating: 1 + 2
Configuration: 4 × 2
Weight:
  (empty) 3495 kg
  (loaded) 5600 kg
Max load: 2105 kg
Load area: 3.15 × 2.2 m
Max towed load: 1150 kg
Length: 5.325 m

Width: 2.32 m
Height:
  (cab, unloaded) 2.345 m
  (cab, loaded) 2.3 m
  (tarpaulin, unloaded) 2.68 m
  (tarpaulin, loaded) 2.535 m
Track:
  (front) 1.76 m
  (rear) 1.54 m
Wheelbase: 2.95 m
Max speed: 98 km/h
Range: 750 km
Fuel consumption: 11.2 l/100 km
Gradient: 27%
Engine: OM 314 4-cylinder diesel developing 85 hp at 1800 rpm
Transmission: manual, 5 forward and 1 reverse gears
Clutch: single dry plate
Steering: recirculating ball
Turning radius: 5.7 m

Suspension: semi-elliptical leaf springs, hydraulic shock absorbers with both axles fitted with torsion bar stabilisers
Tyres: 7.00 R 16 C 10 PR
Brakes:
  (main) air/hydraulic
  (parking) mechanical
Electrical system: 24 V
Batteries: 2 × 12 V

Status
In production. In service with the German Army and other armed forces, including Sweden.

Manufacturer
Daimler-Benz AG, Postfach 202, D-7000 Stuttgart-Untertürkheim, Federal Republic of Germany. Tel: 0711 17 5 5186. Telex: 72524-0 db d. Fax: 0711 17 2244.

IVECO Magirus 75-13 AWM (4 × 4) 2500 kg Truck

Description

There are two versions of the IVECO Magirus 75-13 AWM (4 × 4) 2500 kg truck, one using banjo axles and the other with a longer wheelbase and Portal axles. Both have forward control cabs and a cargo area that can be used to carry 12 men, a 2500 kg load or a shelter/container. These trucks were formerly known as the 130M7FAL.

The forward control cab is all steel and has seating for the driver and two passengers. The cab may be tilted forward for access to the engine and transmission. At the rear the cargo body is also all steel and has tiltable and removable sideboards and a tailgate. Folding benches are provided for 12 men. The load area is covered by a tarpaulin resting on bows. There is a spare wheel holder between the cab and the cargo body. Both versions have a standard 130 litre fuel tank but the version with Portal axles has an optional 200 litre tank.

Other options include a 3000 kg mechanical or hydraulic winch, an anti-roll bar at the rear, an exhaust brake and a roof hatch for the cab. It is also possible to provide a wading kit for depths up to 1.2 m.

Specifications

Cab seating: 1 + 2
Configuration: 4 × 4
Weight:
    (unladen) 4900 kg
    (laden) 7500 kg
Max load: 2600 kg
Towed load: 7500 kg
Length: 5.51 m
Width: 2.4 m
Height:
    (cab, SWB) 2.745 m
    (cab, LWB) 2.835 m
    (tarpaulin, SWB) 3.18 m
    (tarpaulin, LWB) 3.24 m
    (load area, SWB) 1.38 m
    (load area, LWB) 1.44 m
Ground clearance:
    (SWB) 0.26 m
    (LWB) 0.44 m
Track:
    (SWB) 1.852 m
    (LWB) 1.943 m
Wheelbase: 2.85 m or 3.1 m
Angle of approach/departure:
    (SWB) 35°/38°
    (LWB) 39°/50°
Max speed: 83 km/h
Range: 900 km
Fuel capacity: 130 l (200 l optional on LWB)

Gradient: 60%
Side slope: 30%
Fording: 0.8 m (optional 1.2 m)
Engine: Deutz Diesel F 6 L 913 6.128 l 6-cylinder air-cooled developing 130 hp at 2500 rpm
Gearbox: manual, 5 forward and 1 reverse gears
Clutch: single dry disc
Transfer box: 2-speed
Steering: ball and nut, assisted
Turning radius:
    (SWB) 6.7 m
    (LWB) 7.1 m
Suspension: semi-elliptical springs with hydraulic shock absorbers front and rear
Tyres: 12.50 × 20
Brakes:
    (main) drum type, dual circuit air over hydraulic
    (parking) mechanical on rear wheels
Electrical system: 24 V
Batteries: 2 × 12 V, 100 Ah
Alternator: 55 A

Status

In production.

Manufacturer

IVECO Magirus AG, Defence Vehicle Division, Postfach 2740, D-7900 Ulm, Federal Republic of Germany. Tel: 731 1041. Telex: 712 522 im d. Fax: 731 672 18.

IVECO Magirus 75-13 AWM (4 × 4) 2500 kg truck with banjo axles

IVECO Magirus 75-13 AWM (4 × 4) 2500 kg truck with Portal axles

IVECO Magirus 90-13 ANWM (4 × 4) 4000 kg Truck

Description

The IVECO Magirus 90-13 ANWM (4 × 4) 4000 kg truck was formerly known as the 130 D9AL.

The layout of the 90-13 ANWM is orthodox with the engine set forward under a square-cut bonnet. The radiator is usually protected by a grille guard and the bonnet top can be raised to the rear. The all-steel cab has seating for the driver and two passengers and a roof hatch is optional. The cab is soundproofed with cavity corrosion protection. Laminated glass is used for the one-piece windscreen. The cargo body has folding bench seating for 16 men and is covered by a tarpaulin resting on bows. The tailgate and sideboards are both tiltable and removable.

Optional equipment includes a 5000 kg mechanical or hydraulic winch, additional or enlarged fuel tanks, jerrican or extra equipment stowage and a power take-off on the gearbox or transfer box. A wading kit for depths up to 1.2 m can be fitted.

Specifications

Cab seating: 1 + 2
Configuration: 4 × 4
Weight:
    (unladen) 6100 kg
    (laden) 10 100 kg
Max load: 4000 kg
Towed load: 5000 kg
Length: 7.195 m
Width: 2.5 m
Height:
    (air intake) 2.87 m
    (tarpaulin) 3.2 m

IVECO Magirus 90-13 ANWM (4 × 4) 4000 kg truck

    (load area) 1.4 m
Ground clearance: 0.31 m
Track:
    (front) 1.97 m
    (rear) 1.902 m
Wheelbase: 4.2 m
Angle of approach/departure: 42°/31°
Max speed: 82 km/h
Range: 900 km
Fuel capacity: 130 l (optional 200 l or 200 + 130 l)
Gradient: 43%

Side slope: 30%
Fording: 0.8 m (1.2 m optional)
Engine: Deutz Diesel F 6 L 913 6.128 l 6-cylinder air-cooled developing 130 bhp at 2500 rpm
Gearbox: manual with 5 forward and 1 reverse gears
Clutch: single dry disc
Transfer box: 2-speed
Steering: ball and nut, assisted
Turning radius: 9.9 m
Suspension: leaf springs and hydraulic shock absorbers front and rear

Tyres: 13.00 × 20
Brakes:
(main) drum, dual circuit air over hydraulic
(parking) mechanical on rear wheels
Electrical system: 24 V

Batteries: 2 × 12 V, 100 Ah
Alternator: 35 A

Status
In production. In widespread service.

Manufacturer
IVECO Magirus AG, Defence Vehicle Division, Postfach 2740, D-7900 Ulm, Federal Republic of Germany. Tel: 731 1041. Telex: 712 522 im d. Fax: 731 672 18.

IVECO Magirus 110-16 AWM (4 × 4) 5000 kg Truck

Description
The IVECO Magirus 110-16 AWM (4 × 4) 5000 kg truck was formerly known as the 168M11FAL and is available in two forms, one with single tyres on the rear axle and the other with dual tyres and a shorter wheelbase. Both can be used as cargo trucks to carry a 5400 kg or 5500 kg load, a shelter/container or 18 men.

The 110-16 AWM has a forward control cab with an adjustable seat for the driver plus seating for two passengers. The cab is all steel and can tilt forward for engine access. A ventilation flap is provided on the roof and a roof hatch is available as an optional extra. A spare wheel holder is located between the cab and the cargo body which is also all steel with removable or tiltable sides and tailgate. A tarpaulin resting on bows is used to cover the cargo area and folding benches are provided for 18 men.

Optional equipment includes a 5000 kg mechanical or hydraulic winch, stowage for five jerricans, an enlarged fuel tank and an anti-roll bar at the rear.

Variant
IVECO Magirus 110-17 AM (4 × 2) 5000 kg Truck
This is a 4 × 2 version of the 110-16 AWM and was formerly known as the 168M11FL. It is similar to the 4 × 4 models, having dual tyres on the rear axle and a spare wheel stowed under the cargo body.

Status
In production. In widespread service.

Manufacturer
IVECO Magirus AG, Defence Vehicle Division, Postfach 2740, D-7900 Ulm, Federal Republic of Germany. Tel: 731 1041. Telex: 712 522 im d. Fax: 731 672 18.

IVECO Magirus 110-16 AWM (4 × 4) 5000 kg truck with single tyres on rear axle

Specifications

Model	110-16	110-17
Cab seating	1 + 2	1 + 2
Configuration	4 × 4	4 × 2 or 4 × 4
Weight		
(unladen)	6300 kg	6400 kg
(laden)	11 800 kg	11 800 kg
Max load	5500 kg	5400 kg
Towed load	11 800 kg	11 800 kg
Length	7.56 m	7.1 m
Width	2.37 m	2.37 m
Height		
(cab)	2.905 m	2.835 m
(tarpaulin)	3.39 m	3.29 m
(load area)	1.59 m	1.59 m
Ground clearance	0.31 m	0.264 m
Track (front/rear)	1.988/1.988 m	1.92/1.724 m
Wheelbase	4.2 m	3.6 m
Angle of approach/departure	40°/30°	35°/24°
Max speed	85 km/h	80 km/h
Range	600 km	600 km
Fuel capacity	130 l	130 l

Model	110-16	110-17
Max gradient	60%	60%
Side slope	30%	30%
Fording	0.8 m	0.8 m
Engine	Deutz Diesel BF 6 L 913 6.128 l 6-cylinder air-cooled turbocharged developing 168 bhp at 2650 rpm	
Gearbox	manual with 6 forward and 1 reverse gears	
Clutch	single dry disc	single dry disc
Transfer box	2-speed	2-speed
Steering	ball and nut, assisted	
Turning radius	8.8 m	7.9 m
Suspension	leaf springs with hydraulic telescopic shock absorbers front and rear	
Tyres	13.00 × 20 PR-18	10 × 22.5
Brakes		
(main)	drum, independent, dual circuit pneumatic	
(parking)	spring energy brake cylinder	
Electrical system	24 V	24 V
Batteries	2 × 12 V, 100 Ah	2 × 12 V, 125 Ah
Alternator	35 A	35 A

IVECO Magirus 120-19 ANWM (4 × 4) 5000 kg Truck

Description
The IVECO Magirus 120-19 ANWM (4 × 4) 5000 kg truck was formerly known as the 192D12AL and may be regarded as an enlarged version of the 4000 kg 90-13 ANWM. It has a more powerful engine and a longer wheelbase, and a number of different types of body can be fitted.

The standard cargo body version is covered by a tarpaulin resting on bows and has folding bench seating for 18 men. The cab has an adjustable driver's seat and seating for two passengers. The one-piece windscreen is of laminated glass and the cab is soundproofed with cavity corrosion protection. A ventilation flap is provided on the roof and a roof hatch is optional. A spare wheel is carried between the cab and cargo body. The cargo body tailgate and side-boards are both tiltable and removable.

Optional equipment includes a 5000 kg or 8000 kg mechanical or hydraulic winch, an enlarged fuel tank or extra fuel tanks, jerrican or extra equipment stowage and a power take-off on the gearbox or transfer box. A wading kit for depths up to 1.2 m is available.

Specifications
Cab seating: 1 + 2 (up to 18 in rear)
Configuration: 4 × 4
Weight:
(unladen) 7300 kg
(laden) 12 300 kg
Max load: 5000 kg
Towed load: 6000 kg
Length: 8.405 m
Width: 2.5 m
Height:
(air intake) 2.93 m
(tarpaulin) 3.38 m
(load area) 1.58 m
Ground clearance: 0.37 m
Track:
(front) 1.985 m
(rear) 2.03 m
Wheelbase: 4.9 m
Angle of approach/departure: 37°/33°
Max speed: 85 km/h
Fuel capacity: 130 l (optional 200 l or 200 + 130 l)
Max gradient: 60%
Side slope: 30%
Fording: 0.8 m (1.2 m optional)
Engine: Deutz Diesel F6L 413 F 9.572 l 6-cylinder air-cooled developing 192 hp at 2500 rpm
Gearbox: manual with 6 forward and 1 reverse gears
Clutch: single dry disc
Transfer box: 2-speed
Steering: ball and nut, assisted
Turning radius: 12 m
Suspension: leaf springs with hydraulic shock

absorbers front and rear
Tyres: 14.00 × 20
Brakes:
   (main) drum, dual circuit plus exhaust brake
   (parking) failsafe acting on rear wheels via air-
   controlled spring energy cylinder
Electrical system: 24 V
Batteries: 2 × 12 V, 100 Ah
Alternator: 35 A

Status
In production. In widespread service.

Manufacturer
IVECO Magirus AG, Defence Vehicle Division, Post-
fach 2740, D-7900 Ulm, Federal Republic of Germany.
Tel: 731 1041. Telex: 712 522 im d.
Fax: 731 672 18.

IVECO Magirus 120-19 ANWM (4 × 4) 5000 kg truck

IVECO Magirus 160-23 ANWM (6 × 6) 7000 kg Truck

Description
This truck may be regarded as the lengthened and
three-axled version of the lighter 90-13 ANWM and
120-19 ANWM versions. It can be used either in the
basic cargo body form or used to carry a wide variety of
other types of body such as tankers, office or workshop
bodies, and so on. The similar 160-25 ANWM with a
payload capacity of 8000 kg (formerly known as the
256D18AL) is no longer in production.

The layout is orthodox with the engine forward under
a bonnet top that can be raised to the rear. The radiator
grille can be folded forward. The all-steel cab has an
adjustable seat for the driver and seating is provided
for two other passengers. The roof has a ventilation
flap and a roof hatch is optional. Laminated glass is
used for the one-piece windscreen and the cab is
soundproofed with cavity corrosion protection. Two air
intake pipes are located each side of the cab windscreen. A spare wheel holder is located between the
cab and the cargo body. The cargo area is covered by
a tarpaulin resting on bows, has folding benches for 18
men and is all steel with tiltable and removable
sideboards and tailgate.

Optional equipment includes an 8000 kg or 10 000 kg
mechanical or hydraulic winch, an enlarged or extra
fuel tank, stowage for five 20 litre jerricans and a power
take-off on the gearbox or transfer box. A wading kit for
the electrical system is available for depths of up to
1.2 m.

This model was replaced in production by the 240-25
ANWM – see separate entry in this section.

Specifications
Cab seating: 1 + 2 (up to 18 in rear)
Configuration: 6 × 6
Weight:
   (unladen) 9400 kg
   (laden) 16 400 kg
Max load: 7000 kg
Towed load: 12 000 kg
Length: 8.55 m
Width: 2.5 m

IVECO Magirus 160-23 ANWM (6 × 6) 7000 kg truck

Height:
   (air intake) 2.99 m
   (tarpaulin) 3.365 m
   (load area) 1.565 m
Ground clearance: 0.37 m
Track:
   (front) 2.005 m
   (rear) 2.048 m
Wheelbase: 4.2 m + 1.38 m
Angle of approach/departure: 38°/38°
Max speed: 80 km/h
Range: 700 km
Fuel capacity: 200 l (optional 300 l or 300 l plus 200 l)
Max gradient: 60%
Side slope: 30%
Fording: 0.8 m (optional 1.2 m)
Engine: Deutz Diesel F 8 L 413 11.31 l 8-cylinder
air-cooled diesel developing 232 hp at 2650 rpm
Gearbox: manual with 6 forward and 1 reverse gears
Clutch: single dry disc
Transfer box: 2-speed
Steering: ball and nut, assisted

Turning radius: 10.4 m
Suspension:
   (front) single flexibility leaf springs with hydraulic
   telescopic shock absorbers
   (rear) single flexibility leaf springs, reversed, fully
   articulated
Tyres: 14.00 × 20
Brakes:
   (main) drum, dual circuit plus exhaust brake
   (parking) mechanical on rear wheels
Electrical system: 24 V
Batteries: 2 × 12 V, 100 Ah
Alternator: 35 A

Status
Production complete. In widespread service.

Manufacturer
IVECO Magirus AG, Defence Vehicle Division, Post-
fach 2740, D-7900 Ulm, Federal Republic of Germany.
Tel: 731 1041. Telex: 712522 im d.
Fax: 731 672 18.

IVECO Magirus 200-23 ANWM and 210-32 ANWM (6 × 6) 10 000 kg Trucks

Description

There are two basic types of truck under this designation with the main difference between the two being the type and power of engine fitted – the 200-23 has an eight-cylinder 232 hp engine and the 210-32 a ten-cylinder 320 hp engine. Short and long wheelbase models of each version are produced.

The IVECO Magirus 200-23 and 210-32 follow the same basic lines as the IVECO Magirus 160-23 ANWM and 160-25 ANWM and differ only in some weights and dimensions. They can be produced in a number of body types, in addition to the basic cargo body version. The cargo version has seating for up to 18 men in the rear.

This model was replaced in production by the 240-25 ANWM – see separate entry in this section.

Status

Production complete. In widespread service.

IVECO Magirus 200-23 ANWM (6 × 6) 10 000 kg truck

Manufacturer

IVECO Magirus AG, Defence Vehicle Division, Postfach 2740, D-7900 Ulm, Federal Republic of Germany.

Tel: 731 1041. Telex: 712 522 im d. Fax: 731 672 18.

Specifications

(Data for short wheelbase versions; data for long wheelbase in square brackets where different.)

Model	200-23	210-32	Model	200-23	210-32
Cab seating	1 + 2	1 + 2	Side slope	30%	30%
Configuration	6 × 6	6 × 6	Fording	0.8 m	0.8 m
Weight			Engine	Deutz Diesel	Deutz Diesel
(unladen)	10 400 kg	10 700 kg		F 8 L 413F 11.310-l	F 10 L 413F 15.953-l
(laden)	20 400 kg	21 000 kg		8-cylinder	10-cylinder
Max load	10 000 kg	10 300 kg		air-cooled	air-cooled
Towed load	18 000 kg	18 000 kg	Engine output	232 hp at 2650 rpm	320 hp at 2500 rpm
Length	7.495* [9.6] m	7.495 [9.6] m	Gearbox	manual with 6 forward and 1 reverse gears	
Width	2.5 m	2.5 m	Clutch	single dry disc	single dry disc
Height			Transfer box	2-speed	2-speed
(air intake)	2.925 m	2.925 m	Steering	ball and nut, assisted	
(tarpaulin)	3.365 m	3.365 m	Turning radius	11.8 [12.5] m	11.8 [12.5] m
(load area)	1.565 m	1.565 m	Suspension		
Ground clearance	0.335 m	0.305 m	(front)	single flexibility leaf springs with hydraulic shock absorbers	
Track					
(front)	2.005 m	2.005 m	(rear)	single flexibility leaf springs, reversed, fully articulated	
(rear)	2.048 m	2.048 m			
Wheelbase	3.9 m + 1.38 m	3.9 m + 1.38 m	Tyres	14.00 × 20	14.00 × 20
	[5.25 m + 1.38 m]	[5.25 m + 1.38 m]	Brakes		
Angle of approach/departure	32°/60°*	32°/60°*	(main)	drum, dual circuit, exhaust brake	
	[35°/30°]*	[35°/30°]*	(parking)	mechanical on rear wheels	
Max speed	80 [81] km/h	80 [81] km/h	Electrical system	24 V	24 V
Range	600 km	600 km	Batteries	2 × 12 V, 1 Ah	2 × 12 V, 100 Ah
Fuel capacity	200 l	200 l	Alternator	35 A	35 A
Max gradient	60%	60%	* chassis only		

IVECO Magirus 240-25 ANWM (6 × 6) 12 000 kg Truck

Description

The IVECO Magirus 240-25 ANWM (6 × 6) 12 000 kg high mobility truck replaced the earlier 160-23 ANWM and 200-23 ANWM (6 × 6) trucks in production. Short and long wheelbase models are available.

The IVECO Magirus 240-25 follows the same basic lines as the earlier models. Both wheelbase length models can be produced in a number of body types, in addition to the basic cargo body version.

Status

In production.

Manufacturer

IVECO Magirus AG, Defence Vehicle Division, Postfach 2740, D-79 Ulm, Federal Republic of Germany. Tel: 731 1041. Telex: 712 522 im d. Fax: 731 672 18.

Short wheelbase version of IVECO Magirus 240-25 ANWM (6 × 6) 12 000 kg truck

Specifications

Model	SWB	LWB
Cab seating	1 + 2	1 + 2
Configuration	6 × 6	6 × 6
Weight		
(kerb, chassis/cab)	8 800 kg	8 800 kg
(GVW)	24 500 kg	24 500 kg
Max load	12 000 kg	12 000 kg
Towed load	11 500 kg	11 500 kg
Length	8.55 m	9.2 m
Width	2.5 m	2.5 m
Height		
(air intake)	3.088 m	3.088 m
(tarpaulin)	3.365 m	3.365 m
(load area)	1.565 m	1.565 m
Ground clearance	0.37 m	0.37 m
Track		
(front)	2.005 m	2.005 m
(rear)	2.048 m	2.048 m
Wheelbase	4.2 m + 1.38 m	5.25 m + 1.38 m
Angle of approach/departure	38°/38°	35°/30°
Max speed	84 km/h	84 km/h
Range	600 km	600 km

Model	SWB	LWB
Fuel capacity	300 l	300 l
Max gradient	56%	56%
Side slope	30%	30%
Fording	0.8 m	0.8 m
Engine	Deutz Diesel F 8 L 513 13.382 l 8-cylinder air-cooled diesel developing 264 hp at 2300 rpm	
Gearbox	manual with 6 forward and 1 reverse gears	
Clutch	single dry disc	single dry disc
Transfer box	2-speed	2-speed
Steering	ball and nut, assisted	
Turning radius	11.4 m	13.5 m
Suspension		
(front)	semi-elliptic leaf springs with hydraulic shock absorbers	
(rear)	cantilever leaf springs	
Tyres	14.00 R 20	14.00 R 20
Brakes		
(main)	drum, dual circuit, exhaust brake	
(parking)	mechanical on rear wheels	
Electrical system	24 V	24 V

MAN LX 90 (4 × 4) and (6 × 6) High Mobility Off-road Trucks

Description
During 1989 MAN launched the L-mil series, now known as the LX 90 series, to cover the load class range from 2.5 up to 7.5 tonnes. There are 4 × 4 and 6 × 6 versions with permanent all-wheel drive.

The cab is designed for military use and is available with or without a roof hatch. It allows transport by railway and carrying in C-130 and C-160 transport aircraft. The radiator arrangement to the rear of the cab prevents clogging and allows fording of depths up to 1.2 m. Extensive use has been made of corrosion protection.

The frame has newly designed stiff U-profile longitudinal frame rails in combination with tubular cross-sections and soft leaf springs, allowing good handling both on and off roads.

A self-recovery winch allows towing to the front as well as a double line pull to the rear, both without removing the winch cable.

The chassis can be fitted with a cargo box body, a load handling system, a tanker body, shelters for various military systems, or a material handling crane. It can also be configured as a medium recovery vehicle.

Status
In production. Prototypes delivered to Luxembourg and Swiss armies.

Manufacturer
MAN Nutzfahrzeuge AG, Postfach 500620, D-8000 Munich 50, Federal Republic of Germany.
Tel: 89 1480-1. Telex: 211 023.

MAN LX 90 (4 × 4) truck

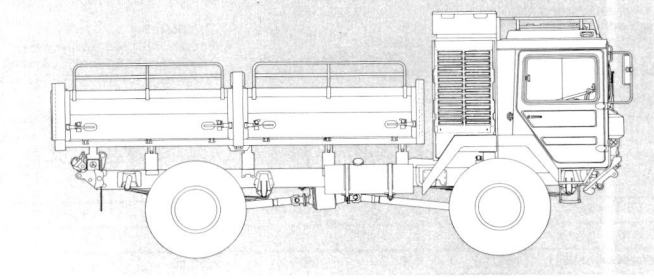

MAN LX 90 (4 × 4) truck (not to 1/76 scale)

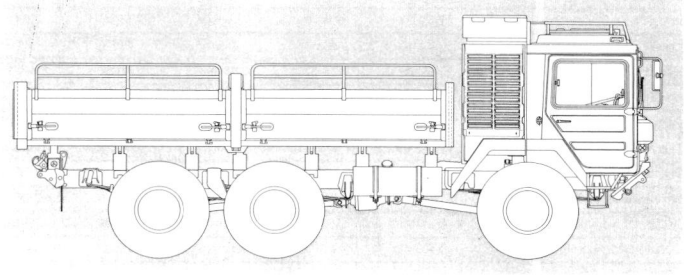

MAN LX 90 (6 × 6) truck (not to 1/76 scale)

Specifications

Wheelbase	3.8 m	4 m	3 m + 1.35 m	3.55 m + 1.35 m
Cab seating	1 + 2	1 + 2	1 + 2	1 + 2
Configuration	4 × 4	4 × 4	6 × 6	6 × 6
Weight				
(unladen)	6700 kg	6850 kg	8000 kg	8200 kg
(laden)	10 700 kg	10 850 kg	16 000 kg	16 200 kg
Chassis capacity	2500 to 4000 kg		4000 to 7500 kg	
Length	6.91 m	7.51 m	7.51 m	8.61 m
Width	2.5 m	2.5 m	2.5 m	2.5 m
Height				
(cab)	2.58 + 0.29 m (detachable)		2.58 + 0.29 m (detachable)	
(load area)	1.38 m	1.38 m	1.38 m	1.38 m
Ground clearance	0.388 m	0.388 m	0.388 m	0.388 m
Track	1.98 m	1.98 m	1.98 m	1.98 m
Wheelbase	3.8 m	4 m	3 m + 1.35 m	3.55 m + 1.35 m
Angle of approach	30°	30°	30°	30°
Max speed, road	90 km/h	90 km/h	90 km/h	90 km/h
Fuel capacity	200 l	200 l	200 l	200 l
Fording, max	1.2 m	1.2 m	1.2 m	1.2 m
Engine	MAN D 0826 6-cylinder in-line watercooled turbocharged and intercooled diesel developing 190 hp, 230 hp or 270 hp			
Gearbox	ZF 9S-75 or Eaton 6109 or optional ZF 5 HP 500 automatic			
Clutch	MF 380 single dry plate or optional ZF Transmatic WSK 380			
Steering	ZF 8097 recirculating ball hydraulic			
Suspension	progressively acting leaf springs and shock absorbers			
Tyres	14.5 R 20 or optional 15.5/80 R 20			
Brakes	dual circuit air			
Electrical system	24 V	24 V	24 V	24 V
Batteries	2 × 12 V, 125 Ah			

Mercedes-Benz LA 911B (4 × 4) 4500 kg Truck

Description

The Mercedes-Benz LA 911B (4 × 4) 4500 kg truck is also known as the LA 1113 and before 1963 was known as the LA 328. It has been in production for many years and is in widespread military use, particularly in Africa and Asia.

The LA 911B is produced in two wheelbase lengths, 3.6 m and 4.2 m. The layout is orthodox with the engine forward under a distinctive curved bonnet and the cab is all steel. The cab has seating for the driver and two passengers with the passenger's bench seat folding down to provide access to the roof hatch. The cargo area can be used to seat up to 24 persons and can be covered by a canvas tilt. A spare wheel is carried under the load area. The electrical system is splashproof and to NATO standard, with an external plug socket.

Various types of bodies can be fitted to the LA 911B. In service are ambulance, workshop, light recovery, firefighting and other bodies. The LA 911B can be used as a light artillery tractor.

Mercedes-Benz LA 911B (4 × 4) 4500 kg truck

Specifications

Cab seating: 1 + 2
Configuration: 4 × 4
Weight:
 (unladen) 5500 kg
 (laden) 10 000 kg
 (GCW) 21 600 kg
Weight on front axle: 4000 kg
Weight on rear axle: 6400 kg
Max load: 4500 kg
Max towed load: 11 000 kg
Length:
 (SWB) 5.98 m
 (LWB) 6.9 m
Width: 2.46 m
Height:
 (cab) 2.71 m
 (tarpaulin) 3.13 m
Ground clearance: 0.34 m
Track: 1.97 m
Wheelbase: 3.6 m or 4.2 m
Angle of approach/departure: 37°/46°
Max speed: 84 km/h
Fuel capacity: 135 l
Gradient: 68%
Fording: 0.9 m
Engine: Mercedes-Benz OM 352 5.675 l 6-cylinder in-line water-cooled diesel developing 130 hp at 2000 rpm or Mercedes-Benz OM 352A 5.675 l 6-cylinder in-line water-cooled turbocharged diesel developing 168 hp at 2000 rpm
Gearbox: Mercedes-Benz G 3/50-5/8.5 with 5 forward and 1 reverse gears
Clutch: single dry disc
Transfer box: Mercedes-Benz VG 500-3W/1.6 2-speed

Steering: recirculating ball (power steering optional)
Turning radius: 8.1 m
Tyres: 12.00 × 20
Brakes: single-circuit hydraulic, compressed air assisted
Electrical system: 24 V
Batteries: 2 × 12 V, 100 Ah
Alternator: 55 A

Status

In production. In military service worldwide.

Manufacturer

Daimler-Benz AG, Postfach 202, D-7000 Stuttgart-Untertürkheim, Federal Republic of Germany.
Tel: 0711 17 5 5186. Telex: 72524-0 db d.
Fax: 0711 17 2244.

Mercedes-Benz Model 1017 (4 × 2) and Model 1017 A (4 × 4) 5000 kg Trucks

Development

These two vehicles were developed by Mercedes-Benz to meet the requirements of the German Army and are essentially standard commercial vehicles with the minimum of modifications to suit them for military use. Adaptations include a modified electrical system, use of low-torsion platform with stowage boxes and adequate structure plus mounting points for van bodies, additional stowage space on the rear wall of the cab for military equipment and installation of an observation hatch in the roof of the cab. The major differences between the 1017 and the 1017 A are that the latter has 4 × 4 drive and larger tyres. Final deliveries were made in 1987. It was replaced in production by the Model 1217 CA (see entry in this section).

Description

The layout of both vehicles is identical with the forward

Mercedes-Benz 1017 A (4 × 4) 5000 kg truck complete with bows and tarpaulin cover (C R Zwart)

Mercedes-Benz 1017 A (4 × 4) 5000 kg truck with bows stowed and tarpaulin cover removed

control cab at the front and the cargo area at the rear.

The parallel ladder chassis is bend-resistant but flexible; the sidemembers are the fish belly type in that the height of the web is tailored to the load acting on the chassis at the respective point. Open hat section crossmembers, cold-riveted to the frame, provide the desired torsional elasticity. With this design the chassis adapts to the surface of the road or track and imposes little stress on the material.

The all-steel forward control cab is noise and temperature insulated and the front rests on two rubber-bushed pivot bearings and its rear end on two vibration-damped spring struts.

The heating system keeps the inside temperature at between −4 and 25°C and the cab has a ventilation system incorporating a blower. Adjustable air inlets ensure well-balanced air distribution and window defrosting.

The platform has a wooden bed with sectional steel seam and is provided with lashing eyelets for pallets and supplies, plus countersunk anchors for the centre seat benches for the transport of troops. The top edges of the drop type wooden sideboards are covered by U-sections and side racks are installed for troop transport. The tarpaulin can be removed and the bows, which are adjustable for height, can be removed and stowed away. The truck can be loaded from the sides, even with the bows installed.

Status

Production complete. In service with Germany, Belgium, Portugal and NATO units.

Manufacturer

Daimler-Benz AG, Postfach 202, D-7000 Stuttgart-Untertürkheim, Federal Republic of Germany.
Tel: 0711 17 5 5186. Telex: 72524-0 db d.
Fax: 0711 17 2244.

Specifications

Model	**1017**	**1017 A**
Cab seating	1 + 1	1 + 1
Configuration	4 × 2	4 × 4
Weight		
(unladen)	6250 kg	6800 kg
(laden)	11 700 kg	12 200 kg
Max load	5450 kg	5400 kg
Max towed load	12 800 kg	12 300 kg
Length	7.19 m	7.19 m
Width	2.47 m	2.47 m
Height (cab, unloaded)	2.7 m	2.88 m
(cab, loaded)	2.665 m	2.843 m
(load area, unloaded)	1.425 m	1.525 m
Load area	5 × 2.38 m	5 × 2.38 m
Ground clearance	0.263 m	0.288 m
Track (front)	1.954 m	2.067 m
Wheelbase	3.6 m	3.6 m
Angle of approach/departure	23°/20°	30°/23°
Max speed	87 km/h	81 km/h
Range	730 km	695 km
Fuel capacity	135 l	135 l
Fuel consumption	18.5 l/100 km	19.4 l/100 km
Gradient (road)	45%	46%
(cross-country)	n/app	80%
Fording	0.5 m	0.5 m
Engine	OM 352 A 6-cylinder turbocharged diesel developing 172 hp at 2800 rpm	
Clutch	hydraulically operated	hydraulically operated
Transfer box	none	2-speed
Steering	hydraulic	hydraulic
Turning radius	7.4 m	8.75 m
Suspension (front and rear)	leaf springs, telescopic shock absorbers and torsion bar stabilisers, rear axle has secondary leaf spring	
Tyres	22.50/6.00 × 25	22.50/7.50 × 22.50
Brakes (main)	hydraulic, dual circuit	hydraulic, dual circuit
(parking)	mechanical	mechanical
(exhaust brake)	standard	standard
Electrical system	24 V	24 V
Batteries	2 × 12 V	2 × 12 V

MAN-Volkswagen Type 8.150 FAE and 9.150 FAE (4 × 4) 3000 kg Trucks

Description

These trucks, originally the Type 8.136 FAE and 9.136 FAE, were developed jointly by MAN and Volkswagen and were first shown during the Spring of 1983. The two models vary in chassis weights and capacities but use the same engine.

In late 1984 the Danish Army ordered more than 725 of the Type 8.136 FAE version at a reported cost of DM45 million for delivery between 1985 and 1989; by late 1990, 989 had been delivered and a further 60 were on order. These trucks were fitted with engines developing 136 hp at 3000 rpm.

In 1987 MAN received an order from the British Army for 42 Type 9.136 FAE vehicles. In early 1988 the engine rating was increased to 150 hp and the British Army ordered 15 units of the new model Type 9.150 FAE. By the end of September 1990 100 units had been delivered.

The Type 8.150 FAE and Type 9.150 FAE (4 × 4) trucks are of conventional layout with all-steel forward control cabs. Seating is provided inside the cab for the driver and one or two passengers while behind the cab is space for a spare wheel and tool stowage. The load area may be covered by a canvas tilt.

MAN-Volkswagen Type 8.136 FAE 3000 kg truck as ordered by Danish Army

Single tyres are provided front and rear and the 4 × 4 drive configuration is permanent. The suspension is based on the use of semi-elliptical springs front and rear that allow a considerable degree of axle articulation.

A winch is located behind the rear axle with the cable leading through rollers mounted on the front bumper. Other items that may be fitted include a material handling crane behind the cab, and the cab may have a roof hatch. A NATO towing hitch is usually fitted. The vehicles for the Danish order are fitted with external engine starting, stowage over the cab, movable running boards, chassis shackles for use when carried on rail cars, and the alternator and fan have been moved to allow fording through water obstacles 1 m deep. Other optional extras include a special oil sump with two pumps to ensure optimum oil flow on up to 60 per cent gradients.

Specifications

(Type 8.150 FAE; data for 9.150 FAE in square brackets where different)

Cab seating: 1 + 1 or 2
Configuration: 4 × 4
Weight:
(empty, 3.1 m WB) 3580 [3670] kg
(empty, 3.5 m WB) 3620 [3710] kg
(loaded) 7490 [8990] kg
Max load: 3330 [3240] kg
Length: 5.92 m
Width: 2.245 m
Height: 2.685 m
Ground clearance:
(front) 0.375 m
(rear) 0.32 m

Wheelbase: 3.1 m or 3.5 m
Track: 1.8 m
Angle of approach/departure: 31°/24°
Max speed: 80.8 km/h
Fuel capacity: 100 l
Max gradient: (with special sump) 60%
Fording: (prepared) 1 m
Engine: D 0826 6.87 l 6-cylinder in-line water-cooled direct injection diesel developing 150 hp at 2700 rpm
Gearbox: VW7 with 5 forward and 1 reverse gears
Transfer box: MAN G 300, 2-speed
Clutch: single dry disc
Steering: ZF Type 8036 hydraulic-assist
Turning circle: 15.5 m
Suspension: (front and rear) semi-elliptic leaf springs with double-action hydraulic shock absorbers

Tyres: 9.00 × 20 S + G, 10.00 × 20, 12.5 R 20 (22PR)
Brakes:
(main) dual circuit air
(parking) mechanical on wheels
Electrical system: 24 V

Status

In production. In service with Danish Army (more than 725 ordered) and British Army (57).

Manufacturer

MAN Nutzfahrzeuge AG, Postfach 500620, D-8000 Munich 50, Federal Republic of Germany. Tel: 89 1480-1. Telex: 211 023.

MAN 11.136 HA (4 × 4) 5000 kg Truck

Description

The MAN 11.136 HA (4 × 4) 5000 kg truck is based on standard commercial components with suitable modifications for military use. MAN delivered 3000 of these vehicles to the Belgian Army which also uses the older MAN 630 L2AE-B series of 5000 kg (4 × 4) trucks.

The chassis consists of U-frame longitudinal members with riveted and bolted crossmembers with four reinforced couplings at the front and trailer coupling, type RU, size K3D, at the rear.

The layout of the vehicle is conventional with the engine at the front, two-door fully enclosed cab in the centre and cargo area at the rear. The cab has a reinforced bonnet, hydraulically cushioned seat for the driver and a buzzer connected to the differential lock that informs the driver when the differential is engaged. The rear cargo body has a steel frame, sheet steel drop sides and tailgate, pinewood floor, removable bows and a tarpaulin cover.

A 4 × 2 model was also available under the designation 11.136 H.

Specifications

Cab seating: 1 + 2
Configuration: 4 × 4
Weight:
(empty) 6000 kg
(loaded) 11 000 kg
Max load: 5000 kg
Load area: 4.6 × 2.35 m
Length: 7.305 m
Width: 2.3 m
Height:
(cab) 2.605 m
(load area) 1 m
Ground clearance:
(front) 0.33 m
(rear) 0.334 m
Track:
(front) 1.82 m
(rear) 1.664 m
Wheelbase: 4.4 m
Max speed: 83.9 km/h
Range: 720 km
Fuel capacity: 200 l
Max gradient: 60%
Fording: 0.75 m
Engine: MAN/Renault model 797/06 6-cylinder water-cooled diesel developing 150 hp (SAE) at 3000 rpm

Gearbox: ZF synchromesh model S 5-35 with 5 forward and 1 reverse gears
Clutch: single dry plate
Transfer box: G 300, 2-speed
Steering: ZF Gemmer worm and roller
Turning radius: 9.65 m
Suspension:
(front) semi-elliptical leaf springs with progressively working hollow rubber springs
(rear) leaf springs with progressively working stepped springs
Tyres: 9.00 × 20
Brakes:
(front) air/hydraulic
(rear) air
(parking) spring loaded on rear wheels
(engine brake) exhaust
Electrical system: 24 V
Batteries: 2 × 12 V, 100 Ah

Status

In production. In service with the Belgian Army (3000).

Manufacturer

MAN Nutzfahrzeuge AG, Postfach 500620, D-8000 Munich 50, Federal Republic of Germany. Tel: 89 1480-1. Telex: 211 023.

Belgian Army MAN 11.136 HA (4 × 4) 5000 kg truck (P Touzin)

Belgian Army MAN 11.136 HA (4 × 4) 5000 kg truck with van body (C R Zwart)

MAN 14.240 HAE and 19.240 HAE (4 × 4) 5000 kg Trucks

Description

The MAN 14.240 HAE (4 × 4) 5000 kg truck was based on standard commercial components with suitable modifications for military use. It may be regarded as a logical progression from the MAN 11.136 HA series (see previous entry). MAN delivered more than 250 of these vehicles to various North African countries.

The chassis consists of U-frame longitudinal members with riveted and bolted crossmembers with one reinforced coupling at the front and a trailer coupling, type RU, size K4D, at the rear.

The layout of the vehicle is conventional with the engine at the front, a two-door fully enclosed cab in the centre and the cargo area at the rear. The cab has a reinforced bonnet, a hydraulically cushioned seat for the driver, and a buzzer connected to the differential lock to inform the driver when the differential is engaged. The rear cargo body has a steel frame, sheet steel drop sides and tailgate, a pinewood floor, removable bows and a tarpaulin cover.

An upgraded version, the 19.240 HAE, is still in production. A 4 × 2 model with the designation 19.240 H was available. Also available were 6 × 6 and 6 × 4 models with payloads of up to 10 000 kg with rear axles single-tyred, or 23 000 kg with twin tyres on the rear axles.

Specifications (14.240 HAE)

Cab seating: 1 + 2
Configuration: 4 × 4
Weight:
(empty) 6600 kg
(loaded) 14 000 kg
Max load: 5000 kg
Load area: 5 × 2.44 m
Length: 8.2 m
Width: 2.5 m
Height: (cab, unladen) 2.863 m
Ground clearance:
(front) 0.44 m
(rear) 0.37 m

MAN 19.240 HAE (4 × 4) truck

Track:
(front) 2.035 m
(rear) 2.078 m
Wheelbase: 5.2 m
Max speed: 80 km/h

Range: approx 800 km
Fuel capacity: 300 l
Max gradient: 60%
Fording: 0.75 m
Engine: MAN model D 2566 6-cylinder water-cooled

diesel developing 240 hp (DIN) at 2200 rpm
Gearbox: ZF synchromesh model S 6-90 with 6 forward and 1 reverse gears
Clutch: single dry plate
Transfer box: G 801, 2-speed
Steering: ZF hydraulic
Turning radius: 9.65 m
Suspension:
(front) semi-elliptic leaf springs with progressively working hollow rubber springs
(rear) leaf springs with progressively working stepped rings
Tyres:
(4 × 4) 14.00 R 20
(4 × 2) 12.00 R 20
Brakes:
(main) air
(parking) spring loaded on rear wheels
(engine) exhaust
Electrical system: 24 V
Batteries: 2 × 12 V, 140 Ah

Status
Production of 19.240 HAE continues; production of 14.240 HAE complete. In service with various North African and South American countries.

Manufacturer
MAN Nutzfahrzeuge AG, Postfach 500620, D-8000 Munich 50, Federal Republic of Germany.
Tel: 89 1480-1. Telex: 211 023.

Mercedes-Benz 1217 CA (4 × 4) 5500 kg Truck

Description
The Mercedes-Benz 1217 CA (4 × 4) 5500 kg truck is a two-axle, cross-country truck designed for the transport of personnel or supplies and as a tractor for light artillery.

The Mercedes-Benz 1217 CA has a forward control cab with seating for the driver and two passengers. The cab is available in two forms, a standard through-cab access model and a medium length cab with even more space. On both, the centre seat has a folding backrest that can be used to gain access to a roof hatch. There is stowage for weapons and other equipment. Both cabs can be tilted forward for engine and other maintenance. Heating and ventilation systems are provided.

The AL3 front axle has differential locks and a planetary hub drive is used on the HL7 back axle.

The cargo body has drop sides and a drop tailgate and may be protected by a cover and tilt. Purpose-built bodies are envisaged for a number of applications including ambulances, communications, fuel and water tankers and for firefighting. A 5000 kg tractive capability hydraulic or mechanical winch may be fitted, with cable control to the front or rear.

Specifications
Cab seating: 1 + 2
Configuration: 4 × 4
Weight:
(kerb) approx 7800 kg
(GVW) 14 000 kg
(GCW) 24 500 kg
Front axle load: 6000 kg
Rear axle load: 8500 kg
Max load: approx 5500 kg
Towed load: 10 500 kg

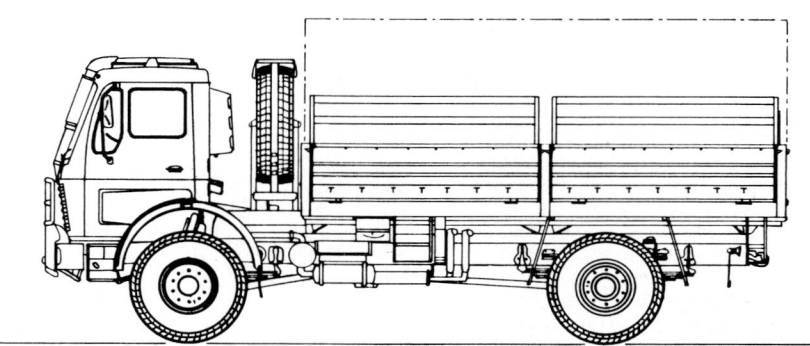

Mercedes-Benz 1217 CA (4 × 4) 5500 kg truck

Load area: 4.5 × 2.43 m
Length: 7.015 m
Width: 2.5 m
Height:
(top of cab hatch) 2.91 m
(tilt) 3.38 m
(load area) 1.527 m
Ground clearance: 0.31 m
Track: 2.09 m
Wheelbase: 3.6 m
Angle of approach/departure: 30°/32°
Max speed:
(road) 85 km/h
(cross-country) 48 km/h
Fuel capacity: 200 l
Max gradient:
(road) 36%
(cross-country) 73%
(road, GCW with trailer) 19%
(cross-country, GCW with trailer) 35%
Fording: 1 m
Engine: Mercedes-Benz OM 366A 5.958 l 6-cylinder in-line turbocharged water-cooled diesel developing

170 hp at 2600 rpm
Transmission: Mercedes-Benz G 3/60-5/7.5 synchromesh with 5 forward and 1 reverse gears
Clutch: single dry disc
Transfer box: Mercedes-Benz VG 500-3W with differential lock, 2-speed
Steering: Mercedes-Benz LS 5 F, power
Turning circle: 16.6 m
Tyres: 13.00 × 20 (14.00 × 20 optional)
Brakes: dual circuit compressed air with automatic load-dependent brake (ALB) pressure control
Electrical system: 24 V
Batteries: 2 × 12 V, 110 Ah

Status
In production.

Manufacturer
Daimler-Benz AG, Postfach 202, D-7000 Stuttgart-Untertürkheim, Federal Republic of Germany.
Tel: 0711 17 5 5186. Telex: 72524-0 db d.
Fax: 0711 17 2244.

Mercedes-Benz 1222 A (4 × 4) 5500 kg Truck

Description
The Mercedes-Benz 1222 A (4 × 4) 5500 kg truck is available in two versions, one with a wheelbase of 3.55 m and the other having a wheelbase of 4.15 m.

Both are powered by the same engine and use the same transmission.

Two cab versions are available, both having seating for the driver and two passengers with the centre seat folding down to provide access to the roof hatch. One is the standard cab and the other the medium-length cab with more internal space for equipment stowage. Both cabs can be tilted forward for engine and

transmission access. The normal body is a cargo platform with drop sides and tailgate that can be protected by a cover over the bows. Other body options are possible, including vehicle-mounted cranes. Mechanical or hydraulic cable winches with tractive capacities up to 5000 kg can be fitted, with cable control possible to front or rear. A spare wheel is located between the cargo body and the cab.

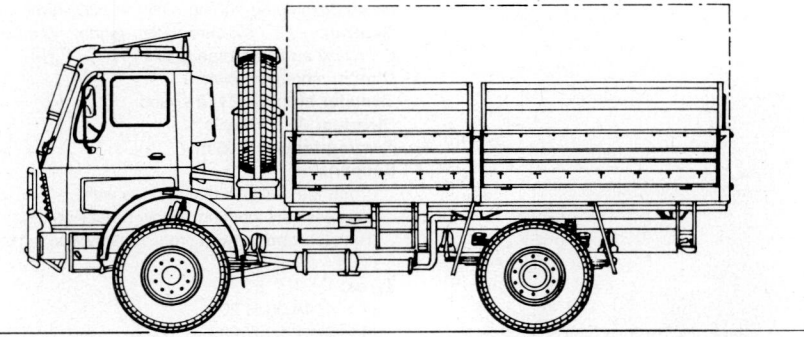

Mercedes-Benz 1222 A (4 × 4) 5500 kg truck

Specifications

(Data for short wheelbase model; data for long wheelbase model in square brackets where different)

Cab seating: 1 + 2
Configuration: 4 × 4
Weight:
  (kerb) approx 8500 kg
  (GVW) 14 000 kg
Front axle load: 6000 kg
Rear axle load: 8500 kg
Max payload: approx 5500 kg
Towed load: 10 500 kg
GCW: 24 500 kg
Load area: 4.35 × 2.5 [4.85 × 2.5] m

Length: 6.87 [7.4] m
Width: 2.5 m
Height:
  (cab) 2.93 m
  (top of tilt) 3.4 m
  (loading platform) 1.537 m
Ground clearance: 0.33 m
Track: 2.091 m
Wheelbase: 3.55 [4.15] m
Angle of approach/departure: 30°/30°
Max speed:
  (road) 93 km/h
  (cross-country) 55 km/h
Fuel capacity: 200 l

Max gradient:
  (road) 50%
  (cross-country) 80%
  (road, GCW with trailer) 26%
  (cross-country, GCW with trailer) 48%
Fording: 1 m
Engine: Mercedes-Benz OM 421 10.964 l V-6 water-cooled diesel developing 216 hp (DIN) at 2300 rpm
Gearbox: Mercedes-Benz G4/95-6/9.0 synchromesh with 6 forward and 1 reverse gears
Clutch: GF 380 single dry disc
Transfer box: Mercedes-Benz VG 900-3W/1.6, 2-speed
Steering: Mercedes-Benz LS 5F, power
Turning circle: 16.8 [19] m
Tyres: 13.00 × 20 XL (option 14.00 × 20 XL)
Brakes: dual circuit compressed air with automatic load-dependent brake (ALB) pressure control
Electrical system: 24 V
Batteries: 2 × 12 V, 110 Ah

Status
In production.

Manufacturer
Daimler-Benz AG, Postfach 202, D-7000 Stuttgart-Untertürkheim, Federal Republic of Germany.
Tel: 0711 17 5 5186. Telex: 72524-0 db d.
Fax: 0711 17 2244.

Mercedes-Benz 1628 A (4 × 4) 7000 kg Truck and 2028 A (6 × 6) 10 000 kg Truck

Description

These two Mercedes-Benz cross-country trucks have been produced for the export market and have many common components. Some civilian model design experience has been incorporated but the design is basically new. See also entry on Mercedes-Benz 2628 A in this section.

Both vehicles use the same design of cab with seating for the driver and two passengers. The centre seat has a folding backrest to allow clear access to the roof-mounted hatch which is provided with a rail grip. There is a medium-length cab available which has extra space for crew equipment. Both cab types can be tilted forward for engine access to an angle of 65°. For normal day-to-day maintenance access flaps are provided. Behind the cab there is spare wheel stowage, and in front of the cab the headlights and radiator grille are protected by heavy duty tubular guards.

All the undersides and major drive components are fully waterproofed for a fording depth of 1 m without preparation and the air intake pipe is routed upwards over the cab roof side. The load area has 500 mm high

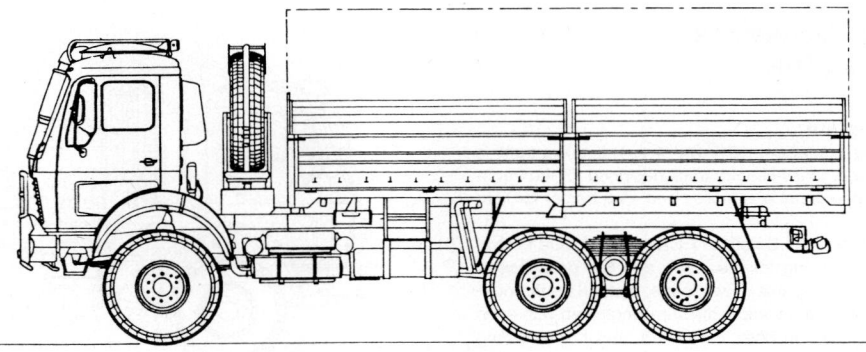

Mercedes-Benz 2028 A (6 × 6) 10 000 kg truck

drop sides and tailgate, and is provided with lash-down points and a canvas tilt. A towing hook for trailers or artillery is provided at the rear. Optional equipment includes a hydraulic 10 000 kg winch with cable control to the front or rear. Various box and cab bodies may be provided, and both models may be produced as tankers, fire tenders or command and communication vehicles.

Single-tyred versions of both trucks are available with tyre pressure regulation systems as an option.

Status
In production. 2028 A in service with Pakistan and the United Arab Emirates.

Manufacturer
Daimler-Benz AG, Postfach 202, D-7000 Stuttgart-Untertürkheim, Federal Republic of Germany.
Tel: 0711 17 5 5186. Telex: 72524-0 db d.
Fax: 0711 17 2244.

Specifications

Model	1628 A	2028 A	Model	1628 A	2028 A
Cab seating	1 + 2	1 + 2	Max speed	91 km/h	91 km/h
Configuration	4 × 4	6 × 6	Fuel capacity	300 l	300 l
Weight (empty)	9000 kg	11 200 kg	Gradient	80%	80%
(loaded)	16 000 kg	22 000 kg	Fording	1.2 m	1.2 m
(front axle load)	7300 kg	7500 kg	Engine	Mercedes-Benz OM 422 V-8 water-cooled	
(rear axle load)	9000 kg	2 × 8000 kg		diesel, 14.618 l, developing 106 bhp at	
Max load	7000 kg	10 000 kg		1200 rpm	
Length	7.43 m	8.3 m	Transmission	ZF 5 S – 111 GP fully synchronised with	
Width	2.5 m	2.5 m		9 forward and 1 reverse gears or	
Height (cab)	3.08 m	3.04 m		optional ZF torque converter system	
(canvas cover)	3.485 m	3.5 m	Turning radius	10.15 m	10.15 m
Load area	4.6 × 2.35 m	5.5 × 2.35 m	Tyres	14.00 × 20 XL	14.00 × 20 XL
Ground clearance	0.435 m	0.435 m	Brakes	dual circuit	dual circuit
Track	2.07 m	2.07 m		compressed air	compressed air
Wheelbase	4.5 m	3.8 m + 1.45 m	Electrical system	24 V	24 V
Angle of approach/departure	32°/42°	32°/46°	Batteries	2 × 12 V	2 × 12 V

MAN 14.240 FAEG (4 × 4) 6000 kg and 20.280 DFAEG (6 × 6) 10 000 kg Trucks

Description

MAN developed the Category III vehicles basing them on the Category I vehicles developed for the German Army. They use the same suspension and drive train technology as the Category I vehicles, torsionally stiff chassis, coil springs, axles with planetary gear hub reduction, but use MAN engines, commercial tilt cabs and allow a high payload; 6000 kg for the 14.240 FAEG (4 × 4) and 10 000 kg for the 20.280 DFAEG (6 × 6).

The chassis consists of hollow section longitudinal members welded with tubular crossmembers. The cab is a MAN two-door all-steel forward control type which can be tilted forward to allow access to the engine for maintenance purposes. The rear cargo area has a steel subframe, aluminium dropsides with two side walls and one tailgate, fixed corner stakes in the front, insertable in the middle and rear, pinewood floor, removable bows and a tarpaulin cover.

Production of these models ceased during 1989.

Irish Army MAN 14.240 FAEG (4 × 4) 6000 kg truck

Status

Production complete. In service with Algeria, Ireland, Oman, Peru, Singapore and Venezuela.

Manufacturer

MAN Nutzfahrzeuge AG, Postfach 500620, D-8000 Munich 50, Federal Republic of Germany. Tel: 89 1480-1. Telex: 211 023.

Specifications

Model	14.240 FAEG	20.280 DFAEG	Model	14.240 FAEG	20.280 DFAEG
Configuration	4 × 4	6 × 6	Hp/rpm	240/2200	280/2200
Weight (empty)	8350 kg	10 300 kg	Gearbox	manual, 6 forward	manual, 6 forward
(loaded)	14 350 kg	20 300 kg		and 1 reverse	and 1 reverse
Max load	6000 kg	10 000 kg		gears	gears
Load area	5 × 2.44 m	6.1 × 2.44 m	Clutch	torque converter	torque converter
Length	7.85 m	8.95 m	Transfer box	MAN G801 with	MAN G801 with
Width	2.49 m	2.49 m		differential lock	differential lock
Height (cab)	3.01 m	3.01 m	Tyres	14.00 × 20	14.00 × 20
Wheelbase	4.5 m	4 m + 1.4 m	Brakes	air over hydraulic dual circuit with	
Angle of approach/departure	40°/43°	40°/40°		spring loaded auxiliary brake and starting	
Max road speed	80 km/h	80 km/h		auxiliary brake (climbing brake), exhaust	
Fuel capacity	310 l	310 l		brake	
Max gradient	limit of adhesion	limit of adhesion	Steering	ZF recirculating	ZF recirculating
Fording	1 m	1 m		ball hydro-steering	ball hydro-steering
Engine	MAN D 2566	MAN D 2566	Suspension	progressive coil springs, hydraulic	
	6-cylinder in-line	6-cylinder in-line		telescopic shock absorbers	
	water-cooled	water-cooled	Electrical system	24 V	24 V
	diesel	diesel	Batteries	2 × 12 V, 110 Ah	2 × 12 V, 110 Ah

MAN 4 × 4, 6 × 6 and 8 × 8 High Mobility Tactical Trucks

Development/Description

In the late 1950s and early 1960s the West German Technical Office for Armament and Military Purchases drew up requirements for a new range (or second generation) of tactical trucks for the West German Army. This range was to have consisted of 4-tonne (4 × 4), 7-tonne (6 × 6) and 10-tonne (8 × 8) vehicles, 4 × 4 and 6 × 6 armoured amphibious load carriers

and an 8 × 8 amphibious reconnaissance vehicle.

Since development of these trucks began in the 1960s there were some changes in the requirements of the army and in 1972 the amphibious specification and the requirement that the vehicles should be powered by a multi-fuel engine were dropped. In 1975 the 4-tonne was uprated to 5-tonne and at the same time its rear cargo platform was lengthened and the wheelbase was increased from 4.3 to 4.5 m.

Category I
In December 1975 MAN was awarded a contract to

build 8385 4 × 4, 6 × 6 and 8 × 8 vehicles at a cost of DM1400 million. The 8 × 8 version was the first model to enter production and first deliveries were made in 1976. Deliveries of the 6 × 6 tipper and the 4 × 4 cargo truck began in 1977. Deliveries of the 6 × 6 cargo truck began in January 1979 and final deliveries were made in 1981. By 1983, 8617 vehicles of all configurations had been delivered to the then West German armed forces. By the end of 1986, 411 had been delivered to the Austrian Army and 82 to the Belgian Army.

This range of vehicles, which was produced at MAN's Watenstedt plant, was known as the Category I (or Kat I) and was designed specifically for cross-country operations and to keep up with mechanised forces operating across country.

Many components of this range, such as axles, engines and gearboxes, are standard commercial components and spare parts can be easily obtained.

Category II
The next generation was the Category II (or Kat II) version which was developed at the request of and in close co-operation with the United States armed forces. By the end of 1986, 534 of these trucks had been delivered to the US armed forces, 157 to France and 42 to Canada.

Category III
In a parallel development the so-called Category III (or Kat III) vehicles were developed. These are similar to the Category I vehicles but are fitted with a cab from the MAN civilian truck range, modified for military use. A total of 1594 Category III trucks was delivered to Algeria (280), Ireland, Oman (95), Peru (165), Singapore (104) and Venezuela (405).

MAN Cat I A1 (8 × 8) high mobility truck

MAN Cat I (4 × 4) 5-tonne truck

Category I A1 extra wide versions
In April 1985 MAN presented the first of a new vehicle, the Category I A1, to the German Federal Office for Military Technology and Procurement (BWB) and to the Test Centre 41. It was planned that there would be 35 test vehicles of all configurations (including the extra wide 8 × 8 version) and versions for Patriot, Roland, MLRS, a folding bridge and a folding roadway, and for the LUER air-surveillance radar. Production of

the new category vehicles began in 1987.

The Category I A1 generation was a development of the Category I with improved performance on and off roads due to higher powered engines and an improved design of frame and cab.

Planned changes introduced on the Category I A1 vehicles included the following:

A hand-tiltable cab, for better access to the engine which can then be removed or installed in about

30 minutes as opposed to the previous 10 hours

A rearrangement of components so that the cab no longer has to be tilted for routine checks

A fully integrated anti-corrosion treatment package for extreme climate conditions and operational use for more than 20 years

A paint finish that fulfils all military requirements including camouflage pattern, infra-red reflection and NBC decontamination needs

Extended use of more commercial components to reduce costs

A range of water-cooled MAN engines with performances of up to 550 hp

All vehicles able to use 16.00 × 20 radial tyres

A removable cab roof to assist rail and air transport

Logistic commonality with earlier vehicles would be maintained.

The layout of all the basic vehicles is almost identical. All vehicles are fitted with a hydraulically tiltable uniform three-man cab specifically designed for military purposes. The plastic roof can support the weight of a man and is fitted with an observation hatch; it can be removed for air transport. A low-torsion frame is used together with coil springs and telescopic shock absorbers. Most vehicles are fitted with a Rotzler winch. All attachments, such as stowage compartments and canister brackets, are fastened to the frame so that different bodies and platforms can be fitted.

Variants
MAN Cat I A1 (4 × 4) truck
This was designed for a chassis carrying capacity up to 7500 kg. It is used as a cargo truck and is able to carry the Dornier military container, in production for the German Army.

MAN Cat I A1 (6 × 6) truck
This truck was designed for a chassis carrying capacity of up to 13 000 kg. The cargo version is also used to tow 155 mm FH-70 howitzers used by the German Army. Specialised versions include a tipper, a bridging truck which transports and launches the German version of the Ribbon Bridge (this has a longer wheelbase) and CL-289 drone carrier. The 110 mm Light Artillery Rocket Systems (LARS) previously mounted on the older Magirus-Deutz chassis have been installed on this MAN (6 × 6) truck chassis. (Full details of the 110 mm LARS are given on pages 722 and 723 of *Jane's Armour and Artillery 1992-93*). The Austrian company Gräf and Stift built 350 6 × 6 versions rated at 10 tonnes for the Austrian Army with a slightly different cab and a hydraulic crane mounted to the rear of the cab. Details of this version are given in this section under Austria.

Variants introduced during 1988 included a mine-laying version for the Belgian Army and a carrier for a Dornier mobile telescopic mast.

MAN Cat I A1 (8 × 8) truck
This truck was designed for a chassis carrying capacity of up to 16 000 kg, and by using 13-tonne axles, up to 25 000 kg. Many of the cargo trucks are fitted with a 1000 kg Atlas hydraulic crane for loading and unloading. The 8 × 8 chassis is also used to carry the German AEG-Telefunken TRMS radar and a shelter-mounted version system has been proposed to carry

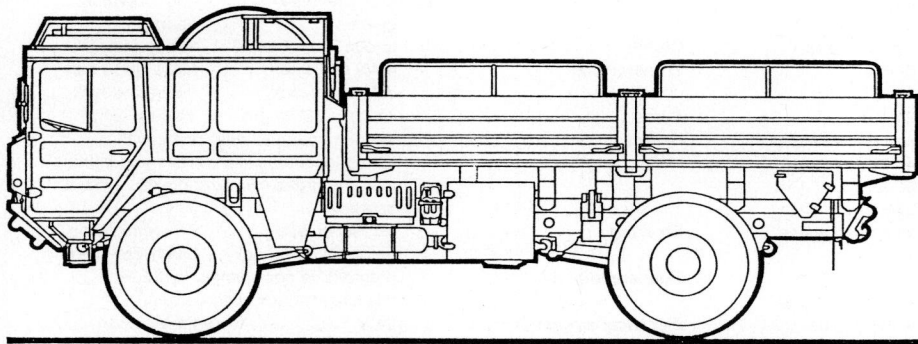

MAN Cat I A1 (4 × 4) truck (not to 1/76th scale)

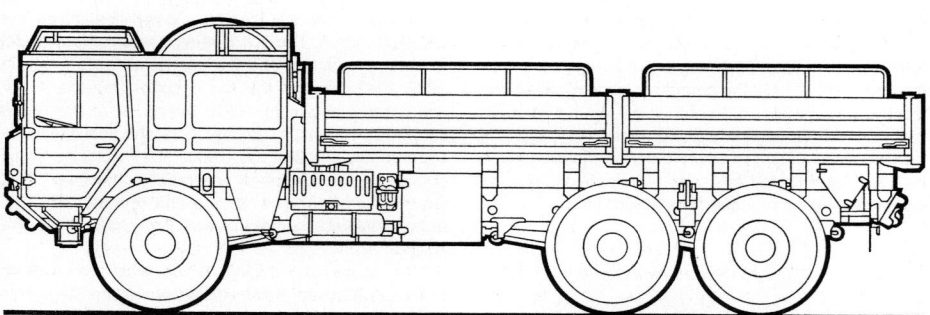

MAN Cat I A1 (6 × 6) truck (not to 1/76th scale)

MAN Cat I A1 (8 × 8) truck (not to 1/76th scale)

MAN Cat I A1 (6 × 6) cargo truck

MAN Cat I A1 (6 × 6) truck carrying Dornier mobile telescopic mast

MAN Cat I A1 (8 × 8) truck with elevating combat platform

Specifications

Model	Cat I A1 4 × 4	Cat I A1 6 × 6	Cat I A1 8 × 8	Cat I A1 8 × 8 Width 2.9 m
Cab seating	1 + 2	1 + 2	1 + 2	1 + 2
Configuration	4 × 4	6 × 6	8 × 8	8 × 8
Weight (empty)	9500 kg	11 300 kg	13 400 kg	12 800 kg
(loaded)	16 000 kg	26 000 kg	32 000 kg	32 000 kg
Chassis carrying capacity	7500 kg	13 500 kg	20 000 kg	20 000 kg
Load area	5.1 × 2.44 m	6.2 × 2.44 m	7.2 × 2.44 m	7.2 × 2.44 m
Length	8.17 m	9.27 m	10.27 m	10.27 m
Width	2.5 m	2.5 m	2.5 m	2.9 m
Height (cab)	2.64 + 0.29 m	2.64 + 0.29 m	2.64 + 0.29 m	2.64 + 0.29 m
Height (load area)	1.54 m	1.54 m	1.54 m	1.54 m
Ground clearance	0.41 m	0.41 m	0.41 m	0.41 m
Track	2.07 m	2.07 m	2.07 m	2.47 m
Wheelbase	4.5 m	4.5 m + 1.5 m	1.93 m + 3.57 m + 1.5 m	
Angle of approach/departure	34°/39°	34°/39°	34°/39°	34°/39°
Max cruising speed (road)	90 km/h	90 km/h	90 km/h	90 km/h
Fuel capacity	400 l	400 l	400 l	400 l
Max gradient	limit of adhesion			
Fording	1.2 m	1.2 m	1.2 m	1.2 m
Engine	range of MAN 6-cylinder in-line diesel, water-cooled with turbocharging or combined intercooling turbocharge system (optional MAN V-10 diesel, water-cooled with intercooling and turbocharging)			
Engine hp (DIN)	performance range from 252 hp up to 550 hp			
Gearbox	range of ZF synchronised gearboxes between 9 and 16 gears with or without integrated transfer case			
Clutch	mechanical or hydraulic converter with lock-up clutch			
Steering	recirculating ball hydro-steering type:			
	ZF 8046	ZF 8046	ZF dual circuit 8096	
Turning radius	9.65 m	10.6 m	13.7 m	13.8 m
Suspension	progressively acting helical springs			
Tyres	14.00 R 20 (optional 16.00 R 20)			
Brakes	air/2 circuit/2 lines			
Electrical system	24 V	24 V	24 V	24 V
Batteries	2 × 12 V, 170 Ah (optional 4 × 12 V, 100 Ah)			

and launch the Dornier Keibitz RPV. The range has been increased by the addition of a truck with a hydraulic crane mounted at the rear. This version has the cargo area reduced to 5.5 × 2.5 m. Other specialised versions include a palletised loading system, and a wrecker equipped with a recovery winch, a towing device and a crane.

MAN has produced a number of special container-body versions. For details of these vehicles see entries in the *Shelters and containers* section.

MAN Cat I A1 (8 × 8) Width 2.9 m
MAN offers an extra wide version of the 8 × 8 with an increased width of 2.9 m for the transport of sensitive loads with high centres of gravity. This extra wide version uses a low-torsioning frame equipped with coil springs, mounted as wide apart as possible, and with telescopic shock absorbers to provide good lateral stability.

MAN has proposed that this chassis, for missile and other tactical applications, could be fitted with four (two each side) hydraulic extended outriggers, combat tyres with an emergency run-flat capability, a central tyre inflation system, a coil spring suspension system with lock out capability, EMP hardening and an onboard camouflage system.

FlaRakRad Roland II
The MAN Cat I A1 (8 × 8) Width 2.9 m chassis is used to carry the shelter body that acts as the command and launching post for the Roland II mobile anti-aircraft weapon system. The vehicle/weapon combination is known as the FlaRakRad Roland II. The German Air Force ordered 68 of these systems, the German Navy 20 and in addition the German Air Force ordered 27 to defend US Air Force bases in Germany.

Patriot
Germany adopted the Patriot (MIM-104) tactical air defence system and mounts the various mobile com-

ponents on various MAN chassis. The 4 × 4 truck is used to carry a Dornier mobile telescopic mast associated with the Patriot system; the mast is 34 m high and carries four dish antennas. The 6 × 6 chassis is used to carry a generator and a hydraulic mast system similar to that carried by the 4 × 4 truck. The (8 × 8) Width 2.9 m chassis is used to carry a radar system with a folding antenna and a four-round Patriot missile launcher.

Elevating combat platform
Using a MAN Cat I A1 chassis as a basis, a prototype of an elevating combat platform was developed in close co-operation with Krauss Maffei and MBB for possible use in anti-tank and anti-helicopter operations. For this project an armoured cab variant is under development to provide a higher degree of protection for the vehicle crew; this will eventually be suitable for use with the entire MAN range.

10 000 kg (8 × 8) trucks for US Army
In October 1980 MAN was awarded a contract by the US Army for the supply of 13 (8 × 8) tractors designated XM1001 and two (8 × 8) recovery vehicles designated XM1002. These were delivered between July and September 1981. In December 1981 an order

was placed by the US Army and Air Force for 251 (8 × 8) vehicles for use with the Pershing II SSM and 214 (8 × 8) vehicles for use with the GLCM. The MAN (8 × 8) truck was also tested by the US Army to meet its requirement for a Heavy Expanded Mobility Tactical Truck, but this contract was subsequently awarded to Oshkosh.

The M1001 (8 × 8) tractor has an Atlas hydraulic crane over the second and third axles with a capacity of 20 000 kg, 2-inch kingpin, 9072 kg self-recovery winch, tools and a tool box.

For details of the M1002 (8 × 8) recovery vehicle see entry in *Recovery vehicles* section.

Status – Category I A1 only
In production. In service with Belgium (23), France (1), German armed forces (657 delivered, 527 on order) and British Army (2 recovery vehicles). See also text for users of other Category vehicles.

Manufacturer
MAN Nutzfahrzeuge AG, Postfach 500620, D-8000 Munich 50, Federal Republic of Germany. Tel: 89 1480-1. Telex: 211 023.

MAN 630 Series of (4 × 4) 5000 kg Trucks

Description

The MAN 630, together with the MB LG 315/46, was the standard 5000 kg truck of the German Army until the introduction of the new generation of tactical trucks. It is in service in two basic models, the MAN 630 L2A with dual rear wheels and the MAN 630 L2AE with single rear wheels.

The layout of the vehicle is conventional with the engine and cab at the front and the cargo area at the rear. The cab has a removable canvas top, windscreen which can be folded forward onto the bonnet and a single door on each side, the tops of which can be removed. The all-steel rear cargo area has a drop tailgate, removable bows and a tarpaulin cover. Some vehicles have been fitted with a winch at the front.

An earlier MAN truck was the 3000 kg MAN 400 L1AE which had an unladen weight of 4480 kg. This was followed by the MAN 415 series of (4 × 4) 4000 kg trucks powered by six-cylinder multi-fuel engines developing 100 bhp and with 4.2 m wheelbases. The MAN 415 is produced in India (with a number of modifications) as the Shaktiman, details of which appear in the Indian section.

Variants include an ambulance which can carry up to four stretcher patients, a decontamination vehicle called the TER-Kfz, the drone carrier for the Canadian AN/USD-501 reconnaissance system, a field kitchen, a radar vehicle for AN/TPS-1E system, a tanker with two fuel tanks in the rear and dispensing equipment, a tipper with a short wheelbase with either single or dual wheels at the rear, a tractor with a wheelbase of 4.1 m and dual rear wheels, and a van.

Specifications

(data in square brackets relate to L2AE where different from the L2A)

Cab seating: 1 + 1
Configuration: 4 × 4
Weight:
 (empty) 7515 [7980] kg
 (loaded) 13 000 [13 200] kg
Load area: 5 × 2.35 m
Length: 7.9 [7.73] m
Width: 2.5 m
Height: (tarpaulin) 2.845 [2.98] m
Ground clearance: 0.35 [0.4] m
Track: (front/rear) 1.922 m/1.763 m [2.506 m/2.506 m]
Wheelbase: 4.6 m
Angle of approach/departure: 32°/45°
Max speed: (road) 66 km/h
Range: 440 km
Fuel capacity: 110 l

Fuel consumption: 25 l/100 km
Max gradient: 60%
Fording: 0.85 m
Engine: MAN Model D 1246 MV3A/W 6-cylinder multi-fuel developing 130 hp at 2000 rpm
Gearbox: manual with 6 forward and 1 reverse gears
Transfer box: 2-speed
Turning radius: 9.75 m
Suspension: semi-elliptical springs with hydraulic shock absorbers
Tyres: 11.00 × 20 [14.00 × 20]
Brakes:
 (main) air
 (parking) mechanical
Electrical system: 24 V
Batteries: 2 × 12 V, 100 Ah

Status

Production complete. In service in Belgium (assembled in Belgium by Ets Hocké and known as the L2AE-B), Germany, India, and several nations in Central and South America, including El Salvador.

Manufacturer

MAN Nutzfahrzeuge AG, Postfach 500620, D-8000 Munich 50, Federal Republic of Germany.
Tel: 89 1480-1. Telex: 211 023.

German Army MAN 630 L2AE 5000 kg truck

Belgian Army MAN 630 L2AE 5000 kg truck (C R Zwart)

Mercedes-Benz 2628 A (6 × 6) 12 000 kg Truck

Development/Description

The Mercedes-Benz 2628 A (6 × 6) 12 000 kg truck was developed along the same lines as the Mercedes-Benz 1628 A and 2028 A trucks (see separate entry) and shares many features and components with them. The Mercedes-Benz 2628 A does however have a much heavier payload and may be used as a tractor for artillery with calibres up to 155 mm. It may also have a materials handling crane located behind the cab.

The 2628 A has an enlarged cab to accommodate the driver and two passengers plus space for other personnel or equipment. A roof hatch is provided. The standard cargo area may be fitted with a canvas tilt and has dimensions of 5.5 × 2.35 m.

The 2628 AS is a 6 × 6 tractor truck intended to tow engineer equipment on a semi-trailer with a gross combination weight of 38 000 kg.

Various purpose-built bodies may be fitted to the 2628 A, one being the Marrel torsion free military platform. The 2628 A can also carry the Marrel Ampliroll AL 160 demountable platform system capable of carrying vehicles as large as the M113 armoured personnel carrier. Other versions can carry tanker or box and cabin bodies for a variety of roles. One option is a side-mounted 10 000 kg hydraulic winch with the cable paying out to front or rear. An automatic tyre pressure adjusting system is also available as an optional extra.

The Mercedes-Benz 2628 A has been produced as a heavy recovery vehicle carrying a Marrel MH 45 or Hägglunds Moelv recovery hamper.

Mercedes-Benz 2628 A (6 × 6) 12 000 kg truck

Specifications

Cab seating: 1 + 2 (space for more)
Configuration: 6 × 6
Weight:
  (empty) approx 11 300 kg
  (loaded) 25 000 kg
  (GCW) 38 000 kg
Weight on front axle: 7500 kg
Weight on rear axle: 2 × 9000 kg
Max load: approx 10 000 kg
Length: 8.3 m
Width: 2.5 m
Height:
  (cab) 3.04 m
  (tarpaulin) 3.5 m
Load area: 5.5 × 2.35 m
Ground clearance: 0.435 m

Track: 2.07 m
Wheelbase: 3.8 m + 1.45 m
Angle of approach/departure: 32°/46°
Max speed: 93 km/h
Fuel capacity: 300 l
Gradient:
  (max) more than 80%
  (with trailer, GCW 38 000 kg, on road) 34%
  (with trailer, GCW 38 000 kg, off road) 66%
Fording: 1.2 m
Engine: Mercedes-Benz OM 422 14.618 l V-8 liquid-cooled direct injection diesel developing 280 hp at 2300 rpm
Transmission: ZF 5 S – 111 G fully synchronised with crawler providing 9 forward and 1 reverse gears or ZF S 6-90 6-speed with torque converter/mechanical clutch (WSK)

Clutch: GF 420 single dry disc
Transfer box: VG 1400 2-speed
Turning radius: 10.15 m
Brakes: dual circuit, compressed air
Tyres: 14.00 × 20 XL
Electrical system: 24 V
Batteries: 2 × 12 V, 110 Ah

Status
In production.

Manufacturer
Daimler-Benz AG, Postfach 202, D-7000 Stuttgart-Untertürkheim, Federal Republic of Germany.
Tel: 0711 17 5 5186. Telex: 72524-0 db d.
Fax: 0711 17 2244.

HUNGARY

Csepel D-562 (4 × 2), D-564 (4 × 4), D-566 (6 × 6), D-566.02 (6 × 6) and D-588 (8 × 8) Trucks

Description

The D-566 (6 × 6) cargo truck appeared in 1970 and entered production the following year. It has a two-door all-steel forward control cab with the cargo area at the rear with a drop tailgate, bows and a tarpaulin cover. A central tyre pressure regulation system is fitted as standard. The D-566.02 is identical to the D-566 but has a 7000 kg capacity winch with 60 m of cable.

The D-562 (4 × 2) and D-564 (4 × 4) vehicles were introduced in 1972 with first production vehicles being completed in 1974. These also have a two-door all-steel forward control cab with the cargo area at the rear with a drop tailgate, drop sides, a tarpaulin cover and bows. Both are provided with a central tyre-pressure regulation system. A dump truck model was produced.

The D-588 was an 8 × 8 truck with a forward control cab and a central tyre-pressure regulation system.

Variants of the D-566 include a recovery vehicle and a shop/van.

Status
The D-566 is in service with the Hungarian Army.

Manufacturer
Csepel Motor Vehicle Plant, Szigethzlem, Hungary.

Specifications

Model	D-562	D-564	D-566
Configuration	4 × 2	4 × 4	6 × 6
Weight (empty)	5200 kg	5400 kg	9000 kg
(loaded, cross-country)	9200 kg	9400 kg	14 000 kg
Load (road)	5000 kg	5000 kg	8000 kg
(cross-country)	4000 kg	4000 kg	5000 kg
Towed load (road)	n/a	n/a	10 000 kg
(cross-country)	n/a	n/a	5000 kg
Length	6.43 m	6.43 m	7.18 m
Width	2.5 m	2.5 m	2.5 m
Height	2.67 m	2.67 m	2.74 m
Ground clearance	n/a	n/a	0.575 m
Track	2 m	2 m	2.05 m
Wheelbase	3.7 m	3.7 m	2.9 m + 1.4 m
Max speed	87.9 km/h	87.9 km/h	80 km/h
Range	n/a	n/a	700 km
Fording	n/a	n/a	1.2 m
Engine model	D-614.33	D-614.33	Raba-MAN
Engine type	6-cylinder water-cooled diesel	6-cylinder water-cooled diesel	6-cylinder water-cooled diesel
Hp/rpm	145/2300	145/2300	200/2200
Gearbox	n/a	n/a	manual, 5 forward and 1 reverse gears
Transfer box	none	n/a	2-speed
Tyres	16.5 × 19.5	16.5 × 19.5	14.00 × 20
Electrical system	24 V	24 V	24 V
Batteries	n/a	n/a	2 × 120 Ah
Generator	n/a	n/a	750 W

Csepel D-566 (6 × 6) recovery vehicle

Csepel D-566 (6 × 6) shop/van

INDIA

Azad (4 × 4) 2500 kg Truck

Description

At least four prototypes of the Azad (4 × 4) 2500 kg truck have been produced. The truck has a forward-mounted steel cab with seating for a driver and at least one passenger and it would appear that the cab can be tilted forward for access to the engine and gearbox. The cab roof appears to have hatches for access to a machine gun roof mounting and the radiator grille is protected by a steel guard mounted on the front bumper; this guard also protects the headlights. The cargo area to the rear can be covered by a canvas tilt and the side and rear flaps either fold downwards or can be removed to enable the Azad to carry a variety of loads, including container bodies. Apart from use as a cargo truck the Azad can be used as a personnel carrier, a tractor for light artillery field pieces, a tanker (fuel or water) or a missile launcher vehicle.

Specifications
Cab seating: 1 + 1 or 2
Configuration: 4 × 4
Weight: (loaded, max) 7500 kg
Max load: 2500 kg
Length: 5.4 m
Width: 2.25 m
Height: (cab roof) 2.45 m
Ground clearance: 0.32 m
Max speed: 84 km/h

Range: 800 km
Gradient: 60°
Fording: 0.8 m
Engine: Perkins P6.354 water-cooled diesel

developing 120 hp at 2800 rpm
Gearbox: ZF AK 5-35 with 5 forward and 1 reverse gears
Transfer box: 2-speed

Steering: power-assisted

Status
Prototypes.

Shaktiman (4 × 4) 4000 kg Truck

Description
The Shaktiman 4000 kg (4 × 4) truck is basically the German MAN 415 L1 AR truck built under licence in India. The main visual difference between the German and Indian vehicle is that the latter has dual rather than single rear wheels. The vehicle entered production at Jabalpur in 1958 and was initially assembled from components supplied by Germany, but as production built up an increasing number of the components were supplied by Indian companies.

The Shaktiman is available in both 4 × 4 and 4 × 2 versions and they can be produced in either hard- or soft-top form. Also available is a version with a deeper chassis frame, a heavy duty suspension and larger tyres for a GVW of 11 000 kg. An artillery tractor version with a separate crew shelter behind the driver's cab is used by the Indian Army to tow 105 mm field guns.

An amphibious vehicle, the Rampar, was developed from the Shaktiman. See entry in the *Amphibians* section for available details.

Specifications
Cab seating: 1 + 2
Configuration: 4 × 4 or 4 × 2

Weight:
  (empty) 5075 kg
  (GVW) 9000 kg
Max load:
  (front axle) 3300 kg
  (rear axle) 6600 kg
Load area: 4.45 × 2.25 m
Length: 7.16 m
Width: 2.35 m
Height:
  (top of cab, loaded) 2.435 m
  (load area) 1.13 m
Ground clearance: 0.308 m
Track:
  (front) 1.824 m
  (rear) 1.632 m
Wheelbase: 4.2 m
Fuel capacity: 300 l
Engine: D 0026 M 8 A 5.88 1 6-cylinder in-line diesel developing 110 hp at 2500 rpm
Gearbox: AK5-35 manual with 5 forward and 1 reverse gears
Clutch: single dry plate
Transfer box: 2-speed
Steering: heavy duty roller
Turning radius: 8.075 m
Suspension: semi-elliptical springs front and rear
Tyres: 8.25 × 20
Brakes:
  (main) hydro-pneumatic dual circuit
  (parking) mechanical
Electrical system: 12 V
Batteries 2 × 12 V, 92 Ah
Alternator 40 A

Status
In production. In service with India and Bangladesh.

Manufacturer
Vehicle Factory, Indian Ordnance Factories, Jabalpur 482009, Madhya Pradesh, India.
Tel: 21969. Telex: 076 219.

Shaktiman (4 × 4) 4000 kg truck

INTERNATIONAL

Percheron (6 × 6) 10 000 kg Truck Heavy Logistic Vehicle Wheeled (HLVW)

Description
In March 1988 the Canadian Department of Defence signed a contract with UTDC Inc of Kingston, Ontario to produce the Heavy Logistic Vehicle Wheeled (HLVW) for the Canadian armed forces.

The UTDC submission was an Austrian Steyr

vehicle, the Steyr 1491.6 × 6 M. (For full details of this vehicle refer to the entry under Austria in this section.) Other submissions came from MAN, Oshkosh (who entered a 6 × 6 version of their 8 × 8 HEMTT) and Scania (the SBAT 111).

The HLVW is based on the Steyr 1491.310/040/ 6 × 6 M and in Canadian service is known as the Percheron. The Percheron differs from the original vehicle in several respects. These include a camouflage net storage space behind the cab, a cold weather start capability, a brush guard, a cargo bay walkway and a

radio installation kit.

There are eight variants of the basic Percheron, produced in the following numbers:
  Basic cargo – 276
  Basic cargo with winch – 147
  Basic cargo with winch and crane – 388
  Recovery – 124
  Tractor – 46
  Dumper – 25
  Bridge transport/flatrack system – 176
  Heavy Mobile Repair Team – 18.

Heavy Mobile Repair Team variant of the Heavy Logistic Vehicle Wheeled (HLVW), the Percheron

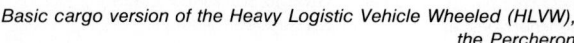
Basic cargo version of the Heavy Logistic Vehicle Wheeled (HLVW), the Percheron

The three cargo variants are essentially similar and have dropping sides and a rear tailgate. The version with the material handling crane has its cargo area reduced in length from 6 to 5 m.

The recovery variant is a combination of the Vulcan recovery unit and the Pitman PK 19000 material handling crane, forming an integrated system. The Vulcan recovery unit consists of a heavy duty hydraulic lift and carry system at the rear together with two stabilising and anchoring legs. There is also a recovery winch with a capacity of 25 000 kg. A special bogie-type suspension is used with this variant.

The dumper has a three-way tipper body with a capacity of 8500 kg.

The tractor can tow loads of up to 25 000 kg with a 12 000 kg fifth wheel capacity. The rear suspension is of the bogie type.

The bridge transporter is used to carry Ribbon Bridge components and is equipped with a Multilift Mark 4 load handling system. The system can also be used to carry cargo flatracks.

The Heavy Mobile Repair Team (HMRT) vehicle is used to provide forward maintenance support for the Canadian Army's Leopard C1 MBT and M109 155 mm self-propelled howitzer units. A Pitman PK 19000 material handling crane is mounted at the rear. This crane has a lifting capacity of 19 000 kg and can lift a Leopard C1 engine pack. The HMRT can carry major assemblies and also carries a workshop area.

Specifications
Cab seating: 1 + 2
Configuration: 6 × 6
Weight:
   (kerb) 9700 kg
   (GVW) 22 000 kg
Max load:
   (without winch) 10 000 kg
   (with winch) 9600 kg
Length: 9.12 m
Width: 2.5 m
Height: (cab) 3.025 m
Ground clearance: (axles) 0.37 m
Track: 2.072 m
Wheelbase: 4 m + 1.4 m
Angle of approach/departure: 31°/35°
Max speed: 95 km/h
Range: 1000 km
Fuel capacity: 400 l
Max gradient: 100%
Fording: 0.8 m
Engine: Steyr model WD 615.98m 9.7 l 6-cylinder in-line direct injection water-cooled turbocharged diesel developing 306 bhp at 2300 rpm
Transmission: ZF WSK 400 +4 S 150 GP hydrodynamic torque converter with single dry disc, synchromesh gearbox with 8 forward and 1 reverse gears
Transfer box: Steyr VG1200 2-speed
Steering: ZF 80 46 hydraulic power
Turning radius: 10.5 m
Suspension: semi-elliptic leaf springs with double-acting hydraulic shock absorbers
Tyres: 14 × 20
Brakes:
   (main) air, dual circuit
   (parking) spring loaded on both rear axles
Electrical system: 24 V
Batteries: 4 × 12 V, 100 Ah

Status
Production for the Canadian armed forces completed by November 1991 (1200 units).

Manufacturer
UTDC Inc, PO Box 70, Station A, Kingston, Ontario, Canada K7M 6P9.
Tel: (613) 384 3100. Fax: (613) 389 6382.
This concern has now closed.

ISRAEL

M-462 ABIR (4 × 4) 1800 kg Multi-purpose Tactical Truck

Description
The M-462 ABIR (4 × 4) 1800 kg multi-purpose tactical truck was designed and developed using the considerable experience gained by Automotive Industries Limited during its involvement with the M-325 Commandcar series of 4 × 4 trucks (see following entry).

The layout of the ABIR is conventional but many new features have been incorporated to improve crew comfort, improve the smoothness of the ride and enhance all-round visibility. The cab is a modern design and can comfortably accommodate the driver and two passengers. The standard cargo body can seat up to 12 passengers under a canvas tilt.

A fully automatic three-speed transmission and integral power steering are provided. Maintenance costs and time are stated to be low.

The standard version of the ABIR can have a canvas top to the cab and a canvas tilt over the cargo area. The cab doors are also canvas and can be readily removed. Metal doors are available as an option together with a hard-top cabin cover and air-conditioning.

Other versions of the ABIR are a cargo version with roll-bars; a version with a shortened cargo area; a reconnaissance vehicle armed with machine guns at front and sides; a TOW ATGW missile carrier; a mine-shielded troop carrier; a communication centre shelter carrier; a command, communications, control and intelligence (C³I) vehicle; a police vehicle with the rear area enclosed with transparent plastic screens; and maxi and mini ambulances. There are also fire tender versions. The Model W-1000 is a special forest firefighting vehicle.

Specifications
Cab seating: 1 + 2
Configuration: 4 × 4
Weight:
   (unladen) 2610 kg
   (fully laden) 4500 kg
Max load: 1800 kg
Towed load: 1800 kg
Length: 5.12 m
Width: 2.04 m
Height: 2.01 m
Ground clearance: 0.26 m
Wheelbase: 3.2 m
Track: 1.715 m
Angle of approach/departure: 52°/30°
Max speed: 110 km/h
Range: 600 km
Fuel capacity: 144 l
Max gradient: 78%
Side slope: 60%
Vertical obstacle: 0.45 m
Fording: 0.76 m
Engine: GM 6.2 l water-cooled diesel developing 145 hp at 3600 rpm or optional Chrysler 318 5.2 l V-8 petrol
Transmission: automatic with 3 forward and 1 reverse speeds or manual with 4 forward and 1 reverse gears or NVG 4500 manual with 5 forward and 1 reverse gears
Transfer box: NP 241 2-speed
Steering: integral power steering
Turning radius: 7.1 m
Suspension:
   (front) semi-elliptic multi-leaf (11 leaves) plus shock absorbers
   (rear) semi-elliptic multi-leaf plus shock absorbers
Tyres: 9.00 × 16 – 10 ply NATO tread
Brakes: hydro/booster power (vacuum booster for petrol engines); rear drum self-aligning, front disc
Electrical system: 24 V
Batteries: 2 × 12 V, 100 Ah
Alternator: 60 A (100 A optional)

Status
In production. In service with the Israel Defence Forces and some other nations.

Manufacturer
Automotive Industries Limited, PO Box 535, Nazareth Illit, 17105 Israel.
Tel: 972 6 558111. Telex: 46217 ail il.
Fax: 972 6 558103.

M-462 ABIR (4 × 4) 1800 kg multi-purpose tactical vehicle fitted with cargo body

M-462 ABIR (4 × 4) configured as police vehicle

M-325 Commandcar (4 × 4) 1800 kg Truck

Description
The first M-325 Commandcars were constructed during 1966 and have remained in production ever since. Although the basic design remains unchanged some innovations have been introduced and several variants now exist. Commandcars are produced for export as well as for use by the Israel Defence Forces.

The M-325 Commandcar is produced using mainly commercial components allied to a locally developed chassis design. The basis is a chassis using a ladder-type frame with a reinforced drop centre section channel siderail. Crossmembers are bolted or riveted to the frame. Carbon steel with a minimum yield strength of 2200 kg/cm is used for the siderails. Dana Spicer axles are used front and rear and a dual hydraulic brake system using Bendix disc brakes is employed. The engine, mounted forward, is a Chrysler in-line petrol OHV 225-2 LC. A Borg & Beck clutch system connects power to a four-speed Model 435D transmission system and NP-200-D transfer case. This has four forward gears and one reverse. There is a New Process two-speed transfer case. A Chelsea 350-series power take-off is located on the left side. The propeller shaft is a Chrysler 5380. Steering is carried out by a Ross 378 worm and roller steering gearbox.

The bonnet and cab are standard for nearly all versions but the cab may be of the open type with a simple canvas hood for weather protection or of the enclosed type for the ambulance and some export versions. Recent changes to the cab involve a more comfortable seat for the driver and a revised 'through the steering wheel' layout for the instrument panel. Most M-325s have a single-piece windscreen that can be folded forward over the bonnet but some variants use a two-part split windscreen so that a machine gun can be mounted for forward use by the passenger. Night driving lights can be fitted and forward of the front bumper a forward-mounted winch may be fitted. This is a Braden AMSU3-10F with a capacity of 4500 kg and 76 m of 11 mm cable. A Donaldson Cyclopac air cleaner is a virtual standard for Middle East operations.

The cargo body is a multi-purpose cargo and personnel carrier with an all-steel, one-piece body with two longitudinal benches facing inwards and containing lockable equipment compartments. For patrol and reconnaissance versions the benches are located centrally and facing outwards. Machine gun and other weapon pintles can be mounted on the sides along with searchlights for night use. A towing hook at the rear allows the M-325 to tow loads up to 1500 kg, including weapons such as 120 mm mortars.

There is a 24 V electrical system, and a distribution panel powerful enough for up to four radios is fitted. Two batteries are located in compartments under the cargo area and may be pulled out on rails for maintenance, whereas earlier models had the batteries behind the cab.

Variants
Basic cargo and personnel carrier
Bench seats are provided for up to 12 passengers in the cargo area. The tilt is light PVC-coated tarpaulin. Weapons may be carried and the towing hook can be used to tow weapons such as a 120 mm mortar or a special trailer known as the MT-100 (see entry in the *Trailers* section for details). This version can be used to carry a communications shelter; for this role a 100 A alternator is used in place of the normal 60 A item.

Patrol and reconnaissance version
This normally uses the Type B body with weapon and searchlight pintles along the sides of the rear area. This version may be used to carry a 1300 litre tank that can be fitted onto the cargo area for carrying fuel or water.

Mine-shielded version
This is a variation of the Type B-bodied patrol and reconnaissance vehicle with the cab and body constructed of heavy duty metal plates and with the cargo body floor strengthened by honeycomb partitions between the floor plates. There are fitted seats for eight men in the rear. The cab and sides are left open and the spare wheel is relocated to the rear. Large roll-bars are fitted over the cab and at the rear. The seats can be removed easily for carrying cargo.

Ambulance
This uses a hard cab and body with access from the cab into the ambulance body. Folding racks for up to four stretchers are provided and up to 12 seated casualties may be carried. A folding seat is provided for an attendant. Ventilation is either a three-speed blower system or a full air-conditioning unit.

Box body
A solid body similar to the ambulance may be used as a mobile workshop, a mobile office or for other similar roles.

Specifications (cargo version, Type A body)
Cab seating: 1 + 1 (up to 12 in rear)
Configuration: 4 × 4
Weight: (loaded) 4500 kg
Max load: 1950 kg
Towed load: 1500 kg
Length: (without winch) 5.073 m
Width: 2.08 m
Height: (top of tilt) 2.37 m
Ground clearance: 0.4 m
Track: 1.7145 m
Wheelbase: 3.2 m
Angle of approach/departure:
(without winch) 62°/33.5°
(with winch) 45°/33.5°
Max speed: 100 km/h
Fuel capacity: 144 l
Max gradient: 73%
Side slope: 70%
Vertical obstacle: 0.45 m
Fording: 0.76 m
Engine: Chrysler 3.687 l 6-cylinder in-line OHV 225-2 LC petrol developing 100 hp at 3600 rpm
Gearbox: manual with 4 forward and 1 reverse gears
Transfer box: NP-200-D 2-speed
Steering: worm and roller, manual
Turning radius: 7.1 m
Suspension: front and rear leaf springs with double-acting shock absorbers
Tyres: 9.00 × 16 – 10 ply
Brakes: hydraulic disc, dual circuit
Electrical system: 24 V
Batteries: 2 × 12 V, 100 Ah
Alternator: 28 V, 60 or 100 Ah

Status
In production. In service with the Israel Defence Forces and some other nations.

Manufacturer
Automotive Industries Limited, PO Box 535, Nazareth Illit, 17105 Israel.
Tel: 972 6 558111. Telex: 46217 ail il.
Fax: 972 6 558103.

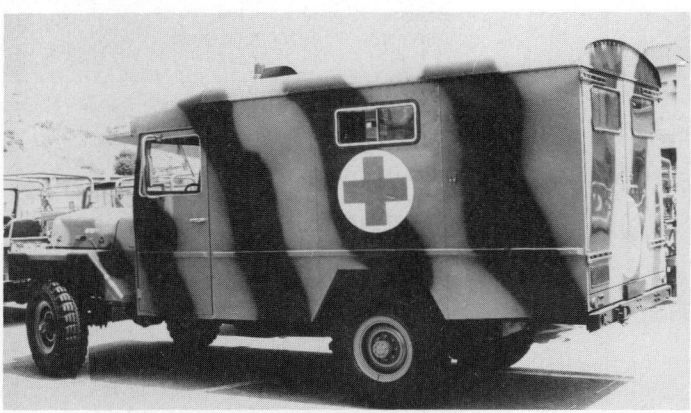

Ambulance version of M-325 Commandcar

M-325 Commandcar with Type B body and machine gun mounted in split front windscreen

ITALY

IVECO FIAT 40-10 WM (4 × 4) 1500 kg Light Truck

Description
The IVECO FIAT 40-10 WM (4 × 4) light truck is a military derivative of the FIAT commercial Daily model and was developed via the interim FIAT 40 PM. The prototypes were produced at FIAT's Brescia factory with the intention of providing a light truck for airborne and other similar formations – production vehicles are manufactured at Bolzano. In its current form the vehicle has a payload of 1500 kg but a gross vehicle weight of 4300 kg, making it ideally suited for many tactical roles as a troop and cargo carrier. It is suitable for mounting various forms of weapon including machine guns, anti-tank weapons and rocket launchers, and can be used as a tractor for light artillery.

The IVECO FIAT 40-10 WM has a conventional layout with the engine at the front and the cargo area to the rear. The semi-forward cab has seating for the driver and two passengers and is normally provided with a soft canvas top; a hard-top is optional. The all-steel cargo area has folding seats along each side facing inwards for 10 men. The tailgate folds down-wards and when down the loading height is 0.98 m.

The bonnet may be removed for engine access and maintenance with routine maintenance operations designed to be kept to a minimum. The FIAT 8142 diesel engine is supercharged and is a military version of a well-established commercial model. The transfer box is of the two ratio chain-type and is controlled by a single lever. The axles are of the single reduction type front and rear, both with locking differentials. Hydraulic power steering is standard. Left- and right-hand steering versions are available.

The standard truck can accommodate an S-250 container shelter at the rear and various other body

IVECO FIAT 40-10 WM (4 × 4) 1500 kg light truck (Bob Morrison – Military Scene)

configurations are possible. A van body is offered as is a four stretcher ambulance body. The same body may also be used as a command and communications centre and various weapons, including a 106 mm recoilless rifle, may be carried in the cargo area. The standard truck can be used to tow a 105 mm light artillery piece. Optional extras include a 2000 kg capacity front winch. Two vehicles can be carried in a C-130 Hercules and a vehicle, stripped down, can be carried with an OTO Melara 105 mm Pack Howitzer in an Alenia G222 transport aircraft.

In October 1991 it was announced that the Canadian armed forces had selected the IVECO FIAT 40-10 WM (4 × 4) light vehicles as the winner of the competition for the Light Support Vehicle Wheeled (LSVW) project. The award value was in the order of C\$200 million, including spares, engineering services and project management.

Approximately 2750 vehicles are to be licence-produced by Western Star Trucks Inc of Kelowna, British Columbia, with production commencing in early 1992 and continuing until early 1994. Configurations include command and control, maintenance and repair, troop carrier and ambulances.

Specifications
Cab seating: 1 + 2 (10 in rear)
Configuration: 4 × 4
Weight:
(empty) 2800 kg
(max) 4300 kg
Max load: 1500 kg
Towed load: (off road) 1500 kg
Load area: 2.075 x 1.88 m
Length: 4.645 m
Width: 2 m

Height:
(top of tilt) 2.38 m
(top of folded windscreen) 1.75 m
(load area) 0.98 m
Track: 1.67 m
Wheelbase: 2.8 m
Angle of approach/departure: 45°/40°
Max speed: over 100 km/h
Max gradient: over 60%
Side slope: over 30%
Range: over 500 km
Fuel capacity: 70 l
Fording: 0.7 m
Engine: FIAT 8142 2.5 l turbocharged 4-cylinder water-cooled diesel developing 103 hp at 3800 rpm
Gearbox: manual with 5 forward and 1 reverse gears
Clutch: single dry plate
Transfer box: 2-speed
Steering: hydraulic power-assist
Turning radius: 6 m
Suspension: independent longitudinal torsion bars at front, leaf spring at rear, telescopic shock absorbers front and rear
Tyres: 9.00 × 16 14PR
Brakes:
(main) disc front, drum rear, split circuit
(parking) mechanical on rear wheels
Electrical system: 24 V
Batteries: 2 × 12 V, 55 Ah
Alternator: 28 V, 30A

Status
In production. In service with Italy (1300), Pakistan (2200) and the Belgian Gendarmerie, Netherlands, Portugal and several other countries. Also serving with EEC organisations operating in the former Yugoslavia. Ordered by Canada (approximately 2750, licence production).

Manufacturer
IVECO SpA, Defence Vehicle Division, Via Volta 6, I-39100 Bolzano, Italy.
Tel: 0471 905111. Telex: 400541.
Fax: 0471 934240.

IVECO FIAT 75-14 WM (4 × 4) 2500-3000 kg Cargo Truck

Description
This vehicle is an improvement of the 75 PM 13 (4 × 4) 2000 kg truck and 90 PM 16 (4 × 4) 4000 kg truck, now in service with the Italian Army with the designation ACL/75 and ACM-80. The new product range has a high degree of standardisation between the two vehicles.

The chassis consists of longitudinal members to which the crossmembers are cold-riveted. The cab is all steel and is of the forward control type. It can be tilted forwards 55° to allow access to the engine. A circular observation hatch is provided in the roof of the cab on the passenger side. The rear cargo area has drop sides and a drop tailgate and if required bows and a tarpaulin cover can be installed.

Optional equipment includes a front- or rear-mounted winch with a capacity of 4000 kg and an air-operated lockable front differential. Left- and right-hand versions are available.

The vehicle can be fitted with a wide range of different bodies and various other types of specialised equipment including aerial cage, bus body, crane, digger, fire appliance, mobile lubrication and greasing unit and a three-way tipper body.

Specifications
Cab seating: 1 + 1 plus up to 12 in rear
Configuration: 4 × 4
Weight:
(kerb) 5250 kg
(loaded) 7750-8250 kg
Max load: 2500-3000 kg
Towed load: 4000 kg
Load area: 3.01 × 2.195 m
Length: 5.178 m

IVECO FIAT 75 PM 14 (4 × 4) 2500 kg truck

Width: 2.3 m
Height:
(cab) 2.646 m
(tarpaulin) 2.96 m
(load area) 1.4 m
Ground clearance: 0.445 m
Track: 1.852 m
Wheelbase: 2.75 m
Angle of approach/departure: 45°/45°
Max speed: over 80 km/h
Range: over 500 km

Fuel capacity: 155 l
Max gradient: over 60%
Max side slope: 30%
Fording: 0.7 m
Engine: Model 8060.05 5.861 l 6-cylinder direct injection water-cooled diesel developing 139 bhp (DIN) at 3000 rpm
Gearbox: manual with 5 forward and 1 reverse gears
Clutch: single dry plate
Transfer box: 2-speed
Steering: recirculating ball with hydraulic servo

Turning radius: 6 m
Suspension: leaf springs (dual at rear) with hydraulic telescopic shock absorbers
Tyres: 12.50 × 20
Brakes:
(main) air-hydraulic drum on all wheels with separate circuits

(parking) on rear wheels
Electrical system: 24 V
Batteries: 2 × 12 V, 110 Ah
Alternator: 28 V, 30 A

Status
In production. In service with the Italian Army as the

ACL/90, Somalia and several other countries.

Manufacturer
IVECO SpA, Defence Vehicle Division, Via Volta 6, I-39100 Bolzano, Italy.
Tel: 0471 905111. Telex: 400541.
Fax: 0471 934240.

IVECO FIAT 90-17 WM (4 × 4) 4000 kg Cargo Truck

Description
This vehicle is an improvement of the 90 PM 16 (4 × 4) 4000 kg truck and the 75 PM 13 vehicle family in service with the Italian Army as the ACM-80 and the ACL/75. The new vehicle range has a high standard-isation rate between the two vehicles.

The chassis consists of longitudinal members to which the crossmembers are cold riveted. The forward control cab is all steel and is of the forward control type. It can be tilted forwards to an angle of 55° to allow access to the engine. There is a circular observation hatch in the roof of the cab on the right side. The rear cargo area has drop sides and a drop tailgate and if required bows and a tarpaulin cover can be installed.

Optional equipment includes a front- or rear-mounted winch with a capacity of 4000 kg, an air-operated lockable front differential and 14.5 R 20 tyres.

Variants produced include a light recovery vehicle (see entry in the *Recovery vehicles* section), a tanker, a mobile workshop, a light artillery tractor and a firefighting vehicle.

IVECO FIAT 90-17 WM (4 × 4) 4000 kg cargo truck

Specifications
Cab seating: 1 + 1 (up to 18 in rear)
Configuration: 4 × 4
Weight:
(kerb) 5740 kg
(loaded) 9740 kg
Max load: (off road) 4000 kg
Towed load: (off road) 4000 kg
Load area: 4.19 × 2.21 m
Length: 6.358 m
Width: 2.3 m
Height:
(cab) 2.646 m
(tarpaulin) 2.96 m
(load area) 1.4 m
Ground clearance: 0.445 m
Track: 1.852 m
Wheelbase: 3.7 m

Angle of approach/departure: 45°/35°
Max speed: over 80 km/h
Range: over 500 km
Fuel capacity: 155 l
Max gradient: over 60%
Max side slope: over 30%
Fording: 0.7 m
Engine: Model 8060.25 5.861 l 6-cylinder super-charged direct injection water-cooled diesel developing 170 hp (DIN) at 3000 rpm
Gearbox: manual with 5 forward and 1 reverse gears
Clutch: single dry plate
Transfer box: 2-speed
Steering: recirculating ball with hydraulic servo
Turning radius: 7.5 m
Suspension: leaf springs (dual at rear) with hydraulic telescopic shock absorbers
Tyres: 12.5 R 20 PR22

Brakes:
(main) air-hydraulic on all wheels with separate circuits
(parking) on rear wheels
Electrical system: 24 V
Batteries: 2 × 12 V, 110 Ah

Status
In production. In service with Italy (as ACM/90), Portugal, Singapore, Somalia (100) and several other countries.

Manufacturer
IVECO SpA, Defence Vehicle Division, Via Volta 6, I-39100 Bolzano, Italy.
Tel: 0471 905111. Telex: 400541.
Fax: 0471 934240.

Astra BM 201 MC1 (4 × 4) 4000 kg Medium Mobility Truck

Description
The Astra BM 201 MC1 chassis is made of high elastic steel and consists of two double C-shaped side-members connected through rigid crossmembers. The two powered axles have double reduction centre bevel gears and planetary final drives. The two-door glass fibre cab with a metal frame can be tilted forwards 48° to allow access to the engine for maintenance.

The rear cargo area has drop sides, drop tailgate, removable bows and a tarpaulin cover. There is also a dump truck model (6 m³) which has 12.00 × 20 tyres, dual at the rear.

Specifications
Cab seating: 1 + 1
Configuration: 4 × 4
Weight:
(empty) 7120 kg
(loaded, cross-country) 11 120 kg
Max load: (cross-country) 4000 kg
Towed load: 2500 kg
Length: 6.6 m
Width: 2.5 m
Height: (cab) 2.85 m
Ground clearance: 0.285 m
Track:
(front) 2 m

Astra BM 201 MC1 (4 × 4) 4000 kg medium mobility truck

(rear) 1.85 m
Wheelbase: 3.45 m
Max road speed: 86.5 km/h
Fuel capacity: 180 l
Max gradient: 60%
Fording: 1.2 m
Engine: FIAT Model 8360 6-cylinder in-line diesel developing 169 hp at 2600 rpm
Gearbox: ZF manual, 6 forward and 1 reverse gears

Clutch: single dry plate
Transfer box: 2-speed
Steering: hydraulic
Turning radius: 8 m
Suspension:
(front) parabolic springs with hydraulic shock absorbers
(rear) semi-elliptical springs with double flexible auxiliary springs
Tyres: 14.00 × 20

Brakes:
(main) air, dual circuit
(parking) mechanical
Electrical system: 24 V
Batteries: 2 × 12 V

Status
In production.

Manufacturer
Astra Veicoli Industriali SpA, Via Caorsana 79, I-29100

Piacenza, Italy.
Tel: 0523 5431. Telex: 530148 astra i.
Fax: 0523 69293.
Astra Veicoli is part of the IVECO organisation.

IVECO FIAT 6602 CM (4 × 4)
6000 kg Cargo Truck

Description
The IVECO FIAT 6602 CM (4 × 4) truck was designed to carry 6000 kg of cargo on both roads and across country and is designated the Autocarro Pesante CP.70 by the Italian Army. Many of the components of the 6602 CM are also used in the 6607 CM (6 × 6) 6000 kg cargo truck (see following entry).

The chassis is of the ladder type with two longitudinal steel channels to which the crossmembers, brackets and spring supports are riveted. The cab is of the forward control type and is of all-steel construction with removable canvas top and side curtains. The windscreen can be folded flat against the front of the cab if not required. The cab is equipped with a heater.

The rear cargo area is of all-steel construction with a wood-lined floor. The drop tailgate has swing-out steps and is removable. Along each side of the cargo area are seats which are folded flat against the sides when not required. The cargo area is covered by removable bows and a tarpaulin cover.

The 9200 kg capacity winch is mounted at the rear and is provided with 60 m of 16 mm diameter cable. The electrical system is waterproof and radio suppressed.

A fuel tanker version is in service.

Specifications
Cab seating: 1 + 1
Configuration: 4 × 4
Weight:
(empty) 7400 kg
(loaded) 13 540 kg
Weight on front axle: (loaded) 4790 kg
Weight on rear axle: (loaded) 8750 kg
Max load: 6140 kg
Towed load:
(road) 10 000 kg
(cross-country) 4000 kg
Load area: 4.28 × 2.23 m
Length: 6.55 m

IVECO FIAT 6602 CM (4 × 4) 6000 kg cargo truck complete with bows and tarpaulin cover

Width: 2.46 m
Height:
(cab) 2.7 m
(tarpaulin) 2.974 m
(load area) 1.417 m
Ground clearance: 0.271 m
Track:
(front) 1.873 m
(rear) 1.785 m
Wheelbase: 3.57 m
Angle of approach/departure: 45°/35°
Max speed: (road) 74 km/h
Range: 700 km
Fuel capacity: 230 l
Max gradient: 60%
Max side slope: 30%
Fording: 0.85 m
Engine: Model 8202.02 6-cylinder in-line liquid-cooled diesel developing 193 hp (DIN) at 2500 rpm
Gearbox: manual with 5 forward and 1 reverse gears
Clutch: single dry plate

Transfer box: 2-speed
Steering: worm and sector, power-assisted
Turning radius: 8.1 m
Suspension: semi-elliptical springs front and rear with double-acting hydraulic shock absorbers on the front axle only
Tyres: 11.00 × 20
Brakes:
(main) air
(parking) mechanical
Electrical system: 24 V
Batteries: 2 × 12 V, 90 Ah

Status
Production complete. In service with the Italian Army.

Manufacturer
IVECO SpA, Defence Vehicle Division, Via Volta 6, I-39100 Bolzano, Italy.
Tel: 0471 905111. Telex: 400541.
Fax: 0471 934240.

IVECO FIAT 6607 CM (6 × 6)
6000 kg Truck

Description
The IVECO FIAT 6607 CM (6 × 6) truck was designed to carry 6000 kg of cargo on both roads and across country. It is designated the Autocarro Pesante CP.70 by the Italian Army and entered service in December 1973. The vehicle is a further development of the FIAT 6602 CM (4 × 4) truck and uses many components of this model.

The ladder-type chassis has longitudinal steel channels to which crossmember brackets and spring supports are riveted. The forward control cab is all steel with a removable canvas top and side curtains. If

required the windscreen can be folded forward flat against the front of the cab. The cab is provided with a heater.

The rear cargo area is all steel with a wood-lined floor and has drop sides and a removable drop tailgate. The worm gear type winch mounted at the rear of the vehicle has a capacity of 9200 kg (first layer) and is provided with 60 m of 16 mm diameter cable. The winch is fitted with an automatic safety brake. The electrical system is waterproof and radio suppressed.

Specifications
Cab seating: 1 + 1
Configuration: 6 × 6
Weight:
(empty) 8830 kg

(loaded) 15 000 kg
Weight on front axle: (loaded) 4620 kg
Weight on rear bogie: (loaded) 10 380 kg
Max load: (road) 6170 kg
Towed load:
(road) 10 000 kg
(cross-country) 4000 kg
Load area: 5.545 × 2.265 m
Length: 7.824 m
Width: 2.43 m
Height:
(cab) 2.699 m
(reduced, top of steering wheel) 2.135 m
(load area) 1.392 m
Ground clearance: (axles) 0.244 m
Track:
(front) 1.873 m
(rear) 1.872 m
Wheelbase: 3.567 m + 1.25 m
Angle of approach/departure: 45°/29°
Max speed: (road) 74 km/h
Range: 750 km
Fuel capacity: 230 l
Max gradient: 60%
Max side slope: 30%
Fording: 0.85 m
Engine: Model 8202.02 6-cylinder in-line liquid-cooled diesel developing 193 hp (DIN) at 2500 rpm
Gearbox: manual with 5 forward and 1 reverse gears
Clutch: single dry plate
Transfer box: 2-speed
Steering: power-assisted, worm and sector
Turning radius: 8.96 m

IVECO FIAT 6607 CM (6 × 6) 6000 kg truck (Italian Army)

Suspension:
(front) semi-elliptical leaf springs and double-acting shock absorbers
(rear) parallelogram torque arm with 2 constant rate leaf springs
Tyres: 11.00 × 20
Brakes:
(main) drum, air-operated, dual circuit

(parking) drum on transfer rear output shaft
Electrical system: 24 V
Batteries: 2 × 12 V, 90 Ah

Status
Production complete. In service with the Italian Army.

Manufacturer
IVECO SpA, Defence Vehicle Division, Via Volta 6, I-39100 Bolzano, Italy.
Tel: 0471 905111. Telex: 400541.
Fax: 0471 934240.

IVECO FIAT 6605 (6 × 6) Series

Development
In the 1960s FIAT built a light artillery tractor (6 × 6) called the Model 6606 (TL65) and a medium artillery tractor (6 × 6) called the Model 6605 (TM65). The TM65 (TM standing for *Trattore Medio*) was powered by a petrol engine and further development resulted in the diesel-engined TM69 which was adopted by the Italian Army. The range consists of the 6605 TM used for towing medium artillery such as the 155 mm FH-70, the 6605 FH used for carrying ammunition, the 6605 AG recovery vehicle and the 6605 A cargo truck.

Description (6605 TM)
The chassis is of the ladder type with two longitudinal pressed steel channels, to which are riveted the crossmembers, brackets and spring supports. The forward control cab is all steel and has a removable canvas top and side screens and a windscreen which can be folded flat against the bonnet. A cab heater and ventilator are standard on all versions. The gap to the rear of the cab and body houses the spare wheel, two water and two fuel containers, tyre chain locker and the exhaust pipe.

The rear cargo area is all steel with a wood-lined floor. The sides consist of two boards, the front a drop type and the rear fixed. The drop tailgate is fitted with integral steps and is removable. The rear cargo area is covered by removable bows and a tarpaulin cover. When not required the bows can be stowed under the central area of the body. The cargo space is divided into three compartments by removable partitions: the first is used for stowing the charges, the second for the projectiles and the rear for stores and the tarpaulin cover.

The transmission consists of a set of gears mounted on four shafts (input, primary, layshaft and reverse). Shifting from each gear is controlled by a lever through a pneumatic servo. Shifting from the high to the low range, or vice versa, is by an electropneumatic control with a preselector switch, interlocked with the clutch pedal. The transfer box is mechanical and consists of helical constant mesh gears mounted on three shafts (input, intermediate and output) of which the input one carries the dog clutch with a lockable divider differential distributing power to front and rear axles.

Mounted at the rear of the vehicle is a worm type winch with a capacity of 10 000 kg which can be used to the front or rear of the truck and has 60 m of 18 mm diameter cable.

Variants
FIAT 6605 FH
This is almost identical to the 6605 TM but has a

Specifications

Model	6605 TM	6605 FH	6605 A
Cab seating	1 + 11	1 + 11	1 + 1
Configuration	6 × 6	6 × 6	6 × 6
Weight (empty)	11 800 kg	12 600 kg	12 000 kg
(loaded)	17 000 kg	19 220 kg	20 500 kg
Max load	5000 kg	6620 kg	8500 kg
Towed load	15 000 kg	15 000 kg	15 000 kg
Length	7.33 m	7.33 m	7.33 m
Width	2.5 m	2.5 m	2.5 m
Height (cab)	2.92 m	2.92 m	2.78 m
(tarpaulin)	2.87 m	2.78 m	3.08 m
(load area)	1.533 m	1.533 m	1.522 m
Ground clearance	0.363 m	0.363 m	0.363 m
Track	2.072 m	2.072 m	2.072 m
Wheelbase	3.217 m + 1.365 m	3.217 m + 1.365 m	3.217 m + 1.365 m
Angle of approach/departure	45°/40°	45°/40°	45°/40°
Max speed (road)	80 km/h	80 km/h	80 km/h
Range	700 km	700 km	700 km
Fuel capacity	360 l	360 l	360 l
Max gradient	60%	60%	60%
Max side slope	20%	20%	20%
Fording	1.5 m	1.5 m	1.5 m
Engine	Model 8212.02.500 6-cylinder in-line water-cooled diesel developing 260 hp at 2200 rpm		
Gearbox	manual with 8 forward and 2 reverse gears		
Clutch	dry, dual plate	dry, dual plate	dry, dual plate
Transfer box	2-speed	2-speed	2-speed
Steering	ZF hydraulic assisted	ZF hydraulic assisted	ZF hydraulic assisted
Turning radius	8 m	8 m	8 m
Suspension (front)	2 semi-elliptical constant rate leaf springs with double-acting hydraulic shock absorbers		
(rear)	rocker and torque arms with 2 constant rate leaf springs		
Tyres	14.00 × 20	14.00 × 20	14.00 × 20
Brakes (main)	drum air-operated on all wheels, dual circuit with connections for trailer braking		
(parking)	drum, hand-operated, mounted on transfer rear output shaft		
Electrical system	24 V	24 V	24 V
Batteries	4 × 12 V, 90 Ah	4 × 12 V, 90 Ah	4 × 12 V, 90 Ah

shorter rear cargo area as a hydraulic crane is mounted between the cab and the cargo area for unloading pallets of ammunition. The prototype was completed in 1974 with first production vehicles completed in 1976.

FIAT 6605 AG
Full details of this recovery vehicle are given in the *Recovery vehicles* section.

FIAT 6605 A
This is the truck version and has a two-man cab with the cargo area at the rear with tiltable troop seats down each side, drop tailgate with integral steps, removable bows and a tarpaulin cover. The prototype was

completed in 1974 with first production vehicles following in 1976.

Status
In service with the Italian Army, Libya and Somalia. Somalia has 10 6605 TM, 200 6605 A, 12 10 500 litre fuel tankers, 10 recovery vehicles, four command posts, five aircraft refuellers and 50 8000 litre water tankers.

Manufacturer
IVECO SpA, Defence Vehicle Division, Via Volta 6, I-39100 Bolzano, Italy.
Tel: 0471 905111. Telex: 400541.
Fax: 0471 934240.

IVECO FIAT 6605 TM69 (6 × 6) artillery tractor fitted with removable cab roof, bows and tarpaulin cover

IVECO FIAT 6605 FH (6 × 6) with hydraulically operated crane mounted to rear of cab

Astra BM 309F (6 × 6) Truck

Description
In 1983 Astra Veicoli introduced a range of 6 × 6 trucks known as the 'Series 300', produced in a variety of wheelbases, engine fits, cabs and configurations. One of these is the BM 309 which underwent evaluation trials for the Italian Army.

The 'Series 300' are produced with two wheelbase lengths, 3.3 m + 1.4 m for tractor trucks and 3.5 m + 1.4 m for cargo and other chassis. Four different engine fits are available (the BM 309 originally had a choice of two engines, a FIAT and a Mercedes), and both 6 × 6 and 6 × 4 configurations are offered. Double and single cabs are available. Numerous other options such as tyre sizes, power take-offs, and so on, are possible. The military version is the BM 309F, details of which are provided in the Specifications.

Specifications
Cab seating: 1 + 1
Configuration: 6 × 6
Weight:
 (kerb with FIAT engine) 10 180 kg
 (kerb with Mercedes engine) 9980 kg
Gross vehicle weight: 33 000 kg
Length: 7.06 m
Width: 2.5 m
Height: (overall) 3.06 m
Ground clearance: 0.385 m
Track:
 (front) 2.045 m
 (rear) 1.829 m
Wheelbase: 3.5 m + 1.4 m
Max speed: 80 km/h
Fuel capacity: 300 l
Max gradient: 40%
Engine: FIAT 8280.02 8-cylinder diesel developing 352 hp at 2400 rpm or
Mercedes OM 423 diesel developing 355 hp at 2300 rpm
Gearbox: ZF 16-S-160 ECOSPLIT, mechanical synchronised, with 16 forward and 2 reverse gears
Steering: hydraulic servo
Turning radius: 9.75 m
Suspension:
 (front) 4-leaf parabolic springs with hydraulic shock absorbers and torsion bar
 (rear) 12-leaf semi-elliptical spring oscillating by pivot system; tandem axle is connected to the main frame by radius rod with rubber silent block
Brakes: dual circuit air
Tyres: 12.00 × 20 or 24
Electrical system: 24 V
Batteries: 2 × 12 V, 143 Ah

Status
In production.

Manufacturer
Astra Veicoli Industriali SpA, Via Caorsana 79, I-29100 Piacenza, Italy.
Tel: 0523 5431. Telex: 530148 astra i.
Fax: 0523 69293.
Astra Veicoli is part of the IVECO organisation.

Chassis of Astra BM 309F (6 × 6) truck

Astra BM 20 Series (6 × 6) 10 000 kg Truck

Description
The Astra BM 20 series two-door glass fibre cab with metal frame can be tilted forwards to 48° allowing access to the engine for maintenance. The cab has seats for the driver and one passenger plus two emergency folding seats. The chassis is made of high elastic steel and consists of two double C-shaped sidemembers connected through rigid crossmembers. The rear cargo area has drop sides, drop tailgate, removable bows and a tarpaulin cover.

Variants
Dump truck
This has a struck capacity of 8.5 m³ and fully loaded weighs 30 000 kg.

Recovery vehicle
Full details of this are given in the *Recovery vehicles* section.

Bridging Boat Carrier BM 20 NB1
This vehicle has the same chassis as the BM 20 N series but with provision for carrying, launching and recovery of a bridging boat. The bridging boat is carried on a platform to the rear of the cab which can be tilted through 45° by means of a hydraulic multi-stage cylinder actuated by a hydraulic pump. The platform enables the launching and loading of the boat without any assistance apart from the driver in the cab. Total weight loaded is 20 300 kg and the length with boat is 10.67 m.

Truck Tractor for Engineer Corps Trailer Workshop BM 20 NC2
This vehicle, which is in service with the Italian Army, has the same chassis as the BM 20 N series but is equipped with a light body with drop sides and a drop tailgate. To the rear of the cab is a hydraulic crane which can lift 2500 kg to a height of 2.1 m.

BM 20 NP1 Mobile Drilling Equipment
This vehicle mounts a Model G21 Geo-Astra drilling rig weighing 13 100 kg and which can drill a 200 mm hole to a depth of 200 m.

BM 20 NR2 Crane Truck
This carries a 20-tonne crane and entered production for the Italian Engineer Corps in 1983. The crane has a full 360° traverse.

Specifications (BM 20 NC2)
Cab seating: 1 + 3
Configuration: 6 × 6
Weight:
 (empty) 11 550 kg
 (loaded, cross-country) 22 100 kg
Max load:
 (road) 15 000 kg
 (cross-country) 10 000 kg
Towed load: (road) 28 000 kg
Length: 7.51 m
Width: 2.5 m
Height: 2.75 m
Ground clearance: 0.265 m
Track:
 (front) 2 m
 (rear) 1.85 m
Wheelbase: 3.485 m + 1.3 m
Max speed: 67.2 km/h
Range: 1000 km
Fuel capacity: 280 l
Max gradient: 60%
Fording: 1.2 m
Engine: FIAT 8210 6-cylinder in-line diesel developing 260 hp at 2200 rpm
Gearbox: ZF manual with 6 forward and 1 reverse gears

BM 20 NC2 (6 × 6) tractor truck for Engineer Corps trailer workshop as used by Italian Army

Astra BM 20 NB1 (6 × 6) bridging boat carrier

Clutch: single dry plate
Transfer box: 2-speed
Steering: hydraulic-assisted
Turning radius: 11 m
Suspension:
 (front) semi-elliptical springs with four rubber
 bumpers and hydraulic shock absorbers
 (rear) oscillating semi-elliptical type springs with
 rocker arm system

Tyres: 12.00 × 20
Brakes:
 (main) air
 (parking) mechanical
Electrical system: 24 V
Batteries: 4 × 12 V

Status
Production complete. The BM 20 NC2 tractor truck for

Engineer Corps trailer workshop is in service with the
Italian Army.

Manufacturer
Astra Veicoli Industriali SpA, Via Caorsana 79, I-29100
Piacenza, Italy.
Tel: 0523 5431. Telex: 530148 astra i.
Fax: 0523 69293.
Astra Veicoli is part of the IVECO organisation.

IVECO FIAT 230-35 WM (6 × 6) 10 000 kg Artillery Truck/Tractor

IVECO FIAT 230-35 WM (6 × 6) 10 000 kg truck

Description
The IVECO FIAT 230-35 WM (6 × 6) 10 000 kg artillery truck/tractor is the only vehicle of its type produced by IVECO FIAT and is the updated version of the former 230 PM 35. An essentially similar vehicle, the 230 PM 26 is no longer available.

The vehicle has a forward control cab for the driver and two passengers. The cab has a canvas roof that can be easily removed and can tilt forward for engine and transmission access. The cargo area is covered with a tarpaulin resting on bows. The tailgate and sideboards are all tiltable and removable and there are folding benches for 22 men. A spare wheel holder is located between the cab and the cargo body.

Options include a 10 000 kg hydraulic winch, sand tyres, a hard-top cab with observation hatch, a power take-off on the gearbox, brake couplings for towing, a spare wheel holder with a tyre handling crane, a towing hook, a 900 kg material handling crane, and a jib for handling artillery trail legs.

The IVECO FIAT 230-35 WM can be produced in a special artillery tractor version with the cargo body divided into two sections. One section is used to carry a gun crew of 10 men while the other section is used to carry ammunition and other supplies up to a weight of 8500 kg. The crew compartment can be made removable if required. The tractor can tow artillery up to a weight of 15 000 kg.

Other variants of this vehicle include a recovery vehicle (refer to *Recovery vehicles* section for details), a tanker, a mobile workshop, a mobile hospital, a logistics vehicle carrying a pallet loading system, and a missile system carrier.

Specifications
Cab seating: 1 + 2 (up to 22 in rear)
Configuration: 6 × 6
Weight:
 (kerb) 13 000 kg
 (GVW) 23 000 kg
Max load: 10 000 kg
Towed load: 15 000 kg
Load area: 5.05 × 2.35 m

Length: 7.762 m
Width: 2.5 m
Height:
 (cab) 3.05 m
 (tarpaulin) 3.43 m
 (load area) 1.58 m
Ground clearance: 0.36 m
Track:
 (front) 2.027 m
 (rear) 2.032 m
Wheelbase: 3.3 m + 1.38 m
Angle of approach/departure: 42°/40°
Max speed: over 80 km/h
Range: over 600 km
Fuel capacity: 300 l
Max gradient: 60%
Side slope: 30%
Fording: 1.2 m
Engine: FIAT 8280.02 17.174 l V-8 water-cooled diesel developing 352 hp at 2400 rpm
Gearbox: ZF Type 4 S 150 GPA, 8 forward and 1 reverse gears
Transmission: torque converter

Transfer box: electro-pneumatically lockable
Steering: recirculating ball, power-assisted
Turning radius: 9.5 m
Suspension:
 (front) single flexibility leaf springs with hydraulic shock absorbers
 (rear) single flexibility leaf springs, reversed, fully articulated
Tyres: 14.00 × 20
Brakes: drum, air-operated
Electrical system: 24 V
Batteries: 2 × 12 V, 143 Ah
Generator: 650 W

Status
In production.

Manufacturer
IVECO SpA, Defence Vehicle Division, Via Volta 6, I-39100 Bolzano, Italy.
Tel: 0471 905111. Telex: 400541.
Fax: 0471 934240.

IVECO FIAT 260-35 WM (6 × 4) and (6 × 6) 10 000 kg Trucks

Description
The IVECO FIAT 260-35 WM series of 6 × 4 and 6 × 6 10 000 kg trucks was developed by the company from standard commercial vehicles. The chassis consists of section sidemembers connected by crossmembers with sheet steel bumper at the front and towing hook and bumper at the rear.

The all-steel two-door fully enclosed cab is of the forward control type and can be tilted forward by one man to give access to the engine for maintenance. The steering wheel and both seats are adjustable and a two-speed electrical ventilating system, combined with a water heater and defroster, is fitted as standard.

The rear cargo body is of sheet steel with wood-lined platform, fixed headboard, tiltable sideboards with folding benches (22 troop seats), tiltable and removable tailgate with tiltable ladders for access to the platform. The body is attached to the chassis by means of elastic brackets with the spare wheel between the cab and the cargo body. Standard equipment includes

IVECO FIAT 260-35 WM (6 × 6) 10 000 kg truck

Specifications

Configuration	6 × 4	6 × 6
Cab seating	1 + 1	1 + 1
Weight (loaded)	24 000 kg	24 000 kg
Max load	12 000 kg	14 000 kg
Towed load	20 000 kg	20 000 kg
Length (excluding body)	8 m	8 m
Width	2.5 m	2.5 m
Height (cab, unloaded)	3.123 m	3.123 m
Ground clearance	0.316 m	0.312 m
Track (front)	2.069 m	1.927 m
(rear)	1.809 m	1.809 m
Wheelbase	3.85 m + 1.38 m	3.85 m + 1.38 m
Angle of approach/departure	28°/22°	33°/27°
Max speed	97 km/h	95 km/h
Range	600 km	600 km
Fuel capacity	300 l	300 l
Max gradient	60%	60%
Side slope	30%	30%
Fording	0.65 m	0.65 m
Engine	FIAT 8280.02 V-8 liquid-cooled diesel developing 352 hp at 2400 rpm	

Configuration	6 × 4	6 × 6
Gearbox	FIAT 12802, 8 forward and 2 reverse gears	ZF 4S-150 GPA combined gearbox and transfer box, 8 forward and 1 reverse gears
Steering	ZF recirculating ball with integral power-assistance	
Turning radius	9.75 m	9.75 m
Suspension (front)	single flexible leaf springs and hydraulic shock absorbers	
(rear)	single flexible leaf springs reversed and hydraulic telescopic shock absorbers	
Tyres	12.00 R 20 PR 18	12.00 R 20 PR 18
Brakes (main)	air	air
(exhaust)	pneumatic, controlled by separate spring-loaded acting on rear axle foot control	
(parking)		
Electrical system	24 V	24 V
Batteries	2 × 12 V, 143 Ah	2 × 12 V, 143 Ah

removable bows and tarpaulin cover, blackout lights, transceiver power input radio suppressed, auxiliary receptacle and master switch, NATO standard 12-point socket for trailer and tyre inflation system.

The 6 × 6 model has a combined gearbox and transfer box split from the engine and converter. The transfer box allows the torque distribution between front axle and rear bogie through a central differential which is pneumatically lockable.

The 6 × 4 model has a steering dead front axle with the 6 × 6 model having steer drive axle with epicyclic hub reduction. Both models have the same high articulation bogie for on/off highway use composed of two drive axles with hub reductions and pneumatically lockable differentials.

Optional equipment includes an OM DF 0.9 torque converter and a 1000 kg jib crane mounted to the cab rear.

The chassis can be used for a variety of other applications including a mobile workshop, water or fuel tanker, artillery tractor and a recovery vehicle. The latter can be fitted with a hydraulically operated crane with a capacity of 12 000 kg and an auxiliary recovery winch.

Status

In production.

Manufacturer

IVECO SpA, Defence Vehicle Division, Via Volta 6, I-39100 Bolzano, Italy.
Tel: 0471 905111. Telex: 400541.
Fax: 0471 934240.

Astra BM 318 (8 × 8) 15 000 kg High Mobility Truck

Description

Developed in response to an Italian Army requirement for a heavy high mobility truck, the Astra BM 318 (8 × 8) 15 000 kg truck was presented to the Italian Ministry of Defence in May 1989.

The BM 318 is of conventional layout with a forward control cab. The frame is formed from two special steel straight C-section members with riveted and bolted crossmembers. The cab is glass fibre on a metal frame and has seating for the driver and two passengers. A machine gun ring mounting is provided on the cab roof and there is internal stowage for rifles, personal equipment and a first aid kit. It is possible to install a radio and an NBC kit. A comprehensive instrument display is provided.

The body is of the fixed type and has a steel fixed front wall. The aluminium side and rear walls can be removed or hinged downwards. The anti-skid floor has provision for mounting ISO containers. Other types of body may be fitted.

A hydraulic materials handling crane is provided with a capacity of 1500 kg at 6 m. Also provided is a 10 000 kg capacity winch for front and rear traction.

Astra BM 318 (8 × 8) 15 000 kg high mobility truck

Specifications

Cab seating: 1 + 2
Configuration: 8 × 8
Weight:
  (empty, with body, crane and winch) 14 500 kg
  (loaded) 32 000 kg
Max load: (with crane and winch) 17 500 kg
Towed load: 16 000 kg
Load area: 7.5 × 2.4 m
Length: 10.4 m
Width: 2.5 m
Height: (cab) 2.898 m
Ground clearance: 0.424 m
Track:
  (1st and 2nd axles) 2.05 m
  (3rd and 4th axles) 2.06 m
Wheelbase: 1.955 m + 3.595 m + 1.45 m
Angle of approach/departure: 45°/40°
Max speed: 96 km/h
Range: 800 km
Fuel capacity: 300 l
Max gradient: 100%
Side slope: 40%
Fording: 1.2 m
Engine: IVECO FIAT 8210.TCA 13.798 l 6-cylinder turbo-intercooler diesel developing 420 hp at 2000 rpm
Transmission: ZF type 6 HP 600 automatic with 6 forward and 1 reverse gears
Transfer box: 2-speed
Steering: ZF Servocom type 8099
Turning radius: 22.6 m
Suspension:
  (front) semi-elliptic leaf springs with 2 double-acting hydraulic shock absorbers and bumpers
  (rear) reversed semi-elliptic leaf springs with centre pin and slider connection to axles, 4 lower reaction rods and 2 upper reaction triangles
Tyres: 14.00 R 20 run-flat
Brakes:
  (main) hydraulic disc
  (parking) on 2nd and 3rd axle

Status

Ready for production.

Manufacturer

Astra Veicoli Industriali SpA, Via Caorsana 79, I-29100 Piacenza, Italy.
Tel: 0523 5431. Telex: 530148 astra i.
Fax: 0523 69293.
Astra Veicoli is part of the IVECO organisation.

JAPAN

Kohkidohsha 1500 kg (4 × 4) High Mobility Vehicle

Description

The term Kohkidohsha translates as high mobility vehicle and it is a 4 × 4 1500 kg vehicle developed as a possible replacement for many existing Type 73 2000 kg and Isuzu 2500 kg trucks currently in Japanese Ground Self-Defence Force service. A request for 85 vehicles was made during 1992, at least nine of which will be configured as Kin-Sam close range air defence missile system carriers.

The Kohkidohsha visually resembles the American M998 HMMWV series (qv) but differs in many respects. It can carry at least four people, including the driver. Power is derived from a 4 litre liquid-cooled 150 hp diesel coupled to an automatic transmission and there is permanent four-wheel drive. Steering is power assisted on all four wheels and independent suspension is provided, also on all four wheels.

Kohkidohsha 1500 kg (4 × 4) high mobility vehicle

Specifications
Cab seating: 1 + 3
Configuration: 4 × 4
Weight: approx 2440 kg
Max load: approx 1500 kg
Length: 4.91 m
Width: 2.15 m

Height: 2.09 m
Ground clearance: 0.4 m
Wheelbase: 3.4 m
Angle of approach/departure: 73°/51°
Max speed: 100 km/h
Engine: 4 l liquid-cooled diesel developing 150 hp
Transmission: automatic

Transfer box: full time four-wheel drive
Steering: power-assisted on all four wheels
Suspension: independent
Tyres: run-flat

Status
Ready for production.

Type 73 (4 × 4) 2000 kg Truck

Description

The Type 73 (4 × 4) 2000 kg truck was standardised in 1973 as the successor to Nissan and Toyota (4 × 4) 750 kg trucks in service since the 1950s.

The Type 73 has an over-engine cab with a steel back and sides up to seat-top height and steel doors with glass windows. The single-piece windscreen can be folded forwards. The roof is a single-piece waterproof tarpaulin that can be fixed in place by removable braces. With the tarpaulin in place a high-capacity heater-blower-defroster system can be used. Seats for the driver and one passenger are provided, each with space for kit stowage behind.

The cargo body is all steel but has wooden side stakes and rails that are held in place by latches and unfold to serve as benches. The tailgate has a built-in step that will unfold when a ring on each side is pulled. A heavy canvas tilt and braces can be used to cover the area which is 3 m long and 1.95 m wide.

Standard equipment includes a rear fender, tool box, canvas tilt and spare tyre and carrier. Optional equipment includes a winch (front-mounted), a power take-off, and a tropical cooling system.

An ambulance version with a fully enclosed cab and rear body has been produced. The truck version has been used to carry mortars.

Type 73 (4 × 4) 2000 kg truck (Kensuke Ebata)

Specifications
Cab seating: 1 + 1
Configuration: 4 × 4
Weight:
  (empty) 3195 kg
  (gross weight, on road) 5355 kg
  (gross weight, off road) 4855 kg
Max load:
  (on road) 2000 kg
  (off road) 1500 kg

Front axle load: (on road, loaded) 2325 kg
Rear axle load: (on road, loaded) 3030 kg
Length: 5.36 m
Width: 2.09 m
Height: 2.49 m
Ground clearance: 0.28 m
Wheelbase: 2.9 m
Track:
  (front) 1.61 m
  (rear) 1.635 m
Angle of approach/departure: 37°/32°
Max speed: 87 km/h
Fuel capacity: 115 l
Max gradient: 60%
Fording: 0.8 m
Engine: Hino DQ100 diesel developing 95 hp at 3000 rpm
Gearbox: 5 forward and 1 reverse gears
Transfer box: 2-speed

Clutch: single dry disc
Steering: recirculating ball
Turning radius: 6.4 m
Suspension: semi-elliptic leaf springs with shock absorbers
Tyres: 8.25 × 20
Brakes: hydraulic with vacuum servo
Electrical system: 24 V
Batteries: 2 × 12 V, 100 Ah
Generator: 400 W

Status
In production. In service with the Japanese Ground Self-Defence Force.

Manufacturer
Toyota Motor Corporation, 4-18, Koraku 1-chome, Bunkyo-ku, Tokyo 112, Japan.
Tel: 81 3 5391 5407. Fax: 81 3 5391 5016.

Isuzu (4 × 4) 2500 kg Trucks

Description
There are two basic production versions of the Isuzu (4 × 4) truck, the TSD45 and the TSD55 with a longer wheelbase (later both became the HTS). Both may be produced in a variety of forms which include numerous commercial configurations. The military versions are usually confined to cargo bodies or flat bed types.

Layout and configuration of the Isuzu trucks are conventional with the engine at the front, the all-steel cab placed centrally and the cargo or payload area at the rear. Cargo bodies may be covered with a tarpaulin. Various standard fittings may be found on nearly all models; military options include power take-offs, towing hooks, radio fixtures, and a tyre inflation device.

One service version has an open flat bed rear with a hydraulic crane that is extended forward over the cab for travelling. Two outriggers on each side of the crane provide stabilisation when the crane is in use. This crane version has the spare tyre stowed under the body rear while the cargo version has it behind the cab.

Status
Production complete. In service with the Japanese Ground Self-Defence Force.

Manufacturer
Isuzu Motors Limited, 22-10, Minami-oi, 6-chome, Shinagawa-ku, Tokyo 140, Japan. Tel: 03 762 1111. Telex: 0246 6689.

Specifications

Model	TSD45	TSD55
Cab seating	1 + 1	1 + 1
Configuration	4 × 4	4 × 4
Weight (empty, cab and chassis)	3825 kg	3880 kg
(max permissible)	12 500 kg	12 500 kg
Length	6.465 m	6.91 m
Width	2.2 m	2.2 m
Height (top of cab)	2.43 m	2.445 m
(load area)	1.03 m	1.045 m
Ground clearance	0.23 m	0.23 m
Track (front)	1.68 m	1.68 m
(rear)	1.74 m	1.74 m
Wheelbase	4 m	4.445 m
Max speed	88 km/h	88 km/h
Fuel capacity	100 or 200 l	100 or 200 l
Engine	6BD1 6-cylinder, in-line, 5.784 l water-cooled diesel developing 160 hp at 3200 rpm	
Gearbox	Isuzu manual with 5 forward and 1 reverse gears	
Transfer box	2-speed	2-speed
Clutch	single dry plate	single dry plate
Steering	recirculating ball	recirculating ball
Turning radius	8.7 m	9.4 m
Suspension	semi-elliptical alloy springs, lever type shock absorbers	
Tyres	8.25 × 20	8.25 × 20
Brakes (standard)	hydraulic with vacuum or optional air-assistance	
(braking)	mechanical	mechanical
Electrical system	24 V	24 V
Batteries	2 × 12 V, 65 Ah	2 × 12 V, 65 Ah

Isuzu (4 × 4) 2500 kg cargo truck from side

Isuzu (4 × 4) 2500 kg cargo truck with crane

Isuzu (6 × 6) 2500 kg Trucks

Description
The first Isuzu 6 × 6 truck completed in 1953 was called the TW and was almost identical in appearance to the American GMC 2½-ton truck of the Second World War. It was subsequently tested in the USA and in 1957 was adopted by the US Army for use in Japan. It was also adopted by the Japanese Self-Defence Force and other countries in the Far East including South Korea, Vietnam and the Philippines. First production vehicles were completed in 1957 and since then many versions have been built, including the TWD20 (1963) and the later TWD25, in both single and dual rear wheel configurations; late versions became the HTW. They can carry 5000 kg of cargo on roads or 2500 kg of cargo across country.

The layout of the vehicle is conventional with the engine at the front, two-door cab in the centre and the cargo area at the rear with fixed sides, drop tailgate, removable bows and a tarpaulin cover. The cab has a canvas top and a windscreen which folds forward onto the bonnet. Some versions, for example the tankers, have a fully enclosed cab. Many vehicles have a winch mounted at the front.

Variants
Air compressor
Mounted on the rear is a compressor unit which is used to power a jack-hammer, concrete breaker and other air-driven tools and also for inflating and deflating inflatable craft. Basic specifications are length 6.595 m, width 2.25 m, height 2.595 m and weight 8070 kg.

Dump truck
Two models are in service, one with a dump body that tips to the rear and the other with a dump body that tips to the sides or rear. Both single and dual rear wheel models are in service and all can be used for carrying troops as removable seats can be fitted down either side. Basic specifications are (with data in square brackets relating to the model with dual rear wheels) length: 6.3 [6.4] m, width 2.22 m, height 2.92 [3.02] m and empty weight 6430 [6390] kg.

Cargo (long wheelbase)
Specifications are length 8.69 m, width 2.4 m, height 2.92 m and empty weight 6860 kg.

Shop/van
There are many variants of this model including

Isuzu (6 × 6) 2500 kg dump truck

Isuzu (6 × 6) general utility tanker

engineering (general), engineering (artillery), engineering (small arms), maintenance (general), maintenance (electric), and maintenance (communications). Basic specifications are length 6.91 m, width 2.44 m, height 3.19 m and empty weight 6500 kg.

Tanker (fuel)
This carries 5000 or 2800 litres.

Tanker (water)
This carries 2800 litres and is fitted with a filtration system. Its basic specifications are length 6.7 m, width 2.3 m, height 2.68 m and empty weight 6320 kg.

Specifications (TWD20)
Configuration: 6 × 6
Cab seating: 1 + 2
Weight:
(empty) 5695 kg
(loaded, road) 10 695 kg

(loaded, cross-country) 8195 kg
Max load:
(road) 5000 kg
(cross-country) 2500 kg
Length: 7.09 m
Width: 2.283 m
Height:
(cab) 2.41 m
(tarpaulin) 2.995 m
Ground clearance: 0.23 m
Track:
(front) 1.585 m
(rear) 1.744 m
Wheelbase: 4 m (first axle to centre of rear bogie)
Max road speed: 85 km/h
Fuel capacity: 100 l
Engine: DA120 6-cylinder water-cooled diesel developing 210 hp at 2200 rpm
Gearbox: manual, 4 forward and 1 reverse gears
Clutch: single dry plate

Transfer box: 2-speed
Turning radius: 9 m
Suspension:
(front) semi-elliptical leaf springs and hydraulic shock absorbers
(rear) semi-elliptical leaf springs and torque rods
Tyres: 7.50 × 20
Brakes:
(main) hydraulic
(parking) mechanical
Electrical system: 24 V

Status
Production complete. In service with the Japanese Ground Self-Defence Force and other armed forces.

Manufacturer
Isuzu Motors Limited, 22-10, Minami-oi, 6-chome, Shinagawa-ku, Tokyo 140, Japan.
Tel: 03 762 1111. Telex: 0246 6689.

Toyota (6 × 6) 2500 kg Trucks

Description
The first model, the FQS, was introduced in 1955 for both civilian and military use and was adopted by the Japanese Self-Defence Force, US Army in Japan and other armies in the Far East. The layout of the vehicle is similar to the Isuzu vehicles in this class and it can carry 5000 kg of cargo on roads or 2500 kg of cargo across country. The six-cylinder diesel engine is

coupled to a manual gearbox with four forward and one reverse gears and a two-speed transfer box. Variants include compressor, dump truck, firefighting vehicle, shop/van, water tanker and a wrecker.

Specifications
Weight: (empty) 5235 kg
Length: 6.85 m
Width: 2.26 m
Height: 2.79 m
Wheelbase: 3.492 m (first axle to centre of rear bogie)

Tyres: 7.50 × 20

Status
Production complete. In service with the Japanese Self-Defence Force and other armed forces in South-East Asia.

Manufacturer
Toyota Motor Company Limited, 1 Toyota-cho, Toyota-shi, Aichi-ken, Japan.
Tel: 0565 28 2121. Telex: 4528371 toyota j.

Type 73 (6 × 6) 3500 kg Truck

Description
The Type 73 (6 × 6) 3500 kg truck was developed by Isuzu from the late 1960s to replace the range of 2500 kg (6 × 6) trucks then used by the Japanese Self-Defence Force. After trials and modifications it was standardised in 1973 as the Type 73 large truck

series and since then it has been produced in large numbers for the JASDF.

The first model was the SKW440 but since then many improvements have been made to the engine, axles, cab, and so on. The latest model is the SKW463.

The forward control cab has a windscreen that can be folded forward onto the bonnet and a removable canvas top. The basic cargo body is all steel and has a drop tailgate, bench troop seats down either side,

removable bows and a tarpaulin cover. This basic model can carry 3500 kg of stores across country or 6000 kg on roads.

There are two basic models, one with single-tyred rear wheels (cargo, tanker, and so on) and the other with dual-tyred rear wheels (dumper and light wrecker).

A 4500 kg capacity winch can be mounted on the front of the vehicle.

Specifications

Model	SKW463M	SKW463M	SKW463MV	SKW463MV	SKW463MV	SKW463MD	SKW463MR	SKW463
Type	Cargo truck	Cargo truck (W/W)	Tanker (utility)	Water Tanker	Crane	Dump truck	Light Wrecker	Cargo (long)
Cab seating	1 + 1	1 + 1	1 + 1	1 + 1	1 + 1	1 + 1	1 + 1	1 + 1
Configuration	6 × 6	6 × 6	6 × 6	6 × 6	6 × 6	6 × 6	6 × 6	6 × 6
Weight								
(empty)	7980 kg	8200 kg	8740 kg	8860 kg	8790 kg	9460 kg	14 200 kg	8270 kg
(loaded, road)	14 140 kg	14 360 kg	14 000 kg	14 020 kg	13 950 kg	14 620 kg	19 160 kg	13 430 kg
(loaded, cross-country)	11 640 kg	11 860 kg	—	—	11 450 kg	12 120 kg	—	11 930 kg
Max load								
(road)	6000 kg	6000 kg	5100 kg	5000 kg	5000 kg	5000 kg	—	5000 kg
(cross-country)	3500 kg	3500 kg	—	—	3500 kg	3500 kg	—	3500 kg
Towed load								
(road)	6000 kg	6000 kg	6000 kg	6000 kg	6000 kg	6000 kg	6000 kg	6000 kg
(cross-country)	4000 kg	4000 kg	4000 kg	4000 kg	4000 kg	4000 kg	4000 kg	4000 kg
Length	7.030 m	7.230 m	7.190 m	6.810 m	7.355 m	7.170 m	7.810 m	8.130 m
Width	2.485 m	2.485 m	2.485 m	2.485 m	2.485 m	2.490 m	2.4890 m	2.485 m
Height	3.080 m	3.080 m	2.865 m	2.890 m	3.250 m	3.295 m	3.060 m	3.080 m
Ground clearance	0.330 m	0.330 m	0.330 m	0.330 m	0.330 m	0.330 m	0.330 m	0.330 m
Track (front)	1.970 m	1.970 m	1.970 m	1.970 m	1.970 m	1.840 m	1.840 m	1.970 m
Wheelbase	3.295 m + 1.310 m	3.295 m + 1.310 m	3.295 m + 1.310 m	3.295 m + 1.310 m	3.295 m + 1.310 m	3.295 m + 1.310 m	3.295 m + 1.310 m	3.295 m + 1.310 m
Max road speed	95 km/h	95 km/h	95 km/h	95 km/h	95 km/h	95 km/h	95 km/h	95 km/h
Range	500 km	500 km	500 km	500 km	500 km	500 km	500 km	500 km
Fording	0.8 m	0.8 m	0.8 m	0.8 m	0.8 m	0.8 m	0.8 m	0.8 m
Turning radius	9.2 m	9.2 m	9.2 m	9.2 m	9.2 m	9.4 m	9.4 m	10.5 m
Fuel capacity	170 l	170 l	170 l	170 l	170 l	170 l	170 l	170 l
Tyres	11.00R20 -14PR	11.00R20 -14PR	11.00R20 -14PR	11.00R20 -14PR	11.00R20 -14PR	11.00R20 -14PR	11.00R20 -14PR	11.00R20 -14PR
Engine	Isuzu 8PD1 V-8 liquid-cooled diesel developing 240 hp at 2300 rpm							
Gearbox	all have a manual gearbox with 5 forward and 1 reverse gears							
Clutch	single dry plate	single dry plate	single dry plate	single dry plate	single dry plate	single dry plate	single dry plate	single dry plate
Transfer box	2-speed	2-speed	2-speed	2-speed	2-speed	2-speed	2-speed	2-speed
Steering	power	power	power	power	power	power	power	power
Brakes	(main) air/hydraulic (parking) mechanical							
Suspension	(front) semi-elliptical spring and hydraulic shock absorber, (rear) semi-elliptical spring							
Electrical system	24 V	24 V	24 V	24 V	24 V	24 V	24 V	24 V

Type 73 (6 × 6) 3500 kg dump truck

Variants

Models with single rear wheels
Truck, Cargo with winch (SKW463M 6 × 6)
This is the base model of the cargo series and can carry 3500 kg of cargo across country and 6000 kg on roads. The base version can be used to carry shelters and has been used to carry radar systems and surface-to-air missile systems (such as the Tan SAM). There is a version with a longer wheelbase.

Tanker, Utility (SKW463MV 6 × 6)
This tanker has a maximum payload of 5100 kg of fuel.

Tanker, Water (SKW463MV 6 × 6)
Carries a tank for 5000 litres of water.

Models with dual rear wheels
Truck, Dump (SKW463MD 6 × 6)
This has an all-steel rear tipping body with a payload of 5000 kg. It can also be used to carry cargo.

Truck, Wrecker, Light (SKW463MR 6 × 6)
See entry in the *Recovery vehicles* section.

Status
In production. In service with the Japanese Ground Self-Defence Force.

Manufacturer
Isuzu Motors Limited, 22-10, Minami-oi, 6-chome, Shinagawa-ku, Tokyo 140, Japan.
Tel: 03 762 1111. Telex: 0246 6689.

Type 73 (6 × 6) water tanker

Hino (6 × 6) 4000 kg Truck

Description
Hino developed a series of 6 × 6 trucks known as the ZC34/44 which can carry 4000 kg of cargo across country or 8000 kg of cargo on roads, and were also available for civilian applications such as tractor trucks. The basic cargo model has a conventional layout with the engine at the front, two-door cab in the centre with a windscreen which folds forward onto the bonnet and a removable canvas top, and the cargo area at the rear with fixed sides, drop tailgate, removable bows and a tarpaulin cover. Some late production models have an all-steel hard-top cab with a fixed windscreen.

Variants
Dump truck
Two models are in service, one that tips to the rear only and a second which tips to both sides and the rear. Basic specifications are length 6.75 m, width 2.41 m, height 2.66 m, empty weight 8710 kg, maximum payload across country 4000 kg and maximum payload on roads 7000 kg.

Water sprinkler
This has a water tank behind the cab fitted with a sprinkler system.

Wrecker
Two models are in service, one with a hydraulically operated and the other with a mechanically operated crane, both with a maximum lifting capacity in the static configuration of 6700 kg and a suspended tow capacity of 4000 kg. Both are fitted with front and rear-mounted winches. Basic specifications are as follows (those in square brackets relate to the model with a hydraulic crane) overall length 8.37 [9.3] m, width 2.45 [2.45] m, height 3.02 [2.88] m, maximum road speed 65 [78] km/h and powered by a six-cylinder water-cooled diesel engine developing 125 [160] hp.

Tractor truck
This is used to tow 6000 kg and 10 000 kg trailers and its basic specifications are length 5.22 m, width 2.37 m, height 2.83 m, empty weight 5460 kg, maximum speed 65 km/h and engine six-cylinder water-cooled diesel developing 140 hp.

Type 67 Rocket Launcher
The chassis is used as the launcher for the 337 mm Type 67 rocket, details of which are given in *Jane's Armour and Artillery 1992-93*, page 733. A 4000 kg truck is also used as a missile resupply vehicle; it carries up to six Type 67 rockets and has a hydraulic crane for loading.

Specifications
Cab seating: 1 + 2
Configuration: 6 × 6
Weight:
(empty) 8040 kg
(loaded, road) 16 040 kg
(loaded, cross-country) 12 040 kg
Max load:
(road) 8000 kg
(cross-country) 4000 kg
Length: 7.69 m
Width: 2.44 m
Height: 2.92 m
Max road speed: 78 km/h
Engine: 6-cylinder water-cooled diesel developing 160 hp at 2400 rpm

Status
Production complete. In service with the Japanese Ground Self-Defence Force.

Manufacturer
Hino Motors Limited, 1-1 Hinodai 3-chome, Hino-shi, Tokyo, Japan.
Telex: 2842141 hinojk j. Fax: 0425 86-5038.

Hino (6 × 6) 4000 kg truck complete with bows and tarpaulin cover (Kensuke Ebata)

Hino (6 × 6) 4000 kg truck towing trailer carrying Nike-Hercules SAM (Kensuke Ebata)

Mitsubishi W121P (6 × 6) 6000 kg Truck

Description

In the 1950s Mitsubishi introduced the Fuso range of 6 × 6 trucks which were based on American Second World War type trucks. In the early 1960s these were replaced in production by the improved 6W series which had a redesigned cab as well as numerous other improvements. Production was completed in 1973.

The layout of all models is similar with the engine at the front and cab in the centre. The cab has a removable canvas top and a windscreen that folds forward onto the bonnet. The rear cargo area has troop seats, drop tailgate, removable bows and a tarpaulin cover. Behind the cab, on the right side, is a winch that can be used to the front or rear.

Variants

Tractor truck
The 6000 kg model is used to tow semi-trailers weighing up to 20 tonnes and the 10 000 kg model for semi-trailers up to 25 000 kg. The 6000 kg model is used by JGSDF Engineer Units and the 10 000 kg by construction battalions and engineer equipment companies. Basic specifications are length 7.57 m, width 2.48 m, height 3 m, weight unloaded 9860 kg, maximum road speed 70 km/h and engine 6-cylinder water-cooled diesel developing 200 hp.

Wrecker
Two models are in service, one with a mechanical and the other with a hydraulic crane and both with front- and rear-mounted winches. Basic specifications are as follows (those in square brackets relate to the model with a hydraulic crane): length overall 9.9 [9.32] m, width 2.48 [2.48] m, height 3.14 [3.01] m, empty weight 13 400 [16 570] kg and maximum road speed 72 km/h.

Specifications

Cab seating: 1 + 1
Configuration: 6 × 6
Weight:
  (empty) 9700 kg
  (loaded, road) 21 700 kg
  (loaded, cross-country) 15 700 kg
Max load:
  (road) 12 000 kg
  (cross-country) 6000 kg
Length: 7.42 m
Width: 2.48 m
Height: 3 m
Max road speed: 72 km/h
Engine: 6-cylinder water-cooled diesel developing 200 hp

Status

Production complete. In service with the Japanese Ground Self-Defence Force.

Manufacturer

Mitsubishi Motors Corporation, 33-8 Shiba 5-chome, Minato-ku, Tokyo, Japan.
Tel: 3 456 1111. Telex: 26639 bisijiko j.

Late production model (6 × 6) 6000 kg truck towing twin 35 mm Oerlikon AA gun (Kensuke Ebata)

Late production model (6 × 6) tractor truck towing dozer on Type 73 special semi-trailer (Kensuke Ebata)

Mitsubishi FW415 (6 × 6) Trucks

Description

The Mitsubishi FW415 series of (6 × 6) trucks was introduced in 1984 when it replaced the FW115 series (see next entry) in production.

The basic FW415 (6 × 6) truck has an all-steel forward-control cab with seating provided for the driver and two passengers. The doors have extra vision panels for the driver and warning lights are set into the upper cab roof. The space immediately behind the cab is used for tool and spare wheel stowage on most models, and a heavy duty fender extends behind the front wheel. The front headlights are set into heavy duty bumpers.

Variants

FW415L heavy duty truck
This is the base model of the FW415 series and has a conventional heavy duty rear cargo deck with provision for a canvas tilt. When not in use the folded tilt supports are stowed forward. The cargo area has a tailgate at the rear and a spare wheel is stowed in the space

Specifications

Model	FW415L	FW415L3	FW415LD	FW415LD1	FW415M	FW415M1
Role	truck	truck w/winch	truck	truck w/winch	drop side	recovery
Cab seating	1 + 2	1 + 2	1 + 2	1 + 2	1 + 2	1 + 2
Configuration	6 × 6	6 × 6	6 × 6	6 × 6	6 × 6	6 × 6
Weight						
(empty)	9580 kg	12 950 kg	10 430 kg	11 070 kg	9860 kg	18 100 kg
(loaded)	19 820 kg	19 670 kg	19 670 kg	19 810 kg	19 850 kg	18 340 kg
Max load (off road)	7000 kg	6000 kg	7000 kg	7000 kg	7000 kg	—
Length	8.18 m	8.59 m	8.135 m	8.135 m	9.215 m	9.32 m
Width	2.49 m	2.49 m	2.49 m	2.49 m	2.49 m	2.49 m
Height	3.05 m	3.05 m	3.1 m	3.1 m	3.1 m	3.23 m
Wheelbase	3.88 m + 1.3 m	3.88 m + 1.3 m	3.88 m + 1.3 m	3.88 m + 1.3 m	4.15 m + 1.3 m	4.15 m + 1.3 m
Max road speed	101 km/h	101 km/h	101 km/h	101 km/h	101 km/h	101 km/h
Engine	Mitsubishi Model 8DC9-1A diesel developing 320 hp at 2200 rpm					

Mitsubishi FW415L3 (6 × 6) heavy duty truck with winch

FW415 variant known as the Prime Mover Medium used to tow the 155 mm FH-70 howitzer (Kensuke Ebata)

between the cab rear and the front of the cargo area. The FW415L can be used as an artillery tractor for weapons with calibres up to 35 mm.

FW415L3 heavy duty truck with winch
This is a version of the FW415L with a 10 000 kg capacity rear-mounted winch and a 2000 kg crane. It can be used as an artillery tractor for light weapons.

FW415LD heavy duty truck
The FW415LD heavy duty truck has an all-steel heavy duty dump body with a cab protector. It is provided with a centrally mounted winch with the controls on each side of the cargo area between the body and the cab rear.

FW415LD1 heavy duty truck
This is a version of the FW415LD with a 6000 kg rear winch.

FW415M drop side truck
This is a lengthened wheelbase version of the FW415L. The length of the cargo area is 6.71 m.

FW415M1 recovery vehicle
See separate entry in the *Recovery vehicles* section.

FW415LR2 truck tractor
See separate entry in the *Tank transporters* section.

Prime Mover Medium
This is a tractor vehicle used to tow 155 mm FH-70 howitzers and is equipped with a 10-tonne crane to handle ammunition stowed on a shortened cargo area.

Status
In production. In service with the Japanese Ground Self-Defence Force.

Manufacturer
Mitsubishi Motors Corporation, 33-8 Shiba 5-chome, Minato-ku, Tokyo, Japan.
Tel: 3 456 1111. Telex: 26639 bisijiko j.

Mitsubishi FW115 (6 × 6) Trucks

Description
The Mitsubishi FW115 series of trucks was introduced in 1979 when it replaced the FW105 series in production. The FW105 series, in its turn, had replaced the earlier FW103 trucks which went out of production in 1979.

The basic FW115 (6 × 6) truck is a forward-control design with an all-steel cab with seats for the driver and two passengers. The doors have extra vision panels for the driver and warning lights are set forward on the roof. The area immediately behind the cab is used for tool and spare wheel stowage on most models, and a heavy duty fender extends behind the front wheel to just forward of the second wheel to protect the fuel tanks, transmission and other engine extensions. A towing hook is usually provided at the rear. The front headlights are set into the heavy duty bumpers.

Variants
FW115 L1 heavy duty truck
This is the base model of the FW115 series and has a conventional heavy duty rear cargo area with provision for a canvas tilt. When not in use the folded tilt supports are stowed forward. The cargo area has a tailgate at the rear and a spare wheel is stowed in the space between the cab rear and the front of the cargo area. The FW115 L1 can be used as an artillery tractor for calibres up to 155 mm.

FW115 LD1 heavy duty truck
The FW115 LD1 heavy duty truck has an all-steel heavy duty cargo body with a protective steel bulkhead protecting the rear of the cab. It is provided with a centrally mounted winch with the controls on each side of the cargo area between the body and the cab rear.

FM115 M1 recovery vehicle
This variant has the rear occupied by a large telescopic crane with a limited provision for traverse. The crane has a large cable-actuated pulley and is secured when travelling. The crane is controlled from the left-hand side and a spare wheel is stowed on the right. A high-capacity winch is located centrally and the cable pays out to the rear. A smaller self-recovery winch is situated under the front bumper on the right-hand side. There are four stabiliser legs for the crane which are located one leg fore and aft of each of the four rear wheels. Their stabilising feet can be lowered directly to the ground in use. Various tool and equipment lockers are provided.

FW115 M2
The FW115 M2 has a lengthened wheelbase and cargo body to carry floating bridge components. The cargo body extends forward to just behind the cab.

FW115 M4
The FW115 M4 has the same lengthened wheelbase and body as the FW115 M2 but is used as a conventional heavy duty cargo truck and is equipped with drop sides. There is provision for a canvas tilt.

Status
Production complete. In service with the Japanese Ground Self-Defence Force.

Manufacturer
Mitsubishi Motors Corporation, 33-8 Shiba 5-chome, Minato-ku, Tokyo, Japan.
Tel: 3 456 1111. Telex: 26639 bisijiko j.

Specifications

Model	FW115 L1	FW115 LD1	FW115 M1	FW115 M2	FW115 M4
Configuration	6 × 6	6 × 6	6 × 6	6 × 6	6 × 6
Weight (empty)	9660 kg	11 300 kg	18 290 kg	11 480 kg	10 130 kg
(loaded)	19 160 kg	19 800 kg	18 530 kg	18 970 kg	19 870 kg
Length	8.39 m	8.135 m	9.32 m	9.205 m	9.285 m
Width	2.49 m	2.49 m	2.49 m	2.49 m	2.49 m
Height	3.05 m	3.1 m	3.23 m	3.05 m	3.09 m
Max road speed	95 km/h	95 km/h	95 km/h	95 km/h	95 km/h

Mitsubishi FW115 M2 (6 × 6) long-bodied floating bridge carrier

Mitsubishi FW115 M4 (6 × 6) drop side truck

Type 74 (6 × 6) 10 000 kg Truck

Description
This is a standard commercial truck modified to meet the requirements of the Japanese Ground Self-Defence Force for a 6 × 6 vehicle with a payload of 10 000 kg. It was standardised in 1974 as the Type 74 special large truck.

The all-steel cab is the forward control type and the rear cargo area has drop sides, drop tailgate, removable bows and a tarpaulin cover. The short model of the Type 74 does not have drop sides. A model of the Type 74 is also used to carry bridging equipment for which special unloading equipment is fitted.

Type 74 (6 × 6) 10 000 kg truck (Kensuke Ebata)

Specifications
(data in square brackets relate to short model where different)
Configuration: 6 × 6
Weight:
   (empty) 9850 [9600] kg

(loaded) 19 850 [19 100] kg
Max load: 10 000 [9500] kg
Length: 9.22 [8.3] m
Width: 2.49 m
Height: 3.055 [3] m
Max road speed: 100 km/h

Engine: 300 hp diesel

Status
In service with the Japanese Ground Self-Defence Force.

KOREA, SOUTH

KM45 (4 × 4) 1¼-ton Truck Series

Description
The Asia Motors KM45 series of (4 × 4) trucks are similar in appearance to the American M715/AM 715 1¼-ton trucks but are fitted with MZBA1 diesel engines and a new power train.

The base model of the series is the KM450 light cargo truck. The driver's cab has a canvas top and seats are provided for the driver and one passenger. The cargo area at the rear can be covered by a canvas tilt and sideboards are usually fitted. Bench seats can be fitted to carry four men along each side. There is a drop tailgate at the rear.

The KM451 is an ambulance with a fully enclosed van body and two outward-opening doors at the rear. The ambulance body has space for up to eight seated casualties or five stretchers and a medical orderly. Weight loaded is 3235 kg, payload 1080 kg and length overall is 5.446 m. Overall height is 2.443 m.

The KM452 also uses a van-type box body but is fitted with windows at the side to allow it to be used as a communications vehicle. Other similar vehicles are the KM453 to KM458, all of them equipped with various office or workshop interiors; for instance the KM458 is a mobile workshop van.

Specifications (KM450 cargo truck)
Cab seating: 1 + 1
Configuration: 4 × 4
Weight:
   (kerb) 2550 kg
   (GVW) 4080 kg
Max load: 1530 kg
Length: 5.328 m
Width: 2.008 m
Height: 2.37 m
Ground clearance: 0.254 m
Track:
   (front) 1.675 m
   (rear) 1.71 m
Wheelbase: 3.2 m
Angle of approach/departure: 45°/25°
Max speed: 105 km/h
Range: (cruising) 450 km
Fuel capacity: 106 l
Max gradient: 75%
Fording: (without kit) 0.76 m
Engine: MZBA1 4.052 l 6-cylinder water-cooled diesel developing 115 hp at 3600 rpm
Gearbox: manual, with 5 forward and 1 reverse gears
Clutch: single dry plate
Transfer box: 2-speed
Steering: ball and nut
Turning radius: 7.1 m
Suspension: (front and rear) semi-elliptical leaf springs with hydraulic double-acting shock absorbers
Tyres: 9.00 × 16
Brakes:
   (main) vacuum-assisted hydraulic
   (parking) mechanical
Electrical system: 24 V
Batteries: 2 × 12 V, 100 Ah
Alternator: 45 A

Status
In production. In service with Republic of Korea armed forces.

Manufacturer
Asia Motors Co Inc, 15 Yoido-dong, Yongdungpo-gu, PO Box 5022, Seoul, Republic of Korea. Tel: 783 1501. Telex: 24374 asiamco k.

KM450 (4 × 4) 1¼-ton cargo truck

KM25 (6 × 6) 2500 kg Truck Series

Description
The KM25 series of 2500 kg (6 × 6) trucks closely follow the appearance of the American M44A2 truck and are fitted with MAN diesel engines and locally produced power trains. They are produced in five basic forms: KM250 cargo truck; KM254 decontamination truck; KM255 1000 gallon fuel tanker; KM256 1200 gallon water tanker; and KM258 shop van.

A 4500 kg capacity winch equipped with 61 m of cable is optional for all models.

Specifications (KM250 cargo truck)
Cab seating: 1 + 2
Configuration: 6 × 6
Weight:
   (kerb) 5790 kg
   (GVW) 10 330 kg
Max load: 4540 kg
Length:
   (without winch) 6.712 m
   (with winch) 7.068 m
Width: 2.438 m
Height:
   (top of tilt) 2.845 m
   (top of cab) 2.467 m

KM250 (6 × 6) 2500 kg truck

Ground clearance: 0.278 m
Track:
   (front) 1.721 m
   (rear) 1.778 m

Wheelbase: 3.911 m
Angle of approach/departure:
   (without winch) 48°/40°
   (with winch) 40°/40°

Max speed: 96 km/h
Range: 560 km
Fuel capacity: 200 l
Max gradient: 75%
Fording: 0.762 m
Engine: MAN DO846HM 7.225 l 6-cylinder water-cooled diesel developing 160 hp at 2500 rpm
Gearbox: manual with 5 forward and 1 reverse gears
Clutch: single dry plate
Transfer box: 2-speed
Steering: cam and twin lever

Turning radius: 10.6 m
Suspension:
(front) semi-elliptical leaf springs with shock absorbers
(rear) semi-elliptical inverted leaf springs
Tyres: 9.00 × 20
Brakes:
(main) air over hydraulic, internal expanding
(parking) dual grip mounted on transfer case
Electrical system: 24 V
Batteries: 2 × 12 V, 100 Ah

Alternator: 60 A

Status
In production. In service with the Republic of Korea armed forces.

Manufacturer
Asia Motors Co Inc, 15 Yoido-dong, Yongdungpo-gu, PO Box 5022, Seoul, Republic of Korea.
Tel: 783 1501. Telex: 24374 asiamco k.

KM50 (6 × 6) 5-ton Truck Series

Description
The KM50 series of 5-ton (6 × 6) trucks are similar in appearance to the American M809 truck chassis but are fitted with MAN diesel engines and locally produced power trains. The KM50 series is produced in at least five forms: KM500 cargo truck; M501 dump truck; KM502 wrecker (see entry in the *Recovery vehicles* section); KM503 tractor truck; and KM507 expansible van.

A 9070 kg capacity winch with 61 m of cable is optional on all models.

Specifications (KM500 cargo truck)
Cab seating: 1 + 2
Configuration: 6 × 6
Weight:
(kerb) 9440 kg
(GVW) 18 690 kg
Max load: 9250 kg
Length:
(without winch) 7.652 m

(with winch) 8.045 m
Width: 2.477 m
Height:
(top of tilt) 2.946 m
(top of cab) 2.68 m
Ground clearance: 0.27 m
Track:
(front) 1.88 m
(rear) 1.829 m
Wheelbase: 4.547 m
Angle of approach/departure:
(without winch) 46°/38°
(with winch) 34°/38°
Max speed: 90 km/h
Range: 563 km
Fuel capacity: 295 l
Max gradient: 75%
Fording: 0.762 m
Engine: MAN D2156 HM 10.35 l 6-cylinder water-cooled diesel developing 236 hp at 2200 rpm
Gearbox: manual with 5 forward and 1 reverse gears
Clutch: single dry plate
Transfer box: 2-speed
Steering: integral power-assist

Turning radius: 12.75 m
Suspension:
(front) semi-elliptical leaf springs with shock absorbers
(rear) semi-elliptical inverted leaf springs
Tyres: 11.00 × 20
Brakes:
(main) air over hydraulic, internal expanding
(parking) dual grip mounted on transfer case
Electrical system: 24 V
Batteries: 2 × 12 V, 100 Ah
Alternator: 60 A

Status
In production. In service with the Republic of Korea armed forces.

Manufacturer
Asia Motors Co Inc, 15 Yoido-dong, Yongdungpo-gu, PO Box 5022, Seoul, Republic of Korea.
Tel: 783 1501. Telex: 24374 asiamco k.

KM500 (6 × 6) 5-ton cargo truck

KM501 (6 × 6) 5-ton dump truck

NETHERLANDS

DAF YA 314 (4 × 4) 3000 kg Truck

Description
The DAF YA 314 (4 × 4) 3000 kg cargo truck was developed in the early 1950s and was in production for the Dutch Army from 1955 to 1965. It has an all steel forward control type cab with a tarpaulin roof that can be folded backwards and a windscreen that can be folded forward of the radiator if required. The doors are removable. The rear cargo body is all steel and has a drop tailgate, five bows and a tarpaulin cover. The wheel arches extend along the length of the cargo body on each side and provide seating when necessary. To enable wider cargo to be carried, wooden

Refuelling version of DAF YA 314 known as YF 324

DAF YA 314 with office or command box body

panels can be inserted between the two wheel arches. Some vehicles are provided with a winch with a capacity of 4000 kg mounted at the front.

Late production models of the YA 314 were designated the YA 324. Variants of this series included a truck-mounted air compressor, bomb carrier for the air force, office/command vehicle, radar towing vehicle, 3000 litre aircraft tanker, three-way tipper, water tanker and a workshop vehicle. The Spanish company of Pegaso built a modified version of this vehicle called the Pegaso 3045D, details of which will be found in this section under Spain.

Specifications
Cab seating: 1 + 1
Configuration: 4 × 4
Weight:
(empty) 4500 kg
(loaded) 7500 kg
Max load: 3000 kg
Towed load: 3000 kg

Load area: 4.2 × 2.15 m
Length: 6.09 m
Width: 2.425 m
Height:
(tarpaulin) 2.785 m
(without windscreen) 2.108 m
(load area) 1.035 m
Ground clearance: 0.36 m
Track: 1.905 m
Wheelbase: 3.6 m
Angle of approach/departure: 40°/35°
Max speed: (road) 76 km/h
Range: 630 km
Fuel capacity: 210 l
Gradient: 40%
Fording: 0.76 m
Engine: Hercules JXC 6-cylinder in-line water-cooled petrol developing 102 bhp (SAE) at 3200 rpm
Gearbox: manual with 4 forward and 1 reverse gears
Transfer box: 2-speed
Turning radius: 9 m

Suspension: semi-elliptical springs with double-acting hydraulic shock absorbers
Tyres: 11.00 × 20
Brakes:
(main) air/hydraulic
(parking) mechanical
Electrical system: 24 V
Generator: 900 W

Status
Production complete. In service with the Dutch Army and Air Force. Being replaced by the DAF YA 4440 and YA 4442 (4 × 4) 4000 kg trucks.

Manufacturer
DAF Military Sales, Hugo van der Goeslaan 1, NL-5643 TW Eindhoven, Netherlands. Tel: 040 143440. Telex: 51085 daf nl. Fax: 040 144318.

DAF YA 4442 DNT (4 × 4) 4000 kg Truck

Description
During December 1985 the Dutch Ministry of Defence ordered 5125 DAF YA 4442 DNT (4 × 4) 4000 kg trucks. After verification trials, production commenced in mid-1988 and will continue until 1994. .

The DAF YA 4442 DNT is virtually identical to the YA 4440 (see following entry) but has a new radiator grill, the F 218 tilt cab front has revised protection, and there are dual or single tyres on the rear wheels. The main change was the fitting of the DAF DNT 620 6-cylinder turbocharged diesel engine matched to a ZF 6-speed fully synchronised gearbox. Changes were also made to the electrical and brake systems.

The DAF YA 4442 DNT is produced in three main forms. The YA 4442 DNT is a general purpose cargo vehicle, the YAL 4442 DNT is a general purpose cargo vehicle with a driver training cab, and the YAK 4442 DNT is a cargo vehicle with a HIAB loading crane. The YAM 4442 is a sub-variant of the YA 4442 produced for the Dutch Marines.

The YF 4442 DNT 'Refueller' was developed by DAF for the Dutch Army and carries a 4000 litre fuel tank and pump unit. A total of 395 was ordered with the last

to be delivered in December 1994.

Specifications (YA 4442 DNT)
Cab seating: 1 + 1 (up to 18 in rear)
Configuration: 4 × 4
Weight:
(empty) 7620 kg
(loaded) 11 750 kg
Front axle, permissible: 6000 kg
Rear axle, permissible: 6750 kg
Max load: 4000 kg
Towed load: 6000 kg
Length: 7.3 m
Width: 2.47 m
Height: 3.42 m
Ground clearance: 0.29 m
Track:
(front) 1.9 m
(rear) 1.8 m
Wheelbase: 4.05 m
Angle of approach/departure: 36°/30°
Max speed: 93 km/h
Range: approx 500 km
Fuel capacity: 200 l
Max gradient: 50%
Side slope: 30%
Fording: 0.9 m

Engine: DAF DNT 6.242 l 6-cylinder in-line turbo-charged diesel developing 172 hp at 2600 rpm
Gearbox: ZF S6-36 synchromesh with 6 forward and 1 reverse gears
Clutch: single dry plate (350 mm)
Transfer box: Steyr VG 450 2-speed
Steering: ZF 8043 hydraulic
Turning radius: approx 9.8 m
Suspension: semi-elliptical springs (8 front, 10 rear) with double-acting shock absorbers
Tyres: 13 × 22.5
Brakes: air, dual circuit plus exhaust brake
Electrical system: 24 V
Batteries: 2 × 12 V, 125 Ah
Alternator: 95 A

Status
Production of 5125 units for the Dutch Ministry of Defence commenced in mid-1988.

Manufacturer
DAF Military Sales, Hugo van der Goeslaan 1, NL-5643 TW Eindhoven, Netherlands. Tel: 040 143440. Telex: 51085 daf nl. Fax: 040 144318.

DAF YF 4442 DNT 'Refueller' produced for Dutch Army

DAF YAK 4442 DNT (4 × 4) 4000 kg truck with loading crane

DAF YA 4440 (4 × 4) 4000 kg Truck

Development
The YA 4440 (4 × 4) 4000 kg medium mobility vehicle was developed by DAF to meet the requirements of the Dutch Army. The first five prototypes were handed over to the Army for trials late in 1974, and late in 1976 the Dutch Army placed an order for 4000 for delivery between 1977 and 1980. Late in 1977 a further order for 2500 was placed, with final deliveries made in mid-

1983. The truck is based on proven commercial components and shared many common components with the DAF YA 2442 (4 × 4) 2-tonne truck (this was developed to prototype stage but not placed in production), including the cab, engine, transfer case and transmission. It was designed to carry 4000 kg of cargo on both roads and across country and tow a trailer with a maximum weight of 4000 kg.

In February 1984 it was announced that Portugal had ordered 300 YA 4440 trucks following tests with four vehicles. The order was stated to be worth 26

million guilders and 35 per cent of the value of the vehicles was offset by assembling the vehicles in Portugal and using some Portuguese components. Starting in July 1984 the first vehicles were assembled in Portugal by EVICAR of Setubal. The order was completed by the end of January 1985.

By the end of 1985 DAF had supplied 7250 YA 4440 trucks to the Dutch Ministry of Defence.

Description
The all-steel cab is of the forward control type and can

DAF YA 4440 (4 × 4) 4000 kg truck carrying specialised container (T Neate)

DAF YAK 4440 (4 × 4) 4000 kg truck fitted with HIAB hydraulic crane and stabilisers (T Neate)

be tilted forward to allow access to the engine for maintenance. The engine is mounted at the front of the chassis and power is transmitted to the two-speed transfer box via the five-speed synchromesh transmission. From the transfer case power is taken to the front and rear axles.

The reinforced cab roof allows the installation of a ring mounting for a light machine gun. The frame which supports this ring is bolted directly to the cab roof over the manhole cover. The rear cargo platform has bows, tarpaulin cover, sideboards and a tailgate which can be quickly removed to enable the truck to carry containers or pallets.

The truck is fitted with air brakes, with the parking brake acting on the front axle, an exhaust brake and a trailer brake. The electrical system is waterproof and radio suppressed.

Optional equipment includes a hydraulic crane to the rear of the cab with a capacity of 7000 kg, stabilisers on each side of the chassis for when the hydraulic crane is being used, automatic transmission, two-man passenger seat in place of the standard one-man seat, and a manually operated crane with a 1000 kg capacity.

The YAL 4440 is used for training drivers and has a four-man tilt cab with seats for the driver under instruction, instructor and two student drivers. In total, 375 of these vehicles were built for the Dutch Army.

DAF delivered for trials 17 models of the YAK 4440 fitted with a hydraulic crane for rapid unloading of ammunition and cargo. They have the same chassis as the YA 4440 but a shorter cargo body with no bows or tarpaulin cover. Immediately behind the cab is a hydraulic crane and stabilisers, either side of the cab rear, which are lowered to the ground before the crane is used. Of the 17 units, eight had a PESCI (P445G) crane and nine a HIAB (850S) crane. Following trials with these prototype vehicles the Dutch Army placed an order for 200 units fitted with the HIAB hydraulic crane.

Specifications
Cab seating: 1 + 1
Configuration: 4 × 4
Weight:
  (empty) 7000 kg
  (loaded) 11 000 kg
Max load: 4000 kg
Towed load: 4000 kg
Length: 7.19 m
Width: 2.44 m
Height:
  (tarpaulin) 3.42 m
  (load area) 1.43 m
Ground clearance: 0.3 m
Track: 1.91 m
Wheelbase: 4.05 m
Angle of approach/departure: 36°/30°
Max speed: (road) 80 km/h
Range: 500 km
Max gradient:
  (without trailer) 50%
  (with loaded trailer) 20%
Max side slope: 30%
Fording: 0.9 m
Engine: DAF DT 615 liquid-cooled 6-cylinder in-line turbocharged diesel developing 153 hp (DIN) at 2400 rpm
Gearbox: ZF S5-35/2 with 5 forward and 1 reverse gears
Clutch: hydraulic, single dry plate
Transfer box: ZF VG 250/2 2-speed
Steering: ZF 8042 hydraulic power-assist
Turning radius: 9 m
Suspension: semi-elliptical springs with double-acting hydraulic shock absorbers on both axles
Tyres: 12.00 × 20
Brakes:
  (main) air, dual circuit (plus exhaust brake)
  (parking) mechanical, also holding brake
Electrical system: 24 V
Batteries: 2 × 12 V, 100 Ah
Alternator: 85 Ah

Status
Production complete. In service with the Dutch Army and Navy and Portuguese Army (300).

Manufacturer
DAF Military Sales, Hugo van der Goeslaan 1, NL-5643 TW Eindhoven, Netherlands.
Tel: 040 143440. Telex: 51085 daf nl.
Fax: 040 144318.

DAF YA 5444 DNT (4 × 4) 5000 kg Truck

Description
The DAF YA 5444 DNT (4 × 4) 5000 kg truck is a further development of the DAF YA 4442 series and designed for logistic operations such as a carrier for generator sets, fuel tanks, munitions, shelters, and so on. The three-seater cab has a purpose-designed reinforced roof with a hatch and provision for a machine gun mounting. Production is in progress with first deliveries going to the Royal Netherlands Air Force. The YA 5444 will eventually replace the YA 5441 and YA 5442 models in service.

Specifications
Cab seating: 1 + 2
Configuration: 4 × 4
Weight:
  (empty) 8400 kg
  (loaded) 13 600 kg
Front axle, permissible: 6000 kg
Rear axle, permissible: 8000 kg
Max load: 5000 kg
Towed load: 6000 kg
Length: 8.2 m
Width: 2.5 m
Height: (cab) 3 m
Ground clearance: 0.26 m

DAF YA 5444 DNT (4 × 4) 5000 kg truck

Track:
  (front) 1.9 m
  (rear) 1.8 m
Wheelbase: 4.05 m

Angle of approach/departure: 36°/20°
Max speed: 95 km/h
Range: approx 500 km
Fuel capacity: 200 l

Max gradient: 50%
Side slope: (static) 30%
Fording: 0.9 m
Engine: DAF DNT 6.242 l 6-cylinder in-line turbo-charged diesel developing 172 hp at 2600 rpm
Gearbox: ZF S6-36 with 6 forward and 1 reverse gears
Clutch: single dry plate (350 mm)
Transfer box: Steyr VG 450 2-speed
Steering: ZF 8043 power-assist

Turning radius: approx 9.8 m
Suspension: semi-elliptic leaf spring (8 front, 10 rear) plus telescopic, hydraulic, double-acting shock absorbers front and rear
Tyres: 10.00 × 20
Brakes:
(main) dual circuit, 2-line air
(parking) spring cylinders on rear axle
Electrical system: 24 V
Batteries: 2 × 12 V, 125 Ah

Alternator: 95 A

Status
In production. In service with the Dutch armed forces.

Manufacturer
DAF Military Sales, Hugo van der Goeslaan 1, NL-5643 TW Eindhoven, Netherlands.
Tel: 040 143440. Telex: 51085 daf nl.
Fax: 040 144318.

DAF YA 5441 and YA 5442 (4 × 4) 5000 kg Trucks

Description
The DAF YA 5441 (4 × 4) 5000 kg truck was designed to carry 5000 kg of cargo on both roads and across country. It was developed from a standard commercial design and uses many components of the YA 4440 (4 × 4) 4000 kg truck, in service with the Dutch Army and Navy. A second production series with slight modifications from the YA 5441 is known as the YA 5442.

The cab is of all-steel type and has a circular observation hatch in the roof. The cab can be tilted forward to allow access to the engine for maintenance. The rear cargo area is of all-steel construction and has drop sides and a drop tailgate with integral steps. Removable bows and a tarpaulin cover are fitted as standard.

The engine is mounted at the front of the vehicle with power being transmitted to the two-speed transfer box

via the five-speed (plus one reverse) synchromesh gearbox. From the transfer case power is transmitted to the front and rear axles.

Standard equipment includes a front bumper with a built-in push/pull pin, rear towing hook, exhaust brake retarder and connections for the brakes on the trailer.

Variants
YAK 5442
The YAK 5442 was produced during 1984 for the Dutch Air Force (16) and is a crane truck mounting a HIAB Type 2027 AVL 20 t/m hydraulic crane over the rear axle. Telescopic outrigger legs on the ends of sliding jibs are provided at each corner of the cargo body area. Some vehicles have 8000 kg recovery winches.

YA 5442 DH
This version uses a naturally aspirating diesel engine.

YA 5442 DT
This variant uses a slightly different cargo body and is

used by Dutch Army Lance missile batteries for logistic support. This vehicle was also produced for issue to the NATO NORTHAG Transport Company.

The basic chassis can be adapted for other specific roles such as water tanker, fuel carrier and radio vehicle. DAF also delivered to the Dutch Air Force a number of 4 × 2 tractor trucks based on the commercial FT 1600 series chassis.

Status
Replaced in production by YA 5444. In service with the Dutch Army, Air Force and Navy and some NATO forces.

Manufacturer
DAF Military Sales, Hugo van der Goeslaan 1, NL-5643 TW Eindhoven, Netherlands.
Tel: 040 143440. Telex: 51085 daf nl.
Fax: 040 144318.

Specifications

Model	YA 5441	YA 5442
Cab seating	1 + 2	1 + 2
Configuration	4 × 4	4 × 4
Weight (empty)	7290 kg	7300 kg
(loaded)	12 290 kg	12 600 kg
Weight on front axle (max load)	4900 kg	4800 kg
Weight on rear axle (max load)	8100 kg	8100 kg
Max load	5000 kg	5000 kg
Towed load	4000 kg	4000 kg
Length	7.54 m	7.54 m
Width	2.47 m	2.44 m
Height (overall)	2.96 m	2.96 m
(load area)	1.3 m	1.28 m
Ground clearance (axle)	0.27 m	0.265 m
(chassis)	0.45 m	0.45 m
Track (front)	1.938 m	1.93 m
(rear)	1.729 m	1.8 m
Wheelbase	3.85 m	3.85 m
Angle of approach/departure	32°/23°	32°/24°
Max speed	80 km/h	80 km/h
Range	500 km	500 km
Fuel capacity	200 l	200 l

Model	YA 5441	YA 5442
Max gradient (without trailer)	59%	60%
(with trailer)	38%	40%
Side slope	30%	30%
Fording	0.6 m	0.6 m
Engine	DAF model DT 615 6-cylinder in-line 6.17 l liquid-cooled turbocharged diesel developing 153 hp at 2400 rpm	
Gearbox	ZF S5-35/2 manual with 5 forward and 1 reverse gears	
Clutch	single dry plate	single dry plate
Transfer box	ZF VG250/2 2-speed	ZF VG250/2 2-speed
Steering	ZF 8065 power-assisted	ZF 8065 power-assisted
Suspension	semi-elliptical springs front and rear with double-acting telescopic shock absorbers front and rear	
Tyres	10.00 × 20	10.00 × 20
Brakes (main)	air, 2-line, dual circuit	air, 2-line, dual circuit
(parking)	spring-brake cylinders on rear axle	
Electrical system	24 V	24 V
Batteries	2 × 12 V, 100 Ah	2 × 12 V, 100 Ah

DAF YAK 5442 with HIAB crane for Dutch Air Force

DAF YA 5442 DT (4 × 4) 5000 kg truck as used by Dutch Army Lance batteries

DAF YAV 2300 DHTD (4 × 4) 7000 kg Truck

Description

The DAF YAV 2300 DHTD (4 × 4) 7000 kg truck is described by DAF as a new generation truck derived from the YAZ 2300 (6 × 6) 10 000 kg series (see next entry). It was designed to meet military specifications but is based mainly upon the use of components from DAF's commercial vehicle range.

In 1984 the Dutch Ministry of Defence placed an order, on behalf of NATO, for 85 of these trucks. Deliveries were made in 1985. Some of these are used as prime movers for the 20-tonne trailers used with NATO's AFCENT Mobile War Headquarters. Some of the vehicles involved are used to carry shelters and electronic equipment.

The basic DAF YAV 2300 DHTD (4 × 4) truck is fitted with a cargo body equipped with a load platform and sideboards – these can be removed to provide a platform for a container/shelter or a fuel distribution unit. The forward control cab is derived from the commercial short F 218 model and has a reinforced roof to allow the installation of a machine gun over the roof hatch. It can be tilted forward for engine and transmission access. The frame uses a ladder-type construction that is partially welded and partially bolted with two U-type reinforced longitudinal members and Omega-type crossmembers.

A spare wheel with a handling winch is provided behind the cab. At the front of the vehicle is located a NATO push/pull pin while the rear is equipped with a 24-tonne towing hook. Two towing and two lifting eyes are provided on the front bumper. A trailer brake system is provided.

YTV 2300

The DAF YTV 2300 is a 4 × 4 tractor intended for towing semi-trailers. Loads towed can include water or fuel tank semi-trailers or light armoured vehicle semi-trailers. An ambulance semi-trailer is another possibility. The YTV 2300 has a 7-tonne capacity fifth wheel (2-in/51 mm) and a kerb weight of 8000 kg. Length overall is 6.1 m, width 2.49 m and height (cab) 3.02 m. Wheelbase is 3.6 m.

Specifications

Cab seating: 1 + 1 or 2
Configuration: 4 × 4
Weight:
(kerb) 10 200 kg
(GVW) 15 500 kg
Max permissible weight on front axle: 6500 kg
Max permissible weight on rear axle: 9000 kg

DAF YAV 2300 DHTD (4 × 4) 7000 kg truck carrying electronics container

Max load:
(road) 7000 kg
(cross-country) 5300 kg
Length: 7.82 m
Width: 2.46 m
Height: (overall) 3.1 m
Load area: 5 × 2.35 m
Ground clearance: 0.32 m
Track:
(front) 1.98 m
(rear) 1.82 m
Wheelbase: 4.5 m
Angle of approach/departure: 30°/30°
Max speed: 88 km/h
Range: (with 300 l fuel tank) 1000 km
Fuel capacity: 300 l
Gradient: 50%
Side slope: 30%
Fording: 0.9 m
Engine: DAF DHTD 825 Mil. 8.25 l 6-cylinder in-line direct injection turbocharged developing 213 hp (ISO) at 2400 rpm
Torque converter: ZF WSK 400/25
Gearbox: ZF 5S-111 GPA with 8 forward and 1 reverse gears
Steering: ZF 8046 hydraulic, power-assisted

Turning radius: min 11 m
Suspension:
(front) DAF trapezium with adjustable KONI hydraulic telescopic double-acting shock absorbers
(rear) DAF trapezium with auxiliary spring and adjustable KONI hydraulic telescopic double-acting shock absorbers
Tyres: 13 R 22.5K (14.75/80 R 20 optional)
Brakes:
(main) dual circuit air-mechanical plus exhaust retarder
(parking) spring-brake cylinders on rear axle
Electrical system: 24 V
Batteries: 2 × 12 V, 125 Ah
Alternator: 55 A

Status

In production. In service with NATO AFCENT HQ.

Manufacturer

DAF Military Sales, Hugo van der Goeslaan 1, NL-5643 TW Eindhoven, Netherlands.
Tel: 040 143440. Telex: 51085 daf nl.
Fax: 040 144318.

DAF YAZ 2300 (6 × 6) 10 000 kg Truck

Development

In mid-1981, following trials with a number of prototypes submitted by several manufacturers, the Dutch Ministry of Defence placed an order with DAF Trucks worth Dfl 236.5 million for a family of new 10 000 kg (6 × 6) trucks to replace the current DAF YA 616 6000 kg (6 × 6) trucks. The YA 2300 series is based on the commercial 2300 range and is powered by a DAF DHS 825 250 hp diesel.

Delivery of the first batch commenced in mid-1983 and was completed during 1985. In 1988 the Dutch Ministry of Defence ordered over 1400 YA 2300 series vehicles. The YA 2300 can be adapted to carry weapon systems and has been selected to carry a coastal defence Sea Skua missile battery being produced by British Aerospace Defence Limited.

Description

The YAZ 2300 (6 × 6) general cargo truck may be taken as typical of the other vehicles in the series. It has a chassis designed as a common ladder-type platform and comprises two U-type and Omega-type crossmembers. The longitudinal members are strengthened over their full length.

DAF YTZ 2301 (6 × 6) truck tractor towing Patriot tactical air defence system missile launcher

Specifications

Model	YAZ 2300 Truck	YKZ 2300 Tipper	YHZ 2300 Tractor	YGZ 2300 Bridging
Cab seating	1 + 2	1 + 2	1 + 2	1 + 2
Configuration	6 × 6	6 × 6	6 × 6	6 × 6
Weight (kerb)	13 500 kg	13 500 kg	12 500 kg	13 700 kg
(max permissible)	27 500 kg	27 500 kg	25 500 kg	20 150 kg
Max load	10 000 kg	14 000 kg	10 000 kg	6500 kg
Max gross combination weight	40 000 kg	40 000 kg	40 000 kg	40 000 kg
Length	9.55 m	8.03 m	7.74 m	8.75 m
Width	2.49 m	2.49 m	2.49 m	3.45 m
Height (overall)	3.59 m	3.54 m	3.59 m	4 m
(load area)	1.5 m	1.5 m	1.63 m	1.55 m
Ground clearance	0.32 m	0.32 m	0.32 m	0.32 m
Track (front)	1.98 m	1.98 m	2.05 m	2.05 m
(rear)	1.82 m	1.82 m	2.01 m	2.1 m
Wheelbase	4.85 m	4.45 m	4.45 m	5.35 m
Angle of approach/departure	30°/20°	30°/30°	30°/32°	30°/20°
Max speed	88 km/h	88 km/h	88 km/h	88 km/h
Range (minimum)	600 km	600 km	600 km	600 km
Fuel capacity	300 l	300 l	300 l	300 l
Gradient	50%	50%	50%	50%
Side slope	30%	30%	30%	30%
Fording	0.75 m	0.75 m	0.75 m	0.75 m
Engine	DAF DHS 825 8.25 l 4-stroke, 6-cylinder in-line direct injection, turbocharged liquid-cooled diesel developing 250 hp at 2400 rpm			
Torque converter	ZF WSK 400/1	ZF WSK 400/1	ZF WSK 400/1	ZF WSK 400/1
Gearbox	ZF 5S-110 GPA with 8 forward and 1 reverse gears. Transfer box is a ZF A 600/3D with lockable differential and is an integral part of the gearbox			
Steering	ZF 8046, hydraulic power-assisted			
Turning radius	11.2 m	11 m	11 m	12 m
Suspension (front)	semi-elliptical springs and hydraulic telescopic double-action shock absorbers			
(rear)	semi-elliptical springs			
Tyres	13 R 22.5	13 R 22.5	14.75 R 20	14.75/80 R 20
Brakes (main)	air, mechanical, 2-line, dual circuit			
(parking)	spring brake	spring brake	spring brake	spring brake
(retarder)	exhaust brake	exhaust brake	exhaust brake	exhaust brake
Electrical system	24 V	24 V	24 V	24 V
Batteries	2 × 12 V, 125 Ah	2 × 12 V, 125 Ah	2 × 12 V, 125 Ah	2 × 12 V, 125 Ah
Alternator	55 A	55 A	55 A	55 A

DAF YTZ 2301 (6 × 6) truck tractor with handling crane in use with Patriot SAM system

The fully enclosed two-door all-steel cab was developed from the civilian F 218 type and can be tilted forward to an angle of 60° allowing access to the engine for maintenance. The cab has a large capacity heating and ventilation system and thermal and sound insulation. The driver's and co-driver's seats are adjustable, with the third seat with foot rest being mounted against the cab rear wall. The cab roof, in the cargo model only, is fitted with an observation hatch on which can be mounted a light machine gun.

The rear cargo area is of aluminium construction and is provided with removable drop sides and a drop tailgate. To the rear of the cab is a hydraulic crane for unloading cargo but, before this is used, stabilisers are lowered to the ground either side of the vehicle to the rear of the cab.

The front axle is a Kirkstall DS 65 and is fitted with stabilisers. The rear bogie is a DAF 2699 T with lockable differentials and a lockable inter-axle differential.

Standard equipment includes a 7- and 12-pole trailer connector, slave connector, trouble light connector at front and rear, standard commercial traffic lighting and blackout lighting according to NATO specifications. At the front is a push/pull NATO pin and at the rear is a 24-tonne towing hook. Optional equipment includes a ZF automatic transmission and a larger four-man fully enclosed cab; when the latter is fitted however the crane is not mounted to the rear of the cab.

Variants

YAZ 2300 Snow Fighting Vehicle
This is a special snow clearing vehicle used by the Dutch Air Force for clearing airfield runways. It is equipped with a de-icing fluid tank, pumping gear and swing-out spray bars. It is possible to fit a snow plough on the front.

YKZ 2300 Tipper
This was developed as the replacement for the DAF YK 616 three-way tipper. It has a maximum payload of 14 000 kg and a kerb weight of 13 500 kg.

YHZ 2300 Artillery Tractor
This variant was ordered by the Dutch Ministry of Defence and production of 78 commenced in 1987. It is used to tow 155 mm M114 and M114/39 howitzers and has seating for 12 men and two 12-round racks for ammunition.

YGZ 2300 Bridging Vehicle
This is in production to carry and launch Ribbon Bridge units using a DAF Special Products system in place of the normal cargo body. The system can also be used to carry and launch rolls of trackway.

YBZ 2300 Recovery Vehicle
This is a special recovery vehicle equipped with a side-mounted hydraulic crane for the recovery of Patriot SAM vehicles and units.

YAZ 2301 Truck
Although described as a general cargo truck, the YAZ 2301 (6 × 6) is used to carry container/shelters associated with the Patriot tactical air defence system.

YTZ 2301 Truck Tractor
This is used to tow the Patriot tactical air defence system missile launcher.

Status

In production. In service with the Dutch Army, Marines and Air Force (Patriot).

Manufacturer

DAF Military Sales, Hugo van der Goeslaan 1, NL-5643 TW Eindhoven, Netherlands.
Tel: 040 143440. Telex: 51085 daf nl.
Fax: 040 144318.

PAKISTAN

Yasoob (6 × 6) 6000 kg Truck

Description
The decision to proceed with the development of an indigenous family of military and commercial trucks was taken by the Pakistan government in July 1989. The first two prototypes of the resultant military truck, named Yasoob after the fastest horse of the Prophet, were handed over to the Pakistan Army for trials during 1990. These vehicles had 40 per cent local value which is expected to increase when full production commences. Components for all major vehicles units such as the engine, transmission, axles and transfer will be manufactured under licence (with provision for buy-back arrangements). Production is scheduled to commence about eight months after the completion of the initial test and trial programmes.

The Yasoob (6 × 6) 6000 kg truck is an all-purpose vehicle intended for general logistic purposes and can be used to tow artillery or trailers. The standard model is a cargo truck with a maximum highway load capacity of 12 000 kg (6000 kg cross country). Layout is conventional with the 8.3 litre diesel engine at the front, a two-door, three seat, fully enclosed cab in the centre and the cargo area with high drop sides and a tailgate at the rear. The cargo area can be covered by bows and a tarpaulin with the bows stowed behind the cab when not in use. Bench seats can be fitted for troop carrying.

The frame uses rolled channel construction with six reinforced crossmembers. The front and rear axles have spiral bevel hub reduction.

Three wheelbase lengths (front axle to rear bogie) are available: 4.3 m, 4.6 m and 5.5 m. The standard cargo version has the 4.6 m wheelbase chassis but there is also a lengthened cargo bed variant which uses the 5.5 m chassis. Van-bodied variants (for command post or mobile stores functions) can be produced for all three wheelbase lengths. Other variants in the Yasoob range include a dump truck, a wrecker and a tractor truck for towing loads up to 25 000 kg; all three use the 4.3 m wheelbase chassis. There will also be fuel or water tanker versions (4.6 m chassis) and a bridging equipment carrier (5.5 m chassis).

Commercial versions of the Yasoob will have gross vehicle weights of from 14 000 to 24 000 kg.

Specifications (standard cargo version)
Cab seating: 1 + 2
Configuration: 6 × 6
Weight:
  (loaded, front axle) 6500 kg
  (loaded, rear bogie) 15 000 kg
  (total) 21 500 kg
Max load:
  (road) 12 000 kg
  (cross-country) 6000 kg
Towed load: 10 000 kg
Length: 7.73 m
Width: 2.5 m
Height:
  (unloaded, overall) 3.1 m
  (reduced) 2.75 m
Ground clearance: 0.335 m
Track:
  (front) 2.063 m
  (rear) 2.112 m
Wheelbase: 4.6 m + 1.4 m
Angle of approach/departure: 40°/35°
Max speed with towed load:
  (road) 80 km/h
  (cross-country) 50 km/h
Range: (cruising) 550 km
Fuel capacity: 270 l
Gradient: (with towed load) 60%
Fording: 0.75 m
Engine: 8.3 l 6-cylinder direct injection diesel developing 240 hp at 2400 rpm
Gearbox: manual with 9 forward and 2 reverse gears
Clutch: twin dry plate
Transfer box: 2-speed
Steering: ZF 8097 power assisted
Turning radius: 12.75 m
Suspension:
  (front) semi-elliptic 8-leaf springs
  (rear) inverted semi-elliptic 13-leaf springs
Tyres: 13.00 R 20
Brakes:
  (main) air
  (parking) spring/air
Electrical system: 24 V
Batteries: 2 × 12 V, 150 Ah
Alternator: 150 A

Status
Prototypes.

Manufacturer
Pakistan state factories.

Yasoob (6 × 6) 6000 kg truck

POLAND

Star 266 (6 × 6) 3500 kg Truck

Description
The Star 266 3500 kg truck was the replacement for the older Star 66 2500 kg range of 6 × 6 trucks. The first prototype was completed in 1971 and production began in 1976. Major improvements over the earlier vehicle are its increased load-carrying capability, more powerful engine, all-steel fully enclosed cab and larger tyres. The cab is of the forward control type and the rear cargo area has removable bows, tarpaulin cover and drop tailgate. A winch with a capacity of 6000 kg is fitted.

A tropical version of the Star 266 is produced. This is similar to the standard model but is 7.07 m long and weighs 7350 kg unladen.

Two mobile workshops are produced using the Star 266 chassis. One is the Model 713 and the other the Model 716. Both use similar workshop bodies but the interior layouts differ slightly, being fitted with lathes, drills, generators, tool benches and a full supply of tools and other equipment. Both vehicles are 7.345 m

Star 266 (6 × 6) 3500 kg truck

long, 2.5 m wide and 3.17 m high overall. The work-shop bodies are produced by Jelczańskie Zakłady Samochodowe.

Specifications
Cab seating: 1 + 2
Configuration: 6 × 6
Weight:
  (empty) 7200 kg
  (loaded) 12 200 kg
Max load: 3500 kg
Towed load: 4000 kg
Length: 6.8 m
Width: 2.5 m
Height:
  (cab) 2.66 m

(tarpaulin) 3 m
Ground clearance: 0.325 m
Track: 1.97 m
Wheelbase: 2.97 m + 1.25 m
Angle of approach/departure: 37°/42.5°
Max speed: (road) 86 km/h
Fuel capacity: 300 l
Range: 800 km
Max gradient: 76%
Fording: 1.8 m
Engine: S-359 6.842 l 6-cylinder water-cooled diesel developing 150 hp at 2800 rpm
Gearbox: ZF S5-45 manual, 5 forward and 1 reverse gears
Clutch: single dry plate
Transfer box: 2-speed

Steering: ZF 8060 with hydraulic servo
Turning radius: 8.5 m
Tyres: 12.00 × 20
Brakes:
  (main) hydraulic
  (parking) mechanical
Electrical system: 24 V

Status
In production. In service with the Polish Army.

Manufacturer
Fabryka Samochodów Ciężarowych, 27-202 Starachowice, Poland.
Tel: 88-31. Telex: 0612571.

Star 28 and Star 200 Series (4 × 2) Trucks

Description
In 1968 the Star 28 and Star 29 entered production as the replacements for the Star 25 and Star 27. The Star 28 is powered by an S-530A1 six-cylinder diesel which develops 100 hp at 2600 rpm and gives the vehicle a maximum road speed of 81 km/h. Payload on roads is 5000 kg. The Star 29 is powered by an S-474 six-cylinder water-cooled petrol engine, which develops 105 hp at 3000 rpm and gives the vehicle a maximum road speed of 81 km/h. Payload on roads is 5000 kg and towed load is 5250 kg.

The Star 28 was replaced by the Star 200 and Star 244 (see following entry). The Star 200 is powered by an S-533 (90 hp) or an S-359 (150 hp) engine and can carry a maximum payload of up to 6000 kg on roads; towed load is 8500 kg. The basic Star 200 is a 4 × 2 general purpose platform truck with a 3.4 m wheelbase; the Star 200L has a 3.9 m wheelbase. Variants include the C200 tractor truck, the A200 produced to carry box bodies, the A200K produced for various utility bodies, the A200A (wheelbase 4.1 m) for bus bodies, and the W200 for tipper bodies.

The Star 200 is powered by an S-359 engine which develops 150 hp at 2800 rpm and is coupled to a ZF S5-45 manual gearbox with five forward and one reverse gears. Brief specifications are length 6.51 m,

width 2.33 m, payload 6000 kg, towed load 8500 kg and maximum road speed 90 km/h.

There are many variants of the Star 28 and Star 200 series including tankers (for example Star 20C, 21C (3500 litres), A3-573 and C-28), tippers (for example W-28) and crane trucks (for example Z-28).

Status
In production.

Manufacturer
Fabryka Samochodów Ciężarowych, 27-202 Starachowice, Poland.
Tel: 88-31. Telex: 0612571.

Star 244 (4 × 4) 5000 kg Truck

Description
The Star 244 (4 × 4) 5000 kg truck series was developed from the 4 × 2 Star 200 series and differs from the earlier model mainly by the addition of front-axle drive and a reduction gear. The Type 359 6.842 litre diesel engine is retained. The forward control all-steel cab was developed in association with Chausson of France.

Variants of the basic Star 244 are the Star 244RS produced primarily for agricultural purposes, the A244 adapted to carry various forms of cross-country bodies, the P244L (wheelbase 3.9 m) for mounting fire truck bodies, and the 3W244 (wheelbase 3 m) for tipper bodies.

Specifications
Configuration: 4 × 4
Weight: (empty) 5500 kg
Max load: 5000 kg
Towed load: 8500 kg
Length: 6.34 m
Width: 2.46 m
Height: (cab) 2.59 m

Ground clearance: 0.28 m
Track:
  (front) 1.9 m
  (rear) 1.8 m
Wheelbase: 3.4 m
Angle of approach/departure: 40°/27°
Engine: S-359 6.842 l 6-cylinder water-cooled diesel developing 150 hp at 2800 rpm
Gearbox: ZF S5-45 manual with 5 forward and 1 reverse gears
Transfer box: 2-speed
Clutch: single dry plate
Steering: ZF 8060 with hydraulic servo
Tyres: 8.25 × 20
Electrical system: 24 V
Batteries: 2 × 12 V, 135 Ah
Alternator: 30 A

Status
In production.

Manufacturer
Fabryka Samochodów Ciężarowych, 27-202 Starachowice, Poland.
Tel: 88-31. Telex: 0612571.

Star 244 (4 × 4) 5000 kg truck (Henry Dodds)

Jelcz Trucks

Description
From 1968 the Zubr (A-80) 4 × 2 trucks were replaced in production by the Jelcz series. The basic model is designated the Jelcz 315, and is powered by an SW 680/49 six-cylinder water-cooled diesel engine which develops 200 hp and gives a maximum road speed of 85 km/h. Payload on roads is 8000 kg and maximum towed load is 14 000 kg. The Jelcz 315A is almost identical and the 315M is the military version with the same payload as the civilian vehicles. The 315MB is the 315M but fitted with a hydraulic crane for loading purposes. The fuel tanker is designated the A3-591 and can carry 8000 litres of fuel.

The 315 has a two-door fully enclosed forward control type cab with the cargo area at the rear with drop sides, drop tailgate, removable bows and a canvas cover.

In 1970 the Jelcz 316 (6 × 2) truck entered production. It is powered by an SW 680/49 six-cylinder diesel developing 200 hp and has a maximum payload of 10 000 kg and towed load of 14 000 kg. The following year the 316E appeared with a 240 hp diesel. The 317 is a 4 × 2 tractor truck and later versions include the 317D with the same engine as the 316 and the 317MD which can tow a semi-trailer weighing up to 22 500 kg. Jelcz dump trucks include the 3W317-821 (4 × 2) and the 640 (6 × 4).

The latest Jelcz truck series is based on the Jelcz 416, a platform truck powered by the SW680/207/2 diesel. This has an updated tilting cab with provision for sleeping accommodation. Variants include the 6 × 2 Jelcz S416, the Jelcz C417K tractor truck and the Jelcz C620D 6 × 2 tractor truck. Firefighting vehicles include the Jelcz 004M and 005M.

Jelcz trucks have been developed in conjunction with Austria, for example the Jelcz 640 (6 × 4) truck which is powered by a Steyr V-8 diesel developing

320 hp at 2600 rpm. Variants of this model include a dump truck (W-640) and a three-sided dump truck (W-640-S).

Specifications (Jelcz 416)
Cab seating: 1 + 1
Configuration: 4 × 2
Weight:
  (empty) 8000 kg
  (loaded) 15 700 kg
Max load: (road) 7700 kg
Towed load: (road) 14 000 kg
Length: 8.675 m
Width: 2.5 m
Height: (tarpaulin) 3.713 m
Track:
  (front) 2.062 m
  (rear) 1.8 m
Wheelbase: 4.9 m
Angle of approach/departure: 35°/14°

Max speed: (road) 92 km/h
Engine: SW 680/207/2 11.1 l 6-cylinder water-cooled diesel developing 235 hp at 2200 rpm
Gearbox: ZF 6-90 manual with 6 forward and 1 reverse gears
Clutch: single dry plate
Steering: ZF 8065 with hydraulic servo
Tyres: 11.00 R 20
Electrical system: 24 V
Batteries: 2 × 12 V, 165 Ah
Alternator: 500 W

Status

In production. The Jelcz 315A is known to be in service with the Polish Army.

Manufacturer

Jelczańskie Zaklady Samochodowe, Jelcz k. Olawy, Poland.
Marketed by POLMOT, Stalingrdzka 23, 03-370 Warsaw, Poland.
Tel: 11 0001. Telex: 813901 pomo pl.

Standard Jelcz 315 (4 × 2) 8000 kg truck with original cab

PORTUGAL

Bravia Gazela (4 × 4) 1134 kg Truck

Description

The Bravia Gazela truck has a conventional layout with the engine at the front, cab in the centre and the cargo area at the rear. The standard cab, which has a windscreen that can be folded forward onto the bonnet and a canvas top, can be replaced by a fully enclosed cab similar to the one on the Bravia Leopardo Mk III 3000 kg (6 × 6) truck.

The cargo area has drop sides and a drop tailgate which can be removed. Fold-up troop seats which are an integral part of the sides can be fitted back-to-back along the centreline of the cargo area so that the troops are facing outwards. Bows and a tarpaulin cover are fitted as standard.

The engine may be a Perkins P.4-236 diesel developing 90 hp or an optional GAZ V-8 developing 180 hp. The Gazela is being produced as a standard cargo truck, an ambulance, a communications shelter carrier, a missile carrier or a water-carrying firefighting vehicle.

Optional equipment includes a Braden winch with a capacity of 4536 kg.

Specifications

Cab seating: 1 + 1
Configuration: 4 × 4
Weight:
(empty without winch) 2494 kg
(empty with winch) 2721 kg
(loaded, cross-country without winch) 3854 kg
(loaded, cross-country with winch) 4081 kg
Max load:
(road) 1360 kg
(cross-country) 1134 kg
Towed load:
(road) 1628 kg
(cross-country) 1288 kg
Length: 5.327 m
Width: 2.159 m
Height:
(overall) 2.413 m

Bravia Gazela (4 × 4) 1134 kg truck with front-mounted winch

(reduced) 1.498 m
Ground clearance: 0.254 m
Track: 1.7 m
Wheelbase: 3.3 m
Angle of approach/departure: 45°/25°
Max speed: 100 km/h
Range:
(Perkins diesel) 450 km
(GAZ petrol) 362 km
Fuel capacity: 106 l
Max gradient: 50%
Fording:
(without preparation) 0.914 m
(with preparation) 1.524 m
Engine: Perkins 4-cylinder turbocharged diesel developing 90 hp at 3300 rpm or GAZ V-8 petrol developing 180 hp at 4000 rpm
Gearbox: manual with 4 forward and 1 reverse gears
Clutch: single dry plate

Transfer box: 2-speed
Steering: recirculating ball
Turning radius: 8.384 m
Suspension: horizontal semi-elliptical springs and direct-acting shock absorbers with hydraulic dampers
Tyres: 9.00 × 16 or 10.50 × 16
Brakes:
(main) hydraulic
(parking) mechanical
Electrical system: 12 or 24 V

Status

In service in Portugal.

Manufacturer

Bravia SARL, Sociedade Luso-Brasiliera de Viaturas e Equipamentos, Estrada Nacional No 10, KM 107 Porto Alto, P-2135 Samora Correia, Portugal.
Tel: 63 93256/7. Telex: 12715 bravia p.

Bravia Leopardo Mk III (6 × 6) 3000 kg Truck

Description

The Leopardo Mk III was designed to carry 3000 kg of cargo across country or up to 6000 kg on roads. Its layout is conventional with the engine at the front, cab in the centre with a windscreen which folds forward onto the bonnet and a removable canvas top, and the cargo area at the rear with hinged seats, drop tailgate, removable bows and a tarpaulin cover. It is available with single or dual rear wheels and tracks can be fitted to the dual rear wheel version to increase cross-country mobility. The vehicle can be delivered with one of three types of engine: model V-8 318-3 petrol developing 202 hp at 2400 rpm; a V-8 361-3 petrol developing 210 hp at 4000 rpm; or a British Perkins diesel type 6-354-2D. Optional equipment includes a fully enclosed cab, Braden model MU2-3 winch with a capacity of 4536 kg, 24 V electrical system, power

Bravia Leopardo III (6 × 6) 3000 kg truck with single rear wheels

Bravia Leopardo III (6 × 6) 3000 kg truck with tracks fitted to rear wheels to increase traction in soft soil

steering and an additional 250 litre fuel tank.

The Leopardo Mk I is a 4 × 2 truck with a 4.179 m wheelbase, gross vehicle weight of 8845 kg and a 10 206 kg gross combination weight. The Leopardo Mk II is also a 4 × 2 truck, with a 4.444 m wheelbase, gross vehicle weight of 10 206 kg and a gross combination weight of 16 330 kg.

Variants include a dump truck, fuel and water tankers, van bodies, a light wrecker and firefighting vehicles.

Specifications (cargo version)
Cab seating: 1 + 2
Configuration: 6 × 6
Weight:
  (empty) 5900 kg
  (loaded, road) 10 400 kg
Max load:
  (road) 6000 kg
  (cross-country) 3000 kg
Length: 6.7 m

Width: 2.4 m
Height:
  (overall) 3.2 m
  (reduced) 2.1 m
Ground clearance: 0.28 m
Track:
  (front) 1.721 m
  (rear) 1.778 m
Wheelbase: 2.9 m
Angle of approach/departure: 47°/40°
Fuel capacity: 227 l
Range: 480 km
Max gradient: 65%
Fording: 0.78 m
Engine: see text
Gearbox: manual, 5 forward and 1 reverse gears
Clutch: single dry plate
Transfer box: 2-speed
Steering: manual
Turning radius: 13 m

Suspension:
  (front) semi-elliptical springs and hydraulic double-acting shock absorbers
  (rear) Hendrickson type with semi-elliptical springs
Tyres:
  (double) 9.00 × 20
  (single) 11.00 × 20
Brakes:
  (main) air over hydraulic
  (parking) mechanical
Electrical system: 24 V

Status
In service with Portuguese armed forces.

Manufacturer
Bravia SARL, Sociedade Luso-Brasileira de Viaturas e Equipamentos, Estrada Nacional No 10, KM 107 Porto Alto, P-2135 Samora Correia, Portugal.
Tel: 63 93256/7. Telex: 12715 bravia p.

Bravia Pantera (6 × 6) 6000 kg Truck

Description
The Pantera was designed to carry 12 000 kg of cargo on roads or 6000 kg of cargo across country. Its layout and appearance are almost identical to the Leopardo Mk III and it has the same wheelbase. It can be delivered with one of four types of engine: Perkins V-8-510 diesel developing 170 hp at 2800 rpm; Perkins V-8-540 diesel developing 180 hp at 2600 rpm; Cummins 378C diesel; or a 361-4 petrol engine. Optional equipment is the same as the Leopardo except that the winch installed is an MU12 rated at 9072 kg. Tracks may be fitted to the dual rear wheels to increase mobility across soft ground.

Variants include a long wheelbase (4.775 m + 1.371 m) cargo truck, dump trucks, a tractor truck, a van-body truck and firefighting vehicles.

Specifications
Cab seating: 1 + 2
Configuration: 6 × 6
Weight:
  (empty) 9733 kg
  (loaded, road) 18 985 kg
Max load:
  (road) 12 000 kg
  (cross-country) 6000 kg
Towed load:
  (road) 13 620 kg
  (cross-country) 6802 kg
Length: (with winch) 7.52 m
Width: 2.464 m
Height:
  (overall) 2.946 m
  (reduced) 2.172 m
Ground clearance: (axles) 0.295 m
Track:
  (front) 1.88 m
  (rear) 1.829 m

Bravia Pantera (6 × 6) 6000 kg truck with front-mounted winch, bows and tarpaulin cover

Wheelbase: 3.86 m + 1.371 m
Angle of approach/departure: 46°/35°
Fuel capacity: 500 l
Range: 746 km
Max gradient:
  (without towed load) 67°
  (with towed load) 42°
Side slope: 20%
Fording: 0.76 m
Engine: see text
Gearbox: manual, with 5 forward and 1 reverse gears
Clutch: single dry plate
Transfer box: 2-speed
Turning radius: 12.75 m
Tyres:
  (double) 11.00 × 20

  (single) 14.00 × 20
Brakes:
  (main) air over hydraulic
  (parking) mechanical
Electrical system: 24 V
Batteries: 4 × 12 V, 100 Ah

Status
In service with Portuguese armed forces.

Manufacturer
Bravia SARL, Sociedade Luso-Brasileira de Viaturas e Equipamentos, Estrada Nacional No 10, KM 107 Porto Alto, P-2135 Samora Correia, Portugal.
Tel: 63 93256/7. Telex: 12715 bravia p.

Bravia Elephant (6 × 6) 10-tonne Truck

Description
Designed to be a cargo truck in the NATO 10-tonne class, the Bravia Elephant resembles similar American trucks and uses an American-style cab. The vehicle layout is entirely conventional.

Known variants include a dump truck, a tractor truck, a bituminous road layer and a concrete mixer carrier.

Specifications
Cab seating: 1 + 1
Configuration: 6 × 6
Weight:
(empty) 13 608 kg
(loaded) 29 484 kg
Max load: (road) 15 786 kg
Length: (with winch) 8.9 m
Width: 2.895 m
Height:
(cab) 2.819 m
(tarpaulin) 3.282 m
(load area) 1.689 m
Ground clearance: 0.523 m
Track: 2.006 m
Wheelbase: 3.847 m + 1.524 m
Angle of approach/departure: 30°/45°
Max speed: 70 km/h
Range: 531 km
Fuel capacity: 736 l
Max gradient: 60%
Fording: 0.76 m
Engine: Detroit Diesel 6V-53T diesel
Gearbox: manual with 5 forward and 1 reverse gears
Clutch: single dry plate
Transfer box: 2-speed
Steering: hydraulic power-assist
Turning radius: 10.97 m
Suspension:
(front) semi-elliptical leaf springs and hydraulic
double-acting shock absorbers
(rear) pair of inverted semi-elliptical springs mounted longitudinally at centre to trunnion arrangement attached to chassis
Tyres: 14.00 × 24
Brakes:
(main) air
(parking) mechanical
Electrical system: 24 V
Batteries: 2 × 12 V

Status
In service with Portuguese armed forces.

Manufacturer
Bravia SARL, Sociedade Luso-Brasileira de Viaturas e Equipamentos, Estrada Nacional No 10, KM 107 Porto Alto, P-2135 Samora Correia, Portugal.
Tel: 63 93256/7. Telex: 12715 bravia p.

ROMANIA

SR-131 Trucks and Variants

Description
The SR-131 Bucegi (4 × 2) truck replaced the SR-101 vehicle in production. It is powered by an SR-211 eight-cylinder diesel engine which develops 140 hp and gives the vehicle a maximum speed of 90 km/h. Payload on roads is 3000 kg. The 4 × 4 model, designated the SR-132 Bucegi, is almost identical and is powered by the same engine. The layout of both vehicles is identical, with the engine at the front, two-door all-steel cab in the centre and the cargo area at the rear with drop sides and a drop tailgate.

Further development of the SR-131/SR-132 vehicles resulted in the SR-113 (4 × 2) and SR-114 (4 × 4)
Carpati trucks powered by the same engine as the earlier vehicles but with a wheelbase of 4 m compared with the earlier vehicle's wheelbase of 3.4 m. The SR-113's payload on roads is 5000 kg and the SR-114's is 4000 kg. Both vehicles are fitted with 9.00 × 20 tyres. The SR-114 is used as a carrier for Romanian Army 21-round BM-21 multiple rocket systems (for details of the BM-21 see *Jane's Armour and Artillery 1992-93*, pages 715 to 717).

Tractor truck models (4 × 2) are designated the SR-116 while dump trucks (4 × 2) include the ABS-116 and AB45-116. Ambulance and van-type versions are also in service. Other Bucegi vehicles include the 7-BA-1 L (4 × 2) 7000 kg truck, 7-BA-1 N (4 × 2) 6000 kg truck and the 18-BTA-1 (4 × 2) tractor truck which can pull a semi-trailer weighing up to 18 000 kg.

The AC-302 is a 4000 litre tanker based on the SR-113 chassis. As far as it is known these are not used by the Romanian Army.

Specifications (SR-132 (4 × 4) truck)
Cab seating: 1 + 2
Configuration: 4 × 4
Weight:
(empty) 3750 kg
(loaded, road) 6750 kg
(loaded, dirt road) 5750 kg
Max load:
(road) 3000 kg
(dirt road) 2000 kg
Towed load:
(road) 3000 kg
(dirt road) 2000 kg
Length: 5.78 m
Width: 2.263 m
Height: (cab) 2.1 m
Ground clearance: 0.27 m
Track: 1.75 m
Wheelbase: 3.4 m
Max speed: (road) 95 km/h
Engine: SR-211 V-8 water-cooled petrol developing 140 hp at 3600 rpm
Gearbox: manual with 4 forward and 1 reverse gears
Transfer box: 2-speed
Tyres: 9.75 × 18

Status
In service with the Romanian Army.

Manufacturer
Red Star Motor Vehicle Plant, Brasov, Romania.

SR-132 Bucegi (4 × 4) truck

DAC 665 T (6 × 6) 5000 kg Truck

Description
The DAC 665 T (6 × 6) 5000 kg truck is the standard truck in its class in the Romanian Army. In appearance it is very similar to the Hungarian D-566 (6 × 6) 5000 kg truck.

The forward control all-steel cab hinges forward to allow access to the engine for maintenance and there is an observation hatch in the roof on the right side. The spare wheel is mounted to the rear of the cab on the right side.

The rear cargo area has a drop tailgate, removable bows and a tarpaulin cover. Bench seats can be fitted. Standard equipment includes a winch and a central tyre-pressure regulation system.

One variant of the DAC 665 T is used to carry a locally produced 122 mm (40-round) multiple rocket launcher. This vehicle caries a crew of up to five and weighs 17 250 kg loaded. A further variant is used as a resupply vehicle for this system and carries two

DAC 665 T (6 × 6) 5000 kg truck chassis carrying 122 mm (40-round) multiple rocket launcher system

launcher reload modules and a rear-mounted MH 90 crane. The crane has a maximum lifting capacity of 6000 kg and a maximum lifting height of 6 m. The resupply vehicle weighs 15 000 kg loaded and can tow a four-wheeled two-axle trailer carrying more rockets that are loaded into empty modules by hand. For full details of this system refer to *Jane's Armour and Artillery 1992-93* pages 736.

Specifications
Cab seating: 1 + 2
Configuration: 6 × 6

Max load:
   (road) 10 000 kg
   (cross-country) 5000 kg
Length: 7.57 m
Width: 2.5 m
Height: 2.85 m
Ground clearance: 0.39 m
Track: 2 m
Wheelbase: 3.095 m + 1.31 m
Range: 450 km
Fuel capacity: 220 l
Gradient: 60%

Fording: 0.65 m
Engine: 6-cylinder, 10.39 l diesel developing 215 hp at 2200 rpm
Gearbox: 10 forward and 2 reverse gears
Tyres: 14.00 × 20

Status
In production. In service with the Romanian Army and Iraq.

Manufacturer
Red Star Motor Vehicle Plant, Brasov, Romania.

ROMAN 12135 DFAE (6 × 6) 10 000 kg Truck

Description
Romania obtained a licence from the German company MAN to build a wide range of 4 × 2, 6 × 2, 6 × 4 and 6 × 6 trucks, which are marketed under the name of the ROMAN (RO: Romania + MAN) series. ROMAN also supplies cabs to Hungary for its Raba series of trucks.

At least one of these vehicles, the ROMAN 12135 DFAE, is used by the Romanian Army. This has a two-door all-steel cab of the forward control type with the cargo area at the rear. The cargo area has a drop tailgate and can be fitted with seats. The civilian model is designated the ROMAN 12135 DF.

Specifications
Configuration: 6 × 6
Weight:
   (empty) 5755 kg
   (loaded) 15 755 kg
Max load: (road) 10 000 kg
Towed load: (road) 4000 kg
Length: 7.005 m
Width: 2.49 m
Height: (cab) 2.91 m
Ground clearance: 0.3 m
Track: 1.912 m

Max speed: (road) 90 km/h
Fuel capacity: 220 l
Engine: Type 797-05 6-cylinder water-cooled diesel developing 135 hp
Tyres: 9.00 × 20

Status
In production. In service with the Romanian Army. Many ROMAN trucks are produced under licence in China, especially for construction purposes.

Manufacturer
Red Star Motor Vehicle Plant, Brasov, Romania.

SERBIA

IMR TARA (4 × 4) 1200 kg Truck

Description
The IMR TARA (Terenski Automobili Rakovica) (4 × 4) truck appears to be based on the Austrian Steyr-Daimler-Puch Pinzgauer light vehicle but the IMR vehicle has a longer wheelbase and numerous body changes.

The IMR TARA uses a forward control cab with the engine located between the driver's and front passenger's positions. An open area to the rear can accommodate two rows of lateral seats for a further six passengers or it can be used to carry cargo. The all-steel cargo body can be covered by a tarpaulin supported on bows. If required the bows can be removed as can the upper parts of the front doors; the windscreen can be folded forwards. The cab area can be heated either by using a system employing the engine coolant or by a Webasco heater.

The vehicle is supplied with a spare wheel, a spare fuel container, a maintenance tool kit, spare parts, engineer tools, NBC equipment and a camouflage net. The vehicle can be screened against radio interference and there is a connection for an infra-red driving or vision system.

Optional equipment includes power steering, a heavy duty air cleaner or air pre-cleaner, 7.50 R 16 XS tyres, a towing pintle, an engine pre-heating system,

snow chains, air-conditioning and a light electric winch.

The IMR TARA can be configured as a personnel carrier with seating for the driver and seven passengers, a minibus, a general utility pick-up (with or without an enlarged crew cab), a van, or as a shelter/container carrier. Other specialised bodies are available according to requirements.

Specifications
Cab seating: 1 + 7
Configuration: 4 × 4
Weight: (GVW) 3500 kg
Max load: up to 1200 kg
Towed load:
   (without brakes) 900 kg
   (with brakes) 1500 kg
Load area: 2.4 × 1.7 m
Length: 4.2 m
Width: 1.85 m
Height: 2.1 m
Ground clearance: 0.295 m
Track: 1.54 m
Wheelbase: 2.4 m
Angle of approach/departure: 45°/50°
Max speed: 105 km/h
Fuel capacity: 70 l
Range: approx 500 km
Max gradient:
   (without trailer) 70%

   (with trailer) 45%
Side slope: 35%
Fording: 0.6 m
Engine: IMR S-54 V 2.45 l 4-cylinder water-cooled in-line diesel developing 75 hp at 4200 rpm
Gearbox: manual with 5 forward and 1 reverse gears
Clutch: single dry plate
Transfer box: 2-speed
Steering: Gemmer mechanical
Turning radius: 6.25 m
Suspension: coil springs with rubber elements and double-action hydraulic shock absorbers
Tyres: 6.50K × 16
Brakes:
   (main) dual circuit hydraulic
   (parking) mechanical on rear axle
Electrical system: 24 V
Batteries: 2 × 12 V, 143 Ah

Status
In production.

Manufacturer
Industrija Motora Rakovica, Patrijarha Dimitrija 7, YU-11 090 Beograd, Serbia.
Tel: 011/591 111. Telex: 11341 YU IMR.
Fax: 011/582 574.

IMR TARA (4 × 4) 1200 kg truck

IMR TARA (4 × 4) 1200 kg truck

TAM 110 T7 BV (4 × 4)
1500/2500 kg Truck

Description

The TAM 110 T7 BV has been referred to as the TAM 1500 and was developed specifically to meet the requirements of the former Yugoslav Army, using the design of the German Magirus-Deutz 130T7FAL (which did not enter production) as a basis. It is the 4 × 4 component of two basically similar vehicles, the other being the TAM 150 T11 BV 6 × 6 vehicle (see following entry). Both vehicles use versions of the TAM 413 engine which was produced in what was then Yugoslavia under licence from Klockner-Humboldt-Deutz.

The two-door all-steel forward control cab has a reinforced PVC material roof which can be removed, as can the side windows. The cab has seating for two and can be tipped forward to an angle of 55° for engine access. The windscreen can be tipped forward over the bonnet if required. Two forms of cab heating are available. The cargo body is of all-steel construction and has two collapsible benches fitted one to each side to seat 12 soldiers. The cargo area has a capacity of 3.31 m³ and is 3.02 m long, 2.12 m wide and the sides are 0.64 m high. A canvas tilt may be fitted.

The engine is mounted forward under the cab as is a 2500 kg capacity winch which can be used to the front or rear. A towing hook is provided at the rear under the downward-opening tailgate. Special equipment carried on the vehicle includes pioneer tools, equipment for the winch and an NBC kit. The vehicle is fitted with radio interference protection and space is provided for the fitment of an infra-red device. There is provision for changing the tyre pressures in the range 0.7 to 3.5 atm while the vehicle is being driven.

A signals vehicle variant houses its signals equipment in a removable container weighing 6700 kg that can be lifted off the vehicle using telescopic support legs. The container is 5.17 m long, 2.34 m wide and 3 m high. A generator may be fitted inside the container.

An ambulance variant has a box-body and can carry up to four stretchers and associated medical equipment. Total weight is 6400 kg.

Specifications

Cab seating: 1 + 1 (up to 12 in rear)
Configuration: 4 × 4
Weight:
  (empty) 4500 kg
  (loaded, road) 7000 kg
  (loaded, off road) 6000 kg
Max load:
  (road) 2500 kg
  (off-road) 1500 kg
Towed load: 1800 kg
Load area: 3.02 × 2.12 m
Length: 4.85 m
Width: 2.275 m
Height: (top of cab) 2.47 m
Ground clearance: 0.3 m
Wheelbase: 2.85 m
Angle of approach/departure: 49°/45°
Max speed:
  (road) 90.8 km/h
  (off-road) 45 km/h

Fuel capacity: 100 l
Max gradient:
  (without trailer) 67%
  (with trailer) 44.5%
Fording: 1 m
Engine: TAM (KHD) F 4 L 413 FR 4-cylinder 6.381 l air-cooled diesel developing 115 hp at 2650 rpm
Gearbox: Z5-35S with 5 forward and 1 reverse gears
Clutch: GF 310 KR hydraulic with single dry plate
Transfer box: R 28 NP 2-speed
Steering: PPT (ZF) 8038 hydraulic
Turning radius: 6.5 m
Suspension: leaf-type springs with rubber buffers and telescopic shock absorbers
Tyres: 12.00 × 18 PR 8
Brakes:
  (main) dual circuit air-hydraulic on all wheels
  (parking) mechanical with air-servo assist on rear wheels
Electrical system: 24 V
Batteries: 2 × 12 V, 110 Ah

Status

In service with the former Yugoslav Army and Saudi Arabia.

Manufacturer

Tovarna Avtomobilov in Motorjev, Maribor, Slovenia. Enquiries to Federal Directorate of Supply and Procurement (SDPR), YU-11005 Beograd, 9 Nemanjina Street, Serbia.
Tel: 621522. Telex: 71000/72566 SDPR YU.
Fax: 38 11 631588/630621.

TAM 110 T7 BV (4 × 4) signals vehicle

TAM 110 T7 BV (4 × 4) 1500/2500 kg truck

TAM 150 T11 BV (6 × 6)
3000/5000 kg Truck

Description

The TAM 150 T11 BV (6 × 6) truck may be regarded as an enlarged version of the TAM 110 T7 BV (4 × 4). It uses the same cab and general layout but the TAM 150 is larger and uses a version of the F 6 L 413F in a V-6 configuration. This engine was built in the former Yugoslavia under licence from Klockner-Humboldt-Deutz.

The TAM 150 T11 BV has a reinforced PVC cab roof which can be removed, as can the side windows. The cab has seating for two and if required the windscreen may be folded forward over the bonnet. The cargo body is all-steel and has collapsible benches along each side to seat 18 men. A downward-opening tailgate is provided. A canvas tilt may be fitted. There is a 5000 kg capacity winch fitted under the cargo body rear which may be used forwards for self-recovery or to the rear. Power for the winch is taken from a reduction gear and a power take-off for tools may be fitted.

Tyre pressures may be altered while the TAM 150 T11 BV is being driven and a rear-mounted hook may be used to tow either a trailer or light artillery such as anti-tank guns.

TAM 150 T11 BV (6 × 6) 3000/5000 kg truck

TAM 150 T11 BV (6 × 6) 3000/5000 kg trucks used to tow anti-tank guns

Specifications

Cab seating: 1 + 1 (up to 18 in rear)
Configuration: 6 × 6
Weight:
  (empty) 6200 kg
  (loaded, road) 11 200 kg
  (loaded, off-road) 9260 kg
Max load:
  (road) 5000 kg
  (off-road) 3600 kg
Towed load: 3600 kg
Load area: 4.17 × 2.12 m
Length: 6.55 m
Width: 2.275 m
Height:
  (max, loaded) 2.82 m
  (cab) 2.42 m
Ground clearance: 0.305 m
Wheelbase: 3.1 m + 1.2 m
Track: 1.86 m

Angle of approach/departure: 48°/40°
Max speed:
  (road) 94.7 km/h
  (off-road) 55.2 km/h
Fuel capacity: 150 l
Max gradient:
  (without trailer) 71%
  (with trailer) 42.8%
Fording: 1 m
Engine: TAM F 6 L 413 F 9.572 l V-6 air-cooled diesel developing 154 hp at 2650 rpm
Gearbox: Z5-35S with 5 forward and 1 reverse gears
Clutch: G 350 KR single dry plate
Transfer box: R 28 NP 2-speed
Steering: PPT (ZF) 8038 hydraulic
Turning radius: 7.6 m
Suspension: leaf-type springs with rubber buffers and telescopic shock absorbers, additional front rubber springs
Tyres: 12.00 × 18 PR 10

Brakes:
  (main) dual circuit air-hydraulic on all wheels
  (parking) mechanical with air-servo assist on rear wheels
Electrical system: 24 V
Batteries: 2 × 12 V, 143 Ah

Status
In service with the former Yugoslav Army and Saudi Arabia.

Manufacturer
Tovarna Avtomobilov in Motorjev, Maribor, Slovenia. Enquiries to Federal Directorate of Supply and Procurement (SDPR), YU-11005 Beograd, 9 Nemanjina Street, Serbia.
Tel: 621522. Telex: 71000/72566 SDPR YU. Fax: 38 11 631588/630621.

TAM 4500/5000/5500/6500 Trucks

Description
The TAM 4500 series of trucks was manufactured in the former Yugoslavia under licence from Magirus-Deutz. The 4500 is powered by an F 4 L 514 four-cylinder air-cooled diesel which develops 85 hp giving the vehicle a maximum road speed of 75 km/h. Payload on roads is 4500 kg. The layout of the vehicle is conventional with the engine at the front, fully enclosed two-door all-steel cab in the centre and the cargo area at the rear with drop sides and a drop tailgate. Suffixes are used to designate different versions: B for forward control, D for 4 × 4 drive, and K for dump truck. The 4500D is the 4 × 4 model used by the former Yugoslav Army and is similar in layout to the civil version but has a different rear cargo area with a drop tailgate. Seats can be installed if required. The forward control version is the TAM 4500B and the dump truck version is the 4500K.

The TAM 5000 is powered by the same engine as the TAM 4500 and was available in two versions: 4 × 2 (TAM 5000) and 4 × 4 (TAM 5000DV). The DV version was developed specifically for the former Yugoslav Army and has a central tyre pressure regulation system. A dump truck model is designated the TAM 5000K (4 × 2).

The TAM 5500 is powered by a V-6 F 4 L 614 air-cooled diesel engine, which develops 85 hp and gives the vehicle a maximum road speed of 85 km/h. Payload is 5000 kg. The dump truck model is the TAM 5500DK (4 × 4) and there is also a tractor truck model.

TAM 4500D truck towing 128 mm M-63 Plamen multiple rocket system launcher

The largest model in the range is the TAM 6500, which can carry 6500 kg, and there is also a dump truck model.

Specifications (TAM 5000DV)
Configuration: 4 × 4
Weight:
  (empty) 4500 kg
  (loaded road) 9500 kg
Max load: (road) 5000 kg
Length: 6.75 m
Width: 2.19 m

Height: (cab) 2.75 m
Wheelbase: 4.2 m
Engine: F 4 4-cylinder air-cooled diesel developing 85 hp at 2300 rpm
Tyres: 12.00 × 18

Status
Production complete. In service with the former Yugoslav Army.

Manufacturer
Tovarna Avtomobilov in Motorjev, Maribor, Slovenia.

FAP 2220 BDS (6 × 4) and FAP 2026 BS (6 × 6) Trucks

Description
The FAP 2220 BDS (6 × 4) truck was originally used for carrying and launching a truck-mounted scissors bridge. This vehicle can be distinguished from the FAP 2026 BS which has a central tyre-pressure regulation system and single rear wheels.

The FAP 2026 BS/AV (6 × 6) was developed specifically for the former Yugoslav Army and features a central tyre-pressure regulation system. The two-door all-steel cab is of the forward control type with the cargo area at the rear with a drop tailgate, removable bows and a tarpaulin cover. The engine for these vehicles was built under licence from British Leyland (now Leyland DAF).

The FAP 2220 BDS and FAP 2026 BS (6 × 6) are used as the chassis for the 128 mm (32-round) M-77 Oganj multiple rocket system. Details of this equipment

FAP 2026 BS (6 × 6) truck

FAP 2026 BS carrying 128 mm (32-round) M-77 Oganj multiple rocket system under canvas cover

are given in *Jane's Armour and Artillery 1992-93*, page 745.

The FAP 2832 BS/AV (8 × 8) 9000 kg truck is described in the following entry in this section.

Specifications (FAP 2026 BS/AV (6 × 6))
Cab seating: 1 + 1 (20 in cargo area)
Configuration: 6 × 6
Weight:
(empty) 11 000 kg
(loaded) 21 000 kg
Weight on front axle: (loaded) 6000 kg
Weight on rear axle: (loaded) 15 000 kg
Max load: 10 000 kg
Max towed load: 7200 kg
Max winch capacity: 10 000 kg
Load area: 4.53 × 2.342 m
Length: 7.72 m
Width: 2.49 m

Height: (top of cab) 3.1 m
Wheelbase: 3.4 m + 1.4 m
Track: 2.02 m
Angle of approach/departure: 40°/40°
Max speed: 80 km/h
Fuel consumption: 33 l/100 km
Range: 600 km
Max gradient:
(less trailer) 60%
(with trailer) 40%
Fording: 0.3 m
Engine: V-8 direct injection water-cooled diesel developing 256 hp at 2500 rpm
Gearbox: 6MS-80 with 6 forward and 1 reverse gears
Clutch: single dry plate
Transfer box: 2-speed
Steering: hydraulic, ball, joint
Turning radius: 11 m
Suspension: leaf springs with additional rubber springs

and telescopic shock absorbers
Tyres: 15.00 × 21
Brakes:
(main) dual circuit air drum type
(parking) mechanical, air-actuated
Electrical system: 24 V
Number of batteries: 2 × 12 V, 143 Ah

Status
In production. In service with the former Yugoslav Army and Saudi Arabia.

Manufacturer
Motor Vehicle Plant, Priboj.
Enquiries to Federal Directorate of Supply and Procurement (SDPR), YU-11005 Beograd, 9 Nemanjina Street, Serbia.
Tel: 621522. Telex: 71000/72566 SDPR YU.
Fax: 38 11 631588/630621.

FAP 2832 BS/AV (8 × 8) 9000 kg Truck

Description
The FAP 2832 BS/AV (8 × 8) 9000 kg truck is the 8 × 8 equivalent of the FAP 6 × 6 trucks (see previous entry). The vehicle has a forward control cab which is identical to that of the FAP 6 × 6 trucks and can be tipped forward for maintenance access. Behind the cab is a spare wheel carried in a handling device. The steel-sided cargo area has a tailgate and is covered by a tilt carried on curved bows. A central tyre pressure system is provided with control from the cab. A winch is a standard fitting and is located at the rear for forward or rear use.

The FAP 2832 BS/AV can be used to tow artillery weighing up to 11 000 kg and can carry a maximum load of 14 000 kg on roads.

The FAP 3232 BDST/AV is a tractor truck version of this vehicle and is covered in an entry in the *Tank transporters* section.

Specifications
Cab seating: 1 + 1
Configuration: 8 × 8
Weight:
(empty) 16 000 kg
(loaded, road) 30 000 kg
(loaded, cross-country) 25 000 kg
Max load:
(road) 14 000 kg
(cross-country) 9000 kg
Towed load: 11 000 kg
Length: 9.02 m

FAP 2832 BS/AV (8 × 8) 9000 kg truck

Width: 2.5 m
Height: (top of tilt) 3.319 m
Ground clearance: 0.38 m
Track: 2.02 m
Wheelbase: 1.5 m + 3.2 m + 1.4 m
Angle of approach/departure: 41°/45°
Range: 600 km
Max gradient: 32%
Fording: 1.2 m
Engine: OM 403 15.95 l V-10 4-stroke diesel developing 320 hp
Gearbox: 8 forward and 1 reverse gears
Clutch: single dry plate
Transfer box: 2-speed
Steering: hydraulic, ball, joint
Turning radius: 13 m
Suspension: parabolic leaf springs
Tyres: 15.00 × 21 T-101

Brakes:
(main) dual circuit air plus exhaust brake
(parking) mechanical with air actuation
Electrical system: 24 V
Batteries: 2 × 12 V, 210 Ah

Status
In production. In service with the former Yugoslav Army.

Manufacturer
Motor Vehicle Plant, Priboj.
Enquiries to Federal Directorate of Supply and Procurement (SDPR), YU-11005 Beograd, 9 Nemanjina Street, Serbia.
Tel: 621522. Telex: 71000/72566 SDPR YU.
Fax: 38 11 631588/630621.

SOUTH AFRICA

SAMIL 20 Mark 2 (4 × 4) 2000 kg Truck

Description
Development of the SAMIL 20 Mark 2 (4 × 4) 2000 kg truck began in 1981 with the vehicle being unveiled in 1985. The SAMIL 20 Mark 2 retains the overall configuration and general appearance of the SAMIL 20 Mark 1 from which it was developed (see next entry) but the basic specification has been substantially altered. The most significant change is that the engine is now a South African manufactured ADE 352N (ADE – Atlantis Diesel Engines) water-cooled diesel weighing 420 kg, and corresponding alterations to the gearbox and transfer box ratios have been introduced. The forward control cab has been altered to become a fully enclosed hard cab. The fuel tank is now constructed using high density polyethelene and the associated piping systems are now made of a nylon-based material. These changes, along with other new locally produced components such as the propshafts, mean that over 90 per cent of the vehicle is local content.

SAMIL 20 Mark 2 (4 × 4) 2000 kg truck

The only body type announced to date is the standard cargo body with removable banks of seating for 12 soldiers. It is expected that many of the various types of body and roles that are associated with the SAMIL 20 Mark 1 (see next entry) will be transferred to the SAMIL 20 Mark 2.

Specifications
Cab seating: 1 + 1
Configuration: 4 × 4
Weight:
  (chassis/cab) 4730 kg
  (loaded) 7700 kg
Max load: 2000 kg
Towed load: 1360 kg
Length: 5.692 m
Width: 2.438 m
Height: 2.82 m
Ground clearance: 0.47 m
Track: (front and rear) 1.852 m
Wheelbase: 2.9 m
Angle of approach/departure: 40°/45°
Max speed: (road) 85.9 km/h

Range: 800 km
Fuel capacity: 200 l
Max gradient: 70%
Side slope: 18°
Fording: 1.2 m at 5 km/h
Engine: ADE 352N 5.675 l 6-cylinder in-line water-cooled direct injection diesel developing 106 hp at 2800 rpm
Gearbox: manual, 5 forward and 1 reverse gears
Transfer box: 2-speed, pneumatic
Clutch: single sintered metal with automatic adjustment
Steering: ball and nut, power-assisted
Turning radius: 6 m
Suspension: semi-elliptic leaf springs with telescopic shock absorbers; stabiliser fitted to rear axle

Tyres: 14.5 × 20 PR 12
Brakes: dual circuit air-assisted hydraulic with spring brakes on rear axle and engine-mounted exhaust retarder
Electrical system: 24 V
Batteries: 2 × 12 V, 118 Ah

Status
In production. In service with South African Defence Forces and Mozambique (4).

Manufacturer
TruckMakers (Pty) Ltd, PO Box 911-255, Rosslyn 0200, South Africa.
Tel: 2712582361. Telex: 3 20297 SA.
Fax: 27125412802.

SAMIL 20 Mark 1 (4 × 4) 2000 kg Trucks

Description
The SAMIL 20 Mark 1 (4 × 4) chassis provides the basis for a wide range of cross-country vehicles. The basic model is a 2000 kg cargo truck. This has a forward control half-cab with a canvas roof and removable side windows. The cargo area has extruded aluminium sides and may be covered with a canvas tilt over a steel framework. A removable bank of wooden seats may be fitted along the centre of the body for 12 fully equipped soldiers. These seats can be stored at the sides when the truck is required to carry cargo. Container lash-down points are provided on the body floor and two fork-lift pockets are in the body frame bottom for lifting purposes. Corner blocks are provided in the four bottom corners to facilitate body mounting on a container-type subframe. A spare wheel is mounted between the cab and the cargo area and a light crane arrangement is provided to allow the wheel to be handled by one man.

Variants
Protected transport
This version has the driver's cab protected against mine blast and small arms fire by a shaped arrangement of armoured plates around the cab and engine. The cargo area is slightly reduced in size from the normal version.

Bulldog
This is a completely armoured personnel and load carrier based on the SAMIL 20 Mark 1. There is a centrally placed cab for the driver. The rear carrying area is enclosed by folding armour plates round the sides. The open-top may be covered by a canvas cover.

Protected troop carrier (Rhino)
This version of the SAMIL 20 Mark 1 has a fully armoured body with a two-man front cab and protection for 10 men in the rear. Access to the rear is by two outward-opening armoured doors at the rear and 13 firing ports are provided along the sides and rear. Armoured glass windows and vision ports are provided. The rear passengers normally face inwards.

Valkiri rocket launcher
The SAMIL 20 Mark 1 is used for the vehicle component of the full production version of the Valkiri multiple artillery rocket system. In this form the SAMIL 20 Mark 1 can be used as the launcher vehicle as well as the meteorological vehicle associated with the system (early versions of the Valkiri system used Unimog light trucks). When in use as the launch vehicle the SAMIL 20 Mark 1 carries 24 launching tubes and when covered with a canvas tilt it is virtually identical to the standard SAMIL 20 Mark 1 truck. Full details of the Valkiri system can be found in *Jane's Armour and Artillery 1992-93*, pages 738 to 740.

Light repair workshop
On this version of the SAMIL 20 Mark 1 the rear area is occupied by a cabin constructed from glass fibre panels reinforced by steel strips and brackets. The rear and sides are flaps that fold upwards for access to the body interior and when raised act as partial weather protection. The interior contains racks for repair equipment.

Container body carrier
When the SAMIL 20 Mark 1 is used as a container body carrier, the container is fixed directly onto the chassis frame and can then carry a payload of up to 2000 kg. The containers may also be used as mobile offices, control or command posts and for radio and other equipment.

Specifications (basic SAMIL 20 Mark 1 truck)
Cab seating: 1 + 1
Configuration: 4 × 4
Weight:
  (chassis/cab) 4580 kg
  (loaded) 7700 kg

Payload: 2000 kg
Length: 5.692 m
Width: 2.438 m
Height: 2.82 m
Ground clearance: 0.47 m
Track: 1.852 m
Wheelbase: 2.9 m
Angle of approach/departure: 40°/40°
Max speed: (road) 90 km/h
Range: 800 km
Fuel capacity: 200 l
Max gradient: 70%
Side slope: 18°
Fording: 1.2 m at 5 km/h
Engine: 6-cylinder 6.128 l air-cooled diesel developing 103.5 hp at 2650 rpm
Gearbox: manual, 5 forward and 1 reverse gears
Transfer box: 2-speed mechanical
Clutch: single sintered metal self-adjusting, hydraulic
Steering: ball and nut, power-assisted
Turning radius: 6 m
Suspension: telescopic hydraulic shock absorbers, leaf springs
Tyres: 14.5 × 20 PR 12
Brakes: dual circuit, air/hydraulic
Electrical system: 24 V
Batteries: 2 × 12 V, 120 Ah

Status
Production complete. In service with the South African Defence Forces.

Manufacturer
TruckMakers (Pty) Ltd, PO Box 911-255, Rosslyn 0200, South Africa.
Tel: 2712582361. Telex: 3 20297 SA.
Fax: 27125412802.

SAMIL 20 Mark 1 (4 × 4) truck

SAMIL 20 Mark 1 (4 × 4) truck

SAMIL 50 Mark 2 (4 × 4) 5000 kg Truck

Description

Development of the SAMIL 50 Mark 2 (4 × 4) 5000 kg truck began in 1981 with the first examples being shown in 1985. The SAMIL 50 Mark 2 was developed from the SAMIL 50 Mark 1 (see next entry) and retains its general configuration. However its basic specification has altered significantly with the most important alteration being the inclusion of a South African produced ADE 409N diesel engine weighing 675 kg, and the transmission has been modified accordingly. The new engine is housed in an enlarged bonnet in front of a new locally produced cab. The front axle has been upgraded to achieve increased durability. Other changes are that the two 200 litre fuel tanks are

manufactured using high density polyethelene and the associated piping is made from a nylon-based material. These changes bring the local content of the vehicle to over 90 per cent.

The SAMIL Mark 2 retains the personnel and general cargo body of the SAMIL Mark 1 with removable bench seating for 32 men, and can be readily converted to carry containers/shelters. It is anticipated that the range of roles and types of body already in use with the SAMIL 50 Mark 1 (see next entry) will be carried over to the SAMIL 50 Mark 2.

Specifications

Cab seating: 1 + 1
Configuration: 4 × 4
Weight:
(chassis/cab) 6060 kg
(loaded) 12 400 kg

Body and payload allowance: 5800 kg
Towed load: 6000 kg
Length: 7.78 m
Width: 2.5 m
Height: 2.955 m
Ground clearance: 0.355 m
Track:
(front) 1.985 m
(rear) 2.03 m
Wheelbase: 4.9 m
Angle of approach/departure: 32°/37°
Max speed: 85 km/h
Range: 1000 km
Fuel capacity: 400 l (200 + 200 l)
Max gradient: 70%
Side slope: 18°
Fording: 1.2 m
Engine: ADE 409N 9.51 l 5-cylinder in-line water-cooled direct injection diesel developing 165 hp at 2200 rpm
Gearbox: manual, 6 forward and 1 reverse gears
Transfer box: 2-speed
Clutch: single sintered metal with automatic adjustment
Steering: ball and nut, power-assisted
Turning radius: 11.5 m
Suspension: semi-elliptic leaf springs and hydraulic telescopic shock absorbers
Tyres: 14.00 × 20 PR 18
Brakes: dual circuit air with spring brakes on rear axle plus exhaust retarder
Electrical system: 24 V
Batteries: 2 × 12 V, 118 Ah

Status

In production. In service with South African Defence Forces and Mozambique (30).

Manufacturer

TruckMakers (Pty) Ltd, PO Box 911-255, Rosslyn 0200, South Africa.
Tel: 2712582361. Telex: 3 20297 SA.
Fax: 27125412802.

SAMIL 50 Mark 2 (4 × 4) 5000 kg truck with basic cargo/personnel body

SAMIL 50 Mark 1 (4 × 4) 4800 kg Trucks

Description

The SAMIL 50 Mark 1 (4 × 4) 4800 kg truck forms the basis for a range of different types of vehicle all using the same chassis. The SAMIL 50 Mark 1 chassis frame is a single-piece channel section with parallel side-members and bolted-in crossmembers and brackets. The engine is mounted at the front with the two-man all-steel cab mounted just to the rear. The cargo area may be covered by a canvas tilt and four removable wooden bench seats may be fitted along the sides and, back-to-back, along the centre. When in use these seats can accommodate 32 fully equipped men. All the body panels are hinged and removable. A spare wheel is mounted inside the body area and is provided with a small winch to handle the wheel. A towing hook is provided at the rear.

Variants

Recovery vehicle
See entry in the *Recovery vehicles* section.

Telecommunications workshop
This version has a glass fibre superstructure to house work tables and drawers for telecommunications repair requirements. Small windows are provided in the sides with burglar proofing bonded to the superstructure. An air conditioner is standard. Access to the rear door is via a ladder which extends to the roof.

Battery charging vehicle
This has a box-type body with side and rear panels hinging upwards if required. Inside there are two sets of battery charging equipment each capable of charging 18 batteries arranged on a bench.

Mobile welding workshop
This follows the same general lines as the battery

charging vehicle but a fully equipped welding workshop is enclosed.

Water tanker
The superstructure of this variant consists of a 4500 litre water tank fitted with a tropical roof. There are five taps each side of the tank from which water can be drawn. At the rear is a single draw-off point and a spray bar for sprinkling. Two sections of armoured hose 75 mm in diameter and 4 m long are stored in boxes alongside the tank. These hoses can be quickly coupled to the rear draw-off point. A water pump capable of passing 500 litres/min for filling or disposal purposes is driven by a power take-off from the gearbox.

Fuel tanker
This variant has an oval-section mild steel fuel tanker body with a capacity of 5000 litres. The tank has a tropical roof cover and three manholes on the top. A 400 litres/min fuel pump is provided and a meter and

SAMIL 50 Mark 1 (4 × 4) truck carrying 4.5 m container shower

SAMIL 50 Mark 1 (4 × 4) 4800 kg truck with standard cargo/personnel body

control platform is situated at the tank rear. Four delivery lines for can filling are provided.

Mobile pantry

On this SAMIL 50 Mark 1 variant the superstructure box body is formed from rigid sandwich sections of foamed polyurethane contained in seamless glass fibre skins with reinforcing members. Internally there are two compartments with the forward section refrigerated and the rear for the stowage of canned and non-perishable goods. Each section has shelves. The front section is equipped with stainless steel trays while the rear section is equipped with bins and baskets for handling and stowage purposes. The temperature can be controlled between −20 and +20°C in the front compartment.

Container shower

The SAMIL 50 can carry a specially developed 4.5 m container shower for use by personnel in field locations. Showers can be provided for eight men at one time with each of the shower heads being individually operated. The container is mounted on twist-locks and equipped with three liquid gas draw-off water heaters, a petrol engine-driven self-priming pumping plant and liquid draw-off gas cylinders mounted outside the front panel. The water-heating compartment is provided with fire protection using an automatic roof-mounted fire extinguisher. Internal lighting is provided by a 12 V battery charged by the pump engine. The shower container is non-stackable and can only be lifted by a fork-lift.

Specifications (basic SAMIL 50 Mark 1 truck)

Cab seating: 1 + 1
Configuration: 4 × 4
Weight:
  (chassis/cab) 6256 kg
  (loaded) 12 400 kg
Body and payload allowance: 5800 kg
Towed load: 6000 kg
Length: 7.78 m
Width: 2.5 m
Height: 2.955 m
Ground clearance: 0.355 m
Track: 2.03 m
Wheelbase: 4.9 m
Angle of approach/departure: 35°/37°
Max speed: (road) 90 km/h
Range: 1000 km
Fuel capacity: 400 l
Max gradient: 70%

Side slope: 18°
Fording: 1.2 m at 5 km/h
Engine: V-6 9.572 l air-cooled diesel developing 157 hp at 2650 rpm
Gearbox: manual, 6 forward and 1 reverse gears
Transfer box: 2-speed
Clutch: self-adjusting, hydraulic
Steering: ball and nut, power-assisted
Turning radius: 11.5 m
Suspension: telescopic hydraulic shock absorbers, leaf springs
Tyres: 14.00 × 20 PR 18
Brakes: duplex compressed air
Electrical system: 24 V
Batteries: 2 × 12 V, 118 Ah

Status

Production complete. In service with the South African Defence Forces.

Manufacturer

TruckMakers (Pty) Ltd, PO Box 911-255, Rosslyn 0200, South Africa.
Tel: 2712582361. Telex: 3 20297 SA.
Fax: 27125412802.

SAMIL 100 (6 × 6) 10 000 kg Trucks

Description

The SAMIL 100 (6 × 6) 10 000 kg truck shares many components with the SAMIL 50 Mark 1, including the cab, and as with the other vehicles in the SAMIL range is used as the basis for a wide range of bodies. The basic SAMIL 100 is a cargo truck with the rear body constructed of pressed steel to form a sturdy unit and fixed to the chassis by spring-loaded mountings for flexibility in off-road conditions. The floor is of 5 mm flat sheet metal with supporting crossmembers fitted with dropout twist locks to transport containers (one 6 m, two 3 m or four 1.5 m). The drop sides and tailgate are bottom-hinged to fold down and are detachable. On the mine-protected versions expanded metal extensions are side-hinged to the support pillar and swing open by removing two pins either side or can be detached by removing all four pins. All support pillars can fold down and are detachable. A 6 t/m elephant trunk-type crane is mounted between the driver's cab and rear body for cargo handling. This crane is fully power-controlled through an arc of 360° and is capable of lifting 1200 kg at a jib length of 5 m.

It is anticipated that a Mark 2 version of this vehicle, along the same lines as the SAMIL 20 and SAMIL 50 Mark 2, will be produced.

Variants

Protected transport

This is the same vehicle as the basic SAMIL 100 but is fitted with an armoured cab and engine cover.

Armoured personnel carrier

This version of the SAMIL 100 has a fully protected cab and engine cover and the rear is fully enclosed in an armoured hull. Seating is provided internally and there are five bullet-resistant vision windows on each side.

Tipper

This is a conventional tipper truck with a 7.5 m³ capacity body and dual-tyred rear wheels.

Water tanker

This follows the same general lines as the SAMIL 50 Mark 1 water tanker but the tank capacity on the SAMIL 100 is 9100 litres. A water pump with a rate of 910 litres/min is provided. The oval-section stainless steel tank has a manhole on the top and is fitted with internal baffles. Spray devices are fitted at the rear and all controls are situated between the cab and the tank.

Fuel tanker

The tank for this variant is subdivided into two baffled compartments and has a capacity of 13 000 litres. Each compartment has its own sump drain and manhole on the top. A 64 mm diameter hose is used to fill containers directly from the tank, and four smaller hoses can be used to fill cans. All controls are on the left-hand side of the tank.

Recovery vehicle

See entry in the *Recovery vehicles* section.

Artillery tractor

Developed to tow the 155 mm G5 howitzer, the SAMIL 100 artillery tractor has a superstructure consisting of a crew compartment, a cargo drop side body, an elephant trunk-type crane and a 10 000 kg winch. The crew compartment provides seating for seven crew members and storage space for their personal equip-ment. A 150 litre hydraulic oil tank is situated under the rearward-facing seats and a 200 litre water tank is located under the forward-facing seats. An observation hatch is fitted centrally in the roof with provision for mounting a machine gun. The cargo drop side body, immediately behind the crew compartment, consists of built-in storage for 60 propellant charges and winching equipment. On top of these compartments storage is provided for 15 projectile pallets, each weighing 189 kg. A canvas cover is provided to cover the cargo body and ground pegs are supplied to allow the cover to be used as a ground shelter. A 360° traverse crane is mounted behind the rear cargo area with a 800 kg lift at a jib length of 3.5 m. It is used mainly to handle the projectile pallets. The hydraulic drag winch located at the rear between the longitudinal chassis members has a 10 000 kg capacity on the first layer with the cable routed front or rear.

Production of this variant has been completed.

Canteen

The canteen box body has a load capability of 8500 kg and consists of front and rear compartments manu-factured from glass fibre and polyurethane sandwich constructed panels. A cooling unit is provided on the front panel of the front compartment which is used for storing cooled products. The rear compartment is fitted with a food warmer, a microwave oven, a till, a mini-safe, a counter, shelves, a potato chip dispenser, a bulk storage compartment, roof lights, ventilation fans and a trickle charger. A service platform and a power plant are fitted and stored under the body.

Cargo panel body

Designed mainly for the transport of perishable prod-ucts, the panel body has a maximum load of 9700 kg.

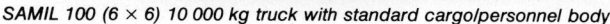

SAMIL 100 (6 × 6) 10 000 kg truck with standard cargo/personnel body

SAMIL 100 (6 × 6) artillery tractor

The body is manufactured from glass fibre and polyurethane sandwich constructed panels. The interior is equipped with lashing eyes and roof lights. There are two rear doors and one side door.

Mobile beer cooler
This box-bodied variant of the basic SAMIL 100 can carry 500 cases (4140 litres) of cooled beer; each case holds 24 cans. The body is manufactured from glass fibre and polyurethane constructed panels. A cooling unit is fitted to the front panel. Roof lights and two rows of four racks each are fitted to the interior to hold the beer cases. A ladder and a platform are provided on the outside to assist in servicing the cooling unit.

Abba
A SAMIL 100 has been fitted with a load handling system. For available details refer to entry in the *Materials handling equipment* section.

Valkiri
The SAMIL 100 chassis has been adapted to act as a carrier for a 40-round version of the Valkiri 127 mm multiple rocket launcher system. The chassis used for this version has its front axle capacity increased from 6500 to 7500 kg and extra fuel tanks are provided. Combat weight of the system is 12 000 kg and length

travelling is 8.53 m. A mineproof cab is used for the five-man crew. For full details of this system refer to *Jane's Armour and Artillery 1992-93* pages 738 and 739.

Specifications (basic SAMIL 100 truck)
Cab seating: 1 + 1
Configuration: 6 × 6
Weight:
(chassis/cab) 9135 kg
(loaded) 24 000 kg
Payload: 10 000 kg
Towed load: 14 000 kg
Length: 10.27 m
Width: 2.5 m
Height: 3.35 m
Ground clearance:
(front axle) 0.355 m
(rear axles) 0.359 m
Track:
(front) 2.002 m
(rear) 2.048 m
Wheelbase: 5.25 m + 1.38 m
Angle of approach/departure: 30°/30°
Max speed: (road) 90 km/h
Range: 800 km
Fuel capacity: 400 l

Max gradient: 70%
Side slope: 18°
Fording: 1.2 m at 5 km/h
Engine: V-10 air-cooled diesel developing 268 hp at 2650 rpm
Gearbox: manual, 6 forward and 1 reverse gears
Transfer box: 2-speed
Clutch: single sintered metal, self-adjusting, hydraulic
Steering: power-assisted, ball and nut
Turning radius: 11.9 m
Suspension: telescopic hydraulic shock absorbers, leaf springs
Tyres: 14.00 × 20 PR 18
Brakes: duplex, compressed air
Electrical system: 24 V
Batteries: 2 × 12 V, 120 Ah

Status
In production. In service with the South African Defence Forces.

Manufacturer
TruckMakers (Pty) Ltd, PO Box 911-255, Rosslyn 0200, South Africa.
Tel: 2712582361. Telex: 3 20297 SA.
Fax: 27125412802.

SPAIN

Santana S-2000 Militar (4 × 4) Light Truck

Description
The first forward control vehicle developed by Land Rover Santana was the Model 1300, first produced in 1967 in both petrol- and diesel-engined versions. From this evolved the S-2000, produced in both military and civil versions. The Model Militar has a payload of 2000 kg and was produced in several forms for military use.

In its basic form as a troop carrier the S-2000 has a forward control cab for the driver and passenger and seating for up to twelve troops in the rear. In the rear area the troops are seated along two outward-facing bench seats along the centre line of the body. The body sides and tailgate can be quickly folded down for easy access and the rear area can be covered by a non-flammable canvas tilt carried on bows. The cab roof may have a hatch and provision for a light machine gun mounting.

The chassis has a stair-type construction with two parallel sidemembers and seven crossmembers welded into position. All the chassis members are rectangular in cross-section and are painted once finished; a special galvanised finish is applied if the vehicle is to be used in a saline environment. There is a six-cylinder 3.5 litre petrol engine but a diesel engine may be fitted.

Several versions of the S-2000 exist and the model is capable of being converted for a number of roles.

Variants
Command post
This version uses a van body with sliding rear windows

and wide rear doors with a concealed rear step. The body is made from duraluminium sheet with insulating panels and fibre panels for the interior. The normal command interior includes a table, two swivelling seats, a document cabinet, lamps, two portable fans and a fire extinguisher. Electrical equipment can be powered by a 42 or 90 A alternator or two auxiliary batteries. An office version can be produced.

Communications version
This version also uses a van body but can contain various radio communication installations.

Mobile workshop
On this version the items of workshop equipment are contained in a series of lockers situated each side of the vehicle rear. The centre area of the rear body is used for equipment stowage and there are lighting masts carried over the lockers. Equipment provided includes a generating set powered from a power take-off and capable of delivering 15 kW, a compressor, welding equipment and electrical, pneumatic and manual tools. One side of the body rear folds down to form a workbench, complete with a vice. A 500 kg crane is also supplied.

Tanker
This version has a rear-mounted tank body that can be used to carry 1600 litres of fuel or water. The tank is 2.2 m long and 0.8 m high and the equipment will vary according to the liquid carried.

Generating set
This carries a 15 kW generator powered from a power take-off on the vehicle. This equipment is used mainly for lighting purposes and carries up to four strings of

lamps or 1000 W halogen lamps together with all the necessary leads and components.

Container carrier
This version is used for the carriage of S-250 and other container/shelters.

A fire tender was also produced.

Specifications
Cab seating: 1 + 1 (up to 12 in rear)
Configuration: 4 × 4
Weight:
(unladen) 2360 kg
(laden) 4360 kg
Max load: 2000 kg
Length: 4.949 m
Width: 1.96 m
Height: 2.235 m
Ground clearance: 0.27 m
Track:
(front) 1.461 m
(rear) 1.486 m
Wheelbase: 2.565 m
Angle of approach/departure: 37°/34°
Fuel capacity: 157 l
Engine: 3.429 l 6-cylinder in-line water-cooled petrol developing 100 hp at 4000 rpm
Gearbox: manual with 4 forward and 1 reverse gears
Clutch: diaphragm and disc, hydraulic
Transfer box: 2-speed
Steering: worm and recirculating ball with power-assist
Turning radius: 6.75 m
Suspension: semi-elliptical underslung springs with double-acting shock absorbers

Basic troop-carrying version of S-2000 (4 × 4) light truck

Flat bed version of S-2000 (4 × 4) light truck carrying S-250 container/shelter

Tyres: 9.00 × 16
Brakes: hydraulic drum, front and rear, dual circuit
Electrical system: 24 V
Batteries:
  (petrol) 2 × 12 V, 57 Ah
  (diesel) 2 × 12 V, 120 Ah

Alternator: 35 A (50 or 90 A optional)

Status
Production complete. In service with the Spanish armed forces and some other nations.

Manufacturer
Land Rover Santana SA, Carretora de Vadallanos, S/N, 23.700 Linares, Spain.
Tel: 34 53 693051. Fax: 34 53 653201.

URO 115 PM 2000 kg (4 × 4) Truck

Description
As a result of trials held between April and late June 1983, a new 2000 kg (4 × 4) tactical truck was introduced to the Spanish armed forces. The only company to submit a vehicle for the competition was URO Vehiculos Especiales SA, which was formed in 1981. This company produced a truck prototype and a 10 vehicle pre-production series resulting in a series of four commercial models, the U-14.09, U-14.10, U-12.08 and U-12.13, each of which was produced in four wheelbase lengths. The model U-12.13 was selected for the competition and, with some improvements, the URO 115 PM was produced. The 115 refers to the horsepower of the engine, a Perkins Military diesel (hence PM).

The first order for the Spanish Army was placed in October 1984.

The URO 115 PM is produced in two wheelbase lengths, 2.8 m and 3.2 m, with the latter version being used for a variety of special bodies including general load carriers, wireless vehicle, four-stretcher ambulance, water tanker, fuel tanker, crane, workshop van, fire tender, tipper, anti-aircraft gun platform and a minibus for 16 passengers plus the driver. A wading version has been proposed.

The driver is seated in an all-metal forward control cab that can be tipped forward to an angle of 55° for engine access. The cab structure uses steel tube for the frame and GRP panels are fitted for insulation. The engine is mounted forward over the front axle which is a URO UED-1 with double reduction gears in the wheel hubs and URO differentials; the rear axle is a URO UET-1. The chassis is attached to the engine and cab at only three points to allow maximum chassis torsion. The suspension uses leaf springs allied to telescopic shock absorbers.

General cargo-carrying versions have either fixed or removable panel bodies and a winch may be fitted at the front.

Specifications
Cab seating: 1 + 1
Configuration: 4 × 4
Weight: (approx) 11 900 kg
Payload: 2000 kg
Towed load: 3500 kg
Length: (chassis)
  (long wheelbase) 5.315 m
  (short wheelbase) 4.915 m
Width: 1.985 m
Height: (cab) 2.55 m
Ground clearance: 0.38 m
Track: (front and rear) 1.555 m
Wheelbase
  (long wheelbase) 3.2 m
  (short wheelbase) 2.8 m
Max speed: 96 km/h
Range: (road) 700 km
Fuel capacity: 180 l
Angle of approach/departure: 44°/60°
Gradient: 100%
Side slope: 40%
Fording: 0.8 m
Engine: Perkins Iberica 6.354.3 5.8 l 6-cylinder in-line water-cooled diesel developing 118 hp
Gearbox: Motor Iberica/Clark-285 V with 5 forward and 1 reverse gears
Transfer box: URO URT-1 2-speed
Clutch: single dry disc
Steering: hydraulic-assist
Turning radius
  (long wheelbase) 8 m
  (short wheelbase) 7.15 m
Suspension: leaf springs plus telescopic shock absorbers
Tyres: 13.80 × 20
Brakes: drums, dual circuit air on all wheels

Front view of URO 115 PM 2000 kg (4 × 4) truck

Electrical system: 24 V
Alternator: 400 VA

Status
In production. In service with the Spanish armed forces.

Manufacturer
Vehiculos Especiales URO SA, Via Edison 17, Poligono del Tambre, Santiago de Compostela, Spain.
Tel: 981 580189.

Pegaso 3045 (4 × 4) 3000 kg Cargo Truck

Description
The Pegaso 3045 (4 × 4) truck was designed by DAF of the Netherlands to meet the requirements of the Spanish Army. While under development it had the DAF designation YA 414, and is basically an improved model of the DAF YA 314 (4 × 4) 3000 kg truck used by the Dutch forces (see entry in this section).

The Pegaso 3045 entered service in 1970 and initial production vehicles used many DAF components, but as production increased more components of Spanish manufacture were used and eventually almost all of the truck was built in Spain.

First production models were powered by a petrol engine coupled to a manual gearbox with five forward and one reverse gears, and had single rear wheels. This was soon replaced in production by the Pegaso 3045D powered by a Pegaso diesel engine built under licence in Spain from British Leyland, a gearbox with six forward and one reverse gears and dual rear wheels. To meet the requirements of the Spanish Marines a special model was developed known as the Pegaso 3045DV which can ford to a maximum depth of 2 m.

The two-door forward control cab is made of steel and has a tarpaulin roof that can be folded backward and a windscreen that can be folded forward onto the radiator. The rear cargo body is all steel and has a drop tailgate, five removable bows and a tarpaulin cover. The wheel arches extend all the way along the cargo body on either side and provide seats when the vehicle is carrying passengers. Wooden panels can be inserted between the wheel arches to enable the vehicle to carry wider loads. A winch with a 4000 kg capacity can be installed.

Variants include a crane truck (Marines use one version and Army use at least two different versions), dump truck, refueller, water carrier and workshop.

Specifications (Pegaso 3045D)
Cab seating: 1 + 1
Configuration: 4 × 4
Weight:
  (empty) 6750 kg
  (loaded, cross-country) 9750 kg
Max load:
  (road) 6000 kg
  (cross-country) 3000 kg

Pegaso 3045D (4 × 4) 3000 kg cargo truck

Pegaso 3045DV (4 × 4) fuel tanker fitted with deep wading equipment

Towed load: 4500 kg
Load area: 4.2 × 2.15 m
Length: 6.47 m
Width: 2.48 m
Height: (cab) 2.617 m
Ground clearance: 0.32 m
Track: 1.9 m
Wheelbase: 3.7 m
Angle of approach/departure: 48°/34°
Max speed: 72 km/h (3045, 90 km/h)
Range: 650 km
Fuel capacity: 260 l
Max gradient: 60%
Fording: 1 m

(3045) 0.7 m
(3045DV) 2 m
Engine: Pegaso Model 9026/13 6-cylinder diesel developing 125 hp at 2400 rpm (3045, DAF 6-cylinder petrol developing 134 hp at 3500 rpm)
Gearbox: manual with 6 forward and 1 reverse gears (3045, manual with 5 forward and 1 reverse gears)
Transfer box: 2-speed
Turning radius: 6.96 m
Suspension: semi-elliptical springs with double-acting hydraulic shock absorbers
Tyres: 11.00 × 20 (3045, 12.00 × 20)
Brakes:
(main) air/hydraulic

(parking) mechanical
Electrical system: 24 V

Status
Production complete. In service with the Spanish armed forces. Also used by Burkina Faso (33), Chile and Nicaragua.

Manufacturer
Pegaso, Empresa Nacional de Autocamiones SA, Defence Division, Avenida de Aragón, 402 – E28022 Madrid, Spain.
Tel: (1) 750 1000. Telex: 46 972 maba e.
Fax: (1) 747 1307.

Pegaso 3046 (4 × 4) Cargo Trucks

Development
The Pegaso 3046 trucks were developed primarily as export/commercial models. The first widely available model was the Pegaso 3046/50 which had a nominal payload of 3000 kg. This was replaced by the Pegaso 3046/10 with a nominal payload of 5000 kg; this model was sold to Egypt. The first contract to export 2650 Pegaso 3046/10 trucks to Egypt was signed in November 1980. In July 1981 a contract was signed for a further 5000 trucks, and a contract for another 4000 trucks was awarded. More than 4000 units were supplied to the Spanish Army and a further 1000 units were delivered to Somalia, Peru and Morocco.

A variant is the Model 7222A which has a 220 hp engine and a longer wheelbase. The 7222 designation is a Pegaso numbering system in which 7 denotes a military vehicle, 2 refers to the number of axles and 22 to the 220 hp of the engine. A workshop-bodied version of the Model 7222A has been produced.

The latest model is the Model 7217 with a Pegaso 170 hp diesel engine. Production of this model commenced in 1987 with 200 units delivered to the Spanish armed forces. The similar Model 7223 has a 125 hp turbocharged engine. The Pegaso BRP 2223 (4 × 4) forest firefighting vehicle was derived from the Model 7223.

Description
The Pegaso 3046/50 and 3046/10 are fundamentally identical. The two-man cab is situated well forward over the engine and has a soft-top which can be removed if required. The two-piece windscreen can be folded forwards over the short bonnet to reduce the vehicle height. In front of the bonnet a large steel frame provides protection for the radiator grill and headlamps

which are set into the bodywork. At the rear the normal load-carrying body is an open cargo/personnel area that can be used to carry 5000 kg of stores or 23 men on bench seats situated along each side. Off-road the maximum load is 3000 kg. For protection against the weather a canvas tilt can be fitted. A spare wheel is carried under the load area on the left-hand side; the corresponding area on the right is occupied by the fuel tank. On some versions the spare wheel is carried behind the cab.

Optional equipment for the 3046/10 includes a metal roof for the cab, a fording kit, a power take-off on the gearbox and a 4500 kg capacity front winch. Versions other than the cargo/personnel type include a tanker, a recovery vehicle with a swivelling crane, an ambulance, a communications post vehicle, a mobile workshop, a refrigerated cold storage vehicle and a command post. Various weapons can be fitted.

Specifications
(Model 3046; data for Model 7217 in square brackets where different)
Cab seating: 1 + 1 (22 in rear)
Configuration: 4 × 4
Weight:
(empty) 7200 [7250] kg
(loaded, on road) 12 200 [13 250] kg
(loaded, off road) 10 200 [11 250] kg
Max payload:
(on road) 5000 kg
(off road) 3000 [4000] kg
Towed load:
(on road) 7500 kg
(off road) 4500 kg
Length: 6.085 [7.05] m
Width:
(cab) 2.4 m
(over rear axle) 2.406 m

Height: (cab) 2.765 [2.755] m
Ground clearance: 0.34 [0.32] m
Track: 1.96 m
Wheelbase: 3.7 [4.14] m
Angle of approach/departure: 49°/49° [49°/36°]
Max speed: 89 [90] km/h
Range: 900 km
Fuel capacity: 350 l
Max gradient: 70%
Side slope: 30%
Engine: Pegaso Model 9100/42, 6-cylinder, in-line, 10.17 l four-stroke diesel developing 170 hp at 2100 rpm
Gearbox: Pegaso Model 8256.10 manual with 6 forward and 1 reverse gears [ZF synchronised with 6 forward and 1 reverse gears]
Clutch: Model 8500.01 single dry disc
Transfer box: Pegaso pneumatic 2-speed
Steering: block, servo-hydraulic
Turning radius: 9.5 [11.3] m
Suspension: semi-elliptical leaf springs and hydraulic shock absorbers, front and rear
Tyres: 13.00 × 20 or 14.00 × 20
Brakes: dual circuit air
Electrical system: 24 V
Batteries: 2 × 12 V, 110 Ah
Alternator: 840 W

Status
In service with Egypt (more than 9000), Morocco, Peru, Somalia and the Spanish armed forces.

Manufacturer
Pegaso, Empresa Nacional de Autocamiones SA, Defence Division, Avenida de Aragón 402, E-28022 Madrid, Spain.
Tel: (1) 750 1000. Telex: 46 972 maba e.
Fax: (1) 747 1307.

Pegaso Model 7217 (4 × 4) 4000 kg cargo truck

Pegaso Model 7217 (4 × 4) 4000 kg cargo truck

Pegaso 3050 (6 × 6) 6000 kg Cargo Truck

Description
The Pegaso 3050 (6 × 6) 6000 kg cargo truck was developed from the earlier Pegaso 3040 (4 × 4) 4000 kg truck and uses the same cab as the Pegaso 3045 (4 × 4) 3000 kg truck. The two-door forward control cab is of steel construction with a tarpaulin roof that can fold back and a windscreen which folds forward onto the radiator. The rear cargo area is all steel and has a drop tailgate, seven removable bows and a tarpaulin cover. Most vehicles have a 6000 kg capacity winch.

Variants
These include a bridging vehicle (for carrying components of the MAN bridge), a dump truck, two recovery vehicles (one with a Bazán Onara crane, one with an IASA crane), shop/van and tractor truck. A Pegaso 3050 was used as a prototype launcher for the Teruel artillery rocket. Forty rockets were carried and the vehicle had an enlarged armoured cab with two rows of seats for the crew.

Basic specifications of the Pegaso 3040 are: weight loaded, road 12 000 kg; weight loaded, cross-country 9000 kg; unladen weight 5000 kg; length 6.78 m; width 2.45 m; height overall 3.2 m; and powered by a six-cylinder diesel engine developing 125 bhp. The Pegaso 3040 is used in small numbers by the Spanish Army and some were sold to the Nigerian Army. The 3040 has a hard-top cab and the earlier 3020 is similar but with a soft-top cab.

Specifications
Cab seating: 1 + 1
Configuration: 6 × 6
Weight:
  (empty) 8500 kg
  (loaded, cross-country) 14 500 kg
Max load:
  (road) 10 000 kg
  (cross-country) 6000 kg
Towed load:
  (road) 14 500 kg
  (cross-country) 7500 kg
Length: 7.2 m
Width: 2.5 m
Height: (cab) 2.64 m
Ground clearance: 0.32 m
Track: 1.9 m
Wheelbase: 3.987 m + 1.426 m
Angle of approach/departure: 48°/44°
Max speed: (road) 68 km/h
Range: 500 km
Fuel capacity: 250 l
Max gradient: 89% (low-range, bottom gear)

Fording: 1 m
Engine: Pegaso model 910/40 6-cylinder in-line diesel developing 170 hp at 2000 rpm
Gearbox: manual with 6 forward and 1 reverse gears
Transfer box: 2-speed
Steering: power-assisted
Suspension:
  (front) semi-elliptical springs and hydraulic shock absorbers
  (rear) oscillating arms and spring common to both axles. Rear axles joined to chassis frame by torsion bars
Tyres: 13.00 × 20
Brakes:
  (main) air/hydraulic
  (parking) mechanical
Electrical system: 24 V
Batteries: 2 × 12 V, 175 Ah

Status
In service with Spanish forces and Nigeria.

Manufacturer
Pegaso, Empresa Nacional de Autocamiones SA, Defence Division, Avenida de Aragón, 402 – E28022 Madrid, Spain.
Tel: (1) 750 1000. Telex: 46 972 maba e.
Fax: (1) 747 1307.

Pegaso 3050 (6 × 6) 6000 kg cargo truck

Pegaso 3050 (6 × 6) recovery vehicle

Pegaso 3055 and Model 7323 (6 × 6) 6000 kg Trucks

Description
The Pegaso 3055 is a 6 × 6 derivative of the Pegaso 3046 (4 × 4) truck. In March 1982 it was announced that the Pegaso 3055 was to be the standard 6000 kg off-road truck chassis for all three Spanish armed services.

The cab of the Pegaso 3055 is the same as that used on the Pegaso 3046. It has a canvas hood as standard with an optional metal top. The cab has seating for the driver and one passenger and if required the hood can be removed and the windscreen folded forward over the short bonnet. The main load-carrying area is at the rear and on the standard cargo/personnel body there is bench seating for 30 men. The engine fitted may have either a 200 hp or 220 hp output, with the latter selected for use with the Spanish armed forces.

The Pegaso 3055 was produced in the following versions: medium truck; medium fuel tanker; medium water tanker; heavy crane; medium tipper truck; firefighting vehicle; tractor; van body for workshops, stores, refrigerated bodies and so on. A tractor truck for use as a tank transporter is in service.

The Pegaso 3055 can be used as an artillery tractor or Teruel artillery rocket launcher (for details refer to *Jane's Armour and Artillery 1992-93* pages 740 to 741) and may be used to carry engineering stores such as bridging components. A 6000 kg winch may be fitted.

The current version of the Pegaso 3055 is the longer-wheelbased Model 7323 powered by a Pegaso 225 hp naturally aspirated diesel engine. The Model 7323 replaced the Model 3055 in production in 1987 (the prototype was completed in 1986) and during 1987 and 1988 more than 1000 units were delivered to Morocco. The Model 7323 is produced as an artillery tractor, a fuel or water tanker, a recovery vehicle with a crane, a mobile workshop, an ambulance, a firefighting vehicle, a tipper and as a multiple rocket launcher carrier. Optional extras include a hard-top cab, a power take-off, run-flat tyres and a 4500 kg winch.

Specifications
(data in square brackets apply to the Model 7323 where it differs from the Pegaso 3055)
Cab seating: 1 + 1 (30 in rear)
Configuration: 6 × 6
Weight:
  (empty) 9000 [9700] kg

Pegaso Model 7323 (6 × 6) 6000 kg truck

(loaded, on road) 19 000 [19 700] kg
(loaded, off road) 15 000 [15 700] kg
Max payload:
(on road) 10 000 kg
(off road) 6000 kg
Towed load:
(on road) 14 500 kg
(off road) 7500 kg
Length: (cab and chassis) 6.956 [7.483] m
Width:
(cab) 2.4 m
(rear wheels) 2.406 m
Height: (cab) 2.71 [2.8] m
Ground clearance: 0.34 [0.32] m
Track: 1.96 [1.93] m
Wheelbase: 3.245 m + 1.484 m [3.7 m + 1.484 m]
Angle of approach/departure: 47°/50°
Max speed: 80 [90] km/h
Range: 550 km

Fuel capacity: 350 l [360 l – 200, 400 and 560 l optional]
Max gradient: 51% [60%]
Side slope: 30%
Fording: 1.1 m [1.9 m with preparation]
Engine: Pegaso model 9220/10 6-cylinder, in-line, 10.518 l 4-stroke, turbocharged diesel developing 200 or 220 hp at 2000 rpm
[Pegaso 10.52 l 6-cylinder naturally aspirated diesel developing 225 hp at 2000 rpm]
Gearbox: Pegaso Model 8256.10.09 manual with 6 forward and 1 reverse gears [ZF with 6 forward and 1 reverse gears]
Transfer box: Pegaso [ZF] pneumatic 2-speed
Clutch: Model 8500.01 single dry disc
Steering: recirculating ball, power-assisted
Turning radius: 10.2 [11.1] m
Suspension:
(front) semi-elliptical leaf springs and telescopic

shock absorbers
(rear) semi-elliptical leaf springs
Tyres: 13.00 × 20 or 14.00 × 20
Brakes: dual circuit air
Electrical system: 24 V
Batteries: 2 × 12 V, 105 Ah
Alternator: 840 [1300] W

Status
Pegaso 3055 production complete. In service with the Spanish armed forces. Model 7323 in production for the Spanish and Moroccan armed forces.

Manufacturer
Pegaso, Empresa Nacional de Autocamiones SA, Defence Division, Avenida de Aragón, 402 – E28022 Madrid, Spain.
Tel: (1) 750 1000. Telex: 46 972 maba e.
Fax: (1) 747 1307.

SWEDEN

Volvo 4140 Series of 4 × 4 and 6 × 6 Cross-country Vehicles

Development
In the early 1960s the Swedish Army Materiel Department drew up its requirements for a new generation of tactical vehicles for the 1970s and 1980s. In 1966 Volvo was awarded the development contract for the Class 1 and 2 vehicles in the 1000 to 2500 kg range and SAAB-Scania the contract for the heavier Class 3 and 4 vehicles, subsequently known as the Scania SBA (4 × 4) and SBAT (6 × 6).

Primary requirements were a high power-to-weight ratio, forward control cab, good angle of approach and departure, high ground clearance, tough suspension, chassis which could be adapted to accept a wide variety of bodies, commercial components to be used wherever possible, ease of repair and maintenance, low training requirement and a minimum total service life cost.

During the development stage it was decided to increase the payload of the 4 × 4 version to 2000 kg and of the 6 × 6 model to 2500 kg. An 8 × 8 version was developed to the prototype stage but was not placed in production.

Description
(4 × 4) 4140/4141 (or C303)
The first prototypes completed in 1966 were powered by a B-20 (94 hp) engine which was subsequently replaced by the more powerful B-30 (145 hp) engine. First deliveries were made to the Swedish Army in 1974.

Two basic models were built, the 4140 cargo and the 4141 fully enclosed, or hard-top. Both have a two-door fully enclosed cab which can be split above the waist line. The cargo model has an all-steel rear cargo area with a drop tailgate, removable bows and a tarpaulin cover. The hard-top model has a fully enclosed steel rear body with an aluminium roof, and a large door at the rear and a door in each side.

Specifications

Model	C303 hard-top	C304 chassis and cab	C306 chassis and cab
Cab seating	1 + 6	1 + 1	1 + 1
Configuration	4 × 4	4 × 4	6 × 6
Weight			
(empty)	2250 kg	1940 kg	2400 kg
(loaded)	3450 kg	3900 kg	5500 kg
Weight on front axle			
(loaded)	1650 kg	1800 kg	1000 kg
Weight on rear axles			
(loaded)	1800 kg	2100 kg	1800 kg
Max load	1200 kg	1960 kg (inc body)	3100 kg (inc body)
Towed load	2500 kg	2500 kg	2500 kg
Load area	2.25 × 1.8 m	n/app	n/app
Length	4.25 m	4.28 m	5.735 m
Width	1.9 m	1.87 m	1.88 m
Height			
(cab)	2.13 m	2.13 m	2.13 m
(load area)	0.83 m	n/app	n/app
Ground clearance	0.386 m	0.386 m	0.386 m
Track	1.54 m	1.54 m	1.54 m
Wheelbase	2.3 m	2.53 m	2.72 m + 1.05 m
Angle of approach/ departure	45°/45°	45°/45°	45°/40°
Max speed			
(road)	120 km/h	100 km/h	90 km/h
Fuel capacity	83 l	125 l	150 l
Max gradient	100%	100%	100%
Max side slope	40%	40%	40%
Fording			
(without preparation)	0.7 m	0.7 m	0.7 m
Engine	Volvo B-30 in-line 6-cylinder OHV petrol developing 125 hp at 4250 rpm		
Gearbox	all have manual gearbox with 4 forward and 1 reverse gears		
Clutch	single dry plate	single dry plate	single dry plate
Transfer box	2-speed	2-speed	2-speed
Steering	all cam and roller type		
Turning radius	5.77 m	5.73 m	8.25 m
Tyres	8.90 × 16	8.90 × 16	8.90 × 16
Electrical system	12 V	12 V	12 V
Battery	1 × 12 V, 60 Ah	1 × 12 V, 60 Ah	1 × 12 V, 60 Ah

Volvo 4143 (6 × 6) in configuration known as Tgb 211A (S Bengtson)

Volvo 4141 (4 × 4) fully enclosed version

All-wheel drive is engaged by a press-button in the high range and automatically when low range is engaged. Both front and rear axles have vacuum-operated mechanical differential locks which can be engaged separately or together. The chassis consists of box sidemembers with tubular crossmembers welded into position. The chassis is torsionally stiff to avoid stressing the superstructure.

The front suspension consists of underslung semi-elliptical leaf springs carried in rubber mountings, hollow-rubber springs and double-acting telescopic shock absorbers. The rear suspension consists of overslung semi-elliptical leaf springs carried in rubber mountings, hollow-rubber springs and double-acting telescopic shock absorbers. The main brakes are vacuum-hydraulic drum-type, dual circuit, with one vacuum cylinder per circuit.

The handbrake is mechanical and acts on the propeller shaft. Optional equipment includes an air-conditioning system, electric engine heater, electric compressor with 10 m of hose for pumping tyres, PTO, protective wooden floor ribs, roof ventilator, tow hook, trailer electrical socket, Webasto engine and passenger area heater and a 2200/3000 kg capacity winch. The basic model is fitted with a thermostatically controlled heater, defroster system and a two-speed blower in the cab with a heater and two-speed blower for the rear compartment.

The C304 (4 × 4) version is almost identical to the C303 but has a wheelbase of 2.53 m.

(6 × 6) 4143 (or C306)
The 6 × 6 model is based on the 4 × 4 model and has the same engine, gearbox, transfer box and cab. The vehicle can be fitted with a variety of bodies including cargo, fully enclosed and ambulance. The cargo model has drop sides, drop tailgate, removable bows and a tarpaulin cover. The fully enclosed body version has a large door in the rear and a door in each side, and can be used for a variety of roles including radio/command.

The front suspension consists of underslung semi-elliptical leaf springs, hollow-rubber springs and double-acting telescopic shock absorbers. The rear suspension is of the double cantilever type with parabolic springs with progressively acting hollow-rubber springs and double-acting telescopic shock absorbers. The main brakes are vacuum-hydraulic drum-type, with the mechanical parking brake operating on the transfer box output shaft. Optional equipment is similar to that available for the 4 × 4 version.

Status
Production complete. In service with the Swedish armed forces and Malaysia (4 × 4 and 6 × 6).

Manufacturer
Volvo Truck Corporation, S-405 08 Göteborg, Sweden. Tel: 46 31 66 60 00. Telex: 27000 volvo s. Fax: 46 31 51 04 65.

Volvo 4151 (4 × 4) Anti-tank Vehicle

Description
The Volvo 4151 was primarily designed to succeed the Volvo L3304 as an anti-tank and reconnaissance vehicle for the Swedish Army. It was not available on the civilian market.

The vehicle shares the mechanical components with the Volvo C303 (4 × 4) cross-country vehicle with a special superstructure supplied by Hägglunds in northern Sweden. This superstructure consists of a metal bodywork up to waist level, and an upper part made from canvas, which can be easily folded down when the 90 mm recoilless rifle is used. When travelling the gun is lowered, but it can easily be raised for use.

The engine is mounted in the forward part of the vehicle and while travelling the crew are protected by an anti-roll bar.

Specifications
In most respects, these are similar to those of the Volvo 4140/C303.

Status
Production complete. In service with the Swedish Army.

Volvo 4151 (4 × 4) anti-tank vehicle armed with a 106 mm recoilless rifle (C F Foss)

Manufacturer
Volvo Truck Corporation, S-405 08 Göteborg, Sweden.

Tel: 46 31 66 60 00. Telex: 27000 volvo s. Fax: 46 31 51 04 65.

Scania SBA 111 4500 kg (4 × 4) and SBAT 111S 6000 kg (6 × 6) Trucks

Development
In the early 1960s the Swedish Army Materiel Department drew up its requirements for a new generation of tactical vehicles for the 1970s and 1980s. Volvo was awarded the contract for the lighter Class 1 and 2 vehicles and Scania the contracts for the heavier Class 3 (4 × 4) and Class 4 (6 × 6) vehicles.

Scania started design work in 1966 and received its first development contract in 1968. Primary requirements of the Swedish Army were for a vehicle which would be easy to handle and maintain, use proved and standardised commercial components wherever possible, be reliable and have a low repair cost and finally have a low total service life cost. The first prototypes were completed early in 1971 with the second series of prototypes being completed late in 1972. The Swedish Army placed its first production order in 1974 for 2000 vehicles (both 4 × 4 and 6 × 6) at a total cost of SEK 225 million for delivery between 1976 and 1979. In 1977 a further 258 vehicles were ordered for the Swedish Air Force and Navy. A total of 2500 vehicles was delivered to the Swedish Army.

A modified version of the SBAT was produced for the Indian Army to tow Bofors 155 mm FH-77B howitzers.

Description
The layout of both vehicles is almost identical, the only major differences being in their engines and configurations. Ninety per cent of the components of both

'Indian Army' version of SBAT 111S 6000 kg (6 × 6) trucks

vehicles are interchangeable.

The chassis consists of two longitudinal U-shaped members with the crossmembers riveted into position.

The two-door forward control cab is all steel and has a hatch in the right side of the roof. The driver's windscreen is hinged at the top and can be opened

Specifications

Model	SBA 111	SBAT 111S
Cab seating	1 + 2	1 + 2
Configuration	4 × 4	6 × 6
Weight		
(empty)	9150 kg	11 650 kg
(loaded, cross-country)	13 700 kg	20 650 kg
Max load		
(cross-country)	4500 kg	6000 kg
(road)	6000 kg	9000 kg
Towed load	6000 kg	12 000 kg
Load area	4.2 × 2.35 m	4.75 × 2.35 m
Length	6.75 m	7.78 m
Width	2.48 m	2.48 m
Height		
(cab)	2.9 m	2.9 m
(load area)	1.472 m	1.472 m
Ground clearance	0.4 m	0.42 m
Track	2.02 m	2.02 m
Wheelbase	4 m	3.55 m + 1.48 m
Angle of approach/ departure	45°/40°	45°/40°
Max speed	85 km/h	85 km/h
Range (road)	600 km	550 km
Fuel capacity	167 l	167 l
Max gradient	60%	60%
Max side slope	40%	40%
Fording	0.8 m	0.8 m
Engine	D11 6-cylinder diesel developing 202 hp at 2200 rpm	DS11 (supercharged) 6-cylinder diesel developing 296 hp at 2200 rpm
Steering	hydraulic	hydraulic
Turning radius	9 m	10.3 m
Suspension	semi-elliptical springs with double-acting hydraulic shock absorbers	
Tyres	14.00 × 20	14.00 × 20
Brakes	air, dual circuit. Hand, spring type operating on front and rear wheels	
Electrical system	24 V	24 V

upward for improved visibility. The cab can be tilted forward to an angle of 55° with the aid of a double-acting hydraulic pump. The grille on the front of the cab opens upwards to allow access to the oil dipstick, oil filter and oil tank for daily checks.

The engines of the two vehicles differ only in that the SBAT (6 × 6) has a turbocharger. The engine is fitted with a special fuel pump which allows the engine to continue running when inclined at an angle of 35°.

The gearbox is of the automatic split type in which two-thirds of the power is always transmitted mechanically. The gearbox consists of the automatic gearbox, distributor gearbox and a torque converter. The main gearbox has six speeds, three hydraulic and three mechanical. The transfer box has one ratio for cross-country operations and another for road operations. Changing up or down to the gear that corresponds to the engine speed and torque requirements is automatic.

All axles on both trucks are identical and each axle has a central bevel gear, hub reduction gears and a differential lock.

The rear platform is torsionally rigid and the basic cargo models have removable drop sides and a drop tailgate.

Both vehicles have an 8000 kg capacity winch mounted on the right side of the chassis driven by a PTO on the transfer box and operated by a switch on the dashboard and a winch brake control in front of the steering wheel. The winch can be used to the front or rear of the vehicle.

Cold weather equipment includes an engine heater, battery heater, fuel pre-heater, starting pilot and connections for starting cables.

Variants

SBA (4 × 4)

This basic model was designed for carrying cargo but some were delivered to the Swedish Army with a 1500 kg hydraulic crane at the rear for unloading. Some have been fitted with bows, canvas cover and bench seats down each side for carrying passengers; others have a small hard-top crew shelter.

SBAT (6 × 6)

The basic model was designed for carrying cargo but other variants include a version with a 5500 kg hydraulic crane mounted to the rear of the cab, which is used for ammunition resupply for the Bofors 155 mm FH-77 howitzer and the 120 mm KARIN towed coast defence gun. The FH-77 and KARIN are towed by an SBAT truck fitted with a fully enclosed cabin for the ten-man crew at the forward end of the platform. Mounted at the rear of the vehicle is a 1500 kg hydraulic crane. A 6 × 6 recovery vehicle was built to the prototype stage but was not ordered by the Swedish Army. The

SBAT 111S (6 × 6) chassis carrying Giraffe radar system

6 × 6 version is used to carry the Giraffe radar system used in conjunction with the Bofors RBS 70 and RBS 90 SAM systems. In March 1989 the Swedish Defence Materiel Administration ordered 83 of these vehicles with options for more.

Crash rescue vehicles
Following trials with two prototype bodies the Swedish armed forces ordered 47 crash rescue vehicles for delivery in 1979. They have a loaded weight of 16 000 kg and are fitted with both firefighting and crash rescue equipment.

Snow-clearing vehicle
This version is based on the chassis of the SBA (4 × 4) truck and used by the Swedish Air Force for clearing snow from airfield runways. Forty-five of these vehicles were ordered at a cost of SEK 12 million. When being driven forward on the road the vehicle is driven from the normal driver's position, but when clearing snow it is driven in reverse from the second cab which faces the rear. Maximum speed when clearing snow is 30 km/h. Steering during snow-clearing operations is by a duplicated hydrostatic steering system which acts on the ordinary steering mechanism of the vehicle. The snow-clearing equipment fitted is a Rolba 1500S, which is of the cut and sling type and with a capacity of 30 to 35 000 kg of snow/minute.

Status

Production complete. In service with Finland (33 SBAs), India (660 SBATs ordered in 1986) and Sweden.

Manufacturer

SAAB-Scania, Scania Division, S-151 87 Södertälje, Sweden.
Tel: 46 8 553 810 00. Telex: 10200 scania s.

Volvo L 4854 and N86 (4 × 4) Trucks

Description

The Volvo L 4854 (4 × 4) truck is basically a standard production Viking truck modified to meet the requirements of the Swedish Army. The first prototype was completed in 1960 and the vehicle was in production for the Army between 1961 and 1963. The L 4854 is known as the Lastterrängbil 939 (cross-country truck) by the Army and is in service in three basic models, the 939 BF with a 5.2 m wheelbase, the 939 AF with a 4.4 m wheelbase and the 939 E with a 4.4 m wheelbase and a longer cab.

The layout of the vehicle is conventional with the engine at the front, cab in the centre and the cargo area at the rear. The two-door all-steel cab has an observation hatch in the roof, over which anti-aircraft machine guns can be mounted. The rear cargo area has drop sides and a drop tailgate. A winch with a capacity of 5000 kg mounted under the right side of the chassis can be used to the front or rear. Both front and rear axles have a hand-operated differential lock. Some L 4854s have been fitted with a HIAB crane to the rear of the cab for unloading.

The Volvo N86 is a later variant of the L 4854 produced only for the Swedish coast artillery and air force. It has a more powerful engine and a revised transmission.

The Swedish armed forces use over 20 variants of the basic L 4854 and more are added as existing vehicles are converted for various roles.

Specifications (L 4854)
Cab seating: 1 + 2
Configuration: 4 × 4
Weight:
(empty) 6720 kg
(loaded, cross-country) 9720 kg
Max load:
(road) 4500 kg
(cross-country) 3000 kg
Length: 7.5 m
Width: 2.28 m

Height: 2.82 m
Ground clearance: 0.25 m
Track:
  (front) 1.83 m
  (rear) 1.74 m
Wheelbase: 4.4 m
Angle of approach/departure: 38°/25°
Max speed: (road) 77 km/h
Range: 300 km
Fuel capacity: 120 l
Engine: Volvo D67C 6-cylinder diesel developing 125 hp at 2400 rpm
Gearbox: Volvo K17 manual with 5 forward and 1 reverse gears
Clutch: single dry plate
Transfer box: 2-speed
Steering: ZF power-assisted
Turning radius: 10 m
Tyres: 10.00 × 20

Status

Production complete. In service with the Swedish armed forces.

Manufacturer

Volvo Truck Corporation, S-405 08 Göteborg, Sweden.
Tel: 46 31 66 60 00. Telex: 27000 volvo s.
Fax: 46 31 51 04 65.

Volvo N86 (4 × 4) truck fitted with personnel shelter as used by coast artillery units

Scania-Vabis (4 × 2) L-36A and L-50 5920 kg Trucks

Description

The Scania-Vabis L-36A is the standard civilian model L 3642 (4 × 2) truck with a minimum of modifications to suit it for military use. A total of 800 were built for the Swedish Army between 1964 and 1967.

The layout of the L-36A is conventional with the engine at the front, all-steel fully enclosed cab in the centre and the cargo area at the rear with drop sides and a drop tailgate. Some vehicles have been fitted with a HIAB crane mounted to the rear of the cab for loading.

A fully enclosed mobile workshop version is in service under the designation of the Materielvardsbil 111. Scania-Vabis also delivered 1500 L50 series 4 × 2 vehicles to the Swedish Army with various bodies. The L-50 is based on the civilian L5042 (4 × 2) truck and has a wheelbase of 4.2 m. Basic specifications are: length 6.5 m; width 2.206 m; height (cab) 2.538 m; powered by a four-cylinder diesel developing 110 hp at 2400 rpm; and tyres 9.00 × 20.

Specifications

Cab seating: 1 + 2
Configuration: 4 × 2
Weight:
  (empty) 4580 kg
  (loaded) 10 500 kg
Max load: 5920 kg
Length: (chassis) 6.59 m
Width: 2.19 m
Height: (cab) 2.76 m
Ground clearance: 0.355 m
Track: 1.85 m
Wheelbase: 4.2 m
Angle of approach/departure: 36°/30°
Max speed: (road) 77 km/h
Range: 450 km
Fuel capacity: 100 l
Engine: Model D5 4-cylinder diesel developing 102 bhp at 2400 rpm
Gearbox: manual model S-5-35 with 5 forward and 1 reverse gears
Clutch: single dry plate
Steering: cam and triple roller
Turning radius: 7.3 m

Suspension:
  (front) semi-elliptical springs and double-acting hydraulic shock absorbers
  (rear) semi-elliptical springs
Tyres: 8.25 × 20
Brakes:
  (main) air
  (parking) mechanical
Electrical system: 24 V
Batteries: 2 × 12 V

Status

Production complete. In service with the Swedish Army.

Manufacturer

Scania-Vabis, now SAAB-Scania, S-151 87 Södertälje, Sweden.
Tel: 46 8 553 810 00. Telex: 10200 scania s.

Scania-Vabis (4 × 2) L-36A 5920 kg truck

Scania-Vabis (4 × 2) L-50 5920 kg truck (C F Foss)

Scania Trucks

Description

The Scania Division of SAAB-Scania builds an extensive range of heavy trucks with a gross vehicle weight of 16 tonnes and upwards, and by drawing on a range of standardised modules a large number of truck models and variants can be built using a strictly limited selection of standard components.

The Scania truck range is powered by three basic diesel engine models with capacities of 8.5, 11 and 14.2 litres. These power plants are available in turbocharged and naturally aspirated variants. The Scania truck engine range features nine engine types covering a power range from 210 to 500 bhp in closely stepped increments.

Three different chassis strength classes are available (M, H and E) with several axle configurations in each class. There is also a range of transmission options such as a manual gearbox with torque converter, a fully automatic transmission, hub reduction and all-wheel drive.

There is also a wide range of cab options of two major types, forward control (P and R) and bonneted (T).

There are about 250 Scania chassis variants including several all-wheel drive off-road models. Gross vehicle weights range from 17 000 kg up to 46 000 kg. Many of the models are all-wheel driven for cross-country operation.

Scania has delivered a large number of special vehicles both to military and civilian customers. Among the former are the Norwegian armed forces, who ordered 1700 Scania vehicles of different types in 1986 at a cost of SEK 750 million. These included the P93 M (4 × 4), the P113 H (6 × 6) and the R143EK (6 × 6) tank transporter. Vehicles are delivered as chassis from Scania with bodies fitted by Norsk Scania-Vabis A/S in Norway. Deliveries will continue until 1994. A total of 255 Scania T 113 HK (6 × 6) trucks plus spare parts were ordered by the Brazilian ENGESA concern. They received locally produced vehicles from Scania's Brazilian subsidiary, provided them with new coachwork and delivered them to Angola. The order was worth SEK 120 million.

One further model is the Scania P113 HK 8 × 6 which is on test with the Swedish and Norwegian armies carrying a Multilift DROPS load handling system. This model has a GVW of 34 000 kg and is powered by a DS11 75 six-cylinder turbocharged diesel developing 310 hp at 2000 rpm.

The data provided in the tables may be taken as typical for only a small portion of the full Scania truck range.

Manufacturer

SAAB-Scania, S-151 87 Södertälje, Sweden.
Tel: 46 8 553 810 00. Telex: 10200 scania s.

Specifications

Model	P93 MK 4 × 4-5T	P93 MK 4 × 4-8T	P93 HK 4 × 4 + 2/S42	P113 HK (6 × 6)
Purpose	truck	truck	bridge carrier	truck, desert version
Cab seating	1 + 2	1 + 2	1 + 2	1 + 2
Configuration	4 × 4	4 × 4	6 × 4	6 × 6
Weight (empty)	9300 kg	9500 kg	13 360 kg	13 400 kg
Max load	5000 kg	8000 kg	11 140 kg	11 540 kg
Length	7 m	8.56 m	8.41 m	7.6 m
Width (loaded)	2.48 m	2.48 m	3.4 m	2.66 m
Height	3.3 m	3.28 m	3.34 m	3.4 m
Ground clearance				
(front)	0.41 m	0.4 m	0.4 m	0.4 m
(rear)	0.41 m	0.335 m	0.285 m	0.335 m
Track				
(front)	2.02 m	2.03 m	2.03 m	2.03 m
(rear)	2.02 m	2.03 m	1.83 m	2.03 m
Wheelbase	4 m	4.6 m	4.6 m + 1.315 m	3.55 m + 1.35 m
Angle of approach/ departure	34°/41°	33°/23°	n/a	n/a
Max speed	90 km/h	105 km/h	90 km/h	90 km/h
Engine type	DS9 diesel	DS9 diesel	DS9 diesel	DS11 diesel
Engine power/rpm	252 hp/2200 rpm	252 hp/2200 rpm	252 hp/2200 rpm	310 hp/2000 rpm
Gearbox	5-speed	5-speed	5-speed	10-speed
Tyres	14.00 × 20	14.00 × 20	13 × 22.5 12.00 × 20	20.00 × 20 rib

Scania P93 M (4 × 4) trucks

Scania P113 HK (8 × 6) truck carrying a Multilift DROPS load handling system

Volvo N10/N12 (6 × 6) Trucks

Description

The Volvo N10 and N12 6 × 6 trucks are heavy duty commercial vehicles that can be used for military purposes. They are produced in both 4 × 4 and 6 × 6 forms but to date the 6 × 6 versions are the only ones known to have been adopted for military use. There is also a choice of rigid rear axles or a Volvo T-ride bogie on 6 × 6 models. The main difference between the two models is that the N10 has a turbocharged and inter-cooled engine while that on the N12 lacks the inter-cooling.

The layout of the N10/N12 is conventional with the engine located forward under a squared-off bonnet, the cab having seating for the driver and at least one passenger, and with the cargo area to the rear. Some vehicles are fitted with a handling crane just behind the cab and the all-steel cargo body has drop sides and a tailgate. Three wheelbase lengths are available, 4.835 m, 5.235 m, and 5.635 m, and there are various chassis lengths.

Gross vehicle weights vary between 16 500 kg to 19 500 kg for the 4 × 4 models and 26 500 kg to 33 500 kg for the 6 × 6 models.

Belgium adopted the N10, with local production being carried out in Belgium by Hocke at Alsemberg. A total of 1228 units will be procured. Of these 683 will be cargo trucks, 78 will have enclosed bodies for offices, maintenance, and so on, 133 will have tipper bodies, 40 units will have the Bennes Amplirol load handling system, 145 will be equipped as recovery vehicles, and

Belgian Army Volvo N10 (6 × 6) truck with cargo body (C R Zwart)

Belgian Army Volvo N10 (6 × 6) truck fitted with crane for use as ammunition resupply vehicle (C R Zwart)

20 will have bodies for the medical services. Manumat cranes fitted to Belgian vehicles have a capacity of 1100 kg and a reach of 5.6 m.

Specifications (N10 6 × 6)
Cab seating: 1 + 1 or 2
Configuration: 6 × 6
Weight: (basic chassis, 5.235 m wheelbase) 9155 kg
Max payload, including superstructure: 17 345 kg
Length: (chassis) 7.992 m
Width: (overall) 2.4 m
Height: (cab) 3.02 m

Wheelbase: 5.235 m
Fuel capacity: 300 l
Engine: 9.6 l 6-cylinder turbocharged and inter-cooled diesel developing 275 hp at 2200 rpm
Gearbox: R1400, 8 forward (plus crawler) and 2 reverse gears
Clutch: KFD214A twin dry plate
Transfer box: FD6 2-speed
Steering: ball and nut, power-assist
Suspension: leaf springs and hydraulic shock absorbers front and rear
Tyres: 12.00 R 20, 14.00 R 20 or 12.00 R 24

Brakes: dual circuit air
Electrical system: 24 V

Status
In production. In service with the Belgian Army (1228 ordered).

Manufacturer
Volvo Truck Corporation, S-405 08 Göteborg, Sweden. Tel: 46 31 66 60 00. Telex: 27000 volvo s. Fax: 46 31 51 04 65.

SWITZERLAND

Bucher DURO (4 × 4) and (6 × 6) Trucks

Description
Development of the Bucher DURO (4 × 4) and (6 × 6) trucks began in 1979 and (4 × 4) prototypes were produced during 1985. The (6 × 6) version was announced in October 1986. Prototypes were tested by the Defence Technology and Procurement Agency of the Swiss Military Department. The vehicle was originally known as the Puma. DURO stands for Dauerhaft, Unabhängig, Robust, Oekonomisch – Durable, Self-reliant, Robust, Economic.

Bucher DURO (4 × 4) and (6 × 6) trucks are constructed using a low-slung, torsion-free chassis with an integral roll stabiliser. The frame is of the ladder type and tubular. Both vehicles use a forward control cab of aluminium construction with reinforced plastic panels. There is seating for the driver and two passengers. Wide-vision windows are provided for all cab occupants and the entire cab can be tilted forward for maintenance access. The rear platform is of aluminium construction with provision for bench seats along each side and there is provision for the body to be covered by a tarpaulin carried on sliding bows. There is space at the rear to carry four or six standard pallets. A 2000 kg trailer may be towed.

The engine for all three models is a Ford 4 litre V-6 with electronic fuel injection although options include a 147 hp six-cylinder or 118 hp four-cylinder diesel engine. An automatic transmission with a torque converter is used. There is permanent all-wheel drive with Torson self-locking differentials. Steering is power-assisted. De Dion rigid axles with patented roll stabilisers are fitted and the hydraulic disc brakes operate with Y-type braking effort distribution. The wheel geometry remains stable under braking conditions and there is no brake fading and no cleaning of brakes after fording.

Two 4 × 4 models are available, one with a 1500 kg capacity and the other being a 2200 kg vehicle. The 6 × 6 model has a 2200 kg capacity.

It is proposed that DURO trucks will be produced in cargo-carrying, personnel or shelter carrier and

Specifications

Model	4 × 4 1.5 t	6 × 6 2 t	4 × 4 2 t
Cab seating	1 + 2	1 + 2	1 + 2
Configuration	4 × 4	6 × 6	4 × 4
Weight			
(cab and chassis)	2400 kg	2800 kg	2700 kg
(total)	4700 kg	5800 kg	5800 kg
Max load	1500 kg	2200 kg	2200 kg
Towed load	2000 kg	2000 kg	2000 kg
Load area inside length	2.61 m	3.74 m	3.74 m
Length	4.74 m	5.87 m	5.87 m
Width	1.96 m	1.96 m	1.96 m
Height (unloaded)	2.55 m	2.55 m	2.55 m
Ground clearance	0.36 m	0.36 m	0.36 m
Track	1.67 m	1.67 m	1.67 m
Wheelbase	2.9 m	2.9 m + 1.13 m	3.8 m
Angle of approach/departure	46°/40°	46°/40°	46°/35°
Max speed	100 km/h	100 km/h	100 km/h
Fuel capacity	100 l	100 l	100 l
Max gradient	100%	80%	80%
Fording	0.76 m	0.76 m	0.76 m
Engine	Ford 4 l V-6 water-cooled with electronic fuel injection developing 161 hp at 4500 rpm		
Transmission	DB W4A 028 automatic with torque converter with 4 forward speeds and 1 reverse		
Transfer box	2-speed	2-speed	2-speed
Steering	ZF power-assist	ZF power-assist	ZF power-assist
Turning radius	12 m	14 m	n/av
Suspension	coil spring with gas pressure shock absorber and roll stabiliser		
Tyres	10.5 R 20	10.5 R 20	10.5 R 20
Brakes	hydraulic disc	hydraulic disc	hydraulic disc
Electrical system	24 V	24 V	24 V

Bucher DURO (6 × 6) 2000 kg truck (right) with (4 × 4) 1500 kg truck (left)

Bucher DURO (4 × 4) 1500 kg truck

Status
Ready for production.

Manufacturer
Bucher-Guyer Limited, Engineering Works, CH-8166, Niederweningen/Zurich, Switzerland.
Tel: 01 857 22 11. Telex: 53199 bgnwg ch.
Fax: 01 857 22 49.

ambulance forms. Other versions proposed include a command and communications vehicle, mobile workshops, a firefighting vehicle and an NBC decontamination vehicle.

Options include an extra cab seat, various tyre types and an exhaust retarder.

It is claimed that the DURO's design would permit local production at relatively low cost for medium production quantities.

Saurer 2DM and Berna 2VM (4 × 4) 4500 kg Trucks

Description
These vehicles were in production for the Swiss Army from 1964 to 1973 and are identical apart from their nameplates. The layout of the vehicles is conventional with the engine at the front, two-door fully enclosed cab in the centre, with a circular observation hatch in the left side of the roof, and the cargo area at the rear with drop sides, drop tailgate, removable bows and a tarpaulin cover. Standard equipment includes a 6000 kg capacity winch with 55 m of cable.

There are two variants in service: two types of tipper truck and a tractor truck for hauling semi-trailers.

Further development by Saurer resulted in the D180N (4 × 4) truck which can carry 9000 kg of cargo on roads or 5000 kg of cargo across country and is powered by a 180 hp diesel with the option of installing a 230 or 250 hp diesel. Deliveries of the D180N were made to the Middle East and South America.

Specifications
Cab seating: 1 + 2
Configuration: 4 × 4
Weight:
(empty) 6900 kg
(loaded) 12 000 kg
Max load: 4900 kg
Load area: 4.1 × 2.18 m
Length: 7.37 m
Width: 2.3 m
Height: 3.2 m
Ground clearance: 0.27 m
Track:
(front) 1.898 m
(rear) 1.711 m
Wheelbase: 4.2 m

Saurer 2DM (4 × 4) 4500 kg truck

Angle of approach/departure: 34°/30°
Max speed: (road) 75 km/h
Fuel capacity: 160 l
Fuel consumption: 35 l/100 km
Engine: Saurer CT3D (or Berna T3) 6-cylinder diesel developing 135 hp at 2200 rpm
Gearbox: manual with 8 forward and 2 reverse gears
Transfer box: 2-speed
Turning radius: 8.51 m
Tyres: 9.00 × 20
Brakes: air + exhaust retarder

Electrical system: 24 V
Batteries: 2 × 12 V

Status
Production complete. In service with the Swiss Army.

Manufacturers
Adolph Saurer Limited, CH-9320 Arbon, Switzerland.
Berna AG, Olten, Bern, Switzerland.

Saurer 6 DM (4 × 4) 6000 kg and 10 DM (6 × 6) 10 000 kg Trucks

Description

During the late 1970s Adolph Saurer Limited started the development of a new family of 6000 and 10 000 kg trucks to meet the requirements of the Swiss Army. The first prototypes, the D250MF (4 × 4) and D3000MF (6 × 6) were completed in 1978. They were subsequently redesignated the 6 DM (4 × 4) and 10 DM (6 × 6). By late 1981 the vehicles had been tested by the Swiss Army and production commenced soon after.

Both vehicles share many common components, including the engine. Both have a two-door fully enclosed all-steel forward control cab with a circular observation hatch in the roof. The rear cargo area is provided with removable drop sides and a drop tailgate, removable bows and a tarpaulin cover. A 10 000 kg capacity hydraulic winch can be fitted.

The chassis is semi-flexible with independent leaf spring suspension with telescopic dampers, with all axles being fitted with differential locks. On both vehicles the front and rear axles are interchangeable.

In-service variants include a 6 × 6 Ribbon Bridge carrier and a crane version.

Status

In service with the Swiss armed forces.

Manufacturer

Adolph Saurer Limited, CH-9320 Arbon, Switzerland.

Specifications

Model	6 DM	10 DM
Configuration	4 × 4	6 × 6
Weight (empty)	10 000 kg	12 000 kg
(loaded)	16 000 kg	22 000 kg
Max load	6000 kg	10 000 kg
Length	7.705 m	8.905 m
Width	2.5 m	2.5 m
Height (cab)	3.335 m	3.46 m
Ground clearance	0.38 m	0.38 m
Wheelbase	4.35 m	4 m + 1.4 m
Track	2.1 m	2.1 m
Angle of approach/departure	40°/40°	40°/40°
Fuel capacity	300 l	300 l
Fording	1.15 m	1.15 m
Engine	Saurer D4KT 6-cylinder in line 4-stroke turbocharged diesel developing 250 hp at 2200 rpm	
Gearbox	ZF S-6 90 with torque converter, retarder and splitter group	
Transfer box	ZF A 800 3D electro-pneumatically lockable	
Turning radius	8.75 m	9.75 m
Axles	Saurer with lockable bevel gear differential	
Tyres	14.00 × 20	14.00 × 20
Brakes (main)	air, dual circuit	air, dual circuit
Electrical system	24 V	24 V

Saurer 10 DM (6 × 6) 10 000 kg truck

TURKEY

MANAS 16.210 FAE (4 × 4) 7500 kg and 26.281 DFAE 13 800 kg Trucks

Description

These heavy duty trucks were originally developed by the German MAN Nutzfahrzeuge AG to meet requirements for front line logistic supply vehicles capable of crossing rough terrain. The two vehicles share many components with the main difference between the two, apart from the differing drive configurations, being the engines. The 16.210 FAE (4 × 4) vehicle is fitted with a MAN D 2565 9.51 litre diesel developing 210 hp (SAE) at 2200 rpm. The 26.281 DFAE (6 × 6) has an 11.41 litre supercharged engine, the MAN D 2566 MKF, developing 308 hp (SAE) at 2200 rpm.

The two vehicles share the same all-steel cab with seating for the driver and two passengers. A roof hatch is provided. The cab can be tilted forward for maintenance. The chassis has longitudinal members of pressed U-profile made of high quality steel. Cross-members are fixed to the main members by rivets or bolts. There is a tow pin at the front and a NATO-type tow hook at the rear; electrical and brake circuits are

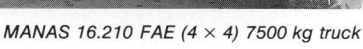

MANAS 16.210 FAE (4 × 4) 7500 kg truck

MANAS 26.281 DFAE (6 × 6) 13 800 kg truck

provided for trailers. A cable winch is located at the centre of the vehicle between the frame members. It has a 5 tonnes pull capacity to the front and 10 tonnes to the rear. The winch has 65 m of cable.

The body is steel and covered with a tarpaulin. Swing-open side and rear walls are provided. A tool box and steps are provided at the rear and there is stowage for extra fuel canisters. A swing-out spare wheel carrier is located behind the cab.

Tipper truck, tanker, snowplough and firefighting versions of both vehicles are available.

Status
In production.

Manufacturer
MAN Kamyon Ve Otobüs AS, Cirpici Yolu 10, Tokapi, Istanbul, Turkey.
Tel: (11) 567 0710. Telex: 22 367 man tr.

Specifications

Model	16.210 FAE	26.281 DFAE
Cab seating	1 + 2	1 + 2
Configuration	4 × 4	6 × 6
Weight (empty)	8930 kg	11 670 kg
(GVW)	16 500 kg	25 500 kg
Max load	7570 kg	13 830 kg
Towed load	15 500 kg	21 000 kg
Length	7.45 m	8.6 m
Width	2.5 m	2.5 m
Height (top of cab)	3.05 m	3.05 m
Ground clearance	0.433 m	0.433 m
Track (front/rear)	2.06 m/2.087 m	2.06 m/2.087 m
Wheelbase	4.2 m	3.825 m + 1.4 m
Angle of approach/departure	33°/35°	33°/33°
Max speed	78 km/h	78 km/h
Range	1000 km	970 km
Fuel capacity	300 l	300 l
Max gradient	60%	60%
Fording	1 m	1 m
Engine	see text	see text
Gearbox	6 forward, 1 reverse	8 forward, 1 reverse
Clutch	single dry plate	single dry plate
Transfer box	G450, 2-speed	GF 420, 2-speed
Steering	ZF 8046	ZF 8046
Tyres	14.00-20 × 18 PR	14.00-20 × 18 PR
Brakes	dual circuit air	dual circuit air
Electrical system	24 V	24 V
Batteries	2 × 12 V, 120 Ah	2 × 12 V, 150 Ah
Alternator	980 W	980 W

UNITED KINGDOM

HUGO (6 × 6) 1500 kg All Terrain Vehicle

Description
Developed from the HUGO (8 × 8) All Terrain Vehicle (see following entry), the HUGO 6 × 6 vehicle uses the same Perkins Phaser 110T 4 litre turbocharged diesel engine coupled to a Land Rover five-speed manual synchromesh gearbox. This vehicle is in service with Portuguese Army paratroop units where it is used to tow a 120 mm mortar while carrying a crew of six and 1 tonne of stores.

The chassis is formed from high press steel box sections, with four box-section crossmembers; the front crossmember forming a strengthened beam at the front end of the vehicle. The hull is mild steel with the driver and co-driver seated over the forward axle on either side of the engine. The vehicle carries a

1500 kg payload both on and off the road. A high load roll cage structure is integral to the vehicle which can be lifted on the roll cage. Steering, using many Land Rover components, is on the front axle.

The vehicle carries the driver and passenger with an optional removable frame seat for eight men. The vehicle can wade fast through 1 m deep water and breathes through a high level air intake. Side loading ramps are standard. Land Rover Defender 110 axles are fitted with automatically engaged cross-axle locks on the two non-steering axles. The vehicle is airportable by a CH-47D or C-130. High flotation tyres offer low ground pressure and high tractability off roads.

Optional extras include a NATO rotating tow hook, an electric winch and a hydraulic power take-off.

Specifications
Seating: 1 + 1 (up to 8 on platform)
Configuration: 6 × 6
Weight: 2740 kg
Ground pressure: (loaded) 0.35 bar
Payload: (standard) 1500 kg
Load area dimensions: 2.2 × 2 m
Length: 4.32 m
Width: 2 m
Height:
(overall) 2.25 m
(cargo bed) 1.075 m
Ground clearance: 0.215 m
Track: 1.603 m
Angle of approach/departure: 45°/45°
Max speed: (road) 109 km/h
Fuel capacity: 80 l
Gradient: 45°
Fording: 1 m
Vertical obstacle: 0.45 m
Trench: 1 m
Engine: Perkins Phaser 110T 4 l 4-cylinder in-line water-cooled turbocharged diesel developing 110 bhp at 2600 rpm
Transmission: manual with 5 synchromesh forward and 1 reverse gears
Transfer box: 2 × 2-speed, one to axles 1 and 3, one to axle 2
Steering: front axle, power-assisted
Turning circle: (kerbs) 11.1 m
Suspension: long travel coil springs, axles located by radius arms with Panhard rods
Tyres: 31 × 15.5 8PR
Brakes: servo-assisted drum all round; transmission handbrake operating on first transfer box
Electrical system: 12 V
Battery: 1 × 12 V, 60 Ah
Alternator: 65 Ah

Status
In service with Portuguese Army (6).

Manufacturer
HUGO All Terrain Vehicles Limited, PO Box 2, Guildford, Surrey GU3 3EH, UK.
Tel: 0483 60516. Fax: 0483 502234.

HUGO (6 × 6) 1500 kg All Terrain Vehicle

HUGO (8 × 8) 2000 kg All Terrain Vehicle

Description

The HUGO (High Utility, Global Operation) 8 × 8 All Terrain Vehicle was extensively developed from the original ESARCO design (for details refer to *Jane's Military Logistics 1989* page 508). While retaining a substantial use of Land Rover components in the suspension, axles and transfer boxes, the engine is now a Perkins Phaser turbocharged diesel coupled to a specially developed Chrysler automatic gearbox.

The chassis was substantially modified to create a robust four-box section, with stronger crossmembers, carrying the axle suspension, engine and body components. The hull is mild steel and both body and hull are extensively corrosion treated, with a further layer of wear resistant paint.

This forward control vehicle has a robust steering layout and utilises a strong built-in roll cage in the four-door, four-seat cab. An occasional seat is available between the rear seats and the cab. Full safety harness is fitted all round.

The front axle is heavily reinforced and the front and rear axles both steer, giving the vehicle great agility off road and directional stability on road. All axles can be locked together using differential locks in the two transfer boxes. The central non-steering pair of axles can also engage a lock on the differential which is selectable and de-selectable, both on the move or stationary.

There is a fully redesigned electrical system allowing easy access to fuses, relays, and so on, from within the cab. The vehicle can fast wade unprepared in over 1 m of water. Disc brakes are fitted all round and are operated by twin servos. Heating/demisting is by use of a fuel burning heater, allowing the heater to be used with the engine switched off. Air-conditioning is an option.

The vehicle will carry 2000 kg both on and off roads, and can tow an additional 2000 kg at the same time. The vehicle can be self-loading with an optional rear-mounted crane and the load deck, which is completely flat, can have a variety of body types, including ambulance, canvas tilt and frame, mobile workshop, hydraulic lift bucket for servicing overhead cables, and other specialised equipment.

HUGO (8 × 8) 2000 kg All Terrain Vehicle

The HUGO was granted full UK type approval during 1991 and is thus certified for unrestricted general use on public highways.

Specifications

Cab seating: 1 + 3 or 4 (up to 10 in rear)
Configuration: 8 × 8
Weight:
(empty) 3550 kg
(loaded) 5550 kg
Max load: 2000 kg
Towed load: 2000 kg
Load area: 2.77 × 2.2 m
Length: 5.37 m
Width: 2.2 m
Height:
(cab/roll bar) 2.36 m
(cargo bed, unladen) 1.17 m
Ground clearance: (under differentials) 0.268 m
Track: 1.779 m
Angle of approach/departure: 45°/45°
Max speed: (road, unladen) 113 km/h
Range: (road) 960 km
Fuel capacity: 136 l

Max gradient: 45°
Side slope: 30°
Fording: 1 m
Engine: Perkins Phaser 110T 4 l 4-cylinder turbocharged diesel developing 110 bhp at 2600 rpm
Gearbox: Chrysler 3-speed automatic
Transfer box: 2 × Land Rover LT230, 2-speed
Steering: Land Rover, power-assisted
Turning circle: (kerbs) 11.1 m
Suspension: coil springs all round with double-acting shock absorbers
Tyres: Trelleborg 305/75-16
Brakes: disc all round
Electrical system: 12 V
Battery: 12 V
Alternator: 60 A

Status

Development complete. Ready for production.

Manufacturer

HUGO All Terrain Vehicles Limited, PO Box 2, Guildford, Surrey GU3 3EH, UK.
Tel: 0483 60516. Fax: 0483 502234.

Stonefield Range of 4 × 4 and 6 × 4 Cross-country Vehicles

Development

The original Stonefield Vehicles was formed in 1974 to investigate the design of military and commercial cross-country vehicles. Its studies covered four main areas: chassis, transmission, suspension and brakes.

The first production 4 × 4 Stonefield vehicles were completed in mid-1978 and in December 1982 it was announced that Malaysia had placed a contract worth £14 million for Stonefield vehicles. The contract was completed in March 1986.

The original Stonefield Vehicles was taken over by Gomba Holdings and became Gomba Stonefield. In May 1986 three of the Gomba Holding companies were taken over to form Stonefield Holdings Limited with one of the companies becoming Stonefield Military Vehicles.

Description

There are two basic versions of the Stonefield range, a 4 × 4 and a 6 × 4, both with the same basic components such as engine and transmission.

The chassis is an all-welded structure of rectangular tubing of varying sizes, the side frame of which extends up to waist rail height. The wheel arches and engine

compartment are integral within the structure. All mountings for the road springs and other components are jig welded to the chassis. Two types of cab are available: a standard fully enclosed two-door cab constructed from square tubing and clad with aluminium panels; and an alternative utility waist level version, with tubular steel hood supports to take a canvas roof with detachable side windows and a fold-flat windscreen. The rear cargo area in the pick-up version has a drop tailgate and can be fitted with bows and a tarpaulin cover if required. Fully enclosed and specialised versions of the Stonefield were available.

The engine is beneath and to the rear of the cab. The transfer box has two speeds and three output shafts,

Stonefield P5000 (6 × 4) 2850 kg truck

Stonefield P5000M (4 × 4) 2000 kg truck

Specifications

Configuration	4 × 4	6 × 4		Configuration	4 × 4	6 × 4
Cab seating	1 + 1 or 2	1 + 1 or 2		Side slope	40°	40°
Weight				Fording	0.78 m	0.78 m
(empty)	2337 kg	2383 kg		Engine	Chrysler 318M V-8 water-cooled petrol	
(loaded)	4337 kg	5034 kg			developing 150 hp at 4000 rpm (other engines	
Max load	2000 kg	2850 kg			optional)	
Towed load	2500 kg	2500 kg		Transmission	Chrysler A727 3 speed automatic with transposer	
Length	4.99 m	5.445 m			box	
Width	1.9 m	1.9 m		Steering	recirculating ball and nut, manual or power	
Height	2.4 m	2.336 m		Turning circle	14.6 m	16.3 m
Ground clearance	0.255 m	0.24 m		Suspension	front and rear semi-elliptic multi-leaf	
Track	1.644 m	1.644 m			springs with hydraulic shock absorbers	
Wheelbase	2.8 m	2.575 m + 0.95 m		Tyres	9.00 × 16	9.00 × 16
Angle of approach/				Brakes	twin circuit vacuum hydraulic	
departure	45°/40°	45°/40°		Electrical system	12 V (or 24 V)	12 V (or 24 V)
Max speed	136 km/h	136 km/h		Battery	1 × 12 V, 68 Ah	1 × 12 V, 68 Ah
Fuel capacity	109 or 160 l	109 or 160 l		Alternator	60 A	60 A

one for each axle and one for a power take-off. The Chrysler engine is a Type 318M V-8 four-stroke petrol developing 150 bhp at 4000 rpm, coupled to a Chrysler A727 automatic transmission (three forward and one reverse gears) and a model A 777 torque converter. The transmission is allied to a unit known as a transposer box which uses two Morse chain drives to provide two speed ratios with a manual change. The transposer box also has a three-speed power take-off.

The third epicyclic differential gives a third of the power to the front wheels and two-thirds to the rear

wheels. This has two major advantages: it allows the transfer from hard to soft terrain without stopping to engage all-wheel drive, and it has an automatic lock-up device which passes power to all wheels when one loses surface adhesion.

Optional equipment includes an air-conditioning system, auxiliary fuel tanks, centrifuge and paper element air filter, external sun visor, flotation tyres, map light, radio, spot lights and directional beam lamps.

Both models were available in a range of forms. The

Malaysian contract was for personnel carriers, ambulances, mortar carriers, communication or command vehicles and general service cargo trucks.

Status

In service with the Malaysian Army.

Manufacturer

Stonefield Holdings Limited, Knight Road, Strood, Rochester, Kent ME2 2AT, UK.

Hotspur One Fifty (6 × 6) Vehicles

Description

The Hotspur One Fifty (6 × 6) light vehicle was formed by converting the Land Rover One Ten (now the Defender 110) to a 6 × 6 or 6 × 4 drive configuration and using V-8 petrol or turbocharged diesel engines. The Hotspur-designed heavy duty drive-through centre axle with a disengage mechanism and a Land Rover rear axle are positioned to carry a 3000 kg payload across country and over soft or difficult terrain. The One Fifty has 90 per cent spares commonality with established Land Rover models.

Optional equipment includes full air-conditioning, auxiliary fuel tanks, CS gas and smoke dischargers, radio equipment, a siren, automatic fire extinguishing equipment, power take-offs, a front-mounted winch, deluxe seating, and 9.00 × 16 run-flat tyres.

Applications for the One Fifty include raid intervention, fire rescue, light pump fire appliances, command vehicle, long distance patrol, light weapon platform or tractor, maintenance vehicle, catering vehicle, EOD, secure transport of valuables, and helicopter servicing. The Hotspur 6384 armoured personnel carrier is based on the One Fifty chassis and is in service with four Middle East countries. During 1986 Hotspur developed the Hotspur Polisec, an armoured internal security vehicle for police and para-military use, also based on the One Fifty chassis.

The Hotspur Desert Patrol Vehicle is based on the One Fifty conversion and was developed for off-road long-range duties in Africa, the Middle and Far East. Standard equipment includes seating for the driver, forward gunner and rear gunner, two machine gun mountings (front and rear), open-top equipment bins on the sides, fuel can racks, and radio equipment. Optional extras include a drop-down front screen, grenade launchers, a winch, sand channels, gun mounts, a heavy duty roll cage and an extra large fuel tank.

Specifications (Desert Patrol Vehicle)

Crew: 2 + 2 to 6
Configuration: 6 × 6
Gross vehicle weight: 5350 kg
Length: 5.86 m
Width: 1.84 m
Height: 2.5 m

Hotspur One Fifty (6 × 6) Desert Patrol Vehicle

Ground clearance: 0.21 m
Track: 1.486 m
Wheelbase: 3.81 m
Angle of approach/departure: 35°/29°
Max speed: (road) 95 km/h
Range: 300 km plus 200 km
Fuel capacity: 85 l plus 68 l
Engine: 3.5 l water-cooled V-8 petrol developing 134 bhp at 4000 rpm
Gearbox: manual, with 5 forward and 1 reverse gears
Clutch: single dry plate, hydraulic
Transfer box: 2-speed
Steering: worm and roller, power-assist
Turning radius: 8.6 m
Suspension:
    (front) dual rate coil springs, live beam axle, double-acting hydraulic dampers

    (rear) A-frame live rear axle, dual rate coil springs, double-acting hydraulic springs
Tyres: 7.50 × 16
Brakes: dual circuit; (front) hydraulic servo-assist disc, (rear) hydraulic servo-assist drum
Electrical system: 12 V

Status

In service with European, African, Middle and Far East countries.

Manufacturer

Hotspur Armoured Products, a Division of Penman Engineering Limited, Heathall, Dumfries DG1 3NY, UK.
Tel: 0387 52784. Telex: 779771.
Fax: 0387 67332.

Reynolds Boughton RB-44 (4 × 4) Truck

Development

The RB-44 was developed as a private venture by the Boughton Group and was originally called the RB-510. In addition to its use as a cargo troop carrier, it can be used for a variety of other roles such as towing a 105 mm artillery piece, the British Aerospace Dynamics Rapier SAM system or the Marconi Command and Control Systems Blindfire radar.

The RB-44 Mark 2 was one of the two final contenders for the British Army's 2-tonne Truck Universal Heavy (TUH) requirement. During mid-1988 it was announced that the RB-44 had been selected as the successful contender. The initial order was for 846 vehicles and the final requirement is expected to entail a total of 1840 vehicles. The first examples entered service with the British Army during 1991.

Description

The Reynolds Boughton RB-44 (4 × 4) truck has a ladder-type bolted chassis which can be fitted with various types of body. A three-seat semi-forward control pressed steel cab is standard, but an extended crew cab conversion is available for carrying extra personnel and equipment. Three wheelbase lengths are available: 3.226, 3.68 and 4.06 m.

The standard production engine is the Perkins Phaser 110MT diesel but other engines may be fitted if required. A Boughton designed and manufactured two-speed transfer box incorporating six- and eight-stud SAE power take-offs capable of between 30 and 90 hp is fitted, and the transfer box provides a permanent 4 × 4 drive configuration incorporating a differential lock.

Conventional semi-elliptical springs are used for the suspension, fitted with double-acting telescopic shock absorbers. Vacuum-assisted brakes, with a dual-servo split system, are fitted front and rear. The front and rear axles have hypo gearing with a ratio of 4.1:1. The front axle's plated capacity is 2500 kg with 2800 kg for the rear.

RB-44 variants include a general service cargo body, soft- and hard-top bodies FFR (including a hard-

Reynolds Boughton RB-44 (4 × 4) truck towing 105 mm Light Gun

topped version for the VIXEN tactical electronic warfare system), a transportable container body FFR, an ambulance and a lubrication body. A front-mounted winch (the Boughton VH8) can be added to any version.

RB-44 Truck, Utility, Heavy (TUH) variants being built for the British Army include general service cargo FFR, soft and hard top and truck container body variants. Reynolds Boughton are undertaking the private venture development of ambulance, command and adminstration, and recovery vehicle variants.

Specifications

Cab seating: 1 + 2 (up to 12 in rear)
Configuration: 4 × 4
Weight:
 (kerb, basic wheelbase chassis) 3000 kg
 (loaded) 5300 kg
Max load: 2250 kg
Towed load: 2200 kg
Length:
 (3.226 m wheelbase) 5.06 m
 (3.68 m wheelbase) 5.65 m
 (4.06 m wheelbase) 6.03 m
Width: 2.1 m
Height: (cab top, laden) 2.348 m
Ground clearance: 0.255 m
Wheelbase: 3.226 m or 3.68 m or 4.06 m
Track: (front and rear) 1.789 m
Angle of approach/departure: 45°/40°
Max speed: 109 km/h

Gradient: 60%
Side slope: 33°
Fording: 0.75 m
Engine: Perkins Phaser 110MT 4-cylinder direct injection diesel developing 109 bhp at 2800 rpm
Gearbox: Spicer T5-250 manual with 5 forward and 1 reverse gears or
Chrysler A727 Torqueflite automatic with 3 forward and 1 reverse gears
Clutch: single plate, hydraulic
Transfer case: Boughton 2-speed
Steering: ZF hydraulic power-assisted
Turning radius: (3.226 m wheelbase) 7.4 m
Suspension: (front and rear) heavy duty leaf springs with AEON rubber assisters and double-action shock absorbers
Tyres: 9.00 × 16 XL or 11.00 × 16 XL or XS
Brakes: hydraulic, servo-assisted, dual line system
Electrical system: 12 V or 12 V with 24 V FFR
Alternator: (12 V) 65 A

Status

In production for the British Army.

Manufacturer

Reynolds Boughton Limited, Bell Lane, Amersham, Buckinghamshire HP6 6PE, UK.
Tel: 0494 764411. Telex: 83132.
Fax: 0494 765218.

British Army Reynolds Boughton RB-44 (4 × 4) truck with hard-top body

Reynolds Boughton RB-44 (4 × 4) truck with winch

Volvo Trucks (GB) M6 (4 × 4) 4000 kg Truck

Description

The Volvo Trucks (GB) M6 (4 × 4) 4000 kg truck is a derivative of the commercial Volvo FL6 range and is called the Highlander. It uses a high level of British components, including the gearbox and axles, to the point where there is over 90 per cent local content. The prototypes used a Volvo FL6 forward control cab with a low roof design and seating for the driver and two passengers. For maintenance the steel cab can be tilted forward 55°. There is provision for a roof hatch and a machine gun mounting. The chassis is a conventional ladder frame and carries the load area

which uses a cargo body with drop sides and a tailgate. The load area can be covered by a tilt stretched over bows. Lockers and a spare wheel are carried on the chassis frame on the right-hand side. A fuel tank is located centrally on the left-hand side and towing pintles are provided front and rear.

The Highlander can be fitted with a winch or a crane. It is airportable in a C-130 transport aircraft.

Specifications

Cab seating: 1 + 1 or 2
Configuration: 4 × 4
Weight:
 (kerb) 5815 kg
 (front axle) 3756 kg
 (rear axle) 2059 kg

Max load: 4000 kg
Length: 6.44 m
Width: 2.368 m
Height:
 (top of cab) 2.654 m
 (platform, unladen) 1.427 m
 (platform, laden) 1.382 m
Ground clearance: 0.325 m
Track: 2 m
Wheelbase: 3.7 m
Fuel capacity: 150 l
Engine: Volvo TD61G 5.48 l 6-cylinder in-line liquid-cooled diesel developing 150 hp at 2800 rpm
Gearbox: ZF S6-36 with 6 forward and 1 reverse gears
Clutch: KF114B 350 mm diaphragm pull-type

Transfer box: ZF VG 250/2 2-speed, provision for PTO
Steering: power-assisted ball and nut
Turning radius: 7.13 m
Suspension:
(front) twin-leaf parabolic springs with telescopic dampers and rubber bump stops
(rear) twin-leaf parabolic springs with telescopic dampers and rubber bump stops with one-leaf helper spring
Tyres: 12.00 R.20 18 PR D002 all-terrain
Brakes: dual line air-actuated dual circuit wedge-operated drum-type
Electrical system: 24 V
Batteries: 110 Ah
Alternator: 55 A

Status
In service with the Royal Swedish Air Force (63).

Manufacturer
Volvo Trucks (GB) Limited, Wedgnock Lane, Warwick CV34 5YH, UK.
Tel: 0926 401777. Telex: 31444.
Fax: 0926 490991.

Volvo Trucks (GB) M6 (4 × 4) 4000 kg truck

Leyland DAF (4 × 4) 4000 kg Truck

Description
This (4 × 4) 4000 kg truck was developed by Leyland DAF under the project number T 244 to participate in the British Army's 4-tonne truck replacement contest along with Volvo (GB) Limited and Bedford. Eight prototypes were handed over to the Ministry of Defence in December 1987 to take part in a series of technical trials. The result of the contest was that in June 1989 Leyland DAF was awarded a contract worth £155 million for 5350 vehicles over a five-year period. The vehicle is produced at the Leyland DAF Assembly Plant in Lancashire using largely British-sourced components, including axles from the Leyland DAF Albion operation in Glasgow, Scotland. The first six production vehicles were handed over for acceptance in July 1990 with deliveries to the Ministry of Defence commencing in early August 1990. The 2000th example was handed over in October 1992.

The Leyland DAF (4 × 4) 4000 kg truck is conventional in layout and design. Some key components used on the vehicle are shared with the commercial Leyland DAF Roadrunner light truck. The T 244 uses the sleeper cab version of the C44 forward control cab which has room for the driver, two passengers and stowage for their full kit. As an alternative, the space provided may be used for driver training (the driver plus four personnel) or radio communications equipment. The cab roof is reinforced to take the weight of two men and has provision for a roof hatch and machine gun installation over an observer's platform inside the cab.

For maintenance the cab can be hydraulically tilted forward 50°.

The vehicle is powered by a Leyland DAF 310 turbocharged diesel engine coupled to a transmission using a five-speed, all-synchromesh gearbox. There is permanent 4 × 4 drive. The axles were specially developed at Leyland DAF's Albion plant in Glasgow. The front axle has a rating of 4850 kg with an offset bowl to reduce overall cab height. The rear axle has a rating of 6800 kg.

Fitments include front end rotating tow hooks, lugs for suspended or supported recovery, and an infra-red reflective paint finish. The vehicle can be carried in a C-130 Hercules transport aircraft.

The body is produced and fitted by Edbro Limited and has a fixed flat platform and bulkhead with provision for interchangeable drop sides, a tailboard, a superstructure and canopy. The flat platform can be used to carry various forms of military equipment including containers, seats, fuel pods, NATO pallets, and so on. A vehicle carrying a 'mini DROPS' load handling system has been developed as a concept exploration vehicle.

Options include left- or right-hand drive, a winch, a hydraulic crane, a tipping body, or a chassis-and-cab-only arrangement. The crane has a capacity of 6.5 t/m while the winch (produced by Reynolds Boughton) has a capacity of 5500 kg front and rear and is provided with 75 m of cable.

The vehicle shares many similarities and components with Leyland DAF's civilian 45 series and Comet trucks.

Specifications
Cab seating: 1 + 2
Configuration: 4 × 4
Weight:
(empty) 6010 kg
(loaded) 10 210 kg
GVW: 10 800 kg
GCW: 16 260 kg
Max load: 4200 kg
Towed load: (on/off road) 8000 kg
Length: 6.65 m
Width: 2.49 m
Height: 3.43 m
Platform height: (unladen) 1.41 m
Ground clearance: 0.32 m
Track: (front and rear) 2.1 m
Wheelbase: 3.95 m
Angle of approach/departure: 41°/38°
Max speed: 89 km/h
Range: approx 500 km
Fuel capacity: 135 l
Max gradient: (fully loaded, with trailer) 33%
Side slope: (static) 33°
Fording: 0.75 m
Engine: Leyland DAF 310 5.9 l 6-cylinder direct injection turbocharged diesel developing 145 hp at 2600 rpm
Gearbox: Turner T5-350 synchromesh with 5 forward and 1 reverse gears
Clutch: servo-assisted self-adjusting single dry plate (330 mm)
Transfer box: Getrag 304 2-speed
Steering: ZF 8045 power-assist

Leyland DAF (4 × 4) 4000 kg truck

Leyland DAF (4 × 4) 4000 kg truck with tipper body

Turning radius: 9 m
Suspension:
(front) 2 taper leaf with telescopic hydraulic double-acting shock absorbers
(rear) dual rate taper leaf with telescopic hydraulic double-acting shock absorbers
Tyres: 12.00 R 20

Brakes:
(main) Girling air-actuated 2-line dual system
(parking) spring actuators on all wheels
Electrical system: 24 V
Batteries: 2 × 12 V, 95 Ah
Alternator: 40 A

Status
In production for the British Army (5350).

Manufacturer
Leyland DAF, Eastern Bypass, Thame, Oxfordshire OX9 3FB, UK.
Tel: 0844 261111. Telex: 838848.
Fax: 0844 217111.

Bedford MT-series (4 × 4) Trucks

Description
The Bedford MT-series (4 × 4) trucks may be regarded as a progressive development of the Bedford MK truck series. There are five models in the series. The MT 12-14, MT 12-18 and MT 12-16 have a nominal payload of 5000 kg while that for the MT 15-18 and MT 15-16 is 8000 kg.

All five vehicles follow the same general lines, with a forward control cab mounted on a flat-topped ladder-type flexible chassis frame capable of accommodating a wide range of bodies. The chassis uses cold squeeze riveted construction and has high yield strength steel channel section sidemembers with 'alligator jaw' intermediate crossmembers. The front and rear axles on the MT 12 vehicles are both Bedford components with fully floating single-speed hypoid interchangeable differentials front and rear; the rear axle on MT 15 vehicles is a Rockwell R144 unit. Tow hooks are provided front and rear.

The cab is all-steel and has a torsion bar tilt arrangement to provide access to the engine and transmission for maintenance; day-to-day checks can be carried out from a point at the rear of the cab. The driver is seated behind a laminated windscreen on a fully adjustable seat while the passenger's seat is fixed. Inertia reel seat belts are provided along with a map reading light. A roof hatch is provided for access to a machine gun mounting with an internal platform for the gunner/observer using the hatch. The cab roof is reinforced to support the weight of two men. There is internal stowage for personal kit, rifles and other equipment.

The engine used with the MT 12-14 is a Perkins Phaser 6.135 naturally aspirating diesel developing 130 bhp. The MT 12-16 and MT 15-16 use a Perkins Phaser 6.160T turbocharged diesel developing 160 bhp; the MT 12-18 and MT 15-18 use the same engine but with inter-cooling and developing 180 bhp. All engines are coupled to a Spicer five-speed all-synchromesh gearbox. Power take-offs can be provided front and rear.

Numerous equipment options are available including different axles gearings, extreme climate modifications for the engine, an exhaust brake and various tyre sizes. Many other options are available.

Specifications
Cab seating: 1 + 1
Configuration: 4 × 4
Weight: (kerb, nominal) 4760 kg
Front axle design weight: 4750 kg
Rear axle design weight: (MT 12/MT 15) 8890 kg/ 10 000 kg
Max load:
(MT 12, nominal) 5000 kg
(MT 15, nominal) 8000 kg
Length: (chassis) 6.53 m

Bedford MT 15-18 (4 × 4) truck

Width: 2.48 m
Height: (top of cab) 2.63 m
Track:
(front) 2.09 m
(rear) 2.05 m
Wheelbase: 3.94 m
Angle of approach/departure: 41°/38°
Max speed:
(MT 12-14) 86 km/h
(MT 12-16/18) 115 km/h
(MT 15-16/18) 115 km/h
Fuel capacity: 109 l
Max gradient: (stop/restart capability)
(MT 12-14) 58%
(MT 12-16) 50%
(MT 12-18) 57%
(MT 15-16) 39%
(MT 15-18) 44%
Engine:
(MT 12-14) Perkins Phaser 6.135 6 l 6-cylinder in-line water-cooled naturally aspirating diesel developing 130 bhp at 2600 rpm
(MT 12-16 and MT 15-16) Perkins Phaser 6.160T 6 l, 6-cylinder, in-line, water-cooled turbocharged diesel developing 160 bhp at 2600 rpm
(MT 12-18 and MT 15-18) Perkins Phaser 6.180Ti 6 l, 6-cylinder, in-line, water-cooled turbocharged and inter-cooled diesel developing 180 bhp at 2600 rpm
Gearbox: Spicer with 5 forward and 1 reverse gears

Clutch: single dry plate
Transfer box: (Bedford) 2-speed
Steering: recirculating ball with integral power-assist
Turning radius: 9 m
Suspension: taper leaf springs with rubber-bushed springs and telescopic hydraulic double-acting shock absorbers front and rear
Tyres:
(MT 12-14/16/18) 12.00 R 20
(MT 15-16/18) 14.75/80 R 20
Brakes:
(MT 12-14/16/18) full air with independent circuits for service and secondary
(MT 15-16/18) air over hydraulic actuation with dual circuits
Electrical system: 24 V
Batteries: 2 × 12 V, 120 Ah
Alternator: 45 A

Status
In production.

Manufacturer
Marshall SPV Limited, Airport Works, Cambridge CB5 8RX, UK.
Tel: 0223 301133. Telex: 81208.
In October 1992 Marshall SPV Limited acquired the product designs and some of the assets of AWD Limited.

Bedford MK (4 × 4) 4000 kg Truck

Development
In the early 1960s the British Army issued a requirement for a 4 × 4 4000 kg (nominal payload) truck to replace the then current Bedford RL. To meet this requirement Austin submitted the FJ (FV 13701), Commer the CB (FV 13901) and Vauxhall the RK (FV 13801). After comparative trials the Vauxhall model, based on its civilian TK (4 × 2) truck, was selected and standardised as the Truck Cargo (Bedford MK 4-tonne 4 × 4).

As from April 1981 Bedford changed the designation of the MK to MJ as the K multi-fuel engine was superseded by the J diesel engine. The designation MK is an abbreviated form of the alpha designation MKP2BMO, MJ being MJP2BMO. B becomes W for winch variants.

In mid-1982 a £46 million order was announced for new MJP trucks fitted with a new 5.42 litre turbocharged diesel engine designated the 5.4/105TD. This series of trucks incorporated many minor modifications to take advantage of the new engine's power, and production of the new model commenced in September 1982.

Production totals for the M-series of vehicles, including both military and civilian models, stood at 48 318 in December 1988 with a further 200 being built between 1989 and 1992, when production ceased in favour of the MT series (see previous entry).

In October 1992 Marshall SPV Limited acquired the product designs and some of the assets of AWD Limited.

Description
The chassis is of the ladder type with six crossmembers, two of 'alligator jaw' design. The all-steel two-door forward control cab has a circular observation

hatch in the roof. Access to the engine for maintenance is via the top-hinged panels on the rear quarters of the cab at either side. The cab rear panel, between the driver's and passenger's seats, is easily removed for engine access.

The all-steel rear cargo area has drop sides and a drop tailgate, which can be removed quickly to provide a platform for the carriage of containers, pallets or the Simon Saro demountable fuel pod. Removable bows and a tarpaulin cover are fitted as standard. A hydraulic crane can be fitted for unloading. Detachable outward-facing seats can be fitted in the centre of the cargo area for carrying passengers. The body of the MJP is manufactured by Marshall of Cambridge (Engineering) Limited.

The MJP2 has a 3.962 m wheelbase but a model with a wheelbase of 3.505 m is also available (MOR1). Power is provided by a 5.42 litre diesel engine in turbocharged or naturally aspirated form.

The basic models of the M-type are designated the FV 13801/FV 13802 or when fitted with a winch the FV 13803/FV 13804. The winch has a capacity of 5080 kg and 76 m of cable. Provision is made for a PTO to be driven from either the front or rear of the transfer box casing. In addition a standard six-stud SAE PTO facing is fitted to the side of the gearbox. The MJP has single rear wheels with either 12.00 × 20 or 13.00 × 20 tyres but dual rear wheels with 9.00 × 20 tyres can be fitted. Standard equipment includes a heater and defroster and stowage racks for small arms.

Variants

Drone carrier (for the Canadian Midge AN/USD-501 reconnaissance drone), dump truck, refueller, mine-proof cab (conversion work carried out by Reynolds Boughton), portable roadway laying vehicle, and with special bodies. The Royal Air Force uses the M-type for carrying bombs and other munitions to support Harrier V/STOL aircraft. Bedford TK trucks (4 × 2) are used for a wide variety of roles by all three British services including driver training vehicles, stores carriers and aircraft refuellers.

Specifications

Cab seating: 1 + 1
Configuration: 4 × 4
Weight:
　(empty) 5129 kg
　(loaded, on road) 11 180 kg
　(loaded, off road) 9650 kg
Weight on front axle: (max load) 4060 kg
Weight on rear axle: (max load) 7620 kg
Max load: (single rear wheels) 6060 kg
Towed load: 4570 kg
Load area: 4.28 × 2.01 m
Length: 6.579 m
Width: 2.489 m
Height:
　(cab) 2.501 m
　(tarpaulin) 3.404 m
Ground clearance: 0.343 m
Track:
　(front) 2.05 m
　(rear) 2.03 m
Wheelbase: 3.962 m
Angle of approach/departure: 41°/38°
Max speed: (road) 77 km/h
Range: 560 km

Fuel capacity: 155 l
Max gradient: 49%
Fording: 0.762 m
Engine: Bedford 5.42 l 6-cylinder naturally aspirated diesel developing 97.9 bhp (gross) at 2600 rpm
Gearbox: manual with 4 forward and 1 reverse gears
Clutch: single dry plate
Transfer box: 2-speed
Steering: semi-irreversible worm and sector
Turning radius: 9 m
Suspension: semi-elliptical springs with telescopic hydraulic double-action shock absorbers
Tyres: 12.00 × 20, 13.00 × 20, or 9.00 × 20
Brakes:
　(main) air/hydraulic
　(parking) mechanical
Electrical system: 24 V
Batteries: 2 × 12 V, 128 Ah

Status

Production complete. In service with Bangladesh, Belgium, Brunei, Indonesia, Ireland, Kenya, Netherlands, Turkey (300), Uganda, United Arab Emirates, United Kingdom and other countries.

Manufacturer

Marshall SPV Limited, Airport Works, Cambridge CB5 8RX, UK.
Tel: 0223 301133. Telex: 81208.
In October 1992 Marshall SPV Limited acquired the product designs and some of the assets of AWD Limited.

Late version of MJP (4 × 4) 4000 kg cargo truck with roof platform capable of supporting weight of two men over cab

Bedford MK (4 × 4) 4000 kg truck

Bedford RL (4 × 4) 4000 kg Truck

Development

To replace Second World War trucks three new 3000 kg (4 × 4) trucks were introduced into the British Army in 1952. These were built by Bedford (the RL), Commer (the Q4) and Ford; all were based on civilian chassis.

The Bedford RL was based on the civilian 7-tonne SLC chassis and the 4 × 4 version was in production from 1952 to 1969, by which time 73 135 had been built for both civil and military use. By the 1960s most of the Commer and Ford trucks had been phased out of service, but the RL remained the standard truck of the British Army in the 3000 kg class until the introduction of the Bedford MK in the late 1960s. In 1968 the RL's capacity was uprated from 3000 to 4000 kg and there are still many in service with the British and other armed forces.

Bedford became AWD Bedford Limited in November 1987. In October 1992 Marshall SPV Limited acquired the product designs and some of the assets of AWD Limited.

Description

The basic RL (L for long) has a wheelbase of 3.962 m and the RS (S for short) has a wheelbase of 3.35 m.

The chassis consists of two deep channel-section sidemembers, tapered towards the front, riveted to five crossmembers. The two-door all-steel forward control cab has an observation hatch in the roof. The rear cargo body is also of steel and has drop sides and a drop tailgate, removable bows and a tarpaulin cover. The following cargo models were built: FV 13101 (not drop side), FV 13105 (drop side), FV 13109 (not drop side), FV 13112 (drop side) and FV 13143 (left-hand drive, not drop side). Many RLs are fitted with a 5000 kg capacity winch.

The engine is mounted between and below the driver's and passenger's seats and is removed through the front of the vehicle after detaching the grille and engine crossbearer. Power is taken from the engine to the gearbox and then via a propeller shaft to the transfer box which is under the chassis in the centre of the vehicle. Power is then taken from the transfer box to the front and rear axles by propeller shafts. The differential and hypoid gear assembly of both the front and rear axles are interchangeable.

Variants

There were many variants of the RL, not all of which are still in service: charging vehicle (FV 13104), 3636 litre fuel tanker (FV 13106), signals vehicle (FV 13110), short wheelbase tipper (FV 13111), motor transport repair vehicle (FV 13113), light recovery vehicle (FV 13115), 1728 litre tanker (FV 13120), flat bed for carrying containers (FV 13136), airportable cargo truck with removable cab top (FV 13142), container truck (FV 13152), dental surgery (FV 13165), and a 4 × 2 aircraft water refueller (FV 13197). The vehicle was also used for carrying the Canadian Midge reconnaissance drone (now mounted on the Bedford MK), the MGB (now also carried on the Bedford MK), the Laird portable roadway (now carried on the Bedford MK), and as a fire engine.

Specifications

Cab seating: 1 + 1
Configuration: 4 × 4
Weight:
　(empty) 4400 kg
　(loaded) 8800 kg
Max load: 4000 kg
Load area: 4.267 × 2.178 m
Length: 6.36 m
Width: 2.39 m
Height:
　(cab) 2.602 m
　(tarpaulin) 3.11 m
Track: 1.854 m
Wheelbase: 3.962 m
Angle of approach/departure: 36°/30°
Max speed: (road) 75 km/h
Range: 400 km
Fuel capacity: 118 l
Max gradient: 33%
Engine: Bedford 6-cylinder OHV petrol developing 130 bhp (gross) at 3200 rpm. (Early models had 110 bhp. Others including 107 bhp 6-cylinder diesel available)
Gearbox: manual with 4 forward and 1 reverse gears
Clutch: single dry plate

Transfer box: 2-speed
Steering: semi-irreversible worm and sector
Turning radius: 9.13 m
Suspension: (front and rear) semi-elliptical springs
with hydraulic double-acting shock absorbers
Tyres: 11.00 × 20
Brakes:
  (main) hydraulic
  (parking) mechanical
Electrical system: 12 V
Battery: 1 × 12 V, 80 Ah
Generator: 230 W

Status

Production complete. In service with Belgium (4 × 2),
Denmark, Ireland, Malta, Netherlands, New Zealand,
Oman, Pakistan and Singapore.

Manufacturer

Marshall SPV Limited, Airport Works, Cambridge CB5
8RX, UK.
Tel: 0223 301133. Telex: 81208.
In October 1992 Marshall SPV Limited acquired the
product designs and some of the assets of AWD
Limited.

Danish Army Bedford RL (4 × 4) 4000 kg truck fitted with forward-sloping windscreen to accommodate cab roof turret ring for 12.7 mm Browning machine gun

Alvis Stalwart (6 × 6) 5000 kg High Mobility Load Carrier

Development

The first Stalwart, called the PV 1, was built as a
private venture by Alvis Limited in 1959. It was based
on the chassis of the FV 652 Salamander (6 × 6)
fire/crash tender used by the Royal Air Force, which in
turn used many components of the FV 601 Saladin and
FV 603 Saracen armoured vehicles. The PV 1 had a
flat bed cargo area at the rear and was not amphibious.
In 1961 a second, fully amphibious, prototype called
the PV 2 was built with drop sides and a drop tailgate to
the rear cargo area. Over 140 vehicles of this configuration were subsequently produced, being known
as the Stalwart Mk 1, FV 620. As a result of trials with
the British Army a number of modifications were
carried out including the installation of a front-mounted
winch and more powerful waterjets, improvement in
cab layout and visibility, reduction in maintenance and
improvement in reliability. Production vehicles were
known as the Alvis Stalwart Mk 2, FV 622 and were
produced from 1966. Production continued until 1971,
when over 1400 Stalwarts had been produced.

Alvis Stalwart Mk 2 (6 × 6) 5000 kg high mobility load carrier converted to use a Perkins Phaser 180 MTi diesel engine

Description

The fully enclosed cab is at the front of the vehicle and
access is via two circular hatches in the roof which
open forward. The driver is seated in the centre of the
cab with a single passenger seat either side. The load
area is at the rear and has drop sides and a drop
tailgate. A tarpaulin cover can be fitted over the load
area if required. The Stalwart can carry 5000 kg of
cargo or 38 fully equipped troops. The engine is under
the cargo area, and engine drive is taken through a
twin dry plate clutch and five-speed gearbox to the
transfer box with a no-spin differential, which transfers
drive direct to each centre bevel box and then via
transmission shafts to the front and rear bevel boxes.
Each wheel houses epicyclic reduction gears and is
connected to its appropriate bevel box by a transmission shaft and two universal joints.

The hydraulically operated winch mounted at the
front of the vehicle has a 4990 kg capacity.

The Stalwart is fully amphibious and is propelled in
the water by two Dowty marine jets driven by a PTO
from the gearbox. Steering is by two levers controlling
vanes on the jet units which can be turned 180° for
reverse thrust. Before entering the water a trim vane is
erected at the front of the vehicle.

The FV 623 is basically the FV 622 fitted with an
Atlas 3001/66 hydraulic crane to the cab rear for
unloading pallets of ammunition, and was used by the
Royal Artillery to supply self-propelled artillery
regiments with ammunition.

The FV 624 is a fitter's vehicle for the Royal
Electrical and Mechanical Engineers.

The Stalwart has been fitted with the Simon Gloster
Saro refuelling pack and has carried the THORN EMI
Ranger barrier defence system.

In 1990 it was announced that AF Budge (Sales)
Limited had developed a conversion package for the
Stalwart with the backing and assistance of Perkins
Engines. The conversion involves the replacement of
the existing engine with a Perkins Phaser 180 MTi
diesel developing 180 hp. Other components involved
in the conversion are a new radiator, a new exhaust
pipe and new air filters. The conversion offers improved
fuel efficiency, an increased operating range and a
reduced fire risk.

Specifications

Cab seating: 1 + 2
Configuration: 6 × 6
Weight:
  (empty) 8970 kg
  (loaded) 14 480 kg
Max load: 5000 kg
Towed load: 10 000 kg
Load area: 3.6 × 2.4 m
Length: 6.356 m
Width: 2.616 m
Height:
  (cab) 2.312 m
  (tarpaulin) 2.64 m
  (load area) 1.5 m
Ground clearance: 0.42 m
Track: 2.04 m
Wheelbase: 1.524 m + 1.524 m
Angle of approach/departure: 44°/40°
Max speed:
  (road) 63 km/h
  (water, empty) 10.2 km/h
  (water, loaded) 9.6 km/h
Range: 515 km
Fuel consumption: 71 l/100 km
Max gradient: 60%
Vertical obstacle: 0.46 m
Trench: 1.52 m
Fording: amphibious
Engine: Rolls-Royce B-81 Mk 8B 8-cylinder water-
cooled petrol developing 220 bhp at 3750 rpm
Gearbox: 5 forward and 5 reverse gears
Clutch: twin plate friction
Transfer box: bevel and helical gear incorporating
reverse and no-spin differential
Steering: recirculating ball, hydraulic-assisted on front
4 wheels
Turning radius: 8.38 m
Suspension: independent all wheels by double wish-
bone and torsion bars; hydraulic telescopic double-
acting shock absorbers
Tyres: 14.00 × 20

Brakes:
(main) air over hydraulic on all wheels
(parking) contracting bands on drums on front bevel boxes
Electrical system: 24 V

Batteries: 2 × 12 V 6 TN, 100 Ah

Status
Production complete. In service with the United Kingdom.

Manufacturer
Alvis Vehicles Limited, The Triangle, Walsgrave, Coventry CV2 2SP, UK.
Tel: 0203 595501. Telex: 31459.
Fax: 0203 598554.

Bedford TM 4-4 (4 × 4) 8000 kg Truck

Development

In the early 1970s the British Army issued a requirement for a new 4 × 4 8000 kg (nominal payload) cargo truck as a part of its Medium Mobility Vehicle Programme. To meet this requirement prototypes were built by Foden, Leyland and Bedford and, after comparative trials, in September 1977 Bedford was awarded a contract worth almost £40 million for 2099 of its model TM 4-4. Production began in September 1980 and first vehicles were delivered to the British Army in April 1981.

In October 1992 Marshall SPV Limited acquired the product designs and some of the assets of AWD Limited.

Description

The basic cargo model is designated the WNV3NPO by Bedford and has a GVW of 17 000 kg and a GTW of 25 000 kg.

The TM 4-4 has a ladder-type chassis with 450 N/mm² yield structural steel channel-section side-members and constant depth and section throughout with special rear crossmembers for drawbar trailer operations. The full width heavy duty front bumper is bolted to the first chassis crossmember. Front towing pintle and brake pipeline couplings for trailer brake operations and vehicle recovery are incorporated.

The front axle is a Kirkstall fully floating, single speed, spiral bevel with 3.857 to 1 hub reduction and overall axle ratio of 5.887 to 1. The rear axle is also a Kirkstall fully floating, single speed, spiral bevel with 3.857 to 1 hub reduction and air-actuated differential lock. Overall axle ratio is 5.887 to 1.

The all-steel two-door forward control cab has an observation hatch in the roof. The cab can be tilted forwards hydraulically through 60° locking in a number of intermediate positions. The hinged front grille provides access to the engine for checking oil and other services such as heater and steering systems. The water level can be checked in the expansion tank at the rear of the cab and fuses can be changed from inside. Standard equipment includes an inter-vehicle starting system, heater and ventilation system and a spare wheel carrier and spare wheel.

The cargo body was built and mounted onto the chassis by Marshall of Cambridge (Engineering) Limited. It is steel with a wooden floor, removable drop sideboards and tailboard, lashing shackles for NATO pallets and longitudinal folding bench seats for personnel. An alternative platform body was available with headboard only. Twistlock attachments or lashing hooks for securing containers are also fitted.

The central roof-mounted hip ring has a glass fibre reinforced cover which is stowed on the rear of the cab when removed. The gunner's platform is centrally mounted in the cab, for use with the hip ring. The roof is reinforced to withstand the load of a light machine gun and two men.

The standard vehicle is equipped with a 24 V electrical system, an exhaust system and fire screening which comply with United Kingdom petroleum-carrying regulations.

Power is transmitted from the engine to the gearbox and then to the transfer case which provides drive to the front and rear hub reduction axles.

The following optional equipment is available for the Bedford TM 4-4: exhaust brake, cab painted in NATO IRR green, ringfeeder drawbar coupling, flitch plates, NATO batteries, cab roof front marker lights, dry charged batteries (for CKD purposes), reverse lamps, rear fog guard lamps, tachograph, steering column lock and electric stop control, mid-mounted winch, Atlas hydraulic crane, inertia reel seat belts for driver and passenger, multi-leaf springs, transfer box differential, transfer box with PTO adaptor, transfer box with differential and PTO adaptor, and military-type cargo body.

Variants

TM 4-4 with tipper body
These have the Bedford designation of WNV6NPO + RPO 585, a wheelbase of 3.883 m, GVW of 16 300 kg and GTW of 24 300 kg. The Edbro military tipper body has a capacity of 6.5 m³. The body can be tipped to an angle of 54° and is of all-steel construction with a three-stage front end ram. The tailgate is hinged at the top and bottom with hydraulic drive via the main gearbox PTO.

TM 4-4 with Atlas self-loading crane
Over 700 of these were delivered to the British Armed Forces and have the Bedford designation of WNV3NPO + RPO 355. Mounted to the cab rear is an Atlas self-loading crane controlled by the operator standing at the hip ring position. The hydraulic crane is driven via the main gearbox PTO and has a slew angle of 193° and the following capabilities: 3650 kg lift at 2.02 m reach, 2140 kg lift at 3.46 m reach and 1700 kg lift at 4.32 m reach.

TM 4-4 with winch
These are fitted with a mid-mounted winch with a capacity of 8000 kg powered from a transfer box from a PTO. The cable is 75 m long and has a minimum speed of 4.5 m/min and a maximum speed of 23 m/min. The controls are air-operated with fairleads and pulleys for front and rear winching capability, band-type winch brake and safety overload cutout. The Bedford designation for this model is WNV3NPO + RPO 414.

Specifications
Cab seating: 1 + 1
Configuration: 4 × 4
Weight:
(empty) 8300 kg
(loaded) 17 000 kg
Max load: 8000 kg
Towed load: 10 000 kg
Length: 6.623 m
Width: 2.476 m
Height:
(cab) 2.997 m
(tarpaulin) 3.454 m
Ground clearance:
(axles) 0.352 m
(mid-wheelbase) 0.47 m
Track:
(front) 2.02 m
(rear) 2.08 m
Wheelbase: 4.325 m
Angle of approach/departure: 41°/38°
Max road speed: 93 km/h
Max range: 500 km
Fuel capacity: 155 l
Gradient: 55.55%
Side slope: (unladen) 43°
Fording: 0.75 m
Engine: Bedford 8.2/205 TD 8.2 l water-cooled direct injection turbocharged diesel developing 206 bhp at 2500 rpm
Gearbox: Spicer T6-47026 manual with 6 forward and 1 reverse gears
Clutch: twin dry plate
Transfer box: Rockwell T226-133, 2-speed
Steering: recirculating ball with integral power assistance
Suspension: (front and rear) semi-elliptical taper leaf springs with hydraulic double-acting telescopic shock absorbers
Tyres: 15.50/80 × 20 radial
Brakes:
(main) air
(parking) air released spring brakes
Electrical system: 24 V

Status
Production complete. In service with Abu Dhabi, Bahrain, Oman and the United Kingdom.

Manufacturer
Marshall SPV Limited, Airport Works, Cambridge CB5 8RX, UK.
Tel: 0223 301133. Telex: 81208.
In October 1992 Marshall SPV Limited acquired the product designs and some of the assets of AWD Limited.

Bedford TM 4-4 (4 × 4) SWB (3.883 m) tipper

Bedford TM 4-4 (4 × 4) 8000 kg truck

JCB 712 12 000 kg Rough Terrain Vehicle

Description

The JCB 712 Rough Terrain Vehicle is a development of the JCB 712 12-tonne articulated (frame steer) dump truck, conceived to carry loads over difficult unprepared terrain. In Rough Terrain Vehicle form the JCB 712 has a payload capacity of 12 000 kg and both 4 × 4 and 4 × 2 configurations are available.

The articulated steer machine offers manoeuvrability and, with wide base tyres, has good flotation characteristics. A compact, all-welded front chassis arrangement and a side-mounted driver station enables the unit to have a high angle of approach (44°). The flat, parallel rear chassis, constructed of folded plate box-section, can be of varying length and is capable of being adapted to suit a variety of load-carrying duties, including the mounting of hydraulic load handling systems.

The front and rear frames are joined together with a large interframe casting providing 36° articulation either side and an oscillating ring which allows all-wheel contact over uneven ground. The vehicle has an electrically operated full power-shift transmission and torque proportioning axles.

A full ROPS/FOPS resiliently mounted cab is fitted as standard.

Specifications

Cab seating: 1
Configuration: 4 × 4 or 4 × 2
Weight:
  (empty) 8400 kg
  (loaded) 21 000 kg
Max load: 12 000 kg
Length: 6.06 to 7.06 m
Width: 2.5 m

Artist's impression of JCB 712 12 000 kg Rough Terrain Vehicle

Height: 3.02 m
Ground clearance: 0.46 m
Track: 1.955 m
Wheelbase: 3.65 m to 4.65 m
Angle of approach: 44°
Max speed: 36 km/h
Engine: Perkins 5.8 l 6-cylinder direct injection diesel developing 109 hp at 2250 rpm
Transmission: Clark 18000 series with integral hydrodynamic single stage torque converter; full power-shift with 6 forward and 3 reverse gears
Steering: hydrostatic, two double-acting cylinders
Turning radius: 6.6 to 7.266 m
Tyres: 20.5 R 25
Brakes:
  (main) dual circuit all hydraulic operating inboard mounted oil immersed, multi-discs on all four wheels (parking/emergency) independent hydraulic operating on rear wheels; fail-safe
Electrical system: 24 V
Batteries: 2 × 12 V, 120 Ah
Alternator: 43 A

Status

Dump truck version in production. Rough Terrain Vehicle variants adapted to suit requirements.

Manufacturer

JCB Military Products Division, Rocester, Staffordshire ST14 5JP, UK.
Tel: 0889 590312. Telex: 36372.
Fax: 0889 590588.

Foden Medium Mobility (6 × 6) Range of Vehicles

Development

The Foden Medium Mobility range of vehicles was developed for use with the FH-70 155 mm howitzer in service with the British, German and Italian armies. The British Army placed a production order for 116 tractors and limbers, with the bodies built by Marshall of Cambridge (Engineering) Limited. Final deliveries to the British Army were made late in 1979.

The Medium Mobility range was designed for both on- and off-road conditions and shares many common components with the Foden Low Mobility range.

Description

The chassis is of bolted construction with a flitch plate and the full width front bumper has a towing jaw. Mounted at the rear is a rigid rear-pulling jaw and there are lift and recovery lugs front and rear.

The forward control cab is identical to that used for the Low Mobility range and the reader is referred to this entry for a description.

The Rolls-Royce engine is coupled to a Fuller gearbox with eight forward and one reverse gears. This has a single control stick and range change with overdrive.

The front axle is a Kirkstall SD.65-11-1 rated at 10 000 kg and fitted with a differential lock. The foremost tandem axle is a Kirkstall D65-111-1AF with an air-operated differential and the rearmost tandem axle is a Kirkstall D65-11-1 with a differential driving head. A cross-axle differential lock is fitted to each of the rear axles and is air-operated with an electrical warning switch which indicates when the lock is engaged. The rear bogie has high articulation for cross-country operations.

The transfer (or auxiliary) gearbox is a Kirkstall AGB7000 which comprises a two-speed, three-shaft, constant mesh helical gearbox with disengageable front-wheel drive. Engagement is pneumatically actuated via spur dogs designed to prevent any possibility of clutch throw-out. Provision for optional high or low ratio live PTO is provided by utilising a duplicate front drive cartridge mounted at the rear of the input shaft.

Various optional engines and transmissions are available.

Variants

Gun tractor
This is used to tow the 155 mm FH-70. The platform comprises two sections of underframe with hardwood boarded floors mounted fore and aft of the Atlas hydraulic crane. Mounted to the rear of the cab is a removable cabin which provides heated accommodation for eight men. Two NATO ammunition pallets are carried both fore and aft of the crane. Stowage for the spare wheel and other gun equipment is provided at the rear of the vehicle. Spare wheels for the gun are stowed on the roof of the cabin.

Gun limber
This is used to carry eight NATO pallets containing 155 mm ammunition for the FH-70. The platform comprises two sections of underframe with hardwood boarded floor mounted fore and aft of the crane.

Recovery vehicle
This uses the 6 × 6 chassis and cab. Full details of this vehicle are given in the *Recovery vehicles* section.

Foden (6 × 6) medium mobility vehicle used as gun tractor for FH-70

Foden (6 × 6) medium mobility vehicle used as FH-70 limber vehicle

Specifications
Cab seating: 1 + 2
Configuration: 6 × 6
Weight:
  (loaded) 27 440 kg
  (chassis and cab) 10 990 kg
Max towed load: 9300 kg
Length: 9.16 m
Width: 2.5 m
Height: 3.75 m
Track:
  (front) 2.029 m
  (rear) 2.032 m
Wheelbase: 3.97 m + 1.516 m
Angle of approach/departure: 40°/29°

Max speed: (road) 104 km/h (tyre limitation 80 km/h)
Fuel capacity: 409 l
Max gradient: 33%
Engine: turbocharged Rolls-Royce 305 Mk III 6-cylinder liquid-cooled diesel developing 305 bhp at 2100 rpm
Gearbox: Fuller with 8 forward and 1 reverse gears
Transfer box: 2-speed
Steering: recirculatory ball with integral power-assistance
Turning radius: 12 m
Suspension:
  (front) semi-elliptical springs
  (rear) 2 springs fully articulated
Tyres: 16.00 × 20

Brakes:
  (main) air
  (parking) mechanical
Electrical system: 24 V
Batteries: 2 × 12 V

Status
Production complete. In service with the British Army.

Manufacturer
Foden Trucks, A Division of PACCAR UK Ltd, Moss Lane, Sandbach, Cheshire CW11 9YW, UK.
Tel: 0270 763244. Fax: 0270 762758.

Bedford TM 6-6 (6 × 6) 14 000 kg Truck

Development
The Bedford TM 6-6 (6 × 6) 14 000 kg truck was developed from the Bedford TM 4-4 (4 × 4) 8000 kg truck (see separate entry in this section), in response to a British Army General Staff Requirement for a cost-effective 6 × 6 vehicle with the same 14-tonne payload as the TM 4-4 and trailer combination (such as 10 standard NATO pallets). The TM 6-6 uses many of the same components as the TM 4-4 and the first pre-test prototype was completed in November 1981. A further four prototypes were built during 1983 and another eight Ministry of Defence validation vehicles were built during 1984 for trials at the RARDE Chertsey and user trials that extended into 1985. Volume production commenced in September 1986 with initial Ministry of Defence contracts for 1045 vehicles.

During 1988 the payload allowance of the TM 6-6 was uprated to 16 000 kg.

In October 1992 Marshall SPV Limited acquired the product designs and some of the assets of AWD Limited.

Description
The cabs of the TM 4-4 and TM 6-6 are identical with the roof having a central hip ring with a detachable cover. The interior layout is also the same as the TM 4-4 except for modifications to controls associated with permanent six-wheel drive and the revised transmission. The roof is reinforced to take the weight of a machine gun and two men. Provision is made for stowage of a rifle at each end of the instrument panel. By using a hydraulic pump the cab can be tilted forward 62° allowing engine maintenance. The engine is the same as that used with the TM 4-4 but the TM 6-6 has an exhaust brake operated from a foot pedal. Features common to both vehicles include the cooling system, exhaust, front axle and suspension, steering wheel and tyres. The electrical and braking systems are modified to suit the 6 × 6 function.

Features of the TM 6-6 designed for ease of operation include the synchroniser engagement of the transfer box for on-the-move ratio changes. This provides more effective use of the transfer box combining the advantages of the wider gear ratio spread with the advantages of a range-change.

A six-link rear bogie suspension provides equalised axle loading on wide wheel centres for optimum traction and large axle articulation through maintenance-free rubber bushed links for good axle control. Tapered-leaf chevron-profile springs provide high durability with substantial weight savings.

Three versions of the TM 6-6 were produced. The load-carrier with a standard cargo body was manufactured by Edbro Limited. This is a basic flat bed with

Bedford TM 6-6 (6 × 6) 14 000 kg truck with flat bed body

body sides, tailboard, tilt and canvas covers. An alternative cargo-bodied version has a centrally mounted hydraulic winch produced by FW Engineering Limited. This can be used for the recovery of loads up to 10 000 kg front and rear. A third variant is a platform body version equipped with an Atlas crane capable of lifting 1400 kg at a radius of 6.55 m. The crane, with controls immediately behind the cab, is only operable when the stabiliser legs are extended. All versions are fitted with a towing pintle and lashing and lifting eyes.

Specifications
Cab seating: 1 + 1
Configuration: 6 × 6
Weight:
  (kerb) 8682 kg
  (loaded) 24 390 kg
Max load: 14 000 kg (max 16 000 kg)
Length: 8.59 m
Width: 2.47 m
Height: (cab) 3.04 m
Ground clearance: (axle) 0.35 m
Track:
  (front) 2.02 m
  (rear) 2.08 m
Wheelbase: (mean) 5 m
Max speed: (road) 89.7 km/h
Fuel capacity: 227 l
Range: 500 km
Side slope: 28°

Fording: 0.75 m
Engine: Bedford 8.2/205TD 8.195 l water-cooled direct injection turbocharged diesel developing 205 bhp at 2500 rpm
Gearbox: ZF S6-80 manual with 6 forward and 1 reverse gears
Transfer box: Kirkstall AGB 42 2-speed with synchronised shift
Clutch: twin dry plate
Steering: recirculating ball with power-assistance
Turning circle: 21.5 m
Suspension:
  (front) semi-elliptical taper leaf springs with telescopic shock absorbers
  (rear) six-leaf bogie-type with chevron-profile springs and telescopic shock absorbers
Tyres: 15.50/80 × 20 radial
Electrical system: 24 V

Status
Production complete. In service with the British Army and Abu Dhabi.

Manufacturer
Marshall SPV Limited, Airport Works, Cambridge CB5 8RX, UK.
Tel: 0223 301133. Telex: 81208.
In October 1992 Marshall SPV Limited acquired the product designs and some of the assets of AWD Limited.

Bedford TM 30-30 (6 × 6) 18 000 kg Truck

Description
The Bedford TM 30-30 (6 × 6) 18 000 kg truck was derived from the TM 6-6 truck (see previous entry) and was developed specifically for the artillery towing role. The vehicle uses some components from the TM 6-6 including the cab, which is also shared by the Bedford

TM 4-4.

The layout of the TM 30-30 is conventional with a forward control cab. Power from a 300 hp Caterpillar 10.5 litre turbocharged and aftercooled diesel is transmitted to the front and rear Kirkstall hub reduction axles via a ZF 16-speed synchromesh gearbox and single-speed transfer box. This drive line, plus cross- and inter-axle differential locks on the rear bogie, provide the tractive effort to tow guns weighing up to 14 tonnes under all conditions.

The TM 30-30 meets fuel and explosives carrying requirements and with specialised bodies can be used for the carriage of ammunition, fuel or water and the loading and unloading of palletised equipment. As a cargo vehicle it can carry 10 standard NATO pallets.

Optional equipment includes a 425 hp Caterpillar engine, 325 or 465 hp Cummins engines, a ZF Transmatic gearbox with WSK 400 torque converter, an Allison automatic transmission, hydraulic self-loading cranes, sand tread tyres and winches.

Specifications

Cab seating: 1 + 1
Configuration: 6 × 6
Weights:
  (unladen) 9300 kg
  (design weight, front axle) 8000 kg
  (design weight, rear axle) 22 000 kg
  (GVW) 30 000 kg
Body and payload capacity: approx 20 700 kg
Towed load: 14 000 kg
Length: (chassis) 8.91 m
Width: (over tyres) 2.47 m
Height: (cab) 3.11 m
Ground clearance: 0.42 m
Track:
  (front) 2 m
  (rear) 2.1 m
Wheelbase:
  (centre of front axle to centre of rear bogie) 5 m
  (between centres of rear axles) 1.61 m
Angle of approach/departure: 38°/30°
Max speed: 90 km/h
Fuel capacity: 2 × 340 l
Gradient: 50%
Engine: Caterpillar 3306B ATAAC 10.487 l 6-cylinder turbocharged diesel developing 300 bhp at 2100 rpm (for options see text)
Gearbox: ZF synchromesh range change splitter giving 16 forward and 2 reverse gears
Transfer box: ZF A800 single-speed
Steering: recirculating ball with power-assist
Suspension: leaf springs and hydraulic shock absorbers front and rear
Tyres: 16 R 20

Bedford TM 30-30 (6 × 6) 18 000 kg truck

Brakes: air
Electrical system: 24 V
Batteries: 2 × 12 V, 120 Ah

Status
In production. In service with Abu Dhabi.

Manufacturer
Marshall SPV Limited, Airport Works, Cambridge CB5 8RX, UK.
Tel: 0223 301133. Telex: 81208.
In October 1992 Marshall SPV Limited acquired the product designs and some of the assets of AWD Limited.

Bedford MTM 40-30 (8 × 8) Multidrive Truck

Description

The Bedford MTM 40-30 (8 × 8) Multidrive truck was developed from the TM 8-8 Multidrive truck first shown in 1988. It has a 27-tonne payload and was designed for on- and off-highway military operations.

The MTM 40-30 features the Multidrive system with which the rear trailer bogie is steered and driven to provide good off-road performance and manoeuvrability, plus the steered rear axles eliminate trailer cut-in for improved mobility in confined locations. The Multidrive trailer can be employed for all manner of loads from stores to light armoured vehicles and is suitable for load handling systems.

The forward control cab used on the MTM 40-30 is similar to that used on the Bedford TM 4-4, TM 6-6 and TM 30-30, and can be tilted forward for engine access. Power is provided by a 300 hp Caterpillar turbocharged diesel driving through a ZF 16-speed gearbox and transfer box. An MTM 40-43 version is available with a 425 hp Caterpillar engine.

Optional equipment includes hydraulic cranes with 3, 4 and 6-tonne capacity, a 10-tonne line pull winch, palletised load handling systems, and a light tank transport platform with loading ramps. Integral fuel and water tanker bodies are available.

An 8 × 6 variant, the 38-tonne MTM 55 tanker, was procured by the British Army. This version is powered by a Caterpillar diesel developing 425 hp and can carry 20 tonnes of fuel or water. The tanker bodywork is by NEI-Thompson and the tanks may be either aluminium or mild steel. It is understood that 26 units were procured.

Specifications

Cab seating: 1 + 1
Configuration: 8 × 8
Weights: (unladen) 14 000 kg
Max load: 27 000 kg
Length: (overall) 11.73 m
Width: (over tyres) 2.47 m
Height: (cab) 3.11 m
Ground clearance: 0.42 m
Wheelbase: 3.93 m + 6.46 m (to centre of rear axle)
Max speed: 90 km/h
Fuel capacity: 2 × 340 l
Gradient: 37%
Engine: Caterpillar 3306B ATAAC 10.487 l 6-cylinder turbocharged diesel developing 300 bhp at 2100 rpm
Gearbox: ZF synchromesh range change splitter giving 16 forward and 2 reverse gears or

ZF Transmatic with WSK 400 torque converter
Transfer box: single-speed
Steering: recirculating ball, power-assist
Turning circle: 17.5 m
Suspension: (tractor unit) leaf springs and hydraulic shock absorbers front and rear
  (trailer) fully articulating 6-link bogie with leaf springs and shock absorbers
Tyres: 16 R 20
Brakes: air
Electrical system: 24 V
Batteries: 2 × 12 V, 120 Ah
Alternator: 45 A

Status
In production. MTM 55 tanker in service with British Army (26).

Manufacturer
Marshall SPV Limited, Airport Works, Cambridge CB5 8RX, UK.
Tel: 0223 301133. Telex: 81208.
In October 1992 Marshall SPV Limited acquired the product designs and some of the assets of AWD Limited.

Bedford MTM 55 (8 × 6) Multidrive tanker

Bedford MTM 40-30 (8 × 8) Multidrive truck carrying two Scorpion reconnaissance vehicles

Foden Low Mobility (8 × 4) and (6 × 4) Range of Vehicles

Development
The Foden Low Mobility range of vehicles was developed to meet a British Army requirement for a vehicle that would operate satisfactorily when laden to its gross vehicle weight on both roads and unsurfaced tracks. The range was based on standard commercial components with emphasis on ease of maintenance. Deliveries to the British Army amounted to 1275 units, of which over 60 per cent were delivered with left-hand drive for use by the British Army in Germany. A total of 15 more 8 × 4 tankers and 10 more 6 × 4 tankers were supplied fitted with GRP cabs and the Foden FF20 rubber rear suspension to update the overall specification.

Description
The vehicles are provided with a circular observation hatch in the centre of the cab roof. Standard cab equipment includes suspension seats, twin heaters/ demisters, sun visors and a visible warning system for air pressure, water temperature level and oil pressure.

The cab has two stages of access for maintenance. The first, for daily and weekly servicing, involves lifting the front grille panel to gain access to power steer and clutch reservoirs, engine oil filter and dipstick, windscreen washer bottle, wiper motor and linkage, cab heater system, air auxiliary feed connections and wiring harness and so on. The second stage involves using a hand-operated pump and ram assembly to tilt the cab forward to an angle of 68° to enable the engine to be removed without removing the cab. The cab can be removed as a complete unit if required, as quick-detachable, multi-point electrical connections are provided.

The front axles on the 8 × 4 versions are rated at 6604 kg; the rear axles have a capacity of 10 160 kg each with single reduction hubs. A third differential is fitted to the foremost differential housing, with provision for a differential lock on both rear axles.

The rear bogie is designed to a rating of 19 500 kg and is fitted to Foden FF20 rubber suspension units with a roll control device and telescopic shock absorbers.

Standard equipment on all models includes full width front bumper with central towing eye, rigid rear pulling jaw and lift and recovery lugs front and rear.

Variants
8 × 4 Cargo
A total of 800 was delivered. These can carry a maximum of 20 000 kg of cargo. The rear cargo body has drop sides, drop tailgate, removable bows and a canvas cover.

8 × 4 Tanker
A total of 256 was delivered. The chassis is fitted with a 22 500 litre tank body which has five compartments, each of which holds 4500 litre of fuel. The tank was manufactured by Thompson Tankers of Bilston, Staffordshire.

8 × 4 Tipper
A total of 70 was delivered. These have a shorter wheelbase than the other two 8 × 4 vehicles and are fitted with an Edbro 11 m³ all-steel end tipping body and an Edbro 6 NC single ram tip gear.

6 × 4 Tanker
A total of 183 was delivered; the tank has a capacity of 12 000 litres. The tank body was manufactured by Charles Roberts (Engineering) Limited of Wakefield, West Yorkshire.

Status
Production complete. In service with the British Army.

Manufacturer
Foden Trucks, A Division of PACCAR UK Ltd, Moss Lane, Sandbach, Cheshire CW11 9YW, UK. Tel: 0270 763244. Fax: 0270 762758.

Specifications

Type	Cargo	Tanker	Tipper	Tanker
Cab seating	1 + 2	1 + 2	1 + 2	1 + 2
Configuration	8 × 4	8 × 4	8 × 4	6 × 4
Weight (loaded)	29 553 kg	28 888 kg	29 705 kg	22 786 kg
(chassis and cab)	9553 kg	9553 kg	9770 kg	9030 kg
Weight on front axle (loaded)	10 000 kg	11 570 kg	10 659 kg	5532 kg
Weight on rear axles (loaded)	19 553 kg	17 318 kg	19 046 kg	17 254 kg
Length	10.278 m	10.27 m	8.69 m	8.75 m
Width	2.497 m	2.502 m	2.497 m	2.497 m
Height	3.317 m	3.25 m	3.319 m	3.214 m
Wheelbase	1.372 m + 3.614 m + 1.516 m	1.372 m + 3.614 m + 1.516 m	1.372 m + 2.522 m + 1.516 m	3.97 m + 1.516 m
Angle of approach/departure	23°/23°	23°/23°	23°/23°	36°/28°
Max speed (road)	76 km/h	76 km/h	76 km/h	87 km/h
Fuel capacity	227 l	227 l	227 l	227 l
Max gradient	31.64%*	31.64%*	31.3%	28.6%
Engine	Rolls-Royce 220 Mk III 6-cylinder liquid diesel developing 220 bhp at 2100 rpm			
Gearbox	Fuller with 9 forward and 1 reverse gears			
Steering	re-circulatory ball with integral power assistance			
Turning radius	12.25 m	12.25 m	10.35 m	11.4 m
Suspension (front)	semi-elliptical springs with telescopic hydraulic dampers			
(rear)	Foden FF20 rubber			
Tyres	11.00 × 20	11.00 × 20	11.00 × 20	12.00 × 20 (front) 14.00 × 20 (rear)
Brakes (main)	2-line air, dual circuit			
(parking)	spring brake chambers on rear axles only. Air brake couplings front and rear for recovery			
Electrical system	24 V	24 V	24 V	24 V
Batteries	2 × 12 V	2 × 12 V	2 × 12 V	2 × 12 V

* At GVW of 24 000 kg

Foden (8 × 4) low mobility tanker

Foden (8 × 4) 16 000 kg low mobility cargo truck (Ministry of Defence)

Scammell Crusader (6 × 4) Tractors

Description

The Scammell Crusader (6 × 4) tractor is basically a standard civilian vehicle adapted to meet military requirements. Two basic military models were produced, both of which are in service with the British Army. The first, known as the 20-tonne payload tractor, has a two-man cab and the second, the 35-tonne tractor, has a three-man cab with provision for two bunks.

20 000 kg (6 × 4) Tractor

The two-door forward control pressed steel cab is mounted on the chassis by two rubber bushed trunnion mountings at the front and two coil springs with integral telescopic dampers at the rear. The military version is powered by a Rolls-Royce Eagle 305 Mk III turbocharged diesel which develops 305 bhp at 2100 rpm coupled to a manual transmission with nine forward and two reverse gears.

35 000 kg (6 × 4) Tractor

The two-door forward control pressed steel cab has two individual seats at the front (one for the driver and one for a passenger) and two seats at the rear. The rear seats convert to bunks. The cab is mounted on the chassis by two rubber bushed trunnion mountings at the front and two coil springs with integral telescopic dampers at the rear. The engine is the same as in the 20 000 kg model but is coupled to an RTO 915 manual gearbox with 15 forward and three reverse gears. Mounted to the rear of the cab is a Plummett capstan model CA80 winch with 120 m of 16 mm cable which has a maximum capacity of 8000 kg at a speed of 27.5 m/min. The winch can be used either to the front or rear and is fitted with an overload warning bell.

Late in 1977 the British Army ordered 130 Scammell Crusader (6 × 4) recovery vehicles. For details see the *Recovery vehicles* section.

Status

Production complete. In service with the British Army.

Specifications

Type	20 000 kg	35 000 kg
Cab seating	1 + 1	1 + 3
Configuration	6 × 4	6 × 4
Weight (empty)	9200 kg	11 095 kg
Towed load	20 000 kg	35 000 kg
Length	6.66 m	6.66 m
Width	2.502 m	2.502 m
Height (overall)	3.3 m	3.3 m
(5th wheel)	1.412 m	1.549 m
Track (front)	2.05 m	2.05 m
(rear)	1.845 m	1.845 m
Wheelbase (1st axle to centre of rear bogie)	3.962 m	3.962 m
Max speed (road)	85 km/h	65 km/h
Range	500 km	500 km
Fuel capacity	318 l	455 l
Max gradient (stop and restart)	24%	20.9%
Engine	Rolls-Royce Eagle 305 Mk III turbocharged diesel developing 305 bhp at 2100 rpm	
Gearbox	manual with 9 forward and 1 reverse gears	manual with 15 forward and 3 reverse gears
Clutch	twin dry plate	twin dry plate
Steering	ball and nut, power-assisted	
Turning radius	9.5 m	9.5 m
Suspension (front)	longitudinal semi-elliptical springs pivoted front with slipper rear ends, and telescopic shock absorbers	
(rear)	fully articulated, inverted longitudinal semi-elliptical springs, trunnion-mounted at centre with slipper rear ends	
Tyres	11.00 × 20	11.00 × 20
Brakes	air on all axles incorporating 3-line brake system	
Electrical system	24 V	24 V
Batteries	4 × 12 V, 100 Ah	4 × 12 V, 100 Ah

Manufacturer

Unipower Vehicles Limited, 34 Greenhill Crescent, Watford Business Park, Watford, Hertfordshire WD1 8QU, UK.
Tel: 0923 816555. Telex: 261760 unitrk g.
Fax: 0923 228621.

Scammell Crusader (6 × 4) 35 000 kg tractor towing RE semi-trailer

British Army Scammell Crusader (6 × 4) tractor carrying German Army Lance vehicle

Unipower M Series (8 × 8) Logistics Support Load Carriers

Description

The Unipower M Series (8 × 8) logistics support load carrier is one element in a series of high mobility vehicles based on the same 8 × 8 IMMLC chassis. The chassis is designed to provide evenly distributed axle loadings for optimum mobility with designed combined axle capacities of 19 tonnes at the front and 20 tonnes at the rear. The specified engine output is 410 bhp giving fully laden performance figures exemplified by a 78 km/h maximum speed and 30 per cent continuous gradient climbing ability.

The general cargo variant, with drop side type bodywork and tilt, is specified with a 20 t/m hydraulic crane and a nett load capacity of 15 tonnes. The chassis could also be used to carry light armoured vehicles, for the launching and recovery of combat support craft or pontoons, and as a platform for mine warfare equipment. The M Series chassis can carry load handling equipment (see entry under *Materials handling equipment*) and may be configured as a tank transporter, heavy recovery vehicle or tanker with a 15 000 litre capacity. There is also a tactical bridging component carrier. The logistic load carrier can be carried in a C-130 transport aircraft without special preparation.

Pre-production M Series 8 × 8 trials vehicle undergoing durability trials

The M Series logistic load carrier is provided with a three-man forward control all-steel welded cab. The driver's seat is adjustable for height, reach and weight while a hatch above the central passenger seat provides access to a machine gun mounting, if required.

The chassis frame bolted construction uses heat treated carbon steel and is of the open channel type with open and tubular crossmembers. Towing facilities are provided front and rear. The front suspension consists of two slipper-ended semi-elliptic parabolic springs per axle. At the rear, two fully articulating semi-elliptical multi-leaf springs are trunnion-mounted on bearings. The rear axles are located longitudinally by upper and lower radius rods and transversally by eight Panhard rods.

The main power plant is a Cummins NTA A430 CELECT turbocharged diesel providing 430 bhp, although other similar power plants may be utilised. The power plant is coupled to a ZF Ecomat fully automatic transmission with a torque converter and a ZF single speed transfer box. Two PTOs are provided on the torque converter.

Standard equipment provided with each vehicle includes a tool kit, a wheel changing kit and two fire extinguishers.

Specifications
Cab seating: 1 + 2
Configuration: 8 × 8
Weight:
(unladen) 16 262 kg
(GVW, actual) 34 000 kg
(GVW, design) 39 000 kg
Length: 10.146 m
Width: 3 m
Height: 2.776 m
Ground clearance: 0.33 m
Wheelbase: 6 m
Angle of approach: 38°
Max speed: (laden) 76 km/h
Fuel capacity: 580 l
Range: 1000 km
Gradient: (restart, laden) 48%
Engine: Cummins NTA A430 CELECT 6-cylinder in-line turbocharged and after-cooled diesel developing 430 hp at 1900 rpm
Transmission: ZF Ecomat 6HP 600 Series III fully automatic providing 6 forward and 2 reverse gears plus ZF 380-30 torque converter
Transfer box: ZF single-speed
Steering: ZF 8098 power-assisted
Suspension:
(front) two slipper-ended semi-elliptic parabolic springs per axle
(rear) two fully articulating semi-elliptical multi-leaf springs trunnion-mounted on bearings
Brakes: air to all axles
Tyres: 24 R 21 XL
Electrical system: 24 V
Batteries: 2 × 12 V, 150 Ah
Alternator: 90 A

Status
Pre-production.

Manufacturer
Unipower Vehicles Limited, 34 Greenhill Crescent, Watford Business Park, Watford, Hertfordshire WD1 8QU, UK.
Tel: 0923 816555. Telex: 261760 unitrk g.
Fax: 0923 228621.

UNITED STATES OF AMERICA

Commercial Utility Cargo Vehicles (CUCV)

Development
Starting in 1981 a 14-month programme known as the 'Special Analysis of Wheeled Vehicle Requirements' (usually abbreviated to just 'WHEELS') was carried out by the US Army Tank Automotive Command. Its objective was to find a commercial vehicle that could be easily procured for US Army use in areas where extreme environmental conditions would not be met and where expensive vehicles were not necessary. The objective was to replace 20 per cent of the M151 Jeeps in use and the bulk of the M880 series of pick-up trucks. The vehicle types chosen would also be used by the US Air Force and Marine Corps.

During the programme the US Army purchased 26 commercial vehicles and subjected them to exhaustive tests at the Aberdeen Proving Grounds, Maryland. The final choice was a General Motors design, the Model K which is one of the GM C/K series, over 9 million of which were produced.

In July 1982, a contract was awarded to General Motors worth $689 million for a total of 53 248 vehicles known as the Commercial Utility Cargo Vehicles (CUCV). First deliveries were made in August 1983 and the initial production programme lasted three years.

Projected procurement was for 57 349 CUCVs for all the armed services with 54 087 for the US Army. Total production at the end of 1986 was 70 889, including FMS. Production ceased in 1987.

The US Marine Corps received 2989 CUCVs of the following types: M1008 – 2194; M1009 – 166; M1010 – 290; M1031 – 95; M1028 – 414.

Specifications

Type	A	B	C	D	E
Function	utility	cargo	ambulance	truck	cargo, shelter carrier
Model	M1009	M1008	M1010	M1031	M1028
GM model number	K10516 Blazer	K30903 Pick-up	K30903 Chassis/cab	K30903 Chassis/cab	K30903 Pick-up
Cab seating	1 + 1 + 3	3	1 + 1	3	3
Configuration	4 × 4	4 × 4	4 × 4	4 × 4	4 × 4
Weight (loaded)	2903 kg	3992 kg	4287 kg	4334 kg	4264 kg
Max payload	544 kg	1315 kg	943 kg	1792 kg	1633 kg
Length	4.873 m	5.607 m	5.784 m	5.408 m	5.607 m
Width	2.022 m	2.062 m	2.062 m	2.062 m	2.062 m
Height (overall)	1.905 m	1.915 m	2.581 m	1.938 m	1.92 m
Track (front)	1.485 m	1.488 m	1.488 m	1.488 m	1.488 m
(rear)	1.382 m	1.438 m	1.438 m	1.438 m	1.438 m
Wheelbase	2.705 m	3.34 m	3.34 m	3.34 m	3.34 m
Fording	0.508 m	0.508 m	0.508 m	0.508 m	0.508 m
Engine	General Motors 6.2 l V-8 diesel developing 135 hp at 36 rpm				
Gearbox	General Motors THM-400 3-speed automatic with 1 reverse				
Transfer box	2-speed	2-speed	2-speed	2-speed	2-speed
Suspension (front)	tapered leaf springs with 1021 kg capacity				
(rear)	semi-elliptical multi-leaf springs with 850, 1588, 1588, 1701, 1701 kg capacity respectively				
Tyres	10.00 × 15	9.50 × 16.5	9.50 × 16.5	9.50 × 16.5	9.50 × 16.5
Electrical system	28 V, 100 Ah	28 V, 100 Ah	28 V, 200 Ah	28 V, 100 Ah	28 V, 100 Ah

Description
The CUCV fleet comprises five types of vehicle, as follows:

Type A, Truck, Utility, Tactical ¾-ton, (4 × 4), M1009

Type B, Truck, Cargo, Tactical 1¼-ton, (4 × 4), M1008

Type C, Truck, Ambulance, Tactical 1¼-ton, (4 × 4), M1010

Type D, Truck, Chassis, Tactical 1¼-ton, (4 × 4), M1031

Type E, Truck, Cargo, Shelter Carrier, Tactical 1¼-ton, (4 × 4), M1028

All five types are based on a common power train but utilise different body and/or chassis variations to fulfil a variety of purposes and having varying payloads to suit their role. All five types have the 6.2 litre diesel engine, automatic transmission and two-speed transfer box.

Truck, Cargo, Tactical 1¼-ton, (4 × 4), M1008 (M Bell)

Truck, Ambulance, Tactical 1¼-ton, (4 × 4), M1010

The rear and front axles are the same in all types other than the Type A. The 28 V electrical system in all types is the same apart from the Type C ambulance which has a system with doubled power.

The five types are all commercial models with the following alterations incorporated: blackout lights; camouflage paint (three colour, NATO); engine diagnostic connector assembly; military markings, including a removable red cross for the Type C ambulance; NBC warfare protection and kit provisions; rear pintle hook; slave-start capability; towing capability; weapon holders; and a winterisation kit to allow operations down to −46°C.

The Type C ambulance version has provision for four stretcher patients or eight seated wounded. An air filter system is also provided along with air-conditioning and extra lighting, including spotlights. The Type E cargo, shelter carrier is equipped with shelter tie-down brackets.

All five types are air-transportable.

Status
Production complete. A total of 70 889 units was delivered to all branches of the American armed forces. The total includes FMS to nations such as Columbia, Grenada, Honduras, Israel, Jamaica, Liberia (M1009), Panama and Taiwan.

Manufacturer
General Motors Truck and Bus Group, Flint, Michigan, USA.

Enquiries to General Motors Corporation, Military Vehicles Operation, 660 South Boulevard East, Pontiac, Michigan 48341-3128, USA.
Tel: (313) 456 5977. Fax: (313) 456 6241.

Commercial Utility Cargo Vehicles II (CUCV II)

Description
Following the completion of production of the original CUCV range (see previous entry), General Motors Corporation, Military Vehicles Operation, has introduced a new range of economical tactical support vehicles known as the CUCV II. The CUCV II range follows the same general lines as the original CUCV range and similar basic General Motors commercial models are involved, but updated and revised to the latest commercial and military specifications. The CUCV II range includes petrol- as well as diesel-engined options.

There are four basic models in the CUCV II range. They are:

The Type A Utility based on the K10516 Yukon and generally similar to the M1009

The Type B Cargo/Troop Carrier based on the K20903 Pick-up and generally similar to the M1008

The Type C Ambulance based on the K30903 Chassis/cab and generally similar to the M1010

The Type E S-250 Shelter Carrier based on the K20903 Pick-up and generally similar to the M1028.

As yet the US Army has not fielded CUCV II vehicles but Types B, C and E have been purchased by TACOM for Foreign Military Sales (FMS).

The military standard options available for CUCV II vary from model to model but include a 24 V electrical system, blackout lighting, a battery booster connector, a radiator brush guard, front and rear tie-downs, a trailer pintle hook and electrical connector, weapon racks and similar specialised items.

Specifications

Type	A	B	C	E
Function	utility	carrier	ambulance	shelter carrier
GM model number	K10516	K20903	K30903	K20903
Cab seating	2 + 3	3 + 8	3 + 4	1 + 2
Configuration	4 × 4	4 × 4	4 × 4	4 × 4
Weight (loaded)	2835 kg	3900 kg	4170 kg	4170 kg
Towed load	1361 kg	1361 kg	n/app	1361 kg
Length	4.902 m	5.669 m	5.9 m	5.669 m
Width	1.957 m	1.95 m	1.961 m	1.95 m
Height (overall)	1.869 m	1.93 m	2.713 m	2.613 m
Ground clearance	0.229 m	0.206 m	0.206 m	0.206 m
Wheelbase	2.832 m	3.34 m	3.34 m	3.34 m
Max speed	88 km/h	88 km/h	88 km/h	88 km/h
Range	400 km	400 km	400 km	400 km
Fording	0.508 m	0.508 m	0.508 m	0.508 m
Engine	GM 5.7 l V-8 petrol developing 210 hp at 4000 rpm			
Transmission	GM THM 4L60E automatic with 4 forward and 1 reverse gears			
Transfer box	2-speed	2-speed	2-speed	2-speed
Suspension (front)	independent heavy duty torsion bar with shock absorbers			
(rear)	two-stage semi-elliptical leaf springs with shock absorbers			
Tyres	16 × 6.5	16 × 6.5	16 × 6.5	16 × 6.5
Electrical system	24 V	24 V	24 V	24 V

The base engine for the CUCV II range is a GM 5.7 litre V-8 petrol developing 210 bhp. Also available is a 5.7 litre V-8 petrol developing 190 bhp or a 7.4 litre V-8 petrol developing 230 bhp. A further option is provided by a 6.2 litre diesel developing 150 bhp. All engines are coupled to General Motors Hydra-Matic automatic transmissions.

One closely allied vehicle to the CUCV II range is the General Motors Pursuit Vehicle. Based on the K20906 Suburban chassis this hard-topped 4 × 4 or 4 × 2 vehicle can carry a 12.7 mm machine gun over a square hatch in the roof. Numbers have reportedly been sold to countries in the Middle East.

Status
In production.

Manufacturer
General Motors Corporation, Military Vehicles Operation, 660 South Boulevard East, Pontiac, Michigan 48341-3128, USA.
Tel: (313) 456 5977. Fax: (313) 456 6241.

M715 (4 × 4) 1¼-ton Truck

Development
The M715 was developed in the 1960s as an interim replacement vehicle for the M37 (4 × 4) ¾-ton truck. The vehicle was developed by the Kaiser Jeep Corporation from its commercial Gladiator (4 × 4) vehicle and after trials with prototypes the company received its first production contract in March 1966. That was for 20 680 vehicles to be delivered over two years at a cost of $90.9 million. First deliveries were made in January 1967 and production continued until 1970 by which time 30 510 had been built. Late in 1969 the company received a contract to build 43 improved vehicles to be tested in competition with the General Motors developed XM705. The company produced an improved model under the designation AM 715, for which there is a separate entry. This series is being replaced by the High Mobility Multi-purpose Wheeled Vehicle (HMMWV).

Description
The layout of the vehicle is conventional with the engine at the front, cab in the centre and cargo/personnel area at the rear. The chassis of the M715 is designated the M724. The cab has a windscreen which can be folded forward onto the bonnet and removable canvas top. The rear cargo area has a drop tailgate, removable bows, a tarpaulin cover and longitudinal folding seats on each side which can seat four men. Many vehicles have a front-mounted winch with a capacity of 3402 kg. Kits available for the M715 include deep fording kit, cargo and crew compartment enclosure kit, engine heater kit, and heaters for both the crew and cargo areas.

Variants
M725 ambulance
This was the replacement for the M43 ambulance. It has a fully enclosed rear van-type body and can carry eight seated patients plus the driver and medical orderly or five stretcher patients plus the driver and medical orderly.

M726 telephone line maintenance vehicle
This was the replacement for the M201 ¾-ton maintenance truck; its rear all-steel body has compartments for stowing tools and spare parts.

M142
This is the standard M715 with the S-250 communications shelter installed in the rear, used for a variety of roles by the US Army and Marine Corps.

Specifications
Cab seating: 1 + 1
Configuration: 4 × 4
Weight:
(empty without winch) 2494 kg
(empty with winch) 2721 kg
(loaded, cross-country without winch) 3854 kg

M715 (4 × 4) 1¼-ton truck

(loaded, cross-country with winch) 4081 kg
Max load:
(road) 1360 kg
(cross-country) 1134 kg
Towed load:
(road) 1628 kg
(cross-country) 1288 kg
Length: 5.327 m
Width: 2.159 m
Height:
(overall) 2.413 m
(reduced) 1.498 m
Ground clearance: 0.254 m
Track: 1.71 m
Wheelbase: 3.2 m

Angle of approach/departure: 45°/25°
Max speed: 96.6 km/h
Range: 362 km
Fuel capacity: 106 l
Gradient: 58%
Fording:
(without preparation) 0.914 m
(with preparation) 1.524 m
Engine: Model OHC 6-230 6-cylinder in-line water-cooled petrol developing 132.5 bhp at 4000 rpm
Gearbox: manual with 4 forward and 1 reverse gears
Transfer box: 2-speed
Steering: recirculating ball
Turning radius: 8.384 m
Suspension: horizontal semi-elliptical springs and

direct acting shock absorbers, with hydraulic dampers
Tyres: 9.00 × 10
Brakes:
(main) hydraulic
(parking) mechanical
Electrical system: 24 V

Status
Production complete. In service with the US forces, Haiti (M715 and M724) and Israel.

Manufacturer
AM General Corporation, 105 N. Niles Avenue, PO Box 7025 South Bend, Indiana 46634-7025, USA. Tel: (219) 284 2942/2911. Fax: (219) 284 2959/2814.

AM 715 Series (4 × 4) 1¼-ton Trucks

Description
When production of the M715 (4 × 4) 1¼-ton truck was completed for the US Army in 1969 AM General developed another version for export called the AM 715. In appearance this is almost identical to the M715 but has a more powerful engine and other small modifications. The chassis is designated the AM 724.

The layout of the AM 715 is conventional with the engine at the front, two-door cab with a removable canvas top, windscreen which folds forward onto the bonnet and side windows which can be wound down in the centre, and the cargo area at the rear with a drop tailgate, stake-type sides, removable bows and a tarpaulin cover. A fold-up bench seat, capable of seating five fully equipped men, is provided down each side of the cargo area. The AM 715 can also carry a standard S-250 military shelter and be used as a command or communications vehicle.

The AM 725 is an ambulance which can carry five stretcher patients plus an attendant. The AM 715C is a weapon carrier (for example TOW), while the AM 715S is a field service vehicle similar to the M726 telephone line maintenance truck.

Specifications
(AM 715; data in square brackets relate to AM 725 where different)
Cab seating: 1 + 2
Configuration: 4 × 4
Weight:
(empty) 2132 [2676] kg
(loaded) 3537 [3583] kg
Weight on front axle: (loaded) 1361 [1383] kg
Weight on rear axle: (loaded) 2177 [2200] kg
Max load: 1134 [726] kg
Towed load: 1288 kg [n/app]
Load area: 2.355 × 1.626 m [n/app]
Length: 5.321 [5.359] m

AM General AM 715 (4 × 4) 1¼-ton cargo truck

Width: 2.032 [2.134] m
Height:
(reduced) 1.36 m [n/app]
(overall) 2.286 [2.451] m
(load area) 0.838 m [n/app]
Ground clearance: (axles) 0.22 [0.21] m
Track:
(front) 1.641 [1.626] m
(rear) 1.674 [1.661] m
Wheelbase: 3.327 [3.319] m
Angle of approach/departure: 41°[32°]/25°
Max speed: (road) 97 km/h
Range: 322 km
Fuel capacity: 72 l
Max gradient: 60%
Fording: 0.457 m
Engine: Model 6-258 6-cylinder in-line OHV petrol developing 150 hp at 3800 rpm
Gearbox: manual, with 4 forward and 1 reverse gears

Clutch: single plate
Transfer box: 2-speed
Steering: recirculating ball
Turning radius: 7.11 [7.32] m
Suspension: horizontal semi-elliptical springs with hydraulic shock absorbers
Tyres: 7.50 × 16
Brakes: front, power; rear, drum (vacuum-assisted)
Electrical system: 12 V
Battery: 1 × 12 V, 63 Ah

Status
Production complete.

Manufacturer
AM General Corporation, 105 N. Niles Avenue, PO Box 7025 South Bend, Indiana 46634-7025, USA. Tel: (219) 284 2942/2911. Fax: (219) 284 2959/2814.

Jeep AM 720 (4 × 4) 1135 kg Light Truck

Description
The Jeep AM 720 (4 × 4) 1135 kg light truck is an updated version of the AM 715 (see previous entry),

which it resembles in general layout and appearance. The AM 720 is based on the commercial J-20 truck and is available with two main types of cargo body known

as the Military Cargo Box or the Townside Cargo Box, with the latter intended more for the civilian market. Either can carry up to 13 men seated on folding

Jeep AM 720 (4 × 4) 1135 kg light truck   *Jeep AM 720 (4 × 4) 1135 kg light truck showing Military Cargo Box body*

benches and can be covered by a vinyl top resting on bows. The cab also has a vinyl top.

Numerous options are available for the AM 720, including various wheelbase lengths and left- or right-hand drive. An electric winch with a capacity of 2832 kg can be fitted and a 24 V conversion kit is available.

This vehicle is licence-produced in Egypt – see separate entry in this section.

Specifications
Cab seating: 1 + 2 (up to 13 in rear)
Configuration: 4 × 4
Weight: (off road)
(unladen) 2175 kg
(laden) 3814 kg
Max load:
(off road) 1135 kg
(on road) 1639 kg

Towed load: 3629 kg
Length: 5.36 m
Width: 2.004 m
Height:
(with cargo top) 2.286 m
(cargo bed) 0.84 m
Ground clearance: 0.208 m
Track:
(front) 1.626 m
(rear) 1.661 m
Wheelbase: (standard) 3.322 m
Angle of approach/departure: 35°/21°
Fuel capacity: 69 l
Fording: 0.457 m
Engine: Model 258 CID 4.2 l 6-cylinder OHV developing 112 hp at 3000 rpm or 5.9 l 8-cylinder developing 144 hp at 3200 rpm
Gearbox: manual, 4 forward and 1 reverse gears

Transfer box: 2-speed
Clutch: single dry disc
Steering: variable ratio power-assisted
Turning radius: 6.78 m
Suspension: longitudinal leaf springs with severe-use shock absorbers
Tyres: 9.50 × 16.5 or 9.00 × 16
Brakes: power, disc front; drum rear
Electrical system: 12 V (24 V optional)

Status
In production. In widespread service.

Manufacturer
Jeep Corporation, International Operations, 27777 Franklin Road, Southfield, Michigan 48034, USA.

M880 (4 × 4) and (4 × 2) 1133 kg Series

Development
In February 1972 the 'WHEELS' (Special Analysis of Wheeled Vehicle Requirements) study was established under the chairmanship of the Assistant Vice Chief of Staff, Army. Its object was to conduct a comprehensive analysis of the US Army's wheeled vehicle needs, fleet management and utilisation. The study was undertaken in three phases, the last of which was completed in April 1973. The study made many recommendations, most of which were implemented. One of the recommendations was that standard commercial vehicles could be used for many of the roles previously undertaken by specialised vehicles. The US Army then had a fleet of 600 000 vehicles and it was expected that 400 000 of these would be replaced by commercial vehicles with few, if any, modifications for Army use.

The first requirement was for a new 1¼-ton 4 × 4 and 4 × 2 series of vehicles. The US Army issued a requirement for 33 759 vehicles and received bids from AM General ($170.5 million), Chevrolet Division of General Motors Corporation ($150.5 million), Ford Motor Corporation ($188.7 million) and the Chrysler Corporation, Dodge Division ($145.7 million). In March 1975 the latter bid was accepted and the contract was awarded to Chrysler. First production vehicles were delivered to the Army in May 1975 and final deliveries were made late in 1978. The range comprised both 4 × 4 (Dodge W200) and 4 × 2 (Dodge D200) vehicles in both pick-up and ambulance versions (about 4000). The pick-up contract price was $3825.16 (retail price in 1975 was about $5200), which included steel-belted radial tyres, maintenance-free battery, rustproofing and lustreless forest green paint. The vehicles were covered by the standard new truck warranty of 19 312 km or 12 months, and repairs were carried out by local Dodge dealers.

Approximately 44 000 M880 series trucks were built between 1975 and 1977. The series is being replaced by the High Mobility Multi-purpose Wheeled Vehicle (HMMWV) and CUCV.

Description
The 4 × 4 cargo model is designated the M880 (Dodge W200 chassis) and the 4 × 2 cargo model is designated the M890 (Dodge D200 chassis). Both are identical in appearance with the engine at the front, fully enclosed two-door all-steel cab in the centre and the cargo area at the rear with a drop tailgate. A bench-type seat for four fully equipped men can be fitted down either side. Mounted at the rear is a swivel tow pintle and a trailer lighting receptacle.

The 4 × 4 ambulance model is designated the M886 (Dodge W200 chassis) and the 4 × 2 ambulance model the M893 (Dodge D200 chassis). They are identical in appearance and the fully enclosed rear body can accommodate four to five stretcher patients and a medical attendant on a jump seat.

Including the basic vehicle, there were 13 members in the family:
M880, Truck, Cargo: 1¼-ton (4 × 4)
M881, Truck, Cargo: 1¼-ton (4 × 4) with 60 A kit

Specifications

Designation (US Army) (Dodge)	M880 W200	M886 W200	M890 D200	M893 D200
Type	cargo	ambulance	cargo	ambulance
Cab seating	1 + 2	1 + 2	1 + 2	1 + 2
Configuration	4 × 4	4 × 4	4 × 2	4 × 2
Weight (empty)	2108 kg	2774 kg	1913 kg	2578 kg
(loaded)	3629 kg	3629 kg	3402 kg	3402 kg
Max load	1133 kg	n/app	1133 kg	n/app
Towed load	1360 kg	n/app	1360 kg	n/app
Length	5.56 m	5.46 m	5.56 m	5.46 m
Width	2.02 m	2.02 m	2.02 m	2.02 m
Height	1.87 m	2.57 m	1.8 m	2.49 m
Wheelbase	3.33 m	3.33 m	3.33 m	3.33 m
Track	1.625 m	1.625 m	1.625 m	1.625 m
Fuel capacity	76 l	76 l	76 l	76 l
Engine	Chrysler V-8 OHV petrol developing 150 hp at 4000 rpm			
Transmission	Loadflite automatic with 3 speeds forward and torque converter			
Transfer box (4 × 4 model only)	New Process model 203 with 2-speed full-time 4 × 4 drive with locking interaxle differential			
Steering	mechanical, recirculating ball			
Turning circle	14.63 m	14.63 m	14.63 m	14.63 m
Suspension	semi-elliptical springs with hydraulic double-acting shock absorbers			
Brakes	power (vacuum/hydraulic), front disc, rear drum			
Electrical system	12 V	12 V	12 V	12 V
Battery	1 × 12 V	1 × 12 V	1 × 12 V	1 × 12 V

M886, Truck Ambulance: 1¼-ton (4 × 4) (C R Zwart)

M882, Truck, Cargo: 1¼-ton (4 × 4) with 60 A kit and communication kit
M883, Truck, Cargo: 1¼-ton (4 × 4) with 60 A and communications shelter tie-down kit
M884, Truck, Cargo: 1¼-ton (4 × 4) with 100 A and communications shelter tie-down kit
M885, Truck, Cargo: 1¼-ton (4 × 4) with communications shelter tie-down kit
M890, Truck, Cargo: 1¼-ton (4 × 2)
M891, Truck, Cargo: 1¼-ton (4 × 2) with 60 A kit
M892, Truck, Cargo: 1¼-ton (4 × 2) with 60 A kit and communications kit
M886, Truck, Ambulance: 1¼-ton (4 × 4)

M893, Truck, Ambulance: 1¼-ton (4 × 2)
M887, Truck, Contact Maintenance: 1¼-ton (4 × 4)
M888, Truck, Telephone Maintenance: 1¼-ton (4 × 4)

Status
Production complete. In service with the US Army and Pakistan.

Manufacturer
Dodge Division of Chrysler Corporation, 7900 Jos Campau Avenue (Hamtramck), Detroit, Michigan 48211, USA.

HMMWV M998 Series Multi-purpose Wheeled Vehicles

Development

Based on the draft specification for the High Mobility Multi-purpose Wheeled Vehicle (HMMWV) issued by the US Army in mid-1979, AM General Corporation designed and built a prototype in the weapons carrier configuration.

The first prototype was completed in August 1980 and was sent to the Nevada Automotive Test Center for extensive trials and by February 1981 the prototype had accumulated 21 000 km of instrumented and dynamic testing.

AM General became one of three contenders awarded a US Army contract for the design and construction of 11 prototype HMMWVs (six weapons carriers and five utility) which were delivered in May 1982. In March 1983 AM General was awarded a $59.8 million contract by the US Army Tank Automotive Command (TACOM) for 2334 HMMWVs, which were then designated the M998 Series (unofficially Hummer). This was the first increment in a five-year contract for 54 973 vehicles worth approximately $1.2 billion. Of these some 39 000 were for the US Army and the remainder were divided between the US Air Force, Navy and the Marine Corps (initially 3123). Production commenced at Mishawaka, Indiana, early in 1985. Contract options for a further 15 000 were exercised to bring the total production by mid-1991 to over 80 000 vehicles, including overseas sales.

In August 1989 the US Army awarded AM General a further multi-year contract worth approximately $1 billion. The contract calls for a further 33 331 vehicles until 1993, with two further option years. Production under the new contract began in January 1990 and production for the US armed forces will continue throughout 1994, by which time the US armed forces will have approximately 84 000 HMMWVs. A further 10 000 units have been ordered by 30 foreign governments, including 2300 units purchased by Saudi Arabia in mid-1991 at a cost of $123 million.

In service the M998 Series HMMWVs replaced some M151 Jeeps, the M274 Mule (830 in service), the M561/M792 Gama Goat (11 000 in service) and the M880 series (40 000 in service), with 20 per cent of the fleet of M151s and many of the M880s being replaced by the Commercial Utility Cargo Vehicle (CUCV).

Description

The HMMWV has 2 × 2 seating on each side of the drive train which is in a midship position allowing the front differential to be raised. This, together with the geared hubs, provides a ground clearance of 0.41 m. The location of the crew on each side of the drive train also allows a low centre of gravity. The windshield frame is strong enough to serve as a roll bar and support for various equipment kits. Other pillars also make the ballistically protected weapon station inherently strong and a steady location on which to mount a variety of weapons such as TOW, 7.62 and

12.7 mm machine guns and the MK19 40 mm grenade launcher. At the rear the cargo bed is large enough to accommodate an S-250 or similar shelter without overhang.

Production versions of the HMMWV can be converted into numerous variants by changing the body configuration. These configurations are:
M998 Cargo/troop carrier without winch
M1038 Cargo/troop carrier with winch
M966 TOW missile carrier, basic armour, without winch
M1036 TOW missile carrier, basic armour, with winch
M1045 TOW missile carrier, supplemental armour, without winch
M1046 TOW missile carrier, supplemental armour, with winch
M1025 Armament carrier, basic armour, without winch
M1026 Armament carrier, basic armour, with winch
M1043 Armament carrier, supplemental armour, without winch
M1044 Armament carrier, supplemental armour, with winch
M997 Maxi-ambulance, 4-litter, basic armour
M1035 Soft-top ambulance, 2-litter
M1037 Shelter carrier, without winch
M1042 Shelter carrier, with winch

In addition to the above, selected application kits are produced as follows:
Cargo/troop carrier, soft-top enclosure (2-door cab) for M998
Cargo/troop carrier, soft-top enclosure (4-door cab) for M998
Cargo/troop carrier, soft-top enclosure (2-door cab, troop seats) for M1038
Cargo/troop carrier, soft-top enclosure (2-door cab, troop/cargo) for M1038
Cargo/troop carrier, soft-top enclosure (4-door cab, cargo) for M1038
Armament carrier, basic armour with M60 7.62 mm machine gun for M1026
Armament carrier, supplemental armour with M2 0.50/ 12.7 mm machine gun for M1044
Armament carrier, supplemental armour with MK19 grenade launcher for M1043
Lightweight weapon station kit for the M998/M1038 (weight 114 kg).

The HMMWV has been adapted for use as a missile launch vehicle. Launch vehicles produced to date include the following:
Pedestal-Mounted Stinger (PMS) carrying eight Stinger surface-to-air missiles and one 12.7 mm machine gun. This became operational with the US Army in 1989-90 and the total requirement is for 273 over a five-year period. For full details refer to *Jane's Land-based Air Defence 1992-93* pages 150 to 153.
LTV Crossbow Pedestal-Mounted Weapon System carrying a variety of air defence or anti-tank systems. For details of this private venture refer to *Jane's Land-based Air Defence 1992-93* pages 153 and 154.
Fibre Optic Guided Missile (FOG-M) System. The HMMWV was selected as the launch vehicle for the Non-Line-of-Sight (NLOS) component of the FOG-M

which was cancelled in December 1990. For details refer to *Jane's Land-based Air Defence 1992-93* pages 154 and 155.
An HMMWV was used for firing trials involving the Hellfire anti-tank guided weapon in a surface-to-surface role.
An HMMWV has been adapted to carry an M40A2 106 mm recoilless rifle for overseas sales.
At least one HMMWV has been used by Alliant Techsystems for trials involving a Light Volcano version of the M139 Volcano multiple delivery mine system – see under *Minelaying equipment* for details.
Stanley Hydraulic Tools of Milwaukie, Oregon, has proposed a combat engineer or first line maintenance vehicle version of the HMMWV equipped with the Stanley Hydraulic Integrated Tool System (HITS) involving 70 different hydraulic tools.
In addition to the above vehicles and kits, further vehicles were used for research and development but were not adopted by the US Army. These were:
RED-T with 25 mm Chain Gun
Armoured squad carrier with MK19 40 mm grenade launcher
Stinger missile team vehicle
Command and control, communications, and intelligence (C^3I) vehicle
70 mm Rapid Deployment Multiple Rocket Weapon System. For details of this system refer to *Jane's Armour and Artillery 1992-93* page 743.

To reduce life cycle and initial procurement costs, standard automotive components are used wherever possible, as in the engine, transmission, transfer case, brakes and steering.

The independent suspension, front and rear, gives good manoeuvrability, ease of handling and part commonality. The geared hubs give 0.41 m ground clearance incorporating raised axles for high speed operations on road and across country. They also provide a 1.92:1 torque output multiplication at the ground.

The suspended carrier front and rear axles are identical, have differentials and are mounted high directly in the chassis frame. The front propeller shaft has double cardan joints and the rear propeller shaft has single cardan joints which, according to AM General, give minimal motion, improved torque characteristics and higher reliability with resultant lower support costs. Vehicle handling is enhanced by the front stabiliser bar being attached to the lower control arms and pivot bracket reducing shock from the lower A-frame member to the chassis.

Acceleration of the HMMWV is such that it can move from a standstill to 48 km/h in 8 seconds and from a standstill to 80 km/h in 24 seconds.

In addition to the above-mentioned variants, AM General has also produced the M1097 'Heavy Hummer' variant (HHV) to increase the GVW to 4536 kg – all existing HMMWV versions can be produced to this level, known as the Heavy Weapons Carrier or Heavy Armament Carrier. The 'heavy' chassis permits a payload increase to 2042 kg in the case of the M1037 – GVW is 4536 kg. The M1097 chassis incorporates

HMMWV M998 with Lightweight Weapon Station and McDonnell Douglas Helicopters 30 mm ASP-30 cannon

Prototype of HMMWV M1097 up-armoured Heavy Armament Carrier armed with GECAL 50 0.50/12.7 mm Gatling Gun

HMMWV M997 Maxi-ambulance with deep water fording kit   *HMMWV M998 cargo/troop carrier*

improved front and rear differentials, a new transfer case, new front and rear propshafts, an improved frame mounting for the steering gear, variable rate rear springs and new lower ball joints. The heavier chassis allows the use of an up-armoured ballistic panel protection kit with 5.56 and 7.62 mm ball protection and permits the carriage of heavy weapons such as the McDonnell Douglas Helicopters ASP-30 30 mm cannon. Production commenced in September 1992.

Modification kits developed by and available directly from AM General include a selective up-armour kit, a brushguard, spare tyre and jerrican carriers, a driveline skid protection kit, a central tyre inflation system (CTIS) and a special desert operations package including secondary oil and fuel filtration, sealed dipsticks, a constant drive fan and enhanced oil filtration. A lightweight weapon station kit is an adaptation of that used on standard HMMWV weapon carriers and weighs 114 kg.

The M1097 HHV was used as the basis for the Hummer Cab-over (4 × 4) 2268 kg cargo truck – see following entry. Civilian and public utility versions of the HMMWV are available.

A high-mobility trailer (HMT) for use with the HMMWV is under development and testing. It will have a capacity of from 680 to 1134 kg and is scheduled to be fielded during 1994.

Three HMMWVs can be carried in a C-130 Hercules transport aircraft, six in a C-141B and 15 in a C-5A Galaxy.

Specifications (M1038 Cargo Troop Carrier w/winch)
Cab seating: 1 + 3
Configuration: 4 × 4
Weight:
 (kerb) 2416 kg
 (GVW) 3493 kg
Max load: 1077 kg
Max towed load: 1542 kg
Length: 4.72 m
Width: 2.16 m
Height: 1.83 m
Ground clearance: 0.41 m
Track: 1.82 m
Wheelbase: 3.29 m
Angle of approach/departure: 47°/45°
Max speed: 105 km/h
Range: 482 km
Fuel capacity: 94.6 l
Max gradient: 60%
Side slope: 40%
Fording: 0.76 m
 (with preparation) 1.52 m
Engine: V-8 6.2 l diesel developing 150 hp at 3600 rpm

Transmission: automatic with 3 forward and 1 reverse gears
Transfer box: 2-speed, full-time 4-wheel drive
Suspension: (front and rear) independent, double A-arm, coil spring
Steering: power-assisted
Turning radius: 7.42 m
Brakes: hydraulic disc front and rear
Tyres: 36 × 12.50-16.5
Electrical system: 24 V
Batteries: 2 × 12 V

Status
In production. In service with US Army, Air Force, Navy and Marine Corps. Some 10 000 vehicles have been sold to 30 friendly foreign countries. Known to be in service with Abu Dhabi (3), Djibouti (10), Luxembourg (29), the Philippines, Saudi Arabia (2300 ordered in 1991), Taiwan and Thailand (150). Civilianised versions have been sold to the Chinese Ministry of Petroleum Exploration, the US Border Patrol and other civilian agencies.

Manufacturer
AM General Corporation, 105 N. Niles Avenue, PO Box 7025 South Bend, Indiana 46634-7025, USA. Tel: (219) 284 2942/2911. Fax: (219) 284 2959/2814.

Hummer Cab-over (4 × 4) 2268 kg Cargo Truck (COCT)

Description
Using many of the components of the M1097 HHV (see previous entry) the Hummer Cab-over (4 × 4) 2268 kg cargo truck (COCT) was developed to meet a possible international requirement for a lightweight high mobility and high capacity truck. The first two prototypes were produced and tested by AM General during 1990. Production is planned for 1994.

The Hummer COCT utilises the basic steel box frame chassis of the M1097 HHV allied to a new forward control three-man cab. The full 4 × 4 drive configuration and front and rear independent suspension of the HMMWV are also retained. The main change is that a new transfer case with power take-off provision is added to the transfer case.

The forward control cab is high and distinctive in appearance and utilises a soft-top and canvas doors. The location of the cab is such that a load area measuring (externally) 3.18 × 2.16 m is available at the rear. This load area may be used for a cargo body with drop sides or for a flat bed capable of carrying shelters and/or containers. Optional equipment includes a central tyre inflation system and a 3629 kg capacity hydraulic winch weighing, in kit form, approximately 136 kg.

The vehicle may be air-transported in C-130, C-141B and C-5A aircraft.

Hummer Cab-over (4 × 4) 2268 kg cargo truck (COCT) carrying shelter/container

Specifications

Cab seating: 1 + 2
Configuration: 4 × 4
Weight:
  (kerb) 3175 kg
  (GVW) 5670 kg
Max load: 2268 kg
Towed load: 1905 kg
Load area: 3.06 × 2.02 m
Length: 5.06 m
Width: 2.16 m
Height: (top of cab) 2.5 m
Ground clearance: 0.41 m
Wheelbase: 3.3 m

Angle of approach/departure: 47°/33.5°
Max speed: 95 km/h
Range: 483 km
Fuel capacity: 182 l
Gradient: 60%
Fording: 0.76 m
Engine: 6.5 l V-8 turbo diesel developing 190 hp
Gearbox: automatic with 3 forward and 1 reverse gears
Transfer box: 2-speed
Steering: power-assisted
Suspension: (front and rear) independent, double A-arm, coil spring
Tyres: 37 × 12.50-16.5

Brakes: hydraulic, disc front and rear
Electrical system: 24 V
Batteries: 2 × 12 V
Alternator: 200 A

Status
Prototypes. US Army testing to commence during 1993.

Manufacturer
AM General Corporation, 105 N. Niles Avenue, PO Box 7025 South Bend, Indiana 46634-7025, USA. Tel: (219) 284 2942/2911. Fax: (219) 284 2959/2814.

Freightliner All Terrain Tow Vehicle (ATTV)

Description
The Freightliner All Terrain Tow Vehicle (ATTV) is a variant of the Small Emplacement Excavator (SEE – see entry under *Field fortifications and related emplacements equipment* section for details) and is under evaluation by the US Air Force.

The ATTV is based on a modified Unimog U 900 chassis and has MS 51118 pintle hooks front and rear; pintle height front and rear is 0.79 m. A steel cab with full ROPS/FOPS protection is provided and can be tilted forward for maintenance. The steel cargo platform has a tailgate and removable sides. The vehicle is used for the ground towing of aircraft and helicopters and can be carried by C-130 cargo aircraft and the CH-47D helicopter. It is also LAPES certified and can be fitted with a hydraulic system for front-mounted tractor attachments.

Freightliner All Terrain Tow Vehicle (ATTV)

Specifications

Cab seating: 1 + 1
Configuration: 4 × 4
Weight:
  (empty) 4040 kg
  (loaded) 5400 kg
Rated load: 1360 kg
Length: 4.64 m
Width: 2.04 m
Height: (overall) 2.46 m
Ground clearance: 0.43 m
Track: 1.63 m
Wheelbase: 2.38 m
Angle of approach/departure: 33°/60°
Max speed: 80 km/h

Fuel capacity: 114 l
Max gradient: 60%
Side slope: 30%
Fording: 0.76 m
Engine: 5.675 l 6-cylinder in-line diesel developing 110 hp
Transmission: fully synchronised with pneumatic pre-select shift providing 16 forward and 8 reverse gears
Clutch: single dry plate
Transfer box: 2-speed
Steering: recirculating ball with integral hydraulic-assist
Suspension:
(front) coil springs, telescopic shock absorbers and stabiliser

(rear) coil springs with helper springs, telescopic shock absorbers and stabiliser
Tyres: 12.5 R 20 12PR multi-purpose low pressure
Brakes:
(main) hydraulic, dual circuit disc with air-assist
(parking) mechanical on rear wheels
Electrical system: 24 V

Status
Under evaluation by the US Air Force.

Manufacturer
Freightliner Corporation, 4747 North Channel Avenue, PO Box 3849, Portland, Oregon 97208, USA. Tel: (503) 735 8000.

Family of Medium Tactical Vehicles (FMTV)

Development
In late 1985 the US Army announced that it was planning to introduce a new family of tactical trucks known as the Family of Medium Tactical Vehicles (FMTV), comprising a Light Medium Tactical Vehicle (LMTV) with a 2½-ton minimum payload, and a Medium Tactical Vehicle (MTV) with a 5-ton minimum payload. The LMTV will replace the current M44 series of trucks while the MTV will replace the M54 and M809 series and will supplement M939 series trucks. The maximum practicable commonality of components between the LMTV and the MTV was requested. The LMTV was to have a 4 × 4 configuration with the MTV being a 6 × 6. The FMTV was to include a light medium tactical vehicle trailer (LMTVT) and a medium tactical vehicle trailer (MTVT).

The programme commenced with the preparation of an FMTV Operational and Organisational (O & O) plan and an FMTV Joint Service Operational Requirement (JSOR) document. A Request for Proposals (RFP) was issued during 1988.

The FMTV will be operated worldwide over various terrains, ranging from paved roads to soft soil, sand, snow and ice. Vehicle operations will be round-the-clock, in all climatic conditions at temperatures down to −50°F. Requirements for the FMTV included the ability to be easily air-transported in the C-130 transport aircraft, helicopter lifting and use of the low altitude parachute extraction system (LAPES). Other requirements were for a diesel engine, a fully automatic shifting transmission, full-time all-wheel drive and radial ply tyres. Both vehicles were to be fitted with a materials handling crane (MHC) on some cargo versions. The MTV crane requirement was a hydraulic system adequate to lift 1134 kg at 4.267 m. That for the LMTV was a hand or electric system adequate to lift 680 kg from ground level to the cargo deck.

The MTV encompasses the following models: cargo, long wheelbase cargo, wrecker, expansible van body, tractor, dump truck, tanker, ambulance and trailer. The LMTV will be produced in cargo, van and tractor forms.

In October 1988 it was announced that three firm-fixed-price contracts for Phase 1 of the FMTV programme had been awarded. The first was a $500 000 increment as part of a $13 515 493 contract awarded to Teledyne Continental Motors. The second contract, again an increment of a contract worth $14.5 million, was awarded to the Tactical Truck Corporation (TTC) formed by General Motors and BMY. A third contract was awarded to Stewart & Stevenson Services of Houston, Texas. Their increment of $500 000 was part of a contract worth $17 204 174, with 20 per cent of the work involved being carried out by Steyr-Daimler-Puch (now Steyr Antriebstechnik) of Austria and based on the Steyr 12 M 18. All three contracts were to be completed by January 1991. The contracts were awarded by the US Army Tank-Automotive Command, Warren, Michigan.

Durability and performance tests with prototypes were conducted at Aberdeen Proving Grounds, Maryland, and at Yuma Proving Grounds, Arizona. Troop evaluation followed.

Following budget allocation and other similar delays it was announced in October 1991 that Stewart & Stevenson had been awarded the FMTV contract (for vehicle details see the following entry). The initial contract was worth $85 million, representing the first year of a five-year buy to be completed by December 1996. Initial plans involved replacing some 11 000 2½- and 5-ton vehicles. Testing of the first 35 production vehicles should commence by the start of 1993.

It is anticipated that the five-year contract will be worth over $1.2 billion and that, if fully implemented, the final value of the FMTV programme could reach $20 billion.

Stewart & Stevenson Family of Medium Tactical Vehicles (FMTV)

Description

In October 1991 it was announced that Stewart & Stevenson had been awarded the contract to produce the US Army's Family of Medium Tactical Vehicles (FMTV). For details of the overall FMTV programme refer to the previous entry.

The Austrian Steyr 12 M 18 truck (for details see entry under Austria in this section) was used as the basis for the Stewart & Stevenson FMTV with much of the development of the 12 M 18 to full FMTV standards being carried out in Austria by Steyr Antriebstechnik. Production of FMTV vehicles is being carried out by Stewart & Stevenson at a dedicated production plant in Sealy, Texas.

The FMTV will be produced in two versions, the Light Medium Tactical Vehicle (LMTV) 2½-ton (4 × 4) and the Medium Tactical Vehicle (MTV) 5-ton (6 × 6). There is over 90 per cent commonality of components and assemblies between the two vehicles, including the same Caterpillar 3116 ATAAC diesel, rated at 225 hp for the LMTV and 290 hp for the MTV. The powerpack was designed for easy and rapid removal

and replacement. Other systems shared by the two vehicles include the transmission, fan system, air system and air compressor, wheels and tyres, starter motor, alternator, front suspension and axle, cab, steering system, exhaust and intake systems, fuel system and cooling. The lowest possible risk and life cycle costs have been achieved by the integration of suitable commercial components where possible.

The basic overall layout of the LMTV and MTV is similar for both vehicles with a forward control cab over the engine. The stamped panel steel cab can be tilted forward for power train maintenance access and has space for the driver and two passengers with enough internal space to allow all three occupants to wear and exchange arctic or NBC clothing. Internal space is also provided for chemical detection equipment and crew equipment. The cab has been tested for roll-over and crash resistance and has a high strength roof structure to support a ring-type machine gun mount over a central roof hatch. All FMTV vehicles share the same waterproofed instrument and control panel. Mounted behind the cab is a spare tyre on an arrangement capable of being handled by light-statured and female personnel.

The Allison MD-D7 automatic seven-speed transmission is coupled to an Allison full-time all-wheel drive

transfer case with a torque bias inter-axle differential. There are traction differentials on front and rear axles. The 'smooth ride' suspension system allows over 254 mm of spring travel. On the MTV the rear suspension uses a combination of bogie and walking beam elements. Radial steel-belted tyres are used with a central tyre inflation system (CTIS). This system has settings for roads, cross-country, air transport, sand/mud/snow and emergency. The controls for the CTIS are mounted in the cab.

On both versions the front axle is a Rockwell Model R-611 Type 1. The LMTV rear axle is a Rockwell Model R-611 Type 2; those for the MTV are a Type 3 and a Type 4. The wrecker and tractor truck versions of the MTV have the Type 5 and Type 6 rear axles.

For helicopter or sling loading the FMTV vehicles make use of a special sliding outrigger system that allows the vehicle to retain the full use of available cargo space and eliminates sling contact with the cargo drop sides. For air transport two vehicles, LMTV or MTV, can be carried without preparation inside a C-130 and four in a C-141B.

FMTV production models are as follows:

M1078 – LMTV Standard Cargo
M1079 – LMTV Van
M1080 – LMTV Chassis

Specifications – LMTV Series

Model	M1078	M1079	M1080	M1081
Type	standard cargo	van	chassis	standard cargo-LAPES
Cab seating	1 + 2	1 + 2	1 + 2	1 + 2
Configuration	4 × 4	4 × 4	4 × 4	4 × 4
Weight (kerb)	7310 kg	8543 kg	6276 kg	6351 kg
Max load	2268 kg	2268 kg	n/app	2268 kg
Towed load	4318 kg	4318 kg	4318 kg	4318 kg
Length	6.4065 m	6.682 m	6.4605 m	6.461 m
Width	2.4 m	2.4 m	2.4 m	2.4 m
Height (overall)	3.1815 m	3.6192 m	3.0586 m	3.181 m
(cab)	2.765 m	2.765 m	2.765 m	2.765 m
(air transport)	2.6 m	2.6 m	2.6 m	2.2 m[1]
Ground clearance (loaded)	0.564 m	0.564 m	0.564 m	0.564 m
Wheelbase	3.9 m	3.9 m	3.9 m	3.9 m
Angle of approach/departure	40°/40°	40°/30°	40°/40°	40°/40°
Max speed	89 km/h	89 km/h	89 km/h	89 km/h
Range (max, loaded)	640 km	640 km	640 km	640 km
Max gradient	60%	60%	60%	60%
Fording (with preparation)	1.538 m	1.538 m	1.538 m	1.538 m
(without preparation)	0.923 m	0.923 m	0.923 m	0.923 m
Engine	Caterpillar 3116 ATAAC 6.6 1 6-cylinder turbocharged and after-cooled diesel developing 225 hp at 2600 rpm			
Transmission	Allison MD-D7 automatic 7-speed			
Transfer case	Allison single-speed			
Steering	power	power	power	power
Suspension	parabolic tapered leaf springs			
Tyres	395 R 20 XML	395 R 20 XML	395 R 20 XML	395 R 20 XML
Electrical system	12/24 V	12/24 V	12/24 V	12/24 V
Alternator	100 A	100 A	100 A	100 A

[1] for air drop

Specifications – MTV Series

Model	M1083	M1084	M1085	M1086	M1088	M1089
Type	cargo	cargo/crane	LWB cargo	LWB cargo/crane	tractor	wrecker
Cab seating	1 + 2	1 + 2	1 + 2	1 + 2	1 + 2	1 + 2
Configuration	6 × 6	6 × 6	6 × 6	6 × 6	6 × 6	6 × 6
Weight (kerb)	8715 kg	10 330 kg	9236 kg	7912 kg	8039 kg	14 892 kg
Max load	4536 kg	4536 kg	4536 kg	4536 kg	n/app	n/app
Towed load	9526 kg	9526 kg	9526 kg	9526 kg	27 538 kg[1]	n/app
Length	6.9335 m	7.8135 m	8.9355 m	9.6895 m	7.1452 m	9.1435 m
Width	2.4 m	2.4 m	2.4 m	2.4 m	2.4 m	2.4 m
Height (overall)	3.1873 m	3.1873 m	3.1815 m	3.1815 m	3.0586 m	3.0586 m
(cab)	2.765 m	2.765 m	2.765 m	2.765 m	2.765 m	2.765 m
(air transport)	2.6 m	2.6 m	2.6 m	2.6 m	2.6 m	2.6 m
Ground clearance	0.564 m	0.564 m	0.564 m	0.564 m	0.564 m	0.564 m
Wheelbase	4.1 m	4.5 m	4.5 m	5.5 m	4.1 m	5.3 m
Approach/departure	40°/63°	40°/38.2°	40°/30°	40°/30°	40°/40°	40°/40°
Max speed	89 km/h	89 km/h	89 km/h	89 km/h	89 km/h	89 km/h
Range (max, loaded)	480 km	480 km	480 km	480 km	480 km	480 km
Max gradient	60%	60%	60%	60%	60%	60%
Fording (with kit)	1.538 m	1.538 m	1.538 m	1.538 m	1.538 m	1.538 m
(without kit)	0.923 m	0.923 m	0.923 m	0.923 m	0.923 m	0.923 m
Engine	Caterpillar 3116 ATAAC 6.6 1 6-cylinder turbocharged and after-cooled diesel developing 290 hp at 2600 rpm					
Transmission	Alison MD-D7 automatic 7-speed					
Transfer case	Allison single-speed					
Steering	power	power	power	power	power	power
Suspension	parabolic tapered leaf springs					
Tyres	395 R 20 XML	395 R 20 XML	395 R 20 XML	395 R 20 XML	395 R 20 XML	395 R 20 XML
Electrical system	12/24 V	12/24 V	12/24 V	12/24 V	12/24 V	12/24 V
Alternator	100 A	100 A	100 A	100 A	100 A	100 A

[1] 27 538 kg on road, 20 867 kg off road

M1081 – LMTV Cargo-LAPES
M1083 – MTV Standard Cargo
M1084 – MTV Standard Cargo with Crane
M1085 – MTV Long Wheelbase Cargo
M1086 – MTV Long Wheelbase Cargo with Crane
M1088 – MTV Tractor Truck
M1089 – MTV Wrecker
M1090 – MTV Dump
M1092 – MTV Chassis

M1093 – MTV Cargo-LAPES
M1094 – MTV Dump-LAPES
M1096 – MTV Long Wheelbase (5.3 m) Chassis
Cargo versions without a dedicated crane may be fitted with an optional electrical loading/unloading crane capable of lifting 680 kg at 1.8 m.
LMTV variants can be fitted with a P-10J winch with a 4990 kg line pull. MTV variants use a DP-515 winch with a 7031 kg line pull.

Status
Preparing for series production. Ordered by US Army.

Manufacturer
Stewart & Stevenson Services Inc, Government Operations, 2707 North Loop West, Houston, Texas 77251-1637, USA.
Tel: (713) 868 7667. Fax: (713) 868 7692.

Stewart & Stevenson 2½-ton (4 × 4) LMTV in M1078 standard cargo truck form   *Stewart & Stevenson 5-ton (6 × 6) MTV in M1083 standard cargo truck form*

Model	M1090	M1092	M1093	M1094	M1096
Type	dump	chassis	cargo-LAPES	dump-LAPES	chassis LWB
Cab seating	1 + 2	1 + 2	1 + 2	1 + 2	1 + 2
Configuration	6 × 6	6 × 6	6 × 6	6 × 6	6 × 6
Weight (kerb)	9037 kg	7609 kg	7684 kg	7684 kg	7692 kg
Max load	4536 kg	n/app	4536 kg	4536 kg	n/app
Towed load	9526 kg	9526 kg	9526 kg	9526 kg	9526 kg
Length	7.1682 m	6.9935 m	6.961 m	7.1693 m	8.204 m
Width	2.4 m	2.4 m	2.4 m	2.4 m	2.4 m
Height (overall)	2.964 m	3.0586 m	3.1873 m	2.9681 m	3.0586 m
(cab)	2.765 m	2.765 m	2.765 m	2.765 m	2.765 m
(air transport)	2.6 m	2.6 m	2.6 m	2.6 m	2.6 m
Ground clearance	0.564 m	0.564 m	0.564 m	0.564 m	0.564 m
Wheelbase	4.1 m	4.1 m	4.1 m	4.1 m	5.3 m
Approach/departure	40°/63°	40°/63°	40°/63°	40°/63°	40°/63°
Max speed	89 km/h	89 km/h	89 km/h	89 km/h	89 km/h
Range (max, loaded)	480 km	480 km	480 km	480 km	480 km
Max gradient	60%	60%	60%	60%	60%
Fording (with kit)	1.538 m	1.538 m	1.538 m	1.538 m	1.538 m
(without kit)	0.923 m	0.923 m	0.923 m	0.923 m	0.923 m
Engine	Caterpillar 3118 ATAAC 6.6 1 6-cylinder turbocharged and after-cooled diesel developing 290 hp at 2600 rpm				
Transmission	Allison MD-D7 automatic 7-speed				
Transfer case	Allison single-speed				
Steering	power	power	power	power	power
Suspension	parabolic tapered leaf springs				
Tyres	395 R 20 XML	395 R 20 XML	395 R 20 XML	395 R 20 XML	395 R 20 XML
Electrical system	12/24 V	12/24 V	12/24 V	12/24 V	2/24 V
Alternator	100 A	100 A	100 A	100 A	100 A

M35/M44A2 (6 × 6) 2½-ton Cargo Truck Series

Development

In the late 1940s Reo and the Truck and Bus Division of General Motors Corporation each developed a new 2½-ton (6 × 6) truck for the US Army to replace wartime vehicles. Reo was awarded the initial production contract for 5000 vehicles and delivered the first vehicle in 1950. Originally it was to have been only an interim solution pending large-scale production of the General Motors design, but as soon as the Korean War broke out it was apparent that Reo alone could not meet the requirements of the Army so the General Motors models were placed in immediate production. They were the M135 with single rear wheels and the M211 with dual rear wheels, but they were phased out of production after the end of the Korean War in favour of the Reo design which was also built by Studebaker and was commonly known as the Eager Beaver.

The first vehicles were powered by a Reo (model OA-331) or Continental (COA-331) petrol engine which developed 146 bhp at 3400 rpm, but later models with the suffix A1 (for example M35A1) were powered by a Continental LDS 427-2 multi-fuel engine. Current models (for example M35A2) have the Continental LD 465-1 multi-fuel engine which develops 140 bhp (gross) at 2600 rpm.

In 1964 the Kaiser Jeep Corporation bought the Studebaker facilities in South Bend, Indiana, and was awarded contracts to build both 2½-ton (6 × 6) and 5-ton (6 × 6) trucks for the US Army.

In 1967 Kaiser Jeep formed the Defense and Government Products Division to handle its government contracts but in 1970 Kaiser Jeep was acquired by American Motors and the Defense and Government Products Division was named the General Products Division of the Jeep Corporation. In 1971 it was renamed the AM General Corporation, then a wholly owned subsidiary of American Motors Corporation.

By early 1980 AM General had produced over

150 000 M35/M44 series 6 × 6 trucks. A product-improved prototype designated the M963 series was developed by the company under contract to the US Army but it did not enter production.

The M963 series was powered by a Caterpillar Model 3208 V-8 diesel developing 210 hp coupled to an Allison MT643 four-speed automatic transmission. New axles gave the vehicle a wider track and larger tyres improved soft soil mobility, allowing single instead of the usual dual rear wheels to be fitted. Other improvements included redesigned suspension, brakes and steering, a forward-tilting bonnet for easier maintenance and a wider three-man cab with a spring-mounted seat for the driver.

By 1988 M35/M44 production was being carried out by AM General Corporation. In that year an order for a further 399 M44A2s was placed for delivery by October 1988. In September 1988 it was announced that AM General would discontinue medium and heavy truck production to concentrate on production of the HMMWV series. The South Bend plant closed in late 1989.

M35A2 2½-ton (6 × 6) cargo/personnel truck with machine gun mounting over cab

M342A2 dump truck

In October 1990 it was announced that the South-eastern Equipment Company Inc of Augusta, Georgia, had been awarded a $10 791 908 contract to rebuild 285 M35A2C trucks. More such contracts were anticipated pending the introduction of the ESP project (see below).

Description

In the 1950s there were two basic models in this series: the M34 with single rear wheels and the M35 with dual rear wheels. The former still remains in service, especially with countries in Europe, the Far East and South America.

The layout of the basic cargo model is conventional with the engine at the front, two-door cab in the centre with a windscreen which can be folded forward onto the bonnet and a removable canvas top, and the cargo area at the rear with a drop tailgate, removable bows, tarpaulin cover and troop seats down either side.

A wide range of kits was available including A-frame, alcohol evaporator, arctic, cargo body closure (arctic), central troop seats, electric brakes, fording, hard-top for cab, hoist and rail for installation in rear of vehicle for carrying out minor repair work, ring mount for machine gun over cab, hot water personnel heater, fuel-burning personnel heater, power plant heater, slave cable and a thermal barrier. Many vehicles are fitted with a 4536 kg capacity winch which can be used to the front or rear of the vehicle, and has 61 m of 13 mm diameter cable with two speeds forward and one speed in reverse.

Variants

Models with single rear wheels

M34: cargo truck with an unladen weight of 5332 kg, chassis designated M44

M47: dump truck with an unladen weight of 6100 kg, chassis designated M57

Truck, maintenance: earth-boring machine and pole setter V18A/MTQ, chassis M44

Truck, maintenance: telephone construction and maintenance V17A/MTQ, chassis M44.

Models with dual rear wheels

M35: this is the basic member of the family and is based on the M45 chassis; the final production model

was designated the M35A2. The M35A2C (chassis M46A2C) is almost identical but has drop sides. Both drop sides and tailgate of this model are interchangeable with those of the M54A2C (5-ton) truck.

M36: this cargo truck is the long wheelbase version of the M35 and its chassis is designated the M36. Final production model was the M36A2

M48: tractor truck for towing semi-trailers, chassis designation M45

M49: fuel tanker, final model the M49A2C (chassis M45A2), has an all-steel tank which holds 4542 litres of fuel for road travel or 2271 litres of fuel for cross-country travel. Fuel can be dispensed by gravity or pumped under pressure at a maximum rate of 303 l/min and the pump can also be used to refill the tank. The tanker can be fitted with bows and a tarpaulin cover to make detection more difficult

M50: water tanker, final model the M50A3, has an aluminium tank which holds 3785 litres of water for road travel or 1893 litres of water for cross-country travel. Water can be dispensed by gravity or pumped under pressure at a maximum rate of 303 l/min and the pump can also be used to refill the tank. The tanker can be fitted with bows and a tarpaulin cover to make detection more difficult

M59: dump truck, chassis designation M58

M60: light wrecker, details of which will be found in the *Recovery vehicles* section

M108: wrecker, details of which will be found in the *Recovery vehicles* section

M109: shop van, chassis designated M45, final production model the M109A3, has a fully enclosed rear body and is used for a variety of roles such as workshop and maintenance

M132: medical van

M185: repair van, M45 chassis; late models were M185A3

M275: tractor truck for towing semi-trailers weighing up to 16 329 kg on roads and up to 7712 kg across country. Late production model was M275A2

M292: shop van with extensible sides

M342: dump truck, final production model was the M342A2 (chassis M45A2G) which can carry 1.9 m³ of soil

M756A2: pipeline maintenance truck (chassis M45A2), fitted with rear winch, PTO and rear- or side-mounted

A-frame, removable cargo rack and sides

M763: telephone maintenance truck

M764: truck, maintenance, earth-boring machine and pole setter, equipped with rear winch, PTO, boring machine. Pole setting is accomplished using derrick tube of boring machine and rear winch.

M44 Extended Service Program (ESP)

In August 1988 it was assessed that the US Army had approximately 65 000 2½-ton trucks in its inventory although none had been acquired since 1977. During December 1990 the US Army Tank-Automotive Command (TACOM) issued a requirement for an Extended Service Program (ESP) involving M44-series vehicles. The intention is to overhaul a portion of the US Army's 2½-ton fleet and equip them with new diesel engines and matching drive trains, upgrade the steering and braking systems, plus some other improvements. In addition to extending vehicle service life ESP will improve fuel economy, enhance off-road performance and reduce servicing costs and exhaust emissions. Fielding of the first ESP vehicle is scheduled for 1995.

Prototype ESP contracts were awarded to AM General Corporation and Cummins Military Services Company on 8 May 1992. Each company was to provide eight vehicles, four with new engines, manual transmissions and other improvements (these will act as baseline vehicles) and four enhanced vehicles with new engines, automatic transmissions and central tyre inflation systems (CTIS). These vehicles were to be delivered to the US Army for pre-production qualification test in October 1992. The tests were scheduled to be completed by March 1993. The RFP solicitation was scheduled for issue in December 1992 with production contract award in September 1993 for the remanufacture of possibly 2000 to 10 000 trucks over the next five years. The AM General baseline vehicle will use a Caterpillar 3116 engine and a ZF manual five-speed transmission. The AM General enhanced vehicle will have an Allison Automatic transmission with four forward speeds as well as AM General's Pneumatic CTI system and larger radial tyres.

Status

Production complete. In service with the US armed forces and many other armed forces including Bolivia,

M50A3 water tanker version of M35A2 2½-ton (6 × 6) truck

M36A2 long wheelbase version of M35A2 2½-ton (6 × 6) truck

Brazil, Chad, El Salvador, Guatemala, Haiti, Honduras, Israel, Djibouti, South Korea, Lebanon, Liberia, Morocco, Pakistan, Panama, Philippines, Saudi Arabia, Senegal, Somalia, Spain (over 2000 of which have been re-engined), Sudan, Taiwan, Thailand, Turkey and Zaïre. An undisclosed number were supplied to the People's Republic of China.

Manufacturer

AM General Corporation, 105 N. Niles Avenue, PO Box 7025 South Bend, Indiana 46634-7025, USA. Tel: (219) 284 2942/2911. Fax: (219) 284 2959/2814.

Specifications

Model	M35A2	M36A2	M49A2C	M50A3	M109A3	M342A2
Type	cargo	cargo	fuel	water	van	dump
Cab seating	1 + 2	1 + 2	1 + 2	1 + 2	1 + 2	1 + 2
Configuration	6 × 6	6 × 6	6 × 6	6 × 6	6 × 6	6 × 6
Weight (empty)	5900 kg	6900 kg	6500 kg	6644 kg	6800 kg	6800 kg
(loaded, road)	10 400 kg	11 500 kg	10 100 kg	10 408 kg	10 200 kg	11 300 kg
Weight on front axle (loaded)	2700 kg	3200 kg	2700 kg	2880 kg	3000 kg	3100 kg
Weight on rear axle (loaded)	7700 kg	8300 kg	7400 kg	7528 kg	7100 kg	8300 kg
Max load (road)	4535 kg	4535 kg	4542 l	3785 l	3401 kg	4535 kg
(cross-country)	2268 kg	2268 kg	2271 l	1893 l	2268 kg	2268 kg
Towed load (road)	4535 kg	4535 kg	4535 kg	4535 kg	3628 kg	4535 kg
(cross-country)	2721 kg	2721 kg	2721 kg	2721 kg	2721 kg	2721 kg
Load area	3.7 × 2.2 m	5.3 × 2.2 m	n/app	n/app	n/app	3.3 × 1.9 m
Length (without winch)	6.7 m	8.4 m	6.7 m	6.7 m	6.8 m	6.6 m
Width	2.4 m	2.4 m	2.4 m	2.4 m	2.4 m	2.4 m
Height (reduced)	2.1 m	2.1 m	2.3 m	2.4 m	3.3 m	2.1 m
(overall)	2.9 m	3.2 m	2.6 m	2.6 m	3.3 m	2.7 m
(load area)	1.32 m	1.4 m	n/app	n/app	1.3 m	1.3 m
Ground clearance (axles)	0.28 m	0.28 m	0.28 m	0.28 m	0.28 m	0.28 m
Track (front/rear)	1.721/1.778 m	1.721/1.778 m	1.721/1.778 m	1.721/1.778 m	1.721/1.778 m	1.721/1.778 m
Wheelbase	3.912 m	4.826 m	3.912 m	3.912 m	3.912 m	3.912 m
Angle of approach/departure	47°/40°	47°/24°	47°/40°	47°/40°	47°/40°	47°/70°
Max speed (road)	90 km/h	90 km/h	90 km/h	90 km/h	90 km/h	90 km/h
Range	480 km	480 km	480 km	480 km	480 km	480 km
Fuel capacity	189 l	189 l	189 l	189 l	189 l	189 l
Max gradient	60%	60%	60%	60%	60%	60%
Fording (without preparation)	0.76 m	0.76 m	0.76 m	0.76 m	0.76 m	0.76 m
(with preparation)	1.98 m	1.98 m	1.98 m	1.98 m	1.52 m	1.83 m
Engine	LDT-465-1C 6-cylinder in-line multi-fuel diesel developing 140 net hp at 2600 rpm					
Gearbox	all have a manual gearbox with 5 forward and 1 reverse gears					
Clutch	single dry plate is fitted to all models					
Transfer box	2-speed	2-speed	2-speed	2-speed	2-speed	2-speed
Steering	all have cam and twin lever type					
Suspension (front/rear)	semi-elliptical springs/semi-elliptical springs inverted					
Tyres	9.00 × 20	9.00 × 20	9.00 × 20	9.00 × 20	9.00 × 20	9.00 × 20
Brakes (main)	air over hydraulic	air over hydraulic	air over hydraulic	air over hydraulic	air over hydraulic	air over hydraulic
(parking)	internal/external	internal/external	internal/external	internal/external	internal/external	internal/external
Electrical system	24 V	24 V	24 V	24 V	24 V	24 V
Batteries	2	2	2	2	2	2

BMY 3-tonne (4 × 4) Truck, Cargo

Description

Following production experience with the M939A2 series of 5-ton 6 × 6 trucks (see entry later in this section), BMY-Wheeled Vehicles Division decided that there is a market for a 4 × 4 3-tonne military truck in many of the less developed parts of the world and among many armed forces where the larger 5-ton 6 × 6 trucks are not required for many logistic or other tasks. In mid-1991 BMY therefore produced prototypes of a 3-tonne 4 × 4 truck embodying M939A2 components and production experience. The US Marine Corps have tested the vehicle to verify its ability to satisfy their helicopter transportability requirements.

The design resembles a twin-axle M939A2 series truck and uses the same general overall layout. The vehicle is provided with the same Cummins 6CTA8.3 diesel engine as the M939A2 series, and the same automatic transmission.

The standard cargo body consists of a flat deck with drop side walls and rails plus a tailgate. A tarpaulin over bows can be provided. ISO securing ties are provided for carrying containers.

For helicopter lift the vehicle can be equipped with forward lifting eyes behind the front bumper and rear lifting eyes positioned on sliding telescopic posts which are locked into position by pins for lifting. Two 3-tonne trucks can be carried in a C-130 without special preparation.

This vehicle can tow a M198 155 mm howitzer.

A central tyre inflation system with four preset pressures is provided as standard. Various supplementary and accessory kits, including a deep wading kit and side-mounted winch, are available.

Prototype of BMY 3-tonne (4 × 4) Truck, Cargo

Specifications

Cab seating: 1 + 2
Configuration: 4 × 4
Weight:
(kerb) 7488 kg
(loaded) 10 482 kg
Max load: 3000 kg
Towed load: 7711 kg
Load area: 3.73 × 2.23 m
Length: 6.922 m
Width: 2.5 m
Height:
(top of cab) 2.213 m
(top of tarpaulin) 3.073 m
(reduced) 2.41 m
(load area, unloaded) 1.44 m
Ground clearance: 0.391 m
Track:
(front) 1.98 m
(rear) 2.07 m
Angle of approach/departure: 46°/29°
Max speed: 89 km/h
Range:
(without towed load) 644 km

(with towed load) 483 km
Gradient: 60%
Fording:
  (without kit) 0.76 m
  (with kit) 1.98 m
Wheelbase: 4.255 m
Engine: Cummins 6CTA8.3 8.3 l 6-cylinder in-line turbocharged aftercooled diesel developing 240 hp at 2100 rpm
Transmission: automatic with 5 forward and 1 reverse gears

Transfer box: 2-speed
Steering: hydraulic with power-assist
Turning radius:
  (right) 11.88 m
  (left) 12.75 m
Suspension: semi-elliptical springs with double-acting hydraulic shock absorbers
Tyres: 14.00 R 20
Brakes: air
Electrical system: 24 V
Batteries: 2 × 12 V, 100 Ah

Alternator: 60 A

Status
Prototypes. Has been tested by US Marine Corps.

Manufacturer
BMY-Wheeled Vehicles Division of HARSCO, 13311 Industrial Parkway, Marysville, Ohio 43040, USA. Tel: (513) 644 0041. Fax: (513) 642 0022.

M54 (6 × 6) 5-ton Cargo Truck Series

Development
The M54 series of 6 × 6 5-ton trucks was developed in the immediate post-Second World War period to replace vehicles in the 4-, 5-, 6- and 7½-ton class. First production models were completed by Diamond T and International Harvester in 1950 with later production being undertaken by Kaiser Jeep (now AM General) and Mack. The first vehicles were powered by a six-cylinder petrol engine, which was replaced by a six-cylinder diesel engine in 1962, in turn replaced by a six-cylinder multi-fuel engine the following year. The multi-fuel engine was a supercharged version of the LD465 as used in the 2½-ton truck, which developed 230 hp but was not successful as it became overheated. The AM General Corporation replaced this with a commercial engine and the series then became known as the M809 range, for which there is a separate entry.

A wide range of kits was developed for the M54 series including A-frame, air brake, electric brake, engine heater, deep fording, hard-top, machine-gun mount, personnel heater, thermal barrier and a front-mounted winch with a capacity of 9072 kg.

Description
The layout of the basic cargo version is conventional with the engine at the front, two-door cab in the centre with a windscreen which can be folded forward onto the bonnet and a removable canvas top, and the welded steel cargo area at the rear with fixed sides, removable side racks, troop seats, removable bows and a tarpaulin cover.

Variants
AM General Retrofit Package
AM General designed a retrofit kit to upgrade M54 Series vehicles to an M809 Series configuration. These kits, produced for the US Marine Corps, include a powerpack, frame, steering system, brake system, fuel and exhaust system, and electrical and sheet metal components to achieve the M809 configuration.

The powerpack includes a Cummins NHC-250 diesel engine, radiator and cooling lines, a 24 V alternator and starter, clutch, flywheel, five-speed transmission and an air cleaner assembly. The frame includes rails and crossmembers for the new powerpack while the steering includes steering gear, a power steering pump, power-assist cylinder and hoses. The brake system includes air reservoir tanks, air and hydraulic lines and couplings, adaptors and mounting hardware. Included in the fuel system are a 295 litre tank, a cold start primer, filters, fuel lines and a new accelerator linkage. Exhaust pipes, a muffler exhaust stack, heat shield, gaskets and other hardware make up the exhaust system and the new electrical system contains wiring harnesses, bulbs and dials, batteries and cables and a new battery box. The kit is complete with a new hood, fenders, instrument panel and other items.

All items in the kit have been fitted to US military vehicles and tested at the Aberdeen Proving Grounds, Maryland.

Specifications

Designation	M51	M52	M54	M55
Type	dump	tractor	cargo	cargo (LWB)
Cab seating	1 + 2	1 + 2	1 + 2	1 + 2
Configuration	6 × 6	6 × 6	6 × 6	6 × 6
Weight (empty)	9970 kg	8616 kg	8732 kg	10 915 kg
(loaded, road)	19 042 kg	19 956 kg	18 119 kg	20 146 kg
Weight on front axle (loaded, road)	4112 kg	—	4347 kg	—
Weight on rear axles (loaded, road)	15 088 kg	—	13 807 kg	—
Max load (road)	9072 kg	n/app	9072 kg	9072 kg
(cross-country)	4536 kg	n/app	4536 kg	4536 kg
Towed load (road)	13 608 kg	24 948 kg	13 608 kg	13 608 kg
(cross-country)	6804 kg	13 608 kg	6804 kg	6804 kg
Load area	3.175 × 2.082 m	n/app	4.267 × 2.235 m	6.15 × 2.235 m
Length	7.146 m	6.933 m	7.974 m	9.797 m
Width	2.463 m	2.463 m	2.463 m	2.463 m
Height (overall)	2.809 m	2.638 m	2.946 m	2.946 m
Ground clearance	0.267 m	0.267 m	0.267 m	0.267 m
Track (front/rear)	1.869/1.828 m	1.869/1.828 m	1.869/1.828 m	1.869/1.828 m
Wheelbase	3.555 m + 1.371 m	3.555 m + 1.371 m	3.86 m + 1.371 m	4.775 m + 1.371 m
Angle of approach/departure	52.5°/69°	52.5°/69°	37°/38°	37°/23°
Max speed (road)	84 km/h	84 km/h	84 km/h	84 km/h
Range	785 km	483 km	344 km	344 km
Fuel capacity	416 l	416 l	295 l	295 l
Max gradient	70%	77%	50%	65%
Fording (without preparation)	0.762 m	0.762 m	0.762 m	0.762 m
(with preparation)	1.981 m	n/app	1.981 m	1.981 m
Gearbox	manual with 5 forward and 1 reverse gears			
Clutch	single dry plate	single dry plate	single dry plate	single dry plate
Brakes	all have hydraulic brakes, air-actuated, and mechanical parking brakes			
Electrical system	24 V	24 V	24 V	24 V
Batteries	2	2	2	2

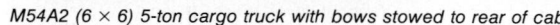

M54A2 (6 × 6) 5-ton cargo truck with bows stowed to rear of cab

M51 (6 × 6) 5-ton dump truck

Truck, Cargo, 5-ton, M41 (6 × 6)
This has single instead of dual rear wheels and can carry 6804 kg of cargo and tow a 13 608 kg trailer on roads or 6804 kg across country. It is powered by a Continental R6602 six-cylinder OHV petrol engine which develops 196 bhp at 2800 rpm, coupled to a five-speed gearbox and a two-speed transfer box.

Truck, Dump, 5-ton, M51 (6 × 6)
This has a rear tipping all-steel dump body and is based on the M61 chassis, and can also be used to carry cargo. The engine is the same as in the M41 and is coupled to a Spicer Model 6352 gearbox, Timken Model T-138 two-speed transfer box and a Spicer WND-61 PTO mounted on the transmission, and powers the front-mounted winch (when fitted) and the hydraulic dump body mechanism. The equivalent vehicle in the M809 series is the M817. The M51A1 has a Mack model ENDT-673 six-cylinder diesel which develops 211 bhp at 2100 rpm and the M51A2 has an LD465 six-cylinder turbocharged multi-fuel which develops 230 hp.

Truck, Tractor, 5-ton, M52 (6 × 6)
The chassis is designated the M61 and is powered by the same engine as the M41. Later models were the M52A1 and M52A2 with diesel and multi-fuel engines respectively. The M52 can tow a semi-trailer weighing up to 11 340 kg on roads or up to 6804 kg across country. The equivalent vehicle in the M809 series is the M818.

Truck, Cargo, 5-ton, M54 (6 × 6)
This is the basic cargo model and its chassis is designated the M40. It has the same engine as the M41 with later models being the M54A1 (diesel) and M54A2 (multi-fuel). The equivalent in the M809 series

is the M813.

Truck, Cargo, 5-ton, M55 (6 × 6)
This is the long wheelbase cargo model of the M54 and is based on the M63 chassis. It has the same engine as the M41 with later models being the M55A1 (diesel) and M55A2 (multi-fuel). The equivalent vehicle in the M809 series is the M814.

Truck, Wrecker, Medium, 5-ton, M62 (6 × 6)
This is based on the M40C chassis with a walking beam rear suspension; details will be found in the *Recovery vehicles* section.

Truck, Cargo, Van, 5-ton, M64 (6 × 6)
This has a fully enclosed rear body.

Truck, Tractor, Wrecker, 5-ton, M246 (6 × 6)
This is based on the M63C chassis and can be used for recovery operations as well as towing trailers. Details will be found in the *Recovery vehicles* section.

Truck, Van, Expansible, 5-ton, M291 (6 × 6)
This is fitted with a fully enclosed rear van body with sides which are extended when the vehicle is stationary. Later models were the M291A1 (diesel) and M291A2 (multi-fuel). The equivalent vehicle in the M809 series is the M820.

Truck, Stake, Bridging, 5-ton, M328 (6 × 6)
This is used to carry bridge components. Later models were the M328A1 (diesel) and M328A2 (multi-fuel). The equivalent vehicle in the M809 series is the M821.

Truck, Wrecker, Medium, 5-ton, M543 (6 × 6)
This is based on the M40C chassis with walking beam rear suspension. Later models are the M543A1 (diesel)

and M543A2 (multi-fuel). The equivalent vehicle in the M809 series is the M816, details of which will be found in the *Recovery vehicles* section.

Truck, Bolster, 5-ton, M748 (6 × 6)
Later models were designated the M748A1 (diesel) and M748A2 (multi-fuel). The equivalent vehicle in the M809 series is the M815.

Chassis, Truck, 5-ton, M139 (6 × 6)
This chassis has been used for a variety of applications. The basic M139 is used for carrying bridging equipment and the M139C was designed to carry the Honest John surface-to-surface rocket. The M139D has a different rear axle and jack bracket supports and both the M139C and M139D are equipped with high reduction axles to increase tractive power and a modified front crossmember.

The Italian CP 56 bridging truck used a chassis very similar to that of the M139.

Status
Production complete. In service with the US Army and most other armies that have received American aid, including South Korea, Spain (many of which have been re-engined), and Turkey.

Manufacturer
Last manufacturer of the M54 series was AM General Corporation, 14250 Plymouth Road, Detroit, Michigan 48232, USA.

Similar vehicles were manufactured in Italy (as the CP 56) and Spain.

M809 (6 × 6) 5-ton Cargo Truck Series

Development
The M809 series of 6 × 6 5-ton cargo trucks is similar to the older M54 series but was fitted with a diesel engine in place of the multi-fuel engine by the AM General Corporation under a product engineering development and test programme.

AM General Corporation started production of the M809 series in 1970 and by the middle of 1980 had completed some 38 000 vehicles. In September 1988 it was announced that AM General would be withdrawing from the production of medium and heavy vehicles and their South Bend plant closed in late 1989.

Further development of the M809 series by AM General, under an engineering contract with the US Army, resulted in the much improved M939 series for which there is a separate entry.

Description
The chassis of the vehicle consists of two rail-type beams with six reinforced crossmembers. Both front and rear axles are of the hypoid, single-speed, double-reduction type. The layout is conventional with the engine at the front, two-door cab in the centre with a windscreen which can be folded flat against the bonnet and a removable canvas top, and the cargo area at the rear. The basic cargo model has an all-steel rear cargo body with drop sides, removable bows, tarpaulin cover

and troop seats down either side which enable 18 fully equipped troops to be carried.

There are three basic chassis in the series, the M809 (used for the M813, M813A1, M816 and M815), the

M810 (used for the M817 and M818) and the M811/ M812 (used for the M814, M819, M820 and M821). A variety of kits is available for the range including A-frame, air brake, closure hard-top, deep water

M813A1 (6 × 6) 5-ton cargo truck fitted with drop side cargo body

M821 carrier for bridge erection boat (C R Zwart)

M809 5-ton (6 × 6) truck fitted with platform body for air compressor

Designation	**M813**	**M813A1**	**M814**	**M817**	**M818**	**M820**
Type	cargo	cargo	cargo (LWB)	dump	tractor	van
Cab seating	1 + 2	1 + 2	1 + 2	1 + 2	1 + 2	1 + 2
Configuration	6 × 6	6 × 6	6 × 6	6 × 6	6 × 6	6 × 6
Weight (empty)	9733 kg	10 043 kg	11 297 kg	10 776 kg	9202 kg	12 474 kg
(loaded, road)	18 985 kg	18 993 kg	20 549 kg	20 028 kg	20 349 kg	29 459 kg
Weight on front axle (loaded)	5015 kg	5016 kg	5326 kg	4981 kg	4950 kg	4936 kg
Weight on rear axles (loaded)	13 969 kg	13 976 kg	15 223 kg	15 047 kg	15 399 kg	14 523 kg
Max load (road)	9070 kg	9070 kg	9070 kg	9070 kg	n/app	6803 kg
(cross-country)	4535 kg	4535 kg	4535 kg	4535 kg	n/app	2268 kg
Towed load (road)	13 620 kg	13 620 kg	13 620 kg	13 620 kg	24 943 kg	13 620 kg
(cross-country)	6802 kg	6802 kg	6802 kg	6802 kg	17 007 kg	6802 kg
Load area	4.3 × 2.2 m	4.3 × 2.2 m	6.2 × 2.2 m	3.2 × 2.1 m	n/app	5.2 × 2.1 m
Length	7.652 m	7.652 m	9.609 m	6.86 m	6.71 m	9.144 m
Width	2.464 m	2.464 m	2.464 m	2.464 m	2.464 m	2.483 m
Height (overall)	2.946 m	2.946 m	2.946 m	2.946 m	2.946 m	3.467 m
(reduced)	2.172 m	2.172 m	2.172 m	2.832 m	2.172 m	3.467 m
(load area)	1.4 m	1.4 m	1.4 m	n/app	n/app	n/app
Ground clearance (axles)	0.295 m	0.295 m	0.295 m	0.295 m	0.295 m	0.295 m
Track (front/rear)	1.88/1.829 m	1.88/1.829 m	1.88/1.829 m	1.9/1.829 m	1.9/1.829 m	1.9/1.829 m
Wheelbase	3.86 m +	3.86 m +	4.775 m+	3.55 m +	3.55 m +	4.775 m+
	1.371 m	1.371 m	1.371 m	1.371 m	1.371 m	1.371 m
Angle of approach/departure	46°/35°	46°/35°	46°/23.5°	34°/69°	45°/69°	46°/24°
Max speed (road)	84 km/h	84 km/h	84 km/h	84 km/h	84 km/h	84 km/h
Range	563 km	563 km	563 km	772 km	563 km	563 km
Fuel capacity	295 l	295 l	295 l	295 l	295 l	295 l
Max gradient (without towed load)	67%	67%	61%	61%	60%	65%
(with towed load)	42%	42%	38%	31%	42%	41%
Max side slope (cross-country)	20%	20%	20%	20%	20%	20%
Fording (without preparation)	0.76 m	0.76 m	0.76 m	0.76 m	0.76 m	0.76 m
(with preparation)	1.98 m	1.98 m	1.98 m	1.98 m	1.98 m	1.98 m
Engine	all powered by an NHC-250 6-cylinder in-line diesel developing 240 hp at 2100 rpm					
Gearbox	all have manual gearbox with 5 forward and 1 reverse gears					
Clutch	single dry plate	single dry plate	single dry plate	single dry plate	single dry plate	single dry plate
Transfer box	2-speed	2-speed	2-speed	2-speed	2-speed	2-speed
Steering	power-assisted	power-assisted	power-assisted	power-assisted	power-assisted	power-assisted
Turning radius	12.75 m	12.75 m	14.3 m	12.75 m	12.75 m	14.53 m
Suspension (front/rear)	semi-elliptical springs/semi-elliptical springs, inverted					
Tyres	11.00 × 20	11.00 × 20	11.00 × 20	11.00 × 20	11.00 × 20	11.00 × 20
Brakes	main, air over hydraulic. Parking, dual grip on transfer case					
Electrical system	24 V	24 V	24 V	24 V	24 V	24 V
Batteries	4	4	4	4	4	4

fording, level wind device, slave receptacle, thermal barrier, water personnel heater, winterisation personnel heater kit and a winterisation powerplant kit. All models except the M820 can be fitted with a winch at the front.

M809 series vehicles can be fitted with the Enhanced Mobility System (EMS) for increased mobility over sand, mud and snow.

Variants
M813 (Cargo Truck, 5-ton, 6 × 6)
This is the basic cargo model and can carry 4535 kg of cargo across country and 9070 kg of cargo on roads. The foldable seats enable 26 fully equipped troops to be carried.

M813A1 (Dropside, Cargo Truck, 5-ton, 6 × 6)
This is similar to the M813 but has drop sides as well as a drop tailgate.

M814 (Long Cargo Truck, 5-ton, 6 × 6)
This is the long wheelbase model and can be delivered with removable bows and a tarpaulin cover.

M815 (Bolster Truck, 5-ton, 6 × 6)
This has the M809 chassis and can carry a maximum load of 4536 kg across country or 9072 kg on roads. Towed load is identical to the M813 cargo truck.

M816 (Wrecker, Truck, 5-ton, 6 × 6)
Details of this vehicle are given in the *Recovery vehicles* section.

M817 (Dump Truck, 5-ton, 6 × 6)
This has an all-steel 3.8 m³ capacity rear dump body which can be fitted with bows and a tarpaulin cover.

M818 (Tractor, Truck, 5-ton, 6 × 6)
This has both a fifth wheel and a pintle tow hook and can tow semi-trailers weighing up to 24 970 kg on roads or 17 025 kg across country.

M819 (Tractor, Wrecker, 5-ton, 6 × 6)
Details of this vehicle are given in the *Recovery vehicles* section.

M820 (Van, Expansible, Truck, 5-ton, 6 × 6)
This is provided with a fully enclosed body at the rear which is 2.1 m wide and 1.9 m high in its normal position. When static, the sides of the van are extended either side and the interior is then 4.2 m wide. Access to the body is via steps at the rear.

M821 (Bridge Transport, 5-ton, 6 × 6)
This is used to carry bridging components and is based on the M812 chassis.

Ribbon Bridge Carrier and Launching Vehicle
An M809 chassis is used to carry and launch the Ribbon Bridge system as well as carrying and launching a bridge erection boat.

Specifications
Specifications relate to a vehicle without winch, with the exception of the M817 which is fitted with a winch as standard equipment. All other vehicles, except M820, can be fitted with a front-mounted winch. When fitted with a front-mounted winch the vehicles have an angle of approach of 34°.

Status
Production complete. In service with the US Army and other armed forces including El Salvador, Honduras, Jamaica, Jordan, South Korea, Lebanon, Liberia, Pakistan, Panama, Philippines, Saudi Arabia, Senegal, Somalia, Spain, Sudan, Taiwan, Thailand and Zaïre. An undisclosed number was supplied to China.

Manufacturer
AM General Corporation, 105 N. Niles Avenue, PO Box 7025 South Bend, Indiana 46634-7025, USA. Tel: (219) 284 2942/2911. Fax: (219) 284 2959/2814.

M939 (6 × 6) 5-ton Cargo Truck

Development
When the M809 was type classified it was intended that a product-improvement programme would be carried out in the areas of transmission, transfer case and brakes. Extensive testing of the M809 series in 1970 had shown that product improvements in these three areas would be most beneficial. The programme was shelved when the US Army withdrew from Vietnam but was reinstituted in 1975.

In October 1979 the M939 (6 × 6) 5-ton cargo truck was type classified for inclusion in US Army field units.

In April 1981 AM General Corporation was awarded a contract for 11 394 M939 trucks, later increased to 22 789, by the US Army Tank-Automotive Command. The total value of the five-year contract eventually reached $1.6 billion. Production began in the first half of 1982 at AM General's plant at South Bend, Indiana. The M939 series became available for export during late 1983.

During the mid-1980s the basic M939 design was upgraded to the M939A1. This version was equipped with 14.00 R 20 'Super Single' tyres with a single tyre replacing the dual biased-ply tyres on the rear axles. Only a limited number of M939A1s were produced.

In May 1986 ARVECO, a joint venture between BMY

Corporation and the General Automotive Corporation, won a contract to produce 15 218 M939A2 vehicles over a five-year period. The initial one-year contract was for 2046 vehicles at a cost of $145 million while the five-year contract was expected to be worth $1 billion. Following contract award BMY acquired the General Automotive Corporation's portion of ARVECO. HARSCO renamed this wholly owned organisation BMY-Wheeled Vehicles Division and began deliveries from its new truck plant in Marysville, Ohio, in early 1987. By late 1990 the base contract quantity was fixed at 17 092 vehicles, with production extending into 1992 following orders from the US Government that included FMS quantities for Saudi Arabia.

AM General Corporation completed its five-year contract in September 1986 but production was extended until April 1987 by the award of a further contract. Production by AM General Corporation ceased in late 1989 when their South Bend plant closed.

Description

The M939 is essentially the existing M809 series improved in three major areas: transmission, transfer case and brake system. The M809's transmission and transfer case were under capacity and mismatched to the engine/axle ratio and performance requirements; there was no way to prevent the engine from over-speeding (rpm too high) or labouring in many gear ratio selections. The M939 has a fully automatic transmission to eliminate these problems, and it also requires less driver training, reduces fuel consumption, is more reliable/durable, lessens driver fatigue and improves safety.

The transfer case is pressure- rather than splash-lubricated. The driver controls the engagement of the front wheels for 6 × 6 drive with an air system, eliminating a mechanical sprag clutch which frequently failed. The transfer case on the M939 can be shifted from either range while the vehicle is moving.

Tests demonstrated that the full air brakes on the M939 have four times the brake shoe life of the air-over-hydraulic brakes on the M809. The air brakes are self-adjusting and backed by fail-safe mechanical spring brakes.

The M939 was the first tactical truck to meet Surgeon General standards for noise in the cab even with the windows open. This was achieved by relocating intake/exhaust ports to behind the cab.

The front-mounted winch is hydraulically driven and stops when overloaded and restarts when the overload is removed. The older mechanically driven winches used on the M809 require shear-pin replacement when similarly overloaded.

The M939 bonnet and bumpers tilt forward so maintenance can be carried out from the ground, whereas even opening the M809's bonnet necessitates climbing onto the bumpers.

Flat tyres are replaced using a boom just behind the cab. The cab holds three personnel, the M809 only two.

The M939 was the first truck built with special connectors for use with the US Army's diagnostic equipment (STE/ICE). This encourages the use of test equipment, reduces maintenance time and eliminates incorrect replacements based on poor diagnosis.

The upgraded M939A2, produced by BMY-Wheeled Vehicles Division (BMY-WVD), incorporates an Eaton central tyre inflation system (CTIS – known as 'Big Foot') integrated with 14.00 R 20 'Super Single' radial tyres. The engine is changed to a Cummins 6CTA8.3 developing 240 hp at 2100 rpm, providing an increase in range to 644 km. Due to the lighter engine the kerb weight is reduced. Modifications were also made to the cooling system.

Specifications

Model	M923A2	M925A2	M927A2	M928A2	M929A2	M930A2
Type	cargo	cargo	LWB cargo	LWB cargo	dump	dump
Winch	no	yes	no	yes	no	yes
Cab seating	1 + 2	1 + 2	1 + 2	1 + 2	1 + 2	1 + 2
Configuration	6 × 6	6 × 6	6 × 6	6 × 6	6 × 6	6 × 6
Weight (kerb)	9494 kg	9993 kg	10 791 kg	11 290 kg	10 805 kg	11 304 kg
(GVW)	14 030 kg	14 529 kg	15 327 kg	15 826 kg	15 340 kg	15 840 kg
Payload	4536 kg	4536 kg	4536 kg	4536 kg	4536 kg	4536 kg
Towed load	6804 kg	6804 kg	6804 kg	6804 kg	6804 kg	6804 kg
Length	7.887 m	8.433 m	9.792 m	10.363 m	6.934 m	7.48 m
Width	2.474 m	2.474 m	2.474 m	2.474 m	2.474 m	2.474 m
Height (overall)	3.073 m	3.073 m	3.063 m	3.063 m	3.175 m	3.175 m
(reduced)	2.385 m	2.385 m	2.375 m	2.375 m	2.375 m	2.375 m
Track (front)	1.98 m	1.98 m	1.98 m	1.98 m	1.98 m	1.98 m
(rear)	2.065 m	2.065 m	2.065 m	2.065 m	2.065 m	2.065 m
Wheelbase	4.547 m	4.547 m	5.461 m	5.461 m	4.242 m	4.242 m
Ground clearance	0.333 m	0.333 m	0.333 m	0.333 m	0.333 m	0.333 m
Fording (normal)	0.76 m	0.76 m	0.76 m	0.76 m	0.76 m	0.76 m
(with kit)	1.98 m	1.98 m	1.98 m	1.98 m	1.98 m	1.98 m
Engine	Cummins 6CTA8.3 8.3 l 6-cylinder in-line turbocharged after-cooled diesel developing 240 hp at 2100 rpm					
Gearbox	Allison MT654CR 5-speed automatic					
Transfer box	2-speed with high ratio 0.732:1, low ratio 1.790:1					
Steering	Ross HFB 64 power-assisted					
Suspension	leaf springs front and rear					
Tyres	14.00 R 20 tread design, all terrain					
Electrical system	24 V	24 V	24 V	24 V	24 V	24 V
Alternator	60 A	60 A	60 A	60 A	60 A	60 A

2000-gallon (6 × 6) hard-sided tanker variant of M939A2 produced by BMY-Wheeled Vehicles Division

M929 (6 × 6) 5-ton dump truck

M924 cargo (6 × 6) 5-ton truck (C R Zwart)

M923 cargo/personnel drop-side (6 × 6) 5-ton truck

Model	M931A2	M932A2	M934A2	M935A2	M936A2
Type	tractor	tractor	exp van	exp van	wrecker
Winch	no	yes	no	no	yes
Cab seating	1 + 2	1 + 2	1 + 2	1 + 2	1 + 2
Configuration	6 × 6	6 × 6	6 × 6	6 × 6	6 × 6
Weight (kerb)	9024 kg	9523 kg	12 717 kg	13 624 kg	16 724 kg
(GVW)	26 034 kg	26 533 kg	14 985 kg	15 892 kg	19 918 kg
Payload	6804 kg[1]	6804 kg[1]	2268 kg	2268 kg	3175 kg
Towed load	6804 kg[2]	6804 kg[2]	6804 kg	6804 kg	9072 kg
Length	6.718 m	7.264 m	9.21 m	9.55 m	9.195 m
Width	2.474 m	2.474 m	2.489 m	2.489 m	2.474 m
Height (overall)	3.078 m	3.078 m	3.614 m	3.609 m	3.048 m
(reduced)	2.39 m	2.39 m	3.614 m	3.609 m	2.756 m
Track (front)	1.98 m	1.98 m	1.98 m	1.98 m	1.98 m
(rear)	2.065 m	2.065 m	2.065 m	2.065 m	2.065 m
Wheelbase	4.242 m	4.242 m	5.461 m	5.461 m	5.547 m
Ground clearance	0.333 m	0.333 m	0.333 m	0.333 m	0.333 m
Fording (normal)	0.76 m	0.76 m	0.76 m	0.76 m	0.76 m
(with kit)	1.98 m	1.98 m	1.98 m	1.98 m	1.98 m
Engine	Cummins 6CTA8.3 8.3 l 6-cylinder in-line turbocharged after-cooled diesel developing 240 hp at 2100 rpm				
Gearbox	Allison MT654CR 5-speed automatic				
Transfer box	2-speed with high ratio 0.732:1, low ratio 1.790:1				
Steering	Ross HFB 64 power-assisted				
Suspension	leaf springs front and rear				
Tyres	14.00 R 20 tread design, all terrain				
Electrical system	24 V	24 V	24 V	24 V	24 V
Alternator	60 A	60 A	60 A	60 A	60 A

[1] on 5th wheel   [2] pintle

Variants

BMY-WVD has developed two M939A2 variants, a 3-tonne 4 × 4 (see separate entry in this section) and a 2000-gallon (9092-litre) hard-sided tanker with a GVW of 19 010 kg. The tanker, which is equipped with a central tyre inflation system (CTIS) provides armed forces with M939 fleets with a POL and water off-road transport capability not previously available.

BMY-WVD is also developing an 8-ton variant of the M944A2 chassis. Using higher rated components from other M939A2 series vehicles, the 8-ton variant provides a basis for such tasks as Ribbon Bridge launcher, medium palletised loads and other operations not currently within the M939A2's capability.

M939 variants are as follows:
M923: drop side cargo
M924: cargo; equivalent to M814
M925: drop side cargo with winch
M926: cargo with winch
M927: long wheelbase cargo
M928: long wheelbase cargo with winch
M929: dump truck; equivalent to M817
M930: dump truck with winch
M931: tractor
M932: tractor with winch
M933: tractor wrecker with winch
M934: expansible body

M935: expansible van body
M936: wrecker with winch
M939: chassis with or without winch
M939: chassis with winch
M940: chassis with winch
M941: chassis without winch
M941: chassis with winch
M942: long wheelbase chassis with or without winch
M943: long wheelbase chassis with winch
M944: long wheelbase chassis
M945: long wheelbase chassis with winch.
M939A2 production models are as follows:
M923A2: drop side cargo without winch
M925A2: drop side cargo with winch
M927A2: long wheelbase cargo without winch
M928A2: long wheelbase cargo with winch
M929A2: dump truck without winch
M930A2: dump truck with winch
M931A2: tractor truck without winch
M932A2: tractor truck with winch
M934A2: expansible van without winch
M935A2: expansible van with hydraulic tailgate
M936A2: wrecker with winch
M942A2: chassis with or without winch
M944A2: chassis without winch
M945A2: chassis with winch.
Also produced are 6822-litre water and fuel tankers

and a cargo truck with a loading/unloading crane.

The following kits are available for the M939 and M939A2 series of trucks: air brake, automatic chemical alarm, deep water fording, bow and tarpaulin cover, electric brake, engine coolant heater, front and rear lifting points, fuel burning heater, hard-top closure, machine gun mount, radiator and hood cover and rifle racks. M939A2 series cargo and dump trucks fitted with a winch can also be fitted with a front-mounted A-frame kit. This can be fitted in the field and has a lifting capacity of up to 1362 kg.

Status

M939A2 in production for the US Army. M923A2/M925A2 ordered by Egypt. M939A2 ordered by Saudi Arabia in February 1991 (2633 at cost of $129.8 million).

Manufacturers

(M939 and M939A1 – production complete) AM General Corporation, 105 N. Niles Avenue, PO Box 7025 South Bend, Indiana 46634-7025, USA.
Tel: (219) 284 2942/2911. Fax: (219) 284 2959/2814.
(M939A2 – in production) BMY-Wheeled Vehicles Division of HARSCO, 13311 Industrial Parkway, Marysville, Ohio 43040, USA.
Tel: (513) 644 0041. Fax: (513) 642 0022.

Standard Trailing Arm Drive Vehicle Series

Description

The Standard Trailing Arm Drive (TAD) vehicles incorporate a trailing arm suspension with all wheels being hydrostatically driven. The number of wheels used on a vehicle is dependent upon the vehicle application and can vary from six to ten. The suspension is vertically adjustable from the driver's position while on the move or stationary. The system enables the driver to raise one wheel individually or all wheels simultaneously to reduce the silhouette in a combat environment, when loading an aircraft or to level the vehicle on a side slope. This feature can also be used to kneel the vehicle forward or rearward. A variety of upper structures or bodies ranging from gun systems to cargo platforms can be integrated with the TAD carrier system with wide variations in weight, size and configuration. The vehicles can turn within their own diagonal length (neutral steer) and can travel at high speed over rough terrain while maintaining the smooth carriage of delicate loads such as electronic equipment.

Variants

Modular Wheeled Carrier
This 8 × 8 weapon carrier can be used to carry a

Standard (8 × 8) Forward Area Multi-purpose Vehicle

demountable 20 mm Vulcan rotary gun system in such a manner that the vehicle can emplace the gun and then be free for other purposes. The vehicle weighs 5448 kg and the maximum speed is 72.4 km/h. Ground clearance can be varied from 102 to 406 mm and the height from 2.26 to 2.565 m. A three-man crew is carried along with 550 rounds of ready-use ammunition for the gun and 1700 rounds in reserve. Length is 5.181 m and width 2.641 m. Two vehicles can be carried in a C-130 transport aircraft.

Forward Area Multi-purpose Vehicle (FAMV)
This multi-purpose 8 × 8 vehicle has the engine mounted under the forward control cab and has a payload capacity of 3175 kg. Central tyre inflation is used on all wheels.

The Medium Combat Truck (MCT) is essentially similar to the FAMV and was used as a concept demonstration vehicle to carry a 105 mm M102

howitzer as part of a programme to develop a light self-propelled artillery weapon for the US Army's Light Infantry Divisions.

Specifications (FAMV)
Cab seating: 1 + 1
Configuration: 8 × 8
Weight:
(empty) 6350 kg
(loaded) 9525 kg
Max load: 3175 kg
Towed load: 8392 kg
Length: 5.64 m
Width: 2.591 m
Height: variable from 2.16 to 2.41 m
Ground clearance: variable from 0.292 to 0.559 m
Max speed: 72.4 km/h
Fuel capacity: 227 l
Max gradient: 60%

Side slope: 40%
Engine: Detroit Diesel 8.2 l 8-cylinder 4-cycle diesel developing 205 hp at 2800 rpm
Transmission: hydrostatic
Steering: pivot or automotive
Suspension: 8-wheel independent trailing arm drive
Tyres: 36/12.5 × 16.5R
Brakes: hydrostatic with power disc

Status
In production.

Manufacturer
Standard Manufacturing Company, Inc, PO Box 210300, 4012 West Illinois Avenue, Dallas, Texas 75211, USA.
Tel: (214) 337 8911. Telex: 73326.

Oshkosh MK48 Series Articulated (8 × 8) Vehicle

Development
During the 1960s Lockheed developed a vehicle known as the Twister which, following US Army trials, evolved into a commercial model known as the Dragon Wagon. After entering into a licence agreement with Lockheed, Oshkosh Truck Corporation developed an articulated high mobility vehicle designated by Oshkosh as the DA series. Four prototypes were delivered to the US Marine Corps during 1981 and 1982.

As a result of extended user trials by the US Marine Corps, an order was placed in September 1983 for 1433 vehicles to be known as the MK48 but based on the DA Series. This was a five-year multi-year contract with the award covering the first programme year requirements of 139 units, the second programme year (148 units), the third programme year (354 units), the fourth programme year (560 units), the fifth programme year (432 units), plus options (878 modules). The total contract value was $301.6 million. The final production total was 1482 vehicles.

Description
The MK48 Series consists of a front and rear body that are connected by a centre articulation joint that provides 64° of powered steering motion co-ordinated with steering of the front axle. Articulated steering provides a 30 per cent shorter turning radius than a conventional truck of the same wheelbase. The articulated joint also provides 6° of roll capability between the front and rear modules. Roll capability and a new six-rod suspension with tapered leaf springs provides superior wheel-to-ground contact for improved off-road capability. The rear body/module can be disconnected and another body/module of a different type quickly connected.

The two-man enclosed cab mounted at the front of the vehicle has an optional roof hatch. The engine is mounted behind the cab and is coupled to a four-speed automatic transmission and a two-speed transfer case which provides full-time all-wheel drive and has driver-controlled lockout. The hydraulic boosted power steering for the front axle co-ordinates with twin hydraulic cylinders astride the articulated joint to induce rear-body yaw and assure a tight turning circle.

Standard equipment includes a voltmeter, diagnostic connector assembly for STE/ICE, blackout lights, suspension seats, winch, material handling crane, towing provision with air and electrical connections, traction control axle differentials, Jacobs engine brake, various axle and transfer ratios, spare tyre and wheel, spotlight, off-road onboard equipment, off-road cab and glass protection kit, and various rear modules. Optional equipment includes 24.00 × 21 radial sand tyres, a strobe beacon, and other special military options.

The MK48 series was produced as part of the US Marine Corps' Logistic Vehicle System (LVS) and includes the following models:
MK48/14: logistics platform truck
MK48/15: recovery vehicle
MK48/16: truck tractor

Oshkosh MK48/14 (8 × 8) vehicle during Operation Desert Storm

Specifications

Model	MK48/14	MK48/15	MK48/16	MK48/17
Type	logistics platform truck	recovery	truck tractor	cargo truck
Cab seating	1 + 1	1 + 1	1 + 1	1 + 1
Configuration	8 × 8	8 × 8	8 × 8	8 × 8
Weight (empty)	18 597 kg	23 133 kg	18 597 kg	21 769 kg
Gross vehicle combination weight				
(on road)	68 040 kg	69 840 kg	85 277 kg	69 840 kg
(off road)	47 628 kg	47 628 kg	47 628 kg	47 628 kg
Payload				
(on road)	20 412 kg	9072 kg[1]	20 866 kg[2]	18 144 kg
(off road)	11 340 kg	n/app	n/app	9072 kg
Length	11.582 m	11.278 m	10.09 m	11.582 m
Width	2.438 m	2.438 m	2.438 m	2.438 m
Height (cab)	2.591 m	2.591 m	2.591 m	2.591 m
Track	2.007 m	2.007 m	2.007 m	2.007 m
Wheelbase	1.524 m + 6.579 m +1.524 m	1.524 m + 6.579 m +1.524 m	1.524 m + 5.817 m +1.524 m	1.524 m + 6.579 m +1.524 m
Angle of approach/ departure	45°/45°	45°/48°	45°/65°	45°/40°
Max speed (road)	84 km/h	84 km/h	84 km/h	84 km/h
Range (cruising)	483 km	483 km	483 km	483 km
Fuel capacity	2 × 284 l	2 × 284 l	2 × 284 l	2 × 284 l
Gradient	60%	60%	60%	60%
Side slope	30%	30%	30%	30%
Fording	1.524 m	1.524 m	1.524 m	1.524 m
Engine	Detroit Diesel 8V-92TA V-8 2-cycle water-cooled 12.06 l diesel developing 445 hp at 2100 rpm			
Gearbox	Allison HT740D 4-speed automatic with torque converter			
Transfer box	Oshkosh 2-speed			
Steering	hydraulic powered yaw steering with power-assist on No 1 axle			
Turning radius	11.7 m	11.7 m	10.4 m	11.7 m
Suspension	leaf springs with steel saddle and 6 torque rods front and rear giving 356 mm wheel travel			
Tyres	16.00 × 21	16.00 × 21	16.00 × 21	16.00 × 21
Electrical system	24 V	24 V	24 V	24 V
Batteries	4 × 12 V	4 × 12 V	4 × 12 V	4 × 12 V
Alternator	24 V, 62 A	24 V, 62 A	24 V, 62 A	24 V, 62 A

[1] towed load 14 515 kg   [2] load on 5th wheel

MK48/17: cargo truck with material handling crane (MHC)
MK48/18: load handling system vehicle.

The MK48/14 logistics platform truck uses a steel flat

deck with standard container lashing points to carry either one 20 ft/6.096 m container, two 10 ft/3.048 m containers or six 6.66 ft/2.03 m containers. The platform length is 6.058 m and loading height is 1.549 m.

The MK48/15 recovery vehicle uses a steel cargo

body. At the rear is a hydraulic crane with a capacity of 4082 kg and a recovery winch with a pull capacity of 27 216 kg.

The MK48/16 truck tractor has a fully oscillating fifth wheel for a 3.5-in/88.9 mm kingpin mounted 1.6 m above ground level. Full trailer air and electrical connections are provided as is a 27 216 kg recovery winch.

The MK48/17 cargo truck has a steel cargo body with fold-down sides and a 4082 kg capacity hydraulic materials handling crane at the rear.

The MK48/18 involves a Reynolds Boughton load handling system mounted on a modified MK14 trailer. For full details refer to the entry in the *Materials handling equipment* section.

Status
Production for US Marine Corps (1433) complete.

Manufacturer
Oshkosh Truck Corporation, PO Box 2566, Oshkosh, Wisconsin 54903-2566, USA.
Tel: (414) 235 9150. Fax: (414) 233 9540.

Oshkosh Heavy Expanded Mobility Tactical Truck (8 × 8) 9979 kg

Development
After evaluating a number of proposals and testing 8 × 8 vehicles submitted by MAN and Pacific Car and Foundry, in May 1981 the US Army Tank-Automotive Command awarded a $251.13 million five-year contract to the Oshkosh Truck Corporation for production of the 10-ton (US) 8 × 8 Heavy Expanded Mobility Tactical Truck (HEMTT). The original HEMTT contract provided for a base quantity of 2140 vehicles and had provisions for an additional 5351 option vehicles. All five-year base quantities, and most of the options, were released under the contract.

At the completion of the original HEMTT five year contract, the US Army Tank-Automotive Command awarded a follow-on contract in April 1987. The follow-on contract provided for a base quantity of 1403 vehicles and had provisions for an additional 1684 option vehicles. All the options have been exercised.

An additional 1449 vehicles were added to this contract in April 1989 by a supplemental agreement. This agreement also contained a provision for 363 option vehicles, since exercised. To date, 6643 vehicles have been funded under the follow-on HEMTT production. Vehicles are manufactured at a rate of four per day to meet the monthly delivery schedule.

To reduce procurement and life cycle costs, the HEMTT features extensive use of commercial automotive components including an Oshkosh truck cab, standard eight-cylinder diesel engine and a standard four-speed automatic transmission. Some of the components used in this vehicle are also found in the LVS (8 × 8) vehicles used by the US Marine Corps (see previous entry).

Description
The chassis is of formed channel bolted construction with Grade 8 bolts, with heat-treated carbon manganese steel being used throughout. The chassis is provided with heavy duty front bumper and skid plate, external hydraulic connection (not on tractor trucks), service and emergency air brake connection, slave start connection and trailer electrical connector.

The two-man, two-door forward control cab is of heavy duty welded steel construction with corrosion resistant skins. Standard equipment includes suspension seats for the driver and passenger, seat belts, heater and defroster, dual sun visors, interior lights, variable speed air windscreen wipers, windscreen washers and electric and air horns. A spare wheel is mounted to the rear of the cab and is provided with a davit to assist in lowering it to the ground.

All models have Oshkosh 46K front tandem axles which are used for steering, single reduction, 32° front turning angle, single cardan joint, closed-type steering ends with an inter-axle driver-controlled differential.

The rear axles, except for those on the M984A1, are Eaton DS-480 single reduction type with driver-controlled differential. The M984A1 has Eaton DS-650 axles with single reduction and driver-controlled differential.

Variants
M977 Cargo Truck
This is the basic member of the family with a light duty materials handling crane at the very rear, produced with and without a self-recovery winch which can be used to the front or rear of the vehicle. The cargo area is 5.4 m long and is provided with drop sides.

M978 Fuel Servicing Truck
9500-litre capacity tanker, produced with or without a self-recovery winch.

Oshkosh M997 (8 × 8) cargo truck

Oshkosh M983 tractor truck towing Patriot tactical air defence system missile launcher

Specifications

Designation	M977	M978	M983	M985
Type	cargo	tanker	tractor	cargo
Cab seating	1 + 1	1 + 1	1 + 1	1 + 1
Configuration	8 × 8	8 × 8	8 × 8	8 × 8
Weight (empty)	17 600 kg	17 305 kg	14 583 kg	17 985 kg
(loaded)	27 080 kg	26 694 kg	27 125 kg	28 168 kg
Length	10.173 m	10.173 m	8.903 m	10.173 m
Width	2.438 m	2.438 m	2.438 m	2.438 m
Height (cab)	2.565 m	2.565 m	2.565 m	2.565 m
Wheelbase	5.334 m	5.334 m	4.597 m	5.334 m
Angle of approach/departure	43°/45°	43°/45°	43°/66°	43°/45°
Max speed	88 km/h	88 km/h	88 km/h	88 km/h
Gradient	60%	60%	60%	60%
Range	483 km	483 km	483 km	483 km
Fuel capacity	589 l	589 l	589 l	589 l
Engine	Detroit Diesel 8V-92TA, V-8 2-stroke 12.06 l diesel developing 445 hp at 2100 rpm			
Gearbox	Allison HT740D automatic with torque converter, 4 forward and 1 reverse gears			
Transfer box	Oshkosh 55000, 2-speed			
Steering	integral hydraulic, main and booster gears			
Suspension	Hendrickson RT340 spring with steel saddle and equalising beams, 250 mm vertical axle travel. M985 rear axle has Hendrickson RT380			
Tyres	16.00 × 20	16.00 × 20	16.00 × 20	16.00 × 20
Brakes (main)	air operated, dual system, internal shoe			
(parking)	spring brakes mounted on Nos 3 and 4 axles			
Electrical system	24 V	24 V	24 V	24 V
Batteries	4 × 12 V	4 × 12 V	4 × 12 V	4 × 12 V

M983 Tractor Truck
Tractor truck with material handling crane and fifth wheel, produced with or without a self-recovery winch.

M984A1 Wrecker
See *Recovery vehicles* section.

M985 Cargo Truck
Similar to M977 but with a heavy duty materials handling crane at rear, produced with or without a self-recovery winch. It is used, with a M989A1 trailer, to support the Multiple Launch Rocket System (MLRS).

10 × 10 PLS Truck
During 1990 it was announced that Oshkosh had been awarded a contract for 2626 10 × 10 Palletized Load System (PLS) trucks based on the HEMTT. For full details refer to the entry in the *Materials handling equipment* section.

US Customs Service HEMTT
The US Customs Service operates a small number of HEMTTs which have been specially modified to act as mobile winch and anchor vehicles for aerosats (non-motorised blimps) equipped with General Electric radar. The vehicles are located along the US-Mexican border to counter drug-smuggling activities. Each vehicle carries a cable drum and winch gear to allow an aerosat to operate at heights up to 4570 m.

Status
In production. In service with the US Army, and in Bahrain, Egypt, Israel, South Korea, Saudi Arabia and Taiwan. Commercial variants have also been sold.

Manufacturer
Oshkosh Truck Corporation, PO Box 2566, Oshkosh, Wisconsin 54903-2566, USA.
Tel: (414) 235 9150. Fax: (414) 233 9540.

Mack RM6866SX (6 × 6) 10 000 kg Truck

Description
The Mack RM6866SX (6 × 6) 10 000 kg truck is one of the 'R' series of Mack 6 × 6 vehicles. It has an all-steel cab with an optional removable roof. Suspension-seating is provided for a driver and one passenger. Left- or right-hand steering can be provided. A heavy duty frame extending from the cab to the rearmost point of the vehicle is fitted. This is constructed in single channel frame rail with a 340 × 83 × 10 mm section. The engine is rated at 250 hp but other

engines up to 400 hp can be fitted; all are turbocharged. The transmission is a Mack design and uses an aluminium case. The 'Maxitorque' transmission is equipped with three counter-shafts equally spaced around the main shaft to provide equal distribution of the torque load on the main shaft. An automatic transmission is available as an option. The Mack differential uses a 'top mount' with a high entry of driveshaft to improve clearance. The bogies use camelback springs and an automatic power divider.

The standard body on the RM6866SX is of the cargo type with drop sides and a tailgate. A hydraulic loading crane may be fitted if required. Bows and a tilt are provided as standard but other body configurations can

be made available.

Specifications
Cab seating: 1 + 1
Configuration: 6 × 6
Weight:
(loaded chassis, front) 7300 kg
(loaded chassis, rear) 17 200 kg
(GVW) 24 500 kg
Length: 8.001 m
Width: 2.463 m
Height: 2.994 m
Wheelbase: (front axle to centre of rear bogie) 4.677 m
Max speed: 84 km/h
Gradient: 60%
Fuel capacity: 359 l
Engine: Mack 6-cylinder turbocharged diesel developing 300 hp
Transmission: Mack TRL1078 5-speed or optional automatic
Clutch: CL697
Transfer case: TC15, 2-speed
Tyres: 11.00 × 22
Brakes:
(front) air wedge type
(rear) air cam type
Electrical system: 12 or 24 V
Batteries: 4 × 12 V

Status
In production. In service with several nations – see also entry under Australia in this section.

Manufacturer
Mack Trucks Inc, Box M, Allentown, Pennsylvania 18105, USA.
Tel: (215) 439 3011. Telex: 847429.
Fax: (215) 439 3308.

Mack RM6866SX (6 × 6) 10 000 kg truck

M915 Series of Trucks

Development
One of the recommendations of the 'WHEELS' study was that the US Army should use commercial trucks wherever practicable. In January 1977 the US Army Automotive Material Readiness Command (TARCOM) issued a request for technical proposals for a series of heavy trucks ranging from 22 680 to 34 019 kg gross vehicle weights. The Army subsequently received technical proposals from six truck manufacturers: AM General Corporation, FWD (Four Wheel Drive) Corporation, General Motors Truck and Coach, International Harvester Corporation, Kenworth Truck Corporation and White Autocar Corporation.

All six manufacturers who responded to the original request qualified to offer priced bids under the second step of the procurement. Bids were opened in June 1977 with AM General Corporation the lowest at $252.8 million for the requirement of 5507 trucks. In June 1977 a contract was awarded to AM General for 5507 trucks and in addition the government had the right to exercise options on an additional 5507 trucks, giving a potential of 11 014 units. The contract was for four years with the first test vehicles (M915 Line Haul Tractor) being delivered early in 1978.

The US Government did not exercise its option on the additional 5507 trucks but in September 1981 awarded AM General a contract for 2511 M915A1 (6 × 4) tractor trucks. This was completed.

The AM General series was based on the Centaur series of trucks built by the Crane Carrier Company of Tulsa, Oklahoma. A licence agreement between AM General and Crane Carriers gave rights to AM General to manufacture and sell vehicles to the US Government.

The contract also required complete after-market support of the M915 including spare part provisioning and a full complement of maintenance and service publications, as well as the training of Army instructors. The Army received warranty covering defects in design, materials and workmanship for a period of 15 months or for 19 312 km. In addition, the Army received 'free time' up to six months, for new vehicles stored in depots.

The latest production versions are the M915A2 and the M916A1. These versions are produced by the Freightliner Corporation who were awarded a contract to produce 797 trucks with a 200 per cent overbuy option.

Description
The series is based on commercial vehicles with the

minimum of modifications to suit them for military use, such as forest green paint, rear-mounted pintle hooks, front and rear tow hooks and blackout lights. There are three basic chassis, 6 × 4 for road use and 6 × 6 and 8 × 6 for both road and cross-country use.

The layout of all vehicles is similar with the engine at the front, two-door all-steel fully enclosed cab in the centre and the fifth wheel or body at the rear.

M915, Tractor, Truck, 14-ton, 6 × 4
This is powered by a Cummins model NTC 400 6-cylinder diesel which develops 400 hp (gross) at 2100 rpm, coupled to a Caterpillar semi-automatic gearbox with 16 forward and 2 reverse gears. The suspension consists of front: Rockwell Asymmetrical leaf pin and shackle, and rear: Hendrickson RTE 380 walking beam.

The M915 is used primarily for the long distance movement of containers and normally tows the 34-ton (US) M872 semi-trailer. It replaced the 5-ton military series tractors and certain commercial tractors used in moving cargo from the port of embarkation to the division rear boundary. M52 and M818 truck tractors will continue to operate from within the division and brigade areas, performing the same types of mission as currently assigned.

M915A1 (6 × 4) 14-ton tractor truck (C R Zwart)

M917 (8 × 6), 20-ton dump truck

M915A1, Tractor, Truck, 14-ton, 6 × 4

In September 1981 AM General Corporation was awarded a contract by the US Army Tank-Automotive Command for 2511 M915A1 (6 × 4) tractor trucks. This contract was worth $130 million with a 100 per cent option for an additional 2511 units. Production began at the company's South Bend plant in January 1983 and continued for 18 months.

The M915A1 is similar to the earlier M915 except that it has an Allison HT 754 CR automatic transmission with five forward and one reverse gears.

Specifications (similar to the M915 except for the following details)
Length: 6.489 m
Width: 2.438 m
Height: 2.984 m
Fording: 0.616 m
Max road speed: 91.7 km/h
Speed on 3% slope: 45 km/h
Max gradient: 18.4%
Fuel capacity: 446 l

M915A2, Tractor, Truck, 14-ton, 6 × 4

This Freightliner Corporation 6 × 4 tractor truck is powered by a Detroit Diesel DDE 12.7 litre unit developing 400 hp at 2100 rpm coupled to an Allison HT-740 automatic transmission. Weight empty is 8481 kg and the vehicle is 7 m long, 2.49 m wide and 3.02 m high overall. Wheelbase is 4.12 m.

The M915A2 contract was awarded to Freightliner on September 20, 1988, and was for 385 units. The first deliveries were made in May 1989 and the first production vehicles entered the US Army's inventory in November 1990 (see also following entry).

M916, Tractor, Truck, 20-ton, 6 × 6

This replaced the M123 (6 × 6) tractor and has the same engine and transmission as the M915 but also has an Oshkosh F-U29 transfer case. Suspension is the same as in the M915 with differential lock-ups on front axle and rear bogie. Mounted to the rear of the cab is a hydraulic winch with a capacity of 20 250 kg.

The M916 is used by units throughout the world as the prime mover for the M172A1 low-bed trailer to transport heavy construction equipment within the theatre of operations. It also operates efficiently hauling the M870 40-ton low-bed semi-trailer when fully loaded; however, a 6-inch fifth-wheel spacer must be used for compatibility with the M870 kingpin height.

M916A1, Tractor Truck, 20-ton, 6 × 6

This Freightliner Corporation 6 × 6 tractor truck is powered by a Detroit Diesel DDE 12.7 litre unit developing 400 hp at 2100 rpm coupled to an Allison HT-740 automatic transmission. Weight empty is 12 594 kg. Length is 7.35 m, width 2.49 m and the height is 3.24 m overall. Wheelbase is 4.41 m.

The M916A1 contract was awarded to Freightliner in September 1988, and was for 393 units. The first deliveries were made in May 1989 and the first production vehicles entered the US Army's inventory in November 1990.

M917, Dump Truck, 20-ton, 8 × 6

This has a rear tipping dump body by Fruehauf which has a heaped capacity of 10.7 m³, and the same engine, gearbox, transfer box and suspension as the M916.

The M917 is used for earthmoving and construction projects, augmenting the current fleet of 20-ton dump

trucks and in some selected units replacing 5-ton dump trucks.

M918, Bituminous Distributor, 1500 gallons, 6 × 6

This has a 56 775 litre bituminous spreader on the rear manufactured by E D Etnyre and Company of Oregon. Engine, transmission, transfer box and suspension are the same as for the M916.

The M918 is used for distributing liquid bitumen for road and airfield construction and is provided with a hydrostatically driven bituminous pump.

M919, Concrete Mobile, 8 cu yd, 8 × 6

This has a concrete mixer to the rear manufactured by the National Concrete Machinery Company of Lancaster, Pennsylvania. The engine, transmission, transfer box and suspension are the same as in the M916. It can transport dry concrete ingredients and water, mix the ingredients in various increments and proportions, and pour the mixed concrete. The M919 is charged with dry ingredients by aggregate bins or scoop loaders and discharges into mixed concrete handling equipment. This vehicle can also be used as a central mix plant where large amounts of concrete are required at a single location.

A M919A1 version is produced by the Freightliner Corporation.

M920, Tractor, Truck, 20-ton, 8 × 6

This has a fifth wheel at the rear and is used to haul semi-trailers. Mounted to the rear of the cab is a hydraulic winch with a capacity of 20 250 kg. The engine, transmission, transfer box and suspension are the same as in the M916.

The M920 will, together with the M916 series,

Specifications

Designation	M915	M916	M917	M918	M919	M920
Type	tractor	tractor	dump truck	bituminous	concrete	tractor
Cab seating	1 + 2	1 + 2	1 + 2	1 + 2	1 + 2	1 + 2
Configuration	6 × 4	6 × 6	8 × 6	6 × 6	8 × 6	8 × 6
Weight (empty)	8446 kg	11 327 kg	14 768 kg	13 535 kg	15 791 kg	12 414 kg
(loaded)	22 213 kg	29 629 kg	33 070 kg	19 789 kg	32 056 kg	30 716 kg
Weight on front axle (loaded)	5443 kg	6543 kg	3775 kg	5600 kg	4511 kg	3864 kg
Weight on rear axles (loaded)	17 236 kg	23 036 kg	33 070 kg	14 210 kg	32 506 kg	30 716 kg
Gross combination weight	47 627 kg	57 153 kg	n/app	n/app	n/app	61 235 kg
Length	6.49 m	7.48 m	8.9 m	8.9 m	9.5 m	8.11 m
Width	2.49 m	2.49 m	2.49 m	2.49 m	2.49 m	2.49 m
Height (cab)	2.93 m	3.25 m	3.25 m	3.25 m	3.25 m	3.25 m
(overall)	3.61 m	3.61 m	3.61 m	3.61 m	3.61 m	3.61 m
Ground clearance	0.254 m	0.305 m	0.305 m	0.295 m	0.305 m	0.295 m
Track (front/rear)	1.99 m/1.82 m	1.98 m/1.85 m	1.98 m/1.85 m	1.98 m/1.85 m	1.98 m/1.85 m	1.98 m/1.85 m
Wheelbase (excluding pusher axle)	4.24 m + 1.32 m	4.72 m + 1.42 m	4.876 m + 1.42 m	4.72 m + 1.42 m	4.876 m + 1.42 m	4.876 m + 1.46 m
Angle of approach	38°	42°	41°	42°	42°	42°
Max speed (road)	107 km/h	103 km/h	107 km/h	103 km/h	107 km/h	103 km/h
(3.9% gradient)	40.2 km/h	40.2 km/h	40.2 km/h	40.2 km/h	40.2 km/h	40.2 km/h
Fuel capacity	416 l	416 l	416 l	416 l	416 l	416 l
Fording	0.51 m	0.73 m	0.61 m	0.61 m	0.61 m	0.61 m
Steering	all have Ross integral power system					
Turning radius	8.15 m	12.2 m	13.65 m	12.2 m	13.65 m	13.65 m
Tyres	10. × 20	11.00 × 24	11.00 × 24	11.00 × 24	11.00 × 24	11.00 × 24
Electrical system (24 V optional)	12 V	12 V	12 V	12 V	12 V	12 V
Batteries	4 × 12 V	4 × 12 V	4 × 12 V	4 × 12 V	4 × 12 V	4 × 12 V

replace the M123, and is used to haul the M870 semi-trailer.

The Freightliner Corporation is producing a Freightliner Military Truck Family based on its M915A2 and M916A1 – see following entry for details.

Note: On the 8 × 6 model the second axle is of the pusher type and can be raised if required.

Status
M915A2 and M916A1 in production. In service with the US Army.

Manufacturers
(M915 and M916 – production complete) AM General Corporation, 105 N. Niles Avenue, PO Box 7025 South Bend, Indiana 46634-7025, USA.
Tel: (219) 284 2942/2911. Fax: (219) 284 2959/2814.
(M915A2 and M916A1 – in production) Freightliner Corporation, 4747 North Channel Avenue, PO Box 3849, Portland, Oregon 97208, USA.
Tel: (503) 735 8000.

Freightliner Military Truck Family

Description
The Freightliner Corporation is producing the Freightliner Military Truck Family based on its M915A2 and M916A1 tractor trucks already in service with the US Army (see previous entry). These two models are included in the Family and, using these two models as a basis, Freightliner is also producing a 6 × 6 wrecker (see entry under *Recovery vehicles* for details of this model), a 60-tonne capacity Medium Equipment Transporter (MET) based on a tractor truck unit, a 6 × 6 dump truck and a mobile concrete mixer – the latter has been type standardised as the M919A2 and is in production.

All vehicles are based on the Detroit Diesel DDE Series 60 12.7 litre engine with microprocessor control and an Allison automatic transmission. All vehicles have a WABCO four-channel anti-lock brake system (ABS) and Ross integral power steering.

Status
In production.

Manufacturer
Freightliner Corporation, 4747 North Channel Avenue, PO Box 3849, Portland, Oregon 97208-3849, USA.
Tel: (503) 735 8000.

Freightliner M916A1, Tractor, Truck, 20-ton, 6 × 6

Freightliner 60-tonne capacity (6 × 6) Medium Equipment Transporter

Specifications

Model	M9152A	M916A1	-	M919A2	-
Type	tractor truck	tractor truck	dump	concrete mixer	MET
Cab seating	1 + 1	1 + 1	1 + 1	1 + 1	1 + 1
Configuration	6 × 4	6 × 6	6 × 6	6 × 6	6 × 6
Weight (kerb)	8481 kg	12 594 kg	13 358 kg	15 442 kg	13 363 kg
Weight on front axle (loaded)	5448 kg	7258 kg	7258 kg	7258 kg	7258 kg
Weight on rear axle (loaded)	18 160 kg	25 587 kg	25 587 kg	25 587 kg	25 587 kg
GCW	47 670 kg	59 020 kg	n/app	n/app	87 317 kg
Length	7 m	7.35 m	7.52 m	9.65 m	7.39 m
Width	2.49 m	2.49 m	2.49 m	2.49 m	2.49 m
Height (cab)	2.76 m	2.97 m	2.97 m	2.97 m	2.97 m
(overall)	3.02 m	3.24 m	3.24 m	3.24 m	3.24 m
Ground clearance	0.23 m	0.23 m	0.23 m	0.23 m	0.23 m
Wheelbase	4.12 m	4.41 m	4.41 m	4.83 m	4.75 m
Angle of approach	27°	37.5°	37.5°	37.5°	37.5°
Max speed (road)	90 km/h	85.3 km/h	85.3 km/h	85.3 km/h	78 km/h
(3% grade)	47 km/h	40.22 km/h	40.22 km/h	40.22 km/h	29 km/h
Fuel capacity	379 l	379 l	379 l	379 l	379 l
Fording	0.51 m	0.51 m	0.51 m	0.51 m	0.51 m
Engine	Detroit Diesel Series 60 12.7 1 6-cylinder diesel developing 400 hp at 2100 rpm[1]				
Transmission	Allison HT-740 automatic with 4 forward and 1 reverse gears[2]				
Steering	Ross power	Ross power	Ross power	Ross power	Ross power
Turning radius	16.44 m	24.21 m	24.21 m	25.1 m	25.4 m
Brakes	air/mechanical	air/mechanical	air/mechanical	air/mechanical	air/mechanical
Tyres	315/80 R 22.5	315/80 R 22.5	315/80 R 22.5	315/80 R 22.5	315/80 R 22.5
Electrical system	12/24 V	12/24 V	12/24 V	12/24 V	12/24 V
Batteries	4 × 12 V	4 × 12 V	4 × 12 V	4 × 12 V	4 × 12 V

[1] Engine on MET develops 450 hp at 2100 rpm
[2] Transmission on MET is Allison CLT-754 automatic with torque converter with 5 forward and 1 reverse gears

Freightliner M915A2, Tractor, Truck, 14-ton, 6 × 4

Freightliner 6 × 6 dump truck

TANK TRANSPORTERS

This section covers prime movers which are used principally for towing semi-trailers carrying MBTs. Many military trucks also exist as tractor trucks, these being used for towing semi-trailers carrying cargo or light armoured vehicles. For example the Berliet TBU-15 is the tractor truck version of the GBU-15 truck and is often used to tow a semi-trailer carrying a light tank. The reader is referred to the *Trucks* section for vehicles of this type. Details of the tank semi-trailers will be found in the *Trailers* section.

AUSTRIA

ÖAF 34.440 VFA (8 × 8) Tank Transporter Tractor

Description

The ÖAF 34.440 VFA (8 × 8) tank transporter tractor was developed by the Österreichische Automobilfabrik ÖAF – Graf und Stift AG to replace existing tank transporters in use with the Austrian Army. The first example was produced in 1983.

The ÖAF 34.440 VFA tractor is equipped with a cab accommodating the driver and five passengers. Behind the cab is a Palfinger Type PK 8200 A crane for use as a truck loader. This crane has a safe working load of 3150 kg at a radius of 2.5 m and 970 kg at 7.7 m. When in use, stability is provided by two hydraulic outriggers, one each side. In the centre of the vehicle there is a Rotzler Treibmatic TR 080 friction-type winch with a capacity of 8000 kg. This winch can operate to the front or rear and can be controlled by a portable hand-held unit. It has 60 m of cable.

Two main winches are used to load tanks onto the trailer. They are Rotzler type 25 000 H/3-367 winches with a capacity of 20 000 kg each. Both are controlled from an elevated platform and both have 50 m of cable. Also controlled from the same platform is an auxiliary winch, a Rotzler KO 22, with a capacity of 600 kg. This is used to pull the heavy cables to the vehicle to be loaded. All the winches and the crane are hydraulic. Power for the 8000 kg winch, the auxiliary winch and the crane is taken from a secondary power take-off on the gearbox. The main recovery winches are powered by a hydraulic pump driven by the main power take-off.

The trailer used with this tractor is a Goldhofer TUAH 8 55/80. It has eight axles and can carry loads of up to 55 000 kg. The loading platform is 10.2 m long and can be varied in width from 3.2 to 3.7 m. It has its own hydraulic system that can be powered by the towing vehicle or an onboard power unit. The hydraulics raise and lower the ramps at both ends of the trailer and the loading stabilisers and can also be used to raise and lower the load platform height.

Specifications (provisional)
Cab seating: 1 + 5
Configuration: 8 × 8
Weight: (loaded) 34 000 kg
Towing capacity: up to 80 000 kg
Length: 8.85 m
Width: 2.5 m
Height: 3.4 m
Max speed: 84 km/h
Fuel capacity: 600 l
Engine: 10-cylinder turbocharged water-cooled diesel developing 440 hp
Gearbox: 8-speed with hydraulic torque converter

Status
In service with the Austrian Army.

Manufacturer
Österreichische Automobilfabrik ÖAF – Graf und Stift AG, Brunner Strasse 72, A-1211 Vienna, Austria.

OAF 34.440 VFA (8 × 8) tank transporter tractor

OAF 34.440 VFA (8 × 8) tank transporter tractor from rear showing main tank recovery winches and control platform

Steyr 1491.330.S34/6 × 6 and 3891/6 × 6 Tractor Trucks

Description

The Steyr 1491.330.S34/6 × 6 tractor truck is based on a heavy duty all-wheel drive commercial vehicle and has been adapted to meet military requirements. It was designed to pull semi-trailers on roads and prepared surfaces up to a weight of 85 000 kg. Most of the components used on this tractor truck are identical to those used on the Steyr 1491/6 × 6 M (see entry in the *Trucks* section).

The forward control cab is all steel, has seating for the driver and two passengers and may be tilted forward 70° for engine access. An observation hatch for the roof is standard and a machine gun may be mounted on the roof. The chassis frame is of the parallel ladder type with an integrated sub-frame for the winch and the fifth wheel. Two hydraulic winches, each with a pulling capacity of 20 000 kg, are mounted behind the cab for loading and off-loading. The vehicle is fully rail-transportable and can be used with all conventional semi-trailers.

Steyr 1491.330.S34/6 × 6 tractor truck

Steyr 3891/6 × 6 tractor truck as produced for Saudi Arabia

A version is also available with 14.00 R 20 MPT tyres, single at the front and dual on the rear axles. This is known as the Steyr 3891/6 × 6 and was produced for delivery to Saudi Arabia.

Specifications
Cab seating: 1 + 2
Configuration: 6 × 6
Weight:
 (kerb) 13 000 kg
 (5th wheel) 21 000 kg
 (GCW) 85 000 kg
Length: 7.051 m
Width: 2.462 m
Height: 3.14 m
Ground clearance: 0.314 m
Wheelbase: 3.4 m + 1.35 m

Max speed: 60 km/h
Fuel capacity: 380 l
Max gradient: (85 t GCW) 25%
Engine: Steyr Model WD 815.74 V-8 water-cooled direct injection turbocharged diesel developing 340 hp at 2200 rpm
Gearbox: ZF 5 S 111 GP manual, synchronised with 8 speeds plus 1 crawler forward and 1 reverse
Transfer box: Steyr VG 1200 2-speed
Steering: ZF 8046 hydraulic power-assist
Turning radius: 9 m
Suspension:
 (front) semi-elliptical leaf springs with shock absorbers
 (rear) two swivel springs
Tyres: 12.00 × 20 (14.00 R 20 MPT optional)

Brakes:
 (main) dual circuit compressed air
 (trailer) two-line compressed air
 (parking) spring energy brake cylinder, air operated
Electrical system: 24 V
Batteries: 2 × 12 V, 135 Ah

Status
In production. Steyr 3891/6 × 6 in service with Saudi Arabia.

Manufacturer
Steyr Nutzfahrzeuge AG, Schönauerstrasse 5, A-4400 Steyr, Austria.
Tel: 7252/585-0. Telex: 28200.
Fax: 7252/46746, 48650.

Steyr 37M42/S38/6 × 6 Tractor Truck

Description
The Steyr 37M42/S38/6 × 6 tractor truck is a derivative of the Steyr 1491 series of truck (see entry under *Trucks* for details) and is used to tow 5th wheel loads of up to 22 000 kg. It can be used as a heavy tractor truck for trailers and semi-trailers with payloads up to 60 tonnes. Two 25-tonne winches are provided to handle disabled vehicles.

Specifications
Cab seating: 1 + 2
Configuration: 6 × 6
Weight:
 (empty) approx 15 000 kg
 (loaded) 37 000 kg
 (gross train weight) 90 000 kg
Weight on front axle: 8000 kg
Weight on rear axle: 2 × 14 500 kg
Max load: 22 000 kg
Length: 7.764 m
Width: 2.072 m
Height: 3.246 m
Ground clearance: 0.38 m
Track: 2.072 m
Wheelbase: 3.8 m + 1.47 m
Angle of approach/departure: 31°/35°
Max speed: approx 80 km/h
Range: approx 500 km
Fuel capacity: 500 l
Gradient: (fully loaded) 34.4%
Side slope: 30%

Steyr 37M42/S38/6 × 6 tractor truck

Fording: 0.8 m
Engine: Steyr WD 815.76 12 l V-8 direct injection, water-cooled, turbocharged, inter-cooled diesel developing 416 hp at 2200 rpm
Gearbox: ZF 4 S 150 GP 8-speed synchromesh
Clutch: WSK 400 torque converter
Transfer box: Steyr VG 2000, 2-speed
Steering: ZF 8046 power-assisted
Turning radius: 10.8 m
Suspension: semi-elliptical springs with shock absorbers at front
Tyres: 14.00 R 20
Brakes: dual circuit, air

Electrical system: 24 V
Batteries: 2 × 12 V, 135 Ah each
Alternator: 28 V, 55 A

Status
In production.

Manufacturer
Steyr Nutzfahrzeuge AG, Schönauerstrasse 5, A-4400 Steyr, Austria.
Tel: 7252/585-0. Telex: 28200.
Fax: 7252/46746, 48650.

CHINA, PEOPLE'S REPUBLIC

Hanyang HY 480 (8 × 8) Tractor Truck

Description
The HY 480 (8 × 8) heavy tractor truck is used for the moving of heavy loads carried on a semi-trailer and uses a standard fifth wheel (88.9 mm) carried between the third and fourth axles at the rear. The cab is of the forward control type with seating for a driver and one passenger and there is room behind the seats for a bunk or seating for four passengers. The cab can be tilted forwards for maintenance access to the engine and other components.

Specifications
Cab seating: 1 + 5
Configuration: 8 × 8

Weight:
 (unladen) 13 900 kg
 (max GVW) 34 000 kg
 (fifth wheel loading) 20 000 kg
Length: 8.595 m
Width: 2.58 m
Height:
 (top of cab) 2.95 m
 (fifth wheel) 1.5 m

Hanyang HY 480 (8 × 8) tractor truck

Hanyang HY 480 (8 × 8) tractor truck

Ground clearance: 0.39 m
Wheelbase: 1.45 m + 3.5 m + 1.45 m
Track: 2.145 m
Max speed: 70 km/h
Max gradient: 35%
Engine: KHD B F 12 L 413FC developing 500 hp at 2500 rpm
Gearbox: 8TBF-150 8/8.14-1

Clutch: YB400
Turning radius: 12 m
Tyres: 14.00 × 20
Electrical system: 24 V

Status
In production.

Manufacturer
Hanyang Special Auto Works, Hanyang Bridge Jianghan Road, Wuhan, Hubei Province, People's Republic of China.

Hanyang HY 473 32.35 (6 × 6) Tractor Truck

Description
The Hanyang HY 473 32.35 (6 × 6) tractor truck is used for the towing of semi-trailers carrying tanks up to about 50 000 kg in weight. It has a forward control cab that can be tilted forward for engine access and the cab is large enough to accommodate bunks behind the seats. Two winch drums are located behind the cab for loading and unloading. This vehicle is used to tow the HY 962 semi-trailer (see entry in the *Trailers* section).

The HY 472 is essentially a similar vehicle intended mainly for commercial use and the HY 960 is a military version with an enlarged crew cab.

Specifications
Cab seating: 1 + 4 to 6
Configuration: 6 × 6
Weight:
 (empty) 12 500 kg
 (5th wheel loading) 19 500 kg
 (GVW) 32 000 kg
 (GCW) 62 000 kg
Length: 7.245 m
Width: 2.58 m
Height:
 (cab) 2.9 m
 (5th wheel) 1.45 m
Ground clearance: 0.34 m
Wheelbase: 3.5 m + 1.35 m
Track:
 (front) 2.05 m

 (rear) 1.92 m
Max speed: 64 km/h
Gradient: 24%
Engine: KHD F 12 L 413F developing 355 hp at 2500 rpm
Gearbox: 9TBF-110 9/13.40-1
Turning radius: 10 m
Tyres: 12.00 × 20
Electrical system: 24 V

Status
In production. In service with the Chinese Army.

Manufacturer
Hanyang Special Auto Works, Hanyang Bridge Jianghan Road, Wuhan, Hubei Province, People's Republic of China.

Hanyang HY 960 (6 × 6) tractor truck with tank transporter semi-trailer (C F Foss)

Hanyang HY 960 (6 × 6) tractor truck (C F Foss)

COMMONWEALTH OF INDEPENDENT STATES

MAZ-535 and MAZ-537 (8 × 8) Series

Description
These 8 × 8 vehicles were seen for the first time in public during a parade held in Moscow in 1964, and are used for a wide variety of roles by the CIS armed forces and for a variety of civil roles. They are closely related to the MAZ-543 (8 × 8) series of trucks.

They all have full 8 × 8 drive with powered steering

on the front two pairs of wheels, central tyre pressure regulation system, cab heater and an engine pre-heater. They are all powered by the same V-12 diesel used in some CIS tanks. In the case of the MAZ-535 the engine has been derated to deliver 375 hp instead of 525 hp as in the MAZ-537.

The MAZ-535A, MAZ-537A and MAZ-537K (which has a small crane) are cargo trucks but are also used to tow trailers or heavy artillery. The other models are used to tow semi-trailers carrying missiles or armoured fighting vehicles. The tractor trucks are normally used

in conjunction with the ChMZAP-5247 and ChMZAP-5247G semi-trailers.

Variants
MAZ-535A: cargo truck
MAZ-537A: cargo truck
MAZ-537K: cargo truck
MAZ-537: tractor truck
MAZ-537D: tractor truck with additional generator to rear of engine compartment
MAZ-537E: tractor truck with generator, winch; can

MAZ-537 (8 × 8) tank transporter (C R Zwart)

MAZ-537 (8 × 8) tank transporter (C R Zwart)

also be used with powered semi-trailer
MAZ-537G: tractor truck with winch
KET-T: heavy recovery version of MAZ-537G fitted with recovery crane, winches, stabilisers and towing gear.

A version of the MAZ-537 carrying a turntable crane has been observed but no details are available.

Status
In production. In service with members of the former

Warsaw Pact as well as Egypt, Finland, Iran, Syria and the former Yugoslavia.

Manufacturer
Minsk Motor Vehicle Plant, Minsk, Belarus.

Specifications

Designation	MAZ-535A	MAZ-537A	MAZ-537
Type	truck	truck	tractor truck
Configuration	8 × 8	8 × 8	8 × 8
Weight (empty)	18 975 kg	22 500 kg	21 600 kg
(loaded)	25 975 kg	37 500 kg	n/app
Weight on front axles (loaded)	n/a	14 890 kg	n/a
Weight on rear axles (loaded)	n/a	22 610 kg	n/a
Max load (road and cross-country)	6000 kg	15 000 kg	n/app
Towed load (road)	50 000 kg	75 000 kg	65 000 kg
(dirt road)	15 000 kg	30 000 kg	25 000 kg
Load area	4.5 × 2.595 m	4.562 × 2.53 m	n/app
Length	8.78 m	9.13 m	8.96 m
Width	2.805 m	2.885 m	2.885 m
Height (cab)	2.915 m	2.8 m	2.88 m
(load area)	1.4 m	1.875 m	n/app
Ground clearance	0.475 m	0.5 m	0.55 m
Track	2.15 m	2.2 m	2.2 m
Wheelbase	1.7 m + 2.35 m	1.7 m + 2.65 m	1.8 m + 2.65 m
	+ 1.7 m	+ 1.7 m	+ 1.7 m
Angle of approach/departure	38°/60°	38°/52°	38°/52°
Max speed (road)	60 km/h	60 km/h	55-60 km/h
Range	650 km	650 km	650 km
Fuel capacity	760 l	840 l	840 l
Fuel consumption	110 l/100 km	125 l/100 km	125 l/100 km
Max gradient	30°	8° (laden)	8° (laden)
Fording	1.3 m	1.3 m	1.3 m
Engine model	D12A-375	D12A-525	D12A-525
Engine type	V-12 water-cooled	V-12 water-cooled	V-12 water-cooled
	diesel developing	diesel developing	diesel developing
	375 hp at 1650 rpm	525 hp at 2100 rpm	525 hp at 2100 rpm
Gearbox	planetary, 3 speeds forward and 1 speed reverse, with smooth start device on low gear and reverse		
Transfer case	manual, 2-speed, with direct drive and reduction gears, pneumatic and manual backup control		
Auxiliary reduction gear transmission	manual, with inter-axle self-locking differential, consisting of spur gear pair		
Torque converter	single stage	single stage	single stage
Overdrive	single-row 3-shaft reduction gear with spur skew gears		
Steering	hydraulic, screw with nut on moving balls and rack engaged with gear quadrant		
Suspension	MAZ-535A, independent, individual, lever torsion bar (rear suspension equaliser, springless on MAZ-535V and MAZ-537), with hydraulic shock absorbers on all wheels. MAZ-537A, independent, individual, lever torsion bar, with hydraulic shock absorbers on both sides of front axle; rear: springless equaliser		
Tyres	18.00 × 24	18.00 × 24	18.00 × 24
Brakes	air/hydraulic	air/hydraulic	air/hydraulic
Electrical system	24 V	24 V	24 V
Batteries	4 × 12-ST-70	4 × 12-ST-70	4 × 12-ST-70
Generator	1500 W	1500 W	1500 W

FRANCE

Renault TRM 700-100 (6 × 6) Tractor Truck

Description

The Renault TRM 700-100 (6 × 6) tractor truck was first shown at the 1987 Satory exhibition and was designed as a tank transporter for the Leclerc MBT. It uses a forward control four-door cab similar to that used on the Renault TRM 10 000 (6 × 6) 10 000 kg truck (see entry in the *Trucks* section) but enlarged to carry the driver and four passengers. The cab can be tilted forward hydraulically for maintenance purposes. The chassis has reinforced pressed steel sidemembers with inner sections connected by crossmembers.

The engine is a Type E9 turbocharged diesel developing 700 hp coupled to an automatic six-speed gearbox (with integrated electronic control and a hydraulic retarder). The transfer box is integral with the gearbox. Hydraulic power-assisted steering is provided. Two optional hydraulic 15-tonne loading winches are located behind the cab.

The TRM 700-100 has been demonstrated towing a Nicolas SFD A6 semi-trailer with a capacity of 70 000 kg.

Renault TRM 700-100 (6 × 6) tractor truck towing Leclerc MBT

Specifications

Cab seating: 1 + 4
Configuration: 6 × 6
Weight:
  (kerb) 13 946 kg
  (GVW) 39 000 kg
  (GTW) 106 000 kg
Towed load: 90 000 kg

Max load on 5th wheel: 23 000 kg
Length: 8.045 m
Width: (overall) 2.68 m

Height: (unloaded) 3.083 m
Ground clearance: (rear axle, loaded) 0.341 m
Wheelbase: 4.325 m + 1.35 m
Track:
(front) 2.12 m
(rear) 2.03 m
Angle of approach: 42°
Max speed: 76 km/h
Fuel capacity: 780 l (2 × 390 l)
Range: 850 km
Max gradient: 20%
Engine: RVI Type E9 16.4 l V-8 turbocharged intercooled diesel developing 700 hp at 2500 rpm

Transmission: Type PS 226 automatic with 6 forward gears and 1 reverse; type WR hydraulic torque converter with lock-up and hydraulic retarder
Transfer box: single-speed
Steering: Type 8098 hydraulic power-assist
Turning radius: 14 m
Suspension:
(front) semi-elliptic leaf springs with auxiliary equaliser spring and hydraulic telescopic shock absorbers
(rear) inverted semi-elliptic leaf springs, oscillating swivels and reaction rods
Tyres: 14.00 R 20

Brakes: dual circuit, air
Electrical system: 24 V
Batteries: 4 × 12 V, 125 Ah
Alternator: 50 A

Status
Pre-production. Under evaluation by French Army.

Manufacturer
Enquiries to Renault Véhicules Industriels, 40 rue Pasteur, BP 302, F-92156 Suresnes Cedex, France.
Tel: (1) 40 99 71 11. Telex: 620567 sdce f.
Fax: (1) 40 99 71 08.

Nicolas Tractomas (6 × 6) and (8 × 8) Tank Transporter Tractor Trucks

Description
The Nicolas Tractomas tractor trucks were designed to be used primarily as tank transporter tractor units for the Nicolas power-axle tank transporter trailers (see entry in the *Trailers* section). There are four models in the basic range, each of which may be equipped with a civil cab or a military cab with increased capacity and seating. All models are equipped with Mercedes OM 424 A diesel engines developing 525 hp at 2300 rpm. The gearboxes used are the Transmatic ZF type. Few details are available on the range but the

performance outlines are shown here.

Specifications (TATT 66 OZ)
Cab seating: 1 + 4 or 5
Configuration: 6 × 6
Weight:
(empty) 23 500 kg
(loaded) 44 500 kg
Length: 8.065 m
Width: 3.3 m
Height:
(cab, loaded) 3.72 m
(5th wheel, loaded) 1.82 m
Wheelbase: 3.79 m + 1.65 m
Track: 2.65 m
Angle of approach: 30°

Max speed: 62 km/h
Gradient: 30%
Fuel capacity: 900 l
Engine: Mercedes OM 424 A V-12 4-cycle water-cooled supercharged diesel developing 525 hp at 2300 rpm
Gearbox: ZF 4S.150.GPA with 8 forward and 1 reverse gears
Converter: ZF WSK 400.59
Steering: hydraulic power-assisted
Turning radius: 10.5 m
Suspension:
(front) leaf springs
(rear) leaf springs, cantilever mounting
Tyres: 18.00 × 25 XS
Brakes: air
Electrical system: 24 V
Batteries: 4 × 6 V, 192 Ah
Alternator: 60 A

Status
Production to customer request. In widespread service.

Manufacturer
Nicolas, F-89290 Champs sur Yonne, France.
Tel: (33) 86 53 30 09. Telex: 800938 f.
Fax: (33) 86 53 79 74.

Performance

Military Model	TA 66 OZ	TA 88 OZ	TATT 66 OZ	TATT 88 OZ
Max load 5th wheel	27 500 kg	33 000 kg	21 000 kg	33 500 kg
Max speed	86 km/h	86 km/h	66.5 km/h	66.5 km/h
(with 60 t trailer load)	67.5 km/h	67.5 km/h	65 km/h	65 km/h
Max gradient				
(at 2300 rpm with locking)	11.8%	11.8%	15.5%	15%
(at 1500 rpm with locking)	14%	14%	18.5%	17.8%
(at 1500 rpm with converter)	32.5%	32.5%	42%	40%
Speed on 10% with 60 t payload	12 km/h	12 km/h	10.2 km/h	10.2 km/h

Nicolas Tractomas TATT 66 OZ towing CS 66 40A semi-trailer

Nicolas Tractomas TATT 66 OZ towing CS 66 40A semi-trailer

Renault R 390 (6 × 4) Tractor Truck

Description
The R 390 (6 × 4) tractor truck is a standard commercial vehicle adapted to meet military requirements. It has been adopted by the French Army for road use and is used in conjunction with the Nicolas STA 43 semi-trailer. The vehicle can be used with other semi-trailers carrying MBTs up to a maximum weight of 55 000 kg.

The chassis consists of two U-shaped sidemembers with five crossmembers welded and riveted into position. The vehicle is fitted with a model KB 2480 cab which is of the two-door forward control type and has seats for the driver, two passengers and two bunks at the rear of the cab. The cab is heated and soundproofed and can be tilted forward to an angle of 70° to allow maintenance work on the engine. Optional equipment includes a hydraulic winch with a capacity of 15 000 kg and 90 m of cable, dividing curtain, elbow rests, heating system, fog lamps, tachograph, radio equipment, blackout lights, searchlight, flashing light, combined air/electric cables and an anti-freeze device for the brake circuit.

The French Army uses a similar version of the Renault R 390 (6 × 4) tractor truck for towing semi-trailers carrying fuel and other supplies. The French Army also uses the Berliet TR 260 (4 × 2) tractor truck for hauling a variety of semi-trailers.

Specifications
Cab seating: 1 + 4
Configuration: 6 × 4
Weight:
(empty) 10 300 kg
(loaded) 34 500 kg
Weight on front axle:
(empty) 5300 kg

Renault R 390 (6 × 4) tractor truck towing Nicolas semi-trailer carrying AMX-30 EBG

(loaded) 6500 kg
Weight on rear bogie:
(empty) 5000 kg
(loaded) 28 000 kg
Max weight on 5th wheel: 24 000 kg
Length: 6.53 m
Width: 2.49 m
Height: 3 m
Ground clearance: 0.303 m
Track:
(front) 2.028 m
(rear) 1.825 m
Wheelbase: 2.95 m + 1.35 m
Angle of approach/departure: 22°/45°
Max speed: 66 km/h

Range: 800 km
Fuel capacity: 650 l
Max gradient: (laden with 70 600 kg gross weight) 15%
Fording: 0.7 m
Engine: Renault model MIVR 08-35-30 8-cylinder water-cooled supercharged diesel developing 390 hp at 2100 rpm
Gearbox: Renault B 9 with 18 forward and 2 reverse gears
Steering: 8065 hydraulic power-assisted
Turning radius: 8.5 m
Suspension:
(front) leaf springs and shock absorbers
(rear) torsion bar stabiliser; rear wheels have

reduction gears in the wheel hubs, differential locking system between axles and wheels
Tyres: 13 × 22.5
Brakes: pneumatic
Electrical system: 24 V
Batteries: 4 × 12 V, 200 Ah

Status
R 390 in production. In service with French Army.

Manufacturer
Enquiries to Renault Véhicules Industriels, 40 rue Pasteur, BP 302, F-92156 Suresnes Cedex, France. Tel: (1) 40 99 71 11. Telex: 620567 sdce f. Fax: (1) 40 99 71 08.

Renault TRM 340.34 T (6 × 6) Tractor Truck

Description
The Renault TRM 340.34 T (6 × 6) tractor truck replaced the earlier TBH 280 (6 × 6) tractor truck in production and is a variant of the TRM 340.34 (6 × 6) 16 000 kg truck (see entry under *Trucks* for details).

The TRM 340.34 was designed for towing semi-trailers both on roads and across country up to a maximum weight of 65 000 kg. The chassis consists of U-shaped sidemembers with the crossmembers bolted into position. The layout of the vehicle is conventional with the engine at the front, cab in the centre and fifth wheel at the rear. The rear bogie has both inter-wheel and inter-axle differential locks.

Optional equipment includes a heating system and a sleeper cab with one bunk. The engine can have a pre-heating system, a heavy duty air filter and a vertical exhaust. A power take-off can be provided on the transfer case. The chassis can be provided with a 3.5-in/89 mm fifth wheel coupling with single or double oscillation. Electrical equipment can include an inter-ference suppressor and blackout lighting. Further options include twin 15-tonne hydraulic winches.

Specifications
Cab seating: 1 + 2
Configuration: 6 × 6
Weight:
(empty) 9905 kg
(loaded) 34 000 kg
(max GCW, on road) 100 000 kg
Weight on front axle:
(empty) 5049 kg
(loaded) 7500 kg
Weight on rear bogie:
(empty) 4856 kg
(loaded) 27 000 kg
Max weight on 5th wheel: 14 500 kg
Length: 7.78 m
Width: 2.49 m
Height:
(cab) 3.005 m
(5th wheel bracket) 1.365 m
Ground clearance: 0.312 m
Track:
(front) 1.91 m
(rear) 1.825 m
Wheelbase: 3.9 m + 1.35 m
Angle of approach: 28°
Max speed: 82 km/h
Range: 700 km
Fuel capacity: 250 l
Gradient: (towing fully laden semi-trailer) 18%

Side slope: 30%
Fording: 0.85 m
Engine: Renault MIDR 06-35-40 6-cylinder turbo-charged and inter-cooled diesel developing 336 hp at 1900 rpm
Gearbox: Type B9 with 8 synchronised forward and 1 reverse gears
Transfer box: Type VG 1200, 2-speed
Steering: Type 8046 hydraulic integral power
Turning radius: 10.8 m
Suspension:
(front) semi-elliptical springs with rubber bump stops and double-acting hydraulic shock absorbers
(rear) trunnion suspension using semi-elliptic leaf springs with axle torque rods
Tyres: 12.00 R 20
Brakes: pneumatic
Electrical system: 24 V
Batteries: 2 × 12 V, 143 Ah

Status
In production.

Manufacturer
Enquiries to Renault Véhicules Industriels, 40 rue Pasteur, BP 302, F-92156 Suresnes Cedex, France. Tel: (1) 40 99 71 11. Telex: 620567 sdce f. Fax: (1) 40 99 71 08.

LOHR DMC Tank Transporter System

Description
The LOHR DMC tank transporter system is described by the manufacturer as a combined tank transporter and recovery vehicle system. It consists of a hydraul-ically powered moving platform carried on the rear of a 6 × 6 open-framed truck chassis. The DMC system can off-load and recover the platform by the combined use of a hydraulic ram, and for recovery a heavy duty hydraulic winch (on the platform) is provided. The platform may be traversed to one side or the other for off-loading or recovery. The forward part of the platform has a raised guard frame to protect the carrier cab and this frame is also used as the carrier for the vehicle spare wheel. The LOHR DMC system has a payload of 16 000 to 18 000 kg. Locking devices at the front and back of the platform anchor the load when transported.

Status
In production.

LOHR DMC system being used to load AMX-10P APC onto IVECO FIAT 260 PM 35 (6 × 6) 10 000 kg truck

Manufacturer
LOHR SA, F-67980 Hangenbieten, France. Tel: 88 38 98 00. Telex: 870082 f. Fax: 88 96 06 36.

GERMANY

MAN (6 × 6) Tractor Trucks

Description
There are three MAN 6 × 6 tractor trucks which all use the same basic chassis, cab and equipment. They are the 32.365 DFAT with a maximum possible towed weight of 105 000 kg; the 40.440 DFAT with a maximum possible towed weight of 130 000 kg; and the 40.521 DFAT with a maximum possible towed weight of 150 000 kg. Differences are found mainly in engine capacity and power (see Specifications table).

All three models have forward control, all-steel cabs that can be tilted forward for engine access. The chassis frames have longitudinal members constructed from pressed U-sections with crossmembers both riveted and bolted in place. The front bumper is reinforced for winch operations. A sub-frame carries the fifth wheel.

All three models can be fitted with ZF gearboxes but the 32.365 may be fitted with optional Fuller RTO 11613, WSK 400, Allison or Renk automatic transmissions (the Specifications table provides the standard gearboxes). All gearboxes are provided with a power take-off.

The power take-off is used to power a 20 000 or 25 000 kg hydraulic winch. Both are equipped with 50 m of 24 mm diameter cable. A mechanical winch is also provided. This may be an Itag-Celle M 240 or M 180, the former with a 24 000 kg capacity and the latter with 18 000 kg capacity. Both have 60 m of 26 mm cable. Power for both is taken from the vehicle's main engine.

Optional extra equipment for all models includes a variable speed governor for the fuel injection pump, a tropical radiator (which raises the cab height by 80 mm), a manual engine throttle, a reinforced transmission, reinforced exhaust and tank brackets, a roof air induction inlet, an upswept exhaust stack, an alternative Jost fifth-wheel coupling, a raised axle bleed system, a spare wheel on the winch guard, a working platform behind the cab, a towing coupling, a battery charging socket and two 60 litre glass fibre water tanks.

Status
Production complete. In service with various countries.

Manufacturer
MAN Nutzfahrzeuge AG, Postfach 500620, D-8000 Munich 50, Federal Republic of Germany.

Tel: 89 1480-1. Telex: 523 211-23.
Fax: 89 150 3972.

Specifications

Model	32.365 DFAT	40.440 DFAT	40.521 DFAT
Cab seating	1 + 2	1 + 2	1 + 2
Configuration	6 × 6	6 × 6	6 × 6
Weight (loaded)	32 000 kg	40 000 kg	40 000 kg
Weight on front axle (loaded)	6700 kg	8500 kg	8500 kg
Weight on rear axle (loaded)	13 000 kg	16 000 kg	16 000 kg
Permissible towed load	80 000 kg	100 000 kg	102 000 kg
Max towed load	105 000 kg	130 000 kg	150 000 kg
Length	7.57 m	7.74 m	8.81 m
Width (cab)	2.5 m	2.5 m	2.5 m
(rear wheels)	2.466 m	2.49 m	2.5 m
Height (cab, loaded)	3.122 m	3.115 m	3.189 m
(5th wheel base plate)	1.15 m	1.338 m	—
Track (front)	1.904 m	2.008 m	1.903 m
(rear)	1.804 m	1.816 m	1.804 m
Wheelbase	3.85 m + 1.35 m	3.825 m + 1.4 m	4 m + 1.4 m
Max speed (road)	65 km/h	78 km/h	79 km/h
(cross-country)	43 km/h	52 km/h	—
Fuel capacity (total)	630 l	630 l	400 l
Max gradient (permissible load)	30%	20.2%	19.7%
Engine	MAN type D 2840 MF V-10 18.272 l diesel developing 365 hp (DIN) at 2500 rpm	MAN type D 2540 MTF V-10 15.953 l diesel developing 440 hp (DIN) at 2300 rpm	MAN type D 2840 LF V-10 18.272 l diesel developing 520 hp (DIN) at 2300 rpm
Gearbox	ZF Synchroma type, 4S-150, 8 forward and 1 reverse gears	ZF Synchroma type, 4S-150, 8 forward and 1 reverse gears	ZF Synchroma type, 16S-190A, 16 forward and 2 reverse gears
Transfer case	MAN type G 801 2-speed	MAN type G 801 2-speed	mounted on gearbox
Clutch	2-plate hydraulic	hydrodynamic torque converter	hydrodynamic torque converter
Steering	ZF hydro-steer type 8046	ZF hydro-steer type 8046	ZF hydro-steer type 8046
Suspension (front)	semi-elliptic leaf springs with hollow rubber springs and telescopic shock absorbers	semi-elliptic leaf springs with hollow rubber springs and telescopic shock absorbers	semi-elliptic leaf springs with hollow rubber springs and telescopic shock absorbers
(rear)	semi-elliptic leaf springs	semi-elliptic leaf springs	semi-elliptic leaf springs
Tyres	12.00 × 24	12.00 × 24	12.00 × 24
Brakes	air, 2-circuit	air, 2-circuit	air, 2-circuit
Electrical system	24 V	24 V	24 V
Batteries	2 × 12 V, 170 Ah	2 × 12 V, 170 Ah	2 × 12 V, 170 Ah

MAN 40.440 DFAT (6 × 6) tractor truck carrying Leopard 1 MBT

MAN 40.440 DFAT (6 × 6) tractor truck carrying Leopard 1 MBT

Mercedes-Benz 2636 AS (6 × 6) Tank Transporter

Description
The Mercedes-Benz 2636 AS (6 × 6) tank transporter is used to tow tank loads of up to 65 000 kg. It has a forward control cab complete with a frontal cab protector and has seating for the driver and two passengers with space for bunks at the rear. An air intake over the cab has a prefilter for use in dusty environments. The V-10 diesel engine powers a torque converter for a 16-speed transmission system and the axles use planetary-gear hub reduction. There are differential locks in the front and rear axles as well as in the transfer case. For maintenance the cab can be tilted forward, and a spare wheel is provided behind the cab complete with a handling device.

The 2636 AS is supplied with a mechanically controlled ITAG Type 241 winch capable of pulling up to 65 000 kg using 60 m of 26 mm diameter cable. As an option a Rotzler Type 2 × 20000 H double-acting hydraulic winch may be supplied.

Specifications
Cab seating: 1 + 2
Configuration: 6 × 6
Weight:
(kerb) approx 11 900 kg
(GCW) 105 000 kg
(5th wheel load) 24 000 kg
Length: (tractor unit) 7.075 m
Width: 2.5 m
Height: (unloaded) 3.195 m
Ground clearance: (rear axle) 0.427 m
Track:
(front) 1.987 m
(rear) 1.804 m
Wheelbase: 3.5 m + 1.45 m
Angle of approach/departure: 35°/47°
Max speed: 79 km/h
Fuel capacity: 400 l
Range: (approx) 1000 km
Gradient:
(GCW 80 000 kg) 38%
(GCW 105 000 kg) 20%
Engine: Mercedes-Benz OM 423 V-10 18.273 l water-cooled 4-stroke diesel developing 355 hp at 2300 rpm

Clutch: torque converter
Transmission: ZF 16 S S-130 16-speed fully synchronised
Transfer case: VG 2000-3W/1.4 2-speed
Steering: power-assisted
Turning circle: 20.3 m
Tyres: 14.00 × 20
Brakes: two-circuit two-line with compressed-air booster plus exhaust brake
Electrical system: 24 V
Batteries: 2 × 12 V, 110 Ah
Alternator: 28 V/55 A

Status

In production. In service with Pakistan (100).

Manufacturer

Daimler-Benz AG, PO Box 60 02 02, D-7000 Stuttgart 60, Federal Republic of Germany.
Tel: 711 17-0. Telex: 725 420.
Fax: 711 2244.

Mercedes-Benz 2636 AS (6 × 6) tank transporter

Mercedes-Benz 3850 AS (6 × 6) Tank Transporter

Description

The Mercedes-Benz 3850 AS (6 × 6) tank transporter may be regarded as a development of the Mercedes-Benz 2636 AS (6 × 6) tank transporter and uses the same engine and many other components. It has a longer wheelbase and can operate at gross combination weights of up to 110 000 kg.

The forward control cab has separate seating for a driver and two passengers plus a folding bench at the rear for a further four passengers. For access to the roof hatch the centre front seat has a forward-folding backrest on which to stand. The cab is mounted at the front on two pivot bearings with flexible rubber sleeves and at the rear on four vibration-damped spring struts. An air-conditioning unit or supplementary heater are optional. The entire cab can be tilted forward for access to the engine and transmission.

Mechanical or hydraulic single or dual-drum winches can be fitted. Both can be operated from the cab or by remote-control. Various types of semi-trailers may be towed but for low-loader trailers a ballast platform on the tractor is necessary.

An automatic transmission is optional as are single sand tyres and a tyre pressure regulation system.

Specifications

Cab seating: 1 + 6
Configuration: 6 × 6
Weight:
  (kerb, without winch) 13 150 kg
  (5th wheel load) 24 850 kg
  (GCW, with semi-trailer) 110 000 kg
  (GCW, with trailer) up to 220 000 kg
Front axle load: 8000 kg
Rear axle load: 2 × 16 000 kg
Length: 7.6 m
Width: 2.765 m
Height: (unloaded) 3.46 m
Ground clearance: (rear axle) 0.39 m
Track:
  (front) 2.07 m
  (rear) 1.965 m
Wheelbase: 3.8 m + 1.45 m

Mercedes-Benz 3850 AS (6 × 6) tank transporter

Angle of approach/departure: 33°/55°
Max speed: 90 km/h
Fuel capacity: 600 l
Range: (approx) 1000 km
Gradient: (GCW 110 000 kg) 32%
Engine: Mercedes-Benz OM 423 LA 18.273 l V-10 water-cooled diesel with inter-cooler developing 500 hp (DIN) at 2300 rpm
Transmission: ZF 16 S 160 A 8-speed fully synchronised or
Allison CLBT 754 automatic with integrated retarder
Clutch: ZF-WSK 400 torque converter
Transfer box: 2-speed
Steering: power-assisted
Turning circle: (tractor) 19.4 m

Tyres: 14.00 × 20 XL (24 × 21 optional)
Brakes: dual-circuit two-line with compressed air booster plus exhaust retarder
Electrical system: 24 V
Batteries: 2 × 12 V, 136 Ah
Alternator: 28 V/55 A

Status

In production.

Manufacturer

Daimler-Benz AG, PO Box 60 02 02, D-7000 Stuttgart 60, Federal Republic of Germany.
Tel: 711 17-0. Telex: 725 420.
Fax: 711 2244.

Mercedes-Benz 4850 A (8 × 8) Tank Transporter

Description

The Mercedes-Benz 4850 A (8 × 8) tank transporter may be regarded as an 8 × 8 version of the Mercedes-Benz 3850 AS (6 × 6) tank transporter. There are two models in the range. The 4050 A has twin 14.00 × 20 R tyres on the rear axles while the 4850 A may have either twin 14.00 × 20 R tyres on the rear axles or

single sand 24 × 21 R tyres on all axles. There are slight weight variations between all three models.

The Mercedes-Benz 4850 A shares many components with the smaller tank transport truck tractors in the Mercedes-Benz range, including the forward control cab which is tiltable for engine access. This has separate seating for the driver and two passengers with a folding bench seat for a further four passengers in the rear. Air-conditioning or extra cabin heaters may be provided and a roof hatch is fitted. The area behind the cab may be occupied by mechanical or hydraulic

drum winches as required and there is also provision for carrying a spare wheel – more spare wheels may be carried on the semi-trailer or trailer. The fifth wheel is located directly over the third tractor axle and may be used to tow a variety of semi-trailers. If low-loader trailers are towed a ballast platform is required.

The fuel tank capacity may be between 400 and 1000 litres, as needed, and another option is an Allison CLBT 754 automatic transmission with an integrated retarder. A tyre pressure regulation system is also optional.

Mercedes-Benz 4850 A (8 × 8) tank transporter fitted with single sand tyres on all axles

Specifications

(Data refer to Model 4850 A with dual rear tyres; data in square brackets refer to version with sand tyres where different)

Cab seating: 1 + 6
Configuration: 8 × 8
Weight:
(kerb) 17 200 [18 100] kg
(5th wheel load) 31 000 [22 000] kg
(GCW, with semi-trailer) 110 000 kg
(GCW, with trailer) up to 220 000 kg
Front axle loads: 2 × 8000 kg
Rear axle loads: 2 × 16 000 [2 × 12 000] kg
Length: 8.435 m
Width: 2.765 m
Height: 3.46 m
Ground clearance: (rear axle) 0.39 m

Track:
(front) 2.07 m
(rear) 1.965 m
Wheelbase: 1.6 m + 2.935 m + 1.48 m
Angle of approach/departure: 35°/60°
Max speed: 90 km/h
Fuel capacity: 400 to 1000 l
Range: variable according to fuel capacity
Gradient: (GCW 110 000 kg) 36%
Engine: Mercedes-Benz OM 423 LA 18.273 l V-10 water-cooled diesel with inter-cooler and two turbochargers developing 500 hp at 2300 rpm
Transmission: ZF 16 S – 190 8-speed fully synchromesh or
Allison CLBT 754 automatic with integrated retarder
Clutch: ZF-WSK 400 torque converter
Transfer box: VG 2000 – 3W, 2-speed

Steering: dual circuit power-assisted
Turning circle: (tractor) 22.5 [26.2] m
Tyres: 14.00 × 20 R [24 × 21 R]
Brakes: dual-circuit compressed air
Electrical system: 24 V
Batteries: 2 × 12 V, 135 Ah
Alternator: 28 V/55 A

Status

In production.

Manufacturer

Daimler-Benz AG, PO Box 60 02 02, D-7000 Stuttgart 60, Federal Republic of Germany.
Tel: 711 17-0. Telex: 725 420.
Fax: 711 2244.

IVECO Magirus 330-40 ANWTM (6 × 6) Tractor Truck

Description

This 6 × 6 tractor truck is based on the IVECO Magirus range of cross-country vehicles. The 330-40 ANWTM was formerly the Magirus 400M33AS. (The IVECO Magirus 330-32 ANWTM is no longer offered.)

The IVECO Magirus 330-40 ANWTM has a turbocharged diesel engine and the same type of cab as that used on the IVECO Magirus cross-country trucks. There is a double articulated fifth wheel located over the rear axles.

Two hydraulic 20 000 kg winches are fitted. Other options are a cab roof hatch, a blackout lighting system and a twin-compartment crew cab. The 330-40 ANWTM may be fitted with special tyres for use over sandy terrain – single 14.00 R 20 at the front and single 24-20.5 at the rear.

Specifications

Cab seating: 1 + 2
Configuration: 6 × 6
Weight:
(kerb) 14 200 kg
(on 5th wheel) 21 500 kg
(GVW) 35 700 kg
(GCW) up to 87 000 kg
Length: 7.86 m
Width:
(over cab) 2.5 m
(over rear wheels) 2.802 m
Height: (top of air intake) 2.965 m
Ground clearance: 0.372 m
Track:
(front) 2.002 m

IVECO Magirus 330-40 ANWTM (6 × 6) tractor truck

(rear) 2.802 m
Wheelbase: 4 m + 1.45 m
Angle of approach/departure: 30°/54°
Max speed: 84 km/h
Range: 800 km

Fuel capacity: (standard) 400 + 300 l
Max gradient: 63%
Side slope: 20%
Fording: 0.8 m
Engine: Deutz Diesel BF 10 L 513 15.953 l 10-cylinder

air-cooled diesel developing 415 hp at 2300 rpm
Gearbox: ZF 4 S-150 GP manual, 8 forward and 1 reverse gears
Transfer box: 2-speed
Clutch: WSK 400 torque converter
Steering: ball and nut, assisted
Turning radius: 11.8 m
Suspension:
(front) semi-elliptic leaf springs, hydraulic shock absorbers

(rear) cantilever leaf springs
Tyres: 14.00 R 20, twin at rear
Brakes:
(main) drum, air on all wheels plus exhaust retarder
(parking) mechanical on rear wheels
Electrical system: 24 V

Status
In production. In widespread service.

Manufacturer
IVECO Magirus AG, Defence Vehicle Division, Postfach 2740, D-7900 Ulm, Federal Republic of Germany. Tel: 49 731 1041. Telex: 712 522 im d. Fax: 49 731 672 18.

Faun FS 42.75/42 (8 × 6) Tractor Truck

Description
The Faun FS 42.75/42 (8 × 6) tractor truck was produced as a replacement for the Faun SLT 50-2 with the then West German Army.

The FS 42.75/42 follows the same overall layout as the SLT 50-2 and has a Faun forward control cab constructed from steel and synthetic materials. Apart from the adjustable driver's seat there is seating for three passengers. There is a roof hatch with provision for a machine gun mounting and internally there is a stowage compartment. All walls are double-skinned and laminated glass is used for all windows. The windscreen is angled forward at an angle of 5°. An engine-driven heater is used to heat the cab interior and a Wabasco heater, independent of the engine, can be used for heating and ventilation when the engine is off.

The chassis use a die-pressed construction with U-shaped members. Lateral and longitudinal supports are bolted or riveted.

The area behind the cab is mainly occupied by a dual 18 600 kg capacity winch assembly provided with a 28 mm diameter cable. The winch speed is adjustable from zero to 24 m/min for loads up to 8500 kg and up to 9 m/min for heavier loads. The fifth wheel is a Jost JSK 38 GL.

The two front axles are used for steering but only the front axle is driven. The rear-driven Starr-planetary axles have a longitudinal differential lock between them and a transverse differential lock can be engaged.

An 8 × 8 version with 24 R 20.5 tyres is available.

Specifications
Cab seating: 1 + 3
Configuration: 8 × 6
Weight:
(empty) 19 700 kg
(loaded) 36 000 or 39 700 kg
(load on 5th wheel) 16 300 or 20 000 kg
(gross train weight) 95 000 kg

Faun FS 42.75/42 (8 × 6) tractor truck towing trailer carrying Leopard 2 MBT

Length: 8.835 m
Width: 3.07 m
Height: 3.02 m
Track:
(front) 2.585 m
(rear) 2.612 m
Wheelbase: 1.5 m + 2.7 m + 1.5 m
Angle of approach/departure: 30°/45°
Max speed: 72 km/h
Fuel capacity: 800 l
Gradient: 50%
Engine: KHD BF 12 L 513 C 19.144 l 12-cylinder air-cooled diesel developing 525 hp at 2300 rpm
Gearbox: ZF Transmatic with torque converter drive clutch ZF WSK 400 and Ecosplit-gearbox 16 S 190 A with 16 forward and 2 reverse gears
Steering: ZF semi-block hydraulic, dual circuit
Turning radius: 11.2 m
Suspension: (front and rear) semi-elliptical leaf springs

and telescopic shock absorbers
Tyres: 18.00 × 22.5 XS PR 20
Brakes:
(main) dual circuit air
(parking) pneumatically operated exhaust valve
Electrical system: 24 V
Batteries: 4 × 12 V
Alternator: 95 A

Status
In production for the German Army.

Manufacturer
Faun GmbH, Postfach 10 01 08, D-8560 Lauf a.d. Pegnitz, Federal Republic of Germany. Tel: 091 23 185-0. Telex: 622990. Fax: 091 23 3085.

Faun SLT 50-2 (8 × 8) Tractor Truck

Development
The development of the SLT 50-2, or Elefant as it is more commonly known, can be traced back to 1965 when West Germany and the USA decided to design a tank transporter known as the Heavy Equipment Transporter (HET) to carry the MBT-70 then under development by both countries. In the USA the Chrysler Corporation was the prime contractor for the tractor while in Germany Faun was responsible for the tractor and Krupp for the trailer. In 1970 the MBT-70 and the HET were cancelled. Further development in the USA resulted in the XM746, which was standardised as the M746 and production was undertaken by Ward La France. Development continued in Germany and the Federal German Army placed an order with Faun for 328 Elefants, the last of which were delivered in 1980. The SLT 50-2 and its semi-trailer can carry any of the AFVs in service with the Federal German Army including the Leopard 2 MBT.

A more powerful model, known as the SLT 50-3, was available powered by a 750 hp engine coupled to a Renk automatic transmission with seven forward gears and one reverse.

Faun SLT 50-2 (8 × 8) Elefant tractor truck towing semi-trailer carrying M48 series MBT

Description
The SLT 50-2 is an 8 × 8 vehicle with powered steering on the front two axles. The fully enclosed cab is of steel and glass fibre construction and has seats

for the driver and three passengers.

The drive train consists of a V-8 diesel engine coupled to a hot-shift transmission and a two-speed transfer case. The front and rear bogies are fitted with a lockable inter-axle differential and each axle has a lockable differential. The front and rear bogies are suspended by torque rods and taper leaf springs arranged in parallel with progressive springing.

Air brakes are provided for both the tractor and semi-trailer and an automatic load-sensitive brake valve ensures equal braking under all load conditions. The parking brake consists of spring-loaded cylinders mounted to the rear wheel brakes. A retarder is connected directly to the gearbox and is also connected via an electric control line to the service brakes of the semi-trailer.

Mounted to the rear of the cab is a dual winch unit, each winch with a capacity of 17 000 kg. Both winches have a winch up mechanism and the right winch can also be used to the front of the vehicle for self-recovery operations. Each winch is provided with 43 m of 28 mm diameter rope; maximum winding speed is 24 m/min at a capacity of 8500 kg or 12 m/min at a capacity of 17 000 kg.

The spare wheel is mounted on the right side of the tractor and a small winch is provided to facilitate handling of the wheel.

Specifications
Cab seating: 1 + 3
Configuration: 8 × 8
Weight:
(empty) 23 030 kg
(on 5th wheel loaded) 18 300 kg
(gross combination weight) 92 000 kg
Length: 8.83 m
(with trailer) 18.82 m
Width: 3.05 m
Height: 2.83 m
(to 5th wheel) 1.55 m
Ground clearance: 0.303 m
Track:
(front) 2.535 m
(rear) 2.593 m
Wheelbase: 1.5 m + 2.7 m + 1.5 m
Angle of approach/departure: 30°/50°
Max speed:
(road, without semi-trailer) 63.5 km/h
(road, with loaded semi-trailer) 40 km/h
(15% gradient with loaded semi-trailer) 9 km/h
Range: 500 km
Fuel capacity: 800 l

Max gradient: (87 500 kg gross combination weight) 30%
Fording: 0.8 m
Engine: MTU MB 837 Ea-500 V-8 diesel developing 730 hp at 2100 rpm
Gearbox: ZF 4 PW 200H2 with 4 forward and 2 reverse gears
Torque converter: ZF 500-10
Transfer box: 2-speed
Steering: ZF semi-block hydraulic
Turning radius: (without trailer) 11.2 m
Tyres: 18.00 × 22.5
Brakes: air
Electrical system: 24 V

Status
Production complete. In service with the German Army.

Manufacturer
Faun GmbH, Postfach 10 01 08, D-8560 Lauf a.d. Pegnitz, Federal Republic of Germany.
Tel: 091 23 185-0. Telex: 622990.
Fax: 091 23 3085.

Faun HZ 40.45/45 (6 × 6) Tractor Truck

Description
The Faun HZ 40.45/45 (6 × 6) tractor truck is a militarised version of a commercial tractor truck in the Faun range adapted for the tank transporter role. The Faun Model Number is 2144.93 Version B.

The vehicle has a conventional layout with the engine forward under a steel frame and reinforced glass fibre panel bonnet, the crew cab placed just to the rear of the front axle and the fifth wheel placed over the two rear axles. The steel cab has three doors, one on the left and two on the right, providing access to two rows of seating for the driver and six passengers. The front row has seating for the driver and two passengers, all on single seats. The rear seating consists of a single padded bench with the central portion tiltable to allow access to a centrally positioned 800 mm diameter roof hatch.

The chassis frame consists of pressed segments with a U-profile design and with crossmembers bolted or riveted to the longitudinal girders. Towing eyes are provided at the front and a NATO trailer coupling with a towing capacity of up to 55 tonnes is located at the rear.

Optional equipment available for the vehicle includes a hydraulic twin-winch providing 2 × 18 tonnes drawbar pull on the first layer. The winches operate to the front or rear and each drum is provided with 55 m of 24 mm diameter cable. Transverse differential locks are available on both rear axles. Also available are a set of six snow chains, up to four spare fuel cans, a combined oil bath air filter, two 6 kg fire extinguishers, a compressed air hose connection for slave filling of the brake system, a slave starting device with 6 m of cable and sliding rails to facilitate connecting a trailer to the fifth wheel.

Specifications
Cab seating: 1 + 6
Configuration: 6 × 6

Faun HZ 40.45/45 (6 × 6) tractor truck

Weight:
(empty) 19 000 kg
(loaded) 45 000 kg
Max fifth wheel load: 26 000 kg
Length: 9 m
Width: 2.75 m
Height: 3.4 m
Wheelbase: 5.4 m
Max speed: 63.6 km/h
Fuel capacity: 2 × 450 l
Max gradient: 44.6%
Engine: Deutz Type BF 12 L 513 C 19.144 l V-12 direct injection air-cooled diesel developing 525 hp at 2300 rpm
Gearbox: Allison Type CL T 754 with 5 forward and 1 reverse gears
Torque converter: Allison Type TC 496
Transfer box: 2-speed
Steering: ZF semi-block steering with working cylinder, primary pump and secondary pump
Turning radius: approx 12.5 m

Suspension:
(front) semi-elliptic leaf springs, longitudinal guide struts for thrust transmission, telescopic shock absorbers
(rear) semi-elliptic leaf springs in floating arrangement, longitudinal guide struts for thrust transmission
Tyres: 14.00 × 24
Brakes:
(main) dual circuit air plus exhaust brake
(parking) operating on rear axles
Electrical system: 24 V
Batteries: 2 × 12 V, 170 Ah

Status
In service with Turkey (40).

Manufacturer
Faun GmbH, Postfach 10 01 08, D-8560 Lauf a.d. Pegnitz, Federal Republic of Germany.
Tel: 091 23 185-0. Telex: 622990.
Fax: 091 23 3085.

TITAN Z 50.816 H 6 × 6/51 (6 × 6) Tank Transporter

Description
The TITAN Z 50.816 H 6 × 6/51 (6 × 6) tank transporter is a military version of a heavy duty civilian tractor designed to carry tanks weighing up to 50 000 kg. It can operate at a gross combination weight of up to 300 000 kg.

The tractor cab has seating for a driver, a co-driver and a further five passengers. The cab is fully insulated

against heat, dust and noise and there is a roof hatch. The tractor uses a heavy duty ladder-type frame with crossmembers, that has been designed to operate on and off roads with very high fifth-wheel loads. A tropical capacity cooling system is fitted with two water radiators. The 3.5-in/89 mm fifth wheel is fully oscillating for cross-country use and there is also a NATO towing hook for loads up to 20 000 kg.

The tractor is provided with two Rotzler 25 000 kg hydraulic double barrel winches each with 55 m of 26 mm diameter rope. One winch is mounted behind the cab for trailer loading with the other at the front for

self-recovery. Spotlights are provided for night operations.

Auxiliary equipment includes a rack for four 20 litre jerricans, a rack for six rifles, two 10 kg fire extinguishers, two lockable tool boxes, a set of entrenching tools, an emergency repair tool-set including a 30 000 kg hydraulic jack, and a tyre inflation hose. An air-conditioning unit may be mounted on the cab roof.

Various types of semi-trailer or trailer may be used with this tractor.

TITAN Z 50.816 H 6 × 6/51 (6 × 6) tank transporter towing special cargo semi-trailer

Fifth wheel load: approx 30 000 kg
Length: approx 10.1 m
Width: approx 3 m
Height: approx 4.05 m
Wheelbase: 5.1 m + 1.6 m
Max speed: approx 75 km/h
Fuel capacity: 1200 l (2 × 600 l)
Range: approx 1400 km
Gradient: (with 180 000 kg GCW) 16%
Fording: 1.2 m
Engine: MWM type TBD 234 21.6 l V-12 water-cooled turbocharged and after-cooled diesel developing 816 hp (DIN) at 2300 rpm
Gearbox: Renk type HS 227 hydraulic power-shift with 7 forward and 1 reverse gears
Transfer box: 2-speed
Steering: ZF, power
Turning radius: (outer) 21.5 m
Tyres: 14.00-24 × 18 XS
Brakes:
    (main) 2-line dual circuit air on all wheels plus exhaust retarder
    (parking) spring-loaded
Electrical system: 24 V
Batteries: 2 × 12 V, 135 Ah
Alternator: 95 A

Variant

TITAN PB 65.520 10 × 10
TITAN has proposed that this 10 × 10 tractor unit could carry a payload of up to 65 000 kg. It is powered by a 530 hp (DIN) engine and can be fitted with an Ampliroll tank carrier and loading system. Overall length is 13 m.

Specifications

Cab seating: 1 + 6
Configuration: 6 × 6
Weight:
    (kerb) approx 20 000 kg
    (GVW) 50 000 kg
    (GCW) 300 000 kg
Front axle load: 14 000 kg
Rear axle loads: 2 × 18 000 kg

Status

In production.

Manufacturer

TITAN Spezialfahrzeuge GmbH, Industriestrasse 5, D-7604 Appenweier, Federal Republic of Germany. Tel: 49 7805 40 40. Telex: 752897. Fax: 49 7805 404 39.

INDIA

Bharat Earth Movers (8 × 8) Tractor Truck

Description

Bharat Earth Movers, a public sector company controlled by the Indian Ministry of Defence, has designed a tractor truck intended for the tank transporter role.

The 8 × 8 vehicle is powered by a 450 hp engine and has a 20-tonne payload and haulage capacity of 80 tonnes. A 27-tonne direct pull recovery winch is provided.

A version with a 60-tonne haulage capacity is envisaged for export sales and the vehicle has been evaluated by the Indian Army.

No further details are available.

Status

Prototypes.

Manufacturer

Bharat Earth Movers Limited, Sheriff Bhatia Towers, 88 M.G. Road, Bangalore-560 001, India.

ITALY

IVECO FIAT 320-45 WTM (6 × 6) Tractor Truck

Description

The IVECO FIAT 320-45 WTM (6 × 6) tractor truck was designed to meet an Italian Army requirement for a vehicle capable of towing a semi-trailer carrying a Leopard 1 MBT both on and off the road as well as having the capability to recover damaged and disabled vehicles. The first prototype was completed in 1978 and the vehicle is in service with the Italian Army as the ATC/81.

The IVECO FIAT 320-45 WTM (6 × 6) tractor tows an OTO Melara-designed, Bartoletti-manufactured trailer, designated the Mod TCS 50 BO. The forward control four-man cab can be tilted forward to give access to the engine for maintenance. Two types of cab are available, one with a fully enclosed hard-top and the other with a windscreen that can be folded forward through 180°, removable door tops and side screens and a canvas roof that folds to the rear.

To the rear of the cab are two winches, each rated at 20 000 kg and with 50 m of cable. The standard 89 mm diameter king-pin is positioned over the two rear axles. The vehicle can be delivered with either single or dual rear wheels.

A variant was designed to operate over sandy terrain. It has a revised wheelbase (3.565 m + 1.45 m) and uses single tyres on all axles (14.00 × 24 at the front and 24 × 20.5 at the rear). Kerb weight is 14 700 kg.

IVECO FIAT 320-45 WTM (6 × 6) tractor truck towing semi-trailer carrying M60A1 MBT

Specifications
Cab seating: 1 + 3
Configuration: 6 × 6
Weight:
  (kerb) 15 420 kg
  (max load on 5th wheel) 20 000 kg
  (gross combination weight) 93 420 kg
Length: 7.52 m
Width: 2.775 m
Height:
  (overall) 3.051 m
  (5th wheel) 1.647 m
Ground clearance: 0.36 m
Track:
  (front) 1.985 m
  (rear) 1.97 m
Wheelbase: 3.6 m + 1.38 m

Angle of approach/departure: 41°/60°
Max speed: 65 km/h
Range: over 600 km
Fuel capacity: 500 l
Gradient: over 30% with semi-trailer
Side slope: 20%
Fording: 0.85 m
Engine: FIAT 8280.22 17.174 l V-8 water-cooled turbocharged diesel developing 450 hp (DIN) at 2400 rpm
Transmission: 8 forward and 1 reverse gears, torque converter, transfer box with lockable torque divider, lockable differential at rear axles
Steering: powered
Turning radius: 9.5 m
Suspension: leaf springs
Tyres: 14.00 × 20

Brakes:
  (main) drum, air operated
  (parking) acting on rear axles
  (exhaust) pneumatic
Electrical system: 24 V
Number of batteries: 2 × 12 V, 143 Ah
Generator: 650 W

Status
In production. In service with the Italian Army and several overseas countries.

Manufacturer
IVECO FIAT SpA, Defence Vehicle Division, Via Volta 6, I-39100 Bolzano, Italy
Tel: 0471 905111. Telex: 400541 ivedvd i.
Fax: 0471 905444.

JAPAN

Mitsubishi Model FW455LRS2 (6 × 6) Truck Tractor

Description
The Mitsubishi Model FW455LRS2 (6 × 6) truck tractor is known to the Japanese Ground Self-Defence Force as the Type 84 truck tractor. It is designed to tow a three-axle semi-trailer carrying a tank with a maximum weight of 40 000 kg.

The Model FW455LRS2 uses a forward control cab of all-steel welded construction with seating for the driver and two passengers. The cab doors have extra vision panels and a ladder is provided for access to stowage space on the cab roof. A flat area behind the cab may be used for more stowage and carries the spare wheel and the fuel tank. The fifth wheel is located directly over the dual rear axles.

Specifications
Cab seating: 1 + 2
Configuration: 6 × 6
Weight:
  (empty) 9500 kg
  (loaded) 26 240 kg
  (on 5th wheel) 16 500 kg
Length: 7.16 m
Width: 2.49 m
Height:
  (cab) 3.51 m
  (5th wheel) 1.47 m
Track:
  (front) 2.005 m

Mitsubishi Model FW455LRS2 (6 × 6) truck tractor

  (rear) 1.845 m
Wheelbase: 3.73 m + 1.3 m
Max speed: 59 km/h
Engine: Mitsubishi 8DC9T2 turbocharged (with intercooler) diesel developing 430 hp at 2200 rpm
Turning radius: 9.6 m
Tyres: 10.00 × 20

Status
In production. In service with Japanese Ground Self-Defence Force.

Manufacturer
Mitsubishi Motors Corporation, 33-8, Shiba 5-chome, Minato-ku, Tokyo, Japan.

Mitsubishi Model NW204JR (6 × 6) Truck Tractor

Description
The Mitsubishi Model NW204JR (6 × 6) truck tractor was designed to tow a three-axle semi-trailer carrying an MBT with a maximum weight of 40 000 kg. The vehicle is designated the Type 73 truck tractor by the Japanese Self-Defence Force. The layout of the vehicle is conventional, with the engine at the front, two-door fully enclosed cab in the centre and the fifth wheel at the rear.

Specifications
Cab seating: 1 + 2
Configuration: 6 × 6
Weight:
  (empty) 9500 kg
  (loaded) 26 240 kg
  (on 5th wheel) 16 500 kg
Length:
  (tractor) 6.835 m
  (tractor and trailer) 16.255 m
Width: 3.29 m

Mitsubishi Model NW204JR (6 × 6) truck tractor towing semi-trailer carrying Type 61 MBT

Height:
  (cab) 2.92 m
  (5th wheel) 1.47 m
Track:
  (front) 1.915 m
  (rear) 1.865 m
Wheelbase: 4.65 m
Max speed: 60 km/h
Engine: Model DED 10-cylinder diesel developing 375 hp at 2500 rpm
Turning radius: 8.9 m

Tyres: 10.00 × 20

Status
Production complete. In service with the Japanese Ground Self-Defence Force.

Manufacturer
Mitsubishi Heavy Industries, 5-1, Marunouchi 2-chome, Chiyoda-ku, Tokyo, Japan.
Tel: 81 3 212 3111. Telex: 22282.
Fax: 81 3 201 6258.

SERBIA

FAP 3232 BDST/AV (8 × 8) Tractor Truck

Description
First shown in 1985, the FAP 3232 BDST/AV (8 × 8) tractor truck is a variant of the FAP 2832 (8 × 8) 9000 kg truck (see entry in *Trucks* section for details). The main change is that in place of the usual truck cargo body there is a fifth wheel coupling for towing semi-trailers weighing up to 65 000 kg and with a payload of 50 000 kg. There are two winches located on the platform behind the cab, one for forward use. In all other respects the FAP 3232 BDST/AV and FAP 2832 truck are identical.

Specifications
Cab seating: 1 + 1
Configuration: 8 × 8
Weight:
  (unloaded) 16 000 kg
  (loaded, on road) 34 000 kg
  (load on 5th wheel) 18 000 kg
Towed load: 65 000 kg
Length: 8.612 m
Width:
  (over tractor unit) 2.5 m
  (over towed load) 3.5 m
Height:
  (cab) 3.335 m
  (5th wheel) 1.9 m
Ground clearance: 0.38 m
Track: 2.02 m
Wheelbase: 1.5 m + 3.2 m + 1.4 m
Angle of approach: 41°
Max speed: 60 km/h
Range: over 600 km
Max gradient: (tractor unit) 32%
Fording: 1.2 m
Engine: OM 403 15.95 l V-10 diesel developing 320 hp
Gearbox: synchronised with auxiliary drive, 8 forward and 1 reverse gears
Clutch: single dry plate
Transfer box: 2-speed
Steering: hydraulic, ball joint
Turning radius: 13 m
Tyres: 15.00 × 21 T-101
Brakes:
  (main) dual circuit air plus exhaust brake
  (parking) mechanical
Electrical system: 24 V
Batteries: 2 × 12 V, 210 Ah
Alternator: 85 A

Status
In service with the former Yugoslav armed forces.

Manufacturer
Sour FAP FAMOS 11 Oktomvri Taz, YU-11000 Beograd, Serbia.
Enquires to Federal Directorate of Supply and Procurement (SDPR), YU-11005 Beograd, 9 Nemanjina Street, Serbia.
Tel: 621522. Telex: 71000/72566 SDPR YU.
Fax: 38 11 631588/630621.

FAP 3232 BDST/AV (8 × 8) tractor trucks towing semi-trailers carrying T-72 MBTs

SPAIN

Kynos Aljiba (8 × 8) Truck Tractor

Description
The Kynos Aljiba (8 × 8) truck tractor was originally developed as a private venture by Kynos SA commencing in 1982 – Kynos SA is a subsidiary of the Agroman Group and normally specialises in construction equipment. The Spanish Ministry of Defence provided some funding and one prototype and three pre-series vehicles were produced. The Spanish Army carried out field trials with one vehicle in May 1985, near Toledo. The first two production vehicles were delivered to the Spanish Marines during mid-1987.

The Aljiba (Quiver) was designed to tow and retrieve MBTs up to a weight of 60 000 kg and is built on a flexible rectangular chassis that is resistant to the stresses imparted when travelling over uneven terrain. The chassis is reinforced by longitudinal members with special crossmembers attached. A swing-arm suspension with leaf springs and trailing arms is employed. The forward control cab is formed from a steel frame mounted on elastic shock absorbers and has seating for the driver, a crewman and three passengers.

The Aljiba is powered by a Deutz 19 litre V-12 turbocharged diesel and uses a ZF semi-automatic gearbox with torque converter. All four axles are driven with the front two being steered, with power-assistance. Each wheel hub has a planetary reduction gear and each pair of axles can be pneumatically locked. The dual circuit pneumatic brakes act on all wheels and the brake circuits are also used to provide air for the de-icing, protection and alarm systems. An air take-off is provided each side of the vehicle for tyre inflation. The special 24-20.5XS-PR16 tyres may be fitted with chains for extra traction and the spare wheel is provided with handling gear.

For recovery the Aljiba is equipped with two 25 000 kg winches with 26 mm cable that normally operate to the rear, but the left-hand winch cable may be routed forward using a pulley fixed to the chassis. Operating speed is 8 m/min.

Kynos Aljiba (8 × 8) tank transporter towing semi-trailer carrying M107 175 mm self-propelled gun

It has been proposed that the Aljiba may also be used to carry out a number of other roles including that of artilllery tractor, logistics carrier, bridging equipment carrier, shelter/containers for command and communications or hospitals and other such roles. It has also been suggested that the vehicle could be used as a missile system carrier. The semi-trailer demonstrated to date has two axles but it is possible that three- or four-axle semi-trailers or trailers could be developed.

Specifications
Cab seating: 1 + 4
Configuration: 8 × 8
Weight:
(empty) 21 100 kg
(max load on chassis) 46 100 kg
Weight on front axles: 13 670 kg
Weight on rear axles: 25 680 kg
(GCW) 96 000 kg
Length:
(tractor) 9.875 m
(tractor and trailer) 22.269 m
Width:
(tractor) 3.3 m
(tractor and trailer) 4.025 m
Height: (overall) 3.278 m
Track: 2.6 m
Wheelbase: 1.524 m + 3.476 m + 1.524 m
Angle of approach/departure: 30°/75°
Max speed: 65 km/h
Fuel capacity: 1000 l (500 + 500 l)
Range:
(road) 1000 km
(off road) 700 km
Gradient:
(tractor unit) 68%
(loaded) 31%
Engine: Deutz BF 12 L 513 FC 19.144 l V-12 turbocharged diesel developing 525 hp at 2300 rpm
Gearbox: ZF 16S-190A with ZF WSK 400 torque converter, 14 forward and 2 reverse gears
Clutch: ZF Transmatic

Transfer box: ZF, single-speed
Steering: power-assisted on front two axles
Turning radius: 13.407 m
Suspension: swing arm with leaf springs and trailing arms; roll bars on front axle
Tyres: 24-20.5XS-PR16
Brakes: dual circuit air on all wheels
Electrical system: 24 V
Batteries: 2 × 12 V, 120 Ah

Status
In production for Spanish Marines.

Manufacturer
Kynos SA, Division de Vehiculos Militares, Carretera San Martin de la Vega 25, E-28041 Madrid, Spain. Tel: 792 4361. Telex: 48826 kynos e.

Pegaso 7345 (6 × 6) Tractor Truck

Description
The Pegaso 7345 (6 × 6) tractor truck was designed to meet a requirement from the Spanish Army for a tank transporter. In 1987 the prototype was approved by the Spanish Army and production and deliveries began in 1988.

The Pegaso 7345 has a forward control cab with seating for the driver and five passengers. The cab can be tilted forward for engine maintenance access. Power is provided by a Pegaso diesel engine developing 450 hp via a synchronised gearbox for a gross combination weight of 90 000 kg. Two winches behind the cab each have a capacity of 20 000 kg.

As well as being produced as a tank transporter the Pegaso 7345 can be produced as a cargo carrier, an artillery tractor, a multiple rocket launcher, and as a bridge transporter.

Specifications
Cab seating: 1 + 5
Configuration: 6 × 6
Weight:
(empty) 15 000 kg
(semi-trailer) 15 000 kg
(GCW) 90 000 kg
(towed load) 75 000 kg
Length: 7.5 m
Width: 2.48 m
Height: 3.4 m
Track: 2.062 m
Wheelbase: 3.815 m + 1.41 m
Max speed: 83 km/h
Range: 900 km
Fuel capacity: 560 l
Max gradient: 30%
Side slope: 30%
Engine: Pegaso 12.8 l turbo inter-cooling diesel with ZF torque converter developing 450 hp at 2200 rpm
Gearbox: ZF synchronised with 16 forward and 2 reverse gears, easy shift

Transfer box: ZF single-speed with torque distributor
Steering: servo-hydraulic
Turning radius: 10.5 m
Suspension:
(front) semi-elliptical leaf springs and shock absorbers
(rear) semi-elliptical leaf springs and Hendrikson type arms
Tyres: 12.00 × 24
Brakes: dual circuit air
Electrical system: 24 V
Batteries: 2 × 12 V, 165 Ah

Status
In production for the Spanish Army.

Manufacturer
Pegaso, Empresa Nacional de Autocamiones SA, Defence Division, Avenida de Aragón 402, E-28022 Madrid, Spain.
Tel: 750 1000. Telex: 46972 maba e.
Fax: 747 1307.

Pegaso 7345 (6 × 6) tractor truck

Pegaso 7345 (6 × 6) tractor truck

SWEDEN

Volvo N12 (6 × 4) Tractor Truck

Description

The Volvo N12 (6 × 4) tractor truck was developed from a commercial vehicle to meet a Swedish Army requirement for a vehicle capable of carrying a Centurion or S-tank and having a large enough cab to accommodate the tank crew of three or four in addition to the crew of the truck.

The protorype was delivered to the Swedish Army in October 1975 for field trials and first production tractor trucks were delivered in April 1977. With the Swedish Army the N12 tows the DAF YTS 10050 semi-trailer although it can also tow other semi-trailers such as the Swedish HAFO H50-3-RLS or the H50-4-RLS, both of which have a maximum payload of 50 000 kg.

The layout of the N12 is conventional with the engine at the front, a fully enclosed four-door all-steel cab in the centre and the fifth wheel at the rear. The vehicle is not fitted with a winch and so cannot recover disabled and damaged vehicles.

The chassis sides are of rolled U-profile and reinforced. The rear axle is a tandem bogie, single reduction with hub reduction, differential lock for wheels and shafts are pneumatically controlled from the cab. The fifth wheel is a Jost JSK 25 pivoting type.

Specifications

Configuration: 6 × 4
Max weight on front axle: 6500 kg
Max weight on rear axle: 26 000 kg
Length: 7.56 m

Volvo N12 (6 × 4) tractor truck towing DAF YTS 10050 semi-trailer carrying Centurion MBT

Width: 2.5 m
Height: (overall) 3.1 m
Track:
  (front) 1.945 m
  (rear) 1.82 m
Wheelbase: 4.2 m + 1.37 m
Fuel capacity: 300 l
Engine: 120 E 6-cylinder turbocharged OHV diesel developing 326 hp at 2200 rpm
Gearbox: manual 8-speed range, supplemented with splinter section which provides 16 forward speeds
Clutch: twin dry plate
Steering: recirculating ball and nut with built-in servo
Tyres: 12.00 × 20
Brakes:
  (main) air, dual circuit
  (parking) air-operated spring brakes operating

directly on front and rear wheels
Suspension:
  (front) semi-elliptical leaf springs with threaded spring bolt in front mounting and slipper-type anchorage at rear. Shock absorbers and hollow rubber springs
  (rear) multi-leaf springs with rubber springs at both ends

Status

In production. In service with the Swedish Army.

Manufacturer

Volvo Truck Corporation, S-405 08 Göteborg, Sweden.
Tel: 46 31 66 60 00. Telex: 27000 volvo s.
Fax: 46 31 51 04 65.

Scania R143 and T143 (6 × 6) and (6 × 4) Tractor Trucks

Description

There are two Scania heavy tractor trucks, the Scania R143EK with a forward control cab and the Scania T143E with a bonnet. Both are designed for towing tank transporter semi-trailers and are similar in weight, capability and overall dimensions but differ in detail according to cab type and the engine fitted.

Both vehicles carry the driver and five passengers and there is provision for carrying the occupants' personal equipment. The forward control model has a four-door cab while the bonneted T model can be equipped with a shorter two-door cab or the four-door version.

Two Sepson MAS 30/30 recovery winches are fitted, each with a capacity of 20 000 kg and equipped with 40 m of 24 mm cable. Other equipment includes two snatch blocks, an electric engine heater, a 12-pin trailer connector, a 24 V emergency connection, a fuel heater, a battery master switch, reversing lights, 24 V sockets front and rear, a 20-tonne hydraulic jack, two

working lights and a rotating beacon.

The first of 19 Scania T143E tractors for the Swedish Army was handed over in March 1990; production of the rest of the batch continued until 1991. The T143Es are used with a four-axle semi-trailer with force-steered rear axles produced by HAFO of Göteborg.

It should be noted that while the gross train weight of the T143E is around 91 tonnes, the maximum peacetime gross train weight on Swedish roads is limited to 86 tonnes.

Specifications (Scania R143EK)

Cab seating: 1 + 5
Configuration: 6 × 6
Weight:
  (kerb) 14 800 kg
  (GVW) 31 200 kg
  (GTW) 100 000 kg
Length: 7.725 m
Width: 2.49 m
Height: 3.44 m
Ground clearance:
  (front) 0.315 m
  (bogie) 0.277 m

Track:
  (front) 2.086 m
  (rear) 1.83 m
Wheelbase: 3.93 m + 1.45 m
Fuel capacity: 400 l
Engine: DSC14 03 diesel developing 450 hp at 1900 rpm
Gearbox: GRH880 10-speed with torque converter
Turning radius: 9.8 m
Tyres: 12.00 × 20 (options 12.00 × 24 or 315/80 × 22.5)
Brakes: dual circuit air
Electrical system: 24 V
Batteries: 2 × 12 V, 160 Ah
Alternator: 55 A

Status

Both models in production. T143E in service with the Swedish Army (19).

Manufacturer

SAAB-Scania AB, Scania Division, S-151 87 Södertälje, Sweden.
Tel: 46 755 81000. Telex: 10200.

Scania T143E (6 × 4) tractor truck carrying Centurion MBT

Scania R143EK (6 × 6) tractor truck carrying Leopard ARV

UNITED KINGDOM

Bedford TT120-40 (6 × 6) Tank Transporter Tractor

Description

In July 1988 Bedford showed for the first time the prototype of its TT120-40 (6 × 6) tank transporter tractor intended for a gross combination weight of 120 tonnes, enabling the 12.5-tonne tractor unit to pull a trailer and payload of 107.5 tonnes. The vehicle was intended to be a prototype for a new range of tank transporters that will be available in 4 × 2, 6 × 4 and 6 × 6 versions with an 8 × 6 variant using the Multi-drive system.

The Bedford TT120-40 (6 × 6) tank transporter is powered by a 400 hp Cummins NTE 400 turbocharged diesel housed under a relatively long squared-off bonnet; the bonnet is hinged forward hydraulically for access to the engine area. The chassis frame is of the flat-topped ladder-type with asymmetric section side-members; cold squeeze riveted contruction is used. Inside the all-steel cab an adjustable suspension seat is provided for the driver and a seat is also provided for a passenger. There is a roof hatch and an internal observer/gunner's platform.

The front axle is a fully floating GKN (Kirkstall) SD66 with a design rating of 8000 kg; the rear bogie is a GKN (Kirkstall) D102 with a design rating of 36 000 kg. The fifth wheel is located over the rear bogie.

Numerous options are available, including a 4.92 m mean wheelbase version in 6 × 4 configuration, a forward control cab-over-engine version, a crew cab with provision for up to seven passengers, dual or triple passenger seats, air-conditioning, various winches, various Cummins or Caterpillar engines, an automatic or ZF driveline and transmission, a central tyre inflation system, various cab roof beacons or spot lights, and numerous other options.

Specifications

Cab seating: 1 + 1
Configuration: 6 × 6 (or 6 × 4)
Weight:
 (kerb) 12 500 kg
 (GVW) 44 000 kg
 (GCW) 120 000 kg
Max trailer and payload weight: approx 107 500 kg

Bedford TT120-40 (6 × 6) tank transporter

Length: 8.25 m
Width: 3.04 m
Height: (cab) 3.16 m
Track: 2.22 m
Wheelbase: (mean) 5.34 m
Angle of approach: 47°
Max speed: 80 km/h
Fuel capacity: 2 × 340 l
Max gradient: 35%
Engine: Cummins NTE 400 14 l 6-cylinder in-line water-cooled turbocharged diesel developing 400 bhp at 2100 rpm
Gearbox: Fuller RT 11609A range change with 9 forward and 2 reverse gears
Transfer box: GKN (Kirkstall) AGB 7000 MK II 2-speed
Steering: recirculating ball with power-assist
Turning radius: 11.5 m
Suspension:
 (front) semi-elliptic multi-leaf springs with rubber

bush eyes and telescopic hydraulic double-acting shock absorbers
 (rear) high articulation Hendrikson RS 700 equalising beam
Tyres: 14.00 R 24
Brakes: dual circuit air
Electrical system: 24 V
Batteries: 2 × 12 V, 120 Ah
Alternator: 35 A

Status

Prototype.

Manufacturer

Marshall SPV Limited, Airport Works, Cambridge CB5 8RX, UK.
Tel: 0223 301133. Telex: 81208.
In October 1992 Marshall SPV Limited acquired the product designs and some of the assets of AWD Limited.

Unipower M Series Tank Transporter

Description

The Unipower M Series tank transporter is part of the Unipower M Series military 8 × 8 family of logistics vehicles and is intended to tow MBTs weighing over 70 tonnes; the vehicle and load combination can be 115 tonnes. The tank transporter version is powered by a 700 bhp engine coupled to an automatic transmission. Twin 25-tonne winches enable the transporter to retrieve and unload immobilised armoured vehicles.

The forward control cab has seating for the driver and four crew, plus space for their equipment. There is a roof hatch with provision for a machine gun mounting. Air-conditioning and an integral heating system are provided. The cab height is low enough to allow the vehicle to be carried in a C-130 transport aircraft.

The M Series tank transporter has permanent 8 × 8 drive and features balanced axle loads and traction distribution. The chassis frame utilises open channel bolted construction while the front suspension and steering, rated at 19 000 kg, employs two slipper-ended semi-elliptic parabolic springs with integral power-assisted steering. The rear suspension is a two-spring high articulation bogie located by Panhard and radius rods, and is rated at 36 000 kg.

The engine is a Cummins KTA 700 19 litre turbo-

charged diesel developing 700 bhp, although other similar units could be installed. The engine is coupled to a fully automatic five-speed automatic transmission and a torque converter.

The fifth wheel is cast steel and is of the double oscillating type. Various types of semi-trailer unit can be towed, including multi-axle models (six or seven rows of beam axles).

Specifications

Cab seating: 1 + 3
Configuration: 8 × 8
Weights: (design on/off road)
 (1st front axle) 9500 kg
 (2nd front axle) 9500 kg
 (1st rear axle) 14 200 kg
 (2nd rear axle) 14 200 kg
 (GVW) 47 400 kg
 (GCW) 115 000 kg
Length: 10.045 m
Width: 2.9 m
Height: 2.776 m
Ground clearance: 0.33 m
Wheelbase: 5.8 m
Angle of approach: 38°
Max speed: 80 km/h
Fuel capacity: 900 l
Range: 1000 km
Gradient: 35%

Engine: Cummins KTA 700 19 l turbocharged and after-cooled diesel developing 700 bhp at 2200 rpm
Transmission: ZF HP1500 fully automatic, 5 forward and 1 reverse gears
Transfer box: 2-speed
Steering: ZF 8098 power-assisted
Suspension:
 (front) 2 slipper-ended semi-elliptical parabolic springs per axle
 (rear) two fully articulated semi-elliptical multi-leaf springs trunnion mounted at centre with slipper ends; axles located by upper and lower radius rods and transversally by Panhard rods
Brakes: air to all axles; dual circuit
Tyres: 24 R 20.5
Electrical system: 24 V
Batteries: 2 × 12 V, 150 Ah
Alternator: 90 A

Status

Available for production.

Manufacturer

Unipower Vehicles Limited, 34 Greenhill Crescent, Watford Business Park, Watford, Hertfordshire WD1 8QU, UK.
Tel: 0923 816555. Telex: 261760 unitrk g.
Fax: 0923 228621.

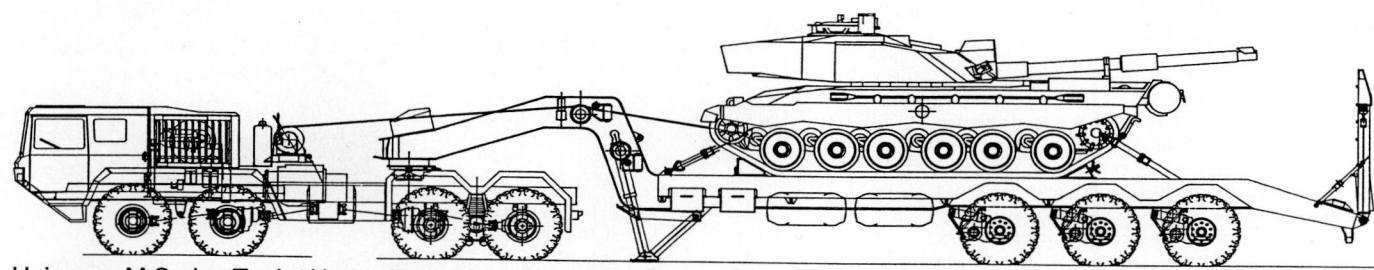

Unipower M Series Tank / Heavy Equipment Transporter (on / off road trailer) (Challenger main battle tank)

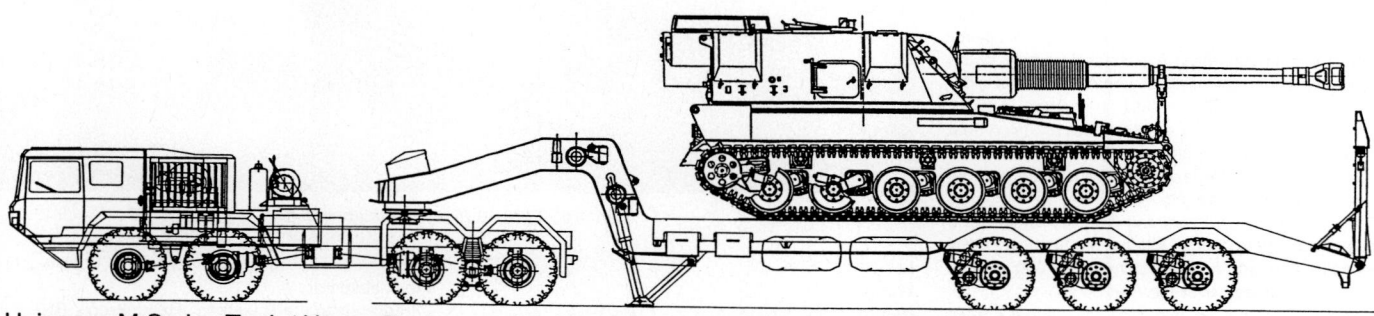

Unipower M Series Tank / Heavy Equipment Transporter (on / off road trailer) (AS90 tracked howitzer)

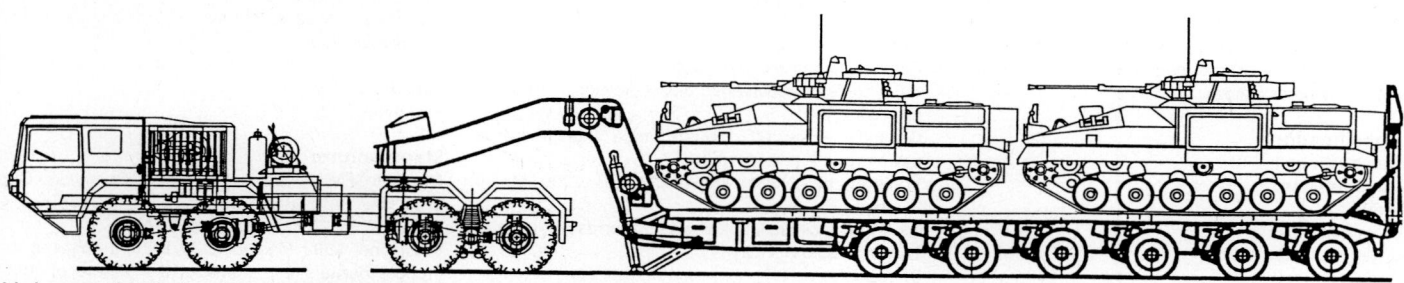

Unipower M Series Tank / Heavy Equipment Transporter (road trailer) (2 x Warrior infantry fighting vehicles)

Drawings of various possible configurations and carrying capabilities of Unipower M Series tank transporter

Unipower Contractor (6 × 4) Tractor Truck

Development

The Scammell (now Unipower) Contractor (6 × 4) vehicle was introduced by Scammell in 1964 and has since been used for a variety of civil and military applications. It is used by the military for hauling semi-trailers carrying MBTs such as the M48/M60, and large numbers were exported, especially to the Middle East and Africa.

Description

The layout of the Contractor is conventional with the engine at the front, two-door fully enclosed all-steel cab in the centre and the fifth wheel at the rear. A wide range of different engines and transmissions is available, according to the role for which the vehicle is required.

Optional equipment includes a larger four-door cab, three-line brake system (standard on British vehicles), engine brake, air-conditioning system, canopy over roof, cab heater and demister, searchlights, seven-pin plug at mid-chassis for semi-trailer, seven-pin plug and socket at front and rear of frame for full trailer, tow hitches front and rear, winch with a capacity of 15 240 kg or a Darlington winch with a capacity of 22 680 kg, and a gearbox oil cooler. The winch has 131 m of cable and an interlock is provided to ensure that a winch brake and cut-out device operate continuously during loading so that overloading is prevented

Australian Army Contractor (6 × 4) tractor truck with semi-trailer (P Handel)

and run-back cannot occur should the engine stop. A maximum pull of 50 800 kg is available by means of suitable sheaving; pull on first layer is 15 240 kg.

The series comprised seven basic models. Gross weights covered were 86 300 kg, 101 600 kg, 111 700 kg, 122 000 kg, 152 400 kg and 182 800 kg for articulated operation, or 111 700 kg, 162 500 kg, 193 000 kg, and 244 000 kg respectively as ballasted tractors for specialised heavy duty haulage. The final

production model had a maximum train weight of 244 000 kg. Standard models were 6 × 4 but 6 × 6 models were also available. Civilian applications include use as dump trucks and for logging.

Specifications

Cab seating: 1 + 2
Configuration: 6 × 4
Weight: (gross combination)

[CT85 C33F48] 86 360 kg
(loaded, tractor truck) 38 530 kg
(empty, tractor truck) 12 567 kg
Weight on front axle: (loaded) 8130 kg
Weight on rear bogie: (loaded) 30 490 kg
Length: 7.773 m
Width: 2.489 m
Height: 2.955 m
Height: (5th wheel) 1.622 m
Track:
(front) 1.991 m
(rear) 1.845 m
Wheelbase: 4.748 m
Max speed:
(loaded) 77.14 km/h [CT85 C33F48] 86 360 kg GCW

Fuel capacity: 636 l
Max gradient:
[GCW 116 840 kg] (loaded) 16.67%
Engine: Cummins NTC 6-cylinder 4-stroke in-line diesel developing 335 bhp (gross) at 2100 rpm
Gearbox: RTO 12515 15 speed forward, 3 reverse, twin countershaft
Clutch: twin dry plate
Steering: power-assisted
Suspension:
(front) longitudinal semi-elliptical leaf springs with telescopic hydraulic dampers
(rear) fully articulated, inverted longitudinal springs, trunnion-mounted at centre
Brakes: air

Electrical system: 24 V
Batteries: 4 × 6 V, 195 Ah

Status
Production complete. The Contractor is known to be in service in Australia, Jordan, Kenya and Libya.

Manufacturer
Unipower Vehicles Limited, 34 Greenhill Crescent, Watford Business Park, Watford, Hertfordshire WD1 8QU, UK.
Tel: 0923 816555. Telex: 261760 unitrk g.
Fax: 0923 228621.

Unipower S24 Contractor Range (6 × 4) and (6 × 6) Transporter Tractors

Development
The S24 range was introduced in 1981 by Scammell, its design based on military and civilian experience gained with the earlier Contractor models.

In May 1988, Unipower Vehicles Limited acquired the design, manufacturing and support rights for the Scammell S24 range, their rear engine crash tenders, Commander, Contractor, Explorer, Super Constructor, Crusader, LDSS, Nubian Major and Thornycroft Antar models.

Description
The S24 Contractor range is available in 6 × 4 and 6 × 6 configuration with left- and right-hand normal control power-assisted steering.

Power outputs range from 400 to 600 bhp utilising Cummins N & K in-line series and Perkins RF CV8 power units, coupled to manual, semi- and fully-automatic transmissions. Sustained performance figures of up to 32 km/h on 1 in 40 gradients at 110 tonne GTW are available with top speeds in the 74 to 80 km/h range.

King-pin imposed loads of 25 to 28 tonnes at unrestricted speeds are available with 12.00 R 24 and 14.00 R 20 tyre equipment on standard and wide track axles. All driving axles of the spiral bevel epicyclic hub reduction type are equipped with inter- and cross-lockable differentials actuated by air pressure from the cab. Front wheel drive variants can be disengaged from the cab via the single-speed transposing box as dictated by terrain considerations.

Dual circuit primary air braking with secondary spring and parking brakes are provided while manual transmission vehicles are equipped with engine brakes and the semi-auto variants have integral hydraulic retarders.

Suspension is of the semi-elliptic leaf spring variety with telescopic hydraulic damping at the front. High

Unipower S24TT8 tractor truck and trailer

ground clearance is achieved by the fully articulating centre trunnion mounted rear springs.

An all-steel bonneted cab accommodates the driver and two passengers whilst the optional extended version can accommodate six seated men.

Dual hydraulically driven, independently operated 20-tonne winches are fitted behind the cab and are supplied with 50 m of 24 mm rope in end drum.

A full set of tools and equipment associated with the transporter role are provided together with up to two spare wheels and tyres.

Specifications (CA45)
Cab seating: 1 + 2 or 1 + 5
Configuration: 6 × 6
Weight laden:
(front axle) 9000 kg
(rear bogie) 36 000 kg
(GVW) 45 000 kg
(GCW) 100 000 kg
Length: 8.475 m
Width: 2.868 m
Height: 3.298 m

Wheelbase: 5.42 m
Max speed: 80 km/h
Fuel capacity: 900 l
Engine: Cummins NTE 400 turbocharged and after-cooled developing 400 bhp at 2100 rpm
Transmission: Eaton Fuller RTX 14615, 15 forward speeds
Clutch: twin plate (394 mm diam)
Transfer box: Unipower single speed
Tyres: 14.00 R 20
Brakes: dual circuit air
Electrical system: 24 V

Status
In service in the Middle East.

Manufacturer
Unipower Vehicles Limited, 34 Greenhill Crescent, Watford Business Park, Watford, Hertfordshire WD1 8QU, UK.
Tel: 0923 816555. Telex: 261760 unitrk g.
Fax: 0923 228621.

Unipower Commander (6 × 4) Tractor Truck

Development
The Unipower (formerly Scammell) Commander tractor truck was developed to meet the requirements of the British Army for a new tractor truck to replace its ageing Thornycroft Antars and to carry the Challenger 1 MBT. Design work on the Commander began in 1976 with the first three prototypes being completed in 1978. Two of them were powered by the Rolls-Royce CV12 TCE diesel and the third by an American Cummins KTA 600 diesel.

In 1981 there was a General Staff Requirement for a vehicle similar to the Commander but as a result of defence spending cuts the GSR was not endorsed at the time. However in late 1982 an order for 125 Commanders for the British Army was placed. The first examples were delivered in late 1983 with production continuing into 1985.

In January 1992 Unipower was awarded a contract

Unipower Commander (6 × 4) tractor truck

for the in-depth repair of an undisclosed pilot quantity of Commander tractor trucks. The contract involved total strip-down and refurbishing, where necessary, with new parts.

Although designed for towing semi-trailers carrying AFVs weighing up to 65 000 kg, the Commander can also be used for high-speed haulage of heavy indivisible loads.

Description

The engine is at the front, all-steel cab in the centre, winch to rear of the cab and the fifth wheel over the bogie at the rear.

The cab is arranged for left-hand drive and incorporates noise insulating material. A two-piece flat glass windscreen with an electric heating element is provided on the driver's side. For crew access large steps are fitted and full interior heating and ventilating equipment is standard. Air-conditioning equipment is optional as are various radio installations. The cab has individual seats for the commander and driver behind which is a bench seat for two men which can be positioned to form two individual bunks, one above the other.

The chassis is of steel channel sidemembers with bolted-in, fabricated and tubular crossmembers. There are heavy duty members at the front and rear for towing, lifting and recovery.

The front axle is a Scammell 12 200 kg capacity steer. Lock angles of 40° give high manoeuvrability.

The rear axle is a Scammell 40 700 kg capability double drive bogie comprising two hub reduction axles linked by a lockable third differential for increased traction on poor surfaces. The fully articulated fifth wheel has an imposed load capacity of 34 600 kg.

A heavy duty Rotzler winch is standard for the Commander for self-loading dead loads and the tractor is fully equipped with recovery fittings. The 20 300 kg line pull horizontal winch has 110 m of 26 mm diameter rope. The winch is fitted with an automatic pay-on gear and has a fail-safe brake. A high rope warning and an automatic overload cut-out is provided. The rope can be led out over the neck of the semi-trailer or through fairleads at the rear of the chassis. Winch controls are mounted behind the cab in a weatherproof enclosure.

Specifications

Cab seating: 1 + 3 or 4
Configuration: 6 × 4
Weight: (empty) 19 920 kg
Weight on front axle: (empty) 9680 kg
Weight on rear bogie: (empty) 10 240 kg
Gross combination weight: 104 000 kg
Length: 9.01 m
Width: 3.25 m
Height: 3.5 m
Wheelbase: 5.03 m
Max speed: (with semi-trailer and 65 t MBT) 61 km/h
Fuel capacity: 817 l
Gradient: 20%

Fording: 0.76 m
Engine: Rolls-Royce CV12 TCE turbocharged 60° V-12 diesel developing 625 bhp at 2100 rpm
Gearbox: Allison CLBT 6061 6-speed epicyclic with torque converter permitting gear changes to be made under power. Hydraulic retarder for speed control on hills to supplement wheel brakes
Steering: hydraulic-assisted
Suspension: leaf springs front and rear with telescopic dampers to front; 2-spring high-articulation rear bogie suspension ensures equal wheel loads
Tyres: 14.00 × 24
Brakes: twin leading show wedge brakes with automatic adjustment on all wheels, operated by 2 air circuits; 2-line couplings for trailer connections and additional couplings for double heading
Electrical system: 24 V
Batteries: 6 × 12 V, 100 Ah

Status

In service with the British Army (125).

Manufacturer

Unipower Vehicles Limited, 34 Greenhill Crescent, Watford Business Park, Watford, Hertfordshire WD1 8QU, UK.
Tel: 0923 816555. Telex: 261760 unitrk g.
Fax: 0923 228621.

UNITED STATES OF AMERICA

M1070 (8 × 8) Heavy Equipment Transporter (HET)

Description

As the result of a US Army requirement to transport the M1A1 Abrams MBT the Oshkosh Truck Corporation was awarded a contract to produce 1044 M1070 Heavy Equipment Transporters (HET); the contract contains an option for a further 522 units. The first year's funding was released in January 1990 with the first of six prototypes being ready for testing in October 1990. Production commenced in July 1992 and will be completed in August 1993. The full contract, with spares, is worth $213.9 million. Production for export customers is forecast to begin during 1993.

The M1070 HET has full 8 × 8 drive and is powered by a Detroit Diesel 8V-92TA diesel developing 500 hp coupled to an Allison five-speed automatic transmission. The single front axle is steered in co-ordination with the rear axle of the rear 'tridem' unit. All axles are Rockwell Model SVI 5MR units with planetary hub reductions and differential locks on the tridem.

The layout is conventional with a large sloping bonnet positioned in front of a fully enclosed cab having seating for the driver and crewman and three passengers. Two 25-ton capacity loading winches are fitted as standard, as is a central tyre inflation system. The fifth wheel has a nominal load capacity of 20 866 kg and a diameter of 3.5 in/89 mm.

The M1070 HET tows the M1000 semi-trailer. The HET is transportable in C-5A and C-17 transport aircraft.

Specifications

Cab seating: 1 + 4
Configuration: 8 × 8
Weight:
  (kerb) 18 598 kg
  (GVW) 39 463 kg

M1070 (8 × 8) Heavy Equipment Transporter (HET) towing M1000 semi-trailer carrying an M1 Abrams MBT

(GCW) 104 963 kg
Load on 5th wheel: (nominal) 21 325 kg
Length: 9.093 m
Width: 2.591 m
Height: 3.662 m
  (5th wheel) 1.616 m
Track: 2.083 m
Wheelbase: 5.461 m
Max speed:
  (secondary road at GCW) 52 km/h
  (3% gradient at GCW) 24 km/h
Range: (cruising) 724 km
Fuel capacity: 946 l
Gradient: (at full GCW) 15%
Fording: 0.711 m
Engine: Detroit Diesel Model 8V-92TA 12.1 l diesel developing 500 hp with DDEC II electronic control system
Transmission: Allison CLT-754 automatic with 5 forward gears and torque converter

Transfer box: Oshkosh 55000 2-speed
Steering: power-assisted with front and rear axle co-ordinated steer
Turning radius: (wall to wall) 11.1 m
Suspension:
  (front) springs and hydraulic shock absorbers front
  (rear) air ride
Tyres: 425/95 R 20 XLZ
Brakes: drum type, air-actuated S-cam
Electrical system: 24 V start, 12 V lighting
Batteries: 4 × 12 V

Status

Production for US Army (1044 plus 522 options) commenced July 1992.

Manufacturer

Oshkosh Truck Corporation, PO Box 2566, Oshkosh, Wisconsin 54903-2566, USA.
Tel: (414) 235 9150. Fax: (414) 233 9540.

M911 (6 × 6) Heavy Equipment Transporter

Development

Early in 1976 the US Army issued a requirement for a truck tractor which would operate at 70 km/h at 86 183 kg, at 22.5 km/h at 86 183 kg on a 3 per cent grade, start and operate at 86 183 kg on a 20 per cent grade, operate in ambient air temperatures of +52°C maximum to −32°C minimum without kits and to −46°C with arctic kits, provide reliability, long service life, and use components with adequate manufacturing life to provide parts backup for the anticipated life cycle of the truck and provide minimum weight, size and cost consistent with other criteria.

In September 1976 Oshkosh was awarded an initial contract for 747 vehicles designated the M911, based on the commercial Oshkosh F2365 truck. A number of export customers purchased the M911 (some with Oshkosh-supplied trailers). Production has continued since 1976.

It is understood that the M911 is under consideration for an Extended Life Program (ESP) which will upgrade the vehicle to enable it to be modernised to extend its operational life while extending its capabilities.

Oshkosh M911 (6 × 6) truck tractor towing an M1 Abrams MBT

Description
The layout of the vehicle is conventional with the engine at the front, all-steel two-door cab in the centre and the fifth wheel at the rear. Standard equipment for the cab includes an adjustable seat for the driver, air-operated variable speed wipers, 22 000 BTU/h hot water heater and defroster.

The brakes have a dual air supply system, one for the front and one for the rear axles. If the air system that supplies the front brakes fails the rear brakes can be operated normally. If the rear system fails, the front system as well as the rear spring chamber will still remain pressurised. A hydraulic retarder operated with a foot control in the transmission can absorb up to 80 per cent of the engine's horsepower.

The main transmission is fully automatic and will automatically upshift or downshift in all ranges above second gear, with a hold in each range. Built-in inhibitors prevent downshift or reverse shift at excessive speeds.

Standard equipment includes two retrieval winches with a capacity of 20 412 kg each, rear decklights, a spare tyre carrier with lift, a rear pintle hook, trailer air and electrical connections, spotlights, fog lights, a hydraulic jack, a tyre inflation hose, an oscillating fifth wheel, splash guards, a radiator and headlight guard, and towing eyes. Optional equipment includes air-conditioning.

Specifications
Cab seating: 1 + 2
Configuration: 6 × 6
Weight:
(kerb) 18 144 kg
(GVW) 39 463 kg
(GCW) 102 514 kg
Load on 5th wheel: (nominal) 20 866 kg
Length: 9.373 m
Width:
(over bumpers) 2.438 m
(rear duals) 2.896 m
Height:
(overall) 3.404 m
(cab) 3.175 m
(5th wheel, no load) 1.626 m
Track:
(front) 2.083 m
(rear) 2.057 m
Wheelbase: 5.207 m + 1.524 m
Max speed:
(road, with GCW) 72 km/h
(3% gradient, fully loaded) 23 km/h
Range:
(no payload, maximum speed) 1344 km
(at 86 183 kg gross combination weight, economical speed) 990 km
Fuel capacity: 757 l
Max gradient: (at full GCW) 20%
Fording: 0.711 m

Engine: Detroit Diesel model 8V-92TA-90 V-8 developing 450 hp at 2100 rpm
Transmission: Allison CLBT-754 automatic with 5 forward and 1 reverse gears and hydraulic retarder
Transfer case: Oshkosh Model 7038 single-speed
Auxiliary transmission: Fuller AT 1202 2-speed
Steering: hydraulic, dual power-assist at front
Turning radius: 13.72 m
Suspension:
(front) Hotchkiss type with semi-elliptical main springs with Berlin eye and semi-elliptical auxiliary spring
(rear) Hendrickson RT-650, steel spring, equalising beam design with 1.524 m spread
Tyres: 14 R 24
Brakes: drum, dual system air S-type
Electrical system: 24 V
Batteries: 4 × 12 V, 100 Ah
Alternator: 65 A

Status
Production for export continuing. In service with the US Army, Greece, Morocco, Oman, Saudi Arabia, Taiwan, Thailand, and Yemen.

Manufacturer
Oshkosh Truck Corporation, PO Box 2566, Oshkosh, Wisconsin 54903-2566, USA.
Tel: (414) 235 9150. Fax: (414) 233 9540.

M746 (8 × 8) 22½-ton Tractor Truck (Heavy Equipment Transporter)

Development
Development of the Heavy Equipment Transporter (HET) can be traced back to 1965 when a contract was issued to the Chrysler Corporation for a joint study, with the then West German companies of Faun and Krupp, for an HET which could carry the MBT-70 tank then under development by both the United States and Germany. The first two American prototypes were completed by Chrysler in 1966 with a German-supplied chassis and cab. The following year they were tested alongside German prototype vehicles. In 1970 the MBT-70 programme was cancelled. The Germans continued development of their vehicle which was standardised as the SLT-50, with production undertaken by Faun. The Americans built a further three prototypes for additional testing under the designation XM746 which was subsequently standardised as the M746. The production contract was awarded to the Ward LaFrance company and first production vehicles were completed in 1975. Production for the US Army continued until 1977.

Description
The fully enclosed all-steel cab is of the forward control type and its overall height can be reduced for air transport. A circular observation hatch is provided in the right side of the roof. Mounted to the rear of the cab are two Pacific Car and Foundry P-60 hydraulic winches, each with a capacity of 27 216 kg and 45.72 m of 25 mm diameter cable, which enable the M746 to recover disabled vehicles without additional assistance.

The power steering operates on the front four wheels. Power is transmitted to all four axles by a five-speed power-shift transmission. The rear axles have no spin differentials. The brakes are automatically adjusted with a fail-safe and anti-skid braking system.

The HET was designed for use with the M747 semi-trailer; full details will be found in the *Trailers* section.

Specifications
Cab seating: 1 + 2
Configuration: 8 × 8
Weight:
(empty) 20 412 kg
(loaded) 39 010 kg

Ward LaFrance M746 (8 × 8) 22½-ton tractor truck from front

Weight on front axles: (loaded) 8460 kg
Weight on rear axles: (loaded) 11 045 kg
Weight on 5th wheel: 20 412 kg
Towed load: 62 143 kg
Length: 8.229 m
Width: 3.048 m

Height:
(cab) 3.048 m
(reduced) 2.514 m
(5th wheel) 1.6 m
Ground clearance: 0.33 m
Track: 2.546 m

Wheelbase: 1.498 m + 1.27 m + 1.498 m
Angle of approach: 30°
Max speed: 62 km/h
(15% gradient) 8 km/h
Range: 322 km
Fuel capacity: 530 l
Fording: 1.219 m
Engine: Detroit Diesel model 12V-71(T) 12-cylinder liquid-cooled diesel developing 600 hp at 2500 rpm
Gearbox: Twin Disc model TADC-51-2012 power-shift with converter, 5 speeds forward and 1 reverse
Transfer box: one-speed drop box
Steering: powered
Suspension: taper leaf bogies with hydraulic shock absorbers
Brakes: air
Electrical system: 24 V
Batteries: 6, total capacity 300 Ah

Status
Production complete. In service with the USA (125) and Morocco (68).

Manufacturer
Ward LaFrance Truck Corporation, Elmira Heights, New York 14903, USA.

Mack RD8226SX 52 000 kg (6 × 6) Tank Transporter

Description
The Mack RD8226SX is the tank transporter component of the Mack RM6006S range of vehicles. It is capable of towing semi-trailers carrying loads up to 52 000 kg and it may be equipped with a crew cab situated behind the normal driver's cab. The engine used with the Mack RD8226SX is the Mack EE9 eight-cylinder diesel developing 500 hp. This is located in the front of the vehicle with the driver's cab central and the fifth wheel to the rear. The Mack RD model has a full-time operating front drive axle. Driver comfort is catered for by an adjustable steering wheel, a convenient-to-view instrument layout and driving seat suspension. Many options are available to suit a wide range of requirements.

Specifications
Cab seating: 1 + 2
Configuration: 6 × 6
Weight:
(loaded chassis, front) 10 400 kg
(loaded chassis, rear) 36 300 kg
(total) 46 700 kg
(GVW) 46 700 kg
(GCW) 92 254 kg
Length: 8.542 m
Width: 2.642 m

Mack RD8226SX 52 000 kg (6 × 6) tank transporter towing semi-trailer carrying M60 tank

Height: 3.734 m
Wheelbase: 5.842 m
Max speed: 79 km/h
Fuel capacity: (total) 832 l
Gradient: 20%
Engine: Mack EE9 8-cylinder turbocharged diesel developing 500 hp
Transmission: T2100 10-speed
Clutch: CLS795
Transfer case: TC152 2-speed with PTO
Suspension: spring type
Tyres: 12.00 × 24

Brakes:
(front) air/hydraulic disc
(rear) air cam
Batteries: 4 × 12 V

Status
In production. In service worldwide.

Manufacturer
Mack Trucks Inc, Box M, Allentown, Pennsylvania 18105, USA.
Tel: (215) 439 3011. Telex: 84-7424.

Navistar International Corporation F5070 (6 × 4) Tank Transporter

Description
The Navistar International Corporation, formerly the International Harvester Company, produces the F5070 (6 × 4) tank transporter which was developed as an MBT and heavy equipment tractor truck from the International Paystar 5000 truck series. The F5070 will tow semi-trailers carrying loads up to 60 000 kg. The engine used is the Cummins Diesel NTC 400 with the option of various Fuller direct transmissions or alternative Allison automatic transmissions. The heavy duty hydraulic winches in dual formation have a capacity of 29 500 kg each and each has 45.72 m of cable. Various drive trains and power units are available to produce various payload and vehicle combination weights. The tractor is usually supplied with an Aztec Products heavy duty FCBLF 6020 semi-trailer.

The F5070 is available with a 6 × 6 configuration. In this form the maximum gross combination weight is 90 720 kg and maximum gradient is 50%.

Navistar International Corporation F5070 (6 × 4) tractor truck

Specifications
Cab seating: 1 + 2
Configuration: 6 × 4
Weight:
    (max gross vehicle weight) 40 824 kg
    (max gross combination weight) 85 180 kg
Length: 8.433 m
Width: 2.594 m
Height: 3.3 m
Track: (rear) 1.887 m
Wheelbase: 5.437 m
Max speed: 84 km/h
Fuel capacity: 1083 l
Max gradient: (loaded) 25.9%
Engine: Cummins Diesel NTC 400 diesel developing

400 hp at 2100 rpm
Gearbox: Fuller 10-speed
Steering: Sheppard dual steering gears
Turning radius: 13.5 m
Suspension:
    (front) leaf springs with torque rods
    (rear) walking beams with leaf springs and torque
    rods
Tyres: 12.00 × 24, 18 ply
Brakes:
    (main) air
    (parking) spring/air release
Electrical system: 24 V
Batteries: 4 × 12 V

Status
In production. In service in the Middle East and elsewhere.

Manufacturer
Navistar International Corporation, 400 North Michigan Avenue, Chicago, Illinois 60611, USA.

AMPHIBIANS

This section covers vehicles designed specifically for amphibious operations, such as crossing inland waterways or carrying cargo from ships offshore on to the beach, or inland. It does not include vehicles which require preparation to make them amphibious nor does it include amphibious over-snow vehicles or tracked prime movers, details of which will be found in their respective sections.

COMMONWEALTH OF INDEPENDENT STATES

PTS, PTS-M and PTS-2 Tracked Amphibious Vehicles

Description
The PTS tracked amphibious vehicle entered service in the mid-1960s as the replacement for the earlier K-61 (GPT) vehicle. The main improvements over the K-61 were its higher water speed and its ability to transport 10 000 kg on land for 3 km in order to reach the water. The PTS-M, which first appeared in 1969, is a modified version while the later (1985) PTS-2 is the replacement for the PTS-M.

PTS and PTS-M
These two vehicles are essentially similar. The crew compartment is at the front of the vehicle and is fully sealed against NBC attack. The crew enter the cab via two circular hatches in the roof. The cargo area is at the rear of the vehicle and vehicles are loaded via the hinged tailgate which also has integral loading ramps. Tie-down points are fitted for securing the vehicle. The engine is under the centre of the cargo compartment with the exhaust exits just above the top of the cargo compartment on each side. The vehicles are propelled in the water by two propellers in tunnels under the rear of the hull and steering is by two rudders at the rear of the hull.

The suspension is of the torsion bar type and consists of six road wheels with the idler at the rear and the drive sprocket at the front.

A winch is mounted at the front of the vehicle and before entering the water a trim vane is erected at the front and the bilge pumps are switched on. The cargo area can be covered by bows and a tarpaulin cover and is sometimes used as an ambulance vehicle. Standard equipment includes infra-red night vision equipment, intercom, radios and a searchlight mounted on the top of the crew compartment.

The vehicles were designed to carry 5000 kg on land or 10 000 kg on water, or up to 70 men. In the ambulance role up to 12 stretchers can be carried in the open cargo area. The PTS-M has also been used to lay portable trackway across beach areas.

The PKP trailer was designed specifically for use with the PTS-M. Basic specifications are: unladen weight 3600 kg, overall length 10.3 m, width (travelling) 2.82 m, height 1.98 m, ground clearance 0.4 m and track 1.89 m. The PKP is a boat-shaped trailer and has two small pontoons pivoted either side which rest on top of the trailer when it is travelling and are swung through 180° and locked in position before entering the water. Loading ramps are provided for loading. The trailer is normally used to carry 122 mm howitzers while the PTS carries the prime mover, for example the Ural-375D. The PKP can be towed at a speed of between 20 and 25 km/h laden or 25 to 30 km/h unladen.

PTS-2
Introduced in 1985, the PTS-2 is based on the chassis of the MT-T heavy tracked transporter which uses suspension components of the T-64 MBT and is

PTS-M tracked amphibious vehicle

PTS-M tracked amphibious vehicle afloat

powered by a V-64-4 diesel derived from that used in the T-72 MBT. The PTS-2 is understood to be the eventual replacement for the PTS-M and has been in service for some time.

The PTS-2 has revised running gear consisting of seven road wheels and four track return rollers; the track links have rubber pads. The driving cab is enlarged and features an NBC protection system, while the trim vane at the bow is slightly curved. The sponson is higher than on earlier models and there is a rectangular exhaust outlet on both sides to accommodate the turbocharged engine mounted amidships. A ramp-like stern is provided. The cargo space is enlarged to 8.3 × 2.6 m and it is understood that the PTS-2 has a higher payload capacity than earlier models.

Variant
The Polish Army has used a number of PTS tracked amphibious vehicles fitted with rocket-propelled mine-clearing equipment in the rear.

Specifications (PTS-M)
Cab seating: 1 + 1 (70 troops in rear)
Weight:
  (empty) 17 700 kg
  (loaded, land) 22 700 kg
  (loaded, water) 27 700 kg
Max load:
  (land) 5000 kg
  (water) 10 000 kg
Load area: 7.9 × 2.6 m

Length: 11.426 m
Width: 3.3 m
Height: 2.6 m
Ground clearance: (loaded) 0.4 m
Track: 2.8 m
Track width: 480 mm
Length of track on ground: 5.63 m
Ground pressure:
  (empty) 0.382 kg/cm^2
  (with 5000 kg load) 0.483 kg/cm^2
  (with 10 000 kg load) 0.582 kg/cm^2
Max speed:
  (land with 5000 kg load) 42 km/h
  (water with 10 000 kg load) 10.6 km/h
Range: up to 300 km
Fuel capacity: 705 l
Max gradient:
  (empty) 60%
  (loaded) 20%
Vertical obstacle: 0.65 m
Trench: 2.5 m
Engine: V-54P diesel developing 211 hp at 1800 rpm

Status
PTS-2 probably still in production. In service with members of the former Warsaw Pact as well as Egypt, Iraq and the former Yugoslavia.

Manufacturer
State factories.

INDIA

Rampar (4 × 4) 3000 kg Amphibious Vehicle

Description
The Rampar (4 × 4) 3000 kg amphibious vehicle was developed at the Indian Vehicle Research and Development Establishment and is a conversion of the Shaktiman (4 × 4) 5000 kg truck (see separate entry in *Trucks* section). It was developed following experiences in the eastern sector during the 1971 Indo-Pakistan War when numerous river crossings were made necessary.

The Rampar can carry up to 22 men or 3000 kg of cargo. The basic Shaktiman is converted by adding a mild steel hull and providing two steering rudders at the rear. Speed in calm water is 10 km/h. The boat hull is conventional with a prominent bow, a cabin for the driver and at least one passenger, and a cargo-carrying/passenger area at the rear. The load area can be covered by a canvas tilt as can the driver's cabin. A trim vane is fitted over the bow. A 4000 kg capacity winch is carried in the bow and a glass fibre trackway may be carried at the rear for use when crossing boggy ground. There is provision for a 7.62 mm machine gun pintle above the passengers' position on the cab. Light armour protection for the hull could be provided.

Specifications
Cab seating: 1 + 1 (22 men in rear)
Configuration: 4 × 4
Weight:
  (empty) 6500 kg
  (loaded) 9500 kg
Length: 8.1 m
Width: 2.3 m
Height: 3 m
Ground clearance: 0.5 m
Max speed:
  (road) 74 km/h
  (water) 10 km/h
Angle of approach/departure: 38°/32°
Engine: 6-cylinder turbocharged diesel developing 125 hp at 2500 rpm
Gearbox: 5 forward and 1 reverse gears
Transfer box: 2-speed

Status
Prototype.

ITALY

IVECO FIAT Model 6640 G (4 × 4) 2000 kg Amphibious Cargo Carrier

Description
This vehicle, announced in 1980, is very similar to the IVECO FIAT Model 6640A (4 × 4) amphibious cargo carrier described in *Jane's Military Logistics 1988* page 573. The 6640 G has a much greater weight due to stronger construction and a slightly longer wheelbase; it has a more powerful diesel engine coupled to automatic transmission and is propelled in the water by a waterjet rather than a propeller as is the earlier vehicle.

The hull of the vehicle is of all-welded aluminium construction with a maximum thickness of 4 mm. The engine compartment is at the front of the hull and is separated from the crew compartment by a fireproof bulkhead. The two-man fully enclosed cab is heated and ventilated. The cargo area is to the rear of the cab and is provided with removable bows and a tarpaulin cover. Folding bench seats for 14 men run along both sides of the cargo area.

The vehicle is propelled in water by its wheels or the waterjet mounted under the hull at the rear; steering in the water is by a rear-mounted rudder linked to the steering wheel. In an emergency the rudder can be operated by hand. Three bilge pumps, one in the bottom of the engine compartment and two below the cargo area, are provided.

As an option, a winch with a capacity of 4500 kg on the first layer can be mounted at the front of the vehicle. A materials handling crane with a capacity of 700 kg can be fitted if required.

The latest version is the IVECO 6640 H which is powered by a 220 hp 5.861 litre engine. The automatic three-speed gearbox is fitted with a torque converter.

Specifications
Cab seating: 1 + 2
Configuration: 4 × 4
Weight:
  (kerb) 6700 kg
  (loaded) 8700 kg
  (on front axle, loaded) 3400 kg
  (on rear axle, loaded) 5300 kg
  (payload) 2000 kg
Load area: 3.21 × 1.95 m
Length: 8.2 m
Width: 2.5 m
Height:
  (cab) 2.7 m (approx)
  (tarpaulin) 3.16 m
Ground clearance: 0.35 m

IVECO FIAT Model 6640 G (4 × 4) 2000 kg amphibious cargo carrier with tarpaulin cover

Track: 1.96 m
Wheelbase: 3.1 m
Angle of approach/departure: 30°/25°
Max speed:
  (road) 100 km/h
  (water, propelled by waterjet) 11 km/h
Range:
  (road) over 600 km
  (water, propelled by waterjet) over 5 h
Max gradient: 60%
Max side slope: 30%
Fording: amphibious
Engine: Model 8062.24 6-cylinder 4-stroke liquid-cooled turbocharged diesel developing 195 hp at 3200 rpm (6640 H, 220 hp at 3000 rpm)
Gearbox: automatic, 3 forward and 1 reverse gears with power take-off for pump-jet
Axle differential carriers: single reduction, spiral bevel drive. Air-operated differential lock at front and rear
Planetary drives: (front and rear) epicyclic gear train in wheel hubs
Steering: power-assisted
Turning radius: (land) 7.5 m
Suspension: (front and rear) independent strut and link type with helical spring and rubber bump stop plus hydraulic shock absorbers
Tyres: 14.5 × 20 PS 12 (13.00 × 20 optional)
Brakes:
  (main) disc, air over hydraulic, dual circuit
  (parking) drum type, mounted on transfer rear output shaft
Electrical system: 24 V
Batteries: 2 × 12 V, 110 Ah

Status
Production as required. During 1984 a total of 17 sold to Italian Ministry of Interior (Direction of Civil Protection) plus a further 21 for Civil Defence.

Manufacturer
IVECO SpA, Defence Vehicle Division, Via Volta 6, I-39100 Bolzano, Italy.
Tel: 0471 905111. Telex: 400541 ivedvd i.
Fax: 0471 905444.

SINGAPORE

SAE Upgraded LARC-V

Description

The Singapore armed forces operate a number of LARC-5 amphibious cargo carriers and Singapore Automotive Engineering (SAE) carried out an upgrading programme on these vehicles. The programme involves the installation of a Cummins V-903-C diesel engine and some other changes, including the option of fitting a hydraulically operated crane. This upgrading programme is being offered to other LARC-5 users as the SAE Upgraded LARC-V and the specifications provided by SAE are given below.

SAE also offers a modification kit for the LARC-5 to convert the vehicle into an amphibious firefighting vehicle.

Specifications

Cab seating: 1 + 2
Configuration: 4 × 4
Weight:
(empty) 8600 kg
(loaded) 13 100 kg
Max load: 4536 kg
Load area: 4.876 × 2.971 m
Length: 10.7 m
Width: 3 m
Height:
(overall) 3.1 m
(reduced) 2.4 m
Ground clearance: 0.61 m
Freeboard:
(amidship, unloaded) 0.35 m
(amidship, loaded) 0.25 m
Track: 2.6 m
Wheelbase: 4.9 m
Angle of approach/departure: 20.7°/26.5°
Max speed:
(road) 44 km/h
(water) 13 km/h
Range:
(land, unloaded) 400 km
(land, loaded) 322 km
(water, unloaded) 65 km
(water, loaded) 56 km
Fuel capacity: 545 l
Max gradient: 60%
Side slope: 20%
Fording: amphibious
Engine: Cummins V-903-C diesel developing 295 bhp at 2600 rpm
Turning radius: 11.124 m
Suspension: rigid
Tyres: 18.00 × 25

Status

Modified vehicles in service with Singapore armed forces.

Manufacturer

Singapore Automotive Engineering, 5 Portsdown Road, Republic of Singapore.
Tel: 4736311. Telex: 25755 sineng rs.
Fax: 4710662.

SPAIN

VAP 3550/1 (4 × 4) 3000 kg Amphibious Vehicle

Description

The VAP 3550/1 (4 × 4) 3000 kg amphibious vehicle was developed by ENASA to meet Spanish Navy requirements for a vehicle which can be launched from LSTs and other amphibious craft offshore, reach the coast under its own power and then travel inland over rough country. VAP is the export name of this vehicle, within Spain it is known as the Pegaso 3550 with the first production batch being known as the 3550/1.

The vehicle uses many automotive components of the ENASA (Pegaso) range of 3045 (4 × 4) 3000 kg and 3050 (6 × 6) 6000 kg trucks of which over 6000 were supplied to the Spanish Army.

The boat-shaped hull of the VAP 3550/1 is made of all-welded 6 mm thick steel plates and is divided into watertight compartments. The driver sits in the semi-enclosed cab, which has an open back, towards the front with two passengers seated on his right. A searchlight that can be operated from within the cab is mounted over the top of the cab. Immediately behind the cab is a hydraulic crane with a maximum lifting capacity of 350 kg.

The cargo area in the centre of the vehicle can be covered with removable bows and a tarpaulin cover. Removable benches for troops can be fitted down either side of the cargo compartment.

The engine compartment is at the rear with the air-outlet, air-inlet louvres and exhaust pipe mounted on the top.

The VAP is fully amphibious, propelled in the water by two waterjets at the rear of the hull immediately behind the second axle. The two single waterjets are driven by a hydraulic system composed of a pump directly connected to the vehicle's engine and two hydraulic motors acting directly on the hydrojets. It features a pressurising system for the mechanical units in contact with the water which operates as soon as the VAP enters the water. When afloat, pivot turns can be accomplished.

The load compartment is equipped with two pumps with a maximum capacity of 6000 l/h and there are two automatic bilge pumps in the hull with a maximum capacity of 3600 l/h. Mounted at the front is an optional winch with a maximum capacity of 4500 kg. Other options include a pintle-mounted 7.62 mm machine gun and smoke launchers.

VAP 3550/1 (4 × 4) 3000 kg amphibious vehicle

Specifications

Cab seating: 1 + 2 (rear, 18 men)
Configuration: 4 × 4
Weight:
(empty) 9500 kg
(loaded) 12 500 kg
Max load: 3000 kg
Load area: 3.2 × 2.05 m
Length: 8.85 m
Width: 2.5 m
Height:
(cab) 2.5 m
(crane) 2.83 m
Ground clearance: 0.32 m
Track: 1.927 m
Wheelbase: 3.45 m
Angle of approach/departure: 33°/27°
Max speed:
(road) 87 km/h
(water) 5.5 kts
Range:
(road) 800 km
(water) 80 km
Fuel capacity: 250 l
Max gradient: 60%
Max side slope: 30%
Fording: amphibious
Engine: Pegaso 9135/5 6.55 l 6-cylinder in-line turbo-charged diesel developing 170 hp at 2600 rpm
Gearbox: Pegaso manual, 6 forward and 1 reverse gears
Clutch: single dry plate
Transfer box: Pegaso 2-speed
Steering: recirculating ball power-assisted
Turning radius: 9 m
Suspension: semi-elliptical springs and hydraulic double-acting shock absorbers, both axles have a self-locking differential case
Tyres: 13.00 × 20
Brakes: drum, dual circuit, air
Electrical system: 24 V
Batteries: 2 × 12 V, 99 Ah
Alternator: 1500 W

Status

Reported ordered by Egypt. Seven delivered to Mexico in 1982. In service with the Spanish Marines.

Manufacturer

Pegaso SA, ENASA, Defence Division, Avenida de Aragón 402, E-28022 Madrid, Spain.
Tel: 750 1000. Telex: 42373 bara e.
Fax: 747 1307.

UNITED KINGDOM

Amphitruck (4 × 4) 3000 kg Amphibious Vehicle

Description

The Amphitruck (4 × 4) 3000 kg amphibious vehicle was designed to be a low cost conversion of an existing road vehicle for the amphibious role. The prototype vehicle is based on the Bedford MJ 1120 and uses a glass reinforced plastic (GRP) hull divided into separate water compartments to reduce free water cross-flow. Propulsion when waterborne is by propeller and steering is via a rudder coupled to the steering wheel. The axles are fitted with differential locks and the front axle has free wheel hubs for use on hard surfaces. The vehicle will float in 1 m depth of water and the draught increases 100 mm for every tonne carried.

The engine is a standard 95 hp Bedford diesel. Detail design consideration has been given to maintenance access and the cab can be removed for transport or tilted (optional). There are removable floor and side panels and there is engine and other access through panels beneath the hull and via the removable wheel arches. All parts, including the chassis, can be removed. The prototype is fitted with 15.00 × 20 tyres but future versions will have 11.00 × 20 tyres.

Amphitruck can provide fully converted vehicles or convert customer's vehicles. Vehicles are delivered with full electrics (including lights), propeller, rudder, bilge pumps, built-in buoyancy, an electric winch, a spare wheel, a canopy, anchor, differential locks, free wheel hubs, keel cooling and so on.

Models other than the Bedford MJ 1120 can be converted and 6 × 6 conversions are possible. Apart from use as an amphibious cargo carrier various other roles are envisaged for the Amphitruck, including acting as a working or ferry platform when coupled to other Amphitruck units.

Specifications (Mark 3)
Cab seating: 1 + 1 or 2
Configuration: 4 × 4
Weight: approx 5000 kg
Max load: 3000 kg plus, depending on water conditions
Length: 9.2 m
Width: 2.46 m
Height: (top of cab, road) 2.46 m
Load area: 5.5 × 2.1 m
Max speed:
 (land) 90 km/h
 (water) 12.5 km/h
Fording: amphibious
Engine: Bedford diesel developing 103 hp at 2600 rpm
Transfer box: 2-speed with PTO
Tyres: 11.00 × 20

Status
Prototypes.

Manufacturer
Amphibious Vehicles Limited, Unit 11, Green Lane, Cadishead, Manchester M30 5BU, UK.
Tel: 061 777 8778. Fax: 061 480 2622.

Amphitruck (4 × 4) 3000 kg amphibious vehicle

UNITED STATES OF AMERICA

LARC-5 (4 × 4) 4545 kg Amphibious Cargo Carrier

Development

The LARC-5 (Lighter, Amphibious, Resupply, Cargo, 5-ton) (4 × 4) was developed by the Borg Warner Corporation from 1958 under the direction of the US Transportation Engineering Command at Fort Eustis, Virginia. The first production contract was awarded to the Adams Division of Le Tourneau Westinghouse in June 1961 and between 1962 and 1968 950 LARC-5s were built. The last manufacturer was ConDiesel Mobile Equipment of Waterbury, Connecticut. The vehicle has been designed to carry 4545 kg of cargo, or 15 to 20 fully equipped troops from ships offshore to the beach, or if required, farther inland, and is issued on the scale of 34 per Army light amphibious company.

Description

The hull of the LARC-5 is of all-welded aluminium construction with reinforced aluminium frames. The cab is at the front of the vehicle and contains, in addition to the operating controls, heater and windscreen defroster, portable lamp and cable, fire extinguisher, fabric cover for the back of the cab, radio, adjustable seat for the driver, two fixed seats for the other crew members and a magnetic compass. The cargo area is in the centre of the vehicle. Fabric curtains reinforced with stranded wire rope can be installed on each side of the cargo deck to protect the cargo.

The transfer transmission compartment is below the cargo deck and contains the transfer transmission, front wheel disconnects, drive shafts and service brakes.

The engine compartment is at the rear and is covered by two watertight hatches. Air is blown out of the compartment through a small grille between the two hatch covers. A fixed fire extinguisher is installed in the engine compartment and is controlled by a pull of a handle on the cargo deck rear bulkhead. Two manual bilge pumps are installed for use if the main hydraulic pump fails. The vehicle is propelled in the water by a three-bladed propeller under the rear of the hull.

Power is transmitted from the engine to a torque converter and hydraulic retarder installed on the flywheel end of the engine. The driver selects either forward or reverse by shifting the forward/reverse transmission lever. The main drive shaft connects the output of the forward/reverse transmission to the transfer transmission. This transmission has two gear ratios (high and low) for land operations and one gear ratio (marine) for water operations. The differential transmission transmits power to the four wheels. With the transmission in low or high range, power is always transmitted to the wheels. A mechanical disconnect can be used to apply power to the rear wheels only for two-wheel drive. Four drive shafts connect the differential transmission to the wheels. A right angle drive assembly is installed at each wheel to apply the driving

LARC-5 (4 × 4) 4545 kg amphibious cargo carrier on amphibious exercises

power to the wheels. This is a gearbox used to apply the rotation of the four-drive shaft to the axle ends of the wheels.

Some vehicles have been fitted with a hydraulically operated boom designed by the ConDiesel Mobile Equipment Division. The boom is 4.51 m long and can lift a maximum load of 2500 kg.

SAE Upgraded LARC-V
See entry under Singapore in this section.

Specifications
Cab seating: 1 + 2
Configuration: 4 × 4
Weight:
  (empty) 9507.5 kg
  (loaded) 14 053 kg
Max load: 4545 kg
Load area: 4.876 × 2.971 m

Length: 10.07 m
Width: 3.05 m
Height:
  (overall) 3.1 m
  (reduced) 2.41 m
Ground clearance: 0.406 m
Track: 2.565 m
Wheelbase: 4.876 m
Angle of approach/departure: 27°/20.7°
Max speed:
  (road) 48.2 km/h
  (water) 13.92 km/h
Range:
  (land, empty) 400 km
  (land, loaded) 322 km
  (water, empty) 65 km
  (water, loaded) 56 km
Fuel capacity: 547.2 l
Max gradient: 60%

Max side slope: 25%
Fording: amphibious
Engine:
  (early vehicles) 8-cylinder petrol developing 300 hp at 3000 rpm
  (late production vehicles) Cummins 4-cycle V-8 diesel developing 300 hp
Turning radius: 13.26 m
Suspension: rigid
Tyres: 18.00 × 25

Status
Production complete. In service with Argentina, Australia (87), France, Germany, Portugal, Singapore, Thailand and the USA.

Manufacturer
ConDiesel Mobile Equipment, 84 Progress Lane, Waterbury, Connecticut 06705, USA.

TRACKED PRIME MOVERS, CARGO CARRIERS AND ARMOURED LOGISTIC VEHICLES

This section excludes tracked vehicles which have been designed specifically for amphibious use (such as the CIS K-61 and PTS-M) or for over-snow use (such as the Swedish Bv 202) details of which will be found in their respective sections.

BRAZIL

TECTRAN VBT-2028 (6 × 6) 10 000 kg Armoured Truck

Description

The TECTRAN VBT-2028 (6 × 6) 10 000 kg armoured truck was developed as a support and launch vehicle for the ASTROS II artillery rocket system. (For details of this system refer to *Jane's Armour and Artillery 1992-93* page 697). With the ASTROS II system the VBT-2028 is used as a launch vehicle (AV-LMU), for ammunition supply (AV-RMD), as a battalion command and control vehicle (AV-VCC), for fire control (AV-UCF) and for mobile workshops. There is also a personnel carrier.

All versions use the same basic 6 × 6 drive configuration chassis with an armoured cab set forward. The cab has a wedge-shaped side profile with well-sloped armour and steel covers for the windows. Air-conditioning is provided for the crew area. A roof hatch is provided with provision for a machine gun mounting and the cab roof can withstand the weight of at least two men. A hydraulic load handling crane and winch are located behind the cab. Four stabiliser legs are lowered when the crane is in use.

The load area can take the form of a conventional cargo body complete with canvas tilt, drop sides and tailgate, but may also be of the flat bed type to carry shelters for the command and control or fire control role. Rocket launch vehicles have an elevating and traverse system located over the rear axles.

Optional equipment includes a tyre pressure regulation system and what is termed a run-flat device.

Specifications
Configuration: 6 × 6
Gross vehicle weight: approx 20 000 kg

TECTRAN VBT-2028 (6 × 6) 10 000 kg armoured truck (left) loading an ASTROS II multiple rocket launcher (right)

Payload: 10 000 kg
Max speed: 90 km/h
Max gradient: 66%
Engine: Mercedes-Benz OM 422 14.618 l V-8 diesel developing 280 hp at 2300 rpm
Transmission: ZF AK 6S/90, 6-speed, with optional torque converter
Clutch: mechanical
Turning radius: 20.3 m
Tyres: 14.00 × 20
Brakes: dual circuit, air
Batteries: 2 × 12 V, 143 Ah

Status
In production. In service with Brazil, Iraq and Saudi Arabia.

Manufacturer
TECTRAN Engenharia, Indústria e Comércio SA, Rodovia Presidente Dutra, Km 155/156, Caixa Postal 165, São José dos Campos, São Paulo, Brazil. Tel: 123 220142. Telex: 39431 ttte br.

CANADA

General Motors LAV (8 × 8) 2470 kg Armoured Logistics Carrier (LAV-L)

Development

The General Motors LAV (8 × 8) 2470 kg armoured logistics carrier, or LAV-L, is one component in a series of vehicles known to the US Marine Corps as Mission-Role-Vehicles (MRVs). These five vehicles (LAV-L, 81 mm mortar carrier, TOW-2 anti-tank, recovery (see entry in *Recovery vehicles* section), and command and control) are all variants of the basic LAV light armoured vehicle and for details of this basic vehicle refer to *Jane's Armour and Artillery 1992-93*, pages 290 to 293. Originally the LAV-L was known as the General Motors (8 × 8) Logistics Vehicle.

The first LAV-L was handed over to the US Marine Corps in August 1985. The delivery of a batch of 94 vehicles began in November 1985 and was completed by August 1986.

Description
The LAV-L is intended to provide the US Marine Corps with mobile logistic support in the field. It uses many components of the basic LAV light armoured vehicle, including the suspension, drive train and hull. On the LAV-L the driver is seated forward to the left of the

General Motors LAV (8 × 8) 2470 kg armoured logistics carrier (LAV-L)

engine compartment under an armoured hatch. When in the closed down position the driver is provided with three wide-vision periscopes. Behind the driver is the raised commander's position which is provided with all-round vision devices for use when the armoured hatch is closed down. This position may be equipped with a pintle for a 7.62 mm M60 machine gun. Also provided are two four-barrel M257 smoke grenade launchers controlled from the commander's position. There is seating behind the commander for a third crew member.

The main cargo-carrying compartment has an unobstructed level floor measuring 2.59 × 1.65 m. Access to the area is via two outward-opening rear doors or through two roof hatches each with dimensions of 1.07 × 1.28 m. To the left rear of the roof hatch is a 500 kg telescopic crane operated from a folding platform over the left rear wheel. When the rear doors are open it is possible to load the cargo area using fork-lift trucks, and internal net stowage and lashing points are provided.

The LAV-L is amphibious and may be airlifted by a heavy helicopter. Extra internal seating can be provided, as can internal hoists and powered tailgates. A standard NATO towing hook is provided.

Specifications
Crew: 3
Configuration: 8 × 8
Weight: (combat) 12 730 kg
Max load: 2470 kg
Length: 5.448 m
Width: 2.5 m
Height: 2.194 m
Max speed:
  (road) 100 km/h
  (water) 10 km/h
Range: 660 km
Gradient: 60%
Side slope: 30%
Vertical obstacle: 0.5 m
Trench: 2.057 m
Fording: amphibious
Engine: Detroit Diesel 6V-53T 6-cylinder diesel developing 275 hp at 2800 rpm
Transmission: Allison MT-653 DR automatic, 5 forward and 1 reverse gears
Transfer case: Rockwell AG-VST (modified)
Steering: power-assisted on front 2 axles
Turning circle: 15.5 m
Suspension:
  (front four wheels) independent coil springs and shock absorbers

(rear four wheels) independent torsion bars and shock absorbers
Tyres: 11.00 × 16 with Hutchinson run-flat inserts
Brakes:
  (main) 8-wheel dual air brake, transmission brake and transfer case lock
  (parking) transmission brake and transfer case lock
Electrical system: 24 V
Batteries: 4 × 12 V
Alternator: 200 A
Armament: 1 × 7.62 mm M60 MG
  2 × 4-barrel smoke dischargers
Ammunition carried: 7.62 mm – 1000 rounds
  smoke grenades – 8 in launchers, 8 spare
Armour
hull front: 8 mm
hull sides: 10 mm

Status
Production complete. In service with US Marine Corps (94).

Manufacturer
Diesel Division, General Motors of Canada Limited, PO Box 5160, London, Ontario, Canada N6A 4N5. Tel: (519) 452 5184. Fax: (519) 452 5688.

CHILE

FAMAE-MOWAG Piraña 8 × 8 Armoured Logistics Carrier

Development
FAMAE of Chile has obtained a licence to produce the 8 × 8 version of the Swiss MOWAG Piranha for the Chilean Army where it is known as the Piraña. A prototype was built as an armoured personnel carrier and several other versions of this basic vehicle are under development, including a 120 mm mortar carrier, a 90 mm anti-tank gun carrier, a command and control vehicle and a repair and recovery vehicle. A riot control version has also been proposed. An armoured logistics carrier has also been developed and is in production for the Chilean Army.

For details of the armoured personnel carrier version of this vehicle refer to *Jane's Armour and Artillery 1992-93* pages 296 and 297. Details of the Swiss MOWAG Piranha will be found on pages 441 to 443.

Description
The FAMAE-MOWAG Piraña 8 × 8 armoured logistics carrier uses the main components of the basic MOWAG Piranha 8 × 8 including the drive train, suspension and hull configuration.

The vehicle has a basic crew of three: driver, commander and loader. The engine is located to the right of the driver and the commander is seated behind him. The commander is provided with all-round vision devices for use when the armoured hatch is closed down. This position may be provided with an external machine gun mounting. The loader is seated behind the commander.

The cargo compartment has an internal capacity of 5 m³. Access to the cargo area is via a single downward-opening rear door or through two roof hatches. The compartment is provided with a 500 kg capacity telescopic crane used to load up to 2500 kg of cargo. It is possible to use a fork-lift truck to load cargo via the rear door.

The Piraña 8 × 8 can be provided with two propeller blades at the rear for amphibious operations and the vehicle may be airlifted by a heavy helicopter.

Specifications
Crew: 3
Configuration: 8 × 8
Weight: (combat) 13 000 kg
Max load: 2500 kg

FAMAE-MOWAG Piraña 8 × 8 armoured logistics carrier showing loading crane

Length: 6.373 m
Width: 2.5 m
Height: (top of hull) 1.85 m
Ground clearance:
  (under differential) 0.39 m
  (under hull) 0.5 m
Track:
  (front) 2.18 m
  (rear) 2.2 m
Wheelbase: 1.1 m + 1.335 m + 1.04 m
Angle of approach/departure: 40°/45°
Max speed:
  (road) 100 km/h
  (water) 10 km/h
Range: (road) 660 km
Fording: amphibious
Gradient: 60%
Side slope: 30%
Vertical obstacle: 0.5 m
Engine: Detroit Diesel Model 6V-53T turbocharged

diesel developing 275 hp at 2800 rpm
Transmission: Allison MT-653 automatic with 5 forward and 1 reverse gears
Steering: power-assisted on front two axles
Turning circle: 15.5 m
Suspension:
  (front) independent coil springs and shock absorbers
  (rear) independent torsion bars and shock absorbers
Brakes: hydraulic/air, dual circuit
Tyres: 11.00 × 16 with run-flat inserts
Electrical system: 24 V

Status
In production for the Chilean Army.

Manufacturer
FAMAE, Fábricas y Maestranzas del Ejército, Avenida Pedro Montt 1606, PO Box 4100, Santiago, Chile. Tel: 5561011. Telex: 242346. Fax: 5550944.

CHINA, PEOPLE'S REPUBLIC

Type 59 Artillery Tractor

Description
This tractor was designed to tow artillery such as the 122 mm Type 54 howitzer or the 122 mm Type 60 gun. The fully enclosed cab at the front of the vehicle has sufficient seats for most of the crew of the gun and has a circular observation hatch in the left side of the roof. The rear cargo area has a stake-type body and a drop tailgate, removable bows and a tarpaulin cover. The suspension is believed to be of the torsion bar type and consists of five road wheels with the drive sprocket at the front and the idler at the rear. The Type 59 may be powered by a V-12 diesel truck engine.

Status
In service with China and Vietnam.

Type 59 artillery tractor towing 57 mm Type 59 anti-aircraft gun

Manufacturer
NORINCO, China North Industries Corporation, 7A Yue Tan Nan Jie, PO Box 2137 Beijing, Beijing, People's Republic of China.
Tel: 867570. Telex: 22339 cnic cn.
Fax: 867840.

Type 60-1 Tracked Artillery Tractor

Description
The Type 60-1 tracked artillery tractor appears to be a close development of the Type 59 artillery tractor with differences occuring in details such as the cab shape.

The Type 60-1 can carry up to 5000 kg of cargo and tow artillery or trailers weighing up to 15 000 kg. The forward control all-steel cab has provision for a driver and an artillery detachment and the roof is equipped with a hatch mounting a 12.7 mm Type 54 machine

gun, the Chinese version of the CIS DShK. There is stowage for the crew's personal equipment in lockers behind the cab and the main cargo area may be covered by bows and a canvas tarpaulin. A winch may be fitted which adds 1000 kg to the vehicle's weight. This has a maximum capacity of 17 000 kg and is equipped with 75 m of cable. The engine starting time in winter with the ambient temperature at −35°C is stated to be 18 minutes. Rubber-covered track links are used.

The Type 60-1 is also used as the carrier for the 273 mm Type 83 multiple rocket system. For details of

this equipment refer to *Jane's Armour and Artillery 1992-93* page 702.

Specifications
Weight:
(with winch) 12 500 kg
(without winch) 11 500 kg
Payload: 5000 kg
Towed load: 15 000 kg
Length: 6.117 m
Width: 2.6 m
Height:
(top of cab) 2.81 m
(top of tilt) 3.015 m
(to horizontal machine gun) 3.26 m
Ground clearance: 0.4 m
Track: 2.15 m
Length of track on ground: 3.248 m
Max speed: 48.8 km/h
Range: 400 km
Max gradient:
(with 5000 kg load) 30°
(with 5000 kg load and 15 000 kg trailer) 15°
Side slope: 26°
Fording: 1 m
Engine: 12150L-1 V-12 water-cooled 4-cycle direct injection diesel developing 300 hp at 1600 rpm

Status
In production. Offered for export.

Manufacturer
NORINCO, China North Industries Corporation, 7A Yue Tan Nan Jie, PO Box 2137 Beijing, Beijing, People's Republic of China.
Tel: 867570. Telex: 22339 cnic cn.
Fax: 867840.

Type 60-1 tracked artillery tractor

COMMONWEALTH OF INDEPENDENT STATES

AT-L and AT-LM Light Tracked Artillery Tractors

Description
The AT-L first appeared in 1953 as the replacement for the M-2 light tracked artillery tractor. When first introduced the vehicle was widely used for towing artillery and mortars including 160 and 240 mm mortars, 122 and 152 mm howitzers and 57 mm anti-aircraft guns. These roles have been mainly taken over by 6 × 6 trucks and although some artillery units still use the vehicles as prime movers they are mainly used for other specialised roles.

The engine of the AT-L is at the front with the three-man cab in the centre and the cargo area at the rear with removable bows, tarpaulin cover and a drop tailgate. The fully enclosed all-steel cab has a three-part windscreen with the two outer windscreens being

hinged at the top. A circular observation hatch is provided in the right side of the cab roof. Seats can be provided for up to 12 men. The suspension is of the torsion bar type and consists of six road wheels with the idler at the rear, the drive sprocket at the front, and three return rollers. In 1956 the AT-LM was introduced. It has five large road wheels, with the drive sprocket at the front, idler at the rear but no track return rollers.

Variants
Electronic versions
The AT-L and AT-LM are widely used for mounting electronic equipment including the Pork Trough (SNAR-2) and Small Yawn (ARSOM-2) radars.

Dozer
The AT-L and AT-LM can both be fitted with the OLT dozer blade on the front of the hull for general clearing work; when being used on soft soil at a speed of 4 km/h

it can clear between 80 and 90 m³/h. See entry in the *Field fortifications and related emplacements equipment* section.

Specifications
Cab seating: 2 + up to 8 in rear
Weight:
(empty) 6300 kg
(loaded) 8300 kg
Max load: 2000 kg
Towed load: 6300 kg
Length: 5.313 m
Width: 2.214 m
Height: (cab) 2.2 m
Ground clearance: 0.35 m
Track: 1.9 m
Track width: 300 mm
Length of track on ground: 3.005 m
Ground pressure: 0.45 kg/cm²

Max speed: (road) 42 km/h
Range: 300 km
Fuel capacity: 300 l
Vertical obstacle: 0.6 m
Trench: 1 m
Fording: 0.6 m (some can ford to 1 m)
Engine: YaMZ-204VKr 4-cylinder water-cooled diesel developing 130 or 135 hp at 2000 rpm

Status
Production complete. In service with members of the former Warsaw Pact and countries in the Middle East and North Africa.

Manufacturer
State factories.

AT-LM light tracked artillery tractor with Pork Trough (SNAR-2) radar

ATS-59G Medium Tracked Artillery Tractor

Description
This was first seen during 1972, towing a 130 mm M-46 field gun. Until its correct designation became known the vehicle was called the M1972. It is essentially an ATS-59 (see following entry) with a redesigned cab. The new tractor has a much larger forward control type cab with the cargo area at the rear. The suspension consists of five large road wheels with the drive sprocket at the front and the idler at the rear. There are no track return rollers.

Specifications
Weight:
    (empty) 13 750 kg
    (loaded) 16 750 kg
Max load: 3000 kg
Max towed load: 14 000 kg
Fuel capacity: 580 l
Ground pressure: 0.55 kg/cm²
Fording: 1.5 m

Status
In service with Egypt, the former Yugoslavia, and members of the former Warsaw Pact.

Manufacturer
State factories.

ATS-59G medium tracked artillery tractor (Josef Spurny)

ATS-59 Medium Tracked Artillery Tractor

Description
The ATS-59 medium tracked artillery tractor appeared in the late 1950s as the replacement for the AT-S tractor, and uses a number of components of the T-54 MBT. The ATS-59 is used for towing artillery such as the 130 mm M-46 field gun.

The layout of the vehicle is unusual, with the engine behind the cab, preventing the full length of the cargo area being used as the engine compartment projects into it. The steel cab has a door in each side and there is a circular hatch in the right side of the roof. The rear cargo area has a tailgate, removable bows and a tarpaulin cover. The suspension consists of five large road wheels with the drive sprocket at the front and the idler at the rear. There are no return rollers.

Some ATS-59s have had the rear cargo area removed and a fifth wheel mounted on the top of the rear chassis for towing semi-trailers carrying the SA-2 surface-to-air missile. The vehicle has also been seen in service fitted with a hydraulically operated dozer blade on the front of the hull. A Polish version of this

ATS-59 medium tracked artillery tractor towing 130 mm M-46 field gun

variant exists. See entry in the *Field fortifications and related emplacements equipment* section.

Specifications
Cab seating: 1 + 1
Weight:
(empty) 13 000 kg
(loaded) 16 000 kg
Max load: 3000 kg
Towed load: 14 000 kg
Length: 6.28 m
Width: 2.78 m
Height:
(cab) 2.3 m

(tarpaulin) 2.5 m
Ground clearance: 0.425 m
Track: 2.25 m
Track width: 525 mm
Ground pressure: 0.52 kg/cm²
Max speed: 39 km/h
Range: 350 km (500 km with long-range tanks)
Vertical obstacle: 1.1 m
Trench: 2.5 m
Max gradient: 50%
Max side slope: 20%
Fording: 1.5 m
Engine: A-650 V-12 water-cooled diesel developing 300 hp at 1700 rpm

Status
Replaced in production by the ATS-59G. Poland produced the ATS-59 after production of the Polish-designed Mazur D-350 medium tracked artillery tractor had been completed. In service with members of the former Warsaw Pact, including Romania, and countries in the Middle East and North Africa.

Manufacturers
State factories.
Heavy Machinery Plant, Labedy, Poland.

MT-S Medium Tracked Transporter

Description
The MT-S medium tracked transporter was developed around the same time as the MT-T heavy tracked transporter (see entry in this section) but does not appear to have been produced in very large numbers in the transporter form. Few details regarding this vehicle have been released but it is believed to be powered by a diesel engine similar to that used by the MT-T. The basic chassis is derived from that used for the 152 mm self-propelled gun-howitzer 2S3 (S-152) Akatsiya and has been used for a number of other applications, including the GMZ minelayer (see entry in the *Minelaying equipment* section). It is also used as a carrier for components of the SA-11 'Gadfly' missile system including the associated radar vehicles.

Specifications (provisional)
Cab seating: 1 + 3
Weight: 23 500 kg
Max payload: 10 200 kg
Length: 7.8 m

Width: 3.34 m
Height: 1.846 m
Engine: diesel developing 710 hp

Status
In service with the CIS.

Manufacturer
State factories.

MT-S medium tracked transporter

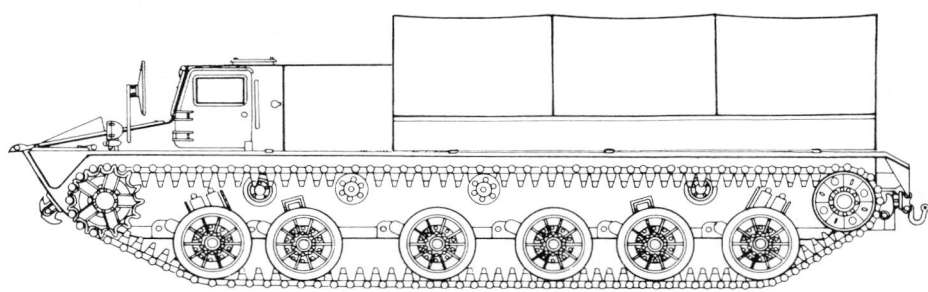
MT-S medium tracked transporter (not to 1/76th scale) (Steve Zaloga)

AT-T Heavy Tracked Artillery Tractor

Description
The AT-T heavy tracked artillery tractor appeared in 1950 and is used to tow heavy artillery such as the 180 mm S-23 gun/howitzer, the 130 mm KS-30 anti-aircraft gun and the 130 mm SM-4-1 mobile coastal gun.

The engine is under the floor of the four-man cab, which is of all-steel construction and has a door either side. The cargo compartment is at the rear and is provided with a drop tailgate, removable bows and a tarpaulin cover. The fuel tanks are under the rear behind the engine and the winch is mounted at the very back.

The suspension is of the torsion bar type and consists of five large road wheels with the drive sprocket at the front and the idler at the rear. There are no track return rollers.

Variants
BAT and BAT-M Dozers
See entry in the *Field fortifications and related emplacements equipment* section.

Radar
The AT-T with a fully enclosed van-type body is used to mount the Track Dish (ARSOM-1). A lengthened version of the AT-T with seven road wheels mounts the Long Track radar.

BTM and MDK-2 Ditching Machines
For details see the *Field fortifications and related emplacements equipment* section.

AT-TA
This is a special version of the basic AT-T with extra wide tracks and other modifications for polar exploration.

Iraqi Army AT-T heavy tracked artillery tractor

Specifications
Cab seating: 1 + 3 (up to 16 in rear)
Weight:
(empty) 20 000 kg
(loaded) 25 000 kg
Max load: 5000 kg
Towed load: 25 000 kg
Length: 6.99 m
Width: 3.14 m
Height: (cab) 2.845 m
Ground clearance: 0.425 m
Track: 2.64 m
Track width: 508 mm
Length of track on ground: 3.836 m
Ground pressure:
(empty) 0.52 kg/cm²
(loaded) 0.68 kg/cm²
Max speed: 35 km/h
Range: 700 km

Fuel: 1415 l
Fuel consumption:
(not towing) 140 l/100 km
(towing) 190 l/100 km
Max gradient: 60%
Vertical obstacle: 1 m
Trench: 2.1 m
Fording: 0.75 m (some can ford to 1 m)
Engine: V-401 V-12 water-cooled diesel developing 415 hp at 1500 rpm

Status
Production complete. In service with members of the former Warsaw Pact, the former Yugoslavia and countries in the Middle East (including Iraq) and North Africa.

Manufacturer
Mzlyshev Transport Machine Plant, Khar'kov, CIS.

MT-T Heavy Tracked Transporter

Description

The MT-T heavy tracked transporter first appeared during the early 1980s and uses suspension components from the T-64 tank. The engine is the V-64-4 diesel derived from that used in the T-72 tank. On the MT-T a forward control cab is located in front of the main drive gear and the large cargo area to the rear can be covered by a canvas tilt.

The chassis of the MT-T is used as the basis for several other vehicles, including the PTS-2 amphibious tracked vehicle (see entry in the *Amphibians* section), the MDK-3 trenching machine and the BAT-2 tractor-mounted bulldozer (see entries in the *Field fortifications and related emplacements equipment* section), and the PMM-2 amphibious bridging and ferry system (see entry in the *Mechanised bridges* section). The MT-T may be used as the basis for the SA-12 'Gladiator'/'Giant' missile system transporter and launcher vehicle.

Specifications (provisional)

Cab seating: 1 + 4 (up to 18 in rear)
Weight: approx 25 000 kg
Max load: 12 000 kg
Towed load: 12 000 kg
Length: 8.63 m
Width: 3.42 m
Height: 2.99 m
Engine: V-64-4 diesel developing 710 hp

Status

In production. In service with the CIS and some members of the former Warsaw Pact.

Manufacturer

State factories.

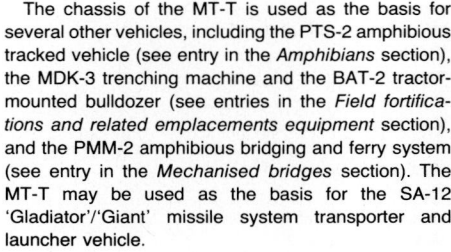

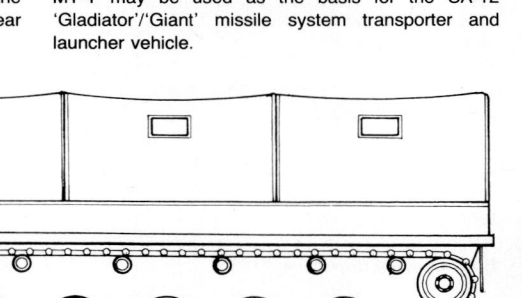

MT-T heavy tracked transporter (not to 1/76th scale) (Steve Zaloga)

MT-T heavy tracked transporter

GM-569 Tracked Tractor

Description

During 1990 the first reports of a GM-569 tracked tractor appeared in technical reports, mainly referring to the vehicle's novel hydromechanical transmission. The GM-569 appears to be a large vehicle, possibly utilising drive components of the T-64 MBT, with a low superstructure over the forward part of the upper hull and a built-up engine compartment at the rear. The driving and crew compartment extends the full width of the front hull. There are six road wheels and four return

rollers. No dimensions, weights or other technical details have yet been released.

The GM-569's hydromechanical transmission is considered to be a considerable improvement over mechanical transmissions and involves a reduction mechanism, a hydraulic torque converter, a planetary gearbox, an equalising block and a hydraulic steering mechanism which imparts good manoeuvrability. Special driving techniques have to be employed to derive the best performance from the system and a column-mounted steering wheel is involved. Pivot turns are possible on hard surfaces. Hydraulically operated and self-adjusting dry plate disc brakes are used when on

the move although a mechanical brake is used for parking. To provide power supplies for the vehicle's various electrical and electronic control systems two AC generators can be powered by a gas turbine engine and there is a reserve system, used only when halted, powered by a reduction take-off from the main engine.

Status

Apparently in production.

Manufacturer

State factories.

FINLAND

Sisu NA-140 All-terrain Vehicle

Description

The Sisu NA-140 was developed for military purposes and the first prototype commenced testing during 1985. Pre-production of 11 units started in Autumn 1986 with full-scale production commencing during 1988. During 1988 the Finnish Defence Ministry placed an order worth $35 million for 112 NA-140s, with first deliveries made during 1989.

The NA-140 is an articulated two-unit vehicle driven by four wide and flexible rubber tracks. The two units are connected by a flexible coupling that also carries the steering assembly and the drive to the rear unit. Power in the standard version is derived from an eight-cylinder diesel engine. Several types have been installed and are available, along with a petrol engine. Articulated hydrostatic power steering is employed.

Both units have a chassis supporting the suspension, tracks and running gear over which are built

light alloy frames for the bodies. Track and road wheel assemblies are interchangeable on both sides. Sisu BTN axles are used throughout, along with disc brakes on both units.

The bodywork is constructed from light reinforced plastic panels. The front unit has four doors and contains the engine. There is provision for the driver and five passengers or 700 kg of cargo. A roof hatch can be provided over the cab front. The rear unit is fully enclosed with a single access door at the rear and can carry up to 12 men or 1300 kg of supplies. Vision blocks can be provided according to customer specifications. Stowage space can be utilised on the roofs of both units. A towing hook on the rear unit allows light weapons to be towed.

The NA-140 can carry a total of 18 men or 2000 kg of supplies and is fully amphibious when loaded. Optional equipment includes a winch with 30 m of cable and a halon fire extinguishing system. The vehicle can also be armoured against small-arms fire and light shell splinters.

Specifications

Cab seating: 1 + 5 (front unit – up to 12 in rear unit)
Weight:
  (empty) 5150 kg
  (loaded) 7200 kg
Max load: 2000 kg
Towed load: 2500 kg
Length:
  (total, overall) 7.65 m
  (front unit) 3.235 m
  (rear unit) 3.45 m
Width: 1.91 m
Height: 2.3 m
Ground clearance: 0.4 m
Track width: 620 mm
Max speed:
  (road) 65 km/h
  (water) 6 km/h
Fuel capacity: 200 l
Max gradient: friction limits
Side slope: 35°
Fording: amphibious when loaded
Engine: GM Powertrain 6.2 l 4-stroke V-8 diesel
Transmission: GM Hydra-matic 3L 80HD automatic with 3 forward and 1 reverse gears
Transfer box: Sisu 2-speed manual
Steering: articulated hydrostatic
Turning radius: 6 m
Suspension: rubber torsion springs
Brakes: disc
Electrical system: 12 or 24 V
Batteries: 2 × 12 V

Status

In production. In service with the Finnish Army and the Ministry of Forestry in the People's Republic of China.

Manufacturer

Oy Sisu-Auto AB, Sisu Defence, PO Box 189, SF-13101 Hämeenlinna, Finland.
Tel: 358 17 5851. Telex: 2315.
Fax: 358 17 197130.

Sisu NA-140 all-terrain vehicle

GERMANY

Kässbohrer Flexmobil FM 23.150K All-terrain Vehicle

Description

The Kässbohrer Flexmobil FM 23.150K is based on the design of the Kässbohrer Pisten Bully, many thousands of which are in use in some 40 countries. The Flexmobil is intended for use as a general load carrier and working vehicle and may be equipped with a load platform covered by a tilt or a passenger body accommodating up to 10 men including the driver. The passenger body has fold-up seats, a roof air-extractor, insulated walls and roof, and a heater.

The Flexmobil uses rubber tracks that can be fitted with bolt-on double steel web plates for difficult terrain such as rock, loose stones or gravel; one width of summer track and two widths of winter tracks, all steel, are available. The main road wheels use a double track guide system and are self-cleaning. There are five road wheels and three track return rollers. A hydrostatic drive is used not only for the transmission but also for steering and braking. An 80 hp power take-off on the hydraulic system can be used to power tools and attachments. A wide range of attachments including snowclearing blades and blowers, cranes and a backhoe may be fitted. The engine may be either a water-cooled Mercedes-Benz or an air-cooled Deutz. Both options are diesels. Also available as an option is a Rotzler 3000 kg winch with 50 m of 11 mm cable. A special towing equipment for winter accessories, such as snow sweeping brushes, can be provided.

The Flexmobil can tow a special tracked trailer with a payload capacity of approximately 2 tonnes. Also available is a semi-trailer that is carried on a fifth wheel

arrangement mounted on the Flexmobil's cargo bed. This has a payload of approximately 4 tonnes.

To transport the Flexmobil over long distances a special single-axle transport trailer, the ETP 9, is available. It is possible to lift the Flexmobil by heavy helicopters such as the CH-53E.

The latest version of the Flexmobil is the FM 23.150K Series 106. This can be fitted with either a KHD BF 6 L 913 152 hp diesel or a Mercedes-Benz OM 366A 150 hp diesel. A modified transmission reduces engine noise and fuel consumption. Other changes are made to the hydraulic drive and steering and the fuel capacity is increased to 165 litres. Various other detail design modifications have been made.

The Thyssen Henschel Breitkettenfahrzeug TH 439 is an armoured personnel carrier version of the Flexmobil FM 23.150K. For details refer to *Jane's Armour and Artillery 1992-93* page 387.

Specifications

Cab seating: (with personnel cab) 1 + 9
Weight:
(with load platform) 4200 kg
(with personnel cab) 4500 kg
(GVW) 5400 kg
Payload: 1200 kg
Load area: 2.2 × 2.2 m
Ground pressure:
(laden) 0.12 kg/cm^2
(unladen) 0.09 kg/cm^2
Length: 4.1 m
Width: 2.3 m
(over summer tracks) 2.4 m
(over winter tracks) 2.5 or 2.7 m

Height:
(to light on roof) 2.5 m
(top of cab) 2.4 m
(load area) 1.03 m
Ground clearance: 0.43 m
Track width:
(summer steel track) 775 mm
(winter steel track) 825 or 925 mm
Track: 1.55 m
Max speed:
(road) 40 km/h
(off-road) 25 km/h
Fuel capacity: 116 l
Gradient: 100%
Side slope: 40%
Fording: 0.8 m
Engine: Mercedes-Benz OM 352A water-cooled 6-cylinder turbocharged diesel developing 150 hp or Deutz BF 6 L 913 air-cooled 6-cylinder turbocharged diesel developing 160 hp
Transmission: hydrostatic
Steering: hydrostatic
Turning radius: on the spot

Status

In production. Has been used by United Nations personnel operating in Lebanon.

Manufacturer

Karl Kässbohrer Fahrzeugwerke GmbH, Postfach 2660, D-7900 Ulm/Donau, Federal Republic of Germany.
Tel: 0561 8011. Telex: 99750 thksr d.
Fax: 0561 801 6733.

Kässbohrer Flexmobil FM 23.150K all-terrain vehicle

Kässbohrer Flexmobil FM 23.150K all-terrain vehicle towing 4-tonne tracked semi-trailer

ITALY

OTO C14 Tracked Cargo Carrier

Description

The OTO C14 is a member of the OTO Melara C13 family of armoured fighting vehicles which includes an armoured personnel carrier, infantry fighting vehicles, an anti-aircraft vehicle, an ambulance and an anti-tank missile carrier (for full details of these vehicles refer to *Jane's Armour and Artillery 1991-92* pages 364 to 365).

The OTO C14 can carry 6500 kg of cargo and has a strengthened suspension to carry this load. The crew consists of a driver and commander and there is seating for three passengers. The driver sits on the left with the commander and passengers seated on a bench seat. The cab is protected by aluminium alloy armour and a 12.7 mm machine gun can be mounted on a pedestal over the cab.

Compared with other vehicles in the C13 family the C14's engine has a transfer to permit the installation of

the transmission parallel to the engine axis to make the pack compact and allow more room for the cargo area behind the cab. The transfer case has two power take-offs. The tracks run on six road wheels each side. The cargo area behind the cab has drop sides and a tailgate that can be removed to carry shelters and containers or for carrying ammunition pallets. A hydraulic handling crane can be mounted at the rear.

The cargo area can also be used for mounting the Istrice minelaying system (see entry under *Minelaying equipment* for details). Other configurations are an artillery ammunition carrier with an overhead gantry for ammunition pallets, a shelter/container carrier, an OTOMAT or ASPIDE missile system launcher, a Selenia SPADA radar carrier and as a rapid intervention firefighting vehicle.

A 10 000 kg capacity winch is mounted in front of the cab. It has 100 m of 20 mm cable and a maximum line speed of 5 m/min. Various tools are also stowed on the front of the cab.

Specifications

Crew: 2 + 3
Weight:
(empty) 12 500 kg
(loaded) 19 000 kg
Towed load: 10 000 kg
Length: 6.67 m
Width: 2.71 m
Height: (top of cab) 2.75 m
Dimensions of cargo compartment: 3.9 × 2.45 m
Ground clearance: 0.4 m
Length of track on ground: 3.482 m
Ground pressure: (loaded) 0.72 kg/cm^2
Max speed: (road) over 65 km/h
Range: approx 500 km
Fuel capacity: 500 l
Gradient: 60%
Side slope: 30%
Vertical obstacle: 0.7 m
Trench: 1.8 m

Fording: 1.5 m
Engine: Isotta Fraschini model V 1286 HTI/ID 38 SS 6
V 9.73 l 90° V-6 supercharged diesel developing
340 hp at 2800 rpm
Transmission: ZF 5 HP 500 automatic, 5 forward and
1 reverse gears with hydrodynamic torque converter
Steering: hydrostatic
Electrical system: 24 V
Batteries: 2 × 12 V, 100 Ah
Armament: 1 × 12.7 mm MG
Armour: aluminium alloy

Status
Prototypes.

Manufacturer
OTO Melara SpA, 15 Via Valdilocchi, I-19100 La
Spezia, Italy.
Tel: 0187 530 111. Telex: 270 368 oto i.
Fax: 0187 530 669.

OTO C14 tracked cargo carrier

JAPAN

Type 73 Tracked Artillery Tractor
Type 87 Tracked Ammunition Carrier

Description
The Type 73 tracked artillery tractor was developed
from 1969 as the replacement for the M4 and M8 high-
speed tractors used by the Japanese Ground Self-
Defence Force. Trials with prototype vehicles were
successfully completed in 1972 and the following year
it was standardised as the Type 73 tracked artillery
tractor, or tractor (prime mover). Production began in
1974 but only a small number were built owing to
restrictions in the defence budget.

The Type 73 has a fully enclosed four-door cab at
the front with the engine in the centre and the
ammunition stowage area at the rear. The suspension
is believed to be of the torsion bar type and consists of

six road wheels with the drive sprocket at the front, the
sixth road wheel acting as the idler. A 12.7 mm/0.50
M2 machine gun is mounted on the roof for anti-aircraft
defence. Some Type 73s have been fitted with a
hydraulically operated dozer blade at the front of the
hull for clearing obstacles and preparing fire positions.
The tractor was used to tow artillery pieces such as the
8-inch/203 mm M115.

The Type 87 tracked ammunition carrier is based on
the Type 73 tracked artillery tractor. Following the
switch from towed to self-propelled artillery by the
Japanese Ground Self-Defence Force, over 100 Type
73s will be converted to Type 87 carriers. The Type 87
can carry up to 50 rounds of 203 mm ammunition and it
is equipped with a crane.

Specifications (Type 73)
Cab seating: 1 + 11
Weight: 19 800 kg

Max towed load: 16 000 kg
Length: 6.13 m
Width: 2.95 m
Height: 2.3 m
Max speed: (road) 45 km/h
Range: 300 km
Gradient: 60%
Engine: Mitsubishi ZF6 6-cylinder air-cooled diesel
developing 400 hp at 2200 rpm

Status
Production complete. In service with the Japanese
Ground Self-Defence Force. Over 100 Type 73 tractors
being converted to Type 87 tracked ammunition
carriers.

Manufacturer
Hitachi Manufacturing Co, Japan.

Type 87 tracked ammunition carrier (Kensuke Ebata)

Type 73 tracked artillery tractor (Kensuke Ebata)

Special Tracked Prime Mover

Description
This vehicle is based on the Type 73 armoured personnel carrier and is used to tow special equipment such as the Type 76 gun locating radar (JMPQ-P7). The vehicle has an enclosed crew cab and probably carries an electrical generator at the rear, but few details are available. For details of the Type 73 APC on which this vehicle is based refer to *Jane's Armour and Artillery 1992-93* pages 405 and 406.

Status
In service with the Japanese Ground Self-Defence Force.

Manufacturer
Mitsubishi Heavy Industries, 5-1, Marunouchi 2-chome, Chiyoda-ku, Tokyo, Japan.
Tel: 81 3 212 3111. Telex: 22282.
Fax: 81 3 201 6258.

Special tracked prime mover towing Type 76 gun locating radar (Kensuke Ebata)

KOREA, SOUTH

Field Artillery Ammunition Support Vehicle

Description
This vehicle is based on the same chassis as the Flying Tiger (Biho) twin 30 mm self-propelled anti-aircraft gun system (for details refer to *Jane's Land-based Air Defence 1992-93* pages 80 and 81). It is intended to supply artillery ammunition support for 155 mm self-propelled batteries and the M109 series of self-propelled howitzers in particular. The vehicle will also have a recovery and towing function.

The Field Artillery Ammunition Support Vehicle follows the same general lines as the American M992 Field Artillery Ammunition Support Vehicle (FAASV) — see separate entry under United States in this section. The vehicle has a crew of four men, three of them located in the raised superstructure. Inside this super-structure, ammunition is located in racks from which it is removed by a stacker mechanism for transfer to the interior of a self-propelled artillery piece via a conveyor system. The stacker mechanism can handle 6 rounds/minute while transferring them via the conveyor to a point 1.6 m left or right of the centre line of the vehicle's rear door; the conveyor can be raised or lowered 1.69 m. The conveyor has a maximum reach distance of 2.73 m. Power for the ammunition transfer system is provided by a 28 V 180 A auxiliary generator.

The Field Artillery Ammunition Support Vehicle uses a torsion bar suspension with six road wheels each side. The track is of the steel double-pin type with detachable rubber pads. There are four shock absorbers each side. Power is provided by a 520 hp Daewoo D2840L diesel.

Specifications
Crew: 4
Weight:
  (kerb) 18 400 kg
  (combat loaded) 26 700 kg
Power-to-weight ratio: 19.5 hp/t
Ground pressure: (combat loaded) 0.7 kg/cm²
Length: 6.47 m
Width: 3.15 m

Daewoo Field Artillery Ammunition Support Vehicle

Height: 3.3 m
Track width: 392 mm
Max speed: 60 km/h
Range: (cruising) 360 km
Fuel capacity: 500 l
Gradient: 60%
Side slope: 30%
Vertical obstacle: 0.7 m
Trench: 2 m
Engine: Daewoo D2840L 10-cylinder turbocharged diesel developing 520 hp
Transmission: GE HMPT500-3 hydromechanical
Suspension: torsion bar

Electrical system: 24 V
Batteries: 4 × 12 V (6TN), 100 Ah
Alternator: 100 A

Status
Prototypes.

Manufacturer
Daewoo Heavy Industries Limited, Special Products Division, 20th Floor, Daewoo Center, 541, 5ga, Namdaemun-ro, Jung-gu, Seoul, South Korea.
Tel: (02) 726 3011. Telex: DHILTD K23301.
Fax: (02) 756 2679.

POLAND

Bumar Labedy 668 High Speed Tractor

Description
The Type 668 high speed tractor developed and produced by the Kombinat Urzadzen Mechanicznych 'Bumar Labedy' at Gliwice as a general purpose tractor unit is capable of fulfilling numerous logistic and other support tasks. It can carry a maximum load of 3000 kg, tow artillery pieces or trailers weighing up to 14 000 kg, and carry up to 12 troops in the cargo area.

The 668 has an all-steel forward control cab located over the engine. Seating is provided for the driver and up to five passengers. A roof hatch is provided on the right-hand side. The cabin is kept at an overpressure for operations in NBC-contaminated environments and extra defrosting equipment can be installed for use in cold environments.

The steel-sided load area located over the engine is used to carry supplies only. Only the rear part of the load area can be configured to carry passengers or supplies. The load area can be covered by a canvas tilt over bows. The towing position at the rear is equipped

Bumar Labedy 668 high speed tractor

with shock absorbers.

The tractor suspension consists of five pairs of torsion bars with shock absorbers on the first and fifth road wheel stations. Power is provided by a V-12 A-650-G diesel via a five-speed gearbox. An engine pre-heater system is provided and the engine may be started by electrical or compressed air systems.

The 668 is provided with a recovery winch with a capacity of 14 700 kg. A version of this vehicle without the winch is known as the 668 BL.

A version of the 668 known as the 668 S is equipped with a front-mounted lattice crane with a lift capacity of 7500 kg and an operating radius of 2.5 m. When fully raised the crane has a height of 7.8 m. The crane can be broken down into three sections for transport on the cargo area.

Other possible variants of the 668 include a fire-fighting vehicle and a cable-laying model capable of pulling a plough which enables cables to be laid to a depth of 0.7 m.

Specifications

Cab seating: 1 + 5 (up to 12 in rear)
Weight: (combat) 13 750 kg

Max load: 3000 kg
Towed load: up to 14 000 kg
Length: 6.28 m
Width: 2.78 m
Height:
  (top of tilt) 2.62 m
  (cab) 2.58 m
  (load area) 1.27 m
Ground clearance: (loaded) 0.42 m
Max speed:
  (cruising) 39 km/h
  (cross-country with towed load) 22-27 km/h
Range: (cross-country with towed load) 500 km
Fuel capacity: 580 l (plus optional 240 l)
Fording:
  (normal) 1.1 m
  (with preparation) 1.5 m
Gradient:
  (without towed load) 35°
  (with towed load) 18°
Side slope: 25°
Engine: A-650-G V-12 diesel developing 295 hp
Transmission: synchromesh, 5 forward and 1 reverse gears
Suspension: independent torsion bar
Electrical system: 24 V
Batteries: 3 × 12 V, 210 Ah
Generator: 2200 W

Status
In production.

Manufacturer
Kombinat Urzadzen Mechanicznych 'Bumar Labedy', 44-109 Gliwice, ul. Mechanikow 9, Poland.
Tel: 04832 345-111. Telex: 036237 zam pl.
Fax: 04832 342-443.

Mazur D-350 Medium Tracked Artillery Tractor

Description
The Mazur was developed in the 1950s and to some extent was based on the CIS AT-S medium tracked artillery tractor. The first prototypes were known as the Mazur D-300; production versions had a more powerful engine and are known as the D-350, although sometimes referred to as the ACS. The Mazur D-350 is used for towing anti-tank guns and heavy artillery up to 152 mm in calibre.

The engine is at the front with the cab in the centre and the cargo area at the rear. The cab has two doors in either side, one at each end of the cab, front windscreens that can be opened horizontally for improved vision and a square hatch in the forward part of the roof. The rear cargo area has a tailgate, removable bows and a tarpaulin cover. The suspension consists of five road wheels with the drive sprocket at the front and the idler at the rear. There are four track return rollers. A 17 000 kg capacity winch and 80 m of cable are fitted as standard.

Mazur D-350 medium tracked artillery tractor towing 100 mm field gun M53

Specifications
Cab seating: 1 + 8
Weight:
  (loaded road) 18 560 kg
  (loaded cross-country) 17 060 kg
Towed load:
  (road) 15 000 kg
  (cross-country) 10 000 kg
Length: 5.81 m
Width: 2.89 m

Height: (cab) 2.695 m
Ground clearance: 0.465 m
Track: 2.448 m
Max speed: 53 km/h
Range: 490 km
Gradient: 50%
Vertical obstacle: 0.6 m
Trench: 1.45 m
Fording: 0.8 m
Engine: D-350 V-12 water-cooled diesel developing

350 hp at 1800 rpm
Gearbox: manual with 5 forward and 1 reverse gears

Status
Production complete, replaced in production in Poland by the ATS-59. In service with Czechoslovakia and Poland.

Manufacturer
Heavy Machinery Plant, Labedy, Poland.

ROMANIA

ABAL Armoured Vehicle for Combat Supply

Description

The ABAL armoured vehicle for combat supply is a variant of the Romanian MLI-84 infantry combat vehicle which is based on the BMP-1 IFV. The ABAL also shares some components and features with the Romanian MLVM mountaineers combat vehicle designed specifically for use in mountainous terrain. For details of both these vehicles refer to *Jane's Armour and Artillery 1992-93* pages 416 and 417.

The ABAL is a turretless armoured tracked carrier with the bulk of its load of ammunition (or other cargo) carried inside the hull, although ammunition may also be carried in ready-use lockers along each side of the upper hull. The maximum payload is 2100 kg, which may be 64 rounds of 100 mm ammunition or 104 rounds of 76 mm ammunition. Other calibre/load combinations can be accommodated.

There are two crewmen and the only vehicle armament carried is a 7.62 mm machine gun mounted to the rear of the driver's position. Other equipment includes an NBC protection system, night driving equipment, firefighting equipment, a nuclear radiation detector and communications equipment.

ABAL armoured vehicle for combat supply

Specifications

Crew: 2
Weight:
  (vehicle) 8400 kg
  (combat) 10 500 kg
Payload: 2100 kg
Towed load: 5400 kg
Power-to-weight ratio: 15.47 hp/t
Ground pressure: 0.49 kg/cm^2
Length: 5.85 m
Width: 2.714 m
Height: 1.9 m
Ground clearance: 0.38 m
Track: 2.3 m
Angle of approach: 27°

Max speed: (road) 48 km/h
Range:
  (roads) 666 km
  (country roads) 500 km
  (cross-country) 383 km
Fuel capacity: 450 l
Fuel consumption:
  (roads) 69 l/100 km
  (country roads) 92 l/100 km
  (cross-country) 120 l/100 km
Fording: 0.6 m
Gradient: 60%
Side slope: 30%
Vertical obstacle: 0.7 m
Trench: 1.5 m

Engine: 4-stroke supercharged diesel
Armament: 1 × 7.62 mm MG
Elevation: −5 to +82°
Traverse: 360°

Status

In production. In service with the Romanian Army.

Marketing Agency

ROMTECHNIKA, 9-11 Drumul Taberei Street, Bucharest, Romania.
Tel: 46 20 87. Telex: 11608 TXKCO.
Fax: 46 03 17.

SOUTH AFRICA

Blesbok (4 × 4) 5000 kg Armoured Freighter

Description

The Blesbok (4 × 4) 5000 kg armoured freighter is a member of the Casspir Mark 11 armoured personnel carrier series and was designed to carry supplies to military and paramilitary forces operating in remote areas. The main user was the South-West African (now Namibian) Police which operates along mechanised infantry lines when on counter-insurgency operations. In total, 160 units were produced. Most vehicles are now operated by the South African Army.

The Blesbok is built on the same chassis as the Casspir Mark 11 which was derived from that of a 15-ton commercial truck. The Blesbok also uses the same protected cab for the driver and passenger, and has many other components of the Casspir. The cab has seating for two men and houses the vehicle's 185 litre fuel tank. The cab has sloped armoured undersides for mine protection and the cab armour is proof against 5.56 and 7.62 mm NATO ball ammunition. The cab roof has a hatch and a small turret for a 7.62 mm machine gun. All windows use 52 mm thick laminated glass. The cab interior is cooled by two impeller fans and both adjustable seats have safety belts.

The open cargo area has drop sides and a tailgate and a tow hook is provided at the rear. Equipment carried includes a 200 litre drinking water tank and two 2.5 kg fire extinguishers. A towing pintle is provided at the front. An optional 1000 litre fuel tank may be carried at the rear.

Variant

Duiker Armoured Tanker
The Duiker armoured tanker is a Blesbok with the cargo area replaced by a 5000 litre diesel fuel tank fitted with a gravity feed system for dispensing fuel,

Blesbok (4 × 4) 5000 kg armoured freighter

Duiker armoured tanker with 5000 litre diesel fuel tank

with an electrical pump as an option. Loaded weight is 13 490 kg. 30 units were produced.

Specifications (Blesbok)
Cab seating: 1 + 1
Configuration: 4 × 4
Weight:
  (empty) 9400 kg
  (loaded) 14 400 kg
Max load: 5000 kg
Length: 7 m
Width: 2.5 m
Height: 3.12 m
Ground clearance: 0.355 m
Wheelbase: 4.3 m
Angle of approach: 46°
Max speed: 87 km/h
Range:
  (road) 850 km
  (cross-country) 560 km
Fuel capacity: 185 l
Max gradient: 60%
Side slope: 30°
Vertical obstacle: 0.5 m
Trench crossing: 0.95 m
Fording: 1 m
Engine: ADE 352 T 5.675 l 6-cylinder vertical in-line direct injection diesel developing 162.5 hp at 2800 rpm
Gearbox: Mercedes-Benz DB 6/3/60 – 5/7.5 synchromesh with 5 forward and 1 reverse gears
Clutch: single dry plate
Transfer box: Mercedes-Benz 2-speed
Steering: ball and nut, power-assisted
Turning radius: 9.15 m
Suspension: semi-elliptic leaf springs mounted on needle roller bearings with telescopic shock absorbers front and rear (double spring pack at rear)
Tyres: 14.00 × 20

Brakes:
  (main) dual circuit pneumatic with engine-mounted exhaust brake
  (parking) mechanical
Electrical system: 12 V
Battery: 1 × 12 V
Alternator: 55 A
Armament: 1 × 7.62 mm MG

Status
In service with the Namibian Police and South African Army.

Manufacturer
TFM (Pty) Limited, PO Box 46131, Orange Grove 2119, South Africa.
Tel: 012 61 2106. Telex: 3-21041.
Fax: 012 61 1462.

SWEDEN

Bandvagn Bv 206 All-terrain Carrier

Development
In 1974 the Swedish Defence Materiel Administration awarded Hägglund and Söner (now Hägglunds Vehicle AB) a contract worth SEK 13 million for the development of a new over-snow/all-terrain vehicle to succeed the Volvo Bv 202 in the Swedish Army. Three batches of vehicles were delivered to the Swedish Army for trials in 1976, 1977 and 1978. Hägglunds was awarded a first production contract in June 1979 from the Swedish Defence Administration. Under this SEK 800 million contract the company delivered pre-production vehicles late in 1980 and began full-scale production in early 1981. Full rate deliveries were made from the middle of 1981 until 1988.

In September 1981 the British Army purchased four Bv 206s for trials in a variety of forms and a further number were purchased to replace Bv 202 vehicles then in service with the Army and Royal Marines; a further order (worth $40 million) for vehicles for the Royal Marines was placed in March 1990. In 1983 the US Army ordered 318 Bv 206s for service in Alaska as the M973 Small Unit Support Vehicle (SUSV – see separate entry in this section). These entered service in 1983-84. During 1988 the US Army placed a new order for a further 390 M973 SUSV vehicles in various forms to enter service during 1989. By 1991 the US Army fleet numbered approximately 1100 vehicles.

The first of a batch of 12 Bv 206Ds for the German Bundeswehr was delivered in mid-1985. A second order for 63 vehicles was awarded during 1989. The Dutch Royal Marines ordered their first batch of Bv 206 vehicles in 1989 and continued to order vehicles with differing configurations during 1991 and 1992 (their total was approximately 200 units by 1992). Around 40 Bv 206 vehicles are used by Dutch United Nation Forces operating in Cambodia.

In October 1992 it was announced that the French Defence Ministry had awarded a contract worth SEK 20 million for an initial batch of Bv 206 vehicles, mainly in ambulance form, for use by the French Army's 27th Mountain Division. It is anticipated that the French Army will eventually purchase as many as 300 to 400 Bv 206 vehicles in different configurations.

Description
The Bv 206 consists of two tracked units linked together with a steering unit, each unit consisting of a chassis with the body mounted on four rubber elements.

Each chassis consists of a central beam, a final drive assembly and two track assemblies. The chassis of the front and rear units are identical except that a two-step drop-down gearbox is mounted in the rear end of the front chassis. The track assemblies are mounted to the central beam by two transversal leaf springs. Each track assembly is built up around a tubular bar which carries the sprocket assembly, road wheels and idler. In each track assembly there are four pairs of road wheels on trailing arms springed by rubber tension springs. The idler at the rear with a tensioning device is also supported by a rubber spring. All four track assemblies of the vehicle are identical and interchangeable. The tracks are rubber with longitudinal textile cord and integral steel profile reinforcements.

Steering is accomplished by changing the direction between the front and rear unit by two hydraulic cylinders, servo-controlled from a conventional steering wheel. The hydraulic system is built up of commercially available components. The steering unit is designed to permit a large freedom of movement between the two bodies.

The engine and transmission are mounted in the front unit. A shaft connects the gearbox with the drop-down gearbox. A disc brake is mounted on this shaft in front of the drop-down gearbox inside the body. Cardan shafts transmit power to the final drives on the front end of both chassis. Early units were fitted with petrol engines but current production examples are fitted with Mercedes-Benz 136 hp diesels.

The bodies are made of glass fibre reinforced plastic (GRP), which is fire-resistant, with PVC foam insulation. Each body is built like a closed box with integrated roll-over protection. Heating of the units is by heat exchangers and the de-icing capacity in the front unit is sufficient to keep the windscreen clear down to a temperature of −40°C. The bodies have holders for lashing cargo in the rear unit and also in the rear part of the front unit. The rear unit is also provided with brackets for carrying four stretchers.

The Bv 206 is fully amphibious being propelled in the

Bv 206 all-terrain carrier configured as a radar vehicle

Bv 206 all-terrain carrier configured for the RBS 90 air defence system

Bv 206 120 mm mortar carrier; the front unit is fitted with a NM 165 Ring Mount for the 0.50/12.7 mm machine gun

Bv 206 all-terrain carrier in service with Pakistan Army

water by its tracks.

Variants

Flat Bed Vehicle
This variant accommodates the driver and five passengers in the front unit. The load capacity is increased to 2350 kg. This variant is available in amphibious and non-amphibious versions.

Anti-tank Vehicle
Anti-tank vehicles may be armed with a Bofors 90 mm recoilless rifle, or a TOW, MILAN or Bofors RBS 56 BILL ATGW on a pivot mount which can be hydraulically raised to the required level. The open-front body is provided with roll-bars which can be quickly lowered. The low profile rear body is designed to withstand the back-blast of the weapon when it is fired and is used for storing ammunition.

RBS 90
The Bofors RBS 90 surface-to-air missile system is carried in two Bv 206s, one carrying the disassembled missile stand and the other the fire control equipment, including early warning radar; the crew is distributed between the two vehicles. For details of this system refer to *Jane's Land-based Air Defence 1992-93* pages 252 and 253.

Command Post/Radio Vehicle
This can accommodate up to six operators in the rear body and driver plus four men in the front body. Door arrangements are identical to the standard carrier version. The vehicle has VHF transceivers in the rear body and all the radios can be operated from the front unit.

Radar and C³I Vehicles
The high payload of the Bv 206 permits the installation of a very wide range of specialist equipment. For instance, a radar vehicle has a special generator and an Ericsson Giraffe 50 AT C-band search radar with an instrumented range of 50 km and a mast height of 7 m. A radio jamming vehicle is equipped with a separate jamming generator driven by the main engine, generating 15 kVA. The antenna is mounted on an 18 m rapidly erected mast.

A radio locating vehicle is equipped with radio intelligence and direction finding systems. The antenna is mounted on an 18 m telescopic mast. Equipment in a radio relay vehicle consists of either VHF or UHF multi-channel radios for automatic relay transmission. The rear vehicle carries spare batteries and a 3 kVA diesel-driven power unit. There is also a 20 m antenna mast for ground or vehicle mounting.

Mortar Carriers
Special shock-absorbing flat beds in various forms enable mortars to be fired from the rear unit of a Bv 206. Mortars tested with this system include Thomson-Brandt and Royal Ordnance 81 mm mortars, with each vehicle carrying approximately 100 rounds of ammunition. A 4.2-inch mortar version carries 60 rounds of ammunition while a 120 mm mortar variant (in both smooth- and rifled-barrelled versions) can carry approximately 30 rounds.

Firefighting Version
The Royal Air Force has three special fire and rescue Bv 206 variants based at RAF Mount Pleasant in the Falkland Islands. These vehicles have their rear units occupied by fire and rescue equipment and are utilised as rapid intervention vehicles in the event of airfield accidents.

Bv 206D
Bv 206 all-terrain carriers used by the German Army are fitted with Mercedes-Benz six-cylinder diesel engines developing 134 bhp at 4600 rpm. The maximum payload is increased to 2120 kg but maximum speed is reduced to 50 km/h.

Bv 208
This is the Swedish Army designation for vehicles fitted with diesel engines.

Bv 206 S
This variant appeared during mid-1990 and is an armoured personnel carrier version of the basic Bv 206. For details refer to entry in *Jane's Armour and Artillery 1992-93* page 440.

Sea Crab
The Sea Crab D500 is an underwater remotely operated vehicle based on the hull, suspension and running gear of the Bv 206. A prototype has been built powered by a 40 kW electrohydraulic power unit with electrical power being delivered by an umbilical cord.

Skorpion-AB
This is an airborne open-topped version of the Bv 206 with the rear unit accommodating a Dynamit Nobel Skorpion mine launching system. It is in the final stages of development for the Swedish Army. For details see Skorpion entry under *Minelaying equipment*.

Ring Mount NM 165
When equipped with a Ring Mount NM 165 the Bv 206 can be armed with either a 0.50/12.7 mm machine gun or a 40 mm MK 19 automatic grenade launcher.

Ambulance/First Aid Station Vehicle
This variant carries a crew of five, four stretchers, a medical specialist and medical equipment. It is provided with a tent which folds onto the rear unit to allow the vehicle to be used as a first aid station. The front unit serves as a surgery while the tent acts as a treatment area for up to eight casualties.

Forward Repair Team Vehicle
A typical example of this variant is provided with a hydraulic crane with a lifting capacity of 1500 kg. A 3600 kg capacity hydraulic winch is mounted at the front. The vehicle carries a repair crew and sufficient spares, tools, and so on, to remain operational for several days. The example quoted is used by the British Army and Royal Marines.

SUSV
See entry under United States in this section.

Other Variants
The Bv 206 has been used for a variety of other roles, not all of them military. Using a hydraulically operated load changer arm the Bv 206 can be used to carry a variety of containers, shelters and various load bodies. The trailer can also be used to carry a light crane or lifting platform and may be configured for a number of special purposes such as a remote area firefighting vehicle, as a mobile workshop or as a field ambulance.

Specifications (cargo carrier)
Cab seating:
  (front unit) 5-6
  (rear unit) 11
Weight:
  (empty) 4490 kg
  (loaded) 6740 kg
Weight of front unit: (empty) 2740 kg
Weight of rear unit: (empty) 1730 kg
Max load: 2250 kg
  (front unit) 610 kg
  (rear unit) 1640 kg
Towed load: 2500 kg
Load area:
  (front unit) 0.81 × 1.4 m
  (rear unit) 2.5 × 1.4 m
Length: 6.9 m
Width: 1.87 or 2 m
Height: 2.4 m
Ground clearance: 0.35 m
Track width: 620 mm
Max speed:
  (road) 52 km/h
  (water) 3 km/h

Max gradient:
(hard surface) 100%
(snow) 30%
Max side slope: 90%
Fording: amphibious
Range: (roads) 300 km
Engine: Mercedes-Benz OM 603.950 2.996 l 6-cylinder diesel developing 136 hp at 4600 rpm (early production) Ford model 2658 E V-6 water-cooled petrol developing 136 bhp at 5200 rpm (could also be fitted with Mercedes-Benz 5-cylinder in-line turbocharged diesel engine developing 125 bhp at 4500 rpm)

Gearbox: Daimler-Benz W4A-040 fully automatic with torque converter, with 4 forward and 1 reverse gears
Transfer box: Hägglunds 2-speed
Steering: articulated hydrostatic
Turning radius: 8 m (6 m with pitch control)
Electrical system: 24 V
Batteries: 2 × 12 V, 105 Ah
Alternator: 55 or 100 A

Status
In production. More than 10 000 ordered or in service.

In service with Brazil, Canada (100), Chile, China, Finland (400), France, Germany, Italy, Netherlands (200), Norway (2200), Pakistan, Spain, Sweden (4500), US Army (approx 1100) and United Kingdom (600 for Army, Royal Marines and Royal Air Force). Singapore ordered 300 units in early 1993.

Manufacturer
Hägglunds Vehicle AB, S-891 82 Örnsköldsvik, Sweden.
Tel: 46 0660 800 00. Telex: 6051 haegg s.
Fax: 46 0600 826 49.

UNITED KINGDOM

Streaker High Mobility Load Carrier

Description

Streaker was developed during 1982 as an addition to the Scorpion/Spartan family of tracked vehicles (for details of these vehicles see *Jane's Armour and Artillery 1992-93*, pages 521 to 527), in order to provide a tracked cargo carrier with a good cross-country performance. It was developed as a result of experience gained in the Falkland Islands campaign as well as a British Army requirement for a vehicle to tow the Bar minelayer. A prototype was built at the end of 1982.

The Streaker is based on the same hull as the Spartan armoured personnel carrier and the Samson armoured recovery vehicle. It has the same automotive layout with the main power plant to the right of the driver and the transmission forward of the driver's position. The engine can be either a Jaguar 4.2 litre petrol engine or a Perkins T6.3544 turbocharged diesel. The transmission is a seven-speed hot shift unit with integral steering. Suspension is through transverse torsion bars and lever arm dampers. The track is of the single-pin, active rubber-bush type, with integral rubber pad and a central horn. The vehicle is fully armoured forward of the load deck, so that the driver has a 'head-down' position with an armoured periscope and an optional night driving sight. Alternatively the hatch can be opened and the seat raised into a 'head-out' driving position. A door at the back of the driver's compartment provides emergency egress to the load deck.

The main load area is a flat bed, 2.75 m long and 2.1 m wide. At each end panels can be hinged out to reveal sponson seating and footwells, and stowage access. Recessed tie-down points are fitted in the decking and along the sides. The drop sides are removable. Maximum payload (including fuel and the deck crew) is 3600 kg. Loading is assisted by an electric winch and by deploying the drop sides as loading ramps. Lights, a towing pintle and so on, are recessed under the decking to allow the vehicle to be reversed right back to a loading platform.

As well as a general cargo carrier, the vehicle is configured for rapid conversion into a variety of specialised roles by the fitting of palletised kits. In a few minutes the vehicle can be adapted for laying anti-tank mines (Bar Mines) or dispensing anti-personnel mines (Ranger). A field refuelling vehicle carrying a refueller

Streaker high mobility load carrier carrying Ranger barrier defence system

unit with a 2730 litre tank has been proposed. This would have an operating laden weight of 8304 kg.

Specifications
Seating: driver under armour, up to 3 deck crew
Weight:
(empty) 5445 kg
(gross laden) 9075 kg
Max load: 3630 kg
Load area: (flat bed) 2.75 × 2.1 m
Length: 4.878 m
Width: 2.21 m
Height: 1.92 m
Ground clearance: approx 0.4 m
Length of track on ground: 2.74 m
Max speed: 80.5 km/h
Range: (road) over 483 km
Fuel capacity: 320 l
Fuel consumption: 1.6 km/l at 48.3 km/h
Gradient: 60%
Vertical obstacle: 0.5 m

Fording: (unprepared) 1.067 m
Angle of approach/departure: 45°/45°
Engine: Jaguar J60 No 1 Mark 100B 4.2 l 6-cylinder in-line petrol developing 190 hp at 4750 rpm or Perkins T6-3544 5.8 l 6-cylinder in-line turbocharged diesel developing 200 hp at 2600 rpm
Transmission: TN15 manual foot-operated with 7 forward and 7 reverse gears
Steering: Merrit system incorporated in gearbox
Suspension: transverse torsion bar, 5 units per side; shock absorbers on front and rear stations
Electrical system: 28 V

Status
Ready for production.

Manufacturer
Alvis Vehicles Limited, The Triangle, Walsgrave, Coventry, West Midlands CV2 2SP, UK.
Tel: 0203 535455. Telex: 31459.
Fax: 0203 539280.

Alvis Stormer High Mobility Load Carrier (HMLC)

Description
Announced in June 1988, the Alvis Stormer high mobility load carrier plays the same part in the Alvis Stormer family of vehicles as does the Streaker in the Scorpion/Spartan family (see previous entry – for full details of the Stormer armoured personnel carrier refer to *Jane's Armour and Artillery 1992-93* pages 452 to 454). It is a flat bed tracked cargo carrier that can be used in a variety of forms, including a platform for scatterable mine systems.

In general terms the Stormer high mobility load carrier (HMLC) follows the same lines as the Streaker but there are six road wheels each side in place of the five on the Streaker. The main load area and payload are increased accordingly. The commander has an armoured compartment surmounted by a cupola, and an overpressure NBC system is provided for the crew.

The Stormer is powered by a Perkins T6/3544 six-cylinder diesel developing 250 bhp coupled to a Self-Changing Gears T300 cross-drive transmission located at the front of the vehicle.

It has been proposed that the Stormer HMLC could be fitted with a hydraulic crane for use in the logistics carrier role, or as a Bar minelaying vehicle. It has also been proposed as the basis for a repair/recovery vehicle with a roof-mounted hydraulic crane.

Alvis Stormer high mobility load carrier carrying Minotaur Vehicle-Launched Scatterable Mine System (VLSMS)

Status
Initial production complete. Under United Kingdom Ministry of Defence evaluation for Vehicle-Launched Scatterable Mine System (VLSMS) role and further production.

Manufacturer
Alvis Vehicles Limited, The Triangle, Walsgrave, Coventry, West Midlands CV2 2SP, UK. Tel: 0203 535455. Telex: 31459. Fax: 0203 539280.

UNITED STATES OF AMERICA

M992 and M992A1 Field Artillery Ammunition Support Vehicle (FAASV)

Development
In 1979 prototypes of three armoured artillery resupply vehicles were tested during HELBAT (Human Engineering Laboratory, Battalion Artillery Test) trials. The BMY Combat Systems vehicle was based on the chassis of the proven M109 155 mm self-propelled howitzer chassis, as was the HEL/AAI vehicle, and was named the M109 Ammunition Delivery System by the company. The FMC Corporation provided a stretched (for example additional road wheel on either side) and armoured M548 tracked vehicle.

Following completion of the initial trials and the Concept Evaluation Test, it was decided that the M109 chassis was most suitable for the Field Artillery Ammunition Support Vehicle, and in August 1980 TACOM issued a request for proposals for the design, construction, test and integrated logistics support for the FAASV. In March 1981 BMY was awarded a contract by TACOM for the supply of five prototype FAASVs under the designation of XM992. These were

delivered during November and December 1981 and underwent DT/OT II trials at Yuma Proving Ground and at Fort Sill until March 1982. Following these trials the XM992 was type classified as the M992 FAASV in the Autumn of 1982.

Research, development, test and evaluation costs for the FAASV up to FY82 amounted to $5.6 million and in FY83 procurement costs totalled $29.7 million for 54 vehicles. FY84 procurement costs were $60 million for 120 vehicles, and FY85 costs were $78.2 million for 170 vehicles. The FY86 figures were $70.2 million for 142 vehicles and for FY87 they were $62.5 million for 141 vehicles. FY88 planning called for $28.7 million for 48 vehicles. Production ceased for a while until 1991 when it was restarted to meet an order for 60 FAASVs, believed to be for Saudi Arabia and worth more than $50 million. In September 1991 a contract for 60 US Army and 20 FMS FAASVs was announced; the contract was worth $42 041 340 and is expected to be completed by the end of April 1993.

The following components are common to the M992 FAASV and the standard M109: hull structure, engine and auxiliary equipment, transmission and drive, complete suspension, commander's and driver's hatches and controls, heating and ventilation system, electrical

components, internal communications equipment and towing provisions.

The M992A1 is basically similar to the M992 but is configured for the support of the 155 mm M109A6 Paladin self-propelled howitzer. See entry under Variants for details.

Description
The hull is made of all-aluminium armour with the driver at the front of the hull on the left, the engine to his right and ammunition stowage at the rear.

The driver has a hinged hatch cover that opens to the rear, in front of which are three M45 periscopes which can be covered by small metal flaps to prevent damage.

The engine is coupled to the General Motors Allison Division XTG-411-4 cross-drive transmission which is at the front of the hull.

The torsion bar suspension consists of seven dual rubber-tyred road wheels with the drive sprocket at the front and the idler at the rear. There are no track return rollers. The tracks are of the single-pin, centre guide type with replaceable rubber pads.

In the forward part of the roof there is a three-part projectile rack removal hatch and behind it is the

US Army M992 FAASV in process of reloading a M109 series 155 mm self-propelled howitzer

US Army M992 FAASV (Pierre Touzin)

commander's cupola. This can be traversed through 360° and has a single-piece hatch cover. A 0.50/ 12.7 mm M2 anti-aircraft machine gun can be mounted at this station.

Prototype FAASVs had a 626 kg capacity crane mounted at the front of the hull but this crane was not fitted to full production vehicles for the US Army (it was, however, fitted to vehicles supplied to Egypt). The 155 mm projectiles are handled in racks of 10 projectiles, for example two horizontal layers of five projectiles each. If required projectiles can also be loaded individually using the powered conveyor to feed the empty racks.

The charges are located in their containers in either side of the FAASV at the rear with fuzes being stowed in the left side of the hull. Ammunition is transferred to the M109 through its lower rear door by a power-operated conveyor at a maximum rate of 6 rounds/ minute, which is higher than the M109's rate of fire. Overhead protection is provided by the large upward-opening powered door of the vehicle. The conveyor has lateral protection from the M109 and M992 lower rear doors. When not in use the conveyor folds up and is stowed inside the vehicle.

The projectiles are transferred from their stowed position in the forward part of the vehicle to the conveyor belt by the X-Y stacker which is part of the ammunition handling system and can be moved vertically and horizontally. The tray of the stacker serves as a working platform for installing fuzes onto the projectiles.

The upward-swinging rear door is hydraulically powered with the smaller lower door opening manually to the right. The commander's adjustable seat is over the rear part of the conveyor belt.

US Army FAASVs are configured to carry storage racks each holding ten 155 mm projectiles plus charges, fuzes and other cargo. For export the following maximum quantities can be carried, according to BMY:

Calibre	155 mm	203 mm
Projectiles	90 or 1	48
Propelling charges	99 or 110	53
Fuzes	104 or 128	56

In the US Army FAASV space has been allocated for special projectiles such as the Martin Marietta Copper-head Cannon-Launched Guided Projectile, the Remote Anti-Armor Mine System (M718/M741) and the Area Denial Artillery Munition (M692/M731).

The auxiliary power unit is located in the forward part of the FAASV's superstructure and supplies hydraulic and electrical power to the vehicle systems as well as charging the batteries. In addition, it can also provide power to the self-propelled howitzer being serviced.

The FAASV also incorporates a number of improvements which are included in the M109A6 Paladin. These include an automatic fire suppression system, NBC VFP protection system, simplified test equipment as fitted to more recent AFVs such as the M1 MBT, M2 IFV and M3 CFV, AN/VIC-1 intercom and an AN/PRC-68 small unit radio. Also fitted are chemical detection and alarm units and chemical decontamination units.

Variants
M992A1
A series of product improvements have been incorporated into the FAASV, leading to the type classification of the M992A1. These improvements include: electrical system enhancements; the integration of a low heat rejection engine and T-154 Track Assembly; removal of the X-Y stacker, plus container stowage and conveyor enhancements; and modification of the upward-swinging rear door adding two small doors to allow conveyor interface with the M109A6 with the rear door closed. These improvements were generated by the US Army's Initial Operational Test and Evaluation (IOTE) of the M109A6 HIP, later named Paladin. The improvements will also increase the operational capabilities of the FAASV with all versions of the M109 series.

M1050
The M1050 is a version of the FAASV for use with 8-in/203 mm howitzer ammunition and is fitted with a stacker device.

Fire Direction Centre Vehicle/Command Post Vehicle (FDCV/CPV)
BMY delivered a fire direction centre vehicle/command post vehicle (FDCV/CPV) based on the chassis of the FAASV to the US Army for trials. This model was fitted with the following equipment: complete hybrid NBC protection system, APU, Magnavox graphic display, Litton TACFIRE digital display terminal, PDP computer, Battery Computer System printer, power distribution system, pocket radio and a PRC-68 radio. Customers for this vehicle in specialised configurations include Egypt (72), Greece (41) and Taiwan (6).

Specifications (M992 FAASV)
Cab seating: 2 (+ 6 passengers)
Weight:
(empty) 19 749 kg
(loaded) 26 105 kg
Max load: 6109 kg
Load area: 3.38 × 3.05 × 2.21 m
Length: 6.67 m
Width: 3.15 m
Height: 3.24 m
Ground clearance: 0.3683 m
Track width: 381 mm
Length of track on ground: 3.962 m
Max speed: (combat loaded, road) 56.3 km/h
Acceleration: (0-48 km/h) 19 s
Range: approx 354 km
Fuel capacity: 511 l
Max gradient: 60%
Max side slope: 40%
Fording: 1.07 m
Vertical obstacle: 0.53 m
Trench: 1.83 m
Engine: Detroit Diesel Model 8V-71T turbocharged, 2-stroke, liquid-cooled 8-cylinder diesel developing 405 bhp at 2350 rpm
Transmission: Allison Transmission Division of General Motors Corporation XTG-411-4 cross-drive with 4 forward and 2 reverse gears
Suspension: torsion bar
Electrical system: 24 V
Batteries: 4 × 12 V 6TN
Alternator: 100 A

Status
In production. In service with Egypt (51 FAASV, 72 FDCV/CPV), Greece (41 FDCV/CPV), Spain (6 FAASV), Taiwan (6 FDCV/CPV), US Army (740 FAASV) and Saudi Arabia (60 FAASV).

Manufacturer
BMY Combat Systems Division of HARSCO, PO Box 15512, York, Pennsylvania 17405-1512, USA. Tel: (717) 225 4781. Fax: (717) 225 4615.

Fighting Vehicle Systems Carrier

Development
The Fighting Vehicle Systems Carrier (XM987) is part of the Bradley Fighting Vehicle Systems (BFVS) family which also includes the M2 Infantry Fighting Vehicle, the M3 Cavalry Fighting Vehicle, and the M993 MLRS carrier, all of which were developed by the FMC Corporation under contract to the US Army. Details of these vehicles are given in *Jane's Armour and Artillery 1992-93*, pages 469 to 474.

The vehicle is a highly mobile armoured carrier used for a wide range of requirements. Major features of the vehicle are its component commonality with the IFV and CFV, overpressure ventilation system, nuclear hardened electrical system, air transportability in the Lockheed C-141 Starlifter transport aircraft, tilt cab to facilitate maintenance and a current payload of 12 700 kg; the vehicle has added gross vehicle weight growth potential through the use of new suspension components in the latest version of the Bradley Fighting Vehicle.

Prototypes of the Fighting Vehicle Systems Carrier were originally built by FMC specifically for use with the General Support Rocket System (now known as the Multiple Launch Rocket System or MLRS), and the first prototype vehicles, under the designation XM993, were delivered to the two competing contractors late in 1978. After trials the Vought system was selected and in June 1980 the company was awarded a $26.9 million contract for 1374 missiles packed in launch containers and 16 self-propelled launcher loaders, to be built by FMC. This vehicle is designated the M993 and 360 of the basic version were produced for the US Army during 1987 with another 350 enhanced systems expected to be built until the end of 1994.

Description
The basic FVS Carrier has a cab-over-powerpack arrangement with the cargo area at the rear.

The aluminium armour plate cab is fitted with noise attenuation materials and large ballistic windows to provide forward and side vision. When used with the MLRS the front windows are fitted with exterior louvres to provide protection during rocket firing and for nuclear survivability. The louvres can be opened or closed individually with levers inside the cab. In a tactical situation the louvres may be rotated to a stowed position on the cab roof. An 'Uparmor Kit' is available for vehicles fitted with the 600 hp engine.

The cab has accommodation for the three-man crew, an overpressure ventilation system, space for radios and provisions and an instrument panel for operating the vehicle. Sufficient space is provided to add a second control panel for weapon system operation.

An overhead hatch above the right-hand seat can be fully opened for use as an airguard, or fixed partially opened for additional ventilation. As an option the cab roof can be fitted with a NATO mount for a 7.62 mm M240 machine gun.

The complete powerpack, which is centered in the vehicle, is interchangeable with the one in the IFV and CFV. It consists of a Cummins 500 or 600 hp diesel engine coupled to a General Electric cross-drive transmission. The powerpack can be removed or installed in 30 minutes without breaking cooling or hydraulic lines and this arrangement enables the powerpack to be operated on the ground outside the vehicle.

The powerpack is wired to accommodate built-in test equipment for rapid fault isolation using RCA's STE/ FVS (Simplified Test Equipment/Fighting Vehicle System), the same test equipment as used in the M1 Abrams MBT.

The powerpack has a negative pressure system where cooling air is drawn through the radiator and is discharged through the exhaust grille above the right sponson. The fuel is carried in two integral tanks under the floor plates at the rear of the vehicle.

The suspension is an elongated version of the IFV/CFV system and each side consists of six dual rubber road wheels, two dual support rollers, two single support rollers, front drive sprocket, raised rear idler and a high return track.

The single-pin track has forged steel blocks, rubber bushings and detachable rubber pads. Track tension is adjusted by a grease-filled cylinder between the hull and idler wheel. Vertical road wheel travel is controlled by high strength steel torsion bars splined to trailing road arms forming a fully independent suspension. Linear hydraulic shock absorbers at the first, second and sixth road wheels stabilise the vehicle on rough terrain.

A suspension lockout system is provided for the MLRS application of the carrier. The lockout is a hydraulically actuated, multi-disc brake mounted concentric with the torsion bar. Lock-out units can be installed at some or all the torsion bar stations depending on the degree of suspension stiffness required. The lock-outs provide platform stability during both launching and loading operations.

In the left rear corner of the cab is the overpressure ventilation system. It consists of a 5-micron dust filter, 3-micron particulate filter, charcoal filter, bypass valve, and an axial-flow fan. Dual positioning of the bypass valve permits air to pass through all three filters or just

Prototype Armored Maintenance Vehicle version of Fighting Vehicle Systems Carrier

XM1070 Electronic Fighting Vehicle System (EFVS) mounted on Fighting Vehicle Systems Carrier

through the dust filter, depending on the mission. As an option this system can be converted to a hybrid system. The present design has an M13A1 NBC unit in the cab. This secondary system provides for the crew's safety if the cabin air inadvertently becomes contaminated during the course of a mission.

Variants

MLRS Carrier
This was the first application for the FVS Carrier, the chassis being designated the M993 for this purpose. Details of the MLRS are given in *Jane's Armour and Artillery 1992-93*, pages 723 to 727.

Cargo Carrier
This is designated the XM987 but is not yet in production.

Armored, Forward-Area, Rearm Vehicle (AFARV)
The US Army tested the prototype of an Armoured, Forward-Area, Rearm Vehicle (AFARV) to resupply armoured and infantry units in the forward battefield area.

That vehicle was fitted with a 1½-ton hydraulic crane to lift pallets of ammunition from trucks to the internal stowage compartment. The crane can also be used to unload pallets. A conveyor system enables the vehicle to offload single rounds of tank ammunition into the tank while the crew remains under the armour protection of the ammunition resupply module. The AFARV can be used to carry 105 and 120 mm tank ammunition as well as TOW and Dragon ATGWs, LAWs and small arms ammunition.

XM-1 Artillery Rearm Module (ARM)
The XM-1 Artillery Rearm Module (ARM) is a General Electric Aerospace project to re-supply self-propelled artillery units operating in forward areas under adverse conditions. It is one component of the projected FARV-A (Fully Integrated/Armored Rearm) programme.

The XM-1 ARM consists of an artillery ammunition module/container carried on the back of an FVSC with an automated transfer arm and conveyer moving ammunition (projectiles and charges) from the module and transferring them into the fighting compartment of a self-propelled artillery vehicle. Transfer rates can be up to 10 items/minute. Operators use a remote handset to input and monitor the ARM while being able to remain under cover provided by the FVSC cab.

General Electric delivered a prototype of the ARM for US Army trials commencing in October 1990. Trials were carried out at Fort Hood using a three-man crew, leading to the XM-1 designation being applied in September 1991.

It is anticipated that the ARM will be carried by other vehicles in addition to the FVS Carrier. General Electric is currently under contract to build and test an ARM II demonstrator capable of handling 20 items/minute.

Armored Maintenance Vehicle
A prototype Armored Maintenance Vehicle (AMV) fitted with a 10-ton crane was built and evaluated by the US Army in 1985. The vehicle was leased to the US Army. See entry in the *Armoured repair vehicles* section.

XM1070 Electronic Fighting Vehicle System (EFVS)
This is an integrated vehicle consisting of an armoured module for electronic systems and operator personnel, an NBC overpressure system for NBC protection, 60 kW onboard primary power unit and a push-button operated automatic 20 m telescopic antenna mast. The vehicle is suitable for mounting the TACJAM, Teampack and Trailblazer systems, for use as a Joint STARS ground station module or as a tactical command post vehicle. A prototype was completed in 1986 and two engineering development models were completed by the end of 1991. Estimated weight of the armoured module is 13 608 kg.

XM4 Command and Control Vehicle
A prototype of a command and control (C^2) vehicle has been built with an armoured module housing equipment and personnel for the command post role, including an NBC protection system. The vehicle, the XM4, is completely self-contained and may also be used as an artillery fire direction centre or air defence battle management operations centre.

Proposed Variants

MLRS resupply vehicle
This vehicle can carry four pods of rockets and a crane for self-loading and unloading.

Armored Resupply Multipurpose System (ARMS)
This is an armoured vehicle capable of reconfiguration in the field for ammunition resupply, refuelling or medical evacuation.

Fuel resupply vehicle
This vehicle can deliver 7570 litres of fuel in one mission, sufficient to supply six M60A1 or five M1 Abrams MBTs.

Firefinder vehicle
For trial purposes an FVS carrier was fitted with the Hughes AN/TPQ-37 Firefinder artillery locating radar. This trials vehicle is being reconfigured.

Corps SAM Carrier
Loral Aeronutronic has proposed a new version of the Chapparal surface-to-air missile (SAM) system, known as the Corps SAM, to be carried on an M987 cargo carrier chassis. For available details refer to *Jane's Land-Based Air Defence 1992-93* page 160.

Armored command, communications and intelligence vehicle
Recovery vehicle

Tactical operations centre
Field artillery ammunition support vehicle
Medical evacuation vehicle

Specifications
Cab seating: 1 + 2
Weight:
(empty) 14 636 or 14 818 kg
(loaded) 25 545 or 30 630 kg
Max load: 10 909 or 15 812 kg
Load area:
(cargo bed between sponsons) 3.96 × 1.78 m
(above sponsons) 3.96 × 2.97 m
Length: 6.97 m
Width: 2.97 m
Height:
(cab) 2.59 m
(chassis) 1.206 m
(top of load area) 1.09 m
Ground clearance: 0.43 m
Track width: 533 mm
Length of track on ground: 4.33 m
Max speed:
(road) 59 km/h
(10% gradient) 26 km/h
Range: (at 40 km/h) 483 km
Fuel capacity: 726 l
Max gradient: 60%
Max side slope: 40%
Fording: 1.02 m
Vertical obstacle: 0.91 m
Trench: 2.36 m
Engine: Cummins VTA-903 14.8 l turbocharged 8-cylinder diesel developing 500 hp at 2400 rpm or Cummins VTA-903T 14.8 l turbocharged 8-cylinder diesel developing 600 hp at 2400 rpm
Transmission: GE HMPT-500-3 hydromechanical
Steering: hydrostatic
Suspension: steel torsion bar
Brakes: multi-disc, oil-cooled
Electrical system: 28 V
Batteries: 4 × 12 V 6TN, 100 Ah
Alternator: 2 × 300 A

Status
In production for the US Army in MLRS role. Ordered for the British Army (71 for MLRS). Also ordered by France (56 for MLRS), Germany (202 for MLRS), Italy (20 for MLRS), Netherlands (21 for MLRS) and Turkey (12 for MLRS).

Manufacturer
FMC Corporation, Defense Systems Division, 881 Martin Avenue, Santa Clara, California 95052, USA.
Tel: (408) 289 0111. Telex: 6714210.
Fax: (408) 289 2150.
Also being produced under licence in Europe for MLRS application.

M548 Tracked Cargo Carrier

Development

The XM548 cargo carrier was designed for the US Army Signal Corps in 1960 using the basic automotive components of the M113 tracked armoured personnel carrier. At that time its primary purpose was to serve as a highly mobile transport carrier for the AN/MPQ-32 Hostile Artillery Radar System. This application did not reach production and a modified version with a diesel engine, designated the XM548E1, was designed using the powerpack and automotive components common to the M113A1 APC. Engineer and service tests on three prototype vehicles were completed late in 1964 and the vehicle was type classified the following year. First production vehicles were completed early in 1966 by the FMC Corporation.

The vehicle is used in the US Army for a wide variety of roles including use as an ammunition resupply vehicle with self-propelled artillery units equipped with the M109 and M110 weapons.

The US Army did not procure any vehicles in FY76 to 1978 but 193 vehicles were bought with FY79 funding of $15.6 million and 242 with 1980 funding of $30 million. The FY82 request was for a further 160 vehicles at $20.9 million. In FY83 FMC produced 29 M548A1 carriers for the US Army plus six for other countries. As of March 1987, 3683 M548s had been purchased by the US Army plus 1295 for export. In total 254 M548A1s were purchased by the US Army with another 18 produced for export.

Description

The engine and crew compartment are at the front of the vehicle and the cab roof, sides, front and rear can be removed for air transport. The cargo compartment has a rear opening that can be secured by two watertight doors. Six hollow aluminium extruded plates bolted in place in either an upper or lower position form the cargo deck. The lower position allows more cargo to be carried or provides leg room for seated passengers. Tie-downs are available for both cargo deck positions. The cargo area can be enclosed using a standard vinyl-coated nylon cover supported by bows.

If required an M66 ring mount for an anti-aircraft machine gun can be mounted over the top of the cab. If this is fitted with a 7.62 mm machine gun, 660 rounds of ammunition are carried, or if fitted with a 12.7 mm/ 0.50 machine gun, 300 rounds of ammunition are carried.

The suspension is of the torsion bar type and consists of five road wheels with the drive sprocket at the front and the idler at the rear. (The M548A1 has hydraulic shock absorbers on the first, second and last road wheel stations.) There are no return rollers. The first and last road wheel stations are provided with a hydraulic shock absorber and the tops of the tracks are covered by a rubber skirt.

The vehicle has the same wheels, sprocket, sprocket carrier, track adjuster, idler, idler wheel, shock absorber and mount, wheels and track as the M113A1 but has a larger diameter torsion bar and the final drive assembly has a different gear ratio.

The M548 is fully amphibious and is propelled in the water by its tracks. On US Army vehicles, however, the amphibious capability has been eliminated. A winch with a 9072 kg capacity is mounted at the front of the vehicle. Optional equipment includes a heater (personnel and cargo areas), heater (engine coolant and battery), and an air brake kit to actuate brakes on the towed trailer, and material handling hoist.

Variants
M1015

First shown in 1982 the XM1015 was a modified version of the M548 intended to carry equipment containers or containerised shelters for electronic systems. It has been used to carry the first production units of the Emerson Electric Company's AN/MSQ-103A Teampack radar monitoring system developed for the US Army under a contract from the US Army Electronics Warfare Laboratories at Fort Monmouth, New Jersey. Teampack is used to monitor ground-based radar systems on the battlefield which include mortar locating, surveillance and air defence radars. The equipment is contained in a shelter carried on the M1015. The M1015 has no provision for a tilt and when carrying the Teampack the vehicle has no provision for a machine gun mounting ring. A telescopic aerial is carried on the vehicle right front. The Teampack containerised shelter has ballistic protection for its contents and crew. The XM1015 was standardised as the M1015. In total, 125 were procured and they also carry the AN/TSQ-114A Trailblazer communications intercept and direction-finding system and the AN/MLQ-34 TACJAM system.

In August 1986 it was announced that the first of 127 Improved M1015 carriers had been ordered at a cost of $21 million. The Improved M1015 has a solid-state engine governor and revised shelter rails. It has a 60 kW generator for powering electronic systems.

Stretched M548A1E1

In 1977 the FMC Corporation completed the prototype of a stretched M548A1E1 about 0.66 m longer than the basic model and with an additional set of road wheels. The standard 210 hp engine was replaced by a turbocharged model developing 300 hp. Other improvements included a transmission that featured hydrostatic steering and a modified cooling system.

M667

This is the basic vehicle for the Lance tactical missile system. The loader transporter is called the M688 and the launch vehicle is the M752. Net weight of the M667 is 6455 kg. The suspension on the M667 can be locked to provide a more stable firing platform.

M730

This has four Chaparral SAMs on a launcher at the rear of the cab. Full details of this system are given in *Jane's Land-Based Air Defence 1992-93*, pages 156 to 159.

Recovery vehicles

A recovery version, known as the XM696, was developed only to the prototype stage.

The Norwegian firm of Hägglunds Moelv AS fitted one of its NM84 wrecker cranes onto an M548 for the Norwegian Army. This crane has a maximum lift capacity of 5000 kg at 3.5 m and a maximum winch pulling capacity of 18 000 kg. Maximum outreach is 5.3 m at which 3400 kg can be lifted.

Rapier SAM system

This was developed by British Aerospace for the Iranian Army, but was adopted by the British Army and consists of a modified M548 with a fully armoured cab. On the rear are eight Rapier SAMs ready to launch. Full details of this system are given in *Jane's Land-Based Air Defence 1992-93*, pages 145 to 147. A standard M548 is used as a missile resupply vehicle and carries battery logistic loads. One version was developed for use by the Forward Area Support Team (FAST). This has a crew of two, a forward-mounted crane, test and repair equipment for forward area maintenance and repair of the Tracked Rapier vehicles.

Radar vehicles

Many countries use the M548 for carrying radars: for example, Contraves of Switzerland has fitted its Skyguard anti-aircraft radar in the rear of the vehicle for trials.

M45

This is used to support the M132A1 flamethrower version of the M113A1 APC; it is not currently in service with the US Army but is held in reserve.

M548A1

This is currently in production and has improved suspension and cooling systems.

M548GA1

This is a low side vehicle that mounts a platform for the German Skorpion mine dispensing system, for details of which the reader is referred to the *Minelaying equipment* section.

M548/S

This was developed to the prototype stage and is essentially an M548A1E1 stretched carrier with an armoured cab and armoured cargo area at the rear. Combat weight with a 5443 kg payload is 15 100 kg. Cargo can be loaded through twin doors at the rear.

LAR-160

AAI Inc of the USA is acting as overall systems integrator to adapt the Israel Military Industries LAR-160 light artillery rocket system to the M548. Also involved are Thiokol (Wasatch Division), Avco Systems Division and Westinghouse, with the intention of providing Rapid Deployment Force units with a long-range artillery rocket system. The LAR-160, which is described in *Jane's Armour and Artillery 1992-93*, pages 730 and 731, has a body diameter of 160 mm, is 3.311 m long and weighs 110 kg at launch. As the body diameter is very similar the LAR-160 can use 155 mm projectile warheads with HE, bomblet and other loads. On the M548 the LAR-160 is packed and fired from 18-rocket launch pod containers (LPCs), two of which can be carried on one vehicle. The LPCs act as transport containers and are discarded once the rockets have been fired. Each LPC weighs 2522 kg and the range is 30 000 m. The weight of an M548 loaded with two LAR-160 LPCs is approximately 12 800 kg.

M548 tracked cargo carrier

M548 tracked cargo carrier of US Army armed with 12.7 mm machine gun
(C R Zwart)

Specifications (M548A1)
Cab seating: 1 + 3
Weight:
(empty) 7439 kg
(loaded) 12 882 kg
Max load: 5443 kg
Towed load: 6350 kg
Load area: 3.32 × 2.45 m
Length: 5.892 m
Width: 2.69 m
Width: (over tracks) 2.54 m
Height:
(excluding MG) 2.71 m
(reduced) 1.94 m
(load area) 1.21 m
Ground clearance: 0.43 m
Track: 2.159 m

Track width: 381 mm
Length of track on ground: 2.82 m
Ground pressure: 0.6 kg/cm^2
Angle of approach/departure: 57°/35°
Max speed:
(road) 64 km/h
(10% gradient) 18.2 km/h
Range: 483 km
Fuel capacity: 397 l
Max gradient: 60%
Max side slope: 30%
Fording: 1 m
Vertical obstacle: 0.609 m
Trench: 1.68 m
Engine: GMC Model 6V-53 6-cylinder liquid-cooled diesel developing 215 hp at 2800 rpm
Gearbox: Allison TX-100-1 3-speed. A torque

converter gives 6 forward and 2 reverse speeds
Suspension: torsion bar
Electrical system: 24 V
Batteries: 2 × 12 V, 6TN, 100 Ah

Status
In production. In service with Australia, Canada, Egypt, Germany, Greece, Israel, Italy, New Zealand, Norway, Spain, Switzerland, Tunisia, United Kingdom and the USA.

Manufacturer
FMC Corporation, Defense Systems Division, 881 Martin Avenue, Santa Clara, California 95052, USA. Tel: (408) 289 0111. Telex: 6714210. Fax: (408) 289 2150.

M973 Small Unit Support Vehicle (SUSV)

Description
During 1983 the US Army Tank-Automotive Command (TACOM) awarded a $24.2 million contract for 268 Bv 206 all-terrain carriers (plus an option for a further 34, later exercised) known as the Small Unit Support Vehicle (SUSV). The contract followed a period of extensive trials carried out using a small batch of vehicles at the Cold Regions Test Center at Fort Greely, Alaska. Most of the vehicles involved in the contract, delivered from Sweden in 1983 and 1984, were issued to the US Army's 172nd Infantry Brigade in Alaska and the Alaskan National Guard. Early M973 SUSVs were powered by 3-litre four-stroke, five-cylinder in-line diesel engines developing 125 hp at 4500 rpm. Vehicles delivered after 1987 are powered by a six-cylinder turbocharged diesel engine developing 136 hp at 4500 rpm.

There are four basic SUSV variants: cargo, ambulance, flat bed, and command and control vehicle.

In 1984 Hägglunds modified a Bv 206 to undertake hot weather trials for the US Army. The changes involved greater engine cooling capacity produced by radiator, water pump and air flow modifications, a new oil cooler, a self-cleaning air filter, transmission modifications (later incorporated into all SUSVs), and dust-proofing of electrical components. The trials were held at Yuma Proving Ground, Arizona, and were completed by early 1985.

In 1988 the US Army ordered a further 390 M973

Bv 206 all-terrain carrier used for trials concerned with M973 Small Unit Support Vehicle (SUSV)

SUSVs from Hägglunds Vehicle AB. These vehicles were delivered during 1989. Continued purchases until 1992 resulted in a total fleet of approximately 1100 vehicles.

For full details of the Bv 206 see separate entry in this section.

Status
In service with US Army.

OVER-SNOW VEHICLES

CANADA

Bombardier BR-100+ Over-snow Vehicle

Description
The Bombardier BR-100+ vehicle was designed specifically for use in marginal terrain such as snow, swamplands and desert. It is an updated version of the Bombardier BR-100 (Bombi).

The chassis is the toboggan type with the fully enclosed three-man safety cab in the centre and the engine at the rear. Entry to the cab is by a forward-opening door in either side. The BR-100+ is delivered with a fully enclosed two-door cab.

The torsion bar suspension consists of four pneumatic tyres (4.60 × 10) either side with the drive sprocket at the front. There are no track return rollers. Two types of track can be fitted: the summer tracks are 711 mm wide and consist of rubber belts with steel crosslinks and the wider (813 mm) winter tracks consist of rubber belts with aluminium crosslinks.

Standard equipment includes an automatic transmission, pusher fan, full instrumentation, differential oil cooler, shoulder and lap seat belts for all three occupants, a heater-defroster, and a lighting system.

Optional equipment includes a spare wheel, tyre and inner tube mounted at the rear of the vehicle, 600 W engine block heater, brush guard, front- or rear-mounted electric winch, pintle hook, hydraulic system, front blade and an all-steel 453 kg payload trailer.

Specifications
Cab seating: 1 + 2
Weight:
(empty) 1500 kg
(loaded) 1950 kg
Max load: 450 kg
Length: 3.15 m
Width:
(with summer tracks) 2 m
(with winter tracks) 2.2 m
Height: 2.01 m

Bombardier BR-100 (Bombi) with fully enclosed cab

Ground clearance: 0.32 m
Track width:
(winter tracks) 813 mm
(summer tracks) 711 mm
Ground pressure:
(summer tracks) 0.1 kg/cm^2
(winter tracks) 0.08 kg/cm^2
Max speed: 22 km/h
Fuel capacity: 45 l
Gradient: up to 75%
Side slope: up to 50%
Engine: Ford 2.3 l 4-cylinder petrol developing 80 hp at 4500 rpm
Gearbox: automatic, 3 forward and 1 reverse gears
Differential: planetary controlled
Steering: manual, through controlled differential
Turning radius: (inside) 1.68 m

Suspension: wheels independently mounted on rubber torsion bar
Brakes:
(main) disc brake on drive line
(parking) locking device on brake disc
Electrical system: 12 V
Battery: 1 × 12 V

Status
In production.

Manufacturer
Bombardier Inc, Industrial Equipment Division, Valcourt, Québec, Canada J0E 2L0.
Tel: (514) 532 2211. Telex: 5832575.

Bombardier Skidozer Over-snow Vehicle

Description
As with other members of the Bombardier range, the Skidozer was designed specifically for use in marginal terrain such as snow, swamplands and desert. There are two basic models in the series, 252G (petrol) and 252D (diesel).

The chassis of the Skidozer is formed of steel on a tubular subframe. The two-man fully enclosed cab at the front of the vehicle has two adjustable seats with safety belts, heater, two front windscreen wipers and thermal windscreens. Entry to the cab is through a large door in either side that opens to the rear.

The Skidozer can carry a maximum payload of 1088 kg and is also available with a four-door ten-man fully enclosed cab that extends to the rear of the vehicle. On the latter model, in addition to the two normal doors, there are two large doors in the rear of the cargo/personnel compartment.

The torsion bar suspension consists of five pneumatic tyres each side and a drive sprocket at the rear. There are no return rollers. Two types of track can be fitted, both of the rubber belt type with steel or aluminium crosslinks and with a width of 740 or 1040 mm.

Standard equipment includes a dry air cleaner, suction-type fan, full instrumentation, differential oil cooler and a lighting system. Optional equipment includes six-way straight blade/six-way U-blade, power steering, two-speed gearbox, hydraulic systems, solid rubber tyres, rotating beacon, block heater and mirrors.

Bombardier Skidozer over-snow vehicle with 12-man cab

Specifications (252G, military version)
Cab seating: 1 + 9
Weight: 3936 kg

Payload: 1088 kg
Length: 4.09 m
Width: (overall) 2.946 m

Height:
(top of lamp) 2.546 m
(top of tilt) 2.35 m
Ground clearance: 0.305 m
Track width: 1.04 m
Max speed: 34.6 km/h
Fuel capacity: 170 l
Gradient: up to 80% with front blade
Side slope: up to 60%
Engine: Ford 6-cylinder petrol developing 124 hp at 3600 rpm
Gearbox: Ford C6 automatic with 3 forward and

1 reverse gears
Differential: planetary controlled
Steering: manual operating through controlled differential
Turning radius: (inside) 3.66 m
Suspension: wheels independently mounted on rubber torsion bar
Brakes:
(main) disc on drive line
(parking) mechanical on drive line
Electrical system: 12 V
Battery: 1 × 12 V, 85 Ah

Alternator: 60 A

Status
In service with Argentina, Canada, Greece, Italy, the Royal Air Force, Turkey (Army, Navy and Air Force) and the US Air Force.

Manufacturer
Bombardier Inc, Industrial Equipment Division, Valcourt, Québec, Canada J0E 2L0.
Tel: (514) 532 2211. Telex: 5832575.

COMMONWEALTH OF INDEPENDENT STATES

GT-SM Tracked Amphibious Over-snow Vehicle

Description
The GT-SM, or GAZ-71 as it is also known, is the replacement for the earlier GT-S tracked vehicle. It is widely used in marshy and snow-covered areas as it has a very low ground pressure and is used for both civil and military roles. The GT-SM has the same load-carrying capability as the earlier vehicle but has a more powerful engine.

The GT-SM is fully amphibious, propelled in the water by its tracks. The engine and cab are at the front of the vehicle, which is enclosed and has a door in either side and two roof hatches. The load area is normally covered by a tarpaulin cover with integral side and rear windows. Entry to the rear is by twin doors in the rear of the hull. The suspension is of the torsion bar type and consists of six large road wheels with the last road wheel acting as the idler, with the drive sprocket at the front. There are no track return rollers.

Specifications
Cab seating: 1 + 1 (up to 10 in rear)
Weight:
(empty) 3750 kg
(loaded) 4750 kg
Max load: 1000 kg
Towed load: 2000 kg
Length: 5.365 m
Width: 2.585 m

GT-SM tracked amphibious over-snow vehicle

Height: 1.74 m
Ground clearance: 0.38 m
Track: 2.18 m
Track width: 390 mm
Length of track on ground: 3.63 m
Ground pressure: 0.17 kg/cm²
Max speed:
(road) 50 km/h
(water) 5-6 km/h
Range: 500 km (estimate)

Fuel capacity: 300 l
Engine: GAZ-71 V-8 water-cooled petrol developing 110 hp

Status
Production complete. In service with the CIS.

Manufacturer
Gor'kiy Motor Vehicle Plant, Gor'kiy, CIS.

GT-T Tracked Amphibious Over-snow Vehicle

Description
The GT-T is the largest in the GT range of tracked amphibious over-snow vehicles. It can carry a maximum of 2000 kg of cargo and tow a trailer weighing up to 4000 kg.

The engine is at the front of the hull and extends rearwards into the crew compartment. The driver is seated on the left side and the vehicle commander on the right, both with a side door, and the commander has a circular hatch in the roof. The load area is at the rear and is usually covered by a tarpaulin cover. Up to ten men can be seated in the rear. An unusual feature of the GT-T is that the fuel tanks are positioned externally above the tracks on each side at the rear.

The torsion bar suspension consists of six road wheels with the idler at the rear and the drive sprocket at the front. The road wheels are similar to those used on the PT-76 light amphibious tank family, and are also used as the basis for the more recent MT-LB multi-purpose tracked vehicle (*Jane's Armour and Artillery 1992-93*, pages 327 to 330).

The GT-T is fully amphibious. Most sources state that it is propelled in the water by its tracks at a speed of between 5 and 6 km/h.

Variants
A number of GT-Ts have had a fifth wheel mounted to the rear of the cab for towing semi-trailers carrying missiles such as the SA-2. They are designated the GT-TS.

Troops boarding GT-T tracked amphibious over-snow vehicles during winter exercises

A number of specialised civilian models have been developed with a fully enclosed cabin at the rear. In 1965 the GT-T maintenance vehicle entered service with the designation MTO-SG. Mounted at the front of the vehicle is an A-frame for changing components and inside the hull rear is a workshop with a petrol-driven power generator, electric drill, electric grinder, arc welding equipment, compression pressure meter and a full set of tools. The A-frame can lift a maximum load of 1500 kg and radios are fitted as standard on all repair vehicles.

A field kitchen version has been produced and a version has been reported carrying a modified aircraft jet engine to carry out NBC decontamination of equipment and vehicles.

Specifications
Cab seating: 1 + 2 (up to 10 in rear)
Weight:
(empty) 8200 kg
(loaded) 10 200 kg
Max load: 2000 kg

Towed load: 4000 kg
Length: 6.34 m
Width: 3.14 m
Height: 2.16 m
Ground clearance: 0.45 m
Track width: 540 mm
Length of track on ground: 3.914 m
Ground pressure: (loaded) 0.24 kg/cm^2

Max speed:
(road) 45.5 km/h
(water) 6 km/h
Range: 500 km
Max gradient: 60%
Engine: 1Z-6 6-cylinder water-cooled diesel developing 192 hp

Status
In service with the CIS.

Manufacturer
State factories.

MT-L Tracked Amphibious Over-snow Vehicle

Development
The MT-L is thought to have been developed at the same time as the GT-T vehicle which is specifically an over-snow vehicle and is also used in swampy areas, whereas the MT-L is not strictly an over-snow vehicle as its ground pressure is 0.42 kg/cm^2 compared with the 0.24 kg/cm^2 of the GT-T.

A special variant of the MT-L, the MT-LV, has a ground pressure of 0.27 kg/cm^2, which puts it in almost the same class as the GT-T. Its major difference from the MT-L is probably wider tracks and hence a lower ground pressure.

The MT-L is the basis for a complete family of full tracked vehicles which replaces unarmoured over-snow vehicles, unarmoured artillery tractors, armoured artillery tractors and even APCs.

The MT-LB multi-purpose tracked vehicle, fully described and illustrated in *Jane's Armour and Artillery 1992-93*, pages 327 to 330, is a member of the family.

Description
The fully enclosed cab is at the front of the hull and can seat eight men including the vehicle commander and the driver. The engine of the MT-L is in the rear part of the cab. Normal means of entry is through the door in either side of the hull, but there is also a roof hatch.

The load area is at the back and is provided with drop tailgate, bows and a tarpaulin cover. The torsion bar suspension consists of six road wheels with the drive sprocket at the front and the idler at the rear. The MT-L can be fitted with extra-wide 565 mm tracks and with an aggressive grouser to facilitate over-snow and soft vehicle operations. This model is designated the MT-LV and has a ground pressure of 0.27 kg/cm^2. There are no track return rollers. The road wheels are similar to those used on members of the PT-76 light amphibious tank family and are also used on the MT-LB with a hydraulic shock absorber being mounted at the first and last road wheel stations.

MT-L tracked amphibious over-snow vehicle

The MT-L is fully amphibious without preparation, being propelled in the water by its tracks at a maximum speed of 6 km/h. A bilge pump is fitted as standard.

Specifications
Cab seating: 1 + 7 (up to 10 in rear)
Weight:
(empty) 8500 kg
(loaded, without trailer) 13 000 kg
(loaded, with trailer) 11 000 kg
Max load:
(without trailer) 4500 kg
(loaded, with trailer) 2500 kg
Towed load: 7000 kg
Length: 6.364 m
Width: 2.85 m
Height: 2.013 m
Ground clearance: 0.4 m
Track width: 350 mm
Length of track on ground: 3.7 m
Track: 2.5 m
Ground pressure: 0.428 kg/cm^2

Max speed:
(road, without trailer) 61.5 km/h
(road, with trailer) 46.8 km/h
(water) 5-6 km/h
Range: 500 km
Max gradient:
(without trailer) 60%
(with trailer) 40%
Side slope: 40%
Engine: YaMZ-238V V-8 diesel developing 230 hp at 2100 rpm
Transmission: manual with 6 forward and 1 reverse gears
Steering: clutch and brake
Suspension: torsion bar
Electrical system: 24 V

Status
In production. In service with the CIS.

Manufacturer
State factories.

DT-10, DT-20 and DT-30 Tracked Over-snow Transporters

Description
The DT-10, DT-20 and DT-30 tracked over-snow transporters are special purpose vehicles developed specifically for arctic use. All are powered by the same diesel engine as the MT-T and MT-S tracked transporters (see entries in *Tracked prime movers, cargo carriers and armoured logistic vehicles* section) rated at 730 hp. The figures behind the DT- denote the total payload of the vehicle involved in tonnes, spread over the tractor unit and a powered trailer driven via a shaft from the tractor unit engine. All three vehicles are fitted with special 1.1 m wide tracks. On the DT-30 the ground pressure resulting from the use of these tracks

DT-20 tracked over-snow transporter with powered trailer

is 0.27 kg/cm^2 and top speed is 37 km/h.

The DT-10 and DT-20 both have four road wheels each side; the DT-30 has six. The DT-20 weighs approximately 27-tonnes while a fully loaded DT-30 weighs 59-tonnes. One DT-30 can carry a full company of men complete with their weapons.

The DT-10P, DT-20P and DT-30P are variants with provision for amphibious operations.

All three vehicles have the same general appearance but vary in scale. Each vehicle has a forward control cab with seating for two or three men, including the driver, and a housing over the cab appears to incorporate NBC collective protection equipment for the cab. The cargo areas on both the tractor unit and the powered trailer have high vertical sides and are covered by tarpaulins.

Status
In production. In service with the CIS.

Manufacturer
State factories.

JAPAN

Type 60 Over-snow Vehicle

Description

In 1952 the Komatsu Manufacturing Company developed the KC-20 over-snow vehicle primarily for civilian use. Further development resulted in the KC-20-35 which entered production in 1960 and is widely used in Japan for civil applications.

The KC-20-35 was followed by the KC-20-3 which, with modifications, was adopted by the Japanese Ground Self-Defence Force in 1960 as the Type 60 Snow Mobile, or Medium Snow Mobile as it is sometimes called. It is widely used in the northern main Japanese island of Hokkaido.

The engine is at the front of the vehicle with the crew and passenger/cargo area at the rear. The windscreen can be folded forwards onto the bonnet and the cargo area has bows, a tarpaulin-type cover with side windows and a drop tailgate at the rear.

The suspension is the bogie/torsion bar type with each side having eight dual road wheels, drive sprocket, idler and two track return rollers.

Specifications
Cab seating: 1 + 9
Weight:
  (empty) 2870 kg
  (loaded) 3770 kg
Max load: 900 kg
Max towed load: 1500 kg
Length: 4.07 m
Width: 1.98 m
Height: 2.05 m
Ground clearance: 0.3 m
Track: 1.34 m
Ground pressure: 0.105 kg/cm^2
Trench: 1.006 m

Type 60 over-snow vehicle (Kensuke Ebata)

Max speed: 36 km/h
Range: 135 km
Fuel capacity: 90 l
Max gradient: 60%
Engine: Toyota 6-cylinder water-cooled petrol developing 105 hp at 3400 rpm
Gearbox: manual, 4 forward and 1 reverse gears
Suspension: bogie/torsion bar
Electrical system: 12 V

Status
Production complete. In service with the Japanese Ground Self-Defence Force.

Manufacturers
Komatsu Manufacturing Company and Ohara Ironworks, Japan.

Type 61 Over-snow Vehicle

Description

To meet the requirements of the Japanese Ground Self-Defence Force the Komatsu company and the Ohara Ironworks built a full tracked over-snow vehicle designated the KC-50-2. The prototype was completed in 1955 and after modification was adopted as the Type 61 Large Snow Mobile in 1961. In addition to being used as a cargo/troop carrier it is also used to tow 105 and 155 mm artillery weapons mounted on skis.

The engine is at the front of the vehicle with the crew and passenger/cargo area at the rear. The engine is fitted with a turbocharger for high altitude operations and aluminium is used wherever possible to save weight. The windscreen can be folded forwards onto the bonnet and the cargo area has a drop tailgate, bows and a tarpaulin cover with side windows.

The suspension is the bogie/torsion bar type with each side having eight dual road wheels, drive sprocket, idler and three track return rollers.

The Type 61 is distinguishable from the Type 60 by its larger size and much deeper engine compartment.

Specifications
Cab seating: 1 + 10
Weight:
  (empty) 5220 kg
  (loaded) 6500 kg
Max load: 1280 kg
Max towed load: 3200 kg
Length: 5.34 m
Width: 2.5 m
Ground clearance: 0.34 m
Track: 1.71 m
Track width: 790 mm

Length of track on ground: 3 m
Ground pressure: 0.135 kg/cm^2
Max speed: 35 km/h
Range: 166 km
Fuel capacity: 160 l
Max gradient: 60%
Trench: 1.5 m
Engine: Isuzu DA-120T 6-cylinder water-cooled diesel developing 155 hp at 2600 rpm
Gearbox: manual, 5 forward and 1 reverse gears
Suspension: bogie/torsion bar

Status
Production complete. In service with the Japanese Ground Self-Defence Force.

Manufacturer
Komatsu Manufacturing Company and Ohara Ironworks, Japan.

SWEDEN

Bandvagn Bv 202 Tracked Over-snow Vehicle

Development

After the Second World War the Swedish Army bought a number of war surplus Studebaker Weasel over-snow vehicles but by the early 1950s they were becoming expensive to maintain. Between 1954 and 1956 the Swedish Ordnance Department evaluated a number of vehicles as possible replacements for the Weasel but none of the vehicles offered met its requirements. In 1956 a number of Swedish companies were approached and asked if they could design an over-snow vehicle, but none showed any interest in the project. In 1957 the Swedish Army started its own project and following trials with test rigs, two prototypes were completed in 1958. These were followed by another batch of 10 vehicles in 1960. In

1960 the completed design was sent out to Swedish companies for competitive bidding. Late in 1961 Volvo was awarded a contract to prepare the design for production. First production vehicles were completed by Bolinder-Munktell in 1962-63.

By early 1980 some 5000 Bv 202s had been delivered, with final deliveries made in 1981.

Description

The Bv 202 consists of two tracked units joined by a universal coupling. The front and rear units have identical subframes and their bodies are of all-welded construction. The front unit contains the engine and transmission at the front and the fully enclosed cab at the rear. The driver is seated on the left with the vehicle commander to his right. The cab is insulated from the engine compartment by aluminium sheets covering a 25 mm compressed layer of mineral wool (rockwool). The cab has a heater as a standard fitting. The rear

unit, which can be fitted with a heater as an optional extra, is provided with a drop tailgate and a tarpaulin cover. A maximum load of 800 to 1000 kg can be carried in the rear unit.

Power from the engine is transmitted to a main gearbox which is combined with a transfer box. Power is transmitted from the transfer box to the drive axles at the front end of both units via propeller shafts.

The suspension system consists of torsion bars with pivoting and bogie arms, and rubber helper springs. The torsion bars are attached to the bottom of the front and rear of each units, for example two torsion bars per unit. This means that each torsion bar carries four wheels, two on each side. The fifth and rear wheel on each side serves as a track tensioning wheel and therefore has an individual rubber suspension system. The five road wheels each side all have pneumatic tyres. The drive sprocket is at the front of each unit and there is a single track return roller. The tracks consist of

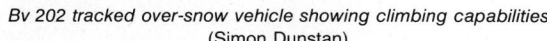
Bv 202 tracked over-snow vehicle showing climbing capabilities
(Simon Dunstan)

Bv 202 tracked over-snow vehicle in typical operating environment

endless rubber bands reinforced with stainless steel wire. They are moulded in one piece and have embedded steel plates which not only provide a meshing surface for the teeth of the drive sprocket, but also serve as retainers for the track guide tongues which are made of light alloy.

The steering system is mounted in the front unit and is of the hydrostatic type. It consists of a hydraulic pump, steering valve, steering wheel and steering cylinder. If the pump pressure should fail for any reason the vehicle can still be steered. The steering cylinder is double-acting and actuates the steering joint in such a way that the two vehicle units are deflected in relation to each other. Apart from lateral steering deflection, the two vehicle units are able to move horizontally in relation to each other by up to 40°. They can also move up to 34° vertically and if necessary can be lifted or lowered in relation to each other by a maximum of 180 mm. The steering joint has two damping units with strong rubber springs, one on the front unit and the other on the rear.

The basic vehicle is fully amphibious, being propelled in the water by its tracks. Standard equipment includes two bilge pumps, jack, tools, towing cable, axe, crowbar, spade and two jerricans. Optional equipment includes a heater for the rear unit, tropical kit, fully enclosed rear unit, cold starting device, torque converter and stowage bin on the roof of the rear unit.

The final model was the Bv 202 Mk 2 which has a more powerful engine and a different transmission. The Bv 203 has a 24 V electrical system, a hard-top for the rear unit and is radio-suppressed.

Specifications
(Bv 202 Mk 1; data in square brackets relate to Bv 202 Mk 2 where different)
Seating:
(front) 1 + 1
(rear) 8-10
Weight:
(empty) 2900 kg
(loaded) 4200 [4400] kg
Max load:
(road) 1000 [1200] kg
(cross-country) 800 [1000] kg
Load area: (rear) 2.3 × 1.56 m
Length: 6.172 [6.175] m
Width: 1.759 m
Height: 2.21 m
Ground clearance: 0.3 [0.28] m
Track: 1.118 m
Ground pressure: 0.85 [0.09] kg/cm²

Max speed:
(road) 39 km/h
(water) 3.3 [3] km/h
Range: 400 km
Fuel capacity: 156 l
Max gradient: 60%
Vertical obstacle: 0.5 m
Engine: Volvo B18 [Volvo B20B]
Engine type: 4-cylinder petrol
Engine hp: 91 [97] bhp at 5300 rpm
Gearbox: manual with 4 forward and 1 reverse gears
Clutch: single dry disc
Transfer box: 2-speed
Steering: power-assisted
Turning radius: 6.8 m
Brakes: hydraulic
Electrical system: 24 V
Batteries: 72 Ah

Status
Production complete. In service with Finland (including Mk 2 version), Netherlands (Marines, 60), Norway and Turkey.

Manufacturer
Volvo BM, S-631 85 Eskilstuna, Sweden.

UNITED STATES OF AMERICA

LMC 1500 Over-snow Vehicle

Description
The LMC 1500 over-snow vehicle replaced the earlier LMC 1450 in production and is available in three versions. One is a two-man cab version with an uncovered cargo area measuring 1.7 × 1.778 m and another a five-man cab with a reduced cargo area measuring 1.122 × 1.7 m. A fully enclosed full cab version with a covered cargo area or seating for the driver and up to seven passengers is also available.

In all forms the LMC 1500 has a maximum load capacity of 1088 kg which is reduced to 454 kg when crossing deep unpacked snow. Two widths of track are available, 711 mm for summer use and 914 mm to enable the vehicle to cross rough terrain as well as snow. The tracks are three-ply rubber with heat-treated steel cleats and steel grousers can be fitted to increase traction over rough ground. The suspension each side is three or four rubber-tyred road wheels with trailing arms and there are no return rollers. The drive sprocket is at the rear.

The driver and passenger are provided with bucket seats and seat belts. Passengers in the five-seat version are also provided with bucket seats but rear passengers on the eight-man version use padded folding benches. The driver and forward passenger are provided with doors and on the cab models a rear door is fitted. All windows use safety glass.

The vehicle is powered by an AMC 258 petrol engine allied to a Chrysler A727 automatic transmission and a torque converter. Steering is provided by a planetary steering differential using two steering levers in front of the driver's seat. The levers actuate a master cylinder which in turn actuates slave cylinders connected by

LMC 1500 over-snow vehicle with roll bars, as delivered to US Navy

linkage to each steering band.
Roll bars may be fitted if required.

Specifications
Crew: 2 + up to 6
Weight: (base vehicle)
(empty, summer tracks) 1950 kg
(empty, wide tracks) 2086 kg
Max load: 1088 kg
Length:
(four axles) 2.972 m

(three axles) 2.667 m
Width:
(cab) 1.71 m
(overall, summer tracks) 2.13 m
(overall, wide tracks) 2.489 m
Height: 2.11 m
Ground clearance: (with differential guard) 0.23 m
Tread width: 1.422 m
Track width: 711 or 914 mm
Max speed: (hard surface) 32 km/h
Fuel capacity: 110 l

Fording: 0.355 m
Gradient: (hard snow) 80%
Vertical obstacle: 0.254 m
Engine: AMC 258 6-cylinder liquid-cooled petrol developing 120 hp at 3500 rpm
Transmission: Chrysler A727 automatic with 3 forward and 1 reverse speeds

Turning radius: 3.048 m
Electrical system: 12 V
Battery: 1 × 12 V, 70 Ah
Alternator: 66 A

Status
In production. In service with US Army (6), Navy (6)

and Marine Corps (2).

Manufacturer
Logan Manufacturing Company, PO Box 407, Logan, Utah 84321, USA.
Tel: (801) 753 0220.

LMC 1200 Over-snow Vehicle

Description
Although designed primarily for over-snow operation, the LMC 1200 can be used over other types of marginal terrain such as swamps. The basic vehicle has a two-man fully enclosed cab at the front of the vehicle and optional roll bars can be fitted to enable it to withstand two times its weight. Entry to the cab is by a door in each side that opens to the front. There is a combined heater and windscreen defroster unit and an optional second heater can be fitted into the cab. In all models seat belts are standard equipment for each crew member and passenger.

Fitted with the standard two-man cab the LMC 1200 has 4.08 m² of uncovered cargo area behind the cab, with a five-man cab it has 2.6 m² of uncovered cargo area and with the fully enclosed 10-man cab, with the bench seats folded, it has 3.9 m².

The engine is in the forward part of the cab which is insulated to decrease noise level. Steering is by a planetary steering differential providing drive to both track systems. The driver has two levers which actuate the hydraulic master cylinder, which in turn actuates the slave cylinders connected by linkage to each steering band.

The suspension each side consists of five rubber-tyred road wheels with the drive sprocket at the rear. There are no track return rollers and the track grousers are of steel alloy. The standard track is 0.914 m wide but the LMC 1200 is also available with 1.152 m tracks.

Specifications (LMC 1200 with 914 mm wide tracks)
Cab seating: 2 + up to 10
Weight: (empty) 2803 kg
Max load: 1361 kg
Normal load: 453-907 kg

LMC 1200 over-snow vehicle with 10-man fully enclosed body

Length: 4.114 m
Width: 2.526 m
Height: 2.108 m
Ground clearance: 0.254 m
Track width: 914 mm
Ground pressure: 0.07 kg/cm²
Max speed: (with outboard reduction gearing) 27 km/h
Fuel capacity: 159 l
Gradient:
  (dirt) 80%
  (snow) 60%
Engine: Ford 6-cylinder petrol developing 124 hp
Gearbox: Ford C-6 automatic, 3 forward and 1 reverse gears

Differential steering: planetary controlled
Turning radius: 4.572 m
Suspension: trailing arms in rubber
Brakes: (parking) double caliper disc
Electrical system: 12 V

Status
Production complete. In service with the US Army (41), Navy (25), Air Force (19), Marine Corps (7) and Coast Guard (13).

Manufacturer
Logan Manufacturing Company, PO Box 407, Logan, Utah 84321, USA.
Tel: (801) 753 0220.

TRAILERS

Within each country, trailers appear in the following order:

    general cargo trailers

tank-carrying trailers and flat bed type trailers used for carrying engineer plant and armoured vehicles

tanker trailers

specialised trailers including those used for carrying missiles, pontoons and radars

AUSTRALIA

Trailer, Cargo, 1-tonne, GS 2-wheel

Description

The Australian Army 1-tonne cargo trailer was developed concurrently with the Trailer, Chassis, Light MC2 (see following entry) to replace existing equipments in service. It is used for the carriage of general cargo, packaged POL, ammunition or missiles and stores. The box-body, with a hinged tailgate, is manufactured from aluminium and is demountable from the trailer chassis.

Specifications
Weight:
  (loaded) 1510 kg
  (empty) 510 kg
Max load: 1000 kg
Length:
  (overall) 3.33 m
  (body internal) 2.18 m
Width:
  (overall) 2.06 m
  (body internal) 1.95 m
Height:
  (overall, loaded) 1.2 m
  (overall, empty) 1.6 m
  (body internal) 0.43 m
  (lunette, loaded) 0.76 m
  (lunette, empty) 0.87 m
  (floor, loaded) 0.72 m
  (floor, empty) 0.83 m

Track: 2 m
Suspension: semi-elliptic leaf springs and rubber bump stops
Brakes: hydraulic override
Tyres: 7.50 × 16
Electrical system: 12 V

Status
In service with the Australian Army.

Agency
Department of Defence (Army Office), Engineering Development Establishment, Private Bag 12, Ascot Vale PO, Victoria, Australia 3032.
Tel: (03) 319 5511. Telex: Army AA30943.
Fax: (03) 318 3421.

Trailer, cargo, 1-tonne, GS 2-wheel

Trailer, cargo, 1-tonne, GS 2-wheel

Trailer, Chassis, Light MC2 (1-tonne)

Description

The Australian Army 1-tonne trailer chassis was developed to meet a requirement for the deployment of 10, 15 and 30 kVA generator sets in the field. Initially two variants were considered, a powered version and an unpowered version. After pilot model trials held in 1972-73 further development of the powered version was discontinued. Procurement detailing for the unpowered trailer began in 1976 and actual procurement was recommended in October 1980. Quantity production commenced in November 1980.

This trailer chassis is used for the carriage of twin-mounted 10 or 15 kVA generators, a single-mounted 30 kVA generator or a hydrogen generator. It complies with all NATO standards and may be towed behind all wheeled vehicles from 1500 kg to 8000 kg capacity. The braking system is a mechanical/electrical override hydraulic system modified to operate with either 12 or 24 V vehicle electrical systems. The trailer meets the requirements of Specification Army (Aust) 5798.

Specifications
Weight:
  (loaded) 1500 kg
  (empty) 500 kg
Length: 3.33 m
Width: 2.06 m
Height:
  (loaded) 0.72 m
  (empty) 0.83 m

Track: 2 m
Tyres: 7.50 × 16
Electrical system: 12 V or 24 V

Status
In service with the Australian Army.

Agency
Department of Defence (Army Office), Engineering Development Establishment, Private Bag 12, Ascot Vale PO, Victoria, Australia 3032.
Tel: (03) 319 5511. Telex: Army AA30943.
Fax: (03) 318 3421.

International Harvester Semi-trailers

Description

In May 1987 it was announced that the Australian Army's existing semi-trailer and prime mover fleet would be replaced by a new fleet of 88 International Harvester SF2670 prime movers (fitted with Cummins NTC 365 engines) and 115 semi-trailers, plus support equipment. The contract was worth A$18 million and over 70 per cent of the total was to be spent in Australia.

The semi-trailers are used for carrying engineer plant, armoured vehicles, cargo and bulk water. They were produced by two subcontractors to International Harvester; Fruehauf at Somerton, Victoria, and Walsh at Toowoomba, Queensland. The Walsh semi-trailers are used to carry tanks and large equipment and are capable of being closed up hydraulically to reduce road width when unloaded. Fruehauf produced the cargo and water tanker semi-trailers and converter dollies.

Status
In service with the Australian Army.

Main Contractor
International Harvester, Dandenong, Victoria, Australia.

AUSTRIA

Goldhofer 25 000 kg Low Bed Trailer

Description
The Austrian Army uses this three-axle, 12-wheel full trailer for the transportation of light AFVs of the Saurer

4K-7F and 4K-4F families and nearly all the engineer material used by the Austrian Army. The trailer is towed by an ÖAF 10-tonne (6 × 6) truck.

Status
Thirty trailers were supplied to the Austrian Army.

Manufacturer
Goldhofer GmbH, Starhembergstrasse 19, A-4020 Linz, Austria.
Tel: 7223 2296. Telex: 2175 512.

CHINA, PEOPLE'S REPUBLIC

Hanyang HY 962 50 000 kg Semi-trailer

Description
This semi-trailer was designed for use with the Hanyang HY 473 tractor truck and has a maximum capacity of 50 000 kg. The semi-trailer has three axles with a total of 12 tyres. Two spare tyres are carried on supports on the top of the gooseneck. Two stabiliser legs at the forward end of the loading platform can be lowered to the ground for support when the tractor truck is removed. The two loading ramps are sprung-loaded to assist in raising and lowering. The 88.9 mm towing pin is a standard component and has a loading capacity of 19 500 kg.

The Hanyang HY 960 is a simplified version of the HY 962 that may not always be fitted with spring-loaded loading ramps. It retains the 50 000 kg loading capacity but is 10.655 m long, 3.2 m wide and 1.994 m high. Its weight when empty is 11 500 kg. The normal tractor truck is the HY 417 F10.

Specifications (HY 962)
Weight: (empty) 12 430 kg
Max payload: 50 000 kg
Axle load: 42 930 kg
Length:
(overall) 10.945 m
(platform) 6.965 m
Width: 3.22 m
Height:
(raised ramps) 2.92 m

HY 962 50 000 kg semi-trailer (C F Foss)

(coupling face) 1.45 m
Wheelbase: 1.19 m + 1.19 m
Track: 2.358 m
Tyres: 10.00 × 20

Status
In production. In service with the Chinese Army.

Manufacturer
Hanyang Special Auto Works, Hanyang Bridge Jianghan Road, Wuhan, Hubei Province, People's Republic of China.

COMMONWEALTH OF INDEPENDENT STATES

GAZ-704 500 kg Trailer

Description
The trailer entered production at the UAZ plant in 1953 and was designed for use with the GAZ-69 and GAZ-69A (4 × 4) vehicles. The trailer has a single axle with 6.50 × 16 tyres. No brakes are provided. The body is of all-steel construction and has a hinged tailgate.

Specifications
Weight:
(loaded) 840 kg
(empty) 340 kg
Max load: 500 kg
Length:
(overall) 2.7 m
(of body) 1.66 m
Width:
(overall) 1.645 m
(of body) 1.07 m

Height:
(overall) 1.15 m
(loading) 0.7 m
Depth: (of body) 0.45 m
Height of drawbar: 0.5 m
Track: 1.44 m

Status
In service with the CIS and other armed forces.

Manufacturer
Ul'yanovsk Automobile Plant, Ul'yanovsk, CIS.

ChMZAP-2303V 20-tonne Heavy Load Trailer

Description
This three-axle heavy load trailer is normally towed by a KrAZ-255B (6 × 6) 7500 kg truck. If required the four-wheeled dolly can be removed and the trailer is then used as a semi-trailer and can be towed by a KrAZ-221 or similar vehicle. The suspension of the dolly consists of semi-elliptical springs with check springs while the rear suspension consists of semi-elliptical springs. The trailer is provided with drum-type air-operated brakes on the rear axle, with a mechanical parking brake operating on one rear axle. Standard

equipment includes loading ramps, guide bars and guide rollers for the tractor winch cable.

Specifications
Weight: (empty) 9750 kg
Max load:
(as trailer) 20 500 kg
(as semi-trailer) 22 000 kg
Length:
(overall) 12.95 m
(of platform) 6.59 m
Width: 3 m
Height:
(overall) 2.09 m
(loading) 1.35 m

Ground clearance: 0.28 m
Track: 1.92 m
Max towing speed:
(road) 50 km/h
(dirt road) 25 km/h
Tyres: 12.00 × 20

Status
In service with the CIS and other armed forces.

Manufacturer
Chelyabinsk Machine Building Plant for Motor Vehicle and Tractor Trailers, Chelyabinsk, CIS.

ChMZAP-5523 Heavy Flat Bed Trailer

Description

This trailer was designed for hauling heavy equipment on both hard surface and dirt roads. The front dolly can be removed enabling the trailer to be used as a semi-trailer. Two hydraulically operated folding ramps are provided at the rear of the hull.

The suspension consists of longitudinal semi-elliptical springs with check springs while the rear bogie is provided with semi-elliptical springs. Drum-type brakes are provided on all eight wheels of the rear axle and a parking brake operates on one of the rear axles.

Specifications (with front dolly)
Weight:
  (loaded) 31 000 kg
  (empty) 9750 kg
  (on front dolly unladen) 3750 kg
  (on rear bogie unladen) 6000 kg
Max load: 21 250 kg
Length:
  (overall) 12.95 m
  (of platform) 6.43 m
Width:
  (overall) 3 m
  (of platform) 3 m
Height:
  (overall) 2.08 m

  (of platform) 1.35 m
Ground clearance: (under axle of rear suspension equaliser arm) 0.28 m
Max towing speed: 50 km/h
Tyres: 12.00 × 20

Status
In service with the CIS and other armed forces.

Manufacturer
Chelyabinsk Machine Building Plant for Motor Vehicle and Tractor Trailers, Chelyabinsk, CIS.

ChMZAP-5524 23-tonne Heavy Load Trailer

Description

The ChMZAP-5524 can be used either as a conventional trailer, or as a semi-trailer with its single-axle four-wheeled bogie removed. Its front suspension consists of semi-elliptical springs with check springs while its rear suspension consists of a bogie with semi-elliptical springs. The trailer is normally towed by a KrAZ-255B (6 × 6) 7500 kg truck or a tractor truck such as the KrAZ-255V (6 × 6) when being used as a semi-trailer.

The ChMZAP-5524A is similar but is extended by 1 m.

Specifications
Weight:
  (loaded) 30 000 kg
  (empty) 6300 kg
Max load:
  (as trailer) 23 700 kg
  (as semi-trailer) 25 500 kg
Length: (overall) 11.36 m
Width: (overall) 2.64 m
Height:
  (overall) 1.6 m

  (loading) 1.09 m
Ground clearance: 0.28 m
Track: 1.92 m
Max towing speed:
  (road) 50 km/h
  (dirt road) 20 km/h
Tyres: 12.00 × 20

Status
In service with the CIS and other armed forces.

Manufacturer
Chelyabinsk Machine Building Plant for Motor Vehicle and Tractor Trailers, Chelyabinsk, CIS.

ChMZAP-5208 40-tonne Heavy Flat Bed Trailer

Description

This trailer entered production at the Chelyabinsk plant in 1957 and was designed for hauling heavy cargo on hard surfaced roads. The trailer has drum-type air-operated brakes on all wheels, with a hydraulic-operated parking brake on the rear axle. Loading ramps, guide bars and load securing gear are also fitted. The ChMZAP-5208 is normally towed by the MAZ-537A (8 × 8) tractor truck.

Specifications
Weight:
  (loaded) 51 000 kg

  (empty) 11 000 kg
  (on front dolly unloaded) 3900 kg
  (on rear bogie unloaded) 7100 kg
Max load: 40 000 kg
Length:
  (overall) 9.33 m
  (of platform) 4.88 m
Width:
  (overall) 3.2 m
  (of platform) 3.2 m
Height:
  (overall) 1.94 m
  (of platform) 1.44 m
Ground clearance: (loaded under front suspension crossmember) 0.35 m
Track: (centre of outer wheels) 2.41 m

Wheelbase:
  (centre of front dolly to centre of rear bogie) 4.75 m
  (rear bogie) 1.19 m
Max towing speed: 40 km/h
Tyres: 8.25 × 20

Status
In service with the CIS and other armed forces.

Manufacturer
Chelyabinsk Machine Building Plant for Motor Vehicle and Tractor Trailers, Chelyabinsk, CIS.

ChMZAP-5247G 50-tonne Heavy Load Semi-trailer

Description

The ChMZAP-5247G 50-tonne semi-trailer is widely used for transporting MBTs such as the T-62 and is towed by the MAZ-537 (8 × 8) tractor truck. All eight wheels have air-operated drum brakes with a mechanical parking brake. Standard equipment includes powered loading ramps, guide bars and load securing gear.

The ChMZAP-5247B is a 45-tonne semi-trailer 14.68 m long and 2.64 m wide. The rear section is not provided with loading ramps and has no incline.

Specifications
Weight:
  (loaded) 68 000 kg
  (empty) 18 000 kg
Max load: 50 000 kg

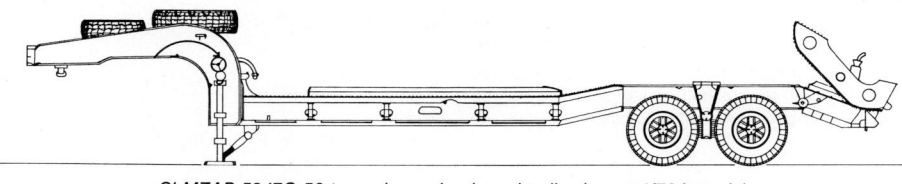

ChMZAP-5247G 50-tonne heavy load semi-trailer (not to 1/76th scale)

Length:
  (overall) 15.23 m
  (of platform) 5.69 m
Width:
  (overall) 3.38 m
  (of platform) 3.23 m
Height:
  (overall) 2.78 m
  (of platform) 1.16 m
Ground clearance: 0.35 m
Track: 2.09 m

Max towing speed: 50 km/h
Tyres: 15.00 × 20
Electrical system: 24 V

Status
In service with members of the former Warsaw Pact and with countries in Africa and the Middle East.

Manufacturer
Chelyabinsk Machine Building Plant for Motor Vehicle and Tractor Trailers, Chelyabinsk, CIS.

ChMZAP-5212 60-tonne Heavy Flat Bed Trailer

Description

This four-axle heavy flat bed trailer was designed for carrying heavy loads on highways, and is normally towed by the MAZ-537A (8 × 8) tractor truck. The trailer is provided with drum brakes, air-operated on all wheels, loading ramps, guide bars and load securing gear.

Specifications
Weight:
(loaded) 74 500 kg
(empty) 14 500 kg
(on front dolly empty) 7340 kg
(on rear bogie empty) 7160 kg
Max load: 60 000 kg
Length:
(overall) 11.37 m
(of load platform) 5.5 m
Width: (overall) 3.3 m
Height:
(overall) 2.07 m
(of load platform) 1.14 m

Ground clearance: (at full load under suspension equalisers) 0.19 m
Track: (on centres of external dual wheels) 2.48 m
Wheelbase: 1.2 m + 4 m + 1.2 m
Max towing speed: 32 km/h
Tyres: 9.00 × 15

Status
In service with the CIS and other armed forces.

Manufacturer
Chelyabinsk Machine Building Plant for Motor Vehicle and Tractor Trailers, Chelyabinsk, CIS.

CIS Trailers

Designation	Type	Unladen weight	Payload	Max tow speed	Length overall	Height overall	Width	Wheelbase	Track	Ground clearance	Load area (l × w)	No of tyres	Electrical system	Towing vehicle(s)
GAZ-704	cargo	340 kg	500 kg	75 km/h	2.56 m	1.15 m	1.645 m	—	1.44 m	0.28 m	1.66 × 1.07 m	2	12 V	GAZ-69, GAZ-69A
UAZ-8109	cargo	350 kg	500 kg	75 km/h	2.785 m	1.19 m	1.72 m	—	1.44 m	0.29 m	1.66 × 1.07 m	2	12 V	UAZ-469, UAZ-469B
TAPZ-755, TAPZ-755A	special	470 kg	1500 kg	80 km/h	3.025 m	0.8 m	2.07 m	—	1.77 m	0.375 m	1.73 × 0.936 m	2 + 1 spare	12 V	GAZ-66
GKB-8302	cargo	950 kg	1200 kg	90 km/h	3.82 m	2.52 m	2.24 m	—	1.82 m	0.35 m	2.153 × 1.82 m	2 + 1 spare	12 V	GAZ-66
GKB-83021	special	650 kg	1500 kg	90 km/h	3.25 m	1.115 m	2.2 m	—	1.82 m	0.35 m	1.685 × 1.56 m	2 + 1 spare	12 V	GAZ-66
IAZP-738	special	570 kg	1500/1800 kg	80 km/h	3.85 m	1.65 m	2.1 m	—	1.77 m	0.378 m	2.285 × 1.87 m	2 + 1 spare	12 V	GAZ-66
IAZP-739	special	470 kg	1000 kg	80 km/h	3.85 m	1.65 m	2.1 m	—	1.77 m	0.355 m	2.285 × 1.87 m	2 + 1 spare	12 V	GAZ-66
GKB-8301	cargo	1610 kg	2500 kg	80 km/h	4.825 m	2.9 m	2.5 m	—	1.89 m	0.36 m	3.225 × 2.325 m	2 + 1 spare	12 V	ZIL-131
GKB-83011	special	1110 kg	3000 kg	80 km/h	4.055 m	1.16 m	2.73 m	—	1.88 m	0.36 m	no platform	2 + 1 spare	12 V	ZIL-131
SMZ-710V	cargo	1500 kg	2000 kg	60 km/h	5.64 m	2.715 m	2.32 m	3.7 m	1.59 m	0.305 m	5.3 × 2.11 m	4 + 1 spare	12 V	ZIL-157K, ZIL-131
SMZ-710B	special	1250 kg	2500 kg	60 km/h	5.64 m	1.13 m	1.89 m	2.4 m	1.59 m	0.305 m	3.95 × 1.89 m	4 + 1 spare	12 V	ZIL-157K, ZIL-131
SMZ-8325	cargo	2030 kg	2100 kg	80 km/h	6.22 m	2.78 m	2.48 m	2.5 m	1.82 m	0.42 m	4.22 × 2.25 m	4 + 1 spare	12 V	ZIL-131
SMZ-8326	special	1650 kg	2500 kg	80 km/h	6.2 m	1.2 m	2.23 m	2.5 m	1.82 m	0.42 m	4.535 × 0.925 m	4 + 1 spare	12 V	ZIL-131
SMZ-810	cargo	2400 kg	4000 kg	50 km/h	6.24 m	2.315 m	2.35 m	2.95 m	1.97 m	0.3 m	4.21 × 2.185 m	4 + 1 spare	12 V	Ural-375D
SMZ-810A	special	1900 kg	4500 kg	50 km/h	6.34 m	1.275 m	2.35 m	2.95 m	1.97 m	0.3 m	4.5 × 1.8 m	4 + 1 spare	12 V	Ural-375D
782V	cargo	3030 kg	4000 kg	75 km/h	6.875 m	2.9 m	2.455 m	2.95 m	2 m	0.35 m	4.87 × 2.3 m	4 + 1 spare	12 V	Ural-4320, Ural-375N
782B	special	2320 kg	4680 kg	75 km/h	6.8 m	1.34 m	2.34 m	2.95 m	2 m	0.35 m	4.93 × 1.8 m	4 + 1 spare	12 V	Ural-4320, Ural-375N
GKB-817	cargo	2540 kg	5500 kg	80 km/h	6.68 m	1.87 m	2.5 m	3 m	1.8 m	0.37 m	4.95 × 2.35 m	4 + 1 spare	12 V	ZIL-130, ZIL-130G
GKB-817A	cargo	2450 kg	5500 kg	80 km/h	6.68 m	1.87 m	2.5 m	3 m	1.8 m	0.37 m	4.95 × 2.35 m	4 + 1 spare	12 V	ZIL-130, ZIL-130G
GKB-817V	special	2640 kg	5400 kg	80 km/h	n/a	n/a	n/a	n/a	1.8 m	0.37 m	n/a	4 + 1 spare	12 V	ZIL-130, ZIL-130G
MAZ-5207VSh	special	2450 kg	6750 kg	50 km/h	6.55 m	1.14 m	2.405 m	3 m	1.97 m	0.31 m	4.91 × 2.405 m	4 + 1 spare	24 V	KrAZ-255B
MAZ-8925	special	3000 kg	7000 kg	85 km/h	7.785 m	1.14 m	2.5 m	3.7 m	1.97 m	0.43 m	5.56 × 1.7 m	4 + 1 spare	24 V	KrAZ-255B
MAZ-8926	cargo	4000 kg	6000/8000 kg	85 km/h	7.71 m	2.79 m	2.5 m	3.7 m	1.97 m	0.43 m	5.5 × 2.365 m	4 + 1 spare	24 V	KrAZ-255B
GKB-8350	cargo	3500 kg	8000 kg	80 km/h	8.29 m	1.81 m	2.5 m	4.34 m	2.315 m	0.38 m	6.1 × 2.315 m	8 + 1 spare	24 V	KamAZ-5320
MAZ-5224V	special	4000 kg	10 500 kg	50 km/h	8.355 m	1.06 m	2.87 m	3.7 m	2.15 m	0.38 m	6.46 × 2.8 m	8 + 2 spare	24 V	KrAZ-255B
MAZ-8950	special	4500 kg	10 500 kg	70 km/h	8.92 m	1.2 m	2.82 m	4.1 m	2.16 m	0.4 m	6.78 × 2.8 m	4 + 1 spare	24 V	KrAZ-255B
MAZ-8378	cargo	5500 kg	14 500 kg	85 km/h	11.57 m	3.735 m	2.5 m	7.375 m	2.365 m	0.43 m	9.67 × 2.365 m	8 + 1 spare	24 V	MAZ-5335, MAZ-5336
ChMZAP-5208	transporter	10 900 kg	40 000 kg	40 km/h	9.33 m	1.74 m	3.2 m	4.13 m	2.55 m	0.26 m	7.43 × 3.2 m	24 + 2 spare	24 V	MAZ-537P
ChMZAP-8386	transporter	13 170 kg	40 000 kg	60 km/h	11.23 m	1.63 m	3.15 m	3.85 + 1.3 m	—	0.25 m	8.2 × 3.15 m	12 + 2 spare	24 V	MAZ-537P

CIS Semi-trailers

Designation	Type	Weight	Payload	Max tow speed	Length overall	Height overall	Width	Coupling to wheelbase	Track	Ground clearance	Load area (l × w)	No of tyres	Electrical system	Towing vehicle(s)
OdAZ-885	cargo	2850 kg	7500 kg	80 km/h	6.385 m	2.03 m	2.455 m	4.43 m	1.79 m	0.315 m	6.08 × 2.22 m	4 + 1 spare	12 V	ZIL-130V1, ZIL-MMZ-164N, KAZ-608, KAZ-606, KAZ-606A
MAZ-5245	cargo	3800 kg	13 500 kg	75 km/h	8.12 m	2.355 m	2.5 m	5.18 m	1.866 m	0.38 m	7.875 × 2.32 m	4	24 V	MAZ-504A
MAZ-93801	cargo	4100 kg	13 500 kg	85 km/h	8.745 m	2.035 m	2.5 m	5.75 m	1.86 m	0.43 m	8.535 × 2.365 m	4 + 1 spare	24 V	MAZ-504A, MAZ-5429
OdAZ-9350	cargo	5500 kg	9500 kg	75 km/h	10.57 m	3.49 m	2.5 m	4.545 + 1.42 m	2 m	0.4 m	10 × 2.335 m	4 + 1 spare	12 V	Ural-4420, Ural-375S
MAZ-938	special	7500 kg	13 000 kg	70 km/h	13.05 m	2.23 m	2.5 m	8.46 + 1.4 m	2.16 m	0.36 m	9.16 × 2.8 m	4	24 V	KrAZ-255V
MAZ-938B	special	7000 kg	13 500 kg	70 km/h	13.05 m	2.23 m	2.5 m	8.46 + 1.4 m	2.16 m	0.36 m	9.16 × 2.8 m	4	24 V	KrAZ-255V
OdAZ-9370	cargo	3700 kg	15 400 kg	80 km/h	9.64 m	2.03 m	2.5 m	6.14 + 1.32 m	1.85 m	0.26 m	9.18 × 2.32 m	8 + 1 spare	24 V	KamAZ-5410
MAZ-5205A	cargo	5700 kg	20 000 kg	80 km/h	10.18 m	3.615 m	2.5 m	5.53 + 1.54 m	1.9 m	0.34 m	9.965 × 2.32 m	8 + 1 spare	24 V	MAZ-504V
OdAZ-9385	cargo	4100 kg	21 000 kg	80 km/h	10.67 m	1.98 m	2.5 m	6.19 + 1.32 m	1.85 m	0.285 m	10.17 × 2.32 m	8 + 1 spare	24 V	KamAZ-54112
MAZ-9397	cargo	6000 kg	21 000 kg	85 km/h	11.465 m	3.715 m	2.5 m	6.5 + 1.54 m	1.79 m	0.35 m	11.24 × 2.4 m	8 + 1 spare	24 V	MAZ-5432
MAZ-941	cargo	6700 kg	25 000 kg	80 km/h	13.22 m	3.755 m	2.5 m	8.85 + 1.54 m	1.86 m	0.42 m	12.795 × 2.365 m	8 + 1 spare	24 V	MAZ-515B
ChMZAP-5524P	special	4400 kg	25 600 kg	68 km/h	9.8 m	1.6 m	2.638 m	4.52 + 1.4 m	1.92 m	0.24 m	n/a	8 + 2 spare	24 V	KrAZ-258
MAZ-9398	cargo	6500 kg	26 500 kg	85 km/h	12.325 m	3.715 m	2.5 m	6.485 + 1.5 + 1.5 m	1.97 m	0.42 m	12.12 × 2.4 m	6 + 1 spare	24 V	MAZ-6422
ChMZAP-5523A	transporter	7000 kg	25 000 kg	70 km/h	12.83 m	n/a	3 m	6.83 + 1.4 m	n/a	0.24 m	6.765 × 3 m	8 + 1 spare	24 V	KrAZ-258
MAZ-5247/ ChMZAP-5247G	transporter	18 000 kg	50 000 kg	50 km/h	15.23 m	2.78 m	3.38 m	10.84 + 1.58 m	2.09 m	0.35 m	n/a	8 + 1 spare	24 V	MAZ-537
ChMZAP-9990	transporter	18 000 kg	52 000 kg	60 km/h	14.42 m	3.19 m	3.15 m	8.4 + 1.3 + 1.3 m	n/a	0.25 m	8.96 × 3.15 m	12 + 2 spare	24 V	MAZ-537

Other CIS trailers

Designation	Type	Manufacturer	Capacity	Unladen weight	Length	Width	Height	Notes
2-ASP-4.5	dump	Nal'chik	4500 kg	2190 kg	5.02 m	2.26 m	2.25 m	Side dump trailer
2-PN-2 (SMZ-710V)	low bed, 2-axle		2000 kg	1500 kg	5.75 m	2.32 m	1.75 m	Towed by ZIL-157K or ZIL-131[1]
2-PN-4 (SMZ-810)	low bed, 2-axle		4000 kg	2400 kg	6.24 m	2.35 m	1.45 m	Towed by Ural-375D[2]
2-PN-6 (MAZ-520)	low bed, 2-axle		6000 kg	3200 kg	6.58 m	2.5 m	1.52 m	Towed by MAZ or KrAZ[3]
GKB-817 (2-P-5)	2-axle	Lugansk, 1967 Petropavlovsk, 1968	5000 kg	2540 kg	6.6 m	2.5 m	2.22 m	Wooden platform with hinged sides towed by Ural-375
GKB-816	2-axle		3000 kg	1500 kg	5.73 m	2.25 m	1.73 m	Towed by ZIL-131
KAZ-717	semi-trailer	Kutaisi, 1965	11 500 kg	4000 kg	7.69 m	2.48 m	1.98 m	Wooden platform, 3 hinged sides
MAZ-524Z	2-axle	Minsk, 1960	6800 kg	3200 kg	6.97 m	2.5 m	2.05 m	MAZ-524ZB has canopy
MAZ-584B	semi-trailer	Mytishchi, 1956 Saransk, 1961	7000 kg	2525 kg	6.3 m	2.46 m	2 m	Hinged side boards and tailgate, towed by ZIL-164A
MAZ-886 (2-P-8)	2-axle	Minsk, 1968	8500 kg	3500 kg	7.12 m	2.5 m	3.31 m	Hinged on 3 sides, fitted canopy and bows, towed by MAZ-500 or KrAZ-255B
MAZ-938	semi-trailer	Minsk	15 000 kg	7500 kg	12.2 m	2.8 m	2.33 m	Towed by KrAZ-255
MAZ-941	semi-trailer	Minsk	24 700 kg	13 700 kg	10.67 m	2.5 m	2.3 m	Towed by MAZ-525
MAZ-5206	flat bed, 2-axle	Minsk	10 000 kg	5400 kg	9.23 m	2.53 m	1.53 m	Towed by wheeled or tracked vehicle
MAZ-5224	low bed, 2-axle	Minsk	10 000 kg	5000 kg	8.04 m	2.68 m	1.77 m	Towed by KrAZ-255B[4]
MAZ-5243	2-axle	Minsk	6800 kg	3200 kg	6.97 m	2.5 m	2.05 m	Towed by MAZ-500 truck
MAZ-5245	semi-trailer	Minsk, 1961	14 000 kg	3800 kg	8.12 m	2.5 m	2.33 m	Towed by MAZ-504[5]
OdAZ-740	semi-trailer	Odessa	23 000 kg	7000 kg	11.33 m	2.5 m	3.45 m	Van type, towed by KrAZ-221B
OdAZ-760	semi-trailer	Odessa	14 000 kg	4800 kg	8.84 m	2.5 m	2.27 m	Towed by Ural-377
OdAZ-784	semi-trailer	Odessa, 1959	7000 kg	2950 kg	8 m	2.57 m	3.3 m	Van type, towed by Kaz-606
OdAZ-794	semi-trailer	Odessa, 1966	7500 kg	3000 kg	6.93 m	2.5 m	3.22 m	Van type
OdAZ-795	semi-trailer	Odessa, 1965	13 250 kg	4200 kg	9.38 m	2.5 m	3.32 m	Van type, towed by MAZ-504
OdAZ-832	semi-trailer	Odessa, 1965	12 000 kg	4000 kg	9.5 m	2.5 m	3.5 m	Van type, towed by MAZ-200V
OdAZ-828	semi-trailer	Odessa	5500 kg	5800 kg	8.46 m	2.37 m	1.97 m	Van type, towed by ZIL-157KV
OdAZ-935	semi-trailer	Odessa, 1965	13 500 kg	4800 kg	9.38 m	2.5 m	3.32 m	Van type, towed by Ural-377S
PAZS-3137	mobile fuelling unit trailer		4200 l	2806 kg	5.99 m	2.31 m	2.84 m	Fitted with pumps and hoses
TAPZ-738 (1-P-1.5)	trailer chassis	Irbitsk	1800 kg	600 kg	3.94 m	2.07 m	1.77 m	Towed by GAZ-53A, GAZ-63 and GAZ-66
TAPZ-739 (1-P-1)	trailer chassis	Irbitsk	1000 kg	500 kg	3.55 m	1.81 m	0.92 m	Towed by GAZ-53A, GAZ-63[6] and GAZ-66
TAPZ-754 V	2-axle	Irbitsk, 1958	4000 kg	1900 kg	6.05 m	2.39 m	2.13 m	Wooden platform, 3 hinged sides, towed by ZIL-164
TAPZ-755 A	trailer chassis	Irbitsk	1500 kg	470 kg	3.03 m	1.82 m	0.93 m	Towed by GAZ-51A, GAZ-53A and GAZ-66[7]
TsV-50	single-axle trailer	Biysk	1000 l	910 kg	3.92 m	1.66 m	2.08 m	Drinking water trailer
PTs-4.2-754V	tanker-trailer	Grabovskiy, 1966	4200 l	2268 kg	6 m	2.28 m	2.75 m	Fitted with dispensing equipment
PTs-6	tanker-trailer	Grabovskiy	6700 l	3700 kg	5.06 m	2.4 m	2.55 m	Fitted with dispensing equipment
VMG-40-51	tanker-trailer		950 l (water) 300 l (oil)		4.2 m	2.13 m	2.28 m	Water and oil, heater fitted
PKhZ	semi-trailer, 2-axle	—	—	—	—	—	—	Field bakery
SP-32	4-axle	—	—	—	—	—	—	Dining hall

1 SMZ-710B trailer chassis is a modified version of 2-PN-2 with 2500 kg load capacity. The 2-PN-2M (SMZ-8325) trailer is used for the PPK material preservation trailer
2 Modified versions of 2-PN-4 are SMZ-810A trailer chassis with 4500 kg load capacity and SMZ-810PA trailer chassis for special bodies
3 Modified version of 2-PN-6 is MAZ-5207VSh trailer chassis with 6750 kg capacity, which is fitted with various types of body, and MAZ-847 dump trailer with 6000 kg capacity
4 Modified version of MAZ-5224 is MAZ-5224V chassis for van bodies
5 MAZ-5245B is provided with canopy. Between 1956 and 1961 plant produced MAZ-5215B semi-trailer with 12 500 kg capacity
6 This chassis is used for 1-P-1 1000 kg cargo trailer. TAPZ-739K chassis is used for KP-125M field kitchen
7 MNUM-50M trailer-mounted pump comprises 3 V 40/25 pump on TAPZ-755A chassis

Manufacturers

Biysk Molmashstroy Plant.
Grabovskiy Specialised Automobile Plant.
Irbitsk Motor Vehicle Trailer Plant, Irbit.
Kutaisi Motor Vehicle Plant, Kutaisi, Georgia.

Lugansk Motor Vehicle Assembly Plant.
Minsk Motor Vehicle Plant, Minsk, Belorussia.
Mytishchi Machine Building Plant, Mytishchi.
Nal'chik Machinery Construction Plant.
Odessa Motor Vehicle Assembly Vehicle Plant,

Odessa, Ukraine.
Petropavlovsk Machine Construction Plant.
Saransk Dump Truck Plant, Saranski.
Zelenokumsk Plant.

CZECHOSLOVAKIA

Czechoslovakian Heavy Transport Trailers P-32, P-46, P-50 and P-80

Status

In service with the Czechoslovak Army. The P-50 is also in service with the German Army.

Manufacturer

Czechoslovak state factories.

Description

These trailers are used for moving construction equipment and armoured vehicles and have unloading ramps at the rear of the trailer.

Tatra 141 (6 × 6) prime mover towing P-32 trailer

Specifications

Model	P-32	P-46	P-50	P-80
Weight (empty)	10 600 kg	10 600 kg	16 200 kg	16 200 kg
(loaded)	50 600 kg	56 600 kg	66 200 kg	79 200 kg
Payload	40 000 kg	46 000 kg	50 000 kg*	63 000 kg**
Length	9.474 m	9.5 m	10.715 m	10.7 m
(of platform)	4.9 m	4.9 m	6.2 m	6.2 m
Width	3.1 m	3.1 m	3.1 m	3.1 m
Height	1.42 m	1.42 m	1.54 m	1.42 m
(of platform)	1 m	1 m	1 m	1 m
Tyres	8.25 × 15	8.25 × 15	8.25 × 15	8.25 × 15
Number of axles	3	4	5	5
Towing speed	40 km/h	40 km/h	40 km/h	40 km/h

*   Can be increased to 63 000 kg if towing speed is reduced to 10 km/h
** Can be increased to 80 000 kg if towing speed is reduced to 10 km/h

FINLAND

Vammas BVK 191W All-Terrain General Purpose Trailer

Description

The Vammas BVK 191W all-terrain general purpose trailer was designed for use with the Swedish Bv 206 and Sisu NA-140 all-terrain vehicles (refer to entries in *the Tracked prime movers, cargo carriers and armoured logistic vehicles* section for information on these vehicles). The 1000 kg payload of the BVK 191W increases the potential payload of both vehicles by 50 per cent but the trailer does not affect the mobility of the tractor vehicle, to the point of being amphibious.

A preliminary series of BVK 191 trailers was trialled by the Finnish Defence Forces beginning in March 1987. Following minor changes to the design, series production of the resultant BVK 191W commenced during 1989.

The BVK 191W has a light but robust construction, having a steel frame with the body and deck made of aluminium. The trailer can be towed across country, marsh, sand, snow and in water as well as roads. It can float when crossing water obstacles, even when fully loaded. The trailer is equipped with both wheels and skis, using an articulated suspension which allows the trailer to remain as level as possible in the most uneven terrain. When using the wide skis and when fully loaded, the ground pressure is as low as that of the tractor vehicle. A special filling is used for the four wheels to reduce damage from rough ground or tree stumps. The cargo area is watertight and can be covered with a tarpaulin. Cargo lashing points, a 76 mm towing eye and a tailgate are fitted.

Specifications

Weight: (empty) 725 kg

Payload: 1000 kg
Length: 4.6 m
Width: 1.89 m
Height: 1.4 m
Cargo area dimensions: 2.8 × 1.7 × 0.7 m
Ground clearance:
  (wheels) 0.6 m
  (skis) 0.44 m
Tyres: 5.00 × 8/10 PR

Status

In production for the Finnish Defence Forces.

Manufacturer

Vammas Limited, PO Box 18, SF-38201 Vammala, Finland.
Tel: 932 1971. Telex: 22283 vammas sf.
Fax: 932 41148.

Vammas BVK 191W all-terrain general purpose trailer

Vammas BVK 191W all-terrain general purpose trailer

FRANCE

LOHR RMTL 1.5 Multi-purpose Trailer

Description

The LOHR RMTL 1.5 (*Remorque Militaire de Transport Logistique*) is a modular design intended to have a GVW of up to 3.1 tonnes, a payload of 1.5 tonnes and a cross-country capability. It is also intended to be transportable by aircraft or helicopter.

The RMTL 1.5 has a multi-leaf spring suspension (a pneumatic suspension is optional) with hydraulic shock absorbers. A single rigid axle is provided with an air drum braking system (two or three lines) and a spare wheel is carried over the drawbar. Other equipment includes a folding drawbar wheel, a tool box, two rear folding legs and a 24 V NATO lighting system.

The RMTL 1.5 can carry a series of modular bodies that includes standard cargo bodies (with optional covers), fuel tanker bodies, generators and other types. Optional equipment includes two side boxes, a platform with four ISO corners, a tilt kit with a tarpaulin, a 1800 litre water tank, and other equipment to meet customer specifications.

Specifications

GVW: up to 3100 kg
Payload: 1500 kg

Length: 3.9 m
Width: 2.5 m
Height: (platform) 1 m
Ground clearance: 0.4 m
Load area: 2.1 × 2.6 m
Tyres: 9.00 R 16 XL tubeless

Status

Prototype delivered to the French Army for trials.

Manufacturer

LOHR SA, F-67980 Hangenbieten, France.
Tel: 88 38 98 00. Telex: 870082 f.
Fax: 88 96 06 36.

Trailor 1100 kg Cross-country Cargo Trailer

Description

The Trailor 1100 kg cross-country cargo trailer is sometimes referred to as the Africa-type trailer and is intended for off-road use in remote areas. The frame of the trailer is constructed from two channel-shaped variable section high tensile steel beams on which a steel-bodied cargo carrier is placed, supported on one-piece crossmembers. The body has steel sides 0.46 m high that can be swung downwards for loading or may be removed altogether. The floor is also steel. To extend the height of the sides expanded metal exten-sions can be fitted to the sides and a tarpaulin cover may be fitted on bows. The axle is a 90 mm square beam and EEC-approved dual air brakes are fitted. Each trailer is equipped with a wheel nut wrench, a spare wheel carrier on the front panel, a tool box, a drinking water tank, a jerrican carrier and a rear stabilising strut. The trailer can be fitted with a fuel bowser or generating plant.

Specifications

Weight:
  (empty) 1400 kg
  (loaded) 2500 kg
Max load: 1100 kg

Length: 4.05 m
Width: 2.2 m
Height:
  (tarpaulin cover) 2.4 m
  (load area) 1 m
  (trail eye) 0.765 m
Load area: 2.71 × 2.06 m
Track: 1.953 m
Suspension: Trailor single-axle type SMU 7 SE with rubber-bushed radius rods, leaf springs and shock absorbers
Brakes: dual circuit air
Tyres: 8.25 × 20 XL
Electrical system: 24 V

Status
In production. In service with several armed forces.

Manufacturer
Trailor SA, 5 Route Nationale 10, Coigniegres, BP 49,
F-78311 Maurepas Cedex, France.
Tel: (1) 30 50 61 26. Telex: 698896 f.
Fax: (1) 30 50 31 32.

Trailor 1100 kg cross-country cargo trailer

ACMAT RM 215S 1500 kg Cargo Trailer

Description
The ACMAT RM 215S series of trailers was designed
for maximum compatibility with the ACMAT range of
vehicles. Each trailer has an integral 200 litre water
tank and the standard specification includes eight
jerricans and two sections of PSP-type sand channel.
The RM 215S trailer is provided with canopy rails.

Specifications
Weight:
   (loaded) 2700 kg
   (empty) 1200 kg
Payload: 1500 kg
Length: (overall) 4.125 m
Width: 2.07 m
Height:
   (top of canopy rails) 2.4 m
   (load area) 1 m
Lunette height: 0.765 m
Internal clearance: (inside canopy) 1.4 m
Track: 1.74 m
Load area: 2.69 × 1.94 m
Suspension: semi-elliptical springs
Tyres: 12.50 × 20

Status
In production.

ACMAT RM 215S 1500 kg cargo trailer

Manufacturer
ACMAT, Ateliers de Construction Mécanique de
l'Atlantique, Le Point du Jour, F-44600 Saint-Nazaire,
France.
Tel: 40 22 33 71. Telex: 700913 f.
Fax: 40 66 30 96.

Titan T6 R2 3800 kg Trailer

Description
This two-axle trailer was designed to carry a maximum
load of 3800 kg or six standard pallets. The chassis is
of all-steel construction. The floor is of light alloy sheet
and has an anti-skid surface and tie-down points. The
ribbed sheet steel sides are of the drop-down type and
can be removed. The tailgate is similar and has an
integral step. The front gate can be removed if
required. Standard equipment includes air-line connection, parking brake on the rear axle, 12-pin (24 V)
socket, tool box, spare wheel and wheel chocks.

Specifications
Weight:
   (empty) 2200 kg
   (loaded) 6000 kg
Max load: 3800 kg
Length:
   (including tow bar) 6.3 m
   (excluding tow bar) 4.3 m
Width: 2.44 m

Titan T6 R2 3800 kg trailer

Height: 1.73 m
   (loading platform) 1.23 m
Ground clearance: 0.4 m
Load area: 4.26 × 2.4 m
Tyres: 10.50 × 20
Track: 1.86 m
Suspension: semi-elliptical springs

Status
In production.

Manufacturer
Titan SA, BP 407, F-69400 Villefranche-sur-Saône,
France.

LOHR RM16 16 000 kg Trailer

Description
This two-axle trailer, known as the *Remorque Grande Capacité de 16 T PTC*, was designed to meet the requirements of the Logistic Transport Squadrons of the French Army. The trailer has drop sides and a drop tailgate which can be quickly removed, bows that can be adjusted to any one of three heights and a quick bache system for the rapid uncovering of the load.

Specifications
Weight:
  (empty) 4280 kg
  (loaded) 16 000 kg
Max load: 11 720 kg
Length of platform: 6.3 m

LOHR 16 000 kg trailer complete with bows and cover

Width of platform: 2.38 m
Tyres: 9.00 × 20

Status
In production. In service with the French Army.

LOHR 16 000 kg trailer with sides and tailgate lowered

Manufacturer
LOHR SA, F-67980 Hangenbieten, France.
Tel: 88 38 98 00. Telex: 870082 f.
Fax: 88 96 06 36.

Trailor 17 500 kg Semi-trailer

Description
This semi-trailer was designed to meet the requirements of the French Army and also meets current TIR requirements. The cargo area has eight drop sides (four each side), doors at the rear, bows and a tarpaulin cover. The floor is of wood and has retractable rings for securing cargo. The trailer is fitted with dual air brakes, one line acting on each of the rear axles, and a mechanical parking brake.

Specifications
Weight:
  (empty) 5500 kg
  (loaded) 23 000 kg
Max load: 17 500 kg
Load area: 11.31 × 2.5 m

Status
In production. In service with the French Army.

Manufacturer
Trailor SA, 5 Route Nationale 10, Coigniegres, BP 49, F-78311 Maurepas Cedex, France.
Tel: (1) 30 50 61 26. Telex: 698896 f.
Fax: (1) 30 50 31 32.

Decauville SRPC 36/46-tonne Tank Transporter Semi-trailer

Description
This semi-trailer was designed for transporting MBTs such as the AMX-30, Leopard 1, T-54/T-55, T-62 and similar tanks. Its chassis consists of two longitudinal girders connected by crossbars and gussets, with a serrated steel sheet covering. Two loading ramps are provided at the rear of the trailer.

The suspension consists of four axles on oscillating balance bars. Air brakes are fitted on all wheels and a mechanical parking brake is provided. Shoe-type stabilisers are provided at the front of the trailer.

Standard equipment includes stowage boxes, front roller, adjustable blocks and a jack. Optional equipment includes hydraulically operated rear loading ramps, rear rollers, shrouded pulley wheels, drinking water tank, jerrican support racks and a camouflage net.

Specifications
Weight:
  (empty) 12 900 kg
  (loaded) 58 900 kg
Max load: 46 000 kg
Length:
  (overall) 12.05 m
  (of platform) 7.35 m

Decauville SRPC 36/46-tonne tank transporter semi-trailer carrying AMX-30 MBT

Width:
  (overall) 3.65 m
  (of loading ramps) 0.62 m
Height: (over loading ramps in vertical position) 2.6 m
Ground clearance:
  (under axles) 0.35 m
  (under front of semi-trailer) 1.65 m
Wheelbase: (from king-pin to centre of rear bogie) 9 m
Max towing speed: 60 km/h

Tyres: 9.00 × 20 or 12.00 × 20

Status
In production. Has been exported to a number of countries in the Middle East.

Manufacturer
Decauville SA, BP 38, F-91102 Corbeil-Essonnes, France.

Decauville SRPC 48/54-tonne Tank Transporter Semi-trailer

Description
This semi-trailer was designed for transporting MBTs such as the Chieftain, Centurion and M60. Its chassis consists of two longitudinal girders connected by crossbars and gussets, with a serrated sheet steel covering. Two loading ramps are provided at the rear of the trailer.

The suspension consists of four axles on oscillating balance bars. Air brakes are fitted on all wheels and a parking brake is provided. Shoe-type stabilisers are provided under the front of the trailer. Standard equipment includes stowage boxes, shackles, front rollers, adjustable blocks and a jack. Optional equipment includes hydraulically operated rear loading ramps, rear rollers, shrouded pulley wheels, drinking water tank, jerrican support racks and a camouflage net.

Decauville SRPC 48/54-tonne tank transporter semi-trailer with M47 MBT

Specifications

Weight:
  (empty) 14 000 kg
  (loaded) 68 000 kg
Max load: 54 000 kg
Length:
  (overall) 12.05 m
  (of platform) 7.35 m

Width:
  (trailer) 3.65 m
  (of loading ramps) 0.62 m
Height: (over loading ramps in vertical position) 2.6 m
Ground clearance:
  (under axles) 0.35 m
  (under front of semi-trailer) 1.65 m
Wheelbase: (from king-pin to centre of rear bogie) 9 m

Max towing speed: 60 km/h
Tyres: 11.00 × 20 or 12.00 × 20

Status
Ready for production.

Manufacturer
Decauville SA, BP 38, F-91102 Corbeil-Essonnes, France.

Fruehauf Medium Tank Transporter Semi-trailer

Description
This semi-trailer was designed for the long distance transport of tanks weighing up to 45 000 kg. The trailer has manually operated 0.6 m wide rear loading ramps, removable track guides and heavy duty manually operated stabilisers mounted towards the front. It can be towed on roads at a maximum speed of 80 km/h.

Specifications
Max load: 45 000 kg
Length:
  (overall) 11.75 m
  (of loading platform) 7.92 m
Width: 3.1 m
King-pin size: 89 mm
Tyres: 8.25 × 15

Status
In production. In service with at least one army outside France.

Manufacturer
Fruehauf France, 2 avenue de l'Aunette, F-91130 Ris-Orangis, France.
Tel: 69 43 30 00. Telex: 601381 f.
Fax: 69 43 33 66.

Fruehauf medium tank transporter semi-trailer

Fruehauf medium tank transporter semi-trailer

Fruehauf Heavy Tank Transporter Semi-trailer

Description
This semi-trailer was designed for carrying tanks weighing up to 60 000 kg. The trailer has manually operated 0.6 m wide rear loading ramps, removable track guides, and heavy duty manually operated stabilisers mounted towards the front of the trailer.

Specifications
Max load: 60 000 kg
Length:
  (overall) 12.5 m
  (of loading platform) 7 m
Width: 3.6 m
King-pin size: 89 mm
Tyres: 12.00 × 20

Fruehauf heavy tank transporter semi-trailer

Status
In production. In service with at least one country outside France.

Manufacturer
Fruehauf France, 2 avenue de l'Aunette, F-91130 Ris-Orangis, France.
Tel: 69 43 30 00. Telex: 601381 f.
Fax: 69 43 33 66.

LOHR SMC Tank Transporter Semi-trailers

Description
There are, among others, three semi-trailers in the LOHR SMC range, the SMC 60 DT (DT – desert), the SMC 60 RD (RD – route et desert) and the SMC 40 PL. The SMC 60 DT has a maximum load of 60 000 kg and uses a hydraulically operated rear ramp. The SMC 60 RD also has a maximum load of 60 000 kg and uses manually lifted ramps. Other differences between the two are the types of tyres fitted and the chassis construction. The SMC 40 PL has a maximum load of 44 000 kg and uses manually lifted ramps.

On all three models the chassis and deck are made of all-welded steel and the suspension consists of twin unsprung walking beams on which are mounted the

LOHR SMC 60 series tank transporter semi-trailer

LOHR SMC 60 RD tank transporter semi-trailer loaded with 155 mm GCT self-propelled gun; the towing vehicle is a Renault R 400 (6 × 6) tractor truck

Specifications

Model	SMC 60 DT	SMC 60 RD	SMC 40 PL
Weight (loaded)	78 500 kg	77 000 kg	60 000 kg
Maximum load	60 000 kg	60 000 kg	44 000 kg
Length	13.05 m	11.55 m	12.93 m
Length of load on deck	7.215 m	6.6 m	7.76 m
Length of overhang at rear	1.9 m	1.75 m	1.52 m
Height of load deck	1.54 m	1.38 m	1.35 m
Width	4.13 m	3.4 m	3.3 m
Tyres	24.00 × 20.5 sand	18.00 × 22.5 sand	13.00 × 20 P
Electrical system	24 V	24 V	24 V

eight tyres. Winch cable guides and rollers are fitted and there are also guide blocks for the tracks of the vehicles being loaded. Spare wheels are carried under the loading deck.

A special version of the SMC semi-trailers, the SMC 60 EM 5 LT, is described in the following entry.

A cargo version of the SMC 60 DT, which remains capable of carrying an AMX-30 MBT, is available.

Status
In production. SMC 60 DT exported to the Middle East and Africa. SMC 60 RD in service with the French Army and several other countries.

Manufacturer
LOHR SA, F-67980 Hangenbieten, France.
Tel: 88 38 98 00. Telex: 870082 f.
Fax: 88 96 06 36.

LOHR SMC 60 EM 5 LT Tank Transporter Semi-trailer

Description
The LOHR SMC 60 EM 5 LT tank transporter semi-trailer was designed to act as a road and rough-terrain transporter semi-trailer for the latest generation of MBTs. It has been tested in the United States as a possible carrier for the M1 Abrams series and by the French Army for the Leclerc.

The chassis consists of a steel heavy duty low bed with two longitudinal girders braced by crossmembers. The all-steel platform is welded to the chassis and the rear part is inclined with square bars for track grips. There are perforations for track guides and blocks, with a roller and pulley located at the rear for the winch cable. Two two-piece loading ramps are provided at the rear, with spring assistance for handling. The running gear is based on 10 pendular hydraulic axles

arranged in five rows, four steerable and one fixed (the forward row). Dual circuit air brakes are provided. Two support legs are provided at the base of the gooseneck. A standard 3.5 in/89 mm king-pin coupling is used.

Standard equipment provided with the semi-trailer includes four track guides and blocks, three lashing rings each side plus two lashing eyes on the gooseneck, a wheel wrench and a 25-tonne capacity hydraulic jack. Optional equipment includes four adjustable chains for the load, three stowage boxes each side of the platform plus another on the gooseneck, a 300 litre water tank, a 300 litre fuel tank in the gooseneck, and heavy duty hydraulic legs on each side. Further optional equipment includes hydraulic loading ramps, an emergency pump, a hydraulic loading/unloading mechanism for a spare wheel, and blackout electrical equipment.

Specifications
Weight: (kerb) 20 000 kg

Max load: 65 000 kg
Length:
(overall, ramps raised) 15.8 m
(platform, useful) 10.08 m
Width:
(overall) 3.6 m
(ramps) 0.96 m
Height: (platform) 1.17 m
Loading angle: 18°
Tyres: 215/75 R 17 5XZA
Electrical system: 24 V

Status
In production.

Manufacturer
LOHR SA, F-67980 Hangenbieten, France.
Tel: 88 38 98 00. Telex: 870082 f.
Fax: 88 96 06 36.

LOHR SMC 60 EM 5 LT tank transporter semi-trailer on tow by Oshkosh M983 (8 × 8) tractor truck

Nicolas Tank Transporter Semi-trailers

Description
Nicolas manufactures a wide range of semi-trailers for military and commercial use and it recently expanded its military range by the introduction of a wide range of tank transporter trailers. The range includes 14 separate models varying in payload from 16 500 kg up to 95 000 kg. The various semi-trailers differ not only in size but also in the number of short axles used, the tyre sizes and the number of tanks that can be carried. Two of the smaller models (the STA D 30.15 and the STA L 30.20) can each carry two light tanks of the AMX-13 type, while the STA 100 can carry two AMX-30 tanks using eight axle units and 32 tyres. The full range of models and their main characteristics can be seen on the Model table.

A typical example from the range is the STA S 60.20.5. This model can be used to carry most models of MBT in service and is mainly constructed from high tensile steel. The loading deck has two central main beams and two siderails connected by welded beams of 'I' section high tensile steel. The steel decking is 2 mm thick, apart from the main channels which are 2 to 8 mm thick. Panels over the twin axles can be

Renault TRH 350 (6 × 4) tractor towing Nicolas STA 43 semi-trailer

removed for access. A 250 mm adjustment for width is possible on the loading ramps which fold upwards for travelling and an optional hydraulic lift mechanism is available. The axles have a 10° oscillation and air brakes are used. One spare wheel is provided with an optional rack for another and a small crane is provided for handling the spare wheel. Optional equipment includes a tool box, cable guides on the gooseneck, lashing chains, blocks, track guides, blackout lighting and fuel and water tanks.

Variants
Nicolas produces a tank transporter semi-trailer with powered rear axles for use with its Tractomas tractor trucks. By varying the type of Tractomas tractor and the type of powered semi-trailer, loads of 40 000, 50 000 or 60 000 kg can be carried. The hydraulically powered axles provide extra traction and power when travelling with loads across country and across soft terrain such as sand. All types can travel at 7 km/h with the power-assist facility selected. All the semi-trailers

List of models

Model	Weight* (empty)	Length*	Height (platform)	Payload*	Load* (5th wheel)	Load* (rear axle)	Axles (pairs)	Tyres (number)
STA 18.15	6000 kg	9.815 m	0.89 m	17 500 kg	7800 kg	15 700 kg	2	8.25 × 15 (8)
STA 18.20	6300 kg	9.815 m	1.1 m	17 500 kg	7800 kg	16 000 kg	2	9.00 × 20 (8)
STA D 30.15	12 000 kg	14.515 m	1.17 m	30 000 kg	15 000 kg	30 000 kg	3	10.00 × 15 (12)
STA L 30.20	10 500 kg	14.615 m	1.29 m	33 000 kg	15 500 kg	28 000 kg	2	12.00 × 20 (8)
STA 45.15	10 600 kg	10.815 m	0.998 m	45 000 kg	19 600 kg	36 000 kg	2	8.25 × 15 (16)
STA 40.20	10 800 kg	10.815 m	1.29 m	38 000 kg	15 800 kg	33 000 kg	2	12.00 × 20 (8)
STA 3 35.15	10 400 kg	11.115 m	0.83 m	40 400 kg	14 000 kg	31 500 kg	3	8.25 × 15 (12)
STA 3 45.22.5	11 200 kg	11.115 m	1.27 m	43 000 kg	17 200 kg	37 000 kg	3	18 × 22.5 (6)
STA 40.24	11 600 kg	11.915 m	1.38 m	40 000 kg	19 600 kg	32 000 kg	2	12.00 × 24 (8)
STA 50.20	12 600 kg	11.915 m	1.39 m	50 600 kg	21 600 kg	42 000 kg	3	12.00 × 20 (12)
STA 3 45.15	11 500 kg	11.115 m	1.17 m	44 500 kg	17 000 kg	39 000 kg	3	10.00 × 15 (12)
STA S 60.20.5	17 000 kg	12.62 m	1.6 m	60 000 kg	21 000 kg	56 000 kg	2	20.5 × 24 (8)
STA 60.20	16 500 kg	11.5 m	1.36 m	58 000 kg	22 500 kg	52 000 kg	2	12.00 × 20 (16)
STA 100	20 000 kg	18.215 m	1.15 m	95 000 kg	27 000 kg	88 000 kg	4	8.25 × 15 (32)

*   approximate figures

use 24 × 20.5 tyres and the number of axles used may be two or three per side.

The hydraulic system used to power the wheels of the semi-trailer is based on the use of a three-part motor produced by Poclain. One part is the cylinder block which supports the hydraulic cylinders and the associated rollers. The rollers controlled by the hydraulic cylinders press on cams on the second part which is the motor casing fastened onto the hub. Pressure on the cam makes the hub and wheel turn. When not in use the rollers are retracted and held away from the cams by springs. The third section of the motor is the timing section. The entire motor can be removed without removal of the wheel or any part of the axle. Power for the motor comes from a multi-cylinder pump on a declutchable power take-off on the gear box. Each cylinder of the pump feeds one axle

motor. The system is operated from a remote-control box carried in the vehicle cab.

Specifications (STA S 60.20.5 only)
Weight:
(empty) 17 000 kg
(on 5th wheel) 21 000 kg
(on axles) 56 000 kg
Max load: 60 000 kg
Max gross weight: 77 000 kg
Length:
(ramp folded) 13.1 m
(loading deck) 7.2 m
(loading ramp) 2.875 m
Width:
(overall) 4.195 m
(gooseneck) 2.5 m

(loading ramps) 0.8 m
Height:
(loading deck) 1.6 m
(fifth wheel) 1.8 m
Wheelbase: (5th wheel to centre of axle unit) 9.12 m
Tyres: 20.5 × 24
Electrical system: 24 V

Status
The company is currently building several hundred STA 45.15 semi-trailers for the French Army.

Manufacturer
Nicolas, PO Box 3, F-89290 Champs-sur-Yonne, France.
Tel: (33) 86 53 30 09. Telex: 800938 f.
Fax: (33) 86 53 79 74.

Titan Tank Transporter Semi-trailers

Description
There are two Titan tank-carrying semi-trailers. The smaller has a capacity of 45 000 kg and was designed

for carrying tanks such as the AMX-30 and Leopard 1, while the larger has a capacity of 55 000 kg.

The chassis consists of two laminated steel main bearers with the crossmembers welded into position. The platform consists of full width steel section crossmembers and siderails covered in chequered steel flooring. Traps give access to the axles. Two

doors in the gooseneck give access to the tool box. The rear loading ramps are in two articulated parts, and a balance spring is fitted to assist in raising the ramps. The ramps are locked once raised.

Standard equipment includes air brake connection, parking brakes on each of the axles, spare wheel holder and tool box in the gooseneck, lashing rings, adjustable track guides and blocks, guide cables, tool kit, 12-pin (24 V) socket, and telescopic, two-speed landing system with separate crank handle controls.

Titan tank transporter semi-trailer with one rear loading ramp lowered

Specifications

Model	45	55
Weight (empty)	14 000 kg	17 000 kg
(loaded)	59 000 kg	72 000 kg
Max load	45 000 kg	55 000 kg
Length (overall)	12.61 m	13.6 m
(of platform)	7.9 m	8.64 m
Width	3.15 m	3.65 m
Height of platform		
(loaded)	1.15 m	1.32 m
King-pin size	89 mm	89 mm
Tyres	9.00 × 20	12.00 × 20

Status
In production.

Manufacturer
Titan SA, BP 407, F-69400 Villefranche-sur-Saône, France.

Trailor Tank Transporter Semi-trailers

Description
There are three Trailor tank transporters and all are similar, differing only in load capacities and tyre sizes. All are of conventional two-axle configuration, with all-steel frames and decks. Three-line air braking and 89 mm king-pins are standard and each trailer also has track guides, chocks and winch cable rollers. The rear loading ramps are spring-balanced and mechanically operated.

Specifications
Model	54T	62T	74T
Length	12.96 m	11.95 m	12.97 m
Width	3.1 m	—	—
Deck length	6.6 m	5.18 m	6.15 m
Capacity	38 000 kg	45 000 kg	55 000 kg
Tyres	7.50 × 15	E20 size	12.00 × 20

Status
In production.

Manufacturer
Trailor SA, 5 Route Nationale 10, Coigniegres, BP 49, F-78311 Maurepas Cedex, France.
Tel: (1) 30 50 61 26. Telex: 698896 f.
Fax: (1) 30 50 31 32.

Trailor 54T tank transporter semi-trailer

Trailor 62T tank transporter semi-trailer

Fruehauf Flat Bed Semi-trailers

Description
Fruehauf France flat bed semi-trailers are produced with varying load-carrying capacities for the transport of general cargoes over long distances. Versions with capacities of between 20 and 60 tonnes are available. Tilt-bodies, cargo vans and container carriers with associated locking and other systems may be adapted to these semi-trailers.

The data provided in the specifications table are for a typical 40-tonne capacity flat bed semi-trailer producing a GVW of 50 tonnes.

Specifications
Max load: 40 000 kg
Length: 12.2 m
Width: 2.5 m
King-pin: 2 in or 3.5 in
Tyres: 12.00 × 20

Status
In production. In service with at least one army outside France.

Fruehauf 40-tonne flat bed semi-trailer

Manufacturer
Fruehauf France, 2 avenue de l'Aunette, F-91130 Ris-Orangis, France.
Tel: 69 43 30 00. Telex: 601381 f.   Fax: 69 43 33 66.

ACMAT ALM Saharian Trailer Model RM 215 SC 1250 litre Tanker

Description
This trailer may be used to carry water, petrol or oil in a 1250 litre steel-plated tank. The tank, together with its associated stowage boxes, is carried in a 2 mm thick steel body on the standard ACMAT ALM Saharian trailer chassis. A Japy manual pump is fitted as standard but for the petrol version a reel with piping and connection pipes are carried. For the water tanker version a filter system is supplied. A 4 litre fire extinguisher is also carried with the petrol tanker version.

Standard fittings carried on all types of trailer include one spare wheel, stowage for eight jerricans, a tool set (in two boxes) and sand channels. Oil and air brakes are standard and a mechanical handbrake is also fitted for parking. A jockey wheel with a diameter of 0.4 m is provided.

ACMAT ALM Saharian trailer Model RM 215 SC

Specifications
Weight:
  (loaded) 2850 kg
  (empty) 1600 kg
Max load: 1250 kg
Capacity of tank: 1250 l
Length: 4.125 m
Width: 2.07 m

Height:
  (overall) 1.915 m
  (lunette) 0.765 m
Track: 1.71 m
Tyres: 12.5 × 20 XL

Status
In production.

Manufacturer
ACMAT, Ateliers de Construction Mécanique de l'Atlantique, Le Point du Jour, F-44600 Saint-Nazaire, France.
Tel: 40 22 33 71. Telex: 700913 f.
Fax: 40 66 30 96.

Fruehauf 20 000 litre Tanker Semi-trailer

Description
This semi-trailer was designed for transporting various fuels including petrol and has remote-controlled drainage pipes with safety valves, pump operated by auxiliary engine, shielded electrical system, manually operated stabilisers mounted towards the front of the trailer and external fully enclosed containers on either side of the tank for stowage of fuel pipes.

A generally similar semi-trailer with an aluminium tank having a capacity of 30 000 litres is also produced. This has a gross weight of 32 000 kg.

Specifications
Capacity: 20 000 l
Length: 9.92 m
Width: 2.5 m
King-pin size: 89 mm
Tyres: 12.00 × 20

Status
In production. In service with the French Army.

Manufacturer
Fruehauf France, 2 avenue de l'Aunette, F-91130 Ris-Orangis, France.
Tel: 69 43 30 00. Telex: 601381 f.
Fax: 69 43 33 66.

Fruehauf 20 000 litre tanker semi-trailer

LOHR SMT 50 D Special Tanker Semi-trailer

Description
This all-terrain tanker semi-trailer was developed specifically for use in desert areas and can carry 50 000 litres of dispensable fuel. The fuel is carried in five 10 000 litre compartments with an additional 2000 litre compartment used to supply fuel for an air-cooled 36 hp auxiliary motor to power a compressor or to provide services for the tractor vehicle. Two 670 l/min fuel pumps are provided and four fuel dispensing nozzles can each deliver 250 l/min; there are manual pumping facilities. There is also a 300 litre water tank. A 12 or 24 V electrical system can be provided.

Specifications
Capacity: 50 000 l
Length:
  (overall) 12.8 m
  (tank) 11.4 m
Width: 4.28 m
Height: 4.8 m

LOHR SMT 50 D special tanker semi-trailer for desert use

Tank diameter: 2.5 m
Tyres: 24 × 20.5 S

Status
In production. In service with at least one nation.

Manufacturer
LOHR SA, F-67980 Hangenbieten, France.
Tel: 88 38 98 00. Telex: 870082 f.
Fax: 88 96 06 36.

Trailor Tanker Semi-trailers

Description
The 30 000 litre tank is of all-aluminium construction and has two compartments, upper and lower. The top of the tank is provided with a non-skid walkway and handrails. The trailer has two-speed manually operated telescopic stabilisers, hoses, hose racks and hose winder, air brakes (one line acting on each axle) and a shielded electrical system.

The 37 500 litre tank is of all-aluminium construction and has five compartments. Other equipment is similar to that fitted to the 30 000 litre tanker.

Specifications

Capacity	30 000 l	37 500 l
Length	10.36 m	12.36 m
Width	2.5 m	2.5 m
Tyres	18.00 × 22.5	18.00 × 22.5

Status
In production. In service with the French Army.

Manufacturer
Trailor SA, 5 Route Nationale 10, Coigniegres, BP 49, F-78311 Maurepas Cedex, France.
Tel: (1) 30 50 61 26. Telex: 698896 f.
Fax: (1) 30 50 31 32.

ACMAT RM 215 SA Workshop Trailer

Description
The ACMAT RM 215 SA is built onto the standard ACMAT trailer as described earlier in this section. The workshop trailer was designed to carry out vehicle field repairs up to fourth echelon level, even in desert areas. Equipment provided with the trailer includes a 13 kVA generator, two 180 litre oil tanks for engine and transmission oils, an air compressor, injection calibrating equipment, a bench-mounted press, engine and transmission oil and grease lines, a work bench with a 125 mm vice, an electric grinder and a vertical drill. Portable equipment includes hydraulic circuit maintenance equipment, battery maintenance equipment, electric and gas welding equipment, two large tool chests and two spare parts cabinets. A mast with floodlights is also supplied.

Specifications
Weight: (operating) 3950 kg
Length: 4.155 m
Width: (travelling) 2.07 m
Height:
(travelling) 2.034 m
(towing eye) 0.765 m
Track: 1.71 m

Status
In production.

Manufacturer
ACMAT, Ateliers de Construction Mécanique de l'Atlantique, Le Point du Jour, F-44600 Saint-Nazaire, France.
Tel: 40 22 33 71. Telex: 700913 f.
Fax: 40 66 30 96.

ACMAT RM 215 SA workshop trailer

ACMAT RM 215 GCR Trailer-mounted Field Kitchen

Description
The RM 215 GCR is an airportable, trailer-mounted field kitchen capable of serving 350 meals in 2 hours. The kitchen equipment is mounted on a standard ACMAT trailer chassis, as described previously in this section.

The kitchen is equipped with four 100 litre cooking containers and may be fired by wood or diesel fuel, depending upon availability. Ovens or heating plates can be substituted for cooking containers. The equipment can also be butane-fired.

In the working position, the kitchen is surrounded by folding walkways and protected by a canvas/nylon canopy. A 400 litre water tank is incorporated in the trailer chassis and four jerricans are also carried. A fuel tank is incorporated and this allows over three hours continuous cooking on all burners. Two utensil cupboards and two working surfaces are also included, and a jib and block are provided for handling cooking pots.

Specifications
On tow
Weight: (laden) 2870 kg
Length: (overall) 4.225 m
Body length: 2.8 m
Height: (overall) 2.4 m
Width: (overall) 2.07 m
Track: 1.71 m
Lunette height: 0.765 m

Working position
Cooking area: 1.7 × 1.25 m
Walking area: 4.12 × 3.45 m
Height above ground: 1 m
Height: (overall) 4.3 m

Status
In production.

Manufacturer
ACMAT, Ateliers de Construction Mécanique de l'Atlantique, Le Point du Jour, F-44600 Saint-Nazaire, France.
Tel: 40 22 33 71. Telex: 700913 f.
Fax: 40 66 30 96.

ACMAT RM 215 GCR trailer-mounted field kitchen in travelling order

ACMAT RM 215 GCR trailer-mounted field kitchen in working configuration

ACMAT Semi-trailers

Description
ACMAT produces a range of semi-trailers for use with its TPK 6.35 TSR truck tractor. These semi-trailers are used to carry standard military shelter/containers and three types have been produced with capacities ranging from 4300 kg to 6000 kg. A 9000 litre fuel or water tank can be installed if necessary. The semi-trailers maintain a high level of commonality with existing ACMAT trucks and trailers and the suspension is the same as that used on the rear suspension of the TPK 6.35 TSR. A 200 litre water tank and a spare wheel are fitted to each semi-trailer. The full NATO specification is respected for the 24 V suppressed electrical system and also for the air transport hold-down points.

Specifications (SR 490)
Weight: (empty) 10 000 kg
Length: 8.53 m
Width: 2.4 m
Height:
(load platform) 1.12 m
(gooseneck) 1.97 m
Track: 1.8 m

Wheelbase:
(fifth wheel to centre of rear bogie) 6.25 m
(between rear axles) 1.22 m

Status
In production.

Manufacturer
ACMAT, Ateliers de Construction Mécanique de L'Atlantique, Le Point du Jour, F-44600 Saint-Nazaire, France.
Tel: 40 22 33 71. Telex: 700913 f.
Fax: 40 66 30 96.

ACMAT semi-trailer carrying communications shelter and towed by TPK 6.35 TSR tractor truck

ARE 2-tonne F2 Ammunition Trailer

Description
The F2 trailer was designed to fill the need for additional ammunition to accompany the 155 mm self-propelled gun Mk F3. It was specifically designed to be towed by the AMX-13 VCA which normally transports the gun detachment and some ammunition. The body is steel and is open at the top, although the sides provide a slight measure of ballistic protection to the contents. Removable racks and cases provide stowage for 30 155 mm projectiles and charges and six hinged cases for storing warhead fuze containers. The rear door is hinged along its base, forming a working platform when open and a watertight seal when closed, allowing the trailer to ford to a depth of about 1 m. The wheels are fitted with bulletproof tyres and are mounted on torsion bars. By removing the ammunition racks the trailer may be used for general cargo.

Specifications
Length: 4.8 m
Width: 2.5 m
Height: 1.465 m
Weight:
(empty) 2500 kg
(loaded) 4400 kg
Capacity: 2.9 m³
Ground clearance: 0.48 m

Status
In service with the French Army, Kuwait, Qatar and Venezuela.

Manufacturer
Creusot-Loire Industrie, Division Mécanique Spécial-isée, Immeuble Ile de France, Cedex 33, F-92070 Paris La Defense, France.
Tel: (1) 49 00 60 50. Telex: 615 638 f.
Fax: (1) 49 00 58 99.

ARE 2-tonne F2 ammunition trailer (ECPA)

LOHR RF 3.5-tonne Refrigerated Container Trailer

Description
This special trailer was designed to carry refrigerated containers for food and other perishable products. It consists of an open side-walled trailer onto which the refrigerated containers can be loaded. The towing bar has a dolly wheel and a towing bar link which can accommodate towing hitch heights from 0.8 to 1.5 m. Two 50 litre tanks are provided to service a carried container. One is located on each side, the left-hand one for fuel and the other for water. Removable steps are provided for access to the container interior. Telescopic stabiliser arms are provided on the towing arm (one) and at the rear (two). A spare wheel is provided.

Specifications
Weight:
(empty) 1090 kg
(loaded) 3870 kg
Length: 4.236 m
Width: 2.23 m
Height: 1.25 m
Track: 1.9 m
Tyres: 11.00 R 16 X type S
Electrical system: 24 V

Status
In production.

LOHR RF 3.5-tonne refrigerated container trailer

Manufacturer
LOHR SA, F-67980 Hangenbieten, France.

Tel: 88 38 98 00. Telex: 870082 f.
Fax: 88 96 06 36.

LOHR CRC 150 Trailer-mounted Field Kitchen

Description

The LOHR CRC 150 trailer-mounted field kitchen is mounted on a single-axle trailer and can cook or reheat meals for up to 150 men at one time. The CRC 150 uses a central kitchen unit arranged around a heater powered by a 2.5 kWA power unit and supplying a cooking pot, a pressure cooker, a grill pan and a bain-marie – a folding chimney is provided. A folding work platform is provided all around the central unit and weather protection is provided by an awning over supports which can be folded down for transport.

There is independent pneumatic suspension on both wheels.

Specifications
Weight: 1450 kg
Length: 3.92 m
Width: 2.06 m
Height: (max) 1.9 m

Status
In production.

Manufacturer
LOHR SA, F-67980 Hangenbieten, France.
Tel: 88 38 98 00. Telex: 870082 f.
Fax: 88 96 06 36.

LOHR CRC 150 trailer-mounted field kitchen

GERMANY

SLT 50-2 Tank Transporter Semi-trailer

Development

In 1965 the then West Germany and the USA agreed on the joint development of a tank transporter for the MBT-70. The firm of Krupp was responsible for the design of the trailer. Even before the cancellation of the MBT-70 project each country had decided to go its own way on the design of the tank transporter, although in major design features the versions of both looked very similar. The SLT 50-2 semi-trailer (*Schwerlasttransporter*, or heavy load carrier) was adopted by the German Army and 328 were produced. The US Army version was standardised as the M747 (qv).

Description

The semi-trailer has four axles, each with two single-tyred steerable wheels. Steering of the wheels is hydraulically controlled and depends on the angle between the tractor and semi-trailer. Each axle is independently suspended on semi-leaf springs which also locate the axles. Swing arms and a connecting linkage provide for load equalisation and an additional mechanism allows the load platform to be lowered by about 0.1 m to the required underpass height of 3.9 m when loaded. All four axles are equipped with air brakes and parking brakes are fitted to two axles.

The load platform has a frame of box construction to resist longitudinal flexing and a bearing surface of sandwich construction. Folding, spring-balanced ramps are fitted and make an angle of only 14° for loading, yet may be lifted by only two men. Cable guides are provided on the trailer gooseneck to assist in winching loads on and off the trailer.

Specifications
Weight: 16 600 kg
Max load: 52 000 kg
Axle loadings:
 (loaded) 13 000 kg
 (unloaded) 3478 kg
Length: (overall) 13.1 m
Width: 3.15 m
Track: 2.65 m
Height: (to top of raised ramps) 3.15 m
Fifth wheel height: (loaded) 1.55 m

Loading platform
Length: 8 m
Height:
 (unloaded) 1.37 m
 (loaded) 1.28 m
 (loaded, lowered) 1.16 m
Ground clearance: 0.31 m
Departure angle: 35°
Turning circle radius: (with SLT 50-2 tractor) 9 m
Tyres: 18.00 × 22.5, 20 PR
Ramps:
 (length) 4.18 m
 (width) 0.75 m each
King-pin: 89 mm

Status
Production complete. In service with the German Army.

Manufacturer
Karl Kässbohrer Fahrzeugwerke GmbH, Postfach 2660, D-7900 Ulm/Donau, Federal Republic of Germany.
Tel: 731 1811. Telex: 712766.

Kärcher TFK 250 Mobile Kitchen Trailer

Description

This tactical field kitchen is a mobile catering unit mounted on a single-axle 3.5-tonne trainer. It uses stainless steel (chrome-nickel 18/10) for the cooking appliances as well as other high quality materials.

The trailer is fitted with the following equipment: 150 litre double-walled GASTRONOM pressure cookers; a 55 litre GASTRONOM pressure frier; an integrated 75 litre GASTRONOM baking area in which two working levels are heated by one burner; a 28 litre hot water generator and tea maker; and a four-unit pressure vapourisation burner that can use diesel oil, light fuel, petrol or kerosene. Using the TFK 250 two cooks can provide meals for 250 men or a single-course meal for 500 men in 2 hours.

The trailer has a cross-country capability and in use is provided with four support legs. The trailer has an integral weather shelter, and four tarpaulins can be opened semi-automatically within seconds.

Specifications
Weight: (unloaded) approx 2075 kg
Load capacity: approx 425 kg
Length: 4.17 m
Width: 2.16 m
Height:
 (overall) 2.62 m
 (working table) 0.96 m
Ground clearance: 0.32 m
Track: 1.908 m

Status
In production. In service with Belgium (air force), China, Germany (1283 on order between 1990 and 1997), Ireland, Luxembourg, NATO headquarters, New Zealand, Norway, Qatar, Saudi Arabia, United Kingdom and USA, plus some nations in the Middle East and Africa.

Manufacturer
Alfred Kärcher GmbH & Co, Alfred Kärcher-Strasse 28-40, D-7057 Winnenden, Federal Republic of Germany.
Tel: 07195 142797. Telex: 724432.
Fax: 07195 142720.

Kärcher TFK 250 mobile kitchen trailer

Kärcher Modular Field Kitchen MFK

Description

The Kärcher modular field kitchen MFK can be assembled to meet a number of field catering needs and can be mounted on a single axle trailer. The design is based on that of the TFK 250 mobile kitchen (see previous entry) but the various cooking modules can be used separately on the ground or as a complete kitchen unit on the trailer.

Equipment carried includes the following: two 125 litre boiling kettles, one single-walled, one double-walled; a 25 litre frying/baking module; a frying pan module; a grill module; a stowage compartment module; lateral stowage compartments equipped with stainless steel working plates; working tables; integral weather protection; two pressure vaporisation burners; a propane burner; and a solid fuel burner. All cooking equipment is to GASTRONOM/DIN 66075 regulations.

Together with their Spanish partner MEISA, Kärcher obtained an order worth about DM 3.5 million from the Spanish Army for approximately 250 MFK field kitchens.

Specifications

Weight:
 (empty) 520 kg
 (loaded) 2000 kg
Width: 2 m
Height:
 (with tilted chimney) 1.38 m
 (with weather shelter) 2.6 m
Electrical system: 24 V

Status

In production. In service with Austrian and German civil defence and emergency rescue organisations, and Spain (approx 250).

Manufacturer

Alfred Kärcher GmbH & Co, Alfred Kärcher-Strasse

Kärcher modular field kitchen MFK

28-40, D-7057 Winnenden, Federal Republic of Germany.   Tel: 07195 142797. Telex: 724432. Fax: 07195 142720.

GREECE

NK AP-130/60 T Tank Transporter Semi-trailer

Description

This tank transporter semi-trailer was designed to carry tanks up to the weight of a Chieftain or Leopard 2, and heavy engineering plant. The chassis frame is formed from two longitudinal 'I' section beams connected by crossmembers and bridges through stress diffusers. The deck is hardwood with the sides, rear area and foredeck covered with 10 mm steel sheet. The suspension is formed from a pair of model MZP 2/14000 walking beam units each side.

The king-pin is a bolted 89 mm Jost unit mounted on a heavy duty upper coupler plate 16 mm thick. Jost also supplies the two model HDK 240T side-operated two-speed loading winches, providing a static capacity of 60 000 kg and a lift capacity of 30 000 kg. Two hydraulically operated loading ramps, each 2.2 m long by 0.7 m wide, are provided. Power for the ramps is provided by a hydraulic pump located on the right-hand side of the trailer.

Equipment carried on the trailer includes two spare wheels mounted on the gooseneck and provided with handling winches. Also carried are two pulley assemblies, cable guides, a set of wheel chocks and two storage boxes under the front deck.

Specifications

Weight: (unloaded) 19 000 kg

NK AP-130/60 T tank transporter semi-trailer carrying M32 armoured recovery vehicle

Max payload: 60 000 kg
Length:
 (overall, ramps lowered) 14.8 m
 (deck) 7.6 m
Width: 3.6 m
Height:
 (overall) 2.75 m
 (king-pin) 1.67 m
Ground clearance: 0.63 m
Tyres: 12.00 × 18 PR
Electrical system: 12/24 V

Status

In production.

Manufacturer

N Kioleides SA, PO Box 51156, 145 10 Kifissia, Athens, Greece.
Tel: 816 1902/3. Telex: 214500 nk gr.
Fax: 816 1739.

INDIA

20-tonne Low Deck Full Trailer

Description
Bharat Earth Movers Limited and Mahindra & Mahindra produce a number of trailers and semi-trailers, among which is a 20-tonne low deck full trailer. Designed for on- and off-road use it has a front and rear suspension that provides a lateral articulation of 200 mm for the equal distribution of the load during off-road operations. The front suspension has two longitudinally mounted beams pivoted in the front and spring supported in the rear, with two single wheels on each beam. The rear suspension has four rear wheels in one row fitted to half axles supported by longitudinally mounted suspension beams pivoted front and rear.

Standard accessories include two spare wheels, lashing shackles, a tool box, plus hinged and extension ramps.

Specifications
Weight: (unladen) 12 050 kg
Payload: 20 000 kg
Bed area: 6 × 3.1 m
Length: (overall) 12.8 m
Width: 3.1 m
Height:
  (overall) 2.259 m
  (platform) 1.1 m
  (drawbar) 0.87 m
Wheelbase: 8.4 m
Tyres:
  (front) 14.00 × 20, 18 PR (4)
  (rear) 9.00 × 20, 14 PR (8)
Electrical system: 24 V

Status
In production.

Manufacturers
Bharat Earth Movers Limited, Sheriff Bhatia Towers, 88 M.G. Road, Bangalore-560 001, India.
Mahindra Engineering & Chemical Products Limited, Mahindra Owen Division, 148 Bombay Pune Road, Pimpri, Pune-411018, India.
Tel: 775045.   Telex: 0146-233 MOL-IN.
Fax: 771286.

Artist's impression of 20-tonne low deck full trailer

ISRAEL

AAI MT-100 1000 kg General Purpose Trailer

Description
The MT-100 1000 kg general purpose trailer was designed for use with the AAI M-325 Commandcar vehicles (see entry in *Trucks* section) but can be used by other vehicles. It has a welded steel chassis with trailing arm suspension using rubber element springs. The MT-100 can be towed on roads at speeds up to 80 km/h and the wheels and tyres are the same as those used on the M-325. Service braking is by means of an overrun unit operating mechanical brakes through a spring damper. A safety chain will operate the brakes if the trailer is released from the towing vehicle and a spring damper is fitted to the towing eye. The electrical system is 24 V connected through a plug for the stop lights, turn signals and side lights.

The trailer may be produced in three forms: a flat bed trailer for carrying special equipment and generators, as a water tank with a capacity of 770 litres constructed from stainless steel, or for general cargo use a welded steel cargo body may be fitted. The latter is supplied with lashing points for the load and a PVC-coated tarpaulin cover if required.

Specifications
Weight: (chassis, unladen) 290 kg
Max load: 1000 kg
Length: 3.2 m

MT-100 trailer with general cargo body and cover in place

Width: 1.95 m
Track: 1.66 m
Fording: 0.76 m
Tyres: 9.00 × 16 – 10 ply
Electrical system: 24 V

Status
Production complete. In service with the Israeli armed forces.

Manufacturer
Automotive Industries Limited, PO Box 535, Nazareth Illit, Israel.
Tel: 06 558111. Telex: 46217 ail il.
Fax: 06 558103.

CST-3 Combat Support Trailer

Description
TAAS – Israel Industries Limited (formerly Israel Military Industries) produces a special combat support trailer known as the CST-3 (Combat Support Trailer 3000 kg) with a payload of 3000 kg. The trailer was designed for use in a number of combat engineer roles and can be towed behind various types of vehicle including armoured personnel carriers, tanks and 5-ton trucks. To accommodate this range of vehicles, the CST-3 is equipped with a special towing arm, and can be towed at speeds of up to 50 km/h across country and 90 km/h on roads.

The sheet metal body is divided into a central cargo area of 5.25 m³ and two 1.5 m³ side stowage compartments. The trailer has its own foldable 500 kg capacity loading and unloading system and can be fitted with removable bows. It can be adapted for a number of roles including the rapid laying of mines using a chute over the rear. An electrical remote-control system is supplied for use with various forms of specialised equipment. A pyrotechnic quick-release system for the towing hitch is available if required.

The trailer body is carried on a single axle with a capacity of 8000 kg. The suspension uses independent trailing arms and rubber torque springs. Air brakes are provided.

Specifications
Weight:
   (empty) 2000 kg
   (loaded, all terrain) 5000 kg
Max load: (all terrain) 3000 kg
Length: 5.3 m
Width: 2.5 m
Height: (unloaded) 1.4 m
Max towing speed:
   (road) 90 km/h
   (cross-country) 50 km/h
Tyres: 14.00 × 20

Status
In production.

Manufacturer
TAAS – Israel Industries Limited, PO Box 1044, Ramat Hasharon 47100, Israel.
Tel: (3) 542 52 22. Telex: 33 719 misbit il.
Fax: (3) 48 96 39.

CST-3 combat support trailer

Urdan ARTRAIL Ammunition Resupply Trailer

Description
The Urdan ARTRAIL ammunition resupply trailer was designed and developed to overcome some of the ammunition resupply problems associated with self-propelled artillery in the field. In essence, the ARTRAIL is a trailer that can be towed into action by a self-propelled artillery system to act as a mobile auxiliary ammunition supply source. The ARTRAIL carries 44 projectiles, propellant charges and fuzes. It has been tested with the M109A2 155 mm self-propelled howitzer system.

The ARTRAIL is a two-wheeled trailer consisting of three units: a stowage compartment for the ammunition, a two-wheeled assembly with a connecting shaft, and a conveyor assembly with two conveyors and one pick-up device.

When required for action the front-mounted doors on the ammunition compartment are swung open. The doors contain the propellant charges and when open reveal the projectiles stowed in horizontal and slightly inclined stowage cradles. Up to eight smoke projectiles are stored vertically in side-mounted compartments. All projectiles may be carried fuzed or unfuzed and there is capacity to carry more fuzes than projectiles to accommodate variations in fire plans.

The conveyor assembly takes the projectile into the self-propelled artillery system fighting compartment by gravity. The conveyor assembly is balanced and easy to raise or lower. Each projectile is released from its stowage cradle in the trailer ammunition compartment by a pick-up device described as a fork-lift, and moves down the conveyor into the fighting compartment to a height of 400 mm above the fighting compartment floor, that is at a height convenient for loading. Propellant charges can be taken direct from their locations in the trailer doors and the vertically stowed projectiles can be moved into the fighting compartment by hand. Up to 10 projectiles can be delivered each minute.

After use, reloading the ARTRAIL takes up to 15 minutes. If required an empty ARTRAIL can be

ARTRAIL ammunition resupply trailer in action with an M109A2 155 mm self-propelled howitzer

unhitched and directly replaced by a loaded unit. ARTRAIL can be located by any 5-ton truck or armoured personnel carrier. The rear door of the self-propelled artillery system involved can be modified to accommodate the ARTRAIL in 30 minutes under field conditions. The transition time for ARTRAIL from road transport to field conditions takes 5 minutes. In action ARTRAIL provides the same degree of protection to its contents as the self-propelled artillery system involved but as an option composite armour can be added to the entire stowage area or to selected sensitive areas.

The ARTRAIL is mounted on a two-wheel assembly fitted with combat tyres, a hydropneumatic suspension and a braking system.

Specifications
Weight:
   (empty) approx 3990 kg
   (loaded) approx 6105 kg
Length: 4.2 m
Width: 3.2 m
Height:
   (empty) 2.5 m
   (loaded) 2.4 m

Status
Development complete. Ready for production.

Manufacturer
Urdan Industries Limited, Industrial Zone, Netanya 42378, Israel.
Tel: 972 53 338074. Telex: 341822 usaf il.
Fax: 972 53 610246.

ITALY

Bartoletti One-axle 1000 kg Cargo Trailer Type B.10

Description

This single-axle trailer has an all-steel body with drop tailgate, canvas supports and canvas cover, leaf spring suspension, 510 mm disc wheels, hydraulic overrun brakes, 12-pole 24 V electric system, standard and blackout lights and a retractable dolly wheel.

Specifications

Weight:
 (empty) 750 kg
 (loaded) 1750 kg
Max load: 1000 kg
Inside length of body: 2.445 m
Inside width of body: 1.165 m
Height of side boards: 0.46 m
Length: 3.72 m
Width: 1.81 m
Height: 1.8 m
Track: 1.51 m
Tyres: 8.25 × 20

Status

In production.

Bartoletti one-axle 1000 kg cargo trailer type B.10 with canvas cover

Manufacturer

E Bartoletti, Via Leonardo Da Vinci 4, I-47100 Forli,
Italy.
Tel: 543 734111. Telex: 550064 barto 1.
Fax: 543 739029.

Bartoletti One-axle 2000 kg Cargo Trailer

Description

This single-axle trailer can be fitted with a variety of different bodies and used for specialised applications such as carrying radar. The trailer has semi-elliptic simple flexible leaf spring suspension with hydraulic dampers, 510 mm disc wheels, compressed air two-line (automatically adjustable) brake booster, 12-pole 24 V electric system, standard and blackout lights, removable screw-type dolly wheel and two stabilisers that can be lowered at the rear.

Specifications

Weight:
 (empty) 1000 kg
 (loaded) 3000 kg
Payload: 2000 kg
Length:
 (including towbar) 4.19 m
 (excluding towbar) 2.3 m
Width: 2.07 m
Chassis width: 1.35 m

Bartoletti one-axle 2000 kg cargo trailer

Height to upper edge of chassis: 1 m
Track: 1.77 m
Tyres: 11.00 × 20

Status

In production.

Manufacturer

E Bartoletti, Via Leonardo Da Vinci 4, I-47100 Forli,
Italy.
Tel: 543 734111. Telex: 550064 barto 1.
Fax: 543 739029.

Bartoletti 3000 kg Light Cargo Trailer Type 2L-30 M

Description

This all-steel trailer has drop sides and a drop tailgate with the front axle mounted on a ball-type turntable, simple flexible semi-elliptic leaf spring suspension, 380 mm spoke wheels, 12-pole 24 V electric system, standard and blackout lights, and a compressed air two-line (automatically adjustable) brake booster.

Specifications

Weight:
 (empty) 1300 kg
 (loaded) 4300 kg
Payload: 3000 kg
Length:
 (including towbar) 4.325 m
 (excluding towbar) 3 m
Width: 1.56 m
Height of deck from ground: (loaded) 0.92 m
Height of sideboards: 0.4 m

Bartoletti 3000 kg light cargo trailer type 2L-30 M

Track: 1.295 m
Tyres: 7.50 × 15

Status

In production.

Manufacturer

E Bartoletti, Via Leonardo Da Vinci 4, I-47100 Forli,
Italy.
Tel: 543 734111. Telex: 550064 barto 1.
Fax: 543 739029.

Bartoletti One-axle Flat Bed Trailer Type B.40 MGB

Description
This single-axle trailer was designed for the transport of components of the British Williams Fairey Medium Girder Bridge. The trailer has semi-elliptic flexible leaf spring suspension, 510 mm disc wheels, compressed air two-line (automatically adjustable) brake booster, 12-pole 24 V electric system, standard and blackout lights and a removable screw-type loading gear. Stabilisers are mounted at the rear of the trailer.

Specifications
Weight:
  (empty) 1600 kg
  (loaded) 5700 kg
Max load: 4100 kg
Length:
  (with towbar) 5.5 m
  (without towbar) 3.6 m
Width: 2.5 m

Bartoletti one-axle flat bed trailer type B.40 MGB

Deck width: 2.31 m
Deck height from ground: (loaded) 1.145 m
Track: 2.05 m
Tyres: 11.00 × R20

Status
In production. In service with the Italian Army.

Manufacturer
E Bartoletti, Via Leonardo Da Vinci 4, I-47100 Forli, Italy.
Tel: 543 734111. Telex: 550064 barto 1.
Fax: 543 739029.

Bartoletti 24 000 kg Container Transport Trailer Type 24 RD

Description
This two-axle trailer has a flat deck designed for the transportation of standard 20 ft ISO containers, or general cargo. The trailer has semi-elliptic double flexible leaf springs on silent blocks with stabilisers, 510 mm disc wheels, 12-pole 24 V electric system, standard and blackout lights and compressed air two-line (automatically adjustable) brake booster.

Specifications
Weight:
  (empty) 4750 kg
  (loaded) 24 000 kg
Payload: 19 250 kg
Length:
  (deck) 6.5 m
  (including towbar) 8.505 m
Width:
  (overall) 2.5 m
  (deck) 2.4 m
Height of deck from ground level: 1.29 m
Tyres: 12.00 × 20 PR 18

Bartoletti 24 000 kg container transport trailer type 24 RD

Status
In production.

Manufacturer
E Bartoletti, Via Leonardo Da Vinci 4, I-47100 Forli, Italy.
Tel: 543 734111. Telex: 550064 barto 1.
Fax: 543 739029.

Bartoletti 1800 litre Water Tanker Type B.10

Description
This single-axle trailer has an 1800 litre capacity drinking water tank, 500 mm diameter safety manhole, gravity outlet through a 65 mm gate valve and 26 mm taps, leaf spring suspension, 510 mm disc wheels, hydraulic overrun brake, 12-pole 24 V electric system with standard blackout lights and a retractable dolly wheel.

Specifications
Weight:
  (empty) 1000 kg
  (loaded) 2800 kg
Max load: 1800 kg
Length: (including towbar) 3.72 m
Width: 1.81 m
Track: 1.51 m
Tyres: 8.25 × 20
Maximum diameter of tank: 1.46 m
Minimum diameter of tank: 0.86 m
Height of tank: 2 m

Status
In production.

Bartoletti 1800 litre water tanker type B.10

Manufacturer
E Bartoletti, Via Leonardo Da Vinci 4, I-47100 Forli, Italy.
Tel: 543 734111. Telex: 550064 barto 1.
Fax: 543 739029.

Bartoletti 8000 litre Fuel Tanker Trailer Type 2M-55

Description
The front axle of this two-axle trailer is mounted on a turntable. The oval section tank is of all-steel construction and is provided with a single 255 mm loading mouth, metric rod and fuel level indicator, remote-controlled foot valve, 80 mm gate valves with quick coupling mouth and standard accessories.

Specifications
Weight:
(empty) 4200 kg
(loaded) 11 000 kg
Max load: 6800 kg
Length:
(including towbar) 7.32 m
(trailer only) 5.75 m
Width: 2.47 m
Height: 2.84 m
Track: 1.727 m
Tyres: 12.00 × 20 PR 18

Status
In production.

Bartoletti 8000 litre fuel tanker trailer type 2M-55

Manufacturer
E Bartoletti, Via Leonardo Da Vinci 4, I-47100 Forli, Italy.
Tel: 543 734111. Telex: 550064 barto 1.
Fax: 543 739029.

Bartoletti 2PX Trailer

Description
The trailer was designed for the transport of tracked vehicles such as armoured fighting vehicles and engineering equipment. The trailer has aligned axles on independent dollies, low bed, steering by means of equaliser and guide arms, sliding rear dollies with jacks, simple flexible semi-elliptical oscillating leaf spring suspension, 510 mm spoke wheels, 12-pole 24 V electric system, standard and blackout lights, compressed air two-line (automatically adjustable) brake booster and rear loading ramps.

Specifications
Weight:
(empty) 7350 kg
(loaded) 27 350 kg
Payload: 20 000 kg
Length:
(including towbar) 9.56 m
(trailer only) 8.3 m
(bed) 4.7 m

Bartoletti 2PX trailer in travelling configuration

Width:
(overall) 2.5 m
(bed) 2.5 m
Height of low bed: (loaded) 0.63 m
Tyres: 11.00 × 20 PR 16

Status
In production.

Manufacturer
E Bartoletti, Via Leonardo Da Vinci 4, I-47100 Forli, Italy.
Tel: 543 734111. Telex: 550064 barto 1.
Fax: 543 739029.

Bartoletti Tank Semi-trailer Type TCS 60 BO

Description
The TCS 60 BO semi-trailer was designed for carrying MBTs weighing up to 60 000 kg and can be towed by tractor trucks such as the IVECO FIAT 320-45 WTM (6 × 6).

The trailer has three axles each with four tyres, lowered chassis with double hydraulically retractable loading ramps at the rear, balanced suspension with semi-elliptical leaf springs and reaction arms, pneumatic retractable forward landing gear and adjustable track guides to suit different types of tracked vehicles. The semi-trailer also has a system of rollers and pulleys for easy loading and unloading of vehicles.

Standard equipment includes 12-pole 24 V electric system with standard and blackout lights, compressed air (two-line), automatically adjustable service brake and parking brake.

Specifications
Weight:
(empty) 20 000 kg
(loaded) 80 000 kg
Payload: 60 000 kg
Length: 11.95 m

Bartoletti tank semi-trailer type TCS 60 BO towed by IVECO FIAT 320-45 WTM (6 × 6) tractor truck

Width: 4 m
Platform height from ground: (loaded) 1.42 m
Length of platform: 7.08 + 0.95 m
Track: 2.6 m
Tyres: 16.00 × 20 XS

Status
In production.

Manufacturer
E Bartoletti, Via Leonardo Da Vinci 4, I-47100 Forli, Italy.
Tel: 543 734111. Telex: 550064 barto 1.
Fax: 543 739029.

Bartoletti TCS 50 BO Tank Transporter Semi-trailer

Description

In the same way as the German SLT 50-2 and American M747 semi-trailers, the Bartoletti TCS 50 BO semi-trailer owes its origins to the US/FRG HET-70 programme and is based on the design of the SLT 50-2. It is intended for the transportation of MBTs of up to 50 000 kg, such as the M60 series, without exceeding a height of 4.5 m from ground level to permit transit through road tunnels. The Bartoletti TCS 50 BO is a four-axle semi-trailer with a lowered chassis and retractable loading ramps. The suspension is a combination of semi-elliptical springs and air springs, and the outer axles can be lifted to reduce tyre wear during unloaded running and to improve manoeuvrability at low speed. Rollers and pulleys are provided to facilitate the loading and unloading of damaged vehicles.

Bartoletti TCS 50 BO tank transporter semi-trailer

Max fifth wheel load: 20 000 kg
Length: 12.42 m
Width: 3.15 m
Track: 2.7 m
Load deck length: 7.67 m
Platform height: (loaded) 1.23 m
Height:
(over folded ramps) 2.93 m
(over spare wheel) 3.12 m
King-pin:
(height) 1.64 m
(diameter) 89 mm
Distance between axle centres: 1.25 m

Tyres: 18 × 22.5 XS
Brakes: dual air
Electrical system: 24 V

Status

In production, under licence from OTO Melara.

Manufacturer

E Bartoletti, Via Leonardo Da Vinci 4, I-47100 Forli, Italy.
Tel: 543 734111. Telex: 550064 barto 1.
Fax: 543 739029.

Specifications

Weight: (unladen) 14 000 kg
Payload: 50 000 kg

Cometto MPS50 Tank Transporter Semi-trailer

Description

On the MPS50 Cometto tank transporter semi-trailers the twin-axle rows may be fitted with either four or eight tyres to assist in weight distribution to suit the payload. An extra pair of tyres may be carried under the loading platform for use as spares; these two spare tyre carriers have lifting devices to assist stowage. The MPS50 is fitted with a five-speed roller and pulley system for loading disabled vehicles and when not on the tractor truck a folding stand is situated to the front of the trailer. The two loading ramps are spring-loaded to provide quick and easy loading and for extra stability two foldable rear stabiliser legs on the ramp hinges may be used. The loading ramps measure 1.7 ×

0.75 m. Sliding track guides are fitted as standard as are load fastening hooks and chains. Accessories include a tool kit and box and a 150 litre water tank.

Specifications

Number of tyres per axle row	4	8
Weight (empty)	16 000 kg	16 600 kg
(loaded)	66 000 kg	77 000 kg
Max load	50 000 kg	60 000 kg
Length (overall)	12.34 m	12.34 m
(loading platform)	7.925 m	7.925 m
Width	3.505 m	3.505 m
Height (loading platform)	1.25—1.3 m	1.25—1.3 m
(5th wheel, approx)	1.5 m	1.5 m
Axle wheelbase	1.5 m	1.5 m
King-pin	89 mm	89 mm
Tyres	18.00 × 22.5	12.00 × 20

Status

In production.

Manufacturer

Cometto Industriale Srl, Via Cuneo 38, I-12011 Borgo S Dalmazzo (Cuneo), Italy.
Tel: 0171 76331. Telex: 210375.

Cometto MPS50 tank transporter semi-trailer carrying M60A1 tank

---

Cometto S53 Tank Transporter Semi-trailer

Description

The S53 is a heavy duty semi-trailer for the transport of tanks and heavy equipment. Its running gear has 20 wheels, suspended independently in five pairs on each side. It is thought that there is provision for raising and steering at least some of the wheels hydraulically to assist manoeuvrability as an auxiliary power unit is mounted on the gooseneck. The operation and stabilisation of the rear loading ramps are also hydraulic.

Cometto S53 tank transporter semi-trailer

Specifications

Weight: 27 000 kg
Payload: 51 000 kg
Load on fifth wheel: 21 500 kg
Length: (overall) 14.77 m
Width: 3.4 m

Load deck height: 1.4 m (can be adjusted by 0.28 m up or down)
Tyres: 18-19.5 × 5

Status

In production.

Manufacturer

Cometto Industriale Srl, Via Cuneo 38, I-12011 Borgo S Dalmazzo (Cuneo), Italy.
Tel: 0171 76331. Telex: 210375.

De Filippi Trailers

De Filippi manufactures a wide range of trailers and semi-trailers, many of which are suited for military use. Brief specifications are given below:

Status
In production.

Manufacturer
Costruzioni Meccaniche A De Filippi SAS,

Via Garibaldi 124, I-12061 Carru' (CN), Italy.
Tel: 0173 75101. Telex: 210175 caruca i.
Fax: 0173 75112.

Model	Type	Payload	Empty weight	Length	Length of platform	Width	Tyres	Number of tyres	Axles	Notes
R-6	full trailer	4300 kg	1700 kg	5.6 m	4 m	2.38 m	7.50 × 15	4	1	
R-10	full trailer	9500 kg	3000 kg	5.8 m	5.6 m	2.5 m	7.50 × 15	8	2	Can be fitted with side panels
R-20	full trailer	13 400 kg	4500 kg	n/a	5.2 m	2.5 m	8.25 × 15	8	2	Fitted with hydraulic loading ramps
R-25	full trailer	19 800 kg	6000 kg	n/a	5.2 m	2.5 m	8.25 × 15	12	3	Fitted with hydraulic loading ramps
R-28N	full trailer	25 400 kg	6600 kg	7.93 m	6 m	2.5 m	8.25 × 15	12	3	
S-36C	semi-trailer	28 100 kg	7900 kg	10 m	6.95 m	2.5 m	8.25 × 15	12	3	side panels
S-36N	semi-trailer	27 600 kg	8400 kg	12.5 m	8.9 m	2.5 m	8.25 × 15	12	3	
R-42	full trailer	33 100 kg	8900 kg	8 m	5.8 m	2.5 m	8.25 × 15	16	4	Fitted with hydraulic loading ramps
S-40	semi-trailer	40 000 kg	10 000 kg	11 m	6.5 m	2.5 m	12.00 × 20	8	2	
S-48	semi-trailer	40 000 kg	9000 kg	10.5 m	7 m	2.5 m	8.25 × 15	12	3	Spring assisted loading ramps
SR-60	semi-trailer	50 000 kg	15 000 kg	12.5 m	9 m	3 m	12.00 × 20	12	3	
S-56	semi-trailer	70 000 kg	15 000 kg	11.3 m	7.4 m	2.5 m	265/7 or 19.5	16	2	Fitted with hydraulic loading ramps

De Filippi R-42 trailer

De Filippi S-48 semi-trailer

KOREA, SOUTH

SsangYong Light Trailers

Description
The SsangYong Motor Company produces five types of light trailer in the ¼- to 1½-ton payload range, including a water tank trailer. All five types are licence-produced versions of US service trailers and the US designation is retained in the Korean designations, prefixed by the letters DA. In nearly every respect the Korean trailers are the same as the US originals but the data quoted by the Korean manufacturer differ from the US specifications and are thus shown here.

Status
In production. In service with the South Korean armed forces.

Specifications
Model	DA-M1	DA-M101	DA-M105	DA-M332	DA-M106
Type	cargo	cargo	cargo	cargo	water tank
Max load	250 kg	750 kg	1500 kg	1500 kg	1500 l
Length	2.735 m	3.78 m	4.23 m	3.76 m	4.23 m
Width	1.545 m	1.87 m	2.105 m	2.413 m	2.06 m
Height	1.31 m	2.17 m	2.413 m	1.532 m	2.26 m
Ground clearance	0.263 m	0.315 m	0.45 m	0.27 m	0.35 m
Track	1.27 m	1.48 m	1.714 m	2.032 m	1.714 m
Tyres	7.00 × 16	7.50 × 20	9.00 × 20	9.00 × 20	9.00 × 20
Electrical system	24 V	24 V	24 V	24 V	24 V

Manufacturer
SsangYong Motor Company Limited, SsangYong Building, 24-1, 2-ka, Jeo-dong, Chung-ku, Seoul, Korea 100-748.

Tel: (02) 273 4181. Telex: 27596 ssymc k.
Fax: (02) 274 5062.

SsangYong Low Bed Semi-trailers

Description
The SsangYong Motor Company produces four types of low bed semi-trailer with capacities of 25 000 kg, 32 000 kg, 40 000 kg and 60 000 kg. All may be used to carry a wide range of military vehicles and equipment ranging from construction equipment to self-propelled artillery and armoured fighting vehicles. All four types have rear-mounted loading ramps with the largest size at least using hydraulic power to lift the ramps after use.

Status
In production.

Manufacturer
SsangYong Motor Company Limited, SsangYong Building, 24-1, 2-ka, Jeo-dong, Chung-ku, Seoul, Korea 100-748.
Tel: (02) 273 4181. Telex: 27596 ssymc k.
Fax: (02) 274 5062.

Specifications
Capacity	25 000 kg	32 000 kg	40 000 kg	60 000 kg	Capacity	25 000 kg	32 000 kg	40 000 kg	60 000 kg
Weight (empty)	7200 kg	9900 kg	11 590 kg	21 000 kg	Offset	3.63 m	4.25 m	4.25 m	4.75 m
Length	10.75 m	11.68 m	11.68 m	12.885 m	Wheelbase	8.73 m	9.75 m	9.67 m	10.49 m
Width	2.98 m	2.98 m	2.98 m	3.64 m	Tyres	9.00 × 20	10.00 × 20	11.00 × 20	11.00 × 20
Height	1.65 m	1.65 m	1.71 m	2.256 m					

NETHERLANDS

DAF tank transporter semi-trailer Type YTS 10050

DAF Tank Transporter Semi-trailer Type YTS 10050

Description

The DAF tank transporter semi-trailer Type YTS 10050 was designed to carry all MBTs currently in service. Provision was made in the design of the semi-trailer to winch disabled tracked vehicles on to and off the trailer with the aid of the winch on the tractor.

The chassis frame consists of two steel box-section girders which form a single welded unit together with the cross-pulley members, outriggers, outer rails, floor plates, fifth-wheel support frame, toolboxes, pulley housing and other components. The king-pin is a standard 89 mm size.

The platform bed is provided with track guides to prevent sideways movement of the tank and these track guides can be adjusted laterally to suit different types of tracked vehicle.

The running gear comprises two separate and identical independently oscillating tandem axle units next to each other, each axle with four sets of twin wheels and tyres. The front and rear axles can oscillate 7° longitudinally in relation to the rocker beam brackets. The transverse oscillation of the wheel axles in relation to the rocker beam is also 7°.

Two ramps at the rear of the trailer can be raised and lowered by two men. Two mechanically operated, pivot-mounted front supports are raised and locked to the main girder at the gooseneck when travelling. As an optional extra, the semi-trailer can be equipped with two hydraulic front supports.

The trailer is fitted with a two-line brake system. Four of the eight diaphragm-type brake chambers are safety actuators with a locking mechanism functioning as a parking brake as well as a service brake. Standard

equipment includes chains and two hydraulic jacks each with a capacity of 25 000 kg. The YTS 10060 semi-trailer is similar to the YTS 10050.

Specifications

Weight:
  (empty) 15 000 kg
  (loaded) 70 000 kg
Max load: 55 000 kg
Length: (overall) 11.72 m
Width:
  (overall) 3.4 m
  (of platform) 3.04 m
Height:
  (top of platform) 1.27 m
  (over loading ramps) 1.81 m

Ground clearance: (under chassis) 0.61 m
Track: 1.78 m
Wheelbase: (king-pin to centre of rear bogie) 8.7 m
Max towing speed: 50 km/h
Tyres: 11.00 × 20

Status

Production complete. In service with Belgium (29), Denmark (14), Netherlands (36), Spain (made under licence) and Sweden (91).

Manufacturer

DAF Military Sales, Hugo van der Goeslaan 1, NL-5643 TW Eindhoven, Netherlands.
Tel: 040 143440. Telex: 51085 daf nl.
Fax: 040 144318.

DAF Tanker Trailer, 2-wheel, 900 litre Type YEW 400

Description

This single-axle two-wheeled trailer was designed for transporting drinking water and has a double-acting hand pump with suction hose, one 26 mm and four 12.7 mm taps and four supporting legs.

Specifications

Weight:
  (empty) 670 kg
  (loaded) 1620 kg
Capacity: 900 l
Length:
  (overall) 3.61 m
  (of tank) 1.55 m
Width:
  (overall) 1.55 m
  (of tank) 1.65 m
Height:
  (overall) 1.6 m
  (to towing eye) 0.89 m
Ground clearance: 0.4 m
Track: 1.5 m
Tyres: 9.00 × 16

Status

Production as required. In service with the Dutch Army.

Manufacturer

DAF Military Sales, Hugo van der Goeslaan 1, NL-5643 TW Eindhoven, Netherlands.
Tel: 040 143440. Telex: 51085 daf nl.
Fax: 040 144318.

DAF tanker trailer, two-wheel, 900 litre type YEW 400 (C R Zwart)

DAF 2500 kg Trailer Type M53 (YEP 600)

Description
This trailer was designed for carrying pontoons for the Engineer Corps of the Netherlands Army. It has mechanical brakes and a single-front support mounted to the rear of the towing lunette. The DAF trailer types YRE 600 and YRI 600 are similar to the YEP 600 but have torsion bar suspension and are used to transport radar and other electronic equipment.

Specifications
Weight:
  (empty) 1280 kg
  (loaded) 3780 kg
Max load: 2500 kg
Length:
  (overall) 4.59 m
  (of mounting) 2.2 m
Width:
  (over wheels) 2.23 m
  (over mounting) 2.08 m
Height: (to top of mounting) 1.2 m
Ground clearance: 0.45 m
Track: 1.97 m
Wheelbase: (towing eye to centre of axle) 3.34 m
Tyres: 9.00 × 20

Status
Production complete. In service with the Dutch Army.

DAF 2500 kg trailer type YEP 600

Manufacturer
DAF Military Sales, Hugo van der Goeslaan 1, NL-5643 TW Eindhoven, Netherlands.
Tel: 040 143440. Telex: 51085 daf nl.
Fax: 040 144318.

NORWAY

Hägglunds Moelv MB 58 Off-road Trailer

Description
The Hägglunds Moelv MB 58 is a general-purpose cargo trailer designed for extreme cross-country operations. The special Hägglunds Moelv pendulum bogie suspension provides excellent cross-country and road performance. The cargo platform is constructed of impregnated pine boards and the drop sides, tailboard and frontboard are plywood. The platform has an area of 9.36 m².

Upon request this trailer may be reinforced for total weights of up to 12 000 kg.

Specifications
Weight: (chassis) 3060 kg
Max load: 6140 kg
Length: 5.47 m
Width: 2.56 m
Height: 2.35 m
Track: 2.03 m

Hägglunds Moelv MB 58 trailer showing pendulum bogie suspension

Tyres: 315/80 × 22.5
Electrical system: 24 V

Status
Production on request.

Manufacturer
Hägglunds Moelv AS, Postboks 244, N-2391 Moelv, Norway.
Tel: 47 65 68500. Telex: 76350 hagmo n.
Fax: 47 65 67056.

Hägglunds Moelv MB 59 All-Terrain Trailer

Description
The Hägglunds Moelv MB 59 is a general-purpose cargo trailer developed to meet tough environmental and terrain conditions. The system is based on the Hägglunds Moelv pendulum bogie system providing good cross-country and on-road travelling capabilities. The materials used are a combination of high tensile steel and aluminium.

The MB 59 can be used on and off roads, over rough terrain, over swamps and in deep snow. The trailer is amphibious carrying a full load and for operations in deep snow the bogie system is fitted with skis. For the latter the lower wheel sections extend below the skis to allow the trailer to be towed from snow to dry road conditions.

The cargo platform may be covered by a canvas or hard-top. The trailer system can be reinforced for total weights of up to 2500 kg.

Hägglunds Moelv MB 59 all-terrain trailer

Specifications
Weight:
  (total) 2000 kg
  (chassis, winter with skis) 900 kg
Max load: 1100 kg
Load area: 1.67 × 2.38 m
Length: 4.2 m
Width: 1.84 m

Height: 1.89 m
Track: 1.546 m
Tyres: 18.5 × 14
Electrical system: 24 V

Status
In production.

Manufacturer
Hägglunds Moelv AS, Postboks 244, N-2391 Moelv, Norway.
Tel: 47 65 68500. Telex: 76350 hagmo n.
Fax: 47 65 67056.

Hägglunds Moelv MB 63 Multi Trailer

Description
The Hägglunds Moelv MB 63 Multi trailer was designed and built specifically for transporting ISO containers and light tracked vehicles. The trailer features a unique system for loading and unloading standard ISO containers and the complete loading platform can be tilted to the rear to enable vehicles to be driven directly onto the platform.

The standard Multi trailer can carry loads up to 9000 kg. To meet special requirements the trailer system can be reinforced for higher total weights.

At the front of the cargo platform are loading ramps to enable tracked vehicles to be driven directly onto the cargo platform. Anchoring fixtures are provided to secure vehicles and general cargo.

The design of the MB 63 Multi is based on the Hägglunds Moelv pendulum bogie system to provide enhanced cross-country and road mobility. The wide interspace between the wheels and the low loading height add to trailer stability, even if the cargo has a high centre of gravity.

Hägglunds Moelv MB 63 Multi trailer

Specifications
Weight:
  (chassis) 3400 kg
  (total) 12 500 kg
Max load: 9100 kg
Length: 8.45 m

Width: 2.5 m
Height: (top of platform) 1.1 m
Track: 2.05 m
Tyres: 285/70-19.5

Status
In production.

Manufacturer
Hägglunds Moelv AS, Postboks 244, N-2391 Moelv, Norway.
Tel: 47 65 68500. Telex: 76350 hagmo n.
Fax: 47 65 67056.

POLAND

Polish Heavy Transport Trailers and Semi-trailers P-40, P-50, NP-40 and PN-600

Description
The P-40 and P-50 are conventional three-axle trailers with folding ramps at the rear of the trailer bed. The NP-40 is a semi-trailer and is towed by the single-axle Zg-201A tractor. The PN-600 is a four-axle full trailer with a single-axle dolly and three axles under the loading platform. There are folding ramps at the rear of the platform.

Specifications

Model	P-40	NP-40	PN-600
Weight			
(empty)	13 575 kg	14 000 kg	13 500 kg
(loaded)	53 575 kg	54 000 kg	73 500 kg
Max load	40 000 kg	40 000 kg	60 000 kg
Length			
(overall)	11.2 m	n/a	11.75 m
(trailer only)	n/a	n/a	9.88 m
Length of			
platform	5.1 m	8.5 m	6.5 m
Width	2.9 m	3.15 m	3.1 m
Height	2 m	n/a	n/a
(to platform)	1 m	n/a	1.1 m

Model	P-40	NP-40	PN-600
Towing speed			
(empty)	15 km/h	40 km/h	80 km/h
(loaded)	—	—	60 km/h
Tyres	—	—	8.25 × 15 (32)

Status
The P-40 and P-50 are known to be in service with the Polish Army. The NP-40 and the PN-600 both have military applications.

Manufacturer (PN-600)
ZREMB Factory, Wroclaw, Poland.

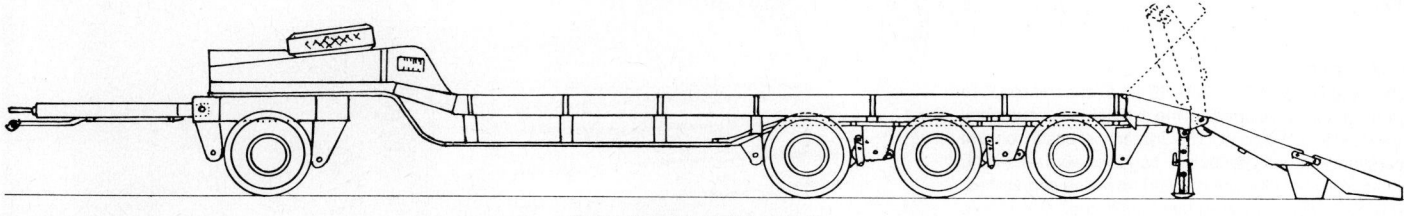

Polish PN-600 60 000 kg trailer

ROMANIA

200-man Field Kitchen Trailer

Description
This singleaxled kitchen trailer was designed to prepare hot food for up to 200 men at one time. The heater for the system may be either diesel oil or petrol and is used to heat up to four boilers, one 120 litre, one 70 litre and two 60 litre. If required, one of the 60 litre boilers may be replaced by a cooking range which will then be in addition to a further two cooking ranges already provided as fixtures.

Along each side of the trailer are two containers, the sides of which can be opened up to form working surfaces. The containers contain various items of kitchen equipment to assist food preparation and serving.

The trailer weighs 1400 kg and is 3.565 m long, 2.08 m wide and 2.28 m high.

Status
In production. In service with the Romanian armed forces. Offered for export sales.

Marketing Agency
ROMTECHNICA, 9-11 Drumul Taberei Street, Bucharest, Romania.
Tel: 46 20 87. Telex: 11608 TXKCO.
Fax: 46 03 17.

200-man field kitchen trailer

SERBIA

FNNPP 50/3U 50 000 kg Low Bed Semi-trailer

Description
The FNNPP 50/3U low bed semi-trailer is normally towed by the FAP 3232 BDST/AV tractor truck (see entry in *Tank transporters* section) but reports indicate that it has also been used by MAZ-537G (8 × 8) tractor trucks, in which combination it is known as the M-60.

The semi-trailer frame is welded and comprises two steel longitudinal 'I' beams with crossmembers and siderails. Fixed to the frame are the axle bogies, loading ramps, spare wheel carriers, air and hydraulic systems and other equipment. The front part of the frame is in the form of a gooseneck while the frame platform is flat with a 20° tapered rear end. The loading ramps are 600 mm wide and are raised and lowered with the assistance of hydraulic pumps. The ramps are laterally movable within limits of 2.5 to 3 m and their upper surface is ribbed steel. The platform is hardwood and the siderails are provided with load securing hooks.

The four axles have a loading of 12 000 kg each. The front axle is fixed and the remainder are steerable. The suspension uses flexible leaf springs supported at their ends by spring hangers. Axle steering is hydro-mechanical and air brakes are used. Load distribution between axles is performed by equalisers. Each axle has four tyres.

Loading can be assisted by using a winch system driven by a power take-off on the tractor. Two pulleys are provided on the gooseneck for this system.

Specifications
Weight:
(empty) 16 000 kg
(loaded) 66 000 kg
Max load: 50 000 kg
Max 5th wheel load: 18 000 kg
Length:
(overall) 12.287 m
(platform) 7.697 m
Width: 3.5 m
Height:
(5th wheel, loaded) 1.83 m
(5th wheel, unloaded) 1.025 m
(platform, loaded) 0.972 m
(platform, unloaded) 1.025 m
Wheelbase:
(axles) 1.245 m + 1.245 m + 1.245 m
(from 5th wheel to bogie centre) 8.7 m
Track: 2.55 m
Tyres: 8.25 × 15
Electrical system: 12 or 24 V

Status
In service with the former Yugoslav armed forces.

Contractor
Federal Directorate of Supply and Procurement (SDPR), YU-11005 Beograd, 9 Nemanjina Street, Serbia.
Tel: 621522. Telex: 71000/72566 sdpr yu.
Fax: 38 11 631588/630621.

FNNPP 50/3U 50 000 kg low bed semi-trailer

MK-100, MK-200 and MK-300 Mobile Kitchen Trailers

Description
The MK series of mobile kitchen trailers consists of all basically similar trailers that differ only in the type of heating fuel system. The MK-100 uses gas contained in cylinders, the MK-200 uses solid fuel or gas from cylinders and the MK-300 has a fuel oil burner. The trailer uses a basic structure built on a sprung steel chassis. Stop and safety brakes are provided and a spare wheel is carried on the drawbar. A variety of towing eyes can be fitted to the drawbar and an adjustable-height jockey wheel is provided close to the eye.

The cooking facilities are provided by an 80 litre capacity boiler and a 40 litre cast iron baking dish. The boiler has an insulated jacket to preserve heat. Compartments and lockers around the sides of the kitchen body are used to store utensils and cooking requirements. There is sufficient space around the main cooking utensils to provide working surfaces. A central flue pipe acts as a fume exhaust for the heating system. When on the move this pipe can be removed and the top surface can be covered by a canopy. Each trailer can cook up to 240 meals at a time.

Specifications
Weight: 550 to 590 kg according to type
Length:
(overall) 3.275 m
(kitchen unit) 2.075 m
(drawbar) 1.2 m
Width:
(overall) 1.34 m
(kitchen unit) 1.286 m
Height:
(travelling) 0.915 m to 1.1 m
(in use) 3.275 m

Status
In service with Algeria.

Contractor
Federal Directorate of Supply and Procurement (SDPR), YU-11005 Beograd, 9 Nemanjina Street, Serbia.
Tel: 621522. Telex: 71000/72566 sdpr yu.
Fax: 38 11 631588/630621.

SOUTH AFRICA

10-tonne Cargo Trailer

Description
This general-purpose cargo trailer is the standard South African Defence Forces load-carrying trailer and can be towed by SAMIL 100 trucks. The trailer is a twin-axled design with 650 kPa air brakes and an all-steel body. There are four downward-opening side panels, two to each side, and steel wire mesh panel extensions are permanently fitted for oversize loads. A spare wheel is carried under the cargo body, and a full set of rear lights is provided.

Specifications
Weight:
(empty) 4200 kg
(fully loaded) 14 200 kg
Payload: 10 000 kg
Length:
(inc towbar) 6.66 m
(body internal) 4.85 m
Height:
(inc cant rails) 2.85 m
(towing eye, coupling) 1 m
(body internal) 0.46 m
Width: (body internal) 2.335 m

10-tonne cargo trailer

Wheelbase: 3.2 m
Track: 2.03 m
Tyres: 12.00 × 20 × 14 ply

Status
In service with the South African Defence Forces.

Manufacturer
Enquiries to Armscor, Private Bag X337, Pretoria 0001, South Africa.
Tel: 012 428 1911. Telex: 30217.
Fax: 012 428 5635.

3-tonne 4-wheel Workshop Trailers

Description
There are a number of these workshop trailers, all basically the same in layout and appearance but differing in equipment and internal layout. A general repair trailer is one of the more numerous types but there are also armourers' workshop, welding workshop and vehicle repair trailers. Each trailer has a fully enclosed body when being towed but once in position, side and rear-mounted flaps are opened upwards to reveal the interior. Once emplaced each trailer is usually covered by a canvas tent with the trailer roof and side flaps supporting the tent roof. The tent, when erected, is 8.5 m long, 5.7 m wide and 2.5 m high. Each trailer has its own 10 kVA 380 V three-phase 50 Hz generator with a convertor supplying 265 V at 200 Hz. A 220 V supply is used for internal lighting and two fans in the trailer roof. The general chassis voltage supply is 24 V from batteries. Air brakes are fitted. The trailers are supplied complete with all the necessary machine and other tools.

Specifications
Weight:
(empty) 3780 kg
(equipped) 5500 kg
Length:
(inc drawbar) 7.765 m
(interior) 5.6 m
Height:
(total) 2.49 m
(interior) 1.28 m
(interior, over gooseneck) 1.06 m
(tow eye) 0.9 m
Width: (overall) 2.3 m
Track: 2.03 m
Tyres: 9.00 × 16 × 12 ply
Electrical system: 24 V

Status
In service with the South African Defence Forces.

Manufacturer
AFRIT (Pty) Ltd, PO Box 911374, Rosslyn 0200, South Africa.
Tel: 012 541 2123. Telex: 32-0439 SA.

3-tonne 4-wheel workshop trailer

2-tonne 4-wheel Shower Unit Trailer

Description
This trailer body is basically the same as that used on the Office Trailer but is fitted with shower facilities for up to eight men at one session. Each shower head can be operated individually but normally an operator controls the shower cycle. Water is pumped from an outside source through a filter unit to three liquid petroleum gas heaters, although any one or two of these heaters can be eliminated if required. Internal lighting is supplied from a 12 V battery and a tunnel tent can be provided for connection from the rear-situated access door to a standard military tent nearby. Air brakes are fitted. The water pump is powered by a petrol/gas-operated engine carried behind an access flap.

Specifications
Weight:
  (empty) 3000 kg
  (equipped) 4000 kg
Length:
  (inc drawbar) 6.65 m
  (internal) 4.79 m
Width: (internal) 2.21 m
Height:
  (total) 3.075 m
  (internal) 2.1 m
Track: 2.03 m
Tyres: 7.50 × 16 × 10 ply
Electrical system: 24 V

Status
In production. In service with the South African Defence Forces.

Manufacturer
Enquiries to Armscor, Private Bag X337, Pretoria 0001, South Africa.
Tel: 012 428 1911. Telex: 30217.
Fax: 012 428 5635.

2-tonne 4-wheel shower unit trailer

250-man Mobile Field Kitchen Trailer

Description
This mobile kitchen unit is mounted on a heavy duty two-wheeled trailer fitted with air brakes. The cooking range, three pressure cookers, griddle plates, oven and hot water tank are enclosed by side flaps which can open upwards to the equipment and provide shelter for the operator. The cooking equipment is heated by gas supplied by low pressure gas cylinders through a vaporiser unit. All the control valves are fitted with flame failure devices and the oven is thermostatically controlled.

The full equipment carried on the trailer includes three pressure cookers, three pans, three gas lights, a poker lighter, four 14 kg liquid withdrawal gas cylinders, two fire extinguishers, a spare wheel and heavy duty jockey wheel, canvas sides and a canvas roof cover, a handbrake, four adjustable corner jacks with levellers and a removable stainless steel worktop with a chopping board on the reverse side. The canvas sides are provided for blackout use at night and for protection in bad weather.

Status
In service with the South African Defence Forces.

Manufacturer
Enquiries to Armscor, Private Bag X337, Pretoria 0001, South Africa.
Tel: 012 428 1911. Telex: 30217.
Fax: 012 428 5635.

250-man mobile field kitchen trailer

Other South African Trailers

Description
South Africa has the ability to produce about 80 types of trailer and semi-trailer. Trailers are produced with capacities from 1000 kg to 16 000 kg and semi-trailers (of which there are nearly 40 types) with capacities from 7000 kg to 60 000 kg. Most of these are produced to match the standard South African Defence Force truck capacities of 1000, 2000, 5000 and 10 000 kg but many are specially produced for specific roles, some of which have been described in the preceding entries. Apart from specialist roles such as training media and office trailers, trailers are also produced for such roles as mobile blood banks, mobile food pantries and corpse embalming.

Status
Most types are available. In service with the South African Defence Forces.

Manufacturer
Enquiries to Armscor, Private Bag X337, Pretoria 0001, South Africa.
Tel: 012 428 1911. Telex: 30217.
Fax: 012 428 5635.

TURKEY

Ibrahim Örs Military Trailers

Description
Ibrahim Örs AS produces a wide range of military and commercial trailers and associated equipment at their Kirikkale facility, including the following military trailers:

Model ORS AR-1, 1000 kg payload single-axle cargo trailer similar to the American M105 series

Model ORS AR-05, 500 kg payload single-axle trailer intended for towing by Jeep-type vehicles

Model ORS AT-2, double-axle fuel tank trailer carrying a 2000 litre tank

Model ORS AR-2, double-axle trailer intended for the carrying of up to 2000 kg of ammunition and similar loads

Model ORS SM-250, mobile kitchen with three cookers and the capacity to cook meals for up to 250 men

Model ORS MV-1, twin-axle mobile van-bodied trailer for use as a mobile darkroom or electronic equipment carrier

Model ORS AS, single-axle water tank trailer carrying up to 2000 litres of drinking water

Model ORS A-7, 750 kg capacity tipping body trailer

Model ORS M3-MTK, carrier for M3 machine guns for Turkish Navy

Model ORS TTR, twin-axle carrier for torpedos

Model ORS PTR, glider container

Model ORS MTR, mine carrier trailer for NATO

Model ORS STR, single-axle water purification trailer

Model ORS BYT, bomb loading trailer for aircraft.

In addition to the above there is also a special electrical generator-carrying single-axle trailer and a stabilised trailer with an elevating servicing platform that can be raised to a height of 8 m.

Status
All the above are in production and in service with the Turkish armed forces.

Manufacturer
Ibrahim Örs AS, GMK Bulvari, Onur Iscçhani Kat:6, No 146, 06440 Kizilay, Ankara, Turkey.
Tel: (4) 118 39 46. Telex: 43 130 iors tr.
Fax: (4) 125 39 25.

Model ORS AS water tank trailer

Model ORS MTR mine-carrying trailer

UNITED KINGDOM

Scottorn 750 kg Trailers

Description
Reynolds Boughton Limited, Scottorn Division, produces many military pattern trailers in various weight capacities. There are two 750 kg trailers: the Bushranger trailer is lighter and simpler than the Military L model, and has a hinged removable tailboard.

Specifications

Model	Bushranger	Military L (510/760 kg)
Weight	279 kg	355 kg
Length		
(overall)	2.695 m	2.795 m
(of cargo area)	1.754 m	1.83 m
Width		
(overall)	1.587 m	1.475 m
(of cargo area)	1.015 m	1.475 m
Height		
(without canopy)	1.015 m	1.015 m
(of towing eye)	0.56 m	0.535 m
Track	1.333 m	1.335 m
Tyres	6.00 × 16	6.00 × 16 (Land Rover wheels)
Suspension	6-leaf semi-elliptic leaf springs	

Status
In production.

Scottorn Military L (510/760 kg) cargo trailer

Manufacturer
Reynolds Boughton Limited, Scottorn Division, Bell Lane, Amersham, Buckinghamshire HP6 6PE, UK.
Tel: 0494 764411. Telex: 83132.
Fax: 0494 765218.

750 kg Cargo Trailer

Description

The FV2381 cargo trailer has a capacity of 750 kg and is of all-welded steel construction. Two stabilising jacks are provided at the rear and an adjustable jockey wheel is fitted in front. The trailer is equipped with lashing points for the load and for a canvas canopy.

Service braking is by means of an overrun unit which operates hydraulic disc brakes and there is also a mechanical parking brake. A hydraulic damper isolates the trailers from shock transmitted from the prime mover, prolonging the operational life of the trailers.

As cargo carriers these trailers meet the NATO requirement of fording to a depth of 0.76 m in fresh or sea water without preparation. The limit for the protection of cargo while wading is 0.61 m. When fully loaded the trailers will normally be towed by any suitable vehicle of up to 1-tonne capacity, and a NATO standard inter-vehicle connector is fitted.

The FV2380 0.75-tonne trailer chassis is identical to the above but without the cargo body. This chassis can be adapted to take a variety of equipment such as water tanks and generators.

The FV2381 trailer is the standard trailer to MVEE Specification 679 and uses the FV2380 0.75-tonne trailer chassis.

Specifications
Weight: 408 kg
Length: 2.85 m
Width: 1.68 m
Track: 1.42 m
Max towing speed:
(road) 72 km/h
(cross-country) 24 km/h
Tyres: 6.50 × 16

Status
In production. This and other similar trailers are in service with the British Army.

Manufacturer
Reynolds Boughton Limited, Scottorn Division, Bell Lane, Amersham, Buckinghamshire HP6 6PE, UK. Tel: 0494 764411. Telex: 83132. Fax: 0494 765218.

750 kg cargo trailer (wide-axle)

Scottorn 1-tonne Trailers

Description

Four 1-tonne trailers are produced by the Scottorn Division of Reynolds Boughton Limited for the military market. They differ in details of construction and in their intended roles. The Bushranger trailer has a hinged tailboard and angular mudguards and uses Land Rover wheels and independent suspension units. Of the 1-tonne general-purpose (GP) trailers, the first model is the simplest, with a one-piece body with the minimum of fittings. The next model has a hinged tailboard and cleats for securing a tarpaulin. The last model is heavier and is intended for use with larger trucks, such as the Bedford 4-tonne or the Mercedes-Benz LA 911 and 1130 models. It has a canopy and a spare wheel.

Status
In production.

Specifications

Model	Bushranger	GP (Model 1)	GP (Model 2)	GP (Model 3)
Length (overall)	2.87 m	2.79 m	2.79 m	n/a
Width	1.71 m	1.86 m	1.86 m	n/a
Height	1.15 m	1.25 m	1.25 m	n/a
Body (length)	1.86 m	1.83 m	1.83 m	n/a
(height)	0.46 m	0.54 m	0.54 m	n/a
(width)	1.12 m	1.22 m	1.22 m	n/a
Weight	n/a	540 kg	550 kg	n/a
Wheels	5-stud	5-stud	5-stud	6-stud; can be made interchangeable with towing vehicle
Tyres	7.50 × 16 (8 ply)	7.50 × 16 (8 ply)	7.50 × 16 (8 ply)	7.50 × 20, 12 ply rating
Suspension	leaf	8-leaf semi-elliptical	8-leaf semi-elliptical	leaf
Brakes	mechanical overrun and parking brakes			single line air

Manufacturer
Reynolds Boughton Limited, Scottorn Division, Bell Lane, Amersham, Buckinghamshire HP6 6PE, UK. Tel: 0494 764411. Telex: 83132. Fax: 0494 765218.

Scottorn 1-tonne general purpose trailer (1st model)

Scottorn 1-tonne general purpose trailer (2nd model)

Scottorn 1-tonne general purpose trailer (3rd model)

Scottorn Military 1000/1250 kg General Purpose Trailer

Description
This trailer is designed for towing by vehicles of the Land Rover class and, as with many other Scottorn trailers, the wheels are interchangeable with the Land Rover. The trailer body is welded and has a removable hinged tailboard. Stop lights, tail lights, direction indicators and an electrical plug are provided to suit the towing vehicle. The square section beam axle is fitted with 9.00 × 16 tyres on Land Rover wheels and is suspended on semi-elliptical leaf springs with shock absorbers and Aeon rubber helper springs. Mechanical overrun and parking brakes are fitted.

Status
In production.

Manufacturer
Reynolds Boughton Limited, Scottorn Division, Bell Lane, Amersham, Buckinghamshire HP6 6PE, UK. Tel: 0494 764411. Telex: 83132. Fax: 0494 765218.

Scottorn Military 1000 kg/1250 kg general-purpose cargo trailer with optional canopy supports

Scottorn Military 1750 kg Cargo Trailer

Description
This trailer was produced to meet the MVEE/LV98 specification for a trailer with a gross weight of 2.8 tonnes. It is conventional in design with a drawbar mounting a standard NATO towing eye and with connections for the hydraulic overrun service brakes and the full military lighting system. The single axle uses a torsion bar and Aeon rubber suspension. A mechanical parking brake is provided. The cargo body has a tailgate.

A light repair workshop unit can be mounted on this trailer. The unit consists of a steel frame with lockers, a fold-out bench, a davit, enclosed working lights and electrical controls. An all-round canvas awning is provided for use in all weathers. This workshop body is in production and in service with the British Army.

Specifications (basic trailer)
Weight:
(unladen) 1040 kg
(gross) 2800 kg
(payload) 1750 kg
Length:
(overall) 3.8 m
(cargo area) 2.425 m
Width:
(overall) 2.425 m
(cargo area) 1.72 m

Height:
(overall) 1.225 m
(cargo area) 0.45 m
Track: 2.09 m
Tyres: 8.25 × 16, 14 ply

Status
In service with the British Ministry of Defence.

Scottorn 1750 kg cargo trailer carrying a light repair workshop

Manufacturer
Reynolds Boughton Limited, Scottorn Division, Bell Lane, Amersham, Buckinghamshire HP6 6PE, UK. Tel: 0494 764411. Telex: 83132. Fax: 0494 765218.

2500 kg Trailers

Description
There are three trailers in the 2500 kg special-purpose trailer range. The base element is the FV2405 Mark 11 Trailer Chassis (2.5-tonne). Then comes the FV2406 Mark 11 Flat Platform Trailer (2.5-tonne) and the FV2406 Mark 11 Trailer Cargo (2.5-tonne).

The FV2406 Mark 11 Flat Platform Trailer (2.5-tonne) was designed primarily for the carriage of a specialist 24/16 kW generator but the trailer is suitable for a wide range of equipment including water tanks, weapon systems, air-conditioning units, and so on. Welded steel construction is used for the chassis with uprated trailing arm suspension using rubber springs. The platform is constructed of exterior grade plywood and incorporates load lashing loops and wear strips. Three stabilising jacks are fitted as is a jockey wheel. Service braking is by means of an overrun unit operating hydraulic brakes through a hydraulic damper linkage to the master cylinder; a mechanical hand-brake is fitted for parking. A spare wheel and carrier

FV2406 Mark 11 flat platform trailer (2.5-tonne)

are fitted to the underside at the rear.
The normal tractor is a 4 × 4, 4-tonne truck. Elec-

trical equipment conforms to EEC regulations, and a NATO inter-vehicle connector is fitted.

Specifications (FV2406)
Weight: (empty) 1089 kg
Max load: 2500 kg
Length: 4.25 m
Width: 2.489 m
Height: (top of mudguard) 1.002 m
Track: 2.242 m

Max towing speed:
(roads) 72 km/h
(rough roads) 24 km/h

Status
In service with the British Army.

Manufacturer
GKN Defence, PO Box 106, Hadley Castle Works, Telford, Shropshire TF1 4QW, UK.
Tel: 0952 244321. Telex: 35248 sanhad g.
Fax: 0952 243910.

Scottorn 1000 to 2500 kg Flat Bed Trailers

Description
There are three Scottorn flat bed trailers, each of which consists of a heavy gauge sheet steel decking mounted on a rolled steel channel chassis with the drawbar provided with a 76 mm NATO towing eye. The trailers are designed to be towed by four-wheel drive vehicles ranging from Land Rovers to 4-tonne trucks. Typical loads could include generators, radar systems or ammunition packs, with the larger trailer carrying either NATO standard pallets or two 150-gallon (682 litre) water tanks. General cargo can be carried when the optional side panels are fitted.

Status
In production.

Manufacturer
Reynolds Boughton Limited, Scottorn Division, Bell Lane, Amersham, Buckinghamshire HP6 6PE, UK.
Tel: 0494 764411. Telex: 83132.
Fax: 0494 765218.

Scottorn flat bed trailer

Specifications

Payload	1000 kg	1750 kg	2500 kg
Weight	400 kg	900 kg	1050 kg
Length (overall)	2.85 m	3.8 m	4.25 m
(deck)	1.8 m	2.25 m	2.25 m
Width (overall)	1.67 m	2.46 m	2.46 m
(deck)	1 m	1.72 m	1.72 m
Track	1.4 m	2.2 m	2.2 m
Tyres	7.50 × 16	8.25 × 16	9.00 × 20

Crane Fruehauf 35-tonne Engineer Plant Semi-trailer (FV3541A)

Description
This is a cranked framed trailer with the vehicle being loaded over the rear suspension. The foredeck is narrow and fitted with tool lockers between the beams. The main frame is of high-tensile steel universal beam 406 × 178 mm on the maindeck with 356 × 171 mm on the foredeck. Frame crossmembers are 152 × 89 mm rolled steel joists with a steel box-section member of 203 × 152 mm at the extreme rear. Suspension is of the unsprung beam type with oscillating axles mounted at the ends of each beam to give full compensation between all wheels. Axles are constructed in solid form and oscillate on the rocker beams on plain bushes. The rear loading ramps are made from steel channel-section with 34.9 mm finished hardwood boards, plus auxiliary ramps. The landing gear is screw-operated with feet fitted at the crank. Rear support jacks are mounted under the tail of the frame to give support while loading.

Specifications
Length:
(overall) 13.98 m
(main deck from base of crank to start of suspension area) 5.51 m

Crane Fruehauf 35-tonne commercial type semi-trailer being towed by Scammell Constructor (6 × 4) tractor

(drop deck, including area over suspension and beavertail) 9.7 m
Width: (overall) 3.2 m
Height: (of platform) 1 m
Ground clearance: (minimum empty) 0.51 m
Slope of ramp: 1 in 5
Bogie wheeltrack: 0.84 m
Wheelbase: (king-pin to centre line of rear bogie) 10.08 m

Status
In production. In service with the British Army.

Manufacturer
Crane Fruehauf, Toftwood, Dereham, Norfolk NR19 1JF, UK.
Tel: 0362 695353. Telex: 97251.

King GTLS38/3F-17.5 25-tonne Lowloader Semi-trailer

Description

The King GTLS38/3F-17.5 25-tonne Lowloader semi-trailer was designed for use as a fork-lift truck transporter. It features a sloping timber deck and a full width hydraulically operated folding neck. This lowers to the ground to form a ramp, thus facilitating loading and unloading.

Various options are available including different types of suspension, rear ramps, winches and outriggers. These allow these semi-trailers to be adapted to suit a wide variety of applications and conditions.

Specifications

Weight: 10 000 kg
Capacity: 25 000 kg
Length: (deck) 8.76 m
Width: 2.49 m
Tyres: 9.5 R 17.5

Status

In service with the British Army.

Manufacturer

King Trailers Limited, Riverside, Market Harborough, Leicestershire LE16 7PX, UK.

Tel: 0858 467361. Telex: 341835 king g.
Fax: 0858 467161.

King GTLS38/3F-17.5 25-tonne Lowloader semi-trailer

Crane Fruehauf Tank Transporter Semi-trailer CF 2000

Description

This semi-trailer was designed to carry MBTs weighing up to 65 000 kg. The chassis is all welded with a mild steel decking welded into position. The suspension consists of heavy duty unsprung rocker beam design with phosphor-bronze bushes on the pivots. The suspension is fitted with bump stops to limit fore and aft oscillation. The semi-trailer has four short axles mounted in two lines of two axles. Each axle is fitted with a taper roller bearing. Brakes are air-operated and a screw-type handbrake operates on one row of axles only. Standard fittings include manually operated rear loading gear, track guides, stowage boxes and tie-down points.

Status

Production complete. In service with several armies including those of Jordan, Kenya, Kuwait and Libya.

Manufacturer

Crane Fruehauf, Toftwood, Dereham, Norfolk

NR19 1JF, UK.
Tel: 0362 695353. Telex: 97251.

Crane Fruehauf tank transporter semi-trailer CF 2000

King 35-tonne Tank Transporter Stepframe Semi-trailer

Description

The King 35-tonne tank transporter stepframe semi-trailer was designed mainly to transport lightweight armoured vehicles and armoured personnel carriers. It can also carry general military plant and machinery and 20-foot/6.096 m ISO containers.

The main load platform is 9.6 m long and 3 m wide, although the latter can be extended to 3.3 m using outriggers. The deck is covered in 8 mm chequer plate and fitted with twistlocks for ISO containers, and attachments for track guides for tracked vehicles.

Machinery is loaded over the rear via a beavertail and 2.5 × 1 m spring-assisted ramps which are wide enough to accommodate various track widths and wheeled vehicles, including a Land Rover.

SAF Triaxle three-leaf parabolic spring suspension is fitted, incorporating one fixed and two king-pin power-steered axles which substantially reduce the turning circle and tyre wear. The semi-trailer is approved for operations in Germany.

King 35-tonne tank transporter stepframe semi-trailer

Specifications
Weight: approx 13 000 kg
Max load: approx 35 000 kg
Length: (overall) 13.885 m
Width: 3 m

Tyres: 9.5 R 17.5

Status
In service with the British Army in Germany (30) via Ryder Truck Rentals.

Manufacturer
King Trailers Limited, Riverside, Market Harborough, Leicestershire LE16 7PX, UK.
Tel: 0858 467361. Telex: 341835 king g.
Fax: 0858 467161.

Scottorn Tanker Trailers

Description

The Scottorn Division of Reynolds Boughton Limited produces a range of tanker trailers of various capacities, of which three are described here. The smallest is a 682 litre (150-gallon) tanker which can be towed by any 750 kg vehicle such as a Land Rover. The other trailers differ in dimensions, capacities and fittings. All models have 3.2 mm welded steel plate tanks with 4.8 mm welded steel plate ends. Transverse baffles are incorporated in the tanks to prevent the liquid from surging. The tanks are filled through a 406 mm manhole with a 254 mm filling aperture, which is fitted with a lockable quick release cover with a pressure/vacuum valve. On the 680 and 1140 litre tankers a drainage pump, fitted with a 40 mm bsp gate valve, is provided at the rear of the tank. The 1350 litre tanker trailer is fitted with a water purification filter. The filtered liquid can be discharged either by gravity feed to four 12.5 mm bibcocks and one 25 mm bibcock, or pumped out by a 25 mm semi-rotary pump with 15 m of 25 mm delivery hose. Similar filtering and pumping arrangements are also available as optional extras for the other trailers.

Status
In production.

Manufacturer
Reynolds Boughton Limited, Scottorn Division, Bell Lane, Amersham, Buckinghamshire HP6 6PE, UK.
Tel: 0494 764411. Telex: 83132.
Fax: 0494 765218.

Scottorn 680 litre tanker trailer

Scottorn Military 1350 litre tanker trailer

Specifications

Type	680 l	1140 l	1350 l
Weight (empty)	350 kg	582 kg	860 kg
Length (overall)	2.49 m	2.794 m	3.404 m
(of tank)	—	1.524 m	1.829 m
Width (overall)	1.65 m	1.85 m	2.11 m
(of tank)	—	1.22 m	1.219 m
Height (overall)	1.12 m	1.473 m	1.524 m
(of towing eye)	—	0.66 m	0.99 m
Track	1.33 m	1.6 m	1.79 m
Tyres	6.00 × 16	7.50 × 16	10.00, 11.00 or 12.00 × 20 or 10.50 × 16
Wheels	5-stud	5-stud	6- or 8-stud to suit towing vehicle
Brakes	mechanical overrun and parking		service brake: mechanical overrun or single-line air brake
Suspension	6-leaf, semi-elliptical	8-leaf, semi-elliptical	semi-elliptical springs with Aeon rubber assists

---

Scottorn 'Flat Top' 2280 – 10 000 litre Tanker Trailers

Description

The Scottorn 'Flat Top' all-steel tanker trailer has been developed over the years to form a comprehensive range of four (and in some cases eight) wheel tankers with a capacity of from 2280 to 10 000 litres (500 to 2200 gallons). The design features an integral chassis and a 'D' shaped tank, allowing the tankers to be used for a variety of purposes. The trailers can be equipped as fuel bowsers, fire tenders, drinking water and foam compound tanks, carrying liquids such as diesel, oil, petrol, water and chemicals. As there is a flat top to the tank there is a capability for storage and for carrying equipment.

Specifications (4560 l (1000 gallon) version)
Weight: 2250 kg
Length: (over drawbar) 5.185 m
Width: 1.83 m
Height: 1.75 m
Track: 1.664 m

Status
In production. In service with the British Ministry of Defence.

Manufacturer
Reynolds Boughton Limited, Scottorn Division, Bell Lane, Amersham, Buckinghamshire HP6 6PE, UK.
Tel: 0494 764411. Telex: 83132.
Fax: 0494 765218.

Scottorn 'Flat Top' tanker trailer

Tecalemit Model SM 6001 Lubricating and Service Unit Trailer

Description

Following extensive tests Tecalemit Garage Equipment Company Limited was awarded a contract to produce 100 mobile lubrication and service unit trailers for the British Army during late 1986. This order was followed by another for 110 units during July 1987 and a further 240 units in 1990.

The self-contained trailers are known as the Model SM 6001 and are intended for towing behind 4000 and 8000 kg trucks. They consist of a single-axle trailer base complete with overrun brakes, lights and a NATO 76 mm towing eye. The base frame is constructed from 100 × 50 × 3 mm folded steel channel-section, welded and decked with 3 mm steel plate. Under-deck bracing gives additional support to equipment carried and also permits lifting by forklift trucks. Four lifting eyes are provided. A 300 kg capacity jockey wheel is positioned on the towing eye A-frame. Two adjustable prop standards are provided for support and stability at the rear end of the trailer.

Carried on the trailer is a diesel-driven air compressor for operating the lubrication pumps, tyre inflation and tools. Also carried are a high pressure grease dispensing system, three low pressure oil dispensing systems, a low pressure transfer pump for filling oil drums, a hand-held penetrating oil sprayer, a tyre inflator, a storage locker, a spare 50 litre oil drum, a 150 litre coolant tank, a 2.5 kg fire extinguisher and a tool box. A bank of four 7.6 m long hoses is provided. The equipment is protected by a canvas canopy with zipped side panels.

Tecalemit Model SM 6001 lubricating and service unit trailer

Specifications

Weight:
(with full lubricant and coolant tank) 1350 kg
(less liquids) 950 kg
(on towing eye, fully laden) 70 kg
Length: (with towing eye) 3.5 m
Width: 1.77 m
Height:
(over canopy) 1.8 m
(towing eye, nominal) 0.8 m
Max towing speed:
(roads) 80.5 km/h
(rough tracks) 32 km/h
Tyres: 6.00 × 16 × 6 PR

Status

In service with the British Army (210).

Manufacturer

Tecalemit Garage Equipment Company Limited, Belliver Industrial Estate, Roborough, Plymouth, Devon PL6 7BW, UK.
Tel: 0752 701212. Telex: 45124.
Fax: 0752 796329.

Scottorn Mobile Servicing 510 kg Lubrication Trailer and Scottorn LAD 510 kg Workshop Trailer

Description

Both trailers are constructed on a chassis fabricated from rolled steel channel. Four retractable snapjack supports are fitted, one at each corner of the body, for added stability when the unit is in use. A tubular support frame is provided for a canvas tilt, which is raised when the unit is in use and lowered for travelling.

The lubrication trailer is fitted with a petrol engined compressor, grease pump, two oil pumps, grease reel, two oil reels, air reel, tyre inflator, penetrating oil reel, static sprayer and a spark plug cleaner. Optional extras include an all-steel canopy and hubs and brakes fully interchangeable with the standard Land Rover. A similar installation is available mounted on a Land Rover Defender 110.

The LAD workshop trailer is provided with a 6 kVA, single-phase, 250 V, 50 Hz alternator set with direct coupled air-cooled diesel engine complete with starter, starter battery and starter battery dynamo, totally enclosed sheet steel switchboard mounted on the alternator and also fitted with a distribution panel incorporating one 30 A fused isolator, one 25 A Nipham output socket and seven output sockets. Equipment includes heavy duty drill, heavy duty grinder, bench grinder and polisher, pillar drill stand, portable air-cooled arc-welding set, portable air compressor, battery charger, two vices and a 9.14 m extension cable.

Scottorn mobile servicing 510 kg lubrication trailer

Specifications

Type	Mobile servicing	LAD workshop
Weight	825 kg	1029 kg
Length (overall)	2.794 m	2.794 m
(of body)	1.829 m	1.829 m
Width	1.525 m	1.624 m
Height (overall)	1.955 m	2.134 m
(over equipment)	1.65 m	n/a
(to towing eye)	0.56 m	0.584 m
Track	1.333 m	1.333 m

Status

In production.

Manufacturer

Reynolds Boughton Limited, Scottorn Division, Bell Lane, Amersham, Buckinghamshire HP6 6PE, UK.
Tel: 0494 764411. Telex: 83132.
Fax: 0494 765218.

1-tonne Special Purpose Trailers

Description

This range of trailers shares the same basic suspension. Welded steel construction is used for the chassis, while the suspension is of the trailing arm type using rubber springs. Service braking is by means of an overrun unit operating hydraulic brakes through a hydraulic damper linkage to the master cylinder, and a mechanical handbrake is fitted for parking.

The trailers are normally towed by vehicles of 250 kg to 1000 kg capacity, except in the case of the FV2415, which is described below.

The electrical equipment and inter-vehicle connector comply with NATO requirements. Optional fitments for the FV2411, FV2412, FV2413 and FV2415 include suspension retraction for airportability, front jockey wheels and support legs.

The trailer, missile resupply, 1-tonne FV2411, was designed to carry spare missiles in their containers for the Rapier SAM system, while the trailer, cargo, 1-tonne FV2412, was designed for the carriage of general cargo and specialist equipment for the Rapier system.

The 1-tonne flat platform trailers FV2413 and FV2415 were designed for the carriage of specialist equipment such as generators for use in conjunction with weapon systems. The two trailers differ from each other in that the FV2415 has a raised and lengthened drawbar to permit towing by a 3- or 4-tonne vehicle, while the FV2413 is normally towed by vehicles of 250 kg to 1000 kg capacity.

The 1-tonne airportable bridge trailer FV2420 was designed to carry sections of the Laird Class 16 airportable bridge. Each trailing suspension arm is retractable to assist in loading and offloading the bridge sections and to reduce the overall height when the trailer is transported by air. The electrical system is mounted on a quickly detachable bar and extension cable enabling it to be mounted either on the rear crossmember of the trailer or on the bottom of the box on the bridge load. The side lamps are mounted on hinged bars to facilitate stacking of trailers. Turnbuckle-type lashing screws are provided for securing the bottom box of the bridge to the chassis. These are also used for lashing stacked trailers together for transport by air.

The flat platform generator trailer FV2421, rated at 1.5 tonnes, was designed primarily for the carriage of a specialist 24/16 kW generator used in conjunction with Electronic Repair Vehicles (ERVs), but is also suitable for a wide range of equipment such as air-conditioning systems and water tanks. Its chassis is fitted with uprated suspension units, and three stabilising jacks and a jockey wheel.

Specifications

Model	FV2411	FV2412	FV2413	FV2415	FV2420	FV2421	FV2425
Weight	534 kg	534 kg	533 kg	533 kg	340 kg	533 kg	447 kg
Length	3.63 m	3.63 m	3.63 m	3.95 m	2.01 m	4.15 m	3.35 m
Width	1.75 m	1.75 m	1.75 m	1.75 m	2.01 m	2.02 m	1.78 m
Height	1.75 m	1.35 m	1.07 m	1.07 m	0.71 m	0.83 m	0.71 m
Track	1.5 m	1.5 m	1.5 m	1.5 m	1.75 m	1.77 m	1.5 m
Towing speed (good roads)	88 km/h	88 km/h	88 km/h	88 km/h	72 km/h	72 km/h	72 km/h
(rough roads)	40 km/h	40 km/h	40 km/h	40 km/h	24 km/h	24 km/h	24 km/h

The FV2425 trailer was designed for the carriage of the THORN EMI Cymbeline mortar locating radar (Radar FA No 15). Four steadying legs are fitted and the suspension may be retracted hydraulically to assist the functioning of the radar.

Status

FV2411/2412: In service with countries using the Rapier SAM system: Australia, Brunei, Indonesia, Iran, Oman, Singapore, Switzerland, Turkey, United Arab Emirates, UK, USA and Zambia.
FV2413/2415: In service with the British Army and other armed forces.

FV2420: In service with Australia, Canada, Nigeria and the UK.
FV2421: In service with the British Army.
FV2425: In service with the British Army and other armed forces.

Manufacturer

GKN Defence, PO Box 106, Hadley Castle Works, Telford, Shropshire TF1 4QW, UK.
Tel: 0952 244321. Telex: 35248 sanhad g.
Fax: 0952 243910.

Australian Army GKN Defence 1-tonne cargo trailer (specialist) (FV2412)
(P Handel)

1-tonne missile resupply trailer (FV2411)

GKN Defence High Mobility Trailer

Description

The GKN Defence High Mobility Trailer was designed to be towed by the Warrior recovery and repair vehicles (see entry in the *Armoured recovery vehicles* section) but can be towed by other vehicles; 45 were ordered for the Warrior repair and recovery role. The trailer has a gross weight of 10 500 kg and is used to carry major assemblies such as a Warrior or Challenger MBT powerpack. It is also being evaluated for carrying ammunition and bridging components.

The High Mobility Trailer is fitted with an air brake system and is provided with a four-damper jacking system to maintain a safe level platform when not connected for towing. It can also traverse 40° side slopes. All controls for the system are contained in a compartment at the front end of the load area. The detachable towing eye is fitted with an umbilical winch to aid single-man coupling to towing vehicles.

This trailer has a high volume and weight capability and is being assessed for other roles such as armoured unit, ammunition and missile resupply and for carrying radars. It can be towed behind tanks, self-propelled artillery, mortar vehicles and other vehicles.

GKN Defence High Mobility Trailer

Specifications
Weight:
(kerb) 5500 kg
(gross) 12 000 kg
Length: 4.94 m
Width: 2.89 m
Height: 1.97 m

Ground clearance: (laden) 0.5 m
Track: 2.49 m
Wheelbase: 1.37 m
Tyres: 14.00 × 20

Status
In service with the British Army (45).

Manufacturer
GKN Defence, PO Box 106, Hadley Castle Works, Telford, Shropshire TF1 4QW, UK.
Tel: 0952 244321. Telex: 35248 sanhad g.
Fax: 0952 243910.

Rubery Owen Medium Girder Bridge Trailer (FV2842)

Description

This trailer was designed to carry palletised loads of the Williams Fairey Medium Girder Bridge (MGB), with a secondary role as a general-purpose flat trailer. The trailer is the single-axle type fitted with semi-elliptical suspension springs with rubber bump stops with wire rope rebound slings. The chassis is constructed of rectangular tubular members on to which an aluminium corrugated decking is fitted. There is a two-line air pressure braking system and a mechanical parking brake. The trailer was designed to be towed on roads at a maximum speed of 56 km/h and across country at a maximum speed of 24 km/h.

Specifications
Weight:
(empty) 1461 kg
(loaded) 4939 kg
Length: (overall) 5.867 m
Width: (overall) 2.565 m
Height:
(overall, loaded) 2.62 m
(overall, empty) 1.02 m
Track: 2.261 m
Tyres: 10.00 × 15, 14 ply rating

Medium Girder Bridge trailer with load of MGB sections

Status
In service with most countries using the Williams Fairey Medium Girder Bridge.

Manufacturer
Defence Equipment Division, Rubery Owen Group Services Limited, Darlaston PO Box 10, Wednesbury, West Midlands WS10 8JD, UK.
Tel: 021 526 3131. Telex: 338236/7.
Fax: 021 526 2869.

Rubery Owen Class 60/70 Trackway Trailer

Description

The Rubery Owen Class 60/70 trackway trailer was developed by Rubery Owen in conjunction with the British Ministry of Defence. A prototype has been built and trialled to meet a British Army requirement for the carriage and deployment of two rolls of Class 60/70 trackway together with their associated accessories. It is capable of accepting asymmetric loads during loading and unloading, or transporting a single centrally located roll of trackway.

Chassis construction is in high tensile steel rectangular hollow section and is carried on a specially developed suspension giving a medium mobility off-road capability. Each walking beam is comprised of a fabricated leading and trailing arm reacting against each other through an integrally mounted square section laminated torsion bar. The whole assembly is carried in bearings and affords considerable wheel movement. Travel is limited by hollow rubber bump stops acting on the suspension arms.

A heavy duty slewing ring is mounted onto the chassis and carries the load platform. This structure is also manufactured from high tensile steel rectangular hollow section and is capable of controlled slewing through an angle of 360° enabling the trackway to be launched or recovered over the rear of the trailer as well as from the sides. Incorporated into the load platform are features that facilitate management of the trackway by a five-man team, if necessary without recourse to external mechanical handling equipment.

The brake system is an air servo-assisted hydraulic system operating on all wheels. The mechanically operated handbrake acts on the rear wheels.

The trailer is capable of being towed by a number of in-service prime movers including both wheeled and

Rubery Owen Class 60/70 trackway trailer on tow behind Combat Engineer Tractor

tracked vehicles. To facilitate coupling a self-aligning drawbar unit embodying a standard 3-in/76.2 mm NATO eye has been incorporated. A mechanical jacking leg is located adjacent to the drawbar for use when the trailer is detached from a prime mover. The trailer is equipped with full lighting conforming to FRG, EEC and UK regulations, inter-vehicle connection being via the standard NATO 12-pin plug.

A rear towing pintle is fitted so that two unladen trailers may be towed in tandem on hard standing. The trailer is equipped with stowage lockers and a spare wheel.

Specifications
Weight:
(unloaded, estimate) 4360 kg
(loaded, estimate) 10 020 kg
Length:
(overall) 6.7 m
(load platform) 4.72 m

Width:
(laden) 2.74 m
(unladen) 2.53 m
Height: (load platform, loaded) 1.215 m
Total wheel movement: (bump free) 0.25 m
Track: 2.2 m
Tyres: Michelin X2A 285/70R × 19.5
Electrical system: 24 V

Status
Prototypes.

Manufacturer
Defence Equipment Division, Rubery Owen Group Services Limited, Darlaston, PO Box 10, Wednesbury, West Midlands WS10 8JD, UK.
Tel: 021 526 3131. Telex: 338236/7.
Fax: 021 526 2869.

Rubery Owen Trailer, Four-wheeled Close-coupled 1000 kg, Medium Mobility

Description

The chassis of this trailer is of welded steel hollow section and is fitted with two torsion bar axle units. The

trailing/leading arm suspension is integral with the axle tubes and comprises laminated square section torsion bars for wheel articulation. A hydraulically damped towing eye minimises towing shock loads. Hydraulic brakes on all four wheels are actuated by the towing eye through an overrun device. For parking a mechanical handbrake operates on the leading axle.

Variants dedicated to the carriage of radar equipment and generator sets have undergone development. Available options include a spare wheel, rugged mudwings, steady legs, levelling jacks and robust longitudinal mounting rails for generator sets.

Specifications
Weight: (unladen) 738 kg
Length: 3.98 m
Width: 1.88 m
Height: (chassis) 0.6 m
Track: 1.67 m

Status
In service with the British Army.

Manufacturer
Defence Equipment Division, Rubery Owen Group Services Limited, Darlaston PO Box 10, Wednesbury, West Midlands WS10 8JD, UK.
Tel: 021 526 3131. Telex: 338236/7.
Fax: 021 526 2869.

Rubery Owen Trailer, 4-wheeled close-coupled 1000 kg, medium mobility

Lolode 8-tonne Recovery Transporter Ground Loading Trailer

Description
Lolode trailers were designed primarily for the recovery of fork-lift trucks. They can be used for the recovery of disabled equipment or plant and machinery with poor gradeability or low ground clearance.

The trailer is fitted with the Lolode ground loading suspension system. A hydraulic device allows the trailer bed to be lowered to the ground to enable equipment to be loaded and unloaded at ground level. The hydraulic system, operated via an electric start petrol-engined powerpack with a handpump backup, then raises the trailer bed and the load up to the travelling position. Locking pins are designed to withstand all imposed loads when towing.

The main load platform measures 4.26 × 1.76 m. The timber deck is overlaid with three strips of 3 mm aluminium tread plate to distribute concentrated loadings. An adjustable height drawbar is fitted so that the trailer does not require uncoupling from the tractive unit when the platform is lowered for loading and unloading. The loading ramp is hydraulically operated.

Provided with the trailer is a 2-tonne capacity manual winch, a toolbox, and a spare wheel and tyre.

Specifications
Weight: 2360 kg
Max load: 5640 kg

Lolode 8-tonne recovery transporter ground loading trailer

Length: (overall) 5.86 m
Width: 2.5 m
Tyres: 215 × 75R 17.5

Status
In service with the British Army (12).

Manufacturer
King Trailers Limited, Riverside, Market Harborough, Leicestershire LE16 7PX, UK.
Tel: 0858 467361. Telex: 341835 king g.
Fax: 0858 467161.

Stead & Wilkins Ammunition Mover SWAM II

Description
The Stead & Wilkins Ammunition Mover SWAM II was originally developed to act as a towed vehicle to carry two unit load containers (ULCs) for towing across rough terrain by vehicles such as self-propelled guns or howitzers, or other similar vehicles. A typical ULC could contain 17 155 mm projectiles and 17 charges and weigh 1320 kg.

The SWAM II has a mild steel chassis made up mainly from rectangular hollow sections. It is towed using a counter-balanced drawbar provided with a damped coupling with a capacity of 3500 kg. The coupling is fitted with a handbrake and an emergency breakaway cable. The twin axle sprung undergear uses a tandem set of leaf springs with a centre rocker beam. There is overrun braking on all four wheels which are fitted with auto-reverse hubs.

The two ULCs are secured in position using four webbing-type straps with a ratchet breaking load of

A Stead & Wilkins Ammunition Mover (SWAM II) on tow behind a M109A2 155 mm self-propelled howitzer

3000 kg/strap. ULCs can be carried back to back or side to side. An optional towing pintle at the rear allows an extra unloaded SWAM II to be towed. Other options include mudguards, an adjustable height drawbar, and a lighting system.

In addition to use as a ULC carrier, the SWAM II can be configured as an emergency water carrier, a heavy duty general purpose trailer with a timber or sheet metal body, a generator or air-conditioning unit carrier, or as a personnel accommodation shelter carrier.

In 1991 the British Ministry of Defence ordered 75 SWAM IIs for use in the air-conditioning unit transport role; these were supplied for use in the Gulf region.

Specifications
Load carrying capacity: 3300 kg
Length overall: 3.95 m
Width: 1.83 m
Height: (with ULC) 1.9 m
Tyres: 7.5 × 15 Avon Ranger 11
Towing speed: (max load, cross-country) 50 km/h
Side slope: (max, with 2 ULCs) 40°

Status
In service with the British Army.

Manufacturer
Stead and Wilkins Fabrications Limited, Jolly Farmers Wharf, Thames Road, Crayford, Dartford, Kent DA1 4HQ, UK.
Tel: 0322 529134. Fax: 0322 550314.

Trailer, Mineclearing Equipment, Giant Viper, No 2 Mk 3 (FV3705)

Description
This trailer was developed specifically as the transport and launch platform for the Giant Viper mine clearance device. It provides a cross-country capability for a payload of some 3000 kg comprising explosive hose and launching rocket. It can be towed by wheeled or tracked vehicles. The chassis is of all-steel welded construction, supported by semi-elliptical leaf springs on the single beam axle.

Specifications
Length: (overall) 5.9 m
Width: (overall) 2.476 m
Height:
  (overall) 2.217 m
  (platform) 1.089 m
Track: 2.134 m
Wheelbase: (axle to towing eye) 3.569 m
Gross vehicle weight: 4460 kg
Brakes: 3-line air system operation 394 mm diameter × 76 mm wide 'S' cam brakes
Tyres: 12.00 × 20 with run-flat capability

Status
In service with the British Army.

Manufacturer
Defence Equipment Division, Rubery Owen Group

Rubery Owen FV3705 Giant Viper trailer

Services Limited, Darlaston PO Box 10, Wednesbury, West Midlands WS10 8JD, UK.
Tel: 021 526 3131. Telex: 338236/7. Fax: 021 526 2869.

King Rapid Runway Repair Mat Carrier Drawbar Trailer

Description
The King rapid runway repair mat carrier drawbar trailer is used for the transport, loading and unloading of rapid runway repair mats. For details of the Rapid Runway Repair System involving the mats refer to the entry in the *Rapid runway repair equipment/portable runways* section.

The 20-tonne gross unit consists of a front and rear bogie connected by a long single spine fitted with hydraulic lifting gear by which the runway repair mat is handled. The front bogie features a turntable steered front axle mounted on two-spring, seven-leaf suspension connected to a 1.83 m drawbar towing facility. The rear bogie has hydraulic override steering complete with a wanderlead control mounted on a ball bearing turntable. The tyres are filled with urethane foam for puncture protection and to provide improved heat resistance.

The 13.41 m central spine has a detachable centre portion to reduce overall length and facilitate aircraft loading. Two hydraulic boosters for unloading and loading operations are fitted either end of the spine and are operated off a fully independent powerpack. Two hydraulically operated jack legs are fitted beneath each booster for stability during operation.

Specifications
Weight: 5000 kg
Capacity: 15 340 kg
Length: (overall) 16.37 m

King rapid runway repair mat carrier drawbar trailer

Width: 2.5 m
Tyres: 8.25 × 15

Status
In service with the British Army (20).

Manufacturer
King Trailers Limited, Riverside, Market Harborough, Leicestershire LE16 7PX, UK.
Tel: 0858 467361. Telex: 341835 king g. Fax: 0858 467161.

Scottorn 125-ration Mobile Kitchen Trailer

Description
The Scottorn kitchen trailer is a self-contained unit housing all the equipment required to prepare and cook meals for up to 125 personnel. It is carried on an all-steel electrically welded chassis formed from rolled steel channel. It uses a 'V' shaped drawbar which is fitted with a 75 mm NATO tow eye and a solid-tyred jockey wheel. The body consists of a sheet steel flooring with internal wheelboxes and a pressed steel skirt forming a shallow body allowing easy removal of stowed equipment. The trailer has a square section axle beam with roller bearing hubs and internal expanding brakes operated by an inertia system. The suspension is semi-elliptic springs with the whole unit mounted on 6.70 × 15 tyres with steel wheels. Two rear chassis props are fitted and other fittings include stop/tail lights and direction indicators, a registration number plate and other plates.

The trailer is equipped with two cooking stands (one two-container, the other three-container), five 6-gallon/22.71 litre cooking containers and a further five insulated containers, four frying pans, three 3-gallon/11.4 litre cooking containers, a vaporising type burner and a stand end plate. All these items are held in their respective travelling positions by quick-release webbing straps.

The trailer can be towed by most light four-wheel drive vehicles of the Land Rover type.

Status
In production.

Manufacturer
Reynolds Boughton Limited, Scottorn Division, Bell Lane, Amersham, Buckinghamshire HP6 6PE, UK. Tel: 0494 764411. Telex: 83132. Fax: 0494 765218.

Scottorn 125-ration mobile kitchen trailer

UNITED STATES OF AMERICA

Trailer, Cargo: ¼-ton, 2-wheel, M416 and M416A1

Description
The M416 single-axle trailer is the replacement for the earlier ¼-ton M100 trailer and is towed by the M151 (4 × 4) light vehicle. The all-welded body, bolted to the M569 chassis, is watertight and will float with a load of 226.8 kg. Two drain holes are provided in the floor of the trailer, which has a support leg and a tarpaulin cover. Its suspension consists of semi-elliptical springs. A mechanical parking brake is fitted as standard.

The M416A1 is the replacement for the earlier M100 and M416 and has an inertia braking system added. The M367 and later M716 are variants used to install and repair electrical transmission lines.

Specifications (M416)
Weight:
(empty) 258 kg
(loaded road) 599 kg
(loaded cross-country) 485 kg
Max load:
(road) 340 kg
(cross-country) 227 kg
Length:
(overall) 2.75 m

Trailer, cargo: ¼-ton, 2-wheel, M416 with non-standard top (Michael Ledford)

(inside body) 2.44 m
Width: 1.54 m
(inside body) 1.04 m
Height: 1.07 m
Depth: (inside body) 0.28 m
Coupling height: 0.58 or 0.66 m
Track: 1.44 m

Wheelbase: 1.87 m
Tyres: 7.00 × 16

Status
In service with the US Army and other armed forces.

Trailer, Amphibious: Cargo, ¼-ton, 2-wheel, M100

Description
The M100 single-axle trailer was designed to carry cargo on both roads and across country or water, and is normally towed by an M151 light vehicle. The body and frame of the trailer are of all-welded construction and are mounted on the trailer chassis M115. Two drain valves are provided in the floor of the trailer. The support leg at the front of the trailer is movable and a mechanical parking brake is provided, the hand lever for operating this being mounted on the right-front body panel. A canvas cover is provided to cover the cargo area and when not required this is stowed in a metal box mounted on the left front body panel.

Specifications
Weight:
(empty) 256 kg
(loaded road) 596 kg
(loaded cross-country) 483 kg

Trailer, amphibious: cargo, ¼-ton, 2-wheel, M100

Max load:
(road) 340 kg
(cross-country) 227 kg

Length:
(overall) 2.68 m
(inside body) 1.83 m

Width:
  (overall) 1.47 m
  (inside body) 0.97 m
Height: 1.07 m
  (to towing eye) 0.69 m

Depth: (inside body) 0.46 m
Ground clearance: 0.35 m
Wheelbase: (towing eye to centre of axle) 1.77 m
Tyres: 7.00 × 16

Status
In service with the US Army. Due to be replaced by M416.

Trailer, Cargo: ¾-ton, 2-wheel, M101 Series

Description

This trailer was designed to transport cargo both on roads and across country. Its body is all steel and is provided with a hinged tailgate, bows and a tarpaulin cover. The drawbar assembly is attached to the front of the chassis and a retractable pivoted front support is attached to the drawbar bracket. The chassis of the M101 trailer is designated the M116.

The latest version is the M101A2. A contract for 2583 of these worth $5 191 434 was awarded to the Kasel Manufacturing Company in November 1987. Production continued until January 1991. In 1988 the UMC Electronics Company of North Haven, Connecticut, was awarded a $4 006 326 firm-fixed-price contract for 1884 M101A2 trailers.

Specifications
Weight:
  (empty) 608 kg
  (loaded road) 1588 kg
  (loaded cross-country) 1288 kg
Max load:
  (road) 1020 kg
  (cross-country) 680 kg
Length:
  (overall) 3.73 m

Trailer, cargo: ¾-ton, 2-wheel, M101

  (inside body) 2.44 m
Width:
  (overall) 1.87 m
  (over wheels) 1.83 m
Height: (over tarpaulin) 2.11 m
Ground clearance: 0.36 m
Track: 1.57 m
Wheelbase: (towing eye to centre of axle) 2.54 m
Tyres: 9.00 × 16

Status
In service with the US Army, and many other armed forces.

Manufacturers
(M101A2) Kasel Manufacturing Company, Ebensburg, Pennsylvania, USA.
  UMC Electronics Company, North Haven, Connecticut, USA.

Trailer, Cargo: 1½-ton, 2-wheel, M105 Series

Description

The M105 single-axle cargo trailer was designed to transport cargo both on roads and across country and is normally towed by a 2½-ton truck. The body of the trailer is of the box type and is provided with lattice-type side extensions, tailgate, bows and a tarpaulin cover (optional). The brakes of the trailer are air-over-hydraulic with a mechanical parking brake.

The M105A1 and M105A2 are slightly smaller than the M105. The body of the M105A2 is wood and steel where the others are steel, and the M105A2 has an optional support leg.

Southwest Mobile Systems produces a mobile clothing repair shop based on the M105A2. Weight complete is 3289 kg.

Specifications
Weight: (empty) 1202 kg
Max load: 1361 kg
Length:
  (overall) 4.2 m
  (inside body) 2.79 m
Width:
  (overall) 2.11 m
  (inside body) 1.88 m
Height:
  (overall) 2.49 m

Trailer, cargo: 1½-ton, 2-wheel, M105 complete with side extensions (Ray Young)

  (to towing eye) 0.87 m
Ground clearance: 0.42 m
Track: 1.71 m
Wheelbase: (towing eye to centre of axle) 2.79 m

Tyres: 9.00 × 20

Status
In service with the US Army and other armed forces.

Trailer, Cargo: ¾-ton, 2-wheel, M104 Series

Description

The M104 trailer was designed for general cargo work and is normally towed by a 2½-ton truck. The trailer has a body of welded plate construction with the wheel housing integral with the body. The body has front and rear tailgates, hinged at the floor line and latched in the closed position by hooks. The chassis is designated

the M102 (for the M104), M102A1 (for the M104A1) and M102A3 (for the M104A2). The M104A2 is identical to the M104 except that it does not have a hinged tailgate.

Specifications
(M104; data in square brackets relate to M104A1 where different)
Weight:
  (empty) 1089 [1238] kg
  (loaded road) 3583 [3733] kg

  (loaded cross-country) 2449 [2599] kg
Max load:
  (road) 2495 kg
  (cross-country) 1360 kg
Length:
  (overall) 4.2 m
  (cargo area) 2.79 m
Width:
  (overall) 2.11 m
  (over wheels) 2.06 m
  (inside body) 1.88 m

Height: 2.52 m
Ground clearance: 0.49 m
Track: 1.77 m
Wheelbase: (towing eye to axle centre) 1.77 m

Tyres: 11.00 × 20
Towing speed:
(road) 80 km/h
(cross-country) 56 km/h

Status
In service with the US Army and other armed forces. The M104 trailers have been replaced in most units by the M105 series.

Semi-trailer, Stake: 6-ton, 2-wheel, M118 and M118A1

Description
The M118 semi-trailer, stake, consists of a stake-type body mounted on an M117 chassis. Mounted towards the front of the trailer is the landing gear assembly. On the left side of the chassis is a box for storing the tarpaulin when not in use. The M118 has commercial-type axles and air brakes but the M118A1 has air-over-hydraulic brakes. For air transport, the suspension assembly of the M118A1 can be removed. These trailers are towed by 2½-ton trucks.

Specifications
Weight: (empty) 3239 kg
Max load:
(road) 7348 kg
(cross-country) 5443 kg
Length:
(overall) 7 m
(inside body) 6.7 m
Width:
(overall) 2.41 m
(over wheels) 2.35 m
Height: 3.37 m
(to coupling) 1.19 m
Ground clearance: 0.49 m

Semi-trailer, stake: 6-ton, 2-wheel, M118 (US Army)

Track: 1.52 m
Wheelbase: (king-pin to centre of rear axle) 5.18 m
Max towing speed:
(road) 80 km/h
(cross-country) 48 km/h

Tyres: 9.00 × 20

Status
In service with the US Army and other armed forces.

Semi-trailer, Van: Cargo, 6-ton, 2-wheel, M119 and M119A1

Description
The M119 semi-trailer van is used for carrying cargo both by road and across country and is normally towed by a 2½-ton truck. The semi-trailer consists of a van body mounted on an M117 chassis. The body of the trailer consists of an angle iron framework covered on the outside with sheet metal and on the inside with plywood panels. The chassis consists of the frame, semi-elliptical springs mounted on an axle which is supported by dual wheels. The M119 has air-operated brakes while the later M119A1 has air-over-hydraulic brakes. Dual mechanically operated landing gear is mounted under the forward part of the chassis.

Specifications
Weight:
(empty) 3257 kg
(loaded road) 10 605 kg
(loaded cross-country) 8700 kg
Max load:
(road) 7348 kg
(cross-country) 5443 kg
Length:
(overall) 6.97 m
(inside body) 6.78 m
Width:
(overall) 2.53 m
(inside body) 2.23 m
Height:
(overall) 3.37 m
(coupling) 1.19 m

Semi-trailer, van: cargo, 6-ton, 2-wheel, M119 (US Army)

Ground clearance: 0.49 m
Track: 1.78 m
Wheelbase: (king-pin to centre of rear axle) 5.18 m
Tyres: 9.00 × 20

Status
In service with the US Army and other armed forces.

Semi-trailer, Stake: 12-ton, 4-wheel, M127, M127A1, M127A1C and M127A2C

Description
This trailer is used to transport general cargo and is towed by a 5-ton tractor truck. The body frame consists of pressed steel siderails, crossmember, and short crossmembers welded together forming one integral unit. The chassis consists of two drop-frame I-section longitudinal frame rails and intermediate crossmembers with an upper fifth wheel plate, king-pin, two axles mounted on a leaf spring suspension and two foot-type landing legs.

The basic M127 has air brakes but all later models have air-over-hydraulic brakes. The M127A1 is provided with chains which support the panels and also lifting rings for hoisting the semi-trailer. The M127A1C has a voltage control box mounted on the underside of the body and the M127A2C has improved landing legs.

Specifications
Weight:
(empty) 6123 kg [M127]
6531 kg [M127A1, M127A1C]
Max load:
(road) 16 329 kg
(cross-country) 10 886 kg
Length:
(overall) 8.75 m
(inside body) 8.53 m
Width:
(overall) 2.46 m
(inside body) 2.26 m
Height: (overall) 2.76 m
Ground clearance: 0.3 m
Track: 1.83 m
Wheelbase: (king-pin to centre of rear bogie) 6.12 m
Max towing speed:
(road) 80 km/h
(cross-country) 48 km/h
Tyres: 11.00 × 20

Semi-trailer, stake: 12-ton, 4-wheel, M127 (US Army)

Status
In service with the US Army and other armed forces.

Trailer, Flat Bed: 10-ton, 4-wheel, M345

Description
The M345 flat bed trailer is used for carrying equipment both by road and across country and can be towed by a 5-ton truck provided it has an air supply.

The trailer is constructed of structural and pressed steel with the two axles forming a bogie unit. The trailer has an air-over-hydraulic brake system that is controlled from the towing vehicle. As the trailer has no parking brakes, chocks are provided to stop the trailer rolling when parked. Swing-mounted landing gear is provided under the front and rear of the trailer.

Trailer, flat bed: 10-ton, 4-wheel, M345 (Larry Provo)

Specifications
Weight:
(empty) 5107 kg
(loaded road) 16 901 kg
(loaded cross-country) 14 179 kg
Max load:
(road) 11 793 kg

(cross-country) 9072 kg
Length:
(overall) 8.38 m
(platform) 7.01 m
Width: 1.93 m
Height: 1.38 m

Track: 1.83 m
Tyres: 11.00 × 20

Status
In service with the US Army. A new 12-ton flat bed trailer is under development.

Semi-trailer, Low Bed: Wrecker, 12-ton, 4-wheel, M270 and M270A1

Description
The M270 semi-trailer is used for general haulage work and is normally towed by an M818 5-ton tractor truck. The semi-trailer has two axles at the rear mounted on a leaf-spring suspension. Mounted under the front of the trailer is a foot-type landing gear, which supports the front of the trailer when not coupled to the towing vehicle.

The M270 is fitted with commercial axles and air brakes while the M270A1 has Ordnance-designed axles and air-over-hydraulic brakes.

Specifications
(M270; data in square brackets relate to M270A1 where different)
Weight:
(empty) 7938 [10 886] kg
(loaded road) 26 082 [29 030] kg
(loaded cross-country) 18 824 [21 773] kg
Max load:
(road) 18 144 kg
(dirt roads and cross-country) 10 886 kg
Length: (overall) 15 [15.17] m
Length of platform: 12.19 m
Width:
(overall) 2.46 m
(over platform) 2.44 m
Height:
(overall) 3.07 m

(over platform) 1.24 m
(to coupling) 1.37 m
Ground clearance: 0.46 m
Track: 1.83 m
Wheelbase: (king-pin to centre of rear bogie) 12.34 m
Tyres: 11.00 × 12
Max towing speed:
(road) 80 km/h
(cross-country) 48 km/h

Status
In service with the US Army.

Manufacturer
Kalyn Incorporated, Gatesville, Texas 76528, USA.

Semi-trailer, Low Bed, 60-ton, M747 (ConDec C2288)

Description
The M747 semi-trailer was originally designed as part of the HET-70 (Heavy Equipment Transporter for the 1970s) project. This was a joint development by Chrysler (USA) and Krupp and Faun of Germany, and was to have transported the MBT-70 tank which was cancelled in January 1970. The M747 was designed for use with the M746 (8 × 8) 22½-ton tractor manufactured by the Ward LaFrance Truck Corporation of New York.

The semi-trailer is equipped with four axles, dual wheels, and high flotation duplex tyres. The

M747 heavy equipment transporter

suspension for the two front axles is a walking beam type and the two rear axles are fitted with an adjustable air ride system which permits equalisation of loading among all four axles under a wide range of payloads. The airlift system, used with the two rearmost axles, raises these axles off the road surface when the vehicle is not loaded or is carrying a light load. Raising the rearmost axles also provides improved manoeuvrability when turning corners and reduces tyre wear.

The semi-trailer is equipped with heavy duty, militarised, air-operated service brakes at all wheel positions. Each wheel is fitted with fail-safe provisions which require an initial build-up to a preset, continuous air supply pressure before normal operations begin. Emergency service provisions are incorporated to provide for all wheel lock-up in the event of a sudden loss of air pressure. The brake system incorporates manual release to override both fail-safe and

emergency service conditions facilitating subsequent movement of the vehicle.

Two removable aluminium loading ramps permit backloading operations without disconnecting the tractor/trailer. Four cable roller assemblies and a snatch block preclude the need of special rigging when winching operations are required to load disabled or trackless vehicles; 28 tie-downs are provided to secure the load.

Specifications
Weight:
(empty) 14 514 kg
(loaded) 69 059 kg
Max load: 54 545 kg
Length:
(overall) 12.954 m
(of platform) 8.05 m

Width:
(overall) 3.48 m
(of platform) 3.048 m
Height:
(overall) 2.71 m
(to platform) 1.17 m
Ground clearance: (under chassis) 0.69 m
Track: 2.54 m
Wheelbase: (king-pin to centre of first bogie) 8.07 m
Tyres: 15.00 × 19.5

Status
Production complete. In service with the US Army and Morocco.

Manufacturer
ConDiesel Mobile Equipment, 84 Progress Lane, Waterbury, Connecticut 06705, USA.

Semi-trailer, Heavy Equipment Transporter, M1000

Description
The Semi-trailer, Heavy Equipment Transporter (HET), M1000, with automatically steered axles, was originally developed as a private venture by Southwest Mobile Systems as a response to a possible US Army requirement for transporting M1 and M1A1 MBTs. This requirement materialised as the XM1000 and the HET was involved in US Army trials that were completed during 1986. A production order for 1066 M1000 units was placed by the US Army in 1989 with Southwest Mobile Systems. An additional 111 units were ordered in 1992.

The M1000 uses hydraulic/mechanical steering that is automatically controlled by the tractor-trailer angle. The semi-trailer has a maximum on- and off-road payload of 70 000 kg and is compatible with existing US Army and Marine Corps prime movers such as the M911, MK48/16 and M1070 tractors. When coupled to an M911 the HET can negotiate intersections of 9.144 m roads in a single pass. There are five axle

lines with two half-width axles per line. Each axle is mounted on a hydraulic pendular suspension providing a ±254 mm stroke, fully equalised. There is lateral oscillation provided to accommodate crowned roads and rough terrain. A hydraulic suspension system is also provided on the pivoting gooseneck to equalise fifth wheel loads. Hydraulics are used for the control of the deck height, gooseneck angle, axle jacking, loading ramps and rear support legs. A diesel powerpack is mounted on the gooseneck in case power is not available from a prime mover. Any axle may be raised without having to remove the payload and the axles can be rotated to allow access to the inboard tyres for ease of changing flat tyres.

The M1000 is being investigated by the US Army Engineer Center as a transporter of heavy engineer equipment.

Specifications
Weight: 22 860kg
Payload: 70 000 kg
Length:
(overall) 15.8 m
(deck) 10.24 m

Width:
(overall) 3.66 m
(deck) 3.05 m
Height:
(deck) 1.074 m ± 0.254 m
(5th wheel) 1.6 m – variable
King-pin: 88.9 mm (3½ in)
Max speed:
(road) 72.4 km/h
(secondary road) 64 km/h
(cross-country) 24 km/h
Tyres: 215/75 R 17.5
Loading ramp angle: 18°

Status
In production for US Army (1177 units).

Manufacturer
Southwest Mobile Systems Corporation, 200 Sidney Street, St Louis, Missouri 63104, USA.
Tel: (314) 771 3950. Fax: (314) 771 1169.

Semi-trailer, Heavy Equipment Transporter (HET) M1000 travelling off-road with an M1A1 Abrams MBT

Semi-trailer, Heavy Equipment Transporter (HET) M1000 being trialled for the transport of engineer vehicles

---

Talbert 64-tonne Tank Transporter Semi-trailer

Description
For use during operations associated with Operations Desert Shield and Desert Storm the US Army procured 150 examples of the Talbert Model T4LW-64M-FG 64-tonne capacity tank transporter semi-trailers. These commercially designed semi-trailers were used for the road transport of either a single M1 Abrams MBT or

two M2/M3 Bradley fighting vehicles.

The Talbert 64-tonne semi-trailer has a usable cargo bed length of 12.041 m and a width of 3.609 m. Maximum towing speed is 88 km/h. The main spring beam suspension consists of four axles, each carrying two road wheels each side. Spring-loaded and balanced loading ramps are provided. The gooseneck has provision for a spare wheel and carrier and a water tank.

A shorter and lighter version of this semi-trailer is available, as is a version with an off-road suspension.

Specifications
Weight: (empty) 18 642 kg
Max load: 64 012 kg
Length:
(overall) 15.773 m
(cargo bed) 12.041 m
Width: 3.609 m
Height:
(5th wheel, loaded) 1.689 m
(overall) 3.359 m
Tyres: 315/80 R 22.5

Status
Available. In service with US Army.

Manufacturer
Talbert Manufacturing Inc, R.R.5, Box 195, Rensselaer, Indiana 47978, USA.
Tel: (219) 866 7141. Fax: (219) 866 5437.

M1 Abrams MBT being loaded onto Talbert 64-tonne tank transporter semi-trailer

Semi-trailer, Flat Bed, 22½-ton, Break Bulk/Container Transporter M871 and Semi-trailer, Flat Bed, 34-ton, Break Bulk/Container Transporter M872/M872A3

Description

The M871 and M872 semi-trailers were procured to carry containers and other military freight in rear areas, and are intended for operation at sustained high speeds on main roads. The M872 is normally operated from a port area as far forward as the Corps General Support Supply Activity (GSSA), while the M871 is used for the transport of containers, shelters and cargo forward from the Corps GSSA to the Division Support Command (DISCOM) or even to user units.

From 1979 Southwest Mobile Systems delivered 3367 M871 units and a further 246 M871A1s were delivered by Shoals America; the total requirement for the M871A2 was understood to be 3420 units. From FY86 a total of 8877 M872 units was purchased, plus a further 346 M872A3 units from Southwest Mobile Systems.

The M871 semi-trailer was designed to carry containers and shelters of up to 6.1 m in length, while the M872 was designed for the carriage of containers up to 12.2 m long. Both can also carry break bulk (loose) items of cargo. The two semi-trailers use many identical components and differ only in length and running gear. Each has a main frame on which the load bed and a headboard are fitted. The M871 is a two-axle trailer while the M872 has a three-axle bogie. Two landing jacks are provided and there are two storage lockers below the load deck. A yard kit is supplied with removable guide assemblies to aid positioning of containers before being secured with twistlock devices. Side racks are also provided with removable side and rear panels and cover plates. The side panels are hinged to allow for the carriage of loose break bulk cargo without spoilage. The M872A3 is the latest production version of the M872. It retains all the original capabilities plus specific features to facilitate the transport of two M113 APCs (there are tie-downs on the platform and lower platform heights to allow a 4 m overhead clearance).

Specifications

Type	M871	M872/M872A3
Weight	7090 kg	8300/8700 kg
Payload	20 412 kg	30 481 kg
Length	9.1 m	12.45 m

Type	M871	M872/M872A3
Width	2.44 m	2.44 m
Deck (length)	9 m	12.3 m
(width)	2.44 m	2.44 m
(height)	1.4 m	1.52/1.4 m
King-pin height	1.27 m	1.27 m
Track	1.79 m	1.8 m
Ground clearance	0.38 m	0.36/0.27 m
Tyres (commercial highway tread)	11.20 × 20, 12 PR	10.00 × 20, 14 PR
Number of tyres	8 + 1 spare	12 + 1 spare
Towing vehicle		
(primary)	M915 line haul tractor	
(secondary)	M818 5-ton tractor	
(terminal)	M878 yard tractor	

Status
In production the US Army and US Air Force. The US Army has a requirement for a total of 3982 M871 and 11 488 M872 semi-trailers.

Manufacturers
M871: Southwest Mobile Systems Corporation.
    M871A2: Dynaweld Inc, Naperville, Illinois, USA.
    M872: Heller Truck Body System, Southwest Mobile Systems Corporation and Theurer-Greenville Corporation.

Semi-trailer, flat bed, 34-ton, break bulk/container transporter M872

Semi-trailer, flat bed, 34-ton, break bulk/container transporter M872A3 carrying two M113 APCs

Trailer, Tank: Water, 1½-ton, 2-wheel, 400-gallon, M106 Series

Description
The M106 single-axle trailer is used to transport, store and distribute drinking water. The aluminium tank has a capacity of 1514 litres and has an elliptical cross-section. The trailer is provided with a hand water pump and a 7.62 m suction hose for filling.

The trailer was designed for fording where the trailer may be completely submerged and is normally towed by a 2½-ton truck, provided the towing vehicle has an air supply.

The M106A1 has a cover plate over the piping between the two welded metal tap boxes at the front of the tank. The M106A2 employs two hydraulic wheel cylinders for each wheel service brake. The M106A1 and M106A2 do not have a support leg, which is fitted only on the M106 trailer.

Specifications
(M106; data in square brackets relate to M106A1 where different)
Weight:
 (empty) 1034 [1070] kg
 (loaded) 2547 [2583] kg
Max load: 1514 l
Length: 4.23 m
Width: 2.36 m
 (over tyres) 2.06 m
Height: 2.03 m
Ground clearance: 0.5 m
Track: 1.77 m
Wheelbase: 2.88 m

Trailer, tank: water, 1½-ton, 2-wheel, 400-gallon, M106 (Ray Young)

Tyres: 11.00 × 20
Max towing speed:
 (road) 80 km/h
 (cross-country) 48 km/h

Fording: complete submergence

Status
In service with the US Army.

Trailer, Tank: Water, 1½-ton, 2-wheel, 400-gallon, M107 Series

Description
The M107 tanker trailer was designed to transport, store and dispense drinking water, and is normally towed by a 2½-ton truck, provided the truck has an air supply.

The trailer has a 1514 litre aluminium water tank with an elliptical cross-section and is fitted with a hand water pump and a 7.62 m suction hose for filling. Brakes on the trailer are of the air-over-hydraulic type, with a mechanical parking brake. The basic M107 is provided with a support leg, which is not fitted to the M107A1 and M107A2.

On the M107A1 and M107A2 there is a cover plate over the piping between the two welded metal tap boxes at the front of the tank, and the castor is raised and locked in a mounting bracket welded to the nose of the chassis frame. The M107A2 also employs two hydraulic wheel cylinders for each wheel service brake.

Specifications
(M107; data in square brackets relate to M107A1 where different)
Weight:
 (empty) 1034 kg
 (loaded) 2546 kg
Max load: 1512 l
Length: (overall) 4.32 [4.14] m
Width: (overall) 2.27 [2.08] m
Height: 1.91 [1.96] m
Ground clearance: 0.41 m
Track: 1.72 m
Max towing speed:
 (road) 88 km/h
 (cross-country) 24 km/h
Tyres: 9.00 × 20
Fording: complete submergence

Status
In service with the US Army and other armed forces.

Trailer, tank: water, 1½-ton, 2-wheel, 400-gallon, M107A1 of Spanish Army

Trailer, Tank: Water, 1½-ton, 2-wheel, 400-gallon M149 Series

Description
This single-axle two-wheeled trailer is used to transport, store and dispense drinking water, and is normally towed by a 2½-ton truck. The trailer has a filling cap on top of the tank and two dispensing taps in boxes in front of the tank. The main brakes are air-over-hydraulic, with a mechanical parking brake also provided. The M149A1 has an improved lighting system. Glass fibre tanks are fitted in all versions except the M149A2, on which the tank is of stainless steel.

Trailer, tank: water, 1½-ton, 2-wheel, 400-gallon, M149

Specifications
Weight: 1288 kg
Max load: 1514 l
Length: 4.09 m
Width: 2.09 m
Height: 1.94 m
    (towing eye) 0.76 to 1.04 m

Ground clearance: 0.43 m
Track: 1.71 m
Wheelbase: (towing eye to centre of axle) 2.87 m
Tyres: 9.00 × 20

Status
In production. In service with the US Army and some other countries including Kenya (M149A2).

Manufacturer
(M149A2) Kogen Industries, Patton, Pennsylvania, USA.

Semi-trailer, Tank, Fuel, 5000-gallon, 4-wheel, M131 Series

Description
The M131 semi-trailer was designed to transport and dispense 18 927 litres of fuel. A cabinet mounted at the rear of the trailer houses the air-cooled auxiliary engine, pump and control equipment. A fire extinguisher is carried on each side of the trailer and there are two stabiliser legs at the front. The M131 series semi-trailers are towed by a 5-ton truck.

The M131 and M131A1 each have three compartments and the other models all have four. The coating of the tanks of the M131 to M131A3C is not corrosion-resistant. The M131A4 (known during development as the XM664) has a corrosion-resistant tank and can carry gasoline, diesel, JP4 and JP5. The M131A4C is similar to the M131A4 but has a complete servicing capability, being provided with a filtration unit, hose reel and meter. The M131E6 (a development model) was configured as an aircraft refueller. The M308 is similar to the M131 series but was designed to carry

Specifications

Type	M131A1	M131A2	M131A3C	M131A4C	M131A5	M131A5C
Weight						
(empty)	6770 kg	5610 kg	6680 kg	7020 kg	5660 kg	7020 kg
(loaded, cross-country)	15 670 kg	14 510 kg	15 580 kg	15 920 kg	14 560 kg	15 920 kg
(loaded, road)	20 620 kg	19 460 kg	20 530 kg	20 870 kg	19 510 kg	20 870 kg
Max load						
(cross-country)	8900 kg	8900 kg	8900 kg	8900 kg	8900 kg	8900 kg
(road)	13 850 kg	13 850 kg	13 850 kg	13 850 kg	13 850 kg	13 850 kg
Length	8.94 m	9.65 m	9.77 m	9.49 m	9.49 m	9.56 m
Width	2.48 m	2.48 m	2.49 m	2.48 m	2.48 m	2.45 m
Height	3.34 m	2.72 m	2.68 m	2.76 m	2.72 m	2.76 m
Coupling height	1.42 m	1.42 m	1.42 m	1.42 m	1.42 m	1.42 m
Ground clearance	0.3 m	0.3 m	0.3 m	0.3 m	0.3 m	0.3 m
Tyres	11.00 × 20	11.00 × 20	11.00 × 20	11.00 × 20	11.00 × 20	11.00 × 20
Max towing speed						
(cross-country)	32 km/h	32 km/h	32 km/h	32 km/h	32 km/h	32 km/h
(road)	84 km/h	84 km/h	84 km/h	84 km/h	84 km/h	84 km/h

4000 gallons (15 140 litres) of water. The M857 series is the replacement for the M131 series of fuel semi-trailers.

Status
Most of the later models are still in service with the US Army.

Semi-trailer, Tank, Fuel, 5000-gallon, 4-wheel, M900 Series, M967, M969, M970

Description
The M900 series of fuel semi-trailers is the replace-ment for the earlier M131 series. It consists of the M967 bulk haul refueller, the M969 automotive refueller and the M970 aircraft refueller.

Status
In service with the US Army and (M970) US Marine Corps. The initial order was for approximately 850 semi-trailers of the M900 series. The FY82 budget included a request for funds for 703 fuel semi-trailers. M900 series semi-trailers have been supplied to Portugal.

Trailer, Ammunition: 1½-ton, 2-wheel, M332

Description
The M332 ammunition trailer consists of a frame supported by an axle assembly with leaf spring suspension. A retractable support is provided at the front end of the trailer. Brakes are air-over-hydraulic and there is also a mechanical parking brake. If required, the top of the trailer can be covered by a tarpaulin which is stowed in a box on the forward part of the trailer when not in use.

Specifications
Weight:
    (empty) 1270 kg
    (loaded) 2630 kg
Max load: 1360 kg
Length: (overall) 3.76 m
Width: (overall) 2.48 m
Height: 1.35 m
    (to towing eye) 0.85 m

Trailer, ammunition: 1½-ton, 2-wheel, M332

Track: 2.03 m
Towing speed:
    (road) 80 km/h
    (cross-country) 40 km/h

Tyres: 9.00 × 20

Status
In service with the US Army.

Chassis, Trailer: 2-ton, 2-wheel, M390 and M390C

Description
These chassis trailers are used with the HAWK SAM system. The M390 is used to transport electronic equipment while the M390C carries three missiles. Each trailer consists of a chassis, deck plate (not on the M390), suspension system, two wheels, air-over-hydraulic brakes, individual handbrakes for each wheel, retractable landing gear, levelling support jacks and a towing eye.

These trailers were also built in the Netherlands by DAF under the designation M390-17 and M390-17C.

Specifications
(M390; data in square brackets relate to M390C where different)
Weight:
    (empty) 1711 [1656] kg
    (loaded) 3525 [3470] kg
Length: 4.77 m
Width:
    (travelling) 2.47 m
    (emplaced) 2.82 m
Height: (without equipment) 0.93 m

Ground clearance: 0.43 m
Track: 2.03 m
Wheelbase: (towing eye to centre of axle) 3.23 m
Tyres: 9.00 × 20
Towing speed:
  (road) 80 km/h
  (cross-country) 40 km/h

Status
In service with countries using the HAWK surface-to-air missile system including Belgium, Denmark, France, Germany, Greece, Iran, Israel, Italy, Japan, Jordan, South Korea, Kuwait, the Netherlands, Saudi Arabia, Spain, Sweden, Taiwan and the USA. Most trailers for European countries were supplied by DAF.

M390C trailer of Japanese Self-Defence Force with three-round pallet of HAWK SAMs

Chassis, Trailer: 1-ton, 2-wheel, M514

Description
The M514 trailer consists of a heavy duty frame supported by an independent trailing arm suspension. Mounted at the front of the chassis is an A-shaped extension on which the retractable swivel castor and towing eye are mounted. The chassis has three levelling jacks, one at the rear and one either side. The brakes are the air-over-hydraulic type with two mechanical handbrakes for parking. This trailer is used with the HAWK SAM system and is used to mount the Radar Set, CW, Acquisition, AN/MPQ-34 and the Radar Set, CW, Illuminator, AN/MPQ-33.

Specifications
Weight:
  (empty) 1034 kg
  (loaded) 2150 kg
Max load: 1116 kg
Length: (without radar) 4.35 m
Width: (without radar) 2.39 m
Height: (without radar) 1.67 m
Ground clearance: 0.36 m
Towing eye height: adjustable from 0.56 to 0.86 m
Track: 2.03 m
Wheelbase: 2.69 m
Tyres: 9.00 × 20
Towing speed:
  (road) 80 km/h
  (cross-country) 40 km/h

Radar set, CW, illuminator, AN/MPQ-33 mounted on Spanish Army M514 1-ton trailer chassis (J I Taibo)

Status
In service with countries using the HAWK SAM system including Belgium, Denmark, France, Germany, Greece, Iran, Israel, Italy, Japan, Jordan, South Korea, Kuwait, the Netherlands, Saudi Arabia, Spain, Sweden, Taiwan and the USA.

Chassis, Trailer, Generator, 2½-ton, 2-wheel, M200A1

Description
The M200A1 trailer was originally a single-axle trailer with two road wheels each side. A total of 1704 basic chassis was procured following the FY82 budget.

While the M200A1 was originally intended to be a mobile platform for electrical generators and similar equipment, the trailer was also used for carrying the M58 MICLIC mineclearing system. However, following operational experience in the Gulf region, it was appreciated that the M200A1 could not carry out its MICLIC tasks due to a general lack of mobility over soft terrain. As a result an initial total of 250 kits was procured to convert the M200A1 trailers to accommodate the Caterpillar Mobil-trac tracked system which considerably reduces the ground pressure of the trailer and enhances its mobility over mud, sand and snow. The first kit conversions were carried out in March 1992 at Army depots.

It is anticipated that the Mobil-trac system will also be applied to other in-service trailers.

Status
In service with the US Army. Mobil-trac system conversions being carried out by US Army depots.

Manufacturer (Mobil-trac system)
Caterpillar Inc, Defense & Federal Products Department, Peoria, Illinois 61629, USA. Tel: (309) 675 6938. Telex: 404435.

Chassis, Trailer, Generator, 2½-ton, 2-wheel, M200A1 carrying a 60 kW generator and with the Caterpillar Mobil-trac system installed

Chassis, Trailer: 3½-ton, 2-wheel, M353

Description
The M353 chassis was designed to mount various types of bodies and other equipment such as generators. It consists of a heavy duty frame supported by an offset axle assembly with leaf spring suspension and has two retractable swivel castors mounted at the front. The trailer has air-over-hydraulic brakes operated from the towing vehicle and a mechanical parking brake. The castors are secured in the raised or lowered positions by gravity pin and chain assembly. The fuel tank for the Patriot system generator is mounted on the M353 trailer.

Chassis, trailer: 3½-ton, 2-wheel, M353 fitted with generator (Michael Ledford)

Specifications
Weight: (empty) 1202 kg
Max load:
  (road) 3629 kg
  (cross-country) 3175 kg
Length: 4.58 m
Width: 2.43 m
Height:
  (overall) 1.23 m

  (to platform) 0.69 m
  (to towing eye) 0.86 or 0.96 m
Track: 2.07 m
Wheelbase: 3.36 m
Tyres: 11.00 × 20
Max towing speed:

  (road) 80 km/h
  (cross-country) 40 km/h

Status
In service with the US Army.

Patriot Missile Semi-trailer M860A1

Description
Under contract to TACOM, Southwest Mobile Systems Corporation was the sole producer of 419 M860A1 semi-trailers for the Patriot air defence guided missile system. In early 1987 Urdan Industries of Israel was awarded a multi-year contract to produce 72 M860A1 semi-trailers per year, 70 per cent of the work to be carried out in Netanya, Israel, and the rest in Lebanon, Pennsylvania. Southwest has completed a technology

transfer programme with the TOKYU Car Corporation of Yokohama, Japan, where M860A1s have been produced since 1987.

The M860A1 semi-trailer is designed to carry either the Patriot missile-launching stations or associated radar equipment, and is constructed to a high degree of precision so that the deck mounting pads for the equipment do not vary more than 0.015 in (0.381 mm) in height over the deck length. A stowage box is situated under the sides of the deck and houses lashing equipment and spares. Two triple-legged joists support the semi-trailer when it is not attached to a

tractor. In use at a firing location, the semi-trailer is removed from the tractor, raised off the ground and levelled by four heavy duty outriggers on the ends of folding stays. These operate under electric power supplied by the tractor truck's 100 A alternator. When on the move, the outriggers are raised vertically and lie alongside the carried load which is in shelter/container form. A panel at the front of the gooseneck connects the semi-trailer electrical system to that of the tractor truck.

Specifications
Weight: (kerb) 10 182 kg
Max load: 12 273 kg
Length: 10.08 m
Width:
  (outriggers up) 2.87 m
  (outriggers down) 6.55 m
Height: (outriggers up) 3 m
Max towing speed:
  (road) 80 km/h
  (cross-country) 32 km/h

Status
In production. In service with the US Army. The Patriot missile system is used by Israel, the Netherlands, Germany and Japan.

Manufacturers
Southwest Mobile Systems Corporation, 200 Sidney Street, St Louis, Missouri 63104, USA.
  Urdan Industries Limited, 30161 Southfield Road, Southfield, Michigan 48076, USA.
  TOKYU Car Corporation, 1 Kamajiya-Cho, Kanazawa-Ku, Yokohama 236, Japan.

M860A1 semi-trailer for Patriot air defence missile system

Chassis, Semi-trailer, Coupleable, MILVAN Container Transporter

Description
The MILVAN chassis forms the basis of a military-owned fleet for the movement of military containers over primary roads in the continental USA but appears to be used primarily to transport refrigerated containers within US Army Europe (USAREUR). It consists of a 6.1 m frame, landing gear and a single-axle bogie, which can be moved along the length of the frame. Two chassis can be coupled together with the bogies under

the rear frame to form a tandem-axle 40 ft semi-trailer. ISO twistlocks are provided.

Specifications

Type	20ft unit	20ft unit, tandem axle	40ft unit, tandem axle
Weight	1814 kg	2654 kg	3629 kg
Length	6.25 m	6.15 m	12.29 m
Width	2.44 m	2.44 m	2.44 m
Height (on landing legs with deck level)	1.36 m	1.36 m	1.36 m

Status
Production complete. A total of 5106 chassis are in service with the US Army.

M989A1 Heavy Expanded Mobility Ammunition Trailer (HEMAT)

Development

The M989A1 Heavy Expanded Mobility Ammunition Trailer (HEMAT – originally the XM989) is intended for the carrying of Multiple Launch Rocket System (MLRS) rocket pods. Other applications include transporting ammunition pallets as well as fuel bladders for aviation refuelling.

A contract was awarded in FY82 for 400 trailers but this contract was suspended in 1985 following the discovery of a stability problem after 353 trailers had been delivered. In 1986 the US Army solicited bids for a new multi-year production phase. Bids were submitted by the Southwest Mobile Systems Corporation, Teledyne Continental Motors, Landoll, and Prototype Development. In 1987 Southwest Mobile Systems was awarded a four-year contract for 1046 M989A1 HEMAT trailers with a 50 per cent option. Testing of the first article units was carried out during 1989. Contract deliveries commenced during 1990.

M989A1 Heavy Expanded Mobility Ammunition Trailer (HEMAT)

Description

The HEMAT is a two-axle trailer with the front axle featuring an Ackerman steering design; the rear axle is stationary. The brakes are air-actuated while the air suspension is designed for on- and off-road mobility. The trailer meets all the requirements for a 0.55*g* lateral stability.

The treated hardwood deck is surrounded by 22 tie-down rings evenly spaced for securing MLRS pods and other payloads up to 10 000 kg. The HEMAT is normally towed by the M985 HEMTT but can be towed by other military or commercial tractors as well as the MLRS launch vehicle. The HEMAT can be air-transported, unloaded, in a C-130 transport aircraft, or loaded by C-141 and C-5 aircraft. It can also be carried, loaded, by a CH-47D helicopter.

Specifications

Weight:
  (gross) 14 091 kg
  (kerb) 4566 kg
Max payload: 10 000 kg
Length: 7.85 m
Width: 2.44 m
Height: 1.45 m
Cargo area: 4.47 × 2.44 m
Ground clearance:
  (bottom of axles) 0.32 m
  (trailer structure) 0.51 m

Wheelbase: 5.94 m
Gradient: 40%
Side slope: 30%
Brakes: air
Suspension: air ride

Status

In production for US Army.

Manufacturer

Southwest Mobile Systems Corporation, 200 Sidney Street, St Louis, Missouri 63104, USA.
Tel: (314) 771 3950. Fax: (314) 771 1169.

Caterpillar Combat Support Trailer

Description

The Caterpillar Combat Support Trailer is intended for off-road employment in forward areas carrying a variety of combat engineer and other supply loads. The trailer uses a Mobil-trac rubber belted two-wheeled undercarriage arrangement that provides up to 24° of vertical articulation over rough terrain while maintaining the level of the flat cargo bed. Air over hydraulic disc brakes are provided on all four wheels.

The trailer has been demonstrated carrying bridging equipment, mineclearing systems and up to 6804 kg of payload. It can be towed by a 5-ton truck or a tracked vehicle such as an M113 APC and may be air-transported in a C-130 transport aircraft.

Specifications

Weight:
  (unloaded) 2721 kg
  (fully loaded) 9525 kg
Payload: 6804 kg
Length: 4.267 m
Width: 2.438 m
Height: 1.09 m
Flat bed dimensions: 4.263 × 2.438 m
Ground clearance: 0.419 m
Wheelbase: 0.914 m
Gradient: (loaded) 60%
Side slope: (loaded) 40%
Vertical obstacle: 0.38 m
Trench: 1.524 m
Towing speed:
  (5-ton truck, paved road) 80 km/h

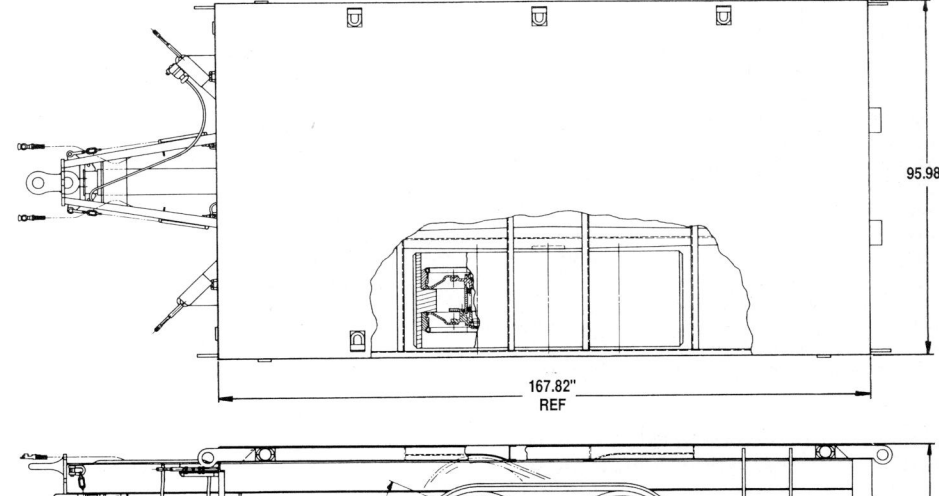

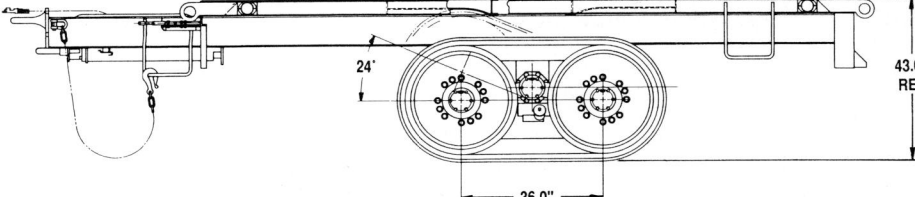

General outline drawing of an early version of the Caterpillar Combat Support Trailer

  (5-ton truck, secondary road) 48 km/h
  (tracked vehicle, cross-country) 32 km/h

Status

Ready for production.

Manufacturer

Caterpillar Inc, Defense & Federal Products Department, Peoria, Illinois 61629, USA.
Tel: (309) 675 6938. Telex: 404435.

Other United States Trailers

Many other trailers are in service, or have been in service, with the US Army. Those listed below include some which have been declared obsolete, but which may still be found in other armies' inventories.

Designation	Notes
Trailer, mount, 20-mm automatic gun, 2-wheel, M42	For M167 towed Vulcan Air Defense System
Chassis, trailer: 1½-ton, 2-wheel, M102	For M104 and M106 trailers
Chassis, trailer: 1½-ton, 2-wheel, M103	For M105 and M107 trailers
Trailer, flat bed, 5-ton, 4-wheel, M106A1	997 units ordered from Utility Tool and Body Company for use as fuel unit carriers to replace M105 series
Trailer, low bed, 3½-ton, 4-wheel, M114	M113 chassis
Chassis, trailer: ¼-ton, 2-wheel, M115	For M100 and M367 trailers
Chassis, trailer: ¾-ton, 2-wheel, M116	For M101 trailer
Chassis, semi-trailer: 6-ton, 2-wheel, M117	For M118, M119 and M508 semi-trailers
Chassis, semi-trailer: 12-ton, 4-wheel, M126	For M127, M128 and M129 semi-trailers
Semi-trailer, van, cargo, 12-ton, 4-wheel, M128 series	Production of 44 M128A2C semi-trailers at a cost of $1.4 m was included in FY82 budget request
Semi-trailer, van, supply, 12-ton, 4-wheel, M129 series	Similar to M128 series but with interior fittings
Trailer, bomb, 2-ton, 4-wheel, M143	M143A1 is shorter
Semi-trailer, van, shop, 6-ton, 2-wheel, M146	M146C has windows
Semi-trailer, low bed, 60-ton, 8-wheel, M162	
Semi-trailer, van, office, 6-ton, 2-wheel, M164	
Dolly, trailer converter, 4-ton, 2-wheel, M196	Converts 3 and 4-ton semi-trailers to full trailers
Dolly, trailer converter: 6-ton, 2-wheel, M197	For 6-ton semi-trailers
Dolly, trailer converter: 8-ton, 4-wheel, M198	For 12-ton semi-trailers
Dolly, trailer converter: 18-ton, 4-wheel, M199	For larger semi-trailers
Trailer, van, fire control mount, 3-ton, 4-wheel, M242	
Trailer, flat bed: fire control/acquisition radar, 2-ton, 4-wheel, M243	
Trailer, van, fire control, 2-ton, 4-wheel, M244	
Tracking station, guided missile, trailer-mounted, M248	
Trailer, van, radar tracking control, M258	Used with Nike-Hercules system
Trailer, van, director station, M259	
Trailer, low bed, antenna mount, M260	
Trailer, flat bed, guided missile, M261	
Trailer, van, launching control, M262	
Chassis, trailer, generator, 2½-ton, 2-wheel, M267	
Trailer, bolster, pole handing, 3½-ton, 2-wheel, M271	M271A1 is later model
Semi-trailer, low bed, 12-ton, wrecker, 4-wheel, M269 and M269A1	
Chassis, semi-trailers, 6-ton, 4-wheel, M295	
Trailer, basic utility, 2½-ton, 2-wheel, M296	
Electrical shop, trailer-mounted, M304	
Semi-trailer, tank, water, 4000-gallon, 4-wheel, M308	Similar to M131 series of fuel semi-trailers
Trailer, cable reel, 3½-ton, 2-wheel, M310	Signal Corps designation was K37-B
Semi-trailer, van, expansible, 6-ton, 4-wheel, M313	
Semi-trailer, refrigerator, 15-ton, 4-wheel, M347	
Semi-trailer van, electronic, 3-ton, 2-wheel, M348	M348A1 and M348A2 are also 3-ton but M348A2C, -D, -F and -G models are 6-ton
Semi-trailer, van, refrigerator, 7½-ton, 2-wheel, M349 series	M349A1 is later model
Dolly, trailer converter, 18-ton, 4-wheel, M354	
Trailer, van, electronic shop, 2½-ton, 4-wheel, M359	
Dolly, trailer converter, 3-ton, 2-wheel, M363	
Dolly, trailer converter, 6-ton, 2-wheel, M364	
Dolly, trailer converter, 10-ton, 2-wheel, M365	
Trailer, maintenance, cable splicer, ¼-ton, 2-wheel, M367	Based on M100 trailer
Semi-trailer, van, electronic, 3-ton, 2-wheel, M373	Contract for 330 M373A2 worth $8 373 120 awarded to Miller Trailers Inc, Bradenton, Florida, August 1989
Trailer, van, electronic shop, 6-ton, 4-wheel, M382	
Trailer, van, electronic shop, 5-ton, 4-wheel, M383	
Semi-trailer, van, dental clinic, 3-ton, 2-wheel, M393	M393A1 is electronic shop
Semi-trailer, van, medical, 3-ton, 2-wheel, M394	
Semi-trailer, van, medical, 6-ton, 2-wheel, M395	
Trailer, antenna, 2-ton, 4-wheel, M406	For Nike-Hercules system
Trailer, guided missile director, M424	For Nike-Hercules system
Trailer, guided missile, tracking station, M428	Used on M242, M244, M248, M258, M259, M260, M261, M262, and M359 trailers
Dolly, trailer, front, M429 series	
Dolly, trailer, rear, M430 series	
Dolly, trailer, front, M431	
Dolly, trailer, rear, M432	Single-wheel dollies with electric brakes
Semi-trailer, van, shop, folding sides, 6-ton, 4-wheel, M447 and M447C	
Trailer, van, shop, folding side, 1½-ton, 2-wheel, M448	

Designation

Chassis, trailer, 2½-ton, 2-wheel, M454

Semi-trailer, maintenance, weapon, mechanical unit, M457
Semi-trailer, maintenance, weapon, electric unit, M458
Semi-trailer, maintenance, weapon, connecting unit, M459
Trailer, air-conditioner, 1½-ton, 2-wheel, M463
Semi-trailer, van, shop, 6-ton, 2-wheel, M508

Semi-trailer, van, electrical, 6-ton, 2-wheel, M513
Laundry unit, trailer-mounted, 80 lb capacity, M532
Bakery oven, trailer-mounted, M533
Chassis, trailer, laundry, 3½-ton, 2-wheel, M536
Chassis, trailer, bakery oven, 2½-ton, 2-wheel, M537
Chassis, trailer, bakery, dough mixing, 1½-ton, 2-wheel, M538
Trailer, van, electronic, 10-ton, 4-wheel, M564
Dolly, trailer, front, electronic shop, M565
Dolly, trailer, rear, electronic shop, M566
Chassis, trailer, ¼-ton, 2-wheel, M569
Semi-trailer, van, 10-ton, electronic, 4-wheel, XM574
Chassis, trailer, 1½-ton, 2-wheel, M580
Trailer, van, electronic, 1½-ton, 2-wheel, M581
Trailer, van, electronic, 2-ton, 4-wheel, M582
Trailer, van, electronic, 2-ton, 4-wheel, M583
Dolly, trailer, front, M584
Dolly, trailer, front, electronic shop, M589
Dolly, trailer, rear, electronic shop, M590
Semi-trailer, tank transporter, jointed, 52½-ton,
16-wheel, M627 ('Trackporter')

Semi-trailer, low bed, 15-ton, 4-wheel, M674

Semi-trailer, van, 15-ton, 4-wheel, M681
Semi-trailer, van, 15-ton, 4-wheel, M682
Semi-trailer, van, 15-ton, 4-wheel, M683
Dolly set, lifting, transportable shelter, M689
Dolly, front, M690
Dolly, rear, M691
Dolly set, lift, M707
Trailer, stake and platform, utility, ¾-ton, M709
Trailer, cable splicer, ¼-ton, 2-wheel, M716
Dolly set, lifting, transportable shelter, M720
Dolly, front, M721
Dolly, rear, M722
Semi-trailer, van, repair parts storage, 6-ton, 4-wheel, M749
Semi-trailer, van, repair, shop, 6-ton, 4-wheel, M750
Trailer, platform, ¾-ton, 2-wheel, M762
Dolly set, lift, MUST, M840
Semi-trailer, low bed, construction equipment transporter,
40-ton, M870

Notes

Mounts AN/MPQ-4 mortar
locating radar
Based on M508 semi-trailer
Based on M508 semi-trailer
Based on M508C semi-trailer

On M119 chassis; basis
of M457 and M458

On M536 chassis
On M537 chassis

For M416 and M716 trailers

Previously designated XM793;
believed to be for foreign
military sales only
For transport of Nike-Hercules
missile

Comprises M690 and M691 dollies
Together form M689 dolly set

Based on M416 trailer
Comprises M721 and M722
dollies; for shelters
S-141/G, S-280/G, S-285/G

Used with MUST hospital

Manufactured by Load King

Recent development model trailers

Designation

Shop equipment, nuclear projectile, semi-trailer mounted, XM21
Trailer, aircraft cargo loading, 3½-ton, 4-wheel, XM712
Trailer, flat bed, tilt loading, 6-ton, 4-wheel, XM714
Semi-trailer, van, telephone, 10-ton, 4-wheel, XM738
Semi-trailer, van, switchboard, 10-ton, 4-wheel, XM739
Trailer, flat bed, tilt loading, ¾-ton, 2-wheel, XM789
Semi-trailer, van, M822E1
Semi-trailer, van, electronic, 10-ton, 4-wheel, XM823
Semi-trailer, van, electronic, 10-ton, 4-wheel, XM824
Dolly set, lift, transportable shelter, general support, XM832
Chassis, semi-trailer, guided missile launching station, 4-wheel,
M869 (for M901)
Semi-trailer, line haul, 22½-ton, M871A2
Launching station, guided missile, semi-trailer mounted,
M901 (Patriot)
Semi-trailer, tank, 12-ton, bulk haul, 5000-gallon, self
load/unload, M967A1
Semi-trailer, tank, 12-ton, fuel dispensing, 5000-gallon
automotive, M969A1
Semi-trailer, tank, 12-ton, fuel dispensing, 5000-gallon
under/over wing aircraft, M970A1
Semi-trailer, van, 10-ton, 4-wheel, XM971
Semi-trailer, tank, potable water, 5000-gallon, 4-wheel, XM972
Semi-trailer, flat bed, 4-wheel, XM974
Semi-trailer, guided missile transport, 4-wheel, M976 (Patriot)
Trailer, flat bed, 5-ton, M979
Trailer, ammunition, 10-ton, M989A1
Semi-trailer, van, 6-ton, 2-wheel, XM990
Semi-trailer, van, 10-ton, 4-wheel, XM991
Semi-trailer, van, 10-ton, 4-wheel, XM995
Semi-trailer, low bed, 70-ton
Semi-trailer, van, repair parts storage, 12-ton, 4-wheel
Dolly set, 7.5-ton, M1022

Notes

For electrical equipment

For GEMSS

For mobile test equipment
For mobile test equipment

Designation	Notes
Trailer, 5-ton, XM1034	For generator used with AN/TSQ-114A tactical intercept system
Trailer, 6-ton, XM1048	For AN/TPQ-37 Firefinder antenna-receiver unit
Trailer, flat bed, 5-ton, 4-wheel, M1061A1	For laundry units, generators and fuel pods
Semi-trailer, tank, 7500-gallon, M1062	Replacement for M967, 727 units ordered from Fruehauf
Semi-trailer, van, 12-ton, 40 ft, XM1063	For electronic equipment
Semi-trailer, 35 ft, XM1065	For ATE
Trailer, flat bed, 7½-ton, XM1073	65 ordered from Utility Tool and Body Company, 1989

MATERIALS HANDLING EQUIPMENT

AUSTRIA

Voest-Alpine TROSS 130 Military Multi-purpose Vehicle

Description

The TROSS 130 was the result of a joint development between the Austrian Army and Voest-Alpine (TROSS stands for Technical and Rear Operation Support System). This military multi-purpose equipment is a four-wheeled, all-wheel steering vehicle with a swivel mount on which the various hydraulically operated attachments, such as a front-loading bucket, lifting forks and a crane, can be fitted using a rapid-change device.

The TROSS 130 has been designed for earthmoving and recovery operations as well as for handling military loads under difficult conditions. All the necessary auxiliary equipment, including a spare wheel and tools, can be carried with the TROSS 130, and with the vehicle's high cruising speed of 62 km/h it is able to travel in convoy with other military vehicles.

The TROSS 130 has an automatic differential lock and a dual circuit brake system. Standard equipment includes an emergency steering system that allows towing of the vehicle after breakdown, a cold starting device, a three-phase dynamo and special military-proof indicator and control instruments. The driver's steel safety cabin is sound insulated and has two adjustable seats, a heater, defroster and stowage for weapons and a full pack. Optional equipment includes air-conditioning, cab ventilation, a tropical roof, a tyre inflation system, blackout lights and an anti infra-red colour scheme.

Specifications

Cab seating: 1 + 1
Weight: 15 950 kg
Length: 8.3 m
Width: 2.65 m
Height: 3.13 m
Ground clearance: 0.435 m
Fording depth: 1 m
Turning radius: 5.35 m
Fuel capacity: 250 l
Max speed: 62 km/h
Max gradient: 70%

Engine: MAN Type D 2565 ME water-cooled diesel developing 160 hp at 2100 rpm
Tyres: 20.5 × 25 EM 16 PR
Electrical system: 24 V
Max load:
(front) 6000 kg
(turning) 4000 kg
Bucket capacity: 1.8 m³
Winch capacity: 8000 kg
Winch cable length: 55 m

Status

In service with the Austrian Army.

Manufacturer

Voest-Alpine AG, A-4010 Linz, Austria.
Marketing and sales enquiries to NORICUM, Maschinenbau und Handel GmbH, PO Box 3, A-4010 Linz, Austria.
Tel: 732 274546. Telex: 22491 nla a.
Fax: 732 585 9290.

TROSS 130 with crane attachment

TROSS 130 with fork-lift attachment

Steyr LBW 1500 Electrohydraulic Tailgate

Description

The Steyr LBW 1500 electrohydraulic tailgate lift is used for the loading and unloading of bulky and heavy loads or equipment onto a platform truck. The hydraulic system pump is driven by an electro-motor from the vehicle batteries. Control may be by a control box in the cab or using a remote-control unit on a cable. The basic carrier vehicle is a standard troop carrier without bench seats or a tailgate. The structure is bolted to the rear section of the chassis frame. Warning lamps are provided in the platform for safety.

The lifting capacity is 1500 kg at 0.5 m.

Status

In production. In service with Austria.

Manufacturer

Steyr Nutzfahrzeuge AG, Schönauerstrasse 5, A-4400 Steyr, Austria.
Tel: 7252/585-0. Telex: 28200.
Fax: 7252/26746, 28650.

The Steyr LBW 1500 electrohydraulic tailgate fitted to a 12 M 18 (4 × 4) truck

BRAZIL

TECTRAN Straddle Carriers

Description

TECTRAN straddle carriers are intended to move bulky loads such as ISO containers across reasonably flat and paved open areas. The exact form of the carrier can be modified to suit customer requirements and the data provided are only a guide.

There are six basic models, as follows:

TT-2000, maximum load, 20 000 kg
TT-3000, maximum load, 30 000 kg
TT-4000, maximum load, 40 000 kg
TT-5000, maximum load, 55 000 kg

The TTC-2020 and TTC-3040 are special ISO container carriers for 20 ft/6.096 m and 40 ft/12.19 m containers respectively.

The TECTRAN straddle carrier is based around a welded steel frame. It uses hydrostatic transmission connected by planetary gears installed in the two rear driving wheel hubs and is highly manoeuvrable, being able to make 360° pivot turns. The driver/operator is seated in a heated, air-conditioned cab over the main engine on the left-hand side of the vehicle and controls two hoists, also driven by a hydrostatic transmission connected to planetary gears installed in the hoist cable drum. The hoists are located in the front and rear arches and are two-speed. Loads can be traversed on a trolley operated by a steel cable and pulley arrangement driven by a hydraulic motor and a worm gear reduction box. Steering is hydraulic, using the 'Orbitrol' system actuating the two rear driving wheels with double-action hydraulic cylinders and with mechanical articulation around each front wheel.

Specifications (TT-2000)

Cab seating: 1
Max length: 5.8 m
Max width: 5.3 to 9.3 m
Inside clear width: 3.5 to 7.5 m
Max height: 5.45 to 8.45 m
Height to hood saddle: 4.75 to 7.5 m
Wheelbase: 4.5 m
Max speed: 8 km/h
Gradient:
  (unloaded) 10%
  (loaded) 4%
Engine: Mercedes-Benz OM-314 developing 76 hp at 2600 rpm
Transmission: hydrostatic
Steering: 'Orbitrol' system
Turning radius: 360° pivot turns
Brakes:
  (service) disc on front wheels, vacuum-assisted
  (parking) drum on rear wheels
Tyres: 14.00 × 24
Hoist speed, full load: 10 m/min
Trolley traverse speed: 45 m/min

Status

In production.

Manufacturer

TECTRAN Engenharia, Indústria e Comércio SA, Rodovia Presidente Dutra, Km 155/156, Caixa Postal 165, CEP 12200 São José dos Campos – SP, Brazil. Tel: 123 220142. Telex: 39431 ttte br.

TECTRAN TT-2000 straddle carrier

TECTRAN TTC-2020 straddle carrier for 20 ft/6.096 m ISO containers

COMMONWEALTH OF INDEPENDENT STATES

Truck-mounted Cranes

Description

Some of the more recent CIS truck-mounted cranes are described briefly here. Many of these are in service with the CIS and other former Warsaw Pact armed forces, but the exact status of many is uncertain.

9T31M1 crane on Ural-375D (6 × 6) truck chassis

Model	Operation	Traverse	Chassis*	Capacity Max load/ radius	Load at max radius	Length	Width	Height	Speed	Remarks
LAZ-690	mechanical	360°	ZIL-164A (ZIL-130) (ZIL-150)	3 t/2.5 m	1 t/5.5 m	8.88 m	2.4 m	3.45 m	45 km/h	Obsolescent
KS-1571	hydraulic	360°	GAZ-53A	4 t/3.3 m	—/9.35 m	—	—	—	—	Military use not confirmed
K-67	electric	360°	MAZ-500 (MAZ-200)	6.3 t/3.5 m	2 t/7.5 m	8.2 m	2.6 m	3.35 m	40 km/h	180 hp engine
K-68	electric	360°	MAZ-200 (MAZ-500)	6.3 t/5.5 m	2 t/7.5 m	8.9 m	2.71 m	3.3 m	40 km/h	Also K-68A

Model	Operation	Traverse	Chassis*	Capacity	Load at	Length	Width	Height	Speed	Remarks
KS-2571	hydraulic	360°	ZIL-130	6.3 t/3.3 m	—/9.8 m	—	—	—	—	Military use not confirmed
8T210	hydraulic	360°	Ural-375D	6.3 t/3.5 m	1.8 t/7.5 m	8.3 m	2.45 m	—	70 km/h	Special military crane originally for missile units
9T31M1	—	360°	Ural-375D							Special military crane for missile units
AK-75	mechanical	360°	ZIL-164A (ZIL-130)	7.5 t/2.8 m	1.65 t/7 m	10.1 m	2.5 m	3.56 m	40 km/h	97 hp engine
KS-3562A	electric	360°	MAZ-500A	10 t/4 m	—	—	—	—	60 km/h	
KS-3571	hydraulic	360°	MAZ-500A	10 t/4 m	—/13.2 m	—	—	5 m	75 km/h	Military use not confirmed
KS-3572	hydraulic	360°	KrAZ-255B	10 t/4 m	—/9.1 m	—	—	—	70 km/h	
K-162	electric	360°	KrAZ-219 KrAZ-257	16 t/3.9 m	2.35 t/10 m	14 m	2.75 m	3.96 m	30 km/h	Also K-162M
KS-4571	hydraulic	360°	KrAZ-257	16 t/3.8 m	—/20.25 m	—	—	—	70 km/h	Military use not confirmed
MPK-30	electric	360°	MAZ-529V	30 t/3.7 m	6 t/27 m	12.8 m	4 m	4.2 m	25 km/h	Articulated, with 2-wheel tractor
8T26	—	—	—	10 t/4.5 m	2 t/9.5 m	—	—	—	40 km/h	Special military crane for missile units
KM-61	mechanical	80°	KrAZ-214 KrAZ-255B	3.2 t/2 m	2 t/2.8 m	—	—	—	—	Used with KMT-5 mineclearing apparatus
KS-2561D	—	360°	—	6.3 t/—	1.5 t/—	—	—	—	—	150 hp engine

* Chassis designation in brackets are older or less common variants.

AK-75 7.5-tonne crane

MPK-30 crane mounted on MAZ-529V chassis

DENMARK

Container Load Trailer (CLT)

Description
The Container Load Trailer (CLT) is a highly mobile container handling system that can be used in various configurations to handle and carry 20 and 40 ft ISO containers, shelters and associated loads. It is particularly suitable for use in remote areas where normal ISO handling equipment is not available. Containers can be handled as end or side loads and the CLT can also be used as a trailer carrying a container or, with a flat bed, other loads. Towing vehicles may be trucks or tracked armoured vehicles such as APCs. The CLT can load and unload two ISO containers from a C-130 Hercules transport aircraft in 20 minutes. The CLT was developed in co-operation with the Danish Army.

The CLT consists of two units; a front section with a steerable unit and drawbar, and a rear unit with a fixed axle. Each unit has two hydraulic primary cylinders and two secondary cylinders. The primary cylinders are used for lifting and the secondary cylinders for extending upper and lower beams when loading or unloading. On each unit there are also two bars which are used for the sideways lifting of filled containers, a hydraulic unit, a tank, petrol or diesel engine, valves, lock fittings, and truck wheels with all-terrain tyres. The front unit has brakes while the rear unit has a rigid axle which can move vertically through a 27° angle.

The CLT can be mounted on the end of any container or shelter with the necessary fittings and lifts using hydraulics alone. Maximum lift height is 1.8 m and the lift capacity for side lifts is up to 25 tonnes; end lift and carrying capacity is also up to 25 tonnes.

Container Load Trailer (CLT) carrying a container as a side load

When not in use the CLT can be stored or transported inside a standard 20 ft ISO container. Weight of each unit is 2850 kg.

Status
In production. In service with the Danish Army and United Nations peace-keeping forces.

Manufacturer
Danish Camp Supply ApS, Virkelyst 11, DK-9400 Norresundby, Denmark.
Tel: 98 19 13 00. Telex: 69 925 camp dk.
Fax: 98 19 07 00.

FRANCE

Renault G 290.26 (6 × 4) VTL Transport Vehicle

Description
In January 1988 the French Army awarded a contract worth FFr 3500 million for 3500 Renault G 290.26 (6 × 4) trucks, 3500 Bennes Marrel Ampliroll 155NB load handling systems, 2500 LOHR RM19 trailers, 12 000 20 ft/6.096 m platforms, and 100 tilt-type semi-trailers. The order will be complete by December 1993. The equipments will be used by about 40 transport regiments and various other army units. The combined logistic package is known as the *Véhicule de Transport Logistique* (VTL).

The Renault G 290.26 is a logistic transport vehicle fitted with a hydraulic loading system produced by Bennes Marrel. The system is capable of loading and unloading platforms carrying loads of up to 16 000 kg. Loading time is 38 seconds and unloading 34 seconds. The system can withstand misaligned loads of up to 10° either side. Apart from the usual cargo-carrying platforms the system can be used with tanker and tipper bodies.

The Renault G 290.26 vehicle can carry a maximum load of 18 000 kg. It is powered by a Type MIDR 06-20-45 turbocharged diesel developing 291 hp at 2100 rpm and has a Type B9 gearbox with nine forward and one reverse gears. The cab has seating for the driver and two passengers. The gross vehicle weight is 26 000 kg.

Status
In production for the French Army Service Corps.

Renault G 290.26 (6 × 4) VTL vehicle using its Bennes Ampliroll system to load a flatrack carrying ammunition

Manufacturers
Renault Véhicules Industriels, 40 rue Pasteur, BP 302, F-92156 Suresnes Cedex, France.
Tel: (1) 47 72 33 33. Telex: 620567 sdce f.
Fax: (1) 40 99 71 08.

Bennes Marrel SA, ZI St Etienne Bouthéon, BP 56, F-42160 Andrezieux-Bouthéon, France.
Tel: 77 36 55 50. Telex: 330657 f.
Fax: 77 55 35 77.

Bennes Marrel Ampliroll System

Description
The Ampliroll system is a load handling system designed to fit any type of truck with a load capacity from 3000 to 25 000 kg. To meet military requirements the systems selected for 6 × 4, 6 × 6 and 8 × 8 trucks generally have a load capacity of between 12 and 20 tonnes.

The Ampliroll system consists of a chassis reinforcing subframe, a central beam to which the tipping rams are hinged, a short hinged connecting arm framework which controls the extent of rearward movement, a telescopic jib sliding in front of the central beams and carrying at its upper end the unit front lifting hook and rear hinges, and incorporating flanged rollers on bronze bushes to centralise the unit. The hydraulic system contains a pump complete with a safety valve and transmission, two main arms providing both the normal tipping action and for lowering the platform, a double-acting ram to actuate the sliding jib beam and a direction and braking valve block actuated from the vehicle cab by a remote servo-control.

Military applications include ammunition handling, either on a flatrack or in an ISO container; fuel handling using the Marrel 9000 or 12 000 litre roll-off fuel tank and filling unit, complete with a hydraulic pump serving five discharge points; mobile shelter handling for field hospitals; and general cargo handling using flatracks with suitable cargo bodies and covers. The system may also be used for vehicle recovery using a multi-

Ampliroll system in use on Renault TRM 10 000 PD (6 × 6) logistic truck

purpose flatrack with adjustable track guides to permit the recovery of light armoured vehicles such as the M113 APC. With some additional components the Ampliroll system can be used to launch floating bridge components (such as the Ribbon Bridge) and their associated bridging boats. Flatracks may also be used to carry engineer equipment or may be converted to carry weapon systems such as air defence weapons. Other flatrack loads could include electrical generators, desalination plant and communication centres. If required, the lifting hook can be used as a crane.

Status
In production. Quantities have been sold for military applications in Europe and Africa. In service with the French Army (see previous entry).

Manufacturer
Bennes Marrel SA, ZI St Etienne Bouthéon, BP 56, F-42160 Andrezieux-Bouthéon, France.
Tel: 77 36 55 50. Telex: 330657 f.
Fax: 77 55 35 77.

LOHR PLM 17 Materials Handling System

Description
The LOHR PLM 17 materials handling system was designed for the transportation of vehicles (wheeled or tracked) and for the logistic transport of ammunition and other combat supplies on 20 ft ISO flatracks. It can be mounted on all types of 6 × 4 and 6 × 6 trucks with a GVW of 26 000 kg and a 300 hp engine, and has been demonstrated on the Renault TRM 10 000

(6 × 6) 10 000 kg truck.

The system uses a hydraulic system to either load a platform onto a truck or unload it onto the ground. It utilises a two-part subframe which bolts onto the vehicle chassis. Two conical rollers located at the rear, centre the platform during loading operations. The loading arm is constructed using two rectangular and longitudinal beams braced by crossmembers and is articulated round the rear part of the frame. A bracket assembly on the loading platform completes the structural system.

The hydraulic system is based on a Leduc L 65 pump operating at a maximum pressure of 400 bars. The pump is mounted on the vehicle gearbox and is directly driven. The hydraulic circuit has three parts for blocking the vehicle suspension, controlling the lifting bracket and the lifting arm. Two cylinders are used, one for the bracket, one for the arm. A tank associated with the hydraulic system contains 100 litres of oil.

The platform is a standard 20 ft/6.096 m DIN unit and is made of beams braced by crossmembers. A total of 12 lashing rings is provided.

Specifications (System on TRM 10 000 truck)
Weight on front axle, loaded: 7480 kg
Weight on rear axle, loaded: 18 520 kg
Weight, total: 26 000 kg
Length: (overall) 9.2 m
Width: 2.5 m
Height:
  (overall) 3.7 m
  (platform, loaded) 1.7 m

Status
Has been proposed for the new logistic all-terrain vehicle for the French Army.

Manufacturer
LOHR SA, F-67980 Hangenbieten, France.
Tel: 88 38 98 00. Telex: 870082 f.
Fax: 88 96 06 36.

LOHR PLM 17 materials handling system in use on Renault TRM 10 000 (6 × 6) truck

LOHR RM 19 Load Handling Trailer

Description
The LOHR RM 19 load handling trailer is part of the French Army's Véhicule de Transport Logistique (VTL) programme. LOHR SA was awarded a contract to produce 2500 RM 19 trailers and 12 000 of the associated 20 ft ISO flatracks for the programme. The RM 19 trailer has two axles with four double-tyred wheels and is so arranged that the VTL prime mover's load handling system can load and off-load flatracks from the trailer. It is possible to erect covers for the complete trailer.

LOHR RM 19 load handling trailer

Specifications
Weight loaded: 19 000 kg
Max load: 13 400 kg
Length: (with flatrack) 8.37 m
Width: 2.5 m
Height: (with loaded flatrack) 1.475 m

Status
In production for the French Army.

Manufacturer
LOHR SA, F-67980 Hangenbieten, France.
Tel: 88 38 98 00. Telex: 870082 f.
Fax: 88 96 06 36.

LOHR RM 22 PLM Load Handling Trailer

Description
The LOHR RM 22 PLM load handling trailer was selected as the trailer component of the US Army's Palletised Loading System (PLS) which involves the Oshkosh M1074 (10 × 10) truck. The US Army ordered 1050 RM 22 trailers in October 1990 and it was anticipated that more would be ordered.

The RM 22 uses a mainframe assembled using electric welding with a secondary frame supporting the front axle on a turning table and the drawbar; a steering lock allows the steering to be fixed when required. Two axles are provided at the rear and braking is on all three axles. Flatracks can be on- and off-loaded from the trailer by the prime mover's load handling system.

LOHR RM 22 PLM load handling trailer on tow by Oshkosh (10 × 10) PLS tractor

Specifications
Weight:
  (kerb) 4050 kg
  (gross) 21 500 kg
Max payload: (with flatrack) 17 950 kg
Length: 8.84 m
Width: 2.49 m

Height: (unloaded) 1.51 m
Ground clearance: 0.46 m
Track: 2.12 m
Wheelbase: 2.81 m + 1.4 m
Max road speed: 90 km/h
Side slope: 30%
Tyres: 13.00 R 20 XL

Status
In production for the US Army.

Manufacturer
LOHR SA, F-67980 Hangenbieten, France.
Tel: 88 38 98 00. Telex: 870082 f.
Fax: 88 96 06 36.

FDI Sambron J24 Series Wheeled Materials Handlers

Description
The FDI Sambron J24 series encompasses a number of rough-terrain materials handlers designed to handle bulk materials, palletised loads or stores such as munitions.

The basic model is the J24 2004S loader with a lift capacity of 2000 kg to a height of 3.6 m. It is powered by a Deutz F 3 L 912 developing 52 hp at 2500 rpm. All other models (L and T ranges) are powered by a Perkins 4.236 diesel and are available in a choice of two capacities (2000 or 2500 kg) with two- or four-wheel drive. Four-wheel drive models are available with straight axles or dropped hub axles for higher ground clearance, with four-wheel steering as an option. The L range has a rigid arm giving lift heights up to 4.6 m. The T range has a telescopic arm which provides a maximum forward reach of 3.81 m ahead of the front wheels, and a maximum lift height of 6.2 m.

All the J24 series vehicles have a dual range hydrostatic transmission. The arm can be fitted with a variety of earthmoving or handling attachments such as buckets, diggers, pallet forks, jibs, clamps and aerial platforms, all secured by quick-fit systems.

Specifications (J24 2504T)
Cab seating: 1
Configuration: 4 × 4
Weight without attachment: 6980 kg
Length:
   (overall, with forks, straight axles) 5.64 m
   (overall, with forks, dropped hub axles) 5.53 m
Width:
   (over body) 2.03 m
   (over wheels, straight axles) 2.05 m
   (over wheels, dropped hub axles) 2.18 m
Height:
   (straight axles) 2.34 m
   (dropped hub axles) 2.51 m
Ground clearance:
   (straight axles) 0.31 m
   (dropped hub axles) 0.46 m
Wheelbase: 1.92 m
Max speed:
   (low range) 10 km/h
   (high range) 25 km/h
Fuel capacity: 100 l
Engine: Perkins 4.236 water-cooled diesel developing
72 hp at 2250 rpm
Transmission: dual range hydrostatic
Steering: hydrostatic
Turning radius:
   (outer, straight axles) 5.36 m
   (outer, dropped hub axles) 5.65 m
Tyres:
   (straight axles) 12.5 × 18
   (dropped hub axles) 16/70 × 20
Brakes: hydrostatic plus inboard wet disc brakes

FDI Sambron J24 2504T wheeled materials handlers awaiting delivery

Max lift height:
   (straight axles) 6.03 m
   (dropped hub axles) 6.2 m
Capacity at max lift height: 2500 kg
Max forward reach:
   (straight axles) 3.81 m
   (dropped hub axles) 3.74 m
Capacity at max forward reach: 1200 kg

Status
In production.

Manufacturer
FDI Sambron, Route de Nantes, BP 71, F-44160
Pontchateau, France.
Tel: 40 00 73 50. Telex: 710788 f.
Fax: 40 00 73 60.

GERMANY

ADK 160 16-tonne Mobile Crane

Description
AD 160 or ADK 160 (for Autodrehkran 160) was the
German designation of a 16-tonne hydraulic crane
mounted on the Czechoslovak Tatra 138 or 148
(6 × 6) chassis. The chassis differ from the standard
truck chassis only in the addition of four stabilising
jacks. The crane, made by CKD, is separately powered
and has a two-section telescopic jib.

Specifications
Chassis: see under Czechoslovakia in the *Trucks*
section *except* max speed: 71 km/h
Weight: (travelling) 24 600 kg
Length: 9.85 m
Width: 2.5 m
   (over extended stabilisers) 4.5 m
Height: 3.4 m
Crane capacity: max 16 000 kg at 3.8 m radius
Traverse: 360°

Tatra ADK 160 mobile crane on Tatra 148 chassis

Status
Believed to be in service with several former Warsaw
Pact armies.

Manufacturers
Chassis: Tatra, Národni Podnik, Kohprivinice, Czecho-
slovakia.
Crane: CKD, Federal Republic of Germany.

Klaus Kranmobil Mobile Container Handling System

Description
The Klaus Kranmobil container handling system has
been in production for over 20 years and is now
produced in two basic forms: double-side operating
(KM 32, KM 26, KM 30 E) or single-side operating (KM
32-293, KM 24 E, KM 13 E). Both types have a lifting
capacity of from 13 to 36 tonnes and can handle
containers or flatracks.

   The Kranmobil system can be used in conjunction
with vehicles or railway trucks and enables the carrier
vehicle to load and off-load loaded containers and
flatracks as required. The larger systems are usually
carried on semi-trailers while the smaller systems can
be carried on large trucks. Containers can be loaded

Specifications

Model	KM 32	KM 26	KM 30 E	KM 24 E	KM 13 E
Loading sides	both	both	both	single	single
Container size	20-40 ft	20 ft	20-40 ft	20 ft	20 ft
Lifting capacity	32 000 kg	26 000 kg	36 000 kg	24 000 kg	13 000 kg
Carrier (typical)	3 axle semi-trailer	2 axle semi-trailer	3 axle semi-trailer	3 axle semi-trailer	8 × 8 truck
Length (approx, with tractor)	17.4 m	12 m	16 m	11 m	9.8 m
Width	2.5 m	2.5 m	2.5 m	2.5 m	2.5 m
Height (approx)	4 m	4 m	4 m	4 m	4 m
Hydraulic circuit (dual circuit)	300 bar	200 bar	270 bar	250 bar	230 bar
Electrical system	24 V	24 V	24 V	24 V	24 V

onto the carrier vehicle or directly onto another vehicle
or railway truck. The double-sided loaders can lift and
load from one side to the other in one sweep if
required. Containers can be stacked two high.

   When operating, the lifter-loader is stabilised by

hydraulically operated stabiliser legs. This enables the
system to be used on unprepared surfaces. The
system can be used with toplift container spreaders,
rope slings or chains. Control is usually carried out by
means of a portable remote-control box.

When not in use the system arms can be folded down or to the side to lower the overall height for air transport.

The Klaus RTE is a towed semi-trailer equipment used to unload flatracks and ISO containers weighing up to 16.5 tonnes from rail cars. The RTE moves along either side of a train, lifts off a flatrack using a special chain-lift device which can be safely used under overhead power cables and places it on the ground nearby. The RTE can handle up to 12 flatracks/hour. The British Army has 30 of these KM 20-298 (RTE) units in service in Germany for their DROPS system.

Status

In production. In widespread use, including with the British Army (over 70 units, including 26 units employed with DROPS system), US Army (12 KM 26-298 for 20 ft ISO containers) and US Air Force in Europe (30 KM 32-298 and 6 KM 26-298).

Manufacturer

Arbau-Klaus GmbH & Co, PO Box 1141, Schlachthof-strasse 46, D-8940 Memmingen, Federal Republic of Germany.
Tel: 083 31 16-0. Telex: 54516 klausm d.
Fax: 083 31 16 212.

Klaus Kranmobil KM 32 container handling system on Mercedes-Benz tractor truck

Klaus Kranmobil KM 20-298 (RTE) load handling system used by British Army as part of DROPS system

POLAND

Polish Truck-mounted Cranes

The following truck-mounted cranes are thought to be in service with the Polish Army:
All models have 360° traverse.

Model	ZS-4	ZSH-6	ZS-25
Chassis	Star 27	Star 66 or 660	special 6 × 6
Capacity (max load)	4000 kg	6300 kg	25 000 kg
(load at max radius)	n/a	1000 kg/3 m	16 000 kg
Weight	7500 kg	10 500 kg	32 000 kg
Length	8.7 m	n/a	n/a
Height	3.02 m	n/a	n/a
Max speed	40 km/h	40 km/h	n/a
Remarks	—	also ZSH-6P	military use not confirmed

Polish ZSH-6 6.3-tonne mobile crane

SOUTH AFRICA

RTS RT 20 Load Handling System

Description

The RTS RT 20 load handling system is an adaptation of an existing commercial load handling system which has been modified to allow it to be mounted on SAMIL 100 (6 × 6) trucks for extended trials with the South African Defence Forces. In its military form the vehicle and load handling system combination is known as the Abba.

The RT 20 has a maximum payload capacity of 20 000 kg although for military purposes the usual maximum load is lower. The general operating principles follow the same general lines as other hydraulically operated load handling systems. The system can be operated by one man for both loading and unloading procedures and to maximise the capacity of the carrier vehicle the system can be used in conjunction with a trailer.

In addition to stores-carrying flatracks, the RT 20

can be used to carry fuel tanks, command centres, containerised medical stations and other similar loads.

A similar system, the RT 8.5, is available with an 8500 kg capacity.

Status

In production. Undergoing evaluation by the South African Defence Forces.

Manufacturer

RTS (Pty) Limited, PO Box 912-1014, Silverton 0127, South Africa.
Tel: 27 12 832373. Fax: 803 6204.

Abba load handling system on SAMIL 100 (6 × 6) truck

Bond Miskruier Rough Terrain Fork-lift Truck

Description

The Bond Miskruier fork-lift truck is a three-wheel rough terrain compact vehicle intended for use in forward areas to handle stores and munitions. The vehicle utilises two front wheels with a single wheel at the rear turning on a turntable and yoke steering assembly operated via a hydrostatic steering valve and a hydraulic rack and pinion. Drive to all three wheels is hydrostatic with power provided by a 2.5 litre ADE 152 diesel.

The driver is seated on the right-hand side of the vehicle on a fully adjustable seat; a tubular roll bar assembly is provided over the driver's position. The driver uses his left hand to operate the fork-lift controls.

The mast assembly has a lift height of 2 m and a side shift of 200 mm. The mast assembly can be tilted 12° back and 6° forward. Lift capacity is 2500 kg at 600 mm load centre.

Optional attachments include a 0.5 m³ bucket, and a 200 to 500 kg capacity rotating grab. Other attachments can be produced to meet customer requirements.

Specifications
Seating: 1
Configuration: 3 × 3
Weight:
  (kerb) 3800 kg
  (loaded) approx 6300 kg
Max load: 2500 kg at 600 mm load centre
Length: 2.73 m
Width: 1.6 m
Height: (overall) 2.184 m
Ground clearance: 0.25 m

Bond Miskruier rough terrain fork-lift truck

Wheelbase: 1.7 m
Max speed: 12 km/h
Engine: ADE 152 2.5 l 3-cylinder in-line diesel developing 46 hp at 2500 rpm
Transmission: hydrostatic
Steering: hydrostatic
Turning radius: 2 m
Tyres: 400 × 15.5 10 ply

Status
In production.

Manufacturer
Bond Industries, 5 Teak Avenue/30 Vulcan Street Klerkindustria, PO Box 914 Klerksdorp 2570, South Africa.
Tel: (018) 462 9737. Fax: (018) 462 5910.

UNITED KINGDOM

Boughton Load Handling System

Description

Reynolds Boughton (Vehicle Division) designed a Load Handling System for the US Marine Corps capable of handling a 20 ft/6.096 m ISO container, Ribbon Bridge sections or a Combat Support Boat. It can be converted to a flat bed body. By late 1992 a total of 320 units had been ordered by the US Marine Corps.

The system is mounted on a modified MK14 trailer coupled to an Oshkosh MK48/18 (8 × 8) truck. A

20 ft/6.096 m ISO container having a payload of 20 tonnes can be loaded to and from ground level onto the back of the vehicle without any additional assistance from other load handling equipment or flatracks. Ribbon Bridge sections can be picked up, launched and recovered in both low and high bank situations. For this facility the load handling system is complemented by a Boughton winch. The Combat Support Boat and cradle can be loaded, launched and recovered by the system and winch.

Conversion of the equipment to a flat bed body requires the insertion of metal floor panels which, when placed in position, make some of the hydraulic functions

inoperable.

The operation of all the hydraulic functions of the Boughton Load Handling System is carried out either by manual lever operation at the side of the vehicle or by a remote-control lead up to 12.2 m in length.

Specifications
Weight: (system only) 5000 kg
Length: 6.5 m
Width:
  (with ISO container) 2.44 m
  (with Ribbon Bridge) 3.3 m
Height: (overall) 1.86 m

US Marine Corps MK48/18 truck fitted with Boughton Load Handling System unloading a fully laden 20 ft/6.096 m ISO container

US Marine Corps MK48/18 truck fitted with Boughton Load Handling System launching a section of Ribbon Bridge

Status
In production. In service with the US Marine Corps (320 units ordered).

Manufacturer
Reynolds Boughton Limited, Vehicle Division, Bell Lane, Amersham, Buckinghamshire HP6 6PE, UK.

Tel: 0494 764411. Telex: 83132.
Fax: 0494 765218.

Boughton DROPS/PLS Hydraulic Loading System

Description
The Boughton DROPS/PLS hydraulic loading system evolved from the original Ampliroll system developed by Bennes Marrel of France. Vehicles modified by Boughton were used by the British Army for trials and development over a period of six years and all equipment was supplied on a single tender basis. The British Army term used for the loading system is DROPS (Demountable Rack Off-loading and Pick-up System). The US Army originally required only the hydraulic loading system but procured the complete Boughton system (see following entries) including trucks and trailers. The US Army uses the term PLS (Palletised Load System).

Development of the system concentrated on improvements in operation on rough terrain, on height and weight reductions and generally militarising the basic commercial concept. 'Retrofit DROPS/PLS' or the fitting of the 'load handling system only' to an existing vehicle is an option for any armed force not requiring maximum performance in terms of mobility, payload or overall cost-effectiveness. The system can be fitted to almost any chassis with varying degrees of effectiveness but even in the worst cases it may be expected to provide some of the basic benefits of the DROPS/PLS concept.

Boughton DROPS/PLS hydraulic loading system fitted to Irish Army Hino truck

The Boughton DROPS/PLS features a hydraulically operated self-loading cargo system designed to improve the productivity of a chassis by reducing turnround times and freeing the chassis from dedicated roles. The system enables a conventional chassis to carry more in payload terms and allows an armed force to increase its total logistic capability by switching chassis from secondary roles to meet peak requirements.

Roles envisaged for the Boughton DROPS/PLS include a flatrack cargo vehicle (especially for carrying pallets of ammunition), a recovery vehicle, a fuel or water tanker, a box-bodied vehicle (command post, ambulance, medical centre or workshop) and for specialist engineer uses such as carrying, launching and recovering bridging pontoons, carrying palletised loads of bridging components and for carrying and laying portable roadways.

Status
In production. In service with Irish, Tanzanian, Thai and US armed forces.

Manufacturer
Hearncrest Boughton Engineering Limited, Bell Lane, Amersham, Buckinghamshire HP6 6PE, UK.
Tel: 0494 764411. Telex: 83132.
Fax: 0494 765218.

Boughton (6 × 6) DROPS/PLS Truck (Heavy PLS)

Description
Experience gained during the British Army trials of the Boughton DROPS system indicated to Boughton that the only satisfactory DROPS/PLS system would be based on a fundamentally new design of truck and trailer. The inherent compromises involved in retrofit solutions and modifications to existing vehicles all involved loss of mobility, loss of payload, some lateral instability, greater complexity, excessive size and less value for money. Accordingly a new design was initiated and the result is a purpose-built Boughton chassis with an integral hydraulic load handling system coupled with a special Boughton DROPS/PLS close-coupled trailer (for details see entry in this section). All the bodies are Boughton designed and built and include numerous features which are patented and patent applied for.

Three sets of prime movers, trailers and bodies were supplied to the US Army in mid-1983 for concept evaluation at Fort Lewis in Washington and were joined by three more complete sets. These vehicles, known as 'Heavy PLS', led to support for the concept and its expansion to incorporate a breakbulk/distribution capability. This gave rise to a need for a smaller truck known as 'Medium PLS' (see following entry).

Boughton (6 × 6) DROPS/PLS truck loading flatrack loaded with COMPODS

The Boughton truck is a 6 × 6 vehicle with a payload of 14 000 kg. The truck was designed to meet the Medium Mobility criteria of the British Army and, when used with the special DROPS/PLS trailer, enables 28 000 kg of payload to be moved into forward areas.

A forward control cab is used with seating for the driver and one or two passengers. Twin hydraulic cylinders under the flatrack are used to power the DROPS/PLS system. The engine is a Perkins diesel developing 450 hp and coupled to an Allison five-speed automatic transmission. During US trials the truck was used as an artillery tractor for the 155 mm M198 howitzer, and during mobility trials the flatrack was used to free the vehicle from muddy locations by unloading the flatrack using the DROPS/PLS system and using the loading system to 'lift' the vehicle free. It is airportable in the C-141 Starlifter with preparation.

Status
Prototypes.

Manufacturer
The Boughton Group (Hearncrest Boughton/Reynolds Boughton/Scottorn/TTB Fabrication), Bell Lane, Amersham, Buckinghamshire HP6 6PE, UK.
Tel: 0494 764411. Telex: 83132.
Fax: 0494 765218.

Boughton (4 × 4) DROPS/PLS Truck (Medium PLS)

Description
Following the performance success of the Boughton (6 × 6) Heavy PLS (see previous entry) and trailers used by the US Army Development and Employment Agency (ADEA) for concept trials since mid-1983, the US Army sought offers for a new 'Medium PLS'. The Medium PLS was to have roughly half the payload of Heavy PLS and a clear preference was stated for achieving this on a 10 ft ISO flatrack, so that two Medium PLS flatracks could be carried 'piggyback' on a Heavy PLS 20 ft flatrack.

The Boughton Group won the competitive tender by producing a new vehicle where the 10 ft Medium PLS body can be handled with 6350 kg of payload on a Medium PLS vehicle weighing only 6350 kg. This preserved the aim of the US Army Light Division logistic planners for a one-to-one payload to weight ratio and achieving the objective of a two-to-one load split with Heavy PLS. The first of 15 leased Medium PLS sets was delivered to the US Army 9th Infantry Division in March 1985 and the remainder soon after, seven with three-man cabs and eight with six-man 'crew cabs'.

The Boughton (4 × 4) Medium PLS was designed to carry a payload of 6350 kg. It is powered by a GM 205 hp engine allied to an Allison automatic transmission. It can tow a 3.05 m long Medium PLS trailer with a 6350 kg useful payload. As the vehicle is 5.893 m long it can fit within 20 ft ISO flatrack dimensions and can be carried on a Heavy PLS flatrack. With preparation and a reduced weight of 5216 kg the vehicle can be carried in a C-130 transport aircraft or slung under a CH-47D Chinook helicopter.

Status
The US Army has 15 vehicles in service.

Manufacturer
The Boughton Group (Hearncrest Boughton/Reynolds Boughton/Scottorn/TTB Fabrication), Bell Lane, Amersham, Buckinghamshire HP6 6PE, UK.
Tel: 0494 764411. Telex: 83132.
Fax: 0494 765218.

Boughton (4 × 4) DROPS/PLS truck (Medium PLS) with six-man crew cab and towing Medium PLS trailer

Leyland DAF (8 × 6) DROPS Logistic Support Vehicle

Description
Two Leyland DAF logistic support vehicles, a 6 × 6 and an 8 × 6, were developed as part of the British Army's DROPS programme and the 8 × 6 version was selected in late 1986 as the DROPS medium mobility load carrier. Under a contract worth £150 million, 1500 units were ordered in April 1989. The first vehicle came off the production line in November 1989 and the first examples entered British Army service in early 1990. The 1000th unit was handed over to the Ministry of Defence in October 1992. A total of 24 has been delivered fitted with Rail Transfer Equipment (RTE).

The 8 × 6 vehicle can carry a 15 000 kg payload with a mobility equivalent to Medium Mobility Load Class. It uses a forward control S26 cab with seating for the driver and a second crew member with space for their kit. A hatch with a machine gun mounting is located in the roof and the cab roof can take the weight of two men. The engine is a Perkins Eagle 350LM six-cylinder turbocharged four-stroke diesel developing 350 bhp. The transmission uses a five-speed fully automatic ZF 6 HP 600 gearbox with a lockable torque converter. Drive to the axles is via a single-speed Leyland DAF auxiliary gearbox. Kirkstall axles are fitted.

The vehicle is fitted with the Multilift Mark 4 load handling system (see separate entry in this section).

Specifications
Cab seating: 1 + 1 or 2
Configuration: 8 × 6
Weight:
  (kerb) 14 038 kg
  (loaded) 32 000 kg
Max load: 15 000 kg (plus flatrack)
Towed load: 20 000 kg
Length: 9.11 m
Width: 2.5 m
Height: 3.18 m
Ground clearance: 0.29 m
Track: 1.99 m
Wheelbase: 5.54 m
Angle of approach/departure: 34°/38°

Max speed: 75 km/h
Range: 500 km
Fuel capacity: 272 l
Max gradient: 61%
Fording: 0.75 m
Engine: Perkins Eagle 350LM 12.17 l 6-cylinder turbocharged diesel developing 350 hp at 2100 rpm
Gearbox: ZF 6 HP 600 with 6 forward and 1 reverse gears
Clutch: lockable torque converter
Transfer box: Leyland DAF single-speed
Steering: ZF 8098 power-assisted
Turning radius: 12.5 m
Suspension: semi-elliptic 3-leaf springs with telescopic hydraulic shock absorbers, double-acting on both front axles only
Tyres: 18 R 22.5 Michelin XL

Brakes:
  (main) air, dual line, dual circuit
  (parking) spring on 3 axles
Electrical system: 24 V
Batteries: 4 × 6TN
Alternator: 30 A

Status
In production. In service with the British Army.

Manufacturer
Leyland DAF, Eastern Bypass, Thame, Oxon OX9 3FB, UK.
Tel: 0844 261111. Telex: 838848.
Fax: 0844 217111.

Leyland DAF (8 × 6) DROPS logistic support vehicle

Foden (8 × 6) DROPS IMMLC Logistic Support Truck

Description

Foden Trucks developed two logistic support trucks for evaluation by the Ministry of Defence in connection with the British Army's DROPS programme. Termed the MMLC (Medium Mobility Load Carrier) and IMMLC (Improved Medium Mobility Load Carrier) they completed concept field trials and the Improved Medium Mobility Load Carrier was selected for production commencing in 1993. Over 400 vehicles are involved.

The 8 × 6 IMMLC vehicles use a 10-tonne capacity forward steering drive axle, a second steer axle also of 10-tonne capacity, and 20-tonne double drive rear bogies, all manufactured by GKN. They are powered by a Perkins (Shrewsbury) 350E Eagle diesel engine using a ZF fully automatic transmission. The load handling system is the Multilift Mark 4 (see separate entry in this section) using flatracks manufactured by Marshall of Cambridge that can carry up to 15 000 kg of palletised military stores.

The vehicle can tow, load and off-load a custom-built drawbar trailer incorporating ISO twistlocks and designed to carry standard 20 ft containers or flatracks.

The IMMLC is built to a width of 2.88 m and is fitted with 20.5 × 25 R tyres.

Status

Over 400 of the IMMLC version ordered for the British Army's DROPS programme.

Manufacturer

Foden Trucks, Division of Paccar UK Limited, Moss Lane, Sandbach, Cheshire CW11 9YW, UK. Tel: 0270 763244. Fax: 0270 762758.

Foden (8 × 6) IMMLC logistic support truck undergoing durability trials

Foden (8 × 6) IMMLC logistic support truck

Unipower M Series (8 × 8) DROPS/PLS Vehicle

Description

The Unipower M Series (8 × 8) DROPS/PLS vehicle is a member of the Unipower M Series of military logistics truck range. The vehicle follows the same general lines as other vehicles in the M Series range (see entries in the *Trucks* and *Tank Transporters* sections) but is fitted with a Multilift Mark 4 load handling system (LHS – see following entry).

As with other vehicles in the Unipower M Series range, the DROPS/PLS vehicle has an all-steel forward control cab with seating for the driver and two passengers – only the driver is needed to operate the load handling system. The vehicle can carry standard flatracks or 10 or 20-foot ISO containers up to a maximum design load of 15 000 kg. The load/unload cycle can be as low as 40 seconds.

The vehicle is powered by a Cummins 430 hp diesel (other units can be used) coupled to an automatic transmission. The chassis frame uses open channel bolted construction with a subframe carrying the load handling system. A combination of flotation tyres and an evenly distributed axle load enables the vehicle to operate effectively over rough terrain in forward areas.

Specifications

Cab seating: 1 + 2
Configuration: 8 × 8
Weight:
  (unladen) 16 262 kg
  (GVW, actual) 34 000 kg
  (GVW, design) 39 000 kg
Length: 10.146 m
Width: 3 m
Height: 2.776 m
Ground clearance: 0.33 m
Wheelbase: 6 m
Angle of approach: 38°
Max speed: (laden) 76 km/h
Fuel capacity: 580 l
Range: 1000 km
Gradient: (restart, laden) 48%
Engine: Cummins NTA A430 CELECT 6-cylinder in-line turbocharged and after-cooled diesel developing 430 hp at 1900 rpm
Transmission: ZF Ecomat 6HP 600 Series III fully automatic providing 6 forward and 2 reverse gears plus ZF 380-30 torque converter

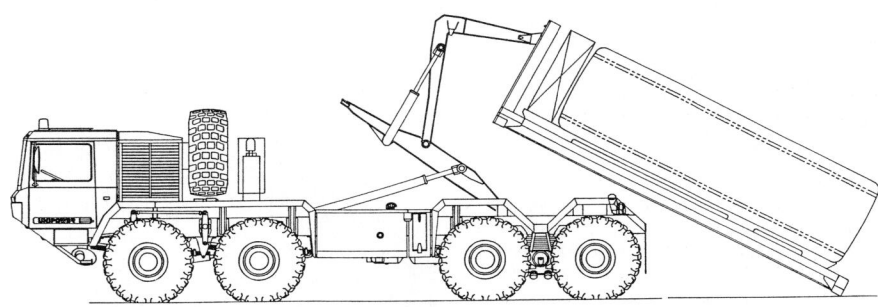

Unipower M Series Multi-role Self-loading / unloading Logistics Truck (liquids tank)

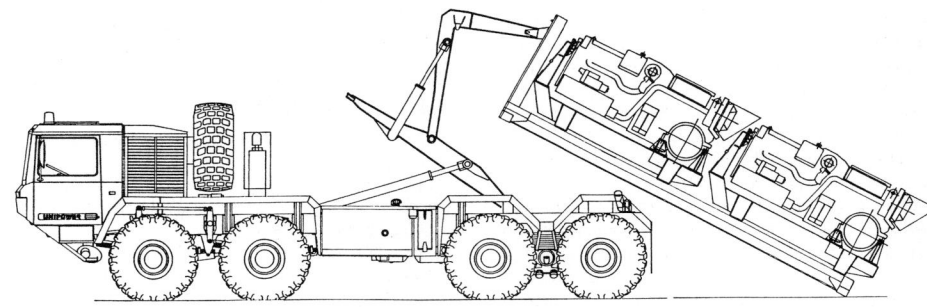

Unipower M Series Multi-role Self-loading / unloading Logistics Truck (armoured vehicle power packs)

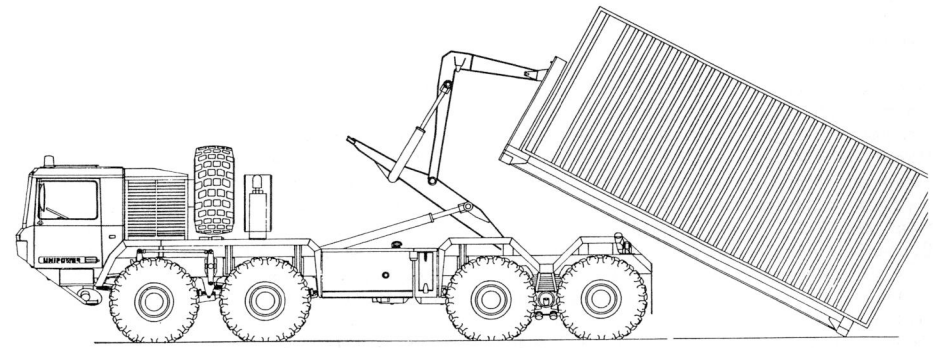

Unipower M Series Multi-role Self-loading / unloading Logistics Truck (20ft ISO container)

Drawings of various operating configurations of Unipower M Series (8 × 8) DROPS/PLS vehicle

Transfer box: ZF single-speed
Steering: ZF 8098 power-assisted
Suspension:
 (front) two slipper-ended semi-elliptic parabolic springs per axle
 (rear) two fully articulating semi-elliptical multi-leaf springs trunnion-mounted on bearings
Brakes: air to all axles
Tyres: 24 R 21 XL
Electrical system: 24 V
Batteries: 2 × 12 V, 150 Ah
Alternator: 90 A

Status
Pre-production.

Manufacturer
Unipower Vehicles Limited, 34 Greenhill Crescent, Watford Business Park, Watford, Hertfordshire WD1 8QU, UK.
Tel: 0923 816555. Telex: 261760 unitrk g.
Fax: 0923 228621.

Pre-production Unipower M Series (8 × 8) DROPS/PLS vehicle

Multilift Load Handling Systems

Description
Multilift Limited is part of Cargotec, a division of the Scandinavian multi-national Partek Corporation. The company has manufactured and supplied load handling equipment to defence forces since the 1950s but it was in the mid-1970s that Multilift commenced its involvement with the British Army's Demountable Rack Off-load Pick-up System (DROPS). Following trials with commercially derived systems it became apparent that a new range of 'off highway' custom-designed products was necessary for military applications. In the early 1980s two high performance systems were developed for a competitive selection programme. In 1984 over 1900 of the Multilift Mark 4 systems were selected for DROPS, with Leyland DAF and Foden being selected to carry 1500 and 400 of the units respectively. Production of the Mark 4 system commenced in 1989 following two years of validation trials with both vehicles.

The Multilift Mark 4 load handling system (LHS) was designed and developed from the outset for off-road military applications. Mounted in a light and flexible 'compression frame', the LHS moving structures (the middle frame and the hook arm) are pivoted on large plain bearings while the operating cylinders utilise spherical bearing. This arrangement, combined with a special 'transit' circuit within the hydraulic system, allows flexibility whilst guaranteeing load security and ensures that no stresses are passed into the truck chassis when manoeuvring over rough terrain. The control system uses automatic single lever operation with two modes of backup for emergencies. A high power-to-weight ratio maximises payload within the vehicle maximum weight.

The Multilift Mark 4 LHS is a high pick-up system used in conjunction with 20-foot/6.096 m ISO flatracks embodying a one-piece hook A-frame. Auto-location is facilitated when the driver lowers the hook arm to its maximum down position, using the joystick control unit located in the cab, and reverses his vehicle towards the flatrack until contact is made with the A-frame. The driver then selects 'lift' and the flatrack is loaded with the hook providing a fail-safe interface. Experienced operators can complete the load/unload cycle in less than one minute. The system can lift loads at its rated lift capacity from 500 mm below ground level.

A rear roller assembly designed to provide lateral strength at the chassis/load handling system interface is provided. The rear rollers are designed to ensure that a misaligned flatrack applies its vertical load to the chassis before the transmission of the horizontal load. All system cylinders, pivots, bearings and grease seals are readily accessible, removable and interchange-

Multilift Mark 4 load handling system (LHS) loading a 20-foot/6.096 m ISO container

able. Slave hydraulics are standard. The complete range of Multilift equipment conforms to NATO interoperability/DIN30722 standards.

The US Army tested 46 competitively procured Kenworth 6 × 6 trucks fitted with Multilift Mark 4 systems as part of its Palletised Load System (PLS) programme. Following concept trials held in 1986, 39 of the trucks were sold to the Canadian armed forces.

In 1988 Multilift, via a Canadian licensee, was awarded a contract for the supply of 133 LHS to be mounted on Steyr/UTDC 6 × 6 vehicles, plus 57 Ribbon Bridge Launchers for the Canadian Army Heavy Logistic Vehicle Wheeled (HLVW) programme. The HLVW LHS is modified from the Mark 4 DROPS system to conform to Canadian requirements. The Ribbon Bridge launching equipment is based on a standard Mark 4 unit to which is added a Bridge Adaptor Pallet (BAP) with all the necessary guides, rollers, locks and winches for Ribbon bridge unit handling; weight of the BAP is 1600 kg. The US Army Research and Development Center at Fort Belvoir purchased one set of this equipment as part of a full-scale test and evaluation contract.

In response to a US Army requirement, a Multilift LHS was fitted to Oshkosh 10 × 10 trucks. This was the Multilift Mark 5, a modified version of the Mark 4 with an airportability feature to support rapid reaction

forces. The Multilift Mark 5 is in production under licence to Oshkosh to meet an order for 2626 M1074 Oshkosh PLS trucks. (For an illustration and details of the vehicle involved refer to the entry under *United States* in this section.)

The Multilift Mark 6 LHS is a further development of the Mark 5, custom-designed and produced to be mounted on an Oshkosh 8 × 8 Heavy Extended Mobility Tactical Transport (HEMTT) truck. This system is being tested for the Improved Ribbon Bridge programme. Using the BAP, a full bridge and combat support boat launching and retrieval is offered. NATO flatracks can also be transported.

One further system, the Multilift Mark 4T, has been selected for use by the Royal Engineers. This system combines the full DROPS/PLS performance characteristics with an additional 25-tonne tipping capacity. The double-acting rams provide a speed and performance comparable with specialised earthmoving vehicles as the engineer skip body can be tipped to angles in excess of 60° in less than 15 seconds. A wide range of engineer logistic tasks and equipment can thus be accommodated. In September 1992 it was announced that an order for 75 Mark 4T systems had been placed, with production commencing during early 1993. The systems will be used on Terex 3066 LC high mobility frame steer dump trucks. A similar vehicle and

Multilift Mark 4T 'tipping' load handling system installed on a Terex 3066 LC high mobility frame steer truck

Multilift Mark 4T 'tipping' load handling system installed on a Terex 3066 LC high mobility frame steer truck

LHS combination has been supplied to the Royal Canadian Engineers.

Specifications (Mark 4 LHS)
Installed weight: 1800 kg
Rated lift capacity: (ground level) 16 500 kg
Overload capacity: (ground level) 20 000 kg
Flatrack or body length: 6.055 m
Flatrack or body width: 2.435 m
Misaligned tolerance: approx 15° either side
Load/unload cycle time: 58 s

Status
In production for British Army's DROPS programme and the US Army's PLS programme. In service with the Canadian, Norwegian and Swedish armed forces.

Manufacturer
Multilift Limited, Government Business Operations, Harlescott Lane, Shrewsbury, Shropshire SY1 3AG, UK.
Tel: 0743 232232. Fax: 0743 369935.

Marshall DROPS Flatracks

Description
In 1983 Marshall SPV Limited was selected by the Ministry of Defence to produce for evaluation a range of DROPS flatracks to be used with the Leyland DAF and Foden DROPS logistic supply vehicles. Each flatrack can carry a payload of 15 000 kg.

The test programme was completed in 1984 and in 1986 interoperability trials were carried out with United Kingdom and German vehicles. In late 1986 it was announced that Marshall SPV was to be a subcontractor to Foden for the supply of over 9000 flatracks for the British Army's DROPS programme. Production is carried out in a purpose-built semi-automated plant with a capacity of more than 2000 units per year.

Status
In production for the British Army's DROPS programme.

Manufacturer
Marshall SPV Limited, Airport Works, Cambridge CB5 8RX, UK.
Tel: 0223 301133. Fax: 02205 3875.

Marshall DROPS flatrack suitable for ammunition or other special purpose loads

Reynolds Boughton MLRS/DROPS Flatrack

Description
This skeletal flatrack transports up to four Multiple Launch Rocket System (MLRS) rocket pods and is capable of interoperability with the complete range of British Army DROPS equipment. Being of ISO configuration it can also be transported on road and rail flat beds, is ship and air transportable and can be carried underslung by helicopters.

A unique feature of the Boughton flatrack is a patented retractable roller which enables the flatrack to be easily manoeuvred on the ground and assists in vehicle-to-vehicle transfer operations.

Status
In production for the British Ministry of Defence.

Manufacturer
Reynolds Boughton Limited, Bell Lane, Amersham, Buckinghamshire HP6 6PE, UK.

Tel: 0494 764411. Telex: 83132.
Fax: 0494 765218.

Reynolds Boughton MLRS/DROPS flatrack

Reynolds Boughton DROPS/MLRS Pallet Trailer

Description
This trailer is a drawbar two-axle close-coupled type of skeletal construction designed specifically for the transportation of ISO-configured flatracks and their loads. The trailer is towed behind a tractive unit fitted with a demountable swap-body system such as the Boughton DROPS/PLS 6 × 6 truck (see separate entry in this section).

The design incorporates a patented telescopic pivoting drawbar. This enables the trailer to be coupled to and uncoupled from the prime mover by one man (the vehicle driver) without assistance. The flatrack can be transferred to and from the trailer with the trailer coupled to the vehicle.

Pallet location sockets and stops are fitted to the rear with standard ISO locks to the front and rear. A 76 mm diameter towing eye is fitted.

The unit is mounted on a Ridewell Dynaflex suspension. Two air line brakes are fitted, together with a full 24 V lighting system.

Specifications
Length:
(drawbar extended) 7.68 m
(drawbar retracted) 6.48 m
Width: 2.438 m
Height:
(laden) 1.2 m
(unladen) 1.25 m
Track: 2.97 m
Departure angle: 30°
Tyres: 16.5 × 22.5.385-65 R 22.5
Electrical system: 24 V

Status
In production for British Ministry of Defence. In service with the US Army (21).

Reynolds Boughton DROPS/PLS pallet trailer

Manufacturer
Reynolds Boughton Limited, Bell Lane, Amersham, Buckinghamshire HP6 6PE, UK.
Tel: 0494 764411. Telex: 83132.
Fax: 0494 765218.

King DROPS DB20/2-19.5 Tandem-axle Drawbar Trailer

Description
The King DROPS DB20/2-19.5 tandem-axle drawbar trailer can combine with either Foden or Leyland DAF 8 × 6 vehicles to make up a DROPS combination. The trailer was designed specifically to carry ammunition flatracks or 20 ft/6.096 m ISO containers and have a payload capacity of 16 500 kg.

King Trailers designed and developed the trailer within the parameters of the British Ministry of Defence's requirements. The design consists of a skeletal construction with built-in guides having a gathering-in facility to allow easy loading of flatracks by DROPS vehicles.

Although the initial production run was for five units the total order, spread over five years, is in the region of 300 trailers.

Specifications
Weight:
(empty) 3400 kg
(fully loaded) 19 900 kg
Payload: 16 500 kg
Length: (overall) 7.73 m
Width: 2.49 m
Tyres: 265 – 70R – 19.5

Status
In production. In service with the British Army.

King DROPS DB20/2-19.5 tandem-axle drawbar trailer and Foden (8 × 6) IMMLC DROPS vehicle

Manufacturer
King Trailers Limited, Riverside, Market Harborough, Leicestershire LE16 7PX, UK.

Tel: 0858 467361. Telex: 341835 king g.
Fax: 0858 467161.

SUPACAT Fork-Lift Pallet Trailer (FLPT)

Description
Designed and developed by SUPACAT Limited in response to a foreseen military requirement, the Fork-Lift Pallet Trailer (FLPT) was developed principally for the SUPACAT (6 × 6) 1000 kg light vehicle (see entry in the *Light vehicles* section for details) but can be used with other vehicles. The FLPT can extend the load moving capacity of the towing vehicle by one or two times. It was developed primarily for military airborne and air mobile operations and can be delivered by helicopter or parachute.

The FLPT has a tilting load platform on which are mounted folding fork-lift forks. The platform and forks are rotated by an electrically or manually operated hydraulic system and the FLPT can self-load and transport a standard pallet weighing up to 1400 kg. Once loaded the pallet lays on its side and is retained by the lifting forks but a tie-down can be used when traversing rough terrain.

The FLPT is light and can be stowed to take up minimum space. The drawbar can be retracted and the forks folded. If required the FLPT can be stowed vertically, with or without a load, and can be self-loaded onto a SUPACAT. The trailer has a rear tow hook to enable one FLPT to be towed behind another in a 'train' when conditions are favourable. As an alternative the FLPT tow hook may be used to tow a mortar or 105 mm Light Gun.

The trailer is fitted with a mesh bed to allow it to be used as a general load carrier or as a stretcher carrier when not carrying pallets.

Specifications
Weight: (unloaded) 382 kg
Load capacity: 1400 kg
Length overall:
(drawbar extended) 2.75 m
(drawbar retracted) 1.9 m
Width: (overall) 2.01 m
Height: (unloaded) 0.95 m
Tyres: 31 × 15.5 × 15 low ground pressure

Status
Available. In service with the British Army.

Manufacturer
SUPACAT Limited, The Airfield, Dunkeswell, Honiton, Devon EX14 0RA, UK.
Tel: 0404 891777. Fax: 0404 891776.

SUPACAT Fork-Lift Pallet Trailer (FLPT) loaded with an ammunition pallet and on tow behind a SUPACAT (6 × 6) 1000 kg light vehicle

TEREX 2366 LC Rough Terrain Load Carrier

Description
The TEREX 2366 LC rough terrain load carrier is a development of the TEREX 2366 articulated (frame steer) dump truck and is intended for logistic support in difficult conditions or for general military applications. It features a swap-body load handling system conforming to the NATO standard for 6 m bodies, for rapid interchangeability of roles and for interoperability with swap-body logistic road vehicles.

As a load carrier the TEREX 2366 LC has a payload of 20 000 kg or 16 000 kg with a 10 000 kg towed load. The frame-steer chassis combines manoeuvrability with the ability to accept extra-wide tyres and to 'duck-walk' through bad going. The rigid welded box-sections of the rear chassis frame permit direct mounting of hydraulic load handling systems without risk of deformation or jamming during rough terrain transit.

The front and rear chassis frames are coupled to provide 45° articulation to each side and full oscillation. This arrangement keeps all four wheels permanently in contact with the ground and assists in the alignment of vehicle and load during the pick-up phase of swap-body operations and in manoeuvring trailed loads by 'nosing'.

A two-man cab with full ROPS/FOPS protection is fitted as standard. The vehicle can accept all known types of proprietary load handling systems. Chassis options include higher engine ratings and full air-conditioning. A range of special bodies includes a bulk materials skip and a boat and pontoon rack. The TEREX 2366 LC can be used as an artillery tractor capable of towing heavy ordnance, for the launch and recovery of combat support craft, for the transport of light armoured vehicles, and as a general-purpose engineering vehicle carrying the bulk materials skip. The load handling system can also be used as a light crane.

Specifications
Cab seating: 1 + 1
Configuration: 6 × 6 or 6 × 4
Weight:
(empty) 16 300 kg
(loaded) 40 000 kg

TEREX 2366 LC rough terrain load carrier

Max load: 20 000 kg
Towed load: (with 16 000 kg payload) 10 000 kg
Length: 10.225 m
Width: 2.73 m
Height: 3.305 m
Ground clearance: 0.44 m
Track: 2.095 m
Wheelbase: 5.015 m + 1.62 m
Angle of approach/departure: 25°/47°
Max speed: 53 km/h
Engine: Deutz BF 6L 513 R 9.572 l turbocharged air-cooled 4-stroke direct injection diesel developing 224 hp (net) at 2300 rpm
Transmission: ZF 6WG 180 with integral hydro-dynamic torque converter close-coupled to power-shift countershaft gearbox providing 6 forward and 3 reverse gears
Steering: hydrostatic
Turning radius: 8 m
Suspension:
(front) axle carried on leading arms of subframe pivoting on main frame with self-levelling air units and hydraulic dampers
(rear) rubber/laminated units between axles and beam ends
Tyres: 25/65 R 25
Brakes:
(main) air-assisted disc on all wheels
(parking) spring-applied, air-released disc on rear driveline
Electrical system: 24 V
Batteries: 2 × 12 V, 175 Ah
Alternator: 55 A

Status
In service with the British Army, fitted with Multilift LHS for use by Royal Engineers (20).

Manufacturer
TEREX Equipment Limited, Newhouse, Motherwell ML1 5RY, UK.
Tel: 0698 732121. Telex: 77141.
Fax: 0698 734046.

Hyster Fork-lift Trucks

Description

Hyster manufactures over 70 lift truck models, from 1 to 48 tonnes capacity, with electric or internal combustion power. The company has three manufacturing plants in Europe; Irvine and Craigavon in the United Kingdom and Nijmegen in the Netherlands.

The Challenger range of trucks is engine-powered pneumatic-tyred trucks ranging from the small H1.25XL trucks which can lift up to 1.25 tonnes at 500 mm, to trucks which can lift up to 48 tonnes at 1.2 m. The Hyster electric lift trucks have advanced design features with all models up to 3000 kg capacity having the option of pneumatic or cushion tyres; models over 3000 kg have cushion tyres. The range starts at 1.25 tonne capacity lift trucks and extends up to trucks with 5.5 tonnes capacity at 600 mm.

Status

In production. Various models in both the Challenger and electric ranges are used by the British armed forces, the US Army and many other defence forces.

Manufacturer

Hyster Europe Limited, PO Box 54, Berk House, Basing View, Basingstoke, Hampshire RG21 2HQ, UK. Tel: 0256 461171. Telex: 858384. Fax: 0256 56733.

Hyster H2.00J lift truck in use by the British Army

Hyster H2.00J lift truck stacking ammunition boxes

Kalmar Climax Fork-lift Trucks

Description

Kalmar Climax produces a wide range of both engine-powered and electric front-loading fork-lift trucks and electric moving mast reach trucks, including the PROTECTION range incorporating 30 years' experience in providing trucks protected to operate in potentially explosive or hazardous atmospheres (for example ammunition handling). The company also supplies side loaders and hand pallet trucks.

Status

In production. The company is registered on the United Kingdom Defence Contractor's list to supply fork-lift trucks to the United Kingdom armed forces. Models are in service with the defence forces of Belgium, Canada, Denmark, Egypt, Norway, the United Kingdom and the USA.

Manufacturer

Kalmar UK Limited, Sandy Lane, Coventry, West Midlands CV1 4DX, UK. Tel: 0203 555355. Telex: 312414. Fax: 0203 229417.

Kalmar Climax Series 2000 Model 2725 'PROTECTION 2' fork-lift truck

Boughton Fork-lifts

Description
Reynolds Boughton Limited manufactures a range of fork-lift attachments for wheeled front end loaders with lift capacities from 1500 to 6000 kg at 0.5 m load centre. Optional features include hydraulic operation carriage side shift, carriage rotation, fork load levelling, and fork spread. Fitment to the loader is either by direct pin mounting to the loader arms or via a quick coupler attachment.

Status
In production. In service with the British Army and French Army.

Manufacturer
Reynolds Boughton Limited, Engineering Division, Bell Lane, Amersham, Buckinghamshire HP6 6PE, UK. Tel: 0494 764411. Telex: 83132. Fax: 0494 765218.

Boughton 1850 kg fork-lift on Muir Hill A5000 front loader

Boughton 4200 kg fork-lift on Case 721 wheeled tractor in service with the British Army

JCB 410M Rough Terrain Fork-lift Truck

Description
The JCB 410M rough terrain fork-lift truck was developed from the JCB 410 articulated loading shovel. A total of 932 units was delivered by the end of 1987, including a quantity of fully winterised vehicles capable of starting up and operating at −40°C.

The JCB 410M is a military rough terrain fork-lift designed specifically to handle NATO pallets. Its lift capacity is 1815 kg. Developed for military use, the 410M has a low profile cab for air-portability and a higher road speed to keep pace with military convoys; it can also be towed at convoy speeds. It has a forward reach capability to allow loading and unloading from one side of a cargo truck or rail wagon. The operator's cab is on the front module to provide good visibility with minimum engine noise and vibration. It has a full three-speed power-shift transmission. Steering is by power-operated centre pivot articulation for increased manoeuvrability, giving a 9.26 m maximum turning circle. The 410M can be fitted with a range of attachments such as buckets, crane hooks, sweepers, and so on, to increase the machine's versatility. A NATO tow hitch is fitted as standard.

JCB 410M rough terrain fork-lift truck

Specifications
Cab seating: 1
Configuration: 4 × 4
Weight: 6850 kg
Operating load: 1815 kg at 0.61 m
Length:
    (overall) 5.625 m
    (without forks) 4.5 m
Height: (top of cab) 2.67 m
Ground clearance: 0.4 m
Track: 1.8 m
Wheelbase: 2.7 m
Angle of approach/departure: 45°/45°
Max speed: 57.02 km/h
Fuel capacity: 95 l
Max gradient: 100 %

Fording: 0.75 m
Engine: Perkins T4.236 3.86 l 4-cylinder direct injection diesel developing 102 hp at 2600 rpm
Transmission: Clark 18000 series full power-shift with 3 forward and 3 reverse gears
Steering: power-assisted
Turning radius: (outside tyres) 9.26 m
Tyres: 15.5/80 × 20R XL
Brakes:
    (main) hydraulic multi-disc
    (parking) axle mounted disc on front differential shaft
Electrical system: 24 V

Batteries: 2 × 12 V, 96 Ah
Alternator: 40 A

Status
In service with the British Army, Royal Navy and Royal Air Force, and the Jordanian armed forces.

Manufacturer
JCB Military Products Division, Rocester, Staffordshire ST14 5JP, UK. Tel: 0889 590312. Telex: 36372. Fax: 0889 590588.

JCB 926 and 930 Rough Terrain Fork-lift Trucks

Description

The JCB 926 and 930 rough terrain fork-lift trucks are basically similar, with the JCB 926 having a lift capacity of 2600 kg and the JCB 930 3000 kg. Both are built around a specially designed chassis and can be fitted with duplex, triplex (heights of 3.6, 5.5 and 6.55 m available) or free lift (4.5 m) masts and both can be produced in 4 × 2 and 4 × 4 configurations. Access to the one-man cab is from either side.

The engine used is a Perkins 4.40 diesel driving through a JCB Syncro-Shuttle gearbox via a torque converter. The JCB epicyclic hub reduction front axle incorporates inboard-mounted oil-immersed multi-disc brakes.

Specifications

(Data relate to JCB 926; data for JCB 930 in square brackets where different)
Cab seating: 1
Configuration: 4 × 2 or 4 × 4

Weight:
(4 × 2) 5955 [6685] kg
(4 × 4) 6025 [6755] kg
Length: (less forks) 3.58 [3.66] m
Width: 2.22 m
Height: (cab) 2.56 m
Track: (front) 1.8 m
Wheelbase:
(4 × 2) 2.06 m
(4 × 4) 2.12 m
Engine: Perkins 4.40 water-cooled 4-cylinder diesel developing 76 hp
Transmission: torque converter with powershuttle reverser and full synchromesh 4-speed gearbox

Status

In production. In service with the defence forces of several countries.

Manufacturer

JCB Military Products Division, Rocester, Staffordshire ST14 5JP, UK.
Tel: 0889 590312. Telex: 36372.
Fax: 0889 590588.

JCB 926 rough terrain fork-lift truck; JCB 930 is visually similar

JCB 'Loadalls'

Description

JCB is the largest producer of variable reach handling machines in the world. Production of the first model, the JCB 520, began in 1977. Machines in the range have lift capacities from 2500 to 4000 kg and lift heights from 5.8 to 10.79 m. The range includes both two- and three-stage telescopic arms.

The Loadalls have the features of conventional rough terrain trucks with the advantage of forward reach which permits 'one side' loading and unloading of road and rail trucks. Telescopic machines can stand back from hazardous areas or soft ground and still lift or place a load accurately.

In the latest range all machines now have four equal-sized wheels which enable them to steer in three modes: all-wheel steer, front wheel steer and crab steer.

All Loadalls are powered by four-cylinder Perkins diesel engines and drive via a torque converter through a JCB synchromesh gearbox and JCB drive axles, which incorporate oil-immersed multi-disc brakes. The single operator all-weather cab meets all ROPS/FOPS requirements.

Specifications (JCB 525-67)

Cab seating: 1
Configuration: 4 × 4
Weight: 6420 kg
Length: (fork carriage) 4.78 m
Width: 2.34 m
Height: (to top of cab) 2.59 m
Ground clearance: (minimum) 0.42 m
Track: (front) 1.9 m
Wheelbase: 2.48 m
Max road speed: 29 km/h

JCB Loadall 525B in service with the Royal Navy

Engine: Perkins 4.40 water-cooled 4-cylinder diesel developing 102 hp
Transmission: full power-shift torque converter with 4 forward and reverse gear ranges
Steering: twin ram hydrostatic power on each axle with 3 steer modes: all-wheel, front wheel and crab
Tyres: (front and rear) 15.5 × 24 traction
Capacity at 0.5 m load centres: 2500 kg at radius of 1.63 m to maximum height of 6.7 m; 835 kg at maximum radius of 3.55 m to maximum height of 6.7 m

Status

In production. In service with the Royal Navy and the defence forces of several countries, including some remotely controlled 'specials'.

Manufacturer

JCB Military Products Division, Rocester, Staffordshire ST14 5JP, UK.
Tel: 0889 590312. Telex: 36372.
Fax: 0889 590588.

BOSS Trucks 700 Series Sideloader

Description

The BOSS range of sideloaders comprises 30 models with capacities between 1600 and 45 000 kg. The Royal Air Force used BOSS 700 series sideloaders with the Bloodhound SAM at missile bases in the United Kingdom. Some of the vehicles are equipped

with a missile handling attachment made by British Aerospace and all are electrically protected to the relevant explosives safety standard. Similar sideloaders are used by the British Army for depot handling of the Lance ballistic artillery missile.

Specifications (700 series sideloader)

Cab seating: 1
Configuration: 4 × 2

Weight: 9625 kg
Length: 5.44 m
Height: 2.92 m
Width: 2.62 m
Ground clearance: 0.23 m
Wheelbase: 3.13 m
Track: 2.25 m
Max road speed: (unladen) 56 km/h
Engine: Ford 2714E diesel

Transmission: torque converter with 3 forward and reverse ratios
Steering: hydrostatic on front axles
Turning radius: 5.5 m
Tyres: 9.00 × 20
Lift height: 3.66 m
Free lift: 0.28 m
Lowered height: 2.92 m
Extended height: 5.03 m
Capacity: (stabilising jacks extended, typical) 6000 kg to 3.66 m lift height

Status
Production complete. In service with the British Army, Swiss Air Force and US Army.

Manufacturer
BOSS Trucks Limited, Grovebury Road, Leighton Buzzard, Bedfordshire LU7 8SR, UK.
Tel: 0525 372031. Telex: 825781.

BOSS Trucks 700 series sideloader with attachment for Bloodhound SAM

Lansing Linde Fork-lift Trucks

Description
Lansing Linde Limited manufactures an extensive range of materials handling equipment ranging from 1 to 42 tonnes capacity in both battery electric and internal combustion engine forms. Products cater for virtually every form of materials handling from hand pallet trucks to the stacking of heavy ISO containers.

Several models have been the subject of Ministry of Defence 'Best Buy' agreements, the reach truck, the sea-going counterbalanced fork-lift truck, and the shipboard pallet truck being the prime examples. The company has also developed machines for use in hazardous atmospheres (gases and dusts) and to handle sensitive and dangerous loads.

The company has production plants in the United Kingdom as well as Germany and France. In the United Kingdom the factories are registered to British Standard (BS) 5750 Pt 1 and have been assessed by the Ministry of Defence to AQAP 1 in quality control systems. Maintenance and spares support services are available, as are training courses for operators,

engineers and instructors.

Status
Numerous models in production and in service worldwide, including with the British armed forces and the US Army, Navy and Air Force.

Manufacturer
Lansing Linde Limited, Kingsclere Road, Basingstoke, Hampshire RG21 2XJ, UK.
Tel: 0256 342000. Telex: 858120 lbba g.
Fax: 0256 342916.

Lansing reach truck working in British Army ammunition handling area in Germany

Lansing H250 container handling truck operating in dock area in Falkland Islands

BOSS FUG 2.5-tonne All-terrain Lift Truck

Development
The BOSS FUG 2.5-tonne all-terrain lift truck was originally designed and produced by Steinbock GmbH of Germany. In 1982 Steinbock GmbH was awarded a DM 83.7 million contract for 199 trucks by the German Government for the Bundeswehr and in 1985 a contract option for a further 378 trucks and spare parts was exercised at an estimated cost of DM 61.1 million. In August 1983 Steinbock became part of the UK LancerBoss Group, now BOSS Trucks Limited, and is wholly owned by it.

Description
The BOSS FUG 2.5-tonne all-terrain lift truck has a lifting capacity of 2500 kg and can be converted for a number of rough terrain materials handling con-

figurations. It can be used as a fork-lift truck, a crane or a bulldozer and can also be used as a tractor by employing front and rear towing points.

The FUG has a full 4 × 4 configuration with the front-lift mast situated centrally at the front between two cabs. These fully enclosed single-seat cabs are for the driver on the left and a passenger on the right; both cabs have heating and soundproofing. The engine takes up much of the area behind the cabs and the area on both sides can be used to carry a variety of materials handling and other equipment. More equipment can be carried in racks under the cabs. The FUG has a road speed of 50 km/h and is equipped with a ZF gearbox with a torque converter and full power-shift for six forward and two reverse gears. There is an automatic differential lock on the front axle.

The front-lift mast can be tilted forward 10° and backwards 18° – when on the road it is carried at a rearwards angle of 40°. There is a side-shift capability of 150 mm in either direction. A crane or dozer blade

attachment can be fitted to the mast.

Specifications
Cab seating: 1 + 1
Configuration: 4 × 4
Weight:
 (unladen) 8260 kg
 (laden) 11 700 kg
Max load: 2500 kg
Length: (overall, with forks) 5.674 m
Width: 2.23 m
Height:
 (top of mast) 2.78 m
 (top of cab) 2.47 m
Ground clearance: 0.43 m
Track: 1.875 m
Wheelbase: 2.5 m
Angle of departure: 45°
Max road speed: approx 50 km/h
Range: approx 500 km

BOSS FUG 2.5-tonne all-terrain lift truck

Gradient: limit of adhesion
Fording: 0.75 m
Engine: KHD F 6 L 913 D diesel developing 106 hp at 2150 rpm
Transmission: ZF 6 WG 120 torque converter and power-shift with 6 forward and 2 reverse gears
Steering: ZF type, full power hydrostatic
Tyres: 14.5 – 20 MPT/PR14
Brakes: two independent hydraulic servo-assisted circuits; drum front, disc rear
Electrical system: 24 V
Batteries: 2 × 12 V, 125 Ah
Forklift unit height: (fork retracted) 2.78 m
Height: (fork extended) 4.64 m
Lift: 3.6 m
Normal free lift: 290 mm
Tilt compensation: ±15°
Side shift: 150 mm each way

Status
In production. In service with German armed forces (577).

Manufacturer
BOSS Trucks Limited, Grovebury Road, Leighton Buzzard, Bedfordshire LU7 8SR, UK.
Tel: 0525 372031. Telex: 825781.

BOSS 'G' Series Rough Terrain Container Handling Front-lift Trucks

Description
BOSS 'G' Series Container Handling Rough Terrain (RT) Front-lifts were specifically designed to handle and transport laden containers up to 25 000 kg on rough surface conditions ranging from relatively poor, uneven surfaces to rough, cross-country terrain.

A choice of two- or four-wheel drive models is available (designated RT and AT respectively, also known as the Bear) sharing many design features. Many major components are used in the orthodox 'G' Series Container Handling Front-lift Series for port operations, with the advantage of spare parts commonality and servicing familiarity for operators.

High flotation tyres, high under-clearances, a long wheelbase and optimum weight distribution combine with the high-power Volvo turbocharged diesel and power-matched Allison power-shift transmission to give good traction and stability, laden or unladen. Panoramic visibility from the operator's offset control centre and the BOSS 'VisionMast' ensure that the driver can see clearly in all weather conditions. A fork-lift may be attached.

A BOSS 20 ft/6.096 m fork-mounted Top-lift Attachment is fitted to the inverted Fork Frame and the all-hydraulic operation allows for effective transportation and stacking of laden containers up to 25 000 kg.

Specifications
Cab seating: 1

BOSS 'G' Series ATCH with container

Configuration: 4 × 2 (RT) or 4 × 4 (AT)
Weight: 46 620 kg
Length: (including top-lift attachment) 10.125 m
Height: 4.99 m
Width: (excluding top-lift attachment) 4.48 m
Wheelbase: 5.5 m
Track: (front axle) 4.05 m
Max road speed: (unladen) 34 km/h
Engine: Volvo TD.120G 11.98 l diesel developing 350 bhp at 2200 rpm
Transmission: Allison CRT5643 (torque converter and power-shift: 3 forward/3 reverse speeds)
Tyres: front, 26.4R × 25; rear, 23.5 × 25.
Capacity: (under top-lift attachment) 25 000 kg

Status
In production. In service with the British Army (4, AT).

Manufacturer
BOSS Trucks Limited, Grovebury Road, Leighton Buzzard, Bedfordshire LU7 8SR, UK.
Tel: 0525 372031. Telex: 825781.

Grove Coles Mobile Cranes

Description
Grove Coles is a well established supplier of cranes and lifting equipment for military purposes and over 40 types of Grove Coles cranes are at present in military use throughout the world. Grove Coles produces the widest range of mobile cranes in the world including industrial, port, all-terrain, rough terrain and truck-mounted, all of which can be used for military purposes, plus specialised military cranes with lifting capacities from 6 to 250 tonnes.

Hydra Truck, Supertruck and Octag
These ranges of truck-mounted telescopic boom cranes have lifting capacities from 12 to 135 tonnes. They

have limited off-road capabilities and are therefore more suited to use in rear areas.

The Hydra Truck 12/14T general duties crane can be made as a special variant for use aboard aircraft carriers.

Hydra Speedcranes
The Speedcrane range consists of conventional truck-mounted telescopic hydraulically operated cranes with lifting capacities from 6 to 9 tonnes. The 4 × 2 chassis makes the Speedcrane range suitable for use in permanent installations.

The Speedcrane 8/9T Mk II is the standard Royal Air Force 7-tonne crane and is in use for general stores handling and aircraft maintenance work in the Royal Air Force and with the Fleet Air Arm, both ashore and aboard.

Hydra Husky, Transit and Ranger
The Husky series of cranes is specifically designed for use on rough terrain and therefore has clear military applications. The Hydra Husky 150T has been the standard Medium Field Support Crane in the British Army for over a decade and is ideally suited to military applications.

The 6/8TCC Airportable Husky, suitable for transportation in the C-130 Hercules transport aircraft, is used in quantity by the former Yugoslav Army.

The Model 315M is the current 'Crane, Field, Medium' used by the Royal Engineers for bridge building and general stores handling from base to forward areas, by the REME for major unit changes on AFVs in the field and for workshop use, and by the RCT and RAOC in their general stores and overall support role along the British Army's line of

Specifications

Model	Hydra Speedcrane 8/9T Mk II	Husky 6/8TCC	Model 315M	Hydra Truck 12/14T	Ranger (Transit) 517	Model 335M	Ranger 520	Ranger 530	Husky 680
Configuration	4 × 2	4 × 4	4 × 4	4 × 2	4 × 4	4 × 2	4 × 4	4 × 4	4 × 4
Traverse	360°	360°	360°	360°	360°	360°	360°	360°	360°
Lifting capacity									
(min radius)	8130 kg/2.45 m	7320 kg/2.8 m	15 000 kg/3 m	12 200 kg/3 m	18 000 kg/3 m	40 800 kg/3.5 m	20 000 kg/3 m	30 000 kg/3 m	75 000 kg/3 m
(max radius)	710 kg/11 m	1650 kg/25 m	2050 kg/10 m	820 kg/15 m	1400 kg/16.5 m	1150 kg/36 m	900 kg/24 m	600 kg/28 m	2560 kg/30 m
Length	6.55 m	7.27 m	9.14 m	8.6 m	8.71 m	15 m	10.7 m	11.08 m	14.63 m
Width	2.44 m	2.5 m	2.5 m	2.5 m	2.5 m	2.9 m	2.5 m	2.75 m	3.65 m
Height	2.82 m	2.67 m	3.6 m	3.26 m	3.62 m	3.9 m	3.4 m	3.66 m	4 m
Weight	13 590 kg	14 860 kg	21 130 kg	16 642 kg	18 430 kg	36 240 kg	21 250 kg	23 970 kg	50 460 kg
Engine	100 hp	158 hp	196 hp	146 hp	160 hp	165 hp	150 hp	240 hp	210 hp
Gears	5 forward, 1 reverse	4 forward, 4 reverse	6 forward, 3 reverse	6 forward, 1 reverse	6 forward, 1 reverse	4 forward, 4 reverse	6 forward, 3 reverse	5 forward, 1 reverse	6 forward, 6 reverse
Max speed	—	—	75 km/h	—	65 km/h	61 km/h	70 km/h	61 km/h	30 km/h

Grove Coles Hydra Husky 6/8TCC being loaded onto an RAF Hercules transport aircraft

Grove Coles 315M, the British Army's Crane, Field, Medium

communications.

The Transit 517 Lightweight is a specially developed version of the 517 for use both on flight decks and in hangar operations on aircraft carriers.

The Ranger series of all-terrain cranes has the on-road performance of a truck crane and the off-road capabilities of a rough terrain crane with lifting capacities from 15 to 30 tonnes, and again is suited to military purposes.

Starlift

The Starlift range of self-propelled, telescopic aerial work platforms can place men and their equipment to working heights from 17 to 27.5 m and at maximum outreach from 13.5 to 24 m. Typical military applications include the maintenance and repair of buildings and aircraft. The standard versions are self-propelled,

but truck-mounted variants are available on such chassis as the military version of the Bedford TK 4 × 2 truck or on the specialised Grove Coles 315M crane chassis.

Status

Various models of Grove Coles Cranes are in service with the British armed forces, the Belgian Air Force, the former Yugoslav Army and numerous other armed forces.

Manufacturer

Grove Coles, Harefield, Uxbridge, Middlesex UB9 6QG, UK.
Tel: 0895 656281. Telex: 53484 cranes g.
Fax: 0895 109242.

Grove Coles Hydra Husky 150T used by the British Army

Joloda Materials and Weapons Handling System

Description

The Joloda materials and weapons handling system uses a skate and track system to manually move and stack 20 ft/6.096 m containers, MILVANS and flatracks up to 20 tonnes in weight into storage buildings and achieve dense-pack storage. The system relies on

manual elevated skates that lift the load which is then rolled into position on a latticework of sunken tracks in the floor of a storage building or weapon shelter.

Loads can be stacked and stored with only 25.4 mm between the loads. The tracks on the floor have a slope of 1/200 towards the doors so that in an emergency the loads can be rolled out by simply elevating the skates. Once outside the storage structure the loads can be handled by fork-lift trucks, cranes or other methods. Inside buildings the Joloda track is inset longitudinally

in lanes, with latitudinal junction crossovers. Sections of portable track are clipped into position on the aprons of the building for initial placement and retrieval from the store. For weapons handling systems with loads of up to 20 tonnes a deep section track with a stainless steel inlay is used.

The Royal Air Force uses a 10-tonne system for the support of Tornado units, moving weaponry in and out of high density storage igloos. During 1988 the US Army completed trials with a 20-tonne system at Fort

McClennan, Alabama. The trials involved the moving and storage of 20 ft MILVANS, PLS flatracks and dummy-loaded MLRS packs. All loads were moved through a 3.05 m door width into Stradley magazines.

Status
In service with the Royal Air Force and trialled by the US Army.

Manufacturer
Joloda plc, Unit 12, Garston Industrial Estate, Blackburne Street, Garston, Liverpool L19 8JA, UK.
Tel: 051 427 8954. Telex: 32641 mds int g.
Fax: 051 427 1393.

A MLRS pack loaded on a Joloda 20-tonne capacity weapons handling system about to enter a magazine during US Army trials

UNITED STATES OF AMERICA

Oshkosh (10 × 10) Palletized Load System (PLS)

Description
The US Army Tank Automotive Command awarded prototype contracts to three contractors for prototype Palletized Load System (PLS) vehicles in January 1989. Each of the three firms involved delivered nine trucks, six trailers and 30 flatracks. Prototype hardware testing began in September 1989. The three firms involved in the programme were the Oshkosh Truck Corporation, the PACCAR Government Group, and General Motors, Military Vehicle Operations.

In September 1990 it was announced that the production contract had been awarded to the Oshkosh Truck Corporation. Oshkosh was awarded a five-year $860 million contract for 2626 PLS trucks, 1050 trailers (a LOHR design, see entry under France in this section for details) and 11 030 flatracks. The contract includes yearly 100 per cent options that, if completely exercised, could bring the contract value to approximately $1.1 billion and involve around 5200 trucks. Production commenced in 1991 and will last until October 1995.

The Oshkosh PLS prime mover is a 10 × 10 full-time all-wheel drive truck. The vehicle has a front tandem unit with two powered steering axles and a rear tridem unit with two powered rigid axles plus one powered steering axle. The 10 × 10 configuration provides optimum turning capability and good weight distribution between all axles to provide mobility and capability above the desired level of the US Army specification. The vehicle is diesel powered with an automatic shift transmission, a two-speed transfer case, and full-time drive to all 10 wheels.

The PLS truck is capable of transporting 16.5-ton of flatrack-mounted cargo, and can tow a PLS trailer loaded with a 16.5 tons flatrack payload.

The PLS truck/trailer design includes an integral self-load/unload capability using the PLS flatrack. Oshkosh selected the Multilift Mark 5 load handling lift system and will licence-produce the system for the PLS contract. A single operator can load or unload a 16.5-ton flatrack in less than one minute without leaving the cab.

The vehicles are air-transportable in C-5A and C-17 cargo aircraft and can be carried in C-130 and C-141 aircraft with preparation.

One half of the trucks involved in the PLS contract will be equipped with a Grove material handling crane with a capacity of 1769 kg at 12.1 m and are designated the M1074. Trucks without the material handling crane, trailers and flatracks are the M1075, M1076 and

Oshkosh (10 × 10) Palletized Load System (PLS) equipped with Multilift Mark 5 load handling system

M1077 respectively.

The US Army initially purchased the PLS for ammunition resupply. Other applications under consideration are for the resupply of MLRS pods, fuel and water tanks, medical shelters, Ribbon Bridge components, portable kitchens, command/control shelters, barrier material and tank ammunition. A PLS Patriot lightweight launcher platform is one further possibility, as is a PLS dump body.

Specifications
Cab seating: 1 + 1
Configuration: 10 × 10
Weights:
 (bare chassis) 16 783 kg
 (kerb, with crane and flatrack) 24 131 kg
 (kerb, without crane, with flatrack) 21 992 kg
 (GVW) 39 290 kg
 (GCW) 62 135 kg
Max PLS payload: 14 696 kg
Length: 10.78 m
Width: 2.44 m
Height: (cab) 2.6 m
 (deck) 1.727 m
Ground clearance: 0.4 m
Track: 1.925 m
Wheelbase: 5.71 m
Angle of approach/departure: 42°/62°
Max speed: (GCW, road) 90.1 km/h
Range: 362 km
Fuel capacity: 379 l
Max gradient: 60%

Fording: 1.2 m
Engine: Detroit Diesel Model 8V-92TA 12.1 l V-8 diesel equipped with electronic control system developing 500 hp at 2100 rpm
Transmission: Allison CLT-755 5-speed automatic with torque converter and equipped with Allison Transmission electronic controls (ATEC)
Transfer box: Oshkosh 55000 Series 2-speed with 30:70 differential
Steering: power-assisted front tandem co-ordinated with power-assisted rear axle steer
Turning circle: (wall to wall) 29.3 m
Suspension: Hendrickson walking beam front and rear with mid-axle equipped with Hendrickson-Turner air ride suspension
Tyres: 16.00 R 20 with central tyre inflation system
Brakes:
 (main) Rockwell wedge drum, air-operated, dual system, internal shoe
 (parking) spring brake mounted on rear tridem axles
Electrical system: 12/24 V
Batteries: 4 × 12 V

Status
Production commenced in early 1992 for the US Army (2626 units).

Manufacturer
Oshkosh Truck Corporation, PO Box 2566, Oshkosh, Wisconsin 54903-2566, USA.
Tel: (414) 235 9150. Fax: (414) 233 9540.

Case Rough Terrain Fork-lift Trucks

Description

The Case M4K-B rough terrain fork-lift truck was designed to load and unload material from ISO containers. The fork free-lift, side-shift and vehicle dimensions allow the fork-lift to enter a container and pick or place loads. Adequate side-shift is provided to place loads against either wall of a container. The M4K-B is towable with standard drawbar and safety equipment. Canopies or cabs are provided with ROPS and FOPS meeting the latest international requirements. Lift and tie-down brackets are standard equipment and are designed for parachute delivery or helicopter transport. The vehicle is fitted with high flotation tyres and standard driving and blackout lights. Other features include hydraulic fork rotation, and front and rear axle disconnects for towing.

The M6K-B articulated rough terrain fork-lift has reach for loading trucks from one side. Features include power rotation, side-shifting and fork spacing. The unit has been tested and is in service in salt water applications, both onshore and shipboard.

The M13K articulated rough terrain fork-lift is designed with the primary mission of loading and unloading cargo aircraft such as the C-130. The forks can be equipped with conveyor ramps which match aircraft cargo systems. The cab, load guard and counterweight may be removed so that the unit can be transported by C-130 aircraft.

The M6K-B and M13K have a parallel linkage system which ensures that the forks remain in a level position throughout the lift arc. The M13K is also equipped with the necessary safety equipment for handling nuclear systems.

* Weight and height can be reduced for aircraft transport in C-130.

Specifications

Model	M4K-B	M6K-B*	M13K*
Cab seating	1	1	1
Configuration	4 × 4	4 × 4	4 × 4
Weight (without load)	4536 kg	9100 kg	10 400 kg
Length	5.35 m	6.25 m	7.35 m
Height (cab/canopy)	2.03 m	3.05 m	3.12 m
Width	2.01 m	2.16 m	2.31 m
Ground clearance	334 mm	406 mm	432 mm
Wheelbase	2.34 m	2.54 m	2.74 m
Engine (diesel)	Case 4-390	Case 6-590	Case A504BD
Hp/rpm (SAE net)	66/2200	90/2200	110/2200
Gearbox	3/3	3/3	4/2
Transmission	full power-shift	full power-shift	full power-shift
Max road speed	35.9 km/h	34.76 km/h	37.49 km/h
Turning radius	n/a	10 m	9.93 m
Brakes (type)	hydraulic disc	air/hydraulic disc	air/hydraulic disc
Tyres	15 × 19.5	15.5 × 25	17.5 × 25
Electrical system	24 V	24 V	24 V
Fork-lift (type)	mast	boom	boom
Lift capacity rated	1814 kg at 610 mm	2722 kg at 610 mm	5897 kg at 1.22 m
Max lift height	2.54 m	3.05 m	1.98 m
Tilt (forward)	11°	30°	10°
(back)	22°	33°	16.5°
Sideshift (left/right)	559 mm/559 mm	1.27 m/1.27 m	none
Fork rotation (total)	22°	21°	none

Status

M4K-B, M6K-B and M13K in production. Over 3000 Case M-series military rough terrain fork-lifts are in service with the US armed forces. The M4K and its predecessor (the MC4000) are no longer in production but remain in service. The M6K and M6K-B are in service with the US Navy. The M13K and M10K are in service with the US Air Force.

Manufacturer

J I Case Company, Government Marketing, 700 State Street, Racine, Wisconsin 53404, USA.

Case M6K-B rough terrain fork-lift truck for US Navy and US Air Force

US Air Force Case M13K loading C-130 transport aircraft

TEREX 72-31 Series Rough Terrain Fork-lift Trucks

Description

TEREX produced two main types of military fork-lift truck for the US armed forces, both derived from the commercial TEREX 72-31 articulated front end loader. One was the TEREX 72-31MP2U/R for the US Marine Corps which was first produced in 1967; production continued until 1972. These were produced as scoop loaders, but once in service, trials demonstrated that the vehicle was capable of acting as a 4545 kg fork-lift vehicle after it was fitted with rear-mounted counterweights and a modified US Air Force 463L fork carriage. The vehicle was then re-classified as a Tractor, Wheeled, Industrial with the capability of use as a fork-lift truck or a loader with a bucket attachment. The US Marine Corps had 418 units. During 1984 a further 92 72-31MP2U units were delivered.

In 1977 it was decided to rebuild these machines to new conditions at the TEREX factory. During the rebuild a Rollover Protective Structure (ROPS), water compatible disc brakes, larger tyres, heavier counterweights and a side-shift fork carriage were fitted as part of a general upgrade package which took place from 1978 to 1981. A total of 369 vehicles was involved.

Another military version of the TEREX 72-31 was the TEREX 72-31F Adverse Terrain Fork-lift Truck (US Air Force Type A/S32 H-15) produced for the US Air Force to use as part of its 463L Material Handling System. As such it has an aluminium half-cab that can be easily removed by two men without tools, and a segmented counterweight system to allow the machine to be airlifted in either a C-130 or C-141 aircraft. The TEREX 72-31F is widely used as the loader for the C-130 transport aircraft and the US Air Force alone has over 300. As with the 72-31M, the vehicle is rated as a 4545 kg payload vehicle but the US Air Force uses the 72-31F at a rating of 6136 kg for short periods.

Status

Production complete. 72-31M is in service with US Marine Corps. 72-31F is in service with the Argentinian, Belgian, Israeli and US air forces.

Specifications

Model	72-31M	72-31F
Used by	USMC	USAF
Cab seating	1	1
Configuration	4 × 4	4 × 4
Weight	15 727 kg	11 766 kg
Operating load	4545 kg	4545 kg
Length	7.2 m	7.2 m
Width	2.624 m	2.489 m
Height	3.086 m	3.01 m
Wheelbase	2.515 m	2.5 m
Ground clearance	0.343 m	0.343 m
Max speed	41.9 km/h	32.9 km/h
Fording	1.524 m	n/a

Model	72-31M	72-31F
Engine	Detroit Diesel 2-cycle Model 4-71N developing 140 hp at 2300 rpm	Detroit Diesel Model 4-53N 2-cycle diesel developing 129 hp at 2800 rpm
Transmission	Allison Power-shift CRT 3331-1 with 3 forward and reverse gears	Allison Twin Turbine Power-shift Model TRT2220-1 with 4 forward and reverse gears
Brakes	air over hydraulic	air over hydraulic
Tyres	20.5 × 25 16PR	17.5 × 25 12PR
Electrical system	24 V	24 V

TEREX 72-31MP2U/R industrial wheeled tractor as used by US Marine Corps

TEREX 72-31F rough terrain fork-lift truck as used by US Air Force

Manufacturer

TEREX Corporation, 5405 Darrow Road, Hudson, Ohio 44236, USA.

All TEREX production is now concentrated at their facility in Scotland.

Military Fork-lift Trucks

Listed below is a *résumé* of the main types of rough terrain fork-lift truck in production in the USA or in service with the armed forces. In most cases both diesel- and petrol-engined versions are in use.

Truck, fork-lift, 2722 kg capacity:
Anthony MLT 6 (MHE-200)
Athey ARTFT-6 (MHE-222)
Chrysler MLT-6CH (MHE-202)
Baker RJF-060-M02 (MHE-164)

Truck, fork-lift, 4536 kg capacity:
Pettibone-Mulliken RTL-10 (MHE-199)
RTL-10-1 (MHE-215)
Clark MR-100 (MHE-165, MHE-173)
MR-100B (MHE-179)

Truck, fork-lift, 1360 kg capacity:
Clark ART-30
IHC Model M10A (MHE 236)
Case Model M4K (MHE 237)

The Clark CR40B rough terrain fork-lift is also in US Army service.

Australian Army Clark 35 AWS (all-wheel steer) fork-lift truck (P Handel)

Variable Reach Rough Terrain Fork-Lift Truck (VRRTFLT)

Development/Description

The US Army has a requirement for a materials handling system that will enable large and heavy ammunition pallets (including MLRS rocket packs) and other large loads to be unpacked from 20 ft (6.096 m) MILVAN containers. To meet this a twin-phase acquisition strategy to replace current rough terrain vertical mast fork-lift trucks was formed. It was decided to procure a Variable Reach Rough Terrain Fork-Lift Truck (VRRTFLT) with a capacity to lift 6000 lb (2722 kg) using a 'shooting boom', which does not require the use of special ramps for loading or unloading open or enclosed trucks. The VRRTFLT is used by US Army conventional ammunition companies and quartermaster, transport and other units.

Phase 1 of the programme covered the period from October 1985 to April 1986 and involved the request for proposals (RFP) and the award of three contracts to produce and deliver four prototypes for competitive tests at Aberdeen Proving Grounds, Maryland.

In 1988 it was announced that the production contract for the VRRTFLT had been awarded to TRAK International of Port Washington, Wisconsin, for their Sky Trak 6000M. Testing was completed in 1989 and the first production units were delivered in 1990; over 300 units were used during Operation Desert Storm. The US Army has selected the VRRTFLT configuration for all future rough terrain materials handling logistic support equipment and the US Marine Corps and US Air Force have also selected the VRRTFLT.

Sky Trak 6000M Variable Reach Rough Terrain Fork-Lift Truck (VRRTFLT)

The VRRTFLT has a one-man enclosed cab. There is a full-time planetary four-wheel drive with dry disc brakes and the front axle is equipped with a 'No-Spin' differential and parking brake. The hydraulically actuated forks are located at the articulating end of a telescopic three-stage welded box-section boom constructed from high strength alloy steel. The maximum reach from the front tyres to the 609 mm load centre is 7.35 m and maximum lift capacity is 4536 kg. Maximum lift height is 10.2 m.

Specifications
Cab seating: 1
Configuration: 4 × 4
Weight: (operating with driver and max fuel) 12 338 kg
Max lift capacity: 4536 kg
Length: (with forks) 7.93 m
Width: 2.59 m
Height: 2.57 m
Ground clearance: (axle) 0.356 m
Track: 2.06 m
Wheelbase: 3.15 m
Speed: 37 km/h

Fuel capacity: 166.6 l
Engine: Cummins 6BT 5.9 l diesel developing 152 hp at 2500 rpm
Transmission: power-shift with 3 forward and reverse speeds
Turning radius: 4.67 m

Max lift capacity: 4536 kg
Max lift height: 10.2 m
Max lift below grade: 0.635 m
Max reach:
   (from front tyres to 609 mm load centre) 7.35 m

(at max height to 609 mm load centre) 4.19 m
Frame tilt: (left or right) 9°

Status
In production for US Army and Air Force.

Manufacturer
TRAK International Inc, 369 W. Western Avenue, Port Washington, Wisconsin 53074, USA.
Tel: (414) 284 5571. Fax: (414) 284 4955.

High Mobility Materiel Handler (HMMH)

Description

The High Mobility Materiel Handler (HMMH) is a development of the Small Emplacement Excavator (SEE – see entry in *Field fortifications and related emplacements equipment* section) and was trialled by the US Army's 9th Infantry Division to test potential equipment for the Rapid Deployment Joint Task Force. The modified U 900 chassis used for the SEE was used as the basis for the HMMH and in June 1982 two units were fitted with front-mounted 1814 kg capacity fork-lifts and 3946 kg capacity cranes on the rear. In mid-1983 a further seven HMMHs were delivered under a lease contract and underwent tests under field conditions.

The front-mounted fork-lift has a maximum lift height of 2.96 m. When the fork-lift is in use the front suspension is mechanically locked. Telescopic stabilisers are used when the rear-mounted hydraulic folding crane is in use. The vehicle retains its normal towing hook.

Data for the HMMH are provided in the Specifications table but data for the standard attachments are as follows.

Fork-lift
Lifting capacity: 1814 kg
Lifting height: 2.69 m
Tilt angle: 18° total
Fork rotation: 15°/15°

Crane
Max lifting capacity: 3846 kg
Max reach: 5.84 m
Lifting height: 8.08 m (max)
Outrigger span: 4.22 m

Specifications
Cab seating: 1 + 1
Configuration: 4 × 4
Max weight: 7190 kg
Length: 5.36 m
Width: 2.39 m
Height: 2.46 m
Ground clearance: 0.43 m

High Mobility Materiel Handler (HMMH)

Track: 1.63 m
Wheelbase: 2.38 m
Angle of approach/departure: 30°/36°
Max speed: (road) 80 km/h
Fuel capacity: 114 l
Max gradient: 60%
Side slope: 30%
Fording: 0.76 m
Engine: OM 352 4-stroke direct injection diesel developing 110 hp at 2800 rpm
Transmission: fully synchromesh, 16 forward and 8 reverse gears
Clutch: single dry plate
Steering: hydraulic power-assisted
Turning circle: 10.9 m
Suspension:
   (front) coil springs, telescopic shock absorbers and

stabiliser; front hydraulic suspension lock-out for use with front-mounted lift
   (rear) coil springs with helper springs, telescopic shock absorbers and stabiliser
Tyres: 12.5 × 20 12PR MPT
Brakes: hydraulic, dual circuit disc
Electrical system: 24 V with blackout drive
Batteries: 2 × 12 V, 100 Ah

Status
In service with US Army (120).

Manufacturer
Freightliner Corporation, 4747 North Channel Avenue, PO Box 3849, Portland, Oregon 97208-3849, USA.
Tel: (503) 735 8000.

Rough Terrain Container Straddle Truck (RTCST)

Description

The Standard Manufacturing Company Inc was awarded a contract by the US Army's Belvoir Research, Development and Engineering Center to develop a Rough Terrain Container Straddle Truck (RTCST). The vehicle acts as a transporter for standard 20 ft/6.096 m ISO containers and uses the Standard Trailing Arm Drive (TAD) suspension.

The main use of the vehicle is for carrying ISO containers weighing as much as 22 680 kg from landing craft, through surf and over beaches. The vehicle can stack two 20 ft ISO containers and when not being used as an ISO container transport it can be reduced in width to 2.59 m for road transport by using a telescoping frame. Hydrostatic drive is transmitted to each of the eight wheels, and the hydrostatic drive can also be used to make the vehicle counter-rotate for pivot steering in tight locations. A central tyre inflation system is used on all wheels.

Specifications
Cab seating: 1
Configuration: 8 × 8
Weight:
   (empty) 41 414 kg
   (GVW) 64 094 kg
Max load: 22 680 kg
Length: 9.906 m
Width: 2.69 to 3.96 m
Height: (top of cab) 3.988 m
Max speed: 40.2 km/h

Fuel capacity: 545 l
Engine: Detroit Diesel 8V-92 turbocharged diesel developing 736 hp
Transmission: hydrostatic
Steering: pivot, automotive type control
Suspension: 8-wheel independent Trailing Arm Drive
Tyres: 16.00 R 25 XS
Brakes: hydrostatic plus power disc

Status
Prototype.

Manufacturer
Standard Manufacturing Company Inc, 4012 W Illinois Avenue, PO Box 210300, Dallas, Texas 75211-0300, USA.
Tel: (214) 337 8911. Telex: 73326.

Rough Terrain Container Straddle Truck (RTCST)

Caterpillar 988 50 000 lb (22 680 kg) Rough Terrain Container Handler

Description
The Rough Terrain Container Handler (RTCH) is a Military Adapted Commercial Item (MACI), consisting of an AH-60 lift mast and carriage mounted on the basic chassis of the Caterpillar 988B Wheeled Loader. It was designed to lift, carry and load containers 20 ft/6.096 m, 35 ft/10.67 m and 40 ft/12.19 m long, up to 9 ft/2.74 m high and up to 50 000 lb/22 680 kg in weight, and can stack them two high or place them on railway wagons or flat bed trucks. The RTCH is equipped with carriage side-shift as well as mast tilt to allow easy positioning of the container, and lifting pins are locked in place when the container is being lifted.

Because the RTCH may have to operate at beach heads, it is capable of wading in sea water up to 1.52 m deep. Special radial tyres provide flotation on sand and traction in mud and the rear axle oscillates to maintain ground contact on all types of terrain.

In competition with three other major manufacturers, Caterpillar was awarded an $89 million contract from the US Army Mobility Equipment Research and Development Command (MERADCOM, now the Belvoir Research, Development and Engineering Center at Fort Belvoir) in September 1978 for the production of 344 units; this contract has been completed. A further contract was awarded by the US Marine Corps at the end of July 1986. This was for 42 units with a contract value of approximately $9.5 million.

RTCH stacking composite container made from two standard US Army 20 ft MILVANs

Specifications
Cab seating: 1
Weight: 46 866 kg
Length: 10.731 m
Width: (over tyres) 3.505 m
Height: (top of cab) 4.115 m
Ground clearance: 0.406 m
Fuel capacity: 624.5 l
Fuel consumption: 23 l/h
Engine: Caterpillar 3408 developing 393 hp at 2100 rpm

Tyres: 35/65-R33
Brakes: hydraulic

Status
In service with the US Marine Corps and US Army (344).

Manufacturer
Caterpillar Inc, Defense Products Department, Peoria, Illinois 61629, USA.
Tel: (309) 675 6938. Telex: 404435.

Truck, Tractor, Yard Type, 4 × 2, M878 and M878A1

Description
The original M878 was a commercially available vehicle primarily used to shuttle semi-trailers within permanent port installations or rail transfer areas. In 1976 28 were ordered for the US Army and an additional 16 in 1977. In 1981 175 examples of a revised model, the M878A1, were procured, bringing the number of Yard Tractors in service up to 219. The M878A1 differs from the original version by having a turbocharged 6V-53T Detroit Diesel engine in place of the original model 6V-53.

The M878 and M878A1 tractors are highly manoeuvrable vehicles with an automatic locking, hydraulic-lift fifth wheel which facilitates semi-trailer coupling and disengagement and allows movement of the semi-trailer or chassis without the need to retract landing legs.

Truck, Tractor, Yard Type, 4 × 2, M878

Specifications (M878A1)
Cab seating: 1
Configuration: 4 × 2
Weight: 7384 kg
Length: 4.64 m

Width: 2.49 m
Height: 2.89 m
Wheelbase: 2.94 m
5th wheel height: 1.21 to 1.63 m
Engine: Detroit Diesel turbocharged 6V-53T

Status
Production complete. In service with the US Army.

Manufacturer
Ottawa Truck Division, Gulf and Western.

Case MC2500 30-ton Rough Terrain Crane

Description
The MC2500 crane was produced by the J I Case Company. The hydraulic winching equipment includes a main and auxiliary winch, and the crane can be used for pile driving and clamshell operations as well as lifting duties. The boom can be lowered below the horizontal to assist in changing attachments. It is mounted on a 4 × 4 carrier which is driven from the crane operator's cab, and steering of both axles is hydraulic with two-wheel, four-wheel or crab steering possible. Four hydraulic outriggers are provided to stabilise the crane when operating.

Specifications
Weight: 32 790 kg
Length: (travelling) 13.29 m
Width:
 (travelling) 2.92 m
 (over outriggers) 5.39 m
Height: (travelling) 3.86 m
Wheelbase: 3.68 m

Crane
Max capacity: 27 200 kg at 3.05 m radius at 10 m boom extension
Boom length: 10 m, 3-section power extension to 24.3 m
Traverse: 360°

Carrier
Engine: Detroit Diesel 6V-53N, with full power-shift transmission giving 6 forward and 6 reverse speeds
Tyres: 26.5 × 25, 20-ply rating
Max speed: (road) 38.6 km/h
Fording depth: 1.52 m
Ground clearance: 0.55 m

Status
Production complete. 210 in service with the US Marine Corps for use in construction, container handling, bridging and recovery of aircraft.

Manufacturer
J I Case Company, Government Marketing, 700 State Street, Racine, Wisconsin 53404, USA.

Case MC2500 crane lifting US Army MILVAN container

Crane, Truck-mounted, Hydraulic, 25-ton (CCE) (Grove TMS 300-5)

Description
The Grove TMS 300-5 25-ton crane is a commercial truck-mounted crane. It consists of a hydraulically operated telescopic crane with a full 360° traverse mounted on an eight-wheeled carrier. The operator controls the crane from an electric control panel in the superstructure cab. Four outriggers are used to stabilise the crane in operation. The crane is used by engineer units in the construction and repair of roads, airfields, pipelines and bridges, and can also be used for port, marine and beach facilities. In addition to lifting, it can also be used for pile-driving and clamshell operations.

Specifications
Weight: 28 250 kg
Length: (travelling) 12.8 m
Width: (travelling) 2.44 m

Crane
Boom length: 2-section hydraulically extended boom with third lattice section, giving total length of 24.4 m
Counterweight: 4310 kg
Capacity: (max) 25 400 kg

Carrier
Configuration: 8 × 4, front 2 axles steering
Engine: GM 6-71N diesel, developing 203 hp (net) at 2100 rpm
Transmission: Fuller Roadranger RTO 613, providing 13 forward and 3 reverse gears

Tyres:
 (front) 11.00 × 14-ply
 (rear) 11.00 × 12-ply

Status
Production complete. 133 in service with the US Army.

Manufacturer
Grove Worldwide, Box 21, Shady Grove, Pennsylvania 17256, USA.
Tel: (717) 597 8121. Telex: 1842308.
Fax: (717) 597 4062.

Harnischfeger MT-250 25-ton truck-mounted hydraulic crane (US Army)

Model M315T 15-ton capacity truck-mounted crane (US Marine Corps)

Grove Mobile Hydraulic Cranes

Description
Grove Worldwide produces a wide range of mobile hydraulic cranes for military and commercial purposes. Most of the military models are basically commercial ones converted for military use. Five main types of hydraulic crane are produced:

1. Truck-mounted cranes from 30 to 140 tons
2. Rough terrain cranes from 20 to 85 tons
3. All-purpose warehouse cranes from 18 to 15.9 tons
4. All-terrain cranes from 20 to 125 tons
5. Hydraulic lattice boom cranes of 134 tons capacity

Grove Worldwide also produces a wide range of aerial work platforms, both scissors and boom type, up to a working height of 35.35 m.

Groves TMS760 60-ton truck crane used by the US Navy

Status

In production and service with the US defence forces and with other armed forces.

Manufacturer

Grove Worldwide, Box 21, Shady Grove, Pennsylvania 17256, USA.

Tel: (717) 597 8121. Telex: 1842308.
Fax: (717) 597 4062.

Grove RT875CC rough terrain container crane, 269 of which were ordered for the US Army with deliveries from 1988 to 1990

Rough Terrain Crane (4 × 4) 5-ton Hanson H-446A

Description

This rough terrain crane was developed to meet the requirements of the US Army by the Hanson Company of Tiffin, Ohio. The telescopic jib has a maximum reach of 7.62 m and can be rotated through a full 360°. A folding stabiliser leg is provided at each corner of the vehicle and most models have a bulldozer blade mounted at the front of the hull. The fully enclosed cab is at the front of the vehicle with the engine at the rear. Gross vehicle weight is 16 647 kg.

Status

In service with the US Army.

Manufacturer

Hanson Machinery Company, Tiffin, Ohio, USA.

Hanson rough terrain crane (4 × 4) 5-ton (Larry Provo)

US Dual Role Cargo Pallet

Description

A cargo pallet designed to fit the US Army's Ribbon Bridge transporter for a dual role as a general cargo carrier was developed by the US Army Mobility Equipment Research and Development Command (MERADCOM) (now the Belvoir Research, Development and Engineering Center at Fort Belvoir).

An M812 5-ton (6 × 6) transporter equipped with a hydraulic boom is used to carry, launch and retrieve complete bays of the Ribbon Bridge. When not performing its bridging mission it can launch and retrieve the specially designed 5.791 × 3.048 m pallet loaded with up to 5 tons (US) of equipment or supplies to double as a cargo hauler.

The second capability to self-load, transport and off-load cargo was added late in the Ribbon Bridge

Cargo pallet in use with Ribbon Bridge transporter showing units being winched back onto truck (US Army)

transporter development when cutbacks in military vehicles made maximum utilisation imperative. R & D pallets were procured, tested and type classified in only eight months. An initial production quantity of 120 pallets was delivered to the US Army in 1977.

Status

In service with the US Army.

FMC Universal Self-Deployable Cargo Handler (USDCH)

Description

The FMC Corporation's Advanced Systems Center developed the Universal Self-Deployable Cargo Handler (USDCH) under contract with the US Army's Belvoir Research, Development and Engineering Center. The programme is sponsored by the US Army Quartermaster School. A prototype vehicle was delivered in July 1989 for testing and evaluation.

The USDCH addresses the US Army's near- and long-term requirements for a rough terrain cargo handler. The vehicle can maintain a road speed of more than 80 km/h to maintain convoy station without additional transport resources. The system has three quick-change attachments for variable load ratings. Advances in man/machine interface and control allow for single-soldier operation.

A FMC-designed USDCH electronics suite allows the operator to safely and efficiently perform material handling functions as the microprocessor hardware and software precisely controls the hydraulic actuators, displays sensor information and monitors system conditions. Steering modes include two-wheel, four-wheel round and four-wheel crab. The system is designed for transport by C-130 transport aircraft.

The USDCH design allows for future enhancements such as remote operation and automatic load engagement.

The USDCH serves as the proof of principle for the All-Terrain Lifter Articulated System (ATLAS).

Specifications

Weight: 14 016 kg
Rated capacity load: 4536 kg
Length overall: 6.91 m
Width: 2.57 m
Height: 2.57 m
Wheelbase: 3.05 m

FMC Universal Self-Deployable Cargo Handler (USDCH)

Max speed: 85 km/h plus
Engine: Detroit Diesel 8.2T turbocharged diesel
Transmission: Funk Series 2000 'Shift-O-Matic' full power-shift 6-speed automatic
Steering: hydraulic with electrohydraulic backup
Max reach: 7.16 m to load centre (1814 kg load)
Lift height: 9.45 m
Frame tilt: 7° each side

Status
Prototype.

Manufacturer
FMC Corporation, Naval Systems Division, 4800 East River Road, PO Box 59043, Minneapolis, Minnesota 55459-0043, USA.
Telex: 290432.

MISCELLANEOUS EQUIPMENT

Field fortifications and related
    emplacements equipment
Bulk fuel storage
    and distribution systems
Water supplies
Camouflage equipment and decoys
Portable roadways
Rapid runway repair equipment/
    portable runways
Shelters and containers
Vehicle bodies
Other equipment

FIELD FORTIFICATIONS AND RELATED EMPLACEMENTS EQUIPMENT

AUSTRIA

PEKAM Modular Shelters

Description

PEKAM Kunststoffentwicklung GmbH produces special resins and heavy duty plastics and devised a modular shelter system using resin-based panel modules that can be assembled into a variety of forms to act as underground shelters. The modules are assembled on the surface into a number of configurations to suit local conditions and then buried. The materials used for the modules can be produced in a variety of strengths and thicknesses and with varying protection factors to the extent that detonating the equivalent of a 155 mm high explosive artillery shell 1.5 m away results in no damage to the shelter.

The use of the resin-based material makes the shelter modules easy to store, carry and assemble. Shelters as small as one- or two-man structures can be assembled by two men but larger shelters can also be produced. Each module weighs approximately 20 kg and a two-man shelter made up from 11 module elements weighs approximately 200 kg. After use they can be dug up, disassembled and re-used. The modules are proof against corrosion and no special tools are required for assembly.

The standard version is constructed from self-extinguishing synthetic materials. A special version uses non-combustible synthetic materials. For extra protection carbon fibre reinforcement can be used.

One development of the basic module is a two-man modular shelter with an integrated fire bay to carry equipment, weapons and ammunition, and with overhead protection that can be opened and closed at will. Two versions of this shelter, with or without an enlarged area at the base, are available.

Also produced is a 6-man group shelter that can be

PEKAM 6-man modular group shelter in assembled form

extended to produce a 9- or 12-man (or much larger) shelter. Also available is an igloo-type underground shelter with a roof 1.83 m in diameter and with a floor diameter of 4.15 m.

A further design for the Austrian Army is a 12- to 18-man structure which may be erected as a single structure or in combinations of two or more units around a gun position or similar structure. The cross-section may be square or arched.

Status
In production.

Manufacturer
PEKAM Kunststoffentwicklung GmbH and Co KG, A-5411 Oberalm 735, Austria.
Tel: 062 45 2308. Fax: 062 46 203475.

CHINA, PEOPLE'S REPUBLIC

NORINCO Trench Digger

Description
The NORINCO trench digger is based on the chassis and hull of the Type 83 152 mm self-propelled gun-howitzer (for details refer to *Jane's Armour and Artillery 1992-93* pages 544 and 545). The vehicle carries a circular trench digging machine similar in appearance to that used on the CIS MDK-2 series of trench digging machines. This digging machine is electrohydraulically lifted upwards and over the hull rear for transport and lowered to behind the vehicle for digging. The top of the hull carries an armoured enclosed cab and a straight dozer blade is carried on the front of the hull.

Power for the digging operation is taken by a multi-purpose gear system from the vehicle main engine, which is mounted in the forward part of the hull together with the transmission. Mechanical and hydraulic safety devices are incorporated.

The superstructure cab is air-conditioned and the driver is provided with an infra-red night vision device and an adjustable shock absorber seat. No armament appears to be carried other than the crew's personal weapons.

The digging machine can remove up to 300 m³/h of soft soil and up to 150 m³/h of harder ground. The maximum digging depth for each digging cup is 0.45 m and the maximum digging depth 3.5 m.

Specifications
Crew: 3
Weight: (combat) 30 000 kg

NORINCO trench digger

Length:
  (travelling) 8.074 m
  (operating) 10 m
Width: 3.6 m
Height:
  (top of digging equipment) 4.195 m
  (cab roof) 2.96 m
Ground clearance: 0.45 m
Track: 2.62 m
Track width: 480 mm
Length of track on ground: 4.601 m
Max speed: (road) 52 km/h
Gradient: 20°

Side slope: 10°
Engine: Type 12150L diesel developing 520 hp

Status
In service with the Chinese Army.

Manufacturer
China North Industries Corporation (NORINCO), 7A Yue Tan Nan Jie, PO Box 2137 Beijing, Beijing, People's Republic of China.
Tel: 867570. Telex: 22339 CNIN CN.
Fax: 867840 Beijing.

Type 82 Tracked Military Bulldozer

Description
Designed from the outset for combat engineer use the Type 82 tracked military bulldozer has a four-man cab. It is fitted with a dozer blade that can be angled about a central point from the concave to convex. The blade is raised and lowered about a point between the second and third road wheels on each side and is actuated vertically by a large hydraulic cylinder in front of the cab. The blade can be removed if required.

The cab is provided with a roof hatch equipped with a mounting for a 12.7 mm anti-aircraft machine gun. The cab is equipped with two infra-red vision systems: one for the driver with a 30° field-of-view; and another for the commander, a Type 85 device with a 76° horizontal field-of-vision and a 20° vertical field-of-view. A roof periscope is also provided.

The area behind the cab and over the engine and transmission covers is used as a general supplies or equipment-carrying area and is provided with steel drop sides. There is no tailgate other than a load restraint frame.

The Type 82 can travel at a maximum speed of 47.4 km/h to enable it to maintain station in convoys – average convoy speed is 32 km/h. When operating, the minimum bulldozing speed is 2.4 km/h and when operating within a distance of 30 m the earthmoving capacity is 262 m³/h. At an operating distance of 50 m this is reduced to 232 m³/h. The Type 82 can operate for periods of between 20 and 25 hours. Maximum push is 16 tonnes.

Specifications
Crew: 4
Weight: (combat) 20 500 kg
Length:
  (with blade) 7.17 m
  (without blade) 5.81 m
Width:
  (operating) 4.33 m
  (travelling) 3.36 m
  (without blade) 2.92 m
Height:
  (to AA MG) 3.21 m
  (top of cab) 2.76 m
Ground clearance: 0.45 m
Track: 2.49 m
Length of track on ground: 3.385 m
Ground pressure: 0.7 kg/cm²
Max speed:
  (road) 47.4 km/h
  (cruising) 32 km/h
  (reverse) 21.5 km/h
Range:
  (road) 400-450 km
  (cross-country) 350-400 km
Fording: 1.3 m
Gradient: 30°
Vertical obstacle: 0.7 m
Trench: 2.6 m
Engine: Type 12150 L-3 diesel developing 430 hp
Batteries: 4 × Type 65
Armament: 1 × 12.7 mm MG
Ammunition: 200 rounds

Dozer blade
Width: 4.33 to 4.4 m
Height: 1.1 m
Lift height: 1 m
Depth of cut: 370 mm

Status
In production. In service with the Chinese armed forces and offered for export.

Manufacturer
China North Industries Corporation (NORINCO), 7A Yue Tan Nan Jie, PO Box 2137 Beijing, Beijing, People's Republic of China.
Tel: 867570. Telex: 22339 CNIN CN.
Fax: 867840 Beijing.

Type 82 tracked military bulldozer

COMMONWEALTH OF INDEPENDENT STATES

BTM Series of High-speed Ditching Machines

Description
The BTM trenching machine consists of the ETR-409 ditching machine mounted on the rear of the AT-T heavy tracked artillery tractor. The equipment can dig a trench 0.8 m wide to a maximum depth of 1.5 m at the rate of 1120 m/h. The BTM-TMG is a variant of the basic BTM and was designed to dig trenches in frozen ground and can dig a trench 0.6 m wide at 100 m/h in frozen soil. The most recent model is the BTM-3, weighing 27 300 kg, and there is also a BTM-TMG2S model, which has a larger ditching machine.

Specifications

Model	BTM	BTM-TMG	BTM-TMG2S
Crew	2	2	2
Weight	26 500 kg	30 000 kg	32 000 kg
Length			
(travelling)	7.35 m	7.6 m	11.5 m
(operating)	10.85 m	—	11.5 m
Width	3.2 m	3.2 m	4.6 m
Height			
(travelling)	4.3 m	4.3 m	4.6 m
(operating)	3.5 m	—	3.2 m
Speed	35 km/h	36 km/h	36 km/h
Cruising range	500 km	400 km	400 km
Fuel capacity	810 l	—	—

Model	BTM	BTM-TMG	BTM-TMG2S
Trench crossing ability	2.1 m	2.1 m	2.1 m
Max vertical obstacle	1 m	1 m	1 m
Gradient	36°	36°	36°
Side slope	17°	17°	17°
Fording depth	0.75 m	0.75 m	0.75 m
Working capacity (0.8 m trench)	1120 m/h	1120 m/h (summer)	—
Depth of trench	1.5 m	—	3 m
Width of trench			
(top)	1.1 m	0.6 m	1.1 m
(bottom)	0.6 m	0.6 m	—
Height of parapet	0.4 m	—	—

BTM digging machine with digger stowed (D C Spaulding)

Rear view of BTM ditching machine showing soil being deposited on each side of completed trench

Note: automotive details are as for the basic AT-T tractor in the *Tracked prime movers, cargo carriers and armoured logistic vehicles* section.

Status
In service with members of the former Warsaw Pact and some Middle Eastern and North African countries.

Manufacturer
State factories.

MDK-2 Series of Trench Digging Machines MDK-2, MDK-2M

Description
The MDK-2 trench digging machine *(maschina dorozhnoy kopatelnoy)* is based on the chassis of the AT-T heavy tracked artillery tractor. The circular digging machine is carried horizontally on the rear of the chassis and is swung 90° into the vertical for ditching operations. The MDK-2 is used for digging weapon trenches and pits for vehicles, guns and other equipment. Depending on the soil conditions, the MDK-2 can dig a maximum of 300 m³/h. The dug ditch has a maximum depth of 4.5 m and is 3.5 m wide at the bottom and 4 m wide at the top. An OTT hydraulically operated dozer blade is mounted at the front of the vehicle. There is also a more recent MDK-2M model.

Specifications
(Data in square brackets relate to MDK-2M where different from MDK-2)
Crew: 2
Weight: 27 000 [28 000] kg
Length:
　(travelling) 8 m
　(operating) 10.23 m
Width:
　(travelling) 4 [3.4] m
　(operating) [4.05] m
Height:
　(travelling) 3.95 m
　(operating) 3.48 m

MDK-2 trench digging machine

Speed: 35 km/h
Max vertical obstacle: 1 [0.65] m
Max gradient: 36°
Side slope: 10°
Working speed: (class 1 and 2 soil) 300 [387] m³/h
Depth of ditch: 4.5 m
Width of ditch:
　(top) 4 m
　(bottom) 3.5 m

Status
In service with members of the former Warsaw Pact and some countries in North Africa and the Middle East. The MDK-2M was known to be in service with the former East German Army.

Manufacturer
State factories.

MDK-3 Trench Digging Machine

Description
The MDK-3 trench digging machine *(maschina dorozhnoy kopatelnoy)* is intended to be the replacement for the MDK-2 and MDK-2M (see previous entry) and is based on the chassis of the MT-T tracked carrier (see entry in the *Tracked prime movers, cargo carriers and armoured logistic vehicles* section).

The MDK-3 chassis, known as the Kharkov engineer chassis, uses suspension elements from the T-64 tank and is powered by the V-64-4 V-12 diesel engine. The cab is armoured, is fitted with a radio and may be fitted with an NBC protection system. At the front of the vehicle is a hydraulically operated dozer blade which can be tilted. Mounted at the rear of the vehicle is a six-bladed digging wheel capable of excavating a trench just under 3 m in depth in a single pass. Hydraulic rams allow the digging wheel to be positioned for excavating; when travelling the digging wheel is positioned horizontally over the chassis rear. When digging the vehicle is driven slowly backwards and spoil is pushed out to one side to form a loose berm alongside the ditch. Digging blades on the wheel are bolted into position and can be changed.

Specifications (provisional)
Crew: 2
Weight: 40 000 kg

MDK-3 trench digging machine (Jane's Intelligence Review)

Length:
　(digger raised) 10 m
　(digger lowered to ground level) 12 m
Width:
　(over hull) 3.2 m
　(over digger) 3.5 m
Height: (digger raised or lowered) 4 m
Max speed: 50 km/h
Range: approx 500 km
Engine: V-64-4 V-12 water-cooled diesel developing 737 hp

Trench digging speed: 200 m/h
Trench width: 3.5 m
Trench depth: 2.9 m

Status
In production. In service with the CIS.

Manufacturer
State factories.

TMK-2 Trench Digging Machine

Description
The TMK-2 trench digging machine is based on the chassis of the MAZ-538 wheeled tractor (using a longer wheelbase) and shares many components with the PKT road-building machine. It has a crew of two: a driver and a digger assembly operator. Both are seated in a cab equipped with radiation warning and navigation equipment plus an air filtration system. External equipment stowage space is provided on the cab roof.

As well as its trench digging function the TMK-2 can be used to clear bushes and scrub, scrape topsoil from contaminated areas and cut approaches and exits for water crossings using a hydraulically operated dozer blade at the front. The main trench digging assembly is located to the rear of the vehicle and consists of a circular cutter that is raised and lowered hydraulically. The assembly has no digging shovels but relies upon cutting teeth that produce a specific pressure on their cutting edges. Excavated earth is lifted upwards and adheres to the wheel assembly by friction before being discharged to both sides once clear of the trench. The fastest trench digging speed possible in soft soil is 1.3 km/h, controlled by a hand wheel in the cab. Maximum digging depth is 1.5 m and the width of the trench can vary from 0.6 to 1.1 m.

The engine has a pre-heating facility to enable it to start at temperatures below −15°C.

Specifications
Crew: 2
Weight: 27 200 kg
Length: 9.75 m
Width: 3.15 m
Height: 4.18 m
Road speed: between 30 and 60 km/h
Operating endurance with full tank: 21 h
Engine: D 12 A 375 A 12-cylinder diesel developing 362 hp
Transmission: hydraulic with 3 forward and 1 reverse gears
Electrical system: 24 V
Batteries: 4 × 24 V, 280 Ah

Status
In service with the CIS and former East German Armies.

Manufacturer
State factories.

TMK-2 trench digging machine in travelling configuration

PZM and PZM-2 Regimental Trench Digging Machines

Description
The PZM regimental trench digging machine is built on the basis of the T-150K wheeled tractor. The more recent PZM-2 is based on the T-155 tractor. The PZM-2 has a roller chain with digging buckets driven mechanically from the main tractor engine. A front-mounted winch is used to propel the machine when digging as the transmission must be disconnected when the excavator is in use. The winch is driven hydromechanically and exerts a 5000 kg pull at a rate of 60 m/h. The digger is raised and lowered by hand.

Status
Both the PZM and the PZM-2 are in service with the CIS.

Manufacturer
State factories.

PZM-2 regimental trench digging machine in travelling order

High Speed Tractor-mounted Bulldozers BAT-1, BAT-M, OLT, OST, OTT

Description
Most of the CIS full-tracked artillery tractors described in the *Tracked prime movers, cargo carriers and armoured logistic vehicles* section can be fitted with bulldozer blades. One vehicle, the BAT, has been specially modified as a bulldozer.

The BAT tractor dozer consists of the AT-T heavy tractor with a large dozer blade mounted at the front of the hull. It is designed for hasty building of roads and approaches to bridges and crossing sites, and for filling in ditches and similar obstacles. It can also fell trees, root out stumps and boulders and dig emplacements. The basic demolition blade can be fitted with attachments to form a V-blade, bulldozer and angledozer, and is provided with routers and a float.

The more recent BAT-M is an improved model and is electrohydraulically operated, whereas the BAT (also known as the BAT-1) is electropneumatically operated. The BAT-M also has a hydraulic crane, and the dozer

BAT-M tractor dozer, showing hydraulic crane

OST dozer on AT-S tractor

Polish hydraulically operated dozer (not OST) on ATS-59 tractor

BAT tractor dozer

Specifications

Model	BAT (BAT-1)	BAT-M	OLT	OST	OTT
Tractor	(integral)	(integral)	AT-L, AT-LM	AT-S*, ATS-59	AT-T
Weight (with blade)	25 300 kg	27 500 kg	7000 kg	13 392 kg	22 000 kg
Length (with blade)	10 m	7 m (travelling)	n/a	n/a	n/a
Width (with blade)	4.78 m	4.85 m	2.5 m	2.8 m	3.5 m
Height (travelling)	2.95 m	—	2.18 m	2.54 m	2.58 m
Max speed	35 km/h	35 km/h	42 km/h	35 km/h	35 km/h
Cruising range	700 km	550 km	300 km	380 km	700 km
Fuel consumption	140-190 l/100 km	140-190 l/100 km	140-190 l/100 km	140-190 l/100 km	140-190 l/100 km
Trench	1.58 m	2.1 m	1 m	1.45 m	2.1 m
Max vertical obstacle	1 m	1 m	0.6 m	0.6 m	1 m
Max gradient	45%	n/a	60°	53°	60°
Fording depth	0.75 m	0.75 m	0.6 m	1 m	0.75 m
Ground pressure	0.65 kg/cm^2	0.71 kg/cm^2	0.45 kg/cm^2	0.58 kg/cm^2	0.68 kg/cm^2
Working speed	1.5-10 km/h (moderate terrain)	1.5-10 km/h	4-6 km/h (moderate terrain)	4 km/h	n/a
Working capacity (depends on soil conditions)	120-140 m^3/h	max 150 m^3/h (excavation) max 200 m^3/h (dozing)	40 m^3/h	80-90 m^3/h (light soil) 40-50 m^3/h (medium soil)	100 m^3/h
Crane capacity	n/app	2000 kg	n/app	n/app	n/app
Winch capacity	n/app	25 000 kg (100 m cable)	n/app	n/app	n/app
Blade control	electropneumatic	electrohydraulic	n/a	cable operated	n/a
Blade angle	n/a	straight (5 m wide) 55° (4 m wide) 110° (4.5 m wide)	n/a	n/a	n/a
Tractive effort	n/a	16 300 kg	n/a	n/a	n/a

*   Data refer to OST dozer on AT-S tractor.

blade can be swung rearwards to improve the vehicle's load distribution when in travelling order.

The BAT tractor dozers should not be confused with the OTT dozer blade mounted on the AT-T tractor, for which data are also given here. Details of the basic tractor chassis are given in the *Tracked prime movers, cargo carriers and armoured logistic vehicles* section.

Status
All the tractor-mounted dozers are in service with the former Warsaw Pact nations. The BAT tractor dozer is also in service with some North African and Middle Eastern countries.

Manufacturers
State factories.

CZECHOSLOVAKIA

DOK Wheeled Engineer Tractor

Description
The DOK (dozer on wheels) is a wheeled engineer tractor designed specifically for military applications. The DOK has an articulated chassis and a rear-mounted diesel engine; drive is electric. An electrically driven winch is located at the rear of the cab. In addition to the normal multi-purpose bucket, a snow plough attachment is also available. The cab is hermetically sealed and has a filtered ventilation system which enables the vehicle to operate in an NBC environment.

There are three variants of the DOK: the DOK-L, DOK-M and DOK-R. The DOK-L has a universal shovel and the DOK-M, a modified DOK-L, has the universal shovel with the addition of a sawtooth edge and a central ridge. The DOK-M also has hydraulic steering, improved brakes and an improved hydraulic system. The DOK-R has a V-shaped blade that can be adjusted to form a straight blade for dozing.

Specifications
Cab seating: 1
Configuration: 4 × 4
Weight: 28 000 kg

DOK-L wheeled engineer tractor

Towed load: 65 000 kg
Length: 10.53 m
Width: 3.15 m
Height: 3.15 m
Ground clearance: 0.45 m
Track: 2.45 m
Wheelbase: 5 m
Max speed: (road) 50 km/h
Range: (cross-country) 250 km
Fuel capacity: 500 l
Engine: T-930-42 V-12 diesel developing 255 hp at 1800 rpm
Tyres: 21 × 28

Status
In service with Czechoslovak and the former East German armed forces. The DOK-M appears to have been used only by the former East German Army.

Manufacturer
Czechoslovak state factories.

DENMARK

Hydrema Multi-purpose Machines

Description
Hydrema multi-purpose machines can be used for combat engineering and logistics tasks, combining the attributes of a 1.2 m^3 front-end loader, an 8-tonne hydraulic excavator and a conventional back-hoe loader. All machines in the range feature high cross-country mobility due to a patented pivot steer system with oscillation in the centre pivot providing automatic load distribution to the four large wheels. Various types of buckets, shovels and other ancillaries can be fitted, including a fork-lift in place of the front shovel. The machines are air-portable in C-130 or similar aircraft and can be carried slung under a CH-47D Chinook helicopter. A road speed of 40 km/h can be achieved with a maximum load.

The product range consists of two models: a hydraulic side-shift model offering 280° of slew with the excavator (purchased by the British Army and deployed by them in Saudi Arabia); and a fixed kingpost model offering a 200° slew with the excavator (purchased by the Danish Army). Winterised versions capable of operating in temperatures down to −40°C are available.

All models are powered by a Perkins 84 hp engine and utilise a ZF power transmission with four forward and three reverse gears. The articulated chassis all have a box-section construction with heavy duty fittings for the Hamworthy axles. Maximum road speed is 30 km/h.

A Hydrema 10-tonne articulated dump truck built on the same major components as the multi-purpose machines has been developed. It has been tested by the British Army.

Status
In production. In service with the British Army and Danish Army. Tested by the French and Canadian armed forces.

Manufacturer
A/S Hydrema, DK-9530 Stovring, Denmark.
Tel: 45 98 37 13 33. Telex: 9381805.
Fax: 45 98 37 22 11.

Hydrema 806 hydraulic side-shift multi-purpose machine ready for delivery

FRANCE

Matenin Trench Digger

Description
The Matenin trench digger was designed for the rapid excavation of trenches and defences in forward areas and can dig straight or curved trenches or one-man foxholes.

The equipment consists of a cross-country 4 × 4 chassis with a forward control cab. The trench digging equipment, mounted on the rear of the chassis, operates in the vertical position and can be swung into the horizontal position for travelling. Digging can be controlled from within the cab of the vehicle or by means of a remote-control system.

The excavator itself consists of chain-driven buckets made of moulded steel with tilting bases, mounted on a boom. A conveyor belt is provided to discharge earth to the right or the left and the boom is fitted with a scraper to clean the bottom of the trench.

The power-shift hydromechanical transmission has six ranges, allowing for road travel, cross-country, digging and winch drive.

There are two models of the Matenin trench digger: the MXD which digs a trench 0.75 m wide and up to 2 m deep, and the Model NX 7B3 which digs a trench 0.6 m wide and 1.8 m deep. Both models can dig a vertical trench on a 15% side slope and have a typical capacity of 250 m³/h.

Specifications
Cab seating: 1 + 2
Configuration: 4 × 4, with locking differentials
Weight:
   (NX7 B3) 14 500 kg
   (MXD) 15 500 kg
Length: 7.6 m
Width: 2.5 m

Matenin trench digger crossing trench

Height:
   (over cab) 2.8 m
   (travelling) 3.6 m
Ground clearance: 0.5 m
Wheelbase: 3 m
Track: 1.98 m
Angle of approach/departure: 38°/34°
Max speed: (road) 70 km/h
Max gradient: 50%
Max side slope: 15%
Fording: 1.2 m
Engine: 6-cylinder water-cooled diesel developing 225 hp at 2300 rpm
Transmission: power-shift hydromechanical, with torque converter and two 4-gear ranges

Steering: power-assisted
Tyres: 16.00 × 25, low pressure
Brakes: air
Winch: driven by hydraulic motor; 5000 kg capacity line pull
Electrical system: 24 V

Status
In production. In service with the French Army and several other armies.

Manufacturer
Etablissements Matenin, 34 avenue des Champs Elysées, F-75008 Paris, France.
Tel: (1) 45 59 22 00. Telex: 801622 f.

MFRD/F1 Mobile Drilling Machine

Description
The MFRD/F1 is a highly mobile drilling machine mounted on a Pinguely rough terrain carrier known as the RTC10. The drilling equipment can be used for a variety of field engineering purposes but the primary role is that of drilling holes into which demolition charges can be placed (MFRD – *moyen de forage rapide de destruction*). The French Army ordered 122 examples of this equipment.

The drilling machine can be used at any angle from the vertical to the horizontal at 7.5° intervals. The drill uses an auger for drilling in soft soils but in rock a bottom hammer is employed. Both have a working

diameter of 220 mm. Maximum drilling depth is 6 m. When drilling through rock the following drilling speeds can be attained:

Limestone	12 m/h
Granite	17 m/h
Schist	32 m/h

The RCT10 rough terrain carrier has a 4 × 4 configuration with a forward drive cab and seating for a driver/operator and one passenger. The drilling rig is carried on the area behind the cab with the gantry pivot overhanging the rear of the vehicle. An air compressor driven from a power take-off on the gearbox delivers 19 m³/min at 7 bars. A 6000 to 8000 kg winch can be fitted.

Specifications
Cab seating: 1 + 1
Configuration: 4 × 4
Weight:
   (total) 16 800 kg
   (front axle) 8300 kg
   (rear axle) 8500 kg
Length:
   (overall, travelling) 9.75 m
   (chassis) 7.565 m
Width: 2.49 m
Height:
   (overall) 2.384 m
   (cab) 2.68 m
Ground clearance: 0.52 m
Wheelbase: 4.1 m

Track:
(front) 1.971 m
(rear) 2.038 m
Angle of approach/departure: 42°40/35°
Fording: 1 m
Vertical obstacle: 0.5 m
Gradient: 50%
Max speed: (road) 70-75 km/h
Range: (road) 600 km
Engine: turbocharged diesel developing 260 hp at 2200 rpm
Transmission: torque converter semi-automatic hydromechanical gearbox with 3 forward and reverse gears
Suspension: double-action leaf springs and hydraulic shock absorbers
Turning radius: 11 m
Tyres: 16.00 × 25

Status
In service with the French Army (122).

Manufacturers
Carrier: HAULOTTE – c/o SOLEM SA, 32 avenue Marcel-Cachin, F-69120 Vaulx en Velin, France.
Drilling equipment: Constructions Industrielles d'Anjou, ZI Ecouflant, F-49000 Angers, France.

MFRD/F1 mobile drilling machine

Mle F1 Foxhole Charge

Description
Intended for the loosening of soil to allow the rapid manual excavation of an infantry foxhole, the Mle F1 foxhole charge consists of three explosive charges, a 50 second delay exploder and detonating fuze.

The three explosive charges are in rod form and are sealed in a plastic tube 1.06 m long and 25 mm in diameter. Three of these charges are driven vertically into the ground 0.6 m apart and connected by detonating fuze to a 50 second delay exploder. After initiating the exploder and the 50 second delay all three charges will detonate together and loosen and partially remove topsoil over a length of 1.8 m and a width of 0.6 m, and to a depth of 1.2 m (all foxhole dimensions approximate).

Each main charge weighs 0.5 kg of which 0.222 kg is explosive.

Status
In production.

Manufacturer
Société d'Armement et d'Etudes Alsetex, 4 rue Tronchet, F-75009 Paris, France.
Tel: (1) 42 65 50 16. Telex: 640961 f.
Fax: (1) 42 65 24 87.

GERMANY

Schaeff HT 11A Backacter on Unimog U84/406 (Erdarbeitsgerät)

Description
The Erdarbeitsgerät (earthwork equipment) is used by non-mechanised units of the German armed forces to enable field defences to be quickly prepared. It consists of a standard commercial backacter mounted on the rear of a Daimler-Benz Unimog cross-country vehicle, which can also be equipped with a bulldozer blade at the front. In medium soil, up to 18 two-man slit trenches (1.6 m long × 0.6 m wide × 1.2 m deep) can be dug in an hour. The backacter is operated from a 30 hp hydraulic pump driven by the vehicle engine and can be speedily disconnected and removed from the vehicle. The entire assembly can be pivoted by the two-man crew through 90° into its travelling position.

Details of the Unimog vehicle can be found in the *Trucks* section. The overall mobility of the vehicle is scarcely affected by the addition of the backacter. It can maintain a road speed of 74 km/h and can be transported in both the Transall C-160 transport aircraft and the CH-53G helicopter.

Status
377 equipments are in service with German armed forces. A similar equipment mounted on the Unimog U 900 is in production for the US Army under the designation SEE (qv).

Manufacturers
Backacter: Schaeff.
Unimog: Daimler-Benz AG, Postfach 600202, D-7000 Stuttgart 60, Federal Republic of Germany.
Tel: 0711/17-5 5186. Telex: 72524-0.
Fax: 0711 17-2244.

Unimog Erdarbeitsgerät in travelling order and in operation (Federal German Ministry of Defence)

Defendress Type S and Type T Battlefield Shelters

Description

The Defendress battlefield shelters are steel drums 1.25 m high and 1.4 m in diameter fitted with a steel floor and an armoured roof. Each shelter can accommodate two men or act as a mortar or light weapon pit. A communication tunnel 1 m in diameter and at least 2 m long can connect each shelter to others nearby. The armoured hatch can be lifted by a hydraulic pump for observation and once raised it can be turned aside for weapon firing. The hatch has a raised rim to allow soil and camouflage to be inserted. To close the hatch it is turned into the lowering position and a position lock

is released; the shelter is then secure. With soil and other top cover the armoured hatch can weigh up to 1400 kg so a manually operated hydraulic pump is provided with a maximum lift capacity of 15 tonnes. One stroke of the pump handle raises the hatch 15 mm and the maximum lift height is 250 mm.

The Defendress Type S is a welded and prefabricated steel structure with a total weight of approximately 850 kg. It is totally sealed and consists of an upright cylinder with a connection for the communication tunnel pipe and a pivoting shaft for the armoured hatch, the removable armoured hatch and the hydraulic system. The Type T shelter uses a prefabricated kit weighing 550 kg that can be assembled by two men using a simple wedge system. The heaviest component weighs 83 kg. Parts include eight steel shell

segments (one of them with a welded pivoting shaft for the hatch), a ground plate with a welded supporting skirt, a top ring, a ring with a pinion connection and support plate for the armoured hatch, the hydraulic system, joining wedges and connection elements for the communication tunnel pipe.

Status
In production.

Manufacturer
Protection and Defence Systems (PDS), Bäckerstrasse 53, D-8000 Munich 60, Federal Republic of Germany. Tel: 089 260 3841. Telex: 522072 is g. Fax: 089 260 3395.

NETHERLANDS

SPIT Prefab Foxhole Twin (PFT)

Description

The SPIT Prefab Foxhole Twin or PFT is a two-man shelter or foxhole, prefabricated from steel components and delivered complete for installation. The kit consists of two identical sections forming the walls of the foxhole and all other necessary accessories including sandbags, a weather cover, and camouflage net. The complete kit weighs 65 kg and uses steel plates with aluminium profiles.

To install the kit two men can carry it to the selected site. A hole approximately 1.9 × 0.7 × 1.3 m is dug and once the foxhole assembly has been constructed it can be placed in the hole and spoil used to in-fill the sides. If required, insulating material such as dry hay, leaves and so on can be used for the in-fill preventing condensation from forming on the interior walls. It is possible to construct the foxhole in such a manner that there are two foxholes at each end with a sheltered centre section covering a stowage area in the form of a shelf. This can then be used for stowing ammunition and provisions. Sandbags can be stowed around the periphery for increased protection. When the PFT is no longer required in one location it can be levered out of the ground using pioneer tools inserted into holes in the sides.

If required, the PFT can be constructed to stand on the ground surface and then filled with soil to provide

increased protection for tactical positions; earth banks may also be formed against the PFT. A special roof container can be used to provide overhead protection for a normal PFT and will be held in place by six struts. It is possible to arrange the struts and roof container to allow weapons to be fired through gaps between the roof and the ground.

Specifications (PFT)
Weight: (kit) approx 65 kg
Length: (assembled) 1.83 m
Width: 0.62 m
Height: 1.4 m

Roof container
Weight: (empty) approx 90 kg
Length: 2.5 m
Width: 1.23 m
Height: 0.3, 0.6 or 0.9 m
Adjustable height: 0.3 m
Max load: 4000 kg

Status
In production.

Manufacturer
Special Projects and International Trading, PO Box 300, NL-6236 ZN Maastricht, Netherlands. Tel: (31) 4402 70182. Telex: 56235 spit nl.

Complete PFT ready for use and showing centre section of roof in place

SWITZERLAND

Type 88 Field Shelter

Description
Developed for use by the Swiss infantry, the Type 88 field shelter can be assembled in the field without special tools or training. The trench for the shelter can be dug by manual or mechanical methods. The cylindrical shelters are 6 m long and have a diameter of 2.5 m. Each shelter consists of 12 2.5 mm thick corrugated steel section fixed by screws to 500 mm-wide hoops. When assembled each shelter has space for 18 seats or 12 bunks and a simple ventilation system is supplied. The shelters can also be used as command or first aid posts.

Status
In production for the Swiss Army (4500 ordered).

Manufacturer
Dr König Company, Dietikon, Switzerland.

Type 88 field shelter assembled in above ground position for demonstration purposes

UNITED KINGDOM

Hesco Bastion Concertainer Defence Wall

Description

The Hesco Bastion Concertainer Defence Wall is a rapidly built solid blast barrier wall constructed from heavy duty corrosion and rot-proof materials, supplied in a collapsed state for easy transport.

A standard NATO pallet holds five Concertainer walls, each of which, when erected and filled, is 10 m long, 1.37 m high and 1.067 m wide. As supplied the walls have no top or bottom and are constructed from heavy duty wire mesh galvanised for corrosion protection. A standard wall has nine compartments formed by panels joined together with spiral spring hinges, also in galvanised wire. The wire sides of each panel are lined with a geo-membrane approximately 0.5 mm thick. Linings are available in camouflage colours to suit arctic, desert, jungle or European environments. A bag of accessories is also supplied.

Once removed from a pallet, collapsed walls are laid horizontally on the ground. Using handles at one end two men can then pull the wall in the desired direction. As the wall is pulled it will concertina from the horizontal to the vertical and become self-supporting. The wall can then be pulled to its maximum length of 10 m for alignment and levelling. Longer walls can be produced by joining erected units together using wire from the accessory bag. Each nine-compartment wall can be shortened or split along the panel lines, before infill, into two or more smaller walls. It is possible to produce walls higher than the standard 1.37 m. Once erected a 10 m Concertainer can be filled with 35 tonnes of infill material, such as sand, mud, gravel, soil or snow, in approximately 17 minutes using a four-

Hesco Bastion Concertainer Defence Wall in use during Operation Granby

in-one mechanical digger.

The protection provided by the Concertainer has been tested using small arms, machine guns, mortars and 30 mm Rarden cannon. During operations in the Gulf during 1991 they were used extensively by the Royal Air Force for the protection of ammunition, fuel, stores and aircraft on four airfields. Concertainers can also be used for the rapid construction of defence or logistic shelters and reservoirs.

Status

In production. In service with the Royal Air Force and throughout the Middle East.

Manufacturer

Hesco Bastion Limited, Unit 37, Knowsthorpe Gate, Cross Green Industrial Estate, Leeds LS9 0NP, UK. Tel: 0532 486633. Telex: 94016703 hesi g. Fax: 0532 483501.

JCB Backhoe Loaders

Description

JCB backhoe loaders are in use worldwide for a number of military and commercial purposes as they have proved to be compact, manoeuvrable and ruggedly built. They can combine the capabilities of a loader and excavator but both the loader arms and excavator arm can be fitted with special attachments to perform the functions of a fork-lift, crane, grader, bulldozer, rock breaker, grab and other special functions.

Armoured cabs can be provided for front line operations such as digging vehicle scrapes, combat trenches, command and first aid posts. All controls can be operated from within the cab. With attachments fitted, JCB backhoe loaders can assist with other combat duties such as clearing debris, repairing roads and runways, mine clearance, bomb disposal, and vehicle recovery.

Military models have been supplied to meet air-portability requirements and some have been specially prepared for air-drops with fold-down cabs. Remote-control facilities can be fitted.

Naturally aspirated or turbocharged engines developing up to 98 hp are available to provide road speeds of up to 47 km/h.

Specifications
Backhoe
Dig depth: up to 6 m
Reach at ground level: (to rear wheel centre) up to 8 m
Bucket width: up to 1.1 m

JCB backhoe loader

Lift capacity: (excluding bucket) up to 1243 kg

Loader
Bucket capacity: up to 1.1 m³
Loadover height: up to 3.1 m
Forward reach at ground level: up to 1.5 m

Fork-lift
Fork capacity: up to 2500 kg
Lift height: up to 2.7 m
Forward reach at ground level: up to 2.7 m

Status

In production. In service with the British Army, the Royal Air Force, and the defence forces of more than 20 countries.

Manufacturer

JCB Military Products Division, Rocester, Staffordshire ST14 5JP, UK.
Tel: 0889 590312. Telex: 36372.
Fax: 0889 590588.

Case 721 Wheeled Loader

Description

In March 1992 the United Kingdom Ministry of Defence placed a £5.6 million order for 62 Model 721 wheeled loaders with J I Case Europe Limited. The 721s are

essentially standard production machines with a number of special attachments specified by the British Army.

The Case 721 has an operating weight of 13 100 kg and is powered by a Case 6T-830 turbocharged diesel driving through an electrically operated power-shift transmission and torque converter. An electronic

warning system in the cab provides warning to the driver for all important vehicle functions.

Each Case 721 wheeled loader is equipped with a quick-hitch coupler enabling the attachment of an interchangeable Boughton 2.02 m³ multi-purpose four-in-one bucket, a front loader mounted ripper and pallet fork attachments. Mounted on the rear of the chassis is a 10-tonne capacity Boughton H10000 hydraulic winch with the rope having a 50-tonne breaking strain. Other attachments include a Morganite automatic safe load indicator device on one of the loader arms, and a Stanley valve is included to allow the hydraulic system to power hand-operated tools. Some vehicles can be equipped with tyre chains.

Specifications
Seating: 1
Configuration: 4 × 4
Weight: (operating) 13 100 kg
Length: (bucket down) 6.83 m
Width: (over tyres) 2.53 m
Height: 3.25 m
Ground clearance: 0.41 m
Wheelbase: 1.98 m
Max speed: 36 km/h
Fuel capacity: 235 l
Engine: Case 6T-830 turbocharged diesel developing 157 hp at 2100 rpm
Transmission: ZF 4WG 180 power-shift with 4 forward and 3 reverse gears
Steering: hydrostatic
Brakes: disc, dual circuit
Tyres: 20.5 × 25
Electrical system: 24 V
Batteries: 2 × 12 V
Alternator: 65 A

Status
In production. In service with the British Army.

Case 721 wheeled loader

Manufacturer
J I Case Europe Limited, PO Box 121, Wheatley Hall Road, Doncaster, South Yorkshire DN2 4PN, UK.

Tel: 0302 733108. Telex: 547242.
Fax: 0302 733165.

JCB 801 Mini Excavator

Description
The JCB 801 Mini Excavator is a manoeuvrable and easily transportable mini excavator with a variety of field engineering applications, including bomb disposal. An extensive range of optional equipment is available including a choice of six buckets, rock breaker pipework, a full or canopy cab and rubber tracks.

Status
In production.

Manufacturer
JCB Military Products Division, Rocester, Staffordshire ST14 5JP, UK.
Tel: 0889 590312. Telex: 36372.
Fax: 0889 590588.

JCB 801 Mini Excavator on its transporter trailer

Light Mobile Digger (LMD)

Description
The Light Mobile Digger (LMD) was designed in the early 1960s by the Military Engineering Experimental Establishment at Christchurch (now RARDE Christchurch) to meet the following requirements: excavation of a continuous slit trench 0.61 m wide and 1.38 m deep, with the ability to dig holes of a lesser depth; the ability to excavate rectangular holes; air-portability in a C-130 aircraft; good road and cross-country performance; and use by all arms at battalion level with the minimum of training. The digger rate depends on the ground conditions but on average ground a trenching speed of 4.57 to 5.49 m/min can be attained, equivalent to 230 to 275 m³/h.

The LMD is based on a modified Thornycroft Nubian chassis. The driver is seated in the cab at the front of the hull on the right side with the engine to his immediate left. Power is transmitted to the rear axles with optional front wheel drive. The digging head is powered by an auxiliary gearbox.

The chassis has two parallel boom arms on vertical pivots approximately midway along the wheelbase. These project to the rear of the chassis and at their rear ends is a horizontal pivot on which the frame accommodating the digging head assembly is mounted. When travelling the digging head assembly is stowed between these booms, and is raised into the vertical position at the chassis rear when required for digging. The boom is locked in either position by hydraulically operated locking pins operating between the boom arms and the chassis and situated aft of the rear road wheels.

The digging head assembly comprises the jib, which carries the digging chains, and soil conveyor, complete with their associated drive units. When in the vertical position this may be raised or lowered in its mounting frame or offset to either side. The excavated material is discharged to either side of the trench. The digging head hydraulic drive incorporates a relief valve system to prevent serious damage should an obstruction be met during excavation. When excavating, the rear springs are locked out to give additional rigidity to the machine.

Light Mobile Digger in action

Specifications
Cab seating: 1
Configuration: 4 × 4
Weight: 9253 kg
Length:
(travelling) 6.59 m
(digging) 7.61 m
Width: 2.31 m
Height:
(travelling) 2.6 m

(ready for digging) 3.34 m
Track: 1.92 m
Wheelbase: 3.56 m
Max speed: (road) 70 km/h
Engine: Rolls-Royce B81 Mark 7D 8-cylinder petrol developing 200 bhp at 3200 rpm
Transmission: 4 forward and 1 reverse gears, plus 2-speed transfer box
Suspension: semi-elliptical with hydraulic piston-type shock absorbers

Tyres: 12.00 × 20
Brakes: air pressure/dual hydraulic
Electrical system: 24 V

Status
Production complete. In service with the British Army.

Manufacturer
Chassis: Transport Equipment (Thornycroft) Limited, Basingstoke, Hampshire, UK (now closed).

Boughton Ulrich Simplex Multi-purpose Bucket

Description
The Boughton Ulrich Simplex multi-purpose bucket is available for most makes of wheeled or crawler loader in capacities from 0.6 to 5.5 m³ and can be mounted either direct on the loader arms or via a quicker-coupler attachment.

Every bucket is designed to match the requirement of each loader model to dig and load, forward dump, doze, back grade, grab, scrape and bottom dump a wide range of materials with maximum efficiency. The buckets are manufactured entirely from high tensile steel with high abrasion resistant cutting edges. The bucket back is fitted with a bolt-on reversible dozer edge and bolt-on dozing skid plates.

Status
In production. In service with the British Army, US Marine Corps, US Air Force, and other armed forces.

Manufacturer
Reynolds Boughton Limited, Engineering Division, Bell Lane, Amersham, Buckinghamshire HP6 6PE, UK.
Tel: 0494 764411. Telex: 83132.
Fax: 0494 765218.

Boughton Ulrich Simplex 1.72 m³ multi-purpose bucket fitted to Volvo 4400 wheeled loader

Boughton Ulrich Simplex 2.1 m³ multi-purpose bucket fitted to Case 721 medium wheeled tractor in service with the British Army

---

Heywood Williams Field Shelter MEXE Mk III

Description
The Field Shelter MEXE Mk III (or Mexeshelter) was developed by the Military Engineering Experimental Establishment at Christchurch (now the RARDE Christchurch), with production and marketing being undertaken by Heywood Williams Limited. The shelter provides protection against conventional attack, near miss nuclear attack and protection against chemical and bacteriological attack. Protection against the first of these two categories is given by the standard shelter with protection against chemical and bacteriological attack being provided by a kit described below.

The Mk III was originally conceived as an underground shelter for Command Posts (CPs), Observation Posts (OPs) and Regimental Aid Posts (RAPs), for use in forward and rear area tactical situations, and for the underground protection of personnel on air stations and in areas not directly related with the tactical battlefield itself. It is also used as a casualty clearing and first aid station in conjunction with triage; storage for medical supplies, including plasma, drugs, dressings; fuel, food and other combat support items; and as temporary magazines for ordnance items. In the Command Post role it is used at battalion and divisional level.

The Mk III consists of four components plus accessories: three metal structural members, pickets, spacers, arches; plus flexible revetting material to

clothe the metal structural members which is held in place by earth backfill. All components are packaged in manportable kits and can be installed by unskilled personnel with no special tools; all work can be accomplished with a pick and shovel. With the use of mechanical equipment such as a bulldozer, scraper or shovel, approximately two hours are required to fully install the Mk III. In addition to the mechanical equipment, approximately 15 man hours of troop labour are required.

The flexible revetting material used to line the walls and roof of the shelter is a PVC-coated jute fabric reinforced with wire. The PVC layer is impermeable and provides an obstacle to chemical agent penetration, and when this is combined with the additional barrier of 450 to 600 mm of soil over the shelter roof, it

MEXE shelter covering prior to earth backfill

Assembling MEXE shelter and showing general construction method

is likely that there will be no hazard in the shelter even with heavy chemical agent contamination on the ground outside. The installation of an NBC filtration unit and liner as outlined below provides the modifications necessary to give chemical protection without the use of respirators and NBC clothing.

The liner, including the airlock, is constructed of translucent reinforced plastic and folds down in similar fashion to a tent. It is self-supporting, even when there is no inflation from the AFU, and takes approximately 6 minutes to inflate. The airlock has easy access 'fold-away' doors and adjustable ports to vary the liner/airlock

pressure. The liner was developed by Driclad Limited of Sittingbourne, Kent, and liners for other configurations of shelter can be made available.

Various tests have been run to evaluate the protection provided by the Mk III in both a projected nuclear and a conventional weapon environment. In the case of a nuclear blast, the results record the protection provided against heat (thermal radiation), nuclear radiation (immediate) and nuclear fall-out. The shelter components were designed to withstand, to a given level, the effects of a 'near miss' weapons blast. The tests were undertaken by American, German and

British forces.

Status
Production complete. In service with British, Canadian, Kuwait and Saudi Arabian armed forces. Evaluated by Belgium and the USA (40 sets purchased).

Manufacturer
Heywood Williams Limited, Military Engineering Division, Bayhall Works, Huddersfield, West Yorkshire HD1 5EJ, UK.
Tel: 0484 710111. Telex: 51544.

UNITED STATES OF AMERICA

Caterpillar 30/30 Engineer Support Tractor

Description
The Caterpillar 30/30 Engineer Support Tractor was designed to act as a high-speed combat support machine intended for use in several forward area roles. It is a self-deployable unit capable of traversing rough terrain and is fitted with a hydraulically operated angled dozer blade at the front. The driver/operator is seated in an air-conditioned forward control cab fitted with bulletproof glass windows. An automatic fire detection and suppression system is provided.

The tracks use the Caterpillar Mobil-trac System with a rubber track hydropneumatic undercarriage that allows on- and off-road travel at speeds of up to 53 km/h. The sound signature is stated to be low. Power is derived from a Caterpillar 3208 diesel.

For drive-on, drive-off transport in a C-130 aircraft, the overall height can be slightly lowered by tilting forward the spotlamp array over the cab.

Specifications
Cab seating: 1
Weight: 15 513 kg
  (dozer blade angled) 2.718 m
  (dozer blade straight) 3.25 m
Height:
  (working) 2.946 m
  (air transport) 2.565 m
Ground clearance: 0.406 m
Track: 1.829 m
Length of track on ground: 2.438 m

Caterpillar 30/30 Engineer Support Tractor

Max speed: 53 km/h
Range: (cruising) 402 km
Fording: 1.19 m
Engine power:
  (travel) 240 hp
  (work) 170 hp
Turning radius: spot turn

Status
Prototype.

Manufacturer
Caterpillar Inc, Defense & Federal Products Department, Peoria, Illinois 61629, USA.
Tel: (309) 675 6938. Telex: 404435.

Small Emplacement Excavator (SEE)

Description
The Small Emplacement Excavator (SEE) Program was initially undertaken by Euclid Inc, a subsidiary of Daimler-Benz AG. This concern was taken over by the Freightliner Corporation. Based on a modified Unimog U 900, the SEE underwent four years of testing and evaluation with the US Army and in 1985 Freightliner was awarded a five-year contract for 922 vehicles with a 200 per cent overbuy option. The first four vehicles were handed over to the US Army in July 1985. Some 170 SEEs were destined for the US Marine Corps.

With the US Army the SEE is issued to all Active and Reserve forces and to the National Guard, and replaced John Deere 410 tractors on a one-to-one basis from FY87 onwards.

The SEE is based on a modified Daimler-Benz Unimog U 900 chassis with a 2.38 m wheelbase. This chassis can be provided with a variety of equipment for digging, loading, lifting, trenching, grading and powering hydraulic tools. The standard attachments are a front-end loader and backhoe. Typical power tools that can be powered by the SEE include a chain saw, a hammer drill and a concrete breaker. The tractor can be equipped with quickly interchangeable attachments such as a backhoe-mounted breaker and tamper for rapid runway repair, a front-mounted sweeper, a snowplough and a winch. In addition the tractor

Small Emplacement Excavator (SEE) in travelling configuration

provides a platform for shelters and other functions.

One SEE was converted by the Research, Development and Engineer Center at Fort Belvoir as an experimental test-bed with a microprocessor-controlled backhoe. The project is intended to increase in-house knowledge of robotic techniques, to create a prototype for proof-of-concept testing and to replace operators in hazardous situations. Full prototype testing and evaluation commenced during FY87.

Data for the SEE are provided in the Specifications table but data for the standard attachments are as follows.

Front End Loader
Bucket width: 2.07 m
Lift height: 2.5 m
Breakout force: 2722 kg
Lift capacity: 1497 kg
Bucket capacity: 0.57 m³

Backhoe
Bucket capacity: 0.2 m³
Digging depth: 4.26 m
Digging radius: 5.39 m
Loading height: 3.35 m
Swing arc: 180°
Digging force: 4536 kg

Variants
All Terrain Tow Vehicle (ATTV)
See entry in the *Trucks* section.

High Mobility Materiel Handler (HMMH)
See entry in the *Materials handling equipment* section.

High Mobility Entrencher (HME)
This variant, originally developed as part of the Tactical Explosive System (TEXS), is equipped with a 2.14 m wide backfill blade and a rear-mounted trenching attachment. Also fitted is an earth auger and a dewatering pump. This version uses a fully synchronised transmission with eight forward and four reverse speeds and a hydrostatic low range drive. The HME can use the full range of power tools used by the SEE, including a concrete breaker.

Data for the standard attachments are as follows.

Backfill blade
Blade width: 2.14 m
Blade height: 0.76 m
Lift height: 0.94 m
Cut below grade: 10 mm

High Mobility Entrencher (HME) showing trench digging arm and auger blades

Angle adjustment: 25° either side

Trencher
Digging width: (standard) 0.2 m
Digging depth: 2.18 m
Speed: variable, hydrostatic drive

Specifications
Cab seating: 1 + 1
Configuration: 4 × 4
Max weight: 7250 kg
Length: 6.35 m
Width: 2.44 m
Height: 2.58 m
Ground clearance: 0.43 m
Track: 1.63 m
Wheelbase: 2.38 m
Angle of approach/departure: 40°/34°
Max speed: (road) 80 km/h
Fuel capacity: 114 l
Max gradient: 60%
Side slope: 30%
Fording: 0.76 m
Engine: OM 352 4-stroke direct injection diesel

developing 110 hp at 2800 rpm
Transmission: fully synchromesh, 16 forward and 8 reverse gears
Clutch: single dry plate
Steering: hydraulic power-assisted
Turning circle: 10.9 m
Suspension:
   (front) coil springs, telescopic shock absorbers and stabiliser
   (rear) coil springs with helper springs, telescopic shock absorbers and stabiliser
Tyres: 12.5 × 20 12PR MPT
Brakes: hydraulic, dual circuit disc
Electrical system: 24 V with blackout drive
Batteries: 2 × 12 V, 100 Ah

Status
SEE in production. In service with US Army and Marine Corps (2206 delivered). HME under development.

Manufacturer
Freightliner Corporation, 4747 North Channel Avenue, PO Box 3849, Portland, Oregon 97208-3849, USA. Tel: (503) 735 8000.

Trench Digging Machines

Description
The US Army uses a number of different types of trench digging machines manufactured by Barber-Greene (model 750), Parsons (model 624VL) and Unit Rig (model 4262). Gar Wood developed a lightweight (7666 kg) airportable trench digging machine in the late 1950s called the model 831 which was followed in the early 1960s by an improved version known as the model 832.

Specifications (Unit Rig 4262)
Configuration: 4 × 4
Weight: 16 330 kg
Length: 8.89 m
Width: 2.44 m
Height: 3.18 m
Fuel capacity: 378.5 l
Engine: IHC UD-691 diesel
Tyres:
   (front) 14.00 × 24
   (rear) 21.00 × 25

Status
In service with the US Army.

US Army Gar Wood 832 trench digger (Larry Provo)

Foxhole Digger Explosive Kit (EXFODA)

Description

Intended to rapidly produce a foxhole-sized crater on the battlefield, the Foxhole Digger Exploder Kit is a standard issue item for the US Army (the term EXFODA is a general title rather than an abbreviation). The kit is issued in a container with an end screw cap. Inside the container is a small rod, two delay fuzes, two cratering charges, string and tape. The container, which has a carrying ring, also acts as the firing spacer for a small spaced charge fixed at one end of the container, opposite the screw cap.

In use, the container is emptied and placed on the selected site with the small rod being tied on to provide stability if required. The shaped charge is Octol with an RDX booster and, once fired, produces a bore hole from 500 to 800 mm deep. The delay fuzes are taped to the cratering charges and lowered into the bore hole. The cratering charge is PBXN-1 with an RDX booster and once the charge is fired it leaves a small crater approximately 1 m in diameter and 800 mm deep. The process of producing a foxhole crater takes a maximum of 5 minutes, and only one man carries out the operation. The kit can be carried by the operator slung from the container carrying ring.

Specifications (kit container packed)
Weight: 1.8 kg
Length: 300 mm
Width: 300 mm
Height: 100 mm

Status
In service with the US Army.

Overhead Foxhole Cover (OFC)

Description

The Overhead Foxhole Cover (OFC) is a US Army standard issue item and is carried and used by an individual soldier. A mylar-coated polyester fabric sheet, it serves to protect a soldier using a foxhole from the effects of the weather. It provides no other form of protection. Along each side of the cover, which is 2.34 m long and 1.625 m wide, are long pockets which are filled with spoil as the foxhole is excavated. The cover is then placed over the foxhole and layered with spoil to camouflage the emplacement. The setting-up process takes 5 minutes.

Status
In production. In service with the US Army.

Parapet Foxhole Cover (PFC)

Description

The Parapet Foxhole Cover is a preformed glass fibre shelter resembling half of a cylinder. It is intended to provide shelter for a one- or two-man position but by itself it can protect against the weather only. If ballistic protection is required the foxhole cover must be covered by about 0.5 m of spoil or earth, a process that takes approximately 15 minutes. Two of the covers can be joined together to provide shelter for a two-man foxhole. When transported the covers can nest within one another requiring less space. This cover is still under development and when complete it is expected to be issued at a rate of 40 per infantry company.

Specifications
Weight: 10 kg
Length: 1.524 m
Width: 0.76 m
Height: 0.457 m

Status
Development.

Foam Overhead Cover Support System (FOCOS)

Description

Also known as Tactical Fighting Emplacement Covers, Foam Overhead Cover Support System (FOCOS) covers are used to provide overhead shelter for tactical fighting positions such as TOW emplacements. The covers are issued in shipping boxes containing fabric bags and the components for producing a plastic foam. The fabric bag for each cover is laid out over the emplacement to be protected and the two foam components are mixed and poured into the bag. As the foam forms inside the bag it hardens into an arch 2.44 m in diameter and 1.524 m long. Additional ballistic protection can then be added in the form of sand bags or spoil. Setting up one cover takes about 1 hour, and can be carried out by two men.

Status
Development.

BULK FUEL STORAGE AND DISTRIBUTION SYSTEMS

AUSTRALIA

Pumping Assembly POL 180 l/min

Description
This Australian Army pump unit replaced the US Barnes pumping assembly. The pump is utilised with the 38 mm POL system and is used in particular for filling and emptying US 1892.5 litre collapsible fabric drums.

Procurement detailing began in 1968 with the recommendation being made in 1974. Trials and testing were conducted in 1976 and as a result further modifications were made. These were completed early in 1978 and manufacture of production models began in May 1978 with completion in September 1978.

The pumping assembly is used as a general-purpose fuel pumping unit. It consists of a 38 mm aluminium pump driven by a diesel engine, 50 m of 38 mm diameter hose, two 38 mm nozzles, an earthing spike and an aluminium carrying case. The top of the carrying case covers the pump and engine and contains all accessories.

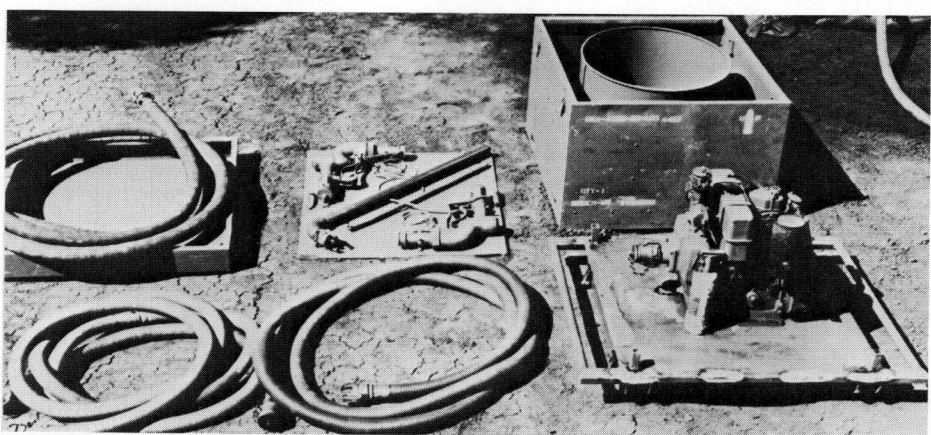

Pumping Assembly POL 180 l/min (Australian Army)

Status
In service with the Australian Army.

Tank and Pump Unit 4.5 m³ Capacity

Description
The Australian Army tank and pump unit is based on two in-service US 1892.5 litre tanks and a 38 mm pump. The Australian requirement was for fitment to a 5000 kg truck. An additional Australian provision was for the use of the equipment in the static role, for example with tanks mounted on a stand.

Procurement detailing began in 1970 and actual procurement was recommended in August 1975. Trials and testing were conducted during 1976 and as a result modified units were tested early in 1978. Manufacture of production models began in June 1978 and was completed by December 1978.

The equipment consists of two 2.25 m³ aluminium tanks and a 30 mm transfer pump. The two tanks and pump unit are fitted on a common base suitable for mounting on a 5000 kg truck. The pump is driven by a diesel engine identical to the 38 mm general-purpose fuel pump. Three types of pump unit are based on functional needs:

Aviation units: the pump is fitted with a filter, separator, air eliminator, flow meter and one hose complete with nozzle and hose reel, all transportable on a 5000 kg truck.

Tank and pump unit 4.5 m³ capacity mounted on rear of 5000 kg (6 × 6) truck (Australian Army)

RAAC: the pump unit is fitted with two hoses complete with nozzles and reels. Transportability as for aviation units.

RAE units: the pump is fitted with two hoses complete with nozzles and reels. The equipment is carried on a 5000 kg truck, or two tanks can be fitted on separate tank stands. Gravity flow fills vehicles whereas the pump unit is used to fill the tanks on the stands.

Status
In service with the Australian Army.

AUSTRIA

Steyr Fuel Tankers

Description
Steyr produces a wide range of fuel tankers based on 4 × 4 and 6 × 6 vehicles. The usual capacity for 4 × 4 medium trucks is 6000 litres (12M and 14M series), 11 000 litres for the 4 × 4 heavy truck (19S series) and 20 000 litres for the 6 × 6.

Vehicles are available with power take-off driven centrifugal pumps for unloading, metering and self-loading operations. Water tankers with a special plastic interior coating are also available.

Specifications (typical)

Chassis type	4 × 4	4 × 4	6 × 6
Length overall	7 m	7.5 m	9 m
Length of tank	4 m	5 m	6 m
Width	2.4 m	2.4 m	2.4 m
Height	2.9 m	3 m	3 m
Capacity	6000 l	11 000 l	20 000 l

Status
In production. In service with Canadian Forces Europe, Ghana, Nigeria and Saudi Arabia.

Manufacturer
Steyr Nutzfahrzeuge AG, Schönauerstrasse 5, A-4400 Steyr, Austria.
Tel: 7252/25351-0. Telex: 28200.
Fax: 7252/26746, 28650.

Steyr 32S29/6 × 6 20 000 litre fuel tanker showing pumping and metering unit

Steyr 19S25/4 × 4 11 000 litre fuel tanker showing pumping and metering unit

COMMONWEALTH OF INDEPENDENT STATES

Fabric Reinforced Rubber Fuel Tanks

Description
This type of fuel tank was introduced into service during 1961 and since then many different types have been produced. The first family of tanks comprised the MR-2.5, MR-4, MR-10 and MR-12. These were all orthodox reinforced rubber fuel tanks and all, except the MR-10, were used to convert flat bed trucks into mobile fuel carriers. The MR-10 was used primarily as a storage tank, not having the internal baffles fitted to the other types.

The latest family of fabric reinforced rubber fuel tanks comprises the MR-4, MR-6, MR-25, MR-50, MR-150 and MR-250. Only the MR-4 and MR-6 are now used for the mobile carrying of fuel and other liquids, and are fitted with metal loading brackets on all corners and diagonal partitions internally. All the tanks have an inspection manhole, filling/draining and air connections, T-pipes and air pipes. Handles are provided for folding, unfolding and handling of each, and these are situated around the periphery of each tank. The MR-150 and MR-250 have underside connectors with elbows and flexible pipes for flushing residual liquids from the tank. When folded each tank has an external pocket into which the various fittings can be stowed.

When transported, each tank is carried inside a cover fitted with loading loops. For storage the tanks may be kept either folded or unfolded under cover, or outdoors under canvas.

Status
The original MR-2.5, MR-4, MR-10 and MR-12 are no longer in production but may be held in reserve. The later MR-4, MR-6, MR-25, MR-50, MR-150 and MR-250 are in production and service.

Manufacturer
State factories.

Specifications

Tank type	MR-4	MR-6	MR-25	MR-50	MR-150	MR-250
Rated capacity	4000 l	6000 l	25 000 l	50 000 l	150 000 l	260 000 l
Length (filled)	3.6 m	3.8 m	9 m	17.6 m	18 m	18 m
Width (filled)	2.6 m	2.5 m	3.7 m	3.7 m	7 m	10 m
Height (filled)	0.65 m	0.9 m	1 m	1 m	1.4 m	1.4 m
Weight (including cover)	125 kg	135 kg	290 kg	580 kg	1050 kg	1450 kg
Number of filling/ draining connectors	1	1	2	2	2	2
Number of air connectors	1	1	1	2	2	2

Fabric reinforced rubber fuel tanks

PMTP-100 Tactical Pipeline

Description
The PMTP-100 tactical POL pipeline is used by the pipeline regiments assigned to each CIS Army front. The pipe is laid in 10 m lengths, each with quick-connect junctions, from tractor-towed trailers which automatically lay the pipes at the rate of 2 to 3 km/h. Once connected the pipes are designed to be easily removed and replaced if damaged, and the entire pipeline can be retrieved for later use. The pipeline capacity is 75 m³ of POL products per hour. Length of the pipeline is dependent on the number of pumping stations and pipe sections available.

Status
In service with former Warsaw Pact forces.

Manufacturer
State factories.

Section of PMTP-100 tactical pipeline

TUM-150 Pipelaying Machine

Description
The TUM-150 pipelaying machine is used by pipe-laying brigades assigned to each Army Front to lay tactical pipelines during offensive operations; it may also be used at divisional level in static situations. The TUM-150 is a trailer-mounted system and lays pipes 6.1 m long while travelling at a speed of 3 km/h. A complete load of 70 pipes is placed on the machine by an onboard hydraulic crane mounted on the forward part of the trailer. The pipes are loaded from the left-hand side in layers of ten and are unloaded into a shallow trench to the rear via a chute located at the lower right-hand side and extending to the rear. A full load of 70 pipes with a total length of 427 m can be laid in approximately 8.5 minutes. With its towing vehicle the TUM-150 has an overall length of approximately 18 m and a width of 3.5 m. The towing vehicle may be a crawler tractor or a 4 × 4 wheeled tractor. Pipes may be loaded into the machine while it is in operation and on tow.

Status
In service with former Warsaw Pact forces.

Manufacturer
State factories.

FRANCE

Trailor 5000 litre Bowser Equipment for AFVs

Description
The Trailor 5000 litre bowser equipment was developed specifically for refuelling tanks and other AFVs in the field and can refuel up to four vehicles at one time. The tank used has an elliptical outline and is manufactured from steel with a Rhomelyte interior lining. The tank has two compartments, one with a capacity of 2000 litres and the other of 3000 litres, and may be filled from either top or bottom. Each compartment has a manhole cover on top and is fitted with safety vents for internal vacuum or pressure. Access to the top of the tank is via ladders and there is a working platform covered with anti-skid and anti-spark coating. The distribution panel at the rear is under a cover which hinges upwards and locks once in place. Inside the cover is a pump driven from the vehicle gearbox power take-off and this embodies a bypass set for an output of 20 000 l/h. Refuelling can be carried out with or without metering.

The full control panel contains a meter, two valves, a manifold linked to four hose reels each with a hose 20 m long (each hose has a diameter of 30 mm and is fitted with a nozzle), a two-way valve for self-filling or bottom filling, a three-way valve, three cabinets for 80 mm diameter hoses, accessories and tools.

The complete equipment may be transported by rail or by C-160 Transall transport aircraft. Cross-country tyres are fitted and the entire equipment may be covered by a full tarpaulin camouflage cover. It is normally carried on a 6 × 6 truck chassis.

Status
In production. In service with the French Army.

Manufacturer
Trailor SA, 5 Route Nationale 10, BP 49, F-78311 Coignières, Maurepas Cedex, France.
Tel: (1) 30 50 61 26. Telex: 698896 f.
Fax: (1) 30 50 31 32.

Distribution panel for Trailor 5000 litre AFV bowser

Fruehauf 18 000 litre Fuel Bowser

Description
This fuel bowser entered service with the French Army during 1983 and uses an 18 000 litre tank mounted on the chassis of a Renault GBH 284 (6 × 4) truck chassis. The tank has three compartments of 11 000, 5000 and 2000 litres. The tank has a special interior coating that enables it to be used for the carrying of diesel fuel, petrol, kerosene and other such hydro-carbon liquids. It is fitted with a discharge pump with a capacity of 50 to 60 m³/h.

Status
In service with the French Army.

Manufacturer
Fruehauf France, avenue de l'Aunette, F-91130 Ris-Orange, France.
Tel: (1) 69 43 30 00. Telex: 601381.
Fax: (1) 69 43 33 66.

Fruehauf 18 000 litre fuel bowser mounted on Renault GBH 284 (6 × 4) truck chassis

Superflexit Flexible Storage and Transport Tanks

Description
The Superflexit Division d'AERAZUR manufactures a range of flexible tanks for transport (capacity 500 to 20 000 litres) and for storage (capacity 500 to 300 000 litres). They are made of high performance synthetic fabrics coated with elastomer to store fuel and other liquids such as water as well as chemicals. The tanks are provided with standard equipment according to French and American specifications but can be equipped to suit customer requirements. All the tanks in the range can be folded when empty and are easy to set up on site. They are resistant to a wide range of climatic conditions.

Superflexit fuel transport tank carried by French Army Berliet GBC 8 KT (6 × 6) 4000 kg truck

Status

In production. In service with the French and some other armed forces.

Manufacturer

Superflexit Division d'AERAZUR, 58 Boulevard Galliéni, F-92137 Issy-les-Moulineaux Cedex, France. Tel: (1) 45 54 92 80. Telex: 270887 f. Fax: (1) 45 54 23 55.

Specifications				
Capacity	**25 000 l**	**80 000 l**	**150 000 l**	**300 000 l**
Weight (empty)	124 kg	287 kg	480 kg	878 kg
Volume (folded)	0.43 m³	0.76 m³	1.25 m³	2.81 m³
Length (empty)	8.1 m	9.1 m	12 m	17.65 m
(full)	7.75 m	9.05 m	11.15 m	17.25 m
Width (empty)	4.25 m	8.2 m	11.5 m	13.7 m
(full)	3.7 m	7.85 m	11.15 m	13.5 m
Height (full)	1.1 m	1.3 m	1.35 m	1.4 m

Superflexit Helicopter Transportable Tanks

Description

These tanks are used to transport fuel or drinking water and can be slung under helicopters. They are manufactured from synthetic fabric coated on each side with elastomer and have capacities of 500, 1000 and 1500 litres. A standard fitting is a 76 mm fill/drain flange on the top but other equipment can be fitted to suit customer specifications.

Status

In production. In service with the French and some other armed forces.

Manufacturer

Superflexit Division d'AERAZUR, 58 Boulevard Galliéni, F-92137 Issy-les-Moulineaux Cedex, France. Tel: (1) 45 54 92 80. Telex: 270887 f. Fax: (1) 45 54 23 55.

Superflexit helicopter transportable tank

Superflexit 20 litre Air-droppable Fuel Containers

Description

Superflexit manufactures a 20 litre flexible fuel container that can be dropped in free fall from helicopters or aircraft flying at altitudes of up to 2000 m. The containers may be dropped individually or in clusters of 20 from a tilting platform.

These containers may also be used to carry drinking water.

Status

In production. In service with the French and some other armed forces.

Manufacturer

Superflexit Division d'AERAZUR, 58 Boulevard Galliéni, F-92137 Issy-les-Moulineaux Cedex, France. Tel: (1) 45 54 92 80. Telex: 270887 f. Fax: (1) 45 54 23 55.

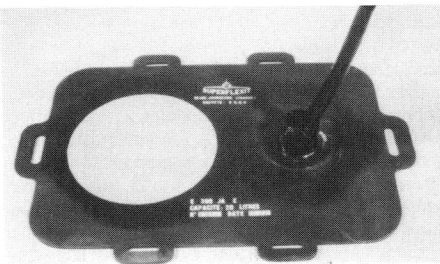

Superflexit 20 litre air-droppable fuel container

Superflexit 20 litre Flexible Jerrican

Description

The Superflexit 20 litre flexible jerricans are containers for fuel or water that require minimum space when empty and are self-supporting when full. The containers are manufactured from rot-proof materials using flexible coated fabric resistant to hydrocarbon. They have been designed for long storage periods and when full can withstand being dropped from heights of up to 10 m. The filler hole allows the use of flexible metallic pouring adaptors used by the French Army. The carrying handles can be arranged to ensure the container remains fully closed up when folded.

Status

In production. In service with the French Army.

Manufacturer

Superflexit Division d'AERAZUR, 58 Boulevard Galliéni, F-92137 Issy-les-Moulineaux Cedex, France. Tel: (1) 45 54 92 80. Telex: 270887 f. Fax: (1) 45 54 23 55.

Full Superflexit 20 litre flexible jerrican

Superflexit Supessence 100 litre Fuel Tank

Description
This self-contained 100 litre fuel tank is intended to increase the range of cargo or troop-carrying vehicles by a coefficient of about 3.5. The principle is that each vehicle can carry up to four of these tanks hooked on the vehicle siderails. Each tank can be placed in position by two men using the integral carrying handles provided and the tank can be filled through a filling port on the top of the tank. The tank is emptied by using a drain hose placed directly into the vehicle main tank.

The tanks are manufactured using coated fabric resistant to hydrocarbons with an interchangeable abrasion resistant cover on the side next to the carrier vehicle. The tank has a self-bracing system that allows it to hold its position when on the ground, even at decreased capacity. The drain hoses can be connected and disconnected to provide the correct refuelling lengths.

Status
In production.

Manufacturer
Superflexit Division d'AERAZUR, 58 Boulevard Galliéni, F-92137 Issy-les-Moulineaux Cedex, France.

Tel: (1) 45 54 92 80. Telex: 270887 f.
Fax: (1) 45 54 23 55.

Superflexit Supessence 100 litre fuel tank being carried by Renault TRM 2000 (4 × 4) 2000 kg truck

Kléber C70 'Commando' Portable Fuel Container

Description
The C70 'Commando' portable fuel container is a flexible drum container that can be towed behind a truck or carried slung from a helicopter. The main body is constructed from rayon cord and is coated with fuel resistant synthetic rubber. There is an abrasion resistant outer cover. The container is fitted with side plates with slinging shackles that can also be attached to a triangular towing bracket. A 2-in/51 mm refuel/defuel port is fitted with an OPW or Guillemin coupling, and a pressure limiting coupler may be supplied. It may be used with a 1.5-in/38 mm hose but there is an adaptor for a 2-in/51 mm hose. This container can withstand dropping from a height of over 4 m.

Specifications
Weight: 125 kg
Diameter: 1.35 m
Width: 1.575 m

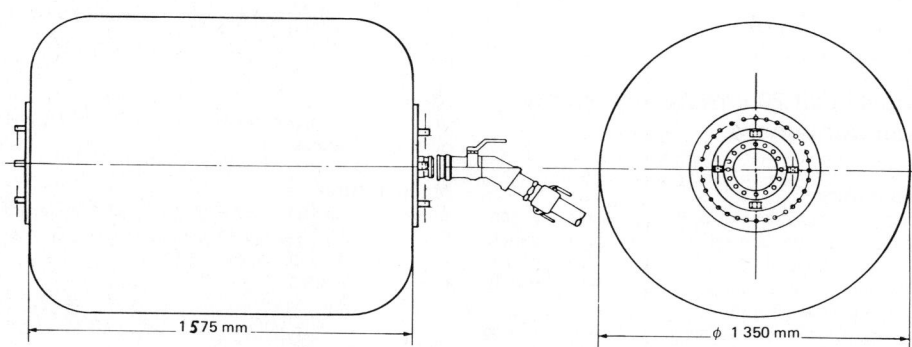

Kléber C70 'Commando' portable fuel container

Capacity: 1900 l
Working pressure: 0.35 bar
Maximum pressure: 2.1 bars

Status
In production for the French Army.

Manufacturer
Kléber Industrie, 143 bis rue Yves Le Coz, BP 554, F-78005 Versailles Cedex, France.
Tel: (1) 39 49 49 50. Telex: 695533 f.
Fax: (1) 39 49 56 47.

Kléber C60 Helicopter Transportable Tanks

Description
The Kléber C60 helicopter-portable tanks are produced in three standard sizes of 500, 1000 and 1500 litres capacity. Each tank has a fuelling/defuelling 40 or 50 mm valve which can be swivelled 360°, a 40 or 50 mm vent, a slinging ring for connection to the helicopter hoist or carriage point, lugs and adjustable harnesses, carrying handles, a bag welded onto the tank wall for carrying the various fittings, and a repair kit. The material used for the construction of the C60 is

designed to resist abrasion and weathering and is strong enough to allow the tank to be dropped from a height of 1 m. The lugs and adjustable harnesses allow the tank to be carried on a truck if required. Apart from fuel the C60 can be used to carry water or other liquids.

Status
In production.

Manufacturer
Kléber Industrie, 143 bis rue Yves Le Coz, BP 554, F-78005 Versailles Cedex, France.
Tel: (1) 39 49 49 50. Telex: 695533 f.
Fax: (1) 39 49 56 47.

Specifications

Capacity	500 l	1000 l	1500 l
Dimensions (empty)	1.45 × 1.45 × 0.155 m	1.8 × 1.8 × 0.155 m	2.15 × 2.15 × 0.155 m
(filled)	1.4 × 1.4 × 0.4 m	1.75 × 1.75 × 0.5 m	2.1 × 2.1 × 0.6 m

Kléber C40 Flexible Storage Tanks

Description

The Kléber C40 range of flexible storage tanks is constructed from rugged, synthetic rubber-coated fabrics and is manufactured in two grades: one for hydrocarbon fuels, and the other for non-toxic liquids. Each grade is equipped with a number of standard fittings that include a stainless steel adaptor for a 50 or 80 mm hose, a bronze valve with a fire-hose type coupling and plug, an over-pressure valve for hydrocarbon grade tanks, a stack pipe with a cap for tanks holding transformer oils, a stainless steel vent pipe, a non-toxic level gauge, and a repair kit.

The C40 tanks are available in a range of capacities from 3000 to 60 000 litres (see Specifications) but tanks with capacities up to 150 000 litres are available on request. Tanks for special liquids are also available.

Status

In production. In service with the French armed forces and some other nations.

Manufacturer

Kléber Industrie, 143 bis rue Yves Le Coz, BP 554, F-78005 Versailles Cedex, France.
Tel: (1) 39 49 49 50. Telex: 695533 f.
Fax: (1) 39 49 56 47.

Specifications

Capacity	Dimensions (empty)	Dimensions full (approx)	Volume (folded)	Weight (with fittings)
3000 l	3.2 × 2.1 m	3.1 × 2 × 0.8 m	0.17 m³	45 kg
4000 l	4.15 × 2.1 m	4.05 × 2 × 0.8 m	0.18 m³	52 kg
	2.8 × 2.8 m	2.7 × 2.7 × 0.95 m	0.18 m³	52 kg
5000 l	5.1 × 2.1 m	5 × 2 × 0.8 m	0.21 m³	60 kg
	3.3 × 2.8 m	3.2 × 2.7 × 0.95 m	0.21 m³	60 kg
8000 l	4.9 × 2.8 m	4.8 × 2.7 × 0.95 m	0.3 m³	65 kg
	3.6 × 3.5 m	3.5 × 3.4 × 1.1 m	0.3 m³	65 kg
10 000 l	5.9 × 2.8 m	5.8 × 2.7 × 0.95 m	0.32 m³	77 kg
	4.3 × 3.5 m	4.2 × 3.4 × 1.1 m	0.32 m³	77 kg
15 000 l	5.9 × 3.5 m	5.8 × 3.4 × 1.1 m	0.34 m³	115 kg
	4.6 × 4.2 m	4.5 × 4.1 × 1.35 m	0.34 m³	115 kg
20 000 l	7.6 × 3.5 m	7.5 × 3.4 × 1.1 m	0.41 m³	135 kg
	5.7 × 4.2 m	5.6 × 4.1 × 1.35 m	0.41 m³	135 kg
25 000 l	6.9 × 4.2 m	6.8 × 4.1 × 1.35 m	0.43 m³	155 kg
	6 × 4.9 m	5.9 × 4.8 × 1.45 m	0.43 m³	155 kg
30 000 l	8.1 × 4.2 m	8 × 4.1 × 1.35 m	0.46 m³	165 kg
	6.8 × 4.9 m	6.7 × 4.8 × 1.45 m	0.46 m³	165 kg
40 000 l	10.5 × 4.2 m	10.4 × 4.1 × 1.35 m	0.5 m³	205 kg
	8.7 × 4.9 m	8.6 × 4.8 × 1.45 m	0.5 m³	205 kg
50 000 l	10.4 × 4.9 m	10.3 × 4.8 × 1.45 m	0.6 m³	225 kg
	8.6 × 5.6 m	8.5 × 5.5 × 1.55 m	0.6 m³	225 kg
60 000 l	10 × 5.6 m	9.9 × 5.5 × 1.55 m	0.7 m³	250 kg
	9 × 6.3 m	8.9 × 6.2 × 1.6 m	0.7 m³	250 kg

PRONAL Flexible Storage and Transport Tanks

Description

PRONAL produces a wide range of flexible tanks for both storage and transport purposes and can produce these tanks to suit any customer requirement. For fuel storage purposes the tanks are constructed from a nitrile-coated nylon fabric. Storage tanks have a 2-in/51 mm inlet/outlet valve on one side and a centrally located vent valve. Transport tanks are similar but have a series of lashing points along each side to allow them to be carried on almost any type of truck.

The figures provided in the Specifications table are not comprehensive, as the tanks can be produced to suit almost any customer requirement. Tanks up to a capacity of 200 000 litres can be produced.

Status

In production. In service with the Belgian, French and Swiss armed forces and some other nations.

Manufacturer

PRONAL SA, Z.I. Roubaix Est, BP 18, F-59115 Leers, France.
Tel: (33) 20 99 75 00. Telex: 132 750 f.
Fax: (33) 20 99 75 20.

Typical PRONAL flexible fuel storage tank

Specifications
Flexible storage tanks

Capacity	Length (empty)	Width (empty)	Height (full)	Weight	Volume (folded)
1000 l	2.44 m	1.37 m	0.65 m	25 kg	0.15 m³
2000 l	2.4 m	2.12 m	1.1 m	35 kg	0.2 m³
5000 l	4.6 m	2.12 m	1.1 m	55 kg	0.25 m³
10 000 l	8.2 m	2.12 m	1.1 m	85 kg	0.4 m³
15 000 l	4.97 m	4.13 m	1.2 m	90 kg	0.45 m³
20 000 l	6.29 m	4.13 m	1.2 m	115 kg	0.55 m³
25 000 l	6.01 m	4.96 m	1.3 m	135 kg	0.65 m³
30 000 l	6.99 m	4.96 m	1.3 m	155 kg	0.75 m³
35 000 l	7.98 m	4.96 m	1.3 m	175 kg	0.85 m³
40 000 l	8.96 m	4.96 m	1.3 m	190 kg	0.95 m³
45 000 l	8.65 m	5.63 m	1.3 m	210 kg	1.05 m³
50 000 l	9.49 m	5.63 m	1.3 m	230 kg	1.15 m³
60 000 l	8.88 m	6.97 m	1.3 m	265 kg	1.3 m³
70 000 l	8.47 m	8.14 m	1.35 m	300 kg	1.5 m³
80 000 l	9.14 m	8.47 m	1.35 m	330 kg	1.65 m³
100 000 l	11.15 m	8.47 m	1.35 m	420 kg	2.1 m³
125 000 l	13.66 m	8.47 m	1.35 m	510 kg	2.55 m³
150 000 l	16.17 m	8.47 m	1.35 m	595 kg	2.95 m³

Transport tanks

Capacity	Length (empty)	Width (empty)	Height (full)	Weight	Volume (folded)
1000 l	1.8 m	1.8 m	0.7 m	30 kg	0.15 m³
2000 l	2.4 m	2.12 m	1.1 m	40 kg	0.2 m³
3000 l	3.15 m	2.12 m	1.1 m	50 kg	0.25 m³
4000 l	3.85 m	2.12 m	1.1 m	60 kg	0.3 m³
5000 l	4.6 m	2.12 m	1.1 m	70 kg	0.35 m³
6000 l	5.3 m	2.12 m	1.1 m	80 kg	0.4 m³
7000 l	6 m	2.12 m	1.1 m	90 kg	0.45 m³
8000 l	6.75 m	2.12 m	1.1 m	100 kg	0.5 m³
9000 l	7.45 m	2.12 m	1.1 m	110 kg	0.55 m³
10 000 l	8.2 m	2.12 m	1.1 m	120 kg	0.6 m³
11 000 l	8.9 m	2.12 m	1.1 m	130 kg	0.65 m³
12 000 l	9.65 m	2.12 m	1.1 m	140 kg	0.7 m³

PRONAL Helitransportable and Towable Flexible Tanks

Description
PRONAL flexible tanks are drum-shaped tanks that can be used to transport hydrocarbon fuels, oils or water. They are made of nylon fabric coated with synthetic nitrile rubber which is anti-ultraviolet radiation treated. There are three capacities – 200, 1000 and 1900 litres – with the material thickness of the two smaller tanks being 5 mm and the largest 9 mm.

The 200 litre tank can be dropped from a height of 12 m and once on the ground is rollable. The two largest tanks can be towed. All three can be carried slung under helicopters. The 200 litre tank has a 0.75-in/19 mm adaptor and vent and a filling pipe with a 0.75-in/19 mm coupling and semi-symmetrical DN 40 connection or Kamlock coupling. The larger tanks have a self-plugging DN 50 adaptor and there is also a filling and emptying pipe with a length of 1.6 m – this is fitted with DN 40 Kamlock connections and caps. Also available for the larger tanks are towing, pushing or lifting bars and turning plates with lift rings.

Status
In production. In service with the French Army and some other nations.

Manufacturer
PRONAL SA, Z.I. Roubaix Est, BP 18, F-59115 Leers, France.
Tel: (33) 20 99 75 00. Telex: 132 750 f.
Fax: (33) 20 99 75 20.

Typical PRONAL helitransportable and towable flexible tank

Specifications

Capacity	200 l	1000 l	1900 l
Diameter	0.6 m	1.1 m	1.35 m
Length	1 m	1.3 m	1.6 m
Weight (empty)	20 kg	85 kg	135 kg
Dimensions folded	0.85 × 0.95 × 0.25 m	1.2 × 1.5 × 0.25 m	1.5 × 1.8 × 0.25 m
Working pressure	0.3 bar	0.3 bar	0.3 bar

PRONAL RSH Helicopter Transportable Tanks

Description
PRONAL RSH (RSH – *reservoirs souples heliport-ables*) tanks are produced in three sizes: 500, 1000 and 1500 litres. A patented design is used in which the tank is supported in a Maltese cross-shaped skirt that immediately spreads the load of the vehicle once it is lifted from its single clip-on ring. Once in flight the skirt passes air through its panels and acts as a drogue to prevent the tank from revolving beneath the carrying helicopter. Each tank has one slinging ring, an outlet with a 2-in/51 mm valve coupling and plug, and a symmetrical Guillemin system. The tanks may be used to carry water.

Status
In production. Approved for use by the French Army air arm.

Manufacturer
PRONAL SA, Z.I. Roubaix Est, BP 18, F-59115 Leers, France.
Tel: (33) 20 99 75 00. Telex: 132 750 f.
Fax: (33) 20 99 75 20.

Puma helicopter carrying PRONAL RSH tank

Specifications

Model	0.5 RSH	1.0 RSH	1.5 RSH
Capacity	500 l	1000 l	1500 l
Weight (tank and fittings)	25 kg	32 kg	40 kg
Dimensions empty	1.4 × 1.4 × 0.15 m	1.8 × 1.8 × 0.15 m	2.2 × 2.2 × 0.15 m
Dimensions loaded (hanging)	1.01 × 1.01 × 1.2 m	1.4 × 1.4 × 1.55 m	1.7 × 1.7 × 1.9 m

GERMANY

German Army POL Handling Equipments

Description
KC 17 Fuel Container
The KC 17 fuel container has a capacity of 17 m³ and was designed to be carried either on railway trucks or on special Tatra 138 (6 × 6) tractor trucks fitted with handling arms. Several KC 17 containers may be combined to form a field POL point.

PSG 160 Pumping Station
This equipment is used to feed field pipeline systems and is normally carried on a 4 × 2 truck. It has an output of up to 130 m³/h.

TOF 72 Pumping Plant
This pumping plant is mounted on a standard single-axle trailer and may be used for pumping various fuels, refuelling combat vehicles with measured quantities of filtered fuel, and for filling jerricans. The designed pumping capacity is up to 18 m³/h.

TOK 63 Pumping Plant
The TOK 63 is mounted on a trolley-type chassis and when fitted with booster equipment it can be used to refuel combat vehicles. The designed pumping capacity is up to 18 m³/h.

Status
All the above were in service with the former East German Army.

Manufacturer
State factories.

KC 17 fuel container being loaded onto Tatra 138 (6 × 6) tractor truck

T 138 CN 22 semi-trailer tanker

FTSB 4.0 and 25 Flexible Fuel Tanks

Description
Designed for use by forward units, these two flexible fuel tanks are constructed from a mixture of rubber-based materials with a nylon weave outer covering. The FTSB 4.0 has a capacity of 4 m³ and is intended for use, free-standing in open locations. The much larger FTSB 25 has a capacity of 25 m³ and is intended for main depot storage, usually behind some form of blast protection. The FTSB has numerous carrying and locating handles stitched into the outer surface and end-mounted valves and other hardware. The FTSB 4.0 has these components mounted on the upper surface.

Status
In service with the former East German Army.

Manufacturer
State factories.

FTSB 4.0 flexible fuel tank

Aluminium Storage Tank

Description
This storage tank was designed for bulk storage of liquids such as oil, petrol or water. Its main advantages are its ease of transportation, short assembly time and its capability of being erected on various types of surface including concrete, earth and sand. The tank consists of 16 sections with tongue-and-groove sealing and an adjustable mast which is used as a roof support when the tank is being erected, as the upper sections are assembled first and the lower sections last. The shell and supporting parts are aluminium with the bottom and roof being a fuel-resistant rubber tarpaulin.

Aluminium storage tank

Close-up of discharge outlet on storage tank

Specifications
Capacity: 450 m³
Diameter: 12 m
Height:
(to eaves) 4.2 m
(filling) 4 m
(overall) 5.3 m

Weight of tank: 8300 kg
Total weight: (with transport frames) 10 780 kg

Status
In production. In service with Argentina, Egypt, Libya and the German Army.

Manufacturer
Kurt Steinborn, Neustrasse 17, D-7830 Emmendingen, Federal Republic of Germany.

ISRAEL

Achidatex Collapsible Fuel Containers

Description
Achidatex produces a range of collapsible containers suitable for the transport and storage of fuels, chemicals and also for drinking water and other potable liquids.

One type of container is the pillow tank, produced in sizes ranging from 250 to 100 000 gallons (1136.5 to 454 600 litres). Similar tanks are also produced for drinking water but the largest of these holds 50 000 gallons (227 300 litres). Also produced are collapsible

tanks for container transport (a standard 20 ft ISO container collapsible tank can carry a payload weighing 18 000 kg). The smallest collapsible containers produced are described as jerry-bags with dimensions (full) of 650 × 450 × 180 mm. They are suitable for fuel or water.

Achidatex collapsible containers are produced in three material types, as follows:

ACH-5, with a base fabric of tyre cord strength polyester yarn. This has a high temperature resistant, tough, resilient coating with a non-extractable plasticiser.

Urethane-coated polyester ACH-7714, a specially formulated and produced membrane fabric for contain-

ing leaded or unleaded petrol, jet fuels, methanol and ethanol.

Polyester membrane fabrics ACH-8028 and 8424, approved by the US Food and Drug Administration for the containment of drinking water and other liquids.

Status
All the above are in production and in service with the Israeli Defence Forces.

Manufacturer
Achidatex, PO Box 2156, Ramat Gan, 52151, Israel.
Tel: (3) 472637. Telex: 371271 achid i.
Fax: (3) 497307.

ITALY

Bartoletti System

Description
The Bartoletti system is used by the Italian Army for the transport and distribution of petrol, diesel and kerosene fuels, and in service is mounted on three different chassis: the IVECO FIAT CM 52, CP 62 and the CP 70. A special model of the CP 70 is also in service fitted with a micro-filter for refuelling light aircraft and helicopters. The tanker is provided with both left and right side service points and a drum filling unit.

The left side service point contains a self-priming centrifugal pump driven by the vehicle engine which can deliver 500 l/min, a 77 mm filter, intake for suction from outside, visual indicator and three operating gate valves for circuit formation. The right hand service point contains a control board with rev counter, pressure gauge, vacuum gauge, two remote-controls, engine accelerator remote-control, volumetric measuring unit, discharge mouth, an intake for closed-cycle connection, set of gate valves, reel with hose, and a 51 mm distributor nozzle. The drum filling unit has four 38 mm gate valves with rapid couplings, four rubber hoses and four distributor nozzles.

Specifications (mounted on CP 70 chassis)
Configuration: 4 × 4
Weight:
(empty) 7960 kg
(loaded) 12 500 kg
Tank capacity:
(petrol) 5800 l
(diesel) 5380 l

Bartoletti system on IVECO FIAT CP 70 (4 × 4) chassis (Italian Army)

(kerosene) 5750 l
Useful load: 4540 kg
Length: 6.554 m
Width: 2.5 m
Height: 2.97 m
Range: 650 km
Fuel capacity: 230 l
Gradient: 60%

Status
In production. In service with the Italian Army.

Manufacturer
E Bartoletti, Via Leonardo da Vinci 4, I-47100, Forli, Italy.
Tel: 61122. Telex: 550064 bartfo 1.

Mobile Fuel Can Filler System

Description
The mobile fuel can filler system is mounted on a two-wheeled trailer and can fill 600 20 litre fuel cans per hour. It has a gross capacity of approximately 2000 litres.

Status
In service with the Italian Army.

Mobile fuel can filler system deployed (Italian Army)

Mobile fuel can filler system in travelling position (Italian Army)

Mobile Fuel Transfer Station

Description
The trailer-mounted mobile fuel transfer station consists of two pumps which can be used together or separately, each with a capacity of approximately 300 l/min, complete with a bypass filter and driven by an electric motor connected to the pump by a V-belt. Equipment provided includes one 5 kW mobile generator to supply electricity to the electric motors for the pumps, one current correction unit (5 kW, 220 V), a full set of attachments including metal pipes and hose for both fuel distribution and filling, and a set of cables and accessories for electrical earthing of the mobile station.

Status
In service with the Italian Army.

Mobile fuel transfer station in travelling position (Italian Army)

SOUTH AFRICA

Static Storage Tanks

Description
Intended for the storage of fuel, oil products and water, these static storage tanks are for use in forward areas. They are made from nylon-reinforced nitrile rubber with abrasion, ozone and sunlight resistant external surfaces. Each tank is fitted with an air vent, quick connection dry-break couplings, an inspection manhole and handles for lifting when empty. Each tank is delivered packed in a wooden crate that also contains a repair kit for on-the-spot repairs. Five sizes are produced (see Specifications table).

Specifications

Capacity	Length*	Width
4500 l	3.64 m	2.64 m
13 000 l	5.08 m	4.11 m
22 000 l	5.38 m	5.44 m
45 000 l	7.06 m	6.91 m
50 000 l	7.49 m	6.91 m

* empty

Status
In production. In service with the South African Defence Forces.

Typical SARMCOL static storage tank

Manufacturer
SARMCOL SA (Pty) Limited.
Enquiries to Armscor, Private Bag X337, Pretoria 0001, South Africa.

Tel: 012 428 1911. Telex: 30217.
Fax: 012 428 5635.

Transportable Fuel Tanks

Description

Produced in sizes up to 10 000 litres, these tanks are intended to convert flat bed or box-body trucks into fuel tankers. They are made of high strength and durable synthetic fibre and rubber materials. The ends of each tank are sealed with special reinforcing metal clamps with a fuelling/defuelling coupling at one end only. A simple manually operated air vent is situated at the top centre of the tank to allow the escape of air which might be present in the tank before filling. A special retaining harness is used made from high tensile nylon webbing to provide a safe and sure anchorage for the tank on standard flat bed trucks. Each tank is delivered in a special wooden crate that contains not only the tank but all its accessories including a repair kit. When not in use the tank may be stored in the crate or rolled up.

A 10 000 litre tank laid flat is 6.7 m long and 2.3 m wide.

Status

In production. In service with the South African Defence Forces.

Manufacturer

SARMCOL SA (Pty) Limited.

Transportable fuel tank on a truck

Enquiries to Armscor, Private Bag X337, Pretoria 0001, South Africa.   Tel: 012 428 1911. Telex: 30217. Fax: 012 428 5635.

Container, Vehicle Fuel Pump Unit, 2-tonne, 1DX

Description

This fuel pump unit is based on a steel construction 1DX ISO container with canvas flaps at the sides and back giving access to a diesel engine-driven pump, filters, suction hoses, meters and delivery hoses. The unit can be used to refuel up to 10 vehicles simultaneously from an outside source or for transferring fuel in bulk. Capacity is 27 000 l/h.

When refuelling, fuel is pumped from an outside source by the engine and a self-priming pump, through the filter system and meter to delivery hoses. The hoses are fitted with automatic shut-off delivery nozzles and when transferring fuel in bulk it is pumped directly to a 64 mm delivery hose.

The container may be carried on a container carrier trailer, a SAMIL 20 (4 × 4) 2000 kg truck fitted with twistlocks, or inside a SAMIL 50 (4 × 4) 4800 kg truck drop side body.

The unit weighs 1800 kg, is 3 m long, 2.44 m wide and 1.45 m high.

Container, Vehicle Fuel Pump Unit, 2-tonne, 1DX

Status

In production. In service with the South African Defence Forces.

Manufacturer

Enquiries to Armscor, Private Bag X337, Pretoria 0001, South Africa.
Tel: 012 428 1911. Telex: 30217.
Fax: 012 428 5635.

TFM Tanktainer

Description

The TFM Tanktainer consists of a steel or stainless steel tank held in a rigid angle frame assembly that conforms to ISO standards and can thus be handled by standard ISO material handling systems; ISO twistlocks are provided. The tank can hold a total of 21 000 litres in three equal compartments, each compartment having a lockable manhole and a sump. Associated piping is 80 mm welded steel and each compartment has a butterfly valve with a locking mechanism and seal. Fire extinguisher brackets are provided close to the discharge valves.

Specifications

Weight: (empty) 4250 kg
Length: 6.058 m
Width: 2.438 m
Height: (steel tank) 2.42 m

Status

In production.

Manufacturer

TFM (Pty) Limited, PO Box 46131, Orange Grove, Transvaal, South Africa.
Tel: 012 316 2106. Fax: 012 316 1462.

TFM Tanktainer ready for delivery

UNITED KINGDOM

Demountable Bulk Fuel Dispensing Unit

Description

The demountable bulk fuel dispensing unit comprises two tanks, one pumping and dispensing pack, a two-tier rack and mounting beams.

The unit was designed for mounting on the Bedford MK (4 × 4) flat bed truck but can be adapted to fit other chassis with suitable capacity. The unit can be removed from the vehicle by a fork-lift truck, crane or, in an emergency, by hand.

The tanks are manufactured from AA5454 aluminium sheet and each tank has a capacity of 2100 litres. Access to the tank interior is through a 406 × 356 mm collar in the top skin. The filler cap assembly incorporates a 254 mm diameter EMCO open-fill quick-release manhole and a single pressure/vacuum vent. A dip point containing a captive dipstick is provided, and the filler cap and dip point are contained within a spillage band. An automatic bottom loading facility fitted to each tank enables loading rates of up to 682 l/min and off-loading rates of 455 l/min to be achieved. A drain plug is provided in the tank bottom skin and each tank is pressure tested to 0.703 kg/cm².

The dispensing equipment may be operated independently of the tanks if desired. The pump set is resiliently mounted inside the dispensing pack frame and is adequately protected against spillage by a firescreen and boxed-in exhaust which meets Ministry of Defence (Army) safety requirements.

A two-tier rack fitted with a drip tray and drain plug is provided. The lower tier of the rack is designed as a roller carriage which can be withdrawn from either side of the vehicle. An Alan Cobham filter/water separator with differential pressure gauge is incorporated in the design.

Two 12.192 m 32 mm diameter smoothbore delivery hoses terminating in automatic shut-off nozzles are stowed on a self-rewind Dean hose reel. Also 10 m of 63.5 mm layflat hose are provided. A cross pumping

Demountable bulk fuel dispensing unit on rear of Bedford MK (4 × 4) 4000 kg truck

off-take complete with an Avery Hardoll 63.5 mm self-sealing coupling for cross pumping to a tanker vehicle is connected to a secondary discharge outlet.

A rigid suction pipe connects at one end to the pump and at the other to bifurcated suction hoses, which connect to the two tanks via the CC41 coupling units. The suction hoses have a bore of 63.5 mm.

The whole equipment is retained on two longitudinal beams mounted on the vehicle platform. The equipment is fully bonded to the vehicle and is capable of being earthed. Two Dean bonding reels are provided each with 12.2 m of bonding cable terminating with crocodile clip type clamps. Two fire extinguishers are mounted on the nearside and offside of the two-tier rack.

Optional equipment includes a manifold assembly box for can filling, comprising 63.5 mm Avery Hardoll hose unit type CC40, 10 m of 38 mm bore hose to BS 3158, five-way manifold, 5 m of 19 mm bore hose to BS 3395 (5 off) and 19 mm automatic shut-off nozzles

(5 off).

The lid of the stowage box acts as holder for the cans during filling.

Specifications
Weight: 1798 kg
Payload: 2967 kg
Length: 3.66 m
Width: 2.44 m
Height: 1.22 m

Status
In service with the British Army and other armed forces.

Manufacturer
Simon Gloster Saro Limited, Gloucester Trading Estate, Hucclecote, Gloucestershire GL3 4AD, UK.
Tel: 0452 371321. Telex: 43134 glosro g.
Fax: 0452 371024.

Avon Flexitanks for Fuel

Description
Avon Technical Products Division produces a range of Flexitanks for transporting and storing fuel. They are made from high-strength polymer-coated fabric and are available in a wide range of sizes. They can be folded, transported and re-used repeatedly and will operate throughout a wide temperature range.

Flexitanks are also supplied for water storage and for details of these tanks see the entry in the *Water supplies* section.

Status
In production. In service with the US Department of Defense.

Manufacturer
Avon Technical Products Division, Bath Road, Melksham, Wiltshire SN12 8AA, UK.
Tel: 0225 791823. Fax: 0225 705585.

Typical Avon Flexitanks

Dunlop Dracone Barges

Description
The idea of the Dracone barge dates from 1956 with the concept of transporting liquids having lower specific gravity than the surrounding water through which the cargo is towed in specially designed flexible containers. Dunlop became involved in the programme during 1963. Since 1965 it has developed the Dracone Barge to the stage where it is now widely used by both military and civil concerns.

The Dracone barge combines strength of construction with good towing capabilities in open waters. Each Dracone barge has a tapered nose and rounded tail section and is moulded in individual seamless units joined to the parallel centre section by circumferential seams. The nose section will withstand a pull of 30 tonnes without damage. Body seams are both stitched and hot vulcanised. The high tensile nylon fabrics used are coated with Neoprene for the outer proofing for resistance to abrasion, sunlight, oils and sea water. On the inside nitrile is normally used for proofing.

Dracone barges can be used to carry a wide range of mineral and vegetable oils and can also be used to transport water. Being flexible, the barges can slide over obstructions without friction when wet and the barge acts as its own shock absorber. For open sea towing a length of tow of approximately 100 m is usual although this can be shortened for towing in sheltered waters or moving in confined anchorages. Nylon tow ropes are used. The towing hose, through which the barge is loaded and discharged, is designed to accept the maximum towing loads with ample safety margins. The smaller sizes can be towed at speeds in excess of 12 knots and the largest can travel at 7 knots. From size D5 and upwards all Dracone barges are fitted with a rear stabiliser to prevent snaking. The power required to tow a Dracone is considerably less than that required for a conventional barge of similar capacity.

Dracones can be launched in number of ways including dropping a rolled unit from a cargo net, pulling a rolled unit from a slipway by a small launch, rolling bodily from a beach or launching over the stern of a vessel. Built-in buoyancy panels keep the barge

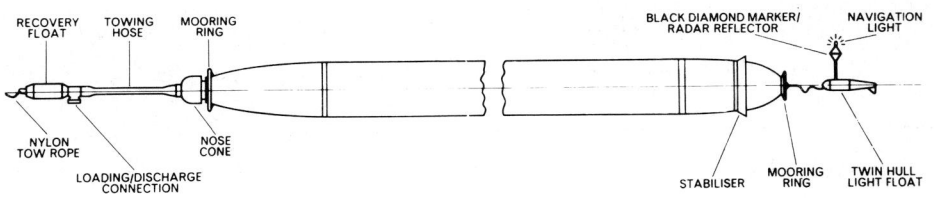

Main components of a typical Dracone barge

afloat even when it is completely empty.

Cargo is loaded and discharged through a length of flexible hose fitted to the nose as an integral part of the tow to make handling easier. Small barges (up to and including the D5) are fitted with a 50 mm bore hose while the larger sizes have a 100 mm hose as standard. Larger bore hoses are available on request. All hoses are supplied in standard lengths of 4.57 m that are bolted together to suit. At the end of the hose is a lightweight corrosion resistant float to which the loading/discharge connection is fitted. A quick-acting coupling can be fitted. Loading can be by gravity or pump.

Empty Dracone barges may be carried as deck cargo but are normally left afloat once launched. A special gripper bar has been developed for recovering empty barges. Little or no maintenance other than cleaning is normally required.

Dracone barges can also be used as alternatives to ship-to-shore pipelines and can be employed as floating fuel reservoirs.

Status
In production and widespread service.

Manufacturer
Dunlop Limited, GRG Division, PO Box 151, Cambridge Street, Manchester M60 1PD, UK.
Tel: 061 236 2131. Telex: 667225 dunman g.
Fax: 061 236 1599.

Specifications

Model	A1	A2	D5	D10	E	F	J	L	O
100% capacity	4.55 m³	9.1 m³	22.75 m³	45.5 m³	100 m³	191 m³	385 m³	519 m³	1100 m³
85% capacity	3.9 m³	7.8 m³	19.3 m³	38.6 m³	85 m³	162 m³	327.25 m³	441 m³	935 m³
Length	7.5 m	14.1 m	15.07 m	31 m	37.64 m	49.2 m	66 m	66 m	91.45 m
Diameter	0.94 m	0.94 m	1.42 m	1.42 m	1.87 m	2.347 m	2.82 m	3.28 m	4.225 m
Weight empty	270 kg	310 kg	430 kg	780 kg	1000 kg	2275 kg	3540 kg	4060 kg	6500 kg
Towing hose bore	50 mm	50 mm	100 mm	100 mm	100 mm	100 mm	100 mm	100 mm	100 mm
Stabiliser	no	no	yes	yes	yes	yes	yes	yes	yes

Dunlop Collapsible Containers

Description
Dunlop collapsible containers can be used to store a wide variety of liquids ranging from petrol, oil and lubricants to water and chemicals for almost any purpose. The range produced is wide but all tanks are constructed from a flexible two-ply textile and polymer laminate. Both sides of the laminate are treated to ensure long life and resistance to abrasions and hard knocks. For extra strength each corner is reinforced by metal clamping bars. Joint reinforcing straps fabricated from panels of vulcanised polymer coated textiles add extra strength to the main structure and all the ports and fittings are constructed from either steel or brass. The filled tanks may be either placed on prepared surfaces or laid on earth or sand foundations. The smaller tanks may be carried on flat bed trucks or the decks of ships. When not in use the collapsible tanks may be cleaned and rolled up for storage ready for re-use.

Status
In production. In service with several armed forces.

Manufacturer
Dunlop Limited, GRG Division, PO Box 151, Cambridge Street, Manchester M60 1PD, UK.
Tel: 061 236 2131. Telex: 667225 dunman g.
Fax: 061 236 1599.

45 000 litre tank intended primarily for petroleum products undergoing final examination before delivery to British Army

Specifications

Tank capacity	225 l	1125 l	2250 l	4500 l	9000 l	11 250 l	22 500 l	45 000 l	90 000 l	135 000 l	225 000 l
Length	2.06 m	1.52 m	2.59 m	4.72 m	4.88 m	5.49 m	9.76 m	10.21 m	11.58 m	17.15 m	18.59 m
Width	0.69 m	2.06 m	2.06 m	2.06 m	3.43 m	3.43 m	3.43 m	4.8 m	7.45 m	8.92 m	11.66 m
Height (filled)	0.38 m	0.79 m	0.79 m	0.79 m	0.91 m	0.91 m	0.91 m	1.22 m	1.22 m	1.07 m	1.22 m

---

UNITED STATES OF AMERICA

Flexcel Liquid Containers

Description
The basis of the Flexcel container is a sausage-shaped storage tank manufactured from acrylonitrile-butadiene synthetic rubber reinforced with nylon tyre cords for the interior bladder and polychloroprene for the strong outer cover. The exterior is fitted with built-in hooks and straps enabling the container to be carried in or on almost any type of vehicle or slung under a helicopter. One end of the container has a shroud containing a hose and a dispensing nozzle plus junctions and refuelling fittings.

There are various sizes of Flexcel container with the most usual being 2.6 m long, 0.356 m wide and weighing 56.7 kg empty. The storage capacity of this version is 55 gallons/250 litres. Other sizes include 30 gallons/113.5 litres and 80 gallons/303 litres.

The Flexcel container is strong enough to be free-dropped from a helicopter even when full. It has been demonstrated being dropped from a helicopter flying at a height of 12.2 m at a speed of 80 knots. When the Flexcel has been dropped from a helicopter or vehicle

Flexcel fuel container being carried on side of M60 MBT

Refuelling nozzle of Flexcel fuel container

it is ready for almost immediate use. The dispenser hose and nozzle are removed from within the shroud and are attached to the Flexcel by a quick-connect device. The vehicle or AFV to be refuelled is then driven onto the Flexcel to provide the refuelling pressure as the nozzle is placed in the vehicle fuel tank. The complete process can take as little as 25 seconds. After use the Flexcel container can be refilled and used again.

The Flexcel can be used for liquids other than fuel and can be used to carry water, decontaminants and other fluids.

Status
In production. In service with US Marine Corps and US Army.

Manufacturer
Teledyne Continental Motors – General Products, 76 Getty Street, Muskegon, Michigan 49442-1238, USA. Tel: (616) 724 2151. Fax: (616) 724 2796.

GTA Superdrums

Description
The GTA Superdrum was designed for the transport of fuel or drinking water. It can be fully collapsed when empty and in use can be rolled, towed, lifted, floated and dropped by helicopter. It is available in 55 gallon (208 litre), 250 gallon (946 litre) and 500 gallon (1893 litre) capacities although other sizes can be produced. The Superdrums have high abrasion and puncture resistance and can be dropped in free fall from a height of 4.5 m. A field repair kit is provided with each unit.

As well as being used as fuel or water tanks, Superdrums can also be used as surface or submerged flotation devices, as pneumatic lifting jacks or ship's fenders, and as storage units for the underwater storage of fuel supplies.

GTA Containers Inc also produces collapsible pillow tanks for fuel and water, storage tanks with capacities of from 3000 gallons (11 356 litres) to 100 000 gallons (378 540 litres), semi-trailer tanks for use on flat bed trucks with capacities of from 3000 to 5000 gallons (11 356 to 18 927 litres), and mini-tanks for use on small trucks with capacities of from 160 gallons (605 litres) to 500 gallons (1893 litres).

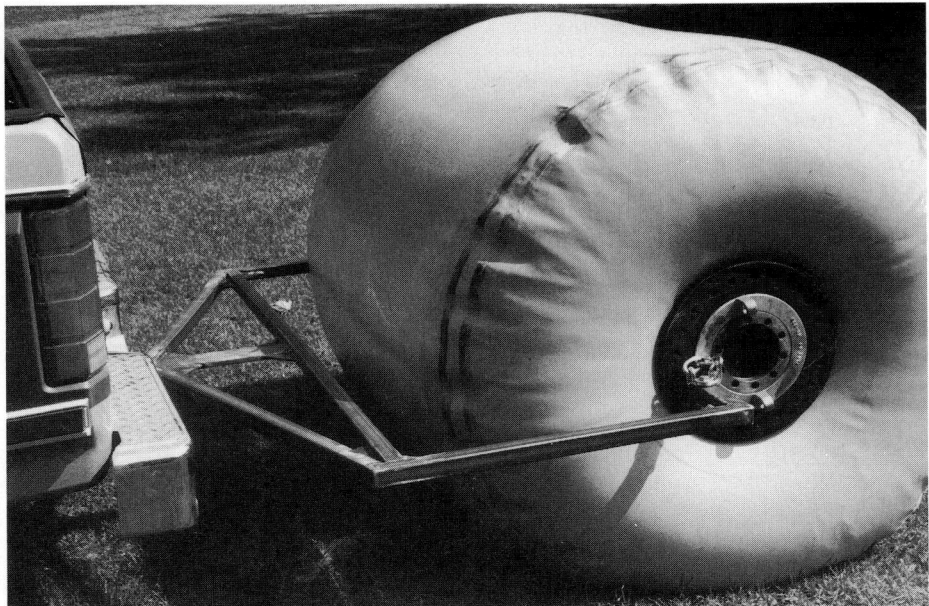

GTA Superdrum on tow

Specifications
Model	GTA-55	GTA-250	GTA-500
Capacity	55 US gal	250 US gal	500 US gal
	208 l	946 l	1893 l
Weight (empty)	15.88 kg	68 kg	72.5 kg
Length	0.86 m	1.52 m	1.52 m
Diameter	0.61 m	1.01 m	1.4 m

Status
In production for the US Army.

Manufacturer
GTA Containers Inc, 1410 W. Napier Street, South Bend, Indiana 46601, USA. Tel: (219) 288 3459. Fax: (219) 289 6060.

Uniroyal Sealdrums

Description
Uniroyal Sealdrums are portable, collapsible rubber containers for storing and transporting POL products, water, liquid chemicals and other fluids. They are circular drums with metal 'hubs' with the bulk of the container being constructed of elastomeric-coated rayon cord. The outer cover is neoprene with the inner lining being a nitrile material. This casing is puncture-resistant and can withstand a minimum of three successive free-fall drops from a height of 3.8 m. Once filled, the Sealdrums are non-vented and hermetically sealed, with extremely low permeability. When empty, Sealdrums collapse to about 15 per cent of their filled size. When filled they can be transported by truck, aircraft or helicopter, and dropped off the rear of a truck or para-dropped. They are the main item in the FARE (see entry in this section), Arctic fuelling and other fuel systems.

There is a Uniroyal range of similar containers known as Sealdbins which are used for the storing and carrying of dry materials.

Uniroyal Sealdrum undergoing trials in South-east Asia

Status
In production. In service with the US Army and many other nations.

Manufacturer
Uniroyal Plastics Co Inc, 312 North Hill Street, Mishawaka, Indiana 46544, USA.

Specifications
Capacity	55 US gal	250 US gal	500 US gal	515 US gal
	208.2 l	946.25 l	1892.5 l	1949.3 l
Length	0.876 m	1.524 m	1.575 m	2.032 m
Diameter	0.597 m	1.016 m	1.349 m	1.168 m
Weight (empty)	22.68 kg	113.4 kg	129.3 kg	129.3 kg

Uniroyal Sealdtanks

Description

Uniroyal Sealdtanks have been in production and use for over 25 years. They are long, bag-type containers that can be used to convert ordinary cargo or closed-body trucks into fuel or other liquid containers by simply unrolling the container in the back of the truck, lashing it down, and filling the container through a valve at one end. When emptied the container can be rolled up onto a special carrying drum by hand. Sealdtanks are heavy duty rubber containers and are produced in two main widths, 2.134 m and 2.235 m. They can be produced in a range of lengths from 4.877 m up to 12.97 m.

Sealdtank undergoing US Army trials

Specifications

Length		Capacity	
		2.134 m	2.235 m
16 ft	4.877 m	5677 l	6302 l
17 ft	5.18 m	6094 l	6737 l
18 ft	5.486 m	6491 l	7172 l
19 ft	5.791 m	6888 l	7607 l
20 ft	6.096 m	7286 l	8043 l
21 ft	6.4 m	7683 l	8478 l
22 ft	6.7 m	8081 l	8913 l
23 ft	7.01 m	8478 l	9349 l
24 ft	7.315 m	8894 l	9784 l
25 ft	7.62 m	9311 l	10 257 l
26 ft	7.925 m	9746 l	10 730 l
27 ft	8.23 m	10 181 l	11 203 l
28 ft	8.534 m	10 617 l	11 676 l
29 ft	8.839 m	11 052 l	12 150 l
30 ft	9.144 m	11 487 l	12 623 l
31 ft	9.45 m	11 941 l	13 115 l

Length		Capacity	
		2.134 m	2.235 m
32 ft	9.75 m	12 395 l	13 607 l
33 ft	10.06 m	12 831 l	14 080 l
34 ft	10.363 m	13 285 l	14 572 l
35 ft	10.67 m	13 758 l	15 083 l
36 ft	10.973 m	14 250 l	15 613 l
37 ft	11.278 m	14 761 l	16 162 l
38 ft	11.58 m	15 291 l	16 728 l
39 ft	11.887 m	15 821 l	17 297 l
40 ft	12.192 m	16 351 l	17 870 l
41 ft	12.97 m	16 880 l	18 435 l

Status

In production.

Manufacturer

Uniroyal Plastics Co Inc, 312 North Hill Street, Mishawaka, Indiana 46544, USA.

Uniroyal Static Storage Tanks

Description

Uniroyal produces a wide range of static storage tanks to store an equally wide range of liquids, including fuel and water (for details of the water tanks see entry in the *Water supplies* section). The tanks intended for fuel use are made from tough polymer-coated nylon fabric. Chafing patches at all fitting and hardware locations provide double-wall thickness and protection. Handles are moulded onto each tank to assist positioning. All the tanks are free-standing. When not in use the tanks can be stored and carried in wooden crates.

Status

In production. In service with US forces and many other nations.

Manufacturer

Uniroyal Plastics Co Inc, 312 North Hill Street, Mishawaka, Indiana 46544, USA.

Specifications

Capacity		Approximate dimensions filled:		
		Width	Length	Height
1000 US gal	3785 l	2.388 m	3.073 m	0.61 m
2000 US gal	7570 l	3.353 m	3.353 m	0.813 m
3000 US gal	11 355 l	3.581 m	4.267 m	0.914 m
5000 US gal	18 925 l	4.47 m	4.623 m	1.118 m
10 000 US gal	37 850 l	6.096 m	6.096 m	1.219 m
15 000 US gal	56 775 l	7.468 m	7.315 m	1.219 m
20 000 US gal	75 700 l	6.7 m	8.23 m	1.727 m
25 000 US gal	94 625 l	6.7 m	10.363 m	1.727 m
50 000 US gal	189 250 l	6.7 m	19.2 m	1.727 m
100 000 US gal	378 500 l	18.136 m	18.212 m	1.219 m

Uniroyal static storage tanks in use by German Army

Uniroyal Bulk Refueller System

Description
The Uniroyal Bulk Refueller System uses standard trucks or other military vehicles for conversion to a bulk fuel tanker and refuelling configuration. The main component of the system is Uniroyal's 250 or 500 US gallon Collapsible Sealdrum. The ancillary equipment, including a pump, hoses and nozzles, can be supplied either separately or together as a unit, mounted and stowed in a small trailer. A Universal Chain Hold-down kit is used to tie one Sealdrum or multiples of Sealdrums to the vehicle, dependent on the vehicle's carrying capacity. Once the refueller arrives at its destination it can either be parked until the fuel has been dispensed, or the fuel-laden Sealdrums can be rolled off the vehicle to release the vehicle for other purposes. When the Sealdrums are empty the vehicle can pick up the collapsed drums, connect the trailer with the ancillary equipment and return to a depot for reassignment.

Status
In production. In service with some NATO and Far East armed forces.

Manufacturer
Uniroyal Plastics Co Inc, 312 North Hill Street, Mishawaka, Indiana 46544, USA.

Uniroyal Bulk Refueller System in use by NATO army

Forward Area Refuelling Equipment (FARE)

Description
FARE is a lightweight, air-transportable refuelling system intended for refuelling helicopters in forward area combat operations. As a secondary function FARE provides a means for safe rapid refuelling of all US Army aircraft ground vehicles and other equipment. FARE was type classified as Standard A and replaced the Pumping Assembly, Flammable Liquid, Bulk Transfer, and Pump Centrifugal, Gas Driven, Base Mounted, 38 mm, 378.5 l/min.

FARE includes: a petrol engine-driven centrifugal pump with a rated capacity of 378.5 l/min at 30.48 m total dynamic head; a lightweight military design filter-separator with a rated capacity of 378.5 l/min; two closed-circuit refuelling nozzles with adaptors for conventional gravity fuelling; 60.96 m of lightweight discharge hose with 50.8 mm nominal inside diameter; 18.28 m of suction hose with 50.8 mm nominal inside diameter; and miscellaneous fittings, valves and accessories.

FARE is capable of dispensing fuel through two nozzles simultaneously at flow rates of up to 189.25 l/

FARE being used in conjunction with standard 1892.5 litre collapsible drums to refuel Bell UH-1 Iroquois helicopter (US Army)

min through each nozzle. The maximum flow rate possible when dispensing fuel through a single nozzle is approximately 302.8 l/min.

Any available bulk fuel storage tank may be used to supply fuel to the FARE – the standard 1892.5 litre (500 US gallon) collapsible drum is the primary source of bulk fuel supply.

Status
In production. In service with the US Army.

Development Agency
US Army Belvoir Research, Development and Engineering Center, Fort Belvoir, Virginia 22060-5606, USA.

Manufacturer
Uniroyal Plastics Co Inc, 312 North Hill Street, Mishawaka, Indiana 46544, USA.

Arctic Fuels Dispensing Equipment (AFDE)

Description
Arctic weather can have many severe effects on orthodox fuelling systems, such as making collapsible fuel storage tanks brittle and liable to split. An increase in fuel viscosity, brought on by cold weather, can make fuels harder to pump and cause engine operating difficulties. To overcome these problems the US Army Research, Development and Engineering Center began development work on a new system of Arctic Fuels Dispensing Equipment (AFDE). The programme introduces a new generation of fuel equipment which is simple, lightweight, air-transportable and collapsible. The fuel tanks and hoses involved are designed for use between −60 and +95°F. They are fabricated from materials based on low-temperature elastomers such as polyurethane and polypropylene. Another AFDE feature is easy starting and improved pumping power made possible by the use of gas turbine engines. Two types of basic installation are envisaged: an AFDE Supply Point with collapsible tanks to store up to 120 000 US gallons of fuel and a pumping capability of 600 US gallons/min, and a Forward Area Refuelling

Artist's impression of arctic fuels dispensing equipment in use (US Army)

Equipment made up of 500 US gallon collapsible fabric drums and a fuel pumping capability of 200 US gallons/min.

Status
Development complete. Production planned.

Development Agency
US Army Belvoir Research, Development and Engineering Center, Fort Belvoir, Virginia 22060-5606, USA.

Fuel System, Supply Point Portable, 60 000 gallon (US) Capacity

Description
The Fuel System, Supply Point Portable is the US Army's primary means of distributing and issuing bulk petroleum to combat units under tactical conditions. The system can handle a total, at any one time, of 60 000 US gallons (227 100 litres) in six 10 000 US gallon (37 850 litre) Uniroyal collapsible bulk fuel static storage tanks. The system consists of two pumping assemblies, two filter/separators, ten 10 000 US gallon (37 850 litre) collapsible tanks, six bottom-loading points for loading tank trucks and semi-trailers, two 500 US gallon (1892.5 litre) Sealdrum filling points and six refuelling points for filling vehicles. There is also a number of 5 US gallon (18.9 litre) cans and 55 US gallon (208 litre) metal drums. The combination and types of filling points can be altered according to local requirements.

Since there are two pumps and filter/separators, this system can be broken down into two 30 000 US gallon (116 250 litre) systems which could then be used to handle two different types of fuel or can be laid out at two different locations.

Part of Fuel System, Supply Point Portable showing hoses and tanks

Status
In production. In service with the US Army and some Far Eastern and European armed forces.

Manufacturer
Uniroyal Plastics Co Inc, 312 North Hill Street, Mishawaka, Indiana 46544, USA.

Bulk Fuel Tank Assembly, 5000-barrel Capacity

Description
This tank provides bulk storage and replaces 10 000- and 55 000-barrel steel tanks. The 5000-barrel tank can be installed rapidly by engineer troops and other troops with construction support. The assembly consists of a pillow-type tank constructed of a lightweight elastomer-coated nylon fabric, positioned within an excavated and lined earthen pit prepared by excavation. Empty weight of the fuel assembly is approximately 1361 kg. When filled to capacity it is 20.72 m long, 20.72 m wide and 2.03 m deep. Continuous re-use of the tank is planned during wartime to the extent of the operational life of the item. It can be drained, recovered and relocated.

Status
In service with the US Army.

Development Agency
US Army Belvoir Research, Development and Engineering Center, Fort Belvoir, Virginia 22060-5606, USA.

Bulk Fuel Tank Assembly (US Army)

Low Profile Tank and Pump Unit

Description
This tank and pump unit is mounted on a 5-ton cargo carrier and consists of two 500-gallon aluminium tanks and a 125 gallons/min electric motor-driven pump, together with the related fuel dispensing equipment mounted on an A-frame. The unit will convert a general-purpose military vehicle into an air-transportable fuel dispensing unit for refuelling military vehicles, ground equipment, aircraft, storage drums and 5-gallon cans. Production of these units began during FY89.

Status
Entered US Army service during FY90.

Development Agency
US Army Belvoir Research, Development and Engineering Center, Fort Belvoir, Virginia 22060-5606, USA.

Automated Pipeline System Construction Equipment

Description
The Automated Pipeline System Construction Equipment is a version of existing commercial pipeline laying equipment adapted for military use. It is intended to be used to construct rapidly high pressure fuel pipelines across country with as few construction personnel as possible.

The equipment is supplied with lengths of 101.6, 152.4 or 203 mm pipe by a tractor-towed semi-trailer. From the semi-trailer the pipes are placed into one half of a special tracked vehicle. From this vehicle half the pipes are lifted by a special vehicle-mounted crane into a hopper on the other half of the equipment. This hopper then automatically delivers the pipes into the pipe-joining mechanism that is situated to one side of the equipment, and from this the jointed pipe is laid onto the ground. Using this equipment it is intended that the pipes will be laid at the rate of 29 to 40 km/day. The equipment is fully self-propelled and apart from the pipe supply component, the personnel to handle the system will be a driver, a crane operator and two others.

Status
Development.

Pipeline Outfit, Petroleum (POP)

Description

Intended to be air-transportable, the Pipeline Outfit, Petroleum (POP) is a simple system for laying fuel-carrying pipelines in undeveloped areas or where existing distribution methods are unusable. The system is intended to carry fuel from shore bases to forward areas. It consists of pre-packed lengths of pipe and handling equipment that can be used with a minimum of training. The main carrying vehicles will be wheeled tractors, each with a side-mounted A-frame jib. The jibs will place the lengths of pipeline roughly in position and then lift them to join the previous pipe section. A following tractor carrying a pipe-joining machine will ensure that the subsequent pipe length fit is secure and leak-free. Once the join has been made the two tractors then progress to the next length.

The pipes involved have diameters of 152.4 mm and 203 mm. The outfit can deploy pipes at the rate of 29 km/day. Once laid, the pipeline system can have a capacity of 27 000 to 30 000 barrels per 20 hour day.

Status

Development.

Hydraulic pipe-joining press used with Pipeline Outfit, Petroleum with carrying wheeled tractor on left

---

Tank, Liquid Storage, Bolted Steel

Description

There are four tank sizes in the Tank, Liquid Storage, Bolted Steel range. The smallest has a capacity of 21 000 US gallons (79 485 litres) with the others having capacities of 42 000 US gallons (158 970 litres), 126 000 US gallons (476 910 litres) and 420 000 US gallons (1 598 700 litres). All the four sizes are intended to be transported to their sites (by air if required) in crates containing preformed steel plates, bolts, gaskets, valves, gauges and various assembly items. On site they can be constructed rapidly into circular steel tanks, fully enclosed and with a central inspection vent cover. An upper surface ladder is provided. Although intended to be for temporary use only they may be used as permanent structures if needed. They can be used for water storage as well as fuel storage.

Status

In service with the US Army: 21 000 US gallon (97), 42 000 US gallon (48), 126 000 US gallon (48), 420 000 US gallon (53).

Specifications

Capacity	21 000 US gal	42 000 US gal	126 000 US gal	420 000 US gal
	79 485 l	158 970 l	476 910 l	1 589 700 l
Weight (empty)	4677 kg	8085 kg	13 442 kg	35 391 kg
Inside diameter	6.566 m	9.06 m	9.06 m	16.758 m
Height	2.44 m	2.438 m	7.363 m	7.379 m

Angus Chemicoil System

Description

The Angus Chemicoil System was designed for the delivery of multi-purpose fuels and chemicals overland in bulk from fixed pipelines and storage points. The system may be used over long distances and may be laid by helicopters or vehicles using a minimum of manpower. It may also be used for ship-to-shore deliveries, aircraft refuelling and marine fuel bunkering. The system can be used with JP-4, JP-5 and JP-8 aircraft fuels, AVGAS, COMBATGAS, and DF-2 and AM-2 diesel fuels.

The pipes used with the Chemicoil system have a high quality, polyurethane inner lining and a circular woven and rot-proof reinforcement which may use copper-coated textile strands for static protection. The cover uses high quality polyurethane that is abrasion, ozone and weather resistant. The covers may be coloured camouflage sand, black, or NATO green. Pipes up to 200 m long may be supplied, with diameters of 25, 38, 45, 51, 63.5, 76, 102 and 152 mm. Pipe with a diameter of 25 mm weighs 0.138 kg/m and 152 mm pipe weighs 1.558 kg/m.

Status

In production. In service with US armed forces and some other nations.

Manufacturer

Angus Fire Armour Corporation, PO Box 879, Angier, North Carolina 27501, USA.
Tel: (919) 639 6151. Telex: 579398.

Chemicoil system in use by NATO forces

680

WATER SUPPLIES

AUSTRALIA

Permutit Water Purification Units

Description
Permutit Australia manufactured 59 CPC 7.5 and CPC 20 trailer-mounted water purification equipments for the Australian Defence Forces and later supplied 16 air-transportable MRO 10 units, used to supply up to 10 000 l/h.

The CPC units use a process of chemical coagulation, settling and filtration to clarify water using a high rate settling technique, and operate on the concept of a low head clarifier using corrugated interceptor plates. Filtration after settling polishes the water while chlorine sterilises it. The units will turn any naturally occurring dirty, muddy, unsafe and undrinkable water into potable water.

The units are self-contained and on arrival on site require levelling using the jacks mounted on the equipment. After hose connection to the water source, potable water is available within 1 hour.

The CPC 20 unit is mounted on a four-wheeled trailer and can produce 20 000 l/h. The CPC 7.5 unit is mounted on a two-wheeled trailer and can produce 7500 l/h.

Water Purification Trailer, Permutit-Boby CPC 20

Status
MRO, CPC 7.5 and CPC 20 in service with the Australian Army and in Papua New Guinea.

Manufacturer
Permutit Australia, PO Box 117, Brookvale, New South Wales 2100, Australia.
Tel: (02) 938 4666. Fax: (02) 938 6569.

CANADA

Zenon Advanced Double Pass Reverse Osmosis Water Purification Unit (ADROWPU)

Description
The Zenon Advanced Double Pass Reverse Osmosis Water Purification Unit (ADROWPU) was designed for field use and can be used to treat water that has been contaminated by NBC agents as well as fresh, brackish and sea water. The ADROWPU employs a double pass reverse osmosis process, that is, a pressure driven membrane separation process that separates dissolved solutes and suspended substances from water. The double pass process is used for NBC contaminant removal and sea water treatment.

The ADROWPU is a fully integrated self-contained system with its own 40 kW diesel power generator and a semi-automatic control system digital controls and instrumentation. Automatic self-cleaning and pre-treatment features are built-in and a pillow tank for storing processed water is provided with each system. Installation time is 20 minutes.

The system is arranged in a self-contained palletised enclosure which enables it to be transported via all modes of military transport, including NATO standard palletised loading systems. The ADROWPU can also fit inside a standard ISO container.

The ADROWPU weighs 6400 kg and measures 5.5 × 2.1 × 1.7 m. It can be operated at temperatures ranging from −40 to +40°C.

Typical ADROWPU outputs are as follows:

Status
In production.

Manufacturer
Zenon Environmental Systems Inc, 845 Harrington Court, Burlington, Ontario, Canada L7N 3P3.
Tel: (416) 639 6320. Telex: 061 8734.
Fax: (416) 639 1812.

Typical outputs (litres/day)

Input water	Fresh	Brackish	Sea
Basic unit:			
Without NBC	84 700	81 520	52 390
With NBC	59 250	58 950	52 390
Expanded unit:			
Without NBC	112 650	108 450	69 680
With NBC	78 830	78 380	69 680

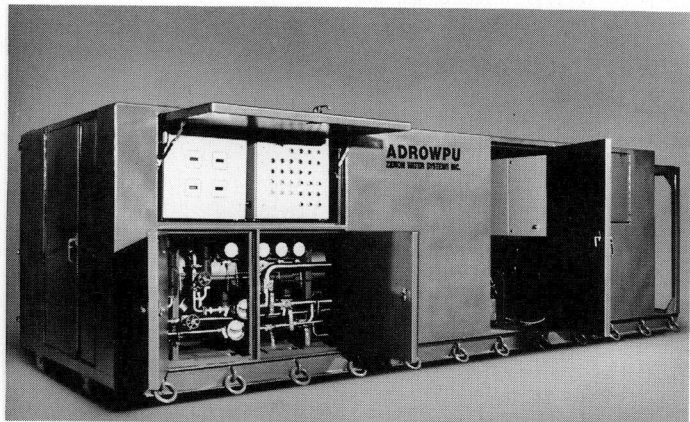

Stand-alone version of Zenon Advanced Double Pass Reverse Osmosis Water Purification Unit (ADROWPU)

Truck-mounted version of Zenon Advanced Double Pass Reverse Osmosis Water Purification Unit (ADROWPU) in travelling configuration

Zenon Seagold Mini-ROWPU Water Purification Modules

Description
The Zenon Seagold Mini-ROWPU family of water purification modules was designed to meet the water purification requirements of mobile rapid-deployment forces. The modules are compact and lightweight and can be used in any terrain to treat fresh, brackish and sea water. The modular system can be configured for double pass operation to treat water contaminated with NBC agents.

There are four main types of Seagold Mini-ROWPU module. They are the Pre-treatment – Screen Filter (PTSF); Pre-treatment – Nanofilter (PTNF); Reverse Osmosis Single Pass treatment (ROSP); and Power Supply Unit (PSU). The latter may be a self-contained petrol unit (PSU/G) or electrical (PSU/E) using a generator. Typical dimensions for each module are 0.6 × 0.6 × 1.5 m.

The PTSF has a typical output of 500 l/h (PTSF-500) while the PTNF output is 500 or 1000 l/h (PTNF-500 or PTNF-1000). A typical ROSP output is 250 l/h (ROSP-250) but ROSP modules connected in parallel can boost output, for example, two ROSP-250 modules placed in parallel and supplied from a PTSF-500 can have an output of 500 l/h. For NBC-contaminated water treatment a typical configuration could be a PTNF-500 feeding two ROSP-250 modules in parallel with their outputs combining to supply a further ROSP-250, thus providing 250 l/h of water free from NBC contamination.

Status
In production.

Manufacturer
Zenon Environmental Systems Inc, 845 Harrington Court, Burlington, Ontario, Canada L7N 3P3. Tel: (416) 639 6320. Telex: 061 8734. Fax: (416) 639 1812.

Stand-alone example of Zenon Seagold Mini-ROWPU water purification modules

COMMONWEALTH OF INDEPENDENT STATES

Mobile Water Desalination Plants OPS and POU

Description
These mobile water desalination plants were produced mainly for use in desert regions and both are mounted on truck chassis. The smallest unit is the POU which is mounted on a ZIL-157 (6 × 6) 2500 kg truck chassis and has an output capacity of 320 l/h. The unit is powered by a petrol engine. The OPS has a capacity of approximately 2000 l/h and is carried on a KrAZ-214 (6 × 6) 7000 kg truck chassis. The process used with the OPS not only distils the water but also purifies it biologically. Power for the OPS is provided by a towed generator.

Status
In service with the CIS.

Manufacturer
State factories.

Mobile water desalination plant OPS

LBU-200 Mobile Well-drilling Equipment

Description
The LBU-200 mobile well-drilling equipment is capable of drilling for water, testing its purity and providing limited storage capacity. The equipment is mounted on three KrAZ-255B (6 × 6) 7500 kg trucks and three 2-PN-6M trailers. One truck is fitted with the drilling rig, while a second carries the LGR-3 laboratory. The third truck, fitted with a hydraulic loading crane, carries hose, purification equipment and other ancillaries. Components of RBD-5000 water tanks are carried on the trailers.

Status
In service with the CIS.

Manufacturer
State factories.

FRANCE

ACMAT UMTE 48 Mobile Water Treatment Unit

Description

The ACMAT UMTE 48 water treatment unit is carried on a standard ACMAT RM 215 S single-axle trailer and can process raw water containing 120 mg/l of suspended matter at the rate of 2 m³/h. The unit is self-contained and automatic under the control of an electronic controller. The system can be used either for plain filtration or filtration with flocculants. If required the unit can be removed from the trailer and placed on a skid mount. Power for the system can be obtained from a 220 V mains supply or from a generator.

Status

In production.

Manufacturer

ACMAT (Ateliers de Construction Mécanique de l'Atlantique), Le Point du Jour, F-44600 Saint-Nazaire, France.
Tel: 40 22 33 71. Telex: 700913 f.
Fax: 40 66 30 96.

ACMAT UMTE 48 water treatment unit

ACMAT UMTE 48 water treatment unit in use

PRONAL Small Capacity Water Storage Tanks

Description

These small capacity tanks are manufactured from polyester fabric coated with non-toxic PVC and are resistant to ultraviolet radiation and all climatic conditions. They are produced in capacities from 20 to 500 litres and the 20-litre size is fitted with carrying handles for use when full. The larger sizes are used laid flat upon the ground. All are fitted with a 19 mm filling and emptying hose and a symmetrical coupling and plug. When not in use they can be rolled up for storage or carrying.

Specifications

Capacity	Length (empty)	Width (empty)	Height (full)	Weight (empty)	Volume (folded)
20 l	0.62 m	0.4 m	0.14 m	1.2 kg	5 dm³
50 l	0.75 m	0.62 m	0.17 m	1.65 kg	6.5 dm³
100 l	1.24 m	0.6 m	0.22 m	2.45 kg	10 dm³
200 l	1.24 m	0.95 m	0.26 m	3.4 kg	12.5 dm³
500 l	1.7 m	1.24 m	0.39 m	5.5 kg	22 dm³

Status

In production. The 20-litre tanks are in service with the Swiss Army.

Manufacturer

PRONAL SA, Z.I. Roubaix Est, BP 18, F-59115 Leers, France.
Tel: (33) 20 99 75 00. Telex: 132 750 f.
Fax: (33) 20 99 75 20.

PRONAL Flexible Open Vat Water Storage Tanks

Description

These open vat tanks are used for the large scale storage of water and other liquids such as decontamination fluids. They have an advantage over conventional storage tanks in that the tank may be filled and emptied very quickly and more than one user point may be employed at any one time. The tanks are placed on circular ground sheets and are filled from an over stand pipe or hose which is usually a 51 mm diameter component. The sides of the tank rise with the volume contained and if required a tarpaulin may be used to cover the contents. The tanks are constructed of polyester fabric coated with PVC.

Specifications

Capacity	Diameter	Height	Weight	Volume (folded)
5000 l	3 m	1 m	40 kg	0.45 m³
10 000 l	4.4 m	1 m	62 kg	0.7 m³

Status

In production.

Manufacturer

PRONAL SA, Z.I. Roubaix Est, BP 18, F-59115 Leers, France.
Tel: (33) 20 99 75 00. Telex: 132 750 f.
Fax: (33) 20 99 75 20.

PRONAL Flexible Water Storage Tanks

Description

PRONAL produces a wide range of flexible water storage tanks to suit specific customer requirements, so examples given in the Specifications table should be regarded as typical rather than applicable to individual cases. The material used for the tanks is a PVC-coated polyester fabric with a weight of 1.1 kg/m². The usual fittings are 51 mm filling/discharging valves and caps which can be connected by adaptors to 51 or 76 mm hoses.

Status

In production. In service with the French armed forces and some other nations.

Manufacturer

PRONAL SA, Z.I. Roubaix Est, BP 18, F-59115 Leers, France.
Tel: (33) 20 99 75 00. Telex: 132 750 f.
Fax: (33) 20 99 75 20.

Specifications

Capacity	Length (empty)	Width (empty)	Height (full)	Weight (empty)	Volume (folded)
1000 l	2.46 m	1.35 m	0.6 m	20 kg	0.09 m³
2000 l	2.46 m	2 m	0.9 m	25 kg	0.11 m³
5000 l	3.69 m	2.5 m	1.1 m	35 kg	0.17 m³
10 000 l	4 m	3.69 m	1.2 m	50 kg	0.25 m³
15 000 l	4.92 m	4.1 m	1.2 m	65 kg	0.3 m³
20 000 l	5 m	4.92 m	1.3 m	75 kg	0.4 m³
25 000 l	6 m	4.92 m	1.3 m	85 kg	0.45 m³
30 000 l	7 m	4.92 m	1.3 m	100 kg	0.5 m³
35 000 l	6.15 m	6.1 m	1.4 m	110 kg	0.55 m³
40 000 l	6.8 m	6.15 m	1.4 m	120 kg	0.6 m³
45 000 l	7.5 m	6.15 m	1.4 m	130 kg	0.65 m³
50 000 l	8.2 m	6.15 m	1.4 m	140 kg	0.7 m³
60 000 l	7.8 m	7.38 m	1.45 m	160 kg	0.8 m³
70 000 l	8.9 m	7.38 m	1.45 m	180 kg	0.9 m³
80 000 l	10 m	7.38 m	1.45 m	200 kg	1 m³
100 000 l	10.4 m	8.61 m	1.45 m	245 kg	1.2 m³
125 000 l	12.7 m	8.61 m	1.45 m	295 kg	1.5 m³
150 000 l	13.05 m	9.84 m	1.45 m	345 kg	1.75 m³
200 000 l	17 m	9.84 m	1.45 m	445 kg	2.25 m³

Individual Water Treatment Equipment

Description

The hand-operated Individual Water Treatment Equipment is intended for use by individual soldiers to remove suspended particles and bacterial, mineral and organic pollution from untreated water sources. Water to be treated is sucked into the system through a flexible tube fitted with a filter; the maximum pumping height is 1 m. The water is then passed through a processing device comprising a disposable cartridge which remains efficient for a maximum of 50 litres with a feed flow rate of approximately 6 l/h. Processed water is recovered directly into a standard water bottle.

The equipment is intended for military use and has an external volume of 1.5 litres and weighs 1.5 kg. Start-up time is less than 1 minute and reversion to the transport mode takes less than 2 minutes.

Status

In production for the French Army.

Manufacturer

SRTI-SODETEG, 9 avenue Réaumur, BP 22, F-92352 Le Plessis Robinson, France.
Tel: (1) 45 37 86 00. Telex: 631096 tcsf f.
Fax: (1) 45 37 88 30.

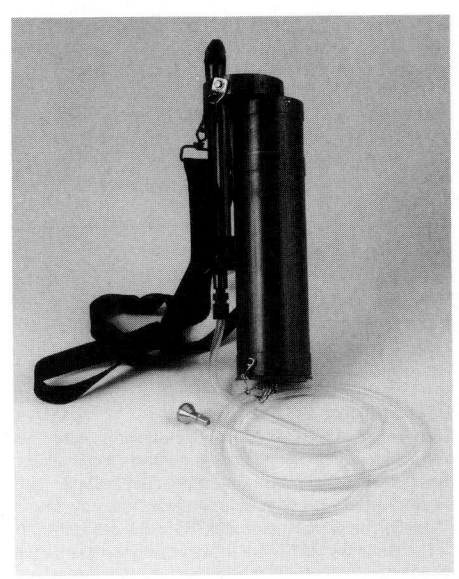

SRTI-SODETEG Individual Water Treatment Equipment

GERMANY

PBU 50M Well-boring Equipment

Description

The PBU 50M well-boring plant is used to sink bored, tube and dug wells. The bored and dug wells are sunk by the rotary boring method and tube wells by the boring and cable drilling methods.

The complete equipment comprises two ZIL-131 (6 × 6) 3500 kg trucks and two twin-axled trailers. One ZIL-131 serves as the drilling vehicle, and the rigs, spares, tools and accessories are carried on the other truck and the two trailers. The normal crew is four men.

The boring equipment is hinged on the rear frame of the drilling vehicle and during transportation it lies horizontally on the vehicle. Hydraulics are used to raise the rig and carry out the drilling, with the power for the two hydraulic pumps and gears coming from the vehicle engine. Two support jacks support the bore frame in the operating position and serve at the same time to align the bore frame.

The drilling vehicle is equipped with a cable winch coupled to a ram. The cable winch is used to raise and lower the drilling tools, the casing for tube wells and the concrete or timber collars for dug wells. The ram enables bores to be sunk by the percussion drill method, the travel of the drilling tool being 1 m at a maximum of 48 actions/minute. Torque transmission to the earth auger is carried out by a rotation gear pivoted at the bore frame which has an interchangeable liner inserted to form the connection with the bore rod. The liner can be disengaged and can be swung into two diametrically opposed directions to allow drilling tools to be connected to the rotation gear. Below the upper mitre gear there is a safety clutch with a shear pin as an overload protection device – normally only one shear pin is used.

Operating controls are located on the left-hand side of the vehicle with an auxiliary drive lever behind the driver's cab. The controls are for the hydraulics, the drilling transmission, the vehicle clutch, the speed regulator, the cable drum, the ram and the cable drum brake. There are also gauges and monitoring instruments behind the driver's cab for the hydraulic fluid pressure, oil and coolant temperatures, the running time and the drill speed. Some of these indicators are duplicated in the driver's cab.

Using the PBU 50M it is possible to sink two bored wells up to 50 m deep and run them simultaneously with each well delivering an average of 2.8 to 4.5 m³/h of water. Borings for dug wells can be made to a depth of 15 m.

Among the drilling tools used by the PBU 50M are augers with an external diameter of 200 mm and a useful length of 2.5 m. Using the PBU 50M it is possible to dig well shafts up to 1 m in diameter.

Status

In service with the former East German Army and possibly some other former Warsaw Pact armed forces.

Manufacturer

(Drilling equipment only): state factories.

Water Filtering Units

Description

The former East German armed forces used three basic forms of water filtering equipment, usually in conjunction with the MSchaK-15 well drilling equipment. The smallest unit is the WFS 1 (Wasserfilter-station 1) which is manportable. The WFS 2 is a trailer-mounted unit, while the WFS 3 is a much larger unit contained in a 6 m long trailer towed by a Tatra 148 truck. The two larger units contain not only water filtering and purification equipment but water sampling and analysis systems. Power for the WFS 3 is taken from a generator mounted on the truck body. The WSF 1 and 2 require external power sources.

Status

In service with the former East German Army.

Manufacturer

State factories.

Kärcher WaterClean 1000 Water Treatment System

Description

The Kärcher WaterClean 1000 water treatment system can continually process water contaminated by NBC agents into water of drinking quality.

The operational capacity of the WaterClean 1000 system is a minimum of 1000 l/h. Various chemicals are added to destroy chemical and biological agents, viruses and bacteria for operating periods of up to 8 hours, after which filters have to be changed and chemicals replaced. The treatment process is fully automatic using a memory-programmable control system with minimal operator intervention. Radioactive ions can be removed using an ion exchanger. If the untreated water contains excess salt a reverse osmosis unit can be used in place of the ion exchanger.

The system, complete with all optional modules, weighs approximately 1430 kg. It is 2.4 m long, 2.145 m wide and 1.7 m high.

Status

In production. Under test in several countries.

Manufacturer

Alfred Kärcher GmbH & Co, Alfred-Kärcher-Strasse 28-40, D-7057 Winnenden, Federal Republic of Germany.
Tel: 07195 14-0. Telex: 724432.
Fax: 07195 14212.

ISRAEL

Aquaport Desalination Plants

Description

Aquaport desalination plants are an advanced type of low temperature evaporator designed to convert sea or brackish water into pure (distilled) water for drinking or industrial purposes. The systems may be used in remote or isolated areas and are designed for simple operation, easy maintenance and low energy consumption. The plants are rugged and of simple mechanical design. They are produced in various standard models with varying capacities. Mobile units can produce up to 150 m^3 a day. The units are all electrical, fully automatic self-contained units and require only push-button operation.

Status

In production.

Manufacturer

IDE Technologies Limited, POB 591, Ra'anana 43104, Israel.
Tel: 052 557 333. Telex: 33590.
Fax: 052 546 542.

NETHERLANDS

Promac Aquaset MLT Mobile Drinking Water Units

Description

The Promac Aquaset MLT mobile drinking water units use a specially developed and patented combination of membrane separation and other purification techniques to produce high quality water from any source of contaminated surface water. Two sets are available.

The Aquaset MLT Mark III was designed to produce clean water from sources polluted by NBC agents, and systems are also available for brackish and sea water feed sources. The first unit was designed and built in co-operation with the TNO PML Netherlands Army Research Laboratory and underwent an initial two-year period of laboratory and field testing.

Several units are operational. The unit is contained in a military container measuring 4.25 × 2.2 × 2.09 m and weighing approximately 4800 kg. The unit is operated by two men and can commence clean water production within 30 minutes of arrival on site. Output is a continuous 3500 l/h. The unit can remain in operation for 30 days without support materials.

The Aquaset MLT Mark I was developed for the Dutch Marines and several units are in operation in Cambodia. The Aquaset Mark I is derived from the Aquaset MLT Mark III but produces 500 l/h and measures 2.5 × 1.32 × 1.36 m. The unit is supplied in an insulated container for operations in cold environments.

Status

In service.

Manufacturer

Promac Watertreatment Division of Promac BV, Schimminck 1, PO Box 22, N-5300 AA Zaltbommel, Netherlands.
Tel: 4180 13855. Fax: 4180 12400.

SERBIA

Hand-operated Water Filters

Description

There are three hand-operated water filters in this range, all employing the same basic principle. Polluted water is hand- or gravity-pumped through a filter element in which particles and bacteria are mechanically separated or absorbed, along with an element of ion exchange, by a multi-layer paper filter insert. The paper insert is saturated/impregnated with active charcoal and other constituents and has to be changed when clogged.

The Hand-operated Filter FR-2 has a capacity of 1 to 2 l/h. Two filter elements can provide up to 2 litres of pure water from NBC polluted water and up to 10 litres from ordinary pollution. Operated by one man, the FR-2 has two filter elements, a pump, a storage vessel, plus hoses and fittings. After filtration the pure water is chlorinated with a tablet. The FR-2 kit is carried in a bag weighing 0.76 kg and measuring 190 × 155 × 88 mm.

The Hand-operated Filter FR-30 has a capacity of 30 l/h and uses three filter elements to provide up to 150 litres of pure water. For ordinary water purification the capacity is 45 l/h, providing up to 1000 litres. The FR-30 is contained in two metal boxes and is operated by one man. A hand-operated reciprocating pump is employed and after purification the water is chlorinated. The complete kit is carried in a haversack and weighs 14.5 kg.

The Hand-operated Filter FR-300/150 has a capacity of 300 l/h for ordinary water purification and 150 l/h for more involved processing. This system uses a process of preliminary treatment (coagulation, hyperchlorination and settling tanks) before filtration through two or four filter columns. The kit can filter NBC agents. The complete kit weighs 132 kg and is packed into three manpack loads.

Status

In service with the former Yugoslav armed forces.

Contractor

Federal Directorate of Supply and Procurement (SDPR), 9 Nemanjina Street, YU-11105 Beograd, Serbia.
Tel: 621522. Telex: 71000/72566 SDPR YU.
Fax: 38 11 631588/630621.

Hand-operated filter FR-2 in use

SOUTH AFRICA

Waterbuffel Water Treatment System

Description
The Waterbuffel (Water Buffalo) water treatment system is carried in a standard 3 m container and can be placed on level ground next to a source of raw water to generate up to 3500 l/h of fresh water. The system includes pre-treatment, filtering and chlorination stages.

Processed water can be stored within storage tanks until it is required.

For transportation the system can be carried on a SAMIL 20 (4 × 4) 2000 kg truck or any 3-tonne flat bed truck. It can also be towed using a set of transporter wheels. The container is equipped with lifting eyes for handling.

Status
In production. In service with the South African

Defence Forces.

Manufacturer
Enquiries to Armscor, Private Bag X337, Pretoria 0001, South Africa.
Tel: 012 428 1911. Telex: 30217.
Fax: 012 428 5635.

Waterbuffel water treatment system in use

Waterbuffel water treatment system container on tow behind a SAMIL 50 (4 × 4) 4800 kg truck

UNITED KINGDOM

Acrokool Nomad Water Filter and Cooling Trailer

Description
The Acrokool Nomad Mark III is a mobile water filter and cooling unit carried on a single-axle trailer. The filters used are Acrokool BF5 filters fitted with five Super Sterasyl silver impregnated ceramic elements with activated carbon cores to remove unpleasant tastes and odours. The water is passed through the filter system by an internal pump driven from the internal petrol/diesel engine, which also drives the cooling unit. The single-cylinder, air-cooled four-stroke engine also drives a generator for battery charging. Fuel for the engine comes from a nominal 24.6 litre tank. The main water tank has a 378.5 litre capacity and the filter/cooling system can supply 94.6 l/h of treated water. The fuel tank will provide the engine with an average non-stop running time of 15 hours.

The trailer unit has two jacks at the rear and a jockey wheel near the towing point. The simple control panel is on the right-hand side facing forward and at the rear are four outlet taps, three for glass-filling and one for filling larger containers. Spare filters are carried in a dustproof box inside the unit housing.

Specifications (shipping dimensions)
Weight: 747 kg
Length: 2.921 m
Width: 1.7272 m
Height: 1.27 m

Status
In production.

Manufacturer
Acrokool Limited, Unit 1, The Shires, Shirehill Industrial Estate, Thaxted Road, Saffron Walden, Essex CB11 3AN, UK.
Tel: 0799 513631. Telex: 81118 lparem g.
Fax: 0799 513635.

Acrokool Nomad water filter and cooling trailer

Acro-Well Water Filtration Systems

Description
The basic Acro-Well is a mobile, self-contained unit for the provision of germ-free drinking water, clean water for domestic uses and the transfer of natural water for irrigation, fire fighting, and so on. The power of the self-priming centrifugal pump is provided by a petrol engine, although diesel or electric units may be used as alternatives.

The Acro-Well will provide germ-free drinking water at the rate of up to 4000 l/h or 5000 l/h of clean water or 50 000 l/h of natural water. It can also be used as a water pump. Included with the equipment are a reinforced suction hose and foot strainer and a 7.62 m minimum length of hose. The pump can lift water from a height of 7.5 m and is fitted with a non-return valve.

There is an SF2/NP2 pre-filter and three BF5/NP5 Super Sterasyl purifiers together with the associated pipework and control valves. The entire unit is mounted on a steel frame with two 0.25 m diameter wheels for mobility and there are two levelling jacks for stability.

Each of the Super Sterasyl filters can be cleaned independently (with supplied brushes) while the unit is operating. Each of these filters uses silver impregnated ceramic elements with activated carbon cores to remove unpleasant tastes and odours, and each filter is contained in a nylon-coated aluminium housing.

The net weight of an Acro-Well unit is 200 kg. Each unit is 1.67 m long, 1.06 m wide and 0.91 m high.

Associated Acro-Well products are as follows:

Mini Acro-Well
The Mini Acro-Well is electrically driven and is completely automatic. It can supply up to 1000 l/h of germ-free drinking water or 4500 l/h of unfiltered water for domestic purposes. The Mini Acro-Well weighs 35 kg and dimensions are length 0.67 m, width 0.45 m and height 0.49 m.

Mini Acro-Well with Pre-filter
This unit is similar to the Mini Acro-Well but has an additional pre-filter to remove suspended solids when dirty water has to be used. It has the same dimensions

and weight as the Mini Acro-Well.

Hand-operated Mini Acro-Well
This is basically a Mini Acro-Well with pre-filter with the electric motor replaced by a hand-operated pump for use in remote areas. The maximum flow rate of this unit is 350 l/h of drinking water and the unit is mounted in a heavy steel frame with roll-over bars and carrying handles. Shipping weight is 80 kg.

Acro-Well Storage Tank
This temporary storage tank can hold up to 9000 litres of water but can also be used to hold other liquids such as fuel oils, or dry materials. It is transported in a robust carrying case and can be erected by one man within minutes. Aluminium alloy extrusions are used to support the chemically resistant PVC coated fabric liner. Options for the tank include a cover and

disposable liners. When erected the tank has a diameter of 3.26 m and is 1.5 m high. When packed in its case the tank weighs 80 kg.

Status
All the above items are in production. The Acro-Well is in service with the British Ministry of Defence in the Falkland Islands and is also used by several armed forces.

Manufacturer
Acrokool Limited, Unit 1, The Shires, Shirehill Industrial Estate, Thaxted Road, Saffron Walden, Essex CB11 3AN, UK.
Tel: 0799 513631. Telex: 81118 lparem g.
Fax: 0799 513635.

Airborne Inflatable Water Tanks

Description
The Airborne inflatable water tanks are widely used for both civil and military applications where the ability to store water or set up an open water relay is required at short notice. The tanks are manportable and each is packed in a valise.

The tank is deployed as follows: the tank is removed from the valise and laid on a flat surface; the ring capping the top of the tank wall, which is formed from a 350 mm diameter tube, is inflated, and floats on the water as the tank is filled, supporting the wall. A webbing strap and buckle keep the filling hose in position while the tank is being filled. The tank has a

cover supported on an inflatable float, which protects the contents from contamination and growth of algae. A water outlet connection is provided at the base of the wall. The tank takes a maximum of 3 minutes to inflate and can be used on inclines of up to 1 in 7.

Other sizes to a maximum capacity of 113 650 litres are available to special order.

Specifications

Capacity	22 730 l	11 365 l	1820 l
Weight	77.18 kg	44 kg	19 kg
Dimension filled (top)	5.02 m	3 m	1.5 m
(base)	5.58 m	3.6 m	1.8 m
(height)	1.4 m	1.4 m	1.1 m
Dimensions packed	1.68 × 0.76 × 0.46 m	1.25 × 0.76 × 0.46 m	0.76 × 0.48 × 0.38 m

Status
In production. In service with the British Army.

Manufacturer
Airborne Industries Limited, Airborne Industrial Estate, Arterial Road, Leigh-on-Sea, Essex SS9 4EF, UK.
Tel: 0702 525265. Telex: 99412 airbrn g.
Fax: 0702 510454.

Airborne inflatable water tank being filled

Filled Airborne inflatable water tank

Reynolds Boughton Water Tanker

Description
Reynolds Boughton (Devon) Limited produces a mobile de-ionising water unit mounted on a 6 × 4 chassis. The unit can produce de-ionised water from any potable water source and has a tank capacity of 11 750 litres. Two outlets deliver or dispose de-ionised water at a rate of 500 l/min. The quality of the de-ionised water is constantly monitored by an automatic onboard system.

Reynolds Boughton also produces a comprehensive range of water (and fuel) tankers of the rigidly mounted, trailer-mounted and demountable DROPS type.

Status
In production. In service with the British Ministry of Defence.

Manufacturer
Reynolds Boughton (Devon) Limited, Winkleigh

Reynolds Boughton water tanker

Airfield, Winkleigh, Devon EX19 8DR, UK.
Tel: 0837 83555. Telex: 42741.
Fax: 0837 83768.

Stellar Water Purification Equipment

Description

Stella-Meta manufactures mobile water purification equipment to treat fresh, saline and NBC contaminated water. Capacities range from the hand-portable ST1 producing 6.8 m³/h through to the Type 10/A5 trailer-mounted unit producing 23 m³/h.

Each Stellar unit typically comprises a pumpset module, a pre-coat filtration module and a sterilising module. The individual units can be used separately when required to provide greater mobility in use.

In addition to the water purification equipment, Stella-Meta is able to supply a complete system of equipment to store and distribute treated water, using the Stellaflex range of flexible tanks (see separate entry in this section).

Equipment is either tubular frame-mounted hand-portable with separate filtration, power and sterilisation modules, or two-wheel trailer-mounted as an option. Sterilisation is carried out with either a stand-alone hypochlorite powder dosing module, or is incorporated into the power source in the form of an electro-chlorinator.

Status

In production. In service with armed forces throughout the world.

Manufacturer

Stella-Meta Filters Limited, Laverstoke Mill, Whitchurch, Hampshire RG28 7NR, UK.
Tel: 0256 895959. Telex: 859605 stella g.
Fax: 0256 892074.

Specifications

Type	AB1A	AB3	ST1
Filter			
Max rated capacity	2.7 m³	4.5 m³	6.8 m³
Type	pre-coat	pre-coat	pre-coat
Weight	47 kg	81 kg	78 kg
Volume	0.23 m³	0.27 m³	0.49 m³
Power Module			
Pump type	positive displacement	centrifugal	centrifugal
Engine type	petrol	diesel	diesel
Weight	73 kg	146 kg	98 kg
Volume	0.25 m³	0.45 m³	0.21 m³
Sterilisation			
Type	sterilant doser	electro-chlorination	sterilant doser
Weight	33 kg	in power module	33 kg
Volume	0.18 m³	in power module	0.22 m³
Frame	tubular	tubular	tubular
Option	trailer	trailer*	trailer

* can be dropped by parachute

Stellar Type ST1 transportable water purification set

Stellar AB3 airportable water purification equipment

Stellar Type AB1A transportable water purification set

Stellar Type 10A/5 Trailer-mounted Water Purification Equipment

Description

The Stellar Type 10A/5 trailer-mounted water purification set has a nominal rated capacity of 23 m³/h of drinking water. It is a self-contained unit with its own diesel engine/pump/alternator set, and incorporates a filter powder pre-treatment plant, hypochlorite steriliser and a Stellar pressure filter with its own cleaning system.

Accessories, tools and spares are stowed within the trailer and bins are provided for storing the filter powder and hypochlorite, an efficient sterilising agent which takes immediate effect in the water.

The unit is so arranged that the pump can be used alone, the pump and filter can be used without the steriliser, or the pump and steriliser can be used without the filter. This saves filter powder and sterilant where filtration and/or sterilising is unnecessary, for example for washing water and similar domestic purposes.

All the equipment is mounted on a four-wheel trailer

Stellar Type 10A/5 trailer-mounted water purification equipment

with suitable bodywork, side and end screens. The side and end screens are mounted on metal frames which are hinged to give protection to the operator.

The Type 10A/5 weighs 2700 kg, with dimensions of 4.5 × 2.3 × 2.2 m.

Status
In production.

Manufacturer
Stella-Meta Filters Limited, Laverstoke Mill, Whitchurch, Hampshire RG28 7NR, UK.
Tel: 0256 895959. Telex: 859605 stella g.
Fax: 0256 892074.

Stellar Saline Water Treatment Units

Description

When brackish or sea water has to be used as a water source Stella-Meta Filters offers two types of equipment to treat both these fluids. Stellar units will convert saline waters to potable fluid that is in accordance with World Health Organisation standards. The complete equipment comprises a low pressure pump, pre-treatment filtration, a high pressure pump, reverse osmosis modules and post sterilisation. All the equipment is mounted on a single trailer chassis and a diesel unit provides the motive power.

Specifications

Type	DS1/A (/B)	DS2/A (/B)	DS3/A (/C)
Sea and brackish			
water flow rate	0.45 m³/h (1.1)	0.9 m³/h (2.4)	2.6 m³/h (5)
Weight	1364 kg	1364 kg	5000 kg
Length	4.2 m	4.2 m	7.07 m
Width	1.88 m	1.88 m	2.41 m
Height	1.83 m	1.83 m	2.78 m

Status
In production. In service in several Middle Eastern countries.

Manufacturer
Stella-Meta Filters Limited, Laverstoke Mill, Whitchurch, Hampshire RG28 7NR, UK.
Tel: 0256 895959. Telex: 859605 stella g.
Fax: 0256 892074.

Stellar NBC Decontamination Water Purification Equipments

Description

The Stellar range of Military Transportable Water Purification Equipment has been augmented to cope with Nuclear, Biological and Chemical (NBC) contamination removal. The treatment process, designed to British Ministry of Defence specifications, includes pre-coat filtration, reverse osmosis, activated carbon treatment and post disinfection capable of removing ionic, organic and bacterial contaminants.

The range of equipments is capable of achieving output capacities of 8.2 m³/h from fresh water or 2.3 m³/h of NBC contaminated water. Variants are available that will also treat sea water. The units can either be fully integral self-contained modules or 'add-on' modules compatible with non-NBC Stellar water purification sets.

The latest equipment entering service with the British Armed Forces is the Type NBC6 with a capacity of up to 2.3 m³/h. The Type NBC6 employs a modular construction incorporating a demountable transfer pump, a Stellasep crossflow microfilter, a slurry feed pump, a diesel-driven high pressure pump, a reverse osmosis module, a final trap activated carbon unit and a post chlorination system. A demountable pump and a pillow tank complete the equipment. The Type NBC6 is mounted in a self-contained space frame unit that can be carried on a truck, trailer, skid base or pallet.

The Type NBC6 was fielded by the British Army during Operation Desert Storm.

Specifications

Type	NBC6(F)	NBC6(SW)
Flow rate	2.3 m³/h	1.8 m³/h
Weight	3300 kg	3300 kg
Length, trailer,		
on tow	4 m	4 m
Width	2.5 m	2.5 m
Height	2.4 m	2.4 m

Status
In production for the British Army.

Manufacturer
Stella-Meta Filters Limited, Laverstoke Mill, Whitchurch, Hampshire RG28 7NR, UK.
Tel: 0256 895959. Telex: 859605 stella g.
Fax: 0256 892074.

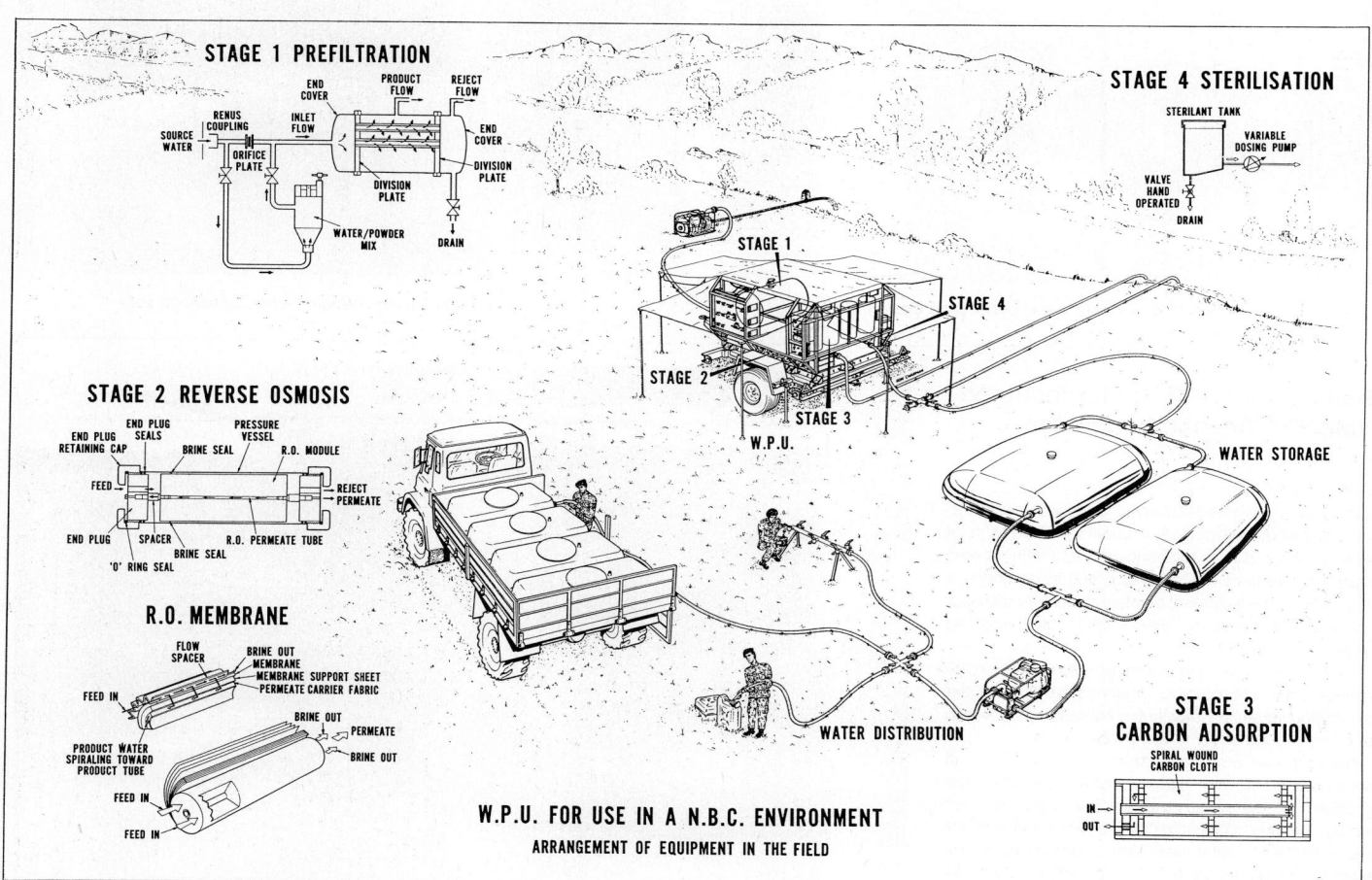

Artist's impression of a typical water processing unit in an NBC environment

Stellar Type NBC6 NBC decontamination water purification equipment for British Army mounted on a two-wheeled trailer

Stellar Type NBC6 NBC decontamination water purification equipment in its modular space frame

Stellaflex Flexible Water Tank Systems

Description

Stella-Meta has developed a complete flexible water tank system enabling the treatment, storage and distribution of drinking water on a totally mobile basis. The Stellaflex flexible tank range is manufactured in materials approved to international standards for drinking water and has been extensively field proven and climatically tested to UK MoD standard 001/issue 2 A1 and B3.

Available sizes range from 2 to 20 m³ in the following types:

Onion tanks or open top tanks where access to stored water is required

Pillow tanks, sealed to prevent contamination of stored water

Flexible tanks for instant transport of stored water on flat bed vehicles.

The tanks are lightweight, foldable and fully transportable when not in use and are manufactured from chemical resistant material.

Status

In production. In service with armed forces worldwide.

Manufacturer

Stella-Meta Filters Limited, Laverstoke Mill, Whitchurch, Hampshire RG28 7NR, UK.
Tel: 0256 895959. Telex: 859605 stella g.
Fax: 0256 892074.

Stellaflex Onion Tank

Stellaflex Pillow Tank in use

Stellaflex flexible water tank in use

Pre-Mac Model PWP and FWP Personal Water Purifiers

Description

The Model PWP personal water purifier was designed for military use in consultation with United Kingdom MoD (Army) medical authorities. It produces safe drinking water from sources in which high levels of bacteria, viral and parasitic contamination are present. It will also remove the organic matter existing in most natural water sources, improving the taste, smell and appearance of the water. The Model PWP can treat at least 500 litres of raw water before replacement and is active for five years.

The Model PWP weighs 500 g, is 140 mm high and 95 mm in diameter. It is made of impact resistant plastics approved for food usage. The unit is available to fit United Kingdom MoD standard water bottles and by means of a simple modification can fit any water bottle. After screwing the unit onto a bottle, raw water is poured into the top chamber. A 1-litre water bottle can be filled in less than 10 minutes, including a 2 minute resting time for final purification.

In the Model PWP a coarse reticulated foam retains large particulate matter and can be removed for cleaning. This is followed by a silver-impregnated activated carbon pre-filter to remove further particulate matter and organic contamination. A primary disinfection chamber contains a resin-iodine complex acting as a contact microbiocide to release iodine at a concentration of 4 parts/million into the water passing through to carry out secondary disinfection in the water bottle. If required, an optional outlet spout can be supplied to remove residual iodine prior to consumption.

With the Model FWP an integral hand pump is employed which is attached directly to a standard

The Pre-Mac Model FWP personal water purifier showing inlet pipe

The Pre-Mac Model PWP personal water purifier in use

water bottle. The FWP uses a four-stage filtering and purifying process. Untreated water is directed into the hand pump via an inlet pipe and passed through a replaceable cartridge assembly. The first stage, pre-filtration, uses silver impregnated carbon materials to remove organic and chemical contamination. This is followed by primary disinfection using an iodine-resin complex acting as a contact microbiocide; the resin also releases a small but controlled amount of iodine into the water. Secondary disinfection is carried out by the residual iodine; this residual is also used to maintain the treated water in a sterile condition. Finally a fine mesh filtration removes particulate matter down to 3 microns in size and the treated water passes into the water bottle.

The flow rate of the Model FWP is 0.5 l/min and a cartridge can be used to process approximately 1000 litres of untreated water. The FWP weighs 0.9 kg, is 210 mm long and has a diameter of 70 mm.

The PWP is marketed in the Far East by Stella-Meta Filters Limited of Whitchurch, Hampshire, UK.

Status
In production. Undergoing trials with the British Army and US Marine Corps.

Manufacturer
Pre-Mac (Kent) Limited, Unit 1, 40 Holden Park Road, Southborough, Tunbridge Wells, Kent TN4 0ER, UK. Tel: 0892 534361. Fax: 0892 515770.

Pre-Mac Model MWP and SWP Personal Water Purifiers

Description
Following on from the technology involved in the PWP and FWP personal water purifiers (see previous entry) Pre-Mac developed the Model MWP to meet operational requirements where size and weight are critical. The Model MWP is a small hand-operated pump unit in which source water is initially filtered to clean the water and remove organic matter as well as chemical contamination. This is followed by disinfection using an iodine-resin complex which acts as a contact microbiocide and also releases a low level of iodine into the water for secondary disinfection. Secondary disinfection occurs during the recommended holding period (3 minutes). The Model MWP will produce 1 litre of water in 5 minutes and its rated capacity is 100 litres. The filtration and disinfection tubes can be changed without using tools.

The Model SWP was designed to meet water treatment requirements in emergency or survival conditions and has a capacity of 25 litres, after which it should be discarded. The water treatment process follows the same lines as the Model MWP.

Specifications

Model	MWP	SWP
Capacity	100 l	25 l
Flow rate	200 ml/min	100 ml/min
Weight	180 g	60 g
Length	135 mm	135 mm
Diameter	45 mm	20 mm

The Pre-Mac Model SWP in use

The Pre-Mac Model MWP in use

Status
In production.

Manufacturer
Pre-Mac (Kent) Limited, Unit 1, 40 Holden Park Road, Southborough, Tunbridge Wells, Kent TN4 0ER, UK. Tel: 0892 534361. Fax: 0892 515770.

Aquastraw 2

Description
The Aquastraw 2 is a simple and disposable emergency device that enables an individual to drink water directly from an untreated source simply by inserting the device into the water source and using it as a drinking straw. The device is compact and light and can be used for up to 24 hours, during which time it is claimed that it will provide a considerable reduction in the biological and other content of the water involved.

Status
In production.

Manufacturer
Domnick Hunter Filters, Durham Road, Birtley, Co Durham DH3 2SF, UK. Tel: 091 410 5121. Telex: 537282. Fax: 091 410 7621.

Aquastraw 2 in use

Airborne Solar Still

Description
The Airborne solar still is an inflatable unit that can produce drinking water from sea water or impure water sources. It is primarily intended for use in emergency situations and is widely used as an integral part of military survival packs.

The solar still consists of an inflatable buoyancy ring that allows the unit to float on water if required. Inside the ring is a black solar collector with a reservoir for impure water underneath. Above the solar collector is a clear cone. Impure water is fed into the solar collector where it evaporates, the water vapour condensing on the inside of the clear cone. The purified water runs down the inside of the cone into a collecting gutter from where it runs into an external collecting bag for use.

The performance of the solar still will depend on the level of solar radiation received which, in turn, is dependent on the geographic location and the local climate. Typical examples are that in the United Kingdom on an average February day the still will produce 0.5 litres. On an average March day in the Indian Ocean it will produce 1.5 litres and on an October day in North Africa, 1.685 litres will be produced.

A typical Airborne solar still has an inflated diameter of 775 mm and a height of 540 mm. Packed weight is 0.85 kg and dimensions packed are 225 × 325 × 35 mm. Instructions for use are printed on the outer waterproof pack.

Status
In production and widespread use.

Manufacturer
Airborne Industries Limited, Airborne Industrial Estate, Arterial Road, Leigh-on-Sea, Essex SS9 4EF, UK. Tel: 0702 525265. Telex: 99412 airbrn g. Fax: 0702 510454.

Avon Flexitanks for Water

Description
These Avon Flexitanks follow the same general lines as those described in the *Bulk fuel storage and distribution systems* section but are intended for water storage only. They are made from high strength polymer-coated fabric and are available in a wide range of sizes. They may be used re-used repeatedly in differing climatic conditions.

Status
In production. In service with the UK Ministry of Defence and US Department of Defense.

Manufacturer
Avon Technical Products Division, Bath Road, Melksham, Wiltshire SN12 8AA, UK. Tel: 0225 791823. Fax: 0225 705585.

UNITED STATES OF AMERICA

600 ft Water Well Drilling System

Description
The US Army's 600 ft (182.9 m) well drilling system supports rapid deployment forces during operations in arid areas of the world where no surface water sources exist. The system includes a drilling machine, support vehicles, a well completion kit and accessories. The system can be loaded for long-range transport into three C-130 transport aircraft. A Navistar F-1954 (6 × 6) support vehicle is used to road transport the system.

The system is used by US Army Active and Reserve drilling units and US Navy construction battalions (Seabees).

Status
In service with the US Army and Navy.

Development Agency
US Army Belvoir Research, Development and Engineering Center, Fort Belvoir, Virginia 22060-5606, USA.

Manufacturer
George E. Failing Company, Enid, Oklahoma, USA.

600 ft Water Well Drilling System drilling machine being carried on a Navistar F-1954 (6 × 6) support vehicle

Tactical Water Distribution System (TWDS)

Description
Intended for use in a Rapid Deployment Force-type situation, the Tactical Water Distribution System (TWDS) is a flexible distribution, storage and receiving system that can issue a maximum of 720 000 US gallons (2 725 200 litres) of water during the course of a 20-hour working day. Using mobile tanks, collapsible containers and static inflatable tanks together with the associated hoses, pipes, pumps and other equipment, the TWDS is designed to distribute water up to 112.4 km. Working pressure is 150 to 200 psi. The basic hardware, apart from the various smaller accessories, is 152.4 mm lightweight layflat hose, 20 000 to 50 000 US gallon (75 700 to 189 250 litre) collapsible tanks and 2271 l/min centrifugal, diesel-driven pumps.

Status
A total of 21 10-mile sets delivered March 1984.

Manufacturers
Tanks: Uniroyal Plastics Co Inc, 312 North Hill Street, Mishawaka, Indiana 46544, USA.

Tactical Water Distribution System undergoing 30-day trials in California

American Fuel Cell and Coated Fabrics Company (Amfuel), Magnolia, Arkansas, USA.

Pipes: Angus Fire Armour Corporation, PO Box 879, Angier, North Carolina 27501, USA.

Forward Area Water Point Supply System (FAWPSS)

Description

The Forward Area Water Point Supply System (FAWPSS) is intended to provide large volumes of drinking water to troops in remote areas where no water supplies of any type are available. Water is delivered to a central point by air, truck or any other local method and from there is distributed as required through a network of tanks, pumps and hose-lines. The complete system consists of six 2271 litre collapsible water drums, one 189 l/min water pump assembly, three suction hose assemblies, six discharge hose assemblies, two valve assemblies, four 'Y' junctions, four dispensing nozzles, one towing and lifting yoke and the associated hoses. The complete system is air-transportable and can be set up by two men. Once in use only one man is required for operation.

Status

In production. In service with US Army.

Manufacturer

Uniroyal Plastics Co Inc, 312 North Hill Street, Mishawaka, Indiana 46544, USA.

Uniroyal Static Water Tanks

Description

Uniroyal produces a wide range of static flexible water tanks for both military and commercial purposes. The tanks produced for water and water-based products are free-standing and made from a chlorobutyl rubber-based material that is fully vulcanised and reinforced with tough nylon basket-weave fabric. These tanks can be placed at almost any location and have double-thickness panels at handling points and positions where hardware is attached. Positioning handles are provided. For transport and storage the tanks can be placed into wooden crates.

Status

In production. In service with the US armed forces.

Specifications

Capacity		Approximate dimensions filled:		
		Width	Length	Height
1000 US gallons	3785 l	2.388 m	3.073 m	0.61 m
2000 US gallons	7570 l	3.353 m	3.353 m	0.813 m
3000 US gallons	11 355 l	3.581 m	4.267 m	0.914 m
5000 US gallons	18 295 l	4.47 m	4.623 m	1.118 m
10 000 US gallons	37 850 l	6.096 m	6.096 m	1.219 m
15 000 US gallons	56 775 l	7.468 m	7.315 m	1.219 m
20 000 US gallons	75 700 l	6.7 m	8.23 m	1.727 m
25 000 US gallons	94 625 l	6.7 m	10.363 m	1.727 m
50 000 US gallons	189 250 l	6.7 m	19.2 m	1.727 m
100 000 US gallons	378 500 l	18.136 m	18.212 m	1.219 m

Manufacturer

Uniroyal Plastics Co Inc, 312 North Hill Street, Mishawaka, Indiana 46544, USA.

Unpacking Uniroyal static flexible tank

Typical Uniroyal static flexible water tank

Uniroyal Collapsible Water Drums

Description

The US Army uses two main types of Uniroyal collapsible water drum that are similar in form to the Uniroyal Sealdrum tanks (see separate entry in *Bulk fuel storage and distribution systems* section). The two models in service are the Uniroyal Model RD105 with a 55 US gallon (208 litre) capacity and the Model RD466 with a 250 US gallon (946 litre) capacity. Both are cylindrical tanks constructed of water-resistant synthetic rubber-coated fabric and can be towed at slow speeds over smooth surfaces for short distances. Both can be airlifted by helicopter.

Specifications

Model	RD105	RD466
Capacity	55 US gal	250 US gal
	208 l	946 l
Length	0.876 m	1.524 m
Diameter	0.597 m	1.016 m
Weight (full)	211.4 kg	1043 kg
(empty)	22.68 kg	93 kg

Status

In service with the US Army.

Manufacturer

Uniroyal Plastics Co Inc, 312 North Hill Street, Mishawaka, Indiana 46544, USA.

11 355 l/h Reverse Osmosis Water Purification Unit (ROWPU)

Description

In August 1984 the Belvoir Research, Development and Engineering Center awarded two contracts for the design, fabrication, assembly and testing of prototype reverse osmosis water purification units (ROWPUs) capable of purifying 11 355 litres (3000 US gallons) of water per hour. Brunswick Corporation Defense Division of Deland, Florida, received a $2 680 060 contract while $3 099 309 was awarded to Aqua-Chem's Water Technologies Division. Each firm produced three prototypes by December 1984 for testing at Aberdeen Proving Ground (Developmental) and Forts Story and Eustis (Operational) during 1985. Testing was completed by late 1986.

In November 1987 it was announced that Aqua-Chem Inc had been awarded a contract for 98 units with deliveries commencing during 1990.

The specifications called for the purification of 11 355 l/h (3000 gallons/h) at 25°C using fresh and brackish water sources, and 7570 l/h at 25°C using sea water sources, both including NBC contamination. The equipments are mounted in standard ISO containers with the NBC treatment unit outside, and may be transported by truck, rail or aircraft. The equipments are designed to be installed or packed up in 90 minutes.

Status
In service with the US Army (98).

Manufacturer
Aqua-Chem Inc, Water Technologies Division, 210 W Capitol Drive, PO Box 421, Milwaukee, Wisconsin 53201, USA.
Tel: (414) 577 2944. Telex: 26679 aqm mil.
Fax: (414) 577 2723.

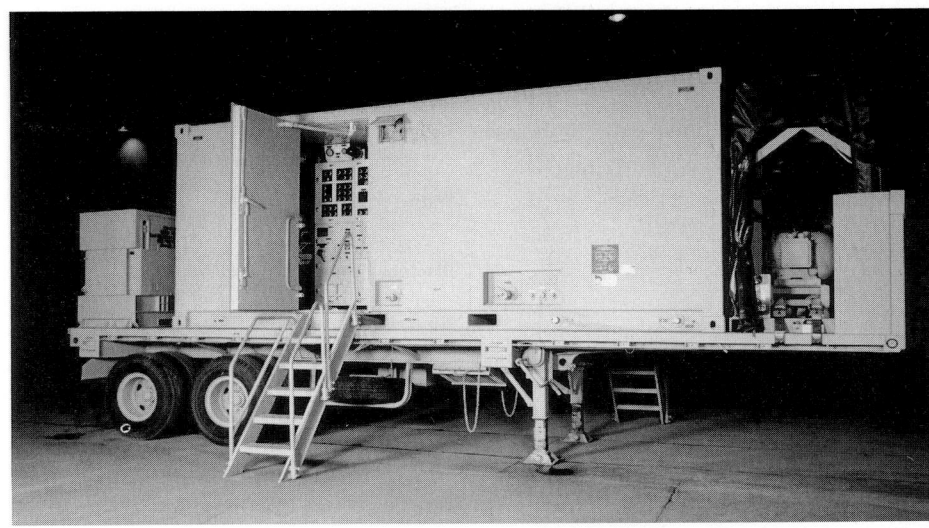

Aqua-Chem 11 355 l/h reverse osmosis water purification unit (ROWPU)

SweetWater Reverse Osmosis Water Purification Units (ROWPUs)

Description

SweetWater is a subsidiary of Marland Environmental Systems Inc which has been producing water purification systems for land and naval use for many years. For land use it produces two reverse osmosis water purification units (ROWPUs), one (the ROWPU 600) with an output capacity of 2271 l/h and the other (the ROWPU 1000) with an output capacity of 3585 l/h; other capacities can be supplied. Both versions can be mounted on skids or four-wheeled trailers.

The equipments are produced to full military specifications. When on trailers they can be used under off-road conditions and they take two men 1 hour to set up once on site. An add-on generator is required for fully self-contained operation.

Specifications

Model	ROWPU 600	ROWPU 1000
Output	2271 l/h	3585 l/h
Feedwater input	132.5 l/min	170.5 l/min
Motor power reqs	20 hp	25 hp
Skid Mount		
Weight (approx)	3240 kg	3600 kg
Length	2.895 m	2.895 m
Width	2.108 m	2.108 m
Height	1.702 m	1.702 m
Model	ROWPU 600	ROWPU 1000
Trailer (optional, less unit)		
Weight (approx)	4500 kg	4500 kg
Length	5.842 m	5.842 m
Width	2.438 m	2.438 m
Height	0.762 m	0.762 m

Status

Both units are in production. In service with several nations. In 1985 the Nigerian armed forces purchased six (plus options for a further six) of the 3585 l/h model.

Manufacturer

Exstar International Corporation, 6502 Windmill Way, Wilmington, North Carolina 28405, USA.
Tel: (919) 452 4737. Fax: (919) 452 4738.

SweetWater Lightweight Trailer-Mount ROWPU System

Description

This equipment was designed to be a lightweight and highly mobile water production unit that can be towed into position by 4 × 4 light vehicles. The unit is mounted on a twin-axled trailer or a skid mounting for ground use and requires only a 20 kW generator for independent operation. An NBC post treatment unit is optional. The unit is designed to provide 27 254 l/day from sea water and 54 508 l/day from fresh and brackish water. Complete, the unit comprises all feedwater pumps, 23 m of deployable hoses and collapsible product and brine tanks. The unit can be deployed in the field by two men in 1 hour.

A skid-mounted unit weighs 2209 kg while a trailer-mounted unit, complete with generator, weighs approximately 4000 kg.

Status

In production.

Manufacturer

Exstar International Corporation, 6502 Windmill Way, Wilmington, North Carolina 28405, USA.
Tel: (919) 452 4737. Fax: (919) 452 4738.

2271 l/h Reverse Osmosis Water Purification System

Description

This equipment was developed by the US Army Mobility Equipment Research and Development Command (MERADCOM) (now the Belvoir Research, Development and Engineering Center) and Univox California Inc, to replace four existing water purification units. A contract was placed in January 1981 with Univox California for 11 units. Total production orders were 455 units at a cost of $55 million.

The 2271 l/h reverse osmosis water purification unit was the first and smallest in a family of multi-purpose units developed for field support. This system replaced the ERDLator, the 568 l/h distillation unit, the CW-BW decontamination kit and the mobile ion exchange unit.

The reverse osmosis (RO) system is capable of producing drinking water from polluted fresh water, sea water, and brackish water, and removing chemical and radiological contaminants from water. Reverse osmosis is the process of pressurising raw water above its osmotic pressure which forces it through a cellulose acetate or polyamide membrane fabricated into a spiral wound element. Eight elements are used in the new unit.

The development of a dry membrane represents a significant advancement in reverse osmosis membrane technology. Unlike commercially available wet

2271 l/h water purification system (US Army)

membranes, the dry membranes can be stored dry and are wet/dry reversible. Incoming water is pre-treated with a polymer to aid filtration before final passage through the RO elements. The unit is mobile and can be air-dropped to forward tactical units, or towed on a trailer. In both cases, it will supply enough water to support at least 2000 men/day.

Specifications
Output: 2271 l/h
Weight:
(on trailer) 7639 kg
(on skid mount) 5121 kg
Feed requirement: 132.4 l/min at 30 psi
Length:
(trailer) 5.8 m
(skid mount) 3 m
Height:
(trailer) 2.4 m
(skid mount) 2.4 m
Width:
(trailer) 2.4 m
(skid mount) 2.4 m
Electrical power consumption: 22 kW

Generator power required: 30 kW

Status
In production. In service with the US Army, Air Force and Marine Corps.

Manufacturer
Univox California Inc, 6551 Loisdale Court, Springfield, Virginia 22150, USA.

Univox Reverse Osmosis Water Purification Units (ROWPUs)

Description
Univox California Inc produces a range of reverse osmosis water purification units (ROWPUs), one of which, the 2271 l/h system, is covered in a separate entry but is included here to provide a complete survey of the range. All the Univox ROWPUs use the same basic system in which water contaminants are removed by pressurising untreated water through a cellulose acetate or polyamide membrane fabricated into a spiral wound element on a drum. A series of these filters completes the process. The units are highly reliable, require only relatively low power sources and are available in different outputs to meet various military and civil requirements. They may be skid-mounted for use from trailers or semi-trailers, or for para-dropping and air transport, or they may be mounted on their own special trailers. If required a special pre-filtration package may be added to each model to provide full NBC treatment.

Skid mount dimensions (all models)
Length: 2.895 m
Height: 1.702 m
Width: 2.108 m

Trailer dimensions (trailer is optional for all models)
Weight: 4500 kg
Length: 5.842 m
Height: 0.762 m

Diagrammatic representation of reverse osmosis process

Width: 2.438 m

Status
In production.

Manufacturer
Univox California Inc, 6551 Loisdale Court, Springfield, Virginia 22150, USA.

Specifications

Model	150S	300S	600S	1000S	ROWPU 600[1]	ROWPU 1000[1]
Output	567 l/h	1135 l/h	2271 l/h	3785 l/h	2271 l/h	3785 l/h
Input (at 30 psi)	37.8 l/min	94.6 l/min	132.5 l/min	170.5 l/min	132.5 l/min	170.5 l/min
Weight on skid mount	2115 kg	2610 kg	2880 kg	3015 kg	3240 kg	3600 kg
Electrical power consumption	6 kW	12 kW	15 kW	19 kW	20 kW	22 kW
Primary motor supplies	7.5 hp	15 hp	20 hp	25 hp	20 hp	25 hp

[1] Includes full NBC filtration

Angus Wellmaster Drop Pipe System

Description
The Angus Wellmaster rising main drop pipe for submersible pumps is in use in many parts of the world and was developed following experiences in the Middle East, where it was found that conventional steel mains have a limited life due to corrosion problems. The Wellmaster pipe uses a composite construction of high strength synthetic polyester and thermoplastic elastomer and can be used at well depths of up to 182.9 m (600 ft). The pipe is corrosion resistant, fast and easy to install or remove, flexible and layflat, and available in lengths up to 182.9 m. The pipe is also easy to transport, store and handle. It is available with internal nominal diameters of 2 in (51 mm), 3 in (76.2 mm) and 4 in (101.6 mm).

Accessories for use with the Wellmaster pipe include stainless steel couplings and adaptors, assembly tools for the couplings, a hose installation set comprising a rotating drum and support frame and two hose clamps, rolls of rubber strapping and studs for power cable retention, and self-lock nylon ties to attach the strapping to the hose ridge.

Wellmaster rising main drop pipe being lowered into well while undergoing evaluation trials held in New Mexico by US Army Belvoir Research, Development and Engineering Center (US Army)

Status
In production. Under procurement by the US Army.

Manufacturer
Angus Fire Armour Corporation, PO Box 879, Angier,

North Carolina 27501, USA.
Tel: (919) 639 6151. Telex: 579398.

Recovery Engineering Hand-operated Watermakers

Description

The Recovery Engineering range of hand-operated watermakers, known as Survivors, combines reverse osmosis and energy recovery technology to make pure drinkable water from salt, brackish or contaminated fresh water. Designed for use as an emergency water supply for naval lifeboats and military units separated from central water supplies, the Survivors are in use by the US Army, Navy and Coast Guard. Three models are available: the Survivor 06, the Survivor 35 and the Survivor 35CS.

To operate any of the Survivors, the user pumps the unit handle back and forth; on the Survivor 06 the unit is operated by lever action with the unit resting on the operator's thigh. This pressurises the feedwater and forces it against a reverse osmosis membrane which allows only pure water molecules to pass through. The units will supply purified water as long as the user pumps.

The Explorer is a pump-type unit that can purify 1 l/min of water without clogging. Weight is 603 g.

Status

In production. In service with US Army, Navy and Coast Guard. Survivor 06 and Survivor 35 in service with the UK armed forces.

Manufacturer

Recovery Engineering Inc, 2229 Edgewood Avenue South, Minneapolis, Minnesota 55426, USA.
Tel: (612) 541 1313. Telex: 290828.
Fax: (612) 541 1230.

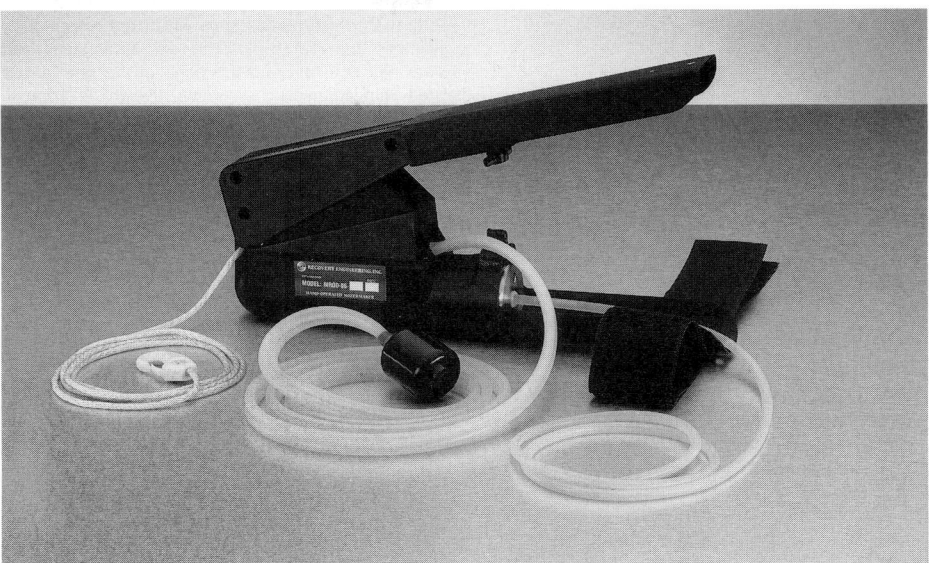

Recovery Engineering Survivor 06 hand-operated watermaker

Specifications

Model	Survivor 06	Survivor 35	Survivor 35CS
Dry weight	1.6 kg	3.2 kg	3.7 kg
Purification rate	1.1 l/h	5.4 l/h	6.41 l/h
Length	200 mm	560 mm	560 mm
Height	130 mm	1.4 m	1.4 m
Width	60 mm	90 mm	90 mm

Potable Water from Engine Gases

Description

Chamberlain GARD has developed a system for the recovery of potable water from the exhaust gases of internal combustion engines. The exhaust gases, which consist primarily of nitrogen, carbon dioxide and water vapour, are passed through a catalytic converter to remove any unburned hydrocarbons. The purified gases are then passed through a condenser and the resultant water is passed through an ion exchange/ polishing column to remove any acidic contaminants.

The basic technology of catalytic conversion of vapours and gases was initiated and developed by GARD under NASA sponsorship for the recovery of potable water from urine and waste water on board spacecraft; the recovery of water from engine exhaust gases is an adaptation of the same technology. Tests using exhaust gases from a small 2.5 hp petrol engine, a large 210 hp diesel engine and a 20 hp diesel-fuelled gas turbine have demonstrated the feasibility of the process and have indicated that the exhaust gases from vehicles and stationary engines, such as electrical power generators, can be catalytically treated to purify water vapour by oxidising the hydrocarbons and other impurities to innocuous gases; the water vapour of the catalytically cleaned-up exhaust can then be condensed. Since the exhaust gases may contain acidic contaminants (such as sulphur dioxide and nitrous oxides) which are partially dissolved in the condensed water, a post-treatment/polishing stage, such as passing the water through an ion exchanger, may be required to make the recovered water potable and more palatable.

Theoretically, approximately one unit of water will be produced per unit of fuel burned. Practically however, 0.66 of a US gallon of water will be produced per US gallon of fuel burned.

Status

Development.

Agency

Chamberlain GARD, A Division of Duchossois Industries Inc, 7449 N Natchez Avenue, Niles, Illinois 60648, USA.
Tel: (708) 647 9000.

CAMOUFLAGE EQUIPMENT AND DECOYS

AUSTRIA

PEKAM CAMNET

Description
The PEKAM CAMNET consists of a basic 80 × 80 mm net which is sewn onto a stranded edging cord. The multi-layer covering is made of hexagonal leaves of PVC-coated polyamide fabric which are attached by synthetic material clips. The net is weather and ultraviolet resistant and the edge of the net can be fitted with connecting elements. Weight is approximately 180 g/m² and the tensile strength is greater than 180 kg. The standard net size is 5 × 5 m although other sizes can be supplied.

Status
In production.

Manufacturer
PEKAM Kunststoffentwicklung GmbH and Co KG, A-5411 Oberalm 735, Austria.
Tel: 06245 2308. Fax: 06245 81162.

BELGIUM

Seyntex Camouflage Nets

Description
Seyntex produces a wide range of camouflage nets manufactured from modern synthetic materials which have been treated to avoid visual detection, even when using reconnaissance equipment such as infra-red optical devices and infra-red photography. For camouflage purposes various shades of net can be produced and the size of net varies making it suitable both for personnel use and for large items of equipment. Seyntex also produces supporting poles and mushrooms for the nets. A quick attach and release system that can raise and lower the nets within 5 seconds is also available.

Status
In production.

Manufacturer
Seyntex nv/sa, Seyntexlaan 1, Industriepark Zuid, B-8880 Tielt, Belgium.
Tel: 32 51 40 24 24. Telex: 81 947.

Seyntex camouflage net being erected over light vehicle

BULGARIA

Camouflage Nets and Materials

Description
The Bulgarian defence industry manufactures a wide variety of camouflage products ranging from personal camouflage to the concealment of major sites against sensor surveillance. Those aspects listed below are only the main headings.

Personal camouflage
Three types of helmet camouflage are available. The Model A is a two-sided fabric cover with a leaf outline while the Model B is a fabric. Both are effective in the visual and near infra-red regions. The Model C is a fabric extending concealment to the radar wave region.

Also available is a range of camouflage clothing that can be supplied in a variety of forms and colours to suit customer requirements. Camouflage creams are available for personal use.

Camouflage nets
A camouflage net system is available, capable of providing protection against the visible, near infra-red and S, X and K radar bands. Made from PVC film elements this net is produced in 3 × 6 m panels. A standard set comprises six panels, 20 fixing elements, a packing bag and six supporting rods.

Camouflage paints
A range of camouflage paints is produced to provide protection of equipment in the visible, near infra-red and radar regions.

The CM-1 series is based on pentaphtalic resins (CM-1A) or epoxy-polyester resins (CM-1B) to provide visual and near infra-red protection.

The CM-2 series provides anti-corrosion and water-proofing as well as concealment against S-, X- and K-band radars. CM-2A is a multi-layer coating based on synthetic rubbers while CM-2B can be used with textiles.

The CM-3 series is a more complex preparation combining the assets of the CM-1 and CM-2 series.

CM-1A, CM-2A and CM-3A paints are not proof against decontamination solutions of the DS2 type.

Anti-radar coatings
Intended to provide protection of tanks and other armoured equipment against S-, X- and K-band radars, anti-radar coatings are available in two forms. Based on the use of rubber blended with various fillers, Type A is a two-layer coating 3 to 4 mm thick and providing 14 to 20 dB attenuation in the X band. Type B is 10 to 14 mm thick and provides radar attenuation of 25 to 30 dB.

A further preparation extends protection to the thermal region. A standard set of this material is provided in sheets measuring 3 × 4 m.

Other products include sets of multi-spectral materials, including the above items, various forms of equipment decoy, and radar-reflecting systems.

Status
In production.

Agency
KINTEX, 66 Anton Ivanov Boulevard, PO Box 209, Bucharest, Bulgaria.
Tel: 66 23 11. Telex: 22471/23243.
Fax: 65 81 91/65 81 01.

DENMARK

CAMTEX Texture Mats

Description
CAMTEX Texture Mats are part of a new generation of camouflage, concealment and deception (CCD) systems developed by the CAMTEX Camouflage Division of GCA APS. The mats are produced using a multispectral material which can be fitted permanently or temporarily on armoured and other vehicles, installations, ships, and helicopters and other aircraft on the ground. When fitted permanently on vehicles they do not impede mobility and minimise time spent on fitting and removing normal camouflage systems.

The texture mats are made of a structured material which has diffuse reflective and absorption properties, including visual spectrum properties such as gloss and shine. The material, which is supplied in mats or rolls and cut to shape for permanent installation, has built-in capabilities against radar, ultraviolet, and near and full infra-red sensors.

Other CCD systems offered by CAMTEX include a Chemical Tone Down Method used to camouflage large fixed installations such as airfields. They also offer a camouflage consultancy service.

Status
In production. In service with NATO nations.

Manufacturer
CAMTEX Camouflage Division, A Division of GCA APS, Store Kongensgade 110A, DK-1264 Copenhagen K, Denmark.
Tel: 45 33 91 15 25. Telex: 52628 gccab dk.
Fax: 45 33 32 25 35.

FINLAND

Protan Camouflage Products

Description
Protan produces a range of camouflage products that includes camouflage nets, umbrellas, trees and vehicle covers. A typical product is the Protan Camouflage Net Summer 25 K. This is made by glueing pieces of PVC-coated fabric of various colours on a polyamide/polyester support net. There is an edge cord sewn around the net and there are cord loops that enable several nets to be joined together. Standard net sizes are 5 × 5 m, 6 × 8 m and 8 × 12 m although net sizes can be produced to customer requirements. The standard colours are light green, dark green and brown. Other colour reflection requirements in visible and near infra-red ranges are available.

The Summer 25 K camouflage net has a weight of 290 g/m² and a thickness of 0.25 mm. Mesh width is 85 × 85 mm ±7 mm.

Status
In production.

Manufacturer
Protan OY Suomi, PO Box 38, SF-70701 Kuopio, Finland.
Tel: 358 71 451399. Telex: 42239 prota sf.
Fax: 358 71 451762.

HUNGARY

The HUNCAM Hungarian Camouflage System

Description
The HUNCAM Hungarian Camouflage System is made up of a number of camouflage materials with special multi-frequency absorption characteristics. These extend into the radar and infra-red spectra and the materials involved may be used for personal camouflage clothing and concealment nets. The main components of the range are as follows:

Camouflage Net RABSORB CND
Made from bulked polyester yarn with varying sizes of mesh, this net has radar-absorption properties and is made in standard sizes of 5 × 5 m, 6 × 6 m and 8 × 12 m. (These sizes apply to all HUNCAM nets.) It is produced in colours to suit customer requirements and has a weight of 160 g/m².

Camouflage Net RABSORB CPV
This net uses pieces of PVC-coated fabric of varying colours and sizes glued onto a polyamide/polyester support net and with an edge cord around the net. Produced in various colours the weight varies between 200 and 300 g/m² according to the exact type of net required.

Camouflage Net RABSORB CNS
This is a lightweight net with a colour-printed surface which may be applied on one or both sides. Weight is between 110 and 180 g/m².

Camouflage Net RABSORB RTN
This net provides both radar and near infra-red thermal camouflage as well as visual camouflage and uses pieces of incised PVC foil interlayered with special additions to produce a three-dimensional texture. The main wavelength efficiency is in the X- and Ku-bands. Weight is 250 to 400 g/m² according to type.

Camouflage Net RABSORB TCN
This net is made from 2 m wide panels with the garnish consisting of incised matt PVC film cemented to the net material, thus providing a three-dimensional effect with infra-red reflection properties. Weight is 200 to 300 g/m², according to type.

Individual Net RABSORB PCN
These nets are intended for use by individual soldiers and are made from incised matt PVC film cemented to a supporting net. This net is normally used together with the Helmet Cover CC made from the same materials.

Camouflage Uniform RABSORB OCS
These uniforms are made from 100 per cent cotton or polyester/cotton fabric. They provide protection against ultraviolet, visual, infra-red and multi-spectrum observation and can be produced in various colours as required.

Camouflage Leaves CV
These are a series of artificial camouflage leaves for attenuating multi-spectral radiation by absorption, reflection and/or scattering. The incised leaves have a thin electrically conductive intermediate layer with particles distributed at intervals and with the two outer layers reflecting visible and near infra-red light. When placed onto supporting cords the leaves use a self-locking system that allows the leaves to be distributed as required. Weight is between 200 and 300 g/m².

Camouflage Trees CT
These are a series of artificial trees using a framework onto which camouflage leaves are distributed. Objects to be concealed are placed behind the trees where they are concealed by the multi-spectral absorption and reflection properties of the materials involved.

Camouflage Paints
There are two types of camouflage paint available. The CP paints are based on a water-soluble polymer and can be removed by water; they are infra-red reflective and seven colours are available. The PCP paints are medium oil alkyd, epoxy or polyurethane based. Both paints provide a matt infra-red reflective finish.

Status
In production. In service with the Hungarian armed forces.

Marketing Agency
IDEX Foreign Trading, Contracting and Engineering Company Limited, PO Box 24, H-1251 Budapest, Hungary.
Tel: (36-1) 115 0090. Telex: 22 4541 idex h.
Fax: (36-1) 135 1393.

ISRAEL

FMS Camouflage Nets

Description

FMS camouflage products are based on a single layer of knitted polyester fabric which provides strong lightweight material that is snag resistant and reversible. Several weights are available for applications from helicopters to large combat vehicles and permanent outdoor structures.

Systems constructed from these products have been extensively tested and yield high performance in the visual, near infra-red, far infra-red and RF region (up to 90 per cent signal reduction). The material is self-extinguishing, water repellent, ultraviolet protected and rot-proof.

Status

In production. In service with the Israeli Defence Forces and several other armed forces.

Manufacturer

FMS Fibrotex Military Systems, PO Box 18064, Tel Aviv 61180, Israel.
Tel: 922 3585. Telex: 381121 fibro il.
Fax: 972 3 9223314.

Preparing FMS camouflage net for use

ITALY

Pirelli Camouflage Nets

Description

Pirelli produces a range of conventional camouflage netting which is delivered in relatively small sections each measuring 4 × 4 m or 6 × 6 m. The net material support is made up of rubber-coated fabric with the addition of a special synthetic and vulcanised elastomer to which various pigments have been added.

This enables the outer surface of the net to be in three or four colours according to requirements while the inner surface is in two shades only in a 60:40 ratio. The nets are not visible to infra-red or ultraviolet photographic reconnaissance and are flame resistant. If required both the support and the rubber-coated net can be provided with further support from a conventional camouflage net. Weight of the supporting net is 500 g/m² while the rubber-coated material weighs 300 g/m².

Status

In production. In service with the Italian armed forces.

Manufacturer

Moldip SpA – Pirelli Group, Via Milano 8, I-20038 Seregno (Milano), Italy.
Tel: 0362 237711. Telex: 330191 pirese i.
Fax: 0362 220412.

SOUTH AFRICA

Alnet Camouflage Nets

Description

The Alnet garnished camouflage net was developed to meet the stringent requirements of the South African Defence Forces and to withstand the extreme climatic conditions of South Africa. In the development stage of producing a net to meet these requirements, a technique of obtaining spectral data of the environment within a region was evolved to the extent that specific colours and disruptive patterns can be produced to resemble the local foliage.

The nets use a basic support net with a square 50 × 50 mm mesh. Low mass, high strength garnishing material is clipped onto the support net to resemble the foliage in the area in which the net is to be deployed. The garnishing material is painted on both sides, one side being for winter use and the other for summer use. Joining rings on the perimeter of each net and the included joining cord and clips allow for the rapid joining and separation of two or more nets – the net sizes can be produced to suit. The nets are flame retardant and provide effective protection in the visual and near infra-red spectra.

Weight of a complete net is 350 g/m². Alnet also produces helmet camouflage nets and shade cloth.

Status

In production. In service with the South African Defence Forces.

Manufacturer

Alnet, PO Box 4995, Cape Town 8000, South Africa.
Tel: 021 542321. Fax: 021 544003.

Ratel MICV about to be covered by Alnet camouflage nets

Ratel MICV covered by Alnet camouflage nets

SWEDEN

BARRACUDA Technologies Camouflage Net Systems

Description
BARRACUDA Technologies AB is a member of the Swedish Incentive Group. With the BARRACUDA product line the company has more than 35 years' experience as a leader in camouflage technology, with sales to more than 40 armed forces around the world.

Standard Camouflage
The BARRACUDA Technologies Standard Camouflage has both visual and near infra-red capabilities that can be adapted to local environments. The net is built up of panels with a PVC garnish chemically or physically attached to a supporting net. The panels are sewn together to form a net of the desired shape and size. A joining system is provided as a standard with each net. The camouflage pattern is designed with computer aid and with a relation between the contrasts to create a colour pattern at both long and short distances.

Other features include adapted near infra-red reflection; dead matt surfaces to avoid shiny nets and to keep colour values even at low angles; resistance to flame, ultraviolet light, heat and cold, water, moisture and so on.

The basic camouflage net can be manufactured in any size and shape. The weight is between 250 and 350 g/m², depending on the variant.

Radar Camouflage
The BARRACUDA Technologies Radar Camouflage net has been in service for several years. When deployed, a substantial reduction of the radar reflection is achieved for the covered equipment. The material used is composed of a PVC foil interlayered with special additions to an approximate weight of 350 g/m². In operational use an attenuation of about 12 dB is obtained against 3 cm radars (X-band, 9.4 GHz). The BARRACUDA Broadband Radar Camouflage net provides similar results but within the frequencies of 5 to 100 GHz, thus providing additional protection against millimetric radars in homing missiles, and so on.

The remaining attenuated echoes from the camouflaged object will then correspond approximately to the ground clutter from the surrounding terrain. All other camouflage parameters are the same as for the standard camouflage net.

Thermal Camouflage
As part of the BARRACUDA system BARRACUDA Technologies developed a system of thermal camouflage for use in the 3-5 and 8-12 micron range. The system makes use of a thermal blanket which blanks out heat from the object covered and uses a thermal net to produce a thermal signature compatible with the normal environment.

The thermal blanket has a low emissive surface in order to create as 'cold' a thermal picture as possible.

A system of regulated vents allows sufficient invisible warm air to escape from within the cover in order to avoid the accumulation of too much heat inside. The blanket material is a reinforced polymer.

The thermal net consists of different polymers in a pattern which, combined with an intermediate layer of metal, creates a blend of warm and cold surfaces as registered by sensors. The thermal net also provides camouflage against both visual and near infra-red reconnaissance.

The finished camouflage material is built from panels. The garnishing material, attached to the net frame, is an incised polymer film containing metal. The panels are sewn together to form a net of the desired shape and size. Computer-generated colour patterns as well as other features described under Standard Camouflage are included in the thermal nets. Edge cord is sewn in place with synthetic fibre thread throughout the entire perimeter of the net.

The complete camouflage is rot- and fireproof. The weight of the net is between 250 and 350 g/m², depending on the variety, and the thermal blanket weighs up to 180 g/m².

Winter Camouflage
BARRACUDA Technologies Winter Camouflage is a self-supporting garnish material which can be supplied in any desired size and shape. The material is a synthetic fabric provided with circular perforations in a pattern to form shade effects on the white surface. The flame resistant material has a high ultraviolet reflection which conforms with real snow. This camouflage can also be provided with radar camouflage or thermal protective characteristics.

TOPCAM
The unique BARRACUDA Technologies TOPCAM concept is intended to be used as a complement to (and in some cases instead of) traditional camouflage nets, mainly to protect equipment from air reconnaissance and strikes. Advantages of the concept include: extremely short times to apply camouflage; the correct camouflage due to fixed positions; an ensured silhouette disruptive effect; guns can remain camouflaged when firing; instantly reversible to allow a two-sided net to function depending on the surrounding terrain; and adaptable thermal capabilities.

ADDCAM
ADDCAM is the first add-on application with thermal deception properties for moving vehicles where each type of vehicle has its own individually designed camouflage. It is a new camouflage concept that reduces the thermal signature of any vehicle and dramatically increases its life expectancy in a combat zone. ADDCAM reduces and changes the thermal signature of the vehicle concerned by making changes both inside and outside the vehicle. The system uses a '3D' top layer and includes colours and patterns adapted to the local terrain in both the visual and the near infra-red spectra.

COVCAM
This military covering material is intended to be used for tarpaulins, mainly made up for trucks, trailers, tents or equipment covers. The material can be manufactured with the same capabilities regarding colour and near infra-red characteristics as the camouflage nets, including a completely matt surface and flame resistance. The computer-generated colour pattern with unlimited repeat length can be made to match the camouflage pattern of different types of vehicle. Two standard weights are available, approximately 350 and 750 g/m², which can be made up to finished covers or delivered in rolls 1.5 m wide.

RAPCAM
BARRACUDA Technologies has introduced its Rapid Camouflage System, known as RAPCAM, which provides an effective and rapidly erected camouflage adapted to the increasing time demands made by modern warfare and using materials that offer full protection against all known sensor systems. RAPCAM, with tailor-made nets, adapted and fixed in position on an object in combination with TOPCAM, reduces the camouflage erection time by 75 to 90 per cent using less personnel. The system is easy to handle in darkness and a crew of three men can conceal a 25 m patrol boat in less than 5 minutes.

Decoys
In co-operation with a customer, BARRACUDA Technologies can provide virtually any type of object as a decoy. Decoys have been produced for the following equipments: AJ 37 Viggen; F-104; MiG-21; F-16; F-18; Improved HAWK SAM; Bailey Bridge; Ribbon Bridge; guns; howitzers; tanks, and so on.

To create the most convincing results the decoys are to 1:1 scale. Each decoy type can be complemented with a radar reflection and/or thermal signature to simulate the real equipment. Other features are correct shapes and colours, stable support construction and a minimum of personnel and time required for erection and relocation.

Accessories and Variations
The nets can be supplied in PVC storage bags for protection against damage during storage and transport. A repair kit is also available. The company can also design netting to suit specific military requirements, for example for use under extreme conditions of heat or cold.

Other camouflage equipment
Other camouflage systems available from BARRACUDA Technologies include harbour camouflage nets, helicopter camouflage nets, naval nets, aircraft decoys and camouflage paint.

Support Poles
BARRACUDA Technologies Support Poles are made of an extruded and reinforced polymer with a dark and dull finish. Each support comprises a telescopic pole

A field howitzer with BARRACUDA Technologies thermal camouflage, including TOPCAM

Command post camouflaged with BARRACUDA Technologies RAPCAM and TOPCAM

with a top spreader. Each pole height is adjustable between 1.5 and 3 m. Maximum load is approximately 50 kg. A three-tapped ground plate ensures stability on any surface.

Status

In production. In service with Australia, Canada, France, India, Japan, Sweden and many other armed forces.

Manufacturer

BARRACUDA Technologies AB, Camouflage Division, Box 160, S-594 00 Gamleby, Sweden.
Tel: 46 493 108 00. Telex: 3934 barfact s.
Fax: 46 493 120 64.

UNITED KINGDOM

Bridport Aviation Products Camouflage and Concealment Equipment and Decoys

Description

Bridport Aviation Products Limited is a division of Bridport-Gundry (UK) Limited – Europe's largest manufacturer of nets and netting – which has been a contractor to the British government for over 200 years. The company specialises in the design, manufacture, supply and installation of modern camouflage and concealment systems for both mobile equipment (vehicles, weapons, fixed-wing aircraft, helicopters and personnel) and fixed installation targets in all types of terrain.

For more than 50 years Bridport Aviation Products has been involved with the innovation, design and manufacture of camouflage material and techniques for the British Armed Forces, the US Air Force and other NATO countries, the Armed Forces of the member countries of the Gulf Co-operation Council, Asean Pact members, various armed forces in Latin America, as well as many other countries worldwide.

Major features of the company's camouflage systems are custom design, flexibility of size, light weight and ease of repair. The company's camouflage nets are manufactured from synthetic materials which are rot- and waterproof and they are lighter than comparable products. The company offers an associated range of support equipment which blends the contours of the camouflage net to the surrounding terrain, and has also developed concealment systems for use with artillery, radar equipment, self-propelled guns, aircraft and helicopters.

Radar scattering camouflage

To complete the multi-spectral range of camouflage, nets can be manufactured to give a broad band attenuation to radar. Bridport Aviation Products continues to extend and improve the capabilities above 90 GHz.

Thermal camouflage

Developed by the United Kingdom Ministry of Defence, thermal camouflage material extends protection into the infra-red (thermal) region of the spectrum. The material used has a special composite construction which reduces thermal emissions from warm or hot objects to a level comparable with their surroundings. Far infra-red emission characteristics can be combined with near infra-red reflectivity and visual colouring in a single continuous membrane system to enable concealment over a wide range of wavelengths. This

camouflage component was designed for low weight and bulk and will not snag in use. It can be incorporated with an incised camouflage set which can be designed and tailored for all vehicles and equipment of any size and shape.

Camouflage net systems

Camouflage net systems degrade hostile surveillance and acquisition system performance primarily by giving the target the optical and textural appearance of its environment. In reducing target recognition and identification probability, immediate attack is less likely and an enemy is less likely to gain a correct assessment of military functions and intentions.

Simple repair procedures involving the attachment of new/replacement garnishing patches with plastic tie-wraps can extend the life of the company's camouflage nets.

Camouflage concealment sets

Purpose designed as complete systems, concealment sets are primarily for use with artillery, aircraft and helicopters, and generally for equipment difficult to camouflage due to bulk or manpower limitations, or for protecting equipment of high tactical value. Specific designs allow artillery to be serviced or fired, radar to operate and aircraft or helicopters to be refuelled and re-armed from concealed positions. Sets are available for 105 and 155 mm artillery (FH-70 and M198 howitzers), 81 and 120 mm mortars, self-propelled guns, the Rapier SAM system and fixed-wing aircraft (F-16, Harrier and Tornado). The company can design and quote for any custom-made set to meet client needs and to match local environmental conditions.

Helicopter sets

The company offers concealment sets for use in forward or rear areas to protect various types of helicopter including the Super Puma and CH-47 Chinook. A specialist design team can develop sets for use with any helicopter.

Camouflage screens

Modern practices for the camouflage of parked aircraft have resulted in the development of a new generation of products including camouflage screens stemming from the desert raschel net produced by Bridport Aviation Products for over 20 years. The screen is based on a two-dimensional lightweight mesh screen which can be produced with a large repeat pattern and may be reversible to suit different areas or climatic changes. Multi-spectral properties are achieved. By the addition of garnish, three-dimensional properties can be enhanced to achieve lower detection ranges.

The screens are snag free and foreign object

damage (FOD) free. Weights are 120 g/m² for the reversible mesh and 170 g/m² for the garnished mesh. The family also includes a version of the screen for use as a false operating surface (FOS).

Ancillary equipment

To achieve effective camouflage it is important for the external net shape to be contoured to match the surrounding terrain. The company's equipment range includes support poles, mushroom caps and ground pegs to help produce natural formations. A quick release system is also available to allow rapid opening for engaging targets or breaking from cover.

Personnel camouflage

The company offers a range of helmet and individual camouflage nets for any type of terrain. The helmet nets are manufactured from synthetic materials to fit most standard helmets and can be supplied with or without garnishing materials.

Fixed installation camouflage

The key to camouflaging air bases and other fixed installations is to deceive oncoming attacking aircraft into targeting systems on non-vital areas. Aircraft shelters are particularly vulnerable to attack due to the easily detected large semi-elliptical shadows created by door areas. Camouflage packages for such installations include the deployment of camouflage nets and screens, decoys and paint schemes for runways, equipment and buildings. A company design team can advise on the camouflage of any fixed installation.

Decoys

Bridport Aviation Products designs and manufactures to client's specific requirements a full range of decoy systems which can authentically duplicate the visual, near infra-red, far infra-red (thermal) and radar signatures of the original equipment. Any MBT, artillery piece or other land vehicle or aircraft (both fixed- and rotary-wing) can. be produced as a full-size realistic decoy which can convince surveillance and guidance systems that the decoy is the real thing. Bridport Aviation Products decoys were operationally proven during Operation Desert Storm.

Status

In production. In service with the British and other armed forces.

Manufacturer

Bridport Aviation Products, The Court, Bridport, Dorset DT6 3QU, UK.
Tel: 0308 56666. Telex: 41132 netsbt g.
Fax: 0308 56605.

Bridport Aviation Products two-dimensional decoy of Chieftain tank in hull down position

Military post under Bridport desert camouflage from distance of 50 m

Airborne Inflatable Dummy Targets

Description

These inflatable dummy targets were developed to provide realistic recognition training to Forward Air Controllers (FACs) directing ground attack aircraft against AFVs and other battle formations. They are used in this role by the Royal Air Force.

At ranges of between 2000 and 3000 m, through binoculars, they are immediately identifiable as armoured vehicles, at 900 to 1000 m they are identifi-able as to type and at a distance of less than 300 m they are identifiable as dummies.

The targets are manufactured in synthetic rubber-coated nylon and consist of a framework of low pressure inflatable tubes which are covered to simulate the vehicle outline. Paint is used to highlight prominent features such as wheels and hatches. Support poles and guys ensure stability. Pressure relief valves are incorporated to limit the pressure to 0.07 kg/cm^2 during inflation or temperature increases.

Inflation is by a small battery-operated blower and can be accomplished in 5 to 8 minutes. The support poles and guys take a further 2 to 3 minutes to position. Several outlet tubes give fast deflation and normally two people can completely deflate, pack and stow a target in 10 minutes. Each target is packed in a valise for ease of handling and storage.

The current range includes the T-72 and T-62 MBT, BMP-1 MICV, BTR-50PK and BTR-60PB APCs, ZSU-23-4 air defence system, and a Rapier SAM system. A 155 mm GCT SPG has been delivered to the French Army. Other AFVs can be designed and the company has designed a T-12 100 mm anti-tank gun dummy target.

Status

In production. In service with the Royal Air Force and French Army.

Manufacturer

Airborne Industries Limited, Airborne Industrial Estate, Arterial Road, Leigh-on-Sea, Essex SS9 4EF, UK.
Tel: 0702 525265. Telex: 99412 airbrn g.
Fax: 0702 510454.

Specifications

Model	T-72	T-62	BMP-1	BTR-60PB
Weight	90 kg	88 kg	76 kg	94 kg
Length (inflated)	9.5 m	9.45 m	6.71 m	7.16 m
Width (inflated)	3.5 m	3.35 m	3.02 m	2.74 m
Height (inflated)	2.45 m	2.29 m	2.44 m	2.44 m
Pack size	all are approximately 1.07 × 0.6 × 0.4 m			

T-62 MBT dummy target by Airborne Industries (Ministry of Defence)

BMP-1 MICV dummy target by Airborne Industries (Ministry of Defence)

UNITED STATES OF AMERICA

Small Area Camouflage Cover (SACC)

Description

The US Army Belvoir Research, Development and Engineering Center at Fort Belvoir has developed a Small Area Camouflage Cover (SACC) designed to conceal individual troops or to be attached together for use over weapon emplacements, combat positions and supply caches. The SACC comes in woodland, desert, arctic and tropical colour versions and provides concealment against visual, near infra-red, radar and ultraviolet light detection (in the case of the arctic SACC). The woodland and tropical SACCs are pat-terned on both sides with a seasonal colour change on the reverse. Desert and arctic are monotone coloured on one side and patterned on the reverse. SACCs are made of incised vinyl-coated scrim cloth, with the exception of the arctic version which is made of unincised spun bonded cloth. Each unit weighs less than 518 g and is small enough (2.13 × 1.37 m) to be folded to fit into a uniform pocket.

Status

Development complete.

Development Agency

Belvoir Research, Development and Engineering Center, Fort Belvoir, Virginia 22060-5606, USA.

Soldier in firing position without camouflage cover

Soldier in firing position with camouflage cover provided by Small Area Camouflage Cover (SACC)

Camouflage Paints and Pattern Painting

Description

Fast drying, dull, high quality alkyd paints are applied by spray gun or brush in patterns to disrupt signature characteristics of vehicles, and to reduce contrast with soil and vegetation in the background. Light green, dark green, forest green, field drab, sand, earth yellow, earth brown, olive drab, black and white colours were provided for blends that counter visual and near infra-red surveillance and target acquisition. Solar and heat reflecting paints and easily removable white coating were also provided for special applications. By January 1977 all US Army tactical equipment was pattern painted.

As the result of a programme that began in August 1978, the US Army turned from alkyd paints to a polyurethane paint. The new finish has a much improved resistance to chemical agents which are unable to penetrate the surface. A surface film is formed which is resistant to the ingress of moisture in any form and thus NBC decontamination can be carried out in the field by washing the affected areas. Once applied the new paint is stated to be far more durable than the alkyd paints. These coatings protect surfaces from absorbing chemical agents and enable soldiers to decontaminate their equipment without breaking down and dissolving the paint.

Three-colour camouflage patterns developed by the Belvoir Research, Development and Engineering Center replaced the four-colour pattern formerly used on tactical equipment. The new pattern is composed of brown, green and black pattern shapes. In theory, the broad patches of colour used will break up the vehicle's silhouette making it harder to identify at a distance as well as blending better with its background at close range.

The US Army decided to adopt the new pattern developed by Germany. By standardising the camouflage used by US and German armies, enemy forces cannot ascertain a vehicle's country of origin by its pattern. After a series of tests, the three-colour German pattern was shown to provide better protection than the four-colour American design. Conversion to the three-colour pattern was carried out in conjunction with the introduction of the new chemical agent resistant coatings also developed by the Belvoir Center.

Status

See text.

Development Agency

Belvoir Research, Development and Engineering Center, Fort Belvoir, Virginia 22060-5606, USA.

Model showing three-colour winter camouflage pattern applied to M1 Abrams MBT

Model showing three-colour winter camouflage pattern applied to M2 Bradley IFV

Teledyne Brown Engineering Camouflage Systems

Description

Teledyne Brown Engineering was awarded an initial camouflage production contract by the US Army in 1987. Since then the equivalent of approximately 160 000 systems has been delivered. The current Teledyne Brown baseline products include the Light-Weight Camouflage Screen System (LWCSS), the personal thermal camouflage system (the Thellie suit), the multi-spectral ultralight camouflage system (Spectralight), and an ultra-lightweight camouflage system (Ultralight). These systems were designed to separately or uniquely satisfy requirements to defeat sensors which operate in the visual, near infra-red and 3-5 and 8-12 microns thermal and RF frequency bands. The systems are adaptable to global requirements for colours.

The LWCSS is processed using a polyester cloth coated by either polyvinyl chloride or a new lighter weight material. Both coatings are custom-treated to resist fungii, ultraviolet rays and other environmental threats while remaining effective in the near infra-red, visual and RF ranges. A finished screen, depending on which coating material is used, weighs about 21.7 to 29.5 kg and will cover approximately 92 m². One system includes a hexagon and a rhombic screen along with repair kits. The LWCSS may be produced to suppress the RF signatures of an asset or be transparent. The transparent system is required when electronic emitting devices are to be camouflaged. A unique thermal suppression system, effective in both the 3-5 and 8-12 micron bands, is available as an adjunct to the LWCSS. The support system for the LWCSS is available separately, consisting of poles, pole caps and stakes. The support system and the LWCSS include all items necessary to camouflage an emplacement, with no need for other materials.

Teledyne Brown has also developed and introduced two multi-spectral camouflage systems, a personal Thellie suit that will effectively defeat the near infra-red 3-5 and 8-12 micron, visual and RF sensors, and a Spectralight camouflage screen system tailored for large areas that provides effective protection from thermal, visual and wideband RF. The latter can be produced with sizes according to requirements.

The Ultralight camouflage screen system has approximately one-third the weight and bulk of the LWCSS. It is available in various colours, sizes and functional characteristics. The system has basically the same performance characteristics as the LWCSS and is particularly suitable for use over emplacements subject to air surveillance.

Status

In production with Woodland LWCSS, Desert Shield LWCSS, Desert Shield Ultralight. In limited production with Thellie suits and Spectralight.

Manufacturer

Teledyne Brown Engineering, Cummings Research Park, Huntsville, Alabama 35807, USA. Tel: (205) 726 3945. Fax: (205) 726 3245.

Brunswick Camouflage and Other Defensive Systems

Description

Brunswick camouflage screens comprise a minimal number of parts and are manufactured from durable synthetics to withstand use and re-use in all environments. Metal fibres distributed throughout the camouflage effectively conceal military equipment from radar systems as described below. Research and development have resulted in colour pigmentations and textures which, in addition to achieving good visual and radar camouflage, provide effective concealment from spectrozal and false colour film combinations, including colour infra-red film.

Three standard colour/texture combinations are available to meet woodland, desert and snow conditions. Each screen has a different colour-texture pattern on each side for greater versatility of application. One side of the woodland screen simulates spring and summer while the reverse simulates autumn. Desert screens simulate both tan and grey desert terrain and the arctic screen provides concealment in total as well as partial snow cover with optimum reflectance in the ultraviolet necessary to preclude detection in this spectral region. Special colour/texture formulations can be developed by Brunswick to meet specific environmental requirements. The screens meet US Military Specifications MIL-C-52771 (ME) and MIL-C-52765 (ME).

Camouflage screens produced by Brunswick have been designed to scatter some of the impinging radar energy, absorb some and allow only enough to be transmitted back to the radar detector to give the military object the same general return as that of the terrain and thus prevent detection. This effect is achieved in the screens by the random dispersion of short, thin steel fibres throughout the garnishing material in combination with selected incising patterns. This combination in the woodland screen results in a proper balance of reflection, absorption, transmission and scatter to achieve the desired simulation of natural woodland surroundings.

Camouflage kits manufactured by Brunswick consist of two subsystems: a screen system and a support system. Each is packed separately in its own vinyl-coated nylon transport case. One screen system consists of a simple hexagon-shaped screen and a rhombic-shaped screen, carrying case and a repair kit. Screen edges are a uniform 4.9 m for joining to make larger screens. Quick disconnect brackets are permanently attached to all screen edges for quick joining. The screens can be quickly disconnected by pulling a lanyard. The support system contains support poles, spikes, spreader assemblies and a carrying case.

The modular concept was designed to meet the

diverse field needs encountered. The rhombic or diamond screen can be used for smaller requirements such as personnel or weapons emplacements while hexagonal nets meet the need for shielding equipment in the ¼- to ½-ton truck range, two- and three-module combinations provide cover for 2½-ton trucks, medium tanks and mobile artillery and regular or irregular configuration module combinations can be assembled to meet almost any installation need.

In October 1990 the US Army ordered 20 000 units of standard lightweight camouflage worth $6.3 million in a new 'Saudi Tan' colour. The order brought the number of lightweight camouflage units produced by Brunswick to over 1 million since 1974.

In 1990 Brunswick introduced a new 'ultralightweight' camouflage with improved radar-scattering and anti-thermal imaging properties. The new camouflage weighs about half as much as standard netting and uses a lightweight garnish cut in a fine pattern and quilted to a fine mesh scrim that is virtually 'snagproof'. The US Army ordered an initial batch of 500 units in 'Saudi Tan' in October 1990, for use with AH-64A Apache helicopters.

Status
In production for the US Army.

Manufacturer
Brunswick Corporation, Defense Division, One Brunswick Plaza, Skokie, Illinois 60076, USA. Tel: (312) 470 4827/8. Telex: 190127. Fax: (312) 470 4938.

Close-up of Brunswick ultra-lightweight camouflage produced for US Army in a 'Saudi Tan' colour

Sullivan Camouflage Screening System

Description
The Sullivan Camouflage Screening System was designed and developed for the US Army. It is designed to be placed over temporarily halted military vehicles, weapons and equipment, and over semi-permanent positions and installations to inhibit location and identification by target acquisition and surveillance systems. The system can also be employed to aid concealment of permanent objects, and objects in a fixed pattern of array which present an obvious target signature. It is effective in the visual, ultraviolet, near infra-red and broadband radar spectrums.

The Sullivan system consists of a basic camouflage screen, a support system, storage/transport case, repair kit and ancillary items.

The basic camouflage screen is made of two parts, one hexagonal-shaped screen and one rhombic-shaped unit interconnected by a quick release system at one edge. The screen is made of synthetic support netting to which is attached specially coated synthetic fabric which has been incised to provide camouflage effective surface texture and colour patterns. It covers approximately 55 m² with a dry weight of 15.5 kg and a packaged volume of 0.113 m³. It is available in woodland, desert and snow colour-pattern-texture combinations, with each combination reversible to provide greater variety of appearance. Colour patterns and reversible combinations can be modified to provide camouflage for specific needs. For example a woodland reversible to tan/grey desert can be easily produced.

Sullivan single desert module deployed

Single screens can be joined along any of their edges to form a large screen of any desired overall size and shape.

The support system is made of reinforced plastic spreaders and telescopic poles which raise the screen above the target in an irregular, domed configuration.

Ancillary items include stakes, ground anchors for use in soft and sandy soil and an instruction sheet.

The system is resistant to mould, rot, fungus, corrosion and colour fading. It is non water-absorbent, and fireproof, and is not adversely affected by petrol or other POL products.

Inflatable decoys
Sullivan Industries also produces inflatable decoys which are valuable both in confusing the enemy as to field strength and in distracting enemy fire. The company has developed its inflatables from original research and development conducted for the US Air Force and US Navy.

The company can design and fabricate inflatable decoys to meet specific customer requirements using a wide variety of synthetic materials. Various degrees of broad spectrum signatures, including ultraviolet, visible, infra-red, radar and so on will simulate tanks or other equipment.

Status
In production. In service with the US Army.

Manufacturer
Sullivan Industries/General Image Engineering Corporation, 1652 West 820 North, Provo, Utah 84601, USA. Tel: (801) 377 9090. Telex: 278007. Fax: (801) 377 9148.

704

PORTABLE ROADWAYS

COMMONWEALTH OF INDEPENDENT STATES

Heavy Portable Roadway Sections

Description
There are three basic forms of portable heavy roadway used by the CIS, two of which make use of the great timber resources of the CIS with timber girders and timber planks on timber ribs. As such there are many different forms and sizes and many are made either by local state factories or by army workshops. Although the sizes may vary, for supply purposes each section using wood planks is estimated to weigh between 160 and 220 kg less crosspieces, and the girders are estimated to weigh between 250 and 300 kg. Road-ways using such timber sections are laid either by hand or by cranes and the rate of laying can vary between 40 and 60 m/h.

The third form of roadway section is manufactured from corrugated steel sheets, each weighing between 100 and 110 kg. Each section measures 2 × 1.05 × 0.08 m, although this may vary. Roadways using these steel sheets can be assembled either by hand or by crane.

Specifications (metal sections only)
Dimensions: 2 × 1.05 × 0.08 m
Wearing quality: 50 000 to 70 000 vehicles

Weight:
(single section) 100-110 kg
(section for 1 km road) 100 000 to 120 000 kg
Number of ZIL-164 trucks: (to transport 1 km of road) 30 to 35
Rate of laying: up to 100 m/h

Status
In service with the former Warsaw Pact forces.

Manufacturer
All types: state factories. Can be assembled in army workshops.

Glued Plywood Roadway Sections – SRDP

Description
The lightest of the CIS types of portable roadway is the SRDP (*Sborno-Razbornoye-Dorozhnoye Pokrytiye*). The basic element of this system is a glued plywood panel measuring 2.5 × 1 × 0.07 m and weighing between 100 and 120 kg. Each panel is held in place by wooden inserts placed into butt-brackets at each end. The panels can be laid to form either strips or wider roadways. They are normally laid by hand with teams of 10 to 12 men, but a mechanical laying method has been developed which enables strips to be laid from amphibious PTS vehicles. This method replaces the wooden end inserts with steel cables and the panels are pre-prepared as they are loaded onto the PTS.

The panels are prepared using methods which have been specially developed to take advantage of the large timber resources of the CIS. The wooden sheets that make up each panel are joined together by phenol-formaldehyde glues and are then rapidly passed to a further process which pressure coats the panels with a layer of bakelite material. The ends are covered by strips of similarly treated plywood and surface gripping strips are added. The panels then require no further maintenance and can be stored in the open if necessary.

Specifications
Panel dimensions: 2.5 × 1 × 0.07 m
Wearing quality: 40 000 to 50 000 vehicles
Weight:
(single panel) 100 to 120 kg
(panels for 1 km road) 80 000 to 100 000 kg
Number of ZIL-164 trucks: (to transport 1 km of road) 25 to 30

Rate of laying: 100 to 150 running m/h

Status
In service with the CIS.

Manufacturer
State factories. Simplified versions may be assembled in army workshops.

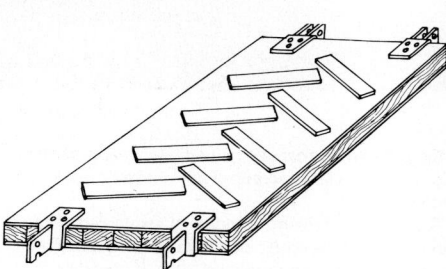

SRDP glued plywood roadway section

SRDP glued plywood roadway in position

CZECHOSLOVAKIA

Truck-mounted Roadway Laying System

Description
This system consists of a Tatra 813 (8 × 8) cross-country truck chassis with two cassettes, each loaded with 40 linked steel plates, behind the cab. The roadway is laid with the vehicle travelling in reverse. As the truck travels backwards, the trackways unfold into the horizontal, pass over rollers and are laid under each of the rear wheels. This system is used by the Czechoslovak Army to prepare exit points of bridges such as the PMP pontoon system.

Status
In service with the Czechoslovak Army.

Manufacturer
Czechoslovak state factories.

Czechoslovak truck-mounted roadway laying system on Tatra 813 (8 × 8) truck chassis showing method of operation

GERMANY

Portable Roadway – Thyssen System

Description
The basis of this heavy portable roadway system is a hexagonal steel plate which is connected to adjoining plates by angled iron brackets. Each plate weighs 23 kg and a standard truck width can be formed by joining nine plates which form a roadway 4.2 m wide. The roadway is constructed by hand and up to eight men can lay 1 m of roadway per minute. To support a 5-tonne truck a mat of 200 plates is necessary, and for a 7-tonne truck, 288 plates. To enable the system to be used for water crossings a method has been evolved in which a completed mat is towed across the water obstacle by a vehicle with a winch. One of the advantages of this system is that it can be assembled under cover and then dragged by winch across the ground to be covered, enabling heavy traffic to be built up rapidly in forward areas.

Status
In production. In service with German forces and the Danish Army.

Thyssen portable roadway system being positioned at river crossing point

Close-up of Thyssen portable roadway system

Krupp Rollmat Matting

Description
Krupp Rollmat matting may be used in conditions where normal road traffic would be unable to move, such as sandy ground or marshy meadowland. Under such conditions the use of this matting enables vehicles up to MLC Class 60 to cross. Rollmat matting may be laid by hand or from special laying units carried on 10 000 kg trucks. The basic element of the matting is a multi-chamber aluminium alloy strip which is 250 mm wide and 57 mm deep. Each element is foam-filled and can be hinge-connected to other elements in varying widths. These widths may be as little as 1 m for walkways to 16 m for the assembly of temporary aircraft landing strips. For the rapid laying of roads from the vehicle-carried laying unit, widths of 4.6 to 5 m are more usual. The weight per square metre of the basic elements is 33 kg. When laid from rolls, lengths may be up to 50 m which will produce a roll diameter of 2.2 m. If required, elements may be joined together to form helicopter landing mats.

Apart from the vehicle-carried laying unit, accessories available for use with Krupp Rollmat include wedge-shaped panels for access ramps, safety dowels, anchors and tools.

Status
In production.

Manufacturer
Krupp Industrietechnik GmbH, Franz-Schubert-Strasse 1-3, Postfach 14 19 60, D-4100 Duisburg 14 (Rheinhausen), Federal Republic of Germany. Tel: 021 35 781. Telex: 0855 486.

Krupp Rollmat matting being rolled out from its laying equipment

Krupp Rollmat matting in use carrying MLC 60 Leopard 2 MBT

GREECE

MICROTECH Class 60 Trackway

Description
The MICROTECH Class 60 Trackway uses the same components and general construction methods as the MICROTECH Runway Repair Decking described in the following section. The trackway is designed for both tracked and wheeled vehicles and is constructed from extruded sections made of heat-treated aluminium alloy. The trackway consists of a number of panels with a tongue on one side and a groove in the other. Each panel has a corrugated shape which together with additional grooves on the section faces provides an anti-slip surface. The panels are provided in 2.3 and 4.6 m lengths which can be easily handled by one man. An end ramp panel section is supplied to enable vehicles to get onto the trackway easily.

The tongue and groove connecting method joins panels together and for a permanent join a large bolt can be added. If the trackway is to be laid on a slope it should be anchored in place using a special chain and shackle assembly. A section handling tool can be supplied for ease of assembly and other accessories include a special towing adaptor.

To produce a standard trackway 40.4 m long and 4.6 m wide a full set as supplied will consist of the

MICROTECH Class 60 trackway in use

following; 185 4.6 m long panels, two ramp panels, four handling tools, four towing adaptors, 380 locking bolts, four strap assemblies, four 18-link welded chains, 24 steel guy stakes and 12 shackles.

The trackway can also be used to construct a mat to cover an area of soft ground for depot, maintenance area and other uses. A standard set can be produced to construct a mat 18.4 m wide and 11.7 m long. The tools and accessories supplied are the same as those used for a standard trackway set but the mat requires 185 4.6 m panels, 54 2.3 m panels and eight ramp panels.

Specifications
Main section width:
   (overall) 242 mm
   (effective) 225 mm
Length:
   (long panel) 4.6 m
   (short panel) 2.3 m
Weight:
   (long panel) 32 kg
   (short panel) 16 kg
Ramp section width:
   (overall) 184 mm
   (effective) 152 mm
Ramp section length: (long panel) 4.6 m
Ramp section weight: (long panel) 45.4 kg
Breaking load: 1465 kg

Status
In production. In service with the Greek armed forces.

Manufacturer
MICROTECH Limited, 167A Patission Street, GR-11252 Athens, Greece.
Tel: (01) 8655030. Fax: (01) 8678541.

INTERNATIONAL

Folding Roadway System

Description
During the late 1960s personnel from France, Germany and Italy undertook a study to improve the crossing of rough terrain by heavy vehicles. These studies led in 1974 to a concept and definition phase conducted by France and Germany. This was completed in late 1982. By then 24 proposals had been submitted of which four were selected for further study. At the beginning of the development phase both participating nations agreed on a design produced by the Trefilunion Usine de Marnaval concern.

This design used a rectangular panel 4.2 m wide and 2.74 m long. The panels consist of a welded round steel bar lattice upon which a thin sheet steel cover is welded. These panels make up the basic components of a folding roadway which is laid using a transport, laying and recovery system developed by Linke-Hofmann-Busch GmbH, a subsidiary of Salzgitter AG. Salzgitter AG developed a parallel system based upon the use of aluminium hexagonal plates, also 4.2 m wide and divided into 2.77 m sections connected by formed hooks and eyes. The hexagonal design was adopted and production is carried out in Germany by Krauss-Maffei and in France by LOHR SA.

The equipment is carried on German Army MAN (8 × 8) 10 000 kg high mobility trucks while the French Army uses the Renault TRM 10 000 (6 × 6) 10 000 kg truck. The MAN truck carries approximately 50 m of roadway while the Renault vehicle originally carried 40 m and used shorter (2.2 m) sections. However a new version of the TRM 10 000 can carry the same 50 m length as the MAN vehicle. The carrying and laying equipment can be mounted onto other existing truck chassis.

The laying mechanism, which weighs 3600 kg, is constructed of welded steel and is supported at three points. A swivel arm is erected hydraulically to guide the belt during the laying and/or recovery process. The laying mechanism can be lowered for rail transport. The main frame is the base for the roadway carrier. It is constructed of torsional elastic steel and consists of individual crossmembers which are hinged to the vehicle chassis and support rails which are bolted to the crossmembers. The roadway sits directly on the roadway carrier which has an upper and lower cradle. To position the roadway the lower cradle can be moved longitudinally, and the upper cradle can rotate 90° in either direction. Both assemblies are of welded steel construction and the lower cradle has a jointed cross-

Folding Roadway System on Renault TRM 10 000 (6 × 6) 10 000 kg truck

shaft axle to compensate for chassis distortion. The launching guide is a tubular steel lattice framework hydraulically pivoted around the top of an upright support. Rollers are mounted on the framework to reduce friction. The upright support is a welded aluminium two-part unit.

In use the carrying truck is backed up to the site to be covered by the roadway. The roadway carrier is then rotated and moved into the laying position. A belt is then attached to the beginning of the folding roadway along with a rope from a rear winch. This rope is used to pull the first roadway sections over the laying frame (bail), thereby unfolding them. Once the first part of the roadway is on the ground the rear winch is disconnected. The vehicle is then placed into reverse and as it moves backwards the roadway unfolds over the laying frame with the laying belt laid centrally under the roadway. The laying process takes approximately 10 minutes for every 50 m of roadway and the roadway can be laid underwater. The recovery process, using the central belt and rear winch, is the reverse of the laying procedure with the carrying truck moving forward one section of plates at a time. The recovery process takes 20 minutes. Laying and recovery involves a vehicle driver and one other man.

Specifications (Roadway – German version)
Total length: 50 m
Length of each section: 2.77 m
Width: (nominal) 4.2 m
Weight:
   (each plate) 10 kg
   (each section) 510 kg
   (50 m roadway) 9200 kg
Continuous load capacity:
   (wheeled) MLC 25
   (tracked) MLC 60

Status
In production for French and German armies.

Manufacturers
LOHR SA, F-67980 Hangenbieten, France.
Tel: 88 38 98 00. Telex: 870082 f.
Fax: 88 96 06 36.
Krauss-Maffei Wehrtechnik GmbH, Krauss-Maffei-Strasse 2, D-8000 Munich 50, Federal Republic of Germany.
Tel: 089 8899-0. Fax: 089 8120190.

SWEDEN

Columbus Mat

Description

The Columbus Mat was designed by Curt F Lundin and is used for a wide variety of civilian and military applications including reinforcement of soft ground to enable tracked or wheeled vehicles to cross difficult country, at river exit points, and as military bridge access mats. It is also used as recovery tracks for aircraft recovery after abortive take-offs and landing overruns. (The Thai Air Force and Scandinavian airports have purchased sets for this purpose.) The standard 5 m mat consists of polythene tubing held together by 15 steel cables. At the ends of the mats there are three tubes 65 mm in diameter and 15 mm thick. The other tubes (71 in all) have an external diameter of 65 mm and are 5.8 mm thick. The cables have 171 threads and a diameter of 8 mm, and the cable ends are drawn in a loop back through the heavy end tube. Coupling links at the cable ends enable mats to be joined end-to-end to form a roadway of any length.

Laying and recovery require no special tools or equipment and the mat can be transported by truck either flat, rolled or folded.

For use by heavy vehicles at water crossings a special system called the Vehicle Mat 2MT was developed. The complete system consists of four mats each with 140 mm outside diameter end tubes and heavy duty cables with coupling links, two steel anchoring beams, four climbing frames, 12 chains, 10 soil anchor frames, 20 soil rod sets plus cables and other accessories. Weight of the complete equipment is 5600 kg. The system was developed in close co-operation with the Swedish Army.

The basic idea is that the mats and the climbing frames, which consist of four Bailey bridge panels, are assembled on the bank on one side of the river and then winched down the river bank by a winch on the far bank. Once in place the mats are held firmly in position by the soil anchor frames which are staked to the ground and connected to the anchoring beam by chains.

Specifications (Basic mat)
Width: 4.5 m (other widths available in 300 mm multiples)
Length: max 15 m (normal standard 5 m)
Weight: 20 kg/m^2

Status
In production. In service with the armed forces of Germany, Norway, Sweden, Switzerland, Thailand, the United Kingdom and the USA. Used with aircraft recovery kits by many countries.

Manufacturer
Vårgårda Plast AB, Columbus Mat Division, S-447 00 Vårgårda, Sweden.

Method of joining two sections of Columbus Vehicle Mat 2MT and showing polythene tube construction

Information and sales: Curt F Lundin, PO Box 1037, S-144 01 Rönninge 1, Sweden.
Tel: 46 753 54677. Telex: 13362 grevtur s.

UNITED KINGDOM

Laird Portable Trackways

Description

The Laird-developed Class 30 and Class 60 Track-ways are both portable non-skid surfaces designed for use on soft ground where conditions would become increasingly difficult with continual traffic and eventually result in the immobilisation of vehicles and mobile equipment. The Trackway can easily be taken up after use, transported elsewhere and relaid. Laird manufactures and supplies all components for these systems. The aluminium alloy (HE 30 TF) section used for the Class 30 and Class 60 Trackways was developed by the British Ministry of Defence in collaboration with the British Aluminium Company Limited, and is fabricated and marketed by Laird.

Class 30 Trackway
The Class 30 Trackway was designed for wheeled vehicles and tracked vehicles with rubber pads and entered service in 1963. Heavier vehicles can use the Trackway when ground conditions are favourable and tanks up to Class 50 may cross the Trackway at an angle provided they do not slew on the track.

The Class 30 Trackway is assembled from a number of extruded aluminium alloy planks with interlocking captive tongue-and-groove joints, forming a continuous non-skid surface 3.35 m wide and normally 32 m long. This standard Trackway length is reeled onto a carriage assembly mounted on the rear of a 6 × 6 or 4 × 4 truck. The spool carrying the length of track is mounted on a frame and turntable assembly which clamps to the truck platform. This arrangement permits the equipment to be stowed within the vehicle dimensions or swung through 90° to the launching and recovery position. The Class 30 Trackway is launched forward over the truck cab using a quickly fitted removable roller frame launching assembly. The track can also be launched over the rear of the truck. The preparation and launching operation can be completed in 10 minutes by a three-man team. The Trackway is recovered over the rear of the vehicle and is rewound onto the spool by ratchet levers. Roller supports clamped to the rear of the truck platform support the track clear of the truck. The recovery operations can be completed in about 15 minutes by a four-man team.

Specifications (Class 30 trackway)
Length: 32-46 m
Width: 3.35 m
Number of planks: 140-201
Weight:
  (per metre run) 68 kg
  (carriage assembly) 760 kg
  (launching assembly) 340 kg
  (recovery equipment) 41 kg
  (total trackway and components) 3325-4280 kg
Individual plank size: 3.35 × 0.23 m

Class 60 Trackway
The heavy duty Class 60 Trackway was designed for both tracked and wheeled vehicles and entered service in 1967. Typical uses include supporting tanks on soft ground and other areas subject to heavy traffic. The Trackway is quickly and easily assembled and the components can be transported in quantity by standard trucks. It was also developed as an instant hard surface for the repair of bomb-damaged airfield runways, for which there is a separate entry in the *Rapid runway repair equipment/portable runways* section.

Class 60 Trackway, 4.6 m wide, can be laid and recovered by a suitably equipped vehicle. Manpower required is a driver and an assistant. Up to 50 m of Trackway can be transported on a detachable spool supported by a swivelling stand with a hydraulic power unit. The Trackway is laid over the rear of the vehicle and under the rear wheels. The weight of the vehicle is supported on its own Trackway during the laying operation as the vehicle reverses. The Trackway is recovered in the exact opposite sequence to laying.

Class 60 Trackway carried by DAF YGZ 2300 (6 × 6) bridging vehicle

British Army Bedford MK (4 × 4) 4000 kg truck carrying Class 30 trackway

Typical military vehicles have a carrying capacity as follows:

    8-tonne, 4 × 4: up to 30 m
    10-tonne, 6 × 6: up to 45 m
    11-tonne and over, 6 × 6: up to 50 m.

The equipment comprises a turntable frame mounted either on the vehicle load platform or directly onto the chassis and supporting a swivelling stand capable of lateral rotation between transit and operating positions. The stand in turn supports a spool on which the Trackway is coiled, guided by rollers and restrained by internally wound ropes. The spool is powered by a hydraulic motor with integral brake, capable of turning the spool in either direction. The motor is powered in turn by a diesel engine/pump unit mounted on the rear end of the spool stand. The hydraulic system also supplies power to rotate the swivelling stand from the transit to the operational position, such as transverse across the truck.

Up to 50 m of Trackway can be laid in approximately 5 minutes. After deploying one length of Trackway an empty spool can be exchanged for a full spool by using a crane. If spare rolls of Trackway are stored on dummy spools and stands, power transfer to the empty vehicle can be effected. If only a limited length of Trackway is required it can be split at a convenient point and the surplus spooled back onto the vehicle. For recovery an approximate guide is that 50 m of clean Trackway can be recovered in 7 minutes by a driver and an assistant.

Specifications (Class 60 applications)
Typical Class 60 mat
Length: 16.46 m
Width: 18.3 m
Area: 301 m^2
Weight:
    (per m^2) 34 kg
    (total) 10 300 kg

Typical Class 60 track
Length: 15.3 m
Width: 4.6 m
Weight:
    (per metre run) 156 kg
    (total) 2385 kg

Laying and recovery equipment
Weight:
    (Trackway) 156 kg/m
    (spool and stand) 2160 kg
    (subframe and turntable) 500 kg
    (rear roller frame) 200 kg

Individual planks

	Long plank	Short plank
Length	4.57 m	2.28 m
Weight	33.07 kg	16.76 kg

Status
In production. In service with many countries including Canada, Germany, Greece, Iraq, Japan, Netherlands, Saudi Arabia, Singapore, United Kingdom and the USA.

Manufacturer
Laird (Anglesey) Limited, Beaumaris, Anglesey, Gwynedd LL58 8HY, UK.
Tel: 0248 810431. Telex: 61295 lrd bms f.
Fax: 0248 810300.

UNITED STATES OF AMERICA

MO-MAT Roadway System

Description
MO-MAT was designed for laying over terrain such as mud, sand and snow to allow the passage of wheeled vehicles. It is also used for a variety of other roles including use as a helicopter pad.

MO-MAT is fabricated from a glass fibre reinforced plastic called Stratoglas, developed by the Stratoglas Division of the Air Logistics Corporation. MO-MAT is moulded into a structural shape resembling that of a waffle with an overall thickness of 16 mm. It is also available in thicknesses of 2.2 and 3.2 mm forming a lattice cross-section 16 mm thick overall and has a durable non-skid material bound to the top surface.

The standard duty MO-MAT (2.2 mm) weighs 4.9 kg/m^2 and the heavy duty MO-MAT (3.2 mm) 7.3 kg/m^2. MO-MAT is supplied in standard panels 3.709 m wide and 14.782 m long. Utility panels 3.709 m wide and 6.6 m long and sheets 3.6 m long and 1.8 m wide are also available. Precision holes are provided around the periphery for interconnecting panels or sheets to any desired length or width. Panels or sheets may also be attached to frames to form a variety of structures.

The MO-MAT panels reduce the ground pressure by spreading the wheel loads over a wider surface area. Excessive crowning of the roadway caused by heavy

MO-MAT roll being held ready for use by US Marine Corps bulldozer (Ray Young)

traffic can be mitigated by doubling the thickness of the roadway — laying one panel on top of the other — or increasing the width of the roadway and spreading the traffic pattern.

The sheets are supplied rolled up on a pallet for ease of transport and can be manually deployed, re-rolled or assembled without the use of special tools or equipment.

Status
Production on receipt of large order. In service with US and other armed forces.

Manufacturer
Air Logistics Corporation, 3600 E Foothill Boulevard, Pasadena, California 81109, USA.
Tel: (818) 795 9971. Fax: (818) 795 2528.

Access/Egress Roadway System (AERS)

Development
The Access/Egress Roadway System (AERS) was developed under the aegis of the Belvoir Research, Development and Engineering Center together with the US Army Waterways Experimental Station in Vicksburg, Mississippi. The system is designed to produce roadways for wheeled and tracked vehicles up to MLC 70 over soils and slopes normally impassable to those vehicles in order to provide access and egress from river-crossing bridges, and in particular the Ribbon Bridge. It is also intended to provide an access or egress roadway for swimming or wading vehicles to cross a water obstacle, and it should also be able to provide a general roadway for heavy traffic moving to and from a bridge point. Following a series of trials involving existing types of matting a contract for an all-new system was awarded in 1981 to PCF Defense Industries of Seattle, Washington, to develop the system for service acceptance.

Four dispensers, each with 25 m of 4 m wide trackway, will be issued to each Ribbon Bridge Company.

Description
The system is designed to be carried on and used from existing 6 × 6 trucks already in service with US Army Ribbon Bridge and Engineer Companies. Each truck will carry a number of corrugated heat-treated steel panels which will be stacked on a stow/supply/dispensing welded aluminium frame mounted directly on the transporter truck. The panels are dispensed from the frame under the control of a powered three-tooth panel movement control, support and dispensing retarder sprocket. A cable and powered winch completes the system.

In use the steel panels are stacked in concertina-fashion on the frame. To dispense the panels the truck may drive directly across the water obstacle dispensing the panels to the rear as it progresses. The connected panels unfold as they are fed outwards. An alternative is to reverse the truck towards the water obstacle dispensing the panels under its wheels as it moves. In this way the following number of men can lay the following track lengths:

Track length	Time	Number of men
15-20 m	15 min	1 Engineer Squad
100-125 m	30 min	10 men
250-300 m	45 min	1 Engineer Platoon

Once laid the system is intended to withstand 2000 to 3000 passes by military traffic, 10% of which will be in the MLC 70 class.

Specifications (panel dimensions)
Length: 4.013 m
Width: 1.295 m
Thickness: 89 mm
Weight: (stack of 35) 4536 kg

Status
Advanced development.

RAPID RUNWAY REPAIR EQUIPMENT/PORTABLE RUNWAYS

FRANCE

DALLEXPRESS Emergency Runway Repair System for Runways and Taxiways

Description

The DALLEXPRESS emergency runway repair system for runways and taxiways was developed by Lafarge Fondu International, a subsidiary of the Lafarge Coppee Group; it is distributed by Automatismes & Techniques Nouvelles (ATN).

The DALLEXPRESS system employs new concrete technologies, producing a concrete slab in a period as short as 30 minutes. With the process a binder in the form of a liquid grout is pumped onto a course of aggregates through which it percolates to occupy all voids and spaces. At the end of the operation the liquid grout entirely covers the aggregate course. The thickness of the finished slab (corresponding to the thickness of the aggregate course) can be adjusted according to traffic requirements. The resultant surface is flat and even and can be matched to the surrounding material by using a broom. Traffic can be resumed 30 to 40 minutes after the application of the grout.

The process can be used over a temperature range of −20 to +50°C. As an example, a transport aircraft of the C-130 Hercules type will require a slab thickness of 370 mm on an aggregate course.

Status
Available.

Manufacturer
ATN SA, Le Clos de Villarceaux, F-78770 Thoiry, France.
Tel: (1) 34 87 55 88. Telex: 696819 f.
Fax: (1) 34 87 40 77.

GREECE

MICROTECH Runway Repair Decking

Description

This runway repair decking is constructed from extruded sections of heat-treated aluminium alloy and consists of panels and accessories that fit together to form a mat. The main sections have been designed to join with a tongue at one end and a groove at the other. Once in position the connections can be locked in place using a large bolt. The sections are supplied in two sizes, each size being manportable. Each section is corrugated in cross-section and has an anti-skid upper surface. Ramp sections can be fitted to the sides or ends of the mat. Special tools in the form of handling picks can be supplied, along with towing adaptors. If required, securing pickets can be used.

To form a standard runway repair decking 18.4 m wide and 11.7 m long the following items are required: 185 long panels, 54 short panels, eight long ramp panels, four handling tools, four towing adaptors, 480 locking devices and 40 expansion bolts. The resultant mat may be rolled for stowage if required.

The MICROTECH runway repair decking can be used, without anchoring, to form a forward area helicopter landing pad that can be rolled up and moved to a new location as required.

The components used for the MICROTECH runway repair decking are the same as those used for the MICROTECH Class 60 Trackway described in the previous section.

Specifications
Main section width:
(overall) 242 mm
(effective) 225 mm
Length:
(long panel) 4.6 m
(short panel) 2.3 m
Weight:
(long panel) 32 kg
(short panel) 16 kg
Ramp section width:
(overall) 184 mm
(effective) 152 mm
Ramp section length: (long panel) 4.6 m
Ramp section weight: (long panel) 45.4 kg
Breaking load: 1465 kg

Status
In production. In service with the Greek Air Force.

Manufacturer
MICROTECH Limited, 167A Patission Street, GR-11252 Athens, Greece.
Tel: (01) 8655030. Fax: (01) 8678541.

Moving rolled repair decking mat using mobile crane

UNITED KINGDOM

Rapid Runway Repair System

Description

This rapid runway repair system is NATO approved and underwent extensive trials by both the British and US Air Forces. It was accepted for service by Britain in 1970 and entered service in 1972.

It is based on the Rapid Runway Repair Mat which consists of an area of interlocking Class 60 aluminium alloy panels, a full description of which is given in the entry for Laird Portable Roadways in the *Portable roadways* section. The mat can be built to any desired size although the 22 × 16 m mat is the accepted size for repairing of bomb craters caused by 340 to 450 kg bombs.

The mat is stowed rolled on special chocks and when required is lifted and transported on a Runway Repair Mat Trolley, enabling the mat to be positioned at the crater site without additional lifting equipment. The laden trolley can be towed by a medium tractor.

Following a strike on a runway, the first task of the repair team is to locate the damage and transfer the information to a runway plan. A minimum operating strip, possibly 1500 m long and 15 m wide, is then plotted to establish the least amount of initial repair

Rapid runway repair mat being laid (Ministry of Defence)

work necessary to restart operations.

The area around the bomb crater is first cleared of debris, and fallback material is taken from inside the crater. The crater is then filled with selected aggregate stockpiled within the perimeter of the airfield. If aggregate is not available crater debris may be used

and pushed back into the crater.

Once the fill has been compacted the damaged area is levelled with a purpose-built screed beam and the repair mat is moved to the site, lowered to the ground and unrolled over the levelled fill. The mat is then tensioned and fastened to the undamaged section of the runway by expanding foundation bolts which pass through the fairing panels. Special fairing panels which enable aircraft to run on to and off the repair mat are connected to each end. The final stage is to clear the area of all loose material with a motorised roller. The complete operation can take as little as 1.5 hours from the time tractors start clearing debris.

To aid concealment the trackway and fairing panels are treated with pylumin, a chemical dip producing a grey/green finish. The Class 60 mat can also be used for aircraft dispersal pads and portable runways.

Status

In production. In service with Greece, Switzerland, Turkey, United Kingdom and other armed forces.

Manufacturer

Laird (Anglesey) Limited, Beaumaris, Anglesey, Gwynedd LL58 8HY, UK.
Tel: 0248 810431. Telex: 61295 lrd bms f.
Fax: 0248 810300.

Airfield Landing Mat

Description

Designed and developed by the MVEE (Christchurch) in conjunction with the British Aluminium Company Limited, the Airfield Landing Mat is usually referred to as the PSA (Prefabricated Surface Aluminium). The standard mat known as the PSA1, which weighs 15 kg/m², is suitable for most freight and passenger aircraft, and for combat aircraft with low-pressure tyres; the maximum tyre pressure is 5.62 kg/cm². The mats are made from aluminium panels and apart from their general use for aircraft landing strip assembly, can also be used for operating pads for aircraft such as the Harrier and also for rapid runway repair.

The Airfield Landing Mat uses six basic components, as follows:

Basic panel. This is 2.74 m long with an effective width of 0.25 m. It is light enough to be carried by one man as the PSA1 panel weighs 9.5 kg. Each panel has slots and lugs to connect it with its neighbouring panels in a brickwork pattern at an angle of 45° to the line of the runway.

Double female panel. This panel is 2.7 m long and 44.5 mm wide. It forms the centre line of the runway from which panels can be laid on both sides.

End anchor panel. This is the same as the basic panel apart from six 25 mm picket holes which provide anchorage.

Picket. The picket is 1.2 m long and 22 mm in diameter. It is made from galvanised steel rod and is used to anchor the end anchor panel. It has a T-shaped head that fits flush into the panel corrugation.

Repair panel. This is a two-part basic panel with a longitudinal interlocking joint. The two halves can be held in place by nine countersunk screws.

Edge restraint device. To prevent the ripple effect that forms when aircraft land and brake on airfield surface mats, the edge restraint device is fitted to the edge of all airfield landing mats. It consists of a fabric strip filled with earth or sand, and with the fabric tied around the filling to form a sausage. The fabric is laid on a connected plywood strip 305 mm wide.

To build a runway, some site preparation is needed to ensure the area is reasonably flat and drained. In wet areas a layer of neoprene-coated nylon fabric (PSN) must be laid. The airfield landing mat can be used by unskilled labour under engineer supervision, and it is possible to lay a complete airfield runway in one or two days. Once laid the mat requires only a minimum of maintenance, but a well-laid and maintained runway can be recovered and re-used with only a minimum of panels needing replacement.

Status

In service with the Royal Air Force and some other countries.

Manufacturer

Laird (Anglesey) Limited, Beaumaris, Anglesey, Gwynedd LL58 8HY, UK.
Tel: 0248 810431. Telex: 61295 lrd bms f.
Fax: 0248 810300.

Laying PSA1 mat (Ministry of Defence)

Fitting end anchor panel to PSA1 mat (Ministry of Defence)

UNITED STATES OF AMERICA

Martin Marietta Aluminium Rapid Runway Repair Kit

Description

The Rapid Runway Repair kit (RRR) was developed by Martin Marietta Aluminium from its AM-2 airfield matting system and is standard equipment with the US Air Force and approved for use by NATO countries. Selected forward operational bases are issued with pre-positioned RRR kits, each base being provided with equipment, tools and portable airfield matting to repair three 340 kg bomb craters within 4 hours.

Each kit provides a patch of AM-2 matting 16.459 m wide and 24.621 m long, containing 35 half mats (0.61 × 1.829 m × 38 mm), 15 full mats (0.61 × 3.65 m × 38 mm) and 18 ramps each 1.829 m long. All components have an anti-skid coating and are packed for shipment and storage in the same manner as the standard AM-2 matting.

The mats have been designed to withstand single wheel loads of up to 13 608 kg each. Half mats are contained in each pallet assembly so that the mats can be laid in a brick-type pattern. This staggered joint arrangement provides the required stability across the mat and the necessary flexibility in the direction of travel. The sides of the mat panels are constructed to interlock with a rotating motion. The end connectors are arranged with the prongs up on one end and down on the other and by properly placing the end connector on one mat over the end connector of another, a continuous layer of matting is formed. Locking couplers are then inserted into the common slot to form a bond between the plates.

There are six main steps in the repair cycle: identifying the craters for repair and establishing a temporary runway centre line; repairing the crater; delivering, stockpiling and placing the selected fill material; assembling the AM-2 matting patch; cleaning, sweeping and painting the new runway and finally placing and anchoring the ramps.

A temporary runway may be a portion of the runway itself, a combination of the parking areas and the taxiway, or other adjacent surfaced area. A temporary runway is normally 15.24 m wide and 1524 m long. All material which has been blown out of the crater is pushed into the crater void and compacted with a dozer. While the crater is being refilled, a grader clears areas on the runway surface for the AM-2 matting assembly. The matting assembly is positioned to allow for a parallel pull over the crater but a sufficient distance away to allow crater repair to continue uninterrupted. When the crater is filled to the final 0.305 m the selected fill is pushed in, compacted and levelled.

The standard patch can be assembled by 17 trained men in less than 1 hour, and when assembled is pulled into place over the filled crater. When the final positioning is made ramps are attached to each end to alleviate the step or contour change between the mat and the runway. Should it become practicable to rebuild the runway, the patch sections may be easily removed, dismantled and stored for future use.

Status
In service with the US Air Force.

Manufacturer
Martin Marietta Aluminium, 19200 South Western Avenue, Torrance, California 90509, USA.
Sales handled by Transaero Inc, 80 Crossways Park Drive, Woodbury, New York 11797, USA.
Tel: (516) 248 0400. Telex: 96 7734.

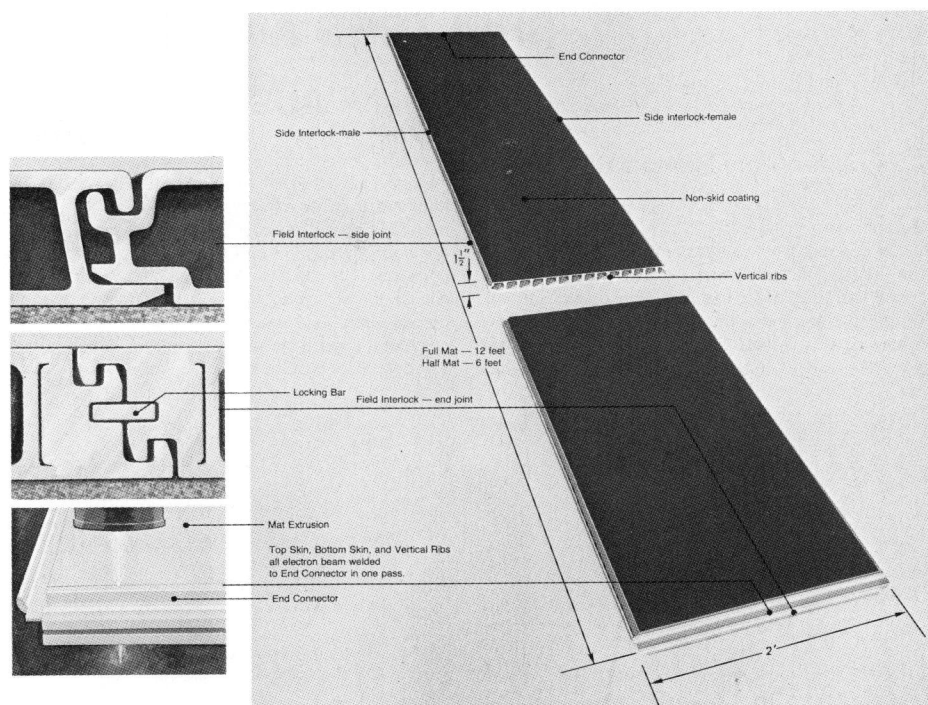

Main components of Martin Marietta aluminium rapid runway repair kit mat

SHELTERS AND CONTAINERS

AUSTRALIA

Australian Army Medical Shelter

Description
Under contract to the Australian Army BONDOR Pty Limited designed an air-transportable medical shelter, one of many types for use in a mobile field hospital. The shelter has the same dimensions as an ISO 1C container. It is rated at 8000 kg and can be stacked two high. The shelter has aluminium-polyurethane wall panels inserted into a structural steel frame. The integral high lift jacks enable the shelter to be dismounted from its carrying vehicle using a hydraulic system or an air line hose from the vehicle. The jacks are normally pushed into the wall housing for transportation. The double doors at both ends provide access for wide loads and the side door is used for normal entry and exit. The shelters are delivered complete apart from air-conditioning, furniture and other such specialised items.

Status
In production.

Manufacturer
BONDOR Pty Limited, 260 Musgrave Road, Coopers Plains, Brisbane, Queensland 4108, Australia.
Tel: 07 277 4044. Telex: AA41214.
Fax: 07 275 1760.

Australian Army medical shelter raised on outrigger legs ready for loading onto truck

Australian Army medical shelter emplaced ready for use

BELGIUM

Baeten Shelters

Description
Often referred to as the Plasti-Baeten Shelter, the Type PB 7601 is made from lightweight non-metallic materials. The basic panel material consists of a 40 mm layer of non-hygroscopic PVC foam covered with a 2.5 mm skin of polyester-reinforced glass fibre. The foam has a density of 60 kg/m^3. The interior floor has strong non-slip surfacing and the underside of the shelter is fitted with two longitudinal aluminium skids 4.4 m long, 32 mm high and 180 mm wide. There is a single door 1.78 m high and 0.8 m wide with blocking devices incorporated. The interior sides can be fitted with up to three windows a side and there is provision for blackout screens. There is an aluminium ladder for access to the shelter when it is carried on a truck and folding handholds to gain access to the shelter roof. Lashing and lifting points are integral. Mains electrical points are provided.

In addition to the above, Baeten also produces a multi-purpose 4-tonne shelter and a 2 or 4-tonne shelter with EMI shielding for the protection of electrical and electronic equipment in the event of high altitude nuclear explosions. Tests have shown that the EMI shelter has an attenuation of over 140 dB and may be built with sandwich panels having an inner and outer skin in polyester or aluminium or a combination of both. Several types have been produced.

Specifications (Type PB 7601)
Length:
  (internal) 4.31 m
  (external) 4.4 m
Width:
  (internal) 2.11 m
  (external) 2.2 m
Height:
  (internal) 1.9 m
  (external) 2 m
Weight: 940 kg
Payload: 3500 kg

Status
In production. In service with the Belgian Army.

Manufacturer
nv Baeten, Autostradweg 1, B-9230 Melle, Belgium.
Tel: 91 52 18 52. Telex: 11087 baeten b.
Fax: 91 52 37 93.

Baeten Shelter Type PB 7601

Baeten non-shielded 4-tonne shelter carried on MAN (4 × 4) truck

FINLAND

Rautaruukki RRC-250 Heavy Duty Container System

Description
The Rautaruukki RRC-250 heavy duty container system uses steel containers complying with ISO standards for stacking and handling. They can be used for transport or storage and can be produced in special forms for carrying explosives, fuels, lubricants, special equipment, and so on. Up to six containers can be connected to a single air-conditioning unit. If required the containers can be supplied painted in camouflage tones according to customer requirements. The containers can have integral loading legs.

Containers can be supplied with the following outer dimensions:

6.055 × 2.5 × 2.65 m
6.055 × 2.6 × 2.65 m
7.15 × 2.5 × 2.75 m

Status
In production.

Manufacturer
Rautaruukki, Transtech Division, Oulu Works, PO Box 217, SF-90101 Oulu, Finland.

FRANCE

Giat Industries Shelters

Description
Giat Industries mass-produces the types of shelters listed below for the French and other armies. They may be delivered bare or fully equipped. The different installations available allow each of these units to respond to the various demands of environment, logistic army, air force and marine employment.

Cadre JVH
This is a mono-shell cabin with PVC, polyester resin and aluminium sandwich panels plus metal reinforcements. It is used by French Army RITA communications system units and also for the Sirocco meteorological station.

Cadre JVA
This shelter uses a metal frame with welded steel components plus plywood facing and thermal insulation. It is used for second and third line mobile mechanical and electronic workshops.

Cadre JVB
Using PVC, resin polyester and aluminium panels, this shelter has an aluminium frame and a door that employs a microwave braided cable surround. It is used in support of the French Army DIADEME programme.

Cadre JVF
This is a specially hardened shelter with sandwich panels continuously welded to an aluminium ISO construction frame. The door uses folded hinges. It is used for the main station of the HADES data transmission system.

Cadre JVG
This is another hardened shelter with high mechanical and thermal performance sandwich panels and continuous welding to provide integrated ballistic and thermal protection. ISO corners are provided and there is a folded hinge door. This shelter is used with various command, control and communication systems.

ATSF
The ATSF (Abri Technique Semi Fixé) is a TEMPEST-hardened shelter proof against the EMP produced by a

A typical Giat Industries shelter carried on a Renault TRM 10 000 (6 × 6) truck

nuclear attack. It has an airlock and is intended to be covered by earth or concrete for complete protection. It has its own integral fire extinguishing system, air-conditioning and NBC system. In 1990 a series of 60 was in production for the French Army for transport by rail.

ATM
The ATM (Abri Technique Mobile) is a 10 ft ISO shelter intended to contain the utilities required by a field hospital, including electrical power generation, the housing of medical gases, air-conditioning and filtering, and other services. There are 100 on order for the French Army. The ATN 20 DD is a variation with extending side walls and ends for use as an operating theatre, and is a 20 ft ISO shelter; 200 are on order for the French Army.

Status
In production. In service with the French Army and some other armies.

Giat Industries JMV shelter

Manufacturer
Giat Industries, 13 route de la Minière, F-78034 Versailles Cedex, France.
Tel: (1) 30 97 37 37. Fax: (1) 30 97 39 00.

LOHR UMC Multi-purpose Shelter

Description
The LOHR UMC (*Unité Mobile de Campagne*) multi-purpose 20 ft shelter was designed to withstand a variety of environments while providing an effective facility for various systems and/or equipment. Applications could include command post, mobile office, communications, workshop, bakery, medical post, and so on.

The UMC shelter is constructed using insulated sandwich panels and stands on four retractable legs, one at each corner and extending 500 mm. The interior can be extended by lowering the side walls to extend the floor area. Tarpaulins then can be used to protect the interior and access platforms are available. The UMC can be handled by fork-lift or various load handling systems.

Specifications
Weight empty: 2900 kg
Length: 6.055 m
Width:
  (closed) 2.435 m
  (open) 4.38 m
Height: 2.435 m

Status
In production. In service with the French Army and several other armies.

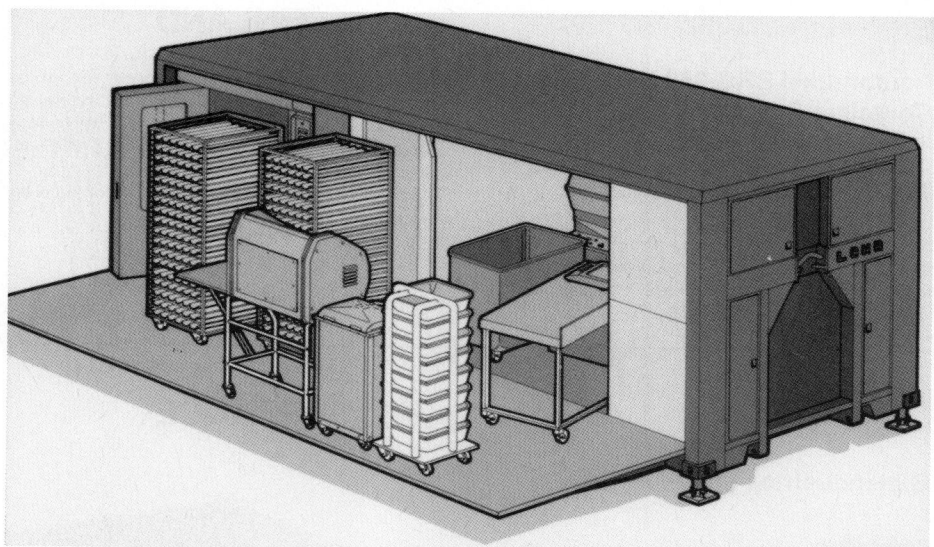

Drawing of LOHR UMC shelter configured as field bakery and with side wall lowered

Manufacturer
LOHR SA, F-67980 Hangenbieten, France.
Tel: 88 38 98 00. Telex: 870082 f.
Fax: 88 96 06 36.

SEH 600 Expandable Modular Shelter

Description
The SEH 600 expandable modular shelter is described as a new generation of shelter intended to be used for a number of roles including an emergency operating theatre. It has an aluminium structure based on the dimensions of a standard 20 ft ISO container with side walls that fold downwards with sealing provided by a series of fan-form side walls. Access to the interior is via double doors at one or both ends and with the side walls folded down the interior has a floor area of

SEH 600 expandable modular shelter with side walls opened

37.5 m². The doors can also be used to connect the shelter to other shelters or structures. The shelter has

high lift jacks at each corner which can be used for loading or unloading and levelling once in position.

When opened the SEH 600 shelter has a width of 6.25 m and a height of 3.02 m. Similar shelters are available in 30 and 40 ft lengths.

Status
In production.

Manufacturer
France Santé Diffusion, 4 avenue Albert de Mun, F-75016 Paris, France.
Tel: 42 23 99 00. Telex: 648772 f.
Fax: 42 54 64 37.

LOHR RMTS 7.5 Container Handling and Carrying Trailer

Description
The LOHR RMTS 7.5 container handling and carrying trailer was designed and developed for the logistic handling and transport of shelter/containers on roads and over rough terrain. The trailer can handle 10 and 20 ft ISO shelters and can be used to load and unload containers into and from C-130 or C-160 transport aircraft. The French Army uses this trailer with mobile field hospital shelters.

There is also an RMTS 10 with a payload of 10 tonnes.

Specifications
Weight:
  (empty) 3000 kg
  (GVW) 11 000 kg
Payload: 8000 kg
Length:
  (overall) 8.67 m
  (folded) 6.535 m
Width: 2.47 m
Max towing speed: (road) 70 km/h
Tyres: 9.5 R 17.5 XTA

Status
In production. In service with French Army.

LOHR RMTS 7.5 container handling and carrying trailer

Manufacturer
LOHR SA, F-67980 Hangenbieten, France.
Tel: 88 38 98 00. Telex: 870082 f.
Fax: 88 96 06 36.

LOHR SLCT 8 Container Handling and Carrying Trailer

Description

The LOHR SLCT 8 container handling and carrying trailer follows the same general lines as the RMTS 7.5 (see previous entry) but uses two carrying axles. It is intended primarily for the transport and handling of 20 ft ISO containers only. For loading and unloading the trailer remains attached to the towing vehicle while the towing bar is hydraulically driven downwards to lower the rear end of the trailer to the ground at an angle of 14°. Containers are loaded onto the trailer using an electrical winch with a pull force of 5440 kg.

Two or three trailers can be stacked for air transport.

Specifications

Weight:
  (empty) 3500 kg
  (GVW) 11 500 kg
Payload: 8000 kg
Length: (overall) 8.68 m

LOHR SLCT 8 container handling and carrying trailer

Width: 2.42 m
Loading height: (unloaded) 0.92 m
Tyres: 305/70 R 19.5 XZA
Electrical system: 12 and 24 V

Status

In production. In service with the French Army and several other armies. On trial with the US Army.

Manufacturer

LOHR SA, F-67980 Hangenbieten, France.
Tel: 88 38 98 00. Telex: 870082 f.
Fax: 88 96 06 36.

GERMANY

MAN/Doll Containers and Container Carriers

Description

MAN Nutzfahrzeuge GmbH and Doll Fahrzeugbau GmbH combined to produce a series of special shelter/containers and carrier vehicles to meet a variety of requirements. The containers have been developed for use on the full range of MAN high mobility military vehicles.

One of the Doll shelters has external dimensions of 6.1 × 2.5 × 2.4 m and a weight of 8000 kg although other Doll shelters can be accommodated on the MAN chassis. The shelter/container has a steel framework with steel covering panels insulated by 50 mm thick sandwich-type foam. A material handling crane may be installed in front of the shelter operating electrically or hydraulically. The shelter roof may be folded backwards for loading and unloading and the entire shelter and crane may be lifted by an overhead crane or gantry. The shelter/container may be fitted to suit customer requirements. Doors, roof walkways, and so on can be fitted to suit customer requirements and various forms of internal and external lighting can be produced.

A special workshop vehicle using the shelter/container concept has been produced using the MAN (8 × 8) carrier vehicle.

Doll also produces two smaller trailer-borne aluminium shelter/containers. One has dimensions of

MAN Type 27.365 VFAE carrying opened Doll workshop shelter/container

2.5 × 2.2 × 2 m and can be carried on a single-axle trailer. It can be produced fully or partially insulated, with RFI shielding and with air-conditioning. It is also possible to fit a generator. A shelter/container produced to similar specifications has dimensions of 3.5 × 2.2 × 2 m and is carried on a twin-axle trailer. Both units can be carried slung from a helicopter. The larger unit can be fitted with stabilising jacks at each corner.

Status

In production. In service with an unspecified nation.

Manufacturers

Doll Fahrzeugbau GmbH, Industriestrasse 13, D-7603 Oppenau, Federal Republic of Germany.
MAN Nutzfahrzeuge GmbH, Postfach 500620, D-8000 München 50, Federal Republic of Germany.
Tel: 089 150 3869. Telex: 523211.

MAN Type 27.365 VFAE carrying special Doll container and material handling crane

Typical Doll 20 ft/6.096 m ISO container converted for workshop use

Zeppelin Shelters

Description
Zeppelin Metallwerke GmbH produces a wide range of containerised shelters for a wide variety of purposes ranging from mobile offices to radar cabins. The entire range is constructed from basic sandwich monocoque with the side walls, roof and floor units all having aluminium skins. The core material is polyurethane foam. Edge framing is made from heat-bonded light metal frame sections. An insulating layer is interposed between the framing sections. All external riveting is air- and watertight, and the corner fittings are replaceable. Skids are mounted lengthwise under the floor unit with each skid being 51 mm high and approximately 100 mm wide. They are riveted or bolted to the integral stiffening members of the floor unit. The shelter door is located in one end wall and mounted on the right-hand side by three heavy duty hinge units. All four corners are rounded and there is a three-point locking device fitted. The flooring is constructed from 17 mm thick marine plywood.

Various optional doors, hatches and windows can be fitted to either end and to the side walls. An air-conditioning unit is available. The shelters can be lifted for transport by four heavy duty jacks that are attached to each corner of the shelter and for some vehicle-carried shelters a special hydraulic jack is used. Most of the Zeppelin shelters are air-transportable.

Status
In production.

Manufacturer
Zeppelin Metallwerke GmbH, Postfach 2540, D-7990 Friedrichshafen 1, Federal Republic of Germany.
Tel: 07541 2021. Telex: 0734323.

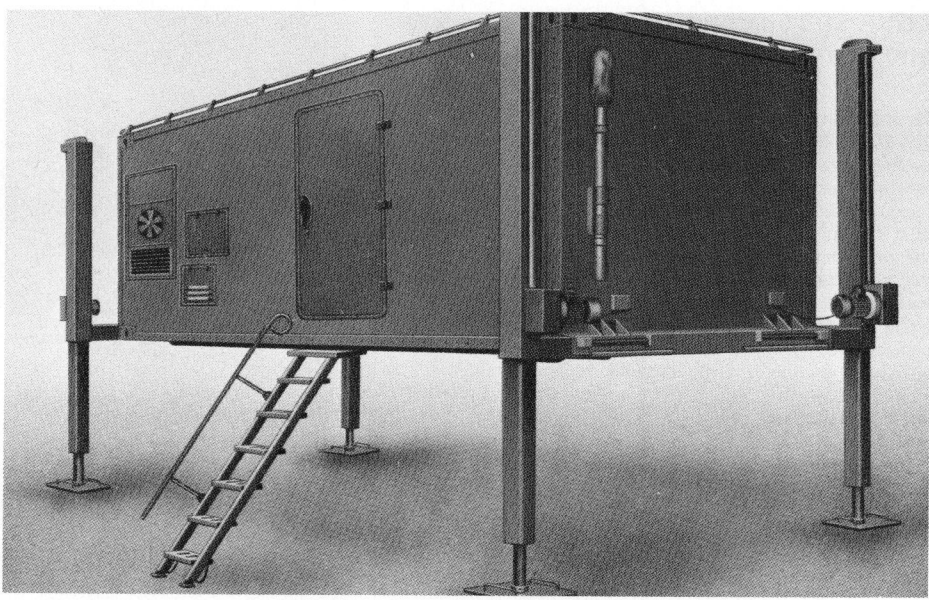

Zeppelin BW III 10 000 kg shelter on lifting jacks

Specifications

Model	BW I	BW II	BW III	BW IV	N 1	N 2	N 3
Weight (empty, approx)	550 kg	900 kg	1500 kg	1400 kg	700 kg	800 kg	400 kg
(max permissible)[1]	2000 kg	4500 kg	10 000 kg	8000 kg	3000 kg	4500 kg	1150 kg
Length (over corner fittings)	2.9 m	4.25 m	6.742 m	6.058 m	3.81 m	3.81 m	2.35 m
(inside clearance)	2.78 m	4.11 m	6.595 m	5.912 m	3.69 m	3.67 m	2.23 m
Width (over corner fittings)	2.05 m	2.2 m	2.438 m	2.438 m	2.08 m	2.08 m	2.05 m
(inside clearance)	1.925 m	2.055 m	2.29 m	2.29 m	1.96 m	1.94 m	1.925 m
Height (over corner fittings)[2]	1.825 m	2.075 m	2.37 m	2.37 m	2.075 m	2.075 m	1.825 m
(inside clearance)	1.695 m	1.905 m	2.2 m	2.2 m	1.93 m	1.91 m	1.675 m

[1]   load evenly distributed
[2]   without skids, skid height +51 mm

Kärcher Container Field Kitchen CFK 250

Description
The Kärcher container field kitchen CFK 250 uses a special water- and sandstorm-proof 20 ft/6.096 m container. It is the only product of its kind in a range that includes container kitchens which cater for 250 up to 1500 people. Units can be provided with and without NBC protection and may be towed as a trailer using a twin-axle trailer arrangement.

The CFK 250 is fully equipped for its role and contains two baking and frying units and two 150 litre pressure cookers, all covered by two 2800 m³/h ventilation hoods. Working tables and shelves are provided along with tables and cupboards, food preparation machines, sinks, water pumps and a hinged table for meal distribution. Also provided is a warm air generator and a 6000 m³/h air-conditioning inlet. A canopy can be erected over the container.

The CFK 250 weighs 6000 kg, is 6.058 m long, 2.438 m wide and 2.438 m high (with canopy).

Status
In production. In service with a NATO headquarters and German border and state police.

Manufacturer
Alfred Kärcher GmbH & Co, Alfred-Kärcher-Strasse 28-40, D-7057 Winnenden, Federal Republic of Germany.
Tel: 07195 14-0. Telex: 724432.
Fax: 07195 14-2720.

Kärcher container field kitchen CFK 250

ITALY

Improved Boneschi Shelters

Description
The Boneschi range of shelters uses a basic container body which is made from light alloy sheets with polyurethane fillings. The framework is of aluminium sections. The overall construction is orthodox and the shelters can be adapted to carry out a wide range of military duties. There are two optional methods of moving the Boneschi shelters, both of them incorporated into the shelter system when required. One is the 'Rolbon' system which has four hand-operated

worm screws and wheels fitted to each corner of the shelter by rolling arms. The other system is the 'Uniborn' lifting system which has four hand-operated worms fitted to each corner by pivoting arms. This latter system enables the shelter to be raised and lowered onto flat bed trucks.

One specialised form of Boneschi shelter is the 'Lifeshelter'. This is a specialised light alloy container which is insulated and enclosing a complete medical unit ready for use. Equipment in the container includes a simple stretcher-type operating table, racks for medical equipment and instruments (all included in the standard kit), oxygen and other such equipment, and

lighting and air-conditioning. The 'Lifeshelter' is air-transportable and is fitted with the 'Uniborn' lifting system for handling. If required, the 'Lifeshelter' can be carried slung under a helicopter.

Status
In production. In service with the Turkish Army.

Manufacturer
Carrozzeria Boneschi srl, Via G Boneschi 1, I-20040 Cambiago (Milan), Italy.
Tel: (2) 95308045. Telex: 334529 boncar i.
Fax: (2) 95308204.

Boneschi shelter loaded onto IVECO FIAT 6601 truck using Uniborn system

Boneschi shelter fitted out as fire control shelter on IVECO FIAT 75 PM (4 × 4) 2000 kg truck

Piaggio Shelters

Description
Piaggio started building military shelters in 1964 and since then has produced shelters for both military and civil purposes. There are now five basic Piaggio shelters with a far larger number being produced for special purposes, but the overall construction remains the same.

Each cabin has eight horizontal angles all in light alloy and four vertical angles in galvanised steel or light alloy. The corner blocks may be standard ISO container type and all the wall and floor or ceiling panels are constructed from a sandwich formed from light alloy sheets 0.8 to 1.6 mm thick with a core of 50 mm thick polyurethane foam. Internal strengthening ribs are fitted and there are three underside skids. The floor has a drain plug, and the end access door is 1.6 m high and 0.8 m wide. Other standard fittings are access steps, roof reinforcement in the centre and an electrical earthing point. A wide range of accessories is available

Specifications

Type	ACE1	ACE2	ACE3	UEO1	UEO2
Length	2.9 m	4.25 m	5 m	2.71 m	3.983 m
Width	2.05 m	2.2 m	2.2 m	1.74 m	1.915 m
Height	1.881 m	2.131 m	2.131 m	1.9 m	2.1 m
Weight	700 kg	900 kg	1200 kg	600 kg	750 kg
Capacity (useful load)	1300 kg	3600 kg	4300 kg	1400 kg	3250 kg

and numerous fits can be produced to suit customer requirements. Piaggio was the first manufacturer to respond to NATO's requirements for EMP shelters (such as shelters protected against electromagnetic pulse from nuclear blast) and in the four year period from 1980 to 1983 Piaggio was the sole supplier of this type of shelter to NATO and NATO affiliated nations. Piaggio EMP shelters differ from conventional shelters in that the outer skin of the cabin is fusion welded to guarantee a flawless electrical continuity. Piaggio also produces a nuclear hardened shelter and a ballistic shelter proof against shell splinters and most small arms projectiles.

Status
Production. In service with the Italian armed forces and several other nations.

Piaggio shelters are produced under special licence agreement by CGEE/Alsthom in France and by Compair Holman Iberica in Spain.

Manufacturer
Industrie Aeronautiche e Meccaniche Rinaldo Piaggio, Via Cibrario 4, I-16154 Genoa, Italy.
Tel: (010) 60041. Telex: 270695 aerpia i.
Fax: (010) 603378.

Piaggio shelters awaiting delivery

Piaggio shelters awaiting delivery

SAI Ambrosini Containers and Shelters

Description
SAI Ambrosini has been manufacturing containers and shelters since 1970 and produces a wide range of specialist containers for military purposes.

The containers are constructed from a sandwich material made up of light aluminium alloy heat bonded to a polyurethane core. Watertight rivets and stainless steel bolts and nuts are used to hold the panels together. All panels have a special lattice of light aluminium struts to absorb stresses from internal and external loads and to provide lashing anchors for internal loads.

SAI Ambrosini also produces a range of air-conditioned containers for special purposes. There are three main models in this range, the smallest with a 4 kW conditioner, then a 9 kW conditioner and the largest has a 20 kW conditioner unit. These units can be used to provide refrigeration if required.

Both standard and cooled containers can be supplied with a range of accessories that includes jacks for lifting and loading, ladders, special or emergency exits and hatches, special electrical looms or lighting and RF suppression. Numerous changes to suit customer requirements can be introduced.

SAI Ambrosini shelters are built to standard dimensions or to special requirements. Air-conditioning units are usually installed and the units can be equipped with mechanical systems for loading and unloading from trucks, including over the sides of drop side trucks. Lifting points are provided and the shelters can be carried on special SAI Ambrosini trailers and trailer systems.

Shelters can be supplied in armoured, RF screened, EMP- and NBC-protected forms. SAI Ambrosini shelters, containers and handling systems can be combined to form the modular SAI Ambrosini Mobile Flight Support System for helicopter unit support.

Examples of SAI Ambrosini logistic shelters and containers

Specifications (containers)
Capacity	3000 kg	5000 kg	8000 kg
Weight	1600 kg	2700 kg	2800 kg
Length	3.25 m	4.55 m	4.55 m
Width	2.1 m	2.2 m	2.3 m

Status
In production. In service with the Italian Army.

Manufacturer
SAI Ambrosini – Società Aeronautica Italiana SpA, Viale Roma 25, I-06065 Passignano sul Trasimeno (PG), Italy.
Tel: (06) 4756774. Fax: (06) 4742909.

SAI Ambrosini Wheel-coupled Shelter and Platform Transporters

Description
To complete its shelter and container systems SAI Ambrosini designed and constructed a wheel-coupled trailer for the transport of shelters and platforms. The wheel-coupling system meets Mil-M-8090F with reference to Mobility Type III, Group C.

The system can be towed by a number of types of military vehicle. The two rolling trains can be coupled independently at the front or rear of the shelter or platform and lift the load for towing. If necessary the load can be lifted to a height of 700 mm for towing through fords or over rough terrain.

When not carrying a load the transporter sections can be connected to form a compact unit for towing.

SAI Ambrosini wheel-coupled shelter and platform transporters

Specifications
Model	TP-3	TP-5	TP-8
Length	2.45 m	3.4 m	3.4 m
Width	2.25 m	2.3 m	2.3 m
Height	1.43 m	1.47 m	1.47 m
Track	1.93 m	2.01 m	2.01 m
Weight	1300 kg	2700 kg	2800 kg
Max capacity	3500 kg	7500 kg	7500 kg

Status
In production. In service with the Italian Army.

Manufacturer
SAI Ambrosini – Società Aeronautica Italiana SpA, Viale Roma 25, I-06065 Passignano sul Trasimeno (PG), Italy.
Tel: (06) 4756774. Fax: (06) 4742909.

SINGAPORE

Mobile Field Hospital

Description
This mobile field hospital was designed to provide a full range of medical facilities in any field or emergency environment. It is based on a specially designed container that can be configured as an operating theatre, X-ray unit, laboratory, blood bank, dental clinic, nursing ward, casualty clearing unit, kitchen, laundry or for other specialised medical purposes.

Each container is fully equipped for its purpose and can be carried into position using a platform truck or a tractor truck with a flat bed semi-trailer. On site the containers are placed on the ground in a suitable formation but each unit can be used independently if required. Power is supplied by towed generators. When not in use the containers can be stacked up to five high.

Each container has external dimensions of length 6.058 m, with width and height both 2.438 m.

Mobile field hospital container towed by Hino tractor truck

Status

In production. In service with the Singapore armed forces.

Manufacturer

Singapore Automotive Engineering Limited (A Singapore Technologies Company), 5 Portsdown Road, Singapore 0513.
Tel: 47366311. Telex: 25755 SINENG RS.
Fax: 4710662.

SOUTH AFRICA

Modular Operating Theatre

Description

This modular operating theatre, based on ICX ISO container dimensions, is constructed from glass fibre panels supported on a steel framework. It has two pairs of access doors while internally it is fully equipped as an operating theatre for all types of medical operations. It uses a 380 V 3-phase electrical system input and a 24 V battery-operated emergency power supply. A penthouse is provided which fits over the theatre to provide accommodation for personnel on either side. The module is transported by means of a specialised semi-trailer.

The module is 6.058 m long, 2.438 m wide and 2.54 m high.

Status

In production for the Surgeon General's arm of the South African Defence Forces.

Manufacturer

Enquiries to Armscor, Private Bag X337, Pretoria 0001, South Africa.
Tel: 012 428 1911. Telex: 30217.
Fax: 012 428 5635.

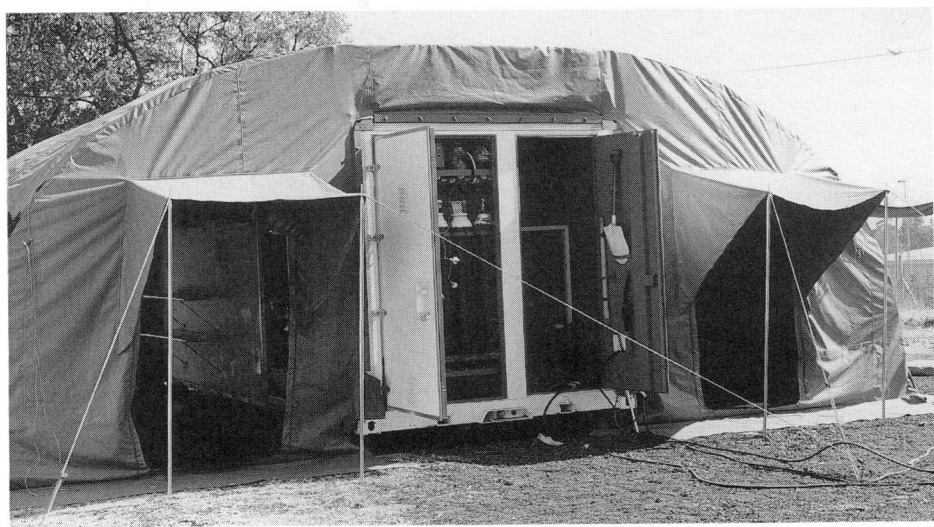
Modular operating theatre in position

SPAIN

EINSA Tactical Operations Centre Type M/PMU-01

Description

This tactical operations centre consists of a number of special containerised shelters, normally four, carried by 4 × 4 all-terrain vehicles that can be configured on site in a number of formations. The tactical operations centre (TOC) shelters are connected to the vehicles by means of a special kit in such a way that each will protrude 1.2 m over the end of the vehicle allowing the shelter doors to remain free from obstruction and to allow variations in the method of interconnecting the shelters. Each shelter has three sliding doors, two at each side rear and the third at the right rear side. Each shelter is supplied with an access ladder that can fit under any door but the variations in positioning the TOC shelters may allow direct access from one shelter to another through the doors. The shelters may also be interconnected to other services including 220 V AC and 24 V DC power lines, intercom telephones and air-conditioning. All doors are equipped for blackout

fittings and each shelter has eight telephone connection points and may be fitted with aerial connection points.

The shelters are constructed from tubular profiles with hooks on the upper surface for crane emplacement. The walls have 40 mm polyester boards for insulation and the roof insulation is 60 mm thick. Each unit has a roof window and some units have side windows as well. Provision is made for air-conditioning and each unit is equipped with an inter-unit closure device. Fittings are supplied for securing camouflage netting.

Extras include quartz wall clocks, fire extinguishers, first aid kits, axes and clothing hooks.

Specifications
Weight: 1200 kg
Length:
  (internal) 5.3 m
  (external) 5.4 m
Width:
  (internal) 2.2 m
  (external) 2.3 m

Minimum height:
  (internal) 2.04 m
  (external) 2.2 m
Maximum height:
  (internal) 2.09 m
  (external) 2.25 m
Volume:
  (internal) 24 m³
  (external) 27.6 m³
Floor surface:
  (internal) 11.8 m²
  (external) 12.4 m²

Status
In production. In service with the Spanish armed forces.

Manufacturer
Equipos Industriales de Manutencion SA (EINSA), Antigua Ctra. de Barcelona, km 27.300, E-28812 Alcala de Henares, Madrid, Spain.
Tel: (1) 880 90 00. Fax: (1) 880 90 86.

Typical EINSA Tactical Operations Centre shelter with side windows

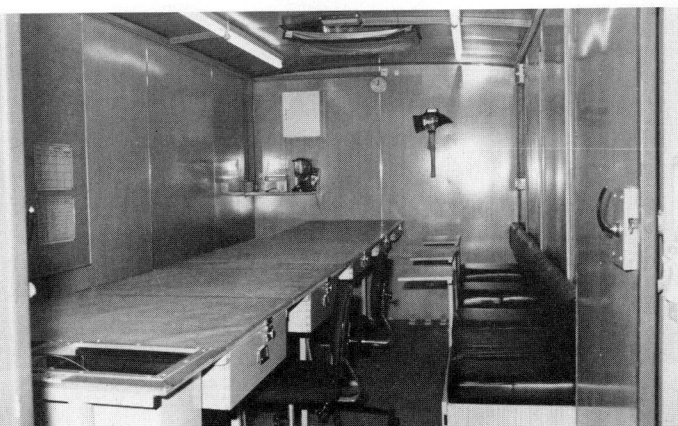
Interior of typical Tactical Operations Centre shelter

UNITED KINGDOM

Marconi ISOLATOR Electronic Equipment Shelters

Description

The Marconi ISOLATOR shelter is a high strength, low weight transportable shelter for both military and commercial applications. It protects electronic equipment from the adverse effects of the environment including the elements, EMI, RFI and NEMP and provides TEMPEST shielding if required.

It is constructed using advanced sandwich panel technology. Finite Element Analysis of the structural design ensures optimum strength, weight and payload ratios at minimum cost. The end product provides the customer with total flexibility in the location of doors, apertures, escape hatches and interface panels.

ISOLATOR shelters have been supplied for many applications including telecommunications, airfield radar and command and control systems. Among these are the Phoenix UAV system for the British Army, the Home Defence Radio System, UKADGE and the British Aerospace electro-optical tracking system.

A lightweight version incorporates many features of the standard shelter but is much lighter and was specifically designed for truck or trailer use.

Status

In production for the British Army, NATO and some overseas defence organisations.

Manufacturer

Marconi Defence Systems (Gateshead), Bill Quay, Gateshead, Tyne and Wear NE10 0UR, UK.
Tel: 091 4950111. Telex: 53312.
Fax: 091 4950144.

Marconi ISOLATOR sandwich panel technology adapted for a vehicle hard-top application

A semi-trailer mounted ISOLATOR shelter with its associated air-conditioning unit for a NATO application

Giltspur Specialist Module Containers

Description

Giltspur Defence Projects is a subdivision of Giltspur Technologies and manages new projects using the experience and resources of the Group. It provides engineering, contract design and development services and has over 30 years' experience in transport, packaging and logistics. It is part of the Unigate Group and has been given the British Ministry of Defence approved status to quality assurance DEF STAN 05-21, 05-24 and 05-32.

Giltspur pioneered the design and manufacture of environmentally controlled ISO shipping containers and was by 1965 the leading company in this field in Europe. In response to the needs of emergency relief planners and military authorities for portable buildings which can be transported and used at short notice,

Giltspur Defence Projects has developed adaptations of standard ISO containers for any type of military or medical application.

Using this approach Giltspur has developed a complete, fully equipped hospital consisting of numerous modules, each specific in its role that can be moved to any location and be operational within minutes of arrival. Acting as prime supplier, Giltspur is responsible for engineering and overall project management, design and build of all containers and all services; the packing, shipping and on-site commissioning of the complete hospital, together with management of commercial aspects such as insurance and contract negotiation.

Using the same formula, radar stations can be moved at will and even complete air bases can be established rapidly in remote areas. Each module can be stored without deterioration for long periods and deployed with minimal preparation. Each unit acts as a unit of accommodation, a secure store and a means of

carrying all its integral equipment and consumables.

Giltspur specialist module containers are available for the following roles: air base medical support module; mobile air base; avionics workshop module; field cooking module; workshop module; field laundry module; field shower module; accommodation module; command module; customs post module; dental module; opthalmic module; navaid (radio) module; and a generator module.

Status

In production. In service with several countries around the world.

Manufacturer

Giltspur Technologies Limited, Giltspur Defence Projects, Nutsey Lane, Salisbury Road, Totton, Southampton SO4 3ZY, UK.
Tel: 0703 865777. Telex: 47526 giltpak g.

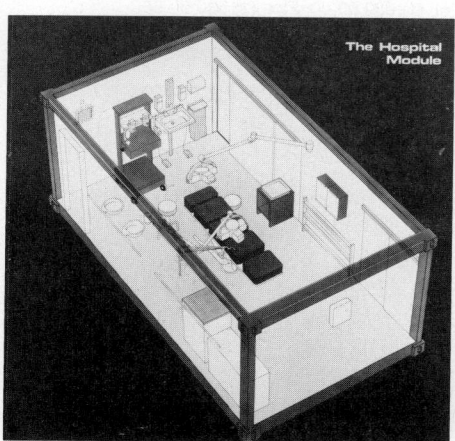

Giltspur airbase medical support module

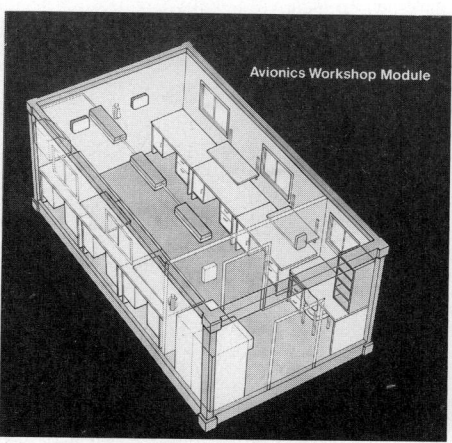

Giltspur avionics workshop module

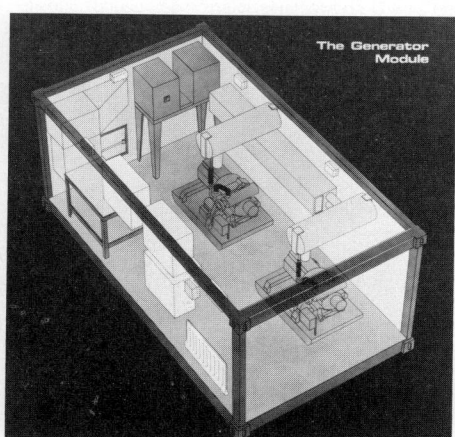

Giltspur power generator module

CB 300 and CB 100 Series of Transportable Shelters

Description

The CB 300 series of transportable shelters was designed by the Ministry of Defence and developed by Marshall SPV from 1962. The Ministry of Defence requirement was for a lightweight, demountable body which would provide the best possible working conditions under extremes of temperature, would have an extended service life under minimal maintenance requirements and would have maximum utilisation by both the Army and the Royal Air Force in mobile and static roles. The first production units were completed in 1964.

The transportable shelter was designed for the operational installation of specialist pneumatic, hydraulic, signals, electronic and similar equipment, for use as specialist repair modules and for use as tactical offices or command posts.

The shelter is constructed of aluminium alloy, is lightweight and fully insulated to provide protected working conditions for personnel and equipment under extremes of temperature. It is weather-sealed and may also be air-conditioned. The basic design concept proved sound but whereas NBC was covered initially, with only minor changes the shelter can be modified to meet EMP and RFI requirements and supplied in armoured or standard form. It was designed to be carried on any flat platform truck or trailer and can be operated dismounted in a static role. It is air-transportable in a Lockheed C-130 transport aircraft. Its modular construction allows doors, windows and access panels to be positioned to meet specific requirements. Strong points in the main framework facilitate the attachment of accessories and equipment, while heavily reinforced corners simplify the fitting of running and handling gear. Typical roles include use as a fuel injection repair shop or machine shop/automotive repair shop, when it has a wide range of installed equipment, including a combined lathe/milling machine, bench drill, battery charger and a range of specialist items and hand tools.

In addition to the CB 300 series, Marshall SPV manufactured the CB 100 range of shelters.

Specifications

Model		CB 100	CB 300
Weight	(empty)	685 kg	from 925 kg[1]
	(loaded)	1703 kg	up to 4500 kg[1]
Length	(external)	1.173 m	4.483 m
	(internal)	0.958 m	4.318 m
Width	(external)	0.835 m	2.489 m
	(internal)	0.88 m	2.324 m
Height	(external)	0.73 m	2.13 m
	(internal)	0.684 m	1.93 m

[1] depending on role

Status

Production complete. In service with the British Armed Forces and Saudi Arabia.

Manufacturer

Marshall SPV Limited, Airport Works, Cambridge CB5 8RX, UK.
Tel: 0223 301133. Fax: 02205 3875.

CB 300 series transportable shelter mounted on Bedford TM 4-4 (4 × 4) 8000 kg truck

Marshall Matrix Shelters

Description

The Matrix family of military shelters produced by Marshall SPV is constructed of sandwich panels formed from a variable range of materials to suit specific applications. The structural sandwich assembly having no intermediate structure is capable of accepting attachments and apertures in any position to suit the required installation.

The panels are contained in a peripheral metal frame. The vertical corners can incorporate locations for the attachment of transfer gear, jacks, ISO corner fittings, running gear, roof access steps and crane or helicopter lift. The fitment of any of these features does not degrade the electrical integrity of the shelter. Aluminium skids can be fitted longitudinally below the shelter floor panel and equipment mounting rails can be fitted to suit individual requirements.

Basic versions of the Matrix shelter are fitted with a single entrance door located in the shelter rear wall but alternative door positions can be offered in sides or ends to suit special installations. Hinged flaps can be fitted to act as escape hatches, power input panels, air-conditioner flaps, and so on. All doors and external flaps can incorporate security fittings.

The standard sandwich panels provide good thermal insulation and various panels are available to provide thermal transmittance figures. The sealing of the shelter enables an efficient overpressure to be created within the container by the fitment of a suitable NBC filtration kit. The shelter, due to its double-skinned insulated structure can provide a high level of RFI and EMP attenuation. Doors and windows can be fitted with metallic gaskets to ensure continuity of the outside skin screening. Shelters required to operate in an EMP/RFI environment can be fitted with input vaults for power and signal cables.

Matrix shelters can be produced in virtually any size as the modular construction system employed means that alternative sizes can be readily accommodated.

Marshall Matrix shelter suitable for installation on a Bedford MK (4 × 4) 4000 kg truck; the shelter can also be trailer-mounted on mobility wheels as shown

Optional features include air-conditioning, equipment lifting gantries, roof antenna mountings, single or double doors, detachable access panels, fixed, sliding or double-glazed windows, window blackout panels, emergency exits, access steps, entrance platforms, underfloor skids, equipment mounting rails and penthouses. Protection can be provided against NBC, EMP, RFI, TEMPEST and various forms of ballistic projectiles.

Systems installations developed for the CB 100 and CB 300 shelters are capable of being installed into the Matrix Series shelters when manufactured to compatible dimensions utilising the same attachment features.

Status

In production for the United Kingdom Ministry of Defence.

Manufacturer

Marshall SPV Limited, Airport Works, Cambridge CB5 8RX, UK.
Tel: 0223 301133. Fax: 02205 3875.

Marshall Matrix 'Drop-In' Shelter

Description
The Marshall Matrix 'Drop-In' transportable shelter was developed to meet the requirements of the electronics and aerospace industry for a small shelter capable of being carried in pick-up truck bodies. It was designed to enable dimensional variations to be made to suit specific requirements.

Construction is based on the use of aluminium-skinned sandwich panels and provides structural strength for the installation of floor- and wall-mounted equipment. It can be fitted with ISO corners and may be carried as external cargo beneath helicopters. The basic shelter provides a high level of attenuation for RFI and EMP shielding due to its double-skinned structure, and conductivity seals are provided around aperture areas.

The shelter permits a 'drop-in' fit to ¾- and 2-tonne trucks and can be produced to fit any suitable pick-up truck.

Status
In production for the British Armed Forces.

Manufacturer
Marshall SPV Limited, Airport Works, Cambridge CB5 8RX, UK.
Tel: 0223 301133. Fax: 02205 3875.

Marshall Matrix 'Drop-In' shelter in use on Reynolds Boughton RB-44 (4 × 4) truck, the British Army's Truck, Utility, Heavy (TUH)

Penman Mobile Shelters and Custom-built Containers

Description
Penman Engineering Limited designs and manufactures a range of shelters and cabins for a variety of uses. Whilst able to build standard NATO tactical shelters, Penman specialises in tailoring specifications to meet the customer's precise needs. The materials and techniques used are fully approved for military applications and are closely controlled by the Quality Assurance Department.

Typical cabin construction comprises sides, roof, floor and end panels manufactured from one-piece aluminium-faced RTM Styrofoam core, and sandwich panels fully bonded together with an extruded aluminium peripheral framework. Doors, windows and escape hatches are located to meet specifications, together with integral stiffening members to suit internal fixtures.

A range of internal layouts can be supplied to meet most military requirements, including command posts, field workshops, communications centres and mobile training units.

Optional equipment for the cabins includes lifting and securing slings, levelling jacks, demount jack legs, power input panels, interior electrical systems, interior partitions and furniture, and RFI screening. Cabins can be supplied on shock-absorbing subframes, demountable frames compatible with DROPS, or rigidly mounted on vehicle chassis or trailers. Cabins can be constructed to meet most military specifications, including armour to various levels.

Status
In production.

Manufacturer
Penman Engineering Limited, Heathhall, Dumfries DG1 3NY, UK.
Tel: 0387 52784. Telex: 779771.
Fax: 0387 67332.

Typical Penman demountable communications cabin on Bedford MK (4 × 4) 4000 kg truck

Penman self-contained mobile workshop

CSC Mobile Workshop Shelter

Description

CSC Specialised Vehicles has supplied the British Ministry of Defence with a number of mechanical workshops installed in transportable shelters, for use by Royal Engineer units worldwide. The workshops contain a comprehensive range of machine tools including a lathe, pillar drill, guillotine and grinding machine. A side-mounted penthouse is provided. The shelters are built using a composite sandwich construction and have been tested extensively at the RARDE Chertsey mobility trials facility.

CSC have also produced command shelters for the Belgian and German armies.

Status

In service with the British Army.

Manufacturer

CSC Specialised Vehicles, Holme Road, Market Weighton, York YO4 3EW, UK.
Tel: 0430 872546. Fax: 0430 872356.

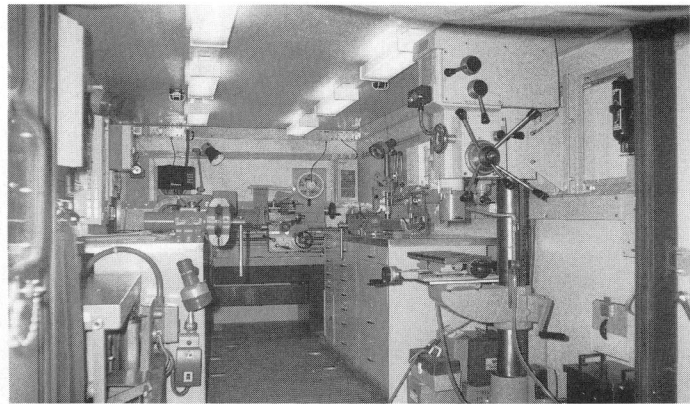

Interior of CSC mobile workshop shelter

CSC mobile workshop shelter

CSC Demountable Shelter Bodies

Description

CSC Specialised Vehicles designed and manufactured a substantial number of demountable shelter bodies for fitting onto Steyr-Daimler-Puch Pinzgauer (6 × 6) 1500 kg vehicles. The vehicles and shelter bodies are used as part of an area communications system for Oman. The shelter bodies were fitted with their electronic equipment by Marconi and Plessey prior to delivery. The contract also included a smaller number of transportable shelters for mounting on flat bed vehicles.

The shelter bodies and shelters were built from an aluminium-faced sandwich construction of CSC design. Onboard generators, air-conditioning and a full electrical installation were provided.

Status

In service with Oman.

Manufacturer

CSC Specialised Vehicles, Holme Road, Market Weighton, York YO4 3EW, UK.
Tel: 0430 872546. Fax: 0430 872356.

CSC demountable shelter body fitted on Steyr-Daimler-Puch Pinzgauer (6 × 6) 1500 kg vehicles of the Omani armed forces

Container Handling Unit (CHU)

Description

The Container Handling Unit (CHU) was developed by Multilift, Government Business Operations. It allows ISO containers to be picked up and transported by vehicles equipped with load handling systems such as the British Army DROPS or the US Army PLS (see entries under *Materials handling equipment* for details of these systems). This enables all types of 20 ft/6.906 m ISO shelter/containers to be efficiently transported without recourse to specialised ISO handling equipment. As no intermediate flatrack is required the payload of the load handling system may also be increased.

The CHU consists of an H-frame which attaches to the end of a container and provides the hook-lift attachment point. The frame attaches to the container using self-aligning upper and lower locking pins, enabling easy deployment by one man. The height of the H-frame is automatically adjustable in use to cater for 2.438 to 2.59 m containers.

A pair of twist locks integral with the rear support section secure the rear end of the container during transit and facilitate loading and unloading. The CHU can be carried on a load handling system when not in use; a stand is provided for storage.

Container Handling Unit (CHU) on a container being handled by the British Army's DROPS

Status
Prototype undergoing trials prior to planned production.

Manufacturer
Multilift Limited, Government Business Operations, Harlescott Lane, Shrewsbury, Shropshire SY1 3AG, UK.
Tel: 0743 232232. Fax: 0743 69935.

UNITED STATES OF AMERICA

Gichner Shelter, Electrical Equipment S-250

Description
The S-250 is a T-shape, non-expansible shelter of adhesive-bonded construction with seamless aluminium interior and exterior skins, extruded aluminium framework structure and a polyurethane foam core. It is used to carry communications, radar, teletype and maintenance electronic equipment and is mounted on the rear of a 1¼- or 1½-ton truck. It can be transported by fixed-wing aircraft, helicopter, rail and ship.

The shelter meets military specifications MIL-S-55541 and is available with RFI integrity.

Specifications
Weight:
  (without RFI kit) 349±9 kg
  (with RFI kit) 355±9 kg
Payload: 862 kg
Interior dimensions:
  (length) 1.628 m
  (width, upper section) 1.908 m
  (width, lower section) 1.333 m
  (height, centre section) 1.79 m
  (height) 1.191 m
Exterior dimensions:
  (length) 1.953 m
  (width, upper section) 1.857 m
  (width, lower section) 2.234 m
  (height) 1.78 m

Status
In production. In service with the US armed forces and other armed forces.

Gichner shelter, electrical equipment S-250

Manufacturer
Gichner Systems Group, 10946 Golden West Drive, Hunt Valley, Maryland 21031, USA.
Tel: (410) 771 9700. Fax: (410) 771 9696.

Gichner Shelter, Electrical Equipment S-280

Description
The S-280 is a rigid rectangular, non-expansible shelter of adhesive-bonded construction consisting of seamless aluminium interior and exterior skins, extruded aluminium framework structure and polyurethane foam core. It is used to carry communications, radar, maintenance equipment and electronic equipment, and is mounted on the rear of a standard 2½-ton truck (for example the M35). It can also be transported by a transporter/mobiliser dolly set (models M720, M832 or M840), fixed-wing aircraft, helicopter, rail or ship.

The shelter meets military specification MIL-S-55286E and is available with RFI integrity.

Specifications
Weight: 612 kg
Payload: 2268 kg
Interior dimensions:
  (length) 3.504 m
  (width) 2.07 m
  (height) 1.959 m
Exterior dimensions:
  (length) 3.733 m
  (width) 2.209 m
  (height) 2.193 m

Status
In production. In service with the US armed forces and other armed forces.

Gichner shelter, electrical equipment S-280

Manufacturer
Gichner Systems Group, 10946 Golden West Drive, Hunt Valley, Maryland 21031, USA.
Tel: (410) 771 9700. Fax: (410) 771 9696.

Gichner HMMWV Compatible Shelters

Description

Gichner Systems Group produces a range of shelters which are compatible with the M998 HMMWV and M1097 'Heavy' HMMWV. The models are as follows:

S-787/G and S-788/G

These shelters are known as the Standard Integrated Command Post Shelters (SICPS) and are produced in SICPS and SICPS-LMS forms. Both are lightweight, high strength enclosures specifically for use on the HMMWV. Construction involves aluminium-faced, honeycomb core, hot-bonded panels. The electromagnetic shielding is a minimum of 60 dB attenuation for electric, magnetic fields and plane wave in the 150 kHz to 10 GHz frequency range. Both shelters can be driven on and off a C-130 Hercules transport aircraft.

The SICPS has been selected by the US Army as its primary electronics platform for wheeled tactical vehicles, and a CUCV version is available.

Weight:
(SICPS, empty) 286 kg
(SICPS-LMS, empty) 268 kg
Exterior dimensions:
(length) 2.59 m
(width) 2.13 m
(height) 1.64 m
Interior dimensions:
(length) 2.53 m
(width) 2.07 m
(height) 1.64 m
Usable interior volume: 8.35 m³

S-710/M

The S-710/M is a lightweight shelter designed specifically for use with the M1037 HMMWV and M1028 CUCV vehicles. The construction techniques and materials are the same as those used for the S-250 and S-280 shelters. RFI integrity in excess of 60 dB per MIL-STD-285 is a standard feature, making this shelter suitable for C³I applications. The dimensions of the shelter allow C-130 transport aircraft drive-on capability when used with either vehicle.

Weight: 308 kg
Payload: 862 kg
Exterior dimensions:
(length) 2.695 m
(width, upper section) 2.148 m
(width, lower section) 1.268 m
(height) 1.753 m
Interior dimensions:
(length) 2.604 m
(width, upper section) 2.057 m
(width, lower section) 1.194 m
(height, centre section) 1.651 m
(height) 1.297 m

GSS 1496 and GSS 1497

Where weight is critical the GSS 1496 and GSS 1497 are the lightest weight shelters for the HMMWV. Both are dimensionally identical and provide good EMI/RFI protection. The GSS 1496 uses paper honeycomb as the core material while the GSS 1497 incorporates the foam and beam construction. A mounting kit for the HMMWV and the CUCV weighs 31.75 kg.

Weights:
(GSS 1496) approx 210 kg
(GSS 1497) approx 233 kg

NOMAD 1 and 2

The NOMAD is the newest shelter design for the Heavy HMMWV variant. When mounted on the HMMWV or CUCV is does not exceed an overall height of 2.59 m and can be driven onto a C-130 or C-141 aircraft. When deployed the shelter roof can be raised to allow a full 2.03 m of interior height. In the extended mode the NOMAD can provide EMI/RFI shielding to 60 dB. The interior dimensions are the same as those for the S-710/M.

Status

All the above are in production.

Manufacturer

Gichner Systems Group, 10946 Golden West Drive, Hunt Valley, Maryland 21031, USA.
Tel: (410) 771 9700. Fax: (410) 771 9696.

Gichner S-787/G SICPS shelter on HMMWV

Gichner GSS 1496 shelter on HMMWV

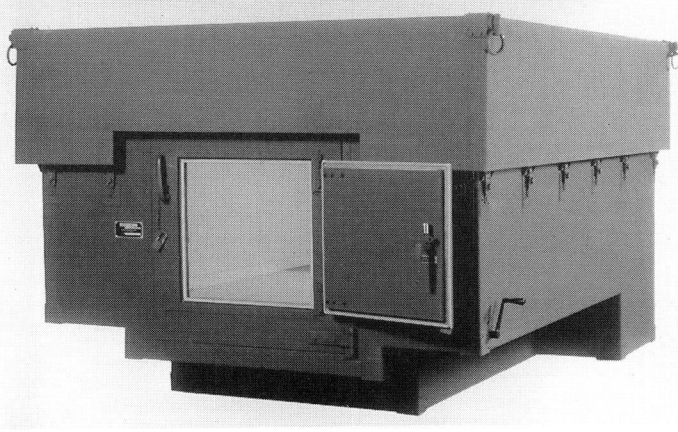

Gichner NOMAD 1 shelter in transport configuration

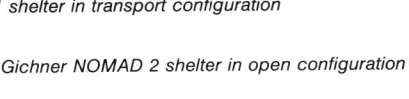

Gichner NOMAD 2 shelter in open configuration

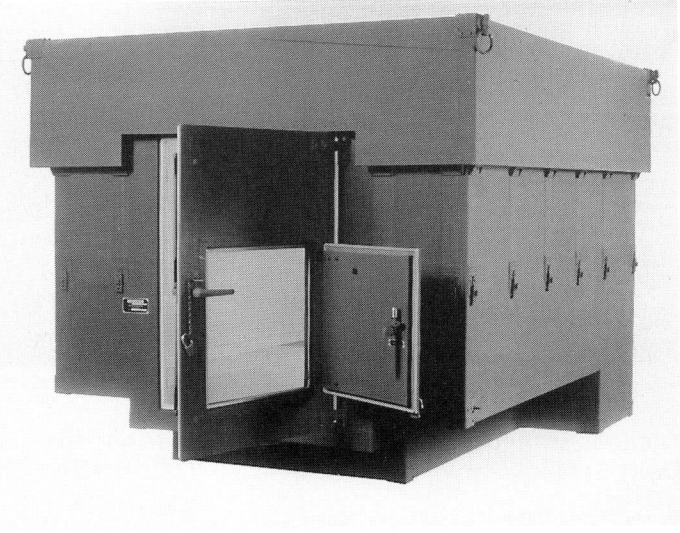

Gichner 20 ft ISO Shelter/Container

Description
This is a rigid rectangular, non-expansible shelter/container of adhesive-bonded sandwich panelling consisting of seamless aluminium exterior skins, extruded aluminium framework structure and a polyurethane foam core. It has integral ISO corner fittings which meet ANSI MH 5.1 requirements. It is used as a multi-purpose electronic equipment enclosure (radar, communication, maintenance, housing, laboratory and so on), with a special butting kit feature and slide-in/slide-out air-conditioner unit optional. Large doors are provided for the installation and removal of equipment.

The shelter/container meets military specification MIL-M-81957 and can be transported by truck, transporter (M1022 end mount or van undercarriage type), fixed-wing aircraft, rail and ship. It is stackable via ISO couplers.

Specifications
Weight: 1996 kg
Payload: 4536 kg
Interior dimensions:
(length) 5.897 m
(width) 2.23 m
(height) 2.141 m
Exterior dimensions:
(length) 6.057 m
(width) 2.438 m
(height, less skids) 2.438 m
(height, with skid for van mobiliser interface) 2.514 m

Gichner 20 ft ISO shelter/container

Status
In production. In service with the US armed forces and other armed forces.

Manufacturer
Gichner Systems Group, 10946 Golden West Drive, Hunt Valley, Maryland 21031, USA.
Tel: (410) 771 9700. Fax: (410) 771 9696.

Gichner Modular Electronic Equipment Shelter GMS-451 Series

Description
The GMS-451 is a rigid rectangular modular side-to-side butting shelter and is of adhesive-bonded sandwich panel construction consisting of seamless interior and exterior skins, extruded aluminium framework structure and a polyurethane foam core. It has removable side panels with GMS shear-loc design.

The shelter, which meets military specification MIL-S-55286 Modified (RFI optional) can be used for a variety of roles including communications, radar, teletype, laboratory, dormitory and hospital. It can be transported by truck, transporter, aircraft, rail or ship.

Specifications

Model	GMS-451	GMS-451-479	GMS-451-537	GMS-451-571
Weight (basic unit)	907 kg	1089 kg	1724 kg	1134 kg
Payload	2268 kg	2722 kg	4536 kg	2722 kg
Interior (length)	3.505 m	4.019 m	5.893 m	4.019 m
(width)	2.032 m	2.07 m	2.286 m	2.286 m
(height)	2.082 m	2.063 m	2.26 m	2.063 m
Exterior (length)	3.733 m	4.242 m	6.096 m	4.241 m
(width)	2.209 m	2.209 m	2.438 m	2.438 m
(height)	2.336 m	2.336 m	2.54 m	2.387 m

Status
In production. In service with the US armed forces and other armed forces.

Manufacturer
Gichner Systems Group, 10946 Golden West Drive, Hunt Valley, Maryland 21031, USA.
Tel: (410) 771 9700. Fax: (410) 771 9696.

Gichner GMS-451-571 seven-shelter complex built for Melpar Division of E-Systems

Interior view of GMS-451 series shelters coupled together

Gichner Transporter/Mobiliser Dolly Sets

Description
Tactical shelters require the use of rugged wheeled devices (end-mounted and van undercarriage type) capable of transporting the shelters via a towing vehicle over rough terrain as well as airfields and roads. This is accomplished via militarised tactical mobilisers of various capacities and types. Listed are two of the standard units available from Gichner.

Status
In production. In service with the US and other armed forces.

Specifications

	Applicable specification	Gross load capacity	Type
M1022	M1022	6804 kg	end-mount
A/M32U-17	CP600530	7711 kg	end-mount

Manufacturer
Gichner Systems Group, 10946 Golden West Drive, Hunt Valley, Maryland 21031, USA.
Tel: (410) 771 9700. Fax: (410) 771 9696.

Gichner Transportable Material Handling Pallet SPA-5000

Description
This pallet provides tactical transport/handling capability for miscellaneous accessory equipment (jacks, air-conditioners, cable reels and generators and so on) used in conjunction with the transportable shelter system.

Its adhesive-bonded sandwich panel constructed base consists of aluminium interior and exterior skins, extruded aluminium framework structure and foam core material.

The pallet, which meets military specification MIL-D-27925, is transportable by truck, transporter/mobiliser dolly set (M720, M832 and M689), fixed-wing aircraft, helicopter, rail and ship.

Specifications
Weight: (with sling) 226.8 kg
Payload: 2268 kg
Payload area: (inside stanchions) 1.831 × 2.352 m
Overall exterior: (including mobiliser brackets and handles) 2.057 × 2.659 m
Standard stanchion height: 0.695 m

Status
In service with the US armed forces.

Manufacturer
Gichner Systems Group, 10946 Golden West Drive, Hunt Valley, Maryland 21031, USA.
Tel: (410) 771 9700. Fax: (410) 771 9696.

Gichner transportable material handling pallet SPA-5000, complete with jacks and air-conditioning equipment

---

Gichner Levelling, Alignment and Lifting Jack Systems

Description
The type of jacking system depends on the basic requirements of the shelter: whether it is fixed or modular/expansible, its gross load and size, jacking height required and its purpose: levelling, truck-loading, or both. Gichner has two basic jack designs which within themselves have been modified to incorporate features which will satisfy all tactical shelter jacking requirements for all tactical military shelters. The two basic types are the fixed type and the roller base type, brief specifications for which are given here.

Status
In production.

Manufacturer
Gichner Systems Group, 10946 Golden West Drive, Hunt Valley, Maryland 21031, USA.
Tel: (410) 771 9700. Fax: (410) 771 9696.

Specifications

Reference	LWJ 25	RBJ 2500	AWJ5000	AWJ5000-AE
Type base	fixed	roller	fixed	fixed
Lift capacity	1134 kg	1134 kg	2268 kg	2268 kg
Travel height	0.457-0.736 m	0.457-0.763 m	1.524 m	1.524 m
General application	S-280	expansible	8 ft × 8 ft × 20 ft modular	truck loading shelter
Approx weight (each)	13.6 kg	14.5 kg	40.9 kg	54.43 kg

Gichner 20 ft shelter with lifting jacks in position

Gichner Transportable Material Handling Pallet SPA-10003

Description
This pallet provides tactical transport/handling capability for miscellaneous equipment (jacks, air-conditioners, cable reels and generators and so on) used in conjunction with the transportable shelter system.

Its adhesive sandwich panel constructed base consists of aluminium interior and exterior skins, extruded aluminium framework structure and foam core material.

The pallet, which meets military specification MIL-D-27925 (modified), is transportable by truck, transporter/mobiliser dolly set (M832 or M689), fixed-wing aircraft, helicopter, rail or ship.

Specifications
Weight: (with sling) 363 kg
Payload: 4538 kg
Payload area: (inside stanchions) 1.872 × 3.342 m
Overall exterior: (including mobiliser brackets and handles, less 463-L rails) 2.085 × 3.768 m
Standard stanchion height: 0.695 m

Status
In service with the US armed forces.

Manufacturer
Gichner Systems Group, 10946 Golden West Drive, Hunt Valley, Maryland 21031, USA.
Tel: (410) 771 9700. Fax: (410) 771 9696.

Gichner transportable material handling pallet SPA-10003

Relocatable Hospital System

Description
Developed in conjunction with the US armed forces, the Relocatable Hospital System was designed for use in outlying or remote locations. It is intended for use in three basic configurations, the smallest of which is a 20-bed configuration. The addition of a single extra ward converts the unit into a 30-bed hospital and the next standard configuration is a 60-bed hospital. The entire system is based on the use of transportable shelters which can be opened out into larger units to form wards, operating theatres and laboratories. Each unit is fully equipped to carry out a certain function and the entire complex is self-sufficient apart from external supplies of water, fuels and expendable supplies. The hospital has its own power generation plant, internal water supply system and material supply centre. The separate units are all interconnected and all entrances have airlocks. Each unit, when transported, is 2.4 × 2.4 × 6 m but in position and opened out the shelter has a floor area of 36.5 m². The shelters are constructed using honeycomb cores and aluminium facings, and each contains all the necessary equipment for its role. All the units have their own integral lighting and air-conditioning with power coming from a generator housed in a standard container. Fuel for the generator and water supplies is kept in collapsible tanks. The 20/30-bed hospital has a 200 kW generator and the 60-bed hospital a 400 kW generator. Support elements such as food service, sanitary facilities, dental units and so on, are available to expand the system.

Status
In production. In service with the US armed forces.

Marketing office
Brunswick Corporation, Defense Division, 150 Johnston Road, Marion, Virginia 24354, USA.
Tel: (703) 783 9636. Fax: (703) 783 9667.

Typical Brunswick Corporation hospital system unit

Typical relocatable hospital system produced by Brunswick Corporation's Defense Division

Brunswick Army Standard Family (ASF) Shelters

Description
Developed by the US Army, the Army Standard Family (ASF) of relocatable/expansible shelters is used by all branches of the US armed forces. These shelters, developed as the standards to be used throughout the 1990s, are available in three configurations – non-expansible, one-side expansible and two-side expansible. All three configurations measure 2.4 × 2.4 × 6 m in the shipping mode. When deployed the one-side and two-side expansible units expand to 4.5 × 6 m and 6.6 × 6 m respectively to provide up to 36.6 m² of floor space. The shelters, constructed of honeycomb core, aluminium-faced panels are highly mobile and can be quickly deployed in the field. Levelling jacks for field deployment are self-contained so that they can be set up on ground slopes of up to 7.5 per cent. No special tools or equipment are required for deployment and a single shelter can be deployed by a crew of four in 10

Brunswick Army Standard Family (ASF) shelters

to 15 minutes.

The shelters conform to ISO shipping container standards which enables them to be transported with any ISO container on container ships. They can be airlifted in aircraft down to C-130 size. Over land they are transported by rail or truck, or by means of a towed dolly developed specifically for this group of shelters. Helicopter lift is also possible. Empty shelters weigh from 1650 kg for a non-expansible version to 3200 kg for a two-sided expansible unit. All shelters are designed to carry an equipment load of up to 4500 kg. They may be used for field hospitals, command and control centres, electronics containers and maintenance shops.

Status
In production. In service with the US armed forces.

Marketing office
Brunswick Corporation, Defense Division, 150 Johnston Road, Marion, Virginia 24354, USA. Tel: (703) 783 9636. Fax: (703) 783 9667.

Brunswick US Marine Corps Shelters

Description
This group of relocatable shelters was developed by the US Marine Corps and consists of 2.4 × 2.4 × 6 m and 2.4 × 2.4 × 3 m units in both standard and EMI-shielded configurations. Also included is a knock-down shelter. In the deployed mode each knock-down unit is 2.4 × 2.4 × 6 m in size; however the units are collapsible for transport and four units in the knock-down configuration can be shipped as one 2.4 m stack. Joining corridors and complexing units are used to connect the units together in a variety of configurations.

The shelters are constructed of honeycomb core, aluminium-faced panels and conform to ISO shipping container standards. Overland movement can be by truck, rail or by towed dolly sets. Helicopter lift and airlift on aircraft as small as the C-130 are also possible. Shelter weights range from 1340 kg for a 2.4 × 2.4 × 3 m unit to 1700 kg for a 2.4 × 2.4 × 6 m unit. The shelters are wired for 120/208 V, three-phase electrics and are designed for a number of functions.

Status
In production. In service with the US Marine Corps.

Brunswick US Marine Corps shelters

Marketing office
Brunswick Corporation, Defense Division, 150 Johnston Road, Marion, Virginia 24354, USA. Tel: (703) 783 9636. Fax: (703) 783 9667.

Craig Standard and ISO Shelters

Description
Craig Systems is one of the largest manufacturers of mobile shelters in the USA and produces a very wide range of standard mobile shelters, shelter vans and accessories. The ISO range of shelters is produced with floors, walls and roofs of single-piece inner and outer aluminium skins with foamed-in-place polyurethane filling. Aluminium extrusions are used for structural strength and for any internal fittings. As with all Craig Systems shelters, the ISO range can be adapted for a wide range of purposes with the internal and external fittings and accessories altered accordingly.

Status
In production. In widespread service.

Manufacturer
Craig Systems, 10 Industrial Way, Amesbury, Massachusetts 01913, USA. Tel: (617) 688 6961. TWX: 710 342 0765.

Specifications

Model	S-138	S-250	S-280	H-376	H-395	H-454	H-556	H-581	H-584	H-586	H-587
Length	2.438 m	1.981 m	3.505 m	3.556 m	3.607 m	6.705 m	5.944 m	1.93 m	2.591 m	3.861 m	3.404 m
Width	1.93 m	1.905 m	2.07 m	2.134 m	1.93 m	2.286 m	2.286 m	1.93 m	1.93 m	1.93 m	1.93 m
Height	1.867 m	1.625 m	1.892 m	2.007 m	1.867 m	2.184 m	2.184 m	1.93 m	1.93 m	1.867 m	1.93 m
Weight	454 kg	347 kg	626.5 kg	726 kg	567.5 kg	1816 kg	1589 kg	390 kg	463 kg	590 kg	545 kg

Craig Model H-833 electronic equipment shelter on Craig Model D-74 1B transporter

Craig S-280 shelter with external air-conditioner mounted on M548 tracked cargo carrier

Craig N-1080 and N-1050 Nuclear Hardened Tactical Shelters

Description

The Craig N-1080 nuclear hardened shelter was developed by Harry Diamond Laboratories together with the Italian Miki SpA to house and shelter complex and expensive equipment that modern armed forces use in the front line. Such equipment includes electronics and various forms of communications equipment, and in some cases the contents of a mobile military shelter can cost millions, whatever the currency involved. To provide such equipment with protection against tactical nuclear weapon effects, the N-1080 was designed. It is a conventional shelter in appearance but the walls, floors and ceiling are Kevlar laminates and many of the fittings are Kevlar extrusions. The door has special blastproof hinges and a Craig V-846 anti-blast valve is fitted above the door. The N-1080 has a specially strengthened air-conditioning and filter unit at the front end of the shelter. The door has an emergency escape hatch, and special corner and lifting castings are provided.

The N-1080 is 3.734 m long, 2.21 m wide and 2.12 m high.

The N-1050 is a smaller nuclear hardened shelter suitable for carrying on small trucks. It is 2.073 m long, 1.994 m wide and 1.717 m high. Weight is 544 kg.

Status

In production.

Manufacturer

Craig Systems, 10 Industrial Way, Amesbury, Massachusetts 01913, USA.
Tel: (617) 688 6961. TWX: 710 342 0765.

Craig N-1080 nuclear hardened shelter

Craig N-1050 nuclear hardened shelter

Craig Shelter Transporters

Description

There are four main types of transporter in the Craig range, the D-741B, D-741Z, D-741 (ISO) and the M-832.

The D-741B transporter consists of front and rear half sections which are permanently attached to the shelter. The payload is up to 7711 kg. The front half is steerable, primarily to facilitate loading large shelters onto cargo aircraft. The D-741B is in service with the US Marine Corps.

The D-741 (ISO) has the same capabilities as the D-741B and is designed for use with ISO shelters.

The D-741Z provides type 'V' mobility without hydraulic cylinders to raise and lower the shelter onto the transporter. A third wheel is provided and the manual system of loading and unloading shelters can be performed with minimal personnel and effort.

The M-832 provides mobility for medium-range payloads up to 4763 kg. The front and rear dolly assemblies are attached to the payload. Hydraulic cylinders permit lowering and raising of the shelter suspension bars and strut assemblies lock the trailer in the raised position for transport. Air-over-hydraulic brakes are provided on all four wheels of the dolly set. Tail, stop and blackout lights are mounted on the rear trailer. The M-832 is used by the US Marine Corps.

Status

In production. In service with the US Army, US Marine Corps and many other armed forces.

Manufacturer

Craig Systems, 10 Industrial Way, Amesbury, Massachusetts 01913, USA.
Tel: (617) 688 6961. TWX: 710 342 0765.

Specifications

Model	D-741Z	M-832	D-741B	D-741 (ISO)
Weight	1361 kg	1664.7 kg	1927.75 kg	2565 kg
Payload (max)	6804 kg	4763 kg	7711 kg	7711 kg
Length	front 1.435 m	3.038 m	front 1.435 m	front 1.448 m
	rear 1.384 m		rear 1.384 m	rear 1.422 m
Width	2.438 m	2.438 m	2.438 m	2.438 m
Height	1.168 m	1.321 m	n/a	2.337 m
Track width	2.438 m	2.134 m	2.134 m	2.134 m
Road clearance	0.432 m	0.432 m	0.432 m	0.432 m
Shelter levelling capability	—	0 to 0.305 m	0 to 0.102 m	—
Shelter lift capability	—	0 to 0.432 m	0 to 0.143 m	0 to 0.635 m
Hydraulic lifting	no	standard	standard	standard
Mechanical lifting	yes	no	no	no
Tyres	11.00 × 20	9.00 × 20	11.00 × 20	11.00 × 20

Craig Model M-832 transporter

Craig Model D-741 (ISO) being used to load shelter into US Air Force C-130 Hercules transport aircraft

Mobile Frame Structures M720 Mobiliser Dolly Set

Description
Mobile Frame Structures manufactures specially engineered trailers and transport equipment including the M720 Mobiliser Dolly Set. This is used by the US Army Tank Automotive Command (TACOM) as the dedicated transport vehicle for the S-280 shelter. The M720 meets the requirements of MIL-M-8090F with reference to Mobility Type III Group C.

Used for the deployment of containerised battlefield communications and radar equipment, the M720 enables the user to easily place containers in field locations. Dolly/shelter combinations can then be moved from location to location and decoupled within minutes. The unloaded dolly can then be used to transport other shelters, eliminating the need for special materials handling equipment.

Generally towed by the M924 or similar 5-ton trucks, the M720 can be loaded and mounted onto a shelter by two men. Braking is air/hydraulic on all wheels and automotive-type steering is used. The hydraulic lift mechanism can be operated independently at each end to mount or level the shelter.

The M720 is rated for a 3-ton payload. Larger shelters than the S-280 require the use of a higher capacity mobiliser which is under development by Mobile Frame Structures.

Mobile Frame Structures M720 mobiliser dolly set

The M720 weighs 1000 kg unladen and has a capacity of 2800 kg. Length is 2.35 m, width 2.43 m and height 2.43 m (0.79 m reduced).

Status
In production and widespread use.

Manufacturer
Mobile Frame Structures Inc, 1408 Calcon Hook Road, Sharon Hill, Pennsylvania 19079, USA.

Brunswick Standardised Integrated Command Post Shelter (SICPS)

Description
The Standardised Integrated Command Post Shelter (SICPS) was specifically designed for the HMMWV and CUCV and, compared to the S-250 formerly used, combines a 30 per cent reduction in weight and a 48 per cent increase in internal volume.

Construction uses two long aluminium-faced honeycomb core hot-bonded panels with the basic box assembled from two U-shaped pieces. The shelter provides EMI and RFI attenuation and has an integral power generator and an environmental control unit incorporating an NBC system. A storage rack is provided over the cab. There is provision for an antenna mast and kits are provided to install the shelter on the HMMWV or CUCV. HMMWV shelters may have single or double rear doors.

In June 1991 Brunswick Defense received a $6.9 million contract from the US Army to design, develop, test and produce prototypes of a nuclear-hardened version of the SICPS to be known as Hardened SICPS. This version will involve the use of fibre-reinforced plastic construction.

Specifications
Weight: (empty) 257 kg
Payload: (for Heavy HMMWV) 1785 kg
Length:
  (exterior) 2.59 m
  (interior) 2.53 m
Width:
  (exterior) 2.13 m
  (interior) 2.07 m
Height:
  (exterior) 1.7 m
  (interior) 1.64 m

Brunswick Standardised Integrated Command Post Shelter (SICPS) on HMMWV

Usable interior volume:
  (HMMWV) 8.35 m³
  (CUCV) 8.72 m³

Status
In production for the US Army.

Marketing office
Brunswick Corporation, Defense Division, 150 Johnston Road, Marion, Virginia 24354, USA. Tel: (703) 783 9636. Fax: (703) 783 9667.

Deployable Rapid Assembly Shelter (DRASH)

Description
The Deployable Rapid Assembly Shelter (DRASH) was developed as a private venture and is in use with the US Marine Corps and Austrian, British and Israeli armed forces. DRASH was developed to meet the requirement for a rugged multi-climate manportable shelter system and can be deployed by four men in less than 5 minutes under practically any weather conditions.

DRASH shelters are manufactured from aluminium alloy tubing connected with plastic hubs. They can fold and pack down to about 2 per cent of their deployed size. Interior and exterior covers are made from state-of-the-art MilSPEC fabrics and are pre-attached to the frames. Tests have shown that repairs to frames and covers can be made in the field by unskilled personnel in less than 5 minutes.

Each DRASH shelter has four entrances and all have universal connectors to join two or more shelters together. Special 'boots' are available to provide a weathertight seal with other types of hard- or soft-wall shelters and with a variety of wheeled and tracked vehicles.

The T-Series of DRASH shelters is exactly the same as the ordinary shelters other than that one end is truncated to allow it to be attached to a vehicle; in this form the internal volume is slightly reduced. Standard shelters can be configured to form command posts or tactical operations centres.

DRASH shelter in use with US Marine Corps HMMWV

DRASH shelter in use with US Army SUSV

Each DRASH shelter has the following equipment as standard: aluminium frame; exterior cover; interior cover; ground cover; flooring; integrated duct interface with plenum; doorways; universal connectors for networking shelters; screened windows with flaps; dual staking/securing system; transport bag; and a repair kit. Other features include light traps for ingress/egress during blackout periods and the capability for rapid camouflage by laying netting lengthways on the shelter before erecting.

DRASH shelters are available in six sizes. Basic features are as follows:

Model 1
Area: 10.5 m²
Dimensions stowed: 1.52 × 0.5 × 0.5 m
Weight: 47-56 kg

Model 2
Area: 15.9 m²
Dimensions stowed: 1.52 × 0.61 × 0.76 m
Weight: 61-70 kg

Model 3
Area: 21.35 m²
Dimensions stowed: 1.52 × 0.61 × 0.91 m
Weight: 75-84 kg

Model 4
Area: 26.7 m²
Dimensions stowed: 1.52 × 0.76 × 1 m
Weight: 88-96 kg

Model 5
Area: 32.1 m²

Dimensions stowed: 1.52 × 0.76 × 1.23 m
Weight: 102-116 kg

Model 6
Area: 37.5 m²
Dimensions stowed: 1.52 × 0.91 × 1.23 m
Weight: 116-125 kg

Status
In production. In service with the Austrian, British and Israeli armed forces and the US Marine Corps.

Manufacturer
Deployable Hospital Systems Inc, 256 Oak Tree Road, Tappan, New York 10983, USA.
Tel: (914) 359 6066. Telex: 825951 usex.
Fax: (914) 365 2114.

VEHICLE BODIES

FRANCE

Trailor Roller Tilt Drop Side Cargo Body

Description
The Trailor rolling tilt drop side cargo body combines the attributes of a drop side cargo body with a rapidly and easily moved tilt cover. It was specifically designed for use with trucks carrying NATO cargo pallets or 20 ft/6.096 m ISO containers and has been fitted to Renault G 260 (6 × 4) trucks. It can also be used on a Trailor 14 400 kg drawbar trailer or with a Trailor 32 000 kg semi-trailer; the latter is in service as a logistics load carrier with the French Army, as is the Renault G 260 truck.

The body has a fixed forward wall in one or two sections. For the latter the lower part is a steel panel with an upper canvas wall. The side and rear drop panels can all be removed as can the side posts. Along the top of the panels are recessed rails in which the rolling tilt can move. Fixed bows are covered by a polyanimide or polyester cover and the tilt is so arranged that one man can rapidly open or close the tilt using only one hand by pulling a handle. When open the bows and cover can be stowed either in the forward or rear position. The cargo floor is manufactured from reinforced timber planks.

Specifications
Length: (internal) 7.42 m
Width: (internal) 2.42 m

Trailor rolling tilt drop side body fitted to Renault G 260 (6 × 4) truck and with two side drop panels open

Height: (under tarpaulin, minimum) 2.1 m
Floor height: (unladen) 1.47 m

Status
In service with the French Army.

Manufacturer
Trailor SA, 5 Route Nationale 10, BP 49, Coignieres, F-78311 Maurepas Cedex, France.
Tel: (1) 30 50 61 26. Telex: 698896 f.
Fax: (1) 30 50 31 32.

GERMANY

Marrel Torsion Free Military Platform

Description
The Marrel torsion free military platform is intended for use on vehicles that have to carry electronic equipment and cargo such as palletised loads over rough terrain. The all-steel body is usually mounted on two swivel joints at the front and rear which allow an optimum turning motion between the mountings and the chassis. This allows the platform to maintain a straight and level position even under extreme off-road conditions.

A typical installation is that used on the Mercedes-Benz 2628 A (6 × 6) 12 000 kg truck. The platform used allows a maximum on-road payload of 13 800 kg with the platform being 5.5 m long and 2.14 m wide. Loading height is 1.7 m. The platform has folding bench seating for 20 men, and is equipped with a storage box for chains and a camouflage net, a spare wheel, a fire extinguisher box, two 20 litre jerrican racks, a tool box, two wheel chocks, a drinking water container, racks for entrenching tools and provision for a winch cable.

Another vehicle that can use a Marrel torsion free military platform is the Mercedes-Benz L 911B/42 (4 × 4) truck. On this vehicle the platform is 4.5 m long, and the loading height is approximately 1.215 m unladen. Folding seating is provided for 18 men.

Status
In production.

Manufacturer
Marrel GmbH, Kruppstrasse 44, D-5603 Wülfrath, Federal Republic of Germany.

Marrel torsion free military platform on Mercedes-Benz 2628 A (6 × 6) 12 000 kg truck

SINGAPORE

Tactical Ambulance Mark II

Description
This tactical ambulance body is built on a Land Rover Defender 110 (4 × 4) chassis. The ambulance body can accommodate a three-man crew (driver, co-driver and one medical attendant) and either four stretcher casualties or six seated casualties.

In this ambulance the stretcher berths can be folded away to form personnel seating. A wash basin with water faucet also folds away to become a bench rest. These features allow the vehicle to be used for general purposes as well as an ambulance.

The body has fresh and waste water tanks, an air extractor, a medical stores stowage area, four hook rails, recessed high/low lighting, a siren, a rotating beacon and ambulance signs.

Status
In production. In service with the Singapore Armed Forces.

Manufacturer
Singapore Automotive Engineering Limited (A Singapore Technologies Company), 5 Portsdown Road, Singapore 0513.
Tel: 4736311. Telex: 25755 SINENG RS.
Fax: 4710662.

Tactical ambulance Mark II

UNITED KINGDOM

Marshall SPV Vehicle Bodies

Description
Marshall SPV is the largest manufacturer of military vehicle bodies in the United Kingdom. The following are typical of the range of military products available.

Ambulances
The range of Marshall 4 × 4 ambulances has been developed over the last 25 years. Over 4000 vehicles have been produced for both the British Ministry of Defence and many overseas customers. The bodywork was designed to suit either the Land Rover Defender 110 or 127 4 × 4 chassis integral body or box body. Designs are available to meet customers' specific requirements.

Interior arrangements offer a capability of accepting up to four stretcher patients or two stretcher patients and four sitting patients, or eight sitting patients. An attendant's seat is fitted and locker space for storage of medical equipment is provided. A wide range of optional equipment can be offered, including air-conditioning, oxygen systems, portable resuscitation equipment and emergency first aid equipment.

Land Rover Conversions
A wide range of conversions and bodies has been

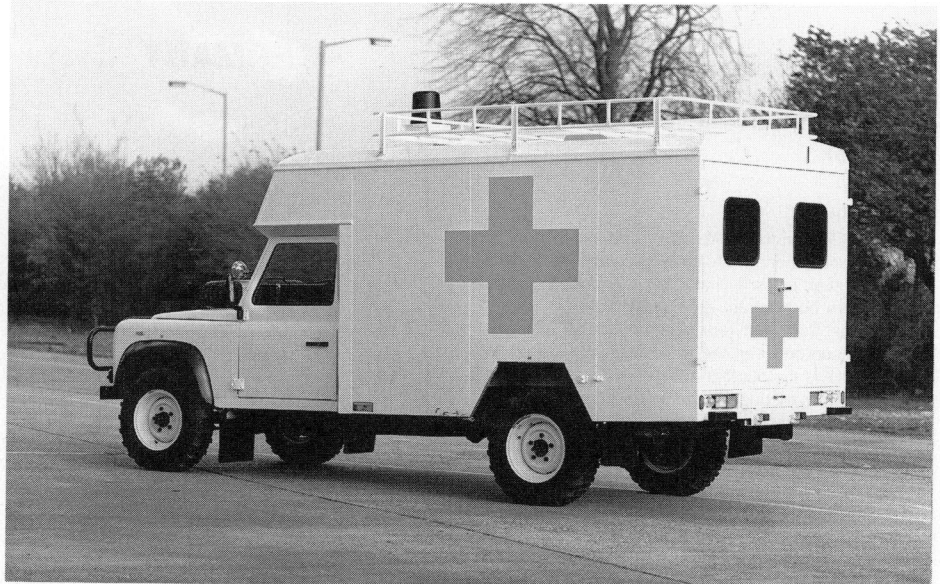

Ambulance built by Marshall SPV using Land Rover Defender 110 (4 × 4)

Bedford TM 4-4 (4 × 4) 8-tonne truck with general service/cargo drop side body

Bedford MK (4 × 4) 4000 kg truck with expansible body with air-conditioning system produced by Marshall SPV

supplied for the Land Rover series. The vehicle has been the base for ambulances (see above), signal vehicles, weapon platforms, radar stations, command posts, workshops, refuelling and missile support vehicles. A cargo-bodied version has been supplied through Land Rover to several overseas territories.

Body General Service/Cargo Drop Side 4-tonne
This was developed from 1967 for the Bedford MK (4 × 4) 4000 kg truck and entered production the following year. Its FVRDE (MVEE) Specification is 9722. The body is capable of being used as a flat platform, fitted with drop sides, as a troop carrier, or for the carriage of a distributed load of 4000 kg. The steel body is of welded construction, with the front bulkhead bolted to forward pillars mounted to the underframe. The hardwood floor is fitted directly to the crossmember. It is protected by steel wearing strips which cover the joints. Rotating flush-fitting lashing rings mounted directly to the crossmember are positioned to provide the most efficient lashing points for lashing down bulky loads. Additional heavy duty lashing points are positioned along the main sides. The four drop sides and tailboards can be removed, and the rear and intermediate pillars unbolted to provide a flat platform. A

tubular steel superstructure is fitted with a tailored tilt cover of cotton-polyester material. Secured to the underframes are two lockers and a carrier for two jerricans. Provision is made on the forward face of the front bulkhead for stowing a pickaxe head and handle, a shovel and a crowbar.

Body General Service 8-tonne
Development of this GS cargo body began during 1974. The body can be used as a flat platform or fitted with drop sides and a tailboard for carrying a distributed load of 8000 kg. Typical loads can be up to six standard pallets, shelters up to 4.5 m long, loose stores, and ISO containers. The body is of welded steel with a hardwood floor, both designed with a view to mass production and providing the maximum protection against corrosion. Rotating flush-fitting lashing rings are secured directly to the body underframe and, with additional lashing points secured to the sides, are positioned to provide an efficient lashing pattern for securing all types of load. The conversion to a flat platform mode is easy and convenient. A tubular steel superstructure and tailboard cotton-polyester tilt cover is supplied. The overall length of the body is 6.637 m and it is 2.5 m wide. The load area measures

4.53 m × 2.145 m.

Marshall Expansible Bodies
The Marshall Expansible Body was developed as an addition to the range of container-based and rigid-mounted bodies produced by Marshall for both the Ministry of Defence and overseas markets. The design allows for the installation of 'special to role' equipment for mechanical or electronic repair, simulation equipment, test and repair workshops, all with almost double the working area of an equivalent box body or shelter. With the body in the closed position the vehicle is within the maximum legal width for use on roads. The body can be expanded by one operator with steadying jacks deployed within 15 minutes. The body can be mounted onto any chassis of suitable payload.

Status
Production as required.

Manufacturer
Marshall SPV Limited, Airport Works, Cambridge CB5 8RX, UK.
Tel: 0223 301133. Fax: 02205 3875.

Pilcher-Greene Ambulances

Description
Since 1956 Pilcher-Greene has produced a range of 4 × 4 ambulances based on the Land Rover. These ambulances are in use in South America, Africa, the Middle East, the Indian subcontinent and the Far East. Production is now concentrated on the Land Rover Defender One Ten. Pilcher-Greene offers a variety of ambulance interior layouts with various fittings to suit customer requirements. Various body types are available ranging from the basic to fully equipped versions complete with air-conditioning and other accessories. Most body types are offered in either aluminium or aluminium with glass-reinforced plastic (GRP) panels.

Series 8303
The Series 8303 is available with a Type S body which has a framework of mild steel, and the sides, tropical roof and the roof itself are constructed from either GRP

or aluminium alloy sheet. Plastic laminates are used on the interior with a vinyl-covered plastic aluminium alloy floor. Large double doors, common to all the Pilcher-Greene bodies, are provided for access. There are five options for the interior fittings and a typical military interior would have provision for four stretcher cases with the stretchers folding to provide seating for up to eight patients. A folding seat could be provided on the cab wall for an attendant. Numerous accessories can be provided.

Series 8404
With the Series 8404 two types of body are available, the Type B and the Type F. With the Type B the Land Rover Defender One Ten cab is retained whereas with the Type F version only the windscreen, sidescreens and doors are retained, the cab roof being custom built as an integral structure with the body. With the Type B body two interior layouts are available while with the Type F four interior layouts are available according to customer choice. A tropical roof is fitted and a full

range of optional extras is available with either model.

Specifications (all 2.77 m wheelbase)

Series	8303	8404	8404
Body type	S	B	F
Weight (approx)	1950 kg	1900 kg	1980 kg
Length (overall)	4.786 m	4.438 m	4.438 m
(body)	2.311 m	1.854 m	1.981 m
Width (overall)	1.908 m	1.79 m	1.79 m
(body)	1.695 m	1.448 m	1.574 m
Height (overall)	2.337 m	2.235 m	2.413 m
(body)	1.536 m	1.321 m	1.524 m

Status
In production and widespread service.

Manufacturer
Pilcher-Greene Limited, Consort Way, Victoria Gardens, Burgess Hill, West Sussex RH15 9NA, UK.
Tel: 0444 235707. Telex: 877102.
Fax: 0444 241730.

Pilcher-Greene Series 8404 ambulance with Type B body

Pilcher-Greene Series 8404 ambulance with Type F body

Edbro Vehicle Bodies and Hydraulic Systems

Description

Approved to AQAP 1 quality assurance standard, Edbro plc is involved in the design and manufacture of vehicle bodywork for all types of material handling to British Ministry of Defence specifications. The manufacturing facility incorporates CAD/CAM and extensive use is made of FE stress analysis in body design. CNC machine tools, friction welding, shot blast, hard chrome plating and low bake ovens for IRR paint schemes feature in the production plant.

In production are flat, cargo, winch and crane bodies for the British Army's Leyland-DAF 4 × 4 4-tonne trucks. Edbro have completed an order for military dump trucks based on the IVECO-Ford 330-25 (6 × 6) chassis. These vehicles, intended for high speed airfield runway repair work, have special features for low temperature operation, including exhaust heated bodywork.

Edbro has previously produced dump bodies and hoists for the British Army's Foden 8 × 4 Low Mobility tipper trucks and Bedford TM 4-4 tippers. The flat cargo and winch bodies fitted to the Bedford TM 6-6 14-tonne vehicles were manufactured by Edbro.

Types of bodywork include flat platform, truck, cargo, winch, crane, tipper, dump truck and dust cart and for over 75 years, since 1916 when the company was founded, Edbro hydraulic systems have featured in automotive applications throughout the world.

Status

In production. In service with the British Army.

Manufacturer

Edbro plc, Lever Street, Bolton, Greater Manchester BL3 6DJ, UK.
Tel: 0204 28888. Telex: 63196 edbroh g.
Fax: 0204 31957.

Edbro cargo body with canvas cover fitted to Leyland-DAF (4 × 4) 4-tonne truck

IVECO-Ford 330-25 (6 × 6) chassis with Edbro DK14 double-acting hoist and 9 m³ steel rock dump body

Reynolds Boughton General Service Cargo Body

Description

The Reynolds Boughton General Service Cargo Body, with winch and crane, was designed to carry general cargo and is mounted on the Bedford WNV3 NSO 4 × 4 8000 kg truck with a wheelbase of 4.32 m. The body is constructed from welded steel and uses an underframe of pressed steel, longitudinal members and cross-bearers. The floor is hardwood, treated with a preservative after machining, with wearing irons over all the joints.

A mid-mounted Boughton H7500 hydraulic winch is fitted enabling self-recovery and recovery in both a forward and rearward direction. An Atlas Model AK 3008A1 hydraulic loader with a capacity of 8 t/m is fitted between the cab and body to permit the self-loading and unloading of cargo.

Specifications

Interior length: 3.914 m
Interior width: 2.332 m
Height of sides: 0.762 m
Floor height: 1.525 m

Status

In production and in service with the British Ministry of Defence. Similar bodies are in service with many overseas armed forces, especially in the Far and Middle East.

Reynolds Boughton General Service Cargo Body with winch and crane

Manufacturer

Reynolds Boughton Limited, Vehicle Division, Bell Lane, Amersham, Buckinghamshire HP6 6PE, UK.

Tel: 0494 764411. Telex: 83132.
Fax: 0494 765218.

Reynolds Boughton General Service Tipper Body

Description

The Reynolds Boughton General Service Tipper Body is of welded construction and is manufactured from high tensile steel. Both under-body and front-end tipping gears are available and bodies are produced to suit a wide variety of general service cargo vehicles.

Status

In production. In service with a number of overseas armed forces, especially in the Far East.

Manufacturer

Reynolds Boughton Limited, Engineering Division, Bell Lane, Amersham, Buckinghamshire HP6 6PE, UK. Tel: 0494 764411. Telex: 83132. Fax: 0494 765218.

Reynolds Boughton general service tipper body

UNITED STATES OF AMERICA

Southwest Special Workshop Bodies

Description

Over the last 20 years Southwest Mobile Systems Corporation has produced almost 3000 special shop bodies of several types and at present produces five workshop body 'sets' as follows:

Set 3 – Contact Maintenance Shop
This is a self-propelled, self-contained, maintenance workshop for wheeled and tracked vehicle maintenance in the field. Early production of this set was mounted on a Dodge chassis with later production (105 units for the US Marine Corps) mounted on the M1031 CUCV, on which the usual onboard generator is replaced by a power take-off driven 12 kW alternator from the vehicle generator. Equipment carried in the body includes the following: a 200 A welder, an air compressor, electric motor driven portable drills, a 3-ton chain hoist, a hydraulic hand jack, ignition timing light, a multimeter, a tachometer, a bench and pipe vice, six electrical test engine adaptors, a comprehensive tool kit and chest, soldering and welding kits, support materials, equipment and supplies, floodlights and masts.

On the CUCV the Set 3 (with vehicle) is 5.41 m long, 2.06 m wide and 1.94 m high when loaded. Weight is 2381 kg.

A lightweight body has been prototyped for fitting to the HMMWV M998 series. A US Army Concept Evaluation Program (CEP) is being sponsored by the Ordnance Corps from Aberdeen, Maryland.

Set 4 – Electrical Repair Shop
This is an electrical repair shop mounted in an M447C Van Semi-trailer ordered by the US Army (158 units). The repair shop is carried in a four-wheel semi-trailer with the steel and aluminium body fitted with benches,

diagnostic equipment, tools, five load banks for electrical power testing of generators, a hydraulic test stand, electrical and other tools and the necessary support supplies. Major equipment carried in the repair shop includes the following: a power supply amplifier, a battery charger, frequency test meters, a petrol engine generating set, a grinding machine, a 1-ton chain hoist, various oscilloscopes and multimeters, a rotary actuator test stand, a variable power transformer, a 2-ton portable hoist trestle, heaters and an air-conditioner. A comprehensive tool kit, containers, measurement devices and various support materials and supplies are all carried inside the repair shop body.

The Set 4 semi-trailer is 8.204 m long, 2.4 m wide and 3.343 m high when loaded. Weight is 10 433 kg.

Set 11 – General-purpose Machine Shop
This is a semi-trailer mounted general-purpose machine shop intended for use in the repair of heavy mechanical equipment such as construction equipment; 128 units were produced for the US Army, US Marine Corps and US Navy Construction Battalions. The unit houses a 300 A welder, an engine lathe with milling, drilling, grinding and slotting attachments, and over 400 tools, test equipments and accessories, plus supplies. The shop contains its own diesel engine-driven 25 kW alternator power generating system, fuel supply and space heater. Large upper side doors provide easy access and open with hydraulic assists. Canvas covers, secured from the raised side and rear doors, can be used to form a spacious heated field repair centre.

Length of the complete semi-trailer is 8.928 m, width 2.502 m and height 3.188 m. Weight is 13 675 kg.

Set 12 – Organisational Repair Shop
This is a truck-mounted organisational level repair set equipped for the inspection, testing, maintenance and repair of vehicles, automotive and other equipment under on- or off-road conditions. The M809 (6 × 6)

5-ton cargo truck was originally used as the chassis for this set while later contracts (240 units for the US Army) utilised the M944 version of the M939 5-ton cargo truck.

The unit contains over 350 separate types of tools, equipment, accessories and supplies. Canvas covers, secured from the raised side and rear doors, can be used to form a spacious heated repair centre. The set's power tools, including a lathe and 300 A welding kit, can be powered by either an external source or from the truck engine through a power take-off driven alternator system. Other major items of equipment carried include a space heater with blower, an electric motor-driven air compressor, floodlights and masts, and other lighting accessories. There is also a small reference library.

Overall length of the set on an M944 chassis is 9.042 m, width is 2.5 m and height 3.175 m. Weight complete is 14 800 kg.

Clothing Repair Shop
This mobile clothing repair shop is used by the US Army (36 units). The shop is carried in a two-wheel M105A2 trailer and is equipped with six clothing machines, one button machine and one darner machine as well as the associated accessories. The set was designed for on- and off-road transport of the equipment, and to allow field set-up of the equipment. Power is provided by a 3 kW power source stored in the shop. Length of the complete trailer is 4.3 m, width 2.11 m and height 2.46 m. Weight is 3289 kg.

Status

In service with the US armed forces.

Manufacturer

Southwest Mobile Systems Corporation, 200 Sidney Street, St Louis, Missouri 63104, USA. Tel: (314) 771 3950. Telex: 434347. Fax: (314) 771 1169.

Set 3 mounted on a Dodge chassis

Set 12 organisational repair shop in travelling configuration on M944 chassis

OTHER EQUIPMENT

GERMANY

Kärcher Hot Air Generator FB 60E

Description
The hot air generator FB 60E was designed to meet the requirements of the German armed forces and is also employed by the medical corps. It is also used for the heating of depots and storage shelters. Other uses include the heating of diesel engines in low temperatures and the pre-flight heating of helicopters and aircraft on the ground.

With the help of a special medical-use extension set clean air and constant temperatures can be achieved in hospital tents without creating turbulence. This is achieved by the use of specially treated and perforated air outlets and distribution ductings. The FB 60E is equipped with a remote thermostat with a built-in sensor accurate to within 0.2°C. In summer the unit can be used to cool tents, shelters, aircraft cockpits and cabins.

All the main components of the FB 60E are installed in a torsionally stiff tubular aluminium frame with pick-up points for fork-lifts or air transport. It can be easily moved by one person using the integral wheels and handles.

The main fan and fuel pump are driven by a central

Kärcher FB 60E hot air generator

220 V motor. Fresh air is sucked in via a radial fan and heated by the burner and heat exchanger. The rated thermal output is 60 kW by a rated air flow of 3000 m³. Fuel consumption is 7.5 l/h.

Optimised combustion is achieved by a specially shaped burner sphere. This and the heat exchanger are made of high-temperature resistant material, both of which are gas-tight welded to ensure that no combustion gases are mixed with the heated fresh air.

Due to its two integrated fuel pre-heaters, the FB 60E is able to work in temperatures down to −30°C. The fuel used can be diesel, diesel-petrol mixtures or kerosene.

Specifications
Weight: 200 kg
Length: 1.72 m
Width: 0.74 m
Height: 0.91 m

Status
In production. In service with the Australian, German and US armed forces.

Manufacturer
Alfred Kärcher GmbH and Co, Alfred-Kärcher-Strasse 28-40, D-7057 Winnenden, Federal Republic of Germany.
Tel: 07195 142797. Telex: 724432.
Fax: 07195 142720.

ISRAEL

Achidatex Protective Equipment Covers

Description
Achidatex produces a three-part protective storage system to meet the exacting requirements of the Israeli Defence Forces with their need for prolonged equipment protection under extremes of climate combined with the need for protected equipment to be ready for virtually immediate use at all times. The main part of the system is a flexible cover with a low moisture vapour transmission rate in the form of a plasticised PVC-coated polyester or nylon fabric sheet combined with an ultra-low permeability grade laminated PVC. These covers can be made to fit a particular item such as a tank or truck or can be loose-fitting to suit a range of equipments. The fabric can be produced in various colours and is resistant to most chemicals or oils. Each cover has a special closure system which is welded to the cover material and this can be sealed either by hand or by means of a special slide which forces the closure system to maintain a seal against all vapours and corrosive materials. The closure can be readily opened for inspection or maintenance and resealed. The covers are re-usable and are resistant to fungi and fire.

To maintain the relative humidity inside the covers various alternatives are available ranging from simple silica gel desiccants to automatic dehumidifiers for covers with an internal volume of more than 90 m³. These automatic equipments operate off a mains supply. Various forms of humidity sensor can be employed ranging from treated papers to meter systems.

Status
In production. In service with the Israeli Armed Forces.

Manufacturer
Achidatex, PO Box 2156, Ramat Gan 52151, Israel.
Tel: 472637. Telex: 371271.

Achidatex covers for multiple stores

Achidatex cover opened to reveal contents

Chemoplast Dry Storage Systems

Description
The Chemoplast dry storage systems use a high-frequency welded cover system in both one-piece cover and tunnel forms.

The one-piece envelope covers are tailor-made to suit specific requirements and can be used in extremes of climate. With these covers the seams generally overlap 20 mm and are formed by continuous heat welding for maximum strength. Extruded closures ensure perfect seals and maximum separation strength. The material has very low water permeability and provides protection against corrosion. Dehumidification by chemical or mechanical means is incorporated. Also provided around high stress areas are padded blankets and reinforced PVC.

The Chemoplast dry storage tunnel system is intended for the bulk storage of high-value products for extended periods. On the tunnel the roof and sides form a single unit supported on a plastic frame system of assorted GRP elements which can be easily assembled and dismantled. An extruded all-around closure ensures top and bottom sealing. The tunnel measures 15 × 2.8 × 2 m and provides a covered

volume of 80 m³, although other sizes can be produced to meet customer requirements.

Status
In production. In service with the Israeli armed forces.

Manufacturer
Chemoplast Limited, PO Box 2110, Afula 18301, Israel.
Tel: (6) 523044/5.
Telex: 451881 attn chemoplast aran il.

Chemoplast dry storage covers in use

An assembled Chemoplast dry storage tunnel

ITALY

Pirelli Protective Covers

Description
Pirelli produces a rubber-coated fabric which is widely used for the protection of equipment in storage and in transit. This fabric can be produced in a wide range of shapes and sizes and has a weight of between 650 and 800 g/m². The fabric, usually coloured olive brown on one side and black on the other, has a minimum tensile strength of 306 kg for every 50 mm and is fire-

resistant. It is also resistant to the effects of extremes of temperature and protection is provided, not only against atmospheric agents, but particularly against NBC attacks and infra-red photographic observations. Contaminated covers can be reclaimed.

One of the various articles produced using this rubber-coated fabric is a cover for use as a weather-defeating barrier on equipment in transit or in storage, but used specifically for Leopard MBTs. It is 8 m long and 4.5 m wide and weighs approximately 25 kg. When packed this cover occupies about 0.15 m³ and in

use is lashed around the equipment to be protected.

Status
In production. In service with the Italian armed forces.

Manufacturer
MOLDIP SpA – Pirelli Group, Via Milano 8, I-20038 Seregno, Italy.
Tel: 0362 237711. Telex: 330191 pirese i.
Fax: 0362 220412.

SWEDEN

Munters Dry Air Method

Description
The Munters dry air method was first used by the Royal Swedish Army during the late 1950s. Since then its use has become widespread for the protection of equipment against depredations caused by moisture in the atmosphere.

The Munters dry air method utilises a dehumidifier that consists of a rotor divided into two zones. The basis of the rotor is manufactured of a special

incombustible glass fibre carrying the desiccant and known as Honeycombe. Moisture is absorbed in one of the zones of the rotor while in another the rotor is dried by hot air, both actions taking place in a constant process. The resultant dry air has a constant low humidity of an even quality.

There are two different systems for dehumidification; closed or open. In a closed system a room is dehumidified to the desired level by recycling the air through the dehumidifier. In an open system air is dehumidified in a single step and the dry air is blown through ducts to ventilate the equipment involved.

Using this system it is possible to dehumidify equipment outdoors using only simple weather protection.

Status
In production for over 30 years. In service with all NATO countries plus Australia, Austria, Finland, France, Israel, Japan, Sweden and Switzerland.

Manufacturer
AB Carl Munters, PO Box 7093, S-191 07 Sollentuna, Sweden.
Tel: 46 31 490775. Fax: 46 31 494914.

The Munters dry air method in use to protect British Army Tracked Rapier fire units

The Munters dry air method in use with a Royal Swedish Air Force AJ-37 Viggen

UNITED KINGDOM

Bog-Cogs

Description

Bog-Cogs are a bolt-on device that can be added to vehicle wheels to improve performance when crossing soft terrain. When fitted to a vehicle they increase flotation and reduce the likelihood of sinking in soft ground, increase traction and increase stability.

Bog-Cogs are moulded in high performance resilient plastic and are attached to vehicle wheels using a special wheel nut and retaining assembly system. Once in place the hollow units add to the width of wheel and the serrated edges provide extra traction, flotation and stability as the tyres sink into soft ground. There is no need to remove the Bog-Cogs once soft conditions have been left behind and a fitted vehicle can continue to travel at speeds of up to 64 km/h.

On each vehicle wheel a Bog-Cog retaining assembly is fitted onto permanently fitted special wheel nuts

Cutaway example of Bog-Cog showing method of attachment

and retained by linch pins. The Bog-Cogs are then offered up to the retaining assembly and a single nut holds them in place. Four Bog-Cogs can be fitted in 5 minutes. A complete kit for a Land Rover-type vehicle consists of four Bog-Cogs (one for each wheel), four flange interfaces with seals, four retaining

assemblies with linch pins, 12 special wheel nuts and one socket spanner and bar. The shipping weight of a complete set for a Toyota Land Cruiser is 70 kg and a set can be carried with the units nested together to reduce storage space.

Bog-Cogs can be fitted to any type of wheeled vehicle and there is no limit, large or small, to the sizes that can be produced. As well as being used on all-wheel drive or all-terrain vehicles Bog-Cogs can be fitted to non-driven axles, trailers and artillery pieces.

Status

In production.

Manufacturer

Wessex (UK) plc, Unit 4, Porsham Close, Belliver Industrial Estate, Plymouth, Devon PL6 7DB, UK. Tel: 0752 766833. Fax: 0752 766811.

Airflex System

Description

Airflex environmental shelters and containers provide efficient and cost-effective long-term protection for military vehicles, weapon systems or support hardware of any configuration, even in the most hostile environment. Equipment protected by the Airflex system may be left in battle-ready condition in forward tactical areas. The system is easy to install, requires no permanent electricity, such as dehumidifiers, and is re-usable indefinitely.

Status

In production. In service with armed forces worldwide.

Manufacturer

MPE Limited, Airflex Division, Brunswick Road, Cobbs Wood Industrial Estate, Ashford, Kent TN23 1EB, UK. Tel: 0233 23404. Telex: 965227.

Airflex shelter protecting Saracen armoured personnel carrier

EPS Driclad Protection and Storage System

Description

The EPS Driclad system is the result of applied research into the causes of corrosion and deterioration of equipment during storage and in transit. It is based on the enclosure of stores or equipment in a dry and clean atmosphere contained within a flexible plastic cover.

The EPS Driclad system was accepted into British Army service in 1965 after extensive trials in Europe and the Far East lasting over two years. The system is now in service with many countries all over the world.

The re-usable covers are an effective barrier to water vapour in extreme conditions of climate,

temperature and humidity. They also provide protection against damage by chemical gases, salt-laden air, sand, dust, fungi and insects. A system can be designed by EPS Driclad for any shape.

The system comprises a dust- and moisture-proof cover with a patented EPS 'Drilok' closure, mechanical dehumidification or a desiccant and a humidity or metering device. Equipment protected by EPS Driclad requires no special building or packing material.

Maintenance requirements are greatly reduced and, in some instances, maintenance procedures become redundant. At certain locations used by the British Army only two technicians were required to keep up to 80 tanks, protected by EPS Driclad, in a state of permanent operational readiness.

Typical uses of the EPS Driclad system include the

protection and preservation of tanks, artillery, helicopters and missiles. It is also used by the Royal Navy in the laying-up of ships and the temporary shore-based protection of ships' stores. Many other items of equipment, large and small, are currently being given short-term and long-term protection against environmental attack.

Status

In production. In service with approximately 40 countries.

Manufacturer

EPS Logistics Technology Limited, Staplehurst Road, Sittingbourne, Kent ME10 1XS, UK. Tel: 0795 424433. Fax: 0795 426970.

EPS Driclad covers being used for long-term protection of tanks

EPS Driclad covers being used to protect HAWK SAMs

Armour Barpack Limited Protective Packaging

Description
One of the base materials used in the Armour Barpack range of military engineered packaging is the Texikoon system. Texikoon covers and shelters protect components and equipment, including complete tanks and aircraft, against chemical gases, sand, dust, salt-laden air, fungi and ultraviolet light. They are designed to allow easy access to the stored equipment and enable simple resealing to restore the controlled environment. They are repeatedly re-usable and cost effective. Texikoon shelters and covers can be manufactured to meet various defence specifications.

An addition to the product range is Storlina, a system which utilises Texikoon with dehumidifiers for the conversion of existing buildings into environmentally controlled warehouses. Storlina is in use by the Ministry of Defence.

Status
In production. In service with the British Armed Forces.

Manufacturer
Armour Barpack Limited, Alma Park, Grantham, Lincolnshire NG31 9SN, UK.
Tel: 0476 62323. Telex: 37551 barpak g.
Fax: 0476 64858.

Texikoon covering Sea King helicopter

Pipe Fascines

Description
Pipe Fascines are a modern development of an ancient combat engineer ploy to provide emergency crossings of gap-type obstacles and were developed to their current standard by the Royal Armament Research and Development Establishment, Christchurch (RARDE(C)). The Pipe Fascine comprises bundles of lightweight plastic pipes chained together in such a way that they take up the shape of the gap, trench or hole into which they are dropped. Vehicles can then cross the gap involved. In contrast to the earlier wood fascines used until the introduction of the Pipe Fascine, the modern unit is much lighter, more durable, does not create dams in wet gaps and can be recovered and re-used many times. It is also easier to store for long periods, is easier to handle and can withstand heavier loads.

The Pipe Fascine used with heavy armoured vehicles is the MAXI. This weighs 2500 kg and can fill a gap 5 m wide for tracked vehicles; more can be added for wider gaps. Vehicles such as the British Army's Chieftain AVRE can carry up to three Pipe Fascines and launch two simultaneously but many other vehicles, such as bulldozers or dump trucks, can carry and launch them.

There is also a MINI Pipe Fascine which weighs 210 kg. These can be carried on the sides of APCs such as the M113, and can be dropped to fill ditches or small gaps for wheeled vehicles, or used in conjunction with MAXI Pipe Fascines.

Status
In production. In service with the Canadian, Dutch, British and US armies.

Manufacturer
PD Technical Mouldings plc, Rotation House, 20 Mayday Road, Thornton Heath, Surrey CR7 7HL, UK.
Tel: 081 689 4336. Fax: 081 683 2491.

Centurion AVRE 165 crossing a MAXI Pipe Fascine

Addenda

RECOVERY VEHICLES

Unipower M Series (8 × 8) Heavy Recovery Vehicle

Description
The Unipower M Series heavy recovery vehicle is a member of the Unipower M Series 8 × 8 military logistics truck range – see entries under *Trucks, Tank Transporters* and *Materials handling equipment* for other vehicles in the M Series family.

The M Series 8 × 8 recovery vehicle was designed to meet the most demanding requirements of engineer and other units operating in forward areas. The vehicle has a specified safe towing performance using a lift-and-tow boom, including the ability to suspend-tow a casualty with a 15-tonne axle load at 1.5 m from the recovery vehicle's rear, and towing (at 30 km/h) a tank/heavy recovery vehicle grossing in excess of 115 tonnes.

The vehicle is provided with a three-man forward control all-steel welded cab. The driver's seat is adjustable for height, reach and weight while a hatch above the central passenger seat provides access to a machine gun mounting, if required.

The chassis frame bolted construction uses heat treated carbon steel and is of the open channel type with open and tubular crossmembers. Towing facilities are provided front and rear. The front suspension consists of two slipper-ended semi-elliptic parabolic springs per axle. At the rear, two fully articulating semi-elliptical multi-leaf springs are trunnion-mounted on bearings. The rear axles are located longitudinally by upper and lower radius rods and transversally by eight Panhard rods.

The main power plant can be provided to suit customer requirements. Available is a Perkins Eagle 400 TX turbocharged diesel developing 400 hp or a higher-powered Cummins KTA 600 developing 600 hp. A further option is a Cummins NTA A430 CELECT turbocharged diesel providing 430 bhp, although other similar power plants may be utilised. The power plant is coupled to a ZF Transmatic transmission with a torque converter and a ZF single-speed transfer box.

The vehicle carries three types of recovery equipment: two 25-tonne winches creating a 50-tonne combined line pull; a 30 t/m hydraulic slewing crane with a four-section telescopic boom; and lift and towing gear.

The integrated recovery equipment is mounted on a full length steel subframe. For the lift and tow gear a

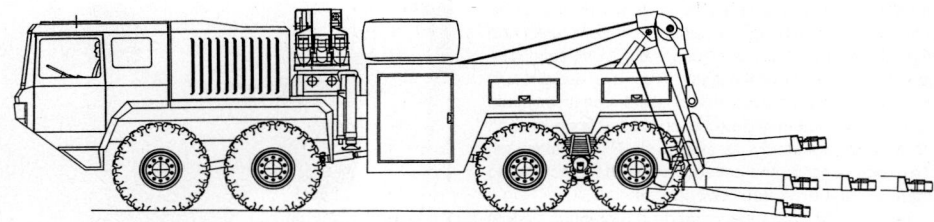

Side-view drawing of Unipower M Series (8 × 8) heavy recovery vehicle

two-piece beam, carrying a three-stage hydraulically extending underlift boom section at its rearmost extremity, is hinged at the forward end of the subframe. Luffing is controlled by hydraulic rams. The underlift boom section is stowed vertically in the travelling mode and when hydraulically unfolded is extended horizontally, as required, under the casualty. Casualty lift is achieved by lifting rams. A cross-head pivot locates the load-bearing forks fitted to the third-stage boom for secure location under the casualty. A range of fitting accessories can be supplied. The main boom extremity is fitted with twin swivelling fairleads through which the winch ropes are fed during winch operations.

The vertically inclined section of the main boom is fitted with two independently powered hydraulically extending stiff legs, each capable of operating independently and equipped with ground anchor spades for winch reaction up to 50 tonnes. The two forward-mounted two-speed hydraulic winches are each rated at 25 tonnes maximum line pull. Each drum is provided with 50 m of 24 mm diameter rope.

A 30 t/m folding hydraulic truck crane is located behind the engine, having a three-section hydraulic telescopic extending boom and vertical support legs. Maximum boom reach is 7 m.

A full range of recovery and winching accessories is carried.

Specifications
Cab seating: 1 + 2
Configuration: 8 × 8
Weight:
(unladen) 27 050 kg
(GCW, design) 140 000 kg
Length: 10.26 m
Width: 3 m
Height: 2.95 m
Ground clearance: 0.33 m
Wheelbase: 6 m
Angle of approach: 38°
Max speed: (laden) 78 km/h
Fuel capacity: 580 l
Range: 900 km
Gradient: (restart, laden) 54%
Engine: Cummins NTA A430 CELECT 6-cylinder in-line turbocharged and after-cooled diesel developing 430 hp at 1900 rpm
Transmission: ZF Transmatic 16 S 220 semi-automatic providing 16 forward and 2 reverse gears plus WSK 400 torque converter
Transfer box: ZF single-speed
Steering: ZF 8098 power-assisted
Suspension:
(front) two slipper-ended semi-elliptic parabolic springs per axle
(rear) two fully articulating semi-elliptical multi-leaf springs trunnion-mounted on bearings
Brakes: air to all axles
Tyres: 24 R 21 XL
Electrical system: 24 V
Batteries: 2 × 12 V, 150 Ah
Alternator: 90 A

Status
Pre-production.

Manufacturer
Unipower Vehicles Limited, 34 Greenhill Crescent, Watford Business Park, Watford, Hertfordshire WD1 8QU, UK.
Tel: 0923 816555. Telex: 261760 unitrk g.
Fax: 0923 228621.

TRUCKS (over 1000 kg)

High Mobility Logistic Vehicle (HMLV)

Description
The High Mobility Logistic Vehicle (HMLV) was developed by Special B Vehicles, a subsidiary of LIW, as a possible ammunition support vehicle for the G6 155 mm self-propelled howitzer (see *Jane's Armour and Artillery 1992-93* pages 583 to 586 for details). By the end of 1992 two prototypes had been produced, differing from each other only in dimensional and other slight details. The name LZN (*Lorry Zonder Naam* – truck without name) has been used for this vehicle although it is an unofficial appellation.

In its G6 ammunition supply form the HMLV is configured to carry up to 160 155 mm projectiles and 175 charges in a specially compartmented cargo body, although the maximum payload is 26 tonnes. Total mass loaded is 45 tonnes, although this can be increased to 55 tonnes. It is intended that one HMLV will provide ammunition supply support for one G6.

The HMLV uses permanent 6 × 6 drive. The air-cooled 525 hp V-12 diesel engine is the same as that used for the G6 self-propelled howitzer while other G6 components include the automatic transmission and

Second prototype of High Mobility Logistic Vehicle (HMLV)

some of the drive components. Longitudinal and transverse differential locks are provided.

The forward control cab overhangs the front of the vehicle due to the location of the fire-protected engine compartment behind the cab. The air-conditioned cab has seating for the driver and four passengers on side by side bucket seats. A two-man cab with space for bunks is projected. A roof hatch is provided on the right-hand side, while the cab can be provided with ballistic protection again 7.62 mm ball projectiles fired from 30 m at a 90° angle of impact.

The chassis frame is a relatively stiff structure formed from steel welded sections in channel and boxed configuration. Semi-elliptical springs with shock absorbers and bump stops are used for the front suspension while the rear suspension is a bogie assembly involving a stack of 21 semi-elliptical spring leaves (each side) with longitudinal arms, wishbones, shock absorbers and bump stops. The tyres have run-flat inserts.

The ammunition supply version of the HMLV carries a 18 t/m hydraulic cantilever crane mounted at the front of the cargo area. The crane has a maximum reach of 8.5 m and a maximum traverse of 280°. The crane also incorporates a 2-tonne hydraulic winch with 35 m of cable and a block and tackle. Two spare wheel carriers are located at the rear. Also provided at the rear is a tow hook with an electrical trailer socket.

A Battery Vehicle variant of the HMLV has been proposed. This will carry G6 spares and equipment, and will be allocated at the rate of one Battery Vehicle for each six-gun G6 battery.

Other roles proposed for the HMLV include a high capacity load carrier, a rapid intervention firefighting vehicle for airfields and similar establishments, a heavy recovery vehicle, a large capacity tanker, a disaster relief tender, and an oil industry support vehicle. Tractor units are also projected.

Specifications
Cab seating: 1 + 4
Configuration: 6 × 6
Weight:
(kerb) 32 000 kg
(loaded) 45 000 kg
Max load:
(as G6 support vehicle) 13 000 kg
(max payload) 26 000 kg
Length: 11.88 m
Width: 3.4 m
Height: 3.74 m
Ground clearance: 0.48 m
Track: 2.81 m
Angle of approach/departure: 35°/35°
Max speed:
(road) 80 km/h
(sand) 30 km/h
Range: 1000 km
Fuel capacity: 1000 l
Fording: 0.6 m
Gradient:
(road) 50%
(sand) 25%
Side slope: 20%

Vertical obstacle: 0.6 m
Trench: 1 m
Engine: V-12 air-cooled twin turbocharged diesel developing 525 hp at 2300 rpm
Transmission: automatic with torque converter, 6 forward and 1 reverse gears
Steering: mechanical with power-assist
Turning circle:
(kerb to kerb) 25 m
(wall to wall) 28 m
(sand) 36 m
Suspension:
(front) semi-elliptical leaf springs, shock absorbers and rubber bump stops
(rear) bogie-mounted semi-elliptical leaf springs (21) with longitudinal arms, wishbones, shock absorbers and rubber bump stops
Brakes: drum with hydro-pneumatic front and pneumatic rear; also parking, transmission and exhaust brakes
Tyres: 21.00 × 25 with run-flat inserts
Electrical system: 24 V
Batteries: 2 × 12 V, 175 Ah
Alternator: 125 A

Status
Prototypes (2).

Manufacturer
LIW, PO Box 7710, Pretoria 0001, South Africa.
Tel: 27 12 620 2494. Fax: 27 12 620 2651.

TRAILERS

Mahindra Owen 500 kg General Service Trailer

Description
The Mahindra Owen 500 kg General Service Trailer is a single-axle trailer with leaf spring suspension and mechanical overrun brakes. Welded steel construction is used for the chassis and the platform is sheet steel. The trailer is fitted with an adjustable draught eye to match pintle hook heights of 500 or 700 mm. The body panels are detachable. Two folding spring-loaded handles are provided for manual handling.

Specifications
Weight:
(empty) 350 kg
(loaded) 850 kg
Max load: 500 kg
Length: (inc tow bar, overall) 2.93 m
Width: (overall) 1.416 m
Height:
(platform) 540 mm
(panel) 455 mm
Track: 1.23 m
Tyres: 6.00 × 15 – 6 ply
Max towing speed:
(road) 80 km/h
(cross-country) 48 km/h

Mahindra Owen 500 kg general service trailer

Status
In production. In service with the Indian Army.

Manufacturer
Mahindra Engineering & Chemical Products Limited,

Mahindra Owen Division, 148 Bombay Pune Road, Pimpri, Pune-411 018, India.
Tel: 775045-6. Telex: 0146-233 MOL-IN.
Fax: 771286.

Mahindra Owen 1000 kg General Service Trailer

Description
The Mahindra Owen 1000 kg General Service Trailer is a single-axle trailer with leaf spring suspension and mechanical overrun brakes. Welded steel construction is used for the chassis and the platform is sheet steel.

The trailer is fitted with an adjustable draught eye to match pintle hook heights of 575 or 775 mm. The body panels are detachable. Two folding spring-loaded handles are provided for manual handling.

Specifications
Weight:
(empty) 780 kg
(loaded) 1780 kg

Max load: 1000 kg
Length: (inc tow bar, overall) 3.555 m
Width: (overall) 1.935 m
Height:
(platform) 700 mm
(panel) 575 mm
Track: 1.65 m
Tyres: 8.25 × 20 – 10 ply

Max towing speed:
  (road) 80 km/h
  (cross-country) 48 km/h

Status
In production. In service with the Indian Army.

Manufacturer
Mahindra Engineering & Chemical Products Limited,
Mahindra Owen Division, 148 Bombay Pune Road,
Pimpri, Pune-411 018, India.
Tel: 775045-6. Telex: 0146-233 MOL-IN.
Fax: 771286.

Mahindra Owen 1000 kg general service trailer

Mahindra Owen 500-litre Water Tanker Trailer

Description
The Mahindra Owen 500-litre Water Tanker Trailer is a single-axle trailer with leaf spring suspension and mechanical overrun brakes. Welded steel construction is used for the chassis. The trailer is fitted with an adjustable draught eye to match pintle hook heights of 500 or 700 mm. Two folding spring-loaded handles are provided for manual handling. The water tank is detachable and is provided with one manhole cover at the top and three dispensing taps at the rear.

A 1000-litre water tanker trailer is also produced.

Specifications
Weight:
  (empty) 360 kg
  (loaded) 860 kg
Length: (inc tow bar, overall) 2.835 m
Width: (overall) 1.41 m
Height: (overall) 1.32 m
Track: 1.225 m
Tyres: 6.00 × 15 – 6 ply
Max towing speed:
  (road) 80 km/h
  (cross-country) 48 km/h
Water tank inside length: 1.075 m
Water tank inside width: 965 m
Water tank inside depth: 510 mm

Mahindra Owen 500-litre water tanker trailer

Status
In production. In service with the Indian Army.

Manufacturer
Mahindra Engineering & Chemical Products Limited,

Mahindra Owen Division, 148 Bombay Pune Road, Pimpri, Pune-411 018, India.
Tel: 775045-6. Telex: 0146-233 MOL-IN.
Fax: 771286.

Mahindra Owen 1000 kg Generator Set Trailer

Description
The Mahindra Owen 1000 kg Generator Set Trailer is a single-axle trailer with leaf spring suspension and mechanical overrun brakes. Welded steel construction is used for the chassis and the platform is sheet steel. The trailer is fitted with an adjustable draught eye to match pintle hook heights of 575 or 775 mm. Two folding spring-loaded handles are provided for manual handling.

Specifications
Weight:
  (empty) 700 kg
  (loaded) 1700 kg
Max load: 1000 kg
Length: (inc tow bar, overall) 3.481 m
Width: (overall) 1.935 m
Height: (platform) 700 mm
Track: 1.65 m

Mahindra Owen 1000 kg generator set trailer

Tyres: 8.25 × 20 – 10 ply
Max towing speed:
(road) 80 km/h
(cross-country) 48 km/h

Status
In production. In service with the Indian Army.

Manufacturer
Mahindra Engineering & Chemical Products Limited,

Mahindra Owen Division, 148 Bombay Pune Road, Pimpri, Pune-411 018, India.
Tel: 775045-6. Telex: 0146-233 MOL-IN.
Fax: 771286.

Mahindra Owen 2000 kg Generator Set Trailer

Description
The Mahindra Owen 2000 kg Generator Set Trailer is a twin-axle trailer with semi-elliptical heavy duty leaf spring suspension and a dual line air brake system. The front axle uses an Ackermann steering arrangement. Welded steel construction is used for the chassis and the platform is sheet steel.

Specifications
Weight:
(empty) 1440 kg
(loaded) 3440 kg
Max load: 2000 kg
Length: (inc tow bar, overall) 6.935 m
Width: (overall) 2.1 m
Height: (platform) 750 mm
Track: 1.7 m
Tyres: 8.25 × 20 – 10 ply
Max towing speed:
(road) 72 km/h
(cross-country) 24 km/h

Status
In production. In service with the Indian Army.

Manufacturer
Mahindra Engineering & Chemical Products Limited,

Mahindra Owen 2000 kg generator set trailer

Mahindra Owen Division, 148 Bombay Pune Road, Pimpri, Pune-411 018, India.

Tel: 775045-6. Telex: 0146-233 MOL-IN.
Fax: 771286.

Mahindra Owen 7500 kg Trailer for Mobile Radar

Description
The Mahindra Owen 7500 kg Trailer for Mobile Radar is a single-axle semi low bed trailer for carrying containerised radar equipment. The trailer has semi-elliptical leaf spring suspension with twin shock absorbers. The braking system consists of a dual line air system plus a manual parking brake. Low alloy welded steel construction is used for the chassis. Removable loading ramps are provided. The loading ramps and

platform are fitted with roller tracks for loading and unloading equipment containers. The trailer has a 50 mm king pin and a 24 V electrical system. A 10 000 kg version of this trailer is produced.

Specifications
Weight:
(empty) 3500 kg
(loaded) 11 050 kg
Length: (overall) 10.175 m
Width: (overall) 2.3 m
Height: (platform) 1.165 m
Track: 1.73 m

Tyres: 9.00 × 20 – 14 ply
Electrical system: 24 V

Status
In production. In service with the Indian Air Force.

Manufacturer
Mahindra Engineering & Chemical Products Limited, Mahindra Owen Division, 148 Bombay Pune Road, Pimpri, Pune-411 018, India.
Tel: 775045-6. Telex: 0146-233 MOL-IN.
Fax: 771286.

Mahindra Owen 50-tonne Heavy Duty Tank Transporter Trailer

Description
The Mahindra Owen 50-tonne Heavy Duty Tank Transporter Trailer is a low deck independent trailer intended for on- and off-road use. The lateral articulation provided on the front axle and the lateral and longitudinal articulation provided on the rear axles give equal load distribution during off-road operations. The trailer is provided with two rows of two in-line axles at the rear and a single axle at the front. There are 24 tyres in all. The chassis is of welded steel construction while the platform is chequered steel plate. Dual line air brakes and manual parking brakes are provided.

The trailer is equipped with rear loading ramps, adjustable track guides, wheel chocks and a roller arrangement for use when winching disabled vehicles onto the platform. Spares wheels and tyres are provided. Standard equipment includes a tool box, a lashing chain, and hydraulic jacks.

Mahindra Owen 50-tonne heavy duty tank transporter trailer

Specifications
Weight:
 (empty) 18 000 kg
 (loaded) 68 000 kg
Max load: 50 000 kg
Length: (overall) 12.705 m
Width: (overall) 3.42 m

Height: (platform) 1.295 m
Wheelbase: 7.1 m
Tyres: 11.00 × 20 – 16 ply
Electrical system: 24 V

Status
In production. In service with the Indian Air Force.

Manufacturer
Mahindra Engineering & Chemical Products Limited, Mahindra Owen Division, 148 Bombay Pune Road, Pimpri, Pune-411 018, India.
Tel: 775045-6. Telex: 0146-233 MOL-IN.
Fax: 771286.

MATERIALS HANDLING EQUIPMENT

Mahindra Manitou Rough Terrain Fork-lift Trucks

Description
The Mahindra Manitou MC and MCE ranges of fork-lift trucks are manufactured in collaboration with Manitou BF of France. The MC range is intended for outdoor use and is available with 2000, 2500, 3000 and 4000 kg capacities while the MCE has both indoor and outdoor functions and is available with 2000, 2500 and 3000 kg capacities.

All trucks are fitted with a four-cylinder 45 hp diesel engine and a mechanical transmission. A duplex mast with a 3.6 m lift height is standard. Free lift and triplex masts are also available, as is a wide range of specialised attachments.

The Indian Ordnance Services have standardised on the 2000 and 3000 kg MC models.

Status
In production. In service with the Indian Ordnance Services.

Manufacturer
Mahindra Engineering & Chemical Products Limited, Mahindra Manitou Division, 148 Bombay Pune Road, Pimpri, Pune-411 018, India.
Tel: 775045-6. Telex: 0146-233 MOL-IN.
Fax: 771286.

Mahindra Manitou rough terrain fork-lift trucks awaiting delivery

FIELD FORTIFICATIONS AND RELATED EMPLACEMENTS EQUIPMENT

Fast Foxholes

Description
The increasing threat which today's 'SMART' weapons pose to ground troops and material, makes finding shelter on the battlefield imperative. Digging foxholes especially in hard or frozen terrain has always required a great deal of manpower.

The Atlas Copco 'Ground Entrenchment Foxhole Explosive System' (GE-FES patent pending) has been developed to produce a foxhole rapidly on the battlefield. Using Atlas Copco Berema Rock drill-breakers, a two-man team can rapidly drive two charge-pipes, insert the charges and blast a foxhole crater 1.8 × 0.7 × 1.8 m (l × w × d). The loose material can then be easily shovelled out.

Atlas Copco Berema Rock drills and breakers are in service with defence forces in over 30 countries.

Status
The GE-FES is in production. In service with Swedish infantry, artillery and tank battalions.

Evaluated by US Army, Belgian Engineer Corps, Dutch Engineer Corps and Miners and Sappers School, Holland.

Manufacturer
Atlas Copco Berema AB, Uddvägen 7, Box 767, Nacka, Sweden.
Tel: 46 (0)8 743 96 00. Fax: 46 (0)8 743 96 50.

Inventory

For ease of reference this is divided up into five key sections: armoured engineer vehicles, recovery vehicles (tracked and wheeled), mechanised bridges (tracked and wheeled), light vehicles and trucks.
In addition to the vehicle type, the following additional information is provided where possible: model number, cross-country payload, configuration, number delivered and the approximate delivery date. It should be noted that the total number normally includes many variants.

Abbreviations used in this section:
ABFS   amphibious bridge and ferry system
AEV   armoured engineer vehicle
ALV   airportable light vehicle
ARV   armoured recovery vehicle
AVLB   armoured vehicle-launched bridge
CEV   combat engineer vehicle
ES   entering service
LAV   Light Armored Vehicle
MB   Mercedes-Benz
PO   Phasing Out of Service
RV   recovery vehicle
RVI   Renault Vehicles Industriels
SDP   Steyr-Daimler-Puch
W   wrecker

AFGHANISTAN

Recovery vehicles
T-54/T-55 ARV

Mechanised bridges
MTU-20 AVLB
MTU AVLB

Light vehicles
UAZ-469B 600 kg (4 × 4)

Trucks
ZIL-131 3500 kg (6 × 6)
Ural-375D 4000 kg (6 × 6)

ALBANIA

Recovery vehicles
T-54/T-55 ARV

Light vehicles
UAZ-469B 600 kg (4 × 4)

Trucks
ZIL-131 3500 kg (6 × 6)

ALGERIA

Recovery vehicles
T-54/T-55 ARV (?)

Light vehicles
UAZ-469B 600 kg (4 × 4)
MB 750 kg (4 × 4) (90)

Trucks
RVI TRM 1200 1200 kg (4 × 4)
Berliet GBC 8 KT 4000 kg (6 × 6)
MB Unimog (4 × 4)
MAN 6000/10 000 kg (280)
RVI TRM 9000 9000 kg (6 × 6) (500)

ANGOLA

Recovery vehicles
T-54/T-55 (?)

Light vehicles
ENGESA EE-12 (4 × 4)
Land Rover (4 × 4)
UAZ-469B 600 kg (4 × 4)

Trucks
ENGESA EE-15 1500 kg (4 × 4)
ENGESA EE-25 2500 kg (6 × 6)
ENGESA EE-50 5000 kg (6 × 6) (255)
MB Unimog (4 × 4)

GAZ-66 2000 kg (4 × 4)
TRM 2000 2000 kg (4 × 4) (85)
ZIL-131 3500 kg (6 × 6)
Ural-375D 4000 kg (6 × 6)

ARGENTINA

Recovery vehicles
SDP 4KH 7FA SB 20 Greif ARV (10)
AMX-13 ARV (?)
VCRT ARV (trials)
AAVR7 ARV (1) (Marines)

Mechanised bridges
AMX-13 AVLB

Light vehicles
LOHR FL 500 (4 × 4)
MB 750 kg (4 × 4) (1200)

Trucks
MB (4 × 4)

AUSTRALIA

Recovery vehicles
Leopard 1 ARV (6)
LAV recovery (8 × 8)
M806A1 light ARV
Mack MC3 heavy wrecker (6 × 6)
M543/M543A1 W (6 × 6)
M816 W (6 × 6)

Mechanised bridges
Biber AVLB (5)

Light vehicles
Land Rover Defender 110 (4 × 4)
Land Rover LWB (4 × 4)
Land Rover 1000 kg (4 × 4) (PO)

Trucks
Land Rover 110 heavy duty (6 × 6) (400) (1989-91)
Ford O913 (4 × 2) (372)
Mack Model RM6866RS 8000 kg (6 × 6) (906)
MB UL 1700 L 4000 kg (4 × 4) (1295) (1982-87)

AUSTRIA

Armoured engineer vehicles
SDP 4KH 7FA AVE (18)

Recovery vehicles
SDP 4KH 7FA SB 20 Greif ARV (50)
M60/M108 W (6 × 6)

Light vehicles
SDP 700 AP (4 × 4)
VW 181 400 kg (4 × 2)
MB 750 kg (4 × 4) (1200)

Trucks
SDP Pinzgauer (4 × 4 and 6 × 6)
SDP 680 M 4500 kg (4 × 4)
SDP 680 M3 3500 kg (6 × 6)
Steyr 480 4000 kg (4 × 2)
SDP 12 M 18 5000 kg (4 × 4) (2000+)
SDP 12 M 21 5000 kg (4 × 4)
G & S LAVI—9F/2H 6000 kg (4 × 4)
G & S ZAVT—9F/1 6000 kg (4 × 4)
G & S ZA-200/1 A 10 000 kg (6 × 6)
OAF 20.320 10 000 kg (6 × 6) (410)
Berliet GBC 8 KT 4000 kg (6 × 6)

BAHRAIN

Recovery vehicles
M88A1 ARV (4)

Light vehicles
Land Rover (4 × 4)

Trucks
Bedford TM 4-4 8000 kg (4 × 4)
Oshkosh HEMET 9979 kg (8 × 8)

BANGLADESH

Recovery vehicles
Type 653 ARV
T-54/T-ARV

Light vehicles
Land Rover (4 × 4)
Mahindra (4 × 4)

Trucks
Bedford MK 4000 kg (4 × 4)

BELGIUM

Armoured engineer vehicles
Leopard 1 AEV (6)

Recovery vehicles
Leopard 1 ARV (36)
M113A1-B-REC ARV
Samson ARV
Berliet TBU 15 CLD W (6 × 6)

Mechanised bridges
Mobile Assault Bridge/Ferry (4 × 4)

Light vehicles
Iltis 500 kg (4 × 4) (2673)
Land Rover ALV 564 kg (4 × 4)
Land Rover Defender 110 (4 × 4)

Trucks
Berliet GBU 15 6000 kg (6 × 6)
MB Unimog (4 × 4)
Bedford MK 4000 kg (4 × 4)
Bedford RL 4000 kg (4 × 4) (PO)
MAN 11.136 HA 5000 kg (4 × 4) (3000)
MAN 630 5000 kg (4 × 4) (PO)
Volvo N10/N12 (6 × 6) (1228)
MAN (8 × 8) (82)

BELIZE

Light vehicles
Land Rover (4 × 4)

Trucks
Bedford MK 4000 kg (4 × 4)

BENIN

Trucks
ACMAT (4 × 4)

BOLIVIA

Recovery vehicles
SDP 4KH 7FA SB 20 Greif ARV
M578 ARV

Trucks
ENGESA EE-25 2500 kg (6 × 6)
M35/M44 2268 kg (6 × 6)

BOTSWANA

Light vehicles
Land Rover (4 × 4)

Trucks
TJ 10 000 kg (82) (1990-91)

BRAZIL

Recovery vehicles
M548 ARV
AAVR7 ARV (1) (Marines)

Bridging systems
XLP-10 AVLB

Light vehicles
X-12 Gurgel series (4 × 2)
ENGESA EE-34 (4 × 4)

Trucks
ENGESA EE-15 1500 kg (4 × 4)
ENGESA EE-25 2500 kg (6 × 6)
ENGESA EE-50 5000 kg (6 × 6)
TEREX UAI M1-50 5000 kg (6 × 6)
MB (4 × 4 and 6 × 6)
M34/M44 2268 kg (6 × 6)

BRUNEI

Recovery vehicles
Samson ARV (1)
Reynolds Boughton RV (4 × 4) (6+)

Light vehicles
Land Rover ALV 564 kg (4 × 4)

Trucks
Bedford MK 4000 kg (4 × 4)

BULGARIA

Recovery vehicles
T-54/T-55 ARV
MTP-1 ARV

Mechanised bridges
BLG-67 AVLB
TMM (6 × 6)
TMM modified (6 × 6)

Light vehicles
UAZ-469B 600 kg (4 × 4)

Trucks
ZIL-157 2500 kg (6 × 6)
ZIL-131 2500 kg (6 × 6)

BURKINA FASO

Light vehicles
Auverland/SAMO (4 × 4)

Trucks
ACMAT (4 × 4)
Pegaso 3045 3000 kg (4 × 4) (33)

BURMA

Light vehicles
Mitsubishi (4 × 4)

BURUNDI

Light vehicles
Auverland/SAMO (4 × 4)

Citroen A FAF (4 × 4)

CAMBODIA

Recovery vehicles
T-54/T-55 ARV

Light vehicles
UAZ-469B 600 kg (4 × 4)

Trucks
ZIL-157 2500 kg (6 × 6)
ZIL-151 2500 kg (6 × 6)

CAMEROON

Light vehicles
Iltis 500 kg (4 × 4)
Auverland/SAMO (4 × 4)

Trucks
ACMAT (4 × 4)

CANADA

Armoured engineer vehicles
Leopard AEV (9)
M113 Engineering Specially Equipped Vehicle (70)

Recovery vehicles
Leopard 1 ARV Taurus (8)
M578 ARV
Huskey repair vehicle (6 × 6) (27)
Bison (8 × 8) MRTV (16)
MAN (6 × 6)
Percheron RV (6 × 6) (124)

Mechanised bridges
Biber AVLB (6)

Light vehicles
Iltis 500 kg (4 × 4) (2500) (1984-85)

Trucks
Chevrolet 1250 kg (4 × 4) (3484)
Bombardier 2500 kg (6 × 6) (2765)
Steyr 8000 kg (4 × 4)
MAN 10 000 kg (8 × 8) (42)
Percheron 10 000 kg (6 × 6) (1200) (1988-91)
IVECO FIAT 40-10 WM 1500 kg (4 × 4) (on order) (2250)

CENTRAL AFRICAN REPUBLIC

Recovery vehicles
T-54/T-55 (?)

Light vehicles
Auverland/SAMO (4 × 4)

CHAD

Light vehicles
Beijing BJ-212/212A (4 × 4)
Auverland/SAMO (4 × 4)

Trucks
ACMAT (4 × 4)
M35/M44 2268 kg (6 × 6)

CHILE

Recovery vehicles
AMX-13 ARV (?)

Trucks
ENGESA EE-15 1500 kg (4 × 4)
ENGESA EE-25 2500 kg (6 × 6)
MB Unimog (4 × 4)
Pegaso 3045 3000 kg (4 × 4)

CHINA, PEOPLE'S REPUBLIC

Recovery vehicles
Type 653/653A ARV
T-54/T-55 ARV

Mechanised bridges
Type 84 AVLB
TMM (6 × 6)
KMM (6 × 6)
Type 84A heavy mechanised bridge

Light vehicles
Beijing BJ-212/212A (4 × 4)

Trucks
M34/M44 2268 kg (6 × 6)
M809 4536 kg (6 × 6)
NJ-230 (4 × 4)
Berliet GBC 8 KT 4000 kg (6 × 6)
Berliet GBU 15 6000 kg (6 × 6)
SDP 1291.280.4 × 4 M 6000 kg (4 × 4)
SDP 1491.6 × 6 M 10 7000 kg (6 × 6)
CA-30 2500 kg (6 × 6)
Dong Feng EQ2080E4DY 2500 kg (6 × 6)
Dong Feng EQ2100E 3500 kg (6 × 6)
Jiefang CA-10 3540 kg (4 × 2)
Jiefang CA-141 5000 kg (4 × 2)
Jiefang CA-1091 5000 kg (4 × 4)
EQD142 6400 kg (4 × 2)
Hongyan CQ 261 8250 kg (6 × 6)
ZIL-157 2500 kg (6 × 6)
ZIL-151 2500 kg (6 × 6)

COLOMBIA

Trucks
ENGESA EE-15 1500 kg (4 × 4)
ENGESA EE-25 2500 kg (6 × 6)
CUCV (4 × 4)

COMMONWEALTH OF INDEPENDENT STATES

Armoured engineer vehicles
IMR-2 CEV (T-72 chassis)
IMR CEV (T-55 chassis)
BAT-2 CEV
IRM engineer reconnaissance vehicle
MT-LB engineer vehicle

Recovery vehicles
BREM-1 ARV (T-72 chassis)
M1977 ARV
T-54/T-55 ARV
BTR-50PK (B) amphibious ARV
BMP-1 light ARV
MTP technical support vehicle (BTR-50P)
MTP-LB technical support vehicle
Ural-375D RV (6 × 6)
Ural-4320 RV (6 × 6)
KET-L RV (6 × 6)

Mechanised bridges
MTU-72 AVLB
MT-55 AVLB
MTU-20 AVLB
MTU AVLB
PMM-2 ABFS

Light vehicles
LuAZ-967M (4 × 4)
UAZ-469B 600 kg (4 × 4)
UAZ-452D 800 kg (4 × 4)
UAZ-3251 800 kg (4 × 4)

Trucks
GAZ-51 2000 kg (4 × 2)
GAZ-63 2000 kg (4 × 4)
GAZ-66 2000 kg (4 × 4)
ZIL-157 2500 kg (4 × 4)
ZIL-151 2500 kg (4 × 4)
GAZ-53 3000 kg (4 × 2)
ZIL-131 3500 kg (6 × 6)
Ural-375 4000 kg (6 × 6)
Ural-4320 4500 kg (6 × 6)
Ural-377 7500 kg (6 × 6)

YaAZ-214 7000 kg (6 × 6)
KrAZ-214 7000 kg (6 × 6)
KrAZ-255B 7500 kg (6 × 6)
KamAZ-5320 8000 kg (6 × 4)
KrAZ-260 9000 kg (6 × 6)
KrAZ-257 12 000 kg (6 × 6)
ZIL-135 (8 × 8)
MAZ-543 (8 × 8)

CONGO

Recovery vehicles
T-54/T-55 AERV (?)

Light vehicles
Auverland/SAMO (4 × 4)

CUBA

Recovery vehicles
T-54/T-55 ARV

Mechanised bridges
MTU-20 AVLB
TMM (6 × 6)
KMM (6 × 6)

Light vehicles
UAZ-469B 600 kg (4 × 4)
GAZ-69/69A 500 kg (4 × 4)

Trucks
GAZ-51 2000 kg (4 × 2)
GAZ-63 2000 kg (4 × 4)
GAZ-66 2000 kg (4 × 4)
ZIL-157 2500 kg (6 × 6)
ZIL-151 2500 kg (6 × 6)

CYPRUS

Recovery vehicles
AMX-30D ARV (2) (1988/1990)
Steyr Type 19S25 (4 × 4) RV
Steyr Type 32S29 (6 × 6) RV

Trucks
MB Unimog
SDP 14 M 14 8000 kg (4 × 4)
Steyr 24 M 12 000 kg (6 × 6)

CZECHOSLOVAKIA

Recovery vehicles
VT-55A ARV
MT-55 ARV
WPT-TOPAS ARV (OT-62A chassis)
VPV ARV (BMP-1 chassis)
AD-90 (6 × 6)

Mechanised bridges
MT-55A AVLB
AM-50 (6 × 6)

Light vehicles
UAZ-469B 600 kg (4 × 4)

Trucks
Praga V3S 3000 kg (6 × 6)
BAZ SNA 4000 kg (6 × 6)
ZIL-131 3500 kg (6 × 6)
Ural-375D 4000 kg (6 × 6)
Tatra 813 7900 kg (8 × 8)
Tatra 815 8000 kg (8 × 8)
Tatra 148 14 580 kg (6 × 6)
Tatra 138 11 850 kg (6 × 6)

Note: This country split into two on 1st January 1993 and it is assumed that this equipment is used by both countries. On the split-up the equipment was split on the ratio of 3:2 (Czech Republic and Slovak Federal Republic)

DENMARK

Recovery vehicles
Centurion ARV (16)
M578 ARV

Mechanised bridges
Centurion AVLB (6)

Light vehicles
VW 181 400 kg (4 × 2)
MB 750 kg (4 × 4) (1300)

Trucks
Bedford RL 4000 kg (4 × 4)
MB Unimog (4 × 4)
MAN 8.136 FAE 3000 kg (4 × 4) (725) (1985-90)

DJIBOUTI

Trucks
ACMAT (4 × 4)
HMMWV 1542 kg (4 × 4) (10)
M34/M44 2268 kg (6 × 6)
M929A1 4536 kg (6 × 6) (89)

DOMINICAN REPUBLIC

Recovery vehicles
AMX-13 ARV (?)

Trucks
M34/M44 2268 kg (6 × 6)

ECUADOR

Recovery vehicles
AMX-13 ARV (?)

Light vehicles
M151 362 kg (4 × 4)

Trucks
M34/M44 2268 kg (6 × 6)

EGYPT

Recovery vehicles
T-54/T-55 ARV
M88A1 ARV (177)
M113 ARV
M578 ARV (43)
BMR 3560.55 ARV (6 × 6)

Mechanised bridges
MTU-20 AVLB
MTU AVLB
KMM (6 × 6)

Light vehicles
M151 (4 × 4)
Jeep (CJ & YJ) (4 × 4)
Santana Model 88 500 kg (4 × 4)
Santana Model 109 1000 kg (4 × 4)
UAZ-469B 600 kg (4 × 4)
GAZ-69/69A 500 kg (4 × 4)
UAZ-452D 800 kg (4 × 4)
Land Rover 1000 kg (4 × 4)
Toyota Land Cruiser (4 × 4)

Trucks
Jeep AM 720 1135 kg (4 × 4)
Jeep J-20 (4 × 4)
MB Unimog (4 × 4)
GAZ-66 2000 kg (4 × 4)
ZIL-131 3500 kg (6 × 6)
Ural-375D 4000 kg (6 × 6)
NASR 4000 kg (4 × 4)
RVI TRM 9000 9000 kg (6 × 6) (50)
Pegaso 3046 3000 kg (4 × 4) (9000+)
M923A2 4540 kg (6 × 6)
Steyr 17 M 29 7000 kg (4 × 4)
Oshkosh HEMET 9979 kg (8 × 8)
Steyr 24 M 12 000 kg (6 × 6)

EL SALVADOR

Recovery vehicles
AMX-13 (?)

Light vehicles
M37 680 kg (4 × 4)

Trucks
M35/M44 2268 kg (6 × 6)
M809 4536 kg (6 × 6)

EQUATORIAL GUINEA

Recovery vehicles
T-54/T-55 ARV (?)

ETHIOPIA

Recovery vehicles
T-54/T-55 ARV (?)

Trucks
ZIL-157 2500 kg (6 × 6)
ZIL-151 2500 kg (6 × 6)

FINLAND

Recovery vehicles
T-54/T-55 ARV

Mechanised bridges
MTU-20 AVLB
MTU AVLB

Light vehicles
GAZ-69/GAZ-69A 500 kg (4 × 4)

Trucks
GAZ-66 2000 kg (4 × 4)
ZIL-131 3500 kg (6 × 6)
SISU A-45 3000 kg (4 × 4)
SISU SA-130 VK 6500 kg (4 × 4)
SISU SA-241 10 000 kg (6 × 6)
Scania SBA 111 4500 kg (4 × 4) (33)

FRANCE

Armoured engineer vehicles
AMX-30 EBG (total requirement 126)
AMX-13 VCG (PO)

Recovery vehicles
AMX-30D ARV (134)
TRM 10 000 CLD RV (6 × 6)
Berliet TBC 8 KT W (6 × 6)
Berliet TBU 15 CLD W (6 × 6)
Brimot TASE RV (4 × 4) (40 required)

Mechanised bridges
AMX-13 AVLB
PAA (4 × 4) (55) (1974-78)
Gillois Series 2 (60)
Gillois Series 1 (4 × 4) (PO)
EFA (4 × 4) (80 being delivered)

Light vehicles
Hotchkiss M201 400 kg (4 × 4) (PO)
LOHR FL 500 500 kg (4 × 4) (300)
Citroen Mehari (4 × 2)
Peugeot P4 750 kg (4 × 4) (12 500) (1983-92)
VW 181 400 kg (4 × 2)
Auverland Type A3 (4 × 4)

Trucks
Peugeot 504 Dangel 1110 kg (4 × 4)
ACMAT (4 × 4)
RVI TRM 1200 1200 kg (4 × 4) (4000+)
SUMB MH 600 BS 1500 kg (4 × 4)
SUMB MH 600 BS 3000 kg (4 × 4)
Simca-Unic F 594 WML 3000 kg (4 × 4)
RVI TRM 2000 2000 kg (4 × 4) (12 000, total requirement)
RVI TRM 4000 4000 kg (4 × 4) (7000)

Berliet GBC 8 KT 4000 kg (6 × 6)
Berliet GBU 15 6000 kg (6 × 6)
RVI TRM 10 000 10 000 kg (5000, total requirement)
MB Unimog
ACMAT 6000 kg (8 × 8)

GABON

Light vehicles
Peugeot P4 750 kg (4 × 4)

Trucks
ACMAT (4 × 4)
ENGESA EE-15 1500 kg (4 × 4)
ENGESA EE-25 2500 kg (6 × 6)

GAMBIA, THE

Light vehicles
M151 (4 × 4)

Trucks
ACMAT (4 × 4)

GERMANY

Armoured engineer vehicles
Pionierpanzer 2 Dachs (137)
Leopard 1 AEV (36)

Recovery vehicles
Buffel ARV (75, delivery from 1991)
Leopard 1 ARV (440)
M88A1 ARV (2)
Faun RTF 15 M RV (4 × 4)
Faun RTF 30-3 M RV (6 × 6)

Mechanised bridges
Biber AVLB (105)
M48 AVLB
M3 (4 × 4) (4 for trials)
M2 (4 × 4)

Light vehicles
Kraka 870 kg (4 × 2) (762) (PO)
VW 181 400 kg (4 × 2)
VW Iltis 500 kg (4 × 4) (8470)
MB 750 kg (4 × 4) (12 000)

Trucks
MB Unimog 2000 kg (4 × 4) (17 000)
MB L 508 PG MA 2150 kg (4 × 2)
Magirus 5000 kg (7000)
MB Model 1017 5450 kg (4 × 2)
MB Model 1017 5450 kg (4 × 4)
MAN 5000 kg (4 × 4) ⎫
MAN 7000 kg (6 × 6) ⎬ (8615)
MAN 10 000 kg (8 × 8) ⎭
MAN 7000 kg (4 × 2) (1500)
MAN 10 000 kg (6 × 4) (2500)
MAN 6300 5000 kg (4 × 4) (PO)

GHANA

Recovery vehicles
Steyr Type 19S25 (4 × 4) RV
Steyr Type 32S29 (6 × 6) RV

Trucks
SDP Pinzgauer
Steyr 17 M 29 7000 kg (4 × 4)

GREECE

Recovery vehicles
Leopard 1 ARV (4)
M88A1 ARV (27)
AMX-30D ARV (14)

Light vehicles
MB 750 kg (4 × 4) (5000)
Namco Pony (4 × 2)

M151 362 kg (4 × 4)
M37 680 kg (4 × 4)

Trucks
M35/M44 2268 kg (6 × 6)
SDP 680 M 4500 kg (4 × 4)
SDP 680 M3 3500 kg (6 × 6)
SDP 14 M 14 8000 kg (4 × 4)

GRENADA

Trucks
CUCV (4 × 4)

GUATEMALA

Light vehicles
M151 362 kg (4 × 4)
MB 750 kg (4 × 4) (50)

Trucks
M35/M44 2268 kg (6 × 6)

GUYANA

Light vehicles
Land Rover ALV 564 kg (4 × 4)

HAITI

Recovery vehicles
Commando V-150 ARV (4 × 4)

Trucks
M715 1360 kg (4 × 4)
M35/M44 2268 kg (6 × 6)

HONDURAS

Trucks
CUCV (4 × 4)
M35/M44 2268 kg (4 × 4)
M809 4536 kg (6 × 6)

HUNGARY

Recovery vehicles
T-54/T-55 ARV

Mechanised bridges
BLG-60 AVLB
MTU AVLB
TMM (6 × 6)

Light vehicles
UAZ-469B 600 kg (4 × 4)

Trucks
Robur 1800 A 1800 kg (4 × 4)
Csepel D-566 5000 kg (6 × 6)
Csepel D-564 4000 kg (4 × 4)

INDIA

Armoured engineer vehicles
Combat Engineer Tractor (15)

Recovery vehicles
T-54/T-55 ARV
WZT-3 ARV

Mechanised bridges
MT-55 AVLB
BLG-60 AVLB
MTU-20 AVLB
Kartik AVLB
AM-50 (6 × 6)

Light vehicles
Mahindra (4 × 4)

Jonga (4 × 4)
Carrier 750 kg (4 × 4)

Trucks
MAN 630 5000 kg (4 × 4)
Shaktiman 4000 kg (4 × 4)
Scania SBAT 111S 6000 kg (6 × 6) (600)
Tatra 813 7900 kg (8 × 8)
Tatra 815 8000 kg (8 × 8)

INDONESIA

Recovery vehicles
AMX-13 ARV (2)
T-54/T-55 ARV

Mechanised bridges
AMX-13 AVLB

Light vehicles
SDP 700 AP (4 × 4) (1000)
Nissan Q4W73 750 kg (4 × 4) (600)
DAF 66 YA 400 kg (4 × 2) (150)
Land Rover ALV 564 kg (4 × 4) (812)
M151 362 kg (4 × 4)

Trucks
MB Unimog (4 × 4)
SDP 680 M 4500 kg (4 × 4) (750)
Bedford MK 4000 kg (4 × 4)
Steyr 17 M 29 7000 kg (4 × 4) (200+)

IRAN

Recovery vehicles
Chieftain ARV
M578 ARV

Mechanised bridges
Chieftain AVLB (14)

Light vehicles
UAZ-469B 600 kg (4 × 4)
Land Rover (4 × 4)
Land Rover 1000 kg (4 × 4)

Trucks
GAZ-66 2000 kg (4 × 4)
M34/M44 2268 kg (6 × 6)

IRAQ

Recovery vehicles
Type 653 ARV
T-54/T-55 ARV
Chieftain ARV
ENGESA EE-11 repair and recovery (6 × 6)

Mechanised bridges
MT-55 AVLB
BLG-60 AVLB (24+)

Light vehicles
Land Rover (4 × 4)
UAZ-469B 600 kg (4 × 4)

Trucks
GAZ-66 2000 kg (4 × 4)
Ural-375D 4000 kg (6 × 6)
MB Unimog (4 × 4)
Scania (4 × 4)
Berliet GBC 8KT 4000 kg (6 × 6)
W 50 LA/A 3000 kg (4 × 4)
L 60 LA/PVB 6200 kg (4 × 4)

IRELAND

Recovery vehicles
Berliet TBU 15 CLD W (6 × 6)

Light vehicles
Land Rover (4 × 4)
Land Rover Defender 110 (4 × 4)

Trucks
ACMAT (4 × 4)
Bedford MK 4000 kg (4 × 4)
Bedford RL 4000 kg (4 × 4)
MAN 6000 kg (4 × 4)

ISRAEL

Recovery vehicles
T-54/T-55 ARV
M88A1 ARV (30)
Centurion Mk 2 ARV

Mechanised bridges
MTU-20 AVLB
MTU AVLB
MAB/F (4 × 4)
M48 AVLB

Light vehicles
M151 362 kg (4 × 4)
M-242 540 kg (6 × 6)

Trucks
M-462 ABIR 1800 kg (4 × 4)
M-325 Commandcar 1800 kg (4 × 4)
CUCV (4 × 4)
M715 1360 kg (4 × 4)
M35/M44 2268 kg (6 × 6)
M54 4536 kg (6 × 6)
Oshkosh HEMET 9979 kg (8 × 8)

ITALY

Armoured engineer vehicles
Leopard 1 AEV (40)
M113 Combat Engineer Support Vehicle

Recovery vehicles
Leopard 1 ARV (69)
IVECO FIAT 6605 RV (6 × 6)

Mechanised bridges
Biber AVLB (64)

Light vehicles
FIAT AR-59 500 kg (4 × 4)
SDP 700 AP (4 × 4)
Fresia F18 400 kg (4 × 4)
FIAT Campagnola 1107AD 750 kg (4 × 4)

Trucks
Leoncino 1000 kg (4 × 4)
CL 51 1800 kg (4 × 4)
IVECO FIAT 40-10 WM 1500 kg (4 × 4) (1300+)
IVECO FIAT 75-14 WM 2500 kg (4 × 4)
IVECO FIAT 90-17 WM 4000 kg (4 × 4)
IVECO FIAT 6601 4000 kg (4 × 4)
IVECO FIAT 6602 6000 kg (4 × 4)
IVECO FIAT 6607 CM 6000 kg (6 × 6)
IVECO FIAT 6605 (6 × 6)

JAMAICA

Light vehicles
Land Rover ALV 564 kg (4 × 4)

Trucks
CUCV (4 × 4)
M809 4536 kg (6 × 6)

JAPAN

Armoured engineer vehicles
Type 67 AEV
Type 75 armoured dozer

Recovery vehicles
Type 90 ARV
Type 78 ARV
Type 70 ARV
Type 73 RV (6 × 6)
Model FW415M1 RV (6 × 6)
Type 73 light wrecker (6 × 6)

Mechanised bridges
Type 67 AVLB
Type 70 pontoon bridge (4 × 4)
Type 81 (6 × 6)

Light vehicles
Mitsubishi (4 × 4)
Nissan Q4W73 750 kg (4 × 4)
Toyota 2FQ15L 750 kg (4 × 4)

Trucks
Type 73 2000 kg (4 × 4)
Isuzu 2500 kg (4 × 4)
Isuzu 2500 kg (6 × 6)
Toyota 2500 kg (6 × 6)
Type 73 3500 kg (6 × 6)
Hino 4000 kg (6 × 6)
Mitsubishi W121P 6000 kg (6 × 6)
Mitsubishi FW415 7000 kg (6 × 6)
Mitsubishi FW115 10 000 kg (6 × 6)
Type 74 10 000 kg (6 × 6)

JORDAN

Recovery vehicles
Chieftain ARV
Centurion Mk 2 ARV
M578 ARV
M88A1 ARV (30)

Light vehicles
Land Rover (4 × 4)

Trucks
M35/M44 2268 kg (6 × 6)
M809 4536 kg (6 × 6)

KENYA

Recovery vehicles
Vickers ARV (7)

Light vehicles
Land Rover (4 × 4)

Trucks
MB Unimog (4 × 4)
Bedford MK 4000 kg (4 × 4)

KOREA, NORTH

Recovery vehicles
T-54/T-55 ARV

Light vehicles
UAZ-469A 600 kg (4 × 4)

Trucks
Victory-58 (4 × 4)
Isuzu (6 × 6)

KOREA, SOUTH

Recovery vehicles
M47 ARV
K-1 ARV (trials)
M88A1 ARV (38)
KIFV ARV
AAVR7 ARV (3) (Marines)
KM502 W (6 × 6)
M816 W (6 × 6)

Mechanised bridges
K-1 AVLB (1) (trials)

Light vehicles
M151 362 kg (4 × 4)
Nissan Q4W73 750 kg (4 × 4)
Toyota 2FQ15L 750 kg (4 × 4)
KM41 series (4 × 4)

Trucks
KM45 family 1530 kg (4 × 4)
KM25 family 2500 kg (6 × 6)

KM50 family 5000 kg (6 × 6)
M35/M44 2268 kg (6 × 6)
M54 4536 kg (6 × 6)
M809 4536 kg (6 × 6)
Oshkosh HEMET 9979 kg (8 × 8)

KUWAIT

Exact status of Kuwaiti vehicles is uncertain.

Recovery vehicles
M88A1 ARV (10 + 44)

Light vehicles
Jeep (YJ) (4 × 4)
MB 750 kg (4 × 4) (400)
Land Rover Defender (4 × 4)

Trucks
MB Unimog (4 × 4)
Steyr 5000 kg (4 × 4)

LEBANON

Recovery vehicles
AMX-13 ARV (18)
M113 ARV

Light vehicles
Land Rover (4 × 4)

Trucks
M35/M44 2268 kg (6 × 6)
M809 4536 kg (6 × 6)

LIBERIA

Light vehicles
M151 362 kg (4 × 4)

Trucks
CUCV (4 × 4)
M35/M44 2268 kg (6 × 6)
M809 4536 kg (6 × 6)

LIBYA

Recovery vehicles
T-54/T-55 ARV

Light vehicles
UAZ-469B 600 kg (4 × 4)
Land Rover APV 564 kg (4 × 4)
Land Rover

Trucks
GAZ-66 2000 kg (4 × 4)
ENGESA EE-25 2500 kg (6 × 6)
Ural-375D 4000 kg (6 × 6)
MB Unimog
IVECO FIAT 6605 (6 × 6)

LUXEMBOURG

Light vehicles
MB 750 kg (4 × 4) (38)
Land Rover 1000 kg (4 × 4) (57)

Trucks
HMMWV 1542 kg (4 × 4) (29)
MAN (4 × 4 and 6 × 6)

MADAGASCAR

Light vehicles
Auverland/SAMO (4 × 4)

MALAYSIA

Recovery vehicles
SIBMAS ARV (6 × 6) (24)
Volvo F10 RV (4 × 4) (30)

Light vehicles
Land Rover (4 × 4)

Trucks
Volvo 4140 (4 × 4)
Volvo 4140 (6 × 6)
Stonefield (4 × 4) (1983-86)
Bedford RL 4000 kg (4 × 4)
MB (4 × 4)

MALTA

Light vehicles
Land Rover (4 × 4)

Trucks
Bedford RL 4000 kg (4 × 4)

MONGOLIA

Recovery vehicles
T-54/T-55 ARV

Light vehicles
UAZ-469 600 kg (4 × 4)

Trucks
Ural-375D 4000 kg (6 × 6)

MOROCCO

Recovery vehicles
SDP 4KH 7FA SB 20 Greif ARV (11)
T-54/T-55 ARV (?)
M578 ARV
M88A1 ARV (18)

Light vehicles
Santana Model 88 500 kg (4 × 4)
Santana Model 109 1000 kg (4 × 4)

Trucks
ACMAT (4 × 4)
RVI TRM 1200 1200 kg (4 × 4)
RVI TRM 2000 2000 kg (4 × 4) (190)
RVI TRM 9000 9000 kg (6 × 6) (1500)
Berliet GBC 8 KT 4000 kg (6 × 6)
MB Unimog (4 × 4)
Pegaso 3046 3000 kg (4 × 4)
Pegaso 7323 6000 kg (6 × 6)
M35/M44 2268 kg (6 × 6)
ACMAT 6000 kg (8 × 8)

MOZAMBIQUE

Recovery vehicles
T-54/T-55 ARV (?)

Light vehicles
UAZ-469 600 kg (4 × 4)
Jonga (4 × 4) (200)

Trucks
MB Unimog (4 × 4)
Ural-375D 4000 kg (6 × 6)
SAMIL 20 2000 kg (4 × 4) (4)
SAMIL 50 5000 kg (4 × 4) (30)

NAMIBIA

Trucks
TRM 2000 2000 kg (4 × 4) (50)

NETHERLANDS

Armoured engineer vehicles
Leopard 1 AEV (25)

Recovery vehicles
Leopard 1 ARV (52)
Buffel ARV (25) (delivery from 1991)
M113 ARV

M578 ARV
DAF YBZ 3300 DKX (6 × 6) HRV (255) (1991-93)
DAF YB 616/626 RV (6 × 6) (266) (PO)

Mechanised bridges
Biber AVLB (25)

Light vehicles
VW 181 400 kg (4 × 2)
MB 750 kg (4 × 4) (3195)
DAF 66 YA 400 kg (4 × 2) (PO)
Land Rover ALV 564 kg (4 × 4)
Land Rover Defender 110 (4 × 4)
M151 362 kg (4 × 4)

Trucks
DAF YA 314 3000 kg (4 × 4) (PO)
DAF YA 4442 DNT 4000 kg (4 × 4) (5125) (1986-93)
DAF YA 4440 4000 kg (4 × 4) (7250) (1977-83)
DAF YA 5444 DNT 5000 kg (4 × 4)
DAF YA 5441/5442 5000 kg (4 × 4)
DAF YA 2300 DHTD 7000 kg (6 × 6) (65) (NATO)
DAF YAZ 2300 10 000 kg (6 × 6) (1400+)
Bedford MK 4000 kg (4 × 4)

NEW ZEALAND

Light vehicles
Land Rover V8 750 kg (4 × 4) (567)

Trucks
MB U 1300 L 1500 kg (4 × 4) (210)
MB UL 1700 L 4000 kg (4 × 4) (412)
MB 2228/4 8000 kg (6 × 4) (118)
Bedford RL 4000 kg (4 × 4)

NICARAGUA

Recovery vehicles
T-54/T-55 ARV

Light vehicles
UAZ-469 600 kg (4 × 4)

Trucks
Pegaso 3045 3000 kg (4 × 4)
Ural-375D 4000 kg (4 × 4)

NIGERIA

Recovery vehicles
SDP 4KH 7FA SB 20 Greif ARV (15)
T-54/T-55 ARV (?)
Vickers ARV (10+)
Steyr Type 19S25 (4 × 4) RV
Steyr Type 32S29 (6 × 6) RV

Mechanised bridges
MTU-20 AVLB
Vickers AVLB (12+)

Light vehicles
Land Rover (4 × 4)
SDP 700 AP (4 × 4)

Trucks
SDP Pinzgauer
SDP 680 M 4500 kg (4 × 4)
MB Unimog (4 × 4)
Steyr 14 M 14 8000 kg (4 × 4)

NORWAY

Recovery vehicles
Leopard 1 ARV (6)
M88A1 ARV (3)
M578 ARV
Scania P113 HK (6 × 6)

Mechanised bridges
Leguan (8 × 8) (26)

Light vehicles
Land Rover (4 × 4)

MB 750 kg (4 × 4) (3500)

Trucks
Scania (4 × 4/6 × 6) (1700) (1986-94)

OMAN

Recovery vehicles
Challenger ARV (4) (1995-96)
Samson (3)
M88A1
Reynolds Boughton 6 t (4 × 4)

Light vehicles
Jeep (CJ) (4 × 4)
Iltis 500 kg (4 × 4)
MB 750 kg (4 × 4)

Trucks
SDP Pinzgauer (6 × 6) (95)
MAN 6000/10 000 kg (95)
Bedford RL 4000 kg (4 × 4) (PO)
Bedford TM 4-4 8000 kg (4 × 4)

PAKISTAN

Recovery vehicles
Type 653 ARV
T-54/T-55 ARV
M88A1 ARV (50)

Mechanised bridges
M48 AVLB
M47M AVLB (trials)

Light vehicles
Beijing BJ-212/212A (4 × 4)
Nispak 400 kg (4 × 4)
M151 362 kg (4 × 4) (1000+)

Trucks
MB Unimog (4 × 4)
IVECO FIAT 40-10 WM 1500 kg (4 × 4) (2200)
M880 series 1133 kg (4 × 4 and 4 × 2)
M35/M44 2268 kg (6 × 6)
RL 4000 kg (4 × 4)
M809 4536 kg (6 × 6)
MB 2028A 10 000 kg (6 × 6)
Steyr 5000 kg (4 × 4)

PANAMA

Trucks
CUCV (4 × 4)
M35/M44 2268 kg (6 × 6)
M809 4536 kg (6 × 6)

PAPUA NEW GUINEA

Light vehicles
Land Rover (4 × 4)

PERU

Recovery vehicles
AMX-13 ARV (?)
T-54/T-55 ARV (?)

Light vehicles
M151 362 kg (4 × 4)

Trucks
MB Unimog (4 × 4)
Pegaso 3046 3000 kg (4 × 4)
MAN 6000/10 000 kg (165)

PHILIPPINES

Recovery vehicles
M578 ARV
M816 W (6 × 6) (36)

Light vehicles
Delta Explorer (4 × 4)
M151 362 kg (4 × 4)

Trucks
CM-125 1250 kg (4 × 4)
HMMWV 1542 kg (4 × 4)
M35/M44 2268 kg (6 × 6)
M809 4536 kg (6 × 6)

POLAND

Armoured engineer vehicles
IWT CEV (T-55 chassis)
MT-LB Engineer Reconnaissance Vehicle

Recovery vehicles
T-54/T-55 ARV
WZT-3 ARV
WPT-TOPAS ARV
MT-LB technical support vehicle

Mechanised bridges
BLG-67M2 AVLB
SMT-1 (6 × 6)

Light vehicles
UAZ-468B 600 kg (4 × 4)

Trucks
Lubin-51 (4 × 2)
Robur LO 1800 A 1800 kg (4 × 4)
Star 66 2500 kg (6 × 6)
Star 266 3500 kg (6 × 6)
Star 244 5000 kg (4 × 4)

PORTUGAL

Recovery vehicles
M88A1 (5)

Light vehicles
Citroën A FAF (4 × 4)
Bravia Comando Mk II 605 kg (4 × 4)
UMM Alter (4 × 4)
UMM 490 1000 kg (4 × 4)
M151 362 kg (4 × 4)
HUGO 1500 kg (6 × 6) (6)

Trucks
Bravia Gazela 1134 kg (4 × 4)
MWG 1500 kg (6 × 6)
Bravia Leopardo 3000 kg (6 × 6)
IVECO FIAT 90-17 WM 4000 kg (4 × 4)
Bravia Pantera 6000 kg (6 × 6)
Bravia Elephant 10 000 kg (6 × 6)
DAF YA 4440 4000 kg (4 × 4) (300) (1984-85)
Berliet GBC 8 KT 4000 kg (4 × 4)
MB Unimog (4 × 4)

QATAR

Recovery vehicles
AMX-30D ARV (1)

Light vehicles
Land Rover

Trucks
TRM 2000 2000 kg (4 × 4) (10)

ROMANIA

Recovery vehicles
T-54/T-55 ARV

Mechanised bridges
MT-55A AVLB
BLG-67M AVLB
BLG-67M2 AVLB

Light vehicles
ARO (4 × 4)
UAZ-469B 600 kg (4 × 4)

Trucks
SR-101 3500 kg (4 × 2)
SR-132 2000 kg (6 × 6)
Ural-375D 4000 kg (6 × 6)
DAC 665 T 5000 kg (6 × 6)
ROMAN 12135 DFAE 10 000 kg (6 × 6)

SAUDI ARABIA

Armoured engineer vehicles
M728 CEV (15)

Recovery vehicles
AMX-30D ARV (57)
M88A1 ARV (47)
M578 ARV (88)
AMX-10 ECH RV
V-150 ARV (4 × 4)
Steyr Type 19S25 (4 × 4) RV
Steyr Type 32S29 (6 × 6) RV
M984A1 (8 × 8) RV

Light vehicles
Land Rover APV 564 kg (4 × 4)
M151 362 kg (4 × 4)

Mechanised bridges
AMX-30 AVLB (12)

Trucks
MB Unimog (4 × 4)
M35/M44 2268 kg (6 × 6)
M809 4536 kg (6 × 6)
HMMWV (4 × 4) (2300) (1992-94)
Oshkosh HEMET 9979 kg (8 × 8)
M939A2 4536 kg (6 × 6) (2633) (1991/1992) (plus 200% option)
RVI TRM 9000 9000 kg (6 × 6) (38)
RVI TRM 10 000 10 000 kg (6 × 6) (67)
TAM 110 T7 BV 1500/2500 kg (4 × 4)
TAM 140 T11 BV 3000/5000 kg (6 × 6)
FAP 2026 BS (6 × 6)

SENEGAL

Light vehicles
M151 362 kg (4 × 4)

Trucks
ACMAT (4 × 4)
M35/M44 2268 kg (6 × 6)
M809 4536 kg (6 × 6)

SERBIA

Armoured engineer vehicles
IWT CEV (equivalent to Soviet IMR)

Recovery vehicles
T-54/T-55 ARV

Mechanised bridges
MT-55 AVLB
TMM (6 × 6)

Light vehicles
MB 750 kg (4 × 4) (500)
Zastava AR-51 500 kg (4 × 4)
FIAT Campagnola 1107 AD 750 kg (4 × 4)
IMR A-0.75 750/1000 kg (4 × 4)

Trucks
SDP Pinzgauer
IMR TATA 1200 kg (4 × 4)
TAM 110 T7 BV 1500/2500 kg (4 × 4)
TAM 150 T11 BV 3000/5000 kg (6 × 6)
TAM 4500 4500 kg (4 × 4)
TAM 5000 5000 kg (4 × 4)
TAM 5500 5500 kg (4 × 4)
TAM 6500 6500 kg (4 × 4)
FAP 2220 BDS (6 × 4)
FAP 2026 BS/AV 10 000 kg (6 × 6)
FAP 2832 BS/AV 9000 kg (6 × 6)

SINGAPORE

Armoured engineer vehicles
M728 CEV (8)

Recovery vehicles
V-200 ARV (4 × 4)
M806A1 ARV
M113A1 fitters

Mechanised bridges
M60 AVLB (12)
M2 system (4 × 4) (36)

Light vehicles
MB 750 kg (4 × 4) (311)
Land Rover 110 (4 × 4)
M151 (4 × 4)

Trucks
MB Unimog (4 × 4)
MB (4 × 4)
MAN 6000/10 000 kg (165)
IVECO FIAT 90-17 4000 kg (4 × 4) (1990/1991)
Bedford RL 4000 kg (4 × 4)

SOMALIA

Recovery vehicles
T-54/T-55 (?)

Light vehicles
M151 362 kg (4 × 4)

Trucks
ACMAT (4 × 4)
M35/M44 2268 kg (6 × 6)
Pegaso 3046 3000 kg (4 × 4)
M809 4536 kg (6 × 6)
IVECO FIAT 90-17 WM 4000 kg (4 × 4) (100)
IVECO FIAT 75-14 WM 2500 kg (4 × 4)
IVECO FIAT 6605 (6 × 6) (291)

SOUTH AFRICA

Recovery vehicles
Olifant ARV (Centurion chassis)
Centurion ARV
Ratel RV (6 × 6)
SAMIL 50 RV (4 × 4)
SAMIL 100 RV (6 × 6)

Light vehicles
Land Rover (6 × 6)
Mitsubishi (4 × 4)
Toyota Land Cruiser (4 × 4)
Jakkals 350 kg (4 × 4)

Trucks
MB Unimog (4 × 4)
Bedford MK 4000 kg (4 × 4)
SAKOM 5000 kg (4 × 2)
SAMIL 20 2000 kg (4 × 4)
SAMIL 50 5000 kg (4 × 4)
SAMIL 100 10 000 kg (6 × 6)

SPAIN

Recovery vehicles
AMX-30D ARV (10)
M88A1 ARV (1)
M578 ARV
AAVR7 (1)
M543 W (6 × 6)

Mechanised bridges
M60 AVLB

Light vehicles
LOHR Fardier (4 × 4)
Citroen Mehari Armee (4 × 2)
Santana Model 88 500 kg (4 × 4)
Santana Model 109 1000 kg (4 × 4)
M151 362 kg (4 × 4)
M37 680 kg (4 × 4)

Trucks
Santana S-2000 2000 kg (4 × 4)
URO 115 PM 2000 kg (4 × 4)
Pegaso 3045 3000 kg (4 × 4)
Pegaso 3046 3000 kg (4 × 4)
Pegaso 3050 6000 kg (6 × 6)
Pegaso 3055 6000 kg (6 × 6)
Pegaso 7323 6000 kg (6 × 6)
M35/M44 2268 kg (6 × 6)
M54 4356 kg (6 × 6)
M809 4536 kg (6 × 6)

SRI LANKA

Light vehicles
Land Rover (4 × 4)
Mahindra

SUDAN

Recovery vehicles
T-54/T-55 ARV
M113 ARV
M88A1 ARV (2)
M3 repair vehicle (4 × 4)

Light vehicles
Land Rover ALV 564 kg (4 × 4)

Trucks
M35/M44 2268 kg (6 × 6)
M809 4536 kg (6 × 6)
SDP Pinzgauer

SWEDEN

Recovery vehicles
Bgbv 82 ARV (24)
Bgbv 81 ARV (Centurion Mk 2)
CV 90 ARV (1) (trials)

Mechanised bridges
Brobv AVLB (17)

Light vehicles
Volvo L3304 (4 × 4)
Volvo L3314 Laplander (4 × 4)

Trucks
MB L 508 DG MA 2105 kg (4 × 2)
Volvo 4140 (4 × 4)
Volvo 4140 (6 × 6)
Volvo 4151 (4 × 4)
Volvo L2204 1500 kg (6 × 6)
Volvo L3154 3000 kg (6 × 6)
Scania SBA 111 4500 kg (4 × 4) ⎫ (2500)
Scania SBAT 111S 6000 kg (6 × 6) ⎭
Volvo L4854 3000 kg (6 × 6)
Scania-Vabis L-36A/L-50 5920 kg (4 × 2) (800+)

SWITZERLAND

Recovery vehicles
Entp Pz 65/88 ARV (Pz 68 chassis)
Entp Pz 56 ARV (Centurion Mk 2) (?)

Mechanised bridges
Bru Pz 68/88 AVLB

Light vehicles
SDP 700 AP (4 × 4)
MB 750 kg (4 × 4) (4100)

Trucks
SDP Pinzgauer (4 × 4 and 6 × 6)
SDP 680 M 4500 kg (4 × 4)
MAN (4 × 4 and 6 × 6)
MOWAG 1500 kg (4 × 4) (1688)
Saurer 2DM 4500 kg (4 × 4)
Berna 2VM 4500 kg (4 × 4)
Saurer 6 DM 6000 kg (4 × 4)
Saurer 10 DM 10 000 kg (6 × 6)

SYRIA

Recovery vehicles
T-54/T-55 ARV

Mechanised bridges
MTU-20 AVLB
MTU AVLB

Light vehicles
UAZ-469B 600 kg (4 × 4)
GAZ-69/69A 500 kg (4 × 4)

Trucks
MB Unimog (4 × 4)
Ural-375D (4 × 4)
GAZ-66 2000 kg (4 × 4)

TAIWAN

Recovery vehicles
M88A1 ARV (37)

Mechanised bridges
M48 AVLB

Light vehicles
M151 362 kg (4 × 4)

Trucks
CUCV (4 × 4)
HMMWV (4 × 4) (2000+)
M35/M44 2268 kg (6 × 6)
M809 4536 kg (6 × 6)
Oshkosh HEMET 9979 kg (8 × 8)

TANZANIA

Recovery vehicles
Vickers ARV (2 or 3) (1990)

Light vehicles
Land Rover (4 × 4)

Trucks
MB Unimog (4 × 4)

THAILAND

Recovery vehicles
Samson ARV
M88A1 ARV (2)
AAVR7 ARV (1) (Marines)
Type 653 ARV

Mechanised bridges
Type 84 AVLB

Light vehicles
Mitsubishi (4 × 4)
M151 362 kg (4 × 4)
M37 680 kg (4 × 4)

Trucks
HMMWV 1542 kg (4 × 4) (150)
M35/M44 2268 kg (6 × 6)
M809 4536 kg (6 × 6)
Dong Feng EQ2080E4DY 2500 kg (6 × 6) (235)
MB (6 × 4)
Steyr 5000 kg (4 × 4)
Steyr 14 M 14 8000 kg (4 × 4)

TOGO

Light vehicles
Peugeot P4 7500 kg (4 × 4)

Trucks
ACMAT (4 × 4)

TUNISIA

Recovery vehicles
M88A1 ARV (6)

Light vehicles
FIAT Campagnola 1107 AD 750 kg (4 × 4) (200)
LOHR Fardier (4 × 4)

Trucks
SDP Pinzgauer
MB Unimog (4 × 4)

TURKEY

Recovery vehicles
Leopard 1 ARV (4)

Light vehicles
Land Rover Defender 110 (4 × 4)
Land Rover Defender 130 (4 × 4)
M151 362 kg (4 × 4)
M37 680 kg (4 × 4)

Trucks
M35/M44 2268 kg (6 × 6)
M54 4536 kg (6 × 6)
MB Unimog (4 × 4)
Bedford MK 4000 kg (4 × 4) (300)
MANAS 16.210 FAE 7500 kg (4 × 4)
MANAS 26.281 DFAE 13 800 kg (6 × 6)

UGANDA

Light vehicles
Land Rover (4 × 4)

Trucks
Bedford MK 4000 kg (4 × 4)
Steyr 14 M 14 8000 kg (4 × 4)

UNITED ARAB EMIRATES

Recovery vehicles
OF-40 ARV (4)
AMX-30D ARV (4)

Light vehicles
Land Rover (4 × 4)
MB 750 kg (4 × 4) (25)

Trucks
HMMWV (4 × 4) (3)
Bedford MK 4000 kg (4 × 4)
Bedford TM 4-4 8000 kg (4 × 4)
Bedford TM 6-6 14 000 kg (6 × 6)
Bedford TM 30-30 18 000 kg (6 × 6)
Berliet GBU 15 6000 kg (6 × 6)
MB 2028 A 10 000 kg (6 × 6)
MB Unimog (4 × 4)

UNITED KINGDOM

Armoured engineer vehicles
Combat Engineer Tractor (141)
Centurion AVRE (165 mm and 105 mm) (PO)
Chieftain AVRE (48) (1992-94)

Recovery vehicles
Challenger ARV (80) (1990-94)
Chieftain ARV
Centurion ARV (107)
M578 ARV
Samson ARV
Saxon ARV (4 × 4) (38)
FV432 ARV
FV434 armoured repair vehicle
Warrior mechanised combat repair vehicle (101)
Warrior mechanised recovery vehicle (39)
MAN RV (8 × 8) (Berlin)
Reynolds Boughton 6 t RV (4 × 4)
Foden RV (6 × 6) (333)
Scammell Crusader RV (6 × 4) (130)

Mechanised bridges
Chieftain AVLB (48)
M3 ABFS (4 × 4) (3 – trials)
M2 ABFS (4 × 4)

Light vehicles
Rolba Goblin 410 kg (4 × 4) (8)
SUPACAT Mk 2 1000 kg (4 × 4) (50)
Land Rover Defender 90 (4 × 4)
Land Rover ALV 564 kg (4 × 4)
Land Rover Defender 110 (4 × 4)
Land Rover 1000 kg (4 × 4) (2500) (PO)

Trucks
MB Unimog (4 × 4)
Reynolds Boughton RB-44 2000 kg (4 × 4) (840)
MAN 9.150 FAE 3000 kg (4 × 4) (57)
Leyland DAF 4000 kg (4 × 4) (5345) (1990-95)
Bedford MK 4000 kg (4 × 4)
Bedford RL 4000 kg (4 × 4) (PO)
Alvis Stalwart 5000 kg (6 × 6)
Foden low mobility (6 × 4 and 8 × 4) (1275)
Foden medium mobility (6 × 6) (116)
Bedford TM 6-6 14 000 kg (1045) (1986-90)
MTM 40-30 Multi-drive (8 × 8) (26) (1991)
Bedford TM 4-4 8000 kg (4 × 4) (2099)

UNITED STATES OF AMERICA

Armoured engineer vehicles
M728 CEV
M9 armoured combat earthmover (434)

Recovery vehicles
M578 ARV
AAVR7 ARV (54) (Marines)
M88A1 ARV (79) (Marines)
M88A1 ARV (2470) (Army)
LAV repair and recovery (45) (Marines)
M60/M108 W (6 × 6)
M62/M246/M543 W (6 × 6)
M816/M819 W (6 × 6)
M984A1 RV (8 × 8)

Mechanised bridges
M48/M60 AVLB

Light vehicles
M151 362 kg (4 × 4)
Fast attack vehicle (4 × 2)
MB 750 kg (4 × 4) (480)

Trucks
CUCV (4 × 4) (60 000)
M715 1360 kg (4 × 4) (PO)
M880 1133 kg (4 × 4, 4 × 2) (PO)
HMMWV (4 × 4) (90 000+)
LMTV 2268 kg (4 × 4) (ES)
MTV 4536 kg (6 × 6) (ES)
M35/M44 2268 kg (6 × 6)
M54 4536 kg (6 × 6)
M809 4536 kg (6 × 6)
M939 4536 kg (6 × 6) (17 092)
Oshkosh MK48 9072 kg (8 × 8) (1433) (Marines)
Oshkosh HEMET 9979 kg (8 × 8) (11 600) (by 1993)

VENEZUELA

Recovery vehicles
AMX-30D ARV (4)
Samson ARV
AAVR7 ARV (1) (Marines)
IVECO FIAT 90 PM 16 W (4 × 4) (60)

Light vehicles
M151 362 kg (4 × 4)

Trucks
M35/M44 2268 kg (6 × 6)
MAN 6000/10 000 kg (405)

VIETNAM

Recovery vehicles
T-54/T-55 ARV

Light vehicles
UAZ-469B 600 kg (4 × 4)
UAZ-69/69A 500 kg (4 × 4)

Trucks
ZIL-157 2500 kg (6 × 6)
ZIL-151 2500 kg (6 × 6)

YEMEN

Recovery vehicles
T-54/T-55 ARV (?)

Light vehicles
Land Rover (4 × 4)
UAZ-469B 600 kg (4 × 4)
UAZ-69/69A 500 kg (4 × 4)

ZAÏRE

Recovery vehicles
M816 W (6 × 6)

Light vehicles
Auverland/SAMO (4 × 4)
M151 362 kg (6 × 6)

Trucks
ACMAT
M35/M44 2268 kg (6 × 6)
M809 4536 kg (6 × 6)

ZAMBIA

Recovery vehicles
T-54/T-55 ARV (?)

Light vehicles
MB 750 kg (4 × 4) (50)
Land Rover (4 × 4)

ZIMBABWE

Recovery vehicles
T-54/T-55 ARV (?)

Light vehicles
Land Rover (4 × 4)

Trucks
Bedford MK 4000 kg (4 × 4)

Manufacturers Index

Pearson mine ploughs 300
Pearson Pathfinder marking device 309
Pearson Surface Mine Plough (SMP) 301

Pegaso, Empresa Nacional de Autocamiones SA, Defence Division
VAP 3550/1 (4 × 4) 3000 kg amphibious vehicle 534
Pegaso 3045 (4 × 4) 3000 kg cargo truck 462
Pegaso 3046 (4 × 4) cargo trucks 463
Pegaso 3050 (6 × 6) 6000 kg cargo truck 464
Pegaso 3055 and Model 7323 (6 × 6) 6000 kg
trucks 464
Pegaso 7345 (6 × 6) truck tractor 523

Penman Engineering Ltd
Penman mobile shelters and custom-built containers ... 722

Penman Engineering Ltd, Hotspur Armoured Products Division
Hotspur One Fifty (6 × 6) vehicles 475

Permutit Australia
Permutit water purification units 680

Peugeot Talbot España
M-47 E2R armoured recovery vehicle 42

Peugeot Talbot España SA, Productos Especiales, Departmento Ventas/Marketing
MAN M47/M48 Leguan armoured bridgelayer 108

Picatinny Arsenal
M24 and M66 off-route anti-tank mines 249

Pilcher-Greene Ltd
Pilcher-Greene ambulances 735

Pinguely see **Creusot-Loire, Pinguely**

Polish state factories
BLG-60, BLG-67 and BLG-67M2 armoured
bridgelayers 106
DMS-65 heavy girder bridge 156
KH-200 bridging boat 171
PP-64 heavy folding pontoon bridge 136
PW-LWD tank-mounted rocket-propelled equipment ... 295
SMT-1 truck-mounted treadway bridge 116
T-54/T-55 armoured recovery vehicles 29
Bailey type panel bridges 156

Pre-Mac (Kent) Ltd
Pre-Mac Model MWP and SWP personal water
purifiers 690
Pre-Mac Model PWP and FWP personal water
purifiers 689

Priboj Motor Vehicle Plant
FAP 2220 BDS (6 × 4) and FAP BS (6 × 6) trucks 456
FAP 2832 BS/AV (8 × 8) 9000 kg truck 457

Promac BV, Watertreatment Division
Promac Aquaset MLT mobile drinking water units 684

Protan OY Suomi
Protan camouflage products 697

Protection and Defence Systems (PDS)
Defendress Type S and Type T battlefield shelters 655

Q

Química Tupan SA
Anti-personnel mine Min AP NM AE T1 181
Anti-tank mine Min AC NM AE T1 182

R

ROMTECHNICA
200-man field kitchen trailer 589

ROMTECHNIKA
ABAL armoured vehicle for combat supply 547

RTK Marine Ltd
RTK combat support boat Type CSB 508 173

RTS (Pty) Ltd
RTS RT 20 load handling system 623

Ramta Structures and Systems, Israel Aircraft Industries Ltd
Ramta Track Width Mine Plough (TWMP) 291
Scatterable Mine Clearing Device (SMCD) 292

Rautaruukki, Transtech Division
Rautaruukki RRC-250 heavy duty container system 713

Recovery Engineering Inc
Recovery Engineering hand-operated watermakers 695

Red Star Motor Vehicle Plant
DAC 665 T (6 × 6) 5000 kg truck 453
ROMAN 12135 DFAE (6 × 6) 10 000 kg truck 454
SR-131 trucks and variants 453

Renault Véhicules Industriels
Berliet GBC 8 KT (6 × 6) 4000 kg truck 403
Berliet GBU 15 (6 × 6) 6000 kg truck 406
Renault B110 Turbo (4 × 4) light vehicle 394
Renault G 290.26 (6 × 4) VTL transport vehicle 620
Renault R 390 (6 × 4) tractor truck 513
Renault TRM 10 000 (6 × 6) 10 000 kg truck 406
Renault TRM 10 000 CLD (6 × 6) heavy wrecker
(vehicle) 68
Renault TRM 160, TRM 180, TRM 200 and TRM 230
(4 × 4) truck series 404
Renault TRM 340.34 (6 × 6) 15 000 kg truck 407
Renault TRM 340.34 T (6 × 6) tractor truck 514
Renault TRM 700-100 (6 × 6) tractor truck 512
Renault TRM 1200 (4 × 4) 1200 kg truck 396
Renault TRM 2000 (4 × 4) 2000 kg truck 397
Renault TRM 4000 (4 × 4) 4000 kg truck 402
Renault TRM 9000 (6 × 6) 9000 kg truck 405
Renault VAB ECH repair vehicle 61
Renault VAB Recovery armoured recovery and repair
vehicle 33

Renault Véhicules Industriels, Automobiles M Berliet
Berliet TBC 8 KT (6 × 6) wrecker 68
Berliet TBU 15 CLD (6 × 6) wrecker 69

Research and Development Center of Mechanical Appliances
SUM-OF tracked minelayer 261

Reynolds Boughton (Devon) Ltd
Reynolds Boughton water tank 686

Reynolds Boughton Ltd
Reynolds Boughton (4 × 4) 6000 kg recovery vehicle 79
Reynolds Boughton DROPS/MLRS pallet trailer 630
Reynolds Boughton MLR/DROPS flatrack 629
Reynolds Boughton RB-44 (4 × 4) truck 476

Reynolds Boughton Ltd, Engineering Division
Boughton fork-lifts 633
Boughton recovery equipment 89
Boughton Ulrich Simplex multi-purpose bucket 658
Boughton winches 88
Reynolds Boughton recovery cranes 88

Reynolds Boughton Ltd, Scottorn Division
FV2381 750 kg cargo trailer 593
Scottorn 1-tonne trailers 593
Scottorn 100 to 2500 kg flat bed trailers 595
Scottorn 125-ration mobile kitchen trailer 603
Scottorn 750 kg trailers 592
Scottorn 'Flat Top' 2280 – 10 000 litre tanker trailers . 597
Scottorn LAD 510 kg workshop trailer 598
Scottorn military 1000/1250 kg general purpose
trailer 594
Scottorn military 1750 kg cargo trailer 594
Scottorn mobile servicing 510 kg lubrication trailer 598
Scottorn tanker trailers 597

Reynolds Boughton Ltd, Vehicle Division
Boughton load handling system 624
Reynolds Boughton general service cargo body 736
Reynolds Boughton general service tipper body 737

Rolba Ltd
Rolba Goblin (4 × 4) 410 kg load carrier 341

Romanian state factories
D-5M mineclearing equipment 296
MC-71 anti-tank mine 232
MAT-62B anti-tank mine 232
MS/3 ambush mine 231
PR-60 heavy pontoon bridge 137
Directional anti-personnel mine 231
Lightweight anti-personnel mine 231

Rotzler GmbH and Company
Rotzler winches 85

Royal Ordnance, Guns & Vehicles Division
Combat Engineer Tractor (FV180) 16

Rubery Owen Group Services Ltd, Defence Equipment Division
Rubery Owen Class 60/70 trackway trailer 600
Rubery Owen medium girder bridge trailer (FV2842) ... 600
Rubery Owen recovery equipment 91
Rubery Owen trailer, four-wheeled close-coupled
1000 kg, medium mobility 600
Trailer, dummy axle, recovery, 1-5 tonne (FV2692) 90
Trailer, mineclearing equipment, Giant Viper, No 2
Mk 3 (FV3705) 602

S

SA Automobiles Citroën
Citroën A FAF 400 kg (4 × 2) and 400 kg (4 × 4) light
vehicles 323
Citroën Méhari Armée 322

SAAB-Scania AB, Scania Division
Scania P113 HK (6 × 6) recovery vehicle 77
Scania R143 and T143 (6 × 6) and (6 × 4) tractor
trucks 524

Scania SBA 111 4500 kg (4 × 4) and SBAT 111S
6000 kg (6 × 6) trucks 466
Scania SBA 111 4500 kg (4 × 4) and SBAT 111S
6000 kg (6 × 6) trucks, model variants 467
Scania trucks 469
Scania-Vabis (4 × 2) L-36A and L-50 5920 kg trucks ... 468

SAI Ambrosini – Societá Aeronautica Italiana SpA
SAI Ambrosini 121 Thruster bridging boat 170
SAI Ambrosini 126 multi-purpose boat 170
SAI Ambrosini bridging boat 169
SAI Ambrosini containers and shelters 718
SAI Ambrosini wheel-coupled shelter and platform
transporters 718

SAKR Factory for Developed Industries
Fateh-1 anti-personnel mineclearing system 288
Gehad-1 anti-tank mineclearing system 289
Mine dispensing system 254

SARMCOL SA (Pty) Ltd
Static storage tanks 671
Transportable fuel tanks 672

SIMA-CEFAR
Anti-personnel mine MGP-30 229

SMAI-Soudure et Mécanique Appliquée Industrielles
SMAI LWV (4 × 4) 800 kg light vehicle 323
SMAI Pick-Up (4 × 4) light vehicle 324

SMI, Military Defence Products, Südsteirische Metallindustrie GmbH
SMI 17/4C giant shotgun 179
SMI 22/7C off-route anti-tank mine 179
SMI directional fragmentation mines 179

SNC Industrial Technologies Inc
C3A2 non-metallic anti-personnel mine (Elsie) 184

SOLEM SA, HAULOTTE
MFRD/F1 mobile drilling machine (carrier) 653

SOMCHEM
Plofadder mineclearing system 297

SOVAMAG
SOVAMAG TC10 (4 × 4) 1000 kg multi-purpose
vehicle 325

SRTI-SODETEG
Individual water treatment equipment 683

SUPACAT Ltd
SUPACAT (6 × 6) light vehicle 342
SUPACAT Fork-Lift Pallet Trailer (FLPT) 630

Sandock-Austral Beperk Ltd
Ratel armoured repair vehicle 63

Saunders-Roe Developments Ltd
Betalight illuminated defile marker 310

Scania-Vabis see **SAAB-Scania**

Schaeff
Schaeff HT 11A backacter on Unimog U84/406
(Erdarbeitsgerät) (backacter) 654

The Second Automobile Works
EQ1110F4D (4 × 2) truck 376
Dong Feng EQ1141G (4 × 2) 8000 kg truck 377
Dong Feng EQ2080E4DY (6 × 6) 2500 kg truck 373
Dong Feng EQ2100E (6 × 6) 3500 kg truck 376

Serbian state factories
Truck-mounted scissors treadway bridge 116

Seyntex nv/sa
Seyntex camouflage nets 696

Shanghai Research Institute of Microwave Technology
Shanghai Research Institute mine detectors 267

Sichuan Automobile Factory
Hongyan CQ 261 (6 × 6) 8250 kg truck 377

Simon Gloster Saro Ltd
Demountable bulk fuel dispensing unit 673

Singapore Automotive Engineering Ltd
SAE upgraded LARC-V 534
Mobile field hospital 718
Tactical ambulance Mark II 734

Singapore Shipbuilding and Engineering Ltd
FBS 60 bridging boat 172
LAB 30 light assault bridge 117
Floating bridge system FBS 60 138
Portable assault bridge PAB 15 156

Sociedade Portuguesa de Explosivos SARL
BPD SB-33 scatterable anti-personnel mine 215

Alphabetical Index

Printed in Great Britain by Butler & Tanner Ltd, Frome and London